The authors

Barbara Donegan is a welfare rights worker at CPAG in Scotland.

Carolyn George is a freelance trainer and writer on welfare rights.

Alison Gillies is a welfare rights worker at CPAG in Scotland.

Daphne Hall is a part-time welfare rights adviser at Bristol City Council, and a freelance trainer and writer on welfare rights.

Henri Krishna is a welfare rights worker at CPAG in Scotland.

Susan Mitchell is a freelance writer on welfare rights.

Simon Osborne is a welfare rights worker at CPAG, based at CPAG in Scotland.

Judith Paterson is CPAG in Scotland's welfare rights co-ordinator.

Jon Shaw is a welfare rights worker at CPAG in Scotland.

Angela Toal is a welfare rights worker at CPAG in Scotland.

Paula Twigg is the director of the Mary Ward Legal Centre.

Rebecca Walker is a freelance trainer and writer on welfare rights.

Martin Williams is a welfare rights worker at CPAG.

Mark Willis is a welfare rights worker at CPAG in Scotland.

Acknowledgements

The authors would like to thank Mark Brough, Sarah Clarke, Liz Dawson, Edward Graham, Barbara Gray, Will Hadwen, David Malcolm, Paul Moorhouse, Kelly Smith and, in particular, Arnie James, for their invaluable contribution to this year's book.

Our thanks are also due to Simon Osborne for acting as the book's content consultant.

We must acknowledge the efforts of the many authors of previous editions of the *National Welfare Benefits Handbook*, the *Rights Guide to Non-Means-Tested Benefits* and the *Jobseeker's Allowance Handbook,* on which this book is based.

Thanks are also due to Nicola Johnston and Alison Key for once again editing and managing the production of the book so efficiently, and to Kathleen Armstrong, Mark Brough and Anne Ketley for proofreading the text. Particular thanks are due to Katherine Dawson and Anne Ketley for producing the index.

We would also like to thank staff at the Department for Work and Pensions, the Child Support Agency, HM Customs and Revenue, HM Courts and Tribunals Service and the Department for Education for their help and co-operation.

Thanks to the staff at KonnectSoft, David Lewis XML Associates and CPI William Clowes for keeping up with our schedules.

The law covered in this book was correct on 1 March 2014 and includes regulations laid up to this date.

Foreword

Welcome to the 2014/15 edition of the *Welfare Benefits and Tax Credits Handbook*.
Universal credit may not have arrived as originally planned, but there is no doubt that we are in a much changed benefits landscape. We are beginning to see the impact of both cuts and changes to rules, such as the benefit cap and the 'bedroom tax'. Families – and the organisations who work with them – are having to make impossible choices in response. But it is also increasingly clear that the big drivers of UK child poverty in the next few years will include the massive cuts to benefits for young children and working families, the breaking of the link between benefits and the retail prices index, the 1 per cent uprating of a number of benefits for three years and, in future, the cap on annually managed expenditure.

The Chancellor's targeting of working-age social security spending will, he hopes, be institutionally locked in through a new annually managed expenditure cap. Labour, too, has advocated such a cap. One simple response is to point out that social security spending has been relatively stable in real terms (as a percentage of GDP) for many years. The part of this spending that is rising is pensioner – not working age – related. Another is to say that we have to recognise that if we want to cut social security spending, we have got to face up to the root causes – poverty pay, unaffordable rents and prohibitive childcare costs. The cap is a device which will punish poor families, the disabled and the sick by rationing decency, if governments duck tackling these fundamentals.

It is against this background of a weakened benefit system that the Institute for Fiscal Studies has published child poverty projections, warning that relative child poverty could rise by 900,000 children to 3.2 million, and absolute child poverty by 1.4 million children to four million, by 2020. Were it not for universal credit, these grim figures would look even worse. Despite this, and the fact that two-thirds of children in poverty live in working families, universal credit's poverty-fighting potential is being degraded by delays, complexities and by reductions in the support it will offer the low paid – for example, most recently, the decision in the 2013 Autumn Statement not to increase the work allowance with the cost of living. As ministers and officials continue to struggle with the significant delivery and IT failings exposed by the National Audit Office in its 2013 report, it is essential that we do not lose sight of the key outcomes universal credit was supposed to deliver: simplification, making work pay and tackling poverty.

The succession of delays to universal credit mean that the system will remain in flux for a number of years to come, with advisers having to deal with a myriad of changing entitlements and systems. This is especially the case at the local level where, in addition to the changing national picture, advisers are grappling with emerging local welfare assistance (which we now hear will be unfunded from 2015) and local council tax support schemes. In the coming year, with support from the Oak Foundation, CPAG will be looking to develop resources on its website to help advisers navigate this complex system of local assistance.

Advice workers have got their work cut out – trying to maximise family incomes in the face of all these pressures. Advisers need to work with local authorities, lawyers and others to continue to provide access to advice in the face of cuts. The effect on living standards will be severe and will have an impact on food and fuel poverty, and levels of housing need. These things are already visible on the ground. The genuine distress and difficulty that is being heaped on so many families is one possible explanation why public support for the government's benefit cuts has fallen, and opposition increased, over the past year. Please use every opportunity to send us evidence about your experience.

In the face of these challenges, CPAG will continue to be a principled and pragmatic voice, and an essential source of expertise to those working hard to help low-income families with children.

Alison Garnham
Chief Executive

Contents

Part 1   Introduction

Provides an overview of the benefits and tax credits system and explains how to use this book. Use this part to find out how to identify which benefits, tax credits or statutory payments you can get and the amount you should receive, and to understand how to use the book to find answers to specific questions about your entitlement.

Part 2   Main means-tested benefits and tax credits

Contains chapters on all the main means-tested benefits and tax credits. Use this part if you are on a low income to check whether you qualify for means-tested benefits or tax credits, and to understand how and when you might be affected by the introduction of universal credit.

Contents

Part 6   **General rules for other benefits**

Outlines the national insurance contribution conditions for contributory benefits, and explains when you may qualify for national insurance credits and the rules on earnings for certain non-means-tested benefits. Use this part to check whether you qualify for contributory benefits and to understand how your earnings may affect your entitlement to non-means-tested benefits.

Part 7   **Special benefit rules**

Explains how particular circumstances, such as going into hospital, affect your entitlement to benefits and statutory payments. Use this part if any of the circumstances apply to you.

Part 8   **Work**

Explains the benefit rules on work and limited capability for work. Use this part to find out how work affects your benefit entitlement, what you may have to do to prepare for and find work in order to get benefit, and what may happen if you do not do so.

Contents

Abbreviations

AA	attendance allowance	IB	incapacity benefit
CA	carer's allowance	ICE	Independent Case Examiner
CAB	Citizens Advice Bureau	IIDB	industrial injuries disablement benefit
CCLT	Complaints, Correspondence and Litigation Team	IS	income support
CJEU	Court of Justice of the European Union	JSA	jobseeker's allowance
CMS	Child Maintenance Service	MA	maternity allowance
CPI	Consumer Prices Index	MS	Medical Service
CRU	Compensation Recovery Unit	NI	national insurance
CSA	Child Support Agency	NICO	National Insurance Contributions Office
CTB	council tax benefit	PAYE	Pay As You Earn
CTC	child tax credit	PC	pension credit
DLA	disability living allowance	PIP	personal independence payment
DWP	Department for Work and Pensions	REA	reduced earnings allowance
EC	European Community	SAAS	Student Awards Agency for Scotland
ECtHR	European Court of Human Rights	SAP	statutory adoption pay
EEA	European Economic Area	SDA	severe disablement allowance
EO	employment officer	SLC	Student Loan Company
ESA	employment and support allowance	SMP	statutory maternity pay
EU	European Union	SPP	statutory paternity pay
EWC	expected week of childbirth	SSP	statutory sick pay
HB	housing benefit	SSPP	statutory shared parental pay
HMCTS	HM Courts and Tribunals Service	TCO	Tax Credit Office
HMRC	HM Revenue and Customs	UC	universal credit
		WTC	working tax credit

Means-tested benefit rates

Income support/income-based jobseeker's allowance
Personal allowances

		£pw
Single	Under 25	57.35
	25 or over	72.40
Lone parent	Under 18	57.35
	18 or over	72.40
Couple	Both under 18	57.35
	Both under 18, certain cases	86.65
	One under 18, one 18–24	57.35
	One under 18, one 25 or over	72.40
	One under 18, certain cases	113.70
	Both 18 or over	113.70

Premiums

Carer		34.20
Disability	Single	31.85
	Couple	45.40
Enhanced disability	Single	15.55
	Couple	22.35
Severe disability	One qualifies	61.10
	Two qualify	122.20
Pensioner	Single (jobseeker's allowance only)	75.95
	Couple	112.80

Children (Pre-6 April 2004 claims with no child tax credit)

Child under 20 personal allowance	66.33
Family premium	17.45
Disabled child premium	59.50
Enhanced disability premium (child)	24.08

Capital limits

	Lower	Upper
Standard	6,000	16,000
Care homes	10,000	16,000

Tariff income £1 per £250 between lower and upper limit

Income-related employment and support allowance

Personal allowances		Assessment phase	Main phase
Single	Under 25	57.35	72.40
	25 or over	72.40	72.40
Lone parent	Under 18	57.35	72.40
	18 or over	72.40	72.40
Couple	Both under 18 (max)	86.65	113.70
	Both 18 or over	113.70	113.70
Components			
Work-related activity		–	28.75
Support		–	35.75
Premiums			
Carer		34.20	34.20
Severe disability (one qualifies)		61.10	61.10
Severe disability (two qualify)		122.20	122.20
Enhanced disability	Single	15.55	15.55
	Couple	22.35	22.35
Pensioner	Single, no component	75.95	–
	Couple, no component	112.80	–
	Single, work-related activity component	–	47.20
	Couple, work-related activity component	–	84.05
	Single, support component	–	40.20
	Couple, support component	–	77.05

Capital limits
As for income support

Pension credit

Guarantee credit

		£pw
Standard minimum guarantee	Single	148.35
	Couple	226.50
Severe disability addition	One qualifies	61.10
	Two qualify	122.20
Carer addition		34.20

Savings credit

Threshold	Single	120.35
	Couple	192.00
Maximum	Single	16.80
	Couple	20.70

Capital disregard
Standard/care homes   10,000
No upper limit
Deemed income £1 per £500 above disregard

Housing benefit
Personal allowances

Single	Under 25	57.35
	Under 25 (on main phase ESA)	72.40
	25 or over	72.40
Lone parent	Under 18	57.35
	Under 18 (on main phase ESA)	72.40
	18 or over	72.40
Couple	Both under 18	86.65
	Both under 18 (claimant on main phase ESA)	113.70
	One or both 18 or over	113.70
Dependent children	Under 20	66.33
Over qualifying age for pension credit	Single under 65	148.35
	Single 65 or over	165.15
	Couple both under 65	226.50
	Couple one or both 65 or over	247.20

Components

Work-related activity	28.75
Support	35.75

Premiums

Carer		34.20
Disability	Single	31.85
	Couple	45.40
Disabled child		59.50
Enhanced disability	Single	15.55
	Couple	22.35
	Child	24.08
Severe disability	One qualifies	61.10
	Two qualify	122.20
Family	Ordinary rate	17.45
	Some lone parents	22.20

Capital limits	Lower	Upper
Standard	6,000	16,000
Care home or over pension credit qualifying age	10,000	16,000

Tariff income £1 per £250 between lower and upper limit,
£1 per £500 for those over qualifying age for pension credit
No upper limit or tariff income for those on pension credit guarantee credit

Social fund payments

Maternity grant		500.00
Cold weather payment		25.00
Winter fuel payment	Under 80	200.00
(over qualifying age for	80 or over	300.00
pension credit)	Care home (under 80)	100.00
	Care home (80 or over)	150.00

Universal credit

Standard allowance

		£pm
Single	Under 25	249.28
	25 or over	314.67
Couple	Both under 25	391.29
	One or both 25 or over	493.95

Elements

First child		274.58
Second and each subsequent child		229.17
Disabled child addition	Lower rate	124.86
	Higher rate	362.92
Limited capability for work		124.86
Limited capability for work-related activity		311.86
Carer		148.61
Childcare costs	One child	up to 532.29
	Two or more children	up to 912.50
	Percentage of childcare costs covered	70%

Capital limits	Lower	Upper
	6,000	16,000

Tariff income £4.35 per £250 between lower and upper limits

Non-means-tested benefit rates

	£pw
Attendance allowance	
Higher rate	81.30
Lower rate	54.45
Bereavement benefits	
Bereavement payment (lump sum)	2,000
Bereavement allowance/widow's pension (55 or over)	111.20
Bereavement allowance/widow's pension (45–54)	33.36–103.42
Widowed parent's allowance/widowed mother's allowance	111.20
Carer's allowance	61.35
Adult dependant (some existing claimants only)	36.10
Child benefit	
Only/eldest child	20.50
Other child(ren)	13.55
Increase for child (some existing claimants only)	
Only/eldest child	8.05
Other child(ren)	11.35
Partner's earnings limit	
Only/eldest child	225.00
Other child(ren)	30.00
Disability living allowance	
Care component	
Highest rate	81.30
Middle rate	54.45
Lowest rate	21.55
Mobility component	
Higher rate	56.75
Lower rate	21.55

Contributory employment and support allowance
Assessment phase
Under 25	57.35
25 or over	72.40

Main phase
16 or over	72.40
Work-related activity component	28.75
Support component	35.75

Guardian's allowance
16.35

Short-term incapacity benefit
Under pension age
Lower rate	78.50
Higher rate	92.95
Adult dependant	47.10

Over pension age
Lower rate	99.90
Higher rate	104.10
Adult dependant	58.20

Long-term incapacity benefit
	104.10
Age addition (under 35)	11.00
Age addition (35–44)	6.15
Adult dependant	60.45

Industrial injuries disablement benefit
20%: £33.20 to 100%: £166.00

Contribution-based jobseeker's allowance
Under 25	57.35
25 or over	72.40

Maternity allowance
Standard rate	138.18

Personal independence payment
Daily living component
Standard rate	54.45
Enhanced rate	81.30

Mobility component
Standard rate	21.55
Enhanced rate	56.75

Retirement pension
Category A	113.10
Adult dependant (some existing claimants only)	64.90

Category B (widow(er)/surviving civil partner)	113.10
Category B (spouse/civil partner)	67.80
Category D	67.80

Severe disablement allowance 73.75

Age addition (under 40)	11.00
Age addition (40–49)	6.15
Age addition (50–59)	6.15
Adult dependant	36.30

Statutory maternity, paternity and adoption pay

Standard rate	138.18

Statutory sick pay 87.55

National insurance contributions

Lower earnings limit	111.00
Primary threshold	153.00
Employee's Class 1 rate	12% of £153 to £805
	2% above £805
Class 2 rate (self-employed)	2.75

Tax credit rates

	£ per day	£ per year
Child tax credit		
Family element	1.50	545
Child element	7.54	2,750
Disabled child element	8.49	3,100
Severely disabled child element	3.44	1,255
Working tax credit		
Basic element	5.32	1,940
Couple element	5.46	1,990
Lone parent element	5.46	1,990
30-hour element	2.20	800
Disabled worker element	8.05	2,935
Severe disability element	3.44	1,255

Childcare element — 70% of eligible weekly childcare costs:

One child	weekly maximum 175
Two or more children	weekly maximum 300

Thresholds

Income threshold	Working tax credit only or with child tax credit	6,420
	Child tax credit only	16,010
Taper		41%
Income decrease disregard		2,500
Income increase disregard		5,000

Part 1

Introduction

Chapter 1

....

How to use this book

This chapter covers:
1. About this *Handbook* (below)
2. Finding out which benefits and tax credits you can get (p6)
3. Working out how much benefit you should receive (p12)
4. Finding answers to specific questions (p12)
5. Finding information on challenging a decision (p13)
6. Finding the law relevant to your situation (p13)
7. Using the index (p14)

---

1. About this *Handbook*

This *Handbook* is a detailed guide to benefits and tax credits. You can use it to identify the benefits and tax credits you may qualify for and the amount you should receive. It explains how to claim benefits and tax credits, how you are paid and how you can challenge decisions. It aims to help you understand how benefits and tax credits interact with each other, and provides information on what other financial help may be available if you are getting benefits or tax credits.

How the book is organised

The book is split into parts, and related chapters are grouped under these parts. For a description of the information covered in each part, see below. For the chapters included in each part, see the table of contents on pvii–xi.

Note: information on jobseeker's allowance (JSA) and employment and support allowance (ESA) is split into two chapters. Chapters on income-based JSA (including joint-claim JSA) and income-related ESA are in Part 2. Chapters on contribution-based JSA and contributory ESA are in Part 5.

1

Part 1: Introduction

Part 2: Main means-tested benefits and tax credits	Use this part if you are on a low income and want to check your entitlement to any of the main means-tested benefits or tax credits – it contains chapters on each of them. Also use this part to find out how and when the introduction of universal credit (UC) will affect you.
Part 3: General rules for means-tested benefits	Use this part, in conjunction with Part 2, to find out who is included in a claim for a means-tested benefit and to work out how much benefit you should get. Similar rules for tax credits are explained in Part 11.
Part 4: Paying for housing	Use this part if you are on a low income and want to check your entitlement to help with certain housing costs, including mortgage interest and rent. It explains the rules on when your rent can be restricted if you are claiming either housing benefit (HB) or UC, and the rules on discretionary housing payments.
Part 5: Other benefits	Use this part to check your entitlement to other benefits and payments. It contains chapters on non-means-tested benefits, including contributory and earnings-replacement benefits, statutory payments, 'passported benefits' and other low-income payments and benefits, arranged in alphabetical order.
Part 6: General rules for other benefits	Use this part to check whether you meet the national insurance (NI) contribution conditions for contributory benefits, to find out whether you qualify for NI credits or to check how your earnings may affect your entitlement to some non-means-tested benefits.
Part 7: Special benefit rules	Use this part if you are 16 or 17 years old, a student, in hospital or a care home, a prisoner, without accommodation or involved in a trade dispute to see how these circumstances affect your benefits, tax credits or statutory payments.
Part 8: Work	Use this part to find out how work affects your benefit entitlement, how limited capability for work is assessed, and the conditions you may be expected to meet to prepare for or find work and what can happen if you do not meet them.

Part 9: Claiming benefits and getting paid	Use this part for general information about claiming and backdating benefits and about how and when you should be paid, and to check whether you are entitled to hardship payments or affected by the benefit cap.
Part 10: Getting a benefit decision changed	Use this part if you are unhappy with a benefit or statutory payment decision and want to know how to challenge it. It covers the different ways to challenge decisions and how to appeal.
Part 11: General rules for tax credits	Use this part to understand the general rules for tax credits, including how your entitlement is worked out, how to make a claim and how to challenge decisions.
Part 12: Immigration and residence rules for benefits and tax credits	Use this part if you are a European Economic Area national or a person subject to immigration control, or if you are going or coming from abroad. It covers how your benefit and tax credit entitlement is affected by these circumstances.
Appendices	Use the appendices to find sources of further information, addresses, useful dates, the earnings limits for NI and an explanation of the abbreviations used in the chapter notes. They also contain the legislation on particular assessments, such as those of limited capability for work, and for personal independence payment and industrial diseases.

How the chapters are organised

To help you locate information easily, many of the *Handbook* chapters follow a similar structure. Each chapter contains the following.
- **Chapter contents:** use this to find the section you need.
- **Key facts:** the key points about the information covered in the chapter.
- **Notes:** notes to the numbered references in the text of the chapter can be found at the end of each chapter. In most cases, these cite the legal source of the information given in the text.

The chapters on particular benefits, tax credits and statutory payments also usually contain the following.
- **Who can claim:** the qualifying rules for the benefit or tax credit concerned.
- **The rules about your age:** any age limits that are relevant.
- **People included in the claim:** who you can claim for, or whether you have to make a joint claim with someone else.

Part 1: Introduction
Chapter 1: How to use this book
2. Finding out which benefits and tax credits you can get

1

- **The amount of benefit or tax credit:** the rules on working out how much benefit or tax credit you should receive, with cross references to rules that are common to more than one benefit or tax credit.
- **Special benefit rules:** to alert you when there are distinct rules that apply to people in particular circumstances – eg, people in hospital.
- **Claims and backdating:** how to claim the benefit or tax credit, who should claim, the information you must provide to support your claim, the date your claim is treated as made, whether a claim for one benefit can be treated as a claim for another, and when claims can be made in advance or backdated.
- **Getting paid:** how and when you are paid, and what to do if your circumstances change.
- **Tax, other benefits and the benefit cap:** whether the benefit or tax credit is taxable, how it interacts with other benefits or tax credits, and whether it is affected by rules on the benefit cap. Plus information on other help you may get.

---

2. Finding out which benefits and tax credits you can get

Step one: do you qualify for any non-means-tested benefits or statutory payments?

What are non-means-tested benefits and statutory payments?

A non-means-tested benefit is a benefit for which it is not necessary to carry out a detailed assessment of your income or capital to work out your entitlement. You may need to meet national insurance contribution conditions to qualify for some non-means-tested benefits ('contributory benefits') and you may qualify for others just because of your circumstances. Certain non-means-tested benefits ('earnings-replacement benefits') and statutory payments are intended to compensate you for loss of earnings. Your entitlement to non-means-tested benefits is not affected by any savings that you have and your income only affects your entitlement to some earnings-replacement benefits.

If you are an employee and are unfit for work or off work because of pregnancy, childbirth or adoption, you may qualify for statutory payments (such as statutory sick pay) from your employer. Your entitlement to statutory payments depends on the level of your past earnings, but it is not affected by any other income or savings you have.

Both jobseeker's allowance (JSA) and employment and support allowance (ESA) have a non-means-tested, contributory element (contribution-based JSA and contributory ESA) and a means-tested element (income-based JSA and income-related ESA). Depending on your circumstances, you may qualify for either or both elements. If you qualify for both, in effect, the means-tested element tops up the contributory element, so check your entitlement to the contributory element first. **Note:** when you come under the universal credit (UC) system (see p19), you cannot qualify for income-based JSA or income-related ESA.

- Use the table below to see which non-means-tested benefits or statutory payments you might get. Check the benefits under all the circumstances that apply to you.
- Check which of these are 'earnings-replacement benefits' (these are marked with an * in the table).
- Turn to the chapter on the benefits you are interested in, looking at any earnings-replacement benefits or statutory payments first. The chapters are listed in alphabetical order in Part 5.
- Check whether you meet the qualifying conditions for the benefit by looking at the section 'Who can claim'. Cross references take you to further details you may need to check.
- Look in the section 'Tax, other benefits and the benefits cap' for details of how the benefit might be affected by other benefits you already get or want to claim. Because of the 'overlapping benefit' rules certain non-means-tested benefits cannot be paid in full at the same time.
- If you think you qualify, use the section 'How to claim' for further information on what to do next.

Your circumstances	Benefits you might get	Chapter
Bereaved	Bereavement payment	Chapter 24
	Widowed parent's allowance*	Chapter 24
	Bereavement allowance*	Chapter 24
Carer	Carer's allowance*	Chapter 25
Pregnant or have a baby	Statutory maternity pay	Chapter 38
	Maternity allowance*	Chapter 34
	Statutory paternity pay	Chapter 38
	Child benefit	Chapter 26
Recently adopted a child	Statutory adoption pay	Chapter 38
	Statutory paternity pay	Chapter 38
	Child benefit	Chapter 26
Responsible for a child	Child benefit	Chapter 26
	Guardian's allowance	Chapter 29
Disabled	Disability living allowance	Chapter 27
	Personal independence payment	Chapter 35
	Attendance allowance	Chapter 23
	Industrial injuries benefits	Chapter 32

Part 1: Introduction
Chapter 1: How to use this book
2. Finding out which benefits and tax credits you can get

1

Unfit for work	Contributory employment and support allowance*	Chapter 28
	Statutory sick pay	Chapter 39
	Industrial injuries benefits	Chapter 32
Pensioner	Retirement pension*	Chapter 36
Unemployed and seeking work, or working part time and seeking more work	Contribution-based jobseeker's allowance*	Chapter 33

Step two: do you qualify for any means-tested benefits and tax credits?

What are means-tested benefits and tax credits?

A means-tested benefit is a benefit for which an assessment of your needs, income and capital is necessary to work out your entitlement. You can only qualify for means-tested benefits if your (and your partner's) income and capital are not too high. Tax credits are also means tested. Your entitlement depends on your assessed needs and the level of your (and your partner's) income. The assessment of the amount you need to live on for means-tested benefits and tax credits may increase if you get certain non-means-tested benefits. You may be entitled to a combination of non-means-tested benefits, a statutory payment, means-tested benefits and tax credits.

You may qualify for more than one means-tested benefit or tax credit, but you cannot get certain means-tested benefits at the same time. If you come under the UC system, see p9.

- Use the table below to see which of the main means-tested benefits and/or tax credits you might get. Check under all the circumstances that apply to you.
- Use Chapter 2 to see whether you come under the UC system and how this affects the benefits you can claim.
- Turn to the chapter on each of the benefits you may qualify for.
- Follow the procedure explained for checking non-means-tested benefits, by looking at the sections 'Who can qualify', 'Tax, other benefits and the benefit cap' and 'How to claim' in the relevant chapters.

Your circumstances	Benefits and other help you might get*	Chapter
Carer	Income support	Chapter 3
Pregnant or recently given birth	Income support	Chapter 3
	Income-related employment and support allowance	Chapter 5
	Child tax credit	Chapter 8
Responsible for a child	Income support (in some circumstances)	Chapter 3
	Child tax credit	Chapter 8

Disabled or unfit for work	Income support (in limited circumstances)	Chapter 3
	Income-related employment and support allowance	Chapter 5
Pensioners or men nearing pension age	Pension credit	Chapter 6
Have a mortgage	Income support	Chapter 3
	Income-based jobseeker's allowance	Chapter 4
	Income-related employment and support allowance	Chapter 5
	Pension credit	Chapter 6
Tenant	Housing benefit	Chapter 7
Working	Working tax credit	Chapter 9
Unemployed and seeking work, or working part time and seeking more work	Income-based jobseeker's allowance	Chapter 4

*UC is being phased in slowly and, when you come under the UC system (see p19), you will not be able to make a claim for income support, income-based jobseeker's allowance, income-related employment and support allowance, housing benefit (unless you live in exempt accommodation), child tax credit or working tax credit. You will be expected to claim UC instead. See Chapter 2 for details.

Step three: can you get any other help?

What further help is there?

If you are entitled to certain benefits or tax credits, you may qualify for other benefits on that basis. These are called 'passported benefits'. Some of these passported benefits can also be awarded on the basis of your circumstances or age, or if you have a low income. Other assistance may be available to people in certain circumstances and may be means tested – eg, help with the cost of council tax.

Entitlement to some of these payments is discretionary.

- Use the tables on pp10–11 to see the other help you may be able to get in your circumstances and to see whether the benefits or tax credits you get help you qualify for any additional 'passported benefits'.
- Use the relevant chapters to check whether you qualify for such help and how to apply.
- Check whether you qualify for council tax reduction (see p827).
- Check Chapter 40 to see if there are any other payments or other kinds of help you might be able to get.

Part 1: Introduction
Chapter 1: How to use this book
2. Finding out which benefits and tax credits you can get

1

Your circumstances	Benefits and other help you might get	Chapter
Bereaved	Funeral expenses payment	Chapter 37
Pregnant or recently given birth	Sure Start maternity grant	Chapter 37
	Health benefits	Chapter 30
	Healthy Start food and vitamins	Chapter 40
Responsible for a child	Free school lunches	Chapter 40
	Health benefits for child	Chapter 30
	Healthy Start food and vitamins	Chapter 40
Disabled or unfit for work	Cold weather payment	Chapter 37
Pensioners or men nearing	Winter fuel payment	Chapter 37
pension age	Cold weather payment	Chapter 37
	Health benefits	Chapter 30
Own a home	Council tax reduction	Chapter 40
Tenant	Council tax reduction	Chapter 40
	Discretionary housing payment	Chapter 21
Not enough money to meet	Budgeting loan	Chapter 37
certain needs	Budgeting advance of universal credit	Chapter 10
	Health benefits	Chapter 30
	Council tax reduction	Chapter 40
	Other payments	Chapter 40

Passported benefit	Passports
Free school lunches (p832)*	Income support
	Income-based jobseeker's allowance
	Income-related employment and support allowance
	Some people on child tax credit
	Guarantee credit of pension credit (England and Wales only)
	Universal credit
Health benefits (Chapter 30)**	Income support
	Income-based jobseeker's allowance
	Income-related employment and support allowance
	Some people on child tax credit
	Some people on working tax credit
	Guarantee credit of pension credit
	Universal credit**

Note: some health benefits are free for everyone in Scotland and Wales.

Sure Start maternity grant (p770)	Income support
	Income-based jobseeker's allowance
	Income-related employment and support allowance
	Pension credit (either or both credits)
	Some people on child tax credit
	Some people on working tax credit
	Universal credit
Social fund funeral expenses payment (p772)	Income support
	Income-based jobseeker's allowance
	Income-related employment and support allowance
	Pension credit (either or both credits)
	Some people on child tax credit
	Some people on working tax credit
	Housing benefit
	Universal credit
Social fund cold weather payment (p778)	Some people on income support
	Some people on income-based jobseeker's allowance
	Some people on income-related employment and support allowance
	Pension credit (either or both credits)
	Some people on universal credit
Social fund budgeting loan (p765)	Income support
	Income-based jobseeker's allowance
	Income-related employment and support allowance
	Pension credit (either or both credits)

* In England, from September 2014, all children in reception and years one and two will be entitled to free school lunches. In Scotland, this is likely to apply to children in P1, P2 and P3 from January 2015.

** At the time of writing, entitlement to UC acts as a passport to health benefits. However, in England it is not known if this will continue to apply after 31 October 2014, and in Wales, after 31 March 2015. See CPAG's online service and *Welfare Rights Bulletin* for updates.

Part 1: Introduction
Chapter 1: How to use this book
4. Finding answers to specific questions

1

3. **Working out how much benefit you should receive**

How much benefit will you get?

The amount you get depends on which benefit you are claiming. Some non-means-tested benefits are paid at different rates depending on your circumstances. The amount of some contributory benefits may depend on your national insurance contribution record (or that of your spouse or civil partner), and some (but not all) non-means-tested earnings-replacement benefits are affected by certain types of income. The amount of means-tested benefits you get always depends on your circumstances and involves a detailed assessment of your needs, your income and your capital. Your entitlement to tax credits also depends on an assessment of your needs and income. Tables of benefit and tax credit rates for 2014/15 are on ppxiii–xx.

- Look at the chapters dealing with the benefit(s) you are interested in, checking the non-means-tested benefits and statutory payments chapters first. This is because any non-means-tested benefits you get may affect the amount of means-tested benefit to which you are entitled.
- If you are not already getting the benefit, check you meet the entitlement conditions and then look at the section 'The amount of benefit'. Follow any relevant cross references for more detailed information about different aspects of the calculation.
- Check the section 'Tax, other benefits and the benefit cap' for additional information on how the benefit or tax credit may be affected by other benefits or tax credits you receive.
- If in doubt, use Appendix 2 for details of where you can get further help.

4. **Finding answers to specific questions**

If you have a specific question about a particular benefit or tax credit, there are various ways to find the information you are looking for.
- Look at the chapter covering the benefit or tax credit you are interested in. Use the chapter contents to direct you to the likely section to check. Cross references in the text direct you to other parts of the book that contain related information.
- Alternatively, use the index to find the page number for the information you need.
- Once you have located information about your question, you can check the law by using the legal references in the notes at the end of the chapter (see p13).

5. Finding information on challenging a decision

Who makes decisions and how can you challenge them?

The Department for Work and Pensions (DWP) is responsible for administering most benefits through Jobcentre Plus, the Pension Service and the Disability and Carers Service. HM Revenue and Customs (HMRC) is responsible for administering tax credits, child benefit and guardian's allowance. HMRC also makes decisions on your national insurance (NI) contribution record and on your entitlement to statutory payments if you and your employer do not agree. Local authorities administer housing benefit, the council tax reduction scheme, certain education benefits and help with community care and in a crisis.

HM Courts and Tribunals Service, which is part of the Ministry of Justice, is responsible for administering benefit and tax credit appeals.

You can request a 'revision' (or, in some cases, a 'supersession') of most decisions, or you may be able to appeal. You are likely to have to apply for a revision before you can appeal. The ways you can challenge a decision, and the procedures and time limits for doing so, depend on the benefit to which the challenge relates and on whether the decision you want to challenge is an initial decision or one that has been made following a revision, supersession or appeal.

- First check whether the decision is correct. See p12 for how to find answers to specific questions.
- If you think it is not, use the chapters in Part 10 or, for tax credits, Chapter 68, to find information on how you may be able to challenge the decision. For decisions relating to NI contributions, see p842.
- Alternatively, look up 'challenging a decision' in the index. The sub-entries under it may help you to find the page number for the type of decision you want to challenge .

6. Finding the law relevant to your situation

How do you find the law?

This *Handbook* provides references to the law (both legislation and relevant cases) and to guidance, to help you trace the source of the information given in the text. In particular, if you are appealing against a decision, it may be helpful to refer to the references given for further information. For a useful introduction to legal sources, see pp1358–62.

- Find the information in the book relevant to the issue you want to check and find the footnote for that information.

Part 1: Introduction
Chapter 1: How to use this book
7. Using the index

1

- Check the note on the relevant footnote at the end of the chapter for the legal reference.
- Check Appendix 14 for an explanation of the abbreviations used in the references.
- See Appendices 2 and 3 for where to find the law and guidance online and for other useful sources of information.

Note: the law referred to in this *Handbook* applies in Great Britain. The equivalent law in Northern Ireland is very similar and, in most cases, has the same effect. Many of the differences are due to the fact that the legislation and the administrative and adjudicating bodies in Northern Ireland are named differently. However, in some cases the differences may be more significant.

7. **Using the index**

The index contains entries in bold type, directing you to the general information on the subject or to the page where the subject is covered more fully. Sub-entries under the bold headings are listed alphabetically and direct you to specific aspects of the subject.

Part 2

Main means-tested benefits and tax credits

Part 2

Main means-tested benefits and tax credits

Chapter 2

Introduction of universal credit

This chapter covers:
1. The introduction of universal credit (below)
2. When you come under the universal credit system (p19)

Key facts
- When you come under the universal credit (UC) system, UC replaces most means-tested benefits and tax credits.
- A 'pathfinder', introducing UC for certain new claimants, started in April 2013 and currently applies in 10 areas. More groups of claimants and more areas in north west England are due to be added during 2014. The government intends that UC will be introduced across the whole of Great Britain during 2016, by which time all new claims will be for UC.
- Existing claims of most means-tested benefits and tax credits are due to be transferred to UC during 2016 and 2017. Existing claimants of income-related employment and support allowance will be transferred later than 2017.
- Official plans for the introduction of UC are subject to change.

1. The introduction of universal credit

Universal credit (UC) is a new benefit that combines means-tested support for adults under the qualifying age for pension credit (PC) and children into one benefit.

When you are able to make a claim for UC, this *Handbook* refers to you as coming under the UC system.

When you come under the UC system (see p19), UC replaces the following means-tested benefits and tax credits:
- income support (IS);
- income-based jobseeker's allowance (JSA);
- income-related employment and support allowance (ESA);
- housing benefit (HB) (except for exempt accommodation – see p416);

Part 2: Main means-tested benefits and tax credits
Chapter 2: Introduction of universal credit
1. The introduction of universal credit

- child tax credit (CTC);
- working tax credit (WTC).

Although UC does not replace PC, if you or your partner are entitled to PC, you cannot come under the UC system (see p19).

Even though you come under the UC system, you can still claim other benefits. So, for example, you can still claim contribution-based JSA, contributory ESA, child benefit and carer's allowance, as well as UC.

Timetable

UC is being introduced more slowly than planned. Originally, it was planned to introduce UC for certain single unemployed claimants without children in 'pathfinder' areas during 2013 and then for all new claimants in Great Britain by 2014, and to have replaced existing claims of the above means-tested benefits and tax credits by 2017.[1] However, due to various problems, including with the required information technology, these plans were changed during 2013.

UC has now been introduced in 10 pathfinder areas. Once 'safely tested', the government plans to introduce UC for new claimants in more areas of north west England by the end of 2014. The type of claimants who can claim UC will also be expanded to include some couples from summer 2014, and families with children from autumn 2014.[2] For more information on the areas in which UC has been introduced, see p20, and for more information on who can claim UC, see p20.

The official 'current planning assumption' is that UC will be fully introduced for new claimants across all areas of Great Britain during 2016. At this point, no new claims for the means-tested benefits and tax credits UC replaces will be possible. The government intends that the 'majority' of existing claims for these benefits and tax credits will be transferred to UC during 2016 and 2017. Current claimants of income-related ESA will not have been transferred by 2017 and the estimated 600,000 to 700,000 people still getting income-related ESA will be transferred at a later date.[3]

Timetable

April 2013	Universal credit pathfinder introduced.
April 2014	Universal credit pathfinder applies in 10 areas.
Summer 2014	New universal credit claims from some couples introduced.
Autumn 2014	New universal credit claims from some families with children introduced.
End 2014	Universal credit pathfinder introduced to more areas in north west England.
2016	Universal credit fully introduced for new claims throughout Great Britain.

| 2016 to 2017 | Most current claims of means-tested benefits and tax credits transferred to claims for universal credit. |
| Post 2017 | Transfer of current claims of income-related employment and support allowance to claims for universal credit. |

Note: the official plans for the introduction of UC are subject to change. The original plans have already been changed significantly, and the official approach is to 'test' and 'learn' from the introduction of UC as it is introduced. The government has confirmed, in particular, that the 'final decisions' on the introduction of UC will be informed by the development of the required information technology.[4] See CPAG's online service and *Welfare Rights Bulletin* for updates.

2. When you come under the universal credit system

You come under the universal credit (UC) system if you:[5]
- live in an area in which UC has been introduced (see p20); *and*
- meet certain personal conditions (see p20); *and*
- you are not already entitled to income support (IS), income-based jobseeker's allowance (JSA), income-related employment and support allowance (ESA), housing benefit (HB), except for exempt (or, from 3 November 2014, specified) accommodation (see p474), pension credit (PC), child tax credit (CTC) or working tax credit (WTC).

If you come under the UC system, you can claim UC. **Note:** you also come under the UC system if you meet the conditions above and you make a new claim for contribution-based JSA or contributory ESA (see p22).

If you come under the UC system, but your circumstances then change (eg, you move to a different area), special rules apply to decide whether you still come under the UC system (see p22).

UC replaces most other means-tested benefits and tax credits, so if you come under the UC system you can no longer qualify for:[6]
- IS;
- income-based JSA. This is abolished in your case if you come under the UC system and you make a new claim for income-based or contribution-based JSA, income-related or contributory ESA, or UC;[7]
- income-related ESA. This is abolished in your case if you come under the UC system and you make a new claim for income-related or contributory ESA, income-based or or contribution-based JSA, or UC;[8]

Part 2: Main means-tested benefits and tax credits
Chapter 2: Introduction of universal credit
2. When you come under the universal credit system

2

- HB, except for exempt (or, from 3 November 2014, specified) accommodation – see p474;
- CTC;
- WTC.

UC does not replace pension credit (PC). However, you only come under the UC system if you and your partner are aged under 60 years and six months (see p21). If you come under the UC system, but later become a member of a couple and your partner is entitled to PC, you no longer come under the UC system (see p22).

Note: even if you are not entitled to UC, if you come under the UC system, you cannot qualify for income-based JSA or income-related ESA.[9]

The areas in which universal credit has been introduced

UC is being introduced on a gradual basis for certain claimants in certain areas of the country. The areas in which UC had been introduced by April 2014 are known as the UC 'pathfinders'. Claimants who live in these areas and also meet the personal conditions for UC (see below) are sometimes referred to as being in the 'pathfinder group'.

UC has currently been introduced in the following postcode areas:
- Ashton-under-Lyne;
- Wigan;
- Warrington;
- Oldham;
- Hammersmith;
- Rugby;
- Inverness;
- Shotton;
- Bath;
- Harrogate.

The government intends to begin expanding the pathfinder in certain areas of north west England by the end of 2014. UC is due to be introduced for all new claimants in all areas of Great Britain during 2016.[10] For details of all the postcode areas in which UC has been introduced, see www.gov.uk/universal-credit/eligibility.

The personal conditions

You must meet certain personal conditions in order to come under the UC system. People who meet these conditions and also live in an area in which UC has been introduced are sometimes referred to as being in the 'pathfinder group'.

To meet the personal conditions for coming under the UC system, the following must apply.[11]

- You must not be entitled to IS, JSA (either contribution-based or income-based), ESA (either contributory or income-related), HB (except for exempt accommodation – see p474), CTC, WTC, incapacity benefit, severe disablement allowance, disability living allowance or personal independence payment.
- You must not have an ongoing appeal for IS, JSA, ESA, HB, CTC or WTC. If an appeal has been determined, there must not be a possibility of a further appeal.
- If you were previously on JSA or ESA, your claim must have stopped more than two weeks before the date of your claim for UC.

In addition, you must:[12]
- be a single person (but note that some couples can claim from summer 2014). See p22 if you become a member of a couple after you have claimed UC;
- be aged at least 18 but less than 60 years and six months;
- be a British citizen who has resided in the UK throughout the two years before your claim for UC without a continuous absence of four weeks or more during that time;
- have a national insurance number, and a bank, building society, Post Office or credit union current account;
- be fit for work – ie, not be covered by a medical certificate or have been found by the DWP to have limited capability for work;
- have capital of less than £6,000.

You must not:
- be pregnant or within 15 weeks of having given birth;
- be working or expecting to earn more than £270 in the next month (if you are under 25) or £330 in the next month (if you are 25 or over);
- be self-employed (ie, have earnings from self-employment) in the month before you claim UC;
- be in education or training, or planning to be in education or training;
- have a child under 16 (or a 'qualifying young person' for whom you are responsible – see p210) living with you some or all of the time, not be a foster parent, not be a carer (except if you are providing care as paid or voluntary employment), or be liable to pay child support maintenance under the Child Support Act 1991. **Note:** some families with children may be able to claim from autumn 2014;
- be homeless, or live in temporary or supported accommodation;
- be an owner-occupier;
- live in the same household as a member of the armed forces who is absent from the household in connection with that role.

Note: the rules on who can claim UC will change during 2014. It is expected that:
- from summer 2014, new claims from couples will be allowed. Initially, this may be limited to certain types of couples – eg, those who are unemployed;

Part 2: Main means-tested benefits and tax credits
Chapter 2: Introduction of universal credit
2. When you come under the universal credit system

- from autumn 2014, new claims from families with children will be allowed. Initially, this may be limited in some way.

These plans are subject to change. See CPAG's online services and *Welfare Rights Bulletin* for updates.

Note: if you claim UC and do not meet the personal conditions, your claim for UC is not allowed. If you claim UC and give incorrect information about your personal conditions, unless you have already been paid UC, if you then claim one of the means-tested benefits or tax credits it replaces within one month, the date of claim is treated as the date you claimed UC. However, if you have already been paid UC, your UC award continues.[13]

Contribution-based jobseeker's allowance and contributory employment and support allowance

If you make a new claim for contribution-based JSA or contributory ESA, you live in an area where UC has been introduced and you meet the personal conditions, you come under the UC system.[14] The rules about claiming and getting paid these benefits (eg, the rules on overpayments, claimant responsibilities and sanctions) may be different from those that apply to people who do not come under the UC system. If you come under the UC system, you must claim UC if you need to 'top up' your contribution-based JSA or contributory ESA.

If your circumstances change

Once you come under the UC system, if you are entitled to UC and continue to satisfy the entitlement conditions (the basic conditions and the financial conditions – see p183), you continue to get UC even if you move to an area in which UC has not been introduced, or you cease to satisfy the personal conditions above.[15] So, for example, if you have a child or you become ill after getting UC, you remain entitled to UC.

If you get contribution-based JSA or contributory ESA and you come under the UC system but are not entitled to UC (eg, because your income is too high), you no longer come under the UC system if you move to an area in which UC has not been introduced or you cease to satisfy the personal conditions.

Couples

You still come under the UC system (and remain entitled to UC) if you cease to satisfy the personal conditions because you have become part of a couple. In this situation, you can be entitled to UC with your partner, provided you satisfy the basic and financial rules of entitlement as a couple. **Note:** these rules may change as more couples come under the UC system. See CPAG's online service and *Welfare Rights Bulletin* for updates.

If your partner was not entitled to UC as a single person, any award s/he has of IS, income-based JSA, income-related ESA, HB (except for exempt accommodation – see p416), WTC or CTC will cease and you are treated as claiming UC as a couple.[16] If your partner was also entitled to UC as a single person, you are entitled to UC as a couple without having to make a claim.[17]

Example

Gareth has been entitled to UC as a single person since June 2014. He meets Jane, and forms a couple with her in August 2014. Jane is entitled to IS as a lone parent (she has a son aged two), as well as CTC and HB. They come under the UC system as a couple and are treated as claiming UC. Gareth and Jane satisfy the basic rules of entitlement for UC as a couple, and are entitled to UC.

Jane's awards of IS, CTC and HB are terminated.

Note: if your new partner is entitled to PC, you no longer come under the UC system (and cannot get UC) unless your partner stops claiming PC.[18] The government has said that couples who are already on PC do not have to move to UC.[19]

If you were entitled to UC as a couple but now separate from your partner, you may still be entitled to UC as a single person (and so remain under the UC system), even if you no longer live in an area in which UC has been introduced or do not meet the personal conditions. Whichever one of you reports the change to the DWP (or who is the first to do so) must make a new claim for UC.[20]

Example

Rose and Nelson were entitled to UC as joint claimants. They separate and Rose, who is pregnant, leaves the area. Nelson notifies the DWP of the fact that they are no longer a couple. Nelson comes under the UC system as a single person and makes a new claim for UC. Rose remains under the UC system and is entitled to UC as a single claimant without having to make a claim, even though she is no longer in an area in which UC has been introduced and does not meet the personal conditions.

If you are not entitled to universal credit

If the change in your circumstances means that you are no longer entitled to UC (eg, because your income is now too high), you still come under the UC system if you continue to live in an area in which UC has been introduced and you satisfy the personal conditions. You may be entitled to UC again in the future – eg, if your income decreases.[21]

If you are not entitled to UC and you no longer live in an area in which UC has been introduced or you no longer satisfy the personal conditions, you no longer

Part 2: Main means-tested benefits and tax credits
Chapter 2: Introduction of universal credit
Notes

come under the UC system and you cannot make a claim for UC. Instead, you can claim the benefits and tax credits that UC replaces.[22]

Notes

1. The introduction of universal credit

1 *Managing the Build-up of Claims to Universal Credit*, DWP Policy Briefing Note 15, November 2011

2 House of Commons, *Hansard*, written ministerial statement on universal credit progress, 5 December 2013; DWP press release, 'Universal credit progress', 5 December 2013

3 House of Lords, *Hansard*, universal credit statement, cols 723-27, 10 December 2013

4 House of Commons, *Hansard*, written ministerial statement on universal credit progress, 5 December 2013; DWP press release, 'Universal credit progress', 5 December 2013

2. When you come under the universal credit system

5 Reg 3 UC(TP) Regs

6 See for example the information at www.gov.uk/universal-credit, and DWP press release, 'Universal credit expands to London', 28 October 2013

7 Art 4 WRA(No.9)O

8 Art 4 WRA(No.9)O

9 Reg 15 UC(TP) Regs. Income-based JSA and income-related ESA are not mentioned, but are abolished for anyone who comes under the UC system and claims UC, or any JSA or ESA, by Art 4 WRA (No.9)O.

10 House of Commons, *Hansard*, written ministerial statement on UC progress, 5 December 2013; DWP press release, 'Universal credit progress', 5 December 2013

11 Reg 7 UC(TP) Regs

12 Regs 5-6 and 8-12 UC(TP) Regs

13 Reg 13 UC(TP) Regs

14 These benefits are not abolished under the UC system and can be claimed under the JSA Regs 2013 and the ESA Regs 2013.

15 Reg 3 UC(TP) Regs only requires that you live in a UC area and satisfy the personal conditions at the time of the claim; HB Circular A13/2013

16 Regs 3(4) and 16 UC(TP) Regs

17 Reg 14(1) UC(TP) Regs; reg 9(7) UC,PIP,JSA&ESA(C&P) Regs; para M1023 ADM

18 Reg 3(2)-(5) UC(TP) Regs; paras M1041-43 ADM

19 House of Commons, *Hansard*, 20 April 2011, col 553

20 Regs 3(2) and 14(1) UC(TP) Regs; reg 9(6) UC,PIP,JSA&ESA(C&P) Regs; paras M1024-25 ADM

21 Art 4 WRA(No.9)O still applies so as to abolish income-based JSA and income-related ESA

22 Art 6 WRA(No.9)O; paras S8041 and V8041 ADM

Chapter 3

Income support

This chapter covers:
1. Who can claim income support (p26)
2. The rules about your age (p32)
3. People included in the claim (p33)
4. The amount of benefit (p33)
5. Special benefit rules (p35)
6. Claims and backdating (p35)
7. Getting paid (p39)
8. Tax, other benefits and the benefit cap (p41)

Key facts

- Income support (IS) is a benefit for people on a low income who are in one of the specific groups of people who can claim.
- IS is a means-tested benefit.
- You do not have to have paid national insurance contributions to qualify.
- You cannot qualify for IS if you (or your partner) are in full-time paid work.
- IS is administered and paid by the DWP.
- If you disagree with an IS decision, you can apply for a revision or a supersession, or appeal against it. You are likely to have to apply for a revision before you can appeal.

Future changes
The government says that, in 2016 you will no longer be able to make a new claim for IS. During 2016 and 2017, the DWP will begin to transfer existing IS claims to universal credit (UC). See p18 for further information.

At some point in the future, you may have to accept a 'claimant commitment' (see p1064) that records what your responsibilities are in return for getting IS. There may be exceptions to this rule.

See CPAG's online service and *Welfare Rights Bulletin* for updates.

Part 2: Main means-tested benefits and tax credits
Chapter 3: Income support
1. Who can claim income support

1. Who can claim income support

You qualify for income support (IS) if:[1]

- you fit into one of the specific groups of people who can claim IS (see pp26–31). Broadly, these are:
  - sick and disabled people;
  - people looking after children and with other responsibilities;
  - carers;
  - pupils, students and people on training courses;
  - other groups – eg, people in custody pending trial or sentence, refugees learning English and some people involved in a trade dispute;
- neither you nor your partner count as being in full-time paid work (see p31 and Chapter 46);
- you are not studying full time. There are exceptions to this rule (see p908). See p903 if you are at school or college in 'relevant education'. See p909 if you are studying part time;
- you are not entitled to jobseeker's allowance (JSA), or employment and support allowance (ESA);
- your partner is not entitled to income-based JSA, joint-claim JSA, income-related ESA or pension credit (PC);
- you are at least 16 and are under the qualifying age for PC (see p78);
- your income is less than your applicable amount (see p33);
- your savings and other capital are worth £16,000 or less. Some capital (in particular, your home) is ignored (see Chapter 17);
- you satisfy the 'habitual residence test' and the 'right to reside test', and are present in Great Britain. To find out if you are exempt from the tests, see Chapter 70. To see if you can claim IS during a temporary absence abroad, see p1578; *and*
- you are not a 'person subject to immigration control' (see p1500). There are exceptions to this rule.

In some cases, you (and your partner if you have one) may be required to attend a work-focused interview (see p1056). If the only reason you are claiming IS is because you are a lone parent and you do not have any children under three, you may be required to undertake work-related activity (see p1061).

Note: if you come under the universal credit (UC) system (see p19), you cannot make a new claim for IS and should claim UC instead.

Groups of people who can claim income support

You can claim IS if you satisfy the other rules for getting IS described above and you fit into one of the groups of people who can claim.[2] If you fit into one of the groups on any day in a benefit week, you count as doing so for the whole week.

Note:

- If you are getting IS on the basis that you fit into one of the groups of people who can claim, but your circumstances change and you no longer fit into that group, check to see if you fit into any of the other groups of people who can claim. If you do, your entitlement to IS continues.[3]
- If you are a member of a couple and you do not fit into one of the groups of people who can claim IS but your partner does, s/he could be the claimant. Whichever one of you claims IS, the other may qualify for national insurance (NI) credits to protect her/his NI record (see Chapter 41).
- In the past there were additional groups of people who could claim IS. If you are getting IS on the basis that you fit into one of these groups (referred to as 'transitional groups' – see p30), you may continue to qualify on this basis.

People who are sick or disabled

You fit into one of the groups of people who can claim IS if any of the following apply to you.[4]

- You are entitled to statutory sick pay (SSP).
- You are incapable of work, but are treated as capable of work because you are disqualified from receiving incapacity benefit (IB) because of misconduct or failure to accept treatment (see p271 of the 2008/09 edition of this *Handbook*).

Some other people who are sick or disabled can still claim, or continue to be entitled to, IS if they are in a transitional group (see p30).

Looking after children and other responsibilities

You fit into one of the groups of people who can claim IS if any of the following apply to you.[5]

- You are a lone parent and have at least one child under five or are under the age of 18 and have a child of any age.
  Your child must be included in your claim (see p210).[6] You do not have to be the child's parent – eg, you could be her/his grandparent.
- You are entitled to and are on 'parental leave' from work under specific provisions; *and*
  - during the period for which you are claiming IS, you are not entitled to a payment of any kind from your employer; *and*
  - you and your child(ren) live in the same household (see p214); *and*
  - you were entitled to working tax credit (WTC), child tax credit (CTC) payable at a higher rate than the family element or housing benefit (HB) on the day before your parental leave began.
- You are entitled to and are on ordinary paternity leave;[7] *and*

Part 2: Main means-tested benefits and tax credits
Chapter 3: Income support
1. Who can claim income support

- you are not entitled to ordinary statutory paternity pay or to a payment of any kind from your employer during the period for which you are claiming IS; *or*
- you were entitled to WTC, CTC payable at a higher rate than the family element or HB on the day before your paternity leave began.

- You are a lone foster parent – ie, you are fostering a child under 16 through a local authority or voluntary organisation, or because of an order or warrant under the Children's Hearings (Scotland) Act 2011, and you are not a member of a couple.
- A child has been placed with you for adoption by an adoption agency and you are not a member of a couple.
- You are pregnant; *and*
  - incapable of work because of your pregnancy. You only have to show that you are incapable of work, not that there is a serious risk to your health or that of your baby;[8] *or*
  - there are 11 weeks or less before the week your baby is due.
- You had a baby not more than 15 weeks ago (including a still birth).

What happens when you can no longer claim as a lone parent?

1. If you were claiming IS as the lone parent of a child of four or over before 21 May 2012, you might be able to continue to receive IS as a lone parent for a period. See p31 for further information about this transitional group.

2. Unless you are under 18, once your only or youngest child turns five, you cannot qualify for IS unless you fit into one of the other groups of people who can claim described in this chapter. Check to see if you fit into any of the other groups (eg, if you are a carer or a lone foster parent of a child under 16). You can continue to qualify for IS on that basis, even if you can no longer qualify as a lone parent.[9]

3. If you no longer qualify for IS, you may qualify for JSA or ESA. If you claim JSA, there are special rules that help you satisfy the jobseeking conditions.

4. Claim CTC for your children. You cannot get allowances and premiums for your children in a new claim for IS or JSA, or with ESA.

You fit into one of the groups of people who claim IS for a temporary period while any of the following apply to you.[10]

- You are looking after a child under 16 because her/his parent or the person who usually looks after her/him is temporarily ill or temporarily away.[11]
- A child under 16 is included in your claim (see p210) and your partner is temporarily out of the UK.
- You are looking after your partner, or a child (this includes a 'qualifying young person') who is included in your claim (see p210), who is temporarily ill.[12]

Carers

You fit into one of the groups of people who can claim IS if you are a carer and any of the following apply to you.[13]

- You receive carer's allowance (CA), or would receive it had it not been restricted under the 'loss of benefit for benefit offences' rules (see p1258).
- The person for whom you care:
  - has claimed attendance allowance (AA), disability living allowance (DLA), personal independence payment (PIP) or armed forces independence payment. You are entitled to IS for up to 26 weeks from the date of that claim or until the claim is decided, whichever comes first; *or*
  - receives AA, the highest or middle rate care component of DLA, either rate of the daily living component of PIP or armed forces independence payment; *or*
  - has been awarded AA, the highest or middle rate care component of DLA or either rate of the daily living component of PIP on an advance claim, but payments have not yet been made.

You must be 'regularly and substantially engaged' in providing care. For CA, this means for at least 35 hours a week. However, to qualify for IS if you do not receive CA, the decision maker must look at the quality and quantity of care you provide. This could be less than 35 hours a week.[14]

If you cease meeting these conditions or stop being a carer, you can continue to claim IS for a further eight weeks. After that, you cannot get IS unless you fit into one of the other groups of people who can claim described in this chapter.

Pupils, students and people on training courses

You fit into one of the groups of people who can claim IS if any of the following apply to you.[15]

- You are a person in 'relevant education' or are a full-time student who can qualify for IS while studying (see p903 or p908). However, if you are a full-time student who only qualifies because you are a lone parent, see p31.
- You are on a course of full-time, non-advanced education (or were accepted or enrolled on it) and you are under 21 or you are 21 but turned 21 while on such a course. This only applies if:
  - you are an orphan and have no one acting as your parent; *or*
  - you have to live away from your parents and any person acting in their place because you are estranged from them, are in physical or moral danger or there is a serious risk to your physical or mental health; *or*
  - you live away from your parents and any person acting in their place, they are unable to support you financially and:
    - they are chronically sick, or are mentally or physically disabled (ie, they could get a disability or a higher pensioner premium, are entitled to ESA including a work-related activity or support component (or would be but

Part 2: Main means-tested benefits and tax credits
Chapter 3: Income support
1. Who can claim income support

for their one-year's entitlement to contributory ESA expiring), or are substantially and permanently disabled); *or*
– they are detained in custody pending trial or sentence or under a sentence from a court; *or*
– they are not allowed to come to Great Britain because they do not have leave to enter under the UK Immigration Rules.

- You are aged 16 to 24 and on a training course provided by the Secretary of State, the Chief Executive of the Skills Funding Agency, the Welsh Ministers or, in Scotland, by a local enterprise company. This does not apply if you are a child for child benefit purposes (see p551).

Some participants on training schemes have the legal status of employees (and are normally given contracts of employment). You do not qualify for IS if you are in full-time paid work; you might qualify for WTC instead.

If you receive a training allowance while on a course, your income may be too high for you to qualify for IS. However, you may qualify if, for example, you are on a lower rate of training allowance or you qualify for a disability premium.

Note: the rules changed on 27 October 2008, 30 December 2009 and 25 January 2010. Before these dates, there were additional groups of full-time students and people in 'relevant education' who could claim and qualify for IS. You may continue to qualify for IS on this basis. See p50 of the 2013/14 edition of this *Handbook* for further information.

Others

You fit into one of the groups of people who can claim IS if any of the following applies to you.[16]

- You **have to go to a court or tribunal** as a JP, juror, witness or party to the proceedings.
- You have been **remanded in custody, or committed in custody**, but only until your trial or until you have been sentenced. You can only get IS for your housing costs (see Chapter 20).
- You are a **refugee who is learning English** in order to obtain employment. You must be on a course for more than 15 hours a week and, at the time the course started, you must have been in Great Britain for a year or less. You can get IS for up to nine months.
- You are not treated as in full-time work because you **qualify for 'mortgage interest run-on'** (see p460 and p996).
- You are involved in a **trade dispute** or have been back at work for 15 days or less following a trade dispute (see p972).

Transitional groups

In the past there were additional groups of people who could claim IS. If you fit into one of these groups (referred to as 'transitional groups'), you may continue to qualify for IS on this basis. You may fit into one of these groups if you are claiming IS:

- 'on the grounds of disability'. See pp50–51 of the 2013/14 edition of this *Handbook* for further information. The DWP intended to transfer people getting IS on the grounds of disability to ESA before April 2014, but may not have transferred all of them. When you are transferred, you should not be worse off; your rate of benefit will be protected until April 2020 (see p662);
- as a disabled worker. See p51 of the 2013/14 edition of this *Handbook* for further information;
- as a lone parent of a child aged five or over (see below).

Claiming income support as a lone parent of a child aged five or over

If you are aged 18 or over, you fit into one of the groups of people who can claim IS if you are a lone parent and your only or youngest child is under five. **Note:** if you are under 18, you can claim IS if you are a lone parent, whatever the age of your child(ren). The age limit for a child was:

- 16, before 24 November 2008;
- 12, before 26 October 2009;
- 10, before 25 October 2010;
- seven, before 21 May 2012.

If you were entitled to IS as a lone parent immediately before these dates, you could continue to receive IS as a lone parent for a period even if your only or youngest child was older than the relevant age limit.[17] See p297 of the 2009/10 edition, p307 of the 2010/11 edition, p315 of the 2011/12 edition and p51 of the 2013/2014 edition of this *Handbook*. Your entitlement could be extended by four weeks if you had claimed CTC, but no decision had been made on your CTC claim by the time you would ordinarily have ceased to qualify for IS.

Special rules apply if you were claiming IS as a lone parent and you were a full-time student or were doing full-time training on an approved course immediately before 21 May 2012. Your only or youngest child must have been aged at least five on 21 May 2012.[18] In this case, you can continue to receive IS as a lone parent, even if your only or youngest child is older than the rules allow. You can claim as a lone parent until there is a break in your claim for IS, or until:

- you cease to be a full-time student or to attend the full-time course; *or*
- if this is sooner, your only or youngest child reaches the age from when your IS would have stopped under the rules that applied when you started your course.

Full-time paid work

You cannot usually qualify for IS if you or your partner are in full-time paid work. If you are the IS claimant, this means 16 hours or more each week. For your

Part 2: Main means-tested benefits and tax credits
Chapter 3: Income support
2. The rules about your age

partner, this means 24 hours or more each week. If you both work fewer hours than this, you can get IS. See Chapter 46 for the rules on work.

In some situations you are treated as *not* in full-time work even if you work more than 16/24 hours (see p995). In others, you are treated as in full-time work when you are not (see p994). See p990 for how your hours are calculated and p989 for what counts as paid work.

Note: if you or your partner have just taken up full-time paid work, you may be able to claim IS for help with your housing costs for the first four weeks. This is known as 'mortgage interest run-on' (see p460).

Would you be better off claiming another benefit instead?

You and your partner might be able to qualify for both WTC and IS because the rules on what counts as full-time paid work for WTC and IS are different. This may apply for example, if:

– you or your partner normally work 16/24 hours or more but are off sick or on maternity, adoption or paternity leave; *or*
– you work less than 16 hours and your partner works at least 16 hours but less than 24 hours each week.

Seek advice to see how you would be better off financially.

If your partner is at least the qualifying age for PC (see p78) and either of you are working 16/24 hours or more each week, your partner might be able to claim PC, or you and your partner may be able to claim WTC (or both if your income is low enough). There is no full-time paid work rule for PC, but earnings are taken into account when working out how much PC you can get.

If you are claiming IS because you are incapable of work, consult the DWP *before* you do any work. For work you may do while you are claiming, see p684 of the 2013/14 edition of this *Handbook*.

---

2. **The rules about your age**

You must be at least 16 to qualify for income support (IS). If you are 16 or 17, there are some issues to consider (see p888). You may instead qualify for jobseeker's allowance (JSA) or employment and support allowance (ESA). Even if you cannot get IS, JSA or ESA, you may qualify for housing benefit.

You cannot claim IS if you are at least the qualifying age for pension credit (PC – see p78). Instead, you can claim PC.

3. **People included in the claim**

If you are single, you claim income support (IS) for yourself. However, if you are a member of a couple, either you can claim IS for both you and your partner or, if your partner also satisfies the qualifying conditions for IS, s/he can claim for you both. The applicable amount that forms part of the calculation of your benefit includes a personal allowance for a couple and can include premiums based on both your and your partner's circumstances. When your benefit is worked out, your partner's income and capital are usually added to yours. See p205 for who counts as a couple.

Your applicable amount that forms part of the calculation of your benefit usually cannot include allowances and premiums for your child(ren) (but see p220). Instead, check to see if you qualify for child tax credit (see Chapter 8). However, there are some situations in which you must show that you are 'responsible' for a child who is living in your household – eg:

- in order to fit into one of the groups of people who can claim IS – eg, to show you are looking after your child who is temporarily ill or that you are a lone parent (see pp27–31);
- to show you are a lone parent so you can benefit from a higher earnings disregard (see p268);
- for some of the rules for help with housing costs (see Chapter 20).

You can count as responsible for any child under 16 and for any qualifying young person – referred to as 'children' in this *Handbook* (see p211 for who counts as a child). You do not have to be the child's parent. For when you count as responsible for a child and when s/he counts as living in your household, see pp212–15.

4. **The amount of benefit**

Income support (IS) tops up your income to a level that is set by the government and which changes every April. The amount you get depends on your needs (your 'applicable amount') and on how much income and capital you have.[19] See Chapter 14 for the rules on income and Chapter 17 for the rules on capital. There are three steps involved in working out your IS.

Step one: calculate your applicable amount

Your applicable amount consists of:

- **a personal allowance** (see p222); *plus*
- **premiums** (see p226) for any special needs; *plus*
- **housing costs**, principally for mortgage interest payments (see Chapter 20).

Part 2: Main means-tested benefits and tax credits
Chapter 3: Income support
4. The amount of benefit

Personal allowances and premiums are increased every April. If you do not currently qualify for IS, you might qualify when the rates go up.

Do you have children?

IS does not include allowances and premiums for your children. Instead, you can claim child tax credit (CTC). However, in some cases, if you are not yet entitled to CTC, you can continue to get allowances and premiums for your children until you claim, or are transferred to, CTC. See p220 for further information. If you *do* get allowances and premiums for your children, there are special rules for the treatment of their income and capital (see p257 and p344).

Step two: calculate your income

This is the amount you have coming in each week from, for instance, other benefits, part-time earnings, working tax credit and maintenance (see Chapter 14). If you have capital over £6,000 (£10,000 if you live in a care home), it also includes your tariff income (see p282).

Step three: deduct income from applicable amount

Example

Mr and Mrs Hughes, aged 27 and 29, have a daughter aged 10. Mr Hughes has been caring for his daughter, who is severely disabled. He gets carer's allowance (CA) of £61.35. Mrs Hughes gets child benefit and CTC, as well as disability living allowance (DLA) for her daughter. The couple have no housing costs to be covered by IS. Their applicable amount is:

Personal allowance	£113.70
Carer premium	£34.20
Total	£147.90

Their income (CA) to be taken into account is £61.35. Child benefit, CTC and DLA are all ignored.

Their IS is £147.90 (applicable amount) *minus* £61.35 (income) = £86.55.

If your income is too high for you to qualify for IS currently, you might qualify once you, your partner or a child included in your claim become entitled to another benefit (a 'qualifying benefit'). Make your claim for IS at the same time as your claim for the qualifying benefit (see p1149).

You might get a reduced amount of IS if:

- you (or, in some cases, your partner) were required to attend a work-focused interview and you failed to do so without good cause; *or*

2

- you are a lone parent without any children under three, you were required to undertake work-related activity and you failed to do so without good cause; *or*
- your IS has been restricted under the 'loss of benefit for benefit offences' rules (see p1258).

Different rules for calculating your benefit can apply if you are in one of the groups to whom special rules apply (see below).

5. **Special benefit rules**

Special rules may apply to:
- 16/17-year-olds (see p888);
- people from abroad (see Chapter 69);
- people who are studying (see Chapter 44);
- people without accommodation, involved in a trade dispute, in hospital or who are prisoners (see Chapter 45);
- people who, or whose partner or children, live in a care home (see p950).

6. **Claims and backdating**

To qualify for income support (IS), you must make a claim for it.[20] The general rules about claims and backdating are in Chapter 53. This section explains the specific rules that apply to IS.

Making a claim

A claim for IS can be made:
- in writing on the form approved by the DWP.[21] Send your completed form to your local Jobcentre Plus office. You may also be able to claim at an alternative office (see p1136). Return the form within one month of your initial contact; *or*
- by telephone on 0800 055 6688 (Welsh 0800 012 1888; textphone 0800 023 4888) Monday to Friday, 8am to 6pm.[22] You are sent a written statement of your circumstances for you to approve and sign.

In practice, the DWP prefers you to start your claim by telephone. There is no rule that says you must start your claim by telephone, but it is best to make your claim in the way the DWP prefers if you can. However, if you claim in writing, keep a copy of your claim form in case queries arise.

Part 2: Main means-tested benefits and tax credits
Chapter 3: Income support
6. Claims and backdating

You must provide any information or evidence required (see p37). You can amend or withdraw your claim before a decision is made (see p1138). If there is a delay in making a claim, you may be able to get a short-term advance (see p1167).

Forms

Get Form A1 from Jobcentre Plus offices or download it at www.gov.uk/income-support/how-to-claim. You may also be able to get the form at your local Citizens Advice Bureau, welfare rights service or advice centre. It is still important to telephone the DWP to let it know you want to claim IS to ensure your date of claim is the earliest possible date (see p37). You are given your date of initial contact to enter on the form.

Note:
- You can make initial contact with the DWP by telephone or letter to say you want to claim. The date of your initial contact is important because it usually determines the date on which your claim is treated as made (see p37).
- If you are claiming IS within 26 weeks of a previous claim, you might be given a shortened claim form. This is known as 'rapid reclaim'.
- You (and your partner) may have to take part in a work-focused interview (see p1056). If you are a lone parent and do not have any children under three, you may have to undertake work-related activity (see p1061).

Housing benefit

You have to make a separate claim to your local authority for housing benefit (HB). If you claim IS by telephone, your HB claim is usually completed at the same time.

If you claim IS on the approved form, you may be given an HB claim form (these are also available at www.gov.uk/housing-benefit/how-to-claim). If you are making a 'rapid reclaim' for IS, you may also be able to make a rapid reclaim for HB.

Who should claim

If you are a single person or a lone parent, you claim on your own behalf. If you are one of a couple, you must choose which one of you claims for you both. See p205 for who counts as a couple. If you have a choice about who can claim and you cannot agree, a decision maker decides.[23]

Can you change who claims?

You can change which partner claims, provided the partner previously claiming agrees.[24] It can be worth swapping who claims, for example, if one of you:
– is about to go abroad or otherwise lose entitlement – eg, becomes a student;
– fits into one of the groups of people who can claim IS but the other does not. You should both seek advice about how to protect your national insurance (NI) record;

   – is working less than 16 hours a week and the other is working between 16 and 24 hours a week (see p987 for what counts as full-time paid work). In this case, you and your partner might also be able to claim working tax credit (WTC). Seek advice to see how you would be better off financially.

If you are unable to manage your own affairs, another person can claim IS for you as your 'appointee' (see p1137).

Information to support your claim

When you claim IS, you must:

- satisfy the NI number requirement (see p1138). If you are a member of a couple, your partner must also usually satisfy this requirement;
- provide proof of your identity, if required (see p1140); *and*
- ensure you have made a valid claim – ie, you must supply information and evidence required on the claim form (see p1140).

It is important that you provide any information or evidence required when you claim – known as the 'evidence requirement'. Until you do, you may not count as having made a valid claim.[25] You should correct any defects in your claim as soon as possible or you might lose benefit.[26] See p1142 for further information about the evidence requirement and to see if you are exempt.

Even if you have provided all that was required when you claimed, you may be asked to provide additional information and evidence relevant to your claim (see p1152). There is a strict time limit for providing this. If you do not do so, the decision maker can decide your claim in the way most adverse to you.

If you have a mortgage, you are given an additional form to give to your lender. It provides details about your mortgage and returns the form to the DWP. If it is not possible to assess your housing costs (see Chapter 20) accurately or your entitlement to the severe disability premium, the decision maker can exclude these from your IS until they can be calculated.[27]

Note: you may be asked to provide information after you are awarded IS. If you fail to do so, your IS could be suspended or even terminated (see p1175).

The date of your claim

Claim as soon as you think you might be entitled to IS; you are usually not entitled to IS for any day before your 'date of claim'.[28] However, in some cases you can claim in advance (see p38) and sometimes your date of claim can be backdated (see p39). If you want this to be done, make this clear when you claim or the DWP might not consider it.

Your **'date of claim'** is usually the earliest of:[29]

Part 2: Main means-tested benefits and tax credits
Chapter 3: Income support
6. Claims and backdating

- the date you first contact a benefit office (eg, you ask to claim IS by telephone or letter or you submit a defective claim) or someone does this on your behalf, so long as a properly completed claim form (if issued) and all the information and evidence required (see p37) are provided within one month; *or*
- the date your properly completed claim form (if issued) and all the information and evidence required are received by the benefit office (or if you may claim at an alternative office (see p1136), that office); *or*
- if you claim by telephone, the date of your call. This includes where you were given time to provide required information or evidence and have done so.[30]

If you claim the wrong benefit

If you claim WTC and you are refused because neither you nor your partner are in full-time paid work for WTC purposes (see p165), your claim for IS can be backdated to the date you claimed WTC.[31] However, you must claim IS within 14 days of the decision refusing your WTC claim. You can ask for your IS claim to start on a later date instead – eg, if your income is currently too high but is due to decrease.

If you claim IS and you should have claimed carer's allowance (CA) instead of or in addition to IS, a decision maker can treat your IS claim as a claim for CA.[32] This could help you qualify for a backdated carer premium.

Claiming in advance

If you do not qualify for IS from the date of your claim (unless this is because you fail the habitual residence test – see p1521) but will do so within the next three months, you can be awarded IS from the first date on which you qualify.[33] This gives the DWP time to ensure you receive benefit as soon as you are entitled. Tell the DWP that you want to claim in advance. You might have to persuade the DWP that it can accept a claim in advance.

You might not currently be entitled to IS, but will be once you (or your partner or a child included in your claim) become entitled to another 'qualifying benefit' – eg, disability living allowance, personal independence payment or CA. You should make your claim for IS at the same time as the claim for the qualifying benefit. If you are:

- refused IS, claim again when you get a decision about the qualifying benefit and ask for your IS to be backdated to the date of your first IS claim or to the date of entitlement to the qualifying benefit, if that is later (see p1149);
- awarded IS, you might be entitled to a higher rate once the outcome of the claim for the qualifying benefit is known. Ask for a revision or a supersession if you think this applies to you (see p1294).

Backdating your claim

It is very important to claim in time. A claim for IS can be backdated for a maximum of three months, but only in exceptional circumstances. See p1146 for the general rules on backdating. Your claim can be backdated for more than three months if:

- you are claiming backdated IS after an award of a qualifying benefit and an earlier IS claim had been refused (see p1149);[34]
- you claimed WTC when you should have claimed IS (see p38).

If you might have qualified for benefit earlier, but did not claim because you were given the wrong information by the DWP or because you were misled by it, you could ask for compensation (see p1382) or complain to the Ombudsman via your MP (see p1387).

Note: if you are entitled to universal credit (UC), you cannot make a backdated claim for IS, even if this is for a period before your entitlement to UC began.[35]

7. Getting paid

Income support (IS) is normally paid by direct credit transfer into your bank (or similar) account (see p1163).[36] If you are unable to open or manage an account, payment can be made by 'simple payment'. If you are unable to act for yourself, payment can be made to someone else on your behalf – called your 'appointee' (see p1137).

When is income support paid?

You are normally paid fortnightly in arrears.[37] The day you are paid depends on your national insurance number (see p1164).[38]

You are paid in advance if you are returning to work after a trade dispute.[39]

IS is a weekly benefit. However, if you are only entitled to IS for part of a week, you are only paid for the part-week.[40]

If you are entitled to less than 10 pence a week, you are not paid IS at all, unless you are receiving another social security benefit which can be paid with IS.[41] If you are entitled to less than £1 a week, a decision maker can decide to pay you at 13-week intervals in arrears.[42]

Your entitlement to IS usually starts from the date of your claim (see p37).[43]

Note:

- Deductions can be made from your IS to pay to third parties (see p1178).
- Your IS might be paid at a reduced rate if you have been sanctioned for failing to take part in a work-focused interview (see p1099) or (if you are a lone parent

and do not have any children under three) to undertake work-related activity (see p1103) or for benefit offences (see p1258).

- If you have forgotten your PIN, see p1163. If your 'simple payment' card has been lost or stolen, or if you have forgotten your memorable date, see p1164. For information on missing payments, see p1164.
- If payment of your IS is delayed, see p1382. You might be able to get a short-term advance (see p1167). If you wish to complain about how your claim has been dealt with, see p1381. You might be able to claim compensation (see p1382).
- If payment of your IS is suspended, see p1175.
- If you are overpaid IS, you might have to repay it (see Chapter 56) and, in some circumstances, you may have to pay a penalty (see p1249). If you have been accused of fraud, see Chapter 57.

Change of circumstances

You must report changes in your circumstances that you have been told you must report, as well as any that you might reasonably be expected to know might affect your right to, the amount of, or the payment of, your benefit. You should do this as soon as possible, preferably in writing. See p1174 for further information.

If you have a mortgage, the DWP can ask your lender about any changes in the amount you owe. If you have this information (eg, from an annual statement you receive from your lender), you must also advise the DWP just in case your lender fails to do so. Make sure the DWP takes this information into account so you are not overpaid IS.

When there has been a relevant change of circumstances, a decision maker looks at your claim again and makes a new decision. To see when your IS is then adjusted, see below.

When your income support is adjusted

As a general rule, if you are paid IS in arrears, your IS is adjusted from the beginning of the week in which the change of circumstances takes effect.[44] There are a number of exceptions including the following.[45]

- If a decision is to your advantage, but you failed to notify the DWP of a change within the time limit (normally one month, but this can be extended – see p1289), your IS is adjusted:
  - if you are paid in arrears, from the beginning of the week in which you notified the change; *or*
  - if you are paid in advance, from the day on which you notified the change if this is the day you are paid benefit. If it is not, your IS is adjusted from the next week.
- Your IS is adjusted from the date of the change of circumstances (or the day on which this is expected to take place) if:

- you are paid IS in arrears and the change of circumstances means you no longer qualify for IS, unless this is because your income is too high;
- you live in a care home for part of the week and are entitled to disability living allowance or personal independence payment when you are staying elsewhere. This means that you can be paid, for example, the severe disability and enhanced disability premiums when you are staying away from the care home. **Note:** a similar rule is not needed if you are entitled to armed forces independence payment as you are paid it whether or not you live in a care home.

8. **Tax, other benefits and the benefit cap**

Tax

Income support (IS) is not taxable except if you are involved in a trade dispute and you are claiming it for your partner.

Means-tested benefits

IS is an automatic passport to maximum housing benefit (HB), but you have to make a separate claim.

You might be able to choose whether to claim IS, income-based jobseeker's allowance or income-related employment and support allowance. If you have a partner, s/he may be able to claim one of these benefits for you and, if s/he is at least the qualifying age for pension credit (PC – see p78), s/he may be able to claim PC for you, instead of your claiming IS. Seek advice about this. You may need to work out how you would be better off financially and the sort of work-focused interviews you have to attend.

Non-means-tested benefits

In some situations, while you are on IS you get national insurance credits (see Chapter 41).

Most non-means-tested benefits are taken into account as income when working out the amount of IS you get. Attendance allowance, disability living allowance, personal independence payment, armed forces independence payment, guardian's allowance and, if you are getting child tax credit (CTC), child benefit are not taken into account. It can be worth claiming non-means-tested benefits. If you or your partner qualify for certain of these, you also qualify for certain premiums (see p226) and, therefore, a higher rate of IS.

You might only qualify for IS once you or your partner, or a child included in your claim, are awarded another benefit, known as a 'qualifying benefit'. To make sure you do not lose out while waiting for the outcome of a claim for a qualifying

Part 2: Main means-tested benefits and tax credits
Chapter 3: Income support
8. Tax, other benefits and the benefit cap

benefit, claim IS at the same time. If your IS claim is refused, once the qualifying benefit is awarded claim IS again and ask for it to be backdated to the date of your first claim (see p1149).

Tax credits

If you work less than 16 hours a week and your partner works at least 16 hours but less than 24 hours a week, you and your partner may be able to claim working tax credit (WTC). Before deciding whether to claim, seek advice to see how you would be better off financially.

If you or your partner have just stopped work or reduced your hours, you might get what is known as 'WTC run-on' for a four-week period (see p172). WTC is taken into account as income when working out your IS, but CTC is not.

IS is an automatic passport to maximum CTC and is usually an automatic passport to maximum WTC.

The benefit cap

In some cases, the total amount of specified benefits you can receive is limited to £350 a week (if you are a single claimant without children) or £500 a week (if you are a lone parent or a member of a couple). This is known as the 'benefit cap'. IS is one of the specified benefits. The benefit cap only applies if you are getting HB. See p1169 for further information.

Passports and other sources of help

If you are entitled to IS, you also qualify for health benefits such as free prescriptions (see Chapter 30) and education benefits such as free school lunches (see p832). You may also qualify for social fund payments (see Chapter 37). You may be entitled to a council tax reduction (see p827).

Financial help on starting work

If you stop getting IS because you or your partner start work, or your earnings or hours in your existing job increase, you may be able to get mortgage interest run-on (if you have a home loan – see p460) and extended payments of HB (if you pay rent – see p136). Your local authority may also provide extended help with council tax. See p838 for information about other financial help you might get.

Notes

1. Who can claim income support

1 s124 SSCBA 1992
2 Reg 4ZA and Sch 1B IS Regs
3 R(IS) 10/05
4 Sch 1B para 7(c) and (d) IS Regs
5 Sch 1B paras 1-2A, 14, 14A and 14B IS Regs
6 CIS/2260/2002
7 The rules on paternity leave are in Part 2 PAL Regs
8 CIS/0542/2001
9 R(IS) 10/05
10 Sch 1B paras 3 and 23 IS Regs
11 CIS/866/2004
12 CIS/4312/2007
13 Sch 1B paras 4-6 IS Regs
14 R(IS) 8/02
15 Sch 1B paras 10-12, 15, 15A and 28 IS Regs
16 Sch 1B paras 9A and 18-22 IS Regs
17 Sch paras 1, 6, 8 and 9 SS(LPMA) Regs; SS(LP) Regs
18 Reg 7 SS(LP) Regs

4. The amount of benefit

19 s124(4) SSCBA 1992

6. Claims and backdating

20 s1 SSAA 1992
21 Reg 4(1A), (5), (6) and (11A) and (11B) SS(C&P) Regs
22 Reg 4(11A) and (11B) SS(C&P) Regs
23 Reg 4(3) SS(C&P) Regs
24 Reg 4(4) SS(C&P) Regs
25 Reg 4(1A), (7A), (9), (12) and (13) SS(C&P) Regs
26 Reg 6(1A) SS(C&P) Regs
27 Reg 13 SS&CS(DA) Regs
28 Reg 19(1) and Sch 4 para 6 SS(C&P) Regs
29 Reg 6(1ZA) and (1A) SS(C&P) Regs; R(IS) 10/06
30 Reg 6(1)(c) and (d) SS(C&P) Regs
31 Reg 6(28) SS(C&P) Regs
32 Reg 9(1) and Sch 1 SS(C&P) Regs; reg 2(3) ESA(TP) Regs
33 Reg 13(1) and (9) SS(C&P) Regs
34 Reg 6(16)-(18) SS(C&P) Regs
35 Reg 15(3) UC(TP) Regs

7. Getting paid

36 Reg 21 SS(C&P) Regs
37 Sch 7 para 1 SS(C&P) Regs
38 Sch 7 para 3(2) SS(C&P) Regs
39 Reg 26(1) and Sch 7 paras 2, 2ZA, 3 and 6(2) SS(C&P) Regs
40 s124(5) and (6) SSCBA 1992; reg 73 IS Regs
41 Reg 26(4) SS(C&P) Regs
42 Sch 7 para 5 SS(C&P) Regs
43 Sch 7 paras 1, 3 and 6(1) SS(C&P) Regs
44 Reg 7 and Sch 3A para 1 SS&CS(DA) Regs
45 Reg 7 and Sch 3A paras 1-6 SS&CS(DA) Regs

Chapter 4

Income-based jobseeker's allowance

This chapter covers:
1. Who can claim income-based jobseeker's allowance (p45)
2. The rules about your age (p51)
3. People included in the claim (p52)
4. The amount of benefit (p52)
5. Special benefit rules (p54)
6. Claims and backdating (p54)
7. Getting paid (p60)
8. Tax, other benefits and the benefit cap (p61)

Note: unless otherwise stated, references to income-based jobseeker's allowance (JSA) in this chapter also refer to joint-claim JSA.

Key facts

- Jobseeker's allowance (JSA) is a benefit for people who are looking for work.
- There are three types of JSA: **contribution-based JSA** (a non-means-tested benefit), **income-based JSA** (a means-tested benefit) and **joint-claim JSA** (paid if you have to make a joint claim with your partner).
- You do not have to have paid national insurance contributions to qualify for income-based JSA or joint-claim JSA.
- You may qualify for income-based JSA or joint-claim JSA even if you do not qualify for contribution-based JSA and vice versa. If you satisfy the conditions for both, you may be able to get your contribution-based JSA topped up with income-based JSA or joint-claim JSA.
- You cannot qualify for income-based JSA or joint-claim JSA if you or your partner are in full-time paid work.
- You must normally be fit for work, satisfy the 'jobseeking conditions' and sign on every fortnight.
- If you lose your job because of misconduct or leave a job voluntarily, you do not take up a job or an employment programme or training scheme opportunity, or you cease to be available for or to actively seek work, you may be 'sanctioned' and your JSA may be paid at a reduced (or nil) rate.

- JSA is administered and paid by the DWP.
- If you disagree with a JSA decision, you can apply for a revision or a supersession, or appeal against it. You are likely to have to seek a revision before you can appeal.

Future changes

The government says that, in 2016, you will no longer be able to make a new claim for income-based JSA. During 2016 and 2017, the DWP will begin to transfer existing income-based JSA claims to universal credit. See p18 for further information.

1. Who can claim income-based jobseeker's allowance

You qualify for jobseeker's allowance (JSA) if:[1]
- you do not count as being in full-time paid work (see p49); *and*
- you do not have limited capability for work. However, in certain circumstances, people who are sick or who have gone abroad for NHS hospital treatment can get JSA (see p50); *and*
- you are not in 'relevant education' (see p903). In addition, if you are a full-time student, you usually cannot get JSA (see p51); *and*
- you satisfy 'jobseeking conditions' – ie, you must:
  - be available for work; *and*
  - be actively seeking work; *and*
  - have a current jobseeker's agreement with the DWP. The DWP calls this a 'claimant commitment';
  See Chapter 48 for full details of these conditions; *and*
- you are below pension age (see p752); *and*
- you are in Great Britain. JSA can continue to be paid in limited circumstances while you are temporarily away (see p1580).

The above conditions apply to all types of JSA. In addition to the conditions above, to qualify for income-based JSA, you must also satisfy extra rules (see p46). **Note:** the extra rules for contribution-based JSA are covered in Chapter 33.

You may qualify for income-based JSA even if you do not qualify for contribution-based JSA. You may qualify for both income-based JSA and contribution-based JSA.

You are not usually entitled to JSA for the first three days of your 'jobseeking period' (see p49). These are known as 'waiting days' (see p53).

Part 2: Main means-tested benefits and tax credits
Chapter 4: Income-based jobseeker's allowance
1. Who can claim income-based jobseeker's allowance

Extra rules for income-based jobseeker's allowance

You qualify for income-based JSA if, in addition to satisfying the rules that apply to all types of JSA (see p45):[2]

- your income is less than your applicable amount (see p52); *and*
- your savings and other capital are worth £16,000 or less. Some capital (in particular your home) is ignored (see Chapter 17); *and*
- your partner does not count as being in full-time paid work (see p49); *and*
- you are aged 18 or over. If you are a 16/17-year-old you might get income-based JSA if you satisfy special rules (see pp888–93); *and*
- if you are a joint-claim couple, at least one of you is aged 18 or over. If one of you is a 16/17-year-old you can get income-based JSA if the member of the couple who is 16/17 satisfies special rules (see pp888–93); *and*
- neither you nor your partner are claiming and entitled to income support (IS), income-related employment and support allowance (ESA) or pension credit (PC), and, if you are not a joint-claim couple (see below), your partner is not claiming and entitled to income-based JSA.

  If you or your partner can qualify for IS, income-related ESA or PC, check whether this would make you better off (see p61); *and*
- you are not a child (this includes some qualifying young people) included in the claim of somone who is entitled to IS or income-based JSA (see p210); *and*
- you satisfy the 'habitual residence test' and the 'right to reside test'. To find out if you are exempt from these tests, see Chapter 70; *and*
- you are not a 'person subject to immigration control' (see p1500). There are exceptions to this rule.

Joint-claim couples

If you are a 'joint claim couple' both you and your partner must usually make a joint claim for JSA and satisfy all the rules for getting income-based JSA. You are a 'joint-claim couple' if you are a member of a couple (see p205) and:[3]

- at least one of you is 18 or over. If one of you is 16 or 17, special rules apply (see p888); *and*
- neither of you is responsible for children in the circumstances described below.

There are exceptions. For the rules on when one of you does not have to satisfy all the conditions, see p47 and, on what happens if one of you does not claim JSA, see p55.

Responsible for children

You do not have to claim joint-claim JSA if you or your partner are responsible for a child (this includes some qualifying young people – see p211). For these purposes, you count as being responsible for a child if:[4]

- you are entitled to child benefit for her/him; *or*
- no one is receiving child benefit for her/him but:

- you count as responsible because s/he usually lives with you; *or*
- you are the only person who has claimed child benefit for her/him, but your claim has not yet been decided; *or*
- someone else is responsible for her/him, but s/he is staying with you so that s/he can attend school; *or*
- you are looking after her/him for the local authority or a voluntary organisation (or, in Scotland only, s/he has been boarded out with you) under specific provisions; *or*
- you are looking after her/him with a view to adoption.

Even if you do not get child benefit for your child and none of the other rules above apply, if you share actual responsibility for the child (eg, with your ex-partner) and are a 'substantial minority carer' (ie, you have the child with you for at least 104 nights a year) following a court decision, you may be able to argue that you should still be regarded as responsible for the child.[5] Seek advice and see CPAG's *Welfare Rights Bulletins* 185 (pp9–11) and 194 (pp5–6).

If, while you are claiming JSA, you and your partner:

- become responsible for a child under 16, you no longer qualify for joint-claim JSA. However, your JSA can continue without interruption if you provide the DWP with evidence of this if required.[6] You and your partner must notify the DWP which of you is to continue claiming income-based JSA for you both;
- stop being responsible for any children, or all the children concerned have either died or reached the age of 16 and are not qualifying young people for child benefit purposes (see p551), you and your partner must claim joint-claim JSA.[7] Your JSA can continue without interruption if the DWP has sufficient information to award you joint-claim JSA and you or your partner have told the DWP which of you has been nominated to receive payment for you both.

Future changes

At some point in the future, couples whose youngest child is five or over will have to make a joint claim for JSA. There may be exceptions. See CPAG's online service and *Welfare Rights Bulletin* for updates.

When joint-claim couples do not have to satisfy all the conditions

If you are a member of a couple who must make a joint claim for JSA (see p46), provided one of you satisfies all the rules for claiming JSA, the two of you can still qualify for joint-claim JSA even if the other does not satisfy the jobseeking conditions or is not in Great Britain. The one who does not satisfy the rules must be below pension age (see p752), not count as being in full-time paid work (see p49) and fit into one of the exempt groups on p48.[8] You must still make a joint claim for JSA and satisfy all the other requirements.

Part 2: Main means-tested benefits and tax credits
Chapter 4: Income-based jobseeker's allowance
1. Who can claim income-based jobseeker's allowance

2

Exempt groups

You fit into an exempt group if, for at least one day in a benefit week, you:[9]

- are studying full time. You must be:
  - a 'qualifying young person' for child benefit purposes (see p551) or a full-time student (see p905). You must normally be in education at the time you and your partner claim JSA, but there are exceptions; *or*
  - someone who can claim IS while in 'relevant education', other than a refugee learning English (see p903).

  You can only fit into this exempt group for one joint claim, unless another one is made because the first ceased when one of you started full-time paid work, was summoned to do jury service or was within a linked period (see p694 – the rules are the same as for contribution-based JSA);[10] *or*
- are a carer who could claim IS (see p29). If you cease meeting this condition or stop being a carer, you continue to fit into an exempt group for a further eight weeks; *or*
- are entitled to statutory sick pay (SSP); *or*
- are incapable of work but are treated as capable of work because you are disqualified from receiving incapacity benefit (IB) – eg, because of misconduct or failure to accept treatment (see p271 of the 2008/09 edition of this *Handbook*); *or*
- have, or are treated as having, limited capability for work or have limited capability for work but are treated as if you do not because you are disqualifed from receiving ESA – eg, because of misconduct or failure to accept treatment (see p617). **Note:** you can qualify for contributory ESA and joint-claim JSA at the same time;[11] *or*
- provide medical evidence to show that you have limited capability for work – ie, a self-certificate (for no longer than seven days) or a current medical certificate from your doctor (the DWP may accept other evidence if it is unreasonable for you to provide this). You are exempt indefinitely on this basis without having to satisfy the work capability assessment; *or*
- are incapable of work, or have limited capability for work, because of your pregnancy. You only have to show that you are incapable of work, or have limited capability for work, not that there is a serious risk to your health or that of your baby;[12] *or*
- are at least the qualifying age for PC (see p78). In practice, this only applies if you are a man at least that age but under 65. In this situation, you might be better off claiming PC rather than JSA; *or*
- are a refugee learning English in order to obtain employment. You must be on a course for more than 15 hours a week and, at the time the course started, you must have been in Great Britain for a year or less. You can only be exempt for nine months on this ground; *or*
- are required to go to court or a tribunal as a justice of the peace, juror, witness or party to the proceedings; *or*

- are not a 'qualifying young person' for child benefit purposes (see p551) and are aged 16–24 and on a training course provided by the Secretary of State or the Skills Funding Agency in England, the Welsh Ministers or a local enterprise company in Scotland; or
- are involved in a trade dispute.

If you fit into some of the exempt groups above, you should also qualify for IS. If you have limited capability for work, you may also qualify for income-related ESA. If you are at least the qualifying age for PC (see p78), you might be able to claim PC. In these cases, you can choose whether to claim IS/income-related ESA/PC or JSA. See p62 for further information before deciding what to do.

Sick and disabled people

The rules changed on 25 January 2010 and again on 1 November 2010. Before these dates, there were other groups of sick and disabled people who were also exempt – eg, if you were incapable of work, registered blind or a disabled student. You may still fit into one of these groups if your claim for JSA was made at a time when these rules applied. See p398 of the 2012/13 edition of this *Handbook* for further information.

Jobseeking periods

A 'jobseeking period' is the period during which you either meet the conditions that apply to all types of JSA (see p45) or do not satisfy the jobseeking conditions but receive hardship payments (see Chapter 55).[13] For what does not count as part of a jobseeking period, see p693. The rules are broadly the same as for contribution-based JSA although, in addition, days for which you have been refused JSA because you have not provided your partner's national insurance number also do not count as part of a jobseeking period. **Note:** periods when you were entitled to contribution-based JSA under the UC system (see p22) are included – eg, if your circumstances change and you are entitled to income-based JSA.[14]

In some cases, two or more jobseeking periods can be linked together and treated as if they were one. Also, certain periods in which you satisfy other conditions ('linked periods') can be linked to a jobseeking period (see p693).[15] This means, for example, that:
- you do not have to serve another three waiting days (see p53) to get JSA;
- if the combined jobseeking periods are at least two years, you might be able to get JSA while attending a qualifying course (see p1029).

Full-time paid work

You cannot usually qualify for income-based JSA if you or your partner are in full-time paid work. If you are the JSA claimant, this means 16 hours or more each

Part 2: Main means-tested benefits and tax credits
Chapter 4: Income-based jobseeker's allowance
1. Who can claim income-based jobseeker's allowance

week.[16] For your partner, this means 24 hours or more each week. All the rules on work are covered in Chapter 46.

If you are a member of a joint-claim couple, you cannot get joint-claim JSA if either one of you is in full-time paid work. If one of you is not working or is working fewer than 16 hours a week, the other can then work up to 24 hours a week. The person working 16 to 24 hours does not have to make a joint claim.[17]

In some situations, you are treated as *not* being in full-time work even if you work more than 16/24 hours (see p995). In others, you are treated as being in full-time work when you are not (see p994). See p990 for how your hours are calculated and p989 for what counts as paid work.

Note: if you or your partner have just taken up full-time paid work, you may be able to claim IS for help with your housing costs for the first four weeks. This is known as 'mortgage interest run-on' (see p460).

Would you be better off claiming another benefit instead?

You and your partner might be able to qualify for both working tax credit (WTC) and JSA because the rules for what counts as full-time paid work for WTC and JSA are different. This may apply, for example, if:

– your partner normally works 16/24 hours or more but is off sick or on maternity, adoption or paternity leave;

– you work less than 16 hours and your partner works at least 16 hours but less than 24 hours each week.

Seek advice to see how you would be better off financially.

If you or your partner are at least the qualifying age for PC and either of you is working 16/24 hours or more each week, you might be able to claim PC or WTC (or both if your income is low enough). There is no full-time paid work rule for PC, but earnings are taken into account when working out how much you can get.

Limited capability for work

To qualify for JSA you must not have 'limited capability for work'.[18] See Chapter 47 for details about the test that decides this. **Note:** if a decision maker has decided that you have (or do not have) limited capability for work for ESA purposes, you are automatically treated as having (or not having) limited capability for work for JSA.[19] You still have to show that you are available for work if you are ill or have a disability, and you may be asked to provide medical evidence that you no longer have limited capability for work, but there are some special rules that allow you to restrict your availability (see p1035).

Even if you have limited capability for work, you do not have to stop claiming JSA in some situations – ie:

• for certain short (two-week) periods; *or*

- if you are temporarily absent from Great Britain to obtain NHS hospital treatment under certain provisions.

See p695 for further information. The rules are the same as for contribution-based JSA.

Full-time training and study

You cannot usually qualify for JSA if you are:
- in relevant education; *or*
- studying full time. This is because you are usually treated as unavailable for work.

To find out if you can claim JSA while studying full or part-time, or while waiting to go back on a course, see Chapter 44.

2. The rules about your age

You cannot usually qualify for:
- **income-based jobseeker's allowance** (JSA) until you are 18. There are special rules that can help you qualify if you are 16 or 17 (see p888). If you do not qualify, check whether you qualify for income support (IS) or employment and support allowance (ESA) instead. Even if you cannot get JSA, IS or ESA, you may qualify for housing benefit;
- **joint-claim JSA** unless you and your partner are both 18. If only one of you is 18 or over, the other must satisfy the conditions for income-based JSA in her/his own right as a 16/17-year-old (see p888).[20] If both of you are under 18, you do not count as a joint-claim couple and so one of you may be able to claim income-based JSA for the other.

You cannot claim any type of JSA if you are pension age or over (see p752). In practice, there is usually no point in remaining on income-based JSA if you are a man of at least the qualifying age for pension credit (PC – see p78) as you qualify for PC because of your age without having to sign on as unemployed. You may also receive automatic national insurance credits (see p858). You (and your partner) should be no worse off on PC than on income-based JSA.

Part 2: Main means-tested benefits and tax credits
Chapter 4: Income-based jobseeker's allowance
4. The amount of benefit

2

3. People included in the claim

If you are single, you claim income-based jobseeker's allowance (JSA) for yourself. If:

- you are a 'joint-claim couple' (see p46), you and your partner must usually both claim joint-claim JSA;
- you are not a 'joint-claim couple', either you claim income-based JSA for both of you or, if your partner meets the qualifying conditions for income-based JSA, s/he claims for you both. Whichever one of you claims JSA, the other may qualify for national insurance (NI) credits in order to protect her/his NI record. See Chapter 41 for more details about NI credits.

If you are a member of a couple, the applicable amount that forms part of the calculation of your benefit includes a personal allowance for a couple and can include premiums based on both your and your partner's circumstances. When your benefit is worked out, your partner's income and capital are usually added to yours.

Your applicable amount usually cannot include allowances and premiums for your child(ren) (but see p220). Instead, check to see if you qualify for child tax credit (see Chapter 8). However, there are some situations in which you must show that you are 'responsible' for a child who is living in your household – eg:

- in order to take advantage of the special rules to help you meet the jobseeking conditions (see Chapter 48);
- to show you are a lone parent so you can benefit from a higher earnings disregard (see p268);
- for some of the rules for help with housing costs if you are an owner-occupier (see Chapter 20).

You can count as responsible for any child under 16 and for any qualifying young person (see p211 for who counts). You do not have to be the child's parent. For when you count as responsible for a child and when s/he counts as living in your household, see pp212–15.

Note: there are different rules about children for deciding whether you must claim joint-claim JSA (see p46).

4. The amount of benefit

After any 'waiting days' (see p53), income-based jobseeker's allowance (JSA) tops up your income to a level set by the government that changes every April. The amount you get depends on your needs (your 'applicable amount') and on how much income (see Chapter 14) and capital (see Chapter 17) you have.[21]

Your applicable amount consists of:

- a **personal allowance** (see p222); *and*
- **premiums** (see p226) for any special needs; *and*
- **housing costs**, principally for mortgage interest payments (see Chapter 20). **Note:** in many cases, you can only get help with housing costs for 104 weeks (see p437).

The way income-based JSA is calculated is the same as for income support (IS – see p33).

Do you have children?

Income-based JSA does not include allowances and premiums for your children. Instead, you can claim child tax credit (CTC). However, in some cases, if you are not yet entitled to CTC, you can continue to get allowances and premiums for your children until you claim or are transferred to CTC (see p220). If you do get allowances and premiums for your children, there are special rules for the treatment of their income and capital (see p257 and p344).

You might get a reduced amount of JSA if:

- you have been sanctioned (see Chapter 51); *or*
- you are a member of a joint-claim couple and your partner has not made a joint claim with you (see p55); *or*
- you have a partner and s/he has failed to attend a work-focused interview without good cause (see p1059). **Note:** this does not apply if you are a 'joint-claim couple' but, if you are, you both usually have to participate in interviews to qualify for JSA; *or*
- you are receiving a hardship payment of income-based JSA (see Chapter 55); *or*
- your JSA has been restricted under the 'loss of benefit for benefit offences' rules (see p1258).

Different rules for calculating your JSA may apply if you are in one of the groups to whom special rules apply (see p54).

Waiting days

You are not entitled to JSA for the first three 'waiting days' (due to increase to seven from October 2014) of any jobseeking period (see p49) unless:[22]

- your claim is linked to a previous claim for JSA so both are treated as part of the same jobseeking period. For joint-claim couples, this includes a previous claim made by either of you separately; *or*
- you (or, for joint-claim couples only, either of you) have been entitled to IS, employment and support allowance (ESA), incapacity benefit or carer's allowance within the 12 weeks before you become entitled to JSA; *or*

Part 2: Main means-tested benefits and tax credits
Chapter 4: Income-based jobseeker's allowance
6. Claims and backdating

- you are the member of a joint-claim couple nominated to be paid JSA and are in receipt of a training allowance; *or*
- you are 16 or 17 and getting JSA under the severe hardship rules (see p892).

In addition, you do not have to serve any waiting days if you swap from claiming IS or ESA to claiming JSA, or you and your partner swap which of you claims IS, ESA or JSA for both of you, and the new claim is for JSA.[23]

If you receive income-based JSA, you are entitled to maximum housing benefit during any waiting days.[24]

5. **Special benefit rules**

Special rules may apply to:
- 16/17-year-olds (see Chapter 43);
- workers who are laid off or working short time (see p1047);
- people from abroad (see Chapter 69);
- people who are studying (see Chapter 44);
- people without accommodation, involved in a trade dispute or in hospital, or who (or whose partner or children) live in a care home (see Chapter 45).

6. **Claims and backdating**

To qualify for jobseeker's allowance (JSA), you must make a claim for it.[25] The general rules about claims and backdating are in Chapter 53.

While you are getting income-based JSA, you must satisfy the jobseeking conditions, and so, as well as giving all the necessary facts about your circumstances, you are expected to participate in:[26]
- an initial interview when you claim (see p56); *and*
- an interview when you sign on (see p1049); *and*
- further interviews as required (see p1052).

Making a claim

Information on how to make a claim for JSA is on pp702–03. Remember that income-based and contribution-based JSA are two types of one benefit. In order to ensure the DWP assesses your entitlement to both, it is important to answer all the relevant questions and provide all the necessary information when making your claim. **Note:**
- If you are 16 or 17 years old, you normally have to register for work and training (see p894).

- If you are claiming JSA within 26 weeks of a previous claim, you may be able to claim without having to give as much detail of your circumstances as is usually required. This is known as 'rapid reclaim'.

Who should claim

For income-based JSA, if you are a single person or a lone parent, you claim on your own behalf. Unless you must make a joint claim for JSA (see below), if you are a member of a couple you must choose which one of you claims for you both. See p205 for who counts as a couple. If you cannot agree who should claim, a decision maker decides.[27] If you are not the person claiming JSA, you may wish to claim national insurance (NI) credits to protect your NI record (see p851) or to gain help from the schemes for assisting people to obtain employment – eg, via the Work Programme (see p1093).

Joint claims for jobseeker's allowance

If you are a joint-claim couple (see p46), you must make a joint claim for JSA.[28] Both of you must usually:

- claim JSA; *and*
- satisfy all the rules for getting income-based JSA (see pp45–46).

There are exceptions. In some cases, one of you does not have to satisfy all the conditions for getting JSA and you can still make a joint claim (see p47). In other cases, you can qualify for income-based JSA even if your partner does not qualify for joint-claim JSA (see below).

If your partner does not qualify for joint-claim jobseeker's allowance

If you are a member of a joint-claim couple and you satisfy all the rules for getting income-based JSA (see pp45–46), in certain circumstances you can qualify for income-based JSA even if your partner does not qualify for joint-claim JSA. This is the case if your partner:[29]

- failed to attend the initial interview (see p56); *or*
- failed to meet the jobseeking conditions (see p1024); *or*
- is subject to immigration control (see p1500); *or*
- is temporarily absent from Great Britain; *or*
- does not satisfy the 'habitual residence test' or the 'right to reside test' (see Chapter 70); *or*
- is over pension age (see p752). In this situation, you both might be better off if your partner were to claim pension credit (PC) for you rather than JSA; *or*
- works 16 or more but under 24 hours a week; *or*
- has claimed maternity allowance or statutory maternity pay; *or*
- is pregnant and there are 11 weeks or less before the week the baby is due; *or*
- was pregnant and her pregnancy ended not more than 28 weeks ago – ie, when her baby was born, or she had a miscarriage; *or*

Part 2: Main means-tested benefits and tax credits
Chapter 4: Income-based jobseeker's allowance
6. Claims and backdating

- is receiving an unemployment benefit from another country under a reciprocal agreement (see p1517); *or*
- is receiving statutory sick pay and was working 16 hours or more a week immediately before s/he became incapable of work.

In the first four cases, your JSA entitlement is calculated as if you were a single claimant.[30] In the remaining cases, JSA entitlement is calculated for both of you in the normal way. In all other respects, you are treated as a couple and, therefore, your partner's income and capital are taken into account.

Information to support your claim

When you claim JSA you must:
- satisfy the NI number requirement (see p1138). If you are a member of a couple, your partner must also usually satisfy this requirement;
- provide proof of your identity, if required (see p1140); *and*
- ensure you have made a valid claim – ie, you must supply information and evidence required on the claim form (see p1140).

It is important that you provide any information or evidence required when you claim. This is known as the 'evidence requirement'. Until you do, you may not count as having made a valid claim.[31] Correct any defects in your claim as soon as possible or you might lose benefit (see p57). The DWP can give you up to one month from the date of your initial contact with Jobcentre Plus, but this is discretionary.[32] See p1142 for the evidence requirement and to see if you are exempt.

Even if you have provided all that was required when you claimed, you may be asked to provide additional information and evidence relevant to your claim (see p1152). There is a strict time limit for providing this. If you do not do so, the decision maker can decide your claim in the way most adverse to you.

If you have a mortgage, you are given an additional form to give to your lender, who provides details about your mortgage and returns the form to the DWP.

Note: you may be asked to provide information after you are awarded JSA. If you fail to do so, your JSA could be suspended, or even terminated (see p1175).

The initial interview

You (or, if you are claiming joint-claim JSA, both you and your partner) must usually attend and participate in an interview (called the 'initial interview' in this chapter).[33] If you do not do so, your date of claim is affected (see p58).

If attending the Jobcentre Plus office would mean that you would have to be away from home for too long, arrangements can be made for your initial interview to be carried out by a visiting employment officer (EO). Your jobseeker's agreement (the DWP calls this a 'claimant commitment') is treated as existing until that has been done.

If you have been sent a claim form, complete it before your interview. If you do not provide all the evidence and information required, your interview might not go ahead unless you are exempt from the evidence requirement (p1143).

At the interview:

- you are told what is expected from you while you are receiving JSA;
- you and the EO discuss what work you are looking for and what you intend to do to find it. What is discussed at your interview forms the basis of your jobseeker's agreement;
- you may be referred to a job vacancy immediately. However, a jobseeker's agreement should still be completed to establish entitlement in case you do not get the job.

The interview also covers what you were doing before you became unemployed and, in particular, why you left your previous job. If the EO thinks that you may have left voluntarily or been dismissed for misconduct (and, therefore, might be liable to be sanctioned – see Chapter 51), you are asked to complete a form explaining your side of the story. The form is passed to the decision maker who may need to make further enquiries before reaching a decision on whether you should be sanctioned.

The date of your claim

You are not usually entitled to benefit for any day before your date of claim.[34] However, in some cases you can claim in advance (see p59) and sometimes your claim can be backdated (see p60). If you want this to be done, you should make this clear when you claim or the DWP might not consider it.

Your **'date of claim'** depends on whether or not you are required to attend an initial interview (see p56). If you (or you and your partner if you are a joint-claim couple) are required to attend an initial interview, your date of claim is usually:

- the date you first contact the Jobcentre Plus office if you (or both of you) attend the interview at the time specified by the DWP and a properly completed claim is provided (on a form or by telephone) with all the information and evidence required. If you (or your partner if you are a joint-claim couple) fail to attend the interview, see p58;[35] *or*
- if you are a joint-claim couple and only one of you is required to attend an initial interview, the earliest of:[36]
  - the date you or your partner first contacted the Jobcentre Plus office, provided a properly completed claim (on a form or by telephone) with all the information and evidence required is provided within one month of your first contact; *or*
  - the date on which a properly completed claim (on a form or by telephone) with all the information and evidence required is received at the Jobcentre Plus office, provided the person who is required to attend an interview does

Part 2: Main means-tested benefits and tax credits
Chapter 4: Income-based jobseeker's allowance
6. Claims and backdating

so. If you (or your partner if you are a joint-claim couple) fail to attend the interview, see below.

2

Forms
In this section, the term 'form' refers to a paper form or a claim form completed online.

If you are not required to attend an initial interview, your date of claim is usually the earliest of:[37]
- the date you first contacted the Jobcentre Plus office, so long as a properly completed claim (on a form or by telephone) with all the information and evidence required is provided within one month of your first contact; *or*
- the date on which a properly completed claim (on a form or by telephone) with all the information and evidence required is received at the Jobcentre Plus office.

The DWP can extend the time you have to provide or make a properly completed claim up to the date one month after the date you first contacted the Jobcentre Plus office to claim JSA.[38] This is discretionary, so provide your claim as required (see above) wherever possible.

Are you a member of a couple?
1. If you are a member of a couple and one of you claims contribution-based JSA but is not entitled to it and a subsequent income-based JSA claim is made by your partner (or you and your partner if you are a joint-claim couple), the date of claim for income-based JSA is the date of the earlier claim for contribution-based JSA.[39]
2. If your partner has been claiming contribution-based JSA, this expires and you claim income-based JSA, the date of claim for your income-based JSA is the day after your partner's entitlement expires.[40]
3. If you claim contribution-based JSA as well as joint-claim JSA, you and your partner are required to attend an initial interview and you do, but your partner does not, you may be able to argue that your date of claim for contribution-based JSA is the date of your initial contact with Jobcentre Plus.

If you fail to attend the initial interview
If you (or your partner if you are a joint-claim couple) fail to attend an initial interview (see p56) at the time specified by the DWP or fail to provide a properly completed claim by the date of the interview and cannot show 'good cause' for this, the rules above do not apply. Instead, so long as a properly completed claim with all the information and evidence required is provided, your date of claim is:

- if you are not a joint-claim couple, the date you eventually go to the Jobcentre Plus office;[41] *or*
- if you are a joint-claim couple and:[42]
  - you are both required to attend an interview, the date one of you eventually goes to the Jobcentre Plus office. However, in this situation, you can only get the single person's rate of JSA until the other attends an interview;[43] *or*
  - only one of you is required to attend an interview, the date the person who is required to attend eventually goes to the Jobcentre Plus office.

'**Good cause**' is not defined. All relevant circumstances must be considered. These may relate to your abilities, or to external factors. The general test is whether there is some factor that would probably cause a reasonable person of your age and experience to act, or fail to act, as you did.[44]

Note: after you have been awarded JSA, you can be required to attend and participate in regular interviews. If you fail to participate in an interview, your entitlement to JSA can end (see p1053) or you may be sanctioned (see p1054).

If you claim the wrong benefit

If you claim working tax credit (WTC) and you are refused because neither you nor your partner are in full-time paid work for WTC purposes (see p165), your claim for JSA can be backdated to the date you claimed WTC.[45] However, you must claim JSA within 14 days of the decision refusing you WTC. You can ask for your JSA claim to start on a later date instead – eg, if your income is currently too high, but is due to decrease.

Claiming in advance

If you do not qualify for JSA from the date of your claim (unless this is because you fail the habitual residence test – see p1521), but will do so within the next three months, you can be awarded JSA from the first date on which you will qualify.[46] This gives the DWP time to ensure you receive benefit as soon as you are entitled. Let the DWP know you want to claim in advance when you claim and at your initial interview. You might have to persuade the DWP that it can accept a claim in advance.

You might not currently be entitled to income-based JSA, but would be once you (or your partner, or a child included in your claim) become entitled to another 'qualifying benefit' – eg, disability living allowance, personal independence payment or carer's allowance. Make your claim for JSA at the same time as the claim for the qualifying benefit. If you are:

- refused JSA, claim again when you get a decision about the qualifying benefit and ask for your JSA to be backdated to the date of your first JSA claim, or to the date of entitlement to the qualifying benefit, if that is later. See p1149 for further information;

Part 2: Main means-tested benefits and tax credits
Chapter 4: Income-based jobseeker's allowance
6. Claims and backdating

- awarded JSA, you might be entitled to a higher rate once the outcome of the claim for the qualifying benefit is known. Apply for a revision or a supersession if you think this applies to you. See p1294 for further information.

Backdating your claim

It is very important to claim in time. A claim for JSA can be backdated for a maximum of three months, but only in exceptional circumstances. The general rules on backdating are covered on p1146. See p1053 for the backdating rules if you make a new claim for JSA when your entitlement ends after you failed to sign on or participate in an interview.

Your claim can be backdated more than three months if:

- you claim JSA after an award of a qualifying benefit and an earlier JSA claim was refused (see p1149); *or*
- you claimed WTC when you should have claimed JSA (see p59).

If you might have qualified for JSA earlier but did not claim because you were given the wrong information or were misled by the DWP, you could ask for compensation (see p1382) or complain to the Ombudsman via your MP (see p1387).

If you want to get your jobseeker's agreement backdated, see p1046.

After you are awarded jobseeker's allowance

Once you have been awarded JSA, in order to continue to receive it you (and if you are a joint-claim couple, you and your partner) have to:

- sign on regularly at the Jobcentre Plus office and attend and participate in regular interviews; *and*
- participate in further interviews as required.

If you fail to participate in interviews, you may be sanctioned (see Chapter 51). See p1048 for further information about the requirements after you are awarded JSA. The rules are the same as for contribution-based JSA. If you fail to sign on or to participate in interviews, your entitlement to JSA can end (see p1051 and p1053). **Note:**

- If you have a partner (and you are not getting joint-claim JSA), s/he might be required to attend a work-focused interview (see p1059). If s/he fails to do so without good cause, your income-based JSA might be paid at a reduced rate.
- In some cases, if you fail to provide information when required to do so, your JSA could be suspended or even terminated (see p1175).

7. **Getting paid**

Information about payment of your jobseeker's allowance (JSA) is on p707. The rules are the same as for contribution-based JSA.

Note: if you and your partner are a joint-claim couple, you must nominate which one of you receives payment for both. If you cannot agree, a decision maker decides.[47] If your JSA is being paid at a reduced rate because one of you has been sanctioned, it is paid to the other member of the couple.[48] Even if you are not the person nominated to receive the JSA, if you separate from your partner and s/he cannot be traced, you can be paid any arrears of JSA that are due.[49]

Change of circumstances

You must report changes in your circumstances that you have been told to report, as well as any that you might reasonably be expected to know might affect your right to, the amount of or the payment of, your benefit, including any that are likely to occur. You should do this as soon as possible, preferably in writing. See p1174 for further information.

If you have a mortgage, the DWP can ask your lender about any changes in the amount you owe during your JSA claim. If you have this information (eg, from an annual statement you receive from your lender), you must also advise the DWP in case your lender fails to do so. Make sure the DWP takes this information into account so you are not overpaid JSA.

When there has been a relevant change of circumstances, a decision maker looks at your claim again and makes a new decision. To see when your JSA is then adjusted, see p709. The rules are the same as for contribution-based JSA.

8. **Tax, other benefits and the benefit cap**

Tax

Jobseeker's allowance (JSA) is taxable.[50] The maximum amount of JSA that is taxable is:
- if you are claiming for yourself, an amount equal to the appropriate personal allowance for a person of your age (see p222); *or*
- if you are a member of a couple, an amount equal to the income-based JSA personal allowance for an adult couple (half this amount if your partner is unable to claim JSA because s/he is involved in a trade dispute).

The tax is not deducted while JSA is being paid but reduces the refund you would otherwise receive through PAYE (Pay As You Earn) when you return to work.

Any refunds of PAYE payments are paid to you at the end of the tax year to which they relate. Any other tax refund is paid only when you stop getting JSA.

Part 2: Main means-tested benefits and tax credits
Chapter 4: Income-based jobseeker's allowance
8. Tax, other benefits and the benefit cap

Means-tested benefits

Income-based JSA is an automatic passport to maximum housing benefit (HB), but you have to make a claim.

If you are getting contribution-based JSA, you may also be entitled to income-based JSA to top this up.

You cannot claim JSA and income support (IS) at the same time. You cannot claim income-based JSA at the same time as pension credit (PC) or income-related employment and support allowance (ESA). If you have a partner, s/he can claim IS, income-related ESA or PC and you might be able to claim contribution-based JSA, but not income-based JSA.

Which benefit should you claim?

In some situations you need to choose whether to claim income-based JSA or IS (or income-related ESA or PC). You should consider the following.

1. The rates of IS, the guarantee credit of PC and income-based JSA are usually the same. The rate of income-related ESA can be higher or lower than the rate of IS, income-based JSA or PC.

2. If you need help with housing costs, see Chapter 20:
– the upper limit for loans can be higher for IS, income-based JSA and income-related ESA than for PC (see p448);
– you might only get help with your housing costs for 104 weeks if you claim income-based JSA (see p437). You can get help indefinitely if you claim IS, income-related ESA or PC.

3. You do not have to sign on or look for work if you are claiming IS, ESA or PC (nor does your partner), although if you claim IS and are the lone parent of a child aged three but under five, or you claim ESA, you may have to undertake work-related activity.

4. You may want to claim JSA or ESA instead of IS in order to receive national insurance (NI) credits (see p851). You might not be entitled to NI credits if you claim IS.

5. If you are sanctioned, you or your partner should claim IS, ESA or PC if you are eligible.

6. If you claim PC:
– there is currently no capital limit and the tariff income rules are more generous;
– you can qualify for the savings credit of PC if your partner is 65 or over;
– there is no rule preventing you or your partner from doing full-time paid work (known as 'remunerative work'), although any earnings are taken into account when working out how much PC you can get.

Non-means-tested benefits

While you are on JSA you are entitled to NI credits (see p851).

Most non-means-tested benefits are taken into account when working out the amount of income-based JSA you can get. Attendance allowance, disability living allowance, personal independence payment, armed forces independence payment, guardian's allowance and, if you are getting child tax credit (CTC), child benefit, are not taken into account. It can be worth claiming non-means-tested benefits. If you or your partner qualify for certain ones of these, you also qualify for certain premiums (see p226) and, therefore, a higher rate of income-based JSA.

You might only qualify for income-based JSA once you (or your partner or a child included in your claim) are awarded another benefit – known as a 'qualifying benefit'. To make sure you do not lose out while waiting for the outcome of a claim for a qualifying benefit, claim JSA at the same time. If your claim for income-based JSA is refused, once the qualifying benefit is awarded claim JSA again and ask for it to be backdated to the date of your first claim (see p1149).

Tax credits

If you work less than 16 hours each week and your partner works at least 16 hours but less than 24 hours each week, you and your partner might be able to claim working tax credit (WTC) as well as, or instead of, income-based JSA. However, before deciding whether to claim, seek advice to see how you would be better off financially.

If you or your partner have just stopped work or reduced your hours, you might get what is known as 'WTC run-on' for a four-week period (see p172).

WTC is taken into account as income when working out your income-based JSA, but CTC is not.

Income-based JSA is an automatic passport to maximum CTC and is usually an automatic passport to maximum WTC.

The benefit cap

In some cases, the total amount of specified benefits you receive is limited to £350 a week (if you are a single claimant without children) or £500 a week (if you are a lone parent or a member of a couple). This is known as the 'benefit cap'. JSA is one of the specified benefits. The benefit cap only applies if you are getting HB. See p1169 for further information.

Passports and other sources of help

If you are entitled to income-based JSA, you also qualify for health benefits, such as free prescriptions (see Chapter 30) and education benefits, such as free school lunches (see p832). You may also qualify for social fund payments (see Chapter 37). You may be entitled to a council tax reduction (see p827).

Financial help on starting work

If you stop getting JSA because you or your partner start work, or your earnings or your hours in your existing job increase, you might be able to get mortgage interest run-on if you have a home loan (see p460) or extended payments of HB if

Part 2: Main means-tested benefits and tax credits
Chapter 4: Income-based jobseeker's allowance
Notes

you pay rent (see p136). Your local authority may also provide extended help with council tax. See p838 for information about other financial help you might get.

Notes

1. Who can claim income-based jobseeker's allowance
1 s1 JSA 1995
2 ss3, 3A and 13 JSA 1995
3 s1(2B) and (4) JSA 1995; reg 3A(1) JSA Regs; CJSA/2633/2004
4 s1(4) JSA 1995; reg 3A(1) JSA Regs
5 *Hockenjos v Secretary of State for Social Security* [2004] EWCA Civ 1749, reported as R(JSA) 1/05 and R(JSA) 2/05
6 Sch 1 para 9A JSA 1995; reg 3B JSA Regs
7 Sch 1 paras 9B and 9C JSA 1995; reg 3C JSA Regs
8 Reg 3D JSA Regs; Sch 1 para 8A JSA 1995
9 Sch A1 JSA Regs
10 Reg 3D(3) and (4) JSA Regs
11 s1(6A) WRA 2007
12 CIS/0542/2001
13 Reg 47(1) and (2) JSA Regs
14 Art 13 WRA(No.9)O; Art 11 WRA(No.11)O
15 Sch 1 para 3 JSA 1995; reg 48 JSA Regs
16 Reg 51 JSA Regs
17 Reg 3E(2)(g) JSA Regs
18 s1(2)(f) JSA 1995
19 Sch 1 para 2 JSA 1995; reg 10 SS&CS(DA) Regs

2. The rules about your age
20 s3A(1)(e) JSA 1995; reg 58 JSA Regs

4. The amount of benefit
21 ss4(3) and (3A) and 13 JSA 1995
22 Sch 1 para 4 JSA 1995; reg 46 JSA Regs; Art 11(2) WRA(No.11)O
23 Reg 14A SS&CS(DA) Regs
24 Reg 2(3)(b) HB Regs

6. Claims and backdating
25 s1 SSAA 1992
26 s8(1) and (1A) JSA 1995; regs 23 and 23A JSA Regs

27 Reg 4(3B)(a) SS(C&P) Regs
28 s1(2B) and (4) JSA 1995; reg 3A(1) JSA Regs; CJSA/2633/2004
29 s1(2C) JSA 1995; reg 3E JSA Regs
30 Sch 5 paras 10, 13A and 17A JSA Regs
31 Reg 4(1A), (7B), (9), (12) and (13) SS(C&P) Regs
32 Reg 6(4AB) SS(C&P) Regs
33 Reg 4(6)(a) SS(C&P) Regs
34 Reg 19(1) and Sch 4 para 1 SS(C&P) Regs
35 Reg 6(1)(c) and (d), (4ZA), (4ZB)(a) and (4A)(a)(i) SS(C&P) Regs
36 Reg 6(4ZC)(a) and (b) SS(C&P) Regs
37 Reg 6(4A)(b) SS(C&P) Regs
38 Reg 6(4AB) SS(C&P) Regs
39 Reg 4(3B)(b) SS(C&P) Regs
40 Reg 4(3B)(c) SS(C&P) Regs
41 Reg 6(4A)(a)(ii) SS(C&P) Regs
42 Reg 6(4ZB)(b) and (4ZC)(c) SS(C&P) Regs
43 Sch 5 para 17A JSA Regs
44 CS/371/1949
45 Reg 6(28) SS(C&P) Regs
46 Reg 13(1) and (9) SS(C&P) Regs

7. Getting paid
47 s3B JSA 1995
48 ss19(7), 19A(10) and 19B(8) JSA 1995
49 Reg 30A SS(C&P) Regs

8. Tax, other benefits and the benefit cap
50 ss671-75 IT(EP)A 2003

Chapter 5

Income-related employment and support allowance

Key facts

- Employment and support allowance (ESA) is a benefit for people who have 'limited capability for work' (ie, they are unable to work because of illness or disability) and who are not entitled to statutory sick pay.
- Entitlement to ESA is assessed by a test called the work capability assessment.
- There are two types of ESA: **contributory ESA**, which is not means tested, and **income-related ESA**, which is means tested.
- You do not have to have paid national insurance contributions to qualify for income-related ESA.
- You may qualify for income-related ESA even if you do not qualify for contributory ESA. You may be able to get your contributory ESA topped up with income-related ESA.
- ESA is administered and paid by the DWP.
- If you disagree with an ESA decision, you can apply for a revision or supersession, or appeal against it. You are likely to have to apply for a revision before you can appeal. All parts of the decision may be looked at.

Future changes

The government says that in 2016, you will no longer be able to make a new claim for income-related ESA. The DWP will begin to transfer existing income-related ESA claims to universal credit after 2017. See p18 for further information.

Part 2: Main means-tested benefits and tax credits
Chapter 5: Income-related employment and support allowance
1. Who can claim employment and support allowance

1. Who can claim employment and support allowance

You qualify for income-related employment and support allowance (ESA) if you satisfy the following basic rules that apply to both income-related and contributory ESA *and* if you satisfy the extra rules for income-related ESA on below.

You satisfy the basic rules for ESA if you:[1]

- have 'limited capability for work' (see p1002); *and*
- are aged 16 or over but under pension age (see p752); *and*
- are in Great Britain (see p71 if you go abroad); *and*
- are not entitled in your own right to statutory sick pay (SSP), income support (IS) or jobseeker's allowance (JSA), and are not in a couple entitled to joint-claim JSA (see p46); *and*
- are not doing any work (unless it is work you are allowed to do while claiming (see p1018)).

You are not usually entitled to ESA for the first three days of your claim (see p1017). You cannot get ESA and certain other benefits at the same time (see p74). Most claimants of ESA (except those in the 'support group' – see p621) are required to take part in work-focused interviews and some can be required to undertake 'work-related activity' (see Chaper 49).

Extra rules for income-related employment and support allowance

You qualify for income-related ESA if, in addition to satisfying the basic rules of entitlement to ESA above:[2]

- your income (see Chapter 14) is less than your applicable amount (see Chapter 12); *and*
- your capital is not over £16,000 (see Chapter 16);[3] *and*
- you are not entitled to pension credit (PC); *and*
- your partner, if you are in a couple (see p205), is not engaged in full-time paid work (p987); *and*
- your partner is not entitled to income-related ESA, income-based JSA, IS or PC in her/his own right; *and*
- you are not 'receiving education', unless you are entitled to disability living allowance (DLA), personal independence payment, armed forces independence payment, or you are a disabled or deaf student who has been transferred from IS to income-related ESA (see p662), in which case you can still qualify for income-related ESA;[4] *and*

- you satisfy the 'right to reside' and 'habitual residence' tests (see Chapter 70);[5] *and*
- you are not a 'person subject to immigration control' (see p1500).[6]

Education

You are in **'education'** if you are a 'qualifying young person' (eg, you are aged under 20 and in full-time, non-advanced education or approved training – see p551) or if you are on a course that is classed as full time.[7] The rules are very similar to those that apply to the definition of full-time courses for IS (see p906). Seek advice if you are unsure.

Note:
- There are certain circumstances in which your partner may be treated as engaged in full-time work or treated as not engaged in it (see Chapter 46).[8]
- When you claim ESA, the DWP first considers your entitlement to contributory ESA (see Chapter 28). If you are entitled to both contributory ESA and income-related ESA, you get the contributory ESA for which you qualify, topped up with income-related ESA.
- If you come under the universal credit (UC) system (see p19), you cannot get income-related ESA and must claim UC instead.

Disqualification from benefit

You can be disqualified from receiving ESA for up to six weeks (or have your benefit paid at a reduced rate if you are a 'person in hardship') in the circumstances described on p617. The rules are the same for both income-related ESA and contributory ESA.

However, if you are absent from Great Britain or you are a prisoner or in detention, the rules for income-related ESA are different from those for contributory ESA.

For income-related ESA, if you are:
- absent from Great Britain, see p1574; *or*
- a prisoner or detained in legal custody, see p961.

2. The rules about your age

To satisfy the basic rules for employment and support allowance, you must be aged at least 16 but under pension age (see p752).

Part 2: Main means-tested benefits and tax credits
Chapter 5: Income-related employment and support allowance
4. The amount of benefit

3. **People included in the claim**

If you are single, you claim income-related employment and support allowance (ESA) for yourself.

If you are a member of a couple (see p205 for who counts), either you claim income-related ESA for both you and your partner or, if your partner meets the qualifying conditions for income-related ESA, s/he can claim for you both instead. The applicable amount that forms part of the calculation of your benefit includes a personal allowance for a couple and can include premiums based on both your and your partner's circumstances. When your benefit is worked out, your partner's income and capital are usually added to yours. Whichever one of you claims ESA, the other may qualify for national insurance (NI) credits in order to protect her/his NI record. See Chapter 41 for more details.

You do not get additional amounts of income-related ESA for your child(ren). Instead, check to see if you qualify for child tax credit (see Chapter 8). However, there are some situations in which you must show that you are 'responsible' for a child who is living in your household – eg:

- in order to take advantage of exemptions from compulsory work-focused interviews and work-related activity (see p1056 and p1061);
- for some of the rules on help with housing costs (see Chapter 20).

You can count as responsible for any child under 16 and for any qualifying young person (referred to as a 'child' in this *Handbook*). You do not have to be the child's parent. For when you count as responsible for a child and when s/he counts as living in your household, see pp212–14.

4. **The amount of benefit**

The amount of income-related employment and support allowance (ESA) you get depends on your needs (your 'applicable amount') and how much income and capital you have.

You are paid a limited amount of ESA during an initial **'assessment phase'**. See p620 for more information (the rules on when the assessment phase applies are the same as for contributory ESA). This usually lasts 13 weeks. After this, there is a **'main phase'**. See p621 (the rules on when the main phase applies are the same as for contributory ESA). During the main phase you get an additional component included in your applicable amount. For the calculation, see p69.

Note:

- If you are appealing against a decison that you do not have limited capability for work and you get ESA pending the outcome of your appeal (see p1015), you are only paid at the assessment phase rate – ie, you do not get an additional component.

- You are entitled to just one award of ESA, but this may be made up of both contributory ESA and income-related ESA.[9] If you are entitled to both types of ESA, the total amount of ESA payable is the same amount as your income-related ESA, but is made up of contributory ESA topped up with income-related ESA.

Calculating income-related employment and support allowance

Income-related ESA is worked out as follows.

Step one: calculate your applicable amount
Your applicable amount consists of:
- in both the assessment phase (see p620) and the main phase (see p621):
  - a **personal allowance** (see p222). Your personal allowance is paid at a lower rate if you are under 25 or, in some cases, if you are under 18 and in the assessment phase (see p620);
  - **premiums** for any special needs (see p226);
  - **housing costs**, principally for mortgage interest payments (see Chapter 20). However, you may have an initial 'waiting period' when your housing costs are not paid (see p453);
- usually in the main phase (see p621) only: either a **support component** (see p621 – the rules are the same as contributory ESA) or a **work-related activity component** (see p622 – the rules are the same as for contributory ESA). In some circumstances (eg, if you are terminally ill), you are also entitled to one of these components during the assessment phase. **Note:** if you are transferred to income-related ESA from income support (IS) paid on the grounds of disability (see p662), the support component or the work-related activity component is included straight away as there is no assessment phase;
- a **'transitional addition'** if you have been transferred to income-related ESA from IS which was paid on the grounds of disability. See p662 for details of the transfer process and p71 for how the transitional addition is calculated.

For more details on applicable amounts, see Chapter 12.

Step two: calculate your income
This is the amount you have coming in each week from, for instance, other benefits, part-time earnings, working tax credit and maintenance (see Chapter 14). If you have capital over £6,000 (£10,000 if you live in a care home), it also includes your tariff income (see p282).

Part 2: Main means-tested benefits and tax credits
Chapter 5: Income-related employment and support allowance
4. The amount of benefit

Step three: deduct income from applicable amount

If your income is less than your applicable amount, your income-related ESA equals the difference between the two. If your income is the same as or more than your applicable amount, you are not entitled to ESA.

Example

Terry is aged 35 when he claims ESA. He lives with his wife, Julie, and six-year-old son, Ray. They get child benefit and child tax credit (CTC). Julie works 10 hours a week and earns £80 a week. Terry is not assessed as being in the support group. He has not paid enough national insurance contributions to get contributory ESA.

Assessment phase

Applicable amount = £113.70 (personal allowance for couple both aged 18 or over)

Income to be taken into account = £60 (child benefit and CTC are ignored; £20 earnings disregard applies)

Terry's income-related ESA during assessment phase is £113.70 *minus* £60 = £53.70

Main phase

Applicable amount = £142.45 (personal allowance of £113.70 for couple both aged 18 or over *plus* work-related activity component of £28.75)

Income to be taken into account (as above) = £60

Terry's income-related ESA during the main phase is £142.45 *minus* £60 = £82.45

Note:
- If you are not currently entitled to ESA because of the level of your income, but will be when either of the additional components are included in your applicable amount, you may be given an 'advance award'. Under this, you are entitled from the point the additional component is awarded, provided you still satisfy the other conditions, without needing to claim again.[10]
- Earnings you receive for 'permitted work' (see p1018) are disregarded when calculating the amount of your income-related ESA.

Your ESA may be reduced if:
- the work-related activity component (see p622) applies to you and you do not comply with the requirement to attend work-focused interviews and work-related activity (see p1056 and p1061); *or*
- you are disqualified from ESA but are a person in 'hardship' (see p617 – the rules are the same as for contributory ESA); *or*
- your ESA is sanctioned because you have committed a benefit offence (see p1258).

Transitional addition

If you have transferred to income-related ESA from IS on the grounds of disability, you may be entitled to a transitional addition in your ESA to top up the amount of your ESA to that of your IS.

When deciding if you qualify for a transitional addition, the decision maker compares the following amounts:[11]

- the IS applicable amount to which you were entitled immediately before the 'effective date' (ie, the date on which your IS was converted to an award of ESA – see p664), minus any part of your applicable amount which was for a child or for housing costs;
- the income-related ESA applicable amount to which you are entitled on the effective date, minus any part of your applicable amount that is for housing costs. Either the work-related activity component or support component is included in the amount.

If the resulting amount of ESA is more than the IS amount, you are not entitled to a transitional addition. If the ESA amount is less than the IS amount, you get the difference between the two amounts as a transitional addition to your income-related ESA. The transitional addition is reduced by the amount of the annual increase in income-related ESA (ignoring any increase in your housing costs) and by increases in your income-related ESA that occur as a result of changes in your circumstances.

If your entitlement to income-related ESA ends, but you then reclaim it, the transitional addition can be included again if:

- your new period of limited capability for work can be linked to the old one (see p1018); or
- you lost entitlement because your partner was in full-time paid work but s/he has subsequently stopped being so, and you reclaim within 12 weeks of your old claim ending.[12]

No transitional addition will be paid after 5 April 2020.

For more details, see p93 of the 2013/14 edition of this *Handbook*.

5. Special benefit rules

Special rules may apply to:

- people in prison or detention (see p958);
- people subject to immigration control (see p1500);
- people in care homes and other special accommodation (see p950);
- people going abroad. A basic rule of entitlement for employment and support allowance is that you must be in Great Britain. However, you can remain

Part 2: Main means-tested benefits and tax credits
Chapter 5: Income-related employment and support allowance
6. Claims and backdating

entitled during a temporary absence in some circumstances, provided you otherwise continue to satisfy the rules (see Chapter 71).[13]

6. Claims and backdating

To be entitled to employment and support allowance (ESA), you must usually make a claim for it.[14] The general rules about claims and backdating are in Chapter 53. Most of the specific rules about claiming ESA are described in Chapter 28. You do not have to make a claim if you have appealed against a decision that you do not have limited capability for work, the appeal has not yet been decided and you wish to claim ESA while continuing with it.[15]

If you make a new claim for incapacity benefit, income support on the grounds of disability or severe disablement allowance, this is treated as a claim for ESA.[16]

In most cases (unless you are recognised as exempt straight away), you are required to attend a medical examination to assess whether you have limited capability for work and limited capability for work-related activity. In addition, unless you are in the 'support group' (see p621), you are usually required to attend compulsory work-focused interviews and, in some cases, carry out work-related activity (see p1057).

Making a claim

For details of how to make a claim for ESA, see p627.

Income-related and contributory ESA are two types of the same benefit. When you claim ESA, in order for the DWP to assess your entitlement to both, it is important to answer all the relevant questions and provide all the necessary information.

Note: if you come under the universal credit (UC) system (see p19), a claim for ESA will be a claim for contributory ESA only, as new claimants must claim UC instead of income-related ESA.

Who should claim

Usually, you must claim ESA on your own behalf. If you are unable to manage your own affairs, another person can claim ESA for you as your 'appointee' (see p1137). For income-related ESA, if you are a member of a couple you should choose which of you claims for you both (bearing in mind that to get ESA the claimant must satisfy the entitlement rules, including having limited capability for work). Whoever is the claimant can be switched later by the other member of the couple claiming income-related ESA and (if s/he is entitled) by both you and your partner confirming in writing that you want the claim to be switched.[17]

If you are employed

If you are employed, see p628. You should normally be paid statutory sick pay (SSP – see Chapter 39) for the first 28 weeks of your limited capability for work.

Information to support your claim

When you claim ESA you must:
- satisfy the national insurance number requirement (see p1138). If you are a member of a couple, your partner must also satisfy this requirement;
- provide proof of your identity, if required (see p1140); *and*
- ensure you have made a valid claim – ie, supply the information or evidence required on the claim form (see p1140).

You may be referred for a medical assessment. If you fail to attend the medical without good cause, your claim can be refused.[18]

For further details about information or evidence (including medical evidence) that you should provide, see p628. The rules described for contributory ESA also apply to income-related ESA.

The date of your claim

The date of your claim is usually the date of your telephone call starting the claim, or the date your claim form is received. Backdating is possible (see p629).

If you claim the wrong benefit

In some circumstances a claim for maternity allowance may be treated as a claim for ESA (or vice versa) or your ESA claim can be treated as made on the date you applied for SSP (see p629).

Claiming in advance

You can claim ESA up to three months in advance if you are not entitled to it now, but will become entitled within 13 weeks of claiming, unless the reason you do not qualify straight away is because you fail the habitual residence test (see p1521).[19]

Backdating your claim

Your claim can be backdated for up to three months before the day you actually claim (see p629).

Starting work when your claim ends

If you start work and later fall sick again, you may be able to benefit from the rules on linking periods of limited capability for work (see p1018). If you have to

Part 2: Main means-tested benefits and tax credits
Chapter 5: Income-related employment and support allowance
8. Tax, other benefits and the benefit cap

claim ESA again within a 12-week linking period, you can return to the same level of ESA that you were previously receiving. **Note:** you may be able to benefit from a 104-week linking rule for housing costs (see p456)

7. Getting paid

As income-related and contributory employment and support allowance (ESA) are two types of the same benefit, the rules described on p630 on getting paid contributory ESA apply equally to income-related ESA.

For details of when your income-related ESA might be paid at a reduced rate, see p70.

Change of circumstances

You must report changes in your circumstances that you have been told to report, as well as any that you might reasonably be expected to know might affect your right to, the amount of, or the payment of, your benefit. You should do this as soon as possible, preferably in writing. See p1174 for further information.

If you have a mortgage, the DWP can ask your lender about any changes in the amount you owe. If you have this information (eg, from an annual statement from your lender), you must also advise the DWP just in case your lender fails to do so. Make sure the DWP takes this information into account so you are not overpaid.

8. Tax, other benefits and the benefit cap

Tax

Income-related employment and support allowance (ESA) is not taxable.[20]

Means-tested benefits

Income-related ESA is an automatic passport to maximum housing benefit (HB), but you must make a separate claim for HB.

You might be able to choose between claiming income-related ESA, income support (IS), income-based jobseeker's allowance (JSA) and pension credit (PC). If you have a partner, s/he may be able to claim one of these benefits for you instead of your claiming income-related ESA. Seek advice about this. You may need to work out how you would be better off financially and the sort of work-focused interviews you have to attend.

Non-means-tested benefits

You can be entitled to income-related ESA and contributory ESA at the same time.

While you are on income-related ESA you get national insurance credits (see Chapter 41).

You are not entitled to ESA if you are entitled to statutory sick pay.[21]

Most non-means-tested benefits are taken into account as income when working out the amount of income-related ESA you get. Attendance allowance, disability living allowance, personal independence payment, guardian's allowance and child benefit are not taken into account. It can be worth claiming non-means-tested benefits. If you or your partner qualify for certain of these, you also qualify for certain premiums and, therefore, a higher rate of income-related ESA.

You cannot claim ESA and JSA in your own right at the same time. If your partner is entitled to contribution-based JSA, you can claim ESA. Your partner's JSA is taken into account when assessing your income for income-related ESA.

Tax credits

If your partner works at least 16 hours but less than 24 hours a week, you and your partner may be able to claim working tax credit (WTC). Before deciding whether to claim, seek advice about how you would be better off financially.

If you or your partner have just stopped work or reduced your hours, you might get what is known as 'WTC run-on' for a four week period (see p172).

WTC is taken into account as income when working out your IS, but child tax credit (CTC) is not. Income-related ESA is an automatic passport to maximum CTC and to maximum WTC.

The benefit cap

In some cases, the total amount of specified benefits you can receive is limited to £350 a week (if you are a single claimant without children) or £500 a week (if you are a lone parent or a member of a couple). This is known as the 'benefit cap'. ESA is one of the specified benefits. The benefit cap only applies if you are getting HB. However, it does not apply if you or your partner receive ESA which includes a support component. See p1169 for further information.

Passports and other sources of help

If you are entitled to income-related ESA, you also qualify for health benefits such as free prescriptions (see Chapter 30) and education benefits such as free school lunches (see p832). You may also qualify for social fund payments (see Chapter 37). You may be entitled to a council tax reduction (see p827).

Part 2: Main means-tested benefits and tax credits
Chapter 5: Income-related employment and support allowance
Notes

Financial help on starting work

If you stop getting income-related ESA because you or your partner start work, or your partner's earnings or hours in her/his existing job increase, you might be able to get mortgage interest run-on if you have a home loan (see p460), or extended payments of HB if you pay rent (see p136). Your local authority may also provide extended help with council tax. See p838 for information about other financial help you might get.

Notes

1. Who can claim employment and support allowance
1 ss1 and 20(1) WRA 2007; reg 40(1) ESA Regs
2 Sch 1 para 6 WRA 2007
3 Reg 110 ESA Regs
4 Reg 18 ESA Regs; Schs 1 para 2 and 2 para 2 ESA(TP)(EA)(No.2) Regs
5 Reg 70 and Sch 5 para 11 ESA Regs
6 s115 IAA 1999
7 Regs 14-17 ESA Regs
8 Regs 41-43 ESA Regs

4. The amount of benefit
9 s6 WRA 2007
10 s5 WRA 2007; reg 146 ESA Regs
11 Regs 9, 11, 12 and 13 ESA(TP)(EA)(No.2) Regs
12 Reg 21 ESA(TP)(EA)(No.2) Regs

5. Special benefit rules
13 Sch 2 paras 5, 6 and 8 WRA 2007; regs 151-155 ESA Regs

6. Claims and backdating
14 s1 SSAA 1992
15 Reg 3(j) SS(C&P) Regs
16 Reg 2 ESA(TP) Regs
17 Reg 4I(1) and (2) SS(C&P) Regs
18 s19 SSA 1998; reg 23 ESA Regs
19 Reg 13(9) SS(C&P) Regs

8. Tax, other benefits and the benefit cap
20 s677 IT(EP)A 2003
21 s20 WRA 2007

Chapter 6

• •

Pension credit

This chapter covers:
1. Who can claim pension credit (below)
2. The rules about your age (p78)
3. People included in the claim (p78)
4. The amount of pension credit (p79)
5. Special benefit rules (p84)
6. Claims and backdating (p85)
7. Getting paid (p88)
8. Tax, other benefits and the benefit cap (p91)

Key facts
- Pension credit (PC) is a benefit for people on a low income who are at least the qualifying age.
- Women can claim PC when they reach pension age. Men can claim when they reach what would be the pension age for a woman with the same date of birth.
- There are two types of PC: **guarantee credit** ensures a minimum level of income and **savings credit** is intended to 'reward' you for making provision for your retirement, such as savings or occupational pensions. You can be entitled to either guarantee credit, savings credit or both.
- PC is a means-tested benefit.
- You do not have to have paid national insurance contributions to qualify.
- You can qualify for PC whether you are in or out of work.
- PC is administered and paid by the Pension Service, which is part of the DWP.
- If you disagree with a PC decision, you can apply for a revision or supersession, or appeal against it. You are likely to have to apply for a revision before you can appeal.

---

1. Who can claim pension credit

Guarantee credit

You qualify for guarantee credit if:[1]
- you have reached the qualifying age (see p78);[2]

Part 2: Main means-tested benefits and tax credits
Chapter 6: Pension credit
3. People included in the claim

- you are in Great Britain (with exceptions for periods of temporary absence) and satisfy the 'habitual residence' test and the 'right to reside' test (see Chapter 70);[3]
- your partner (if you have one) is not entitled to PC;[4]
- you have no income or your income is below the appropriate minimum guarantee (see p79);[5]
- you are not a 'person subject to immigration control', although there are exceptions to this rule (see p1504).[6]

Savings credit

You qualify for savings credit if:[7]
- you or your partner are 65 or over;[8]
- you are in Great Britain (with exceptions for periods of temporary absence) and satisfy the 'habitual residence' test and the 'right to reside' test (see Chapter 70);[9]
- your partner (if you have one) is not entitled to PC;[10]
- you are not a 'person subject to immigration control', although there are exceptions to this rule (see p1504);[11]
- you have 'qualifying income' that exceeds the 'savings credit threshold' but is not so high that it produces a nil award (see p82).[12]

2. The rules about your age

Entitlement to pension credit for both men and women is linked to the minimum qualifying age at which a woman can receive state retirement pension.[13] The qualifying age is rising steadily to 66 (by 2020) and will eventually go up to 68.[14] When you reach the qualifying age depends on your date of birth. **Note:** this applies to both men and women.
- If your date of birth is before 6 April 1950, your qualifying age is 60.
- If your date of birth is between 6 April 1950 and 5 December 1953 inclusive, see Appendix 5 to find your qualifying age.
- If your date of birth is after 5 December 1953, your qualifying age is 65 or over. To check your pension age, see www.gov.uk/calculate-state-pension.

In addition, you or your partner must be 65 or over in order to qualify for the savings credit element.[15]

3. People included in the claim

If you are single, you claim pension credit (PC) for yourself. If you are a member of a couple, either you claim PC for both you and your partner or, if your partner also meets the qualifying conditions for PC, s/he can claim for you both. The 'appropriate minimum guarantee' that forms part of the calculation of your benefit includes an allowance for a couple and can include additional amounts based on both your and your partner's circumstances. When your benefit is worked out, your partner's income and capital are usually added to yours. See p205 for who counts as a couple. Whichever one of you claims PC, if the other is not yet pension age, s/he may qualify for national insurance (NI) credits in order to protect her/his NI record. See Chapter 41 for more details about NI credits. If you are a man under age 65, see in particular p858.

Your appropriate minimum guarantee that forms part of the calculation of your benefit cannot include allowances and premiums for your child(ren). Instead, check to see if you qualify for child tax credit (see Chapter 8).

4. The amount of pension credit

The amount of pension credit (PC) you receive depends on whether you are single or a member of a couple, or have any disabilities, caring responsibilities or eligible housing costs. The maximum amount of guarantee credit you could receive is reduced by your income (subject to any applicable disregards). For savings credit, the rules are slightly more complicated (see p82). For information on income and capital, see Chapters 15 and 18. However, for information on qualifying income for savings credit, see p82.

Guarantee credit

Your maximum guarantee credit is known as the 'appropriate minimum guarantee'[16] and is made up of:
- standard minimum guarantee; *and*
- where applicable, additional amounts.

Standard minimum guarantee

If you do not have any additional needs, you receive an award of PC which ensures that your weekly income is brought up to one of the following standard minimum guarantee levels.

Single person[17]	£148.35
Couple[18]	£226.50
Each additional spouse in a polygamous marriage[19]	£78.15

Part 2: Main means-tested benefits and tax credits
Chapter 6: Pension credit
4. The amount of pension credit

2

Additional amounts

If you have additional needs (eg, a disability, caring responsibilities or housing costs), your award brings income to the level of the standard minimum guarantee plus additional amounts. These broadly correspond to the premiums and housing costs payable with income support (IS), with an additional transitional amount to ensure that those in receipt of IS, income-based jobseeker's allowance (JSA) or income-related employment and support allowance (ESA) at the time they first become entitled to PC are not worse off as a result of moving onto PC.

Additional amounts		
Severe disability[20] The qualifying rules are broadly the same as for the IS severe disability premium (see p233).	£61.10	£122.20 (if both partners qualify)
Carer[21] The rules are the same as those for the IS carer premium (see p237).	£34.20	£34.20 (for each partner who qualifies)
Housing costs[22] These provisions broadly mirror those for IS, but with some exceptions.	See Chapter 20	
Transitional[23]	See below	

Transitional amount

If you are in receipt of IS, income-based JSA or income-related ESA immediately before you first become entitled to PC, in order to ensure you are not worse off by moving onto PC, your appropriate minimum guarantee may include a transitional amount.[24] You are eligible for this extra amount if, on the day you first become entitled to PC, your IS, income-based JSA or income-related ESA applicable amount (less any amounts for dependent children) exceeds your appropriate minimum guarantee.

The transitional amount reduces over time by any increase in your appropriate minimum guarantee and ceases when you or your partner stop being entitled to PC (disregarding any break in entitlement of less than eight weeks).[25]

When your appropriate minimum guarantee may be reduced

Your appropriate minimum guarantee may be reduced in certain circumstances. The most important of these are if:[26]
- you are a couple and one of you is a 'person subject to immigration control' (see p1507);
- you are a prisoner (see p961);
- your partner is abroad (see p1582);

- you are a member of a religious order. In this case, your applicable amount is nil.

The guarantee credit calculation

Step one: calculate your appropriate minimum guarantee
This consists of:
- standard minimum guarantee for you and your partner, if you have one; *plus*
- additional amounts for any special needs and/or housing costs.

Step two: calculate your income
This is the amount you have coming in each week – eg, from benefits, private pensions and earnings.[27] Not all income counts (eg, disability living allowance (DLA), personal independence payment (PIP), attendance allowance (AA), child tax credit and child benefit are disregarded in full) and some income is subject to disregards (see Chapter 15). See also p89 for assessed income periods. If you have capital over £10,000, you are treated as having £1 for every £500 (or part of £500) capital that exceeds £10,000.[28]

Step three: deduct income from appropriate minimum guarantee
The amount of your guarantee credit is your appropriate minimum guarantee less any relevant income you have.[29] If your income is above the appropriate minimum guarantee, you do not qualify for any guarantee credit, but you might qualify for some savings credit. You may qualify for guarantee credit if you or your partner become entitled to a qualifying benefit, like AA, which may increase the amount of your appropriate minimum guarantee.

Examples

Barbara is single and aged 68. She is in receipt of AA. She lives alone and no one gets carer's allowance (CA) for looking after her. She lives in rented accommodation.

Her appropriate minimum guarantee is:

Standard minimum guarantee (single person rate)	£148.35
Severe disability additional amount	£61.10
Total	£209.45

Her weekly income is her basic state pension of £113.10. AA is ignored as income.

She is therefore entitled to £96.35 guarantee credit to bring her total income up to £209.45.

She is not entitled to any savings credit as she does not have any qualifying income above the savings credit threshold (see p82).

She is also entitled to maximum housing benefit (HB) and any other passported benefits that may apply.

Part 2: Main means-tested benefits and tax credits
Chapter 6: Pension credit
4. The amount of pension credit

· ·

Maria and Geoff are a couple. Maria is 62 and Geoff is 67. Their 24-year-old daughter lives with them and she is in receipt of income-based JSA. They have eligible weekly housing costs of £40. Maria receives the middle rate care component of DLA and Geoff gets AA. Their appropriate minimum guarantee is:

Standard minimum guarantee (couple rate)	£226.50
Eligible housing costs	£40.00
Total	£266.50

Their joint weekly income for calculating PC is £273.90, made up of basic state pension of £180.90 (Maria £67.80, Geoff £113.10), occupational pension of £90 and £3 deemed income from £11,500 savings. DLA and AA are ignored as income.

They are not entitled to any guarantee credit because their income exceeds their appropriate minimum guarantee of £266.50. Their appropriate minimum guarantee does not include a severe disability addition because their 24-year-old daughter lives with them. However, they are entitled to some savings credit as they have qualifying income above the savings credit threshold (see below).

· ·

Savings credit

In order to qualify for this element of PC you must have qualifying income above the **savings credit threshold** of:[30]

Single person	£120.35
Couple	£192.00

'**Qualifying income**' for this purpose is all income that counts for guarantee credit (see Chapter 15) except:[31]
- working tax credit;
- incapacity benefit (IB);
- contributory ESA;
- contribution-based JSA;
- severe disablement allowance;
- maternity allowance;
- maintenance payments for you, or your partner, from a spouse or former spouse.

The amount of savings credit to which you are entitled is subject to a maximum figure, known as the '**maximum savings credit**'.[32]

Single person	£16.80
Couple	£20.70

The savings credit calculation

To calculate savings credit, follow the steps below.[33] If you have already calculated whether you are entitled to the guarantee credit, you have already worked out the amounts in Steps one and two. If you are entitled to the guarantee credit, you only need to follow Steps one to four below.

Step one: calculate your total income

This is any income that counts for PC purposes and includes qualifying income.

Step two: calculate your appropriate minimum guarantee

This is the standard minimum guarantee plus any additional amounts.

Step three: calculate 60 per cent of any qualifying income above the threshold

This is 60 per cent of all your income that counts for guarantee credit, other than non-qualifying income listed on p82, above the savings credit threshold of £120.35 (if you are single) or £192 (if you are a couple). The figure you calculate is the maximum savings credit you can receive, but it is subject to a cap: you cannot get more than £16.80 if you are single, or £20.70 if you are a couple. If the figure you get is more than the cap, use the relevant maximum figure instead.

Step four: compare total income with appropriate minimum guarantee

If your total income (Step one) is less than your appropriate minimum guarantee (Step two) **the amount at Step three is your savings credit**. If your total income is more than your appropriate minimum guarantee, go to Step five.

Step five: calculate 40 per cent of total income above your appropriate minimum guarantee

This is 40 per cent of your total income, not just qualifying income, above your appropriate minimum guarantee.

Step six: deduct amount at Step five from amount at Step three

This is your savings credit.

If you cannot deduct it because it is more than the amount at Step three, you do not get any savings credit.

Examples
Terry and Julie are a couple over 65. They have a total weekly income of £215.90 made up of £180.90 basic state pension and £35 personal pension – all of this is qualifying income.
Step one: their total income is £215.90.
Step two: their appropriate minimum guarantee is £226.50 (standard minimum guarantee with no additional amounts).

Part 2: Main means-tested benefits and tax credits
Chapter 6: Pension credit
5. Special benefit rules

Step three: their total qualifying income of £215.90 exceeds the savings credit threshold of £192 by £23.90.

£23.90 x 60% = £14.34

Step four: their total income (Step one) is less than their appropriate minimum guarantee (Step two) so the amount in Step three (£14.34) is their savings credit.

They also qualify for guarantee credit of £10.60 to bring their income to the standard minimum guarantee (£226.50) for a couple. Their total income is £240.84 (£215.90 + £10.60 guarantee credit + £14.34 savings credit).

They may also be entitled to maximum HB and other passported benefits (see p93).

Angelina and Michael are a couple. Michael is 67 and Angelina is 58. They have a total weekly income of £298.25, made up of £113.10 state pension, £80 private pension, £101.15 contributory ESA for Angelina, and £4 deemed income from £12,000 savings. They have eligible housing costs of £15 a week.

Step one: their total income is £298.25.

Step two: their appropriate minimum guarantee is £241.50 (£226.50 standard minimum guarantee + housing costs of £15).

Step three: their total qualifying income of £197.10 (state pension, private pension and deemed income from savings – ESA is not qualifying income) exceeds the savings credit threshold of £192 by £5.10.

£5.10 x 60% = £3.06

Step four: their total income (Step one) is more than their appropriate minimum guarantee (Step two) so proceed to Step five.

Step five: their total income of £298.25 exceeds their appropriate minimum guarantee of £241.50 by £56.75.

£56.75 x 40% = £22.70

Step six: the amount at Step five (£22.70) cannot be deducted from the amount at Step three (£3.06) so they are not entitled to savings credit.

They are also not entitled to guarantee credit as their income is greater than their appropriate minimum guarantee.

---

5. **Special benefit rules**

Special rules may apply to:
- people subject to immigration control (see p1500);
- people in hospital (see p941);
- people in care homes and other special accommodation (see p950);
- prisoners (see p958).

You are not entitled to any pension credit if you are a member of, and are fully maintained by, a religious order.[34]

6. **Claims and backdating**

To be entitled to pension credit (PC) you must make a claim for it.[35] The general rules about claims and backdating are covered in Chapter 53. This section explains the specific rules that apply to PC.

Making a claim

A claim can be made:[36]

- by telephone. Call the Pension Service on 0800 99 1234 (textphone 0800 169 0133) from 8am to 6pm, Monday to Friday. If you choose not to claim by telephone, you are sent a claim form (PC1) to complete;
- in writing on the approved form. This can be obtained by telephone or downloaded from www.gov.uk/pension-credit/how-to-claim. To find out where to send the completed form, call the Pension Service on 0845 606 0265 (0845 606 0275 in Welsh), or check on www.gov.uk/find-pension-centre. You may be able to take or send the form to a local authority housing benefit (HB) office, an 'alternative office' (see p1136) or or, in England, a county council.

If you apply in writing, keep a copy of your claim form in case queries arise.

You must provide any information or evidence required (see p86). In certain circumstances, the DWP may accept a written application not on the approved form (see p1140). You can amend or withdraw your claim before a decision is made (see p1138). If there is a delay in dealing with your claim, you may be able to get a short-term advance of benefit (see p1167).

If you are under 65 and have been awarded the guarantee credit, when you turn 65 you are contacted to assess whether you are entitled to any savings credit and whether you should be given an assessed income period (see p89). The Pension Service either telephones you and completes the form over the telephone or sends you the form to complete. You must provide the information requested as part of this review within one month of being asked to do so.[37]

Who should claim

If you are a single person, you must claim on your own behalf. If you are one of a couple, you must choose which one of you claims for you both (see p205). If you cannot agree who should claim, a decision maker decides.[38]

You can swap who claims as long as the partner previously claiming agrees. It may be worthwhile doing so – eg, if one of you is about to go abroad.

If you are unable to manage your own affairs, another person can claim PC for you as your 'appointee' (see p1137).

Part 2: Main means-tested benefits and tax credits
Chapter 6: Pension credit
6. Claims and backdating

Information to support your claim

When you claim PC, you must:
- satisfy the national insurance number requirement (see p1138). If you are a member of a couple, your partner must also usually satisfy this requirement;
- provide proof of your identity, if required (see p1140); *and*
- ensure you have made a valid claim – ie, you must supply information and evidence required on the claim form (see p1140).

Even if you have provided all that was required when you claimed, you may be asked to provide additional information and evidence relevant to your claim (see p1152). There is a strict time limit for providing this. If you do not do so, the decision maker can decide your claim in the way most unfavourable to you.

Information and evidence relevant to your claim include specific details of any personal pension scheme to which you belong.[39] Additionally, you may be required to provide, within one month of being notified of the requirement, information and evidence of any likely future changes in circumstances that are needed to enable the decision maker to decide whether to apply an assessed income period and, if so, the length of that period.[40]

When you claim you are asked about your circumstances, including information about any income or savings and any housing costs you or your partner have. If further information or verification is needed, a letter is sent for you to complete, sign and return with any requested verification.

If the claim was made in writing to the local authority or, in England, to the county council, the local authority or county council can accept and obtain information and evidence, and give advice about the PC claim.

For claims made in the advance period (the four months before you reach the qualifying age) the one-month time limit starts from the day after the advance period ends.[41]

Once your claim has been decided, you are sent a statement of details, setting out the information on which the award is based. You are asked to check this and report any omissions or changes.

Note: you may be asked to provide information after you are awarded PC. If you fail to do so, your PC could be suspended or even terminated (see p1175).

The date of your claim

Claim as soon as you think you might be entitled to PC. You are not usually entitled to PC for any day before your date of claim. However, you can claim PC in advance before you qualify (see p87) and your date of claim can be backdated (see p87).

Your **'date of claim'** (unless the backdating rules apply) is:[42]

- the date your written or telephone claim, properly completed with all the required information and evidence, is received at the appropriate office (the DWP, local authority HB office or county council); *or*
- the date your 'defective claim' (ie, a claim that is not valid because it was not properly completed with all the required information and evidence) is received at the appropriate office and you correct the defect within one month (or a longer period that the DWP considers reasonable) of being notified of the defect; *or*
- the date you notify the appropriate office of your intention to claim, and you submit a properly completed claim with all the required information and evidence within one month of this date.

If you are making an advance claim for PC before you have reached the qualifying age and your claim is defective, you may correct it at any time before the end of the advance period.[43]

Claiming in advance

You can make an advance claim for PC to give the DWP time to ensure you receive your benefit as soon as you become entitled. However, you cannot make an advance claim if the reason you do not qualify straight away is because you fail the habitual residence test (see p1521). PC can be claimed up to four months before you qualify, whether this is before you reach the qualifying age and know you will be entitled when you reach that age *or* after you reach the qualifying age when you know you will have a future entitlement – eg, because of a drop in income.[44] The date of claim is the date you qualify.[45]

Backdating your claim

It is important that you claim in time because PC can only be backdated for up to three months. Your claim can be backdated if you satisfy the qualifying conditions over the period for which you require backdating – you do not have to show why your claim was late.[46] If you want your claim to be backdated, it is important that you request this as claims are not automatically backdated. You can do so on Part 10 of the claim form. If you make a telephone claim, you should be asked about the date from which you want your claim to start.

If you claim backdated PC within three months of being awarded a qualifying benefit and an earlier PC claim was refused because you did not get a qualifying benefit (see p1149) at that time, your PC can be backdated to the date of your earlier PC claim or the date when the qualifying benefit was first payable, whichever is later.[47]

For general rules on backdating, see p1144.

7. Getting paid

Payment of pension credit (PC) is normally made by direct credit transfer into a bank (or similar) account (see p1163). If you are unable to open or manage an account, payment can be made by 'simple payment' (see p1163). If you are unable to act for yourself, PC can be paid to someone else on your behalf, called your appointee (see p1137).

When is pension credit paid?

	Qualifying age on or after 6 April 2010	Qualifying age before 6 April 2010
When is PC paid?	The day you are paid depends on your national insurance number (see p1164).[48]	Monday, or the same day as your retirement pension is paid.[49]
How often is PC paid?	Weekly, fortnightly or four-weekly in arrears.	Weekly in advance. If you were entitled to income support (IS) immediately before 6 October 2003 and paid in arrears, PC is also paid in arrears.[50]

If you are entitled to less than 10 pence a week, you are not paid PC, unless you are receiving another social security benefit that can be paid with PC,[51] although you will still have an underlying entitlement. If your entitlement is less than £1 a week, a decision maker can decide to pay you quarterly in arrears.

There may be a delay between the date of your claim and the date PC becomes payable. This is because payment does not normally start until the first payday following the claim.[52] There are exceptions to this rule.[53]

Note:
- Deductions can be made from your PC to pay to third parties (see p1178).
- Your PC might be paid at a reduced rate if you have been sanctioned for benefit offences (see p1258).
- If you have forgotten your PIN, see p1163. If your 'simple payment' card has been lost or stolen, or if you have forgotten your memorable date, see p1164. For information on missing payments, see p1164.
- If payment of your PC is delayed, see p1382. You might be able to get a short-term advance (see p1167). If you wish to complain about how your claim has been dealt with, see p1383. You might be able to claim compensation (see p1382).

- If payment of your PC is suspended, see p1175.
- If you are overpaid PC, you might have to repay it (see Chapter 56) and, in some circumstances, you may have to pay a penalty (see p1249). If you have been accused of fraud, see Chapter 53.

Change of circumstances

You must report changes in your circumstances that you have been told to report, as well as any that you might reasonably be expected to know might affect your right to, the amount of, or the payment of your benefit. You should do this as soon as possible, preferably in writing. See p1174 for further information.

See below for the circumstances that do not need to be reported during the assessed income period.

If there are any changes to the amount of housing costs you owe or the interest payable, your lender is required to report these to the DWP.[54] If you have this information, you must also inform the DWP in case your lender fails to do so. To avoid an overpayment, make sure that the DWP takes this information into account.

If there has been a relevant change of circumstances, a decision maker looks at your claim again and makes a new decision. To find out when the new decision takes effect, see p1287.

When your pension credit is adjusted

Generally, your PC is adjusted from the day the change occurs or is expected to occur, if this is the day you are paid benefit. If it is not, your PC is adjusted from the start of the next benefit week.[55]

However, there are a few exceptions to this general rule.[56]

Assessed income period

An assessed income period is a set period during which you are not required to report any changes in certain types of your income, known as 'retirement provision'.[57]

'Retirement provision' means income from:[58]
- retirement pension (other than one payable under the Social Security Contributions and Benefits Act 1992);
- an annuity (other than retirement pension income);
- capital.

The effect of this is that if you have an increase in, or subsequently start to receive, retirement provision during your assessed income period, you do not have to report this to the DWP. All other income changes that affect your PC entitlement must be reported to the DWP as soon as they occur. During the assessed income period your PC entitlement may change as a result of 'deemed increases in retirement provision' (see below).

An assessed income period is only set if you or your partner are 65 or over. Also, an assessed income period is not made if:[59]

- you are a member of a couple and one of you is under 60; *or*
- you have been awarded PC, or your PC has been increased, because an element of your retirement provision that is due to be paid has temporarily stopped; *or*
- you have failed to provide sufficient information, as requested by the DWP at the end of the assessed income period, to enable the DWP to determine whether your retirement provision will vary throughout the 12 months that follow the day the previous assessed income period ends. If the assessed income period has expired and the DWP already has enough information to set a new period, it may do so automatically. You are sent notification of the income and circumstances on which the new assessed income period has been based and are asked to inform the DWP if these have changed.[60]

An assessed income period can be set for five years or for an indefinite period if you are aged 75 or over.[61] If the amount assessed as your retirement provision seems unlikely to represent your typical retirement provision throughout the following 12 months, an assessed income period is made for less than five years or not at all.[62] If you have asked for your claim to be backdated (see p87), when deciding whether your retirement provision is likely to be typical throughout the 12 months, the decision maker looks at the 12 months starting with the date from when your claim is backdated, as opposed to the date you make your claim.[63]

Deemed increases in retirement provision

During an assessed income period your PC entitlement may change as a result of a deemed increase in retirement provision. If the terms of your retirement provision provide for periodic increases and the date and amount of such increases, and the DWP is informed of these, the increase is in line with these terms.[64] Otherwise, the increase is in line with the social security uprating for additional pensions.[65] There is no deemed increase if your retirement provision arrangements do not provide for periodic increases in the amount payable.[66] If your retirement provision includes income from capital, it is deemed not to change unless it is capital that counts as having a tariff income.[67] In that case, it may be deemed to increase or decrease in line with any changes made to the tariff income rules – currently £1 for every £500 (or part of £500) over £10,000.

If the adjustment to your retirement provision results in a change in the amount of PC to which you are entitled, the DWP amends your PC payment automatically.[68] This takes effect from the start of the benefit week if the increase or uprating date also falls on that day. In all other cases, it takes effect from the start of the next benefit week.[69] However, if the period for which the first increase in retirement provision is paid is not the same length as the period of the last regular payment, the adjustment takes effect from the date of the second payment of the increased amount if that falls on the same day as the start of the benefit week; otherwise, from the start of the next benefit week.

Example

Ruth's occupational pension is paid at the end of each month. Her last payment was made on 31 March 2014. An annual increase of 1.8 per cent takes effect on 16 April 2014 and is first included in the payment on 30 April 2014.

The period from 16 April to 30 April (15 days) is not the same length as the last regular payment (one month), so any resulting adjustment to Ruth's PC is not applied until the start of the benefit week following the second payment of the increased amount.

Decreases in retirement provision

If your retirement provision decreases during an assessed income period, you can report this and your PC is adjusted. This does not end the period, but instead your PC award is adjusted via a supersession.[70] It is in your interest to report decreases in order to gain from any increased PC during a current assessed income period, otherwise you have to wait until the reassessment at the end of the period and any PC adjustment only applies from the start of your next assessed income period.

When an assessed income period ends

Your assessed income period comes to an end if:[71]

- you become a member of a couple;
- you cease to be a member of a couple;
- you or your partner reaches the age of 65;
- you are no longer entitled to PC;
- you are single and enter a care home on a permanent basis;
- payments of retirement provision due to you stop temporarily or are less than the amount due, and your PC award is superseded as a result.

8. Tax, other benefits and the benefit cap

Tax

Pension credit (PC) is not taxable.

Means-tested benefits

The guarantee credit of PC is an automatic passport to maximum housing benefit (HB), but you have to make a separate claim. If you are only entitled to the savings

Part 2: Main means-tested benefits and tax credits
Chapter 6: Pension credit
8. Tax, other benefits and the benefit cap

credit, your HB claim is subject to a standard calculation. The Pension Service provides the local authority with the assessed income figure (the figure the DWP used to work out your PC entitlement). The local authority modifies this to take certain income into account – eg, savings credit.[72] Although savings credit counts as income for HB, the HB applicable amount for people aged 65 or over is increased by an amount equal to the maximum savings credit (see p82) to minimise any loss in HB as a result of having more qualifying income (see Chapter 12).

The £16,000 capital limit for HB does not apply if you receive the guarantee credit (with or without the savings credit). It does apply if you only receive the savings credit.

If you are a man aged between the qualifying age for PC (see p78) and 65, you can choose between claiming income-based jobseeker's allowance (JSA) or PC. When deciding which benefit to claim, you should be aware of the different rules for these two benefits to ensure you will be better off. For example, there is no capital limit or 16-hour work rule for PC, but there is for income-based JSA. Similarly, if you are a man aged between the qualifying age for PC (see p78) and 65, you can choose between claiming employment and support allowance (ESA) and PC, or, in some situations, between claiming contributory ESA and PC. However, regardless of age, no one can get income-related ESA and PC at the same time. Also, if you are a member of a couple and you claim PC, your partner cannot be entitled to income-related ESA. You may want to seek advice about any 'better-off' considerations.

PC continues after the introduction of universal credit (UC) if you do not come under the UC system (see p19). However, you cannot get both PC and UC at the same time. If you are a couple and one of you is over the qualifying age for PC, current rules prevent you from coming under the UC system (see p19).

Non-means-tested benefits

Some non-means-tested benefits are taken into account as income when calculating entitlement to PC. Others have a £10 disregard and some are disregarded entirely. See Chapter 15 for details.

Qualifying for certain non-means-tested benefits can help you qualify for more PC. For example, if you get carer's allowance, you may be entitled to a carer addition with your appropriate minimum guarantee.

Tax credits

PC acts as a passport to maximum tax credits, although you need to make a separate claim.[73] Child tax credit (CTC) does not count as income when calculating PC, but working tax credit does.[74]

The benefit cap

In some cases, the total amount of specified benefits you receive is limited to £350 a week (if you are a single claimant without children) or £500 a week (if you are a lone parent or a member of a couple). This is known as the 'benefit cap'. PC is *not* one of the specified benefits. The benefit cap does not normally apply if you are at least the qualifying age for PC. The benefit cap only applies if you are getting HB. See p1169 for further information.

Passports and other sources of help

If you are entitled to PC, you may also be eligible for:
- a Christmas bonus (see p835);
- health benefits if you are getting the guarantee credit of PC (see Chapter 30);
- free school lunches if you are getting the guarantee credit of PC. This only applies in England and Wales – claimants in Scotland can qualify via CTC (see p832);
- social fund payments if you receive either or both elements of PC (see Chapter 37);
- council tax reduction from your local authority (see p827);
- home insulation grants and discretionary grants from the local authority towards the cost of home improvements (see p837).

Notes

1. Who can claim pension credit
1 s2 SPCA 2002
2 s1(6) SPCA 2002
3 s1(2)(a) SPCA 2002; regs 2-4 SPC Regs
4 s4(1) SPCA 2002
5 s2(2) SPCA 2002; reg 6 SPC Regs
6 s4(2) SPCA 2002
7 s3 SPCA 2002
8 s3(1) SPCA 2002
9 s1(2)(a) SPCA 2002; regs 2-4 SPC Regs
10 s4(1) SPCA 2002
11 s4(2) SPCA 2002
12 s3(2)-(4) SPCA 2002

2. The rules about your age
13 s1(6) SPCA 2002
14 s126 and Sch 4 PA 1995
15 s3(1) SPCA 2002

4. The amount of pension credit
16 s2(3) SPCA 2002
17 Reg 6(1)(b) SPC Regs
18 Reg 6(1)(a) SPC Regs
19 Reg 6 and Sch 3 para 1(5) SPC Regs
20 Reg 6(4) and (5) SPC Regs
21 Reg 6(6)(a) SPC Regs
22 Reg 6(6)(c) SPC Regs
23 Reg 6(6)(b) SPC Regs
24 Reg 6(6)(b) and Sch 1 para 6 SPC Regs
25 Sch 1 para 6(8) and (9) SPC Regs
26 Reg 6(2)(b) and (3) SPC Regs
27 s15 SPCA 2002; regs 14-24 SPC Regs
28 Reg 15(6) SPC Regs
29 s2(2) SPCA 2002
30 Reg 7(2) SPC Regs
31 Reg 9 SPC Regs

• •

32 s3(7) SPCA 2002; reg 7(1)(a) SPC Regs
33 s3(3) SPCA 2002; reg 7(1)(b) and (c)
     SPC Regs

5. Special benefit rules
34 ss2(9) and 3(8) SPCA 2002; regs 6(2)(b)
     and 7(3)(b) SPC Regs

6. Claims and backdating
35 s1 SSAA 1992
36 Reg 4D SS(C&P) Regs
37 Reg 7(1B) SS(C&P) Regs
38 Reg 4D(7) SS(C&P) Regs
39 Reg 7(4) SS(C&P) Regs
40 Reg 7(1A) and (1B) SS(C&P) Regs
41 Reg 7(1C) SS(C&P) Regs
42 Reg 4F SS(C&P) Regs
43 Regs 4D(12) and 4E(3) SS(C&P) Regs
44 Regs 4E and 13D(4) SS(C&P) Regs
45 Reg 13D SS(C&P) Regs
46 Reg 19(2) and (3) SS(C&P) Regs
47 Reg 6(16) SS(C&P) Regs

7. Getting paid
48 Reg 26BA SS(C&P) Regs
49 Reg 26B SS(C&P) Regs
50 Reg 36(6) SPC(CTMP) Regs
51 Reg 13 SPC Regs
52 Reg 16A(1) and (4) SS(C&P) Regs
53 Reg 16A(2) SS(C&P) Regs
54 Sch 9A para 10 SS(C&P) Regs
55 Reg 7 and Sch 3B para 1(b) SS&CS(DA)
     Regs
56 Reg 7 and Sch 3B SS&CS(DA) Regs
57 ss6-10 SPCA 2002; regs 10-12 SPC Regs
58 s7(6) SPCA 2002
59 Reg 10(1) SPC Regs
60 Reg 32(6) SS(C&P) Regs; Memo DMG
     23/08
61 s9(1) SPCA 2002
62 s9(2) SPCA 2002
63 para 83045 DMG
64 Reg 10(4) SPC Regs
65 Reg 10(6) SPC Regs
66 Reg 10(2)(a) SPC Regs
67 Reg 10(2)(b) and (7) SPC Regs
68 s10 SPCA 2002
69 Reg 10(5)-(7) SPC Regs
70 s8 SPCA 2002
71 s9(4) SPCA 2002; reg 12 SPC Regs

8. Tax, other benefits and the benefit cap
72 Reg 27 HB(SPC) Regs
73 s7(2) TCA 2002; reg 4(d) TC(ITDR) Regs
74 s15(1)(b) SPCA 2002

Chapter 7

Housing benefit

This chapter covers:

Key facts

- Housing benefit (HB) is a benefit for people on a low income who pay rent.
- The amount of your HB is not necessarily the amount of rent you have to pay. It might be restricted under one of the rent restriction schemes.
- HB is a means-tested benefit.
- You do not have to have paid national insurance contributions to qualify.
- You can qualify for HB whether you are in or out of work.
- If you need extra financial assistance to meet housing costs, you can claim discretionary housing payments to top up your HB.
- A 'benefit cap' may be applied if the total amount of certain benefits you receive exceeds a specified amount and your HB can be reduced.
- HB is administered and paid by local authorities, although it is a national scheme and the rules are mainly determined by DWP regulations.
- If you disagree with an HB decision, you can apply for a revision or a supersession, or appeal against it. You do not have to apply for a revision before you can appeal.

Future changes

The government says that, in 2016, you will no longer be able to make a new claim for HB. The DWP will begin to transfer existing HB claims to universal credit after 2017. See p18 for further information. See CPAG's online service and *Welfare Rights Bulletin* for updates.

Part 2: Main means-tested benefits and tax credits
Chapter 7: Housing benefit
1. Who can claim housing benefit

1. Who can claim housing benefit

You qualify for housing benefit (HB) if:[1]

- your income is low enough (see Chapters 14 and 15);
- unless you or your partner are getting the guarantee credit of pension credit (PC), your savings and other capital are worth £16,000 or less (see Chapters 17 and 18);[2]
- the payments you make can be met by HB (see below);
- you or your partner count as liable to pay rent (see p98);
- the payments you make are for the home in which you normally live (see p102) or you are only temporarily absent from it;
- you satisfy the 'right to reside test' and the 'habitual residence test' (see Chapter 70); *and*
- you are not a 'person subject to immigration control' (see p1500). There are exceptions to this rule.

Are you the qualifying age for pension credit?

The HB rules for people who are at least the qualifying age for PC (see p78) who are not (and whose partners are not) on income support (IS), income-based jobseeker's allowance (JSA) or income-related employment and support allowance (ESA) (or universal credit – UC) are more generous than those for other HB claimants. The different rules for income, capital and applicable amounts are covered in other chapters.

Note: if you come under the UC system (see p19), you cannot make a new claim for HB, unless this is for exempt accommodation (see p416). If you live in 'exempt accommodation', you can get HB for the rent you pay even if you are getting UC. From 3 November 2014, you can get HB for other 'specified accommodation' (see p1171).

Payments that can be met by housing benefit

HB can meet rent and other types of payment, such as payments as a licensee and payments for bed and breakfast and hostel accommodation. In this *Handbook*, we refer to any payments you make as 'rent'. Some types of payment cannot be met by HB (see p97). HB can meet:[3]

- rent paid in respect of a tenancy. This can include rent or ground rent payable in respect of a lease of 21 years or less.[4] If your lease is for longer than 21 years, the rent or ground rent may be met by IS, income-based JSA, income-related ESA or PC (see p444);
- payments in respect of a licence or other permission to occupy premises;

- 'mesne profits' (in Scotland, 'violent profits'), including payments made if you remain in occupation when a tenancy has been ended;
- other payments for the use and occupation of premises (including boat licence and mooring permit fees if you live in a houseboat[5]);
- payments for eligible service charges (see p114);
- rent, including mooring charges, for a houseboat;
- site rent for a caravan or mobile home (but not a tent, although that might be met through IS, income-based JSA, income-related ESA or PC – see p444);
- rent paid on a garage or land (unless used for business purposes). Either you must be making a reasonable effort to end your liability for it, or you must have been unable to rent your home without it;[6]
- contributions made by a resident of a charity's almshouse;
- payments made under a rental purchase agreement under which the purchase price is paid in more than one instalment and you do not finally own your home until all, or an agreed part of, the purchase price has been paid;
- in Scotland, payments in respect of croft land.

The payment must be in return for your occupation of the home. This usually means that the payments must be made to the person who has the right to let you occupy it, or someone acting on her/his behalf. Payments to someone else might qualify for HB. This depends on, for example, whether you have a valid tenancy agreement with that person.[7]

Payments that cannot be met by housing benefit

HB cannot meet payments:[8]
- by an owner or under a long tenancy (ie, you own your accommodation or have a lease of more than 21 years), unless you have a shared ownership tenancy (ie, you are buying part of your house or flat and renting the rest), in which case you can get HB on the part you rent. You are treated as the owner of the property if you have the right to sell it, even though you may not be able to do so without the consent of other joint owners;[9]
- you make for a dwelling owned (or part-owned) by your partner;
- by a Crown tenant;
- under a co-ownership scheme under which you receive a payment related to the value of the accommodation when you leave;
- under a hire purchase (eg, for the purchase of a mobile home), credit sale or a conditional sale agreement except to the extent that it is in respect of land.

In all of the above cases (other than the second), the payments might be met by IS, income-based JSA, income-related ESA or PC instead. In the second case, the payments you make to your partner cannot be met by IS, income-based JSA, income-related ESA or PC, but certain loans and other housing costs you (or your

Part 2: Main means-tested benefits and tax credits
Chapter 7: Housing benefit
1. Who can claim housing benefit

partner) have might be met by those benefits. See Chapter 20 for further information.

In addition, HB cannot meet payments if you are getting IS, income-based JSA or income-related ESA for these.[10] However, if you are now getting your housing costs met through IS, income-based JSA or income-related ESA but were previously getting HB for the same accommodation, your HB continues for your first four weeks on IS, income-based JSA or income-related ESA.[11] Remember that, if you buy a home and immediately before that you were renting accommodation and getting HB, your full housing costs might not be met (see p442).

Note: if you live in a care home, you usually cannot get HB for the rent you pay to the home (see p955).

Liability to pay rent

To qualify for HB you must count as liable to pay rent. You count as liable if either you or your partner are liable.[12] You also count as liable if you are treated as liable – ie:[13]

- you have to pay rent in order to continue to live in your home because the liable person is not doing so; *and*
  - your former partner is liable to make the payments; *or*
  - you are not the former partner of the liable person and it is reasonable to treat you as liable.[14]
  It does not matter whether or not the landlord is prepared to transfer the tenancy to you or wants to evict you. If you are a local authority tenant and the local authority refuses to accept your HB claim, point out that the eligibility rules for HB and for transferring local authority tenancies are quite separate. If the local authority refuses your claim, request a revision or appeal; *or*
- your landlord allows you a rent-free period as compensation for carrying out repairs or redecoration which s/he would otherwise have had to carry out (for a maximum of eight benefit weeks in a rent free period). If you expect the work to last longer, arrange with your landlord to schedule the work in periods of eight weeks or less, separated by at least one complete benefit week where you resume paying rent; *or*
- you are the partner of a full-time student who is treated as not liable to pay rent (see p99). This means that you can qualify for HB even if your partner cannot.

Even if you fall into one of these categories, you can still be treated as not being liable to pay rent, and so not entitled to HB, in certain circumstances (see pp99–102).

If you pay your rent in advance, you are still treated as liable to pay it, even if you paid it before claiming HB.[15]

What 'liable' means

For you to be 'liable' to pay rent, your agreement must be legally enforceable.[16] It is not enough if you only have a moral obligation, such as a promise to pay something whenever you can afford to do so. You can count as liable to pay rent even if someone else has been paying it on your behalf, or if your landlord has failed to provide notice of an address for the purposes of s48 of the Landlord and Tenant Act 1987 so rent is treated as not being due.[17] You can be liable to pay rent by yourself or you can be jointly liable to do so (see below).

If you have a **written agreement** with your landlord, the local authority uses this to decide if you are liable to pay rent and whether the liability is a genuine part of the agreement. Even if the local authority accepts this, it might still treat you as not liable to pay rent (see below).[18]

Your agreement can be enforceable even if it is **not in writing**. The fact that you have made a firm promise to pay money to your landlord in return for your occupation of the property should be sufficient to allow you to claim HB. If the local authority refuses to accept that you have a legal liability unless you produce a written agreement, a rent book or some other evidence in writing, argue that this is wrong and seek a revision or appeal.[19]

16/17-year-olds

People under 18 can be liable to pay rent and, therefore, entitled to HB, if there is an intention to create legal relations, regardless of the precise wording of the agreement. If you are under 16, an adult or a social services department is generally responsible for the rent, but HB departments should not decide HB entitlement based on what they think the social services department ought to provide.

Joint liability

If you are a member of a couple (see p205 for who counts) and are jointly liable for the rent, only one of you can claim HB.[20]

The way a group of single people living together and paying rent to their landlord is treated depends on how many of you are liable under the agreement. If all, or some, of you have joint liability for the rent, you can each make a separate claim and be paid HB on your share (unless the local authority thinks the joint tenancy has been created to take advantage of the HB scheme – see p101).

People treated as not liable to pay rent

Even if you or your partner are liable to pay rent, or you count as liable, you can be treated as though you are not liable to pay rent. In this case, you cannot qualify for HB. This applies if you are in any of the situations below.[21]

- You are a full-time **student** and you are not in one of the categories of student who can qualify for HB (see pp915–16). This does not apply if you are at least

Part 2: Main means-tested benefits and tax credits
Chapter 7: Housing benefit
1. Who can claim housing benefit

the qualifying age for PC (see p78) and neither you nor your partner are getting IS or income-based JSA, income-related ESA (or UC).

• You **do not satisfy the habitual residence test** (see p1521).
• You are a member of, and are fully maintained by, a **religious order.**[22]
• You are living in a **care home** or an **independent hospital** (but see p955).[23]
• You **pay rent to someone who also lives in the dwelling and who is a close relative** of you or your partner (see p101 for who counts).[24] Your landlord might be regarded as living in your dwelling if you share some accommodation with her/him, other than a bathroom, toilet or a hall or passageway.[25] It all depends on the facts. It does not matter if you use the accommodation at different times or if you pay to use it.[26]
• Your **agreement to pay rent is not on a commercial basis.**[27] In deciding whether or not your agreement is commercial, the local authority must look at the whole agreement, taking into account all the circumstances. It must consider, among other things:[28]
    – whether your agreement includes terms that are not legally enforceable. DWP guidance suggests that this might arise, for example, where a tenant does household chores. However, if you do chores in exchange for a lower rent, it could be considered commercial;
    – your agreement to pay rent. The rent does not have to be a market rent. Your agreement can count as commercial even if your landlord is not collecting the full contractual rent from you – eg, if it is not being met by HB because of the rent restriction rules (see Chapter 19);
    – your relationship to your landlord. However, just because you are a relative of, or have a close friendship with, her/him, or s/he provides you with care and support, does not mean that your agreement is non-commercial.
• You are **renting from:**[29]
    – any ex-partner of yours and the home is your former joint home with that ex-partner; *or*
    – any ex-partner of your partner and the home is your partner's former joint home with that ex-partner.
• You or your partner are **responsible for a child (under 16) of your landlord.**[30] Being responsible for a child means more than caring for her/him. It only applies in situations where the child is included in your HB claim (see p210).[31]
• You, your partner, your ex-partner, your partner's ex-partner or a close relative of you or your partner who lives with you is either:[32]
    – a **director or employee of a company which is your landlord;** *or*
    – a **trustee or beneficiary of a trust which is your landlord.**
    However, you should be treated as liable if you can show the arrangement was not intended to take advantage of the HB scheme (see p101).
• You are renting accommodation from a trustee of a trust, of which your **child (under 16)** (or your partner's child) **is a beneficiary.**

- You were **previously the non-dependant** (see p116) of someone who lived, and continues to live, in the accommodation. This should not apply to you if you can show that the agreement was not created to take advantage of the HB scheme (see below).[33]
- You or your current partner **previously owned, or had a long tenancy** in (ie, a lease of more than 21 years), the accommodation and less than five years have passed since you last owned it (or the tenancy ceased).[34]

  This rule does not apply if you can show that you could not have continued to occupy the accommodation without giving up ownership (or the tenancy) – eg, if the lender was seeking possession of your home. Whether you were legally or practically compelled to give up ownership or the tenancy is relevant, but your motivation for doing so is not.[35] You may need to show that you have taken steps to explore alternatives.[36]
- You or your partner are employed by your landlord and are **occupying your accommodation as a condition of employment.** This should not apply if you continue to live in the accommodation after ceasing employment.
- Where none of the above apply, the local authority considers that your **liability to pay rent has been created to take advantage of the HB scheme** (see below).

Close relatives

A **'close relative'** is a parent, parent-in-law (including a civil partner's parent), son, son-in-law (including a son's civil partner), daughter, daughter-in-law (including a daughter's civil partner), brother, sister, step-parent (including a parent's civil partner), stepson (including a civil partner's son), stepdaughter (including a civil partner's daughter), or the partners of any of these.[37] It also includes half-brothers and sisters.[38] Relations with in-laws or step-relatives are severed by divorce (or dissolution of a civil partnership) but arguably not by death – eg, a stepchild is still a stepchild after the death of her/his mother.[39]

Agreements taking advantage of the housing benefit scheme

For your agreement to count as 'taking advantage of the HB scheme', it must amount to an abuse of the scheme or to taking improper advantage of it. It must be shown that the main reason you entered into the agreement was to obtain HB.[40] All the circumstances should be taken into account, including what your landlord has to say.[41] An agreement can count as taking advantage of the HB scheme even if it was created from the best of motives.[42] Bear the following in mind.

- Your agreement does not take advantage of the HB scheme just because your landlord is your parent[43] or because you hope to be able to claim HB to help you with your rent – ie, if your main purpose is to get accommodation, not to obtain HB.[44]

Part 2: Main means-tested benefits and tax credits
Chapter 7: Housing benefit
1. Who can claim housing benefit

- You should not be seen as taking advantage of the HB scheme just because you seek to find out what rent can be covered by HB before moving in.
- Tenants of a landlord who deliberately charges high rents to try and get them paid by HB may be affected by this provision, even if they had no such intention themselves. However, the fact that a landlord sets a high rent does not in itself mean that the liability takes advantage of the HB scheme.[45]
- If your landlord is going to evict you if you cannot get HB, this suggests that the agreement does *not* take advantage of the HB scheme.[46]

Occupying accommodation as your home

HB is paid for the home in which you and your partner and any children included in your claim (see p210) normally live.[47] You cannot usually be paid for any other home. However, there are special rules if you:
- have just moved into your home (see below);
- are temporarily absent from home (see p103);
- are liable to pay rent on more than one home (see p105);
- are in certain other situations (see p106).

Note:
- If you occupy more than one property or room as your home (eg, because you have a large family and rent adjacent flats, or have a live-in carer and rent two adjacent rooms in shared accommodation), you can argue that both properties or rooms count as part of your home – ie, that you only have one home.[48]
- If you have to live in an approved bail or probation hostel or are a prisoner on temporary release, you are treated as not occupying the accommodation in which you are staying as your home.[49] This means you cannot qualify for HB for any rent you pay there.

Moving home

If you have **just moved into your home** but were liable to pay rent before moving in, you can get HB on your new home for a period of up to four weeks before you moved in.[50] Before moving, you must either have claimed HB or have notified the local authority of the move to the new home. If you have given up your previous home and have no other home, you can argue that the date you move in is the date you move your furniture and belongings in.[51]

You can only qualify under this rule if your delay in moving was reasonable, *and*:
- you were waiting for 'local welfare provision' (see p103) or a social fund payment for a need connected with the move – eg, removal expenses or to help you set up home. This only applies if:
  - you have a child of five or under living with you; *or*
  - you are at least the qualifying age for PC (see p78) and neither you nor your partner are getting IS, income-based JSA or income-related ESA (or UC); *or*

- you are under the qualifying age for PC (see p78), or you or your partner are getting IS, income-based JSA or income-related ESA (or UC), and you qualify for a disability, severe disability or disabled child premium, or a support or work-related activity component; *or*
- you were waiting for adaptations to be finished to meet needs you, your partner or a child included in your claim (see p210) have because of a disability. The adaptations do not have to involve a change to the fabric or structure of the dwelling, but must be reasonably required and have a clear connection to the disability needs;[52] *or*
- you became liable to make payments on your new home while you were a hospital patient or in 'residential accommodation' (see p105 for the meaning).

Local welfare provision

'**Local welfare provision**' means occasional financial or other assistance provided by a local authority, the Welsh Ministers or the Scottish Ministers, or people authorised by them.[53] The assistance must be:

- to meet, or to help to meet, an immediate short-term need due to exceptional circumstances or to avoid a risk to a person's wellbeing;
- to enable someone to establish or maintain a settled home if s/he has been (or without assistance might be) in prison, hospital, residential care or another institution, or homeless or living an unsettled way of life.

Your HB is not actually paid until you move in. If an earlier claim for HB you made before you moved in was turned down, you must claim again within four weeks of moving to qualify.

In addition, if you are **not liable to pay rent in your new accommodation** (eg, if you are in prison or hospital), you can get HB for up to four weeks for your former home if you:[54]

- were liable for rent on it immediately before moving into your new accommodation and continue to be liable – eg, because you have to give notice to your landlord; *and*
- could not reasonably have avoided liability for rent on your former home.

If you are obliged to pay rent for your old home as well as your new accommodation, you can only get HB for one of these unless you are covered by the rules described on pp105–06.[55]

Temporary absence from home

If you are temporarily absent from your normal home, your HB can continue to be paid for a period if you have not rented out your home and you intend to return to it. You can argue that you count as temporarily absent from home even

Part 2: Main means-tested benefits and tax credits
Chapter 7: Housing benefit
1. Who can claim housing benefit

if you have not yet stayed there – eg, you move your furniture and belongings in, but then have to go into hospital.[56]

You can get HB for up to:

- **13 weeks** while you are away, whatever the reason. You must be unlikely to be away for longer than this;[57]
- **52 weeks** if you fit into any of the groups below. You must be unlikely to be away for longer than this (or, in exceptional circumstances, unlikely to be away for substantially longer than this).[58]

The 13 and 52 weeks both run from the date you leave home. If, for example, you have been away from home for 10 weeks and then have grounds to continue to get HB for 52 weeks, you only get HB for the balance: 42 weeks. However, a new period of absence starts if you return home for even a short stay. A stay of at least 24 hours may be enough.[59] This does not apply, however, if you are a prisoner on temporary release.[60]

Your intention to return, and whether or not you are unlikely to be away for longer than 13/52 weeks should be considered initially based on the circumstances on the date you leave your home, unless you are in residential accommodation for a trial period (see p105).[61] If, at any time after that date, you no longer intend to return or it becomes likely that you will be away from home for more than the 13/52 weeks, your entitlement can be reconsidered.[62]

Note: if you have someone living with you who is temporarily absent (eg, s/he is a student who is away during term time), the local authority may use these rules to decide if s/he is a non-dependant (see p116).[63]

Housing benefit for up to 52 weeks

You can get HB for up to 52 weeks for your normal home if you are unlikely to be away for longer than this (or, in exceptional circumstances, unlikely to be away for substantially longer than this) and one of the following applies.[64]

- You are a remand prisoner held in custody pending trial or sentence. Once you are sentenced, you no longer qualify for HB under this rule but might still qualify under the 13-week rule. The 13 weeks run from the date you were first in prison, so any time you spend in prison awaiting trial or sentence counts towards the 13 weeks. **Note:** you are treated as still in custody if you are a prisoner on temporary release.[65]
- You are required to live in an approved hostel or at an address away from your normal home as a condition of bail.
- You are resident in a hospital or similar institution as a patient. **Note:** you cannot get HB after you have been resident in hospital for 52 weeks, even if this is because you are seriously mentally ill.[66]
- You, your partner or a 'dependent child' under 16 are undergoing medical treatment or medically approved convalescence in the UK or abroad, other than in residential accommodation (see p105 for the meaning). Dependent

child is not defined in the rules, so could include children who are not included in your claim.

- You are providing, or receiving, 'medically approved' care (ie, certified by a medical practitioner) in the UK or abroad. If you are receiving the care, you cannot be in residential accommodation (see below for the meaning).
- You are caring for a child under 16 whose parent or guardian is away from home receiving medically approved care or medical treatment.
- You are undertaking a training course (see below for the meaning) in the UK or abroad.
- You are a student. You must not fall into the first category under 'Other situations' on p106, or be entitled to HB on two homes (see below).
- You are in residential accommodation (see below) for short-term or respite care.
- You are in 'residential accommodation' (see below) for a trial period to see if it suits your needs. On the date you enter the accommodation, you must intend to return home if it is not suitable.[67] You can only get HB for up to 13 weeks.[68] If the accommodation does not suit your needs, you can have further trial periods in other accommodation provided you are not away from home for more than 52 weeks in total.
- You are away from home because of a fear of violence. You need not have experienced actual violence, but you must be in fear of violence in your home or from a former partner, or a child or qualifying young person formerly included in your claim. The first category includes violence by neighbours and racial attacks on your home. See below if you need to claim for two homes and p106 if you do not intend to return to your former home.

There must be some causal link between your absence from home and being in one of the situations above.[69]

Definitions[70]

'**Residential accommodation**' means a care home, an independent hospital or an Abbeyfield Home. It also means an establishment managed or provided by a body incorporated by Royal Charter or constituted by an Act of Parliament, other than a local social services authority.

A '**training course**' is a course of training or instruction provided by or on behalf of, or approved by, a government department, the Secretary of State, Skills Development Scotland, Scottish Enterprise or Highlands and Islands Enterprise.

Housing benefit for more than one home

You can usually only get HB for one home. **Note:** if you occupy more than one property as a home (eg, you rent adjacent flats because you have a large family or

Part 2: Main means-tested benefits and tax credits
Chapter 7: Housing benefit
1. Who can claim housing benefit

two adjacent rooms in shared accommodation because you have a live-in carer), you can argue that you only have one home.[71]

If you occupy two homes, you can get HB for both:

- for up to **four weeks**, if:[72]
  - you have moved into a new home and you could not reasonably avoid having to pay rent on your old home.[73] The local authority must consider the reasons why you had to move quickly. For example, if you were forced to move quickly to take advantage of better accommodation, you may not have been able to avoid leaving without giving notice; *or*
  - you qualify for HB on a new home because a move was delayed while you were adapting your new home to meet needs you, your partner or child included in your claim have because of disability (see p103). You can get HB on both homes for the four weeks prior to the date you move. The adaptations do not have to involve a change to the fabric or structure of the dwelling, but must be reasonably required and have a clear connection to the disability needs;[74]
- for up to **52 weeks**, if you have left your home because of a fear of violence (see p105 for the meaning). You must intend to return to your former home, and it must be reasonable for you to receive payments for both homes. The payments can be either HB or UC. For example, if your temporary home counts as exempt accommodation (see p416), you can get HB for it, and HB or a UC housing costs element for the rent you pay for your normal home;[75]
- **indefinitely**, if:[76]
  - you are a member of a couple and you or your partner are a student eligible for HB (see p915) or are on a training course (see p105 for the meaning), it is necessary for you to live apart and it is reasonable for you to receive HB for both homes;
  - the local authority has housed you in more than one home because your family is large.

Other situations

If you have left your home because of a **fear of violence** (see p105) and you do not intend to return, you can get HB for four weeks for your former home.[77] This only applies if your liability to pay rent was unavoidable – eg, you should have given your landlord notice, but had to leave in a hurry because of the violence.

If you have **two homes**, and you are only liable to pay for one of them, you are treated as occupying the home for which you pay and therefore get HB for that home, even when you are not there. This only applies if:

- you are a single claimant or a lone parent, and you are either a student eligible for HB (see p915) or are on a training course (see p105 for the meaning), and you live in one home during periods of study or training and another home at other times – eg, for vacations;[78] *or*

- you had to move into temporary accommodation because essential repairs are being carried out on your main home.[79] 'Essential repairs' means basic works rather than luxuries, but they need not be crucial to making the house habitable.[80]

Note: you cannot get HB under this rule if you pay rent for both homes, or if you pay rent for one and a mortgage on the other.

2. The rules about your age

There are no lower or upper age limits for claiming housing benefit (HB). However, if you are:
- **under 16**, there may be a question about whether you have a legally enforceable liability for rent (see p99);
- **16 or 17** and have been looked after by a local authority, you cannot usually claim HB. See p886 for further information;
- a **single claimant under 35** and are living in private rented accommodation, the amount of your rent that can be met by HB is usually restricted to the 'single room rent' or the local housing allowance for one-bedroom shared accommodation (see Chapter 19);
- at least **the qualifying age for pension credit** (see p78) and neither you nor your partner are getting income support, income-based jobseeker's allowance, income-related employment and support allowance or universal credit, more generous rules apply.

3. People included in the claim

You claim housing benefit (HB) for yourself. However, if you are a member of a couple, you or your partner must claim HB for you both. The applicable amount that forms part of the calculation of your benefit includes a personal allowance for a couple and can include premiums based on both your and your partner's circumstances. When your benefit is worked out, your partner's income and capital are usually added to yours. See p205 for who counts as a couple.

Sometimes you need to know when a child is included in your claim. A child is included in your claim if s/he lives in your household and you or your partner count as 'responsible' for her/him.[81] See p211 for who counts as a child (this includes some qualifying young people). You do not have to be the child's parent. For when you count as responsible for a child, and when s/he counts as living in your household, see pp212–15.

Your applicable amount includes allowances and premiums for child(ren) included in your claim. You should also check to see if you qualify for child tax

Part 2: Main means-tested benefits and tax credits
Chapter 7: Housing benefit
4. The amount of benefit

credit (see Chapter 8). There are additional situations in which you must show that your child(ren) are included in your claim – eg:

- to show you are a lone parent so you can benefit from a higher earnings disregard (see p268 and p309);
- to qualify for a disregard of earnings for childcare costs (see p270 and p311);
- for some of the rules about the size of accommodation or the number of bedrooms you are allowed (see Chapter 19).

4. The amount of benefit

The amount of housing benefit (HB) you get depends on:

- your 'applicable amount' (see Chapter 12). This is made up of personal allowances, as well as premiums and components for any special needs. It may include a transitional addition if you or your partner were transferred to contributory employment and support allowance (ESA) from income support (IS) 'on the grounds of disability', incapacity benefit (IB) or severe disablement allowance (SDA), or are appealing a decision not to transfer you to ESA (see p243);
- your 'maximum HB' (see below); *and*
- how much income and capital you have (see Chapters 14, 15, 17 and 18).

Maximum housing benefit

Your '**maximum HB**' is your 'eligible rent' (see p111), calculated on a weekly basis, minus any deductions made for your non-dependants (see p116).[82] The amount depends on whether your 'eligible rent' is restricted (see Chapter 19).

Example

Mr and Mrs Feinstein and their adult son live together in a two-bedroom flat rented from the local authority. They are allowed two bedrooms under the social sector rules. Mr Feinstein is the sole tenant. The rent is £100 a week. This does not include any service charges. Their son earns £150 a week gross.

Eligible rent is the contractual rent	£100.00
Minus non-dependant deduction (see p118)	£32.45
Maximum HB	**£67.55**

If you do not qualify for HB currently, you may qualify when:

- the benefit rates go up every April; *or*
- you or your partner reach:
  - the qualifying age for pension credit (PC – see p78). If neither you nor your partner are on IS, income-based jobseeker's allowance (JSA) or income-

related ESA (or universal credit – UC), your applicable amount is higher and the income and capital rules are also more generous; *or*
- 65. Your personal allowance is increased by the equivalent of the amount of the maximum savings credit of PC, whether or not you receive this, if neither you nor your partner are on IS, income-based JSA or income-related ESA (or UC).

If your income is too high for you to qualify for HB currently, you might qualify once you (or your partner or a child included in your claim) become entitled to another benefit (a 'qualifying benefit' – see p127).

If you need extra financial assistance to meet your housing costs, you might be entitled to discretionary housing payments (see Chapter 21).

Remember that if you or your partner:
- stop getting IS, income-based JSA, ESA, IB or SDA because of starting work or increasing your hours or your earnings, you may be entitled to extended payments of HB (see p136);
- stop getting IS, income-based JSA or income-related ESA because you or your partner are moving onto PC, you may be able to continue to receive HB at the same rate for four weeks. See p135 for information about continuing payments on PC;
- have been incapable of work but move into work or training, you might count as a 'welfare-to-work beneficiary'. This means you retain entitlement to the disability premium if you become incapable of work again within 104 weeks. See p686 of the 2013/14 edition of this *Handbook* for further information.

Note: you might get a reduced amount of HB if:
- you are affected by the 'benefit cap' (see p1169); *or*
- your HB is restricted because of a benefit offence (see p1258).

If you are on a means-tested benefit

Being on **IS, income-based JSA, income-related ESA** or **the guarantee credit of PC** (or **UC**) is an automatic passport to maximum HB (once you have made a claim for HB). You, therefore, do not need to work out your applicable amount, income or capital.[83] HB equals 'maximum HB' (see p108). **Note:** if you are on UC, you can only qualify for HB for exempt accommodation (see p416).

For these purposes, you are treated as being on:[84]
- income-based JSA:
  - when you satisfy the conditions of entitlement but are not being paid it because of a sanction (see p1083);
  - on your waiting days (see p53); *and*
  - when it is not paid because of the benefit offence rules (see p1258);
- income-related ESA:

Part 2: Main means-tested benefits and tax credits
Chapter 7: Housing benefit
4. The amount of benefit

- when you satisfy the conditions of entitlement but are not being paid it because you are disqualified for the reasons on p67, during a temporary absence abroad or because you are a prisoner;
        - on your waiting days (see p1017);
- UC on any day you are entitled to it, whether or not it is being paid to you.

Example

Glen and his partner Craig are the joint housing association tenants of a two-bedroom flat. Glen's aunt lives with them. They pay rent of £150 a week. They receive income-based JSA while they are looking for work. Glen's aunt receives IS. Glen claims HB. They are allowed two bedrooms under the social sector rules.

Eligible rent and, therefore, maximum HB is £150 a week.

Glen's aunt counts as a non-dependant and so £14.15 a week is deducted.

Therefore, Glen's maximum HB is £135.85 week (£150 – £14.15).

Because they receive income-based JSA, Glen's HB is £135.85 week.

If you are not on a means-tested benefit

If you are **not on IS, income-based JSA, income-related ESA or the guarantee credit of PC (or UC)**, you need to follow the steps below to calculate your HB.

- **Step one:** check that your capital is not too high (see Chapters 17 and 18).
- **Step two:** work out your maximum HB (see p108 for the meaning).
- **Step three:** work out your applicable amount (see Chapter 12).
- **Step four:** work out your income (see Chapters 14 and 15, but also p923 if you are a student and p305 if you are getting the savings credit of PC).
- **Step five:** calculate HB.
    - If your **income is less than or equal to your applicable amount**, HB equals maximum HB.
    - If your **income is greater than your applicable amount**, work out the difference. HB equals maximum HB minus 65 per cent of the difference between your income and your applicable amount.

Examples

Mr Jopling is aged 45. He is unemployed and gets contribution-based JSA of £72.40 a week. Mrs Jopling is aged 46. She works 21 hours a week. She is paid £180 a week after deductions of tax and national insurance (NI) contributions. The couple are joint private tenants who pay £120 rent a week. Mrs Jopling claims HB. Her eligible rent is £108 a week because rent restriction rules have been applied.

Mr and Mrs Jopling have no non-dependants. Therefore, her maximum HB is £108 a week. Mrs Jopling's applicable amount is £113.70 (the standard rate for a couple).

Income to be taken into account is Mr Jopling's JSA and Mrs Jopling's earnings of £170 a week (because £10 of her earnings are disregarded – see p269). £72.40 + £170 = £242.40.

The difference between her income and her applicable amount is £128.70 a week.

65% x £128.70 = £83.65 a week.

Mrs Jopling's HB is, therefore, £108 – £83.65 = £24.35 a week.

Mr Haralambous is 63 years old. He receives contributory ESA including a support component, totalling £108.10 a week. His weekly income from his private pension is £45. His total weekly income is therefore £153.10 (£108.10 + £45). He is a sole tenant of his one-bedroom council flat. His rent of £100 a week includes his heating and hot water. His eligible rent is £69.25 a week because £27.55 and £3.20 are deducted from his contractual rent for heating and hot water. This is also his maximum HB because he does not have any non-dependants.

His applicable amount is £148.35 (adult personal allowance for a single person at least the qualifying age for PC but under 65).

The difference between his income and his applicable amount is £4.75.

65% x £4.75 = £3.09 a week.

Mr Haralambous's HB is, therefore, £69.25 – £3.09 = £66.16 a week.

Eligible rent

Your 'eligible rent' is the amount of your rent used to calculate your HB. It may be lower than the actual amount of rent you pay. Unless any of the rent restriction rules apply to you, your eligible rent is your contractual rent, minus any ineligible charges (see p112).[85] If any of the rent restriction rules apply to you, your eligible rent is usually your 'maximum rent' as determined under those rules – ie, your contractual rent, minus any amount above the level to which your rent is restricted. See Chapter 19 for details of all the rent restriction schemes and how your maximum rent (and, therefore, your eligible rent) is worked out.

If none of the rent restriction rules apply, the local authority has general powers to decrease your eligible rent to an amount it considers appropriate (see p395).

Remember the following.

- If you are in shared accommodation, your eligible rent might be apportioned between you and the people with whom you share (see below).
- If the rent you pay covers both residential and other accommodation (eg, for business use), your HB only covers the rent you pay for the residential accommodation.[86]

If you live in shared accommodation

Unless the local housing allowance or social sector rules apply to you (see p395 and p403), if you share accommodation with people other than your partner and children included in your claim and are jointly liable for the rent with them, the local authority apportions the eligible rent between you. It considers:[87]

- the number of jointly liable people in the property (including any students who are treated as not liable to pay rent);[88] and

Part 2: Main means-tested benefits and tax credits
Chapter 7: Housing benefit
4. The amount of benefit

2

- the proportion of the rent actually paid by each liable person; *and*
- any other relevant circumstances, such as:
  - the number of rooms occupied by each jointly liable person;
  - whether any formal or informal agreement exists between you regarding the use and occupation of the home; *and*
  - if one of the jointly liable people has left the accommodation, the demands being made by the landlord on those who remain, or the possibility of finding other accommodation.

In some circumstances, it could be appropriate to apportion the whole of the rent to you even if you are jointly liable.[89]

If the rent includes any ineligible service charges, these are apportioned between you on the same basis as the rent. If only one of you is liable for the rent, that person is treated as the tenant and the other(s) might count as a non-dependant(s) (see p116).

Example

Sarah and Maude are friends who rent a two-bedroom housing association flat. They are joint tenants and pay rent of £100 a week. Sarah claims HB. The eligible rent is apportioned between them and Sarah's HB is based on £50 (£100 divided by two).

If the local housing allowance or social sector rules apply to you, although it is not necessary to apportion the eligible rent if you are jointly liable for it with people other than your partner or children included in your claim, the local authority *does* apportion your 'cap rent' (under the local housing allowance rules) or your maximum rent (under the social sector rules).[90] See Chapter 19 for details.

Ineligible charges

The local authority deducts ineligible charges when it works out your eligible rent. Note, however, that, if the local reference rent rules or the local housing allowance rules apply, an adjustment on account of ineligible charges is instead generally made when the rent officer makes determinations.

Ineligible charges include:
- water charges;[91]
- most fuel charges (see p113); *and*
- some service charges (see p114), including charges for meals.

Remember that, in addition, you cannot get HB for:
- payments for any part of your accommodation that is used exclusively for business purposes;[92]
- rent supplements charged to clear your rent arrears.[93]

Fuel charges

Fuel charges are ineligible unless they are for communal areas (see p114).[94] If your fuel charge is:

- specified on your rent book or is **readily identifiable** from your agreement with your landlord, the full amount of the charge is ineligible.[95] However, if your fuel charge is considered to be unrealistically low in relation to the fuel provided, a flat-rate amount is ineligible instead (see below). This is also the case if your total fuel charge is specified but contains an unknown amount for communal areas. If you are a local authority tenant, it is assumed that your fuel charges are always specified or readily identifiable.[96]
- **not readily identifiable**, a flat-rate amount is ineligible. The amounts are:[97]

If you and your family occupy more than one room:

For heating (other than hot water)	£27.55
For hot water	£3.20
For lighting	£2.20
For cooking	£3.20

If you and your family occupy one room only:

For heating alone, or heating combined with either hot water or lighting or both	£16.48
For cooking	£3.20

These amounts are added together where fuel is supplied for more than one purpose. If you are a joint tenant, all the amounts are apportioned according to your share of the rent (see p111).

Note: the local authority must notify you if flat-rate fuel amounts have been used in calculating your HB. It must explain that, if you can produce evidence from which the actual or approximate amount of your fuel charge can be estimated, the flat-rate amounts may be varied accordingly.

Do you occupy one room only?

The lower amounts apply if the accommodation you and your partner and children occupy consists of one room only (see above). This is not defined, but the decision maker is likely to say this means that, if you only occupy one room but share the use of other rooms (such as a communal lounge), the higher amounts apply.[98] Argue that bathrooms, toilets and shared kitchens are not rooms you occupy. If you are forced to live in one room because the other room(s) in your accommodation are, in practice, unfit to live in (eg, because of severe mould or dampness), argue that the lower amounts apply.

Part 2: Main means-tested benefits and tax credits
Chapter 7: Housing benefit
4. The amount of benefit

Fuel for communal areas

If you pay a service charge for the use of fuel in communal areas, and that charge is separately identified from any other charge for fuel used within your accommodation, it may be included as part of your eligible rent.[99] Communal areas include access areas like halls and passageways, but not rooms in common use, except those in sheltered accommodation – eg, a shared TV lounge or dining room.[100] If you pay a charge for the provision of a heating system (eg, regular boiler maintenance), this is also eligible if the amount is separately identified from any other fuel charge you pay.[101]

Service charges

Service charges are only covered by HB if payment is a condition of occupying the accommodation rather than an optional extra.[102] Eligible and ineligible service charges are listed below. If the local authority regards any of the eligible charges as excessive, it estimates a reasonable amount given the cost of comparable services.[103] If you are in supported accommodation, see p115.

Eligible services

The following services are eligible for HB:

- services for the provision of adequate accommodation, including some warden and caretaker services, gardens, children's play areas, lifts, entry phones, communal telephone costs, portering and rubbish removal.[104] This can include upkeep of a communal garden.[105] TV and radio relay charges are covered – eg, satellite or cable, including free-to-view UK channels;[106]
- laundry facilities (eg, a laundry room in an apartment block), but not charges for the provision of personal laundry;[107]
- furniture and household equipment, but not if there is an agreement that the furniture will eventually become yours;[108]
- cleaning of the outside of windows where neither you nor any member of your household are able to clean them yourself and cleaning of rooms and windows in communal areas, unless payment for these is made by your local authority or the Welsh Ministers.[109]

Ineligible services

The following services are not eligible for HB:[110]

- food, including prepared meals (see p115);
- sports facilities;
- TV rental, licence and subscription fees (but see above);
- transport;
- personal laundry service;
- provision of an emergency alarm system;
- medical expenses;
- nursing and personal care;

- counselling and other support services;
- any other charge not connected with the provision of adequate accommodation and not specifically included in the list of eligible charges on p114.

The amount of the charge specified in your rent agreement is not eligible for HB, although local authorities can substitute their own estimate if they consider the amount to be unreasonably low.[111] If the amount is not specified in your rent agreement, the local authority estimates how much is fairly attributable to the service, given the cost of comparable services.[112]

Charges for meals

If your housing costs include an amount for meals, set amounts are ineligible regardless of the actual cost.[113] These are:

If at least three meals a day are provided:

For the claimant, partner and each child aged 16 or over included in the claim £26.55

For each child aged under 16 included in the claim £13.45

If breakfast only is provided:

For the claimant, partner and each child included in the claim £3.25

In all other cases (part board):

For the claimant, partner and each child aged 16 or over included in the claim £17.65

For each child aged under 16 included in the claim £8.90

A child is treated as having reached the age of 16 on the first Monday in September following her/his 16th birthday.

Note: the standard amounts are also ineligible for everyone who has meals paid for by you – eg, a non-dependant.[114]

Service charges in supported accommodation

If you live in supported accommodation, HB can help with your rent. However, HB is not available for the support services provided with your accommodation. Instead, the local authority funds these – eg, via your landlord or a voluntary organisation.

In some cases, your local authority can charge you for the support services you get. A means test is used to determine how much you have to pay.

Calculating a weekly amount of housing benefit

HB is always paid for a specific benefit week – a period of seven consecutive days beginning with a Monday and ending on a Sunday.[115] If you pay rent at different intervals (eg, monthly or daily), the amount has to be converted to a weekly figure before HB can be calculated.[116]

Part 2: Main means-tested benefits and tax credits
Chapter 7: Housing benefit
4. The amount of benefit

Rent-free periods

If you have a regular rent-free period (eg, you pay rent on a 48-week rent year), you get no HB during your rent-free period. Your applicable amount, weekly income, non-dependant deductions, the set deductions for meals and fuel charges and the minimum amount payable (but not your eligible rent) are adjusted.[117]

Note: this does not apply if your landlord has temporarily waived the rent in return for you doing repairs (see p98).

Deductions for non-dependants

If other people normally live with you in your home, other than your partner and children included in your claim (called 'non-dependants'), a set deduction is usually made from your HB.[118] This is because it is assumed the non-dependant makes a contribution towards your outgoings, whether or not s/he does so. Examples of non-dependants are adult sons or daughters, or elderly relatives who share your home.

Non-dependant deductions: checklist

1. Do you have a non-dependant – ie, someone who normally lives with you? If not, no deduction can be made.
2. Even if you have a non-dependant, must a deduction be made?
3. If a non-dependant deduction must be made, what is the correct amount of the deduction?

Who counts as a non-dependant

A person only counts as your non-dependant if s/he normally lives with you.[119] So, for example, if someone is only staying with you temporarily but has a home elsewhere, or is homeless and is only using your address as a postal address, s/he should not count as a non-dependant. If you think the local authority has wrongly assumed that a person is your non-dependant, ask for a revision or appeal. Note: some people do not count as non-dependants even if they normally live with you (see p117).

A person is only **living with you** if s/he has her/his home with you and shares some accommodation with you.[120] This includes sharing the kitchen (unless it is only used by someone else to prepare food for her/him[121]), but not a bathroom, lavatory or a communal area such as a hall, passageway or a room in common use in sheltered accommodation. If other areas of the house are shared, the person is treated as living with you. This is the case even if you only use them at different times, so long as you have a shared right to use them and are living in the same household (see p215 for the meaning of 'household').[122] A person who is separately liable to pay rent to your landlord does not count as living with you.

A person should only count as **normally living with you** if s/he has been there long enough to regard your home as her/his normal home.[123] Factors to be taken into account to decide whether a person is normally living with you include:[124]

- the relationship between you;
- how much time s/he spends at your address;
- where s/he has her/his post sent;
- where s/he keeps her/his clothes and personal belongings;
- whether her/his stay or absence from your address is temporary or permanent. The local authority may use the temporary absence rules on p103 to work this out;[125]
- whether s/he has another place that could be regarded as home and if, for instance, s/he pays rent or water charges there or s/he just travels around.

People who do not count as non-dependants

The following people do *not* count as non-dependants, and no non-dependant deduction is made for them, even if they normally live with you:[126]

- your partner;
- a child or qualifying young person included in your claim;
- a child or qualifying young person living with you who does not count as a member of your household (see p214) – eg, a foster child, or someone placed with you prior to adoption;
- someone who is employed by a charitable or voluntary organisation as a resident carer for you or your partner and who you pay for the service. This can also apply if a public body pays on your behalf;
- any person, or a member of her/his household, to whom you or your partner are liable to pay rent on a commercial basis;
- someone who jointly occupies your home and is either a co-owner or jointly liable with you or your partner to make payments in respect of occupying it. You do not jointly occupy the home with someone unless you made a joint agreement with your landlord to occupy the home. The mere fact that you live in the same home does not make you joint occupiers;[127]
- someone who is liable to pay rent on a commercial basis to you or your partner. However, although no non-dependant deduction can be made for her/him, the rent s/he pays can count as your income (see p280 and p314).

If the person comes within the last three categories above, s/he *does* count as a non-dependant if s/he is treated as not liable for rent under the rules explained on pp99–101 (unless s/he is a student or a 'person subject to immigration control', or s/he has failed the 'habitual residence test').[128]

Part 2: Main means-tested benefits and tax credits
Chapter 7: Housing benefit
4. The amount of benefit

When no non-dependant deduction is made

Even if you have a non-dependant, no non-dependant deduction is made for her/him if either you or your partner:[129]

- are registered blind (certified blind in Scotland) or have regained your eyesight within the last 28 weeks; *or*
- receive attendance allowance (AA) (or equivalent benefits paid because of injury at work or a war injury), the care component of disability living allowance (DLA), the daily living component of personal independence payment (PIP) or armed forces independence payment.

No deduction is made in respect of any non-dependant who is:[130]

- staying with you but whose normal home is elsewhere;
- receiving a training allowance in connection with youth training under specified provisions;[131]
- a full-time student during her/his period of study. This includes those getting JSA who count as full-time students while on a specified scheme for assisting people to obtain employment (see p1093). **Note:** no deduction is made during the summer vacation but, if you or your partner are under 65, only if the student is not in full-time work;
- not living with you because s/he is a member of the armed forces and is deployed on operations, no matter how long s/he has been away;
- in hospital for more than 52 weeks. Separate stays in hospital which are not more than 28 days apart are added together when calculating the 52 weeks;
- in prison;
- under 18 years old;[132]
- under 25 and:
  - on IS, income-based JSA or income-related ESA which does not include a work-related activity or support component. S/he can be treated as on income-based JSA or income-related ESA for these purposes (see p109);[133]
  - entitled to UC, provided s/he does not have any earned income;
- on PC.

The amount of deductions

If you have a non-dependant living with you who is 18 or over, and for whom a deduction must be made, a fixed amount is deducted from your HB, whatever s/he pays you. A deduction is made for every non-dependant living in your household, except in the case of a non-dependant couple (see p120).

Unless your non-dependant is in full-time paid work, a £14.15 deduction is made each week. If your non-dependant is in full-time paid work, the amount of the deduction depends on her/his gross weekly income as follows.[134]

Circumstances of the non-dependant	Deduction
Aged 18 or over and in full-time paid work with a weekly gross income of:	
£406 or more	£91.15
£326–£405.99	£83.05
£245–£325.99	£72.95
£188–£244.99	£44.55
£128–£187.99	£32.45
All others (for whom a deduction is made)	£14.15

The rules on full-time paid work are in Chapter 46. Remember the following.

- A non-dependant who is not in (or is treated as not in) full-time paid work does not attract the higher levels of deduction even if her/his weekly gross income is £128 or more.
- If someone is on IS, income-based JSA or income-related ESA (see p109) for more than three days in a benefit week, s/he does not count as being in full-time paid work in that week.[135] This means the lower deduction (£14.15) is made (or, in some cases, no deduction).

Gross income includes wages before tax and NI are deducted, plus any other income the non-dependant has (apart from AA (or equivalent benefits paid because of injury at work or a war injury), DLA, PIP, armed forces independence payment and payments from any of the Macfarlane Trusts, the Eileen Trust, MFET Ltd, the Skipton Fund, the Caxton Foundation, the London Bombings Relief Charitable Fund, the Fund and the Independent Living Fund (2006)).[136]

Do you know your non-dependant's income?

You should try to provide information to show which deduction applies. However, if you do not know your non-dependant's income, ask the local authority to consider the circumstances – eg, if your non-dependant is doing a job which is normally very low paid. The local authority should not assume the worst – eg, that your non-dependant is earning the highest amount. It should assess what the likely level of her/his income is on the evidence available.[137]

If you are 65 or over

If you or your partner are 65 or over and a non-dependant moves in with you, so a deduction should be made, or there has been a change of circumstances in respect of a non-dependant, the effect of this can be delayed for 26 weeks (see p142).

Part 2: Main means-tested benefits and tax credits
Chapter 7: Housing benefit
5. Special benefit rules

2

Non-dependant couples

Only one deduction is made for a couple (or the members of a polygamous marriage) who are non-dependants. The deduction made is the highest that would have been made if they were treated as individuals.[138] For the purpose of deciding which income band applies (see p119), their joint income counts, even if only one of them is in full-time work.[139]

Non-dependants of joint occupiers

If you share a non-dependant with any other joint occupiers, the deduction is divided between you, taking into account the proportion of housing costs paid by each.[140] If the person is a non-dependant of only one of you, the full deduction is made from that person's benefit. No apportionment is made between the members of a couple (or polygamous marriage).

Income and capital of a non-dependant is greater than yours

Normally, the income and capital of any non-dependant is only relevant when deciding which non-dependant deduction applies. However, unless you are on IS, income-based JSA, income-related ESA or the guarantee credit of PC, your HB entitlement is assessed on the basis of your non-dependant's income and capital rather than your own if:[141]
- the income and capital of your non-dependant are both greater than yours; *and*
- the local authority is satisfied you have made an arrangement with your non-dependant to take advantage of the HB scheme (see p101 for what this means).

Any income and capital normally treated as belonging to you is completely ignored, but the rest of the calculation proceeds as normal.

Extra benefit for war pensioners

The local authority has the power to pay extra HB to people getting certain war pensions, by disregarding some or all of the pension as income, rather than just disregarding £10.[142] See p275 and p313 for further information.

---

5. **Special benefit rules**

Special rules may apply to:
- people who are studying (see p915);
- people subject to immigration control (see p1500);
- 16/17-year-olds formerly looked after by a local authority (see p886);
- prisoners (see pp961–62);
- people in care homes and other similar accommodation (see p955).

6. Claims and backdating

To be entitled to housing benefit (HB) you must make a claim for it.[143] Some of the general rules about claims are in Chapter 53. This section explains the specific rules that apply to HB. Claim HB as soon as you think you might be entitled to it or you may lose benefit. The rules about backdating are explained on p128.

If you want to claim discretionary housing payments, you must claim separately (see Chapter 21).

Making a claim

A claim for HB must normally be made in writing on a properly completed claim form.[144] See p124 for information about where to claim. Note that if you are claiming another benefit (ie, income support (IS), income-based jobseeker's allowance (JSA), employment and support allowance (ESA), incapacity benefit (IB) or pension credit (PC)), you can claim HB at the same time (see p122).

You may also be able to claim:
- by telephone if:
  – your local authority has published a number for this purpose.[145] The local authority may then provide a written statement of your circumstances. For your claim to be valid, you must approve this statement. Note that, even if you cannot claim by telephone, if you telephone to ask to be sent a claim form and you return it within one month, your claim is backdated to the date of your call (see p126); *or*
  – you are claiming IS, JSA, ESA, IB or PC by telephone;
- by electronic communication (eg, online or by email), if your local authority has authorised it (by a Chief Executive's Direction).[146]

If you claim in writing, keep a copy in case queries arise. **Note:** the local authority can treat any written document (eg, a letter) as a claim for benefit, so long as the written information and evidence you provide is sufficient.[147]

You must provide any information and evidence required (see p125). You can amend or withdraw your claim before a decision is made (see p123).

Forms

Claim forms are available from your local authority or to download at www.gov.uk/housing-benefit/how-to-claim.[148]

Note:
- Make your claim as soon as you can so you do not lose benefit. However, ensure your claim is accepted as valid (see p122).

Part 2: Main means-tested benefits and tax credits
Chapter 7: Housing benefit
6. Claims and backdating

- If you are claiming HB within a set number of weeks of a previous entitlement ending, you might be given a shortened claim form. This is known as 'rapid reclaim' (see p124).

If you are claiming another benefit

You may be able to make your claim for HB with your claim for another benefit if:
- you are claiming IS, JSA, ESA, IB or PC by telephone;
- you are claiming IS, income-based JSA or PC on a written claim form;
- you are providing evidence or information or notifying a change of circumstances in connection with your IS, JSA, ESA, IB or PC claim.

If you are **claiming IS, JSA, ESA, IB or PC by telephone**, your HB claim is usually completed at the same time.[149] The DWP takes your details over the telephone and sends you a statement of your circumstances to check, sign and return to the Jobcentre Plus office, along with evidence to support your claim. Your HB claim is forwarded to the local authority. You can claim HB by telephone to the DWP (using the number specified for this purpose) at any time before a decision is made on your claim for IS, JSA, ESA, IB or PC. **Note:** if the local authority or DWP provides a written statement of your circumstances, you must approve this for your claim to be valid.[150]

If you are **claiming IS, income-based JSA or PC on a written claim form**, you are given an HB claim form with the IS/JSA/PC form to complete and return to the local authority. The local authority may ask you to complete its own form. You should do this as soon as possible.

If the DWP agrees, you can claim HB **when you are providing evidence or information that is required, or notifying a change of circumstances, in connection with your claim for IS, JSA, ESA, IB or PC.**[151] You can do this at any time before a decision is made on the award of benefit to which the evidence, information or change of circumstances relates. Although the rules do not say so, the intention is that you can make your claim for HB by telephone in this situation.[152] The local authority or DWP might ask you for further information and evidence (see p125).

Making sure your claim is valid

Where possible, your claim for HB should be accompanied by all the information and evidence needed to assess it.[153] Your claim is 'defective' if you:
- do not complete your claim form properly or you claim in writing, but not on the claim form (eg, by letter or by electronic communication), and do not provide sufficient information and evidence;
- claim by telephone and do not provide all the information required by the local authority or DWP during the telephone call.

It is very important that you provide any information or evidence required. Until you do, you may not count as having made a valid claim. However, you should not delay your claim just because you do not have all the evidence ready to send.

If you have:[154]

- not completed the claim form properly, the local authority can return it to you to do so. However, if you sent or gave your claim form to the DWP, it can ask you to provide the local authority with information needed to complete the form; *or*
- claimed in writing, but not on the claim form (eg, by letter or electronic communication), the local authority can send you a claim form to complete properly; *or*
- claimed by telephone to the local authority, the local authority must give you an opportunity to provide the information required; *or*
- claimed by telephone to the DWP, the DWP can give you an opportunity to provide the information required. However, if the DWP does not do so, the local authority *must* give you an opportunity to provide the information, unless it thinks it already has sufficient information.

If you return the form completed properly or provide the information or evidence within one month, your claim is treated as though it was received on the date of your original claim.[155] The local authority can allow you longer than one month if it thinks this reasonable. Note that if you claimed HB by telephone to the DWP, and you do not provide the information required within the time limit, the local authority can still treat your claim as though it was received on the date of your original claim if it thinks it already has sufficient information.

Note:

- If your claim is not accepted as valid, you should be given a decision saying so. You can appeal against the decision.
- Even if you provide all the information required with your claim, the local authority (or DWP) might ask you to provide further evidence or information (see p125).

Amending or withdrawing your claim

You may amend your claim at any time before a decision is made. You can do this by writing to the local authority, by telephone to the local authority or the DWP or by any other manner the local authority or DWP decides or accepts.[156] If you amend your claim by telephone, you must do this to the number specified by the local authority or DWP. Amendments are treated as though they were part of your original claim.

You may withdraw your claim at any time before a decision is made.[157] You must do this by writing to the local authority or, if you made your claim by telephone to the local authority, by telephone to the local authority. A notice to withdraw your claim takes effect from the day it is received.

Part 2: Main means-tested benefits and tax credits
Chapter 7: Housing benefit
6. Claims and backdating

Rapid reclaim

You may be able to complete a shortened HB claim form (known as 'rapid reclaim') if your circumstances have not changed since the last time you were claiming HB, and:[158]

- you are reclaiming within 26 weeks, are also reclaiming IS, JSA or IB and are entitled to IS, income-based JSA or IB; *or*
- you are reclaiming within 12 weeks and you are also reclaiming ESA.

You are given the shortened form by the Jobcentre Plus office but you must send your HB claim to the local authority, *not* to the DWP.

Where to make your claim

If you claim **in writing**, you must usually send or give your HB claim to the local authority's designated office for the receipt of HB claims.[159] The address is usually on the claim form or a notice accompanying it. You can also send or give your claim to:[160]

- if you or your partner are also claiming IS, JSA, ESA, IB or PC, either your DWP office or the local authority's designated office for HB claims. If you send your HB claim to the DWP, unless it is on the same form as your IS, JSA, ESA, IB or PC claim, the DWP must forward it to the local authority.[161]
  It may speed up your claim if you send your HB form direct to the local authority. The local authority then verifies your entitlement to IS, JSA, ESA or IB before assessing your HB; *or*
- a county council office, if your local authority has arranged for claims to be received there; *or*
- if you are at least the qualifying age for PC (see p78), any 'authorised office' – ie, an office nominated by the DWP and authorised by the local authority for receiving HB claims.

Keep a copy of your claim form wherever possible. Ask for confirmation that you have delivered it to the relevant office.

If your local authority has authorised it and you are claiming **by electronic communication**, check the correct address for this with your local authority.[162]

If you are allowed to claim **by telephone**, you must make your claim to the telephone number published or specified for this purpose.[163]

Who should claim

If you are a single person or a lone parent, you claim HB on your own behalf. If you are a member of a couple, you can decide between you who should claim. If you cannot agree who should claim, the local authority can decide for you.[164]

Who should you choose to make the claim?

If you are a member of a couple, the choice of claimant may affect the level of HB you receive – eg, if one of you is a full-time student and not eligible for HB (see p915) or if one of you is getting ESA and the other is getting disability living allowance (DLA). In addition, if you are considering changing the claim to your partner's name, check whether this could result in your becoming subject to harsher rent restriction rules (see Chapter 19) or losing entitlement to any premiums or components (see Chapter 12).

If a person is either temporarily or permanently unable to manage her/his own affairs, the local authority must accept a claim made by someone formally appointed to act legally on her/his behalf.[165]

If no one has been formally appointed to look after a claimant's affairs, the local authority can decide to make someone aged over 18 an appointee who can act on her/his behalf.[166] For the purpose of the claim, an appointee has the responsibility of exercising all rights and duties as though s/he were the claimant.[167]

You can write to ask to be an appointee, and can resign after giving four weeks' notice. The local authority may terminate any appointment at any time.[168] If someone is given a formal legal appointment, that person automatically takes over from the person appointed by the local authority.[169]

Information to support your claim

When you claim HB, you must:
- satisfy the national insurance (NI) number requirement (see below and p1138), unless you are living in a hostel. If you are a member of a couple, your partner must also usually satisfy this requirement;
- provide proof of your identity, if required; *and*
- ensure your claim is valid – ie, you must provide information and evidence required with the claim (see p122).

Even if you have provided all that was required when you claimed, the local authority (or DWP) might ask you to provide additional evidence or information relevant to your claim. You must then supply this within one month, or longer if the local authority thinks this is reasonable.[170]

If you or your partner are getting IS or JSA and have notified the DWP that you have started work, the DWP can ask you to provide the local authority with any information or evidence it needs to decide whether you continue to be entitled to HB.[171] This only applies if, as a result of the change, your entitlement to IS or JSA will end or, if you are getting contribution-based JSA, the amount will reduce.

If you have claimed HB in association with a claim for IS, income-based JSA or PC and the DWP has accepted that you satisfy the NI number requirement, the local authority can accept that it is also satisfied for HB purposes.[172] If your claim is for contribution-based JSA, contributory ESA or IB, the local authority may still need to verify your partner's NI number and identity.

Part 2: Main means-tested benefits and tax credits
Chapter 7: Housing benefit
6. Claims and backdating

The local authority may ask you to provide information after you are awarded HB. If you fail to do so, your HB could be suspended or even terminated (see p1175). **Note:** you must actually have been notified; proof of posting to your last known address is not sufficient.[173]

The date of your claim

Claim as soon as you think you might be entitled to HB. You are not usually entitled to HB for any day before your date of claim. Your date of claim is important because it affects the date from which your entitlement to HB starts (see p135). Remember: your date of claim is not necessarily the date it is received by the local authority. It can be an earlier date (see below). In some cases, you can claim in advance (see p127) and in some cases your claim can be backdated (see p128).

Your '**date of claim**' is usually the earliest of:[174]

- the date you first notify a designated office, DWP office or authorised office (see p124) (or county council office, if the local authority has arranged for claims there) that you want to claim HB (eg, by telephone, in person or where someone does this on your behalf), if a properly completed claim is received in one of those offices within one month. The one-month period can be extended if the local authority thinks it is reasonable; *or*
- the date your valid claim is received by the designated office, DWP office or authorised office (see p124) (or county council office, if the local authority has arranged for claims there).

There are exceptions to the rule if:[175]

- you or your partner have successfully claimed IS, income-based JSA, income-related ESA or the guarantee credit of PC and your HB claim is made within one month of that claim being received by the DWP. Your claim is treated as made on the first day of entitlement to IS, income-based JSA, income-related ESA or PC (including the waiting days for JSA or ESA). For example, if your claim for IS is backdated, your date of claim for HB purposes is the date to which your IS claim is backdated;[176]
- you or your partner are on IS, income-based JSA, income-related ESA or the guarantee credit of PC (or universal credit – UC), have just become liable to pay rent and your HB claim reaches the local authority's designated office or DWP office within one month of your becoming liable. Your claim is treated as having been made on the date that you first became liable;
- you have separated from your partner or s/he has died and s/he was claiming HB for you on the date this happened and you claim within one month of this. Your claim is treated as having been made on the date you separated or your partner died.

Note: if you claim UC, there are two further exceptions.

- If you are awarded UC and you claim HB within one month of your UC claim or, if you are someone who does not have to make a claim for UC, within one month of being notified that you were awarded UC, your HB claim is treated as made on the first day of entitlement to UC.[177] **Note:** you can only qualify for HB for exempt accommodation (see p416).
- If you gave incorrect information (eg, about your personal circumstances), you did not actually come under the UC system (see p19) on the date of your UC claim and the DWP discovers this before a decision is made, or after a decision has been made but before you have been paid any UC, you must be informed that you are not entitled to UC. If you then claim HB within one month of this and your date of claim under the rules described above (or under the rules for backdating) is after the date you claimed UC, your HB claim is treated as made on the date you claimed UC.[178]

Claiming in advance

You can claim HB in advance if:

- you become liable for rent for the first time but cannot move into your accommodation until after your liability begins. You must claim HB as soon as you are liable. Once you move in, you may be able to receive HB for up to four weeks prior to moving in (see p102);
- you are not entitled to HB now, but will become entitled within 13 weeks of claiming (17 weeks if you or your partner will be the qualifying age for PC (see p78) within 17 weeks), unless the reason you do not qualify straight away is because you fail the 'habitual residence test' (see p1521). The local authority can treat your claim as having been made in the benefit week immediately before you are first entitled.[179] If this happens, you do not need to make a further claim later.

Housing benefit after an award of a qualifying benefit

You might not be entitled to HB currently, but would be once you, your partner, or a child or qualifying young person included in your claim become entitled to another 'qualifying benefit' – eg, DLA, personal independence payment or carer's allowance. Alternatively, you might be entitled to a higher rate of benefit once the qualifying benefit is awarded. If you are already entitled to HB when the qualifying benefit is awarded, see p1278, p1285 and p1294.

Do you only qualify for housing benefit when a qualifying benefit is awarded?

If you only qualify for HB when a qualifying benefit is awarded, the rules operate in an unfair way.

1. You should claim HB while waiting to hear about the claim for a qualifying benefit.

2. If you do not qualify for HB, ask the local authority to wait to make a decision on your claim until the award of the qualifying benefit is made (known as 'stockpiling' your claim).

Part 2: Main means-tested benefits and tax credits
Chapter 7: Housing benefit
6. Claims and backdating

If the local authority refuses, argue that its failure to delay making a decision on your claim was an 'error of law' and, therefore, that there are grounds for an 'any time' revision (see p1275).[180]

3. If you are refused HB but are then awarded a qualifying benefit, claim again and ask for your claim to be backdated. Argue that you have good cause for your late claim (see p129).

4. If you lose benefit because of the way the rules operate, ask your local authority for compensation to cover the period before your fresh HB claim.

Backdating your claim

It is very important to claim in time. Even if your claim is backdated, the arrears of HB you can get are limited. Your claim can be backdated:

- for up to three months if you are at least the qualifying age for PC and neither you nor your partner are on IS, income-based JSA or income-related ESA (or UC) (see below);
- for up to six months if you are not yet the qualifying age for PC or you or your partner are on IS, income-based JSA or income-related ESA (or UC), but you must show good cause for your late claim (see p129).

For backdated HB to be considered, you must ask for HB for a past period. Do this as soon as possible, preferably at the same time as your claim for HB. Any backdated HB is calculated on the basis of your circumstances and the HB rules as they were over the backdating period.

If you would have been entitled to HB for an earlier period than the backdating rules allow, you could:

- ask for an any time revision if there are grounds (see p1275);
- ask for compensation from the local authority if you were given wrong information or misled by it (see p1382);
- complain to the Ombudsman (see p1388).

If you only qualify for HB when a qualifying benefit is awarded, see p127.

Note: if you are entitled to UC, you cannot claim HB (other than for exempt accommodation) even if this is for a period before you were entitled to UC.[181]

Three months' backdating

If you are at least the qualifying age for PC and neither you nor your partner are on IS, income-based JSA or income-related ESA (or UC), your claim for HB can be backdated for up to three months.[182] This applies whatever the reasons were for your delay in claiming and even if you do not ask for HB for a past period until some time after you make your claim for HB. You only need to show that you qualified for HB during that period.

You can get backdated HB for the three months before the date of your HB claim (see p126) – eg, the date your claim was received or the date you notified the local authority that you wanted to claim HB.[183] However, if you or your partner successfully claimed the guarantee credit of PC and your claim for HB is received within one month of your PC claim being received by the DWP, your entitlement to HB cannot begin earlier than three months before your claim for PC was made (or treated as made).

Six months' backdating

Your claim for HB can be backdated for up to six months, provided you are not yet the qualifying age for PC or, if you are at least that age, provided neither you nor your partner are on IS, income-based JSA or income-related ESA (or UC).[184]

You must show that you qualified for HB during the period *and* prove you had continuous 'good cause' for your failure to claim or to ask for backdated HB (see below). You can only get backdated HB from the latest of the following:[185]

- the day from which you had continuous good cause for your late claim; *or*
- the day six months before the date of your HB claim (see p126) – eg, six months before the date your claim was received or the date you notified the local authority that you wanted to claim HB; *or*
- the day six months before you asked for backdated HB.

Example

Rose claimed HB on 1 April, within one month of a successful claim for IS (made on 14 March 2014). She asked for backdated HB on 8 April 2014.

The local authority accepts that she had continuous good cause for her late claim from 23 February 2010.

Her claim for HB is treated as made on 14 March 2014 (the first day of entitlement to IS – see p126). Six months before that date is 14 September 2013.

The day six months before she asked for backdated HB is 8 October 2013.

Rose gets backdated HB from 8 October 2013, the latest of the three relevant dates.

Good cause for claiming late

You count as having '**good cause**' for your late claim if you can show there is something that would probably have caused a reasonable person of your age and experience to act (or fail to act) as you did, having regard to all the circumstances (including your state of health and the information which you received and which you might have obtained).[186] The more reasonable your behaviour in not claiming earlier given your circumstances, the more likely it is that you have good cause.[187] It is your mental age, not your chronological age, that is relevant.[188] If you have a mental health problem that makes you act unreasonably, that must be borne in mind.[189] If you have difficulty communicating in English or understanding documents, or have little knowledge of the benefits system, this

Part 2: Main means-tested benefits and tax credits
Chapter 7: Housing benefit
6. Claims and backdating

should be taken into account, but these are not usually good cause in themselves.[190]

If you choose not to claim but later change your mind, you still have to show you have good cause for your late claim. The longer you have delayed in claiming, the harder this may be.[191] However, you may be able to show you have good cause – eg, if the reason you did not claim earlier was because you were making real efforts to find work to avoid relying on benefits, and you only chose not to claim for a limited period.

Good cause for making a late claim: examples

1. You sought advice about your rights, but were misled by someone on whom you were entitled to rely – eg, officers from the local authority or the DWP or independent advisers such as solicitors, Citizens Advice Bureaux, trade union officials or accountants.[192] Relying on the advice of work colleagues, friends, or even a doctor, is not enough.[193] The enquiries that you made need not have been specific, provided the situation is such that you ought to have been told about your possible entitlement.

2. You did not seek advice about your rights because you misunderstood them (eg, you reasonably believed you did not need to make a claim), you mistakenly thought that you understood them or you mistakenly thought that you had no entitlement and there was nothing for you to enquire about.[194] Generally, you are expected to find out about your rights, but if it was reasonable for you to form one of these views, you can still have good cause.

3. The delay was due to something beyond your control (eg, the failure of the post or of someone you asked to help with your claim), provided you checked whether the claim arrived in good time.[195]

4. You were unable to claim because of physical or mental ill health.[196] However, you might reasonably be expected to seek the assistance of friends or relatives if available.

5. You only qualify for HB when a qualifying benefit is awarded (see p127).

Notice of the decision

If you are a person affected by an HB decision, you must be notified of it by the local authority without delay if it is a decision on a claim (within 14 days in other cases) or as soon as 'reasonably practicable'.[197] You can request reasons for a decision. Your request must be in writing and it must be signed by you.[198]

You are a person affected by a decision if you are:[199]

- a claimant;
- someone acting for a claimant who is unable to act for her/himself – eg, an appointee;
- someone from whom the local authority decides to recover an overpayment (including a landlord); *or*

- a landlord or agent if the decision concerns whether or not to make a direct payment of HB to you.[200]

Information a decision notice should contain

The local authority must include a minimum amount of information in its decision notice and may also include other relevant information.[201] If the decision is one against which you have a right of appeal (see p1307), you must be informed of:[202]

- your right to appeal against the decision; *and*
- your right to a written statement of reasons for the decision (if this is not already included – see p1156).

The information that must be provided varies with the particular circumstances of your case and includes the following (where relevant).[203]

- The normal weekly amount of HB to which you are entitled, including the amount of any non-dependant deductions and fuel deductions. You must be told why fuel deductions have been made and that they can be varied if you provide evidence of the actual amount involved.
- Your weekly eligible rent (see p111).
- If you are a private tenant, the day your HB will be paid and whether payment will be made weekly or monthly.
- The date on which your entitlement starts.
- In some cases, how your applicable amount is calculated, how your income has been assessed and the amount of capital the local authority has taken into account. If the income and capital of a non-dependant has been used instead of yours to calculate your HB (see p120), you must be informed of this and the reasons why.
- If your claim was:
  - successful, your duty to notify the local authority of any change in circumstances which might affect your entitlement and the kinds of changes that should be reported;
  - unsuccessful, a statement explaining exactly why you are not entitled.
- If it has been decided to pay your HB direct to your landlord, information saying how much is to be paid to her/him and when payments will start. If recovery of an overpayment (see p1239) is made from a landlord's tenant other than the one who was overpaid, the tenant from whose HB the recovery is made is treated as if the full payment of HB had been made.[204]

7. **Getting paid**

How payment of housing benefit (HB) is made depends on whether you are the tenant of the housing authority responsible for paying HB (a local authority) or a private or housing association tenant (see below). If you are unable to act for yourself, payment can be made to someone else on your behalf (see p133). In some circumstances, payment can be made to your landlord (see p133). **Note:** no HB is payable if the amount would be less than 50 pence a week.[205]

When is housing benefit paid?

You are normally paid in arrears at intervals of a week, two weeks, four weeks or a month, depending on when your rent is usually due. HB can also be paid at longer intervals if you agree.[206] If you are a private or housing association tenant, the local authority can pay your rent allowance weekly to avoid an overpayment or if you are liable to pay rent weekly and it is in your interests for HB to be paid weekly.[207]

Different rules apply if HB is paid direct to your landlord.[208]
Note:
- Your HB might be paid at a reduced rate if you have been sanctioned for benefit offences (see p1258).
- If payment of your HB is delayed, see p139. You might be able to get a 'payment on account' (see p139). If you wish to complain about how your claim has been dealt with, see p1385. You might be able to claim compensation (see p1382).
- If payment of your HB is suspended, see p1175.
- If you are overpaid HB, you might have to repay it (see Chapter 56) and, in some circumstances, you may have to pay a penalty (see p1249). If you have been accused of fraud, see Chapter 57.

How your benefit is paid

If **your landlord is the housing authority** responsible for paying HB, your HB is paid in the form of a reduction in your rent. This is called a 'rent rebate'.[209]

If **you are a private or housing association tenant**, you receive HB in the form of a 'rent allowance'.[210] If you live in a caravan, mobile home or houseboat, this applies even if you are also liable to make payments to a local authority – eg, for site or mooring fees. HB is normally paid to you although, in some cases, it may be paid direct to your landlord or to someone acting on your behalf (see p133).

Note: if your rent allowance is:
- less than £1 a week, the local authority can choose to pay your benefit up to six months in arrears;[211]
- more than £2 a week, you can insist on two-weekly payments, unless HB is paid direct to your landlord.[212]

The local authority has the discretion to pay you by whatever method it chooses but, in doing so, it must have regard to your 'reasonable needs and convenience'.[213]

It should not insist on payment into a bank account if you do not have one (but it may encourage you to open one), nor should it make you collect it if it is difficult to reach the office by public transport.[214] If it does, complain to your local councillor. If that has no effect, ask your MP to take up the matter (see p1387) and also complain to the Ombudsman (see p1388).

If the local authority refuses to replace a payment which has never arrived, you could threaten to sue in the county court (sheriff court in Scotland).

Payment to someone acting on your behalf

If an appointee or some other person legally empowered to act for a claimant has claimed HB on her/his behalf, that person can also receive the payments.[215]

If you are able to claim HB for yourself, you can still nominate an agent to receive or collect it for you. To do this you must make a written request to the local authority. Anyone you nominate must be aged 18 or over.[216]

If a claimant dies, any unpaid HB may be paid to her/his personal representative or, if there is none, to her/his next of kin aged 16 or over.[217] A written application must be received by the local authority within 12 months of the claimant's death. The local authority may allow longer. If HB was being paid to the landlord prior to the claimant's death, the local authority can pay any outstanding HB to clear remaining rent due.

Payment direct to a landlord

Your HB can be paid direct to your landlord (or the person to whom you pay rent) but only in specific circumstances. Your landlord could contact the local authority about this.[218] The local authority can suspend payment while it makes enquiries about who should be paid your HB.[219] If the local authority is suspicious of your landlord, see p134.

If you have just claimed HB or the local authority has done a supersession of your award, and the local authority thinks you have not already paid your rent and that it would be in the interests of the 'efficient administration' of HB, it can make the first payment to your landlord.[220]

Both you and your landlord should be notified if HB is to be paid to your landlord. If it is *not* in your interests to have HB paid direct to your landlord, it is worth trying to persuade the local authority to withhold it rather than paying it to your landlord. *Always* seek advice before you do so.

When payment must be made to your landlord

The local authority *must* pay your HB, including payments on account (see p139),[221] direct to your landlord (or the person to whom you pay rent) if:[222]

- you or your partner are on income support (IS), jobseeker's allowance (JSA), employment and support allowance (ESA) or pension credit (PC) and the DWP has decided to pay part of that benefit to your landlord for arrears (see p1182); or

- you have rent arrears equivalent to eight weeks' rent or more, unless the local authority considers it to be in your overriding interest not to make direct payments. Once your arrears have been reduced to less than eight weeks' rent, compulsory direct payments stop. The local authority may then choose to continue direct payments on a discretionary basis (see below).

Payment to your landlord on a discretionary basis

Unless the local housing allowance rules apply to you (see p395), the local authority may pay your HB direct to your landlord (or the person to whom you pay rent):[223]

- if you have requested or agreed to direct payments; or
- without your agreement, if it decides that direct payments are in the best interests of you and your family.

If the local housing allowance rules apply to you (see p395), the local authority may pay your HB direct to your landlord (or the person to whom you pay rent) if it:[224]

- thinks you are likely to have difficulty managing your own financial affairs or that it is improbable that you will pay your rent. The local authority can make direct payments (for a maximum of eight weeks) while it considers the situation; or
- thinks it will help you to secure or to keep accommodation. **Note:** the government's intention is that this should only apply if the rent is at a level you can afford; or
- has already made direct payments during your current award of HB in any of the situations when direct payments must be made (see p133).

Whether or not the local housing allowance rules apply to you, the local authority may also pay your HB direct to your landlord (or the person to whom you pay rent) without your agreement if you have left the address for which you were getting HB and there are rent arrears. In this case, direct payments of any unpaid HB due in respect of that accommodation can be made, up to the total of the outstanding arrears.[225]

When the local authority is suspicious about a landlord

If HB is being paid to a landlord, or a request is made for payment to a landlord, and the local authority suspects impropriety on the part of the landlord, it may require the landlord (or her/his agent) to provide information which must then be provided within four weeks (plus a further four weeks in specified circumstances).[226] The local authority may also refuse to make direct payments where it 'is not satisfied that the landlord is a fit and proper person'.[227]

However, direct payments may be made if:[228]

- the requirements for discretionary direct payments are met; or

- the local authority is satisfied that it is in the best interests of you and your family.

If the local authority decides not to make payments to your landlord, it can make payments to you (including sending you a cheque payable to the landlord, or paying you in the presence of your landlord) or to a trusted third party, such as a social worker or solicitor.[229]

When your entitlement starts

Your entitlement to HB starts:[230]
- if you became liable for rent in the first of the weeks for which you are claiming, from the Monday of that week. This includes where you become liable for daily payments in a hostel or accommodation provided by the local authority on a short-term lease or because you are homeless. This means that your HB starts on the same day your liability actually begins;[231] or
- in all other cases, from the Monday following your date of claim, or following the date from which you are trated as claiming if your claim is backdated (see pp126–30).

Continuing payments

There are two situations when your HB can continue to be paid at the same rate, even though your entitlement might otherwise have changed. If you stop claiming:
- IS, income-based JSA or income-related ESA because you or your partner are moving onto PC, you may be able to continue to receive HB at the same rate for four weeks (see below);
- IS, income-based JSA, income-related or contributory ESA, incapacity benefit (IB) or severe disablement allowance (SDA) because you or your partner start work or increase your hours or earnings, you may be entitled to extended payments of HB (see p136).

Continuing payments on claiming pension credit

To avoid problems caused by delays in reassessing your HB when you move from IS, income-based JSA or income-related ESA onto PC, provided you otherwise continue to qualify for HB, you continue to receive it, normally at the same rate as before this happened (but see p136). You qualify for continuing payments if:[232]
- your partner has claimed PC and the DWP has certified this; or
- your IS, income-based JSA or income-related ESA ceased because you reached the qualifying age for PC (see p78) or, if you were getting income-based JSA or income-related ESA beyond that age, this ceased because you turned 65. The

DWP must certify this and that you are required to claim or have claimed PC (or are treated as having done so).

You get continuing payments for:[233]
- a period of four weeks from the day after your IS, income-based JSA or income-related ESA ceases; or
- if the four-week period ends other than on a Sunday, until the Sunday after the end of the four-week period.

Note: your maximum HB (see p108 for the meaning) is recalculated if your rent increases or there is a change in the non-dependant deductions (see p116) that should be made.[234]

Extended payments of housing benefit

If you or your partner are on IS, income-based JSA, income-related or contributory ESA, IB or SDA and your entitlement ends because you (or your partner) start work or increase your hours or pay, you may be entitled to continue to receive the same amount of HB as you did before your entitlement ended. These extended payments of HB are paid for up to four weeks. You do not have to make a fresh claim for HB (but you must report the change in your circumstances).

You can apply for a revision or supersession of an extended payments decision or appeal against it (see Chapters 58 and 59).

Who can claim extended payments

You qualify for extended payments of HB if you are getting HB and:
- you or your partner:[235]
  - were entitled to IS, income-based JSA or income-related ESA and your entitlement ended because you (or your partner) started work (including self-employed work) or increased your hours or pay. However, you cannot qualify if, immediately before your entitlement to IS ended, you were getting mortgage interest run-on (see p460); and
  - had been continuously entitled to, and in receipt of, either IS, contribution-based or income-based JSA or income-related ESA, or a combination of these, for at least 26 weeks; or
- unless you are getting PC, you or your partner:[236]
  - were not entitled to or in receipt of IS, income-based JSA or income-related ESA; and
  - were entitled to and in receipt of contributory ESA, IB or SDA and your entitlement ended because you or your partner started work (including self-employed work) or increased your hours or pay; and
  - had been continuously entitled to, and in receipt of, contributory ESA, IB or SDA, or a combination of these, for at least 26 weeks.

The end of your entitlement to IS, income-based JSA, ESA, IB or SDA is a change in your circumstances that you must report to the local authority (see p139). Bear the following in mind.

- Although a failure to report this change does not affect your entitlement to extended payments of HB, this could result in an overpayment of HB at the end of the extended payment period.
- You could be entitled to a higher rate of HB than you were before your entitlement to IS/JSA/ESA/IB/SDA ended. Report the change as soon as possible so it can be taken into account.
- If you are claiming IS, JSA, ESA, IB or SDA and you start work or your hours or pay change, you must notify the DWP of the change to avoid an overpayment of those benefits.

If you move home, you can still qualify for extended payments of HB, as long as the day you moved was in the same week, or the week before, you or your partner started work or increased your hours or pay.[237] See below for how the amount of the extended payments can be affected.

Amount of the extended payments and how long they last
Extended payments of HB are paid for four weeks unless:[238]
- any of the weeks count as rent-free periods (see p116); *or*
- your liability to pay rent ceases altogether within the four weeks.

The weekly amount of your extended payments (unless you move into local authority accommodation in a different local authority area – see p138) is the higher of:[239]
- the amount of HB you got in the last (non-rent-free) week before your entitlement to IS/JSA/ESA/IB/SDA ceased. However, if the benefit cap was applied (see p1169), it is the amount of HB you would have got – ie, the amount before any reduction was made; *or*
- the amount of HB to which you would be entitled based on your new circumstances; *or*
- if you are a member of a couple, the amount of HB to which your partner would be entitled if s/he claimed based on her/his circumstances.

Note: report any changes in your circumstances during the four-week period. This is because the weekly amount you get is then the highest of the above amounts.[240]

Example
Jill is a local authority tenant with a non-dependant. Her rent is £102 a week. She was getting HB of £69.55 in the week before her entitlement to IS ceased, because a non-dependant deduction of £32.45 was made. Her weekly HB entitlement based on her

2

circumstances in work is £54.37. Her extended payments are therefore £69.55 a week. In the second week of the four-week period, Jill's non-dependant moves out. Her weekly entitlement based on her circumstances in work is now £86.82, because a non-dependant deduction is no longer made. Her extended payments are now £86.82 for the remainder of the four-week period. This is also Jill's HB entitlement from the end of the period.

You may qualify for extended payments of HB on two homes (see p105). However, if your liability to pay rent for either of these ceases within the four-week period, the amount of your extended payments is reduced by the amount of HB payable for that home.[241]

If you were being paid discretionary housing payments (see Chapter 21), ask for these to continue for the extended payment period.

If you **move into local authority accommodation in a different local authority area**, the weekly amount of your extended payments of HB is the amount of HB you got in the last (non-rent-free) week before your entitlement to IS/JSA/ESA/IB/SDA ceased – ie, the amount you got at your old address.[242] The extended payments can be paid to you or to the new local authority landlord. If you or your partner claim HB at your new address, the amount you or your partner get is reduced by the weekly amount of the extended payments. The effect of this is that, if your new HB entitlement is higher, your extended payments can be 'topped up'.

Note: if you move house in any other circumstances (eg, to private rented or housing association accommodation, or within the same local authority area), your extended payments are worked out under the normal rules (see p136). If you also claim HB at your new address, it does not appear that the local authority can reduce the amount of HB you get by the weekly amount of your extended payments.[243] It is not clear if this was the intention.

Claims

You do not have to make a claim for extended payments of HB; they should be paid automatically.[244] However, let your local authority know that your or your partner's entitlement to IS, income-based JSA, ESA, IB or SDA has ceased.

Ongoing entitlement to housing benefit

Your entitlement to HB continues until at least the end of the extended payment period.[245] Entitlement to HB can continue after that if you qualify under the normal rules, but at the weekly rate based on your new circumstances. You do not have to make a fresh claim. Your HB entitlement will be continuous. This means if you have a form of transitional protection that requires continuous entitlement, your transitional protection continues.

Note: unless you move to local authority accommodation in a different local authority area, if your partner claims HB this cannot be paid to her/him while you are getting extended payments of HB.[246]

Delays and complaints

The local authority must make a decision on your claim, tell you in writing what the decision is, and pay you any HB to which you are entitled within 14 days or, if that is not reasonably practicable, as soon as possible after that.[247] If you consider a delay is unreasonable, write to the HB manager and threaten to complain to the Ombudsman (see p1388). In serious cases, you may want to seek advice on whether you have grounds for judicial review (see p1351).

Payments on account

If you are a private or housing association tenant and the local authority has not been able to assess your HB within the required period, the local authority must normally make a 'payment on account' (sometimes called an interim payment) while your claim is being sorted out.[248] The local authority should automatically do this. You do not have to request a payment on account.[249] Bear the following in mind.

- Payments on account are not discretionary. The local authority *must* pay you an amount which it considers reasonable, given what it knows about your circumstances.
- Payments on account can only be refused if it is clear that you will not be entitled to HB or the reason for the delay is that you have been asked for information or evidence in support of your claim and you have failed, without good cause, to provide it (see p125).[250] If the delay has been caused by a third party (eg, the rent officer, your bank or employer), this does not affect your right to a payment on account.
- The local authority must notify you of the amount of a payment on account and that it can recover any overpayment which occurs if your actual HB entitlement is different from the payment.[251]
- If your payment on account is less than your actual entitlement, your future HB can be adjusted to take account of the underpayment.[252]
- If the local authority has not made a payment on account, complain. You could also complain to the Ombudsman (see p1388).

Change of circumstances

It is your duty to report any change in your circumstances which you might reasonably be expected to know might affect your right to, the amount of, or payment of, your HB.[253] You should do this promptly to the office handling your claim:

- in writing; *or*

- by telephone (unless the local authority says you must report it in writing), but only if your local authority has published a telephone number for this purpose or allows you to claim HB by telephone (see p121);
- electronically – eg, by email, if your local authority authorises it.[254]

However, it is always best to report a change in writing and keep a copy in case of a dispute in the future.

You may report a change in your circumstances to the DWP, instead of the local authority, if the DWP has provided a telephone number for this purpose, and:[255]

- you or your partner are getting IS or JSA; and
- the change of circumstances is that you or your partner have started work; and
- as a result of the change, entitlement to IS or JSA will end or, if you or your partner are getting contribution-based JSA, the amount will reduce.

If the change is a birth or a death, there is a special rule (sometimes called 'Tell Us Once'). You can report such a change in person at a local authority (and, in England, a county council) office, if such an office has been specified for reporting these changes.[256] If the change is a death, you can notify it to the DWP electronically, or by telephone if a number has been specified for that purpose. Check with your local authority (eg, at the registrar's office) to see if it provides this service.

If you do not report a change promptly, any resulting overpayment may be recoverable from you (see Chapter 56) and, in some circumstances, you may have to pay a penalty (see p1249). If you are considered to have acted knowingly or dishonestly, you may also be guilty of an offence (see Chapter 57). Remember:

- the local authority must tell you in writing about the changes you have to report;[257]
- it is important to report changes to the right department. Your duty to notify changes is to the HB department, not to the local authority as a whole;[258]
- if your benefit is paid to someone else on your behalf, the duty to report any relevant changes also extends to her/him.[259]

If in doubt, always report changes in circumstances. If you think that the local authority might not have taken a change into account, you should check with it.

If you do not get pension credit

If you do not get PC, you must report:[260]

- any change to your rent, unless you are a local authority tenant;
- entitlement to IS, income-based JSA or income-related ESA ending. Do not assume that the DWP does this on your behalf;
- any change that results in a child or young person no longer being included in your claim (see p210).

You must also report other changes that you 'might reasonably be expected to know' could affect your HB, such as changes to:

- your family income or capital;
- the number of boarders or sub-tenants you have or the payments made by them;
- the number or circumstances of any non-dependants that may affect the level of deductions made to your benefit (see p116);
- any absence from your home which is, or is likely to be, for more than 13 weeks;
- your status – eg, marriage, civil partnership, cohabitation, separation or divorce.

If you get pension credit

If you get PC, you must report:[261]

- any change to your tenancy, apart from changes in your rent if you are a local authority tenant;
- any changes affecting a non-dependant normally living with you or with whom you normally live;
- any absence from your home which is, or is likely to be, for more than 13 weeks.

If you are only getting the savings credit of PC, you must also report:[262]

- changes affecting a child under 16 who lives with you that could affect how much HB you get. You need not report changes in the child's age;
- any changes to your capital that do or could take it above £16,000;
- any changes in the income or capital of a non-dependant of yours, if your HB has been assessed on the basis of this instead of your own (see p120), and whether s/he has stopped or resumed living with you;
- any changes in the income or capital of your partner that have not been taken into account since the determination of your PC award, and whether your partner has stopped or resumed living with you.

Note: if you are on PC, these are the only changes you have to report to the local authority.[263] Other relevant changes in your circumstances should be passed to the local authority by the DWP.

Other changes

There may be other changes which the local authority requires you to report, depending on the particular circumstances of your case. The need to report these additional changes must be drawn to your attention at the time you claim and also if you are asked for further information.[264] This is important because you only have a duty to report changes that you 'might reasonably be expected to know' could affect your HB.[265]

You do not have to report:[266]
- any changes in your rent if you are a local authority tenant;
- changes in the ages of your children, or of non-dependants, unless the change results in a child or young person ceasing to be included in your claim.[267]

When changes in circumstances take effect

If you report a change in circumstances before the local authority has assessed your HB claim, your claim is assessed on the basis of the revised information you have provided.

If a change of circumstances takes place once HB has been awarded, the local authority must establish the date on which that change occurred.[268]

In most cases, a change takes effect from the Monday after the change occurred.[269] This applies whether or not a decision is advantageous to you. However, if you are liable to pay rent on a daily basis (eg, in a hostel) and the change means you are no longer entitled to HB, it takes effect on the day it occurs.[270]

Exceptions

There are a number of exceptions to the general rule described above, which include the following.
- If the change is one you are required to notify to the local authority (other than one relating to your having to take part in a work-focused interview or, if you are on PC, one of the additional exceptions to the rules described below), it is advantageous to you and you fail to notify the change within the one-month time limit (or any longer period allowed by the local authority – see p1290), the date of notification is treated as if that is the date the change occurred.
- A payment of income (or arrears of income) for a past period, other than benefit or arrears of benefit, is taken into account from the date it would have been taken into account had it been paid to you on time.[271] Note that arrears of some benefits, working tax credit, child tax credit and discretionary housing payments count as capital and can be disregarded for a period after they are paid (see p355 and p382).
- If you or your partner are at least 65 and either a non-dependant comes to live with you or there is a change so that a higher non-dependant deduction should be made, the effect of this can be delayed for 26 weeks.[272] This does not apply if you or your partner are getting IS, income-based JSA or income-related ESA (or universal credit).

Note: there are other exceptions. These include if there is a change in your rent, if you move to a new home or if you become (or cease to be) entitled to HB for more than one home.[273] In addition, there are exceptions if you or your partner become entitled to ESA which includes a work-related activity or support component.[274]

There are additional exceptions to the rules described above **if you are on PC** and the amount of this changes because of a change in your circumstances or the correction of an official error (see p1276), and this means there is a change in the amount of HB you can be paid. This includes where you are only getting the savings credit of PC and the change is as a result of a change in the DWP assessment of your income or savings.[275]

Special rules apply if two or more changes occurring in the same benefit week would normally take effect in different benefit weeks.[276]

8. Tax, other benefits and the benefit cap

Tax

Housing benefit (HB) is not taxable.

Means-tested benefits

Entitlement to income support (IS), income-based jobseeker's allowance (JSA), income-related employment and support allowance (ESA), the guarantee credit of pension credit (PC) or universal credit (UC) acts as an automatic passport to maximum HB (see p109) because all of your income and capital are ignored.

Non-means-tested benefits

Most non-means-tested benefits are taken into account as income when working out the amount of HB you get. Attendance allowance, disability living allowance, personal independence payment, guardian's allowance and child benefit are not taken into account. It can still be worth claiming non-means-tested benefits. If you, your partner or your child(ren) qualify for certain of these, you also qualify for certain premiums and components (see Chapter 12) and potentially a higher rate of HB. If you think you might qualify, seek advice to see if you would be better off.

You may only qualify for HB once you or your partner, or a child or qualifying young person included in your claim, are awarded another benefit (known as a 'qualifying benefit'). You may be entitled to a higher rate of HB once the qualifying benefit is awarded (see p127).

Tax credits

Working tax credit counts as income when working out your HB. So does child tax credit, unless you are at least the qualifying age for PC (see p78) and neither you nor your partner are on IS, income-based JSA or income-related ESA (or UC).

The benefit cap

In some cases, the total amount of specified benefits you receive is limited to £350 a week (if you are a single claimant without children) or £500 a week (if you are a lone parent or a member of a couple). This is known as the 'benefit cap'. The benefit cap only applies if you are getting HB. HB is one of the specified benefits, but HB for specified accommodation is ignored. See p1169 for further information.

Passports and other sources of help

If you have been awarded HB, you may qualify for a social fund funeral expenses payment (see Chapter 37). You may be entitled to council a tax reduction (see p827).

Financial help on starting work

If you stop getting IS, income-based JSA, income-related or contributory ESA, incapacity benefit or severe disablement allowance because you or your partner start work or your hours or earnings in your existing job increase, you may be entitled to extended payments of HB. You might also be able to get mortgage interest run-on if you have a home loan (see p460). Your local authority may also help with extended help with council tax. See p838 for information about other financial help you might get.

Notes

1. **Who can claim housing benefit**
   1 s130 SSCBA 1992; s115 IAA 1999; reg 10 HB Regs; reg 10 HB(SPC) Regs
   2 Reg 26 HB(SPC) Regs
   3 Regs 11(1) and 12(1) HB Regs; regs 11(1) and 12(1) HB(SPC) Regs
   4 CH/3110/2003; R(H) 3/07
   5 CH/844/2002; R(H) 9/08
   6 Reg 2(4)(a) HB Regs; reg 2(4)(a) HB(SPC) Regs
   7 *R v Cambridge CC ex parte Thomas,* 10 February 1995 (QBD); CH/2959/2006
   8 Reg 12(2) HB Regs; reg 12(2) HB(SPC) Regs
   9 Reg 2(1) HB Regs and reg 2(1) HB(SPC) Regs, definition of 'long tenancy' and 'owner'; CH/2258/2004; *Burton v New Forest District Council* [2004] EWCA Civ 1510, reported as R(H) 7/05; R(H) 3/07; CH/3586/2005; R(H) 8/07; *CR v Wycombe District Council* [2009] UKUT 19 (AAC)
   10 Reg 11(2) HB Regs
   11 Reg 11(4) HB Regs
   12 Reg 8(1)(a) and (b) HB Regs; reg 8(1)(a) and (b) HB(SPC) Regs
   13 Reg 8(1)(c)-(e) HB Regs; reg 8(1)(c)-(e) HB(SPC) Regs
   14 CSHB/606/2005
   15 Reg 8(2) HB Regs; reg 8(2) HB(SPC) Regs

16 *R v Rugby BC HBRB ex parte Harrison*
[1994] 28 HLR 36 (QBD); CH/2959/
2006
17 CH/3579/2003; CH/257/2005
18 R(H) 3/03
19 *R v Poole BC ex parte Ross* [1995] 28 HLR
351 (QBD); *R v Warrington BC ex parte
Williams* [1997] 29 HLR 872 (QBD)
20 s134(2) SSCBA 1992; reg 82(1) HB
Regs; reg 63(1) HB(SPC) Regs
21 Regs 9, 10 and 56 HB Regs; regs 9
and 10 HB(SPC) Regs
22 *Scott v SSWP* [2011] EWCA Civ 103
23 Reg 9(4) HB Regs; reg 9(4) HB(SPC)
Regs; CH/1326/2004; CH/1328/2004
24 CH/542/2006; R(H) 5/06 decided that
the rule did not conflict with the Human
Rights Act.
25 Reg 3(4) HB Regs; reg 3(4) HB(SPC)
Regs; R(H) 5/06; CPC/1446/2008; *RK v
SSWP* [2008] UKUT 34 (AAC)
26 *Thamesdown BC v Goonery* [1995] 1 CLY
2600 (CA)
27 R(H) 1/03; CH/1171/2002; CH/2899/
2005
28 Reg 9(2) HB Regs; reg 9(2) HB(SPC)
Regs; *R v Poole BC ex parte Ross* [1995]
28 HLR 351 (QBD); CH/1076/2002;
CH/296/2004; CH/1097/2004; paras
A3/3.258-65 GM
29 *DH v Kirklees MBC and SSWP (HB)* [2011]
UKUT 301 (AAC); [2012] AACR 16
30 *R (Tucker) v Secretary of State* [2001]
EWCA Div 1646, unreported (EWCA).
The Court decided that the rule did not
conflict with the Human Rights Act.
31 para A3/3.269 GM
32 Reg 9(3) HB Regs; reg 9(3)
HB(SPC) Regs; *SD v London Borough of
Brent* [2009] UKUT 7 (AAC)
33 Reg 9(3) HB Regs; reg 9(3) HB(SPC)
Regs
34 Reg 2(1) HB Regs and reg 2(1) HB(SPC)
Regs. Both, definition of 'owner' and
'long tenancy'; CH/1278/2002; CH/
0296/2003; *MH v Wirral MBC* [2009]
UKUT 60 (AAC); *Bradford MDC v MRC
(HB)* [2010] UKUT 315 (AAC);
Nottingham CC v CJ (HB) [2011] UKUT
392 (AAC)
35 CH/3853/2001; CH/396/2002; R(H) 6/
07; *KH v Sheffield CC* [2008] UKUT 11
(AAC)
36 *CH v Wakefield DC* [2009] UKUT 20
(AAC)
37 Reg 2(1) HB Regs; reg 2(1) HB(SPC)
Regs
38 R(SB) 27/87

39 paras A3/3.243-45 GM
40 *R v Solihull MBC ex parte Simpson* [1995]
1 FLR 140 (CA); CH/39/2007
41 *R (Mackay) v Barking and Dagenham
HBRB* [2001] EWHC Admin 234 (HC)
42 CH/2258/2004
43 *R (Mackay) v Barking and Dagenham
HBRB* [2001] EWHC Admin 234 (HC)
44 *R v Sutton LBC HBRB ex parte Keegan*
[1992] 27 HLR 92 (QBD)
45 *R v Manchester CC ex parte Baragrove
Properties Ltd* [1991] 23 HLR 337 (QBD);
R v Gloucestershire CC ex parte Dadds
[1997] 29 HLR 700 (QBD); CH/39/2007
46 *R v Poole BC ex parte Ross* [1995] 28 HLR
351 (QBD)
47 s130(1) SSCBA 1992; reg 7(1) and (2)
HB Regs; reg 7(1) and (2) HB(SPC) Regs
48 R(H) 5/09; *Birmingham City Council v IB*
[2009] UKUT 116 (AAC)
49 Reg 7(5), (14) and (15)(c) HB Regs;
reg 7(5), (14) and (15)(c) HB(SPC) Regs
50 Reg 7(8) HB Regs; reg 7(8) HB(SPC)
Regs
51 R(H) 9/05
52 *Bury MBC v DC (HB)* [2011] UKUT 43
(AAC); *R (Mahmoudi) v LB Lewisham
and Another* [2014] EWCA Civ 284, 6
February 2014
53 Reg 2(1) HB Regs; reg 2(1) HB(SPC)
Regs
54 Reg 7(7) HB Regs; reg 7(7) HB(SPC)
Regs; para A3/3.430 GM
55 CH/2201/2002
56 R(H) 9/05
57 Reg 7(13) HB Regs; reg 7(13) HB(SPC)
Regs
58 Reg 7(16) and (16A) HB Regs; reg 7(16)
and (16A) HB(SPC) Regs
59 *R v Penwith DC ex parte Burt* [1988] 22
HLR 292 (QBD); para A3/3.460 GM
60 Reg 7(14) and (15)(a) HB Regs;
reg 7(14) and (15)(a) HB(SPC) Regs
61 CH/1237/2004
62 CH/3893/2004
63 R(H) 8/09; *SK v South Hams DC (HB)*
[2010] UKUT 129 (AAC); [2010] AACR
40
64 Reg 7(16) and (16A) HB Regs; reg 7(16)
and (16A) HB(SPC) Regs
65 Reg 7(14) and (15)(b) HB Regs;
reg 7(14) and (15)(b) HB(SPC) Regs;
CSH/499/2006
66 *Obrey and Others v SSWP* [2013] EWCA
Civ 1584, 5 December 2013
67 *SSWP v Selby DC and Bowman* [2006]
EWCA Civ 271, reported as R(H) 4/06

68 Reg 7(11) HB Regs; reg 7(11) HB(SPC) Regs
69 *Torbay BC v RF* [2010] UKUT 7 (AAC); [2010] AACR 26
70 Reg 7(18) HB Regs; reg 7(18) HB(SPC) Regs
71 R(H) 5/09; *Birmingham CC v IB* [2009] UKUT 116 (AAC)
72 Reg 7(6)(d) and (e) HB Regs; reg 7(6)(d) and (e) HB(SPC) Regs
73 CH/1911/2006
74 *R (Mahmoudi) v LB Lewisham and Another* [2014] EWCA Civ 284, 6 February 2014
75 Reg 7(6)(a) HB Regs; reg 7(6)(a) HB(SPC) Regs
76 Reg 7(6)(b) and (c) HB Regs; reg 7(6)(b) and (c) HB(SPC) Regs
77 Reg 7(10) HB Regs; reg 7(10) HB(SPC) Regs
78 Reg 7(3) HB Regs; reg 7(3) HB(SPC) Regs
79 Reg 7(4) HB Regs; reg 7(4) HB(SPC) Regs
80 R(SB) 10/81

3. People included in the claim
81 s137(1) SSCBA 1992

4. The amount of benefit
82 Reg 70 HB Regs; reg 50 HB(SPC) Regs
83 s130(3) SSCBA 1992; Schs 4 para 12, 5 para 4 and 6 para 5 HB Regs; reg 26 HB(SPC) Regs; *R v Penwith DC ex parte Menear* [1991] 24 HLR 120 (QBD); *R v South Ribble DC HBRB ex parte Hamilton* [2000] 33 HLR 104 (CA)
84 Reg 2(3), (3A) and (3B) HB Regs; reg 2(3) and (3A) HB(SPC) Regs
85 Reg 12B(2) HB Regs; reg 12B(2) HB(SPC) Regs
86 Regs 12B(3) and 12C(2) HB Regs; regs 12B(3) and 12C(2) HB(SPC) Regs; reg 12(4) HB Regs and reg 12(4) HB(SPC) Regs as set out in Sch 3 para 5 HB&CTB(CP) Regs
87 Regs 12B(4) and 12C(2) HB Regs; regs 12B(4) and 12C(2) HB(SPC) Regs; reg 12(5) HB Regs and reg 12(5) HB(SPC) Regs as set out in Sch 3 para 5 HB&CTB(CP) Regs; CH/3376/2002
88 *R (Naghshbandi) v Camden LBC* [2002] EWCA Civ 1038, *The Times*, 5 August 2002, unreported (CA)
89 CH/3376/2002
90 Regs B13(2) and 13D(12) HB Regs; regs 13B(2) and 13D(12) HB(SPC) Regs

91 Reg 12B(2) HB Regs; reg 12B(2) HB(SPC) Regs; reg 12(3) HB Regs and reg 12(3) HB(SPC) Regs as set out in Sch 3 para 5 HB&CTB(CP) Regs; *R v Bristol City Council ex parte Jacobs* [1999] 32 HLR 82 (QBD)
92 Regs 12B(3) and 12C(2) HB Regs; regs 12B(3) and 12C(2) HB(SPC) Regs; reg 12(4) HB Regs and reg 12(4) HB(SPC) Regs as set out in Sch 3 para 5 HB&CTB(CP) Regs
93 Reg 11(3) HB Regs; reg 11(2) HB(SPC) Regs
94 Sch 1 para 5 HB Regs; Sch 1 para 5 HB(SPC) Regs
95 Sch 1 para 6(1) HB Regs; Sch 1 para 6(1) HB(SPC) Regs
96 Sch 1 para 6(1)(a) HB Regs; Sch 1 para 6(1)(a) HB(SPC) Regs
97 Sch 1 para 6(2) and (3) HB Regs; Sch 1 para 6(2) and (3) HB(SPC) Regs
98 paras A4/4.912-913 GM
99 Sch 1 paras 5 and 6(1)(b) HB Regs; Sch 1 paras 5 and 6(1)(b) HB(SPC) Regs
100 Sch 1 para 8 HB Regs; Sch 1 para 8 HB(SPC) Regs. For the meaning of 'sheltered accommodation', see *Oxford CC v Basey* [2012] EWCA Civ 115; [2012] AACR 38.
101 Sch 1 para 8 HB Regs; Sch 1 para 8 HB(SPC) Regs
102 Reg 12(1)(e) HB Regs; reg 12(1)(e) HB(SPC) Regs
103 Sch 1 para 4 HB Regs; Sch 1 para 4 HB(SPC) Regs
104 para A4/4.730 GM
105 *CP and others v Aylesbury Vale DC v SSWP (HB)* [2011] UKUT 22 (AAC)
106 Sch 1 para 1(a)(iii) HB Regs; Sch 1 para 1(a)(iii) HB(SPC) Regs
107 Sch 1 para 1(a)(ii) HB Regs; Sch 1 para 1(a)(ii) HB(SPC) Regs
108 Sch 1 para 1(b) HB Regs; Sch 1 para 1(b) HB(SPC) Regs
109 Sch 1 para 1(a)(iv) HB Regs; Sch 1 para 1(a)(iv) HB(SPC) Regs
110 Reg 12B(2)(b) and Sch 1 para 1 HB Regs; reg 12B(2)(b) and Sch 1 para 1 HB(SPC) Regs; reg 12(3)(b) HB Regs and reg 12(3)(b) HB(SPC) Regs as set out in Sch 3 para 5 HB&CTB(CP) Regs
111 Reg 12B(2)(c) and Sch 1 para 3(2) HB Regs; reg 12B(2)(c) and Sch 1 para 3(2) HB(SPC) Regs; reg 12(3)(c) HB Regs and reg 12(3)(c) HB(SPC) Regs as set out in Sch 3 para 5 HB&CTB(CP) Regs
112 Sch 1 para 3 HB Regs; Sch 1 para 3 HB(SPC) Regs

113 Sch 1 paras 1(a)(i) and 2(1) HB Regs; Sch 1 paras 1(a)(i) and 2(1) HB(SPC) Regs

114 Sch 1 para 2(6) and (7) HB Regs; Sch 1 para 2(6) and (7) HB(SPC) Regs

115 Reg 2(1) HB Regs; reg 2(1) HB(SPC) Regs

116 Reg 80 HB Regs; reg 61 HB(SPC) Regs

117 Reg 81(3) and Sch 1 para 7(2) HB Regs; reg 62(3) and Sch 1 para 7(2) HB(SPC) Regs

118 Reg 70 HB Regs; reg 50 HB(SPC) Regs

119 Reg 3(1) HB Regs; reg 3(1) HB(SPC) Regs

120 Reg 3(4) and Sch 1 para 8 HB Regs; reg 3(4) and Sch 1 para 8 HB(SPC) Regs; CPC/1446/2008; *AM v SSWP (IS)* [2011] UKUT 387 (AAC)

121 CSIS/185/1995

122 *Thamesdown BC v Goonery* [1995] 1 CLY 2600 (CA); *RK v SSWP* [2008] UKUT 34 (AAC)

123 CIS/14850/1996

124 para A5/5.521 GM

125 R(H) 8/09; *SK v South Hams DC (HB)* [2010] UKUT 129 (AAC); [2010] AACR 40

126 Reg 3(2) HB Regs; reg 3(2) HB(SPC) Regs

127 *R v Chesterfield BC ex parte Fullwood* [1993] 26 HLR 126 (CA)

128 Reg 3(3) HB Regs; reg 3(3) HB(SPC) Regs

129 Regs 2(1), definition of 'attendance allowance', and 74(6) HB Regs; regs 2(1), definition of 'attendance allowance', and 55(6) HB(SPC) Regs

130 Reg 74(7) and (10) HB Regs; reg 55(7) and (9) HB(SPC) Regs

131 s2 Employment and Training Act 1973; s2 Enterprise and New Towns (Scotland) Act 1990

132 Reg 74(1) HB Regs; reg 55(1) HB(SPC) Regs

133 Regs 2(3) and 74(8) HB Regs; regs 2(3) and 55(8) HB(SPC) Regs

134 Reg 74(1) and (2) HB Regs; reg 55(1) and (2) HB(SPC) Regs

135 Reg 6(6) HB Regs; reg 6(6) HB(SPC) Regs

136 Reg 74(9) HB Regs; reg 55(10) HB(SPC) Regs

137 CH/48/2006

138 Reg 74(3) HB Regs; reg 55(3) HB(SPC) Regs

139 Reg 74(4) HB Regs; reg 55(4) HB(SPC) Regs

140 Reg 74(5) HB Regs; reg 55(5) HB(SPC) Regs

141 Reg 26 HB Regs; reg 24 HB(SPC) Regs

142 s134(8) and (14) SSAA 1992; Sch Housing Benefit and Council Tax Benefit (War Pension Disregards) Regulations 2007, No.1619

6. Claims and backdating

143 s1 SSAA 1992

144 Reg 83(1) and (9) HB Regs; reg 64(2) and (10) HB(SPC) Regs

145 Reg 83(4A) and (4B) HB Regs; reg 64(5A) and (5C) HB(SPC) Regs

146 Reg 83A and Sch 11 HB Regs; reg 64A and Sch 10 HB(SPC) Regs

147 Reg 83(1) HB Regs; reg 64(2) HB(SPC) Regs

148 Reg 83(2) HB Regs; reg 64(3) HB(SPC) Regs

149 Reg 83(4AA) and (4AB) HB Regs; reg 64(5B) and (5BA) HB(SPC) Regs

150 Reg 83(4BA) HB Regs; reg 64(5AA) HB(SPC) Regs

151 Reg 83(4AC)-(4AE) HB Regs; reg 64(5BB)-(5BD) HB(SPC) Regs

152 Explanatory memorandum to SI 2008 No.299

153 Reg 83(1), (4C), (6) and (9) HB Regs; reg 64(2), (5D), (7) and (10) HB(SPC) Regs

154 Reg 83(4D), (4DA), (7) and (7A) HB Regs; reg 64(5E), (5EA), (8) and (8A) HB(SPC) Regs

155 Reg 83(4E), (4F), (8) and (8A) HB Regs; reg 64(5F), (5G), (9) and (9A) HB(SPC) Regs

156 Reg 87(1) and (3) HB Regs; reg 68(1) and (3) HB(SPC) Regs

157 Reg 87(4)-(6) HB Regs; reg 68(4)-(6) HB(SPC) Regs

158 paras A2/2.560-65 GM

159 Reg 83(4)(b) HB Regs; reg 64(5)(b) HB(SPC) Regs

160 Regs 2, definition of 'appropriate DWP office', and 83(4)(a), (f) and (g) and (13) HB Regs; regs 2, definition of 'appropriate DWP office', and 64(5)(a), (f) and (g) and (14) HB(SPC) Regs

161 Reg 83(4)(c) HB Regs; reg 64(5)(c) HB(SPC) Regs

162 Reg 83A and Sch 11 HB Regs; reg 64A and Sch 10 HB(SPC) Regs

163 Reg 83(4A) and (4AA) HB Regs; reg 64(5A) and (5B) HB(SPC) Regs

164 Reg 82(1) HB Regs; reg 63(1) HB(SPC) Regs; CH/2995/2006

165 Reg 82(2) HB Regs; reg 63(2) HB(SPC) Regs
166 Reg 82(3) and (5) HB Regs; reg 63(3) and (5) HB(SPC) Regs
167 Reg 82(6) HB Regs; reg 63(6) HB(SPC) Regs
168 Reg 82(4) HB Regs; reg 63(4) HB(SPC) Regs
169 Reg 82(4)(c) HB Regs; reg 63(4)(c) HB(SPC) Regs
170 Reg 86(1) HB Regs; reg 67(1) HB(SPC) Regs
171 Reg 86(1A) HB Regs; reg 67(1A) HB(SPC) Regs
172 para A1/1.300 GM
173 *AA v LB Hounslow* [2008] UKUT 13 (AAC)
174 Regs 83(5)(d) and (e) and 85(1) HB Regs; regs 64(6)(d) and (e) and 66(1) HB(SPC) Regs
175 Reg 83(5)(a)-(c) HB Regs; reg 64(6)(a)-(c) HB(SPC) Regs
176 *Leicester CC v LG* [2009] UKUT 155 (AAC)
177 Reg 83(5)(aa) HB Regs
178 Reg 13 UC(TP) Regs
179 Reg 83(10) and (11) HB Regs; reg 64(11) and (12) HB(SPC) Regs
180 CG/1479/1999; CIS/217/1999
181 Reg 15(3)-(5) UC(TP) Regs
182 Reg 64(1) HB(SPC) Regs
183 Regs 57 and 64(1), (1A) and (6) HB(SPC) Regs; *Leicester CC v LG* [2009] UKUT 155 (AAC)
184 Reg 83(12) HB Regs
185 Reg 83(12A) HB Regs
186 R(S) 2/63 (T); CH/2659/2002; CH/474/2002; CH/393/2003; A2/Annex A GM
187 *UH v LB Islington (HB)* [2010] UKUT 64 (AAC)
188 CH/393/2003
189 CH/474/2002
190 R(G) 1/75
191 *FR v Broadband DC* [2012] UKUT 449 (AAC)
192 R(SB) 6/83; CS/50/1950; R(U) 9/74; CI/146/1991; CI/142/1993; FC/39/1993; *R v Canterbury CC ex parte Goodman*, 11 July 1995, unreported (QBD)
193 R(U) 5/56; R(S) 5/56
194 CI/37/1995
195 R(P) 2/85
196 R(S) 10/59; R(SB) 17/83
197 Reg 90 HB Regs; reg 71 HB(SPC) Regs; reg 10 HB&CTB(DA) Regs
198 Reg 90(2) HB Regs; reg 71(2) HB(SPC) Regs; reg 10 HB&CTB(DA) Regs
199 Reg 3 HB&CTB(DA) Regs
200 CH/180/2006

201 Reg 90 and Sch 9 HB Regs; reg 71 and Sch 8 HB(SPC) Regs
202 Reg 10(1) HB&CTB(DA) Regs
203 Sch 9 paras 9-15 HB Regs; Sch 8 paras 9-15 HB(SPC) Regs
204 Sch 9 paras 11 and 12 HB Regs; Sch 8 paras 11 and 12 HB(SPC) Regs

7. Getting paid
205 Reg 75 HB Regs; reg 56 HB(SPC) Regs
206 Reg 92(1) and (6) HB Regs; reg 73(1) and (6) HB(SPC) Regs
207 Reg 92(6) HB Regs; reg 73(6) HB(SPC) Regs
208 Reg 92(3) and (4) HB Regs; reg 73(3) and (4) HB(SPC) Regs
209 s134(1A) SSAA 1992
210 s134(1B) SSAA 1992; regs 91A and 94(1) HB Regs; regs 72A and 75(1) HB(SPC) Regs
211 Reg 91(2) HB Regs; reg 72(2) HB(SPC) Regs
212 Reg 92(5) HB Regs; reg 73(5) HB(SPC) Regs
213 Reg 91(1)(b) HB Regs; reg 72(1)(b) HB(SPC) Regs
214 para A6/6.120 GM
215 Reg 94(2) HB Regs; reg 75(2) HB(SPC) Regs
216 Reg 94(3) HB Regs; reg 75(3) HB(SPC) Regs
217 Reg 97 HB Regs; reg 78 HB(SPC) Regs
218 *R v Haringey LBC ex parte Azad Ayub* [1992] 25 HLR 566 (QBD)
219 R(H) 1/08
220 Reg 96(2) HB Regs; reg 77(2) HB(SPC) Regs
221 *R v Haringey LBC ex parte Azad Ayub* [1992] 25 HLR 566 (QBD)
222 Reg 95 HB Regs; reg 76 HB(SPC) Regs; Sch 9 SS(C&P) Regs
223 Reg 96(1)(a) and (b) and (3A)(a) HB Regs; reg 77(1)(a) and (b) and (3A)(a) HB(SPC) Regs
224 Regs 95(2A) and 96(3A)(b) HB Regs; regs 76(2A) and 77(3A)(b) HB(SPC) Regs
225 Regs 95(2A) and 96(1)(c) HB Regs; regs 76(2A) and 77(1)(c) HB(SPC) Regs
226 s126A SSAA 1992; regs 118-120 HB Regs; regs 99-101 HB(SPC) Regs
227 Regs 95(3) and 96(3) HB Regs; regs 76(3) and 77(3) HB(SPC) Regs
228 Reg 96(3) HB Regs; reg 77(3) HB(SPC) Regs
229 para A6/6.212 GM
230 Reg 76 HB Regs; reg 57 HB(SPC) Regs; R(H) 9/07

Chapter 8

Child tax credit

This chapter covers:
1. Who can claim child tax credit (below)
2. The rules about your age (p156)
3. People included in the claim (p157)
4. The amount of child tax credit (p157)
5. Claims and backdating (p158)
6. Getting paid (p160)
7. Tax, other benefits and the benefit cap (p161)

Key facts

- Child tax credit (CTC) is paid to families with children or qualifying young people.
- You do not have to have paid national insurance contributions to qualify.
- CTC is paid whether or not you or your partner are working.
- CTC does not count as income for income support, income-based jobseeker's allowance, income-related employment and support allowance or pension credit (PC) purposes and can be paid in addition to these benefits.
- CTC is administered and paid by HM Revenue and Customs.
- If you disagree with a CTC decision, you can apply for a revision, or appeal against it. You must apply for a review before you can appeal.

Future changes

The government says that, in 2016, you will no longer be able to make a new claim for CTC. Amounts for children are included in universal credit (UC) and will be included in pension credit (PC). During 2016 and 2017, the DWP will begin to transfer existing CTC claims to UC (or PC). See p18 for further information.

1. Who can claim child tax credit

You qualify for child tax credit (CTC) if:[1]
- you (or your partner) are 'responsible' for at least one dependent child – including some qualifying young people (see p151);

- your income is sufficiently low (see Chapter 64);
- you are 'present' and 'ordinarily resident' in the UK. You can be treated as present and ordinarily resident in the UK in some circumstances – eg, if you are temporarily away. You can be treated as not being in the UK if you claim CTC for the first time on or after 1 May 2004 and do not have a 'right to reside'. See Chapter 70 for further information;
- you are not a 'person subject to immigration control' (see Chapter 69).

Note:
- Although full-time paid work does not affect your entitlement to CTC, income from work affects the amount you can be paid.
- If you come under the universal credit (UC) system (see p19), you cannot make a new claim for CTC and should claim UC instead.

Children

To qualify for CTC, you must be 'responsible' for at least one child or qualifying young person.[2] The terms 'child' or 'children' in this chapter also refer to qualifying young people. You do not have to be the child's parent. You could, for example, be the grandparent, sister or brother. See p153 for when you count as responsible for a child and p155 for when you do not count as responsible.

If you are entitled to CTC for a child (or would have been had you made a claim) and the child dies, you continue to be entitled to CTC for the child for eight weeks immediately following her/his death (or to the date your child would have turned 20 if this is earlier).[3] After this period, you may still continue to qualify for CTC if you are responsible for any other child(ren) and still satisfy the means test.

Who counts as a child

Someone counts as a child until her/his 16th birthday.[4] In some circumstances, a young person aged under 20 also counts as a child. HM Revenue and Customs (HMRC) refers to her/him as a **'qualifying young person'**.

A young person counts as a child during any period:[5]
- from her/his 16th birthday until 31 August following that birthday, whether or not s/he is in full-time non-advanced education or 'approved training' (but see p153 for when s/he may not count as a child);
- from 1 September following her/his 16th birthday (or from 31 August if s/he turns 16 on that date), while s/he is under 20 and in:
  - full-time non-advanced education (see p152). This does not apply if s/he is getting the education because of her/his employment. A young person counts as in full-time education during any gaps between the ending of one course and the start of another, if s/he is enrolled on and commences the other course; *or*

Part 2: Main means-tested benefits and tax credits
Chapter 8: Child tax credit
1. Who can claim child tax credit

2

- approved training (see p554 for what counts) or has been enrolled on or accepted to undertake approved training. This does not apply if s/he is getting the training by means of a contract of employment.

The course or approved training must have begun before s/he reached 19, or s/he must have been enrolled on or accepted to undertake the course or approved training before that age. **Note:** there is no equivalent to the child benefit 'terminal date rule' (see p555) so, unless the young person is under 18 and the rule below applies, s/he cannot count as a child once the course or training ends. Therefore, ensure you notify HMRC when the course or training ends;

- from 1 September following her/his 16th birthday (or from 31 August if s/he turns 16 on that date), while s/he is under 18, has ceased full-time education or approved training (see p554) and it is not more than 20 weeks since s/he did so. S/he must notify HMRC within three months of ceasing full-time education or approved training that s/he has registered for work or training with a qualifying body – eg, the place where your local authority provides careers advice for young people or the Ministry of Defence. This rule can apply again if s/he goes back into full-time education or approved training and ceases again.

What should you do when your child turns 16?

Notify HMRC in the September after your child's 16th birthday if s/he is staying on in non-advanced education or approved training. In England, this applies even though the school participation age is rising to 17, and then to 18.

When working out whether a young person counts as in full-time education or approved training, HMRC ignores:[6]

- an interruption of up to six months, whether it began before or after the young person turned 16; *and*
- an interruption of any length which is due to the young person's illness or disability 'of the mind or body'.

The interruption is only ignored if HMRC thinks it is reasonable to do so.

You should notify HMRC if the above applies to ensure that you continue to get CTC for your child.

Full-time and non-advanced education[7]

'Education' means education at a school or college or (if receiving the education before the age of 16) elsewhere, if approved by HMRC.

Education counts as **'full time'** if it is for more than 12 hours a week, on average, in normal term time, including instruction or tuition, supervised study, exams, practical work and experiments or projects provided for in the curriculum but excluding meal breaks and unsupervised study.

For examples of what counts as '**non-advanced**' education, see p553.

When a young person does not count as a child

A young person cannot count as a child during any period following her/his 16th birthday:[8]

- in which, having ceased full-time education or approved training, s/he is in full-time paid work. This means work of 24 hours or more per week. For information about:
  - what counts as paid work, see p166;
  - how the hours are calculated, see p166;
  - situations when the young person is not treated as in full-time paid work, see p172.

  The rules are the same as for working tax credit (WTC).

  Remember that, even if a young person has *not* started full-time paid work, s/he cannot count as a child from 1 September after her/his 16th birthday if s/he has ceased full-time education or 'approved training' and has not registered for work or training with a qualifying body – eg, the place where your local authority provides careers advice for young people or the Ministry of Defence; *or*
- in which s/he gets income support (IS), income-based jobseeker's allowance (JSA), income-related employment and support allowance (ESA) or universal credit (UC) in her/his own right. **Note:** you might not count as responsible for a child aged 16 or over if s/he gets CTC or contributory ESA in her/his own right (see p155).

Being responsible for a child

For tax credit purposes, a child can only count as the responsibility of one claimant (or joint-claim couple).[9] You are treated as 'responsible' for a child if:[10]

- s/he normally lives with you. HMRC calls this the 'normally living with test'; *or*
- you have the main responsibility for her/him. HMRC calls this the 'main responsibility test'. This test only applies if you and another person (or couple) make competing claims for CTC for the same child.

Note:

- Entitlement to child benefit is not a specific factor in working out who is responsible for a child for CTC purposes.
- If a child for whom you are treated as responsible has a child of her/his own (eg, your grandchild) who normally lives with her/him, you also count as

Part 2: Main means-tested benefits and tax credits
Chapter 8: Child tax credit
1. Who can claim child tax credit

responsible for that child, but not if your child is 16 or over and is awarded CTC in her/his own right.[11]

2 The 'normally living with test'

The rules do not define when a child counts as 'normally living with' you. HMRC says it means that your child 'regularly, usually, typically' lives with you and that this allows for temporary or occasional absences.[12] So if your child counts as normally living with you, s/he should also count as doing so even if s/he is away from home – eg, because s/he is away at school or for a temporary period on holiday or in hospital. You can argue that a child is normally living with you if s/he spends more time with you than with anyone else.[13]

Your child can count as normally living with you even if s/he also lives with someone else or only lives with you for part of the week, and lives for part of the week with someone else – eg, her/his other parent. This means that more than one person could claim CTC for the same child. However, CTC can only be paid to one claimant (or joint-claim couple). If more than one claims, see the 'main responsibility' test below.

The 'main responsibility' test

If you (and your partner) and at least one other person (or couple) with whom the child also normally lives claim CTC for the same child, you only qualify for CTC for the child if you can show you have the 'main responsibility' for her/him. The main responsibility test applies if:[14]

- your child normally lives with *both* you *and*:
  - at least one other person in another household – eg, with you and with the child's other parent from whom you have separated; *or*
  - someone who is not your partner in the same household – eg, with you and with the child's grandparent where you live together.

  It also applies if it is a combination of these situations. 'Household' is not defined. See p215 for ideas about what might count as a household; *and*
- you and at least one of the other people with whom your child normally lives claim CTC.

You and the other CTC claimant(s) can decide which of you should count as having main responsibility. If you cannot agree, a decision maker decides.[15] You can challenge the decision (see p156).

'**Main responsibility**' is not defined in the rules. The decision maker is likely to consider things like:[16]

- whether any court orders exist that set out where your child is to live or who is to care for her/him;
- who pays for your child's food and clothes and who is responsible for giving her/him pocket money;

- with whom your child normally lives, where the majority of her/his clothes and toys are kept and who does her/his laundry;
- who is the main contact or registered address for the school or college, nursery or childcare provider or for healthcare and who takes most responsiblity for your child when s/he is at school;[17]
- who arranges appointments to see a doctor.

Even though you may be sharing responsibility for a child and s/he normally lives with you for part of the week, the rules might not treat you as having the main responsibility. There is currently no provision for allowing CTC to be split between parents if a child divides her/his time between their homes. Even if you share actual responsibility for the child (eg, you share responsibility with your ex-partner) and are a 'substantial minority carer' (ie, you have the child with you for at least 104 nights a year), you cannot argue that you should be regarded as responsible for the child.[18]

Do you share responsibility for a child?

If you share responsibility for your child(ren) equally with other CTC claimant(s), it may be difficult to decide who has the main responsibility.

If you and another claimant have more than one child, you can each claim CTC for different children – eg, if you have two children, you could claim for one and the other claimant could claim for the other.

You might be able to argue that the decision maker should regard you as having the main responsibility if you would be entitled to more CTC than the other claimant(s).[19]

When you do not count as responsible for a child

Even if a child normally lives with you or, if the main responsibility test applies, you have the main responsibility for her/him, you do *not* count as responsible for the child and cannot qualify for CTC for her/him during any period when s/he is:[20]

- provided with or placed in accommodation and the accommodation or the child's maintenance is funded wholly or partly by the local authority under specified provisions or out of other public funds. This includes children staying with foster carers who get foster payments for them from the local authority. This does not apply if your child is staying in certain forms of residential accommodation and this is only necessary because your child has a disability or because her/his health would be significantly impaired or further impaired if s/he were not staying in the accommodation. You must have been treated as responsible for her/him immediately before s/he went into the accommodation;[21] *or*
- being looked after by a local authority and has been placed with you because you want to adopt her/him. This only applies if the local authority is paying

Part 2: Main means-tested benefits and tax credits
Chapter 8: Child tax credit
2. The rules about your age

for the child's accommodation or maintenance or both under specified provisions; *or*
- in custody. This only applies if your child:
  - is serving a life or unlimited sentence; *or*
  - is serving a term of more than four months; *or*
  - has been detained 'during Her Majesty's pleasure'; *or*
- at least 16 and:
  - is awarded CTC in her/his own right for a child for whom s/he is responsible; *or*
  - receives WTC in her/his own right (including in a joint claim); *or*
  - is entitled to and receiving contributory ESA in her/his own right; *or*
  - is married, in a civil partnership or living with someone as a couple and her/his partner is not in full-time non-advanced education or approved training (see p152 and p554 for what counts); *or*
  - is your partner and and you are living with her/him.

Note: a young person does not count as a child if s/he gets IS, income-based JSA, income-related ESA or UC in her/his own right (see p153).

Challenging a decision

HMRC might say that:
- your child does not normally live with you or that you are not the person with main responsibility for her/him so you are not entitled to CTC;
- someone else has claimed CTC for your child(ren) and now satisfies the 'main reponsibility test' when you have been getting CTC for the same child(ren). In this case, your entitlement to CTC ends and you may have been overpaid.

If you think a decision is wrong and it affects your tax credits, you can appeal.[22] See Chapter 68 for more information about revisions and appeals. **Note:** you must apply for a review before you can appeal.

It is possible that the DWP, the local authority and HMRC might reach different conclusions about whether your child(ren) can be included in your claims. If so, you should appeal *all* the decisions with which you disagree.

2. **The rules about your age**

You (and your partner) must be aged at least 16 to qualify for child tax credit (CTC).[23] There is no upper age limit. If you are under 16, someone else (eg, your parent or the adult with whom you normally live) may be able to claim CTC for you *and* your child.

3. People included in the claim

You can only qualify for child tax credit (CTC) if you are responsible for one or more children. Some qualifying young people continue to count as children until they are 20. See pp151–56 for who counts as a child and when you count as responsible for her/him.

If you are single, you claim CTC yourself.[24] However, if you are a member of a couple, you must claim CTC jointly with your partner.[25] For information about who counts as a couple for tax credit purposes, see p1438. The rules are the same as for working tax credit. **Note:** if you claim jointly with your partner, but then cease to count as a couple (or you claim as a single person, but then become a member of a couple), your entitlement to CTC ends. You should therefore report this change in your circumstances and claim tax credits as a single person (or a couple) immediately.

If you are a couple:
• when working out how much CTC you get, your partner's income is added to yours (see Chapter 64);
• CTC is paid to the person who is the main carer for your children (see p1447).

4. The amount of child tax credit

The amount of child tax credit (CTC) you get depends on:
• your maximum CTC. This is made up of a combination of 'elements':
  – child element (£2,750 a year) – one for each child;
  – disabled child element (£3,100 a year) – one for each child who qualifies;
  – severely disabled child element (£1,255 a year) – one for each child who qualifies;
  – family element (£545 a year).
  For details of how you qualify for the above elements, see Chapter 63.
• how much income you have; *and*
• the 'income threshold figure' that applies to you.

The elements and thresholds can be increased every April. If you do not qualify for CTC currently, you might qualify if the rates go up.

If you are on a means-tested benefit

Being on income support (IS), income-based jobseeker's allowance (JSA), income-related employment and support allowance (ESA) or pension credit (PC) is an automatic passport to maximum CTC.[26] You, therefore, do not need to work out your income or capital. In these circumstances, CTC equals maximum CTC.

Part 2: Main means-tested benefits and tax credits
Chapter 8: Child tax credit
5. Claims and backdating

If you are not on a means-tested benefit

If you are not on IS, income-based JSA, income-related ESA or PC, follow the steps below to calculate your CTC.

- **Step one:** work out your 'relevant period' (see p1399).
- **Step two:** work out your maximum entitlement (your maximum CTC) for the relevant period (see p1400).
- **Step three:** work out your 'relevant income' (see Chapter 64 and p1411).
- **Step four:** compare your income with the 'income threshold figure' for the relevant period. This is currently £16,010 a year if you are entitled to CTC only, or £6,420 a year if you are entitled to CTC and your maximum amount of tax credits includes working tax credit (WTC) elements.[27] See p1412 for further information.
- **Step five:** calculate your CTC entitlement for the relevant period (see p1412). If your income is less than the 'income threshold figure', CTC equals your maximum CTC. If your income exceeds the 'income threshold figure', your maximum CTC is reduced by 41 per cent of the excess.

You may also be entitled to WTC. Full details of both calculations are in Chapter 63.

5. Claims and backdating

The general rules on claiming, backdating and how your claim can be be renewed at the end of the year are in Chapter 65. This section gives an outline of the rules on claims for child tax credit (CTC).

Making a claim

Your first claim for CTC must usually be made in writing on the form approved or authorised by HM Revenue and Customs (HMRC).[28] You use the same form for CTC and for working tax credit (WTC). See p1440 for information about how and where to make a claim. Keep a copy of your claim form in case queries arise.

You can amend or withdraw your claim before you are given notice of the decision on it.[29]

Who should claim

If you are a member of a couple, you must make a joint claim with your partner. If you are not a member of a couple, you claim yourself. For information about who counts as a couple for tax credit purposes, see p1438. If you cannot make your claim yourself, an 'appointee' (see p1440) can claim on your behalf.

Information to support your claim

When you claim CTC, you must:[30]
- satisfy the national insurance (NI) number requirement (see p1442);
- provide proof of your identity, if required;
- supply information to support your claim (see p1442).

It is important that you provide all the information required. If you do not do so, a decision might not be made on your claim. If HMRC requires further information before it makes a decision on your claim, see p1444 for details of the time you must be given to provide the information and what happens if you fail to do so.

When to claim

The general rule is that your claim runs from the date it is received by HMRC.[31] You cannot make a claim in advance of the tax year for which you are claiming. However, you may be able to get your claim backdated.

Is your income too high?
Awards of CTC are always based on annual income. HMRC bases the initial award of CTC on your (and your partner's) *previous* tax year's income. If you think your income may be too high to qualify for CTC currently, you can make a 'protective claim' so that you do not lose out if you expect your income to fall (see p1441).

Backdating your claim

It is important to claim in time. A claim for CTC can usually only be backdated for a maximum of 31 days.[32] See p1446 for further information.

Note: if you are waiting to hear whether your child or qualifying young person is entitled to disability living allowance (DLA), personal independence payment (PIP) or armed forces independence payment, you should claim CTC, even if you will not qualify for CTC until the disabled child element or severely disabled child element can be included. If you do not qualify, you are given a 'nil award'. A special rule then allows your entitlement to these elements to be backdated for more than one month (see p1447). You must notify HMRC within one month of the date the DLA, PIP or armed forces independence payment is awarded.

Renewal awards

At the end of the tax year in which you claimed CTC, you (and your partner), receive a 'final notice' from HMRC asking you to confirm that your income and your household circumstances are as stated for the previous tax year. This is known as the 'annual review' (see p1455). You must reply within a strict time limit. HMRC then makes a final decision, based on your actual income during the

Part 2: Main means-tested benefits and tax credits
Chapter 8: Child tax credit
6. Getting paid

• •

tax year. It decides whether you were entitled to CTC and, if so, the amount of your award. HMRC also uses the information about your income and household circumstances for the previous tax year to renew your award for the next tax year.[33] **Note:** if you have a 'nil award', you may be given notice that your claim will not be renewed unless you specifically request this.

6. Getting paid

This section gives an outline of the rules about payment of child tax credit (CTC). For more information about getting paid, see p1447.

CTC is normally paid by direct credit transfer into the bank (or similar) account of whoever is deemed to be the main carer of your children (see p1447). If you are unable to act for yourself, payment can be made to someone else on your behalf – called your 'appointee' (see p1440).[34]

• •

When is child tax credit paid?
You are paid every week or every four weeks, whichever is more convenient for you, although HM Revenue and Customs (HMRC) can decide how often.[35]

• •

You can be paid by cheque while your account arrangements are finalised.

If your award of CTC (or the combination of CTC and working tax credit (WTC)) is £2 a week or less, it is paid in a single lump sum into your account to cover the whole year.[36] **Note:** if your entitlement to CTC (or the combination of CTC and WTC) is less than £26 for the whole of the tax year, no award is made and you are not paid at all.[37]

Note:

*   Even if you have been sanctioned for a benefit offence, your CTC cannot be paid at a reduced rate.
*   If you have forgotten your PIN, see p1163. The issues are the same as for benefits.
*   If payment of your CTC is delayed and this is causing hardship, ask HMRC to make a 'next day/same day payment'. If you wish to complain about how your claim has been dealt with, see p1384. You might be able to claim compensation (see p1382).
*   If payment of your CTC is postponed, see p1449.
*   If you are overpaid CTC, you might have to repay it (see Chapter 66). In some cases, interest can be added to the overpayment. In some circumstances you may have to pay a penalty (see p1476). If you have been accused of fraud, see Chapter 67.

• • • •

· ·

Length of award

Your award of CTC runs from the date your claim is received by HMRC (or from the date to which your claim can be backdated) to the end of the tax year.[38] However, changes in your circumstances can be taken into account during the tax year. In some cases, you *must* report changes of circumstances. See below and Chapter 65 for details.

Change of circumstances

Your award of CTC is made on the basis of your (and your partner's) previous year's income and your personal circumstances on the date of your claim. If your current year's income or your personal circumstances change, your award of CTC can be amended. Remember the following.

- There are some changes you *must* report to HMRC (see p1450). If you fail to do so within one month, you might be given a financial penalty. Some changes end your entitlement to CTC and you must make a fresh claim.
- Unless it is a change that you must report, it is optional to report changes that affect your maximum entitlement to CTC – eg, when you have a baby or if one of your children stops getting disability living allowance (see p1451). However, changes that increase your maximum entitlement to CTC can generally only be backdated one month from when you notify HMRC. Changes that decrease your entitlement may result in an overpayment.
- It is optional to report changes in your income (see p1452). These are always taken into account at the end of the tax year, but you may want to consider reporting these sooner to avoid an overpayment or underpayment of CTC.

7. Tax, other benefits and the benefit cap

Tax

Child tax credit (CTC) is not taxable.

Means-tested benefits

CTC is not taken into account as income for income support (IS), income-based jobseeker's allowance (JSA), income-related employment and support allowance (ESA) or pension credit (PC).

Unless you are on IS, income-based JSA or income-related ESA or are at least the qualifying age for PC (see p78), the amount of CTC you are paid *is* taken into account as income for housing benefit (HB).

If you get arrears of CTC, these count as capital for means-tested benefits and can be disregarded in some circumstances (see p355 and p382).

Part 2: Main means-tested benefits and tax credits
Chapter 8: Child tax credit
7. Tax, other benefits and the benefit cap

Non-means-tested benefits

CTC can be paid in addition to any non-means-tested benefits to which you (or your partner) are entitled, including child benefit, but see Chapter 64 for which of these benefits may be taken into account as income for CTC. If your child qualifies for disability living allowance (DLA), personal independence payment (PIP) or armed forces independence payment, you might qualify for the disabled child or severely disabled child elements of CTC and the income from DLA, PIP or armed forces independence payment is ignored.

Tax credits

If you are in full-time paid work, you might qualify for working tax credit (WTC). WTC can be paid in addition to CTC.

The benefit cap

In some cases, the total amount of specified benefits you receive is limited to £350 a week (if you are a single claimant without children) or £500 a week (if you are a lone parent or a member of a couple). This is known as the 'benefit cap'. CTC is one of the specified benefits. The benefit cap only applies if you are getting HB. See p1169 for further information.

Passports and other sources of help

If you are entitled to CTC, you may also qualify for:
- health benefits such as free prescriptions (see Chapter 30). You do not have to satisfy the means test if you are getting CTC and your gross annual income is no more than a set amount; *and*
- education benefits such as free school lunches (see p832).

You may also qualify for a Sure Start maternity grant or a social fund funeral expenses payment. If you have a low income, you may be entitled to a council tax reduction (see p827).

Notes

1. Who can claim child tax credit

1 ss3(3) and (7), 8 and 42 TCA 2002; regs 3-5 CTC Regs; reg 3 TC(R) Regs; reg 3 TC(Imm) Regs
2 s8(1) TCA 2002
3 s8(5) TCA 2002; reg 6 CTC Regs
4 s8(3) TCA 2002; reg 2(1), definition of 'child', CTC Regs
5 s8(4) TCA 2002; regs 2, definition of 'qualifying young person' and 'full-time education', 4 and 5(1)-(3A) CTC Regs
6 Reg 5(7) CTC Regs
7 Regs 2(1), definition of 'advanced education' and 'full-time education', and 5(5) and (6) CTC Regs
8 Regs 2, definition of 'remunerative work', and 5(4) CTC Regs
9 Reg 3(1) rule 2.2 CTC Regs
10 s8(2) TCA 2002; reg 3(1) rules 1 and 2 CTC Regs
11 Reg 3(1) rule 4 Case D and (2) CTC Regs
12 para 02202 TCTM
13 CFC/1537/1995
14 Reg 3(1) rule 2 CTC Regs
15 Reg 3 rule 3 CTC Regs
16 para 02204 TCTM
17 *KN v HMRC* [2009] UKUT 79 (AAC)
18 *Humphreys v HMRC* [2012] UKSC 18, 16 May 2012; [2012] AACR 46
19 CTC/4390/2004. However, the judge in *CM v HMRC (TC)* [2010] UKUT 400 (AAC) disagreed that this was a legitimate consideration.
20 Reg 3(1) rule 4.1 CTC Regs
21 Reg 3(1) rule 4.2 CTC Regs; reg 9 CB Regs
22 CTC/2090/2004

2. The rules about your age

23 s3(3) TCA 2002

3. People included in the claim

24 s3(3)(b) TCA 2002
25 s3(3)(a) and (5A) TCA 2002; reg 2(1) CTC Regs; CTC/3864/2004; R(TC) 1/07

4. The amount of child tax credit

26 ss7(2) and 13 TCA 2002; reg 4 TC(ITDR) Regs
27 Reg 3(2) and (3) TC(ITDR) Regs

5. Claims and backdating

28 Reg 5 TC(CN) Regs
29 Reg 5(7) TC(CN) Regs; R(IS) 3/05
30 Reg 5(3)-(6) TC(CN) Regs
31 s5(2) TCA 2002
32 Reg 7 TC(CN) Regs
33 Regs 11 and 12 TC(CN) Regs

6. Getting paid

34 s24(3) TCA 2002; reg 6 TC(PC) Regs
35 Regs 8 and 13 TC(PC) Regs
36 Reg 10 TC(PC) Regs
37 Reg 9 TC(ITDR) Regs
38 s5(2) TCA 2002

Chapter 9

Working tax credit

This chapter covers:
1. Who can claim working tax credit (below)
2. The rules about your age (p174)
3. People included in the claim (p174)
4. The amount of working tax credit (p175)
5. Claims and backdating (p176)
6. Getting paid (p178)
7. Tax, other benefits and the benefit cap (p180)

Key facts
- Working tax credit (WTC) is paid to low-paid workers. It tops up your wages if you are in full-time paid work (known as 'remunerative work').
- You do not have to have paid national insurance contributions to qualify.
- WTC is administered and paid by HM Revenue and Customs.
- If you disagree with a WTC decision, you can apply for a revision, or appeal against it. You must apply for a review before you can appeal.

Future changes

The government says that, in 2016, you will no longer be able to make a new claim for WTC. During 2016 and 2017, the DWP will begin to transfer existing WTC claims to universal credit. See p18 for further information.

1. Who can claim working tax credit

You qualify for working tax credit (WTC) if:[1]
- you (or your partner) are in full-time paid work (see p165);
- your income is sufficiently low (see Chapter 64);
- you are 'present' and 'ordinarily resident' in the UK. You can be treated as present and ordinarily resident in the UK in some circumstances – eg, if you are away temporarily. See Chapter 70 for further information;
- you are not a 'person subject to immigration control' (see Chapter 69).

Note: if you come under the universal credit (UC) system (see p19), you cannot make a new claim for WTC and should claim UC instead.

Full-time paid work

To qualify for WTC, you or your partner must be in full-time paid work. HM Revenue and Customs (HMRC) calls this 'remunerative work'.[2] See below for what counts as full-time work, p166 for what counts as paid work and for how your hours are calculated. 'Work' includes self-employment and work which is done from home.

In some circumstances, you may be treated as not being in full-time paid work even if you are (see p172). In others, you may be treated as if you are in full-time paid work when you are not (see p170). If you are unsure whether you are in full-time paid work, see p169.

Income from work affects your entitlement to WTC. This means that, although your (or your partner's) hours of work are high enough for you to qualify, you might not satisfy the means test.

If neither you nor your partner are in full-time paid work, you may be able to claim income support (IS), jobseeker's allowance (JSA) or employment and support allowance (ESA). You may be able to choose whether to claim IS/JSA/ESA or WTC. In some situations, you may be able to claim both IS/JSA/ESA and WTC – eg, if you are a 'term-time only' worker or are off sick and getting statutory sick pay (SSP). This is because different rules on what counts as full-time paid work apply. See p998 for information about what you should consider.

What counts as full-time work

You count as being in full-time work if any of the following apply.[3]

- You work at least **30 hours** a week and you are 25 or over.
- You work at least **16 hours** a week and:
  - you have a physical or mental disability which puts you at a disadvantage in getting a job and you qualify for a disabled worker element; *or*
  - you are 60 or over; *or*
  - you are a single claimant and are responsible for at least one child or qualifying young person (see p153); *or*
  - you are a member of a couple, you (or your partner) are responsible for at least one child or qualifying young person (see p153) and your partner counts as incapacitated for the purposes of the childcare element (see p1406), is entitled to carer's allowance (CA), is a hospital inpatient or is in prison.
- You and your partner's combined hours of work are at least **24 hours** a week, and you (or your partner) are responsible for at least one child or qualifying young person (see p153). One of you must do at least 16 hours a week. If only one of you works, that person must work at least 24 hours a week.

Part 2: Main means-tested benefits and tax credits
Chapter 9: Working tax credit
1. Who can claim working tax credit

If you are under 25, you can only qualify for WTC if you work at least 16 hours a week and qualify for a disabled worker element, or you are responsible for a child in the circumstances on p165.

If your circumstances change and you are no longer responsible for a child or qualifying young person, or no longer qualify for a disabled worker element, unless you are 60 or over, you may have to increase your weekly hours to 30 or more to continue to qualify for WTC. See Chapter 65 for more information on changes of circumstances and when you must report them.

At the date of your claim, you must be working or have accepted an offer of work which is expected to start within seven days.[4] In the latter case, you only count as being in full-time paid work when the work begins. The work must be expected to continue for at least four weeks after you make your claim (or if you have accepted an offer of work, after the work starts).[5]

Note:

- You can continue to count as being in full-time work for four weeks after you leave work, or your hours reduce to less than the number you (or your partner) need to do. See p172 for information about what is known as 'WTC run-on'.
- If you normally work sufficient hours a week, but are off sick or on maternity, paternity or adoption leave, you may be able to claim WTC as you can be treated as in full-time paid work (see p170). You may also be able to claim IS, JSA or ESA.

What counts as paid work

'Paid work' includes work for which you are paid or expect to be paid.[6] Payment of a benefit (eg, CA) does not count for these purposes. The information on p989 about what counts as paid work for means-tested benefits also applies to WTC.

How your hours are calculated

How you calculate your hours depends on whether you are employed or self-employed.[7]

- If you are employed, include all the hours:
  - you normally work under your contract, if you are an apprentice or employee; *or*
  - you normally perform in the office in which you are employed, if you are an office holder. This includes if you are in an elective office or are a company director; *or*
  - for which you are normally paid by the employment agency with whom you have a contract, if you are an agency worker.
- If you are self-employed, include all the hours you normally do for payment or for which you expect to be paid.

Paid meal and refreshment breaks count towards the total hours you work.[8] Also included is any time allowed for visits to a hospital, clinic or other establishment, but only if this is to treat or monitor your disability and if you are paid, or expect to be paid, for the time.[9] Your total hours from more than one job are added together.

Periods when you are on a customary or paid holiday from work are ignored when calculating your hours.[10] Likewise, unpaid meal and refreshment breaks are ignored.

Employed and self-employed[11]

You count as 'employed' if you are employed under a contract of service or apprenticeship and your earnings are taxable as employment income under certain provisions of the Income Tax (Earnings and Pensions) Act 2003. You count as 'self-employed' if you are carrying out a trade, profession or vocation.

Hours you normally work

Whether you are employed or self-employed, the measure for WTC purposes is the number of hours you normally work.[12] 'Normally' is not defined in the WTC rules. HMRC says you should calculate your hours based on what you 'regularly, usually or typically' do and that the number of hours you normally work might not be the number of hours specified in your contract of employment.[13] The hours that are relevant are those you *actually* work. If you routinely do paid overtime, argue that these are hours you normally work and that they should be included. See p168 if your hours fluctuate.

Example

Harriet is a cashier in a supermarket. Her partner stays at home to look after their children. She is contracted to work 21 hours a week over a three-day week but she does 3.5 hours overtime almost every week. She gets an unpaid half-hour lunch break. When Harriet and her partner claim WTC, she has just returned from two weeks' paid holiday.

Harriet normally works 21 + 3.5 = 24.5 hours a week. Unpaid lunch breaks and the time she was on paid holiday are not taken into account. As Harriet and her partner are responsible for children, one of them needs to work at least 16 hours a week and between them, they need to work at least 24 hours a week. Harriet therefore counts as being in full-time paid work.

When working out your normal hours if you are self-employed, HMRC says you can include not only the hours you spend providing orders or services but also those that are necessary to your self-employment – eg, trips to wholesalers and retailers, visits to potential clients, time spent on advertising or canvassing, cleaning the business or vehicles used as part of the business, bookkeeping and research work.[14]

Part 2: Main means-tested benefits and tax credits
Chapter 9: Working tax credit
1. Who can claim working tax credit

If your hours fluctuate

Working out the number of hours you normally work is straightforward if:

- you do the same number of hours each and every week; *or*
- your hours vary, but you always do at least enough hours each week to count as being in full-time paid work.

However, if your weekly hours fluctuate, it can be more complicated. Unless you are a term-time only worker (see below), there is no rule on how to average your hours. Working out the number of hours you normally work is a question of judgement. If you have a regular pattern of work (a recognised work cycle), HMRC says the hours you normally work are those that reflect an overall view of the pattern of your hours over a representative period, or over a year.[15] For example, if you always work two weeks on and two weeks off, you could argue that your hours should be averaged over a four-week period.

If you are in any doubt about what your normal hours are, contact HMRC and seek advice. If you are unsure whether you are in full-time paid work, see p169.

Examples

Shane works in a residential project. He works three weeks on and one week off. When he is on, he works 40 hours a week. His average hours are 40 x 3 ÷ 4 = 30 hours a week. Shane can try to argue that he normally works 30 hours or more a week. As Shane is aged 45, does not have a physical or mental disability and has no children, he must work at least 30 hours a week. He therefore counts as being in full-time paid work.

Narindar is contracted to do 15 hours a week. However, she gets regular overtime of three hours every other week. Her average hours are 15 + 18 ÷ 2 = 16.5 hours. Narindar can try to argue that she normally works 16 hours or more a week. As Narindar is a lone parent, she need only work 16 hours or more a week. She therefore counts as being in full-time paid work.

Appeal if you think your average hours have been calculated unfairly. You should first work out whether you are better off claiming IS/JSA/ESA or WTC (see p998).

Term-time only workers

A term-time only worker rule applies if:[16]

- you work in a school, an educational establishment or other place of employment; *and*
- you have a recognisable 'work cycle' that lasts for a year; *and*
- your 'work cycle' includes periods of school holidays or similar vacations during which you do not work.

If the term-time only worker rule applies, periods when you are not working are ignored when deciding whether you are in full-time paid work. In practice, if the hours of work you do during term time mean you are in full-time paid work during term time, you also count as being in full-time paid work over the holidays. You should be able to claim WTC during this period if your normal hours of work each week are sufficient during term time. Because the way hours are calculated is different for JSA and ESA, if you are not paid for the holidays, you may also be able to claim JSA (or if you have a partner, s/he may also be able to claim income-related ESA) during these periods if you satisfy the other qualifying conditions (see Chapter 46).

Example

Dee is 35 years old and has no children. She is a cleaner at a local college and works 35 hours a week, 32 weeks of the year. She does not work (and is not paid) when the students are on study leave and on holiday. The periods when Dee does not work are ignored. She is in full-time paid work during term time because she works 30 hours or more a week. She therefore counts as being in full-time paid work throughout the year and can claim WTC.

Note:

- It may not be clear whether you have a work cycle that lasts a year – eg, if you have only started your job recently or have a fixed-term contract that finishes at the end of the school term, or are employed on a casual or relief basis.[17] If you have an indefinite contract to work in term time only, you can argue that you have a yearly work cycle from the start.[18]
- If you work casually or intermittently (eg, you are a seasonal worker who works in the summer but you are unemployed the rest of the year), HMRC might say your work cycle is that part of the year in which you are working and that you do not count as in full-time work when you are unemployed.[19]

If you are unsure whether you are in full-time paid work

If you are unsure if the number of hours you normally work are sufficient at the date of your claim, contact HMRC and seek advice. Bear in mind that a claim for WTC can be backdated for 31 days automatically (see p1446), so there is scope to postpone claiming WTC until you are certain. If time is running out and you are still uncertain, consider making a claim to protect your position.

If you are refused WTC because neither you nor your partner are in full-time paid work for WTC purposes and within 14 days of that decision you claim IS or JSA, your claim for IS or JSA can be backdated to the date you claimed WTC.[20] This rule does not apply to ESA. However, your ESA claim can be backdated for up to three months.

Part 2: Main means-tested benefits and tax credits
Chapter 9: Working tax credit
1. Who can claim working tax credit

Have your circumstances changed?

1. If you are uncertain about whether you (or your partner) are still in full-time paid work (eg, your weekly hours change), keep a record of the hours you work each week. If you (and your partner) no longer normally work sufficient hours a week, you are no longer entitled to WTC.

2. If you have a partner and are getting a childcare element because both of you are in full-time paid work and it appears that one of you no longer normally works 16 hours a week, you may no longer be entitled to a childcare element (see p1405). You must report your change in hours to HMRC within one month (see Chapter 65).

3. If you are no longer responsible for a child or qualifying young person (you must report this to HMRC within one month) or no longer qualify for a disabled worker element, unless you are 60 or over you may now have to increase your hours to continue to qualify for WTC.

4. If you no longer count as being in full-time paid work, check to see whether you (or your partner) qualify for IS, JSA or ESA and make a claim if this is possible. Remember that claims for IS and JSA can only be backdated in limited circumstances.

5. Whether or not you are in full-time paid work, check to see if you qualify for pension credit (PC). There is no full-time paid work rule for PC, but earnings and WTC count as income.

6. If you (and your partner) no longer work sufficient hours to qualify for WTC, you may be able to claim universal credit (UC) if you come under the UC system (see p19) and are not entitled to CTC.

7. If your hours change, but you still count as being in full-time paid work, the amount of WTC to which you are entitled could be affected by:
- a change in your earnings. If these increase, you may wish to report this to HMRC to avoid an overpayment at the end of the year. If these decrease, you may get increased WTC if you report the change. You may wish to consider waiting until the end of the year (see p1452);
- whether or not you are entitled to have a 30-hour element included in calculating your WTC. If your entitlement decreases, you must report your change in hours to HMRC within one month. Any increase in your entitlement to WTC can only be backdated one month from the date you notify HMRC of the change.

People treated as being in full-time paid work

You or your partner are treated as being in full-time paid work in a number of situations.

Maternity, paternity or adoption leave

You or your partner are treated as being in full-time paid work during any period when:[21]
- you are being paid statutory maternity pay (SMP), statutory paternity pay (SPP), statutory adoption pay (SAP) or maternity allowance (MA); *or*

- you are absent from work during ordinary maternity leave, ordinary paternity leave or ordinary adoption leave, or during the first 13 weeks of additional maternity or adoption leave; *or*
- you are absent from work during additional paternity leave, but only during the period in which you would have been paid additional SPP had you qualified.

If you are an employee, you are treated as in full-time paid work from the start of the period, provided you are in full-time paid work for WTC purposes immediately before the period begins. However, if this is not the case (eg, you are under 25, or are 25 or over but working less than 30 hours a week, and the child you and your partner are having or adopting is your first), you are treated as in full-time paid work from the date of birth (or adoption) provided you would have counted as in full-time paid work had you been responsible for a child or qualifying young person immediately before the period begins.[22]

If you are self-employed, you count as in full-time paid work during any period when the above would have applied had the work done in the week before the period began been as an employee.

If you do not return to work when your SMP, SPP, SAP or MA ceases or your leave ends, you are no longer treated as being in full-time paid work under this rule.

Note: you should consider letting HMRC know if you are in any of the above situations. This is because any MA is ignored as income for WTC, as is the first £100 a week of any SMP, SPP and SAP.

Periods of ill health

You or your partner are treated as being in full-time paid work during any period when:[23]

- you are being paid SSP or short-term lower rate incapacity benefit (IB). Note that short-term lower rate IB is ignored as income for WTC; *or*
- you are:
  - being paid IS because you are entitled to SSP, are disqualified from IB because of misconduct or failure to accept treatment or are incapable of work because of pregnancy; *or*
  - being paid ESA; *or*
  - getting national insurance (NI) credits because you are incapable of work or have limited capability for work.

This only applies for 28 weeks.

You must have been in full-time paid work for WTC purposes immediately before the period began. You may be able to argue that you can continue to be treated as in full-time paid work if you start to receive ESA or NI credits immediately after your entitlement to SSP ends.

Part 2: Main means-tested benefits and tax credits
Chapter 9: Working tax credit
1. Who can claim working tax credit

If you are self-employed, you count as in full-time paid work during any period when the above would have applied had the work done in the week before the period began been as an employee.

If you do not return to work when your SSP or short-term lower rate IB ceases (or if you are being paid IS or ESA, after 28 weeks), you no longer count as being in full-time paid work under this rule.

Working tax credit run-on

If you or your partner stop work or reduce your hours, you can get what is known as 'WTC run-on'. You are treated as being in full-time paid work for the four weeks immediately after you stop work, or your hours reduce to less than the number you (or your partner) must do to count as in full-time paid work.[24] This means you continue to qualify for:

- WTC for the four-week period, even if you would otherwise no longer count as in full-time paid work;
- all the elements you were previously getting for that period – eg, the 30-hour element and the childcare element, even if the reduction in hours means you would otherwise lose entitlement to these.

Note: you must report the change in your circumstances to HMRC within one month.

Other situations

You or your partner are treated as being in full-time paid work:

- if you were in full-time paid work within the past seven days.[25] This means you can make a new claim or continue to qualify for WTC – eg, during a short period between jobs or when you are on jury service;
- during any period when you are on strike or are suspended from work while complaints or allegations against you are investigated, so long as you were in full-time paid work for WTC purposes immediately before the start of the period. You must not be on strike for longer than 10 consecutive days when you should be working.[26]

People treated as not being in full-time paid work

You or your partner are treated as *not* being in full-time paid work during any period during which you are receiving pay in lieu of notice after you stop work, unless you continue to qualify under the four-week 'run-on' rule (see above).[27] In addition, you or your partner are treated as *not* being in full-time paid work if:[28]

- you are a **volunteer**, or are working for a charity or voluntary organisation and are giving your services free (except for your expenses);
- you are **providing care** for someone who is staying with you temporarily but who is not normally a member of your household; *and*

- the only payment you receive is from a health authority, a local authority, a voluntary organisation, a clinical commissioning group or the person her/himself for caring for her/him; *and*
- the payment is disregarded as a tax-free payment under HMRC's 'rent-a-room' scheme (see p1430);

Note that if you are an adult placement carer who has *not* opted for the 'rent-a-room' scheme, you *can* count as in full-time paid work;[29]

- you are **working on a training scheme** and are being paid a training allowance (see below) unless the training allowance or the money you are being paid by the DWP is subject to income tax as a profit from work;[30]
- the only payment you receive, or expect to receive, is a **sports award** from a sports council;
- you are working while you are a **sentenced or remand prisoner**. This means you cannot qualify for WTC even if the work you do is outside the prison – eg, while you are on temporary release.

Training allowance

A '**training allowance**' is an allowance paid to maintain you or a member of your family:[31]
- by a government department or by or on behalf of the Secretary of State, Scottish Enterprise or the Highlands and Islands Enterprise; *and*
- for the period or part of a period during which you are on a course provided or approved by or under arrangements made by any of the above.

Allowances paid to, or in respect of, you by a government department or by the Scottish government are not included if these are paid because you are a trainee teacher or on a full-time course of education, unless this is under arrangements made under s2 of the Employment and Training Act 1973.

Students

You are not excluded from claiming WTC simply because you are a student. However, you must do sufficient hours of paid work in addition to your studies or during the holidays and the work must be expected to last for four weeks.

Is the work part of your course?

1. If you are paid in return for the work you do (eg, you are paid by an employer during a work placement), you can argue that you are in full-time paid work.

2. Any work you do in studying for a degree or other qualification does not count as full-time paid work – any grant or loan you receive is not paid in return for work done on the course.

3. You are not considered to be in full-time paid work if you are a student nurse because the NHS bursary and other grants or loans you get are not payments for work done on the course and do not count as income for tax credit purposes.[32]

Part 2: Main means-tested benefits and tax credits
Chapter 9: Working tax credit
3. People included in the claim

When calculating how much WTC you can get, student loans and most other student income is disregarded. See p1427 for what income counts.

Foster carers

If you are working sufficient hours as a foster carer, you can qualify for WTC. HMRC generally treats foster carers as self-employed. It says that the hours of work you declare on your claim form should be accepted.[33] If you do more than one job, the total hours are added together, so if you are doing work in addition to foster caring, the hours from the other work can be added to those spent foster caring.

Fostering allowances that qualify for tax relief are generally ignored when calculating your WTC. See p1432 for further information.

Would you be better off claiming another benefit instead?

For IS and JSA, if you or your partner are (or for income-related ESA, your partner is) a foster carer (or, in Scotland only, a kinship carer) receiving a payment for looking after a child from a local authority or voluntary organisation, you are (or s/he is) treated as *not* being in full-time paid work (see p995). You may therefore wish to consider how you would be better off financially.

2. The rules about your age

You (and your partner) must be aged at least 16 to make a claim for working tax credit (WTC).[34] There is no upper age limit.

If you are under 25, you can only qualify for WTC if you work at least 16 hours and you are a disabled worker or are responsible for a child in the circumstances described on p165.

3. People included in the claim

If you are single, you claim working tax credit (WTC) for yourself.[35] However, if you are a member of a couple (see p1438), you must claim WTC jointly with your partner.[36] WTC includes elements for you and your partner and for the special needs of either of you (see Chapter 63). When working out how much WTC you get, your partner's income is added to yours (see Chapter 64). **Note:** if you claim jointly with your partner but then cease to count as a couple (or you claim as a single person but then become a member of a couple), your entitlement to WTC ends. You should therefore report this change in your circumstances and claim tax credits as a single person (or a couple) immediately.

If you are responsible for at least one child or qualifying young person:

- you (or your partner) need only do paid work of 16 hours a week to qualify for WTC (although if you are a member of a couple, in most cases your combined hours must be at least 24 a week);
- if you are a couple and one of you works at least 16 hours a week, your hours of work can be added to those of your partner to enable you to qualify for the 30-hour element (see p1403);
- you (and your partner) might qualify for the childcare element of WTC if you pay for childcare.

See p151 for who counts as a child or qualifying young person. The rules are the same as for child tax credit (CTC).[37] The terms 'child' or 'children' in this chapter include qualifying young people.

For when you count as responsible for a child, see p153. HM Revenue and Customs uses the same test as for CTC.[38]

4. The amount of working tax credit

The amount of working tax credit (WTC) you get depends on:
- your maximum WTC. This is made up of a combination of 'elements':
  - basic element (£1,940 a year);
  - disabled worker element (£2,935 a year). More than one can be included if you are a member of a couple and you both qualify;
  - lone parent/couple element (£1,990 a year);
  - 30-hour element (£800 a year);
  - severe disability element (£1,255 a year). More than one can be included if you are a member of a couple and you both qualify;
  - childcare element.
  For details of how you qualify for the above elements, see Chapter 63.
- how much income you have; *and*
- the 'income threshold figure'.

The elements and threshold can be increased every April. If you do not qualify for WTC currently, you might qualify if the rates go up.

If you are on a means-tested benefit

Being on income support (IS), income-based jobseeker's allowance (JSA), income-related employment and support allowance (ESA) or pension credit (PC) is an automatic passport to maximum WTC.[39] You therefore do not need to work out

Part 2: Main means-tested benefits and tax credits
Chapter 9: Working tax credit
5. Claims and backdating

your income and capital. In these circumstances, WTC equals maximum WTC. **Note:** this does not apply while you are getting 'WTC run-on' (see p172).

> ### *Can you claim a means-tested benefit with working tax credit?*
> There are not many situations in which you can claim IS, income-based JSA or income-related ESA at the same time as WTC. This is because you cannot claim IS or JSA if you or your partner are in full-time paid work for IS/JSA purposes, and you cannot claim income-related ESA if you do *any* work (unless this is work you may do while claiming) or if your partner is in full-time paid work for ESA purposes. However, you might be able to claim both – eg, if you (or your partner) are a 'term-time only' worker or are off sick. It does not matter how many hours you (or your partner) work for PC. However, WTC counts in full as income for IS, income-based JSA, income-related ESA and PC.

If you are not on a means-tested benefit

If you are not on IS, income-based JSA, income-related ESA or PC, you need to follow the steps below to calculate your WTC.
- **Step one:** work out your 'relevant period' (see p1399).
- **Step two:** work out your maximum entitlement (your maximum WTC) for the relevant period (see p1411).
- **Step three:** work out your 'relevant income' (see Chapter 64 and p1411).
- **Step four:** compare your income with the 'income threshold figure' for the relevant period – currently £6,420 a year for WTC.[40]
- **Step five:** calculate your WTC entitlement for the relevant period (see p1412). If your income is less than the 'income threshold figure', WTC equals your maximum WTC. If your income exceeds the 'income threshold figure', your maximum WTC is reduced by 41 per cent of the excess.

You may also be entitled to child tax credit. Full details of both calculations are in Chapter 63.

5. **Claims and backdating**

The general rules on claiming, backdating and how your claim can be renewed at the end of the year are in Chapter 65. This section gives an outline of the rules on claims for working tax credit (WTC).

Making a claim

Your first claim for WTC must usually be made in writing on the form approved or authorised by HM Revenue and Customs (HMRC). You use the same form for

WTC and for child tax credit (CTC). See p1440 for more information about how and where to make a claim. Keep a copy of your claim form in case queries arise.

You can amend or withdraw your claim before you are given notice of the decision on it.[41]

Who should claim

If you are a member of a couple, you must make a joint claim with your partner. If you are not a member of a couple, you claim for yourself. For information about who counts as a couple for tax credit purposes, see p1438. If you cannot make your claim yourself, an 'appointee' (see p1440) can claim on your behalf.

Information to support your claim

When you claim WTC, you must:[42]
- satisfy the national insurance number (NI) requirement (see p1442);
- provide proof of your identity, if required;
- supply information to support your claim (see p1442).

It is important that you provide all the information required. If you do not do so, a decision might not be made on your claim. If HMRC requires further information before it makes a decision on your claim, see p1444 for details of the time you must be given to provide the information and what happens if you fail to do so.

When to claim

The general rule is that your claim runs from the date it is received by HMRC.[43] You cannot make a claim in advance of the tax year in which you are claiming, but you *can* claim WTC in advance of starting work, provided you expect to start work within seven days and will be entitled to WTC within seven days of starting work.[44] However, you may be able to get your claim backdated.

Is your income currently too high?

Awards of WTC are always based on annual income. HMRC bases the initial award of WTC on your (and your partner's) *previous* tax year's income. If you think your income may be too high to qualify for WTC currently, you can make a 'protective claim' so you do not lose out if your income is expected to fall (see p1441).

Backdating your claim

It is very important to claim in time. A claim for WTC can usually only be backdated for a maximum of 31 days.[45] See p1446 for further information.

Note: there is a special backdating rule if you claim WTC when you are awarded a qualifying benefit – eg, disability living allowance, personal independence

Part 2: Main means-tested benefits and tax credits
Chapter 9: Working tax credit
6. Getting paid

payment or armed forces independence payment (see p1447). Under this rule, your WTC can be backdated more than 31 days.

Renewal awards

At the end of the tax year in which you claimed WTC, you (and your partner if you are a member of a couple) receive a 'final notice' from HMRC asking you to confirm that your income and your household circumstances are as stated for the previous tax year. This is known as the 'annual review' (see p1455). You must reply within a strict time limit. HMRC then makes a final decision, based on your actual income during the tax year. It decides whether you were entitled to WTC and, if so, the amount of your award. HMRC also uses the information about your income and household circumstances for the previous tax year to renew your award for the next tax year.[46] **Note:** if you have a 'nil award', you may be given notice that your claim will not be renewed unless you specifically request this.

6. **Getting paid**

This section gives an outline of the rules on payment of working tax credit (WTC). For more information about getting paid, see p1447.

WTC is normally paid by direct credit transfer into your bank (or similar) account. If you make a joint claim, any WTC to which you are entitled towards your childcare expenses is paid to whoever is decided to be the main carer of your child(ren) (see p1447). If you are unable to act for yourself, payment can be made to someone on your behalf – called your 'appointee' (see p1440).[47]

When is working tax credit paid?
You are paid every week or every four weeks, whichever is more convenient for you, although HM Revenue and Customs (HMRC) can decide how often.[48]

You can be paid by cheque while your account arrangements are finalised.

If your award of WTC (or the combination of WTC and child tax credit (CTC)) is £2 a week or less, it is paid in a single lump sum into your account to cover the whole year.[49] **Note:** if your entitlement to WTC (or the combination of WTC and CTC) is less than £26 for the whole of the tax year, no award is made and you are not paid at all.[50]

Note:

- You can be disqualified from being paid WTC if you have committed a benefit offence (see p1261).
- If you have forgotten your PIN, see p1163. The issues are the same as for benefits.

- If payment of your WTC is delayed and this is causing hardship, ask HMRC to make a 'next day/same day payment'. If you wish to complain about how your claim has been dealt with, see p1384. You might be able to claim compensation (see p1382).
- If payment of your WTC is postponed, see p1449.
- If you are overpaid WTC, you might have to repay it (see Chapter 66). In some cases, interest can be added to the overpayment. In some circumstances you may have to pay a penalty (see p1476). If you have been accused of fraud, see Chapter 67.

Length of award

Your award of WTC runs from the date your claim is received by HMRC (or from the date to which your claim can be backdated) to the end of the tax year.[51] However, changes in your circumstances can be taken into account during the tax year. **Note:** in some cases, you *must* report changes of circumstance. See below and Chapter 65 for details.

Change of circumstances

Your award of WTC is made on the basis of your (and your partner's) previous year's income and your personal circumstances on the date of your claim. If your current year's income or your personal circumstances change, your award of WTC can be amended. Remember the following.

- There are some changes you *must* report to HMRC (see p1450). If you fail to do so within one month, you might be given a financial penalty. Some changes end your entitlement to WTC and you have to make a fresh claim.
- Unless it is a change that you must report, it is optional to report changes that affect your maximum entitlement to WTC – eg, when your hours increase to 30 or more so you would qualify for a 30-hour element (see p1451). However, changes that increase your maximum entitlement to WTC can generally only be backdated one month from when you notify HMRC. Changes that decrease entitlement may result in an overpayment.
- It is optional to report changes in your income (see p1452). These are always taken into account at the end of the tax year, but you may want to consider reporting them sooner to avoid an overpayment or underpayment of WTC.

If you are claiming WTC and you only qualify for the lone parent or childcare element because you (or your partner) are responsible for a child and the child dies, you are paid WTC for a further eight weeks (or to the date your child would have turned 20 if this is earlier) as if this had not happened.[52] This is only the case if you would have continued to qualify for the element but for the child's death. After that period, you may continue to qualify for WTC – eg, if you still satisfy the means test and work sufficient hours to count as in full-time paid work.

Part 2: Main means-tested benefits and tax credits
Chapter 9: Working tax credit
7. Tax, other benefits and the benefit cap

7. Tax, other benefits and the benefit cap

Tax

Working tax credit (WTC) is not taxable.

Means-tested benefits

WTC counts as income for income support (IS), income-based jobseeker's allowance (JSA), income-related employment and support allowance (ESA), pension credit (PC) and housing benefit (HB). Also note the following.

- You may be able to claim IS/income-based JSA/income-related ESA or WTC, for example, if your partner works more than 16 but less than 24 hours a week. You may be able to claim both IS/income-based JSA/income-related ESA and WTC at the same time in some circumstances (see p998).
- There is no rule that prevents you or your partner doing full-time paid work while claiming PC, so you can claim WTC at the same time as PC.
- In some cases, if you are an owner occupier and have to pay housing costs (see Chapter 20), you might be better off financially if you claim IS, income-based JSA, income-related ESA or PC.
- If you qualify for HB, you might get an additional earnings disregard (see p270 and p311).

If you get arrears of WTC, these count as capital for means-tested benefits and can be disregarded in some circumstances (see p355 and p382).

Non-means-tested benefits

In some situations, while you are receiving WTC you get national insurance credits. See p858 for further details.

WTC can be paid in addition to any non-means-tested benefits to which you (or your partner) are entitled, but see Chapter 64 for which of these benefits may be taken into account as income for WTC. Qualifying for certain non-means-tested benefits means you may also qualify for the disabled worker element or severe disability element of WTC.

Tax credits

If you have dependent children (including a 'qualifying young person'), you might qualify for child tax credit (CTC). CTC can be paid in addition to WTC.

The benefit cap

In some cases, the total amount of specified benefits you receive is limited to £350 a week (if you are a single claimant without children) or £500 a week (if you are a lone parent or a member of a couple). This is known as the 'benefit cap'. WTC is *not* one of the specified benefits. The benefit cap only applies if you are getting HB. However, the benefit cap does *not* apply if you or your partner are entitled to WTC. See p1169 for further information.

Passports and other sources of help

If you are entitled to WTC, you may also qualify for health benefits, such as free prescriptions (see Chapter 30). You do not have to satisfy the means test if your gross annual income is no more than a set amount and you are getting WTC which includes a disabled worker element or a severe disability element, or CTC with your WTC.

You may also qualify for free school lunches (see p832) and a Sure Start maternity grant or a social fund funeral expenses payment. You may be entitled to a council tax reduction (see p827).

Notes

1. Who can claim working tax credit
1 ss3(3) and (7), 10 and 42 TCA 2002; regs 4-8 WTC(EMR) Regs; reg 3 TC(R) Regs; reg 3 TC(Imm) Regs
2 s10(1) TCA 2002
3 Reg 4(1) (second condition) WTC(EMR) Regs
4 Reg 4(1) (first condition) WTC(EMR) Regs
5 Reg 4(1) (third condition) WTC(EMR) Regs
6 Reg 4(1) (fourth condition) WTC(EMR) Regs
7 Reg 4(3) WTC(EMR) Regs
8 Reg 4(4)(b) WTC(EMR) Regs
9 Reg 4(5) WTC(EMR) Regs
10 Reg 4(4)(a) WTC(EMR) Regs
11 Reg 2(1) WTC(EMR) Regs
12 Reg 4(3) WTC(EMR) Regs
13 paras 02451-52 TCTM
14 para 02453 TCTM
15 para 02457 TCTM
16 Reg 7 WTC(EMR) Regs; *Stafford and Banks v CAO* [2001] UKHL 33 (HL), reported as R(IS) 15/01
17 R(JSA) 8/03; CIS/914/1997; CJSA/2759/1998

18 R(JSA) 5/02
19 R(JSA) 1/07; *Saunderson v SSWP* [2012] ScotCS CSIH10
20 Reg 6(28) SS(C&P) Regs
21 Reg 5 WTC(EMR) Regs
22 Reg 5A WTC(EMR) Regs
23 Reg 6 WTC(EMR) Regs
24 Reg 7D WTC(EMR) Regs
25 Reg 8 WTC(EMR) Regs
26 Regs 7A and 7B WTC(EMR) Regs
27 Reg 7C WTC(EMR) Regs
28 Reg 4(2) WTC(EMR) Regs
29 para 02440 TCTM
30 Reg 4(2)(c) and (d) and (2A) WTC(EMR) Regs
31 Reg 2(1) WTC(EMR) Regs
32 R(FIS) 1/83; R(FIS) 1/86; para 02431 TCTM
33 para 02440 TCTM

2. The rules about your age
34 s3(3) TCA 2002

3. People included in the claim
35 s3(3)(b) TCA 2002
36 s3(3)(a) and (5A) TCA 2002; CTC/3864/2004; R(TC) 1/07

Part 2: Main means-tested benefits and tax credits
Chapter 9: Working tax credit
Notes

● ●

2

37 Reg 2 WTC(EMR) Regs, definition of
    'child' and 'qualifying young person'
38 Reg 2(2) WTC(EMR) Regs

4. The amount of working tax credit
39 ss7(2) and 13 TCA 2002; reg 4 TC(ITDR)
    Regs
40 Reg 3(2) TC(ITDR) Regs

5. Claims and backdating
41 Reg 5(7) TC(CN) Regs; R(IS) 5/05
42 Reg 5(3)-(6) TC(CN) Regs
43 s5(2) TCA 2002
44 Reg 10 TC(CN) Regs
45 Reg 7 TC(CN) Regs
46 Regs 11 and 12 TC(CN) Regs

6. Getting paid
47 s24(3) TCA 2002; reg 6 TC(PC) Regs
48 Regs 8 and 13 TC(PC) Regs
49 Reg 10 TC(PC) Regs
50 Reg 9 TC(ITDR) Regs
51 s5(2) TCA 2002
52 Reg 19 WTC(EMR) Regs; reg 6 CTC Regs

Chapter 10

Universal credit

This chapter covers:
1. Who can claim universal credit (below)
2. The rules about your age (p185)
3. People included in the claim (p186)
4. The amount of benefit (p186)
5. Special benefit rules (p191)
6. Claims and backdating (p191)
7. Getting paid (p194)
8. Tax, other benefits and the benefit cap (p199)

Key facts

- Universal credit (UC) is a new benefit for people on a low income who are in or out of work (including those who are sick or a carer).
- UC replaces income support, income-based jobseeker's allowance, income-related employment and support allowance, housing benefit, child tax credit and working tax credit.
- UC is being introduced gradually for certain new claimants in 'pathfinder' areas. Eventually, it will be introduced nationwide. The way in which UC is introduced may change during 2014.
- UC is a means-tested benefit.
- You do not have to have paid national insurance contributions to qualify.
- A 'benefit cap' may be applied if the total amount of certain benefits you receive exceeds a specified amount and your UC can be reduced.
- UC is administered and paid by the DWP.
- If you disagree with a UC decision, you can apply for a revision or supersession, or appeal against it. Usually, you must apply for a revision before you can appeal.

1. Who can claim universal credit

You qualify for universal credit (UC) if you:
- come under the UC system (see p19); *and*

Part 2: Main means-tested benefits and tax credits
Chapter 10: Universal credit
1. Who can claim universal credit

- you satisfy the **'basic conditions'** – ie:[1]
  - you are aged 18 or over and under the qualifying age for pension credit (PC). Note, however, that some 16/17-year-olds can get UC (see p896);
  - you are not 'receiving education', although there are some exceptions (see p185);
  - you satisfy the 'habitual residence test' and the 'right to reside test' (see Chapter 70), and are in, or treated as in, Great Britain (see Chapters 70 and 71);
  - you are not a 'person subject to immigration control' (see p1499);
  - you have accepted a 'claimant commitment' (see p185); *and*
- you satisfy the **'financial conditions'** – ie:[2]
  - your income is not too high;
  - your savings and other capital are £16,000 or less.

Couples

If you are a member of a couple (see p205), usually you must make a joint claim. Both of you must satisfy the basic conditions and (on a joint basis) the financial conditions for UC.[3]

However, both of you do *not* need to meet all the basic conditions (and you can get UC as a couple in the normal way) if one of you is:[4]

- over the qualifying age for PC. **Note:** you do not come under the UC system in this situation and so cannot make a claim for UC (see p19); *or*
- 'receiving education' (but see below if one of you is 16 or 17).

Even though you are a member of a couple and one of you does not satisfy the conditions for UC, there are limited circumstances in which you can make a claim as a single person. In this situation, your UC amounts are for a single person, but your income and capital are still assessed jointly. You can claim as a single person if your partner is:[5]

- aged 16 or 17 and is not someone who can get UC as an under-18-year-old (see p896 for who can); *or*
- not in (or treated as in) Great Britain, including if s/he has failed the habitual residence or right to reside test (see Chapter 70); *or*
- a 'person subject to immigration control' (see Chapter 69); *or*
- a prisoner or serving a sentence while detained in hospital, or is a member of a religious order and is fully maintained by the order.

You can also claim as a single person if you are in a polygamous marriage and:[6]

- your spouse is still married to someone else from an earlier marriage; *and*
- the other person in the earlier marriage is still living in the same household as your spouse.

Who cannot claim universal credit

Initially, UC is only for new claimants who come under the UC system. For when you come under the UC system, see p19.

In general, if you are already getting income support (IS), income-based jobseeker's allowance (JSA), income-related employment and support allowance (ESA), housing benefit (HB), child tax credit (CTC) or working tax credit (WTC), you do not come under the UC system straight away and you cannot get UC until your claim is transferred to UC. For details, see Chapter 2.

If you are a prisoner or serving a sentence while detained in hospital, or you are a member of a religious order and are fully maintained by the order, generally you are not entitled to UC (see p191).

Receiving education

Generally, you cannot claim UC if you are 'receiving education'. The basic rule is that if you are a qualifying young person (see p551) or undertaking full-time education, study or training, you are regarded as 'receiving education'.[7] There are exceptions – eg, for some disabled people and for those without parental support or with children. For full details, see Chapter 44.

If you are a member of a couple making a joint claim and one of you is receiving education (and not eligible for UC) but the other is not, you may still be entitled to UC as a couple (see p183).

The claimant commitment

A basic condition of entitlement to UC is that you (and your partner, if you are making a joint claim) accept a 'claimant commitment'. This is an agreement that you will meet certain requirements.[8] The claimant commitment sets out what you must do to receive your UC, and you must agree to this. If you do not, your benefit may be sanctioned – ie, paid at a reduced rate. See Chapter 50 for further details on benefit sanctions.

If either you or your partner do not accept the claimant commitment, UC is not awarded, unless you 'lack the capacity' to accept or if there are exceptional circumstances and the DWP accepts that it would be unreasonable to expect you to accept a claimant commitment.[9]

2. The rules about your age

In most cases, you (and your partner, if you are making a joint claim) must be 18 or over to claim universal credit (UC). Some 16/17-year-olds can claim UC – eg, those without parental support or who have children (see Chapter 43).[10]

You must be under the qualifying age for pension credit (PC – see p78).[11] If you are in a couple and one of you is over the qualifying age for PC, when you come

Part 2: Main means-tested benefits and tax credits
Chapter 10: Universal credit
4. The amount of benefit

under the UC system (see p19), you cannot claim PC and must claim UC instead.[12] The government has said that couples in this situation who are already on PC do not have to move to UC.[13]

3. People included in the claim

If you are single, you claim universal credit (UC) for yourself. If you are a member of a couple, you and your partner must usually make a joint claim for UC (see p192).[14]

See p205 for who counts as a couple.

Your maximum amount (see Chapter 13), which forms part of the calculation of your benefit, includes elements for your child(ren), including an element for childcare costs. There are also other situations in which you must show that you are 'responsible' for a child – eg:

- in order to take advantage of the special rules to help you meet the claimant responsibilities (see p1061 and p1066);
- so you can benefit from a higher work allowance when calculating your UC entitlement (see p188);
- for some of the rules for the housing costs element (see Chapter 22).

You can count as responsible for any child under 16 and for any 'qualifying young person' (see p211 for who counts as a child).[15] You do not have to be the child's parent. For when you count as responsible for a child, see p212.

4. The amount of benefit

Universal credit (UC) is a means-tested benefit. The amount you get is calculated over a monthly 'assessment period' (see below). The amount of UC you get depends on your family circumstances and:

- your 'maximum amount' of UC. This is made up of a standard allowance and various 'elements'; *and*
- how much capital and income you have.

As your income increases, your UC award will reduce.

Assessment period

The **'assessment period'** is one calendar month, beginning with the first date of entitlement to UC.[16] Each subsequent assessment period (ie, a calendar month) usually begins on the same day of the month except if:

– the first day of entitlement to UC falls on the 31st of the month, in which case each assessment period begins on the last day of the month;

– the first day of entitlement to UC falls on the 29th or 30th of the month, in which case each assessment period begins on the 29th or 30th. In February, it begins on the 27th (or in a leap year, on the 28th);

– your entitlement has started before the actual date of claim because of the backdating rules, the first assessment period begins on the first day of entitlement and ends on the day before the date of claim.

Examples

Danny claims UC on 5 July. His UC entitlement starts on that date, so his monthly assessment period is from the 5th of each month until the 4th inclusive. His next monthly assessment period begins on 5 August.

Carmen claims UC on 31 July. Her first monthly assessment period is from 31 July until 30 August inclusive. Her next assessment period begins on 31 August, and the one after that begins on 30 September.

Calculating universal credit

Your UC is worked out in the following way.
- **Step one:** calculate your maximum amount. See Chapter 13 for details of this.
- **Step two:** work out your earnings and how much can be ignored.
- **Step three:** work out your other income and how much can be ignored.
- **Step four:** calculate your total income.
- **Step five:** calculate your UC entitlement.

Step one: calculate your maximum amount

Your maximum UC is made up of the total (worked out on a monthly basis) of:[17]
- a standard allowance – for a single claimant or a couple (see p250);
- a child element for each child, with an increase for disabled and severely disabled children (see p250);
- a limited capability for work (see p251) or a limited capability work-related activity element (p252) for an adult who is too ill to work;
- a carer element for someone looking after a severely disabled person (see p252);
- a housing costs element for renters or owner-occupiers (see Chapter 22);
- a childcare costs element (see p253).

Example

Gail and Joe are a couple both aged over 25. They have two children. Gail works; Joe is ill and has limited capability for work. They do not have housing or childcare costs.

Gail and Joe's maximum amount for UC is calculated as follows:

Part 2: Main means-tested benefits and tax credits
Chapter 10: Universal credit
4. The amount of benefit

2

Standard allowance	£493.95
Child element (first child)	£274.58
Child element (second child)	£229.17
Limited capability for work element	£124.86
Total	**£1,122.56**

Step two: work out your earnings and how much can be ignored

See Chapter 16 for how to work out your earnings (called 'earned income' for UC).

Once you have established your earnings, work out how much can be ignored when calculating your UC. This is done by comparing your earnings with a set amount, called a 'work allowance' (see below).

If your earnings do not exceed the work allowance, they are all ignored. If your earnings are more than your work allowance, 65 per cent of the excess is taken into account as income.[18]

The way your earnings reduce the amount of your UC is sometimes called the 'taper' – ie, the rate at which your UC will taper away as your earnings increase. The work allowance rules mean that, as your earnings rise above the level that is disregarded, your UC reduces by 65 pence for every extra pound you earn.

The work allowance

The work allowance is set at one of two levels. A **higher work allowance** applies if your UC does not include a housing costs element (see Chapter 22). A **lower work allowance** applies if your UC includes a housing costs element. In either case, there are different set amounts of the work allowance, depending on whether you are a couple (p205), have responsibility for a child (including a qualifying young person) (p210) or have limited capability for work (Chapter 47). The highest work allowance that may apply to you is used.

Higher work allowance	
Single	
Not responsible for a child	£111
Responsible for one or more children	£734
Has limited capability for work	£647
Couple	
Neither responsible for a child	£111
Responsible for one or more children	£536
One or both have limited capability for work	£647

Lower work allowance

Single

Not responsible for a child	£111
Responsible for one or more children	£263
Has limited capability for work	£192

Couple

Not responsible for a child	£111
Responsible for one or more children	£222
One or both have limited capability for work	£192

Examples

Anne is a lone parent with a child aged six. She rents her home and is entitled to the housing costs element in her UC. She has a part-time job from which her earned income for UC over her assessment period is £300.

At least some of Anne's earnings are ignored. Because she has a housing costs element, Anne's work allowance is set at the lower level for a single person with a child – £263. Anne's earned income exceeds her work allowance by £37 (£300 – £263). Sixty-five per cent of this excess is £24.05. Therefore, £24.05 of Anne's earned income is taken into account when calculating her UC.

Gail and Joe are a couple with two children. They have a mortgage, but are not entitled to the housing costs element because Gail has earned income from work. Joe is ill and has limited capability for work. Gail's earned income for UC over their assessment period is £1,200.

At least some of Gail's earnings are ignored. Because they do not have housing costs included, Gail and Joe's work allowance is set at the higher level for a couple with one or both partners having limited capability for work – £647 (ie, the highest that could apply). Their earned income exceeds their work allowance by £553 (£1,200 – £647). Sixty-five per cent of this excess is £359.45. So £359.45 of Gail and Joe's earned income is taken into account when calculating their UC.

Step three: work out your other income and how much can be ignored

See Chapter 16 for how to work out your other income and how much can be ignored.

If you have other income (eg, other benefits), unless it is ignored it affects your UC by reducing it pound for pound. This is in addition to any reductions from your earnings.

Part 2: Main means-tested benefits and tax credits
Chapter 10: Universal credit
4. The amount of benefit

2

Income from capital

If you and your partner have more than £16,000 capital, you cannot get UC. If you have more than £6,000 but £16,000 or less, you count as having an income of £4.35 a month for every £250, or part of £250, over £6,000.[19] This assumed monthly income is sometimes referred to as 'tariff income'.

For how to calculate your capital, including assumed monthly income, see Chapter 17.

Step four: calculate your total income

Add the income that is to be taken into account under Steps two and three.

Step five: calculate your universal credit entitlement

Deduct your total income to be taken into account (Step four) from your maximum UC (Step one).

Note: if you are transferred from a means-tested benefit or tax credit to UC, you may also be entitled to transitional protection (see below). Note however that the transfer process is not expected to begin until 2016.

Example

Gail and Joe are a couple both aged over 25, with two children. Gail works and earns £1,200 in their monthly assessment period. Joe is ill and has limited capability for work. He gets fortnightly payments of contributory employment and support allowance (ESA) of £202.30. For UC purposes, this is converted to a monthly figure of £438.32. They do not have housing costs or childcare costs included in their UC. They have savings of £5,000.

Their total income to be taken into account under Step four is £359.45 in earned income, plus £438.32 contributory ESA during their monthly assessment period = £797.77

Their maximum UC under Step one = £1,122.56

Their monthly UC entitlement = £1,122.56 – £797.77 = £324.79

Transitional protection

From some point in 2016, claimants with existing awards of means-tested benefits and tax credits will begin to have their claims transferred to claims for UC. If you are transferred to UC and your UC maximum amount is less than the amount you were getting on the benefit you were transferred from, your UC includes transitional protection in the form of an additional amount to make up the difference. **Note:** at the time this *Handbook* was written, the date when the transfer of existing claims would begin and the rules on transitional protection had not been finalised. See CPAG's online service or *Welfare Rights Bulletin* for updates. The following is based on information published by the DWP.[20]

Transitional protection applies if you have your benefit or tax credit claim transferred to UC and, at the point of transfer, 'the total household UC entitlement' would otherwise be lower than your 'total existing award of benefit and tax credit'. **Note:** it is understood that this refers to means-tested benefits, not all benefits.

Transitional protection can only apply if your claim is transferred by the DWP as part of the 'managed migration' process. It does not apply if you must claim UC after a change of circumstances.

5. Special benefit rules

Special rules may apply to:[21]
- prisoners (see p962);[22]
- people serving a sentence of imprisonment while detained in hospital (see p962);
- people who are members of a religious order and wholly maintained by their order. They are not entitled to universal credit;
- people from abroad and 'people subject to immigration control' (see p183);
- 16/17-year-olds (see p896);
- people who are studying (see p185).

6. Claims and backdating

In most cases, to be entitled to universal credit (UC), you must make a claim for it. The general rules about claims and backdating are covered in Chapter 53. This section explains the specific rules that apply to UC.

You do not have to make a claim for UC (and you keep the same assessment period as before) if:[23]
- you were refused UC because your earnings were too high, or lost entitlement because of an increase in your earnings; *and*
- it is not more than six months since your claim, or since your entitlement stopped; *and*
- your circumstances have changed and you provide details of your earnings to the DWP.

You also do not need to make a new claim (and keep the same assessment period as before) if:[24]
- you were entitled as a single claimant, are now part of a couple and your partner was also entitled to UC as a single claimant. Although you do not need to make a new joint claim, you must tell the DWP that you are now part of a couple; *or*
- you are now a member of a couple and either you or your partner (but not both of you) was entitled to UC as a single claimant and that award has now been terminated; *or*

Part 2: Main means-tested benefits and tax credits
Chapter 10: Universal credit
6. Claims and backdating

2

- you were a member of a couple making a joint claim but have now ceased to be a couple and your former partner has reported that you have ceased to be a couple. If you are the first to tell the DWP that you are no longer a couple, you must make a new claim.

Making a claim

In most cases, claims for UC must be made online at www.gov.uk/apply-universal-credit. A claim can be made by telephone if the DWP has provided a number for this and is willing to accept a claim in this way.[25]

If you do not have internet access, the DWP says you can access the internet at your local Jobcentre. If you need support (eg, if you cannot use a computer), a one-to-one telephone service is available on 0845 600 0723 (textphone 0845 600 0743) and a DWP adviser completes an online form on your behalf. **Note:** these calls are not free of charge.[26] In exceptional circumstances, if you are unable to use either a computer or the telephone, the DWP may make a home visit to help you claim. Your local council may have support services that can help you with online claims, as well as things like monthly budgeting (UC is normally paid monthly).

You must provide any information or evidence required (see below). You can amend or withdraw your claim before a decision is made (see p1138). If there is a delay in making a claim, you may be able to get a short-term advance of UC (see p1167).

Forms

There are no paper claim forms for UC. The claim form is only available online.

Who should claim

If you are single, you claim on your own behalf, as a single person. If you are a member of a couple, you must normally make a joint claim with your partner.[27] For when you count as a couple, see p186. If you are a member of a couple and one of you does not satisfy the conditions for UC, you can claim as a single person (although your income and capital are assessed jointly with your partner) in certain circumstances (see p184). The DWP treats your joint claim as one made by a single person.[28]

If you are unable to manage your own affairs, another person can claim UC for you as your 'appointee' (see p1137).[29]

Information to support your claim

When you claim UC, you must:
- satisfy the national number requirement (see p1138). If you are claiming as a couple, your partner must also satisfy this;

- provide proof of your identity if required (see p1140). In practice, the DWP tries to verify your identity as you make your online claim, but if it cannot do this, you may be asked to produce documentation;
- supply information and evidence required for the claim and, after you have claimed, additional information and evidence relevant to your claim (see p1140). The DWP intends that, in most cases, both partners must agree the claim before an award can be made. There is a strict time limit for supplying information and evidence.

It is important that you provide any information or evidence required when you claim. In practice, it is not possible to make an online claim for UC if there is missing or incomplete essential information.

If your claim is regarded as 'defective', you might not count as having made a valid claim (see p1143).[30]

Information and evidence you must provide includes details of your and your partner's income and savings and the circumstances of you, your partner and dependent children. If you are working for an employer, the DWP uses a 'real-time information system' to obtain information about your earnings. Your employer is required to send information to HM Revenue and Customs (HMRC) every time your wages are paid.

The date of your claim

You should claim UC as soon as you think you might be entitled. In some cases, you can claim in advance (see p194) and sometimes your claim can be backdated (see p194).

Your date of claim is usually the date on which your online claim is received by the DWP.[31] If you received help from the DWP in making the claim before you claimed online, your date of claim is the date you notified the DWP that you intended to make it. If you claim by telephone, your date of claim is the date on which the claim is 'properly completed', or earlier if you previously notified your intention to claim and the claim is made within a month of that.

If your claim is regarded as 'defective' (see p1140), your date of claim is the date you made the claim, provided the defect is corrected within one month (or longer, if considered reasonable) of the date you were informed of the defect. In practice, the DWP expects relatively few defective claims, as it will not be possible to make an online claim without essential information.

If you claim the wrong benefit

There are no rules for when a claim for another benefit can be treated as a claim for UC. You should claim UC as soon as you can and, if necessary, ask for the claim to be backdated.

Claiming in advance

If you claim UC when you are not yet entitled, but the DWP thinks that you will be entitled within one month of the day you claimed, it can make an advance award. If this applies, your claim is treated as made on the first day on which you are entitled to UC.[32] However, the DWP intends to accept advance claims only in very limited circumstances – eg, from prisoners who are to be released within a month. Otherwise, the intention is that a partially completed online claim can be left open for a time until it can be submitted at the appropriate time.[33]

Backdating your claim

A claim for UC can only be backdated for a maximum of one month, and only if one or more circumstances applied that meant you could not reasonably have claimed earlier. If you are making a joint claim, both you and your partner must satisfy this rule. Your claim can be backdated if:[34]

- you were previously getting another benefit and you were not notified that your entitlement was going to end before it did;
- you have a disability (the rules do not define this);
- you were unwell and that meant you could not claim online or by telephone on time, and you have now supplied medical evidence showing that you were unwell;
- you could not claim online because of a system failure or planned system maintenance, and you have now claimed on the first day that the system was working;
- you had a joint claim for UC but this terminated because you stopped being a couple, you were the first to report that you ceased to be a couple and you have now reclaimed UC as a single person;
- you made a joint claim for UC and this was either turned down or awarded but later terminated because your partner did not accept the claimant commitment, but you have now ceased to be a couple and you have reclaimed UC as a single person.

If you might have qualified for benefit earlier, but did not claim because you were given the wrong information by the DWP or because you were misled by it, you could ask for compensation (see p1382) or complain to the Ombudsman through your MP (see p1387).

---

7. Getting paid

Universal credit (UC) is normally paid directly into your bank or building society account. If you are unable to open or manage an account, payment can be made by 'simple payment' (see p1163). If you are unable to act for yourself, payment can be made to someone else on your behalf – called your 'appointee' (see p1162).

When is universal credit paid?

You are normally paid within seven days of the end of an assessment period. UC is paid monthly, in arrears.[35]

Your award is assessed over an 'assessment period' of one calendar month, beginning from your date of claim (see p186).[36] UC should normally be paid directly into your account within seven days of the last day of the monthly assessment period or, if this is not possible, 'as soon as reasonably practicable' thereafter.[37] Note that this means that you are likely to have to wait for a month and up to seven days for your first payment. If you are in financial need in the meantime, or if there is a delay in subsequent payments, you may be able to get a short-term advance of UC (see p1167). Otherwise you may be able to get help from your local authority (see p829).

If you find monthly payments difficult to budget for, or having your UC housing costs for rent paid to you rather than to your landlord is leading to serious arrears, it may be possible to be paid more frequently through alternative payment arrangements. This is discretionary (there is no right of appeal). You must show that you cannot manage the monthly payment arrangements and, as a result, there is a risk of financial harm to you or to someone in your family. According to government guidance, the following applies.[38]

- You cannot decide that alternative payment arrangements should apply. The DWP must be satisfied that they should apply, based on your inability to cope with monthly payment and on your circumstances.
- Alternative payment arrangements are considered in the following order of priority:
    - paying rent directly to your landlord to safeguard your home;
    - more frequent payment – ie, two payments a month, rather than just one. Exceptionally, more frequent payments can be considered;
    - splitting payment between the partners in a couple in specific situations – eg, if one partner is mismanaging the UC award or if there is domestic violence.
- The DWP splits claimants into those with circumstances with a 'high likely need' for alternative payments and those with 'less likely need'. You are in high likely need if you:
    - have drug, alcohol and other addiction problems;
    - have learning difficulties;
    - have severe debt problems;
    - are living in temporary or supported accommodation;
    - are homeless;

- have experienced domestic violence or abuse;
- have a mental health condition;
- are currently in rent arrears or at threat of eviction or repossession;
- are aged 16 or 17 or have left local authority care;
- are a family with multiple and complex needs.

You are in less likely need if you:
- have no bank account;
- have third-party deductions in place – eg, for utility arrears;
- are a refugee or asylum seeker;
- have a history of rent arrears;
- were previously homeless or living in supported accommodation;
- have a physical disability;
- have just left prison or hospital;
- are recently beareaved;
- have problems with language skills;
- are an ex-servicewoman/man;
- are not in education, employment or training.

Couples can decide which partner is paid. The DWP can decide that the other partner should be paid instead or can split the payments between you if it considers it to be in your interests, the interests of a child for whom you are responsible (see p212), or the interests of a severely disabled person and your UC includes a carer element (see p252).[39]

If you need a loan for an item you cannot afford, you can ask for a 'budgeting advance' of UC (see p197).

Your UC can be paid in whole or in part to another person on your behalf, if the DWP considers this is necessary to protect your interests, or those of your partner, a child for whom you are responsible (see p212) or a severely disabled person and your UC includes a carer element (p252).[40]

Note:
- Deductions can be made from your UC to pay third parties – eg, the housing costs element to cover mortgage interest is paid directly to your mortgage lender (see p1178). The housing costs element to cover rent is normally paid to you rather than your landlord, unless paying your landlord would be in your interest (see above). Official guidance says that your landlord can request that payment is made to her/him, and that request will be granted automatically if your rent is over two months in arrears.[41]
- Your UC might be paid at a reduced rate if you have been sanctioned under the UC system (see Chapter 52) or committed a benefit offence (see p1258).
- If you have forgotten your PIN, see p1163. If your 'simple payment' card is lost or stolen or if you have forgotten your memorable date, see p1164. For information on missing payments, see p1164.

- If payment of your UC is delayed, see p1382. You might be able to get a short-term advance (p1167). If you wish to complain about how your claim has been dealt with, see p1381. You might be able to claim compensation (see p1382).
- If payment of your UC is suspended, see p1175.
- If you are overpaid UC, you might have to repay it (see Chapter 56) and, in some circumstances, you may have to pay a penalty (see p1249). If you have been accused of fraud, see Chapter 57.

Budgeting advances

Budgeting advances are extra amounts of UC, which must be repaid, usually by deductions from future payments of your UC. They are intended to help you with expenses – eg, buying essential furniture or household equipment. Budgeting advances are discretionary. If you are refused a budgeting advance, you do not have a right to appeal against this decision.

If you are awarded a budgeting advance, the DWP must send you notice in writing that you will have it deducted from subsequent payments of your UC and that, if it is not deducted, you must otherwise repay it. The same rules apply to deductions from your UC that apply to the recovery of overpayments on p1230.

To get a budgeting advance:[42]

- you must apply for one; *and*
- you (or your partner if you are a couple) must be getting UC and (unless the expense is 'necessarily related' to employment) have been getting UC (or income support, income-based jobseeker's allowance, income-related employment and support allowance or pension credit) for a continuous period of at least six months when the claim is made; *and*
- you satisfy the 'earnings condition' and the 'recovery condition' (see below).

The earnings and recovery conditions

The 'earnings condition'. If you are not a member of a couple, your earnings from work must not exceed £2,600 in the period covered by the previous six complete monthly assessment periods. If you are a member of a couple, your joint earnings from work must not exceed £3,600 in this period. In these rules, if you are self-employed then your actual earned income is taken into account, not any assumed minimum income under the 'minimum income floor' (see p329).

The 'recovery condition'. There must be no outstanding budgeting advance (ie, which has not yet been recovered) paid to you (or your partner) and the DWP is satisfied that the budgeting advance can reasonably be expected to be recovered, taking into account all your debts and other liabilities.

The minimum amount of a budgeting advance is £100. The maximum payable is:

- if you are single and not responsible for a child, £348;

- if you are in a couple and not responsible for a child, £464;
- if you are responsible for a child and either single or in a couple, £812.

For when you are responsible for a child, see p210.

If your capital (or your joint capital if you are a couple) is over £1,000, the budgeting advance is reduced by the amount the capital exceeds £1,000. For how your capital is calculated, see Chapter 17.

Change of circumstances

You must report changes in your circumstances that you have been told you must report, as well as any that you might reasonably be expected to know might affect your right to, the amount of, or the payment of, your benefit. You should do this as soon as possible, preferably in writing. See p1174 for further information.

If you are working and being taxed through PAYE, the DWP should get information about changes in your earnings automatically from HM Revenue and Customs through the 'real-time information system'. However, this does not change your responsibilities and, if your employer has not reported your earnings, you must report them yourself.[43] Check with your employer that your earnings are being reported as you are paid. If you are self-employed, you must always report your earnings.

When you notify the DWP of a change of circumstances, the decision on your UC is changed by a supersession. The general rule is that a supersession takes effect from the first day of the monthly assessment period in which the change occurred or is expected to occur.[44] So a change that actually occurs partway through a monthly assessment period can be treated as having occurred on the first day of the period. For full details, see p1287. Note the following exceptions, when a supersession can take effect from a different date.

- If the change of circumstance is that you or someone included in your claim has become entitled to a 'qualifying benefit' or the rate of it has changed, see p1292.
- If you are required by the DWP to report your earnings and your earnings decrease, the superesession takes effect from the first day of the assessment period in which the decrease occurred.[45]
- If the change of circumstance is about your limited capability for work and you did not report the change, see p1288.
- A change of circumstance which is advantageous to you is only backdated to the start of the assessment period in which it occurred if you report it before the end of that assessment period, unless the time allowed is extended. Otherwise, the change applies from the start of the assessment period in which you reported it. For full details, see p1288.

Examples

Terry, a lone parent with one child, is entitled to maximum UC of £589.25 a month – ie, a standard allowance of £314.67, plus a child element of £274.58. His assessment period begins on 5 October. Halfway through this assessment period, Terry stops being responsible for a child as his son goes to live with his mother, and so Terry is no longer entitled to the child element. His maximum UC entitlement reduces to £314.67 a month. This change is not advantageous to Terry, but is backdated to the start of the assessment period – ie, to 5 October. This includes a period before he lost entitlement to the child element.

However, Terry is not overpaid UC as he does not get paid until seven days after the end of the assessment period on 4 November. So Terry gets paid just £314.67 for the whole of the assessment period in which the change occurred.

Julie is entitled to maximum UC of £314.67 per month – ie, a standard allowance. Towards the end of her monthly assessment period, she has a child and her maximum UC entitlement increases by £274.58 – ie, it now includes a child element. The change is advantageous to Julie. She reports the change before the end of the assessment period and it is backdated to the start of the assessment period – ie, including a period before she had her child. When Julie gets paid (after the end of the assessment period in which the change occurred), she gets the additional £274.58 for the whole period. If Julie did not report the change until the start of her next assessment period, it may only have applied from the start of that period.

8. Tax, other benefits and the benefit cap

Tax

Universal credit (UC) is not taxable.

Means-tested benefits and tax credits

If you come under the UC system (see p19), you cannot qualify for income support, income-based jobseeker's allowance (JSA), income-related employment and support allowance (ESA), housing benefit (except for exempt accommodation – see p416), child tax credit or working tax credit. If your partner is claiming one of these benefits and you come under the UC system, you claim UC as a couple instead (see p22). If you are already getting one of the above benefits when UC is introduced, your claim will be transferred to a claim for UC at some point from 2016.

You cannot get pension credit (PC) at the same time as UC because of the rules about your age (see p185). If you are in a couple and one of you has reached the

Part 2: Main means-tested benefits and tax credits
Chapter 10: Universal credit
8. Tax, other benefits and the benefit cap

qualifying age for PC, the current rules prevent you from coming under the UC system (see p19).

Non-means-tested benefits

For the rules on entitlement to national insurance credits for people on UC, see p852.

When you come under the UC system (see p19), you can still claim contribution-based JSA or contributory ESA, but they are taken into account in full as income for UC (and so reduce your UC entitlement).

You can also claim other non-means-tested benefits at the same time as UC, including:

- bereavement benefits;
- carer's allowance (CA);
- child benefit;
- guardian's allowance;
- disability living allowance (DLA);
- personal independence payment;
- statutory sick pay;
- statutory maternity, paternity and adoption pay;
- maternity allowance;
- industrial injuries benefits.

For how non-means-tested benefits are treated when working out your income for UC, see Chapter 16.

It can be worth claiming non-means-tested benefit. For example, if you get CA, you may be entitled to a carer element in your UC (see p252). If your child gets DLA, you may be entitled to a disabled child addition (see p250).

The benefit cap

In some cases, the total amount of specified benefits you receive is limited to £350 a week (if you are a single claimant without children) or £500 a week (if you are a lone parent or a member of a couple). This is known as the 'benefit cap'. UC is one of the specified benefits. The benefit cap only applies if you are getting UC. See p1169 for further information.

Passports and other sources of help

At the time this *Handbook* was written, only limited information was available on the ways in which UC will be a qualifying benefit for 'passported' benefits during 2014/15.[46] See Chapter 30 for details on health benefits, Chapter 40 for other payments including Healthy Start food and vitamins and free school lunches. See CPAG's online service and *Welfare Rights Bulletin* for updates.

If you are entitled to UC, you may be entitled to a Sure Start maternity grant, a funeral expenses payment or cold weather payments from the social fund (see Chapter 37). You may be entitled to a council tax reduction (see p827).

Notes

1. Who can claim universal credit
1   ss3 and 4 WRA 2012; reg 9 UC Regs
2   s5 WRA 2012
3   ss3 and 4 WRA 2012
4   Reg 3(2) UC Regs
5   Reg 3(3) UC Regs
6   Reg 3(4) UC Regs
7   Reg 12 UC Regs
8   s14 WRA 2012
9   Reg 16 UC Regs

2. The rules about your age
10 s4(3) WRA 2012; reg 8 UC Regs
11 s4(4) WRA 2012
12 Sch 2 para 64 WRA 2012
13 House of Commons, *Hansard*, 28 April 2011, col 553

3. People included in the claim
14 s2 WRA 2012
15 s10 WRA 2012

4. The amount of benefit
16 Reg 17 UC Regs
17 s8 WRA 2012
18 Reg 22 UC Regs
19 DWP, *21st Century Welfare*, Cm 7913, July 2010, para 8
20 *Transitional Protection and Universal Credit*, DWP Briefing Note, 10 December 2012, via www.gov.uk/government/publications/transitional-protection-universal-credit-policy-briefing-note

5. Special benefit rules
21 Reg 19 UC Regs
22 Reg 19(2) UC Regs

6. Claims and backdating
23 Reg 6 UC,PIP,JSA&ESA(C&P) Regs; reg 21(3) UC Regs
24 Reg 9(6)-(8) UC,PIP,JSA&ESA(C&P) Regs; reg 21(3) UC Regs
25 Reg 8 UC,PIP,JSA&ESA(C&P) Regs
26 'Claim universal credit', via www.gov.uk/apply-universal-credit
27 s2 WRA 2012
28 Reg 9 UC,PIP,JSA&ESA(C&P) Regs
29 Reg 51 UC,PIP,JSA&ESA(C&P) Regs
30 Reg 8(3) UC,PIP,JSA&ESA(C&P) Regs
31 Reg 10 UC,PIP,JSA&ESA(C&P) Regs
32 s98 WRA 2012; reg 32 UC,PIP,JSA&ESA(C&P) Regs
33 para A 2048 ADM
34 Reg 26 UC,PIP,JSA&ESA(C&P) Regs

7. Getting paid
35 Reg 47 UC,PIP,JSA&ESA(C&P) Regs
36 s7 WRA 2012; reg 21 UC Regs
37 Reg 47(2) UC,PIP,JSA&ESA(C&P) Regs
38 *Universal Credit Guidance on Personal Budgeting Support*, DWP, 11 February 2013
39 Reg 47(6) UC,PIP,JSA&ESA(C&P) Regs
40 Reg 58 UC,PIP,JSA&ESA(C&P) Regs
41 HB Circular A13/2013
42 Regs 12-15 SS(PAB) Regs
43 Reg 61 UC Regs
44 Sch 1 para 20 UC,PIP,JSA&ESA(DA) Regs
45 Sch 1 para 22 UC,PIP,JSA&ESA(DA) Regs

8. Tax, other benefits and the benefit cap
46 The basic power for passporting is in Sch 2 para 39 WRA 2012

Part 3

General rules for means-tested benefits

Chapter 11

People included in the claim

This chapter covers:
1. Couples (below)
2. Children (p210)
3. Households (p215)

This chapter covers the rules for means-tested benefits. For child tax credit and working tax credit, see Chapters 9 and 10.

Key facts

- Whether you count as a member of a couple or have children included in your claim can be relevant for all the means-tested benefits.
- You count as a member of a couple if you are married or in a civil partnership and are living in the same household with your partner. You also count as a couple if you are not married or in a civil partnership, but are living with your partner as if you were husband and wife or as civil partners.
- A child or 'qualifying young person' can be included in your claim if you are 'responsible' for her/him. For all benefits except universal credit (UC), s/he must also live your 'household'. For UC, s/he must 'normally live' with you.
- You can continue to count as a couple, and children and young people can continue to be included in your claim, while you are living apart temporarily.

1. Couples

You and your partner count as a 'couple' for means-tested benefit purposes if you are both 16 or over and you are:[1]
- married or civil partners and members of the same household; *or*
- not married or civil partners but 'living together as a married couple'.

Note: currently, the rule is slightly different in Scotland. People who are not married or civil partners but who are living together count as a couple for means-tested benefit purposes if they are 'living together as husband and wife' or 'living together as civil partners'. The test for whether a couple are living together is the

Part 3: General rules for means-tested benefits
Chapter 11: People included in the claim
1. Couples

same as that described below. When same-sex marriages are introduced in Scotland (expected in autumn 2014), the Scottish rule is expected to be aligned with that in England and Wales. See CPAG's online service and *Welfare Rights Bulletin* for updates.

For when you count as living in the same 'household', see p215. **Note:** for pension credit (PC) only, if your partner is a 'person subject to immigration control' (see p1500), you are treated as not being members of the same household and so do not count as a couple.[2]

Spouse or civil partner

Being married to someone does not necessarily mean that you cannot be treated as part of a couple with someone else instead.[3]

You count as **'polygamously married'** if you are married to more than one person and your marriages took place in a country that permits polygamy.[4] For employment and support allowance (ESA) only, you and all your partners must also be living in the same household (see p215). There are special rules if you are polygamously married (see p526).[5] These specify that for benefits other than universal credit (UC), any income and capital of any polygamous partners are taken into account, but an increased amount of benefit is allowed to take into account their needs. For UC, there are rules that allow one person in a polygamous marriage to claim as a single person (see p192).

You count as someone's **civil partner** if you are both of the same sex and have been registered as her/his civil partner.[6]

Living together as a married couple

You count as a couple if you are 'living together as' a married couple. We refer to this as 'cohabiting' in this *Handbook*. You can be living together as a married couple if you and your partner are in a different sex relationship or same-sex relationship.[7]

Note: at the time this *Handbook* was written, this rule was slightly different in Scotland (see p205).

If you are awarded income support (IS), income-based jobseeker's allowance (JSA) or income-related ESA, the local authority should not make a separate decision about whether you are cohabiting when considering your claim for housing benefit (HB).[8] However, if the local authority thinks that the benefit claim on which your HB claim is based is fraudulent, it can decide that you are not entitled to HB.[9] If you have not been awarded IS, income-based JSA, income-related ESA or PC, the local authority must consider whether you are cohabiting and may reach a different conclusion from that of the DWP.[10]

The factors on p207 are used as 'signposts' to determine whether or not you are cohabiting.[11] No one factor, in itself, is conclusive, as it is your overall relationship and your particular circumstances that are looked at.[12] Caselaw says that the 'emotional aspect' of the relationship (your interdependence, devotion, love and affection) should be considered in addition to the factors below.[13] This does not necessarily conflict with the factors but, like your individual circumstances, should not be regarded as conclusive. For example, if your partner stays with you for three nights or more a week, you should not automatically be treated as living together as a couple.

Cohabiting: some relevant factors
1. Do you live in the same household? See below.
2. Do you have a sexual relationship? See below.
3. What are your financial arrangements? See below.
4. Is your relationship stable? See p208.
5. Do you have children? See p208.
6. How do you appear in public? See p208.

Living in the same household

If you live in the same household, you may be treated as cohabiting. For what counts as a 'household', see p215.

Even if you *do* share a household, you may not be cohabiting. It is essential to look at *why* two people are in the same household.[14] For example, if you are living in the same household for 'care, companionship and mutual convenience', you can argue that you are not 'living together as husband and wife'.[15]

Being in a sexual relationship

In practice, a decision maker may not ask you about the existence of a sexual relationship, in which case s/he only has the information if you volunteer it. However, if you are appealing about whether you are a member of a couple, the First-tier Tribunal may well ask you about this.[16] If you do not have a sexual relationship, you should make this known (and perhaps offer to show your separate sleeping arrangements).

Having a sexual relationship is not sufficient, by itself, to prove you are cohabiting. If you have never had a sexual relationship, there is a strong (but not necessarily conclusive) presumption that you are not cohabiting.[17] A couple who abstain from a sexual relationship before marriage should not be counted as cohabiting until they are formally married.[18]

Your financial arrangements

If one person is supported by the other or your household expenses are shared, this may be treated as evidence that you are cohabiting. However, it is important to consider how expenses are shared. There is a difference between, on the one hand, paying a fixed weekly contribution or rigidly sharing bills 50/50 (which

Part 3: General rules for means-tested benefits
Chapter 11: People included in the claim
1. Couples

does *not* suggest cohabitation) and, on the other hand, a common fund for income and expenditure (which might).

The financial relationship between lodger and landlord often comes under scrutiny. Decision makers sometimes claim that the payments are too high or too low and so indicate that the relationship is not purely financial. It is important to explain how the payments came to be as they are. There may also be many motives for having a lodger, apart from purely commercial ones or cohabitation (eg, for company or security) and so friendship between a lodger and landlord does not mean they are cohabiting.

A stable relationship

Marriage and civil partnership are expected to be stable and lasting and so an occasional or brief association should not be regarded as cohabitation. However, the fact that your relationship is stable does not make it cohabitation – eg, you can have a stable landlord or lodger relationship, but not be cohabiting.

The way you spend your time together, the activities you do together and the things you do for each other are relevant, so questions about how you spend your holidays and how you organise the shopping, the laundry and cleaning may be important.

Children

If you have had a child together and live in the same household as the other parent, there is a strong (but not conclusive) presumption of cohabitation.

Your appearance in public

Decision makers may check the electoral roll and claims for other benefits to see if you present yourselves as a couple. Many couples retain their separate single identities publicly. If you do not have a committed emotional loving relationship that is publicly acknowledged, you can argue that you are not living together as a married couple.[19]

Couples living apart

If you **separate permanently** (ie, you do not intend to resume living with your partner), you no longer count as a couple.[20] When deciding whether you intend to resume living together or not, your intention must be 'unqualified' – ie, it must not depend on something over which you have no control, such as the right of entry to the UK being granted by the Home Office[21] or the offer of a suitable job.[22]

If you and your partner are **living apart temporarily**, you continue to count as a couple because you are still treated as members of the same household.[23] Your former household need not have been in this country.[24] However, there are exceptions to this rule (see p209).

Note: if you and your partner continue to count as a couple while you are temporarily living apart, your partner's income and capital continue to be treated as yours. However, in certain situations your benefit (except UC) is calculated in a different way (see p221).

Exceptions

Even if you and your partner are only living apart temporarily, **you no longer count as a couple** if:

- for **IS, income-based JSA, income-related ESA, PC** and **HB**, you are likely to be separated for more than 52 weeks. However, you still count as a couple if you are unlikely to be separated for 'substantially' longer than 52 weeks and there are exceptional circumstances, such as a stay in hospital, or if you have no control over the length of the absence;[25]
- for **UC**, you have been separated (or expect to be separated) for more than six months.[26] If either you or your partner go abroad, see p1584. If your partner is a prisoner, serving a sentence while in hospital or a member of a religious order who is fully maintained by that order, you cannot get UC as a couple, but you can claim as a single person;
- for **IS, income-based JSA, income-related ESA** and **PC**:[27]
  - either of you are in custody;
  - either of you are released on temporary licence from prison;
  - either of you are a compulsory patient detained in hospital under the mental health provisions;
  - either of you are staying permanently in a care home, an Abbeyfield Home or an independent hospital;
  - you are abroad and do not qualify for benefit while temporarily absent from Great Britain. For when you qualify while temporarily absent and for when your partner is abroad, see p1578 (for IS), p1580 (for income-based JSA), p1574 (for income-related ESA) and p1582 (for PC).

Challenging a decision that you are a couple

Your benefit may be stopped or adjusted if the decision maker decides you are a member of a couple.

The decision maker might decide that you are cohabiting if someone regularly stays overnight, even though you might have none of the long-term commitments generally associated with marriage or a civil partnership. Couples with no sexual relationship who live together (eg, as landlord and lodger or as flat sharers) also sometimes fall foul of the rule. People who provide mutual support and share household expenses are not necessarily cohabiting.[28]

If you disagree with a decision that you are a couple, you can apply for a revision or supersession (see Chapter 58), or appeal to the First-tier Tribunal (see Chapter 59). You must usually apply for a revision before you can appeal.

Part 3: General rules for means-tested benefits
Chapter 11: People included in the claim
2. Children

How do you show that you are not a couple?

1. Consider carefully what evidence to submit:

– if you are married or in a civil partnership, to show that you are not living in the same household with your spouse or civil partner;

– if you are not married or in a civil partnership, in relation to each of the six questions on p206, the emotional aspect of your relationship and any other matters you consider relevant.

2. Provide evidence if the other person has another address[29] (eg, a rent book and other household bills), receipts for board and lodging, statements from friends and relatives, or evidence of a formal separation, divorce proceedings or a dissolution application or order.

You do not have to prove that you are not a couple when you first claim benefit, but you must provide any information that is reasonably required to decide your claim.[30] Neither party has the burden of proof in this situation – a decision should simply be made on all the evidence available.[31] In contrast, if your benefit as a single person is stopped because it is alleged that you are a couple, the burden of proof is on the decision maker to prove that you are.[32]

If your benefit is stopped because it is decided that you are a couple, challenge the decision and reapply immediately if your circumstances change. Also apply for any other benefits for which you might qualify – eg, HB, as the local authority may reach a different decision to the DWP.[33] You should apply for other benefits for which you previously automatically qualified – eg, health benefits (see Chapter 30).

If you are still entitled to a means-tested benefit as a couple, you should be paid on that basis.

2. **Children**

Note: even though a child counts as part of your family and may be included in your benefit claim, you can only get additional amounts of money for her/him in certain circumstances (see p211).

A child (see p211 for who counts) counts as part of your family for benefit purposes and is included in your claim if:

- for income support (IS), income-based jobseeker's allowance (JSA), income-related employment and support allowance (ESA) and housing benefit (HB):
  - you or your partner are 'responsible' for her/him (see p212); *and*
  - s/he is living in your 'household' (see p214);[34]
- for universal credit (UC), you or your partner are 'responsible' for her/him – ie, s/he 'normally lives' with you (see p212).[35]

You do not have to be the child's parent.

A child stops being included in your claim when you no longer fulfil the conditions described above or s/he no longer counts as a child (see below).

Note: children are not included in claims for pension credit (PC). Instead, you must claim child tax credit (CTC) for the child (see Chapter 8).

If a child is included in your claim and counts as part of your family for benefit purposes, you can get an additional amount included in your HB and UC. You can only get an additional amount for a child in your IS or income-based JSA if:

- you already have a current claim for IS or income-based JSA that began before 6 April 2004; *and*
- you had a child included in that claim before 6 April 2004 and you have not been awarded CTC.

ESA does not include additional amounts for children.[36]

Who counts as a child

A person usually counts as a child if:[37]

- s/he is aged under 16; *or*
- s/he is aged 16 or over but under 20 and counts as a 'qualifying young person' for child benefit purposes. This includes, for example, most young people who are at school or college full time studying for GCSEs or A levels (or equivalent), or who are doing approved training. See p550 for who counts as a qualifying young person. A young person can continue to count as a child after s/he has left school or training until the 'terminal date' (see p555) or the end of the child benefit 'extension period' (see p552); *or*
- for UC, s/he is aged 16 or over but under 20 and counts as a 'qualifying young person' under the UC rules. This includes most young people studying for GCSEs or A levels or who are doing approved training. Specifically, it means someone who:[38]
    - is aged 16 but who has not reached the 1 September following her/his 16th birthday; *or*
    - is aged 16–19 but who has not yet reached the 1 September following her/his 19th birthday, and has been accepted for (or has enrolled on) approved training or non-advanced education at school or college, or another institution approved by the Secretary of State (see p212). During term time there must be more than 12 hours on average a week of tuition, practical work, supervised study and examinations. Meal breaks and unsupervised study are not included.

Note: a 19-year-old must have started (or been accepted for or enrolled on) the education or training before reaching 19 in order to count as a qualifying young person.

Part 3: General rules for means-tested benefits
Chapter 11: People included in the claim
2. Children

Definitions for universal credit

A course is **'non-advanced'** if it is below the level of 'advanced education'. Courses that count as advanced education include university degrees and other courses above GCSE, A level, GNVQ and Scottish National Qualifications above higher or advanced higher level.[39] See p553 for more examples of advanced and non-advanced courses.

'Approved training' is training that is approved by the DWP and provided under s2(1) of the Employment and Training Act 1973 or s2(3) of the Enterprise and New Towns (Scotland) Act 1990.

Who does not count as a child

A person does *not* count as a child if:[40]

- s/he is getting certain benefits or tax credits in her/his own right and so does not count as a qualifying young person (see p556 for details). For IS and income-based JSA, s/he may not count as a child if s/he is entitled to one of these benefits but is not getting it – eg, because it has been suspended; *or*
- s/he is excluded from entitlement to IS, income-based JSA and HB because s/he is aged 16 or 17, has left local authority care on or after 1 October 2001 and certain other conditions apply (see p883); *or*
- for UC, s/he is receiving UC, ESA or JSA in her/his own right.

Responsibility for a child

For IS, income-based JSA (but not joint-claim JSA), income-related ESA and HB, a child is included in your claim if you are 'responsible' for her/him and s/he is living in your 'household'. For UC, a child is included in your claim if you are 'responsible' for her/him.

- You are treated as 'responsible' for a child for **IS** if you get child benefit for her/him (see Chapter 26).[41] If no one gets child benefit, you are responsible if you are the only one who has applied for it. In all other cases, the person responsible is the person with whom the child usually lives.[42] However, if you are a 'substantial minority carer' (see below), you may be able to argue that you should be regarded as responsible for the child, even if you do not get child benefit.[43] If a child for whom you are responsible gets child benefit for another child, you are also responsible for that child.[44]
- You are treated as 'responsible' for a child for **JSA**, if either you get child benefit for her/him or, if no one gets child benefit for her/him, the child 'usually lives' with you or you are the only person who has applied for child benefit.[45] If you share responsibility for the child (eg, with your ex-partner), even if you do not get child benefit for her/him, you might be regarded as responsible for her/him if you are the 'substantial minority carer' – ie, you have the child with you for at least 104 nights a year.[46] Seek advice if necessary (see Appendix 2). If a child for whom you are responsible gets child benefit for another child, you

are also responsible for that child. **Note:** the rules for when you count as responsible for a child for the purposes of deciding whether you must claim joint-claim JSA are different (see p46).[47]

- You are treated as 'responsible' for a child for **ESA** if s/he 'usually lives' with you. This is not defined in the rules.[48]

- You are treated as 'responsible' for a child for **HB** if the child is 'normally living' with you.[49] This means that s/he spends more time with you than with anyone else.[50] If it is unclear in whose household the child lives, or if s/he spends an equal amount of time with two parents in different homes (this may not mean literally three and a half days with each parent[51]), you are treated as having responsibility if:[52]
  - you get child benefit for her/him (see Chapter 26);
  - no one gets child benefit, but you have applied for it;
  - no one has applied for child benefit, or both of you have applied, but you appear to have the most responsibility.

  Note: if you are a 'substantial minority carer' (see p212), you may be able to argue that you should be regarded as responsible for the child, even if you do not get child benefit.[53]

- You are treated as 'responsible' for a child for **UC** if s/he 'normally lives' with you. Although the UC rules do not say so, this is likely to mean that s/he spends more time with you than with anyone else. If the child normally lives with two (or more) people who are not a couple (eg, if s/he lives in the homes of separated parents), the person who is responsible is whoever has the 'main responsibility'. In this situation, the people concerned can agree who this is. The DWP can decide otherwise or, if there is no agreement, decide which person has the main responsibility.[54] You cannot be treated as responsible for a child during any period in which s/he is:[55]
  - looked after by a local authority, except planned short breaks in local authority care to provide respite care for the person who normally looks after her/him, and except if the child is living with you and you are her/his parent or (unless you are a foster parent) someone with parental responsibility for her/him; *or*
  - a prisoner; *or*
  - temporarily absent from your household (see p215) and has been absent for more than six months, including if this is for medical treatment abroad; *or*
  - (after one month) absent from Great Britain for a reason other than medical treatment.

For HB, it is only necessary to look at who gets child benefit when it is unclear in whose household the child *normally* lives. For IS, it is essential to look first at who gets child benefit, and only if this is not decisive is it relevant to look at where the child *usually* lives. This difference may, for example, mean that, in some

Part 3: General rules for means-tested benefits
Chapter 11: People included in the claim
2. Children

situations, one parent may be able to claim IS for a child while the other parent can claim HB for the same child at the same time.

A child can only be the responsibility of one person in any week for IS, income-based JSA and HB.[56] The rules for ESA do not expressly say this but, in any case, a person can only be responsible for a child if s/he usually lives with her/him. If benefit is paid for a child, it cannot be split between parents if a child divides her/his time equally between their two homes. The person who has main responsibility for the child has the child included in her/his claim for UC.

Living in the same household

In addition to being responsible for her/him, a child is only included in your claim if s/he is a member of the same household. If you count as responsible for a child, s/he is usually treated as a member of your household, despite any temporary absence. For exceptions to the rule, see below. For what 'household' means, see p215.

Note: for UC, the test is simply whether you are 'responsible' for the child.

When a child does not count as a member of your household

A child does *not* count as a member of your household if:[57]
- for **IS, JSA, ESA** and **HB**, s/he is not living with you and:
  – has no intention of resuming living with you; *or*
  – is likely to be absent for more than 52 weeks, unless there are exceptional circumstances, such as being in hospital, or if you have no control over the length of absence and the absence is unlikely to be substantially longer than 52 weeks;
- for **IS, JSA, ESA** and **HB**:
  – s/he is being fostered by you or your partner following a formal placement by social services. This does not apply if you are fostering privately or if social services has made a less formal arrangement for the child to live with you;
  – s/he is living with you or your partner prior to adoption and has been placed by social services or an adoption agency;
  – s/he is boarded out with you or your partner, whether or not with a view to adoption (for JSA, ESA and HB only);
  – s/he has been placed with someone else prior to adoption;
  – s/he is in the care of, or being looked after by, the local authority and not living with you. However, s/he counts as a member of your household on the days when s/he comes home – eg, for the weekend or a holiday.[58] Make sure you tell the decision maker in good time. For HB, your child counts as a member of the household for all that week whether s/he returns for all or only part of it;[59]
- for **IS, JSA** and **ESA**, s/he is not living with you and:
  – has been in hospital or in a local authority home (for non-temporary accommodation) for more than 12 weeks and has not been in regular contact

with you or other members of your household. The 12 weeks run from the date s/he went into hospital or the home, or from the date you claim IS/JSA/ESA, if later.[60] However, the 12 weeks run from the date s/he went into the hospital or home if:[61]

- you were getting income-based JSA immediately before your claim for IS; *or*
- you were getting IS or income-related ESA immediately before your claim for JSA; *or*
- you were getting IS or income-based JSA immediately before your claim for ESA;
  - is in custody. Note that a child can still be included in your claim for any periods s/he spends at home;[62]
  - has been abroad for more than four weeks, or for more than eight weeks (26 weeks for ESA) to get medical treatment.[63] The four-/eight-/26-week period runs from the day s/he went abroad, or from the day you claim IS/JSA/ESA, if later. However, the four-/eight-/26-week period is calculated from the day after the child went abroad if:[64]
    - you were getting income-based JSA immediately before your claim for IS; *or*
    - you were getting IS or income-related ESA immediately before your claim for JSA; *or*
    - you were getting IS or income-based JSA immediately before your claim for ESA;
- for **IS** and **income-based JSA**, s/he is living with you and away from her/his parental or usual home in order to attend school. The child is not included in your claim, but remains a member of her/his parent's household.[65]

3. Households

The term '**household**' is not defined. Whether you should be treated as members of the same household is decided on the particular facts of your case. In all cases, you must spend the major part of your time in the same household. **Note:** for pension credit only, if your partner is a 'person subject to immigration control' (see p1500), you are treated as *not* being members of the same household and so do not count as a couple.[66]

A house or flat can contain a number of separate households and if one person has exclusive occupation of separate accommodation from another, s/he is not considered to be living in the same household. Physical presence is not, in itself, conclusive. There must be a 'particular kind of tie' binding two people together in a domestic establishment. So, for example, a husband and wife may be in separate households in the same care or nursing home.[67] A household must also involve

Part 3: General rules for means-tested benefits
Chapter 11: People included in the claim
3. Households

two or more people living together as a unit and enjoying a reasonable level of independence and self-sufficiency. In one case, it was held that a married couple sharing a room in a residential home because they needed help organising their personal care and domestic activities were not self-sufficient and did not live in a domestic establishment, and therefore did not share a household.[68]

Is there a separate household?

If you think you should not be treated as a member of the same household as someone, check whether you can show that you maintain separate households.

A separate household might exist if there are:
– independent arrangements for storing and cooking food;
– independent financial arrangements;
– separate eating arrangements;
– no evidence of family life;
– separate commitments for housing costs, even if the liability is to another person in the same premises.

You cannot be a member of more than one household at the same time.[69] So if you are a member of one couple, you cannot also be treated as part of another. If two people maintain separate homes (ie, they each have a separate address where they usually live), they cannot share the same household.[70] Even if you have the right to occupy only part of a room, you may have your own household.[71]

If you are separated from your partner, but living under the same roof, you should not be treated as a couple if you are maintaining separate households.[72] If your relationship has only recently broken down, continuing financial support and shared responsibilities and liabilities may be particularly inconclusive, especially if there is evidence that you are taking active steps to live apart. The way people live and their attitudes may be more significant. Any 'mere hope' of a reconciliation is not a 'reasonable expectation' if at least one partner has accepted that the relationship is at an end.[73]

Note: if you are still married or in a civil partnership, a shared attitude that the relationship is at an end may not be enough to show there is no shared household.[74]

Notes

1. **Couples**
   1 s137(1) SSCBA 1992; CFC/7/1992
   IS Reg 2(1) IS Regs
   JSA s35(1) JSA 1995; reg 1(3) JSA Regs
   ESA Sch 1 para 6(5) and (6) WRA 2007;
   reg 2(1) ESA Regs
   PC s17(1) SPCA 2002; reg 1(2) SPC
   Regs
   HB Reg 2(1) HB Regs; reg 2(1) HB(SPC)
   Regs
   UC s39 WRA 2012
   2 Reg 5(1)(h) SPC Regs
   3 R(SB) 8/85
   4 **IS** Reg 2(1) IS Regs
   JSA Reg 1(3) JSA Regs
   ESA Reg 2(1) ESA Regs
   PC s12 SPCA 2002
   HB Reg 2(1) HB Regs; reg 2(1) HB(SPC)
   Regs
   UC Reg 3(5) UC Regs
   5 **IS** Regs 18 and 23 IS Regs
   JSA Regs 84 and 88(4) and (5) JSA Regs
   ESA Regs 68 and 83 ESA Regs
   PC Reg 8 and Sch 3 SPC Regs
   HB Regs 23 and 25 HB Regs; regs 22
   and 23 HB(SPC) Regs
   UC Reg 3(4) and (5) UC Regs
   6 s1 CPA 2004
   7 **IS** Reg 2(1) IS Regs
   JSA s35(1A) JSA 1995; reg 1(3) JSA Regs
   ESA Sch 1 para 6(6) WRA 2007; reg 2(1)
   ESA Regs
   PC s17(1A) SPCA 2002; reg 1(2) SPC
   Regs
   HB Reg 2(1) HB Regs; reg 2(1) HB(SPC)
   Regs
   IS/HB s137(1A) SSCBA 1992
   UC s39 WRA 2012
   8 *R v Penwith DC HBRB ex parte Menear* 24
   HLR 120, 11 October 1991; however,
   AM v Chelmsford Borough Council (HB)
   [2013] 245 (AAC) suggests that this only
   applies to the assessment of income and
   capital, and not to cohabitation
   questions.
   9 *R v South Ribble BC HBRB ex parte
   Hamilton*, 24 January 2000 (CA)
   10 CH/4014/2007
   11 *Crake and Butterworth v SBC* [1982] 1 All
   ER 498
   12 R(SB) 17/81; R(G) 3/71; CIS/87/1993
   13 *PP v Basildon District Council (HB)* [2013]
   UKUT 0505 (AAC)
   14 *Crake and Butterworth v SBC,* quoted in
   R(SB) 35/85
   15 R(SB) 35/85
   16 CIS/87/1993; CIS/2559/2002
   17 CIS/87/1993
   18 CSB/150/1985
   19 *JP v SSWP (IS)* [2014] UKUT 0017 (AAC)
   20 **IS** Reg 16(2)(a) IS Regs
   JSA Reg 78(2)(a) JSA Regs
   ESA Reg 156(3)(a) ESA Regs
   PC Reg 5(1)(a)(i) SPC Regs
   HB Reg 21(2)(a) HB Regs; reg 21(2)(a)
   HB(SPC) Regs
   UC Reg 3(6) UC Regs
   21 CIS/508/1992; CIS/13805/1996
   22 CIS/484/1993
   23 **IS** Reg 16(1) IS Regs
   JSA Reg 78(1) JSA Regs
   ESA Reg 156(2) ESA Regs
   PC Reg 5(2) SPC Regs
   HB Reg 21(1) HB Regs; reg 21(1)
   HB(SPC) Regs
   UC Reg 3(6) UC Regs
   24 CIS/508/1992
   25 **IS** Reg 16(2) IS Regs
   JSA Reg 78(2) JSA Regs
   ESA Reg 156(3) ESA Regs
   PC Reg 5(1)(a) SPC Regs
   HB Reg 21(2) HB Regs; reg 21(2)
   HB(SPC) Regs
   26 Reg 3(6) UC Regs
   27 **IS** Reg 16(3) IS Regs
   JSA Reg 78(3) JSA Regs
   ESA Reg 156(4) ESA Regs. This wrongly
   refers to Chapter 4, but correctly refers
   to the rules on temporary absence from
   Great Britain.
   PC Reg 5(1)(b)-(d) and (f) SPC Regs
   28 CSSB/145/1983
   29 R(SB) 13/82
   30 **IS/ESA/PC** Reg 7(1) SS(C&P) Regs
   JSA Reg 24 JSA Regs
   HB Reg 86 HB Regs; reg 67 HB(SPC)
   Regs
   UC Reg 37 UC,PIP,JSA&ESA(C&P) Regs
   31 CIS/317/1994

Part 3: General rules for means-tested benefits
Chapter 11: People included in the claim
Notes

32 R(I) 1/71
33 R(H) 9/04

2. Children

34 s137 SSCBA 1992
JSA s35 JSA 1995; reg 77 JSA Regs
ESA Reg 2(1), definition of 'family', ESA Regs
35 s10 WRA 2012; reg 4(2) UC Regs
36 Reg 1 SS(WTCCTC)(CA) Regs
37 **IS** Reg 14 IS Regs
JSA s35 JSA 1995; regs 1(3) and 76 JSA Regs
ESA Reg 2(1) ESA Regs
HB Reg 19 HB Regs; reg 19 HB(SPC) Regs
IS/HB s137 SSCBA 1992
UC s40 WRA 2012; regs 2 and 5 UC Regs
38 Reg 5 UC Regs
39 Reg 12(3) UC Regs
40 **IS** Reg 14(2) IS Regs
JSA Reg 76(2) JSA Regs
ESA Reg 2(1) ESA Regs, definition of 'young person'
HB Reg 19(2) HB Regs; reg 19(2) HB(SPC) Regs
UC Reg 5(5) UC Regs
All para 2208 DMG. This does not refer to IB, contributory ESA or tax credits, which arguably should also be included in the list.
41 Reg 15(1) IS Regs
42 Reg 15(2) IS Regs
43 *Hockenjos v Secretary of State for Social Security* [2004] EWCA Civ 1749, reported as R(JSA) 2/05, applies only to JSA. However, it may support arguments concerning IS based on the HRA 1998. Note that, in the context of CTC, the argument has been rejected by *Humphreys v HMRC* [2010] EWCA Civ 56.
44 Reg 15(1A) IS Regs
45 Reg 77(1)-(3) JSA Regs
46 Reg 77 JSA Regs, as applied in *Hockenjos v Secretary of State for Social Security* [2004] EWCA Civ 1749, reported as R(JSA) 2/05. However, see also CJSA/2507/2002
47 Reg 77(2) JSA Regs
48 Reg 156(10) ESA Regs
49 Reg 20(1) HB Regs; reg 20(1) HB(SPC) Regs
50 CFC/1537/1995
51 CFC/1537/1995
52 Reg 20(2) HB Regs; reg 20(2) HB(SPC) Regs

53 *Hockenjos v Secretary of State for Social Security* [2004] EWCA Civ 1749, reported as R(JSA) 1/05, applies only to JSA. However, it may support arguments concerning HB based on the HRA 1998. Note that, in the context of CTC, the argument has been rejected by *Humphreys v HMRC* [2010] EWCA Civ 56.
54 Reg 4 UC Regs
55 Reg 4(6) and (7) UC Regs
56 **IS** Reg 15(4) IS Regs
JSA s3(1)(d) JSA 1995; reg 77(5) JSA Regs
HB Reg 20(3) HB Regs; reg 20(3) HB(SPC) Regs
57 **IS** Reg 16 IS Regs
JSA Reg 78 JSA Regs
ESA Reg 156 ESA Regs
HB Reg 21 HB Regs; reg 21 HB(SPC) Regs
58 **IS** Regs 15(3) and 16(6) IS Regs
JSA Regs 77(4) and 78(7) JSA Regs
ESA Reg 156(8) ESA Regs
59 Reg 21(5) HB Regs; reg 21(5) HB(SPC) Regs
60 **IS** Reg 16(5)(b) IS Regs
JSA Reg 78(5)(c) JSA Regs
ESA Reg 156(6)(c) ESA Regs
61 **IS** Reg 16(5A) IS Regs
JSA Reg 78(6) JSA Regs
ESA Reg 156(7) ESA Regs
62 **IS** Regs 15(3) and 16(6) IS Regs
JSA Regs 77(4) and 78(5)(i) and (7) JSA Regs
ESA Reg 156(6)(h) and (8) ESA Regs
63 **IS** Reg 16(5)(a) and (aa) IS Regs
JSA Reg 78(5)(a) and (b) JSA Regs
ESA Reg 156(6)(a) and (b) ESA Regs
64 **IS** Reg 16(5A) IS Regs
JSA Reg 78(6) JSA Regs
ESA Reg 156(7) ESA Regs
65 **IS** Reg 16(7) IS Regs
JSA Reg 78(8) JSA Regs

3. Households

66 Reg 5(1)(h) SPC Regs
67 *Santos v Santos* [1972] 2 All ER 246; CIS/671/1992; CIS/81/1993
68 CIS/4935/1997
69 R(SB) 8/85
70 R(SB) 4/83
71 CSB/463/1986
72 para 11018 DMG
73 CIS/72/1994
74 CIS/2900/1998

Chapter 12

....

Applicable amounts

This chapter covers:
1. What is the applicable amount (below)
2. Personal allowances (p222)
3. Premiums (p226)
4. Components (p241)
5. Transitional addition (p243)

This chapter explains the amounts allowed for meeting your needs when calculating your entitlement to income support, income-based jobseeker's allowance, income-related employment and support allowance and housing benefit. The rules for pension credit (PC) are mainly dealt with in Chapter 6. However, the additional amounts in the guarantee credit of PC for claimants who are severely disabled or who are carers have rules which are similar to those for the severe disability premium and carer premium, and are dealt with in this chapter (see p233 and p237). The rules for the universal credit maximum amount are in Chapter 11.

Key facts

- Applicable amounts are used in means-tested benefits to help calculate the amount of benefit to which you are entitled.
- Applicable amounts differ according to the benefit you are claiming. They comprise personal allowances, premiums, housing costs and, in some cases, components. You may have one or more of these included.
- In some cases, if you were on a benefit for incapacity for work and have been transferred to employment and support allowance (ESA), your applicable amount for income-related ESA and housing benefit can also include a transitional addition.

---

1. What is the applicable amount

Your applicable amount for income support (IS), income-based jobseeker's allowance (JSA) and income-related employment and support allowance (ESA) is

Part 3: General rules for means tested benefits
Chapter 12: Applicable amounts
1. What is the applicable amount

the amount you are expected to live on each week. Your applicable amount for housing benefit (HB) is the amount used to see how much help you need with your rent. This chapter explains how to work out your applicable amount for these benefits. For the way your benefit is calculated, see p33 for IS, p696 for income-based JSA, p69 for income-related ESA and p108 for HB.

What is included in your applicable amount

Your applicable amount is made up of:

- **personal allowances**: the amount the law says you need for living expenses (see p222);
- **premiums**: the amount given for certain extra needs you or your partner or children may have (see p226);
- for income-related ESA and, in some circumstances, for HB, **a support or work-related activity component** (see p241);
- for IS, income-based JSA and income-related ESA only, **housing costs** (see Chapter 20);
- for income-related ESA and HB only, any **transitional addition** following the transfer of your incapacity benefit (IB), severe disablement allowance (SDA) or IS on the grounds of disability claim to ESA (see p243).

Can you get allowances and premiums for children?

IS and income-based JSA have not included allowances and premiums for children since 6 April 2004. However, you may continue to have these included if:[1]

– you have a claim which began before 6 April 2004; *and*

– you had a child included in the claim before 6 April 2004; *and*

– you have not yet been awarded child tax credit (CTC).

In these circumstances, personal allowances and premiums for children continue to be included in your claim (and amounts for a new child can be added) until you claim and are awarded CTC, or you are automatically transferred to CTC. When this transfer process will begin is yet to be announced. It is possible that the DWP may wait until your claim is transferred to universal credit instead. See p18 for details of when this is likely to be, and see CPAG's online service and *Welfare Rights Bulletin* for updates.

When your applicable amount may be reduced

Your applicable amount may be reduced in certain circumstances. The most important of these are if:

- for IS and income-based JSA only, you are involved in a trade dispute (see p972);
- you are a couple and one of you is a 'person subject to immigration control' (see p1507);

- for IS, income-based JSA and income-related ESA only, you are without accommodation (see p969);
- you are a prisoner (see p961 and p962);
- your partner or child is abroad. For IS, see p1579, for JSA, see p1581, for ESA, see p1575 and for HB, see p1576;
- your child is in custody, or is being looked after by the local authority, for part of the week. The family premium and the disabled child premium may be affected (see p228);
- for IS, income-based JSA and income-related ESA only, you or your partner are a patient in hospital for 52 weeks or more (see pp946–49);
- you are a member of a religious order. In this case, your applicable amount is nil.[2]

Note: for information about when your pension credit 'appropriate minumum guarantee' may be reduced, see p80.

Couples temporarily living apart

In many cases, you continue to count as a couple while you are temporarily living apart from your partner (see p208). If you *do* count as a couple, your applicable amount continues to be calculated as for a couple. However, if your partner is abroad, see above.

For IS, income-based JSA and income-related ESA only, your applicable amount is calculated as if you were single claimants, if this amount would be higher than your usual couple rate and:

- one of you is at home or in hospital, or in local authority residential accommodation or a care home;[3] *and*
- the other is:
  - resident in a care home, independent hospital or Abbeyfield Home, but not counted as a patient; *or*
  - in a home for the rehabilitation of people with an addiction to alcohol or drugs; *or*
  - in Polish resettlement accommodation; *or*
  - on a government training course and has to live away from home; *or*
  - in an approved probation or bail hostel.

If you have housing costs that can be included (see Chapter 20), your applicable amount includes these.

Your income and capital are calculated in the normal way for a couple.

2. Personal allowances

The amount of your personal allowance for income support (IS), income-based jobseeker's allowance (JSA), income-related employment and support allowance (ESA) and housing benefit (HB) depends on your age and whether you are claiming as a single person or a couple. For HB and, in some circumstances, for IS and income-based JSA, you also get an allowance for each child included in your claim.

If you are polygamously married (see p205), you receive an extra amount for each additional spouse in your household. However, unless you are entitled to joint-claim JSA, if any additional spouse is under the age of 18, you only receive an extra amount for her/him if:[4]

- for IS, income-based JSA and income-related ESA, s/he is either responsible for a child (see p212) or would otherwise meet the special conditions for qualifying for JSA as a 16/17-year-old (see p888); *or*
- for IS and income-related ESA, s/he would qualify for that benefit in her/his own right were s/he not a member of a polygamous marriage.

Personal allowances for children

In some circumstances, personal allowances for children are included in your applicable amount. You get one personal allowance for each child. **Note:**
- HB includes personal allowances for children.
- IS, income-based JSA and income-related ESA do *not* usually include personal allowances for children. However, if you have been claiming IS or income-based JSA since before 6 April 2004, these can sometimes be included (see p220).

For when children are included in your claim, see p210. See p211 for who counts as a child.

Note: your child's income and capital do not affect the amount of HB to which you are entitled. However, if you are still entitled to a personal allowance for your child in your IS or income-based JSA, you do not get an allowance for a child if s/he has over £3,000 capital. See p257 for how a child's income may affect IS or income-based JSA.

Rates of personal allowances for people aged 18 or over

Note:
- Some 16/17-year-olds may also be entitled to these rates (see p224).
- In some cases, your applicable amount may be reduced (see p220).

- In some cases, your applicable amount is calculated differently if you are a couple but are temporarily living apart (see p221).
- Some allowances refer to the qualifying age for pension credit (PC).[5] For this, see p78.

	IS/JSA/ESA/HB	HB only – claimant or partner is qualifying age for PC or over and not claiming IS, income-based JSA or income-related ESA
Single claimant:		
Aged 18–24	£57.35	
Aged 25 or over	£72.40	
Aged 18 or over and ESA includes (or would include) a support or work-related activity component (see p241) (ESA/HB only)	£72.40	
Aged between qualifying age for PC and 64 inclusive		£148.35
Aged 65 or over		£165.15
Lone parent:		
Aged 18 or over	£72.40	
Couple:		
Both aged 18 or over	£113.70	
One or both aged between qualifying age for PC and 64 inclusive		£226.50
One or both aged 65 or over		£247.20
One aged under 18 (some IS/JSA/ESA cases only – see p224 – and all HB cases)	£113.70	
One aged under 18 (other IS/JSA/ESA cases – see p224):		
either	£72.40	
or	£57.35	
Polygamous marriages, each additional qualifying partner living in the same household:[6]		
Partner aged 18 or over, or under 18 in certain circumstances (see p222)	£41.30	
Claimant and all partners aged under 65		£78.15
One or more aged 65 or over		£82.05

Rates of personal allowances for 16/17-year-olds

- For IS and income-based JSA, if you are single and aged 16 or 17 (including if you are a lone parent), you get the same rate as single 18–24-year-olds – ie, £57.35. If you are in a couple (unless one of the special circumstances below applies) and your partner is also aged under 18, you get £57.35. If your partner is aged 18 or over, see the table below.
- For income-related ESA, you get £57.35 or, if your ESA includes the support or work-related activity component, £72.40. If you are in a couple (unless in one of the special circumstances on p224) and your partner is also under 18, the same applies.
- For HB, if you are single (including if you are a lone parent), you get the same rate as 18–24-year-olds (ie, £57.35), unless you are entitled to ESA and qualify for either the support or work-related activity component (see p241), in which case you get £72.40. If you are in a couple and your partner is also under 18, you get £86.65. If your partner is aged 18 or over, or if you are entitled to ESA including either component, you get £113.70. For this purpose, you count as qualifying for an ESA component even if your actual award of ESA is nil – eg, because you are only entitled to national insurance contribution credits.

Note:
- Most 16/17-year-olds who have previously been looked after by a local authority cannot claim IS/JSA or HB (see p883).
- In some cases, your applicable amount may be reduced (see p220).
- In some cases, your applicable amount is calculated differently if you are a couple but are temporarily living apart (see p221).

Young couples in special circumstances

Note: the following rules apply to IS, income-based JSA and income-related ESA only.[7]

If you are a young couple, the amount of personal allowance paid depends on your ages and whether one or both of you are entitled to IS, income-based JSA (including JSA severe hardship payments – see p892) or income-related ESA, or you would be if you were a single person. The amount of your allowance in ESA can also depend on whether you qualify for the support or work-related activity component (see p241). For some couples, the personal allowance may be no more than that for a single person.

Age	£pw
Both aged 16–17, higher rate:	
ESA assessment phase	86.65
ESA main phase	113.70
IS/JSA	86.65

Both aged 16–17, lower rate:

ESA assessment phase	57.35
ESA main phase	57.35
IS/JSA	57.35

One aged 16–17, one 18 or over, higher rate:

ESA assessment phase	113.70
ESA main phase	113.70
IS/JSA	113.70

One aged 16–17, one 25 or over, lower rate:

ESA assessment phase	72.40
ESA main phase	72.40
IS/JSA	72.40

One aged 16–17, one 18–24, lower rate:

ESA assessment phase	57.35
ESA main phase	72.40
IS/JSA	57.35

If both of you are aged 16 or 17, you get the higher rate if:

- for IS:
  - one is responsible for a child; *or*
  - *both* of you would qualify for IS or income-related ESA if you were not a couple; *or*
  - the claimant's partner would qualify for income-based JSA or JSA severe hardship payments if s/he were single;
- for JSA:
  - one is responsible for a child; *or*
  - both of you would still qualify for income-based JSA if you were not a couple; *or*
  - the claimant would still qualify for income-based JSA and her/his partner would still qualify for IS or income-related ESA if you were not a couple, or you would both qualify for JSA severe hardship payments if you were single; *or*
  - one would qualify for JSA severe hardship payments and the other for income-based JSA, IS or income-related ESA if s/he were single; *or*
  - you are married or civil partners and you both qualify for income-based JSA or one does and the other is registered for work or training;
- for ESA:
  - one is responsible for a child; *or*
  - both of you would qualify for income-related ESA if you were not a couple; *or*
  - the claimant's partner would still qualify for IS if s/he were single; *or*

- the claimant's partner would qualify for income-based JSA or JSA severe hardship payments as a single person.

The higher rate is paid at the main phase rate if the claimant qualifies for a support or work-related activity component (see pp621–22). Otherwise, it is paid at the assessment phase rate.

If one of you is aged 16 or 17 and the other is 18 or over, you get the higher rate personal allowance if:

- for IS, the younger partner qualifies for IS or income-related ESA (or would do so if s/he were not a member of a couple) *or* income-based JSA or JSA severe hardship payments (see below);
- for JSA, the younger partner is treated as responsible for a child, or qualifies for income-based JSA or JSA severe hardship payments, or either IS (or s/he would do so were s/he not a member of a couple) or income-related ESA (were s/he to make a claim);
- for ESA, the younger partner would either qualify for IS or income-related ESA (were s/he not a member of a couple), or for income-based JSA or JSA severe hardship payments. It is paid at the same rate in the assessment phase and main phase.

Qualifying for jobseeker's allowance
For these purposes, if you are under 18, you qualify for:
– income-based JSA, if you meet the rules for income-based JSA described on p889;
– JSA severe hardship payments, if you are subject to a severe hardship direction (see p892).

Rate of personal allowance for children

For HB (and for IS and income-based JSA if still included), there is one rate of personal allowance for children who are included in your claim – £66.33. You get one personal allowance for each child. **Note:** you cannot get personal allowances for children in joint-claim JSA, as you cannot claim this type of JSA if you have children.

3. Premiums

Premiums are added to your personal allowances and are intended to help with the extra expenses of age or having a disability or, in some circumstances, children.

- **Family premium:** for housing benefit (HB) and some income support (IS) and income-based jobseeker's allowance (JSA) claims (see p228). Not for income-related employment and support allowance (ESA).

- **Disabled child premium:** for HB and some IS and income-based JSA claims (see p228). Not for income-related ESA.
- **Disability premium:** for IS, income-based JSA and HB (see p229). Not for income-related ESA.
- **Enhanced disability premium:** for IS, income-based JSA, income-related ESA and HB (see p231).
- **Pensioner premium:** for IS, income-based JSA and income-related ESA (see p231). Not for HB.
- **Higher pensioner premium:** for IS and income-based JSA (see p232). Not for income-related ESA or HB.
- **Severe disability premium:** for IS, income-based JSA, income-related ESA and HB. A similar allowance applies to the guarantee credit of pension credit (PC – see p233).
- **Carer premium:** for IS, income-based JSA, income-related ESA and HB. A similar allowance applies to the guarantee credit of PC (see p237).

Note: if you or your partner have reached the qualifying age for PC (see p78) and are not getting IS, income-based JSA, income-related ESA or universal credit, your HB can only include the family, disabled child, enhanced disability for a child, severe disability and carer premiums.[8] In these circumstances, your HB cannot include a disability premium.

See p239 for information about backdating premiums. See p238 for the premium rates.

Premiums for children

In some circumstances, certain premiums can be included in your applicable amount if you have children included in your claim. These are the family premium, disabled child premium and the child rate of the enhanced disability premium. **Note:**

- **HB** can include these premiums.
- **IS, income-based JSA** and **income-related ESA** cannot include these premiums. However, if you have been claiming IS or income-based JSA since before 6 April 2004, see p220.

For when children are included in your claim, see p210. See p211 for who counts as a child.

Note: your child's income and capital do not affect the amount of your HB. However, if you are still entitled to premiums for children in your IS or income-based JSA, you do not get a premium (except a family premium) for a child who has over £3,000 capital. See p257 for how a child's income may affect IS or income-based JSA.

Family premium

You are entitled to a family premium in your HB and, if applicable, your IS and income-based JSA, if at least one child is included in your claim (see p210).[9] The premium is paid even if you are not the parent of the child. For IS and income-based JSA, you are only entitled to a family premium in certain circumstances (see p227). If you are entitled, a family premium is included even if you do not receive a personal allowance in your IS or income-based JSA for any child because s/he has capital over £3,000. Income-related ESA does not include a family premium.

Only one family premium is payable, regardless of how many children you have.

If a child who is being looked after by a local authority or who is in custody comes home for part of a week, your IS or income-based JSA includes a proportion of the weekly premium, based on the number of days the child is with you.[10] You can be paid the full premium in your HB if your child who is being looked after by a local authority is part of your household for any part of the week, provided the local authority thinks this is reasonable, given how often and for how long the child is at home with you.[11]

Disabled child premium

You are entitled to a disabled child premium in your HB and, if applicable, your IS and income-based JSA, for each child included in your claim who gets disability living allowance (DLA), personal independence payment (PIP) or armed forces independence payment if s/he is at least 16 (or extra-statutory payments to compensate for non-payment of DLA or PIP), or who is blind.[12] You are only entitled to the premium in IS and income-based JSA in certain circumstances (see p220). Income-related ESA does not include a disabled child premium.

A child is treated as blind if s/he is registered as blind, and for the first 28 weeks after s/he has been taken off the register on regaining her/his sight.[13] If DLA or PIP stops because s/he has gone into hospital, see p946.

If your child is looked after by the local authority or is in custody for part of the week, the disabled child premium is affected in the same way as the family premium (see above).

Note: your child's capital does not affect the amount of your HB.[14] For IS and income-based JSA, if your child has over £3,000 capital or has been in hospital for more than 52 weeks, you do not get this premium.[15]

If your child dies

If your child dies, you may be able to continue receiving the disabled child premium for eight weeks.[16] This applies if:

- you get child benefit for the child following her/his death (see p568); and
- you were getting the disabled child premium for that child in your applicable amount immediately before her/his death.

Disability premium

Income-related ESA does not include a disability premium.

The way in which you can get a disability premium depends on whether or not you have a partner (see p205). In either case, the person who satisfies the qualifying conditions must be under the qualifying age for PC (see p78). For IS and income-based JSA, if you or your partner have reached the qualifying age for PC, you may get the higher pensioner premium instead (see p232). There is a single rate and a couple rate, which applies if both of you satify the conditions.

You qualify for a disability premium if none of the exclusions (p230) apply and one of the following applies.[17]

- You (or your partner) are getting a qualifying benefit.These are:[18]
  - DLA (see Chapter 27), PIP (see Chapter 35), armed forces independence payment or an equivalent benefit paid to meet attendance needs because of an injury at work (see Chapter 32) or a war injury;[19]
  - attendance allowance (AA), DLA or PIP if you (or your partner) were getting one of these benefits, but payment was suspended when one of you became a hospital patient.[20] In the case of IS and income-based JSA only, you or your partner must previously have qualified for a disability premium;
  - for IS and income-based JSA, your partner or, for joint-claim JSA, you or your partner, IB paid at the long-term rate which stopped at pension age for income-based JSA (including joint-claim JSA)[21] or when retirement pension became payable for IS. For IS, you must have been continuously entitled to IS or income-based JSA since that time.[22] If it was your partner who reached pension age or began receiving a retirement pension, s/he must still be alive.[23] You or your partner must have previously qualified for a disability premium;[24]
  - war pensioner's mobility supplement;
  - the disabled worker element or severe disability element of working tax credit (WTC);
  - severe disablement allowance (SDA). For IS and HB you must be getting SDA; for income-based JSA your partner must be getting it. For joint claim JSA, either you or your partnermust be getting it;
  - an NHS invalid trike or private car (for you or your partner) because of a disability;[25]
  - extra-statutory payments to compensate you or your partner for not getting any of the above benefits.[26]

  Once you qualify for the disability premium, you or your partner are treated as still getting a qualifying benefit if you no longer receive it because of the overlapping benefit rules (see p1165).[27]
- You (or your partner) are registered as **blind** with a local authority. If you (or your partner) regain your sight, you still qualify for 28 weeks after being taken off the register.

- For joint-claim JSA only, either you or your partner have (or are treated as having) 'limited capability for work' (see p1003) for a continuous qualifying period of:
  - 196 days if you or s/he are 'terminally ill'; *or*
  - 364 days in all other cases.

  For this purpose, gaps in your periods of limited capability for work that last no more than 12 weeks are ignored.[28]

If you undertake training

If you go on a government training course or receive a training allowance for any period, you keep the disability premium even though you may stop receiving one of the qualifying benefits, or cease to be entitled to statutory sick pay (SSP) during the course, provided you continue to be entitled to IS, income-based JSA or HB. After the course, the premium continues if you are getting a qualifying benefit, remain entitled to SSP (for IS only), or remain incapable of work.[29]

Exclusions

You may not be entitled to the disability premium in your IS or income-based JSA once you or your partner have been receiving free treatment as a hospital inpatient for more than 52 weeks (see p941).

You cannot get a disability premium in your HB on any grounds if:

- you have, or are treated as having, limited capability for work.[30] This applies even if you would otherwise qualify for the premium – eg, if you (or your partner) get DLA, PIP or are registered blind. If your partner is the HB claimant and s/he does not have (and is not treated as having) limited capability for work, the disability premium can be included;[31] *or*
- you have reached the qualifying age for PC and neither you nor your partner are getting IS, income-based JSA, or income-related ESA.

Do you have limited capability for work?
1. If you claim ESA or national insurance credits on the basis of limited capability for work and you are a member of a couple, it may be beneficial for your partner to be the HB claimant instead of you in order for the disability premium to be be included in your applicable amount. Local authorities are advised to tell you if this is the case.[32]
2. If you have (or are treated as having) limited capability for work, although you cannot qualify for a disability premium, you may qualify for either the support or work-related activity component in your applicable amount, although this is not normally until after the 'assessment phase' has ended (see p621).
3. If your partner has limited capability for work, but you do not, you can still qualify for the disability premium, which is paid at the couple rate. However, if the disability premium is awarded, you cannot qualify for a support or work-related activity component in your applicable amount.

Enhanced disability premium

The enhanced disability premium can be paid in respect of disabled children and disabled adults.[33]

For HB, you qualify for one enhanced disability premium for each child included in your claim who receives the highest rate care component of DLA (or extra-statutory payments to compensate for non-payment of this), the enhanced rate of the daily living component of PIP, or armed forces independence payment.

For IS and income-based JSA, you are only entitled to the child rate of this premium in certain circumstances (see p220). If your child dies, the premium continues for eight weeks if you or your partner continue to get child benefit for her/him (see p568).

Income-related ESA does not include the child rate of this premium (although you can qualify for the adult rate).

For IS, income-based JSA, income-related ESA and HB, you are entitled to an enhanced disability premium for an adult (at the single or couple rate) if either:

- you or your partner receive the highest rate care component of DLA, the enhanced rate of the daily living component of PIP or armed forces independence payment. If it is your partner who satisfies this, s/he must be under the qualifying age for PC; *or*
- for income-related ESA, you qualify for the support component (see p621); *or*
- for HB, the decision maker has determined that you have, or can be treated as having, limited capability for work-related activity (see p1008).

This premium can be paid in addition to both the disability and severe disability premiums (see p238). For more details of the premiums with which the enhanced disability premium can be paid, see p238.

Once you or your partner reach the qualifying age for PC (see p78), you are paid the pensioner premium (or the higher personal allowance in HB) instead.

In most cases, you (or your partner or child) are treated as receiving the highest rate of the DLA care component or the enhanced rate of the daily living component of PIP during any period when DLA or PIP is suspended while you are in hospital.

However, the following people cannot qualify:

- for the child rate, for IS and income-based JSA only, children who have been in hospital for more than 52 weeks, or who have more than £3,000 in capital;[34]
- some people who have been in hospital for more than 52 weeks or, in some cases, if their partner has (see p947).

Pensioner premiums

There is a pensioner premium and a higher pensioner premium. They are paid at the same rate.[35]

You qualify for a pensioner premium if:

- your partner has reached the qualifying age for PC (see p78). This applies to IS, income-based JSA and income-related ESA; *or*
- you have reached the qualifying age for PC. This applies to men claiming income-based JSA and income-related ESA. Women of the same age must claim PC instead of income-based JSA or income-related ESA.

You qualify for a higher pensioner premium instead of a pensioner premium in IS or income-based JSA if:

- your partner is aged 80 or over; *or*
- you or your partner are sick or disabled and certain conditions are satisfied (see below).

There are no pensioner premiums in HB; you get a higher personal allowance instead.

Although paid at the same rate as the pensioner premium, qualifying for the higher pensioner premium may be important – eg, because it qualifies you for a £20 earnings disregard (see p268) or because it meets one of the qualifying conditions for the disabled worker element of WTC (see p1403). For joint-claim JSA, there is no pensioner premium or higher pensioner premium on age grounds if your partner is aged 75 or over.

These premiums are paid at a single or couple rate. The couple rate of the premium is included in your applicable amount even if only one partner fulfils the condition. The rate of the pensioner premium in income-related ESA depends on whether or not you are entitled to the work-related activity or support component (see p241) and whether you are a member of a couple.

Higher pensioner premium

You qualify for the higher pensioner premium in IS or income-based JSA if:[36]

- for IS and income-based JSA, your partner is aged 80 or over;
- for IS, your partner has, or for income-based JSA you or your partner have, reached the qualifying age for PC (see p78) and receive a qualifying benefit (eg, AA, DLA, PIP or SDA), are registered blind, or have an NHS trike or a private car allowance. If your AA, DLA or PIP stops because you go into hospital, see p944. If you are getting SDA, see p233;
- for income-based JSA, you (or, for joint-claim JSA, you or your partner) were getting a disability premium as part of your IS or income-based JSA before you reached the qualifying age for PC (see p78) and you have continued to claim income-based JSA since then. You must have been getting a disability premium at some time during the eight weeks (104 weeks if you are a 'welfare-to-work beneficiary'[37]) before you reached the qualifying age for PC and have received IS or JSA continuously since then.[38] You are treated as being

continuously entitled to benefit if there is a break in your entitlement of eight (or 104) weeks or less, which includes the day you reached the qualifying age for PC;

- for IS, you were getting a disability premium as part of your IS or income-based JSA at some time in the eight weeks (104 weeks if you are a 'welfare-to-work beneficiary') before your partner reached the qualifying age for PC (see p78) and have continued to get IS since then. You are treated as being continuously entitled to benefit if there is a break in your entitlement of eight (or 104) weeks or less, including the day your partner reached the qualifying age for PC.[39]

Note: you may not be entitled to the higher pensioner premium once you or your partner have been receiving free treatment as a hospital inpatient for more than 52 weeks (see p947).

In the case of couples, the person who was the benefit claimant before s/he reached the qualifying age for PC must continue to claim after that, but the claimant does not need to have been the person who qualified for the disability premium.

If you get SDA when you reach 65, you are awarded it for life.[40] This also applies even if it ceases to be paid because you get retirement pension at a higher rate.[41]

Severe disability premium and pension credit additional amount

You qualify for a severe disability premium or for the additional amount for severe disability in the guarantee credit of PC if *all* the following apply to you.[42]

- You receive a **qualifying benefit** (see p234). If you are a couple for IS, income-based JSA, income-related ESA and HB, your partner must also be getting a qualifying benefit, or be registered blind (or treated as blind because it is no more than 28 weeks since s/he stopped being registered).[43] For PC, both of you must be getting a qualifying benefit or one must be getting a qualifying benefit and the other registered blind or treated as blind. For PC only, either partner can be the claimant.[44] If you are a member of a couple, you and your partner are treated as getting any of these benefits while one or both of you are in hospital, but only if you are not claiming the premium or additional amount for severe disability on the basis that your partner (or you, for PC) is blind or treated as blind.[45] For IS, income-based JSA, income-related ESA and HB, the benefit must be paid for you or your partner; receipt of benefit for someone else (eg, a child) does not count.[46] It is probably intended that the same rule should apply to PC.
- No non-dependant aged 18 or over (eg, an adult son or daughter or parent) is 'normally residing with you' (see p235). It does not matter whose house it is.[47] For IS, income-based JSA, income-related ESA, PC and HB, someone is only

counted as residing with you if you share accommodation, apart from a bathroom, lavatory or a communal area such as a hall, passageway or a room in common use in sheltered accommodation. If s/he is separately liable to make payments for the accommodation to the landlord, s/he does not count as residing with you.[48]

- No one gets carer's allowance (CA) for looking after you or, if you are a couple, no one gets CA for both of you (but see p945 if you and/or your partner go into hospital). If you are a member of a couple and someone gets CA for one (but not both) of you, but you are both disabled, you can get the severe disability premium at the single person's rate. Only actual receipt of CA counts (except if it is not paid because of the loss of benefit rules – see p1258).[49] No account is taken of any underlying entitlement to CA if it is awarded but not paid because of the overlapping benefit rules, or of any extra-statutory payments to compensate for its not being paid. Similarly, no account is taken of any backdated payments or arrears of CA.[50] Also argue that no account should be taken of any overpaid CA, if you have been denied the premium because of a CA overpayment, it should be repaid to you (see p238).

Receiving a qualifying benefit
A **'qualifying benefit'** is either AA, the middle or highest rate care component of DLA, the daily living component of PIP, armed forces independence payment, constant attendance allowance, or exceptionally severe disablement allowance (or the equivalent war pension). You are **'treated as receiving'** a qualifying benefit if you receive an extra-statutory payment to compensate you for not receiving that benefit.[51]

Couples

You get the couple rate if both you and your partner get a qualifying benefit and no one gets CA for either of you. If CA is paid for one of you, or if your partner does not get a qualifying benefit but is registered blind (or treated as blind), you get the single rate. In polygamous marriages, the single rate is awarded for each eligible spouse who gets a qualifying benefit while CA is not paid. **Note:**

- You and/or your partner are treated as getting a qualifying benefit, even though it has stopped because you/your partner have been in hospital for more than four weeks, but the severe disability premium is paid at the single person rate only. Similarly, for IS, income-based JSA, income-related ESA and HB, if you are a couple, you are treated as receiving CA even though you are no longer getting it because the person for whom you care has been in hospital for more than four weeks.[52]
- For couples on IS, JSA and income-related ESA only, if you or your partner temporarily move into a care home, you still count as a couple but your applicable amount is calculated in a different way (see p221).[53] If your applicable amount is calculated as if you and your partner were single

claimants, this means that, if the person who stays at home gets a qualifying benefit, a severe disability premium is included in the applicable amount of that person.

- For PC, if you or your partner temporarily move into a care home, you still count as a couple if you have not been apart for substantially more than 52 weeks (see p955). So, once the partner in the care home loses her/his AA or DLA care component, no severe disability premium can be paid for either of you, even if the partner at home gets a qualifying benefit.

Non-dependants

Non-dependants are adults living with you who are not included in your benefit claim (eg, adult son or daughter, or a parent), but who are regarded as being able to contribute towards your household costs.

The following people who live with you do *not* count as non-dependants.[54]

For IS, income-based JSA, income-related ESA, HB and PC:
- anyone aged under 18;
- anyone else who receives a qualifying benefit for the severe disability premium (see p233);[55]
- anyone who is registered blind (or treated as blind);[56]
- anyone staying in your home who normally lives elsewhere. In deciding whether someone normally lives with you or elsewhere, it may be relevant to consider:
  - why the residence started;
  - the relationship and its history, if any, between those concerned;
  - the motivations involved;
  - the purpose for which residence has been taken up;
  - the duration of the residencey and whether there is any other home in which residence is, or could be, taken up;[57]
- any person (and, for IS, income-based JSA, income-related ESA and PC only, her/his partner) employed by a charitable or voluntary body as a resident carer for you or your partner if you pay a charge for that service (even if the charge is only nominal).[58] **Note:** these rules do not apply to a live-in carer employed directly by you (even if, for example, you are paying her/him from direct payments made to you by social services for that purpose under the Health and Social Care Act 2001).

For IS, income-based JSA, income-related ESA and HB:
- any member of your 'family' (see p237 for who counts). This may include any child under the age of 20 (see p210) as well as your partner, although your partner must be getting a qualifying benefit (or would be if s/he were not in hospital), or be registered or treated as blind (see p27), for you to get the severe disability premium (see p233);

- any child or qualifying young person who is living with you but who is not a member of your household (see p214).[59]

For IS, income-based JSA, income-related ESA and PC:
- any person (or her/his partner) who jointly occupies (see p237) your home and is either the co-owner with you or your partner, or jointly liable with you or your partner, to make payments to a landlord for occupying it. If this person is a close relative (see p237), however, s/he *does* count as a non-dependant *unless* the co-ownership or joint liability to make payments to a landlord existed either before 11 April 1988 or by the time you or your partner first moved in;
- any person (or any member of her/his household) who is liable to pay you or your partner on a commercial basis (see p237) for occupying the dwelling (eg, tenants or licensees), unless s/he is a close relative of you or your partner;
- any person (or any member of her/his household) to whom you or your partner are liable to make such payments on a commercial basis, unless s/he is a close relative of you or your partner.

For PC:
- any child or qualifying young person.[60]

Note: for IS, income-based JSA, income-related ESA and PC, if someone comes to live with you in order to look after you (or your partner) and has not lived with you before, your severe disability premium or amount for severe disability remains in payment for the first 12 weeks after the carer moves in, even if s/he would otherwise count as a non-dependant.[61] After that, you lose the premium or the amount for severe disability. The carer should then consider claiming CA (see Chapter 25).

For HB:[62]
- any person who jointly occupies your home and is either the co-owner with you or your partner, or liable with you or your partner to make payments for occupying it. A joint occupier who was a non-dependant at any time within the previous eight weeks counts as a non-dependant if the local authority thinks that the change of arrangements was created to take advantage of the HB scheme;
- any person who is liable to pay you or your partner on a commercial basis for occupying the dwelling unless s/he is a close relative of you or your partner, or if the local authority thinks that the rent or other agreement has been created to take advantage of the HB scheme (but this cannot apply if the person was otherwise liable to pay rent for the accommodation at any time during the eight weeks before the agreement was made);
- any person, or any member of her/his household, to whom you or your partner are liable to make payments for your accommodation on a commercial basis unless s/he is a close relative of you or your partner.

Definitions

'Close relative' is a parent, parent-in-law (including a civil partner's parent), son, son-in-law (including a son's civil partner), daughter, daughter-in-law (including a daughter's civil partner), brother, sister, step-parent (including a parent's civil partner), stepson (including a civil partner's son), stepdaughter (including a civil partner's daughter), or the partners of any of these.[63]

'Member of the family' means your partner and any child who lives in your household and for whom you or your partner count as 'responsible' (see p210).[64]

'Jointly occupies' has a legal meaning. It is a legal relationship involving occupation by two or more people (whether as owner-occupiers, tenants or licensees), with one and the same legal right.[65] It does not exist if people merely have equal access to different parts of the premises.

'Commercial basis' has no legal meaning, and there is no requirement for there to be an intention to make a profit.[66] It may be sufficient if a 'reasonable' charge is made, even if this does not fully cover the cost of the accommodation and meals being provided.[67] The reasonableness of the charge made should be judged solely against the cost of occupying the dwelling, disregarding the additional costs of providing food, clothing and care for the claimant.[68] A useful, but not conclusive, test to apply is to consider whether the same arrangement *might* have been entered into with a lodger rather than with the claimant.[69] It is not relevant whether the non-dependant depends financially on the charge being paid or if s/he would take action against the claimant if s/he did not pay.[70] These last two matters are relevant to whether there is a *liability*.

'Liability' means a legal or contractual liability, although there is no requirement that any arrangements need be in writing.[71]

Carer premium and pension credit additional amount

You qualify for a carer premium, or an additional amount in PC, if you or your partner are entitled to CA (see Chapter 25).[72]

You are entitled to CA even if you do not receive it because of the overlapping benefit rules (see p1165) – eg, you get contributory ESA or retirement pension instead.

If the person you or your partner are getting CA for dies, or you or your partner stop being entitled to CA for another reason, your entitlement to a carer premium continues for a further eight weeks. The eight-week period runs from the Sunday after the death (or from the date of the death, if the death occurs on a Sunday). In other cases, it runs from the date entitlement to CA stops. If you first claim IS, income-based JSA, income-related ESA or (if you or your partner are below the qualifying age for PC) HB after the CA stops, you continue to qualify for a carer premium for eight weeks after the death or, if it stops for another reason, after entitlement to CA stops.[73]

A double rate premium is awarded if both you and your partner satisfy the conditions for it.

Should you claim carer's allowance?

1. Before claiming CA, you should consider how your claim might affect the entitlement to the severe disability premium, or the amount for severe disability in the guarantee credit of PC (see p233), of the disabled person for whom you care – particularly if the only financial advantage to you as the carer is the amount of the carer premium, which may be worth considerably less than the severe disability premium (but see p233 for the rules on notional income).

2. Any backdated award of CA does not affect a disabled person's entitlement to the severe disability premium or the amount for severe disability in the guarantee credit of PC.[74] You may be able to take advantage of this rule so that you are paid CA or the carer premium for the same period in which the disabled person has already received a severe disability premium or an amount for severe disability in PC.

3. Although the severe disability premium or amount for severe disability is not payable throughout any period during which a carer is receiving CA, if you are a carer and it is later decided that you have been overpaid CA, the disabled person should ask for the decision refusing her/him the severe disability premium or the amount for severe disability to be revised. You must be both entitled to *and* in receipt of CA for the severe disability premium not to be payable.[75]

4. Other than for HB, if payment of CA stops, the severe disability premium can be backdated to the date the CA stopped.[76]

Rates of premiums

Rates of premiums

The following premiums can be paid in addition to any other premium, except that the enhanced disability premium cannot be paid in addition to the pensioner or higher pensioner premium.[77]

Family premium	£17.45
Disabled child premium	£59.50
(for each qualifying child)	
Severe disability premium	
Single (or one partner qualifies)	£61.10
Couple (both partners qualify)	£122.20
Carer premium	
Single (or one partner qualifies)	£34.20
Couple (both partners qualify)	£68.40

Enhanced disability premium

Child (for each qualifying child)	£24.08
Single	£15.55
Couple (one or both partner(s) qualify)	£22.35

Only one of the following premiums can be paid. If you qualify for more than one, you get the highest:[78]

Family premium for HB (lone parent increase)	£4.75
Disability premium	
Single	£31.85
Couple	£45.40
Pensioner and higher pensioner premium for IS/ income-based JSA	
Single (income-based JSA only; not payable in IS)	£75.95
Couple	£112.80
Pensioner premium for income-related ESA	
Claimant entitled to support component:	
Single	£40.20
Couple	£77.05
Claimant entitled to work-related activity component:	
Single	£47.20
Couple	£84.05
Claimant not entitled to either component:	
Single	£75.95
Couple	£112.80

Note: the lone parent increase to the family premium is only payable in HB if you were entitled to it on 5 April 1998 and certain changes in your circumstances do not occur. For more information, see p793 of the 2011/12 edition of this *Handbook*.[79]

Backdating premiums

To qualify for the disability, enhanced disability, higher pensioner, severe disability, disabled child or carer premium, you or your partner or child must usually have been awarded a 'qualifying benefit' that applies to each premium. The date you can begin to get your premium may, therefore, depend on the date from which your qualifying benefit is awarded. However, because of the time it may take to deal with your claim for the qualifying benefit, or if your claim is backdated (see p1144) or initially refused but awarded some time later after a revision (see p1270), supersession (see p1281) or appeal (see p1303), you may not get your premium straight away and you may have to apply for it to be backdated.

If you are already getting benefit

If you are already getting IS, JSA, ESA, HB or pension credit (PC), you should ask for your award of this benefit either to be revised or superseded and for your premium to be backdated to the date from which the qualifying benefit is awarded, or to when you first got (or claimed) IS, JSA, ESA, HB or PC, if that is later. There is no limit to the period for which arrears can be paid to you.[80]

If you were refused benefit

If you have previously claimed IS or income-based JSA, but your claim was refused because at the time you or your partner or child did not get the qualifying benefit for the premium (see p1149), you should make another IS or income-based JSA claim once the qualifying benefit is awarded. To get full backdating you should have claimed the qualifying benefit before, or no later than 10 days after, the first IS or income-based JSA claim. You must then make your second claim for IS or income-based JSA within three months of the decision awarding the qualifying benefit. The second claim, including the premium, is backdated to the date of the first IS or income-based JSA claim, or to the date from which the qualifying benefit was awarded if that is later.[81] If the qualifying benefit is initially refused, or awarded at a lower rate than you need for the premium, but is later decided in your favour, to get full backdating you must make your second IS or income-based JSA claim within three months of the date the qualifying benefit is decided in your favour on revision, supersession or appeal.[82]

A new claim for income-related ESA can be backdated for a maximum of three months; you do not need to establish a reason for the backdating.

For HB, you may be limited to a maximum of six months' or three months' backdating, depending on your age (see p127).

Note: for the backdating rules for PC, see p87.

If you lose entitlement to benefit

If you lose your existing IS or income-based JSA as a result of having your (or your partner or child's) qualifying benefit stopped or reduced, or while you are waiting for a claim for a qualifying benefit to be decided, and that qualifying benefit is then awarded, or reinstated on a revision, supersession or appeal (or you make a later claim for the qualifying benefit), you should make a new claim for IS or income-based JSA. Provided you claim within three months of the favourable decision on the qualifying benefit, your IS or income-based JSA is fully backdated to the date your entitlement previously ended, or to the date from when the qualifying benefit is payable if that is later.[83]

If you lose your HB because you lose entitlement to a qualifying benefit, the decision ending your HB can be revised if the qualifying benefit is reinstated. Your HB can be fully backdated in this situation. You must tell the local authority that you have had your qualifying benefit reinstated, but you do not need to make a fresh claim for HB.[84]

4. Components

Your applicable amount for income-related employment and support allowance (ESA) and, in certain circumstances, housing benefit (HB) may include either:[85]
- a support component (see below); *or*
- a work-related activity component (see below).

You cannot be awarded both these components at the same time.

For **HB**, you can qualify for one of these components if either you or your partner meet the conditions for it and have limited capability for work. It does not matter if a claim for ESA is refused, or if your entitlement has stopped because of the rules on how long contributory ESA can be paid.

To qualify for a component in income-related ESA, you must meet the conditions. **Note:**
- These components cannot be included in your applicable amount for income support (IS), income-based jobseeker's allowance (JSA) or pension credit (PC).
- You cannot qualify for a component in your HB applicable amount if you have reached the qualifying age for PC (see p78).
- For income-related ESA, if you or your partner have been receiving free treatment as a hospital inpatient for a continuous period of more than 52 weeks, you cannot qualify for either component.[86]

Support component

In order to qualify for a support component with your income-related ESA, you must meet the conditions for the component described on p621. The rules are the same as for contributory ESA.

You qualify for a support component in your HB if:[87]
- you or your partner have claimed ESA and, unless you are terminally ill in the circumstances detailed on p242, the ESA assessment phase has ended (see p621); *and*
- you are not entitled to a disability premium (p229); *and*
- the decision maker has determined that either you or your partner have limited capability for work-related activity (see p1008 – the rules are the same as for contributory ESA).

Work-related activity component

In order to qualify for a work-related activity component with your income-related ESA, you must meet the conditions for the component described on p622. The rules are the same as for contributory ESA.

You qualify for a work-related activity component in your HB if:[88]

- you or your partner have claimed ESA and, unless you are terminally ill in the circumstances detailed below, the ESA assessment phase has ended (see p620); *and*
- you are not entitled to a disability premium (p229); *and*
- the decision maker has determined that you or your partner have, or can be treated as having, limited capability for work (see p1002).

If you are **terminally ill** (ie, you have a progressive disease because of which your death can reasonably be expected within six months) and you have either claimed ESA expressly on this ground, or have asked for a revision or supersession and have said that you are terminally ill, it is not necessary for the assessment phase to have ended for you to qualify for either the support or work-related activity component.

You keep the maximum work-related activity component in HB even if you lose it in ESA because of a sanction.[89] The full, unsanctioned amount of ESA continues to be taken into account as your income.

Rates of components

You can only be entitled to one component. There is no higher rate of the support or work-related component paid for couples.

For income-related ESA, your applicable amount includes either the support or work-related activity component if you are the claimant and you meet the conditions for that component (see p241). If you have a partner and both you and your partner have limited capability for work, you can choose which of you is the claimant. If only one of you qualifies for a component, it may be beneficial for that person to be the claimant. If in doubt, seek advice.

For HB, you qualify for either a support or work-related activity component if either you or your partner satisfy the conditions for the component (see p241). If you qualify for one component and your partner qualifies for the other, the component for which *you* qualify is awarded.[90]

Rates of components[91]

Support component	£35.75
Work-related activity component	£28.75

Backdating components

For income-related ESA, your entitlement to either the support or work-related activity component normally starts once the 'assessment phase' has ended (see p620 – the rules are the same as for contributory ESA). The assessment phase is usually expected to last for the first 13 weeks of your claim. Earlier periods on ESA may be linked to your current one when calculating the length of your claim (see p1018). However, if your assessment phase ends later than this, your entitlement to a component can be backdated to the beginning of the 14th week of your claim.[92] If you make a claim, or request a revision or supersession of your entitlement, expressly on the grounds of being terminally ill (see p621 – the rules are the same as for contributory ESA), you do not have to wait for the assessment phase to end to qualify for the support component, but can qualify either from the date of your claim, or from the date on which you became terminally ill if that is later.[93]

If you are getting HB and you become entitled to a support or work-related activity component, you qualify for that component in your applicable amount from the Monday on or after your entitlement to the component began. However, if your HB entitlement starts after the date your entitlement to the component began, you qualify for the component in your HB applicable amount from the date your entitlement to HB began.[94]

If you only become entitled to HB once a component is awarded to you, you should claim (or reclaim) HB as promptly as you can since you can only get a maximum of six months' backdating (see p128).

5. Transitional addition

If you are claiming incapacity benefit (IB), severe disablement allowance (SDA) or income support (IS) 'on the grounds of disability', your claim will have been (or, if not done so by April 2014, will soon be) transferred to employment and support allowance (ESA) and your entitlement will be reassessed (see p662 for details). When this happens, you may have a transitional addition included in your applicable amount for income-related ESA or housing benefit (HB).

Income-related employment and support allowance

If your claim for IS on grounds of disability is transferred to an award of income-related ESA and your ESA is worth less than your IS, you are entitled to a transitional addition of ESA. This transitional addition is calculated by comparing your IS applicable amount with your applicable amount for ESA. If you are entitled to a transitional addition, it is included as part of your ESA applicable amount. See p71 for details.

Housing benefit

If your claim for IB or SDA has been transferred to contributory ESA (see p662):

- you may no longer be entitled to the disability premium in your HB applicable amount, as this is not paid if you are the claimant and have limited capability for work;

- if your HB applicable amount would be reduced because of the transfer of your (or your partner's) IB or SDA claim to contributory ESA, it includes a transitional addition to make up the difference and ensure that you do not immediately lose out.[95]

A transitional addition is not necessary if:[96]
- you (or your partner) are transferred to income-related ESA. In this case, you are entitled to maximum HB; or
- you (or your partner) are over the qualifying age for pension credit (p78). In this case, your applicable amount is not affected by the transfer to ESA.

You are entitled to a transitional addition in your HB if:[97]
- you (or your partner) have been transferred to contributory ESA and, on the date of the transfer, your HB applicable amount is reduced as a result; or
- on transfer to ESA, you (or your partner) are found not to have limited capability for work, you have appealed against this and you are entitled to contributory ESA pending the appeal (see p1014), and your HB applicable amount is reduced as a result. If you win your appeal, the transitional addition is recalculated (because your contributory ESA applicable amount may now include a component).[98]

The amount of the transitional addition is the amount by which your old HB applicable amount exceeds your new HB applicable amount, following the transfer from IB or SDA to contributory ESA. All the parts of the applicable amount that apply to your claim, including personal allowances, premiums and the support or work-related activity component, are taken into account.[99]

The transitional addition is not permanent. It is reduced by annual increases to your HB and any other changes of circumstances that increase your applicable amount – eg, the birth of a child, or becoming a member of a couple. The transitional addition is reduced by the amount of the increase.[100] It is not affected by changes in your income or the number of non-dependants.

Your transitional addition ends on 5 April 2020, or earlier if:[101]
- the transitional addition ends because it is reduced to nil by annual increases or other changes in your circumstances; or
- you (or your partner) stop being entitled to contributory ESA; or
- your award of HB is terminated; or
- you (or your partner) become entitled to income-related ESA, or to income-based jobseeker's allowance or IS.

Once ended, your transitional addition can be included again if:[102]
- it ended because you (or your partner) stopped being entitled to contributory ESA or because your HB award was terminated; and
- you (or your partner) become entitled to contributory ESA or to HB again; and

- in the case of a new award of HB, this is within 12 weeks of the transitional addition ending or, in the case of a new contributory ESA award, within 12 weeks of the transitional addition ending.

If your transitional addition is included again, the amount is what it would have been had it not ended, allowing for reductions as a result of increases to your applicable amount that have occurred in the meantime.

Notes

1. What is the applicable amount
1 Reg 1(3) and (7) SS(WTCCTC)(CA) Regs
2 **IS** Reg 21 and Sch 7 para 7 IS Regs
  JSA Regs 85 and 86C and Schs 5 para 4 and 5A para 3 JSA Regs
  ESA Reg 69 and Sch 5 para 2 ESA Regs
3 **IS** Reg 21 and Sch 7 para 9 IS Regs
  JSA Regs 85 and 86C and Schs 5 para 5 and 5A para 4 JSA Regs
  ESA Reg 69 and Sch 5 para 4 ESA Regs

2. Personal allowances
4 **IS** Reg 18(2) IS Regs
  JSA Reg 84(2) JSA Regs
  ESA Reg 68(2) ESA Regs
5 **IS** Sch 2 Part 1 IS Regs
  JSA Sch 1 Part 1 JSA Regs
  ESA Sch 4 Part 1 ESA Regs
  HB Sch 3 Part 1 HB Regs; Sch 3 Part 1 HB(SPC) Regs
6 **IS** Reg 18(1)(b) IS Regs
  JSA Regs 84(1)(b) and 86B(b) JSA Regs
  ESA Reg 68(1)(b) ESA Regs
  HB Reg 23(b) HB Regs; Sch 3 para 1 HB(SPC) Regs
7 **IS** Sch 2 para 1(3) IS Regs
  JSA Sch 1 para 1(3) JSA Regs
  ESA Sch 4 para 1(3) ESA Regs

3. Premiums
8 Sch 3 paras 3 and 6-9 HB(SPC) Regs
9 **IS** Sch 2 para 3 IS Regs
  JSA Sch 1 para 4 JSA Regs
  HB Sch 3 para 3 HB Regs; Sch 3 para 3 HB(SPC) Regs

10 **IS** Regs 15(3) and 16(6) IS Regs
  JSA Regs 74(4) and 78(7) JSA Regs
11 Reg 21(4)-(5) HB Regs; reg 21(4)-(5) HB(SPC) Regs
12 **IS** Sch 2 paras 14 and 15(6) IS Regs
  JSA Sch 1 para 16 JSA Regs
  HB Sch 3 paras 16 and 20(7) HB Regs; Sch 3 paras 8 and 12(3) HB(SPC) Regs
13 **IS** Sch 2 paras 12(1)(a)(iii) and (2) and 14(c) IS Regs
  JSA Sch 1 para 14(1)(h) and (2) JSA Regs
  HB Sch 3 paras 13(1)(a)(v) and (2) and 16(c) HB Regs; Sch 3 para 8(b) HB(SPC) Regs
14 Reg 25(3) HB Regs; reg 23(3) HB(SPC) Regs
15 **IS** Sch 2 para 14(2)(a) IS Regs
  JSA Sch 1 para 16(2)(a) JSA Regs
16 **IS** Sch 2 para 14 IS Regs
  JSA Sch 1 para 16 JSA Regs
  HB Sch 3 para 16 HB Regs; Sch 3 para 8 HB(SPC) Regs
17 **IS** Sch 2 para 11 IS Regs
  JSA Sch 1 paras 13, 14, 20G and 20H JSA Regs
  HB Sch 3 para 12 HB Regs
18 **IS** Sch 2 para 12(1)(a)(i) IS Regs
  JSA Sch 1 paras 14(1)(a)-(d) and 20H(1)(a)-(d) JSA Regs
  HB Sch 3 para 13(1)(a)(i) HB Regs
19 **IS** Reg 2(1) IS Regs
  JSA Reg 1(3) JSA Regs
  HB Reg 2(1) HB Regs
  All Definition of 'attendance allowance'

● ●

20 **IS** Sch 2 para 12(1)(d) IS Regs
 JSA Sch 1 paras 14(1)(g)(ii) and
 20H(1)(h)(ii) JSA Regs
 HB Sch 3 para 13(1)(a)(iii) HB Regs
21 R(IS) 7/02
22 **IS** Sch 2 para 12(1)(c)(i) IS Regs
 JSA Sch 1 paras 14(1)(g)(i) and
 20H(1)(h)(i) JSA Regs
 HB Sch 3 para 13(1)(a)(ii) HB Regs
23 **IS** Sch 2 para 12(1)(c)(i) IS Regs
 JSA Sch 1 paras 14(1)(g)(i) and
 20H(1)(h)(i) JSA Regs
24 **IS** Sch 2 para 12(1)(c) IS Regs
 JSA Sch 1 paras 14(1)(g) and 20H(1)(h)
 JSA Regs
25 **IS** Sch 2 para 12(1)(a)(ii) IS Regs
 JSA Sch 1 paras 14(1)(e) and (f) and
 20H(1)(f) and (g) JSA Regs
 HB Sch 3 para 13(1)(a)(iv) HB Regs
26 **IS** Sch 2 para 14A IS Regs
 JSA Sch 1 paras 18 and 20K JSA Regs
 HB Sch 3 para 18 HB Regs
27 **IS** Sch 2 para 7(1)(a) IS Regs
 JSA Sch 1 paras 8(1)(a) and 20D(1)(a)
 JSA Regs
 HB Sch 3 para 7(1)(a) HB Regs
28 Sch 1 para 20H(1)(ee) JSA Regs
29 **IS** Sch 2 paras 7(1)(b) and 12(5) IS Regs
 JSA Sch 1 paras 8(1)(b) and 20D(b) JSA
 Regs
 HB Sch 3 paras 7(1)(b) and 13(5) HB
 Regs
30 The rules only refer to the 'claimant'.
31 Sch 3 para 13(9) HB Regs
32 HB/CTB Circular A11/2008
33 **IS** Sch 2 para 13A IS Regs
 JSA Sch 1 paras 15A and 20IA JSA Regs
 ESA Sch 4 para 7 ESA Regs
 HB Sch 3 para 15 HB Regs; Sch 3 para 7
 HB(SPC) Regs
34 **IS** Sch 2 para 13A IS Regs
 JSA Sch 1 para 15A JSA Regs
35 **IS** Sch 2 paras 9 and 9A IS Regs
 JSA Sch 1 paras 10, 11, 20E and 20F JSA
 Regs
 ESA Sch 4 para 5 ESA Regs
36 **IS** Sch 2 para 10 IS Regs
 JSA Sch 1 paras 12 and 20F JSA Regs
37 Sch 1 paras 12(3) and 20F(3) JSA Regs
38 Sch 1 paras 12(1)(a)(ii) and (c)(ii) and
 (2) and 20F(1)(b) and (2) JSA Regs
39 Sch 2 para 10(1)(b)(ii), (3) and (4) IS
 Regs; reg 32 IS(JSACA) Regs
40 CIS/458/1992
41 **IS** Sch 2 para 7(1)(a) IS Regs
 JSA Sch 1 paras 8(1)(a) and 20D(1)(a)
 JSA Regs

42 **IS** Sch 2 para 13 IS Regs
 JSA Sch 1 paras 15 and 20I JSA Regs
 ESA Sch 4 para 6 ESA Regs
 PC Reg 6(4) and Sch 1 paras 1-2 SPC
 Regs
 HB Sch 3 para 14 HB Regs; Sch 3 para 6
 HB(SPC) Regs
43 **IS** Sch 2 para 13(2A) IS Regs
 JSA Sch 1 para 15(3) and 20I(2) JSA
 Regs
 ESA Sch 4 para 6(3) and (9) ESA Regs
 HB Sch 3 para 14(3) HB Regs; Sch 3 para
 6(3) HB(SPC) Regs
44 Sch 1 para 11(b) and (c) SPC Regs
45 **IS** Sch 2 para 13(3A)(a) IS Regs
 JSA Sch 1 paras 15(5)(a) and 20I(4)(a)
 JSA Regs
 ESA Sch 4 para 6(5)(a) ESA Regs
 PC Sch 1 para 1(2)(b) SPC Regs
 HB Sch 3 para 14(5) HB Regs; Sch 3 para
 6(7) HB(SPC) Regs
46 **IS** Sch 2 para 14B IS Regs
 JSA Sch 1 paras 19 and 20L JSA Regs
 ESA Sch 4 para 10 ESA Regs
 HB Sch 3 para 19 HB Regs; Sch 3 para
 11 HB(SPC) Regs
 See also R(IS) 10/94, upheld in *Rider v
 CAO, The Times*, 30 January 1996 (CA)
47 *Bate v CAO* [1996] 2 All ER 790 (HL),
 reported as R(IS) 12/96
48 **IS** Reg 3(4) and (5) IS Regs
 JSA Reg 2(6) and (7) JSA Regs
 ESA Reg 71(6) ESA Regs
 HB Reg 3(4) HB Regs; Sch 3 para 6(7)
 HB(SPC) Regs
49 **IS** Sch 2 para 13(2)(a)(iii) and (b) IS Regs
 JSA Sch 1 paras 15(1)(c) and (2)(d) and
 20I(1)(d) JSA Regs
 ESA Sch 4 para 6(2)(a)(iii) and (b) ESA
 Regs
 PC Sch 1 para 1(1)(a)(iii) SPC Regs
 HB Sch 3 para 14(2)(a)(iii) and (b) HB
 Regs; Sch 3 para 6(2)(a)(iii) and (b)
 HB(SPC) Regs
50 **IS** Sch 2 para 13(3ZA) IS Regs
 JSA Sch 1 paras 15(7) and 20I(6) JSA
 Regs
 ESA Sch 4 para 6(6) ESA Regs
 PC Sch 1 para 2(c) SPC Regs
 HB Sch 3 para 13(6) HB Regs; Sch 3 para
 6(8) HB(SPC) Regs
51 **IS** Sch 2 para 14A IS Regs
 JSA Sch 1 paras 18 and 20K JSA Regs
 ESA Sch 4 para 9 ESA Regs
 PC Sch 1 para 1(2)(a)(ii) SPC Regs
 HB Sch 3 para 18 HB Regs; Sch 3 para
 10 HB(SPC) Regs

52 **IS** Sch 2 para 13(3A) IS Regs
JSA Sch 1 paras 15(5) and 20I(4) JSA Regs
ESA Sch 4 para 6(5) ESA Regs
PC Reg 6(5) and Sch 1 para 1(2)(b) SPC Regs
HB Sch 3 para 14(5) HB Regs; Sch 3 para 6(7) HB(SPC) Regs

53 **IS** Reg 16(1) and Sch 7 para 9 IS Regs
JSA Reg 78(1) and Sch 5 para 5 JSA Regs
ESA Reg 156 and Sch 5 para 4 ESA Regs

54 **IS** Reg 3 and Sch 2 para 13 IS Regs
JSA Reg 2 and Sch 1 paras 15 and 20I JSA Regs
ESA Reg 71 and Sch 4 para 6 ESA Regs
PC Sch 1 para 2 SPC Regs
HB Reg 3 HB Regs; reg 3 HB(SPC) Regs

55 **IS** Sch 2 para 13(3)(a) IS Regs
JSA Sch 1 paras 15(4)(a) and 20I(3)(a) JSA Regs
ESA Sch 4 para 6(4)(a) ESA Regs
PC Sch 1 para 2(2)(a) SPC Regs
HB Sch 3 para 13(4) HB Regs; Sch 3 para 6(6) HB(SPC) Regs

56 **IS** Sch 2 para 13(3)(d) IS Regs
JSA Sch 1 paras 14(1)(h) and (2), 15(4)(c), 20H(1)(i) and (3) and 20I(3)(c) JSA Regs
ESA Sch 4 para 6(4)(c) and (9) ESA Regs
PC Sch 1 para 2(2)(b) and (c) SPC Regs
HB Sch 3 para 14(4)(b) HB Regs; Sch 3 para 6(6)(b) HB(SPC) Regs

57 CIS/14850/1996 para 10

58 **IS** Reg 3(2)(c) and (d) IS Regs
JSA Reg 2(2)(c) and (d) JSA Regs
ESA Reg 71(2)(c) and (d) ESA Regs
PC Sch 1 para 2(d) and (e) SPC Regs
HB Reg 3(2)(f) HB Regs; reg 3(2)(f) HB(SPC) Regs

59 **IS** Reg 3(2)(b) IS Regs
JSA Reg 2(2)(b) JSA Regs
ESA Reg 71(2)(b) ESA Regs
HB Reg 3(2)(c) HB Regs; reg 3(2)(c) HB(SPC) Regs

60 **PC** Sch 1 para 2(2)(f) SPC Regs

61 **IS** Sch 2 para 13(3)(c) and (4) IS Regs
JSA Sch 1 paras 15(4)(b) and (6) and 20I(3)(b) and (5) JSA Regs
ESA Sch 4 para 6(4)(b) and (7) ESA Regs
PC Sch 1 para 2(3)-(4) SPC Regs

62 Regs 3 and 9(1) HB Regs; regs 3 and 9(1) HB(SPC) Regs

63 **IS** Reg 2(1) IS Regs
JSA Reg 1(3) JSA Regs
ESA Reg 2(1) ESA Regs
HB Reg 2(1) HB Regs; reg 2(1) HB(SPC) Regs
All Definition of 'close relative'

64 **IS/HB** s137(1) SSCBA 1992
JSA s35(1) JSA 1995
ESA Reg 2(1) ESA Regs

65 *Bate v CAO* [1996] 2 All ER 790 (HL)

66 R(IS) 11/98, tribunal of commissioners

67 CSIS/43/1989

68 CIS/754/1991 and R(IS) 11/98, para 12

69 R(IS) 11/98, para 8

70 R(IS) 11/98, paras 10 and 11

71 CIS/754/1991

72 **IS** Sch 2 para 14ZA IS Regs
JSA Sch 1 paras 17 and 20J JSA Regs
ESA Sch 4 para 8 ESA Regs
PC Reg 6(6)(a) and Sch 1 para 4 SPC Regs
HB Sch 3 para 17 HB Regs; Sch 3 para 9 HB(SPC) Regs

73 **IS** Sch 2 paras 7 and 14ZA(3) and (4) IS Regs
JSA Sch 1 paras 8, 17(3) and (4) and 20J(3) and (3A) JSA Regs
ESA Sch 4 para 8(2)-(4) ESA Regs
PC Sch 1 para 4(2) and (3) SPC Regs
HB Sch 3 paras 7 and 17(3) and (4) HB Regs; Sch 3 paras 5 and 9(3) HB(SPC) Regs

74 **IS** Sch 2 para 13(3ZA) IS Regs
JSA Sch 1 paras 15(7) and 20I(6) JSA Regs
ESA Sch 4 para 6(6) ESA Regs
PC Sch 1 para 1(2)(c) SPC Regs
HB Sch 3 para 14(6) HB Regs; Sch 3 para 6(8) HB(SPC) Regs

75 **IS** Sch 2 para 13(2)(a)(iii) and (b) IS Regs
JSA Sch 1 paras 15(1)(c) and (2)(d) and 20I(1)(d) JSA Regs
ESA Sch 4 para 6(2)(a)(iii) and (b) ESA Regs
PC Sch 1 para 1(1)(ii), (b) and (c)(iv) SPC Regs
HB Sch 3 para 14(2)(a)(iii) and (b) HB Regs; Sch 3 para 6(2)(a)(iii) and (b) HB(SPC) Regs

76 Reg 7(2)(bc) SS&CS(DA) Regs

77 **IS** Sch 2 para 6(2) IS Regs
JSA Sch 1 paras 7(2) and 20C(2) JSA Regs
ESA Sch 4 para 3 ESA Regs
HB Sch 3 para 6 HB Regs

78 **IS** Sch 2 para 5 IS Regs
JSA Sch 1 paras 6 and 20B JSA Regs
HB Sch 3 para 5 HB Regs

79 Sch 3 para 3 HB Regs

80 **IS/JSA/ESA** Regs 3(7) and 6(2)(e) SS&CS(DA) Regs
HB Regs 4(7B) and 7(2)(i) HB&CTB(DA) Regs

81 Reg 6(16)-(18) SS(C&P) Regs

• •

82 Reg 6(26) SS(C&P) Regs
83 Reg 6(19), (20) and (30) SS(C&P) Regs
84 Reg 4(7C) HB&CTB(DA) Regs

4. Components
85 **ESA** s4(2), (4) and (5) WRA 2007
    HB Reg 22 and Sch 3 paras 21-24 HB
    Regs
86 Reg 69(2) and Sch 5 para 13 ESA Regs
87 Sch 3 paras 22 and 24 HB Regs
88 Sch 3 para 23 HB Regs
89 Because there is no provision to remove
    it in these circumstances.
90 Sch 3 para 22(2) HB Regs
91 **ESA** Sch 4 paras 12 and 13 ESA Regs
    HB Sch 3 paras 25 and 26 HB Regs
92 Regs 6(2)(r) and 7(38) SS&CS(DA) Regs
93 Reg 7(1)(a) ESA Regs; regs
    3(9)(c), 6(2)(a) and 7(2)(be)
    SS&CS(DA) Regs
94 Regs 4(7B), 7(2)(o) and 8(14D)
    HB&CTB(DA) Regs

5. Transitional addition
95 Sch 3 paras 27 and 30 HB Regs
96 HB/CTB Circular A14/2010, paras 21-23
97 Sch 3 para 27(1) HB Regs
98 HB/CTB Circular A14/2010, para 28 and
    Annex C
99 Sch 3 para 30 HB Regs
100 Sch 3 para 31 HB Regs; HB/CTB Circular
    A14/2010, paras 32-33
101 Sch 3 para 27(2) HB Regs
102 Sch 3 paras 28 and 29 HB Regs

Chapter 13

•••

Universal credit maximum amount

This chapter covers:
1. What is the maximum amount (below)
2. The standard allowance (p250)
3. Elements (p250)

Key facts
- Together with your income and capital, the maximum amount of universal credit (UC) is used to calculate the amount of UC to which you are entitled.
- The maximum amount comprises a standard allowance plus one or more elements, depending on your circumstances.
- The maximum amount is similar, but not identical, to the applicable amount used to calculate other means-tested benefits, such as income support and income-based jobseeker's allowance.

---

1. What is the maximum amount

Your maximum universal credit (UC) is made up of the total of:
- a standard allowance – either for a single claimant or a couple making a joint claim (see p250);
- a child element for each child, with an increase for disabled and severely disabled children (see p250);
- an element for an adult who is ill and assessed as having limited capability for work (see p251) or an element for an adult who is assessed as having limited capability for work and also too ill to engage in work-related activity (see p252);
- a carer element for someone caring for a severely disabled person (see p252);
- a childcare costs element (see p253);
- a housing costs element for help with your rent or mortgage interest costs (see p255).

Part 3: General rules for means tested benefits
Chapter 13: Universal credit maximum amount
3. Elements

2. The standard allowance

A standard allowance is always included in your universal credit (UC) maximum amount. The amount depends on your age and whether you are claiming as a single person or making a joint claim as a couple with your partner (see p192).[1]

If you are a member of a couple, but one of you is temporarily absent from the household for more than six months, you stop being treated as a couple (see p209). Even if you do not stop being treated as a couple under this rule, your UC is affected if one of you goes abroad and cannot be treated as in Great Britain while temporarily absent (see p1584).

If you are making a joint claim with your partner and your partner dies, your standard allowance continues at the joint claim rate for the remainder of the monthly UC assessment period (see p186) in which the death occured, and for the next two assessment periods. The rest of your maximum amount is also unaffected during this period.[2]

Note: if one member of a couple does not satisfy the rules of entitlement for UC, the other partner may be able to claim as a single person (see p192). In this case, the standard allowance for a single claimant is used.

Rates of standard allowance

Single claimant	*per month*
Under 25	£249.28
25 or over	£314.67
Joint claimants	
Both under 25	£391.29
One or both 25 or over	£493.95

3. Elements

Child element

A child element is included in your maximum amount for each child for whom you are responsible. The child must be aged under 16, or 16–19 and a 'qualifying young person' for universal credit (UC) purposes (see p211).[3]

You are 'responsible' for a child if s/he is normally living with you (see p210).[4]

There is a higher rate of the child element for the eldest or only child.

If the child is disabled, the child element is increased by a 'disabled child addition'. A lower level is included if s/he is entitled to disability living allowance (DLA) or personal independence payment (PIP). A higher level is included if s/he is entitled to DLA care component at the highest rate, the daily living component of PIP at the enhanced rate, or is registered blind.[5]

If your child dies, you continue to get the child element included in your maximum amount for the remainder of the monthly UC assessment period in which the death occurred, and for the next two assessment periods. The rest of your maximum amount is also unaffected during this period.[6]

Rates of child element

	per month
First child	£274.58
Second/subsequent child	£229.17
Disabled child addition	
Lower rate	£124.86
Higher rate	£362.92

Limited capability for work element

A limited capability for work element is included in your maximum amount if you (or your partner in a joint claim) have limited capability for work.

If you (or your partner in a joint claim) are also entitled to the limited capability for work-related activity element (see p252), you receive that instead – you cannot get both elements. For the tests of limited capability for work and limited capability for work-related activity, see Chapter 47. **Note:** if you work and earn at least an amount equal to a certain earnings threshold, you are usually treated as *not* having limited capability for work (see p1004).

If you are making a joint claim with your partner, only one limited capability for work element can be included, even if you both meet the conditions.[7] If you were previously getting UC as a single person but then form a couple with someone who was not entitled to UC, but who was getting employment and support allowance (ESA) that included the work-related activity component (see p622), the limited capability for work element is included in your joint UC award.[8] However, if your partner's assessment phase for ESA (see p620) lasted less than 13 weeks, the limited capability for work element is not included in your joint UC award immediately. Instead, you must wait until 13 weeks has passed since your partner's ESA assessment phase began. The element is then included from the start of your next UC assessment period.[9]

Rate of limited capability for work element

	per month
Limited capability for work	£124.86

Limited capability for work-related activity element

A limited capability for work-related activity element is included in your maximum amount if you (or your partner in a joint claim) have been assessed as

Part 3: General rules for means tested benefits
Chapter 13: Universal credit maximum amount
3. Elements

having limited capability for work-related activity.[10] For how this is assessed, see p1008 – the rules are very similar to those that apply for ESA.

If this element can be included in your claim, you get this instead of the limited capability for work element.[11]

If you are making a joint claim with your partner, only one limited capability for work-related activity element can be included, even if you both meet the conditions.[12] If you were previously getting UC as a single person but then form a couple with someone who was not entitled to UC, but who was getting ESA that included the support component (see p621), the limited capability for work-related activity element is included in your joint UC award.[13] However, if your partner's assessment phase for ESA (see p620) lasted less than 13 weeks, the limited capability for work-related activity element is not included in your joint UC award immediately. Instead, you must wait until 13 weeks has passed since your partner's ESA assessment phase began. The element is then included from the start of your next UC assessment period.[14]

Rate of limited capability for work-related activity element

	per month
Limited capability for work-related activity	£311.86

Carer element

A carer element is included in your maximum amount if you have 'regular and substantial' caring responsibilities for a severely disabled person. This means that you satisfy, or would satisfy were it not for the level of your earnings, the conditions for carer's allowance (CA) – eg, you are caring for at least 35 hours a week (see p540). You do not have to have claimed CA. **Note:** you do not qualify for the carer element if you have any earnings from your caring responsibilities.[15]

If you are making a joint claim, you can get two carer elements if both you and your partner satisfy the conditions, provided you are not caring for the same person. If you are both caring for the same person, you get one carer element. You can decide between you which partner should be entitled – eg, if it is necessary for your partner to be entitled to the carer element so that you can also get the limited capability for work or limited capability for work-related activity element. If you do not decide which one of you should be entitled to the carer element, the DWP will decide for you.[16]

If the person you care for dies, the carer element continues for the rest of the monthly UC assessment period in which the death occurred, and for the next two assessment periods. The rest of your maximum amount is also unaffected during this period.[17]

Rate of carer element

	per month
Carer	£148.61

Childcare costs element

A childcare costs element is included in your maximum amount if you are working (or have an offer of work) and you have childcare costs for recognised childcare – eg, a registered childminder.

The amount of the element is 70 per cent of your childcare costs, up to a maximum of £532.29 a month for one child and £912.50 a month for two or more children.[18] **Note:** at some point in the future, the amount will increase to 85 per cent. See CPAG's online service and *Welfare Rights Bulletin* for updates.

To get the childcare costs element you must be in paid work (there are no minimum hours) or have an offer of paid work that is due to start before the end of your next monthly assessment period for UC (see p186).[19] If you are a member of a couple, your partner must also be in paid work, unless s/he cannot provide childcare her/himself because s/he has limited capability for work (see Chapter 47), or s/he is caring for a severely disabled person and gets (or would be entitled to) CA (see p539), or s/he is temporarily absent from your household. **Note:** you stop counting as a couple if your partner is (or is expected to be) absent from Great Britain for more than six months.[20] If your partner is temporarily absent abroad, see p1569.

You are treated as still in paid work if you are getting statutory sick pay, statutory maternity pay, ordinary and additional statutory paternity pay, statutory adoption pay or maternity allowance. You are also treated as still in paid work if your work ended during the assessment period concerned or in the previous one. In effect, you continue to get childcare costs for one month after your work ends.[21]

In addition, you must meet all the following conditions.[22]

- You pay charges for 'relevant childcare' (see p254) for a child for whom you are responsible – ie, s/he normally lives with you.
- The child is aged under 16 or has not reached the 1st September following her/his 16th birthday.
- The childcare charges are to enable you to do paid work (or were to enable you to do paid work but that work has stopped).
- You report the charges to the DWP no later than the end of the monthly UC assessment period following the assessment period in which the charges were paid.

Part 3: General rules for means tested benefits
Chapter 13: Universal credit maximum amount
3. Elements

Relevant childcare

'Relevant childcare' means care for a child provided by the following.

In England:[23]
- a registered childcare provider – ie, someone registered with OFSTED under Part 3 of the Childcare Act 2006; or
- a school on school premises out of school hours (or at any time regarding a child who has not reached compulsory school age); or
- an official domiciliary care provider – ie, one registered with the Care Quality Commission.

In Scotland:[24]
- a registered childminder or similar provider of daycare – ie, registered as such under the Public Services Reform (Scotland) Act 2010; or
- a childcare agency under the Public Services Reform (Scotland) Act 2010; or
- a local authority registered to provide childminding or daycare under the Public Services Reform (Scotland) Act 2010.

In Wales:[25]
- a registered childminder or daycare provider – ie, registered under Part 2 of the Children and Families (Wales) Measure 2010; or
- someone providing daycare that would count for registration, were it not for the fact that it is provided in a care home, hospital, children's home, residential family centre or school; or
- someone providing childcare under a Welsh Assembly scheme for tax credit purposes; or
- out of school hours, a school on school premises or a local authority; or
- an official domiciliary care worker – ie, under the Domiciliary Care Agencies (Wales) Regulations 2004; or
- a foster parent (but not for the child who s/he is fostering) if, were it not for the fact that the child is too old, the childcare would count as registered childcare or daycare – ie, under Part 2 of the Children and Families (Wales) Measure 2010.

The following **does not count** as relevant childcare:[26]
- care provided by a 'close relative' of the child (ie, parent, parent-in-law, son, daughter, son-in-law, daughter-in-law, stepson, stepdaughter, stepbrother, stepsister, and a partner of any of these) wholly or mainly in the child's home;[27]
- care provided by a foster parent, foster carer or kinship carer for a child who the person is fostering or looking after as a kinship carer.

Rates of childcare costs element

	per month
Maximum for one child	£532.29
Maximum for two or more children	£912.50

Housing costs element

A housing costs element is included in your maximum amount for qualifying housing costs. Housing costs can be either rent or owner-occupier payments. See Chapter 22 for when you are entitled and the amount of your housing costs element.

Notes

2. **The standard allowance**
   1 Reg 36 UC Regs
   2 Reg 37 UC Regs

3. **Elements**
   3 Reg 24 UC Regs
   4 Reg 4 UC Regs
   5 Reg 24 UC Regs
   6 Reg 37 UC Regs
   7 Reg 27(4) UC Regs
   8 Reg 23(4) UC(TP) Regs
   9 Reg 24(3) UC(TP) Regs
   10 Reg 27 UC Regs
   11 Reg 27(1) UC Regs
   12 Reg 27(4) UC Regs
   13 Reg 23(5) and (6) UC(TP) Regs
   14 Reg 24(3) UC(TP) Regs
   15 Regs 29 and 30 UC Regs
   16 Reg 29(2) and (3) UC Regs
   17 Reg 37 UC Regs
   18 Regs 34 and 36 UC Regs
   19 Reg 32 UC Regs
   20 Reg 3(6) UC Regs
   21 Reg 32(2) UC Regs
   22 Reg 33 UC Regs
   23 Reg 35(2) UC Regs
   24 Reg 35(3) UC Regs
   25 Reg 35(4) UC Regs
   26 Reg 35(7) UC Regs
   27 Reg 2, definition of 'close relative', UC Regs

Chapter 14

Income: under pension credit age

This chapter covers:
1. Whose income counts (p257)
2. What counts as income (p257)
3. Earnings (p258)
4. Income other than earnings (p273)
5. Notional income (p288)
6. Working out weekly income (p291)

This chapter explains the rules for working out your weekly income for income support, income-based jobseeker's allowance (JSA) and income-related employment and support allowance. It also explains the income rules for housing benefit (HB) if you and your partner are under the qualifying age for pension credit (PC). For the rules for PC and for HB for those over the qualifying age for PC, see Chapter 15. For the rules on universal credit, see Chapter 16; for tax credits, see Chapter 64; for non-means-tested benefits, see Chapter 42; and for health benefits, see Chapter 30.

Note: unless otherwise stated, references to income-based JSA in this chapter also refer to joint-claim JSA.

Key facts
- Your entitlement to income support (IS), income-based jobseeker's allowance (JSA), income-related employment and support allowance (ESA) and housing benefit (HB) and the amount you get depends on how much income you have.
- Your own income counts and, if you are a member of a couple, your partner's income also counts. The income of your child is ignored for new claims and for most existing claims.
- Some income may be completely or partly ignored, or it may count in full.
- Some income may be treated as capital and some capital may be treated as income.
- If you get IS, income-based JSA or income-related ESA, you are entitled to the maximum HB, so you do not need to work out your income again for HB.

1. Whose income counts

Your income counts, and if you are a member of a couple, so does your partner's (see below). The income of your dependent children may affect your income support (IS) or income-based jobseeker's allowance (JSA) if you have been on benefit since before 6 April 2004 (see below).

Income of a partner

If you are a member of a couple (see p205), your partner's income is added to yours.[1]

Note: for housing benefit (HB), if you or your partner are getting IS, income-based JSA or income-related employment and support allowance (ESA), all of your (and your partner's) income is ignored.[2]

If you or your partner are under 18 and because of this, for IS, income-based JSA or income-related ESA, the rate of the normal personal allowance for a couple of £113.70 is reduced to £72.40 or £57.35 (see p224), an amount of income equivalent to the reduction is ignored.[3]

Income of a dependent child

Maintenance paid to or for a child is usually disregarded (see p276).

The income of a dependent child does *not* affect your means-tested benefit with one exception that applies to IS and income-based JSA.[4]

The exception where income of a dependent child may affect IS and income-based JSA applies if you have been getting benefit since before 6 April 2004 with a child included in your claim and you do not yet have an award of child tax credit (CTC). Once CTC is awarded, amounts for children are no longer included in your IS or income-based JSA and any income of a dependent child is ignored.

Even when you can still have a child included in your IS or JSA claim, if s/he has capital of over £3,000, you do not get benefit for her/him[5] (although you can still get a family premium) and her/his income is not counted as yours.[6] If your child has capital of £3,000 or less, any income is treated as yours but some may be disregarded – eg, earnings from part-time work of less than 16 hours a week or from any work if s/he is still at school or college. See p903, p927 and p935 of the 2012/13 edition of this *Handbook* for details.[7]

2. What counts as income

All income is taken into account for income support (IS), income-based jobseeker's allowance (JSA) and income-related employment and support allowance (ESA) unless it is specifically disregarded.

Part 3: General rules for means tested benefits
Chapter 14: Income: under pension credit age
3. Earnings

If you get IS, income-based JSA or income-related ESA, all your income is ignored for housing benefit (HB). All income is also ignored for HB if you come under the universal credit (UC) system and, exceptionally, can get HB and UC together. Otherwise, all income is taken into account for HB other than income that is specifically disregarded.

The way income from employment and self-employment is treated is explained below and on p264. Some of your earnings are disregarded (see p267). Most other types of income are taken into account, less any tax due on them.[8] For HB, changes in tax and national insurance rates and in the maximum rate of child tax credit or working tax credit may be ignored for up to 30 weeks (for earnings, see p259).[9]

Income only counts if it is paid to you for your own use, and does not count if you cannot prevent it being paid to a third party (eg, under an attachment of earnings order), although other payments for you made to a third party might count (see p290).[10]

Income is converted into a weekly amount (see p292).

Income or capital?

The difference between income and capital is not defined. Payments of income are normally made in respect of a specified period or periods and form, or are intended to form, part of a regular series of payments.[11] In this way, payments of income can usually be distinguished from payments of capital. However, sometimes a one-off payment can be income depending on what it is paid for – eg, a settlement for underpaid wages under equal pay legislation.[12] Some income is treated as capital (see p349) and some capital is treated as income (see p282).

3. Earnings

How earnings are treated depends on whether you are an employed earner (see below) or are self-employed (see p264). In either case, some of your earnings can be disregarded (see p267).

Earnings of employed earners

This section explains how any earnings received by you or your partner and, in some cases, a dependent child (see p257) are treated. The same rules apply to your (but not your partner's or child's) earnings if you are claiming contribution-based jobseeker's allowance (JSA – see p697). For the rules on earnings for non-means-tested benefits, see Chapter 42.

To work out how earnings are taken into account:

- check whether the payments count as earnings (see p260). In some cases, payments are treated as capital, as income other than earnings, or ignored altogether;
- calculate net earnings (see below);
- work out weekly net earnings (see p291);
- deduct the appropriate weekly earnings disregard (usually £5, £10, £20 or £25 – see p267) and, for housing benefit (HB), the additional earnings disregard (see p270) and disregard for childcare costs (see p270);
- for HB, the amount worked out as above is your weekly income from earnings in the benefit assessment. For income support (IS), income-based JSA and income-related employment and support allowance (ESA), work out the period covered by payments of earnings (see p293). Normally a payment counts from the date it is due to be paid and for the length of time it has been paid – eg, a month's wages count for a month, starting from the day they are due, at the weekly rate as calculated (see p291).

There are special rules for how payments affect benefit when you leave a job (see p261).

Calculating net earnings from employment

Both your 'gross' earnings and 'net' earnings must be calculated so that a proper assessment can be made of your income from employment.

Gross and net earnings

'**Gross earnings**' means the amount of earnings received from your employer less deductions for any expenses wholly, necessarily and exclusively incurred by you in order to carry out the duties of your employment.[13] See p260 for what counts as earnings and for examples of expenses that can be deducted.

'**Net earnings**' means your gross earnings less any deductions made for:[14]

– income tax;

– Class 1 national insurance (NI) contributions (but not Class 3 voluntary contributions[15]);

– half of any contribution you make towards a personal or occupational pension scheme.

For HB, if your earnings are estimated, the amount of tax and NI you would expect to pay on those earnings is estimated. This amount, plus half of any pension contribution you are paying, is then deducted.[16]

For HB, the local authority has the discretion to ignore changes in tax or NI contributions and the maximum rate of working tax credit (WTC) or child tax credit (CTC) for up to 30 benefit weeks. This can be used, for example, if Budget changes are not reflected in your actual income until several months later. When the changes are eventually taken into account and your benefit entitlement is

Part 3: General rules for means tested benefits
Chapter 14: Income: under pension credit age
3. Earnings

either increased or reduced accordingly, you are not treated as having been underpaid or overpaid benefit during the period of the delay.[17]

What counts as earnings

'Earnings' means 'any remuneration or profit derived from ... employment'. As well as your wages, this includes:[18]

- any bonus or commission (including tips);
- holiday pay (but see p261 if your job ends or you are off work);
- for HB, any statutory sick pay (SSP) or contractual sick pay.[19] For IS, income-based JSA and income-related ESA, all sick pay is treated as income other than earnings and, therefore, does not attract an earnings disregard and is counted in full less any tax, Class 1 NI contributions and half of any pension contributions;[20]
- for HB, any statutory maternity pay (SMP), statutory paternity pay (SPP) or statutory adoption pay (SAP), or any other payment made to you by your employer while you are on maternity, paternity or adoption leave.[21] For IS, income-based JSA and income-related ESA, all maternity, paternity or adoption pay is treated as income other than earnings and therefore does not attract an earnings disregard and is counted in full less any tax that is payable, Class 1 NI contributions and half of any pension contributions;[22]
- any payments made by your employer for expenses not 'wholly, exclusively and necessarily' incurred in carrying out your job, including any travel expenses to and from work, and any payments made to you for looking after members of your family. The latter can apply if you are looking after your child, even if they cannot be included in your claim for IS, income-based JSA or income-related ESA;
- a retainer (eg, payments during the school holidays if you work for the school meals service[23]) or a guarantee payment – eg, if you are working short time or laid off;[24]
- certain compensation payments in respect of the termination of your employment, including employment tribunal awards and pay in lieu of notice (see p261 for the way these are treated when you stop work). For IS/JSA/income-related ESA, compensatory refunds of contributions to an occupational scheme[25] are not treated as earnings;
- an equal pay settlement – eg, through a 'single-status agreement';[26]
- any payment of a non-cash voucher which is liable for Class 1 NI contributions.[27] Non-cash vouchers that are *not* liable for contributions are classed as payments in kind (see below).[28]

What does not count as earnings

Examples of payments not counted as earnings include the following.

- Payments in kind (eg, petrol) are ignored[29] unless you are on IS or income-based JSA and involved in a trade dispute (see p971), although the notional income rules may be applied instead (see p288).[30] Although non-cash vouchers which are liable for Class 1 NI contributions are not treated as payments in kind, vouchers which are not liable for contributions (eg, certain childcare and charitable vouchers) are treated as payments in kind and these are disregarded.[31]

- The value of any free accommodation provided as part of your job should be ignored.[32]
- An advance of earnings or a loan from your employer is treated as capital[33] (although it is still treated as earnings for IS or income-based JSA if you or your partner are involved in a trade dispute, or have been back at work after a dispute for no longer than 15 days).[34]
- Payments towards expenses that are 'wholly, exclusively and necessarily' incurred during the course of your work, such as travelling expenses, are ignored.[35] For example, deductions could be made for:
  - tools or work equipment;
  - special clothing or uniform;[36]
  - telephone costs (including rental);[37]
  - postage;
  - fuel costs (including standing charges);
  - secretarial expenses;[38]
  - running a car (including petrol, tax, insurance, repairs and maintenance and rental on a leased car).[39]

  If any expenditure serves a dual purpose for both business and private use, it should be apportioned as appropriate to the circumstances (and any determination by HM Revenue and Customs normally followed).[40]
- If you are a local councillor, travelling expenses and subsistence payments are (and basic allowances may be[41]) ignored as expenses 'wholly, exclusively and necessarily' incurred in your work.
- Earnings payable abroad which cannot be brought into Britain (eg, because of exchange control regulations) are ignored.[42] **Note:** if your earnings are paid in another currency, any bank charges for converting them into sterling are deducted before taking them into account.[43]
- Any occupational pension[44] counts as income other than earnings and the net amount is taken into account in full.[45] See p698 (and p623) for the occupational pension rules for contribution-based JSA (and contributory ESA).
- If you are a member of a territorial or reserve force, earnings while on annual continuous training are disregarded for up to 15 days a year to allow you to keep a minimum 10 pence a week IS, JSA or income-related ESA entitlement.[46]

Payments when you stop work

When you stop work and claim benefit, your final earnings are usually ignored with some exceptions. If you were claiming benefit while working, final earnings are generally taken into account.

Part 3: General rules for means tested benefits
Chapter 14: Income: under pension credit age
3. Earnings

Your job ends before benefit starts

If your employment ends before your entitlement to benefit begins, any payments that count as earnings (see p260), including wages, holiday pay (but see below) and pay in lieu of notice, are ignored for that benefit, except for the following payments, which are taken into account.[47]

- A retainer counts as earnings.
- If you were in full-time paid work, certain employment tribunal awards (and 'out-of-court' settlements) count as earnings, including:
  - compensation because of unfair dismissal;[48]
  - a 'protective' award when an employer fails to comply with redundancy procedures and, for JSA, a compensatory award in respect of trade union activity;[49]
  - for IS, income-related ESA and HB, pay under a continuation of contract award or for arrears of pay in respect of a reinstatement or re-engagement order.[50]

If you were in part-time work, these are all ignored for IS, income-related ESA and HB but count for JSA.

- Guarantee payments for workless days or while suspended on medical or maternity grounds count as earnings, including when awarded by an employment tribunal.[51]
- Arrears of sick pay, maternity, paternity and adoption pay (statutory or contractual) or lump-sum advance payments are taken into account for IS, JSA and income-related ESA as income, without any earnings disregard, from when they are paid for the same length of time covered by the arrears. For HB, they are ignored.[52]
- Statutory redundancy pay counts as capital.[53]
- Contractual redundancy pay (deducting an amount for statutory entitlement) is ignored completely for JSA.[54] For IS, income-related ESA and HB, it counts as capital unless, for IS and income-related ESA, you work part time and have not been paid all pay in lieu of notice due, in which case it is ignored.[55]
- Some redundancy schemes make periodic payments after leaving work. These are treated as income other than earnings.[56]
- Ex gratia payments and other kinds of compensation (other than employment tribunal awards) are treated in the same way as contractual redundancy pay.
- Holiday pay is usually ignored. However, if your job ends, it counts as capital if your contract provides for it to be payable more than four weeks after termination of employment – eg, in some cases if you leave without giving notice.[57]

For what counts as 'full-time paid work', see p987. For this rule, the IS definition also applies to income-related ESA (except for term-time workers whose hours are assessed under the JSA rule).[58]

Note: these rules only apply to benefits you claim after employment ends. So, for example, if you are already getting HB when you leave your job, but not IS, JSA or income-related ESA, your final earnings are disregarded for IS/JSA/income-related ESA in this way, but not for HB. See below for how final payments are treated when you are already getting benefit.

Example

Gina is made redundant from a full-time job on 31 May and leaves with one month's wages, her full four weeks' pay in lieu of notice, contractual redundancy pay of £5,000 and three days' holiday pay. All are due to be paid on 31 May. She claims IS and HB after her job ends. Final wages, pay in lieu of notice and holiday pay are ignored. Redundancy pay is treated as capital. Her capital is below the limit and she is entitled to benefit from 1 June.

You stop work but your job has not ended

If you stop work before your benefit begins but your employment has not ended (eg, you go on sick leave or maternity leave), statutory and contractual sick pay, maternity, paternity and adoption pay are taken into account as income without any earnings disregard for IS, JSA and income-related ESA.[59] For HB, they count as earnings with the usual disregard.[60] If holiday pay is due to be paid more than four weeks after you stopped work, it is treated as capital (unless, for IS/JSA, you are involved in a trade dispute). If it is paid less than four weeks after you stopped work, it is ignored.[61] All other payments that count as earnings are ignored, except for a retainer or guarantee payments for workless days or for medical or maternity suspension.[62]

Note: these rules only apply to benefits you claim after you stop work. If, for example, you are already getting HB when you stop work, but not IS/JSA/income-related ESA, your final earnings are ignored in this way for IS/JSA/income-related ESA, but not for HB.

If you are suspended from work, any earnings are taken into account as normal.

You were working while claiming benefit

If your job ends or you stop work before your entitlement to benefit begins, any payments that count as earnings are ignored with some exceptions, as described on p262. If, however, you were claiming benefit while you were in work, any payments made to you when that job ends are taken into account as earnings as follows.[63] For IS, JSA and income-related ESA, some different kinds of payments count consecutively in the order below,[64] but for HB final earnings are averaged as normal.

- Final earnings are taken into account as normal (including wages, bonuses and expenses that count as earnings).

Part 3: General rules for means tested benefits
Chapter 14: Income: under pension credit age
3. Earnings

- For IS, income-related ESA and HB, pay in lieu of notice is taken into account; for IS and income-related ESA, final earnings are taken into account first, followed by pay in lieu of notice.
- Contractual redundancy pay, ex gratia payments and other types of compensation (other than employment tribunal awards) above the level of entitlement to statutory redundancy pay:
  - for IS and income-related ESA, are treated as capital if you work out your notice or get full pay in lieu of notice. Otherwise, they are taken into account as earnings for one week only;
  - for JSA, are treated as earnings, together with pay in lieu of notice, up until the end of the fixed-term contract, if you had one, or until the end of the notice period (sometimes longer if the employer says it covers a longer period). For JSA, if none of the payment covers pay in lieu of notice or early termination of a fixed-term contract, the total of these payments covers a standard number of weeks arrived at by dividing the payment by the weekly maximum statutory redundancy (£464) if this is shorter than the notice period;
  - for HB, are treated as capital except for any amount representing loss of income which is taken into account as earnings.
- Holiday pay normally counts as earnings. However, it counts as capital if it is payable more than four weeks after employment ends or is interrupted – eg, if you are off sick before your employment ends. For IS, JSA and income-related ESA, it counts for the number of weeks covered by the holiday pay (not the number of working weeks[65]) starting after the period covered by other payments listed in the above three bullet points.
- An employment tribunal award (eg, for unfair dismissal) is taken into account as earnings.
- Arrears of sick pay, maternity, paternity and adoption pay count as earnings for HB, and as income other than earnings for IS, JSA and income-related ESA.[66]
- Statutory redundancy payments are treated as capital.

Example
Neelam has been getting HB while working part time. She earned £50 a week. She finishes work on 16 July and on that day is given £60, made up of £30 final wages and £30 holiday pay. For HB, the £60 wages and holiday pay are taken into account as normal, deducting the earnings disregard. She claims JSA on 17 July. For JSA, her final wages and holiday pay are ignored so none of the £60 is taken into account. Her JSA starts on 20 July after the three waiting days.

Earnings from self-employment

This section explains how any earnings from self-employment received by you or your partner and, in some cases, a dependent child (see p257) are treated. The same rules apply to your (but not your partner's or child's) earnings if you are claiming contribution-based JSA (see p697). For the rules on earnings for non-means-tested benefits, see Chapter 42.

To work out how earnings are taken into account:
- calculate net earnings (see below);
- work out your average earnings (see p266);
- deduct the appropriate weekly earnings disregard (usually £5, £10, £20 or £25 – see p267) and, for HB (if you qualify), the additional earnings disregard (see p270) and disregard for childcare costs (see p270).

Calculating net earnings

Your '**net profit**' over the period before your claim must be worked out. This consists of your self-employed earnings *minus*:[67]
- reasonable expenses (see below); *and*
- income tax and NI contributions; *and*
- half of any premium paid in respect of a personal pension scheme contract which is eligible for tax relief.[68]

Drawings from capital do not count as income whether the business is in profit or not.[69] If you receive payments for board and lodging charges, these do not count as earnings[70] but as other income (less any disregards, see p281).

If you are getting help with your business under a DWP scheme and this is classed as the 'self-employment route' (eg, the New Enterprise Allowance), income and expenses are treated differently (see p283).

Reasonable expenses

Expenses must be reasonable and 'wholly and exclusively' incurred for the purposes of your business.[71] This involves similar considerations to those that apply in the allowances permitted in the assessment of 'gross' earnings of employed earners. If a car or telephone, for example, is used partly for business and partly for private purposes, the costs of it can be apportioned and the amount attributable to business use can be deducted.[72]

Reasonable expenses include:[73]
- repayments of capital on loans for replacing equipment and machinery;
- repayment of capital on loans for, and income spent on, the repair of a business asset except where this is covered by insurance;
- interest on a loan taken out for the purposes of the business;
- excess of VAT paid over VAT received.

Reasonable expenses do not include:[74]
- any capital expenditure;
- depreciation;

Part 3: General rules for means tested benefits
Chapter 14: Income: under pension credit age
3. Earnings

- money for setting up or expanding the business – eg, the cost of adapting the business premises;
- any loss incurred before the beginning of the current assessment period. If the business makes a loss, the net profit is nil. The losses of one business cannot be offset against the profit of any other business in which you are engaged, or against your earnings as an employee[75] (although where two businesses or employments share expenses, these may be apportioned and offset);[76]
- capital repayments on loans taken out for business purposes;
- business entertainment expenses;
- for HB, debts (other than proven bad debts) – but the expenses of recovering a debt can be deducted.

Working out average earnings from self-employment

For **IS**, **income-based JSA** and **income-related ESA**, the weekly amount is the average of earnings:[77]

- over a period of any one year (normally the last year for which accounts are available);
- over a more appropriate period where you have recently taken up self-employment or there has been a change which will affect your business or for any other reason if a different period may enable any part or all of your income and expenditure to be calculated more accurately.

For **HB**, the amount of your weekly earnings is averaged out over an 'appropriate' period (usually based on your last year's trading accounts), which must not be longer than a year.[78]

For **all benefits**, if your earnings are royalties, copyright payments or payments under the Public Lending Right Scheme, the amount of earnings is divided by the weekly amount of benefit that would be payable if you had not received this income plus the amount that would be disregarded from those earnings (for income-related ESA, any contributory ESA that would be payable without this income is also taken into account).[79] For IS, income-based JSA and income-related ESA, you are not entitled to benefit for the resulting number of weeks. For HB, earnings are taken into account for the resulting number of weeks.

If you stop doing self-employed work, any earnings from that work are disregarded except for royalties and copyright and Public Lending Right Scheme payments.[80]

Childminders

Childminders, in practice, are always treated as self-employed. Your net profit is deemed to be one-third of your earnings less income tax, your NI contributions and half of personal pension scheme contributions (see p265).[81] The rest of your earnings are completely ignored.

Disregarded earnings

Some of your earnings from employment or self-employment are disregarded and do not affect your benefit. The amount of the 'disregard' depends on your circumstances. For IS, income-based JSA and HB, the three main levels of disregard are £25, £20 or £5/£10. For HB, there is an additional disregard depending on the hours you work, a childcare costs disregard (see p270) and a permitted work disregard.

For income-related ESA, the main level of disregard is £20. However, different rules apply if you are doing 'permitted work' (see below).

For the amount of disregarded earnings for contribution-based JSA, see p1018.

Disregards for income-related employment and support allowance

Permitted work disregard

- All your earnings are disregarded from '**permitted work**' (see p1019) up to whichever earnings limit applies: £20 or £101. (Only £20 can be disregarded from self-employed earnings from royalties, copyright payments or Public Lending Right Scheme payments.)[82]
- If your earnings are less than the £20 or £101 limit, up to £20 of what is left can be disregarded from your partner's earnings.[83]

Note: earnings for permitted work (for both contributory and income-related ESA) are assessed in the same way as earnings are generally for income-related ESA described in this chapter.[84]

£20 disregard

Twenty pounds of your earnings (including those of your partner) is disregarded if:[85]
- you are doing work you may do while claiming ESA (see p1018), but only if it is:
  - as a councillor; *or*
  - as a disability member of the First-tier Tribunal. If you are also doing 'permitted work', instead of the £20 disregard, any unused permitted work disregard up to £20 can be deducted from these tribunal earnings; *or*
  - during an emergency to protect someone or to prevent serious damage to property or livestock; *or*
  - while receiving assistance in pursuing self-employment under a government scheme;
- your partner is in part-time employment of under 24 hours a week (but if you are doing permitted work, see above);
- your partner would be treated as not being in full-time paid work for IS purposes (other than if this is because of qualifying for mortgage interest run-on). See the list on p995; *or*

Part 3: General rules for means tested benefits
Chapter 14: Income: under pension credit age
3. Earnings

• your partner is working but does not count as being in full-time paid work because s/he:
  - is childminding in her/his home; *or*
  - is a carer (under the rules for who can claim IS, see p29); *or*
  - is receiving assistance under the 'self-employment route' – eg, New Enterprise Allowance; *or*
  - is an auxiliary coastguard, part-time firefighter, part-time member of a lifeboat crew or member of the Territorial Army; *or*
  - is working as a councillor; *or*
  - would not qualify for JSA on the grounds that s/he has been involved in a trade dispute (see p971), or it is the first 15 days following her/his return to work after having been involved in a trade dispute.

Disregards for other means-tested benefits

£25 disregard

Lone parents on HB have £25 of their earnings ignored.[86] This does not apply to anyone claiming IS, income-based JSA or income-related ESA.

£20 disregard

For IS, income-based JSA and HB, £20 of your earnings (including those of your partner) is disregarded if:

• for IS or income-based JSA, you are a lone parent;[87]
• you or your partner qualify for a disability premium (see p229).[88] For IS and income-based JSA, you are treated as qualifying for the premium if you would do so but for the fact that you are in hospital;
• for HB, you or your partner qualify for a severe disability premium, or the work-related activity or support component (see p233 and p241);[89]
• you or your partner qualify for a carer premium (see p237). The disregard applies to the carer's earnings. For a couple, if both partners get the carer premium, £20 is disregarded from their combined earnings. If you are the carer and the claimant and your earnings are less than £20, up to £5 (£10 for HB) of the disregard can be used on your partner's earnings (or all of what is left of it if your partner's earnings are from one of the services listed below) – but the total disregard cannot be more than £20;[90]
• you or your partner are an auxiliary coastguard, part-time firefighter, part-time member of a lifeboat crew or member of the Territorial Army.[91] If you earn less than £20 for doing any of these services, you can use up to £5 (for HB up to £10, if you have a partner) of the disregard on another job[92] or on a partner's earnings from another job;[93]
• for IS and income-based JSA only, you are a member of a couple, your benefit would include a disability premium but for the fact that one of you qualifies for the higher pensioner premium (see p232), and one of you is under the

qualifying age for PC (see p78) and either of you are in employment. You are treated as qualifying for the higher pensioner premium if you would do so but for the fact that you are in hospital;[94]

- for IS and income-based JSA only, you or your partner qualify for the higher pensioner premium (see p232) and, immediately before reaching the qualifying age for PC (see p78), you or your partner were in part-time employment and you were entitled to a £20 disregard because of qualifying for a disability premium. Since reaching the qualifying age for PC, you or your partner must have continued in part-time employment, although breaks of up to eight weeks when you were not getting IS, income-based JSA or income-related ESA are ignored. You are treated as qualifying for the higher pensioner premium even if you are in hospital.[95]

If you qualify under more than one category, you still have a maximum of only £20 of your earnings disregarded.

Basic £5 or £10 disregard

For IS, income-based JSA and HB, if you do not qualify for a £25 or £20 disregard (or, for HB, the permitted work disregard), £5 of your earnings is disregarded if you are single. If you claim as a member of a couple, £10 of your total earnings is disregarded – whether or not you are both working.[96]

Permitted work disregard for housing benefit

If you or your partner are doing 'permitted work' (see p1019) and getting contributory ESA, incapacity benefit (IB), severe disablement allowance (SDA) or NI credits for limited capability for work or incapacity, the permitted work earnings limit for that benefit or credit (either £20 or £101) is also disregarded from earnings for HB.[97] This is instead of the usual disregard of £5, £10, £20 or £25.

For couples, this permitted work disregard applies if either you or your partner are doing permitted work. If earnings from permitted work are less than the limit, you can use up the rest:

- on your partner's earnings, up to a maximum of £20 or up to the limit if s/he is also doing permitted work, but there is only one disregard between you; *or*
- on your own earnings from other work (see p1018 for other work you may do while claiming one of these benefits). If you are a lone parent, the £25 disregard applies instead of the £20 permitted work disregard.

Note: there is also an earnings disregard for permitted work for income-related ESA but not for IS.

Part 3: General rules for means tested benefits
Chapter 14: Income: under pension credit age
3. Earnings

Additional disregard for housing benefit

For **HB only**, whichever earnings disregard applies is increased by £17.10 if:[98]

- you or your partner receive the 30-hour element as part of your (or your partner's) WTC (see p1403); *or*
- you or your partner are aged 25 or over and work 30 hours a week or more on average; *or*
- you or your partner work 16 hours or more a week on average and your HB includes the family premium (see p228); *or*
- you are a lone parent and work 16 hours or more a week on average; *or*
- you or your partner work 16 hours or more a week on average and your HB includes the disability premium (see p229), or the work-related activity component or the support component (see p241). For couples, the partner for whom the premium/component is awarded must be working 16 hours a week or more on average.

The additional earnings disregard does not apply if your total earnings are less than the total of £17.10 plus any earnings disregard and childcare costs disregard (see below). In this case, £17.10 is disregarded from any WTC which is awarded to you or your partner, but the earnings disregard is not increased.

Note: as with the ordinary earnings disregards, only one additional disregard can be allowed from your (or your partner's) earnings.

Example
Owen and Mia are a couple with one child aged eight. Owen gets contributory ESA and HB. Mia works part time for 16 hours a week earning £101.
The amount of Mia's earnings taken into account for HB is £63.90 a week. From her £101 wages, £20 is disregarded because Owen's ESA includes a work-related activity component, and £17.10 is disregarded because they have a child and Mia works enough hours for the additional disregard.

Childcare costs for housing benefit

Note: for **IS, income-based JSA** and **income-related ESA**, no allowance is made for any childcare charges you may have to pay.

For **HB**, an allowance of up to £175 a week for one child, or up to £300 a week for two or more children, can be deducted from your (or your partner's) earnings (from employment or self-employment) for childcare costs if you are:[99]

- a lone parent working 16 hours a week or more; *or*
- a couple and both of you work 16 hours a week or more, or one of you works 16 hours a week or more and the other is 'incapacitated' (see p272), or is in hospital or prison.

Lone parents and couples can still make this deduction for childcare costs if they are off work sick, although for lone parents it stops after 28 weeks (see p272).

If you or your partner (if you have one) also get WTC or CTC, in some circumstances your earnings (and, if applicable, those of your partner) and the WTC/CTC are added together before the deduction for childcare costs is made. This applies if your earnings, once other HB deductions have been taken off, are less than the deduction for childcare costs.[100]

The childcare allowance only applies to charges you pay for certain types of childcare provided for any child(ren) in your family under the age of 15 (or 16 if s/he is disabled). A child is not treated as having reached the age of 15/16 until the day before the first Monday in September following her/his 15th/16th birthday.[101] A child is defined as disabled if s/he is:[102]

- in receipt of disability living allowance (DLA), personal independence payment (PIP), armed forces independence payment, or payment has been suspended because s/he is a hospital inpatient; *or*
- registered as blind, or was taken off the register before the first Monday in September following her/his 16th birthday, but no more than one year and 28 weeks before then.

The childcare must be provided:[103]

- by a registered childminder or other registered childcare provider (such as a nursery or local authority daycare service); *or*
- out of school hours for children between the ages of eight and 15/16, by a school on school premises or a local authority – eg, an out-of-hours or holiday play scheme; *or*
- by another relevant childcare provider (see p1407 – these are the same as for WTC).

You cannot include charges for care provided by a relative of the child in the child's own home even if s/he is a registered childminder, nor charges paid by you to your partner or by your partner to you for a child in your family. Charges for compulsory education do not count.

If you or your partner are on maternity, paternity or adoption leave, you are treated as working, and so are able to deduct childcare charges if you (or your partner):[104]

- were working in the week immediately before the maternity, paternity or adoption leave began; *and*
- are entitled to SMP, SPP, SAP or maternity allowance (MA) (see Chapters 38 and 34), or are getting IS because you are on paternity leave.

You are no longer treated as working and thus cannot get childcare charges deducted when:

- the maternity, paternity or adoption leave comes to an end; *or*

Part 3: General rules for means tested benefits
Chapter 14: Income: under pension credit age
3. Earnings

- if you are not receiving the childcare element of WTC, you or your partner stop getting SMP, SPP, SAP or MA, or IS because you are on paternity leave; *or*
- if you are receiving the childcare element of WTC when you stop getting SMP, SPP, SAP or MA or IS because you are on paternity leave, you stop getting the childcare element of WTC.

You can deduct charges for childcare for the new child in your family while you are still on maternity, paternity or adoption leave.

Childcare costs and ill health or disability

Provided you were working at least 16 hours a week immediately before you started getting one of the following benefits, you can still deduct charges for childcare while off work sick for the first 28 weeks while you are getting:[105]

- SSP;
- ESA;
- NI credits for limited capability for work.

After 28 weeks, lone parents who are off work sick can no longer deduct childcare charges, but couples can do so (before or after 28 weeks) if one of them works 16 hours or more a week and the other is treated as 'incapacitated'.

Incapacitated

You (or your partner) are treated as **'incapacitated'** if:[106]

– you get ESA which includes a support or work-related activity component; *or*

– you get short-term higher rate or long-term IB; *or*

– you get SDA; *or*

– you get attendance allowance, DLA, PIP, armed forces independence payment or constant attendance allowance (or an equivalent award under the war pensions or industrial injuries schemes) or you would receive one of these benefits but for the fact that you (or your partner) are in hospital; *or*

– you have an invalid carriage or similar vehicle; *or*

– your HB includes a disability premium, support component or work-related activity component for the incapacitated person's incapacity or limited capability for work; *or*

– you (but not your partner) have been treated either as having limited capability for work or as incapable of work for a continuous period of 196 days or more (disregarding any break of up to 84 or 56 days respectively).

Calculating childcare costs

The costs to be taken into account are estimated over whatever period, not exceeding a year, that will give the best estimate of the average weekly charge based on information to be provided by the childminder or care provider.

Points to note

- These rules do *not* apply to IS, JSA or income-related ESA and *only* apply to HB. There are also separate childcare costs rules for non-means-tested benefits (see p879).
- The maximum amount that can be deducted for one child is £175, even if the actual cost of your childcare is more. Even if you have to pay for childcare for more than two children or the actual cost is more, £300 is the maximum.
- The costs of any childcare outside the child's home provided by a relative (other than your partner – but a former partner, who may even be the child's parent, is not excluded) may be allowed, provided s/he is a registered childminder.
- It is not necessary for the childcare to be provided only while you are at work, nor for it to be work-related, and there is no requirement for the charges to be reasonable.

4. Income other than earnings

As well as income from earnings, most other forms of income are taken into account in full less any tax due. To work out the weekly income to take into account, check whether the payment can be disregarded in part or in full, deduct any tax due and work out the weekly amount (see p291). Where a taxable benefit or other unearned income is not taxed at source and you have not yet had a tax assessment, ask HM Revenue and Customs (HMRC) for a forecast of tax due on that income; otherwise the DWP itself needs to calculate how much tax to deduct.[107]

Benefits and tax credits

Benefits and tax credits that are taken into account

The following count in full:

- carer's allowance (CA);
- child tax credit (CTC) counts in full for housing benefit (HB), but is disregarded for income support (IS), income-based jobseeker's allowance (JSA) and income-related employment and support allowance (ESA). See p276 if your CTC is reduced to recover a tax credit overpayment;
- child's payment under the Armed Forces Forces Compensation Scheme (but if it is paid for a dependent child it is usually ignored – see p257);
- contribution-based JSA;
- contributory ESA. If ESA is paid at a reduced rate because of a sanction, it is still the full rate that counts;[108]
- incapacity benefit (IB) and severe disablement allowance (SDA);

Part 3: General rules for means tested benefits
Chapter 14: Income: under pension credit age
4. Income other than earnings

- industrial injuries benefits, except constant attendance allowance and exceptionally severe disablement allowance which are disregarded;
- maternity allowance (MA);
- retirement pensions;
- statutory sick pay (SSP), statutory maternity pay (SMP), statutory paternity pay (SPP) and statutory adoption pay (SAP) count for IS, income-based JSA and income-related ESA only, less any Class 1 national insurance (NI) contributions and half of any pension contributions and any tax.[109] These are treated as earnings for HB and, therefore, may benefit from an earnings disregard (see p267);[110]
- widow's pension, bereavement allowance and industrial death benefit;
- working tax credit (WTC) is taken into account (but see p276 if a tax credit overpayment is being deducted):
  - for IS, income-based JSA and income-related ESA;
  - for HB, except for those whose earnings are too low to use the whole £17.10 additional full-time earnings disregard (see p270). In this case, £17.10 is disregarded from your WTC instead of your earnings. You must satisfy the conditions for the additional earnings disregard and have earnings of less than £17.10 plus whichever other earnings disregard applies plus any childcare costs disregard.[111]

Benefits and tax credits that are not taken into account

The following are ignored completely:
- armed forces independence payment;
- attendance allowance (AA);[112]
- child benefit.[113] However, for IS and income-based JSA, it is taken into account if you have been getting IS or income-based JSA since before 6 April 2004 with a child already included in your claim (ie, you still have amounts for children in your claim) and you do not yet have an award of CTC. In this case, child benefit continues to be taken into account until your CTC award begins;[114]
- Christmas bonus;[115]
- constant attendance allowance, exceptionally severe disablement allowance or severe disablement occupational allowance paid because of an injury at work or a war injury;[116]
- CTC is ignored completely for IS, income-based JSA and income-related ESA.[117] CTC is taken into account in full for HB;
- disability living allowance (DLA) care component and mobility component;[118]
- guardian's allowance;[119]
- HB;[120]
- IS, income-based JSA and income-related ESA are ignored for HB.[121] There are special HB rules for these claimants (see p109);
- mobility supplement under the War Pensions Scheme;[122]

- personal independence payment (PIP) daily living component and mobility component;[123]
- any extra-statutory payment made to you to compensate for non-payment of IS, income-based JSA, income-related ESA, universal credit, mobility supplement, AA, DLA or PIP;[124]
- social fund payments and replacement local welfare provision (see p829).[125] They are also disregarded as capital indefinitely;[126]
- any supplementary payments to war widows, widowers or surviving civil partners for pre-1973 service;[127]
- any increase for a child dependant is ignored for IS or income-based JSA if you get CTC and for income-related ESA. For all benefits, any increase for adult or child dependants who are not members of your family paid with a benefit (eg, IB or retirement pension) or a service pension is ignored;[128]
- any payment made by the DWP to compensate for the loss of HB;[129]
- any payment in consequence of a reduction in liability for council tax, including from a council tax reduction scheme.[130]

Benefits that are partly taken into account

For HB only, widowed mother's allowance and widowed parent's allowance have £15 ignored.[131]

The following benefits have £10 ignored:[132]

- for IS, income-based JSA and income-related ESA only, widowed mother's allowance and widowed parent's allowance;
- war disablement pension;
- guaranteed income payment and survivor's guaranteed income payment under the Armed Forces Forces Compensation Scheme (or if another pension reduces the payment to below £10, ignore the remainder from the pension);
- war widow's, widower's or surviving civil partner's pension;
- an extra-statutory payment made instead of the above pensions;
- similar payments made by another country;
- a pension from Germany or Austria paid to the victims of Nazi persecution.

Even if you have more than two payments which attract a £10 disregard, only £20 in all can be ignored.[133] However, the £10 disregard allowed on the payments above is in addition to the total disregard of any mobility supplement or AA (ie, constant attendance allowance, exceptionally severe disablement allowance and severe disablement occupational allowance) paid as part of a war disablement pension.

The £10 disregard may overlap with other disregards such as on student loans and access funds (see p928 and p932) when a combined maximum of £20 is allowed.

Local authorities are given a limited discretion to increase the £10 disregard on war disablement, war widows' or widowers' pensions and the guaranteed income

Part 3: General rules for means tested benefits
Chapter 14: Income: under pension credit age
4. Income other than earnings

payment and survivor's guaranteed income payment, when assessing income for HB.[134] Some local authorities disregard the full amount of these pensions, and some do not increase the disregard at all, so check your own local authority's policy. It has been held that a local authority must at least consider the nature and purpose of such pensions when deciding whether or not to disregard them, and the courts have indicated that it may be appropriate to apply a disregard to retrospective awards.[135]

Benefit delays

Problems can arise where a decision maker tries to take into account a benefit you are not receiving (such as child benefit) because it has been delayed. In such a case, the benefit should not be treated as income possessed by you. For IS, income-based JSA and income-related ESA, you should get your full benefit and leave the DWP to deduct the difference from arrears of the delayed benefit when it is eventually awarded.[136]

For the treatment of payments of arrears of certain benefits and tax credits, see p355.

Tax credit overpayments

For **HB**, if a tax credit overpayment is being recovered, it is the amount of your tax credit award less any reduction to recover the overpayment that is taken into account.[137] Because HB entitlement is based on the amount of tax credits you are actually paid at the time, local authorities do not treat you as having been underpaid HB for the earlier period when tax credits were being overpaid, so your HB award is not revised for that period.[138]

For **IS, income-based JSA** and **income-related ESA**, the rules are less clear, but the intention seems to be to take into account the actual award paid – eg, after any overpayment has been deducted.[139]

Maintenance payments

If you get **child maintenance** for a child who is a member of your family, it is all ignored if it is made by the child's parent (who is not your partner) or by another 'liable relative' (see p277).[140]

Child maintenance payments include:
- any payment made voluntarily;
- payments under a court order or consent order;
- child support maintenance (assessed by the Child Support Agency or Child Maintenance Service);
- in Scotland, payments under a registered maintenance agreement.

Note: arrears of regular child support maintenance should count as income not capital.[141]

Other kinds of maintenance

If you get another kind of maintenance payment from a former partner – eg, maintenance for yourself:[142]

- £15 is ignored for HB if you have a family premium included in your HB (if you get maintenance from more than one person only £15 of the total is ignored);
- for other benefits, it is regarded as a 'liable relative' payment and usually counts in full (see below).

Liable relative

A **'liable relative'** is:[143]

– a spouse, civil partner, former spouse or civil partner; or

– parent of a child who is a member of your family; or

– someone who can reasonably be treated as the child's father because of the financial support he makes.

For IS, income-based JSA and income-related ESA, any payment from a liable relative other than child maintenance is taken into account in full as income, whether it is paid regularly or as a lump sum, with some exceptions as follows.[144]

- Payments made directly to someone else and not to you (ie, to a third party) are taken into account as maintenance if they are for certain normal living expenses (food, clothing, footwear), for certain bills (fuel, council tax, water charges), for rent met by HB or for housing costs met by IS, JSA or ESA (such as mortgage interest payments). Payments for other kinds of expenses such as mortgage capital repayments paid directly to the mortgage lender or TV license payments paid directly are ignored.[145] This means it can be better for you if your ex-partner pays these other kinds of expenses directly rather than to you. If you use your maintenance payments to pay the mortgage yourself, all of it is taken into account as your income, not just the amount for mortgage interest, so you will get less benefit.
- Payments in kind are ignored – eg, food, holidays, clothing (although not if you are involved in a trade dispute).
- Gifts of up to £250 in total in any period of 52 weeks (eg, a birthday and Christmas present) are not taken into account as maintenance but may count as capital.
- If you have already spent a payment before the DWP makes its decision about the effect on your benefit, then the payment is ignored as long as you did not deliberately get rid of the money in order to claim or increase your benefit (the issues are the same as the deprivation of income/capital rule on p359).
- A payment from a 'disposition of property' because of divorce, separation, nullity or dissolution of a civil partnership is not taken into account as maintenance (so is not treated as income) but would normally count as capital. This applies, for example, where your former partner buys out your interest in

Part 3: General rules for means tested benefits
Chapter 14: Income: under pension credit age
4. Income other than earnings

a home so you get a lump sum settlement instead of a share of the property itself.[146]

- Payments for a child who is not a member of your household (eg, the child is looked after by the local authority and is not living with you, or is in custody) do not count as maintenance but they will nevertheless count as your income if you keep the money or spend it on yourself, but they should be ignored if you spend the money on the child.[147]
- A payment made after the liable relative has died no longer counts as maintenance (so is not automatically treated as income) but would still be taken into account as income or capital under the normal rules.

If you get payments towards maintenance from someone who is not a liable relative (eg, a grandparent), this normally counts as a voluntary payment and is ignored (see p279).

If you pay maintenance

If you *pay* maintenance to a former partner or a child not living with you, your payments are not disregarded for the purpose of calculating your income for any benefits.[148]

Student loans and grants

For the special rules on the treatment of student grants and loans and other payments made to students, see Chapter 44.

Adoption, fostering, guardianship and residence order payments

Adoption allowance

An adoption allowance is disregarded in full except in the two cases below.[149]

- If the adoption allowance is paid for a child who is not a member of your family (eg, because the adoption order has not yet been granted), it is fully disregarded in England.[150] In Scotland and Wales, any amount you spend on the child is disregarded and any you keep or use for yourself is taken into account.[151]
- For IS and income-based JSA, if you have been getting benefit since before 6 April 2004 with a child included in your claim and do not yet have an award of CTC, the adoption allowance is taken into account in full up to the level of the adopted child's personal allowance and any disabled child premium.[152] Above that level it is ignored. If the child has capital over £3,000, you get no benefit for that child and all the adoption allowance is disregarded.[153] Seek advice to check whether you would be better off claiming CTC instead.

Fostering allowance

The way a fostering allowance is treated depends on whether the arrangement is official or private. If a child is placed or boarded out with you by the local authority or a voluntary organisation under specific legal provisions,[154] the child is not counted as a member of your family (see p214) and any fostering allowances you receive while the child is placed with you should be ignored altogether.[155] If the fostering arrangement is a private one, any money you receive from the child's parent(s) is counted as maintenance (see p276). If the money is not from the child's parent(s), you should probably be treated as a childminder (see p266).

Residence order allowance and similar payments

If you are paid a residence order allowance by the local authority (in England and Wales), this is treated in the same way as an adoption allowance (see p278).[156] Any payments made by the biological parents count as maintenance (see p276). In Scotland, kinship care payments can be made under different legal provisions. If made under s22 of the Children (Scotland) Act 1995 or reg 33 of the Looked After Children (Scotland) Regulations 2009, they are ignored altogether, but if made under s50 of the Children Act 1975, they are treated in the same way as an adoption allowance.[157]

Special guardianship allowance

The law treats a special guardianship allowance, payable in England and Wales for a child who is a member of your family, in the same way as an adoption allowance (see p278), but official guidance advises that it should be fully disregarded for IS and income-based JSA.[158]

Charitable, voluntary and personal injury payments

Payments from the Macfarlane Trust and similar funds

Any payments from the following funds, including payments in kind, are disregarded in full:[159]
- the Macfarlane Trusts, the Fund, the Eileen Trust, the Skipton Fund, the Caxton Foundation or MFET Ltd (for people infected with HIV or hepatitis C through blood products and NHS treatment);
- the Independent Living Funds.

Payments can still be disregarded if you give them to certain relatives or they inherit them from you after your death. Also disregarded are payments from the London Bombings Relief Fund, although these are generally made as lump-sum capital payments.

Any income or capital that derives from any such payments is also disregarded.

Part 3: General rules for means tested benefits
Chapter 14: Income: under pension credit age
4. Income other than earnings

Other payments

Most other charitable or voluntary payments that are made irregularly and are intended to be made irregularly are treated as capital and are unlikely to affect your claim unless they take your capital above the limit.[160] However, if you are on IS or income-based JSA, they count as income if you are involved in a trade dispute and, for IS only, for the first 15 days following your return to work after a dispute (see p971).[161]

Payments made on a regular basis

Charitable and voluntary payments and certain personal injury payments (see below) are ignored if they are made, or are due to be made, regularly.[162]

A '**voluntary payment**' is one given without getting anything back in return.[163]

For IS and income-based JSA, these payments are not disregarded where you are involved in a trade dispute and, for IS only, for the first 15 days following your return to work after a trade dispute.

Payments from a former partner, or the parent of your child, are dealt with as maintenance (see p276).

The **personal injury payments** that qualify under the above rules are:[164]

- payments from a trust fund set up out of money paid because of any personal injury to you; *or*
- payments under an annuity purchased either under an agreement or court order set up because of any personal injury to you, or from money paid because of any personal injury to you; *or*
- payments you get under an agreement or court order because of any personal injury to you. This does not include an occupational pension – eg, if you have retired early because of personal injury.[165]

See also p290 for payments made to someone else on your behalf and p287 for payments disregarded under miscellaneous income.

Concessionary coal to former British Coal workers and their surviving partners is ignored (except to strikers). Cash in lieu of coal counts in full.[166]

Income from tenants and lodgers

How income from tenants is treated depends on whether or not you live in the same property.

Lettings without board

If you let out a room(s) in your home to tenants, sub-tenants or licensees under a formal contractual arrangement, £20 of your weekly charge for each tenant, sub-tenant or licensee (and her/his family) is ignored.[167] The balance counts as income.

If someone shares your home under an informal arrangement, any payment s/he makes to you for living and accommodation costs is ignored,[168] but a non-dependant deduction may be made from any HB or housing costs paid with IS/income-based JSA/income-related ESA (see p116 and p450).

Boarders

If you have a boarder(s) on a commercial basis in your own home, and the boarder or any member of her/his family is not a close relative of yours, the first £20 of the weekly charge is ignored and half of any balance remaining is then taken into account as your income.[169] For HB, this applies even if the boarder is a close relative and it is not a commercial arrangement. However, there might still be a non-dependant deduction for her/him (see p116). This disregard applies for each boarder you have. The charge must normally include at least some meals.[170] If you have a business partner, even though your gross income includes just your share of the weekly charge to boarders, you still get the full disregard of £20 plus half the excess for each boarder.[171]

Note: if you let part of your home, any income left after applying the above disregards may be considered to be intended to be used to meet any housing costs of your own which are not met by IS, income-based JSA, income-related ESA or HB, and may, therefore, be offset accordingly (see p285).[172]

Tenants in other properties

If you have a freehold interest in a property other than your home and you let it out, the rent is normally treated as capital.[173] This rule also applies if you have a leasehold interest in another property which you are sub-letting. The full rent would count initially (as well as the capital value of the property itself) but if you spend some on a debt that is immediately repayable (eg, a mortgage) after a period (eg, a month for monthly paid rent), only what remains continues to count as capital. If you spend it on something else to deliberately increase your benefit, the notional capital rules could treat you as still having the money (see p359).[174]

The rent is treated as income if the property you let is in one of the categories where the capital value is disregarded (see p351) and, in this case, the expenses listed below are deducted from the income.

Income from capital

In general, actual income generated from capital (eg, interest on savings) is ignored as income[175] but counts as *capital*[176] from the date you are due to receive it. However, income derived from the following categories of disregarded capital (see p350) is treated as income:[177]

- your home;
- your former home, if you are estranged, divorced or your civil partnership has ended;

Part 3: General rules for means tested benefits
Chapter 14: Income: under pension credit age
4. Income other than earnings

- property which you have acquired for occupation as your home but into which you have not yet been able to move;
- property which you intend to occupy as your home but which needs essential repairs or alterations;
- property occupied wholly or partly by a partner or relative of any member of your family who has reached the qualifying age for PC (see p78) or is incapacitated;
- property occupied by your former partner, but not if you are estranged, divorced or your civil partnership has ended;
- property for sale;
- property which you are taking legal steps to obtain to occupy as your home;
- your business assets;
- a trust of personal injury compensation.

Some expenses are deducted from this income. Income from any of the above categories (other than your current home, business assets or a personal injuries trust) is ignored up to the amount of the total mortgage repayments (ie, capital and interest, and any payments that are a condition of the mortgage such as insurance or an endowment policy),[178] council tax and water charges paid in respect of the property for the same period over which the income is received.[179]

Tariff income from capital

If your capital is over a certain level, you are treated as having an assumed income from it, called your '**tariff income**'. You are assumed to have an income of £1 for every £250, or part of £250, by which your capital exceeds £6,000 but does not exceed £16,000.[180]

For IS, income-based JSA, income-related ESA and HB, if you are in a care home or similar accommodation (see p343), tariff income applies between £10,000 and £16,000.

Capital that counts as income

Sometimes the rules treat capital as though it is income.

The following count as income:
- instalments of capital outstanding when you claim benefit, if they would bring you over the capital limit. For IS, income-based JSA and income-related ESA, the instalments to be counted are any outstanding, either when your benefit claim is decided, or when you are first due to be paid benefit, whichever is earlier or at the date of any subsequent supersession.[181] For HB, it is any instalments outstanding when your claim is made or treated as made, or when your benefit is revised or superseded.[182] The outstanding instalments count as income by spreading them over the number of weeks between each instalment;[183]
- any payment from an annuity[184] (see p284 for when this is disregarded);

- any professional and career development loan paid under s2 of the Employment and Training Act 1973 (see p931);[185]
- for IS only, a tax refund if you or your partner have returned to work after a trade dispute (see p971);[186]
- periodic payments made under an agreement or court order for any personal injury to you (see p279 for when these are disregarded);[187]
- some lump sums from liable relatives (see p277).

Capital which is counted as income cannot also be treated as producing a tariff income (see p282).[188]

Sometimes you may find that withdrawals from a capital sum are treated as income.[189] This is most likely if the sum was intended to help cover living expenses over a particular period – eg, a bank loan taken out by a mature student. If this is not the intended use of any capital sum, dispute the decision. Even if the sum is intended for living expenses, argue that, unless it is actually paid in instalments, it should be treated as capital.[190] A loan that you have an obligation to repay immediately should not be treated as your income (or capital), however it is paid.[191]

Income tax refunds

PAYE refunds (employed earners) and tax refunds under Schedule D (self-employed) are treated as capital.[192]

For IS and JSA, tax refunds paid during a trade dispute are treated as income and taken into account.[193] For IS only, if you or your partner have returned to work after a trade dispute (see p971), tax refunds are treated as income and are taken into account in full.[194]

Income from employment and training programmes

Payments from employment or training programmes under s2 of the Employment and Training Act 1973 or s2 of the Enterprise and New Towns (Scotland) Act 1990 are treated as follows.[195]

The following payments are taken into account:
- for ESA, those made as a substitute for ESA or JSA; for other benefits, payments made as a substitute for IS, JSA or ESA – eg, a training allowance;
- those intended for certain living costs while you are participating in a scheme to enhance your employment prospects. Payments for food, ordinary clothing or footwear, fuel, rent met by HB, housing costs met by IS, JSA or income-related ESA, council tax or water charges are all taken into account.

All other payments are disregarded – eg:
- travel expenses;
- training premium;

Part 3: General rules for means tested benefits
Chapter 14: Income: under pension credit age
4. Income other than earnings

- childcare expenses;
- special needs payments;
- expenses for participating in a specified scheme for assisting people to obtain employment (see p1093);[196]
- New Enterprise Allowance weekly allowance.

For ESA, any payment for expenses incurred in complying with a requirement to undertake work-related activity (see p1061) are ignored.[197]

If you have been getting help under the 'self-employment route' (eg, for JSA and HB, the New Enterprise Allowance), any payments to meet expenses 'wholly and necessarily' incurred while trading, or used for the repayment of a loan necessary for the business, are also disregarded if they are from a special account set up for this programme).[198] Income built up in your special account while you are getting this help, for HB, is treated as capital.[199] For IS/JSA/ESA, at the end of the programme, this is treated as income and spread over the same number of weeks in the future for which you have been receiving assistance, less any income tax due on the profits and an earnings disregard appropriate to your circumstances (see p267).[200]

Occupational pensions and annuities

The following income is **taken into account in full:**
- an occupational pension (except for any discretionary payment from a hardship fund) or income from a personal pension;[201]
- payments from an annuity, except (for IS, income-based JSA and income-related ESA only) payments under an annuity purchased either under an agreement or court order set up because of any personal injury to you, or from money paid because of any personal injury to you (see p280). However, in the case of home income plans, income from the annuity equal to the interest payable on the loan with which the annuity was bought is ignored if:[202]
  - you used at least 90 per cent of the loan made to you to buy the annuity; *and*
  - the annuity will end when you and your partner die; *and*
  - you or your partner are responsible for paying the interest on the loan; *and*
  - you (if you took out the loan), or your partner (if s/he did), were at least 65 at the time the loan was made; *and*
  - the loan is secured on a property which you or your partner own or in which you have an interest, and the property on which the loan is secured is your home, or that of your partner.

  If the interest on the loan is payable after income tax has been deducted, it is an amount equal to the net interest payment that is disregarded; otherwise it is the gross amount of the interest payment.

Mortgage and insurance payments

The following income is ignored:

- for IS, income-based JSA and income-related ESA only, payments you receive under a mortgage protection policy on your home count as income up to the level of the housing costs included in your 'applicable amount'. If the payments are higher than this, disregarded from the excess is whatever you use to pay:[203]
  - the interest on a qualifying loan which is not met by the DWP – eg, if the interest on the loan is higher than the DWP's standard interest rate;
  - capital repayments on a qualifying loan; *and*
  - any premiums you pay on the policy and any buildings insurance policy on your home.

  Any amount of the mortgage protection policy payments left over counts as your income;

- for IS, income-based JSA and income-related ESA only, and as long as you have not already used insurance payments for the same purpose, any money you receive which is given, and which you use, to make:[204]
  - payments under a secured loan which do not qualify under the housing costs rules (see Chapter 20);
  - interest payments which are not met under the housing costs rules, even though some interest payments under the loan may be met;
  - capital repayments on a qualifying loan;
  - payments of premiums on an insurance policy which you took out to insure against the risk of not being able to make the payments in the above three categories, and premiums on a building insurance policy;
  - payment of any rent that is not covered by HB (see Chapter 7);
  - payment of the part of your accommodation charge in a care home that exceeds that payable by a local authority.

  If you are using maintenance from a former partner or parent of your child (but not child maintenance which is disregarded whatever you use it for) to pay these costs, it may be taken into account as a 'liable relative payment' unless paid directly to someone else (eg, a lender). See p277;

- for HB only, payments you receive under an insurance policy to insure against the risk of being unable to maintain payments on a loan secured on your home. However, anything you get above the total of the following counts as your income:[205]
  - the amount you use to maintain your payments; *and*
  - any premium you pay for the policy; *and*
  - any premium for an insurance policy to insure against loss or damage to your home;

- payments you receive under an insurance policy to insure against the risk of being unable to maintain hire purchase or similar payments or other loan

Part 3: General rules for means tested benefits
Chapter 14: Income: under pension credit age
4. Income other than earnings

payments – eg, credit card debts. However, anything you get above the amount you use to make your payments and the premium for the policy counts as your income.[206]

Social services, community care and other payments

The following payments are ignored:

- local welfare provision to meet an immediate short-term need or establish or maintain a settled home in certain circumstances. This replaced social fund community care grants and crisis loans;[207]
- a payment from a local authority under ss17, 23B, 23C or 24A of the Children Act 1989, or, in Scotland, a payment under s12 of the Social Work (Scotland) Act 1968 or under ss22, 29 or 30 of the Children (Scotland) Act 1995 – ie, payments to assist children in need or young people who have been in care or who have been looked after.[208] For IS and income-based JSA, such payments are not ignored if you or your partner are involved in or, for IS only, have returned to work after a trade dispute (see p971);
- a payment from a local authority under s23C of the Children Act 1989 or ss22 or 29 of the Children (Scotland) Act 1995 to someone formerly in your care as a child or young person who has passed it on to you, and who is now aged 18 or over but continues to live with you. For IS and income-based JSA, such payments are not ignored if you or your partner are involved in or, for IS only, have returned to work after a trade dispute (see p971);[209]
- any community care or healthcare direct payments. Local authorities or the NHS pay these to disabled people or carers to buy their own services instead of providing services directly. A direct payment is not ignored as income of the person you pay for services even if this is your partner;[210]
- any payment you or your partner receive for looking after a person temporarily in your care if it is paid under community care arrangements by a health authority, clinical commissioning group or NHS Commissioning Board, local health board, local authority, voluntary organisation or by the person being looked after.[211] Any HB paid to you by a local authority for that person is not ignored, although see p280 for other possible disregards;
- payments under the Supporting People programme for support services to help you live independently are ignored indefinitely.[212] Landlords receiving such payments for providing the services do not benefit from this disregard, although other disregards may apply (see p280);
- if you live in a care home and the local authority arranged your place, local authority payments towards your fees are ignored for IS, JSA and income-related ESA. If the local authority did not arrange your place, any payment intended and used for your maintenance is fully disregarded if it is a voluntary or charitable payment, and partly disregarded if not – up to the difference between the care home fees and your applicable amount;[213]

- a lump-sum payment from the local authority to enable you to make adaptations to your home for a disabled child. This is treated as capital and ignored.[214]

Miscellaneous income

The following income is ignored:
- education maintenance allowances and 16 to 19 bursary fund payments (paid in England).[215] These are paid to some young people staying on at school or other non-advanced education;
- any payment to cover your expenses if you are working as an unpaid volunteer, or working unpaid for a charity or voluntary organisation;[216]
- payments in kind (unless, for IS or income-based JSA, you or your partner are involved in a trade dispute, see p971).[217] These may include food, fuel, cigarettes,[218] clothing, holidays, gifts, accommodation, transport or nursery education vouchers (but see p288 for the rules on notional income and p260 for the rules on non-cash vouchers paid as earnings). Items for essential living needs provided from the UK Border Agency to an asylum-seeking partner are ignored for IS, income-based JSA and income-related ESA;
- a payment (other than a training allowance) to a disabled person under the Disabled Persons (Employment) Act 1944 to assist her/him to obtain or retain employment;[219]
- any payments, other than for loss of earnings or a benefit, made to jurors or witnesses for attending at court;[220]
- Victoria Cross or George Cross payments or similar awards;[221]
- income paid outside the UK which cannot be transferred here;[222]
- if income is paid in another currency, any bank charges for converting the payment into sterling;[223]
- fares to hospital and refunds for prescription or dental charges;[224]
- payments instead of milk tokens and vitamins, or Healthy Start food vouchers;[225]
- payments to assist prison visits;[226]
- for HB, if you make a parental contribution to a student's grant or loan, an equal amount of any 'unearned' income you have for the period the grant or loan is paid. If your 'unearned' income does not cover the contribution, the balance can be disregarded from your earnings. If you are a parent of a student under 25 in advanced education who does not get a grant or loan (or who only gets a smaller discretionary award) and you contribute to her/his living expenses, the amount of your 'unearned' income that is ignored is the amount equal to your contribution up to a maximum of £57.35 (less the weekly amount of any discretionary award the student has). This is only ignored during the student's term. Again, any balance can be disregarded from your earnings;[227]

Part 3: General rules for means tested benefits
Chapter 14: Income: under pension credit age
5. Notional income

- a sports award made by UK Sport out of National Lottery funds for living expenses is taken into account. This covers food, ordinary clothing or footwear, fuel, council tax, water charges and rent (less any non-dependant deductions) for which HB could be payable or housing costs that could be met by IS, income-based JSA or income-related ESA. Payments for anything else are ignored – eg, sportswear and dietary supplements to enhance performance;[228]
- any discretionary housing payments paid by a local authority;[229]
- any payment for expenses if you are being consulted as a service user by a health, care or housing body that provides statutory services (expenses do not count as earnings either).[230]

5. **Notional income**

You may, in certain circumstances, be treated as having income even if you do not possess it, or have used it up.

Deliberately getting rid of income

If you deliberately get rid of income in order to claim or increase your benefit, you are treated as though you are still in receipt of the income.[231] The basic issues involved are the same as those for the deprivation of capital (see p359). **Note:** the rule can only apply if the purpose of the deprivation is to gain benefit for *yourself* (or your family). It should not apply if, for example, you stop claiming carer's allowance (CA) solely so that another person (who is not a member of your family) can become entitled to the severe disability premium (see p233).[232] However, if you do not claim a benefit which would clearly be paid if you did, it may be argued that you have failed to apply for income (see below). The rule still applies if you move from one benefit to another in the case of income support (IS), jobseeker's allowance (JSA) and employment and support allowance (ESA). For example, if you got rid of income to increase your ESA and then claim JSA instead, you are still treated as having the income for your JSA claim.

Failing to apply for income

If you fail to apply for income to which you are entitled without having to fulfil further conditions, you are deemed to have received it from the date you could have obtained it.[233]

This does not include, for example, income from:
- a discretionary trust; *or*
- a trust set up from money paid as a result of a personal injury; *or*
- funds administered by a court as a result of a personal injury; *or*
- a rehabilitation allowance made under the Employment and Training Act 1973; *or*

• •

- JSA (for IS, JSA and ESA) or ESA (for ESA only); *or*
- if you are under the qualifying age for pension credit (see p78), a personal or occupational pension scheme or payments from the Pension Protection Fund. However, for IS, income-based JSA and income-related ESA, if you or your partner have reached that age, you are treated as receiving income in certain circumstances if you defer or fail to claim your pension or purchase an annuity;[234] *or*
- working tax credit and child tax credit (CTC).[235]

For other income or benefits, it must still be certain that it would be paid upon application (and the rule ceases to apply as soon as a claim is made[236]). It may, therefore, be difficult to establish that there is 'no doubt' that CA, for example, would be paid to a carer who does not wish to claim it because of the effect on another person's severe disability premium (see p233).[237]

Income due to you that has not been paid

This applies to IS, income-based JSA and income-related ESA only.[238] You are treated as possessing any income owing to you. Examples of when this rule may apply could include:
- when wages are legally due to you but are not paid; *or*
- an occupational pension payment that is due but has not been received, unless the pension scheme has insufficient funds.[239]

This rule should not apply if:
- any social security benefit has been delayed; *or*
- you are waiting for a late payment of a government training allowance or a benefit from a European Economic Area country; *or*
- money is due to you from a discretionary trust, or a trust set up from money paid as a result of a personal injury; *or*
- you are owed earnings when your job has ended because of redundancy but these have not been paid to you.[240]

The income must be due to *you* (or your family) and for your own benefit.[241]

Unpaid wages

This applies to IS, income-based JSA and income-related ESA only. If you have wages due to you, but you do not yet know the exact amount or you have no proof of what they will be, you are treated as having a wage similar to that normally paid for that type of work in that area.[242] If your wages cannot be estimated, you might qualify for an interim payment (see p1167).[243]

Part 3: General rules for means tested benefits
Chapter 14: Income: under pension credit age
5. Notional income

Income paid to someone else on your behalf

If money is paid to someone on your behalf (eg, a landlord for your rent), this can count as notional income.[244] Even if it does count as notional income, it is still subject to the usual disregards that would apply if it were actual income – eg, a voluntary or charitable payment of income is ignored whether it is paid directly to you or to someone else on your behalf. See p364 for a description of these third-party rules – the notional income rules are the same as those for notional capital.

Income in kind given to a third party for you is ignored (eg, a food parcel used to prepare meals for you), unless, for IS or income-based JSA, you or your partner are involved in a trade dispute. However, money given to someone who uses it to buy you goods or services counts as notional income under the usual rules.

Income paid to you for someone else

If you or your partner get a payment for somebody not in the 'family' (eg, a relative living with you), it counts as your income if you keep any of it yourself or spend it on yourself or your partner unless it is – eg:[245]

- from the Macfarlane Trusts or one of the similar funds listed on p279;
- concessionary coal under the Coal Industry Act 1994;
- a payment for an approved employment-related course of education, or specified scheme for assisting people to obtain employment (see p1093);
- income in kind (eg, a food parcel given to you to make meals for someone else), although it does count for IS or income-based JSA if you or your partner are involved in a trade dispute.

Cheap or unpaid labour

If you are helping another person or an organisation by doing work of a kind which would normally command a wage, or a higher wage, you are deemed to receive a wage similar to that normally paid for that kind of job in that area.[246]

The burden of proving that the kind of work you do is something for which an employer would pay, and what the comparable wages are, lies with the decision maker.[247]

The rule does not apply if:[248]

- you are on an unpaid approved work placement or work experience; *or*
- you are on a government employment or training programme with no training allowance or only travel or meals expenses; *or*
- you can show that the person (including a limited company[249]) cannot, in fact, afford to pay, or pay more; *or*
- you work for a charitable or voluntary organisation or as a volunteer, and it is accepted that it is reasonable for you to give your services free of charge.[250] A 'volunteer' is someone who, without any legal obligation, performs a service for another person without expecting payment.

Sometimes it may also be reasonable to do a job free of charge from a sense of community duty, particularly if the job would otherwise remain undone, and there would be no financial profit to an employer.[251]

If you are caring for a sick or disabled relative, it is usually accepted that it is reasonable to do this free of charge rather than expecting her/him to pay you from benefits. However, if you need to show that it is reasonable, you should take into account:[252]

- how much care you give;
- the expectations you both have;
- your housing arrangements;
- whether you gave up work to care;
- the risk of your losing entitlement to CA if you were paid, or to a social services assessment of your needs;
- whether your relative would actually pay you.

It may also be reasonable to provide such support out of family duty.[253]

---

6. Working out weekly income

For housing benefit (HB), to assess your current normal weekly income you should do the following.

- Average your earnings over a past period (see p292 for earnings from employment and p266 for self-employed earnings).
- Estimate income other than earnings (see p273 for what income counts) by looking at an appropriate period of up to 52 weeks. The period chosen must give an accurate assessment of your income.[254] Child tax credit and working tax credit (WTC) are taken into account instalment by instalment – eg, if paid weekly or four-weekly, each instalment counts for the seven or 28 days ending on the day it is due to be paid.
- For earnings from employment and income other than earnings, convert income into a weekly amount if necessary (see p292).
- Deduct the appropriate earnings disregard(s) (see p267).

For income support (IS), income-based jobseeker's allowance (JSA) and income-related employment and support allowance (ESA), as well as working out weekly income, you also need to know the period that payments cover. These rules apply to earnings from employment and income other than earnings (see p266 for how self-employed earnings are assessed).

- Work out the period covered by the income (see p293).
- Work out the date from which to start taking the income into account (see p294).

Part 3: General rules for means tested benefits
Chapter 14: Income: under pension credit age
6. Working out weekly income

- Convert income into a weekly amount if necessary (see below). There are special rules covering variable income (see p293), payments for less than a week (see p293) and overlapping payments (see p293).

Averaging earnings for housing benefit

For HB, earnings as an employee are usually averaged out over:
- the previous five weeks if you are paid weekly; *or*
- two months if you are paid monthly.[255]

If your earnings vary, or if there is likely to be, or has recently been, a change (eg, you usually do overtime but have not done so recently, or you are about to get a pay rise), the local authority may average them over a different period if this is likely to give a more accurate picture of what you are going to earn.[256]

If you are on strike, the local authority should not take into account your pre-strike earnings and average them out over the strike period.[257]

If you have only just started work and your earnings cannot be averaged over the normal period (ie, five weeks or two months), an estimate is made, based on any earnings you have been paid so far if these are likely to reflect your future average wage. If you have not yet been paid or your initial earnings do not represent what you will normally earn, your employer must provide an estimate of your average weekly earnings.[258] Remember that if you start work after having been on certain benefits, you may get four weeks' extended payments of HB at the same amount (see p136). If your earnings change during your award, your new weekly average figure is estimated on the basis of what you are likely to earn over whatever period (up to 52 weeks) best allows an accurate estimate.[259] If averaging does not result in a weekly figure, the amount is converted (see below).

Converting income into a weekly amount

IS, income-based JSA, income-related ESA and HB are all calculated on a weekly basis, so your earnings and other income have to be converted into a weekly amount if necessary.

The following rules apply to income from employment and income other than earnings.[260] For income from self-employment, see p264.

To convert income to a weekly amount:
- if the payment is for less than a week, it is treated as the weekly amount;
- if the payment is for a month, multiply by 12 and divide by 52;
- for IS, income-based JSA and income-related ESA, multiply a payment for three months by four and divide by 52;
- for IS, income-based JSA and income-related ESA, divide a payment for a year by 52 (unless it is a WTC payment in which case divide by 365 and multiply by seven);

- for all four benefits, for any other period, divide the payment by the number of days in the period then multiply by seven.

If you work on certain days but are paid monthly, it is necessary to decide whether the payment is for the days worked or for the whole month. This generally depends on the terms of your contract of employment,[261] but may depend on how your employer has arranged to make payments to you.[262]

Variable income

For IS, income-based JSA and income-related ESA, if your income fluctuates or your earnings vary because you do not work every week, your weekly income may be averaged over the cycle, if there is an identifiable one, or, if there is not, over five weeks, or over another period if this would be more accurate.[263] If the cycle involves periods when you do no work, those periods are included in the cycle, but not other absences – eg, holidays or sickness.

Part weeks

For IS, income-based JSA and income-related ESA, there are rules about the calculation of income for part weeks.

- If income covering a period up to a week is paid before your first benefit week and part of it is counted for that week, or if, in any case, you are paid for a period of a week or more and only part of it is counted in a particular benefit week, multiply the whole payment by the number of days it covers in the benefit week, then divide the result by the total number of days covered by the payment.[264]
- If any payment of maternity allowance (MA) falls partly into the benefit week, only the amount paid for those days is taken into account. For any payment of IS, JSA or ESA, that amount is the weekly amount multiplied by the number of days in the part week and divided by seven.[265]

Overlapping payments

For IS, income-based JSA or income-related ESA, if you have regularly received a certain kind of payment of income from one source and in a particular benefit week you receive that payment and another of the same kind from the same source (eg, if your employer first pays you sick pay in arrears and this then overlaps with a payment in advance), the maximum amount to be taken into account is the one paid first.[266]

This does not apply if the second payment was due to be taken into account in another week, but the overlapping week is the first in which it could practically be counted (see p294).

The period covered by a payment

For IS, income-based JSA and income-related ESA, there are special rules for deciding the length of the period for which, and the date from which, payments

Part 3: General rules for means tested benefits
Chapter 14: Income: under pension credit age
6. Working out weekly income

of earnings and other income count. These rules are designed to give a clearer indication of how you are expected to make use of any earnings or other income you receive for each week of your claim for IS, income-based JSA or income-related ESA. These rules, however, do not apply to self-employed earnings (see p264).

- If a payment of income is made for an identifiable period, it is taken into account for a period of equal length.[267] For example, a week's part-time earnings are taken into account for a week. If you are paid monthly, the payments are taken into account for the number of weeks between the date you are treated as having been paid and the date you are next due to be paid.
- If the payment does not relate to a particular period, the amount of the payment is divided by the amount of the weekly IS, income-based JSA or income-related ESA to which you would otherwise be entitled. If part of the payment should be disregarded, the amount of IS, income-based JSA or income-related ESA is increased by the appropriate disregard. The result of this calculation is the number of weeks that you are not entitled to IS, income-based JSA or income-related ESA.[268]

Example
Conor receives £950 net earnings for work which cannot be attributed to any specific period of time. He and his partner are both aged 28. Their rent is met by HB. Conor's income-based JSA is £113.70. As a couple they are entitled to a £10 earnings disregard.
Divide £950 by the weekly JSA (£113.70) plus the disregard (£10).
950 ÷ 123.70 = 7.6799
This is seven weeks, with 0.6799 x £123.70 left over = £84.10
This means that Conor is not entitled to income-based JSA for seven weeks and the remaining £84.10 (less a £10 earnings disregard, leaving £74.10) is taken into account in calculating his benefit for the following week.

Payments made on leaving a job, if not ignored, are taken into account for a forward period (see p261).

The date from when a payment is counted

For IS, income-based JSA and income-related ESA, the date from when a payment of earnings and/or other income counts depends on when it was due to be paid. If it was due to be paid before you claimed IS, income-based JSA or income-related ESA, it counts from the date on which it was due to be paid.[269] Otherwise it is treated as paid on the first day of the benefit week in which it is due, or on the first day of the first benefit week after that in which it is practicable to take it into account.[270]

Payments of IS, JSA, ESA, universal credit, MA, and ESA are treated as paid on a daily basis for each day for which they are paid.[271]

The 'benefit week' for JSA, and usually also for IS and ESA although this may vary, is normally the seven days ending with the day allocated to you according to your national insurance number (also your payday).[272]

The date that a payment is due may well be different from the date of actual payment. Earnings are due on the employee's normal payday. If the contract of employment does not reveal the date of due payment, and there is no evidence to indicate otherwise, the date the payment was received should be taken as the date it was due.[273] If your contract of employment is terminated without proper notice, outstanding wages, wages in hand, holiday pay and any pay in lieu of notice are due on the last day of employment and are treated as paid on that day, even if this does not happen (although these are usually disregarded).[274]

If you receive compensation (eg, in a sex discrimination equal pay case), there is disagreement as to whether the relevant date is the date when the earnings in question were due to be paid[275] or when the compensation was awarded.[276]

For the treatment of payments at the end of a job, see p261.

Notes

1. Whose income counts

1 **IS/HB** s136(1) SSCBA 1992
JSA s13(2) JSA 1995
ESA Sch 1 para 6(2) WRA 2007; reg 83 ESA Regs
2 **HB** Schs 4 para 12 and 5 para 4 HB Regs
3 **IS** Reg 23(4) IS Regs
JSA Reg 88(3) JSA Regs
ESA Reg 83(4) ESA Regs
4 **IS** Reg 23(2) IS Regs
JSA Reg 88(2) JSA Regs
ESA Reg 83(2) ESA Regs
HB Reg 25(3) HB Regs
5 **IS** Reg 17(b) IS Regs
JSA Reg 83(b) JSA Regs
6 **IS** Reg 44(5) IS Regs
JSA Reg 106(5) JSA Regs
7 **IS** Reg 44(4) and Sch 8 para 15 IS Regs
JSA Reg 106(4) and Sch 6 para 18 JSA Regs
Both Reg 1 SS(WTCCTC)(CA) Regs

2. What counts as income

8 **IS** Reg 40 and Sch 9 para 1 IS Regs
JSA Reg 103(1) and (2) and Sch 7 para 1 JSA Regs
ESA Reg 104 and Sch 8 para 1 ESA Regs
HB Reg 40 and Sch 5 para 1 HB Regs
9 Reg 34 HB Regs
10 R(IS) 4/01
11 *R v SBC ex parte Singer* [1973] 1 WLR 713
12 *Minter v Kingston Upon Hull City Council and Potter v SSWP* [2011] EWCA Civ 1155

3. Earnings

13 *Parsons v Hogg* [1985] 2 All ER 897 (CA), appendix to R(FIS) 4/85
14 **IS** Reg 36(3) IS Regs
JSA Reg 99(1) and (4) JSA Regs; reg 59(1) and (3) JSA Regs 2013
ESA Reg 96(3) ESA Regs; reg 81(2) ESA Regs 2013
HB Reg 36(3) HB Regs
15 CIS/521/1990

Part 3: General rules for means tested benefits
Chapter 14: Income: under pension credit age
Notes

16 Regs 29(2) and 36(6) HB Regs
17 Reg 34 HB Regs; para BW2.34 GM
18 **IS** Reg 35(1) IS Regs
JSA Reg 98(1) JSA Regs; reg 58(1) JSA Regs 2013
ESA Reg 95(1) ESA Regs; reg 80(1) ESA Regs 2013
HB Reg 35(1) HB Regs
All R(SB) 21/86
19 Reg 35(1)(i)-(j) HB Regs
20 **IS** Regs 35(2)(b) and 40(4) and Sch 9 paras 1, 4 and 4A IS Regs
JSA Regs 98(2)(c) and 103(6) and Sch 7 paras 1, 4 and 5 JSA Regs; reg 58(2)(c) JSA Regs 2013
ESA Regs 95(2)(b) and 104(8) and Sch 8 paras 1, 4 and 5 ESA Regs; reg 80(2)(b) ESA Regs 2013
21 Reg 35(1)(i)-(j) HB Regs
22 **IS** Regs 35(2)(b) and 40(4) and Sch 9 paras 1 and 4 IS Regs
JSA Regs 98(2)(c) and 103(6) and Sch 7 paras 1 and 4 JSA Regs; reg 58(2)(c) JSA Regs 2013
ESA Regs 95(2)(b) and 104(8) and Sch 8 paras 1 and 4 ESA Regs; reg 80(2)(b) ESA Regs 2013
23 **IS** Reg 35(1)(e) IS Regs
JSA Reg 98(1)(d) JSA Regs; reg 58(1)(d) JSA Regs 2013
ESA Reg 95(1)(e) ESA Regs; reg 80(1)(e) ESA Regs 2013
HB Reg 35(1)(e) HB Regs
24 R(IS) 9/95
25 **IS** Reg 35(3)(a)(iv) IS Regs
JSA Reg 98(3)(d) JSA Regs; reg 67(4)(d) JSA Regs 2013
ESA Reg 95(4) ESA Regs, definition of 'compensation'; reg 80(4) ESA Regs 2013
26 *Minter v Kingston Upon Hull City Council and Potter v SSWP* [2011] EWCA Civ 1155
27 **IS** Reg 35(1)(j) IS Regs
JSA Reg 98(1)(h) JSA Regs; reg 58(1)(i) JSA Regs 2013
ESA Reg 95(1)(k) ESA Regs; reg 80(1)(k) ESA Regs 2013
HB Reg 35(1)(k) HB Regs
28 **IS** Reg 35(2A) IS Regs
JSA Reg 98(2A) JSA Regs; reg 58(3) JSA Regs 2013
ESA Reg 95(3) ESA Regs; reg 80(3) ESA Regs 2013
HB Reg 35(3) HB Regs

29 **IS** Reg 35(2)(a) and Sch 9 para 21 IS Regs
JSA Reg 98(2)(a) and Sch 7 para 22 JSA Regs; reg 58(2)(a) JSA Regs 2013
ESA Reg 95(2)(a) and Sch 8 para 22 ESA Regs; reg 80(2)(a) ESA Regs 2013
HB Reg 35(2)(a) and Sch 5 para 23 HB Regs
30 CIS/11482/1995
31 para 26096 DMG
32 **IS** Reg 35(2)(a) IS Regs
JSA Reg 98(2)(a) JSA Regs; reg 58(2)(a) JSA Regs 2013
ESA Reg 95(2)(a) ESA Regs; reg 80(2)(a) ESA Regs 2013
HB Reg 35(2)(a) HB Regs
All para 26040 DMG
33 **IS** Reg 48(5) IS Regs
JSA Reg 110(5) JSA Regs
ESA Reg 112(5) ESA Regs
HB Reg 46(5) HB Regs
34 **IS** Reg 48(6) IS Regs
JSA Reg 110(6) JSA Regs
35 **IS** Reg 35(2)(c) IS Regs
JSA Reg 98(2)(d) JSA Regs; reg 58(2)(d) JSA Regs 2013
ESA Reg 95(2)(c) ESA Regs; reg 80(2)(c) ESA Regs 2013
HB Reg 35(2)(b) HB Regs
36 R(FC) 1/90
37 CFC/26/1989
38 R(FIS) 4/85
39 R(IS) 13/91; R(IS) 16/93; CFC/26/1989
40 R(FIS) 4/85; R(FC) 1/91; R(IS) 13/91
41 CIS/77/1993; CIS/89/1989
42 **IS** Sch 8 para 11 IS Regs
JSA Sch 6 para 14 JSA Regs; Sch para 9 JSA Regs 2013
ESA Sch 7 para 9 ESA Regs
HB Sch 4 para 13 HB Regs
43 **IS** Sch 8 para 12 IS Regs
JSA Sch 6 para 15 JSA Regs; Sch para 10 JSA Regs 2013
ESA Sch 7 para 10 ESA Regs
HB Sch 4 para 14 HB Regs
44 **IS** Reg 35(2)(d) IS Regs
JSA Reg 98(2)(e) JSA Regs; reg 58(2)(e) JSA Regs 2013
ESA Reg 95(2)(d) ESA Regs; reg 80(2)(d) ESA Regs 2013
HB Reg 35(2)(c) HB Regs
45 **IS** Reg 40(4) and Sch 9 para 1 IS Regs
JSA Reg 103(6) and Sch 7 para 1 JSA Regs
ESA Reg 104(8) and Sch 8 para 1 ESA Regs
HB Reg 40(10) and Sch 5 para 1 HB Regs

46 **IS** Sch 8 para 15A IS Regs
JSA Sch 6 para 19 JSA Regs
ESA Sch 7 para 11A ESA Regs

47 **IS** Sch 8 paras 1(1)(a) and (2) and 2 IS Regs
JSA Sch 6 paras 1(1)(a) and (2) and 2 JSA Regs; Sch paras 1(1)(a) and (2) and 2 JSA Regs 2013
ESA Sch 7 paras 1(1)(a) and (2) and 2 ESA Regs
HB Sch 4 paras 1b) and 2(b)(i) HB Regs

48 **IS** Reg 35(1)(g) IS Regs
JSA Reg 98(1)(f) JSA Regs; reg 58(1)(f) JSA Regs 2013
ESA Reg 95(1)(g) ESA Regs
HB Reg 35(1)(g) HB Regs

49 **IS** Reg 35(1)(h) IS Regs
JSA Reg 98(1)(g) JSA Regs; reg 58(1)(h) JSA Regs 2013
ESA Reg 95(1)(i) ESA Regs
HB Reg 35(1)(h) HB Regs

50 **IS** Reg 35(1)(h) IS Regs
ESA Reg 95(1)(i) ESA Regs
HB Reg 35(1)(h) HB Regs

51 **IS** Sch 8 paras 1(1)(a), (2)(a)(ii), (2)(b)(ii) and 2 IS Regs
JSA Sch 6 paras 1(1)(a), (2)(a)(ii), (2)(b)(ii) and 2 JSA Regs; Sch paras 1(1)(a), 2(a)(ii), 2(b)(ii) and 2 JSA Regs 2013
ESA Sch 7 paras 1(1)(a), (2)(a)(ii), (2)(b)(ii) and 2 ESA Regs
HB Sch 4 paras 1(b)(i)(bb), (b)(ii)(bb) and 2 HB Regs

52 **IS** Regs 35(2)(b) and 40(4) and Sch 9 paras 4 and 4A IS Regs; R(IS) 8/99
JSA Regs 98(2)(c) and 103(6) and Sch 7 paras 4 and 5 JSA Regs; reg 58(2)(c) JSA Regs 2013
ESA Regs 95(2)(b) and 104(8) and Sch 8 paras 4 and 5 ESA Regs
HB Reg 35(1)(i) to (j) and Sch 4 paras 1(b) and 2(b)(i) HB Regs

53 **IS** Reg 35(3)(a)(iii) IS Regs
JSA Reg 98(2)(f) JSA Regs; reg 58(2)(f) JSA Regs 2013
ESA Reg 95(4) ESA Regs, definition of 'compensation'
HB because not listed as earnings in reg 35 HB Regs

54 Regs 98(1)(b), (3) and 104(4) and Sch 6 para 1(1) JSA Regs

55 **IS** Reg 35(1)(i) and (3) and Sch 8 paras 1(1)(a) and 2 IS Regs
JSA Reg 98(1)(b) and Sch 6 paras 1(1)(a) and 2 JSA Regs; reg 58(1)(b) and Sch paras 1(1)(a) and 2 JSA Regs 2013
ESA Reg 95(1)(j) and (4) and Sch 7 paras 1(1)(a) and 2 ESA Regs
HB Reg 35 HB Regs
All CJSA/82/98

56 **IS** Reg 35(1)(b) IS Regs
JSA Regs 98(2)(b) and 103(6)(a) JSA Regs; reg 58(2)(b) JSA Regs 2013
ESA Reg 95(1)(b) ESA Regs
HB Reg 35(1)(b) HB Regs

57 **IS** Regs 35(1)(d) and 48(3) IS Regs
JSA Regs 98(1)(c) and 110(3) JSA Regs; reg 58(1)(c) JSA Regs 2013
ESA Regs 95(1)(d) and 112(3) ESA Regs
HB Regs 35(1)(d) and 46(3) HB Regs

58 Sch 7 para 14 ESA Regs

59 **IS** Regs 35(2)(b) and 40(4) IS Regs
JSA Regs 98(2)(c) and 103(6) JSA Regs; reg 58(2)(c) JSA Regs 2013
ESA Regs 95(2)(b) and 104(8) ESA Regs

60 Reg 35(1)(i) to (j) and Sch 4 paras 1(c) and 2(b)(ii) HB Regs

61 **IS** Regs 35(1)(d) and 48(3) and Sch 8 paras 1(1)(b) and 2 IS Regs
JSA Regs 98(1)(c) and 110(3) and Sch 6 paras 1(1)(b) and 2 JSA Regs; reg 58(1)(c) and Sch paras 1(1)(b) and 2 JSA Regs 2013
ESA Regs 95(1)(d) and 112(3) and Sch 7 paras 1(1)(b) and 2 ESA Regs
HB Regs 35(1)(d) and 46(3) and Sch 4 paras 1(c) and 2(b)(ii) HB Regs

62 **IS** Sch 8 paras 1(1)(b) and 2 IS Regs
JSA Sch 6 paras 1(1)(b) and 2 JSA Regs; Sch paras 1(1)(b) and 2 JSA Regs 2013
ESA Sch 7 paras 1(1)(b) and 2 ESA Regs
HB Sch 4 paras 1(c) and 2(b)(ii) HB Regs

63 **IS** Reg 35 IS Regs
JSA Reg 98 JSA Regs; reg 58 JSA Regs 2013
ESA Reg 95 ESA Regs
HB Reg 35 HB Regs

64 **IS** Reg 29(4) and (4C) IS Regs
JSA Reg 94(4) JSA Regs; reg 54(6) JSA Regs 2013
ESA Reg 91(6) and (8) ESA Regs

65 R(JSA) 1/06

66 **IS** Regs 35(2)(b) and 40(4) IS Regs
JSA Regs 98(2)(c) and 103(6) JSA Regs; reg 58(2)(c) JSA Regs 2013
ESA Regs 95(2)(b) and 104(8) ESA Regs

Part 3: General rules for means tested benefits
Chapter 14: Income: under pension credit age
Notes

• •

67 **IS** Regs 37(1) and 38(3) IS Regs
JSA Regs 100(1) and 101(4) JSA Regs;
regs 60(1) and 61(3) JSA Regs 2013
ESA Regs 97(1) and 98(3) ESA Regs;
regs 82(1) and 83(2) ESA Regs 2013
HB Regs 37 and 38(3) HB Regs

68 **IS** Reg 2(1) IS Regs
JSA s35(1) JSA 1995
ESA Reg 2(1) ESA Regs; reg 2(1) ESA
Regs 2013
HB Regs 2(1) and 38(11) and (12) HB
Regs

69 *AR v Bradford Metropolitan District
Council* [2008] UKUT 30 (AAC), reported
as R(H) 6/09

70 **IS** Reg 37(2)(a) IS Regs
JSA Reg 100(2)(a) JSA Regs; reg 60(2)(a)
JSA Regs 2013
ESA Reg 97(2)(a) ESA Regs; reg 82(2)(a)
ESA Regs 2013
HB Sch 5 para 42 HB Regs

71 **IS** Reg 38(3)(a), (4), (7) and (8)(a) IS
Regs
JSA Reg 101(4) and (8) JSA Regs; regs
61(3) and (7) JSA Regs 2013
ESA Reg 98(3)(a), (4), (7) and (8)(a) ESA
Regs; reg 83(2)(a), (3), (6) and (7)(a)
ESA Regs 2013
HB Reg 38(3)(a), (4), (7) and (8)(a) HB
Regs

72 R(IS) 13/91; R(FC) 1/91; CFC/26/1989

73 **IS** Reg 38(6) and (8)(b) IS Regs
JSA Reg 101(7) and (9) JSA Regs; reg
61(6) and (8) JSA Regs 2013
ESA Reg 98(6) and (8)(b) ESA Regs; reg
83(5) and (7)(b) ESA Regs 2013
HB Reg 38(6) and (8)(b) HB Regs

74 **IS** Reg 38(5) IS Regs
JSA Reg 101(6) and (8) JSA Regs; reg
61(5) and (7) JSA Regs 2013
ESA Reg 98(5) ESA Regs; reg 83(4) ESA
Regs 2013
HB Reg 38(5) HB Regs

75 **IS** Reg 38(11) IS Regs
JSA Reg 101(12) JSA Regs; reg 61(11)
JSA Regs 2013
ESA Reg 98(11) ESA Regs; reg 83(10)
ESA Regs 2013
HB Reg 38(10) HB Regs
All R(FC) 1/93

76 CFC/836/1995

77 **IS** Regs 30 and 38(10) IS Regs; R(JSA) 1/
09; *GM v SSWP (JSA)* [2010] UKUT 221
(AAC); [2011] AACR 9
JSA Regs 95 and 101(11) JSA Regs; regs
55 and 61(10) JSA Regs 2013
ESA Regs 92 and 98(10) ESA Regs; regs
77 and 83(9) ESA Regs 2013

78 Regs 30(1) and 33(2) HB Regs

79 **IS** Reg 30(2) IS Regs
JSA Reg 95(2) JSA Regs; reg 55(2) JSA
Regs 2013
ESA Reg 92(2) ESA Regs
HB Reg 37(3) and (4) HB Regs

80 **IS** Sch 8 para 3 IS Regs
JSA Sch 6 para 4 JSA Regs; Sch para 4
JSA Regs 2013
ESA Sch 7 para 4 ESA Regs
HB Sch 4 para 2A HB Regs

81 **IS** Reg 38(9) IS Regs
JSA Reg 101(10) JSA Regs; reg 61(9) JSA
Regs 2013
ESA Reg 98(9) ESA Regs; reg 83(8) ESA
Regs 2013
HB Reg 38(9) HB Regs

82 Sch 7 paras 5 and 5A ESA Regs

83 Sch 7 para 6 ESA Regs

84 Reg 88 ESA Regs; reg 39(5) ESA Regs
2013

85 Sch 7 paras 7 and 14 ESA Regs

86 Sch 4 para 4 HB Regs

87 **IS** Sch 8 para 5 IS Regs
JSA Sch 6 para 6 JSA Regs

88 **IS** Sch 8 para 4(2) IS Regs
JSA Schs 6 para 5(1) and (2) and 6A
para 1(1) and (2) JSA Regs
HB Sch 4 para 3(2) HB Regs

89 Sch 4 para 3(2) HB Regs

90 **IS** Sch 8 paras 6A and 6B IS Regs
JSA Schs 6 paras 7 and 8, and 6A para 2
JSA Regs
HB Sch 4 paras 5 and 6 HB Regs

91 **IS** Sch 8 para 7(1) IS Regs
JSA Schs 6 para 9(1) and 6A para 3 JSA
Regs
HB Sch 4 para 8(1) HB Regs

92 **IS** Sch 8 para 8 IS Regs
JSA Schs 6 para 10 and 6A para 4 JSA
Regs
HB Sch 4 para 9 HB Regs

93 **IS** Sch 8 para 7(2) IS Regs
JSA Schs 6 paras 9-10 and 6A paras 3
and 4 JSA Regs
HB Sch 4 para 8(2)(b) HB Regs

94 **IS** Sch 8 para 4(3) IS Regs
JSA Sch 6 para 5(3) and 6A para 1(3)
JSA Regs

95 **IS** Sch 8 para 4(4) and (7) IS Regs
JSA Schs 6 para 5(4) and (7) and 6A
para 1(4) and (5) JSA Regs

96 **IS** Sch 8 paras 6 and 9 IS Regs
JSA Schs 6 paras 11 and 12, and 6A
para 6 JSA Regs
HB Sch 4 paras 7 and 10 HB Regs

97 Sch 4 para 10A HB Regs

98 Sch 4 para 17 HB Regs

99 Regs 27(1)(c) and 28 HB Regs; reg 30(1)(c) HB(SPC) Regs
100 Reg 27(2) HB Regs; reg 30(2) HB(SPC) Regs
101 Reg 28(6) HB Regs; reg 31(6) HB(SPC) Regs
102 Reg 28(13) HB Regs; reg 31(13) HB(SPC) Regs
103 Reg 28(6)-(8) HB Regs; reg 31(6)-(8) HB(SPC) Regs
104 Reg 28(14) HB Regs; reg 31(14) HB(SPC) Regs
105 Reg 28(2)-(4) HB Regs; reg 31(2)-(4) HB(SPC) Regs
106 Reg 28(11), (12) and (12A) HB Regs; reg 31(11), (12) and (12A) HB(SPC) Regs

4. Income other than earnings
107 R(IS) 4/05
108 **IS** Reg 40(6) IS Regs
    JSA Reg 103(5B) JSA Regs
    HB Reg 40(5A) HB Regs
109 **IS** Reg 35(2) and Sch 9 para 4 IS Regs
    JSA Sch 7 para 5 JSA Regs
    ESA Reg 95(2) and Sch 8 para 4 ESA Regs
110 Reg 35(1)(i) HB Regs
111 Sch 5 para 56 HB Regs
112 **IS** Sch 9 para 9 IS Regs
    JSA Sch 7 para 10 JSA Regs
    ESA Sch 8 para 11 ESA Regs
    HB Sch 5 para 9 HB Regs
113 **IS** Sch 9 para 5B(2) IS Regs
    JSA Sch 7 para 6B(2) JSA Regs
    ESA Sch 8 para 7(2) ESA Regs
    HB Sch 5 para 65 HB Regs
114 **IS** Reg 7(4)-(6) SS(WTCCTC)(CA) Regs
    JSA Reg 8(3)-(5) SS(WTCCTC)(CA) Regs
115 **IS** Sch 9 para 33 IS Regs
    JSA Sch 7 para 35 JSA Regs
    ESA Sch 8 para 37 ESA Regs
    HB Sch 5 para 32 HB Regs
116 **IS** Sch 9 para 9 IS Regs
    JSA Sch 7 para 10 JSA Regs
    ESA Sch 8 para 11 ESA Regs
    HB Sch 5 paras 6 and 9 HB Regs
117 **IS** Sch 9 para 5B(1) IS Regs
    JSA Sch 7 para 6B(1) JSA Regs
    ESA Sch 8 para 7(1) ESA Regs
118 **IS** Sch 9 paras 6 and 9 IS Regs
    JSA Sch 7 paras 7 and 10 JSA Regs
    ESA Sch 8 paras 8 and 11 ESA Regs
    HB Sch 5 para 6 HB Regs
119 **IS** Sch 9 para 5A(1) IS Regs
    JSA Sch 7 para 6A(1) JSA Regs
    ESA Sch 8 para 6 ESA Regs
    HB Sch 5 para 50 HB Regs

120 **IS** Sch 9 paras 5 and 52 IS Regs
    JSA Sch 7 paras 6 and 51 JSA Regs
    ESA Sch 8 paras 64 and 65 ESA Regs
    HB Sch 5 para 51 HB Regs
121 Sch 5 para 4 HB Regs
122 **IS** Sch 9 para 8 IS Regs
    JSA Sch 7 para 9 JSA Regs
    ESA Sch 8 para 10 ESA Regs
    HB Sch 5 para 8 HB Regs
123 **IS** Sch 9 paras 6 and 9 IS Regs
    JSA Sch 7 paras 7 and 10 JSA Regs
    ESA Sch 8 paras 8 and 11 ESA Regs
    HB Sch 5 para 6 HB Regs
124 **IS** Sch 9 paras 7 and 8 IS Regs
    JSA Sch 7 paras 8 and 9 JSA Regs
    ESA Sch 8 paras 9 and 10 ESA Regs
    HB Sch 5 paras 7 and 8 HB Regs
125 **IS** Sch 9 paras 31 and 31A IS Regs
    JSA Sch 7 paras 33 and 33A JSA Regs
    ESA Sch 8 paras 35 and 35A ESA Regs
    HB Sch 5 paras 31 and 31A HB Regs
126 **IS** Sch 10 para 18 IS Regs
    JSA Sch 8 para 23 JSA Regs
    ESA Sch 9 para 23 ESA Regs
    HB Sch 6 para 20 HB Regs
127 **IS** Sch 9 paras 54-56 IS Regs
    JSA Sch 7 paras 53-55 JSA Regs
    ESA Sch 8 paras 49, 51 and 52 ESA Regs
    HB Sch 5 paras 53-55 HB Regs
128 **IS** Sch 9 paras 5B(3) and 53 IS Regs
    JSA Sch 7 paras 6B(3) and 52 JSA Regs
    ESA Sch 8 paras 7(3) and 50 ESA Regs
    HB Sch 5 para 52 HB Regs
129 **IS** Sch 9 para 40 IS Regs
    JSA Sch 7 para 42 JSA Regs
    ESA Sch 8 para 42 ESA Regs
    HB Sch 5 para 36 HB Regs
130 **IS** Sch 9 para 46 IS Regs
    JSA Sch 7 para 45 JSA Regs
    ESA Sch 8 para 44 ESA Regs
    HB Sch 5 para 41 HB Regs
131 Sch 5 para 16 HB Regs
132 **IS** Sch 9 para 16 IS Regs
    JSA Sch 7 para 17 JSA Regs
    ESA Sch 8 para 17 ESA Regs
    HB Sch 5 para 15 HB Regs; Sch Part 2 HB&CTB(WPD) Regs
133 **IS** Sch 9 para 36 IS Regs
    ESA Sch 8 para 39 ESA Regs
    JSA Sch 7 para 38 JSA Regs
    HB Sch 5 para 34 HB Regs
134 ss134(8)and 139(6) SSAA 1992; reg 40(3)-(4A) HB Regs
135 *R v South Hams District Council ex parte Ash, The Times,* 27 May 1999
136 s74(2) SSAA 1992
137 Regs 32 and 40(6) HB Regs; reg 32 HB(SPC) Regs

Part 3: General rules for means tested benefits
Chapter 14: Income: under pension credit age
Notes

138 CH/1450/2005
139 CIS/1064/2004 seems to lend weight to this approach.
140 **IS** Sch 9 para 73 IS Regs
JSA Sch 7 para 70 JSA Regs
ESA Sch 8 para 60 ESA Regs
HB Sch 5 para 47A HB Regs
141 *KW v Lancaster City Council v SSWP (HB)* [2011] UKUT 266 (AAC)
142 Sch 5 para 47 HB Regs
143 **IS** Reg 54 IS Regs
JSA Reg 117 JSA Regs
ESA Reg 119 ESA Regs
144 **IS** Regs 54 and 55 IS Regs
JSA Regs 117 and 118 JSA Regs
ESA Regs 119 and 120 ESA Regs
145 **IS** Reg 42(4)(a) IS Regs
JSA Reg 105(10)(a) JSA Regs
ESA Reg 107(3)(c) ESA Regs
146 R(SB) 1/89
147 **IS** Reg 42(4)(b) IS Regs
JSA Reg 105(10)(b) JSA Regs
ESA Reg 107(4) ESA Regs
148 CIS/683/1993
149 **IS** Sch 9 para 25(1)(a) and (1A) IS Regs
JSA Sch 7 para 26(1)(a) and (1A) JSA Regs
ESA Sch 8 para 26(1)(a) and (2) ESA Regs
HB Sch 5 para 25(1)(a) and (2) HB Regs
150 **IS** Sch 9 para 25(1A) IS Regs
JSA Sch 7 para 26(1A) JSA Regs
ESA Sch 8 para 26(2) ESA Regs
HB Sch 5 para 25(2) HB Regs
151 **IS** Reg 42(4)(b) IS Regs
JSA Reg 105(10)(b) JSA Regs
ESA Reg 107(4) ESA Regs
HB Reg 42(6)(c) HB Regs
All para 28174 DMG
152 **IS** Sch 9 para 25(1)(a) and (2)(b) IS Regs
JSA Sch 7 para 26(1)(a) and (2)(b) JSA Regs
153 **IS** Sch 9 para 25(2)(a) IS Regs
JSA Sch 7 para 26(2)(a) JSA Regs
Both Reg 1 and Schs 1 para 23(c) and 2 para 23(c) SS(WTCCTC)(CA) Regs
154 That is, under ss23(2)(a) or 59(1)(a) CA 1989 or (in Scotland) s26 C(S)A 1995 or regs 33 or 51 Looked After Children (Scotland) Regulations 2009
155 **IS** Sch 9 para 26 IS Regs
JSA Sch 7 para 27 JSA Regs
ESA Sch 8 para 28 ESA Regs
HB Sch 5 para 26 HB Regs
156 **IS** Sch 9 para 25(1)(c) and (2) IS Regs
JSA Sch 7 para 26(1)(c) and (2) JSA Regs
ESA Sch 8 para 26(1)(b) ESA Regs
HB Sch 5 para 25(1)(ba) HB Regs

157 **IS** Sch 9 paras 25(1)(ba), 26((a)(iii) and 28(1)(c) IS Regs
JSA Sch 7 paras 26(1)(ba), 27(a)(iii) and 29(1)(c) JSA Regs
ESA Sch 8 paras 26(1)(b), 28(a)(iii) and 30(1)(c) ESA Regs
HB Sch 5 paras 25(1)(ba), 26(a)(iii) and 28 HB Regs
158 **IS** Sch 9 para 25(1)(e) IS Regs; para 28402 DMG
JSA Sch 7 para 26(1)(e) JSA Regs; para 28402 DMG
ESA Sch 8 para 26(1)(d) ESA Regs
HB Sch 5 para 25(1)(d) HB Regs
159 **IS** Sch 9 para 39 IS Regs
JSA Sch 7 para 41(1) JSA Regs
ESA Sch 8 para 41 ESA Regs
HB Sch 5 para 35 HB Regs
160 **IS** Reg 48(9) IS Regs
JSA Reg 110(9) JSA Regs
ESA Reg 112(7) ESA Regs
HB Reg 46(6) HB Regs
161 **IS** Reg 48(10)(a) IS Regs
JSA Reg 110(10) JSA Regs
162 **IS** Sch 9 para 15 IS Regs
JSA Sch 7 para 15 JSA Regs
ESA Sch 8 para 16 ESA Regs
HB Sch 5 para 14 HB Regs
163 R(H) 5/05 explains the difference between a loan and a voluntary payment.
164 **IS** Sch 9 para 15(5A) IS Regs
JSA Sch 7 para 15(5A) JSA Regs
ESA Sch 8 para 16(3) ESA Regs
HB Sch 5 para 14 HB Regs
165 *Malekout v SSWP* [2010] EWCA Civ 162; [2010] AACR 28
166 para 28102 DMG
167 **IS** Sch 9 para 19 IS Regs
JSA Sch 7 para 20 JSA Regs
ESA Sch 8 para 20 ESA Regs
HB Sch 5 para 22 HB Regs
168 **IS** Sch 9 para 18 IS Regs
JSA Sch 7 para 19 JSA Regs
ESA Sch 8 para 19 ESA Regs
HB Sch 5 para 21 HB Regs
169 **IS** Sch 9 para 20 IS Regs
JSA Sch 7 para 21 JSA Regs
ESA Sch 8 para 21 ESA Regs
HB Sch 5 para 42 HB Regs
170 **IS** Reg 2(1) IS Regs
JSA Reg 1(3) JSA Regs
ESA Reg 2(1) ESA Regs
HB Sch 5 para 42(2) HB Regs
IS/JSA/HB definition of 'board and lodging accommodation'
ESA definition of 'board and lodging'
171 CIS/521/2002

172 CIS/13059/1996
173 **IS** Reg 48(4) IS Regs
   JSA Reg 110(4) JSA Regs
   ESA Reg 112(4) ESA Regs
   HB Reg 46(4) HB Regs
   All *CAO v Palfrey and Others, The Times*,
   17 February 1995; R(IS) 26/95
174 CIS/563/1991
175 **IS** Sch 9 para 22(1) IS Regs
   JSA Sch 7 para 23 JSA Regs
   ESA Sch 8 para 23(1) ESA Regs
   HB Sch 5 para 17(1) HB Regs
176 **IS** Reg 48(4) IS Regs
   JSA Reg 110(4) JSA Regs
   ESA Reg 112(4) ESA Regs
   HB Reg 46(4) HB Regs
177 **IS** Sch 9 para 22(1) IS Regs
   JSA Sch 7 para 23(2) JSA Regs
   ESA Sch 8 para 23(2) ESA Regs
   HB Sch 5 para 17(1) HB Regs
178 CFC/13/1993
179 **IS** Sch 9 para 22(2) IS Regs
   JSA Sch 7 para 23(2) and (3) JSA Regs
   ESA Sch 8 para 23(2) and (3) ESA Regs
   HB Sch 5 para 17(2) HB Regs
180 **IS** Reg 53 IS Regs
   JSA Reg 116 JSA Regs
   ESA Reg 118 ESA Regs
   HB Reg 52 HB Regs
181 **IS** Reg 41(1) IS Regs
   JSA Reg 104(1) JSA Regs
   ESA Reg 105(1) ESA Regs
182 Reg 41(1) HB Regs
183 **IS** Reg 29(2) IS Regs
   JSA Reg 94(2) JSA Regs
   ESA Reg 91(2) ESA Regs
   HB Reg 33 HB Regs
184 **IS** Reg 41(2) IS Regs
   JSA Reg 104(2) JSA Regs
   ESA Reg 105(2) ESA Regs
   HB Reg 41(2) HB Regs
185 **IS** Reg 41(6) IS Regs
   JSA Reg 104(5) JSA Regs
   ESA Reg 105(4) ESA Regs
   HB Reg 41(4) HB Regs
186 Regs 41(4) and 48(2) IS Regs
187 **IS** Reg 41(7) IS Regs
   JSA Reg 104(6) JSA Regs
   ESA Reg 105(5) ESA Regs
   HB Reg 41(5) HB Regs
188 **IS** Sch 10 para 20 IS Regs
   JSA Sch 8 para 25 JSA Regs
   ESA Sch 9 para 25 ESA Regs
   HB Sch 6 para 22 HB Regs
189 *R v SBC ex parte Singer* [1973] 1 All ER
   931; *R v Oxford County Council ex parte
   Jack* [1984] 17 HLR 419; *R v West Dorset
   DC ex parte Poupard* [1988] 20 HLR 295

190 R(H) 8/08
191 *Leeves v Chief Adjudication Officer* [1998]
   EWCA 1706, reported as R(IS) 5/99; CIS/
   2287/2008
192 **IS** Reg 48(2) IS Regs
   JSA Reg 110(2) JSA Regs
   ESA Reg 112(2) ESA Regs
   HB Reg 46(2) HB Regs
193 **IS** s126(5) SSCBA 1992
   JSA s5(2)(c) JSA 1995
194 Regs 41(4) and 48(2) IS Regs
195 **IS** Sch 9 para 13 IS Regs
   JSA Sch 7 para 14 JSA Regs
   ESA Sch 8 para 15 ESA Regs
   HB Sch 5 para 13 HB Regs
196 **IS** Sch 9 para 1A IS Regs
   JSA Sch 7 paras A2 and A3 JSA Regs
   ESA Sch 8 para 1A ESA Regs
   HB Sch 5 paras A2 and A3 HB Regs
197 Sch 8 para 15A ESA Regs
198 **IS** Sch 9 para 64 IS Regs
   JSA Sch 7 para 62 JSA Regs
   ESA Sch 8 para 55 ESA Regs
   HB Sch 5 para 58 HB Regs
199 Reg 46(7) HB Regs
200 **IS** Regs 39C and 39D IS Regs
   JSA Regs 102C and 102D JSA Regs
   ESA Regs 102 and 103 ESA Regs
201 **IS** Reg 40(4) IS Regs
   JSA Regs 98(2)(e) and 103(6) JSA Regs
   ESA Reg 104(8) ESA Regs
   HB Reg 40(10) HB Regs
   All definition of 'occupational pension'
   in reg 2(1) of each of these Regs or reg 1
   for JSA
202 **IS** Reg 41(2) and Sch 9 para 17 IS Regs
   JSA Reg 104(2) and Sch 7 para 18 JSA
   Regs
   ESA Reg 105(2) and Sch 8 para 18 ESA
   Regs
   HB Reg 41(2) HB Regs
203 **IS** Sch 9 para 29 IS Regs; para 28240
   DMG
   JSA Sch 7 para 30 JSA Regs
   ESA Sch 8 para 31 ESA Regs
204 **IS** Sch 9 para 30 IS Regs
   JSA Sch 7 para 31 JSA Regs
   ESA Sch 8 para 32 ESA Regs
   All R(IS) 13/01
205 Sch 5 para 29 HB Regs
206 **IS** Sch 9 para 30ZA IS Regs
   JSA Sch 7 para 31A JSA Regs
   ESA Sch 8 para 33 ESA Regs
   HB Sch 5 para 29 HB Regs
207 **IS** Sch 9 para 31A IS Regs
   JSA Sch 7 para 33A JSA Regs
   ESA Sch 8 para 35A ESA Regs
   HB Sch 5 para 31A HB regs

Part 3: General rules for means tested benefits
Chapter 14: Income: under pension credit age
Notes

208 **IS** Sch 9 para 28 IS Regs
JSA Sch 7 para 29 JSA Regs
ESA Sch 8 para 30 ESA Regs
HB Sch 5 para 28 HB Regs
209 **IS** Sch 9 para 28(2) and (5) IS Regs
JSA Sch 7 para 29(2) and (5) JSA Regs
ESA Sch 8 para 30(2) and (3) ESA Regs
HB Sch 5 para 28A HB Regs
210 **IS** Sch 9 para 58 IS Regs
JSA Sch 7 para 56 JSA Regs
ESA Sch 8 para 53 ESA Regs
HB Sch 5 para 57 HB Regs
All *Casewell v SSWP* [2008] EWCA Civ
524, reported as R(IS) 7/08
211 **IS** Sch 9 para 27 IS Regs
JSA Sch 7 para 28 JSA Regs
ESA Sch 8 para 29 ESA Regs
HB Sch 5 para 27 HB Regs
212 **IS** Sch 9 para 76 IS Regs
JSA Sch 7 para 72 JSA Regs
ESA Sch 8 para 63 ESA Regs
HB Sch 5 para 63 HB Regs
213 **IS** Sch 9 paras 15, 30A and 66 IS Regs
JSA Sch 7 paras 15, 32 and 64 JSA Regs
ESA Sch 8 paras 16, 34 and 56 ESA Regs
214 **IS** Sch 10 para 8(b) IS Regs
JSA Sch 8 para 13(b) JSA Regs
ESA Sch 9 para 12(b) ESA Regs
HB Sch 6 para 10(b) HB Regs
215 **IS** Sch 9 para 11 IS Regs
JSA Sch 7 para 12 JSA Regs
ESA Sch 8 para 13 ESA Regs
HB Sch 5 para 11 HB Regs
216 **IS** Sch 9 para 2 IS Regs
JSA Sch 7 para 2 JSA Regs
ESA Sch 8 para 2 ESA Regs
HB Sch 5 para 2 HB Regs
217 **IS** Sch 9 para 21 IS Regs
JSA Sch 7 para 22 JSA Regs
ESA Sch 8 para 22 ESA Regs
HB Sch 5 para 23 HB Regs
218 para BW2 Annex B para 13 GM
219 **IS** Sch 9 para 51 IS Regs
JSA Sch 7 para 50 JSA Regs
ESA Sch 8 para 48 ESA Regs
HB Sch 5 para 49 HB Regs
220 **IS** Sch 9 para 43 IS Regs
JSA Sch 7 para 43 JSA Regs
ESA Sch 8 para 43 ESA Regs
HB Sch 5 para 39 HB Regs
221 **IS** Sch 9 para 10 IS Regs
JSA Sch 7 para 11 JSA Regs
ESA Sch 8 para 12 ESA Regs
HB Sch 5 para 10 HB Regs
222 **IS** Sch 9 para 23 IS Regs
JSA Sch 7 para 24 JSA Regs
ESA Sch 8 para 24 ESA Regs
HB Sch 5 para 24 HB Regs

223 **IS** Sch 9 para 24 IS Regs
JSA Sch 7 para 25 JSA Regs
ESA Sch 8 para 25 ESA Regs
HB Sch 5 para 33 HB Regs
224 **IS** Sch 9 para 48 IS Regs
JSA Sch 7 para 47 JSA Regs
ESA Sch 8 para 45 ESA Regs
HB Sch 5 para 44 HB Regs
225 **IS** Sch 9 para 49 IS Regs
JSA Sch 7 para 48 JSA Regs
ESA Sch 8 para 46 ESA Regs
HB Sch 5 para 45 HB Regs
226 **IS** Sch 9 para 50 IS Regs
JSA Sch 7 para 49 JSA Regs
ESA Sch 8 para 47 ESA Regs
HB Sch 5 para 46 HB Regs
227 Schs 4 para 11 and 5 paras 19 and 20 HB
Regs
228 **IS** Sch 9 para 69 IS Regs
JSA Sch 7 para 67 JSA Regs
ESA Sch 8 para 57 ESA Regs
HB Sch 5 para 59 HB Regs
229 **IS** Sch 9 para 75 IS Regs
JSA Sch 7 para 71 JSA Regs
ESA Sch 8 para 62 ESA Regs
HB Sch 5 para 62 HB Regs
230 **IS** Sch 9 para 2A IS Regs
JSA Sch 7 para 2A JSA Regs
ESA Sch 8 para 2A ESA Regs
HB Sch 5 para 2A HB Regs

5. **Notional income**
231 **IS** Reg 42(1) IS Regs
JSA Reg 105(1) JSA Regs
ESA Reg 106(1) ESA Regs
HB Reg 42(1) HB Regs
232 paras 28608-16 DMG; see also CIS/
15052/1996
233 **IS** Reg 42(2) IS Regs
JSA Reg 105(2) JSA Regs
ESA Reg 106(2) ESA Regs
HB Reg 42(2) HB Regs
234 **IS** Reg 42(2ZA) and (2A) IS Regs
JSA Reg 105(2B) and (3) JSA Regs
ESA Reg 106(3) and (4) ESA Regs
235 **IS** Reg 42(2)(e)-(f) IS Regs
JSA Reg 105(2)(d) JSA Regs
ESA Reg 106(2)(e) and (f) ESA Regs
HB Reg 42(2)(f)-(g) HB Regs
236 CIS/16271/1996
237 paras 28608-16 DMG
238 **IS** Reg 42(3) IS Regs
JSA Reg 105(6) JSA Regs
ESA Reg 107(1) ESA Regs
239 **IS** Reg 42(3A) and (3B) IS Regs
JSA Reg 105(7)(a), (8) and (9) JSA Regs
ESA Reg 107(2)(a) and (b) ESA Regs

240 **IS** Reg 42(3C) IS Regs
JSA Reg 105(7)(d) JSA Regs
ESA Reg 107(2)(c) ESA Regs
241 CIS/15052/1996, para 10
242 **IS** Reg 42(5) IS Regs
JSA Reg 105(12) JSA Regs
ESA Reg 108(1) ESA Regs
243 Reg 2 SS(PAOR) Regs
244 **IS** Reg 42(4)(a) IS Regs
JSA Reg 105(10)(a) JSA Regs
ESA Reg 107(3) ESA Regs
HB Reg 42(6)(b) HB Regs
245 **IS** Regs 42(4)(b) and (4ZA) IS Regs
JSA Regs 105(10)(b) and (10A) JSA Regs
ESA Regs 107(4) and (5) ESA Regs
HB Regs 42(6)(c) and (7) HB Regs
246 **IS** Reg 42(6) IS Regs; CIS/191/1991
JSA Reg 105(13) JSA Regs
ESA Reg 108(3) ESA Regs
HB Reg 42(9) HB Regs
247 R(SB) 13/86
248 **IS** Reg 42(6A) IS Regs
JSA Reg 105(13A) JSA Regs
ESA Reg 108(4) ESA Regs
HB Reg 42(10) HB Regs
249 R(SB) 13/86
250 **IS** Reg 42(6A)(a) IS Regs
JSA Reg 105(13A)(a) JSA Regs
ESA Reg 108(4)(a) ESA Regs
HB Reg 42(10)(a) HB Regs
251 CIS/147/1993
252 *Sharrock v CAO*, 26 March 1991 (CA);
CIS/93/1991; CIS/422/1992; CIS/701/
1994
253 CIS/93/1991

6. Working out weekly income

254 Reg 31 HB Regs
255 Reg 29(1)(a) HB Regs
256 Reg 29(1)(b) HB Regs; para BW2/W2.53
GM
257 *R v HBRB of the London Borough of Ealing
ex parte Saville* [1986] 18 HLR 349
258 Reg 29(2) HB Regs
259 Reg 29(3) HB Regs
260 **IS** Reg 32(1) IS Regs
JSA Reg 97 JSA Regs; reg 57 JSA Regs
2013
ESA Reg 94(1) ESA Regs; reg 79(1) ESA
Regs 2013
HB Reg 33 HB Regs
261 R(IS) 3/93
262 R(IS) 10/95
263 **IS** Reg 32(6) IS Regs
JSA Reg 97(6) JSA Regs; reg 57(5) JSA
Regs 2013
ESA Reg 94(6) ESA Regs; reg 79(5)(b)
ESA Regs 2013

264 **IS** Reg 32(2) and (3) IS Regs
JSA Reg 97(2) and (3) JSA Regs; reg
57(2) and (3) JSA Regs 2013
ESA Reg 94(2) and (3) ESA Regs; reg
79(2) and (3) ESA Regs 2013
265 **IS** Reg 32(4) IS Regs
JSA Reg 97(4) JSA Regs
ESA Reg 94(4) ESA Regs
266 **IS** Reg 32(5) and Sch 8 para 10 IS Regs
JSA Reg 97(5) and Sch 6 para 13 JSA
Regs; reg 57(4) and Sch para 8 JSA Regs
2013
ESA Reg 94(5) and Sch 7 para 8 ESA
Regs; reg 79(4) ESA Regs 2013
267 **IS** Reg 29(2) IS Regs
JSA Reg 94(2) JSA Regs; reg 54(2) JSA
Regs 2013
ESA Reg 91(2) ESA Regs; reg 76(2) ESA
Regs 2013
268 **IS** Reg 29(2)(b) IS Regs
JSA Reg 94(2)(b) JSA Regs; reg 54(2)(c)
JSA Regs 2013
ESA Reg 91(2)(c) ESA Regs; reg 76(2)(c)
ESA Regs 2013
269 **IS** Reg 31(1)(a) IS Regs
JSA Reg 96(1)(a) JSA Regs; reg 56(a) JSA
Regs 2013
ESA Reg 93(1)(a) ESA Regs; reg 78(a)
ESA Regs 2013
270 **IS** Reg 31(1)(b) IS Regs
JSA Reg 96(1)(b) JSA Regs; reg 56(b) JSA
Regs 2013
ESA Reg 93(1)(b) ESA Regs; reg 78(b)
ESA Regs 2013
271 **IS** Reg 31(2) IS Regs
JSA Reg 96(2) JSA Regs
ESA Reg 93(2) ESA Regs
272 **IS** Reg 2(1) IS Regs
JSA Reg 1(3) JSA Regs; reg 2(2) JSA Regs
2013
ESA Reg 2(1) ESA Regs; reg 2 ESA Regs
2013
273 R(SB) 33/83
274 R(SB) 22/84; R(SB) 11/85
275 CIS/590/1993
276 *SSWP v JP (JSA)* [2010] UKUT 90 (AAC)

Chapter 15

Income: over pension credit age

This chapter covers:
1. Whose income counts (p305)
2. What counts as income (p305)
3. Earnings (p306)
4. Income other than earnings (p312)
5. Notional income (p318)
6. Working out weekly income (p320)

This chapter explains the rules for working out your weekly income for pension credit (PC) and for housing benefit (HB) if you or your partner are over the qualifying age for PC and neither of you are on income support (IS), income-based jobseeker's allowance (JSA), income-related employment and support allowance (ESA) or universal credit (UC). See Chapter 14 for the rules for IS, income-based JSA and income-related ESA and for HB if you and your partner are under the qualifying age for PC. See Chapter16 for the rules for universal credit. **Note**: whenever HB is referred to in this chapter, this only applies to the rules for people over the qualifying age for PC.

Key facts
- Your entitlement to pension credit (PC) and housing benefit (HB) and the amount you get depends on how much income you have.
- Your own income counts and, if you are a member of a couple, your partner's income also counts.
- Some income may be completely or partly ignored, or it may count in full.
- If you get the guarantee credit of PC, you are entitled to maximum HB, so you do not need to work out your income again for HB.

1. Whose income counts

If you are a member of a couple (see p205), your partner's income is added to yours.[1]

The income of a dependent child does *not* affect pension credit or housing benefit.[2]

2. What counts as income

Pension credit

For pension credit (PC), **'income'** means:[3]

- earnings (see p307 and p309);
- certain benefits and tax credits, including state retirement pensions and war pensions (see p312);
- maintenance (see p314);
- income from tenants and lodgers (see p314);
- income from capital (see p315);
- other specified miscellaneous income, including occupational and personal pensions (see p316);
- notional income (see p318);
- any income paid in lieu of the above.

For each type of income, some income is taken into account and some is ignored in the assessment of PC. If the rules do not specify a type of income as being included in the assessment, it is ignored and does not affect your benefit.

For the rules on qualifying income for the savings credit and the 'assessed income period', see Chapter 6.

Housing benefit

How your income affects your entitlement to housing benefit (HB) depends on whether you are getting PC and, if you are, which type of PC.

If you get pension credit guarantee credit

If you (or your partner) are getting the guarantee credit of PC, all of your (and your partner's) income is ignored.[4] This is because entitlement to guarantee credit of PC acts as a passport to maximum HB.

If you get pension credit savings credit

If you (or your partner) are only getting the savings credit of PC, your income for HB purposes is the income (and capital) figure used by the DWP to work out your PC, *plus*:[5]

Part 3: General rules for means tested benefits
Chapter 15: Income: over pension credit age
3. Earnings

- the amount of savings credit of PC;
- any income (and capital) of your partner which was not taken into account in the PC calculation – eg, if a partner abroad is no longer included for PC but is for HB; *and*
- any income of a non-dependant, but only in the very limited circumstances when her/his income can be treated as yours under the HB rules (see p120);[6]

minus:[7]

- any childcare charges earnings disregard (see p311);
- the higher amount disregarded, where applicable, for:
  - lone parent earnings (see p309);
  - payments of maintenance (see p314);
- any additional full-time earnings disregard (see p311);
- any earnings disregarded from permitted work (see p311);
- any discretionary increase to the £10 disregard for war pensions, and war widows' and widowers' pensions (see p313).

If you do not get pension credit

If you or your partner are over the qualifying age for PC (see p78) and are not getting the guarantee or savings credit of PC (or income support, income-based jobseeker's allowance, income-related employment and support allowance or universal credit), income is defined in the same way as for PC (see p305).[8] Some income is taken into account and some disregarded but the rules are not always the same as for PC. The differences are explained in the relevant sections below.

Net weekly income

The income that is taken into account is the amount after deducting any tax or national insurance (NI) contributions.[9]

For HB, the local authority may ignore changes (eg, Budget changes) in tax or NI contributions and the maximum rate of tax credits for up to 30 benefit weeks. When the changes are eventually taken into account, you are not treated as having been underpaid or overpaid benefit during the period of the delay.[10]

Once you have worked out what income should be taken into account, this is converted into a weekly amount (see p320) and the total taken into account in the benefit assessment. See p321 for the date from when a payment is counted. Chapters 6 and 7 explain how income affects the amount of PC or HB you get.

3. Earnings

How earnings are treated depends on whether you are an employed earner (see p307) or are self-employed (see p309). In either case, some of your earnings can be disregarded (see p309).

Earnings of employed earners

Calculating net earnings from employment

It is your 'net earnings' that are taken into account in the assessment. See p320 for how earnings are converted into a weekly amount.

Net earnings

'Net earnings' means your 'gross earnings' *minus*:[11]

– any deductions made for income tax; *and*

– Class 1 national insurance (NI) contributions; *and*

– half of any contribution you make towards a personal or occupational pension scheme.

'Gross earnings' means the amount of earnings received from your employer less deductions for any expenses 'wholly, exclusively and necessarily incurred' by you in order to carry out the duties of your employment.[12] A range of deductions may be made.

If your earnings are estimated for housing benefit (HB), the amount of tax and NI you would expect to pay on those earnings is estimated and deducted, together with half of any pension contributions you are paying.[13]

What counts as earnings

'Earnings' means 'any remuneration or profit derived from ... employment'. As well as your wages, this includes:[14]

- any bonus or commission (including tips);
- holiday pay – but this is ignored if your employment ends before your pension credit (PC) or HB entitlement starts;
- statutory sick pay and contractual sick pay,[15] statutory maternity pay, statutory paternity pay or statutory adoption pay or any other payment made to you by your employer while you are on maternity leave;[16]
- any payments made by your employer for expenses not wholly, exclusively and necessarily incurred in carrying out your job, including any travel expenses to and from work, and any payments made to you for looking after members of your family;
- pay in lieu of notice, or pay in lieu of remuneration except for periodic payments following redundancy. However, all earnings, including pay in lieu, are ignored if your employment ends before your PC or HB entitlement starts;
- a retainer fee (eg, payment during the school holidays if you work for the school meals service[17]) or a guarantee payment;[18]
- an equal pay settlement – eg, through a 'single status agreement';[19]
- any payment of a non-cash voucher which is liable for Class 1 NI contributions.[20] Non-cash vouchers that are not liable for contributions (eg, certain childcare and charitable vouchers) are classed as payments in kind and ignored.[21]

Part 3: General rules for means tested benefits
Chapter 15: Income: over pension credit age
3. Earnings

What does not count as earnings

The following are examples of payments not counted as earnings.

- If you become entitled to HB or PC after your employment ends, all earnings are disregarded except certain royalties.[22]
- Payments in kind (eg, petrol) are ignored.[23]
- An advance of earnings or a loan from your employer is treated as capital, according to PC guidance.[24]
- The value of free accommodation provided as part of your job is ignored, according to PC guidance.[25]
- Payments towards expenses that are wholly, exclusively and necessarily incurred, such as travelling expenses during the course of your work, are ignored.[26]
- If you are a local councillor, travelling expenses and subsistence payments are (and basic allowances may be[27]) ignored as expenses wholly, exclusively and necessarily incurred in your work.
- If your earnings are paid in another currency, any bank charges for converting them into sterling are deducted before taking them into account.[28]
- The net amount of any occupational pension,[29] although not counted as earnings (and therefore having no earnings disregard), is still taken into account in full.[30]
- Any compensation payments made by an employment tribunal for unfair dismissal or unlawful discrimination do not count as earnings.[31]

Payments at the end of a job

Redundancy payments are treated as capital.[32]

If you leave a job, any earnings should be disregarded except certain copyright royalties, payments for patents, trademarks or under the Public Lending Rights Scheme.[33]

However, these rules only apply if you leave your job before you claim benefit. If you are already getting HB or PC when you leave your job, your earnings are not disregarded for that benefit.

For PC, any final payment is treated as paid on the date your next regular payment of earnings would have been paid and taken into account for the same period unless the final payment is higher than the normal amount. If it is higher, it is taken into account over the corresponding multiple of the regular payment period with any remainder counting for a further payment period.[34]

Example
Sandra has been getting PC and working part time. She earns £25 a week, paid on a Friday. She finishes work on Wednesday 7 August and on that day is given £35 made up of £15 final wages and £20 holiday pay. This £35 is treated as paid on Friday 9 August and taken into account for two benefit weeks: £25 in the first week and the remaining £10 in the second week.

Earnings from self-employment

Calculating net earnings

Your **'net profit'** over the period before your claim must be worked out. This consists of your self-employed earnings *minus*:[35]

- reasonable expenses (see p265 – the rules are the same as those for people under the qualifying age for PC except that expenses relating to debts are not excluded); *and*
- income tax and NI contributions; *and*
- half of any premium paid in respect of a personal pension scheme which is eligible for tax relief.[36] You must supply certain information about the scheme or annuity contract to the DWP or local authority if requested.[37]

If you receive payments for board and lodging charges, these do not count as earnings, but as other income (less any disregards – see p315).[38]

Working out average earnings from self-employment

The weekly amount is the average of earnings:[39]

- over a period of one year (normally the last year for which accounts are available);
- over a more appropriate period where you have recently taken up self-employment or there has been a change which will affect your business.

Childminders

Childminders, in practice, are always treated as self-employed. Your net profit is deemed to be one-third of your earnings less income tax, your NI contributions and half of certain pension contributions.[40] The rest of your earnings are completely ignored.

Disregarded earnings

Some of your earnings from employment or self-employment are disregarded and do not affect your PC or HB. The amount of the disregard depends on your circumstances. The three main levels of disregard are £25, £20 or £5/£10. Additional disregards may apply to HB in special circumstances, including if you have childcare costs.

£25 disregard

Lone parents on HB have £25 of their earnings ignored.[41] This does not apply to PC.

£20 disregard

For PC, £20 of your earnings (including those of your partner, if any) are disregarded if:

Part 3: General rules for means tested benefits
Chapter 15: Income: over pension credit age
3. Earnings

- you are a lone parent;[42]
- you or your partner qualify for an additional amount of PC for a carer (see p237). For a couple, if both partners get the additional amount, £20 is disregarded from their combined earnings;[43]
- you or your partner are in receipt of:[44]
  - employment and support allowance (ESA), long-term incapacity benefit (IB), severe disablement allowance (SDA); *or*
  - attendance allowance (AA), disability living allowance (DLA), personal independence payment (PIP), armed forces independence payment or a mobility supplement; *or*
  - the disability or severe disability element of working tax credit (WTC);
- you or your partner are registered or certified as blind;[45]
- you or your partner previously had a £20 earnings disregard in your income support, income-based jobseeker's allowance or income-related ESA and that benefit ended no more than eight weeks before PC entitlement began (the disregard ends if you have a break in employment of more than eight weeks) or, immediately before reaching pension age, there was a £20 disregard in your PC because you or your partner were getting IB or SDA. You cannot get this disregard if you have more than an eight-week break in your PC claim;[46]
- you or your partner are an auxiliary coastguard, part-time firefighter, part-time lifeboat crew or in the Territorial Army.[47] If earnings are less than £20 a week, what is left over can be disregarded from your, or your partner's, earnings from any other employment.

For HB, £20 of your earnings are disregarded if:
- you or your partner qualify for a carer premium. For a couple, if both partners get the carer premium, £20 is disregarded from their combined earnings;[48]
- you or your partner are in receipt of:[49]
  - ESA with a work-related activity or support component, long-term IB or SDA; *or*
  - AA, DLA, PIP, armed forces independence payment or a mobility supplement; *or*
  - the disability or severe disability element of WTC;
- you or your partner are registered or certified as blind;[50]
- you or your partner have (or are treated as having) limited capability for work and the assessment phase has ended;[51]
- you or your partner are (or are treated as) incapable of work and have been for a continuous period of 364 days (196 days if you are terminally ill);[52]
- you or your partner had a £20 earnings disregard in your HB or council tax benefit (CTB) in the eight weeks before you or your partner reached the qualifying age for PC. You cannot get this disregard if you have more than an eight-week break in your employment or in your HB claim (or previously, CTB claim);[53]

• you or your partner are an auxiliary coastguard, part-time firefighter, part-time lifeboat crew or in the Territorial Army. If earnings are less than £20 a week, what is left can be disregarded from your or your partner's earnings from other employment.[54]

Note: if you qualify under more than one category, you still have a maximum of only £20 of your earnings disregarded.

Permitted work disregard for housing benefit
For HB only, £20 or £101 is disregarded from earnings if you or your partner are doing 'permitted work' in the circumstances described on p269.[55]

Basic £5 or £10 disregard
If you do not qualify for a £25 or £20 disregard (or for HB, a permitted work disregard), £5 of your earnings is disregarded if you are single. If you claim as a member of a couple, £10 of your total income is disregarded, whether or not you are both working.[56]

Additional disregard for housing benefit
For HB only, whichever earnings disregard applies is increased by £17.10 if:[57]
• you or your partner receive the 30-hour element as part of your (or your partner's) WTC (see p1403); or
• you or your partner work 30 hours a week or more on average; or
• you or your partner work 16 hours or more a week on average and your HB includes the family premium (see p228); or
• you are a lone parent and work 16 hours or more a week on average; or
• you or your partner work 16 hours or more a week on average and one or both of you get long-term IB, ESA which includes a support or work-related activity component, SDA, AA, DLA, PIP, armed forces independence payment, a mobility supplement or the disabled worker or severe disability element in your WTC, or you are registered blind or have been incapable of work for 364 days (196 days if terminally ill). For couples, the partner who is disabled is the one who must be working 16 hours a week or more on average.

The only exception is where your total earnings are less than the total of £17.10, plus any earnings disregard and childcare costs disregard (see below). In this case, £17.10 is disregarded from any WTC awarded to you or your partner, but the earnings disregard is not increased.
Note: as with the ordinary earnings disregards, only one additional disregard can be allowed from your (or your partner's) earnings.

Childcare costs for housing benefit
For HB only, an allowance of up to £175 a week for one child, or up to £300 a week for two or more children, can be deducted from your (or your partner's)

Part 3: General rules for means tested benefits
Chapter 15: Income: over pension credit age
4. Income other than earnings

earnings (from employment or self-employment) for childcare costs in certain circumstances.[58] The rules are the same as those for people under the qualifying age for PC (see p270), except you can also have an allowance deducted if you are a couple and one of you works 16 hours or more a week and the other is aged 80 or over. There is no allowance for childcare costs for PC.

4. Income other than earnings

Benefits and tax credits

Some benefits and tax credits are taken into account as income and others are disregarded wholly or partly.

Benefits and tax credits that are taken into account

The following benefits and tax credits are taken into account:
- carer's allowance (CA);
- a war orphan's pension, dependant's allowance or payment under the Armed Forces Compensation Scheme for someone whose parent died and who is still eligible as an adult because of disability;[59]
- contribution-based jobseeker's allowance (JSA);
- incapacity benefit (IB) and severe disablement allowance (SDA);
- contributory employment and support allowance (ESA). If ESA is paid at a reduced rate because of a sanction, it is still the full rate that counts;[60]
- industrial injuries benefits, except constant attendance allowance and exceptionally severe disablement allowance, which are disregarded;
- maternity allowance (MA);
- retirement pensions;
- statutory sick pay (SSP), statutory maternity pay (SMP), statutory paternity pay (SPP) and statutory adoption pay (SAP). These are treated as earnings and therefore may benefit from an earnings disregard (see p309);[61]
- widow's pension, bereavement allowance and industrial death benefit;
- working tax credit (WTC). However, for housing benefit (HB), if your earnings are too low to use the whole £17.10 additional full-time earnings disregard (see p311), £17.10 is disregarded from your WTC instead of your earnings.[62] If a tax credit overpayment is being recovered from your WTC award, it is the amount of the WTC award less the overpayment that is taken into account for pension credit and HB;
- foreign social security benefits which are similar to the benefits listed above.[63]

Benefits and tax credits that are not taken into account

The following benefits and tax credits are ignored completely:[64]
- armed forces independence payment;

- attendance allowance (AA);[65]
- bereavement payments. These are taken into account as capital;[66]
- child benefit;[67]
- child tax credit (CTC);[68]
- Christmas bonus (see p835);[69]
- constant attendance allowance, exceptionally severe disablement allowance or severe disablement occupational allowance paid because of an injury at work or a war injury;[70]
- disability living allowance (DLA) care component and mobility component;[71]
- guardian's allowance;[72]
- HB;[73]
- mobility supplement under the War Pensions Scheme;[74]
- personal independence payment;[75]
- social fund payments[76] and local welfare provision replacing community care grants and crisis loans;
- supplementary payments to pre-1973 war widows or widowers;[77]
- increases for child dependants. Increases for adult dependants are only ignored if the dependant is not your partner.[78]

Benefits that are partly taken into account

The following benefits have £15 ignored:

- for HB only, widowed mother's allowance and widowed parent's allowance.[79]

The following benefits have £10 ignored:

- for pension credit (PC) only, widowed mother's allowance and widowed parent's allowance;[80]
- war disablement pension;[81]
- guaranteed income payment and survivor's guaranteed income payment under the Armed Forces Compensation Scheme (if reduced to under £10 by another pension, the remainder is disregarded from the pension);[82]
- war widow's, widower's or surviving civil partner's pension;[83]
- an extra-statutory payment made instead of the above pensions;[84]
- similar payments made by another country;[85]
- a pension from Germany or Austria paid to the victims of Nazi persecution.[86]

The £10 disregard allowed on these war pensions is additional to the total disregard of any mobility supplement or AA (ie, constant attendance allowance, exceptionally severe disablement allowance and severe disablement occupational allowance) paid as part of a war disablement pension.

Note: local authorities have discretion to increase the £10 disregard on war disablement, war widows' or widowers' pensions and on the guaranteed income payment and survivor's guaranteed income payment, when assessing income for HB.[87] Some local authorities disregard the full amount of these pensions, and

Part 3: General rules for means tested benefits
Chapter 15: Income: over pension credit age
4. Income other than earnings

some do not increase the disregard at all, so you should check your own local authority's policy. It has been held that a local authority must at least consider the nature and purpose of such pensions when deciding whether or not to disregard them, and the courts have indicated that it may be appropriate to apply a disregard to retrospective awards.[88]

Benefit delays

If you have made a claim for benefit but have not yet been paid, the benefit should not be treated as income possessed by you. For PC, you should get your full benefit and leave the DWP to deduct the difference from arrears of the delayed benefit when it is eventually awarded.[89]

For the treatment of payments of arrears of certain benefits and tax credits, see p382.

Maintenance payments

For HB, if you have a family premium included in your HB, £15 of any maintenance payments for you or your partner made by your (or your partner's) spouse/civil partner or former spouse/civil partner is disregarded.[90] If you receive maintenance from more than one person, only £15 of the total is disregarded. Other kinds of maintenance (eg, for a child) do not count as income and are ignored completely.[91]

For PC, any maintenance payments for you or your partner made by your (or your partner's) spouse/civil partner or former spouse/civil partner count in full as income. Maintenance for a child is ignored completely.[92]

If you *pay* maintenance to a former partner or a child not living with you, your payments are not disregarded for the purpose of calculating your income for PC or HB.[93] Even if you are on PC, you may still have to pay child support maintenance.

Income from tenants and lodgers

How income from tenants is treated depends on whether or not you live in the same property.

Lettings without board

If you own or are the tenant of your home, and you rent out a room(s) under an agreement, £20 of your weekly charge for each person is ignored. The balance is taken into account.[94]

If someone shares your home under an informal arrangement and is not paying rent under an agreement, any money s/he does pay is ignored,[95] but a non-dependant deduction may be made from any HB or housing costs paid with PC.

Boarders

If you have a boarder(s) on a commercial basis in your own home who is not a close relative (see p430), the first £20 of the weekly charge is ignored. Half of any balance remaining is taken into account as your income.[96]

For HB, this applies even if the boarder is a close relative or it is not a commercial arrangement (and there could be a non-dependant deduction). For PC in these circumstances, all the payment the boarder gives you is ignored, although there could be a non-dependant deduction from any housing costs paid with PC.[97]

This disregard applies for each boarder you have. The charge must normally include at least some meals.[98] If you have a business partner, even though your gross income includes just your share of the weekly charge to boarders, you still get the full disregard of £20 plus half the excess for each boarder.[99]

Tenants in other properties

Rent from a property other than your home is not taken into account as income.[100] Instead, the value of the property counts as capital and therefore is treated as producing a 'deemed income' (see p316). If the value of the property can be disregarded (see p379), both the rent and the capital value are ignored (there is no deemed income).[101]

Income from capital

The general rule is that capital (unless disregarded) is assumed to provide a set rate of income called 'deemed income' (see p316). Actual income generated from capital is ignored as income with the exception of the following types of capital.[102] In these cases, any actual income (but no deemed income) is taken into account.[103] **Note:** for HB, it is only taken into account in these cases if the total capital listed below is worth more than £10,000.[104]

Actual income from the following capital is taken into account:
* the value of the right to receive a payment in the future of:
  – income under a life interest or life rent;
  – rent, unless you only have a reversionary (ie, future) interest in the property. For the way the actual rent is treated, see p314;
  – the surrender value or income under an annuity;
* property held in a trust, but not charitable trusts or, for PC, trusts set up out of payments from personal injury to you or your partner or, for HB, from the Independent Living Funds, Macfarlane Trusts, the Fund, the Eileen Trust, MFET Ltd, the Skipton Fund, the Caxton Foundation or the London Bombings Relief Charitable Fund. Income from a discretionary trust can be ignored in some circumstances (see p317).

Part 3: General rules for means tested benefits
Chapter 15: Income: over pension credit age
4. Income other than earnings

If deemed income is taken into account, actual income from the same capital is ignored.[105]

There are no rules that treat capital of any kind as though it were income.

Deemed income

There is no upper capital limit for PC. If you have capital above £10,000, you are treated as having an assumed income of £1 for every £500, or part of £500, by which your capital exceeds £10,000.[106]

For HB, the following applies.

*   If you or your partner are getting the guarantee credit of PC, all of your (and your partner's) capital is ignored.[107]
*   In any other case, there is a capital limit of £16,000.[108] If you have capital above £10,000, you are treated as having an assumed income of £1 for every £500, or part of £500, of capital between £10,000.01 and £16,000.[109]

For PC and HB , you are not treated as having deemed income on capital that is disregarded (see p379).

Example
Samuel, aged 72, has savings of £12,000. Deemed income is taken into account for PC (he gets savings credit only) and HB of £4 a week for each benefit. Any interest from the savings is ignored as income.

Occupational and personal pensions

The following income is taken into account:[110]

*   an occupational pension;
*   income from a personal pension;
*   income from a retirement annuity contract (including an annuity purchased for you or transferred to you on divorce);
*   payments from a former employer for early retirement on the grounds of ill health or disability, unless this was under a court order or settlement of a claim;[111]
*   overseas pension;
*   Civil List Act pension;[112]
*   payment under an equity release scheme.[113] This provides regular payments from a loan secured on your home. For some home income plans where you buy an annuity, interest on the loan can be disregarded (see p317);
*   payments from the Financial Assistance Scheme and periodic payments from the Pension Protection Fund (these help some people with underfunded occupational schemes whose employer has gone out of business).

Some charitable trusts provide discretionary income to people retired from specific occupations. This is ignored for PC and HB.[114]

Specified miscellaneous income

Any income from copyright royalties, payments for patents, trademarks or under the Public Lending Rights Scheme are counted in full. Add the payments to your earnings (if any) if you are the first owner of the copyright or patent or author of the book and deduct the appropriate earnings disregards on p309.[115]

The following income is ignored:
- income paid outside the UK which cannot be transferred here;[116]
- if income is paid in another currency, any bank charges for converting the payment into sterling;[117]
- income from an annuity is normally taken into account. However, an amount equal to the interest payable on the loan with which the annuity was bought is ignored if:[118]
  - you used at least 90 per cent of the loan made to you to buy the annuity; *and*
  - the annuity will end when you and your partner die; *and*
  - you or your partner are responsible for paying the interest on the loan; *and*
  - you (if you took out the loan) or your partner (if s/he did) were at least 65 at the time the loan was made; *and*
  - the loan is secured on a property which you or your partner own or have an interest in, and the property on which the loan is secured is your home or your partner's home.

  If the interest on the loan is payable after income tax has been deducted, it is an amount equal to the net interest payment that is disregarded, otherwise it is the gross amount of the interest payment;
- any discretionary payment made to you by trustees is ignored altogether, *except* where the payment is for the purpose of:
  - obtaining food, ordinary clothing or footwear, or household fuel; *or*
  - paying rent, council tax or water charges for which you or your partner (if any) are liable. 'Rent' means eligible rent under the HB rules, less any non-dependant deductions; *or*
  - meeting housing costs which could be met by the PC rules.

  In this case, £20 of the payment is disregarded, or if the payment is less than £20, the whole of the payment is disregarded.[119] If this disregard overlaps with certain other disregards (eg, certain war pensions), a combined maximum of £20 is allowed.[120] **Note:** this is a weekly disregard so payments spread over different or successive benefit weeks attract a £20 disregard for each.

  School uniforms and sportswear are examples of clothing and footwear that are not ordinary;
- periodic payments made to you or your partner under an agreement entered into in settlement of a claim for any injury to you or your partner;[121]

Part 3: General rules for means tested benefits
Chapter 15: Income: over pension credit age
5. Notional income

- any payment ordered by a court to be made to you or your partner because of an accident, injury or disease you or your partner (or, for HB only, your child) have.[122]

Other income

Only income that is specified in the rules can affect your benefit. This income is listed on p305 and described on p317. Any other kind of income is ignored. The following are examples of income that is ignored and does not affect your benefit.
- **Student loans and grants** are disregarded.[123]
- For HB only, see p287 if you make a **parental contribution** to a student's grant or loan or towards your under-25-year-old child's expenses in advanced education.
- **Adoption allowances, fostering allowances, residence order payments** and **kinship care payments** are disregarded in full.[124]
- **Charitable and voluntary payments** are not taken into account as income, so if a charity or a person gives you voluntary payments, these do not reduce your benefit. **Note:** maintenance payments can affect your benefit (see p314).
- Payments for expenses if you are being consulted as a **service user** by certain public bodies are ignored. Other payments count as earnings but if you choose not to take them or have them paid to someone else on your behalf, they will not count as your notional income.[125]

5. Notional income

In certain circumstances, you may be treated as having income that you do not possess.

If you are working but earning less than the going rate, there are no rules to treat you as though your wages were higher than those you actually get, as there are for other means-tested benefits.

Deliberately getting rid of income

If you deliberately get rid of income in order to claim or increase your benefit, you are treated as though you are still in receipt of the income.[126] The basic issues involved are the same as those for the deprivation of capital (see p384). If you deferred your retirement pension to get extra increments, then take a lump sum instead, you are not treated as still having the increments (see below for what happens if you fail to apply for or defer your pension). **Note:** the rule can only apply if the purpose of the deprivation is to gain benefit for *yourself* (or your partner). It should not apply if, for example, you stop claiming carer's allowance (CA) solely so that another person (who is not your partner) can become entitled to a severe disability premium (see p233).[127] However, if you do not claim a benefit which would clearly be paid if you did, it may be argued that you have failed to apply for income (see below).

Failing to apply for income

Sometimes you can be treated as having pension income even though you have not applied for it.[128] There are no rules to treat you as having any other income, such as another benefit, that you could have applied for but did not.

If you defer your Category A or B pension, graduated retirement benefit or any shared additional pension paid on divorce, you are *not* treated as having that income for housing benefit (HB) before you actually claim it. However, for pension credit (PC), you *are* treated as having that income. The amount that counts for PC is the pension to which you would expect to be entitled were you to claim, less any overlapping benefit you get – eg, CA. If you have deferred claiming your pension for at least 12 months, the amount is based on your taking the lump-sum option (there is a choice when claiming a deferred pension to take a lump sum or to take extra pension income). To take account of the time it can take to process claims, you are only treated as having this income from the date you could expect to get it were you to make a claim.

For PC and HB, you are treated as having any amount of Category C or D pension and age addition to which you might expect to be entitled if you were to claim. For PC, any overlapping benefit you get is deducted.

You are treated as having any income from an occupational pension you have elected to defer beyond the scheme's retirement age,[129] as though you had claimed it (for PC, taking account of the time it might take to process and deducting any overlapping benefit). If you have reached the qualifying age for PC and are entitled to money-purchase benefits under an occupational or personal pension scheme and you fail to purchase an annuity (because you defer or do not apply), you are treated as having the amount of income you have foregone. If your scheme does not allow income withdrawal, you are treated as having income you could have received if you had chosen a different kind of scheme. However, if you give up a small occupational or personal pension in favour of a lump sum within the 'trivial commutation' limit (your pension provider can advise on this), you are not treated as having that income.[130]

Income paid to someone else on your behalf

Any money that counts as income and is paid to someone on your behalf is normally treated as being yours and is then either taken into account or ignored as income under the rules described in this chapter. The exception is for payments of income made under an occupational or personal pension scheme (or, for HB only, from the Pension Protection Fund) if you or your partner are bankrupt (or the subject of a sequestration order). In this case, if the payment is made to the trustee or other person acting on your creditors' behalf and you (and your partner) have no income other than the payment made, it is not treated as being yours.[131]

Part 3: General rules for means tested benefits
Chapter 15: Income: over pension credit age
6. Working out weekly income

6. **Working out weekly income**

To assess your weekly income:
- work out whether income is taken into account, or fully or partly disregarded (see p305);
- if income varies, work out average income (see below);
- convert into a weekly amount if necessary (see below);
- add any deemed weekly income from capital (see p316).

Variable income

If your earnings vary because you do not work the same hours every week, your weekly income may be averaged over the cycle, if there is an identifiable one.[132] If you do not work a recognisable cycle or your income fluctuates, your income is worked out on the basis of:[133]
- the last two payments before your claim was made or treated as made (or, where applicable, before your claim was superseded) if those payments are at least one month apart; *or*
- the last four payments before your claim was made or treated as made (or, where applicable, before your claim was superseded) if the last two payments are less than a month apart; *or*
- calculating (or estimating for HB) any other payments that would give a more accurate figure for your average weekly income.

In all cases, if the cycle involves periods when you do no work, those periods are included in the cycle, but not other absences – eg, holidays, sickness.

The payment is treated as if made for a period of a year if you are entitled to:[134]
- royalties or other sums for the use of any copyright, patent or trademark; *or*
- payments for any book registered under the Public Lending Rights Scheme 1982; *or*
- payments made on an occasional basis.

Converting income into a weekly amount

Pension credit (PC) and housing benefit (HB) are calculated on a weekly basis, so your earnings and other income have to be converted into a weekly amount if necessary. The following rules apply to income from employment and other income.[135] For income from self-employment, see p309.
- If the payment is for less than a week, it is treated as the weekly amount.
- If the payment is for a month, multiply by 12 and divide by 52.
- Multiply a payment for three months by four and divide by 52.
- Divide a payment for a year by 52.
- Multiply payments for any other periods by seven and divide by the number of days in the period.

The date from when a payment is counted

For PC, at the start of a claim or a new 'assessed income period' (see p89), the total weekly income is taken into account from the first day of the first 'benefit week' or new assessed income period.[136] A **'benefit week'** is the seven days ending on the day PC is payable if paid in arrears, or starting on that day if paid in advance.[137]

The general rule is that benefits are treated as paid on the last day of the PC benefit week in which the benefit is payable, but on the first day if the benefit is paid in advance.[138] Some benefits are treated slightly differently. Contribution-based jobseeker's allowance, contributory employment and support allowance and maternity allowance are treated as paid on the day that benefit is payable.

For other types of income, the general rule is that changes to income take effect from the first day of the benefit week in which the change takes place.[139] If that is not practicable, the change is put into effect from the start of the next benefit week. However, if there is a change to the amount of deemed income from capital or an increase in working tax credit, the change is put into effect from the benefit week that starts on or after the change takes place.[140]

Notes

1. Whose income counts
1 **PC** s5 SPCA 2002
   HB s136(1) SSCBA 1992
2 Reg 23(3) HB(SPC) Regs

2. What counts as income
3 s15 SPCA 2002; reg 15 SPC Regs
4 Regs 25 and 26 HB(SPC) Regs
5 Reg 27(4) HB(SPC) Regs
6 Reg 24 HB(SPC) Regs
7 Reg 27(4) HB(SPC) Regs
8 Reg 29 HB(SPC) Regs
9 **PC** Reg 17(10) SPC Regs
   HB Reg 33(12) HB(SPC) Regs
10 Reg 34 HB(SPC) Regs

3. Earnings
11 **PC** Regs 17(10) and 17A(4A) SPC Regs
   HB Reg 36(2) and (4) HB(SPC) Regs
12 *Parsons v Hogg* [1985] 2 All ER 897 (CA), appendix to R(FIS) 4/85
13 Reg 36(5) HB(SPC) Regs
14 **PC** Reg 17A(2) SPC Regs
   HB Reg 35(1) HB(SPC) Regs

15 **PC** Reg 17A(h) and (k) SPC Regs
   HB Reg 35(1)(h) and (k) HB(SPC) Regs
16 **PC** Reg 17A(h)-(k) SPC Regs
   HB Reg 35(1)(h)-(k) HB(SPC) Regs
17 **PC** Reg 17A(2)(e) SPC Regs
   HB Reg 35(1)(e) HB(SPC) Regs
18 R(IS) 9/95
19 *Minter v Kingston Upon Hull CC and Potter v SSWP* [2011] EWCA Civ 1155
20 **PC** Reg 17A(2)(g) SPC Regs
   HB Reg 35(1)(g) HB(SPC) Regs
21 **PC** Reg 17A(4) SPC Regs
   HB Reg 35(3) HB(SPC) Regs
22 **PC** Sch 6 para 6 SPC Regs
   HB Sch 4 para 8 HB(SPC) Regs
23 **PC** Reg 17A(3)(a) SPC Regs
   HB Reg 35(2)(a) HB(SPC) Regs
24 para 86058 DMG
25 para 86054 DMG
26 **PC** Reg 17A(3)(b) SPC Regs
   HB Reg 35(2)(b) HB(SPC) Regs
27 CIS/77/1993; CIS/89/1989
28 **PC** Sch 6 para 7 SPC Regs
   HB Sch 4 para 10 HB(SPC) Regs

Part 3: General rules for means tested benefits
Chapter 15: Income: over pension credit age
Notes

. . . .

3

29 **PC** Reg 17A(3)(c) SPC Regs
     HB Reg 35(2)(c) HB(SPC) Regs
30 **PC** s15(1)(c) SPCA 2002
     HB Reg 29(1)(c) HB(SPC) Regs
31 **PC** Reg 17A(3)(e) SPC Regs
     HB Reg 35(2)(e) HB(SPC) Regs
32 para 86162 DMG
33 **PC** Sch 6 para 6 SPC Regs
     HB Sch 4 para 8 HB(SPC) Regs
34 Reg 17ZA SPC Regs
35 **PC** Reg 17B(5) SPC Regs; reg 13(1) and
     (4) SSB(CE) Regs
     HB Reg 39(1)-(3) HB(SPC) Regs
36 **PC** Reg 17B(1) SPC Regs; regs 2 and
     13(4) SSB(CE) Regs
     HB Regs 2(1) and 39(2) and (11)
     HB(SPC) Regs
37 Reg 32(3) SS(C&P) Regs
     HB Reg 67(5) HB(SPC) Regs
38 **PC** Reg 17B(4)(b) SPC Regs; reg 12(2)
     SSB(CE) Regs
     HB Reg 38(2)(a) HB(SPC) Regs
39 **PC** Reg 17B SPC Regs; reg 11(1)
     SSB(CE) Regs
     HB Reg 37(1) HB(SPC) Regs
40 **PC** Reg 17B(5)(b) SPC Regs; reg 13(10)
     SSB(CE) Regs
     HB Reg 39(8) HB(SPC) Regs
41 Sch 4 para 2 HB(SPC) Regs
42 Sch 6 para 1 SPC Regs
43 Sch 6 paras 3 and 4A SPC Regs
44 Sch 6 para 4(1)(a) SPC Regs
45 Sch 6 para 4(1)(b) SPC Regs
46 Sch 6 para 4(2)-(4) SPC Regs
47 Sch 6 para 2 SPC Regs
48 Sch 4 para 4 HB(SPC) Regs
49 Sch 4 para 5(1)(a) HB(SPC) Regs
50 Sch 4 para 5(1)(b) HB(SPC) Regs
51 Sch 4 para 5(1)(d) HB(SPC) Regs
52 Sch 4 para 5(1)(c) HB(SPC) Regs
53 Sch 4 para 5(2) HB(SPC) Regs
54 Sch 4 para 3 HB(SPC) Regs
55 Sch 4 para 5A HB(SPC) Regs
56 **PC** Sch 6 para 5 SPC Regs
     HB Sch 4 para 7 HB(SPC) Regs
57 Sch 4 para 9 HB(SPC) Regs
58 Reg 30(1)(c) HB(SPC) Regs

4. Income other than earnings
59 **PC** Reg 15(5)(a) and (ab) SPC Regs
     HB Reg 29(1)(h) and (l) HB(SPC) Regs
60 **PC** Reg 15(3) SPC Regs
     HB Reg 29(3) HB(SPC) Regs
61 **PC** Reg 17A(2)(h)-(j) SPC Regs
     HB Reg 35(1)(h)-(j) HB(SPC) Regs
62 **PC** s15(1)(b) SPCA 2002
     HB Sch 5 para 21 HB(SPC) Regs

63 **PC** Reg 15(2) SPC Regs
     HB Reg 29(1)(k) HB(SPC) Regs
64 **PC** Reg 15(1) SPC Regs
     HB Reg 29(1)(j) HB(SPC) Regs
65 **PC** Reg 15(1)(b) SPC Regs
     HB Reg 29(1)(j)(ii) HB(SPC) Regs
66 **PC** Reg 15(1)(n) SPC Regs
     HB Reg 29(1)(j)(xiii) HB(SPC) Regs
67 Reg 15(1)(j) SPC Regs
68 s15 SPCA 2002
69 **PC** Reg 15(1)(k) SPC Regs
     HB Reg 29(1)(j)(x) HB(SPC) Regs
70 **PC** Reg 15(1)(c) and (e) and Sch 4 para
     2 SPC Regs
     HB Reg 29(1)(j)(iii) and (v) and Sch 5
     para 2 HB(SPC) Regs
71 **PC** Reg 15(1)(a) SPC Regs
     HB Reg 29(1)(j)(i) HB(SPC) Regs
72 **PC** Reg 15(1)(g) SPC Regs
     HB Reg 29(1)(j)(vii) HB(SPC) Regs
73 **PC** Reg 15(1)(l) and (m) SPC Regs
     HB Reg 29(1)(j)(xi) and (xii) HB(SPC)
     Regs
74 **PC** Sch 4 para 3 SPC Regs
     HB Sch 5 para 3 HB(SPC) Regs
75 **PC** Reg 15(1)(aa) SPC Regs
     HB Reg 29(ia) HB(SPC) Regs
76 **PC** Reg 15(1)(i) SPC Regs
     HB Reg 29(1)(j)(ix) HB(SPC) Regs
77 **PC** Sch 4 paras 4-6 SPC Regs
     HB Sch 5 paras 4-6 HB(SPC) Regs
78 **PC** Reg 15(1)(h) SPC Regs
     HB Reg 29(1)(j)(viii) HB(SPC) Regs
79 Sch 5 paras 7 and 8 HB(SPC) Regs
80 Sch 4 paras 7 and 7A SPC Regs
81 **PC** Sch 4 para 1(a) SPC Regs
     HB Sch 5 para 1(a) HB(SPC) Regs; Sch
     Part 1 HB&CTB(WPD) Regs
82 **PC** Sch 4 para 1(cc) SPC Regs
     HB Sch 5 para 1(d) HB(SPC) Regs
83 **PC** Sch 4 para 1(b), (ba) and (c) SPC
     Regs
     HB Sch 5 para 1(b) and (c) HB(SPC)
     Regs; Sch Part 1 HB&CTB(WPD) Regs
84 **PC** Sch 4 para 1(d) SPC Regs
     HB Sch 5 para 1(e) HB(SPC) Regs
85 **PC** Sch 4 para 1(e) SPC Regs
     HB Sch 5 para 1(f) HB(SPC) Regs
86 **PC** Sch 4 para 1(f) SPC Regs
     HB Sch 5 para 1(g) HB(SPC) Regs
87 ss134(8) and 139(6) SSAA 1992
88 *R v South Hams District Council ex parte
     Ash, The Times,* 27 May 1999
89 s74(2) SSAA 1992
90 Sch 5 para 20 HB(SPC) Regs
91 Reg 29(1)(o) HB(SPC) Regs
92 Reg 15(5)(d) SPC Regs
93 CIS/683/1993

Chapter 15

Income: over pension credit age

94 **PC** Sch 4 para 9 SPC Regs
   HB Sch 5 para 10 HB(SPC) Regs
95 **PC** Income from capital under s15(1)(i)
   SPCA 2002 would count but is ignored
   under regs 15(6) and 17(8), Sch 5 para
   1A and Sch 4 para 18 SPC Regs
   HB Reg 29(1)(i) HB(SPC) Regs
96 **PC** Sch 4 para 8 SPC Regs
   HB Sch 5 para 9 HB(SPC) Regs
97 Reg 15(6) and Sch 4 para 18 SPC Regs
98 **PC** Reg 1(2) SPC Regs
   HB Reg 2(1) HB(SPC) Regs
   Both definition of 'board and lodging
   accommodation'
99 CIS/521/2002
100 **PC** s15(1)(i) SPCA 2002; Sch 4 para 18
   SPC Regs
   HB Reg 29(1)(i) and Sch 5 para 22
   HB(SPC) Regs
101 **PC** Reg 17(8) SPC Regs
   HB Regs 29(1)(i) and 44(2) HB(SPC)
   Regs
102 **PC** Sch 4 para 18 SPC Regs
   HB Sch 5 para 22 HB(SPC) Regs
103 **PC** s15(1)(i) SPCA 2002; reg 15(6) and
   Sch 4 para 18 SPC Regs
   HB Reg 29(1)(i) HB(SPC) Regs
104 Sch 5 para 24 HB(SPC) Regs
105 **PC** Sch 4 para 18 SPC Regs
   HB Sch 5 para 22 HB(SPC) Regs
106 s15(2) SPCA 2002; reg 15(6) SPC Regs
107 Regs 25 and 26 HB(SPC) Regs
108 Reg 43 HB(SPC) Regs
109 Reg 29(2) HB(SPC) Regs
110 **PC** ss15(1)(c) and 16(1) SPCA 2002; reg
   16 SPC Regs
   HB Reg 29(1)(c) HB(SPC) Regs
111 **PC** Reg 16 SPC Regs
   HB Reg 29(1)(s) HB(SPC) Regs
112 **PC** Reg 16 SPC Regs
   HB Reg 29(1)(t) HB(SPC) Regs
113 **PC** Reg 16 SPC Regs
   HB Reg 29(1)(w) HB(SPC) Regs
114 para 85136 DMG
115 **PC** Reg 17(9) SPC Regs
   HB Reg 33(8) HB(SPC) Regs
116 **PC** Sch 4 para 15 SPC Regs
   HB Sch 5 para 16 HB(SPC) Regs
117 **PC** Sch 4 para 16 SPC Regs
   HB Sch 5 para 17 HB(SPC) Regs
118 **PC** Sch 4 para 10 SPC Regs
   HB Sch 5 para 11 HB(SPC) Regs
119 **PC** Sch 4 para 11 SPC Regs
   HB Sch 5 para 12 HB(SPC) Regs
120 **PC** Sch 4 para 11(3)(b) SPC Regs
   HB Sch 5 para 12(3) HB(SPC) Regs
121 **PC** Sch 4 para 14 SPC Regs
   HB Sch 5 para 15 HB(SPC) Regs

122 **PC** Sch 4 para 13 SPC Regs
   HB Sch 5 para 14 HB(SPC) Regs
123 The rules do not include grants and
   loans in the definition of 'income'.
124 **PC** s15 SPCA 2002; regs 15 and 17B(4)
   SPC Regs
   HB Regs 29 and 38(2) HB(SPC) Regs
125 **PC** Regs 17A(3)(f), 18(7A) and 24(2)
   SPC Regs
   HB Regs 35(2)(f), 41(8C) and 42(3)
   HB(SPC) Regs

5. Notional income
126 **PC** Reg 18(6) SPC Regs
   HB Reg 41(8) HB(SPC) Regs
127 paras 28608-16 DMG; see also CIS/
   15052/1996
128 **PC** Reg 18(1)-(5) SPC Regs
   HB Reg 41(1)-(7) HB(SPC) Regs
129 para 85453 DMG
130 **PC** Reg 18(9) SPC Regs
   HB Reg 41(11) HB(SPC) Regs
131 **PC** Reg 24 SPC Regs
   HB Reg 42 HB(SPC) Regs

6. Working out weekly income
132 **PC** Reg 17(2)(b)(i) SPC Regs
   HB Reg 33(2)(b)(i) HB(SPC) Regs
133 **PC** Reg 17(2)(b)(ii) SPC Regs
   HB Reg 33(2)(b)(ii) HB(SPC) Regs
134 **PC** Reg 17(4) SPC Regs
   HB Reg 33(4) HB(SPC) Regs
135 **PC** Reg 17(1) SPC Regs
   HB Reg 33(1) HB(SPC) Regs
136 para 85030 DMG
137 Reg 1(2) SPC Regs
138 Reg 13B SPC Regs
139 Sch 3B para 2 SS&CS(DA) Regs
140 Sch 3B paras 1(b) and 3 SS&CS(DA)
   Regs

3

Chapter 16

Income: universal credit

This chapter covers:
1. Whose income counts (below)
2. What income counts (p325)
3. Earned income (p326)
4. Income other than earnings (p333)
5. Working out monthly income (p338)

Key facts
- Your entitlement to universal credit (UC) and how much you get depends on your income.
- Your own income counts and, if you are a member of a couple, your partner's income also counts.
- Your earnings from employment and self-employment are taken into account on a monthly basis over each 'assessment period'.
- If earnings from self-employment are low, your UC award may be worked out on more earnings than you get, based on the number of hours the DWP expects you to work.
- Certain other kinds of income are also taken into account.

1. Whose income counts

Only your own income counts in working out your universal credit (UC) award if you are single.[1]

Couples normally make a joint claim and your UC award is worked out using your income and your partner's income added together.[2]

However, there are some situations in which one member of a couple qualifies for UC but the other does not – eg, in certain circumstances where your partner is under age 18, does not meet residence tests, is out of the country or is in prison (see p184). In these cases, you make a single claim. You do not get any amount for your partner in the UC award, but your partner's income (and capital) is still added to yours when working out the award.[3]

Children's income is ignored.

2. What income counts

The amount of universal credit (UC) you are entitled to depends on how much income you have.

Income for UC means:[4]

- earned income from employment (see p326) and self-employment (see p327);[5] *and*
- certain income other than earnings:[6]
  - certain benefits (see p333);
  - maintenance for you or your partner but not for a child (see p334);
  - student loan and grants (see p920 for how much of the loan counts and which grants are ignored);
  - certain income from employment and training schemes (see p334);
  - occupational and personal pensions (see p335);
  - certain insurance payments (see p335);
  - income from an annuity (seep335);
  - income from a trust (see p336 for which types are ignored);
  - assumed income from savings and other capital (see p336);
  - sports awards from UK Sport (see p337);
  - miscellaneous income (see p337);
  - capital treated as income (see below).

You may in certain circumstances be treated as having income that you do not actually have. This is called 'notional income'. See p332 for when you can be treated as having notional earned income and p338 for notional income other than earnings. If a type of income is not specified in the rules as being included for UC, then it is ignored and does not affect your award. See p338 for some examples of income that is ignored.

Income is taken into account month by month for each assessment period (see p186). You can keep a certain amount of earnings from employment and self-employment, known as your 'work allowance', before your award is affected. Above that level, as your earnings go up, the amount of UC you get goes down: 65 per cent of the amount above the work allowance is deducted from the maximum amount of UC (see p188). The whole of income other than earnings, if it is taken into account, is deducted from the maximum amount of UC. See p189 for how your UC award is worked out.

Income or capital?

Any amounts that are paid regularly and by reference to a specific period are treated as income and not as capital.[7] This is so even if payments might otherwise be regarded as capital or as being part capital – eg, payments under an annuity are treated as income.

Part 3: General rules for means tested benefits
Chapter 16: Income: universal credit
3. Earned income

This is also the case if you have a lump sum which is payable by instalments. Each instalment is treated as income, but only while your capital remains above the £16,000 upper limit for getting UC. Once what is left of the lump sum, added to any other capital you have, is below this limit, then each instalment is treated as capital.[8]

3. Earned income

How earnings are treated depends on whether you are employed (see below) or self-employed (see p327).

Employed earnings

To work out the amount of earnings from employment to take into account:
- check whether the payment counts as earnings (see below);
- work out monthly earnings for the assessment period (see p338);
- calculate net earnings for the assessment period (see p327).

The amount worked out as above is your monthly earnings from employment that is used in the universal credit (UC) assessment. If you also have self-employed earnings, these are also worked out (see p327) and added to your monthly employed earnings to give your total earned income. See p188 for how much of your earnings you can keep (the 'work allowance') before your UC award is reduced.

What counts as earnings

'Earnings' means 'remuneration or profits derived from... employment'. This includes:[9]
- wages and overtime pay;
- tips, bonuses, and commission;
- fees;
- holiday pay;
- statutory sick pay or other sick pay from your employer;
- statutory maternity pay, ordinary and additional statutory paternity pay, statutory adoption pay or other pay from your employer while you are on maternity, paternity or adoption leave.

The DWP usually gets information on your earnings from the records your employer sends to HM Revenue and Customs (HMRC) each time you are paid (see p339). So what counts for earnings for UC is normally what is recorded on PAYE records and is defined in terms of what counts as taxable income. However, there are differences, and not all kinds of taxable income count for UC purposes.

What does not count as earnings

Types of income not taken into account as earnings for UC include the following (some of which are taxable):[10]

- expenses incurred 'wholly, exclusively and necessarily' in the course of your employment;[11]
- certain taxable and tax exempt expenses and allowances – eg, mileage allowance, homeworkers' additional expenses (these are usually listed on HMRC Form P11D which your employer gives you);[12]
- expenses if you are a service user (or her/his carer) being consulted by a health, social care or social housing body providing statutory services or one undertaking research or monitoring to improve these services;[13]
- benefits in kind – eg, salary sacrifice scheme, non-cash vouchers (eg, for childcare), living accommodation connected with work, cars and car fuel benefits, parking or meals;[14]
- allowances for special types of employment – eg, certain armed forces allowances, free coal to miners or allowances in lieu of coal, offshore oil and gas workers' travel, subsistence and accommodation allowances.[15]

Earnings when you stop work

Your final earnings when you stop work are taken into account in the assessment period in which they are paid.[16] This includes arrears of pay, pay in lieu of notice and accrued holiday pay.[17] The following lump-sum payments are taken into account as capital:[18]

- redundancy pay, both statutory and contractual;
- employment tribunal awards for unfair dismissal;
- pay in lieu of notice for damages for breach of contract.

Working out net earnings

From your monthly earnings for the assessment period, deduct the following payments you make in that period:[19]

- income tax;
- Class 1 national insurance (NI) contributions;
- any contribution you make towards a personal or occupational pension scheme. If you pay contributions through your employer, your payslips should show your wages after the contributions have been deducted, so there is no further deduction to make.

Also deduct any charity payments under a payroll giving scheme.

Self-employed earnings

To work out the amount of your self-employed earnings to take into account in the UC assessment:[20]

- work out your actual receipts for the assessment period (see p328);

Part 3: General rules for means tested benefits
Chapter 16: Income: universal credit
3. Earned income

- deduct permitted expenses from your receipts (see below). This gives your gross profit;
- from the gross profit worked out as above (or your share of the gross profit if you are in a business partnership), deduct any payment made in the assessment period for:
  - income tax;
  - Class 2 or Class 4 NI contributions;
  - contributions made by you to a personal or occupational pension (but not if these have already been deducted from employed earnings).

Check whether the amount worked out as above (adding earnings from employment if you have any) is above the set minimum level of earnings (see p329). This is set at the national minimum wage for the number of hours the DWP expects you to work. If your earnings are below this level and you are in 'gainful self-employment', you are usually treated as having earnings equal to the minimum level. There are exceptions if you have recently started in self-employment or the DWP does not expect you to work.

Receipts from self-employment

The starting point to work out how much self-employed earnings are taken into account is the actual amount of receipts into the business in the assessment period – eg, sales, takings, payment for work.[21] Include:[22]
- any refund of income tax, VAT or NI contributions for the self-employment;
- receipts in kind – ie, the value of the goods or service you provided for which you accepted payment in kind.[23]

To work out gross profit, from these receipts, deduct the permitted expenses below.

Permitted expenses

Expenses must be reasonable and 'wholly and exclusively' incurred for purposes of your business.[24] Reasonable expenses may include:[25]
- regular costs – eg, rent, wages, utilities and insurance;
- stock purchase;
- stationery and advertising;
- repairs of business assets;
- transport (but see below for flat-rate deductions);
- equipment purchase and hire;
- up to £41 repayment of interest on a loan – eg, for an overdraft or credit card;
- VAT.

These are just examples. The deduction allowed is usually the actual amount of permitted expenses paid in the assessment period. However, there are flat-rate deductions for the use of a vehicle that you can choose to include instead of the actual expense of buying and using the vehicle:[26]

- for a motorcycle, 24 pence a mile;
- for a car, van or other vehicle, 45 pence a mile for the first 833 miles, then 25 pence a mile after that (for a car, you must use this rate rather than the actual expense).

If an expense has been incurred partly for business and partly for private purposes, the expense can be apportioned and the part that is identifiably for business deducted.[27] There are set deductions for the following.[28]

- If you use your own home for 'income-generating activities' for the business, instead of deducting actual expenses, there is a flat-rate deduction which depends on the number of hours spent in the assessment period. Activities include providing services to customers, business administration, sales and marketing, but do not include being on call.[29] The deduction is:
  - £10 for work of at least 25 hours but no more than 50 hours in the month;
  - £18 for work of more than 50 hours but no more than 100 hours;
  - £26 for more than 100 hours.
- If you live in premises that you use mainly for your business, then from the expenses relating to the premises deduct an amount depending on the number of people living there:
  - £350 if you live there alone;
  - £500 if you live there with one other person;
  - £650 if you live there with two or more other people.

Example
Margo runs a guest house. She and her partner, Jerry, live in the guest house. Margo works out her expenses as £1,500 for the monthly assessment period for the whole house. She finds it difficult to say which expenses are for the business. Instead of apportioning expenses for business and personal use, she deducts £500 from the £1,500 for the whole house. The expenses allowed are £1,000.

Minimum level of earnings

If your main work is self-employment but your earnings are low, your UC may be worked out on earnings higher than you actually have. This is called the 'minimum income floor' and is generally at the level of the national minimum wage for the number of hours the DWP expects you to work, usually 35 hours a week. This applies if:[30]

- you are in 'gainful self-employment' (see p331);
- you are not in a 'start-up' period (see p332);
- you have to meet all work-related requirements (see p1073). This is set out in your claimant commitment agreement that the DWP gives you when you

Part 3: General rules for means tested benefits
Chapter 16: Income: universal credit
3. Earned income

claim UC. If you are not subject to any work-related requirements, or just subject to work-focused interviews or work preparation, your actual earnings from self-employment are taken into account however low; *and*

- your earned income from self-employment, together with earnings from employment, if any, in the assessment period is less than the minimum income floor.

The minimum income floor

The 'minimum income floor' is equal to 35 hours a week at the minimum wage for your age (see Appendix 12). In some circumstances (eg, for some carers, disabled people and foster carers), the number of 'expected hours' is lower (see p1069). It is worked out monthly (ie, multiplied by 52 and divided by 12), deducting a notional appropriate amount for income tax and NI contributions.[31]

If you are single, your earnings are treated as being at the minimum income floor. This also means that you will have no work-related requirements to fulfil because it is based on the same individual 'earnings threshold' used to decide work-related requirements – see p1076).

If you are in a couple and the minimum income floor applies to you, normally your combined earnings for the UC assessment will be your partner's earnings added to the minimum income floor for you. However, you cannot be treated as having combined earnings of more than a certain amount. This amount is the same as the joint earnings threshold for couples used to decide if there are any work-related requirements to fulfil explained on p1076 but with a notional amount for tax and NI contributions deducted.[32]

- If your actual combined earnings are above the joint earnings threshold, it is your actual earnings that count in the UC assessment with no minimum income floor.
- If your actual combined earnings (ie, ignoring the minimum income floor) are below the joint earnings threshold, but adding your partner's actual earnings to the minimum income floor for your earnings would take you over the threshold, your combined earnings are treated as being equal to the joint earnings threshold with a notional amount for tax and NI contributions deducted.

Examples

Jake has a window cleaning business. He is single. For the current assessment period he declares earnings of £300. The DWP works out Jake's minimum income floor to be £920.02 a month (35 hours a week x £6.31 x 52 divided by 12, less £37 for notional tax and NI contributions). Jake's UC award for the assessment period is worked out on earnings of £920.02.

Maja and Jan are a couple. Jan is a self-employed builder and Maja works part time in a shop. They have a two-year-old child and Maja is the 'responsible carer'. Jan declares earnings of £500 and Maja £600. The DWP works out Jan's minimum income floor to be £920.02 a month (35 hours a week x £6.31 x 52 divided by 12, less £37 for tax and NI contributions).

Jan and Maja's actual combined earnings are £1,100 (£500 plus £600).

This is below their joint earnings threshold of £1,357.51 (£920.02 for Jan plus £437.49 for Maja (16 hours a week x £6.31 x 52 divided by 12 with no tax or NI contribution deduction at this earnings level)).

Adding Jan's minimum income floor to Maja's actual earnings gives £1,520.02 (£920.02 plus £600). This is above their joint earnings threshold of £1,357.51.

The amount of combined earnings taken into account is therefore limited to £1,357.51.

Gainful self-employment

When you claim UC or when you declare to the DWP that you are self-employed, you are asked to attend a 'gateway' interview if you are someone who has to meet all work-related requirements. You will be asked to bring evidence that you are in gainful self-employment which means that:[33]

- the self-employment is your main employment – ie, it is your only employment or, if you also work for an employer, you normally spend more hours or have more earnings from your self-employment; *and*
- your earnings count as self-employed earnings – ie, they are not employed earnings and are from carrying out a 'trade, profession or vocation'.[34] If it is not clear whether you are employed or self-employed, the DWP may look at a number of factors including whether you pay your own tax, whether your work is supervised and whether you can decide your own hours;[35] *and*
- your self-employment is 'organised, developed, regular and carried on in expectation of profit' – eg, whether you work for financial gain, how many hours you do, whether you have a business plan or have taken steps to get work, what work is arranged, whether you are registered as self-employed with HMRC, and whether you advertise your business.[36]

The DWP may decide that you are in gainful self-employment even though you are off sick and not able to do any work or you have no income at all from your business at present. If you disagree with a decision to apply a minimum income floor, you can ask for a revision and then appeal. You may argue, for example, that your self-employment is no longer organised or regular and you no longer have an expectation of profit. If you are off sick and your weekly earnings are below 16 times the hourly rate of the minimum wage (see Appendix 12), send in medical certificates so that the DWP can assess whether you have limited capability for work (see p1004 for how your earnings affect this assessment). If

Part 3: General rules for means tested benefits
Chapter 16: Income: universal credit
3. Earned income

you do, only your actual earnings should be taken into account (because you should no longer be subject to all work-related requirements – see p329).

If your business is new, but the DWP decides that it does count as gainful self-employment, you will then have a start-up period before the minimum income floor applies (see below).

If you are not in gainful self-employment, you still have to report your earnings and these are taken into account in your UC award but there is no minimum income floor applied.

Start-up period

If you are self-employed, during a 'start-up period' your UC is worked out on your actual earnings no matter how low. The minimum income floor does not apply.

This start-up period of 12 months starts from the beginning of the assessment period in which the DWP decides you are in gainful self-employment so long as you began your self-employment (as your main employment) at some point in the 12 months before that.[37] You must also be taking active steps to increase your earnings to the level of your individual earnings threshold – ie, the level that means you no longer have to meet work-related requirements (see p1076). The DWP can end the start-up period if it decides you are no longer taking active steps to increase your earnings or are no longer in gainful self-employment.

Once you have had one start-up period, you cannot have another one for the same self-employment. However, if you have stopped that work and started new self-employed work, you can have a new start-up period, but only if more than five years have passed since the start of the earlier period.

Notional earned income

You can be treated as having earnings from employment or self-employment that you do not actually have in the two circumstances below.

Deliberately getting rid of income to claim or increase benefit

If you deliberately get rid of income in order to claim or increase your UC, you are treated as though you still have that income.[38] In particular, this applies if you did actually get UC or more UC, and the DWP believes that this was a foreseeable result and was what you intended. Even if it is your employer who has arranged for you to lose income, you are still caught by this rule if you or your employer intended you to get UC or more UC by doing so.

Cheap or unpaid labour

If you are doing work for somebody or for an organisation for free or for less than the going rate (eg, you are working for a relative), you are treated as though you had earnings that would be reasonable for that work.[39] The comparison is with what the pay would be for similar work in the same location.

You are not treated as having more income than you receive for that work if:[40]

- the person cannot afford to pay you, or pay you more than s/he does;
- you work for a charitable or voluntary organisation or as a volunteer and it is accepted that it is reasonable for you to give your services free of charge or at less than the going rate;
- you are on a government-approved employment or training programme;
- you are a service user who is being consulted about provision of services by certain public bodies.

4. Income other than earnings

Only the specified types of income other than earnings are taken into account for universal credit (UC). These are listed on p325 and explained in more detail below. This kind of income reduces your UC pound for pound. Any other kind of income that is not earnings is ignored.

Benefits

Some benefits are taken into account as income while others are disregarded.

Benefits that are taken into account
The following benefits count in full:[41]
- bereavement allowance;
- carer's allowance;
- employment and support allowance;
- incapacity benefit;
- industrial injuries benefit except constant attendance allowance and exceptionally severe disablement allowance which are disregarded;
- jobseeker's allowance;
- maternity allowance;
- retirement pensions;
- severe disablement allowance;
- statutory sick pay, statutory maternity pay, statutory paternity pay and statutory adoption pay are treated as earnings and so may benefit from the work allowance;
- widow's pension, widowed mother's allowance, widowed parent's allowance;
- foreign social security benefits that are similar to the benefits listed above.

Benefits that are not taken into account
All other benefits are ignored – eg:
- armed forces independence payment;
- attendance allowance;
- bereavement payment (but it counts as capital);

Part 3: General rules for means tested benefits
Chapter 16: Income: universal credit
4. Income other than earnings

- child benefit;
- disability living allowance;
- guaranteed income payment and surviving guaranteed income payment under the Armed Forces Compensation Scheme;
- guardian's allowance;
- industrial injuries constant attendance allowance, exceptionally severe disablement allowance;
- personal independence payment;
- war disablement pension;
- war widows', widowers' or surviving civil partners' pensions.

Maintenance payments

Maintenance for a child is ignored completely.

Any maintenance for you or your partner made by your or your partner's spouse/civil partner or former spouse/civil partner under a court order or under a maintenance agreement counts in full as income.

If a former partner makes payments directly to a third party (eg, your mortgage lender), this should not count as your income.[42] However, if there is income available to you which you choose not to access, you could be caught by the 'notional income' rules (see p338).

If you *pay* maintenance to a former partner or a child not living with you, your payments are not disregarded when working out your income for UC.

Student loans and grants

For the special rules on the treatment of student loans, grants and other payments made to students, see Chapter 44.

Employment and training schemes

Payments from employment or training programmes under s2 of the Employment and Training Act 1973 or s2 of the Enterprise and New Towns (Scotland) Act 1990 are treated as follows.[43]

The following payments are taken into account:

- those made as a substitute for UC – eg, a training allowance;
- those intended for certain living costs. Payments for food, ordinary clothing or footwear, fuel, rent or other housing costs including council tax are all taken into account.

All other payments are disregarded – eg:

- travel expenses;
- training premium;
- childcare expenses;
- special needs payments.

Occupational and personal pensions

The following income is taken into account:[44]

- an occupational pension;
- income from a personal pension;
- income from a retirement annuity contract (including an annuity purchased for you or transferred to you on divorce);
- payments from a former employer for early retirement on the grounds of ill health or disability, unless this was under a court order or settlement of a claim;
- overseas pension;
- Civil List Act pension;
- payment under an equity release scheme. This provides regular payments from a loan secured on your home;
- payments from the Financial Assistance Scheme and periodic payments from the Pension Protection Fund (these help some people with underfunded occupational schemes whose employer has gone out of business).

Some charitable trusts provide discretionary income to people retired from specific occupations. This is ignored for UC.[45]

Insurance payments

There are two types of insurance policy payments that count as income:[46]

- illness, accident or redundancy insurance. Payments under a policy to insure against these risks are taken into account in full;
- mortgage protection policy and other loan protection policies for a loan secured on the home you live in. Payments under a policy to insure against the risk of being unable to maintain payments on a mortgage or loan secured on your home are taken into account if:
  - the payment is to pay interest on the mortgage or loan. The whole payment for interest counts even if your interest is more than the standard rate included in your UC. Any part of the payment for another purpose is ignored – eg, for capital repayment or policy premium; *and*
  - you have a housing element included in your UC for the mortgage or loan. If you or your partner have some earned income, your UC does not include a housing element so the whole of any mortgage protection payment you get is ignored.

Income from an annuity

Income from an annuity is taken into account with the exception of income from an annuity bought from personal injury compensation, which is ignored.[47] An annuity is usually when you pay a lump sum to an insurance company, often on retirement, with the capital built up in your personal pension, which then pays

Part 3: General rules for means tested benefits
Chapter 16: Income: universal credit
4. Income other than earnings

you an income for the rest of your life. It may also be through a home income plan where the annuity is bought with a loan secured on the home.

Income from trusts, personal injury payments and special compensation schemes

If you get an amount awarded to you because of a personal injury to you, it can be disregarded in certain circumstances.[48]

- You receive the compensation in regular payments. They are disregarded as income.
- The compensation is in a trust. Both the capital value of the trust and any income from the trust is ignored. For more about trusts, see p346 and about how payments from personal injury trusts or other trusts are treated, see pp347–48.
- The compensation was used to buy an annuity. Payments under the annuity are ignored.
- The compensation is administered by the court on your behalf or can only be used by direction of the court. The capital is ignored and regular payments are disregarded as income.
- If the compensation is not used in one of the ways above, it is disregarded as capital for 12 months. This gives you a chance to spend some or all of it, or to put it in a trust or buy an annuity.

Income from a trust that is not set up from personal injury compensation is taken into account, whether it is a discretionary trust or other type of trust.

Special compensation schemes

Any payment of income or capital from certain special schemes approved or set up by government are ignored if they are:[49]

- to support people with a disability to live independently – eg, the Independent Living Fund;
- for those with variant CJD (Creuzfeldt-Jacob disease) or infected from contaminated blood products – eg, the MacFarlane Trusts;
- compensation for the London bombings of July 2005;
- World War Two compensation (rather than a war pension).

Income from capital

If you have capital over £16,000, you are not entitled to UC. If your capital is below this level, it can affect the amount of income that is taken into account. This is either because you have actual income from the capital, such as income from a trust, or because it is assumed that the capital is giving you a certain amount of income.

Assumed monthly income

If your capital is over £6,000 but not more than £16,000, you are treated as having a certain amount of income from it. This assumed monthly income is set at the rate of £4.35 a month for every £250, or part of £250, between £6,000.01 and £16,000.[50]

Example
Nuala and Ian have savings of £9,100. They are treated as having an income of £56.55 a month from their savings. £9,100 – £6,000 = £3,100. £3,100 divided by £250 = 12.4 (ie, 12 x £250 plus part of £250). 13 x £4.35 = £56.55.

In working out how much capital you have, some capital is disregarded (see p350). You are not treated as having an assumed monthly income from disregarded capital.[51]

Note: the lower limit is £6,000 in all circumstances, even if you are in a care home (the lower capital limit is £10,000 for other means-tested benefits).

Actual income from capital

If your capital is treated as giving you an assumed monthly income as above, any actual income you might have from the same capital is treated as part of your capital from the day it is due to be paid to you.[52] For example, if you own a property other than the home you live in, rent is taken into account not as income but as capital and added to the capital value of the property itself (see also p338).

There are two types of capital where actual income is specifically taken into account. This applies to income from an annuity and income from a trust (unless the income is disregarded because the annuity or trust is from personal injury compensation, see p335 and p336). In these two cases, the capital is not also treated as giving you an assumed monthly income.[53] For example, if you have income from a trust (one that was *not* set up from a personal injury payment) it counts as your income, but the capital value of the trust is not also treated as giving you an assumed monthly income (see p348 for more about how trusts are treated).

Sports awards

A sports award from UK Sport out of National Lottery funds for living expenses is taken into account. This covers food, ordinary clothing and footwear, fuel, rent, housing costs and council tax for you, your partner or dependent child.[54] Amounts for anything else are ignored – eg, sportswear.

Specified miscellaneous income

If a type of income is not listed in the rules as being taken into account (p325), it is ignored for UC. The category of 'miscellaneous income' only includes unearned

Part 3: General rules for means tested benefits
Chapter 16: Income: universal credit
5. Working out monthly income

income that is taxable under the HM Revenue and Customs 'sweep-up' provisions in Part 5 of the Income Tax (Trading and Other Income) Act 2005.[55] This includes copyright royalties if your writing does not amount to a trade or profession and unusual tax situations – eg, tax avoidance schemes.

Notional income other than earnings

You may be treated as having income even if you do not actually have it.[56] This only applies to income that would be available to you if you applied for it.

However, you cannot be treated as having another benefit that you have not applied for, with the exception of retirement pension.

If you are over pension credit (PC) age, you may be treated as having pension income even though you have not applied for it. The rules are the same as those for PC on p319. If you are under PC age, you can choose not to apply for pension income without your UC award being affected.

The rules on notional earned income are on p332.

Other income

Only income specified in the rules and described above can affect your UC. Any other kind of income is ignored – eg:

- adoption allowance, fostering allowance, residence order payment and kinship care payment;
- support from a charity – eg, if you get income from a benevolent fund;
- voluntary payments – eg, if a family member gives you regular money. However, if it is voluntary maintenance for you (rather than for a child which is always ignored) from a separated or former spouse or civil partner, this is taken into account;
- payments to third parties – eg, if a family member pays your phone bill for you;
- rental income from a room you let in your own home. This is because actual income that comes from capital that is disregarded (the value of the home you live in is disregarded) is not in the list of income that is taken into account. On the other hand, if you rent out a property that you do not live in, the capital value of that property is taken into account and the rent is treated not as income but as capital. This is because actual income that comes from capital that is *not* disregarded is generally treated as capital (see p337).

5. Working out monthly income

Universal credit (UC) is paid in arrears for the monthly assessment period (see p186) just past. Awards are worked out month by month. Your award is adjusted as your earnings or other income go up or down but always for a whole assessment period.[57] UC awards are not adjusted for income changes part way through the monthly assessment period. See p198 for reporting changes in your earnings and when this affects your award.

Monthly earned income

When you first claim, the DWP can make a decision on whether you qualify for UC based on an estimate of your earnings.[58] At the end of the first assessment period, your award will be based instead on your actual earnings.[59]

The amount of earnings used to work out your UC award for each assessment period is based on the actual amount you received in that assessment period.[60] There is no averaging from one month to the next.

If you are **employed**, your employer is required to report your earnings to HM Revenue and Customs every time you are paid. This is called '**real-time information**'. The employed earnings figure used in the UC assessment is taken from the amount in the report/s received by the DWP in that assessment period.[61]

If your employer does not report your earnings or reports late, the DWP may ask you to give this information instead (called 'self-reporting').[62] If you do not report this information as required, the award can be based on an estimate of earnings for the assessment period, but may be suspended (see p1175).[63]

If you think the DWP has used the wrong earnings figure, you can ask for a formal decision and then ask for the decision to be revised.[64]

If you are **self-employed**, you must report your earnings every month. Your UC award is based on the actual amount received in the assessment period and the actual amounts paid out in, for example, tax and expenses. The way you work out your earnings for the assessment period is explained on p327. If you do not report your earnings in time, your UC award may be suspended and, after another month, your entitlement terminated.

Monthly income other than earnings

Each type of income you have that is not earnings is worked out as a monthly amount – eg:[65]

- multiply weekly payments by 52 and divide by 12;
- multiply fortnightly payments by 26 and divide by 12;
- multiply payments for four weeks by 13 and divide by 12;
- multiply payments for three months by four and divide by 12;
- a payment of income for a whole year is divided by 12.

If your income varies and there is a cycle that can be identified, you take one cycle and convert that as above into a monthly amount. If there is no cycle to the income, it is worked out by taking three months of income, or another period if

Part 3: General rules for means tested benefits
Chapter 16: Income: universal credit
Notes
• •

that would give a more accurate picture, and calculating an average monthly amount as above.

Note: there are different rules for working out student income (see p920).

• •

Example

Dan gets contributory employment and support allowance (ESA) of £202.30 every two weeks. The amount of ESA taken into account in his UC award is £438.32 (£202.30 x 26 divided by 12).

• •

Notes

• •

1. Whose income counts
1 s8(4)(a) WRA 2012
2 s8(4)(b) and Sch 1 para 4(5) WRA 2012; reg 22(1) UC Regs
3 Regs 3(3) and (6) and 22(3) UC Regs

2. What income counts
4 s8(3) WRA 2012
5 Reg 52 UC Regs
6 Reg 66 UC Regs
7 Reg 46(3) UC Regs
8 Reg 46(4) UC Regs

3. Earned income
9 Reg 55(2) and (4) UC Regs; HMRC, *Employment Income Manual*, para 00520
10 Reg 55(2) and (3)(a) UC Regs
11 Part 5, Chapter 2, s336 IT(EP)A 2003
12 Part 4 IT(EP)A 2003
13 Regs 53(2) and 55(3)(b) UC Regs
14 Part 3, Chapters 2 to 11 and Part 4, Chapter 6 IT(EP)A 2003
15 Part 4, Chapter 8 IT(EP)A 2003
16 Reg 54(1) UC Regs
17 Reg 55(2) UC Regs; these are 'general earnings' under s7(3) IT(EP)A 2003 – HMRC, *Employment Income Manual*, para 12850
18 Reg 55(2) UC Regs; these come under s401 IT(EP)A 2003 and are therefore not 'general earnings' under s7(3) – HMRC, *Employment Income Manual*, paras 12960 and 13005
19 Reg 55(5) UC Regs

20 Reg 57 UC Regs
21 Regs 54 and 57(3) UC Regs
22 Reg 57(4) UC Regs
23 para H4184 ADM
24 Reg 58(1) UC Regs
25 Reg 58(2) and (3) UC Regs; para H4214 ADM
26 Reg 59(2) UC Regs
27 Reg 58(1)(b) UC Regs
28 Reg 59(3) and (4) UC Regs
29 para H4241 ADM
30 Reg 62(1) and (5) UC Regs
31 Reg 62(2) UC Regs
32 Reg 62(3) and (4) UC Regs
33 Reg 64 UC Regs
34 Reg 57(1) UC Regs
35 para H4016 ADM
36 para H4050 ADM
37 Reg 63 UC Regs
38 Reg 60(1) and (2) UC Regs
39 Reg 60(3) UC Regs
40 Reg 60(4) UC Regs

4. Income other than earnings
41 Reg 66(1)(a) and (b) UC Regs; reg 28(1) UC(TP) Regs
42 Because there is no rule to treat payments to a third party as yours; DWP email to CPAG, 7 February 2013
43 Reg 66(1)(f) UC Regs
44 Reg 67 UC Regs; reg 16 SPC Regs
45 Because this type of income is not in the list of income that counts under reg 66 UC Regs.

46 Reg 66(1)(h) UC Regs
47 Reg 66(1)(i) UC Regs
48 Reg 75 UC Regs
49 Reg 76 UC Regs
50 Reg 72(1) UC Regs
51 Reg 72(2) UC Regs
52 Reg 72(3) UC Regs
53 Reg 72(2) UC Regs
54 Reg 66(1)(g) UC Regs
55 Reg 66(1)(m) UC Regs; Part 5 Income Tax (Trading and Other Income) Act 2005
56 Reg 74 UC Regs

5. Working out monthly income
57 Sch 1 paras 20-30 UC,PIP,JSA&ESA(DA) Regs
58 Reg 54(2)(a) UC Regs
59 para H3011 ADM
60 Reg 54 UC Regs
61 Reg 61(1) UC Regs
62 Reg 61(2) UC Regs
63 Reg 54(2)(b) UC Regs
64 Reg 41 UC,PIP,JSA&ESA(DA) Regs
65 Reg 73 UC Regs

Chapter 17

Capital: under pension credit age

3

This chapter covers:
1. The capital limits (p343)
2. Whose capital counts (p344)
3. What counts as capital (p344)
4. Disregarded capital (p350)
5. Notional capital (p359)
6. How capital is valued (p366)

This chapter explains how capital affects your entitlement to income support, income-based jobseeker's allowance, income-related employment and support allowance and universal credit. It also applies to housing benefit (HB) if you and your partner are under the qualifying age for pension credit (PC). Chapter 18 explains the rules for PC and for HB if you or your partner are over the qualifying age for PC. For the capital limits for health benefits, see Chapter 30. There are no capital rules for non-means-tested benefits.

Key facts
- If you have more than £16,000 capital, you are not entitled to income support (IS), income-based jobseeker's allowance (JSA), income-related employment and support allowance (ESA), housing benefit (HB) or universal credit (UC).
- If you have capital above a lower limit, your benefit is affected because this is assumed to give you a certain income, often called 'tariff income'.
- Some kinds of capital are ignored when working out your benefit – eg, the value of the home in which you live.
- Getting IS, income-based JSA, income-related ESA or UC means the amount of your HB is automatically the maximum, so there is no need to work out your capital again for HB (although usually you would not get UC and HB together).

1. The capital limits

There is a lower and upper limit.[1]
* The lower limit is £6,000.
* The upper limit is £16,000.

If you have over £16,000 of capital, you are not entitled to benefit. The first £6,000 is ignored and does not affect your weekly benefit. If you have between £6,000.01 and £16,000, you may be entitled to benefit, but it is assumed that you have some income from your capital (known as 'tariff income' or for universal credit (UC), as 'assumed monthly income').

This 'tariff income' (see p282) is assumed to be £1 a week for every £250, or part of £250, of your capital within these limits. For UC, this assumed monthly income (see p336) is £4.35 a month for every £250, or part of £250, of your capital within these limits.

The lower limit is £10,000 if you live in a care home (see below), except for UC when it is always £6,000.

Whichever limit applies, some capital is disregarded (see p350), but you may also be treated as having some capital which you do not actually have (see p359).

Care homes

If you live permanently in a care home (see p955):
* the lower limit is £10,000 except for UC;
* the lower limit is £6,000 for UC;
* the upper limit is £16,000.

Tariff income starts above £10,000 or, for UC, above £6,000.

For housing benefit (HB),[2] the £10,000 lower limit applies if you live permanently in one of the limited categories of care home for which HB is payable (see p955). Some temporary absences (see p103) are ignored.

Example

Colin gets income-related employment and support allowance (ESA). He has £8,100 in savings. He is assumed to have tariff income of £9 a week. Colin moves permanently into a care home. Because his savings are below the £10,000 limit, they are now disregarded entirely. A few months later he sells his home and gets £80,000. As a result he is no longer entitled to income-related ESA.

Part 3: General rules for means tested benefits
Chapter 17: Capital: under pension credit age
3. What counts as capital

2. Whose capital counts

Your partner's capital

If you are a member of a couple (see p205), your partner's capital is added to yours.[3]

If your partner is a 'person subject to immigration control', her/his capital is added to yours even if you are not paid benefit for her/him (see p1507). For universal credit, in the limited circumstances for couples in which you must make a single claim rather than a joint claim, your partner's capital is still added to yours (see p184).[4]

Your child's capital

Your child's capital is not added to yours and does not affect your benefit.[5] However, if you are still entitled to have amounts for children included in your income support or income-based jobseeker's allowance (ie, your benefit award includes a child, it began before 6 April 2004 and you have not yet been awarded child tax credit), your child's capital is not added to yours. However, if your child's capital is over £3,000, you cannot get benefit included for her/ him (although the family premium is still payable – see p228).[6] If this applies, any income of the child is not counted as yours.[7]

3. What counts as capital

All your capital is taken into account, unless it is disregarded (see p350) or is treated as income (see p359).

The term 'capital' is not defined. In general, it means lump-sum or one-off payments rather than a series of payments – eg, it includes savings, property and statutory redundancy payments.[8] For how other payments when you stop work are treated, see p261, and for universal credit (UC), see p327.

Capital payments can normally be distinguished from income because they are not payable for any specified period(s) and they are not part of a regular series of payments (although capital can be paid by instalments).[9]

Note: some capital is treated as income (see p282 and p325) and some income is treated as capital (see p349).

Savings

Your savings generally count as capital – eg, cash you have at home, premium bonds, stocks and shares, unit trusts and money in a bank account or building society.

There is no provision to disregard money put aside to pay bills.[10] If your savings are just below the capital limit, you could pay bills by monthly direct debit or use a budget account to keep your capital below the limit.

For income support (IS), income-based jobseeker's allowance (JSA), income-related employment and support allowance (ESA) and housing benefit (HB), your savings from past earnings can only be treated as capital when all relevant debts, including tax liabilities, have been deducted.[11] Savings from other past income (including benefits – see p355) are treated as capital after the period for which the income was paid has lapsed – eg, a weekly payment of child benefit becomes capital a week after it is paid and a monthly occupational pension becomes capital after a month.[12]

Fixed-term investments

Capital held in fixed-term investments counts. However, if it is presently unobtainable, it may have little or no value. If you can convert the investment into a form that lets you access it, or you sell your interest, or raise a loan through a reputable bank using the asset as security, its value counts. If it takes time to produce evidence about the nature and value of the investment, you may be able to get a short-term advance of IS, JSA, ESA or UC (see p1167) or a payment on account of HB (see p139).

Property and land

Any property or land that you own counts as capital. Many types of property are disregarded (see p350). See also 'proprietary estoppel' on p347.

Loans

A loan to you usually counts as money you possess. In the following situations, you can argue that a loan should not count as your capital:

- a loan granted on condition that you only use the interest but do not touch the capital because the capital element has never been at your disposal;[13]
- money you have been paid to be used for a particular purpose on condition that the money must be returned if not used in that way;[14]
- property you have bought on behalf of someone else who is paying the mortgage;[15]
- money held in your bank account on behalf of another person, which is to be returned to her/him at a future date;[16]
- when you get the loan, you are under an immediate obligation to repay it.[17]

See p282 if you find that a loan is taken into account as income even though it is paid as a lump sum.

If you lend money to someone, it could still count as your 'notional capital' (see p359) depending on your reasons for lending it. You will normally have a

Part 3: General rules for means tested benefits
Chapter 17: Capital: under pension credit age
3. What counts as capital

legal right to be repaid and that right itself could have a capital value, although the value would normally be less than the amount loaned, and could be nil if you have no expectation of getting the money back.[18]

Trusts

A trust is a way of owning an asset. In theory, the asset is split into two notional parts: the legal title owned by the trustee and the beneficial interest owned by the beneficiary. A trustee (if not also a beneficiary) can never have use of the asset, only the responsibility of looking after it. An adult beneficiary can ask for the asset at any time. Anything can be held on trust – eg, money, houses and shares.

If you are the adult beneficiary of:

* a non-discretionary trust, you can obtain the asset from the trustee at any time. You effectively own the asset and so its market value counts as your capital;
* a discretionary trust, you cannot insist on receiving payments from it. Payments are at the discretion of the trustee within the terms of the trust. The trust asset itself does not normally count as your capital because you cannot demand payment (of either income or capital);[19]
* a trust which gives you the right to receive payments in the future (eg, on reaching 25) has a current capital value, unless disregarded (see p355).

If you transfer an asset into a trust in order to increase benefit entitlement, it could still count as yours under the 'notional capital' rules (see p360).

If you only have a life interest (in Scotland, a life rent) in an asset (ie, you have the right to enjoy an asset in your lifetime, but the asset passes to someone else when you die), the value of your right to receive income from the asset is disregarded but not the income itself if you get any (see p355 – there is no special rule for UC).[20]

If the beneficiary is under 18, even with a non-discretionary trust, s/he has no right to payment until s/he is 18 (16 in Scotland, or later if that is what the trust stipulates). Her/his interest may nevertheless have a current value.

Do you hold an asset for someone else?

There may be a trust even without a formal trust deed.[21] If you hold an asset as a trustee, it is not part of your capital.

You are only a trustee if either:

– someone gives you an asset on the express condition that you hold it for someone else (or use it for her/his benefit); or

– you have expressed a clear intention that your own asset is for someone else's benefit and renounced its use for yourself.[22]

It is not enough just to intend to give someone an asset; you usually must transfer it in a particular way for there to be a trust. However, if you lead someone to believe that you are transferring your interest in some property or land to her/him, but fail to do so (eg, it is never properly conveyed) and that person acts on the belief that s/he has ownership (eg, s/he improves or repairs it, or takes on a mortgage), it would then be unfair if s/he were to lose out if you insisted that you were still the owner.[23] In this case, you can argue the capital asset has been transferred to her/him and you are like a trustee. Thus, when claiming benefit, you can insist that it is not your capital asset, but the other person's. This is referred to as 'proprietary estoppel'.

If money (or another asset) is given to you to be used for a special purpose, it may be possible to argue that it should not count as your capital.[24]

Payments of personal injury compensation

A payment that does not come from a trust and is made because of personal injury to you or your partner is disregarded for 52 weeks.[25] This gives you time to spend some or all of the payment, or put it into a trust or annuity, before your benefit is affected. The 52 weeks start from when you receive the payment (for UC, this is defined as when it is paid to you). As you spend it, the disregard goes down to the level of the payment you have left. A subsequent payment for the same injury is not disregarded unless it is put into a trust.

If a trust fund has been set up out of money paid because of a personal injury to yourself or your partner, its value is ignored without time limit.[26] See p348 for how income and capital payments from trust funds are treated.

If the personal injury was to your partner and s/he has since died, you cannot carry over the remainder of the 52-week disregard, or if the payment is in a trust fund, it is no longer ignored.[27] If the personal injury was to a child, income or capital belonging to the child does not count as yours, so compensation paid for the child should not affect your benefit. However, if you still get amounts for a child included in your IS or JSA (see p344), the value of a personal injury trust for a child is not ignored.

For the payment to be disregarded, it is not necessary for the trust to be set up by a formal deed. The important point is that the person who is awarded the compensation should not be able to have any direct access to it.

In this context, 'personal injury' includes not only accidental and criminal injuries, but also any disease and injury as a result of a disease.[28]

Trust funds administered by a court

The value of a trust fund is also ignored if damages are awarded for personal injury and the money is paid into a special fund administered by a court – eg, the Court of Protection.[29] As well as ignoring the capital value, income from these funds is also ignored.[30] This also applies if the fund is for children to compensate for the death of a parent (except for UC).

Note: the notional income and capital rules (see p288 and p359) do not apply to trusts or funds administered by a court that have been set up as a result of a personal injury (although there is no specific exclusion for UC).

Part 3: General rules for means tested benefits
Chapter 17: Capital: under pension credit age
3. What counts as capital

Payments from trust funds

Whether your money is in a discretionary or non-discretionary trust can make a difference to how your benefits are affected. If the trust is set up from money for a personal injury, the rules are more generous.

How payments are treated: general rule

The general rule (which does not apply to UC) is that payments made from a trust fund *not* set up from money for a personal injury to you or your partner:

- from a discretionary trust count as income or capital depending on the nature of the payment.[31] Capital payments are taken into account in full, but income from the trust is generally treated as a voluntary payment and is ignored;[32]
- from a non-discretionary trust count in full as capital, whatever the nature of the payment.[33]

Payments made to you from a discretionary or non-discretionary trust set up from money for a personal injury to you or your partner are treated either as income or capital depending on the nature of the payment. Income is disregarded, but capital payments count in full.[34]

Trustees may have a discretion to use such funds to purchase items that would normally be disregarded as capital, such as personal possessions (eg, a wheelchair, car or new furniture) or to arrange payments that would normally be disregarded as income – eg, ineligible housing costs. Similarly, they may have discretion to clear debts or pay for a holiday, leisure items or educational or medical needs. See p279 for the treatment of voluntary payments and p279 and p290 for the treatment of payments made to third parties.

How payments are treated: universal credit

If you have money in a trust from a personal injury to you or your partner, income from the trust is disregarded.[35] This also means that any regular payment is disregarded if it is paid for a particular period even if, for example, you get it just once a year.[36] However, a lump sum from the trust that is not for a particular period is taken into account as capital. It should not affect your benefit if trustees give you regular payments, pay your bills or, instead of giving you a lump sum, buy you something that would be disregarded because it is a personal possession – eg, furniture or a car. The value of the capital from personal injury money in the trust itself is disregarded.

If you have a trust *not* from money from a personal injury to you or your partner, payments from the trust are taken into account in full, whether they are income or capital.[37]

Note:

- Putting money in a discretionary trust has the advantage of the value of the trust itself being disregarded. Note, however, that if you transfer money into a trust in order to get more UC, it can still count as yours under the notional capital rules (see p359).

- You are treated as having access to the capital in a non-discretionary trust and so it counts as your capital. If this takes you over the £16,000 capital limit, you are not entitled to UC. However, you are not treated as having an assumed monthly income from the capital.[38]
- There is no difference between a discretionary and non-discretionary trust in the way that payments to you from the trust are treated. In either case, they are taken into account. Generally, regular payments for a particular period are treated as income while a lump sum is treated as capital.[39]
- If trustees of a discretionary trust choose to pay your bills directly or buy you something that is disregarded (eg, because it is a personal possession), this should not affect your benefit.

Money held by your solicitor

Money held by your solicitor normally counts as your capital. This includes compensation payments, other than for personal injury, before a trust fund has been set up.[40] A payment for personal injury to you or your partner is ignored for 52 weeks from when you receive it (see p347). If it is sent to your solicitor first, it is likely the 52 weeks will start from when the solicitor receives it. If you have had legal aid and your solicitor is holding money back while working out the statutory charge to be deducted for legal costs, it does not count as your capital, as it is not possible to identify the capital which belongs to you until any statutory charge has been quantified and deducted.[41]

Income treated as capital

Certain payments which appear to be income are treated as capital. The general rule (which does not apply to UC) is that the following payments are treated as capital:[42]

- income from capital (eg, interest on a bank account) and income from property let to tenants (see p280). However, income from the first five disregarded property bullet points listed on p351, trust funds administered by a court (see p347), income from the home of a partner, former partner or relative in the circumstances described on p353, income from the home in which you normally live and income from business assets or personal injury trusts count as income not capital;
- a lump sum or 'bounty' paid to you not more than once a year as a part-time firefighter, part-time member of a lifeboat crew, auxiliary coastguard or member of the Territorial Army;
- the following payments:
  - an advance of earnings or loan from your employer;

Part 3: General rules for means tested benefits
Chapter 17: Capital: under pension credit age
4. Disregarded capital

- holiday pay which is not payable until more than four weeks after your employment ends or is interrupted;
- income tax refunds;
- irregular (one-off) charitable or voluntary payments.

This does not apply to IS or income-based JSA if you are involved in a trade dispute, or to IS if you are returning to work after a dispute (see p971);

- for IS, income-based JSA and income-related ESA only, a discharge grant paid on release from prison;
- for IS and income-based JSA only, arrears of residence order payments from a local authority;
- for HB only, any arrears of child tax credit or working tax credit;[43]
- for HB only, the gross receipts from work carried out under New Enterprise Allowance.

For UC, actual income from capital (unless the capital is disregarded – see below) is treated as capital from the day it is due to be paid – eg, interest on savings or rent from a property that is not your home.[44] This avoids double counting income from capital, which is also treated as giving you an assumed monthly income (see p343).

Example
Gordon has £7,000 savings, which give him interest of £8 a month. His UC assessment takes into account an assumed monthly income from his savings of £17.40 (£4.35 a month for each £250 above the £6,000 lower capital limit) and his actual £8 interest is added to his capital.

4. **Disregarded capital**

Your home

If you own the home in which you normally live, its value is ignored.[45]

This disregard applies to any home in which you are treated as normally living – eg, because you are only temporarily living away from it (see p431). If you own more than one property, only the one that you normally occupy is disregarded under this rule.[46]

Exceptionally, for means-tested benefits other than universal credit (UC), two separate properties can be regarded as a single home as though one was an annexe of the other, if you personally (rather than a member of your family) normally occupy both properties.[47] This is more likely for a large family, but you could argue that it should apply if neither property on its own meets your family's needs

– eg, if you are a carer living between two properties.[48] The UC rules are not quite the same, but you could argue that the same should apply.

Your home includes any garage, garden, outbuildings and land belonging to the property, including croft land.[49]

When the value of the property is disregarded

The value of the property can be disregarded, even if you do not normally live in it, in the following circumstances.

- **If you have left your former home following a marriage or relationship breakdown**, the value of the property is ignored for 26 weeks (six months for UC) from the date you left. It may also be disregarded for longer if any of the steps below are taken. If it is occupied by your former partner who is a lone parent, its value is ignored as long as s/he lives there.[50]

- **If you have sought legal advice or have started legal proceedings in order to occupy property** as your home, its value is ignored for 26 weeks (six months for UC) from the date you first took either of these steps.[51] The 26 weeks can be extended if it is reasonable to do so, if you need longer to move in.

- **If you are taking reasonable steps to dispose of a property**, its value is ignored for 26 weeks (six months for UC) from the date you *first* took such steps (which may start before you claim benefit).[52] The steps you take must be 'reasonable', so, for instance, advertising at an unrealistic sale price does not count. Placing the property with an estate agent or contacting a possible buyer should count,[53] as might taking ancillary proceedings to resolve financial issues in a divorce.[54] The disregard can continue beyond 26 weeks, even for years if it is reasonable – eg, if a court orders that the former matrimonial home should not be sold until the children are grown up. Taking a property off the market and putting it on again does not necessarily begin a new 26-week period, but it may do if the second attempt to sell is quite separate.[55]

- **If you are carrying out essential repairs or alterations** which are needed so that you can occupy a property as your home, the value of the property is ignored for UC for six months from the date you began the repairs or, for other benefits, for 26 weeks from the date you first began to take steps to carry them out.[56] 'Steps' may include applying for planning permission or a grant or loan to make the property habitable, employing an architect or finding someone to do the work.[57] If you cannot move into the property within that period because the work is not finished, its value can be disregarded for as long as is necessary to allow the work to be carried out.

- **If you have acquired a property and intend to live there** as your home but have not yet moved in, its value is ignored for UC for six months from the date you acquired it or for longer if that is reasonable.[58] For other benefits, it is ignored if you intend to live there within 26 weeks of acquiring it.[59] If you cannot move in by then, the value of the property can be ignored for as long as seems reasonable.

Part 3: General rules for means tested benefits
Chapter 17: Capital: under pension credit age
4. Disregarded capital

- **If you sell your home** and intend to use the money from the sale to buy another home, the capital is ignored for 26 weeks from the date of the sale (for UC, six months from the date you received the money).[60] This also applies even if you do not actually own the home but, for a price, you surrender your tenancy rights to a landlord.[61] If you need longer to complete a purchase, your capital can continue to be ignored if it is reasonable to do so. You do not have to have decided within the 26 weeks to buy a particular property. It is sufficient if you intend to use the proceeds to buy some other home within the 26-week (or extended) period,[62] although your 'intention' must involve more than a mere 'hope' or 'aspiration'.[63] There must be an element of 'certainty' which may be shown by evidence of a practical commitment to another purchase, although this need not involve any binding obligation.[64] If you intend to use only part of the proceeds of sale to buy another home, only that part is disregarded even if, for example, you have put the rest of the money aside to renovate your new home.[65]
- **If your home is damaged or you lose it altogether**, any payment in consequence of that, including compensation, which is to be used for its repair, or for acquiring another home, is ignored for 26 weeks. For UC, an insurance policy payment is ignored for six months from the date it is received, but not other kinds of payments.[66] In either case, it can be ignored for longer if it is reasonable to do so.
- **If you have taken out a loan or been given money for the express purpose of essential repairs or alterations (for UC) or repairs or improvements (for other benefits)** to your home, it is ignored for 26 weeks (six months for UC), or longer if it is reasonable to do so.[67] If it is a condition of the loan that it must be returned if the improvements are not carried out, you should argue that it should be ignored altogether.[68]
- **If you have deposited money with a housing association as a condition of occupying your home**, this is ignored indefinitely.[69] If money which was deposited for this purpose is now to be used to buy another home, this is ignored for 26 weeks (six months for UC), or longer if reasonable, in order to allow you to complete the purchase.[70]
- **Grants made to buy a home are ignored for UC for six months, and are ignored for other benefits for up to 26 weeks if made to local authority tenants to buy a home or do repairs or alterations to it.** They can be ignored for longer, if reasonable, to allow completion of the purchase or the repairs/ alterations. **Note:** the repairs or alterations must be required to make the property fit for occupation as your home.[71]

When considering whether it is reasonable to extend the period of any disregard, all the circumstances should be considered – eg, your personal circumstances, any efforts made by you to use or dispose of the home[72] and the general state of the market. In practice, periods of around 18 months are not considered unusual.

It is possible for property to be ignored under more than one of the paragraphs on pp351–52 in succession.[73]

Some income generated from property which is disregarded is ignored (see p281).

The home of a partner, former partner or relative

The value of a home (see p350) is ignored if it is occupied as her/his home by:[74]

- someone over the qualifying age for pension credit (PC – see p78), or who has limited capability for work or is incapacitated (see below), who is:
  - a relative of yours or of your partner or dependent child; or
  - your spouse or civil partner, provided you are still treated as living in the same household (see p205), or your cohabitee, provided you are still treated as living together as husband and wife or civil partners (see p206);
- for UC (instead of the rule above), a close relative who is over the qualifying age for PC or has limited capability for work;
- your former partner from whom you are not estranged but are living apart (and are, therefore, not treated as still living together or as living in the same household) – eg, if one of you is living in a care home;
- your former partner from whom you are estranged and who is a lone parent. If your former partner is not a lone parent, the value of the home is ignored for 26 weeks (six months for UC) from the date you ceased to live in the home. You are 'estranged' if you are living apart because your relationship has broken down, even if the separation is amicable.[75]

Definitions
'**Incapacitated**' is not defined, but guidance suggests it refers to someone who is getting an incapacity or disability benefit, or who is sufficiently incapacitated to qualify for one of those benefits.[76] However, you should argue for a broader interpretation, if necessary.

'**Close relative**' includes: a parent, son, daughter, step-parent, stepson, stepdaughter, parent-in-law, son-in-law, daughter-in-law, brother or sister, or a partner of any of these people.[77] It also includes half-brothers and sisters and adopted children.[78]

'**Relative**' is a close relative or a grandparent or grandchild, uncle, aunt, nephew or niece.[79]

Personal possessions

All personal possessions, including jewellery, furniture or a car, are ignored.[80] A personal possession has been defined as any physical asset not used for business purposes, other than land.[81] For example, in one case, a static caravan on a non-residential site was treated as a personal possession. However, a home that you own but do not live in would not normally be a personal possession but would

Part 3: General rules for means tested benefits
Chapter 17: Capital: under pension credit age
4. Disregarded capital

count as capital (see p351). Personal possessions are not ignored if you have bought them in order to be able to claim or get more benefit. In this case, the sale value, rather than the purchase price, is counted as actual capital and the difference is treated as notional capital (see p359).[82]

Compensation (or for UC, an insurance payment) for damage to, or the loss of, any personal possessions, which is to be used for their repair or replacement, is ignored for six months, or longer if reasonable.[83]

Business assets

If you are self-employed, your business assets are ignored for as long as you continue to work in that business.[84]

If you cannot work because of incapacity, the disregard runs for 26 weeks from the date of claim if you intend to work in the business again when you are able, or for longer if reasonable in the circumstances.[85] For UC, the disregard runs for six months from when you stopped work if you can reasonably expect to work in the business again when you recover, or for longer if reasonable in the circumstances.[86]

If you stop working in the business, you are allowed a reasonable time to sell these assets without their value affecting your benefit. For UC, the assets are ignored for six months, provided you are taking reasonable steps to sell them, or longer if reasonable.[87] It is sometimes difficult to distinguish between personal and business assets. The test is whether the assets are 'part of the fund employed and risked in the business'.[88] If the assets of a business partnership (eg, plant and machinery) have been sold but the partnership has not yet been dissolved, the proceeds of sale can still count as business assets.[89] **Note:** letting a single house does not constitute a business.[90] For the treatment of business assets if you are taking part in New Enterprise Allowance, see p358.

Personal pension schemes

The value of a fund held in a personal pension scheme is ignored.[91] For UC, it is intended to ignore these funds although there is no specific rule.[92] Note that the value of the right to receive an occupational or personal pension is also ignored.

Insurance policy and annuity surrender values

The surrender value of a life assurance policy is ignored.[93] Some investments include an element of life insurance – eg, endowment policies. If the policy terms include how the payment on death is calculated, the whole investment is ignored.[94] However, you cannot choose to put money in such an investment in order to increase your benefit entitlement because you are likely to be caught by the notional capital rule if you do (see p359).

For benefits other than UC, the surrender value of any annuity is also ignored (see p282 and p343),[95] as is the value of the right to receive any payment under an annuity. Any payment under the annuity counts as income[96] (but see p284 for when this is ignored).

Future interest in property

For benefits other than UC, a future interest in most kinds of property is ignored.[97] A '**future interest**' is one which will only revert to you, or become yours for the first time, when some future event occurs – eg, where someone else has a life interest in a fund and you are only entitled to it after that person has died.

However, this does not include a freehold or leasehold interest in property which has been let *by you* to tenants. If you did not let the property to the tenant (eg, because the tenancy was entered into before you bought the property), your interest in the property should be ignored as a future interest in the normal way.

The right to receive a payment in the future

If you know that you will receive a payment in the future, you could sell your right to it at any time so it has a market value and therefore constitutes an actual capital resource. For benefits other than UC, the value of this is ignored if it is a right to receive:

- income under a life interest or, in Scotland, a life rent;[98]
- an occupational or personal pension (this is also ignored for UC);[99]
- any rent if you are not the freeholder or leaseholder.[100] Any actual income which this right generates for you and which is not disregarded as income can be taken into account as income;
- any payment under an annuity (see p287).[101] Any actual income generated by this right and which is not disregarded as income can be taken into account as income;
- any earnings or income that is ignored because it is frozen abroad;[102]
- any outstanding instalments if capital is being paid by instalments;[103]
- any payment under a trust fund set up with money paid because of a personal injury to you or your partner.[104]

Benefits and other payments

Arrears of benefits and tax credits

The **general rule** (except for UC) is that arrears of specified benefits and other payments (see p356) are ignored for:[105]

- 52 weeks after they are received by you; *or*
- longer in some cases of official error. If arrears are £5,000 or more and are paid to compensate for an official error (see p1276), they are ignored until the end of your (or your partner's) award. If you or your partner then reclaim the same benefit (ie, income support (IS), income-based jobseeker's allowance (JSA), income-related employment and support allowance (ESA) or housing benefit (HB)), or move from IS, income-based JSA or income-related ESA to another of

Part 3: General rules for means tested benefits
Chapter 17: Capital: under pension credit age
4. Disregarded capital

these three benefits, they continue to be ignored for the whole of this next and any subsequent awards if there is no gap between awards.[106]

Arrears of the following benefits are ignored under the above general rule: attendance allowance (AA), mobility supplement, disability living allowance (DLA), personal independence payment (PIP), IS, income-based JSA, income-related ESA, UC, HB, council tax benefit (CTB), child tax credit (CTC), working tax credit (WTC) and discretionary housing payments, or concessionary payments instead of any of these.

Also ignored for 52 weeks from the date you receive the payment are:
- arrears of certain payments to war widows, widowers and surviving civil partners;[107]
- fares to hospital, payments for prescriptions and dental charges;[108]
- payments in lieu of milk tokens, vitamins or Healthy Start food vouchers;[109]
- payments to assist prison visits.[110]

For UC, arrears of certain benefits, and any compensation you get for late payment of these, are ignored for 12 months from when you receive them.[111] This applies to:
- UC;
- any benefit that is ignored as income for UC – eg, child benefit and DLA (see p333);
- IS, income-based JSA, income-related ESA, HB, CTB, CTC and WTC.

Other payments

The following payments are ignored (for UC, only where specified):
- social fund payments[112] and replacement local welfare provision (for UC these are ignored for 12 months);[113]
- refunds of council tax liability (ignored for 52 weeks from the date you receive the arrears);[114]
- a payment to a disabled person under the Disabled Persons (Employment) Act 1944 (other than a training allowance or training bonus) to assist with employment, or a local authority payment to assist blind homeworkers;[115]
- any payments made to holders of the Victoria or George Cross (these are also ignored for UC);[116]
- any payments to compensate for the loss of entitlement to HB;[117]
- payments under the Supporting People programme.[118]

Charitable and personal injury payments

- **Charitable payments.** For means-tested benefits other than UC, any payment in kind by a charity is ignored.[119]
- **Personal injury payments.** A personal injury payment can be disregarded for 52 weeks after you first receive it and when it is held in a trust (see p347).

- **Special compensation schemes.** Any payment of capital (or income) from certain special schemes approved or set up by the government are ignored if they are:[120]
  - from the Independent Living Fund or, for UC, to support people with a disability to live independently;
  - for you or your partner who has variant CJD (Creutzfeldt-Jacob disease). If you are the parent of someone with variant CJD, the payment is ignored for two years. For a dependent child of someone with variant CJD, the payment is ignored for benefits other than UC until s/he reaches 20, finishes full-time education or for two years, whichever is later;
  - in respect of someone infected from contaminated blood products (eg, the MacFarlane Trusts, the Fund, the Skipton Fund, the Caxton Foundation, the Eileen Trust and MFET Ltd). If you give money from the payment to your partner or, for benefits other than UC, to your dependent child, it is ignored for her/his benefit claim indefinitely. If you have no partner or children and you give the money to your parent, it is ignored for two years;
  - compensation for the London bombings of July 2005;
  - World War Two compensation (rather than a war pension).

Funeral plan payments

The value of any funeral plan contract is ignored indefinitely for UC but not other benefits.[121] A funeral plan contract is a contract under which:
- you make payments to another person to ensure you are provided with a funeral; *and*
- the sole purpose of the plan is to provide a funeral.

Social services, community care and other payments

The following payments for children and families from a local authority are ignored for all benefits (they are ignored for 12 months for UC):[122]
- in England and Wales, payments under s17 of the Children Act 1989;
- in Scotland, payments under s12 of the Social Work (Scotland) Act 1968 or, for HB, under s22 of the Children (Scotland) Act 1995.

Payments made by local authorities to young people who have previously been looked after by the local authority are also ignored. These are:
- in England and Wales, payments under ss23B, 23C or 24A of the Children Act 1989;
- in Scotland, payments under ss29 or 30 of the Children (Scotland) Act 1995.

For UC only, any payment made in the last 12 months by a local authority to meet welfare needs related to old age or disability is ignored, unless it is for certain

Part 3: General rules for means tested benefits
Chapter 17: Capital: under pension credit age
4. Disregarded capital

living expenses (food, fuel, clothing, footwear, rent, housing costs or council tax for you, your partner or dependent child).[123]

For benefits other than UC, certain payments under s23C of the Children Act 1989 or s29 of the Children (Scotland) Act 1995 are not only ignored as the young person's capital, but also as yours if s/he passes it to you, provided s/he was in your care, is still living with you and is aged 18 or over.

However, if you or your partner are involved in a trade dispute, these payments count as income for IS and income-based JSA. They also count for IS if made during the first 15 days of a return to work after a dispute.

Also ignored indefinitely for benefits other than UC are:

- local welfare provision to meet an immediate short-term need or establish or maintain a settled home in certain circumstances. This replaced social fund community care grants and crisis loans;[124]
- community care or healthcare direct payments;[125]
- special guardianship allowances (payable in England and Wales);[126]
- payments under ss2, 3 or 4 of the Adoption and Children Act 2002.[127]

Employment and training programme payments

For benefits other than UC, some payments are ignored for 52 weeks from the date they are received:[128]

- payment for travel or other expenses from a specified scheme for assisting people to obtain employment (see p1093);
- for income-related ESA, payment for travel or other expenses for undertaking required work-related activity;
- payment under s2 of the Employment and Training Act 1973 or s2 of the Enterprise and New Towns (Scotland) Act 1990;
- capital acquired for the purpose of participating under the 'self-employment route' (eg, for income-based JSA and HB, New Enterprise Allowance).[129] Any capital acquired is ignored for as long as you are receiving assistance for taking part in the programme and, after you have ceased trading, for as long as is reasonable in order to dispose of the assets.[130]

For when employment and training programme payments are treated as income, notional income and notional capital, see p283, p290 and p364.

Miscellaneous payments

The following payments are disregarded for benefits other than UC:

- a sports award made by the UK Sport National Lottery funds, except for any part of the award which is made for ordinary living expenses (see p288). It is disregarded for 26 weeks;[131]
- an education maintenance allowance, or a 16 to 19 bursary fund payment (paid in England), are ignored indefinitely;[132]

- for IS, income-based JSA and income-related ESA, any payments made to jurors or witnesses for attending at court, except for payments for loss of earnings or benefit.[133]

Capital treated as income

Some payments which appear to be capital are treated as income, not as capital (see p282 and p325).[134]

---

5. Notional capital

In certain circumstances, you are treated as having capital that you do not have. This is called '**notional capital**'.[135] There is a similar rule for notional income (see p288, p332 and p338). Notional capital counts in the same way as capital you do have, except that a 'diminishing notional capital rule' (see p362) may be applied so that the value of the notional capital you are treated as having is considered to reduce over time.

For benefits other than universal credit (UC), you may be treated as having notional capital if:
- you deliberately deprive yourself of capital in order to claim or increase benefit (see below);
- you fail to apply for capital which is available to you (see p363);
- someone makes a payment of capital to a third party on your behalf or on behalf of a member of your family (see p364);
- you (or a member of your family) receive a payment of capital on behalf of a third party and you (or the member of your family) use or keep the capital (see p365);
- you are a sole trader or a partner in a business which is a limited company (see p365).

Note: the 'diminishing notional capital rule' (see p362) can only apply if you are treated as having notional capital under the first bullet point.

For UC only, you may be treated as having notional capital if:
- you deliberately deprive yourself of capital in order to claim or increase the amount of your UC (see below);
- you are a sole trader or a partner in a business (see p365).

Deliberately getting rid of capital

If you deliberately get rid of capital in order to claim or increase your benefit, you are treated as still having it.[136] The same applies if your partner got rid of capital, even if s/he did so before you became a couple.[137] You are likely to be affected by this rule if, at the time of using up your money, you knew that you might qualify

Part 3: General rules for means tested benefits
Chapter 17: Capital: under pension credit age
5. Notional capital

for benefit (or more benefit), or qualify more quickly as a result. It should not be used if you knew nothing about the effect of using up your capital (eg, you did not know about the capital limit for claiming benefit)[138] or if you have been using up your capital at a rate which is reasonable in the circumstances. Knowledge of capital limits can be inferred from a reasonable familiarity with the benefit system as a claimant,[139] but, if you fail to make enquiries about the capital limit, this does not constitute an intention to secure benefit. This is because you cannot have the intention if you do not know about the capital rules.[140]

In practice, arguing successfully that you have not deprived yourself of capital to get or increase benefit may depend on whether you can show that you would have spent the money in the way you did (eg, to pay off debts or reduce your mortgage) regardless of the effect on your benefit entitlement. If this is unclear, the burden of proving that you did it to get benefit lies with the decision maker.

Your intentions

Even if you did know about the capital limits, it still has to be shown that you intended to obtain, retain or increase your benefit.[141] For example, in one case, a claimant faced repossession of his home and transferred ownership to his daughter (who he feared would otherwise be made homeless), despite having been warned by DWP staff that he would be disqualified from benefit if he did so. It was held that, under the circumstances, he had not disposed of the property with the intention of gaining benefit.[142] The longer the period that has elapsed since the disposal of the capital, the less likely it is for the purpose of obtaining benefit.[143] However, no matter how long it has been since you may have disposed of an asset, there is no set 'safe' period after which the benefit can be claimed without the need for further enquiry.[144]

If you use up your resources, you may have more than one motive for doing so. Even if qualifying for benefit is only a lesser motive for your actions and the main motive is something quite different (eg, ensuring your home is in good condition by spending capital on necessary repairs and improvements), you may still be counted as having deprived yourself of a resource in order to gain benefit.[145]

Examples of the kinds of expenditure that could be caught by the rule are an expensive holiday and putting money in trust[146] (although note that for income support (IS), income-based jobseeker's allowance (JSA) and income-related employment and support allowance (ESA), putting money in trust for yourself does not constitute deprivation if the capital being put in trust came from compensation paid for a personal injury[147]). However, the test is not what the money has been spent on, but your intention behind the expenditure.

For UC, if the reason you used up your capital was to buy goods or services, you must show why that was reasonable in the circumstances. If the expenditure was reasonable, you are not treated as having deprived yourself of capital.[148]

Paying off debts and bankruptcy

For benefits other than UC, if you pay off a debt which you are required by law to repay immediately, you may not be counted as having deprived yourself of capital in order to gain benefit.[149] It is the facts of your case that are important: if you paid off an immediately repayable debt when you thought it would not be recalled for some time, it may be that you will be held to have deprived yourself of money in order to get benefit. However, even if you pay off a debt that you are not required by law to repay immediately, the decision maker must still prove that you did so in order to get benefit – again, it is the facts of your case that are important.[150]

For UC, you are allowed to repay or reduce a debt. This does not count as depriving yourself of capital.[151]

If you are declared bankrupt, you cannot spend your capital without court approval and cannot normally be held to have deprived yourself of it if you do. Capital you have (but cannot spend) does not count for benefit purposes from the date of the bankruptcy order.[152] However, if you deliberately go bankrupt, or do not take reasonable steps to discharge the bankruptcy, in order to get benefit, your capital can still count as notional capital.

Calculation of notional capital

Notional capital is generally calculated in the same way as actual capital and the same disregards usually apply.[153] However, you may not be able to rely on the 26-week (or longer) disregard you would otherwise be allowed to take steps to dispose of a property, even if the new owner is trying to sell it (but there is conflicting caselaw on this).[154]

Other points on deprivation of capital

If you have intentionally deprived yourself of capital in order to get IS, it does not necessarily follow that you also intended to get housing benefit (HB). Similarly, deprivation of capital to get income-based JSA cannot be treated as a deprivation for IS, although deprivation for IS can be treated as deprivation for income-based JSA, and deprivation for IS or income-based JSA can be treated as deprivation for income-related ESA. Each decision maker must reach her/his own decision on each benefit. This may result in different conclusions being drawn for each benefit. Even if intent is found in two different benefits, there may be different views about the amount of capital that has been intentionally disposed of.

However, if you are held to have deprived yourself of capital for the purposes of claiming HB and you then submit a successful claim for IS, income-based JSA or income-related ESA, the local authority should put the notional capital rules for HB on hold for as long as the other benefit remains in payment.[155]

Part 3: General rules for means tested benefits
Chapter 17: Capital: under pension credit age
5. Notional capital

The diminishing notional capital rule

The 'diminishing notional capital rule' provides a way of working out how your notional capital may be treated as spent. It only applies if you have deliberately deprived yourself of capital.[156]

Diminishing notional capital: general rule

These rules apply to benefits other than UC (see p363 for this). The diminishing notional capital rule starts to operate from the first week after the week in which it is decided that notional capital is to be taken into account.

- If your benefit has been refused because of notional capital, the amount of notional capital is reduced by the amount of IS, income-based JSA or income-related ESA you would have had if notional capital had not been taken into account for that benefit. In each case, if you would also have had HB or more HB without the notional capital, then this extra HB also reduces the amount of notional capital for the other means-tested benefit claimed.[157] Notional capital for an HB claim that has been refused is reduced by the amount of HB you would have had, and any IS, income-based JSA or income-related ESA you would have had, if notional capital had not been taken into account.[158] Make sure you claim the benefit you would otherwise have got so that the reduction in notional capital is worked out correctly.
- If your benefit is reduced because of tariff income from your notional capital, that capital is diminished by the amount of that reduction each week. For example, if your notional capital is £6,750 (and you have no other capital), giving a tariff income of £3 a week, the reduction is £3 a week until it reaches £6,500, when it will be £2 and so on. For HB, the amount of your notional capital is also reduced by the amount of IS, income-based JSA or income-related ESA you would have had if no notional capital had been taken into account.
- The reduction in your notional capital is calculated on a weekly basis. However, if your benefit has been stopped altogether because of the notional capital rule, the weekly amount by which your notional capital is reduced is fixed for at least 26 weeks. Even if the amount of benefit to which you would have been entitled increases during this period, there will be no change in the amount by which the capital is reduced. However, guidance for HB states that, in circumstances not related to capital (eg, you have had a baby), a new assessment can be made.[159] If you reclaim benefit 26 weeks or more after your previous claim, your benefit entitlement can be recalculated from the week after your second claim. If it is more than it was previously, the weekly amount by which your notional capital is reduced is increased, but the weekly reduction stays the same as in the earlier assessment if your benefit entitlement remains unchanged or is less than it was before. You do not have to reclaim at the end of every 26-week period, but there can be no recalculation unless and until you

do. Once the amount of reduction has been recalculated in this way, it is again fixed for the same period. Ask the DWP for a forecast of when your notional capital will reduce to a point when a fresh claim might succeed. The onus is on you to reclaim when it is to your advantage to do so – ie, when you may qualify for an increased assessment or because you have requalified for benefit.[160] If you delay, you may lose out, as new assessments cannot take effect before you reclaim. However, if you reclaim too soon, you must wait until the fixed periods have lapsed before you can apply for a fresh determination.

- If you have both actual and notional capital, you may have to use your actual capital to meet your living expenses. There is no reason why this should affect the amount by which your notional capital is diminished, even if this effectively results in double counting. Any reduction in your actual capital should be taken into account in calculating any tariff income arising from your combined actual and notional capital, unless you have spent it at such a rate and in such a way that it raises questions of intent, when you may find that the notional capital rules are applied all over again.

Diminishing notional capital: universal credit

Notional capital is added to any actual capital you may have. This may reduce your UC award because of assumed monthly income from capital being included in the assessment (see p337), or end it altogether. The notional capital amount is not fixed, but reduced over time at a set rate. This rate is based on how much your UC is reduced because of the notional capital.

If you are treated as having notional capital of:[161]

- over £16,000 and your UC entitlement stops, in the following month the amount of UC you would have received but for the notional capital is deducted from the amount of notional capital;
- between £6,000 and £16,000, in the following month the amount of the assumed monthly income from that notional capital is deducted from the amount of notional capital.

Notional capital is reduced in the same way in each subsequent month. If your UC stops altogether, make a fresh claim when you think you might become entitled. Ask the DWP to tell you how long it will be before a new claim might succeed. If you have both actual and notional capital, you may need to spend your actual capital to meet living expenses.

Failing to apply for capital

For benefits other than UC, you are expected to apply for any capital that is due to you. If you would get capital if you applied for it, you are treated as having that capital.[162] Examples of failing to apply include when money is held by a court

Part 3: General rules for means tested benefits
Chapter 17: Capital: under pension credit age
5. Notional capital

which could be released if you applied, or an unclaimed premium bond win. You are only treated as having such capital from the date you could obtain it.

This rule does not apply if you do not apply for:

- capital from a discretionary trust; *or*
- capital from a trust (or fund administered by a court) set up from money paid as a result of a personal injury; *or*
- capital from a personal pension scheme or, if you are under the qualifying age for pension credit (see p78), from an occupational pension scheme or payment from the Pension Protection Fund; *or*
- a loan which you could only get if you gave your home or other disregarded capital (see p350) as security; *or*
- for HB only, child tax credit or working tax credit.[163]

Capital payments made to a third party on your behalf

If someone pays an amount to a third party (eg, a fuel company or a building society) for you or your partner (or a child for HB, or for IS or income-based JSA if children are still included in your claim – see p344), this may count as your capital for benefits other than UC. It counts if the payment is to cover:[164]

- certain normal living expenses – ie, food, household fuel, council tax, water charges or ordinary clothing or footwear. School uniforms and sportswear are not ordinary clothing,[165] nor are special shoes needed because of a disability.[166] Payments made, for instance, for food or clothes for you or your partner count as yours. However, since a child's capital is not counted as belonging to you, a payment to, for example, a clothes shop for your child should count as the child's notional capital and not yours, and, in most cases, is ignored;
- rent for which HB could be payable (less any non-dependant deductions);
- for IS, income-based JSA and income-related ESA only, housing costs which could be met by IS, income-based JSA or income-related ESA.

Payments to a third party do *not* count as yours if they are:[167]

- for other kinds of expenses (eg, a TV licence or mortgage capital repayments) unless they come from a benefit or pension (see below);
- from the Macfarlane Trusts or similar funds listed on p357;
- for participating in a specified scheme for assisting people to obtain employment (see p1093).

Payments from an occupational or personal pension scheme or from the Pension Protection Fund to a third party count as yours regardless of whether or not the payments are used, or intended to be used, for ordinary living expenses.[168] They are disregarded, however, if:

- you (or your partner) are bankrupt (or the subject of a sequestration order), the payment is made to the trustee or other person acting on your creditors' behalf and you and your partner (or your family for HB, and for IS or income-based JSA if amounts for children are still included in your claim – see p344) have no income other than the payment made;[169] *or*

- the payments do nothing to support you financially and, therefore, do not reduce or remove your need to be supported by IS, income-based JSA, income-related ESA or HB – eg, deductions from an occupational pension made under an attachment of earnings order.[170]

For IS, income-based JSA and income-related ESA only, payments *derived* from certain social security benefits (including war disablement pensions, war widows' pensions and Armed Forces Compensation Scheme payments) and paid to a third party count:[171]

- as yours if you are entitled to the benefit; *and*
- as your partner's if s/he is entitled to the benefit.

For IS, income-based JSA and income-related ESA, there are different rules if you could be liable to pay maintenance (see p276).

Capital payments made to you for a third party

For benefits other than UC, if you or your partner get a payment for someone not in your family (eg, a relative who does not have a bank account), it only counts as yours if it is kept or used by you.[172] For HB, and for IS or income-based JSA if amounts for children are still included in your claim (see p344), the same also applies to payments received by a member of your family for someone not in the family. Payments from the Macfarlane Trusts and similar funds listed on p357, or a specified scheme for assisting people to obtain employment (see p1093), do not count at all. Payments from pension schemes paid for a third party are disregarded in the same circumstances as described on p364.

Companies run by sole traders or a few partners

Normally, if you hold shares in a company, their value is taken into account. If, however, your influence in the company is such that you are like a sole trader or like a partner in a small partnership, you are treated accordingly. For IS, income-based JSA, income-related ESA and UC, the value of your shareholding is ignored but you are treated as having a proportionate share of the capital of the company.[173] However, these company assets are not taken into account while you are doing any work on the company's business,[174] even if you only do a little work for the company – eg, taking messages.[175] It has, however, been held that a 'sleeping partner' in a business managed and worked exclusively by others may not benefit from this disregard. As well as having a financial commitment to the business, you must also be involved or engaged in it in some practical sense as an earner.[176]

Part 3: General rules for means tested benefits
Chapter 17: Capital: under pension credit age
6. How capital is valued

For HB, the local authority has a discretion about whether to apply the same rules as for IS. If it decides to, it must apply them all.[177]

Note: for UC, income from the company, or your share of it, is regarded as your self-employed earnings. If this is your main employment, it counts as 'gainful employment', so that you can be treated as having a minimum level of earnings from that employment if your actual earnings are low (see p329).[178] You may also have employed earnings as a director or employee.

6. **How capital is valued**

Market value

Your capital is valued at its current market or surrender value.[179] This means the amount of money you could raise by selling it or raising a loan against it. The test is the price that would be paid by a willing buyer to a willing seller on a particular date.[180] So if an asset is difficult or impossible to realise, its market value should be very heavily discounted or even nil.[181] In the case of a house, an estate agent's figure for a quick sale is a more appropriate valuation than the district valuer's figure for a sale within three months.[182] It is not uncommon for an unrealistic assessment to be made of the value of your capital. You should consider challenging any decision you disagree with (see Chapters 58 and 59).

Expenses of sale

If there would be expenses involved in selling your capital, 10 per cent is deducted from its value (before any debts are deducted) for the cost of sale.[183]

Debts

Deductions are made from the 'gross' value of your capital for any debt or mortgage secured on it.[184] If a creditor (eg, a bank) holds the land certificate to your property as security for a loan and has registered notice of deposit of the land certificate at the Land Registry, this counts as a debt secured on your property.[185] If a single mortgage is secured on a house and land, and the value of the house is disregarded for benefit purposes, the whole of the mortgage can be deducted when calculating the value of the land.[186]

If you have debts which are not secured against your capital (eg, tax liabilities), these cannot be offset against the value of your capital.[187] However, once you have repaid your debts, your capital may well be reduced. You can be penalised if you deliberately get rid of capital in order to get benefit (see p359).

If you are overdrawn at the bank and have savings in another account at the same bank, the amount of the overdraft should be deducted from your savings if the terms of the accounts allow the bank to make these transfers.[188]

Capital that is jointly owned under a joint tenancy

If you jointly own any capital asset (except as a partner in a company – see p365) under a joint tenancy, you are treated as owning an equal share of the asset with all other owners.[189] For example, if two of you own the asset, you are each treated as having a 50 per cent share of it. However, for universal credit (UC), if you can show that you own unequal shares, only the value of the share you own is taken into account.[190]

Note: this rule does not apply, however, if you jointly own the capital asset as 'tenants in common'.[191] The key differences between a joint tenancy and a tenancy in common are that, with a joint tenancy, each co-owner owns the whole of the capital asset jointly and severally. If one of the joint tenants were to die, her/his interest in the asset would pass automatically to the other joint tenant(s). With a tenancy in common, each co-owner owns a discrete share in the asset and this share can be passed on by the deceased on her/his death to whomever s/he wishes.

If the rule does apply, the value of your deemed share should be calculated in the same way as your actual capital. However, it is only the value of your deemed share looked at in isolation that counts, and this will usually be worth less than the same proportion of the value of the whole asset. If the asset is a house, for example, the value of any deemed share may be very small or even worthless, particularly if the house is occupied and there is a possibility that the sale of the property cannot be forced. This is because even a willing buyer could not be expected to pay much for an asset s/he would have difficulty making use of.[192] Whether a sale can be forced depends on individual circumstances, and valuations should take into account legal costs and the length of time it could take to gain possession of the property.[193] A valuation should set out details of the valuer's expertise (where relevant), describe the property in sufficient detail to show that all factors relevant to its value have been taken into account, and state any assumptions on which it is based.[194] You may need to challenge any decision (see Chapters 58 and 59) based on an inadequate valuation.

The rule applies regardless of whether the capital asset in question is in the UK or abroad. See p368 for the rules that apply to assets abroad.[195]

If the rule does not apply to you because you jointly own the capital asset under a tenancy in common, it is your actual share in the asset that has to be valued.

Treatment of assets after a relationship breakdown

When partners separate, assets, such as their former home or a bank account, may be in joint or sole names. For example, if a bank account is in joint names, under the rule about jointly owned capital, you and your former partner are treated as having a 50 per cent share each (see above) unless, for UC, you can show that you actually own a different share. On the other hand, a former partner may have a

Part 3: General rules for means tested benefits
Chapter 17: Capital: under pension credit age
6. How capital is valued

right to some, or all, of an asset that is in your sole name – eg, s/he may have deposited most of the money in a bank account in your name. If this is established, you may be treated as not entitled to the whole of the account but as holding part of it as trustee for your former partner.[196] If an asset such as the matrimonial home belongs to your former partner and you have no share in it, you cannot be treated as having any interest in it under the Matrimonial Causes Act 1973 unless you take divorce or separation proceedings and get a property order.[197]

Shares

Shares are valued at their current market value less 10 per cent for the cost of sale, and after deducting any 'lien' held by brokers for sums owed for the cost of their acquisition and any commission.[198] Market value should be calculated in accordance with guidance from HM Revenue and Customs, based on the bid price plus a quarter of the difference between this and the offer price.[199] Fluctuations in price between routine reviews of your case are normally ignored. If you have a minority holding of shares in a company, the value of the shares should be based on what you could realise on them, and not by valuing the entire share capital of the company and attributing to you an amount calculated according to the proportion of shares held.[200] For UC, there are no special rules about valuing shares.

Unit trusts

These are valued on the basis of the 'bid' price quoted in newspapers. No deduction is allowed for the cost of sale because this is already included in the 'bid' price.[201]

The right to receive a payment in the future

The value of any such right that is not ignored (see p355) is its market value – what a willing buyer will pay to a willing seller.[202] For something which is not yet realisable, this may be very small.

Overseas assets

If you have assets abroad and there are no exchange controls or other prohibitions that would prevent you transferring your capital to this country, your assets are valued at their current market or surrender value in that country.[203] If there are problems getting benefit because it is difficult to get the assets valued, you may be able to get a short-term advance of UC, income support, income-based jobseeker's allowance or income-related employment and support allowance (see p1167), or a 'payment on account' of housing benefit (see p139).

If you are not allowed to transfer the full value of your capital to this country, you are treated as having capital equal to the amount that a willing buyer in this country would give for those assets.[204] It seems likely that the price such a person (if there is one) would be willing to pay may bear little relation to the actual value of the assets.

Ten per cent is deducted if there are expenses of sale, and deductions are made for any debts or mortgage secured on the assets abroad. If the capital is realised in a currency other than sterling, charges payable for converting the payment are also deducted.[205]

Notes

1. The capital limits
1 **IS** Regs 45 and 53 IS Regs
   JSA Regs 107 and 116 JSA Regs
   ESA Regs 110 and 118 ESA Regs
   HB Regs 43 and 52 HB Regs
   UC Regs 18 and 72 UC Regs
2 Reg 52(3)-(5), (8) and (9) HB Regs

2. Whose capital counts
3 **IS/HB** s136(1) SSCBA 1992
   JSA s13(2) JSA 1995
   ESA Sch 1 para 6(2) WRA 2007
   UC s5(2) WRA 2012
4 Reg 18(2) UC Regs
5 **IS** Reg 23(2) IS Regs
   JSA Reg 88(2) JSA Regs
   ESA Reg 83(2) ESA Regs
   HB Reg 25(3) HB Regs
   UC s5 WRA 2012
6 **IS** Reg 17(1)(b) IS Regs
   JSA Reg 83(b) JSA Regs
7 **IS** Reg 44(5) IS Regs
   JSA Reg 106(5) JSA Regs

3. What counts as capital
8 para BW1.71 GM; para 29020 DMG
9 *R v SBC ex parte Singer* [1973] 1 WLR 713
10 R(IS) 3/93
11 R(SB) 2/83; R(SB) 35/83; R(IS) 3/93
12 R(IS) 3/93 para 22
13 R(SB) 12/86
14 R(SB) 53/83; R(SB) 1/85
15 R(SB) 49/83
16 R(SB) 12/86; for how this works in Scotland, see *JK v SSWP (JSA)* [2010] UKUT 437 (AAC); [2011] AACR 26

17 CIS/2287/2008
18 *JC v SSWP* [2009] UKUT 22 (AAC)
19 *Gartside v Inland Revenue Commissioners* [1968] 1 All ER 121; [1968] AC 553
20 **IS** Sch 10 para 13 IS Regs
   JSA Sch 8 para 18 JSA Regs
   ESA Sch 9 para 18 ESA Regs
   HB Sch 6 para 15 HB Regs
21 R(SB) 1/85; CIS/30/1993; *SB v SSWP (IS)* [2012] UKUT 252 (AAC)
22 R(IS) 1/90; CSIS/639/2006
23 R(SB) 23/85; CSIS/639/2006
24 *Barclays Bank v Quistclose Investments Ltd* [1970] AC 567; R(SB) 49/83; CFC/21/1989
25 **IS** Sch 10 para 12A IS Regs
   JSA Sch 8 para 17A JSA Regs
   ESA Sch 9 para 17 ESA Regs
   HB Sch 6 para 14A HB Regs
   UC Reg 75(6) UC Regs
26 **IS** Sch 10 para 12 IS Regs
   JSA Sch 8 para 18 JSA Regs
   ESA Sch 9 para 16 ESA Regs
   HB Sch 6 para 14 HB Regs
   UC Reg 75(4) UC Regs
27 R(IS) 3/03
28 R(SB) 2/89; *KQ v SSWP (IS)* [2011] UKUT 102 (AAC); [2011] AACR 43
29 **IS** Sch 10 paras 44 and 45 IS Regs
   JSA Sch 8 paras 42 and 43 JSA Regs
   ESA Sch 9 paras 43 and 44 ESA Regs
   HB Sch 6 paras 45 and 46 HB Regs
   UC Reg 75(5) UC Regs
   All R(IS) 9/04; *CP v SSWP (IS)* [2011] UKUT 157 (AAC)

Part 3: General rules for means tested benefits
Chapter 17: Capital: under pension credit age
Notes

30 **IS** Sch 9 paras 15 and 22 IS Regs
JSA Sch 7 paras 15 and 23 JSA Regs
ESA Sch 8 paras 16 and 23 ESA Regs
HB Sch 5 paras 14 and 17 HB Regs
UC Reg 75(5) UC Regs
31 CIS/25/1989
32 **IS** Sch 9 para 15 IS Regs
JSA Sch 7 para 15 JSA Regs
ESA Sch 8 para 16 ESA Regs
HB Sch 5 para 14 HB Regs
All para 29239 DMG
33 **IS** Reg 48(4) IS Regs
JSA Reg 110(4) JSA Regs
ESA Reg 112(4) ESA Regs
HB Reg 46(4) HB Regs
34 **IS** Sch 9 para 15 IS Regs
JSA Sch 7 para 15 JSA Regs
ESA Sch 8 para 16 ESA Regs
HB Sch 5 para 14 HB Regs
35 Reg 75(4) UC Regs
36 Reg 46(3) UC Regs
37 Regs 46, 48 and 66(1)(j) UC Regs
38 Reg 72(2) UC Regs
39 Reg 46(3) UC Regs
40 *Thomas v CAO*, appendix to R(SB) 17/87
41 CIS/984/2002
42 **IS** Reg 48 IS Regs
JSA Reg 110 JSA Regs
ESA Reg 112 ESA Regs
HB Reg 46 HB Regs
43 Reg 46(9) HB Regs
44 Reg 72(3) UC Regs

4. Disregarded capital
45 **IS** Sch 10 para 1 IS Regs
JSA Sch 8 para 1 JSA Regs
ESA Sch 9 para 1 ESA Regs
HB Sch 6 para 1 HB Regs
UC Sch 10 para 1 UC Regs
46 **IS** Sch 10 para 1 IS Regs
JSA Sch 8 para 1 JSA Regs
ESA Sch 9 para 1 ESA Regs
HB Sch 6 para 1 HB Regs
UC Schs 3 para 1(1) and 10 para 1(2)
UC Regs
47 R(JSA) 9/03; R(SB) 10/89
48 *MM v SSWP (IS)* [2012] UKUT 358 (AAC)
49 **IS** Reg 2(1), definition of 'dwelling
occupied as the home' IS Regs; R(SB) 3/
84; CIS/427/1991 and R(IS) 3/96
JSA Reg 1(3), definition of 'dwelling
occupied as the home', JSA Regs
ESA Reg 2(1), definition of 'dwelling
occupied as the home', ESA Regs
HB Sch 6 para 1 HB Regs
UC Sch 3 paras 1(4) and 2 UC Regs

50 **IS** Sch 10 para 25 IS Regs
JSA Sch 8 para 5 JSA Regs
ESA Sch 9 para 5 ESA Regs
HB Sch 6 para 25 HB Regs
UC Reg 48(2) and Sch 10 para 5 UC
Regs
51 **IS** Sch 10 para 27 IS Regs
JSA Sch 8 para 7 JSA Regs
ESA Sch 9 para 7 ESA Regs
HB Sch 6 para 27 HB Regs
UC Reg 48(2) and Sch 10 para 4(1)(b)
and (2) UC Regs
52 **IS** Sch 10 para 26 IS Regs
JSA Sch 8 para 6 JSA Regs
ESA Sch 9 para 6 ESA Regs
HB Sch 6 para 26 HB Regs
UC Reg 48(2) and Sch 10 para 6 UC
Regs
All CIS/6908/1995; R(IS) 4/97
53 R(SB) 32/83
54 R(IS) 5/05
55 *SP v SSWP* [2009] UKUT 255 (AAC)
56 **IS** Sch 10 para 28 IS Regs
JSA Sch 8 para 8 JSA Regs
ESA Sch 9 para 8 ESA Regs
HB Sch 6 para 28 HB Regs
UC Reg 48(2) and Sch 10 para 4(1)(c)
UC Regs
57 *R v London Borough of Tower Hamlets
Review Board ex parte Kapur*, 12 June
2000, unreported
58 Reg 48(2) and Sch 10 para 4(1)(a) UC
Regs
59 **IS** Sch 10 para 2 IS Regs
JSA Sch 8 para 2 JSA Regs
ESA Sch 9 para 2 ESA Regs
HB Sch 6 para 2 HB Regs
60 **IS** Sch 10 para 3 IS Regs
JSA Sch 8 para 3 JSA Regs
ESA Sch 9 para 3 ESA Regs
HB Sch 6 para 3 HB Regs
UC Reg 48(2) and Sch 10 para 13(a) UC
Regs
61 R(IS) 6/95
62 R(IS) 7/01
63 CIS/685/1992
64 CIS/8475/1995; CIS/15984/1996
65 R(SB) 14/85
66 **IS** Sch 10 para 8(a) IS Regs
JSA Sch 8 para 13(a) JSA Regs
ESA Sch 9 para 12(a) ESA Regs
HB Sch 6 para 10(a) HB Regs
UC Reg 48(2) and Sch 10 para 14 UC
Regs

67 **IS** Sch 10 para 8(b) IS Regs
JSA Sch 8 para 13(b) JSA Regs
ESA Sch 9 para 12(b) ESA Regs
HB Sch 6 para 10(b) HB Regs
UC Reg 48(2) and Sch 10 para 15 UC
Regs
68 *Barclays Bank v Quistclose Investments Ltd*
[1970] AC 567; CSB/975/1985
69 **IS** Sch 10 para 9(a) IS Regs
JSA Sch 8 para 14(a) JSA Regs
ESA Sch 9 para 13(a) ESA Regs
HB Sch 6 para 11(a) HB Regs
UC Sch 10 para 12 UC Regs
70 **IS** Sch 10 para 9(b) IS Regs
JSA Sch 8 para 14(b) JSA Regs
ESA Sch 9 para 13(b) ESA Regs
HB Sch 6 para 11(b) HB Regs
UC Reg 48(2) and Sch 10 para 13(b) UC
Regs
71 **IS** Sch 10 para 37 IS Regs
JSA Sch 8 para 9 JSA Regs
ESA Sch 9 para 36 ESA Regs
HB Sch 6 para 38 HB Regs
UC Reg 48(2) and Sch 10 para 13(c) UC
Regs
72 CIS/4757/2003
73 CIS/6908/1995
74 **IS** Sch 10 paras 4 and 25 IS Regs
JSA Sch 8 paras 4 and 5 JSA Regs
ESA Sch 9 paras 4 and 5 ESA Regs
HB Sch 6 paras 4 and 25 HB Regs
UC Sch 10 paras 2, 3 and 5 UC Regs
75 R(IS) 5/05; CH/3777/2007
76 **HB** BW1/Annex A/A1.01 GM
Other benefits para 29437 DMG
77 Reg 2 UC Regs
78 CSB/209/1986; CSB/1149/1986; R(SB)
22/87
79 **IS** Reg 2(1) IS Regs
JSA Reg 1(3) JSA Regs
ESA Reg 2(1) ESA Regs
HB Reg 2(1) HB Regs
80 **IS** Sch 10 para 10 IS Regs
JSA Sch 8 para 15 JSA Regs
ESA Sch 9 para 14 ESA Regs
HB Sch 6 para 12 HB Regs
UC Reg 46(2) UC Regs
81 R(H) 7/08
82 CIS/494/1990 and CIS/2208/2003
83 **IS** Sch 10 para 8(a) IS Regs
JSA Sch 8 para 13(a) JSA Regs
ESA Sch 9 para 12(a) ESA Regs
HB Sch 6 para 10(a) HB Regs
UC Reg 48(2) and Sch 10 para 14 UC
Regs

84 **IS** Sch 10 para 6(1) IS Regs
JSA Sch 8 para 11(1) JSA Regs
ESA Sch 9 para 10(1) ESA Regs
HB Sch 6 para 8(1) HB Regs
UC Sch 10 para 7 UC Regs
85 **IS** Sch 10 para 6(2) IS Regs
JSA Sch 8 para 11(2) JSA Regs
ESA Sch 9 para 10(2) ESA Regs
HB Sch 6 para 8(2) HB Regs
86 Reg 48(2) and Sch 10 para 8(b) UC Regs
87 Reg 48(2) and Sch 10 para 8(a) UC Regs
88 R(SB) 4/85
89 CIS/5481/1997
90 CFC/15/1990
91 **IS** Sch 10 para 23A IS Regs
JSA Sch 8 paras 28 and 29 JSA Regs
ESA Sch 9 paras 28 and 29 ESA Regs
HB Sch 6 para 32 HB Regs
UC Sch 10 para 10 UC Regs; the
disregard for the actual value of the fund
is not in the regulations, but it is
intended to be disregarded.
92 Email from DWP to CPAG, 7 February
2013
93 **IS** Sch 10 para 15 IS Regs
JSA Sch 8 para 20 JSA Regs
ESA Sch 9 para 20 ESA Regs
HB Sch 6 para 17 HB Regs
94 R(IS) 7/98
95 **IS** Sch 10 para 11 IS Regs
JSA Sch 8 para 16 JSA Regs
ESA Sch 9 para 15 ESA Regs
HB Sch 6 para 13 HB Regs
96 **IS** Reg 41(2) IS Regs
JSA Reg 104(2) JSA Regs
ESA Reg 105(2) ESA Regs
HB Reg 41(2) HB Regs
All *Beattie v Secretary of State for Social
Security* [2001] EWCA Civ 498,
TheTimes, 3 May 2001, upholding CIS/
114/1999, reported as R(IS) 10/01
97 **IS** Sch 10 para 5 IS Regs
JSA Sch 8 para 10 JSA Regs
ESA Sch 9 para 9 ESA Regs
HB Sch 6 para 7 HB Regs
98 **IS** Sch 10 para 13 IS Regs
JSA Sch 8 para 18 JSA Regs
ESA Sch 9 para 18 ESA Regs
HB Sch 6 para 15 HB Regs
99 **IS** Sch 10 para 23 IS Regs
JSA Sch 8 para 28 JSA Regs
ESA Sch 9 para 28 ESA Regs
HB Sch 6 para 31 HB Regs
UC Sch 10 para 10 UC Regs
100 **IS** Sch 10 para 24 IS Regs
JSA Sch 8 para 30 JSA Regs
ESA Sch 9 para 30 ESA Regs
HB Sch 6 para 33 HB Regs

Part 3: General rules for means tested benefits
Chapter 17: Capital: under pension credit age
Notes

101 **IS** Sch 10 para 11 IS Regs
JSA Sch 8 para 16 JSA Regs
ESA Sch 9 para 15 ESA Regs
HB Sch 6 para 13 HB Regs

102 **IS** Sch 10 para 14 IS Regs
JSA Sch 8 para 19 JSA Regs
ESA Sch 9 para 19 ESA Regs
HB Sch 6 para 16 HB Regs

103 **IS** Sch 10 para 16 IS Regs
JSA Sch 8 para 21 JSA Regs
ESA Sch 9 para 21 ESA Regs
HB Sch 6 para 18 HB Regs

104 **IS** Sch 10 para 12 IS Regs
JSA Sch 8 para 17 JSA Regs
ESA Sch 9 para 16 ESA Regs
HB Sch 6 para 14 HB Regs

105 **IS** Sch 10 para 7 IS Regs
JSA Sch 8 para 12 JSA Regs
ESA Sch 9 para 11 ESA Regs
HB Sch 6 para 9 HB Regs

106 **IS** Sch 10 para 7(2) IS Regs
JSA Sch 8 para 12(2) JSA Regs
ESA Sch 9 para 11(2) ESA Regs
HB Sch 6 para 9(2) HB Regs

107 **IS** Sch 10 para 41 IS Regs
JSA Sch 8 para 39 JSA Regs
ESA Sch 9 para 40 ESA Regs
HB Sch 6 para 9 HB Regs

108 **IS** Sch 10 para 38 IS Regs
JSA Sch 8 para 36 JSA Regs
ESA Sch 9 para 37 ESA Regs
HB Sch 6 para 40 HB Regs

109 **IS** Sch 10 para 39 IS Regs
JSA Sch 8 para 37 JSA Regs
ESA Sch 9 para 38 ESA Regs
HB Sch 6 para 41 HB Regs

110 **IS** Sch 10 para 40 IS Regs
JSA Sch 8 para 38 JSA Regs
ESA Sch 9 para 39 ESA Regs
HB Sch 6 para 42 HB Regs

111 Sch 10 para 18 UC Regs

112 **IS** Sch 10 para 18 IS Regs
JSA Sch 8 para 23 JSA Regs
ESA Sch 9 para 23 ESA Regs
HB Sch 6 para 20 HB Regs
UC Sch 10 para 16 UC Regs

113 **IS** Sch 10 para 18A IS Regs
JSA Sch 8 para 23A JSA Regs
ESA Sch 9 para 23A ESA Regs
HB Sch 6 para 20A HB Regs

114 **IS** Sch 10 para 36 IS Regs
JSA Sch 8 para 35 JSA Regs
ESA Sch 9 para 35 ESA Regs
HB Sch 6 para 37 HB Regs

115 **IS** Sch 10 paras 42 and 43 IS Regs
JSA Sch 8 paras 40 and 41 JSA Regs
ESA Sch 9 paras 41 and 42 ESA Regs
HB Sch 6 paras 43 and 44 HB Regs

116 **IS** Sch 10 para 46 IS Regs
JSA Sch 8 para 44 JSA Regs
ESA Sch 9 para 45 ESA Regs
HB Sch 6 para 47 HB Regs
UC Sch 10 para 19 UC Regs

117 **IS** Sch 10 para 31 IS Regs
JSA Sch 8 para 33 JSA Regs
ESA Sch 9 para 33 ESA Regs
HB Sch 6 para 30 HB Regs

118 **IS** Sch 10 para 66 IS Regs
JSA Sch 8 para 59 JSA Regs
ESA Sch 9 para 55 ESA Regs
HB Sch 6 para 57 HB Regs

119 **IS** Sch 10 para 29 IS Regs
JSA Sch 8 para 31 JSA Regs
ESA Sch 9 para 31 ESA Regs
HB Sch 6 para 34 HB Regs

120 **IS** Sch 10 para 22 IS Regs
JSA Sch 8 para 27 JSA Regs
ESA Sch 9 para 27 ESA Regs
HB Sch 6 para 24 HB Regs
UC Reg 76 UC Regs

121 Sch 10 para 11 UC Regs

122 **IS** Sch 10 para 17 IS Regs
JSA Sch 8 para 22 JSA Regs
ESA Sch 9 para 22 ESA Regs
HB Sch 6 para 19 HB Regs
UC Sch 10 para 17 UC Regs

123 **UC** Sch 10 para 17(1)(b) UC Regs

124 **IS** Sch 10 para 18A IS Regs
JSA Sch 8 para 23A JSA Regs
ESA Sch 9 para 23A ESA Regs
HB Sch 6 para 20A HB Regs

125 **IS** Sch 10 para 67 IS Regs
JSA Sch 8 para 60 JSA Regs
ESA Sch 9 para 56 ESA Regs
HB Sch 6 para 58 HB Regs

126 **IS** Sch 10 para 68A IS Regs
JSA Sch 8 para 61A JSA Regs
ESA Sch 9 para 58 ESA Regs
HB Sch 6 para 60 HB Regs

127 **IS** Sch 10 para 68 IS Regs
JSA Sch 8 para 61 JSA Regs
ESA Sch 9 para 57 ESA Regs
HB Sch 6 para 59 HB Regs

128 **IS** Sch 10 paras 1A and 30 IS Regs
JSA Sch 8 paras A2, A3 and 32 JSA Regs
ESA Sch 9 paras 1A, 32 and 32A ESA Regs
HB Sch 6 paras A2, A3 and 35 HB Regs

129 **IS** Sch 10 para 52 IS Regs
JSA Sch 8 para 47 JSA Regs
ESA Sch 9 para 46 ESA Regs
HB Sch 6 para 49 HB Regs

130 **IS** Sch 10 para 6(3) and (4) IS Regs
JSA Sch 8 para 11(3) and (4) JSA Regs
ESA Sch 9 para 10(3) and (4) ESA Regs
HB Sch 6 para 8(3) and (4) HB Regs

131 **IS** Sch 10 para 56 IS Regs
JSA Sch 8 para 51 JSA Regs
ESA Sch 9 para 47 ESA Regs
HB Sch 6 para 50 HB Regs
132 **IS** Sch 10 para 63 IS Regs
JSA Sch 8 para 52 JSA Regs
ESA Sch 9 para 52 ESA Regs
HB Sch 6 para 51 HB Regs
133 **IS** Sch 10 para 34 IS Regs
JSA Sch 8 para 34 JSA Regs
ESA Sch 9 para 34 ESA Regs
134 **IS** Sch 10 para 20 IS Regs
JSA Sch 8 para 25 JSA Regs
ESA Sch 9 para 25 ESA Regs
HB Sch 6 para 22 HB Regs

5. Notional capital
135 **IS** Reg 51(6) IS Regs
JSA Reg 113(6) JSA Regs
ESA Reg 115(8) ESA Regs
HB Reg 49(6) HB Regs
UC Regs 50(1) and 77(2) UC Regs
136 **IS** Reg 51(1) IS Regs
JSA Reg 113(1) JSA Regs
ESA Reg 115(1) ESA Regs
HB Reg 49(1) HB Regs
UC Reg 50(1) UC Regs
137 R(IS) 7/07
138 CIS/124/1990; CSB/1198/1989
139 R(SB) 9/91
140 CIS/124/1990
141 CIS/40/1989
142 CIS/621/1991. See also CJSA/3937/2002
143 CIS/264/1989
144 R(IS) 7/98, para 12(3)
145 R(SB) 38/85; R(IS) 1/91; R(H) 1/06
146 para BW1.714 GM
147 **IS** Reg 51(1)(a) IS Regs
JSA Reg 113(1)(a) JSA Regs
ESA Reg 115(1)(a) ESA Regs
148 Reg 50(2)(b) UC Regs
149 R(SB) 12/91; *Verna Jones v SSWP* [2003] EWCA Civ 964, 10 July 2003, unreported (CA)
150 CIS/2627/1995; *Verna Jones v SSWP* [2003] EWCA Civ 964, 10 July 2003, unreported (CA)
151 Reg 50(2)(a) UC Regs
152 *KS v SSWP* [2009] UKUT 122 (AAC); [2010] AACR3
153 **IS** Reg 51(6) IS Regs
JSA Reg 113(6) JSA Regs
ESA Reg 115(8) ESA Regs
HB Reg 49(7) HB Regs

154 CIS/30/1993, but other commissioners have taken a different view (see for example, CIS/25/1990 and CIS/81/1991)
155 para BW1.831 GM
156 **IS** Reg 51A(1) IS Regs
JSA Reg 114(1) JSA Regs
ESA Reg 116(1) ESA Regs
HB Reg 49(1) HB Regs
UC Reg 50(3) UC Regs
157 **IS** Reg 51A IS Regs
JSA Reg 114 JSA Regs
ESA Reg 116 ESA Regs
158 Reg 49 HB Regs
159 para BW1.795 GM
160 R(IS) 9/92
161 Reg 50(3) UC Regs
162 **IS** Reg 51(2) IS Regs
JSA Reg 113(2) JSA Regs
ESA Reg 115(2) ESA Regs
HB Reg 49(2) HB Regs
163 Reg 49(2) HB Regs
164 **IS** Reg 51(3)(a)(ii) and (8) IS Regs
JSA Reg 113(3)(a)(ii) and (8) JSA Regs
ESA Regs 2(1) and 115(3)(c) ESA Regs
HB Reg 49(3)(a) and (7) HB Regs
165 **IS** Reg 51(8) IS Regs
JSA Reg 113(8) JSA Regs
ESA Reg 2(1) ESA Regs
HB Reg 49(7)(b) HB Regs
166 para 29867 DMG
167 **IS** Reg 51(3)(a)(ii), (3A)(a) and (ba) IS Regs
JSA Reg 113(3)(a)(ii), (3A)(a), (bb) and (bc) JSA Regs
ESA Reg 115(3)(c), (5)(a) and (ba) ESA Regs
HB Reg 49(3)(b), (4)(a), (bb) and (bc) HB Regs
168 **IS** Reg 51(3)(a)(ia) IS Regs
JSA Reg 113(3)(a)(ia) JSA Regs
ESA Reg 115(3)(b) ESA Regs
HB Reg 49(3)(a) HB Regs
169 **IS** Reg 51(3A)(c) IS Regs
JSA Reg 113(3A)(c) JSA Regs
ESA Reg 115(5)(c) ESA Regs
HB Reg 49(4)(c) HB Regs
170 R(IS) 4/01
171 **IS** Reg 51(3)(a)(i) IS Regs
JSA Reg 113(3)(a)(i) JSA Regs
ESA Reg 115(3)(a) ESA Regs
172 **IS** Reg 51(3)(b) IS Regs
JSA Reg 113(3)(b) JSA Regs
ESA Reg 115(4) ESA Regs
HB Reg 49(3)(c) HB Regs

Part 3: General rules for means tested benefits
Chapter 17: Capital: under pension credit age
Notes
• •

173 **IS** Reg 51(4) IS Regs
  JSA Reg 113(4) JSA Regs
  ESA Reg 115(6) ESA Regs
  HB Reg 49(5) HB Regs
  UC Reg 77(1) and (2) UC Regs
174 **IS** Reg 51(5) IS Regs
  JSA Reg 113(5) JSA Regs
  ESA Reg 115(7) ESA Regs
  HB Reg 49(6) HB Regs
  UC Reg 77(3)(a) UC Regs
175 para 29879 DMG; see also R(IS) 13/93
176 R(IS) 14/98
177 Reg 49(5) HB Regs
178 Reg 77(3) UC Regs

6. How capital is valued
179 **IS** Reg 49(a) IS Regs
  JSA Reg 111(a) JSA Regs
  ESA Reg 113 ESA Regs
  HB Reg 47(a) HB Regs
  UC Reg 49(1) UC Regs
180 R(SB) 57/83; R(SB) 6/84
181 R(SB) 18/83
182 R(SB) 6/84
183 **IS** Reg 49(a) IS Regs
  JSA Reg 111(a) JSA Regs
  ESA Reg 113(a) ESA Regs
  HB Reg 47(a) HB Regs
  UC Reg 49(1) UC Regs
184 **IS** Reg 49(b) IS Regs
  JSA Reg 111(b) JSA Regs
  ESA Reg 113(b) ESA Regs
  HB Reg 47(b) HB Regs
  UC Reg 49(1)(b) UC Regs
185 CIS/255/1989
186 R(SB) 27/84
187 R(SB) 2/83; R(SB) 31/83
188 *JRL v SSWP (JSA)* [2011] UKUT 63 (AAC);
  [2011] AACR 30
189 **IS** Reg 52 IS Regs
  JSA Reg 115 JSA Regs
  ESA Reg 117 ESA Regs
  HB Reg 51 HB Regs
  UC Reg 47 UC Regs
190 Reg 47 UC Regs
191 *Hourigan v SSWP* [2002] EWCA Civ 1890
  reported as R(IS) 4/03
192 CIS/15936/1996; CIS/263/1997; CIS/
  3283/1997 (joint decision); R(IS) 26/95
193 R(IS) 3/96
194 R(JSA) 1/02
195 CIS/2575/1997
196 R(IS) 2/93
197 R(IS) 1/03
198 **IS** Reg 49(a) IS Regs
  JSA Reg 111(a) JSA Regs
  ESA Reg 113 ESA Regs
  HB Reg 47(a) HB Regs

199 R(IS) 18/95; paras 29665-70 DMG
200 R(SB) 18/83; R(IS) 2/90
201 **IS/JSA** para 29681 DMG
  HB BW1/1.530 GM
202 *Peters v CAO* (appendix to R(SB) 3/89)
203 **IS** Reg 50(a) IS Regs
  JSA Reg 112(a) JSA Regs
  ESA Reg 114(a) ESA Regs
  HB Reg 48(a) HB Regs
  UC Reg 49(2)(a) UC Regs
204 **IS** Reg 50(b) IS Regs
  JSA Reg 112(b) JSA Regs
  ESA Reg 114(b) ESA Regs
  HB Reg 48(b) HB Regs
  UC Reg 49(2)(b) UC Regs
205 **IS** Sch 10 para 21 IS Regs
  JSA Sch 8 para 26 JSA Regs
  ESA Sch 9 para 26 ESA Regs
  HB Sch 6 para 23 HB Regs
  UC Reg 49(3) UC Regs

Chapter 18

Capital: over pension credit age

This chapter explains the rules for working out your capital for pension credit (PC) and for housing benefit (HB) if you or your partner are over the qualifying age for PC and neither of you are on income support (IS), income-based jobseeker's allowance (JSA), income-related employment and support allowance (ESA) or universal credit (UC). If you do get IS, income-based JSA, income-related ESA or UC, your capital is ignored for HB. Chapter 17 explains the rules for universal credit, IS, income-based JSA, income-related ESA, and for HB if you and your partner are under the qualifying age for PC.

Key facts

- There is no capital limit for pension credit (PC).
- Generally, you are not eligible for housing benefit (HB) if your total capital is over £16,000. However, if you get the guarantee credit of PC, there is no capital limit for HB because all your capital is ignored.
- If you have capital over £10,000, this affects the amount of PC or HB you get because it is assumed to give you a certain income, called 'deemed income'.
- Capital includes your and your partner's savings, investments and property. Some kinds of capital are ignored when working out your PC or HB – eg, if you own the home in which you live.
- If you deliberately get rid of capital in order to get more benefit, you are treated as still having it. This is called 'notional capital'.

Part 3: General rules for means tested benefits
Chapter 18: Capital: over pension credit age
2. The capital limits

1. How capital is taken into account

Unlike other benefits, **for pension credit (PC)** there is no upper limit on the amount of capital you can have, beyond which you are excluded from benefit. Instead, your capital above the lower limit of £10,000 is taken into account.

* Actual income from capital (eg, interest or regular payments) is only taken into account for some specific kinds of capital.[1] This includes the value of the right to receive certain kinds of payment in the future, and capital in a trust unless the trust is set up out of personal injury payments to you or your partner or is a charitable trust (see p315).

* Any other capital, unless it is specifically disregarded, is assumed to provide you with a set rate of income called 'deemed income' (see p316). Some capital can be ignored for a period of time or ignored permanently. If deemed income is taken into account, any actual income (eg, interest) is ignored.

If any actual income is taken into account (eg, payments from a trust), the capital is ignored when working out how much deemed income to include.

For **housing benefit (HB)**, there is an upper capital limit. If your capital is over £16,000, you are not eligible for HB unless you get PC guarantee credit. Capital between the lower limit of £10,000 and the upper limit is taken into account in the assessment in the same way as described above for PC.

Examples
Liz is 85 and has savings of £20,000. Deemed income of £20 a week is taken into account for PC but actual interest from her savings is ignored.

Pranav is 67 and has £20,000 in a non-discretionary trust. He gets £40 a week income from the trust. Actual income of £40 is taken into account for PC but no deemed income on top.

2. The capital limits

Pension credit

For pension credit (PC), the lower limit is £10,000. There is no upper capital limit.

Capital of £10,000 or less is ignored. If you have capital above £10,000, you are treated as having a deemed income of £1 for every £500, or part of £500, by which your capital exceeds £10,000.[2]

Housing benefit

For housing benefit (HB):
* the lower limit is £10,000;
* the upper limit is £16,000.[3]

If you have over £16,000, you are not entitled to benefit. The first £10,000 is ignored. If you have capital above £10,000, you are treated as having a deemed income of £1 for every £500, or part of £500, by which your capital exceeds that amount.[4]

If you get the guarantee credit of PC, all your and your partner's capital (and income) is ignored for HB.[5] This is because entitlement to PC guarantee credit acts as a passport to maximum HB. Because PC has no upper capital limit, you can get maximum HB even with capital above £16,000.

If you get the savings credit of PC but not the guarantee credit, the following applies.[6]

- Your capital for HB purposes is the capital figure worked out by the DWP for your PC. This is modified to include any capital belonging to your partner which was not taken into account in the PC calculation – eg, if a partner abroad is no longer included for PC but is for HB. If this is over £16,000, you are not entitled to HB.

- For PC savings credit during an 'assessed income period', an increase in capital does not affect your PC, but may affect HB. If capital rises above £16,000 (worked out by the local authority under the HB rules), you are no longer entitled to HB. If capital increases but is still less than £16,000, the local authority must continue to use the DWP capital figure.

Example
Amy is 66 and a widow. She has a state pension and a personal pension. She gets HB and the savings credit of PC but not the guarantee credit. Her PC award letter shows that her assessed income period ends in June 2018. She inherits £20,000. Her HB stops but her PC is not affected until June 2018.

3. **Whose capital counts**

Your partner's capital is added to yours.[7]

The capital of any dependent child does not affect your pension credit or housing benefit.

4. **What counts as capital**

The term 'capital' is not defined. In general, it means lump-sum or one-off payments rather than a series of payments – eg, savings, investments and property.[8]

Part 3: General rules for means tested benefits
Chapter 18: Capital: over pension credit age
4. What counts as capital

Savings

Your savings generally count as capital – eg, cash you have at home, premium bonds, stocks and shares, unit trusts and money in a bank account.

Savings from past income (including benefits – see p382) are treated as capital after the period for which the income was paid has lapsed. There is no provision to disregard money put aside to pay bills.[9] If your savings are just below the capital limit, you could pay bills by monthly direct debit or use a budget account to keep your capital below the limit.

Fixed-term investments

Capital held in fixed-term investments counts. However, if it is presently unobtainable, it may have little or no value. If you can convert the investment into a realisable form, sell your interest, or raise a loan through a reputable bank using the asset as security, its value counts. If it takes time to produce evidence about the nature and value of the investment, you may be able to get a short-term advance of pension credit (see p1167), or a payment on account of housing benefit (see p139).[10]

Property and land

Any property or land that you own counts as capital. Many types of property are disregarded (see p379). See also 'proprietary estoppel' on p347.

Loans

A loan to you usually counts as money you possess. However, in some limited circumstances you can argue that a loan should be disregarded (see p345). If you lend someone money, see p345.

Trusts

Money or property held in a trust for you or your partner is ignored when working out deemed income (see p376). You are not assumed to have a fixed income from the trust.[11] This applies to both discretionary and non-discretionary trusts. However, payments actually made from the trust can be taken into account. If made regularly, payments are treated as income. For discretionary trusts, regular payments are either disregarded in full or in part (see p317). If payments are not made regularly, they are taken into account as capital.

The rules are different if the trust is set up from personal injury payments. Payments made from certain charitable trusts are specifically ignored (see p383).

Payments of personal injury compensation

Any money paid because of a personal injury to you or your partner is ignored whether or not it has been placed into a trust.[12] Neither deemed income (see p376) nor actual income from the fund is taken into account. The capital value is not ignored if it was paid in respect of someone who is no longer a member of your family – eg, because s/he has died.[13] 'Personal injury' includes not only accidental and criminal injury but also any disease and injury as a result of a disease.[14]

Trust funds administered by a court

The value of a trust fund is also ignored where damages are awarded in respect of personal injury and the money paid into a special fund to be administered by a court – eg, the Court of Protection. Payments from these funds are ignored completely, both as capital and income.[15]

5. Disregarded capital

Some kinds of capital are ignored in the assessment of pension credit (PC) and housing benefit (HB).

Your home

If you own the home you normally live in, its value is ignored.[16] The value of your home is disregarded for the purposes of the deemed income rule (see p376).[17]

Your '**home**' includes any garage, garden, outbuildings and land, together with any premises that you do not occupy as your home but which it is impractical or unreasonable to sell separately – eg, croft land.[18] This disregard applies to any home in which you are treated as normally living – eg, because you are only temporarily living away from it (see p431). However, if you own more than one property, only the value of the one normally occupied is disregarded under this rule.[19] Exceptionally, two separate properties can be regarded as a single home, as though one was an annexe of the other, if you personally (rather than a member of your family) normally occupy both properties.[20] This is most likely to be the case for a large family, but other situations are possible where neither property on its own caters for a family's needs – eg, if there is a carer living between two properties.[21]

When the value of your home is disregarded

The value of the property can be disregarded, even if you do not normally live in it, in the following circumstances.

- **If you have left your former home following a marriage or relationship breakdown**, the value of the property is ignored for 26 weeks from the date

Part 3: General rules for means tested benefits
Chapter 18: Capital: over pension credit age
5. Disregarded capital

you left. It may also be disregarded for longer if any of the steps below are taken. If it is occupied by your former partner who is a lone parent, its value is ignored as long as s/he lives there.[22]

- **If you have sought legal advice or have started legal proceedings in order to occupy property as your home**, its value is ignored for 26 weeks from the date you first took either of these steps.[23] The 26 weeks can be extended, if it is reasonable to do so, if you need longer to move into the property.

- **If you are taking reasonable steps to dispose of any property**, its value is ignored for 26 weeks from the date you first took such steps (which may start before you claimed benefit).[24] See p351 for more details.

- **If you are carrying out essential repairs or alterations which are needed so that you can occupy a property as your home**, the value of the property is ignored for 26 weeks from the date you first began to take steps to carry them out.[25] See p351 for more details.

- **If you have acquired a property for occupation as your home but have not yet moved in**, its value is ignored if you intend to live there within 26 weeks of acquiring it.[26] If you cannot move in by then, the value of the property can be ignored for as long as seems reasonable.

- **Any amounts paid to you or deposited in your name for the sole purpose of buying a home for you to live in or carrying out essential repairs or alterations to your home or the home you intend to occupy** are ignored for a year from the date you were paid them.[27] This includes money from the sale of a home that you earmark to buy another place to live in. For PC, if there is an assessed income period (p89) that extends beyond the year's disregard, the rules provide for the disregard to last until the end of that period. However, it is not clear how this applies in all cases. For example, it would not apply if your PC entitlement or assessed income period began only after the year's disregard had expired. Arguably, it should apply in other cases where there is an assessed income period.[28]

- **Any compensation paid under an insurance policy because of loss or damage to your home** is ignored for a year from the date it is paid to you.[29] For PC, if there is an assessed income period, it can be disregarded until the end of that period in the same way as explained in the bullet point above.

When considering whether to increase the period of any disregard, all the circumstances should be considered – eg, your personal circumstances, any efforts made by you to use or dispose of the home[30] and the general state of the market. In practice, periods of around 18 months are not considered unusual.

It is possible for property to be ignored under more than one of the above paragraphs in succession.[31]

The home of a former partner or relative

The value of a home (see p379) is ignored if it is occupied wholly or partly as her/his home by:[32]
- a relative of yours or your partner (see p353 for who this includes) who is over the qualifying age for PC (see p78) or is incapacitated (see below);[33]
- your former partner from whom you are not estranged, divorced or out of a civil partnership – eg, if one of you is living in a care home;
- your former partner from whom you are estranged, divorced or out of a civil partnership if s/he is a lone parent. If s/he is not a lone parent, the value of the home is ignored for 26 weeks from the date you ceased to live in the home.[34]

Incapacitated

'Incapacitated' is not defined, but guidance suggests it refers to someone who is getting an incapacity or disability benefit, or who is sufficiently incapacitated to qualify for one of those benefits.[35] However, you should argue for a broader interpretation, if necessary.

Personal possessions

All personal possessions, including items such as jewellery, furniture or a car, are ignored.[36]

Compensation paid under an insurance policy for damage to or loss of your personal possessions is ignored for a year from the date you were paid the compensation or, for PC only, until the end of the assessed income period (if there is one) if that is longer.[37]

Business assets

If you are self-employed, your business assets are ignored for as long as you continue to work in that business.[38] If you cannot work because of physical or mental illness, but intend to work in the business when you are able, the disregard operates for 26 weeks from the date of claim, or for longer if reasonable in the circumstances.[39] For more about this, see p354.

Insurance policy and annuity surrender values

The surrender value of any life assurance policy is ignored.[40] Some investments include an element of life insurance – eg, endowment policies. If the policy terms include how the payment on death is calculated, the whole investment is ignored.[41] However, you cannot choose to put money into such an investment in order to increase your benefit entitlement because you are likely to be caught by the notional capital rule if you do (see p384).

The surrender value of any annuity is also ignored for the purposes of the deemed income rule (see p316). Any actual income the surrender value generates

Part 3: General rules for means tested benefits
Chapter 18: Capital: over pension credit age
5. Disregarded capital

for you, and which is not disregarded as income, can be taken into account as income.[42] Any payment under the annuity counts as income (but see p317 for when this is ignored).[43]

Future interests in property

A future interest in most kinds of property is ignored.[44] A **'future interest'** is one which will only revert to you, or become yours for the first time, when some future event occurs. For more about this, see below.

The right to receive a payment in the future

If you know you will receive a payment in the future, you could sell your right to that payment at any time so it has a market value and therefore constitutes an actual capital resource. The value of this is ignored for some types of payment (these are the first four bullet points listed on p355).[45]

Benefits and other payments

Arrears of specified benefits (see below) are ignored:[46]
- for one year after they are received by you; *or*
- for PC if there is an assessed income period that extends beyond the year's disregard (p89). The rules provide for the disregard to last until the end of that period. However, it is not clear how this applies in all cases. For example, it would not apply if your PC entitlement or assessed income period began only after the year's disregard had expired.[47] Arguably, it should apply in other cases where there is an assessed income period;[48] *or*
- for the remainder of the PC or HB award if the payment is £5,000 or more for arrears or late payment of a specified benefit (see below), which was made to compensate for an official error, and which you received in full since becoming entitled to PC or HB. If you got the compensation before then, it is still disregarded if your current award follows immediately from a previous award of income support (IS), income-based jobseeker's allowance (JSA), income-related employment and support allowance (ESA), universal credit (UC), HB or council tax benefit (CTB) (or PC for current awards of HB) in which the compensation was disregarded, or it is still being disregarded in an award of one of those benefits.

Specified benefits

The **'specified benefits'** are:
- attendance allowance, disability living allowance, personal independence payment, armed forces independence payment, income-based JSA, income-related ESA, IS, UC, PC, HB, CTB, child tax credit, constant attendance allowance and exceptionally severe disablement allowance; *or*

- for PC only, child benefit and social fund payments; *or*
- for HB only, working tax credit and discretionary housing payments; *or*
- concessionary payments (ie, compensation) made instead of any of the above benefits or payments made in lieu of any of these benefits.

Also ignored for one year (or for PC, to the end of the assessed income period) from when you get the payments are:

- local welfare provision payments that replaced social fund community care grants and crisis loans;
- refunds of council tax liability, including from the council tax reduction scheme;
- payments under the Supporting People programme;
- arrears of a supplementary pension to war widows, widowers or surviving civil partners for pre-1973 service.

Ignored indefinitely are:[49]

- the lump-sum state retirement pension if you deferred your pension and chose a lump sum rather than increased income;
- community care or health direct payments.

Charitable and personal injury payments

- **Personal injury payments.** Any money paid because of a personal injury to you or your partner is ignored (see p379).
- **Special compensation schemes.** Any payment of capital (or income) from certain special schemes approved or set up by government are ignored if they are:[50]
  - from the Independent Living Fund (to support people with a disability to live independently);
  - for you or your partner who has variant CJD (Creutzfeldt-Jakob disease). If you are the parent of someone with variant CJD, the payment is ignored for two years;
  - from the MacFarlane Trusts, the Fund, the Skipton Fund, the Caxton Foundation, the Eileen Trust and MFET Ltd (for those infected from contaminated blood products). You can give money from the payment to your partner and it is ignored indefinitely in her/his benefit claim or, if you have no partner or children, to your parent and it is ignored for two years;
  - compensation for the London bombings of July 2005;
  - World War Two compensation (rather than a war pension) if you, your partner or deceased spouse or civil partner were interned as a prisoner of war in Japan, lost a child, suffered injury or forced labour or lost property.

Part 3: General rules for means tested benefits
Chapter 18: Capital: over pension credit age
6. Notional capital

Funeral plan payments

The value of any funeral plan contract is ignored indefinitely.[51]
A funeral plan contract is a contract under which:
* you make at least one payment to another person;
* that person undertakes to ensure you are provided with a funeral; *and*
* the sole purpose of the plan is to ensure you are provided with a funeral.

Payments in other currencies

Any payment in a currency other than sterling is taken into account after
disregarding banking charges or commission payable on conversion.[52]

6. Notional capital

In certain circumstances, you are treated as having capital which you do not have.
This is called **'notional capital'**.[53] There is a similar rule for notional income (see
p318).
You are treated as having notional capital if you:
* deliberately deprive yourself of capital in order to claim or increase benefit (see
  below);
* are in a position like a sole trader or a partner in a business (see p385).

Notional capital counts in the same way as capital you do have except that a
'diminishing notional capital rule' (see p362) may be applied so that the value of
the notional capital you are treated as having is considered to reduce over time.

Deliberately getting rid of capital

If you deliberately get rid of capital in order to claim or increase your benefit, you
are treated as still having it.[54] You are not treated as having deprived yourself of
capital if:
* you pay off or reduce a debt which you owe; *or*
* you pay for goods or services if the purchase of those goods or services was
  reasonable in the circumstances of your case.

Diminishing notional capital

The diminishing notional capital rule applies if you are treated as having notional
capital because of depriving yourself of capital.
If you are getting pension credit (PC), the amount of the notional capital goes
down each week by the extra PC you are losing because of the notional capital.[55]
For example, if your notional capital is £11,000, you have £2 a week less PC

because of 'deemed income' (see p316) so £2 a week is deducted from the notional capital until it reaches £10,500 when it will be £1 a week.

If you are not getting any PC, notional capital goes down, not just by the amount of PC you would have had, but also by any additional housing benefit (HB) you would have had if notional capital had not been taken into account. Ask the DWP for a forecast of when it is worth claiming again. If in doubt, you can claim every 26 weeks (but not more often).

For HB, the same rule applies to reduce your notional capital except that, not only is it reduced by the amount of HB you are losing because of the notional capital, it is also reduced by any PC you would have been entitled to (or income-based jobseeker's allowance or income-related employment and support allowance) whether or not you are currently getting HB.[56]

Companies run by sole traders or a few partners

Normally, if you hold shares in a company, their value is taken into account. If, however, your influence in the company is such that you are like a sole trader or partner in a small partnership, you are treated accordingly. The value of your shareholding is ignored, but you are treated as possessing a proportionate share of the capital of the company.[57] This does not apply while you are doing any work on the company's business, even if you do very little work for the company – eg, taking messages.[58] It has, however, been held that a 'sleeping partner' in a business managed and worked exclusively by others may not benefit from this disregard. As well as having a financial commitment to the business, you must also be involved or engaged in it in some practical sense as an earner.[59]

7. How capital is valued

There are a number of issues to consider when valuing capital.

- **Market value.** Capital is valued at its current market or surrender value,[60] which could be very low if it is difficult to sell. See p366 for more information.
- **Expenses of sale.** If there would be expenses involved in selling your capital, 10 per cent is deducted from its value for the cost of sale.[61]
- **Debts.** Deductions are made from the 'gross' value of your capital for any debt or mortgage secured on it.[62] For more information, see p366.
- **Capital that is jointly owned under a joint tenancy.** If you jointly own any capital asset (except as a partner in a company, when the rules explained above apply instead) under a joint tenancy, you are treated as owning an equal share of the asset with all other owners.[63] For example, if two of you own the asset, you are each treated as having a 50 per cent share of it. This rule does not apply, however, if you jointly own the capital asset as tenants in common.[64] For more information, see p367.

Part 3: General rules for means tested benefits
Chapter 18: Capital: over pension credit age
Notes

- **Treatment of assets after a relationship breakdown.** There are no specific rules about this, but there is some guidance and caselaw – see p367.
- **Shares** are valued at their current market value less 10 per cent for the cost of sale and after deducting any 'lien' held by brokers for sums owed for the cost of their acquisition and any commission.[65] See p368 for more details.
- **Unit trusts** are valued on the basis of the 'bid' price quoted in newspapers. No deduction is allowed for the cost of sale because this is already included in the 'bid' price.[66]
- **The right to receive a payment in the future.** The value that is not ignored (see p382) is its market value – what a willing buyer would pay to a willing seller.[67] For something which is not yet realisable, this may be very small.
- **Overseas assets.** If you have assets abroad, and there are no exchange controls or other prohibitions that would prevent you transferring your capital to this country, your assets are valued at their current market or surrender value in that country.[68] If you are not allowed to transfer your capital, you are treated as having capital equal to the amount that a willing buyer in this country would give (which might not be very much).[69] Deduct any debts or mortgage secured on the assets, 10 per cent for any expenses of sale and any charges for converting the payment into sterling.[70]

Notes

1. How capital is taken into account
1 **PC** s15 SPCA 2002; Sch 5 paras 24-28 SPC Regs
HB Reg 29(1)(i) and Sch 6 paras 27-30 HB(SPC) Regs

2. The capital limits
2 s15(2) SPCA 2002; reg 15(6) SPC Regs
3 Reg 43 HB(SPC) Regs
4 Reg 29(2) HB(SPC) Regs
5 Reg 26 HB(SPC) Regs
6 Reg 27 HB(SPC) Regs

3. Whose capital counts
7 **PC** s5 SPCA 2002
HB s136(1) SSCBA 1992

4. What counts as capital
8 BP1/P1.71 GM
9 R(IS) 3/93

10 **PC** Reg 2 SS(PAOR) Regs
HB Reg 74(1) HB(SPC) Regs
11 **PC** Sch 5 para 28 SPC Regs
HB Sch 6 para 30 HB(SPC) Regs
12 **PC** Sch 5 para 16(1) SPC Regs
HB Sch 6 para 17(1) HB(SPC) Regs
13 R(IS) 3/03
14 R(SB) 2/89
15 **PC** Schs 4 paras 13 and 14, and 5 para 16(2) SPC Regs
HB Schs 5 paras 14 and 15, and 6 para 17(2) HB(SPC) Regs

5. Disregarded capital
16 **PC** Sch 5 para 1A SPC Regs
HB Sch 6 para 26 HB(SPC) Regs
17 **PC** Reg 17(8) SPC Regs
HB Reg 33(11) HB(SPC) Regs

18 **PC** Reg 1(2) SPC Regs
HB Reg 2(1) HB(SPC) Regs
Both Definition of 'dwelling occupied as the home'
19 **PC** Sch 5 para 1A SPC Regs
HB Sch 6 para 26 HB(SPC) Regs
20 R(JSA) 9/03; R(SB) 10/89
21 *MM v SSWP (IS)* [2012] UKUT 358 (AAC)
22 **PC** Sch 5 para 6(1) SPC Regs
HB Sch 6 para 6(1) HB(SPC) Regs
23 **PC** Sch 5 para 2 SPC Regs
HB Sch 6 para 2 HB(SPC) Regs
24 **PC** Sch 5 para 7 SPC Regs
HB Sch 6 para 7 HB(SPC) Regs
Both CIS/6908/1995; R(IS) 4/97
25 **PC** Sch 5 para 3 SPC Regs
HB Sch 6 para 3 HB(SPC) Regs
26 **PC** Sch 5 para 1 SPC Regs
HB Sch 6 para 1 HB(SPC) Regs
27 **PC** Sch 5 paras 17 and 19 SPC Regs
HB Sch 6 paras 18 and 20 HB(SPC) Regs
DG v SSWP (SPC) [2010] UKUT 241 (AAC)
28 But see CPC/0206/2005 and CPC/1928/2005, which suggest an assessed income period could be reduced on revision.
29 **PC** Sch 5 paras 17 and 18 SPC Regs
HB Sch 6 paras 18 and 19 HB(SPC) Regs
30 CIS/4757/2003
31 CIS/6908/1995
32 **PC** Sch 5 para 4 SPC Regs
HB Sch 6 para 4 HB(SPC) Regs
33 **PC** Reg 1(2) SPC Regs
HB Reg 2(1) HB(SPC) Regs
Both definition of 'close relative'
34 **PC** Sch 5 para 6 SPC Regs
HB Sch 6 para 6 HB(SPC) Regs
35 **PC** para 84444 DMG
HB para BP1/ Annex A/ A1.01 GM
36 **PC** Sch 5 para 8 SPC Regs
HB Sch 6 para 8 HB(SPC) Regs
37 **PC** Sch 5 paras 17 and 18 SPC Regs
HB Sch 6 paras 18 and 19 HB(SPC) Regs
38 **PC** Sch 5 para 9 SPC Regs
HB Sch 6 para 9 HB(SPC) Regs
39 **PC** Sch 5 para 9A SPC Regs
HB Sch 6 para 10 HB(SPC) Regs
40 **PC** Sch 5 para 10 SPC Regs
HB Sch 6 para 11 HB(SPC) Regs
41 R(IS) 7/98
42 **PC** Sch 5 para 26 SPC Regs
HB Sch 6 para 29 HB Regs
43 **PC** s15(1)(d) SPCA 2002
HB Reg 29(1)(d) HB(SPC) Regs
Both R(IS) 10/01
44 **PC** Sch 5 para 5 SPC Regs
HB Sch 6 para 5 HB(SPC) Regs

45 **PC** Sch 5 paras 22 and 24 to 26 SPC Regs
HB Sch 6 paras 24 and 27 to 29 HB(SPC) Regs
46 **PC** Sch 5 paras 17, 20, 20A and 20B SPC Regs
HB Sch 6 paras 18, 21, 22 and 26B HB(SPC) Regs
47 *DG v SSWP (SPC)* [2010] UKUT 241 (AAC)
48 But see CPC/0206/2005 and CPC/1928/2005, which suggest that an assessed income period could be reduced on revision in some cases.
49 **PC** Sch 5 paras 23A and 23C SPC Regs
HB Sch 6 paras 26A and 26D HB(SPC) Regs
50 **PC** Sch 5 paras 12-15 SPC Regs
HB Sch 6 paras 13-16 HB(SPC) Regs
51 **PC** Sch 5 para 11 SPC Regs
HB Sch 6 para 12 HB(SPC) Regs
52 **PC** Sch 5 para 21 SPC Regs
HB Sch 6 para 23 HB(SPC) Regs

6. Notional capital
53 **PC** Reg 21 SPC Regs
HB Reg 47 HB(SPC) Regs
54 **PC** Reg 21(1) SPC Regs
HB Reg 47(1) HB(SPC) Regs
55 Reg 22 SPC Regs
56 Reg 48 HB(SPC) Regs
57 **PC** Reg 21(3) and (4) SPC Regs
HB Reg 47(3) and (4) HB(SPC) Regs
58 R(IS) 13/93
59 R(IS) 14/98

7. How capital is valued
60 **PC** Reg 19(a) SPC Regs
HB Reg 45(a) HB(SPC) Regs
61 **PC** Reg 19(a) SPC Regs
HB Reg 45(a) HB(SPC) Regs
62 **PC** Reg 19(b) SPC Regs
HB Reg 45(a) HB(SPC) Regs
63 **PC** Reg 23 SPC Regs
HB Reg 49 HB(SPC) Regs
64 R(IS) 4/03
65 **PC** Reg 19(a) SPC Regs
HB Reg 45(a) HB(SPC) Regs
66 **PC** para 84772 DMG
HB BP1/P1.530 GM
67 *Peters v CAO* (appendix to R(SB) 3/89)
68 **PC** Reg 20(a) SPC Regs
HB Reg 46(a) HB(SPC) Regs
69 **PC** Reg 20 SPC Regs
HB Reg 46(b) HB(SPC) Regs
70 **PC** Sch 5 para 21 SPC Regs
HB Sch 6 para 23 HB(SPC) Regs

3

Part 4

Paying for housing

Chapter 19

Rent restrictions

This chapter covers:
1. Which rent restriction rules apply (below)
2. The local housing allowance rules (p395)
3. The social sector rules (p403)
4. The local reference rent rules (p407)
5. The pre-January 1996 rules (p416)
6. Delay before a rent restriction is applied (p421)
7. Challenging a rent restriction (p422)

This chapter covers the rent restriction rules for housing benefit (HB). The rent restriction rules for the universal credit (UC) housing costs element are covered in Chapter 22. However, the rules about local housing allowances for UC are broadly the same as for HB, so reference is made to this chapter where relevant.

Key facts
- If you are a private tenant (or, in some other exceptional cases, a housing association tenant), the rent used to calculate your housing benefit (HB) may be restricted and your HB may be based on a rent lower than the one you are liable to pay. There are three schemes: the local housing allowance rules, the local reference rent rules and the pre-January 1996 rules.
- If you are a local authority or housing association tenant (except if you live in temporary accommodation) and your home is larger than the rules allow, the rent used to calculate your HB may be restricted under the social sector rules.
- If your rent is restricted, you might be able to get discretionary housing payments from your local authority to help with any shortfall.

1. Which rent restriction rules apply

Whatever kind of tenancy you have, rent restriction rules may apply. There are four rent restriction schemes.
- The **local housing allowance rules** (see p395): your housing benefit (HB) is based on the local housing allowance that is appropriate for you.

Part 4: Paying for housing
Chapter 19: Rent restrictions
1. Which rent restriction rules apply

- The **social sector rules**, sometimes called the 'bedroom tax' (see p403): a deduction may be made from your HB if you are considered to have too many bedrooms.
- The **local reference rent rules** (see p407): your HB is based on a rent officer's 'determinations'.
- The **pre-January 1996 rules** (see p416): your HB may be restricted if your home is too large or your rent is too high.

You need to work out whether any of the above rent restriction rules apply to you and, if so, which set of rules applies. This depends on the type of tenancy you have and, in some cases, when you claim HB or how long you have lived in your home.

- If you are a **private tenant**, the local housing allowance rules, the local reference rent rules or the pre-January 1996 rules may apply.
- If you are a **housing association tenant**, the local reference rent rules or, in exceptional cases, the pre-January 1996 rules or the local housing allowance rules may apply. If none of these apply, the social sector rules may apply.
- If you are a **local authority tenant**, the pre-January 1996 rules may in exceptional cases apply. If these do not apply, the social sector rules may apply. **Note:** the social sector rules *never* apply if you or your partner are at least the qualifying age for pension credit (PC).

To work out whether any of the rent restriction rules apply and, if so, which ones, see below if you are a private or a housing association tenant and p394 if you are a local authority tenant.

Are you thinking of moving home?

If you are claiming HB and are considering a move, or there will be a break in your claim, check whether the rules that will apply to you are more or less favourable than at present. In some cases, you can apply to the local authority to find out the rent figure that will be used to calculate your HB (see p414). You can also find out the current rate of the appropriate local housing allowance (see p401).

Private and housing association tenants

Work out which rent restriction rules apply if you are a private or housing association tenant as follows.

- Check whether your tenancy is an excluded tenancy (see p393). If it is and you are:
  - a private tenant, none of the rent restriction rules apply;
  - a housing association tenant, the local housing allowance, the local reference rent and the pre-January 1996 rules do not apply, but the social sector rules may apply (see p403).

- If your tenancy is *not* an excluded tenancy; *and*
  - you make a new claim for HB or move on or after 7 April 2008, follow the steps on p394 to see if the pre-January 1996 rules, the local reference rent rules or the local housing allowance rules apply. **Note:** the local housing allowance rules and the pre-January 1996 rules generally only apply to private tenants; *or*
  - if your rent was already being restricted before 7 April 2008, it may continue to be restricted under the same rules (see p394);
- If you are a housing association tenant and the local housing allowance rules, the local reference rent rules and the pre-January 1996 rules do not apply, check whether the social sector rules apply (see p403).

Excluded tenancies

If you are claiming HB and have an 'excluded tenancy', the local housing allowance rules, the local reference rent rules and the pre-January 1996 rules do not apply to you. However, if your landlord is a registered housing association, the social sector rules may apply to you (see p403).

The following are excluded tenancies:[1]

- a **regulated or protected tenancy** – ie, a tenancy entered into before 15 January 1989 or, in Scotland, 2 January 1989;
- a tenancy in an **approved bail or probation hostel**. However, if you are required to live in such a hostel, you cannot qualify for HB towards the rent you pay to the hostel (see p102);
- a **housing action trust tenancy**;
- a **former local authority or new town letting** which has been transferred to a new owner, unless there has been a rent increase since the transfer; *and*
  - the local authority considers your rent to be unreasonably high; *or*
  - if the transfer took place before 7 October 2002 only, the local authority considers your accommodation to be unreasonably large.
  If this is the case, the local reference rent rules apply;
- a **shared ownership tenancy** (ie, you are buying part of your house or flat and renting the rest), unless this is with a private landlord, in which case the local housing allowance rules may apply (see p395);
- a **letting by a registered housing association**[2], by a **county council** (if you live in a caravan or mobile home provided on a travellers' site[3]) or a **in a caravan, mobile home or houseboat** (if you are also liable to make payments to a local authority – eg, for site or mooring fees).
  However, your tenancy is not excluded if the local authority considers your rent to be unreasonably high or, if you or your partner are at least the qualifying age for PC and neither of you are getting income support, income-based jobseeker's allowance or income-related employment and support allowance (or UC), your accommodation to be unreasonably large. In both cases, the local reference rent rules apply (see p407).

Part 4: Paying for housing
Chapter 19: Rent restrictions
1. Which rent restriction rules apply

Claiming or moving on or after 7 April 2008

If your tenancy is *not* an excluded tenancy (see p393) and you make a new claim for HB on or after 7 April 2008 (or you have a current claim and move on or after that date), work out which rent restriction rules apply as follows.

* Do you live in 'exempt accommodation'? If so, the pre-January 1996 rules apply. In limited cases, they also apply if you are an 'exempt claimant'. See p416 for further information.
* Does your rent include board and attendance, or do you live in a hostel, houseboat, mobile home or caravan? If so, the local reference rent rules apply (see p407). They *may* also apply if the local authority considers your rent to be unreasonably high or your accommodation to be unreasonably large and:
  – your landlord is a registered housing association; *or*
  – your tenancy is a former local authority or new town letting that has been transferred to a new owner; *or*
  – your landlord is a county council and you live in a caravan or mobile home provided on a travellers' site;[4] *or*
  – you live in a caravan, mobile home or houseboat, and you are also liable to make payments to a local authority – eg, for site or mooring fees.
* In all other cases, the local housing allowance rules may apply (see p395).

Housing benefit was restricted before 7 April 2008

The government intends that, if your HB was being restricted under any of the rules that applied before 7 April 2008, it continues to be restricted under these rules until there is a break in your claim or you move to a new home. If any of the rent restriction rules apply to you at that point, your HB is restricted under the rules that then apply.

Example
Daniel lives in a private rented flat with his partner and child. He has been getting HB since October 2005. This was being restricted under the local reference rent rules. When his partner had a baby in 2013, they moved to a two-bedroom private rented house. The local authority reassessed Daniel's HB claim using the local housing allowance rules.

Local authority tenants

If you are a local authority tenant, the social sector rules may apply if neither you nor your partner are at least the qualifying age for PC (see p403). If you are at least the qualifying age for PC, the pre-January 1996 rules may, in exceptional cases, apply (see p416). **Note:** before 3 March 2014, the pre-January 1996 rules could apply to any claimants of any age. See p403 for further information.

Discretion to decrease eligible rent for housing benefit

If none of the rent restriction rules apply to you, the local authority still has discretion to decrease your eligible rent to an amount it considers 'appropriate'. The local authority may say that this is also the case if the local housing allowance or the local reference rent rules apply.[5] However, you can argue that the local authority can only use its discretion to decrease your eligible rent if it has been determined under the normal HB rules.[6] It should have evidence which justifies its doing so and must exercise its discretion properly. All the circumstances should be taken into account, including your health and financial circumstances, the special housing-related needs of anyone occupying your home and whether alternative accommodation is available to HB claimants.[7] Local authorities should rarely use their powers to decrease your HB in this way. If your HB is reduced under this rule, ask for a revision or appeal (see Chapters 58 and 59).

Note: if the social sector rules apply to you, the local authority can decrease your maximum rent under a similar rule (see p407).

2. The local housing allowance rules

If the local housing allowance rules apply, they determine the amount of rent that is used to calculate your housing benefit (HB). Your HB is based on the local housing allowance that is appropriate for you (see below).

The local housing allowance rules apply if, on or after 7 April 2008, you:[8]

- claim HB; *or*
- move to a new home while you are entitled to HB; *or*
- live in a former Pathfinder area and the pilot local housing allowance rules applied to you before that date. In this case, you may have transitional protection (see p422).

These rules can apply if you are a private tenant, including if you have a shared ownership tenancy with a private landlord. They can also apply if you are a housing association tenant, but not if your landlord is a registered social landlord (in Wales or Scotland) or a non-profit or profit-making registered provider of social housing (in England). In the latter case, your accommodation must be available at a rent below the market rate.[9] **Note:**

- These rules *never* apply if you are a local authority tenant.
- These rules do *not* apply if you have an 'excluded tenancy', or the local reference rent or the pre-January 1996 rules apply (see p392).

Which local housing allowance is appropriate

The local housing allowance that is appropriate for you depends on the area where you live and the category of dwelling that applies to you. To establish the

Part 4: Paying for housing
Chapter 19: Rent restrictions
2. The local housing allowance rules

category of dwelling that applies (see p398), you must first know how many bedrooms you are allowed under what are known as the 'size criteria' (see below).

Note: for the universal credit (UC) housing costs element, if you have a private landlord or you live in specified temporary accommodation, the rules on the categories of dwelling (see p398) and the local housing allowance rates (see p400) are broadly the same as for HB. These sections and the footnotes, therefore, also refer to UC rules.

The number of bedrooms you are allowed

For HB, you are allowed (up to a maximum of four bedrooms):[10]
- one bedroom for each of the following 'occupiers', each coming only into the first category for which s/he is eligible:
  - a couple (see p205 for who counts);
  - a person who is not a child – ie, someone aged 16 or over;
  - a 'child who cannot share a bedroom'. **Note:** you are only allowed a bedroom for her/him if you have a bedroom in your home that is additional to those you would be allowed if s/he *were* able to share a bedroom;
  - two children under 16 of the same sex;
  - two children under 10;
  - a child; *and*
- one or two additional bedrooms in specified situations (see p397).

Definitions

'Occupiers' are:[11]
- you and anyone else living in the dwelling (other than a joint tenant who is not a member of your household);
- your (or your partner's) son, daughter, stepson or stepdaughter who is in the armed forces deployed on operations who lived with you before being deployed, provided s/he intends to return home.

'Occupiers' therefore include not only your partner and children, but also other people – eg, a joint tenant who *is* a member of your household, a non-dependant or a live-in carer, but not a foster child or child placed with you for adoption under specified provisions.[12]

You can argue that someone is an 'occupier' if s/he normally lives with you, but is temporarily away.[13] However, if you share the care of a child, the child is considered to be occupying the home of the parent with whom s/he normally lives.[14]

To count as a **'child who cannot share a bedroom'**:[15]
- the child must be under 16 and must be entitled to the middle or highest rate of disability living allowance (DLA) care component, whether or not it is being paid; *and*
- the local authority must be satisfied that because of her/his disability, the child cannot reasonably share a bedroom with another child.

Examples
Bill and Sarah have two sons, both under age 10. Sarah's nephew, aged 20, lives with them. They claim HB. They are allowed three bedrooms under the size criteria: one for Bill and Sarah, one for the sons and one for the nephew. Appropriate local housing allowance: dwelling with three bedrooms.

Terry is his father's carer. They live together in the same household and are joint tenants. Terry claims HB. He is allowed two bedrooms under the size criteria: one for Terry and one for his father. Appropriate local housing allowance: dwelling with two bedrooms.

Note: for the size criteria for UC, see p492.

Additional bedrooms
You are allowed one additional bedroom if you satisfy one of the following conditions. If you satisfy both, you are allowed two additional bedrooms.[16]

- You (or your partner) are a 'person who requires overnight care' (see below for who counts). You are allowed one additional bedroom for a non-resident carer. Even if both of you require overnight care, only one additional bedroom is allowed.

- You (or your partner) are a 'qualifying parent or carer' – ie, certain foster parents and people with whom a child has been placed for adoption (see below for who counts). You are allowed one additional bedroom. This applies even if, for example, you have more than one foster child or child placed with you for adoption, or if both you and your partner are a 'qualifying parent or carer'.

The rules do not allow additional bedrooms for any other reason. In addition, before 4 December 2013, an additional bedroom might not have been allowed (when it should have been) for a severely disabled child who cannot share a bedroom. You should appeal if you are affected and think you should be allowed more bedrooms – eg, to store equipment required because of a severe disability, for a disabled child or non-dependant who requires overnight care or for a partner unable to share a bedroom with you because of a severe disability.[17]

Definitions
You (or your partner) are a **'person who requires overnight care'** if:[18]
- you (or s/he) are getting attendance allowance (AA), the middle or highest rate of DLA care component, either rate of the daily living component of personal independence payment (PIP) or armed forces independence payment; *or*
- you (or s/he) have provided the local authority with sufficient certificates, documents, information or evidence to satisfy it that overnight care is required; *and*
- whichever of the above applies, it has been arranged for one or more people who do not live with you to provide overnight care and to stay overnight regularly in your home for

Part 4: Paying for housing
Chapter 19: Rent restrictions
2. The local housing allowance rules

this purpose, and to be provided with the use of a bedroom additional to those used by other people who live with you. You must satisfy the local authority that you (or s/he) reasonably require this care.

You can count as a person who requires overnight care even if you are not living in your home, provided you can be treated as occupying it – eg, while you are temporarily absent.

You count as a **'qualifying parent or carer'** if:[19]

– a child has been placed with you (or your partner) for adoption under specified provisions; or

– you (or your partner) are a foster parent (in Scotland this includes foster and kinship carers). This applies even though you do not currently have a child placed with you, as long as you have become an approved foster parent, or have fostered a child, within the last 52 weeks.

To come within the definition, you must have a bedroom in your home that is additional to those used by the other people living in your home.

Example
Seamus and Elaine are the foster parents of two children. Their non-dependent son, aged 24, lives with them. They are allowed three bedrooms under the size criteria: one for Seamus and Sarah, one for their son and one additional room because they are each a 'qualifying parent or carer'. Appropriate local housing allowance: dwelling with three bedrooms.

Categories of dwelling

The category of dwelling that applies to you depends on how many bedrooms you are allowed (see p396) and whether you are living in shared accommodation.

One-bedroom shared accommodation

The category of dwelling that applies is one-bedroom shared accommodation if:[20]

- even if you do not live in shared accommodation, you are under 35, are a single claimant without children and do not have a non-dependant living with you (see p116 for HB and p494 for UC). See p399 for exceptions. **Note:** for UC, this category also applies if you are a member of a couple but are claiming as a single person (see p184); or

- for HB only, you (and your partner) live in shared accommodation and are only allowed one bedroom under the size criteria. You count as living in shared accommodation if you do not have the exclusive use of at least two rooms, or the exclusive use of one room as well as the exclusive use of a bathroom, a toilet and a kitchen or facilities for cooking. See p399 for exceptions.

There are **exceptions** to the rule and this category of dwelling does not apply (even if you live in shared accommodation) if:

- you (or, for HB, your partner):[21]
  - qualify for a severe disability premium (for HB) or are getting AA, the middle or highest rate of the DLA care component, the daily living component of PIP or armed forces independence payment (for UC); *or*
  - for HB only, are under the age of 22 and:
    - were looked after (in the care of), or under the supervision of, a local authority under specific legal provisions after you turned 16; *or*
    - ceased to be subject to a compulsory supervision order under s83 of the Children's Hearings (Scotland) Act 2011 which had continued after you turned 16. **Note:** there are exceptions; *or*
  - are under the age of 22 and were provided with accommodation by the local authority under specified provisions. For UC only, you must be at least 18 and must have been living in the accommodation on your 16th birthday. **Note:** in some cases, you cannot claim HB, or get the UC housing costs element, if you were previously looked after by a local authority (see p886); *or*
- you are a single claimant aged under 35 and are:[22]
  - for HB only, a 'person who requires overnight care' (see p397). **Note:** for UC, this exception is not needed because you are exempt if you are getting AA, the middle or highest rate of DLA care component, the daily living component of PIP or armed forces independence payment; *or*
  - for HB only, a 'qualifying parent or carer' (see p398); *or*
  - at least 25; *and*
    - have been living in a homeless hostel for three months or more (this does not have to be continuous) and while living in such a hostel you have accepted support services to assist you in being rehabilitated or resettled in the community; *or*
    - are an offender subject to specific multi-agency risk management arrangements.

One-bedroom self-contained accommodation

The category of dwelling that applies is one-bedroom self-contained accommodation if you are allowed one bedroom under the size criteria (see p396).[23] For UC only, it must be reasonable for you to occupy this category of accommodation.[24]

For HB only, you must have:

- the exclusive use of at least two rooms; *or*
- the exclusive use of one room as well as the exclusive use of a bathroom, a toilet and a kitchen or facilities for cooking.

Part 4: Paying for housing
Chapter 19: Rent restrictions
2. The local housing allowance rules

Rooms

'Room' means a bedroom or a 'room suitable for living in', other than one you share with someone who is not a member of your household, a non-dependant or someone who pays rent to you or your partner.

Note: if you are a single claimant under 35, this category of dwelling applies, even if you do not live in shared accommodation, unless any of the exceptions listed on p398 apply.

Dwellings with two or more bedrooms

If you are allowed more than one bedroom under the size criteria, the category of dwelling that applies is that for a dwelling with the number of bedrooms you are allowed (see p396 for HB and p492 for UC), up to a maximum of four bedrooms.[25] For UC only, it must be reasonable for you to occupy this category of accommodation, taking into account the number of people in your 'extended benefit unit' (see p494 for who counts).[26] So this category applies, for example, if you are a lone parent or a member of a couple with children, you have a non-dependant living with you, you are a 'person who requires overnight care' or a 'qualifying parent or carer' (see p397 for who counts) or (for HB) you are a joint tenant with someone who is a member of your household.

Local housing allowance rates

Local housing allowances for each category of dwelling are set by the rent officer annually. New rates take effect every 15 January (or the first Tuesday following if that day is not a Tuesday). A local housing allowance is usually the lowest of two figures:[27]

- the amount of rent at the 30th percentile point of local market rents for assured tenancies in a 'broad rental market area'; *or*
- the previous year's local housing allowance rate increased by 1 per cent.

However, for some categories of dwelling in some specified areas (eg, where rents are known to be higher), a local housing allowance is the previous year's local housing allowance rate increased by 4 per cent, up to a set maximum.[28]

Broad rental market area[29]

A **'broad rental market area'** is an area where you could reasonably be expected to live, taking into account the facilities and services for health, education, recreation, banking and shopping, and the travel distance by public and private transport. It must contain a variety of kinds of residential accommodation and types of lettings, and have sufficient private rented housing to ensure that the local housing allowance for the categories of dwelling in the area is representative of the rents that a landlord might reasonably be expected to obtain in that area.

If you are considering renting accommodation

If you are considering renting accommodation privately and are likely to claim benefit, you might want to find out the rent figure that will be used to calculate it. If you are already claiming benefit, you may wish to find out the rent figure that will be used when your claim is reassessed (usually annually).

If the local housing allowance rules apply to you, check what category of dwelling applies to you (see p398) and work out the appropriate local housing allowance.

You can check the amount of the appropriate local housing allowance at www.gov.uk/housing-benefit/what-youll-get. **Note:** local housing allowances are updated annually (usually taking effect on 15 January) and can go down as well as up.

Maximum rent

Your 'maximum rent' for HB purposes is the appropriate local housing allowance for you or, if lower, your 'cap rent'.[30] The local authority might call this your 'maximum rent (LHA)'. The 'eligible rent' used to calculate your HB (see p111) is your maximum rent.[31]

Your **'cap rent'** is the rent you are liable, or treated as liable, to pay for your home (including service charges).[32] If you share accommodation with anyone other than your partner or your children included in your claim and you are jointly liable for the rent with her/him, the local authority apportions the cap rent between you.

Example
Phil, aged 28, shares a privately rented house with four friends. Phil claims HB. The rent is £300 a week. His cap rent is £60 (£300÷5).

The local authority may say it has general discretion to decrease your cap rent to an amount it considers appropriate (but see p395).
Note:
• If you share accommodation with someone other than your partner or a child included in your claim and are jointly liable for the rent with her/him (eg, you are joint tenants), your maximum rent is based on the local housing allowance that applies to you (see p398), subject to the cap rent rule.
• A rent restriction can be delayed in specified circumstances (see p421).

Part 4: Paying for housing
Chapter 19: Rent restrictions
2. The local housing allowance rules

Example

Terry, aged 40, lives with his father in the same household. They are joint tenants. The rent for the flat is £300 a week. Terry works part time and earns £100 a week after deductions of tax and national insurance contributions. He claims HB.

The appropriate local housing allowance is that for two-bedroom accommodation (£250).

Terry's cap rent is £150 (£300÷2). His maximum rent (and his eligible rent) is therefore £150 as this figure is lower than the local housing allowance.

Terry has no non-dependants. Therefore, his maximum HB is £150.

His applicable amount is £72.40 (the standard amount for a single person aged 25 or over).

His income to be taken into account is £95 a week (£5 of his earnings are disregarded).

The difference between his income and his applicable amount is, therefore, £22.60.

65% x £22.60 = £14.69 a week.

Terry's HB is therefore £150 – £14.69 = £135.31 a week.

How long a maximum rent applies

Your maximum rent is based on the appropriate local housing allowance when your claim is assessed. Your HB is paid on this basis until the next time the local authority assesses your claim.[33] This is usually only annually, even if the amount of the allowance changes. When the local authority reassesses your claim, it uses the local housing allowance that is then appropriate. Some changes of circumstances can lead to an earlier reassessment – eg, if:[34]

- there is a change in the category of dwelling that applies to you (see p398) – ie, you are allowed more or fewer bedrooms because, for instance, someone has moved in with you or has moved out, or your child has reached aged 16 and is allowed her/his own bedroom; *or*
- your partner or a child included in your claim (see p210) (or a relative of yours or your partner who lives in the same accommodation as you without a separate right to do so) dies; *or*
- there is a change that affects the amount of your cap rent – eg, your rent goes up or down; *or*
- you move to a new home.

Your maximum rent is then based on the local housing allowance that is appropriate for you on the date of the change.[35] However, you may qualify for a protected rate of HB (transitional protection) if you live in a former pathfinder area (see p422).

Example

Cleo rents a three-bedroom house from a private landlord. She pays £170 a week rent. She has one son, aged seven. Appropriate local housing allowance: dwelling with two bedrooms. When she claims income support and HB, the local housing allowance for two-bedroom accommodation is £105. Cleo's maximum rent (and eligible rent) is £105. Cleo has no non-dependants, so this is also her maximum HB and, therefore, her weekly HB.

Cleo's Aunt Sue comes to live with her. As there has been a change in the category of dwelling that applies to Cleo (this is now three-bedroom accommodation), the local authority reassesses her claim. The local housing allowance for three-bedroom accommodation is now £158. Cleo's maximum rent (and eligible rent) is £158. Aunt Sue is on incapacity benefit so a non-dependant deduction of £14.15 must be made. Cleo's maximum HB and, therefore, her HB is £143.85 a week (£158 – £14.15).

3. The social sector rules

If the social sector rules apply, they determine the amount of rent that is used to calculate your housing benefit (HB). Broadly, a deduction is made from your HB if the number of bedrooms you are allowed under what are known as the 'size criteria' (see p404) is lower than the number of bedrooms in your home.

If you are a 'social sector' tenant (ie, you are not a private tenant), the social sector rules may apply if you are living in accommodation that has more bedrooms than the rules allow.[36] These are commonly referred to as the 'bedroom tax', or by the DWP as the 'removal of the spare room subsidy'.

There are exceptions. The social sector rules do *not* apply if:[37]

- you or your partner are at least the qualifying age for pension credit (see p78);
- the local housing allowance rules, the local reference rent rules or the pre-January 1996 rules apply (see p395, p407 and p416). **Note:** the pre-January 1996 rules can only apply in exceptional cases (but see below). The local housing allowance rules and the local reference rent rules *never* apply if you are a local authority tenant;
- your tenancy is one of the excluded tenancies listed on p393 other than the last one, and your landlord is *not* a registered housing association or the local authority;
- you have a shared ownership tenancy – ie, you are buying part of your house or flat and renting the rest;
- your rent is for mooring charges for a houseboat or for caravan or mobile home site fees;
- you live in specified types of temporary accommodation for homeless people provided by a local authority or a registered housing association.

Do the pre-January 1996 rules apply to you?

If the pre-January 1996 rules apply to you (ie, you are an 'exempt claimant' or live in 'exempt accommodation'), the social sector rules do *not* apply. Since 3 March 2014, if you are a local authority or housing association tenant, you can only count as an 'exempt

Part 4: Paying for housing
Chapter 19: Rent restrictions
3. The social sector rules

claimant' in exceptional cases. See p416 for further information. However, note the following.

1. Before 3 March 2014, your local authority may have applied the social sector rules in error to some claimants who were 'exempt claimants'. It should try to identify those affected from its records, but this might not be possible – eg, if the records are no longer available.

2. If you think the pre-January 1996 rules applied to you before 3 March 2014 (ie, you were an 'exempt claimant' under the rules that then applied), but your HB was reduced under the social sector rules, ask your local authority to revise the decision to reduce your HB and ask it to pay you all the arrears due. Provide as much evidence as you can to enable the local authority to do this. Alternatively, you can appeal against the decision to reduce your HB if you are within the time limit.

The number of bedrooms you are allowed

You are allowed:[38]
- one bedroom for each of the following people who occupy your home (see below), each coming only into the first category for which s/he is eligible:
  - a couple (see p205 for who counts);
  - a person who is not a child – ie, someone aged 16 or over;
  - a 'child who cannot share a bedroom' (see p396 for who counts);
  - two children under 16 of the same sex;
  - two children under 10;
  - a child; *and*
- one or more additional bedrooms in specified circumstances (see p405).

Note: unlike with the local housing allowance rules, there is no maximum number of bedrooms.

People who occupy your home

1. This means anyone who the local authority is satisfied occupies your dwelling as a home[39] and can, therefore, include people other than your partner or children included in your claim – eg, your non-dependants or a live-in carer, but not a foster child or child placed with you for adoption under specified provisions.[40]

2. The local authority must include a member of the armed forces deployed on operations if s/he is your (or your partner's) son, daughter, stepson or stepdaughter who lived with you before being deployed and s/he intends to return home.

3. You can argue that someone counts as occupying your home if s/he normally lives with you but is temporarily away.[41] However, if you share the care of a child, the child is considered to be occupying the home of only one parent – the parent with whom the child normally lives.[42]

Additional bedrooms

You are allowed one additional bedroom if you satisfy one of the following conditions. If you satisfy both, you are allowed two additional bedrooms.[43]

- You (or your partner) are a 'person who requires overnight care' (see p397 for who counts). Even if both of you require overnight care, only one additional bedroom is allowed.

- You (or your partner) are a 'qualifying parent or carer' – ie, certain foster parents and people with whom a child has been placed for adoption (see p398 for who counts). Even if, for example, you (or your partner) have more than one foster child, only one bedroom is allowed.

In addition, if you are jointly liable for the rent with someone other than your partner (eg, a joint tenant), you are allowed an additional bedroom for her/him if s/he (or her/his partner) is a 'person who requires overnight care' or a 'qualifying parent or carer' (see p397 for who counts).[44] You are allowed two additional bedrooms if s/he satisfies both conditions.

The rules do not allow additional bedrooms for any reason other than those shown above. In addition, before 4 December 2013, an additional bedroom might not have been allowed (when it should have been) for a severely disabled child who cannot share a bedroom. You should appeal if you are (or were) affected and think you should be allowed more bedrooms – eg, to store equipment required because of a severe disability, or for a disabled child or non-dependant who requires overnight care, or for a partner unable to share a bedroom with you because of a severe disability.[45]

Examples
Angus lives with his wife and child in a four-bedroom council house. He claims HB. Angus is a 'person who requires overnight care'. Under the social sector rules, he is allowed three bedrooms, one for himself and his wife, one for his child and one for a non-resident carer. He, therefore, has one too many bedrooms and the social sector rules apply.

Bill, an approved foster parent, shares a four-bedroom council house with his mother and father. His foster daughter lives with them. Bill's mother is severely disabled and requires, and receives, overnight care. Bill and his father are joint tenants. Bill claims HB. Under the size criteria, Bill is allowed two bedrooms: one for him and one for his mother and father. However, he is allowed one additional bedroom because he is a 'qualifying parent or carer' and one additional bedroom because his mother is a 'person who requires overnight care'. So he is allowed a total of four bedrooms. For the purposes of the social sector rules, he does not have too many bedrooms.

Part 4: Paying for housing
Chapter 19: Rent restrictions
3. The social sector rules

Maximum rent

If the social sector rules apply, the 'eligible rent' used to calculate your HB is your 'maximum rent'. The local authority might call this your 'maximum rent (social sector)'.[46] Your 'maximum rent' is determined under the following steps.[47] **Note:** if you are a joint tenant, see p407.

- **Step one:** work out how many bedrooms you are allowed for all the people who occupy your home (see p404).
- **Step two:** calculate your eligible rent under the normal rules (see p111). This is the contractual rent for the whole dwelling, minus any ineligible service charges. If the number of bedrooms in your home is the same as or lower than the number in Step one, this is your maximum rent.
- **Step three:** if the number of bedrooms in your home is greater than the number of bedrooms in Step one, your maximum rent is the amount in Step two, reduced by:
  - 14 per cent, if you have one too many bedrooms; *or*
  - 25 per cent if you have two or more too many bedrooms.

Bedrooms

'Bedroom' is not defined in the rules. It is the ordinary meaning of the word that is relevant – ie, a room is a bedroom if it is furnished and used for sleeping in. You can try to argue that the local authority should not count a room in your home as a bedroom and, therefore, that your HB should not be reduced (or reduced as much) under these rules. Suggest that the local authority should, for example, take into account:

– the size of the room – eg, if it is too small to fit a single bed;
– your personal use of the room – eg, if you use the room to store equipment you need because of a severe disability;
– whether your home has been converted or adapted – eg, if two small bedrooms have been converted into one big bedroom.

Note:
- If it appears to the local authority that the amount in Step three is still too high to be met by HB, it has a general discretion to reduce your maximum rent further.[48]
- A restriction can be delayed in specified circumstances (see p421).

Example

Raj and Indira rent a two-bedroom flat from a housing association. Their rent is £140 a week. Raj works part time and earns £200 a week after deductions of tax and national insurance. Indira claims HB. Under the size criteria, they are allowed one bedroom. They, therefore, have one too many bedrooms.

14% x £140 = £19.60. Therefore, Indira's maximum rent (and her eligible rent) is £120.40 (£140 – £19.60). She has no non-dependants. Therefore, her maximum HB is £120.40.

Her applicable amount is £113.70 (the standard amount for a couple).

The income to be taken into account is £190 a week (£10 of Raj's earnings are disregarded).

The difference between income and her applicable amount is, therefore, £76.30.

65% x £76.30 = £49.60 a week.

Indira's HB is, therefore, £120.40 – £49.60 = £70.80 a week.

If you are a joint tenant

If more than one person is liable for the rent (eg, you are a joint tenant with someone other than your partner), the local authority apportions the amount in Step two or Step three (as the case may be) between you, taking into account all the circumstances, including the number of people and the proportion of rent each pays.

Example

Sam and Dave are joint tenants of a four-bedroom council house. Their rent is £210 a week. Sam is an approved foster parent. Sam pays £140 and Dave pays £70. Dave loses his job and claims income-based jobseeker's allowance (JSA) and HB. Under the size criteria, he is allowed three bedrooms: one for himself, one for Sam and an additional room because Sam counts as a 'qualifying parent or carer'. He, therefore, has one too many bedrooms.

14% x £210 = £29.4

£210 – £29.40 = £180.60

Dave pays one-third of the rent, so the local authority apportions the maximum rent accordingly. One-third of £180.60 = £60.20

Therefore, Dave's maximum rent (and his eligible rent) is £60.20. He has no non-dependants. Therefore his maximum HB is £60.20.

Because Dave gets income-based JSA, he is automatically passported to maximum HB. His HB is therefore £60.20.

Note: if Sam also claims HB, his maximum rent (and eligible rent and maximum HB) is two-thirds of £180.60 = £120.40.

4. The local reference rent rules

If the local reference rent rules apply, they determine the amount of rent that is used to calculate your housing benefit (HB). Your HB is based on a rent officer's 'determinations' (see p408).

The local reference rent rules apply to you if, on or after 7 April 2008, you claim HB, or move to a new home while you are entitled to HB, and:[49]

Part 4: Paying for housing
Chapter 19: Rent restrictions
4. The local reference rent rules

- you live in a hostel, houseboat, mobile home or caravan; *or*
- your rent includes board and attendance; *or*
- your landlord is a registered housing association or is a county council (if you live in a caravan or mobile home provided on a travellers' site[50]), or you are renting a caravan, mobile home or houseboat (where you are also liable to make payments to a local authority – eg, for the site or mooring fees). However, this only applies if the local authority considers your rent to be unreasonably high (or, in some cases, your accommodation unreasonably large). Otherwise, you have an 'excluded tenancy' (see p393); *or*
- your tenancy was a local authority or new town letting, but it has been transferred to a new owner. However, this only applies if there has been a rent increase since the transfer; *and*
  - the local authority considers your rent to be unreasonably high; *or*
  - if the transfer took place before 7 October 2002, the local authority considers your accommodation to be unreasonably large.

  Otherwise, you have an 'excluded tenancy' (see p393).

Note:
- These rules can also apply to other tenants, but only if you were entitled to HB immediately before 7 April 2008 under the local reference rent rules that then applied. See below for further information.
- These rules *never* apply if you are a local authority tenant.
- These rules do *not* apply if you have an 'excluded tenancy', or if the local housing allowance or the pre-January 1996 rules apply (see p392).

If you were getting housing benefit before 7 April 2008

Even if you are not someone to whom the current local reference rent rules would apply (eg, you rent a private house or flat), if you were entitled to HB immediately before 7 April 2008 and the local reference rent rules applied to you, they continue to do so until you make a new claim for HB (ie, after a break in your claim) or you move to a new home.[51] If any rent restriction rules still apply to you at that point, your HB is restricted under the rules that are then applicable.

The local reference rent rules continue to apply to you even following any of the changes of circumstances listed below, and then when the local authority has to apply to the rent officer for determinations every 52 weeks thereafter.[52]

The rent officer's determinations

When the local reference rent rules apply, the local authority must apply to the rent officer and ask her/him to make 'determinations'. The rent officer makes determinations about the rent for your home (see p409), comparing it with the rent for other private sector tenancies in the area. The rent officer also makes determinations that indicate the average rents for specific types of accommodation (see p412).

The local authority must apply to the rent officer if:[53]

- you make a new claim for HB or move to a new home while you are entitled to HB; *or*
- a previous reference to the rent officer was made in respect of your claim 52 weeks or more ago; *or*
- there has been one of the following changes of circumstances since a rent officer's determination:[54]
  - the number of occupiers has changed (except in a hostel). Argue this does not apply if someone who normally lives with you is only away temporarily;[55] *or*
  - there has been a substantial change in the condition of the dwelling or the terms of the tenancy (other than a rent increase); *or*
  - there has been an increase in the rent under a term of the tenancy, unless the previous determination was a significantly high, size-related or exceptionally high rent determination;[56]
  - a size-related rent determination was made and there has since been a change in the composition of the household, or a child living with you has reached the age of 10 or 16; *or*
  - you or your partner become, or cease to be, a 'person who requires overnight care' or a 'qualifying parent or carer' (see p397 for who counts), or a child becomes, or stops being, a 'child who cannot share a bedroom' (see p396 for who counts) and this affects the size of accommodation you are allowed under the size criteria (see p410); *or*
- your HB was being restricted under the local housing allowance rules, but these no longer apply – eg, if the home you rent was sold to a housing association and the local reference rent rules apply instead.

The local authority *cannot* apply to the rent officer for determinations if:

- a rent officer determination has been made for the same tenancy (or a tenancy in the same dwelling) on substantially the same terms within the last 52 weeks.[57] This means that a determination made for a previous tenant may be valid for your HB claim. A new referral *is* needed if you are a young individual and no single room rent determination has yet been made (see p412);
- you live in a hostel and a rent officer determination has been made for similar accommodation in the hostel, sleeping the same number of people as yours, within the last 12 months and there has been no change of circumstances in respect of that accommodation.[58]

Determinations about the rent for your home

The rent officer makes the following determinations about the rent for your home.

- A '**significantly high rent determination**' if your rent is significantly higher than that paid for similar tenancies and dwellings in the vicinity – ie, the

Part 4: Paying for housing
Chapter 19: Rent restrictions
4. The local reference rent rules

immediate area around your home. This is the amount your landlord might reasonably be paid for your tenancy.[59]

- An **'exceptionally high rent determination'** if s/he considers the 'rent payable' for your home to be exceptionally high. This is the highest amount your landlord might reasonably be paid for an assured tenancy in the neighbourhood for a home that is the same size as yours (or the size you are allowed under the size criteria).[60]

- A **'size-related rent determination'** if your accommodation is larger than you are allowed under the size criteria (see below). This is the amount your landlord might reasonably be paid for a similar tenancy of an appropriate size for you in the vicinity.[61] 'Vicinity' means the immediate area around your home or, if there is no dwelling in that area of a size you are allowed under the size criteria, the nearest area where there is one.[62] **Note:** if you are a single person under 35, the rent officer must also identify a single room rent (see p412).

The rent officer uses these determinations to identify the **'claim-related rent'**. The 'claim-related rent' is the lowest of the determinations above or, if no such determination was made, the rent you are supposed to pay.[63]

Definitions

A **'neighbourhood'** is:[64]

– the part of the town or city where your home is located that is a distinct area of residential accommodation; *or*

– if you do not live in a town or city, the area surrounding your home that is a distinct area of residential accommodation, which includes homes of the same size as yours (or of a size you are allowed under the size criteria – see below).

'Rent payable' means the size-related rent determination (see below) or, if there is no such determination, the significantly high rent determination (if there is one) or, in any other case, the rent you are supposed to pay.

The size of accommodation you are allowed

Under the 'size criteria', the rent officer allows you one bedroom or 'room suitable for living in' for each of the following occupiers, each coming only into the first category for which s/he is eligible:[65]

- a couple (see p205 for who counts);
- a person who is not a child – ie, someone aged 16 or over;
- two children under 16 of the same sex;
- a 'child who cannot share a bedroom' (see p396 for who counts). **Note:** you are only allowed a bedroom for her/him if you have a bedroom in your home that is additional to those you would be allowed if s/he *were* able to share a bedroom;
- two children under 10;
- a child.

You are allowed an additional bedroom (or 'room suitable for living in') if you satisfy one of the following conditions. If you satisfy both conditions, you are allowed two additional bedrooms (or rooms suitable for living in).[66]

- You (or your partner) are a 'person who requires overnight care' (see p397 for who counts). Even if both you and your partner require overnight care, only one additional room is allowed.

- You (or your partner) are a 'qualifying parent or carer' (see p398 for who counts). Even if both you and your partner are a 'qualifying parent or carer', or if, for example, you have more than one foster child, only one additional room is allowed.

Note: unlike with the local housing allowance rules, there is no maximum number of bedrooms.

You are also allowed the following number of 'rooms suitable for living in'.

Number of occupiers	Number of rooms
Fewer than four	One
Four to six	Two
Seven or more	Three

If any of the rooms in your home are not suitable for living in (eg, because of their size or lack of ventilation), argue that they should be ignored.

Occupiers

A person counts as an **'occupier'** if the local authority includes her/him on the form used to refer your tenancy to the rent officer.[67] This can include people other than your partner or children included in your claim – eg, your non-dependants or a live-in carer, but not a foster child or a child placed with you for adoption under specified provisions.[68] This also includes your (or your partner's) son, daughter, stepson or stepdaughter who lives with you and who is in the armed forces, even when s/he is deployed on operations, provided s/he intends to return home.

You can argue that someone is an occupier if s/he normally lives with you, but is temporarily away.[69] However, if you share the care of a child, the child is considered to be occupying the home of only one parent – the parent with whom s/he normally lives.[70]

Example

Alice and Len have three children: two sons, 12 and 14, and a daughter, 17. They are allowed one room for themselves, one for their sons and one for their daughter – three bedrooms, as well as two other 'rooms suitable for living in'. They are, therefore, allowed five rooms, as well as a kitchen, bathroom and toilet.

Part 4: Paying for housing
Chapter 19: Rent restrictions
4. The local reference rent rules

Determinations that indicate average rents

The rent officer makes determinations that indicate the average rents for specific types of accommodation in a 'broad rental market area'. These are as follows.

* The **'local reference rent'** is the mid-point of 'reasonable market rents' for assured tenancies in the broad rental market area appropriate to the size of property in which you live (or the size you are allowed under the size criteria – see p410).[71] This is only provided if the claim-related rent (see p409) exceeds it.[72]

* The **'single room rent'** is the mid-point of 'reasonable market rents' for assured tenancies in the broad rental market area in which the tenant has exclusive use of one bedroom only, and other than that only shares a living room, kitchen, a toilet and bathroom, and makes no payment for board and attendance.[73] It is only provided if you are a 'young individual' (see below).

Broad rental market area

A **'broad rental market area'** is the area where you could reasonably be expected to live, taking into account the facilities and services for health, education, recreation, banking and shopping, and the travel distance by public and private transport. It must contain a variety of residential accommodation and types of lettings, and have sufficient private rented housing to ensure that the local reference rents for tenancies in the area are representative of the rents that a landlord might reasonably be expected to obtain in that area.[74]

Young individuals

If you are a 'young individual' (generally a single claimant under the age of 35), in most cases the rent officer identifies a single room rent.[75] Your 'maximum rent' (see p413) is based on this figure unless you have a non-dependant living with you (see p116) or you:[76]

* qualify for a severe disability premium as part of your applicable amount; *or*
* are a housing association tenant; *or*
* are under the age of 22; *and*
  – were looked after (in the care of), or under the supervision of a local authority under specific legal provisions after you turned 16 or were provided with accommodation by the local authority under s20 of the Children Act 1989; *or*
  – ceased to be subject to a compulsory supervision order under s83 of the Children's Hearings (Scotland) Act 2011 which had continued after you turned 16. **Note:** there are exceptions; *or*
* are a 'person who requires overnight care' (see p397 for who counts); *or*
* are a 'qualifying parent or carer' (see p398 for who counts); *or*
* are at least 25; *and*

– have been living in a homeless hostel for three months or more (this does not have to be continuous) and while living in such a hostel have accepted support services to assist you in being rehabilitated or resettled in the community; *or*

– are an offender subject to specific multi-agency risk management arrangements.

Service charges in rent officer determinations

The local authority notifies the rent officer of the amount of rent you are supposed to pay, whether this includes service charges and the amount of the charges that can and cannot be met by HB (see p112).[77] The claim-related rent (see p409) does not include ineligible charges unless you live in one-room accommodation and the landlord provides substantial board and attendance. In this case, the claim-related rent and local reference rent (though not the single room rent) include charges for meals.[78]

Maximum rent

If the local reference rent rules apply, your 'maximum rent' for HB purposes and, therefore, your 'eligible rent' (see p111), is usually the lowest of the rent officer's determinations, even if the rent you pay is higher.[79]

Your 'maximum rent' is:[80]

* the lowest of the claim-related rent, the local reference rent or, if you are a 'young individual' (see p412) and it is relevant, the single room rent; *or*
* if you have been continuously entitled to, and in receipt of, HB for the same property since 5 October 1997, the local reference rent plus half the difference between the local reference rent and the claim-related rent.[81] If you or your partner are a 'welfare-to-work beneficiary', breaks in your claim of up to 52 weeks are ignored. For information about who counts as a welfare-to-work beneficiary, see p686 of the 2013/14 edition of this *Handbook*.

Example

Jo and Louis are a couple who rent a three-bedroom mobile home with a living room and separate dining room. They pay rent of £120 a week. The rent officer decides that the accommodation is too big and that the rent is too high, so makes significantly high and size-related rent determinations. S/he notifies the local authority of a claim-related rent of £90 and a local reference rent of £80. Their maximum rent is therefore £80 a week.

Note:

* If you are in shared accommodation, your maximum rent can be apportioned between you and the people with whom you share. It only covers the rent you pay for residential accommodation.[82]

Part 4: Paying for housing
Chapter 19: Rent restrictions
4. The local reference rent rules

- A rent restriction can be delayed in specified circumstances (see p421).
- If you are considering renting accommodation to which the local reference rent rules apply and you are likely to claim HB, you can apply to the local authority for a pre-tenancy determination (see below).

How long a maximum rent applies

Once your maximum rent is set, your HB is paid on the basis of this until the next time the local authority refers your claim to the rent officer (usually annually). However, if you negotiate with your landlord and s/he agrees a new rent which is lower than the maximum rent, your HB is recalculated using your new rent.[83]

If you are considering renting accommodation

If you are considering renting accommodation privately and are likely to claim HB, you might want to find out the rent figure that will be used to calculate it. If you are already claiming HB, you may wish to find out the rent figure that will be used when your claim is reassessed (usually annually).

If you want to claim HB and the local reference rent rules apply to you, you can apply to the local authority for a **pre-tenancy determination**.[84] You can also apply if you are already receiving HB and your tenancy is due for renewal. Your current tenancy agreement must have started at least 11 months before your request.[85] The procedure is as follows.

- You must apply in writing on the form approved by your local authority. Both you and your prospective landlord must sign it.[86] The local authority must forward your request to the rent officer within two days of receipt.[87]
- The rent officer must send you, the prospective landlord and the local authority her/his determinations within five working days (unless s/he needs more information from the local authority) or as soon as is practicable after that.[88] If the rent officer needs further information, the five days run from the date this is received.

A pre-tenancy determination is usually valid for a year.[89] So, if someone else applied for a pre-tenancy determination for your accommodation in the previous 12 months, it also applies to you.

You cannot appeal against a pre-tenancy determination. However, if you accept the tenancy and claim HB, you can ask for it to be redetermined. If you subsequently negotiate a lower rent with your landlord which is lower than your 'maximum rent', your HB is recalculated using your new rent.[90]

Challenging a rent restriction

You cannot appeal against a rent officer's determination. However, the local authority *can* ask for it to be redetermined on your behalf.[91]

Do you want a redetermination?

1. You must apply to the local authority in writing no later than one month after the date you are notified of its decision on your HB claim.

2. The local authority must apply to the rent officer for a redetermination and pass any representations you make or evidence you supply to her/him within seven days.

3. The rent officer must notify the local authority of her/his decision within 20 working days.[92]

It is not easy to challenge rent officers, but it may still be possible. If, for example, the rent officer has said that your rent is significantly high, s/he might reconsider this if you provide evidence of similar tenancies where tenants who are not on HB are paying the same rent as you.

The rent officer's redetermination might reduce your maximum rent, so consider your position carefully before requesting a redetermination – you could end up with less HB. However, if the redetermination:[93]

- reduces your maximum rent (see p413), it only applies from the Monday after the date of redetermination, so you have not been overpaid;
- increases your maximum rent, it applies from the date of the original decision and you should be paid any HB arrears.

In practice, if you ask for revision or appeal against an HB decision and this relates, in whole or in part, to the rent officer's determinations, the local authority should apply for a redetermination.[94] The local authority can ask for a rent officer redetermination even if you have not done so, and must do in some circumstances.[95] If there has been a property-related error, the rent officer can send a substitute determination automatically.[96] You can ask for a redetermination in any of these situations. Otherwise, you are limited to one request for a rent officer determination.[97]

Note: you can appeal against local authority decisions about your award of HB which involve rent officer determinations – ie, you can challenge the factual basis on which the rent officer made a determination, such as whether you are a 'young individual' or whether someone occupies accommodation with you.[98] If you are in doubt, you may want to appeal *and* ask for a redetermination.

Part 4: Paying for housing
Chapter 19: Rent restrictions
5. The pre-January 1996 rules

5. The pre-January 1996 rules

Before January 1996, the rent restriction rules were less harsh than the rules that replaced them. These pre-January 1996 rules still apply if are claiming housing benefit (HB) and you live in 'exempt accommodation' or if you are an 'exempt claimant'.

Note: you generally cannot qualify for HB if you come under the universal credit (UC) system (see p19). However, if you live in exempt accommodation, the help you get with your rent is not provided in UC. Instead, you can claim HB for the rent you pay and the pre-January 1996 rules may apply.

Exempt accommodation

The pre-January 1996 rules apply to you if you live in 'exempt accommodation' – ie, if it is:[99]
* temporary accommodation for people without a settled way of life, funded by the Resettlement Agency; *or*
* accommodation provided by a housing association, non-metropolitan county council, registered charity or voluntary organisation where that body, or a person acting on its behalf, also provides you with care, support or supervision.[100] You must need the care, support or supervision and it must be more than a token or minimal amount.[101] **Note:** if the person (or body) providing the care, support or supervision has a contract with the local authority to provide these, but is not providing the accommodation, the decision maker is likely to say it is not exempt accommodation.[102]

Exempt claimants

The pre-January 1996 rules apply to you if you are an 'exempt claimant'. You are an exempt claimant if you are a private tenant (or, in exceptional cases, a local authority or housing association tenant – see p417) and you:[103]
* have been continuously entitled to and in receipt of HB since 1 January 1996; *and*
* continue to occupy the same property as your home (except if you are forced to move because fire, flood or natural catastrophe makes it uninhabitable).

You are *not* an exempt claimant if you are a local authority or registered housing association tenant unless:[104]
* you (or your partner) are at least the qualifying age for pension credit (PC – see p78); *or*

- the pre-January 1996 rules applied to you on or before 31 March 2013 – ie, using these rules, the local authority:
  - restricted your rent; *or*
  - decided that your accommodation was too large or your rent was too high, but did not restrict your rent because the rules for those in a protected group applied (see p419), or the restriction was delayed for either of the reasons on p421.

Note: all local authority and registered housing association tenants could count as exempt claimants before 3 March 2014. Your local authority may have applied the social sector rules to you in error before that date. See p403 for information.

If you are an exempt claimant, provided when you make a new claim you are *not* someone to whom the local housing allowance rules apply (see p395):[105]

- breaks in your HB claim of up to four weeks are ignored (52 weeks if you or your partner are a 'welfare-to-work beneficiary'. For information about who counts as a welfare-to-work beneficiary, see p686 of the 2013/14 edition of this *Handbook*);
- an exemption can be transferred to you if you claim HB because:
  - an exempt claimant dies and you are a member of her/his family, or a relative (see p422 for who counts) occupying the same accommodation without a separate right to do so. You must continue to occupy the same property and claim within four weeks of the death;
  - your partner (who was exempt) has been detained in custody and is not entitled to HB under the temporary absence rules (see p103). You must continue to occupy the same property and claim within four weeks of her/his detention;
  - your former partner (who was exempt) has left the dwelling and you are no longer living together as husband and wife. This should also apply if you are no longer living together as civil partners. You must continue to occupy the same property and claim within four weeks of the date s/he left.

The exemption can only be transferred if either the exempt claimant was in receipt of HB at the time s/he died (or left the dwelling) or had become a 'welfare-to-work beneficiary' (see above) within the previous 52 weeks.[106] If the exemption cannot be transferred, other rent restriction rules may apply when you make a new claim (see p391).

Note: if you are thinking of making *any* changes to your claim, check whether this would mean you are no longer an exempt claimant and, therefore, the local reference rent rules, the local housing allowance rules or the social sector rules apply.

Part 4: Paying for housing
Chapter 19: Rent restrictions
5. The pre-January 1996 rules

When your rent can be restricted

The local authority must restrict your 'eligible rent' if it decides your accommodation is unreasonably large or your rent is unreasonably high (see below).[107] If you are in a 'protected group' (see p419), this only applies if:[108]
- cheaper suitable alternative accommodation is available to you; *and*
- it is reasonable to expect you to move.

Note: a rent restriction can be delayed in some circumstances (see p421).

Is your accommodation unreasonably large?

Your accommodation counts as unreasonably large if it is larger than is reasonably needed for you and anyone else who occupies the accommodation (including non-dependants and sub-tenants), taking account of suitable alternative accommodation occupied by other households of the same size.[109] The important question is the size of home you need, rather than the size of home you want.[110]

The needs of everyone living in your accommodation, whether or not they are part of your family, must be considered – eg, you might need additional space because someone has a disability, or lives elsewhere but regularly visits you.

Is your rent unreasonably high?

Your rent can count as too high if it is unreasonably high compared with that for suitable alternative accommodation elsewhere.[111] 'Rent' includes, among other things, any service charges or licence fees you must pay.[112] In making this comparison, the local authority must consider the full range of rents that could be paid for such accommodation and not just the cheapest.[113] If your rent is within the range or just above it, the local authority may find it difficult to justify finding your rent to be unreasonably high.[114]

Note: when deciding whether your rent is unreasonably high, the local authority may ask a rent officer to assess a reasonable rent for your property, but the figures are not binding. The local authority (not the rent officer) must decide whether your rent is unreasonably high, using different criteria from that used by the rent officer.[115]

Suitable alternative accommodation

It is not sufficient for the local authority to show that cheaper or smaller alternative accommodation exists; it must also be 'suitable' for the age and health of all the people that the local authority must take into account, having regard to the nature of the accommodation and the facilities available.[116] The local authority must consider these factors, even if you do not raise your housing needs yourself.[117]

Who must the local authority take into account?

The local authority must take into account: you, your partner, any child(ren) included in your claim and any relative (see p422 for who counts) of yours or your partner who lives in the same dwelling as you without a separate right to do so.[118]

The local authority must compare your home with 'alternative accommodation'.

- It cannot just compare homes with the same number of bedrooms; some effort must be made to establish what other facilities are available.[119]
- It must compare your home with other properties offering the same security of tenure. For example, if you have an assured tenancy, the local authority may not rely on comparisons with accommodation that is let on assured shorthold tenancies, or with council or housing association properties.[120]
- It does not have to exclude properties which you cannot take because the landlord wants a deposit that you cannot afford.[121] However, if you are in a 'protected group', you might be able to argue that the accommodation is not available to you (see below).
- It should not make comparisons with other parts of the country where accommodation costs differ widely from local ones, but it may compare your property with one in a less expensive area within a city.[122]

Are you in a protected group?

If the local authority decides that your rent or the size of your accommodation is unreasonable, it must consider whether you are in a 'protected group'.[123] If you are, it cannot restrict your rent unless cheaper suitable alternative accommodation is available (see below) and it is reasonable to expect you to move (see p420).

You are in a protected group if any of the people the local authority must take into account:

- are at least the qualifying age for PC (see p78); *or*
- satisfy any of the tests for being incapable of work or for having limited capability for work, or can be treated as incapable of or as having limited capability for work;[124] *or*
- have a child (this includes a 'qualifying young person') living with them for whom they are responsible (see p212).

Cheaper suitable alternative accommodation

The local authority must prove that suitable alternative accommodation exists and is actually available to you. It does not need to refer to specific properties, but must have sufficient evidence to show there is an active housing market with accommodation of a suitable type, rent and location for you.[125]

Part 4: Paying for housing
Chapter 19: Rent restrictions
5. The pre-January 1996 rules

In considering whether accommodation is 'available', the local authority must take into account personal factors, such as whether you can afford to pay a deposit.[126] If the local authority produces a list of properties that it says are available to you, try to show that they are not available because of your personal circumstances.[127]

Is it reasonable to expect you to move?

The local authority must show that it is reasonable to expect you to move. It must take into account the adverse effects of a move on:[128]

* your ability to retain your job; *and*
* the education of any child or young person living with you. In considering this, the local authority must justify any decision that it is reasonable to make the child travel to or move school.[129]

The local authority may say that it does not need to consider any other factors, such as your health.[130] However, if there are good reasons why you cannot move other than those listed above, try to argue that alternative accommodation cannot be suitable.[131]

Maximum rent

Your 'maximum rent' for HB purposes (and your 'eligible rent' – see p111) is normally your contractual rent minus ineligible services. If you are in shared accommodation, this can be apportioned between you and the people with whom you share. It only covers the rent you pay for residential accommodation.[132]

However, if the local authority decides your 'eligible rent' should be restricted, it reduces it to the amount it considers appropriate.[133] It must take into account the cost of suitable alternative accommodation and other circumstances that are reasonably relevant to the decision – eg, pregnancy, the difficulty of finding other suitable accommodation and whether the local authority would have to rehouse you if you had to move.[134]

The local authority should not be unduly influenced by the amount of subsidy it is paid by the government, but it can take this into account when deciding on a reasonable level of rent. It cannot be reduced below that payable for suitable alternative accommodation.[135]

Note: a rent restriction can be delayed in specified circumstances (see p421).

Rent increases

If your landlord increases your rent, the local authority cannot increase your eligible rent by the full amount if it decides that:[136]

* the increase is unreasonably high compared with increases in suitable alternative accommodation. The local authority must consider the amount of the increase, as well as what your rent was and what your rent will be,

and compare it with the rent in the suitable alternative accommodation.[137] It should also consider, for example, the quality of the accommodation, your age and state of health, whether you would have to move if the increase is not met and how a move would affect you;[138] *or*

- the increase is unreasonable because a previous increase occurred within the preceding 12 months.

If the local authority considers a rent increase to be unreasonable, it may refuse to meet all of that increase or meet only so much of it as it considers appropriate. If your rent has been increased for the second time in under 12 months but is still below the market level for suitable alternative accommodation, or the increase reflects improvements made to your accommodation, argue for the full amount to be allowed.

6. Delay before a rent restriction is applied

In some situations, a reduction in your housing benefit (HB) (a rent restriction) can be delayed. A rent restriction can be delayed:

- in specified circumstances (see below);
- if the local housing allowance rules apply and you qualify for 'transitional protection' (see p422).

When a rent restriction can be delayed

A rent restriction can be delayed if:

- a member of your family (or a relative of you or your partner who lived in the same accommodation as you without a separate right to do so) dies and you still live there (temporary absences of up to 13 weeks are allowed). In most cases, no restriction is made for 12 months from the date of death;[139]
- you, or a member of your family (or a relative of you or your partner who lives in the same dwelling as you without a separate right to do so) could meet the costs of the dwelling when you took them on (this could include other bills as well as the rent). In most cases, no restriction is made for 13 weeks, provided neither you nor your partner were entitled to HB in the 52 weeks before your current award of HB.[140]

Under the local housing allowance and social sector rules, your eligible rent can change before the end of the 12-month/13-week period if your eligible rent as calculated under these rules is now the same or higher, or you move to a new home or another member of your family (or relative) dies.[141] **Note:** if the local housing alllowance rules apply and you qualify for transitional protection, different rules may apply after a member of your family or a relative dies.

Part 4: Paying for housing
Chapter 19: Rent restrictions
7. Challenging a rent restriction

Definitions[142]

'**Family**' means you, your partner and any child or qualifying young person for whom you or your partner are responsible and who lives in your household.

'**Relative**' means a close relative (see p101 for who counts) or a grandparent, grandchild, uncle, aunt, nephew or niece.

Example

Mr and Mrs Connor and their four-year-old son live in a private three-bedroom flat. They pay rent of £225 a week. Until her recent death, Mr Connor's mother lived with them. Mr Connor's maximum rent (and hence his eligible rent) was being restricted to the local housing allowance for a three-bedroom property (£190).

When he notifies the local authority of the death of his mother, his new maximum rent (and eligible rent) is the local housing allowance for a two-bedroom property (£150). However, the decrease is delayed for 12 months.

Mr Connor gets income support. Before his mother's death his HB was £175.85 a week (£190 *minus* a non-dependant deduction of £14.15).

For 12 months from his mother's date of death, his HB is £190 a week.

Transitional protection

When HB rules change, you could be entitled to a lower rate of HB than you were before the rule changes. In some cases, your old (higher) rate of HB can be protected for a period. This is called transitional protection. The local housing allowance rules were piloted in 18 'pathfinder' areas from late 2003 until 7 April 2008. The pilot rules were more generous than the current local housing allowance rules. If you live in a former pathfinder area, you may still have transitional protection. See pp282–83 of the 2011/12 edition of this *Handbook* for further information. In the past, there were other situations when you could qualify for transitional protection – ie, if:

- your HB was calculated on the basis of the local housing allowance rules immediately before 1 April 2011; *or*
- you were at least 25 but not yet 35 and your HB was calculated on the basis of the local housing allowance for one-bedroom self-contained accommodation before 1 January 2012.

See pp317–18 of the 2012/13 edition of this *Handbook* for details.

7. **Challenging a rent restriction**

If the **local housing allowance rules** apply, you cannot appeal against the amount of the local housing allowance. However, you *can* appeal against local authority decisions about your award of housing benefit which involve the local housing allowance – ie, you can challenge the factual basis on which a particular local housing allowance was used, such as whether the local housing allowance for one-bedroom shared accommodation applies to you or whether someone occupies accommodation with you.[143]

If the **social sector or the pre-January 1996 rules** apply and you disagree with the local authority's decision to apply a rent restriction (eg, if you think the social sector rules do not apply in your case) or with the amount of the restriction (eg, if you think you should be allowed a higher number of bedrooms), you can ask for a revision or appeal (see Chapters 58 and 59).

If the **local reference rent rules** apply, see p415.

Notes

1. Which rent restriction rules apply

1 Regs 13C(5)(a) and (c) and 14(2)(b) and Sch 2 paras 3-13 HB Regs; regs 13C(5)(a) and (c) and 14(2)(b) and Sch 2 paras 3-13 HB(SPC) Regs
2 Reg 2(1) and Sch 2 para 3(1A)HB Regs. Note that in England this means a 'private registered provider of social housing', but if the provider is profit-making, only if the housing is available at a rent below the market rate.
3 The law refers to 'gypsies and travellers' – Sch 2 para 3 HB Regs; Sch 2 para 3 HB(SPC) Regs
4 The law refers to 'gypsies and travellers' - Sch 2 para 3 HB Regs; Sch 2 para 3 HB(SPC) Regs
5 Regs 12C(2) and (3) and 13D(12) HB Regs; regs 12C(2) and 13D(12) HB(SPC) Regs
6 Reg 12B(6) HB Regs; reg 12B(6) HB(SPC) Regs; *AA v Chesterfield BC* [2011] UKUT 156 (AAC)
7 *R on the application of Laali v Westminster CC* [2002] HLR 179 (HC); *R v Macclesfield BC HBRB ex parte Temsemani* [1999] unreported (QBD); A4 Annex B GM

2. The local housing allowance rules

8 Reg 13C(1), (2)(a)-(c) and (5) HB Regs; reg 13C(1), (2)(a)-(c) and (5) HB(SPC) Regs
9 Reg 13C(5)(a) HB Regs; reg 13C(5)(a) HB(SPC) Regs
10 Reg 13D(2)(c) and (3) HB Regs; reg 13D(2)(c) and (3) HB(SPC) Regs
11 Reg 13D(12) HB Regs; reg 13D(12) HB(SPC) Regs. Both, definition of 'occupiers'
12 Reg 21(3) HB Regs; reg 21(3) HB(SPC) Regs; *AA v Chesterfield BC and SSWP (HB)* [2011] UKUT 156 (AAC)
13 R(H) 8/09; *SK v South Hams DC (HB)* [2010] UKUT 129 (AAC); [2010] AACR 40
14 *R v Swale BC HBRB ex parte Marchant* [1999] 1 FLR 1087 (QBD); [2000] 1 FLR 246 (CA)
15 Reg 2(1) HB Regs
16 Reg 13D(3A) and (3B) HB Regs; reg 13D(2A) and (3B) HB(SPC) Regs
17 *Burnip v Birmingham CC and others* [2012] EWCA Civ 629, 15 May 2012. A judicial review is pending on the basis that the rules discriminate unlawfully against disabled children who need overnight care.
18 Reg 2(1) HB Regs; reg 2(1) HB(SPC) Regs

19 Reg 2(1) HB Regs; reg 2(1) HB(SPC) Regs
20 **HB** Reg 13D(2)(a) HB Regs; reg 13D(2)(a) HB(SPC) Regs
    UC Sch 4 paras 27 and 28 UC Regs
21 **HB** Regs 2(1)(b)-(f) and (i) and 13D(2)(a) HB Regs; reg 13D(2)(a) and (12) HB(SPC) Regs
    UC Sch 4 para 29(2), (3) and (5) UC Regs
22 **HB** Reg 2(1), (1A)-(1C) HB Regs
    UC Sch 4 para 29(4) and (6)-(10) UC Regs
23 **HB** Reg 13D(2)(b) HB Regs; reg 13D(2)(b) HB(SPC) Regs
    UC Sch 4 paras 8 and 25(2) UC Regs
24 Sch 4 para 8(1) UC Regs
25 **HB** Reg 13D(2)(c) HB Regs; reg 13D(2)(c) HB(SPC) Regs
    UC Sch 4 paras 8, 25(2) and 26 UC Regs
26 Sch 4 para 8(1) UC Regs
27 **HB** Reg 13D(1) HB Regs; reg 13D(1) HB(SPC) Regs; Art 4B(2A), (2B) and (4) and Sch 3B RO(HBF)O; Art 4B(2A), (2B) and (4) and Sch 3B RO(HBF)(S)O
    UC Sch 4 para 25(2) and (5) UC Regs; Art 4 and Sch 1 RO(UCF)O
28 **HB** Sch 3B paras 2(2) and (9) and 6 RO(HBF)O; Sch 3B paras 2(2) and (9) and 6 RO(HBF)(S)O
    UC Sch 1 paras 2(2)(a), 4 and 6 RO(UCF)O
29 **HB** Sch 3B paras 4 and 5 RO(HBF)O; Sch 3B paras 4 and 5 RO(HBF)(S)O
    UC Art 3 RO(UCF)O
30 Reg 13D(5) HB Regs; reg 13D(5) HB(SPC) Regs
31 Reg 12D(2)(a) HB Regs; reg 12D(2)(a) HB(SPC) Regs
32 Reg 13D(4) and (12) HB Regs; reg 13D(4) and (12) HB(SPC) Regs
33 Regs 12D(2) and 13C(3) HB Regs; regs 12D(2) and 13C(3) HB(SPC) Regs
34 Regs 2, definition of 'linked person', 12D(2)(b) and 13C(2)(d) HB Regs; regs 2, definition of 'linked person', 12D(2)(b) and 13C(2)(d) HB(SPC) Regs
35 Reg 13D(1) and (12) HB Regs; reg 13D(1) and (12) HB(SPC) Regs. Both, definition of 'relevant date'

3. **The social sector rules**
36 Reg A13(1) HB Regs
37 Regs 2(1), definition of 'registered housing association', and A13(1)-(4) HB Regs
38 Reg B13(5) and (8) HB Regs
39 Reg B13(5) and (8) HB Regs
40 Reg 21(3) HB Regs; reg 21(3) HB(SPC) Regs
41 R(H) 8/09; *SK v South Hams DC (HB)* [2010] UKUT 129 (AAC); [2010] AACR 40
42 *R v Swale BC HBRB ex parte Marchant* [1999] 1 FLR 1087 (QBD); [2000] 1 FLR 246 (CA)
43 Reg B13(6), (7) and (9) HB Regs
44 Reg B13(6), (7) and (9) HB Regs
45 *Burnip v Birmingham CC and others* [2012] EWCA Civ 629, 15 May 2012. A judicial review is also pending on the basis that the rules discriminate unlawfully against disabled children who need overnight care.
46 Reg 12BA HB Regs
47 Reg B13(2) HB Regs
48 Reg B13(4) HB Regs

4. **The local reference rent rules**
49 Regs 13(1), 13C(5)(a)-(e) and (6) and 14(1) HB Regs; regs 13(1), 13C(5)(a)-(e) and (6) and 14(1) HB(SPC) Regs
50 The law refers to 'gypsies and travellers' – Sch 2 para 3 HB Regs; Sch 2 para 3 HB(SPC) Regs
51 Reg 13C(2)(a)-(c) HB Regs; reg 13C(2)(a)-(c) HB(SPC) Regs
52 Regs 13(1) and 14(1)(c), (f) and (g) and (8) HB Regs; regs 13(1) and 14(1)(c), (f) and (g) and (8) HB(SPC) Regs
53 Reg 14(1) and (8) HB Regs; reg 14(1) and (8) HB(SPC) Regs
54 Sch 2 para 2(3)(a)-(d) and (f)-(h) HB Regs; Sch 2 para 2(3)(a)-(d), (f) and (g) HB(SPC) Regs
55 R(H) 8/09; *SK v South Hams DC (HB)* [2010] UKUT 129 (AAC); [2010] AACR 40
56 CH/1556/2006; CH/3590/2007
57 Sch 2 para 2(1) and (2) HB Regs; Sch 2 para 2(1) and (2) HB(SPC) Regs
58 Reg 14(2)(a) and (7) HB Regs; reg 14(2)(a) and (7) HB(SPC) Regs
59 Sch 1 para 1 RO(HBF)O; Sch 1 para 1 RO(HBF)(S)O
60 Sch 1 para 3 RO(HBF)O; Sch 1 para 3 RO(HBF)(S)O

61 Sch 1 para 2 RO(HBF)O; Sch 1 para 2 RO(HBF)(S)O

62 Sch 1 para 1(4) RO(HBF)O; Sch 1 para 1(4) RO(HBF)(S)O

63 Sch 1 para 6 RO(HBF)O; Sch 1 para 6 RO(HBF)(S)O

64 Sch 1 para 3(5) RO(HBF)O; Sch 1 para 3(5) RO(HBF)(S)O

65 Sch 2 para 1 RO(HBF)O; Sch 2 para 1 RO(HBF)(S)O

66 Sch 2 paras 1A and 1B RO(HBF)O; Sch 2 paras 1A and 1B RO(HBF)(S)O

67 Art 2(1) RO(HBF)O; Art 2(1) RO(HBF)(S)O. Both, definition of 'occupier'

68 Reg 21(3) HB Regs; reg 21(3) HB(SPC) Regs

69 R(H) 8/09; *SK v South Hams DC (HB)* [2010] UKUT 129 (AAC); [2010] AACR 40

70 *R v Swale BC HBRB ex parte Marchant* [1999] 1 FLR 1087 (QBD); [2000] 1 FLR 246 (CA)

71 Sch 1 para 4 RO(HBF)O; Sch 1 para 4 RO(HBF)(S)O

72 Sch 1 para 9(2) RO(HBF)O; Sch 1 para 9(2) RO(HBF)(S)O

73 Sch 1 para 5 RO(HBF)O; Sch 1 para 5 RO(HBF)(S)O

74 Sch 1 para 4(6) and (7) RO(HBF)O; Sch 1 para 4(6) and (7) RO(HBF)(S)O

75 Reg 13(5) HB Regs

76 Regs 2(1), definition of 'young individual', and 13(6) HB Regs

77 Reg 114A(6) and (8)(a) HB Regs

78 Sch 1 paras 5(2)(c) and 7(1) RO(HBF)O; Sch 1 paras 5(2)(c) and 7(1) RO(HBF)(S)O

79 Reg 12C HB Regs; reg 12C HB(SPC) Regs

80 Reg 13(2), (3) and (5) HB Regs; reg 13(2) and (3) HB(SPC) Regs

81 Reg 13(4) HB Regs; reg 13(4) HB(SPC) Regs; Sch 3 para 8 HB&CTB(CP) Regs

82 Reg 12C(2) and (3) HB Regs; reg 12C(2) HB (SPC) Regs

83 Reg 13ZB(1) HB Regs; reg 13ZB(1) HB(SPC) Regs

84 Reg 14(1)(e) and (2) HB Regs; reg 14(1)(e) and (2) HB(SPC) Regs

85 Reg 14(8) HB Regs; reg 14(8) HB(SPC) Regs. Both, definition of 'prospective occupier'

86 Reg 14(1)(e) and (8) HB Regs; reg 14(1)(e) and (8) HB(SPC) Regs. Both, definition of 'specified matters'

87 Reg 14(5) HB Regs; reg 14(5) HB(SPC) Regs

88 Art 2(1) RO(HBF)O; Art 2(1) RO(HBF)(S)O. Both, definition of 'relevant period'

89 Reg 14(4)(b) and Sch 2 para 2(2)(b) HB Regs; reg 14(4)(b) and Sch 2 para 2(2)(b) HB(SPC) Regs

90 Reg 13ZB(2)-(4) HB Regs; reg 13ZB(2)-(4) HB(SPC) Regs

91 Reg 16 HB Regs; reg 16 HB(SPC) Regs

92 Arts 2(1), definition of 'relevant period', and 4 and Sch 3 RO(HBF)O; Arts 2(1), definition of 'relevant period', and 4 and Sch 3 RO(HBF)(S)O

93 Regs 16(5) and 79(1) HB Regs; regs 16(5) and 59(1) HB(SPC) Regs; reg 8(2) and (6) HB&CTB(DA) Regs

94 Reg 16(1)(b) HB Regs; reg 16(1)(b) HB(SPC) Regs

95 Regs 15 and 17 HB Regs; regs 15 and 17 HB(SPC) Regs

96 HB/CTB Circular G5/2005

97 Regs 16(3) and (4) and 18 HB Regs; regs 16(3) and (4) and 18 HB(SPC) Regs

98 *SK v South Hams DC (HB)* [2010] UKUT 129 (AAC); [2010] AACR 40; *LB Bexley v LD (HB)* [2010] UKUT 79 (AAC)

5. The pre-January 1996 rules

99 Regs 13C(5)(b) HB Regs; reg 13C(5)(b) HB(SPC) Regs; Sch 3 para 4(1)(b) and (10) HB&CTB(CP) Regs; CH/1289/2007

100 R(H) 7/07; R(H) 4/09; CH/3900/2005; CH/2726/2008; *East Hertfordshire DC v KT* [2009] UKUT 12 (AAC); *Bristol CC v AW* [2009] UKUT 109 (AAC)

101 R(H) 7/07; CH/1289/2007; *Salford CC v PF* [2009] UKUT 150 (AAC)

102 R(H) 2/07

103 Sch 3 para 4(1)(a), (2), (3) and (4) HB&CTB(CP) Regs

104 Reg 2(1), definition of 'registered housing association', HB Regs; Sch 3 para 4(2)(aa) HB&CTB(CP) Regs

105 Reg 13C HB Regs; reg 13C HB(SPC) Regs; Sch 3 para 4(2)(a) and (b), (5), (6), (9) and (10) HB&CTB(CP) Regs

106 Sch 3 para 4(10), definition of 'previous beneficiary', HB&CTB(CP) Regs

107 Reg 13(3) HB Regs and reg 13(3) HB(SPC) Regs as set out in Sch 3 para 5(2) HB&CTB(CP) Regs

108 Reg 13(4) HB Regs and reg 13(4) HB(SPC) Regs as set out in Sch 3 para 5(2) HB&CTB(CP) Regs

109 Reg 13(3)(a) HB Regs and reg 13(3)(a) HB(SPC) Regs as set out in Sch 3 para 5(2) HB&CTB(CP) Regs

110 *R v Kensington and Chelsea RBC HBRB ex parte Pirie* [1997] 26 March, unreported (QBD)

111 Reg 13(3)(b) HB Regs and reg 13(3)(b) HB(SPC) Regs as set out in Sch 3 para 5(2) HB&CTB(CP) Regs; *R v Kensington and Chelsea RBC ex parte Abou-Jaoude*, 10 May 1996, unreported (QBD); *SS v Birmingham City Council and SSWP (HB)* [2013] UKUT 418 (AAC)

112 *R v Beverley DC HBRB ex parte Hare* [1995] 27 HLR 637 (QBD)

113 *Macleod v Banff and Buchan District HBRB* [1988] SLT 753 (CS); *Malcolm v Tweedale District HBRB* [1994] SLT 1212 (CS); CH/4970/2002

114 *R v Kensington and Chelsea RBC ex parte Abou-Jaoude*, 10 May 1996, ureported (QBD); *R v Coventry CC ex parte Waite*, 7 July 1995, unreported (QBD)

115 *R v Kensington and Chelsea RBC HBRB ex parte Sheikh*, 14 January 1997, unreported (QBD)

116 Reg 13(9) HB Regs and reg 13(9) HB(SPC) Regs as set out in Sch 3 para 5(2) HB&CTB(CP) Regs

117 R(H) 2/05

118 Reg 13(10) and (11) HB Regs and reg 13(10) and (11) HB(SPC) Regs as set out in Sch 3 para 5(2) HB&CTB(CP) Regs

119 *R v Lambeth LBC HBRB ex parte Harrington*, 22 November 1996, unreported (QBD)

120 Reg 13(9)(a) HB Regs and reg 13(9)(a) HB(SPC) Regs as set out in Sch 3 para 5(2) HB&CTB(CP) Regs; *R v Kensington and Chelsea RBC ex parte Pirie*, 26 March 1997, unreported (QBD); *R v Coventry CC ex parte Waite*, 7 July 1995, unreported (QBD)

121 *R v Waltham Forest LBC ex parte Holder* [1996] 29 HLR 71 (QBD); *R v Slough BC ex parte Green*, 15 November 1996, unreported (QBD)

122 *R v Waltham Forest LBC ex parte Holder* [1996] 29 HLR 71 (QBD); *R v Kensington and Chelsea RBC HBRB ex parte Sheikh*, 14 January 1997, unreported (QBD)

123 Reg 13(4) HB Regs and reg 13(4) HB(SPC) Regs as set out in Sch 3 para 5(2) HB&CTB(CP) Regs

124 R(H) 3/06

125 *R v East Devon DC HBRB ex parte Gibson* [1993] 25 HLR 487 (QBD); CH/4306/2003

126 *R v Waltham Forest LBC ex parte Holder* [1996] 29 HLR 71 (QBD)

127 *R v Oadby and Wigston DC ex parte Dickman* [1995] 28 HLR 806 (QBD)

128 Reg 13(9)(b) HB Regs and reg 13(9)(b) HB(SPC) Regs as set out in Sch 3 para 5(2) HB&CTB(CP) Regs

129 *R v Kensington and Chelsea RBC HBRB ex parte Sheikh*, 14 January 1997, unreported (QBD)

130 *R v Kensington and Chelsea RBC HBRB ex parte Carney* [1997] Crown Office Digest 124 (QBD)

131 *R v Camden LBC HBRB ex p W* [1999] 21 May, unreported, QBD; *R v Westminster CC HBRB ex p Pallas* [1997], unreported, 23 September, (QBD)

132 Reg 12(3)-(5) HB Regs and reg 12(3)-(5) HB(SPC) Regs as set out in Sch 3 para 5(1) HB&CTB(CP) Regs

133 Reg 13(3) HB Regs and reg 13(3) HB(SPC) Regs as set out in Sch 3 para 5(1) HB&CTB(CP) Regs

134 *R v City of Westminster HBRB ex parte Mehanne* [1992] 2 All ER 317 (CA)

135 *R v Brent LBC HBRB ex parte Connery* [1989] 22 HLR 40 (QBD)

136 Reg 13ZA HB Regs and reg 13ZA HB(SPC) Regs as set out in Sch 3 para 5(3) HB&CTB(CP) Regs

137 *BM v Cheshire West and Cheshire Council* [2009] UKUT 162 (AAC)

138 CH/2214/2003

6. Delay before a rent restriction is applied

139 Regs 2(1), definitions of 'reckonable rent' and 'linked person', 12BA(3)-(5), 12D(3), (4) and (8) and 13ZA(1) and (2) HB Regs; regs 2(1), definitions of 'reckonable rent' and 'linked person, 12D(3), (4) and (8) and 13ZA(1) and (2) HB(SPC) Regs; reg 13(5) HB Regs and reg 13(5) HB(SPC) Regs as set out in Sch 3 para 5(2) HB&CTB(CP) Regs

140 Regs 12BA(6)-(8), 12D(5), (6) and (8)
and 13ZA(3) and (4) HB
Regs; regs 12D(5), (6) and (8) and
13|ZA(3) and (4) HB(SPC) Regs;
reg 13(7) and (8) HB Regs and reg 13(7)
and (8) HB(SPC) Regs as set out in Sch 3
para 5(2) HB&CTB(CP) Regs
141 Regs 12BA(5) and (8), 12D(7) HB
Regs; reg 12D(7) HB(SPC) Regs
142 Reg 2(1) HB Regs; reg 2(1) HB(SPC)
Regs

7. Challenging a rent restriction
143 *LB Bexley v LD (HB)* [2010] UKUT 79
(AAC); *SK v South Hams DC (HB)* [2010]
UKUT 129 (AAC); [2010] AACR 40

Chapter 20

Housing costs

This chapter covers:
1. When you can get help with housing costs (p429)
2. Modified rules (p435)
3. The type of housing costs that can be met (p437)
4. Calculating the amount of housing costs (p445)
5. Waiting periods (p453)
6. Linking rules (p456)
7. Mortgage interest run-on (p460)

This chapter covers the housing costs rules for income support, income-based jobseeker's allowance, income-related employment and support allowance and pension credit. It does not cover the housing costs rules for universal credit (see Chapter 22) or the rules for help with your rent in housing benefit (see Chapter 7).

Key facts
- If you own or are buying your home, income support (IS), income-based jobseeker's allowance (JSA), income-related employment and support allowance (ESA) and pension credit can include help with a variety of housing payments, including mortgage payments and loans for repairs and improvements.
- The amount of help you get is not based on what you pay your lender. It is calculated in a special way using a standard rate of interest.
- The help you get is usually paid directly to your lender.
- You might not get full help with your housing costs in IS, JSA and ESA during an initial 'waiting period'.
- In some cases, if you are getting JSA, you can only get help with your housing costs for 104 weeks.

1. When you can get help with housing costs

You can get help with your housing costs if:[1]
- you or your partner are liable to pay the housing costs (see below), or for income support (IS) and income-based jobseeker's allowance (JSA) only, a child or qualifying young person included in your claim (see p210) is liable to pay them;
- the housing costs are for the home in which you normally live (see p430);
- they are a type of housing cost that can be met (see p437).

Liable to pay housing costs

You count as liable to pay housing costs if:[2]
- **either you, or your partner, are liable** to pay them. However, you do not count as liable to pay housing costs if you pay these to someone who is a member of your household (see p215 for the meaning of 'household'). If you or your partner share liability with someone, you might only get help with your share of the housing costs. However, if the other person is not paying her/his share, you can argue that you should get help with the full amount;[3]
- **you are treated as liable** to pay them. You are treated as liable if:
  - you share the costs with other members of your household; *and*
  - at least one of those with whom you share is liable.

  You can be paid for your share,[4] provided the people with whom you share are not 'close relatives' (see p430 for who counts) of you or your partner and it is reasonable to treat you as sharing responsibility for the costs;
- **someone else is liable to pay them but is not paying** so you have to meet the cost yourself in order to continue to live in your home. You must show that it is reasonable for you to pay instead – eg, if you have given up your home to live with and care for someone and s/he has now gone into a care home, or if you have separated from your partner (even if you have not lived in the home continuously since your partner left[5]).

If you are not required to pay any housing costs currently (eg, if you do not have to pay under the terms of your mortgage), you cannot receive IS, income-based JSA, income-related employment and support allowance (ESA) or pension credit (PC) for housing costs. This applies to special mortgage schemes for pensioners where the mortgage is repaid from your estate when you die rather than by your making regular monthly payments.[6]

For IS and JSA only, if you are on strike, your partner or a child or qualifying young person included in your claim (see p210) who is not affected by the strike is treated as liable for your housing costs.[7]

Part 4: Paying for housing
Chapter 20: Housing costs
1. When you can get help with housing costs

Close relative

'**Close relative**' means a parent, parent-in-law (including a civil partner's parent), son, son-in-law (including a son's civil partner), daughter, daughter-in-law (including a daughter's civil partner), brother, sister, step-parent (including a parent's civil partner), stepson (including a civil partner's son) or stepdaughter (including a civil partner's daughter), or the partners of any of these. 'Sister' or 'brother' includes a half-sister or half-brother. An adopted child ceases to be related to her/his birth family on adoption and becomes the relative of her/his adoptive family.[8]

Costs for the home in which you normally live

You can get help with housing costs for the home in which you and your partner (and for IS, JSA and ESA only, your children) normally live.[9] You cannot usually be paid for any other home. Even if you are liable to pay the mortgage on a property, if you have no immediate intention of living there you cannot get help with the cost.[10]

If you live permanently in a care home, an independent hospital or, for IS, JSA and ESA only, an Abbeyfield Home, you cannot get help with housing costs for your former home.[11] If you are only staying in the accommodation temporarily, you might get help with the housing costs on your normal home (see p431).

Your home

Your '**home**' is defined as the building, or part of the building, in which you live. This includes any garage, garden, outbuildings and other premises and land which it is not reasonable or practicable to sell separately.[12] You can argue that a home can consist of more than one building if you occupy more than one dwelling – eg, because your family is too large for one.[13]

There are special rules if you:
- have just moved into your home (see below);
- are temporarily absent from home (see p431);
- are liable to pay housing costs on more than one home (see p434).

Moving home

If you have just moved into your home but were liable to pay housing costs before moving in, your IS, income-based JSA, income-related ESA or PC can include help with these costs for up to four weeks before you moved in if your delay in moving was reasonable, you claimed IS, JSA, income-related ESA or PC before moving in, and:[14]

- you were waiting for adaptations to be finished to meet the disability needs of you or your partner: *or*
  - for IS, JSA and ESA, a child or qualifying young person included in your claim (see p210); *or*
  - for PC, someone under 20 for whom you or your partner are responsible ('responsible' is not defined in the rules).

  The adaptations do not need to involve a change to the fabric or structure of the dwelling, but must be reasonably required and have a clear connection to the disability;[15] *or*
- you became responsible for the housing costs while you were in hospital, or were in a care home or an independent hospital (or, for IS, JSA and ESA only, in an Abbeyfield Home); *or*
- you were waiting for 'local welfare provision' (see below) or a social fund payment for a need connected with the move – eg, for removal expenses or items to help you set up home (see Chapter 37). In addition you must:
  - for IS, JSA and ESA only, have a child aged five or under living with you, or be getting child tax credit for a child of any age which includes a disabled child or severely disabled child element; *or*
  - for IS and JSA only, qualify for a disability, severe disability, disabled child or pensioner premium; *or*
  - for ESA only, be getting ESA including a work-related or support component, or qualify for a severe disability or pensioner premium.

* *

Local welfare provision

'**Local welfare provision**' means occasional financial or other assistance provided by a local authority, the Welsh Ministers or the Scottish Ministers, or people authorised by them.[16] The assistance must be:

– to meet, or to help to meet, an immediate short-term need due to exceptional circumstances or to avoid a risk to a person's wellbeing; *or*

– to enable someone to establish or maintain a settled home if s/he has been (or without assistance might be) in prison, hospital, residential care or another institution, or homeless or living an unsettled way of life.

* *

The amount for housing costs is not actually included until you move in. If the earlier IS, JSA, ESA or PC claim you made before you moved was turned down, you must claim again within four weeks of moving in to qualify.

Temporary absence from home

If you are temporarily absent from home but are still entitled to IS, income-based JSA, income-related ESA or PC, have not rented out your home and intend to return, help with your housing costs continues to be paid for a period. You can

Part 4: Paying for housing
Chapter 20: Housing costs
1. When you can get help with housing costs

argue that you count as temporarily absent even if you have not yet stayed there – eg, you move your furniture and belongings in but then have to go into hospital.[17]

You can get help with housing costs for up to:

- **13 weeks** while you are away, whatever the reason. You must be unlikely to be away for longer than this.[18]
- **52 weeks** if you fit into one of the groups below. You must be unlikely to be away for longer than this (or, in exceptional circumstances, unlikely to be away for substantially longer than this).[19]

The 13- and 52-week periods run from the date you leave home. If, for example, you have been away from home for 10 weeks and then have grounds to continue to get help with housing costs for 52 weeks, you only get this for the balance: 42 weeks. However, a new period of absence starts if you return home even for a short stay – eg, a day or a weekend.[20]

Your intention to return, and whether or not you are unlikely to be away for longer than 13/52 weeks, should be considered initially based on the circumstances on the date you leave your home, unless you are in a care home, independent hospital (or, for IS, JSA or ESA, an Abbeyfield Home) for a trial period (see p433).[21] If at any time after that date, you no longer intend to return or it becomes likely that you will be away from home for more than the 13/52 weeks, your entitlement can be reconsidered.[22]

Note: if you have someone living with you who is temporarily absent (eg, a student who is away during term time), the DWP may use these rules to decide if s/he is a non-dependant (see p450).[23]

If you have to live in temporary accommodation while essential repairs are done to your normal home and you only have to pay for housing costs for one of the homes, your IS, income-based JSA, income-related ESA or PC covers these costs.[24] This is not subject to the normal limits on temporary absence from home.[25] If you have to pay housing costs for both homes, you may be able to claim IS, income-based JSA, income-related ESA or PC for both for up to four weeks (see p434). After that, you are only paid for one home. This could be your normal home if you are unlikely to be away for more than 13/52, weeks or your temporary home if you will be away for longer.

Housing costs for up to 52 weeks

You can get help with your housing costs for up to **52 weeks** if you are unlikely to be away for longer than this (or, in exceptional circumstances, unlikely to be away for substantially longer than this) and:[26]

- you are resident in a **hospital** or a similar institution. If you are claiming JSA, this must be during a two-week period of sickness (see p50) – ie, you are treated as capable of work for JSA purposes. If you are sick for longer than this, claim IS, income-related ESA or PC. **Note:** you cannot get help with housing costs after you have been resident in hospital for 52 weeks even if this is because you are seriously mentally ill;[27]

- as long as it is not in a care home or an independent hospital (or, for IS, JSA and ESA only, an Abbeyfield Home):
  - you are **receiving care** (approved by a doctor) in the UK or abroad;
  - you or your partner or a dependent child (for PC a dependant under 20) are **receiving medical treatment or convalescing** in the UK or abroad (approved by a doctor);
- you are **attending a 'training course'** away from home in the UK or abroad (see p434 for the meaning);
- you are required to live in an approved hostel or an address away from your normal home as a **condition of bail**;
- for IS, ESA and PC only, you are **in prison on remand** pending trial or sentence. You can argue that this applies even if you are simultaneously serving another sentence.[28]
  If you were claiming JSA before going into prison, you must instead claim IS, income-related ESA or PC to cover your housing costs. Once you are sentenced, you are no longer entitled to IS, ESA or PC;
- you are in a **care home or an independent hospital** (or, for IS, JSA and ESA only, an Abbeyfield Home) for short-term or respite care;
- you are in a **care home or an independent hospital** (or, for IS, JSA and ESA only, an Abbeyfield Home) **for a trial period** to see if it suits your needs. On the date you enter the accommodation, you must intend to return home if it is not suitable.[29] You can only get your housing costs met for up to 13 weeks.[30] If the accommodation does not suit your needs, you can have further trial periods in other homes, as long as you are not away from home for more than 52 weeks in total;
- you are **providing care** for someone living in the UK or abroad (approved by a doctor);
- you are **caring for a child under 16** (or, for PC only, someone under 20) whose parent or guardian is receiving medical treatment or care (approved by a doctor) away from home;
- you are away from home because of a **fear of violence** (see p434 if you need to claim for two homes and for what counts as violence);
- you are a **full-time student** (see p905); *and*
  - living apart from your partner but cannot get help with housing costs for two homes (see p434); *or*
  - a single claimant or a lone parent who is liable to pay housing costs on both a term-time and a home address.

There must be some causal link between your absence from home and being in one of the situations above.[31]

Part 4: Paying for housing
Chapter 20: Housing costs
1. When you can get help with housing costs

Training course
A **'training course'** is a course of training or instruction provided by, approved by, on behalf of, or by arrangement with, a government department, the Secretary of State, Skills Development Scotland, Scottish Enterprise or Highlands and Islands Enterprise.[32]

Housing costs for more than one home

In most cases, you can only get help with the housing costs for one home. If you occupy more than one dwelling as a home (eg, because you have a large family), you can argue that you only have one home.[33]

If you have to pay housing costs for two homes, you *can* get IS, income-based JSA, income-related ESA or PC for both:[34]

- for up to **four weeks** if you have moved into a new home and cannot avoid having to pay for the other one as well;[35]
- **indefinitely** if you left your home because of a fear of violence. Provided you left home because of this and are still away from home because of this, it does not matter if you were away from home for some other reason during this period – eg, because you were in prison.[36] You have to show that it is reasonable for you to get payment for two homes. Thus, if you do not intend to return home or someone else is paying the mortgage, you might not get IS, income-based JSA, income-related ESA or PC for both homes.

'Violence' means violence against you and not caused by you.[37] For the purpose of these rules, it must be fear of violence:[38]
  – in your home. Fear of a racial attack should be covered, provided the attack would take place in your home. Remember that your garden and garage, for example, count (see p430); *or*
  – from a former partner; *or*
  – for IS, JSA and ESA, from a child or qualifying young person who is no longer included in your claim; *or*
  – for PC, from a close relative (see p430 for who counts);
- **indefinitely** if you are one of a couple and you or your partner are a full-time student or on a training course and living away from your home (see below).

If you have to live in temporary accommodation while essential repairs are done to your normal home and you only have to pay for housing costs for one of the homes, see p432.

If you have to live away from your normal home because you or your partner are a **full-time student** (see p905) or on a **training course** (see above for what counts):
- if you are one of a couple and have to live apart, you can get help with housing costs for both of your homes if it is reasonable for you to get help with both;[39]
- if you are a single person or lone parent and must pay housing costs for *either* your normal home *or* your term-time accommodation but not both, you can get help with housing costs for the home for which you pay.[40]

If neither of the above applies, you may only get help with your usual home for up to 52 weeks during a temporary absence (see p431).[41]

If you have been getting help with housing costs for your term-time accommodation and you stop living there during a vacation, you cannot continue to get this unless you are away because you are in hospital.[42]

2. Modified rules

Modified rules were introduced on 5 January 2009 to help those affected by the recession and to assist them in retaining their homes. They will continue to apply until at least 31 March 2016. If the modified rules apply to you:

- the upper limit for your loans is £200,000 (see p448); *and*
- if you have to serve a waiting period before housing costs can be met, a 13-week waiting period applies (see p455); *and*
- if you are claiming jobseeker's allowance (JSA), there may be a 104-week limit on the time you can get help with housing costs for your mortgage or loan for repairs and improvements (see p437).

The modified rules apply if your claim for income support (IS), or any type of JSA or employment and support allowance (ESA) is (or was) made after 4 January 2009. They can apply even if your income is too high for you to qualify for IS, income-based JSA or income-related ESA until help with housing costs is included – ie, if you have to serve a waiting period, you do not have to be receiving IS, JSA or ESA during that period.

You must meet *at least one* of the following conditions.[43]

- This is your **first claim** – ie, neither you nor your partner have ever been awarded IS, ESA or JSA in the past, nor have either of you received pension credit (PC) at any time before your claim was made (or treated as made).

  You cannot meet this condition if you are treated as being in continuous receipt of the benefit you are now claiming under the linking rules on pp456–60 for a period beginning on or before 4 January 2009 and ending immediately before the date your claim is made (or treated as made).

- There is a **gap between a previous claim and your current claim** – ie, you or your partner have been awarded IS, JSA or ESA in the past, but you did not receive IS, JSA, ESA or PC, and your partner did not receive PC, immediately before your current claim was made (or treated as made).

  You cannot meet this condition if you are treated as being in continuous receipt of IS, JSA or ESA under the linking rules on pp456–60 during the gap – ie, during the period beginning when you were last receiving IS, ESA or JSA (whether on your own or as a member of a couple) and ending immediately before the date your current claim is made (or treated as made).

- You (or your partner) were **receiving PC** before your (or her/his) claim for IS, ESA or JSA was made or treated as made. However, you cannot meet this condition if you or your partner were getting PC which included help with housing costs in the 12 weeks or less (26 weeks or less in some cases) before becoming entitled to IS, income-based JSA or income-related ESA in the circumstances described on p447.
- The **modified rules have applied** to you before on a previous claim.

The modified rules also apply if you were entitled to IS, contribution-based or income-based JSA or contributory or income-related ESA on 4 January 2009 but were still in a 26- or 39-week waiting period (see p455).

Examples
Martin claims IS on 1 April 2014 when he has to give up work to care for his disabled son. He has never claimed or been entitled to IS, JSA or ESA before. The modified rules apply. Full help with housing costs is included after a 13-week waiting period and his upper limit is £200,000. He can get help with his housing costs indefinitely.

Julia was claiming and entitled to IS until she returned to work in December 2008. She was made redundant in March 2014 and claimed JSA. The modified rules apply. Full help with housing costs is included after a 13-week waiting period and her upper limit is £200,000, but she can only get help with housing costs for 104 weeks. This is because, although she was entitled to IS in the past, she is not treated as receiving IS, JSA or ESA between the end of her IS claim and her claim for JSA.

Ruth received IS as a lone parent until her youngest child turned 10 on 1 July 2010. She then claims JSA. When she was claiming IS, the 39-week waiting period applied to her. The modified rules do not apply when she claims JSA because she was receiving IS immediately before her claim for JSA was made. Help with housing costs is included straight away; weeks when she was receiving IS count towards her 39-week waiting period and she had received IS for more than 39 weeks. She can get help with her housing costs indefinitely, but her upper limit for loans is £100,000.

Edwina is a lone parent. She claimed IS on 11 February 2014 when she and her partner separated. She had never claimed or been entitled to IS, JSA or ESA before. However, her former partner had claimed IS for her for a few years until they separated. The modified rules do not apply because she is treated as receiving IS immediately before her entitlement began (see p458). Although her mortgage was taken out in 2005, because she was abandoned by her partner, the 26-week waiting period applies (see p455 – 'couples and former couples') and her upper limit for loans is £100,000. The weeks when her partner was receiving IS for her count towards the 26 weeks so she can get help with her housing costs straight away.

Note: different rules applied between 5 January 2009 and 5 January 2010. For full details, see pp833–34 of the 2009/10 edition of this *Handbook*.

Limit on the time you can get help with housing costs

If you are claiming income-based JSA and the modified rules apply to you (see p435), you can no longer get help with mortgages, other home loans or loans for repairs and improvements (see p438 and p443) once you have been getting help with either or both of these types of housing costs for 104 weeks.[44] The earliest the 104 weeks can start is 4 January 2009. The DWP only counts the weeks when help with housing costs is included in your applicable amount. The following are ignored:

- weeks in your 13-week waiting period;
- weeks in which your upper limit is £100,000 (see p448);
- if you have claimed JSA before, weeks when help with housing costs was included in your applicable amount in your previous claim. This only applies if you are *not* treated as receiving JSA continuously during the period between your previous and current claims under the linking rules described on pp456–60.

Example

Jim claims JSA. After he serves his 13-week waiting period, he gets help with his housing costs for 30 weeks. His JSA stops when he takes a temporary job for 10 weeks. When he claims JSA again, help with housing costs can only be included in his applicable amount for a further 74 weeks (104 – 30). This is because he is treated as receiving JSA during the 10-week gap between claims.

This rule does not apply and you can get help with your housing costs indefinitely if:

- you are claiming JSA and the modified rules do not apply to you; *or*
- you or your partner were claiming and entitled to IS or ESA and this was no more than 12 weeks before your entitlement to JSA started. However, any entitlement to IS which is 'mortgage interest run-on' (see p460) is ignored if you or your partner were getting JSA immediately before this;[45] *or*
- you are claiming IS, ESA or PC.

3. The type of housing costs that can be met

Your income support (IS), income-based jobseeker's allowance (JSA), income-related employment and support allowance (ESA) or pension credit (PC) can include help with:

Part 4: Paying for housing
Chapter 20: Housing costs
3. The type of housing costs that can be met

- mortgages and other loans for house purchase (see below);
- loans used to pay for certain repairs and improvements or to meet a service charge for these (see p443);
- 'other housing costs' – eg, ground rent, payments under co-ownership schemes and service charges (see p444).

Note: if you are a tenant, you cannot get IS, income-based JSA, income-related ESA or PC for your rent.[46] Rent is covered by housing benefit (HB). If you come under the universal credit (UC) system (see p19), help with rent is covered by UC unless it is for exempt accommodation, in which case it is covered by HB.

Mortgages and loans

An amount for qualifying home loan payments can be included in your IS, income-based JSA or income-related ESA applicable amount and in your PC appropriate minimum guarantee. However, restrictions might be made if you took out or increased the loan while entitled to IS, JSA, income-related ESA or PC (see p439).

You must have a home loan – eg, a mortgage, a hire purchase agreement or other loan to help you buy your home.[47]

Payment of your IS, income-based JSA, income-related ESA or PC housing costs is usually made direct to the lender.

Loans that qualify

Your loan qualifies if it was:[48]
- **taken out to buy the home in which you normally live.** Loans taken out to buy an existing property, as well as those to pay for materials and labour to build your own home, are covered. If all or part of your loan was not taken out with the immediate intention of paying for your home (eg, it was to buy a car or set up a business), or is for deferred interest, you cannot get help with the loan (or part of the loan) even if it is secured on your home (but see p445 for the rules about housing costs that are no longer paid);[49] *or*
- **taken out to buy an additional interest in the home in which you normally live** – eg:[50]
  - by buying out your ex-partner's share in your home after you separate. However, if your ex-partner has registered a right to occupy your home (a 'Class F land charge') you cannot get help with a loan to pay her/him to remove it;[51]
  - by purchasing the freehold on a leasehold property;[52]
  - by buying your partner's share from a trustee if s/he is bankrupt;[53]
  - by buying out sitting tenants;[54] *or*

- **taken out to repay a loan which itself would have qualified.** However, if the second loan is also for things that do not qualify for help (eg, to pay debts or for a holiday), you only get help with the amount of the original loan.

Example

Mr Clay took out a mortgage of £60,000. £45,000 was to pay off a mortgage to buy his home and £15,000 was to pay off business debts. He gets help with the loan of £45,000.

Note:
- Loans for costs necessary to help you buy your home or an additional interest (eg, search, valuation or legal fees and stamp duty) are covered.[55]
- If your home is used for both business and domestic purposes, you can only get help with the loan for the part where you live.[56]
- Even if a loan qualifies, you cannot get help for a loan with IS, income-based JSA or income-related ESA if the loan is interest-free. It may be possible to argue that you can get help with an interest-free loan with PC.[57]
- The rules for help with mortgages and loans changed on 2 October 1995. If you took out your loan before that date, you might still be able to get help under the old, more favourable, rules (see p445).

Taking out or increasing loans while entitled to benefit

Even if your loan qualifies (see above), you cannot usually get help with it if the loan was incurred (eg, it was taken out or increased) during a 'relevant period' (see below for what counts) and this was after 1 October 1995 (for IS and PC), 7 October 1996 (for JSA) or 27 October 2008 (for ESA).[58] **Note:** the rule can also apply if the loan was incurred before these dates (see 'other dates' below).

The DWP is likely to say that this rule even applies if you are awarded backdated IS, income-based JSA, income-related ESA or PC for the day on which you became liable for or increased your loan.[59]

Other dates

You cannot get help with a loan incurred during a 'relevant period':[60]
- after 2 May 1994, if you did not qualify for IS for the loan in the 26 weeks before 2 October 1995 (for IS, ESA and PC) or in the 26 weeks before 7 October 1996 (for JSA), or (for ESA) you did not qualify for IS or PC for the loan after 1 October 1995 or JSA for the loan after 7 October 1996;
- for IS and PC only, in the 26 weeks before 2 October 1995 when you were not entitled to IS, but you or your partner became entitled to IS or income-based JSA after 1 October 1995 and within 26 weeks of your or your partner's IS ceasing. This does not apply to loans for which you were getting IS without restriction before 2 October 1995;
- for JSA only, in the 26 weeks before 7 October 1996 when you were not entitled to IS, but you or your partner became entitled to JSA after 6 October 1996 and within 26

Part 4: Paying for housing
Chapter 20: Housing costs
3. The type of housing costs that can be met

weeks of your or your partner's IS ceasing. This does not apply to loans for which you were getting IS without restriction before 7 October 1996;

– for ESA only, in the 26 weeks before 27 October 2008 when you were not entitled to IS, income-based JSA or PC, but you or your partner became entitled to income-related ESA after 27 October 2008 and within 26 weeks of your or your partner's IS, income-based JSA or PC ceasing. This does not apply to loans for which you were getting IS without restriction before 27 October 2008.

Relevant periods

A **'relevant period'** is a period:

- for IS:[61]
  - when you were entitled to IS, income-based JSA or income-related ESA; *or*
  - when you were living as a member of the family (see below for who counts) of someone who was entitled to IS, income-based JSA or income-related ESA; *or*
  - of up to 26 weeks between two of either of the types of period above.
- for JSA:[62]
  - when you were entitled to IS, JSA or income-related ESA; *or*
  - when you were living as a member of the family (see below for who counts) of someone who was entitled to IS, JSA or income-related ESA; *or*
  - of up to 26 weeks between two of either of the types of period above.

  Note: official guidance suggests that the DWP might only apply this rule if you (or the family member with whom you were living) were entitled to IS, *income-based* JSA or income-related ESA;[63]
- for ESA and PC:[64]
  - when you were entitled to IS, income-based JSA, income-related ESA or PC; *or*
  - when your partner was entitled to IS, income-based JSA, income-related ESA or PC; *or*
  - of up to 26 weeks between two of either of the types of period above.

For these purposes, you and your partner are *not* treated as entitled to IS, JSA or income-related ESA under the linking rules described on pp456–60.[65]

Member of the family

'Member of the family' means your partner (if you are a member of a couple) and any child or qualifying young person who lives in your household and for whom you or your partner count as responsible (see p212). If you are included in someone else's claim for a relevant benefit – eg, s/he is your mother or father, you are a member of her/his family.

Note: if you become liable for the loan during a period of 26 weeks or more between two relevant periods, you *can* get help with the cost.

Full help with a new or increased loan

You *can* get help with a loan even if you took it out during a relevant period (see p440), if you:

- took out or increased your loan to buy a home which is better suited than your former home to the **special needs of a 'disabled person'** (see below).[66] There is no rule that says you must buy the home or take out the loan within a certain time before or after the disabled person moves in.[67] However, there must be a link between the purchase of the home, the loan and the move.[68] The person must qualify as disabled at the time the loan is taken out.[69] S/he does not have to be a member of your family or to have previously lived with you;
- increased your loan and moved to a new home because you needed to provide separate sleeping accommodation for a **boy and a girl aged 10 or over** but under 20 and (for IS, ESA or JSA) for whom you or your partner are responsible and who live with you or (for PC) who live with you and who you or your partner are looking after.[70] You can argue that this should apply if both children will be 10 or over in the reasonably near future.[71]

Disabled person

A **'disabled person'** is:[72]

- someone getting ESA (for IS, JSA and PC) or someone to whom ESA is payable (for ESA) that includes a work-related activity or support component, or someone who would get contributory ESA with the work-related activity component, but her/his entitlement has ended because of the rules on how long ESA can be paid;
- for IS, JSA and ESA, a child or young person who counts as disabled or severely disabled for the child tax credit disabled child or severely disabled child element;
- for IS and JSA, someone for whom you (or someone living with you) are getting a disabled child, disability, enhanced pensioner or higher pensioner premium (or who would get one of these premiums if s/he were on IS or JSA);
- for ESA and PC, someone who would qualify for a disability premium if s/he were on IS and someone who is 75 or over;
- for PC, anyone under 20 for whom you or your partner are responsible ('responsible' is not defined in the rules) and to whom disability living allowance, personal independence payment or armed forces independence payment is payable (or would be payable were s/he not a patient) or who is registered blind (certified blind, in Scotland), or anyone who would qualify for a higher pensioner premium if s/he were on IS;
- someone entitled to UC that includes a limited capability for work or limited capability for work-related activity element. This also applies if one of these elements would be included but for a carer element being included, or if the person is a member of a couple, both with limited capability for work, but for only one of those elements being included (see p251 and p252).

Part 4: Paying for housing
Chapter 20: Housing costs
3. The type of housing costs that can be met

A person continues to count as a disabled person even if, under the incapacity or capability for work rules, s/he is either disqualified from receiving benefit or is treated as capable of work or as not having limited capability for work. For IS, JSA and PC, this includes if s/he is disqualified from receiving ESA while a prisoner or because of her/his absence abroad.

Restricted help with a new or increased loan

You *can* get help with a loan even if you took it out during a relevant period (see p440), but the amount you get might be restricted in the following situations. You can get help if you:[73]

- took out a loan to pay off an original home loan – eg, you have remortgaged your home; *or*
- paid off an original loan (this can be a home loan, or a loan for repairs or improvements), and have now taken out a new loan for a new property, even if this is some time later – eg, you have moved home.

The original loan must have qualified (see p438 and p443) during the relevant period. Unless the loan is one for which you can get full help (see p441), you can only get help with the amount of the original loan and cannot get help with any increase. So if your original mortgage was £30,000 and you took out a new loan for £35,000, you can only get housing costs on £30,000 of the second loan.

Are you divorced or separated from your partner?

If, following divorce or separation, you buy your former partner's share of your home, you cannot get help with the mortgage for that share. Similarly, if you take out a loan or increase an existing loan to buy a home after separation, the restriction, in principle, applies. However, you can argue that each of you should be entitled to help with housing costs up to the amount of the loan you were liable to pay when you were together – eg, if you were liable to pay £50,000 when you were together, you should each be entitled to help with housing costs on a mortgage of up to £50,000 when you separate.[74]

You *can* get help if you buy a home and the week before:

- you were in **rented accommodation and getting HB**. To begin with, you only get the amount of HB to which you were entitled plus any 'other housing costs' (see p444) you were already getting;[75]
- you were **only getting other housing costs** (see p444) paid with your IS, income-based JSA, income-related ESA or PC – eg, as ground rent.[76] To begin with, you only get the amount you had been getting for those other costs.

In both cases, you get any subsequent increases in the standard rate of interest (see p446) or the other housing costs and do not lose these if the interest rate or costs go down again.[77]

Loans for repairs and improvements

IS, income-based JSA, income-related ESA and PC do not meet the cost of repairs and improvements to your home or the cost of service charges for these (although service charges for *minor* repairs and maintenance *can* be covered as other housing costs – see p444). However, if you take out a loan to pay for specified types of repairs and improvements (see below) or a service charge (or to pay off an earlier loan taken out for this purpose), you can get help with this.[78]

You must use the loan for the repairs and improvements or service charge within six months (longer if this is reasonable). A bank overdraft that is taken out to pay for the repairs and improvements counts as a loan.[79]

Repairs and improvements that qualify

You can only get help with loans for repairs or improvements undertaken to maintain the fitness of your current home,[80] or any part of the building in which it is contained, for human habitation.[81] This includes loans towards the cost of necessary survey work.[82] In addition, the loan must be for specified repairs and improvements – ie, for:[83]

- providing a bath, shower, toilet, wash basin and the necessary plumbing for these, and the provision of hot water not connected to a central heating system;[84]
- repairs to your heating system;
- damp-proof measures (you can argue this includes repairs to a roof[85]);
- providing:
  - ventilation and natural lighting;
  - drainage facilities;
  - facilities for preparing and cooking food (but not for storing it);[86]
  - home insulation;
  - electric lighting and sockets;
  - storage facilities for fuel or refuse;
- repairing unsafe structural defects;
- adaptations for a disabled person (see p441 for who counts);
- providing separate sleeping accommodation for children of different sexes aged 10 or over but under 20 for whom you or your partner are responsible and who live with you. For PC, 'responsible' is not defined in the rules. For IS, JSA and ESA, see p212.

  You can argue that this should apply if both children will be 10 or over in the reasonably near future.[87]

If your loan is also for other repairs and improvements, you can only get help with the proportion which relates to any of the items listed above.

Part 4: Paying for housing
Chapter 20: Housing costs
3. The type of housing costs that can be met

Note:
- The rules for help with loans for repairs and improvements changed on 2 October 1995. If you took out your loan before then, you might still be able to get help under the old, more favourable, rules (see p445).
- Payment of your IS, income-based JSA, income-related ESA or PC housing costs is usually made directly to the lender.

Help with other housing costs

You are paid the normal weekly charge for all 'other housing costs' covered by IS, income-based JSA, income-related ESA and PC.[88] These are:
- service charges (see below). Note that some service charges are excluded;
- rent or ground rent if you have a lease of more than 21 years. If your lease is of 21 years or less, the rent or ground rent might be met by HB instead (see p96);[89]
- rent charge payments;
- payments under a co-ownership scheme;
- rent if you are a Crown tenant (minus any water charges[90]);
- payments for a tent and its pitch if that is your home.

If you pay your other housing costs annually or irregularly, the weekly amount is worked out by dividing what is payable for the year by 52.[91]

If your other housing costs have been waived because you or your partner (or, for IS, JSA or ESA only, a child or qualifying young person included in your claim – see p210 for who counts) have paid for repairs or redecoration that are not your responsibility, you can still get IS, income-based JSA, income-related ESA or PC for them for up to eight weeks.[92]

Charges that cannot be met
The following charges cannot be met:[93]
- fuel, if this is included in your other housing costs. If there is no specific charge for fuel, set deductions are made:

Heating	£27.55	Lighting	£2.20
Hot water	£3.20	Cooking	£3.20

- amounts for repairs and improvements listed on p443. You are expected to take out a loan to pay for these and can claim help with this;[94]
- ineligible services listed on p114. These are the same as for HB.[95]

Service charges
A 'service' is something that is agreed and arranged on your behalf and for which you are required to pay. So, for example, if you own a flat and the freeholder arranges for the exterior of the building to be painted, for which you have to pay

a share of the cost, your IS, income-based JSA, income-related ESA or PC includes this as a service charge. Some service charges are ineligible (see p114 – the rules are the same as for HB). Some service charges can only be met if they relate to the provision of 'adequate accommodation'.[96] Bear the following in mind.

- Service charges to cover minor repairs and maintenance are eligible. However, those to cover any of the repairs and improvements listed on p443 are not.[97]
- Payments for support services are not eligible. Instead, you can get help with these through your local authority (see p115).
- House insurance paid under the terms of your lease can be a service charge, but insurance required by a bank as a condition of your mortgage is not.[98]
- Services provided by an authority that you arrange yourself are not covered. Thus, charges for water and sewerage paid to a water company are not met.[99]

Old rules: housing costs that are no longer paid

You can continue to get help with certain types of housing costs that could be paid with IS before 2 October 1995, but which can no longer be paid with IS, income-based JSA or income-related ESA. These are:[100]

- accumulated arrears of interest;
- interest on a secured loan that was not for house purchase, taken out when you were one of a couple, where your partner had left and could not (or would not) pay the cost, or had died;
- interest on a loan for repairs and improvements under the pre-2 October 1995 rules.

See p484 of the 2013/14 edition of this *Handbook* for further information.

---

4. Calculating the amount of housing costs

Once you have worked out which housing costs can be met by income support (IS), income-based jobseeker's allowance (JSA), income-related employment and support allowance (ESA) or pension credit (PC), you can calculate the amount you get.

- **Step one:** calculate the weekly amount for:
  - home loans;
  - loans for repairs and improvements;
  - 'other housing costs'.
  Remember to deduct any restrictions being made because you took out your loan or increased it while entitled to IS, JSA, income-related ESA or PC (see p439), because your loan is above the upper limit (see p448) or because your housing costs are excessive (see p448).
- **Step two:** add these amounts together.

Part 4: Paying for housing
Chapter 20: Housing costs
4. Calculating the amount of housing costs

- **Step three:** deduct any amounts for other people living in your home (known as non-dependants – see p450).

For IS, JSA and ESA only, a reduced amount might also be paid during a 'waiting period' in the early weeks of your claim (see p453).

Note: you might only get a share of the housing costs if you share liability or are treated as liable because you share the costs with someone (see p429).

Loans

The amounts included in your benefit for loans for house purchase, and for repairs and improvements, are calculated with a formula, using a standard rate of interest (see below). They do not always cover the whole of your loan payments. You cannot get help with associated insurance premiums – eg, if you have an endowment mortgage, you do not get the insurance element paid.

There can be a limit on the amount that can be paid. If the total of your loans is more than an upper limit (usually £100,000 or £200,000), the amount might only be calculated using this figure (see p448). Whether or not your loans are lower than the upper limit, if your housing costs are still thought to be excessive they may be restricted (see p448).

Note: if the amount of benefit you get for your housing costs is actually more than the interest you must pay on your loan(s), your lender must first apply the excess to any arrears you have, then to repaying the loan itelf.[101]

The formula

The weekly amount for loans is worked out using a special formula.[102] A standard rate of interest is used, not what you actually have to pay, even if this is higher or lower. At the time of writing the **standard rate of interest** was 3.63 per cent.[103]

The amount of your loans that qualify (see p438 and p443), less any restrictions that have been made (see p442 and p448), is multiplied by the standard rate of interest. This figure is divided by 52 to reach a weekly amount.

Example
Mr and Mrs Khan have a repayment mortgage and a loan for repairs and improvements. The outstanding loans of £30,000 and £5,000 qualify. They also have a loan for a conservatory. This does not qualify. They pay interest at the rate of 6.1%.
£30,000 x 3.63% (standard interest rate) = £1,089
£5,000 x 3.63% = £181.50
Their weekly IS help with housing costs is (£1,089 ÷ 52) + (£181.50 ÷ 52) = £24.43

The standard rate of interest is set by the DWP and can be varied. You can find out the current rate at www.gov.uk/support-for-mortgage-interest.

Note: the rules for calculating housing costs changed on 2 October 1995. If you were on IS both on and after 1 October 1995, you may get an extra payment (called an 'add-back') to make up the loss.[104] See pp810–11 of the 2008/09 edition of this *Handbook* for more details.

When housing costs are recalculated

Even if there is a reduction in the amount of your outstanding loan, your IS, income-based JSA, income-related ESA or PC for housing costs is usually only recalculated annually, on the anniversary of the date these were first met by your benefit.[105] However, if you are getting PC, you or your partner are at least 65, and a non-dependant has come to live with you (or your non-dependant's circumstances have changed) and this means the amount for housing costs to which you are entitled reduces, this is recalculated 26 weeks after the date of the change (or, if there is more than one change in respect of the same non-dependant, the first of these).[106]

If you or your partner were getting (or treated as getting) IS, income-based JSA, income-related ESA or PC which included help with housing costs in the 12 weeks or less before becoming entitled to another of these benefits, the same amount is met as was met when you were getting the other benefit, unless there has been a change of circumstances affecting the calculation , other than a reduction in the amount of your outstanding loan.[107] For IS, JSA and ESA, the 12 weeks is extended to 26 weeks if you or your partner reclaimed IS, income-based JSA, income-related ESA or PC within 26 weeks of a previous claim during which help with housing costs was included and you have been receiving payments under an employment insurance policy which has since run out.

If your housing costs are not met in full

If you do not have enough money to pay your lender, you may be in danger of losing your home, particularly if you are on benefit for a long time. Inform your lender and discuss how to resolve the situation. Your lender may be prepared to accept interest-only payments for a while. Seek independent debt advice. Note:

- You may be able to increase your income by taking in lodgers (but see p280 and p314).
- Some payments made directly to the lender by relatives, friends or a charity towards your housing costs that are not being met can be ignored when calculating your entitlement to IS, income-based JSA or income-related ESA.[108]
- If you get charitable or voluntary payments, these are ignored as income (see p280 and p318).

Ultimately, you may have to sell your home and buy somewhere cheaper. If you move out and put your house up for sale, the capital value of your property can be disregarded for a period while you take reasonable steps to sell it (see

Part 4: Paying for housing
Chapter 20: Housing costs
4. Calculating the amount of housing costs

p351 and p379).[109] If you rent it out while trying to sell, see p281 and p315 for how the income is treated.

Restrictions if your housing costs are too high

The amount of benefit you get for housing costs can be restricted if your:
* loans exceed an upper limit (see below); *or*
* total housing costs are considered excessive (see below.

The upper limit

If the total of your loans is more than an upper limit, your housing costs might not be met in full.[110] This includes all mortgages taken out to buy your home and also any loans for repairs and improvements. The restriction is applied proportionately to each loan. If a loan was taken out to adapt your home for a disabled person (see p441 for who counts), it is ignored when working out if your loans exceed the upper limit. If you are getting help with the housing costs for more than one home (see p434), you can be paid up to the limit for each.[111]

Your upper limit is:
* £200,000 if you are claiming IS, JSA or ESA and the modified rules described on p435 apply to you. See below if you become entitled to PC; *or*
* £100,000 in most other cases.

If you are entitled to IS, JSA or ESA with an upper limit of £200,000, but you then claim PC, this upper limit continues to apply if:[112]
* the modified rules described on p435 applied to you (or your partner); *and*
* you (or your partner) were entitled to IS, JSA or ESA no more than 12 weeks before you became entitled to PC (or, where your claim for PC is backdated, before the date you claimed PC); *and*
* immediately before your (or your partner's) entitlement to IS, JSA or ESA ended, your (or her/his) applicable amount included an amount for a mortgage (or other house purchase loan) or a loan for repairs and improvements.

Note: see pp838–39 of the 2011/12 edition of this *Handbook* for details of the old limits which may still apply to some loans taken out before 10 April 1995.

Excessive housing costs

Whether or not an upper limit applies to you (see above), the amount of benefit you get for housing costs can be restricted if:[113]
* your home (excluding any part which you let) is too big for you, your partner and:
  – for IS and JSA, any children or qualifying young people included in your claim and any non-dependants (see p450) (including foster children);
  – for ESA and PC, anyone under 20 living with you and any other non-dependants (see p450).

When deciding if your home is too big, a comparison is made with other suitable accommodation given the size of your household. Everyone's needs must be considered – eg, if someone needs extra space because of a disability, or you have a child or relative in a care home who regularly comes to stay with you, your need for a large home may be justified; *or*

- the area in which you live is more expensive than other areas where there is suitable accommodation. The area should not be chosen on too wide a basis. 'Area' means something more confined, restricted and compact than a locality or district. It might be a neighbourhood or even a large block of flats;[114] *or*
- the outgoings on your home which are met by IS, income-based JSA, income-related ESA or PC are higher than those in other suitable accommodation in the area.

The capital value of your home cannot be taken into account.[115] **Note:** in some situations, no restriction should be made (see below).

If it is appropriate to restrict the amount of benefit you get for your housing costs, the amount you get is based on the amount of loan you would need in order to get suitable alternative accommodation.[116] This must be assessed in practical and realistic terms.

Any loans that are repayable on the sale of your home which would leave you with less money to purchase another home should be taken into account.[117]

If the equity in your property was sufficient to buy a new home outright, without a loan, your housing costs could be nil.[118]

When no restriction should be made
No restriction can be made, even if suitable accommodation is available, if it is not reasonable for you (and your partner) to look for cheaper accommodation. Account should be taken of:[119]

- the general level of housing costs in the area and whether suitable accommodation is available. This means that property must be generally available, not necessarily available to you personally;[120]
- your family circumstances (for IS and JSA) or your circumstances and those of the people who live with you (for ESA and PC) – eg, your employment prospects, the age and health of your family members and whether the move would have a detrimental effect on a child's or young person's education if s/he were to change schools.

These are not the only situations which count.[121] A move may not be reasonable if:

- the size of your family would make it difficult to find accommodation;
- you need to be near relatives or friends to provide (or receive) care or support;
- you have moved a number of times recently;

Part 4: Paying for housing
Chapter 20: Housing costs
4. Calculating the amount of housing costs

- it would be difficult to sell your property,[122] you have negative equity or selling would cause you financial hardship;[123]
- you have lived in your home for many years and it is now too large because you are separated or divorced, your children have left home or your partner has died;
- before your claim you were advised by the DWP that your housing costs would not be restricted;[124]
- you could not get another mortgage on a property.[125]

Even if it is reasonable for you to move, a restriction can be delayed in certain circumstances (see below).

Delaying a restriction

The amount of benefit you get for housing costs cannot be restricted for 26 weeks if you (or your partner) were able to meet your housing costs when they were first taken on, and for a further 26 weeks if you are trying to find cheaper accommodation.[126] Periods of 12 weeks or less when you stop getting IS, income-based JSA, income-related ESA or PC, and some other specified periods, can be included when calculating the 26 weeks.[127]

Deductions for non-dependants

If other people normally live with you in your home who are not part of your family for benefit purposes (called 'non-dependants'), a set deduction is usually made from the amount of benefit for housing costs.[128] This is because it is assumed the non-dependant makes a contribution towards your outgoings, whether or not s/he does so. Examples of non-dependants are adult sons or daughters, or elderly relatives who share your home.

For whether someone may count as normally living with you, see p116. What needs to be considered is the same as for housing benefit (HB).

The DWP may use the rules on p431 to work out if someone is only temporarily absent from your home.[129] If you think the DWP has wrongly assumed that a person is normally living with you, ask for a revision or appeal (see Chapters 58 and 59). You are likely to have to apply for a revision before you can appeal.

People who are not non-dependants

No deduction is made if the person living with you is not treated as a non-dependant (although any rent or lodging charges s/he pays to you affect the amount of your IS, income-based JSA, income-related ESA or PC – see p280 and p314). The following people do not count as non-dependants even if they normally live with you:[130]

- your partner and:
  - for IS, JSA and ESA only, any child or qualifying young person included in your claim and any child or qualifying young person living with you who

does not count as a member of your household (see p214) – eg, a foster child or a child placed with you prior to adoption;
- for PC only, anyone under 20 for whom you or your partner are responsible ('responsible' is not defined in the rules);
- someone who is liable to pay you, or your partner, in order to live in your home (eg, a sub-tenant, licensee or boarder) along with other members of her/his household. This does not apply if the person is a close relative of yours or your partner (see p430 for who counts).
The payment must be on a commercial basis. A low charge does not necessarily mean that the arrangement is not commercial. You do not have to make a profit. An arrangement between friends can be commercial;[131]
- for IS, JSA and ESA only, someone other than a close relative (see p430 for who counts) to whom you, or your partner, are liable to make payments on a commercial basis (ie, as a sub-tenant, licensee or boarder) in order to live in her/his property. Other members of her/his household also do not count as non-dependants;
- someone who jointly occupies your home and is a co-owner or joint tenant with you or your partner. Your joint occupier's partner is also not a non-dependant. For IS, JSA and ESA only, close relatives (see p430 for who counts) who jointly occupy your home are treated as non-dependants unless they had joint liability before 11 April 1988 or joint liability existed on or before the date you first lived in the property (or your partner did if s/he is the joint owner/tenant). However, no non-dependant deduction is made for them even though they are non-dependants (see below);
- someone who is employed by a charitable or voluntary organisation as a resident carer for you, or your partner, and who you pay for that service (even if the charge is nominal). If the carer's partner lives in your home, s/he also does not count as a non-dependant.

When no deduction is made

Even if you have a non-dependant in your home, no deduction is made for her/him if you (or your partner):[132]
- are registered blind (certified blind in Scotland);
- get attendance allowance (AA) (or equivalent benefits paid because of injury at work or a war injury), the care component of disability living allowance (DLA), the daily living component of personal independence payment (PIP) or armed forces independence payment.

In addition, no deduction is made for a non-dependant:[133]
- who is staying with you but whose normal home is elsewhere;
- for whom a deduction is already being made from your HB;
- who is 16 or 17 years old;
- who is under 25 years old and who is:

Part 4: Paying for housing
Chapter 20: Housing costs
4. Calculating the amount of housing costs

- getting IS, income-based JSA or income-related ESA which does not include a work-related activity or support component (see Chapter 5); *or*
        - entitled to universal credit, provided s/he does not have any earned income;
- who is getting PC;
- who gets a training allowance in connection with youth training under specific provisions;[134]
- who is a full-time student during her/his period of study (see p905). This includes those getting JSA who count as full-time students while on a specified government scheme for assisting people to obtain employment (see p1093).[135] **Note:** no deduction is made during the summer vacation but, unless you are getting PC and you or your partner are 65 or over, only if the student is not in full-time paid work (see p987);
- who is not living with you at present because s/he:
    - has been in hospital for more than 52 weeks. Separate stays in hospital which are not more than 28 days apart are added together when calculating the 52 weeks;
    - is a prisoner (see p962 for who counts);
- for IS, JSA and ESA only, who is a close relative (see p430 for who counts) and a co-owner or joint tenant with you, or your partner. For PC, no deduction is made because co-owners and joint tenants do not count as non-dependants, even if they are close relatives.

The amount of the deduction

If you have a non-dependant living with you who is 18 or over and for whom a deduction must be made, a fixed amount is deducted, whatever s/he pays you. Unless your non-dependant is in full-time paid work, a £14.15 deduction is made each week. If your non-dependant is in full-time paid work, the amount of the deduction depends on her/his gross weekly income.[136]

Gross weekly income	Weekly non-dependant deduction
£406 or more	£91.15
£326–£405.99	£83.05
£245–£325.99	£72.95
£188–£244.99	£44.55
£128–£187.99	£32.45
Less than £128	£14.15

The rules on full-time paid work are covered in Chapter 46. **Note:**
- A non-dependant who is not in (or is treated as not in) full-time paid work does not attract the higher level of deduction even if her/his gross weekly income is £128 or more.

- For PC, if someone is getting IS or income-based JSA for more than three days in a benefit week, s/he does not count as in full-time paid work in that week.[137] This means the lower deduction (£14.15) is made (or, in some cases, no deduction is made).

Gross income includes wages before tax and national insurance are deducted, plus any other income the non-dependant has (but not AA (or equivalent benefits paid because of injury at work or a war injury), DLA, PIP, armed forces independence payment or certain payments from the Macfarlane Trusts, the Eileen Trust, MFET Ltd, the Fund or the Independent Living Fund (2006), the London Bombings Relief Charitable Fund, the Skipton Fund and the Caxton Foundation, or, for PC only, payments in kind).[138]

Do you know your non-dependant's income?
You should try to provide information to show which deduction applies. However, if you do not know your non-dependant's income, ask the DWP to consider the circumstances – eg, if your non-dependant is doing a job which is normally very poorly paid. **Note:** the DWP should not assume that your non-dependant is earning the highest amount. It should assess the likely level of your non-dependant's earnings on the evidence available.[139]

A deduction is made for each non-dependant in your home. However, if you have a non-dependant couple and a non-dependant deduction applies to both members, only one deduction is made – the highest applicable. The couple's joint income counts.

If you are a joint owner with someone other than your partner, any deductions are shared proportionally between you and the other owner(s).

5. Waiting periods

Even if you qualify for help with your housing costs, these are not usually met until you have been entitled (or treated as entitled) to income support (IS), jobseeker's allowance (JSA) or employment and support allowance (ESA) for a number of weeks (13, 26 or 39 weeks as the case may be). This is known as a 'waiting period'.[140] **Note:** if you claim pension credit (PC), there is no waiting period and you get help with your housing costs straight away.

While in your waiting period, if you are entitled to some IS, JSA or ESA even though housing costs are not included in your applicable amount, the decision maker should do a supersession when your waiting period ends, and your housing costs are then included from the end of that period.[141] However, even if you are *not* entitled to some IS, JSA or ESA during your waiting period, help with your housing costs can still be included when it ends if you are *treated* as entitled to IS, JSA or ESA during the period. In some cases, you have to make a fresh claim for IS, income-based JSA or income-related ESA (when sufficient weeks have passed). For information about when you can be treated as entitled to IS, JSA or ESA, see the linking rules on pp456–60.

Help with your housing costs can be **included straight away** (without a waiting period) if:[142]

- you can be treated as entitled to IS, JSA or ESA for sufficient weeks during the period before your claim;
- you have already been entitled to IS, JSA or ESA for sufficient weeks when you agree to pay your loan or other housing costs (but see p439 for the rules restricting the amount you can get if you take out or increase a loan while entitled to benefit or in a period between claims);
- you were getting help with your housing costs when your IS, JSA or ESA ceased because you:
  - became a 'work or training beneficiary' (see p457) or a 'welfare-to-work beneficiary' (see p686 of the 2013/14 edition of this *Handbook*); *or*
  - started full-time paid work or training for work or self-employment, or increased your hours or your pay (so long as you qualify for a longer linking period – see p460).
  This only applies if you claim IS, income-based JSA or income-related ESA again within 104 weeks (if you are a 'work or training beneficiary' or a 'welfare-to-work beneficiary') or 52 weeks (if you qualify for a longer linking period);
- your partner is at least the qualifying age for PC (see p78) or, for JSA only, you are at least that age;
- you are claiming for payments as a Crown tenant, under a co-ownership scheme or for a tent.

In addition, if you (or your partner) reclaim IS, income-based JSA or income-related ESA within 26 weeks of a previous award of benefit which included help with housing costs and you (or s/he) have been receiving payments under an employment insurance policy which has since run out, periods between those claims are ignored when calculating the waiting periods.[143] Because the number of weeks in the previous claim can be added to the number of weeks in your current claim for that benefit, this means that you can requalify for help with housing costs sooner.

All other claimants get a reduced amount of help initially. You are expected to use mortgage payment protection policy payments, savings or income to meet any shortfall. If you do not have enough to pay the shortfall, discuss with your lender how you can protect your home.

The 13-week waiting period

If the modified rules described on p435 apply to you, your waiting period is 13 weeks.[144] You get nothing for the first 13 weeks, then full help with housing costs after you have been entitled (or treated as entitled) to IS, JSA or ESA for 13 weeks.

Note: if the 13-week waiting period applies:

- the upper limit for your loans is £200,000 (see p448); *and*
- if you are claiming JSA, you may only be able to get help with housing costs for your mortgage (or other loan for house purchase), or loan for repairs and improvements, for a maximum of 104 weeks (see p437).

The 26-week and 39-week waiting periods

If the modified rules described on p435 do *not* apply to you, a 26- or 39-week waiting period applies. If one of these waiting periods applies:

- the upper limit for your loans is usually £100,000 (see p448); *and*
- even if you are claiming income-based JSA, there is no limit on the number of weeks you can get help with housing costs for your mortgage (or other loan for house purchase) or loan for repairs and improvements.

Note: in practical terms, if you make a new claim for IS, JSA or ESA and the modified rules described on p435 do not apply, in most cases you will have already served your 26- or 39-week waiting period so housing cost should be included in your applicable amount straight away.

The **26-week waiting period** applies if you:[145]

- agreed to pay your loan or other housing costs before 2 October 1995 (the DWP calls these 'existing housing costs'); *or*
- agreed to pay your loan after 1 October 1995, but it replaced a loan you agreed to pay before that date. You must have been liable for the housing costs under both the old and the new agreements and the new loan must be for the same (or lower) amount as the earlier loan; *or*
- are exempt from the 39-week waiting period – eg, because you are a lone parent whose partner abandoned you or died, or a carer, or you have been refused payments under a mortgage payment protection policy because of a pre-existing medical condition or because you are HIV positive or, for IS and income-related ESA only, you are in prison awaiting trial or sentence.[146] For full details of who is exempt from the 39-week waiting period, see p846 of the 2011/12 edition of this *Handbook*.

No housing costs are included in your applicable amount until you have been entitled (or treated as entitled) to IS, JSA or ESA for eight weeks, 50 per cent are included for the next 18 weeks and full housing costs are included after you have been entitled (or treated as entitled) to IS, JSA or ESA for 26 weeks.

Unless the 26-week waiting period applies, the **39-week waiting period** applies if you agreed to pay your loan or other housing costs after 1 October 1995 (the DWP calls these 'new housing costs').[147] No housing costs are included in your applicable amount until you have been entitled (or treated as entitled) to IS, JSA or ESA for 39 weeks.

If you have two loans or agreements to pay other housing costs and one was agreed before and one after 1 October 1995, the relevant waiting periods apply to each.[148]

4

6. Linking rules

You are treated as entitled to or receiving income support (IS), income-based jobseeker's allowance (JSA) or income-related employment and support allowance (ESA) for certain periods, even though you were not actually entitled to or receiving it. These are known as 'linking rules'.

- Periods when you are treated as entitled to IS, income-based JSA or income-related ESA can count towards your waiting period (see p453), so you can get full help with housing costs earlier.
- The modified rules on p435 do not apply to you if you are treated as receiving IS, income-based JSA or income-related ESA during the specified period, so for example, the £200,000 upper limit for loans does not apply.
- Periods that count towards the 104-week maximum time for help with housing costs with JSA link, if you are treated as receiving JSA continuously between them (see p437), so the weeks in the linked periods are added together.
- You can continue to get help with certain types of housing costs that are no longer met (see p445) if there is a break in your claim.

General rules

You are treated as entitled to and receiving:[149]

- IS for any period when you were entitled to or receiving income-based JSA or income-related ESA;
- JSA for any period when you were entitled to or receiving IS or income-related ESA;
- income-related ESA for any period when you were entitled to or receiving IS, income-based JSA or pension credit (PC);
- IS or JSA for any period when you were receiving JSA as a 'joint-claim couple' (see p46);
- IS, JSA or income-related ESA during a period of no more than 12 weeks between two periods when:

- for IS and JSA, you were entitled to, receiving, or treated as receiving, IS, JSA or income-related ESA, or were treated as entitled to one of these while your income or capital was too high in the circumstances described below; *or*
- for ESA, you were entitled to, receiving, or treated as receiving, IS, income-based JSA, income-related ESA or PC, or were treated as entitled to one of these while your income or capital was too high in the circumstances described on p457.

The 12 weeks is extended to 104 weeks if you or your partner are a 'work or training beneficiary' (see below) or a 'welfare-to-work beneficiary' (see p686 of the 2013/14 edition of this *Handbook*), or to 52 weeks if you qualify for a longer linking period (see p460);

- IS or JSA during any period for which you are awarded IS, JSA or income-related ESA after a revision, supersession or appeal;
- income-related ESA during any period for which you are awarded IS, income-based JSA, income-related ESA or PC after a revision, supersession or appeal.

Work or training beneficiary

You count as a work or training beneficiary during a period of up to 104 weeks that links two periods of limited capability for work if:[150]

- you stopped being entitled to benefit or another 'advantage' (eg, national insurance (NI) credits) to which you were entitled on the basis that you had limited capability for work; *and*
- you had limited capability for work for more than 13 weeks in the most recent past period of limited capability for work. If that period started when you were transferred from incapacity benefit (IB)/severe disablement allowance/IS on grounds of disability to ESA (see p662), it does not matter if it was 13 weeks or less; *and*
- within a month of your entitlement to the benefit or advantage ceasing, you start paid work (other than work you may do while claiming – see p1018) or training.

Even if you satisfy these conditions, you are not a work or training beneficiary if your most recent past period of limited capability for work ended because you were found not to have limited capability for work – ie, you failed the work capability assessment.

Income or capital is too high

If, when you claimed, you were not entitled to IS, income-based JSA or income-related ESA (or, for ESA only, to PC) because your income was too high or your capital was over £16,000, you can be treated as entitled to IS, income-based JSA or income-related ESA for a period of up to 39 weeks. This includes if your contribution-based JSA was the same as, or higher than, your income-based JSA applicable amount (or your contributory ESA was the same as or higher than your income-related ESA applicable amount).

This applies if, on all the days in the period, you are:[151]

- entitled to contribution-based JSA, statutory sick pay, IB or contributory ESA (or NI credits for unemployment, incapacity or limited capability). A previous claim for IS, *income-based* JSA or *income-related* ESA is not required;[152] *or*
- for IS only, treated as receiving IS or income-based JSA.[153]

This also applies if you are a lone parent or a carer (see below for who counts).[154] In this case, you or someone claiming on your behalf must have previously claimed and been refused IS or income-based JSA or (for IS and JSA only) contribution-based JSA or (for JSA and ESA only) income-related ESA or (for ESA only) PC. However, this rule does not apply if, during the 39-week period:

- for IS and JSA, you or your partner count as being in full-time paid work (see p987), or you are a full-time student who cannot claim IS or JSA (see p905); *or*
- for ESA, you count as being in paid work, your partner counts as being in full-time paid work (see p987) or you are in full-time education and are getting disability living allowance, personal independence payment or armed forces independence payment; *or*
- you are temporarily absent from Great Britain other than:
  - for IS and ESA, during the first four weeks of absence in specified circumstances or if you are away solely because you are accompanying a dependent child for medical treatment; *or*
  - for JSA, in circumstances in which you would normally continue to qualify for JSA (see p1580).

Carer

You count as a **'carer'** if:

– for IS and ESA, you are someone who would qualify for IS as a carer (see p29); *or*

– for JSA, you have caring responsibilities and are, therefore, allowed to restrict the hours you are available for work (see p1036).

If these rules apply and you were not entitled to IS, income-based JSA or income-related ESA only because your income was too high and you were getting payments under a mortgage payment protection policy, you are treated as entitled to IS, income-based JSA or income-related ESA for *any* period for which the payments were made.[155] This could be longer than 39 weeks.

Couples and former couples

You are treated as entitled to and receiving IS, income-based JSA or income-related ESA during the time when:[156]

- your former partner was receiving, or was treated as receiving, IS, income-based JSA (but, for IS and JSA, not joint-claim JSA), income-related ESA or PC for you both, provided you claim IS, income-based JSA or income-related ESA within 12 weeks of separating (104 weeks if you are a 'work or training beneficiary' (see p457) or a 'welfare-to-work beneficiary' (see p686 of the 2013/14 edition of this Handbook), or 52 weeks if you qualify for a longer linking period – see p460);
- your partner was receiving, or was treated as receiving, IS, income-based JSA or income-related ESA (or, for ESA only, PC) on her/his own, provided you make a claim for IS, income-based JSA or income-related ESA within 12 weeks of becoming a couple (or a 'joint-claim couple' – see p46). Unless you are a joint-claim couple, the time limit is 104 weeks if you or your partner are a 'work or training beneficiary' (see p457) or a 'welfare-to-work beneficiary', or 52 weeks if you qualify for a longer linking period (see p460);
- your partner was receiving or treated as receiving IS, income-based JSA (but, for IS and JSA, not joint-claim JSA) or income-related ESA (or, for ESA only, PC) for you both, if you take over the claiming role.

Employment and training schemes

You are treated as entitled to and receiving IS, income-based JSA or income-related ESA during periods when you stop receiving IS, income-based JSA or income-related ESA (or, for ESA only, PC) because you or your partner are on training under specific provisions or an employment training rehabilitation course.[157]

Note: before 22 October 2012, you could be treated as entitled to and receiving IS, income-based JSA or income-related ESA during periods when you or your partner were on specified New Deal programmes or schemes. See p499 of the 2013/14 edition of this *Handbook* for details.

Former claimant's family

You are treated as entitled to and receiving IS, income-based JSA or income-related ESA during the time when someone who was not your partner (the 'former claimant' – eg, your parent or an adult acting as your parent) was entitled to:[158]
- IS or income-based JSA;
- for JSA and ESA only, income-related ESA; *or*
- for ESA only, PC.

In all cases, you and a child or young person must have counted as a member of the former claimant's family and the child or young person must now count as a member of *your* family (see p440 for who counts). You must make a claim for IS, income-based JSA or income-related ESA within 12 weeks of the former claimant's entitlement ceasing. So, for example, this applies if your mother or father was

Part 4: Paying for housing
Chapter 20: Housing costs
7. Mortgage interest run-on

claiming benefit for you and your child, but you are now claiming IS, income-based JSA or income-related ESA. **Note:** the 12 weeks can be extended to 104 weeks if you are a 'work or training beneficiary' (see p457) or a 'welfare-to-work-beneficiary (see p686 of the 2013/14 edition of this *Handbook*), or 52 weeks if you qualify for a longer linking period (see below).

Longer linking periods

Some of the 12-week periods and time limits above are extended to 52 weeks – referred to in this *Handbook* as 'longer linking periods'. You qualify for a longer linking period if you stop getting IS, JSA or income-related ESA because:[159]
- you or your partner:
  - start work or increase your hours; *or*
  - are taking steps to get work under certain training schemes; *or*
  - are getting assistance in pursuing self-employment while on a training course funded under specific provisions;[160] *and*
- as a result, your earnings or your income are too high, or (for IS and JSA) you or your partner count as being in full-time paid work, or (for ESA) you count as being in paid work or your partner counts as in full-time paid work (see p987).

You only qualify for a longer linking period if, immediately before the day your entitlement to IS, income-based JSA or income-related ESA ceased, you had served enough of your waiting period (see p453) so that help with housing costs:[161]
- was included in your IS, income-based JSA or income-related ESA (in full or in part); *or*
- would have been included but for a non-dependant deduction (see p450).

7. **Mortgage interest run-on**

When you (or your partner) return to work or increase your hours and so count as being in full-time paid work, you no longer qualify for income support (IS), income-based jobseeker's allowance (JSA) or income-related employment and support allowance (ESA). However, you might qualify for mortgage interest run-on. If you do, you are paid IS for your housing costs for the first four weeks after you go into full-time paid work, even if the benefit you were claiming was income-based JSA or income-related ESA.

Note:
- You do not have to make a claim to qualify for mortgage interest run-on; it is paid automatically.[162] However, you must let the DWP know you are starting full-time paid work.
- Mortgage interest run-on is not taxable.

- Mortgage interest run-on is a payment of IS, and IS is included in the 'benefit cap' (see p1169). You might get health benefits (see Chapter 30) and education benefits (see p832) and qualify for social fund payments.

Who can claim mortgage interest run-on

You qualify for mortgage interest run-on if:[163]
- you or your partner take up a new job or increase your weekly hours of work and so count as being in full-time paid work (see p987). You must expect the work to last for at least five weeks; *and*
- throughout the 26 weeks before the day you count as being in full-time paid work, you or your partner were receiving IS, income-based JSA or income-related ESA. Periods when you were receiving mortgage interest run-on do not count towards the 26 weeks;[164] *and*
- on the day before you or your partner commenced the work, your IS, income-based JSA or income-related ESA applicable amount included help with any of the following housing costs:
  – mortgages and other home purchase loans (see p438); *or*
  – loans for repairs and improvements (see p443); *or*
  – 'other housing costs' (see p444); *and*
- you or your partner are still liable to pay the housing costs.

If you qualify, you are paid IS for the housing costs for the first four weeks of full-time paid work.[165] Mortgage interest run-on is paid to you, *not* directly to your lender.[166]

The amount of mortgage interest run-on

You are paid the lowest of:[167]
- the weekly amount of IS, income-based JSA or income-related ESA for housing costs that you were getting immediately before you or your partner took up full-time paid work. See p445 for how these costs are calculated; *or*
- your or your partner's IS, income-based JSA or income-related ESA entitlement in the week before you took up full-time paid work (or the amount to which you would have been entitled had you not been getting a training allowance).

Your earnings from the full-time paid work and any other income you get are disregarded.[168] All of your capital is also disregarded.[169]

Your mortgage interest run-on can be adjusted if specified changes occur.[170]

Notes

1. When you can get help with housing costs

1 **IS** Regs 17(1)(e) and 18(1)(f) and Sch 3 para 1 IS Regs
JSA Regs 83(7), 84(1)(g) and 86A(d) and Sch 2 para 1 JSA Regs
ESA Regs 67(1)(c) and 69(1)(d) and Sch 6 para 1 ESA Regs
PC Reg 6(6)(c) and Sch 2 para 1 SPC Regs
2 **IS** Sch 3 paras 2 and 5(5) IS Regs
JSA Sch 2 paras 2 and 5(5) JSA Regs
ESA Sch 6 paras 4 and 7(5) ESA Regs
PC Sch 2 paras 3 and 6(5) SPC Regs
3 R(IS) 4/00
4 R(IS) 4/95
5 *Ewens v Secretary of State for Social Security*, reported as R(IS) 8/01
6 CIS/636/1992, confirmed by the Court of Appeal in *Brain v CAO*, 2 December 1993
7 **IS** Sch 3 para 2(2) IS Regs
JSA Sch 2 para 2(2) JSA Regs
8 **IS** Reg 2(1) IS Regs
JSA Reg 1(3) JSA Regs
ESA Reg 2(1) ESA Regs
PC Reg 1(2) SPC Regs
All R(SB) 22/87
9 **IS** Sch 3 para 3(1) IS Regs
JSA Sch 2 para 3(1) JSA Regs
ESA Sch 6 para 5(1) ESA Regs
PC Sch 2 para 4(1) SPC Regs
10 CIS/297/1994
11 **IS** Sch 3 para 4(1)(b) IS Regs
JSA Sch 2 para 4(1)(b) JSA Regs
ESA Sch 6 para 6(1)(b) ESA Regs
PC Sch 2 para 5(1)(b) SPC Regs
12 **IS** Reg 2(1) IS Regs
JSA Reg 1(3) JSA Regs
ESA Reg 2(1) ESA Regs
PC Reg 1(2) SPC Regs
All Definition of 'dwelling occupied as the home'; s137(1) SSCBA 1992 and reg 2(1) ESA Regs, definition of 'dwelling'
13 *SSWP v Mohamed Miah*, reported as R(JSA) 9/03; R(H) 5/09
14 **IS** Sch 3 para 3(7) and (13) IS Regs
JSA Sch 2 para 3(7) and (13) JSA Regs
ESA Sch 6 para 5(7) and (13) ESA Regs
PC Sch 2 para 4(7) SPC Regs
15 *Mahmoudi v LB Lewisham and Another*, EWCA, 6 February 2014
16 **IS** Reg 2(1) IS Regs
JSA Reg 1(3) JSA Regs
ESA Reg 2(1) ESA Regs
PC Reg 1(2) PC Regs
17 R(H) 9/05
18 **IS** Sch 3 para 3(10) IS Regs
JSA Sch 2 para 3(10) JSA Regs
ESA Sch 6 para 5(10) ESA Regs
PC Sch 2 para 4(10) SPC Regs
19 **IS** Sch 3 para 3(11)-(13) IS Regs
JSA Sch 2 para 3(11)-(13) JSA Regs
ESA Sch 6 para 5(11)-(13) ESA Regs
PC Sch 2 para 4(11)-(13) SPC Regs
20 *R v Penwith DC ex parte Burt* [1990] 22 HLR 292 (QBD)
21 CH/1237/2004
22 CH/3893/2004
23 R(H) 8/09; *SK v South Hams DC (HB)* [2010] UKUT 129 (AAC); [2010] AACR 40
24 **IS** Sch 3 para 3(5) IS Regs
JSA Sch 2 para 3(5) JSA Regs
ESA Sch 6 para 5(5) ESA Regs
PC Sch 2 para 4(5) SPC Regs
25 CIS/719/1994
26 **IS** Sch 3 para 3(11)-(13) IS Regs
JSA Sch 2 para 3(11)-(13) JSA Regs
ESA Sch 6 para 5(11)-(13) ESA Regs
PC Sch 2 para 4(11)-(13) SPC Regs
27 *Obrey and Others v SSWP* [2013] EWCA Civ 1584, 5 December 2013
28 *MR v Bournemouth BC (HB)* [2011] UKUT 284 (AAC)
29 *SSWP v Selby DC and Bowman* [2006] EWCA Civ 271, reported as R(H) 4/06
30 **IS** Sch 3 para 3(8) and (9) IS Regs
JSA Sch 2 para 3(8) and (9) JSA Regs
ESA Sch 6 para 5(8) and (9) ESA Regs
PC Sch 2 para 4(8) and (9) SPC Regs
31 *Torbay Borough Council v RF* [2010] UKUT 7 (AAC); [2010] AACR 26
32 **IS** Sch 3 para 3(13) IS Regs
JSA Sch 2 para 3(13) JSA Regs
ESA Sch 6 para 5 (13) ESA Regs
PC Sch 2 para 4(13) SPC Regs
33 R(H) 5/09

Chapter 20

34 **IS** Sch 3 para 3(6) IS Regs
  JSA Sch 2 para 3(6) JSA Regs
  ESA Sch 6 para 5(6) ESA Regs
  PC Sch 2 para 4(6) SPC Regs
35 CH/1911/2006
36 CIS/543/1993
37 CIS/339/1993
38 **IS** Sch 3 para 3(6)(a) IS Regs
  JSA Sch 2 para 3(6)(a) JSA Regs
  ESA Sch 6 para 5(6)(a) ESA Regs
  PC Sch 2 para 4(6)(a) SPC Regs
39 **IS** Sch 3 para 3(6)(b) IS Regs
  JSA Sch 2 para 3(6)(b) JSA Regs
  ESA Sch 6 para 5(6)(b) ESA Regs
  PC Sch 2 para 4(6)(b) SPC Regs
40 **IS** Sch 3 para 3(3) IS Regs
  JSA Sch 2 para 3(3) JSA Regs
  ESA Sch 6 para 5(3) ESA Regs
  PC Sch 2 para 4(3) SPC Regs
41 **IS** Sch 3 para 3(11)(c)(viii) IS Regs
  JSA Sch 2 para 3(11)(c)(viii) JSA Regs
  ESA Sch 6 para 5(11)(c)(viii) ESA Regs
  PC Sch 2 para 4(11)(c)(viii) SPC Regs
42 **IS** Sch 3 para 3(4) IS Regs
  JSA Sch 2 para 3(4) JSA Regs
  ESA Sch 6 para 5(4) ESA Regs
  PC Sch 2 para 4(4) SPC Regs

2. Modified rules
43 Regs 1, definition of 'relevant benefit', and 8 SS(HCSA)(A&M) Regs
44 Regs 3, 6(a), 7, 8 and 11(b) SS(HCSA)(A&M) Regs; Sch 2 para 4A JSA Regs
45 Sch 2 para 4A(3) and (4) JSA Regs, as inserted by reg 6 SS(HCSA)(A&M) Regs; Sch 2 para 4A(6) and (7) JSA Regs, as inserted by reg 11 SS(HCSA)(A&M) Regs

3. The type of housing costs that can be met
46 **IS** Sch 3 para 4(1)(a) IS Regs
  JSA Sch 2 para 4(1)(a) JSA Regs
  ESA Sch 6 para 6(1)(a) ESA Regs
  PC Sch 2 para 5(1)(a) SPC Regs
47 CIS/14483/1996
48 **IS** Sch 3 para 15 IS Regs
  JSA Sch 2 para 14 JSA Regs
  ESA Sch 6 para 16 ESA Regs
  PC Sch 2 para 11 SPC Regs
49 R(IS) 14/01; CPC/3322/2007
50 R(IS) 11/94
51 R(IS) 4/95
52 R(IS) 7/93
53 R(IS) 6/94
54 R(IS) 24/95
55 R(IS) 11/94

56 **IS** Sch 3 para 5 IS Regs
  JSA Sch 2 para 5 JSA Regs
  ESA Sch 6 para 7 ESA Regs
  PC Sch 2 para 6 SPC Regs
57 *RV v SSWP(IS)* [2013] UKUT 273 (AAC)
58 **IS** Sch 3 para 4(2)-(4) IS Regs
  JSA Sch 2 para 4(2)-(4) JSA Regs
  ESA Sch 6 para 6(2)-(4) ESA Regs
  PC Sch 2 para 5(2)-(4) SPC Regs
  All *Saleem v Secretary of State for Social Security*, reported as R(IS) 5/01; *SSWP v Mohammed* [2011] EWCA Civ 1358
59 CPC/3226/2005; CPC/3992/2007; CIS/88/2008
60 **IS** Sch 3 para 4(2) and (3) IS Regs
  JSA Sch 2 para 4(2) and (3) JSA Regs
  ESA Sch 6 para 6(2) and (3) ESA Regs
  PC Sch 2 para 5(2) and (3) SPC Regs
61 Sch 3 para 4(4) IS Regs; reg 32 IS(JSACA) Regs
62 Sch 2 paras 4(4) and 18(1)(c) JSA Regs
63 para 23466 DMG
64 **ESA** Sch 6 para 6(4) ESA Regs
  PC Sch 2 para 5(2) and (4) SPC Regs
65 **IS** Sch 3 para 4(4B) IS Regs
  JSA Sch 2 para 4(4B) JSA Regs
  ESA Sch 6 para 6(6) ESA Regs
66 **IS** Sch 3 paras 1(3) and (4) and 4(9) IS Regs
  JSA Sch 2 paras 1(3) and (4) and 4(9) JSA Regs
  ESA Sch 6 paras 1(3) and (4) and 6(11) ESA Regs
  PC Sch 2 paras 1(2)(a) and (3) and 5(10) SPC Regs
  All R(IS) 12/08
67 CIS/3295/2003
68 *Ahmed v SSWP* [2011] EWCA Civ 1186, reported as [2012] AACR 23
69 R(IS) 20/98
70 **IS** Sch 3 para 4(10) IS Regs
  JSA Sch 2 para 4(10) JSA Regs
  ESA Sch 6 para 6(12) ESA Regs
  PC Sch 2 para 5(11) SPC Regs
  All *Saleem v Secretary of State for Social Security*, reported as R(IS) 5/01; CIS/1068/2003
71 CIS/14657/1996; *SSWP v CA* [2009] UKUT 13 (AAC)
72 **IS** Sch 3 para 1(3) and (4) IS Regs
  JSA Sch 2 para 1(3) and (4) JSA Regs
  ESA Sch 6 para 1(3) and (4) ESA Regs
  PC Sch 2 para 1(2)(a) and (3) SPC Regs

73 **IS** Sch 3 para 4(6) IS Regs
JSA Sch 2 para 4(6) JSA Regs
ESA Sch 6 para 6(8) ESA Regs
PC Sch 2 para 5(7) SPC Regs
All *AH v SSWP (IS)* [2010] UKUT 353
(AAC)
74 CIS/11293/1995
75 **IS** Sch 3 para 4(8) IS Regs
JSA Sch 2 para 4(8) JSA Regs
ESA Sch 6 para 6(10) ESA Regs
PC Sch 2 para 5(9) SPC Regs
All CIS/4712/2002
76 **IS** Sch 3 para 4(11) IS Regs
JSA Sch 2 para 4(11) JSA Regs
ESA Sch 6 para 6(13) ESA Regs
PC Sch 2 para 5(12) SPC Regs
77 R(IS) 8/94
78 **IS** Sch 3 para 16 IS Regs
JSA Sch 2 para 15 JSA Regs
ESA Sch 6 para 17 ESA Regs
PC Sch 2 para 12 SPC Regs
All CIS/1480/2005
79 R(IS) 22/98
80 R(IS) 5/96
81 *SSWP v AR (IS)* [2012] UKUT 308 (AAC);
JT v SSWP [2013] UKUT 194 (AAC)
82 CIS/14657/1996
83 **IS** Sch 3 para 16(2) IS Regs
JSA Sch 2 para 15(2) JSA Regs
ESA Sch 6 para 17(2) ESA Regs
PC Sch 2 para 12(2) SPC Regs
84 *KW v SSWP (IS)* [2012] UKUT 180 (AAC)
85 CIS/2132/1998; R(IS) 2/07; *SSWP v AR
(IS)* [2012] UKUT 308 (AAC)
86 R(IS) 16/98; *DC v SSWP (JSA)* [2010]
UKUT 459 (AAC)
87 CIS/14657/1996; *SSWP v CA* [2009]
UKUT 13 (AAC)
88 **IS** Sch 3 para 17(1) IS Regs
JSA Sch 2 para 16(1) JSA Regs
ESA Sch 6 para 18(1) ESA Regs
PC Sch 2 para 13(1) SPC Regs
89 CH/3110/2003; R(H) 3/07
90 **IS** Sch 3 para 17(5) IS Regs
JSA Sch 2 para 16(5) JSA Regs
ESA Sch 6 para 18(5) ESA Regs
PC Sch 2 para 13(5) SPC Regs
91 **IS** Sch 3 para 17(3) IS Regs
JSA Sch 2 para 16(3) JSA Regs
ESA Sch 6 para 18(3) ESA Regs
PC Sch 2 para 13(3) SPC Regs
92 **IS** Sch 3 para 17(4) IS Regs
JSA Sch 2 para 16(4) JSA Regs
ESA Sch 6 para 18(4) ESA Regs
PC Sch 2 para 13(4) SPC Regs

93 **IS** Sch 3 para 17(2) IS Regs
JSA Sch 2 para 16(2) JSA Regs
ESA Sch 6 para 18(2) ESA Regs
PC Sch 2 para 13(2) SPC Regs
94 CIS/15036/1996; CIS/488/2008
95 **IS** Sch 3 para 17(2)(b) IS Regs
JSA Sch 2 para 16(2)(b) JSA Regs
ESA Sch 6 para 18(2)(b) ESA Regs
PC Sch 2 para 13(2)(b) SPC Regs
96 R(IS) 4/91; CIS/1460/1995; CIS/15036/
1996
97 **IS** Sch 3 para 17(2)(c) IS Regs
JSA Sch 2 para 16(2)(c) JSA Regs
ESA Sch 6 para 18(2)(c) ESA Regs
PC Sch 2 para 13(2)(c) SPC Regs
98 R(IS) 4/92; R(IS) 19/93
99 CIS/4/1988
100 Reg 3 IS(AT) Regs; Sch 6 para 20(2) ESA
Regs

4. Calculating the amount of housing costs

101 Regs 34A and 34B and Sch 9A para 4A
SS(C&P) Regs
102 **IS** Sch 3 para 10 IS Regs
JSA Sch 2 para 9 JSA Regs
ESA Sch 6 para 11 ESA Regs
PC Sch 2 para 7(1) SPC Regs
103 **IS** Sch 3 para 12 IS Regs
JSA Sch 2 para 11 JSA Regs
ESA Sch 6 para 13 ESA Regs
PC Sch 2 para 9 SPC Regs
104 **IS** Sch 3 para 7 IS Regs
JSA Sch 2 para 18 JSA Regs
ESA Sch 6 para 20(1)(b) ESA Regs
105 **IS** Sch 3 paras 6(1A) and (1B) and 8(1A)
and (1B) IS Regs; reg 7(14) and (23) and
Sch 3A paras 12 and 13 SS&CS(DA)
Regs
JSA Sch 2 paras 6(2) and 7(2)-(2B) JSA
Regs; reg 7(18) and (23) and Sch 3A
paras 12 and 13 SS&CS(DA) Regs
ESA Sch 6 paras 8(2) and (3) and 9(2)
and (3) ESA Regs; reg 7(17D) and (23)
and Sch 3C paras 9 and 10 SS&CS(DA)
Regs
PC Sch 2 para 7(2) and (4C) SPC Regs;
reg 7(17A) SS&CS(DA) Regs
106 Reg 7(17B) and (17C) SS&CS(DA) Regs
107 **IS** Sch 3 para 1A IS Regs
JSA Sch 2 para 1A JSA Regs
ESA Sch 6 para 3 ESA Regs
PC Sch 2 para 7(4A)-(5) SPC Regs
108 **IS** Reg 42(4)(a)(ii) IS Regs
JSA Reg 105(10)(a)(ii) JSA Regs
ESA Reg 107(3)(c) ESA Regs

109 **IS** Sch 10 para 26 IS Regs
JSA Sch 8 para 6 JSA Regs
ESA Sch 9 para 6 ESA Regs
PC Sch 5 para 7 SPC Regs

110 **IS** Sch 3 para 11(4) and (5) IS Regs
JSA Sch 2 para 10(3) and (4) JSA Regs
ESA Sch 6 para 12(3) and (4) ESA Regs
PC Sch 2 para 8(1) and (2) SPC Regs
All Regs 3-6 and 8-11 SS(HCSA)(A&M)
Regs

111 **IS** Sch 3 para 11(6) IS Regs
JSA Sch 2 para 10(5) JSA Regs
ESA Sch 6 para 12(5) ESA Regs
PC Sch 2 para 8(3) SPC Regs

112 Reg 12 SS(HCSA)(A&M) Regs

113 **IS** Sch 3 para 13 IS Regs
JSA Sch 2 para 12 JSA Regs
ESA Sch 6 para 14 ESA Regs
PC Sch 2 para 10 SPC Regs

114 R(IS) 12/91

115 **IS** Sch 3 para 13(2) IS Regs
JSA Sch 2 para 12(2) JSA Regs
ESA Sch 6 para 14(2) ESA Regs
PC Sch 2 para 10(2) SPC Regs

116 **IS** Sch 3 para 13(3) IS Regs
JSA Sch 2 para 12(3) JSA Regs
ESA Sch 6 para 14(3) ESA Regs
PC Sch 2 para 10(3) SPC Regs

117 CJSA/2683/2002

118 R(IS) 9/91; CJSA/2536/2000

119 **IS** Sch 3 para 13(4) and (5) IS Regs
JSA Sch 2 para 12(4) and (5) JSA Regs
ESA Sch 6 para 14(4) and (5) ESA Regs
PC Sch 2 para 10(4) and (5) SPC Regs

120 R(SB) 7/89

121 R(SB) 6/89; R(SB) 7/89

122 R(IS) 10/93

123 CIS/347/1992

124 CSB/617/1988. This case has been
reported as R(SB) 4/89, but the reported
version omits the relevant paragraphs.

125 R(SB) 7/89

126 **IS** Sch 3 para 13(6) IS Regs
JSA Sch 2 para 12(6) JSA Regs
ESA Sch 6 para 14(6) and (10) ESA Regs
PC Sch 2 para 10(6) SPC Regs
All *Secretary of State for Social Security v
Julien,* reported as R(IS) 13/92; R(SB) 7/
89; CIS/104/1991; CJSA/2536/2000

127 **IS** Sch 3 paras 13(7) and (9) and
14(15) IS Regs
JSA Sch 2 paras 12(7) and (9) and
18(1)(c) JSA Regs
ESA Sch 6 paras 14(7), (9) and (10) and
20(1)(c) ESA Regs
PC Sch 2 para 10(7), (9) and (10) SPC
Regs

128 **IS** Reg 3 and Sch 3 para 18 IS Regs
JSA Reg 2 and Sch 2 para 17 JSA Regs
ESA Reg 71 and Sch 6 para 19 ESA Regs
PC Sch 2 paras 1(4)-(9) and 14 SPC Regs

129 R(H) 8/09; *SK v South Hams DC (HB)*
[2010] UKUT 129 (AAC); [2010] AACR
40

130 **IS** Reg 3 IS Regs
JSA Reg 2 JSA Regs
ESA Reg 71 ESA Regs
PC Sch 2 para 1(4)-(7) SPC Regs

131 CSB/1163/1988

132 **IS** Sch 3 para 18(6) IS Regs
JSA Sch 2 para 17(6) JSA Regs
ESA Sch 6 para 19(6) ESA Regs
PC Sch 2 para 14(6) SPC Regs

133 **IS** Sch 3 para 18(7) IS Regs
JSA Sch 2 para 17(7) JSA Regs
ESA Sch 6 para 19(7) ESA Regs
PC Sch 2 para 14(7) SPC Regs

134 Made under s2 ETA 1973 or s2
Enterprise and New Towns (Scotland)
Act 1990 or by the Secretary of State for
people enlisted in HM Forces for any
special term of service specified in
regulations made under s2 Armed
Forces Act 1966.

135 Reg 3 JSA(SAPOE) Regs

136 **IS** Sch 3 para 18(1) and (2) IS Regs
JSA Sch 2 para 17(1) and (2) JSA Regs
ESA Sch 6 para 19(1) and (2) ESA Regs
PC Sch 2 para 14(1) and (2) SPC Regs

137 Sch 2 para 2(6) SPC Regs

138 **IS** Sch 3 para 18(8) IS Regs
JSA Sch 2 para 17(8) JSA Regs
ESA Sch 6 para 19(8) ESA Regs
PC Sch 2 para 14(8) SPC Regs

139 CH/48/2006

5. Waiting periods

140 **IS** Sch 3 paras 6 and 8 IS Regs
JSA Sch 2 paras 6 and 7 JSA Regs
ESA Sch 6 paras 8 and 9 ESA Regs
All SS(HCSA)(A&M) Regs

141 *SK v SSWP* [2013] UKUT 138 (AAC)

142 **IS** Sch 3 para 9 IS Regs
JSA Sch 2 para 8 JSA Regs
ESA Sch 6 para 10 ESA Regs
All SS(HCSA)(A&M) Regs

143 **IS** Sch 3 para 14(8) and (9) IS Regs; regs
5(d) and 10(h) SS(HCSA)(A&M) Regs
JSA Sch 2 para 13(10) and (11) JSA
Regs; regs 6(e) and 11(i)
SS(HCSA)(A&M) Regs
ESA Sch 6 para 15(13) and (14) ESA
Regs; regs 4(d) and 9(h)
SS(HCSA)(A&M) Regs
All Regs 3 and 8 SS(HCSA)(A&M) Regs

144 Regs 3-6 and 9-11 SS(HCSA)(A&M)
     Regs
145 **IS** Sch 3 paras 1(2), 6 and 8(2)-(5) IS
     Regs
     JSA Sch 2 paras 1(2), 6 and 7(3)-(6) JSA
     Regs
     ESA Sch 6 paras 1(2), 8 and 9(4)-(7) ESA
     Regs
     All CJSA/2028/2000
146 **IS** Sch 3 para 8(2)-(5) IS Regs
     JSA Sch 2 para 7(3)-(6) JSA Regs
     ESA Sch 6 para 9(4)-(7) ESA Regs
147 **IS** Sch 3 paras 1(2) and 8 IS Regs
     JSA Sch 2 paras 1(2) and 7 JSA Regs
     ESA Sch 6 paras 1(2) and 9 ESA Regs
     All CJSA/2028/2000
148 **IS** Sch 3 para 11(2) IS Regs
     JSA Sch 2 para 10(1) JSA Regs
     ESA Sch 6 para 12(1) ESA Regs

6. Linking rules
149 **IS** Sch 3 para 14(1)(a), (3A) and (15) IS
     Regs; reg 32 IS(JSACA) Regs
     JSA Sch 2 paras 13(1)(a), (2A) and
     (4) and 18(1)(c) JSA Regs
     ESA Sch 6 paras 15 (1)(a), (5), (15) and
     (16) and 20(1)(c) ESA Regs
150 Sch 6 para 1(3A)-(3C) ESA Regs
151 **IS** Sch 3 para 14(4) and (5) IS Regs; reg
     32 IS(JSACA) Regs
     JSA Sch 2 paras 13(5) and (6) and
     18(1)(c) JSA Regs; reg 32 IS(JSACA) Regs
     ESA Sch 6 paras 2(9), 15(8) and (9) and
     20(1)(c) ESA Regs
     All CIS/621/2004
152 CJSA/4613/2001
153 Sch 3 para 14(5)(c) IS Regs; reg 32
     IS(JSACA) Regs
154 **IS** Sch 3 para 14(4), (5A) and (5B) IS
     Regs; reg 32 IS(JSACA) Regs
     JSA Sch 2 paras 13(7) and (8) and
     18(1)(c) JSA Regs; reg 32 IS(JSACA) Regs
     ESA Sch 6 paras 2(9), 15(8), (10) and
     (11) and 20(1)(c) ESA Regs
     All CIS/621/2004
155 **IS** Sch 3 para 14(6) IS Regs
     JSA Sch 2 para 13(9) JSA Regs
     ESA Sch 6 para 15(12) ESA Regs
156 **IS** Sch 3 para 14(1)(c), (d) and (e),
     (3A), (14) and (15) IS Regs
     JSA Sch 2 paras 13(1)(c), (d), (dd) and
     (e), (4) and (16) and 18(1)(c) JSA Regs
     ESA Sch 6 paras 15(1)(c), (d) and (e),
     (15) and (19) and 20(1)(c) ESA Regs

157 **IS** Sch 3 para 14(3), (3A) and (15) IS
     Regs
     JSA Sch 2 paras 13(3), (4) and
     18(1)(c) JSA Regs
     ESA Sch 6 paras 15(3), (5) and 20(1)(c)
     ESA Regs
158 **IS** Sch 3 para 14(1)(f) and (3A) IS Regs
     JSA Sch 2 para 13(1)(f) and (4) JSA Regs
     ESA Sch 6 paras 15(1)(g) and (5) and
     20(1)(c) ESA Regs
159 **IS** Sch 3 para 14(11) and (12) IS Regs
     JSA Sch 2 para 13(13) and (14) JSA Regs
     ESA Sch 6 paras 2(9) and 15(16) and
     (17) ESA Regs
160 Schemes mentioned in reg 19(1)(r)(i)-
     (iii) JSA Regs
161 **IS** Sch 3 para 14(13) IS Regs
     JSA Sch 2 para 13(15) JSA Regs
     ESA Sch 6 para 15(18) ESA Regs

7. Mortgage interest run-on
162 Reg 3(h) SS(C&P) Regs
163 Reg 6(5) and (8) IS Regs
164 Reg 6(7) IS Regs
165 Reg 6(6) IS Regs
166 Sch 9A para 3(9) SS(C&P) Regs
167 Sch 7 para 19A(1) IS Regs
168 Schs 8 para 15C and 9 para 74 IS Regs
169 Sch 10 para 62 IS Regs
170 Sch 7 para 19A(2) and (3) IS Regs

Chapter 21

Discretionary housing payments

This chapter covers:
1. Who can claim discretionary housing payments (below)
2. The rules about your age (p468)
3. People included in the claim (p469)
4. The amount of discretionary housing payments (p469)
5. Claims, decisions and getting paid (p469)
6. Tax, other benefits and the benefit cap (p470)

Key facts

- Discretionary housing payments are extra payments that can be made by your local authority if you need help to meet your housing costs.
- You must be entitled to housing benefit or universal credit to get discretionary housing payments.
- You do not have a 'right' to discretionary housing payments. They are paid from a cash-limited budget allocated to your local authority by the government.
- You cannot appeal to the First-tier Tribunal against a discretionary housing payment decision, but you can ask the local authority for a review.

1. Who can claim discretionary housing payments

A local authority can pay you discretionary housing payments if you are entitled to:[1]
- housing benefit (HB); *or*
- universal credit (UC) that includes a housing costs element for rent payments, or that would include one but for the fact that you live in 'exempt accommodation' (see p474).

You must also appear to the local authority to require financial assistance in addition to the benefit to which you are entitled in order to meet your housing

Part 4: Paying for housing
Chapter 21: Discretionary housing payments
2. The rules about your age

costs (including rent in advance, deposits and removal expenses). You might get discretionary housing payments, for example, if your HB or UC is being paid at a reduced rate because of the benefit cap, or under any of the rent restriction rules in Chapter 19.

The local authority has discretion on whether to pay you, the amount to pay you (within certain limits) and over what period to pay you.[2] The DWP provides guidance to local authorities at www.dwp.gov.uk/docs/dhpguide.pdf.

Note: if you are only liable to pay council tax (and not rent), you are not eligible for discretionary housing payments. This means that, even if you get help with your council tax from your local authority (a council tax reduction), if you are not entitled to HB or UC you cannot get discretionary housing payments.

When discretionary housing payments cannot be made

Discretionary housing payments *cannot* be made to you if your need for financial assistance arises as a consequence of:[3]

- ineligible service charges under the HB (see p114) or the UC scheme (p476);
- water and sewerage charges;
- liability for council tax;
- your rent payments increasing to cover arrears of rent, service charges or other unpaid charges;
- a reduced benefit decision because you refused to co-operate in pursuing maintenance for your child(ren);
- your benefit being reduced because you refused to take part in a work-focused interview;
- your jobseeker's allowance (JSA) or UC being paid at a reduced (or nil) rate because you have been sanctioned under specified rules;
- if you are 16 or 17, your severe hardship payments of JSA (see p892) being reduced because you gave up a place on a training scheme or failed to attend without a good reason;
- your benefit being suspended;
- a reduction in your benefit because an overpayment of HB, UC or council tax benefit is being recovered;
- your benefit being restricted because of a benefit offence (see p1258).

2. The rules about your age

There are no lower or upper age limits for discretionary housing payments.

3. People included in the claim

You claim discretionary housing payments for yourself. However, your needs as well as those of your child(ren) and your partner should be taken into account in deciding if you can be paid them.

4. The amount of discretionary housing payments

Discretionary housing payments are normally paid in weekly amounts. The local authority can decide how long you can be paid and how far your payments can be backdated.[4] However, it can only pay discretionary housing payments for periods during which you are (or were) entitled to housing benefit (HB) or universal credit (UC).

You cannot be paid more than:[5]

- if you are entitled to HB and your discretionary housing payments are calculated as a weekly amount, an amount to meet your rent and other payments listed on p96, less any amounts paid for ineligible service charges and rent-free periods; *or*
- if you are entitled to UC and your discretionary housing payments are calculated as a monthly amount, the amount of your housing costs element for rent payments or, if you are in exempt accommodation, the amount of your rent payments (other than the rent payments for 'exempt accommodation') and service charge payments that can be included in your housing costs element.

However, there is no restriction on one-off payments – eg, for rent in advance or a deposit. Larger amounts can, therefore, be paid by way of a lump sum.

Note: if you are getting UC, ensure the local authority knows how much rent you are liable to pay, and if your housing costs element is a lower amount than this (see p485).

5. Claims, decisions and getting paid

Ask your local authority how to make a claim for discretionary housing payments. The local authority may accept a claim from you, or from someone acting on your behalf, as long as you are entitled to housing benefit (or universal credit).[6] Your local authority does not have to insist your claim is made in writing, but it decides what 'form or manner' your claim should take.[7]

Part 4: Paying for housing
Chapter 21: Discretionary housing payments
6. Tax, other benefits and the benefit cap

Note:

- You must provide grounds for your claim and provide any other information that the local authority specifies.[8] If you want your claim to be backdated, tell the local authority.
- You must be given written notice of the local authority's decision on your claim and the reasons for its decision as soon as is 'reasonably practicable'.[9]
- The local authority can pay you or, if reasonable, someone else where appropriate.[10]
- It is your duty to report any change in your circumstances that may be relevant to payment of your discretionary housing payments continuing.[11]

Getting a decision changed

You do not have a right of appeal to the First-tier Tribunal against a discretionary housing payment decision. However, you do have the right to ask the local authority for a review of its decision.[12] You are entitled to written notice of, and reasons for, the review decision as soon as is 'reasonably practicable'.[13] You might be able to challenge a review decision by judicial review (see p1351).

---

6. **Tax, other benefits and the benefit cap**

Discretionary housing payments are not taxable.

Discretionary housing payments are disregarded as income and capital for income support, jobseeker's allowance, income-related employment and support allowance, pension credit, housing benefit, universal credit, working tax credit and child tax credit purposes.[14]

The benefit cap

In some cases, the total amount of specified benefits you receive is limited to £350 a week (if you are a single claimant without children) or £500 a week (if you are a lone parent or a member of a couple). This is known as the 'benefit cap'. Discretionary housing payments are *not* one of the specified benefits. See p1169 for further information.

Notes

1. Who can claim discretionary housing payments
1 s69 CSPSSA 2000; reg 2(1) DFA Regs
2 Reg 2(2) DFA Regs
3 Reg 3 DFA Regs

4. The amount of discretionary housing payments
4 Reg 5 DFA Regs
5 Reg 4 DFA Regs

5. Claims, decisions and getting paid
6 Reg 6 DFA Regs
7 Reg 6(1)(a) DFA Regs
8 Reg 7 DFA Regs
9 Reg 6(3) DFA Regs
10 Reg 6(2) DFA Regs
11 Reg 7(b) DFA Regs
12 Reg 8 DFA Regs
13 Reg 6(3) DFA Regs

6. Tax, other benefits and the benefit cap
14 **IS** Schs 9 para 75 and 10 para 7(1)(d) IS Regs
JSA Schs 7 para 71 and 8 para 12(1)(d) JSA Regs
ESA Schs 8 para 62 and 9 para 11(1)(c) ESA Regs
PC Reg 15 SPC Regs
HB Schs 5 para 62 and 6 para 9(1)(d) HB Regs; reg 29 HB(SPC) Regs
UC Reg 66 UC Regs

Chapter 22

Universal credit housing costs

This chapter covers:
1. When you get a housing costs element (below)
2. Payments that can be met (p474)
3. Liability for payments (p478)
4. Occupying the accommodation as a home (p481)
5. The rules about your age (p485)
6. The amount for rented accommodation (p485)
7. The amount for owner-occupiers (p498)

Key facts
- Your universal credit can include a housing costs element if you are renting accommodation, are an owner-occupier or if you pay service charges.
- The amount of your housing costs element is not necessarily the same as the amount of rent, loan or service charges you are liable to pay.
- If you are a private tenant (or you live in certain types of temporary accommodation), the rent used to calculate your housing costs element is based on a local housing allowance for a property with the number of bedrooms the rules allow.
- If you are a social rented sector tenant (eg, your landlord is a local authority or housing association) and your home has more bedrooms than the rules allow, your housing costs element is reduced by a percentage.
- You cannot get a housing costs element for owner-occupier payments if you (or your partner) have any earned income, however low your earnings are.
- You might not get a housing costs element for owner-occupier payments during an initial 'waiting period'.
- If you need extra financial assistance to meet your housing costs, you may be able to claim discretionary housing payments from your local authority.

1. When you get a housing costs element

Your universal credit (UC) maximum amount can include a housing costs element to provide help with your rent payments (see p474) or help with the costs of buying your home (owner-occupier payments – see p475). It can also include some service charge payments (see p476). You qualify for a housing costs element if:[1]

- your accommodation is in Great Britain; *and*
- your accommodation is residential – ie, not for a business; *and*
- you or your partner are liable to make eligible payments for the accommodation and you occupy it as your home. For:
  - the payments that can be met, see p474;
  - when you count as liable to make payments, see p478. **Note:** in some cases, you can be treated as liable. In other cases you can be treated as *not* liable, even if you are;
  - when you count as occupying accommodation as your home, see p481.

The accommodation can comprise the whole of a building or part of a building – eg, a flat in a block, a bedsit in a house or a room in a shared house. You can get a housing costs element whether or not the accommodation comprises separate and self-contained premises.[2]

Note:
- If a housing costs element is included in your UC maximum amount, a lower work allowance may apply (see p188) – ie, a higher amount of your earnings are taken into account. In practice, this can only apply if you live in rented accommodation; if you are an owner-occupier you cannot get a housing costs element if you (or your partner) have *any* earned income.
- If you have a shared ownership tenancy (ie, you are buying part of your home and renting the rest), your housing costs element can include your rent and owner-occupier payments, as well as any service charge payments you make.[3]

When you cannot get a housing costs element

Even if you satisfy the payment, liability and occupation conditions, your UC maximum amount *cannot* include a housing costs element:
- for rent payments, if you are 16 or 17 and were previously looked after by a local authority (see p886);[4]
- for owner-occupier payments, during an assessment period in which you (or your partner) have any earned income (see p326), however much your earnings are.[5] The nature and duration of the work is not relevant – eg, it does not matter if your job is part time or temporary. **Note:** this only applies for the owner-occupier payments you make, so if you have a shared-ownership tenancy, you can get a housing costs element for your rent and your service charge payments.[6]
- if you live in 'exempt accommodation' (see p474), for the rent you pay for that accommodation. Instead, you can get housing benefit (HB).

Part 4: Paying for housing
Chapter 22: Universal credit housing costs
2. Payments that can be met

Exempt accommodation

If you live in 'exempt accommodation', the help you get with your rent for that accommodation is *not* provided via a UC housing costs element. For the foreseeable future, you can get HB instead (see Chapter 7).

Exempt accommodation

You live in **'exempt accommodation'** if it is:[7]

– temporary accommodation for people without a settled way of life, funded by the Resettlement Agency; *or*

– accommodation provided by an upper-tier county council, a housing association, a registered charity or a voluntary organisation. The body providing the accommodation, or a person acting on its behalf, must also provide you with care, support or supervision.[8] You must need this and it must be more than a token or minimal amount.[9] **Note:** if the person (or body) providing the care, support or supervision has a contract with the local authority to provide these, but is not providing the accommodation, the decision maker is likely to say it is not exempt accommodation.[10]

From 3 November 2014, you will also be able to get HB for other types of 'specified accommodation'. The definition is the same as for the benefit cap (see p1171).

---

2. Payments that can be met

To qualify for a housing costs element, the payments you make must be eligible. This is called the 'payment condition' in this *Handbook*. There are three types of eligible payments:

- rent payments (see below);
- owner-occupier payments (see p475); *and*
- service charge payments (see p476).

A housing costs element can include any of the eligible payments that you make. **Note:** if you have a shared ownership tenancy (ie, you are buying part of your home and renting the rest), your housing costs element can include rent and owner-occupier payments, as well as the service charge payments you make.[11]

Rent payments

Eligible rent payments include the rent you pay to your landlord, but can also include other types of payment, such as payments as a licensee and for bed and breakfast or hostel accommodation. Some types of payment cannot be met (see below). **Note:** if you live in 'exempt accommodation', such as supported accommodation, you cannot get a housing costs element for the rent you pay for that accommodation, but can get housing benefit for this (see p474).

The eligible payments are:[12]
- rent payments;
- payments for a licence or permission to occupy accommodation;
- mooring charges payable for a houseboat;
- site rent for a caravan or mobile home (but not for a tent); *and*
- contributions made by a resident of a charity's almshouse towards its maintenance and the essential services in it. The almshouse must be provided by a housing association.

In this *Handbook*, we refer to any of these payments as 'rent payments'. **Note:**
- Some types of payment are not eligible (see below).
- The amount of your housing costs element is restricted if you are a private tenant or live in temporary accommodation and your rent is higher than the rules allow (see p486) or, if you are a social rented sector tenant and your home has more bedrooms than the rules allow (see p489).

Payments that are not eligible

The following types of payments are not eligible, and cannot be included in your housing costs element:[13]
- ground rent;
- payments for a tent and its pitch;
- payments for an approved hostel – eg, a bail or probation hostel;
- payments made for 'exempt accommodation' or, from 3 November 2014, for other 'specified accommodation' (but see p474); *and*
- payments made for a care home.

Care homes

'**Care home**' means a care home (in England and Wales), a care home service (in Scotland) or an independent hospital.[14]

Owner-occupier payments

The eligible payments are:[15]
- interest payments on a loan that is secured on the accommodation you occupy, or are treated as occupying, as a home (see p481), whatever the purpose of the loan; *and*
- payments made under alternative finance arrangements to enable you to acquire an interest in the accommodation you occupy, or are treated as occupying, as a home (see p481) – eg, for a Sharia-compliant mortgage.

Part 4: Paying for housing
Chapter 22: Universal credit housing costs
2. Payments that can be met

In this *Handbook*, we refer to any of these payments as 'owner-occupier payments'. You cannot get help with associated insurance premiums – eg, if you have an endowment mortgage, you do not get the insurance element paid.

Service charge payments

The eligible payments are payments:[16]
- for the costs of, or charges for, services or facilities for the use or benefit of people occupying the accommodation; *or*
- fairly attributable to the costs of, or charges for, services or facilities connected with accommodation that are available for the use or benefit of people occupying the accommodation.

In this *Handbook*, we refer to any of these payments as 'service charge payments'. Note:
- Some types of payment are not eligible (see below).
- If you live in social rented sector accommodation (other than temporary accommodation), or you are getting a housing costs element for owner-occupier payments, there are extra conditions that must be satisfied. In addition, the rules specify categories of payments that are eligible (see p477).

The service charge payments do not have to be separately identified – eg, in your tenancy agreement. It does not matter if they are paid in addition to, or as part of, your rent, or if they are made under the same or a different agreement to that under which you occupy your home.

Payments that are not eligible

Payments are not eligible service charge payments and cannot be included in your housing costs element if:[17]
- you have taken out a loan to make the payments that is secured on the accommodation you occupy, or are treated as occupying, as a home. However, payments you make on the loan may qualify as owner-occupier payments (see p475); *or*
- the services or facilities to which the payments relate are for someone occupying a tent, approved premises (eg, a bail or probation hostel), a care home (see p475) or 'exempt accommodation' (but see p474).

Extra conditions for service charge payments

If you live in social rented sector accommodation (other than temporary accommodation – see p487 for what counts), or you are getting a housing costs element for owner-occupier payments, service charge payments are only eligible if you must make them as a condition of occupying your accommodation – eg, as part of your tenancy agreement, not as an optional extra.[18] The costs and charges must be reasonable and must be for services and facilities that are reasonable to provide.[19]

The payments must fit into one of the following categories.[20]

- **Payments to maintain the general standard of accommodation** – ie, for:
  - cleaning the outside of windows on the upper floors of a multi-storey building; *or*
  - internal or external maintenance or repair of the accommodation. The payments must be separately identifiable. You must occupy the accommodation under a shared ownership tenancy or be getting a housing costs element for owner-occupier payments.
- **Payments for the general upkeep of communal areas** – ie, for:
  - the ongoing maintenance of internal or external areas; *or*
  - the supply of water, fuel or any other service or facility relating to the common use of internal or external areas – eg, litter removal, laundry facilities and children's play areas.

  'Internal and external areas' include communal gardens, tenant parking, laundry rooms and children's play areas.
- **Payments for basic communal services.** They must be for the provision, ongoing maintenance, cleaning or repair of basic services generally available to everyone living in the accommodation – eg, refuse collection, communal lifts, secure building access, fire alarm systems or wireless or television aerials to receive a service free of charge. The DWP says it should also include payments for someone employed to provide an eligible service charge (eg, a concierge, groundskeeper or caretaker), as well as the costs of managing and administering eligible services.[21]
- **Accommodation-specific charges.** These must be for essential items specific to the particular accommodation you occupy – eg, for furniture or domestic appliances.

However, the service charge payments *cannot* be included in your housing costs element if they are:[22]

- for services or facilities for which public funding is available, whether or not you are entitled to such funding;
- connected to the use of an asset which will result in the transfer of that asset, or any interest in it – eg, payments for furniture and equipment that will eventually become yours;
- for food, medical services or personal services (including personal care).

Part 4: Paying for housing
Chapter 22: Universal credit housing costs
3. Liability for payments

3. **Liability for payments**

To qualify for a housing costs element, you (or your partner) must be liable to make eligible payments on a commercial basis, or you (or s/he) must be treated as liable (see below).[23] This is called the 'liability condition' in this *Handbook*.

For what 'liable' may mean in respect of rent payments, see p99. The issues are the same as for housing benefit.

In deciding if your agreement is on a commercial basis, the DWP must look at the whole agreement, taking all the circumstances into account. The DWP should consider, among other things:[24]

- whether your agreement includes terms that are not legally enforceable. This might arise, for example, if you do household chores. However, if you do chores in exchange for a lower rent, it could be considered commercial;
- your agreement to pay rent. The rent does not have to be a market rent. Your agreement can count as commercial even if your landlord is not collecting the full contractual rent from you – eg, if it is not being met in full because of the way your housing costs element is calculated;
- your relationship to the person to whom you are liable. However, just because s/he is a relative or close friend, or s/he provides you with care and support does not mean that your agreement is non-commercial.

Note:

- There are situations in which you (or your partner) are treated as *not* liable to make payments, even if you are (see p479).
- If you are jointly liable to make payments with someone (other than your partner or your child) and you are in rented accommodation, the way your housing costs element is calculated takes this into account (see p488 and p490).

People treated as liable to make payments

You (or your partner) are treated as liable to make payments:[25]

- if a child or qualifying young person for whom you (or your partner) are responsible (see p213) is liable to make the payments;
- if you are a member of a couple but you are claiming universal credit (UC) as a single person and your partner is liable to make the payments;
- if someone else is liable to make the payments but is not doing so and you must make the payments yourself in order to continue to live in your home (see p479);

- if payments are waived by the person to whom you are liable (eg, your landlord) as reasonable compensation for your carrying out reasonable repairs or redecoration which s/he would otherwise have had to carry out; *or*
- during rent-free periods (for rent and service charge payments only).

Another person is liable but is not paying

You (or your partner) are treated as liable to make payments if someone else is liable to make them but is not doing so, and you have to make the payments yourself to continue to live in your home.[26] In addition, you must show that:

- it would be unreasonable to expect you to make other arrangements; *and*
- it is reasonable to treat you as liable. In deciding what is reasonable for owner-occupier payments, the DWP can take into account the fact that the liable person may benefit from your making the payments.

This might apply, for example, if you have given up your home to live with and care for someone and s/he has now gone into a care home, or if you have separated from your partner (even if you have not lived in the home continuously since your partner left).[27]

For rent payments, it does not matter whether or not the landlord is prepared to transfer the tenancy to you or wants to evict you. If the DWP refuses to treat you as liable, point out that the eligibility rules for the housing costs element and the rules for transferring tenancies are separate. If you are refused the housing costs element, ask for a revision or appeal. **Note:** you are likely to have to apply for a revision before you can appeal.

People treated as not liable to make payments

Even if you are liable, or treated as liable, to make payments, you can be treated as though you are *not* liable. In this case, the payments cannot be included in your housing costs element. This applies if you are in specified situations (see p480) and also if the DWP considers the liability to be 'contrived' (see p481). In addition, you are treated as not liable to make:

- rent, owner-occupier or service charge payments if they are for an increase in the amount that you would otherwise be liable to pay, which is as a result of outstanding arrears of any payment or charge for your accommodation, or for accommodation you previously occupied, or for any other unpaid payment or charge;[28]
- service charge payments, if you are liable to make them to someone who lives in your household (see p215 for the meaning) and you are not liable to make rent or owner-occupier payments.[29]

For other situations in which you are treated as not liable to make rent and service charge payments, or to make owner-occupier and service charge payments, see p480.

Part 4: Paying for housing
Chapter 22: Universal credit housing costs
3. Liability for payments

Rent and service charge payments

You are treated as not liable to make rent payments if you are liable to make them to:[30]

- **someone who also lives in the accommodation**, and who is:[31]
  - your partner, or a child or qualifying young person for whom you (or your partner) are responsible (see p212); *or*
  - a close relative of yours or your partner, or of a child or qualifying young person for whom you (or your partner) are responsible (see p212).

  If you are liable to pay service charge payments to the person, you are also treated as not liable for those payments;
- **a trustee of a trust** and the trustees or beneficiaries of that trust include:
  - you, your partner or a child or qualifying young person for whom you (or your partner) are responsible (see p212); *or*
  - a close relative of yours or your partner, or of a child or qualifying young person for whom you (or your partner) are responsible (see p212).

  If you are liable to pay service charge payments to a trustee of the same trust or of another trust whose trustees or beneficiaries include any of the people listed above, you are also treated as not liable for those payments;
- **a company** and the owners or directors of the company include:
  - you, your partner or a qualifying young person for whom you (or your partner) are responsible (see p212); *or*
  - a close relative of yours or your partner, or of a qualifying young person for whom you (or your partner) are responsible (see p212). The close relative must live with you in the accommodation.

  If you are liable to pay service charge payments to the same company, or a company whose owners or directors include any of the people listed above, you are also treated as not liable for those payments.

Close relative

A '**close relative**'is a parent, parent-in-law (including a civil partner's parent), son, son-in-law (including a son's civil partner), daughter, daughter-in-law (including a daughter's civil partner), brother, sister, step-parent (including a parent's civil partner), stepson (including a civil partner's son), stepdaughter (including a civil partner's daughter), or the partners of any of these.[32] It also includes half-brothers and sisters.[33] Relations with in-laws or step-relatives are severed by divorce (or dissolution of a civil partnership) but arguably not by death – eg, a stepchild is still a stepchild after the death of her/his mother.

Owner-occupier and service charge payments

You are treated as not liable to make owner-occupier payments if you are liable to make them to someone who lives in your household (see p215 for the meaning).[34] If you are liable to pay service charge payments to the same person, you are also treated as not liable for those payments.

Contrived agreements

Even if none of the specified situations above apply, you may still be treated as not liable to make rent, owner-occupier or service charge payments if your liability was 'contrived' to get the housing costs element included in your UC, or to increase the amount of your housing costs element.[35] For your agreement to count as contrived, it must amount to an abuse of the UC scheme or to taking improper advantage of it – ie, that the main reason you entered into the agreement to make payments was to obtain or increase your UC housing costs element.[36] All the circumstances should be taken into account when deciding whether this is the case, including what your landlord or other person you are liable to pay has to say.[37] An agreement can count as contrived even if it was created from the best of motives.[38] Bear the following in mind.

- Your agreement should not count as contrived just because the person you are liable to pay is your parent[39] or because you hope to be able to claim UC to help you with your rent or mortgage – ie, if your main purpose is to get accommodation, not to obtain the UC housing costs element.[40]
- You should not be regarded as having a contrived agreement just because you try to find out what payments can be covered by UC – eg, before moving in.
- Tenants of a landlord who deliberately charges high rents to have them paid by UC may be affected by this provision, even if they had no such intention themselves. However, the fact that a landlord sets a high rent does not, in itself, mean that the liability is contrived.[41]
- If your landlord will evict you if you cannot get the UC housing costs element, or get it increased, this suggests that the agreement is *not* contrived.[42]

4. Occupying the accommodation as a home

To qualify for the universal credit (UC) housing costs element, you must normally occupy the accommodation for which you make eligible payments as your home.[43] This is called the 'occupation condition' in this *Handbook*. You cannot usually get a housing costs element for any other home. However, there are special rules if you:

- have just moved into your home (see below);
- are temporarily absent from home (see p482);
- are liable to make payments for more than one dwelling (see p483);
- have left your previous home because of a fear of domestic violence (see p484);
- are in temporary accommodation while repairs are carried out on your home (see p484).

Moving home

If you have moved into new accommodation, you are treated as occupying it for up to one month before you moved in, provided you met the payment condition

Part 4: Paying for housing
Chapter 22: Universal credit housing costs
4. Occupying the accommodation as a home

(see p474) and the liability condition (see p478) for the accommodation immediately before you moved in. This applies in the following circumstances.[44]

- There was a delay in moving into your accommodation, this was reasonable, and was necessary to enable the accommodation to be adapted to meet needs you, your partner or a child or qualifying young person for whom you (or your partner) are responsible (see p212) have because of a disability. The adaptations do not need to involve a change to the fabric or structure of the dwelling, but must be reasonably required and have a clear connection to the disability needs.[45] The person with the needs must be getting the middle or higher rate of disability living allowance (DLA) care component, attendance allowance (AA), armed forces independence payment or the daily living component of personal independence payment (PIP).

  Note: in these circumstances you may also qualify for a housing costs element for your former home (see p483), or for housing benefit (HB) for your former home if it was 'exempt accommodation' (see p105).

- You became liable to make payments on your new accommodation while you were a patient or were living in a care home (see p475 for the meaning).

Patient

For these purposes, you are a **'patient'** if you are undergoing medical or other treatment as an inpatient in any hospital or similar institution.[46] You do not have to be receiving the treatment free of charge.

Temporary absence from home

If you are only temporarily absent from the accommodation you normally occupy as a home, you can continue to be treated as occupying it for a period. You can argue that you count as temporarily absent from accommodation even if you have not yet stayed there – eg, you move your furniture and belongings in, but then have to go into hospital.[47] A new period of absence starts if you return home for even a short stay. A stay of at least 24 hours may be enough.[48]

You are treated as occupying your normal home:[49]

- **indefinitely** if you have to live in other accommodation because repairs are being carried out on your normal home (but see p484);

- for up to **12 months** if you are living away from your normal home because of a fear of domestic violence (see p484). In these circumstances, you may also qualify for a housing costs element for your current home (see p484). **Note:** you are no longer treated as occupying your normal home when your absence has lasted, or is expected to last, longer than 12 months;

- for up to **six months** in any other circumstances, whatever the reason for your absence. You are no longer treated as occupying your normal home when your absence has lasted, or is expected to last, longer than six months. **Note:** if you are a prisoner or are on temporary release from prison, you can get a housing costs element under this rule while you are temporarily absent from home, but only if you were entitled to UC as a single person immediately before you became a prisoner, your UC included a housing costs element and your prison sentence is not expected to last more than six months.[50] If you are a member of a couple, your partner may be able to continue to claim UC with a housing costs element in your absence.

Note:
• The decision whether or not your absence from home is expected to last longer than the time allowed should be initially based on the circumstances on the date you leave your home.[51] If at any time after the date you left home you no longer intend to return, or it becomes likely that you will be away from home for more than the the time allowed, your entitlement can be reconsidered.[52]
• If you are temporarily absent from Great Britain for longer than a set period, your entitlement to UC may be affected. See p1584 for further information.

More than one dwelling

You cannot usually be treated as occupying accommodation which consists of more than one dwelling.[53] If you do, to decide which dwelling you normally occupy as your home, the DWP must consider all the circumstances, including the people who live with you in each dwelling.

You can get the housing costs element for two dwellings:
• for up to **one month**, if there was a delay in moving into your new accommodation, this was reasonable, and was necessary to enable the accommodation to be adapted to meet needs you, your partner or a child or qualifying young person for whom you (or your partner) are responsible (see p212) have because of a disability.[54] The adaptations must involve a change to the fabric or structure of the dwelling, not just decorating or furnishing it.[55] You can only get a housing costs element for both your previous and your new accommodation if you have moved into your new accommodation, and:
  – the person with the needs gets the middle or higher rate of DLA care component, AA, armed forces independence payment or the daily living component of PIP; *and*
  – immediately before you moved, you qualified for a housing costs element for your previous accommodation and you satisfied the payment condition (see p474) and the liability condition (see p478) for your new accommodation.
  Note: if you are only liable to make payments for your new accommodation, you may qualify for a housing costs element for that accommodation (see p481);
• for up to **12 months**, if you are living away from your normal home because of a fear of domestic violence. See p484 for how you can qualify;

Part 4: Paying for housing
Chapter 22: Universal credit housing costs
4. Occupying the accommodation as a home

- **indefinitely**, if you have been housed in two dwellings by a 'provider of social housing'.[56] This must be because of the number of children and qualifying young people who live with you. You must normally occupy both dwellings with the children or qualifying young people for whom you (or your partner) are responsible (see p212). You must meet the payment condition (see p474) and the liability condition (see p478) for both dwellings.

Provider of social housing

A 'provider of social housing' is a local authority, a non-profit registered provider of social housing, a profit-making registered provider of social housing (if you have been housed in social housing) or a registered social landlord.[57]

Domestic violence

If you are living in accommodation other than your normal home, and it is unreasonable to expect you to return to that home because of a reasonable fear of violence against you or any child or qualifying young person for whom you are responsible (see p212):[58]

- you are treated as occupying both the accommodation you are living in, and the accommodation you normally live in, for up to 12 months if:
  - you meet the payment condition (see p474) and the liability condition (see p478) for both your current accommodation and your normal home; *and*
  - it is reasonable to include an amount for the payments for both homes in your housing costs element; *or*
- if you only meet the payment condition and the liability condition for one of the homes, you are treated as occupying that home. This could be your current accommodation or your normal home. It must be reasonable to include an amount for the payments for that accommodation in your housing costs element. **Note:** if one of the homes is 'exempt accommodation' (see p474), you can qualify for HB for the exempt accommodation and can get a housing costs element for the other home.

You must fear violence in your normal home, or from a former partner, and must intend to return to your normal home.

Note: you are no longer treated as occupying your normal home when your absence has lasted, or is expected to last, longer than 12 months.[59]

Temporary accommodation while repairs are carried out

If you are required to move into temporary accommodation because essential repairs are being carried out on your normal home, but you intend to return to that home, and you:[60]

- only meet the payment condition (see p474) and the liability condition (see p478) for one of the homes, you are treated as occupying that home and you get a housing costs element for the payments you make in respect of it indefinitely; *or*
- meet the payment condition (see p474) and the liability condition (see p478) for both homes, you are treated as occupying your normal home and you get a housing costs element for the payments you make for that home indefinitely.

'Essential repairs' means basic works rather than luxuries, but they need not be crucial to make the house habitable.[61]

5. The rules about your age

You must be aged at least 18 and under the qualifying age for pension credit (see p78) to qualify for universal credit (UC). Some 16/17-year-olds may be able to qualify (see p896). If you qualify for UC and satisfy the rules in this chapter, you can get a housing costs element. **Note:** if you are:

- 16 or 17 and were previously looked after by a local authority (see p886), you cannot qualify for a housing costs element for rent payments;[62]
- a single claimant under 35 without children, and are living in private rented or temporary accommodation, the amount of your housing costs element for rent payments may be restricted to the local housing allowance for one-bedroom shared accommodation, even if you live in larger accommodation (see p398).

6. The amount for rented accommodation

If you live in rented accommodation, how you calculate the amount of your housing costs element depends on whether you are a private tenant (or live in temporary accommodation) (see p486) or whether you are a social rented sector tenant (unless you live in temporary accommodation) (see p489). In all cases, to calculate your housing costs element, you must first work out the following.

- The monthly equivalent of your rent payments, if these are paid other than calendar monthly.[63] For example, if you pay your rent:
  - weekly, multiply by 52 and divide by 12;
  - two-weekly, multiply by 26 and divide by 12;
  - four-weekly, multiply by 13 and divide by 12;
  - three-monthly, multiply by four and divide by 12;
  - annually, divide by 12.

  If you have a regular rent-free period, to work out the monthly equivalent divide the total payments you make over the year by 12 – eg, if you have four

Part 4: Paying for housing
Chapter 22: Universal credit housing costs
6. The amount for rented accommodation

rent-free weeks each year and so only pay rent for 48 weeks, divide the total of the 48-week payments by 12.
- The number of bedrooms you are allowed under the size criteria (see p492).
- Who counts as a member of your 'extended benefit unit' (broadly, the people who live with you in your accommodation – see p494).

Note:
- Your housing costs element is calculated for each assessment period during which you qualify for universal credit (UC).
- If a housing costs element is included in your UC maximum amount, a lower work allowance may apply (ie, a higher amount of your earnings are taken into account) – see p188.
- Special rules apply if you qualify for a housing costs element for more than one dwelling (see p497).
- If you are a joint tenant, the housing costs element calculation takes this into account (see p488 and p490).
- If you have a shared ownership tenancy (ie, you are buying part of your home and renting the rest), your housing costs element can include both the rent and owner-occupier payments you make (see p498).[64] Your service charge payments are calculated as for rent payments.
- You and other people in your 'extended benefit unit' (see p494) can continue to be included in working out how many bedrooms you are allowed under the size criteria while absent from home for a temporary period (see p482 and p495).[65]
- If your partner or a child or qualifying young person for whom you (or your partner) was responsible (see p212), a non-dependant or a severely disabled person for whom you were caring dies, your UC continues to be calculated as if s/he has not died for the assessment period in which the death occurred and the following two assessment periods. This means, for example, that if you are no longer allowed as many bedrooms under the size criteria, this does not affect your housing costs element until after the three assessment periods.[66]
- Your housing costs element, is normally paid to you. However, payment can be made to another person (eg, your landlord) if it appears to the DWP to be necessary to protect your interests, those of your partner or any child or adult for whom you get UC, or those of a severely disabled person for whom you are caring and in respect of whom you get a carer element.[67]

Private tenancies and temporary accommodation

If you are a private tenant, or you live in temporary accommodation, your housing costs element is calculated as follows.[68]
- **Step one:** work out your core rent (see p487) and your cap rent (see p488).
- **Step two:** if your extended benefit unit (see p494) includes any non-dependants, deduct any housing costs contribution that applies (see p496)

from the lowest of your core rent or your cap rent. This is the amount of your housing costs element. It can never be lower than nil – ie, no further reduction can be made to your UC award.[69]

Note: if you qualify for a housing costs element for more than one dwelling, special rules apply (see p497).

Temporary accommodation

Your accommodation is **'temporary accommodation'** if you live in specified homeless accommodation that does not count as 'exempt accommodation' (see p474) and your rent is payable to a local authority or a provider of social housing (see p484 for the meaning).[70] **Note:** if you live in 'exempt accommodation' you may qualify for housing benefit (HB) for the rent you pay there.

Examples

Hannah, aged 24, is a joint tenant of a private flat with three friends. The rent for the flat is £1,000 a month, including services. She is the only member of her extended benefit unit; her joint tenants do not count as non-dependants.

Step one: Hannah's core rent is £1,000 ÷ 4 x 1 = £250 a month.

Hannah's cap rent is the local housing allowance for one-bedroom shared accommodation. In her area this is £240 a month. Her cap rent is lower than her core rent.

Step two: Hannah's housing costs element is, therefore, £240.

Patrick and Isla rent a three-bedroom private flat. They pay £150 a week. Their rent includes service charge payments for the communal lift. Patrick's uncle Gerald lives with them. Gerald is in full-time work.

Step one: Patrick and Isla's core rent is £150 x 52 ÷ 12 = £650 a month. Their cap rent is the local housing allowance for two-bedroom accommodation (under the size criteria, they are allowed one bedroom for themselves and one bedroom for Gerald). In their area, the local housing allowance rate is £520 a month. Their cap rent is lower than their core rent.

Step two: Patrick and Isla's extended benefit unit includes one non-dependant. Their housing costs element is therefore £451.32 (£520 - £68.68 housing costs contribution).

Core rent

If you are **solely liable** to make payments, your 'core rent' is the sum of all the eligible rent and service charge payments that you are liable (or treated as liable) to make for your home – ie, the amounts you actually pay.[71] If you pay your rent or service charges other than calendar monthly, you must work out the monthly equivalent.

Part 4: Paying for housing
Chapter 22: Universal credit housing costs
6. The amount for rented accommodation

If you are **jointly liable** to make payments with someone, different rules apply. Your core rent is worked out using the following steps.[72]

- **Step one:** work out the sum of all of the eligible rent and service charge payments for which you and your joint tenant(s) are liable, for the whole of the accommodation, using the monthly equivalents.
- **Step two:** if:
  - the only people who are jointly liable are in the list of 'relevant family members' below (eg, only you and your partner are liable), your core rent is the amount in Step one; *or*
  - one or more people in the list of relevant family members below are jointly liable with one or more others who are not relevant family members (eg, you and a friend are joint tenants), divide the amount in Step one by the total number of people who are liable and multiply by the number of relevant family members who are liable. This is your core rent. However, if the DWP is satisfied that it would be unreasonable to take this amount as your core rent, it must apportion the amount in a manner it considers appropriate, taking into account the number of people who are jointly liable and the amount of the rent and service charge payments for which each is liable.

If you qualify for a housing costs element for **more than one home** and this is because you have been housed in two dwellings because of the number of your children (see p484), your housing costs element is calculated using a single calculation.[73] All the eligible rent payments and service charge payments are taken into account.

Relevant family members

The **'relevant family members'** (the DWP may call these 'listed persons') are you, your partner and any child or qualifying young person for whom you (or your partner) are responsible (see p212).[74]

Example

Jan and her partner Lois are joint tenants of a two-bedroom private flat with a friend.

Step one: The rent for the flat is £120 a week. The monthly equivalent is £120 x 52 ÷ 12 = £520

Step two: Jan and her partner are jointly liable with a person who is not a 'relevant family member'. Their core rent is therefore £520 ÷ 3 (the number of joint tenants) x 2 (the number of relevant family members) = £346.67 a month.

Cap rent

Your 'cap rent' is normally the local housing allowance for the category of dwelling that applies to you, in the area where you live.[75]

This depends on how many bedrooms you are allowed under the size criteria (see p492), to a maximum of four bedrooms. To work out which category of dwelling applies, see p398. The rules are the same as for HB. See p400 for information about the local housing allowance rates. The rules are the same as for HB.

Note: your housing costs element is based on the local housing allowance that is appropriate at the time your housing costs element is calculated.[76]

If you qualify for a housing costs element for **more than one home**, and this is because you have been housed in two dwellings because of the number of your children (see p484), your housing costs element is calculated using a single calculation.[77] If the cap rents for the two dwellings are different (eg, because they are in different areas), the lowest amount at the time your housing costs element is first calculated is used.[78] Your housing costs element continues to be calculated on the basis of the cap rent for that dwelling until you move to other accommodation.

Example

Phil and Holly have been housed by the local authority in temporary accommodation. They have been housed in two dwellings because they have five children: two girls aged 15 and 17, and three boys aged 12, 14 and 20. Holly's mother lives with them. Under the size criteria, they are allowed six bedrooms: one bedroom for Phil and Holly, one bedroom each for the two girls, one bedroom for the youngest boys, one bedroom for the oldest boy and one bedroom for Holly's mother. Their cap rent is limited to the local housing allowance for a four-bedroom dwelling. For one dwelling, this is £950 a month and for the other, which is in a different area, this is £1,000 a month. Their cap rent is therefore £950.
Note: their core rent is the sum of the eligible payments they make for *both* dwellings.

Social rented sector tenancies

You are a 'social rented sector' tenant if you pay your rent to a 'provider of social housing' (see p484).[79] If you are a social rented sector tenant (other than if you live in specified temporary accommodation – see p487) and you are **solely liable** to make payments, your housing costs element is worked out as follows.[80]

- **Step one:** work out the number of bedrooms you are allowed under the size criteria (see p492).
- **Step two:** work out the amount of your eligible rent payments (see p474).[81] If you pay your rent other than calendar monthly, work out the monthly equivalent (see p485).
- **Step three:** work out the amount of your eligible service charge payments (see p476).[82] Deduct any amount that relates to the supply of a 'commodity' to your accommodation – eg, for water or fuel. If you pay your service charges other than calendar monthly, work out the monthly equivalent (see p485).

Part 4: Paying for housing
Chapter 22: Universal credit housing costs
6. The amount for rented accommodation

- **Step four:** total the payments in Step two and Step three. Unless Step five or Step six apply, this is your housing costs element.
- **Step five:** if the number of bedrooms in your home is greater than the number of bedrooms you are allowed under the size criteria (see p492), reduce the amount in Step four by:[83]
  - 14 per cent, if you have one too many bedrooms; *or*
  - 25 per cent if you have two or more too many bedrooms.

  Note: this does not apply if you have a shared ownership tenancy.

  Unless Step six applies, this is your housing costs element.
- **Step six:** if your extended benefit unit includes any non-dependants, deduct any housing costs contribution that applies (see p496), from the amount in Step four or Step five as appropriate.[84] This is your housing costs element.

Bedrooms

'**Bedroom**' is not defined in the rules. It is the ordinary meaning of the word that is relevant – ie, a room is a bedroom if it is furnished and used for sleeping in. You can try to argue that the DWP should not count a room in your home as a bedroom, and therefore that your rent and service charge payments should not be reduced (or reduced as much) under these rules. Suggest that the DWP should, for example, take into account:

– the size of the room – eg, if it is too small to fit a single bed;

– your personal use of the room – eg, if you use the room to store equipment you need because of a severe disability;

– whether your home has been converted or adapted – eg, if two small bedrooms have been converted into one big bedroom.

If you are **jointly liable** to make payments with someone, different rules apply.[85] Work out the total of the monthly equivalent of the eligible rent and service charge payments for which you and your joint tenant(s) are liable, for the whole of the dwelling. Then, if:

- the only people who are jointly liable are in the list of relevant family members on p488 (eg, you and your partner are the only joint tenants), a reduction is made as under Step five above (unless you have a shared ownership tenancy) if the number of bedrooms in your home is greater than the number you are allowed under the size criteria; *or*
- one or more people in the list of relevant family members on p488 are jointly liable with one or more others who are not relevant family members (eg, you and a friend are joint tenants), divide the total rent and service charge payments by the total number of people who are liable and multiply by the number of relevant family members who are liable to get the amount that can be included. However, if the DWP is satisfied that it would be unreasonable to

take this amount as your rent, it must apportion the amount in a manner it considers appropriate, taking into account the number of jointly liable people and the amount of the rent and service charge payments for which each is liable. **Note:** no reduction is made as under Step five. It is not known if this is an error or the intention.

If your extended benefit unit includes any non-dependants, deduct any housing costs contribution that applies (see p496).[86]

Note:

- In all cases, your housing costs element can never be lower than nil – ie, no further reduction can be made to your UC award.[87]
- If you qualify for a housing costs element for more than one dwelling, special rules apply (see p497). In addition, if you have been housed in two dwellings by a provider of social housing because of the number of your children (see p484), your housing costs element is calculated using a single calculation.[88] All the eligible payments for both dwellings are taken into account, and the number of bedrooms you are treated as having is the total number in both dwellings.

Examples

Kirsty rents a four-bedroom house from the local authority. She and her partner live there with their 14-year-old daughter. Their rent is £125 a week. They have four rent-free weeks every year. Their 'extended benefit unit' does not include any non-dependants.

Step one: They are allowed two bedrooms under the size criteria: one bedroom for Kirsty and her partner and one bedroom for their daughter.

Step two: The monthly equivalent of their rent payments is £125 x 48 ÷ 12 = £500.

Step three: They do not have any service charge payments.

Step four: The total payment is £500 a month.

Step five: They have two bedrooms too many. The amount in Step four must be reduced by 25 per cent. 25 per cent of £500 = £125. £500 – £125 = £375

Their housing costs element is therefore £375 a month.

Len is the joint tenant of a three-bedroom housing association flat with his friend. The rent is £180 a week.

The monthly equivalent of the rent payments is £180 x 52 ÷ 12 = £780 a month.

They do not have any service charge payments.

The total payment is £780 a month.

Len is the only relevant family member. The amount that can be included in his housing costs element is therefore £780 ÷ 2 (the number of joint tenants) x 1 (the number of relevant family members) = £390 a month.

Len's 'extended benefit unit' does not include any non-dependants. His housing costs element is therefore £390 a month.

Part 4: Paying for housing
Chapter 22: Universal credit housing costs
6. The amount for rented accommodation

Your housing costs element may be lower if the DWP thinks your rent or service charge payments are higher than it is reasonable for a housing costs element to meet.[89] In this case, the DWP can apply to the rent officer. If the rent officer thinks that your landlord could reasonably have expected to get a lower amount of rent than what you pay, the lower amount is used to calculate your housing costs element, unless the DWP is satisfied that this is not appropriate.

The number of bedrooms you are allowed

If you live in rented accommodation, to calculate your housing costs element you need to know how many bedrooms you are allowed under what is known as the 'size criteria'. This depends on the number, ages and gender of the people who count as members of your 'extended benefit unit' (see p494).

You are allowed:[90]

- one bedroom for each of the following members of your extended benefit unit (see p494):
  - you (and your partner if you are a member of a couple);
  - a qualifying young person for whom you (or your partner) are responsible (see p212);
  - a non-dependant aged at least 16 (see p494 for who counts);
  - two children under 16 of the same sex;
  - two children under 10;
  - any other child under 16.

  If a member of your extended benefit unit fits into more than one category, s/he is treated as being in the category that results in the lowest number of bedrooms; *and*
- one or more additional bedrooms in specified situations (see p493).

Note:
- If you are a private tenant (or you live in specified temporary accommodation), the maximum number of bedrooms you are allowed (including any additional bedrooms) is four. If you are a social sector tenant, there is no maximum number of bedrooms.
- People can be treated as part of your extended benefit unit during a temporary absence from home (see p495). In some cases, this only applies for a period.

Example
Michael and Barbara have two daughters, aged 10 and 13, and two sons, aged 15 and 22. The 10-year-old daughter is severely disabled and is unable to share a bedroom because of this. Michael's parents live with them. They claim UC. Under the size criteria, they are allowed one bedroom for Michael and Barbara, one bedroom for the daughters, one bedroom each for the sons and one bedroom for each of Michael's parents. They are allowed an additional bedroom for their 10-year-old daughter. They are therefore allowed a total of seven bedrooms. If they are private tenants or live in specified temporary

accommodation, their housing costs element is calculated based on a four-bedroom property – the maximum allowed. If they are social sector tenants, their housing costs element is not restricted unless they have more than seven bedrooms.

Additional bedrooms

In addition to the number of bedrooms you are allowed (see above), you are allowed one or more additional bedrooms if you satisfy one of the following conditions. If you satisfy more than one of the conditions, you are allowed the total number of additional bedrooms to which you are entitled under each condition you satisfy.[91]

- You are allowed one additional bedroom for a non-resident carer if you (or your partner) need, and have arranged for, someone to stay overnight and provide care regularly.[92] You (or your partner) must get getting attendance allowance (AA), the middle or highest rate of disability living allowance (DLA) care component, the daily living component of personal independence payment (PIP) or armed forces independence payment. Even if both you and your partner require overnight care, only one additional bedroom is allowed.
- You (or your partner) or another member of your extended benefit unit (eg, a non-dependant) are responsible for a child under 16, who would normally be expected to share a bedroom under the size criteria above, but cannot reasonably do so because of her/his disability. The child must be getting the middle or highest rate of DLA care component. If more than one child qualifies, you are allowed as many additional bedrooms as you need to ensure that each has her/his own bedroom.
- You are allowed one additional bedroom if you (or your partner) have a child placed with you for adoption or you are a foster parent (in Scotland this includes foster and kinship carers). If you are a foster parent, you meet this condition even if you do not currently have a child placed with you, provided you have become an approved foster carer, or have fostered a child, within the last 12 months. You are only allowed one bedroom even if, for example, you have more than one foster child, or if both you and your partner are foster parents or adopters.

Example
Jim is the foster parent of two sisters aged 10 and 16. He has two sons aged 10 and 12, one of whom is getting the middle rate of DLA care component and cannot share a bedroom because of his disability. Under the size criteria, Jim is allowed one bedroom for himself, and would normally be allowed one bedroom for his two sons. However, he is allowed one additional bedroom for his disabled son, and one additional bedroom because he is a foster parent. He is therefore allowed a total of four bedrooms.

Part 4: Paying for housing
Chapter 22: Universal credit housing costs
6. The amount for rented accommodation

The rules do not allow additional bedrooms for any other reason than those shown above. In addition, before 4 December 2013, an additional bedroom might not have been allowed (when it should have been) for a severely disabled child who could not share a bedroom. You should appeal if you are (or were) affected, and think you should be allowed more bedrooms than shown above – eg, to store equipment required because of a severe disability, or for a disabled child who needs overnight care, or for a partner who is unable to share a bedroom with you because of severe disabilities.[93] **Note:** you are likely to have to apply for a revision before you can appeal.

Extended benefit unit

The members of your extended benefit unit are:[94]
* you;
* your partner;
* any child or qualifying young person for whom you (or your partner) are responsible (see p212);
* any non-dependant (see below for who counts).

Note: people can continue to count as a member of your extended benefit unit for the purposes of working out how many bedrooms you are allowed under the size criteria while absent from home for a temporary period (see p495).

Who counts as a non-dependant
Other people who normally live in your accommodation with you (other than your partner and any children are called 'non-dependants'.
Examples of non-dependants are adult sons or daughters, or elderly relatives who share your home.

A person only counts as your non-dependant if s/he normally lives with you (and your partner) in your accommodation.[95] So, for example, if someone is only staying with you temporarily but has a home elsewhere, or is homeless and is only using your address as a postal address, s/he should not count as a non-dependant. If you think the DWP has wrongly assumed that a person is your non-dependant, ask for a revision or appeal. **Note:** some people do not count as non-dependants even if they live with you (see p495).

A person is only 'living with you' if s/he has her/his home with you and shares some accommodation with you.[96] This includes sharing the kitchen (unless it is only used by someone else to prepare food for her/him[97]). A person living with you in your accommodation who is separately liable to pay rent to your landlord does not count as a non-dependant (see p495).

A person should only count as 'normally living with you' if s/he has been there long enough to regard your home as her/his normal home.[98]

A number of factors should be taken into account to decide whether a person normally lives with you, including:

- the relationship between you;
- how much time s/he spends at your address;
- where her/his post is sent;
- where s/he keeps her/his clothes and personal belongings;
- whether her/his stay or absence from your address is temporary or permanent, and if s/he is absent temporarily, how long the absence has lasted (see below);
- whether s/he has another place that could be regarded as home and if, for instance, s/he pays rent there or s/he just travels around.

4

People who are not non-dependants

The following people do *not* count as non-dependants and no deduction for housing costs contributions is made for them, even if they normally live with you in your accommodation:[99]

- your partner;
- a child or qualifying young person for whom you (or your partner) are responsible (see p212);
- a child or qualifying young person for whom no one in your extended benefit unit (see p494) is responsible;
- if you (or your partner) are a foster parent, your foster child(ren);
- someone to whom you (or your partner) are liable to make rent or service charge payments, and any member of her/his household – eg, your resident landlord and her/his family;
- someone who has already been treated as the non-dependant of another UC claimant, if the other claimant is also liable to make rent or service charge payments for the accommodation you occupy. A deduction is only made from the housing costs element of one claimant (or pair of joint claimants);
- someone who is liable to make rent or service charge payments on a commercial basis for the accommodation you occupy, whether this is to you or your partner, or to another person – eg, s/he is your lodger or sub-tenant, or a joint tenant.

Temporary absence from home

When determining how many bedrooms you are allowed under the size criteria, people can continue to be included in your extended benefit unit while temporarily absent from your home.[100]

You (or your partner) are included during:[101]

- the one- (or two-) month period you (or your partner) continue to qualify for UC while temporarily absent from Great Britain (see p1584); *or*
- the first six months you (or your partner) are a prisoner, provided immediately before becoming a prisoner, you were getting a housing costs element and your (or your partner's) sentence is not expected to last longer than six months.

Part 4: Paying for housing
Chapter 22: Universal credit housing costs
6. The amount for rented accommodation

If immediately before the start of the period of absence, s/he was included in your extended benefit unit and you were getting a housing costs element, **your child or qualifying young person** is included:[102]
- during the first six months of her/his absence if s/he is:
  – being looked after by the local authority; *or*
  – a prisoner, provided s/he has not been sentenced to a term of custody that is expected to last longer than six months;
- in any other case, for the period you continue to be treated as responsible for her/him while s/he is absent from your household (see p213).

If, immediately before the start of the period of absence, s/he was included in your extended benefit unit, **your non-dependant** is included:[103]
- indefinitely, if s/he is your (or your partner's) son, daughter, stepson or stepdaughter who is a member of the armed forces deployed on operations;
- during the one- (or two-) month period s/he continues (or would have continued) to qualify for UC while temporarily absent from Great Britain (see p1584);
- during the first six months of her/his absence if s/he is:
  – temporarily absent from Great Britain to receive medical treatment or convalescence or to take her/his partner, child or a qualifying young person for medical treatment or convalescence (see p1584);
  – a prisoner, provided her/his sentence is not expected to last longer than six months;
- in any other case, for up to six months. However, s/he is no longer included if the absence lasts (or is expected to last) longer than six months.

Note: other than if your non-dependant is a member of the armed forces deployed on operations, you must also have been getting a housing costs element immediately before the start of the period.

Housing costs contributions

If you have a 'non-dependant' living with you (see p494), a set deduction is usually made from your housing costs element for rent payments.[104] This is because it is assumed that the non-dependant makes a contribution towards your outgoings, whether or not s/he does so. The DWP calls these deductions 'housing costs contributions'. They are also known as 'non-dependant deductions'. In some circumstances, no deductions are made (see below).

No housing costs contribution

Even if you have a non-dependant, no deduction is made for any housing costs contribution if you (or your partner):[105]
- are registered blind; *or*

- receive AA (or equivalent benefits paid because of injury at work or a war injury), the middle or highest rate care component of DLA, the daily living component of PIP or armed forces independence payment, or would receive one of these but for being in hospital.

No deduction for a housing costs contribution is made in respect of any non-dependant who is:[106]
- staying with you but who does not live with you in your accommodation – ie, her/his home is elsewhere;
- receiving AA, the middle or highest rate of DLA care component, the daily living component of PIP or armed forces independence payment, or who would receive it but for being in hospital;
- receiving carer's allowance;
- receiving pension credit;
- a prisoner;
- under 21 years old;
- your (or your partner's) son, daughter, stepson or stepdaughter who is in the armed forces and is deployed on operations. **Note:** this only applies if s/he lived with you immediately before leaving, and intends to live with you at the end of the operations;
- responsible for a child under five.

The amount of the deduction

If a deduction for a housing costs contribution must be made, it is made for every non-dependant who is a member of your extended benefit unit (see p494).[107] The deduction is a fixed amount of £68.68 for the assessment period, whatever her/his income and whatever s/he pays you.[108]

Special rules: more than one dwelling

If you qualify for a housing costs element for more than one dwelling, and this is because:
- you have been **housed in two dwellings** by a provider of social housing because of the number of your children (see p484), your housing costs element is calculated using a single calculation.[109] All the eligible payments for both dwellings are taken into account, and the number of bedrooms you are treated as having is the total number in both dwellings. Your housing costs element is calculated as for social rented sector tenancies (see p489) if you pay rent to a social sector landlord for both dwellings and neither is temporary accommodation. Otherwise, your housing costs element is calculated as for private sector tenancies (see p486);
- there was a **delay in moving** into your home because of adaptations for a disabled person and you qualify for a housing costs element for both your old and your new accommodation (see p483), amounts are calculated for each

Part 4: Paying for housing
Chapter 22: Universal credit housing costs
7. The amount for owner-occupiers

home as for social rented sector or private sector tenancies (as appropriate) and your housing costs element is the total of these.[110] However, a housing costs contribution for a non-dependant (see p496) is only deducted from the rent payments for your old home;
* you are living away from your normal accommodation because of a fear of **domestic violence** and qualify for a housing costs element for both your current and your normal home (see p484), amounts are calculated for each home as for social rented sector or private sector tenancies (as appropriate) and your housing costs element is the total of these.[111] However, housing costs contributions from non-dependants (see p496) are only deducted from the rent payments for the home you are occupying.

7. The amount for owner-occupiers

If you are an owner-occupier, your housing costs element can include an amount for owner-occupier payments and service charge payments. The amount you get for owner-occupier payments is not the amount you pay, but is calculated using a formula. Remember that owner-occupier payments include both loan interest payments and alternative finance payments (see p475).

Once you have worked out which owner-occupier and service charge payments are eligible, the amount of your housing costs element is worked out as follows.[112]
* **Step one:** calculate the amount of eligible owner-occupier payments (see p499).
* **Step two:** calculate the amount of eligible service charge payments (see p502).
* **Step three:** add these amounts together. This is the amount of your housing costs element.

Note:
* Your housing costs element is calculated for each assessment period during which you qualify for universal credit (UC).
* You cannot get a housing costs element if you (or your partner) have any earned income, however much your earnings are.
* If you have a shared ownership tenancy (ie, you are buying part of your home and renting the rest), your housing costs element can also include an amount for the rent payments you make (see p485). In this case, your service charge payments are calculated as for rented accommodation.[113]
* You may only qualify for a housing costs element after a 'waiting period' (see p500).
* If your partner or a child or qualifying young person for whom you (or your partner) were responsible (see p212), or a severely disabled person for whom you were caring, dies, your UC continues to be calculated as if s/he has not died for the assessment period in which the death occurred and the following

two assessment periods. This means, for example, that her/his absence from your home does not affect your housing costs element until after the three assessment periods.[114]

- Your housing costs element is normally made directly to your lender.[115]

How your owner-occupier payments are calculated

The amount for owner-occupier payments included in your housing costs element for an assessment period is worked out using a special formula and a standard rate. It is not what you are actually liable to pay, even if this is higher or lower.[116]

At the time of writing, the standard rate was 3.63 per cent. **Note:** the standard rate is set by the DWP and can be varied. You can find out the current rate at www.gov.uk/support-for-mortgage-interest or see CPAG's online service or *Welfare Rights Bulletin* for updates.

There can be a limit on the amount of housing costs that can be paid. If the total of your loans is more than an upper limit, your loan interest payments and alternative finance payments are calculated using your upper limit (see below).

Loan interest payments

For loan interest payments (see p475), the amount of capital outstanding on your loan(s) that qualifies (or if lower, your upper limit) is multiplied by the standard rate (see above).[117] This figure is divided by 12 to reach a monthly amount. The **upper limit** for loans is normally £200,000. However, if any loan (or part of a loan) was taken out to make necessary adaptations to your accommodation to meet needs you, your partner or a child or qualifying young person for whom you (or your partner) are responsible have because of a disability:[118]

- the amount of any loan (or part of a loan) for the adaptations is disregarded in working out whether your total loans exceed £200,000; *and*
- your upper limit is £200,000 plus the amount of the loan(s) (or parts of a loan) for the adaptations.

Example

Jim and Ina Blair have a repayment mortgage and a loan for adaptations for their child's disability needs. The total outstanding is £300,000, £5,000 of which is for the adaptations. £5,000 is disregarded when working out whether their loan exceeds £200,000.

£300,000 − £5,000 = £295,000

This amount is restricted to £200,000.

£200,000 + £5,000 = £205,000

£205,000 x 3.63% (standard rate) = £7,441.50

Their housing costs element for the assessment period is £7,441.50 ÷ 12 = £620.13

Part 4: Paying for housing
Chapter 22: Universal credit housing costs
7. The amount for owner-occupiers

Alternative finance payments

For alternative finance payments (see p475), the purchase price of the accommodation to which the payments relate (or if lower, £200,000), is multiplied by the standard rate (see p499).[119] This figure is divided by 12 to reach a monthly amount. **Note:** the 'purchase price' is the price paid by a party other than you to acquire an interest in the accommodation, minus the amount of any initial payment made by you in connection with acquiring that interest and any payments made before a housing costs element was included in your UC.

4

> *Example*
> Imran's home was purchased for £125,000 with the help of a Sharia-compliant mortgage. He made an initial payment of £8,000.
> £125,000 – £8,000 (the initial payment) = £117,000
> £117,000 x 3.63% (standard rate) = £4,247.10
> His housing costs element for the assessment period is £4,247.10 ÷ 12 = £353.93

When your housing costs element is recalculated

Even if there is a change in the amount of your outstanding loan(s) or alternative finance payments, your housing costs element is only recalculated annually, on the anniversary of the date the housing costs element was first included in your UC.[120]

The waiting period

A housing costs element for owner-occupier payments (and for service charge payments if you also make these) normally cannot be included for a period (called a 'waiting period' in this *Handbook*, but the DWP may call it a 'qualifying period'). If:[121]

- you have a new award of UC (ie, you claim for the first time or claim after a break in your entitlement to UC), a housing costs element cannot be included until there have been three consecutive assessment periods in relation to which you have been receiving UC and, were it not for the waiting period rule, you would otherwise qualify for a housing costs element;
- a housing costs element ceases to be included in your UC award for any reason (eg, because you have earnings from a temporary job) but your entitlement to UC continues, a housing costs element cannot be included again until there have been three consecutive assessment periods in relation to which, were it not for the waiting period rule, you would otherwise qualify for a housing costs element.

A housing costs element is included from the start of the next assessment period. If you cease to qualify for a housing costs element for any reason during a waiting period, the waiting period stops running.[122] A new waiting period starts again from the beginning under whichever of the rules above that apply.

Example

Claire makes a claim for UC. She is unemployed at the time and has no income. She is an owner-occupier and (but for having to serve a waiting period) she qualifies for a housing costs element. She must wait three consecutive assessment periods before a housing costs element can be included in her UC. After she has been receiving UC for two months, Claire gets a temporary job. When it ends, she claims, and is awarded, UC again. A housing costs element is included once she has been receiving UC for a further three consecutive assessment periods.

Note: If you have a shared ownership tenancy (ie, you are buying part of your home and renting the rest), your housing costs element can include the rent and service charge payments you make during your waiting period for the owner-occupier payments.

Exceptions

There are limited exceptions to the general waiting period rule.

- If you come under the UC system (see p19) and you are entitled to contribution-based jobseeker's allowance (JSA) or contributory employment and support allowance (ESA) immediately before your award of UC starts, any period when you were only receiving one of those benefits may be treated as an assessment period (or part of an assessment period) that counts towards your waiting period.[123]
- If you (or a former partner) were getting income support (IS), income-based JSA or income-related ESA and this ended within one month of your becoming entitled to UC or, if you are a joint UC claimant, when you became a couple:[124]
  - if your IS/JSA/ESA included help with housing costs (see Chapter 20), you do not have to serve a waiting period, and your UC award can include a housing costs element straight away; *or*
  - if your (or your former partner's) IS/JSA/ESA did not yet include help with housing costs because you were serving a waiting period (see p453), your UC waiting period is reduced by the amount of time you were entitled to IS/JSA/ESA (including time in which you were treated as entitled under the linking rules – see p456), as well as any time between the date IS/JSA/ESA ended and the date you become entitled to UC.
- If an award of UC made while you were a joint claimant ended because you (and your now former partner) ceased to be a couple, you meet the occupation condition for the same home you occupied with your former partner and you are awarded UC:[125]

Part 4: Paying for housing
Chapter 22: Universal credit housing costs
7. The amount for owner-occupiers

– if a housing costs element was not yet included in your joint award of UC, any assessment period (or part of an assessment period) in respect of which you had been receiving UC counts towards the waiting period for your new award. For example, if you and your former partner had been receiving UC for 45 days, a housing costs element can be included once you have been receiving UC for three assessment periods, minus 45 days;

– if a housing costs element was included in your joint award of UC, you do not have to serve another waiting period; a housing costs element is included straight away.

This can also apply to your former partner – ie, if s/he continues to occupy the same accommodation and also claims, and is awarded, UC.

Service charge payments

If you are an owner-occupier and you make service charge payments, an amount for eligible service charge payments (see p476) is included in your housing costs element whether or not you also make owner-occupier payments.[126] The amount for service charge payments is calculated as follows.[127]

- **Step one:** work out the amount of each eligible service charge payment.
- **Step two:** work out the period for which each eligible service charge payment is payable, and if payments are made other than calendar monthly, work out the monthly equivalent. For example, if you pay your service charge:
  – weekly, multiply by 52 and divide by 12;
  – two-weekly, multiply by 26 and divide by 12;
  – four-weekly, multiply by 13 and divide by 12;
  – three-monthly, multiply by four and divide by 12;
  – annually, divide by 12.
- **Step three:** add all the monthly amounts together. This is the amount of service charge payments that can be included in your housing costs element.

Note: if you have a regular service charge-free period, divide the total payments you make for the year by 12. For example, if you have eight weeks each year when you do not have to pay service charges and so only pay service charges for 44 weeks, add up the payments you make over 44 weeks and divide by 12.

If your housing costs are not met in full

If you do not have enough money to pay your housing costs, you may be in danger of losing your home, particularly if you are on UC for a long time. You should inform your lender and discuss how to resolve the situation. Your lender may be prepared to accept interest-only payments for a while. It is important to discuss this in order to avoid falling into arrears and risk losing your home. Seek independent debt advice.

Ultimately, you may have to sell your home and buy somewhere cheaper. If you move out and put your house up for sale, the capital value of your property can be disregarded for a period while you take reasonable steps to sell it (see p351). If you rent it while trying to sell, see Chapter 16 for how the income is treated.

Notes

1. When you get a housing costs element
1 s11 WRA 2012; regs 25 and 26 UC Regs
2 s11(2)(c) WRA 2012
3 Reg 25(4)-(6) UC Regs
4 Reg 8 and Sch 4 para 4 UC Regs
5 Sch 5 para 4(1) and (2) UC Regs
6 Reg 26(5) and Sch 5 para 4(3) UC Regs
7 Sch 1 para 1 UC Regs
8 R(H) 7/07; R(H) 4/09; CH/3900/2005; CH/2726/2008; *East Hertfordshire DC v KT* [2009] UKUT 12 (AAC); *Bristol CC v AW* [2009] UKUT 109 (AAC)
9 R(H) 7/07; CH/1289/2007; *Salford CC v PF* [2009] UKUT 150 (AAC)
10 R(H) 2/07

2. Payments that can be met
11 Reg 25(4)-(6) UC Regs
12 Reg 25(2)(a) and Sch 1 para 2 UC Regs
13 Sch 1 paras 2 and 3 UC Regs
14 Sch 1 para 1 UC Regs
15 Reg 25(2)(b) and Sch 1 paras 4-6 UC Regs
16 Reg 25(2)(c) and Sch 1 para 7(1), (2) and (4) UC Regs
17 Sch 1 para 7(1) and (3) UC Regs
18 Sch 1 para 8(3) UC Regs
19 Sch 1 para 8(5) UC Regs
20 Sch 1 para 8(4) UC Regs
21 *Universal Credit Service Charges: guidance for landlords*, draft DWP guidance
22 Sch 1 para 8(6) UC Regs

3. Liability for payments
23 Reg 25(3) UC Regs
24 *R v Poole BC ex parte Ross* [1995] 28 HLR 351 (QBD); CH/1076/2002; CH/296/2004; CH/1097/2004
25 Sch 2 paras 1-4 UC Regs

26 Sch 2 para 2 UC Regs
27 *Ewens v Secretary of State for Social Security*, reported as R(IS) 8/01
28 Sch 2 para 9 UC Regs
29 Sch 2 para 8(3) UC Regs
30 Sch 2 paras 5-7 UC Regs
31 CH/542/2006; R(H) 5/06 decided that the similar HB rule did not conflict with the Human Rights Act.
32 Reg 2 UC Regs
33 R(SB) 27/87
34 Sch 2 para 8(1) and (2) UC Regs
35 Sch 2 para 10 UC Regs
36 *R v Solihull MBC ex parte Simpson* [1995] 1 FLR 140 (CA); CH/39/2007
37 *R (Mackay) v Barking and Dagenham HBRB* [2001] EWHC Admin 234 (HC)
38 CH/2258/2004
39 *R (Mackay) v Barking and Dagenham HBRB* [2001] EWHC Admin 234 (HC)
40 *R v Sutton LBC HBRB ex parte Keegan* [1992] 27 HLR 92 (QBD)
41 *R v Manchester CC ex parte Baragrove Properties Ltd* [1991] 23 HLR 337 (QBD); *R v Gloucestershire CC ex parte Dadds* [1997] 29 HLR 700 (QBD); CH/39/2007
42 *R v Poole BC ex parte Ross* [1995] 28 HLR 351 (QBD)

4. Occupying the accommodation as a home
43 Reg 25(4) and Sch 3 paras 1(1) and 2 UC Regs
44 Sch 3 paras 7 and 8 UC Regs
45 *Bury MBC v DC (HB)* [2011] UKUT 43 (AAC); *Mahmoudi v LB Lewisham and Another*, EWCA, 6 February 2014
46 Sch 3 para 8(3) UC Regs
47 R(H) 9/05

Part 4: Paying for housing
Chapter 22: Universal credit housing costs
Notes

48 *R v Penwith DC ex parte Burt* [1988] 22 HLR 292 (QBD)
49 Sch 3 para 9 UC Regs
50 Regs 2 and 19(1)(b), (2) and (3) UC Regs
51 CH/1237/2004
52 CH/3893/2004
53 Sch 3 para 1(2)-(4) UC Regs
54 Sch 3 para 5 UC Regs
55 CH/1363/2006; R(H) 4/07; *Bury MBC v DC (HB)* [2011] UKUT 43 (AAC); *DM v LB Lewisham and SSWP (HB)* [2013] UKUT 26 (AAC)
56 Sch 3 para 4 UC Regs
57 Schs 3 para 4(3) and 4 para 2 UC Regs
58 Sch 3 para 6 UC Regs
59 Sch 3 para 9(3) UC Regs
60 Sch 3 paras 3 and 9(2) UC Regs
61 R(SB) 10/81

5. The rules about your age
62 Reg 8 and Sch 4 para 4 UC Regs

6. The amount for rented accommodation
63 Sch 4 para 7 UC Regs
64 Reg 26(4)-(6) UC Regs
65 Sch 4 para 11 UC Regs
66 Reg 37 UC Regs
67 Reg 58(1) UC, PIP, JSA&ESA(C&P) Regs
68 Reg 26(2) and Sch 4 para 22 UC Regs
69 Sch 4 para 14(3) UC Regs
70 Sch 4 para 21 UC Regs
71 Sch 4 paras 3(1), 6 and 23 UC Regs
72 Sch 4 paras 3(1), 6 and 24 UC Regs
73 Sch 4 para 17 UC Regs
74 Sch 4 para 2 UC Regs
75 Sch 4 paras 25(1), (2) and (5) and 26 UC Regs
76 Sch 4 para 25(5), definition of 'relevant time', UC Regs
77 Sch 4 para 17 UC Regs
78 Sch 4 para 25(3) and (4) UC Regs
79 Sch 4 para 2 UC Regs
80 Sch 4 paras 3, 6, 30-34 and 36 UC Regs
81 Sch 4 para 34 UC Regs
82 Sch 4 paras 31 and 34 UC Regs
83 Sch 4 paras 34 and 36 UC Regs
84 Sch 4 para 33 UC Regs
85 Sch 4 paras 3, 6, 30-33 and 36 UC Regs
86 Sch 4 para 33 UC Regs
87 Sch 4 para 14(3) UC Regs
88 Sch 4 para 17 UC Regs
89 Sch 4 para 32 UC Regs
90 Sch 4 paras 2, 8 and 10 UC Regs
91 Reg 2 and Sch 4 paras 2 and 12 UC Regs

92 Reg 2, definition of 'attendance allowance' and Sch 4 para 12(3) UC Regs
93 *Burnip v Birmingham CC and others* [2012] EWCA Civ 629, 15 May 2012. A judicial review is also pending on the basis that the rules discriminate unlawfully against disabled children who need overnight care.
94 Sch 4 para 9(1) UC Regs
95 Sch 4 para 9(2) UC Regs
96 *AM v SSWP (IS)* [2011] UKUT 387 (AAC)
97 CSIS/185/1995
98 CIS/14850/1996
99 Sch 4 para 9(2) UC Regs
100 Sch 4 para 11 UC Regs
101 Sch 4 para 11(3) UC Regs
102 Sch 4 para 11(2) UC Regs
103 Sch 4 para 11(5) and (6) UC Regs
104 Sch 4 paras 13, 22 and 33 UC Regs
105 Sch 4 para 15 UC Regs
106 Sch 4 para 16 UC Regs
107 Sch 4 para 13 UC Regs
108 Sch 4 para 14(1) UC Regs
109 Sch 4 para 17 UC Regs
110 Sch 4 para 18 UC Regs
111 Sch 4 para 19 UC Regs

7. The amount for owner-occupiers
112 Reg 26(3) and Sch 5 paras 8-11 and 13 UC Regs
113 Reg 26(4)-(6) UC Regs
114 Reg 37 UC Regs
115 Reg 59 and Sch 5 UC, PIP, JSA&ESA(C&P) Regs
116 Sch 5 para 12 UC Regs
117 Sch 5 para 10 UC Regs
118 Sch 5 para 10(2) and (3) UC Regs
119 Sch 5 paras 1(2) and 11 UC regs
120 Sch 5 paras 10(4) and 11(4) UC Regs
121 Sch 5 para 5(1) and (2) UC Regs
122 Sch 5 para 5(3) UC Regs
123 Reg 2, definitions of 'JSA' and 'ESA', and Sch 5 para 6 UC Regs
124 Reg 29 UC(TP) Regs
125 Sch 5 paras 1(2) and 7 UC Regs
126 Reg 26(3) UC Regs
127 Sch 5 para 13 UC Regs

Part 5

Other benefits

Chapter 23

Attendance allowance

This chapter covers:
1. Who can claim attendance allowance (below)
2. The rules about your age (p508)
3. People included in the claim (p509)
4. The amount of benefit (p509)
5. Special benefit rules (p509)
6. Claims and backdating (p510)
7. Getting paid (p514)
8. Tax, other benefits and the benefit cap (p515)

Key facts

- Attendance allowance (AA) is a benefit for people with disabilities who have attention or supervision needs and who are aged 65 or over when they claim.
- AA is a non-means-tested benefit.
- You can qualify for AA whether or not you work.
- You do not have to have paid national insurance contributions to qualify.
- AA can be paid in addition to other benefits and is disregarded as income for means-tested benefits and tax credits.
- AA is administered and paid by the DWP's Disability and Carers Service.
- If you disagree with an AA decision, you can apply for a revision or supersession, or appeal against it. You are likely to have to apply for a revision before you can appeal.

1. Who can claim attendance allowance

You qualify for attendance allowance (AA) if:[1]
- you satisfy the residence conditions (see p1555);
- you are not a 'person subject to immigration control', although there are exceptions to this (see p1500);
- you are aged 65 or over when you first claim (see p508);
- you are not in hospital (see p944) or residential care (see p950);
- you satisfy the disability conditions (see p508);

• you are not entitled to the care component of disability living allowance (DLA) (see Chapter 27) or personal independence payment (see Chapter 35).

The disability conditions

AA can be paid at either a lower rate or a higher rate, depending on your care and supervision needs.

You get the lower rate of AA if you satisfy one of the daytime disability conditions *or* one of the night-time disability conditions.[2] This is the same disability test as for the middle rate of the care component of DLA.

You may also get the lower rate of AA if you undergo renal dialysis (see p510).

You get the higher rate of AA if you satisfy one of the daytime disability conditions *and* one of the night-time disability conditions.[3] This is the same disability test as for the highest rate of the care component of DLA.

You also get the higher rate of AA if you are terminally ill (see p510).

The **daytime disability conditions** are that you are so severely disabled, physically or mentally, that throughout the day you need:[4]

• frequent attention from another person in connection with your bodily functions; *or*
• continual supervision in order to avoid substantial danger to yourself or others.

The **night-time disability conditions** are that you are so severely disabled, physically or mentally, that at night you need:[5]

• prolonged or repeated attention from another person in connection with your bodily functions; *or*
• another person to be awake for a prolonged period or at frequent intervals to watch over you in order to avoid substantial danger to yourself or others.

See Chapter 27 for further details.

Unless you are terminally ill, you must have satisfied the disability conditions for six months before the first day of entitlement.[6]

---

2. **The rules about your age**

You can only claim attendance allowance (AA) if you are aged 65 or over. If you are approaching your 65th birthday, it may be better to claim personal independence payment (PIP) if you can rather than AA, since PIP has a mobility component in addition to a daily living component (see Chapter 35). Because the disability tests for PIP are different from those for AA, it may be worth making a claim for AA after you reach 65 if your claim for PIP is refused. Seek specialist advice if this applies to you.

Note: if you are getting either disability living allowance (DLA) or PIP when you turn 65, your award continues. You can renew your award of either benefit, and cannot claim AA while you still get it. This also means that you can claim, or continue to receive, the mobility component after you reach 65 in certain circumstances if you continue to satisfy the relevant disability conditions (see p591 for DLA and p733 for PIP).

See p591 if you need to renew or change a DLA award after you are 65 and p732 if you need to renew or change an award of PIP after you are 65. If you are 65 or over and have received DLA or PIP within the last 12 months, see p596 for DLA and p732 for PIP.

Future changes

From 2018, the minimum age at which you can claim AA is likely to change in line with pension age (see p752).

3. People included in the claim

You claim attendance allowance (AA) for yourself. You cannot claim any increase in your AA for your partner or child(ren). However, your partner may qualify for AA or personal independence payment (PIP) or have an existing award of disability living allowance (DLA) in her/his own right. Your child(ren) may qualify for DLA in their own right. See Chapter 27 for information about DLA and Chapter 35 for PIP.

4. The amount of benefit

Attendance allowance is paid at one of two weekly rates:[7]
- the lower rate is £54.45;
- the higher rate is £81.30.

5. Special benefit rules

Special rules may apply to:
- people on renal dialysis (see p510);
- people who are terminally ill (see p593);
- people subject to immigration control (see Chapter 69);
- people who have come from or are going abroad (see Chapters 70, 71 and 72);
- people in care homes or other special accommodation (see p951);
- people in hospital or a hospice (see p944);
- prisoners (see p959).

People on renal dialysis

If you are undergoing renal dialysis on a kidney machine, special rules may apply that entitle you to the lower rate of attendance allowance (AA).[8] The rules are the same as for disability living allowance (see p592).

People who are terminally ill

You are regarded as **'terminally ill'** if you have a progressive disease and can reasonably be expected to die within six months as a result.[9] This does not mean that it must be more likely than not that you will die within this period. It simply means that death within six months would not be unexpected.

If you are terminally ill, you are automatically treated as satisfying the conditions for the higher rate of AA. This is paid straight away without your having to serve the six-month qualifying period.[10]

These claims are referred to as 'claims under the special rules'.

See p511 for how to make a special rules claim.

The special rules apply only if your claim, or a request for a revision or supersession of an existing claim, expressly states that you are terminally ill.[11]

The DWP can supersede your award if your condition or prognosis improves so that you are no longer regarded as 'terminally ill'.

6. Claims and backdating

To be entitled to attendance allowance (AA), you must make a claim for it.[12] The general rules about claims and backdating are in Chapter 53. This section explains the specific rules that apply to AA.

Making a claim

A claim for AA must be in writing. You can do this by completing:
- the approved form (AA1A). Send it to the disability benefits office covering your region or any DWP office. You may also be able to take or send it to an 'alternative office' (see p1136). In practice, it is nearly always best to post the form to the disability benefits office;
- an online application form at www.gov.uk.

Note: the success of an AA claim can often depend on how well you have completed the claim form, so try to include all the information that is relevant and use extra pages if necessary. You will find useful tips on completing the form in the section about the disability living allowance (DLA) form for adults on pp598–99. However, problems you have with cooking a meal or walking out of doors may not be relevant to your claim for AA. Keep a copy of your claim form in case queries arise.

You must provide any information or evidence required (see below). In certain circumstances, the DWP may accept a written application which is not on the approved form.[13] You can amend or withdraw your claim before a decision is made (see p1138).

Claims for terminally ill people are made in a different way (see below).

Forms

Get Form AA1A from the AA Service Centre on 0845 605 6055 or 0345 605 6055 (textphone 0845 604 5312).

It is best to request a form from the DWP, as it should be date stamped. You have six weeks from the date of your request to return it.[14] Keep a record of the date you asked for the form. The DWP may complete a checklist to assess your 'potential benefit entitlement'. This is not part of the claim process and you should always be sent a claim pack.

Claim packs are also available from Citizens Advice Bureaux and other advice agencies and can be downloaded at www.gov.uk. These packs are not date stamped, so you must send in the completed form as soon as possible to secure your date of claim. This is the date on which your form is received by the DWP (see p512).

Who should claim

You normally claim AA for yourself. A claim for a person unable to manage her/his own affairs is made by an appointee (see p1137).

Claiming for terminally ill people

To claim under the special rules for terminal illness (see p510) you must provide Form DS1500, completed by your GP or consultant, detailing your medical condition. You do not need to fill in the parts of the AA claim form relating to your need for personal care.

When the decision maker receives Form DS1500, s/he makes an assessment on whether you meet the special rules. If s/he decides you do not, you can claim in the normal way or appeal the decision.

Someone else is allowed to make a claim, or to apply for a revision or supersession or to appeal, on behalf of a terminally ill person without her/his knowledge or permission.[15]

Information to support your claim

When you claim AA, you must:
- satisfy the national insurance (NI) number requirement (see p1138);

- provide proof of your identity, if required (see p1140); *and*
- ensure you have made a valid claim – ie, you must complete your claim properly and provide any information or evidence required when you claim (see p1140).

Even if you have provided all that was required when you claimed, you may be asked to provide additional information and evidence relevant to your claim (see p1152). There is a strict time limit for providing this. If you do not do so, the decision maker can decide your claim in the way most adverse to you.

Note: you may be asked to provide information after you are awarded AA. If you fail to do so, your AA could be suspended or even terminated (see p1175).

See p596 for the evidence you might want to provide to help support your claim.

The date of your claim

Claim as soon as you think you might be entitled to AA; you are not usually entitled to AA for any day before your date of claim. However, in some cases you can claim in advance (see below).

The date of your claim is the date your request for a claim pack is received by the DWP or 'alternative office' (see p1136), provided you return the properly completed form within six weeks of the date of your request.[16] If the DWP has issued a form without date stamping it, write and explain when and where it was issued and ask to be paid from that date or six weeks before you sent it in.[17] There is also some discretion to extend the six-week deadline, so if you return the form late explain why.

If you are using a claim form issued by an advice agency or downloaded from the internet, your date of claim is the date your completed form is received by the DWP.

If you claim the wrong benefit

A claim for DLA or personal independence payment (PIP) can be treated as a claim for AA and vice versa, but only if it appears to the decision maker that you are not entitled to the benefit you claimed (see p1144). A claim for an increase of industrial injuries disablement benefit where constant attendance is needed can be treated as a claim for AA and vice versa (see p1144).[18]

Claiming in advance

A claim for AA can be made before you have satisfied the six-month qualifying period for AA (see p508),[19] or any other qualifying condition. Provided you claim no more than six months before you would qualify for AA, a decision can be made on your claim in advance of your date of entitlement.

Renewal claims

AA can be awarded for fixed periods (see p514). Renewal claims can be invited up to six months before your old award expires. It is important that you return your completed renewal claim form before your old award expires as no backdating is possible.

Decision makers normally treat your renewal claim as a new claim, beginning on the day after your old award runs out.[20] However, they may use the information you give in the renewal claim to revise or supersede your existing award, in which case your entitlement may be changed earlier.[21] If you think you have a strong case for an increased award, return your renewal form early and ask for a revision or supersession. If this is not the case, it is advisable to return the form nearer the date your current award runs out.

If your AA award has ended, you can reclaim the same rate within two years without having to serve the standard six-month qualifying period again.[22] If you are over 65 and have an existing award of DLA or PIP, see p591 for the rules on reclaiming or claiming a new rate of DLA, and p732 for PIP.

How your claim is dealt with

Claims are initially dealt with at a specified office dealing with your region. A decision maker can award AA on the basis of your claim form alone, but may choose to contact someone you have named on the form for more information. It is a good idea to include details of all the medical professionals and other people who know and understand your needs and, if possible, enclose evidence from them. If the decision maker cannot get enough information, s/he may also arrange for you to be given a medical examination by a healthcare professional acting on behalf of the DWP, who will sometimes visit you at home.

If you refuse a medical examination 'without good cause', the decision maker must decide your claim against you.[23]

The decision maker may telephone you to ask for further information. If you do not want to be telephoned, write this clearly on the claim form.

The DWP aims to deal with new claims for AA within 40 working days. Claims made under the special rules for terminal illness (see p510) should be decided more quickly.[24]

Backdating your claim

It is very important to claim as soon as you think you might qualify. A claim for AA *cannot* be backdated.[25]

If you might have qualified for benefit earlier but did not claim because you were given the wrong information or were misled by the DWP, you could ask for a compensation payment (see p1382) or complain to the Ombudsman through your MP (see p1387).

7. **Getting paid**

Payment of attendance allowance (AA) is normally made by direct credit transfer into your bank (or similar) account (see p1163).[26] If you are unable to open or manage an account, it may be possible to be paid by 'simple payment' (see p1163). If you are unable to act for yourself, AA can also be paid to someone else on your behalf, called your 'appointee' (see p1137).

When is attendance allowance paid?
You are normally paid on a Monday, but the DWP can vary the payday.[27] AA is normally paid every four weeks in arrears. However, AA can be paid:
– at shorter intervals in individual cases;[28]
– weekly in advance.
If you leave hospital or a care home and expect to return within 28 days, AA can be paid at a daily rate for days at home.[29]

Note:
- If you are claiming other DWP benefits, AA may be paid in a single payment with them instead.
- Even if you have been sanctioned for a benefit offence (see p1258), you must be paid your AA.
- If you have forgotten your PIN, see p1163. If your 'simple payment' card has been lost or stolen, or if you have forgotten your memorable date, see p1164. For information on missing payments, see p1164.
- If payment of your AA is delayed, see p1382. If you wish to complain about how your claim has been dealt with, see p1383. You might be able to claim compensation (see p1382).
- If payment of your AA is suspended, see p1175.
- If you have been overpaid AA, you might have to repay it (see Chapter 56) and, in some circumstances you may have to pay a penalty (see p1249). If you have been accused of fraud, see Chapter 57.

Length of awards

Awards of AA can be made for either fixed or indefinite periods.[30] The length of an award depends on how long a decision maker estimates your current needs may last. If you have an indefinite award, you will not have to make a renewal claim at any stage, but it is always open to the DWP to reduce or stop your award if it has grounds to revise or supersede it.

There is no legal minimum length for an award.[31] If you think benefit should be awarded for longer, perhaps because your condition is such that your care needs will not decrease, you can consider asking for a revision (see p1270). Bear in mind that, if you challenge the length of your award, the rate of your award may also be reconsidered. If your award is for a limited period, you will be invited to make a renewal claim up to six months before the award runs out (see p513).

Awards under the special rules for terminal illness are normally made for a fixed period of three years (see p510).

Change of circumstances

You must report changes in your circumstances that you have been told to report, as well as any that you might reasonably be expected to know might affect your right to, the amount of, or payment of your benefit. You should do this as soon as possible, preferably in writing. See p1174 for further information.

If your condition deteriorates so that you become eligible for a higher rate, benefit can be backdated to the first payday after the end of the six-month qualifying period, provided you tell the DWP no later than a month after completing the qualifying period. If payment of (but not entitlement to) AA has stopped – eg, while you are in hospital or a care home, still notify the DWP so that the correct rate is paid when payment resumes. If you do not report a change of circumstances within the month, benefit can still be backdated if you do so within 13 months and there were special circumstances that meant it was not practical to report the change earlier.[32]

If your condition improves so that you do not qualify for the higher rate or you lose benefit altogether, the new decision usually takes effect from the date you tell the DWP of the improvement, or from the date of the decision if the DWP changed it without your asking.[33] It would only take effect from an earlier date (and cause an overpayment) if you should have realised earlier that the change should have been reported. It is accepted that it is difficult for claimants to realise when a gradual improvement begins to affect benefit entitlement.[34]

8. Tax, other benefits and the benefit cap

Tax

Attendance allowance (AA) is not taxable.[35]

Means-tested benefits

AA is not taken into account as income when calculating any of the means-tested benefits. AA is paid on top of these benefits.

If your partner is entitled to AA, your income support (IS), income-based jobseeker's allowance (JSA) and, unless you have reached the qualifying age for state pension credit (PC), housing benefit (HB) includes the disability premium (see p229) (or, for IS and JSA only, higher pensioner premium – see p232 – if either of you have reached the qualifying age for PC). If your partner receives AA, a severe disability premium is included in your IS, income-based JSA or income-related employment and support allowance (ESA) if you meet the other conditions for that premium. A severe disability premium is included in your HB, or an addition for severe disability is included in the guarantee credit of PC, if you receive AA and meet the other conditions for that premium or addition. For further information, see p233.

If you or your partner are entitled to AA, non-dependant deductions (see p450) are not made from your HB or from any housing costs included in IS, income-based JSA, income-related ESA and the guarantee credit of PC that either of you get. No housing costs contributions from a non-dependant are made from your universal credit (UC) housing costs if you, your partner or the non-dependant receive AA (see p496).

Non-means-tested benefits

AA may be paid in addition to any other non-means-tested benefits except that it 'overlaps' with armed forces independence payment and constant attendance allowance under the industrial injuries scheme (see p679) or war pensions scheme.[36] See p1165 for details of the overlapping benefits rules. You cannot claim AA if you are entitled to personal independence payment or the care component of disability living allowance.[37]

If you are receiving AA and someone regularly looks after you, that person may be entitled to carer's allowance (CA – see Chapter 25). However, your entitlement to a severe disability premium (or severe disability additional amount) can be affected if s/he receives CA.

Tax credits

AA is ignored as income when calculating child tax credit (CTC) and working tax credit (WTC). An award of AA at any rate counts as a qualifying benefit for the disabled worker element of WTC. If you or your partner get the higher rate of AA, a severe disability element is included in WTC (see Chapter 63).

The benefit cap

In some cases, the total amount of specified benefits you receive is limited to £350 a week (if you are a single claimant without children) or £500 a week (if you are a lone parent or a member of a couple). This is known as the 'benefit cap'. AA is *not* one of the specified benefits. The benefit cap only applies if you are getting HB or UC. The benefit cap does *not* apply if you or your partner receive AA, or are entitled to AA but it is not payable because you (or s/he) are in hospital or a care home. See p1169 for further information.

Passports and other sources of help

You qualify for a Christmas bonus if you receive AA at any rate (see p835). You may qualify for council tax reduction (see p827).

If any member of your household receives AA at any rate, you may get a grant for help with insulation and other energy efficiency measures in your home (see p837).

Notes

1. Who can claim attendance allowance
1 ss64, 65 and 66 SSCBA 1992; reg 2 SS(AA) Regs
2 s65(3) SSCBA 1992
3 s65(3) SSCBA 1992
4 s64(2) SSCBA 1992
5 s64(3) SSCBA 1992
6 ss65(1)(b) and 66(1)(a)(ii) SSCBA 1992

4. The amount of benefit
7 Sch 4 Part III SSCBA 1992

5. Special benefit rules
8 s65(2) SSCBA 1992; reg 5 SS(AA) Regs
9 s66(2)(a) SSCBA 1992
10 s66(1) SSCBA 1992
11 Regs 3(9)(b) and 6(6)(c) SS&CS(DA) Regs

6. Claims and backdating
12 s1 SSAA 1992
13 Reg 4(1) SS(C&P) Regs
14 Reg 6(8), (8A) and (9) SS(C&P) Regs
15 s66(2)(b) SSCBA 1992; regs 3(9)(b), 6(6)(c) and 25(b) SS&CS(DA) Regs
16 Reg 6(8), (8A) and (9) SS(C&P) Regs
17 Reg 6(8A) SS(C&P) Regs
18 Reg 9(1) and Sch 1 SS(C&P) Regs; reg 25(3) and (4) UC,PIP,JSA&ESA(C&P) Regs
19 s65(6) SSCBA 1992
20 Reg 13C SS(C&P) Regs
21 CDLA/14895/1996
22 s65(1)(b) SSCBA 1992; reg 3 SS(AA) Regs
23 s19(3) SSA 1998

24 www.gov.uk/attendance-allowance/how-to-claim
25 s65(4) SSCBA 1992

7. Getting paid
26 Reg 21 SS(C&P) Regs
27 Reg 22(3) and Sch 6 SS(C&P) Regs
28 Reg 22 SS(C&P) Regs
29 Reg 25 SS(C&P) Regs
30 s65(1)(a) SSCBA 1992
31 R(DLA) 11/02
32 Regs 7(9)(b) and 8 SS&CS(DA) Regs
33 s10(5) SSA 1998
34 Reg 7(2)(c) SS&CS(DA) Regs; *RD v SSWP (DLA)* [2011] UKUT 95 (AAC); *DC v SSWP (DLA)* [2011] UKUT 336 (AAC)

8. Tax, other benefits and the benefit cap
35 s677 IT(EP)A 2003
36 Sch 1 para 5 SS(OB) Regs
37 s64(1) and (1A) SSCBA 1992

Chapter 24

Bereavement benefits

This chapter covers:
1. Bereavement payment (p519)
2. Widowed parent's allowance (p520)
3. Bereavement allowance (p523)
4. Definition of terms (p525)
5. Special benefit rules (p528)
6. Claims and backdating (p530)
7. Getting paid (p534)
8. Tax, other benefits and the benefit cap (p535)

Key facts

- Bereavement benefits are paid to widows, widowers or surviving civil partners.
- To qualify for a bereavement benefit, your late spouse or civil partner must have satisfied the national insurance (NI) contribution conditions or died as a result of an industrial accident or disease.
- There are three main bereavement benefits: a lump-sum **bereavement payment**, **widowed parent's allowance** for people with children or for pregnant women and **bereavement allowance** for people who were at least 45 when their spouse or civil partner died.
- Bereavement benefits are non-means-tested benefits.
- You can qualify for bereavement benefits whether you are in or out of work.
- Bereavement benefits are administered and paid by the DWP.
- If you disagree with a bereavement benefit decision, you can apply for a revision or supersession, or appeal against it. You are likely to have to apply for a revision before you can appeal.

Future changes

From April 2016 at the earliest, the government plans to replace bereavement payment, widowed parent's allowance and bereavement allowance with a new benefit, 'bereavement support payment', for people under pension age whose spouse or civil partner dies on or after the date the new payment is introduced. Under the plans, bereavement support payment will have a single NI contribution condition, like that for bereavement payment (see p864), although only Class 1 and 2 NI contributions will count towards this condition. It is planned that bereavement support payment will be paid as a

* *

lump sum with monthly instalments for a year, that it will be paid at a higher rate if you are pregnant or are entitled to child benefit, and that it will be ignored for a year when calculating entitlement to universal credit.[1] See CPAG's online service and *Welfare Rights Bulletin* for updates.

* *

1. Bereavement payment

A bereavement payment is a one-off, lump-sum payment that can be paid in addition to widowed parent's allowance or bereavement allowance.

Who can claim a bereavement payment

You qualify for a bereavement payment if:[2]
- you are either:
  - a widow or widower (see p525) and your spouse died on or after 9 April 2001; *or*
  - a surviving civil partner (see p525); *and*
- your late spouse or civil partner either:
  - satisfied the national insurance contribution conditions (see p864); *or*
  - died as the result of an industrial injury or disease (see p528); *and*
- when your spouse or civil partner died, you were either:
  - under pension age (see p752); *or*
  - pension age or over and your spouse or civil partner was not entitled to a Category A retirement pension when s/he died; *and*
- you claim within the time limits if you must make a claim to qualify (see below).

See p520 if you were living with someone else when your spouse or civil partner died.

Time limit

To qualify for a bereavement payment, you must make a claim within 12 months of your spouse's or civil partner's death, unless one of the following applies.[3]
- If you were receiving retirement pension on the date your spouse or civil partner died, the 12-month time limit does not apply as you do not need to make a claim in order to qualify for a bereavement payment.[4] This rule has applied since 30 October 2008. See p26 of the 2011/12 edition of this *Handbook* for details of the rule before this date.
- If you were not aware that your spouse or civil partner had died, the normal 12-month time limit can be extended (see p533).

Disqualification

Your entitlement to a bereavement payment is not affected if you marry or enter into a civil partnership after the death of your late spouse or civil partner. However, a bereavement payment is not paid to you if, at the time of your spouse's or civil partner's death, you were cohabiting with someone else (see p527).[5]

If your spouse or civil partner was not in Great Britain at the time s/he died, you cannot always qualify for a bereavement payment – see p1553 for details.[6]

The rules about your age

There is no lower age limit for entitlement to a bereavement payment. Anyone who is legally old enough to marry or form a civil partnership may qualify.

For the upper age limit for qualifying for a bereavement payment, see p519.

People included in the claim

You claim a bereavement payment for yourself. You cannot claim any increase to a bereavement payment for your child(ren).

The amount of bereavement payment

A bereavement payment is a lump sum of £2,000.[7]

See p530 for details of how to claim a bereavement payment.

---

2. Widowed parent's allowance

Widowed parent's allowance is a weekly benefit. You cannot receive widowed parent's allowance and bereavement allowance at the same time, but you may qualify for bereavement allowance after your entitlement to widowed parent's allowance ends (see p523).

In addition to your widowed parent's allowance, you may also qualify for a bereavement payment (see p519).

Who can claim widowed parent's allowance

You qualify for widowed parent's allowance if:[8]
* you are either:
    – a widow or widower (see p525) whose spouse died on or after 9 April 2001; *or*
    – a surviving civil partner (see p525); *or*
    – a widower whose wife died before 9 April 2001 (if you are a widow whose husband died before this date, see p528); *and*
* you are under pension age (see p752); *and*

- your late spouse or civil partner either:
  - satisfied the national insurance (NI) contribution conditions (see p866); *or*
  - died as the result of an industrial injury or disease (see p528); *and*
- you are either:
  - entitled to child benefit (or treated as entitled to child benefit) for at least one eligible child (see below); *or*
  - a widow and you are pregnant by your late husband; *or*
  - a widow or a surviving civil partner and you were residing with your late husband or civil partner immediately before her/his death and you are pregnant as a result of artificial insemination by a donor or in vitro fertilisation which was carried out before her/his death. **Note:** when legislation allowing same-sex marriages comes into force in England and Wales from 13 March 2014 (similar legislation is expected in Scotland from autumn 2014), it is likely that entitlement will be extended to surviving members of same-sex marriages in this situation. See CPAG's online service and *Welfare Rights Bulletin* for updates.

Eligible child

The term 'child' in this chapter means both a 'child' and a 'qualifying young person'. The definitions of child and qualifying young person used for child benefit also apply to widowed parent's allowance (see p551).

A child only counts as an eligible child if *either*:[9]
- s/he is your and your late spouse's (or late civil partner's) son or daughter; *or*
- you were residing with your late spouse or civil partner immediately before s/he died and you were entitled, or treated as entitled (see below), to child benefit for the child at that time; *or*
- immediately before s/he died, your late spouse or civil partner was entitled, or treated as entitled, to child benefit for the child.

If you and your spouse or civil partner were living apart at the time of her/his death, you can still be considered to have been residing with her/him if your separation was only intended to be temporary.[10]

Note: if you got an increase for a dependent child in your widowed parent's allowance, or in another non-means-tested benefit, on 5 April 2003, a child who does not live with you can only count as an eligible child if, in addition to one of the above applying, you contribute £16.35 a week to the cost of supporting her/him (on top of the contribution you must make to qualify for child benefit for her/him).[11]

Can you be treated as entitled to child benefit?

1. You still count as entitled to child benefit if child benefit has been awarded to you, but you have elected for it not to be paid to avoid the high-income child benefit charge (see p568).

2. If you were residing together, you are treated as entitled to any child benefit to which your late spouse was entitled, and vice versa.[12]

3. You or your late spouse or civil partner can be treated as entitled to child benefit if you would have been entitled to it had you claimed it, and had the child in question not been abroad.[13]

4. In certain circumstances, if you were not residing with your late spouse or civil partner at the time of her/his death, s/he can be treated as having been entitled to child benefit for a child. This may apply if, before your marriage or civil partnership, you were previously widowed or your civil partner had died. If you need to rely on this rule, seek advice.[14]

Disqualification and suspension

Entitlement to widowed parent's allowance ends if you marry or enter into a civil partnership. You cannot requalify for it even if you subsequently get divorced or if your civil partnership is dissolved. It is suspended if you are cohabiting (see p527), but can be reinstated if you stop cohabiting.[15]

The rules about your age

There is no lower age limit for widowed parent's allowance. Anyone who is legally old enough to have married or formed a civil partnership may qualify. Widowed parent's allowance cannot be paid once you reach pension age (see p752), but you may then qualify for a Category A or B retirement pension (see p748).

People included in the claim

You claim widowed parent's allowance for yourself. You cannot claim an increase for a partner. See above for the effect of marriage, entering into a civil partnership or cohabiting on your entitlement to widowed parent's allowance. You cannot usually claim an increase for your child(ren).

Can you get increases for children?

You may still be entitled to an increase in your widowed parent's allowance for a child if you were entitled to it on 5 April 2003 and your entitlement has continued since that date. If the increase stops being paid for no more than 58 days, you may continue to qualify. If your entitlement to the increase ends because you stop being entitled to widowed parent's allowance, in certain circumstances you may be able to requalify after a longer period. See p745 of the 2012/13 edition of this *Handbook* for further details. For other rules relating to entitlement to the increase, see p50 and pp746–48 of the 2002/03 edition of this *Handbook*.[16]

The amount of widowed parent's allowance

Widowed parent's allowance is made up of:

- a basic widowed parent's allowance. The full weekly rate of this is £111.20, but it may be paid at a reduced rate if your late spouse's or civil partner's NI contribution record was incomplete (see below);
- an additional earnings-related payment based on your late spouse's or civil partner's earnings under the additional state pension scheme, if her/his NI contribution record qualifies you for this (see p760). You may be entitled to this even if her/his contribution record is not sufficient for you to qualify for basic widowed parent's allowance.[17]

See pxvii for the amount of an increase for a child, if you are still entitled to this.

Reduction in the basic widowed parent's allowance

You get a reduced rate of basic widowed parent's allowance if your spouse's or civil partner's NI contribution record was incomplete (see p867).[18] You may be able to increase your entitlement by paying Class 3 NI contributions on your spouse's or civil partner's behalf (which you may do even though s/he has died – contact HM Revenue and Customs' National Insurance Enquiries helpline on 0300 200 3500 or textphone 0300 200 3519 about this). See p848 for further details and p849 for certain time limits for making such payments.

3. Bereavement allowance

Bereavement allowance is a weekly benefit paid for up to 52 weeks. You cannot receive bereavement allowance and widowed parent's allowance at the same time, but you may qualify for bereavement allowance when your entitlement to widowed parent's allowance stops.

In addition to qualifying for bereavement allowance, you may also be entitled to a bereavement payment (see p519).

Who can claim bereavement allowance

You qualify for bereavement allowance if:[19]

- you are either:
  - a widow or widower (see p525) and your spouse died on or after 9 April 2001; *or*
  - a surviving civil partner (see p525); *and*
- you were at least 45 years old when your spouse or civil partner died; *and*
- you are under pension age (see p752); *and*
- not more than 52 weeks have passed since your spouse or civil partner died; *and*

- your late spouse or civil partner either:
  - satisfied the national insurance (NI) contribution conditions (see p866); *or*
  - died as the result of an industrial injury or disease (see p528).

Disqualification and suspension

Entitlement to bereavement allowance ends if you marry or enter into a civil partnership. You cannot requalify for it even if you subsequently get divorced or your civil partnership is dissolved. It is suspended if you are cohabiting (see p527), but can be reinstated if you stop cohabiting.[20]

The rules about your age

You must be 45 or over at the time your spouse or civil partner died to qualify for bereavement allowance. The allowance is reduced if you were under 55 when s/he died (see below).

You cannot receive bereavement allowance if you are pension age or over (see p752). However, you may qualify for retirement pension based on your own or your late spouse's or civil partner's NI contributions (see Chapter 36).

People included in the claim

You claim bereavement allowance for yourself. You cannot get an increase for a partner (see above for the effect of marriage, entering into a civil partnership or cohabiting on your entitlement to bereavement allowance) or for your child(ren). If you have a dependent child you may get widowed parent's allowance rather than bereavement allowance.

The amount of bereavement allowance

The full weekly rate of bereavement allowance is £111.20.[21]

Your bereavement allowance may be reduced, as described below, if:
- your late spouse's or civil partner's NI contribution record was incomplete; *or*
- you were under 55 when s/he died.

Your late spouse's or civil partner's contribution record

If your late spouse's or civil partner's NI contribution record was not complete, the amount of basic bereavement allowance you receive is reduced proportionately (see p867). You may be able to increase your entitlement by paying Class 3 NI contributions on your spouse's or civil partner's behalf (see p523).

Your age

Your bereavement allowance is reduced if you were under 55 when your spouse or civil partner died.[22] For each year, or part of a year, you were under 55, the bereavement allowance you would otherwise have received is reduced by 7 per cent. This percentage reduction remains the same for as long as you receive bereavement allowance.

If your spouse or civil partner had a complete NI contribution record, the amount you would receive is as follows.

Age when spouse or civil partner died	Rate of bereavement allowance (£pw)
54	103.42
53	95.63
52	87.85
51	80.06
50	72.28
49	64.50
48	56.71
47	48.93
46	41.14
45	33.36

4. Definition of terms

Who counts as a widow, widower or surviving civil partner

To qualify for bereavement benefits, you must be a widow, widower or surviving civil partner. For this to apply, you must have been married to your spouse, or in a civil partnership with your partner, at the date of her/his death, and the marriage or civil partnership must have been valid under UK law.

Note:

• If you have been bereaved more than once, your entitlement depends on the national insurance (NI) contribution record of your most recent spouse or civil partner.

• If, following the death of your spouse or civil partner, you marry or enter into a civil partnership, you lose all entitlement to widowed parent's allowance and bereavement allowance based on your previous spouse's or civil partner's NI contribution record.[23]

• A **void** marriage or civil partnership (eg, one in which at least one of the partners was not eligible to marry or form a civil partnership) is invalid and, from a legal point of view, is treated as if it never existed.[24] In England and Wales a **voidable** marriage or civil partnership is treated as having been valid until a decree absolute of annulment is pronounced.[25] Questions about the validity of marriages or civil partnerships are decided by a special unit at the DWP. If a question arises over the validity of your marriage or civil partnership, seek advice.

• In England and Wales, from 29 March 2014 when same-sex couples are able to marry, you are also considered a widow if your wife dies, and a widower if your husband dies. Provided you were married at the date of her/his death and the marriage was valid, you are entitled to bereavement benefits if you meet the usual qualifying conditions. Until same-sex marriages are introduced in Scotland (likely to be in autumn 2014) same-sex marriages under the law of England and Wales are treated as civil partnerships in Scotland.[26] See CPAG's online service and *Welfare Rights Bulletin* for updates.

Marriage by 'cohabitation with habit and repute'

In Scotland (but not the rest of Great Britain[27]) you can also be a widow or widower if you were married by '**cohabitation with habit and repute**', even if you did not go through a formal wedding ceremony. However, this only applies if your cohabitation with habit and repute began before 4 May 2006.[28] If it began on or after 4 May 2006, except in very rare cases, you are not treated as married.[29] To be considered married by cohabitation with habit and repute, your relationship must have been like that of a husband and wife and must have been more than simply living together – there must have been something about it which meant that it could be inferred that you and your partner consented to marriage and nothing existed which would have prevented a valid marriage taking place – eg, neither of you were married to someone else.[30] In addition, your relationship must have been such that other people generally believed that you were married.[31]

Separation, divorce and dissolution

If you were divorced when your former spouse died, or if your civil partnership had been dissolved when your former civil partner died, you are not a widow, widower or surviving civil partner.

A divorce only becomes effective when the decree absolute is pronounced (a decree of divorce, in Scotland), and a civil partnership is dissolved when a final dissolution order is issued (a decree of dissolution, in Scotland). If you were in the process of obtaining a divorce or of dissolving your civil partnership but your spouse or civil partner died before it was finalised, you are still a widow, widower or surviving civil partner (and so may be entitled to bereavement benefits). This is the case even if you were judicially separated.

Note: your entitlement to bereavement benefits will be affected if the DWP disputes the validity of an earlier divorce or dissolution of a civil partnership. In this circumstance, seek advice.

Polygamous marriages

If your marriage was polygamous, you are not usually entitled to bereavement benefits following the death of your spouse. This is because, as a general rule, the law in England, Wales and Scotland does not treat you as legally married unless your marriage is a monogamous one.[32]

Note:

- If your marriage was *formerly* polygamous rather than actually polygamous when your spouse died (ie, if, when your late spouse died, any other spouses had already died or been divorced), you can qualify.
- A marriage is only considered polygamous, if the law of the country where the marriage takes place permits either party to have another wife or husband.[33]
- Whether your marriage is considered polygamous depends on whether you were your spouse's first wife or husband and on where you and your spouse were 'domiciled' at the time of your marriage and any subsequent marriage. In general terms, 'domicile' means the country in which you have chosen to make your permanent home.[34] In particular, no one who is domiciled in England or Wales is allowed to contract a polygamous marriage anywhere in the world even if the local law allows it.[35]

Example

At the time of their wedding, Shaznaz and her husband were domiciled in Pakistan and were married under Islamic law. After the wedding they came to live in England, made their permanent home here and had no intention of returning to live in Pakistan at any time. Later, her husband returned temporarily to Pakistan and married a second wife. As her husband was domiciled in England rather than Pakistan at the time of the second marriage, English law does not recognise the second marriage and, therefore, regards Shaznaz as her late husband's only wife. Provided she meets the other conditions of entitlement, she is entitled to bereavement benefits.[36] If her husband had re-acquired domicile in Pakistan at the time of his second marriage, and his second wife was still alive, both marriages would be polygamous, and neither wife could claim bereavement benefits.[37]

Proving that your spouse or civil partner is dead

It is up to you to prove to the DWP that your spouse or civil partner is dead and that you were married or were civil partners when s/he died.

Normally this is straightforward (see p531 for the information expected). However, if your spouse or civil partner is missing and you think that s/he has died, it may be difficult to establish your entitlement to bereavement benefits. If you are in this situation, seek advice.[38] See p533 for details of backdating benefit if you were unaware of your spouse's or civil partner's death.

Cohabitation

A bereavement payment is not paid to you if you are cohabiting with someone else at the time of your spouse's or civil partner's death.

Your widowed parent's allowance or bereavement allowance is suspended if you begin cohabiting, but becomes payable again if the cohabitation ends.[39]

In England and Wales, 'cohabiting' means living with someone as if you are a married couple. In Scotland, it means living with someone of the opposite sex as if you are husband and wife, or living with someone of the same sex as if you are civil partners. However, it is expected that this definition will be changed to correspond with that for England and Wales when legislation allowing same-sex marriages comes into force in Scotland (likely to be in autumn 2014).[40]

Deciding whether or not you are cohabiting may not be straightforward. For futher information, see p206.

If the DWP decides that you are cohabiting and you do not agree, you can challenge its decision (see Chapters 58 and 59).

Industrial accident or disease

The meaning of 'industrial accident or disease' is discussed on p668 and p671. To qualify for bereavement benefits, the industrial accident or disease must have been a cause of death, but it need not have been a direct cause or the only cause.[41]

5. **Special benefit rules**

Special rules may apply to:
* widows whose husbands died before 9 April 2001 (see below);
* widowers whose wives died before 9 April 2001 (see p529);
* people who have obtained a gender recognition certificate (see p529);
* people who are abroad (see p1571);
* people in prison or detention (see p959).

Widows whose husbands died before 9 April 2001

If you are a widow whose husband died before 9 April 2001, you are not entitled to bereavement benefits but instead may qualify for widowed mother's allowance or widow's pension.

For an explanation of the main qualifying conditions for widows' benefits, see the 2000/01 edition of this *Handbook*. See pxvii for the current rates of widows' benefits.

If you satisfy the qualifying conditions, you can get widowed mother's allowance for as long as you have an eligible child, as there is no upper age limit. A 'child' is someone who counts as a child or qualifying young person for child benefit purposes.

If your entitlement to widowed mother's allowance ends, or if you are not entitled to widowed mother's allowance, you may qualify for a widow's pension. This can be paid until you reach 65 if you satisfy the qualifying conditions.

Once you reach pension age, you may be entitled to both retirement pension and either widow's pension or widowed mother's allowance. Because of the overlapping benefit rules, you cannot receive both benefits in full at the same time, but see p132 of the 2000/01 edition of this *Handbook* if you are in this position.

Note: if you qualify for Category B retirement pension on the basis of being a widow (see Chapter 36), once you qualify your entitlement continues even if you marry or form a civil partnership. Therefore, it may be financially beneficial to delay your marriage or partnership until after pension age (see p750).

Widowers whose wives died before 9 April 2001

If you are a widower and your wife died before 9 April 2001, you may be in a less favourable position than a widow whose husband died before 9 April 2001 because there were no widowers' benefits equivalent to the widows' benefits available to women. This has been challenged on the basis that it breached the non-discrimination principle contained in the European Convention on Human Rights.[42] For a discussion of the decisions in these cases and their consequences, see CPAG's *Welfare Rights Bulletin* 198. If you are over pension age, you may qualify for a Category B retirement pension based on your late wife's national insurance (NI) contribution record (see p749).

People who have obtained a gender recognition certificate

If you have annulled or dissolved an existing marriage or civil partnership (which, at the time of writing, you must do in order to obtain a full gender recognition certificate), you are not entitled to bereavement benefits on the basis of your former spouse's or former civil partner's NI contribution record, if s/he subsequently dies. However, in England and Wales, it is expected that from some time in 2014 you will be able to obtain a full gender recognition certificate while preserving your marriage or, in certain circumstances, your civil partnership. It will also be possible to convert a civil partnership into a marriage. Such changes are also planned in Scotland.[43] See CPAG's online service and *Welfare Rights Bulletin* for updates.

If you were still married or in a civil partnership at the time of your spouse's or civil partner's death, you may qualify for bereavement benefits, even if after the death you obtain a gender recognition certificate. However, when the full certificate is issued, any entitlement to widow's pension ends. Widowed mother's allowance also ends, but you can qualify for widowed parent's allowance instead.[44]

6. Claims and backdating

To qualify for bereavement benefits, you must usually make a claim (but see below for an exception).[45] The general rules about claims and backdating are in Chapter 53. This section explains the specific rules that apply to bereavement benefits.

Making a claim

If you were receiving retirement pension when your spouse or civil partner died, you do not need to make a claim in order to qualify for a bereavement payment. However, it is advisable to ensure that the DWP is aware of the death by telephoning the Bereavement Service (see below).

If this does not apply, you must make a claim to qualify for a bereavement payment. To qualify for widowed parent's allowance or bereavement allowance you must always make a claim. Your claim can be made:[46]

- by phoning the DWP's Bereavement Service (tel: 0845 606 0265, or 0845 606 0275 for Welsh speakers; textphone: 0845 606 0285). After giving information on the phone, you are sent a statement to approve, sign and return; *or*
- in writing, normally on the approved form (see below). Send your claim form to the address on the form. Alternatively, if you have reached the qualifying age for pension credit (PC – see p78), you may also be able to take or send your claim to a designated local authority or English county council office or other 'alternative office' (see p1136).

If you claim in writing, you must complete the form in accordance with the instructions. Keep a copy of your claim in case queries arise. If you claim by phone, you must provide all the information needed to decide the claim (see p531).[47]

In certain circumstances, the decision maker may accept a written application which is not on the approved form, although if you claim in this way you will usually be sent the approved form to complete (see p1140).[48] You can amend or withdraw your claim before a decision is made (see p1138). If there is a delay in dealing with your claim, you may be able to get a short-term advance of benefit (see p1167).

Forms

Form BB1 is the approved claim form for bereavement payment, widowed parent's allowance and bereavement allowance. When you register the death you are normally given a Certificate of Registration of Death. If you complete the form on the certificate and send it to the DWP, you should be sent Form BB1. Alternatively, you can get it by phoning Jobcentre Plus (tel: 0800 055 6688, or 0800 012 1888 for Welsh speakers; textphone: 0800 023 4888) or online (www.gov.uk).

Who should claim

You must normally claim bereavement benefits yourself. If you are unable to manage your own affairs, another person can claim bereavement benefits for you as your 'appointee' (see p1137).

Information to support your claim

When you claim bereavement benefits, you must:
- satisfy the 'national insurance number requirement' (see p1138), unless you qualify for only a bereavement payment and are not required to make a claim to receive it (see p530);
- provide proof of your identity, if required (see p1140); *and*
- ensure you have made a valid claim by supplying the information requested on the claim form if your claim is in writing, or over the phone if it is a telephone claim (see p1140).

You are normally expected to provide proof of your spouse's or civil partner's death. When you register the death you usually get a Certificate of Registration of Death. You can complete the back of the Certificate and send it to the DWP as proof, or provide a death certificate. Alternatively, if you have reported the death to a local office under the 'Tell Us Once' arrangements (see p1137), you are given a reference number, which you can use as proof of death when you make a claim through the Bereavement Service (see p530). If you do not have proof that your spouse or civil partner has died, see p527.

You are also usually expected to provide your marriage or civil partnership certificate.[49] Caselaw has given guidance on assessing evidence from countries where reliable documentary proof of life events such as marriage may not be available.[50]

Even if you have provided all that was required when you claimed, you may be asked to provide additional information and evidence relevant to your claim (see p1152). There is a strict time limit for providing this. If you do not do so, the decision maker can decide your claim in the way most adverse to you.

Note: you may be asked to provide information after you are awarded bereavement benefit. If you do not do so, your benefit could be suspended or even terminated (see p1175).

The date of your claim

The date of your claim determines the date from which you are paid widowed parent's allowance or bereavement allowance (see p534) and whether you qualify for a bereavement payment (if you are required to make a claim in order to qualify – see p530). The date of your claim is normally:[51]
- if you claim by telephone (see p530), the date of your phone call; *or*

- the date your written claim is received at a DWP or Jobcentre Plus office (but see below); *or*
- if you have reached the qualifying age for PC (see p78) and submit your claim to a designated local authority, English county council or other 'alternative office' (see p1136), the date it is received by that office.

If your claim is 'defective' because you did not give all the information needed on the phone or your claim form was not completed correctly, or if you made a written claim that was not on the correct form, you may be asked to provide further information or to complete the correct form. Provided this additional information or form is received by the DWP within a month of the DWP first telling you of the defect or of the DWP supplying you with the correct form (or longer if the decision maker thinks that the delay is reasonable), your claim can be treated as having been made on the date that the initial claim was received.[52]

In some circumstances, you can claim before you qualify for bereavement benefits (see below) or the date of your claim can be backdated (see below).

See p533 if you claim late because you did not know that your spouse or civil partner had died.

If you claim the wrong benefit

The decision maker can treat a claim for retirement pension as a claim for bereavement benefits and vice versa.[53] This may help you qualify for a bereavement payment (although see p530 for when you can qualify without making a claim). A claim for retirement pension may also allow you to get your widowed parent's allowance or bereavement allowance backdated for more than the normal three months (see below). However, you cannot get widowed parent's allowance or bereavement allowance for any period when you are over pension age. See p1144 for details of interchanging claims in this way.

Claiming in advance

You can claim bereavement benefits up to three months before you expect to qualify. In most circumstances, you will not know of your need to claim benefit in advance, but this may be relevant if, for example, you know that you will no longer be cohabiting.[54]

Backdating your claim

A claim for a **bereavement payment** must usually be made within 12 months of your spouse's or civil partner's death, unless:

- you were not aware that s/he had died (see p533); *or*
- you are not required to make a claim in order to qualify for a bereavement payment (see p530).

There is no time limit for claiming **widowed parent's allowance** or **bereavement allowance**, and payment of these benefits can be backdated for up to three months before the date you make your claim, provided you satisfy the qualifying conditions over that period. You do not need to show reasons why your claim was late. If you were not aware of your spouse's or civil partner's death, you may be able to get your claim backdated further (see below). However, remember that bereavement allowance is only payable for the 52-week period running from the date your spouse or civil partner died.

If you might have qualified for benefit earlier but did not claim because you were given the wrong information or were misled by the DWP, you could ask for compensation (see p1382) or complain to the Independent Case Examiner or Ombudsman through your MP (see p1384 and p1387).

See p532 if you claimed retirement pension instead of bereavement benefits.

If you were unaware of your spouse's or civil partner's death

If you were not aware that your spouse or civil partner had died (eg, if s/he had been missing, or you had lost touch), the time limit for claiming a bereavement payment and the normal three-month time limit on backdating of widowed parent's allowance and bereavement allowance can be extended.

Your claim can be backdated to the date your spouse or civil partner died or is presumed to have died, provided you meet the other conditions of entitlement over that period and:[55]

- her/his death has been difficult to establish but s/he has been found to have died or is presumed to have died (whether or not her/his body has been found or identified); *and*
- you claim bereavement benefit within 12 months of the death or presumed death.

The time limit for claiming may be extended further if it is more than 12 months since your spouse or civil partner died, or since the date that s/he is presumed to have died and either:

- her/his body has not been found or identified (or if it has, you were not aware of this); *and*
- the decision maker has decided that your spouse or civil partner has died or is presumed dead; *and*
- you claim within 12 months of that decision;

or

- your spouse's or civil partner's body has been found or identified and you learn this within 12 months of the discovery or identification; *and*
- you claim within 12 months of finding out about her/his death.

In the former situation, bereavement benefits can be backdated to the date of death or the date of the presumed death. In the latter situation, bereavement benefits can only be backdated for a maximum of two years. This is because you must claim within 12 months of finding out about your spouse's or civil partner's death and, in turn, you must have learnt about your spouse's or civil partner's death within 12 months of her/his body being identified.[56]

7. **Getting paid**

Payment of a bereavement payment, widowed parent's allowance or bereavement allowance is normally made by direct credit transfer into your bank (or similar) account (see p1163).[57] If you are unable to open or manage an account, the DWP may agree to pay you by 'simple payment' (see p1163). If you cannot act for yourself, bereavement benefits can be paid to someone else on your behalf, called your 'appointee' (see p1137). If it is necessary to protect your interests (or, if you get an increase in your widowed parent's allowance for a child, the interests of the child), all or part of your benefit can be paid to someone else.[58]

When are widowed parent's allowance and bereavement allowance paid?
The day you are paid depends on your national insurance number (see p1164). You are normally paid fortnightly in arrears. However, the DWP may choose to pay you weekly in advance or in arrears or, if you agree, every four or 13 weeks in arrears.[59]
Payments run from the date your entitlement starts. This is usually the date of your claim (see p531).[60]

If the amount of benefit to which you are entitled is less than £5 a week, the decision maker can decide how often you are paid, although you must be paid at least once a year.[61]

If your entitlement to widowed parent's allowance or bereavement allowance ends and you are paid in arrears, your benefit should be paid up to (and including) the last day on which you qualify for that benefit. If you are paid in advance and your entitlement ends, payment of benefit continues up to, but not including, the following payday unless your entitlement ends on a payday, in which case your benefit is paid up to, but not including, that day.[62] Widowed parent's allowance and bereavement allowance are daily benefits. Payments can be made for part weeks at the beginning and, if you are paid in arrears, at the end of your claim. The daily rate is calculated as one-seventh of the weekly rate of benefit.[63]

Note:
• Your widowed parent's allowance or bereavement allowance might be paid at a reduced rate in certain circumstances (see p523 and p524).
• You might not be paid widowed parent's allowance or bereavement allowance if you have been sanctioned for a benefit offence (see p1258).

- If you have forgotten your PIN, see p1163. If your 'simple payment' card has been lost or stolen, or if you have forgotten your memorable date, see p1164. For information on missing payments, see p1164.
- If payment of your bereavement benefit is delayed, see p1382. You might be able to get a short-term advance (see p1167). If you wish to complain about how your claim has been dealt with, see p1383. You might be able to claim compensation (see p1382).
- If payment of your widowed parent's allowance or bereavement allowance is suspended, see p1175.
- If you are overpaid a bereavement benefit, you might have to repay it (see Chapter 56) and, in some circumstances, you may have to pay a penalty (see p1249). If you have been accused of fraud, see Chapter 57.

Change of circumstances

You must report changes in your circumstances that you have been told to report, as well as any that you might reasonably be expected to know might affect your right to, the amount of, or the payment of, your benefit. You should do this as soon as possible, preferably in writing. See p1174 for further information.

If a change of circumstances affects your entitlement to widowed parent's allowance or bereavement allowance, before your benefit can be stopped or adjusted, the decision maker should first revise or supersede the earlier decision on your entitlement (see Chapter 58).[64] The date from which a new decision takes effect following such a supersession normally depends on whether or not it is advantageous to you and whether you reported the change in time (see p1287).

8. Tax, other benefits and the benefit cap

Tax

A bereavement payment is not taxable. Widowed parent's allowance and bereavement allowance are taxable, except for any increase to widowed parent's allowance for children.[65]

Means-tested benefits

A bereavement payment is counted as capital for all means-tested benefits. For means-tested benefits other than universal credit (UC),
widowed parent's allowance and bereavement allowance count as income, less any tax payable on them. However:

- £10 of your weekly widowed parent's allowance is ignored when calculating your entitlement to income support (IS),[66] income-based jobseeker's allowance (JSA),[67] income-related employment and support allowance (ESA)[68] and pension credit (PC);[69]

- an increase in your widowed parent's allowance for a child is ignored when calculating your entitlement to income-related ESA and PC, and may be ignored when calculating your entitlement to IS and income-based JSA (see p275 and p313);
- when calculating your entitlement to housing benefit (HB), £15 of your weekly widowed parent's allowance is ignored.[70] However, if you are getting the savings credit (and not the guarantee credit) of PC, the income used to calculate your HB is that used by the DWP to calculate your entitlement to PC (which includes only a £10 disregard from your widowed parent's allowance – see p305);
- bereavement allowance is counted in full as income when calculating your entitlement to IS, income-based JSA, income-related ESA, PC and HB.

Widowed parent's allowance and bereavement allowance count in full as income for UC.[71]

If your partner was entitled to HB when s/he died and you claim HB within a month of her/his death, your HB claim can be treated as having been made on the date your partner died (see p126) and, in some circumstances, it can be backdated further (see p128).

Non-means-tested benefits

Your entitlement to non-means-tested benefits is not affected by your entitlement to a bereavement payment.

Widowed parent's allowance and bereavement allowance are affected by the overlapping benefit rules and so you may not get these benefits in full if another earnings-replacement benefit is being paid to you (see p1165).

If you receive an increase in your widowed parent's allowance for a child, the overlapping benefit rules may also affect you. If you receive child benefit for the same child, see p1167. If the increase is for a child for whom you get guardian's allowance, the increase in your widowed parent's allowance is not paid.[72]

Once you reach pension age, you may qualify for a Category A or B retirement pension on the basis of your late spouse's or civil partner's national insurance (NI) contribution record (see p748).

When your bereavement benefit stops, you may qualify for NI credits for contributory ESA and contribution-based JSA (see p858).[73]

Tax credits

A bereavement payment is ignored when calculating your entitlement to working tax credit (WTC) and child tax credit (CTC). Widowed parent's allowance counts in full as pension income for WTC and CTC (it may be possible to ignore some of your pension income – see p1428). Bereavement allowance counts in full as benefit income (see p1423).

The benefit cap

In some cases, the total amount of specified benefits you receive is limited to £350 a week (if you are a single claimant without children) or £500 a week (if you are a lone parent or a member of a couple). This is known as the 'benefit cap'. Bereavement allowance, widowed parent's allowance, widowed mother's allowance and widow's pension are specified benefits. The benefit cap only applies if you are getting HB or UC. H
owever, £15 of your weekly widowed parent's allowance or widowed mother's allowance is ignored if the cap is applied through your HB. See p1169 for further information.

Passports and other sources of help

If you are entitled to widowed parent's allowance, you are also entitled to a Christmas bonus (see p835).

In some circumstances, you may qualify for a social fund grant for funeral expenses (see p772). If you have a low income, you may be entitled to council tax reduction (see p827).

For advice about preparing funerals and registering deaths, see www.gov.uk. Alternatively, consult the DWP's *What to Do After a Death in England or Wales* (www.gov.uk) or the Scottish government leaflet, *What to Do After a Death in Scotland* (www.scotland.gov.uk/familylaw).

Notes

1 Pensions Bill 2013

1. Bereavement payment
2 ss36 and 60(2) and (3) SSCBA 1992; regs 3(da) and 19(3A) SS(C&P) Regs
3 Reg 19(3A) SS(C&P) Regs
4 Reg 3(da) SS(C&P) Regs
5 s36(2) SSCBA 1992
6 Reg 4(2B) SSB(PA) Regs
7 Sch 4 Part II SSCBA 1992

2. Widowed parent's allowance
8 ss39A and 60(2) and (3) SSCBA 1992
9 ss39A(3), 77(5) and 122(5) SSCBA 1992
10 Reg 2(4) SSB(PRT) Regs

11 Arts 2(3)(b) and 3(3) Welfare Reform Act 2007 (Commencement No.7, Transitional and Savings Provisions) Order 2008, No.2101
12 s122(4) SSCBA 1992
13 Reg 16ZA SS(WB&RP) Regs
14 Reg 16ZA(2) SS(WB&RP) Regs
15 s39A(4), (4A) and (5) SSCBA 1992
16 ss80(5) and 81 SSCBA 1992; art 3 TCA(No.3)O; regs 4A(4) and 4B SSB(Dep) Regs
17 Reg 6(2) SS(WB&RP) Regs
18 Reg 6 SS(WB&RP) Regs

3. Bereavement allowance
19 ss39B and 60(2) and (3) SSCBA 1992
20 s39B(4), (4A) and (5) SSCBA 1992

21 ss39C and 44 SSCBA 1992
22 s39C(5) SSCBA 1992

4. **Definition of terms**
23 ss39A(4) and (4A) and 39B(4) and (4A)
    SSCBA 1992
24 R(G) 2/63
25 R(G) 1/73
26 Marriage (Same Sex Couples) Act 2013;
    Marriage and Civil Partnership
    (Scotland) Act 2014; art 5 Marriage
    (Same Sex Couples) Act 2013
    (Consequential and Contrary Provisions
    and Scotland) Order 2014, No.560
27 But see *CAO v Bath, The Times,* 28
    October 1999 (CA), reported as R(G) 1/
    00; R(G) 2/70
28 R(G) 5/83; s3 Family Law (Scotland) Act
    2006; The Family Law (Scotland) Act
    2006 (Commencement, Transitional
    Provisions and Savings) Order 2006,
    No.212
29 paras 10215-16 DMG
30 R(G) 1/71
31 CSG/7/1995; CSG/681/2003; but see
    also CSG/648/2007
32 *Hyde v Hyde* [1866]; reg 2 SSFA(PM)
    Regs
33 Reg 1(2) SSFA(PM) Regs
34 R(S) 2/92
35 s11(3) MCA 1973
36 R(G) 1/95
37 R(G) 1/93; R(P) 2/06
38 paras 10466-96 DMG
39 ss39A(5) and 39B(5) SSCBA 1992
40 Marriage (Same Sex Couples) Act 2013;
    Marriage and Civil Partnership
    (Scotland) Act 2014
41 CI/142/1949; R(I) 14/51

5. **Special benefit rules**
42 *Willis v United Kingdom,* No.36042/97,
    11 June 2002,
    unreported (ECtHR); *Runkee and White v
    United Kingdom,* Nos.42949/98 and
    53134/99, 10 May 2007,
    unreported (ECtHR)
43 Marriage (Same Sex Couples) Act 2013;
    Marriage and Civil Partnership
    (Scotland) Act 2014
44 Sch 5 paras 3-5 GRA 2004

6. **Claims and backdating**
45 s1 SSAA 1992
46 s1 SSAA 1992; reg 4(1), (6)(b), (6A),
    (6B) and (11) SS(C&P) Regs
47 Reg 4(8) and (12) SS(C&P) Regs
48 Reg 4(1) and (7ZA) SS(C&P) Regs

49 Reg 7(1) SS(C&P) Regs
50 CP/4062/2004; see also CP/891/
    2008 and *AR v SSWP* [2012] UKUT 467
    (AAC)
51 Reg 6(1) and (1ZA) SS(C&P) Regs
52 Regs 4(7), (7ZA), (8), (12) and (13) and
    6(1) SS(C&P) Regs
53 Reg 9(1) and Sch 1 Part I SS(C&P) Regs
54 Reg 13 SS(C&P) Regs
55 Reg 19(3B) SS(C&P) Regs
56 CG/7235/1995

7. **Getting paid**
57 Reg 21 SS(C&P) Regs
58 Reg 34(1) SS(C&P) Regs
59 Reg 22A SS(C&P) Regs
60 Reg 22B(1) SS(C&P) Regs
61 Reg 22(2) SS(C&P) Regs
62 Regs 16(2C) and 22B(3) and (4)
    SS(C&P) Regs
63 Reg 22B(6) SS(C&P) Regs
64 Reg 17 SS(C&P) Regs

8. **Tax, other benefits and the benefit cap**
65 ss577-79, 661 and 676 IT(EP)A 2003
66 Reg 40 and Sch 9 para 16(h) IS Regs
67 Reg 103 and Sch 7 para 17(e) JSA Regs
68 Sch 8 para 17(i) ESA Regs
69 Sch IV para 7 SPC Regs
70 Reg 40 and Sch 5 para 16 HB Regs; reg
    29 and Sch 5 paras 7 and 8 HB(SPC)
    Regs
71 Regs 22 and 66 UC Regs
72 Reg 7(4) SS(OB) Regs
73 Reg 8C SS(Cr) Regs

Chapter 25

Carer's allowance

This chapter covers:
1. Who can claim carer's allowance (below)
2. The rules about your age (p541)
3. People included in the claim (p542)
4. The amount of benefit (p542)
5. Special benefit rules (p542)
6. Claims and backdating (p543)
7. Getting paid (p546)
8. Tax, other benefits and the benefit cap (p547)

Key facts
- Carer's allowance (CA) is paid to people who care for someone who is severely disabled.
- CA is a non-means-tested benefit.
- You do not have to have paid national insurance contributions to qualify.
- You can qualify for CA whether you are in or out of work, but you must not earn more than £100 in a week.
- CA can be paid in addition to other benefits and tax credits, but the overlapping benefit rules may apply. CA counts as income for means-tested benefits.
- CA is administered and paid by the DWP's Carer's Allowance Unit.
- If you disagree with a CA decision, you can apply for a revision or a supersession, or appeal against it. You are likely to have to apply for a revision before you can appeal.

1. Who can claim carer's allowance

You qualify for carer's allowance (CA) if:[1]
- you are caring for a 'severely disabled person' (see p540 for the meaning). You do not have to be the person's relative, nor do you have to live with her/him;
- the care you give is regular and substantial (see p540);
- you are not gainfully employed (see p541 for what counts);
- you are not in full-time education (see p922 for what counts);

Part 5: Other benefits
Chapter 25: Carer's allowance
1. Who can claim carer's allowance

- you are aged 16 or over;
- you satisfy the residence conditions (see p1555);
- you are not a 'person subject to immigration control' (see p1500).

Who counts as a severely disabled person?

In this chapter, when we refer to a '**severely disabled person**' we mean a person to whom either attendance allowance (AA), the highest or middle rate of disability living allowance (DLA) care component, either rate of the daily living component of personal independence payment (PIP), armed forces independence payment or constant attendance allowance in respect of an industrial or war disablement (see p679) is payable.[2]

Note:[3]
- Only one person can qualify for CA for caring for the same disabled person. If you cannot agree on who this should be, the DWP decides.
- Even if you care for two or more disabled people, you can only qualify for one award of CA for the same day.

Regularly and substantially caring

To qualify for CA you must be engaged in 'regularly and substantially' caring for a severely disabled person. You satisfy this requirement during any week in which you are (or are likely to be) engaged and regularly engaged in caring for her/him for 35 hours or more.[4] For CA, a week runs from Sunday to Saturday.[5] Caring can include supervision as well as assistance. If some of the time is spent preparing for the disabled person to come to stay with you or clearing up after her/his visit, this can also count towards the 35 hours.[6]

Note:
- You cannot average the hours in one week with those in another – eg, if you care 35 hours or more in some weeks and fewer than 35 in others.[7] You must care for at least 35 hours in the week in question.
- If you are caring for two or more disabled people, you can only qualify for CA if you are caring for at least one of them for 35 hours or more a week.[8] You cannot add together the hours you are caring for all of them to make up the 35.

Breaks from caring

Once you have been caring for a severely disabled person for a while, you can take a temporary break from caring and continue to qualify for CA. This applies if you have been providing care for at least 35 hours a week in 22 of the last 26 weeks (or for at least 14 of the last 26 weeks, and the reason you did not provide care for 22 weeks was that either you or the disabled person were in hospital or in a similar institution). Weeks before you claimed CA can be counted. This means you can have a four-week break from caring in any period of six months, or a 12-week break if one of you was in hospital or in a similar institution (see p942 for what counts) for at least eight weeks.[9] Note, however, that CA stops if the AA, DLA, PIP or constant attendance allowance of the person for whom you are caring stops because s/he is in hospital or in a similar institution (see Chapter 45).[10]

If the person receiving care dies

If the person you care for dies, you continue to be entitled to CA for a further eight weeks, even though you are no longer providing care, providing you satisfy the other qualifying conditions. The eight weeks run from the Sunday following the death, or from the day of the death if this was a Sunday.[11]

Gainfully employed

You cannot qualify for CA if you are 'gainfully employed'. You count as gainfully employed in a week (and cannot qualify for CA in that week) if your earnings in the previous week (from employment and self-employment) were more than £100.[12] This is due to increase to £102 a week from May 2014. For the way earnings are calculated, see p874. Your earnings are ignored if you are working during a period when you are not actually caring for the severely disabled person – eg, because s/he is in hospital or you are on a four-week break from caring (see p540).[13] If you stop work and then claim CA, your final earnings generally do not affect your entitlement to CA (see p874).

2. The rules about your age

You can claim carer's allowance (CA) if you are aged 16 or over.[14] There is no upper age limit. However, because of the overlapping benefits rules, if you receive retirement pension you might not be paid CA, even if you qualify (see p1165). Even if you are not paid CA, you may qualify for a carer premium (pension credit additional amount) with your means-tested benefits (see p237) or a carer element with your universal credit (see p252). **Note:** these rules were different in the past – eg, before 28 October 2002, there was an upper age limit. See p551 of the 2013/14 edition of this *Handbook* for further information.

Part 5: Other benefits
Chapter 25: Carer's allowance
5. Special benefit rules

3. **People included in the claim**

You claim carer's allowance (CA) for yourself.

You now cannot normally claim any increase in your CA for your partner or children.

Can you get an increase for an adult or child?

You may continue to qualify for an increase in your CA for:

– your spouse or civil partner, or for someone who cares for your child, if you were entitled to the increase before 6 April 2010 (but see below for when it may end);

– a child, if you were entitled to the increase before 6 April 2003 and your entitlement has continued since that date.

If an increase for a child stops being paid for no more than 58 days you may continue to qualify for the increase.[15] If your entitlement to the increase ends because you stop being entitled to CA, you may be able to requalify. If you are a member of a couple, you might not get an increase for a child if your partner's earnings are at or above the earnings limit for the increase. See p745 of the 2012/13 edition of this *Handbook* for further details, and pxvii for the current earnings limits. For other rules relating to entitlement to the increase see pp746–48 of the 2002/03 edition. See p552 of the 2013/14 edition for when an increase for an adult may end.

4. **The amount of benefit**

Carer's allowance (CA) is paid at a weekly rate of £61.35.[16]

If you are still entitled to an increase in your CA for an adult or for a child, see pxvii for the amounts.

Note: if you are a member of a couple, your CA might be paid at a reduced rate if your partner fails to take part in a work-focused interview (see p1059).

5. **Special benefit rules**

Special rules may apply if:

• you have come from or are going abroad (see Chapters 69 to 72);
• you, or the person you are caring for, are in hospital (see p945);
• the person you are caring for goes into a care home or other similar accommodation (see p954);
• you, or the person you are caring for, is a prisoner (see p959).

6. Claims and backdating

To be entitled to carer's allowance (CA), you must make a claim for it.[17] The general rules on claims and backdating are in Chapter 53. This section explains the specific rules that apply to CA.

If you are claiming a means-tested benefit, see p547 before claiming CA, as the effect of CA on your other benefits (and possibly those of the person for whom you care) means it is not always advisable for you to claim it.

Making a claim

A claim for CA must be made in writing. You can do this by completing:
- the approved form. Send it to the Carer's Allowance Unit, Palatine House, Lancaster Road, Preston PR1 1HB. You may also be able to make your claim by taking or sending it to an 'alternative office' (see p1136); *or*
- an online application form at www.dwp.gov.uk/carersallowance.

Keep a copy of your claim form in case queries arise.

You must provide any information or evidence required (see below). In certain circumstances, the DWP may accept a written application not on the approved form.[18] You can amend or withdraw your claim before a decision is made (see p1138). If there is a delay in making a claim, you may be able to get a short-term advance of benefit (see p1167).

Forms

Get Form DS700 (DS700SP if you get retirement pension) from your local Jobcentre Plus office, DWP office or telephone contact centre or from www.gov.uk or the Carer's Allowance Unit by email at cau.customer-services@dwp.gsi.gov.uk or by telephone on 0845 608 4321 (textphone 0845 604 5312; text relay 18001 0845 608 4321) .

Who should claim

You must normally claim CA on your own behalf. However, if you are unable to manage your own affairs, another person can claim CA for you as your 'appointee' (see p1137).

Before claiming, you should be aware of how CA affects your entitlement to means-tested benefits and the means-tested benefit entitlement of the person for whom you care (see p547).

Information to support your claim

When you claim CA, you must:
- satisfy the 'national insurance (NI) number requirement' (see p1138);

Part 5: Other benefits
Chapter 25: Carer's allowance
6. Claims and backdating

- provide proof of your identity, if required (see p1140); *and*
- ensure you have made a valid claim – ie, you must supply information and evidence required with the claim (see p1140).

The CA claim forms contain a declaration to be completed by the person for whom you care or the person acting for her/him. This asks for confirmation that you provide 35 hours' care a week and explains that her/his benefit may be affected if your claim is successful. Even if this declaration is not completed, the DWP should still make a decision on your claim, although failure to return it is likely to lead to a delay in the decision and, if it raises questions about the level of care you provide, may result in a refusal of your claim.

Even if you have provided all that was required when you claimed, you may be asked to provide additional information and evidence (such as proof of your earnings) relevant to your claim (see p1152). There is a strict time limit for providing this. If you do not do so, the decision maker can decide your claim in the way most adverse to you.

Note: you may be asked to provide information after you are awarded CA. If you fail to do so, your CA could be suspended or even terminated (see p1175).

The date of your claim

Claim as soon as you think you might be entitled to CA; you are not usually entitled to CA for any day before your date of claim. The date of your claim is important as it determines the date from which you are awarded CA. In some cases, you can claim in advance (see p545) and sometimes your claim can be backdated (see p545). If you want this to be done, make this clear when you claim or the DWP might not consider it.

Your **'date of claim'** is usually the date on which your completed claim form is received by the DWP or a designated 'alternative office' (see p1136).[19] However, if you make a claim for CA in writing, but not on the approved form, or if the claim form you submit is incomplete, you may be asked to provide further information or to complete the approved form properly. As long as this additional information or the form is returned within a month of its being sent back to you (or longer if the decision maker thinks it is reasonable – see p1141), the decision maker must treat your claim as made on the date your initial written claim or form was received.[20] If you submit your claim online, your date of claim is usually the date it is received, although a decision maker has the discretion to treat it as having been received on an earlier or later date than this.[21]

If you claim the wrong benefit

If you claim income support (IS) when you should have claimed CA (either in addition to or instead of IS), a decision maker can treat your IS claim as a claim for CA (see p1144).[22] This applies even if you claim IS 'on the grounds of disability' (see p30) on or after 27 October 2008. This rule may enable you to get round the strict time limits on backdating (see below).

Claiming in advance

You can claim CA up to three months before you qualify.[23] This gives the DWP time to ensure you receive benefit as soon as you are entitled. The decision maker can award benefit from a future date if s/he believes you will satisfy all the CA qualifying conditions on that date. You may want to consider claiming in advance – eg, if you are currently earning more than £100 a week, but you plan to stop work or reduce your hours.

Backdating your claim

It is very important to claim in time. A claim for CA can usually only be backdated for a maximum of three months.[24] You must satisfy the qualifying conditions over that period. You do not have to show any reasons why your claim was late.

Your claim can be backdated for more than three months if:[25]

- you claim CA within three months of a decision to award a 'qualifying benefit' to the person for whom you care (including a decision made by the First-tier Tribunal, the Upper Tribunal or a court). Your CA is backdated to the first day of the benefit week in which the qualifying benefit is payable. However, if the decision awarding the qualifying benefit was made following a renewal claim where a fixed period award has ended or is due to end, your CA is only backdated to the first day of the benefit week in which the renewal award became payable; or

- your CA stopped because the 'qualifying benefit' of the person for whom you care was reduced or stopped (including where a fixed-term award for the qualifying benefit came to an end) or where payment of attendance allowance (AA) or disability living allowance (DLA) stopped because the person for whom you care goes into hospital, a care home or other similar accommodation. If you make a further claim within three months of the decision to reinstate the qualifying benefit, or of payment starting again, your CA is backdated to the date that your earlier claim ended or the date from which the qualifying benefit was re-awarded or became payable again, whichever is later.

A **'qualifying benefit'** is either AA, the middle or highest rate DLA care component, either rate of the daily living component of personal independence payment, armed forces independence payment or constant attendance allowance.

If you might have qualified for benefit earlier but did not claim because you were given the wrong information by the DWP or because you were misled by it, you could ask for compensation (see p1382) or complain to the Ombudsman via your MP (see p1387).

7. **Getting paid**

Payment of carer's allowance (CA) is normally made by direct credit transfer into your bank (or similar) account.[26] If you are unable to open or manage an account, payment can be made by 'simple payment' (see p1163). If you are unable to act for yourself, CA can be paid to someone else on your behalf – called your 'appointee' (see p1137).

When is carer's allowance paid?

You are paid on a Monday (or Wednesday if the person for whom you care receives constant attendance allowance with an industrial injuries benefit or war pension).[27] CA is paid weekly in advance or four-weekly in arrears (13-weekly in arrears if you agree).[28]

Payments normally run from the first payday (ie, Monday or Wednesday) after the date of your claim, unless the date of your claim is on your payday, when they run from that day.

Note:

- CA awards can be made for a fixed or indefinite period.[29]
- Deductions can be made from your CA to repay certain loans (see p1185), and in some cases to pay child support maintenance (see p1185).
- You might not be paid CA if you have been sanctioned for benefit offences (see p1258).
- If you have forgotten your PIN, see p1163. If you have lost your 'simple payment' card, or you have forgotten your memorable date, see p1164. For information about missing payments, see p1164.
- If payment of your CA is delayed, see p1382. You might be able to get a short-term advance (see p1167). If you wish to complain about how your claim has been dealt with, see p1383. You might be able to claim compensation (see p1382).
- If payment of your CA is suspended, see p1175.
- If you are overpaid CA, you might have to repay it (see Chapter 56) and, in some circumstances, you may have to pay a penalty (see p1249). If you have been accused of fraud, see Chapter 57.

Change of circumstances

You must report changes in your circumstances that you have been told to report, as well as any that you might reasonably be expected to know might affect your right to, the amount of, or the payment of, your benefit. You should do this as soon as possible, preferably in writing. See p1174 for further information. **Note:** you can also notify your change of circumstances online at www.dwp.gov.uk/carersallowance.[30]

When there has been a relevant change of circumstances, a decision maker looks at your claim again and makes a new decision. To find out the date from which the new decision takes effect, see p1287.

8. Tax, other benefits and the benefit cap

Tax

Carer's allowance (CA) (including an increase in your CA for your spouse, civil partner, or someone who cares for your child, if you still receive this) is taxable.[31] However, increases for children (if you are still receiving them) are not taxable.

Means-tested benefits

Before you claim CA, consider how your claim might affect your entitlement to means-tested benefits. If in doubt, seek advice.

If you are awarded CA and the person for whom you care has a severe disability premium/additional amount included in her/his income support (IS), income-based jobseeker's allowance (JSA), income-related employment and support allowance (ESA), pension credit (PC) or housing benefit (HB), her/his entitlement to that premium/additional amount can be affected (see p238). Bear in mind that the severe disability premium/additional amount is worth more than the carer premium/additional amount.

If you receive CA, you come within one of the groups of people who can claim IS.

If you are a member of a 'joint-claim couple' claiming income-based JSA, you are not required to satisfy the jobseeking conditions (see Chapter 48) if you are a carer who could claim IS (see p29). You may wish to consider claiming IS or PC instead of income-based JSA.

If you are claiming universal credit (UC), you do not have to meet any of the work-related requirements (see p1073) if you qualify for CA, or you would do but for the fact that your earnings are higher than £100 a week.

Income

CA counts in full as income for all means-tested benefits. However, in some cases an increase in your CA for an adult or child can be ignored when calculating your means-tested benefits. See p312 for PC and HB if you are at least the qualifying age for PC, and p274 for all other means-tested benefits.

CA counts as qualifying income for the savings credit of PC (see p82).

Note:
- For IS, income-based JSA and income-related ESA, and, if you are under the qualifying age for PC, HB, if you choose *not* to claim CA and the DWP decides

Part 5: Other benefits
Chapter 25: Carer's allowance
8. Tax, other benefits and the benefit cap

that you failed to apply for it deliberately, you may be treated as if you receive it.

- For all means-tested benefits other than UC, if you give up your claim for CA, you can be treated as if you receive it if the DWP decides that you deliberately deprived yourself of it in order to qualify for, or increase your entitlement to, benefit for yourself or your family (but see p288 and p318).

The amount of means-tested benefits

If you receive CA (or are entitled but do not receive it because of the overlapping benefit rules – see p1165), a carer premium/additional amount is included in your IS, income-based JSA, income-related ESA, PC and HB.

If you are claiming UC, and:

- you are a member of a couple, you can get a childcare costs element if one of you is in paid work and the other is not in paid work, is unable to provide childcare and qualifies for CA;
- you (or your partner) qualify for CA, or would do but for the fact that your (or her/his) earnings are higher than £100 a week, a carer element is included in your UC maximum amount. However, if you:
  - have limited capability for work *and* are a carer, your UC cannot include both a limited capability for work element and a carer element for the same person;
  - are a single claimant with limited capability for work-related activity, your UC includes a limited capability for work-related activity element instead of a carer element;
  - are a member of a couple, your UC includes the limited capability for work-related activity element if one has not already been included for your partner. However, if a limited capability for work-related activity element has been included for you, a carer element can be included for your partner if s/he satisfies the conditions, whether or not s/he would also qualify for a limited capability for work-related activity element.

You may need to work out how you would be better off financially.

Non-means-tested benefits

For each week you receive CA, you can get national insurance credits (see p855).

CA is subject to the overlapping benefit rules, which means that you may not be paid CA in full if another earnings-replacement benefit (eg, retirement pension) is paid to you (see p1165).

Tax credits

CA counts in full as income for tax credits. Remember, however, that you cannot get CA if you are in gainful employment (see p541).

If you are a member of a couple with at least one child or qualifying young person, and one of you is entitled to CA, the other only has to work 16 hours a week to qualify for working tax credit (WTC) (see p165). You may also qualify for the childcare element of WTC (see p1405).

The benefit cap

In some cases, the total amount of specified benefits you receive is limited to £350 a week (if you are a single claimant without children) or £500 a week (if you are a lone parent or a member of a couple). This is known as the 'benefit cap'. CA is one of the specified benefits. The benefit cap only applies if you are getting HB or UC. See p1169 for further information.

Passports and other sources of help

If you get CA (or would get it but for the overlapping benefit rules), you are entitled to a Christmas bonus (see p835). You may be able to get help, support and services from your local authority; ask for a carer's assessment. If you have a low income, you may be entitled to council tax reduction (see p827).

Notes

1. Who can claim carer's allowance
1 s70 SSCBA 1992; reg 9(1) SS(ICA) Regs
2 s70(2) SSCBA 1992; reg 3 SS(ICA) Regs
3 s70(7) SSCBA 1992
4 Reg 4(1) SS(ICA) Regs
5 s122 SSCBA 1992
6 CG/6/1990
7 R(G) 3/91
8 Reg 4(1A) SS(ICA) Regs
9 Reg 4(2) SS(ICA) Regs
10 *SSWP v Pridding* [2002] EWCA Civ 306
11 s70(1A) SSCBA 1992
12 Reg 8(1) SS(ICA) Regs
13 Reg 8(2) SS(ICA) Regs

2. The rules about your age
14 s70(3) SSCBA 1992

3. People included in the claim
15 Art 3 TCA(No.3)O

4. The amount of benefit
16 Sch 4 SSCBA 1992

6. Claims and backdating
17 s1 SSAA 1992
18 Reg 4(1) SS(C&P) Regs
19 Reg 6(1)(a) and (1ZA) SS(C&P) Regs
20 Reg 6(1)(b) SS(C&P) Regs
21 Reg 4ZC and Sch 9ZC para 4(1) and (2) SS(C&P) Regs
22 Reg 9(1) and Sch 1 SS(C&P) Regs
23 Reg 13 SS(C&P) Regs
24 Reg 19 SS(C&P) Regs
25 Reg 6(16)-(22), (33) and (34) SS(C&P) Regs

7. Getting paid
26 Reg 21 SS(C&P) Regs
27 Reg 22(3) and Sch 6 SS(C&P) Regs
28 Reg 22(1) SS(C&P) Regs
29 Reg 17 SS(C&P) Regs
30 Reg 32ZA SS(C&P) Regs

8. Tax, other benefits and the benefit cap
31 ss660, 661 and 676 IT(EP)A 2003

Chapter 26

Child benefit

This chapter covers:
1. Who can claim child benefit (below)
2. The rules about your age (p561)
3. People included in the claim (p561)
4. The amount of benefit (p561)
5. Special benefit rules (p561)
6. Claims and backdating (p563)
7. Getting paid (p566)
8. Tax, other benefits and the benefit cap (p568)

Key facts
- You may be entitled to child benefit if you are responsible for a child or qualifying young person.
- You do not need to be the child's parent to qualify and the child does not need to live with you.
- Child benefit is a non-means-tested benefit.
- You do not need to have paid national insurance contributions to qualify.
- You can qualify for child benefit whether you are in or out of work.
- If your income is over £50,000 in a tax year, you may be liable to pay tax in respect of child benefit, known as a 'high-income child benefit charge'.
- Child benefit is administered and paid by HM Revenue and Customs.
- If you disagree with a child benefit decision, you can apply for a revision or a supersession, or you may be able to appeal against it. You have to apply for a revision before you can appeal.

1. Who can claim child benefit

You qualify for child benefit for a child if:[1]
- s/he counts as a 'child' or 'qualifying young person' (see p551). **Note:** in the rest of this chapter the term 'child' is used for both a child and a qualifying young person; *and*
- you are responsible for the child because *either*:

- s/he lives with you (see p556); *or*
- you contribute to the cost of supporting her/him (see p557) at a rate of at least the amount of child benefit for that child; *and*
- you have priority over other potential claimants (see p558); *and*
- you and the child satisfy the presence and residence conditions (see p1519, p1527 and p1554); *and*
- you are not a 'person subject to immigration control', although there are exceptions to this (see p1500 and p1505).

In some circumstances, even if you meet the qualifying conditions above, you will not get child benefit (see p560).

If your child has died, see p568.

Note: you may be liable to pay tax in respect of child benefit if you have income of more than £50,000 in a tax year (see p568).

Who counts as a child

Anyone aged under 16 is a '**child**' for child benefit purposes. Provided you meet the other qualifying conditions, child benefit can be paid for her/him.[2] Child benefit can continue be paid for a child after s/he reaches 16 for as long as s/he counts as a 'qualifying young person'.

Who counts as a qualifying young person

A '**qualifying young person**' is someone who:[3]
- is aged 16 and has left relevant education (see p552) or training. S/he can count as a qualifying young person up to and including 31 August after her/his 16th birthday, or, if her/his birthday is on 31 August, up to and including the day after her/his 16th birthday;[4] *or*
- is aged 16 or 17, has left education or training and meets the conditions for being a qualifying young person during an 'extension period' (see p552); *or*
- is aged 16 or over and under 20 and meets the conditions for being a qualifying young person while on a course of full-time non-advanced education or approved training, or while enrolled or accepted on such a course (see p553 and p554); *or*
- is aged 16 or over and under 20 and has left relevant education (see p552) or approved training and has not passed the end of the week that includes her/his 'terminal date' (see p555).

If more than one of the above grounds apply to your child, s/he counts as a qualifying young person until the last date that applies.[5]

Relevant education
'Relevant education' is education that is full time and non-advanced. For the meaning of non-advanced education, see p553. In deciding whether your child is in relevant education, HM Revenue and Customs (HMRC) considers that the definition of 'full time' given on p553 applies, but this is not stated in the legislation.

If child benefit for your child stops because s/he no longer counts as a qualifying young person, but s/he later becomes a qualifying young person once more, you can get child benefit for her/him again if you make a new claim (but see p555 if there is just a temporary interruption in meeting the above conditions).

In the rest of this chapter we use the term 'child' to mean both young people aged under 16 and qualifying young people aged 16 or over. See p556 for who cannot count as a qualifying young person.

The extension period

If a child is aged 16 or 17 and has left education or training, s/he continues to count as a qualifying young person, and so you can continue to qualify for child benefit for her/him, during an **'extension period'** if:[6]

- s/he is registered as available for work, education or training with the Careers Service or a specified body; *and*
- s/he is not in remunerative work – ie, s/he is not working for 24 hours a week or more for payment, or in expectation of payment; *and*
- s/he is not in education or training. If s/he is, s/he may still count as qualifying young person on that basis (see p553 and p554); *and*
- you were entitled to child benefit for her/him immediately before the extension period started; *and*
- you apply in writing (or by another method, such as by telephone, if HMRC accepts this) within three months of the date your child's education or training finished.

In this context, 'education' and 'training' are not defined and so may mean any kind of part-time or full-time education or training.

The extension period starts from the Monday after your child's course of education or training ends and lasts for 20 weeks from that date. If your child reaches 18 during the extension period, unless s/he counts as a qualifying young person on another ground (see p551), your child benefit for her/him will end from the first child benefit payday on or after the date s/he reaches 18.[7]

If your child's ability to satisfy the above conditions is interrupted, see p555.

See p560 for circumstances when you cannot get child benefit for a child.

Full-time non-advanced education

A child aged 16 or over but under 20 counts as a qualifying young person if:[8]
- s/he is attending a full-time course of non-advanced education which s/he started, or was enrolled or accepted on, before reaching 19 (but see p554); *or*
- having previously been on a course of full-time non-advanced education, s/he is enrolled or accepted on another such course.

The course must:
- not be provided as a result of your child's employment or because of an office s/he holds (but see p555); *and*
- be provided:
  - at a school or college; *or*
  - elsewhere (such as at home), but only if a decision maker approves the education and your child was being educated in this way before reaching 16.

HMRC states that a course provided as part of the 16–19 Study Programme in England can also be treated as full-time non-advanced education, even if it is not provided at a school or college.[9]

If your child finishes a course of full-time non-advanced education before s/he is 20, you may still qualify for child benefit for a period after her/his course ends (see p555). You may also still qualify for child benefit for her/him if s/he counts as a qualifying young person on another ground (see p551).[10]

See p555 if your child's education is interrupted and p560 for circumstances when you cannot get child benefit for a child.

Full-time education

A course of education counts as **'full time'** if it is for an average of more than 12 hours a week during term time, including tuition, supervised study, exams and practical work, but excluding meal breaks and unsupervised study.[11]

'Supervised' study requires the close proximity of a teacher or tutor to enforce discipline, and provide encouragement and help.[12]

Examples of non-advanced and advanced courses[13]

Non-advanced courses	Advanced courses
GCSEs	A university degree
AS and A levels	NVQ level 4
NVQ and SVQ level 3 and below	Higher National Diploma (HND) or
International Baccalaureate	Higher National Certificate (HNC)
Scottish National Qualifications (up to	Diploma of Higher Education
higher or advanced higher level)	A teaching qualification
BTEC and OCR Nationals	SVQ level 4 and above

Approved training

A child aged 16 or over but under 20, counts as a qualifying young person if:[14]

- s/he is on a course of approved training, which s/he started, or was enrolled or accepted on, before s/he reached 19 (but see below); *or*
- s/he was on a course of full-time non-advanced education or approved training and is now enrolled or accepted on a course of approved training.

The course must not be provided under a contract of employment (but see p555). 'Approved training' includes:[15]

- in England, Foundation Learning courses or Access to Apprenticeships;
- in Scotland, Get Ready for Work or the Employability Fund;
- in Wales, Traineeships or Foundation Apprenticeships.

See p555 if your child's training is interrupted.

If your child leaves approved training before reaching 20, you may still qualify for child benefit for a period after s/he leaves (see p555). You may also still qualify for child benefit for her/him if she counts as a qualifying young person on another ground (see p551).[16]

See p560 for circumstances when you cannot get child benefit for a child.

Can you get child benefit for a 19-year-old who starts a course?

If a young person is due to start a new course of full-time non-advanced education or approved training *after* reaching 19 and arrangements for the course mean that s/he is not able to enrol on it before becoming 19:

– consider approaching the course provider to see if s/he can be accepted on the course before her/his 19th birthday. If s/he can be, s/he counts as a qualifying young person while on the course;

– if not, provided s/he has been in *continuous* full-time, non-advanced education since before her/his 19th birthday, HMRC states that s/he should be treated as having begun the course before reaching 19 and so will be a qualifying young person while on it.

In either of these situations, provided you meet the other qualifying conditions, you can get child benefit for her/him while s/he is on the course and until the end of the week that includes the first terminal date falling after the course or training ends (unless s/he is 20 before that date – see p555).

However, even if s/he does not count as a qualifying young person while on the new course, provided s/he is under 20:

– s/he can count as a qualifying young person from the date s/he is enrolled or accepted on the course until the date the new course starts; *and*

– arguably, s/he can count as a qualifying young person for a period after s/he leaves such a course under the 'terminal date rule' (see p555).[17]

If you satisfy the other qualifying conditions, but are refused child benefit for a 19-year-old in these circumstances, seek advice.

The 'terminal date rule'

If your child leaves relevant education (see p552) or approved training before reaching 20, s/he continues to count as a qualifying young person until either:[18]

- her/his 'terminal date' if this falls on a Sunday, or until the first Sunday after her/his 'terminal date' (see below); *or*
- if s/he reaches 20 on or before that date:
  - the Sunday on which her/his 20th birthday falls (if it falls on a Sunday); *or*
  - the Sunday before her/his 20th birthday (if it falls on a Monday); *or*
  - the first Sunday after her/his 20th birthday (if it falls on any other day).

Terminal date

Your child's **'terminal date'** is the first of the following dates that falls after the date her/his relevant education or approved training finished:

- the last day in February; *or*
- 31 May; *or*
- 31 August; *or*
- 30 November.

Note:

- If, after leaving a course of relevant education, a child returns to sit an external examination in connection with this course, s/he is treated as still being in relevant education until the date of the last exam, provided s/he was entered for the exam before leaving the course.[19]
- A child who has taken the Higher or Advanced Higher Certificate in Scotland is treated as being in relevant education until the date a comparable course in England or Wales would end, if this is later.[20] This is because exams are often taken earlier in Scotland than in England and Wales.
- A child cannot count as a qualifying young person on the grounds of being on a course of full-time non-advanced education or approved training (or on the grounds of being enrolled or accepted on such a course) if the course is provided as a result of her/his job. However, as long as s/he is under 20, it may be arguable that s/he can count as a qualifying young person from the date s/he leaves such a course under the terminal date rule. This is because the rules on terminal dates do not exclude young people whose course was provided under an employment contract (but see p560 if your child is working).
- See p560 for circumstances when you cannot get child benefit for a child.

Interruptions

Any break in a child's being able to satisfy the conditions for being a qualifying young person can be ignored:[21]

- for up to six months (whether or not the interruption began before or after the child was 16) if it is 'reasonable' in the circumstances; *or*

- indefinitely if it is caused by the child having a physical or mental illness or disability and the length of the absence is 'reasonable', given the circumstances.

In practical terms, this means a child can still be considered to be a qualifying young person during the interruption.

HMRC states that this rule only applies when there is an interruption in a child's ability to attend a course of education or training (eg, because of ill health), but arguably the rule can also apply to 16/17-year-olds during the extension period.

However, an interruption cannot be ignored if, immediately after the interruption, a child starts, or is likely to start:[22]

- a training course which is not 'approved training'; *or*
- a course of advanced education; *or*
- education connected to her/his employment.

Who does not count as a qualifying young person

A 16–19-year-old cannot count as a qualifying young person, and so you cannot receive child benefit for her/him, if s/he receives in her/his own right:[23]

- income support (see Chapter 3);
- income-based jobseeker's allowance (see Chapter 4);
- employment and support allowance (see Chapters 5 and 28);
- working tax credit (see Chapter 9) or child tax credit (see Chapter 8);
- universal credit (see Chapter 10).

Responsible for a child

You are only entitled to child benefit for a child if you are responsible for her/him. You count as responsible for a child in any week in which you:[24]

- have the child living with you (see below); *or*
- contribute to the cost of supporting the child (see p557).

A child 'living with' you

To be living with you, the child 'must live in the same house or other residence as [you] and also be carrying on there with [you] a settled course of daily living'.[25] This does not mean the same as 'residing together' or 'presence under the same roof'.[26] A child may be 'living with' you even while away. There are special rules if your child is looked after by a local authority (see p562).

Living apart

Even if you and your child are living apart, provided s/he lived with you in the past, your child is treated as living with you if you have not lived separately for more than 56 days in the last 16 weeks.[27] When calculating whether a child has been apart from you for 56 days, certain days of absence are ignored. These are days when the child is away only to:[28]

- receive education or training (HMRC states that this rule applies only if the child is away receiving full-time non-advanced education or approved training); *or*
- stay in certain types of residential accommodation, if this is necessary only because of the child's disability or because her/his health would be 'significantly impaired or further impaired' were s/he not staying in the accommodation (but see below); *or*
- receive inpatient treatment in a hospital or similar institution (but see below).

In the latter two situations, a maximum of 12 consecutive weeks' absence can be ignored, unless you are regularly incurring expenditure in respect of the child, when the period of absence can be ignored indefinitely.[29] If you are making visits, or giving the child pocket money, this condition is likely to be satisfied. Two or more periods in hospital or residential accommodation separated by 28 days or less are treated as one when calculating the 12-week period.

However, even if a child is not living with you, you may still qualify for child benefit for her/him if you are contributing to the cost of supporting her/him.

See p1572 if your child is abroad.

Example

Amy's son was in hospital for 18 weeks. She regularly took him food, drinks and comics. On being discharged, he stayed with his grandmother for a month to convalesce before returning home. Amy is entitled to child benefit for her son while he was away. He is treated as still living with her while in hospital as she was regularly incurring expenditure for him. He also counts as still living with her while staying with his grandmother as he was not considered to be absent from home for more than 56 days in the previous 16 weeks. The period he was in hospital is ignored when calculating the 56-day period.

Contributing to the cost of supporting a child

If a child is not living with you, you can still qualify for child benefit if you contribute to the cost of supporting her/him. To satisfy this condition, you must contribute at least the amount of child benefit that would be payable for the child (see p561).[30]

Note:

- Contributions must be regular, although the odd hiccup may be ignored.[31]
- Payments in kind rather than cash may be counted.[32]
- If you reside with your spouse or civil partner, any contribution made by one of you may be treated as a contribution by the other.[33]
- If you and another person(s) each contribute less than the amount of child benefit payable for the child, but your total contributions are at least equal to the amount of child benefit payable, one of you is treated as contributing the whole sum. If you do not agree on which one of you it is to be, HMRC decides.[34] If you qualify for child benefit on this basis, once benefit has been

awarded, you alone must actually contribute at least the amount of child benefit paid for the child in order to continue to be entitled.

Priority between claimants

Potentially, it is possible for more than one person to be entitled to child benefit for the same child – eg, when a child is living with one parent and maintained by the other. However, only one person can be awarded child benefit for a particular child. There is an order of priority for who receives child benefit when two or more people have claimed it and would otherwise be entitled.[35]

No one is entitled to child benefit without making a claim and the priority rules do not apply unless at least two people have claimed child benefit for the same child and both of them would qualify for it.[36] In this situation, claimants take priority in the following order:[37]

- a person with whom the child lives (who has priority over a person who counts as responsible for a child only because s/he is contributing to the cost of supporting the child);
- a wife, if a husband and wife are residing together (see p560);
- a parent (including a step-parent). A 'parent' means a child's 'legal parent', not just her/his biological parent. So it can include an adoptive parent or someone who has 'legal parental responsibility';[38]
- the mother (including a stepmother), if the parents are residing together but are not husband and wife (see p560);
- in any other case, a person agreed by those entitled;
- if there is no agreement, a person selected by a decision maker at HMRC (in which case there is no appeal against the decision[39] – but see p1308).

Even if a new claim takes priority over an existing claim, child benefit continues to be paid on the existing claim for the three weeks following the week in which the new claim is made, unless the existing claimant withdraws her/his claim before this or stops being entitled to child benefit for another reason.[40] In addition, even if your claim has priority, you normally cannot receive child benefit for a period before you made your claim during which it has already been paid to someone else for the same child (see p567).

If you have claimed child benefit, but you want someone who has equal or lower priority to you to receive it instead, contact the Child Benefit Office (see Appendix 1).[41]

It may be important to concede priority to your partner if you spend periods abroad, as entitlement to child benefit normally stops if you have been abroad for more than eight weeks (or 12 weeks in some circumstances – see p1572).

Separation and the priority rules

Problems can arise when there are competing child benefit claims from parents who have just separated. Even if the child only lives with one parent, s/he also may be treated as still living with the other parent for a period, under the rules described on p556 (usually until s/he has been absent from that parent for 56 days in the last 16 weeks). If you are in this situation and your child lives with you, but is still treated as living with her/his other parent, both of you are potentially entitled to child benefit for the child. If neither of you is willing to withdraw your claim, the priority rules apply (see p558).

In these circumstances, the parent already getting child benefit continues to qualify for it for the first three weeks after the week in which the competing child benefit claim is made. After that, if you and the other parent are no longer considered to be residing together, the priority rules indicate that for any period when the child lives with you and can also still be treated as living with her/his other parent, HMRC decides who receives child benefit unless you and the child's other parent can agree on who should get it. However, a commissioner's decision conflicts with this interpretation. It concerned a man whose children were living with him following his separation from their mother, his wife, who made a child benefit claim for them when she was already receiving it. The decision clarifies the situation for similar cases and is binding on them.[42]

Note: if your ex-partner has been getting child benefit for a period before you made your competing claim, see p567.

Do you share the care of a child?

If you share the care of your child with her/his other parent from whom you have separated, both of you may be potentially entitled to child benefit for her/him. If you cannot agree on who should receive it, HMRC uses its discretion to decide to whom it is reasonable to pay the benefit. This usually involves deciding who has the greater responsibility of care. In deciding how best to present your case to HMRC, consider the following questions.

1. How many hours each week do each of you care for the child?
2. What are the terms of any court orders?
3. Where are the child's possessions kept?
4. At which address is the child registered with services, such as school and her/his doctor?
5. What contributions do each of you make towards the cost of bringing up the child? (Although this may not be conclusive if the resources of one parent are greater than the other.)
6. What impact might the decision have on each parent?
7. Are there other children of the same relationship for whom child benefit is paid? For example, in one case, the High Court held that where two parents had nearly equal responsibility for the care of their two children, it was not unreasonable for the decision maker to decide that each parent should receive child benefit in respect of one child.[43]
These are just examples of the issues HMRC might consider – each case depends on its circumstances.

Residing together

It may be important to decide whether a couple are 'residing together' (or 'residing with' each other)[44] if two people make a claim for child benefit for the same child (see p558) or if child benefit is claimed for someone who is married.

If you are married, in a civil partnership or are a parent of a child, you and your spouse/your civil partner/the other parent of your child are still treated as residing together, even if you are apart, if:[45]

- your absence from each other is not likely to be permanent; *or*
- the reason for the absence is only because one or both of you is receiving care or treatment as an inpatient in either a hospital or a similar institution (that caters for people with mental health problems), whether this is likely to be temporary or permanent.

Even if you have not lived together, you can be treated as residing together if your absence from each other is not likely to be permanent.[46]

It is possible to be absent from one another while you are living under the same roof if you are maintaining separate households.[47]

When you cannot get child benefit

You cannot get child benefit for a child if:[48]

- s/he is married, in a civil partnership or cohabiting, unless the child's spouse, civil partner or partner is in relevant education or approved training, or unless the child is not residing with her/his spouse or civil partner (see above). However, the child's spouse, civil partner or partner can never be the claimant even in these circumstances. (S/he counts as cohabiting if s/he is living with her/his partner as if they were married or civil partners);[49] *or*
- in certain circumstances, s/he works for 24 hours a week or more (see below); *or*
- s/he is a 16–19-year-old and is receiving certain benefits (see p556); *or*
- s/he has spent more than eight consecutive weeks (but see p562) either:
  – in prison or other custody; *or*
  – being looked after by the local authority.

16–19-year-olds who work

If your child is under 16, your entitlement to child benefit for her/him is unaffected by any work that s/he does.

If your child is 16 or over and only counts as a qualifying young person under the 'terminal date' rule (see p555), child benefit is not payable for her/him if s/he works for 24 hours or more a week and the work is done for payment, or in the expectation of payment. Also, a 16/17-year-old who does such work cannot count as a qualifying young person on the grounds of being in an extension period (see p552).[50]

However, if your child is a qualifying young person on any other ground (see p551), any work s/he does should not affect your entitlement to child benefit.

2. The rules about your age

There is no upper or lower age limit for entitlement to child benefit.

3. People included in the claim

You claim child benefit for each child for whom you are responsible (only one person can receive child benefit for a particular child). You cannot claim any increase in child benefit for your partner or for any other dependants you have.

4. The amount of benefit

Child benefit is payable at the following weekly rates.[51]

	£pw
Eldest eligible child	20.50
Other children (each)	13.55

The higher rate of child benefit is normally paid for the eldest (or only) child in a family.[52]

If you live with your partner and each of you has children from a previous relationship for whom you receive separate child benefit, you do not both receive the higher rate of child benefit. Instead, the higher rate is paid to the person who has the eldest child.[53]

5. Special benefit rules

Special rules may apply if:
- your child is being looked after by a local authority, or is in prison or detention (see p562);
- you or your child have come from abroad or are going abroad (see p1554 and p1572);
- you are subject to immigration control (see p1499);
- you are in prison (see p960).

Prison, detention or looked after by the local authority

Special rules apply if your child is:[54]

- being looked after by a local authority and is provided with, or placed in, accommodation under certain legislation and at least part of the cost of either the accommodation or the child's maintenance is paid from local authority or public funds (but see below); or
- subject to a compulsory supervision order and living in residential accommodation under certain legislation; or
- in prison or another form of detention, such as a detention centre or young offenders' institution, as a result of criminal proceedings or non-payment of a penalty imposed on conviction.

If any of these circumstances apply to your child and have done so for at least one day a week in the last eight consecutive weeks, you cannot be entitled to child benefit for her/him after the eight-week period. However, there are some exceptions to this rule.

Exceptions

- You are not excluded from entitlement to child benefit for a child on the grounds that s/he is being looked after by the local authority if the child is placed in residential accommodation by the local authority because s/he has a disability or because her/his health would be significantly impaired or further impaired were s/he not in the accommodation.[55] If your child is living away from you in these circumstances, see p556.
- As child benefit only stops after the child has been looked after by the local authority, subject to a supervision order or in prison for at least one day a week in the last eight consecutive weeks, if s/he ceases to be in one of these situations for at least a week (ie, from Monday to Sunday), the eight-week period should start again if s/he is subsequently looked after by the local authority, subject to a supervision order or placed in prison once more.
- You continue to get child benefit after the first eight weeks provided the child 'ordinarily' lives with you throughout at least one whole day each week (which, in practice, means at least two nights – see p563) even if s/he is not actually at home in that particular week.[56]
- After the first eight weeks' absence, even if the child continues to be looked after by the local authority, subject to a supervision order or in prison and does not 'ordinarily' live with you for at least one day a week, you still qualify for child benefit when the child comes to stay with you for a week or more.[57]
- If the child is detained in a hospital or a similar institution because of mental health problems, s/he is treated as if she is in prison only if s/he was taken there from prison (or another place of detention), and the date that s/he would have been expected to be released under her/his sentence has not passed. Otherwise,

s/he is not considered to be in prison and so you can continue to get child benefit, provided you meet the normal qualifying conditions.[58]

- If the child has been detained in custody but, at the conclusion of criminal proceedings, is not sentenced to a term of imprisonment or detention, or detention and training, you are entitled to child benefit for her/him for the period of her/his earlier detention.[59]

A '**week**' means seven days beginning with a Monday.[60] A '**day**' means from midnight to midnight.[61] Because the child must live with you 'throughout' the day,[62] this means that, in practice, s/he has to stay with you for two nights to be regarded as living with you for one day.

Fostering and adoption

- *You* cannot qualify for child benefit for a child if, for any day in a week, the local authority has arranged for her/him to be placed with you under placement, looking after or fostering arrangements and the local authority is paying you an allowance towards the cost of her/his accommodation or maintenance under ss22C(10) or 23 of the Children Act 1989 or reg 33 of the Looked After Children (Scotland) Regulations 2009.[63]
- *No one* can qualify for child benefit for a child if s/he has been placed for adoption in the house of her/his prospective adopters and the local authority is making a payment for the child's accommodation or maintenance under the above provisions.[64]

If these circumstances do not apply, the normal rules on entitlement apply, including the rules on children who are being looked after by the local authority described on p562 (and the exceptions to these rules described on p562).

Your entitlement to child benefit is not affected if you are looking after a child under private fostering arrangements.

6. Claims and backdating

To be entitled to child benefit, you must make a claim for it.[65] The general rules about claims and backdating are in Chapter 53. This section explains the specific rules that apply to child benefit. Child benefit is administered and paid by HM Revenue and Customs (HMRC) through its Child Benefit Office.

Making a claim

A claim for child benefit should be made in writing. You can do this by completing:[66]

- the approved form; *or*

- the approved online form. This can be completed online, printed, signed and sent by post (see below).

Send your claim to the Child Benefit Office (see Appendix 1). Alternatively, if your claim is made immediately following the birth of the child, you may be able to submit your claim through a specified local office under the 'Tell Us Once' scheme. Details should be available when you register the birth.

Keep a copy of your claim form in case queries arise. You must provide any information and evidence required (see below).[67] HMRC has the discretion to accept claims made in another way. However, as it is unlikely to accept any claim not made in writing, it is always best to claim in writing, using the approved form whenever possible. You can amend or withdraw your claim before it is assessed (see p1138). If there is a delay in dealing with your claim, you may be able to get an interim payment (see p1169).

Forms
The approved form is Form CH2, which you can get from the Child Benefit Office (see Appendix 1). To download the form, or to complete the online form, go to www.gov.uk.

Who should claim

You must normally make a claim for child benefit yourself. If you are unable to manage your own affairs, another person can claim child benefit for you as your 'appointee' (see p1137).

If someone else makes a claim on her/his own behalf for child benefit for the same child, you are only entitled to child benefit for that child if you have priority over the other claimant. See p558 for details of priority between claimants.

Information to support your claim

When you claim child benefit you must:
- satisfy the 'national insurance (NI) number requirement' (see p1138);
- provide proof of your identity, if required (see p1140); *and*
- ensure you have made a valid claim – to do so you must supply the information requested on the claim form (see p1140).

HMRC usually needs to see an original copy of your child's birth or adoption certificate. You can either send this to the Child Benefit Office or HMRC states that you can take it to your local Jobcentre Plus office, where a copy can be made and verified and the verified copy can be sent to the Child Benefit Office.[68] However, if your claim is made through a local office under the 'Tell Us Once' scheme (see above), you do not need to send your child's birth certificate to HMRC.

Even if you have provided all that was required when you claimed, you may be asked to provide additional information and evidence relevant to your claim (see p1152).[69] There is a time limit for providing this. If you do not do so, the decision maker can decide your claim in the way most adverse to you.

Note: you may be asked to provide information after you are awarded child benefit. If you fail to do so, your child benefit could be suspended, or even terminated (see p1175).

The date of your claim

The date of your claim is important as it determines the date from when you will be paid (see p566). The date of your claim is normally the date it is received at the Child Benefit Office. If HMRC has stated, in writing, that another office can receive child benefit claims (eg, offices operating under the 'Tell Us Once' scheme – see p564), the date of claim can be the date the claim is received by that office.[70] However, you can ask for the date of your claim to be backdated for up to three months before the date it is received (see p566).

If the claim form you submit is not completed correctly or you make a written claim which is not on the approved form, you may be asked to provide further information or to complete the approved form. Provided this additional information or form is received by the Child Benefit Office (or by any other office that can receive it) within one month of its being sent back to you (or longer if the decision maker thinks the delay is reasonable), your claim is treated as having been made on the date the initial claim was received.[71]

In some circumstances, you can claim before you qualify for child benefit (see below).

If you claim the wrong benefit

The decision maker has the discretion to treat a claim for guardian's allowance (see Chapter 29) as a claim for child benefit for the same child.[72] This may allow you to get your child benefit backdated for up to three months before the date you claimed guardian's allowance, if you satisfy the qualifying conditions for child benefit over that period. However, see p567 if someone else has been getting child benefit for the child. See p1144 for details of interchanging claims in this way.[73]

Claiming in advance

If you do not qualify for child benefit when you make your claim but will qualify for it within the three months after your claim is made, the decision maker has the discretion to award child benefit in advance and can treat your date of claim as the date you start to qualify for child benefit.[74]

Backdating your claim

You should make a claim for child benefit within three months of becoming entitled to it. If you claim late, you can only receive up to three months' arrears (although there are special rules if you were getting child benefit and move between Great Britain and Northern Ireland, or if you have been recognised as a refugee – see p1512).[75] You do not have to show any reason why your claim was late. However, if someone else who is also entitled to child benefit for the same child has already been receiving it, you are not entitled to arrears for the same period (but see p567). Instead, if your claim takes priority (see p558), you are paid child benefit from the fourth week after the week in which you claim, unless the other person withdraws her/his claim before then.[76]

If you might have qualified for child benefit earlier but did not claim because you were given the wrong information or misled by the DWP or HMRC, you could ask for compensation (see p1382) or complain to the Ombudsman through your MP (see p1387).

See p565 for when a claim for another benefit can be treated as a claim for child benefit.

7. Getting paid

Child benefit is normally paid by direct credit transfer into your bank (or similar) account (see p1163). If you are unable to open or manage an account, HM Revenue and Customs (HMRC) may agree to make payments by cheque. Alternatively, you can ask for payment to be made into your partner's account or into an account you hold jointly with your partner.[77] If you are unable to act for yourself, child benefit can be paid to someone else on your behalf (called your 'appointee' – see p1137). Part or all of your child benefit can be paid to someone else if that is necessary to protect your interests, or the interests of the child.[78]

When is child benefit paid?
You are normally paid on a Monday (or on a Tuesday), although the decision maker has discretion to choose any day of the week as your normal payday. Child benefit is usually paid four-weekly for three weeks in arrears and one week in advance. Payment begins from the Monday after the date of your claim (see p565) or, if the date of your claim is on a Monday, from the date of your claim (but see p567 if someone else has been getting child benefit for the child).[79]

In some circumstances, weekly payments of child benefit can be made – eg, if:[80]
• you are a lone parent; *or*

- you or your partner get income support, income-based jobseeker's allowance, income-related employment and support allowance, pension credit or universal credit. **Note:** 'partner' is your spouse or your civil partner, unless you are permanently separated from her/him, or someone with whom you live as if you were husband and wife or civil partners. When legislation allowing same-sex marriages comes into force (in England and Wales from 13 March 2014; in Scotland probably in autumn 2014), HMRC states that this definition will cover spouses of the same sex, and partners of the same sex who live together as if they were married. See CPAG's online service and *Welfare Rights Bulletin* for updates; *or*
- the decision maker is satisfied that the four-weekly payment 'is causing hardship'.

Child benefit is a weekly benefit, which means that it cannot be paid for periods of less than a week.

If your entitlement ends, payment of child benefit normally continues up to, but not including, the following Monday. However, if your entitlement ends on a Monday, your benefit is normally paid up to, but not including, that day.

Has someone else been getting child benefit?

If you make a claim for child benefit and someone else is already getting it for that child, you only receive child benefit if your claim has priority over the existing claimant (see p558). In these circumstances, your benefit normally starts from the beginning of the fourth week after the week in which you claim, unless the existing claimant withdraws her/his claim before this or stops qualifying for child benefit for another reason. However, even if your claim has priority, you are not entitled to child benefit for a period *before* your claim was made if it already been paid to someone else for the same child for that period, unless:[81]

- the decision maker (or, if the decision has been made following an appeal, the First-tier Tribunal or Upper Tribunal) has decided that the child benefit paid is recoverable because the person has failed to disclose or misrepresented a material fact (see p1219) and no appeal against that decision has been made within the time limit; *or*
- the child benefit has been repaid.

Note:
- Even if you have been sanctioned for a benefit offence, you must be paid child benefit.
- If you have forgotten your PIN, see p1163. If a cheque is lost or stolen, see p1164.
- If payment of your child benefit is delayed (see p1382), you might be able to get an interim payment (see p1169). If you wish to complain about how your

claim has been dealt with, see Chapter 61. You might be able to claim compensation (see p1382).

* If payment of your child benefit is suspended, see p1175.
* If you are overpaid child benefit, you might have to repay it (see Chapter 56) and, in some circumstances, you may have to pay a penalty (see p1249). If you have been accused of fraud, see Chapter 57.

Change of circumstances

You must report any change in your circumstances that you are told to report, as well as any that you might reasonably be expected to know might affect your right to, the amount of, or the payment of your benefit. You should do this as soon as possible, preferably in writing. See p1174 for further information.

Note: you can also report changes of circumstances online (go to www.gov.uk).

Child benefit is normally awarded for an indefinite period (unless your circumstances are likely to change shortly after the award). Before your child benefit can be stopped or adjusted following a change in your circumstances, the decision maker must look at your claim again and make a new decision (see Chapter 58).[82] For the date from which the new decision takes effect, see p1287.

If your child dies

If your child dies and you were entitled to child benefit for her/him in the week in which s/he died (or you would have been had s/he not died in the same week s/he was born), child benefit continues to be paid for the following eight weeks, or until the Monday after s/he would have been 20, if this falls within the eight-week period. If your partner got child benefit for the child and s/he also dies, you are entitled to child benefit for the eight-week period. This only applies if you were living with your partner at the time s/he died. See p567 for the meaning of partner.[83]

8. **Tax, other benefits and the benefit cap**

Tax

If your income in a tax year is over £50,000, you are liable to pay tax on your 'taxable child benefit' for that year. This is called the 'high-income child benefit charge'. **Note:** it is only your individual income that is counted – it is not combined with that of your partner.

As well as child benefit to which you are entitled for any week which starts in the tax year, your taxable child benefit may include child benefit to which your partner is entitled (but only for weeks throughout which you were partners) and child benefit to which someone else is entitled for a child that does not live with her/him but lives with you (but only if neither that person nor her/his partner is liable for the charge themselves).[84]

If both you and your partner have income of over £50,000, in respect of child benefit paid for weeks throughout which you were partners, whoever has the highest income is liable for the charge. If you are liable for the charge, you must declare this to HMRC by including details on a self-assessment tax form. There are time limits for doing so. See p582 of the 2013/14 edition of this *Handbook* for further details of the charge.

Note:[85]

- The high-income child benefit charge is 1 per cent of your taxable child benefit for each complete £100 income you have over £50,000 in a tax year, so if your income is over £60,000 in a tax year, the charge equals the amount of taxable child benefit awarded.
- Any child benefit awarded for a child for a period after s/he has died is not included in your taxable child benefit.
- When calculating your income, certain tax reliefs can be deducted.

Electing not to be paid child benefit

You (or your partner, if s/he is the claimant) can ask HMRC not to pay child benefit to avoid liability for the high-income child benefit charge. In some circumstances, HMRC may not agree to this – eg, if deductions are being made from your benefit to collect an overpayment of child benefit.[86]

If you elect not to be paid (rather than just not claiming child benefit, or ending or withdrawing your claim), your underlying entitlement to child benefit continues and so you (or someone with whom you reside or who cares for your child) may still qualify for national insurance (NI) credits (see p852 and p854) and you may qualify for guardian's allowance or widowed parent's allowance if you meet the conditions. For these reasons, consider claiming child benefit for each of your children, even if you do not want the benefit to be paid.

Note: if, after electing not to receive child benefit, you realise your child benefit for the tax year would have been more than the charge for that year, you have up to two years after the end of the tax year to ask for child benefit to be paid for that year.

Means-tested benefits and tax credits

Means-tested benefits can be paid in addition to child benefit.

Usually, any child benefit you get is ignored when calculating your entitlement to income support and income-based jobseeker's allowance.[87] However, see p274 for when child benefit is taken into account.[88]

Child benefit is also ignored when calculating entitlement to employment and support allowance, pension credit (PC), housing benefit (HB), working tax credit, child tax credit and universal credit (UC).[89]

Non-means-tested benefits

If you get an increase in a non-means-tested benefit for a child, the increase is reduced if you also receive child benefit for that child paid at the rate for the eldest eligible child – ie, £20.50 (see p1167). Increases for children were abolished on 6 April 2003, but some people continue to receive them.

If you are awarded child benefit for a child aged under 12, you or, in some circumstances, someone who resides with you or cares for your child, can qualify for NI credits (see p852 and p854). You may also be able to build up entitlement to additional state pension see p760).

Your entitlement to any other non-means-tested benefit is not affected by your entitlement to child benefit.

The benefit cap

In some cases, the total amount of specified benefits you receive is limited to £350 a week (if you are a single claimant without children) or £500 a week (if you are a lone parent or a member of a couple). This is known as the 'benefit cap'. Child benefit is one of the specified benefits. The benefit cap only applies if you are getting HB or UC. See p1169 for further information.

Passports and other sources of help

For details of the qualifying conditions for free school lunches, see p832.

You may be entitled to council tax reduction (see p827).

Children and young people under 19 may qualify for health benefits (see Chapter 30). Young people between the ages of 16 and 19 who are in non-advanced education may qualify for financial help with their studies (see p833).

Notes

1. **Who can claim child benefit**
   1 ss141, 142, 143, 144, and 146 SSCBA 1992; s115 IAA 1999; reg 23 CB Regs
   2 s142(1) SSCBA 1992
   3 s142(2) SSCBA 1992; regs 2-7 CB Regs

4 If a child's 16th birthday falls on 31 August, HMRC states s/he is only a qualifying young person up to and including that day, but arguably, this is not correct; 07030 CBTM; reg 4(3) CB Regs

5   Reg 2(2) CB Regs
6   Reg 5 CB Regs
7   Reg 14 CB&GA(Admin) Regs; reg 5(3) CB Regs
8   Reg 3 CB Regs
9   07020 CBTM
10 Regs 2(2), 3, 4, 5, 6 and 7 CB Regs
11 Reg 1(3) CB Regs
12 R(F) 1/93, but see also *Flemming v SSWP* [2002] EWCA Civ 641, reported as R(G) 2/02; *SSWP v Deane* [2010] EWCA Civ 699
13 Reg 1(3) CB Regs
14 Reg 3(2)(c), (d) and (4) CB Regs
15 Reg 1(3) CB Regs; 07024 CBTM
16 Regs 2(2) and 7 CB Regs
17 As there is no requirement in the terminal date rules that a course must be started before the age of 19.
18 Reg 7(1) and (2) CB Regs
19 Reg 7(2)2.1 CB Regs
20 Reg 7(2)1.3 CB Regs
21 Reg 6(2) and (3) CB Regs
22 Reg 6(4) CB Regs
23 Regs 2(4) and 8 CB Regs
24 s143 SSCBA 1992
25 R(F) 2/81
26 R(F) 2/79
27 s143(2) SSCBA 1992
28 s143(3) SSCBA 1992; reg 9 CB Regs
29 s143(3)(b) and (c) and (4) SSCBA 1992; reg 10 CB Regs
30 s143(1)(b) SSCBA 1992
31 R(U) 14/62
32 R(U) 3/66
33 Reg 11(4) CB Regs
34 Reg 11 CB Regs
35 s144(3) and Sch 10 SSCBA 1992
36 s13(1) SSAA 1992
37 Sch 10 SSCBA 1992
38 s147(3) SSCBA 1992; R(F) 1/08
39 Sch 2 para 4 SSA 1998
40 Sch 10 para 1 SSCBA 1992
41 Regs 14 and 15 CB Regs
42 CF/1771/2003
43 *R (on the application of Ford) v Board of Inland Revenue* [2005] EWHC Admin 1109, 19 May 2005; see also *R (Chester) v Secretary of State for Social Security* [2001] EWHC Admin 1119, 7 December 2001, unreported
44 *Grove v Insurance Officer,* reported as an appendix to R(F) 4/85
45 s147(4) SSCBA 1992; regs 1(3) and 34 CB Regs
46 R(F) 4/85
47 R(F) 3/81

48 Sch 9 paras 1 and 3 SSCBA 1992; regs 8, 12,13 and 16 CB Regs
49 But see *KW v HMRC (CB)* [2011] UKUT 489 (AAC)
50 Regs 1(3), 5(2)(c) and 7(3) CB Regs

4. The amount of benefit
51 Reg 2(1) CB(R) Regs
52 Reg 2(1) CB(R) Regs
53 Reg 2(2) CB(R) Regs

5. Special benefit rules
54 s147(2) and Sch 9 para 1 SSCBA 1992; regs 16-19 CB Regs
55 Regs 9 and 18(b) CB Regs
56 Reg 16(1)(b)(iv) CB Regs
57 Reg 16(1)(b)(i)-(iii) CB Regs
58 Reg 17(2)-(5) CB Regs
59 Regs 1(3) and 17(1) CB Regs
60 s147(1) SSCBA 1992
61 R(F) 3/85
62 Reg 16(2) CB Regs
63 Reg 16(3) CB Regs
64 Reg 16(4) and (5) CB Regs

6. Claims and backdating
65 s13 SSAA 1992
66 Regs 2, definition of 'writing', and 5 CB&GA(Admin) Regs
67 Reg 7 CB&GA(Admin) Regs
68 Regs 3(2) and 5(5) CB&GA(AA) Regs
69 Reg 7 CB&GA(Admin) Regs
70 Reg 5(3) CB&GA(Admin) Regs
71 Reg 10 CB&GA(Admin) Regs
72 Reg 11 CB&GA(Admin) Regs
73 See also reg 9(2) and Sch 1 SS(C&P) Regs
74 Reg 12 CB&GA(Admin) Regs
75 Reg 6 CB&GA(Admin) Regs
76 Sch 10, para 1 SSCBA 1992

7. Getting paid
77 Regs 16 and 17 CB&GA(Admin) Regs
78 Reg 33 CB&GA(Admin) Regs
79 Reg 13 CB&GA(Admin) Regs
80 Regs 18(3), 19 and 20(1) and (2) CB&GA(Admin) Regs
81 Sch 10, para 1 SSCBA 1992; s13(2) SSAA 1992; reg 38 CB Regs; CF/2826/2007
82 Reg 15 CB&GA(Admin) Regs
83 s145A SSCBA 1992; reg 20 CB Regs

• •

8. **Tax, other benefits and the benefit cap**

84 ss681B, 681D and 681H IT(EP)A 2003
85 ss681C, 681E and 681H IT(EP)A 2003
86 s13A SSAA 1992; directions given by the
    commissioners for HMRC on elections
    not to receive child benefit
87 Sch 9 para 5B IS Regs; Sch 7 para 6B JSA
    Regs
88 Reg 40 IS Regs; reg 103 JSA Regs; regs
    1, 7 and 8 SS(WTCCTC)(CA) Regs
89 **ESA** Reg 104(2) and Sch 8 para 7(2) ESA
    Regs
    PC Regs 9 and 15(1)(j) SPC Regs
    HB Reg 40 and Sch 5 para 65 HB Regs;
    regs 27 and 29 HB(SPC) Regs
    UC Reg 66 UC Regs
    TC Reg 7 TC(DCI) Regs

Chapter 27

· ·

Disability living allowance

This chapter covers:

New claims for disability living allowance (DLA) can only be made for children under 16. People aged 16 to 64 who have a disability can claim personal independence payment (PIP). However, many adults who already receive DLA will continue to receive it for some time and can currently renew their claims, apply for revisions or supersessions of decisions and appeal against decisions. This chapter therefore continues to include information about DLA for adults, as well as for children. If you are over 16 and were under 65 on 8 April 2013 and were already getting DLA, the government intends that you will be invited to claim PIP by 2018 and your DLA will end. See Chapter 35 for more about PIP and see CPAG's online service and *Welfare Rights Bulletin* for updates.

Key facts

- Disability living allowance (DLA) is a benefit for people with disabilities who need help getting around and/or with supervision or attention needs.
- You must be under 16 to make a new claim.
- DLA has two separate components: a care component and a mobility component. However, it is a single benefit for which you only have to make one claim. Each component can be paid at different rates.
- DLA is a non-means-tested benefit.
- You can qualify for DLA whether you are in or out of work.
- You do not have to have paid national insurance contributions to qualify.

· · · ·

Part 5: Other benefits
Chapter 27: Disability living allowance
1. Disability living allowance mobility component

- DLA can be paid in addition to other benefits and is disregarded as income for means-tested benefits and tax credits.
- DLA is administered and paid by the DWP's Disability and Carers Service.
- If you disagree with a DLA decision, you can apply for a revision or a supersession, or appeal against it. You are likely to have to apply for a revision before you can appeal.

1. Disability living allowance mobility component

Disability living allowance (DLA) mobility component is for people who have difficulties when walking. There is a higher rate and a lower rate.

Who can claim

You qualify for DLA mobility component if:[1]
- you satisfy the residence conditions (see p1555);
- you are not a 'person subject to immigration control', although there are exceptions to this rule (see p1500);
- you satisfy the age rules – ie, you are under the age of 16 when you first claim (but see p605 for how the introduction of personal independence payment affects you if you are 16 or over and are already getting DLA) and:
  - for the higher rate you must be aged three or over;
  - for the lower rate you must be aged five or over;
- you are not in hospital (although sometimes DLA mobility component is paid in hospital – see p944);
- you satisfy the 'disability conditions' for either the higher rate (see p575) or the lower rate (see p579);
- you have satisfied the disability conditions throughout the three months immediately before your award begins (see p596 if you are reclaiming within two years) and you are likely to continue to satisfy them for the next six months *or* you are terminally ill (see p593);
- you are likely to be able to 'benefit from enhanced facilities for locomotion' (see below).

To benefit from enhanced facilities for locomotion
To qualify for either rate of the DLA mobility component, you must be able to '**benefit from enhanced facilities for locomotion**'. This means you must be able to make outdoor journeys from time to time. It is not essential that you are interested in or enjoy going out, provided it would be beneficial for you to do so. For example, you can get DLA mobility component even if you have to be carried to a car for a ride.[2]

Disability conditions for the higher rate mobility component

You qualify for the higher rate mobility component if:[3]
- you have a disability from a physical cause that means you are unable, or virtually unable, to walk (see below); *or*
- you are both deaf and blind (see p577); *or*
- you are blind or severely visually impaired (see p577); *or*
- you were born without feet or are a double amputee (see p578); *or*
- you are 'severely mentally impaired', have 'severe behavioural problems' and qualify for the highest rate of DLA care component (see p578).

'Unable or virtually unable to walk'
You are eligible for the higher rate if:[4]
- you are unable to walk; *or*
- your ability to walk outdoors is so limited in terms of the distance, speed, length of time, or the manner in which you can make progress on foot without severe discomfort that you are virtually unable to walk; *or*
- the exertion required to walk would constitute a danger to your life or be likely to lead to a serious deterioration in your health.

Your personal circumstances, such as the location of your home or job, should not be taken into account. It is not, for instance, relevant if you live a long way from your nearest bus stop,[5] or if you cannot use public transport.

Physical disability
Your inability, or virtual inability, to walk must have a physical cause.[6] There can be a physical cause, such as pain or dizziness, even without a medically diagnosed origin. It does not matter if the original cause was mental, provided a current physical impairment affects your walking. For example, if you have severe depression and your muscles have atrophied, making you virtually unable to walk, you could qualify. Myalgic encephalomyelitis (ME), or chronic fatigue syndrome, should be accepted as having a physical origin unless there is evidence that your mobility restrictions are purely psychological.[7] If your walking is impaired by weakness due to anorexia nervosa, the cause is physical.[8] A child's discomfort from chronic diarrhoea might make her vitually unable to walk.[9] Your inability to make any progress on foot because of behavioural problems may qualify if the cause is physical – eg, Down's syndrome or autism are both accepted as disorders of development of the brain.[10]

Unable to walk
You are unable to walk if you cannot move your body along by alternate, weight-bearing steps of the feet.[11]

Part 5: Other benefits
Chapter 27: Disability living allowance
1. Disability living allowance mobility component

Prostheses, aids and medication

Your ability to walk is considered taking into account any prosthesis or artificial aid you use, or that would be suitable for you.[12] You may not qualify if you are able to walk with a stick or crutches. However, if you have one leg and no artificial limb suitable to use, you are regarded as 'unable to walk', even if you can get around on crutches.[13] If you have no feet, you qualify automatically (see p578).[14]

Any medication you normally and reasonably use is taken into account – eg, it may not be practical to carry a bulky nebuliser.[15] However, you should not be expected to undergo surgery. If you do not take medicines or treatment because of alcoholism or your mental health, your walking should be assessed as you are now, not how you might be if you accepted any treatment.[16]

Outdoors

The test is how you cope with the terrain and environment normally encountered outdoors. If you have problems with your balance on uneven pavements and roads, or if you have a lung or other condition which is made worse by wind or rain, these should be taken into account.[17] Walking indoors (eg, in a supermarket) is not necessarily an indication of your ability to walk outdoors.[18]

Distance

The law does not require a specific distance to be used when determining your inability to walk. In practice, you may be refused benefit if you state that you can walk more than 50 metres. However, your walking speed, the time it takes you to cover the distance and your manner of walking are also relevant, so give details about these on the claim form. Caselaw says that walking speeds of less than 60 metres per minute are slow, so if you cannot walk this fast without severe discomfort, you should say so.[19]

Without severe discomfort

Any walking that you can achieve only with severe discomfort should be ignored when considering whether you are virtually unable to walk.[20] This is a lesser test than 'severe pain or distress.'[21] If, when you walk, you feel severe discomfort (eg, pain or breathlessness brought on by walking), make this clear.[22] You may be able to walk a distance without severe discomfort, a further distance that causes you severe discomfort, and then have to stop altogether. The test is how far you can walk before going any further causes you severe discomfort. You should state this distance on the claim form, rather than how far you can walk before you actually have to stop. If you can walk further without severe discomfort after a brief rest, this could be taken into account.[23]

If you are in severe discomfort before you start to walk, even if the pain gets no worse, you should count as being virtually unable to walk, provided your disability affects the physical act of walking – eg, if you have an injured foot.[24] You do not, however, count as being virtually unable to walk if something unconnected with walking (eg, a skin condition affected by sunlight) causes the discomfort.[25]

The exertion required to walk

You can qualify for the higher rate mobility component if the exertion required to walk endangers your health. If the deterioration of your health is sudden, you must show that you would never recover, or recovery would take a significant period of time (eg, 12 months) or would require some form of medical intervention. So, a person with ME who needs a few days' rest after walking would not satisfy this test.[26] The fact that walking may cause you stress, or lead to a deterioration in mental health, does not count.[27]

Blind and deaf

You are treated as being unable to walk if:

- the degree of disablement resulting from your loss of vision is 100 per cent; *and*
- the degree of disablement resulting from your loss of hearing is 80 per cent on a scale where 100 per cent represents absolute deafness;[28] *and*
- the combined effect of the blindness and deafness means that you are unable to walk to any intended or required destination while outdoors without the help of another person.[29]

The regulations do not specify how to assess the degree of disablement, but caselaw suggests that the industrial injury provisions should be used (see p674).[30] So 100 per cent disablement through 'loss of vision' means 'loss of sight to such an extent as to render the claimant unable to perform any work for which eyesight is essential'.[31] This is the definition used when someone is registered blind.

If your level of hearing loss, averaged between both ears at 1, 2 and 3 kHz, is at least 87 decibels, you will satisfy the 80 per cent disablement test.[32] You may be required to undertake a hearing test. The assessment of your hearing ability takes into account any hearing aid you use or could reasonably be expected to use.[33]

Blind or severely visually impaired

You must have been certified blind or severely sight impaired and have combined visual accuity, in both eyes, on the 'Snellen scale', while using appropriate corrective lenses if necessary, of:[34]

- less than 3/60; *or*
- 3/60 or more, but less than 6/60, if you have a complete loss of peripheral vision and a central visual field of no more than 10 degrees.

'Appropriate' corrective lenses are ones that you can wear without discomfort.[35]

Part 5: Other benefits
Chapter 27: Disability living allowance
1. Disability living allowance mobility component

People without feet

If you do not have feet or legs (missing from the ankle or above), you are automatically treated as being unable to walk,[36] even if you can walk with prostheses.

Severe mental impairment and behavioural problems

If you have severe behavioural difficulties, you qualify for the higher rate mobility component if:[37]

- you are 'severely mentally impaired' – ie, you have arrested development, or incomplete physical development, of the brain, which results in severe impairment of intelligence and social functioning; *and*
- you display severe behavioural problems – ie:
  - you exhibit extreme disruptive behaviour; *and*
  - you regularly require someone else to intervene and physically restrain you to prevent you causing injury to yourself or others or damage to property; *and*
  - you are so unpredictable that another person has to be present and watching over you whenever you are awake;[38] *and*
- you qualify for the highest rate of the DLA care component.

If you do not meet all the above elements, you might still qualify for the higher rate mobility component because your disability prevents you from walking effectively, so that you are virtually unable to walk (see p575).[39]

Arrested or incomplete development

'Arrested or incomplete development' must occur before the brain reaches its final development. Medical opinion suggests this is at or before the age of 30. Someone with a degenerative condition which occurs after the brain has fully developed would not qualify under this route.[40] The age at which your illness began is significant, and you must also have a severe impairment of intelligence *and* of social functioning.[41]

Severe impairment of intelligence

An IQ of 55 or less is generally accepted as a 'severe impairment of intelligence'. However, some people may have a higher IQ but be unable to apply it practically.[42] Your 'degree of judgement in relation to everyday living' should also be taken into account.[43] For example, an autistic child with no awareness of danger may have severely impaired intelligence even if her/his IQ is over 55.[44]

Physical restraint

Physical restraint may involve as little as a hand on the arm. You do not need to show that any force is used.[45] If the presence of someone who watches over you is enough to prevent you from being disruptive, or a specially adapted environment allows you to be safely left alone, you may not pass the test. However, the decision maker should not focus only on how you are outdoors or in a structured safe environment, and must consider your need for, and the nature of, intervention in all environments.[46] Involuntary behaviour, such as falls due to seizures, can be classed as 'disruptive'.[47]

Disability condition for the lower rate mobility component

You qualify for the lower rate mobility component if you can walk but are 'so severely disabled physically or mentally' that you cannot get around outdoors 'without guidance or supervision from another person most of the time'.[48] **Note:** there is an extra test if you are claiming on behalf of a child under 16 (see below).

Any ability you may have to use familar routes without guidance or supervision should be ignored.[49] Entitlement to the lower rate mobility component is based on an assessment of your need for supervision or guidance, rather than any physical difficulty you have walking, which might qualify you for the higher rate component.[50]

The additional test for children

For the lower rate mobility component for a child, in addition to the usual guidance or supervision condition (see p580) you must also show that *either*:[51]

- your child requires substantially more guidance or supervision than children of her/his age in 'normal' physical and mental health; *or*
- children of the same age in 'normal' physical and mental health would not require such guidance or supervision.

For example, children with visual impairments or learning disabilities may need adults to hold or guide them, or to watch over them in situations in which most children of a similar age would only require someone to acccompany them. Similarly, a young deaf child may need someone to stay within touching distance, whereas a hearing child would not.[52]

As all young children require some guidance or supervision outdoors, it can be difficult to explain what is 'substantially in excess' of the norm. It may be either because of the extra time you devote to these tasks or the degree of supervision the child requires.[53]

The comparison should be with an 'average child' – ie, a child of average intelligence whose behaviour is neither particularly good nor bad.[54]

See p600 for tips on answering the mobility questions on the DLA claim form for a child.

Note: this extra test does not apply to the higher rate mobility component.

Fear and anxiety

You can qualify for the lower rate mobility component on the basis of a mental as well as a physical disablement. If you have an anxiety disorder and need the help

Part 5: Other benefits
Chapter 27: Disability living allowance
1. Disability living allowance mobility component

of an escort to overcome your fear of going outside, you are likely to satisfy the 'guidance or supervision' requirement.[55] There is conflicting caselaw, but if no amount of reassurance can persuade you to go outside, you may not qualify.[56] However, if you can just manage a walk into your garden, this could be enough to qualify.[57]

Any fear or anxiety that stops you going out on your own must be a symptom of mental disability in order to count. Fear and anxiety arising from a physical disability, such as a rational fear of having to cope with incontinence while alone, is not sufficient, although you may still have a physical need for supervision.[58] If your physical disability causes you such fear or anxiety that you can be said to be mentally disabled, you may qualify.

Guidance

'Guidance' can take a number of different forms. It can mean physically leading or directing you, giving oral suggestions or persuasion, helping you avoid obstacles or places that upset you, or leading or persuading you when you become disorientated or have a panic attack. Even if your companion only intervenes occasionally, s/he could still be guiding 'most of the time' if you would otherwise not know when to change direction. If you are visually impaired and use a guide dog or a cane, you may still need guidance to follow directions, avoid obstacles or cross roads. If you are deaf and your main method of communication is sign language, you may require guidance in unfamiliar places if you are unable to ask for or follow directions. However, you may not qualify if you can study maps, read street signs or communicate with passers by.[59]

Supervision

'Supervision' can vary. It can be precautionary (eg, accompanying and watching over you) in order to monitor your physical, mental or emotional state in case you need more assistance to continue walking. It can also be monitoring the route ahead for obstacles, dangers, places or situations which might upset you. Supervision can also be more active, such as encouraging, persuading or cajoling you, talking to you to take your mind off your fears,[60] or distracting you from possibly alarming situations through conversation.[61]

Unlike the 'continual supervision' condition for the DLA care component, you do not need to require supervision to prevent 'substantial danger'.[62] If you qualify for the care component because you require continual supervision, you may also qualify for the lower rate mobility component.[63] However, this is not automatic; your eligibility must be assessed on the mobility criteria alone.[64]

The supervision does not need to improve your walking ability, but should enable you to 'take advantage of the faculty of walking'. It is enough that supervision helps, even if it does not remove risks completely or if you may not always respond well to the person providing it.[65] If you need to have someone with you (eg, to provide help in the event of seizures or a severe asthma attack),[66] even though you have no difficulty getting about, you can qualify for the lower rate mobility component.[67]

---

2. Disability living allowance care component

Disability living allowance (DLA) care component is for people with attention or supervision needs.

Who can claim

You qualify for the DLA care component if:[68]
- you satisfy the residence conditions (see p1555);
- you are not a 'person subject to immigration control', although there are some exceptions (see p1500);
- you are under the age of 16 when you first claim (see p590) (but see p605 for how the introduction of personal independence payment affects you if you are 16 or over and are already getting DLA);
- you are not in hospital (see p944) or residential care (see p950);
- you satisfy the 'disability' conditions for the lower, middle or higher rate of the care component (see p582). You do not need to satisfy the disability conditions if you are terminally ill (see p593) or, in certain circumstances, if you undergo renal dialysis (see p592);
- if you are under 16, you satisfy the additional disability test for children (see below) *or* you are terminally ill;
- you have satisfied the disability conditions throughout the three months immediately before your award begins (see p596 if you are reclaiming within two years) and you are likely to continue to satisfy them for the next six months *or* you are terminally ill (see p593).

The additional test for children

For the DLA care component, you must show that either:[69]
- the child has attention or supervision requirements 'substantially in excess of the normal requirements' of a child of the same age; *or*
- the child has substantial attention or supervision requirements which younger children in 'normal' physical and mental health may also have, but which children of the same age and in 'normal' physical and mental health would not have. If this is due to 'developmental delay', see p583.

These extra tests do not apply if you are claiming DLA care component for a child who is terminally ill.[70]

As all young children require assistance throughout the day, it can be difficult to explain how you are providing attention or supervision that is 'substantially in excess' of what is normally required. It may be either because of the extra time

Part 5: Other benefits
Chapter 27: Disability living allowance
2. Disability living allowance care component

you devote to these tasks, or the degree of attention or supervision which is required.[71] A disabled child might require intensive help with eating, whereas children of the same age might be expected to eat unaided or only need certain foods cut up. Similarly, a disabled child could require supevision to avoid dangers that children would usually be expected to deal with themselves by that particular age. The comparison should be with an 'average child' – ie, a child of average intelligence whose behaviour is neither particularly good nor bad.[72]

See p599 for tips on completing the DLA claim form for a child.

The disability conditions

You qualify for the **lowest rate care component** if:[73]
* you are 16 or over and you are so severely disabled, physically or mentally, that you cannot prepare a cooked main meal for yourself if you have the ingredients (the 'cooking test' – see p583); *or*
* you are so severely disabled, physically or mentally that you require (see p585) attention from another person for a significant portion of the day (whether during a single period or a number of periods) in connection with your bodily functions (see p585 and p588).

You qualify for the **middle rate care component** if:
* you satisfy one of the daytime disability conditions (see below) *or* one of the night-time disability conditions (see below);[74] *or*
* you undergo renal dialysis in certain circumstances (see p592).[75]

You qualify for the **highest rate care component** if:
* you satisfy one of the daytime disability conditions (see below) *and* one of the night-time disability conditions (see below);[76] *or*
* you are terminally ill (see p593).[77]

The **daytime disability conditions** are that you are so severely disabled, physically or mentally, that you require (see p585):[78]
* frequent attention from another person throughout the day in connection with your bodily functions (see p585); *or*
* continual supervision throughout the day in order to avoid substantial danger to yourself or others (see p589).

The **night-time disability conditions** are that you are so severely disabled, physically or mentally, that you require (see p585):[79]
* prolonged or repeated attention from another person at night (see p589) in connection with your bodily functions (see p585); *or*
* another person to be awake at night for a prolonged period or at frequent intervals to watch over you (see p590) in order to avoid substantial danger to yourself or others.

'So severely disabled physically or mentally'

To qualify, you must be 'so severely disabled physically or mentally' that you need attention or supervision. You do not need to have a specific medical condition. What is important is that you are so disabled that you have care needs.[80] However, medical evidence can still be important to establish that you are disabled and what your care needs are.[81]

Problems sometimes arise if, for example, a child has behavioural problems or a developmental delay that have not been attributed to a disability. In one case, it was ruled that what is key is whether you have the physical or mental power to control the behaviour.[82]

Care needs resulting from any medical condition caused or made worse by alcohol should be taken into account, whether or not you can control your drinking. The transitory effects of intoxication, such as incontinence or vomiting, can also be considered for the care component (and the lower rate, but not higher rate, mobility component) if the consumption of alcohol is because of a medical condition that means you cannot realistically stop drinking.[83]

The cooking test

You qualify for the lowest rate care component if you can show that you are so severely disabled, physically or mentally, that you cannot prepare a cooked main meal for yourself if you have the ingredients. **Note:** this test does not apply to children under the age of 16.[84]

The meal looked at is a labour-intensive main meal for one person, freshly cooked on a traditional cooker (although if you use a microwave, this is not proof that you cannot prepare a cooked main meal).[85] It is a hypothetical test about what you can reasonably do – it does not matter whether you actually do or do not cook,[86] or even have never learnt to do so.[87] It is a broad test of your ability – it does not necessarily matter if there are some days when your ability is more or less than it is the rest of the time.[88]

You must show that your disability makes you unable to perform the tasks that are needed to cook a main meal. You need to explain about your ability to plan, prepare and cook it – eg, to:
- peel and chop vegetables;
- use taps;
- use cooking utensils;
- use a cooker, but not necesssarily the oven;
- lift hot or heavy pans;
- drain vegetables;
- tell if food is cooked properly.

Part 5: Other benefits
Chapter 27: Disability living allowance
2. Disability living allowance care component

In order to cook a main meal, you must be able to manage both physical tasks (eg, lifting, carrying, bending and using kitchen equipment) and mental tasks such as concentrating and planning.

- If you have a visual impairment or learning difficulties, you should qualify if you are unable to read labels or cooking instructions, check whether vegetables have been adequately prepared and washed, or see whether food is properly cooked.
- If you have a mental condition and lack the motivation or concentration to cook, you should satisfy the test.[89]
- You may qualify if you can perform some of the individual cooking tasks (eg, chopping meat or vegetables) but do not have the stamina, concentration or ability to co-ordinate tasks to prepare an entire meal. For example, if you have chronic back pain and cannot stand for long periods, it may not be reasonable to expect you to prepare a meal and wait for it to cook while sitting down.[90]
- You may qualify if breathing difficulties in a hot, steamy kitchen or nausea stop you cooking.[91]

Kitchen equipment, aids and adaptations

The cooking test is a hypothetical test of what you can or cannot reasonably do, so it is arguable that it is not appropriate or reasonable to consider whether your kitchen is (or could be) specially adapted.[92] You should qualify if the only 'cooking' you do is using a microwave to heat up convenience food. In general, the test is not about whether using aids and adaptations could overcome any difficulties you have.[93] However, cooking aids and adaptations may be taken into account if it is 'reasonable' to do so – eg, if you could readily obtain them.[94] You should also be able to cook a 'sufficiently wide range of meals'.[95] If it is suggested that you use a slotted spoon instead of draining vegetables from the pan, explain any difficulties you might still have lifting pans of water on and off the cooker. Although a perching stool may be useful to relieve fatigue or discomfort (if it is suitable for you to use one in your circumstances[96]), you must still be sufficiently agile and mobile to cook a meal.[97]

Reasonableness

Only people who can 'reasonably' be expected to prepare a cooked main meal should be regarded as being able to do so. What is reasonable depends on your circumstances. For example, if you have blackouts or seizures, it may be dangerous and unreasonable for you to cook and so you should qualify. In one case, a person with haemophilia was judged to be at risk and to experience anxiety when cooking, but not to the extent that it was unreasonable for him to prepare a cooked main meal.[98]

Attention and supervision

'Requires'

To satisfy the attention or supervision conditions, you must show that you 'require this assistance' from another person. The assistance must be 'reasonably required' rather than 'medically required'.[99] For example, if you are incontinent and need help changing your bedding, this help should count as 'reasonably required', even if not actually required to protect your skin.

Reasonably requires attention

Attention must be 'reasonably required to enable' you 'as far as reasonably possible to live a normal life'. Having a social life, recreation and cultural activities are part of normal life. If you are blind, it is therefore, reasonable for you to have someone read newspapers, describe television pictures, or guide you during social outings. Similarly, if you have learning disabilities, it is reasonable for you to travel to, or take part in, social and recreational pursuits. Your age and interests should be taken into account when deciding what is reasonable.[100]

Reasonably requires supervision

The requirement for supervision need only be reasonable. You are not expected to avoid every risk of harm in order to avoid the need for supervision. You can avoid most risks by staying in a chair all day, but that may be totally unreasonable.[101] It is not reasonable to expect you to avoid all situations in which you might fall.[102]

When considering your need for continual supervision (see p589), you can argue that the fact that supervision is provided shows it is needed. You may reasonably require supervision even if you do not receive it. Be clear about the difficulties you have when your needs are not met, and about what help you think you need.[103]

Refusing medical treatment

Refusing medical treatment may affect whether or not you qualify. If treatment you have been offered by your doctor would remove the need for help, the attention or supervision you get may not be reasonably required. However, it may not be 'reasonably appropriate' for you to take the treatment – eg, because of the side effects.[104] Attention or supervision should be accepted as reasonable if your psychiatric condition causes you to refuse treatment, or you refuse invasive surgery.[105]

Attention

The attention you require must be in connection with 'bodily functions'. These have been defined as the normal action of any organ of the body, or a number of organs acting together.

Part 5: Other benefits
Chapter 27: Disability living allowance
2. Disability living allowance care component

The attention is in connection with your bodily functions if it is a substitute method of providing what the bodily function would provide were it not impaired.[106] For example, guiding a blind person so that s/he is able to walk outside should be treated as attention with the bodily function of 'seeing', rather than of 'walking'. A guide assists with 'seeing' by acting 'as the eyes' of a blind person. Shopping or cleaning do not qualify because they are not normal actions or purposes of an organ or set of organs 'but merely things which a body can do if the relevant bodily functions... are working normally'.[107]

'**Attention**' is defined as 'a service of a close and intimate nature ... involving personal contact carried out in the presence of the disabled person'.[108] The attention must be in connection with the bodily function. So helping someone to drink counts; carrying the drinks to where s/he is sitting does not.[109] Although attention must usually involve personal contact, it need not be *physical* contact. Contact established by the spoken word may count if, for example, you are blind.[110] Thus, reading, describing or giving verbal instructions can be attention.

Similarly, if you would neglect yourself unless cajoled or stimulated to do routine tasks, you may require attention in the form of active stimulation.[111] Spoken reassurance counts, provided your carer is required to be physically in the same place as you. Reassurance provided over the telephone and other types of support not in your physical presence do not qualify as attention,[112] although they may indicate a need for attention where help cannot be provided otherwise.[113]

Attention or supervision?

'**Attention**' involves a service of an 'active nature'[114] whereas '**supervision**' is passive and 'may be precautionary or anticipatory, yet never result in intervention'.[115] However, where supervision does lead to intervention, it becomes attention, so the two categories can overlap. If you need to be supervised because you are likely to fall and injure yourself, you receive attention when your carer gives you a steadying hand or warns you of an obstacle.[116] If attention is frequent, you qualify for the middle rate care component, even if the supervision is not 'continual' throughout the day. Sometimes an act can be both supervision and attention. It is, therefore, important to emphasise the full extent of your needs without trying to fit them neatly into either category at the expense of leaving things out.

Communication

Communication is made up of a 'bundle' of bodily functions, including functions of the brain (such as language processing, or comprehension) or the senses (such as hearing). You need to identify what bodily function is impaired and what attention is needed from another person in connection with that bodily function.[117] If you are profoundly deaf, you may need an interpreter because you cannot hear spoken language,[118] or extra effort may be required to initiate a two-way conversation.[119]

Explaining written information to someone with poor literacy skills as a result of deafness[120] or a learning disability may also qualify.[121]

Domestic duties

Although attention must normally be carried out in your presence, a period of attention can also include incidental activities that could take place without you. For example, if a carer strips a soiled bed at night, the additional tasks of wringing out the sheets or hanging them up to dry could count as attention if done on the spot, as would cleaning a soiled carpet in the event of incontinence.[122] Taking the washing away or doing the cleaning at a different time does not qualify as attention.

Domestic tasks performed by a carer outside your presence do not normally count as attention. There is conflicting caselaw on whether assistance to perform domestic tasks yourself is attention that is reasonably required.[123] If you are blind and someone helps you cook by reading cooking instructions to you, this is assistance with the bodily function of 'seeing' and can count as attention.[124] Similarly, if you have a learning disability and go shopping, you may need help to communicate your requirements. Argue that if you are able to shop or cook for yourself with help, this is part of what constitutes a 'normal life' (see the definition of 'requires' on p585).[125]

Childcare

Help you have that enables you to look after your children can also count as attention.[126] For example, lifting or holding your baby for feeding is a sufficiently intimate service.[127] It will help if you can identify the bodily function in connection with which you need attention. Similarly, assistance to take part in outdoor activities with your children allows you to lead a normal social life.[128] However, while help provided to you counts as attention, help given directly to your child does not.[129]

Special diets

Attention only counts if it needs to be given in your physical presence, so it is often difficult to include help with food preparation. Arguably though, this type of help may count as attention if it forms part of a broader sequence of care tasks. For example, the various parts of the process of regulating the blood sugar levels of a diabetic child, some of which require personal contact and some of which do not, should all be treated as attention because they are integral elements of an overall regime.[130] A person with a learning disability or an eating disorder might need similar help to eat properly.

Part 5: Other benefits
Chapter 27: Disability living allowance
2. Disability living allowance care component

Night and day

Someone who needs help using the toilet at 3am, when most people are asleep, clearly needs that help at night. Problems can arise when children or adults need supervision or attention in the late evening or early morning.

'**Night**' has been defined as 'that period of inactivity' which begins when 'the household, as it were, closes down for the night'.[131] The pattern of activities of each household needs to be taken into account. If a carer stays up into the small hours to help you but would otherwise go to bed earlier, that should count as night care.[132] Similarly, if a carer gets up early in the morning to help you rather than rise later with the rest of the household, that should count as night care.[133] If you live alone and go to bed unusually late or get up unusually early, your 'night' may be assumed to begin at a more average time of 11pm or to end at 7am.[134] The definition of 'night' for a child is the same as for an adult, so that attention given to a child in the evening before the adults have gone to bed counts only towards satisfying the day condition.[135]

'Attention... for a significant portion of the day'

If you can show that you need attention for a 'significant portion of the day', you qualify for the lowest rate care component.[136] A significant portion of the day can be either one period or a number of periods – eg, you could need help with activities connected with getting up, such as dressing and washing, at the beginning of the day, and with activities connected with going to bed, such as undressing and washing, at the end of the day, but are otherwise able to care for yourself without help. Help at night does not count for the lower rate.[137]

The term 'a significant portion of the day' is often taken to mean an hour or thereabouts.[138] However, if your carer spends less time than that in total but has to give help for a number of short periods, that might qualify.[139]

If your carer does not have much time available or the help s/he gives is in spells of particularly concentrated activity, less than an hour's help may be enough. Factors like the amount, importance or effect of the attention may be taken into account.[140]

Frequent attention throughout the day

To satisfy the day attention condition, you must show that you need frequent attention throughout the day.[141] If you only need help at the beginning and end of the day, you are unlikely to satisfy the test. A frequent need might include help with toileting (eg, to reach the toilet, use a commode or deal with zips) or help to walk inside your home. These are both examples of activities that most people usually engage in frequently. Most people who satisfy this condition do so by virtue of a range of different types of care needs. Whether the help you need is 'frequent' should be considered as a whole, looking at the number of times you need help over a period of time.[142] However, if the spread is uneven and you do not need help for lengthy periods, this should not necessarily disqualify you.[143]

Prolonged or repeated attention at night

The help you need during the night must be either prolonged or repeated.[144] There is no clear definition of 'prolonged'. An assumption that 20 minutes is prolonged has been accepted as a reasonable starting point, but shorter periods should also be considered.[145] 'Repeated' simply means twice or more.[146]

Because sleeping is a 'bodily function', soothing a child back to sleep counts as giving attention in connection with a bodily function.[147]

Continual supervision

You satisfy the daytime supervision condition if you require another person to provide 'continual supervision' throughout the day to avoid the risk of substantial danger to yourself or to others.[148] Supervision can be precautionary and anticipatory. It does not necessarily involve direct intervention. The supervision test has four aspects.[149]

- **There must be a substantial danger to yourself or someone else as a result of your medical condition.** What constitutes a 'substantial danger' must be decided on the facts of each case. For example, if an elderly person falls, this is more likely to constitute a 'substantial danger' than if a younger person falls but only sustains minor bruises. What causes the fall may also be relevant. A person who loses consciousness would not be able to do anything to save her/himself.
- **The substantial danger must be one against which it is reasonable to guard.** This involves weighing the remoteness of the risk and the seriousness of the consequences should it arise. While the risk of a house catching fire may be remote, the consequences of leaving a disabled person who is unable to move alone in a house which did catch fire would be catastrophic. Thus, it can be argued that you reasonably require continual supervision.[150] Similarly, the consequences of allowing a child to run out onto the road could be dire even though such an incident may be isolated.[151] In assessing the likelihood of danger, the decision maker must look at what has happened in the past as well as what may happen in the future.[152]
- **There must be a need for the supervision.** What counts is the level of supervision you 'reasonably require' (see p585). If you have mental health problems, you may need supervision to help prevent you harming yourself. If you are at risk of committing suicide, it would be wrong to suggest that no amount of supervision would prevent a determined suicide attempt and supervision is, therefore, not required. The correct approach is to decide whether supervision would result in 'a real reduction in the risk of harm' to you.[153]

Part 5: Other benefits
Chapter 27: Disability living allowance
3. The rules about your age

- **The supervision must be continual.** This is something less than 'continuous', but supervision which is required only occasionally or spasmodically is insufficient.[154] If you can safely be left alone for a few hours, the supervision may not be continual.[155] However, the fact that, for example, a child may need less supervision in a safe structured environment such as school, does not mean that continual supervision is not required.[156] If it is unavoidable that your carer leaves you alone for a period, you still qualify if you can show that you are at risk during this time. If you are liable to epileptic fits without warning, you may need continual supervision, although attention for the period between the fits is not required.[157] Even if you have warning of the fits so that you can prevent yourself from falling, you may require continual supervision if you suffer from prolonged periods of confusion, or need monitoring to make sure you have come out of the seizure safely afterwards.[158]

Watching over

You satisfy the night-time supervision condition if you need someone to be awake to watch over you at night to avoid the risk of substantial danger to yourself or others.[159] The person watching over you must be awake for a 'prolonged period' or 'at frequent intervals'. DWP guidance suggests a 'prolonged period' may mean 20 minutes or more[160] and the term 'at frequent intervals' means more than twice.

---

3. **The rules about your age**

New claims for disability living allowance (DLA) can now only be made for children under 16.

The higher rate mobility component can be paid from age three onwards and the lower rate mobility component from age five.[161] The three months before the child reaches this age can form the qualifying period (see p581), enabling payment to be made from her/his birthday.

There is no lower age limit for DLA care component. However, a baby must still meet the qualifying conditions for three months before DLA becomes payable, unless s/he is terminally ill.[162]

Children under the age of 16 cannot qualify for the lowest rate care component via the cooking test (see p583). A child can only qualify for the lowest rate if s/he requires attention for a 'significant portion of the day' (see p588).[163]

Note: children aged under 16 must satisfy an additional test for the DLA care component (see p581) and the lower rate mobility component (see p579).

See p605 for how the introduction of personal independence payment (PIP) affects your DLA renewal claim if you are 16 or over.

Aged over 65

If you are 65 or over and have not received DLA in the previous 12 months, you must claim attendance allowance (AA – see Chapter 23).

Before the introduction of PIP, the upper age limit for claiming either component of DLA was usually 65. See p605 for details of how the introduction of PIP affects you if you already get DLA.

Although you had to be under 65 to claim, once DLA was awarded, it could be paid beyond the age of 65. If you turned 65 before 8 April 2013, this continues to apply to you and you are unaffected by the introduction of PIP. You can renew an award (including an award of the mobility component or the lowest rate care component) that expires after you are 65, provided you reclaim within a year of the previous award ending.[164]

If your condition changes after you reach the age of 65, you cannot qualify for either rate of the mobility component or the lowest rate of the care component for the first time.

However, you can be awarded either rate of the mobility component or the lowest rate of the care component after reaching the age of 65 if you have an existing award of another component of DLA and you ask for a revision or supersession of that award after you are 65. You must show that you have satisfied the disability conditions for the new component since you were 64 or younger.[165]

If your condition changes, you can move to the middle or highest rate care component. You must show that you have met the qualifying conditions for the middle or highest rate for six months (not three months) before it can be awarded. This is because the rules about qualifying periods for those in receipt of DLA care component over the age of 65 are the same as for AA.[166] If it has been over a year since your previous award ended, you must claim AA instead of DLA.

If you turned 65 on or after 8 April 2013, you can continue to receive DLA until you are required to make a claim for PIP (see p605). This includes renewing an award, if you are notified in writing by the DWP that you must do so. It also includes asking for a revision or supersession of your award if your condition changes.

If you turned 65 on or after 8 April 2013 and have received DLA within the last 12 months, you can choose to claim PIP or AA.[167]

4. People included in the claim

You claim disability living allowance (DLA) for yourself. You cannot claim any increase in your DLA for your partner or child(ren). However, your partner may qualify for DLA, personal independence payment (PIP) (see Chapter 35) or attendance allowance (see Chapter 23) in her/his own right. Your child may qualify for DLA (or PIP if s/he is 16 or over) in her/his own right.

Part 5: Other benefits
Chapter 27: Disability living allowance
6. Special benefit rules

5. **The amount of benefit**

Disability living allowance (DLA) mobility component is paid at one of two weekly rates:[168]
* the lower rate is £21.55;
* the higher rate is £56.75.

DLA care component is paid at one of three weekly rates:[169]
* the lowest rate is £21.55;
* the middle rate is £54.45;
* the highest rate is £81.30.

6. **Special benefit rules**

Special rules may apply to:
* people on renal dialysis (see below);
* people who are terminally ill (see p593);
* people subject to immigration control (see p1500);
* people who have gone abroad (see p1573);
* people in care homes or other special accommodation (see p951);
* people in hospital or a hospice (see p944);
* prisoners (see p959).

People on renal dialysis

If you are undergoing renal dialysis on a kidney machine, special rules may apply that entitle you to the middle rate of disability living allowance (DLA) care component.[170]

To qualify, you must have treatment regularly for two or more sessions a week. The dialysis must normally require the attendance or supervision of another person.

If you dialyse in hospital as an outpatient, you must not have help from any member of the staff. Others who dialyse in hospital do not qualify by this special route but can count these spells of hospital dialysis towards the qualifying periods. This helps those who alternate between dialysis in hospital and at home to get DLA care component more quickly for the times they dialyse at home. Even if you do not qualify under this route, you may qualify under the ordinary conditions.

People who are terminally ill

If you are terminally ill, you are automatically treated as satisfying the conditions for the highest rate if the DLA care component and you do not need to satisfy the three-month qualifying period.[171]

You do not automatically get DLA mobility component. You must satisfy the usual disability conditions (except the three-month qualifying period) and the 'forward test' (see p574) until the anticipated date of your death.[172] The definition of 'terminally ill' is the same as for attendance allowance (see p510).[173]

Claims from people who are terminally ill are referred to as 'claims under the special rules'. The special rules only apply if your claim, or a revision or supersession request, expressly states that you are terminally ill.[174] The DWP can supersede your award if your condition or prognosis improves so that you are no longer regarded as terminally ill.

7. Claims and backdating

To be entitled to disability living allowance (DLA), you must make a claim for it.[175] The general rules about claims and backdating are in Chapter 53. This section explains the specific rules that apply to DLA.

Note: the success of a DLA claim can often depend on how well you have completed the claim form. See p596 for further information.

Making a claim

A claim for DLA must be in writing. You can do this by completing:

- the approved form. Send it to the disability benefits office covering your region or any DWP office. You may also be able to take or send it to an 'alternative office' (see p1136). In practice, it is usually best to post the form to the disability benefits centre;
- an online application form at www.gov.uk.

Keep a copy of your claim form in case queries arise.

You must provide any information or evidence required (see p594). In certain circumstances, the DWP may accept a written application which is not on the approved form (see p1140).[176] You can amend or withdraw your claim before a decision is made (see p1138).

Claims for terminally ill people are made in a different way (see p594).

Forms

Get Form DLA1A or DLA1A Child (for those under 16) from a DWP office or an 'alternative office' (see p1136), or the DLA helpline 0845 712 3456 (textphone 0845 722 4433).

Part 5: Other benefits
Chapter 27: Disability living allowance
7. Claims and backdating

It is best to request a form from the DWP, as it should be date stamped. You have six weeks from the date of your request to return it.[177] Keep a record of the date you asked for the form. The DWP may complete a checklist to assess your 'potential benefit entitlement'. This is not part of the claim process and you should always be sent a claim pack.

Claim packs are also available from Citizens Advice Bureau or other advice agencies and can be downloaded at www.gov.uk. These packs are not date stamped so you must send in the completed form as soon as possible to secure your date of claim. This is the date on which your form is received by the DWP (see p595).

Who should claim

You normally claim DLA for yourself. A claim for a child under 16 or a person unable to manage her/his own affairs is made by an appointee (see p603 and p1137).

Claiming for terminally ill people

If you are claiming the highest rate care component under the 'special rules' on the basis of terminal illness (see p593), you must provide Form DS1500, completed by your GP or consultant, detailing your medical condition. You do not need to fill in the parts of the claim form relating to your need for personal care. If you also wish to claim DLA mobility component, you must answer all the relevant questions. The decision maker makes an assessment of whether you meet the special rules. If the decision maker decides you do not, you can claim in the normal way or appeal that decision.

It is possible for someone acting on behalf of a terminally ill person to make a claim under the special rules, or to request a revision or supersession or to appeal, without that person's knowledge or permission.[178]

Information to support your claim

When you claim DLA, you must:
- satisfy the national insurance (NI) number requirement (see p1138). This does not apply if you are claiming DLA on behalf of a child under 16;[179]
- provide proof of your identity, if required (see p1140); *and*
- ensure you have made a valid claim – ie, you must complete your claim properly and provide any information or evidence required when you claim (see p1140).

Even if you have provided all that was required when you claimed, you may be asked to provide additional information and evidence relevant to your claim (see p1152). There is a strict time limit for providing this. If you do not do so, the decision maker can decide your claim in the way most adverse to you.

Note: you may be asked to provide information after you are awarded DLA. If you fail to do so, your DLA could be suspended or even terminated (see p1175).

The date of your claim

Claim as soon as you think you might be entitled to DLA; you are not usually entitled to DLA for any day before your date of claim. The date of your claim is the date your request for a claim pack is received by the DWP or an 'alternative office' (see p1136), provided you return the properly completed form within six weeks of the date of your request.[180] If the DWP has issued a form without date stamping it, write and explain when and where it was issued and ask to be paid from that date or six weeks before you sent it in.[181] There is also some discretion to extend the six-week deadline, so if you return the form late explain why.[182]

If you are using a claim form issued by an advice agency or downloaded from the internet, your date of claim is the date your completed form is received by the DWP.

If you claim the wrong benefit

A claim for attendance allowance (AA) can be treated as a claim for DLA and vice versa. A claim for personal independence payment can be treated as a claim for DLA and vice versa, but only if the decision maker thinks that you are not entitled to the benefit you actually claimed. A claim for an increase of industrial injuries disablement benefit where constant attendance is needed can be treated as a claim for DLA and vice versa. See p1144 for the rules.[183]

Claiming in advance

A claim for DLA can be made before you have satisfied the three-month qualifying period for DLA[184] (see p574 and p581), or any other qualifying condition. Provided you claim no more than three months before you would qualify for DLA, a decision can be made on your claim in advance of your date of entitlement.

Renewal claims

DLA can be awarded for fixed periods (see p602). Renewal claims can be invited up to six months before your old award expires. It is important that you send back your completed renewal claim form before your old award expires as no backdating is possible.

Decision makers normally treat your renewal claim as a new claim beginning on the day after your old award runs out.[185] However, they may use the information you give in the renewal claim to revise or supersede your existing award, in which case your entitlement may be changed earlier.[186] If you think you have a strong case for an increased award, return your renewal form early and ask for a revision or supersession. If this is not the case, it is advisable to return the form nearer the date your current award runs out, but in time for a decision to be made before it does run out.

Part 5: Other benefits
Chapter 27: Disability living allowance
7. Claims and backdating

Reclaiming under age 65

Following the introduction of PIP, unless you had reached 65 before 8 April 2013 or you are under 16, you may be required to claim PIP instead of renewing your DLA claim. See p605 for more details. People reclaiming DLA under the age of 65 do not have to serve the three-month qualifying period again, provided they meet all the other qualifying conditions for the rate they previously received. This is because the qualifying period is taken to be the last three months of the previous award.[187] However, if you qualify for a different rate when you reclaim, you do have to serve the standard qualifying period.

Reclaiming over age 65

If your DLA award ended after you reached 65 and you reclaim the same rate within one year, you can be paid without having to serve the standard qualifying period again. If you qualify for another rate (see p591), you do have to serve the qualifying period again. If it has been over a year since your previous award ended, you must claim AA instead of DLA care component, and you cannot reclaim DLA mobility component.[188] The qualifying period is three months for DLA mobility component or six months for DLA care component, unless you have already completed a three-month qualifying period by the time you turned 65.[189] **Note:** if you turned 65 on or after 8 April 2013, you may be required to claim PIP instead of reclaiming DLA. See p605 for more details.

Completing the claim form

If you find it difficult to complete the form, the DWP can help you by telephone or, in some circumstances, can send a visiting officer to your home. Most advice agencies can also help.

The DLA claim form is long and concerns different aspects of your care and mobility. Fill in all the pages that are relevant. If the same difficulties apply on more than one page, repeat the information or refer back to earlier in the form. There is space to include details of people who know about your difficulties – include carers and support workers as well as medical professionals.

What evidence should you provide?

When making a claim, and especially when preparing for an appeal, you should ensure that you have as much evidence as possible to support what you say in your claim pack. This can include any of the following.

Evidence that you provide yourself:

About your care needs. Often the easiest way for a decision maker or First-tier Tribunal to get a picture of your care needs and their pattern is for you to keep a diary for a week or a month. You should use this to record variations in your condition and the help you need. This can be particularly useful if you have unpredictable care needs or experience irregular events, such as seizures or falls, which mean that you need supervision. Usually this is best presented as a table, using a row for each date and three or four columns to record the help you need. You can also ask your carer or a friend or family member to keep a diary for you, or write letters in support of your claim or appeal.

About your walking ability. Get someone to walk outdoors with you to measure the distance you can walk without severe discomfort, then write a description of the time it takes you to walk this far. It may help to give an example of the distance – eg, 'I can walk past five houses – about 40 metres.'
Describe the terrain. Is it rough? Are there steps or slopes which present you with problems?
Explain what sort of discomfort you experience (eg, pain or breathlessness) and how it changes as you walk.
Describe your manner of walking – eg, you may have problems with balance, or you may walk with a limp, drag your feet or shuffle.
Say if you need to stop to rest. Try to explain how far you can walk before you need to stop, and for how long you need to rest. Bear in mind that if you can walk a further distance without severe discomfort after a brief rest, it is the total distance that counts.
It might help to download a map or satellite picture from the internet and measure the distances on it.
Ask someone to go somewhere unfamiliar with you and help you describe all the difficulty you have.

Evidence from third parties:
Doctors' reports. These could be reports which have already been provided by specialists to your GP. Often hospital doctors will send you copies of reports when they write them. You can ask your GP for copies of any reports you do not have from your medical records. Alternatively, ask your GP or specialist to write a specific letter for your claim or appeal. Your doctor may charge for writing reports and providing copies from your records. It is not usually worth providing hospital appointment letters and other routine documents which do not comment on your diagnosis, treatment or disability. The DWP may request a specific report from your GP. It can help to make an appointment to discuss the problems you have day to day before this is written.

Reports from other medical professionals. Reports from physiotherapists, psychiatric and other specialist nurses and occupational therapists can often provide more detailed information about your disability and how it affects your day-to-day life than reports from doctors, who only discuss your symptoms and treatment.

Social services and educational reports. If you have had a social care needs assessment, this can be very helpful. A statement of special educational needs may provide useful supporting evidence of the extra help your child needs in school. If you are studying, a disabled student's allowance assessment can be useful.

Part 5: Other benefits
Chapter 27: Disability living allowance
7. Claims and backdating

DWP medical services assessments. The DWP's decisions can often be based on reports prepared by doctors or other healthcare professionals employed by Atos Healthcare, either to assess your limited capability for work for employment and support allowance (ESA – see p1003) or specifically to assess your entitlement to DLA. Caselaw suggests that these should not necessarily be preferred to your own evidence or to that of your doctor and that ESA reports can often be inappropriate for DLA. You should examine any report carefully and explain why any unhelpful findings or assessments are wrong. It helps to have a witness present when you are examined. If the DWP is relying on an ESA report and an adverse decision based on it has been overturned on appeal, it is important to point this out. If, however, the ATOS healthcare professional's report supports your claim, you should highlight this.

5. The claim pack for adults

The DLA form asks about your mobility problems, your supervision and attention needs, and your ability to cook a main meal. Do not worry if a lot of the questions do not apply to you. You can, for example, qualify for the lowest rate of the care component because of the problems you have cooking a main meal (see p583), which only takes up one page of the claim pack.

- **Give as much detail as you can.** Do not feel bound by the size of the boxes. If you need extra space to explain your situation, use a separate piece of paper. There is a statement to be completed by someone who knows you. If your doctor fills this in, s/he should not charge you.[190] If you do not have anyone who can complete it, leave it blank.
- **Unmet care needs.** If you are not receiving any help from another person, it can be difficult to describe your attention or supervision needs. Many disabled people struggle to perform daily tasks on their own. If you do not have a carer, you should still describe your problems. Consider whether certain activities cause you pain, or make you dizzy, tired or breathless. If you take a long time to perform particular tasks, explain this. Also say if you are not able to perform a particular activity adequately – eg, if you cannot bend to reach your feet when washing.
- **Aids and adaptions.** If a decision maker thinks that you can use a particular aid or adaptation, s/he may decide you do not need attention or supervision. For example, if you have a commode, s/he may conclude you do not need someone to help you get to the toilet at night. Therefore, try to explain how useful any equipment actually is and whether you still need help from another person in spite of the equipment. If, for instance, you have had a bath rail fitted, but find it very difficult to climb in or out of a bath, explain this.
- **Frequency, variability and duration.** You are asked throughout the form to estimate how long you need help for, and how often. You should explain:

- **how long you need help for**, to show that you need attention for a 'significant portion of the day' (see p588), or you need 'prolonged' attention at night (see p589);
- **how often you need help**, to show that you need 'frequent attention throughout the day' (see p588) or 'watching over' repeatedly during the night (see p590);
- **how many days a week you need help**, to establish your overall needs, particularly if you have a variable or fluctuating condition. If your condition does not vary but you only receive help on certain days, say that you need help seven days a week. It is the help you need, not the help you get, that counts. If you only have problems a few days a week, you will not necessarily be refused DLA.[191] Explain fully the help you need on your 'bad' days but include the help you need on your 'good' days as well so that you give an overall picture.

- **Walking outdoors.** The section on 'getting about outdoors' is for the DLA mobility component. See p575 and p579 and the tactics on p596 for how to describe your walking ability.
- **Mental disabilities.** There is no specific section about your mental health. There is a section on 'communicating with other people', where you should mention problems caused by anxiety, intrusive thoughts or anger, or learning difficulties. Questions throughout the claim pack ask if you need encouraging or reminding to attend to your bodily functions. The section on 'the help you need when you go out' may also be appropriate if you need assistance to undertake social, leisure and recreational activities. At the end of the form there is a page to 'tell us anything else you think we should know'. It often helps to summarise here your mental health problems and explain any other attention or supervision needs you have.
- **Sensory impairments.** The section on 'communicating with other people' applies to deaf claimants who may need an interpreter or other help with communicating or reading, or blind people who need to have newspapers or correspondence read to them (see p585). Blind people who need someone to tell them if they have stains on their clothes or if their hands are clean should explain these problems in the 'dressing' and 'washing' sections. It is important that people with sensory impairments complete the section on 'the help you need when you go out during the day or in the evening' to explain the help needed to undertake social and recreational activities. If you need extra help because you are working or studying, include this.

The claim pack for children

The claim pack for children is different from the adult form. However, some issues, such as how to answer the questions on frequency, variability and duration of needs, are similar to those faced by people filling in the adult pack (see p598).

Part 5: Other benefits
Chapter 27: Disability living allowance
7. Claims and backdating

Therefore, if you are completing a child's pack, read that section and the tactics on p596. The following issues are specific to claiming for children.

- **When the child is in bed at night.** Only the needs your child has after the rest of the household has gone to bed count as night-time needs (see p588).
- **Mobility.** Children can only qualify for DLA mobility component from the age of three, but problems with getting around may indicate care or supervision needs, so explain these. It can be difficult to explain how a disabled child requires 'substantially more' guidance or supervision outdoors in order to qualify for the lower rate mobility component (see p579). This is because most young children do not go out, at least in unfamiliar places, on their own. A child with a sensory impairment or learning disability may require much more direct or close supervision than a non-disabled child.[192] Whereas a child may normally be allowed to walk in the presence of an adult, a disabled child may require an adult to hold or guide her/him. Also, a 'familiar route' may be a hazardous obstacle course to a child whose sight is impaired. It may help to make comparisons with siblings or classmates. A child with attention deficit disorder may need to be accompanied to school or to local shops, whereas other children might be allowed to go alone.[193]
- **Extra attention or supervision.** When explaining about your child's 'extra' requirements, bear in mind that they must be 'substantially in excess' of those required by a non-disabled child of the same age (see p581). Disabled children may need extra help to develop daily living skills, language and social skills. For example, babies with sensory impairments may require more physical stimulation to aid parental bonding and develop communication skills. A disabled child may need help to use toys, or may need to be coaxed to explore her/his environment. Children with learning or sensory disabilities require extra help to develop daily living or language skills. They may also develop these skills later than other children. Similarly, you may let a non-disabled child play outdoors and instruct her/him not to cross roads. You may be able to supervise the child indirectly without having to watch her/him all the time. However, you may have to supervise directly a child with sensory impairments or behavioural problems, or confine her/him indoors.
- **About the child's development.** The questions on development are extremely important to show that disabled children need extra care or supervision. You may not know exactly when a child should be crawling, walking, speaking, using the toilet independently and feeding her/himself. If you are not sure, ask your health visitor or paediatrician. For example, most children pick up and eat food by 8–12 months. Therefore, if you are still feeding a child after 12 months, you are providing attention that a non-disabled child of the same age would not need. It often helps to make comparisons with other children you know.

When completing renewal forms, bear in mind that the decision maker may suppose that your child no longer needs the same help as s/he did when s/he was younger. However, it is wrong to assume that all disabled children develop in the same way.

- **School-age children.** Disabled children, particularly those with sensory impairments or learning disabilities, usually require extra help with their school work. Extra help in the classroom or with homework can count towards a child's attention needs, provided you can show it is in connection with a bodily function (see p585).[194] Straightforward teaching would probably not be sufficiently intimate to qualify,[195] but additional help (eg, because of dyslexia) may count.[196]
- **Communicating.** Prelingual deaf children, whose first language is British Sign Language, may need help to understand or communicate in written or spoken English. Blind children will not only need help to understand written information, but may also need help to learn Braille. Children with learning difficulties may need help to express themselves or understand other people.

How your claim is dealt with

Claims are initially dealt with at a specified office dealing with your region. A decision maker can award DLA on the basis of your claim form alone, but may choose to contact someone you have named on the form for more information. It is a good idea to include details of all the medical professionals and other people who know and understand your needs, and, if possible, enclose evidence from them. If the decision maker cannot get sufficient information, s/he may also arrange for you to be given a medical examination by a healthcare professional acting on behalf of the DWP, who will sometimes visit you at home.

If you refuse a medical examination 'without good cause', the decision maker must decide your claim against you.[197]

The decision maker may telephone you to ask for further information. If you do not want to be telephoned, write this clearly on the claim form.

The DWP aims to deal with new claims for DLA within 40 working days. Claims made under the special rules for terminal illness (see p593) should be decided more quickly. If you disagree with the decision, you can ask for a revision or make an appeal (see Chapters 58 and 59). You may have to apply for a revision of a decision before you can appeal (see p1270). See p596 for suggestions about the evidence you can use to support a claim, revision or appeal.

Backdating your claim

It is very important to claim in time. A claim for DLA *cannot* be backdated.[198]

If you might have qualified for benefit earlier but did not claim because you were given the wrong information or were misled by the DWP, you could ask for a compensation payment (see p1382) or complain to the Ombudsman through your MP (see p1387).

8. **Getting paid**

Payment of disability living allowance (DLA) is normally made by direct credit transfer into your bank (or similar) account (see p1163).[199] For payment to children, see p603. If you are unable to open or manage an account, it may be possible to be paid by 'simple payment' (see p1163). Payment can also be made to someone else on your behalf, called your 'appointee' (see p1137), if you are unable to act for yourself.

When is disability living allowance paid?

You are normally paid on a Wednesday, but the DWP can vary the payday.[200] DLA is usually paid every four weeks in arrears. However:

– DLA can be paid at shorter intervals in individual cases;[201]
– DLA under the special rules for terminal illness can be paid weekly.

If you leave hospital or a care home and expect to return within 28 days, DLA can be paid at a daily rate for days at home.[202]

Note:

- If you are claiming other DWP benefits, DLA may be paid in a single payment with them instead.
- The higher rate of the DLA mobility component can be paid directly to Motability if you are buying a car through the scheme (see p610).
- Even if you have been sanctioned for a benefit offence (see p1258), you must be paid your DLA.
- If you have forgotten your PIN, see p1163. If your simple payment card has been lost or stolen, or if you have forgotten your memorable date, see p1164. For information on missing payments, see p1164.
- If payment of your DLA is delayed, see p1382. If you wish to complain about how your claim has been dealt with, see p1383. You might be able to claim compensation (see p1382).
- If payment of your DLA is suspended, see p1175.If you have been overpaid DLA, you might have to repay it (see Chapter 56) and, in some circumstances you may have to pay a penalty (see p1249). If you have been accused of fraud, see Chapter 57.

Length of awards

Awards of DLA can be made for either fixed or indefinite periods.[203] The length of an award depends on how long a decision maker estimates your current needs may last. If you have an indefinite award, you do not have to make a renewal claim at any stage, but it is always open to the DWP to reduce or stop your award if it has grounds to revise or supersede it.

In practice, awards are usually made for at least six months because of the DLA requirement that you should satisfy the disability conditions for the next six months. However, there is no legal minimum length for an award.[204] If you think benefit should be awarded for longer, perhaps because your condition is such that your care or mobility needs will not decrease, consider asking for a revision (see p1270). Bear in mind that if you challenge the length of your award, the rate of your award may also be reconsidered. If your award is for a limited period, you will be invited to make a renewal claim up to six months before the award runs out (see p595).

A 'special rules' award on the basis of terminal illness is normally made for a fixed period of three years. If there is already a mobility award in place, the length of the special rules award may be adjusted to finish at the same time as the mobility award.

Although DLA has two components, there can only be a single DLA award, consisting of one or both components. You can have an indefinite award of one component combined with a limited period award of the other. However, although components can be awarded for fixed periods starting at different times, both fixed award periods must be aligned to end on the same day.[205]

Payment to children

DLA for a child under the age of 16 is usually paid to an adult with whom s/he is living, whom the DWP appoints to act on her/his behalf (often called an 'appointee'). This is normally the child's parent.[206] Children cannot make valid claims on their own behalf.[207]

The allowance can continue to be paid to the appointee in some circumstances when the child and appointee are not living together, including during a temporary separation of up to 12 weeks, or when the child is absent at a boarding school or in hospital (although other rules may mean that payment stops – see p941). DLA ceases to be paid to the appointee immediately when the child is in the care of a local authority or any similar arrangement, unless the arrangement is not intended to last for more than 12 weeks.[208]

Change of circumstances

You must report any change in your circumstances that you have been told you must report, as well as any that you might reasonably be expected to know might affect your right to, the amount of, or payment of your benefit. You should do this as soon as possible, preferably in writing. See p1174 for further information.

If your condition deteriorates so that you become eligible for a higher rate or another component, benefit can be backdated to the first payday after the end of the three-month qualifying period, provided you tell the DWP no later than a month after completing the qualifying period. If payment of (but not entitlement to) DLA has stopped (eg, while you are in hospital or a care home), still notify the

DWP so that the correct rate is paid when payment resumes. If you do not report a change of circumstances within the month, benefit can still be backdated if you do so within 13 months and there were 'special circumstances' that meant it was not practical to report the change earlier.[209]

If your condition improves so that you should drop down a rate, lose a component or lose benefit altogether, the new decision normally takes effect from the date you tell the DWP of the improvement, or from the date of the decision if the DWP changed it without your asking.[210] It would only take effect from an earlier date (and cause an overpayment) if you should have realised earlier that the change should have been reported. It is accepted that it may be difficult for claimants to realise when a gradual improvement begins to affect benefit entitlement.[211]

5 'Right payment' and 'correctness' programmes

The DWP checks existing DLA awards as part of a '**right payment programme**'.

This applies to people on all rates of DLA, including those originally awarded DLA 'for life' or indefinitely. You are exempt if your award has been looked at in the last 12 months, if you have been awarded benefit on the basis of terminal illness (see p593) or if no DLA is being paid – eg, because you are in hospital (see Chapter 45).

The DWP contacts you by sending a postal questionnaire (DLA300). You have a duty to supply any information requested that may affect benefit entitlement.[212] If you do not respond, the DWP may notify you that your benefit will be suspended if you do not reply within 14 days.[213] This time limit can be extended if necessary to arrange for someone to help you complete the questionnaire.[214] If you still have not complied after your benefit has been suspended for a month, your award is terminated.[215]

As part of the initial investigation into an existing award, the DWP can require you to have a medical examination.[216] If you fail, without good cause, to have a medical examination on two consecutive occasions, your benefit can be suspended.[217] If, after your benefit has been suspended for one month, you still have not had a medical examination, your benefit can be terminated.[218]

Further checks on claimants who have been reported to the fraud hotline, but where there is not enough evidence to justify a fraud investigation, may be made under a '**correctness programme**'. If you are being checked under this programme, you will be sent Form DLA80.

9. Transfers to personal independence payment

Following the introduction of personal independence payment (PIP), new claims for disability living allowance (DLA) can now only be made for children under 16. People aged 16 to 64 who have a disability can claim PIP (see Chapter 35).

PIP is gradually replacing DLA for all working age people. The transfer process began on 28 October 2013 in certain areas.[219]

You do not need to do anything until you are notified in writing by the DWP. You will be invited to claim PIP and your DLA will end (see p608).

Note: if you get DLA and you turned 65 on or before 8 April 2013, you are not affected by this process and continue to receive DLA for as long as you meet the qualifying conditions.[220] If you are claiming DLA for a child, you are not affected by the transfer to PIP until s/he reaches 16.[221]

If you live in one of the specified areas (see below), are of working age and already get DLA, you are invited to claim PIP when your DLA award expires instead of making a renewal claim for DLA. You must be invited to claim PIP if you live in one of the specified areas (see below) and on or after the date the transfer process started in your area:[222]

- you turn 16 (unless you get DLA under the 'special rules' on the basis of terminal illness – see p593); *or*
- you report a change in your circumstances relevant to the level of your DLA award (unless the change is that you are leaving Great Britain).

If either of these conditions apply to you, the DWP must invite you to claim PIP as soon as possible.

If you are over 16 and being transferred from DLA to PIP, the DWP can extend your fixed-term award of DLA if it will expire before a decision can be made on your PIP entitlement.[223] If you are about to turn 16 and your award is due to end on the day before your 16th birthday or within the following six months, it is extended until the day before you turn 17 or, if earlier, the day your DLA ends under the rules on transferring to PIP.[224] These extensions are to give you time to claim PIP and have a decision made on your entitlement.

Specified areas

At the time of writing, you are invited to claim PIP rather than renew your DLA award if you live in the following postcode areas:[225]

B, CA, CF, CH1, CH4, CH5, CH6, CH7, CH8, CV, DE, DG, DL, DY, EH, GL16, HG, HR, IP, LA, LD, LE, LL, LN, ML, NG, NN, NP, NR, PE, SA, ST, SY, TD, TF, WR, WS, WV and YO.

Note: these areas can be extended without further regulations. See CPAG's online service or *Welfare Rights Bulletin* for updates.

Part 5: Other benefits
Chapter 27: Disability living allowance
9. Transfers to personal independence payment

The DWP can invite you to claim PIP even if you live outside a specified area, although at the time of writing this *Handbook* it has not announced any plans to do so. You should check any letters about your DLA carefully to see whether you have been asked to claim PIP.

You can still make a renewal claim (and so continue to get DLA) if the DWP writes to you and tells you to renew your existing award of DLA as it is going to run out.[226]

If you live in one of the specified areas and have already been sent a DLA renewal claim pack (see p595) before the transfer process began, you should return it as soon as possible.

If you live in a specified area and were under 65 on 8 April 2013, you can choose to claim PIP, even if you are entitled to DLA and have not been sent a letter telling you to claim PIP.[227]

Should you claim personal independence payment?

1. If you have received a letter saying that you must claim PIP, you should do so straight away. If you do not, your DLA award will end (see p608).

2. If you have *not* been sent a letter telling you to claim PIP, you should seek specialist advice before claiming PIP, to help you decide whether it is a good idea to do so. This is because the entitlement conditions are completely different and you may not qualify for PIP at all. If you claim PIP, your DLA award ends. Once you have claimed PIP, you cannot change your mind.[228]

3. The DWP has said that, if you already get the higher rate mobility component and highest rate care component of DLA and have not been sent a letter telling you to claim PIP, it will advise you not to proceed with a claim for PIP unless you report that your condition has improved.[229]

If you get DLA under the 'special rules' on the basis of terminal illness (see p593), you will be invited to claim PIP at the end of your current award. If this is after October 2015, you will be invited to claim PIP some time after October 2015 along with most people who get DLA (see below).[230]

If you are claiming DLA for a child who does not live in one of the specified areas, s/he continues to receive DLA after her/his 16th birthday. The DWP says that, if the award is due to expire on or around her/his 16th birthday, the child's eligibility for DLA under the rules that apply to adults will be checked.[231]

Future changes

Most people who get DLA will be invited to claim PIP from October 2015, and the transfer process is expected to take until 2018 to complete.

From October 2015, the DWP intends to randomly select all remaining people aged 16 or over who get DLA and invite them to claim PIP. It intends that, if you have an indefinite award under the 'special rules' or a fixed term award that is due to expire after September

2017, you will be reassessed towards the end of the transition period. The DWP says that, if you have turned 65 since 8 April 2013, when PIP was introduced, you will be selected as early as possible in the process. In this case, you will be assessed for PIP as if you were under 65 and so you will have access to all the components and rates of PIP. The DWP says that, if you are not awarded any rate of PIP, your claim for PIP will be treated as a claim for attendance allowance (see Chapter 23) and the DWP will consider whether you qualify for it.[232]

Claims for personal independence payment

If you are sent a written invitation to claim PIP, this must inform you that you have 28 days to make a claim and tell you how to do so. The letter must also tell you that, if you do not claim PIP, your DLA award will end and when this will happen.[233]

You should make a claim for PIP, following the instructions in the letter, as soon as possible because your DLA award will end, whether you claim PIP or not.[234]

The 28-day time limit can be extended, if the DWP thinks it is reasonable to do so.[235]

If you do not claim PIP within this time, your DLA award is suspended from your next payment day.[236] You must be sent a letter explaining that your award has been suspended and will be terminated if you do not claim PIP within 28 days of the date on which it was suspended.[237] If you do so, your award of DLA is reinstated. If you still do not claim PIP, your DLA award ends from the date it was suspended.[238] You should make a new claim for PIP if you satisfy the rules of entitlement (see p726).

If you get DLA and have been invited to claim PIP or are in the process of claiming PIP and notify the DWP of a change of circumstances that may affect your entitlement to DLA, this is treated as a change of circumstances affecting your entitlement to PIP.[239]

Once you make a claim for PIP, the assessment process is the same as for a new claim (see p735).

If you do not provide information needed to assess your entitlement to PIP (see p736) and do not have a good reason, your PIP claim will be refused. If this happens, your DLA award ends 14 days after the first DLA payday following the decision refusing your PIP claim.[240] If you are later awarded PIP (eg, because you win an appeal against the decision that you do not have good reason), your PIP award starts from the day after your DLA award ended.[241]

These rules apply if you choose to claim PIP as well as if you are notified that your DLA will stop and invited to claim PIP.[242]

Part 5: Other benefits
Chapter 27: Disability living allowance
10. Tax, other benefits and the benefit cap

When your disability living allowance ends

If you make a claim for PIP, your DLA award continues until a decision is made on your PIP claim. Your DLA award then ends four weeks after the next DLA payday after the decision is made on your PIP claim, whether you are awarded PIP or not. If you are entitled to PIP, your entitlement starts from the day after your DLA award ends.[243] If you withdraw your claim, or notify the DWP that you do not wish to claim PIP when invited to do so, your DLA award ends 14 days after the first DLA payday following the date you notified the DWP.[244] You must be notified in writing of the date your DLA award ends and the start date of any PIP award.[245]

If you have a claim for DLA refused and then claim PIP, but the refusal of DLA is overturned on a revision or appeal before the PIP decision is made, similar rules apply. Your DLA award ends four weeks after the next DLA payday after the decision is made on your PIP claim, whether you are awarded PIP or not.[246]

If you have a 'blue badge' and are refused PIP, you can continue to use the badge until its expiry date.[247]

---

10. Tax, other benefits and the benefit cap

Tax

Disability living allowance (DLA) is not taxable.[248]

Means-tested benefits

DLA is not taken into account as income when calculating any of the means-tested benefits. DLA is paid on top of these benefits, and getting DLA can increase the amount of them.

If your child is entitled to DLA, your housing benefit (HB) includes a disabled child premium (see p228). If s/he gets the highest rate care component, your HB includes an enhanced disability premium (see p231). These premiums are also included in your income support (IS) and income-based jobseeker's allowance (JSA) if you do not yet get child tax credit (CTC). If your child is entitled to DLA and you come under the universal credit (UC) system (see p19), you can be paid a disabled child addition in your UC. This is paid at the higher rate if s/he is entitled to the highest rate of the care component (see p250).

If you or your partner are entitled to DLA, your IS, income-based JSA, and, unless you have reached the qualifying age for pension credit (PC), HB include the disability premium (see p229) (or for IS and JSA only, higher pensioner premium – see p232 – if either of you have reached the qualifying age for PC). If you or your partner are entitled to the highest rate of the DLA care component and aged under the qualifying age for PC, you also get an enhanced disability premium (see p231). This is also paid with income-related employment and support allowance (ESA – see p231). A severe disability premium/addition is included in IS, income-based JSA, income-related ESA, the guarantee credit of PC and HB, if you receive the highest or middle rate of the DLA care component and meet the other conditions for that premium/addition (see p233).

If you or your partner are entitled to the DLA care component, non-dependant deductions (see p450) are *not* made from any housing costs covered by your HB or IS, income-based JSA, income-related ESA or the guarantee credit of PC. No housing costs contributions from a non-dependant are taken into account when calculating your UC housing costs if you, your partner or the non-dependant receive the DLA middle or highest rate care component (see p496).

If you or your partner have reached the qualifying age for PC but you must claim UC because the other person has not yet reached this age, and the person over the qualifying age for PC is entitled to DLA, you qualify for the limited capability for work element in your UC award (see p1004). If the person over the qualifying age for PC is entitled to the highest rate of the DLA care component, you get the limited capability for work-related activity element in your UC award instead (see p1008).

Non-means-tested benefits

DLA may be paid in addition to any other non-means-tested benefits, except that:
- DLA overlaps with armed forces independence payment;[249]
- DLA care component overlaps with attendance allowance (AA) and constant attendance allowance under the industrial injuries scheme (see p679) or war pensions scheme;[250] *and*
- DLA mobility component overlaps with the war pensioners' mobility supplement payable under the war pensions scheme.[251]

See p1165 for details of the overlapping benefits rules.

You cannot be paid both DLA and personal independence payment (see p726).

If you are receiving the highest or middle rate of the DLA care component and someone regularly looks after you, that person may be entitled to carer's allowance (CA – see Chapter 25). However, your entitlement to a severe disability premium (or additional amount) can be affected if s/he receives CA.

Tax credits

DLA is ignored as income when calculating CTC and working tax credit (WTC). A disabled child element is included in CTC for each child who gets DLA (at any rate). If s/he gets the highest rate of the DLA care component, you get a severely disabled child element in CTC. An award of DLA at any rate counts as a qualifying benefit for the disabled worker element in WTC. If you or your partner get the highest rate care component, a severe disability element is included in WTC. See Chapter 63 for futher information.

Part 5: Other benefits
Chapter 27: Disability living allowance
10. Tax, other benefits and the benefit cap

The benefit cap

In some cases, the total amount of specified benefits you receive is limited to £350 a week (if you are a single claimant without children) or £500 a week (if you are a lone parent or a member of a couple). This is known as the 'benefit cap'. DLA is *not* one of the specified benefits. The benefit cap only applies if you are getting HB or UC. The benefit cap does *not* apply if you, your partner or child receive DLA (or are entitled to DLA, but it is not payable because you, or s/he, are in hospital or a care home). See p1169 for further information.

Passports and other sources of help

You qualify for a Christmas bonus if you receive DLA at any rate (see p835). If you are on a low income, you may be entitled to council tax reduction (see p827).

If you get the higher rate of DLA mobility component, you or your carer can be exempt from paying road tax on a car used solely by you or for you. Contact the Disability Living Allowance Unit (see Appendix 1) for an exemption certificate.

If you get the higher rate of the mobility component, you should qualify for the blue badge scheme of parking concessions, which operates throughout Great Britain and the European Economic Area (with certain local variations). Contact your local authority for further information.

If any member of your household receives DLA at any rate, you can get a grant for help with insulation and other energy efficiency measures in your home (see p837) and may be entitled to other benefits, such as concessionary travel.

Motability

Motability is a charity that runs a scheme to help you lease or buy a car if you receive the higher rate of DLA mobility component for a period of 12 months or more (see p574).

DLA mobility component is paid directly to Motability.[252] You may also have to make extra payments. For further information, telephone 0300 456 4566 or visit www.motability.co.uk.

Notes

1. Disability living allowance mobility component

1 ss 71(6) and 73 SSCBA 1992
2 CM/5/1986; *BP v SSWP* [2009] UKUT 90 (AAC)
3 s73 SSCBA 1992; reg 12(1)(b) SS(DLA) Regs
4 Reg 12(1)(a) SS(DLA) Regs
5 R(M) 3/78
6 Reg 12(1)(a) SS(DLA) Regs; R(M) 2/78; R(DLA) 4/06
7 CDLA/2822/1999; CDLA/4329/2001
8 CDLA/1525/2008
9 *MMF v SSWP (DLA)* [2012] UKUT 312 (AAC)
10 R(M) 3/86; CSDLA/202/2007; CDLA/3839/2007; *DM v SSWP (DLA)* [2010] UKUT 375 (AAC)
11 R(M) 2/89; CDLA/97/2001; *Sandhu v SSWP* [2010] EWCA Civ 962
12 Reg 12(4) SS(DLA) Regs
13 R(M) 2/89
14 Reg 12(1)(b) SS(DLA) Regs
15 CDLA/3188/2002; *HJ v SSWP (DLA)* [2010] UKUT 307 (AAC)
16 R(M) 1/95; CSDLA/171/1998
17 CM/208/1989
18 *JK v SSWP (DLA)* [2010] UKUT 197 (AAC)
19 CDLA/1389/1997; CDLA/2195/2008
20 R(M) 1/81
21 R(M) 2/92
22 R(M) 1/83
23 CM/267/93; CDLA/608/1994; R(DLA) 4/03
24 R(DLA) 4/04
25 *Hewitt and Diment v CAO* 29 June 1998 (CA), reported as R(DLA) 6/99
26 R(M) 1/98; CDLA/3941/2005 interpreted 'exertion' to mean the activity of walking 'however slight the exertion'.
27 *KS v SSWP (DLA)* [2013] UKUT 390 (AAC)
28 Reg 12(2) SS(DLA) Regs
29 Reg 12(3) SS(DLA) Regs
30 R(DLA) 3/95
31 Sch 2 SS(GB) Regs
32 Reg 34(2) and Sch 3 Parts II & III SS(IIPD) Regs
33 Reg 12(2)(b) SS(DLA) Regs
34 s73 (1AB) SSCBA 1992; reg 12(1A) SS(DLA) Regs
35 *NC v SSWP (DLA)* [2012] UKUT 384 (AAC)
36 Reg 12(1)(b) SS(DLA) Regs
37 s73(3) SSCBA 1992; reg 12(5) and (6) SS(DLA) Regs
38 *JH v SSWP (DLA)* [2010] UKUT 456 (AAC); *AH v SSWP (DLA)* [2012] UKUT 387 (AAC); *SSWP v MG (DLA)* [2012] UKUT 429 (AAC)
39 R(M) 3/86; CSDLA/202/2007
40 R(DLA) 2/96
41 R(DLA) 3/98
42 *M (a child) v CAO* 29 October 1999 (CA), reported as R(DLA) 1/00
43 CDLA/95/1995
44 CDLA/3215/2001
45 CDLA/2054/1998
46 R(DLA) 7/02; R(DLA) 9/02; CDLA/3244/2001; CDLA/2955/2008; *SSWP v DM (DLA)* [2010] UKUT 318 (AAC); *SSWP v MG (DLA)* [2012] UKUT 429 (AAC)
47 *TV v SSWP (DLA)* [2013] UKUT 364 (AAC)
48 s73(1)(d) SSCBA 1992
49 R(DLA) 6/03
50 CDLA/42/1994
51 s73(4A) SSCBA 1992
52 CDLA/2268/1999
53 CSDLA/76/1998
54 CA/92/1992
55 CDLA/42/1994; R(DLA) 3/04
56 CDLA/2364/1995, but see CDLA/42/1994
57 CDLA/2142/2005
58 Reg 12(7) and (8) SS(DLA) Regs; R(DLA) 3/04; CDLA/2409/2003; R(DLA) 6/05; *SSWP v DC (DLA)* [2011] UKUT 235 (AAC)
59 R(DLA) 4/01
60 R(DLA) 3/04
61 CDLA/42/1994
62 CDLA/42/1994
63 CDLA/42/1994; CDLA/3360/1995; CSDLA/591/1997; CDLA/2643/1998
64 R(DLA) 4/01
65 *IN v SSWP (DLA)* [2013] UKUT 249 (AAC)
66 R(DLA) 6/05
67 R(DLA) 4/01

2. Disability living allowance care component

68 ss71(6) and 72 SSCBA 1992
69 s72(1A)(b) SSCBA 1992
70 s72(5) SSCBA 1992
71 CA/92/1992; CDLA/4806/2002; CSDLA/91/2003; CDLA/4100/2004
72 CA/92/1992
73 s72(1)(a) and (4)(c) SSCBA 1992
74 s72(4)(b) SSCBA 1992
75 Reg 7 SS(DLA) Regs
76 s72(4)(a) SSCBA 1992
77 s72(5) SSCBA 1992
78 s72(1)(b) SSCBA 1992
79 s72(1)(c) SSCBA 1992
80 R(DLA) 3/06, tribunal of commissioners
81 CDLA/4475/04
82 R(DLA) 3/06, tribunal of commissioners
83 R(DLA) 6/06, tribunal of commissioners
84 s72(1A)(a) SSCBA 1992
85 CDLA/1212/2005; CDLA/2367/2004
86 *SSWP v Moyna* [2003] (HL), reported as R(DLA) 7/03
87 *R v Secretary of State for Social Security ex parte Armstrong* [1996] (CA)
88 *Moyna v SSWP* [2003] (HL), reported as R(DLA) 7/03
89 CSDLA/80/1996
90 CDLA/7374/1995; R(DLA) 8/02
91 CDLA/20/1994; CDLA/4214/2002; R(DLA) 1/08; CDLA/2991/2007
92 R(DLA) 2/95, which nonetheless allows for the use of 'certain devices to assist' which may form part of 'normal reasonable facilities' for cooking. However, CDLA/1212/2005 held, following R(DLA) 7/03 (cooking test is a notional test and a thought experiment), that it is not relevant to the tests whether a claimant does or does not have a microwave oven or other standard equipment.
93 *CA v SSWP (DLA)* [2013] UKUT 168 (AAC)
94 CDLA/20/1994; R(DLA) 2/95 insists on a traditional cooker, but note CDLA/770/2000, which allows fresh food to be prepared in a microwave. See also CDLA/3778/2002 and *KS v SSWP (DLA)* [2011] UKUT 29 (AAC) for use of a slow cooker.
95 CDLA/17329/1996 and CDLA/770/2000, both of which would appear to give more weight to the use of special cooking aids than R(DLA) 2/95; *KS v SSWP (DLA)* [2011] UKUT 29 (AAC)
96 *JF v SSWP (DLA)* [2012] UKUT 335 (AAC)
97 CDLA/1714/2005
98 R(DLA) 1/97
99 R(A) 3/86 and *Mallinson v Secretary of State for Social Security*, 21 April 1994 (HL), reported as R(A) 3/94
100 *Secretary of State for Social Security v Fairey* (aka *Halliday*), 21 May 1997 (HL), reported as R(A) 2/98
101 R(A) 3/89
102 R(A) 5/90
103 See for example, R(A) 3/86 and *R v Secretary of State for Social Services ex parte Connolly* [1986] 1 WLR 421 (CA)
104 CDLA/3925/1997; *HJ v SSWP (DLA)* [2010] UKUT 307 (AAC)
105 R(DLA) 10/02
106 *Mallinson v Secretary of State for Social Security*, 21 April 1994 (HL), reported as R(A) 3/94
107 *R v National Insurance Commissioner ex parte Secretary of State for Social Services* [1981] 1 WLR 1017 (CA), also reported as R(A) 2/80
108 Reg 10C SS(DLA) Regs; *R v National Insurance Commissioner ex parte Secretary of State for Social Services* [1981] 1 WLR 1017 (CA), also reported as R(A) 2/80
109 R(A) 1/06
110 *Mallinson v Secretary of State for Social Security*, 21 April 1994 (HL), reported as R(A) 3/94
111 CA/177/1988; CDLA/14696/1996; R(DLA) 1/07, tribunal of commissioners
112 Reg 10C SS(DLA) Regs
113 CDLA/4333/2004; *HP v SSWP (DLA)* [2013] UKUT 248 (AAC)
114 R(A) 3/74
115 R(A) 2/75
116 CA/86/1987
117 R(DLA) 1/07, tribunal of commissioners
118 *R v Social Security Commissioner ex parte Butler*, February 1984, unreported and *Secretary of State for Social Security v Fairey* (aka *Halliday*), 21 May 1997 (HL), reported as R(A) 2/98
119 *Secretary of State for Social Security v Fairey* (aka *Halliday*), 21 May 1997 (HL), reported as R(A) 2/98; R(DLA) 1/02; R(DLA) 2/02; R(DLA) 3/02; *SSWP v PV (DLA)* [2010] UKUT 33 (AAC)
120 R(DLA) 2/02
121 CDLA/3607/2001
122 *Cockburn v CAO and Another*, 21 May 1997 (HL), reported as R(A) 2/98; *Ramsden v SSWP*, 31 January 2003 (CA), reported as R(DLA) 2/03

123 CDLA/267/1994, CDLA/11652/1995,
CDLA/3711/1995, CDLA/12381/1996,
CDLA/16996/1996, CDLA/16129/1996
and CDLA/4352/1999 are useful, but
conflict with CSDLA/281/1996 and
CSDLA/314/1997
124 CDLA/267/1994
125 *Secretary of State for Social Security v
Fairey* (aka *Halliday*), 21 May 1997 (HL),
reported as R(A) 2/98
126 CDLA/16129/1996, CDLA/16996/1996
and CDLA/4352/1999 are helpful, but
conflict with CSDLA/314/1997
127 CDLA/4352/1999 and CDLA/5216/
1998, the latter being more restrictive
128 CDLA/4352/1999
129 CDLA/5216/1998
130 R(DLA) 1/98
131 *R v National Insurance Commissioner ex
parte Secretary of State for Social Services*
[1974] 1 WLR 1290 (DC), also reported
as R(A) 4/74
132 CDLA/2852/2002
133 CDLA/997/2003
134 R(A) 1/04
135 R(A) 1/78
136 s72(1)(a)(i) SSCBA 1992
137 R(DLA) 8/02
138 CDLA/58/1993
139 CSDLA/29/1994
140 *Ramsden v SSWP*, 31 January 2003 (CA),
reported as R(DLA) 2/03
141 s72(1)(b)(i) SSCBA 1992
142 R(DLA) 5/05
143 CA/140/1985
144 s72(1)(c)(i) SSCBA 1992
145 R(DLA) 5/05
146 R(DLA) 5/05
147 R(A) 3/78
148 s72(1)(b)(ii) SSCBA 1992
149 R(A) 1/83
150 R(A) 2/89
151 CA/15/1979, approved in R(A) 1/83
152 CA/33/1984
153 R(A) 3/92
154 R(A) 1/73
155 R(A) 2/75
156 *CP v SSWP (DLA)* [2013] UKUT 230
(AAC)
157 *Moran v Secretary of State for Social
Services, The Times,* 14 March 1987
(CA), reported as R(A) 1/88
158 R(A) 5/81
159 s72(1)(c)(ii) SSCBA 1992
160 para 61165 DMG

3. The rules about your age
161 s73(1A) SSCBA 1992
162 s72(2) and (5) SSCBA 1992
163 s72(1A)(a) SSCBA 1992
164 Sch 1 paras 3(3), 5(3), 6 and 7 SS(DLA)
Regs; see also CSDLA/388/2000
165 Sch 1 para 1(3) SS(DLA) Regs
166 Sch 1 para 3(2) SS(DLA) Regs
167 Reg 27(3) PIP(TP) Regs

5. The amount of benefit
168 Reg 4(2) SS(DLA) Regs
169 Reg 4(1) SS(DLA) Regs

6. Special benefit rules
170 Reg 7 SS(DLA) Regs
171 s72(5) SSCBA 1992
172 s73(9)(b)(ii) and (12) SSCBA 1992
173 ss72(5) and 66(1) and (2) SSCBA 1992
174 ss72(5) and 73(12) SSCBA 1992; regs
3(9)(b) and 6(6)(c) SS&CS(DA) Regs

7. Claims and backdating
175 s1 SSAA 1992
176 Reg 4(1) SS(C&P) Regs
177 Reg 6(8), (8A) and (9) SS(C&P) Regs
178 Regs 3(9)(b), 6(6)(c) and 25(b)
SS&CS(DA) Regs
179 Reg 1A SS(DLA) Regs
180 Reg 6(8), (8A) and (9) SS(C&P) Regs
181 Reg 6(8A) SS(C&P) Regs
182 Reg 6(9) SS(C&P) Regs
183 Reg 9(1) and Sch 1 SS(C&P) Regs; reg
25(3) and (4) UC,PIP,JSA&ESA (C&P)
Regs
184 Reg 13A(1) SS(C&P) Regs
185 Reg 13C SS(C&P) Regs
186 CDLA/14895/1996
187 Regs 6 and 11 SS(DLA) Regs
188 Regs 6 and 11 and Sch 1 paras 3 and 5
SS(DLA) Regs
189 Reg 6(3) and (4) SS(DLA) Regs
190 *DWP Medical (Factual) Reports: a guide to
completion*, DWP, September 2013
191 R(A) 2/74; see also *Moyna v SSWP*, 31
July 2003 (HL), reported as R(DLA) 7/03
192 CDLA/2268/1999
193 CDLA/4806/2002
194 *SSWP v Hughes (a minor)*, reported
as R(DLA) 1/04
195 CDLA/1983/2006
196 *KM v SSWP (DLA)* [2013] UKUT 159
(AAC), three-judge tribunal
197 s19(3) SSA 1998
198 s76(1) SSCBA 1992

8. Getting paid
199 Reg 21 SS(C&P) Regs
200 Reg 22(3) and Sch 6 SS(C&P) Regs

201 Reg 22 SS(C&P) Regs
202 Reg 25 SS(C&P) Regs
203 s71(3) SSCBA 1992
204 R(DLA) 11/02
205 s71(3) SSCBA 1992; CDLA/2887/2008
206 Reg 43 SS(C&P) Regs
207 CDLA/1326/1995
208 Reg 43 SS(C&P) Regs
209 Reg 7(9) SS&CS(DA) Regs
210 s10(5) SSA 1998
211 Reg 7(2)(c) SS&CS(DA) Regs; *RD v SSWP (DLA)* [2011] UKUT 95 (AAC); *DC v SSWP (DLA)* [2011] UKUT 336 (AAC)
212 Reg 32(1) SS(C&P) Regs
213 Reg 17 SS&CS(DA) Regs
214 Reg 17(4)(a)(ii) SS&CS(DA) Regs
215 Reg 18 SS&CS(DA) Regs
216 Reg 19(1) SS&CS(DA) Regs
217 Reg 19(2) SS&CS(DA) Regs
218 Reg 19(3) and (4) SS&CS(DA) Regs

9. Transfers to personal independence payment
219 Regs 3 and 4 PIP(TP) Regs
220 Reg 4(1)(a) PIP(TP) Regs
221 Reg 5(1) PIP(TP) Regs
222 Reg 3 PIP(TP) Regs
223 Reg 19 PIP(TP) Regs
224 Reg 18 PIP(TP) Regs
225 https://www.gov.uk/government/publications/pip-postcode-map-uk
226 Reg 22 PIP(TP) Regs
227 Reg 4 PIP(TP) Regs
228 Regs 12, 13 and 15 PIP(TP) Regs
229 *Reassessing Existing DLA Claimants for PIP*, DWP factsheet, 18 December 2013, available from www.gov.uk
230 *Reassessing Existing DLA Claimants for PIP*, DWP factsheet, 18 December 2013, available from www.gov.uk
231 *Reassessing Existing DLA Claimants for PIP*, DWP factsheet, 18 December 2013, available from www.gov.uk
232 *Reassessing Existing DLA Claimants for PIP*, DWP factsheet, 18 December 2013, available from www.gov.uk
233 Regs 3 and 7 PIP(TP) Regs
234 Regs 9, 11 and 17 PIP(TP) Regs
235 Reg 8(4) PIP(TP) Regs
236 Reg 9 PIP(TP) Regs
237 Reg 10 PIP(TP) Regs
238 Reg 11 PIP(TP) Regs
239 Reg 20 PIP(TP) Regs
240 Reg 13(1) PIP(TP) Regs
241 Regs 13(2) and 17(2)(b) PIP(TP) Regs
242 Reg 12 PIP(TP) Regs
243 Reg 17 PIP(TP) Regs
244 Regs 14 and 15 PIP(TP) Regs

245 Reg 17(1) and (3) PIP(TP) Regs
246 Regs 17(4) and (5) and 30 PIP(TP) Regs
247 **E** Reg 31 PIP(TP) Regs
    W Reg 9A Disabled Persons' (Badges for Motor Vehicles)(Wales) Regulations 2000, No.1786
    S Reg 9(1A) Disabled Persons' (Badges for Motor Vehicles)(Scotland) Regulations 2000, No.59

10. Tax, other benefits and the benefit cap
248 s677 IT(EP)A 2003
249 Reg 24C Armed Forces and Reserve Forces (Compensation Scheme) Order 2011, No.517
250 Sch 1 para 5 SS(OB) Regs
251 Reg 42(1)(b)(ii) SS(C&P) Regs
252 Regs 44, 45 and 46 SS(C&P) Regs

Chapter 28

Contributory employment and support allowance

This chapter covers:
1. Who can claim employment and support allowance (p616)
2. The rules about your age (p618)
3. People included in the claim (p618)
4. The amount of benefit (p619)
5. Special benefit rules (p626)
6. Claims and backdating (p626)
7. Getting paid (p630)
8. Tax, other benefits and the benefit cap (p631)

Key facts

- Employment and support allowance (ESA) is a benefit for people who have 'limited capability for work' (ie, they are unable to work because of illness or disability) and who are not entitled to statutory sick pay.
- Entitlement to ESA is assessed by a test called the 'work capability assessment'.
- There are two types of ESA: **contributory ESA** (which is not means tested, but you have to satisfy a national insurance contributions test) and **income-related ESA** (which is means tested).
- In some cases, contributory ESA is paid for a maximum of 365 days.
- If you qualify for income-related ESA as well as contributory ESA, you may be able to get your contributory ESA topped up with income-related ESA.
- ESA is administered and paid by the DWP.
- If you disagree with an ESA decision, you can apply for a revision or supersession, or appeal against it. You are likely to have to apply for a revision before you can appeal. All parts of the decision may be looked at.

Part 5: Other benefits
Chapter 28: Contributory employment and support allowance
1. Who can claim employment and support allowance

1. **Who can claim employment and support allowance**

You qualify for contributory employment and support allowance (ESA) if you satisfy the following basic rules (which apply to both contributory and income-related ESA), and you satisfy the extra rules for contributory ESA below.

You satisfy the basic rules for ESA if you:[1]

- have 'limited capability for work' (see p1002); *and*
- are aged 16 or over but under pension age (see p752); *and*
- are in Great Britain (see p626 if you go abroad); *and*
- are not entitled in your own right to income support (IS) or jobseeker's allowance (JSA), and are not in a couple entitled to joint-claim JSA (see p46). However, you can get contributory ESA if you are entitled to joint-claim JSA and do not have to satisfy all the JSA conditions (see p47); *and*
- are not entitled to statutory sick pay (SSP); *and*
- are not engaged in any work, whether it is paid or unpaid, unless it is work you are allowed to do while claiming ('permitted work' – see p1019).

You are not usually entitled to ESA for the first three days of your claim (see p1017). You cannot get ESA and certain other benefits at the same time (see p631). Most claimants of ESA (except those in the 'support group' – see p621) are required to take part in work-focused interviews and some can be required to undertake 'work-related activity'. If you come under the universal credit (UC) system (see p19), you must also accept a claimant commitment. See Chapter 50 for details.

Note: in the future it is expected that you must be entitled to work in the UK (and not prevented from taking up work under immigration provisions) to qualify for contributory ESA.[2] There may be exceptions. See CPAG's online service and *Welfare Rights Bulletin* for updates.

Extra rules for contributory employment and support allowance

As well as satisfying the basic rules for ESA above, you qualify for contributory ESA if:[3]

- you satisfy the national insurance (NI) contribution conditions (see p861); *or*
- you were getting incapacity benefit or severe disablement allowance and you have been transferred to contributory ESA (see p662); *or*
- you satisfied the conditions for ESA in youth and you remain entitled (see p617).

Note: you may get income-related ESA if you do not qualify for contributory ESA, or you may be entitled to income-related ESA to top up your contributory ESA. If you come under the UC system (see p19), you cannot get income-related ESA and must claim UC instead.

Employment and support allowance in youth

ESA in youth was a form of contributory ESA for which you did not need to satisfy the NI contribution conditions. You must have been under a certain age when your limited capability for work began.

ESA in youth was abolished for new claimants from 1 May 2012.[4] For details of the rules, see Chapter 10 of the 2012/13 edition of this *Handbook*. If you were already getting ESA in youth when it was abolished, it stops after you have been getting it for a year, beginning on your first day of entitlement. Days when you receive the support component (see p621) are ignored.

If you lose entitlement to ESA in youth because you have received it for a year, but have still got limited capability for work and are put in the support group because your condition has worsened, you can requalify for contributory ESA without having to satisfy the NI contribution conditions.[5] If you are not in the support group, you may be able to get contributory ESA if you satisfy the usual rules, including the NI contribution conditions. You may also be entitled to income-related ESA or, if you come under the UC system (see p19), UC.

Disqualification from benefit

You can be disqualified from receiving ESA for up to six weeks if you:[6]
- have 'limited capability for work' because of your own misconduct (but not, for example, if this is due to pregnancy or a sexually transmitted disease); *or*
- have failed without 'good cause' to accept medical treatment (excluding vaccination, inoculation or major surgery) recommended by a doctor treating you and which would be likely to overcome your limited capability for work; *or*
- have failed without 'good cause' to stop engaging in behaviour that would 'retard' your recovery; *or*
- are absent from your home without telling the DWP where you may be found without 'good cause'.

'**Good cause**' is not defined.

You will not be disqualified if you inform the DWP of your circumstances and you are considered to be a person in hardship – ie, if you are:[7]
- pregnant, or a member of your family is pregnant;
- a single claimant aged under 18, or a member of a couple and both of you are aged under 18;
- responsible (or your partner is responsible) for a child who lives with you. This does not apply to contributory ESA if you come under the UC system (see p19);
- entitled (or your partner is entitled) to attendance allowance (AA), the highest or middle rate of the care component of DLA, the daily living component

Part 5: Other benefits
Chapter 28: Contributory employment and support allowance
4. The amount of benefit

of personal independence payment (PIP) or armed forces independence payment;

- waiting (or your partner is waiting) for a decision on a claim for AA, DLA, PIP or armed forces independence payment;
- caring (or your partner is caring) for someone who is entitled to AA, the middle or highest rate care component of DLA, the daily living component of PIP or armed forces independence payment (or who is waiting for a decision on a claim for AA, DLA, PIP or armed forces independence payment);
- at least the qualifying age for pension credit (see p78), or your partner is;
- at risk of hardship (or a member of your family is at risk) if ESA is not paid to you, including if there is a 'substantial risk' that you will not have sufficient essential items such as food, clothing and heating.

Although you are not disqualified in these situations, your ESA is paid at a reduced rate. You will get 80 per cent of your basic allowance in contributory ESA, or 80 per cent of your personal allowance in income-related ESA (see p222).[8]

You can also be disqualified from receiving contributory ESA during any period in which you are:
- absent from Great Britain (see p1574); *or*
- a prisoner or detained in legal custody (see Chapter 45).

2. **The rules about your age**

To satisfy the basic rules for employment and support allowance, you must be aged at least 16 but under pension age (see p752).

3. **People included in the claim**

You claim contributory employment and support allowance (ESA) for yourself. You cannot claim any increases in your contributory ESA for your partner or children. If you have a partner, you may qualify for income-related ESA (Chapter 5) as well as contributory ESA. You may also qualify for child tax credit (CTC) for any children that you have (see Chapter 8). If you come under the universal credit (UC) system (see p19), you cannot make a new claim for income-related ESA or CTC. Instead, you claim UC which includes amounts for your partner and children.

4. **The amount of benefit**

You are paid a 'basic allowance' of employment and support allowance (ESA) during an initial 'assessment phase' (see p620). Usually, this lasts 13 weeks. After this, during the 'main phase' (see p621), you also get an additional component of ESA.

There are no age-related additions or increases in contributory ESA for other adults or children.

The amount of contributory ESA you are paid depends on:
- whether you are in the assessment phase or the main phase;
- which of the two additional components you get during the main phase. These are the 'support component' (see p621) and the 'work-related activity component' (see p622);
- whether you are entitled to a transitional addition of contributory ESA because you have been transferred from incapacity benefit (IB) or severe disablement allowance (SDA) (see p662).

Your contributory ESA may be reduced if:
- you get a pension or a councillor's allowance (see p623); or
- the work-related activity component (see p622) applies to you and you do not comply with requirements to attend work-focused interviews and carry out work-related activity (see Chapter 49); or
- your ESA is sanctioned because you have committed a benefit offence (see p1258).

Note:
- If you are appealing against a decison that you do not have limited capability for work and get ESA pending your appeal being heard (see p1015), you are paid at the assessment phase rate – ie, you get the basic allowance only.
- You may also be entitled to income-related ESA. If you are, your contributory ESA is topped up by your income-related ESA. If you come under the universal credit (UC) system (see p19), you cannot get income-related ESA, but you may be entitled to UC as well as contributory ESA.

Calculating your contributory employment and support allowance

Contributory ESA is worked out as follows.
- Add together the basic allowance and the amount of any component to which you are entitled, as follows.
  - In the assessment phase (see p620), you are normally only entitled to a basic allowance.[9] This is £57.35 if you are under 25 or £72.40 if you are 25 or over. In some circumstances, such as if you are terminally ill, you are also entitled to either a support component or a work-related activity component while still in the assessment phase (see p621 and p622).
  - After the assessment phase is over and you are in the main phase of ESA (see p621), you are entitled to a basic allowance of £72.40 irrespective of your age, plus one of two additional components: either a support component of

Part 5: Other benefits
Chapter 28: Contributory employment and support allowance
4. The amount of benefit

£35.75 a week (see p621) or a work-related activity component of £28.75 a week (see p622).

- Deduct from this sum an amount for certain pension payments or for a councillor's allowance, if applicable (see p623).
- Add any transitional addition to which you are entitled if you have been transferred to ESA from IB or SDA. See p662 for details of the transfer process and p624 for how the transitional addition is calculated.[10]

Note: when calculating your ESA entitlement after you have been transferred to contributory ESA from IB or SDA (see p662), the support component or the work-related activity component is included straight away, as the assessment phase does not apply.

The assessment phase

The first weeks of your entitlement to ESA are known as the 'assessment phase'. This applies to both contributory and income-related ESA. During this phase, usually your ESA does not include an additional component. You just get a basic allowance of contributory ESA, the amount of which depends on your age. The assessment phase normally ends after 13 weeks.[11]

If the assessment phase lasts longer than 13 weeks, the component is backdated to the 14th week of your claim.[12]

During the assessment phase the DWP gathers further information relevant to your claim. If, after 13 weeks, the DWP has not yet assessed whether you have limited capability for work and you have not been treated as having limited capability for work, the assessment phase does not end until the DWP has decided whether you have limited capability for work. If you are appealing against a decision that you do not have limited capability for work and are getting ESA pending your appeal (see p1015), the assessment phase does not usually end until the First-tier Tribunal has made its decision. However, if you experience a new condition or your condition significantly worsens before your appeal is heard, a new determination on your limited capability for work can be made and it is possible for the assessment phase to end.[13]

In some circumstances, your assessment phase is taken to begin on the first day of a period of previous entitlement to ESA (of either kind), so that some or all of the 13 weeks are treated as already served.[14] This happens if your current period of limited capability for work is linked to a previous one (see p1018) in which you were entitled to ESA but the assessment phase had not ended. In these circumstances, your assessment phase ends when your combined entitlement from the previous and current ESA awards amounts to 13 weeks. If the assessment phase ended in your earlier linked claim (or you were entitled to ESA for more than 13 weeks), the work-related activity or support component is payable from the start of your current claim.

Main phase

The assessment phase is followed by a 'main phase', in which one of the two additional components (a support component or work-related activity component) is added to your basic allowance. The basic allowance of contributory ESA is paid at the rate of £72.40, irrespective of your age.

Support component

The support component is one of the additional components that can be included in your entitlement to both contributory and income-related ESA.[15]

In most cases, you are entitled to the support component if:

- the assessment phase (see p620) has ended (but see below); *and*
- you are assessed as having 'limited capability for work-related activity' (see p1007).

If this applies, the DWP describes you as being in the 'support group'. The DWP decides whether or not you have limited capability for work-related activity as part of the work capability assessment (see p1003). You can appeal if you do not agree with the DWP's decision. If the First-tier Tribunal finds that you have limited capability for work for the purpose of the work capability assessment, it should generally also consider whether you have limited capability for work-related activity.[16]

If you are in the support group, you do not have to take part in work-focused interviews or associated activity as a condition of getting benefit.[17]

Note: if you are transferred from IB or SDA to contributory ESA, or from IS on the grounds of disability to income-related ESA (see p662), the support component is included straight away, as the assessment phase does not apply.

You are entitled to the support component before the assessment phase (p620) has ended if:[18]

- you are terminally ill (ie, you have a progressive disease, because of which your death can reasonably be expected within six months) and have either claimed ESA on these grounds, or asked for a revision or supersession and have said that you are terminally ill. In this case, you qualify for the support component automatically and it is included straight away; *or*
- your period of limited capability for work is linked under the 12-week linking rule (see p1018) to an earlier period in which you were entitled to ESA, you were entitled to the support component in that earlier claim and the claim did not end because you were found fit for work – ie, you did not fail the work capability assessment. In this case, the component can be included straight away; *or*
- your period of limited capability for work is linked under the 12-week linking rule (see p1018) to an earlier period in which you were entitled to ESA, you were entitled to the support component in that earlier claim or the award lasted for more than 13 weeks and it ended either because you failed the work

Part 5: Other benefits
Chapter 28: Contributory employment and support allowance
4. The amount of benefit

capability assessment or before you could be assessed. In this case, you can only get the component again once you have been assessed as passing the work capability assessment, although it is dated from the start of your second award; *or*

- your ESA entitlement has started within 12 weeks of your losing entitlement to IS, when your IS ended it included the disability premium, and the sole reason for your losing entitlement to IS was because you are a lone parent and your youngest child no longer met the age rules (see p27). In this case, once you are entitled to the support component, it is included straight away; *or*
- you have requalified for contributory ESA after having previously lost it because of the rules on how long it can be paid (see p625).

Work-related activity component

The work-related activity component is an additional component that can be included as part of your entitlement to both contributory and income-related ESA.[19] If it is included, the DWP describes you as being in the 'work-related activity group'. This also means that you may be required to take part in work-focused interviews and undertake work-related activity (see Chapters 49 and 50). You are put in the work-related activity group if you are not in the support group.

You are entitled to the work-related activity component if:

- the assessment phase (see p620) has ended (but see below); *and*
- you are not assessed as having 'limited capability for work-related activity' (see p1007) – ie, you are not entitled to the support component; *and*
- you comply with the requirement to attend work-focused interviews and associated activity (see p1057). If you do not, your ESA may be reduced.

Note: if you are being transferred from IB or SDA to contributory ESA or from IS on the grounds of disability to income-related ESA (see p662), the work-related activity component is included straight away, as the assessment phase does not apply.

You are entitled to the work-related activity component before the assessment phase has ended if:[20]

- your period of limited capability for work is linked under the 12-week linking rule (see p1018) to an earlier period in which you were entitled to ESA, you were entitled to the component in this earlier claim and it did not end because you were found fit for work – ie, you did not fail the work capability assessment. In this case, the component can be included straight away; *or*
- your period of limited capability for work is linked under the 12-week linking rule (see p1018) to an earlier period in which you were entitled to ESA, you were entitled to the component or that award lasted 13 weeks or longer, and it ended either because you failed the work capability assessssment or before you could be assessed. In this case, you can only get the component again once you

have been assessed as passing the work capability assessment, although it is dated from the start of your second award; *or*

- your ESA entitlement started within 12 weeks of your losing entitlement to IS, when your IS ended it included the disability premium and the sole reason for your losing entitlement to IS was that you are a lone parent and your youngest child no longer met the age rules (see p27).

Deductions for pension payments and councillor's allowance

A deduction is made from your contributory ESA if you receive certain pension payments of over £85 a week and/or if you are a local councillor and your net allowances exceed £101 a week.[21]

Pension payments that are taken into account for contributory ESA are periodic payments made under:[22]

- any personal, occupational or public service pension scheme; *and*
- any permanent health insurance policy arranged by your employer that provides payments in connection with ill health or disability after your employment ends. However, if you contributed more than 50 per cent of the pension premiums, the amount you receive from this kind of pension is ignored; *and*
- the Pension Protection Fund and the Financial Assistance scheme.

If the total amount of the gross pension payments you receive is more than £85 a week, your contributory ESA is reduced by half the pension payments above £85.

Other types of pension payments (including one-off lump-sum payments) are ignored. The following types of payment are also ignored:[23]

- arguably, any part of your pension paid directly to an ex-spouse or ex-civil partner by the pension scheme trustees under a court order, although the DWP may not accept this;[24]
- any payments you receive as a result of the death of the pension holder;
- any shortfall in your pension if it cannot be paid in full because the pension scheme is in deficit or has insufficient funds;
- payments under a pension scheme for death as a result of military or war service under s639(2) of the Income Tax (Earnings and Pensions) Act 2003, or a guaranteed income payment.

Note: if you are transferred from IB to ESA (see p662) and your pension payment was ignored immediately before the transfer, it continues to be ignored in your ESA.[25] This includes if your IB was not reduced because you were entitled to the highest rate of disability living allowance care component, if you were transferred from SDA to long-term IB, and if you were transferred from invalidity benefit to long-term IB.

If you are a local councillor and your net allowances are more than £101 a week (the limit usually increases in October), your contributory ESA is reduced by

Part 5: Other benefits
Chapter 28: Contributory employment and support allowance
4. The amount of benefit

the amount by which the net allowances exceed £101.[26] A basic allowance or special responsibilities allowance is converted into a weekly amount in a set way – eg, if paid monthly, it is multiplied by 12 and divided by 52. Any payments for expenses are ignored and any other expenses are deducted from the allowance if they are incurred in the relevant week in connection with your council duties. Tax and national insurance (NI) contributions are not deducted.[27]

Transitional addition in contributory employment and support allowance

If you have transferred to contributory ESA from IB or SDA, you may be entitled to a transitional addition in your ESA.

When deciding whether you qualify for a transitional addition, the decision maker compares the following amounts:[28]

- the amount of IB or SDA to which you were entitled immediately before the 'effective date'. This is the date on which your IB or SDA was converted into an award of ESA (see p664). Any increases you received in your IB or SDA for an adult or child are included in the amount. However, the adult increase is no longer included if you no longer satisfy the conditons for getting it, and the child increase is no longer included if you stop getting child benefit for the child. Most deductions made from IB or SDA are ignored;
- the amount of contributory ESA to which you are entitled on the effective date. The work-related activity component or support component is included in the amount.

If the amount of ESA is more than the amount of IB or SDA, you are not entitled to a transitional addition. If the amount of ESA is less than the amount of IB or SDA, you get the difference between the two amounts as a transitional addition, added to your contributory ESA. The transitional addition is reduced by the amount of the annual increase in contributory ESA (ignoring any increase in your housing costs) and by increases in your contributory ESA as a result of changes in your circumstances.

If your entitlement to contributory ESA ends but you requalify for it, the transitional addition can be included again if your new period of limited capability for work can be linked to the old one (see p1018).[29] However, the transitional addition in your contributory ESA cannot be transferred to income-related ESA.

No transitional addition will be paid after 5 April 2020.

For more details, see p638 of 2013/14 edition of this *Handbook*.

Duration of contributory employment and support allowance

Contributory ESA is only paid for 365 days. However, any time when you have limited capability for work-related activity (p1007) is ignored when calculating the 365 days – ie, time spent in the 'support group'. In effect, once you have received contributory ESA for a year and have not been entitled to the support component, you lose your entitlement to contributory ESA. You may, however, be entitled to income-related ESA. The following applies. [30]

- The time limit applies to all new claims of contributory ESA from 1 May 2012.
- If you were already getting contributory ESA on 1 May 2012, any days when you got the work-related activity component are taken into account when calculating the one-year period – ie, if you already had a year or more of contributory ESA on 1 May 2012, your entitlement would have ended immediately.
- Time spent in the assessment phase is taken into account when calculating the 365-day period, except if you were assessed as having limited capability for work-related activity (p1007) and put in the support group.
- If you are appealing about not being in the support group, days when you get ESA while you are appealing are taken into account when calculating the one-year period. This time is then ignored if your appeal is successful.
- If you have been transferred from IB or SDA to contributory ESA, your one-year period is calculated from the date your award was converted to contributory ESA.

You can requalify for contributory ESA again if:
- you remain assessed or treated as having limited capability for work, and you are also assessed as having limited capability for work-related activity for the support component (see p1007); *or*
- the tax years used to decide whether you satisfy the NI contribution conditions (see p861) include at least one year which is later than the last of the relevant tax years which applied to your previous entitlement, and you satisfy the NI contribution conditions again. If you continue to have limited capability for work and still get income-related ESA, under the linking rules (p1018) the tax years remain the same as those that applied to your previous entitlement, so you cannot requalify in this way. However, if you have a break in your ESA entitlement *altogether* (ie, of both contributory and income-related ESA) of more than 12 weeks, you start a new period of limited capability for work and the linking rules do not apply.

Part 5: Other benefits
Chapter 28: Contributory employment and support allowance
6. Claims and backdating

Example
Ravi is aged 24. He has worked since leaving school and has a full NI contribution record, but has had to leave his job because of ill health. He gets the standard rate of the daily livng component of personal independence payment. He is not assessed as being in the support group. As Ravi's wife works full time, he is not entitled to any income-related ESA.
ESA during assessment phase = £57.35 (basic allowance for someone aged under 25).
ESA during main phase = £101.15 (basic allowance of £72.40 *plus* work-related activity component of £28.75). Because Ravi is not in the support group, his award of contributory ESA, which began in July 2013, is limited to one year.
The relevant tax years for the NI contribution conditions are 2010/11 and 2011/12.
After a year of payment, Ravi's contributory ESA stops on 1 July 2014. His condition has not changed and he still does not qualify for the support component. He still has limited capability for work. As his ESA has stopped completely (ie, he is not entitled to income-related ESA either), after 12 weeks Ravi may requalify for contributory ESA. This is because when he makes a new claim for ESA he starts a new period of limited capability for work which does not link to his previous one. One of the relevant tax years that applies to the new claim (2012/13) is later than the years that applied to Ravi's previous claim. However, he must still satisfy the NI contribution conditions again using the new relevant tax years.

5. **Special benefit rules**

Special rules may apply to:
- people in prison or detention (see Chapter 45);
- people still on employment and support allowance in youth (see p1503);
- people subject to immigration control (see p1500);
- people going abroad. A basic rule of entitlement is that you are in Great Britain. However, you can remain entitled during a temporary absence in some circumstances, provided you otherwise continue to satisfy the rules (see Chapter 71).[31]

6. **Claims and backdating**

The general rules about claims and backdating are in Chapter 53. This section explains the specific rules that apply to both contributory and income-related employment and support allowance (ESA). To be entitled to ESA, you must usually make a claim for it. However, you do not need to make a claim if you have appealed against a decision that you do not have limited capability for work, the appeal has not yet been decided and you wish to claim ESA while continuing with it.[32]

If you make a new claim for incapacity benefit (IB), income support (IS) on the grounds of disability or severe disablement allowance (SDA) for a period beginning on or after 27 October 2008, this is treated as a claim for ESA.[33]

In most cases (unless you are recognised as exempt straight away), you are required to attend a medical examination to assess whether you have limited capability for work (p1003) or limited capability for work-related activity (p1007). Also, unless you are in the 'support group' (see p621), you are usually required to attend compulsory work-focused interviews and, in some cases, carry out work-related activity (see p1057).

Note: if you are refused contributory ESA because you do not meet the national insurance (NI) contribution conditions, in some cases it may be worth claiming at a later date that falls in a different benefit year (see p861).

Making a claim

Contributory and income-related ESA are two types of the same benefit. When you claim ESA, in order for the DWP to assess your entitlement to both types, it is important to answer all the relevant questions and provide all the necessary information.

A claim for ESA can be made:[34]

- by telephone. This is usually the way the DWP prefers you to claim. Phone a Jobcentre Plus contact centre (Monday–Friday, 8am–6pm, telephone: 0800 055 6688; Welsh language: 0800 012 1888; textphone: 0800 023 4888). However, the DWP may require you to use a claim form; *or*
- in writing by completing the approved claim form. A form can be downloaded from www.gov.uk/employment-support-allowance/how-to-claim, where an online claim form is also available. Send the completed form to your local Jobcentre Plus office. If the DWP has arranged for a local authority to receive claims for ESA, you can also send it to the local authority housing benefit office.

Note: you do not have to start your claim by telephone, but it is best to make your claim in the way the DWP prefers if you can. If you claim in writing, keep a copy of your claim form in case queries arise.

You must provide any information or evidence required (see p628). You can amend or withdraw your claim before a decision is made (see p1138). If there is a delay in deciding your claim, you may be able to get a short-term advance of benefit (see p1167).

Note: if you come under the universal credit (UC) system (see p19), a claim for ESA will be a claim for contributory ESA only, and you must claim UC instead of income-related ESA.

Part 5: Other benefits
Chapter 28: Contributory employment and support allowance
6. Claims and backdating

Who should claim

You claim contributory ESA on your own behalf. However, if you are unable to manage your own affairs, another person can claim ESA for you as your 'appointee' (see p1137).

If you are employed

If you are employed, you should normally be paid statutory sick pay (SSP – see Chapter 39) for the first 28 weeks of your limited capability for work. If your employer thinks that you are not entitled to SSP or if your entitlement to SSP has run out, it should complete and give you Form SSP1 and you should claim ESA. You are normally expected to include Form SSP1 and a medical certificate with your claim. If your employer refuses you SSP on the grounds that you are not entitled to it, your claim for ESA can be backdated to the date of your SSP claim (see p629). If you disagree with your employer's decision not to pay SSP, you can refer the matter to HM Revenue and Customs (HMRC – see Chapter 60), but do not delay claiming ESA. If you have asked HMRC to decide whether you are entitled to SSP, tell the DWP this when you claim ESA.

Information to support your claim

When you claim ESA you must:
- satisfy the NI number requirement (see p1138); *and*
- provide proof of your identity, if required (see p1140); *and*
- ensure you have made a valid claim – ie, you must supply information or evidence required on the claim form.

For the first seven days of your limited capability for work, the DWP should accept a self-certificate as medical evidence. After seven days, you must provide a medical certificate from your doctor. If it is unreasonable to expect you to provide this, the DWP can accept other evidence if that is sufficient.[35]

You may be referred by the DWP for a medical assessment. If you fail to attend the medical without good cause, your claim can be refused.[36]

Even if you have provided all that was required when you claimed, you may be asked to provide additional information and evidence relevant to your claim – eg, a medical certificate from your doctor (see p1152). There is a strict time limit for providing this. If you do not do so, the decision maker can decide your claim in the way most adverse to you.

Note: you may be asked to provide information after you are awarded ESA. If you fail to do so, your ESA could be suspended or even terminated (see p1175).

The date of your claim

You are not usually entitled to ESA for any day before your date of claim. Unless it is backdated (see below), the date of your claim is usually the date of your telephone call, or the date your claim form is received at a DWP office (or a local authority office – see p627).[37] However, if you notify the DWP that you intend to send in a claim form and you send in a properly completed form within one month, your date of claim is the date of your notification of intent to claim. Remember that, in any case, your claim can be backdated for up to three months (see below). If your claim (either by phone or claim form) is considered defective, the DWP must advise you of this. If you correct the defect within one month of the date the defect was first pointed out to you (or longer, if considered reasonable), your date of claim is still the date you first made the claim.[38]

If you claim the wrong benefit

If your employer has decided that you are not entitled to SSP and you claim ESA within three months of being notified in writing of this, your ESA claim is treated as having been made on the date of your SSP claim.[39]

A claim for maternity allowance (MA) can be treated as a claim for ESA and vice versa.[40] If your MA claim is accepted as a claim for ESA, your ESA can be backdated for up to three months before the date you claimed MA if you satisfy the qualifying conditions during that period (see p1144).

Claiming in advance

You can claim ESA up to three months before the date on which you qualify for it.[41]

Backdating your claim

Your claim can be backdated for up to three months before the day you actually claim – ie, for time during this period when you were entitled to ESA. You should state from which date you are claiming in that period and ask for it to be backdated. You do not need special reasons for backdating.[42]

Starting work when your claim ends

If you start work, you may be able to benefit from the rules for linking periods of limited capability for work should you fall sick again later (see p1018). If this is the case, provided you claim ESA again within a 12-week linking period, you return to the same level of ESA that you previously received.

7. **Getting paid**

Note: this section applies to both contributory and income-related employment and suport allowance (ESA).

Payment of ESA is normally made by direct credit transfer into your bank (or similar) account (see p1163). If you are unable to open or manage an account, payment can be made by 'simple payment' (see p1163).

Payment may be made to someone else on your behalf (your 'appointee' – see p1137) if you are unable to act for yourself.

When is employment and support allowance paid?

The day you are paid depends on your national insurance number (see p1164).[43] ESA is usually paid fortnightly in arrears, although it can be paid at different intervals, including at a daily rate of one-seventh of the weekly amount.[44]

Note:

- Your contributory ESA might be paid at a reduced rate in some circumstances (see p619).
- Deductions can be made from your ESA to pay to third parties (see p1178).
- You might not be paid ESA, or it might be paid at a reduced rate, if you have been sanctioned for a benefit offence (see p1258). **Note:** you may also be sanctioned for other reasons (see Chapters 51 and 52).
- If you have forgotten your PIN, see p1163. If your 'simple payment' card is lost or stolen, or you have forgotten your memorable date, see p1164. For information on missing payments, see p1164.
- If payment of your ESA is delayed, see p1382. You might be able to get a short-term advance (see p1167). If you wish to complain about how your claim has been dealt with, see p1382. You might be able to claim compensation (see p1382).
- If payment of your ESA is suspended, see p1175. This includes if you have failed to supply evidence of your limited capability for work.
- If you are overpaid ESA, you might have to repay it (see Chapter 56) and, in some circumstances, you may have to pay a penalty (see p1249). If you have been accused of fraud, see Chapter 57.

Change of circumstances

You must report changes in your circumstances that you have been told you must report, as well as any that you might reasonably be expected to know might affect your right to, the amount of, or the payment of your benefit. You should do this as soon as possible, preferably in writing. See p1174 for further information.

When your employment and support allowance is adjusted

The general rule is that your ESA is adjusted from the beginning of the week in which the change of circumstances takes effect.[45] However, there are exceptions to this general rule – eg, if you have notified the DWP that you are terminally ill or if you have failed to notify it of a change about your limited capability for work that you should have (see p1287).[46]

8. Tax, other benefits and the benefit cap

Tax

Contributory employment and support allowance (ESA), including ESA in youth, is taxable.[47] **Note**: if you have been transferred from incapacity benefit (IB) or severe disablement allowance (SDA) to contributory ESA (see p662), your contributory ESA is taxable (even if your IB/SDA was not). This includes any contributory ESA paid as a transitional addition.[48]

Means-tested benefits

Your contributory ESA counts as income for the purposes of means-tested benefits if you do not get income-related ESA. If you are getting contributory ESA, you may also be entitled to income-related ESA to top this up or, if you are at least the qualifying age for pension credit (PC), to PC to top this up. If you come under the universal credit (UC) system (see p19), you may be entitled to UC to top up your contributory ESA.

You cannot claim ESA and income support (IS) in your own right at the same time.[49] If it is possible for you to claim either ESA or IS (eg, if you are also a lone parent or a carer), you must decide which benefit to claim. Seek advice about this, as it affects the amount of benefit you get and the sort of work-focused interviews you have to attend.

You cannot claim ESA and income-related jobseeker's allowance (JSA) in your own right, including as part of a joint-claim couple, at the same time. However you can get contributory ESA if you are part of a JSA joint-claim couple and you do not have to satisfy all the JSA conditions (see p47).[50] If your *partner* is entitled in her/his own right to income-based JSA (and it is not joint-claim JSA – eg, because you have a dependent child), you can get contributory ESA at the same time.

You can get ESA and housing benefit (HB) at the same time. You may be entitled to an additional component as part of your HB (see p241). If you are transferred from IB or SDA to contributory ESA (see p662) and do not get income-related ESA, you may get a transitional addition in your HB (see p243).

Part 5: Other benefits
Chapter 28: Contributory employment and support allowance
8. Tax, other benefits and the benefit cap

Non-means-tested benefits

While you are on contributory ESA, you may be entitled to national insurance credits (see Chapter 41).

Contributory ESA is affected by the rules on overlapping benefits (see p1165), which means that you may not be paid it in full if another earnings-replacement benefit is paid to you.

You are not entitled to ESA if you are entitled to statutory sick pay.[51] You can still get contributory ESA if you get statutory maternity pay (SMP), statutory adoption pay (SAP) or ordinary statutory paternity pay (SPP). You can get contributory ESA and additional SPP if the amount of the additional SPP is less than the amount of ESA. Your ESA is reduced by the amount of the SMP, SAP or additional SPP you get.[52]

You cannot claim ESA and contribution-based JSA in your own right at the same time. If your partner is entitled to contribution-based JSA, you can claim ESA.

Tax credits

If you are getting contributory ESA and your partner works, you may be entitled to working tax credit (WTC – see Chapter 10). ESA counts as a 'qualifying benefit' for the disability element of WTC (see p1403).

The benefit cap

In some cases, the total amount of specified benefits you receive is limited to £350 a week (if you are a single claimant without children) or £500 a week (if you are a lone parent or a member of a couple). This is known as the 'benefit cap'. ESA is one of the specified benefits. The benefit cap only applies if you are getting HB or UC. However, the benefit cap does not apply if you or your partner receive ESA which includes a support component. See p1169 for further information.

Passports and other sources of help

If you receive contributory ESA you may be eligible for a Christmas bonus (see p835).

You might also qualify for health benefits such as free prescriptions (see Chapter 30), and education benefits such as free school lunches (see p832).

You might be entitled to council tax reduction (see p827).

Financial help on starting work

If you stop getting contributory ESA because you start work, you might be able to get extended payments of HB if you pay rent (see p136). Your local authority may provide extended help with council tax. See p838 for information about other financial help you might get.

Notes

1. Who can claim employment and support allowance

1 ss1 and 20(1) WRA 2007; reg 40(1) and (7) ESA Regs; reg 37(1) and (8) ESA Regs 2013
2 s62 WRA 2012 (not yet in force)
3 Sch 1 paras 1-4 WRA 2007
4 s53 WRA 2012; s1(3A) WRA 2007
5 s52 WRA 2012; Memo DMG 13/12, paras 24 and 30
6 s18 WRA 2007; reg 157 ESA Regs; reg 93 ESA Regs 2013
7 Regs 157(3) and 158 ESA Regs; reg 94 ESA Regs 2013
8 Sch 5 para 14 ESA Regs; reg 63 ESA Regs 2013

4. The amount of benefit

9 s2(1)(a) WRA 2007; regs 7 and 67(2) and Sch 4 para 1(1)(b) and (c) ESA Regs; regs 7 and 62(1) ESA Regs 2013
10 s2(2) and (3) WRA 2007; reg 67(2) and (3) and Sch 4 paras 1(a), 12 and 13 ESA Regs; Sch 2 para 12 ESA(TP)(EA)(No.2) Regs
11 s24(2) WRA 2007; reg 4 ESA Regs; reg 5 ESA Regs 2013
12 Reg 7(38) SS&CS(DA) Regs; reg 35(7) UC,PIP,JSA&ESA(DA) Regs
13 Regs 4, 5 and 147A ESA Regs; regs 5, 6 and 87 ESA Regs 2013
14 Regs 5 and 6 ESA Regs; regs 6 and 7 ESA Regs 2013
15 ss2(2) and 4(4) WRA 2007
16 *PM v SSWP (ESA)* [2012] UKUT 188 (AAC)
17 Reg 54 ESA Regs; ss11 and 11D WRA 2007
18 Reg 7 ESA Regs; reg 7 ESA Regs 2013
19 ss2(3) and 4(5) WRA 2007
20 Reg 7 ESA Regs; Reg 7 ESA Regs 2013
21 Regs 72-79 ESA Regs; regs 64-72 ESA Regs 2013
22 s3 WRA 2007; regs 72, 72A and 74 ESA Regs; regs 64, 65 and 67 ESA Regs 2013
23 Reg 75 ESA Regs; reg 68 ESA Regs 2013
24 R(IB) 1/04 applied this to IB, but guidance at para 44750 DMG on ESA instructs decision makers to take the opposite approach.
25 Sch 1 para 11 and Sch 2 para 14 ESA(TP)(EA)(No.2) Regs
26 Regs 76(1), 79 and 94(1) ESA Regs; regs 69, 72 and 79 ESA Regs 2013
27 R(IB) 3/01
28 Regs 9, 10, 12 and 13 ESA(TP)(EA)(No.2) Regs
29 Reg 16 ESA(TP)(EA)(No.2) Regs
30 ss51 and 52 WRA 2012; ss1A and 1B WRA 2007

5. Special benefit rules

31 Sch 2 paras 5, 6 and 8 WRA 2007; regs 151-55 ESA Regs

6. Claims and backdating

32 Reg 3(j) SS(C&P) Regs; reg 7 ESA Regs 2013
33 Reg 2 ESA(TP) Regs
34 Regs 4G and 4H SS(C&P) Regs; regs 13 and 15 ESA Regs 2013
35 Regs 2 and 5 SS(ME) Regs
36 s19 SSA 1998; reg 23 ESA Regs
37 Reg 6(1F) SS(C&P) Regs; regs 14 and 16 UC,PIP,JSA&ESA(C&P) Regs
38 Regs 4G(5) and 4H(6) and (7) SS(C&P) Regs; regs 13(5) and 15(4) UC,PIP,JSA&ESA(C&P) Regs
39 Reg 10(1A) SS(C&P) Regs; reg 17 UC,PIP,JSA&ESA(C&P) Regs
40 Reg 9 and Sch 1 SS(C&P) Regs; reg 25 UC,PIP,JSA&ESA(C&P) Regs
41 Reg 13(9) SS(C&P) Regs; reg 34 UC,PIP,JSA&ESA(C&P) Regs
42 Reg 19 and Sch 4 para 16 SS(C&P) Regs; reg 28 UC,PIP,JSA&ESA(C&P) Regs

7. Getting paid

43 Reg 26C(2) SS(C&P) Regs; reg 51 UC,PIP,JSA&ESA(C&P) Regs
44 Reg 26C SS(C&P) Regs; reg 51(5) UC,PIP,JSA&ESA(C&P) Regs
45 Reg 7(2)(a) and Sch 3C SS&CS(DA) Regs; reg 35 and Sch 1 para 1 UC,PIP,JSA&ESA(C&P) Regs
46 Reg 7(2) and (25) and Sch 3C SS&CS(DA) Regs; reg 35 and Sch 1 paras 6 and 9 UC,PIP,JSA&ESA(C&P) Regs

8. Tax, other benefits and the benefit cap
47 ss658(4) and 661(1) IT(EP)A 2003
48 Sch 2 para 6A ESA(TP)(EA)(No.2) Regs
49 s1(3)(e) WRA 2007
50 s1(3)(f) WRA 2007
51 s20 WRA 2007
52 Regs 80-82 ESA Regs; regs 73-75 ESA
    Regs 2013

5

Chapter 29

Guardian's allowance

This chapter covers:
1. Who can claim guardian's allowance (below)
2. The rules about your age (p638)
3. People included in the claim (p638)
4. The amount of benefit (p639)
5. Special benefit rules (p639)
6. Claims and backdating (p639)
7. Getting paid (p641)
8. Tax, other benefits and the benefit cap (p642)

Key facts
- Guardian's allowance may be paid to you if you are responsible for a child or young person and either both her/his parents have died or, in some circumstances, one of her/his parents has died.
- You do not have to be the child's legal guardian to qualify.
- Guardian's allowance is a non-means-tested benefit.
- You do not need to have paid national insurance contributions to qualify.
- You can get guardian's allowance whether you are in or out of work.
- Guardian's allowance can be paid in addition to other benefits and tax credits, but the overlapping benefit rules may apply. It is ignored when calculating your income for means-tested benefits.
- Guardian's allowance is administered and paid by HM Revenue and Customs.
- If you disagree with a guardian's allowance decision, you can apply for a revision or a supersession, or you may be able to appeal against it. You have to apply for a revision before you can appeal.

1. Who can claim guardian's allowance

You qualify for a guardian's allowance if:[1]
- you are entitled, or treated as entitled, to child benefit for a 'child' or a 'qualifying young person' (see p636); *and*
- the child is an 'eligible child' (see p636) and either:

Part 5: Other benefits
Chapter 29: Guardian's allowance
1. Who can claim guardian's allowance

- s/he is living with you (see p556). A child who is absent from home may still be treated as living with you in the circumstances described on p556; *or*
- you or, if you are residing with your spouse or civil partner, you and/or your spouse or civil partner make contributions to the cost of providing for the child at the rate of at least £16.35 a week in addition to any payment you are making to qualify you for child benefit for the child (see below and p557); *and*
- the residence conditions are satisfied (see p1557).

Even if you are not making contributions to the cost of providing for the child, you can be treated as if you are if you give a written undertaking to make the contributions once benefit is paid to you. Any decision to pay you guardian's allowance on this basis may be revised if you do not actually make contributions once benefit is paid to you.[2]

If a child for whom you get guardian's allowance dies, see p642.

Treated as entitled to child benefit

To qualify for guardian's allowance you must either be entitled, or treated as entitled, to child benefit for the child. If you are not entitled to child benefit, you are treated as being entitled to it if:[3]

- you are residing with your spouse or civil partner and s/he is entitled to child benefit for the child; *or*
- you are living in Great Britain and would have been entitled to child benefit for the child had you (or your spouse or civil partner, if you reside with her/ him) not been getting a family benefit from another country.

You can also be treated as entitled to child benefit for a specific week (normally this is the week before your entitlement to child benefit begins, or before your spouse's or civil partner's entitlement begins if you reside with her/him). This allows your guardian's allowance to start from the date child benefit for the child starts.[4]

Note: you still count as entitled to child benefit even if you have elected not to receive it to avoid the high-income child benefit charge (see p568).

A child or qualifying young person

The rules on who counts as a 'child' or a 'qualifying young person' for guardian's allowance are the same as those for child benefit (see p551). In this chapter, the term 'child' is used to refer to both children and qualifying young people.

Eligible children

A child is an **'eligible child'** if:[5]

- both the child's parents (or, if s/he has been adopted, her/his adoptive parents) have died; *or*

- one of the child's parents (or, if s/he has been adopted, one of her/his adoptive parents) has died and:
  - at the time of the death you did not know the whereabouts of the other and you have not been able to trace her/him (see below); *or*
  - the other is sentenced to a term of imprisonment or is detained in hospital by a court order (but see p638); *or*
- when the child was born her/his parents were unmarried, the mother of the child is dead and the paternity of the child has not been clearly established (but see below if the child has been adopted); *or*
- the child was adopted by only one person and that person has died; *or*
- the child's parents (or, if the child has been adopted, her/his adoptive parents) were divorced or their civil partnership had been dissolved, one parent has died and, at the time of her/his death, the other parent:
  - did not have custody of the child or hold a residence order in respect of the child; *and*
  - was not maintaining the child (and was not liable for maintenance of the child under a court order or under a child support maintenance assessment or calculation).

You cannot qualify for guardian's allowance if you are the surviving parent of a child (but see below if the child has been adopted, or if you are a step-parent).

Parents, adoptive parents and step-parents

A parent of a child cannot qualify for guardian's allowance for that child unless one of the following exceptions apply.[6]

- If a child is adopted, because her/his adoptive parents count as parents, one of her/his biological parents can claim guardian's allowance if the qualifying conditions are met.
- Adoptive parents can continue to receive guardian's allowance if they were entitled to it immediately before the adoption.
- A step-parent generally does not count as a parent for guardian's allowance and so may be entitled to guardian's allowance for a stepchild.[7]

Missing parents

If one of the child's parents is dead, you may qualify for guardian's allowance if, at the date of the death, you did not know the whereabouts of the other parent and since then you have failed to discover her/his whereabouts despite making reasonable efforts to do so – eg, asking known relatives and friends and checking old addresses.[8] It may not be necessary to make such efforts if you can show there is a danger that you or the child might experience harm or undue distress if you try to trace the missing parent – eg, if the surviving parent is a threat to your or the child's physical safety or emotional wellbeing.[9]

Part 5: Other benefits
Chapter 29: Guardian's allowance
3. People included in the claim

If contact has been made with a surviving parent since the death of the other parent (but before the decision on the claim), guardian's allowance cannot be paid, as the whereabouts of the surviving parent was known.[10] This applies even if the contact was only fleeting, such as at the funeral, and even if the surviving parent subsequently disappears.

If such contact has not been made, but you are able to communicate with the surviving parent in some way, this is likely to be sufficient to show that the whereabouts of that parent is known.[11] As 'whereabouts' is not the same as an address, merely showing that you do not know where the surviving parent lives may not be sufficient for you to qualify if you know the locality in which s/he is based. However, the locality must be sufficiently defined – if all that is known is that the surviving parent is in a large urban area, you could argue that her/his whereabouts is unknown.

Prison sentences

If one of the child's parents is dead and the other is in prison, you are only entitled to guardian's allowance if the surviving parent is:[12]

- serving a sentence of imprisonment or detention and, at the date of the death, has at least two years of that sentence remaining; *or*
- detained in hospital by order of a court under specified legislation.

A sentence of imprisonment or detention includes detention in a young offenders' institution and detention and training orders, but does not include any period of imprisonment for contempt of court. There are detailed rules for calculating whether the length of a sentence amounts to two years, so seek advice if you are affected by these rules. Guardian's allowance is reduced if the parent in prison contributes to the cost of providing for the child.[13]

2. **The rules about your age**

There is no upper or lower age limit for entitlement to guardian's allowance.

3. **People included in the claim**

You claim guardian's allowance for each eligible child (only one person can qualify for guardian's allowance for a particular child). You cannot get an increase in guardian's allowance for your partner or any other dependants you have.

4. The amount of benefit

Guardian's allowance of £16.35 a week is payable for each eligible child.[14]

5. Special benefit rules

Special rules may apply if:
- you or the eligible child are going abroad (see p1576) or coming from abroad (see p1557);
- the eligible child is in legal custody (see p960);
- the eligible child's parents were born outside the UK (see p1557).

6. Claims and backdating

To be entitled to guardian's allowance, you must make a claim for it.[15] The general rules about claims and backdating are in Chapter 53. This section explains the specific rules that apply to guardian's allowance. Guardian's allowance is administered and paid by HM Revenue and Customs (HMRC).

Making a claim

Claim guardian's allowance in writing on the approved form.[16] Send your claim to the Guardian's Allowance Unit at the Child Benefit Office of HMRC (see Appendix 1). Keep a copy of your claim in case queries arise.

You must provide any information or evidence required (see p640).[17] HMRC has the discretion to accept claims made in another way. However, as HMRC is unlikely to accept a claim that is not made in writing, it is always best to claim in writing, using the approved form whenever possible. You can amend or withdraw your claim before it is assessed by writing to the Guardian's Allowance Unit.[18] If there is a delay in dealing with your claim, you may be able to get an interim payment (see p1169).

Forms
The approved form is Form BG1, which you can get from the Guardian's Allowance Unit (telephone: 0300 200 3101; textphone: 0300 200 3103) or download from www.gov.uk.

Who should claim

You must normally claim guardian's allowance yourself. However, if you are unable to manage your own affairs, another person can claim guardian's allowance for you as your 'appointee' (see p1137).

Part 5: Other benefits
Chapter 29: Guardian's allowance
6. Claims and backdating

If you are a married woman and you live with your husband, it is you, rather than your husband, who is entitled to guardian's allowance.[19]

Information to support your claim

When you claim guardian's allowance, you must:
- satisfy the 'national insurance number requirement' (see p1138);
- provide proof of your identity, if required (see p1140); *and*
- ensure you have made a valid claim – to do so you must supply the information requested on the claim form (see p1140).

HMRC usually needs to see documents such as an original copy of the child's birth or adoption certificate, and a death certificate if a parent has died.[20]

Even if you have provided all that was required when you claimed, you may be asked to provide additional information and evidence relevant to your claim (see p1152). There is a strict time limit for providing this. If you do not do so, the decision maker can decide your claim in the way most adverse to you.

Note: you may be asked to provide information after you are awarded guardian's allowance. If you do not do so, your guardian's allowance could be suspended or even terminated (see p1175).

The date of your claim

The date of your claim is important as it determines the date from when you are paid guardian's allowance (see p641). The date of your claim is normally the date it is received at the Child Benefit Office or at another office that HMRC has stated in writing can receive guardian's allowance claims. However, you can ask for the date of your claim to be backdated (see p641).[21]

If you submit a claim form that has not been completed correctly, or you make a written claim that is not on the approved form, you may be asked to provide further information or to complete the approved form. If this additional information or form is received by the Child Benefit Office (or by another other office that HMRC has stated in writing can receive it) within one month of its being sent back to you (or longer, if the decision maker thinks the delay is reasonable), your claim is treated as having been made on the date the initial claim was received.[22]

In some circumstances, you can claim before you qualify for guardian's allowance (see p641).

If you claim the wrong benefit

The decision maker can treat a claim for child benefit for a child as a claim for guardian's allowance for the same child.[23] If your child benefit claim is accepted as a claim for guardian's allowance, your claim can be backdated for up to three months from the date you claimed child benefit, if you satisfy the qualifying conditions for guardian's allowance over that period (see p1144).

Claiming in advance

You can claim guardian's allowance up to three months in advance. If you qualify for it within the three months after your claim is made, the decision maker has the discretion to treat your date of claim as the date you start to qualify for guardian's allowance.[24]

Backdating claims

Your claim for guardian's allowance can be backdated for up to three months from the date that you make your claim if you satisfy the qualifying conditions over that period.[25] You do not have to show any reason why your claim was late. There are special rules if you were getting guardian's allowance and move between Great Britain and Northern Ireland or if you have been recognised as a refugee (see p1512).[26]

If you might have qualified for benefit for an even earlier period, but did not claim because you were given the wrong information or were misled by HMRC or the DWP, you could ask for compensation (see p1382) or complain to the Ombudsman through your MP (see p1387). If you claimed child benefit instead of guardian's allowance, see p640.

7. Getting paid

Payment of guardian's allowance is normally made by direct credit transfer into your bank (or similar) account (see p1163). If you are unable to open or manage an account, HM Revenue and Customs (HMRC) may agree to make payment by cheque (see p1163). Alternatively, you can ask for payment to be made into your partner's account or into an account held jointly with your partner.[27] If you are unable to act for yourself, guardian's allowance can be paid to someone else on your behalf, called your appointee (see p1137). If you also receive child benefit, guardian's allowance is paid at the same time and in the same way as your child benefit (see p566).[28] If it is necessary to protect your interests, or the interests of the child for whom you get guardian's allowance, all or part of your benefit can be paid to someone else.[29]

When is guardian's allowance paid?
You are normally paid on the same day as your child benefit is paid for the same four-week period (see p566). Payment begins from the first Monday after the date of your claim (see p640), unless the date of your claim is a Monday, when it starts on that day.[30]

Part 5: Other benefits
Chapter 29: Guardian's allowance
8. Tax, other benefits and the benefit cap

Guardian's allowance is a weekly benefit so cannot be paid for a period of less than a week.

If your entitlement to guardian's allowance ends, payment continues up to, but not including, the following payday (normally either Monday or Tuesday), unless your entitlement ends on a payday, when your benefit is paid up to, but not including, that day.[31]

Note:

- Even if you have been sanctioned for a benefit offence (see p1258), you must be paid your guardian's allowance.
- If you have forgotten your PIN, see p1163. If a cheque is lost or stolen, see p1164.
- If payment of your guardian's allowance is delayed, you might be able to get an interim payment (see p1169).
- If you wish to complain about how your claim has been dealt with, see Chapter 61. You might be able to get compensation (see p1382).
- If payment of your guardian's allowance is suspended, see p1175.
- If you are overpaid guardian's allowance, you might have to repay it (see Chapter 56) and, in some circumstances, you may have to pay a penalty (see p1249). If you have been accused of fraud, see Chapter 57.

Change of circumstances

You must report any change in your circumstances that you have been told you must report, as well as any that you might reasonably be expected to know might affect your right to, the amount of, or the payment of your benefit. You should do this as soon as possible, preferably in writing. See p1174 for further information. **Note:** you can also report changes of circumstances online at www.gov.uk. The online forms can be used for both child benefit and guardian's allowance.

The rules about when your benefit is adjusted following a change in your circumstances are the same as those for child benefit (see p568).

If a child dies

If a child for whom you are receiving child benefit dies, you can qualify for guardian's allowance for the eight-week period that child benefit remains in payment for that child (see p568), if you meet the normal qualifying conditions for guardian's allowance over that time (other than the condition that the child either is living with you, or you are contributing to her/his maintenance).[32]

8. **Tax, other benefits and the benefit cap**

Tax

Guardian's allowance is not taxable.[33]

Means-tested benefits and tax credits

Guardian's allowance is ignored when calculating your entitlement to means-tested benefits and tax credits.

Non-means-tested benefits

Although increases in non-means-tested benefits for children were abolished on 6 April 2003, some people continue to be entitled to them. You cannot get such an increase for a child for whom you get guardian's allowance because of the overlapping benefit rules.[34] Otherwise, guardian's allowance can be paid in addition to any other non-means-tested benefit.

Entitlement to guardian's allowance does not qualify you for national insurance (NI) credits. However, you (or, in some circumstances your partner or a family member providing childcare) may qualify for NI credits if you are entitled to child benefit for a child aged under 12 (see p852 and p854).

The benefit cap

In some cases, the total amount of specified benefits you receive is limited to £350 a week (if you are a single claimant without children) or £500 a week (if you are a lone parent or a member of a couple). This is known as the 'benefit cap'. Guardian's allowance is one of the specified benefits. The benefit cap only applies if you are getting housing benefit or universal credit. See p1169 for further information.

Passports and other sources of help

For details of whether you qualify for free school lunches for your children, see p832. You may be entitled to council tax reduction (see p827). Children and young people under 19 may qualify for health benefits (see Chapter 30).

Notes

1. Who can claim guardian's allowance
1 ss77 and 122(5) SSCBA 1992
2 Reg 5 SSB(Dep) Regs
3 s122(4) SSCBA 1992; reg 4A SSB(Dep) Regs
4 Reg 4A(1)(b) and (3) SSB(Dep) Regs
5 s77(2) and (8)(a) SSCBA 1992; regs 4-7 GA(Gen) Regs
6 s77(10) and (11) SSCBA 1992; regs 4 and 6(2) GA(Gen) Regs; R(G) 4/83 (appendix)
7 CBTM 12010; but see also R(F)1/08
8 s77(2)(b) SSCBA 1992
9 12090 CBTM
10 CG/60/1992; R(G) 2/83; CSG/8/1992
11 CG/60/1992; CF/2735/2003

• •

12 Reg 7 GA(Gen) Regs
13 s77(8)(c) SSCBA 1992; reg 8 GA(Gen)
    Regs

4. The amount of benefit
14 Sch 4 Part III SSCBA 1992

6. Claims and backdating
15 s1 SSAA 1992
16 Reg 5(1) CB&GA(Admin) Regs
17 Regs 7 and 10 CB&GA(Admin) Regs
18 Reg 8 and 9 CB&GA(Admin) Regs
19 s77(9) SSCBA 1992
20 Reg 7 CB&GA(Admin) Regs
21 Regs 5(3) and 6 CB&GA(Admin) Regs
22 Reg 10 CB&GA(Admin) Regs
23 Reg 11 CB&GA(Admin) Regs
24 Reg 12 CB&GA(Admin) Regs
25 Reg 6(1) CB&GA(Admin) Regs
26 Reg 6(2) CB&GA(Admin) Regs

7. Getting paid
27 Regs 16, 17 and 34 CB&GA(Admin)
    Regs
28 Regs 16(3),17(2) and 18(4)
    CB&GA(Admin) Regs
29 Reg 33 CB&GA(Admin) Regs
30 Reg 13 CB&GA(Admin) Regs
31 Reg 14 CB&GA(Admin) Regs
32 s145A(4) SSCBA 1992

8. Tax, other benefits and the benefit cap
33 s677 IT(EP)A 2003
34 Reg 7(4) SS(OB) Regs

Chapter 30

Health benefits

This chapter covers:
1. Who can claim health benefits (below)
2. Prescriptions (p650)
3. Dental treatment and dentures (p652)
4. Sight tests and glasses (p652)
5. Wigs and fabric supports (p653)
6. Fares to receive NHS treatment (p654)
7. Claims and refunds (p654)

Key facts
- Health benefits provide help with the costs of NHS prescriptions, dental treatment, sight tests and glasses, and wigs and fabric supports, as well as fares to receive NHS treatment.
- In some cases, you can get items or services free of charge. In some cases, you can get partial help.
- Health benefits are administered by the NHS Business Services Authority.

1. Who can claim health benefits

Although the NHS generally provides free healthcare, there are fixed charges for some items and services such as prescriptions, dental treatment, sight tests and glasses, and wigs and fabric supports. You may also have fares to pay to get to hospital or another establishment for NHS treatment. However, you may qualify for full help with the charges and fares (ie, you may get the items or services free of charge) or you may get partial help.

In some cases, you must make a claim (see p654). If you pay for an item or service that you could have received free, or at a reduced cost, you can apply for a refund (see p657).

Full help

You qualify for full help with charges and fares if you:
- are in an exempt group (see p646); *or*

- satisfy specific conditions; these depend on the item or service. See p650 for prescriptions, p652 for dental treatment and dentures, p652 for sight tests and glasses, p653 for wigs and fabric supports and p654 for fares to receive NHS treatment; *or*
- qualify under the low income scheme (see p647).

Even if you are not in one of the exempt groups, if you are:
- a war disablement pensioner, you may qualify for free prescriptions and wigs and fabric supports. You may also be able to claim money back for dental treatment, fares to hospital, sight tests, glasses or contact lenses. You must have a valid war pension exemption certificate, and you must need the items or treatment, or to travel, because of your war disability. See p655 for where to claim;
- a hospital inpatient, all medication and NHS treatment is provided free of charge (including glasses and contact lenses if prescribed through the Hospital Eye Service). If you are an outpatient or are at a walk-in centre, medication taken and treatment given while you are in the hospital or walk-in centre is also provided without charge (but you may be charged for dentures and bridges).

Exempt groups

You qualify for full help with charges and fares if you are in an exempt group. You are in an exempt group if:[1]
- you, or a member of your family (see p647 for who counts), are receiving:
  - income support (IS), income-based jobseeker's allowance (JSA), income-related employment and support allowance (ESA) or the guarantee credit of pension credit (PC);
  - child tax credit (CTC) and are not eligible for working tax credit (WTC) – eg, you do not work sufficient hours to qualify; *or*
  - CTC and WTC; *or*
  - WTC including a disabled worker or severe disability element; *or*
  - universal credit (UC). **Note:** at the time this *Handbook* was written, it was not known whether UC would be a qualifying benefit after 31 October 2014 (in England), or after 31 March 2015 (in Wales). See CPAG's online service and *Welfare Rights Bulletin* for updates.

  If the qualifying income is tax credits, this only applies if your gross annual income for tax credit purposes does not exceed £15,276.

  Members of your family are also exempt;
- you, or a member of your family, are an asylum seeker or a dependant of an asylum seeker who is receiving asylum support (see p1511). Dependants for whom you are claiming asylum support count as members of your family;

- you are aged 16 or 17 and are receiving support from a local authority after being looked after (in Scotland, receiving support under s29(1) of the Children (Scotland) Act 1995 after leaving care). This does not appear to apply for sight tests in England and Wales or for vouchers for glasses and contact lenses in England.

Note: you may also qualify for full help with particular charges if you satisfy conditions – eg, because of your age, health or medical condition. See the sections on each type of charge below. You may also qualify for full or partial help with charges under the low income scheme (see below).

Member of the family
'**Family**' means you and your partner and any child or qualifying young person included in your claim for the qualifying benefit or tax credit (see p210 for means-tested benefits and p151 for tax credits).

Partial help

Even if you do not qualify for full help with charges and fares, you may still qualify for partial help under the low income scheme (see below).

The low income scheme

You (and members of your family – see above) may be entitled to full or partial help with NHS charges under the low income scheme, even if you do not qualify on other grounds. You must make a claim (see p654). The low income scheme is administered by the NHS Business Services Authority (see Appendix 1).

You (and members of your family) qualify for full help under the low income scheme if:

- you have capital of less than £16,000 (or if you live permanently in a care home, £23,250).[2] Your capital is calculated as for IS (see Chapter 17); *and*
- your income (see p649) does not exceed your 'requirements' (see p648) by more than 50 per cent of the current cost of an English prescription (currently 50 per cent of £8.05 = £4.02).[3] If your income exceeds your requirements by more than this amount, see below to find out if you qualify for partial help with charges.

Partial help with items and services

If you do not qualify for full help with NHS charges, you (and members of your family – see above) may qualify for partial help with these under the low income scheme. You may qualify for:[4]

- reduced-cost dental treatment (including check-ups) and appliances (including dentures); *and*
- reduced-cost sight tests. There is no set charge for sight tests, so it is worth shopping around if you are not entitled to a free test; *and*
- vouchers towards the cost of glasses and contact lenses; *and*
- in England, reduced-cost wigs and fabric supports (these are free in Wales and Scotland); *and*
- partial help with fares to receive NHS treatment.

Note: in England, you cannot qualify for reduced-cost prescriptions under the low income scheme, only free prescriptions. If you cannot qualify for free prescriptions, see p651 for information about pre-payment certificates. In Wales and Scotland, prescriptions are free of charge.

You are expected to pay up to a set amount towards the charges. The set amount is:[5]

- for dental charges and charges for wigs and fabric supports, three times the amount by which your income exceeds your requirements (your 'excess income');
- for glasses or lenses, twice the amount of your excess income;
- for a sight test or fares to receive NHS treatment, the amount of your excess income.

Example

Martin's income exceeds his requirements by £6 so he cannot qualify for full help under the low income scheme. However, he may get partial help. He has to pay the first £18 of dental charges and charges for wigs and fabric supports, the first £6 of the cost of a sight test, the first £12 towards the cost of glasses and lenses and the first £6 of his fares to receive NHS treatment. If he lives in England, he has to pay the full cost of prescriptions.

Calculating your requirements

Your 'requirements' are similar to the IS 'applicable amount' (see Chapter 12). The most significant elements and differences are set out below. There are no reductions in the applicable amounts of people who are subject to immigration control or not habitually resident in the UK, or for students, people engaged in a trade dispute or people without accommodation.

Your requirements are made up of the following elements.[6]

- **Personal allowance(s):**

Single person aged under 25	£57.35
Single person aged under 25, entitled to ESA work-related activity or support component, or incapable of work for at least 28 weeks starting on or after 27 October 2008	£72.40

Single person aged 25–59 or lone parent aged under 60	£72.40
Single person or lone parent aged 60 or over	£148.35
Couples, both partners aged under 60	£113.70
Couples, one or both partners aged 60 or over	£226.50

- **Premiums:** the disability, enhanced disability, severe disability and carer premiums are added to your requirements if you would qualify for them under the IS rules (see p226).

  A disability premium can also be included if you or your partner have been incapable of work for 28 weeks. It can also be included if you (or your partner) have been awarded ESA which includes a work-related activity or support component, or if you (or s/he) have been getting ESA for at least 28 weeks. You (and your partner) must be under 60. If you are a single claimant or a lone parent, the amount of the disability premium is increased to £35.75 if you qualify for an ESA support component or if you are getting disability living allowance (DLA) middle or highest rate care component, either rate of the daily living component of personal independence payment (PIP) or armed forces independence payment and have been getting ESA, or have been incapable of work, for at least 28 weeks starting on or after 27 October 2008.

  An enhanced disability premium can be included if you (or your partner) are getting DLA highest rate care component, the enhanced rate of the daily living component of PIP, armed forces independence payment or ESA which includes a support component. You (and your partner) must be under 60.
- **Weekly council tax.**
- **Weekly rent** *less* **any housing benefit** (HB) and any non-dependant deductions, broadly as the deductions apply under the rules on IS housing costs (see p450). Deductions for fuel and ineligible service charges are made in accordance with HB rules.
- **Weekly mortgage interest and capital payments on loans** secured on a home, to buy a home, or to adapt a home for the special needs of a disabled person, and payments on an endowment policy relating to the purchase of a home. Some other housing costs can be included. Deductions are made for non-dependants.

If you live permanently in a care home, your requirements are your weekly accommodation charge, including meals and services, and a personal expenses allowance. Remember that if your place is being funded by a local authority (fully or in part), you are exempt from some charges.

Calculating your income

Your income is calculated as for IS (see Chapter 14), with modifications. These include the following.[7]

- Your income is normally taken into account in the week in which it is paid. If you are affected by a trade dispute, your normal earnings are taken into account.
- You are entitled to an earnings disregard of £20 if you would qualify for a disability premium (see p229), or if you or your partner are aged 60 or over.
- If you (or your partner) are doing permitted work while claiming ESA (see p1019), the amount of earnings that can be disregarded is the same as for income-related ESA (see p267). If you *and* your partner are both doing permitted work, the disregard is applied to your joint income.
- The full amount of your (or your partner's) contributory ESA is taken into account, even if it is paid at a reduced rate because you failed to take part in a work-focused interview. This does not appear to apply if you come under the UC system (see p19).
- Regular liable relative payments (see p277) count as weekly income. Irregular payments are averaged over the 13 weeks prior to your claim. Lump-sum payments are treated as capital.
- Student loans and grants are divided by 52, unless you are in your final year or are doing a one-year course, in which case the loan is divided by the number of weeks you are studying. The £10 disregard from student loans only applies if you are eligible for a premium, you receive an allowance because of deafness, or you are not a student but your partner is. In addition, in England and Wales, sums in excess of a specified amount of a maintenance grant and certain loans paid to Scottish students studying in England or Wales are disregarded. Also, where a voluntary payment is taken into account, up to £20 of it is disregarded.
- Insurance policy payments for housing costs that cannot be met by IS count as income, but payments for unsecured loans for repairs and improvements (including premiums) are ignored.
- If you live permanently in residential or nursing care:
  – in Wales, no tariff income is taken into account;
  – in England and Scotland, the lower threshold for tariff income is £14,250.
  Remember that if your place is being funded by a local authority (in full or in part), you are exempt from some charges.
- The savings credit of PC is ignored as income.

2. **Prescriptions**

Prescriptions are free in Scotland and Wales. You qualify for free prescriptions in England (and you can get an English prescription free of charge in Scotland and Wales) if:[8]

- you are in one of the exempt groups listed on p646; *or*
- you qualify under the low income scheme (see p647); *or*
- you are aged 60 or over; *or*

- you are aged under 16, or you are under 19 and in full-time education; *or*
- you are pregnant or have given birth in the last 12 months; *or*
- you are a permanent resident in a care home and your place is being partly or wholly funded by a local authority; *or*
- you have:
  - a continuing physical disability, which prevents you leaving your home except with the help of another person;
  - epilepsy requiring continuous anti-convulsive therapy;
  - a permanent fistula, including a caecostomy, ileostomy, laryngostomy or colostomy, needing continuous surgical dressing or an appliance;
  - diabetes mellitus (except where treatment is by diet alone);
  - diabetes insipidus and other forms of hypopituitarism;
  - myxoedema;
  - hypoparathyroidism;
  - forms of hypoadrenalism (including Addison's disease), for which specific substitution therapy is essential;
  - myasthenia gravis; *or*
- you are prescribed or given specific medicines in respect of a pandemic disease.

Prescriptions are also free in England if you are undergoing treatment for cancer, the effects of cancer or the effects of cancer treatment. They are also free if you are in prison or a young offenders' institution or other secure accommodation (or were given the prescription while you were) and if you are detained under the Immigration Act 1971 or s62 of the Nationality, Immigration and Asylum Act 2002.

Pre-payment certificates

In England, if you are not exempt from charges and you need more than three prescription items in three months or 13 items in a year, you can save money by buying a pre-payment certificate.

Apply online, by post, by telephone or at a registered chemist on Form FP95, which you can get from chemists, some surgeries and relevant health bodies. You can also get the form from www.nhsbsa.nhs.uk/healthcosts/2131.aspx or telephone: 0300 330 1341. You can pay by credit or debit card or in monthly instalments by direct debit.

A refund can be claimed in certain circumstances – eg, if you buy a pre-payment certificate and then qualify for free prescriptions.

3. **Dental treatment and dentures**

NHS dental check-ups are free in Scotland. In England, Wales and Scotland you qualify for free NHS dental treatment (including check-ups) and appliances (including dentures) if, when your treatment is arranged or charges are made:[9]

- you are in one of the exempt groups listed on p646; *or*
- you qualify under the low income scheme (see p647); *or*
- you are under 18, or you are under 19 and in full-time education; *or*
- in Wales, for free check ups only, you are under 25 or are 60 or over; *or*
- you are pregnant or have given birth within the last 12 months; *or*
- you are a permanent resident in a care home and your place is being partly or wholly funded by a local authority; *or*
- in England and Wales, you are in prison or a young offenders' institution; *or*
- you are a patient of the Community Dental Service (available if you have difficulty getting treatment because of a disability or for other reasons – contact your health authority for details) or an NHS Hospital Dental Service. Note, however, that there may be a charge for dentures and bridges.

4. **Sight tests and glasses**

Free sight tests

NHS sight tests are free in Scotland. In England and Wales you qualify for a free NHS sight test if:[10]

- you are in one of the exempt groups listed on p646; *or*
- you qualify under the low income scheme (see p647); *or*
- you are aged 60 or over; *or*
- you are under 16, or you are under 19 and in full-time education; *or*
- you are registered blind or partially sighted; *or*
- you have been prescribed complex or powerful lenses; *or*
- you have been diagnosed as having diabetes or glaucoma or are at risk of getting glaucoma; *or*
- you are aged 40 or over and are the parent, brother, sister or child of someone with glaucoma; *or*
- you are a patient of the Hospital Eye Service; *or*
- in England, you are on leave from prison or a young offenders' institution.

Vouchers for glasses and contact lenses

If you are given a prescription for glasses following an eye test, you may be entitled to a voucher that you can use to buy glasses or contact lenses if you need these for the first time, or because your previous ones have worn out through fair wear and tear, or your new prescription differs from your old one. You qualify if:[11]

- you are in one of the exempt groups listed on p646; *or*
- you qualify under the low income scheme (see p647); *or*
- you are under 16, or under 19 and in full-time education; *or*
- you are a Hospital Eye Service patient needing frequent changes of glasses or contact lenses; *or*
- in England, you are on leave from prison or a young offenders' institution; *or*
- you have been prescribed complex or powerful lenses.

In addition, you may be entitled to a voucher when your glasses or lenses need to be replaced or repaired if, because of illness (illness or disability in Scotland), you have lost or damaged them and the cost of repair or replacement is not covered by insurance or warranty. This only applies if:[12]

- you are under 16, or under 19 and in full-time education; *or*
- you, or a member of your family (see p647 for who counts), are exempt from charges because you are receiving income support, income-based jobseeker's allowance, income-related employment and support allowance, the guarantee credit of pension credit, universal credit (UC) or tax credits. **Note:** at the time this *Handbook* was written, it was not known if UC would be a qualifying benefit after 31 October 2014 (in England) or 31 March 2015 (in Wales). See CPAG's online service and *Welfare Rights Bulletin* for updates; *or*
- you qualify under the low income scheme (see p647); *or*
- you have been prescribed complex or powerful lenses.

You can redeem the voucher at any supplier when you buy your glasses or contact lenses (or have glasses repaired). Vouchers are, however, only valid for two years.[13] Vouchers might not cover the full cost of the glasses or lenses you choose to buy. Prices vary; you may need to shop around if you do not want to pay the extra cost.

5. Wigs and fabric supports

Wigs and fabric supports are free in Scotland and Wales. You qualify for free wigs and fabric supports in England if:[14]

- you are in one of the exempt groups listed on p646; *or*
- you qualify under the low income scheme (see p647); *or*
- you are a hospital in-patient; *or*
- you are aged under 16, or under 19 and in full-time education; *or*
- you are a permanent resident in a care home and your place is being partly or wholly funded by a local authority; *or*
- you are in prison or a young offenders' institution or are detained under the Immigration Act 1971 or s62 of the Nationality, Immigration and Asylum Act 2002.

6. **Fares to receive NHS treatment**

You qualify for full help with your fares to attend a hospital or any other establishment for NHS treatment or services if:[15]

- you are in one of the exempt groups listed on p646; *or*
- you qualify under the low income scheme (see p647); *or*
- you are a permanent resident in a care home and your place is being partly or wholly funded by a local authority; *or*
- you live in the Isles of Scilly or the Scottish Islands or Highlands and have to travel more than a specified distance. Special rules (including maximum costs) apply.[16]

The travel expenses of a companion can also be covered – eg, if your child is attending a hospital and you need to accompany her/him, or if you need to be accompanied for medical reasons. You get help with the cost of travelling by the cheapest means of transport that is reasonable and, in Scotland, if necessary, the cost of overnight accommodation. This usually means standard-class public transport. If you have to travel by car or taxi, you should be paid a mileage allowance and road and toll charges, or taxi fares.

Claim at the place where you receive NHS treatment. You may be able to request payment in advance of travelling if this is necessary.

Travel expenses can be covered if you are travelling abroad to receive NHS treatment if the means and cost of travel, as well as any requirements for a companion, have been agreed in advance with the health service body that has arranged the treatment. In England and Wales, you are entitled to payment for the cost of travel to and from the airport, ferry port or international train station if you are in one of the above groups. You are also entitled to payment or repayment of onward travelling expenses to the treatment centre, whether or not you fall within one of the above groups. In Scotland, the rules do not specify what can be covered.

7. **Claims and refunds**

In some situations, you do not have to make a claim for help with charges.

- If you are exempt on the grounds of your age, receipt of a qualifying benefit or because you are a full-time student under 19, complete the back of the prescription form (if required), or complete the appropriate form at your dentist, optician or hospital.
- If you are an asylum seeker receiving asylum support, an HC2 certificate is issued by the UK Border Agency. If you have queries, telephone 0845 602 1739.

- You need an exemption certificate (which you should be sent automatically) if you are exempt because you receive tax credits. This could be up to eight weeks after you are awarded tax credits. If you have not yet received your exemption certificate, sign the prescription form, or other appropriate form, to say you do not have to pay and use your tax credits award notice as proof.
- If you are exempt because you are pregnant or have given birth in the last 12 months, you need an exemption certificate. Obtain one by completing a form, which you can get from your doctor, midwife or health visitor.
- If you are entitled to free prescriptions because you have one of the conditions listed on p650 or you are undergoing treatment for cancer, the effects of cancer or the effects of cancer treatment, you need an exemption certificate. Apply on Form FP92A, which you can get from your doctor, hospital or pharmacist.

In other cases, you must make a claim. To claim under the low income scheme, see below. **Note:** if you are a war disablement pensioner, contact the Service Personnel and Veterans Agency, Norcross, Freepost NAT18006, Thornton Cleveleys, Lancashire FY5 3WP, telephone: 0800 169 2277.

Claiming under the low income scheme

To get full or partial help with charges and fares under the low income scheme, you must make a claim. This includes if you are an asylum seeker, but you are not receiving asylum support. If you *are* receiving asylum support, see above. This also includes if you are exempt because you live in a care home or you are aged 16 or 17 and were formerly looked after by a local authority.

Claim on Form HC1 available from Jobcentre Plus offices or NHS hospitals, some chemists, GP practices, dentists, opticians or advice centres. At www.nhsbsa.nhs.uk you can request a form be sent to you (for England only) or, for Scotland, you can download it. You can also get a form by telephoning 0300 330 1343 (in England), 0845 850 1166 (in Scotland) or 0845 603 1108 (in Wales). Another person can apply on your behalf if you are unable to act for yourself.

If you live in a care home or you are aged 16 or 17 and were previously looked after by a local authority, you can use a shorter Form HC1(SC).

Getting a certificate and when it expires
If you qualify for:
- full help, you are sent an HC2 certificate;
- partial help, you are sent an HC3 certificate which tells you the contribution you must make towards the charges.

Certificates are normally valid for 12 months. However, they are usually valid for:[17]

• five years if you are a single person aged 65 or over, or one of a couple, one aged 60 or over and the other aged 65 or over. This only applies if you do not receive earnings, or payments from an occupational pension, a personal pension or an annuity, and you do not have a dependent child or young person as a member of your household; *or*

• six months from the date of claim if you are receiving asylum support; *or*

• until the end of your course or the start of the next academic year if you are a full-time student.

Make a repeat claim on Form HC1 shortly before the expiry date. If you have a five-year certificate, you must notify the issuing authority of any changes in the composition of your family or household. In other cases, changes of circumstances (eg, starting work and increases in income) do not affect the validity of a certificate. However, if the change could result in increased help (eg, your income has *decreased*), you can reapply for a fresh assessment before the certificate expires.

Proof of entitlement

You are normally asked for proof that you are entitled to full or partial help with charges, although you should not be denied an item or service if you are unable to provide the required evidence. If you have an HC2 or HC3 certificate, show this to the dentist, optician, hospital or pharmacist (you may also have to enter details on the appropriate form). In other cases, you may need to show evidence of your date of birth, student status or exemption certificate.

Overpayments and fraud

If you receive help to which you were not entitled, you can be issued with a penalty notice requiring you to pay the charge you should have paid plus a penalty, unless you can show that you did not act 'wrongfully' or with 'any lack of care'. The penalty can be increased if you do not pay it within 28 days, and court proceedings can be taken to recover the debt. Anyone wrongly claiming help with charges on your behalf can be liable to pay a penalty charge. You can also be prosecuted if you obtain help wrongly, on the basis of a false statement or representation.[18]

Delays and complaints

For general queries, telephone 0300 330 1343. You can ask for a formal review of the decision on your claim by writing to the Review Section at the NHS Business Services Authority. See Appendix 1 for the address.

If there are delays in obtaining a certificate, you can complain to the customer services manager. If necessary, you could pay for the treatment or items you need then try to obtain a refund (see p657).

Refunds

If you pay for an item or service that you could have got free, or at reduced cost, you can apply for a refund. Do this within three months of paying the charge, although the time limit can, in some cases, be extended if you can show good cause for applying late – eg, you were ill.[19]

Apply for a refund of a prescription charge (in England) on Form FP57, which you must obtain when you pay as one cannot be supplied later. For other items and services, apply on the relevant Form HC5. Get the forms by telephoning 0300 330 1343, or from a Jobcentre Plus office or NHS hospital. You must submit a receipt or other documents to show that you have paid the charge. If you need an HC2 or HC3 certificate and have not applied for one, send a Form HC1 with your application for a refund.

Notes

1. Who can claim health benefits

1 **E** Regs 2-5 NHS(TERC) Regs; reg 3 POS Regs; reg 8 NHS(OCP) Regs 2013
S Regs 2 and 4 NHS(TERC)(S) Regs; regs 3 and 8 NHS(OCP)(S) Regs
W Regs 2-5 NHS(TERC)(W) Regs; reg 13 NHS(GOS) Regs; regs 3 and 8 NHS(OCP) Regs

2 **E** Sch 1 Table A NHS(TERC) Regs
S Sch Part 1 NHS(TERC)(S) Regs
W Sch 1 Table A NHS(TERC)(W) Regs

3 **E** Reg 5(2)(e) and (f) NHS(TERC) Regs; reg 3(2)(c) and (d) POS Regs; regs 3(2) and 8(3)(b) and (c) NHS(OCP) Regs 2013
S Reg 4(2)(c) and (d) NHS(TERC)(S) Regs; regs 3(2) and 8(3)(e) and (f) NHS(OCP)(S) Regs
W Reg 5(2)(e) NHS(TERC)(W) Regs; reg 13(2)(e) and (f) NHS(GOS) Regs; regs 3(2) and 8(3)(e) and (f) NHS(OCP) Regs

4 **E** Reg 6 NHS(TERC) Regs; regs 3 and 8 NHS(OCP) Regs 2013
S Reg 5 NHS(TERC)(S) Regs; regs 3 and 8 NHS(OCP)(S) Regs
W Reg 6 NHS(TERC)(W) Regs; regs 3 and 8 NHS(OCP) Regs

5 **E** Reg 6 NHS(TERC) Regs; regs 7, 15 and 20 NHS(OCP) Regs 2013
S Reg 5 NHS(TERC)(S) Regs; regs 14 and 19 NHS(OCP)(S) Regs
W Reg 6 NHS(TERC)(W) Regs; regs 7, 14 and 19 NHS(OCP) Regs

6 **E** Reg 17 and Sch 1 Table B NHS(TERC) Regs
S Reg 8 and Sch Part 2 NHS(TERC)(S) Regs
W Reg 16 and Sch 1 Table B NHS(TERC)(W) Regs

7 **E** Reg 16 and Sch 1 Table A NHS(TERC) Regs
S Reg 8 and Sch Part 1 NHS(TERC)(S) Regs
W Reg 15 and Sch 1 Table A NHS(TERC)(W) Regs

2. Prescriptions

8 **E** Regs 7, 7A and 7B NHS(CDA) Regs; regs 4 and 5 NHS(TERC) Regs
S Regs 3 and 4 NHS(FP&CDA)(S) Regs
W Regs 3, 4 and 8 NHS(FP&CDA)(W) Regs; regs 4 and 5 NHS(TERC)(W) Regs

• •

3. Dental treatment and dentures
9 **E** s177 NHSA 2006; regs 3 and 7 and
Sch 5 NHS(DC) Regs; regs 4 and 5
NHS(TERC) Regs
S Sch 11 NHS(S)A 1978; reg 5 and Sch 2
NHS(DC)(S) Regs; regs 3 and
4 NHS(TERC)(S) Regs
W s126 NHS(W)A 2006; regs 3 and 7
and Sch 5 NHS(DC)(W) Regs; regs 4 and
5 NHS(TERC)(W) Regs

4. Sight tests and glasses
10 **E** Reg 3 POS Regs; regs 3 and 8
NHS(OCP) Regs 2013
W Reg 13 NHS(GOS) Regs; regs 3 and 8
NHS(OCP) Regs
11 **E** Regs 8 and 9 NHS(OCP) Regs 2013
S Regs 8 and 9 NHS(OCP)(S) Regs
W Regs 8 and 9 NHS(OCP) Regs
12 **E** Regs 8 and 16 NHS(OCP) Regs 2013
S Regs 8 and 15 NHS(OCP)(S) Regs
W Regs 8 and 15 NHS(OCP) Regs
13 **E** Reg 12(1) NHS(OCP) Regs 2013
S Reg 12(1) NHS(OCP)(S) Regs
W Reg 12(1) NHS(OCP) Regs

5. Wigs and fabric supports
14 **E** Regs 5(3), 7, 7A and 7B NHS(CDA)
Regs; regs 4 and 5 NHS(TERC) Regs
S Regs 3 and 4 NHS(FP&CDA)(S) Regs
W Regs 3, 4 and 8 NHS(FP&CDA)(W)
Regs

6. Fares to receive NHS treatment
15 **E** s183(a) NHSA 2006; regs 3 and 5
NHS(TERC) Regs
S s75A(1)(b) NHS(S)A 1978; regs 3 and
4 NHS(TERC)(S) Regs
W s131(a) NHS(W)A 2006; regs 3 and 5
NHS(TERC)(W) Regs
16 **E** Reg 9 NHS(TERC) Regs
S Reg 7 NHS(TERC)(S) Regs

7. Claims and refunds
17 **E** Reg 8 NHS(TERC) Regs
S Reg 10 NHS(TERC)(S) Regs
W Reg 8 NHS(TERC)(W) Regs
18 **E** ss193 and 194 NHSA 2006
S ss99ZA and 99ZB NHS(S)A 1978
W ss141 and 142 NHS(W)A 2006
19 **E** Reg 11 NHS(TERC) Regs; reg 10
NHS(CDA) Regs; regs 6 and 24
NHS(OCP) Regs 2013
S Reg 11 NHS(TERC)(S) Regs; reg
5 NHS(FP&CDA)(S) Regs; reg
20 NHS(OCP)(S) Regs
W Reg 10 NHS(TERC)(W) Regs; regs
3(10) and 11A NHS(FP&CDA)(W) Regs;
regs 6 and 20 NHS(OCP) Regs

Chapter 31

Incapacity benefit and severe disablement allowance

This chapter covers:
1. Incapacity benefit (below)
2. Severe disablement allowance (p661)
3. Transferring to employment and support allowance (see p662)

Key facts
- Incapacity benefit (IB) and severe disablement allowance (SDA) are benefits for people who are incapable of work.
- IB was abolished on 27 October 2008. If you are already getting IB, you can continue to receive it. You cannot normally make a new claim for IB, although some people who are getting income support (IS) 'on the grounds of disability' can still do so.
- SDA was abolished on 6 April 2001. No new claims can be made, although some people entitled to it before this date can continue to receive it.
- If you cannot work because of sickness or disability, you must usually claim employment and support allowance (ESA). Most IB or SDA claims will have been transferred to ESA by 31 March 2014.

1. Incapacity benefit

Incapacity benefit (IB) was abolished on 27 October 2008. You can only be entitled to IB now if:[1]
- you are already entitled and you continue to meet the qualifying conditions (see p660); or
- you are entitled to income support (IS) 'on the grounds of disability' (see p27), claim IB and meet the qualifying conditions on p660.

Note: if you are already getting IB, you continue to do so until your entitlement is reassessed under the work capability assessment and you are transferred to employment and support allowance (ESA). This process was largely completed by April 2014, but a few remaining cases may not be transferred until later in 2014. You are not reassessed if you reached pension age before 6 April 2014 (see p662).

Who is still entitled

You still qualify for IB if:
- you are already entitled to IB or are getting IS 'on the grounds of disability'; *and*
- you are assessed or treated as incapable of work (see p683 of the 2013/14 edition of this *Handbook* for details); *and*
- you are within a 'period of incapacity for work'; *and*
- for short-term IB, you are not more than five years above pension age and, for long-term IB, you are not over pension age (see p752); *and*
- you are not entitled to statutory sick pay (SSP – see Chapter 39).

In addition:
- you must have paid (or been credited with) sufficient national insurance (NI) contributions (see p735 of the 2008/09 edition of this *Handbook* for more information) at the start of your claim; *or*
- you qualify as someone who became incapable of work in youth; *or*
- you are no more than five years over pension age (see p752), your period of incapacity for work began before you reached pension age, and you would qualify for a Category B retirement pension as a widow, widower or surviving civil partner, or a Category A retirement pension had you not deferred claiming it or 'de-retired' (see Chapter 36). **Note:** this provision only allows you to qualify for short-term IB; *or*
- your spouse died before 9 April 2001 and you qualify as a widow or widower.

Special rules may apply if:
- you are a widow or widower;
- you have been incapable of work since 12 April 1995;
- you are coming from or going abroad (see Chapters 69, 70 and 71);
- you are in prison or detention (see Chapter 45).

For more details, see p674 of the 2013/14 edition of this *Handbook*.

The amount of benefit

IB is paid at three rates: a lower rate of short-term IB for the first 28 weeks of entitlement, a higher rate of short-term IB after 28 weeks, then long-term IB after 52 weeks of entitlement.

	Under pension age £pw	Pension age or over £pw
Long-term IB		
Claimant	104.10	–
Increase for an adult	60.45	–
Short-term IB (higher rate)		
Claimant	92.95	104.10
Increase for an adult	47.10	58.20
Short-term IB (lower rate)		
Claimant	78.50	99.90
Increase for an adult	47.10	58.20

You may be able to claim an increase in your IB for an adult (your spouse or civil partner, or someone who cares for your child). See pp681-83 of the 2013/14 edition of this *Handbook* for details. The increase is not paid if the adult has earnings above a certain limit. In 2014/15, the increase is not paid if s/he is earning more than £72.40 a week or, if you are not residing with her/him or the increase is of the lower rate of short-term IB, s/he is earning more than the amount of the increase that would apply.

Once you are entitled to long-term IB, you are paid an age-related addition if you were under 45 on the first day of your period of incapacity for work. It is paid at two rates, depending on your age on this day. See p677 of the 2013/14 edition of this *Handbook* for full details.

Age	£pw
Under 35	11.00
Under 45	6.15

2. Severe disablement allowance

Severe disablement allownce (SDA) was abolished on 6 April 2001, but certain people entitled to it before that date can continue to receive it.

Note: if you are already getting SDA, you continue to do so until your entitlement is reassessed under the work capability assessment and you are transferred to employment and support allowance (ESA). This process was largely completed by April 2014, but a few remaining cases may not be transferred until later in 2014. **Note:** you are not reassessed if you reached pension age before 6 April 2014 (see p662).

Part 5: Other benefits
Chapter 31: Incapacity benefit and severe disablement allowance
3. Transferring to employment and support allowance

Who is still entitled

You still qualify for SDA if:[2]

- you were getting SDA before 31 January 2011 and there has been no break in your entitlement since that date; *and*
- you continue to meet the qualifying conditions, including being incapable of work or treated as incapable of work (see p683 of the 2013/14 edition of this *Handbook* for details);[3] *and*
- either you reached pension age before 6 April 2014 or no decision has yet been made on converting your SDA to ESA (see below).

See Chapter 4 of the 2000/01 edition of this *Handbook* for the qualifying conditions for SDA and for more information, see p679 of the 2013/14 edition of this *Handbook*.

The amount of benefit

The current basic rate of SDA is £73.75 a week. You may also be entitled to an age addition (see pxix for amounts).

You may be able to claim an increase in your SDA for an adult (£36.30 a week). Increases for children and young people were abolished on 6 April 2003, but some people can continue to qualify for them. If you qualify, you are paid £11.35 for the eldest child and £8.05 for each other child. For full details see p679–82 of the 2013/14 edition of this *Handbook*.

---

3. **Transferring to employment and support allowance**

If you were claiming incapacity benefit (IB), severe disablement allowance (SDA) or income support (IS) 'on the grounds of disability' when employment and support allowance (ESA) was introduced on 27 October 2008 and have remained entitled, your claim continues as an 'existing award'. However, unless you reached pension age before 6 April 2014, at some time the decision maker will decide whether your entitlement to IB, SDA or IS can be converted to an award of ESA. This process was largely completed by April 2014, but it is expected that a few remaining cases will be decided later in 2014. You do not need to make a claim for ESA.[4] At the end of this process, people claiming national insurance (NI) contribution credits on the grounds of incapacity for work will have their entitlement reassessed to see if they qualify for NI credits on the grounds of 'limited capability for work'.

The reassessment process

If you reached pension age (see p752) before 6 April 2014, your existing award is not reassessed.

If you will reach pension age on or after 6 April 2014, the reassessment of your existing award is usually triggered by the date you are next due to be assessed for incapacity for work under the personal capability assessment.

If you are exempt from this assessment, the DWP decides a date. In both cases, you are sent a notice telling you that you will be reassessed for ESA. You will also get a telephone call about this. The notice must contain certain information.

During the reassessment, the decision maker considers whether you satisfy the basic rules for ESA (other than the condition that you must not be entitled to IS – see p616), including having limited capability for work under the work capability assessment (see Chapter 47). You are sent a questionnaire (ESA50) about limited capability for work and may be required to attend a medical. Your entitlement to your existing award continues while you are being reassessed.

The decision maker then decides if your existing award can be converted to ESA. This is known as a 'conversion decision'.

Note:
- If, as well as being entitled to IS on the grounds of disability, you are entitled to IS on another ground (eg, as a carer), you can remain on IS rather than transfer to ESA. Tell the DWP that you wish to remain on IS before your award is due to end. However, if you remain on IS, your IS does not include the disability premium for incapacity for work.
- If you get IS on the grounds of disability as well as IB or SDA, the decision on whether to transfer you to ESA applies to both your IS and your IB or SDA. If you qualify for IS on another ground (see p26) and want to continue to get IS rather than transfer to ESA, your entitlement to IB or SDA ends.[5]
- If you do not return the questionnaire or attend a medical and you do not have good cause, you lose your entitlement to benefit (see p1009 and p1011).

The conversion decision

If the decision maker decides that:
- you have limited capability for work and you meet the basic rules of entitlement to ESA (see p66), you are transferred to ESA and your IB, SDA or IS stops. If the amount of your IB, SDA or IS is more than the amount of ESA to which you are entitled, you qualify for a transitional addition to ensure your income does not decrease (see p71 and p624);
- you do not have limited capability for work or you do not meet the basic rules of entitlement to ESA, or if you do not return the questionnaire or attend the medical and you do not have good cause, your entitlement to IB, SDA or IS stops and you are not awarded ESA. You can challenge this decision.

Part 5: Other benefits
Chapter 31: Incapacity benefit and severe disablement allowance
3. Transferring to employment and support allowance

Note: in deciding whether you meet the basic rules of entitlement to ESA described on p66, the condition that you must not be entitled to IS is ignored.

Before you are sent this conversion decision, you are likely to get a telephone call to advise you of it.

The exact date your existing award is converted to ESA or is ended if you do not qualify for ESA is known as the 'effective date'. This depends on the day your IB, SDA or IS is paid and is two to four weeks after the date on which you are notified of the conversion decision.

Note:

- If you are a disabled or deaf student being transferred from IS, the usual requirement not to be in education (see p66) does not apply to you – ie, you can get ESA while in education even if you do not get disability living allowance.[6]
- You can appeal against the conversion decision, including about whether you have limited capability for work and whether you are put in the work-related activity group or the support group for ESA. Usually you must request a revision first (see Chapters 58 and 59).
- If you are appealing against a decision that you have failed the work capability assessment (ie, that you do not have limited capability for work – see p1003), you are entitled to ESA at the 'assessment phase' rate if you have submitted a medical certificate.[7] You do not need to make a claim for ESA while appealing.
- A conversion decision can be revised before the effective date (ie, before the actual date on which the conversion to ESA is made, or your IB, SDA or IS otherwise stops), or it can be revised or superseded in the usual way on or after the effective date.[8]

If you are awarded employment and support allowance

If you are transferred to ESA, the transfer is automatic; you do not need to do anything.

Awards of IB and SDA are converted into awards of contributory ESA (without your needing to satisfy the NI contribution conditions for contributory ESA). Awards of IS are converted into awards of income-related ESA. If you are transferred to contributory ESA, you may also be entitled to income-related ESA.

If you are transferred to ESA, you must meet all the usual ESA rules, such as those on permitted work, work-focused interviews and tax. This applies even if your IB was not taxable because you were transferred to it in 1995 from invalidity benefit.[9]

Note:

- If you are transferred to ESA, the work-related activity component or support component is included in your ESA straight away.

• You may be entitled to a transitional addition in your ESA to ensure that the amount of benefit you receive does not decrease. See p71 (for income-related ESA) and p624 (for contributory ESA) for further details.

• If you are awarded contributory ESA, you can only get this for a maximum of 365 days from the date your IB or SDA is converted (although certain days can be ignored – see p625).

Notes

1. Incapacity benefit
1 Reg 2 ESA(TP) Regs

2. Severe disablement allowance
2 Art 4 WRPA(No.9)O; reg 2 ESA(TP) Regs; reg 24 ESA(TP)(EA)(No.2) Regs
3 s68 SSCBA 1992; reg 4 WRPA(No.9)O

3. Transferring to employment and support allowance
4 Reg 3(1) SS(C&P) Regs
5 Regs 10, 11 and 15(2A) ESA(TP)(EA)(No.2) Regs
6 Sch 1 para 2 and Sch 2 para 2 ESA(TP)(EA)(No.2) Regs
7 Regs 7 and 13-15 and Sch 2 paras 5 and 10 ESA(TP)(EA)(No.2) Regs
8 Regs 6 and 16 ESA(TP)(EA)(No.2) Regs
9 Reg 16 ESA(TP)(EA)(No.2) Regs

Chapter 32

Industrial injuries benefits

This chapter covers:
1. Who can claim industrial injuries benefits (below)
2. Industrial injuries disablement benefit (p677)
3. Reduced earnings allowance (p679)
4. Retirement allowance (p683)
5. Special benefit rules (p683)
6. Claims and backdating (p683)
7. Getting paid (p686)
8. Tax, other benefits and the benefit cap (p686)

Key facts
- Industrial injuries benefits are paid if you are disabled as a result of an accident at work or a disease caused by your job (but not if this is self-employment).
- The main industrial injuries benefit is **disablement benefit**, but you may also qualify for **reduced earnings allowance** or **retirement allowance**.
- All industrial injuries benefits are non-means-tested benefits.
- You do not have to have paid national insurance contributions to qualify.
- You can qualify whether you are in or out of work.
- Industrial injuries benefits are administered and paid by the DWP.
- If you disagree with an industrial injuries benefit decision, you can apply for a revision or a supersession, or appeal against it. You are likely to have to apply for a revision before you can appeal.

1. Who can claim industrial injuries benefits

You qualify for industrial injuries benefits if you satisfy the '**industrial injury condition**' – ie:[1]
- you have had a 'personal injury' in an 'industrial accident' (see p668) or you have a 'prescribed industrial disease' (see p671); *and*
- at the time of the injury you were an employed earner (see p667); *and*
- as a result of that accident or disease you have had a 'loss of faculty' (see p673); *and*
- as a result of that 'loss of faculty' you are 'disabled'.

Industrial injuries benefits include industrial injuries disablement benefit (IIDB), reduced earnings allowance (REA) and retirement allowance. You can only qualify for REA or retirement allowance if your accident or disease occurred before October 1990.

If you have been injured by your work, you may also have the right to sue your employer. Legal help may be available and you may be able to get a free consultation with a solicitor. Your right to compensation from your employer is separate from your rights to benefit under the industrial injuries scheme (although your compensation may be reduced if you have received benefits from the DWP – see p1191).

Employed earners

You can only claim industrial injuries benefits if you were an 'employed earner' (see p844) and your accident or disease was caused by your employment.[2] If you are self-employed, you are excluded from the scheme.

If you pay, or ought to pay, Class 1 national insurance (NI) contributions (see p844) as an employed earner you can qualify for industrial injuries benefits. This includes if you pay Class 1 (and, in the case of volunteer development workers, Class 2 – see p845) contributions while abroad.[3]

You can also qualify if your earnings are too low to pay contributions. You are also treated as an employed earner if you are an apprentice, mine inspector or rescue worker, special constable, taxi driver, office cleaner, agency worker, minister of religion, lecturer, member of an aircrew, mariner or, in some situations, an offshore oil or gas worker.[4]

From 31 October 2013, you can be treated as an employed earner if you are participating in a government course or training scheme which forms part of a mandatory work scheme. The person or organisation providing the training is treated as the employer for the purposes of making a claim for benefit.[5]

You are treated as *not* being an employed earner if:[6]

- you are employed by your spouse or civil partner and either your employment is not for the purpose of her/his business or profession (eg, if your partner employs you as her/his carer) or your earnings are normally below the lower earnings limit (see p844); *or*
- you are employed by a close relative (parent, step-parent, grandparent, son, daughter, stepchild, grandchild, brother, sister, half-brother or half-sister) in a private house where you both live, and your employment is not for your relative's trade or business carried out there; *or*
- you are a member of, or a civilian employed by, visiting armed forces, unless you are normally resident in the UK.

Part 5: Other benefits
Chapter 32: Industrial injuries benefits
1. Who can claim industrial injuries benefits

Personal injury

Personal injury includes the obvious, such as broken legs or arms, but also covers the less obvious, such as strains and psychological injury.[7] So an assault at work causing slight physical injury might cause a far greater injury to the mind by resulting in agoraphobia or a breakdown. In difficult cases, the question is whether or not you have experienced a physiological or psychological change for the worse. It is not enough just to be in pain if the pain is merely a symptom of an existing condition and does not make that condition substantially worse.[8] The damage must be to you or part of you. Dislocation of an artificial hip joint counts as a personal injury,[9] but damage to a pair of spectacles does not.[10]

5 Accident

The term **'accident'** has been defined as an unlooked-for mishap or occurrence.[11] However, an accident need only be unexpected from your point of view.[12] It does not matter if it could have been anticipated by an expert. If you do a heavy or dangerous job where accidents are common, a resulting injury is just as much an accident as if your job is sedentary and comparatively safe. A heart attack can be an injury but there needs to be some external event or series of events causing it, such as heavy lifting or work-related stress.[13] Deliberate acts by third parties can be accidents – eg, assaults on security workers or on staff in shops and hospitals.[14]

An accident is 'industrial' if you can show a connection with your work. This connection is established if the accident arose 'out of and in the course of your employment'.[15] Remember that, despite the name, it is not only industrial workers who can have 'industrial accidents'; all employees can. For example, if you are an office worker and a badly loaded filing cabinet tilts and falls on you, this should count as an 'industrial accident'. There need not be a dramatic event; any accident sustained while you are doing your job can qualify – eg, spilling a hot drink and scalding yourself. An illness brought on by conversation could count as being caused by an industrial accident.[16]

Accident or process?

Benefit is payable for an 'accident', but not for a 'process' (unless it causes a 'prescribed disease' – see p671). To fall from a ladder and break your leg is an 'accident', but to work for many years as a heavy manual worker and have a sore back is a cumulative 'process', as is breathing in dust over many years.[17] However, sometimes a series of events, over a period of time, can be treated as an 'accident' for benefit purposes – see example on p669.[18] The cumulative effect of a series of incidents can also result in an accident.[19] Furthermore, you should not be excluded from entitlement to benefit simply because you cannot identify which incidents caused the injury.[20]

Example

Cyril's job is trimming excess rubber from hot water bottles with a pair of scissors. A particularly hard batch of rubber comes through and each cut requires greater strength. Over two or three days he suffers a strain injury in his hand. The series of cuts constitutes a series of 'accidents' that meets the definition.

It is easier to establish the series of events as an accident if the period of time is fairly short,[21] or if it is noticed at an identifiable moment.[22] An accident is proved if you can establish that an identifiable occurrence must have happened, even if it is impossible to prove when.[23]

In the course of employment

The accident (see p668) must arise 'in the course of employment'. Difficulties arise when work rules are broken, or when you do something not directly connected with work.

Generally, when you arrive at your employer's workplace and are on her/his private property, you are 'in the course of your employment'. You do not have to have clocked in or have reported to your actual workplace. If you arrive early to get ready for work or to have a meal in the canteen[24] you are covered, although if you arrive early to play a game of pool you are not.[25] You are probably covered during breaks from working if you remain on the employer's property,[26] but probably not if you go elsewhere. So if, during a tea break, you go to a local shop to buy a snack, you are outside the course of your employment.[27] If you are allowed to have a snack either at home or at work while still on duty, you are covered.[28]

While at work most activities are considered to be 'in the course of employment'.[29] Smoking,[30] chatting[31] or sharing sweets[32] are all 'reasonably incidental' to the employment, provided they are not done in breach of instructions.[33] Even if you were doing something in breach of instructions, you are still covered if the accident would have been taken as arising out of, and in the course of, your employment if you had not been acting in breach of those orders and what you were doing was done for the purposes of, or in connection with, your employment.[34]

Example

Clara works as a labourer in a paper factory where there is an absolute ban on riding on the load of a forklift truck. She is seen riding on the load, falls off and is injured. Usually she would not be covered, but she saw the load was slipping and rode on the truck in order to hold it on. This was done for the purposes of her employment and so on this occasion she is covered.

Part 5: Other benefits
Chapter 32: Industrial injuries benefits
1. Who can claim industrial injuries benefits

Even if you are at home, depending on your contract, you may be covered. This may even include a person on sick leave.[35]

In putting forward your claim (see p683) or arguing your case at an appeal (see Chapter 59), you should consider all aspects of your employment, including the wording of your contract and the degree of flexibility in the arrangements between you and your employer.[36]

Accidents while travelling

Accidents while travelling have been a source of much dispute. You are not in the course of your employment (see p669) during ordinary journeys to and from work, unless you are travelling on transport operated by or on behalf of your employer, or arranged by your employer, and not being operated in the ordinary course of a public transport service.[37]

Many employees have no set place of work – eg, lorry drivers, local authority home helps, gas and electricity company employees. Obviously a lorry driver is at work when driving her/his lorry, but gas company workers travelling directly from home to their first job of the day are not always in the course of employment (see p669), even if driving a company van. It depends on the circumstances, including the rules for the use of the van.[38] In one case, a home help was found to be in the course of her employment travelling between jobs, but not going to the first job or from the last. This is because she became engaged in her employment once she started at the first job and remained engaged until the end of the day.[39]

Some employees with no fixed hours of work may be regarded as covered from the moment of leaving home.[40] Some cases have eased the rules on travelling – eg, to conferences or meetings. Thus, you can be treated as being at your place of work whilst attending a meeting at a site where you do not work.[41] You must look at all the factors when deciding whether or not you were in the course of your employment. For example, a police officer who had to travel about 40 miles from home to a training course was in the course of his employment while travelling.[42] Provided you go reasonably directly, with no marked deviation from a proper route, and do not embark on activities unrelated to the journey, you may be covered.

One important factor in deciding whether you are in the course of your employment is whether you receive wages for travelling.[43] However, if you receive a flat-rate travelling allowance as compensation for having to work at a workplace other than your normal base, this may not be enough to make your journey to your alternative workplace part of your work.[44]

Out of employment

As well as arising in the course of your employment (see p669), the accident (see p668) must arise 'out of' your employment, so that in some way the employment contributed to it. The fact that you suffered a detached retina at work is not sufficient to show it arose 'out of' the employment, but medical evidence which shows that it was caused by sudden head movements while inspecting a production line enables you to establish that an industrial accident (see p668) took place. An unexplained fracture while walking at work is not an industrial accident,[45] but it is if you slip and the fracture occurs while you are falling onto the ground. You are covered even if you are more susceptible to injury because, for example, your bones are brittle[46] or your eyes are weak.

Example

Joe, a farm worker, suffers sudden pain in the groin while doing his normal job of digging. It is found that a previous hernia, which had been surgically repaired, has given way again. The decision maker says that this could have happened at any time and so did not arise 'out of' the employment. Joe's doctor says it could have happened at any time but probably did so at that time because of the heavy digging. The First-tier Tribunal awards him benefit.

An accident also arises out of your employment if it arises in the course of employment (see p669) and it is caused by:[47]
- another's misconduct, 'skylarking' or negligence; *or*
- the behaviour or presence of an animal (including a bird, fish or insect); *or*
- your being struck by any object or by lightning.

In all cases, you must not have directly or indirectly contributed to the accident happening by your conduct, either outside your employment or by any act not incidental to the employment.

An accident is deemed to arise out of, and in the course of, your employment if you are helping people in an emergency, or trying to save property at or near where you are employed.[48]

Prescribed industrial disease

It is necessary for the disease to be a **'prescribed industrial disease'**. This means it is on a list,[49] set out in regulations, of diseases that are known to have a link to a particular 'prescribed' occupation (see p672).[50] Each prescribed disease has a statutory definition and you must fit within that. It is not sufficient simply to have a medical diagnosis that you have a particular condition.[51] From time to time new diseases are added to the list. However, you cannot claim for a disease for any period before it was added to the list.[52] Each prescribed industrial disease has a letter and number to identify it – eg, prescribed disease A12 is carpal tunnel syndrome and prescribed disease D1 is pneumoconiosis. The complete list is in Appendix 7.

If the DWP accepts that you have a prescribed industrial disease, other diseases which result from it are included when assessing your 'loss of faculty' and disablement.[53] See p673 for how your disablement is assessed.

Part 5: Other benefits
Chapter 32: Industrial injuries benefits
1. Who can claim industrial injuries benefits

Prescribed occupations

Different diseases are 'prescribed' for different types of jobs because different jobs have different health risks. To qualify for benefit on grounds of a prescribed industrial disease, you must have a disease which on the list and prove that:

- you have worked in one or more of the jobs for which that disease is prescribed ('prescribed occupations'); *and*
- your job caused the disease.

If the DWP refuses to accept that you have worked in a prescribed occupation, you should obtain advice, preferably from your trade union, or from an advice agency. An expert's report may help to prove your case.

Time limits

For most prescribed diseases, you do not have to have worked in a prescribed occupation for any minimum length of time. You can also claim at any time, even if it is many years since you worked in that occupation. However, there are exceptions to these general rules. For example, if you have occupational deafness (prescribed disease A10), you must have worked in a prescribed occupation for 10 years and claim within five years of having done so.[54] If you have occupational asthma (prescribed disease D7), you must claim within 10 years of working in a prescribed occupation.[55] If you have coal miners' chronic bronchitis or emphysema (prescribed disease D12), you must have been working in a prescribed occupation for 20 years.[56] If you have cataracts (prescribed disease A2), you must have worked in a prescribed occupation for five years or more in aggregate.[57] See Appendix 7 for more examples.

Cause

You must show that the prescribed disease is caused by your occupation. For some diseases, it is assumed that, if you have the disease within one month of last working in the prescribed occupation (see p672), the occupation caused the disease. This is not assumed for others, such as carpal tunnel syndrome (prescribed disease A12) and dermatitis (prescribed disease D5), and you must establish the link 'on a balance of probabilities' – ie, that it is more likely than not that there is a connection.[58] The DWP investigates the connection issue, and you may need to ask your GP or consultant for a report linking the disease to your occupation.

There are different time conditions for occupational deafness (prescribed disease A10), tuberculosis (prescribed disease B5), pneumoconiosis (prescribed disease D1), byssinosis (prescribed disease D2), chronic bronchitis or emphysema (prescribed disease D12) and diseases due to chemical agents.[59]

Example
Connie, a hospital cleaner, uses a new cleaning material. A rash develops on her hands and she has to give up her job. The medical evidence shows that the cleaning material could

5

have caused the problem, but so could several things with which Connie had been in contact outside work. There is a strong argument that the cleaning material caused the rash because the rash developed so soon after using it.

Onset and recrudescence

The **'onset'** (date of starting) of a prescribed disease is taken as the date of the first day you had a relevant 'loss of faculty' (see below). In deafness cases, it is the later of either the date you first experienced the loss of faculty or the date you successfully claimed benefit.[60]

In diseases other than deafness, asthma and respiratory conditions, you can improve and then worsen again. It is important to know whether it is a **'recrudescence'** (fresh outbreak of the existing disease) or a completely new attack. The first is deemed to be a continuation of the existing prescribed disease;[61] with the second, you have to wait 15 weeks before disablement benefit can be claimed. If a further attack starts during a current period of assessment, it is assumed to be a recrudescence unless proved otherwise.

Loss of faculty and disablement

In addition to showing the link between your injury or disease and your occupation, you must also establish that you have had a 'loss of faculty' and are 'disabled'.

'Loss of faculty' is the damage or impairment of part of the body or mind caused by the industrial accident or disease. **'Disability'** is the inability to do something as a result of that damage or impairment. **'Disablement'** is the total of all of your disabilities which, taken together, amount to a disablement. This disablement is expressed as a percentage.

In assessing your disablement, the decision maker considers three questions.
- Has the relevant industrial accident (see p668) or prescribed disease (see p671) resulted in a loss of faculty (see below)?
- What is the extent of disablement resulting from a loss of faculty (this is expressed as a percentage – see p674)?
- What period is to be taken into account by the assessment (see p677)?

A loss of faculty

A **'loss of faculty'** is an 'impairment of the proper functioning of part of the body or mind'[62] caused by an accident or disease. A 'loss of faculty' is not the same as disablement. It includes disfigurement, even if the disfigurement is not accompanied by a loss of physical faculty.[63] A decision that there has been a personal injury resulting from an industrial accident (see p668) does not prevent a decision maker or the First-tier Tribunal from finding that there is no loss of faculty.[64]

Part 5: Other benefits
Chapter 32: Industrial injuries benefits
1. Who can claim industrial injuries benefits

The extent of disablement

In order to qualify for disablement benefit (see p677), generally you must reach a threshold of at least 14 per cent disablement. However, a finding of at least 1 per cent may permit a claim for REA (see p679).

The extent of your disablement is assessed on a percentage basis. Any assessment between 14 and 19 per cent is treated as being 20 per cent.[65] If the total disablement from all industrial accidents and diseases is more than 20 per cent, it is rounded to the nearest multiple of 10 per cent, with multiples of 5 per cent being rounded upwards.[66] For example, an assessment of 22 per cent is rounded down to 20 per cent, an assessment of 25 per cent is rounded up to 30 per cent, as is an assessment of 26 per cent.

Some assessments of disablement are set out in regulations.[67] These are known as 'prescribed degrees of disablement' and include various amputations (eg, loss of a hand or a leg) and degrees of hearing loss (see Appendix 6). However, even in these cases, the decision maker must take into account the real disablement resulting from an injury and increase or decrease the figure to arrive at a reasonable assessment[68] – eg, the loss of a right hand is more disabling for a right-handed person than for a left-handed person. The full extent of your disablement caused by the injury must be taken into account. A further disablement or condition which arises at a later date, but which can be shown to be caused by the industrial accident, must be included in the assessment.[69]

Impaired function of the pleura, pericardium or peritoneum caused by diffuse mesothelioma automatically has an assessment of 100 per cent disablement.[70]

Apart from age, sex and physical and mental condition, your personal circumstances must be ignored, so that particular problems you may have, like the location of your office, or the distance to the nearest bus stop, are not taken into account.

Your disablement should be assessed by comparing you with a person of the same age and sex whose physical and mental condition is 'normal'.[71]

When there is no prescribed degree of disablement, reference may be made to the prescribed percentages to help with the assessment.[72] Although you may suggest that your assessment should be a particular percentage, the decision maker comes to her/his own judgement.[73]

What happens at the assessment?

It is important that you are straightforward with the examining healthcare professional. There are checks to establish that your symptoms are consistent with the injury, and that your movements are consistent with the disablement you claim you have. Therefore, how you walk into the room and how you undress are also considered. Make sure that the person examining you is aware of all the things that you now cannot do as a result of your injury or disease.

Offsets if your disability has more than one cause

If a disability has more than one cause, the rules for the assessment are complex. If a disability is congenital or arose before an industrial one, it is deducted from the total disability.[74] The reduction is often called the 'offset'. The procedure on offsets is complex and frequently leads to disputes. Mistakes are sometimes made because the decision maker incorrectly offsets for medical conditions that have not caused any disability.

Examples

Sam loses a hand, which would normally be 60 per cent, but he had previously lost the index finger. So 14 per cent is deducted, leaving 46 per cent (rounded up to 50 per cent).

Sian has a back injury as a result of an industrial accident. A decision maker has reduced her assessment by 5 per cent on the grounds of a pre-existing disability of which she knew nothing. Many people have spines that are slightly curved as a result of lifting things. The decision maker may have looked at an X-ray, correctly considered that her curved spine was not due to the relevant accident and then incorrectly reduced her assessment.

In the second example, the decision maker should have considered whether the pre-existing loss of faculty (see p673), the curved spine, really had (or would have) led to disablement that would have occurred even if the industrial accident (see p668) had not happened. S/he should have considered, among other things, whether the loss of faculty led to disablement before the industrial accident occurred. There is no physical disablement if you do not have any pain or restriction of movement and it is, therefore, wrong to reduce your assessment unless there is a good reason for deciding that disablement would have arisen during the period of assessment even if the industrial accident had not occurred.

In the second example, depending on the medical opinion:

- there might be no offset; *or*
- it might be appropriate to make a life award (see p677) with some uniform offset over the whole period in respect of any future back problems Sian is likely to have; *or*
- it might be appropriate to make a stepped assessment, making no offset initially but bringing one in at some future date, or applying different levels of offset for different parts of the period covered by the award.[75]

No reduction is made if your injury is one for which the regulations award 100 per cent and this is considered a reasonable assessment for the industrial accident.[76]

The decision maker should also bear in mind that, even if you had a pre-existing problem which caused a disability, the accident may worsen the effects

Part 5: Other benefits
Chapter 32: Industrial injuries benefits
1. Who can claim industrial injuries benefits

of it, as well as cause a new problem. In such a case, the assessment should reflect the increase in the original problem as well as the new disability.[77]

If another disability arose after an industrial accident, the decision maker first has to assess the disablement arising from the industrial injury. If it is less than 11 per cent, any disability from the other cause is ignored; if it is more than 11 per cent, any extra disablement caused by the effect of the industrial injury on the other disability is added.[78]

Examples

Ali loses a little finger in an industrial accident and is assessed as 7 per cent disabled as a result. He then loses the other fingers of that hand in a non-industrial accident. He continues to be assessed as 7 per cent disabled because of the industrial accident.

Paul loses the middle, ring and little fingers of one hand in an industrial accident and is assessed as 30 per cent disabled as a result. He then loses the index finger of that hand in a non-industrial accident. His total disablement is now 50 per cent. But loss of the index finger only would have been 14 per cent. The disablement resulting from his industrial accident may, therefore, be reassessed at 36 per cent (50 per cent *minus* 14 per cent), which is rounded up to 40 per cent.

Two or more industrial accidents or diseases

If you have more than one industrial accident, the percentages of disablement (see p673 and Appendix 6) can be added together and may entitle you to benefit, even if neither accident would do so on its own. If you have two or more industrial accidents, you may end up in a situation where the second or later accident is made worse by the interaction with the effect of the previous accident(s). Your most recent assessment should include an increase for any such interaction.[79] This also applies if an industrial disease (see p671) interacts with the effects of an industrial accident.

Example

Steve has a fall at work and seriously injures his left leg. He receives a life assessment of 10 per cent. Years later, he has a further fall and seriously injures the other leg. He is assessed as 10 per cent disabled for that accident, with a further 5 per cent for the extra disability he has as a result of the interaction between the two injuries. The total of 25 per cent is rounded up, resulting in payment of a 30 per cent pension.

There are special rules if you have pneumoconiosis. The rules allow for certain conditions to be taken into account in order to increase the assessment, even though these conditions did not arise from the pneumoconiosis. Any effect of tuberculosis is assessed with the effects of the pneumoconiosis.[80] If your disability is assessed at 50 per cent because of the pneumoconiosis, any additional disability because of chronic bronchitis or emphysema is added.[81] If you have made such a claim for pneumoconiosis, you cannot then make a separate claim for chronic bronchitis or emphysema.[82]

The period covered by the assessment

The decision maker or the First-tier Tribunal decides how long you are likely to be affected by a relevant loss of faculty and how long you have already been affected (see p673). Percentage assessments are usually made for six months, or for one or two years, or are given for life,[83] but definite dates must be given.

An assessment is either final or provisional.[84] You get a provisional assessment when there is doubt about what will happen in the future, and you are automatically called for another assessment at the end of the period.[85] Life assessments are final.

If you are given a final assessment for a fixed period, this means that the decision maker believes you will no longer be affected by your accident or disease by the end of that period. If you think that the effects of the accident or disease will last for longer, consider an appeal against that assessment (see Chapter 59).

If your condition deteriorates during a period of assessment, or if you still have a disability at the end of a period for which you have been given a final assessment, you should apply for a supersession (see p1281).

An assessment of disablement for occupational deafness is for life.[86]

2. Industrial injuries disablement benefit

The main benefit linked to industrial accidents and diseases is industrial injuries disablement benefit (IIDB). You may qualify for additional amounts of benefit paid as increases to IIDB. These are:
- constant attendance allowance (see p679);
- reduced earnings allowance (see p679);
- exceptionally severe disablement allowance (see p679).[87]

Who can claim industrial injuries disablement benefit

You qualify for IIDB if:[88]
- you satisfy the industrial injury condition (see p666) as a result of one or more industrial accidents (see p668) or prescribed diseases (see p671); *and*
- your resulting disablement is assessed as being at least 14 per cent (1 per cent in the case of pneumoconiosis, byssinosis and diffuse mesothelioma) (see p674 and Appendix 6); *and*

Part 5: Other benefits
Chapter 32: Industrial injuries benefits
2. Industrial injuries disablement benefit

- 90 days (excluding Sundays) have elapsed since the date of the accident or of the onset of the prescribed disease or injury (those who have the prescribed disease of mesothelioma can be paid without serving this waiting period).

Disqualification

You may be disqualified for up to six weeks if you do not provide the required information or notify changes in your circumstances, or do not have a medical examination or treatment. You cannot, however, be disqualified for refusing to have an operation, unless it is a minor one.[89]

The rules about your age

There are no specific age rules or requirement to have paid national insurance contributions. You simply must be under a contract of employment. Therefore, a child who is working is covered, as well as a person over pension age. If the contract under which you work is illegal, you must ask the DWP to make a decision that you are covered by the scheme.[90]

People included in the claim

You claim industrial injuries benefits for yourself. You cannot claim any increases for an adult or your child(ren) unless you are getting unemployability supplement (abolished for new claims after 5 April 1987).

The amount of benefit

The amount of benefit you get depends on the extent of your disablement.[91] See p674 for how this is assessed.

Extent of disablement	Benefit per week
	£
100%	166.00
90%	149.40
80%	132.80
70%	116.20
60%	99.60
50%	83.00
40%	66.40
30%	49.80
11% – 20%	33.20

Since 1 October 1986, IIDB can be paid if the assessment of your disablement is at least 14 per cent,[92] except in the cases of pneumoconiosis, byssinosis and diffuse mesothelioma, when it must be at least 1 per cent.[93] Before 1 October 1986, IIDB

was paid for an assessment of disablement of at least 1 per cent. The old rules are still in force for claims made before this date.[94] If you are getting a payment as a result of such a small percentage assessment, see p176 of the 17th edition of CPAG's *Rights Guide to Non-Means-Tested Benefits.*
You might be able to get an increase of benefit (see below).

Increases of industrial injuries disablement benefit
You get increased IIDB if you qualify for constant attendance allowance or exceptionally severe disablement allowance.

Constant attendance allowance
You qualify for constant attendance allowance if:[95]
* you are entitled to industrial injuries disablement benefit based on a degree of disablement assessed at 100 per cent; *and*
* you require constant attendance as a result of the relevant loss of faculty (see p673).

Disablement as a result of pre-1948 industrial accidents and diseases, war injuries and injuries incurred while on police or fire duty, may be taken into account in considering the degree of your disablement.
There are two rates: the higher weekly rate is £132.80 and the intermediate weekly rate is £66.40, but this can be increased to £99.60 a week in certain circumstances.

Exceptionally severe disablement allowance
This is paid at the weekly rate of £66.40 if you are entitled to constant attendance allowance (or would be if you were not in hospital) at the higher or intermediate rate and you are likely to remain so permanently.[96]

3. Reduced earnings allowance

Reduced earnings allowance (REA) is available if you had an accident or started to have a disease before 1 October 1990. A successful first claim can still be made now if you had an accident or disease before this date.
The amount of REA you get depends on whether your current earnings, or earnings in a job which it is considered you could do, are less than the current earnings in your previous 'regular occupation' (see p681).

Who can claim reduced earnings allowance
You qualify for REA if:[97]
* you satisfy the industrial injury condition (see p666) because of an industrial accident (see p668) before 1 October 1990 or an industrial disease (see p671), the onset of which was before that date (see p673); *and*

Part 5: Other benefits
Chapter 32: Industrial injuries benefits
3. Reduced earnings allowance

- your resulting disablement is assessed as being at least 1 per cent (see p673 and Appendix 6); *and*
- as a result of a relevant loss of faculty, *either*:
  - you are incapable and likely to remain permanently incapable of following your regular occupation (see p681) and are incapable of following employment of an equivalent standard (see p682) which is suitable in your case (the 'permanent condition' – see p681); *or*
  - you are, and have been at all times since the end of the 90-day qualifying period for disablement benefit, incapable of following your regular occupation or employment of an equivalent standard (see p682) which is suitable in your case ('the continuing condition' – see p681).

If you were entitled to REA on 30 October 1990 and you then lost entitlement to it for one or more days, you cannot regain entitlement to it for the same accident or prescribed disease. However, if you were not entitled to REA until after 30 October 1990, breaks in entitlement (eg, because of a temporary improvement in your condition) do not prevent you from re-qualifying.[98]

If you have reached pension age and you gave up regular employment on or after 10 April 1989, and you were entitled to REA on the day before you gave up that employment, this ends your entitlement to REA.[99] If you have given up regular employment, you receive retirement allowance instead (see p683). This is paid to you at a lower rate.

Regular employment

'Regular employment' means working for an average of 10 hours or more a week within a period of five or more weeks of such employment.[100]

However, some claimants have been successful in claiming REA after pension age and retaining REA rather than moving onto the lower rate of retirement allowance (see p683). This is on the basis that the law allows a person who is over pension age and claiming REA for the first time to be paid REA rather than retirement allowance.[101]

If you were entitled to REA on either 10 April 1988 or 9 April 1989, and on that date you were over pension age and were retired, or were treated as retired, you remain entitled to the allowance for life. For the meaning of 'retired or treated as retired' in this context, see p69 of the 12th edition of CPAG's *Rights Guide to Non-Means-Tested Benefits*.

If you are claiming on the basis of an industrial disease, it (or the extension of an existing category of prescribed diseases) must have been added to the list of prescribed diseases before 10 October 1994.[102]

The permanent and continuing conditions

Only incapacity at the time of your claim and in the future are relevant for the **'permanent condition'**. The phrase 'likely to remain permanently incapable' relates only to your 'regular occupation' (see p681) and not to 'employment of an equivalent standard' (see p682), so you do not need to prove that you are likely to remain incapable of employment of an equivalent standard, just that you are unlikely to be able to perform your usual job. If you have pneumoconiosis and you are advised not to work by a decision maker, you are deemed not to be able to work at your own occupation or employment of an equivalent standard unless there is evidence to the contrary from someone other than the decision maker – eg, your GP.[103]

Only incapacity at the time of your claim and in the past is relevant for the **'continuing condition'**. However, if you returned to work but were 'sheltered' by your colleagues, you can still argue that you were 'incapable' of following your regular occupation (see below).[104] If you have worked since the end of the 90-day period, but the work was for rehabilitation, testing or training, it can be disregarded provided it was for a total period of six months or less, approved by the Secretary of State or done on medical advice. If you have given up work because of your pneumoconiosis on the advice of a decision maker, you are deemed to have been continuously incapable of following that regular occupation.[105]

Regular occupation

Deciding what is your 'regular occupation' involves looking at your work history (part time[106] as well as full time) and the content of the job, as opposed to its title. For example, in one case, a docker still employed to work as a docker but unable to earn as much because he was unable to do the full range of his duties was found incapable of his regular occupation.[107]

If an accident occurs when you have just started a new job, that job may be treated as your regular occupation. Your intentions and prospects must be considered.[108] But a stop-gap occupation, taken on during poor health, is not treated as your regular occupation.[109] If you are a full-time student, any part-time work you were in at the time of the accident counts as your regular occupation.[110] Any employment that is subsidiary to your usual or main job does not count. If you would have been promoted by the time of your claim, but for the accident, the promoted position may count as your regular occupation.

It is possible to make a number of separate claims for REA. If you had a number of industrial accidents and had to downgrade your employment each time, you can be compensated for each. The crucial point is whether each accident has led to a change in your regular occupation.[111]

If you have a prescribed disease (see p671) and, because of this, gave up a job before you applied for benefit, it may count as your regular occupation.[112]

Part 5: Other benefits
Chapter 32: Industrial injuries benefits
3. Reduced earnings allowance

Suitable employment of an equivalent standard

Suitability is judged by looking at your education, experience, training, work history and general health.[113] Only an employed earner's employment can be treated as suitable, so self-employed work is not considered.[114] The question is whether the employment is of an equivalent standard. The usual earnings of people employed in what is considered suitable employment are compared with the usual earnings of those employed in the regular occupation.[115] The earnings in both occupations must be assessed, taking into account bonuses, overtime if normally paid[116] and benefits in kind.

If your regular occupation (see p681) was part time, full-time work is not of an equivalent standard even if you are medically fit to undertake it. However, if there are no jobs of the same number of hours, different work for a similar number of hours may be regarded as equivalent.[117]

The rules about your age

There is no specific age rule for REA but you must have been an employed earner. REA is paid until you reach pension age, when it is replaced with retirement allowance (see p683). If you are now over pension age, but have never claimed REA even though you meet the conditions for entitlement, you are not excluded from claiming REA. If you are considering making a claim for REA and you are about to reach pension age, seek advice before delaying a claim for REA.

People included in the claim

You claim REA for yourself. You cannot get any increase in your REA for your partner or child(ren).

The amount of benefit

The amount of REA you get is the amount by which your current earnings, or earnings in a job which it is considered you could do, are less than the current earnings in your previous regular occupation (see p681).[118] Earnings include overtime.

If you are unemployed, the DWP's healthcare professional is asked for your limitations, a DWP disability employment adviser is asked what job s/he thinks you could do and Jobcentre Plus is asked to quote a wage which such a job would pay in your area.

Once the first assessment has been made, the amount is usually increased in line with earnings in that industry or workplace, unless that regular occupation (see p681) has ceased to exist.[119] In this case, it is calculated as rising in line with the nearest 'occupational group' as defined by the DWP. You can ask for a fresh assessment to take into account your prospects of advancement, but you must show that promotion would have happened (eg, at the end of a period of employment or training), not just that it may have happened had you been particularly diligent.[120]

The maximum amount of reduced earnings allowance

The maximum amount you can receive for any one award is £66.40 a week.[121] The total you can receive from industrial injuries disablement benefit (IIDB) and REA (whether for one or more awards) is 140 per cent of the standard rate of IIDB.[122]

If you were over pension age and retired before 6 April 1987, your allowance is reduced if it would otherwise mean you would be receiving more than 100 per cent disablement benefit.[123] If you qualified for REA and were retired or treated as retired on either 10 April 1988 or 9 April 1989, you continue to receive the allowance at the same 'frozen' rate. Its value, therefore, erodes over time.

4. Retirement allowance

Retirement allowance is a reduced rate of reduced earnings allowance (REA – see p679) for people over pension age, paid for life.

You qualify for retirement allowance if:[124]
- you are over pension age (see p752);
- you have given up regular employment (see p681);
- you were entitled to REA at a rate of at least £2 a week (in total, if you had more than one award) immediately before you gave up regular employment;
- you are not entitled to REA.

You can only get one award of retirement allowance, even if you had more than one award of REA.[125]

The amount of retirement allowance you get is £16.60 a week or 25 per cent of the amount of REA you were receiving, whichever is the lower. There are no increases for dependants.

5. Special benefit rules

Special rules may apply to:
- prisoners (see p960);
- people going abroad (see Chapter 71).

6. Claims and backdating

To be entitled to industrial injuries benefits, you must usually make a claim.[126] The general rules about claims and backdating are in Chapter 53. This section explains the specific rules that apply to industrial injuries benefits.

Part 5: Other benefits
Chapter 32: Industrial injuries benefits
6. Claims and backdating

Making a claim

Claims for industrial injuries benefits other than retirement allowance (see below) must be made in writing.[127] You do this by completing the approved form and sending it to your regional industrial injuries disablement benefit (IIDB) delivery centre (Scotland, North West England, East of England, South East England and London, tel: 0845 603 1358, textphone: 0845 608 8551; Yorkshire and the Humber, North East England, East and West Midlands, South West England and Wales, tel: 0845 758 5433, textphone: 0845 608 8551). Keep a copy of your claim form in case queries arise.

You must provide any information or evidence required (see p684). In certain circumstances, the DWP may accept a written application not on the approved form.[128] You can amend or withdraw your claim before a decision is made (see p1138). If there is a delay in making a claim, you may be able to get a short-term advance of benefit (see p1167).

Note: you do not have to make a claim for retirement allowance.[129]

Forms

There are different forms depending on the benefit claimed and on the type of accident or disease. Get them from your regional industrial injuries disablement benefit delivery centre or from www.gov.uk.[130]

Who should claim

You claim for yourself. If you are unable to manage your own affairs, another person can claim industrial injuries benefits for you as your 'appointee' (see p1137).

Information to support your claim

When you claim industrial injuries benefits, you must:
- satisfy the national insurance number requirement (see p1138);
- provide proof of your identity, if required (see p1140); *and*
- ensure you have made a valid claim – ie, you must supply information and evidence required on the claim form (see p1140).

Even if you have provided all that was required when you claimed, you may be asked to provide additional information and evidence relevant to your claim (see p1152). There is a strict time limit for providing this. If you do not do so, the decision maker can decide your claim in the way most adverse to you.

Note: you may be asked to provide information after you are awarded industrial injuries benefits. If you fail to do so, your benefit could be suspended or even terminated (see p1175).

The date of your claim

Claim as soon as you think you might be entitled to benefit; you are not usually entitled to benefit for any day before your date of claim. However, in some cases you can claim in advance (see below) and sometimes your claim can be backdated (see below).

The date of your claim is the date it is received at the regional IIDB delivery centre.

If you claim the wrong benefit

In some circumstances, it is possible for a claim for one benefit to be treated as a claim for a different benefit (see p1144). However, for industrial injuries benefits it is only possible to 'interchange' constant attendance allowance with disability living allowance, personal independence payment and attendance allowance.

Claiming in advance

An advance claim can be made for IIDB if you have had an accident or have a prescribed disease and you are within the 90-day waiting period. Otherwise it is not possible to claim industrial injuries benefits in advance.

Renewal claims

Assessments can be provisional or final, and for a limited period or for life. A provisional assessment means that the decision maker considers that your medical condition has not yet settled down, and might get worse or better. At the end of a provisional assessment, you are invited to be re-examined. A final assessment means that the decision maker believes that your condition has settled down and your case is dealt with once and for all. At the end of a period of award, you must therefore apply for a renewal of benefit.

If you are awarded IIDB for a particular disease, you may recover at some point but subsequently have a further attack. If there is a continuation (or recrudescence) of the old disease, you do not have to wait 15 weeks before gaining entitlement to IIDB.

Backdating claims

It is important to claim in time. Your claim can be backdated for up to three months if you satisfy the qualifying conditions over that period. You do not have to show any reasons why your claim was late. The rules on backdating are covered on p1146.

If you might have qualified for benefit earlier but did not claim because you were given the wrong information or were misled by the DWP, ask for compensation (see p1382) or complain to the Ombudsman via your MP (see p1387).

Part 5: Other benefits
Chapter 32: Industrial injuries benefits
8. Tax, other benefits and the benefit cap

7. Getting paid

Payment of industrial injuries benefits is normally made by direct credit transfer into a bank (or similar) account (see p1163). If you are unable to open or manage an account, payment can be made by 'simple payment' (see p1163). If you are unable to act for yourself, benefit can be paid to someone else on your behalf, called your 'appointee' (see p1137).

> ***When are industrial injuries benefits paid?***
> You are paid on a Wednesday,[131] weekly in advance.[132]

Note:
- You might not be paid your industrial injuries benefit if you have been sanctioned for a benefit offence (see p1258).
- If you have forgotten your PIN, see p1163. If your 'simple payment' card has been lost or stolen, or if you have forgotten your memorable date, see p1164. For information on missing payments, see p1164.
- If payment of your industrial injuries benefit is delayed, see p1382. You might be able to get a short-term advance (see p1167). If you wish to complain about how your claim has been dealt with, see p1383. You might be able to claim compensation (see p1382).
- If payment of your industrial injuries benefit is suspended, see p1175.
- If you are overpaid industrial injuries benefit, you might have to repay it (see Chapter 56) and, in some circumstances, you may have to pay a penalty (see p1249). If you have been accused of fraud, see Chapter 57.

Change of circumstances

You must report any change of circumstances that you have been told you must report, as well as any that you might reasonably be expected to know might affect your right to, the amount of, or the payment of your benefit. You should do this as soon as possible, preferably in writing. See p1174 for further information.

8. Tax, other benefits and the benefit cap

Tax

Industrial injuries benefits are not taxable.[133]

Means-tested benefits

Industrial injuries disablement benefit, reduced earnings allowance and retirement allowance are taken into account in full for all the means-tested benefits. Constant attendance allowance and exceptionally severe disablement allowance are disregarded.

Non-means-tested benefits

In general, the overlapping benefits rule does not apply to industrial injuries benefits. It is possible, for example, to receive full disablement benefit as well as full employment and support allowance.

Carer's allowance (see Chapter 25) may be paid to someone who is 'regularly and substantially caring' for you while you are receiving constant attendance allowance (see p679).[134]

If your spouse or civil partner died as a result of an industrial accident or disease, you may qualify for a bereavement benefit even though the national insurance contribution conditions are not satisfied (see p523).[135]

Tax credits

Industrial injuries benefits are ignored as income for tax credits.

The benefit cap

In some cases, the total amount of specified benefits you receive is limited to £350 a week (if you are a single claimant without children) or £500 a week (if you are a lone parent or a member of a couple). This is known as the 'benefit cap'. Industrial injuries benefits are *not* specified benefits. The benefit cap only applies if you are getting housing benefit or universal credit. The benefit cap does *not* apply if you or your partner get industrial injuries disablement benefit, reduced earnings allowance or retirement allowance. See p1169 for further information.

Passports and other sources of help

You qualify for a Christmas bonus if you receive disablement benefit, but only if it includes unemployability supplement or constant attendance allowance (see p835). If you are on a low income, you may be entitled to council tax reduction (see p827).

If you have (or you are a dependant of someone who has died and who had) pneumoconiosis (including asbestosis, silicosis and kaolinosis), byssinosis, diffuse mesothelioma, diffuse pleural thickening, or primary carcinoma of the lung if accompanied by asbestosis or diffuse pleural thickening, and you cannot get compensation from your employer (eg, because s/he has ceased trading), or you do not have a realistic chance of obtaining damages from that employer, you may be able to get a one-off lump-sum payment in addition to any industrial injuries benefit.[136] From 1 October 2008 you can be entitled to a one-off lump-sum payment from the DWP for diffuse mesothelioma (including if you are a dependant of someone who had that condition immediately before they died), without the need to have worked.[137] The time limit for claiming is 12 months (from the date of diagnosis or death) and the time limit may be extended if there is good cause. All these lump-sum payments may be recovered (ie, deducted) from compensation (see p1192).

Notes

1. Who can claim industrial injuries benefits
1 s94(1) SSCBA 1992
2 ss94(1) and 108(1) SSCBA 1992
3 Reg 10C (5) and (6) SSB(PA) Regs
4 Regs 2, 4 and 6 SS(EEEIIP) Regs
5 Regs 2 and 3 IIB(ETSC) Regs 2013; s95A SSCBA 1992
6 Reg 3 SS(EEEIIP) Regs
7 R(I) 49/52
8 R(I) 1/76
9 R(I) 5/81
10 R(I) 1/82
11 *Fenton v Thorley* [1903] AC 443 (HL)
12 CI/123/1949
13 *Jones v Secretary of State for Social Services* [1972] AC 944 (HL), also reported as an appendix to R(I) 3/69; *SSWP v Scullion* [2010] EWCA Civ 310
14 *Trim Joint District School Board of Management v Kelly* [1914] AC 667 (HL)
15 s94(1) SSCBA 1992
16 CI/105/1998; CI/142/2006
17 *Roberts v Dorothea Slate Quarries Co. Ltd* [1948] 2 All ER 201 (HL)
18 R(I) 24/54; R(I) 43/55
19 CI/3370/1999
20 *Mullen v SSWP* [2002] SC 251; SLT 149; SCLR 475; GWD 3-121, IH (2DIV)
21 R(I) 43/61; R(I) 4/62
22 R(I) 18/54
23 CI/159/1950
24 *R v National Insurance Commissioner ex parte East* [1976] ICR 206 (DC), also reported as an appendix to R(I) 16/75
25 R(I) 1/59

26 *R v Industrial Injuries Commissioner ex parte AEU* [1966] 2 QB 31 (CA), also reported as an appendix to R(I) 4/66
27 R(I) 10/81
28 *R v National Insurance Commissioner ex parte Reed* (DC), reported as an appendix to R(I) 7/80
29 s94(3) SSCBA 1992
30 *R v Industrial Injuries Commissioner ex parte AEU* [1966] 2 QB 31 (CA), also reported as an appendix to R(I) 4/66
31 R(I) 46/53
32 R(I) 17/63
33 *R v Industrial Injuries Commissioner ex parte AEU* [1966] 2 QB 31 (CA), also reported as an appendix to R(I) 4/66
34 s98 SSCBA 1992; CI/210/1950
35 R(I) 1/99
36 *Nancollas v Insurance Officer* [1985] 1 All ER 833 (CA), also reported as an appendix to R(I) 7/85
37 s99 SSCBA 1992
38 R(I) 1/88
39 R(I) 12/75
40 R(I) 4/70
41 R(I)1/93
42 *Nancollas v Insurance Officer; Ball v Insurance Officer* [1985] 1 All ER 833 (CA), also reported as an appendix to R(I) 7/85
43 *Smith v Stages* [1989] 2 WLR 529 (HL)
44 R(I) 1/91
45 R(I) 6/82
46 R(I) 12/52
47 s101 SSCBA 1992
48 s100 SSCBA 1992
49 Sch 1 SS(IIPD) Regs
50 Reg 2 SS(IIPD) Regs
51 R(I) 3/03

52 R(I) 2/03; R(I) 4/96
53 Reg 3 SS(IIPD) Regs
54 Regs 2(c) and 25 SS(IIPD) Regs
55 Reg 36 SS(IIPD) Regs
56 Sch 1 SS(IIPD) Regs
57 Reg 2(e) SS(IIPD) Regs
58 Reg 4(1) SS(IIPD) Regs
59 Reg 4(1) SS(IIPD) Regs
60 Reg 6(2)(c) SS(IIPD) Regs
61 Reg 7 SS(IIPD) Regs
62 *Jones v Secretary of State for Social Services* [1972] AC 944 (HL), also reported as an appendix to R(I) 3/69
63 CI/499/2000; s122(1) SSCBA 1992
64 s30 SSA 1998
65 s103(3) SSCBA 1992
66 s103(2) and (3) SSCBA 1992; regs 15A and 15B SS(IIPD) Regs
67 Sch 2 SS(GB) Regs; Sch 3 SS(IIPD) Regs
68 Reg 11(6) SS(GB) Regs
69 *JL and DO v SSWP (II)* [2011] UKUT 294 (AAC); [2012] AACR 15
70 Reg 20A SS(IIPD) Regs
71 Sch 6 para 1 SSCBA 1992
72 Reg 11(8) SS(GB) Regs; R(I) 5/95; R(I) 1/04
73 CI/636/1993, although the commissioner said that, where there are specific submissions backed with expert medical evidence on the percentage assessment, it would be an error of law to arrive at a different figure without giving reasons for this.
74 Reg 11(3) SS(GB) Regs
75 CI/34/1993
76 Reg 11(7) SS(GB) Regs
77 R(I) 3/91, which contains a definitive survey of the situations when reg 11 SS(GB) Regs applies
78 Reg 11(4) SS(GB) Regs
79 R(I) 3/91
80 Reg 21 SS(IIPD) Regs
81 Reg 22 SS(IIPD) Regs
82 Reg 2(d) SS(IIPD) Regs
83 Sch 6 para 6 SSCBA 1992
84 Sch 6 para 7 SSCBA 1992
85 Sch 6 para 6(2)(b) SSCBA 1992
86 Reg 29 SS(IIPD) Regs

2. Industrial injuries disablement benefit
87 Sch 7, Part VI, para 14(1A) SSCBA 1992
88 ss103 and 108 SSCBA 1992
89 Reg 40 SS(GB) Regs
90 s97 SSCBA 1992
91 Sch 4 SSCBA 1992
92 s103(1)
93 Reg 20(1) SS (IIPD) Regs

94 Sch 7 para 9(1)(a) SSCBA 1992; reg 14 SS(II&D)MP Regs
95 s104 SSCBA 1992
96 s105 SSCBA 1992

3. Reduced earnings allowance
97 Sch 7 paras 11 and 12(1), (2) and (7) SSCBA 1992
98 Sch 7 para 11(2) SSCBA 1992
99 Sch 7 para 13(1) SSCBA 1992
100 Reg 2 SS(II)(RE) Regs; R(I) 3/93; *SSWP v NH (II)* [2010] UKUT 84 (AAC)
101 Sch 7 paras 11 and 13(1) SSCBA 1992; SS(II)(RE) Regs
102 Sch 7 para 11(1)(b) SSCBA 1992
103 Reg 23(a) SS(IIPD) Regs
104 R(I) 39/51; R(I) 26/53
105 Reg 23(b) SS(IIPD) Regs
106 *R v National Insurance Commissioner ex parte Mellors* [1971] 2 QB 401 (CA), also reported as an appendix to R(I) 7/69
107 R(I) 28/51
108 R(I) 65/54
109 CI/80/1949
110 Reg 2 SS(II&D)MP Regs
111 *Hagan v Secretary of State for Social Security* [2001] EWCA Civ 1452, reported in R(I) 2/02
112 Reg 17 SS(IIPD) Regs
113 R(I) 22/61
114 Sch 7 para 11(5)(b) SSCBA 1992
115 *R v National Insurance Commissioner ex parte Mellors* [1971] 2 QB 401, [1971] 1 All ER 740
116 R(I) 7/51; R(I) 1/72
117 R(I) 3/83
118 Sch 7 para 11(10) SSCBA 1992
119 Sch 7 para 11(14) SSCBA 1992
120 Sch 7 para 11(6) SSCBA 1992
121 Regs 2 and 3 Social Security (Industrial Injuries) (Reduced Earnings Allowance and Transitional) Regulations 1987, No.415; Sch 7 para 11(13) SSCBA 1992
122 Sch 7 para 11(10) SSCBA 1992
123 Sch 7 para 11(11) SSCBA 1992

4. Retirement allowance
124 Sch 7 para 13 SSCBA 1992
125 *TA v SSWP (II)* [2010] UKUT 101 (AAC)

6. Claims and backdating
126 s1 SSAA 1992
127 Reg 4(1) SS(C&P) Regs
128 Reg 4(1) SS(C&P) Regs
129 Reg 3(e) SS(C&P) Regs
130 s68(1) WRA 2012

7. **Getting paid**
131 Sch 6 para 3 SS(C&P) Regs
132 Reg 22 SS(C&P) Regs

8. **Tax, other benefits and the benefit cap**
133 s667 IT(EP)A 2003
134 Regs 14, 17 and 21 SS(IB)(T) Regs
135 s60(2) and (3) SSCBA 1992
136 Pneumoconiosis etc (Workers'
      Compensation) Act 1979
137 Part 4 CMOPA 2008

Chapter 33

Contribution-based jobseeker's allowance

This chapter covers:

Key facts

- Jobseeker's allowance (JSA) is a benefit for people who are looking for work.
- There are three types of JSA: **income-based JSA** (a means-tested benefit), **joint-claim JSA** (a means-tested benefit paid if you must make a joint claim with your partner) and **contribution-based JSA** (a non-means-tested benefit).
- You must have paid sufficient national insurance contributions in the last two tax years to qualify for contribution-based JSA.
- You cannot qualify for contribution-based JSA if you are in full-time paid work.
- You must normally be fit for work, satisfy the 'jobseeking conditions' (or meet work-related requirements) and sign on every fortnight.
- If you leave your job voluntarily or lose your job because of misconduct, if you do not take up a job or an employment programme or training scheme opportunity, or if you cease to be available for or to actively seek work, you may be 'sanctioned' and your JSA may be paid at a reduced (or nil) rate.
- JSA is administered and paid by the DWP.
- If you disagree with a JSA decision, you can apply for a revision or a supersession, or appeal against it. You are likely to have to apply for a revision before you can appeal.

Part 5: Other benefits
Chapter 33: Contribution-based jobseeker's allowance
1. Who can claim jobseeker's allowance

1. **Who can claim jobseeker's allowance**

You qualify for jobseeker's allowance (JSA) if:[1]

* you do not count as being in full-time paid work (see p694); *and*
* you do not have limited capability for work. However, in certain circumstances, people who are sick or who have gone abroad for NHS hospital treatment can get JSA (see p695); *and*
* you are not in 'relevant education' (see p903). In addition, if you are a full-time student you usually cannot get JSA (see Chapter 44); *and*
* you do not come under the universal credit (UC) system (see p19) and you satisfy 'jobseeking conditions' – ie, you must:
  – be available for work; *and*
  – be actively seeking work; *and*
  – have a current jobseeker's agreement (the DWP calls this a 'claimant commitment').

  Your entitlement ends if you fail to do so and, in some cases, you can be given a sanction if you claim again. See Chapter 48 for full details of these conditions; *and*

* you come under the UC system (see p19) and you accept a claimant commitment. **Note:** while you are entitled to JSA, you can be required to meet work-related requirements which have been imposed on you – ie:[2]
  – work-focused interviews;
  – work preparation;
  – work search;
  – work availability.

  You can be given a sanction if you fail to do so. See Chapter 50 for full details of these requirements; *and*

* you are below pension age (see p752); *and*
* you are in Great Britain. JSA can continue to be paid in limited circumstances while you are temporarily away (see p1580). Contribution-based JSA can be 'exported' if you are unemployed and looking for work in a European Economic Area country (see p1582).

The above conditions apply to all types of JSA. In addition, to qualify for contribution-based JSA, you must satisfy extra rules (see p693).

You are not usually entitled to JSA for the first three days of your 'jobseeking period' (see p693). These are known as 'waiting days' (see p697).

Note: in the future, it is expected that you must be entitled to work in the UK (and not prevented from taking up work under immigration provisions) to qualify for contribution-based JSA.[3] There may be exceptions. See CPAG's online service and *Welfare Rights Bulletin* for updates.

Extra rules for contribution-based jobseeker's allowance

To get contribution-based JSA, in addition to satisfying the rules that apply to all types of JSA (see p692), you must:[4]
- satisfy the contribution conditions (see p861). This depends on your record of national insurance (NI) contributions and credits in the two tax years immediately before the benefit year in which your jobseeking period begins (or in which a period linked to a jobseeking period begins, if earlier). For example, if you claim JSA immediately after a period of limited capability for work, the contribution test is applied using the date on which you first had limited capability for work; *and*
- not be claiming and entitled to income support (IS); *and*
- not have earnings above a 'prescribed amount' (see p698). If you have earnings below this amount, your JSA is reduced to take account of them.

Jobseeking periods

You are not usually entitled to JSA for the first three days of your 'jobseeking period'. These are known as 'waiting days' (see p697).

A **'jobseeking period'** is the period during which you either meet the conditions that apply to all types of JSA (see p692) or you do not satisfy the jobseeking conditions but receive JSA hardship payments (see Chapter 55).[5] Periods when you are entitled to JSA both before and after you come under the UC system (see p19) are included.[6]

Note: if you are a man of at least the qualifying age for pension credit (PC – see p78) but under 65, special rules apply which mean that in some circumstances your jobseeking period continues even though you do not satisfy the jobseeking conditions.[7]

What does not count as part of a jobseeking period

The following do not count as part of a jobseeking period:[8]
- days for which you do not claim (or are not treated as claiming) JSA;
- if you do not come under the UC system (see p19), days for which you lost your entitlement to JSA because you failed to participate in an interview when required or to 'sign on';
- a period for which you claimed backdated benefit which has been refused;
- any week (Sunday to Saturday) for which you are not entitled to JSA because you were involved in a trade dispute for all or part of that week;
- days on which you are not entitled to JSA because you have not provided your NI number (see p1138).

Linked jobseeking periods

In some cases, two or more jobseeking periods can be linked together and treated as if they were one period. Also, certain periods in which you satisfy other

Part 5: Other benefits
Chapter 33: Contribution-based jobseeker's allowance
1. Who can claim jobseeker's allowance

conditions ('linked periods' – see below) can be linked to a jobseeking period. This means, for example, that:

- the question of whether you satisfy the NI contribution conditions for contribution-based JSA is decided by looking at your situation at the beginning of the first jobseeking period (or a period linked to a jobseeking period if earlier) and not at the beginning of your current claim;[9]
- you do not have to serve another three waiting days (see p697) to get JSA;
- if the jobseeking periods together are longer than 182 days, you cannot get any more contribution-based JSA (see p700).

Two jobseeking periods are treated as linked if they are separated by one or any combination of the following:[10]

- any period of no more than 12 weeks; *or*
- a period during which you are doing jury service; *or*
- a 'linked period' (see below); *or*
- any period of no more than 12 weeks which comes between two linked periods or between a jobseeking period and a 'linked period'.

Linked periods

A **'linked period'** is any period during which you:[11]

- are entitled to carer's allowance (CA), but only if this allows you to get contribution-based JSA when you would not otherwise satisfy the contribution conditions; *or*
- are incapable of work or treated as incapable of work; *or*
- have, or are treated as having, limited capability for work (see Chapter 47); *or*
- are entitled to maternity allowance; *or*
- are undergoing training for which a training allowance is payable.

You cannot argue that a period spent taking time out of work to look after children is a linked period for these purposes.[12]

Full-time paid work

You cannot usually qualify for contribution-based JSA if you are in full-time paid work. This means 16 hours or more each week.[13] All the rules on work are covered in Chapter 46.

In some situations, you are treated as *not* in full-time work even if you work more than 16 hours (see p995). In others, you are treated as in full-time work when you are not (see p994). See p990 for how your hours are calculated and p989 for what counts as paid work.

If your partner is not in full-time paid work, you (or s/he) may qualify for a means-tested benefit to top up your contribution-based JSA. If your partner is in full-time paid work, you (and s/he) may qualify for working tax credit (WTC) or, if you come under the UC system (see p19), UC.

Note: if you or your partner have just taken up full-time paid work, you may be able to claim income support (IS) for help with your housing costs for the first four weeks. This is known as 'mortgage interest run-on' (see p460).

Limited capability for work

To qualify for JSA you must not have 'limited capability for work'.[14] See Chapter 47 for details about the test that decides this. **Note:** if a decision maker has decided for the purpose of employment and support allowance (ESA) or UC that you have (or do not have) limited capability for work, you are automatically treated as having (or not having) limited capability for work for JSA.[15] You still have to show that you are available for work if you are ill or have a disability and you may be asked to provide medical evidence that you no longer have limited capability for work. However, there are special rules that allow you to restrict your availability (see p1035). If you come under the UC system, there are special rules to help you meet the work-related requirements (see p1071).

Periods of sickness when you can claim jobseeker's allowance

Even if you have limited capability for work (or are incapable of work), you do not have to stop claiming JSA in some situations. You are treated as not having limited capability for work (or as capable of work), if the only reason why you would not otherwise qualify for JSA is that:

- you are unable to work because you are sick (you can claim for up to two weeks – see below), unless you have stated in writing that you are going to claim or have claimed ESA or, if you do not come under the UC system (see p19), incapacity benefit, severe disablement allowance or IS;[16] *or*
- you are unable to work because you are sick and are temporarily absent from Great Britain for the purpose of getting NHS hospital treatment under certain provisions (you can claim for an indefinite period), unless you have stated in writing before the period of temporary absence abroad begins that you have claimed ESA immediately before the beginning of the period.[17]

You must make a written declaration that you will be unfit for work from a specific date or for a specific period on a form available at the Jobcentre Plus office.[18]

You are treated as available for and actively seeking work during the period of sickness.[19] If you come under the UC system, you do not have to meet a work search requirement and a special rule helps you meet the work availability requirement.[20]

Two-week periods of sickness

You are allowed up to two two-week periods of sickness in a jobseeking period (see p693) or, if your jobseeking period has lasted more than 12 months, in any successive 12-month period.[21] The two-weeks can start before, and end after, you come under the UC system (see p19).[22] If you are sick more often than this, or for

Part 5: Other benefits
Chapter 33: Contribution-based jobseeker's allowance
4. The amount of benefit

a longer period, you must claim ESA or PC (or UC) instead of JSA for the time you are unable to work.

The rules on two-week periods of sickness do not apply to you if you were getting statutory sick pay in the eight weeks before you were sick.[23] Instead, you can claim benefit on the basis of having limited capability for work without having to serve any 'waiting days' (see p1017).

2. The rules about your age

There is no minimum age for entitlement to contribution-based jobseeker's allowance (JSA) but, in practice, because you can only qualify if you have paid, or been credited with, sufficient national insurance contributions in the two tax years before the benefit year in which you claim, you are unlikely to qualify before you are 18. You cannot claim any type of JSA if you are pension age or over (see p752).

3. People included in the claim

You claim contribution-based jobseeker's allowance (JSA) for yourself. You cannot claim any increases for your partner or child(ren). However, you may qualify for income-based JSA (or joint-claim JSA) as well as contribution-based JSA. You may also qualify for child tax credit for any children you have (see Chapter 8). If you come under the universal credit (UC) system (see p19), you may qualify for UC as well as contribution-based JSA.

4. The amount of benefit

After any waiting days (see p697), contribution-based jobseeker's allowance (JSA) is paid at the following weekly rates.[24]

Age of claimant	£pw
Under 25	57.35
25 or over	72.40

You are not paid an allowance for your partner or children.

These amounts are reduced penny for penny if you receive certain pension payments of more than £50 in any week or any part-time earnings. For more on how these types of income affect contribution-based JSA, see p697. Other types of income and any capital, including any earnings and capital of your partner, do not affect your contribution-based JSA.

Note:

- Contribution-based JSA is paid for a limited period only (see p700).
- You can claim income-based JSA (including joint-claim JSA) to top up your contribution-based JSA if you satisfy the means test. If you come under the universal credit (UC) system, you can instead claim UC to top up your contribution-based JSA.
- Your JSA might be paid at a reduced (or nil) rate if you are sanctioned (see Chapters 51 and 52) or if your JSA has been restricted because you have committed a benefit offence (see p1258).

Waiting days

You are not entitled to JSA for the first three 'waiting days' (due to increase to seven from October 2014) of any jobseeking period (see p693) unless:[25]

- your claim is linked to a previous claim for JSA so both are treated as part of the same jobseeking period; *or*
- you have been entitled to income support (IS), employment and support allowance (ESA), incapacity benefit or carer's allowance within the 12 weeks before you become entitled to JSA.

In addition, you do not have to serve any waiting days if you swap from claiming IS or ESA to claiming JSA.[26] **Note:** this does not apply if you come under the UC system (see p19).

Income for contribution-based jobseeker's allowance

Any earnings and pension payments you receive can affect your entitlement to contribution-based JSA.[27] Any other income you receive does not affect your contribution-based JSA (but see p1165 for the rules on overlapping benefits). Similarly, any savings you have do not affect your entitlement to contribution-based JSA. **Note:** the income and savings of your partner and children do *not* affect your contribution-based JSA, but do affect income-based JSA, joint-claim JSA and UC.

Earnings

Earnings can affect your entitlement to contribution-based JSA. The rules on the following are the same as for income-based JSA (see Chapter 14):

- what counts as earnings (p260). However, if you come under the UC system (see p19), earnings include additional paternity pay;
- calculating net earnings from employment (p259);
- payments when you stop work (p261);
- calculating net earnings from self-employment (p265);

Part 5: Other benefits
Chapter 33: Contribution-based jobseeker's allowance
4. The amount of benefit

- working out average earnings from self-employment (p266);
- childminders (p266);
- how weekly earnings from employment are assessed (p291);
- converting income into a weekly amount (p292);
- the period covered by a payment (p293); *and*
- the date from when a payment is counted (p294).

Different rules apply to:
- disregarded earnings. For contribution-based JSA, £5 a week of your earnings is disregarded. However, if you are an auxiliary coastguard, a part-time firefighter, a part-time lifeboat crew member or a member of the territorial or reserve forces, £20 a week is disregarded.[28] If you earn less than £20 for doing any of these services, you can use up to £5 of the disregard on earnings from another job.
- how earnings affect your contribution-based JSA (see below).

How earnings affect your contribution-based jobseeker's allowance

Your benefit is reduced by the full amount of any earnings you receive over the amount of disregarded earnings.[29] You are not entitled to contribution-based JSA for any week in which your earnings exceed a 'prescribed amount'.[30] However, the days in any week when your earnings exceed the prescribed amount do not count towards your maximum 182 days of contribution-based JSA (see p700).

The **prescribed amount** is not the same for everyone. It is calculated by adding together the amount of the relevant earnings disregard and the rate of contribution-based JSA paid to someone your age (see p696), and then deducting one penny.[31]

Example
Maggie, aged 35, is entitled to contribution-based JSA of £72.40 a week. She works part time. Her earnings disregard is £5 a week. Applying the formula: (£72.40 + £5) – £0.01 = £77.39. If Maggie earns more than £77.39 a week, she is not entitled to contribution-based JSA.

Pension payments

Certain pension payments you receive may also affect your contribution-based JSA.[32] Your contribution-based JSA is reduced by the amount of your weekly pension (or, if you get more than one pension, of the total of your weekly pensions) *above* £50 a week, regardless of your age – ie, £50 a week of your pension payments is ignored.[33]

Pension payments

'**Pension payments**' are periodic payments made under a personal pension scheme, any scheme operated by a former employer for making payments connected with the ending of your employment under an occupational pension scheme or a public service pension scheme, and Pension Protection Fund and Financial Assistance Scheme payments.[34]

This definition of pension payments should cover most periodic pension payments from your former employer (including contractual redundancy/early retirement payments[35]). The amount of pension payments taken into account is the gross amount before tax is deducted, converted into a weekly amount.[36]

Any pension payments you receive because of the death of a person who was a member of a pension scheme are ignored when calculating your contribution-based JSA.[37] For example, if your late partner was a member of a scheme, any payment made to you following her/his death does not affect your contribution-based JSA.

Any pension payment you receive is counted from the first day of the benefit week in which the payment is made to you.[38]

Example

Brian claims JSA and is entitled to contribution-based JSA from Wednesday 30 April 2014. His benefit week begins on a Friday. He starts receiving a personal pension of £68 a week from Monday 5 May 2014. £18 a week is deducted from his contribution-based JSA (£68 – £50) from the benefit week starting Friday 2 May 2014.

If your pension is increased when you are on contribution-based JSA, the change should be taken into account from the first day of the benefit week in which the increase is paid.[39]

How does your pension affect your entitlement?

1. The amount of your pension payments may mean that you are not paid any JSA. However, unless your earnings also exceed the prescribed amount (see p698), you remain *entitled* to contribution-based JSA (provided you also satisfy the other conditions for getting JSA).

2. Any day on which you are entitled to JSA (even if it is not paid) counts towards your 182 days' entitlement to contribution-based JSA (see p700). A combination of earnings and pension payments may mean that you are not paid any JSA, even though you may remain entitled to it.

Part 5: Other benefits
Chapter 33: Contribution-based jobseeker's allowance
4. The amount of benefit

Duration of contribution-based jobseeker's allowance

You cannot receive more than 182 days of contribution-based JSA in any jobseeking period (see p693) or in two or more jobseeking periods if your entitlement is based on national insurance (NI) contributions in the same two contribution years.[40] The 182 days can include days both before and after you come under the UC system (see p19).[41] You can have another 182 days of contribution-based JSA for a later claim if:[42]

* you satisfy the contribution conditions; *and*
* at least one of the two contribution years used to decide whether you satisfy the contribution conditions is later than the second contribution year used to decide your previous entitlement. This can only apply if you are in a later jobseeking period than the one during which you exhausted your entitlement to contribution-based JSA. **Note:** if you are a man aged at least the qualifying age for pension credit (PC – see p78) but under 65, there are special rules that deem your jobseeking period to continue when it would end under the normal rules, so making it difficult for you to requalify for contribution-based JSA.[43]

Each day for which you are entitled to contribution-based JSA, even if you are not paid, counts towards the 182-day total. This includes days when the amount of JSA you are paid has been reduced to nil because you have been sanctioned, or because you are getting a pension or a combination of pension and earnings. Because JSA is a weekly benefit, you are entitled on Saturdays and Sundays.

Days on which you are *not* entitled to contribution-based JSA can also count towards the 182-day total. This applies to days within a jobseeking period (both before and after you come under the UC system) on which you are not entitled to contribution-based JSA because:[44]

* you are entitled to IS or your earnings are above the prescribed amount (see p697), and your contribution-based JSA is not payable either because you have been sanctioned (see Chapters 51 and 52) or because you have committed a benefit offence; *or*
* you do not meet the jobseeking conditions *and* you are receiving a JSA hardship payment (see p1200).

Days on which you are not entitled to JSA and which do *not* count towards the 182-day total include:

* waiting days (see p697);
* days in any benefit week in which you are not entitled to JSA because you earn more than the prescribed amount (see p698), but see above if you have been sanctioned;
* days when you are refused contribution-based JSA because you do not meet the jobseeking conditions and you are *not* getting a JSA hardship payment.

Note: if you are a laid-off or short-time worker (see p1047), days you claim contribution-based JSA count towards your 182 days of entitlement, even if your benefit is reduced to take account of your earnings from work. So, if you think you are likely to become fully unemployed in the near future and you are not claiming income-based JSA, you might gain more JSA overall by not claiming it until you are fully unemployed. However, if your earnings drop below the lower earnings limit (see Appendix 8), you cease to be treated as paying NI contributions. You may then wish to claim JSA, which entitles you to NI credits.

5. Special benefit rules

Special rules may apply to:
- people who are laid off or working short time (see p1047);
- people going abroad (see Chapter 71);
- people who are are studying (see Chapter 44);
- people involved in a trade dispute (see Chapter 45).

6. Claims and backdating

To qualify for jobseeker's allowance (JSA) you must make a claim for it.[45] The general rules about claims and backdating are in Chapter 53. This section explains the specific rules that apply to JSA.

Note: in rare cases, it may be beneficial for you to delay your claim for contribution-based JSA so that you can draw on a different year's record of national insurance (NI) contributions.

While you are getting JSA, to check whether you satisfy all the requirements, as well as giving all the necessary facts about your circumstances, you are expected to attend and participate in an initial interview when you claim (see p703). If you fail to attend, your date of claim is affected (see p705). You are also expected to attend and participate in:
- an interview when you sign on (see p1049) and further interviews as required (see p1049); *or*
- if you come under the universal credit (UC) system (see p19), work-focused interviews (see p1067) and other interviews connected to work-related requirements (see p1072).

If you fail to sign on, your entitlement to JSA could end (see p1051 and p1053). If you fail to participate in an interview, your entitlement to JSA could end, or you could be sanctioned (see p1054, p1093 and p1127).

For further information about:

Part 5: Other benefits
Chapter 33: Contribution-based jobseeker's allowance
6. Claims and backdating

- requirements after you are awarded JSA, see p1048 or, if you come under the UC system, see p1072 and p1067;
- the officers who deal with JSA claims, see p1151.

Making a claim

You can start your claim for JSA:
- in writing on the form approved by the DWP;[46] *or*
- by telephone, if the DWP agrees, on 0800 055 6688 (Welsh 0800 012 1888; textphone 0800 023 4888), Monday to Friday, 8am to 6pm. You are sent a written statement of your circumstances to approve, sign and to return to the DWP;[47] *or*
- online at www.gov.uk/jobseekers-allowance/how-to-claim.[48]

You must normally attend the Jobcentre Plus office to complete your claim at an initial interview (see p703).[49]

In practice, the DWP prefers you to start your claim online. There is no rule that says you must start your claim online, but it is best to make your claim in the way the DWP prefers if you can.

Note: if you come under the UC system (see p19), you can only claim in writing or by telephone if you are *not* required to attend an initial interview.[50]

If you claim in writing, keep a copy of your claim in case queries arise.

You may be sent or given a form to complete about the work you will be looking for and how you intend to go about getting it. The information you give forms the basis of your jobseeker's agreement (or claimant commitment).

You must provide information or evidence as required (see p703). You can amend or withdraw your claim before a decision is made (see p1138). If there is a delay in making your claim, you may be able to get a short-term advance (see p1167).

Note: income-based and contribution-based JSA are two types of one benefit. If you want the DWP to assess your entitlement to both, answer all the relevant questions and provide all the necessary information when making your claim.

Forms

JSA claim forms are only available from Jobcentre Plus offices. If you do not come under the UC system (see p19), one must be provided free of charge if you notify the DWP of your intention to claim.[51] Seek advice if you are unable to claim online or use a telephone and the Jobcentre Plus office tells you that you cannot start your claim in any other way.

Note: you can make initial contact with the DWP by telephone or letter to say you want to claim. The date of your initial contact is important because it usually determines the date on which your claim is treated as made (see p704).

Housing benefit

You must make a claim to your local authority for housing benefit (HB). If you claim JSA by telephone, your HB claim is usually completed at the same time.

If you claim JSA on the approved form, you may be given a claim form for HB (or it is available at www.gov.uk/housing-benefit/how-to-claim).

Claiming national insurance credits

If you are claiming NI credits but not JSA (see p851), the normal claim procedures for getting JSA apply to you.

Who should claim

You claim contribution-based JSA on your own behalf.

Information to support your claim

When you claim JSA you must:
- satisfy the NI number requirement (see p1138);
- provide proof of your identity, if required (see p1140); *and*
- ensure you have made a valid claim – ie, you must supply information and evidence required on the claim form (see p1140).

It is important that you provide any information or evidence required by the instructions on the claim form. Until you do, you may not count as having made a valid claim.[52] Correct any defects in your claim within one month of your initial contact with Jobcentre Plus or you might lose benefit (see p704). You must also normally satisfy a specific 'evidence requirement'. See p1142 for this and to see if you are exempt. **Note:** the evidence requirement does not apply if you come under the UC system (see p19).

Even if you have provided all that was required when you claimed, you may be asked to provide additional information and evidence relevant to your claim (see p1152). There is a strict time limit for provividing this. If you do not do so, the decision maker can decide your claim in the way most adverse to you.

Note: you may be asked to provide information after you are awarded JSA. If you do not do so, your JSA could be suspended or even terminated (see p1175).

The initial interview

You must usually attend and participate in an initial interview.[53] If you do not do so, your date of claim is affected (see p705).

If attending the Jobcentre Plus office would mean that you would have to be away from home for too long, arrangements can be made for your interview to be carried out by a visiting employment officer (EO). Your jobseeker's agreement (the DWP calls this a 'claimant commitment') is treated as existing until that has been done.

Part 5: Other benefits
Chapter 33: Contribution-based jobseeker's allowance
6. Claims and backdating

If you have been sent a claim form, complete it before your interview. If you do not provide all the evidence and information required, your interview might not go ahead unless you are exempt from the evidence requirement (p1143).

At the interview:

- you are told what is expected from you while you are receiving JSA. This is incorporated into your jobseeker's agreement (or claimant commitment if you come under the UC system);

- you and your adviser discuss what work you are looking for and what you intend to do to find it. This forms the basis of your jobseeker's agreement (or claimant commitment);

- you may be referred to a job vacancy immediately. However, a jobseeker's agreement (or claimant commitment) should still be completed to establish entitlement in case you do not get the job.

The interview also covers what you were doing before you became unemployed and, in particular, why you left your previous job. If the EO thinks that you may have left voluntarily or been dismissed for misconduct (and, therefore, might be liable to be sanctioned – see Chapters 51 and 52), you are asked to complete a form explaining your side of the story. The form is passed to the decision maker who may need to make further enquiries before reaching a decision on whether you should be sanctioned.

The date of your claim

You are not usually entitled to JSA for any day before your date of claim.[54] However, in some cases you can claim in advance (see p705) and sometimes your claim can be backdated (see p706). If you want this to be done, you should make this clear when you claim or the DWP might not consider it.

Your 'date of claim' depends on whether or not you are required to attend an initial interview (see p703):

- If you are required to attend an initial interview, your date of claim is the date you first contact the Jobcentre Plus office if you attend your initial interview at the time specified by the DWP and a properly completed claim is provided (on a form or by telephone) with all the information and evidence required. The DWP can extend the time you have to provide or make a properly completed claim up to the date one month after the date of first contact. This is discretionary, so provide your claim as required wherever possible. If you do not attend your initial interview, see p705;[55] *or*

- If you are not required to attend an initial interview, your date of claim is the earliest of:[56]

    - the date you first contact the Jobcentre Plus office, so long as a properly completed claim (on a form or by telephone) with all the information and evidence required is provided within one month of your first contact; *or*

- the date on which a properly completed claim (on a form or by telephone) with all the information and evidence required is received at the Jobcentre Plus office.

Note: if you are a member of a couple and one of you claims contribution-based JSA but is not entitled to it and a subsequent income-based JSA claim is made by your partner (or you and your partner if you are a joint-claim couple), the date of claim for income-based JSA is the date of the earlier claim for contribution-based JSA.[57] If your partner has been claiming contribution-based JSA, this expires and you claim income-based JSA, the date of claim for your income-based JSA is the day after your partner's entitlement expires.[58]

Forms
In this section, the term **'form'** refers to a paper form or a claim form completed online.

If you do not attend the initial interview

If you do not attend your initial interview at the time specified by the DWP, or you fail to provide a properly completed claim by the date of the interview and cannot show good cause for this, the rules above do not apply. Instead, so long as a properly completed claim with all the information and evidence required is provided, your date of claim is the date you eventually go to the Jobcentre Plus office.[59]

'Good cause' is not defined. All relevant circumstances must be considered. These may relate to your abilities, or to external factors. The general test is whether there is some factor that would probably cause a reasonable person of your age and experience to act, or fail to act, as you did.[60]

Note: after you have been awarded JSA, you can be required to attend and participate in regular interviews. If you fail to participate in an interview, your entitlement to JSA can end or you may be sanctioned.

If you claim the wrong benefit

If you claim working tax credit (WTC) but are refused because neither you nor your partner are in full-time paid work for WTC purposes (see p165), your claim for JSA can be backdated to the date you claimed WTC.[61] However, you must claim JSA within 14 days of the decision refusing you WTC. You can ask for your JSA claim to start on a later date instead – eg, if your earnings are currently too high, but are due to decrease.

Claiming in advance

If you do not qualify for JSA from the date of your claim, but will do so within the next three months, you can be awarded JSA from the first date on which you will

Part 5: Other benefits
Chapter 33: Contribution-based jobseeker's allowance
6. Claims and backdating

qualify.[62] This gives the DWP time to ensure you receive benefit as soon as you are entitled. Let the DWP know you want to claim in advance when you claim and at your initial interview. You might have to persuade the DWP that it can accept a claim in advance.

You might only qualify for contribution-based JSA currently but would also be entitled to income-based JSA once you or your partner (or a child who can be included in your claim) become entitled to another 'qualifying benefit' – eg, disability living allowance, personal independence payment or carer's allowance. Tell the DWP you want your entitlement to income-based JSA to be considered at the same time as the claim for the qualifying benefit. See p1294 for further information about revisions and supersessions in this situation.

5 Backdating your claim

It is very important to claim in time. A claim for JSA can be backdated for a maximum of three months, but only in exceptional circumstances. The general rules on backdating are covered on p1146. See p1053 for the backdating rules if you make a new claim for JSA after your entitlement ended when you failed to sign on or participate in an interview. **Note:** these rules do not apply if you come under the UC system (see p19).

If you might have qualified for JSA earlier but did not claim because you were given the wrong information or were misled by the DWP, you could ask for compensation (see p1382) or complain to the Ombudsman through your MP (see p1387).

If you want to get your jobseeker's agreement backdated, see p1046.

After you are awarded jobseeker's allowance

Once you have been awarded JSA, in order to continue to receive it you must:
- attend and participate in regular interviews; *and*
- confirm that you continue to qualify for JSA – eg, by signing on.

If you do not sign on or participate in interviews, your entitlement to JSA can end (see p1051 and p1053). In some cases, if you fail to participate in interviews, you may be sanctioned.

You can be required to meet the jobseeking conditions (or, if you come under the UC system, work-related requirements) and you can be sanctioned if you fail to do so. See Chapters 48 and 49 for further information about the requirements after you are awarded JSA, and Chapters 51 and 52 for information about sanctions.

Note: you may be asked to provide information after you are awarded JSA. If you do not do so, your JSA could be suspended or even terminated (see p1175).

Referral to job, training or employment scheme vacancies

While you are claiming JSA, you may be referred to job vacancies.

You risk being sanctioned if, without a good reason, you refuse to apply for a job vacancy. Alternatively, you could be issued with a jobseeker's direction or be required to meet a work preparation requirement (eg, to take some action to improve your job prospects), and risk being sanctioned if you refuse or fail to to do so. Refusing to apply for a job or vacancy on a scheme or programme may also raise doubts about whether you are available for work.

If you are not considered ready for a job, you are likely to be referred to a place on a training or employment scheme – eg, Work Experience or the Work Programme. You can be sanctioned for not attending or for leaving early.

See Chapters 51 and 52 for information about sanctions.

Referral to a disability employment adviser

If you have a disability that affects your search for work, you may be eligible for specialist help from the DWP, including being referred to a disability employment adviser. Every Jobcentre Plus office has a disability adviser who is responsible for good practice relating to disabled people.

You may want to ask to be referred to an adviser if, for example:

- you think the service from the Jobcentre Plus office is not meeting your needs; or
- your health problem or disability has worsened significantly, or you have a new disability or health problem and need specialist help; or
- you need new skills in order to do a job; or
- you need practical help with looking for a job – eg, help in getting to interviews or identifying specialist equipment; or
- you are not clear about the effect your disability has on the job options open to you.

7. Getting paid

Jobseeker's allowance (JSA) is normally paid by direct credit transfer into your bank (or similar) account (see p1163). If you are unable to open or manage an account, payment can be made by 'simple payment' (see p1163). If you are unable to act for yourself, payment can be made to someone else on your behalf – called your 'appointee' (see p1137). **Note:** the rules in this section apply to all types of JSA.

When is jobseeker's allowance paid?

The day you are paid depends on your national insurance (NI) number (see p1164). JSA is normally paid fortnightly in arrears.[63]

JSA is a weekly benefit, although in some cases it can be paid for part weeks.[64] Most questions about entitlement are decided in relation to a particular 'benefit week' – ie, the period of seven days ending on the day of the week allocated to you according to your NI number.[65]

If you are entitled to less than 10p a week, you are not paid JSA at all,[66] but you are still eligible for NI credits (see p851). If you are entitled to less than £1 a week, a decision maker can decide to pay you at longer intervals of not more than 13 weeks.[67]

Note:

- Deductions can be made from your JSA to pay to third parties (see p1178).
- Your JSA might be paid at a reduced (or nil) rate if you have been sanctioned for a benefit offence (see p1258). **Note:** you may also be sanctioned for other reasons (see Chapters 51 and 52).
- If you have forgotten your PIN, see p1163. If your 'simple payment' card has been lost or stolen, or if you have forgotten your memorable date, see p1164. For information on missing payments, see p1164.
- If payment of your JSA is delayed, see p1382. You might be able to get a short-term advance (see p1167). If you wish to complain about how your claim has been dealt with, see p1383. You might be able to claim compensation (see p1382).
- If payment of your JSA is suspended, see p1175.
- If you are overpaid JSA, you might have to repay it (see Chapter 56) and, in some circumstances, you may have to pay a penalty (see p1249). If you have been accused of fraud, see Chapter 57.

Change of circumstances

You must report changes in your circumstances that you have been told you must report, as well as any that you might reasonably be expected to know might affect your right to, the amount of, or the payment of, your benefit, including any that are likely to occur. You should do this as soon as possible, preferably in writing. See p1174 for further information.

If you have a mortgage and are claiming income-based JSA in addition to contribution-based JSA, the DWP can ask your lender about any changes in the amount you owe during your JSA claim. If you have this information (eg, from an annual statement you receive from your lender), you must also advise the DWP in case your lender fails to do so. Make sure the DWP takes this information into account so you are not overpaid JSA.

When there has been a relevant change of circumstances, a decision maker looks at your claim again and makes a new decision. To see when your JSA is then adjusted, see p709.

When your jobseeker's allowance is adjusted

As a general rule, your JSA is adjusted from the first day of the benefit week in which the change occurs or is expected to do so.[68] There are a number of exceptions to this rule.[69] In particular, if a decision is to your advantage, but you failed to notify the DWP of a change within the time limit (normally one month, but this can be extended – see p1289), your JSA is adjusted:

- if you are paid in arrears, from the first day of the benefit week in which you notified the change; or
- if you are paid in advance, from the day on which you notified the change, if this is the first day of the benefit week. If it is not, your JSA is adjusted from the next week.

8. Tax, other benefits and the benefit cap

Tax

Jobseeker's allowance (JSA) is taxable.[70] The maximum amount of JSA that is taxable is an amount equal to the appropriate personal allowance for a person of your age (see p696). The tax is not deducted while JSA is being paid, but reduces the refund you would otherwise receive through Pay As You Earn (PAYE) when you return to work.

Any tax refunds of PAYE payments are paid to you at the end of the tax year to which they relate. Any other tax refund is paid only when you stop getting JSA.

Means-tested benefits

If you are getting contribution-based JSA, you may also be entitled to income-based JSA (or, if you are at least the qualifying age for pension credit (PC) (see p78), to PC) to top this up. If you come under the universal credit (UC) system (see p19), you may be entitled to UC instead of income-based JSA to top up your contribution-based JSA.

Your contribution-based JSA counts as income for the purposes of means-tested benefits unless you get income-based JSA, PC or UC, in which case it is ignored for housing benefit (HB) purposes.

You cannot claim JSA and income support (IS) at the same time. If you have a partner, s/he can claim IS, income-related employment and support allowance or PC and you can claim contribution-based JSA (but not income-based JSA).

Non-means-tested benefits

While you are on JSA you are entitled to national insurance credits (see p851). Contribution-based JSA is affected by the overlapping benefit rules (see p1165).

Part 5: Other benefits
Chapter 33: Contribution-based jobseeker's allowance
8. Tax, other benefits and the benefit cap

Tax credits

Even if you work less than 16 hours each week, if you have a partner and s/he works sufficient hours, you and your partner might be able to claim working tax credit (WTC).

If you or your partner have just stopped work or reduced your hours, you might get what is known as 'WTC run-on' for a four-week period (see p172).

The benefit cap

In some cases, the total amount of specified benefits you receive is limited to £350 a week (if you are a single claimant without children) or £500 a week (if you are a lone parent or a member of a couple). This is known as the 'benefit cap'. JSA is one of the specified benefits. The benefit cap only applies if you are getting HB or UC. See p1169 for further information.

Passports and other sources of help

If you are entitled to income-based JSA or UC in addition to contribution-based JSA, you also qualify for health benefits such as free prescriptions (see Chapter 30) and education benefits such as free school lunches (see p832). You may qualify for council tax reduction (see p827). You may also qualify for social fund payments (see Chapter 37).

Financial help on starting work

If you stop getting income-based JSA because you or your partner start work, or your earnings or hours in your existing job increase, you might be able to get mortgage interest run-on (if you have a home loan – see p460), or extended payments of HB (if you pay rent – see p136). Your local authority may provide extended help with council tax. See p838 for information about other financial help you might get.

Notes

1. Who can claim jobseeker's allowance
1 s1 JSA 1995
2 ss6-6I JSA 1995
3 s61 WRA 2012 (not yet in forece)
4 s2 JSA 1995
5 Reg 47(1) and (2) JSA Regs; reg 37(1) JSA Regs 2013
6 Arts 12 and 13 WRA(No.9)O; Arts 10(2) and 11(2) WRA(No.11)O
7 Reg 49 JSA Regs; reg 40 JSA Regs 2013
8 Reg 47(3) JSA Regs; reg 37(2) JSA Regs 2013
9 s2(1) and (4) JSA 1995
10 Reg 48 JSA Regs; reg 39 JSA Regs 2013
11 Reg 48(2) and (3) JSA Regs; reg 39(2) and (4) JSA Regs 2013
12 LE v SSWP [2009] UKUT 166 (AAC). The judge decided that the rule indirectly discriminated against women but that the discrimination was justified.
13 Reg 51 JSA Regs; reg 42 JSA Regs 2013
14 s1(2)(f) JSA 1995
15 Sch 1 para 2 JSA 1995; reg 10 SS&CS(DA) Regs; reg 10 UC,PIP,JSA&ESA(DA) Regs
16 Reg 55(1) JSA Regs; reg 46(1) JSA Regs 2013
17 Reg 55A(1) JSA Regs; reg 47(1) JSA Regs 2013
18 Regs 55(2) and 55A(2) JSA Regs; regs 46(2) and 47(2) JSA Regs 2013
19 Regs 14(1)(ll) and 19(1)(ll) JSA Regs
20 Reg 16 JSA Regs 2013
21 Reg 55(3) JSA Regs; reg 46(3) JSA Regs 2013
22 Arts 10(2) and 11(2) WRA(No.11)O
23 Reg 55(4) JSA Regs; reg 46(4) JSA Regs 2013

4. The amount of benefit
24 s4(1) and (2) JSA 1995; reg 79 JSA Regs; reg 49 JSA Regs 2013
25 Sch 1 para 4 JSA 1995; reg 46 JSA Regs; reg 36 JSA Regs 2013; Arts 10(2) and 11(2) WRA(No.11)O
26 Reg 14A(4) SS&CS(DA) Regs
27 s4(1) JSA 1995
28 Regs 99(3) and 101(3) and Sch 6 JSA Regs; regs 59(2) and 61(2) and Sch JSA Regs 2013
29 Reg 80 JSA Regs; reg 50 JSA Regs 2013
30 s2(1)(c) JSA 1995; reg 56(1) and (2) JSA Regs; reg 48 JSA Regs 2013
31 Reg 56(1) JSA Regs; reg 48 JSA Regs 2013
32 s4(1) JSA 1995
33 Reg 81(1) JSA Regs; reg 51(1) JSA Regs 2013
34 ss4(1) and 35(1) JSA 1995
35 R(JSA) 1/01
36 Reg 81 JSA Regs; reg 51 JSA Regs 2013; R(U) 8/83
37 Reg 81(2)(c) and (d) JSA Regs; reg 51(4) JSA Regs 2013
38 Reg 81(1A) JSA Regs; reg 51(2) JSA Regs 2013
39 Reg 81(1B) JSA Regs; reg 51(3) JSA Regs 2013
40 s5(1) JSA 1995
41 Arts 10(2) and 11(2) WRA(N0.11)O
42 s5(2) JSA 1995
43 Reg 49 JSA Regs; reg 40 JSA Regs 2013
44 Reg 47(2) and (4) JSA Regs; reg 37(3) JSA Regs 2013; Arts 12 and 13 WRA(No.9)O; Arts 10(2) and 11(2) WRA(No.11)O

6. Claims and backdating
45 s1 SSAA 1992
46 Reg 4(1A) SS(C&P) Regs; reg 21 UC,PIP,JSA&ESA(C&P) Regs
47 Reg 4(11A) and (11B) SS(C&P) Regs; reg 23 UC,PIP,JSA&ESA(C&P) Regs
48 Reg 4ZC SS(C&P) Regs; reg 3 and Sch 2 UC,PIP,JSA&ESA(C&P) Regs
49 Reg 4(6)(a) SS(C&P) Regs; reg 19 UC,PIP,JSA&ESA(C&P) Regs
50 Regs 21(1) and 23(1) UC,PIP,JSA&ESA(C&P) Regs
51 Reg 4(5) SS(C&P) Regs
52 Reg 4(1A), (7B), (9), (12) and (13) SS(C&P) Regs; regs 21 and 23 UC,PIP,JSA&ESA(C&P) Regs
53 Reg 4(6)(a) SS(C&P) Regs; reg 19 UC,PIP,JSA&ESA(C&P) Regs
54 Reg 19(1) and Sch 4 para 1 SS(C&P) Regs; reg 29(1) UC, PIP,JSA&ESA(C&P) Regs

• •

55 Reg 6(1)(c) and (d), (4A)(a)(i) and (4AB)
SS(C&P) Regs; reg 20
UC,PIP,JSA&ESA(C&P) Regs
56 Reg 6(4A)(b) SS(C&P) Regs; regs 22 and
24 UC,PIP,JSA&ESA(C&P) Regs
57 Reg 4(3B)(b) SS(C&P) Regs
58 Reg 4(3B)(c) SS(C&P) Regs
59 Reg 6(4A)(a)(ii) SS(C&P) Regs; reg 20(2)
UC,PIP,JSA&ESA(C&P) Regs
60 CS/371/1949
61 Reg 6(28) SS(C&P) Regs
62 Reg 13(1) and (9) SS(C&P) Regs; reg 34
UC,PIP,JSA&ESA(C&P) Regs

7. Getting paid
63 Reg 26A SS(C&P) Regs; reg 52
UC,PIP,JSA&ESA(C&P) Regs
64 s1(3) JSA 1995; reg 150 JSA Regs; reg 64
JSA Regs 2013
65 Reg 1(3) JSA Regs; reg 2(2) JSA Regs
2013
66 Reg 87A JSA Regs ; reg 52 JSA Regs 2013
67 Reg 26A(3) SS(C&P) Regs; reg 52(3)
UC,PIP,JSA&ESA(C&P) Regs
68 Reg 7 and Sch 3A para 7 SS&CS(DA)
Regs; reg 35 and Sch 1
UC,PIP,JSA&ESA(DA) Regs
69 Reg 7 and Sch 3A paras 8-13
SS&CS(DA) Regs; reg 35 and Sch 1 Part
1 UC,PIP,JSA&ESA(DA) Regs

8. Tax, other benefits and the benefit cap
70 ss671-75 IT(EP)A 2003

Chapter 34

Maternity allowance

This chapter covers:
1. Who can claim maternity allowance (p714)
2. The rules about your age (p718)
3. People included in the claim (p718)
4. The amount of benefit (p718)
5. Special benefit rules (p719)
6. Claims and backdating (p719)
7. Getting paid (p722)
8. Tax, other benefits and the benefit cap (p723)

Key facts

- You may qualify for maternity allowance (MA) if you are pregnant or have recently given birth and you are not entitled to statutory maternity pay.
- You may qualify for MA if you are, or have been, employed or self-employed. If not, you may qualify if you have helped your spouse or civil partner with her/his self-employment.
- Depending on the type of MA you get, it is paid for a maximum of 39 or 14 weeks.
- MA is a non-means-tested benefit.
- You do not need to have paid national insurance contributions to qualify.
- You may not be able to get MA and another earnings-replacement benefit at the same time because of the overlapping benefit rules.
- If you qualify for MA on the basis of your employment or self-employment, going back to work early may allow your partner to qualify for additional statutory paternity pay from her/his employer instead.
- MA is administered and paid by the DWP.
- If you disagree with a decision on MA, you can apply for a revision or supersession, or appeal against it. You are likely to have to apply for a revision before you can appeal.

Future changes

The government plans to introduce a new statutory scheme of parental leave and pay from April 2015 (see p783). Under the plan, if you qualify for MA on the basis of your employment or self-Employment, you may be able to reduce the length of time over which you get MA in order for the child's other parent (or, in some circumstances, your partner) to get statutory shared parental pay (SSPP) from her/his employer. The maximum combined total number of weeks over which MA and SSPP can be awarded will be 39.[1]

1. **Who can claim maternity allowance**

You may qualify for maternity allowance (MA) if:
* you are, or have been, employed or self-employed (see below); or
* your expected week of childbirth (EWC – see p715) starts on or after 27 July 2014 and you have helped your spouse or civil partner with her/his self-employment (see p717).

Note: it is expected that from some point in the future you will have to be entitled to work in the UK (and not prevented from taking up work under immigration provisions) to qualify for MA.[2] There may be exceptions. See CPAG's online service and *Welfare Rights Bulletin* for updates.

Your own employment or self-employment

You qualify for MA on the basis of your own employment or self-employment if you:[3]
* are pregnant or have recently given birth, and you are within your 'maternity allowance period'; *and*
* satisfy the employment condition (see p715); *and*
* satisfy the earnings condition (see p715); *and*
* are not entitled to statutory maternity pay (SMP).

In certain circumstances, you may be disqualified from receiving MA – eg, if you work during your MA period. See p716 for details.

Maternity allowance period

MA awarded on the basis of your own employment or self-employment can only be paid during the MA period.[4] This is a period of 39 consecutive weeks that normally starts on the day your maternity pay period would have begun had you been entitled to statutory maternity pay (SMP – see p794). However:[5]
* if you are not employed or self-employed at the beginning of the 11th week before your EWC (see p715), your MA period starts from the beginning of that week (but if your baby was born before this, it starts from the day after the birth); *and*
* if you are not entitled to MA during the 11th week before your EWC, but you become entitled to it before your baby is born (perhaps because you then meet

the earnings or employment condition), provided you have stopped work, the earliest day on which your MA period can start is the day you become entitled to MA and the latest it can start is the day after the birth.

Expected week of childbirth
The '**expected week of childbirth**' is the week, starting on a Sunday, in which your baby is due to be born

Employment condition
To qualify for MA on this basis, you must have been an employed earner or self-employed earner for at least 26 weeks in the 66 weeks immediately before your EWC. This 66-week period is known as the '**test period**'.[6] If you are an employed or self-employed earner for just part of a week, the whole of that week counts. The 26 weeks do not need to be consecutive and you do not need to have worked in the same job for the whole period. You need only show that you have been an employed and/or self-employed earner for any part of each of the 26 weeks. For the meaning of employed and self-employed earner, see p844.

See p719 if you have worked abroad.

Example
Rita's baby is due on Saturday 12 July 2014.
Rita's EWC begins on Sunday 6 July 2014 and her 66-week 'test period' runs from Sunday 31 March 2013 to Saturday 5 July 2014.

Appendix 4 contains a table of relevant dates for 2014/15.

Earnings condition
To qualify for MA on the basis of your own employment or self-employment, your average weekly earnings in 13 weeks of your test period (or, if you are self-employed, the average weekly earnings you are treated as having) must be at least equal to the MA threshold of £30 a week (for how earnings are averaged, see p716).[7]

Earnings from employment
If you are employed, your gross earnings are used to calculate your average weekly earnings. What counts as earnings for MA purposes is the same as for SMP (see p791).[8] If you get a backdated pay rise for the period over which your earnings are averaged, this is included in the calculation.[9]

Earnings from self-employment

If you are self-employed, you are treated as earning a certain amount and this figure is used to calculate your average weekly earnings, irrespective of the amount you actually earn. For each week for which:[10]

- you have a national insurance (NI) small earnings exception certificate (see p845), you are treated as having earnings equal to the MA threshold (£30 a week);

- you do not have a small earnings exception certificate and have paid a Class 2 NI contribution, you are treated as having earnings of an amount 90 per cent of which is equal to the maximum amount of MA that can be paid for that week. From 7 April 2014, as the maximum amount of MA is £138.18, you are treated as having earnings of £153.54 a week. (Between 8 April 2013 and 6 April 2014 you would have been treated as having weekly earnings of £151.98.) If you have paid a Class 2 contribution for at least 13 weeks in your 66-week test period, you will qualify for MA of £138.18 a week.[11]

Calculating average earnings

Your average weekly earnings are calculated as follows.[12]

- If you have paid Class 2 contributions as a self-employed person for at least 13 weeks in your 66-week test period, no calculation is needed – you automatically qualify for MA of £138.18 a week. Weeks for which you have a NI small earnings exception do not count in this case, even if you pay voluntary Class 2 contributions for those weeks.

- Otherwise, add together your earnings in the 13 weeks in your 66-week test period when your earnings are highest and divide the total by 13. Remember for weeks in which you are self-employed and you have a small earnings exception, you are treated as earning £30 a week. For weeks in which you have more than one job, the earnings from all your jobs, including earnings you are treated as having from self-employment, are counted.

In both cases, the 13 weeks do not need to be consecutive. If you are not paid weekly, work out your weekly earnings by dividing the payments you receive by the nearest number of weeks in the period for which they are paid.[13]

More than one job

If you get SMP, you cannot receive MA for the same week for the same baby, even if you have more than one job or have been self-employed as well as employed.

Disqualification from benefit

If you are entitled to MA on the basis of your own employment or self-employment, you are disqualified from receiving it for a period if:[14]

- you work for more than 10 days during your MA period. Both employed and self-employed work counts and the 10 days do not need to be consecutive. If you work for part of a day, it counts as a full day. (If you work for 10 days or less, your MA is unaffected, even if you are paid for that work.) Inform the DWP if you work during your MA period (see p723);

- without good cause, you do not take 'due care of your health' or answer 'reasonable enquiries' from the DWP about whether you are doing so. The enquiries should not relate to any medical examination, treatment or advice you have or have not been given;
- before the birth of your baby you fail to attend a medical examination without good cause. You must have been given written notice of the examination at least three days beforehand by the DWP or someone acting on its behalf.

The question of whether or not you have good cause for your behaviour depends on your circumstances.

The DWP can disqualify you for as long as is reasonable given the circumstances. However, if you are disqualified because:

- you have worked for more than 10 days, the disqualification must be for at least the number of days that you worked in excess of those 10 days;
- you have not attended a medical examination, the disqualification cannot continue once you have given birth.

You can challenge the DWP's decision on whether you have good cause or on the length of the disqualification period (see Chapters 58 and 59).

Note: if you are employed and on maternity leave, working for more than 10 days may affect your continued entitlement to leave. If you do not want your maternity leave to end, seek employment advice before agreeing to such work.

Your spouse's or civil partner's self-employment

If your EWC begins on or after 27 July 2014 and you do not qualify for MA on the basis of your own employment or self-employment, you may qualify if you have helped your spouse or civil partner with her/his self-employment. This applies if:[15]

- you are pregnant and have reached the start of the 11th week before your EWC (or you have had your baby) and you are within your 14-week qualifying period (see p718); and
- your spouse or civil partner was a self-employed earner in at least 26 weeks in the 66 weeks immediately before your EWC and s/he is liable to pay Class 2 NI contributions for those 26 weeks; and
- for at least part of each of these 26 weeks you took part in, or assisted, your spouse or civil partner with her/his self-employment, but you were not employed by, or in partnership with, her/him; and
- you are not entitled to SMP for the same week and same pregnancy.

The DWP intends that you will be disqualified from receiving MA on this basis for any week in which you do any work, unless it is in an emergency. You will also be disqualified for a period if you do not take 'due care of your health' or answer 'reasonable enquiries' from the DWP about this and you do not have good cause (see p716) or if, before the birth, you fail to attend a medical examination without good cause.

Note: at the time of writing, the rules on disqualification from MA in these circumstances had not been finalised. Some of this information may therefore be subject to change. See CPAG's online service and *Welfare Rights Bulletin* for updates.

14-week qualifying period

MA awarded on this basis can only be paid in the qualifying period. This is the period of up to 14 consecutive weeks starting from:[16]

- the start of the 11th week before your EWC, if you stopped working with your spouse or civil partner before this date; *or*
- the day after you stop working with your spouse or civil partner, if you do so at any time from the start of the 11th week before your EWC but before the start of the fourth week before your EWC; *or*
- the day after you stop working with your spouse or civil partner (or you refrain from working with her/him if this is at least in part because of your pregnancy or childbirth), if you either stop or refrain from work during the period that runs from the start of the fourth week before your EWC until the day you have your baby; *or*
- if none of the above apply, the day after you have your baby.

Note: 'stopping work' means either stopping permanently or until after the birth.

2. The rules about your age

There are no upper or lower age limits for receiving maternity allowance.

3. People included in the claim

You claim maternity allowance for yourself. You cannot claim any increase for your partner or child(ren).

4. The amount of benefit

If you qualify for maternity allowance (MA) on the basis of your own employment or self-employment, it can only be paid during the 39-week MA period (see p714).

The amount you receive is either 90 per cent of your average weekly earnings or £138.18 a week, whichever is less.[17] See p716 for how your average earnings are calculated.

If you qualify because you help with your spouse's or civil partner's self-employment, MA is only payable during the 14-week qualifying period. The amount you receive is £27 a week (but see p718).

5. Special benefit rules

Special rules may apply to:
- people in prison or legal custody (see p959);
- people who go abroad (see Chapter 71).

There are also special rules if you have been employed abroad.
- If, following a period of employment abroad, you have returned to Great Britain and you remained ordinarily resident in Great Britain while you were away, you may be able to rely on periods of employment abroad to satisfy the employment and earnings condition for maternity allowance (MA).[18]
- In some circumstances, you may be able to rely on periods you have worked in other European Economic Area countries to qualify for MA (see p1559).

6. Claims and backdating

To be entitled to maternity allowance (MA), you must make a claim for it.[19] The general rules about claims and backdating are in Chapter 53. This section explains the specific rules that apply to MA.

If you are (or have recently been) employed, you may be entitled to statutory maternity pay (SMP – see Chapter 38) from your employer (or ex-employer) instead of MA. If you were employed in the 15th week before your expected week of childbirth (EWC), the DWP expects you to have applied for statutory maternity pay (SMP) from your employer. If your employer (or ex-employer) has decided you are not entitled to SMP, it should give you Form SMP1 explaining why and you must send this to the DWP to support your claim for MA. If you disagree with your employer's decision, or your employer fails to give you a decision, also ask HM Revenue and Customs (HMRC) to make a decision on your entitlement to SMP (see Chapter 60).

Making a claim

A claim for MA must be made in writing, normally on the approved form. Send your completed form to the DWP office which deals with claims for MA. The relevant address is included on the form or you can get it by telephoning Jobcentre Plus, or from your local Jobcentre Plus office. Keep a copy of your claim form in case queries arise. Your claim will not be accepted unless it is received after the 15th week before your EWC.[20]

You must complete the form in accordance with the instructions on it. See below for the information and evidence you can be expected to provide in connection with your claim. The decision maker at the DWP may accept a written application not on the approved form.[21] You can amend or withdraw your claim before a decision is made (see p1138). If there is a delay in dealing with your claim, you may be able to get a short-term advance of benefit (see p1167).

Forms

The approved form is Form MA1, which you can get by telephoning the Jobcentre Plus national contact centre (0800 055 6688; textphone: 0800 023 4888) or from www.gov.uk.

Who should claim

You must normally claim MA for yourself. However, if you are unable to manage your own affairs, another person can claim MA for you as your 'appointee' (see p1137).

Information to support your claim

When you claim MA, you must:
- satisfy the national insurance number requirement (see p1138);
- provide proof of your identity, if required (see p1140); *and*
- ensure you have made a valid claim. To do so, you must supply the information requested on the claim form (see p1140).

You must provide evidence, normally a certificate from your doctor or a registered midwife, giving the expected date of birth of your child (Form MAT B1) and, if you are claiming MA after your baby is born, giving the date of the baby's birth.[22] This certificate is not accepted as evidence of your EWC if it is issued before the 20th week before your EWC. If you cannot obtain a MAT B1, the DWP can accept other evidence of the expected or actual date of birth, if this is sufficient in the circumstances.

If you have been employed, the DWP also expects you to provide pay slips or some other written proof of your earnings and an SMP1 form from any employer for whom you worked during the 15th week before your EWC.

Do not delay sending your claim for MA because you are waiting for your SMP1 or evidence of your earnings; you can send these in later.

Even if you have provided all that was required when you claimed, you may be asked to provide additional information and evidence relevant to your claim (see p1152). There is a strict time limit for providing this. If you do not do so, the decision maker can decide your claim in the way most adverse to you.

Note: you may be asked to provide information after you are awarded MA. If you do not do so, your MA could be suspended or even terminated (see p1175).

The date of your claim

The date of your claim determines the date from when you are paid MA. The date of your claim is normally the date it is received at a DWP office.[23]

If the claim form you submit is 'defective' because it has not been completed correctly, or you make a written claim which is not on the approved form, you may be asked to provide further information or to complete the approved form. Provided the additional information or form is received by the DWP within a month of its first telling you of the defect or supplying you with the correct form (or longer if the decision maker thinks that the delay is reasonable), your claim is treated as made on the date the initial claim was received (see p1140).[24] In some circumstances, you can claim before you qualify for MA (see below) or the date of your claim can be backdated (see p722).

If you claim the wrong benefit

A claim for employment and support allowance (ESA) may also (or instead) be treated as a claim for MA and vice versa (see p1144).[25] This may allow you to get your claim for MA backdated for more than the usual three months.

If your employer (or former employer) has decided that you are not entitled to SMP and you claim MA within three months of being notified of your employer's decision in writing, your claim for MA is treated as having been made either on the date on which you gave your employer notice of when you wanted the maternity pay period to start or at the beginning of the 14th week before your EWC, whichever is later.[26]

Claiming in advance

You cannot make a claim for MA until after the 15th week before your EWC (ie, until week 26 of pregnancy) but you should claim as soon as possible after that.[27] However, if you qualify for MA on the basis of your own employment or self-employment, it may be worth waiting a few weeks before claiming if this means you will have higher average earnings, and these would increase the amount of your MA. If you plan to stop work after the 11th week before the EWC and you claim while you are still working, the DWP sends you Form BM25A, notifying you of your entitlement and asking to be informed of the date you stop work.

Backdating your claim

A claim for MA can be backdated for up to three months if you satisfy the qualifying conditions over that period. You do not have to show any reasons why your claim was late.[28]

If you might have qualified for benefit earlier but did not claim because you were given the wrong information or were misled by the DWP, you could ask for compensation (see p1382) or complain to the Independent Case Examiner or to the Ombudsman through your MP (see p1384 and p1387).

If you claimed ESA instead of MA, or if you have been refused SMP, see p721.

7. **Getting paid**

Payment of maternity allowance (MA) is normally made by direct credit transfer into your bank (or similar) account (see p1163). If you are unable to open or manage an account, payment can be made by 'simple payment' (see p1163). Alternatively, MA can be paid into your partner's account or into an account you hold jointly with your partner. In some circumstances, your MA can be paid to someone else on your behalf (see p1162), including, if you are unable to act for yourself, an appointee (see p1137).

When is maternity allowance paid?
The day you are paid depends on your national insurance number (see p1164). MA is normally paid fortnightly in arrears.[29]

MA is a daily benefit, which means that it can be paid for periods of less than a week. The daily rate is one-seventh of the weekly amount.[30]

Note:
- Even if you have been sanctioned for a benefit offence (see p1258), you must be paid your MA.
- If you have forgotten your PIN, see p1163. If your 'simple payment' card has been lost or stolen, or if you have forgotten your memorable date, see p1164. For information on missing payments, see p1164.
- If payment of your MA is delayed, see p1382. You might be able to get a short-term advance (see p1167). If you wish to complain about how your claim has been dealt with, see Chapter 61. You might be able to claim compensation (see p1382).
- If payment of your MA is suspended, see p1175.
- If you are overpaid MA, you might have to repay it (see Chapter 56) and, in some circumstances, you may have to pay a penalty (see p1249). If you have been accused of fraud, see Chapter 57.

Change of circumstances

You must report any change in your circumstances that you have been told you must report, as well as any that you might reasonably be expected to know might affect your right to, the amount of, or the payment of, your benefit. You should do this as soon as possible, preferably in writing. See p1174 for further information.

If the change affects your entitlement to MA, a decision maker looks at your claim again and makes a new decision (see p1281). The date from which the new decision takes effect depends on whether or not it is advantageous to you and whether you reported the change in time (see p1287).

8. Tax, other benefits and the benefit cap

Note: the information given below on how maternity allowance (MA) interacts with other benefits applies to MA awarded on the basis of your own employment or self-employment. At the time of writing, details were not available of how other benefits will be affected by MA awarded on the basis of your spouse's or civil partner's self-employment (see p718).

Tax

MA is not taxable.[31]

Means-tested benefits

In some circumstances, being pregnant or on maternity leave may allow you to qualify for income support (IS – see p27). Alternatively, you may qualify for income-related employment and support allowance (ESA – see Chapter 5) as you are treated as having limited capability for work during the MA period or, in certain circumstances, if you are pregnant (see p1004). If you are treated as having limited capability for work you cannot qualify for jobseeker's allowance (JSA). It is not possible to qualify for both IS and ESA at the same time, so if you are unsure which you would be better off claiming, seek advice.

Although you cannot qualify for JSA during a MA period (see p714), if your partner is not in full-time paid work s/he may qualify. If you are a member of a couple who would normally have to make a joint claim for JSA and you get MA on the basis of your own employment or self-employment, you may not need to make a joint claim for your partner to qualify for income-based JSA (see p46 and p55).

If you come under the universal credit (UC) system (see p19), instead of claiming IS or income-based ESA to top up your MA, or your partner claiming income-based JSA (UC – see Chapter 10). The

MA you get is taken into account in full when calculating your entitlement to IS, income-based JSA, income-related ESA, housing benefit (HB) and UC.

For pension credit (PC – see Chapter 7), any MA you receive counts as income, but is ignored when calculating your qualifying income for the savings credit of PC.[32]

Non-means-tested benefits

MA is affected by the overlapping benefit rules (see p1165).

You cannot get contribution-based JSA (see Chapter 33) or statutory sick pay (SSP) during your MA period if you are entitled to MA. If the father of your baby (or your partner, if your partner is not the father) would be entitled to additional statutory paternity pay (SPP), you may choose to resume work before the end of your MA period, in order to let her/him get additional statutory paternity leave and pay (see p786). **Note:** from April 2015 the government plans to introduce statutory shared parental leave and pay, which will replace additional statutory paternity leave and pay (see p713).

You can get national insurance credits for each week in your MA period in which you get MA (because you are treated as having limited capability for work in those weeks – see p852).

You may qualify for both MA and contributory ESA (because you can be treated as having limited capability for work if you are entitled to MA during your MA period, see p1004) but you cannot receive both benefits in full because of the overlapping benefit rules. A claim for MA may be treated as a claim for ESA (see p1144).

Tax credits

You may qualify for working tax credit (WTC – see Chapter 9) as well as MA because sometimes you can be treated as in full-time work for WTC purposes while getting MA (see p170).

If you are entitled to WTC, you may be able to get help with the cost of childcare for your new baby, as well as for any other children for whom you are responsible, before you resume work (see p1405).

MA (including that paid on the basis you help your spouse or civil partner with her/his self-employment) is ignored when calculating your entitlement to WTC and child tax credit.

The benefit cap

In some cases, the total amount of specified benefits you receive is limited to £350 a week (if you are a single claimant without children) or £500 a week (if you are a lone parent or a member of a couple). This is known as the 'benefit cap'. MA is one of the specified benefits. The benefit cap only applies if you are getting HB or UC. See p1169 for further information.

Passports and other sources of help

For details of whether you may qualify for:

- a Sure Start maternity grant from the social fund, see p770;
- certain health service benefits, see Chapter 30;
- Healthy Start food vouchers and vitamins, see p829;
- council tax reduction, see p827.

Notes

1 Children and Families Act 2014

1. Who can claim maternity allowance
2 s63 WRA 2012 (not yet in force)
3 s35 SSCBA 1992
4 ss35(2) and 165 SSCBA 1992; reg 2(2) SMP Regs
5 ss35(2) and 165 SSCBA 1992; reg 2 SMP Regs; reg 3 SS(MatA) Regs
6 s35(1)(b) SSCBA 1992
7 ss35(1)(c) and (6A) and 35A(4) SSCBA 1992
8 s35A(4)(a) SSCBA 1992; reg 2 SS(MatA)(E) Regs
9 Reg 6(2) SS(MatA)(E) Regs
10 Reg 3 SS(MatA)(E) Regs
11 s35A(5)(c), (5A) and (5B) SSCBA 1992; reg 5 SS(MatA)(E) Regs
12 Regs 4 and 6 SS(MatA)(E) Regs
13 Reg 6(3) SS(MatA)(E) Regs
14 Reg 2 SS(MatA) Regs
15 s35B(1) and (2) SSCBA 1992
16 s35B(4)–(8) SSCBA 1992

4. The amount of benefit
17 ss35(1) and 35A SSCBA 1992

5. Special benefit rules
18 SS(MatA)(WA) Regs

6. Claims and backdating
19 s1 SSAA 1992
20 Reg 14(1) SS(C&P) Regs
21 Reg 4(1) SS(C&P) Regs
22 Reg 2(3) SS(ME) Regs
23 Reg 6(1) SS(C&P) Regs
24 Regs 4(7) and (7ZA) and 6(1) SS(C&P) Regs

25 Regs 9 and 11 and Sch 1 Part I SS(C&P) Regs; regs 18 and 25 UC,PIP,JSA&ESA(C&P) Regs
26 Reg 10(3) and (4) SS(C&P) Regs
27 Reg 14 SS(C&P) Regs
28 Reg 19(2) SS(C&P) Regs

7. Getting paid
29 Reg 24 SS(C&P) Regs
30 s35(5) SSCBA 1992

8. Tax, other benefits and the benefit cap
31 s677 IT(EP)A 2003
32 Regs 9 and 15(1) SPC Regs

5

Chapter 35

Personal independence payment

Key facts

- Personal independence payment (PIP) is a benefit for adults with disabilities who need help getting around and/or help with daily living activities.
- PIP has a daily living component and a mobility component. You can qualify for one or both of the components.
- PIP is a non-means-tested benefit.
- You do not have to have paid national insurance contributions to qualify.
- You can qualify for PIP whether you are in or out of work.
- PIP is administered and paid by the DWP.
- If you disagree with a PIP decision, you can apply for a revision or supersession, or appeal against it. You must apply for a revision before you can appeal.

1. Who can claim personal independence payment

You qualify for personal independence payment (PIP) if:
- you are aged 16 or over[1] and, in most cases, under 65 (see p732);[2]
- you are not a 'person subject to immigration control', although there are some exceptions to this (see p1499);[3]
- you satisfy the residence conditions (see Chapter 70);[4]

- you satisfy the disability conditions for the 'daily living component' (see below), the 'mobility component' (see below) or both;
- in some parts of the country, you are not currently getting disability living allowance (DLA – see p605).

Disability conditions for the daily living component

In addition to satisfying the basic conditions above, you qualify for the daily living component if:[5]

- your ability to undertake 'daily living activities' is limited by your physical or mental condition (for the standard rate), or it is severely limited by your physical or mental condition or you are terminally ill (for the enhanced rate); *and*
- unless you are terminally ill (see p734), you have met the disability conditions for three months and are expected to continue to meet them for a further nine months (known as the 'required period condition' – see p731).

You are assessed against 10 daily living activities:[6]

- preparing food;
- taking nutrition;
- managing therapy or monitoring a health condition;
- washing and bathing;
- managing toilet needs or incontinence;
- dressing and undressing;
- communicating verbally;
- reading and understanding signs, symbols and words;
- engaging with other people face to face;
- making budgeting decisions.

For details of the activities, see Appendix 13. To work out whether you are likely to qualify for the daily living component, see p728.

Disability conditions for the mobility component

In addition to satisfying the basic conditions above, you qualify for the mobility component if:[7]

- your ability to undertake 'mobility activities' is limited by your physical or mental condition (for the standard rate) or it is severely limited by your physical or mental condition (for the enhanced rate); *and*
- unless you are terminally ill (see p734), you have met the disability conditions for three months and are expected to continue to meet them for a further nine months (known as the 'required period condition' – see p731).

You are assessed against two mobility activities:[8]

Part 5: Other benefits
Chapter 35: Personal independence payment
1. Who can claim personal independence payment

- planning and following journeys; *and*
- moving around.

For details of the activities, see Appendix 13. To work out whether you are likely to qualify for the mobility component, see below.

How your disability is assessed

This section explains the rules on how you satisfy the disability conditions. See p736 for the process used to assess your entitlement. Your ability to undertake daily living and/or mobility activities is assessed by a points-based test, which considers how your physical or mental condition affects your ability to undertake a set list of specific activities.[9]

Under each of the daily living and mobility activities, there is a list of statements (called 'descriptors'), which describe different types and levels of help needed with the activity. Each descriptor has a points score, and you are awarded one descriptor for each activity. Descriptors that describe a greater limitation in undertaking the activity score more points. For example, you score more points if you need *assistance* to prepare a simple meal than if you can do so yourself with *prompting* from another person. See p731 for how to decide which descriptor you should be awarded if your needs vary.

For the full list of activities, descriptors and points, see Appendix 13.

Your entitlement to a component is assessed by:

- adding up the descriptors that you satisfy for each activity relevant to that component; *and*
- comparing your total score with a 'threshold' for entitlement to the standard and enhanced rates of the component. The threshold is eight points for the standard rate of a component, and 12 points for the enhanced rate.[10]

Definitions of terms used in the assessment

Many of the terms used in the PIP assessment criteria are defined in the regulations, which restricts their meaning.[11] It is important to consider these restricted meanings as they affect which descriptors you satisfy. Some of the most important examples are listed below. For the full list of definitions, see Appendix 13.

'**Stand**' means to stand upright with at least one biological foot on the ground. This means that, if you have had both feet amputated, you are treated as unable to stand and score 12 points for the moving around activity in the mobility component assessment.

'**Cook**' means to heat food at or above waist height. Your ability to bend down is not relevant to your ability to cook (although it could be relevant to other activities, such as dressing and undressing, or washing and bathing).

'**Read**' includes reading signs, symbols or words, but does not include reading Braille. This means that if you have a severe visual impairment which means that you can *only* read Braille, you are assessed as unable to read.

Types of help that may score points in the assessment

The assessment of your ability to undertake daily living activities distinguishes between different kinds of help that you may need. The terms used across most of the activities are:[12]

- assistance;
- supervision;
- prompting; *and*
- use of an aid or appliance.

For most of the daily living activities, the highest scoring descriptor is awarded if you cannot undertake the activity at all, even with the kinds of help listed above.

The mobility activities are structured differently. The 'moving around' activity awards a different points score depending on how far you can 'stand and then move'. The 'planning and following journeys' activity considers whether you experience 'overwhelming psychological distress', or whether you need 'another person, orientation aid or assistance dog' to help you make journeys.

For both daily living and mobility activities, whether you can undertake activities 'reliably' with these kinds of help must also be considered (see p730).

Assistance, supervision and prompting[13]

'**Assistance**' means physical help from another person with completing some part of an activity. It does not include giving verbal instructions, which counts as 'prompting' instead.

'**Supervision**' means the continuous presence of another person throughout the activity to ensure your safety. The definition used is deliberately different from the definition that applies to disability living allowance (DLA) (see p589), so existing DLA caselaw is unlikely to be helpful in arguing that you require supervision for the purposes of the PIP assessment.

'**Prompting**' means that another person needs to remind or encourage you to carry out an activity, or explain how to do it. The definition does not say that the person prompting you has to be in your presence. This means that prompting by telephone could potentially allow you to score points in the assessment, if you need this help to carry out an activity.

Aids and appliances

You can score points in the assessment if you do not need help from another person, but can only manage an activity 'using an aid or appliance'. The definition of this is something that improves, provides or replaces a function (including a prosthetic limb) – eg, a walking stick, modified cutlery or kitchen utensils needed because of your disability, or adaptations to your home such as grab rails in the shower and a shower seat.[14] If you do not use an aid or appliance when you are assessed, it is taken into account if you could 'reasonably be expected' to use one to help you with the activity.[15]

Part 5: Other benefits
Chapter 35: Personal independence payment
1. Who can claim personal independence payment

> *Could you use an aid or appliance?*
>
> When you could reasonably be expected to use an aid or appliance is not set out in the regulations. Guidance to health professionals suggests that the factors taken into account include:[16]
>
> – whether you have an aid or appliance (and its cost and availability if you do not);
> – your ability to use and store the aid or appliance;
> – what medical advice you would get about using one.
>
> If you are assessed as needing an aid or appliance and you think that this is not reasonable, you can ask for a revision of the decision (see p1270). Try to obtain supporting evidence showing that it is not reasonable for you to use it.

An aid or appliance is not necessarily something that only people with disabilities or health problems use. However, to be awarded points in the assessment because you need to use an aid or appliance, you must need to use it because of your physical or mental condition.

> *Example*
>
> Bill has arthritis in his hands and cannot use a manual tin opener. He uses an electric tin opener and can potentially score points for needing to use an aid or appliance to prepare food, even though an electric tin opener is an appliance that someone without Bill's difficulties might use.

Managing an activity reliably

You are only assessed as being able to undertake an activity at a level described by a descriptor if you can complete it 'reliably'. This means that you are only awarded a particular descriptor (rather than a higher scoring one) if you can undertake the activity at that level:[17]

- safely, in a way that is unlikely to cause harm to you or to anyone else either during or after the activity;
- to an acceptable standard;
- repeatedly – ie, as often as it is reasonably required; *and*
- within a reasonable time period – ie, in no more than twice the maximum time normally taken by someone with no health problems or disabilities to complete the activity.

This leaves a lot of discretion to the decision maker, so you may need to ask for a revision and then appeal, and argue that you cannot undertake activities reliably.

If a descriptor applies to you at some point in a day (ie, 24 hours), you should be awarded points for it, provided this applies on sufficient days in the 'required period' (see p731).

The required period

Usually, you must have met the disability conditions for at least three months before the date you are awarded PIP and be expected to meet them for a further nine months after that date.[18] This is called the 'required period'. If, when you claim PIP, your daily living or mobility needs have not yet lasted for three months, you can be awarded PIP in advance if the decision maker believes that you will satisfy the required period condition in the future.[19]

There is no required period for either component if you claim PIP on the grounds that you have a terminal illness (see p734).[20]

If you claim PIP as part of the transfer from DLA (see p605) or you ceased to be entitled to DLA less than two years ago (one year ago if you are over 65), you do not have to satisfy the three-month past period test. Your needs must still be expected to last for nine months at the date of your claim.[21]

A special rule applies if you used to get PIP and your award ended less than two years ago (one year if you are over 65). If you are reclaiming on the basis of substantially the same condition(s) or a condition that has developed as a result of your previous condition, the three-month past period test relates to the last three months of your previous award. So, if you met the disability conditions for a component during that period, you qualify for PIP from the date of your new claim. Your needs must be expected to last for nine months at the date of your new claim.[22]

Once you have been awarded PIP, your needs must be expected to last for nine months throughout the length of your award.[23] If this is no longer the case, you should report this as a change of circumstances. Seek advice if you think your condition may have improved to the extent that your award could be affected.

Fluctuating conditions

The assessment takes account of changes in your condition. The descriptor within each activity that is applied to you is decided as follows.[24]

- If only one descriptor applies to you for more than 50 per cent of the days in the required period (see above), that descriptor is used.
- If two or more descriptors each apply to you for more than 50 per cent of the days in the required period, the one that scores the most points is used.
- If neither of the above bullet points apply, but the number of days on which you satisfy two or more scoring descriptors totals more than 50 per cent of the days in the required period, the scoring descriptor that applies most often is used. If two descriptors apply on the same number of days, the highest scoring one is used.

Example

Aisha makes a new claim for PIP. The required period is 365 days. On 65 days of the period, she cannot engage with other people, as she has severe depression and anxiety. On 50 days, she needs specialist support to engage with anyone. On a further 100 days, she can

Part 5: Other benefits
Chapter 35: Personal independence payment
2. The rules about your age

manage with prompting and encouragement from a friend or family member. On 150 days she can engage with other people unaided.

The third bullet point on p731 applies, as no single descriptor is satisfied on over half of the days in the required period. Aisha is awarded descriptor 9b (see Appendix 13), as she satisfies one or other scoring descriptor in that activity on 215 days of the required period, and this is the scoring descriptor that applies most often. She needs to score at leat six points from the other daily living activities to be entitled to the daily living component .

It can be very difficult to decide which descriptors you satisfy if your condition fluctuates. It may be helpful for you to keep a diary over several weeks to help explain how your condition affects you.

2. **The rules about your age**

You must be aged 16 or over to claim personal independence payment (PIP).[25] The upper age limit for making a new claim is normally 65.[26] However, there are several exceptions to this upper age limit.

- If you have made a claim for PIP which has not yet been decided when you turn 65, an award can be made to you.[27]
- If you are getting PIP when you reach 65, your existing award continues until its end date, provided you still meet the entitlement conditions.[28]
- If you were previously entitled to either PIP or disability living allowance (DLA), you can claim PIP within one year of your previous award ending despite being over the age of 65. This rule also applies to a renewal claim for PIP made after you turn 65. If you were entitled to DLA, you must have been under 65 on 8 April 2013.[29] If you used to be entitled to PIP, this rule only applies if your new claim is on the basis of the same disability or health problem(s) as your former award, or a new condition that has developed as a result of the original one.[30]
- If you get DLA and are now 65 or over, but were under 65 on 8 April 2013, you can claim PIP if you live in an area in which DLA claims are being transferred to PIP.[31] See p607 if you are in this situation and thinking about claiming PIP.

Future changes
The upper age limit for claiming PIP will gradually increase from 65 to 66 between 2018 and 2020.

Mobility component for people over 65

If you are entitled to the mobility component when you reach your 65th birthday, you continue to get it for as long as your award of PIP lasts, provided you continue to meet the rules on entitlement. However, if you make a new claim (including a renewal claim), special rules apply.

- You only qualify for the enhanced rate of the mobility component if you meet the normal entitlement conditions for that rate and you got the enhanced rate in an award which ended less than one year before you claim.[32]
- You qualify for the standard rate if you meet the normal entitlement conditions and got either rate of the mobility component in an award which ended less than one year before you claim.[33]

In either case, your entitlement must be on the basis of the same condition(s) as your former award, or a new condition that has developed as a result of the original one.[34]

If your existing award of PIP is revised or superseded because of a change that happens after you reach 65, you can only be awarded the mobility component if you currently get it, or ceased to get it less than a year before the date on which the decision takes effect.[35] Also, to continue to get the mobility component at the same rate, your entitlement must be based on substantially the same condition(s) as those for which you were previously awarded it.[36] You can move from the enhanced rate to the standard rate (even if your mobility needs result from a new condition),[37] but you cannot qualify for the standard rate for the first time or move from the standard rate to the enhanced rate.[38]

There are no restrictions on your entitlement to the mobility component because of your age if you were under 65 on 8 April 2013 and either you get DLA and are claiming PIP as part of the transfer process (see p605) or you stopped getting DLA less than a year ago.[39]

3. People included in the claim

You claim personal indendence payment (PIP) for yourself. You cannot claim any increase in your PIP for your partner or child(ren). However, your partner may qualify for PIP, attendance allowance (AA) or disability living allowance (DLA) in her/his own right. Your child may qualify for DLA, or for PIP in her/his own right when s/he turns 16. See Chapter 23 for information about AA and Chapter 27 for information about DLA.

Part 5: Other benefits
Chapter 35: Personal independence payment
5. Special benefit rules

4. **The amount of benefit**

The daily living component of personal independence payment (PIP) is paid at one of two weekly rates:[40]
- the standard rate is £54.45;
- the enhanced rate is £81.30.

The mobility component of PIP is paid at one of two weekly rates:[41]
- the standard rate is £21.55;
- the enhanced rate is £56.75.

5. **Special benefit rules**

Special rules apply to:
- people who are terminally ill (see below);
- people in hospital (see p941);
- people in residential care (see p951);
- prisoners (see p959);
- people who have come from or are going abroad (see Chapters 70 and 71);
- people 'subject to immigration control' (see Chapter 69).

Terminal illness

You are regarded as 'terminally ill' if you have a progressive disease and can reasonably be expected to die within six months as a result of that disease.[42] If you claim personal independence payment (PIP) and you are terminally ill, you are automatically treated as satisfying the disability conditions for the enhanced rate of the daily living component, and you do not have to satisfy the required period condition (see p731) – ie, you can get PIP as soon as you are accepted as terminally ill.[43] You still have to satisfy the disability conditions for the mobility component, but the required period condition is waived.[44] If you are claiming PIP because you are terminally ill, it does not matter how long you have lived in the UK.[45] However, there are other residence and presence tests that you must satisfy. See p1555 for more details.

Someone else can make a claim for PIP on behalf of a terminally ill person without her/his knowledge or authority.[46]

Note: the process of claiming PIP is different for terminally ill claimants (see p735).

6. Claims and backdating

To be entitled to personal independence payment (PIP), you must make a claim for it.[47] The general rules about claims and backdating are in Chapter 53. This section explains the specific rules that apply to PIP.

Note: if you currently get disability living allowance or have recently been refused it, you should think carefully about whether to claim PIP or not (see p606).

Making a claim

A claim for PIP must be made either by telephone or in writing by completing an approved form (this includes completing an online claim form when this service is introduced).[48] Claims for PIP are normally made by telephone.[49] If you are unable to make a claim by phone, you can ask for a paper claim form to be sent to you.[50] An online claims facility may be introduced from some time in 2015. See CPAG's online service and *Welfare Rights Bulletin* for updates.

> **Forms**
>
> The easiest way to make a claim or get a claim form (PIP1) sent to you is by phoning 0800 917 2222 (textphone 0800 917 7777). Before sending you a claim form, the DWP must accept that you cannot claim by phone. You *cannot* get a claim form at your local disablity benefits centre, Citizens Advice Bureau, welfare rights service or advice centre. If you cannot use the phone and there is no one to help you, write asking for a claim form to Personal Independence Payment New Claims, Post Handling Site B, Wolverhampton WV99 1AH. This will delay your date of claim. Unless you have clearly explained why you are unable to claim by phone, the DWP may phone you to try to take a telephone claim from you.

People who are terminally ill

The process of claiming and being assessed is different for people who are terminally ill. You should explain that your claim is on the grounds of terminal illness when making it. Your GP or hospital consultant should also complete Form DS1500, giving details of your medical condition.

You are asked questions about your mobility needs as part of your claim. If you are accepted as terminally ill, you are not asked to complete a separate questionnaire, or attend a face-to-face consultation, although the DWP still gets advice about the decision on your claim from a health professional.[51]

Someone else can claim PIP on behalf of a person who is terminally ill without her/his knowledge or authority.[52]

If you have claimed PIP on someone else's behalf, you can also ask for a revision or supersession (see p1267), or appeal against the decision without her/his knowedge or authority.[53]

Part 5: Other benefits
Chapter 35: Personal independence payment
6. Claims and backdating

Who should claim

A claim for PIP should be made by the person entitled to it. However, if you are unable to manage your own affairs, another person can claim PIP for you as your 'appointee' (see p1137). A claim can also be made on behalf of someone who is terminally ill without her/his knowledge or permission (see p735).

Information to support your claim

When you claim PIP, you must:
* satisfy the national insurance (NI) number requirement (see p1138); *and*
* provide proof of your identity, if required (see p1140).

It is important that you complete your claim properly and provide any information or evidence required when you claim. Until you do, you may not count as having made a valid claim. See p1140 for further information about valid claims.

You must provide any information required to support your claim. There is then an evidence-gathering process to help the decision maker decide whether you satisfy the disability conditions for the two components (see p727).

The assessment process

You may be required to:[54]
* provide information or evidence about your ability to undertake daily living or mobility activities (normally in the form of a questionnaire); *and*
* attend and participate in a consultation with a health professional.

The majority of claims involve a face-to-face consultation with a health professional, who is also responsible for gathering other evidence from someone who knows you, if s/he thinks this is needed. S/he then advises the DWP decision maker, who makes a decision on your claim.

The questionnaire

Once the DWP decides that you meet the basic eligibility conditions for PIP, you are sent a questionnaire asking for more information about how your disability or health problem affects you. You are asked specific questions relating to the 10 daily living activities and the two mobility activities set out in Appendix 13.

How should you complete the questionnaire?
1. Read the notes on the form before answering the questions. It may be helpful to draft your answers on a separate sheet of paper first.
2. Many advice agencies can help you to complete benefit forms.
If you have any difficulties with English or with reading and writing, you should always get help to complete the form.

3. If someone else fills in the questionnaire for you, or you are only able to do so yourself slowly, or with pain, explain this.

4. Compare the draft of your answers with the list in Appendix 13 to work out your likely score. Your answers should not be exaggerated, but check that you have not underestimated any of your problems and that you have given all the detail you can.

5. Remember that many of the terms in the assessment have special definitions (see p728). For example, 'dressing and undressing' includes your ability to manage putting on or taking off shoes and socks.

6. If you have good and bad days, explain this. You may need different types of help (see p729) with an activity on different days. If so, try to explain how often you need each kind of help, as this is also relevant to the points that you score (see p731).

7. List any aids or appliances (see p729) that you need to help you complete an activity, and any problems that you have using them.

8. If an activity takes you a long time, puts you at risk, or you can only complete it to a low standard, explain this (see p730).

9. If you eventually have to appeal, the First-tier Tribunal may be less likely to believe your account of the effects of your health problems or disability if you did not mention them on the questionnaire. It is a good idea to ask someone who knows you well to check that your answers explain fully the help you need.

10. If you have any additional information that is relevant to your difficulties with daily living or mobility activities, you can send this with the questionnaire. This might include a report from an occupational therapist or consultant, information from your doctor or a support worker, or a statement from a friend or family member. If you are unsure whether evidence is helpful or not, check carefully how closely the content corresponds to the activities in the assessment.

11. Always make a copy of your questionnaire with your answers before returning it to the DWP, and keep a copy of any additional information that you send with it.

On receiving your completed questionnaire, the DWP sends it to a health professional who decides what other evidence s/he thinks is needed to decide your claim. This is likely to include asking you to participate in a consultation (see p738).

If you do not return the questionnaire

Usually, you have one month from the day it was sent to you to return the questionnaire. You may be allowed longer, if this is considered to be reasonable by the decision maker.[55] If you do not return the questionnaire, your claim is refused, unless you can show that you have a good reason for not returning it.[56] In deciding whether you have a good reason, the decision maker must take into account the state of your health and/or the nature of your disability.[57] Any other reasons can also be considered. Guidance suggests that if the DWP knows that you have a mental or cognitive impairment and you do not return the

Part 5: Other benefits
Chapter 35: Personal independence payment
6. Claims and backdating

questionnaire, your claim will not be disallowed, but instead referred to a health professional.[58] However, the regulations do not mention this, so you should always try to return the questionnaire if you are able to do so.

If you are late in completing the questionnaire, contact the DWP immediately and explain why, and ask for an extension of time. You should complete and return it as soon as possible. If your claim is refused because you have failed to return the questionnaire without a good reason, write to the DWP explaining your reasons and ask for a revision of the decision (see p1280). You should also make a new claim in case your request is unsuccessful.

The consultation

You can be asked to participate in a consultation with a health professional to help the decision maker assess how you are affected by your condition(s).

Who assesses you?

Two companies are contracted by the DWP to carry out PIP consultations. Broadly speaking, if you live in Scotland, Northern England, London, Southern England or East Anglia, the contractor is Atos. If you live in the Midlands, Wales or Northern Ireland, it is Capita. There is a more detailed map showing postcode areas covered by each, available at www.gov.uk/government/publications/pip-postcode-map-uk.

Atos or Capita should contact you to explain what you need to do. You can find more information from www.capita-pip.co.uk or www.atoshealthcare.com/pip.

Before deciding whether you need to have a consultation, the health professional decides whether to ask for evidence from someone who knows you. It is possible that a health professional will prepare a report for the decision maker without the need for a consultation.[59]

Most people have a consultation as part of the process of claiming PIP. It could be by telephone or face to face (either in an assessment centre or in your own home).[60] You can take someone to the consultation to support you, and s/he can also give information to the health professional.[61] In order to produce a report for the decision maker, the health professional asks you questions about your condition and how you manage the different daily living and mobility activities set out in Appendix 13.

What should you do at the consultation?

1. Tell the health professional as much as possible about how you are affected by your condition(s).

2. Remember that the assessment report can also include informal observations of your behaviour – eg, your ability to walk from the waiting area and whether you have attended the consultation by yourself.

3. If you have had to take additional painkillers to attend the consultation, explain this, and also what you can and cannot do taking your normal dose.

4. If you have good and bad days, make sure that you explain this, and how your needs are different on a bad day. This is especially important if you are assessed on a good day.

5. If you are not fluent in English, it is vital that someone who is fluent in English attends with you. Contact the assessment provider as soon as possible if you want an interpreter arranged.

If you do not participate in a consultation

If you do not participate in the consultation (including if you do not attend an assessment centre) and you do not have a good reason, your claim is refused.[62] You must have been sent written notice of the date and time of the consultation (and, for face-to-face consultations, the location of the assessment centre) at least seven days in advance, unless you agreed to accept less notice.[63] If you have agreed to receive information from the DWP by email, 'written notice' includes notice sent to you by email.[64]

In deciding whether you have good reason for not participating in the consultation, the state of your health and/or the nature of your disability must be considered.[65] Anything else that stopped you from participating may also be relevant.

If your claim is refused because you did not participate in a consultation without good reason, write to the DWP and explain why you were unable to participate, and ask for a revision of the decision (see p1280). You should also make a new claim in case your request is unsuccessful.

The date of your claim

Generally, if you are not already getting disability living allowance (DLA), claim PIP as soon as you think you might be entitled. If you get DLA, see p606 to help you decide whether to claim PIP. If you claim by telephone, your date of claim is the date of your phone call.[66] If your claim is considered 'defective', the DWP must advise you of this.[67] If you correct the defect within one month (or longer if considered reasonable), your date of claim is still the date you first made the claim.[68]

If you claim the wrong benefit

If you have claimed PIP but the decision maker thinks that you are not entitled to it, your claim can be treated as a claim for DLA or attendance allowance (AA).[69] If you have claimed AA or DLA but the decision maker thinks that you are not entitled to it, your claim for that benefit can be treated as a claim for PIP.[70] See p1144 for further information.

In either case, your claim is treated as having been made on the day you claimed the first benefit.[71]

Claiming in advance

You can claim PIP in advance if, at the time you make a claim, you do not satisfy the 'required period condition' (see p731), but will do so within three months of the date your claim is decided.[72] If you already get PIP, you can make a renewal claim up to six months before your award ends.[73]

Backdating your claim

You cannot backdate your claim for PIP, even if you would have qualified had you claimed sooner.[74]

7. **Getting paid**

Payment of personal independence payment (PIP) is normally made by direct credit transfer into your bank (or similar) account (see p1163). If you are unable to open or manage an account, it may be possible to be paid by 'simple payment' (see p1163). Payment can also be made to someone else on your behalf, called your 'appointee' (see p1137), if you are unable to act for yourself. Also, payment may be made to someone else on your behalf if the decision maker thinks that it is needed to protect your interests.[75]

When is personal independence payment paid?

PIP is usually paid on the same day of the week as the decision was made on your claim (unless this was a Saturday or Sunday). The day on which you are paid can be changed by the DWP.[76] PIP is usually paid every four weeks in arrears. If you are terminally ill, PIP can be paid weekly in advance.[77]

Note: the enhanced rate of the mobility component can be paid directly to the Motability scheme (see p744) if you are buying or leasing a car through the scheme.[78]

- Even if you have been sanctioned for a benefit offence (see p1258), you must be paid PIP.
- If you have forgotten your PIN, see p1163. If your 'simple payment' card has been lost or stolen, or if you have forgotten your memorable date, see p1164. For information on missing payments, see p1164.

- If payment of your PIP is delayed, see p1382. If you wish to complain about how your claim has been dealt with, see p1383. You might be able to claim compensation (see p1382).
- If payment of your PIP is suspended, see p1175.
- If you are overpaid PIP, you might have to repay it (see Chapter 56) and, in some circumstances, you may have to pay a penalty (see p1249). If you have been accused of fraud, see Chapter 57.

Length of awards

Awards of PIP are normally made for a fixed period – eg, one, two or five years. The length of award depends on how likely your needs are to change over time. If you are awarded PIP for a short period, you should be reminded to reclaim PIP before your award ends if your needs have not changed.[79] If you are awarded it for longer, your case should be referred for review by a health professional a year before it is due to end.[80] It is intended that the process of reviewing your award will be similar to the process of assessing new claims (see p736). You can make a new claim for PIP up to six months before your award is due to end.[81]

Indefinite awards can sometimes be made. The decision maker must follow official guidance when making an indefinite award.[82] It is likely that indefinite awards will also be periodically reviewed to check that they are still correct.[83]

If you think that PIP should have been awarded for a longer period, you can ask for the decision about the length of your award to be revised (see p1270). However, if you do this, it is possible that the decision maker could also reconsider the amount of benefit that you have been awarded.

Note: the DWP can choose to reassess your entitlement to PIP at any time after it has been awarded.[84]

Change of circumstances

You must report any changes in your circumstances that you have been told you must report, as well as any that you might reasonably be expected to know might affect your right to, the amount of, or the payment of, your benefit. You should do this as soon as possible, preferably in writing. See p1174 for further information.

If there has been a relevant change of circumstances, a decision maker looks at your claim again and makes a new decision. To find out the date from which the new decision takes effect, see p1287.

8. Tax, other benefits and the benefit cap

Tax

Personal independence payment (PIP) is not taxable.[85]

Part 5: Other benefits
Chapter 35: Personal independence payment
8. Tax, other benefits and the benefit cap

Means-tested benefits

PIP is not taken into account as income when calculating any of the means-tested benefits. PIP is paid on top of these benefits, and getting PIP can increase the amount you get.

If you or your partner are entitled to PIP, your income support (IS), income-based jobseeker's allowance (JSA) and, unless you have reached the qualifying age for pension credit (PC), housing benefit (HB) includes the disability premium (see p229) (or, for IS and JSA only, higher pensioner premium (see p232) if either of you have reached the qualifying age for PC). If you or your partner are entitled to the enhanced rate of the daily living component and are under the qualifying age for PC, you also get an enhanced disability premium. This is also paid with income-related employment and support allowance (ESA – see p231). A severe disability premium/addition is included in IS, income-based JSA, income-related ESA, the guarantee credit of PC and HB if you receive either rate of the daily living component and meet the other conditions for that premium. For further information, see p233.

If your child is entitled to PIP and still counts as part of your household, your HB includes a disabled child premium (see p228). If s/he gets the enhanced rate of the daily living component, your HB includes an enhanced disability premium. These premiums are also included in IS and income-based JSA if you do not yet get child tax credit (CTC). If your child is entitled to PIP and still counts as part of your household, if you come under the universal credit (UC) system (see p19), your UC includes a disabled child addition. This is paid at the higher rate if s/he is entitled to the enhanced rate of the daily living component (see p250).

If you or your partner are entitled to PIP daily living component, non-dependant deductions (see p450) are not made from any housing costs included in your HB, IS, income-based JSA, income-related ESA and the guarantee credit of PC. No housing costs contributions from a non-dependant are taken into account when calculating your UC housing costs if you, your partner or the non-dependant receive the daily living component (see p496).

If you or your partner have reached the qualifying age for PC but you must claim UC because the other person has not yet reached this age, and the person over PC age is entitled to PIP, you qualify for a limited capability for work element in your UC award (see p251). If the person over PC age is entitled to the enhanced rate of the daily living component, you get the limited capability for work-related activity element in your UC award instead (see p252).

Non-means-tested benefits

PIP may be paid in addition to any other non-means-tested benefits, except that:
- if you are entitled to PIP, you cannot claim disability living allowance[86] or attendance allowance;[87]
- PIP overlaps with armed forces independence payment (see p835);[88]

- PIP daily living component overlaps with constant attendance allowance under the industrial injuries scheme (see p679) or war pensions scheme;[89]
- PIP mobility component overlaps with the war pensioners' mobility supplement payable under the war pensions scheme, or grants for the use of a vehicle from the NHS.[90]

If you are receiving the daily living component of PIP and someone regularly looks after you, that person may be entitled to carer's allowance (CA – see Chapter 25). However, your entitlement to a severe disability premium (or additional amount in PC) can be affected if s/he receives CA, so you should always seek advice.

Tax credits

PIP is ignored as income when calculating CTC and working tax credit (WTC).[91] A disabled child element is included in CTC for each child who gets PIP (at any rate). If s/he gets the enhanced rate of the daily living component, you also get a severely disabled child element in your CTC. An award of PIP at any rate counts as a qualifying benefit for the disabled worker element in WTC. If you or your partner get the enhanced rate of the daily living component, a severe disability element is included in WTC. See Chapter 63 for further information.

The benefit cap

In some cases, the total amount of specified benefits you receive is limited to £350 a week (if you are a single claimant without children) or £500 a week (if you are a lone parent or a member of a couple). This is known as the 'benefit cap'. PIP is *not* one of the specified benefits. The benefit cap only applies if you are getting HB or UC. The benefit cap does *not* apply if you or your partner or child receive PIP, or are entitled to PIP but it is not payable because you (or s/he) are in hospital or a care home. See p1169 for further information.

Passports and other sources of help

You qualify for a Christmas bonus if you receive PIP (see p835).[92]

If you get PIP, you may be entitled to other 'passported' benefits such as a 'blue badge' or a concessionary travel card. Contact your local authority for more information.

If you get the PIP mobility component and you or your carer have a car used only by you or for you, your vehicle excise duty (road tax) is reduced. If you get the enhanced rate of the PIP mobility component, you are exempt from the duty; if you get the standard rate, you get a 50 per cent reduction.

If you have a low income, you may be entitled to council tax reduction (see p827).

Motability

Motability is a charity that runs a scheme to help you lease or buy a car if you receive the enhanced rate of the PIP mobility component and have 12 months or more left to run on your award.

PIP mobility component is paid directly to Motability.[93] You may also have to make extra payments. For further information, telephone 0300 456 4566 or visit www.motability.co.uk.

Notes

5

1. Who can claim personal independence payment
1 Reg 5 PIP(TP) Regs
2 s83 WRA 2012; Part 6 SS(PIP) Regs
3 s115(1) IAA 1999
4 ss77(3) and 84 WRA 2012; Part 4 SS(PIP) Regs
5 s78 WRA 2012
6 Sch 1 Part 2 SS(PIP) Regs
7 s79 WRA 2012
8 Sch 1 Part 3 SS(PIP) Regs
9 Part 2 and Sch 1 SS(PIP) Regs
10 Regs 5 and 6 SS(PIP) Regs
11 Sch 1 Part 1 SS(PIP) Regs
12 Sch 1 SS(PIP) Regs
13 Sch 1 Part 1 SS(PIP) Regs
14 Reg 2 SS(PIP) Regs
15 Reg 4(2) SS(PIP) Regs
16 DWP, *PIP Assessment Guide*, 4 July 2013, p76
17 Reg 4(2A) and (4) SS(PIP) Regs
18 Regs 12-14 SS(PIP) Regs
19 Reg 33(1) UC,PIP,JSA&ESA(C&P) Regs
20 s82(2) and (3) WRA 2012
21 Reg 23 PIP(TP) Regs
22 Regs 15 and 26 SS(PIP) Regs
23 Reg 14(b) SS(PIP) Regs
24 Reg 7 SS(PIP) Regs

2. The rules about your age
25 Reg 5 PIP(TP) Regs
26 s83(2) WRA 2012
27 Reg 25(b) SS(PIP) Regs
28 Reg 25(a) SS(PIP) Regs
29 Reg 27(3) PIP(TP) Regs
30 Regs 15 and 26 SS(PIP) Regs
31 Regs 4 and 27 PIP(TP) Regs

32 Reg 26(2)(c)(i) SS(PIP) Regs
33 Reg 26(2)(c)(ii) and (d) SS(PIP) Regs
34 Regs 15 and 26 SS(PIP) Regs
35 Reg 27 SS(PIP) Regs
36 Reg 27(3)(a)(ii) and (3)(b) SS(PIP) Regs
37 Reg 27(3) SS(PIP) Regs
38 Reg 27(3)(a)(i) and (4) SS(PIP) Regs
39 This is because the definitions of 'previous award' and 'component' in reg 2 SS(PIP) Regs mean that regs 15 and 26 of those regulations only apply to people making a claim for PIP after the age of 65 who have had a previous PIP award.

4. The amount of benefit
40 Reg 24(1) SS(PIP) Regs
41 Reg 24(2) SS(PIP) Regs

5. Special benefit rules
42 s82(4) WRA 2012
43 s82(2) WRA 2012
44 s82(3) WRA 2012
45 Reg 21 SS(PIP) Regs
46 s82(5) WRA 2012

6. Claims and backdating
47 s1 SSAA 1992
48 Regs 2 and 11(1) UC,PIP,JSA&ESA(C&P) Regs
49 DWP, *Personal Independence Payment: the claimant journey*, 28 October 2013
50 DWP, *Personal Independence Payment: the claimant journey*, 28 October 2013
51 DWP, *PIP Assessment Guide*, 4 July 2013, pp21-25
52 s82(5) WRA 2012

53 Reg 49(c) UC,PIP,JSA&ESA(DA) Regs
54 s80(3)-(6) WRA 2012; regs 8 and 9
SS(PIP) Regs
55 Reg 8(1) and (2) SS(PIP) Regs
56 Reg 8(3) SS(PIP) Regs
57 Reg 10 SS(PIP) Regs
58 DWP, *PIP Assessment Guide*, 4 July 2013,
p56
59 DWP, *PIP Assessment Guide*, 4 July 2013,
p26
60 Reg 9(1) SS(PIP) Regs
61 DWP, *PIP Assessment Guide*, 4 July 2013,
p37
62 Reg 9(2) SS(PIP) Regs
63 Reg 9(3) SS(PIP) Regs
64 Reg 9(4) SS(PIP) Regs
65 Reg 10 SS(PIP) Regs
66 Reg 12 UC,PIP,JSA&ESA(C&P) Regs
67 Reg 11(5) UC,PIP,JSA&ESA(C&P) Regs
68 Reg 11(6) UC,PIP,JSA&ESA(C&P) Regs
69 Reg 25(3) UC,PIP,JSA&ESA(C&P) Regs
70 Reg 25(4) UC,PIP,JSA&ESA(C&P) Regs
71 Reg 25(5) UC,PIP,JSA&ESA(C&P) Regs
72 Reg 33(1) UC,PIP,JSA&ESA(C&P) Regs
73 Reg 33(2) UC,PIP,JSA&ESA(C&P) Regs
74 Reg 27 UC,PIP,JSA&ESA(C&P) Regs

7. Getting paid
75 Reg 58(2) UC,PIP,JSA&ESA(C&P) Regs
76 Reg 49 UC,PIP,JSA&ESA(C&P) Regs
77 Reg 48(2) UC,PIP,JSA&ESA(C&P) Regs
78 Reg 62 UC,PIP,JSA&ESA(C&P) Regs
79 para P2063 ADM
80 para P2061 ADM
81 Reg 33(2) UC,PIP,JSA&ESA(C&P) Regs
82 s88(2) and (3) WRA 2012. At the time of
writing, the guidance had not been
made public.
83 para P2063 ADM
84 Reg 11 SS(PIP) Regs

8. Tax, other benefits and the benefit cap
85 s677(1) IT(EP)A 2003
86 Reg 22(1) PIP(TP) Regs
87 s64(1) and (1A) SSCBA 1992
88 Sch 1 para 5a SS(OB) Regs
89 Sch 1 para 5 SS(OB) Regs
90 Reg 61 UC,PIP,JSA&ESA(C&P) Regs
91 Reg 7(3) TC(DCI) Regs
92 s150(1)(bb) SSCBA 1992
93 Regs 62, 63 and
64 UC,PIP,JSA&ESA(C&P) Regs

Chapter 36

. . . .

Retirement pensions

This chapter covers:

This chapter covers the rules that apply to people who become eligible for state retirement pension on or after 6 April 2010. For details of the rules for people claiming pensions before this date, see the 2009/10 edition of this *Handbook*. For details of the changes to the contribution conditions, see Chapter 41.

Key facts

- State retirement pension is a non-means-tested, contributory benefit, paid to people who have reached pension age.
- There are different categories of state retirement pension: **Category A**, based on your national insurance (NI) contribution record, **Category B**, based on your spouse's or civil partner's NI contribution record, and **Category D**, which is non-contributory.
- You can qualify whether or not you are in or out of work.
- Retirement pension is affected by the overlapping benefit rules.
- Retirement pension is administered and paid by the Pension Service, which is part of the DWP.
- If you disagree with a decision on your retirement pension, you can apply for a revision or a supersession, or appeal against it. You are likely to have to apply for a revision before you can appeal.

* *

Future changes

At the time of writing, a Pensions Bill was going through Parliament. This proposes to replace the current state pension system with a single-tier, flat-rate pension from 6 April 2016. It will apply to future pensioners only.

* *

---

1. Who can claim a retirement pension

There are three main categories of retirement pension:
- Category A retirement pension, based on your own national insurance (NI) contribution record;
- Category B retirement pension, based on your spouse's or civil partner's (or late spouse's or civil partner's) NI record;
- Category D retirement pension, a non-contributory pension payable to those over 80.

The type of pension you receive largely depends on your contribution record. See Chapter 41 for full details of the contribution conditions for pensions.

You can get a retirement pension when you reach pension age (see p752).

You do not automatically become entitled to your retirement pension just by reaching pension age. You must claim, unless you fall within the exceptions on p756. If you do not claim, you are treated as having deferred your retirement (see p751).

You do not have to retire from work. If you decide to carry on working, your earnings do not reduce the pension you receive. However, the amount of tax you pay may increase because state retirement pension is taxable.

There are some groups of claimants to whom special rules apply (see p754).

Under the Gender Recognition Act 2004, if you are a transgender person and have been granted a full gender recognition certificate, your retirement pension is paid on the basis of your acquired gender. For periods before 6 April 2005, your retirement pension is also based on your acquired gender if you have undergone gender reassignment surgery, on the basis that, under the European Equal Treatment Directive (Directive 79/9), it would be discriminatory not to do so.[1]

* *

Same-sex marriages and retirement pensions

The Marriage (Same Sex Couples) Act 2013 provides for same-sex marriages in England and Wales. Same-sex marriages in Scotland are expected to be possible from autumn 2014. References to marriage in this chapter also apply to same-sex marriages. See CPAG's online service and *Welfare Rights Bulletin* for updates.

The Act contains special rules on entitlement to Category B retirement pension and graduated retirement pension if you are a woman married to a woman who was previously your husband but, at the time of writing, these were not yet in force.[2]

Category A retirement pension

You qualify for a Category A pension if:[3]
- you satisfy the contribution conditions (see p866) on the basis of your own contribution record. If you do not satisfy the contribution conditions, you may qualify based on the contributions of your late or former spouse or civil partner; *and*
- you are over pension age.

Category B retirement pension

You qualify for a Category B pension if:[4]
- you were married or had a civil partner when you reached pension age (or married or formed a civil partnership after that age); *or*
- you are a widow, widower or surviving civil partner; *or*
- you were entitled to widowed parent's allowance immediately before reaching pension age and have not remarried or formed a new civil partnership;[5] *or*
- in certain circumstances (see p749), you were entitled to widowed parent's allowance or bereavement allowance before reaching pension age.[6]

Married people and civil partners

If you are married or have a civil partner (but see exceptions below), you are entitled to a Category B retirement pension if:
- you and your spouse or civil partner have both reached pension age; *and*
- your spouse or civil partner satisfies the relevant contribution conditions.

For married men, civil partners, and those in same sex-marriages, entitlement is restricted to those whose wives, civil partners or same-sex spouses were born on or after 6 April 1950.

Widows, widowers and surviving civil partners

If you are a widow, widower or surviving civil partner, your entitlement depends on:
- whether you became a widow, widower or surviving civil partner before or after reaching pension age; *and*
- the date on which you became a widow, widower or surviving civil partner.

Women widowed after pension age

You are entitled to a Category B retirement pension based on your late husband's contributions if:[7]

- you were married to him when he died; *and*
- he satisfied the relevant contribution conditions.

Men widowed after pension age

If you are a man widowed after reaching pension age before 6 April 2010, you are entitled to a Category B retirement pension based on your late wife's contributions if:[8]

- she died on or after 6 April 1979 and you were married to her when she died; *and*
- both of you had reached pension age when she died; *and*
- she satisfied the relevant contribution conditions.

If you are a man widowed after reaching pension age on or after 6 April 2010, you are entitled to a Category B retirement pension based on your late wife's contributions if:[9]

- you were married to her when she died; *and*
- she satisfied the relevant contribution conditions.

Surviving civil partners and surviving spouses of a same-sex marriage after pension age

If you reached pension age before 6 April 2010 and your civil partner or same-sex spouse dies, you are entitled to a Category B retirement pension based on your late civil partner's or late spouse's contributions if:[10]

- you were civil partners or married; *and*
- you had both reached pension age when your civil partner or spouse died; *and*
- your civil partner or spouse satisfied the relevant contribution conditions.

If you reached pension age on or after 6 April 2010 and your civil partner or same-sex spouse dies, you are entitled to a Category B retirement pension on your late civil partner's or late spouse's contributions if:[11]

- you were civil partners or married; *and*
- your civil partner or spouse satisfied the relevant contribution conditions.

Widowed people and surviving civil partners before pension age

If you were widowed on or after 9 April 2001, or you are a person who becomes a surviving civil partner on or after 5 December 2005, and you have now reached pension age, you are entitled to a Category B retirement pension based on the contributions of your late spouse or civil partner if:[12]

- because of the death of your late spouse or civil partner, you were entitled to bereavement allowance at any time before reaching pension age, or widowed parent's allowance at any time when you are over age 45 but not immediately before reaching pension age; *and*

• following the death of your spouse or civil partner, you have not remarried or formed a new civil partnership.

When Category B retirement pension can be paid

Once you qualify for a Category B retirement pension, it is paid for life. It does not cease if you live with a new partner, remarry or form a civil partnership.[13] If you are approaching pension age and considering remarriage, assess your position and, if necessary, take advice. There may be financial benefits in postponing any wedding or civil partnership so that you are still a widow, widower or surviving civil partner immediately before attaining pension age. Seek financial advice before deciding what to do.

Category D retirement pension

You qualify for a Category D pension if:[14]

• you are aged 80 or over;

• you were ordinarily resident in Great Britain (see p1519) on the day you reached the age of 80;

• you have been resident in Great Britain for a period of at least 10 years in any continuous period of 20 years immediately before you reached the age of 80; *and*

• you are entitled either to no other retirement pension or to an amount of retirement pension less than the current rate of a Category D retirement pension.

Graduated retirement benefit

'Graduated retirement benefit' is an increase in the weekly rate of retirement pension. However, although described as an increase in pension rate, graduated retirement benefit can be paid to a person over pension age who is not entitled to a retirement pension because s/he does not satisfy the NI contribution conditions.[15] Between 1961 and 6 April 1975, those paying flat-rate Class 1 contributions also paid graduated contributions. Payment of graduated contributions ceased on 5 April 1975.

You are also entitled to an age addition of 25 pence a week if you are over 80 and receiving graduated retirement benefit even if you are not receiving any other retirement pension.[16]

If you are a widow, you may add half of your husband's entitlement to your own. A widower may also add half his wife's entitlement to his own.[17] From 5 December 2005, this rule also applies to surviving civil partners. The Marriage (Same Sex Couples) Act 2013 makes provision to extend entitlement to the surviving spouse of a same-sex marriage on the same terms as currently apply to widowers and surviving civil partners. Widowers, surviving civil partners and surviving spouses of same-sex marriages who reach state pension age before 6 April 2010 can only inherit graduated retirement benefit if both parties are over state pension age when the spouse or civil partner dies. This restriction does not apply to widows.

If you are entitled to only a very small amount, however, you receive a lump-sum payment instead of weekly payments. Graduated retirement pension is increased if you defer entitlement to a retirement pension (see below).[18]

Deferring your retirement pension

Once you have reached pension age, you are allowed to defer your entitlement to a Category A or Category B retirement pension. In return for doing so, you later become entitled to a higher rate of pension or a lump sum.[19]

The same applies to graduated retirement benefit (see p750).[20] You can choose to defer your pension before you claim it or, if you are already claiming your pension, you can choose to stop getting it in order to get more later on – but you can only do this once.[21] To stop claiming, you must notify the Pension Service by telephone or in writing.[22] You can choose to have a higher rate of pension or the same rate of pension paid with a one-off lump sum. To get a lump sum, you have to defer your pension for 12 months or more. For periods in which you defer your pension after 6 April 2005, your pension is increased by one-fifth of 1 per cent for each week of deferment (10.4 per cent for each year). For example, if you defer your pension for 12 months, it would increase by 10.4 per cent, which would be approximately £1 for every £10 of state pension. You are not entitled to any increase unless you defer your pension for long enough to earn an increase of at least 1 per cent.[23] A one-off lump sum is based on the amount of pension that you would have received had you not deferred your claim, plus interest.[24] If you choose a lump sum and the capital rules for people over pension age apply (see Chapter 18), it is ignored as capital indefinitely for pension credit (PC) and housing benefit (see p382). However, periods on PC affect the deferred amount (see p752). The DWP publishes *State Pension Deferral: your guide*, available from www.gov.uk/deferring-state-pension.

The amounts that are increased in this way include any additional pension under the additional state pension scheme (see p760), an incapacity increase and any increase resulting from your late spouse's or civil partner's deferment, but not increases for dependants or age additions.[25]

You may be entitled to claim the extra pension accrued from your late spouse's or late civil partner's deferment when you claim your own pension, provided you were still married or in the civil partnership at the time s/he died and you have not remarried or formed a new civil partnership before you reach pension age.[26] If you are a man or in a civil partnership, you must also be over pension age at the time your wife or civil partner dies. However, this condition does not apply to widowers and civil partners who reached pension age on or after 6 April 2010. If you were under pension age when your wife or civil partner died and you reached pension age before 6 April 2010, you can claim up to three months of your late wife's or civil partner's deferred pension, but not a lump sum.[27]

You do not receive an increase in pension for any period that you receive any other contributory benefit, severe disablement allowance, carer's allowance or maternity allowance,[28] nor for any day when you would have been disqualified from receiving a Category A or B retirement pension because you were in prison.

In addition, for periods on or after 6 April 2011, you cannot gain an increase in pension for any period in which you are in receipt of PC or your partner is in receipt of PC, universal credit, income support, income-based jobseeker's allowance or income-related employment and support allowance. If you are receiving a means-tested benefit, deferring your retirement pension may lead to a problem under the notional income rules. These sometimes entitle the DWP to treat you as if you were claiming your pension when your entitlement to benefit is calculated, even if you are not. For further details of the notional income rules, see p288.

2. **The rules about your age**

Category A or B pension can be claimed when you reach pension age. Category D pension can be claimed if you are over 80.

If you are a man, your pension age is currently 65, and if you are a woman, your pension age is between 60 and 65, depending on your date of birth (see Appendix 5).

If you are a married man born after 5 April 1945 or a widower whose late wife was born after 5 April 1950, the rules for Category B retirement pension are the same as those that currently apply to women.[29]

Pension age from 2016

Pension age for both men and women is being equalised between April 2016 and November 2018.

Women born on after 6 November 1953 will reach pension age at 65 and those born between 6 April 1950 and 5 November 1953 will reach it at an age between 60 and 65. From December 2018, the pension age for men and women will rise to 66 by October 2020. The current rules provide for the pension age to rise to 67 between 2034 and 2036, but a Pensions Bill going through Parliament at the time of writing provides for this rise to occur between 2026 and 2028.[30]

3. People included in the claim

You cannot normally claim an increase in your retirement pension for your partner or child(ren). See Chapter 33 of the 2012/13 edition and pp746 of the 2002/03 edition of this *Handbook* for details of those who continue to qualify for an increase.

4. The amount of benefit

The following amounts may be reduced if the national insurance contribution conditions are not satisfied (see p865).[31]

Category A retirement pension

Category A retirement pension is paid at a weekly rate of £113.10.[32] In addition, you may receive:

- an age addition of 25 pence a week if you are over 80;
- graduated retirement benefit based on earnings between 1961 and 1975 (see p750);
- an additional state pension if you reached pension age after 5 April 1979 (see p760);
- a higher pension if you deferred entitlement to pension (see p751);
- an amount equal to the age-related addition to long-term incapacity benefit if you were receiving this within eight weeks (104 weeks if you are a 'welfare-to-work beneficiary') of reaching pension age (see p747).[33] If you have an additional state pension, this amount is offset against it.[34]

Note: if you are still entitled to an increase in your Category A retirement pension for an adult or for a child, see pxviii for the amounts.

Category B retirement pension for a spouse or civil partner

Category B retirement pension is paid at the weekly rate of £67.80.[35] In addition, you may receive:

- an age addition of 25 pence a week if you are over 80;
- a higher pension from deferring entitlement to pension (see p751).

Note: if you are still entitled to an increase in your Category B retirement pension for a child, see pxviii for the amounts.

Category B retirement pension for a widow, widower or civil partner

Category B retirement pension is paid at the weekly rate of £113.10.[36] In addition, you may receive:

- an age addition of 25 pence a week if you are over 80;
- graduated retirement benefit based on your late spouse's/civil partner's graduated contributions between 1961 and 1975 (see below);
- a higher pension if your late spouse/civil partner deferred entitlement to pension (see p751);
- an additional state pension based on earnings after 5 April 1979 (see p760).

Note: if you are still entitled to an increase in your retirement pension for a child dependant, see pxviii for the amount.

Category D retirement pension

Category D retirement pension is paid at a weekly rate of £67.80.[37] You also receive an age addition of 25 pence a week because you are over 80.

Graduated retirement benefit

The amount of graduated retirement benefit you can receive depends on the amount of graduated contributions paid on earnings between 1961 and 1975.

5. Special benefit rules

Special rules may apply to:

- people coming from or going abroad (see below);
- people who are divorced or have a former civil partner (see p755);
- prisoners (see p958).

People coming from or going abroad

If you have lived elsewhere than the UK during your working life, your pension may be affected – eg, it may be paid at a reduced rate. However, there are reciprocal arrangements with many countries that may help you qualify for a full pension. If you have worked in another European Economic Area (EEA) state, you may benefit from European Union law (see p1589). Your employment in another EEA state counts towards your national insurance contribution record to entitle you to retirement pension. If you are not an EEA national, you may still be able to benefit from a reciprocal agreement or an association or co-operation agreement (see p1517).

If you are going to live abroad, you can take your pension with you to any other country. However, unless you are moving to live in another EEA state or a country with which the UK has a reciprocal agreement for pensions, the amount of state retirement pension you receive is frozen at the rate at which it was paid when you went abroad.

Divorced people and former civil partners

If you are divorced or have ended a civil partnership and you cannot qualify for a Category A pension on the basis of your own contributions, you may qualify by using the contributions of your former spouse or civil partner. You can replace them with your own, either for all the years in your working life up to and including the one in which your marriage or civil partnership ended or for all the years during which you were married or in a civil partnership.

If your former spouse's or civil partner's contribution record was incomplete, you may not be able to receive a full pension, but you may still receive a higher amount than you would have qualified for on your own contributions.

You may qualify if:[38]

- you have been divorced or your civil partnership has ended; *or*
- your marriage was not void (see p525) and has been annulled by a court; *and either*
  - your decree absolute of divorce, civil partnership dissolution or nullity is dated after you reach pension age; *or*
  - your decree absolute of divorce, civil partnership dissolution or nullity is dated before you reach pension age and you do not remarry or form a new civil partnership before you reach that age.

6. Claims and backdating

To be entitled to a retirement pension, you must usually make a claim for it.[39] The general rules about claims and backdating are in Chapter 53. This section explains the specific rules that apply to retirement pensions.

You can request a statement of the amount of pension that you will receive by writing to the Future Pension Centre, The Pension Service 9, Mail Handling Site A, Wolverhampton WV98 1LU, by calling 0845 300 0168 (textphone 0845 300 0169) or at www.gov.uk/state-pension-statement.

Note: you can defer claiming your retirement pension. In return for doing so, you later become entitled to a higher rate of pension or a lump sum (see p751). You can also stop claiming your retirement pension.

Making a claim

You must usually make a claim for retirement pension (unless you come within the exceptions below). A claim for retirement pension can be made:[40]

- in writing by completing the approved form. Send it to the Pension Service. You may also be able to make your claim by taking or sending it to an alternative office (see p1136); *or*
- by telephone on 0800 731 7898 (textphone 0800 731 7339); *or*
- online at www.gov.uk/claim-state-pension-online.

If you claim in writing, keep a copy of your claim form in case queries arise.

You must provide any information or evidence required (see p757). In certain circumstances, the DWP may accept a written application not on the approved form.[41] You can amend or withdraw your claim before a decision is made (see p1138). If there is a delay in making a claim, you may be able to get a short-term advance of benefit (see p1167).

Note: you do not have to make a claim for a Category A or B pension if you have received written notification from the DWP that you do not need to claim (see below). However, if you defer your claim, or stop claiming, you do need to make a claim (see p751). There are other exceptions to the rule on claiming (see below).

Forms

The retirement pension form (BR1) is normally sent to you by the DWP about four months before you reach pension age. Otherwise, you can get it from the state pension claim line on 0800 731 7898 (textphone 0800 731 7339) or at www.gov.uk.

Exceptions to the rule on claiming

- You do not need to make a claim for a Category A or B retirement pension if, eight weeks before you reach pension age, you were in receipt of income support, jobseeker's allowance, employment and support allowance, incapacity benefit (IB) or pension credit and you were not entitled to or waiting for a decision on a claim for carer's allowance, short-term IB, severe disablement allowance, widowed mother's allowance or widow's pension. You also must have received notification from the DWP (by two weeks before you reach pension age), stating that you need not make a claim.[42] If this applies but you defer your entitlement to a Category A or B retirement pension, you will, however, need to make a claim once you decide to stop deferring your pension.[43]
- If you are a widow, you do not need to make a claim for Category A or B retirement pension if either:
  - you are over 65 when you stop getting widowed mother's allowance or widowed parent's allowance; *or*
  - you are getting a widow's pension or bereavement allowance immediately before your 65th birthday.

- You do not need to make a claim for Category A retirement pension if you are entitled to another retirement pension and you get divorced or your civil partnership is dissolved.[44] You need not claim your Category B retirement pension if you are entitled to either or both a Category A retirement pension or graduated retirement benefit, and you marry or enter into a civil partnership, or your spouse or civil partner becomes entitled to a Category A retirement pension or (from 13 July 2009) s/he dies while entitled to such a pension.[45]
- You do not need to make a claim for Category D retirement pension if you were 'ordinarily resident' in Great Britain (see p1519) on your 80th birthday and you are already receiving another retirement pension.[46]

Who should claim

You must normally claim retirement pension on your own behalf. However, if you are unable to manage your own affairs, another person can claim retirement pension for you as your 'appointee' (see p1137).

Information to support your claim

When you claim retirement pension, you must prove you have reached pension age. You must also:
- satisfy the national insurance number requirement (see p1138);
- provide proof of your identity, if required (see p1140); *and*
- ensure you have made a valid claim – ie, you must supply all the information and evidence required relevant to your claim (see p1140).

Even if you have provided all that was required when you claimed, you may be asked to provide additional information and evidence relevant to your claim (see p1152). There is a strict time limit for providing this. If you do not do so, the decision maker can decide your claim in the way most adverse to you.

You may be asked to provide information after you are awarded a retirement pension. If you fail to do so, your retirement pension could be suspended or even terminated (see p1175).

Proving your age

It is up to you to prove you have reached pension age. For most claimants, it is sufficient to produce your birth certificate, but problems can occur if you were born in a country which did not have a formal system of registering births. Other evidence which can prove your birth date includes:
- passport or identity card;
- school or health records;
- army records;
- statements from people who know you.

The date of your claim

You are not usually entitled to benefit for any day before your date of claim. However, in some cases you can claim in advance (see below), and sometimes your date of claim can be backdated (see below).

The date of your claim is:[47]

- the date your written or telephone claim, properly completed with all the required evidence and information, is received at the appropriate office (the DWP, local authority housing benefit office or other designated office). In this case, a claim made by telephone is the date of the telephone call. **Note:** telephone claims cannot be made at designated offices; *or*

- the date your 'defective claim' (ie, not properly completed with all the required information and evidence) is received at the appropriate office and you correct the defect within one month (or a longer period that the DWP considers reasonable) of being notified of the defect.

If you claim the wrong benefit

In certain circumstances, if you have claimed the wrong benefit, it is possible for your claim to be interchanged with another benefit.[48] For retirement pensions, this interchange is only possible with widows' benefits or bereavement benefits.

Claiming in advance

Claims for retirement pensions may be made up to, but no more than, four months in advance.[49] You should take advantage of this, as it can take a long time to sort out your contribution record.

Backdating your claim

It is very important to claim in time, because the maximum period for backdating is 12 months. You cannot backdate your claim for any period before the date you would have first become entitled to your pension.[50] You do not have to show any reasons why your claim is late. The rules on backdating are covered on p1144. In some limited circumstances, if you were not notified that your contribution record was insufficient for the years 1996 to 2002, it is possible for the claim to be backdated beyond the 12-month period to 1 October 1998.[51] If you claim more than 12 months after you became entitled to your pension, you are treated as having deferred your retirement.[52] You may want to consider the impact on your deferral amount and options when requesting backdating. If you backdate your claim, it will reduce the amount of time you had deferred claiming your pension, which will reduce the amount of your weekly increase and lump sum. It could also mean that you no longer have the option to get a lump sum, because you must have deferred your pension for at least 12 months to get a lump sum.[53] Weigh up the financial implications of your options when considering backdating – if necessary, seek advice.

If you might have qualified for benefit earlier but did not claim because you were given the wrong information or were misled by the DWP, you could ask for compensation (see p1382) or complain to the Ombudsman via your MP (see p1386).

7. Getting paid

Payment of retirement pension is normally made by direct credit transfer into a bank (or similar) account (see p1163). If you are unable to open or manage an account, payment can be made by 'simple payment' (see p1163). Payment can also be made to someone else on your behalf – called your 'appointee' (see p1137).

When is retirement pension paid?
The day you are paid depends on your national insurance number (see p1164).[54] Retirement pension is paid weekly, fortnightly or four-weekly in arrears.

If you reached pension age before 6 April 2010, you are paid in advance on a Monday or a Thursday, depending on your circumstances.[55]

Note:
- Deductions can be made from your retirement pension to pay third parties (see p1178).
- Even if you have been sanctioned for benefit offences (see p1258), you must be paid your retirement pension.
- If you have forgotten your PIN, see p1163. If your 'simple payment' card has been lost or stolen, or if you have forgotten your memorable date, see p1164. For information on missing payments, see p1164.
- If payment of your retirement pension is delayed, see p1382. You might be able to get a short-term advance (see p1167). If you wish to complain about how your claim has been dealt with, see p1383. You might be able to claim compensation (see p1382).
- If payment of your retirement pension is suspended, see p1175.
- If you are overpaid retirement pension, you might have to repay it (see Chapter 56) and, in some circumstances, you may have to pay a penalty (see p1249). If you have been accused of fraud, see Chapter 57.

Change of circumstances

You must report changes in your circumstances that you have been told you must report, as well as any that you might reasonably be expected to know might affect your right to, the amount of, or the payment of, your retirement pension. You should do this as soon as possible, preferably in writing. See p1174 for further information.

8. **The additional state pension scheme**

Most employees pay national insurance (NI) contributions that give entitlement to the basic state retirement pension. Those employees, but not the self-employed, can also earn additional pension. The additional state pension provides for earnings-related pensions to be paid to people who have paid (or whose late spouses/civil partners have paid) Class 1 contributions in excess of the minimum required for entitlement to basic state retirement pension. For earnings-related additions to invalidity benefit and incapacity benefit, see p284 of the 2006/07 edition of this *Handbook*.

The rules for the additional state pension were subject to major changes in April 2002. Before this date, the additional state pension was calculated under the state earnings-related pension scheme (SERPS). The rules since April 2002 are based on the state second pension – a simplified and more generous version of SERPS. In particular, under the new scheme, certain low-paid employees are deemed to have a minimum level of earnings.

If a couple divorces, it is possible to apply for a share of any additional pension.[56]

You are not in the additional state pension scheme if you are either contracted out by your employer or covered by an appropriate personal or stakeholder pension scheme. If you are contracted out by your employer, you and your employer pay NI contributions at a lower rate (see p844).[57] From 6 April 2012, you cannot contract out of the additional state pension scheme on a defined contribution (or money purchase) basis. You can only contract out through a defined benefit (or salary-related) pension scheme.[58] If you are in a personal, stakeholder or occupational scheme that contracts out on a defined contribution basis, you will automatically be brought back into the additional state pension scheme. You can continue to pay into your personal and stakeholder pension, but you will no longer receive a rebate on your NI contributions. Contact your employer for how this may affect your occupational pension.

Calculating the additional state pension

Future changes

The government proposes to replace the basic and additional state pension with a single-tier, flat-rate pension from April 2016. This will apply to future pensioners only.

The additional pension is calculated by adding together:
- the amount of additional pension accrued under the rules up to 6 April 2002 (under the previous scheme of SERPS); *and*
- the amount of additional pension accrued under the additional state pension (the state second pension).

The additional state pension depends on your earnings factor in each relevant year in which you have paid contributions (or for Category B retirement pensions, your spouse's or civil partner's earnings factor in each relevant year in which s/he has paid contributions). The additional state pension is calculated on the basis of 'accrual bands' related to surpluses in your earnings factor (see p861). From 2010/11, there were two accrual bands: a lower one for earnings below the lower earnings threshold (see p844) and an upper one for earnings above the lower earnings threshold.[59] From 6 April 2012, earnings in the lower accrual band are treated as producing a flat-rate amount (currently £92, equivalent to £1.77 a week), which is increased annually.[60] The upper accrual band will continue but will not be increased. Therefore, eventually the two accrual bands will have the same value, leaving a flat-rate amount with the additional earnings-related element of the additional state pension ceasing to accrue from around 2030. This change to the accrual bands is part of previous plans to make both tiers of the state pension into flat-rate amounts. However, the government intends to replace the two-tier system of basic and additional state pension with a single-tier, flat-rate pension from 2016.

A pension statement gives you a calculation of the amount of additional pension to which you are entitled at current values, and an estimate of the additional pension you will receive should you continue working.

Claimants who reached pension age before 6 April 1999

If you reached pension age before 6 April 1999 (ie, if you are a man who was born before 6 April 1934 or a woman born before 6 April 1939), the rules were generally more favourable. For an example of how this worked in practice, see p244 of the 21st edition of CPAG's *Rights Guide to Non-Means-Tested Benefits*.

Payment to widows, widowers and surviving civil partners

At present, a widow, widower or surviving civil partner who is eligible for a basic state retirement pension based on her/his spouse's/civil partner's contributions can, in certain circumstances, also receive any additional state pension based on her/his spouse's/civil partner's contributions.

It was originally intended that people whose spouses/civil partners died after 5 April 2000 would only inherit a maximum of 50 per cent of that spouse's additional state pension entitlement. However, because of a failure by the (then) Department of Social Security to advise people about the change, the government decided not to implement the change to inherited additional state pensions from

SERPS until 6 October 2002 and to phase the reduction over a period of 10 years rather than introduce an immediate 50 per cent cut. This phased reduction only applies to the additional pension inherited under the SERPS scheme. Any additional pension derived from the state second pension scheme is only inheritable at 50 per cent. The percentage of the deceased person's additional state pension entitlement from SERPS which can be inherited by her/his surviving spouse/civil partner is reduced if the deceased person reached pensionable age from 5 October 2002 as follows.[61]

Date when deceased person reached pensionable age	Maximum % of additional pension passing to surviving spouse or civil partner
6.10.02 to 5.10.04	90%
6.10.04 to 5.10.06	80%
6.10.06 to 5.10.08	70%
6.10.08 to 5.10.10	60%
6.10.10 onwards	50%

Note: it is the date on which the deceased person reached pension age which is important for this purpose, not the date on which s/he died.

People who are able to prove that they were given incorrect or incomplete information about the reduction in inherited SERPS additional pension, and who have experienced financial loss as a result, may also be able to claim compensation for maladministration (see p1382).

The maximum amount of inherited additional pension from state second pension is 50 per cent.

In certain circumstances, a widow, widower or surviving civil partner may be entitled to an additional pension based on both her/his own contributions and those of her/his spouse.[62]

9. **Tax, other benefits and the benefit cap**

Tax

Retirement pensions are taxable (including an increase in your Category A retirement pension for your spouse or someone who cares for your child, if you still receive this).[63] However, increases for children (if you are still receiving them) are not taxable.

Means-tested benefits

Retirement pensions are taken fully into account for the purposes of means-tested benefits, but pensioners receive a higher rate of some means-tested benefits. You may qualify for pension credit (PC) to top up your retirement pension income (see p77).

Non-means-tested benefits

Retirement pensions are affected by the overlapping benefit rules (see p1165).

Retirement pensions overlap with contribution-based jobseeker's allowance, incapacity benefit, contributory employment and support allowance, severe disablement allowance, carer's allowance, maternity allowance, widowed parent's allowance and bereavement allowance.

There are special rules if you are entitled to both a Category A and Category B retirement pension.

Tax credits

Retirement pensions are partially taken into account as income for tax credits (see Chapter 64).

The benefit cap

In some cases, the total amount of specified benefits you receive is limited to £350 a week (if you are a single claimant without children) or £500 a week (if you are a lone parent or a member of a couple). This is known as the 'benefit cap'. Retirement pension is *not* one of the specified benefits. The benefit cap only applies if you are getting housing benefit if you are below PC age or universal credit. See p1169 for further information.

Passports and other sources of help

You qualify for a Christmas bonus if you receive retirement pension (see p835). People aged 60 or over qualify for free prescriptions and eye tests regardless of their income. If you are on a low income, you may be entitled to council tax reduction (see p827).

Notes

1. Who can claim a retirement pension
1 *Timbrell v SSWP* [2010] EWCA Civ 701; [2011] AACR 13; R(P) 1/09; R(P) 2/09; *MP v SSWP (RP)* [2009] UKUT 205(AAC); [2010] AACR 13
2 Sch 4 paras 11-14 Marriage (Same Sex Couples) Act 2013
3 ss44(1) and 48 SSCBA 1992
4 ss48A, 48B and 48BB and Sch 3 Part I para 5 SSCBA 1992
5 s48BB(1) and (2) SSCBA 1992
6 s48BB(3) and (4) SSCBA 1992
7 s48B(1) SSCBA 1992
8 s51(1)(a) SSCBA 1992
9 s48B(1) SSCBA 1992
10 s51(1A)(b) SSCBA 1992
11 s48B(1A) SSCBA 1992
12 s48BB SSCBA 1992
13 ss48C(1) and 51(4) SSCBA 1992
14 s78(3) SSCBA 1992; reg 10 SS(WB&RP) Regs
15 s36(7) NIA 1965, as kept in force by Sch 1 SS(GRB) No.2 Regs
16 Reg 17(1)(h) and (3) SS(WB&RP) Regs
17 s37 NIA 1965, as kept in force by Sch 1 SS(GRB) No.2 Regs
18 s36(4) NIA 1965, as kept in force by Sch 1 SS(GRB) No.2 Regs
19 s55 and Sch 5 SSCBA 1992
20 Sch 2 SS(GRB) No.2 Regs
21 s54 SSCBA 1992 and reg 2(2) SS(WB&RP) Regs
22 Reg 2(3) SS(WB&RP) Regs
23 Sch 5 para 1(2) SSCBA 1992
24 Sch 5 para A1 SSCBA 1992; SS(DRPSAPGRB)(MP) Regs
25 Sch 5 para 2(5) SSCBA 1992
26 Sch 5 para 4 SSCBA 1992
27 Reg 30(5B)-(5G) SS(C&P) Regs
28 Reg 4(1)(b)(i) SS(WB&RP) Regs

2. The rules about your age
29 ss48A-48C SSCBA 1992, as inserted by Sch 4 para 3 PA 1995
30 s126 and Sch 4 PA 1995

4. The amount of benefit
31 Reg 6(3) SS(WB&RP) Regs
32 ss44(4) and 45 SSCBA 1992

33 ss30B(7) and 47(1) SSCBA 1992; reg 3A SS(WB&RP) Regs
34 s47(2) SSCBA 1992
35 s48A and Sch 4 SSCBA 1992
36 s48B SSCBA 1992
37 s78(6) and Sch 4 para 7 SSCBA 1992

5. Special benefit rules
38 s48 SSCBA 1992; regs 1(3) and (3A), 8 and 8A SS(WB&RP) Regs

6. Claims and backdating
39 s1 SSAA 1992
40 Reg 4 SS(C&P) Regs
41 Reg 4(1) SS(C&P) Regs
42 Reg 3(za) SS(C&P) Regs
43 Reg 3A(4) SS(C&P) Regs
44 Reg 3(ca) SS(C&P) Regs
45 Reg 3(cb) SS(C&P) Regs
46 Reg 3(b) SS(C&P) Regs
47 Reg 6 SS(C&P) Regs
48 Reg 9(1) and Sch 1 SS(C&P) Regs
49 Reg 15 SS(C&P) Regs
50 Reg 19 and Sch 4 para 13 SS(C&P) Regs
51 Reg 6(31) and (32) SS(C&P) Regs
52 s55(3)(a) SSCBA 1992
53 *RM v SSWP (RP)* [2013] UKUT 416 (AAC); CP/712/2013

7. Getting paid
54 Reg 22C SS(C&P) Regs
55 Reg 22 and Sch 6 para 5 SS(C&P) Regs

8. The additional state pension scheme
56 s47 WRPA 1999
57 s41 PSA 1993
58 s15 PA 2007; reg 2 Pensions Act 2007 (Commencement No.4) Order 2011, No.1267
59 s45(2)(c) and Sch 4A SSCBA 1992
60 s45(2)(d) and Sch 4B SSCBA 1992
61 The Social Security (Inherited SERPS) Regulations 2001, No.1085
62 s52(3) SSCBA 1992

9. Tax, other benefits and the benefit cap
63 s677 Income Tax (Earnings and Pensions) Act 2003

Chapter 37

Social fund payments

This chapter covers:
1. Budgeting loans (below)
2. Sure Start maternity grants (below)
3. Funeral expenses payments (p772)
4. Cold weather payments (p778)
5. Winter fuel payments (p779)
6. Tax, other benefits and the benefits cap (p781)

5

Key facts
- The social fund covers one-off loans and payments for specific expenses or circumstances.
- Budgeting loans are interest-free loans. Sure Start maternity grants, funeral expenses payments, cold weather payments and winter fuel payments are non-repayable.
- Social fund loans and payments are administered and paid by the DWP. If you disagree with a budgeting loan decision, there is an internal review system and then a further review to the Independent Case Examiner.
- If you disagree with a decision on a Sure Start maternity grant, funeral expenses payment, cold weather payment or winter fuel payment, you can apply for a revision or appeal against it. You are likely to have to apply for a revision before you can appeal.

---

1. Budgeting loans

To be eligible for a budgeting loan, you must satisfy all the following conditions, which are laid down in legally binding directions. **Note:** if you come under the universal credit (UC) system (see p19), you cannot apply for a budgeting loan and must apply for a budgeting advance of your UC payments instead (see p197).
- **You must be in receipt of a 'qualifying benefit'** when your budgeting loan application is determined.[1] Qualifying benefits are: income support (IS), income-based jobseeker's allowance (JSA), income-related employment and

support allowance (ESA) and pension credit (PC) (guarantee or savings credit). Payments on account and hardship payments are included. You are treated as being in receipt of a qualifying benefit if it is being paid to you, or to an appointee on your behalf. You are eligible if you receive a backdated award of a qualifying benefit, covering the date your application is determined. The High Court has held that you are not 'in receipt of' a qualifying benefit if your partner or another member of your family is the claimant.[2] If you are a member of a 'joint-claim couple', you are only eligible for a budgeting loan if you are the partner being paid JSA.

- **You and/or your partner, between you, must have been receiving a qualifying benefit throughout the 26 weeks before the date on which your application is determined**, disregarding any number of breaks of 28 days or less.[3] A period covered by a payment of arrears should count, as should any benefit received while in Northern Ireland. The three waiting days at the start of a claim for JSA or ESA (see p697 and p1017) do not count. More than one partner could help you satisfy the qualifying period.
- **You must not have too much capital.**[4] Any budgeting loan award is reduced by the amount of capital you have in excess of £1,000 (£2,000 if you or your partner are 61 or over). Capital is calculated as for the qualifying benefit that you are receiving (see Chapters 17 and 18). Payments made from the Family Fund to you, your partner or child, and refugee integration loans are ignored. Capital held by your child(ren) should be disregarded.
- **You, or your partner, must not be involved in a trade dispute** (see p971).[5]
- **You must not be a 'person subject to immigration control'** (there are exceptions to this rule) – see p1500.
- **The loan must be for one or more of the following categories of allowable expenses:**[6]
  - furniture and household equipment;
  - clothing and footwear;
  - maternity expenses;
  - funeral expenses;
  - rent in advance and/or removal expenses to secure fresh accommodation;
  - improvement, maintenance and security of the home;
  - travelling expenses;
  - expenses associated with seeking or re-entering work;
  - hire purchase and other debts for any of the above items.

  You are required to tick the category of expense for which you need the loan on the application form. You are not required to specify the particular items you need – eg, a bed or a winter coat.
- **The loan must be a minimum of £100 and a maximum of £1,500.**[7] You must state how much you are asking for on your application.
- **You must be likely to be able to repay the loan** (see p768).[8]

The amount

The amount of loan you are offered depends on the following factors.[9]

- The amount you request. You are not offered more than you ask for, but you may be offered less because of the factors below.
- The legal minimum and maximum amounts and the capital rules. You cannot be offered a loan of less than £100 or more than £1,500. The amount of your award is also reduced if you have too much capital.
- The weighting of your application and the baseline figure (see below).
- The amount of any outstanding social fund loan debt you or your partner have.
  - If you have no outstanding social fund loans, you are offered the maximum amount appropriate to the weighting of your application, or the amount you have requested, if this is lower.
  - If you have an outstanding social fund loan debt, the maximum amount you can borrow is reduced by this amount.
- The amount you are likely to be able to repay. Generally, this is the amount you can repay within 104 weeks (see p768).

Weighting applications and the baseline figure[10]

The '**weighting**' is:

– one for single people;

– one and one-third for couples without children;

– two and one-third for families (including lone parents) with children.

The '**baseline figure**' is the amount determined by the Secretary of State that a single person should receive. The maximum payable for applications with a higher weighting is calculated by multiplying this baseline figure by the weighting of the application. If, for example, the baseline figure is £300, the maximum payable for an application with a weighting of one and one-third is £400. The baseline figure may vary over the course of the year.

Although decisions are legally made by decision makers, decision making is largely an automated process, with weightings and awards automatically calculated by computer.

Applying and getting paid

An application for a budgeting loan should normally be made to your local Jobcentre Plus office.

Applications must be made in writing, either on the approved Form SF500, or in some other written form, accepted by the Secretary of State.

You can get the application forms from your local DWP office, or download them from www.gov.uk.

An application can be made on your behalf by another person, provided you give your written consent (this is not necessary, however, if an appointee is acting for you).[11]

Your application is treated as made on the day it is received by the DWP.[12] If your application was incomplete and you comply with a request for additional information, your application is treated as made on the day it was originally received.[13]

Payments are generally made into the account into which your qualifying benefit is paid or, if you do not have an account, in the same way as your qualifying benefit is paid.

Challenging a decision

Decisions are made by decision makers in accordance with the weighting critieria and your ability to repay (see p767). You should receive a written decision on your application, with an explanation if it has been refused or partly refused, together with a notification of your right to request a review.

If you are unhappy with a budgeting loan decision, you can ask for a review. This is carried out by a different decision maker. However, a decision is only likely to be changed if it was based on incorrect information about your circumstances, or if the amount you are allowed to borrow has increased.

You must apply for a review of a decision by writing to the office where the decision was made within 28 days of the date the decision was issued to you.[14] Your application must include your grounds for requesting a review.[15] If someone is making an application on your behalf, it must be accompanied by your written authority (unless the person is your appointee – see p1137).[16]

Late applications can be accepted for 'special reasons'.[17] Special reasons are not defined. They could include reasons why the application is late – eg, ill health, a domestic crisis or wrong advice.

However, if your application is out of time, it may be quicker to submit a new application.

If a decision is not wholly revised in your favour, the reviewing officer must either telephone or write to you to explain why and ask further questions if necessary.

If you are still unhappy with the decision, you can ask the Independent Case Examiner (see Appendix 1) to undertake a second-tier review.[18] You should do this within 28 days, although the time limit may be extended if there are special reasons.

Repayments

All loans must be repaid to the DWP.[19]

The decision maker may give you more than one option for repaying a loan, depending on whether you have any other outstanding social fund loans and your other financial commitments. S/he may offer an option of a higher loan with an increased repayment rate, but you cannot be asked to repay at a rate higher than 20 per cent of your IS, income-based JSA or income-related ESA applicable amount or PC appropriate minimum guarantee plus any child tax credit or child benefit you receive. The loan must be repaid within 104 weeks.

You receive a written decision on your application for a budgeting loan with details of any loan offers and repayment terms. You have 14 days from the date the decision was sent to return the declaration agreeing to one of the offers made to you. This time limit can be extended for 'special reasons'.[20]

Note: the rules for the repayment of budgeting loans also apply to any outstanding crisis loans you may still have.

Methods of repayment

Budgeting loans are nearly always recovered by direct deductions from benefit, although you can make a payment at any time to pay off, partially or wholly, the debt. Deductions can only be made from the following benefits:[21]

* IS;
* JSA (contribution-based or income-based);
* ESA (contributory or income-related);
* PC;
* incapacity benefit;
* severe disablement allowance;
* carer's allowance;
* disablement benefit, reduced earnings allowance and industrial death benefit;
* bereavement benefits (excluding the lump-sum bereavement payment) and widows' benefits;
* retirement pensions;
* maternity allowance.

If you have an outstanding budgeting loan when you come under the UC system (see p19), the deductions you were having made from your qualifying benefit continue to be deducted from your UC.

Deductions can also be made from increases of benefit for age and dependants, and additional benefit under the additional state pension scheme.

A loan can be legally recovered from:[22]

* you (the applicant) or the person who the loan was for;
* your partner, if you are living together as a couple (as defined for IS purposes – see p205);
* a person who is liable to maintain either the person who made the application or the person on whose behalf it was made.

Rescheduling repayment terms

You cannot request a review of a decision relating to repayment terms or recovery. If you have accepted a loan, however, and the repayment terms are

Part 5: Other benefits
Chapter 37: Social fund payments
2. Sure Start maternity grants

causing hardship (eg, because your financial situation has deteriorated), you can ask the DWP to reschedule the loan by lowering the weekly repayment rate.

2. Sure Start maternity grants

You qualify for a Sure Start maternity grant if you satisfy all of the following rules.
* **You or your partner have been awarded one of the following qualifying benefits** (including payments on account and hardship payments) in respect of the day you claim a maternity grant:[23]
    - income support (IS);
    - income-based jobseeker's allowance;
    - income-related employment and support allowance;
    - child tax credit paid at a rate exceeding the family element (see p1401);
    - working tax credit including the disabled worker or severe disability element (see p1403);
    - pension credit (guarantee or savings credit);
    - universal credit.

You are eligible if you receive a backdated award of a qualifying benefit covering the date you claim a maternity grant. If you are waiting for a decision on a claim for a qualifying benefit, the DWP may defer making a decision on your maternity grant claim until the qualifying benefit claim has been decided. If your claim for a maternity grant is refused while you are waiting for a decision on a claim for a qualifying benefit, you should reclaim a maternity grant within three months of being awarded the qualifying benefit. **Note:** if you do not claim a maternity grant within the time limits (see p771), a backdated award of a qualifying benefit does not qualify you for a grant. If you are not entitled to a qualifying benefit in your own right because you are under 16 (or under 19 and in 'relevant education' – see p903), a member of your family can claim a maternity grant for you if s/he is getting a qualifying benefit in respect of you.
* **One of the following applies:**[24]
    - you or a member of your family are pregnant or have given birth in the last three months (including stillbirth after 24 weeks of pregnancy);
    - you are the parent (but not the mother) of a child who is less than 12 months old, you are responsible for the child and are not the mother's partner;
    - you are the guardian of a child who is less than 12 months old;
    - you or your partner have a child who is less than 12 months old placed with you for adoption and you are responsible for the child;
    - you have adopted a child who is less than 12 months old under a recognised adoption which takes place outside the UK;
    - you or your partner have been granted a residence order or adoption order for a child who is less than 12 months old;

– you and your spouse have been granted a parental order allowing you to have a child by a surrogate mother.

In the last six cases, you are entitled to a payment even if one has already been made to the birth mother or a member of her family.[25]

- **There is no other member of your family who is under 16 at the time of claim**. However, a grant can be awarded for each child of a multiple birth provided there is no other child under 16. If there is a child or children under 16 and you have a multiple birth, a grant can be awarded for the number of children in the multiple birth less one, or, if any of the other children in the family are the result of the same pregnancy, then less the number in that pregnancy. For example, if you give birth to triplets and already have twins under 16 in your family, one grant will be awarded. If you are under 20 and another member of your family claims for you, the grant is payable, provided you do not have other children under 16.[26]
- **You or your partner are not involved in a trade dispute** (see p971), unless specified circumstances apply.[27]
- **You claim within the time limits** (see below).
- **You have received health and welfare advice from a healthcare professional** (see below).[28]
- **You are not a 'person subject to immigration control'** (there are exceptions to this rule) – see p1500.

The terms 'partner' and 'family' in the above rules have almost the same meanings as they do for IS purposes (see Chapter 11).[29]

The amount

You are entitled to a grant of £500 for each child or expected child.[30] The payment is not affected by any capital you have.

Claiming and getting paid

Claim on Form SF100, which you can get from your local Jobcentre Plus office or from www.gov.uk. There are strict time limits for claiming. You can claim a maternity grant at any time from 11 weeks before the first day of your expected week of childbirth until three months after the actual date of the birth. If you adopt a child, have a residence order for a child, or have a child by a surrogate mother, you can claim up to three months following the date of the adoption, residence order or parental order, subject to the child being under 12 months when the claim is made. There is no provision for claiming outside the time limits.[31]

The back of your claim form must be signed by a healthcare professional (ie, midwife, health visitor or doctor) to confirm that you have received health and welfare advice on your baby or your maternal health.

Part 5: Other benefits
Chapter 37: Social fund payments
3. Funeral expenses payments

Your date of claim is normally the date your form is received by the DWP.[32] If you make a written claim in some other way, you should be sent the appropriate form to complete. If you return it within one month, or such longer period as the Secretary of State considers reasonable, your date of claim is the date the DWP received your initial application.[33] See p770 for when your claim can be backdated if you are subsequently awarded a qualifying benefit.

If you claim before the birth, you need to submit a maternity certificate (MAT B1), a note from your doctor or midwife or an antenatal clinic appointment card showing your expected date of childbirth. If you claim after your child is born, you are usually asked for a maternity, birth or adoption certificate.

If you are overpaid a maternity grant, you may have to repay it (see Chapter 56) and, in some circumstances, you may have to pay a penalty (see p1249).

3. **Funeral expenses payments**

You qualify for a funeral expenses payment if you satisfy all of the following rules.
* **You or your partner** (see p205) **have been awarded one of the following qualifying benefits** (including payments on account and hardship payments) in respect of the day you claim a funeral payment:[34]
  - income support (IS);
  - income-based jobseeker's allowance;
  - income-related employment and support allowance;
  - housing benefit (HB);
  - child tax credit paid at a rate which exceeds the family element (see p1400);
  - working tax credit which includes the disabled worker or severe disability element (see p1402);
  - pension credit (guarantee or savings credit);
  - universal credit.

  You are eligible if you receive a backdated award of a qualifying benefit which covers the date you claim a funeral payment. If you are waiting for a decision on a claim for a qualifying benefit, the DWP may defer making a decision on a claim for a funeral payment until the qualifying benefit claim has been decided. If your claim for a funeral payment is refused while you are waiting for a decision on a claim for a qualifying benefit, reclaim within three months of being awarded the qualifying benefit. **Note:** if you do not claim a funeral payment within the time limit, a backdated award of a qualifying benefit will not qualify you for a grant.
* **You or your partner are in one of the categories of eligible people** listed on p773 who can be treated as responsible for the funeral expenses.

- **You or your partner accept responsibility for funeral expenses** (see p775).[35] If you are claiming as a 'close relative' or 'close friend', it must also be reasonable for you to accept responsibility.
- **The funeral (ie, burial or cremation) takes place in the UK,**[36] unless you or your partner are covered by specified European Union legislation, in which case the funeral can take place in any European Economic Area (EEA) state or Switzerland (see p776).[37]
- **A social fund funeral payment has not already been made in respect of the deceased** (but the amount of a previous award can be revised up to the maximum allowed under the rules).[38]
- **The deceased was 'ordinarily resident' in the UK when s/he died** (see p1519).[39]
- **You are not a 'person subject to immigration control'** (there are exceptions to this rule) – see p1500.
- **You claim within the time limits** (see p777).

Eligible people

You are only eligible for a funeral payment if you or your partner fall into one of the following categories of people who can be treated as responsible for the funeral costs.[40] See p774 for definitions of the terms used.

- You were the 'partner' of the deceased when s/he died.
- The deceased was a 'child' for whom you were responsible when s/he died and there is no 'absent parent', or there is an absent parent but s/he (or her/his partner) was getting a qualifying benefit (see p772) when the child died. If there is an absent parent who was not getting a qualifying benefit when the child died, you may qualify for a payment as a close relative of the deceased. If the deceased was a stillborn child, you are eligible for a funeral payment if you were the parent or the parent's partner, and it does not matter whether there is an absent parent.
- You were a parent, son or daughter of the deceased and it is reasonable for you to accept responsibility for the funeral expenses (see p775).
- You were another 'close relative' or a 'close friend' of the deceased and it is reasonable for you to accept responsibility for the funeral expenses (see p775), and you are not excluded by the rules below.

Definitions[41]

'Child' is defined as for IS purposes (see p210). You are 'responsible' for a child if you get, or could get, child benefit for her/him (see p212).

'Stillborn child' means a child born dead after 24 weeks of pregnancy.

'Absent parent' means a parent of a deceased child, where the child:

– was not living in that parent's household at the date of death; *and*
– was living with another person who was responsible for her/him.

Part 5: Other benefits
Chapter 37: Social fund payments
3. Funeral expenses payments

> 'Close relative' means parent, parent-in-law, son, son-in-law, daughter, daughter-in-law, step-parent, stepson, stepson-in-law, stepdaughter, stepdaughter-in-law, brother, brother-in-law, sister, sister-in-law.
>
> 'Close friend' is not defined in the law. It can include a relative who is not a close relative – eg, a grandparent or grandchild.[42]
>
> 'Partner' has the same meaning as for IS (see p205). You also count as a partner, however, if you were living in a care home when the deceased died and:
> – you and your spouse or civil partner were living in the same home; *or*
> – you were a member of a couple before one or both of you moved into such a home.[43]
> This rule is designed to enable a surviving partner to claim a funeral payment if one or both partners were in a home at the date of death.

Exclusion of certain close relatives and friends

If you claim as a close relative or close friend of the deceased (see p775), you cannot get a payment if:

- the deceased had a partner (unless that partner died before the funeral without making a claim for a funeral payment);[44]
- the deceased was a child or stillborn child and a responsible person or parent is able to claim a funeral payment under the rules set out above;[45]
- there is a parent, son or daughter of the deceased, apart from:[46]
  - anyone under the age of 18;
  - anyone aged 18 or 19 who counts as a qualifying young person for child benefit purposes (see p551);
  - anyone who (or whose partner) has been awarded a qualifying benefit (see p772);
  - anyone estranged from the deceased when s/he died ('estranged' is not defined, but has connotations of emotional disharmony);[47]
  - students aged 18 on a full-time course of advanced education (see p905), or aged 19 to pension age on any full-time course;
  - members of a religious order which fully maintains them;
  - prisoners (including those in youth custody or a remand centre) who (or whose partners) were getting a qualifying benefit immediately before being detained;
  - inpatients receiving free treatment in a hospital or similar institution, who (or whose partners) were getting a qualifying benefit immediately before becoming a patient;
  - asylum seekers receiving asylum support from the UK Border Agency or a local authority (see p1511);
  - anyone who is ordinarily resident (see p1519) outside the UK;
- there is a close relative of the deceased who was in *closer contact* with the deceased than you were, taking into account the nature and extent of such contact;[48]

- there is a close relative of the deceased who was in *equally close contact* with the deceased as you were and who (or whose partner) is not getting a qualifying benefit (see p772).[49]

Note: the last two bullet points do not apply if the close relative was under the age of 18 when the deceased died, or was a student, member of a religious order, prisoner, inpatient or asylum seeker as set out above, or was ordinarily resident outside the UK.[50]

If you are refused a payment on this ground, the DWP (not you) must establish there is another close relative who is not getting a qualifying benefit.[51]

Examples

Jane is not entitled to a funeral payment because, although she looked after her brother for many years before he died, he had a son who is not getting a qualifying benefit (see p772). Although the son rarely saw his father, they were not estranged.

Yuri is entitled to a funeral payment when his close friend Robert dies because, although Robert had two surviving close relatives, a son and a sister-in-law, the son is getting HB and Yuri was in closer contact with Robert than either of them were.

Accepting responsibility for funeral costs

To qualify for a funeral payment, you or your partner must 'accept responsibility' for funeral expenses.[52] The key factor is whether you are liable to pay the costs of a funeral, rather than whether you have made the arrangements.[53]

If the funeral director's account or contract is in your name, you should normally be treated as having accepted responsibility. If the account or contract is in someone else's name (or another person has paid the bill), you can still be 'responsible' if:

- s/he is acting as your agent – eg, because you are too distressed to act on your own behalf;[54] *or*
- s/he transfers liability to you, prior to full payment, with the consent of the funeral director.[55]

If you are a close relative (see p774) or close friend of the deceased, it must also be 'reasonable' for you to accept responsibility for the funeral expenses, in the light of the nature and extent of your contact with the deceased.[56] In one case, it was held reasonable for a person to have accepted responsibility for his father's funeral even though he had not seen him for 24 years. This did not erase the contact they had had in the previous 30 years.[57]

Part 5: Other benefits
Chapter 37: Social fund payments
3. Funeral expenses payments

European Economic Area nationals

You can get a funeral payment for a funeral that takes place in any member state of the EEA or Switzerland (see p1590) if:[58]
- you are a 'worker' or self-employed, or you retain that status; *or*
- you are a member of the family of a worker – ie:
  - her/his spouse or civil partner;
  - the worker's/spouse's/civil partner's child, grandchild or other descendant who is either under 21 or dependent;
  - a dependent relative of the worker, spouse or civil partner in the ascending line – eg, a parent or grandparent; *or*
- you have a permanent right to reside in the UK.

For more details on the benefit rights of EEA nationals, see Chapter 72.

If you have ever been refused a payment for a funeral that took place in an EEA state and you satisfied the above rules, you should ask for a revision (see p1275).

The amount

You are entitled to a payment that is sufficient to cover:[59]
- the necessary costs of purchasing a new burial plot with the exclusive right of burial in it and necessary burial fees. The burial of ashes following cremation is not, however, covered;
- the necessary cremation fees, including medical references, certificates and removing a pacemaker (restricted to £20 if not carried out by a doctor);
- the costs of documentation necessary for the release of the deceased's assets;
- the reasonable cost of transport for the portion of journeys in excess of 80 kilometres (50 miles), undertaken to:
  - transport the body within the UK to a funeral director's premises or to a place of rest;
  - transport the coffin and bearers in a hearse and the mourners in another vehicle from the funeral director's premises or place of rest to the funeral. The cost of this plus burial in an existing plot cannot exceed the cost of such transport plus the purchase and burial costs of a new plot;[60]
- the necessary expenses of one return journey for the responsible person to arrange or attend the funeral. The maximum allowed is the cost of a return journey from home to the place where the burial or cremation costs are incurred;
- up to £700 for any other funeral expenses – eg, funeral director's fees, religious costs, flowers and other transport costs.

Note:
- The cost of any items or services provided under a pre-paid funeral plan or equivalent arrangement cannot be met. Expenses not covered by the plan can

be met if they fall into the above categories, but the maximum allowed under the last category is restricted to £120.[61]

- Costs relating to religious requirements cannot be included in the amount allowed for burial and transport.[62]
- If the amount awarded does not cover your funeral expenses, you may be able to claim a budgeting loan (see p765).

Deductions from awards

The following are deducted from an award of a funeral payment:[63]

- the deceased's assets available to you or a member of your family (defined as for IS purposes) without probate or letters of administration. However, if you have a joint account with the deceased, those assets become yours at the point of death and cannot be deducted.[64] Assets at the date of death count, even if you have spent or distributed them before your claim for a funeral payment.[65] However, arrears of most benefits and tax credits payable to the deceased at the date of death are excluded from the assets;[66]
- a lump sum legally due to you or a member of your family from an insurance policy, occupational pension scheme, burial club or equivalent source on the death of the deceased;
- any contribution towards funeral expenses made to you or a member of your family by a charity, or a relative of yours or of the deceased;
- a funeral grant paid by the government for a war disablement pensioner;
- an amount paid or payable under a pre-paid funeral plan or equivalent arrangement (whether or not the plan was fully paid).

Any capital you have apart from the above has no effect on the amount of the funeral payment. Any payments from the Macfarlane Trust, the Macfarlane (Special Payments) Trusts, MFET Ltd, the Fund, the Eileen Trust, the CJD Trusts, the Skipton Fund, the Caxton Foundation or the London Bombings Relief Charitable Fund are not deducted from an award of a funeral payment.[67]

Claiming and getting paid

Claim on Form SF200, which you can get from your local Jobcentre Plus office or from www.gov.uk or by telephone (via the Bereavement Service on 0845 606 0265; textphone 0845 606 0285). There are strict time limits for claiming. You can claim at any time from the date of death to up to three months after the date of the funeral.[68] There is no provision for late claims. See below for details of the date your claim is treated as made.

When completing the form, bear in mind the rules about accepting responsibility for the funeral expenses and your contact with the deceased.

Your date of claim is normally the date the form is received by the DWP or the date you make your phone claim.[69] If you do not complete Form SF200 properly or apply in writing but not on the form, you should be sent the form to complete

Part 5: Other benefits
Chapter 37: Social fund payments
4. Cold weather payments

or correct. If you submit it within one month, or a longer period if the Secretary of State considers this reasonable, your claim is treated as being made on the date you originally applied.[70] See p772 for when your claim can be backdated if you are subsequently awarded a qualifying benefit.

Payment is normally made directly to the funeral director, unless you have already paid the bill.[71]

If you are overpaid a funeral payment, you might have to repay it (see Chapter 56) and, in some circumstances, you may have to pay a penalty (see p1249). However, see below for recovery from the deceased's estate.

Recovery from the deceased's estate

The Secretary of State is entitled to recover funeral expenses payments from the deceased's estate and normally seeks to do so.[72] Funeral expenses are a first charge on the estate and have priority over anything else (although there may be insufficient assets for full repayment).[73]

4. Cold weather payments

You qualify for a cold weather if you satisfy all the following rules.
- A period of cold weather has been forecast or recorded for the area in which your normal home is situated (see p779).[74]
- You have been awarded pension credit (guarantee or savings credit) for at least one day during the period of cold weather. You also qualify if you have been awarded income support (IS), income-based jobseeker's allowance (JSA), income-related employment and support allowance (ESA) or universal credit (UC) for at least one day during the period of cold weather[75] and:
  - your IS or income-based JSA applicable amount includes a disability, severe disability, enhanced disability, disabled child, pensioner or higher pensioner premium (see p226); or
  - your income-related ESA applicable amount includes the pensioner premium, severe disability premium, enhanced disability premium, or the work-related activity or support component; or
  - your UC includes an increase for a disabled or severely disabled child; or
  - your UC includes the limited capability for work or limited capability for work-related activity element (or would do but for the fact that it includes a carer element) and you are not in employment or gainful self-employment during the period of cold weather or on the day it is forecast; or
  - you are responsible for a child under five; or
  - you are getting child tax credit which includes a disability or severe disability element (see p1400).

- You are not living in a care home.[76]
- You are not a 'person subject to immigration control' (there are exceptions to this rule) – see p1500.

Period of cold weather
A 'period of cold weather' is seven consecutive days during which the average of the mean daily temperature, as forecast or recorded for that period at your designated local weather station, is equal to or below zero degrees celsius.[77]

The amount

The sum of £25 is paid for each week of cold weather.[78]

Claiming and getting paid

You do not need to make a claim for a cold weather payment. The DWP should automatically pay you if you qualify. Your district DWP should publicise when there are periods of cold weather in your area. If you do not receive payment and you think you are entitled, submit a written claim and ask for a written decision. A payment cannot be made more than 26 weeks from the last day of the winter period (1 November to 31 March) in which the cold weather period fell.[79] If you are overpaid a cold weather payment, you might have to repay it (see Chapter 56) and, in some circumstances, you may have to pay a penalty (see p1249).

A payment cannot be made more than 26 weeks from the last day of the winter period (1 November to 31 March) in which the cold weather period fell.[80]

---

5. Winter fuel payments

You qualify for a winter fuel payment if you satisfy all the following rules.[81]
- You are at least the qualifying age for pension credit (PC – see p78) in the 'qualifying week'.
- You are ordinarily resident in Great Britain (see p1519) or you are habitually resident in another European Economic Area country or in Switzerland, are covered by the European Union co-ordination rules and can demonstrate a 'sufficient link to the UK social security system' (see Chapter 72).
- You claim in time (see p780), if a claim is required.
- You are not excluded from a payment under the rules on p780.

The qualifying week
The 'qualifying week' is the week beginning on the third Monday in September.

Part 5: Other benefits
Chapter 37: Social fund payments
5. Winter fuel payments

Who cannot get a winter fuel payment

You are excluded from entitlement to a payment if, throughout the qualifying week (see p779):[82]

- you are serving a custodial sentence;
- you have been receiving free inpatient treatment for more than 52 weeks in a hospital or similar institution (see p942);
- you are receiving PC, income-based jobseeker's allowance (JSA) or income-related employment and support allowance (ESA) and you are living in residential care;[83]
- you are a 'person subject to immigration control', although there are exceptions to this rule (see p1500).

Residential care

You count as **'living in residential care'** if you are living in a care home (ie, an independent home which is registered or exempt from registration, or a local authority home which provides board) throughout the qualifying week and the 12 preceding weeks, disregarding temporary absences.

The amount

Subject to the rules below, you are entitled to a winter fuel payment of:

- £200 if you are aged between the qualifying age for PC and 79 (inclusive) in the qualifying week (see p779); *or*
- £300 if you are aged 80 or over in the qualifying week.[84]

If you do not get PC, income-based JSA or income-related ESA and you share your accommodation with another qualifying person (whether as a partner or friend), you get £100 if you are both aged between the qualifying age for PC and 79 or £150 if you are both aged 80 or over. If only one of you is aged 80 or over, s/he gets £200 and the other person gets £100.

If you get PC, income-based JSA or income-related ESA, you (and your partner if you have one) get £200 if one or both of you is aged between the qualifying age for PC and 79, or £300 if one or both of you is aged 80 or over, regardless of whether there is anyone else in your household who qualifies.[85]

If you are living in residential care (see above) in the qualifying week and are not getting PC, income-based JSA or income-related ESA, you are entitled to a payment of £100 if you are aged between the qualifying age for PC and 79, or £150 if you are aged 80 or over.[86]

Claiming and getting paid

You should automatically receive a payment without having to make a claim if you received a payment the previous year, or if you are getting retirement pension or any other social security benefit (apart from child benefit and housing benefit) in the qualifying week.[87]

Otherwise, you must claim a winter fuel payment on or before 31 March following the qualifying week.[88] To ensure you receive your payment before Christmas, submit your claim before the qualifying week. A claim can be accepted in any written format but it is best to use the designated form, which you can get from the winter fuel payments helpline on 0845 915 1515 (local rate) (textphone: 0845 601 5613) or from www.gov.uk. From 2014, you may also be able to claim by telephone. See www.gov.uk/winter-fuel-payment for details.

You should get a written decision. To be entitled for the winters from 1997/98 to 1999/2000 you must have claimed on or before 31 March 2014.

If you are a member of a couple and your partner is receiving income support, the payment can be made to either of you (even though your partner is under the qualifying age for PC – see p752).[89]

The government aims to make payments between mid-November and Christmas.

6. Tax, other benefits and the benefits cap

Social fund loans and payments are not taxable.

They are disregarded as income and capital for the purposes of means-tested benefits and tax credits, and do not affect entitlement to any non-means-tested benefits.

In some cases, the total amount of specified benefits you receive is limited to £350 a week (if you are a single claimant without children) or £500 a week (if you are a lone parent or a member of a couple). This is known as the 'benefit cap'. Social fund loans and payments are *not* one of the specified benefits. The benefit cap only applies if you are getting housing benefit or universal credit.

Notes

1. **Budgeting loans**
   1 Dir 8 BLG
   2 *R v SFI ex parte Davey*, 19 October 1998, unreported (HC)
   3 Dir 8 BLG
   4 Dir 9 BLG
   5 Dir 8 BLG
   6 Dir 2 BLG
   7 Dir 53 BLG
   8 Dir 11 BLG
   9 Dir 53 BLG
   10 Dir 52 BLG

• •

11 Reg 5 SF(AM) Regs
12 Reg 6(2) SF(AM) Regs
13 Reg 6(3) and (4) SF(AM) Regs
14 Reg 2(1)(a) and (2)(a) SF(AR) Regs
15 Reg 2(4) SF(AR) Regs
16 Reg 2(6) SF(AR) Regs
17 Reg 2(3) SF(AR) Regs
18 Para 60 Part 4 BLG
19 s78(1) SSAA 1992
20 Reg 7(5) and (6) SF(AM) Regs
21 Reg 3 SF(RDB) Regs
22 s78(3) SSAA 1992

2. Sure Start maternity grants
23 Reg 5(2) SFM&FE Regs
24 Reg 5(3) SFM&FE Regs
25 Reg 3A SFM&FE Regs
26 Reg 5A SFM&FE Regs
27 Reg 6 SFM&FE Regs
28 Reg 5(4) SFM&FE Regs
29 Reg 3(1) and (2) SFM&FE Regs
30 Reg 5(1) SFM&FE Regs
31 Reg 19 and Sch 4 para 8 SS(C&P) Regs
32 Reg 6(1)(a) SS(C&P) Regs
33 Regs 4(7) and 6(1)(b) SS(C&P) Regs

3. Funeral expenses payments
34 Reg 7(3) and (4) SFM&FE Regs
35 Reg 7(7) SFM&FE Regs
36 Reg 7(9)(b) SFM&FE Regs
37 Reg 7(9)(a) SFM&FE Regs
38 Reg 4(1) and (2) SFM&FE Regs
39 Reg 7(5) SFM&FE Regs
40 Reg 7(8)(a)-(e) SFM&FE Regs
41 Reg 3(1) SFM&FE Regs
42 CIS/788/2003
43 Reg 3(2) SFM&FE Regs
44 Regs 7(8)(e) and 8(4) SFM&FE Regs
45 Reg 7(8)(e) SFM&FE Regs; R(IS) 7/04
46 Reg 8(1) and (2) SFM&FE Regs
47 R(SB) 2/87
48 Reg 8(7)(a) SFM&FE Regs
49 Reg 8(7)(b) SFM&FE Regs
50 Reg 8(8) SFM&FE Regs
51 *Kerr v Department for Social Development
    (NI)* [2004] All ER(D) 65; [2004] UKHL
    23
52 Reg 7(7) SFM&FE Regs
53 CSB/488/1982
54 CIS/12344/1996; R(IS) 6/98
55 CIS/85/1991
56 Reg 7(8)(e) SFM&FE Regs
57 CIS/12783/1996
58 Reg 7(10) SFM&FE Regs
59 Reg 9(1), (2) and (3) SFM&FE Regs
60 Reg 9(8) SFM&FE Regs
61 Reg 9(10) SFM&FE Regs
62 Reg 9(7) SFM&FE Regs

63 Reg 10(1) SFM&FE Regs
64 para 39404 DMG
65 R(IS) 14/91
66 Reg 10(1A) SFM&FE Regs
67 Reg 10(2) SFM&FE Regs
68 Sch 4 para 9 SS(C&P) Regs
69 Reg 6(1)(a) SS(C&P) Regs
70 Regs 4(7) and 6(1)(b) SS(C&P) Regs
71 Reg 35(2) SS(C&P) Regs
72 s78(4) SSAA 1992; CIS/616/1990
73 R(SB) 18/84

4. Cold weather payments
74 Reg 2(1) and (2) SFCWP Regs
75 Reg 1A(2) and (3) SFCWP Regs
76 Reg 1A(4) SFCWP Regs
77 Reg 1(2) SFCWP Regs
78 Reg 3 SFCWP Regs
79 Reg 2(6) SFCWP Regs
80 Reg 2(6) SFCWP Regs

5. Winter fuel payments
81 Reg 2 SFWFP Regs
82 Reg 3 SFWFP Regs
83 Reg 1(2) and (3) SFWFP Regs
84 Reg 2 SFWFP Regs
85 Reg 2(1)(ii)(aa), (2) and (3) SFWFP Regs
86 Reg 2(2)(b) SFWFP Regs
87 Reg 4 SFWFP Regs
88 Reg 3(1)(b) and (2) SFWFP Regs
89 Reg 36(2) SS(C&P) Regs

Chapter 38

Statutory maternity, paternity and adoption pay

This chapter covers:
1. Who is entitled (p784)
2. The rules about your age (p793)
3. People included in the claim (p794)
4. The amount of benefit (p794)
5. Special benefit rules (p796)
6. Claims and backdating (p800)
7. Getting paid (p804)
8. Tax, other benefits and the benefit cap (p805)

There are two types of statutory paternity pay (SPP): ordinary SPP and additional SPP. In this chapter, when the term 'SPP' is used the rules described apply to both ordinary and additional SPP, unless stated otherwise. Similarly, the rules apply to SPP paid for a birth and SPP paid for an adoption, unless stated otherwise.

Key facts

- **Statutory maternity pay (SMP), statutory paternity pay (SPP)** and **statutory adoption pay (SAP)** are payments made to certain employees by their employers.
- You may be entitled to SMP if you are pregnant or have recently given birth. You may be entitled to SPP if you are the father of a baby, if your partner has recently given birth, if s/he is adopting a child, or if you are jointly adopting a child with her/him. You may be entitled to SAP if you are adopting or jointly adopting a child.
- SMP, SPP and SAP are not means-tested, although each has an employment and an earnings condition.
- You do not have to have paid national insurance contributions to qualify, but you must have had earnings at a certain level.
- You do not need to intend to return to work to qualify for SMP, SPP or SAP (although for additional SPP, the person getting maternity allowance (MA),

Part 5: Other benefits
Chapter 38: Statutory maternity, paternity and adoption pay
1. Who is entitled

SMP or SAP must have done so). You do not have to repay SMP, SPP or SAP, even if you do not return to work.

- You may be entitled to more maternity, paternity or adoption pay under your employment contract.
- If you disagree with your employer's decision on your entitlement, or if your employer has failed to make a decision, you can challenge this.

Future changes

The government plans to introduce a new scheme of statutory shared parental pay (SSPP) for employees to replace additional SPP.[1] This is likely to affect you if your expected week of childbirth starts on or after 5 April 2015, or if you have been notified of an adoption match or have a child placed for adoption on or after this date. Under the plans, if you reduce the length of time over which you get SMP or SAP, you and your partner may qualify for SSPP from your respective employers (or, for SSPP in respect of a birth, you and your child's father or your partner may qualify). Alternatively, if you get MA on the basis of your employment or self-employment and you reduce the length of time over which MA is paid, your child's father or your partner may qualify for SSPP, although you cannot. You can only qualify for SSPP if you meet an employment and earnings condition similar to that for additional SPP and if your partner meets an employment or self employment and earnings condition similar to that for MA. It is proposed that you will be able to request consecutive or non-consecutive weeks of SSPP, and that if both of you qualify, you will be able to request SSPP for different, or the same, weeks. However, it is intended that the combined total number of weeks for which SSPP can be paid is 39 minus the number of weeks over which SMP, MA or SAP has been paid, and that those weeks must fall within a year of the birth or adoption placement. The government also plans to pay SAP at an earnings-related rate for the first six weeks to correspond with arrangements for SMP, and to allow local authority foster carers in England who have been approved as prospective adopters and who have a child placed with them to qualify for either SAP or ordinary SPP and SSPP. See CPAG's online service and *Welfare Rights Bulletin* for updates.

1. **Who is entitled**

The table on p785 details which statutory payment you may qualify for, given your circumstances.

Only women can qualify for statutory maternity pay (SMP); men or women can qualify for statutory adoption pay (SAP) or statutory paternity pay (SPP).

Note: it is expected that from some point in the future you will have to be entitled to work in the UK (and not prevented from working under immigration provisions) to qualify for SMP, SPP or SAP. There may be exceptions.[2] See CPAG's online service and *Welfare Rights Bulletin* for updates.

Event	Circumstances	Benefit you may qualify for
Adoption	You are the sole adopter	SAP
	You and your partner are jointly adopting a child	SAP or SPP (adoption)
	Your partner is the adopter	Ordinary SPP (adoption)
Birth	You are the mother of the baby	SMP or maternity allowance (MA)
	You are the father of the baby or the partner of the mother	SPP (birth)

If you are jointly adopting a child with your partner (see p788 for the meaning of partner), you can choose whether to request SPP or SAP from your employer (you cannot get both for the same adoption). Your partner may be able to qualify for ordinary SPP while you get SAP or vice versa. However, you cannot both qualify for SAP for the same adoption and you can only receive additional SPP (adoption) if your partner was getting SAP.[3]

There are some groups of people to whom special rules apply (see p796).

Appendix 4 contains a table of relevant dates for SMP and SPP (birth) for all the weeks in 2014/15.

Statutory maternity pay

You qualify for SMP if you:[4]
- are pregnant and within the 11 weeks before your 'expected week of childbirth' (see below), or you have recently given birth; *and*
- satisfy the continuous employment rule (see p788); *and*
- satisfy the earnings condition (see p790); *and*
- have given the appropriate notice and information (see p800); *and*
- are not carrying out work for the employer paying you SMP (but see p792); *and*
- do not work for other employers after the birth (but see p793 for an exception).

Expected week of childbirth

The '**expected week of childbirth**' (EWC) is the week, starting on a Sunday, in which your baby is due to be born.

Part 5: Other benefits
Chapter 38: Statutory maternity, paternity and adoption pay
1. Who is entitled

Statutory paternity pay

Statutory paternity pay terminology

'**Ordinary SPP**' is paid for one or two weeks usually at some time in the eight weeks after the birth or adoption. It can be paid whether or not your partner is entitled to MA, SMP or SAP.

Entitlement to '**additional SPP**' depends on the other parent of the child giving up her/his MA, SMP or SAP. It can usually only be paid from 20 weeks after the birth or adoption (see p795). You may qualify for both ordinary SPP and additional SPP for the same birth or adoption.

'**SPP (birth)**' is SPP that you qualify for on the basis of either your partner giving birth to a child, or you being the father of a child.

'**SPP (adoption)**' is SPP that you qualify for on the basis that a child has been, or is to be, placed with your partner for adoption, or with you and your partner for joint adoption.

See p784 for the relationship between SPP and SAP. See p806 if you are entitled to statutory sick pay (SSP).

You qualify for SPP if:[5]

- you satisfy the continuous employment rule (see p788); *and*
- you satisfy the earnings condition (see p790); *and*
- you satisfy the particular conditions for either SPP (birth) or SPP (adoption) (see p787); *and*
- you have given your employer the required notice and information including, for additional SPP, a declaration from the mother or other adopter of the child (see p801); *and*
- you are not carrying out work for the employer paying you SPP (but see p792); *and*
- you do not do any work for other employers (but see p793 for an exception); *and*
- for additional SPP:[6]
  - the baby's mother has been entitled to MA on the basis of her own employment or self-employment (see Chapter 34) or SMP or your partner has been entitled to SAP; *and*
  - at least two weeks before the MA period, maternity pay period or adoption pay period is due to end, payment of MA, SMP or SAP stops as a result of her/him returning to work . This can be as a result of returning to work for the same employer or for another employer and, for MA, it also can be as a result of self-employment (see p716 and p792) . The return to work must occur at least two weeks after the birth or adoption placement (but see p795 for the earliest date on which your additional SPP can start).

You only qualify for additional SPP if the baby's mother (for additional SPP (birth)) or your partner (for additional SPP (adoption)) has returned to work and stopped getting MA, SMP or SAP (HMRC states that s/he can request that her/his MA, SMP or SAP stops, even if s/he has not used up her 10 'keeping in touch days' – see p716 and p792). If her/his MA/SMP or SAP stops, but s/he s/he does not return to work immediately (eg, because s/he takes sick leave or annual leave directly after ending her/his period of maternity leave or adoption leave), you will not qualify for additional SPP until s/he does return to work. However, once s/he has returned to work and stopped getting MA, SMP or SAP, if s/he takes any subsequent period of leave, your additional SPP is unaffected.

Note: if the child's mother or adopter dies, the qualifying conditions for additional SPP are modified (see p798).

Statutory paternity pay (birth)

You qualify for SPP (birth) if, as well as satisfying the general conditions for SPP outlined above, you satisfy the following particular conditions:
- while receiving SPP you intend to care for the child or, for ordinary SPP, to support the child's mother;
  and either
- you are the child's father and you have, or you expect to have, responsibility for her/his upbringing (for additional SPP this must be, apart from the mother's responsibility, the main responsibility); *or*
- you are the partner (see p788) of the child's mother and you have, or you expect to have (apart from the mother's responsibility), the main responsibility for the child's upbringing.

Statutory paternity pay (adoption)

You qualify for SPP (adoption) if, as well as satisfying the general conditions for SPP outlined above, you satisfy the following particular conditions:
- your partner (see p788) is adopting a child, or you and your partner are jointly adopting a child. For additional SPP, both you and your partner must have been matched with the child for adoption; *and*
- while receiving SPP you intend to care for the child or, for ordinary SPP, to support the person adopting the child; *and*
- for ordinary SPP only, you have, or you expect to have (along with the adopter or the other adopter), the main responsibility for the upbringing of the child; *and*
- the adoption is under UK law (if the child is adopted from abroad, see p799); *and*
- you have not elected to receive SAP.

Part 5: Other benefits
Chapter 38: Statutory maternity, paternity and adoption pay
1. Who is entitled

Partner

You count as the **'partner'** of the adopter or of the child's mother if either:[7]

– you are her/his spouse or civil partner; *or*

– you live with her/him and the child in an 'enduring family relationship'. In this situation, however, a parent, grandparent, sister, brother, aunt, uncle, half-sister or half-brother cannot count as your partner and, if you are adopted, neither can your adoptive parents.

Statutory adoption pay

See p785 for the relationship between SPP and SAP. See p806 if you are entitled to SSP.

You qualify for SAP if:[8]

- a child has been, or is expected to be, placed with you for adoption under UK law (but see p799 if the child is adopted from abroad); *and*
- you satisfy the continuous employment rule (see below); *and*
- you satisfy the earnings condition (see p790); *and*
- you have given the required notice and information (see p803); *and*
- you have not elected to receive ordinary SPP. **Note:** you cannot get ordinary or additional SPP if you have elected to receive SAP; *and*
- your co-adopter is not claiming SAP, if you have jointly adopted the child; *and*
- you are not carrying out work for the employer paying you SAP (but see p792); *and*
- you do not do any work for other employers (but see p793 for an exception).

Continuous employment rule

To satisfy the continuous employment rule:[9]

- you must have been employed by your employer (see p789) for a continuous period of at least 26 weeks ending with:
  - for **SMP** and **SPP (birth)**, the 15th week before the EWC (see p785); *or*
  - for **SPP (adoption)** and **SAP**, the week in which you are notified that you have (or, for ordinary SPP, the adopter has) been matched with a child for adoption (see below);
- for **ordinary SPP**, you must also have been continuously employed by that same employer from the end of:
  - the 15th week before the EWC until the day that the child is born (for ordinary SPP (birth)); *or*
  - the week in which the adopter was notified of being matched with a child until the day of the adoption placement (for ordinary SPP (adoption)); *or*
- for **additional SPP**, you must also have been continuously employed by that same employer over the period from:
  - the 15th week before the EWC (for additional SPP (birth)); *or*

– the week in which you were notified of being matched with a child (for additional SPP (adoption)),

until the week before your additional paternity pay period begins (see p795).

Matched for adoption

You are '**matched for adoption**' when an adoption agency or society decides that you would be a suitable adoptive parent for a particular child. It should be able to provide you with a matching certificate to verify this. The date you are notified of a match is the date you receive the adoption agency's notification rather than the date it is sent.[10]

See p797 if your employer has dismissed you 'solely or mainly' to avoid paying you SMP, SPP or SAP.

See p790 if there have been breaks in your employment.

Note:

- For a birth, if the baby is born in or before the 15th week before the EWC, you satisfy the continuous employment rule if you would have done so, for both SMP and ordinary SPP (birth), had the baby been born on the expected date or, for additional SPP (birth), had the baby been born after the 15th week before the EWC. In this situation, to qualify for additional SPP, you must also be continuously employed by the same employer from the date of the baby's birth until the week before your additional paternity pay period begins.[11]
- For SMP, if you are employed for only part of the 15th week before your EWC, the whole week still counts towards your period of continuous employment.[12]
- For SAP, if you are employed for only part of the week in which you receive the notification of a match, the whole week still counts.[13]

Employed by an employer

To satisfy the continuous employment rule, you must have been continuously employed by an employer who was liable to pay secondary Class 1 national insurance (NI) contributions for you, or who would have been liable to pay them had your earnings been high enough (see p844), or had you been older (if you are under 16).[14]

If you count as an 'employed earner' for NI purposes (see p844), you normally count as an employee for SMP, SPP and SAP.[15]

You do not need to have a written contract of employment to count as an employee. Your employer cannot restrict your right to SMP, SPP or SAP by its own rules or contract with you and cannot require you to contribute towards the cost of SMP, SPP or SAP.[16] Periods of employment for the same employer in another European Economic Area state may count towards your period of continuous employment.[17] However, even if you are an employee you may not be entitled to

Part 5: Other benefits
Chapter 38: Statutory maternity, paternity and adoption pay
1. Who is entitled

SMP, SPP or SAP if your employer is based outside Great Britain (see p1584).[18] See p1583 if you are employed abroad.

Breaks in employment

For SMP, SPP and SAP, if you return to work for the same employer following a break in your employment, certain weeks when you were not employed can still count towards your 26 weeks of continuous employment. These include weeks in which, for all or part of the week, you were:[19]

- incapable of work because of sickness or injury, unless your incapacity lasted for more than 26 consecutive weeks;
- absent because your employer temporarily had no work to offer you – eg, you are an agency worker and the agency is unable to find you work in any particular week;
- absent from work, but because of an arrangement or custom, you are regarded as continuing in employment – eg, on public holidays or an annual shutdown, or if you are a teacher employed on a term-by-term contract;
- for SMP only, absent from work wholly or partly because of pregnancy or childbirth if there were no more than 26 weeks between your contracts with your employer, and you were employed by your employer both before and after you had your baby but not during the period of your absence;
- for SMP only, absent from work while on paternity, adoption or parental leave.

If it is your employer's practice to offer work for separate periods of six months or less, at least twice a year, to people who have worked for them before, in some circumstances if you are off work because of illness or pregnancy, you do not have to have returned to work in order to benefit from the above rules.[20]

Note: the above rules are only relevant when there is a *break* in your employment with your employer. So, for example, more than 26 weeks' sickness absence should count towards your continuous employment if you remain employed by your employer while off sick.

If your employment is legally transferred from one employer to another, your employment is unbroken.[21] If you have been reinstated or re-engaged following an unfair dismissal claim, any period between your dismissal and reinstatement or re-engagement counts towards your 26 weeks' continuous employment.[22]

See p976 if your continuity of employment is affected by a strike and p797 if you have been dismissed by your employer.

The earnings condition

To qualify for SMP, SPP or SAP, your average gross weekly earnings during the 'relevant period' (see below) must be at least equal to the lower earnings limit for NI contributions.[23] The lower earnings limit used is the one in force at the end of:

- the 15th week before the EWC (see p785) (unless your baby is born before or during the 15th week before the EWC), for **SMP** or **SPP (birth)**;[24]

- the week in which you or the adopter are notified by the adoption agency of being matched with the child (see p789), for **SAP** and **SPP (adoption)**.

For the tax year 2014/15 the lower earnings limit is £111 a week (see Appendix 8 for the amounts for other years). If your average weekly earnings during the relevant period fall below the lower earnings limit (eg, because you are sick and receiving just SSP), you will not qualify for SMP, SPP or SAP.

See p797 if you have been dismissed.

Relevant period

For **SMP** and **SPP (birth)** the **'relevant period'** is the period between:[25]
- your last normal payday that falls either in or before the 15th week before the EWC (see p785) or before the week in which the baby is born, whichever is earlier; *and*
- the day after your last normal payday falling at least eight weeks before that.

For **SAP** and **SPP (adoption)**, the **'relevant period'** is the period between:
- your last normal payday that falls in or before the week in which you or the adopter are notified of being matched with a child for adoption (see p789); *and*
- the day after your last normal payday falling at least eight weeks before that.

For this purpose, a week runs from Sunday to Saturday. If you are paid at intervals of one or more calendar months, your average earnings are calculated by dividing your earnings by the number of calendar months in the relevant period (to the nearest whole number), multiplying by 12 and dividing by 52.

What counts as earnings

As well as your gross wages, bonuses and any overtime pay you receive during the relevant period, your earnings include payments such as:[26]
- SSP, SMP, SAP and SPP;
- arrears of pay following reinstatement or re-engagement in your job or a continuation of your contract of employment under the Employment Rights Act 1996.

Certain payments (eg, some payments in kind) are ignored.[27]

Pay rises

For **SMP**, if you are awarded a pay rise that affects your wages for any part of the period running from the first day of your relevant period (see above) until the last day of your statutory maternity leave, your employer should reassess your average earnings over the relevant period to take account of this increase (even if the pay rise did not actually increase your wages for any week in the relevant period). If you would have been awarded a pay rise but for being on maternity leave, you are still treated as receiving it. For these purposes 'statutory maternity leave' includes both ordinary and additional maternity leave under the Employment Rights Act

Part 5: Other benefits
Chapter 38: Statutory maternity, paternity and adoption pay
1. Who is entitled

1996. Your employer should recalculate your average weekly earnings as if your earnings in each of the weeks of your relevant period included the increase, and pay any arrears of SMP due to you.[28] If you become entitled to SMP as a result of the pay rise, your employer should deduct any payments of MA that you have received for the same period from the SMP you are owed.[29]

For **SPP** and **SAP**, only a backdated pay rise that is paid in respect of the relevant period is included in the calculation of your average earnings. Your employer should recalculate your average weekly earnings following the rise and pay any arrears of SPP or SAP due to you.[30]

Working during your statutory maternity, paternity or adoption pay period

Your entitlement to SMP, SPP or SAP is not affected by work you do on a self-employed basis during your maternity, paternity or adoption pay period (as long as no Class 1 NI contributions are payable on your earnings from that work), but your entitlement might be affected if you work for an employer.

Working for the employer who is paying you

You can do up to 10 days' work for the employer who pays you **SMP**, **additional SPP** or **SAP** during your maternity, additional paternity or adoption pay period without your entitlement to those payments being affected. These 10 days (called 'keeping in touch days') do not have to be consecutive, but if you work for only part of a day, it still counts as a full day of work.

However:[31]

- you lose a week's SMP or SAP for every week in which you do any work for that employer in excess of those 10 days. This applies even if you only work for part of the week;
- if you do any work for the employer who is liable to pay you additional SPP in excess of the 10 'keeping in touch days', your additional paternity pay period will end and so your additional SPP stops.

If you do *any* work for the employer who is paying you **ordinary SPP** during the ordinary paternity pay period, that employer is not liable to pay you ordinary SPP for the week in which you work.[32]

The above rules apply even if you are working for the employer under a new contract which did not exist before your maternity, paternity or adoption pay period began.

Note:

- If you intend to work for more than 10 days for the employer who is paying you SMP or SAP, this may affect your continued entitlement to maternity or adoption leave (and so may also affect your entitlement to SMP or SAP for the remainder of the maternity or adoption pay period). If you do not want to bring your period of leave to an end, seek employment advice before agreeing to such work. For additional SPP, such work would bring your period of additional paternity leave to an end.

- If more than one employer is liable to pay you SMP, ordinary SPP or SAP, unless the payments are just one award apportioned between your employers (see p796), any work you do for one of those employers does not affect your entitlement to SMP, ordinary SPP or SAP from the other.
- For SMP, if you return to work for your employer but you are subsequently off work sick during the maternity pay period, you are not entitled to SSP. Instead, you can get SMP for each week in which you are off work for a whole week. If your partner or the father of your child gets additional SPP (birth) in respect of the child for whom you receive SMP, s/he should inform her/his employer, in writing, of a change of circumstances such as reinstatement of your SMP. If you are in this situation, and her/his additional SPP is affected, seek advice.

5

Working for another employer

The general rule is that if you work for another employer, who is not liable to pay you SMP, SPP or SAP, while on maternity, paternity or adoption leave, you cannot get SMP, SPP or SAP for the week in which you work and for the remainder of your maternity, paternity or adoption pay period.[33]

However, this is subject to two exceptions.

- For SMP, if the work is done while you are on maternity leave but before your baby is born, your entitlement to SMP is unaffected.[34]
- Your SMP, SPP or SAP is not affected by any work that you do for an employer who is not liable to pay you SMP, SPP or SAP if you also worked for that employer in the:
  - 15th week before the EWC, for SMP and SPP (birth); or
  - week in which you or the adopter were notified that you had been matched with a child for adoption, for ordinary SPP (adoption) and SAP; or
  - 15th week before the expected week of the child's placement for adoption, for additional SPP (adoption).[35]

Notify the employer paying you SMP, SPP or SAP of any work that you do for another employer within seven days of the first day in your maternity, paternity or adoption pay period on which you do such work. For SPP and SAP, your employer has the right to request this information in writing.[36]

2. The rules about your age

There are no upper or lower age limits for statutory maternity pay, statutory paternity pay or statutory adoption pay.

Part 5: Other benefits
Chapter 38: Statutory maternity, paternity and adoption pay
4. The amount of benefit

3. **People included in the claim**

You claim statutory maternity pay, statutory paternity pay or statutory adoption pay for yourself. You cannot claim any increase for your partner or child(ren).

4. **The amount of benefit**

	Period of payment	Gross amount[37]
Statutory maternity pay (SMP)	39 weeks: first six weeks	90% of average weekly earnings
	Remaining 33 weeks (see below)	Lesser of £138.18 or 90% of average weekly earnings
Statutory paternity pay (SPP)	Two weeks for ordinary SPP and normally up to 19 weeks for additional SPP (see p795)	Lesser of £138.18 or 90% of average weekly earnings
Statutory adoption pay (SAP)	39 weeks	Lesser of £138.18 or 90% of average weekly earnings

Period of payment

Statutory maternity pay

SMP can only be paid during the '**maternity pay period**'.[38] This is a period of 39 consecutive weeks which starts from, at the earliest, the beginning of the 11th week before the expected week of childbirth (EWC – see p785), unless your baby is born before this, and at the latest, the day after your baby is born. Within these limits, you can normally choose when your maternity pay period begins by notifying your employer of when you want your SMP to start. However, if you have to stop work earlier than planned, your maternity pay period may begin earlier. If:

- your baby is born before the 11th week before the EWC, or before the date you had arranged to start your SMP, your maternity pay period will begin on the day after the birth;
- you are off work because of your pregnancy on or after the start of the fourth week before your EWC but not later than the day after you have your baby, your SMP will start on the day after the first day of such absence in that period. This does not apply if your absence is not related to your pregnancy;
- you leave your job, see p797.

If your baby is born earlier or later than expected but after your maternity pay period has begun, your maternity pay period is not extended or reduced. If your maternity pay period starts earlier than you intended because of an early birth, the 39 weeks runs from the date your maternity pay starts.

Statutory paternity pay

Ordinary statutory paternity pay

Ordinary SPP can be paid for a maximum of two consecutive weeks (called the **'ordinary paternity pay period'**), although you can choose to receive it for just one week.[39] The earliest ordinary SPP can be paid is from the child's date of birth or the date of the child's placement for adoption, and the latest is eight weeks after those dates. If the child is born before the EWC (see p785), the latest ordinary SPP (birth) can be paid is eight weeks after the first day of the EWC (but see p792 if you work during your paternity pay period).[40]

As long as you request that your ordinary SPP be paid within this period and you give your employer sufficient notice of when you want it to be paid (see p801), you can choose to start your ordinary paternity pay period either on:[41]

- a particular date; *or*
- the day of the baby's birth, or the day of the child's placement for adoption (without specifying an actual date). If you are at work on that day, your ordinary paternity pay period will begin on the next day; *or*
- a day falling a certain number of days after that (without specifying an actual date).

Additional statutory paternity pay

Additional SPP can only be paid during the **'additional paternity pay period'**. Usually, the earliest your additional paternity pay period can start is from:[42]

- 20 weeks after the birth (or from the date the mother's maternity allowance (MA) or SMP stopped as a result of her return to work, if this is later), for additional SPP (birth); *or*
- 20 weeks after the adoption placement (or from the date your partner's SAP stopped as a result of her/his return to work, if this is later), for additional SPP (adoption).

The latest the additional paternity pay period can end is the date the mother's or adopter's 39-week maternity allowance period, maternity pay period or adoption pay period ends (see p714, p794 and p796). You can choose the number of weeks for which you want to be paid additional SPP within this period. The dates when your additional paternity pay period can start and end generally mean that the maximum period for which you can get additional SPP is 19 weeks.[43] If the mother or adopter has died, in some circumstances the additional paternity pay period can start earlier, and additional SPP can therefore be paid for longer (see p798).

See p792 if you work during your paternity pay period. See p797 if you give up or lose your job.

Part 5: Other benefits
Chapter 38: Statutory maternity, paternity and adoption pay
5. Special benefit rules

Statutory adoption pay

SAP can only be paid during the **'adoption pay period'**.[44] This is a period of 39 consecutive weeks which normally begins, at the earliest, 14 days before the day you expect the child to be placed with you and, at the latest, on the date of placement. As long as you request that your SAP starts within these time limits and give your employer the required period of notice (see p803), you can choose whether you want your adoption pay period to begin either:[45]

- on a particular date (but if the child is placed with you before that date, then the adoption pay period will begin on the date of placement); or
- on the day of placement (without specifying an actual date). If you are working on that day, your adoption pay period will begin on the next day.

See p792 if you work during your adoption pay period. See p797 if you give up or lose your job.

Your adoption pay period may end early if the child either:[46]

- is returned to the adoption agency (in Scotland, to the adoption agency or society) after being placed with you; or
- dies, if this happens after being placed with you for adoption; or
- is not actually placed with you but your adoption pay period has already begun.

In these circumstances, your adoption pay period ends eight weeks after the end of the week the child is returned, or dies, or that you are notified that the placement is not to take place, if this is earlier than it would have otherwise ended. In this situation, a week runs from Sunday to Saturday.

More than one job

If you satisfy the conditions of entitlement to SMP, SPP or SAP with more than one employer (or under two or more contracts with the same employer), you can get SMP, SPP or SAP from each job (although if your earnings from any of your jobs are aggregated when calculating your liability to pay national insurance contributions, those jobs are counted as one and the amount of SMP, SPP or SAP your employers have to pay is apportioned between them).[47]

If you are both employed and self-employed, you may get SMP even if you continue to work on a self-employed basis while receiving it, but if you get SMP you cannot also get MA for the same period in respect of the same pregnancy.[48]

5. **Special benefit rules**

Special rules may apply to:

- people in prison or detention (see p958);

- people who are abroad (see p1583);
- people who give up their job or who have been dismissed (see below);
- people involved in a trade dispute (see p976);
- you if your baby is stillborn, you have had a multiple birth or adopted more than one child (see p798);
- people applying for additional statutory paternity pay (SPP) following the death of the mother or adopter (see p798);
- people who have adopted a child from abroad (see p799).

If you give up your job or are dismissed

Your employer is still liable to pay you statutory maternity pay (SMP), SPP or statutory adoption pay (SAP) if:

- after your maternity, paternity or adoption pay period has started, you give up your job, are dismissed or your job ends (but see p1379 if your employer is insolvent);[49] *or*
- your employer dismisses you at any time provided the dismissal was 'solely or mainly' to avoid paying SMP, SPP or SAP and you had been employed by that employer for at least eight continuous weeks. This also applies to additional SPP if the employer is solely or mainly trying to avoid paying you ordinary SPP and vice versa. The amount of your SMP, SPP or SAP is calculated using your average earnings for the eight-week period ending with the last day for which you were paid;[50] *or*
- you satisfy the qualifying conditions for SMP, SPP or SAP and your job ends for any reason at any time after:[51]
  - the beginning of the 15th week before your expected week of childbirth (EWC), for SMP; *or*
  - the day on which the child is born, for ordinary SPP (birth); *or*
  - the day on which the child is placed for adoption, for ordinary SPP (adoption); *or*
  - the beginning of the week before your additional paternity pay period begins, for additional SPP; *or*
  - the beginning of the week in which you were notified of being matched with a child for adoption, for SAP.

For SMP, if your job ends at any time after the start of the 15th week before your EWC or, for SAP, if it ends before the adoption pay period is due to start, you are not required to have given your employer notice of your intention to take maternity or adoption leave, although you still need to give your employer information to support your entitlement to SMP or SAP as detailed on p800 and p803 – eg, evidence of the expected date of birth for SMP.[52]

If you qualify for SMP but your job ends before your maternity pay period was due to start, your SMP will start at the beginning of the 11th week before your

Part 5: Other benefits
Chapter 38: Statutory maternity, paternity and adoption pay
5. Special benefit rules

EWC or, if your job ends after this, on the day after you finish work, unless your baby is born before these dates.[53] If you qualify for SAP but your job ends before your adoption pay period was due to start, it will start 14 days before the expected date of placement or, if your job ends after this, on the day after you finish work, unless your child is placed with you before this.[54]

If you are dismissed while pregnant or on maternity, paternity or adoption leave, seek advice about your right to claim unfair dismissal.

If you start work for another employer after giving up your job or being dismissed, see p793.

Stillbirths, multiple births and adoptions

If your baby is stillborn after 24 weeks of pregnancy, SMP and ordinary SPP (birth) are payable in the same way as for a live birth, so if you have a still-birth certificate you can qualify.[55] If the baby is stillborn before you have completed 24 weeks of pregnancy, this is treated as a miscarriage and SMP and SPP (birth) are not payable. You may qualify for statutory sick pay (SSP – see Chapter 39) or employment and support allowance (ESA – see Chapter 6 and Chapter 28) if you are unfit for work. If the baby is born alive but then dies (even after only a moment), this is a live birth and you can get SMP or ordinary SPP (birth) even if it happens before 24 weeks of pregnancy. Additional SPP (birth) is not payable if your baby has died in any of these circumstances.

No extra SMP, SPP or SAP is payable if you or your partner give birth to more than one baby, or have more than one child placed with you for adoption, unless this happens as part of a different adoption arrangement.[56]

Additional statutory paternity pay following the death of mother or adopter

If the mother of the child (for additional SPP (birth)) or your partner (for additional SPP (adoption)) dies before the end of her/his maternity allowance period, maternity pay period or adoption pay period, you may still qualify for additional SPP. In this situation, the normal rules for additional SPP apply with the following modifications.

If the death occurs:
- after your additional paternity pay period has begun, and you inform your employer of this in writing as soon as reasonably practicable, you can amend the date on which you want your additional paternity pay period to end, although the latest it can end is the date the maternity allowance period, maternity pay period or adoption pay period would have ended;[57]
- before your additional paternity pay period has begun, the earliest your additional paternity pay period can begin is the date of death, and the latest it can end is the date that, had s/he not died, the mother's maternity allowance period or maternity pay period or your partner's adoption pay period would

have ended. Within these limits, the maximum period for which you can receive additional SPP is 39 weeks.[58] It is not necessary for the mother or your partner to have returned to work, or even have started getting maternity allowance (MA), SMP or SAP, for you to qualify, provided that had s/he lived, you both would have met the qualifying conditions.[59]

If the death occurred before your additional paternity pay period had begun, the rules about the notice and information you must give your employer (see p802) and the time limits for providing this are modified. You must notify your employer (not necessarily in writing) of the date you want your additional SPP to begin and provide further information to your employer in writing. Use Form SC10, available from HMRC's website, to give the necessary information. The notice and information must be given as soon as reasonably practicable after the death, but no longer than eight weeks after (but if you cannot provide the information at the same time that you give your employer notice of the date you want your additional SPP to start, you are treated as if you had done so if you provide it as soon as practicable after that). If you provide the notice and information within these time limits, you can qualify from the date the mother or your partner died. If you do not do so within this time, you can still qualify, but you must give the information to your employer at least six weeks' before the date you have notified that you want your additional SPP to start.[60]

If you are adopting a child from abroad

If you are adopting a child from abroad you may be entitled to SPP (adoption) or SAP. To qualify you must satisfy the normal rules of entitlement for SPP (adoption) or SAP described in this chapter but with certain modifications. Although you must have 'official notification' that you have been approved for adoption from UK authorities (see below), you will not have been matched with a child for adoption by UK authorities under UK law, and it is primarily the rules that refer to the date of placement and the date of notification of being matched for adoption (both of which do not apply to overseas adoptions) that are modified.[61] Use Form SC5 (for ordinary SPP), Form SC9 (for additional SPP) or Form SC6 (for SAP), available from www.gov.uk, to apply for SPP or SAP from your employer for an overseas adoption. If a placement is made under UK law, the normal rules of entitlement to SPP and SAP apply.

Official notification

'**Official notification**' for an overseas adoption is a written notification issued by or on behalf of a relevant UK authority stating that it has issued, or is going to issue, a certificate to the overseas authority confirming that you are approved for adoption (sometimes called a Certificate of Eligibility and Suitability to Adopt).

Part 5: Other benefits
Chapter 38: Statutory maternity, paternity and adoption pay
6. Claims and backdating

6. **Claims and backdating**

Making a claim

It is not necessary for you to complete a claim form to qualify for statutory maternity pay (SMP), statutory paternity pay (SPP) or statutory adoption pay (SAP), but you must give your employer certain notice and information.

Notification sent to your employer in a properly addressed and pre-paid letter is treated as having been given on the day it is posted.[62]

There are different notice requirements for statutory maternity, paternity and adoption leave. If your employer offers its own maternity, paternity or adoption pay scheme as well as SMP, SPP or SAP, the notice requirements for this scheme may also be different. Check this with your employer.

Notice and information for statutory maternity pay

To qualify for SMP, you must give your employer:

- notice (in writing if your employer requests this) of the date from which you want to get SMP. This notice must be given at least 28 days before you expect payment to start or, if that is not practicable, as soon as reasonably practicable after that.[63] See p794 for when it is possible for your SMP to start; *and*
- evidence of the expected date of birth (normally a MAT B1 form issued by your doctor or registered midwife – see below). You must provide this evidence no more than three weeks after the start of your maternity pay period. This time limit can be extended to the end of the 13th week of the maternity pay period if you have good cause for the delay.[64]

The terms 'as soon as reasonably practicable' and 'good cause' are not defined in the regulations – you must show that any delay was reasonable, given your circumstances.

If you give your employer less notice than this or you do not provide the above evidence within the time limit, your employer may not pay you SMP. If you think your employer's decision is wrong, you can challenge it (see Chapter 60).

The earliest you can be issued with a MAT B1 form is the start of the 20th week before your expected week of childbirth (EWC). If you do not have a MAT B1, your employer can accept other medical evidence, but it must be substantially like Form MAT B1.[65]

If your employment ends in or after the 15th week before your baby is due, see p797.

If your baby is born early

If your baby is born before your maternity leave has started, your maternity pay period normally begins on the day after you had your baby rather than the day that you planned.

To qualify for SMP, you must inform your employer (in writing if your employer requests this) of the date on which your baby was born if either:

- your baby is born during or before the 15th week before your EWC; *or*
- you had informed your employer of the date from which you wanted your SMP to start, but the baby was born before that date.

You must do this within four weeks of the birth or, if that is not practicable, as soon as reasonably practicable after that.[66]

In addition, if your baby is born before you intended to start your maternity pay period, you must give your employer evidence of the week in which you had the baby (eg, a birth certificate, or a MAT B1 form if the child's date of birth is given on this) and of the expected date of birth, within three weeks of the start of your maternity pay period. This time limit can be extended to the end of the 13th week of the maternity pay period if you have good cause for the delay.[67]

Notice and information for statutory paternity pay

To qualify for SPP, you must give your employer certain notice and information.

Ordinary statutory paternity pay

To qualify for ordinary SPP, you must give your employer, in writing:[68]

- notice of when you want your ordinary SPP to start (see p795 for when it can start) and whether you want to get it for one or two weeks; *and*
- the particular information required for either SPP (birth) (see p802) or SPP (adoption) (see p802).

You must give your employer this notice and information at least 28 days before you want your ordinary SPP to start or, if this is not practicable, as soon as is reasonably practicable after that date. If you do not, your ordinary SPP can start later, once the necessary notice has been given, as long as payment would still fall within the period for which ordinary SPP can be paid (see p795).

To provide the above notice and information to your employer, you may use Form SC3 for ordinary SPP (birth) or Form SC4 for ordinary SPP (adoption), available from www.gov.uk.

In addition, if you notified your employer that you want to start your paternity pay period:[69]

- on the day the child is born or is placed with you for adoption, or on a day falling a certain number of days after that, you must tell your employer the actual date of birth or placement, as soon as is reasonably practicable after that date;
- on a specific date, but the child is not born or placed with you until after that date, you must give your employer notice of the new date on which you want your paternity pay period to start, as soon as is reasonably practicable.

Part 5: Other benefits
Chapter 38: Statutory maternity, paternity and adoption pay
6. Claims and backdating

Additional statutory paternity pay

To qualify for additional SPP, you must give your employer, in writing:[70]

- notice of when you want your additional SPP to start and end (see p795 for when it can start and the latest it can end); *and*
- the particular information required for either SPP (birth) (see p802) or SPP (adoption) (see below); *and*
- a signed declaration from the child's mother (for additional SPP (birth)) or from your partner (for additional SPP (adoption)) giving certain information (such as the date s/he intends to return to work and the start date of her/his maternity allowance, maternity or adoption pay period). Use the declaration on the appropriate form (see below) to ensure s/he provides the necessary information.

You must give your employer this notice and information at least eight weeks before your additional paternity pay period is to start. If you do not, your additional SPP can start later, once the necessary notice has been given, as long as payment would still fall within the additional paternity pay period (see p795).

To provide the above notice and information to your employer, you may use Form SC7 for additional SPP (birth) or Form SC8 for additional SPP (adoption), available from www.gov.uk.

Within 28 days of receiving the above information, your employer has the right to request certain other information from you (such as a copy of the child's birth certificate, for additional SPP (birth) or a document from the adoption agency, for additional SPP (adoption)), which you must provide within 28 days of the request.[71]

Note: these rules are modified if the child's mother or adopter dies.

Statutory paternity pay (birth)

The particular information that you must also give your employer, in writing, in order to qualify for ordinary or additional SPP (birth) is:

- the EWC (and, if the child has already been born or for additional SPP, the date of birth); *and*
- a declaration stating that you meet the conditions specific to SPP (birth) described on p787 – eg, that you are the partner of the child's mother and will have main responsibility for her/his upbringing.

Statutory paternity pay (adoption)

The particular information that you must also give your employer, in writing, in order to qualify for ordinary and additional SPP (adoption) is:

- the date you expect the child to be placed for adoption or the date s/he was placed if the placement has already happened (for additional SPP (adoption) you only need to provide the latter date); *and*
- the date on which the adopter (or you, for additional SPP) was notified of the adoption match (see p789); *and*

- a declaration stating that, for ordinary SPP, you meet the first three of the particular conditions specific to SPP (adoption) described on p787 or, for additional SPP, that you meet the first two of those conditions.

Notice and information for statutory adoption pay

To qualify for SAP you must give your employer:[72]

- notice (in writing if your employer requests this) of:
  - when you want your SAP to start (see p796 for when it can start); *and*
  - the date on which you expect the child to be placed with you for adoption; *and*
- a written declaration that you want to receive SAP rather than SPP; *and*
- documents from the adoption agency giving certain information, including the date on which the child is expected to be (or was) placed with you and the date on which it informed you of this.

  The 'matching certificate' provided by the adoption agency or adoption society will give this information.

This notice and information must be given at least 28 days before your adoption pay period is due to start or, if this is not practicable, as soon as is reasonably practicable after that date, otherwise your employer may not pay you SAP. In this situation, it may be possible to argue that your SAP should start later, once the necessary time limit for providing the notice or information has passed, as long as payment would still fall within the adoption pay period (see p796). This may mean, however, that you might not be entitled to SAP for a full 39 weeks. If you are in this position, seek advice. If you think your employer's decision is wrong, you can challenge it (see Chapter 60).

In addition to the above notice, if you choose to start your adoption pay period on the day the child is placed with you, you must give your employer further notice of the date on which the placement occurs as soon as is reasonably practicable.[73]

If your employment ends before your adoption pay period begins, see p797.

Who should claim

If you are entitled to SMP, SPP or SAP but are not well enough to deal with your own affairs, HM Revenue and Customs (HMRC) can appoint someone else to act for you.[74] This person is your 'appointee' (see p1137). For further information contact HMRC's employees' enquiry line (tel: 0300 200 3500; textphone: 0300 200 3519).

If you claim the wrong benefit

If you are sick with a pregnancy-related illness in the four weeks before the week your baby is due, your employer can start your maternity leave (even if it is sooner than you had planned) and pay you SMP rather than statutory sick pay. It cannot do this if your illness is *not* pregnancy-related.[75]

You may get a claim for MA backdated if your employer has informed you that you are not entitled to SMP (see p721).

Backdating your entitlement

To qualify for additional SPP, you must give your employer eight weeks' notice of when you want payment to start (but see p798 if the baby's mother or your partner has died). For SMP, ordinary SPP or SAP, you must normally give your employer at least 28 days' notice or your notice must be given as soon as is reasonably practicable after that date. Provided you gave notice as soon as was reasonably practicable, your SMP, ordinary SPP or SAP should be paid from the day you have chosen to start your maternity, ordinary paternity or adoption pay period. To qualify you must also give your employer the information and evidence detailed on pp800–01 within the time limits outlined on those pages.

'As soon as was reasonably practicable' is not defined in the regulations. You must show that your delay was reasonable given your circumstances. If you disagree with your employer's decision, you can ask HMRC to make a decision on your entitlement (see Chapter 60).

7. Getting paid

Statutory maternity pay (SMP), statutory paternity pay (SPP) and statutory adoption pay (SAP) are usually paid by your employer in the same way and at the same intervals as your normal wages or salary.[76] See p794 for the period over which you can be paid.

Note:

- If you are also entitled to contractual maternity, paternity or adoption pay from your employer, SMP, SPP or SAP will form part of your payments. Your employer can offset any payment of SMP, SPP or SAP from its contractual liability to pay you for the same period.[77]
- Your employer cannot pay you SMP, SPP or SAP by making a payment in kind, or by providing board and lodging, a service or some other facility.[78]
- If you become entitled to SMP because of a pay rise, your employer can deduct any maternity allowance (MA) that you received for the same period from the SMP you are owed.[79]
- If your entitlement has been decided by a decision maker from HM Revenue and Customs (HMRC), or by the First-tier Tribunal or Upper Tribunal, your employer may be required to pay you within a certain time limit (see p1379). If your employer cannot or will not pay you, see p1379 for when payment can be made by HMRC.

- The rules on overpayments described in Chapter 56 do not apply to SMP, SPP or SAP. If your employer thinks it has overpaid you SMP, SPP or SAP, it may attempt to recover the sum it has overpaid by making a deduction from your wages. If this happens, seek advice. If your employer decides that you have been paid SMP in error, consider claiming MA. You may be able to get this backdated (see p721).
- If your employer becomes insolvent, see p1379.
- For additional SPP and SAP, HMRC, not your employer, pays you if you are entitled for a period after you were imprisoned or detained (see p958), or while you were in detention, if you were subsequently released without charge, found not guilty or given a non-custodial sentence.[80]

Change of circumstances

You must keep your employer informed of any change of circumstances that may affect your entitlement, such as starting work for someone else during the maternity, paternity or adoption pay period.[81] It is advisable to do this in writing, but for additional SPP, you *must* write to your employer to inform it of certain changes – eg, if the mother of the child (for additional SPP (birth)) or your partner (for additional SPP (adoption)) no longer intends to return to work.[82]

8. Tax, other benefits and the benefit cap

Tax

Statutory maternity pay (SMP), statutory paternity pay (SPP) and statutory adoption pay (SAP) are treated as earnings and you pay tax and national insurance (NI) contributions as appropriate.[83]

Means-tested benefits

In some circumstances, being pregnant or on maternity, paternity or adoption leave may allow you to qualify for income support (IS – see p27). In certain situations, you can be treated as having limited capability for work while you are pregnant (see p1004) and so may qualify for income-related employment and support allowance (ESA). If you have limited capability for work, you do not qualify for income-based jobseeker's allowance (JSA). You also cannot qualify for income-based JSA if you are getting SMP or if you are on paternity or adoption leave, because you are treated as unavailable for work. However, your partner may qualify for JSA.[84] If you are a member of a 'joint-claim couple' for JSA (see p46) and you are pregnant, in some circumstances you do not need to meet all the conditions to qualify (see p47) and, in some circumstance (including if you get SMP), only your partner needs to claim.

Part 5: Other benefits
Chapter 38: Statutory maternity, paternity and adoption pay
8. Tax, other benefits and the benefit cap

If you are unsure whether you would be better off if you claim IS or income-related ESA, or if your partner claims income-based JSA, seek advice.

If you are getting SMP, SPP or SAP, you may be able to get an allowance for childcare costs deducted from your earnings when calculating your entitlement to housing benefit (HB – see p270).

If you come under the universal credit (UC) system (see p19), you cannot make a new claim for income-related ESA or IS and your partner cannot make a new claim for income-based JSA. Instead you may qualify for UC.

Your SMP, SPP or SAP is taken into account for IS, income-related ESA and income-based JSA (see p273).

SMP, SPP and SAP are treated as earnings for pension credit and HB (see p258 and p307). When calculating your entitlement to UC, SMP, SPP and SAP are treated as earnings and your net earnings are taken into account (see p326 and, for deductions that are made from earnings, p327).

Non-means-tested benefits

Unless you come under the UC system, you cannot get contribution-based JSA if you are receiving SMP or if you are on ordinary or additional paternity or adoption leave, as you are treated as unavailable for work (see p1032). At the time of writing, if you come under the UC system, provided you do not have limited capability for work and are not treated as having limited capability for work (see p1004), you may qualify for contribution-based JSA while getting SMP, SPP or SAP. As you would have to accept a claimant commitment to qualify for JSA (see p1064), seek advice before claiming if you are still employed – the DWP may contact your employer and this may jeopardise your employment.

You cannot get statutory sick pay (SSP) when you are receiving SMP. See p820 for how your SSP entitlement is affected if you are pregnant. You cannot receive SPP or SAP for any week in which you are entitled to SSP.[85]

If you are getting SMP, additional SPP or SAP, you may qualify for NI credits (see p857). It is important to claim credits in order to protect your future entitlement to contributory benefits.

Employment and support allowance

You can qualify for contributory ESA as well as ordinary SPP if you satisfy the conditions for contributory ESA during your ordinary paternity pay period.

You can only qualify for contributory ESA while you are getting SMP, additional SPP or SAP if you have limited capability for work (or you can be treated as having limited capability for work – see p1004) and if, on the day before your maternity, additional paternity or adoption pay period began:[86]

• you had (or could be treated as having) limited capability for work; *and*
• you satisfied the NI contribution conditions for contributory ESA.

However, if you are entitled to contributory ESA and either SMP, additional SPP or SAP, your contributory ESA is reduced by the amount of SMP, additional SPP or SAP you receive for the same week.

If you are pregnant or have recently given birth, in some circumstances you can be treated as having limited capability for work (see p1004).

Tax credits

If you get SMP, SPP or SAP, you may be entitled to working tax credit (WTC – see Chapter 9) as in some circumstances you can be treated as in full-time work when getting one of these payments (or for some periods when you are on maternity, paternity or adoption leave – see p170).

If you are entitled to WTC, you may be able to get help with the cost of childcare, even before you return to work (see p1405).

You may also qualify for child tax credit (CTC – see Chapter 8).

The first £100 of your weekly SMP, SPP or SAP is ignored when calculating your entitlement to WTC and CTC, and any SMP, SPP or SAP you receive over £100 is counted as employment income.

The benefit cap

In some cases, the total amount of specified benefits you receive is limited to £350 a week (if you are a single claimant without children) or £500 a week (if you are a lone parent or a member of a couple). This is known as the 'benefit cap'. SMP, SPP and SAP are *not* specified benefits. The benefit cap only applies if you are getting HB or UC. See p1169 for further information.

Passports and other sources of help

For details of:
- Sure Start maternity grants from the social fund, see p770. In some circumstances you may qualify for a maternity grant even if you are not the mother of the child;
- free prescriptions and free NHS dental treatment, see Chapter 30;
- Healthy Start food vouchers and vitamins, see p829;
- council tax reduction, see p827.

Notes

1 Children and Families Act 2014;
Statutory Shared Parental Pay (General)
Regulations (draft)

1. Who is entitled
2 s63 WRA 2012
3 **OSPP** s171ZB(4) SSCBA 1992
ASPP s171ZEB(2)(e) and (4) SSCBA
1992
SAP s171ZL(4) and (4A) SSCBA 1992
4 ss164 and 165 SSCBA 1992
5 **OSPP** ss171ZA(2) and (3), 171ZB(2)
and (3), 171ZC and 171ZE(4)-(7)
SSCBA 1992; regs 4 and 11 SPPSAP(G)
Regs; reg 4(2)(b) and (c) PAL Regs
ASPP ss171ZEA(2) and (3) and
171ZEB(2)-(4) SSCBA 1992; regs 4 and
12 ASPP(G) Regs
6 Regs 3, 4(1)(b), 6, 12(1)(b), 13 and 19
ASPP(G) Regs
7 **OSPP** Regs 4 and 11 SPPSAP(G) Regs;
reg 2 PAL Regs
ASPP Regs 2, 4(2)(a) and 12(2)(a)
ASPP(G) Regs
8 s171ZL(2)-(4) SSCBA 1992; reg 3(2)
SPPSAP(G) Regs
9 **SMP** s164(2)(a) SSCBA 1992
OSPP ss171ZA(2)(b) and (d) and (3)
and 171ZB(2)(b) and (d) and (3)
ASPP ss171ZEA(2)(b) and
171ZEB(2)(b) SSCBA 1992; regs 4(3)
and (4) and 12(3) and (4) ASPP(G) Regs
SAP s171ZL(2)(b) and (3) SSCBA 1992
10 **OSPP&SAP** Reg 2(2)(b) SPPSAP(G)
Regs
ASPP Reg 2(5)(b) ASPP(G) Regs
11 **SMP** Reg 4(2)(a) SMP Regs
SPP Reg 5(a) SPPSAP(G) Regs; reg 5(a)
and (c) ASPP(G) Regs
12 Reg 11(4) SMP Regs
13 Reg 33(4) SPPSAP(G) Regs
14 **SMP** s171(1) SSCBA 1992; reg 17 SMP
Regs
SPP&SAP ss171ZJ(1) and (2) and
171ZS(1) and (2) SSCBA 1992; reg 32
SPPSAP(G) Regs; reg 24 ASPP(G) Regs
15 **SMP** Reg 17 SMP Regs
OSPP&SAP Reg 32 SPPSAP(G) Regs
ASPP Reg 24 ASPP(G) Regs

16 **SMP** s164(6) and (7) SSCBA 1992
SPP s171ZF SSCBA 1992
SAP s171ZO SSCBA 1992
17 **SMP** Regs 2 and 5 SMP(PAM) Regs
SPP&SAP Regs 3, 5 and 6
SPPSAP(PAM) Regs; reg 4(4) and (5)
OSPP(A)ASPP(A)&SAP(AO)(PAM) Regs
18 **SMP** Reg 17(3) SMP Regs
OSPP&SAP Reg 32(3) SPPSAP(G) Regs
ASPP Reg 24(4) ASPP(G) Regs
19 **SMP** Reg 11(1) SMP Regs
OSPP&SAP Reg 33 SPPSAP(G) Regs
ASPP Reg 25 ASPP(G) Regs
20 **SMP** Reg 11(3A) SMP Regs
OSPP&SAP Reg 33(3) SPPSAP(G) Regs
ASPP Reg 25(3) ASPP(G) Regs
21 **SMP** Reg 14 SMP Regs
OSPP&SAP Reg 36 SPPSAP(G) Regs
ASPP Reg 28 ASPP(G) Regs
22 **SMP** Reg 12 SMP Regs
OSPP&SAP Reg 34 SPPSAP(G) Regs
ASPP Reg 26 ASPP(G) Regs
23 **SMP** ss164(2)(b) and 171(4) SSCBA
1992
SPP ss171ZA(2)(c), 171ZB(2)(c),
171ZEA(2)(c), 171ZEB(2)(c) and
171ZJ(6)-(8) SSCBA 1992;regs 4(3)(b)
and (4) and 12(3)(b) and (4) ASPP(G)
Regs
SAP ss171ZL(2)(d) and 171ZS(6)-(8)
SSCBA 1992
24 **SMP** s164(2)(b) SSCBA 1992; reg
4(2)(b) SMP Regs
OSPP s171ZA(2)(c) and (3) SSCBA
1992; reg 5(b) SPPSAP(G) Regs
ASPP Reg 5(1)(b) ASPP(G) Regs
25 **SMP** Reg 21 SMP Regs
SPP Reg 40 SPPSAP(G) Regs; reg 32
ASPP(G) Regs
26 **SMP** Reg 20 SMP Regs
OSPP&SAP Reg 39 SPPSAP(G) Regs
ASPP Reg 31 ASPP(G) Regs
27 **SMP** Reg 20(2)(a) SMP Regs
OSPP&SAP Reg 39(2)(a) SPPSAP(G)
Regs
ASPP Reg 31(2)(a) ASPP(G) Regs
28 Reg 21(7) SMP Regs
29 Reg 21B SMP Regs
30 **OSPP&SAP** Reg 40(7) SPPSAP(G) Regs
ASPP Reg 32(7) ASPP(G) Regs

31 **SMP** s165(4) and (5) SSCBA 1992; reg
9A SMP Regs
ASPP 171ZEE(7) and (8)
SSCBA 1992; reg 20(4) ASPP(G) Regs
SAP 171ZN(3) and (4) SSCBA 1992; reg
27A SPPSAP(G) Regs
32 s171ZE(5) and (6) SSCBA 1992
33 **SMP** s165(6) SSCBA 1992; reg 8(2)
SMP Regs
OSPP s171ZE(7) SSCBA 1992; reg
17(1) SPPSAP(G) Regs
ASPP s171ZEE(7) and (8) SSCBA
1992; reg 20(1) ASPP(G) Regs
SAP s171ZN(5) SSCBA 1992; reg 26(1)
SPPSAP(G) Regs
34 s165(6) SSCBA 1992
35 **SMP** Reg 8(1) SMP Regs
SPP Regs 10 and 16 SPPSAP(G)
Regs; regs 11 and 18 ASPP(G) Regs
SAP 25 SPPSAP(G) Regs
36 **SMP** Reg 24 SMP Regs
SPP Reg 17(2) and (3) SPPSAP(G)
Regs; reg 20(2) and (3) ASPP(G) Regs
SAP Reg 26(2) and (3) SPPSAP(G) Regs

4. The amount of benefit
37 **SMP** s166 SSCBA 1992
SPP Reg 2 SPPSAP(WR) Regs; reg 2
ASPP(WR) Regs
SAP Reg 3 SPPSAP(WR) Regs
38 s165 SSCBA 1992; reg 2 SMP Regs; reg
1(2) SMPSS(MA) Regs
39 s171ZE(2) SSCBA 1992; reg 12(3)
SPPSAP(G) Regs
40 s171ZE(3) SSCBA 1992; regs 8 and 14
SPPSAP(G) Regs
41 Regs 6 and 12 SPPSAP(G) Regs
42 s171ZEE(2)-(5) SSCBA 1992; regs 7
and 14 ASPP(G) Regs
43 s171ZEE(4) SSCBA 1992; regs 7(1) and
(3) and 14 (1) and (3) ASPP(G) Regs
44 Reg 21 SPPSAP(G) Regs
45 s171ZN(2) SSCBA 1992; reg 21
SPPSAP(G) Regs
46 Reg 22 SPPSAP(G) Regs
47 **SMP** s164(3) SSCBA 1992; reg 18 SMP
Regs
OSPP&SAP ss171ZD(1) and 171ZM(1)
SSCBA 1992; reg 38 SPPSAP(G) Regs
ASPP s171ZED(1) SSCBA 1992; reg 30
ASPP(G) Regs
48 s35(1)(d) SSCBA 1992

5. Special benefit rules
49 **SMP** s164(2)(a) and (3) SSCBA 1992
OSPP s171ZD SSCBA 1992
ASPP s171ZED SSCBA 1992
SAP s171ZM SSCBA 1992
50 **SMP** s164(8) SSCBA 1992; reg 3(1)
SMP Regs
OSPP s171ZD(2) SSCBA 1992; reg 20
SPPSAP(G) Regs
ASPP s171ZED(2) SSCBA 1992; reg 23
ASPP(G) Regs
SAP s171ZM(2) SSCBA 1992; reg 30
SPPSAP(G) Regs
51 **SMP** s164(2)(a) SSCBA 1992
OSPP ss171ZA(2)(b) and
(d) and 171ZB(2)(b) and (d) SSCBA
1992
ASPP ss171ZEA(2)(b) and
(d) and 171ZEB(2)(b) and
(d) SSCBA 1992; regs 4(3) and 12(3)
ASPP(G) Regs
SAP s171ZL(2)(b) and (3) SSCBA 1992
52 **SMP** Regs 22 and 23(4) and (5) SMP
Regs
SAP Regs 24 and 29 SPPSAP(G) Regs
53 s165(2) SSCBA 1992; reg 2(5) SMP Regs
54 Reg 29 SPPSAP(G) Regs
55 **SMP** s171(1) SSCBA 1992
OSPP s171ZA(5) SSCBA 1992
56 **SMP** s171(1) SSCBA 1992
OSPP ss171ZA(4) and 171ZB(6) SSCBA
1992
ASPP ss171ZEA(4) and 171ZEB(5)
SSCBA 1992
SAP 171ZL(5) SSCBA 1992
57 Regs 7(4) and (5) and 14(4) and (5)
ASPP(G) Regs
58 Regs 9(1)(b)-(e), (2) and
(3) and 16(1)(b)-(e), (2) and (3)
ASPP(G) Regs
59 Regs 9 and 16 ASPP(G) Regs
60 Regs 9(1)(a)(ii), 10, 16(1)(a)(ii) and 17
ASPP(G) Regs
61 SSCBA(AAO) Regs; SPP(A)&SAP(AO)
(No.2) Regs; ASPP(AO) Regs; Statutory
Paternity Pay (Adoption) and Statutory
Adoption Pay (Adoptions from
Overseas) (Administration) Regulations
2003, No.1192

6. Claims and backdating
62 **SMP** Regs 22(4) and 23(3) SMP Regs
OSPP&SAP Reg 47 SPPSAP(G) Regs
ASPP Reg 39 ASPP(G) Regs
63 s164(4) and (5) SSCBA 1992
64 Reg 22 SMP Regs
65 Reg 2 SMP(ME) Regs
66 Reg 23 SMP Regs

67 Reg 22 SMP Regs
68 s171ZC(1) and (3)(c) SSCBA 1992; regs
    9 and 15 SPPSAP(G) Regs
69 Regs 7 and 13 SPPSAP(G) Regs
70 s171ZEC(1) and (3)(c) SSCBA
    1992; regs 8 and 15 ASPP(G) Regs
71 Regs 8(3) and (5) and 15(3) and (5)
    ASPP(G) Regs
72 s171ZL(6) and (7) SSCBA 1992; regs 23
    and 24 SPPSAP(G) Regs
73 Reg 23 SPPSAP(G) Regs
74 **SMP** Reg 31 SMP Regs
    OSPP&SAP Reg 46 SPPSAP(G) Regs
    ASPP Reg 38 ASPP(G) Regs
75 Sch 11 para 2(h) SSCBA 1992; reg 2(4)
    SMP Regs

7. Getting paid
76 **SMP** Reg 27 SMP Regs
    OSPP&SAP Reg 41 SPPSAP(G) Regs
    ASPP Reg 33 ASPP(G) Regs
77 **SMP** Sch 13 para 3 SSCBA 1992
    SPP s171ZG(2) SSCBA 1992; reg 22
    ASPP(G) Regs
    SAP s171ZP(5) SSCBA 1992
78 **SMP** Reg 27 SMP Regs
    OSPP&SAP Reg 41 SPPSAP(G) Regs
    ASPP Reg 33 ASPP(G) Regs
79 Reg 21B SMP Regs
80 **ASPP** Reg 36 ASPP(G) Regs
    SAP Reg 44 SPPSAP(G) Regs
81 **SMP** Reg 24 SMP Regs
    SPP Reg 17(2) SPPSAP(G) Regs; reg
    20(2) ASPP(G) Regs
    SAP Reg 26(2) SPPSAP(G) Regs
82 Regs 8(7) and 15(7) ASPP(G) Regs

8. Tax, other benefits and the benefit cap
83 s4(1)(a)(ii)-(v) SSCBA 1992
84 Reg 15(bc) and (c) JSA Regs
85 **SPP** Reg 18(a)SPPSAP(G) Regs; reg
    21(1)(a) ASPP(G) Regs
    SAP Reg 27(1)(a) SPPSAP(G) Regs
86 s20(2)-(5), (6) and (7) WRA 2007; regs
    80-82 ESA Regs; regs 73-75 ESA Regs
    2013

Chapter 39

. . . .

Statutory sick pay

This chapter covers:
1. Who is entitled to statutory sick pay (below)
2. The rules about your age (p818)
3. People included in the claim (p818)
4. The amount of benefit (p818)
5. Special benefit rules (p819)
6. Claims and backdating (p820)
7. Getting paid (p823)
8. Tax, other benefits and the benefit cap (p823)

Key facts

- Statutory sick pay (SSP) is paid by employers to certain employees who are unfit for work.
- SSP can be paid for up to 28 weeks.
- SSP is a non-means-tested benefit.
- Your entitlement to SSP is not based on your national insurance contribution record, but your usual earnings must be above a certain amount to qualify.
- If you qualify, SSP is the minimum amount your employer should pay while you are sick. You may be entitled to more under your contract.
- In some circumstances, you may qualify for SSP even if you have been dismissed by your employer.
- If you disagree with your employer's decision on your entitlement to SSP, or if your employer has failed to make a decision, you can challenge this.

---

1. Who is entitled to statutory sick pay

You qualify for statutory sick pay (SSP) if:[1]
- you are an employee (see p812); *and*
- you are incapable of work (see p812); *and*
- you are within a period of incapacity for work (see p814); *and*
- you are within your period of entitlement to SSP (see p814); *and*
- the day is a qualifying day (see p817); *and*

Part 5: Other benefits
Chapter 39: Statutory sick pay
1. Who is entitled to statutory sick pay

- your normal earnings are equal to or more than the lower earnings limit for national insurance (NI) contributions (see p816).

There are some groups of people to whom special rules apply (see p819). Certain people do not qualify for SSP (see p815). See below if your employer has dismissed you solely or mainly to avoid paying SSP.

Note: it is expected that from some point in the future you will have to be entitled to work in the UK (and not be prevented from taking up work under immigration provisions) to qualify for SSP.[2] There may be exceptions. See CPAG's online service and *Welfare Rights Bulletin* for updates.

Employees

To be entitled to SSP you must be an employee. If you count as an 'employed earner' for NI purposes (see p844), or if you would but for being under the age of 16, then you normally count as an employee for SSP purposes (so, for example, you may count as an employee if you are an agency worker).

You do not have to have a written contract of employment. It is the fact that you are employed that matters. Your right to SSP cannot be taken away by any document, whether you sign it or not. If your employer dismisses you to avoid paying SSP, see below.[3]

However, even if you are an employee, you are treated as if you are not (and so your employer does not have to pay you SSP) if your employer is:

- not resident and not present in Great Britain, and does not have a place of business in Great Britain (and is not treated as having one); *or*
- exempt from social security legislation because of an international treaty.[4]

See p815 for details of other employees who are not entitled to SSP.

Dismissal from work

If your employer dismisses you during your period of entitlement to SSP solely or mainly to avoid paying you SSP, it is still liable to pay you SSP. In these circumstances, your employer should continue to pay you SSP until either your period of entitlement to SSP ends or until your contract would have ended had you not been dismissed, whichever occurs first.[5] If your employer dismisses you for another reason (ie, not solely or mainly to avoid paying you SSP), you will not normally be entitled to SSP from that employer once your contract ends.

Incapable of work

To qualify for SSP, you must be 'incapable of work'. This has a meaning specific to SSP. Other tests, such as that of 'limited capability for work' described in Chapter 47, do not apply to SSP.

To be **'incapable of work'** for SSP purposes, you must be:[6]

- incapable of doing work that you could reasonably be expected to do under the terms of your contract because you have a specific disease, or a physical or mental disablement; *or*
- treated as incapable of such work (see p814).

Usually, after seven days of absence your employer will expect you to provide a medical certificate from a doctor (see below and p822) as evidence of your incapacity for work.

Medical certificates

On a medical certificate, also called a 'statement of fitness to work' or 'fit note', your doctor can state either that you are not fit for work, or that you 'may be fit for work taking account of the following advice'. These statements are not related to your specific job. If your doctor thinks you may be fit for some work, s/he can include a description of the effects of your condition on your ability to work and specify whether s/he thinks you may benefit from a phased return to work, altered hours, amended duties or workplace adaptations to facilitate your return to work.[7] If your employer does not agree to such altered arrangements, it can treat the fit note as evidence that you are not fit for work. However, it is for your employer to decide whether it accepts that you are incapable of work and if it does not, it will not pay you SSP. If you disagree, you can challenge your employer's decision (see Chapter 60). If you are only fit for work if your duties are changed to such an extent that it would not be reasonable to expect you to do them given the terms of your contract (whether these are written down or not), you may be able to argue that you still qualify for SSP. However, seek independent advice on your employment situation before refusing to accept a change in your duties.

If your employer doubts your incapacity for work, it can seek further advice. For example, it may consult its own medical officer (if it has one), your doctor (with your permission) or HM Revenue and Customs (HMRC). If your employer requests HMRC's help, HMRC may involve its Medical Service (MS) and, with your permission, the MS may contact your doctor and may arrange for you to have a medical examinination with a MS doctor (or other healthcare professional). Your employer is then given only the MS's view on whether you are fit for work in the job you do.

Note: a new government-funded independent service, called the Health and Work Service, is expected to be introduced in some areas, possibly from October 2014. This will provide occupational health advice to employers, employees and GPs. Once it is operational in your area, your GP (or employer) may refer you for an occupational health assessment and a return-to-work plan if you have been sick for four weeks or more. The service is not expected to be available nationally before April 2015.

Part 5: Other benefits
Chapter 39: Statutory sick pay
1. Who is entitled to statutory sick pay

If your employer requests HMRC's help in deciding whether you are capable of work, once the Health and Work Service is available in your area HMRC may advise your employer to use this first.

It is still up to your employer to decide whether to pay SSP, although you can challenge this decision (see Chapter 60).

Treated as incapable of work

Even if you are not actually incapable of work, your employer (or HMRC – see Chapter 60) may treat you as incapable of work if:[8]

- you have been officially excluded or prevented from working because you have (or it is suspected that you have) an infection, disease or contamination detailed under public health legislation, or you have been in contact with a case of such an infection, disease or contamination; *or*
- you are under medical care in connection with a specific disease or physical or mental disablement; *and*
  - a doctor has stated that as a precautionary measure or in order to convalesce you should not work; *and*
  - you do not go in to work for your employer.

If you are incapable of work for just part of a day, you must be treated as incapable of work for the whole day provided you do not do any work on that day. If you are a shift worker and you are incapable of work for part of a day but you do some work on that day, you should still be treated as incapable of work for the whole day if you only finish a shift that began the day before and you do not do any work on a shift that starts on that day and ends the next.

Period of incapacity for work

For SSP to be paid, you must be within a 'period of incapacity for work'. This is defined as four or more consecutive days of incapacity for work (see p812).[9] This means that you can only qualify for SSP if you are incapable of work for at least four days in a row. Every day of the week (including Sunday[10]) counts, even if it is not a day on which you would normally work. Days of incapacity for work which fall before or after the period covered by your contract can still be included in your period of incapacity for work (but see p817 if you have not yet started work).[11]

Two or more periods of incapacity for work are 'linked' and treated as a single period if they are separated by eight weeks or less.[12]

Period of entitlement to statutory sick pay

You only qualify for SSP if you are within 'a period of entitlement'. In certain circumstances, a period of entitlement cannot arise and so you will not qualify for SSP (see p815).

When entitlement to statutory sick pay starts

A period of entitlement normally starts on the first day of your period of incapacity for work, unless your contract of employment starts either during your period of incapacity for work or between two linked periods of incapacity for work.[13]

When entitlement to statutory sick pay ends

A period of entitlement to SSP ends (and so your SSP stops) if:[14]

- your period of incapacity for work ends (see p814); *or*
- you reach your maximum 28 weeks' entitlement to SSP from a particular employer (see p819); *or*
- your contract of employment ends (unless it has been brought to an end by your employer solely or mainly to avoid paying SSP – see p812); *or*
- in certain circumstances, you are pregnant or have just had a baby (see p820); *or*
- you reach the third anniversary of the start of the period of entitlement; *or*
- you are imprisoned or detained in legal custody (see p958).

Two or more periods of incapacity for work that are separated by eight weeks or less are linked and treated as a single period.[15] This is why it may be possible for you to have a period of entitlement which lasts for three years and not to have exhausted your 28 weeks' entitlement to SSP over that period.

If you have received your maximum 28 weeks' entitlement to SSP from a particular employer and you are still incapable of work, see p819.

If your employer stops paying you SSP because it decides your period of entitlement has ended, see p822.

When statutory sick pay is not paid

In certain circumstances a period of entitlement to SSP cannot arise. As a result, you do not qualify for any SSP during your period of incapacity for work.

A period of entitlement cannot arise if:[16]

- your normal weekly earnings are below the lower earnings limit (see p816); *or*
- at some time in the 85 days before the date on which your period of entitlement would have begun you were entitled to employment and support allowance (ESA) or, in some circumstances, you would have been entitled. This only applies if you made a claim for ESA or for another benefit that was treated as a claim for ESA. If it applies and you have limited capability for work, you may qualify for ESA instead of SSP; *or*
- at the time when your period of entitlement would have begun there is a strike at your workplace (but see p976); *or*
- you have not yet started work under your contract of employment (but see p817 if you had an earlier contract with the same employer); *or*

Part 5: Other benefits
Chapter 39: Statutory sick pay
1. Who is entitled to statutory sick pay

- at the time when your period of entitlement would have begun you were entitled to statutory maternity pay (SMP) or maternity allowance (see p820); *or*
- you are within the period immediately before or after you give birth (see p820); *or*
- you are in prison or legal custody (see p958).

If your employer decides not to pay you SSP on any of the above grounds, see p822.

Note:

- If you qualified for either incapacity benefit or severe disablement allowance in the 57 days before your period of entitlement to SSP would have started (or earlier than this if you were a 'welfare to work beneficiary'), you may not qualify for SSP. Instead, if you have limited capability for work, you may qualify for ESA. See p619 of the 2012/13 edition of this *Handbook* for details.
- If you are not entitled to work in the UK, see p812.

People with low earnings

You cannot get SSP if your 'normal weekly earnings' are less than the lower earnings limit for NI contributions (£111 a week in the tax year 2014/15 – see p844).

Your **'normal weekly earnings'** are calculated by averaging your gross earnings from your employer (ie, before tax and NI contributions are deducted) over the period between:[17]

- your last normal payday before your period of entitlement to SSP began (see below); *and*
- the day after the last normal payday that falls at least eight weeks before this.

Only payments actually made in this period count, even if in theory you should have been paid more.[18] However, if your employer has unlawfully withheld *all* of your wages for the period over which your earnings are averaged, you should not be excluded from entitlement to SSP on the basis you have low earnings if you otherwise would have qualified.[19]

If you are paid every one or more calendar months, your average earnings are calculated by dividing your earnings over the above period by the number of calendar months in the period (to the nearest whole number), multiplying by 12 and dividing by 52. If you are paid at other intervals and the period is not an exact number of weeks, the average is calculated by dividing your earnings by the number of days in the above period and multiplying by seven.

As well as your wages, your gross earnings include certain other payments, such as:[20]

- SSP, SMP, statutory paternity pay and statutory adoption pay;
- maternity pay;

• arrears of pay following reinstatement or re-engagement in your job or a continuation of a contract of employment under particular legislation.

Certain payments (eg, some payments in kind) are ignored.[21]
There are special rules to calculate your earnings if you have not been employed sufficiently long to have been paid wages over this eight-week period.[22]
See p819 if you have more than one job.

People who have not yet started work

If you have agreed to work for an employer but have not started work when your period of incapacity for work begins, you are not entitled to SSP from that employer for any day during your period of incapacity for work, unless your current contract of employment can be linked to a previous one with the same employer in which you did some work. Your employment is linked if there are eight weeks or less between the date your new contract starts and the date your last contract with the employer ended.[23] You do not have to have written contracts for this to apply.

Qualifying days

You can only be entitled to SSP for 'qualifying days'. SSP is not paid for your first three qualifying days, which are known as 'waiting days' (see p818).[24]
Qualifying days are usually those days of the week on which you normally work. However, other days may be selected as qualifying days by agreement between you and your employer if they would better reflect your contract of employment – eg, if you work a complicated shift pattern.
For this purpose, a week begins on Sunday and there must be a minimum of one qualifying day in each week.[25]
Any agreement to choose days that relate to the days you are incapable of work, or to the period of entitlement to SSP, are ignored. If you and your employer cannot agree which days are qualifying days, they are presumed to be:

• the days on which it is agreed that you are required to work; *or*
• Wednesday, if it is agreed that you are not required to work on any day in that week – eg, offshore oil workers, who may work two weeks 'on' and then two weeks 'off'; *or*
• if you cannot agree about which days you are or are not required to work, every day in the week, except days on which you and your employer agree that no employee works (if you can agree at least to that extent).[26]

Required to work
'**Required to work**' means required by the terms of your contract of employment.[27] Days when you can choose whether or not to work do not count – eg, voluntary overtime shifts.

Part 5: Other benefits
Chapter 39: Statutory sick pay
4. The amount of benefit

Waiting days

SSP is not paid for the first three qualifying days (see p817) in a period of entitlement.[28] These are called **'waiting days'** and, as they must be qualifying days, they will not necessarily be the first three days of your sickness.

If your period of incapacity for work can be linked to an earlier one in your period of entitlement with the same employer (see p814), any waiting days you served in the earlier linked period(s) do not have to be served again. So you can get SSP from your first qualifying day if your present period of incapacity for work is linked to an earlier one in which you served three waiting days.

2. **The rules about your age**

There are no lower or upper age limits for entitlement to statutory sick pay.

3. **People included in the claim**

You claim statutory sick pay for yourself. You cannot claim any increases for your partner or child(ren).

4. **The amount of benefit**

Statutory sick pay (SSP) is not paid for the first three qualifying days in a period of entitlement (see above). After that, it is payable at a rate of £87.55 a week. If you qualify, the weekly amount of SSP is the same irrespective of the number of hours you normally work for your employer when you are not sick.[29]

SSP is a daily benefit so it can be paid for periods of less than a week. The daily rate is calculated by dividing the weekly amount of SSP by the number of qualifying days you have in that week (a week for these purposes runs from Sunday to Saturday).[30]

Example

Zofia is employed in a shop and works four days a week (Wednesday to Saturday). After injuring her hand, she is incapable of work for just over two weeks. In the week of her injury, she works on Wednsday and is off sick for the rest of the week. Her period of entitlement to SSP begins on Thursday, the first day of her absence, but she is not entitled to SSP for that week as the first three qualifying days in her period of entitlement (Thursday to Saturday) are waiting days. As she is incapable of work for all her qualifying days in the next week she gets £87.55 SSP. In the following week she is off sick on Wednesday, Thursday and Friday and returns to work on Saturday. She receives £65.67 SSP (£87.55 divided by her four qualifying days to give a daily rate paid for three days).

People with more than one job

If you cannot work, you are entitled to SSP from any job for which you fulfil the qualifying conditions. So, you could get payments of SSP for each of two contracts with the same employer (eg, if you are both a daytime teacher and an evening tutor with a local authority) or payments from two separate employers. However, if the earnings from any of your different jobs are added together when calculating your liability to pay Class 1 NI contributions (which usually means you contribute less than if they had been treated separately), you can only receive a total of £87.55 a week from those jobs. Your employers' liability to pay you SSP is apportioned by agreement between them or, if they cannot agree, in accordance with their proportion of your combined earnings.[31]

It is possible for you to be unable to work on one contract and be entitled to SSP, but at the same time be able to work on a different contract – eg, if you perform different tasks for each.

Maximum entitlement to statutory sick pay

You are entitled to a maximum of 28 weeks of SSP from a particular employer in any one period of entitlement (see p814) – ie, 28 times the weekly rate of SSP.[32]

SSP you received from your employer in any previous linked periods of incapacity for work in the same period of entitlement counts in calculating the 28-week maximum. Previous periods of incapacity for work are linked to your current one if they are separated by eight weeks or less.[33] Once you have reached your maximum 28 weeks' entitlement with a particular employer, you cannot qualify for SSP again from that employer in respect of the same contract, until your current period of incapacity for work ends and a new one arises. This usually means more than eight weeks must separate the end of your last period of incapacity for work and the start of your present one (but see p815 if you got employment and support allowance (ESA) in the intervening period).

If you are still incapable of work after you have received your 28-week entitlement to SSP, consider claiming ESA (see Chapters 5 and 28).

5. Special benefit rules

Special rules may apply to:
- people who are abroad (see p1583);
- women who are pregnant or who have recently given birth (see p820);
- people involved in a trade dispute (see p976);
- people in prison or detention (see p958).

Part 5: Other benefits
Chapter 39: Statutory sick pay
6. Claims and backdating

Women who are pregnant or who have recently given birth

If you are entitled to statutory maternity pay (SMP) or maternity allowance (MA), you cannot get statutory sick pay (SSP) during the maternity pay period or the MA period (nor, likely, during the 14-week MA qualifying period if you get MA because you helped with your spouse's or civil partner's self-employment).[34] Within the limits set out on p714, p718 and p794 (and unless your baby is born early), you can choose when your maternity pay or MA period begins. So, for example, your employer cannot insist that you claim SMP or MA at the earliest possible date in order to limit the period for which SSP is paid.

Even if you are not entitled to SMP or MA:[35]

- you cannot get SSP (because a period of entitlement cannot arise) if your period of incapacity for work started at some time during the 18 weeks which run from the first of the following dates:
  - the beginning of the week in which you had your baby (but see below); *or*
  - if you are incapable of work either wholly or partly because of your pregnancy on a day that falls in the four weeks before your 'expected week of childbirth' (see p785), the beginning of the week that contains the first such day;
- if SSP is already being paid to you (because your period of entitlement started before the above period, or because your incapacity for work was not initially linked to your pregnancy), it will stop from the first of the following dates:[36]
  - the first day falling on or after the beginning of the fourth week before your expected week of childbirth when you are incapable of work wholly or partly because of your pregnancy; *or*
  - the date on which you have your baby.

In this situation, a week begins on a Sunday. If your baby is stillborn before you have completed 24 weeks of pregnancy, you qualify for SSP if you satisfy the other conditions of entitlement.

6. Claims and backdating

To qualify for statutory sick pay (SSP), you must notify your employer of your incapacity for work, rather than notifying the DWP or HM Revenue and Customs (HMRC).

Making a claim

You do not need to complete a claim form to qualify for SSP, just inform your employer that you are sick (see p821). Your employer should then decide whether you are entitled to SSP.

Telling your employer that you are sick

Your employer can decide both the time within which it wants to be notified of your sickness absence and the way that it should be told. Your employer must take reasonable steps to inform you of how and when it wants to be notified of your absence.[37] However, your employer cannot insist that you notify it of your sickness:[38]

- earlier than the first qualifying day (which is not necessarily your first day of sickness – see p817), or by a specific time on the first qualifying day;
- personally;
- by providing medical evidence;
- more than once a week;
- on a printed form or other document it provides.

Time limits

The following time limits apply for notifying your employer of your absence.[39]

- You must notify your employer of your absence within the time limit set by your employer, if your employer has taken reasonable steps to inform you of this time limit (unless it requires you to give notice earlier than the first qualifying day).
- If your employer has not taken reasonable steps to inform you, or if it has made no arrangements about the notification it requires, you must notify your employer of your incapacity for work in writing on or before the seventh day after your first qualifying day (see p817).
- This seven-day time limit, or your employer's time limit, can be extended by one month if you have good cause for the delay. What amounts to 'good cause' is not defined in the regulations, but you must show that your delay was reasonable given the circumstances.
- If it is not practical for you to inform your employer within that time, the time limit can be extended further, provided you have notified it as soon as is reasonably practicable and you have notified it on or before the 91st day after your first qualifying day.

Notice sent in a properly addressed pre-paid letter is treated as having been given on the day it was posted. If you do not notify your employer of your absence within the above time limits, you can still be entitled to SSP (and qualify for a total of 28 weeks' payment in your period of entitlement if you are off work for that long), but your entitlement starts from a later date.[40]

Information to support your claim

Your employer can require you to provide 'such information as may reasonably be required' to determine your claim for SSP.[41]

Part 5: Other benefits
Chapter 39: Statutory sick pay
6. Claims and backdating

Medical evidence

For the first seven days of your incapacity for work, your employer cannot insist that you obtain a medical certificate, as you are only required to provide a self-certificate as evidence of your incapacity for work.[42] After the first seven days, an employer would usually expect you to provide a medical certificate from a doctor. If you provide a certificate from someone else, such as an osteopath or chiropractor, this can be accepted if your employer considers it sufficient to show that you are incapable of work.[43] Whatever type of medical evidence you provide, it is up to your employer to decide whether or not to accept it. See Chapter 60 if you want to challenge your employer's decision. See p813 for further details of medical certificates.

5 Who should claim

As your employer cannot insist that you personally notify it of your incapacity for work, someone else can notify your employer on your behalf.

If you are not well enough to be able to deal with your own affairs, HMRC can appoint someone else to act for you (an 'appointee' – see p1137). For further information contact HMRC's National Insurance Enquiries helpline (tel: 0300 200 3500; textphone: 0300 200 3519).

If you claim the wrong benefit

A claim for another benefit cannot be treated as a claim for SSP. However, if you have notified your employer of your sickness, but you are not entitled to SSP, you may be able to get a claim for employment and support allowance (ESA) backdated more than the usual three months (see p629).

Backdating your entitlement

To qualify for SSP, you must notify your employer of your sickness (see p821). Even if you have not notified your employer promptly, your entitlement can still be backdated if you do so within the time limits on p821.

If statutory sick pay ends or is refused

If your employer decides that you are not entitled to SSP or stops paying you, it should provide you with a statement (usually on Form SSP1) within certain time limits, giving you the reasons for its decision.[44] If you do not agree with your employer's decision, see Chapter 60 for how to challenge it.

Whether or not you agree with your employer's decision, you should consider claiming other benefits. If you are not well enough to work, consider claiming ESA (see Chapters 5 and 28). The DWP usually asks HMRC to make a decision on your entitlement to SSP before it makes a decision on your claim for ESA.

7. Getting paid

Statutory sick pay (SSP) is usually paid in the same way and at the same intervals as your wages or salary.

SSP is a daily benefit, so, if you qualify for it, it can be paid for periods of less than a week. See p818 for the way the daily rate is calculated.

Note:

- If you are entitled to contractual sick pay from your employer, SSP forms part of your weekly pay. Your employer can offset any payment of SSP from its liability to pay you contractual sick pay for the same period.[45]
- Your employer cannot pay you SSP by making a payment in kind or by providing board and lodging, a service or other facilities.[46]
- Deductions that can be made from your wages (eg, union subscriptions) can also be made from your SSP.[47]
- If your entitlement to SSP has been decided by HM Revenue and Customs (HMRC) or by the First-tier Tribunal or Upper Tribunal, your employer may be required to pay your SSP within a certain time limit (see p1379).
- If your employer cannot or will not pay you, see p1379 for details of when payment of SSP can be made by HMRC.
- The rules on overpayments and recovery of overpaid benefit described in Chapter 56 do not apply to SSP. If your employer pays you SSP and later decides that you were not entitled to it, it may attempt to recover the sum it considers overpaid by making a deduction from your wages. If this happens, seek advice. If your employer decides that you have been overpaid SSP in error, consider claiming employment and support allowance (ESA). You may be able to get your claim backdated (see p629).

Change of circumstances

Notify your employer of any change in your circumstances that might affect your entitlement to SSP.

8. Tax, other benefits and the benefit cap

Tax

Statutory sick pay (SSP) is treated like any other earnings. You pay tax and, depending on the amount of your earnings in the same week, national insurance (NI) contributions by Pay As You Earn in the normal way.[48]

Means-tested benefits

You cannot qualify for employment and support allowance (ESA) during your period of entitlement to SSP.[49] However, for the linking rules for payment of

Part 5: Other benefits
Chapter 39: Statutory sick pay
8. Tax, other benefits and the benefit cap

housing costs in income-related ESA, in some circumstances you may be *treated* as getting it while you get SSP. This also applies to income support (IS) and income-based jobseeker's allowance (JSA). See p458 for more details.

Entitlement to SSP may allow you to qualify for IS (see p27). Alternatively, if your partner is not in full-time paid work, s/he may qualify for JSA. If you are a 'joint-claim couple' for JSA and you get SSP, you may not need to make a joint claim for your partner to qualify for income-based JSA for you both (see p56). If you have to make a joint claim, you do not need to satisfy all the usual conditions for joint-claim JSA if you get SSP (see p47).

SSP is taken into account when calculating your entitlement to IS and income-based JSA (see p273). It is treated as earnings for pension credit (PC) and housing benefit (HB). See Chapters 14 or 15 for details.

If you get SSP, you may also qualify for a deduction from your earnings (which include your SSP) for certain childcare charges when calculating your entitlement to HB (see p270).

If you come under the universal credit (UC) system (see p19), you may qualify for UC as well as SSP. SSP is treated as employed earnings for UC. When calculating your entitlement to UC, your net earnings are taken into account, so certain amounts may be deducted before applying the work allowance (see p327 and p188). For the purpose of qualifying for help with the cost of childcare in your UC, you can be treated as still in paid work while getting SSP (see p253).

Non-means-tested benefits

You cannot get ESA, statutory paternity pay (SPP) or statutory adoption pay (SAP) while you are getting SSP.[50]

You cannot qualify for SSP while you are getting maternity allowance (MA) or statutory maternity pay (SMP).[51]

SSP counts towards the earnings condition for MA, SMP, SPP and SAP, and counts as earnings for carer's allowance, increases in non-means-tested benefits for dependants and reduced earnings allowance and so may affect your entitlement to these benefits.

Payment of SSP does not affect your entitlement to other non-means-tested benefits.

Unless you have other earnings such as occupational sick pay, you do not have to pay NI contributions while on SSP as the weekly rate of SSP is below the NI lower earnings limit. Instead, you are entitled to Class 1 NI credits (see p852).[52]

Tax credits

In some circumstances, you can be treated as being in full-time work for working tax credit (WTC – see Chapter 9) while you are getting SSP (see p170). It is not necessary for you to have claimed WTC before you became ill, so if you are not getting WTC, perhaps because your income was too high before you went on SSP, check whether you can qualify for it now. Also, in some circumstances, entitlement to SSP can help you to qualify for the disabled worker element and/or a childcare element in your WTC (see p1403 and p1405).[53]

For WTC and child tax credit, any SSP you receive during the course of the tax year is taken into account as employment income (see p1424).

The benefit cap

In some cases, the total amount of specified benefits you receive is limited to £350 a week (if you are a single claimant without children) or £500 a week (if you are a lone parent or a member of a couple). This is known as the 'benefit cap'. SSP is *not* a specified benefit. The benefit cap only applies if you are getting HB or UC. The benefit cap does not apply if you or your partner have worked recently. This may include when you (or s/he) were receiving SSP. See p1169 for further information.

Passports and other sources of help

If you are on a low income, you might be entitled to certain health benefits (see Chapter 30). You may be entitled to council tax reduction (see p827).

Notes

1. Who is entitled to statutory sick pay
1 ss151-155 and Schs 11 and 12 SSCBA 1992
2 s63 WRA 2012
3 ss151 and 163(1) SSCBA 1992; regs 4 and 16 SSP Regs
4 Reg 16(2) SSP Regs
5 Reg 4 SSP Regs
6 s151(4) SSCBA 1992
7 Sch 1 SSP(ME) Regs
8 Reg 2 SSP Regs
9 s152(2) SSCBA 1992
10 s152(5) SSCBA 1992
11 s152(6) SSCBA 1992
12 s152(3) SSCBA 1992
13 s153(2), (7) and (8) SSCBA 1992
14 ss153(2) and (12) and 155 SSCBA 1992; reg 3(1), (3) and (4) SSP Regs
15 s152(3) SSCBA 1992

16 s153(3) and Sch 11 SSCBA 1992; reg 3 SSP Regs
17 s163(2) SSCBA 1992; regs 17 and 19 SSP Regs
18 CSSP/2/1984; CSSP/3/1984
19 *Seaton v HMRC* [2011] UKUT 297 (TCC)
20 Reg 17 SSP Regs
21 Reg 17(2) SSP Regs
22 Reg 19(7) and (8) SSP Regs
23 Sch 11 para 6 SSCBA 1992
24 ss154 and 155(1) SSCBA 1992
25 s154(3) SSCBA 1992
26 Reg 5(2) and (3) SSP Regs
27 R(SSP) 1/85
28 s155(1) SSCBA 1992

4. The amount of benefit
29 s157 SSCBA 1992
30 s157(3) SSCBA 1992
31 Regs 20 and 21 SSP Regs

32 s155(2)-(4) SSCBA 1992
33 s152(3) SSCBA 1992

5. Special benefit rules
34 s153(2)(d) and (12) SSCBA 1992
35 Reg 3(5) SSP Regs
36 Reg 3(4) SSP Regs

6. Claims and backdating
37 Reg 7(1) and (4) SSP Regs
38 Reg 7(1), (4) and (5) SSP Regs
39 Reg 7(1)-(3) SSP Regs
40 s156(3) SSCBA 1992
41 s14(1) SSAA 1992
42 Reg 2(2) SSP(ME) Regs
43 Reg 2(1)(b) SSP(ME) Regs
44 Reg 15 SSP Regs

7. Getting paid
45 Sch 12 para 2 SSCBA 1992
46 Reg 8 SSP Regs
47 s151(3) SSCBA 1992

8. Tax, other benefits and the benefit cap
48 s4(1) SSCBA 1992
49 s20(1) WRA 2007
50 s20(1) WRA 2007; regs 18 and 27
    SPPSAP(G) Regs; reg 21(1)(a) ASPP(G)
    Regs
51 s153(2)(d) and (12) SSCBA 1992
52 Reg 8B(2)(iii) SS(Cr) Regs
53 Regs 6, 9 and 13 WTC(EMR) Regs

Chapter 40

* *

Other payments

This chapter covers:
1. Council tax reduction (below)
2. Local welfare assistance schemes (p829)
3. Healthy Start food and vitamins (p829)
4. Education benefits (p832)
5. Free milk for children (p834)
6. Payments for ill health and disability caused by service in the armed forces (p834)
7. Christmas bonus (p835)
8. Other financial help (p836)

Key facts

- There are a number of payments you may be able to get in addition to your benefits. For some of these you must be receiving a 'qualifying benefit'.
- You may be able to get financial help from your local authority – eg, your council tax may be reduced, you may qualify for help under its welfare assistance scheme or your child may be able to get help with certain costs of education, such as free school lunches.
- Under the Healthy Start scheme, you can get vouchers for milk, fruit and vegetables, and coupons for free vitamins. Free milk is also available to children in daycare under the welfare food scheme.
- You can get a £10 Christmas bonus if you are entitled to a qualifying benefit in the relevant week.
- Other sources of financial help are available – eg, if you are on a low income, starting work, have children, are an older person, have an illness or disability, need help with home improvements or have other special needs.

---

1. Council tax reduction

If you need help to pay your council tax, you might be able to get a reduction under your local authority's council tax reduction scheme. **Note:** a council tax reduction is *not* a social security benefit or a tax credit and the rules for benefits and tax credits in this *Handbook* do not apply.

In:[1]

- England and Wales, local authorities may devise their own local schemes which must meet minimum requirements. However, if a local authority does not adopt its own scheme, a default scheme applies. Check with your local authority whether it has its own local scheme or whether the default scheme applies;
- Scotland, there is a national scheme, administered by local authorities.

The rules for all the schemes, along with some commentary, are in CPAG's *Housing Benefit and Council Tax Reduction Legislation* 2013/14.

Some of the minimum requirements that must be met in all the local schemes for people who are at least the qualifying age for pension credit (PC), the default schemes in England and Wales, and in the national scheme in Scotland are as follows. Unless indicated, these are *not* minimum requirements for the local schemes in England and Wales for people under the qualifying age for PC.

- To qualify for a council tax reduction, you:
  - must be liable for council tax on the dwelling in which you are a resident. Some temporary absences from home are allowed;
  - must make an application for a council tax reduction;
  - must not be subject to immigration control (see p1500) and you must satisfy the habitual residence test (see p1521).
  Note: the above are also minimum requirements for the local schemes in England and Wales for people under the qualifying age for PC.
- Some students are excluded from getting a council tax reduction.
- Council tax reduction is means tested – ie, the amount you get depends on your income. However, if you or your partner are getting the guarantee credit of PC, all your income is ignored. If you are under the qualifying age for PC and you or your partner are getting income support, income-based jobseeker's allowance or income-related employment and support allowance, all your income is ignored. **Note:** this is also a minimum requirement for local schemes in Wales for people under the qualifying age for PC.
- There is a capital limit (currently £16,000). However, if you or your partner are getting the guarantee credit of PC, all your capital is ignored. **Note:** this is also a minimum requirement for local schemes in Wales for people under the qualifying age for PC.
- You may be able to get extended help for a period if you take up paid work, more paid work or better paid work.
- In England and Scotland, but not in Wales, there is an alternative maximum council tax (known as 'second adult rebate') designed to help you if you share your home with anyone on a low income.
- Applications for a council tax reduction can be backdated in some circumstances. **Note:** this is also a minimum requirement for local schemes in England and Wales for people under the qualifying age for PC.

- If you disagree with a council tax reduction decision, you can appeal to a valuation tribunal. **Note:** this is also a minimum requirement for local schemes in England and Wales for people under the qualifying age for PC.

Check with your local authority to find out whether you qualify for a council tax reduction. Ensure the rules are being applied correctly in your case. If your local authority has adopted its own scheme, check that the scheme meets the minimum requirements. If you think your local scheme may be unlawful, irrational or discriminatory, seek specialist advice.

2. Local welfare assistance schemes

Help may be available under local welfare assistance schemes set up by your local authority (in England) or by the devolved administrations (in Wales and Scotland). The DWP may refer to this as 'local welfare provision'.

You may qualify if you need help, for example:
- with immediate short-term needs in a crisis – eg, if you do not have sufficient resources, or you need help with expenses in an emergency or as a result of a disaster, such as a fire or flood in your home;
- to establish yourself in the community following a stay in institutional or residential accommodation, or to help you remain in the community;
- to set up a home in the community as part of a planned resettlement programme;
- to ease exceptional pressure on your family;
- to enable you to care for a prisoner or young offender on temporary release;
- with certain travel expenses – eg, to visit someone in hospital, to attend a funeral, to ease a domestic crisis, to visit a child living with her/his other parent or to move to suitable accommodation.

In England, the local scheme is entirely at your local authority's discretion. Check with your local authority to find out what help is available, whether you qualify and how to apply.

In Wales, the Welsh Social Fund offers 'emergency assistance grants'. It links with credit unions to provide loans for those who are not eligible for a grant.

In Scotland, the Scottish Welfare Fund provides 'community care grants' and 'crisis grants'. These are administered by local authorities, which have some local discretion.

3. Healthy Start food and vitamins

If you qualify for Healthy Start food and vitamins, you get free vitamins as well as vouchers that can be used to buy specified types of food.

Healthy Start food

If you qualify for Healthy Start food, you:[2]
- get fixed-value vouchers (worth £3.10 each) that can be exchanged for 'Healthy Start food' at registered food outlets; *or*
- you are paid an amount equal to the value of the vouchers to which you are entitled, if there is no registered food outlet within a reasonable distance of your home.

Healthy Start food

'Healthy Start food' means liquid cow's milk and cow's milk-based infant formula, fresh or frozen fruit and vegetables including loose, pre-packed, whole, sliced, chopped or mixed fruit or vegetables (but not fruit or vegetables to which fat, salt, sugar, flavouring or any other ingredients have been added).[3]

Who can claim Healthy Start food

You qualify for Healthy Start food vouchers:[4]
- if you are **pregnant** and have been for more than 10 weeks, and you are:
  - 18 or over and are entitled to (or are a member of the family of someone who is entitled to) a 'qualifying benefit' (see p831);
  - under 18, whether or not you are entitled to a qualifying benefit (but not if you are excluded from these because you are a 'person subject to immigration control' – see p1500); *or*
- if you are **a mother** who has 'parental responsibility' for a child and:
  - you are 18 or over and either your child is under one or it is less than a year since her/his expected date of birth. This means you can continue to qualify for vouchers for a period after your child is one – ie, if s/he was born prematurely. You must be entitled to (or be a member of the family of someone who is entitled to) a qualifying benefit other than income-related employment and support allowance (ESA); *or*
  - it is less than four months since your baby's expected date of birth and you have not yet notified Healthy Start that s/he was born. You must have been getting a qualifying benefit before your baby was born. This allows your entitlement to vouchers to continue until you notify the birth. Once you do, you can then qualify under the rule above (if you are 18 or over). **Note:** as long as you provided the notification within the four-month period, you can also get extra vouchers for your child from her/his date of birth.
  If you qualify for vouchers for more than one child under this rule (eg, you have twins), you get a voucher for each. If you do not have parental responsibility but would otherwise qualify for vouchers, your child qualifies instead of you;

- for **a child under four** who is a member of your family. You or a member of the family must be entitled to a qualifying benefit (see below) other than income-related ESA.

In practical terms, this means that each week you get one voucher for each of your children aged between one and four, two vouchers for each of your children under one (or within one year of their expected date of birth), plus one voucher if you are pregnant.

Example

Vera is 17 weeks pregnant. She has three children: twin girls aged two and a boy aged seven. She is getting IS. She qualifies for a voucher because she is more than 10 weeks pregnant. Her twins each qualify for a voucher as they are under four. Her son does not qualify for a voucher. Vera gets three vouchers each week totaling £9.30. When the baby is born, Vera will still be entitled to a voucher because she will be a mother of a child under one. The baby will also be entitled to a voucher. She will then get four vouchers each week, totalling £12.40.

Definitions

The **'qualifying benefits'** are income support, income-based jobseeker's allowance, income-related ESA (in some cases). Child tax credit (CTC) is also a qualifying benefit, provided that gross income for CTC purposes does not exceed £16,190 and there is no entitlement to working tax credit (WTC), other than if this is during the four-week WTC run-on period (see p172). **Note:** it is understood that universal credit was to be a qualifying benefit from some point in October 2013, but there was to be an earnings threshold. At the time of writing, the rules had not yet been amended. See CPAG's online service and *Welfare Rights Bulletin* for updates.

'Parental responsibility' means parental responsibility as defined in s3(1) of the Children Act 1989 (in England or Wales) or s1(1) of the Children (Scotland) Act 1995 (in Scotland).[5] **'Family'** means a person and her/his partner and any child or qualifying young person who is a member of her/his household and for whom s/he or her/his partner counts as responsible.[6] So for example, if you are not entitled to a qualifying benefit, but are included in your mother's or father's claim for one of these, you can qualify for Healthy Start food vouchers.

If you are an asylum seeker receiving asylum support, you receive an extra amount to help you buy healthy food if you are pregnant or have a child under three.

Claims

You must make an initial claim for Healthy Start food vouchers in writing and must provide specified information and evidence.[7] You can:

- complete the form in the Healthy Start leaflet (HS01), available from midwives, health visitors, maternity clinics and some doctors' surgeries or from 0845 607 6823;
- download a form or complete it online and print it off at www.healthystart.nhs.uk;
- email yourself a form from www.healthystart.nhs.uk.

The form must be countersigned by a health professional (eg, a midwife or health visitor) who certifies when your baby is due (if you are pregnant) and that you have been given appropriate advice about healthy eating and breastfeeding. If you are under 16, your claim must also be signed by your parent or carer. Send the completed form to: Healthy Start Issuing Unit, Freepost RRTR-SYAE-JKCR, PO Box 1067, Warrington WA55 1EG.

If you are getting Healthy Start food vouchers while you are pregnant and then inform Healthy Start of your baby's birth by telephone while s/he is under four months old, you can get extra vouchers for her/him from her/his date of birth.[8] You may need to make a claim for CTC for her/him (or add her/him to your existing claim) to ensure that you continue to get the vouchers.

If you do not get vouchers to which you think you are entitled, or have any other problems with these, contact the Healthy Start helpline on 0845 607 6823.

Healthy Start vitamins

If you qualify for Healthy Start food vouchers, you also qualify for Healthy Start vitamins.[9] Mothers and pregnant women are entitled to 56 vitamin tablets and children under four to 10 millilitres of vitamin drops every eight weeks. Ask your local health professional what the local arrangements are for getting your free vitamins.

You do not have to make a separate claim for Healthy Start vitamins; you are sent Healthy Start vitamin coupons with your Healthy Start food vouchers. However, you must show evidence to the vitamin supplier that you are entitled (ie, the letter to which your most recent Healthy Start vouchers were attached) and, if requested, proof of your child's age.[10]

4. **Education benefits**

Financial help is available from your local authority if you are in school or are a student, or if you have children in school or college.

Free school lunches

Children are entitled to free school lunches if their families receive:[11]

- income support (IS), income-based jobseeker's allowance or income-related employment and support allowance (ESA);

- child tax credit (CTC) and have annual taxable income of £16,190 (in Scotland, £16,010) or less. However, this does not apply if the family is entitled to working tax credit (WTC) unless:
  - this is during the four-week 'WTC run-on' period (see p172); or
  - in Scotland only, the WTC award is based on annual taxable income of £6,420 or less – ie, the family gets maximum WTC;
- universal credit (UC);
- in England and Wales only, guarantee credit of pension credit (PC). PC claimants in Scotland may qualify if they receive CTC, as above.

Also entitled are:
- 16–18-year-olds receiving the above benefits or tax credits in their own right;
- asylum seekers in receipt of support provided under Part VI of the Immigration and Asylum Act 1999.

Note:
- In Scotland, free school lunches may be more widely available during the first three years of primary school. This is likely to apply across Scotland from January 2015. Check with your local authority.
- In England, the government says that from September 2014, free school lunches will be provided to all primary school children in reception, and years one and two.

School transport and school clothes

Local authorities must provide **free transport to school** for pupils aged five to 16 if it is considered necessary to enable that pupil to get to the 'nearest suitable school'. This applies if the pupil lives more than a set distance from that school. However, if there is no safe walking route, a pupil must be given free transport no matter how far away s/he lives from the nearest suitable school. Free school transport must also be be provided to pupils with special educational needs and to those whose parents are on a low income – ie, if they qualify for free school lunches or their parents are on the maximum rate of WTC.

Local authorities can give **grants for school uniforms and other school clothes**. Each authority determines its own eligibility rules. Some school governing bodies or parents' associations also provide help with school clothing

Education maintenance allowance and 16 to 19 bursaries

Education maintenance allowance is a means-tested payment for young people aged 16 to 19 from Wales and Scotland who stay on in further education. Payments are made directly to the young person and are conditional on regular course attendance. The young person receives a weekly allowance during term time. The amount depends on the household income. For further details, see www.emascotland.com or www.studentfinancewales.co.uk.

16 to 19 bursaries are payments for young people aged 16 to 19 who stay on in further education or training in England. These are available through the school, college or training provider. Certain young people in need (eg, young people in care, care leavers, young people who get IS or UC, or who get ESA and either disability living allowance or personal independence payment) can get the maximum bursary. Discretionary bursaries are available to those in financial difficulty. See www.gov.uk/1619-bursary-fund for further information.

Neither payment counts as income for any benefits or tax credits the parent may be getting. They are also not affected by any income the young person has from part-time work.

Note: if you are a student, to find out what help is available to finance your studies contact your local authority or college or university, or see www.gov.uk/student-finance. Also see CPAG's *Student Support and Benefits Handbook* and *Benefits for Students in Scotland Handbook*.

5. **Free milk for children**

Children under five are entitled to 189–200 millilitres of free milk on each day they are looked after for two hours or more:[12]
- by a registered childminder or daycare provider; *or*
- in a school, playcentre or workplace nursery which is exempt from registration; *or*
- in local authority daycare.

Children under one are allowed fresh or dried milk. This is provided by the welfare food scheme.

6. **Payments for ill health and disability caused by service in the armed forces**

If you are a former member of the armed forces, you can claim under the following schemes, administered by the Ministry of Defence.

You can qualify for **war pension disablement benefits** if you have ill health or a disablement caused by service before 6 April 2005. The degree of your disablement is assessed on a percentage scale, with 100 per cent being the level of disablement that qualifies for the maximum award. If you are assessed at 20 per cent or more, you receive a pension and if you are assessed at under 20 per cent you receive a lump sum (gratuity). You can also qualify for a number of supplementary allowances. Two of these are particularly important.

- **Constant attendance allowance.** You qualify for this if your disablement is assessed at 80 per cent or more and because of your disablement you require 'constant attendance'. This has the same meaning as either 'attention' or 'supervision' for attendance allowance (AA) or disability living allowance (DLA) care component. The allowance is paid at four different rates depending on the number of hours for which you require constant attendance and whether this is in the daytime or at night. If you claim AA or DLA care component, any constant attendance allowance to which you are entitled is deducted from these benefits. **Note:** the top two rates of constant attendance allowance are considerably more than the highest rates of AA or DLA care component.

- **Mobility supplement.** You qualify for this if your disablement is assessed at 40 per cent or more and because of your disablement your ability to walk is 'of little or no practical use'. This is, in effect, the same test as for the higher rate mobility component of DLA. There is a single rate of benefit, which is the same as for the DLA higher rate mobility component. If you claim DLA mobility component, any mobility supplement to which you are entitled is deducted. **Note:** unlike DLA, there is no upper age limit for claiming mobility supplement.

You can qualify for help under the **Armed Forces Compensation Scheme** if you have ill health or a disablement caused by service on or after 6 April 2005. The main benefit is a lump-sum payment. To qualify, you must have had an injury or ill health that comes within one of the specified 'descriptors'. Each descriptor is assigned to a 'tariff level', running from one (highest) to 15, which determines the amount payable. If you receive an award of at least tariff level 11, you also qualify for a 'guaranteed income payment', calculated as a percentage of your salary on the day your service in the armed forces ended. Awards are at 30, 50, 75 or 100 per cent, depending on your tariff level.

When the scheme was introduced in 2005, it did not include any equivalent of the supplementary allowances payable with war pension disablement benefits and no special provision was made for attention or mobility needs. However, in April 2013 armed forces independence payment was introduced for those entitled to a guaranteed income payment at the 50 per cent rate or more. It is payable at a rate equivalent to the total of the enhanced rates of both the daily living and mobility components of personal independence payment.

7. Christmas bonus

You qualify for a Christmas bonus of £10 if you are entitled (or treated as entitled) to any of the qualifying benefits for at least part of the 'relevant week' (even if the benefit is paid later).[13] The relevant week is usually the week beginning with the first Monday in December.[14]

Qualifying benefits[15]

Armed forces independence payment, attendance allowance, disability living allowance, carer's allowance, disablement benefit (if it includes unemployability supplement or constant attendance allowance), contributory employment and support allowance which includes either the support or the work-related activity component, long-term incapacity benefit, industrial death benefit for widows or widowers, mobility supplement, retirement pension, pension credit (PC), personal independence payment, severe disablement allowance, war disablement pension (if you are at least pension age – see p752),[16] war widow's or surviving civil partner's pension, widowed mother's allowance, widowed parent's allowance or widow's pension.

You may also qualify for an extra bonus for your partner (a further £10) if s/he has not received a bonus in her/his own right, and:[17]

- you are both at least pension age (see p752) and you are entitled, or may be treated as entitled, to an increase of one of the qualifying benefits in respect of her/him; *or*
- you are both at least the qualifying age for PC (see p78) and the only qualifying benefit you get is PC.

The bonus is not taxable and has no effect on other benefits or tax credits.

It is paid automatically. However, you should contact the DWP if you have not obtained your bonus within a year. Otherwise, your right is lost.[18]

8. **Other financial help**

This *Handbook* is mainly concerned with information about social security benefits and tax credits. However, there is other financial help to which you may be entitled, especially if you are on a low income, have children, have an illness, disability or other special needs, or are an older person.

See the *Disability Rights Handbook*, published by Disability Rights UK, for help for those with care needs.

Food banks

If you are experiencing severe financial hardship (eg, caused by debt or benefit delays), you may be able to get vouchers for food which can be redeemed at a 'food bank'. One voucher can be exchanged for three days' food. Vouchers are available from frontline care professionals such as doctors and social workers. Jobcentre Plus staff may also give out vouchers. Further information and details of where there are food banks is available at www.trusselltrust.org.

You may be able to get help with food or meals through local community groups which are part of the Fareshare network. Further information is available at www.fareshare.org.uk.

Repairs, improvements and energy efficiency

Your local authority may be able to provide you with a grant to help with the cost of improving your home. The main types of grant available are:
* home improvement grants; *and*
* disabled facilities grants.

You may also be able to get:
* assistance from a home improvement agency (a local not-for-profit organisation) to repair, improve, maintain or adapt your home, sometimes called 'care and repair' or 'staying put' schemes, or with small repairs, safety checks and odd jobs from a handyperson service. For information see, in England, www.foundations.uk.com, in Wales, www.careandrepair.org.uk and in Scotland, www.careandrepairscotland.co.uk.
* a grant for help with insulation and other energy efficiency measures in your home. Help with fuel bills may also be available. Different schemes operate in England, Wales and Scotland. For further information, contact the Energy Savings Advice Service on 0300 123 1234 (calls charged at standard national rates) or at energysavingtrust.org.uk. For more details, see CPAG's *Fuel Rights Handbook*.

Special funds for sick or disabled people

A range of help is available for people with an illness or disability to assist with things like paying for care services in their own home, equipment, holidays, furniture and transport needs, and for people with haemophilia or HIV contracted via haemophilia treatment. Grants are also available for practical support to help people do their jobs – eg, to pay for specialist equipment and travel.

For more information, see the *Disability Rights Handbook*, published by Disability Rights UK.

Help from social services

Local authority social services departments have statutory duties to provide a range of practical and financial help to families, children, young people, older people, people with disabilities and asylum seekers.

Charities

There are many charities that provide various types of help to people in need. Your local authority social services department or local advice centre may know of appropriate charities that could assist you, or you can consult publications, such as *A Guide to Grants for Individuals in Need* and the *Charities Digest*, in your local library. The organisation turn2us has a website (www.turn2us.org.uk) with an A-Z of all the charities that can provide financial help. In many cases, applications for support can be made directly from the website.

Financial help when starting work

If you or your partner start working full time, you might be entitled to some financial support, administered by Jobcentre Plus, to help your transition into work after a period of time on benefit. Check with your Jobcentre Plus office or employment scheme or programme provider to see what is available. Do this before you start work because you may have to apply before your job starts or within a short period of it starting. Some information is available at www.gov.uk/moving-from-benefits-to-work/overview.

Notes

1. **Council tax reduction**
   1 **E** CTRS(DS)E Regs; CTRS(PR)E Regs
   W CTRS(DS)W Regs; CTRSPR(W) Regs
   S CTR(S) Regs; CTR(SPC)S Regs

3. **Healthy Start food and vitamins**
   2 Regs 5(2) and 8 HSS&WF(A) Regs
   3 Regs 2(1) and 5(1) and Sch 3 HSS&WF(A) Regs; HSS(DHSF)(W) Regs
   4 Reg 3 HSS&WF(A) Regs
   5 Reg 2(1) HSS&WF(A) Regs
   6 Reg 2(1) HSS&WF(A) Regs
   7 Reg 4 and Sch 2 HSS&WF(A) Regs
   8 Reg 4(2) HSS&WF(A) Regs
   9 Reg 3 HSS&WF(A) Regs
   10 Reg 8A HSS&WF(A) Regs

4. **Education benefits**
   11 **E** s512ZB Education Act 1996; The Education (Free School Lunches)(Prescribed Tax Credits)(England) Order 2003, No.383
   W s512ZB Education Act 1996; The Education (Free School Lunches)(Prescribed Tax Credits)(Wales) Order 2003, No.879 (W.110)
   S s53(3) Education (Scotland) Act 1980; The Education (School Lunches) (Scotland) Regulations 2009, No.178

5. **Free milk for children**
   12 Reg 18 WF Regs

7. **Christmas bonus**
   13 ss148(1) and 149(1) SSCBA 1992
   14 s150(4) SSCBA 1992
   15 s150(1) SSCBA 1992
   16 s149(4) SSCBA 1992
   17 ss148(2) and (5) and 150(2) SSCBA 1992
   18 Reg 38 SS(C&P) Regs

Part 6

General rules for other benefits

Chapter 41

National insurance contributions

This chapter covers:
1. Contributions and contributory benefits (p842)
2. Paid contributions (p843)
3. National insurance credits (p850)
4. Contribution conditions for benefits (p860)

This chapter explains the national insurance (NI) contribution rules relevant to contributory benefits. For details of the NI number requirement that applies to most benefits, see p1138.

Key facts

- Entitlement to contributory benefits, and sometimes the amount paid, depends on your national insurance (NI) contribution record. In the case of Category B retirement pension and bereavement benefits, it depends on the contribution record of your spouse or civil partner, or your late spouse or civil partner.
- If you are employed or self-employed, you may be liable to pay NI contributions. If you are not liable to pay contributions, in some circumstances you can be awarded NI 'credits' or you may be able to pay contributions voluntarily.
- There are different types of NI contributions (called 'classes'). Not all classes of NI contributions or all types of NI credits count for all contributory benefits.
- NI contributions are collected by HM Revenue and Customs.

Future changes

The government plans to introduce:[1]

– a 'single-tier state pension' to replace basic state retirement pension and additional state pension for people who reach pension age on or after 6 April 2016. Under the plans, to qualify for the full amount of the new pension, you will have to meet the contribution condition in at least 35 years (rather than the current 30). If you have fewer qualifying years, but at least the minimum number (likely to be between seven and 10), the pension

Part 6: General rules for other benefits
Chapter 41: National insurance contributions
1. Contributions and contributory benefits

will be reduced proportionately. Once it is introduced, you will only be able to build up entitlement to the single-tier pension through your own NI contributions or credits, and not those of your spouse or civil partner. There will be transitional arrangements to recognise contributions made before the introduction of the single-tier pension;
- a 'bereavement support payment' to replace bereavement payment, widowed parent's allowance and bereavement allowance from April 2016 at the earliest (see p518);
- Class 3A voluntary NI contributions from October 2015. You will be able to pay these contributions over a limited period, to top up your additional state pension, if you reach pension age before 6 April 2016.

1. Contributions and contributory benefits

Benefits that have national insurance (NI) contribution conditions are:
- contribution-based jobseeker's allowance (JSA);
- contributory employment and support allowance (ESA);
- bereavement benefits;
- Category A and B retirement pension.

These are known as '**contributory benefits**'. Widows' benefits (see p528) and incapacity benefit (IB – see p659) are also contributory benefits.

Entitlement to contributory benefits normally depends on the NI contribution conditions being met. For the detailed rules on the contribution conditions for contributory benefits, see pp860–67.

In some circumstances, you may be liable to pay NI contributions or, if you are not, in order to help you meet the contribution conditions for some contributory benefits you may either be credited with earnings or with contributions, or you can choose to pay contributions. For details of NI 'credits', see p850.

Note:
- It may be possible for you to rely on the contributions you have paid in other European Economic Area states to qualify for contributory benefits (see p1598).
- Your NI contribution record is based on the NI contributions you have paid, or the NI credits you have received, for each tax year – ie, 6 April to 5 April.
- If you are self-employed, your entitlement to maternity allowance, and the amount you receive, may be affected by whether you have paid Class 2 NI contributions or have been exempted from paying them on the grounds of low earnings (see p716).

How decisions are made

Most decisions on NI contributions are made by an officer of HM Revenue and Customs (HMRC). Appeals against such decisions can be decided by an HMRC review or by the First-tier Tribunal (Tax).[2] The process is similar to appealing against an HMRC decision on your entitlement to a statutory payment (see p1374).

Decisions relating to entitlement to NI credits are made either by HMRC or the DWP, depending on the type of NI credit under consideration.

If you disagree with a decision on your entitlement to NI credits, you can apply for a revision or supersession of the decision (see Chapter 58). You can also appeal, although, before you can do so, you normally must first have applied for a revision. Your appeal is decided by the First-tier Tribunal (Social Security and Child Support) (see Chapter 59).[3]

2. Paid contributions

There are six different types ('classes') of paid national insurance (NI) contribution.[4] Only three of these (Classes 1, 2 and 3) can help you to qualify for contributory benefits, and only Class 1 contributions count for *all* contributory benefits.

If you are an 'employed earner', depending on the amount you earn, you may be liable to pay Class 1 contributions. If you are a 'self-employed earner', you are normally liable to pay Class 2 contributions unless you are exempted (and you may also be liable for Class 4 contributions). If you are not liable to pay contributions, you may choose to pay Class 2 (if you are self-employed) or 3 contributions voluntarily. These are known as 'voluntary contributions'.

Note:
- You are not liable for Class 1 or 2 contributions if you are under 16 or over pension age (see p752).[5]
- You cannot pay Class 3 contributions if you are under 16 (and sometimes if you are 17 or 18) or for the tax year in which you reach pension age or any subsequent tax year.[6]
- Although the amount of Class 1 or 4 contributions you pay depends on your earnings, you do not necessarily gain more benefit by paying higher contributions.

Class of contribution	Payable by	Giving entitlement to
Class 1	Employed earners and their employers	All benefits with contribution conditions
Class 1A and 1B	Employers of employed earners	No benefits
Class 2	Self-employed earners	All benefits with contribution conditions except contribution-based jobseeker's allowance (JSA)

Part 6: General rules for other benefits
Chapter 41: National insurance contributions
2. Paid contributions

| Class 3 | Voluntary contributors | Bereavement benefits and retirement pensions |
| Class 4 | Self-employed earners | No benefits |

Employed earners and self-employed earners

Your liability to pay Class 1, 2 or 4 NI contributions depends on whether you are an employed or self-employed earner.[7]

It is normally clear whether you are employed or self-employed. If there is a dispute, it usually concerns whether you are employed under a *contract of service* (in which case you are an employee) or a *contract for services* (in which case you are self-employed).[8] **Note:**

- To be an employed or self-employed earner you must be 'gainfully employed'.
- Office holders, including people in elective office, who receive earnings are classed as employed earners. Office holders include judges and registrars of births, marriages and deaths.
- Certain people are deemed to be employed earners. These include office cleaners, many agency workers and people employed by their spouse or civil partner for the purposes of their spouse's or civil partner's employment.[9]
- Examiners, moderators and invigilators are deemed to be self-employed.[10]
- If you have two or more jobs, it is possible to be both employed and self-employed.
- You do not have to pay NI contributions on earnings from certain kinds of employment – eg, if you are employed by your spouse or civil partner and it is not for the purpose of her/his employment, or you are employed in your home by a close relative who lives with you and the job is not for a trade or business that is carried out there.[11]

Class 1 contributions

Class 1 contributions have two elements: primary Class 1 contributions (paid by employed earners) and secondary Class 1 contributions (paid by employers).[12]

The amount of primary Class 1 contributions you pay depends on the amount you earn in relation to the upper and lower earnings limit set for the tax year, and to the amount of that year's 'primary threshold'. See Appendix 8 for details of the earnings limits and primary threshold for this year and earlier years. If your earnings are equal to or below the primary threshold (£153 a week in 2014/15), you do not have to pay NI contributions on them. If they are between the lower earnings limit (£111 a week in 2014/15) and the primary threshold, you are treated as if you had paid Class 1 NI contributions on those earnings.[13]

If you earn more than the primary threshold, you are liable to pay Class 1 contributions of 12 per cent of your earnings between the primary threshold and upper earnings limit (£805 a week in 2014/15), plus 2 per cent of the earnings you have above the upper earnings limit.[14] If you are contracted out of the additional state pension scheme (see p760) or if you are a married woman or widow with reduced liability for contributions (see p846) you pay lower Class 1 contributions.[15]

Note:

- It is your employer's responsibility to deduct your Class 1 contributions from your earnings and pay them with its own contributions to HM Revenue and Customs (HMRC).[16] If your employer has failed to pay your Class 1 contributions to HMRC, you are treated as though they had been paid, unless you have been negligent, or consented to or connived in that arrangement.[17]
- If you have more than one job, the basic rule is that your liability to pay Class 1 contributions is calculated for each job as if the other(s) did not exist, although the total you pay is subject to a maximum.[18] There are some exceptions to this rule – eg, if you have two different jobs for the same employer or employers who carry on business in association with each other, earnings from these jobs are normally added together and your NI contributions are based on your total earnings, to stop employers avoiding NI liability.[19]
- The percentage rates of Class 1 contributions changed on 6 April 2011. For the rates for earlier tax years, see previous editions of this *Handbook*.

Class 2 contributions

You must pay Class 2 contributions if you are a self-employed earner (see p844), unless you are exempt from liability. The main grounds for being exempt are that you receive certain benefits (eg, maternity allowance for the week to which the contribution relates, or carer's allowance for at least part of that week) or that you have obtained a certificate of exception because your earnings from self-employment are below a certain level (£5,885 a year in 2014/15). This is also known as a '**small earnings exception**'.[20] Certain expenses are deducted when calculating your earnings.[21]

Even if you are exempt from liability to pay Class 2 contributions, you may still choose to pay them to protect your NI contribution record (see p848).[22]

Class 2 contributions are payable at a flat rate.[23] The current and previous year's rates are:

2013/14	£2.70 a week
2014/15	£2.75 a week

To apply for a small earnings exception, complete Form CF10, available from www.gov.uk or by telephoning HMRC (tel: 0300 200 3505; textphone: 0300 200 3519).[24]

Part 6: General rules for other benefits
Chapter 41: National insurance contributions
2. Paid contributions

Note:
- Married women and widows with reduced liability for contributions (see p846) are not liable for Class 2 contributions.[25]
- Volunteer development workers employed abroad and share fishermen pay Class 2 contributions at special rates which count towards contribution-based JSA, unlike other Class 2 contributions.[26]
- If you are self-employed and also have a job as an employed earner, you may be liable to pay both Class 1 and Class 2 contributions, subject to a maximum.[27]

Class 3 contributions

Payments of Class 3 contributions are voluntary.[28] They give entitlement only to bereavement benefits and retirement pension and are not payable if your earnings factor is otherwise sufficient in that tax year to meet the contribution condition for those benefits (see p861).[29] To help you decide whether to pay Class 3 contributions, see p848, but be aware, under government proposals, Class 3 contributions will not count towards the contribution conditions for the new 'bereavement support payment' which is likely to replace bereavement benefits for new claimants from April 2016 (see p518).

Class 3 contributions are paid at a flat rate. The current and previous year's rates are:[30]

2013/14	£13.55 a week
2014/15	£13.90 a week

Pre-1975 contributions

The present contribution system was introduced on 6 April 1975. Between 5 July 1948 and 5 April 1975, Class 1 contributions were paid by a 'flat-rate stamp' in the same way as Class 2 and Class 3 contributions.

Before 6 April 1975, contribution years were not the same as tax years, as they are now. Transitional arrangements in both 1948 and 1975 may have resulted in your having a contribution year that was not 12 months long, which may explain what would otherwise be anomalies in your contribution record.

Reduced liability for married women and widows

Women who were married or widowed on 6 April 1977 could choose to pay reduced Class 1 or no Class 2 contributions, provided they applied to do so before 12 May 1977.[31]

If you 'elected' to pay at this reduced rate, you can continue to do so until you either apply to pay the full rate again (called 'revoking an election') or until the right to pay reduced contributions is automatically lost.[32]

There are disadvantages to reduced liability – eg, if you have reduced liability, you will not qualify for most kinds of NI credits, and reduced contributions do not entitle you to contributory benefits. However, it is worth thinking carefully about your position, and getting independent advice (see Appendix 2), if you are considering giving it up. Once lost, the right cannot be reclaimed.

See p773 of the 2012/13 edition of this *Handbook* for what to consider if you are deciding whether to revoke your election to pay at a reduced rate, but be aware of the government's plans to introduce a new single-tier state pension to replace the current basic retirement pension and additional state pension (see p841) for people who reach pension age on or after 6 April 2016. Transitional arrangements will include some protection for certain women who have paid a reduced rate of contribution prior to the date the single-tier state pension is introduced.[33]

To revoke your election, complete the form in HMRC leaflet CF9 for married women or CF9A for widows (available from HMRC's website).

Coming from abroad and going abroad

The rules on liability for NI contributions when you have come to the UK from abroad or if you go abroad are complex. In particular, the rules described below may not apply if you are covered by the European Union co-ordination rules (see p1592) or if you move from or to a country which has a reciprocal agreement with the UK (see p1517).

If you have come from abroad and are employed or self-employed in Great Britain you may be liable for Class 1 or 2 (and 4) contributions.[34] If you are self-employed but not liable to pay contributions, you may be able to pay Class 2 contributions voluntarily. If you are not liable to pay contributions, you can choose to pay Class 3 contributions if you are resident in Great Britain throughout the course of the tax year in respect of which you wish to pay contributions and, in some circumstances, even if you have not been resident for the whole tax year.[35]

If you are working abroad as an employee and your employer has a place of business in Britain, in some circumstances for the first year you must still pay Class 1 contributions. If you are not liable, or are no longer liable, to pay Class 1 contributions, it may be worth paying Class 3 contributions (see p848).[36]

If you are self-employed outside Great Britain, you may pay Class 2 contributions if you wish, provided you were employed or self-employed immediately before you left Britain and either:

- you have been resident in Great Britain for a continuous period of at least three years at some time in the past; *or*
- you have paid contributions producing an earnings factor of at least 52 times the lower earnings limit in each of three years in the past (see p861 and Appendix 8 for the meaning of these terms). Each set of 52 flat-rate contributions paid before April 1975 counts as satisfying that condition in respect of one year.[37]

Certain volunteer development workers who are employed abroad may also be allowed to pay Class 2 contributions.[38]

Part 6: General rules for other benefits
Chapter 41: National insurance contributions
2. Paid contributions

Normally, Class 3 contributions may be paid while you are abroad if you satisfy either of the conditions which would allow you to pay Class 2 contributions (but you do not need to have been employed or self-employed before you left Britain or while abroad). You may also pay them if you paid Class 1 contributions for the first year you were employed abroad.[39]

For information on payment of NI contributions while abroad, see www.gov.uk or telephone HMRC's NI helpline for non-UK residents (tel: 0300 200 3506, or from abroad: 44 191 203 7010).

The meaning of 'resident' is explained on p1519.

Note: Northern Ireland and Isle of Man contributions count towards British benefits, as do contributions paid in other countries in some circumstances. In particular, this may apply if you have paid contributions in the European Economic Area (see p1589). You may also be entitled to benefits from other countries while you are in this country.

6 Improving your contribution record

If there are years for which you do not have a full contribution record, it may be beneficial to pay voluntary Class 2 contributions (if you are self-employed but not liable to pay Class 2 contributions – see p845) or Class 3 contributions (see p846). These are called 'voluntary contributions'. Before paying voluntary contributions in respect of a tax year, check whether you qualify for NI credits in that year. (In any event, you are not entitled to pay Class 3 contributions if you would instead be entitled to Class 3 credits – see p850.[40])

You can request a state pension statement to help you decide whether to pay voluntary contributions by telephoning the Future Pension Centre (tel: 0845 300 0168 or textphone: 0845 300 0169), by post using Form BR19, or online at www.gov.uk/state-pension-statement. **Note:** if you reach pension age on or after 6 April 2016, until the planned changes to state pension are finalised it may not be possible to obtain an accurate statement.

Should you make voluntary contributions?

1. Both Class 2 and 3 contributions count for bereavement benefits and Category A and B retirement pension and may help you (or, in the case of bereavement benefits or Category B retirement pension, your spouse or civil partner) qualify for those benefits or qualify for a higher rate of benefit. Voluntary Class 2 contributions also count for contributory employment and support allowance (ESA).

2. From April 2016 at the earliest, the government plans to replace bereavement benefits with bereavement support payment (see p518). This change will affect people whose spouse or civil partner dies after the date the new benefit is introduced. Class 3 contributions and NI credits will not count for bereavement support payment.

3. Consider the cost of paying the contributions and compare this to the additional amount of benefit that might be awarded. When doing so, be aware of the proposed future changes to bereavement benefits (see p518) and retirement pension (see p841).

4. Voluntary contributions may be paid on behalf of a contributor after her/his death, provided they are paid no later than s/he would have been allowed to pay them.[41]

5. Contributions paid late do not always count for benefit purposes (see below).

6. If you have overpaid contributions for a particular year, or have paid voluntary contributions in error, you may be able to get a refund.[42]

7. Seek advice before paying voluntary contributions for years in which you have paid contributions abroad. In some cases, these can count towards British benefits (see p847).

8. If in doubt about paying the contributions, seek advice.

Late payment of contributions

If you are liable for Class 1 contributions but your employer failed to pay these to HMRC or has paid them late, you are treated as if the contributions had been paid – normally on the date they were due to be paid – unless you have been negligent or consented or connived in the failure to pay.[43]

Otherwise, contributions which are paid late normally cannot help you to qualify for contributory benefits for any period before you pay the contributions. However, late-paid contributions can count towards your benefit entitlement for the period *after* they have been paid if they are paid:[44]

- for Class 1 contributions, before the end of the second tax year after the tax year for which the contributions are paid; *or*
- for Class 2 or 3 contributions, before the end of the sixth tax year after the tax year for which they are paid (although special rules apply if you make late payments of Class 2 contributions through Pay As You Earn); *or*
- for Class 3 contributions (for any tax year in which, for at least six months, you were a full-time apprentice, in full-time education or training or a prisoner, and for the year before and after such a year in which you met this condition for less than six months), before the end of the sixth complete tax year after the end of a period of education, apprenticeship or imprisonment.

Even if paid within these time limits, contributions paid late also cannot count for the second contribution condition for contribution-based JSA and contributory ESA unless they were either paid before the start of the relevant benefit year (see p861) or, if they were paid after this, until six weeks after they have been paid.[45] Only in limited circumstances can contributions which are paid after the above time limits count for benefit purposes.[46] For example:

- If you reach pension age between 6 April 2008 and 5 April 2015 you can pay additional Class 3 contributions for any six tax years (but not tax years before 1975/76), provided that you already have at least 20 years which count as

Part 6: General rules for other benefits
Chapter 41: National insurance contributions
3. National insurance credits

qualifying years for retirement pension. If you reached pension age before 6 April 2010, years of home responsibilities protection can count towards the 20 years (see p867) but at least one of those 20 years must consist of paid (not just credited) contributions. You must pay the additional contributions within six years of reaching pension age. If you pay them on or after 6 April 2011, they will count for benefit purposes from the date that they are paid.[47]

- If you reach pension age on or after 6 April 2016, you have until 5 April 2023 to pay voluntary contributions for any of the tax years from 2006/07 to 2015/16 (although you may pay more if you pay them after 5 April 2019).[48]

---

3. **National insurance credits**

In some circumstances, you can be 'credited' with earnings (sometimes known as Class 1 credits) or with Class 3 contributions. 'Credits' can only help you satisfy:

- the second contribution condition for benefits with two contribution conditions – ie, contribution-based jobseeker's allowance (JSA), contributory employment and support allowance (ESA), widowed parent's allowance, bereavement allowance and, when entitlement is based on the 'old contribution conditions', Category A and B retirement pensions (see p866);
- the single contribution condition for Category A and B retirement pensions, if this applies to you (see p865).

Not all types of credits count for all of these contributory benefits, although many Class 1 credits do. Class 3 credits only count for Category A and B retirement pensions, widowed parent's allowance and bereavement allowance.
Note:
- You can only receive sufficient credits in any tax year to meet the contribution condition for that year.[49]
- Credits cannot help you to satisfy the first contribution condition for benefits with two contribution conditions or to qualify for a bereavement payment, which has a single contribution condition.
- If you are a married woman with reduced liability for contributions (see p846), you can only qualify for credits for universal credit (UC), for certain parents and carers (see p852), for family members providing childcare (see p854), for official error (see p859), starting credits (but see p856) or credits following bereavement (see p858). You are not entitled to other types of credits.[50]
- In some circumstances, you may be able to get 'earnings factor credits' which may help you build up entitlement to additional state pension (see p760).[51] The rules for earnings factor credits are not described in this chapter.

Enquiries about credits can be made to the NI Helpline (tel: 0300 200 3500; textphone: 0300 200 3519).

Credits for unemployment

These credits can help you meet the contribution conditions for all contributory benefits except bereavement payment.

You can be credited with earnings equal to the lower earnings limit for either:[52]

- each complete week (ie, the seven days from Sunday to Saturday) for which you receive JSA (or for which you would have received JSA but for the loss of benefit for benefit offences rules – see p1258); *or*
- each complete week in which you are not entitled to UC (to be entitled, you normally must have claimed it) and for which you satisfy or can be treated as satisfying the following qualifying conditions for JSA – ie, that you:
  - are not engaged in full-time paid work (see p987); *and*
  - are not in relevant education (see p903); *and*
  - do not have limited capability for work (see Chapter 47); *and*
  - are under pension age; *and*
  - are either available for and actively seeking work (see p1025 and p1038) or, if you come under the UC system, satisfy the work search and work availability requirements (see p1068 and p1070), or you would have satisfied these conditions in that week but for having limited capability for work (see p695) or being incapable of work for part of the week.

You may also qualify for credits for weeks before 29 October 2013 in which you would have satisfied the above conditions for JSA but were treated as in full-time paid work because you received a compensation payment. See p885–86 of the 2013/14 edition of this *Handbook* for details.

These credits are awarded automatically if you get JSA, otherwise you must apply in writing to Jobcentre Plus, either on the first day for which you are claiming them or within a reasonable period of time after that. You must provide the DWP with the evidence it requires to show that you satisfy the conditions.

Even if you are not entitled to JSA, it may be important to continue to 'sign on' at the Jobcentre Plus office in order to get credits for unemployment, and protect your right to contributory benefits.

However, you will not get credits for weeks in which:[53]

- you would not have been entitled to JSA (whether or not you actually claimed it) because you are involved in a trade dispute; *or*
- your JSA is reduced (or not paid) because you are subject to a sanction. See p1084 and p1116 for the circumstances when this may apply; *or*
- you are receiving hardship payments of income-based or joint-claim JSA (see p1199); *or*
- you are a 16/17-year-old receiving JSA severe hardship payments (see p892).

Part 6: General rules for other benefits
Chapter 41: National insurance contributions
3. National insurance credits

Credits for limited capability for work or incapacity for work

These credits can help you meet the contribution conditions for all contributory benefits (except bereavement payment).

You can be credited with earnings equal to the lower earnings limit for each complete week during which you either:[54]

- were entitled to statutory sick pay (SSP); *or*
- had limited capability for work; *or*
- would have had limited capability for work had you been entitled to contributory ESA (even if the reason you are not entitled to contributory ESA is because of the 365-day limit – see p625) or had you claimed ESA or maternity allowance (MA); *or*
- were incapable of work or could be treated as incapable of work, or you would have been had you made a claim for incapacity benefit (IB) or MA. For information on incapacity for work, see p683 of the 2013/14 edition of this *Handbook*.

You cannot qualify for these credits for weeks in which you are entitled to UC, unless you are also entitled to ESA, SSP, MA, IB or severe disablement allowance in those weeks (to be entitled to UC, you normally must claim it). You also cannot qualify for credits for days on which you were treated as not having limited capability for work (see p1004) or not being incapable of work (or on which you would have been, had you otherwise been entitled to ESA or IB).

These credits are awarded automatically if you get ESA or MA, otherwise you must apply to Jobcentre Plus before the end of the benefit year (ie, by the first Saturday in January – see p861) following the tax year in which you are entitled to the credit. This time limit can be extended if it is considered reasonable to do so, given your circumstances.[55]

Credits for universal credit

These credits can help you meet the contribution conditions for Category A and B retirement pensions, widowed parent's alllowance and bereavement allowance. They are awarded automatically.

If you are entitled to UC for at least part of a week, you can be credited with a Class 3 contribution for that week.[56]

Credits for certain parents and carers

These credits can help you meet the contribution conditions for Category A and B retirement pensions, widowed parent's allowance and bereavement allowance.

These credits replace **home responsibilities protection** for the tax years from 6 April 2010. For how previous years' home responsibilities protection is treated, see p854 and p867. You can be credited with a Class 3 contribution for each week which falls after 6 April 2010 if:

- for any part of the week, you are awarded child benefit for a child under the age of 12;[57] *or*
- you reside with someone who, for any part of the week, is awarded child benefit for a child aged under 12; *and*
  - you share responsibility with that person for a child under 12; *and*
  - in the tax year to which the credit relates, the person awarded child benefit has paid or been credited with NI contributions with an earnings factor of more than 52 times that year's lower earnings limit (see Appendix 8 and p861). In calculating this, any credits s/he gets on the basis of the child benefit award are ignored;[58] *or*
- in that week you are caring for someone for at least 20 hours, or for more than one person for a total of at least 20 hours and:[59]
  - the person(s) for whom you care is entitled to a qualifying benefit (see below); *or*
  - the decision maker considers that the level of care provided is appropriate. You can continue to qualify for these credits for 12 weeks after the week in which you stop satisfying this condition – this allows you to have breaks in caring of up to 12 weeks without losing credits; *or*
- in that week you satisfy the conditions for carers who may qualify for income support (IS) described on p29 (the rules do not state that you must get IS to qualify for credits in this situation);[60] *or*
- for any part of the week, you are an approved foster carer (including a kinship carer in Scotland);[61] *or*
- the week falls in the 12 weeks:[62]
  - before the date you become entitled to CA; *or*
  - following the week you stop being entitled to CA (unless you already qualify for credits for CA for that week – see p855).

For these purposes, a '**qualifying benefit**' includes the daily living component of personal independence payment, attendance allowance, the middle or highest rate of disability living allowance care component, armed forces independence payment, constant attendance allowance in respect of an industrial or war disablement and certain payments under the Pneumoconiosis, Byssinosis and Miscellaneous Diseases Benefits Scheme or Workmen's Compensation (Supple-mentation) Scheme.[63]

Unless you are entitled on the basis that you are awarded child benefit for a child under 12, you will only qualify for these credits if you are ordinarily resident in Great Britain and not in prison or in legal custody.[64]

If you get child benefit, income support or carer's allowance, the credits are awarded automatically. If you qualify because you are caring for someone for at least 20 hours, apply to the DWP (see Appendix 1) using a carer's credit application form (Form CC1), otherwise apply to HMRC (see Appendix 1) on Form CF411A. Both forms are available via www.gov.uk. Your application must be received

Part 6: General rules for other benefits
Chapter 41: National insurance contributions
3. National insurance credits

before the end of the tax year following the tax year to which the credits relate. This time limit can be extended if the DWP or HMRC consider it reasonable in the circumstances.

Note: you can qualify for these credits on the basis of an award of child benefit even if you (or the person with whom you reside) have elected not to receive the child benefit because of the high-income child benefit charge (see p569).

Credits for home responsibilities protection

Home responsibilities protection, which helped you satisfy the second contribution condition for retirement pension, bereavement allowance and widowed parent's allowance, was abolished on 6 April 2010 and was replaced with NI credits for certain parents and carers (see p852). Years of home responsibilities protection which were awarded for tax years up to and including 2009/10 either still help you meet the second contribution condition for these benefits (see p867) or are converted to NI credits, as described below. Home responsibilities protection was not awarded for years before 6 April 1978.

Any year of home responsibilities protection which you received for the tax years up to and including 2009/10 is converted into 52 Class 3 NI contributions:

- for Category A and B retirement pensions, if the 'single contribution condition' is used to determine your entitlement (see p865);
- for widowed parent's allowance and bereavement allowance, if the contributor died on or after 6 April 2010.

However:

- for Category A and B retirement pensions, this conversion can only be done for a maximum of 22 tax years;
- for widowed parent's allowance and bereavement allowance, it can only be done for half the requisite number of years needed to qualify for a full basic widowed parent's allowance or bereavement allowance (see p866).[65]

Credits for family members providing childcare

These credits can help you meet the contribution conditions for:

- Category A retirement pension and Category B retirement pension for spouses and civil partners, if the contributor (see p860) reaches pension age on or after 6 April 2012;
- Category B retirement pension for widows, widowers and surviving civil partners, widowed parent's allowance and bereavement allowance, if the contributor died on or after 6 April 2012 (and, for Category B pension, did not reach pension age before that date).

From 6 April 2011, you can be credited with a Class 3 contribution for each week during which you provide childcare for a child aged under 12, if:[66]

- you are a specified 'family member' of the child (you do not need to be a blood relative and many ex-family members count – see below); *and*
- someone has been awarded child benefit for the child for that week and, in the tax year in which the week falls, her/his contribution record is sufficient for the year to count as a qualifying year for retirement pension (see p865). In calculating this, any credits s/he gets on the grounds of receiving child benefit for a child under 12 are ignored; *and*
- you are not entitled to credits on the basis of being a parent or carer (see p852); *and*
- you are ordinarily resident in Great Britain.

There is no set number of hours for which you must care for the child to qualify and no time limit for claiming. Only one person can qualify for these credits for a particular week for the same child. However, if childcare is shared, it may be possible for someone else to get credits for different weeks in a tax year or, if you look after more than one child, for you each to get credits for the same week in respect of one of the children.

You must apply to HMRC for these credits after the end of the tax year in question. Use Form CA9176 (for specified adult childcare credits) available via www.gov.uk/national-insurance-credits.

Note: if you satisfy the qualifying conditions, you can still get these credits even if the person entitled to child benefit elects not to receive it because of the high-income child benefit charge (see p569).

Family member

You count as a specified **'family member'** if you are:[67]

– the child's parent, grandparent, great or great-great-grandparent, sibling, aunt or uncle (including if you are an adopted, step- or half-sibling of the child or of the child's parent);

– a spouse or civil partner, or former spouse or civil partner, of any of the above relatives;

– a partner or former partner of any of the above (including, for instance, a former partner of a former spouse of one of the above relatives);

– a son or daughter of any of the above;

– a spouse, civil partner or partner (or former spouse, civil partner or partner) of the child's first cousin.

A **'partner'** is someone with whom the relative lives as if they were husband and wife or civil partners. This definition is likely to include someone with whom the relative lives as if they were married following the introduction of same sex-marriages.

Credits for carer's allowance

These credits can help you meet the contribution conditions for all contributory benefits (except bereavement payment). They are awarded automatically.

Part 6: General rules for other benefits
Chapter 41: National insurance contributions
3. National insurance credits

You can be credited with earnings equal to the lower earnings limit for each week in which you receive CA (see Chapter 25), or would receive it but for the loss of benefit for benefit offences rules (see p1258).[68] You also receive credits if the only reason that you do not receive CA is because you are receiving a bereavement benefit or widow's benefit instead.

If you are looking after a disabled person but are not entitled to these credits, you may qualify for credits for certain carers (see p852).

Starting credits

These credits can help you meet the contribution conditions for Category A and B retirement pensions, widowed parent's allowance and bereavement allowance. They are awarded automatically.

You can receive Class 3 credits for the tax years in which you reach the age of 16, 17 and 18 if you would otherwise have had an insufficient contribution record for those years to count towards the contribution conditions for the above benefits.[69]

However, for Category A and B retirement pensions, you can only qualify for these credits:

- for tax years falling before 6 April 2010; *and*
- if you had to make an application for an NI number to be allocated to you, if your application for an NI number was made before 6 April 2010.

No credits were made under this provision for years before 6 April 1975.

Education and training credits

These credits can help you meet the contribution conditions for either contribution-based JSA and contributory ESA or, in certain cases, for all contributory benefits (except bereavement payment).

For the purpose of qualifying for contribution-based JSA and contributory ESA, you can be credited with earnings equal to the lower earnings limit for either one of the two complete tax years that fall before the relevant benefit year (see p861), if:

- for any part of those tax years you were on:[70]
  - a course of full-time training, including training to acquire occupational or vocational skills (or, if you are disabled, a part-time course of at least 15 hours a week); *or*
  - a course of full-time education; *or*
  - an apprenticeship; *and*
- in the other tax year in which you must satisfy the second contribution condition for the benefit (see p863), you have an earnings factor of 50 times the lower earnings limit without relying on this provision; *and*
- you are at least 18 or will become 18 during the tax year in question; *and*

- you were under 21 when the course or apprenticeship started; *and*
- your course of education, training or apprenticeship has finished.

You can receive credits which count for all contributory benefits (except a bereavement payment) for each week in which you were not entitled to UC (to be entitled, you normally must have claimed it) and in which you are undertaking a training course approved by a DWP decision maker if:[71]

- the training is full time (at least 15 hours a week if you are disabled) or it is an introductory course; *and*
- the training is not part of your job; *and*
- the training is intended to last for one year or less (except in certain circumstances if it is a course for disabled people); *and*
- you were 18 or over at the beginning of the tax year in which the week falls.

In any case, if the course was arranged by Jobcentre Plus, you get the credits automatically, otherwise you must apply to HMRC's NI Contributions and Employer Office (see Appendix 1).

Credits for statutory maternity, additional paternity and adoption pay

These credits can help you meet the contribution conditions for all contributory benefits (except bereavement payment).

You can be credited with earnings equal to the lower earnings limit for each week for which you receive statutory maternity pay, additional statutory paternity pay or statutory adoption pay.[72]

To apply for these credits, write to HMRC's NI Contributions and Employer Office (see Appendix 1). Your application must be received before the end of the benefit year (see p861) following the tax year in which the week falls, but this time limit may be extended if it is reasonable to do so.

Credits for jury service

These credits can help you meet the contribution conditions for all contributory benefits (except bereavement payment).

You are entitled to be credited with earnings equal to the lower earnings limit for each week after 6 April 1988 during which you spend at least part of the week on jury service, unless you are self-employed in that week.[73]

To apply for these credits, write to HMRC's NI Contributions and Employer Office (see Appendix 1). Your application must be received before the end of the benefit year (see p861) following the tax year in which the week falls (or such further period as is reasonable).

Part 6: General rules for other benefits
Chapter 41: National insurance contributions
3. National insurance credits

Credits following bereavement

These credits help you meet the contribution conditions for contribution-based JSA and contributory ESA. They should be awarded automatically.

If your entitlement to a bereavement benefit has ended, you can be credited with sufficient earnings for each year up to and including the one in which your bereavement benefit stopped to enable you to satisfy the second contribution condition for contribution-based JSA or contributory ESA (but see note below).[74]

For the purpose of satisfying the second contribution condition for contributory ESA, you are also entitled to credits for each year up to and including the one in which your entitlement to widow's allowance (abolished in April 1988) or widowed mother's allowance ceased (but see note below).[75]

Note: you cannot qualify for credits following bereavement if your entitlement to widows' or bereavement benefits stopped because you married or entered into a civil partnership, or if you started cohabiting (see p527).[76]

Credits for men born before 6 October 1954

These credits can help you meet the contribution conditions for all contributory benefits (except bereavement payment). They are awarded automatically.

If you are a man who was born before 6 April 1954, you can be credited with earnings (known as 'autocredits') from the tax year in which you would have reached pension age had you been a woman (see Appendix 5) up to, but not including, the tax year in which you reach the age of 65.[77] You cannot qualify for these credits for any year in which you were abroad for more than 182 days. Also, if you are self-employed, you must either:

- be liable for at least one Class 2 contribution in any of the above tax years; *or*
- have a small earnings exception (see p845) for at least one week in any of the above tax years,

to qualify for credits for the other weeks in that year.

Credits for tax credits

These credits can help you meet the contribution conditions for Category A or B retirement pension, widowed parent's allowance and bereavement allowance and, in some circumstances, all contributory benefits (apart from bereavement payment). They are awarded automatically.

For each week for which you receive, for any part of the week, the disabled worker element or severe disability element of working tax credit (WTC), you are entitled to be credited with earnings equal to the lower earnings limit. These credits count for all contributory benefits (apart from bereavement payment).

Alternatively, for each week for which you are paid WTC (without the disabled worker element or the severe disability element), you are credited with earnings equal to the lower earnings limit to help you satisfy the contribution conditions for Category A or B retirement pension, widowed parent's allowance and bereavement allowance. In this case, if WTC was paid to you as a member of a couple but only one of you has earnings, the credits will be awarded to that person; otherwise they are awarded to the person to whom WTC is paid.

You can only qualify for either of these credits during any week in which you were either:[78]

- employed and earning less than the lower earnings limit for that year; *or*
- self-employed but not liable to pay Class 2 contributions because you have a small earnings exception (see p845).

If you used to get working families' tax credit, disabled person's tax credit, family credit or disability working allowance, see the 1999/00 and 2002/03 editions of this *Handbook* for details of similar credits.

Credits for a quashed conviction

These credits can help you meet the contribution conditions for all contributory benefits (apart from bereavement payment).

If you were imprisoned or detained in legal custody after being convicted of an offence, and that conviction has subsequently been quashed by the courts, you can be credited with earnings for each week during at least part of which you were imprisoned or detained.[79]

To apply for these credits, write to HMRC's NI Contributions and Employer Office (see Appendix 1). Application by email may also be accepted.

Credits for official error

These credits can help you meet the contribution conditions for Category A or B retirement pension (when the 'old contribution conditions' for retirement pension apply – see p866), contribution-based JSA and incapacity benefit. They were awarded automatically.

Some people were credited with earnings for the tax years from 1993/94 to 2007/08 following an official error arising from discrepancies between the DWP and HMRC computer systems.[80] See the 2009/10 edition of this *Handbook* for details.

Credits for service families

These credits can help you meet the contribution conditions for all contributory benefits (apart from bereavement payment).

From 6 April 2010, you can be credited with earnings equal to that year's lower earnings limit for each week during any part of which you were:[81]

- the spouse or civil partner of a member of the armed forces (or someone treated as such for the purpose of occupying accommodation); and
- accompanying, or were treated as accompanying, her/him on an assignment outside the UK.

Part 6: General rules for other benefits
Chapter 41: National insurance contributions
4. Contribution conditions for benefits

You must usually apply for these credits on the approved form (Form MODCA1, available via www.gov.uk), once you have a confirmed date for the end of the overseas posting and before the end of the tax year following the tax year in which the overseas assignment ended. This time limit can be extended if it is reasonable given your circumstances.

The decision maker has discretion to accept an application made before you receive confirmation of the end date of the overseas assignment. If your application is accepted, you can be awarded credits for the period before your application, but you have to make a further application under these rules for credits for any subsequent period.

4. **Contribution conditions for benefits**

Entitlement to contributory benefits normally depends on the national insurance (NI) contribution conditions being met. For contribution-based jobseeker's allowance (JSA) and contributory employment and support allowance (ESA) (unless you can qualify for contributory ESA without satisfying the contribution conditions), your entitlement is based on your own NI contribution record. For other contributory benefits, the relevant '**contributor**' is:

- for Category A retirement pension, you or, in certain circumstances, your late spouse or civil partner, or your former spouse or civil partner (see p748);
- for Category B retirement pension, your spouse or civil partner, or your late spouse or civil partner (but see p748 for the detailed entitlement rules);
- for bereavement payment, widowed parent's allowance or bereavement allowance, your late spouse or civil partner.

You may be credited with earnings or contributions to fill gaps in your contribution record (see p850). These credits can only count towards the second contribution condition for benefits which have two contribution conditions, or towards the single contribution condition for Category A or B retirement pension (see p865).

In some circumstances, you may be able to combine your own contribution record with that of your late spouse or civil partner, or your former spouse or civil partner, to qualify for a Category A retirement pension (see p748).

It may be possible for you to rely on the contributions you have paid in other European Economic Area states to qualify for contributory benefits (see p1589).

Note: when it is introduced, the government plans that you will only be able to build up your entitlement to the new single-tier state pension on the basis of your own contribution record (see p841).

Earnings factors

Payment of Class 1, 2 and 3 contributions gives rise to an 'earnings factor', which is used to calculate your entitlement to contributory benefits (including the additional pension payable under the additional state pension scheme – see p760).

For Class 1 contributions, the earnings factor is the amount of earnings, excluding those earnings above the upper earnings limit (or above the upper accrual point for additional state pension), on which those contributions have been paid. Each Class 2 or 3 contribution gives rise to an earnings factor equal to that year's lower earnings limit (see Appendix 8).[82]

If you (or, for benefits which do not rely on your own contribution record, the relevant contributor – see p860) have been credited with earnings or Class 3 contributions, these NI credits count towards the earnings factor to help you meet the contribution conditions for certain contributory benefits (see p850).[83]

In some circumstances, you also can be deemed to have an earnings factor sufficient to help you build up entitlement to additional state pension.[84]

Jobseeker's allowance and employment and support allowance

Contribution-based JSA and contributory ESA have two contribution conditions. These conditions relate to particular tax years falling before the 'relevant benefit year'. In some situations, you can qualify for contributory ESA without having to satisfy the contribution conditions. In other situations, the first contribution condition is modified to make it easier to meet.

Relevant benefit year

A 'benefit year' is almost the same as a calendar year and runs from the first Sunday in January.[85]

The 'relevant benefit year' for contribution-based JSA is the benefit year in which the jobseeking period began or, if earlier, the benefit year in which a period that is linked to the jobseeking period began (see p693).[86]

The 'relevant benefit year' for contributory ESA is the benefit year in which your current period of limited capability for work started. However, if you otherwise would not meet the contribution conditions for contributory ESA, your relevant benefit year can instead be any benefit year which includes any part of your current period of limited capability for work (or any part of any period(s) of limited capability for work that can be linked to your current period – see p1017). Note: a period of limited capability for work cannot include a period which falls before the three-month time limit for backdating an ESA claim.[87]

Part 6: General rules for other benefits
Chapter 41: National insurance contributions
4. Contribution conditions for benefits

When the contribution conditions do not apply

You can qualify for contributory ESA without having to satisfy the contribution conditions if:[88]

- your contributory ESA (this includes ESA in youth) ended because you had received it for 365 days in the circumstances described on p625, you continued to have (or be treated as having) limited capability for work after your entitlement ended and you now have, or are treated as having, limited capability for work-related activity (see p1007). In this situation, you can qualify for contributory ESA again without having to satisfy the contribution conditions; or

- you are transferred to contributory ESA, having previously received incapacity benefit (IB) or severe disablement allowance (SDA) (see p662). In this situation, when you are transferred, the contribution conditions for contributory ESA are waived (but, if your contributory ESA is subsequently stopped because of the 365-day limit and you want to reclaim it, you will have to meet the usual contribution conditions to get contributory ESA again unless the previous bullet point applies); or

- you were getting IB or SDA but, following a determination that you do not have limited capability for work, your IB or SDA is not converted into contributory ESA and you have appealed against the decision (you are likely to have to have applied for a revision first). In this situation, you are treated as satisfying the contribution conditions for contributory ESA while you are pursuing your appeal (see p1015).

The first condition

In one of the last two complete tax years before the relevant benefit year (see p861), you must have paid contributions on earnings (in respect of Class 1 contributions), or have paid contributions producing an earnings factor (in respect of Class 2 contributions), of at least 26 times that year's lower earnings limit (eg, £2,886 in 2014/15 – 26 x £111). For contribution-based JSA, only Class 1 contributions count towards meeting this condition (unless you are a share fisherman or volunteer development worker, when special Class 2 contributions also count). For ESA, both Class 1 and Class 2 contributions count.[89]

In calculating the earnings on which you paid Class 1 contributions, you cannot include any earnings above the lower earnings limit, so you must have worked for at least 26 weeks in one of the last two tax years before your relevant benefit year to meet this condition. The 26 weeks do not need to be consecutive but must fall in a single tax year.

Note:
- The first contribution condition can be relaxed in some circumstances (see below).
- The contributions must be paid before the week for which contribution-based JSA or contributory ESA is claimed.

- A widow can be treated as satisfying the first NI contribution condition for contributory ESA if she was entitled to widowed mother's allowance but her entitlement has ended (this does not apply if her entitlement ended because she married or entered into a civil partnership, or if payment stopped because she started cohabiting).[90] She may also be credited with contributions to satisfy the second condition (see p858). This help with the first contribution condition for contributory ESA does not extend to widows, widowers or surviving civil partners who lose entitlement to bereavement benefits.

When the first condition is relaxed

In some situations, the first contribution condition is relaxed, so that sufficient contributions paid in *any* one tax year are enough to satisfy the condition, as long as they were paid before the week for which you are claiming the benefit.

For contribution-based JSA and contributory ESA, this applies if you were entitled to credits for service families (see p859) in at least one week in the tax year before the relevant benefit year (see p861).[91]

For contributory ESA, it also applies if you:[92]

- were entitled to carer's allowance (CA) in the last complete tax year before the relevant benefit year (even if it was not paid because of the overlapping benefit rules – see p1165);
- were entitled to NI credits for a quashed conviction at some time in any tax year before the relevant benefit year (or you would have been entitled to such credits had you claimed them);
- were in full-time paid work (see p165) for more than two years immediately before your period of limited capability for work began and you were entitled to working tax credit which included a disabled worker or severe disability element (see p1403 and p1405).

The second condition

In each of the last two complete tax years ending before the relevant benefit year (see p861), you must have paid contributions, or received NI credits, which produced an earnings factor of at least 50 times the lower earnings limit. Only certain NI credits count towards meeting this condition (eg, credited Class 3 contributions do not – see pp850–59) and, to count, any paid contributions must be Class 1 contributions (or special Class 2 contributions) for contribution-based JSA, or Class 1 or 2 contributions for contributory ESA.[93]

Note: if you want to claim contributory ESA again after a previous award ended because of the 365-day limit, in some circumstances you can requalify without having to satisfy the contribution conditions (see p862). If these circumstances do not apply, normally you only requalify if you satisfy the contribution conditions and if one of the tax years in which you satisfy the second contribution condition falls after the last tax year you relied on to meet the condition for your earlier claim (see p625). The only exception to this is if you did not have to meet

Part 6: General rules for other benefits
Chapter 41: National insurance contributions
4. Contribution conditions for benefits

the contribution conditions when you were previously awarded contributory ESA because either you were transferred from IB or SDA, or you were getting ESA in youth. In this situation, the usual contribution conditions apply to your new claim for contributory ESA.[94]

The timing of your claim

In rare cases, it may be beneficial for you to delay a claim for contribution-based JSA so that you can draw on a different year's contribution record. This is because the years in which you must meet the contribution conditions depend on the benefit year in which your jobseeking period starts. So, for example, if your current jobseeking period is not linked to an earlier one (see p693) and you claim before Sunday 5 January 2014, you must meet the second contribution condition in the tax years 2010/11 and 2011/12 whereas, if you claim on 5 January 2014, you must meet it in 2011/12 and 2012/13.

Any day for which you do not claim does not count as part of your jobseeking period (see p693),[95] so it is easy to postpone when that period begins. However, if you claim and are refused benefit because the contribution conditions are not satisfied, your jobseeking period will have started. You would then normally have to wait for more than 12 weeks to make a fresh claim. The 12-week gap would break the jobseeking period.

The situation is different for contributory ESA. If your claim for contributory ESA is refused only on the grounds that you do not meet the contribution conditions, in some cases it can be worth putting in a later claim that falls in a different benefit year (see p861). However, if a previous award of contributory ESA ended because of the 365-day limit and you are making a new claim, see p863.

Example

Shanti lives with her partner who works full time. Shanti was self-employed and paid Class 2 NI contributions throughout the tax years 2011/12 and 2012/13 (in the tax year 2010/11 she did not pay NI contributions or get NI credits). In December 2013 she became ill and claimed contributory ESA for the first time. The relevant benefit year (see p861) was 2013 and the two complete tax years falling before that are 2010/11 and 2011/12. Having no contributions or credits for 2010/11, Shanti was refused contributory ESA. If she claims again in the 2014 benefit year (which started on 5 January 2014), the contributions she paid in 2011/12 and 2012/13 are counted and she may qualify for contributory ESA. The rules allow 2014 to count as her relevant benefit year as part of her period of limited capability for work falls in that year.

Bereavement payment

In any one tax year before your late spouse or civil partner reached pension age (or before s/he died, if s/he died before reaching pension age), s/he must have paid Class 1, 2 or 3 NI contributions which produced an earnings factor (see p861) of at least 25 times that year's lower earnings limit (eg, £2,775 in 2014/15 – 25 x £111).[96]

If your late spouse or civil partner only became liable to pay contributions in either the last complete tax year before the benefit year in which s/he reached pension age or in which s/he died (if s/he died before reaching pension age), or in the tax year before that, the sum of any contributions paid in *any* year may be counted.

In certain circumstances, the contribution condition for bereavement payment is treated as having been satisfied if your late spouse or civil partner had previously successfully claimed and met the first contribution condition for maternity allowance (MA) or IB. (MA no longer has contribution conditions, although it did for women whose expected week of childbirth fell before 20 August 2000.[97])

The payment of 25 flat-rate contributions in a contribution year before 6 April 1975 also satisfies the contribution condition.[98]

Category A and B retirement pensions from 6 April 2010

If the single contribution condition for Category A and B retirement pension applies (see below), the contributor must have paid Class 1, 2 or 3 NI contributions or received NI credits which produced an earnings factor (see p861) of at least 52 times that year's lower earnings limit (eg, £5,772 in 2014/15 – 52 x £111) in at least one tax year during her/his working life (but, to qualify for a *full* basic Category A or B retirement pension, s/he must have met this condition in 30 such tax years – see below). Most, but not all, kinds of NI credits can be counted (see pp850–59).[99]

For Category A retirement pension, the 'contributor' is normally you – for further information, and for who counts as the contributor for Category B pension, see p860.

A reduced rate of the basic pension is awarded if the contribution condition is met for less than 30 years, as long as the condition is met in at least one year. You qualify for one-thirtieth of the basic weekly pension for each year in which the contribution condition is satisfied. Any additional state pension to which you are entitled is also paid.[100]

The **'single contribution condition'** applies if:[101]

- for Category A retirement pension, and for Category B pension for spouses and civil partners (see p748), the contributor reaches pension age on or after 6 April 2010; *or*
- for Category B retirement pension for widows, widowers and surviving civil partners (see p748), the contributor (ie, your late spouse or civil partner) had not reached pension age before 6 April 2010 and died on or after that date.

If the single contribution condition does not apply, see p866 for the 'old contribution conditions' for Category A and B retirement pensions.

Part 6: General rules for other benefits
Chapter 41: National insurance contributions
4. Contribution conditions for benefits

Note: once changes in legislation come into force (in England and Wales, this is expected to be before the end of 2014) allowing people to obtain a full gender recognition certificate while remaining married, in some circumstances the single contribution condition may also apply if you are a woman claiming Category B retirement pension on the basis of your wife's contributions, even if she reached pension age before 6 April 2010.[102]

Category A and B retirement pension before 6 April 2010, widowed parent's allowance and bereavement allowance

Entitlement to Category A or B retirement pension will still be assessed on the basis of the 'old contribution conditions', rather than the single contribution condition described above, if the contributor reached pension age before 6 April 2010 or, for Category B retirement pension based on the contribution record of a late spouse or civil partner, if s/he reached pension age or died before 6 April 2010 (but see the note above for an exception).

There are two contribution conditions for widowed parent's allowance and bereavement allowance and, if the old contribution conditions apply, for Category A or B retirement pension.

The first condition

In any one tax year before s/he died or reached pension age, the contributor (see p860) must have paid Class 1, 2 or 3 contributions which produced an earnings factor (see p861) of at least 52 times that year's lower earnings limit (eg, £5,772 in 2014/15 – 52 x £111).[103] The payment of 50 flat-rate contributions for any time before 6 April 1975 also satisfies this condition.[104]

The first condition is deemed to be satisfied if the contributor was receiving the support or work-related activity component of ESA (see p621 and p622) or long-term IB either:

- in the year in which s/he died (if s/he died before reaching pension age) or in which s/he reached pension age; *or*
- in the preceding year.[105]

The second condition

In the requisite number of tax years during the contributor's (see p860) working life s/he must have paid Class 1, 2 or 3 contributions, or received NI credits, which produced an earnings factor of at least 52 times that year's lower earnings limit (eg, £5,772 in 2014/15 – 52 x £111).[106] Most, but not all, NI credits count towards meeting this condition (see pp850–59), as do contributions paid before 6 April 1975.

The requisite number of years needed to satisfy this condition depends on the length of the contributor's 'working life'. Your 'working life' is the period inclusive of the tax year in which you reach the age of 16 up to, but excluding, the year in

which you reach pension age or in which you die (if earlier).[107] If you were over 16 on 5 July 1948, your working life may have started on a different date.[108]
The requisite number of years is then calculated as follows.[109]

Length of 'working life'	Requisite number of years
1–10 years	Length of working life minus one
11–20 years	Length of working life minus two
21–30 years	Length of working life minus three
31–40 years	Length of working life minus four
41–50 years	Length of working life minus five

Note:
- A reduced rate of benefit may be paid if you have not met the second contribution condition for the requisite number of years.
- In some circumstances, past years of home responsibilities protection may reduce the requisite number of years over which you must meet the second contribution condition (see below).
- To calculate the number of years before 6 April 1975 in which you satisfied the contribution condition, add together all the contributions paid or credited before 6 April 1975, and divide the answer by 50. If that does not produce a whole number, round the result up, as long as that does not produce a number greater than the number of years of your working life before 6 April 1975.

Home responsibilities protection

Home responsibilities protection was abolished on 6 April 2010. However, you can still rely on years of home responsibilities protection which were awarded for the tax years up to and including the 2009/10 tax year to meet the second contribution condition for:
- widowed parent's allowance and bereavement allowance, if your late spouse or civil partner died before 6 April 2010; *or*
- Category A and B retirement pensions, if the old contribution conditions apply.

See the 2009/10 edition of this *Handbook* for further details. If the conditions in the bullet points above do not apply, past years of home responsibilities protection are converted into NI credits (see p854).

Reduced benefit because of insufficient contributions

Benefit can be paid at a reduced rate if the second contribution condition is not satisfied for the requisite number of years, provided it is satisfied in at least 25 per cent of the requisite number. The benefit is paid at a percentage of the amount which would otherwise be paid. The percentage is calculated by expressing the

Part 6: General rules for other benefits
Chapter 41: National insurance contributions
Notes

number of years in which the condition is satisfied as a percentage of the requisite number of years and rounding it up to the nearest whole number.[110] Thus, if you are a widow and your husband's working life was 12 years, so that the requisite number of years is 10, and he only satisfied the condition in eight years, you receive 80 per cent of the standard rate of widowed parent's allowance or bereavement allowance.

If you still qualify for them, increases for adult dependants are reduced in the same proportion, but increases for children are paid in full.[111]

It may be possible for you to pay Class 3 contributions (see p848) to increase the number of years in which the second contribution condition is satisfied. Whether this is worthwhile will depend on the length of time for which benefit will be paid (remember, for example, that you can only be entitled to bereavement allowance for a maximum of 52 weeks), the amount of the Class 3 contributions you will need to pay, and the amount of benefit to which such payment will entitle you. If in doubt, seek advice.

Notes

1 Pensions Bill 2013

1. Contributions and contributory benefits
2 s11 SSC(TF)A 1999; Part III SSC(DA) Regs; Arts 6 (c)(i) and 7 First-tier Tribunal and Upper Tribunal (Chambers) Order 2010, No.2655
3 Sch 3 para 17 SSA 1998; s17 SSC(TF)A 1999; Arts 2-4 National Insurance Contribution Credits (Transfer of Functions) Order 2009, No.1377

2. Paid contributions
4 s1(2) SSCBA 1992
5 ss6(1) and (3) and 11(1) and (2) SSCBA 1992
6 s13 SSCBA 1992; regs 48(1) and 49(1)(f) and (2A)-(2C) SS(Con) Regs
7 s2(1) SSCBA 1992
8 *Ready Mix Concrete South East Ltd v Ministry of Pensions and National Insurance* [1968] 2 QB 497 (QBD); *Global Plant v Secretary of State for Health and Social Security* [1971] 3 All ER 385 (QBD)

9 Sch 1 paras 1-5A SS(CatE) Regs; *ITV Services Ltd v HMRC* [2012] UKUT 47 (TCC)
10 Sch 1 paras 6 SS(CatE) Regs
11 Sch 1 paras 7-12 SS(CatE) Regs
12 ss6 and 7 SSCBA 1992
13 ss6 and 6A SSCBA 1992
14 s8 SSCBA 1992
15 ss8 and 41 PSA 1993; reg 131 SS(Con) Regs
16 Sch 1 para 3 SSCBA 1992
17 Reg 60 SS(Con) Regs
18 Regs 13, 14, 15 and 21 SS(Con) Regs
19 Sch 1 para 1 SSCBA 1992; regs 13, 14, 15 and 21 SS(Con) Regs
20 s11 SSCBA 1992; regs 43 and 46 SS(Con) Regs
21 Reg 45 SS(Con) Regs
22 Regs 43 and 46 SS(Con) Regs
23 s11(1) SSCBA 1992
24 s11(5) SSCBA 1992; regs 44 and 47 SS(Con) Regs
25 Reg 127(1) SS(Con) Regs
26 Regs 125, 149, 151 and 152 SS(Con) Regs

27 Reg 21 SS(Con) Regs
28 s13 SSCBA 1992
29 s14 SSCBA 1992; reg 49 SS(Con) Regs
30 s13(1) SSCBA 1992
31 Reg 127 SS(Con) Regs
32 Regs 128(1) and 130 SS(Con) Regs
33 Pensions Bill 2013
34 ss2(1), 6 and 11 SSCBA 1992; reg 145(1)(a), (c), (d) and (2) SS(Con) Regs
35 Reg 145(1)(c) and (e) SS(Con) Regs
36 Reg 146 SS(Con) Regs
37 Regs 147 and 148 SS(Con) Regs
38 Regs 149 and 151 SS(Con) Regs
39 Regs 146(2)(b), 147 and 148 SS(Con) Regs
40 Regs 43(3), 46, 48 and 49 SS(Con) Regs
41 Reg 62 SS(Con) Regs
42 Regs 52, 52A and 56 SS(Con) Regs; *Clifford Bonner and Others v HMRC* [2010] UKUT 450 (TCC); see also www.hmrc.gov.uk/nic/vc3-important.htm
43 Reg 60 SS(Con) Regs; reg 5 SS(CTCNIN) Regs
44 Reg 4 SS(CTCNIN) Regs; reg 48(3)(b) SS(Con) Regs
45 Reg 4(7) and (8) SS(CTCNIN) Regs
46 Regs 50 and 61 SS(Con) Regs; regs 4(11), 5A, 6, 6A and 6B SS(CTCNIN) Regs
47 s13A SSCBA 1992; reg 3(8D) SS&CS(DA) Regs; reg 6C SS(CTCNIN) Regs
48 Regs 50C and 61B SS(Con) Regs

3. National insurance credits
49 Reg 3 SS(Cr) Regs
50 Regs 7(3), 7A(2)(b), 7B(3), 7C(4), 8(2)(b), 8A(5)(e), 8B(3), 9B(3), 9C(4), 9D(4) and 9E(8) SS(Cr) Regs
51 s44C SSCBA 1992
52 Reg 8A SS(Cr) Regs
53 Reg 8A(5) SS(Cr) Regs
54 Reg 8B SS(Cr) Regs
55 Reg 8B(4) SS(Cr) Regs
56 Reg 8G SS(Cr) Regs
57 s23A(2) and (3)(a) SSCBA 1992
58 s23A(2) and (3)(c) SSCBA 1992; regs 2, 5(1)(a), 6 and 9 SS(CCPC) Regs
59 s23A(2) and (3)(c) SSCBA 1992; regs 5(1)(b), 7(1)(c), 10 and 11 SS(CCPC) Regs
60 s23A(2) and (3)(c) SSCBA 1992; reg 5(1)(c) SS(CCPC) Regs
61 s23A(2) and (3)(b) SSCBA 1992; regs 4 and 9 SS(CCPC) Regs
62 Reg 7 SS(CCPC) Regs
63 Reg 2 SS(CCPC) Regs

64 Reg 8 SS(CCPC) Regs
65 s23A(5)-(7) SSCBA 1992
66 Reg 9F SS(Cr) Regs
67 Sch SS(Cr) Regs
68 Reg 7A SS(Cr) Regs
69 Reg 4 SS(Cr) Regs
70 Reg 8 SS(Cr) Regs
71 Reg 7 SS(Cr) Regs
72 Reg 9C SS(Cr) Regs
73 Reg 9B SS(Cr) Regs
74 Reg 8C SS(Cr) Regs
75 Reg 3(1)(b) SSB(MW&WSP) Regs
76 HMRC includes same-sex cohabitees in this exclusion because cohabitation stops payment not entitlement to the benefit.
77 Reg 9A SS(Cr) Regs
78 Regs 7B and 7C SS(Cr) Regs
79 Reg 9D SS(Cr) Regs
80 Regs 8D, 8E and 8F SS(Cr) Regs
81 Reg 9E SS(Cr) Regs

4. Contribution conditions for benefits
82 s22 SSCBA 1992; Sch 1 SS(EF) Regs
83 s22(5) and (5A) SSCBA 1992
84 ss44A, 44B and 44C SSCBA 1992
85 s21(6) SSCBA 1992; s2(4) JSA 1995; Sch 1 para 3 WRA 2007
86 s2(4) JSA 1995
87 Sch 1 para 3(1)(f) WRA 2007; regs 2(1) and 13 ESA Regs; reg 2 and 14 ESA Regs 2013
88 s1B WRA 2007; Sch 2 paras 2 and 15 ESA(TP)(EA)(No.2) Regs
89 **JSA** ss1(2)(d) and 2 JSA 1995; regs 45A, 158 and 167 JSA Regs; regs 34, 69 and 75 JSA Regs 2013
   ESA Sch 1 para 1 WRA 2007; reg 7A ESA Regs; reg 8 ESA Regs 2013
90 Reg 3(1) SSB(MW&WSP) Regs
91 Reg 45B JSA Regs; reg 8(2)(ca) ESA Regs; reg 35 JSA Regs 2013; reg 9(2)(d) ESA Regs 2013
92 Reg 8 ESA Regs; reg 9 ESA Regs 2013
93 s2 JSA 1995; Sch 1 para 2 WRA 2007; regs 158 and 167 JSA Regs; regs 69 and 75 JSA Regs 2013
94 s1A WRA 2007
95 Reg 47(3)(a) JSA Regs; reg 37(2)(a) JSA Regs 2013
96 s21and Sch 3 para 4 SSCBA 1992
97 Sch 3 paras 7 and 9 SSCBA 1992
98 Reg 13(1) SS(STB)(T) Regs
99 s122(1), definition of 'qualifying earnings factor', and Sch 3 para 5A SSCBA 1992
100 Reg 6A SS(WB&RP) Regs
101 Sch 3 para 5A(1) SSCBA 1992

Part 6: General rules for other benefits
Chapter 41: National insurance contributions
Notes

102 Sch 4 paras 11 and 12 M(SSC)A 2013
103 Sch 3 para 5 SSCBA 1992
104 Reg 6 SS(WBRP&OB)(T) Regs
105 Sch 3 para 5(6) and (6A) SSCBA 1992
106 Sch 3 para 5(3) SSCBA 1992
107 Sch 3 para 5(8) SSCBA 1992
108 Reg 7(7) SS(WBRP&OB)(T) Regs; s20
    and Sch 3 para 5(5) SSCBA 1992
109 Sch 3 para 5(5) SSCBA 1992
110 Reg 6 SS(WB&RP) Regs
111 s60(4)-(6) SSCBA 1992; reg 6(3)
    SS(WB&RP) Regs

6

Chapter 42

Earnings

This chapter covers:
1. Earnings and non-means-tested benefits (below)
2. Disregarded earnings (p877)
3. Deductions from earnings (p878)

This chapter covers the rules on calculating earnings for carer's allowance and for increases for a child or an adult in your non-means-tested benefits. It does *not* cover the income rules for contribution-based jobseeker's allowance (see p697) or for contributory employment and support allowance (ESA – see p623). For the permitted work earnings rules for ESA, see p1020. For the permitted work earnings rules for incapacity benefit and severe disablement allowance, see Chapter 44 in the 2013/14 edition of this *Handbook*. For the income rules for means-tested benefits, see Chapters 14, 15 and 16.

Key facts
- Your own earnings from employment or self-employment may affect your entitlement to carer's allowance.
- Whether you can get an increase in a non-means-tested benefit for an adult or child may be affected by the earnings (including certain pension payments) of your partner or of the adult for whom you claim the increase.
- Some earnings can be disregarded and, in some circumstances, childcare costs or care costs can be deducted when calculating earnings.

---

1. Earnings and non-means-tested benefits

This chapter explains the general rules on how:
- your earnings are calculated when assessing your entitlement to carer's allowance (CA). See p541 for details of how earnings affect your entitlement;
- the earnings of an adult for whom you claim an increase in your CA or retirement pension are calculated. You are only entitled to an increase if that adult's earnings are not too high;
- the earnings of your partner are calculated if you are entitled to an increase for a child in your CA, retirement pension or widowed parent's allowance. If you

Part 6: General rules for other benefits
Chapter 42: Earnings
1. Earnings and non-means-tested benefits

are getting an increase and are a member of a couple, it is not paid if your partner's earnings are too high.

In respect of a claim for an increase in your non-means-tested benefit for an adult or child, certain pension payments your partner or the adult receives may count as earnings (see below). For how earnings affect these increases, see p542 for CA, p753 for retirement pensions and p522 for widowed parent's allowance.

Note: your entitlement to certain non-means-tested benefits may also be affected by the overlapping benefit rules (see p1165).

When pension payments count as earnings

Pension payments are included in the assessment of the earnings of:
- an adult for whom you claim an increase in your non-means-tested benefit;
- your partner, if you are a member of a couple and are claiming an increase in your non-means-tested benefit for a child.

You may not get an increase if the adult's or your partner's earnings are too high. Pension payments *you* receive do not count as your earnings when assessing your entitlement to CA.

Occupational or personal pension payments count if they are periodic, made in connection with the end of employment (including from the Pension Protection Fund), and arranged:[1]
- by an employer; *or*
- out of money, some or all of which is from an employer; *or*
- under an approved personal pension scheme, including if you are self-employed, or under a statutory scheme.

This includes schemes for early retirement on health or other grounds or, in some cases, voluntary redundancy.[2]

Lump-sum or pension payments on redundancy which are not related to a specific period are not included, even if you choose a lump sum instead of a periodic payment.[3] The gross amount of pension paid counts, less any deductions for income tax and any compulsory reductions made by the pension scheme to acquire additional pension rights.[4] A payment is converted into weekly amounts[5] and counted from the first day of the benefit week in which it is made.

Earnings from employment

To work out how earnings from employment affect entitlement:
- check whether the payment counts as earnings (see p873) and whether it can be disregarded (see p877);
- work out weekly net earnings (see p874);

- work out the date from which earnings count and the period they cover (see p875);
- apply the earnings rule for the benefit you are claiming. See p541 for CA, and, for an increase for a child or adult, see the chapter for the non-means-tested benefit for which you are claiming the increase.

What counts as earnings

For employees (including people employed by a limited company in which they have shares), 'earnings' mean 'any remuneration or profit derived from… employment'. The main type of income which counts as earnings is, therefore, your wages. The following are also included:[6]
- any bonus or commission (including tips);
- holiday pay (but not if it is payable more than four weeks after a job ends or is interrupted);
- compensation for unfair dismissal and certain other types of compensation under the Employment Rights Act 1996 or under trade union legislation;
- an equal pay settlement;[7]
- any payments made by an employer for expenses not 'wholly, exclusively and necessarily' incurred in carrying out the job, including any travel expenses to and from work, and any payments made to an employee for the cost of arranging care for members of her/his family;
- a retainer (eg, this may be paid during the school holidays to people who work for the school meals service) or a guarantee payment (ie, payment for a workless period under the Employment Rights Act 1996);[8]
- statutory or occupational maternity pay, paternity pay (during ordinary paternity leave), adoption pay and sick pay;
- certain payments at the end of a job (see p874).

This list is not exhaustive and other payments derived from employment may also count as earnings.[9]

Note: it is the pay actually received which should be taken into account rather than what someone is legally entitled to,[10] so if you receive less than the national minimum wage, it is that lesser amount that counts as 'earnings'.

What does not count as earnings

The following are examples of payments that *do not* count as earnings:
- periodic payments made as part of a redundancy scheme;[11]
- except in respect of increases for dependants, occupational pension payments;[12]
- payments towards expenses that are 'wholly, exclusively and necessarily' incurred in the performance of employment, such as travelling expenses during the course of work.[13]

See p877 for other examples.

Part 6: General rules for other benefits
Chapter 42: Earnings
1. Earnings and non-means-tested benefits

Payments when you stop work

If you stop work before you claim, final earnings generally do not affect your benefit. Similarly, if you claim an increase in your non-means-tested benefit for an adult or child after the adult or your partner stops work, her/his final earnings generally do not affect your entitlement. As long as benefit entitlement begins after the employment ends, earnings disregarded are:[14]

- final wages, paid or due, including bonus, commission, tips and expenses that count as earnings;
- holiday pay;
- pay in lieu of notice;
- pay in lieu of remuneration – eg, loss of earnings payment to a councillor;
- statutory or contractual redundancy pay and other compensation payments (other than from an employment tribunal complaint).

Certain final payments *are* taken into account (unless they are paid on retirement to someone who is over pension age):[15]

- maternity pay, paternity pay (during ordinary paternity leave), adoption pay and sick pay;
- employment tribunal award or settlement of a complaint to a tribunal or court – ie, compensation for unfair dismissal and certain other types of compensation under the Employment Rights Act 1996 or under trade union legislation;
- a retainer.

If you are already entitled to CA or an increase in your non-means-tested benefit for a child or an adult when a job ends, final earnings at the end of that employment are not disregarded.

Calculating net earnings from employment

'Earnings' are net earnings. **'Net' earnings** are 'gross' earnings less any deductions made for income tax, Class 1 national insurance (NI) contributions (but not Class 3 voluntary contributions[16]) and half of any contribution made towards a personal or occupational pension scheme.[17] It is the amount of weekly earnings that is important. So, for example, monthly earnings are multiplied by 12 and divided by 52 to arrive at a weekly figure.[18] If payment is for a period of less than a week, it is treated as a payment for a week.[19]

If earnings fluctuate and have changed more than once, or the employment is such that an employee does not work every week, weekly earnings may be averaged as follows:[20]

- If there is a regular pattern of work, weekly earnings are averaged over one complete 'cycle' of work. This includes periods when no work is done if this forms part of the regular pattern of work – eg, if you regularly work three weeks on and one week off, earnings are averaged over four weeks.

- In any other case, earnings are averaged over five weeks, or whatever other period will enable the average weekly earnings to be assessed more accurately.[21]

The date from which earnings from employment are counted

Earnings are usually treated as having been received on the first day of the benefit week in which they are due to be paid (or the following week for an increase in CA for an adult, or in retirement pension if s/he does not live with you).[22]

Benefit week

The 'benefit week' is the seven days corresponding to the week for which the particular benefit you are claiming is paid.[23]

The date that a payment is due may well be different from the date of actual payment. Earnings are due on your normal payday. If the contract of employment does not say when the payment is due and there is no evidence to suggest differently, the date the payment was received should be taken as the date it was due.[24]

If a contract of employment is terminated without proper notice, outstanding wages, wages in hand, holiday pay and any pay in lieu of notice are due on the last day of employment and are treated as paid on that day, even if this does not happen.[25] See p874 for when these final payments are disregarded. If an employment tribunal awards compensation for loss of earnings (eg, for being dismissed in circumstances constituting sex discrimination, or an equal pay settlement), there is disagreement about whether the relevant date is the date when the earnings were due to be paid, or when the compensation was awarded.[26]

The period covered by earnings from employment

Earnings count for a future period starting from the date worked out above. The length of that period is worked out as follows.[27]

- If a payment of income is made for a particular period, it is taken into account for the number of benefit weeks corresponding to that period. For example, a week's part-time earnings are taken into account for a week. For monthly payments, earnings are taken into account for the number of weeks between the date they are treated as paid and the date the next monthly earnings are treated as paid. If a payment is for a particular period but is a one-off (eg, holiday pay on leaving a job if the final payments count – see p874), it is taken into account for the number of weeks from the date it is due to the date the next normal monthly earnings would be treated as paid.[28]
- If the payment does not relate to a particular period, it is divided by the amount of the weekly earnings limit plus one penny, and then rounded down to the nearest whole number. If part of the payment should be disregarded (see p877), the weekly earnings limit is increased (for the purpose of this calculation only)

Part 6: General rules for other benefits
Chapter 42: Earnings
1. Earnings and non-means-tested benefits

by the amount of the appropriate disregard. The result of this calculation is the number of full weeks for which you will not get benefit (see the example below).

- If two payments of different types of earnings are made (eg, wages and holiday pay) and the periods worked out as above overlap, they are taken into account consecutively.[29]

Example

Bob receives a Category A retirement pension with an increase for his wife, who lives with him. She receives £700 net earnings for work which cannot be attributed to any particular period of time. The £700 figure includes a tax refund of £150 paid through the PAYE system.

The earnings limit for the increase is £72.40.

The £150 tax refund is disregarded.

The period over which the income is taken into account is:

£700 ÷ (£72.40 + £0.01 + £150)

= £700 ÷ 222.41 = 3.15 weeks

This means that Bob is not entitled to an increase for his wife for three weeks.

Earnings from self-employment

Weekly earnings from self-employment (including any allowance from a DWP scheme to assist with the business[30]) are averaged over a period of a year unless:[31]

- you (or for an increase in your non-means-tested benefit for an adult or child, the adult or your partner) have recently become self-employed; *or*
- there has been a change which is likely to affect the normal pattern of the business.

In either case, earnings are averaged over whatever other period the decision maker considers will give the most accurate figure. This means that when you first claim, you should provide an up-to-date set of accounts.

For royalties or similar payments (eg, from copyrights), the period for which these payments count is calculated in a similar way to that for payments made for unspecified periods to employees.[32]

For the way earnings of childminders, members of a partnership or share fishermen are calculated, see below. Otherwise, it is the net profit from self-employment that is used. '**Net profit**' is calculated by taking the earnings from self-employment over the period and deducting:[33]

- expenses incurred during the period wholly and exclusively for the purposes of the business. If a car or telephone, for example, is used partly for business and partly for private purposes, the costs of it can be apportioned and the amount attributable to business use can be deducted.[34] Certain expenses cannot be deducted, including business entertainment, repayment of capital on a business loan, capital expenditure and depreciation, or providing board and lodging or renting a room in your home;

- income tax and NI contributions;[35] *and*
- half of any contributions made during the period towards a personal pension scheme or retirement annuity contract.

Childminders are always treated as self-employed and net profit is deemed to be one-third of the earnings from childminding less income tax, NI contributions and half of certain pension contributions.[36] The rest of the earnings are completely ignored.

For members of a partnership or share fishermen, it is the relevant share of the 'net profit' that is used, and expenses incurred wholly and exclusively for the purposes of the business are deducted before calculating the share of the profits. After that, income tax, NI contributions and half of any premiums paid in respect of a personal pension or under a retirement annuity contract are deducted from the share.[37]

Notional earnings

You (or for an increase in your non-means-tested benefit for a child or adult, your partner or the adult) are treated as having 'notional earnings' if it is not possible to work out actual earnings from employment or self-employment when your claim is decided.[38] This may apply if, for example, the job is new and pay depends on performance, or it is a new business and there is no way of calculating what the profits of that business will be. If so, the 'notional earnings' are an amount that is considered reasonable, taking into account the number of hours worked and the earnings paid for comparable work in the area.

Estimates of the appropriate deductions for income tax and NI contributions and half of any occupational or personal pension contributions are deducted from notional earnings, as are any earnings disregards or, where relevant, allowances for childcare or care costs.

2. Disregarded earnings

Some income, which might otherwise be classed as earnings, is specifically disregarded and does not affect your benefit. Some care and childcare costs can also be disregarded. The same earnings disregards apply whether the earnings are from employment or self-employment.

When calculating earnings, the following amounts can be disregarded. (**Note:** if it is for an increase to your non-means-tested benefit for a child or adult, it is

Part 6: General rules for other benefits
Chapter 42: Earnings
3. Deductions from earnings

your partner's or that adult's earnings which are relevant and the disregards below refer to payments made and income received by her/him):[39]

- any payment made to you by someone who normally lives with you on an informal or non-contractual basis as part of her/his contribution towards shared living expenses;
- the first £20 a week of any income for renting out room(s) in your home;
- the first £20 of any income you receive each week for providing board and lodging in your home. If you get more than £20 a week, 50 per cent of the excess is also disregarded. This disregard applies to each person who lodges with you – eg, if you are providing bed and breakfast accommodation and in one week five different people each stay for one night and pay £20 each, the full £100 is disregarded;
- payments from a local authority or voluntary organisation for fostering or accommodating a child under formal arrangements;
- payments from a health authority, clinical commissioning group, local authority or voluntary organisation for providing temporary care. There is no set time after which care is no longer temporary;[40]
- income tax refunds;
- if you are an employee, any loan or advance of earnings from your employer;
- certain bounty payments made to part-time firefighters, auxiliary coastguards, members of the territorial or reserve armed forces and part-time lifeboat crews;
- unless you are abroad yourself, earnings payable abroad which cannot be brought into Great Britain – eg, because of exchange control regulations;
- unless you are abroad yourself, any bank charges for converting earnings paid in another currency into sterling.

3. **Deductions from earnings**

In some circumstances:
- the cost of childcare or the cost of looking after the person you care for, up to a maximum amount, can be deducted from your earnings when assessing your entitlement to carer's allowance (CA) (see below);
- the cost of childcare up to a maximum amount (see p879) can be deducted when assessing the earnings of the adult or your partner for an increase in your non-means-tested benefit for an adult or child (including an increase in your CA).

Care costs and carer's allowance

If you are getting CA and, because of your work, have to pay for someone (other than a 'close relative') to look after the severely disabled person you care for or to look after a child under 16 for whom you or your partner are getting child benefit, those care costs can be deducted when your earnings are calculated (in addition to any disregarded earnings).[41] The maximum deduction is 50 per cent of the figure which would otherwise be your net earnings. Any disregarded income is deducted from your net earnings before calculating the 50 per cent figure.

'**Close relative**' means a parent, son, daughter, brother, sister or partner (see p205) of you or the severely disabled person for whom you care. There is, therefore, no restriction on charges paid to someone who is only a close relative of the child being looked after – eg, the parent of the child if you are not married and s/he is not also your partner.

Childcare costs

In respect of an increase in your non-means-tested benefit for an adult or child, up to £60 a week of childcare costs may be deducted from the earnings of the adult or your partner, if s/he is:[42]

- a lone parent; *or*
- a member of a couple if both members of the couple are working (full or part time); *or*
- a member of a couple if the other member of the couple is incapacitated (see below).

To qualify for the deduction, s/he must be paying childcare costs for a child in the family who is under the age of 11. Childcare costs paid by the adult to her/his partner, or by the adult's partner to her/him, do not count. Nor do costs in respect of compulsory education. The childcare must be provided:[43]

- by a registered childminder or other registered childcare provider (such as a nursery or after-school club for the under-eights); *or*
- for children aged eight or over but under 11, by a school on school premises or by a local authority – eg, an out-of-hours or holiday play scheme; *or*
- by a childcare scheme operating on Crown property; *or*
- in schools or establishments exempt from registration.

Incapacitated

Someone counts as '**incapacitated**' if:[44]

– s/he is getting long-term incapacity benefit, severe disablement allowance, attendance allowance, disability living allowance (or an equivalent award under the war pensions or industrial injuries schemes), personal independence payment, armed forces independence payment, or would do were s/he not a hospital inpatient; *or*

– s/he is provided with an invalid carriage or other vehicle by the NHS; *or*

– s/he or her/his partner is getting housing benefit (HB) and either childcare costs have been allowed for under the rules on HB (see p270) or a disability premium for the partner has been awarded.

Note: these rules have not been amended to allow someone to count as 'incapacitated' if s/he receives employment and support allowance.

To calculate childcare costs:[45]
- monthly charges over the previous year are added up and divided by 52;
- weekly (or other non-monthly) charges are averaged over the last four weeks if the child is not yet school age, otherwise a formula is used to average costs over term time and holidays;
- if you have just started to use childcare, the DWP uses an estimate from the childcare provider or from you.

Notes

1. Earnings and non-means-tested benefits
1 s89 SSCBA 1992; Sch 2 para 9 SSB(Dep) Regs
2 CP/7/1987
3 R(U) 5/85
4 Reg 10(4)(a) SSB(CE) Regs; R(U) 4/83; para 15286 DMG
5 Reg 9A SSB(Dep) Regs; para 15290 DMG
6 Reg 9 SSB(CE) Regs
7 Minter v Kingston Upon Hull CC and Potter v SSWP [2011] EWCA Civ 1155
8 CIS/743/1992
9 R(IS) 9/95; CIS/743/1992
10 R(IB) 7/03
11 Reg 9(1)(b) SSB(CE) Regs
12 Reg 2(1) SSB(CE) Regs
13 Reg 9(3) SSB(CE) Regs; Parsons v Hogg [1985] 2 All ER 897 (CA), appendix to R(FIS) 4/85
14 Sch 1 para 12 SSB(CE) Regs
15 Sch 1 para 12(2) SSB(CE) Regs
16 CIS/521/1990
17 Reg 10(4) SSB(CE) Regs
18 Regs 6(1) and 8(1)(b)(i) SSB(CE) Regs
19 Reg 8(1)(a) SSB(CE) Regs
20 Reg 8(3) SSB(CE) Regs
21 CG/4941/2003
22 Reg 7(b) SSB(CE) Regs
23 Reg 2(1) SSB(CE) Regs
24 R(SB) 33/83
25 R(SB) 22/84; R(SB) 11/85
26 CIS/590/1993; SSWP v JP (JSA) [2010] UKUT 90 (AAC)
27 Reg 6(2) SSB(CE) Regs
28 Cotton v SSWP [2009] EWCA Civ 1333; [2010] AACR 17
29 Reg 6(3) SSB(CE) Regs; Cotton v SSWP [2009] EWCA Civ 1333; [2010] AACR 17
30 Reg 12(1) SSB(CE) Regs
31 Reg 11(1) SSB(CE) Regs
32 Reg 11(2) SSB(CE) Regs
33 Reg 13(1)(a) and (b), (4) and (5) SSB(CE) Regs
34 R(IS) 13/91; R(FC) 1/91; CTC/26/1989
35 See also reg 14 SSB(CE) Regs
36 Reg 13(10) SSB(CE) Regs
37 Reg 13(5) SSB(CE) Regs
38 Reg 4(1) and (3) SSB(CE) Regs and R(IB) 7/03, disapplying reg 4(2) of these Regs

2. Disregarded earnings
39 Sch 1 SSB(CE) Regs
40 CG/1752/2006

3. Deductions from earnings
41 Regs 10(3) and 13(3) and Sch 3 SSB(CE) Regs
42 Regs 10(2) and 13(2) and Sch 2 SSB(CE) Regs
43 Sch 2 para 2 SSB(CE) Regs
44 Sch 2 para 8 SSB(CE) Regs
45 Sch 2 paras 4-7 SSB(CE) Regs

Part 7

Special benefit rules

Chapter 43

Benefits for 16/17-year-olds

This chapter covers:
1. Benefits you can claim (below)
2. 16/17-year-olds previously looked after by a local authority (p886)
3. Claiming income support (p888)
4. Claiming jobseeker's allowance (p888)
5. Claiming universal credit (p896)
6. Sanctions (p897)

Key facts

- Being 16 or 17 does not, in itself, prevent you from qualifying for most of the benefits and tax credits in this *Handbook*. However, there are issues you must consider.
- In many cases, you cannot get means-tested benefits if you are studying full time at school or college. Other benefits may also be affected.
- If you cannot qualify for benefits or tax credits in your own right, someone else may be able to include you in her/his claim.
- You might not qualify for income support, income-based jobseeker's allowance (JSA), housing benefit or universal credit (UC) if you were previously looked after by a local authority.
- You must satisfy special rules to qualify for income-based JSA or UC. There are also special rules about sanctions.

1. Benefits you can claim

If you are 16 or 17, you can qualify for any of the benefits for people of working age or the tax credits in this *Handbook*, other than bereavement allowance and statutory adoption pay. However:

- you can only qualify for jobseeker's allowance (JSA) in specified circumstances (see pp888–93). If you cannot qualify under the ordinary rules, you may qualify for income-based JSA on a discretionary basis if you would otherwise experience severe hardship ('severe hardship payments');
- you can only qualify for universal credit (UC) in specified circumstances (see p896);

Part 7: Special benefit rules
Chapter 43: Benefits for 16/17-year-olds
1. Benefits you can claim

- you might not be able to qualify for income support (IS), income-based JSA, housing benefit (HB) or UC (or, if you qualify for UC, the housing costs element for rent payments) if you were previously looked after by a local authority (see p886).

You may also qualify for health benefits (eg, free prescriptions, dental treatment and sight tests) in your own right. Otherwise, you may qualify for these if you are included in someone else's claim. See Chapter 30 for further information.

If you are pregnant, you can qualify for Healthy Start food and vitamins, even if you are not entitled to a qualifying benefit or tax credit (see p829). Check whether you and your baby can continue to qualify once the baby is born – eg, if a member of your family is entitled to a qualifying benefit or tax credit, even if you are not.

Note: if you do not qualify for benefits and tax credits in your own right, someone else may be able to include you in her/his claim (see below).

General issues

If you are 16 or 17, you should consider the following.
- If you qualify for JSA or UC, there are some special rules about sanctions (see p897).
- In many cases, you cannot get means-tested benefits if you are at school or college. Other benefits may also be affected. If you are studying or on training, see p885.
- The rate of some benefits (IS, JSA, employment and support allowance (ESA), UC and HB) you get can be lower than for older claimants. For UC, the rate of benefit is the rate for claimants under 25. See p224 for the other benefits.

Someone else claims benefit for you

If you cannot qualify for benefits and tax credits in your own right, someone else may be able to include you in her/his claim.
- S/he can qualify for child benefit and child tax credit (CTC) for you if you count as a 'qualifying young person' (eg, you are in, or are enrolled to undertake, full-time non-advanced education or approved training) and s/he is treated as 'responsible' for you (see p551, p151 and p211). If s/he comes under the UC system (see p19), s/he can qualify for UC in the same circumstances.
- Her/his HB can include an allowance and premiums for you if you count as a qualifying young person and s/he is responsible for you and you live in the same household (see p213). In some cases, allowances and premiums for you can continue to be included in IS and income-based JSA (see p220).
- S/he may be able to continue to receive an increase in a non-means-tested benefit for you.

- If you are pregnant, s/he can claim a Sure Start maternity grant for you if s/he has been awarded a qualifying benefit (see p770), even if s/he still has dependent children of her/his own.
- You may qualify for free school lunches if the person claiming for you receives a qualifying benefit or tax credit (see p832).

Studying and training

If you are studying full time, your entitlement to carer's allowance (CA), IS, JSA, ESA, UC and HB might be affected. See Chapter 44 for the special rules if you are studying full or part time.

To find out what help is available to finance your studies, contact your local authority or college. Also see CPAG's *Student Support and Benefits Handbook* and *Benefits for Students in Scotland Handbook*. **Note:** education maintenance allowance and payments from the 16 to 19 bursary fund are paid in addition to your benefits. However, student support (eg, grants and loans for study at university) can be taken into account as income when working out the amount of your means-tested benefits.

If you are receiving IS, income-based JSA, income-related ESA, CTC or UC, you may qualify for free school lunches (see p832).

If you are in full-time non-advanced education, and you do not have any parental support, you are likely to qualify for IS (see p908) and so do not have to satisfy any jobseeking conditions. If you come under the UC system (see p19), you do not have to meet any work-related requirements for UC and contributory ESA in similar circumstances.

You may fit into one of the groups of people who can claim IS if you are on a specified training course (see p29). In most cases, if you are getting a training allowance, you can get income-based JSA without having to satisfy the jobseeking conditions (see p1024).

Note:
- If you are in full-time non-advanced education or 'approved training', you may count as a qualifying young person for someone else's benefit or tax credits claim.
- If you qualify for a means-tested benefit while you are getting training, some payments you receive (eg, a training allowance) can be taken into account when working out the amount you get (see p283 and p334).
- If you receive a training allowance:
  – you might be treated as not having limited capability for work for ESA purposes (see p1004). If this happens, you cannot qualify for ESA;
  – in some cases, if you are also getting a non-means-tested benefit (eg, contribution-based JSA, contributory ESA or CA), this is reduced by the amount of the training allowance. See p1166 for information about the overlapping benefit rules.

Part 7: Special benefit rules
Chapter 43: Benefits for 16/17-year-olds
2. 16/17-year-olds previously looked after by a local authority

Paying for housing

If you are living in private rented accommodation, the amount of rent used to calculate your HB (or your UC housing costs element) might be restricted, based on the rent for one-bedroom shared accommodation, even if you are living in larger accommodation (see p398 and p412). **Note:** you might not be able to qualify for HB (or the housing costs element of UC for rent payments) if you were previously looked after by a local authority (see below).

If you are living with someone else who is claiming HB or help with her/his housing costs as an owner-occupier paid with IS, income-based JSA, income-related ESA or pension credit (PC) (or the UC housing costs element for rent payments), no non-dependant deduction can be made for you (see p118, p497 and p451). The rule is not needed for the UC housing costs element for owner-occupier payments as no non-dependant deductions are made.

2. 16/17-year-olds previously looked after by a local authority

You cannot qualify for income support (IS), income-based jobseeker's allowance (JSA) or housing benefit (HB) if you are aged 16 or 17 and were previously looked after by a local authority.[1] There are exceptions to the rules (see p887). If these rules apply to you:

- your local authority must assess and meet your needs for maintenance, accommodation and support; *and*
- you cannot be treated as a member of the family of a person claiming IS, income-based JSA, income-related employment and support allowance (ESA) or HB, so, for example, s/he cannot get allowances and premiums for you with her/his HB.[2]

Being looked after

Being '**looked after**' means, for example, that you were subject to a care, supervision or permanence order or, in England and Wales, provided with accommodation by the local authority under specified functions.

Note:
- If you were previously looked after by a local authority you *can* qualify for ESA and, in most cases, for universal credit (UC – see p896).[3] However, no housing costs element for rent payments can be included in the calculation of your UC.[4]
- In England and Wales, you are not excluded from IS, income-based JSA or HB if you have been in a family placement (eg, living with your parent, someone

with parental responsibility for you or someone who had a residence order for you before you were looked after) for at least six months (unless the placement has broken down).[5]

- If you are being looked after by a local authority, you cannot be included in another person's claim for IS, income-based JSA or income-related ESA if you are not living with her/him. For UC purposes, you generally cannot be treated as the responsibility of a person, so, for example, s/he cannot get elements for you in her/his UC.[6]

- Local DWP and social services offices should liaise to ensure any disputes about who is responsible for supporting you are quickly resolved. If you are refused both benefit and social services support, seek specialist advice.

When you count as previously looked after

For these purposes, you are treated as previously looked after by a local authority if you are 16 or 17 and:[7]

- you were looked after by a local authority (and, in Scotland, were provided with accommodation) for at least 13 weeks. The 13-week period must start after your 14th birthday and end after you turn 16 (in England or Wales) or school-leaving age (in Scotland). The local authority must be obliged to provide you with aftercare services;[8] or

- in England or Wales, you are not subject to a care order, but you were in hospital, or detained in a remand centre or a young offenders' or similar institution when you became 16 and, immediately before you were in hospital or detained, you were looked after by a local authority (in Wales, accommodated) for at least 13 weeks since your 14th birthday.[9]

The 13 weeks do not have to be continuous. Some pre-planned short-term placements, after which you return to the care of your parent, or person acting as your parent, do not count towards the 13 weeks.[10]

Exceptions

Even if you were previously looked after by a local authority, you *can* qualify for IS or income-based JSA (but not HB) if you are in one of the following groups of people who can claim IS (see p26) – ie, you are:[11]

- a lone parent of a child under five;
- a lone foster parent;
- getting statutory sick pay, incapable of work but treated as capable or appealing against an incapacity for work decision;
- a lone parent in 'relevant education'.

In Scotland, you are not excluded if you are living with your family or another person who has parental responsibility for you (unless you are receiving regular

Part 7: Special benefit rules
Chapter 43: Benefits for 16/17-year-olds
4. Claiming jobseeker's allowance

financial assistance from the local authority under s29(1) of the Children (Scotland) Act 1995.[12]

---

3. Claiming income support

If you are 16 or 17 you are entitled to income support (IS) in your own right if you satisfy the normal rules of entitlement described in Chapter 3.[13] You must be in one of the groups of people who can claim IS.[14] You should not have your claim refused or be turned away by the DWP simply because of your age.

However, you should remember the following.

- If you have been looked after by a local authority, you usually cannot claim IS. Instead, your local authority should support and accommodate you. See p887 for exceptions to the rules.
- In many cases, you cannot get IS if you are at school or college. See p903 to find out if you *can* qualify.
- In certain circumstances, you may satisfy the rules for IS *and* income-based jobseeker's allowance (JSA). It is usually better to claim IS because you do not have to be available for and actively seeking work and training and therefore risk benefit sanctions (see Chapter 48). You can still look for work. If you claim IS rather than JSA, however, you might not receive national insurance credits (see Chapter 41).

---

4. Claiming jobseeker's allowance

If you are aged 16 or 17 you can qualify for:

- **contribution-based jobseeker's allowance (JSA)** if you satisfy the contribution conditions;
- **income-based JSA** if you satisfy the basic rules of entitlement and you are entitled to it under the rules described below;
- **joint-claim JSA** if you satisfy the basic rules of entitlement, one of you is 18 or over and the other would qualify for income-based JSA under the rules described below.[15] Usually, you both have to satisfy all the conditions for entitlement to JSA, but see p47 for the exceptions. If both of you are under 18, you do not count as a joint-claim couple and so one of you may be able to claim income-based JSA for the other.

Note: if you are claiming any type of JSA, you may be able to get hardship payments if you are sanctioned or there is a doubt about your meeting the jobseeking conditions (see Chapter 55).

When you cannot qualify

You cannot qualify for income-based JSA if you:[16]
- come under the universal credit (UC) system (see p19); *or*
- are included in the claim of someone who is claiming income support (IS) or income-based JSA. But note that you cannot be included in someone's claim for income-based JSA if you are (or would be) entitled to JSA;[17] *or*
- qualify for contribution-based JSA; *or*
- were previously looked after by a local authority in the circumstances described on pp886–87. There are exceptions to those rules.

Remember that, in most cases, you cannot qualify for JSA if you are in 'relevant education' (see p903). Note that you continue to count as in relevant education for a period after it ends (during the child benefit 'extension period') if someone is claiming child benefit for you during that period. If no one is claiming child benefit for you during that period, you can claim JSA if you satisfy the rules on pp890–91.

When you can qualify

You can qualify for income-based JSA while you are 16 or 17 if you are a person who can claim:
- at any time before age 18 (see below); *or*
- during the child benefit extension period (see p890); *or*
- during other limited periods (see p891); *or*
- on a discretionary basis – ie, you are awarded severe hardship payments (see p892).

You must satisfy all the other rules of entitlement to income-based JSA. You must register for work and training, and must usually show that you are actively seeking both of these. There are special rules for calculating your JSA applicable amount if you are a member of a couple (see p224).

Qualifying at any time before age 18

You can qualify for income-based JSA at any time before you are 18 if you satisfy the normal conditions of entitlement and:[18]
- you come within one of the groups of people who can claim IS (see pp26–31). In this case, you can choose whether to claim JSA or IS. It is usually better to claim IS because you do not have to be available for and actively seeking work and training and therefore risk benefit sanctions (see Chapter 48). You can still look for work. If you claim IS rather than JSA, however, you might not receive national insurance credits (see Chapter 41); *or*
- you have limited capability for work (see Chapter 47). In this case, you may qualify for employment and support allowance (ESA) instead of JSA; *or*

Part 7: Special benefit rules
Chapter 43: Benefits for 16/17-year-olds
4. Claiming jobseeker's allowance

- you are one of a couple and at least one child under 16 can be included in your claim (see p210).

Qualifying during the child benefit extension period

You qualify for income-based JSA during a period of 20 weeks after leaving education or training (called the 'child benefit extension period' – see p552), if:[19]

- you are **married or in a civil partnership** and:
  - your partner is 18 or over; or
  - your partner is under 18, does not qualify for contribution-based JSA, and was not previously looked after by a local authority in the circumstances described on pp886–87 and s/he:
    - is registered for work and training; or
    - is treated as being responsible for a child under 16 who is a member of her/his household (see p210); or
    - is laid off or on short-time working and is available for work under the special rules described on p1047; or
    - is temporarily absent from Great Britain and is taking a child who is included in your claim (see p210) abroad for treatment (for the first eight weeks of the absence); or
    - is incapable of work and training because of a physical or mental condition and a doctor confirms s/he is likely to be for at least 12 months; or
    - fits into certain of the groups of people who can claim IS – ie, people with childcare responsibilities and carers (other than those on parental or paternity leave), or who are pregnant, pupils, students (other than in most cases disabled or deaf students) and people on training courses, refugees learning English, or certain people who are subject to immigration control.

  In many of these cases your partner can claim either JSA or IS (or, if s/he has limited capability for work, ESA), but this allows you to be the claimant instead; or
- you are an **orphan with no one acting as your parent** – eg, a foster carer or any other person with parental responsibility for you; or
- you are **living away from your parents and any person acting as your parent** and:
  - immediately before you were 16 you were in custody or being looked after by a local authority who placed you with someone other than a close relative; or
  - you are living elsewhere:
    - as part of a programme of resettlement or rehabilitation under the supervision of the probation service or a local authority; or
    - to avoid physical or sexual abuse; or

- because you need special accommodation because of mental or physical illness or disability; *or*
- your parents are unable to support you financially and they are in custody or unable to enter Great Britain (eg, because of UK immigration rules) or are 'chronically sick or mentally or physically disabled'; *or*
- this is because you are estranged from them (see p904 for the meaning), you are in physical or moral danger, or there is a serious risk to your physical or mental health.

Close relative

'**Close relative**' means parent, step-parent, parent-in-law, parent of a civil partner, son, stepson, son-in-law, son of a civil partner, daughter, stepdaughter, daughter-in-law, daughter of a civil partner, brother, sister or the partner of any of these.[20]

Qualifying during other limited periods

Even if you are not someone who qualifies for income-based JSA at any time before you are 18 (see p889), you may be able to claim it for a limited period.

- You can qualify after the end of the child benefit extension period (see p552) if:[21]
  - you are in one of the groups of people who can claim income-based JSA during that period and you are **discharged from custody or detention** after it ends (for up to eight weeks from the day of discharge); *or*
  - you have to live away from your parents and anyone acting as your parent **following a stay in accommodation provided by a local authority** in England or Wales under specified provisions (for up to eight weeks from the date of leaving the accommodation, whether before or after the end of the extension period). If you leave less than eight weeks before the end of the extension period, you first get income-based JSA under the rules on p890, and then your benefit can continue under this rule until the end of the eight-week period. Remember that some people cannot claim JSA when they stop being looked after by a local authority (see p886).
- You can qualify during any period that you are **laid off or are on short-time working** and are available for work under the special rules described on p1048.[22]
- If you have **accepted an offer to enlist in the armed forces** within eight weeks of the offer being made and were not in employment or training when it was made, you can qualify for income-based JSA until you are due to enlist. However, this does not apply if you have ever been sanctioned in certain specified situations – eg, because you failed to accept a place on a a training scheme or employment programme, or lost a place (or a job) through misconduct.[23]

Part 7: Special benefit rules
Chapter 43: Benefits for 16/17-year-olds
4. Claiming jobseeker's allowance

Qualifying for severe hardship payments

If you do not qualify for income-based JSA under any of the rules for 16/17-year-olds above, or for IS, you can still be paid income-based JSA on a discretionary basis if severe hardship will result if you are not paid.[24] These are referred to as 'severe hardship payments' in this *Handbook*. You must have registered for training, but you must not be receiving any training.

Remember that:

- severe hardship payments are payments of JSA, so you are automatically eligible for other benefits – eg, housing benefit (see p61);
- there are special rules about sanctions that only apply to severe hardship payments (see p899).

You must have a **'severe hardship direction'** to get severe hardship payments. Authorised staff in the Jobcentre Plus office can consider whether to issue one, but must refer your case to the Under Eighteens Support Team (UEST) for a decision, if their decision is likely to be negative.[25] A decision should be made within 24 hours.

If you are one of a couple and you are only getting income-based JSA at one of the lower couple rates (see p224), you may be eligible for a higher couple rate if a severe hardship direction is made in respect of your partner.

All your circumstances should be considered. The factors that should be taken into account include:[26]

- your financial circumstances, including your income, capital and outgoings;
- whether the person with whom you live is on a means-tested benefit;
- whether you are homeless or at risk of eviction if severe hardship payments are not paid;
- whether you have any health problems, are pregnant or are vulnerable and at risk for any reason and whether you have access to food and accommodation.

How do you get a severe hardship direction?

1. Provide as much evidence as you can to show that you will experience severe hardship without JSA. Explain fully why your parents are not supporting you or why they should not be expected to continue to do so and, if relevant, why it could be damaging if they were to be contacted. The DWP should accept this. You should not be refused a severe hardship direction just because you are living at home.

2. If the DWP wants to contact a responsible third party, such as a relative, social worker, youth worker or recognised voluntary worker, to corroborate what you have said, it must ask your permission.[27] If you refuse this without good reason, your case is referred direct to the UEST. If you have written evidence from, or are accompanied by, a responsible third party, further enquiries of, or contact with, your parents may not be necessary.

3. If there is difficulty in obtaining evidence from your parents or a third party, the interviewing officer should consider a short-term severe hardship direction. You can then receive severe hardship payments while further enquiries are made.

Once a severe hardship direction is issued, the normal rules and procedures for claiming income-based JSA apply. Severe hardship payments are paid in arrears. If you need money urgently, you could apply for a short-term advance (see p1167).

A severe hardship direction normally lasts for eight weeks but it can be longer or shorter than this – eg, it may be shorter if you are starting work or training soon, or evidence to support your application is not easily available.[28]

When your severe hardship direction ends, you can apply for it to be renewed. However, if your severe hardship direction is revoked, you can no longer get severe hardship payments. A direction can (but does not have to) be revoked if:[29]

- your circumstances have changed and you would no longer experience severe hardship if you did not receive severe hardship payments; *or*
- the direction was given in ignorance of, or because of a mistake about, a material fact and but for this, it would not have been given. Any overpayment may be recoverable (see Chapter 56);[30] *or*
- you failed to follow up an opportunity of a place on a training scheme or rejected an offer of a place and cannot show a 'good reason' for having done so. 'Good reason' is not defined in the rules. If your severe hardship direction is revoked on this ground, you can apply for another one straight away but if one is made, your severe hardship payments are reduced for a two-week period. See p899 for further information about severe hardship payment sanctions.

Jobseeking conditions

If you are 16 or 17, in general you are subject to the same jobseeking conditions as people aged 18 or over. However, there are some important differences.

Note: for contribution-based JSA, if you come under the UC system (see p19), you are subject to the same work-related requirements as people aged 18 or over (see p1066).

Availability for work

Usually you can restrict your availability to jobs where the employer provides 'suitable training'.[31] You do not have to show that you have a reasonable prospect of securing employment (see p1034) despite this restriction.

You *cannot* restrict your availability to jobs offering suitable training if:

- you have been sanctioned in specified circumstances either under the normal JSA rules or under the special rules for severe hardship payments; *or*
- you are claiming JSA under the special rules for people laid off or on short-time working (see p1047); *or*
- you are claiming under the special rules for people waiting to enlist in the armed forces (see p891).

Part 7: Special benefit rules
Chapter 43: Benefits for 16/17-year-olds
4. Claiming jobseeker's allowance

Suitable training

Deciding whether training is '**suitable training**' involves considering factors such as your personal abilities and skills, your preference and the preference of your training provider, the level of qualification you are aiming for, the length of the training, how easily you can travel to the training and how soon the training will begin.[32]

If you have only worked for a short time but you received training for that type of work or obtained relevant qualifications, you could argue that you have a usual occupation and so should be given a 'permitted period' (see p1035).

Actively seeking work and training

If you are 16 or 17:[33]
- you are required to actively seek both work *and* training;
- you are expected to take more than one step during a week (at least one to find work and one to find training) unless taking one step is all that it is reasonable for you to do;
- in addition to the normal list of activities that count as a step (see p1039), the activities of seeking training and seeking full-time education also count.

For this purpose, training means 'suitable training' (see above).

These exceptions do not apply if you are claiming under the special rules for people laid off or on short-time working or for people waiting to enlist in the armed forces (see p1047 and p891). The first two exceptions do not apply if you have been sanctioned under specified provisions either under the normal JSA rules or under the special rules for severe hardship payments.

Jobseeker's agreement

If you are 16 or 17, in general, your jobseeker's agreement is the same as those for people aged 18 or over, although it places an emphasis on training. However, it must explain the rules about sanctions for claimants under 18 (including when JSA is payable at a reduced rate), unless you are claiming JSA because you are laid off or are on short-time working (see p1047) or you have accepted an offer to enlist in the armed forces.[34] **Note:** the DWP calls your jobseeker's agreement a 'claimant commitment'. However, all the rules about jobseeker's agreements still apply (see p1043).

Claiming jobseeker's allowance if you are 16 or 17

If you are claiming JSA, the normal rules about claims and payments apply. However, to claim JSA, including severe hardship payments, you must first register for both work and training at the place specified by the DWP. This may be at the Jobcentre Plus office itself, or where the local authority provides careers advice (see below).[35] Ask the Jobcentre Plus office where to register if you are in any doubt. **Note:**

- You do not have to register if you are claiming under the special rules for people laid off or on short-time working (see p1047) or if you have accepted an offer to enlist in the armed forces (see p891).[36]
- You must register at the Jobcentre Plus office if you are unable to register at the specified place because there is an emergency affecting it, such as a strike or a fire, or you would experience hardship because of the extra time it would take to register there.[37]

Local authority careers advice

The DWP refers to the places that provide careers advice to young people as 'local authority youth services'. Your local authority may call its service Connexions or the Careers Service in England, Careers Wales in Wales and Skills Development Scotland or Careers Scotland in Scotland.

If you are claiming severe hardship payments, remember to state this when you claim JSA. Always insist on your right to make a claim under the severe hardship rules and refuse to be turned away. You must have a severe hardship direction (see p892).

Challenging a jobseeker's allowance decision

You can challenge a decision about whether you satisfy the rules for entitlement to JSA in the usual way. See Chapters 58 and 59 for further information.

For severe hardship payments only, you *cannot* appeal against the decision about whether:[38]

- you would experience severe hardship;
- to issue or revoke a severe hardship direction or how long it should last;
- a certificate of 'good reason' should be issued (see p898).

However, you can ask for a revision or seek a supersession of a decision against which you do not have a right of appeal (see p1279 and p1285). You do not have to show specific grounds in this situation. Any reasons you give for disagreeing with the decision should be considered. You can also ask for a review of a decision not to issue a severe hardship direction.[39]

In addition, you can complain to your MP. You might be able to apply for a judicial review (see p1351). If, for example, you obtain more evidence of your hardship, you could also make a new claim.

Part 7: Special benefit rules
Chapter 43: Benefits for 16/17-year-olds
5. Claiming universal credit

5. **Claiming universal credit**

Normally, you must be at least 18 years old to qualify for universal credit (UC). However, if you are aged 16 or 17 and you come under the UC system (see p19), you can qualify for UC if you satisfy the other basic rules of entitlement and you fit into one of the groups of 16/17-year-olds who can claim (see below).[40] **Note:**

- You may be able to get hardship payments if you are sanctioned (see Chapter 55).
- You must meet the same work-related requirements as people aged 18 or over (see Chapter 50), but there are exceptions – eg, if you are in non-advanced education and have no parental support.
- If you are given a high, medium or low level sanction, shorter sanction periods apply and for any level of sanction, the amount by which your benefit is reduced is lower than for older claimants (see Chapter 52).
- The normal rules about claims and payments apply (see p191).
- You can challenge a decision about UC in the usual way (see Chapters 58 and 59).

16/17-year-olds who can qualify for universal credit

You can qualify for UC if you satisfy the other basic rules of entitlement and any of the following applies to you.[41]

- You have limited capability for work, or you have submitted a medical certificate saying you are not fit for work and you are waiting for an assessment of your capability for work.
- You have 'regular and substantial caring responsibilities for a severely disabled person' – ie, you qualify for carer's allowance (CA – see Chapter 25), or would do but for the fact that your earnings are too high.[42] This does not apply if you receive earnings from those caring responsiblities. You do not have to claim CA. **Note:** you cannot qualify under this rule if you were previously looked after by a local authority (see p887).
- You are responsible for a child aged under 16. See p212 for when you count as responsible.
- You are a member of a couple and your partner satisfies the basic rules of entitlement for UC and is responsible for a child (see p212 – this includes some qualifying young people).
- You are pregnant and there are 11 weeks or less before the week your baby is due. **Note:** you cannot qualify under this rule if you were previously looked after by a local authority (see p887).
- You had a baby (or your baby was still born) not more than 15 weeks ago. **Note:** you cannot qualify under this rule if you were previously looked after by a local authority (see p887).

- You are without 'parental support' (this includes support from someone acting in place of your parent – eg, a foster parent or a local authority). For these purposes, you are treated as without parental support if:[43]
  - you are an orphan – ie, you do not have any parents; *or*
  - you have to live away from your parents because you are estranged from them (see p904 for the meaning of 'estrangement') or there is a serious risk to your physical or mental health or you would experience significant harm if you lived with them; *or*
  - you are living away from your parents and they are unable to support you financially because they have a physical or mental impairment, or they are in custody, or they are prohibited from entering Great Britain – eg, because of the UK Immigration Rules.

  Note: you cannot qualify under this rule if you were previously looked after by a local authority (see p887).

Note:

- If you are a member of a couple and one of you is either 18 or over or satisfies the rules above, but the other does not, the one who is 18 or over or who satisfies the above rules can claim UC as a single person, but the other partner's income and capital are taken into account.[44]
- In many cases, you cannot get UC if you are at school or college. See p918 to find out if you *can* qualify.

6. Sanctions

While you are claiming benefit, there are a number of situations when you may be 'sanctioned', including if you fail to attend and participate in work-focused interviews, you fail to participate in training schemes or employment programmes, or you voluntarily leave a job or lose a job because of misconduct. If you are sanctioned, your benefit can be paid at a reduced rate for a period. In some cases, you cannot be sanctioned if you can show you have a good reason for acting as you did. See Chapters 51 and 52 for all the rules about sanctions and which benefits are affected.

If you are aged 16 or 17, you can generally be sanctioned in the same way as claimants aged 18 and over. However, if you are sanctioned and:

- you are receiving income-based jobseeker's allowance (JSA), including under the severe hardship rules, special rules apply for good reason (see p898), sanction periods are shorter (see p899) and the amount by which your benefit can be reduced is lower than for older claimants (see p900);
- you are receiving universal credit (UC), shorter sanction periods apply for high, medium and low level sanctions (see p1122, p1126 and p1127), and the

Part 7: Special benefit rules
Chapter 43: Benefits for 16/17-year-olds
6. Sanctions

amount by which your benefit can be reduced is lower than for older claimants (see p1117).

If you are 16 or 17, you may apply for hardship payments (see Chapter 55) in the same way as people aged 18 and over.

Jobseeker's allowance: good reason

Certain JSA sanctions do not apply if you can show a 'good reason' for acting or failing to act as you did. If you are receiving income-based JSA, when deciding whether you have a good reason, there are special rules for 16/17-year-olds that apply to some training schemes and employment programmes, and employment-related sanctions.

Training scheme and employment programme sanctions

If you give up a place on a training scheme or employment programme or do not apply for, do not accept, or 'neglect to avail' yourself of, a place on one, in addition to any other ground on which you can argue you have a good reason, you have this automatically if:[45]

- it is the first time that you have acted or failed to act in a way that could lead to this type of sanction (under the normal or severe hardship payment rules); *and*
- while claiming JSA, you have never failed to pursue a training opportunity without a good reason, or to complete a training course; *and*
- you were a 'new jobseeker':
  - when you first started the scheme or programme, if a sanction is being considered because you gave up a place; *or*
  - at the time of the act or omission, if the sanction is for another reason.

New jobseeker

You are a **'new jobseeker'** if, since you left full-time education, you have *never:*[46]
– worked for 16 hours or more a week or done a complete training course; *or*
– lost a place on a training scheme or employment programme because of misconduct, or (unless you had a good reason) failed to complete a training course or given up a place on a scheme or programme.

A different system of training-related sanctions applies if you are getting severe hardship payments (see p892).[47] In practice, this system adopts the same approach as above – ie, you are only sanctioned if it is the second time you have done something connected with a training scheme or employment programme that deserves a sanction, unless you lost a place on a course because of misconduct or you were not a new jobseeker at the relevant time.

Under the severe hardship sanction rules, if you fail to attend or give up a place on a training scheme, but you had a good reason for this, explain the circumstances fully to the DWP. If it is satisfied that you had a good reason, it must issue a '**certificate of good reason**' and give you a copy as proof.[48]

Employment-related sanctions

If you have 'neglected to avail' yourself of a reasonable opportunity of a job (see p1089), or refused or failed to apply for a notified job vacancy (see p1088), in addition to any other ground on which you can argue you have a good reason, you have an automatic good reason if your employer did not offer you suitable training (see p894 for what counts).[49] This rule does not apply if your JSA has been reduced in the past for the same reason, or:

- your JSA has been reduced in the past because you were given a training or employment scheme sanction (under the normal or the severe hardship payments rules); *or*
- your JSA has been stopped in the past because you lost a job because of misconduct or left a job voluntarily without a good reason (see p1088); *or*
- you are claiming under the special rules for 16/17-year-olds who are on short-time working, have been laid off or have accepted a firm offer to join the armed forces (see p891).

Sanction periods and amount of jobseeker's allowance payable

If you are receiving income-based JSA, a fixed sanction period of two weeks applies if:[50]

- you lost a place on a training scheme or employment programme because of misconduct; *or*
- without a good reason, you:
  - refused or failed to carry out a jobseeker's direction; *or*
  - gave up a place on a training scheme or employment programme or failed to apply for or to accept, or neglected to avail yourself of, a place on one; *or*
  - refused or failed to apply for or to accept a job, or neglected to avail yourself of a job opportunity; *or*
  - you failed to participate in an interview as required (see p1093).

During the sanction period you continue to be paid JSA, but at a reduced rate (see p900). If you stop claiming JSA before the two weeks is over and then claim again, you are paid JSA at the reduced rate for the remainder of the two-week period. If you reach the age of 18 before the end of your two-week sanction, the sanction ends and you are paid the full rate of JSA for an 18-year-old.

If you are getting a training scheme sanction under the special system for severe hardship payments (see p898), your JSA is paid at a reduced rate for two

Part 7: Special benefit rules
Chapter 43: Benefits for 16/17-year-olds
Notes

weeks.[51] If your severe hardship direction is revoked, you can apply for severe hardship payments again immediately, but they are paid at a reduced rate for two weeks.

Note: if you are being sanctioned for any other reason, the ordinary sanction periods and amounts of JSA apply. You might qualify for hardship payments (see Chapter 55).

Reduced rates of jobseeker's allowance

If you are given a sanction under the rules described above, your JSA is reduced by 40 per cent of the single person's (or lone parent's) personal allowance, even if you are a member of a couple, or by 20 per cent if you are pregnant or seriously ill.[52] Your JSA is also only reduced by 20 per cent if you are sanctioned under the normal rules (not the severe hardship rules) and your partner (or a child in your claim) is pregnant or seriously ill. 'Seriously ill' is not defined.

7 Notes

2. 16/17-year-olds previously looked after by a local authority

1 **IS** Reg 4ZA(3A) IS Regs
   JSA Reg 57, definition of 'young person', JSA Regs
   IS/JSA/HB ss6 and 8(6) C(LC)A 2000; C(LC)SSB(S) Regs
   UC Reg 8(4) UC Regs
2 **IS** Reg 14(2)(c) IS Regs
   JSA Reg 76(2)(d) JSA Regs
   ESA Reg 2(1), definition of 'young person', ESA Regs
   HB Reg 19(2)(c) HB Regs; reg 19(2)(c) HB(SPC) Regs
3 The C(LC)A 2000 was not amended to exclude previously looked-after young people from entitlement to ESA or UC.
4 Sch 4 para 4 UC Regs
5 Reg 3(5) and (6) CL(E) Regs; reg 4(4)-(6) C(LC)(W) Regs
6 Reg 4(6)(a) UC Regs
7 **IS** Reg 4ZA(3A) IS Regs
   JSA Reg 57, definition of 'young person', JSA Regs
   IS/JSA/HB ss6 and 8(6) C(LC)A 2000; C(LC)SSB(S) Regs
   UC Reg 8(4) UC Regs

8 s6 C(LC)A 2000; reg 3 CL(E) Regs; reg 40(1) CPP&CR(E) Regs; regs 3 and 4 C(LC)(W) Regs; C(LC)SSB(S) Regs
9 Reg 3 CL(E) Regs; reg 4(1) and (2) C(LC)(W) Regs
10 ss6 and 8(6) C(LC)A 2000; regs 40(2) and 48 CPP&CR(E) Regs; reg 3(3) CL(E) Regs; regs 3(2) and 4(2A) C(LC)(W) Regs; reg 2(4)(a) C(LC)SSB(S) Regs
11 Reg 2 C(LC)SSB Regs; reg 2(3) C(LC)SSB(S) Regs. Note that the C(LC)SSB Regs have been amended to include entitlement to income-related ESA, but this is not needed because the C(LC)A 2000 was not amended.
12 Reg 2(2) C(LC)SSB(S) Regs

3. Claiming income support
13 s124(1)(a) SSCBA 1992
14 s124(1)(e) SSCBA 1992; Sch 1B IS Regs

4. Claiming jobseeker's allowance
15 s3A(1)(d) and (e) JSA 1995
16 ss3(1)(c) and (d) and 3A(1)(b) and (c) JSA 1995; reg 57(1), definition of 'young person', JSA Regs

17 Reg 76(2)(b) JSA Regs
18 ss3(1)(f)(iii) and 3A(1)(e)(ii) JSA 1995;
   reg 61(1)(b), (c) and (g) and (2)(b) JSA
   Regs
19 ss3(1)(f)(iii) and 3A(1)(e)(ii) JSA
   1995; regs 57 and 59 JSA Regs
20 Reg 1(3) JSA Regs
21 ss3(1)(f)(iii) and 3A(1)(e)(ii) JSA 1995;
   reg 60 JSA Regs
22 Reg 61(1)(a) and (2)(a) JSA Regs
23 Reg 61(1)(f) and (2)(e) JSA Regs
24 ss3(1)(f)(ii), 3A(1)(e)(i) and 16 JSA 1995
25 DWP guidance, *Making a Severe
   Hardship Decision*, para 121
   (www.gov.uk/government/
   publications/jsa-for-16-to-17-year-olds-
   guidance-for-dwp-staff-making-a-
   severe-hardship-decision)
26 DWP guidance, *Making a Severe
   Hardship Decision*, paras 42-68, 106-120
   and 209-12 (www.gov.uk/government/
   publications/jsa-for-16-to-17-year-olds-
   guidance-for-dwp-staff-making-a-
   severe-hardship-decision)
27 DWP guidance, *Making a Severe
   Hardship Decision*, paras 5-41
   (www.gov.uk/government/
   publications/jsa-for-16-to-17-year-olds-
   guidance-for-dwp-staff-making-a-
   severe-hardship-decision)
28 s16(2) and (4) JSA 1995; DWP guidance,
   Making a Severe Hardship Decision, para
   137 (www.gov.uk/government/
   publications/jsa-for-16-to-17-year-olds-
   guidance-for-dwp-staff-making-a-
   severe-hardship-decision)
29 s16(3) JSA 1995
30 s71A SSAA 1992
31 Reg 64(2) and (3) JSA Regs
32 Reg 57(1) JSA Regs
33 Regs 65 and 65A JSA Regs
34 Reg 66 JSA Regs
35 Reg 62 JSA Regs
36 Reg 62(1) JSA Regs
37 Reg 62(2) JSA Regs
38 Sch 2 para 1(a) SSA 1998
39 DWP guidance, *Making a Severe
   Hardship Decision*, paras 124-25
   (www.gov.uk/government/
   publications/jsa-for-16-to-17-year-olds-
   guidance-for-dwp-staff-making-a-
   severe-hardship-decision)

5. Claiming universal credit
40 s4(1)(a) and (3) WRA 2012
41 Reg 8(1) and (2) UC Regs
42 Reg 30 UC Regs

43 Reg 8(3) and (4) UC Regs
44 Reg 3(3) UC Regs

6. Sanctions
45 Reg 67(1) JSA Regs
46 Reg 67(3) JSA Regs
47 ss16(3)(b), 17(1), (1A) and (3) and
   20(2)(b) JSA 1995; reg 63 JSA Regs
48 s17(4) JSA 1995
49 Reg 67(2) JSA Regs
50 Reg 68 JSA Regs
51 ss16(3)(b), 17(3) and 20(2)(b) JSA
   1995; reg 63 JSA Regs
52 Regs 63(1) and (3) and 68(1) and (2) JSA
   Regs

Chapter 44

Benefits for students

This chapter covers:
1. Income support and jobseeker's allowance (p903)
2. Employment and support allowance (p912)
3. Housing benefit (p915)
4. Universal credit (p918)
5. Other benefits (p922)
6. Calculating income from grants and loans (p923)
7. Giving up, changing or taking time out from your course (p933)

England, Scotland and Wales have separate education systems. The same terms (eg, further, higher and advanced education) are often used within the education systems of all three countries, but they can have different technical meanings. Terms are used in the benefit rules to define different levels of education (eg, relevant, non-advanced and advanced) for benefit purposes. However, these terms are not generally used by educational institutions.

Only the benefits covered in this chapter are potentially affected if you are studying.

Key facts
- If you are a part-time student, your benefits are not usually affected by your studying, although there are extra conditions to meet for jobseeker's allowance.
- Most full-time students are excluded from claiming means-tested benefits. There are some exceptions, including for parents, disabled students and some young people on further education courses.
- Even if you can claim means-tested benefits, most student funding counts as income and reduces or stops your benefit.
- If you are a full-time student and are taking time off your course but have not abandoned it completely, you still count as a student and cannot usually claim benefits.
- Child tax credit, working tax credit and certain benefits, including maternity allowance, statutory sick pay, child benefit, disability living allowance and personal independence payment, have no special rules for full-time students, so you can claim these in the same way as anyone else.

1. Income support and jobseeker's allowance

If you are studying, you may count as being in 'relevant education' (see below), or as a 'full-time student' (see p905). You cannot usually qualify for income support (IS) or jobseeker's allowance (JSA) (either contribution-based or income-based). There are some exceptions, however, which are outlined in this section. You may also be able to qualify if you are studying part time (see p909).

Note: this section deals with the rules for income-based JSA, and for contribution-based JSA if claiming under the current system. The rules are different for contribution-based JSA if you come under the universal credit system (see p923).

Relevant education

If you are in relevant education, you can only qualify for IS in some circumstances and you cannot usually qualify for JSA (see pp903–04).[1]

You count as in **'relevant education'** if you are a 'qualifying young person' for child benefit purposes (see p551) – ie, you are under 20 and in full-time, non-advanced education or approved training on which you were accepted, enrolled or started when you were under 19.[2] For these purposes, 'full time' means more than 12 hours a week in term time, not including meal breaks and unsupervised study. 'Non-advanced' means anything below degree, HNC or HND level.

Note: you can continue to count as in relevant education for a period after your education or training ends – eg, if you have enrolled on another course or during what is known as the child benefit 'extension period' (see p551).

When you turn 20, you are no longer treated as being in relevant education even if you are still studying. However, you may then count as a 'full-time student' (see p905). You can qualify for IS or JSA if you are in one of the categories of full-time students who can claim (see pp908–09).

Entitlement to income support while in relevant education

You can qualify for IS while in relevant education if:[3]

- you are the parent of a child for whom you are treated as responsible and who is a member of your household (see p212); *or*
- you are a refugee who is learning English to obtain employment (see p30); *or*
- you are an orphan and have no one acting in place of your parents; *or*
- you have left local authority care and you have to live away from your parents and any person acting in their place (see p904). **Note:** if you are a care leaver aged 16 or 17 (see p886), you can only qualify for IS while you are in relevant education if you are a lone parent and treated as responsible for a child;[4] *or*
- you have to live away from your parents and any person acting in their place (see p904) because:

Part 7: Special benefit rules
Chapter 44: Benefits for students
1. Income support and jobseeker's allowance

- you are estranged from them; *or*
- you are in physical or moral danger; *or*
- there is a serious risk to your physical or mental health.

The physical or moral danger does not have to be caused by your parents. Therefore, a young person who is a refugee and cannot rejoin her/his parents can claim IS while at school;[5] *or*

• you live apart from your parents and any person acting in their place, they are unable to support you and:
- they are in prison; *or*
- they are unable to come to Britain because they do not have leave to enter under the UK Immigration Rules;[6] *or*
- they are chronically sick, or are mentally or physically disabled. This covers people who could get a disability premium or higher pensioner premium, get employment and support allowance (ESA) including a work-related or support component (or who would be entitled to contributory ESA including a work-related component but this has stopped being paid after 52 weeks), have an armed forces grant for car costs because of disability, or who are substantially and permanently disabled.

You may be able to claim IS under some of the above rules beyond age 20 if you are in one of the groups of full-time students who can claim (see p908).

Definitions
A '**person acting in place of your parents**' can include a local authority or voluntary organisation if you are being cared for by them, or foster carers, but only until you leave care.[7] It does not include a person who is your sponsor under the Immigration Rules.[8] In the last bullet point above, however, a person acting in place of your parents includes the person with whom you are placed, but does not expressly include the local authority.[9]
'**Estrangement**' implies emotional disharmony,[10] where you have no desire to have any prolonged contact with your parents or they feel similarly towards you. It is possible to be estranged even though your parents are providing some financial support or you still have some contact with them. If you are being cared for by a local authority, it is also possible to be estranged from the local authority. If you are, you could qualify for IS if you have to live away from accommodation provided by a local authority.[11]

Entitlement to jobseeker's allowance while in relevant education

You cannot qualify for JSA while in relevant education unless you are someone who can qualify for IS while in relevant education (see p903),[12] or you are treated as not being in relevant education. If you *can* qualify for IS while in relevant education (see p903), it may be better for you to claim IS.

So long as you do not count as a full-time student (see p905), you do not count as being in relevant education for JSA and may therefore qualify for benefit if you are on a non-advanced course, or one that does not count as a full-time course under the rules for full-time students, and:[13]

- you previously ceased relevant education and it is after your 'terminal date' for child benefit purposes (see p555); *and*
- you got JSA, incapacity benefit (IB), ESA or IS on the grounds that you were incapable of work, or were on a course of 'training':
  - for at least three months immediately before the date you started the course; *or*
  - for at least three out of the last six months immediately before you started the course and for any remaining part of the six months you were working full time or earning too much to qualify for benefit.

All of the three- or six-month period must fall after your terminal date. You do not count as being in relevant education either during your course or after you have left it.[14]

When someone else is entitled to benefits for you

If you cannot qualify for IS or JSA because you are in relevant education, someone else may be able to get child benefit, child tax credit (CTC) and working tax credit (WTC) if s/he is treated as 'responsible' for you. In some circumstances, you may count as both a person who can qualify for IS while in relevant education and as a person for whom someone else can qualify for child benefit and CTC. Seek advice on how you would be better off financially.

When you leave relevant education

Once you have left relevant education, you may be able to qualify for IS or JSA if you satisfy the rules for getting those benefits (see Chapters 3 and 4). Remember, you can continue to count as being in relevant education for a period after your education or training ends – eg, if you have enrolled on another course or during the child benefit 'extension period' (see p552). While you continue to be treated as in relevant education, you are only entitled to IS in the circumstances outlined on p903.

Full-time students

If you are a full-time student, you cannot usually qualify for IS or JSA for the duration of your course, including vacations.[15] See p908 for exceptions to this rule. See p933 if you give up, change or take time out of your course and p909 if you are studying part time.

You count as a full-time student if you are not in relevant education (p903), you are not getting a training allowance, and:[16]

- you are under 19 and attending or undertaking a full-time course of 'advanced education'. '**Advanced education**' means degree or postgraduate-level qualifications, teaching courses, diplomas of higher education, HND or HNC

Part 7: Special benefit rules
Chapter 44: Benefits for students
1. Income support and jobseeker's allowance

of the Business Technology Education Council or the Scottish Qualifications Authority and all other courses above advanced GNVQ or equivalent, OND, A levels or a Scottish national qualification (higher or advanced level). See below for what counts as a full-time course; *or*

* you are 19 or over but under pension age (see p752) and attending or undertaking a full-time course of study. If your course is full time, you are treated as a full-time student regardless of the level of the course, unless you are aged under 20 and can still be treated as in 'relevant education' (see p903). See below for what counts as a full-time course; *or*

* you are on a sandwich course (see p907).

You are treated as a student until either the last day of your course or until you abandon or are dismissed from it.[17] The **'last day of the course'** is the date on which the last day of the final academic year is officially scheduled to fall.[18]

For JSA, the period of study includes periods during which you are doing work connected to the course, even if this is after the normal end of your study.[19]

Full-time courses

If your course is funded by the Secretary of State under s14 of the Education Act 2002, the Chief Executive of the Skills Funding Agency, the Welsh government or Scottish Ministers, the definition of 'full time' depends on your personal pattern of attendance on the course. For all other courses, the term 'full time' applies to the course as a whole, not your personal pattern of attendance. However, for such courses, the rules contain no definition of when it is classed as a full-time course.

In **England and Wales**, your course counts as full time and you are treated as a full-time student if:[20]

* it is totally or partly funded by the Secretary of State under s14 of the Education Act 2002, the Chief Executive of the Skills Funding Agency or the Welsh government and your personal 'learning agreement' involves more than 16 hours of 'guided learning' each week. Courses include academic or vocational courses leading to a recognised qualification. The Secretary of State/ Chief Executive of the Skills Funding Agency and the Welsh government also fund basic literacy and numeracy courses, English as a Second Language programmes, Access and similar courses that prepare you to move on to qualification-bearing courses, and courses developing independent living skills for people with learning difficulties. The number of guided learning hours you do each week is set out in your learning agreement. This is signed by you and the college. The DWP uses this agreement to decide whether or not you are on a full-time course;[21] *or*

* it is not funded by the Secretary of State under s14 of the Education Act 2002/ Chief Executive of the Skills Funding Agency or the Welsh government and is a 'full-time course of study'.

In **Scotland,** your course counts as full time and you are treated as a full-time student if:[22]

- it is totally or partly funded by the Scottish Ministers at a college of further education, is not higher education *and* your personal learning document states that your course:
  - involves more than 16 hours a week of classroom-based or workshop-based programmed learning under the guidance of a teacher; *or*
  - involves more than 21 hours' study a week, 16 hours or less of which involve classroom-based or workshop-based programmed learning, and the rest of which involve using structured learning packages with the help of a teacher. The number of hours of 'learning' you do each week is set out in your learning document. This is signed by you and the college. The DWP uses this document to decide whether or not you are on a full-time course; *or*
- it is a course of higher education which is funded in whole or in part by Scottish Ministers and is a full-time course of study; *or*
- it is not funded by the Scottish Ministers and is a full-time course of study.

Sandwich courses

A course is a 'sandwich course' if it consists of alternate periods of full-time study at your educational institution and periods of industrial, professional or work experience organised so that, taking the course as a whole, you attend the periods of full-time study for an average of at least 18 weeks in each year.[23] This does not apply if it is a course of initial teacher training. If your periods of full-time study and work experience alternate within any week of your course, the days of full-time study are aggregated with each other and with any weeks of full-time study to determine the number of weeks of full-time study in each year.

Work experience includes periods of employment abroad for modern language students whose course is at least half composed of modern language study.

Health-related courses

If you attend a health-related course for which you are entitled to receive an NHS bursary, you are treated as a full-time or part-time student as appropriate, and not an employee.[24]

Modular courses

A modular course is one that consists of two or more modules and your college or university requires you to complete successfully a specific number of modules before it considers you to have completed the course.[25] You are treated as a full-time student if you are currently attending part of a modular course that would be classed as a full-time course.[26] You are treated as a full-time student for the period beginning on the day your course is defined as a full-time course and ending on the last day on which you are registered with your college or university as attending or undertaking that part of your course. This includes any vacations in

Part 7: Special benefit rules
Chapter 44: Benefits for students
1. Income support and jobseeker's allowance

that period, or the vacation immediately following that part of your course, unless that vacation follows the last day on which you are required to attend or undertake your course, or on such earlier date that you finally abandon or are dismissed from that part of the course.[27]

If you have failed examinations or failed to complete successfully a module relating to a period when the course was classed as a full-time course, any period in which you attend or undertake the course in order to retake those examinations or modules is classed as part of the full-time course and you are treated as a full-time student (even if your college or university registers you as a part-time student during your re-sit period).[28]

Because the rules do not provide a definition of what is a full-time course, unless funded by the Secretary of State under s14 of the Education Act 2002, the Chief Executive of the Skills Funding Agency or Scottish Ministers (see p907), you may be able to argue that you are not attending a full-time course, regardless of your attendance, if your course is not defined as full time or part time by your college or university.[29]

Other courses

If your course does not automatically count as full time under the rules above, whether it counts as a 'full-time course of study' depends on the college or university. Definitions are often based on local custom and practice within education institutions. The college or university's definition is not absolutely final, but if you want to challenge it, you will have to produce a good argument showing why it should not be accepted.[30] If your course is only for a few hours each week, argue that it is not full time. However, a course could be full time even though you only have to attend a few lectures a week.[31]

Full-time students entitled to income support

Even if you are a full-time student, you can qualify for IS (although most student funding counts as income) if you are:[32]

- a lone parent under age 18 (regardless of the age of your child/ren), or a lone parent of a child under five. **Note:** the age limit was reduced from seven from 21 May 2012. There is some transitional protection to IS for lone parents who were full-time students in receipt of IS before the age limit reduced (see p31); *or*
- a lone foster carer of a child under 16; *or*
- single, or are one of a couple and both of you are full-time students and:
  - you fit into one of the groups of people who can claim IS (see Chapter 3); *and*
  - you (or, if you are one of a couple, either one or both of you) are responsible for a child or young person (see p556); *and*
  - it is the summer vacation;
- a refugee who is learning English to obtain employment (see p30); *or*

- in, enrolled on or accepted for full-time non-advanced education and you are aged under 21, or you are 21 and you reached that age while in such education. In addition, you must:
  - have no parents (or anyone acting in their place); *or*
  - have to live away from your parents (or anyone acting in their place) because you are estranged from them, or are in physical or moral danger or there is a serious risk to your physical or mental health; *or*
  - be living away from your parents (or anyone acting in their place) and they cannot support you financially and they are:
    - chronically sick or mentally or physically disabled; *or*
    - detained in custody pending trial or sentence or having been sentenced; *or*
    - prohibited from entering or re-entering Great Britain.

Full-time students entitled to jobseeker's allowance

Even if you are a full-time student, you can qualify for JSA (although most student funding counts as income) if you are:

- single and responsible for a child or, if you are one of a couple, both of you are full-time students and either one or both of you is responsible for a child (see p556). This exception only applies during the summer vacation and if you are actually available for work, or treated as available because you are on either of the courses in the next bullet point;[33] *or*
- on an employment-related course of up to two weeks that has been approved in advance by the DWP,[34] or a Venture Trust training programme of up to four weeks.[35] In either case, only one course is allowed in any 12-month period; *or*
- participating in a scheme for assisting people to obtain employment (eg, Skills Conditionality – see p1093) – ie, you have been required to attend full-time training under it;[36] *or*
- aged 25 or over and on a qualifying course (see p1028);[37]
- waiting to go back to your course, having taken approved time out because of an illness or caring responsibility and that has now come to an end (see p933).

Maintaining two homes

In some cases, if you qualify for IS, income-based JSA or housing benefit, you may be entitled to help with the costs of more than one home if you have to live away from your normal home to attend a course. For further details, see p105 and p434.

Part-time students

If you are studying but are not in relevant education (see p903) or attending a full-time course (see p906), you are treated as attending a part-time course and classed as a part-time student.

Part 7: Special benefit rules
Chapter 44: Benefits for students
1. Income support and jobseeker's allowance

Entitlement to income support while studying part time

You can get IS while studying part time if you are not on a full-time course and you satisfy the other rules for getting IS (see Chapter 3).

If you are currently studying part time on a course you previously attended full time, the DWP may argue that you are attending a full-time course and should, therefore, be treated as a full-time student. It may be possible to challenge this interpretation.[38] Seek specialist advice if you are in this situation.

Entitlement to jobseeker's allowance while studying part time

You count as a part-time student if your course is not full time.[39] You can qualify for JSA while studying part time if you meet the jobseeking conditions – ie, you are available for work, actively seeking work and you have a valid jobseeker's agreement or claimant commitment (see Chapter 48). If you have agreed restrictions with the DWP on the hours that you are available for work, there are special rules that can help you claim JSA and study part time (see p911).

When you claim JSA, you may be asked to fill in a 'student questionnaire'. Your answers are taken into account when deciding whether you are available for and actively seeking work. The DWP needs to be satisfied that you are genuinely available for and actively seeking work while you are studying part time.

Availability for work and part-time study

Your availability for work should not be affected by your part-time course if your hours of study or training are at times outside your agreed pattern of availability (see p1036) – ie, they do not clash with the times you are willing and able to work. If the hours of your course *do* clash with the times you say you are available for work (as set out in your jobseeker's agreement or claimant commitment – see p1043), you are only accepted as available for work if either:[40]

- you are able to rearrange the hours of the course or study to fit around your job; *or*
- you are willing and able to give up the course should a job become available.

Deciding whether you are available for work

A number of factors should be considered when deciding whether you are available for work while you are studying part time. If, for example, it appears you are not willing or able to give up your course or that you cannot confine your study to times that would fit in with employment, you are treated as not being available for work. The factors that may be relevant include:[41]

- where you are studying or training away from home, whether you can be contacted if a job becomes available;
- the extent of your efforts to find employment;
- how important the successful completion of the course is to your future career, including whether it will enhance your chances of finding employment;
- whether you gave up a job or training to do the course;

- the days and hours you are required to attend the course;
- whether the times of attendance could be altered to fit in with any job you might obtain or whether successful completion of the course is possible if you miss some of the scheduled attendances;
- the duration of the study or training;
- whether a fee was paid and, if so, the amount and whether any of the fee could be refunded or transferred if you abandoned or interrupted your studies. If you have paid a fee, it may be more difficult (depending on the amount) to convince the DWP that you are prepared to abandon the course;
- whether you received a grant and, if so, the source, the amount and whether you would have to repay any or all of it if you interrupted or abandoned the course.

The guidance for decision makers states that where a number of claimants are following the same course, some may be able to show that they are available, but others may not.[42] The DWP should not operate a blanket policy of treating all students on the same course as not being available. Equally, you cannot assume that you will be treated as available if other people on your course are getting JSA. Each claim should be considered individually. The DWP assumes that you may be less willing to leave a course if you are near its end or as the chance of obtaining a qualification approaches.[43]

Restricted availability for work and part-time study

There are special rules that can help you qualify for JSA if you are a part-time student. These say that, in certain circumstances, the fact that you are on your course is ignored when deciding whether you are available for work if the hours of your course fall wholly or partly within the times you say you are available for work. However, you still have to be available for and actively seeking work during the rest of the week when you are not on your course.

These rules apply to you if you are a part-time student, and you are willing and able to rearrange the hours of your course to take up a job and the restrictions on your hours of availability have been agreed with the DWP because:[44]

- of your physical or mental condition (see p1035); *or*
- of your caring responsibilities (see p1036); *or*
- you are working 'short time' (see p1047); *or*
- they leave you available for work for at least 40 hours a week (see p1036).

You must also satisfy one of two conditions.

- For the three months immediately before the date you started the course, you were unemployed and getting JSA, or incapable of work and getting IS, IB or ESA, or you were on a course of 'training'.
- In the six months immediately before you started the course, you were unemployed and getting JSA, or incapable of work and getting IS, IB or ESA, or

Part 7: Special benefit rules
Chapter 44: Benefits for students
2. Employment and support allowance

you were on a course of training for a total of at least three months and, for any remaining part of the six months, you were working full time or earning too much to qualify for benefit.

The three-month and six-month periods can only begin after you have reached your terminal date (see p555) and are treated as having ceased to be in relevant education (see p555).

Training

'**Training**' means training for which young people aged under 18 are eligible, or for which a person aged 18–24 may be eligible, provided or arranged by the Secretary of State under s14 of the Education Act 2002 or the Chief Executive of the Skills Funding Agency, the Welsh government or Skills Development Scotland.[45]

Calculating income and capital

The normal rules for assessing your income and capital apply if you are a student (see Chapters 14 and 17). However, there are special rules for assessing the amount of money available from grants, loans and other types of financial support that apply to students (see p923), including people claiming IS while in 'relevant education'.[46] These rules do not apply if you are receiving a training allowance. For which student grants or loans do not count as income, see p926 and p928.

2. Employment and support allowance

Whether you can qualify for employment and support allowance (ESA) while studying depends on your age and the type of ESA you want to claim. You can qualify for contributory ESA (see p616), unless it is contributory ESA in youth (see p617), and you are 'receiving full-time education' (see below). You cannot qualify for income-related ESA if you are 'receiving education' unless you are getting disability living allowance (DLA), personal independence payment (PIP – see p913) or armed forces independence payment. There are some exceptions to the rules. You may be able to qualify if you are studying part time (see p914).

Note: in certain circumstances, if you are attending a training course and are paid a training allowance, you cannot qualify for ESA because you do not count as having limited capability for work (see p1004).[47]

Contributory employment and support allowance in youth

Note: contributory ESA in youth was abolished for new claims from 1 May 2012.

You cannot continue to get contributory ESA in youth (see p617) if you are 'receiving full-time education'.[48] You count as receiving 'full-time education' if:[49]

- you are at least 16 but under 19; *and*
- you attend a course of education for 21 hours or more a week. 'Course of education' is not defined in the rules, so can include both non-advanced and advanced courses. When calculating the 21 hours, any instruction or tuition that is not suitable for people of the same age as you who do not have a disability is ignored. Both the course content and the method of teaching must be taken into account in deciding this.[50]

Temporary interruptions of education are disregarded.

You *can* continue to get contributory ESA in youth even if you are studying if you are:

- under 19 and attending a course of education for less than 21 hours a week; *or*
- 19 or over. In this case, it does not matter how many hours you study. However, the rules are different for income-related ESA.

Income-related employment and support allowance

Unless you are getting DLA, PIP or armed forces independence payment, you cannot qualify for income-related ESA if you are 'receiving education'.[51] You cannot usually qualify for the duration of your course, including vacations. See p914 if you have finished studying and p933 if you give up, change or take time out from your course.

For income-related ESA purposes, you count as 'receiving education' if you are:

- a 'qualifying young person' for child benefit purposes (see p551);[52] *or*
- undertaking a 'course of study'.[53] The DWP may refer to you as a 'full-time student'. The definition is the same as the definition of full-time student for income support (IS) and jobseeker's allowance (JSA) (see p905). A course of study is the same as a full-time course for IS and JSA, and, for ESA, also includes a sandwich course (see p906).

Note: the term **'full-time student'** is used in the rest of this chapter to refer to someone who is receiving education for income-related ESA purposes.

Note also: unless you are a 'qualifying young person' for child benefit purposes, if you qualify for income-related ESA as a full-time student because you are getting DLA, PIP or armed forces independence payment you automatically count as having limited capability for work (see p1004).[54]

Unless it is a modular course (see p907) or you are a qualifying young person for child benefit purposes (see p551), you are treated as a full-time student from the date you start to undertake your course until the last day of the course, or until you abandon it or are dismissed from it.[55] The last day of the course is the last day of the final academic term.[56]

Part 7: Special benefit rules
Chapter 44: Benefits for students
2. Employment and support allowance

Maintaining two homes

In some cases, if you are a full-time student and you qualify for income-related ESA or housing benefit, you may be entitled to help with the costs of more than one home if you have to live away from your normal home to attend a course. For further details, see p105 and p434.

When you stop being a full-time student

Once you stop being a full-time student (see p913), you may be able to claim income-related ESA (see Chapter 5). However, bear the following in mind.

* If you were a 'qualifying young person' for child benefit purposes (eg, you were under 20 and on a full-time course of non-advanced education – see p551), you continue to count as a qualifying young person for a period after your education or training ends – eg, if you have enrolled on another course or during the child benefit 'extension period' (see p552). While you continue to be treated as a qualifying young person, you can only qualify for income-related ESA if you are receiving DLA, PIP or armed forces independence payment. If you cannot qualify for ESA in your own right, your parents may be able to continue to claim child benefit and tax credits for you.
* If you counted as a full-time student other than because you were a 'qualifying young person' for child benefit purposes (see p551), you continue to be treated as a full-time student until the last day of your course, or until you abandon the course or are dismissed from it (see p933).

Studying part time

You can qualify for ESA if you are studying part time. The definition of part-time study is different for contributory ESA and for income-related ESA.

You can continue to get **contributory ESA in youth** if you are under 19 and attending a course of education for less than 21 hours a week. Remember that if you are 19 or over, it does not matter how many hours you study; you can qualify for contributory ESA if you are studying part time *or* full time.

You can qualify for **income-related ESA** if you do not count as a full-time student under the rules described on p913.

When someone else is entitled to benefits for you

If you are under 20, a 'qualifying young person' for child benefit purposes (see p551) and cannot qualify for ESA because you are 'receiving full-time education' (see p912) or are a full-time student (see p913), someone else may be able to qualify for child benefit, child tax credit (CTC) and working tax credit if s/he is treated as 'responsible' for you. In some circumstances, you may count as both a person who can qualify for ESA and a person for whom someone else can qualify for child benefit and CTC. Seek advice on how you would be better off financially.

3. Housing benefit

Note: if you have reached the qualifying age for pension credit (PC – see p78) and neither you nor your partner are in receipt of income support (IS), income-based jobseeker's allowance (JSA) or income-related employment and support allowance (ESA), the student rules for housing benefit (HB) do not apply and there are no restrictions on your studying and qualifying for HB.[57]

Whether you can claim HB (see Chapter 7) depends on whether you are classed as a full-time or a part-time student.

Full-time students

If you are a full-time student (see p905), you cannot usually qualify for HB, but there are some exceptions – eg, students with children and young people in non-advanced education (see below).

The rules for deciding if you are a full-time student are similar to the rules for IS and JSA (see p905), except that there is no separate rule in HB if you are in 'relevant education' (see p903).

Part-time students

You may be able to qualify for HB if you are studying part time. The rules for deciding whether you are a part-time student are similar to the rules for IS and JSA (see p909), except that there is no separate rule in HB if you are in 'relevant education' (see p903).

Partners of students

If your partner is not a student, s/he can qualify for HB if s/he meets the qualifying conditions.[58] The claim is assessed in the normal way, except that the rules about being away from term-time accommodation (see p916) apply to your partner's claim.[59] Additionally, the special rules for assessing any income you receive from grants, loans and other types of financial support for students apply (see p923).

Full-time students entitled to housing benefit

You can qualify for HB (although most student funding counts as income) if:[60]
- you are on IS, income-based JSA or income-related ESA or universal credit (UC) except if your UC includes an amount for UC housing costs (see Chapter 22); *or*
- you are under 21, not following a course of higher education (higher education includes degree courses, teacher training, HND, HNC and postgraduate courses), or are aged 21 and you reached that age while on such a course and are still on it, or you are a child or a 'qualifying young person' for child benefit purposes (see p551); *or*

Part 7: Special benefit rules
Chapter 44: Benefits for students
3. Housing benefit

- you and your partner are both full-time students and either or both of you are responsible for a child or qualifying young person (see p551). Note that, unlike for IS and JSA, this provision applies throughout the year; or
- you are a lone parent with a dependent child or qualifying young person aged under 20 (see p551); or
- you are a lone foster carer and the child has been formally placed with you; or
- you meet the conditions for the disability premium (see p229). **Note:** you cannot qualify for a disability premium if you have limited capability for work; or
- you have been (or have been treated as) incapable of work (see p683 of the 2013/14 edition of this *Handbook*) for 196 days (28 weeks); or
- you have had (or have been treated as having) limited capability for work (see p1002) for 196 days (28 weeks). Two or more periods are joined to form a single period if they are separated by 12 weeks or less. **Note:** claims from 27 October 2008 are assessed under these rules rather than the incapacity for work rules in the bullet point above, unless, broadly, you already get incapacity benefit or IS because of incapacity for work; or
- you meet the conditions for the severe disability premium (see p233); or
- you qualify for a disabled students' allowance because you are deaf; or
- you are waiting to go back to your course, having taken approved time out because of an illness or caring responsibility and this has now come to an end (see p934).

Note: even if you are a full-time student who fits one of the exception categories listed above, you still cannot qualify for HB if the circumstances under the two headings below apply to you.

Being away from your term-time accommodation

Even if you are a full-time student who can qualify for HB (see p915), if your main reason for occupying your home is to enable you to attend your course, you cannot qualify for HB on that home for any full week when you are absent from it outside your period of study (see p925).[61]

This rule does not apply if:
- you are away from home because you are in hospital;[62]
- the main reason for occupying your home is *not* to enable you to attend your course but for some other purpose – eg, to provide a home for your children or for yourself because you do not have a home elsewhere where you normally live when you are not attending your course. If this applies, any absences outside your period of study are dealt with under the temporary absence rules (see p103).

Accommodation rented from an educational establishment

If you are a full-time student who can qualify for HB (see p915), you can usually get HB even if you rent your accommodation from your educational establishment.[63] If you are a part-time student, this rule applies if you would be able to qualify for HB if you were treated as a full-time student.

You cannot, however, get HB if you are a:

- full-time student waiting to go back to your course, having taken approved time out because of illness or caring responsibilities (see p934) and your illness or caring responsibilities have not yet ended; or
- part-time student whose only basis of entitlement to HB if you were a full-time student would be that you are receiving IS, income-based JSA or income-related ESA.

The above two exceptions do not apply if:

- your educational establishment itself rents the accommodation from a third party other than on a long lease or where the third party is an education authority providing the accommodation as part of its functions; or
- the accommodation is owned by a separate legal body – eg, a company established to build halls of residence.

You cannot get HB if the local authority decides that your educational establishment has arranged for your accommodation to be provided by a person or body other than itself in order to take advantage of the HB scheme.

Living in different accommodation during term time

The rules about claiming HB for two homes are explained on p105.

If you are one of a couple and receive HB for two homes, the assessment of HB for each home is based on your joint income and your applicable amount as a couple.

Calculating housing benefit

If you or your partner are on IS, income-based JSA, income-related ESA or the guarantee credit of PC, you are entitled to maximum HB (see Chapter 7).

If you are not on IS, income-based JSA, income-related ESA or the guarantee credit of PC but you or your partner are eligible for HB, your entitlement is calculated in the same way as for other claimants (see Chapters 14 and 17), except that there are special rules for assessing the amount of money available from grants, loans and other types of financial support for students (see p923). Note that, for courses lasting more than one year, in many cases loans and grants are not counted as income over the summer vacation. You may find, therefore, that your HB entitlement is higher over this period, or that you are only entitled to HB during the summer vacation, and that you need to make a new claim or check that your entitlement is reviewed at that time (see p924 for grant income and p928 for loans).

Part 7: Special benefit rules
Chapter 44: Benefits for students
4. Universal credit

Payments

Students are covered by all the normal rules on the administration and payment of HB (see Chapter 8). However, there is a provision that can apply specifically to students. The local authority may decide to pay a rent allowance once each term, although students have the same right as other claimants to insist on fortnightly payments if their entitlement is more than £2 a week.[64]

4. Universal credit

Universal credit (UC) is being introduced gradually over the next few years. For more information about when you come under the UC system, see p19.

Undertaking a course of study (the law refers to this as 'receiving education') may mean that you are not eligible for UC, unless you are in one of the groups of people for whom an exception is made (see p919). In general, these are students with children, some disabled students and young students in non-advanced education who have no parental support.

Receiving education

If you are receiving education, in most cases you are not eligible for UC.[65] There are exceptions, so that even if you are receiving education you may still be eligible (see p919).

You are 'receiving education' if you are:[66]
* a 'qualifying young person'. You must be on, or accepted on, a course of non-advanced education or approved training of at least 12 hours a week, and you must have been enrolled on, accepted on or have started the course before you turned 19. You can continue to be a qualifying young person until 31 August after your 19th birthday (see p211);[67] or
* on a full-time course of advanced education. This is education above the level of advanced GNVQ, general certificate of education (advanced) or a Scottish national qualification (higher or advanced higher), and includes degree level or postgraduate level courses, and higher national diplomas; or
* on another full-time course of study or training for which a loan or grant is provided for your maintenance.

Note: if none of the above apply, but you are on a course that is not compatible with your work-related requirements (see p919), you are treated as if you are receiving education.[68]

You count as receiving education from the start to the end of your course, or sooner if you abandon it or are dismissed from it.[69] The rules for when you count as a student if you are on a modular course are the same as those for income support (see p907).

Entitlement to universal credit while receiving education

You are eligible for UC while receiving education (although most student funding counts as income) if you are:[70]

- under 21 on a non-advanced course (or you are aged 21 and turned 21 on the course) and are 'without parental support' (see below);
- responsible for a child or qualifying young person (p211);
- a single foster parent;
- a member of a couple, both of you are full-time students and one of you is responsible for a child or is a foster parent;
- assessed as having limited capability for work (see p1002) and you also get attendance allowance, disability living allowance (DLA) or personal independence payment;
- over the qualifying age for pension credit (see p78);
- a student with a partner who is not a student;[71]
- waiting to return to your course after taking time out because of illness or caring responsibilities (see p922).[72]

Without parental support

'Without parental support' means you are not looked after by a local authority and you:[73]

– have no parent; *or*

– cannot live with your parents because you are estranged from them, or because there is a serious risk to your physical or mental health, or you would suffer significant harm if you lived with them; *or*

– are living away from your parents, and they cannot support you financially because they are ill or disabled, in prison or not allowed to enter Britain.

'Parent' includes someone acting in place of a parent.

When someone else can claim for you

If you cannot get UC yourself, someone may be able to claim for you if you are a 'qualifying young person' – ie, generally, if you are under 20 and in non-advanced education (see p211).

Work-related requirements

Most people claiming UC have work-related requirements as a condition of getting benefit, which may involve undertaking work-related activity, or looking for work (see p1066). However, you have no work-related requirements if you are receiving education and are:[74]

- under 21 (or 21 and you turned 21 on your course) in non-advanced education and 'without parental support' (see above); *or*
- in receipt of student income which is taken into account for UC – ie, a student loan, or a grant for maintenance (see p920).

Part 7: Special benefit rules
Chapter 44: Benefits for students
4. Universal credit

Note: even if you do not fit into one of the above groups, you may have no work-related requirements under the general rules – eg, if you are responsible for a child under one or if you are severely disabled (see p1073).

If you are on a full-time course but do not get a loan or grant, you may therefore be subject to all work-related requirements, and must be available for and actively seeking work (see p1073). This is more likely to be the case if you are in non-advanced education or on a postgraduate course, as there may be no student loan available, and grants for maintenance are limited.

Studying part time

If you are on a part-time course, you may still be treated as 'receiving education' if the course is not compatible with your work-related requirements.[75] So if you are subject to all work-related requirements, you must show that you meet these despite being on a part-time course. In some cases, it may be possible to argue that the course should be seen as 'voluntary work preparation', and therefore reduce your work search requirements (see p1068).[76]

If you are on a part-time course that is accepted as being compatible with your work-related requirements, you can get UC.

Student income and universal credit

If you (or your partner) have student income, it may count as income for UC. The rules below set out what student income counts, and how it is assessed.[77]

You are counted as having student income if you are undertaking a course and have a student loan or grant in respect of that course.[78]

Student loans

Student loans for maintenance[79] count as income if you could get a loan by taking 'reasonable steps', even if you choose not to apply for one. The maximum loan you could be entitled to is taken into account as income.

This is the case even if the loan is reduced because of an assessed parental (or partner) contribution, or if part of the loan is replaced by a grant. In Scotland, a student loan includes a young student's bursary.[80]

A grant paid for the same period as the loan is disregarded unless it is for the maintenance of someone who is part of your UC claim (eg, a partner or a child) or for rent payments that are met by UC.[81]

Grants

If you do not get a loan but receive a grant, the grant income is taken into account for UC (subject to the disregards below). If you get a loan, see above for what grant income is taken into account. The term 'grant' means an educational grant or award. It does not include a student loan or a grant paid to someone under 21 in non-advanced education to enable them to finish a course.[82]

This means that education maintenance allowance payments and 16 to 19 bursary fund payments do not count as student income.

Access or discretionary fund payments are likely to count as student income (as an 'educational grant'), unless they can be disregarded under the rules below. Grant income is completely disregarded if you do not get a loan and it is a payment:[83]

- for tuition fees or exams;
- in respect of your disability;
- for extra costs for residential study away from your usual place of study during term time;
- to pay for the costs of your normal home (if you live somewhere else during your course), unless these are met by your UC;
- for the maintenance of someone who is not included in your UC claim;
- for books, equipment, course travel costs or childcare costs.

Calculating student income

UC is paid for an 'assessment period' of one month (see p194). Student income counts as income in assessment periods that fall during the course, as well as in the assessment period in which the course, and any subsequent year of the course, begins.[84] Student income is ignored in the assessment period in which the last week of the course or the start of the long vacation falls. The long vacation is the longest holiday, lasting at least a month, in a course which is at least two years long. Student income is also ignored in any other assessment period that falls completely within the long vacation.[85]

In each assessment period, £110 of student income is disregarded.

To work out how much of your student income is taken into account:

Step one: calculate your annual loan or grant or, if the course lasts for less than a year, the amount of loan or grant for the course.

Step two: work out how many assessment periods apply for that year, or for the course if it is less than a year long.

Step three: divide the amount from step one by the number of assessment periods in step two.

Step four: deduct £110.

Example

Susan gets a student loan of £5,555. Year one of her course runs from 6 October 2014 to 22 May 2015. Her assessment periods run from the third of the month to the second of the following month. Her loan counts as income for seven assessment periods.

£5,555 ÷ 7 = £793.57

£793.57 − £110 = £683.57

Susan's UC is calculated on student income of £683.57 a month from 3 October 2014 to 2 May 2015.

Part 7: Special benefit rules
Chapter 44: Benefits for students
5. Other benefits

Taking time out from your course

During a period of temporary absence from your course, you usually still count as receiving education, so the student rules apply. Therefore, if you take time out because you have to re-sit exams or because you are ill, you still count as receiving education and are only eligible for UC if you are in one of the groups that is exempt – eg, you are a parent.

You do not count as 'receiving education' and can claim UC if you have taken time out from your course because of illness or caring responsibilities, you have now recovered or your caring responsibilities have ended, you are not eligible for a grant or student loan, and you are waiting to return to your course.[86] Your institution must have agreed to your taking time out, and you must have recovered from your illness or your caring responsibilities must have ended within the last year.

Note: if you leave your course completely, you no longer count as receiving education, so the normal UC rules apply. Student income is taken into account up to the end of the assessment period before the one in which you leave the course.

5. **Other benefits**

Carer's allowance

You cannot qualify for carer's allowance (CA – see Chapter 25) if you are in full-time education.[87] Usually, if the course you are attending is described by the university, college or school as full time, you are regarded as being in full-time education, although there may be exceptions – eg, if you are exempted from parts of the course.[88] So the actual hours you attend may not be crucial; but if you are attending for 21 hours a week or more (as specified by the institution), you are treated as being in full-time education. When calculating the 21 hours, you include only hours spent in 'supervised study' (see below). You ignore any time spent on meal breaks or unsupervised study undertaken on or off the premises of the educational establishment.[89]

You are treated as still in full-time education during vacations and any temporary interruption of the course, but not if you have abandoned the course or been dismissed from it.

Supervised study

'Supervised study' does not depend on whether your supervisor (ie, teacher, tutor, lecturer) is present with you.[90] If your study is directed to your course of education and the curriculum of your course and it is undertaken to meet the reasonable requirements of your course, it normally counts as supervised study. It counts regardless of whether that study is undertaken on or off the premises of the educational institution you attend.

• •

'**Unsupervised study**' means work beyond the reasonable requirements of your course. In assessing your hours of attendance, evidence from your educational institution about the amount of time you are expected to study to complete your course is important.

• •

Contribution-based jobseeker's allowance

If you come under the universal credit (UC) system (see p19) and are claiming contribution-based jobseeker's allowance (JSA), the rules in this section apply, not the rules on p905.

Students who are in 'relevant education' cannot claim contribution-based JSA. You are in relevant education in the same way that you count as 'receiving education' for UC.

You are in relevant education if you are:[91]
- a qualifying young person (see p551);
- on a full-time course of advanced education;
- on another full-time course for which a loan or grant is provided for your maintenance;
- on a course which is not compatible with your work-related requirements.

Note: you can claim contribution-based JSA, even if you are in relevant education, if you took time out because of illness or caring responsibilities, you have now recovered or the caring responsibilities have ended, and you are waiting to rejoin your course.

National insurance credits

You may be able to receive national insurance credits (see Chapter 41) for a tax year in which you were on a full-time course.

6. Calculating income from grants and loans

Note: the rules in this section apply to the calculation of income support (IS), income-based jobseeker's allowance (JSA), income-related employment and support allowance (ESA) and housing benefit (HB). They apply if you are a part-time or a full-time student. For the rules on *entitlement* to these benefits if you are studying, see the relevant section in this chapter. If you are claiming universal credit, the rules are different (see p920).

If you (or your partner) are a student, some of your (or your partner's) income from a grant, a loan and certain other forms of financial support for students is taken into account when calculating the amount of your benefit under the special rules set out below.[92] Your other income and capital are dealt with under the normal rules (see Chapter 15 and 17).

Part 7: Special benefit rules
Chapter 44: Benefits for students
6. Calculating income from grants and loans

The DWP has issued guidance to decision makers concerning the treatment of various types of financial support to students. Often this guidance only covers some of the benefits to which this section refers. For example, guidance may have been issued for HB purposes, but no equivalent guidance has been issued for IS, JSA or ESA. In addition, the legislation and guidance may not cover all sources of student support across the UK, particularly as new sources of support are introduced. You should, therefore, check the current position.

Note:

- The information in this section applies to support available to new students for the academic year 2013/14. For the treatment of grant and loan income for students who started their course in previous academic years, see the relevant edition of this *Handbook*.
- Grant and loan income does not affect your contribution-based JSA or contributory ESA.
- Any student income you have from a grant or loan is not taken into account as income if you are claiming HB and you:
  - are getting IS, income-based JSA, income-related ESA or the guarantee credit of pension credit (PC); *or*
  - have reached the qualifying age for PC (see p78) and you (or your partner) are not getting IS, income-based JSA or income-related ESA.[93]

Student support

There are many types of financial support available to students attending a course at school or a sixth-form or further education college, or who are undergraduates (including certain courses below degree level) or postgraduates. These are paid in the form of either a grant or a loan. Some types of grant or loan are available to all students who meet the conditions of entitlement; others are available on a discretionary basis. The support available to students varies, depending on whether you live in England, Wales, Scotland or Northern Ireland. For more information, see www.gov.uk/student-finance or CPAG's *Student Support and Benefits Handbook*, or, for Scottish students studying in Scotland, see CPAG's *Benefits for Students in Scotland Handbook*.

Grants

The term **'grant'**[94] includes any kind of educational grant or award, bursary (such as those paid by the NHS for certain health-related courses), scholarship, studentship, exhibition or supplementary allowance. It does not include payments from access funds (see p931), education maintenance allowances or similar payments (or the equivalent in Scotland, Wales and Northern Ireland).

Some grants are ignored as income (see p926) and others are taken into account. When calculating income from a grant, special rules and disregards apply.

If you are assessed as entitled to a parental or partner's contribution to your grant, it counts as income whether or not it has been paid to you.[95] However, only the amount of contribution you actually receive counts if:

- for IS, you are a lone parent, a lone foster carer or a disabled student (see p908); *or*
- for JSA, you qualify for a disability premium (see p229); *or*
- for ESA, you are a lone parent or a full-time student who gets disability living allowance (DLA) (see p913).

General rules on calculating grant income

Your grant income is apportioned:[96]

- if it is payable for your period of study (unless you are attending a sandwich course), over the number of benefit weeks in your period of study;
- if it is payable for a period other than your period of study, over the number of benefit weeks in the period for which the grant is payable.

In most cases, the former applies and your grant income is assessed over a period starting from the 'benefit week' which coincides with (or immediately follows) the first day of your 'period of study' (see below) and ending with the benefit week, the last day of which coincides with (or immediately precedes) the last day of your period of study. In this context, '**benefit week**' means the week for which benefit is paid.[97]

This means your grant income is apportioned over the number of complete benefit weeks in your period of study. Any part weeks at the beginning or end of that period are ignored. **Note:** this rule does not apply to an NHS bursary (see p926).

Period of study

'**Period of study**' means:[98]

– for a course of one year or less, from the start of the course to the last day of the course;

– for a course of more than one year, in the first and subsequent years (but not the final year), from the start of the course, or the start of the year of the course to:

– if the grant is payable for a period of 12 months, the day before the start of the next year of the course; *or*

– in any other case, the day before the start of your normal summer vacation;

– in the final year of a course lasting more than one year, from the start of the final year of the course and ending with the last day of the course.

If you are attending a **sandwich course**, your grant income is taken into account over a different period. Any periods spent on placement or work experience in your period of study are excluded and your grant is apportioned over the remaining benefit weeks in your period of study. **Note:** this only applies if your

Part 7: Special benefit rules
Chapter 44: Benefits for students
6. Calculating income from grants and loans

grant is payable for your period of study. If your grant is payable for a different period, it is taken into account over the number of benefit weeks in the period for which it is payable.

Specific types of grant income

Postgraduate awards made by research councils and the British Academy are apportioned over the number of benefit weeks in the period for which they are payable (usually a calendar year).

NHS bursaries paid to students in England, Wales and Scotland are paid in monthly instalments. They should be taken into account over 52 or 53 weeks (if there are 53 benefit weeks, including part weeks, in the year).[99] If you are studying for an undergraduate diploma or degree or postgraduate qualification in **social work**, you may be eligible for a non-means-tested bursary administered by the NHS in England, the Care Council for Wales or the Scottish Social Services Council. The bursary or grant counts in full as grant income and is apportioned according to the rules above.

If you receive a **supplementary allowance** for an adult dependant as part of a student loan (or you could have received one had you taken reasonable steps to apply for one), the allowance is apportioned over the same period as a student loan (see p928).

If you receive a supplementary allowance from any other source, but you do not receive a student loan (or could not have received one even if you had taken reasonable steps to apply for one), it is apportioned over the same period as 'basic' grant income (see p924).[100] If you receive a supplementary allowance for an adult dependant as part of an NHS bursary, this is apportioned over 52 or 53 weeks.[101]

Note: students on health-related courses, except nursing and midwifery diploma courses, may be eligible for supplementary allowances for an adult dependant under both an NHS bursary and (reduced-rate) student loan. These separate allowances for an adult dependant are, therefore, taken into account over different periods.

In Scotland, a **care leavers' grant** of up to £105 a week towards accommodation, which is paid during the long vacation only, is taken fully into account as income for each week in which it is paid.

The **Scottish young person's bursary** is apportioned in the same way as the student loan (see p928).

Grant income that is ignored

The following grant income is ignored:[102]

- any allowance for tuition and examination fees;
- disabled students' allowance;
- any allowance to meet the cost of residential study away from your normal educational establishment during term time;

- any allowance for the cost of your normal home (away from college) but, for IS, JSA and ESA, only to the extent that your rent is not met by HB;
- any amount for a partner or child living abroad;
- for IS/JSA/ESA only, any amount intended to maintain a dependent child (unless you still have amounts for children included in your IS/JSA and do not get child tax credit);
- any amount intended for the childcare costs of a dependent child;
- any amount intended for the cost of books and equipment;
- any amount intended for travel costs related to course attendance;
- parents' learning allowance;
- higher education grant;[103]
- special support grant;[104]
- if you have been required to make a contribution to your own grant (eg, because you have other income, such as maintenance), an amount equivalent to that contribution is disregarded.[105] In the case of a couple, the amount of any contribution that one member has been assessed to pay to her/his partner who is a student is disregarded from the non-student's income;[106]
- an education maintenance allowance, 16 to 19 bursary or similar payments, including a Care to Learn payment, a further education Welsh Assembly learning grant or Passport to Study grant;[107]
- higher education bursary for care leavers.

In addition to the amounts ignored under the rules above, the following fixed sums are ignored.[108] These disregards apply only to the grant you receive for your period of study and not to any supplementary allowances you may be paid during the long vacation.[109]

- A fixed amount of £390 for books and equipment (2013/14 academic year). If your grant includes a specific amount to cover the cost of books and equipment, that amount is ignored in addition to this fixed amount.
- A fixed amount of £303 for the cost of travel (2013/14 academic year). If your grant includes a specific amount to cover the cost of travel expenses for attendance on your course, that amount is ignored in addition to this fixed amount. If your actual travel costs are higher than any sum specified in your grant for travel (which is ignored under the rules above) plus this fixed amount, the additional costs are not ignored and are taken into account.[110]

Note:
- If you also receive a student loan, the above two fixed sums are not disregarded when calculating your grant income, but are disregarded from your loan income instead (see p928).
- For the purpose of these fixed amounts, the 2013/14 academic year began on 1 August 2013 if your period of study (see p925) began in August 2013. If your period of study began on or after 1 September 2013, the fixed sums apply from

Part 7: Special benefit rules
Chapter 44: Benefits for students
6. Calculating income from grants and loans

that date. At the time of writing, the amounts for 2014/15 were not available. See CPAG's online service and *Welfare Rights Bulletin* for updates.

Loans

A loan is treated as income but is subject to special rules and disregards. Note that some supplementary allowances paid under the student loan provisions are paid as non-repayable grants and are treated as grant income (see p924).

Calculating income from a student loan

How your, or your partner's, student loan is treated depends on whether your course lasts for one year or less, or for a longer period.[111] The maximum amount of available loan is taken into account even if you do not apply for a loan or for the maximum amount,[112] unless, for ESA only, you are taking time out for ill health and are not receiving a student loan.[113]

You are treated as having a parental or partner's contribution to your loan whether or not it has been paid to you. However, only the amount of contribution you actually receive counts if:[114]

- for IS, you are a lone parent, a lone foster carer or a disabled student (see p908); *or*
- for JSA, you qualify for a disability premium (see p229); *or*
- for ESA, you are a full-time student who gets DLA (see p913).

A student loan paid to a student on a Postgraduate Certificate in Education course is treated in the same way as student loans and supplementary allowances for undergraduate students.

Dependants' grants are taken into account over the same period as the student loan if you have a student loan or you are eligible for one.[115]

If you attend a nursing or midwifery diploma course, no loan income should be taken into account as a student loan is not available for these courses. If you are on another health-related course, only the lower maximum loan rate should be taken into account.

Loan income that is ignored

The following are ignored.

- Loans paid for tuition fees (known as a 'fee loan' or a 'fee contribution loan').[116]
- If you have been required to make a contribution to your own loan (eg, because you have other income, such as maintenance), an amount equivalent to that contribution is disregarded as income.[117] In the case of a couple, the amount of any contribution that one member has been assessed to pay to her/his partner who is a student is disregarded from the non-student's income.[118]

Once any of the above income has been deducted from your loan income, also ignored is a fixed amount of:[119]

- £390 for the cost of books and equipment (2013/14 academic year); *and*
- £303 for the cost of travel (2013/14 academic year).

If your actual costs are higher than the amounts for books and equipment and travel, any additional costs cannot be ignored.[120]

Note:

- If you also receive a grant, the two fixed sums above are ignored from your loan income rather than your grant income (see p926).
- For the purpose of the above fixed amounts, the 2013/14 academic year began on 1 August 2013 if your period of study (see p925) began in August 2013. If your period of study began on or after 1 September 2013, the fixed sums apply from that date.

At the time of writing, the amounts for 2014/15 were not available. See CPAG's online service and *Welfare Rights Bulletin* for updates.

Ten pounds a week is ignored for each week in the period over which your loan income is taken into account (see below). This amount may overlap with other disregards applied to certain war pensions (see p275) and access funds (see p931). A combined maximum sum of £20 a week can be ignored.

The period over which loan income is taken into account

Academic year

The rules give a definition of an 'academic year' for the purposes of calculating student loan income. This definition may be different from the actual academic year of the education institution you attend.

Academic year

'Academic year' means a period of 12 months beginning on 1 January, 1 April, 1 July or 1 September according to whether your course begins in the winter, the spring, the summer or the autumn respectively. If you are required to begin attending your course during August or September and to continue attending through the autumn, the academic year of your course is treated as beginning in the autumn rather than summer – ie, from 1 September.[121]

Benefit weeks

Loan income is apportioned over a period of 'benefit weeks'.

The first benefit week may fall before the start of your actual academic year and the last benefit week may fall either before or after the last day of your academic year (academic years vary between educational institutions). This may mean your benefit is recalculated several times depending on when your actual academic

Part 7: Special benefit rules
Chapter 44: Benefits for students
6. Calculating income from grants and loans

year falls in relation to the relevant benefit weeks. You need to make a new claim or check that your entitlement is revised at these times.

If you are required to start attending your course in August, or your course is for less than one academic year, the period begins with the benefit week, the first day of which coincides with, or immediately follows, the first day of the course.[122]

If your academic year does not start on 1 September, your loan payable for that academic year is apportioned equally between the benefit weeks in the period beginning with the benefit week, the first day of which coincides with, or immediately follows, the first day of that academic year and ending with the benefit week, the last day of which coincides with, or immediately precedes, the last day of that academic year. Excluded from that are any benefit weeks falling entirely within the quarter during which, in the opinion of the decision maker, your longest vacation falls.[123]

Quarters

'**Quarter**' means one of the periods from 1 January to 31 March, 1 April to 30 June, 1 July to 31 August, or 1 September to 31 December.[124]

In the first, or only, year of your course your loan income (calculated under the rules below) is ignored for each benefit week that falls before the start of your 'period of study' (the first day of the first term). This is because you cannot be treated as a student until you actually start your course.[125]

A course lasting for one academic year or less

Your loan is apportioned over the benefit weeks beginning with the benefit week, the first day of which coincides with, or immediately follows, the first day of the 'academic year' (or, if a course begins in August, from the first day of the first benefit week on or after the first day of the course) and ending with the benefit week, the last day of which coincides with, or immediately follows, the last day of the course.

A course lasting for more than one academic year

Unless it is your final year (see p931), your loan is apportioned over the period from the earlier of:
- the first day of the first benefit week in September; *or*
- the first benefit week, the first day of which coincides with, or immediately follows, the first day of the autumn term.

It is taken into account until the last day of the benefit week that coincides with, or immediately precedes, the last day of June.

Final year of a course

Your loan is taken into account over the period beginning with either:

- if the final academic year starts on 1 September, the benefit week, the first day of which coincides with, or immediately follows, the earlier of 1 September or the first day of the autumn term; *or*
- the benefit week, the first day of which coincides with, or immediately follows, the first day of the academic year.

It is taken into account until the benefit week, the last day of which coincides with, or immediately precedes, the last day of the course.

Calculating income from other types of loan

Professional and career development loans paid under s2 of the Employment and Training Act 1973 are treated as income.[126] However, this income is ignored except where it is intended to meet 'daily living expenses' and your course or education has not been completed.[127]

Any financial support you receive that is paid in the form of a loan (other than a student loan or a professional and career development loan), including a loan received from an overseas source, does not count as a student loan or a grant.[128] It is taken into account as 'other income' (see p273).

Payments from access funds

Access funds (which include the Learner Support Fund available to some students in further education, the Financial Contingency Fund in Wales, the Access to Learning Fund offered by higher education institutions in England, the 16 to 19 bursary fund in England and discretionary funds in Scotland) are administered by colleges and universities.[129] Individual educational institutions may call all or part of these funds by other names – eg, access bursary, mature students' bursary and childcare support. Payments from access funds should be distinguished from payments with similar names from other sources – ie, hardship loans.

How a payment from access funds is treated depends on whether it is paid as a single lump sum, in instalments or to bridge the period before you start your course or receive a student loan payment.

A single lump-sum payment

A single lump-sum payment is treated as capital but is disregarded for 52 weeks if the payment is intended for and used for any items, expenses or charges which you or your partner may incur (other than 'daily living expenses').[130] However, if the payment is intended for but not used for these items, expenses or charges, it is

Part 7: Special benefit rules
Chapter 44: Benefits for students
6. Calculating income from grants and loans

taken into account as capital immediately. A single lump-sum payment made for 'daily living expenses' counts as capital immediately.

Daily living expenses
'Daily living expenses' are:
– food;
– ordinary clothing or footwear – ie, for normal daily use, but not including school uniforms or that are used solely for sporting activities;
– household fuel;
– for IS/JSA/ESA only, rent for which HB is payable;
– for HB, your 'eligible rent', minus any non-dependant deductions;
– for IS/JSA/ESA only, housing costs met by IS, income-based JSA or income-related ESA;
– council tax;
– water charges.

Payments made in instalments

Payments made in instalments are treated as income, but are disregarded in full.[131] However, if the payment is intended and used for daily living expenses (see above), it is taken into account as income for each week it is intended to cover, except for the first £20 a week, which is disregarded. This amount may overlap with other disregards applied to certain war pensions (see p275) and student loans (see p928). A combined maximum sum of £20 a week can be ignored.

Payments before course starts or student loan received

A payment (whether paid as a single payment or in instalments) is ignored, even if it is for 'daily living expenses', if it is made:[132]
- on or after whichever is the earlier of 1 September or the first day of your course, if it is intended to bridge the period before you receive your student loan; *or*
- before the first day of your course, if it is made in anticipation of your becoming a student.

Other sources of income intended to cover study costs

If you receive a payment from any source other than a grant or student loan, which is intended to cover items or expenses that would be ignored when calculating grant income, the payment made from that other source for those items or expenses is also ignored.[133] You must show that the payment is necessary for you to be able to attend the course. Any sum paid, which is not necessary (or is likely to exceed the sum necessary) for you to attend the course, counts as income. For example, if your grant or student loan does not cover all your tuition fees, any money received from another source such as a parent, intended to make up the difference, is ignored as income. However, if the amount you receive is greater than is likely to be necessary to pay the difference, the amount above that sum counts as income.

Student support once you have completed your course

For IS/JSA/ESA only, any grant income, student loan, assessed contribution made by a parent or spouse/civil partner as part of the loan or grant, or a professional and career development loan that you received no longer counts as income once you have completed the course.[134] However, as most (but not all) types of student support are not taken into account for a period after your course is due to end, it should also be ignored as income for HB once you have completed the course.

Presumably, any student financial support you have left once you have completed your course counts as capital (see Chapter 17) as there are no provisions to disregard it under the rules about capital.

---

7. Giving up, changing or taking time out from your course

Note: this section only applies to income support (IS), jobseeker's allowance (JSA), income-related employment and support allowance (ESA) and housing benefit (HB). However, this section does *not* apply if (for IS and JSA) you are (or were) in 'relevant education' (see p903), or (for ESA) you are (or were) a 'qualifying young person' for child benefit purposes (see p913). See p905 for information about qualifying for IS or JSA when you leave relevant education. See p914 for information about qualifying for income-related ESA when you are no longer a qualifying young person for child benefit purposes. There is no equivalent rule for HB. For universal credit rules if you are taking time out, see p922.

If you abandon your course or are dismissed from it, you can qualify for IS, JSA or income-related ESA from the day after that date so long as you satisfy the other rules for getting these benefits (see Chapters 3, 4 and 5). If you are on a sandwich course (see p907), or your course includes a compulsory or optional period on placement, you count as a full-time student during the sandwich or placement period, even if you have been unable to find a placement or your placement comes to an end prematurely.[135]

If you attend a course at an educational institution that provides training or instruction to enable you to take examinations set and marked by an entirely different and unconnected body (ie, a professional institution) and you abandon or take time out from it because you fail the examinations set by the other body (or you finish the course at the educational institution but fail the exams), you may be able to argue that you are not a student from the date you left the course at your educational institution even if you intend to re-sit the examinations set by the other body at a later date.[136]

Part 7: Special benefit rules
Chapter 44: Benefits for students
7. Giving up, changing or taking time out from your course

If you are taking time out of your course for any other reason and for however long a period, you cannot qualify for IS, JSA or income-related ESA during your period of absence,[137] except in the limited circumstances set out below (but if you are taking time out from a modular or similar course, see also p907).

You may retain entitlement to some student support on a statutory or discretionary basis – eg, through student loans or hardship funds. You should seek specialist advice.

If you complete one course and start a different course, you are not treated as a student in any period between the courses.[138]

Changing from full-time to part-time attendance

If, for personal reasons, you have to change from full-time to part-time attendance on a 'traditional' full-time course, you may be able to argue that you have abandoned your full-time course and are registered on a part-time course and, therefore, that you are not a full-time student.[139]

If, because of exam failure or any other reason, you change to a different course, or your college requires you to change the level of course (eg, from A level to GCSE) and this involves a change from full-time to part-time study, argue that you are a part-time student.[140]

However, changing your attendance may affect your entitlement to any student support you may be receiving. Seek advice on this before acting.

Time out to be a carer

If you are a full-time student and you have taken time out from your course to care for someone, you cannot qualify for IS, JSA or income-related ESA unless you are someone who can qualify while studying (see p908, p909 and p913). However, you can qualify for JSA and HB, but not IS or income-related ESA, when your caring responsibilities have come to an end.[141] **Note:** the rules do not provide a definition of caring responsibilities or when they come to an end. You can then qualify for a maximum period of one year, provided you are not eligible for a student grant or loan during the period, until whichever is the earlier of:

- the day you rejoin your course; *or*
- the first day from which your educational institution has agreed you can rejoin your course.

This means that you may not qualify for benefit for the whole of the period after your caring responsibilities end until the date you actually rejoin your course.

Time out because of illness

If you are a full-time student and you have taken time out from your course because you are ill, you cannot qualify for income-related ESA unless you get disability living allowance, personal independence payment or armed forces independence payment.

Once your illness has ended, you can qualify for JSA and HB. The rules are the same as for when caring responsibilities have ended (see p934).

Time out because you are pregnant

If you are a full-time student and you have taken time out from your course because you are pregnant, you cannot qualify for IS, JSA or income-related ESA, unless you are someone who can qualify while studying (see p908, p909 and p913). It has been decided that, for JSA, this provision does not *directly* discriminate against women under European Union (EU) law.[142] It was also subsequently decided that it does not *indirectly* discriminate against women under EU law, and that it is not incompatible with the Human Rights Act.[143] **Note:**

- Check to see whether you qualify for statutory maternity pay or maternity allowance.
- Once your baby is born, you may then qualify for IS (eg, if you are a lone parent) or you or your partner may qualify for HB.

Calculating income from grants and loans

Grants

For IS, income-based JSA and income-related ESA, if you cease to be a full-time student before your course finishes, any grant you have received is taken into account as if you were still a student (see p924) until the earliest of:[144]

- the date you repay the grant; *or*
- the last date of the academic term or vacation in which you ceased to be a full-time student; *or*
- if the grant is paid in instalments, the day before the next instalment would have been paid had you still been a full-time student.

For HB it is not taken into account as if you were still a student.[145] Instead, it is taken into account until the grant provider asks you to repay it. Until then, it should be calculated over an appropriate period.[146] It could be argued that your grant should be taken into account as income only to the end of the period which your last instalment was meant to cover.

Loans

For income-related ESA, if you suspend attendance on your course because of illness or disability and this is confirmed in writing by the educational institution, you are not treated as having any part of a student loan which has not been paid to you.

If you abandon or are dismissed from your course before it finishes, there are special rules on how your student loan is treated for IS, income-based JSA, income-related ESA and HB.

Part 7: Special benefit rules
Chapter 44: Benefits for students
7. Giving up, changing or taking time out from your course

If you abandon your course before you have received the final instalment of your student loan, it is taken into account using the formula:[147]

$$\frac{A - (B \times C)}{D}$$

A = the maximum amount of student loan available to you (see p928), including any amount paid as a grant intended to maintain your dependants, that you would have received had you remained a student until *the last day of the academic term* in which you abandoned or were dismissed from your course, less any disregards that apply (see p928). This amount is the 'relevant payment'. If, however, you were paid in two or more instalments in a quarter (eg, monthly, as is currently the case for Scottish students studying in Scotland), A = the relevant payment that you would have received calculated in the same way, except that it is the amount that you would have received had you remained a student up until *the day you abandoned or were dismissed from your course.*

B = the number of benefit weeks immediately following the benefit week which includes the first day of your academic year to the benefit week immediately before that which includes the day on which you abandoned or were dismissed from your course (for HB, calculate up until the week that includes the one in which you left the course).

C = the weekly amount of student loan for the academic year which would have been taken into account to calculate your benefit under the normal rules (see p928) but without applying the £10 a week disregard (see p928). This applies regardless of whether you were actually entitled to benefit before you abandoned or were dismissed from your course.

D = the number of benefit weeks beginning with the benefit week which includes the day on which you abandoned or were dismissed from your course and ending with the benefit week which includes the last day of the last 'quarter' (see p931) for which your relevant payment (see A) would have been payable to you had you remained on your course, or to the day before you would have been due your next loan payment, if earlier.

Example

Bhavna abandons her three-year degree course at a university outside London on 31 October 2014 during the first term of her second year. Her benefit week starts on a Tuesday. Her assumed maximum loan income would have been taken into account for 43 weeks (first complete benefit week in September to last complete benefit week in June).

Note: the following disregard figures are from 2013/14, because, at the time of writing, the 2014/15 figures were not finalised. However, the student loan amounts and dates are for the 2014/15 academic year.

Step one: calculate the relevant payment

Loan instalment paid for first term	£1,833.15
less deduction for books and travel	£693.00
Total taken into account	**£1,140.15**

Step two: calculate the benefit weeks prior to leaving the course
2 September 2014 to 27 October 2014   = 8 weeks

Step three: calculate maximum loan for the academic year

Maximum loan	£5,555
less deduction for books and travel	£693
Total loan	£4,862
Weekly amount (£4,862 divided by 43 weeks)	= **£113.07**

Step four: calculate complete benefit weeks from the benefit week including the date of abandonment to the end of the benefit week including the end of the quarter
28 October 2014 to 5 January 2015   = 10 weeks

$$\frac{1,140.15 - (8 \times 113.07)}{10} = \pounds23.56$$

Therefore, £23.56 a week is taken into account from 28 October 2014 to 5 January 2015 (10 weeks) and nothing thereafter.

Note: this formula can result in a nil loan income figure depending on the exact date in your term that you abandon, or are dismissed from, your course.

If you voluntarily repay your student loan, for IS, income-based JSA and income-related ESA you are treated as still having that loan income calculated under the above rules.[148] However, for all the benefits, guidance to decision makers says you should not be treated as having any loan income if the Student Loans Company demands you repay the loan instalment immediately.[149]

Notes

1. **Income support and jobseeker's allowance**
   1 s124(1)(d) SSCBA 1992; s1(2)(g) JSA 1995
   2 **IS** Reg 12 IS Regs
      JSA Reg 54 JSA Regs
   3 Regs 4ZA and 13(2)(a)-(e) IS Regs
   4 Reg 2(1)(b)(i)&(ii) C(LC)SSB Regs; reg 13(2)(a) and (b) IS Regs; para 30524 DMG
   5 R(IS) 9/94
   6 R(IS) 9/94
   7 CIS/11766/1996
   8 R(IS) 9/94
   9 Reg 13(3)(a)(ii) IS Regs
   10 R(SB) 2/87
   11 CIS/11441/1995
   12 s1(2)(g) JSA 1995; regs 54, 57(2) and (4)(a) and 61(1)(c) JSA Regs
   13 Reg 54(3)-(5) JSA Regs
   14 Reg 54(3) and (4) JSA Regs
   15 **IS** Reg 4ZA(2) IS Regs
      JSA Reg 15(a) JSA Regs

Part 7: Special benefit rules
Chapter 44: Benefits for students
Notes

16 **IS** Reg 61(1) IS Regs
   JSA Reg 1(3) JSA Regs
   Both Definition of 'full-time student'
17 **IS** Reg 2(1), definition of 'period of
   study', IS Regs
   JSA Reg 1(3A) JSA Regs
   HB Reg 53(2)(b) HB Regs
18 **IS** Reg 61(1), definition of 'last day of the
   course', IS Regs
   JSA Reg 130, definition of 'last day of
   the course', JSA Regs
   HB Reg 53(1), definition of 'last day of
   the course', HB Regs
19 Reg 4, definition of 'period of study', JSA
   Regs
20 **IS** Reg 61(1), definitions of 'full-time
   course of advanced education' and 'full-
   time course of study', IS Regs; para
   30148 DMG
   JSA Reg 1(3), definition of 'full-time
   student', JSA Regs - the definition of 'full-
   time course' is found within that
   definition
   HB Reg 53(1), definition of 'full-time
   course of study', HB Regs
21 paras 30197-98 DMG
22 **IS** Reg 61, definitions of 'full-time course
   of advanced education' and 'full-time
   course of study', IS Regs; paras 30149
   DMG
   JSA Reg 1(3), definition of 'full-time
   student', JSA Regs, - the definition of
   'full-time course' is found within that
   definition
   HB Reg 53(1), definitions of 'full-time
   course of study' and 'higher education',
   HB Regs
23 **IS** Reg 61(1) IS Regs
   JSA Reg 1(3) JSA Regs
   HB Reg 53(1) HB Regs
   All definition of 'sandwich course'
24 R(IS) 19/98
25 **IS** Reg 61(4) IS Regs
   JSA Reg 1(3C) JSA Regs
   HB Reg 53(4) HB Regs
26 **IS** Reg 61(2)(a) IS Regs
   JSA Reg 1(3A)(a) JSA Regs
   HB Reg 53(2)(a) HB Regs
27 **IS** Reg 61(3)(b) IS Regs
   JSA Reg 1(3B)(b) JSA Regs
   HB Reg 53(3)(b) HB Regs
28 **IS** Reg 61(3)(a) IS Regs
   JSA Reg 1(3B)(a) JSA Regs
   HB Reg 53(3)(a) HB Regs
29 R(IS) 15/98; R(IS) 7/99; CJSA/836/
   1998; R(IS)1/00; *Chief Adjudication
   Officer v Webber* [1997] 4 All ER 274
30 R(SB) 40/83; R(SB) 41/83

31 **IS** Reg 61, definitions of 'full-time course
   of advanced education' and 'full-time
   course of study', IS Regs
   JSA Reg 1(3), definition of 'full-time
   student', JSA Regs - the definition of 'full-
   time course' is found within that
   definition
32 Reg 4ZA and Sch 1B IS Regs
33 Reg 15(2) and (3) JSA Regs
34 Reg 14(1)(a) JSA Regs
35 Reg 14(1)(k) JSA Regs
36 Reg 7(2) JSA(SAPOE) Regs
37 Regs 17A and 21A JSA Regs
38 CIS/152/1994; R(IS) 15/98; CJSA/836/
   1998; R(IS) 1/00
39 Reg 1(3), definition of 'part-time
   student', JSA Regs
40 para 21241 DMG
41 para 21242 DMG
42 para 21243 DMG
43 para 21244 DMG
44 Reg 11 JSA Regs
45 Reg 11(3) JSA Regs
46 Regs 2(1) and 61(1), definitions of
   'student' and 'course of study', IS Regs

2. Employment and support allowance
47 Reg 32(2) and (3) ESA Regs
48 Sch 1 para 4(1)(b) WRA 2007
49 Reg 12 ESA Regs
50 R(S) 2/87 was not about ESA, but
   the rule is very similar.
51 Sch 1 para 6(1)(g) WRA 2007; reg 18
   ESA Regs
52 Reg 15 ESA Regs
53 Reg 14 ESA Regs
54 Regs 14 and 33(2) ESA Regs
55 Reg 17(1)(b) ESA Regs
56 Reg 2(1) ESA Regs

3. Housing benefit
57 There are no student rules in the
   HB(SPC) Regs.
58 Reg 8(1)(e) HB Regs
59 Reg 58 HB Regs
60 Reg 56(2) HB Regs
61 Reg 55(1) HB Regs
62 Reg 55(2) HB Regs
63 Reg 57 HB Regs
64 Reg 92(7) HB Regs

4. Universal credit
65 s4(1)(d) WRA 2012
66 Reg 12 UC Regs
67 Reg 5 UC Regs
68 Reg 12(4) UC Regs
69 Reg 13 UC Regs
70 Reg 14 UC Regs

71 Reg 3(2)(b) UC Regs
72 Reg 13(4) UC Regs
73 Reg 8(3) UC Regs
74 Reg 89 UC Regs
75 Reg 12(4) UC Regs
76 Reg 95(4) UC Regs
77 Regs 68-71 UC Regs
78 Reg 68(1) UC Regs
79 Reg 68(7) UC Regs
80 Reg 68(7) UC Regs
81 Reg 68(3) UC Regs
82 Reg 68(7) UC Regs
83 Reg 70 UC Regs
84 Reg 68(1) UC Regs
85 Reg 68(7) UC Regs
86 Reg 13(4) UC Regs

5. Other benefits
87 Reg 5 SS(ICA) Regs
88 *SSWP v Deane* [2010] EWCA Civ 699
89 Reg 5(2) SS(ICA) Regs
90 R(G) 2/02
91 Reg 45 JSA Regs 2013

6. Calculating income from grants and loans
92 **IS** Regs 2(1) and 61(1) IS Regs
   JSA Regs 1(3) and 130 JSA Regs
   ESA Reg 131 ESA Regs
   HB Reg 53(1) HB Regs
   IS/HB definition of 'student'
   JSA/ESA definition of 'full-time student'
   IS/JSA/HB definition of 'course of study'
93 Reg 29 HB(SPC) Regs
94 **IS** Reg 61(1) IS Regs
   JSA Reg 130 JSA Regs
   ESA Reg 131(1) ESA Regs
   HB Reg 53(1) HB Regs
   All definition of 'grant'
95 **IS** Reg 61(1) IS Regs
   JSA Reg 130 JSA Regs
   ESA Reg 131(1) ESA Regs
   HB Reg 53(1) HB Regs
   All definition of 'grant income'
96 **IS** Reg 62(3) IS Regs
   JSA Reg 131(4) JSA Regs
   ESA Reg 132(4) ESA Regs
   HB Reg 59(5) HB Regs
97 Sch 7 para 4 SS(C&P)Regs
98 **IS** Reg 61(1) IS Regs
   JSA Reg 1(3) JSA Regs
   ESA Reg 131(1) ESA Regs
   HB Reg 53 HB Regs
   All definition of 'period of study'

99 **IS** Reg 62(3A) IS Regs
   JSA Reg 131(5) JSA Regs
   ESA Reg 132(5) ESA Regs
   HB Reg 59(6) HB Regs
100 **IS** Reg 62(3) IS Regs
   JSA Reg 131(4) JSA Regs
   ESA Reg 132(4) ESA Regs
   HB Reg 59(5) HB Regs
101 **IS** Reg 62(3A) IS Regs; R(IS)15/95
   JSA Reg 131(5) JSA Regs
   ESA Reg 132(5) ESA Regs
   HB Reg 59(6) HB Regs
102 **IS** Reg 62(2) and (2A) IS Regs
   JSA Reg 131(2) and (3) JSA Regs
   ESA Reg 132(2) and (3) ESA Regs
   HB Reg 59(2) and (3) HB Regs
103 **IS/JSA** para 30328 DMG
   ESA para 51918 DMG
   HB paras C2/2.165-66 GM
104 **IS/JSA** paras 30329-30 DMG
   ESA paras 51919-20 DMG
   HB paras C2/2.170-73 GM
105 **IS** Reg 67A IS Regs
   JSA Reg 137A JSA Regs
   ESA Reg 141 ESA Regs
   HB Reg 67 HB Regs
106 **IS** Reg 67 IS Regs
   JSA Reg 137 JSA Regs
   ESA Reg 140 ESA Regs
   HB Reg 66 HB Regs
107 **IS** Schs 9 para 11 and 10 para 63 IS Regs
   JSA Schs 7 para 12 and 8 para 52 JSA Regs
   ESA Schs 8 para 13 and 9 para 52 ESA Regs
   HB Schs 5 para 11 and 6 para 51 HB Regs
108 **IS** Reg 62(2A) IS Regs
   JSA Reg 131(3) JSA Regs
   ESA Reg 132(3) ESA Regs
   HB Reg 59(3) HB Regs
109 CIS/91/1994
110 R(IS) 7/95
111 **IS** Reg 61(1) IS Regs
   JSA Reg 130 JSA Regs
   ESA Reg 131(1) ESA Regs
   HB Reg 53(1) HB Regs
   All definition of 'student loan'
112 **IS** Reg 66A(3) and (4) IS Regs
   JSA Reg 136(3) and (4) JSA Regs
   ESA Reg 137(4) and (5) ESA Regs
   HB Reg 64(3) and (4) HB Regs
113 Reg 137(4A) ESA Regs
114 **IS** Reg 66A(4) IS Regs
   ESA Reg 137(5) ESA Regs
   JSA Reg 136(4) JSA Regs

Part 7: Special benefit rules
Chapter 44: Benefits for students
Notes

115 **IS** Reg 62(3B) IS Regs
    ESA Reg 132(6) ESA Regs
    HB Reg 59(7) HB Regs
116 **IS** Reg 66C IS Regs
    JSA Reg 136B JSA Regs
    ESA Reg 139 ESA Regs
    HB Reg 64A HB Regs
117 **IS** Reg 67A IS Regs
    JSA Reg 137A JSA Regs
    ESA Reg 141 ESA Regs
    HB Reg 67 HB Regs
118 **IS** Reg 67 IS Regs
    JSA Reg 137 JSA Regs
    ESA Reg 140 ESA Regs
    HB Reg 66 HB Regs
119 **IS** Reg 66A(2) and (5) IS Regs
    JSA Reg 136(2) and (5) JSA Regs
    ESA Reg 137(3) and (6) ESA Regs
    HB Reg 64(2) and (5) HB Regs
120 R(IS) 7/95
121 **IS** Reg 61(1) IS Regs
    JSA Reg 130 JSA Regs
    ESA Reg 131(1) ESA Regs
    HB Reg 53(1) HB Regs
    All definition of 'academic year'
122 **IS** Reg 66A(2)(a) IS Regs
    JSA Reg 136(2)(a) JSA Regs
    ESA Reg 137(3)(a) ESA Regs
    HB Reg 64(2)(a) HB Regs
123 **IS** Reg 66A(2)(aa) IS Regs
    JSA Reg 136(2)(aa) JSA Regs
    ESA Reg 137(3)(b) ESA Regs
    HB Reg 64(2)(b) HB Regs
124 **IS** Reg 66A(2)(aa) IS Regs
    JSA Reg 136(2)(aa) JSA Regs
    ESA Regs 104(6) and 137(3)(c) ESA Regs
    HB Reg 64(2)(b) HB Regs
    All The Education (Student Support)
    (No.2) Regulations 2008, No.1582
125 CIS/3734/2004
126 **IS** Reg 41(6) IS Regs
    JSA Reg 104(5) JSA Regs
    ESA Reg 105(4) ESA Regs
    HB Reg 41(4) HB Regs
127 **IS** Sch 9 para 13 IS Regs
    JSA Sch 7 para 14 JSA Regs
    ESA Sch 8 para 15 ESA Regs
    HB Sch 5 para 13 HB Regs
128 R(IS) 16/95
129 **IS** Reg 61(1) IS Regs
    JSA Reg 130 JSA Regs
    ESA Reg 131(1) ESA Regs
    HB Reg 53(1) HB Regs
    All definition of 'access funds'

130 **IS** Reg 68(3) and (4) IS Regs
    JSA Reg 138(3) and (4) JSA Regs
    ESA Regs 2(1) and 142(3) ESA Regs
    HB Regs 2(1) and 68(3) and (4) HB Regs
131 **IS** Reg 66B IS Regs
    JSA Reg 136A JSA Regs
    ESA Regs 2(1) and 138 ESA Regs
    HB Regs 2(1) and 65 HB Regs
132 **IS** Reg 66B(4) IS Regs
    JSA Reg 136A(4) JSA Regs
    ESA Reg 138(4) ESA Regs
    HB Reg 65(5) HB Regs
133 **IS** Reg 66(1) IS Regs
    JSA Reg 135(1) JSA Regs
    ESA Reg 136(1) ESA Regs
    HB Reg 63 HB Regs
134 **IS** Sch 9 paras 13 and 61 IS Regs
    JSA Sch 7 paras 14 and 59 JSA Regs
    ESA Sch 8 paras 15 and 54 ESA Regs

7. Giving up, changing or taking time out from your course
135 CIS/368/1992; R(IS) 6/97
136 R(JSA) 2/02; CJSA/1965/2008
137 R(IS) 7/99
138 R(IS) 1/96
139 paras 30230-33 DMG; paras C2/2.41-42 GM
140 CIS/152/1994; R(IS) 15/98
141 **JSA** Reg 1(3D) and (3E) JSA Regs
    HB Reg 56(6) and (7) HB Regs
142 R(JSA) 3/02
143 *CM v SSWP* [2009] UKUT 43 (AAC); R(IS) 7/09
144 **IS** Regs 29(2B) and 32(6A) IS Regs
    JSA Regs 94(2B) and 97(7) JSA Regs
    ESA Regs 91(4) and 94(7) ESA Regs
145 para C2/2.425 GM
146 *Leeves v Chief Adjudication Officer*, reported as R(IS)5/99; reg 31(1) HB Regs
147 **IS** Reg 40(3A), (3AA), (3AAA) and (3AB) IS Regs
    JSA Reg 103(5), (5ZA), (5AZA) and (5ZB) JSA Regs
    ESA Reg 104(4)-(6) ESA Regs
    HB Reg 40(7)-(9) HB Regs
148 Reg 6(6)(a) SS&CS(DA) Regs; CJSA/549/03
149 para 30470 DMG; para C2/2.421 GM

Chapter 45

Benefits in hospital, prison and other special circumstances

This chapter covers:
1. Hospital patients (below)
2. People in care homes and similar accommodation (p950)
3. Prisoners (p958)
4. Paying for your normal home (p967)
5. People without accommodation (p969)
6. People involved in a trade dispute (p971)

People coming from or going abroad are covered in Chapters 69, 70 and 71. Benefits for 16/17-year-olds are covered in Chapter 43. People who are studying are covered in Chapter 44.

Key facts
- Many benefits are affected if you (or your partner, child or a non-dependant) are away from your normal home for a period because you are in hospital, a care home or prison.
- Some benefits are affected if you or your partner are involved in a trade dispute. In some cases, benefit is no longer paid; in others, it is paid at a reduced rate.
- Income support, income-based jobseeker's allowance and income-related employment and support allowance are paid at a reduced rate if you do not have accommodation.

1. Hospital patients

Many benefits are affected after you, your partner or child have been in hospital for a period. In some cases, benefit is no longer paid. In other cases, it is paid at a reduced rate. Until the period has passed, your benefits are paid as normal.

Part 7: Special benefit rules
Chapter 45: Benefits in hospital, prison and other special circumstances
1. Hospital patients

You can arrange for someone else to collect your benefit while you are in hospital and if you are unable to manage your affairs, someone else can act as your appointee.

Always inform the DWP (and local authority) promptly if your benefits may be affected by the rules described below to avoid being overpaid or underpaid.

Who counts as a patient

You count as a **'patient'** if you are being maintained free of charge while undergoing medical or other treatment as an inpatient in a hospital or 'similar institution' and the treatment is funded by the NHS, or the hospital (or similar institution) is maintained and administered by the Defence Council.[1] You should *not* count as a patient if you are getting treatment as a private patient, you are meeting the cost of your treatment in a private hospital or your placement is funded by a local authority.[2]

Note: the universal credit (UC) rules do not use the term 'patient' in the same way as the rules for other benefits. However, your UC may be affected if you (or your partner or child) have been absent from home in hospital for a period (see p949).

Definitions
'Hospitals' include all NHS hospitals, armed forces hospitals and special hospitals such as Broadmoor and Rampton. Prison hospital wings, however, do not count as hospitals.[3]
A **'similar institution'** is not defined in the rules, but can include some care homes, hospices and rehabilitation units that provide medical or nursing care.[4]
'Medical or other treatment' is treatment by a doctor, dentist or professionally qualified or trained nurse, or by someone under the supervision of such a person.[5]

If you are in a care home, you do not count as a patient merely because the NHS is contributing to the cost of your nursing care. However, if your nursing needs are more than merely incidental and ancillary to any other care needs you may have, the NHS should meet the care home costs in full. In this case, you may count as a patient. The NHS body concerned should make an assessment to see if you come under this rule. If it decides that you do, you are only treated as a patient for benefit purposes from the day of the decision.[6] However, if you are *not* getting medical or other treatment at the care home, but get this elsewhere (eg, at an out-patient clinic), you do not count as a patient, but you may be affected by the rules for care homes (see p951).[7]

Note: if you are detained in hospital serving a sentence of imprisonment under certain provisions, you may be treated as a prisoner for benefit purposes, not a patient (see p963).

When you count as a patient

You count as a patient from the day after the day you enter hospital (or a similar institution) up to and including:

- for attendance allowance (AA), disability living allowance (DLA) and personal independence payment (PIP), the day before the day you leave. However, for PIP only, if you go immediately from hospital (or a similar institution) to a care home or to prison, you count as a patient up to and including the day you leave;[8] *or*
- for other benefits, the day you leave.[9]

Example

Hilda is claiming DLA and income support (IS). She is taken ill and admitted to hospital on 1 January. After successful treatment, she is discharged on 21 January.

For DLA purposes, she counts as a patient from 2 January up to and including 20 January = 19 days.

For IS purposes, she counts as a patient from 2 January up to and including 21 January = 20 days.

Social fund payments

Social fund payments are generally not affected if you are a patient. However, you cannot get a winter fuel payment if you have been a patient for more than 52 weeks.[10] The definition of 'patient' is the same as for other benefits (see p942).

Jobseeker's allowance

You cannot qualify for jobseeker's allowance (JSA) if you have limited capability for work. So if you are in hospital for a period, you may have to claim employment and support allowance (ESA) or pension credit (PC) instead of JSA (or UC if you come under the UC system – see p19). If you are a member of a couple, your partner may have to claim IS, JSA, ESA or PC instead of you. However, if you are unable to work because you are sick, you can be treated as not having limited capability for work and as available for and actively seeking work:

- for two weeks;
- indefinitely, if you are absent from Great Briain for NHS hospital treatment.

See p695 for further information. The rules are the same for all types of JSA.

Note: if you come under the UC system (see p19) and are getting contribution-based JSA, during the periods above you are exempt from the work search requirement and you only have to be willing and able to take up work or attend an interview when you get out of hospital.

The amount of your income-based JSA can be affected if you or your partner or child are a patient for a period. See p946 for how means-tested benefits are affected

Part 7: Special benefit rules
Chapter 45: Benefits in hospital, prison and other special circumstances
1. Hospital patients

after 28 (or 84 days) and pp947–49 for how means-tested benefits are affected after 52 weeks. **Note:** if *you* are the patient, the rules are only relevant in the limited circumstances in which you can qualify for JSA while you are in hospital – eg, when you are abroad for NHS hospital treatment.

Benefits affected after 28 or 84 days

Payment of AA, DLA and PIP can be affected after you have been a patient for 28 (or 84 days). Entitlement to child benefit can be affected after your child has been a patient for 84 days. For information on how carer's allowance (CA) and means-tested benefits might then be affected, see pp945–46.

Attendance allowance, disability living allowance and personal independence payment

You are not paid:[11]

- AA, DLA or PIP after you have been a patient for **28 days**; *or*
- DLA for a child under 16 after s/he has been a patient for **84 days**.

Entitlement to AA, DLA or PIP continues even though payment ends. Therefore, payment can begin again following discharge from hospital. This can be at a daily rate if re-admission is expected within 28 days.[12]

There is a 28-day 'linking rule'. This means that:[13]

- different periods spent as a patient separated by 28 days or less are linked together and treated as one period; *and*
- periods spent as a resident in a care home (or, for PIP only, as a prisoner) link with periods spent as a patient if they are 28 days or less apart.

Example

Horace is claiming AA. He goes into hospital for an operation on 16 July and is discharged on 30 July. He counts as a patient from 17 July up to and including 29 July = 13 days. His AA is not affected by his stay in hospital.

Horace has to go back into hospital for further treatment on 10 August. He counts as a patient again from 11 August. As there are 28 days or less between his discharge and re-admission, the two spells in hospital are linked. When he has been a patient for a further 15 days, he cannot be paid AA.

Note:

- If you are awarded AA, DLA or PIP while you are a patient, payment cannot begin until you are discharged.[14]
- You can continue to be paid the mobility component of DLA while you are a patient if:[15]
  - you were a patient on 8 April 2013 and had a Motability agreement (see p610), but only until the agreement ends or, if earlier, 8 April 2016. You are

paid the amount payable under the agreement. If you leave hospital and become a patient again more than 28 days later, this rule no longer applies; *or*

– you have been a patient since 31 July 1995 (other than if you are 'sectioned' under the Mental Health Acts). You are paid at the lower rate (even if you would otherwise qualify for the higher rate). This transitional protection ends if you cease to be a patient for more than 28 consecutive days.

- If you are terminally ill, you can be paid AA, DLA or PIP while you are in a hospice, so long as the DWP has been informed that you are terminally ill.[16] In most cases, the DWP must be informed in writing.
- You continue to be exempt from the 'benefit cap' (see p1169) even if you, your partner or a child included in your claim are no longer receiving AA, DLA or PIP after being a patient for 28/84 days.[17]

Child benefit

Your entitlement to child benefit can be affected if your child is absent from home for a period. However, periods of up to 84 days when your child is receiving inpatient treatment in a hospital or similar institution are ignored. There are rules that can help you retain your entitlement to child benefit when your child has been absent from home in hospital for 84 days or more (see p556). If your child benefit entitlement *does* end, reclaim when s/he is discharged and returns home.

How other benefits are affected

If payment of AA, DLA or PIP or entitlement to child benefit ends, CA and means-tested benefits may be affected.

Carer's allowance

You no longer qualify for CA when the person you care for no longer receives AA, DLA or PIP – ie, after s/he has been a patient for 28 (or 84) days. If the person you care for is discharged and payment of AA, the DLA care component or the daily living component of PIP resumes, you can reclaim CA if you again satisfy the rules for entitlement. Your claim can be backdated to the date from which the AA or DLA is payable.[18] **Note:** this backdating rule does not apply when PIP becomes payable again. It is not known whether this is an error or the government's intention. See CPAG's online service and *Welfare Rights Bulletin* for updates.

Once you have been caring for a disabled person for a period, a temporary break in caring does not affect your CA (see p540), including if you (or the person you care for) are a patient. You can remain entitled to CA for up to 12 weeks in any period of 26 weeks. This can be useful if you (or the person you care for) are in and out of hospital. However, if the person you care for has been a patient for a total of 28 (or 84) days, s/he can no longer be paid AA, DLA or PIP (see above). Your entitlement to CA then ends, even if you have not yet had a break of 12 weeks.

Part 7: Special benefit rules
Chapter 45: Benefits in hospital, prison and other special circumstances
1. Hospital patients
. . . .

Means-tested benefits

When payment of your (or your partner's) AA, DLA or PIP stops:[19]

- if you are a single claimant, you are no longer entitled to the IS/JSA/ESA/HB severe disability premium (or severe disability additional amount for PC);
- if you are a member of a couple and you are getting the IS/JSA/ESA/HB severe disability premium (or additional amount for PC), you (or your partner) are treated as getting AA, DLA or PIP if the only reason you (or s/he) do not get it is that you (or s/he) are a patient. Your carer is treated as getting CA if s/he would be entitled to and receiving it, but for the fact that you (or your partner) have been a patient for longer than 28 days.[20] In this situation, you can therefore continue to qualify for the premium/additional amount. In all cases, it is paid at the single person's rate.

Entitlement to the disability premium (for IS, JSA and HB), the enhanced disability premium (for IS, JSA, ESA and HB) and the higher pensioner premium (for IS and JSA) are not affected by the payment of AA, DLA or PIP stopping.[21] However, these premiums can be affected once you (or your partner) have been a patient for 52 weeks (see p947).

Note: for IS only, if you are only in hospital for part of the week and are entitled to PIP when you are staying elsewhere, you can be paid, for example, the severe disability and enhanced disability premiums when you are staying away from the hospital from the date the change occurs (or is expected to occur).[22]

When payment of your child's DLA or PIP stops:

- entitlement to the disabled child and enhanced disability premiums in HB (and IS or income-based JSA if still included) is not affected, so long as s/he continues to be included in your claim (see p210).[23] However, for IS and income-based JSA, these premiums (if still included) *are* affected once your child has been a patient for 52 weeks (see p947);
- the UC disabled child addition to the child element is not affected.[24]

Note: if child benefit stops because your child is no longer living with you, this may affect whether s/he is included in your claim (see p210). If s/he is no longer included, you can no longer get personal allowances and premiums for her/him in your HB (or IS or income-based JSA if still included), or a UC child element.

If you no longer satisfy the conditions of entitlement for CA because the AA, DLA or PIP of the person you care for stops:

- the IS/JSA/ESA/HB carer premium (or carer additional amount for PC) can continue to be paid for up to eight weeks after CA entitlement stops (see p237). After that, you are no longer entitled to a carer premium (or additional amount). If you lose your CA because *you* are a patient, the person you were caring for may become entitled to the severe disability premium (or additional amount);
- you are no longer entitled to the UC carer element.[25]

Benefits affected after 52 weeks

Some benefits are affected after you, your partner or child (or a non-dependant, or an adult for whom you are getting an increase in a non-means-tested benefit) have been a patient for more than 52 weeks. See below for means-tested benefits other than UC, p949 for non-means-tested benefits and p949 for how UC is affected.

Means-tested benefits

For IS, JSA, ESA, PC and HB, you still count as a couple while you and your partner are only temporarily apart. However, you no longer count as a couple if you are likely to be separated for more than 52 weeks or, in exceptional circumstances, such as a stay in hospital, substantially more than 52 weeks.[26] If you no longer count as a couple, your means-tested benefits are assessed as if you are a single claimant (or lone parent).

If your child has been in hospital for a period, s/he may no longer count as a member of your houshold (see p214) and is no longer included in your claim.

Note:

- HB and help with your housing costs may no longer be payable once you have been away from home for a period. For information about paying for your normal home while you are a patient, see p967.
- If you have a non-dependant living with you and s/he has been a patient for 52 weeks, non-dependant deductions made for her/him stop (see p969).
- For HB , if you are a member of a couple, a deduction for childcare charges can be made from earnings if one of you is in full-time paid work and the other is in hospital (see p270 and p311).

The rate of IS, income-based JSA or income-related ESA may be lower if you (or your partner or child) have been a patient for a continuous period of more than 52 weeks, because you are no longer entitled to certain premiums. You may have already lost the severe disability and carer premiums after 28 (or 84) days (see p946). HB is likewise affected, but only if you are not (or are no longer) entitled to IS, income-based JSA or income-related ESA.

There are no 'linking rules' with these provisions. This means that, if you are discharged from hospital and then are re-admitted, a new period as a patient starts and you can again be entitled to IS, income-based JSA, income-related ESA or HB premiums at the rate you were getting before admission to hospital.

Premiums and components: single claimants and lone parents

If you are a single claimant or a lone parent and you have been a patient for more than 52 weeks:[27]

- the disability premium is not included in your IS or income-based JSA, the higher pensioner premium is not included in your income-based JSA and the enhanced disability premium is not included in your IS, income-based JSA or

Part 7: Special benefit rules
Chapter 45: Benefits in hospital, prison and other special circumstances
1. Hospital patients

income-related ESA applicable amount. The work-related activity component and the support component are not included in your income-related ESA applicable amount. **Note:** if you qualify, the pensioner premium *is* included in your income-based JSA applicable amount;

- HB may be paid at a reduced rate. The enhanced disability premium is not included in your applicable amount.[28] However, the disability premium (or the work-related activity or support component) can still be included.

Premiums and components: couples

If you are a member of a couple and:

- both you and your partner have been a patient for more than 52 weeks, the higher pensioner and enhanced disability premiums are not included in your IS, income-based JSA or income-related ESA applicable amount and the disability premium is not included in your IS or income-based JSA applicable amount. The work-related component and the support component are not included in your income-related ESA applicable amount. **Note:** the pensioner premium *is* included in your IS applicable amount if your partner qualifies or in your income-based JSA or income-related ESA applicable amount if you or your partner qualifies;[29]
- both you and your partner have been a patient for more than 52 weeks, HB may be paid at a reduced rate. The enhanced disability premium is not included in your applicable amount.[30] However, the disability premium can still be included.
- only one of you has been a patient for more than 52 weeks:
  - for IS and income-based JSA, you are paid the normal rate, but without any of the premiums that are only included in your applicable amount for the one who is the patient, other than the pensioner premium;[31]
  - for income-related ESA, you are paid the normal rate if you are the patient. However, if your partner is the patient, you are paid the normal rate less any premiums and any work-related activity or support component.[32] In the latter case, you are better off if you can be assessed as a single claimant or lone parent (see p947).

Premiums: children

If you have a child and you (or s/he) are a patient, s/he may no longer be included in your claim once you (or s/he) have been away from home for a period (see p210). If this happens, you can no longer get allowances and premiums for your child with HB (and IS or income-based JSA, if still included). However, if s/he is still included in your claim:

- you are paid the normal rate of HB. Your entitlement to the disabled child and enhanced disability premiums is not affected if you or your child has been a patient for more than 52 weeks;[33]

- if your child is the patient, your IS or income-based JSA still includes amounts and premiums for your child (see p220) and you are paid the normal rate, less any disabled child premium and enhanced disability premium included in your applicable amount for your child.[34]

Non-means-tested benefits

Contributory ESA may be paid at a reduced rate if you have been a patient for a continuous period of more than 52 weeks. You are paid the normal rate, less any work-related activity or support component.[35] **Note:** in practical terms, if you are in the 'work-related activity group' once you have been receiving contributory ESA for a year, you are not paid any contributory ESA (see p625).

Increases for an adult or a child

If you are still entitled to an increase in a non-means-tested benefit for an adult or child (eg, with CA or incapacity benefit), this is no longer payable once you (or both you and the adult or child) have been a patient for 52 weeks, unless you apply to the DWP to pay the increase on your behalf to:[36]

- the person for whom the increase is paid; *or*
- someone else approved by the DWP. The DWP must be satisfied that the payment will be used for the benefit of:
  - the person for whom the increase is paid, if you are a patient; *or*
  - at least one of your children, if both you and the person are patients.

There are no 'linking rules' with this provision. This means that if you (or the person for whom you are paid the increase) are discharged from hospital and are then re-admitted, a new period as a patient starts and you can be paid the increase again. Remember that if an increase for a child stops being paid for more than 58 days, you might lose your entitlement to it. If you cease to satisfy the conditions for an increase for an adult, you may lose your entitlement to it. See the chapter in this *Handbook* about the benefit you are claiming.

Universal credit

Your UC is generally calculated in the usual way until you (or your partner or child) have been in hospital for more than six months. You may already have lost the carer element (see p946) or the disabled child addition. UC may also be affected if a non-dependant has been in hospital for more than six months (see p969).

Couples

You and your partner continue to count as a couple while one of you is temporarily absent from the household, including when one of you is in hospital. You must continue to make a joint claim with your partner and UC is paid as normal. If the one who is not in hospital is working, you may qualify for a

Part 7: Special benefit rules
Chapter 45: Benefits in hospital, prison and other special circumstances
2. People in care homes and similar accommodation

childcare costs element (see p253). However, if the absence exceeds (or is expected to exceed) six months, you no longer count as a couple.[37] If you no longer count as a couple:

- you can no longer make a joint claim for UC;
- the calculation of your benefit no longer includes amounts for your partner;
- if you live in rented accommodation, the amount of your housing costs element may be affected (see p969).

Children

A child continues to be included in your claim while s/he is temporarily absent from your household because s/he is in hospital. However, s/he is no longer included in your claim if the absence exceeds (or is expected to exceed) six months.[38] If your child is no longer included in your claim:

- the calculation of your benefit no longer includes amounts for her/him;
- if you live in rented accommodation, the amount of your housing costs element may be affected (see p969);
- the work-related requirements you must meet may change (see Chapter 50).

2. People in care homes and similar accommodation

Most benefits are paid as normal if you live in a care home or similar type of accommodation. However, some benefits are no longer payable and some might be paid at a reduced rate. **Note:** if your place in a care home is funded by the NHS, you may count as a 'patient'. In this case, your benefits are affected by the rules for patients instead.

Always inform the DWP (and local authority) promptly if your benefits may be affected by the rules described below, to avoid being overpaid or underpaid.

Care homes and similar accommodation
There is not sufficient space in this *Handbook* to cover the different kinds of care homes and similar accommodation, and the funding arrangements for people living in them. Some homes are run by local authorities and some are independent. You may be able to get help from the local authority with your care home fees, or you may have to pay these yourself. What help you can get to pay for your place depends on whether it is funded by the NHS or by the local authority. Local authority help is means tested, so you may have to contribute part of the cost.

Attendance allowance, disability living allowance and personal independence payment

You cannot usually be paid attendance allowance (AA), disability living allowance (DLA) care component or the daily living component of personal independence payment (PIP) once you have been a resident in a care home for a period of 28 days if any of the 'costs of any qualifying services' provided for you are borne out of public or local funds under specified provisions (see p952).[39] Until then, AA, DLA care component and PIP daily living component are paid as normal. See below for exceptions to these rules.

You count as in a care home if it is an establishment that provides you with accommodation as well as nursing or personal care.[40]

Note:
- DLA *mobility* component and PIP *mobility* component, and armed forces independence payment, are paid as normal however long you are a resident in a care home.
- If you are awarded AA, the care component of DLA or the daily living component of PIP while you are resident in a care home, you cannot be paid for the time you stay in the accommodation.[41]

Entitlement to AA, DLA or PIP continues even though payment ends. Therefore, payment can begin again when you are no longer resident in a care home. If you expect to return within 28 days, you can be paid at a daily rate from when you leave.[42]

Note: you continue to be exempt from the 'benefit cap' (see p1169) even if you or your partner or child are no longer receiving AA, DLA or PIP after being resident in a care home for 28 days.[43]

'**Qualifying services**' means the costs of accommodation, board and personal care.[44] For AA and DLA, the 'costs of any qualifying services' does *not* include the cost of:[45]
- domiciliary services (including personal care) provided in a private dwelling;
- improvements to, or furniture or equipment provided for:
  - a private dwelling because of the needs of a disabled person;
  - a care home, for which a grant or payment was made out of public funds, except where the grant or payment is of a regular or repeated nature;
- social and recreational activities outside the care home;
- buying or running a motor vehicle used in connection with any qualifying service provided in the care home.

Note:
- If the NHS provides nursing services in a care home and your nursing needs are more than merely incidental and ancillary to other care needs, you are treated as a 'patient' for AA, DLA and PIP purposes (see p942).[46]

Part 7: Special benefit rules
Chapter 45: Benefits in hospital, prison and other special circumstances
2. People in care homes and similar accommodation

- If the local authority pays for the services, it assesses what you must pay towards the costs, using a means test that takes account of your income and capital. You may lose AA, DLA or PIP even though you are meeting some of the costs yourself. There are exceptions to the rules (see below). If you are self-funding, see p953.
- If you think the DWP has refused payment of AA, DLA or PIP wrongly, you can apply for a revision or appeal against the refusal. **Note:** you are likely to have to apply for a revision before you can appeal.

Specified provisions

The '**specified provisions**' are:[47]

– Part III of the National Assistance Act 1948, sections 59 and 59A of the Social Work (Scotland) Act 1968, the Mental Health (Care and Treatment) (Scotland) Act 2003, the Community Care and Health (Scotland) Act 2002, the Mental Health Act 1983 and section 57 of the Health and Social Care Act 2001; *or*

– any other Acts relating to people with disabilities or (in the case of DLA and PIP only) young people, education or training – eg, in some special residential schools.

In most cases, a local authority pays for the services in a care home under one of these provisions, but it is always worth checking. Local authorities also have powers to provide accommodation under housing legislation and the Local Government Act 1972, in which case AA, DLA and PIP are not affected.[48] **Note:** the First-tier Tribunal is entitled to decide that your placement is being funded under a different legal power than the one the local authority has stated.[49]

Exceptions to the rules

There are exceptions to the rules. You can continue to be paid AA, the care component of DLA and the daily living component of PIP even *after* 28 days, if:

- you are terminally ill and are in a hospice, so long as the DWP has been informed that you are terminally ill. In most cases, the DWP must be informed in writing;[50] *or*
- for DLA and PIP only, you are a student and the cost of your accommodation is wholly or partly met from a student grant or loan, or from a grant made to education institutions under specified legislation;[51] *or*
- you are under 16 (for DLA) and being looked after by a local authority, or under 18 (for DLA and PIP) and receiving services from your local authority because of your disability or health, but only if you have been placed by the local authority in a private dwelling with a family, a relative or some other suitable person;[52] *or*
- for DLA and PIP, your accommodation is outside the UK and the costs of any qualifying services are being borne by a local authority under specified legislation relating to education – eg, at the Higashi School.[53]

If you are self-funding

You can continue to be paid AA, the care component of DLA and the daily living component of PIP even *after* 28 days if you are meeting the whole costs of all the 'qualifying services' from your own resources, or with the help of another person or a charity – known as 'self-funding'.[54] This applies whether you are in an independent or local authority home. You count as self-funding even if:

- you are claiming benefits such as income support (IS), employment and support allowance (ESA), pension credit (PC), universal credit (UC), AA, DLA or PIP; *or*
- a local authority has arranged and contracted to pay for your placement, so long as you are paying the whole costs of all the 'qualifying services'.

This also applies if a local authority is temporarily funding your placement while you sell a property – eg, your former home, or where you have entered into what is known as a 'deferred payment agreement'. You must be liable and able to repay the local authority in full when the property is sold, or when payment under the deferred agreement falls due (known as 'retrospective self-funding').[55]

Are you likely to become self-funding?

If you move into a care home and are initially receiving help with the fees from the local authority, the DWP should suspend payment of your AA, DLA or PIP if you are likely to become self-funding in the future (eg, if you are only getting local authority help while you sell your former home, or your capital is likely to increase above the limit of the local authority's means test). When you repay the local authority and become self-funding, payment can resume and any arrears can be paid to you. However, if the DWP terminated payment of your AA, DLA or PIP and refuses to pay you arrears when you become self-funding, you can argue that the decision to terminate payment should be revised on the grounds of 'official error'.[56]

When you count as being a resident in a care home

The general rule is that you do not count as a resident in a care home on the day you enter and the day you leave.[57] However, if you:[58]

- are a patient in a hospital or similar institution (or, for PIP only, a prisoner) and enter a care home, you count as a resident in the care home from:
  - for benefits other than PIP, the day you enter;
  - for PIP, the day after the day you enter; *and*
- leave a care home and enter a hospital or similar institution as a patient (or, for PIP only, become a prisoner), you cease to count as a resident in the care home on the day after you leave.

There is a 28-day 'linking rule'. This means that different periods as a resident in a care home separated by 28 days or less link together for the purpose of calculating

Part 7: Special benefit rules
Chapter 45: Benefits in hospital, prison and other special circumstances
2. People in care homes and similar accommodation

the 28 days for which you can continue to be paid AA, the care component of DLA or the daily living component of PIP. Periods spent as a patient in a hospital or similar institution (or, for PIP only, as a prisoner) also count towards the 28-day limit on payment if they are separated by 28 days or less from periods when you are resident in a care home in the circumstances described above.[59]

It can be important to plan periods of respite care in the light of the linking rules so that you can continue to be paid AA, the DLA care component and the daily living component of PIP for as long as possible. This also enables your carer to keep her/his carer's allowance (CA).

How other benefits are affected

If payment of AA, DLA care component or the daily living component of PIP to the person you care for stops, CA is affected in the same way as for hospital patients (see p945). Remember that the carer premium (carer's additional amount for PC) can continue to be paid for up to eight weeks after CA stops (see p237). However, if you no longer satisfy the conditions of entitlement for CA, you are no longer entitled to the UC carer element.[60]

Once payment of AA, DLA care component or PIP daily living component stops because you have been resident in a care home for 28 days, you are no longer entitled to the severe disability premium with IS, income-based jobseeker's allowance (JSA), income-related ESA or housing benefit (HB) (or severe disability additional amount for PC). In addition, you may no longer be entitled to the disability, enhanced disability or higher pensioner premium if the only reason you qualified was because you were receiving AA, DLA care component or PIP daily living component.

Note:
- For IS and ESA only, if you only live in a care home part of the week and are entitled to DLA when you are staying elsewhere, you can be paid, for example, the severe disability and enhanced disability premiums when you are staying away from the care home from the date the change occurs (or is expected to occur).[61] For ESA, this also applies if you are entitled to PIP when you are staying elsewhere.
- For ESA only, you qualify for the enhanced disability premium if you are getting the ESA support component, even if you are not receiving DLA care component or PIP daily living component.
- if you are still being paid AA, DLA care component or PIP daily living component (eg, because you have not yet been in a care home for 28 days), you may be entitled to a severe disability premium, even if you were not before – eg, if you are no longer treated as living with a non-dependant or a partner.

If your partner or child is living in a care home, see p556 for how child benefit may be affected, p956 for how your means-tested benefits (other than UC) are affected and p957 for how your UC is affected.

Means-tested benefits

How your IS, income-based JSA, income-related ESA, PC and HB are affected depends on whether you (or your partner or child) are temporarily or permanently living in a care home. If you are in a care home (on either basis), these benefits are generally calculated in the usual way but, if payment of your AA, DLA care component or PIP daily living component stops, you may no longer be entitled to certain premiums (see p954). For information about paying for your normal home, see p967.

Care homes

For IS, JSA, ESA, PC and HB, when the term 'care home' is used, it means:[62]
– a care home (a care home service in Scotland) as defined in s3 of the Care Standards Act 2000 or paragraph 2 of Schedule 12 to the Public Services Reform (Scotland) Act 2010. So long as the home comes within the definition, it counts as a care home even if it also has some other function, such as an educational institution;[63]
– an Abbeyfield Home run by the Abbeyfield Society or affiliates of that society;
– an independent hospital (an independent healthcare service in Scotland) as defined in s275 of the National Health Service Act 2006 (in England) other than a health service hospital, s2 of the Care Standards Act 2000 (in Wales) or s10F(1)(a) and (b) of the National Health Service (Scotland) Act 1978 (in Scotland).
If you are not sure if you live in a relevant home, seek advice.

Note:
- If you have a partner, you may no longer count as a couple if you (or your partner) are resident in a care home. If your child is resident in a care home, s/he may no longer be included in your claim (see p956).
- For PC, if you have an 'assessed income period' (see p89), it comes to an end if you do not have a partner and are provided with accommodation in a care home (other than in an Abbeyfield Home) on a permanent basis. This means your income may be subject to reassessment.[64]

Housing benefit for your care home

You cannot usually get HB for the rent you pay to your care home.[65] For these purposes, a care home does *not* include an Abbeyfield Home. There are exceptions if you were entitled to HB for your care home when the rules changed at various times in the past and you have transitional protection.[66]

Note: if you are on a placement under the Adult Placement Scheme (a scheme similar to fostering, but for adults) living with an approved carer, the normal conditions of entitlement to HB apply.[67] You *can* get HB for the rent you pay.

Part 7: Special benefit rules
Chapter 45: Benefits in hospital, prison and other special circumstances
2. People in care homes and similar accommodation

Tariff income

For IS, income-based JSA, income-related ESA and, if you and your partner are under the qualifying age for PC (see p78), HB, if you are permanently resident in a care home the threshold for calculating your tariff income is increased to £10,000 (see p343). This also applies if you live in Polish resettlement accommodation (certain care homes for Polish people who came to the UK as refugees after the Second World War). Some temporary absences from the care home or resettlement accommodation are ignored.[68] For HB, the £10,000 threshold is only relevant (and only applies) in the limited situations in which you can get HB while living in a care home. For PC and, if you or your partner are at least the qualifying age for PC, HB, the threshold is always £10,000 (see p376).

Partners and children

If **you or your partner** move into a care home:

*   **permanently** (for PC only, other than to an Abbeyfield Home), you no longer count as a couple.[69] This also applies if you and your partner are both in care homes permanently, even if you are in the same home and the same room.[70] If you do not count as a couple, your benefit, and that of your partner, is calculated as if you are single claimants;
*   **temporarily**, you still count as a couple if you intend to live together again. This only applies if you are unlikely to be apart for more than 52 weeks or, in exceptional circumstances, substantially longer than 52 weeks.[71] If you still count as a couple:
    *   for PC and HB, your benefit continues to be assessed under the normal rules. This means that, once the person in the care home stops getting AA, DLA care component or PIP daily living component, no severe disability premium (or additional amount) for either of you can be included in your applicable amount;
    *   for IS, income-based JSA and income-related ESA, your applicable amount is calculated in a special way. You receive the amount for two single claimants if this is higher than the amount you receive as a couple. This can include the severe disability premium in respect of either or both of you, as if you were single claimants, even if you are not normally entitled to it at home.[72]

If child benefit stops because **your child** lives in a care home or is being looked after by a local authority, this may affect whether s/he is included in your claim (see p210). If your child is no longer included, you can no longer get a personal allowance and premiums for her/him in your HB (or your IS or income-based JSA, if still included – see p220). Entitlement to premiums for your child is also affected if s/he is no longer paid DLA or PIP.

Universal credit

How your UC is affected depends on whether you (or your partner or child) are temporarily or permanently living in a care home and, if only temporarily, the length of time you (or s/he) have been absent from your household. If the absence is temporary, your UC is generally calculated in the usual way until you (or your partner or child) have been (or are expected to be) living in a care home for more than six months. UC may also be affected if a non-dependant has been living in a care home for more than six months (see p969).

For the definition of 'care home', see p955. The meaning is the same as for other means-tested benefits, but it does not include an Abbeyfield Home.[73] **Note:** you cannot get the UC housing costs element for the rent you pay to your care home.[74]

Couples

You and your partner continue to count as a couple while one of you is temporarily absent from the household, including when one of you is in a care home. You must continue to make a joint claim and UC is paid as normal. If the one who is not living in a care home is working, you may qualify for the childcare costs element (see p253). However, if the absence is permanent or it exceeds (or is likely to exceed) six months, you no longer count as a couple.[75] If you no longer count as a couple:

- you can no longer make a joint claim for UC;
- the calculation of your benefit no longer includes amounts for your partner;
- if you live in rented accommodation, the amount of your housing costs element may be affected (see p969).

Children

A child continues to be included in your claim while s/he is temporarily absent from your household because s/he is in a care home. However, s/he is no longer included in your claim if the absence exceeds (or is expected to exceed) six months.[76] If your child is no longer included in your claim:

- the calculation of your benefit no longer includes amounts for her/him;
- if you live in rented accommodation, the amount of your housing costs element may be affected (see p969);
- the work-related requirements you must meet may change (see Chapter 50).

Social fund payments

Some social fund payments are affected if you are in a care home. You cannot get:
- a cold weather payment if you are in a care home (see p955 for the meaning) or Polish resettlement accommodation, unless you are responsible for a child under five or you are getting child tax credit which includes a disabled child or severely disabled child element. **Note:** you are *not* exempt from this rule simply

Part 7: Special benefit rules
Chapter 45: Benefits in hospital, prison and other special circumstances
3. Prisoners

because you are getting UC which includes an increase for a disabled or severely disabled child. It is not known it this is an error or the intention;[77]
* a winter fuel payment if you are getting income-based JSA, income-related ESA or PC and are (and for a period have been) in a care home or Polish resettlement accommodation (see p780).[78]

3. Prisoners

Most benefits are affected if you are a prisoner. Some are not payable, some are suspended and some are only payable for a temporary period. There are issues to consider if you are given an alternative sentence to prison.

Always inform the DWP (and local authority) as soon as you, or a member of your family, enter or leave prison to avoid any underpayment or overpayment of benefit. If you are being held on remand and are then sentenced, notifiy the benefit authorities as soon as this happens. Do *not* assume that the prison will do this for you.

Non-means-tested benefits

You are disqualified from getting most non-means-tested benefits while you are a prisoner. For statutory sick pay (SSP), statutory maternity pay (SMP), statutory adoption pay (SAP) and statutory paternity pay (SPP), see below. For other non-means-tested benefits, see p959. In some cases, payment of your benefit is only suspended pending the outcome of your trial or sentence (see p960). For benefits that are payable, see p960.

Note: non-means-tested benefits (other than SSP, SMP, SAP and SPP) are not affected if you are detained, as a result of a criminal conviction, in a hospital or similar institution as a person with a mental disorder, unless this is under specified provisions (see p963).[79] However, check whether your benefit is affected under the special rules for hospital patients instead.

Statutory sick, maternity, adoption and paternity pay

If you are detained in legal custody or sentenced to a term of imprisonment (except if the sentence is suspended) you:[80]
* are not entitled to SSP. In addition, you are not entitled during any subsequent period during the same period of incapacity for work;
* cannot be paid SMP or ordinary SPP for the whole of your maternity or paternity pay period (see p794), even if you are released from prison during it. If you cannot be paid SMP, check to see if you can be paid maternity allowance (MA) instead.

However, you are paid SAP or additional SPP for any period during which you are detained in custody if you are subsequently released without charge or after being found not guilty, or you are convicted but do not receive a custodial sentence. Payment of SAP or additional SPP should also resume for any period of entitlement subsequent to your release.

Note: you do not count as in legal custody if you are on bail, or living in approved premises (eg, a bail or probation hostel), or are simply helping the police with their enquiries.

Other non-means-tested benefits

If you count as a prisoner you cannot be paid attendance allowance (AA), bereavement benefits, disability living allowance (DLA), carer's allowance (CA), contributory employment and support allowance (ESA), incapacity benefit (IB), MA, reduced earnings allowance (REA), retirement allowance, retirement pension or severe disablement allowance (SDA).[81] However, see p960 to check if your benefit is only suspended pending trial or sentence.

You are paid **personal independence payment** (PIP) for the first 28 days that you count as a prisoner, whatever the outcome of the proceedings against you.[82] However, this does not apply if you are awarded PIP while you are a prisoner.[83] There is a 'linking rule' that means that different periods spent as a prisoner separated by one year or less are linked together and treated as one period.[84] Periods spent in a care home or hospital are also linked with periods spent as a prisoner (see p944 and p953).

You cannot be paid an **increase in CA, IB, retirement pension or SDA for your spouse or civil partner** if s/he is a prisoner.[85] Your entitlement to an increase in these benefits for an adult looking after a child ends if the adult is a prisoner.[86] If your entitlement ends, you might not be able to claim it again. See the chapter in this *Handbook* about the benefit you are claiming for information. This rule is not relevant for the other benefits listed above as there are no increases for a spouse/civil partner/adult caring for a child.

For non-means-tested benefits that are payable, see p960.

Prisoners

You count as a '**prisoner**' if you are imprisoned or detained in legal custody (in Great Britain or abroad) in connection with criminal proceedings – ie, not for civil offences.[87] You therefore do *not* count as a prisoner and benefits are payable, provided you satisfy the normal rules of entitlement, if you are:

– on bail, or living in approved premises – eg, a bail or probation hostel;
– released on parole, temporary licence or under a home detention curfew (electronic tagging).

Note: there are issues for **contribution-based jobseeker's allowance** (JSA) while you are in prison. If you:

Part 7: Special benefit rules
Chapter 45: Benefits in hospital, prison and other special circumstances
3. Prisoners

- do not come under the universal credit (UC) system (see p19), you are unable to satisfy the jobseeking conditions. In addition, you are treated as unavailable for work if you are a prisoner on temporary release. This means you cannot qualify for (and therefore cannot be paid) JSA. However, unless you count as a prisoner, you are treated as available for and actively seeking work during temporary police detention (legal custody in Scotland) of up to 96 hours (see Chapter 48);
- come under the UC system, you are unable to meet the work-related requirements. In addition, you are treated as not having met the work availability requirement if you are a prisoner on temporary release under specified provisions.[88] However, you may be able to satisfy the DWP that you should not have to meet a work search requirement during temporary police detention (legal custody in Scotland) (see p1080).

Benefits suspended

If you are a remand prisoner awaiting trial or sentence, payment of contributory ESA, IB, SDA, AA, DLA, CA, MA, REA, retirement pension, retirement allowance and bereavement benefits is suspended pending the outcome. An increase of CA, IB, retirement pension or SDA for your spouse or civil partner is suspended if s/he is a remand prisoner. If you (or s/he) subsequently receive a sentence of imprisonment or detention (including a suspended sentence), you are not paid the benefits for the whole period you are in prison.[89]

If you (or your spouse or civil partner) do not receive a sentence of imprisonment or detention, or your conviction is quashed, full arrears of any of the benefits that have been withheld are payable when you are released.[90] Arrears are only payable if the normal conditions of entitlement for benefit were met while you (or your spouse/civil partner) were a remand prisoner. For the purpose of entitlement to an increase in your benefit for a spouse or civil partner, you should be treated as still 'residing with' her/him while s/he is in prison, unless your marriage/partnership has broken down and your separation is likely to be permanent.[91]

Benefits payable

You are entitled to **disablement benefit** (but not any of the increases discussed on p679) for periods when you are a prisoner. However, you are not paid until you are released and you can only get a maximum of 12 months' arrears.[92] If you are in prison for more than a year, you should be paid for the 12-month period which gives you the most benefit.[93] You are entitled to full arrears for any period you were on remand, if you are not subsequently sentenced to imprisonment or detention.[94]

You are entitled to **child benefit** and **guardian's allowance**:[95]

- while you are a prisoner. You must continue to be 'responsible' for the child (see p556). If you are in prison for some time, you may want to arrange for child benefit to be paid to the person looking after your child;
- while your child is a prisoner, but entitlement to child benefit usually ends after eight weeks.[96] There are exceptions to the rules (see p562). Full arrears are payable at the end of any period of remand if your child is not sentenced to imprisonment or detention. Once entitlement to child benefit ends, entitlement to guardian's allowance in respect of the child also ends.

Note: if child benefit stops because your child is a prisoner, this may affect whether you can get an increase for her/him with your non-means-tested benefits, and personal allowances and premiums for her/him with your housing benefit (HB) (and income support (IS) or income-based JSA if still included). If you lose the increase in your non-means-tested benefits (or the allowance and premiums included in your IS or income-based JSA), you may no longer qualify for these. For increases for a child, see the chapter in this *Handbook* about the benefit you are claiming. For IS and JSA, see p220.

Means-tested benefits

For means-tested benefits other than UC, if you count as a prisoner:
- you cannot qualify for income-based JSA as you are unable to satisfy the jobseeking conditions. If you need help with your housing costs for your home, you must claim IS, income-related ESA or pension credit (PC) for this (see p968);
- you can qualify for IS, income-related ESA and the PC guarantee credit for up to 52 weeks while you are detained in custody awaiting trial or sentence. However, you only get the amount for help with your housing costs (see p968). Once you have been sentenced, you are no longer entitled to any IS, income-related ESA or PC;[97]
- you can qualify for HB for a period while you are a prisoner (see p968);
- you cannot get any savings credit of PC;[98]
- you may be entitled to the PC severe disability additional amount if you do not receive a sentence of imprisonment and you are given arrears of AA or DLA on your release.[99]

If you have a **non-dependant** who is a prisoner, no non-dependant deduction is made for her/him.[100] However, for HB you may no longer qualify for a bedroom for her/him after a period. See p116 and p450 for further information about non-dependant deductions.

Part 7: Special benefit rules
Chapter 45: Benefits in hospital, prison and other special circumstances
3. Prisoners

For information about UC if you (or your partner or child) are a prisoner, see below.

Prisoners

For IS, JSA, ESA, PC and HB, you count as a **'prisoner'** if you are:[101]

– detained in custody (eg, in prison or a young offenders' institution) awaiting trial or sentence (on remand) or following a sentence of imprisonment; *or*

– on temporary release under specific provisions (this does not include parole licence).

You do not count as a prisoner if you are detained in hospital under specific mental health provisions (but see p963 if you received a prison sentence as a result of a criminal conviction). Check to see if your benefit is affected by the special rules for hospital patients instead. In addition, you do not count as a prisoner if you are:

- released on licence or parole; *or*
- on bail or living in approved premises – eg, a bail or probation hostel; *or*
- released under a home detention curfew (electronic tagging).

If you are a prisoner and have a partner or children, or if your partner (or child) is a prisoner, see below.

Partners and children

If you have a **partner** and one of you is a prisoner:

- you no longer count as a couple for IS, income-based JSA, income-related ESA or PC purposes;[102]
- you continue to count as a couple for HB purposes, so long as you intend to live together again and the prisoner is unlikely to be away for substantially longer than 52 weeks.[103] If the one who is not a prisoner is working, s/he may be able to have childcare costs deducted from her/his earnings (see p270 and p311).[104]

If you no longer count as a couple, the one who is *not* a prisoner can claim benefit as a single person (or lone parent).

If child benefit stops because **your child** is a prisoner, s/he might no longer be included in your claim. If s/he is no longer included in your claim, entitlement to a personal allowance and premiums for her/him with your HB (and with your IS or income-based JSA if they are still included – see p220) might be affected.

Universal credit

If you count as a prisoner, you can qualify for UC for up to six months. However, you only get the amount of the UC housing costs element. See p968 for details.

If your partner or a child included in your claim is a prisoner, see below. If you have a non-dependant who is a prisoner, no deduction is made from your housing costs element for housing costs contributions (see p496), but you may no longer qualify for a bedroom for her/him after a period (see p495).[105]

Prisoners

For UC, you count as a '**prisoner**' if you are:[106]
- detained in custody (eg, in prison or a young offenders' institution) awaiting trial or sentence (on remand) or following a sentence of imprisonment; *or*
- on temporary release under specific provisions (this does not include parole licence).

You do not count as a prisoner if you are detained in hospital under specific mental health provisions unless you are serving a prison sentence as a result of a criminal conviction (see below). See p949 to see how your benefit may be affected if you (or your partner or a child) are in hospital. In addition, you do not count as a prisoner if you are:
- released on licence or parole; *or*
- on bail or living in approved premises – eg, a bail or probation hostel; *or*
- released under a home detention curfew (electronic tagging).

Couples

If you are a member of a couple and one of you is a prisoner, or is serving a prison sentence while detained in hospital, the other member of the couple can claim UC as a single claimant, however long the term of imprisonment.[107] So long as you still count as a couple, your and your partner's income and capital are still assessed jointly, but the amount of your UC is that for a single person. If the one who is not a prisoner is working, you may qualify for a childcare costs element (see p253). In any case, if the absence from the household exceeds (or is expected to exceed) six months, you no longer count as a couple.[108] The amount of your housing costs element for rent payments may be affected (see p967).

Children

If your child is a prisoner, s/he can no longer be included in your claim (see p213).[109] If your child is no longer included in your claim:
- the calculation of your benefit no longer includes amounts for her/him;
- the amount of your housing costs element for rent payments may be affected (see p967);
- the work-related requirements you must meet may change (see Chapter 50).

Person with a mental disorder

For non-means-tested benefits (other than contribution-based JSA, SSP, SMP, SAP and SPP) and for IS, income-related ESA, PC and UC, special rules apply if,

Part 7: Special benefit rules
Chapter 45: Benefits in hospital, prison and other special circumstances
3. Prisoners

although you received a prison sentence as a result of a criminal conviction, you are currently detained in a hospital or similar institution as a person with a mental disorder under ss45A or 47 of the Mental Health Act 1983, s59A of the Criminal Procedure (Scotland) Act 1995 or s136 of the Mental Health (Care and Treatment) (Scotland) Act 2003. This applies if you are:[110]

* ordered to be detained in hospital by a court after you are convicted, where the court specifies a length of sentence; *or*
* sent to prison, but later transferred to hospital by order.

In this case, although you are a patient, you are treated as a prisoner, but only until you would have been entitled to be released under your original sentence or, if you are held under an indeterminate sentence (eg, you are a life prisoner), until your release is authorised.[111] After that, if you are still in hospital, your benefit might be affected under the rules that apply to hospital patients (see p941).

Note:

* There is no specific rule for JSA. However, in this situation you are not able to satisfy the jobseeking conditions (or if you come under the UC system, to meet work-related requirements).
* It appears that this rule applies to contributory ESA, but the rules are contradictory.[112]
* If you are detained in a hospital or similar institution under provisions other than those listed above (eg, you were convicted of a criminal offence but were ordered to be detained in hospital and were not given a prison sentence), you might be paid non-means-tested benefits, or you may qualify for IS, ESA, PC or UC. However, check to see if your benefit is affected under the rules that apply to hospital patients.

Social fund payments

You cannot get a winter fuel payment if you are serving a custodial sentence (see p780). You cannot get other social fund payments if you are not getting a qualifying benefit (see Chapter 37).[113]

Community sentences

You might be given a community sentence that involves punishment or supervision in the community. Although you do not count as a prisoner, you should bear the following in mind.

* There might be a question as to whether you satisfy the jobseeking conditions for JSA (or, if you come under the UC system (see p19), meet the work-related requirements for JSA or UC). Seek advice if you think you have been wrongly refused.

- If you undertake basic skills training and are treated as a full-time student, this may affect your entitlement to benefits (see Chapter 44).
- Argue that the notional income rules for means-tested benefits should not apply where you participate in unpaid work as part of your sentence (see p290).

If you are on bail or living in approved premises

Your non-means-tested benefits are paid as normal if you are on bail or living in approved premises (eg, a bail or probation hostel) or other accommodation as a condition of bail. However, special rules can apply for means-tested benefits.

For **IS, income-based JSA, income-related ESA, PC and HB**, if you have a partner and you are temporarily separated because one of you is living away from home, you still count as a couple if you intend to live together again, but only if you are unlikely to be apart for more than 52 weeks or, in exceptional circumstances, substantially longer than 52 weeks.[114] For IS, income-based JSA and income-related ESA only, if one of you is living in an approved bail or probation hostel, your applicable amount is calculated in a special way – at either the single rate for each of you added together, or the couple rate, whichever is the greater.[115]

For **UC**, you and your partner continue to count as a couple while one of you is temporarily absent from the household. You must continue to make a joint claim and UC is paid as normal. However, if the absence exceeds (or is expected to exceed) six months, you no longer count as a couple.[116] If you no longer count as a couple you can no longer make a joint claim for UC and the calculation of your benefit no longer includes amounts for your partner.

If you are required to live away from home in an approved bail or probation hostel:
- you cannot get HB for the rent you pay for the hostel;[117]
- you can continue to get HB and help with your housing costs paid with IS, income-based JSA, income-related ESA or PC for your normal home. These are paid for up to 52 weeks, provided you intend to return home and you are unlikely to be away for longer than this (or, in exceptional circumstances, substantially longer than this);[118]
- you cannot get the UC housing costs element for the hostel.[119] You can get the housing costs element for your normal home for up to six months so long as you are not expected to be away for longer.[120]

If you are no longer entitled to help with housing costs paid with IS, income-based JSA, income-related ESA or PC, to HB for your normal home, or to the UC housing costs element, these can be paid to another person if s/he is (or can be treated as) liable (see p478, p429 and p98).

Part 7: Special benefit rules
Chapter 45: Benefits in hospital, prison and other special circumstances
3. Prisoners

Benefits on release

If you are **temporarily released** (on temporary licence), you no longer count as a prisoner for non-means-tested benefits. You still count as a prisoner for means-tested benefits.

When you are **permanently released** from prison, you should claim any benefits to which you are entitled as soon as possible. The prison gives you a discharge form that can help you prove your identity. You may also be interviewed by a DWP liaison officer before you leave prison, who should point out which benefits you might be able to claim.

- As IS, income-based JSA, income-related ESA and UC are generally paid in arrears, you may need to apply for a budgeting advance (see p197) or a short-term advance (see p1167).
- For JSA, you are treated as satisfying the jobseeking conditions for the first seven days after your release.[121] **Note:** this does not apply if you come under the UC system (see p19).
- If you are at least 25 and are an offender who is subject to multi-agency risk management arrangements, you are exempt from the private sector rent restriction rules for single claimants under 35 (see p399 and p412).
- You may receive a discharge grant from the Prison Service, which counts as capital for IS, income-based JSA and income-related ESA purposes.[122] The rules do not say how it should be treated for HB, PC or UC.
- If you are released without being sentenced to imprisonment or detention, you should receive any arrears of your non-means-tested benefits that were suspended (see p960).
- If you are released following the quashing of a conviction, you are entitled to national insurance credits for the period you were imprisoned or detained (see p859).

Help with travelling expenses

The Prison Service can help you with travelling expenses when you are temporarily or permanently released from prison.

The Assisted Prison Visits Unit can help a partner or close relative (or another person if s/he is your only visitor) with the cost of visiting you in prison, or the cost of someone bringing your children to visit you. S/he must be getting 'qualifying income'.

Application forms are available at www.gov.uk, from the prison and from the Assisted Prison Visits Unit, PO Box 2152, Birmingham B15 1SD (tel: 0300 063 2100, Monday to Friday, 9am to 5pm). You can also email assisted.prison.visits@noms.gsi.gov.uk.

Qualifying income

'Qualifying income' is IS, income-based JSA, income-related ESA, PC and UC, and health benefits on low-income grounds, as well as child tax credit (CTC) or working tax credit (WTC). The WTC must include a disabled worker element, or you must be getting CTC and WTC.

---

4. Paying for your normal home

You may need to pay for your normal home if you are away from home for a temporary period – eg, you are in hospital either as an NHS or a private patient or in a care home, or you are a prisoner. If your partner, child or a non-dependant are away from home for any of these reasons, see p969.

If you are temporarily in hospital or a care home you may no longer qualify for:

- housing benefit (HB), or help with your housing costs with your income support (IS), income-based jobseeker's allowance (JSA), income-related employment and support allowance (ESA) or pension credit (PC) once you have been absent (or are likely to be absent) from home for more than 52 weeks or, in exceptional circumstances, substantially longer than 52 weeks (see p103 and p431);
- the universal credit (UC) housing costs element if your absence from home exceeds (or is expected to exceed) six months (see p482).

Note:

- Another person (eg, your partner) might be able to qualify for these instead of you if s/he is (or can be treated as) liable (see p478, p98 and p429).
- There are no 'linking rules' with these provisions. This means that, if a new period as a patient or in a care home starts, you can again be entitled to HB, help with housing costs paid with IS, income-based JSA, income-related ESA or PC or the UC housing costs element – eg, if you are discharged from hospital and then are re-admitted.
- You can be treated as occupying, but temporarily absent from, a new dwelling, even if you have not yet stayed there, if you move your furniture and belongings in but cannot move in yourself – eg, because you have to go into hospital.[123]
- For HB and help with your housing costs (paid with IS, income-based JSA, income-related ESA or PC), there are special rules if you are a temporary resident in a care home for a trial period. If you intend to return home, you can get these for a period (see p105 and p433).[124]

Part 7: Special benefit rules
Chapter 45: Benefits in hospital, prison and other special circumstances
4. Paying for your normal home

- HB, help with your housing costs with IS, income-based JSA, income-related ESA and PC and the UC housing costs element are no longer payable for your former home if you are away from it permanently – eg, once you are a permanent resident in a care home.

Prisoners

While you are detained in custody **awaiting trial or sentence**, you can get HB and help with your housing costs (paid with IS, income-related ESA or PC) for your normal home. These are paid for up to 52 weeks, so long as you intend to return home and you are unlikely to be away for longer than this (or, in exceptional circumstances, substantially longer than this).[125] You cannot get help with your housing costs with income-based JSA and must claim IS, income-related ESA or PC for this. Note that you fit into one of the groups of people who can claim IS in this situation (see p30).

If you are serving a **custodial sentence**, you may be able to get HB for up to 13 weeks, so long as you are unlikely to be away from your normal home for longer than this – ie, you are serving a short sentence.[126] The 13 weeks run from the date you were first in prison.[127] So any time you spend in prison awaiting trial or sentence counts towards the 13 weeks. If you are serving a sentence of more than 13 weeks, you may still be entitled to HB, as prisoners serving short sentences are often released early under a home detention curfew (electronic tagging).

For UC, if you are a prisoner, whether you are awaiting trial or sentence or are serving a custodial sentence, you can qualify for a UC housing costs element for up to six months for your normal home. However, you can only qualify *following* a sentence of imprisonment if you have not been sentenced to a term that is expected to go beyond the six-month period from when you first went into prison. You can only get the housing costs element if you were entitled to UC as a single person before becoming a prisoner and this included that element.[128]

Note:

- You should report any change in your circumstances as soon as possible – ie, when you are remanded in custody, are serving a custodial sentence or are being released from custody.
- If you do not qualify for HB for 52 or 13 weeks under the rules described above, you can continue to get HB for a former home for up to four benefit weeks if you are still liable to pay rent for it, and you could not reasonably have avoided this liability – eg, because your tenancy agreement required you to give notice.[129]
- Housing costs (paid with IS, income-based JSA, income-related ESA or PC), HB and the UC housing costs element can be paid to another person (eg, your partner), if s/he is (or can be treated as) liable (see p429, p478 and p98).

If you are not already getting IS, income-related ESA, PC or HB when you go into prison, you should make a claim to protect your position. These benefits can only be backdated for a limited period. See the chapter in this *Handbook* about the benefit you want to claim for details.

Are you on temporary release from prison?

1. You are treated as a prisoner during periods of temporary release under specific provisions.[130] This means that, even if you return home, you are still treated as if you are away from home.

2. If you are a convicted prisoner, you are not entitled to IS, income-based JSA, income-related ESA or PC and cannot get help with your housing costs.

3. For HB, you are still treated as if you are away from home and these periods count towards the 13/52 weeks for which HB may be payable.[131]

4. These periods count towards the six months for which the UC housing costs element may be payable.

Partners, children and non-dependants

If your partner, your child or a non-dependant is away from home because s/he is in hospital or a care home, or s/he is a prisoner, this could affect the amount of your HB, help with housing costs with your IS, income-based JSA, income-related ESA or PC or UC housing costs element. This could apply, for example, if s/he no longer counts as living with you or, for UC, s/he no longer counts as a member of your extended benefit unit (see p494). Bear the following in mind.

- If you live in rented accommodation, you may no longer be allowed the same number of bedrooms under the size criteria (see p396, p404, p410 and p492) and your HB or UC housing costs element may be reduced. For UC, this only applies if your partner or child or a non-dependant is absent (or expected to be absent) from home for more than six months.[132]

- For IS, JSA, ESA and PC, help with housing costs might be restricted if your costs are considered to be excessive because your home is too large (see p448).

- If your non-dependant is the one who is absent, check whether a a deduction for housing costs contributions or a non-dependant deduction should still be made for her/him (see p116, p450 and p496).

5. People without accommodation

Entitlement to non-means-tested benefits and pension credit (PC) is unaffected if you do not have accommodation. However, income support (IS), income-based jobseeker's allowance (JSA) and income-related employment and support allowance (ESA) are paid at a reduced rate (see p971).

If you become homeless and have no money, you can apply for a budgeting advance or a short-term advance (see p197 and p1167). It is possible to get help at any time in an emergency.

Part 7: Special benefit rules
Chapter 45: Benefits in hospital, prison and other special circumstances
5. People without accommodation

If you are homeless, the local authority may have a duty to assist you with accommodation or advice. A child or young person may be entitled to help from social services.

Note:

- Even if you are homeless, you have to satisfy jobseeking conditions to qualify for JSA or, if you come under the universal credit (UC) system (see p19), accept a claimant commitment to qualify for JSA, contributory ESA or UC. See below for some issues to consider.

- If you are at least 25, have been living in a homeless hostel for at least three months and have accepted rehabilitation or resettlement support, you are exempt from the private sector UC and housing benefit (HB) rent restriction rules for single people under 35.

- You can qualify for help with payments for a tent and its pitch (if that is your home) with IS, income-based JSA, income-related ESA and PC (see p444). You cannot get a UC housing costs element for rent payments you make for a tent or the site on which a tent stands.[133]

Jobseeking conditions and claimant responsibilities

Even if you are homeless, to qualify for JSA you must satisfy jobseeking conditions (see Chapter 48). If you come under the UC system (see p19), to qualify for contribution-based JSA, contributory ESA or UC, you must accept a claimant commitment and, to avoid being sanctioned, meet any work-related requirements that have been imposed on you (see Chapter 50).

Being homeless may reduce your prospects of finding work, but personal circumstances that reduce your chances of being employed should not prevent you getting JSA or UC. You can be available for work even if you do not have accommodation, but it must be possible for you to be contacted at short notice if you are to satisfy the requirement that you are willing and able to take up any job immediately, or after the amount of notice allowed (see p1070 and p1026). You may satisfy this requirement by daily visits to the Jobcentre Plus office, or a drop-in centre or support group where a message can be left for you – eg, to notify you of vacancies.

Note:

- The fact that you are homeless should be taken into account when deciding whether you are actively seeking work. For JSA if you come under the UC system, in deciding what steps it is reasonable for you to take to find work, the DWP is specifically required to take into account the fact that you have no accommodation and the steps you need to take (and took) to find a home.[134]

- If you come under the UC system, the DWP can agree deductions from your expected hours of work search for time you spend dealing with a domestic emergency or other temporary circumstances – eg, if you are homeless.[135] See p1069 for further information.

Income support, income-based jobseeker's allowance and income-related employment and support allowance

The amount of your IS, income-based JSA and income-related ESA may be lower than normal if you are a person 'without accommodation'.[136] You get the personal allowance for you (and your partner), but do not get any premiums.[137] In addition, for income-related ESA, you do not get either the work-related activity or support component.

Having no fixed address is *not* the same as having no accommodation. If you have accommodation, but are staying in different places on different nights (eg, with different friends or relatives), your IS, income-based JSA or income-related ESA should be paid as normal.[138]

Accommodation

'**Accommodation**' is not defined in the rules and should be interpreted widely and flexibly. The DWP says that, to count as having accommodation, you must have 'an effective shelter from the elements which is capable of being heated; and in which occupants can sit, lie down, cook and eat; and which is reasonably suited for continuous occupation. The site of the accommodation may alter from day to day, but it is still accommodation if the structure is habitable.'[139] Examples include tents, caravans and other substantial shelters. However, the DWP is likely to say that cardboard boxes, bus shelters, sleeping bags and cars do not qualify.[140]

Note: if you are temporarily absent from the accommodation you normally occupy as your home, even if you are living a lifestyle as though you have no accommodation (eg, you are sleeping rough), you should be treated as having accommodation.[141]

6. People involved in a trade dispute

If you (or your partner) are involved in a trade dispute, income support (IS), jobseeker's allowance (JSA) and universal credit (UC) are affected, as well as benefits paid by your employer, increases for an adult paid with non-means-tested benefits and some social fund payments. You can still qualify for housing benefit (HB), income-related employment and support allowance (ESA) and pension credit (PC), but there are issues to consider (see p977). **Note:**

- Trade dispute law is complex. If there is any doubt whether you are involved in one, seek specialist advice.
- If you need financial help when you return to work after a trade dispute, you may qualify for an IS loan for the first 15 days (see p978).

Part 7: Special benefit rules
Chapter 45: Benefits in hospital, prison and other special circumstances
6. People involved in a trade dispute

Income support and jobseeker's allowance

You can qualify for IS while you are involved in a trade dispute, and for the first 15 days after you return to work. This is because you fit into one of the groups of people who can claim (see p30).[142]

You are not entitled to JSA (including hardship payments) for the whole of any week (seven days from Sunday) if you (or if you are a joint-claim couple, both of you) are involved in a trade dispute for one or more days during that week.[143] Weeks when you are not entitled to JSA do not count as part of your 'jobseeking period' (see p693).[144] This means, for instance, that they do not count towards your 26 weeks' entitlement to contribution-based JSA. If you have a partner and only one of you is involved in a trade dispute, unless you are a joint-claim couple (see p46), the one who is not involved can claim income-based JSA. If you are a joint-claim couple, you can both claim income-based JSA;[145] the one involved in the trade dispute does not have to satisfy the jobseeking conditions.

For IS, you are (and, for IS and income-based JSA, your partner is) treated as being in full-time paid work for the first seven days you are involved in a trade dispute.

You (and your partner) cannot qualify for IS or income-based JSA for that period.[146] This does not apply if your partner was already entitled to IS or income-based JSA, or you were already entitled to IS, when you became involved in the dispute. If the trade dispute causes a series of stoppages, this only applies for seven days from the start of the first stoppage.[147] After the seven-day period, you are not treated as being in full-time paid work, but your IS or your partner's IS or income-based JSA is calculated under special rules (see p974).[148]

Trade disputes

A '**trade dispute**' is any dispute between employers and employees or between employees and employees connected with terms or conditions of employment, or the employment or non-employment of anyone.[149] Note that what counts as a trade dispute here goes beyond what counts as lawful industrial action for employment law purposes.

You count as **involved in a trade dispute** if:[150]

- you are not working because of a 'stoppage of work' caused by a trade dispute at your 'place of work' (see p973). This applies until the stoppage ends, even if you are not a party to the dispute or your contract has been terminated as part of the dispute (but see p973);[151] *or*
- you withdraw your labour to further a trade dispute, whether or not there is a stoppage of work at your place of work.

For IS and income-based JSA, you can be awarded benefit at a reduced rate, pending a decision on whether you are involved in a trade dispute.[152] You cannot appeal to the First-tier Tribunal against this decision.[153] However, the decision maker should then carry out a revision of the decision once full information and evidence is available and you can appeal to the First-tier Tribunal against the new decision.

Stoppage of work and place of work

A 'stoppage of work' could be due to a strike, lock-out or any other stoppage caused by a trade dispute. The stoppage does not have to involve everybody, or stop all work.[154] The DWP says that there is no 'stoppage' if normal work continues through the employment of replacement workers or reorganisation.[155]

'Place of work' means the place or premises where you are employed, but it does not include a separate department carrying out a different branch of work, which is commonly undertaken as a separate business elsewhere – eg, a colliery canteen worker laid off during a miners' strike was not 'involved in a trade dispute at her place of work'.[156] It can be difficult to establish that separate branches are separate businesses.[157]

You do *not* count as being involved in a trade dispute:

- if you can prove you are not directly interested in the dispute – ie, you will not be affected by its outcome.[158] This could apply if your terms and conditions will not be affected by the outcome of the dispute or your employment has permanently ended and you will not gain anything from the dispute. However, it may be difficult to convince the DWP that your employment has permanently ended; when a dispute is settled, it is common for the employer to agree to re-employ those who were dismissed during its course;[159] *or*
- if you can prove that during a stoppage of work:[160]
  - you have been made redundant; *or*
  - you have become genuinely employed elsewhere – ie, not just to avoid the trade dispute rules;[161] *or*
  - if you genuinely resume employment with your employer and then leave for a reason other than the trade dispute (but note that if you are claiming JSA you may be sanctioned if you leave – see p1088 and p1125).

For income-based JSA (if your partner is claiming) and IS, even if you are (or count as) involved in a trade dispute, the special rules for those involved in a trade dispute do not apply during a period:[162]

- when you have limited capability for work (see Chapter 47) (or are incapable of work – see Chapter 31); *or*
- from the sixth week before the week you are due to have a baby to the end of the seventh week after the week the baby is born; *or*
- from the day you return to work with the same employer, even if the dispute is continuing or you are doing a different job.

Part 7: Special benefit rules
Chapter 45: Benefits in hospital, prison and other special circumstances
6. People involved in a trade dispute

The amount of income support or income-based jobseeker's allowance

Even if you qualify for IS or income-based JSA while you (or your partner) are involved in a trade dispute, special rules reduce the amount that is payable. Your applicable amount is calculated in a special way and it is assumed that you have a set level of strike pay. Certain income is taken into account even if it would be disregarded were you (or your partner) not involved in a trade dispute. **Note:** if you are entitled to IS of less than £5 a week, you are only paid if you are receiving another benefit that can be paid together with IS as a single payment.[163]

Applicable amount

Your IS or income-based JSA applicable amount is calculated as follows.

If you are a single claimant, or a member of a couple (without children) both involved in a trade dispute:
- your applicable amount for IS is reduced to nil;[164]
- you are not entitled to any JSA.

If you are a lone parent, or a member of a couple (with children) both involved in a trade dispute:
- your IS applicable amount only includes:[165]
  - personal allowances for your children, the family premium and any premiums for your children (if still included). If these are not still included, you should claim child tax credit (CTC) if you are not already doing so; *and*
  - housing costs;
- you are not entitled to any JSA. You should claim CTC for your children if you are not already doing so.

If you are a member of a couple (with or without children) and only one of you is involved in a trade dispute, your applicable amount only includes:[166]
- half the normal personal allowance for a couple and half of any premiums paid at the couple rate;
- any premiums payable solely in respect of the person *not* involved in the trade dispute;
- personal allowances for your children, the family premium and premiums for your children (if still included). If these are not still included, you should claim CTC if you are not already doing so; *and*
- housing costs.

Actual and assumed strike pay

If you (or your partner) are involved in a trade dispute, £40 a week is deducted from your IS or income-based JSA as 'assumed strike pay', whether or not you or your partner actually receive any payments.[167] Any payments you or your partner actually receive from a trade union in excess of £40 a week count as income;

payments of up to £40 are ignored. If you and your partner are both involved in a trade dispute, only £40 in total is ignored.[168]

Example

Cliff is on strike. His partner is not involved in the dispute. Their only income is £45 a week strike pay.

Applicable amount	£56.80 (half normal amount)
less income	£5.00 (strike pay over £40)
	= £51.80
less	£40.00 (assumed strike pay)
IS payable =	**£11.80**

Other income and capital

For IS and income-based JSA, other income and capital are treated as normal except that the following payments are taken into account in full as income:[169]

- any refunds of income tax paid or due under the PAYE rules;
- any payment received or due because you are not working – eg, a loan or grant from social services, if this is made to help with a need that has arisen since you stopped work;[170]
- if you still get allowances and premiums for your children in your IS or JSA, payments made under the Children Act 1989 or Children (Scotland) Act 1995 to promote the welfare of children. Otherwise they count in full as capital;
- charitable or voluntary payments and certain personal injury payments (see p280), except any payments from the Macfarlane Trusts, the Eileen Trust, MFET Ltd, the Skipton Fund, the Caxton Foundation, the Fund or the Independent Living Fund (2006);
- payments in kind (except payments from the above trusts or funds) paid to the person involved in the trade dispute or to a third party (unless for items allowable under the notional income and capital rules – see p290 and p364);
- holiday pay payable more than four weeks after your employment is terminated or interrupted (subject to any earnings disregard);
- an advance of earnings or a loan from an employer (subject to any earnings disregard).

Universal credit

Being involved in a trade dispute does not affect your entitlement to UC. However, if you (or your partner) have withdrawn your labour in support of a trade dispute, you are treated as having the same earnings you would have received were it not for the trade dispute, even if you are not getting these.[171] This does not apply if your contract of service has been terminated. **Note:** any strike pay you receive (eg, from your trade union) does not count as income.[172]

Part 7: Special benefit rules
Chapter 45: Benefits in hospital, prison and other special circumstances
6. People involved in a trade dispute

Benefits paid by your employer

You cannot qualify for **statutory sick pay** (SSP) if you are not within a 'period of entitlement'. A period of entitlement cannot arise if, on the date it would begin, there is a stoppage of work because of a trade dispute at your place of work (ie, you became incapable of work during the trade dispute), unless you can prove that you did not have a direct interest in the dispute on or before that date.[173] You are not entitled to SSP throughout your period of sickness, even if the trade dispute ends. You might, however, qualify for IS or ESA. **Note:** you can continue to qualify for SSP if you were already entitled to SSP when the trade dispute began.

'Stoppage of work' and 'trade dispute' are not defined in the SSP rules. However, an overtime ban or working to grade does not count as a stoppage of work.[174] For what might count as a stoppage of work and place of work, see p973.

Statutory maternity, paternity and adoption pay

To qualify for statutory maternity pay (SMP), statutory paternity pay (SPP) or statutory adoption pay (SAP), you must have been employed for a continuous period of at least 26 weeks ending on a specified date (the 'continuous employment rule' – see p788). For the purpose of this rule, any week in which you are not working because of a stoppage of work because of a trade dispute at your place of work does not break your continuity of employment.[175] However, unless you can prove that you at no time had a direct interest in the trade dispute:

- any such week does *not* count towards the total of 26 weeks' employment you need to qualify for SMP, SPP or SAP; *and*
- if you are dismissed during the stoppage of work, your continuity of employment ends on the day you stopped work.

This could mean that you cannot qualify for SMP, SPP or SAP.

For information about the meaning of 'trade dispute', 'stoppage of work' and 'place of work', see p973. The rules are the same as for JSA.[176]

Increases for an adult in non-means-tested benefits

You are not entitled to an increase of incapacity benefit (IB), severe disablement allowance (SDA), carer's allowance (CA) or Category A retirement pension for an adult who is involved in a trade dispute.[177] For information about what counts as being involved in a trade dispute, see p972. The rules are the same as for JSA. If the adult returns to work, you can only reclaim an increase for her/him with IB and SDA. **Note:** you cannot make a new claim for an increase for an adult with CA or Category A retirement pension. If you are getting an increase in one of those benefits and lose your entitlement to it, you cannot claim it again.

Chapter 45

Benefits in hospital, prison and other special circumstances

Social fund payments

Involvement in a trade dispute has no effect on entitlement to a funeral expenses, cold weather or winter fuel payment. However, other social fund payments are affected. You cannot qualify for a budgeting loan if you or your partner are involved in a trade dispute.[178] For Sure Start maternity grants, see below.

For information about when you count as involved in a trade dispute, see p972. The rules are the same as for JSA.

You do not count as being involved in a trade dispute during a period when you are incapable of work, or from the sixth week before the week you are due to have a baby to the end of the seventh week after the week the baby is born.[179]

Sure Start maternity grant

If you or your partner are involved in a trade dispute, your entitlement to a Sure Start maternity grant is not affected if your qualifying benefit is income-related ESA, UC or PC. However, you can only qualify for a Sure Start maternity grant if your qualifying benefit is:[180]

- IS or income-based JSA, if the trade dispute has been going on for at least six weeks when you claim a maternity grant; *or*
- CTC or working tax credit, if you claimed the relevant tax credit before the trade dispute began.

Housing benefit, income-related employment and support allowance and pension credit

There are no rules that reduce the amount of your HB, income-related ESA and PC if you or your partner are involved in a trade dispute. However, bear the following in mind.

- For income-related ESA, your partner is treated as not in full-time paid work if s/he is involved in a trade dispute, and for the first 15 days following her/his return to work after having been involved in a trade dispute.[181]
- For HB and PC, it does not matter if you or your partner are treated as in full-time paid work. See Chapter 46 for further information.
- You may become entitled to HB, income-related ESA or PC (or an increased amount of these) if your (or your partner's) income drops because of a trade dispute.
- For HB, if your earnings are reduced due to a trade dispute, the local authority should take this into account and not just consider your pre-strike earnings.[182] Your earnings can be averaged over a different period than normal if this results in a more accurate estimate (see p292 and p320).
- For income-related ESA and PC, you can apply to have your award reassessed under the rules on variable earnings (see p293 and p320).

Part 7: Special benefit rules
Chapter 45: Benefits in hospital, prison and other special circumstances
6. People involved in a trade dispute

Non-dependants

Non-dependant deductions made from your IS, JSA, ESA or PC housing costs and from HB are usually higher if your non-dependant is in full-time paid work. However, if your non-dependant is involved in a trade dispute, this may mean that the non-dependant deduction should be reduced. See p118, p452 and p995 for further information.

Income support loans on return to work

If you return to work with the same employer, whether or not the trade dispute has ended, you can qualify for IS in the form of a loan for the first 15 days back at work.[183] You fit into one of the groups of people who can claim IS and are not treated as being in full-time paid work for this period.[184] However, if you are a member of a couple, you are not entitled to IS if your partner is in full-time paid work.[185] See Chapter 46 for what counts as full-time paid work.

Your income and capital are calculated as if you were still involved in the trade dispute, except that the rules about actual and assumed strike pay do not apply, nor do those on the treatment of payments you get because the person involved in the trade dispute was not working.[186]

Repayment of the loan

Any IS paid during your first 15 days back at work can be recovered by deductions from your earnings.[187] If this is not practical (eg, because you are currently unemployed), it can be recovered directly from you.[188] The rules specify the amount of earnings you must be left with after deductions are made to repay your IS loan and the calculations your employer must make if your earnings come above that level on a particular payday.[189]

Your employer normally starts to make deductions from your earnings from the first payday after receiving a deduction notice from the DWP.[190] Your employer *cannot* make a deduction if you satisfy her/him that you did not receive the IS loan. Your employer has to report this development to the DWP.[191] The deduction notice expires automatically after 26 weeks.

You must tell the DWP within 10 working days if you leave a job or start another while part of your IS loan remains unpaid.[192] It is a criminal offence to fail to do so.[193] It is also a criminal offence for your employer to fail to keep records of deductions and supply the DWP with these.[194] If your employer fails to make a deduction (or makes too low a deduction) which should have been made from your pay, the DWP can recover the amount from your employer instead.[195]

Notes

1. Hospital patients

1 **PIP** s86 WRA 2012; reg 29(2) SS(PIP) Regs
   Other benefits Reg 2(4) SS(HIP) Regs; reg 6 SS(AA) Regs; regs 8 and 12A SS(DLA) Regs; NHSA 2006; NHS(W)A 2006; NHS(S)A 1978; NHSCCA 1990
   All *SSWP v TR (DLA)* [2013] UKUT 622 (AAC)
2 para 18059 DMG
3 paras 18028-33 DMG
4 *White v CAO, The Times,* 2 August 1993 (CA); *Botchett v CAO, The Times,* 8 May 1996, 2 CCLR 121 (CA); *R v North and East Devon Health Authority ex parte Coughlan* [1999] 2 CCLR 285 (CA)
5 *SSWP v Slavin* [2011] EWCA Civ 1515; [2012] AACR 30
6 para 18067 DMG
7 R(DLA) 2/06; *SSWP v Slavin* [2011] EWCA Civ 1515; [2012] AACR 30
8 **AA** Reg 6(2A) SS(AA) Regs
   DLA Regs 8(2A) and 12A(2A) SS(DLA) Regs
   PIP Reg 32(2) SS(PIP) Regs
9 Reg 2(5) SS(HIP) Regs
10 Regs 1(2), definition of 'free in-patient treatment', and 3 SFWFP Regs
11 **AA** Regs 6 and 8(1) SS(AA) Regs
   DLA Regs 8, 10(1), 12A and 12B(1) SS(DLA) Regs
   PIP Regs 29 and 30(1) SS(PIP) Regs
   All *AM v SSWP* [2013] UKUT 27 (AAC)
12 **AA/DLA** Reg 25 SS(C&P) Regs
   PIP Reg 50 UC,PIP,JSA&ESA(C&P) Regs
13 **AA** Reg 8(2) SS(AA) Regs
   DLA Regs 10(5) and 12B(3) SS(DLA) Regs
   PIP Reg 32(4) and (5) SS(PIP) Regs
14 **AA** Reg 8(3) SS(AA) Regs
   DLA Regs 10(3) and 12B(2) SS(DLA) Regs
   PIP Reg 30(2) SS(PIP) Regs
15 Regs 12B(3)-(8B) and 12C(1) and (2) SS(DLA) Regs
16 **AA** Reg 8(4) and (5) SS(AA) Regs
   DLA Regs 10(6) and (7) and 12B(9A) and (12) SS(DLA) Regs
   PIP Reg 30(3) and (4) SS(PIP) Regs

17 **HB** Reg 75F(1)(f) HB Regs
   UC Reg 83(1)(h) UC Regs
18 Reg 6(19)-(21) SS(C&P) Regs
19 **IS** Sch 2 paras 13(3A) and 15(5)(b)(i) IS Regs
   JSA Sch 1 paras 15(5) and 20(6)(b)(i) JSA Regs
   ESA Sch 4 paras 6(5) and 11(2)(b)(i) ESA Regs
   PC Reg 6(5) and Sch 1 para 1(2)(b) SPC Regs
   HB Sch 3 paras 14(5) and 20(6)(b)(i) HB Regs; Sch 3 paras 6(7) and 12(1)(b)(i) HB(SPC) Regs
20 Note that there is no such deeming rule in the PC Regs. It is not needed because the PC Regs set out the benefit rates in a different way than for other benefits.
21 **IS** Sch 2 paras 12(1)(d) and 13A(1) IS Regs
   JSA Sch 1 paras 14(1)(g)(ii) and 15A(1) JSA Regs
   ESA Sch 4 para 7 ESA Regs
   HB Sch 3 paras 13(1)(a)(iii) and 15(1) HB Regs; Sch 3 para 7 HB(SPC) Regs
22 Sch 3A para 3(i) SS&CS(DA) Regs
23 **IS** Sch 2 paras 13A(1) and 14(1)(a) IS Regs
   JSA Sch 1 paras 15A(1) and 16(1)(a) JSA Regs
   HB Sch 3 paras 15(1) and 16(a) HB Regs; Sch 3 paras 7 and 8(a) HB(SPC) Regs
24 Reg 24 UC Regs
25 Regs 29(1) and 30 UC Regs
26 **IS** Reg 16(1) and (2) IS Regs
   JSA Reg 78(1)-(2) JSA Regs
   ESA Reg 156(1)-(3) ESA Regs
   PC Reg 5(1)(a) SPC Regs
   HB Reg 21(1) and (2) HB Regs; reg 21(1) and (2) HB(SPC) Regs
27 **IS** Reg 2(1), definition of 'long-term patient', and Sch 2 paras 11(2)(a) and 13A(2)(b) IS Regs
   JSA Reg 1(3), definition of 'long-term patient', and Sch 1 paras 12(5)(a), 13(2)(a) and 15A(2)(b) JSA Regs
   ESA Schs 4 para 7(2)(a) and 5 para 13 ESA Regs
   HB Sch 3 para 15(2) HB Regs

Part 7: Special benefit rules
Chapter 45: Benefits in hospital, prison and other special circumstances
Notes

28 Sch 3 para 15(2) HB Regs
29 **IS** Reg 2(1), definition of 'long-term patient', and Sch 2 paras 10(6), 11(2)(b) and 13A(2)(c) IS Regs
JSA Reg 1(3), definition of 'long-term patient', and Sch 1 paras 12(5)(b), 13(2)(b), 15A(2)(c), 20F(5), 20G(2)(b) and 20IA(2)(b) JSA Regs
ESA Schs 4 para 7(2)(b) and 5 para 13 ESA Regs
30 Sch 3 para 15(2) HB Regs
31 **IS** Reg 2(1), definition of 'long-term patient', and Sch 2 paras 10(6), 11(2)(c) and 13A(2)(d) IS Regs
JSA Reg 1(3), definition of 'long-term patient', and Sch 1 paras 12(5)(c), 13(2)(c), 15A(2)(c), 20F(5), 20(G)(a) and 20IA(2)(a) JSA Regs
32 Sch 5 para 13 ESA Regs. The difference of treatment appears to be a drafting error.
33 Sch 3 paras 15(1) and 16(a) HB Regs; Sch 3 paras 7 and 8(a) HB(SPC) Regs
34 **IS** Reg 2(1), definition of 'long-term patient', and Sch 2 paras 13A(2)(a) and 14(2) IS Regs
JSA Reg 1(3), definition of 'long-term patient', and Sch 1 paras 15A(2)(a) and 16(2) JSA Regs
35 Sch 5 para 13 ESA Regs; reg 63(1) ESA Regs 2013
36 Reg 2(2) and (3) SS(HIP) Regs
37 s39 WRA 2012; reg 3(6) UC Regs
38 s10 WRA 2012; reg 4(7) UC Regs

2. People in care homes and similar accommodation
39 **AA/DLA** ss67(2) and 72(8) SSCBA 1992; regs 7 and 8(1) SS(AA) Regs; regs 9 and 10(1) SS(DLA) Regs
PIP s85 WRA 2012; regs 28 and 30(1) SS(PIP) Regs
40 ss67(3) and 72(9) SSCBA 1992; s85(3) WRA 2012
41 **AA** Reg 8(3) SS(AA) Regs
DLA Reg 10(3) SS(DLA) Regs
PIP Reg 30(2) SS(PIP) Regs
42 **AA/DLA** Reg 25 SS(C&P) Regs
PIP Reg 50 UC,PIP,JSA&ESA(C&P) Regs
43 **UC** Reg 83(1)(h) UC Regs
HB Reg 75F(1)(f) HB Regs
44 **AA/DLA** ss67(4) and 72(10) SSCBA 1992
PIP s85(4) WRA 2012
45 Reg 7(3) SS(AA) Regs; reg 9(6) SS(DLA) Regs
46 R(DLA) 2/06

47 **AA** Reg 7(2) SS(AA) Regs
DLA Reg 9(2) SS(DLA) Regs
PIP Reg 28(2)-(4) SS(PIP) Regs
48 CDLA/1465/1998; CDLA/2127/2000
49 CA/2985/1997
50 **AA** Reg 8(4) and (5) SS(AA) Regs
DLA Reg 10(6) and (7) SS(DLA) Regs
PIP Reg 30(3) SS(PIP) Regs
51 **DLA** Reg 9(3) SS(DLA) Regs
PIP Reg 28(2)(f) SS(PIP) Regs
52 **DLA** Reg 9(4)(a) and (b) and (5) SS(DLA) Regs
PIP Reg 28(3)(a) and (4) SS(PIP) Regs
53 **DLA** Reg 9(4)(c) SS(DLA) Regs
PIP Reg 28(3)(b) SS(PIP) Regs
54 **AA** Reg 8(6) SS(AA) Regs
DLA Reg 10(8) SS(DLA) Regs
PIP Reg 30(5) SS(PIP) Regs
Steane v CAO and Secretary of State, 24 July 1996 (CA), reported as R(A) 3/96
55 R(A) 1/02; CA/3800/2006; *CAO v Creighton and others*, 15 December 1999 (NICA), reported as R 1/00 (AA); *SSWP v DA* [2009] UKUT 214 (AAC)
56 *SSWP v JL (DLA)* [2011] UKUT 293 (AAC)
57 **AA** Reg 7(4) SS(AA) Regs
DLA Reg 9(7) SS(DLA) Regs
PIP Reg 32(1) and (2) SS(PIP) Regs
58 **AA** Reg 7(5) and (6) SS(AA) Regs
DLA Reg 9(8) and (9) SS(DLA) Regs
PIP Reg 32(3) SS(PIP) Regs
59 **AA** Reg 8(2) SS(AA) Regs
DLA Reg 10(5) SS(DLA) Regs
PIP Reg 32(4) SS(PIP) Regs
60 Regs 29(1) and 30 UC Regs
61 **IS** Sch 3A para 3(h) and (i) SS&CS(DA) Regs
ESA Sch 3C para 3(f) and (g) SS&CS(DA) Regs
62 **IS** Reg 2(1) IS Regs
JSA Reg 1(3) JSA Regs
ESA Reg 2(1) ESA Regs
PC Reg 1(2) SPC Regs
HB Reg 2(1) HB Regs; reg 2(1) HB(SPC) Regs
63 *SA v SSWP (IS)* [2010] UKUT 345 (AAC); [2011] AACR 16
64 Reg 12(c) SPC Regs
65 Reg 9(1)(k) HB Regs; reg 9(1)(k) HB(SPC) Regs
66 Sch 3 para 9 HB&CTB(CP) Regs
67 HB/CTB Circular A20/05
68 **IS** Reg 53(1A), (1B) and (1C) IS Regs
JSA Reg 116(1A), (1B) and (1C) JSA Regs
ESA Reg 118(2), (3) and (4) ESA Regs
HB Reg 52(3)-(5), (8) and (9) HB Regs

69 **IS** Reg 16(3)(e) IS Regs
   JSA Reg 78(3)(d) JSA Regs
   ESA Reg 156(4)(d) ESA Regs
   PC Reg 5(1)(b) SPC Regs
   HB Reg 21(2) HB Regs; reg 21(2)
   HB(SPC) Regs
70 Appendix to CIS/4934/1997; CIS/4965/
   1997; CIS/5232/1997; CIS/3767/1997
71 **IS** Reg 16(1) and (2) IS Regs
   JSA Reg 78(1)-(2) JSA Regs
   ESA Reg 156(1)-(3) ESA Regs
   PC Reg 5(1)(a) SPC Regs
   HB Reg 21(1) and (2) HB Regs; reg
   21(1) and (2) HB(SPC) Regs
72 **IS** Sch 7 paras 9 and 10 IS Regs
   JSA Schs 5 paras 5 and 6 and 5A paras 4
   and 5 JSA Regs
   ESA Sch 5 paras 4 and 5 ESA Regs
   All CIS/1544/2001
73 Sch 1 para 1 UC Regs
74 Sch 1 para 3(d) UC Regs
75 s39 WRA 2012; reg 3(6) UC Regs
76 s10 WRA 2012; reg 4(7) UC Regs
77 Reg 1A(4) and (5) SFCWP Regs
78 Regs 1 and 2 SFWFP Regs

3. Prisoners
79 **ESA** Reg 160(3) ESA Regs; reg 96(3) ESA
   Regs 2013
   PIP Reg 31(3) and (4) SS(PIP) Regs
   Other benefits Reg 2(3) SS(GB) Regs
80 Reg 3(1) and (2) SSP Regs; reg 9 SMP
   Regs; regs 18(c) and 27(1)(c) SPPSAP(G)
   Regs; reg 21(1)(c) ASPP(G) Regs
81 **ESA** s18(4)(b) WRA 2007; reg 160 ESA
   Regs; reg 96 ESA Regs 2013
   Other benefits s113(1)(b) SSCBA
   1992; reg 2 SS(GB) Regs
82 s87 WRA 2012; reg 31(1) SS(PIP) Regs
83 Reg 31(2) SS(PIP) Regs
84 Reg 32(1) and (5) SS(PIP) Regs
85 s113(1)(b) SSCBA 1992
86 Regs 10(2)(d) and 12 and Sch 2 para
   7(b)(ii) SSB(Dep) Regs; reg 14 SS(IB-ID)
   Regs
87 **ESA** s18(4)(b) WRA 2007; reg 160(6)
   ESA Regs
   PIP s87 WRA 2012
   Other benefits s113(1)(b) and Sch 9
   para 1 SSCBA 1992; reg 2(9) and (10)
   SS(GB) Regs; reg 10(2)(d) and Sch 2
   para 7(b)(ii) SSB(Dep) Regs; R(S) 8/79
88 Reg 13(1)(b) JSA Regs 2013

89 **ESA** Reg 160(1), (2) and (5)(c) ESA
   Regs; reg 96(1), (2) and (6)(c) ESA Regs
   2013
   Other benefits Reg 2(2) and (8)(c)
   SS(GB) Regs; reg 14 SS(ICA) Regs
   All R(S) 1/71
90 **ESA** Reg 161 ESA Regs; reg 97 ESA Regs
   2013
   Other benefits Reg 3 SS(GB) Regs; reg
   14 SS(ICA) Regs
91 CS/541/1950
92 Regs 2(6) and (7) and 3(1) SS(GB) Regs
93 Reg 2(7) SS(GB) Regs; para 12091 DMG
94 Reg 2(2) and (7) SS(GB) Regs
95 **CB** s113(1)(b) SSCBA 1992. Child
   benefit is not in Parts 2-5 of that Act.
   GA Reg 2(5) SS(GB) Regs
96 Sch 9 para 1(a) SSCBA 1992; regs 16
   and 17 CB Regs
97 **IS** Schs 1B para 22, 3 para 3(11) and
   (12) and 7 para 8 IS Regs
   ESA Schs 5 para 3 and 6 para 5(11) and
   (12) ESA Regs
   PC Reg 6(2)(a), (3), (6)(c), (7), (9) and
   (10) SPC Regs
98 Reg 7(3) SPC Regs
99 Reg 6(3)(b) and (4) SPC Regs
100 **IS** Sch 3 para 18(7)(g) IS Regs
   JSA Sch 2 para 17(7)(g) JSA Regs
   ESA Sch 6 para 19(7)(g) ESA Regs
   PC Sch 2 para 14(7)(e) SPC Regs
   HB Reg 74(7)(f) HB Regs; reg 55(7)(f)
   HB(SPC) Regs
101 **IS** Reg 21(3) IS Regs
   JSA Reg 85(4) JSA Regs
   ESA Reg 69(2) ESA Regs
   PC Reg 1(2) SPC Regs
   HB Reg 7(14) and (16)(c)(i) HB Regs;
   reg 7(14) and (16)(c)(i) HB(SPC) Regs
102 **IS** Reg 16(3)(b) IS Regs
   JSA Reg 78(3)(b) JSA Regs
   ESA Reg 156(4) ESA Regs
   PC Reg 5(1)(c)(ii) and (iii) SPC Regs
103 Reg 21(2) HB Regs; reg 21(2) HB(SPC)
   Regs
104 Reg 28 HB Regs; reg 31 HB(SPC) Regs
105 Sch 4 paras 11 and 16(2)(h) UC Regs
106 Reg 2(1) UC Regs
107 Regs 3(3)(c) and 19(1)(c) UC Regs
108 s39 WRA 2012; reg 3(6) UC Regs
109 Reg 4(6)(b) UC Regs

Part 7: Special benefit rules
Chapter 45: Benefits in hospital, prison and other special circumstances
Notes

110 **IS** Reg 21(3ZA)-(3ZC) and Sch 7 para 2A
IS Regs
ESA Regs 69(3)-(5), 160(3)-(4A) and
Sch 5 para 12 ESA Regs; reg 96(3)-(5)
ESA Regs 2013
PC Reg 8 and Sch 3 para 2 SPC Regs
PIP Reg 31(3) and (4) SS(PIP) Regs
UC Reg 19(1)(c) and (4) UC Regs
Other benefits Reg 2(3), (4) and (4A)
SS(GB) Regs
All CSS/239/2007; *JB v SSWP (IS)* [2010]
UKUT 263 (AAC)
111 **IS** Reg 21(3ZA)-(3ZC) and Sch 7 para 2A
IS Regs
ESA Regs 69(3)-(5), 160(3)-(4A) and
Sch 5 para 12 ESA Regs; reg 96(3)-(5)
ESA Regs 2013
PC Reg 8 and Sch 3 para 2 SPC Regs
PIP Reg 31(3) and (4) SS(PIP) Regs
UC Reg 19(1)(c) and (4) UC Regs
Other benefits Reg 2(3)-(4A) SS(GB)
Regs
All CSS/239/2007; *JB v SSWP (IS)* [2010]
UKUT 263 (AAC)
112 Sch 5 para 12 ESA Regs and reg 63 ESA
Regs 2013 suggest the rule does not
apply, but this may be a drafting error.
113 Note that *Stewart v SSWP* [2011] EWCA
Civ 907, 29 July 2011, decided that
exclusion of prisoners from entitlement
to a funeral expenses payment did not
breach the Human Rights Act 1998.
114 **IS** Reg 16(2) IS Regs
JSA Reg 78(2) JSA Regs
ESA Reg 156(3) ESA Regs
PC Reg 5(1)(a) SPC Regs
HB Reg 21(1) and (2) HB Regs; reg
21(1) and (2) HB(SPC) Regs
115 **IS** Sch 7 para 9(a)(v) IS Regs
JSA Schs 5 para 5(a)(vi) and 5A para
4(a)(vi) JSA Regs
ESA Sch 5 para 4(a)(v) ESA Regs
116 s39 WRA 2012; reg 3(6) UC Regs
117 Reg 7(5) HB Regs; reg 7(5) HB(SPC)
Regs
118 **IS** Sch 3 para 3(11)(c)(i) and (12) IS Regs
JSA Sch 2 para 2(11)(c)(i) and (12) JSA
Regs
ESA Sch 6 para 5(11)(c)(i) and (12) ESA
Regs
PC Sch 2 para 4(11)(c)(i) and (12) SPC
Regs
HB Reg 7(16)(c)(i) and (17) HB Regs;
reg 7(16)(c)(i) and (17) HB(SPC) Regs
119 Schs 1 paras 1 and 3(c) and 3 para 1(1)
UC Regs
120 Sch 3 para 9 UC Regs

121 Regs 14(1)(h) and 19(1)(h) JSA Regs
122 **IS** Reg 48(7) IS Regs
JSA Reg 110(7) JSA Regs
ESA Reg 112(6) ESA Regs

4. Paying for your normal home
123 R(H) 9/05
124 **IS** Sch 3 para 3(8)-(12) IS Regs
JSA Sch 2 para 3(8)-(12) JSA Regs
ESA Sch 6 para 5(8)-(12) ESA Regs
PC Sch 2 para 4(8)-(12) SPC Regs
HB Reg 7(11)-(13), (16) and (17) HB
Regs; reg 7(11)-(13), (16) and (17)
HB(SPC) Regs
125 **IS** Schs 1B para 22, 3 para 3(11) and
(12) and 7 para 8 IS Regs
ESA Schs 5 para 3 and 6 para 5(11) and
(12) ESA Regs
PC Reg 6(2)(a), (3), (6)(c), (7), (9) and
(10) and Sch 2 para 4(11) and (12) SPC
Regs
HB Reg 7(16)(c)(i) and (17) HB Regs;
reg 7(16)(c)(i) and (17) HB(SPC) Regs
126 Reg 7(13) HB Regs; reg 7(13) HB(SPC)
Regs
127 CSH/499/2006
128 Reg 19 UC Regs
129 Reg 7(7) HB Regs; reg 7(7) HB(SPC)
Regs; paras A3/3.430-32 GM
130 **IS** Reg 21(3) and Sch 7 para 8(a) IS Regs
JSA Reg 85(4) JSA Regs
ESA Reg 69(2) and Sch 5 para 3(a) ESA
Regs
PC Regs 1(2) and 6 SPC Regs
UC Reg 2(1) UC Regs
131 Reg 7(14) and (15) HB Regs; reg 7(14)
and (15) HB(SPC) Regs; R(IS) 17/93
132 Sch 4 para 11 UC Regs

5. People without accommodation
133 Sch 1 paras 1 and 3(b) UC Regs
134 Reg 18(3)(j) JSA Regs
135 **JSA** Regs 4(1) and 12(2) and (3) JSA
Regs 2013
UC Reg 95(2) UC Regs
136 This rule was challenged under the
Human Rights Act, but the Court
decided the rules did not conflict with it:
R(RJM) v SSWP [2008] UKHL 63
137 **IS** Sch 7 para 6 IS Regs
JSA Schs 5 para 3 and 5A para 2 JSA
Regs
ESA Sch 5 para 1 ESA Regs
138 paras 24157 and 54157 DMG
139 paras 24158-59 and 54158-59 DMG
140 paras 24159-60 and 54159-60
DMG; R(IS) 23/98
141 paras 24162 and 54162 DMG

6. People involved in a trade dispute

142 Sch 1B para 20 IS Regs
143 ss14, 15A and 35(1), definition of 'week', JSA 1995
144 Reg 47(3)(e) JSA Regs; reg 37(2)(d) JSA Regs 2013
145 ss15 and 15A JSA 1995; reg 3D and Sch A1 para 17 JSA Regs
146 **IS** Reg 5(4) IS Regs
     JSA Reg 52(2) and (2A) JSA Regs
147 paras 32678-79 DMG
148 **IS** Reg 6(4)(b) IS Regs
     JSA Reg 53(g) and (gg) JSA Regs
149 s126 SSCBA 1992; ss14 and 35(1), definition of 'trade dispute', JSA 1995
150 s14(1) and (2) JSA 1995
151 R(U) 1/65; paras 32121-25 and 32160-61 DMG
152 Regs 13(2)(a)(i) and 15(a)(i) SS&CS(DA) Regs
153 Sch 2 paras 13 and 19 SS&CS(DA) Regs
154 R(U) 7/58; R(U) 1/87
155 para 32107 DMG
156 s14(4) and (5) JSA 1995; CU/66/1986(T)
157 R(U) 4/62; R(U) 1/70
158 s14(1)(b) JSA 1995
159 *Presho v Insurance Officer* [1984] (HL) (see R(U) 1/84); *Cartlidge v CAO* [1986] 2 All ER 1 (CA); R(U) 1/87
160 s14(3) JSA 1995
161 R(U) 6/74
162 **IS** ss126(1) and (2) and 127(a) SSCBA 1992
     JSA s15(4) JSA 1995; reg 171 JSA Regs
163 Reg 26(4) SS(C&P) Regs
164 s126(3)(a) and (d)(i) SSCBA 1992
165 s126(3)(b) and (d)(ii) SSCBA 1992
166 **IS** s126(3)(c) SSCBA 1992
     JSA ss15(2)(a) and (b) and 15A(4) and (5) JSA 1995
167 **IS** s126(5)(b) and (7) SSCBA 1992
     JSA ss15(2)(d) and 15A(5) JSA 1995; reg 172 JSA Regs
168 **IS** Sch 9 para 34 IS Regs
     JSA Sch 7 para 36 JSA Regs
169 **IS** s126(5)(a) SSCBA 1992; regs 35(1)(d), 41(3), 42(4), 48(2), (5), (6), (9), (10)(a) and (c) and Sch 9 paras 15(3)(b), 21, 28 and 39 and Sch 10 paras 17 and 22 IS Regs
     JSA ss15(2)(c) and 15A(5) JSA 1995; regs 98(1)(c), 104(3), 105(10) 110(2), (5), (6), (9) and (10)(a) and (c) Sch 7 paras 15(3)(b), 22, 29 and 41 and Sch 8 paras 22 and 27 JSA Regs
170 R(SB) 29/85
171 Regs 2 and 56 UC Regs
172 Reg 66 UC Regs
173 Sch 11 paras 2(g) and 7 SSCBA 1992
174 R(SSP) 1/86
175 **SMP** Reg 13 SMP Regs
     SPP/SAP Reg 35 SPPSAP(G) Regs; reg 27 ASPP(G) Regs; s35 JSA 1995
176 Note, however, that reg 13 SMP Regs was not amended when the JSA 1995 came into force.
177 s91 SSCBA 1992; s14 JSA 1995
178 **SF** Dir 8(1)(b); s14 JSA 1995
179 s126(1) and (2) SSCBA 1992; s14 JSA 1995; reg 171 JSA Regs; reg 3 SFM&FE Regs; SF Dir 8
180 Regs 3(1) and 6 SFM&FE Regs; s126 SSCBA 1992; s14 JSA 1995
181 Reg 43(2)(b)
182 *R v HBRB London Borough of Ealing ex parte Saville* [1986] HLR 349
183 s127 SSCBA 1992
184 Reg 6(4)(b) and Sch 1B para 20 IS Regs
185 s127(b) SSCBA 1992
186 s127(a) SSCBA 1992; regs 35(1)(d), 41(3) and (4), 42(4) and 48(6) and (10) and Schs 9 paras 15, 21, 28 and 39 and 10 para 17 IS Regs
187 s127(c) SSCBA 1992; reg 18 SS(PAOR) Regs
188 Regs 19(3)-(5) and 26 SS(PAOR) Regs
189 Regs 19(3)-(5) SS(PAOR) Regs
190 Regs 20, 21 and 22(5) and (6) SS(PAOR) Regs
191 Reg 27(3) SS(PAOR) Regs
192 Reg 28 SS(PAOR) Regs
193 Reg 29 SS(PAOR) Regs
194 Regs 27 and 29 SS(PAOR) Regs
195 Reg 27(5) SS(PAOR) Regs

Part 8

Work

Chapter 46

Work and benefits

This chapter covers:
1. The full-time paid work rule (below)
2. People treated as in full-time paid work (p994)
3. People treated as not in full-time paid work (p995)
4. Self-employed people (p996)
5. Universal credit (p997)
6. Non-means-tested benefits (p998)
7. Working tax credit and means-tested benefits (p998)

Key facts

- You cannot usually qualify for income support (IS) or income-based jobseeker's allowance (JSA) if you or your partner are in full-time paid work, or for income-related employment and support allowance (ESA) if your partner is in full-time paid work. You cannot qualify for contribution-based JSA if you are in full-time paid work.
- You cannot qualify for IS on the basis that you are incapable of work or any type of ESA if you do any work, unless it is work you are permitted to do while claiming.
- Your eligibility for housing benefit and pension credit is not affected if you or your partner are in full-time paid work.
- Your eligibility for universal credit is not affected if you or your partner are in full-time paid work. However, you cannot get a housing costs element for owner-occupier payments if you or your partner have any earnings, no matter how low these are, or how many hours you work.
- Earnings affect the amount of all of your means-tested benefits.
- Entitlement to some non-means-tested benefits and tax credits is affected by issues to do with work and employment.

---

1. The full-time paid work rule

Work affects income support (IS), jobseeker's allowance (JSA), employment and support allowance (ESA), housing benefit (HB) and pension credit (PC) in different

Part 8: Work
Chapter 46: Work and benefits
1. The full-time paid work rule

ways. If you are in any paid work, unless it is work that you can do while claiming (see p1018), you are not entitled to ESA. This is called 'paid work' in this *Handbook*.[1]

If you or your partner (or a non-dependant) work full time and are paid for the work, you count as being in what the DWP calls 'remunerative work'. This is called 'full-time paid work' in this *Handbook*.

- If you are in full-time paid work, you cannot usually qualify for IS or JSA.[2] **Note:** you cannot qualify for IS based on your incapacity for work in any week in which you do *any* work (even if it is part time), unless it is work you can do while claiming. See p684 of the 2013/14 edition of this *Handbook* for further information about the work you may do.
- If your partner is in full-time paid work, you cannot usually qualify for IS, *income-based* JSA or *income-related* ESA.[3] Your partner's working hours do not affect your entitlement to *contribution-based* JSA or *contributory* ESA.
- Your eligibility for HB and PC is not affected if you or your partner are in full-time paid work. For HB, however, this can affect the way your income is calculated – eg, whether you can get an additional earnings disregard (see p270 and p311) or a childcare costs disregard (see p270 and p311).
- In some situations, a child who is aged 16 or over who does paid work for 24 hours a week or more does not count as a qualifying young person who can be included in your claim (see p210 and p552). In this case, you might not be able to get an allowance or premiums in your HB for her/him (or, if still included, in your IS or income-based JSA).
- If you have a non-dependant living with you, the amount of the non-dependant deduction made from your IS, income-based JSA, income-related ESA or PC housing costs, and from your HB, can be higher if your non-dependant is in full-time paid work (see p452 and p118).

See p989 for what counts as paid work and p990 for how the hours are calculated. 'Work' includes self-employment and work which is done from home. In some circumstances you may be treated as not in full-time paid work even if you are (see p995). In others, you may be treated as if you are in full-time paid work when you are not (see p994).

Note: income from work is taken into account for all the means-tested benefits and you might not satisfy the means test.

Example
Della works 15 hours a week and so can qualify for IS unless her income is too high. For HB, it does not matter how many hours she works. However, if she is not getting IS, her income may affect the amount she can get.

If you or your partner are in full-time paid work, you might be able to claim working tax credit (WTC). The rules on what counts as full-time paid work for WTC are different from those for IS, JSA and ESA. So you may be able to choose whether to claim IS/JSA/ESA or WTC. You may be able to claim both IS/JSA/ESA/PC and WTC. For IS and JSA, if you are a single claimant, this only applies in limited situations – eg, if you are a 'term-time only' worker or you are off sick and getting statutory sick pay. For ESA, this only applies if your partner counts as in full-time paid work for WTC purposes; you cannot qualify for ESA if *you* work, unless it is work you can do while claiming (see p1018). See p998 for factors to consider.

What counts as full-time work

For IS, JSA and HB, **you** count as in 'full-time work' if you work 16 hours or more a week.[4] **Your partner** counts as in 'full-time work':
- for IS, income-based JSA (but not joint-claim JSA) and income-related ESA, if s/he works 24 hours or more a week;[5]
- for HB, if s/he works 16 hours or more a week.[6]

For IS, JSA, ESA, PC and HB, **your non-dependant** counts as in full-time paid work if s/he works 16 hours or more a week.[7]

See p990 for how the hours are calculated.

Note:
- For ESA, there is no rule for when *you* count as in full-time work because you cannot qualify for ESA if you do *any* number of hours of work, unless it is work you can do while claiming (see p1018).
- For PC, there is no rule for when you or your partner count as in full-time work because it does not matter how many hours you (or s/he) work(s).
- For joint-claim JSA, you do not have to make a joint claim with your partner if s/he works 16 or more but less than 24 hours a week.[8]
- For HB, you and your partner may have to work more than 16 hours to benefit from an additional earnings disregard (see p270 and p311).

What counts as paid work

'Paid work' includes work for which you are paid or expect to be paid – ie, you expect to get payment for the work you are doing, now or at some date in the future, even if no payment is finally made.[9] The question of whether or not you are paid or are working in expectation of payment has to be decided at the time the work is done, not, for example, at the end of the year or accounting period.[10]

Note:
- You must have a real likelihood of getting payment, not just a hope or desire to make money – eg, a self-employed writer who has never sold a manuscript

Part 8: Work
Chapter 46: Work and benefits
1. The full-time paid work rule

and has no publication agreement may be working without real expectation of payment and so is not in paid work even if s/he spends a lot of time writing.[11]

- Some of the initial work necessary to set up a business may not count as paid work if it is unpaid preparatory work done in the hope of further work that will be paid.[12]
- If you have a business but it is not yet making money or has ceased to make a profit, you may count as working in expectation of payment if you are making drawings against future profit or if the business is likely to yield profit in the future. Ultimately, it depends on how viable your business is. If there is no realistic possibility of it yielding a profit, the decision maker is likely to want to know why you are working for nothing.[13]
- Paid work includes work for which you receive payment in kind – eg, free meals or accommodation or free produce for farmworkers.[14]

How your hours are calculated

When calculating your (or your partner's or non-dependant's) hours, include all the hours you (or s/he) actually work(s) for which payment is made or which are worked in expectation of payment. If you do more than one job, add the total hours from each together. If routine paid overtime is done, include those hours. If work is casual or intermittent (eg, you are a seasonal worker who works in the summer but you are unemployed the rest of the year), you can argue that it is only the hours when you are in work that are relevant (but see p992 for 'term-time only' workers).[15] Your word should be accepted unless there is reason for doubt. Bear in mind that:

- if your hours fluctuate, the rules specify how your hours are averaged (see p991);
- for IS, JSA and income-related ESA only, paid lunch hours and breaks count towards the total hours;[16]
- for PC and HB, the rules do not say how to calculate the hours of work unless these fluctuate. However, for PC, the DWP says you should only count the hours for which payment is made or which are worked in expectation of payment, including overtime, but not including paid breaks – eg, lunch or tea breaks;[17]
- for JSA only, the hours that you (or your partner or non-dependant) spend caring for someone in a situation in which it would be possible to qualify for IS as a carer (see p29) are ignored unless you are employed and are being paid to act as a carer.[18] For IS and ESA, although hours spent caring are not ignored, you and your partner (for IS), and your partner (for ESA), are treated as not in full-time paid work in this situation (see p995).

If you are unsure if you (or your partner) are in full-time paid work, see p993. Appeal if you think the average hours have been calculated unfairly if this means you cannot claim the benefit or tax credit you want. Work out first whether you are better off claiming IS/JSA/ESA or WTC (see p998). Likewise, appeal if your non-dependant's hours have been calculated unfairly and the DWP or local authority is making a non-dependant deduction that is too high. **Note:** you are likely to have to apply for a revision before you can appeal.

If your hours fluctuate

If your (or your partner's or your non-dependant's) hours fluctuate, an average of the weekly hours is calculated as follows.

Regular pattern of work

If there is a regular pattern of work (a 'work cycle'), the average hours worked throughout each cycle is used – eg, if you regularly work three weeks on and one week off, your hours are the average over the four-week period (the 'work cycle').[19]

Weeks when you are on paid holiday, or are absent from work without a good reason or because you are off sick or on maternity, paternity or adoption leave, are disregarded – ie, they do not count as zero-hours weeks when calculating the average hours.[20]

Note:

- If you work casually or intermittently (eg, you are a seasonal worker and work in the summer but you are unemployed during the rest of the year), you can argue that your work cycle is that part of the year in which you are in work and that you do not count as in work when you are unemployed.[21]
- If you (or your partner or non-dependant) are in work and have a work cycle that lasts a year with periods in which you do not work (eg, in an educational establishment):
  - for JSA and ESA, this rule applies. In practice, if the average hours of work you (or your partner) do over the whole cycle means you (or your partner) are not in full-time paid work, you can claim JSA or income-related ESA. However, you may only qualify during periods when your income is sufficiently low – eg, during unpaid summer holidays. You could also claim WTC if you (or your partner) work sufficient hours each week during term time;
  - for IS, PC and HB, the 'term-time only' worker rule applies (see p992).

Example

Sheila is a school meals worker. She works 20 hours a week, 38 weeks of the year. She gets four weeks' paid holiday, but otherwise is not paid when she is not working at the school. Her average hours are calculated as follows:

20 hours x 38 weeks = 760 hours. 52 weeks – 4 weeks' paid holiday = 48 weeks.

760 hours ÷ 48 weeks = 15.84 average hours a week.

Part 8: Work
Chapter 46: Work and benefits
1. The full-time paid work rule

Sheila can claim JSA if her income is low enough as she is not in full-time paid work for JSA purposes. She might also qualify for WTC. She cannot qualify for IS as the term-time only worker rule applies and her hours during term time are too high.

No regular pattern of work

If there is no regular pattern of work (no recognisable work cycle), an average of your hours is used. This is the average over the five weeks immediately before the date of your claim (or of a supersession decision for IS, JSA and, in respect of your partner's hours only, income-related ESA), or the average over a longer or a shorter period if this would give a fairer average.[22] The five-week period may not be appropriate if the average is distorted – eg, if you have done a short period of overtime that is not typical, or you have been off sick.[23]

No work pattern yet established

If you (or your partner or non-dependant) have not yet established a pattern of work (a work cycle), the number of hours or average number of hours you are expected to work each week is used.[24] This may apply, for example, if you have just started work or your working arrangements have changed and your previous work cycle no longer applies. Once there is sufficient evidence to calculate your average hours, the decision can be revised or superseded.

'Term-time only' workers

For IS, PC and HB, if you have a regular pattern of work (a recognisable work cycle) that lasts for a year (eg, in a school or an educational establishment where you have periods of school holidays or similar vacations when you do not work), the 'term-time only' worker rule applies. The average number of hours in the periods when you are actually working (eg, during term time) determines whether you are in full-time paid work throughout the year.[25] People who work in schools, colleges or similar institutions and have long periods in which they do not work are affected by this rule.

In practice, if your average hours of work during term time mean you are in full-time paid work during term time, you also count as being in full-time paid work over the school holidays, even if you do no work and are not paid. This means:

- if you or your partner count as in full-time paid work, you cannot claim IS during the school holidays. You might be able to claim JSA or ESA. You can claim WTC if you normally work sufficient hours each week (see Chapter 9);[26]
- if your non-dependant counts as in full-time paid work, higher rate non-dependant deductions may be made from your HB or your IS, JSA or ESA housing costs (see p118 and p452).

This rule can also apply to other seasonal workers. However, if you work casually or intermittently and are unemployed the rest of the year, you can argue that this rule does not apply to you.[27] If your contract comes to an end before a period of absence from work, you should not count as a term-time only worker, unless you are expected to start work again and there is some commitment by you and your employer that this will happen.[28]

Sometimes it might not be clear whether you have a work cycle that lasts a year – eg, if you have only started your job recently or have a fixed-term contract that finishes at the end of the school term, or you are employed on a casual or relief basis.[29] It takes time before it can be said that you have a yearly work cycle.[30] However, if you have an indefinite contract to work in term time only, the decision maker is likely to say that you have a yearly work cycle from the start.[31]

If you are unsure whether you are in full-time paid work

If you are unsure whether you or your partner are working for 16/24 hours or more a week, you should make a claim in any event. If your situation then changes or it becomes clearer that the hours are low enough, provide details of the hours you (or your partner) have worked since you claimed. Provided you do this before the decision maker makes a decision, s/he should take the new information into account. If you are refused benefit because your hours were too high, but later your circumstances change, make a fresh claim.

Alternatively, if you are refused WTC because you or your partner do not count as in full-time paid work for WTC purposes and within 14 days of that decision you claim IS (or, if you do not come under the universal credit system, JSA), your claim for IS or JSA can be backdated to the date you claimed WTC.[32] This rule does not apply to ESA. However, your ESA claim can be backdated for up to three months.

If your (or your partner's) circumstances change while you are claiming:

- IS, JSA or ESA, you may be uncertain about whether you (or your partner) now count as in full-time paid work – eg, if your average weekly hours change or you are now getting regular overtime. If it appears that you (or your partner) are now working 16/24 hours or more a week, report this to the DWP to avoid an overpayment. Also check to see if you qualify for WTC. Remember, you cannot qualify for ESA if *you* do *any* paid work, unless it is work you can do while claiming (see p1018);
- HB, report this to the local authority. A change in your hours of work might affect your entitlement to an additional earnings, or a childcare costs, disregard.

In all cases, increases or decreases in your earnings can affect the amount of benefit to which you are entitled.

Part 8: Work
Chapter 46: Work and benefits
2. People treated as in full-time paid work

If your non-dependant's circumstances change while you are claiming HB (or help with housing costs in IS, JSA, ESA or PC), report this to the local authority (or DWP) to enable your non-dependant deduction to be adjusted.

2. People treated as in full-time paid work

You or your partner can be treated as being in full-time paid work, even if you are not, if:

- for income support (IS), jobseeker's allowance (JSA) and housing benefit (HB), you or your partner (or for employment and support allowance (ESA), your partner) normally work full time, but are off work because of a **recognised, customary or other holiday** and there is a common intention that the employment will be resumed once the holiday is over.[33] Whether you count as on holiday depends on your contractual or legal entitlement to holiday. You can argue that you only count as on holiday if you are paid for it.[34] However, for JSA, even if you do not count as in full-time paid work because you are on unpaid leave, you are likely to have difficulty persuading the DWP that you are available for and actively seeking work (see Chapters 48 and 49). For IS and HB, in some cases, if you are a full-time 'term-time only' worker and your cycle of work lasts a year, you are treated as in full-time work during the school holidays (see p992);
- for IS, JSA and HB, you or your partner (or, for ESA, your partner) are **absent from full-time paid work without a good reason**.[35] All your circumstances should be taken into account. Whether or not your employer has authorised the absence is not conclusive, although if it is authorised, it is likely that you have a good reason;
- for IS and JSA, you or your partner stopped full-time paid work, but you are still **within the period covered by payment in lieu of earnings or wages, or certain holiday pay** (unless they can be disregarded). For ESA, this rule applies if you stopped paid work or if your partner stopped full-time paid work.[36]
  Note: most earnings and payments *are* disregarded if the employment ends before entitlement to IS, JSA or ESA starts. You (or your partner) are *not* treated as in full-time paid work and you can claim IS, JSA or ESA as soon as the work finishes. See p261 for details on payments when you stop work.

For IS, JSA, PC and HB, **your non-dependant** can also be treated as in full-time paid work under the rules above. For ESA, your non-dependant can also be treated as in full-time paid work if s/he normally works full time but is off work because of a recognised, customary or other holiday, or s/he is away from work 'without good cause'.

Note: you or your partner can be treated as in full-time paid work for the first seven days you (or s/he) are **involved in a trade dispute**. See Chapter 45 for further information about entitlement to, and the amount of, IS or JSA during a trade dispute.

---

3. People treated as not in full-time paid work

There are situations when you (or your partner or non-dependant) are treated as not in full-time paid work, even if you actually are. For income support (IS), jobseeker's allowance (JSA) and employment and support allowance (ESA), see below. For housing benefit (HB) and pension credit (PC), see p996.

Income support, jobseeker's allowance and employment and support allowance

For IS and JSA, you (and for IS, income-based JSA and income-related ESA, your partner and your non-dependant) are treated as *not* being in full-time paid work if you (or s/he) are on **maternity, adoption or paternity leave or are absent from work because you are sick,** even if when you are not on leave or off sick you normally work 16/24 hours or more each week.[37] For IS, ESA and JSA, this applies during both ordinary and additional paternity leave. **Note:** for contribution-based JSA if you come under the universal credit (UC) system (see p19), it only applies while you are on *ordinary* paternity leave.[38]

In addition, you (and your partner and your non-dependant) are treated as not being in full-time paid work in so far as you (or s/he):[39]

- are working on a training scheme and are **being paid a training allowance** under specific provisions;
- for JSA only, are **on Work Experience** or, if you do not come under the UC system, are participating in **Mandatory Work Activity** (see p1091) or a specified scheme for assisting people to obtain employment (see p1093) – eg, the Work Programme, Skills Conditionality or the sector-based work academy;
- are **a volunteer** (other than for a relative) or are working for a charity or voluntary organisation and are giving your services free (except for your expenses);
- are **providing care** for someone:
  - who is staying with you but who is not normally a member of your household and you receive payments from a health authority, local authority or voluntary organisation, or from the person concerned under s26(3A) of the National Assistance Act 1948 for caring for her/him;
  - for IS and ESA, in the circumstances described on p29. This means that any hours of work you do are ignored, not just the hours you spend caring. **Note:** for JSA, the hours you spend caring are ignored in this situation (see p990);
- are a **foster carer** (or, in Scotland only, **a kinship carer**) receiving a payment from a local authority or voluntary organisation for a child you are looking

Part 8: Work
Chapter 46: Work and benefits
3. People treated as not in full-time paid work

after. Note that for working tax credit (WTC) purposes, you can count as being in full-time paid work (see p174);
- work as a **part-time firefighter, auxiliary coastguard, member of the Territorial Army or reserve forces, or member of a lifeboat crew;**
- are performing duties as a **local authority councillor;**
- for IS and ESA only, are working as a **childminder** in your (or her/his) home;
- are engaged in an activity for which you (or s/he) receive, or expect to receive, a **sports award** from UK Sport and no other payment is made (or is expected to be made);
- for IS only, **qualify for mortgage interest run-on** (see p460);
- are doing **work in connection with your course of education as a student.**[40]

Note:
- For ESA, *you* do not count as in paid work if you are doing work you can do while claiming (see p1018).
- You, your partner or your non-dependant can also be treated as not in full-time paid work if you (or s/he) are **involved in a trade dispute** or, for IS or ESA, have recently returned to work following one. See Chapter 45 for further information about entitlement to, and the amount of, IS or JSA during a trade dispute.
- Before 25 January 2010, you, your partner or non-dependant could be treated as not being in full-time paid work if you (or s/he) were in employment while living in a care home, an Abbeyfield home or an independent hospital, or if you (or s/he) were disabled and because of this your earnings or hours were 75 per cent lower than would have been expected for a person without a disability in a comparable job. See pp694–95 of the 2011/12 edition of this *Handbook* for further information.

Housing benefit and pension credit

You (or your partner or non-dependant) are treated as *not* being in full-time paid work if:[41]
- you (or s/he) are **on maternity, adoption or paternity leave or are absent from work because you are sick,** even if when you are not on leave or off sick you normally work 16 hours or more each week. However, for HB, you and your partner *can* count as in full-time paid work on such leave to enable you to get an earnings disregard for childcare costs (see p270 and p311);
- the only payment you (or s/he) receive is a **sports award** from UK Sport.

In addition, you (or your partner or non-dependant) are treated as *not* being in full-time paid work in a benefit week, if in that week you (or s/he) are on IS or income-based JSA (or for HB only, income-related ESA) for more than three days.[42]

4. Self-employed people

Some self-employed people may work long hours for little financial reward, sometimes even making a loss. Nevertheless, if you work in expectation of payment, it counts as paid work. The DWP counts payments from the business to meet living expenses (in cash or in kind) as payment for work unless the drawings are from the business capital.[43] If you simply invest in a business and do not help to run it, you are not treated as self-employed.[44]

Note:

- If you do sufficient hours of paid work you count as in full-time paid work.
- It may be difficult to establish whether or not you are in full-time paid work – eg, if there are periods when you have no work, or if you only work part of the year (eg, seasonally) on a regular basis. Whether or not you are in work depends on whether you are carrying out activities in connection with self-employment. Whether or not you are in full-time paid work depends on how many hours you are doing in expectation of payment (using the rules described earlier in this chapter). During periods when you are not in work, or if you have ceased trading, you should not count as in paid work.[45]
- When calculating the number of hours you work each week, the decision maker counts all those necessary to run your business, including time you spend visiting potential customers, providing estimates, advertising or canvassing, bookkeeping and making trips to wholesalers and retailers, cleaning the business premises and doing research work – eg, if you are a writer.[46] The hours spent on services for which you are paid count, as well as other time which is essential for your business – eg, preparation time or unsuccessfully soliciting new customers.[47] The decision maker should accept your statement about the hours you work unless there is a reason for doubt.[48]

5. Universal credit

You can qualify for universal credit (UC) whether or not you or your partner are in paid work. Bear the following in mind.

- Income from work is taken into account in working out how much UC you get.
- You might not have to satisfy any work-related requirements if you have sufficient earnings (see p1076).
- You (and your partner) must satisfy a work condition to get a childcare costs element (see p253).
- You cannot get a UC housing costs element for owner-occupier payments if you have any earnings, no matter how low these are, or how many hours

Part 8: Work
Chapter 46: Work and benefits
7. Working tax credit and means-tested benefits

you work (see Chapter 22). You *can* get a housing costs element for rent payments.
- If you are getting UC and have earnings above a set amount, you are exempt from the 'benefit cap' (see p1171).

6. **Non-means-tested benefits**

Entitlement to some non-means-tested benefits is affected by issues to do with work and employment. For the rules for a specific benefit, see the relevant chapter in this *Handbook*, but a summary of these is as follows.
- You cannot qualify for:
  - carer's allowance if you are 'gainfully employed' – ie, you earn more than a set amount each week;
  - benefits based on your incapacity for work or limited capability for work (eg, incapacity benefit or contributory employment and support allowance) in any week you do any work unless this is work you can do while claiming – called 'permitted work';
  - contribution-based jobseeker's allowance if you are in full-time paid work. The rules described in this chapter apply.
- To qualify for
  - industrial injuries benefits, you must have been an employed earner when you had an accident or contracted a disease;
  - maternity allowance, you must satisfy an employment condition.
- Statutory sick pay, statutory maternity pay, statutory paternity pay and statutory adoption pay are linked to you being employed (not self-employed) and in some cases you can get them even if your employment ends.
- You might not qualify for benefits for your child (ie, child benefit or guardian's allowance) if she is aged 16 or over and does paid work for 24 hours a week or more.
- Additions for an adult are affected by the adult's earnings.

Deciding whether you are an employed earner or self-employed affects both your national insurance contributions (see Chapter 41) and the way your income from earnings is assessed (see Chapter 42).

7. **Working tax credit and means-tested benefits**

Because of differences in the work rules for working tax credit (WTC) and income support (IS), jobseeker's allowance (JSA) and employment and support allowance

(ESA), you may be able to choose whether to claim WTC or IS/JSA/ESA. In some cases, you may qualify for both WTC and IS/JSA/ESA. Because decision makers at the DWP and HM Revenue and Customs interpret the rules differently, you may be refused WTC *and* IS, JSA or ESA. If this happens, appeal against both decisions and ask for the appeals to be heard together or consecutively so the First-tier Tribunal can decide which benefit or tax credit is appropriate. The work rules for WTC are in Chapter 9. Bear the following in mind.

- You might be able to qualify for WTC *or* IS/income-based JSA/income-related ESA if you have a partner and s/he works 16 hours or more but less than 24 hours a week.[49] There is no limit on the number of hours your partner can work if you are getting contribution-based JSA or contributory ESA.
- If you or your partner are (for IS), or your partner is (for ESA), a **childminder** working from home, or you or your partner are (for IS and JSA) or your partner is (for ESA) a **foster carer** (or, in Scotland only, a **kinship carer**), you (or s/he) are treated as not in full-time paid work (see p995). You may, therefore, be able to claim either IS/JSA/ESA or WTC if you (or your partner) work 16 hours or more a week. There are also generous rules on the calculation of income (see Chapter 14).
- In some situations you might be able to claim both IS/income-based JSA/ income-related ESA and WTC. For example, if you are a single claimant, you might be able to claim IS or income-based JSA and WTC if you are a 'term-time only' worker or are off sick and getting statutory sick pay. If you are a member of a couple, you might be able to claim income-related ESA and WTC if your partner is working 16 or more, but less than 24, hours a week. However, whether you can be paid IS, income-based JSA or income-related ESA with WTC depends on your income.

Note:
- WTC counts in full as income for IS, income-based JSA and income-related ESA.
- Only taxable contributory ESA and contribution-based JSA count as income for WTC (see p631 and p709). IS, income-based JSA and income-related ESA are disregarded.[50]

Which means-tested benefit or tax credit should you claim?

1. If you can choose between claiming IS, JSA or ESA and WTC, check which passported benefits you lose or gain (see p9).

2. You get free school lunches if you are getting IS, income-based JSA or income-related ESA, but (generally) not if you are getting WTC (see p832).

3. If you claim IS, JSA or ESA, you can get help with your housing costs (see Chapter 20). You cannot get help with housing costs with WTC.

4. There is a capital limit for IS, income-based JSA and income-related ESA, but not for WTC.

5. You can get help with your childcare costs if you claim WTC, but not with IS, JSA or ESA.

6. If you and your partner are responsible for any children and one of you works at least 16 hours a week, your hours are added together to work out if you can get a 30-hour element in your WTC (see p1403).

Notes

1. The full-time paid work rule

1 Sch 1 para 6(1)(e) WRA 2007; regs 40 and 41 ESA Regs; reg 37 ESA Regs 2013
2 s124(1)(c) SSCBA 1992; s1(2)(e) JSA 1995
3 s124(1)(c) SSCBA 1992; s3(1)(e) JSA 1995; Sch 1 para 6(1)(f) WRA 2007
4 **IS** Reg 5 IS Regs
 JSA Reg 51 JSA Regs; reg 42 JSA Regs 2013
 HB Reg 6(1) HB Regs; reg 6(1) HB(SPC) Regs
5 **IS** Reg 5(1A) IS Regs
 JSA Reg 51(1)(b) JSA Regs
 ESA Reg 42(1) ESA Regs
6 Reg 6(1) HB Regs; reg 6(1) HB(SPC) Regs
7 **IS** Regs 2(1) and 5 IS Regs
 JSA Reg 51(1)(c) JSA Regs
 ESA Sch 6 para 2(1) ESA Regs
 PC Sch 2 para 2(1) SPC Regs
 HB Reg 6(1) HB Regs; reg 6(1) HB(SPC) Regs
8 Reg 3E(2)(g) JSA Regs
9 R(IS) 5/95; *Fiore v CAO*, 20 June 1995
10 *CAO v Ellis*, 15 February 1995 (CA), reported as R(IS) 22/95; CTC/626/2001
11 R(IS) 1/93
12 *Kevin Smith v CAO*, 11 October 1994 (CA), reported as R(IS) 21/95
13 *CAO v Ellis*, 15 February 1995 (CA), reported as R(IS) 22/95; CIS/434/1994
14 CFC/33/1993; R(FIS) 1/83
15 R(JSA) 1/07; *Saunderson v SSWP* [2012] ScotCS CSIH 10, 28 December 2012

16 **IS** Reg 5(7) IS Regs
 JSA Reg 51(3)(a) JSA Regs; reg 42(3)(a) JSA Regs 2013
 ESA Regs 42(2) and 45(9) and Sch 6 para 2(7) ESA Regs
17 Ch78 App5 paras 21, 23, 30 and 47 DMG
18 Reg 51(3)(c) JSA Regs; reg 42(3)(c) JSA Regs 2013
19 **IS** Reg 5(2)(b)(i) IS Regs
 JSA Reg 51(2)(b)(i) JSA Regs; reg 43(2)(b)(i) JSA Regs 2013
 ESA Regs 42(2) and 45(8)(b)(i) and Sch 6 para 2(2)(a) ESA Regs
 PC Sch 2 para 2(4) SPC Regs
 HB Reg 6(2)(a) HB Regs; reg 6(2)(a) HB(SPC) Regs
20 R(JSA) 5/03
21 R(JSA) 1/07; *Saunderson v SSWP* [2012] ScotCS CSIH 10, 28 December 2012
22 para 20322 DMG
 IS Reg 5(2)(b)(ii) IS Regs
 JSA Reg 51(2)(b)(ii) JSA Regs; reg 42(2)(b)(ii) JSA Regs 2013
 ESA Regs 42(2) and 45(8)(b)(ii) and Sch 6 para 2(2)(b) ESA Regs
 PC Sch 2 para 2(2)(b) SPC Regs
 HB Reg 6(2)(b) HB Regs; reg 6(2)(b) HB(SPC) Regs
23 CFC/2963/2001
24 **IS** Reg 5(2)(a) IS Regs
 JSA Reg 51(2)(a) JSA Regs; reg 42(2)(a) JSA Regs 2013
 ESA Regs 42(2) and 45(8)(a) and Sch 6 para 2(3) ESA Regs
 PC Sch 2 para 2(4) SPC Regs
 HB Reg 6(4) HB Regs; reg 6(4) HB(SPC) Regs
 All R(IS) 8/95

8

Chapter 46

25 **IS** Regs 2(2)(b)(i) and 5(3B) IS Regs
PC Sch 2 para 2(3) SPC Regs
HB Reg 6(3) HB Regs; reg 6(3) HB(SPC) Regs
All *Stafford and Banks v CAO* [2001] UKHL 33 (HL), reported as R(IS) 15/01
26 Reg 7 WTC(EMR) Regs
27 R(JSA) 1/07; *Saunderson v SSWP* [2012] ScotCS CSIH 10, 28 December 2012
28 CJSA/3832/2006
29 R(JSA) 8/03
30 CIS/914/1997; CJSA/2759/1998
31 R(JSA) 5/02
32 Reg 6(28) SS(C&P) Regs

2. People treated as in full-time paid work
33 **IS** Reg 5(3) IS Regs
JSA Reg 52(1) JSA Regs; reg 43(1) JSA Regs 2013
ESA Reg 42(3) and Sch 6 para 2(4) ESA Regs
PC Sch 2 para 2(5) SPC Regs
HB Reg 6(5) HB Regs; reg 6(5) HB(SPC) Regs
All R(U) 1/62
34 R(JSA) 5/03; para 20309 and Ch78 App 5 paras 73 and 74 DMG
35 **IS** Reg 5(3) IS Regs
JSA Reg 52(1) JSA Regs; reg 43(1) JSA Regs 2013
ESA Reg 42(3) and Sch 6 para 2(4) ESA Regs
PC Sch 2 para 2(5) SPC Regs
HB Reg 6(5) HB Regs; reg 6(5) HB(SPC) Regs
36 **IS** Reg 5(5) and (5A) IS Regs
JSA Reg 52(3) and (3A) JSA Regs; reg 43(2) and (3) JSA Regs 2013
ESA Regs 41(2) and (3) and 42(4) and (5) ESA Regs

3. People treated as not in full-time paid work
37 **IS** Reg 5(3A) IS Regs
JSA Reg 52(1) JSA Regs; reg 43(1) JSA Regs 2013
ESA Reg 43(3) and Sch 6 para 2(5) ESA Regs
All CIS/621/2004
38 Reg 2(1), definition of 'paternity leave', JSA Regs 2013,
39 **IS** Reg 6(1) and (5) IS Regs
JSA Reg 53(a)-(f) and (i)-(m) JSA Regs; reg 44 JSA Regs 2013
ESA Reg 43 and Sch 6 para 2(6) and (8) ESA Regs
40 R(FIS) 1/86; CDWA/1/1992

41 **PC** Sch 2 para 2(7) and (8) SPC Regs
HB Reg 6(7) and (8) HB Regs; reg 6(7) and (8) HB(SPC) Regs
42 **PC** Sch 2 para 2(6) SPC Regs
HB Reg 6(6) HB Regs; reg 6(6) HB(SPC) Regs

4. Self-employed people
43 para 20238 DMG
44 CIS/649/1992
45 R(JSA) 1/09; *GM v SSWP (JSA)* [2010] UKUT 221 (AAC); [2012] AACR 9; *Saunderson v SSWP* [2012] ScotCS CSIH 10, 28 December 2012
46 para 20265 DMG
47 R(FIS) 6/85; *Kazantzis v CAO* [1999], reported as R(IS) 13/99
48 para 20267 DMG

7. Working tax credit and means-tested benefits
49 **IS** Reg 5(1A) IS Regs
JSA Reg 51(1)(b) JSA Regs
ESA Reg 42(1) ESA Regs
50 Reg 7(3) Table 3 paras 13, 16, 17 and 26 TC(DCI) Regs

Chapter 47

Limited capability for work

This chapter covers:
1. The work capability assessment (p1003)
2. Challenging a decision (p1013)
3. Periods of limited capability for work, waiting days and linking rules (p1017)
4. Work you can do while claiming (p1018)

If you come under the universal credit (UC) system (see p19) and have limited capability for work, the work capability assessment determines whether you are entitled to extra amounts (elements) in your UC. You cannot currently make a new claim for UC if you have limited capability for work. This is not expected to change until 2015 or 2016 at the earliest and so this chapter does not cover the detailed rules for UC. However, you may be getting UC and then have limited capability for work. Most of the rules on the work capability assessment for employment and support allowance outlined in this chapter are the same for UC. Where the UC rules are different, this is indicated. For more details, see Chapter 49 of the 2013/14 edition of this *Handbook,* and see CPAG's online service and *Welfare Rights Bulletin* for updates.

Key facts
- If you are too disabled or ill to work and are assessed as having 'limited capability for work', you may be entitled to employment and support allowance (ESA), national insurance credits and, in some circumstances, to an additional amount in your housing benefit (HB).
- Your capability for work is assessed by a test called the 'work capability assessment'.
- The work capability assessment also tests whether you have 'limited capability for work-related activity'. If so, you are placed in the 'support group' for ESA and may be entitled to an additional amount of HB.
- If you come under the universal credit system, the work capability assessement tests whether you have limited capability for work and limited capability for work-related activity.
- In general, you cannot work and have limited capability for work at the same time, although certain kinds of work are allowed.

* If you disagree with the decision about your limited capability for work or work-related activity, you can apply for a revision or supersession, or appeal against it. Usually, you must apply for a revision before you can appeal.

1. The work capability assessment

Whether or not you have 'limited capability for work' is determined by a test called the work capability assessment. If you do not have, or are not treated as having, limited capability for work, you are not entitled to income-related or contributory employment and support allowance (ESA), national insurance credits (NI) credits for limited capability for work (see Chapter 41) or, if you have claimed ESA and housing benefit (HB), to a work-related activity component in your HB (see p241). In all these cases, whether you have limited capability for work is decided under the ESA rules.

The work capability assessment is also used to determine whether you have limited capability for work or limited capability for work-related activity for universal credit (UC). The UC rules are similar to the ESA rules, but there are some differences.

The work capability assessment establishes:[1]

* whether your capability for work is limited by your physical or mental condition; *and if so*
* whether the limitation is such that it is not reasonable to require you to work.

The rules say that this means 'an assessment of the extent to which [a person] who has some specific disease or bodily or mental disablement' is capable of performing specified activities, or is incapable of performing them.[2] If you have certain limitations in performing these activities, you score points in the assessment. The activities, limitations and points are in Appendix 10.

You satisfy the work capability assessment if you score sufficient points in the assessment (see p1006) or, you do not score sufficient points, but you have exceptional circumstances (see p1007). You also satisfy the work capability assessment if you are treated as having limited capability for work (see p1004).

Note: you may be treated as not having limited capability for work, even if you satisfy the work capability assessment (see p1004).

The work capability assessment also determines whether you have 'limited capability for work-related activity' (see p1008). This is a different test, used to decide whether you should be in the support group for ESA (see p621) and, if you have claimed both ESA and HB, whether you are entitled to a support component as part of your HB (see p241). In either case, whether you have limited capability for work-related activity is decided under the ESA rules.

Part 8: Work
Chapter 47: Limited capability for work
1. The work capability assessment

Treated as not having limited capability for work

You are treated as not having limited capability for work (ie, to have failed the work capability assessment), even if you have been assessed as satisfying it, if you:[3]

- do any work, except certain types or work you can do while claiming (see p1018); *or*
- are disqualified from receiving contributory ESA for more than six weeks because you are a prisoner. If this applies, but you are entitled to income-related ESA (ie, pending trial or sentence pending conviction), you are only treated as not having limited capability for work after your entitlement has ended;[4] *or*
- attend a training course and receive a training allowance or premium, unless your ESA claim is for a period beginning after you stopped attending the course, or if the training allowance or premium was only for travelling or meal expenses;[5] *or*
- are (or were) a member of the armed forces and the day in question is a day of sickness absence from duty;[6] *or*
- do not return the ESA50 questionnaire (see p1009) or attend the medical (see p1010) while the work capability assessment applies to you, and you do not have a good cause (see p1009 and p1011).

Note: these rules are different for UC. See p1041 of the 2013/14 edition of this *Handbook* for more details.

Treated as having limited capability for work

You can be treated as automatically having limited capability for work in certain circumstances. Sometimes this is called being 'exempt'. If you are not exempt and do not score enough points, you may also be treated as having limited capability for work in exceptional circumstances (see p1007). **Note:** the UC rules are slightly different. See the 2013/14 edition of this *Handbook* for more details.

You are treated as having limited capability for work if:[7]

- you have applied for ESA and provided a current medical certificate, but the work capability assessment has not yet been carried out. This rule usually does not apply if, within the last six months, you have failed the assessment or been treated as failing it because you have not returned the ESA50 questionnaire or attended the medical (see p1009) and you do not have good cause. The six months run from the date of the original decision, not from any later decision of the First-tier Tribunal.[8] Even if it is within these six months, however, you can still be treated as having limited capability for work if you have a new condition, your condition has significantly worsened, or if you failed to return the questionnaire but have now returned it; *or*
- a specific circumstance applies to you – ie, you are:[9]

- entitled to the support component on the basis that you meet one of the eating and drinking descriptors in the test of limited capability for work-related activity (see p1007);
- terminally ill;
- receiving chemotherapy or radiotherapy treatment for cancer, recovering from such treatment or are likely to receive such treament within six months from the date the DWP determines whether or not you pass the work capability assessment. In any of these circumstances, the DWP must be satisfied that you should be treated as having limited capability for work. The decision maker should look at the medical evidence to see if your cancer treatment has side effects which are likely to limit your ability to do all forms of work;[10]
- given official notice not to work because of being in contact with an infectious disease;
- pregnant and there is a serious risk to your health or your baby's health if you do not refrain from work;
- pregnant or have recently given birth, you are not entitled to maternity allowance (MA) or statutory maternity pay, you have a medical certificate giving the expected or actual date of birth, and you are within the period beginning with the first day of the sixth week before the expected week of childbirth (or the actual day of childbirth if earlier) and ending on the 14th day after you have the baby;
- in the MA period and entitled to MA;
- an inpatient in hospital where you have been medically advised to stay for at least 24 hours, or are recovering from treatment as an inpatient (and the DWP is satified that your condition remains sufficiently serious), including if you are attending a residential programme of rehabilitation for drug or alcohol addiction;
- receiving plasmapheresis or radiotherapy, regular weekly treatment for haemodialysis for chronic renal failure, or regular weekly treatment for total parenteral nutrition for gross impairment of enteric function, or are recovering from such treatment (and the DWP is satisfied that you should continue to be treated as having limited capability for work). In the first week of such treatment, you must be receiving it or recovering from it for at least two days. You continue to be treated as having limited capability for work if your treatment later goes down to one day a week. However, you cannot get income-related ESA in any week in which you work (apart from work you can do while claiming – see p1018), although you can claim contributory ESA for the days of treatment and recovery;[11]
- on any day on which you are entitled to statutory sick pay for the purpose of the 196-day qualifying period (see p617) for ESA in youth;
- for income-related ESA only, if you are in education, you are not a 'qualifying young person' (see p551) and you are eligible for income-related ESA because

Part 8: Work
Chapter 47: Limited capability for work
1. The work capability assessment

you receive disability living allowance (DLA), personal independence payment (PIP) or armed forces independent payment.

Scoring points

The assessment is carried out without referring to any job and does not take into account your education or training, or any language or literacy problems. It is a test of your ability to perform certain activities, taking account of a 'specific bodily disease or disablement' or a 'specific mental illness or disablement', and the direct results of medical treatment (from a registered doctor) for these.[12] There are two lists of activities: one physical, one mental. Under each activity, there is a further list of statements, called 'descriptors', which describe different levels of difficulty in carrying out the activity. Attached to each descriptor is a points score. You are awarded the highest scoring descriptor in each activity that applies to you, taking into account your ability when wearing or using any aid, appliance or prosthesis that you normally wear or use, or any aid or applicance that you could reasonably be expected to wear or use.[13] For the full list of activities, descriptors and points, see Appendix 10.

To satisfy the test, you must score a total of 15 points or more. The points can be scored in one or more activities, and scores from the physical and mental activities can be combined. For example, you can score nine points in the physical test and six points in the mental test, which, combined, give a total of 15 and so satisfy the test. To score points in the physical test, your incapacity must arise from a 'specific bodily disease or disablement', and to score points in the mental test, your incapacity must arise from a 'specific mental illness or disablement'.[14]

Good days and bad days, pain and tiredness

Generally, what counts is your capability as it is 'most of the time'. If you cannot repeat an activity without a reasonable degree of regularity, you should be considered unable to perform it. The following points should apply.
- Your ability to perform an activity with some degree of repetition should be considered and a 'broad brush' approach applied, rather than just a day-by-day approach.[15]
- A descriptor should apply to you if you cannot perform the activity most of the time. The severity of your condition, the frequency of your good and bad days and the unpredictability of the bad days are all relevant. So, if in a normal week you would have three bad days when a particular descriptor would apply to you, and four good days when it would nearly apply, that descriptor may apply to you, especially if your condition on the bad days is very bad.[16]
- If you have long periods of remission, you may be considered capable of work during these periods. This depends on the severity of your condition and on the length of your periods of ill health and your periods of remission.[17]

- Pain, fatigue and the increasing difficulty you may have in performing an activity on a repeated basis compared with someone in good health should be taken into account.[18] 'Pain' may include nausea and dizziness.[19] The decision maker (or First-tier Tribunal) should consider whether you can perform the activity without too much discomfort and whether you can repeat the activity within a reasonable time.
- Any risk to your health in peforming an activity should be considered, particularly if carrying it out is against medical advice. If the risk is sufficiently serious, you may be considered incapable of the activity.[20]

Exceptional circumstances

If you do not score enough points to satisfy the work capability assessment, you are treated as doing so if:[21]

- you have an uncontrolled or uncontrollable life-threatening disease, and there is medical evidence to show this. There must be reasonable cause for the disease not to be controllable by a recognised therapeutic procedure; or
- because of your illness, there would be a substantial risk to the mental or physical health of any person were you to be found not to have limited capability for work. The 'substantial risk' is one that could arise from the sort of work you may be expected to do, or from the journey to or from work, although it is not necessary to go into the detail of individual job descriptions or potential jobseeker's agreements. Arguably, the risk could also arise from broad factors such as (if you have a mental health problem) apprehension caused by the need to look for work.[22] However, this exceptional circumstance does not apply to you if the risk could be significantly reduced by reasonable adjustments in your workplace, or by your taking medication prescribed by your doctor.

Limited capability for work-related activity assessment

The work capability assessment includes an assessment of whether you have limited capability for work-related activity. This is a different test to that of limited capability for work. This test is to decide whether you are in the support group for ESA (see p621). If you have claimed HB as well as ESA, it is used to decide if you are entitled to a support component in your HB (see p241). It is also used to decide whether you are entitled to a limited capability for work-related activity element in your UC. For all these, you must have, or be treated as having, limited capability for work-related activity. See p1009 for details of the assessment.

You may automatically count as having limited capability for work-related activity, or you may be required to complete a questionnaire and/or attend a medical. If you do not return the questionnaire or take part in the medical and do not have 'good cause' ('good reason' for UC), you are treated as not having limited capability for work-related activity.

Part 8: Work
Chapter 47: Limited capability for work
1. The work capability assessment

When deciding if you have good cause (and, in practice, if you have 'good reason' for UC), the decision maker must take into account:[23]
- whether you were outside Great Britain at the time you were notified;
- your state of health;
- the nature of any disability you have;
- any other matter s/he thinks appropriate.

Limited capability for work-related activity

In order to have limited capability for work-related activity, your mental or physical condition must be such that one or more statements (or 'descriptors') describing a severe limitation in certain activities could be applied to you. For the activities and descriptors, see Appendix 11.

A descriptor applies if it applies to you for the majority of the time(s) you try to do the activity described. You are assessed wearing any prosthesis that you are normally fitted with or wear, and/or using any aid or appliance that you normally wear or use, or could reasonably be expected to wear or use.[24]

Some descriptors in Appendix 11 are about physical incapacity. To have them applied to you, your incapacity must arise from 'a specific bodily disease or disablement'. Other descriptors are about mental incapacity. To have them applied to you, your incapacity must arise from 'a specific mental illness or disablement'.[25]

The DWP may retest you to find out if there has been a relevant change of circumstances, to see if a previous finding was wrong or mistaken, or (for ESA only) if it is three months or more since your last test.[26]

You may be required to complete a questionnaire and/or attend a medical examination.

Treated as having limited capability for work-related activity

You are treated as having limited capability for work-related activity if:[27]
- you have a terminal illness; *or*
- you are receiving chemotherapy or radiotherapy treatment for cancer, or recovering from that treatment, or you are likely to receive such treatment within six months from the date the DWP determines whether or not you have limited capability for work-related activity. In any of these circumstances, the DWP must be satisfied that you have limited capability for work-related activity. The decision maker should look at the medical evidence to see if your cancer treatment has side effects which are likely to limit your ability to do all forms of work;[28] *or*
- because of a specific disease or disablement there would be a substantial risk to your mental or physical health or to the mental or physical health of someone else if you were found not to have limited capability for work-related activity; *or*
- you are pregnant and there would be a serious risk of damage to your health or to your baby's health if you do not refrain from work-related activity.

Note: the rules for UC are similar, but there are some additional circumstances. See p1046 of the 2013/14 edition of this *Handbook* for more details.

The work capability assessment process

Information is sought from your doctor and, unless you are treated as having limited capability for work (see p1004), you are sent a questionnaire (ESA50) to complete. In most cases, you are required to attend a medical examination with a doctor (or other approved healthcare professional) from the DWP Medical Service (MS). For advice about the questionnaire and medical, see below and p1010.

As part of the assessment, the doctor (or other approved healthcare professional) also carries out an assessment of whether you have limited capability for work-related activity.

The questionnaire

Unless it is already accepted that you have limited capability for work, or you are treated as having limited capability for work, you are sent a questionnaire (ESA50) to complete.

How do you complete the questionnaire?

1. Read the notes on the form before answering the questions. It may be helpful to draft your answers on a separate sheet of paper first.

2. If someone has to complete the questionnaire for you, or if you can only do so yourself slowly or with pain, explain this.

3. Make sure to list all your symptoms. If you have to appeal, the First-tier Tribunal may be less likely to believe you have symptoms if you did not mention them on the questionnaire. Ask someone who knows you well to check your answers.

4. If you have good and bad days, explain this. If your condition varies, tick the box that indicates this, but ensure that you then give a fuller answer in the space provided. If possible, give a rough estimate of how often you could perform the activity and how often you could not.

5. Compare the draft of your answers with the list in Appendix 10 and work out your score. Your answers should not be exaggerated, but check that you have not underestimated any of your problems and that you have given all the detail you can.

6. If you have any difficulties with English or with reading and writing, get independent help before you submit the form.

7. If someone has helped you fill out the form, include her/his details at the end where the form asks about this.

8. Always make a copy of your questionnaire with your answers before returning it to the DWP.

You have four weeks from the date the questionnaire is sent to complete and return it. If you do not return it within this time, a reminder must be sent to you

Part 8: Work
Chapter 47: Limited capability for work
1. The work capability assessment

at least three weeks after the questionnaire was sent. You must then be given a further week from the date the reminder was sent to return the questionnaire. If you still do not return it in time, you are treated as capable of work unless you can show that you had good cause (for UC, 'good reason') for not returning it on time.[29]

'Good cause'

When deciding whether you have '**good cause**', the decision maker must consider all the circumstances, including whether you were outside Great Britain at the relevant time, your state of health and the nature of your disability. In practice, the same sort of issues should be taken into account when deciding whether you have 'good reason' for UC.[30]

If you are late in completing and returning the questionnaire, do so as soon as you can and explain why you were late. If your benefit stops because you are considered not to have had good cause (good reason for UC), but you think you did, write to the DWP explaining this. You should also make a fresh claim for benefit. If the decision maker decides that you did not have good cause (good reason for UC), you can appeal, although usually you will have to have had a revision first (see Chapter 59).

On receiving your completed questionnaire, the decision maker considers whether you should be treated as having limited capability for work or if you clearly score enough points to satisfy the test. If neither of these apply, your case is referred to the MS for a medical examination to be arranged.

Medical examinations

You may be required to attend a medical examination as part of the work capability assessment. Bear in mind the following.

- If you fail to attend a medical examination without good cause (for UC, good reason), you are treated as not having limited capability for work.
- If you cannot attend the medical, contact the MS immediately to explain why and ask for another appointment.
- If you are too ill to travel, ask to be examined at home.
- You can claim your travel expenses for going to the medical. If you have to attend by taxi or minicab, the DWP will not pay your fares unless you get them to agree this before you travel.
- You can take a friend or adviser to the medical with you.

In order to complete the medical report, the medical examiner asks about your condition and assesses whether, in her/his opinion, you have limited capability for work. S/he considers your abilities in each of the specific areas of activity as set out in Appendix 10. The medical examiner should consider all the information and reach a judgement on the basis of:

- your answers to the questions on the questionnaire;
- what you tell her/him;
- the results of the examination and any tests s/he may carry out;
- your appearance and behaviour during the assessment. This does not just mean during the examination itself. For example, when the MS examiner greets you in the waiting area, s/he may assess your ability to rise from a chair and walk, and whether you have been able to get to the medical on your own.

The medical examiner asks about your typical day and uses the information to assess your ability to perform the activities in the work capability assessment. S/he then completes a report (an ESA85) indicating which descriptors s/he thinks apply to you and sends it to the decision maker.

What should you tell the medical examiner?

1. Tell the medical examiner how your condition affects you in as much detail as possible.

2. Take the medicines and other aids you are taking or using with you. This may lead the examiner to ask you questions s/he would not otherwise have thought to ask.

3. If you have taken additional painkillers in order to attend the medical, explain this and what you can and cannot do on your normal dosage.

4. The place where the medical takes place is likely to be a very artificial environment and there is only limited time. Tell the examiner if this affects your abilities – eg, if you can bend once or twice at the medical, but cannot do so on a repeated basis or you would start to experience pain if you did.

5. If you have good and bad days and are seen on a good day, tell the examiner what your condition is like on a bad day.

6. When asked about the activities you perform on a typical day, explain how your condition affects your ability to do day-to-day activities such as shopping, washing, dressing and watching TV.

7. If you are not fluent in English, take someone with a good knowledge of English with you. Alternatively, the MS should be able to provide (and pay for) an interpreter if you request one.[31]

If you believe you were treated unfairly at the medical, you can make a complaint. Ask the MS for its leaflet on this.

Failing to attend a medical examination

If you do not attend a medical examination without good cause ('good reason' for UC), you are treated as not having limited capability for work – ie, you will fail the work capability assessment. You must have been sent notice of the date and time

Part 8: Work
Chapter 47: Limited capability for work
1. The work capability assessment

of the medical at least seven days beforehand, unless you agreed to accept less than this.[32]

'Good cause'

When deciding whether you have '**good cause**', the decision maker must consider all the circumstances, including those that apply to the questionnaire (see p1009). 'Good cause' may also include being too ill or distressed on the day of the medical, or wishing to be examined by someone of the same sex and this was not possible. You may also be able to show that you had good cause if your refusal to attend was based on a firm religious conviction.[33] In practice, the same sort of things should be taken into account when deciding whether you have 'good reason' for UC.

If your benefit stops because you are considered not to have good cause for failing to attend the medical, but you think you did, write to the DWP explaining this. You should also make a fresh claim for benefit. If the decision maker does not accept that you had good cause, consider appealing, but note that you must usually apply for a revision first (see Chapter 59).

The decision

The decision on whether or not you have limited capability for work is made by a DWP decision maker. If you have had a medical examination, the medical report (the ESA85) is sent to the decision maker. The decision maker can disagree with the medical report, although in practice this is unusual. The medical examiner includes in the medical report a suggested date when the work capability assessment should be applied to you again in order to retest your capability. You do not have the right of appeal about how often you are retested.

If the decision maker does not consider that you have limited capability for work, you are not entitled to ESA and your claim is refused. If you have been getting ESA, your award is revised or superseded (see Chapter 58) and your benefit is stopped.

What should you do next?

1. If you have been refused ESA (but do not want to challenge the decision) and do not have a job to return to, you can sign on and claim jobseeker's allowance (JSA). Claim as soon as possible, as backdating is possible only in limited circumstances (see p1146). If you come under the UC system (see p19), you cannot get income-related JSA and must claim UC instead. You may still be able to get contribution-based JSA.

2. Remember that if you want to claim ESA again, special rules apply if it is within six months of the decision that you do not have limited capability for work (see p1004). However, if you can satisfy these rules and your new period of limited capability for work is not more than 12 weeks after the end of a previous one, the periods are linked so that, for example, you can be entitled to your former rate of ESA straight away (see p1017).

3. If you think you are not well enough to work, you may be able to challenge the decision by appealing to the First-tier Tribunal, although usually you must apply for a revision first (see Chapter 59).

4. If you do challenge the decision, you cannot get ESA while your request for a revision is being considered. You may be entitled to another benefit, such as JSA or income support (IS), instead. Once you have appealed, if you have also submitted a medical certificate, you can get ESA again (instead of JSA or IS) pending the appeal.

2. Challenging a decision

You can challenge a decision by applying for a revision or supersession (see Chapter 58), or by making an appeal (see Chapter 59), although usually you must apply for a revision first.

Initially, the DWP makes a 'determination' on your limited capability for work.[34] The determination should then be incorporated into a decision about your entitlement to benefit or national insurance (NI) credits for limited capability for work. It is not until this is included in a decision that you have the right of appeal.[35]

The First-tier Tribunal considers your appeal. It must be made up of at least one legally qualified person and one medically qualified person (see p1320). It reconsiders the issue of whether you have limited capability for work or not. The First-tier Tribunal does not have to follow either the ESA85 medical report or the decision maker's decision.

Note: when you appeal against a decision, you enable the whole decision to be looked at again if it is considered right to do so. For example, you may be appealing about limited capability for work, but the First-tier Tribunal may go on to look at whether or not you should be in the support group for employment and support allowance (ESA). Or you may be appealing about whether you should be in the support group, but the First-tier Tribunal may want to reconsider whether you have limited capability for work. This could result in your losing some, or even all, of your entitlement.

For more about First-tier Tribunal hearings, see Chapter 59.

Are you appealing?

1. Get advice from one of the organisations listed in Appendix 2.

2. Remember that there are only certain circumstances in which you can work and still be regarded as having limited capability for work (see p1003). If you work while you are appealing, you may lose entitlement to benefit, even if you eventually win your appeal.

3. Request a copy of the medical evidence that the DWP holds on your file, including a copy of the medical examiner's report (the ESA85). If you appeal, a copy of the medical

Part 8: Work
Chapter 47: Limited capability for work
2. Challenging a decision

report should be included in the appeal papers that the DWP sends to you and HM Courts and Tribunals Service.

4. Request an oral hearing of your appeal. This will give the First-tier Tribunal the opportunity to hear from you first hand about how your condition affects you, and what happened at the medical examination.

5. Discuss your limited capability for work with your own doctor. In practice, it can be very difficult to win an appeal if your GP or consultant does not support you.

6. Get medical evidence to support your appeal if you can. Medical evidence is not formally required, but tribunals often look for it. This could be from your GP or your consultant, or from both. It is more helpful if this comments on the things at issue in your appeal rather than just sets out your diagnosis and treatment. If your doctor has been treating you on a regular basis for many years, s/he should say so, so that there is no doubt that s/he is fully aware of your medical history. Check to see whether your doctor insists on charging you.

7. If you cannot get medical evidence yourself, ask the First-tier Tribunal to obtain this. This is a discretionary decision. There is no charge, but you do not have any control over who does the medical, and the report belongs to the First-tier Tribunal not you.[36] Consider using previous medical reports if you passed the work capability assessment and consider getting evidence from other sources – eg, a community nurse or an occupational therapist.

8. The First-tier Tribunal should make a decision based on all the evidence – medical and non-medical. If necessary, point out that the First-tier Tribunal can prefer your own or your doctor's evidence to that of the medical service doctor.[37]

9. Medical Service medical reports are in electronic form. These can frequently have inconsistencies or errors in them. The First-tier Tribunal must deal with any discrepancies and take these into account when considering the weight to be given to different sources of evidence.[38]

10. The First-tier Tribunal cannot carry out its own examination of you.[39] However, be aware that it may observe your conduct in the room – eg, how you walk or sit.

11. Ask a person who lives with you or who knows you well to attend the hearing to describe the day-to-day problems you have.

12. Take a list of any medication you are taking to the hearing.

Getting benefit while challenging a decision

A decision can be challenged by applying for a revision or a supersession (see Chapter 58) or by making an appeal. If you want to appeal against a decision, you must usually apply for a revision first (see Chapter 59). If you are challenging a decision that you do not have limited capability for work, you cannot get ESA while your request for a revision is being considered. During this period, you may be entitled to another benefit – eg, jobseeker's allowance (JSA) or income support (IS) instead.

Once you have appealed against a decision that you do not have limited capability for work, you can claim ESA pending the outcome of the appeal or, if you cannot get ESA pending the appeal, JSA. In limited circumstances, it may be possible to claim IS instead of ESA.

If you come under the universal credit (UC) system (see p19), you cannot get IS, income-based JSA or income-related ESA, but you may still be entitlted to some UC. You may also be able to get contribution-based JSA or contributory ESA.

Employment and support allowance

If you appeal against a decision on your limited capability for work and have submitted a medical certificate (except if you are being treated as not having limited capability because you did not return the questionnaire or attend the medical – see p1009 and p1011), you are entitled to ESA until the First-tier Tribunal makes its decision. In this chapter, this is referred to as 'ESA pending an appeal'. You must usually have had a revision before you can appeal (see p1305). You cannot get ESA while your request for a revision is being considered. However, the government has said that your ESA pending appeal can cover the period when your request for a revision was being considered.[40]

If you have limited capability for work but are appealing about whether or not you should be put in the support group, you remain entitled to ESA while your request for a revision is being considered and while your appeal is pending, although this does not include the support component.

Are you appealing against a decision that you do not have limited capability for work?

1. To get ESA pending an appeal, you must continue to submit medical certificates.[41]

2. Your ESA does not include the work-related component or support component, although it can include any premiums and housing costs to which you are entitled.[42] You do not have to reclaim ESA.[43]

3. You are treated as having limited capability for work while you are appealing, so usually the DWP does not assess you in this period. However, if you develop a new condition or your condition significantly worsens, the DWP can assess you again. If it determines that you have limited capability for work, you can get ESA in the normal way (including either of the additional components) from that point on. The First-tier Tribunal still considers your appeal for the period up until then. Even if the DWP determines that you do not have limited capability for work, you remain entitled to ESA pending the appeal.[44]

4. If your appeal is successful, the original decision about your limited capability for work is changed so that you are entitled to ESA. Your ESA continues in the normal way, and you can qualify for an additional component.

5. If your appeal is successful but the DWP considers that your condition improved while the appeal was pending, it could decide that you do not have limited capability for work now.[45] You can appeal against this decision, and should be able to get ESA pending the appeal again.[46]

Part 8: Work
Chapter 47: Limited capability for work
2. Challenging a decision

6. If you lose your appeal, the original decision that you do not have limited capability for work is not changed. From the week after the week in which the First-tier Tribunal notifies the DWP of its decision, the DWP treats you as not having had limited capability for work while you were getting ESA pending your appeal.[47] Your entitlement to ESA therefore stops, although you keep the ESA that was paid to you pending the appeal. Although you can appeal against the decison to treat you as not having limited capability for work, the prospect of success is likely to be limited, as the rules allow the DWP to do this when you have lost your appeal. In order to continue to get ESA in this situation, whether you appeal or not, you must make a fresh claim.[48]

7. If you make a fresh claim for ESA within six months of the original decison that you failed the work capability assessment, you cannot be treated as having limited capability for work unless your condition has significantly worsened or you have a new condition. So you will not be entitled to ESA if you are within six months of failing the work capability assessment – ie, the original decision you appealed against (see p1004). However, if it is six months or more since the original decision, you should be able to reclaim and get ESA if you have a medical certificate. The DWP then reapplies the work capability assessment.

Jobseeker's allowance

You may be able to claim JSA while you are waiting for your request for a revision to be considered.

Once you have appealed, instead of claiming ESA pending an appeal, you may be able to claim JSA, at least until the First-tier Tribunal makes its decision. This may be an attractive option if you cannot get ESA because you did not attend the medical and you have decided not to make a fresh claim for ESA.

In both cases, to get JSA you must sign on as available for and actively seeking work (see p1025 and p1038), and must be prepared to accept any reasonable work within your limitations, even while the appeal is pending. You can place restrictions on your availability if these are reasonable in light of your condition (see p1033). If you win your appeal and you are entitled to ESA, your JSA award is removed and you should get arrears of ESA if they are worth more than the JSA you received.[49]

Income support

You may be able to claim IS (see Chapter 3) while you are waiting for your request for a revision to be considered.

Once you have appealed, instead of getting ESA pending an appeal or JSA, in limited circumstances you may be entitled to claim IS – eg, as a lone parent or carer (see p26).

In both cases, you cannot claim IS on the grounds of disability, including incapacity for work. Even if you can get IS, you are not entitled to any disability premium on the basis of incapacity for work. You do not have to sign on as available for and actively seeking work in order to get IS. However, unless you win your appeal, you are not entitled to NI credits for limited capability for work. Therefore, you should check to see how to protect your NI contribution record while on IS (see Chapter 41). Seek advice if necessary. If you win your appeal, you cannot remain entitled to both ESA and to IS at the same time. Normally, your award of IS is removed and you should get arrears of ESA if they are worth more than the IS you received.

If your condition worsens

If your condition has significantly worsened since the decision, or you have a new condition, and you have not already claimed ESA pending the appeal (see above), you could make a fresh claim for ESA. In this situation, you should be treated as having limited capability for work until a new work capability assessment is carried out, even if is within six months of the decision that you do not have limited capability for work (see p1004). If you have already claimed ESA pending the appeal, you could inform the DWP and ask it to make a determination on your limited capability for work. If the DWP thinks that you still fail the work capability assessment, your entitlement to ESA after the appeal has been decided could be affected, even if you win your appeal. **Note:** these rules are slightly different for UC. See p1055 of the 2013/14 edition of this *Handbook* for details.

---

3. Periods of limited capability for work, waiting days and linking rules

For employment and support allowance (ESA), a 'period of limited capability for work' generally means a period in which you have, or are treated as having, limited capability for work. Except for ESA in youth, it does not include any period not covered by your claim for ESA.[50] However, see the linking rules on p1018. For universal credit (UC), there are no rules on periods of limited capability for work.

You are not entitled to ESA for three '**waiting days**' at the beginning of your period of limited capability for work.[51] (**Note:** from October 2014, the number of waiting days is due to increase to seven.) This does not apply if:

- your entitlement to ESA starts within 12 weeks of your entitlement to income support, incapacity benefit, severe disablement allowance, pension credit, jobseeker's allowance, carer's allowance, statutory sick pay or maternity allowance coming to an end; *or*
- you are a member of a couple and one of you has already served the waiting days for a claim for income-related ESA, and that person gives up her/his claim so the other member of the couple can claim it instead; *or*
- you have requalified for contributory ESA on the basis of being put in the support group, having previously lost entitlement because of the rules on how long you can be paid contributory ESA (see p625); *or*

Part 8: Work
Chapter 47: Limited capability for work
4. Work you can do while claiming

- you are terminally ill, or you have been discharged from Her Majesty's forces and three or more days before the discharge were days of sickness absence.

Linking rules

Different periods of limited capability for work can be joined or 'linked' to form one continuous period. The effect is that you are treated as having had limited capability for work throughout the whole of the linked period. Different periods are linked if they are not more than 12 weeks apart.[52] **Note:** a 104-week linking rule applies to housing costs for 'work or training beneficiaries' (see p457).

If periods of limited capability for work are linked, it means that:

- the question of whether or not you satisfy the national insurance contribution conditions for ESA may be decided at the beginning of the first period (see p861);[53]
- you do not have to serve further 'waiting days' (see p1017) before becoming entitled to ESA because you have already served them;
- you may be entitled to one of the additional ESA components straight away, or once you have been reassessed as passing the work capability assessment;
- for the purposes of the rules on housing costs, certain linking rules apply (see p456), including linking ESA claims not more than 104 weeks apart if you are a 'welfare-to-work or training beneficiary'.

4. **Work you can do while claiming**

The general rule is that you cannot work and be entitled to employment and support allowance (ESA) at the same time.[54] With certain exceptions (see below), in any week in which you work (paid or unpaid), you are not entitled to ESA and you are treated as not having limited capability for work, even if it has previously been decided that you do.[55]

However, you are only treated as not entitled to ESA on the actual days that you work, rather than the whole week, if you work:

- during the first week of your claim; *or*
- during the last week in which you had limited capability for work or were treated as having limited capability for work.[56]

It is arguable that work that is so minimal that it can be regarded as trivial or negligible[57] should be ignored.

Certain work, however, is allowed. For how earnings from this may affect income-related ESA, see Chapter 14. Note that earnings under the 'permitted work' rules (see p1019) under the relevant earnings limit are ignored.

The following kinds of work are allowed:[58]

- work as a local councillor;

- work (for a maximum of one day or two half days a week) as a member of the First-tier Tribunal if you have been appointed because of your experience of disability issues;
- domestic work (eg, cooking and cleaning) in your own home;
- the care of a 'relative' (ie, a grandparent, grandchild, uncle, aunt, nephew, niece, and including 'close relatives' – ie, parent, parent-in-law, son, son-in-law, daughter, daughter-in-law, step-parent, stepson, stepdaughter, brother, sister, or the partner of any of these);
- caring for another person living with you under specific legislation relating to accommodating children or temporarily caring for someone else where you are paid for this;
- work you do to protect someone or prevent serious damage to property or livestock during an emergency;
- work done while receiving assistance in pursuing self-employment under s2 of the Employment and Training Act 1973 or s2 of the Enterprise and New Towns (Scotland) Act 1990 (test-trading);
- voluntary work that is not for a relative (ie, any of the people, including close relatives mentioned in the fourth bullet above), the only payment you receive is to cover your reasonable expenses and it is considered reasonable for you to work free of charge;
- work done in the course of a work placement (unpaid practical work experience with an employer) approved in writing by the DWP before the placement starts;
- for contributory ESA, any work you do in a week in which you are treated as having limited capability for work because you are having certain regular treatment (eg, haemodialysis for chronic renal failure) or are recovering from that treatment (see p1004);[59]
- 'permitted work' (see below).

Note: these rules do not apply to universal credit (UC). For UC, if you earn more than a set weekly amount from work, you are treated as not having limited capability for work – ie, even if you have passed the work capability assessment. See p1004.

Permitted work

'Permitted work' (sometimes called 'exempt' work) is work of any kind, which you can do:[60]

- as part of a treatment programme done under medical supervision while you are in hospital or regularly attending hospital as an outpatient, provided you do not earn more than £101 a week; *or*
- for an unlimited period, provided you do not earn more than £20 a week. This is called the 'permitted work lower limit'; *or*

Part 8: Work
Chapter 47: Limited capability for work
4. Work you can do while claiming

- for an unlimited period, provided you do not earn more than £101 a week and you are in 'supported (sometimes called 'supervised') work' (see below); *or*
- for up to 52 weeks, or indefinitely in certain circumstances, provided you work, on average, for less than 16 hours a week and do not earn more than £101 a week. This is called the 'permitted work higher limit'. For how your hours are calculated, see p990.

Supported work

'Supported work' is work which is supervised by someone employed by a public or local authority, or by a voluntary organisation or community interest company, whose job it is to find work for people with disabilities. This could include work in a sheltered workshop or with help from social services. The DWP usually says that you need not have the person working alongside you, although the support should be ongoing and regular. Where possible, check in advance that the DWP agrees that the work counts as supported work.

If your earnings in any week are higher than the relevant limit, you are not entitled to ESA for that week.[61] Your earnings are worked out for this purpose in the same way as for income-related ESA (see p258), except that only your own earnings count, not those of your partner. Only your earnings count, not any other kind of income.

Although there are no special rules, you should inform the DWP as soon as possible about any permitted work you do. Under the general benefit rules, you are required to report changes in circumstances that you might reasonably be expected to know might affect your benefit. Also note that if the particular activities you carry out in your work suggest to the DWP that your limited capability might have changed, it might reassess this.

Note: the amounts referred to in the first, third and fourth bullet points above are usually increased in October. See CPAG's online service and *Welfare Rights Bulletin* for updates.

Permitted work higher limit

You can usually undertake work, earning under the permitted work higher limit, for up to 52 weeks. If you are treated as having limited capability for work-related activity (ie, you are in the support group – see p621), you can do this work indefinitely. Otherwise, after 52 weeks have passed since you started work (whether or not you actually work for all the 52 weeks), you can do more work which falls under the permitted work higher limit if:

- since the beginning of the last 52-week period of such work, you have ceased to be entitled to ESA or national insurance credits for limited capability for work for a continuous period lasting more than 12 weeks; *or*
- a further 52 weeks have passed.

Notes

1. The work capability assessment

1 s8(1) WRA 2007
2 **ESA** Reg 19 ESA Regs; reg 15 ESA Regs 2013
UC Reg 39 UC Regs
3 Reg 44 ESA Regs; reg 37 ESA Regs 2013
4 Reg 159 ESA Regs; reg 95 ESA Regs 2013
5 Reg 32(2) ESA Regs; reg 27 ESA Regs 2013
6 Reg 32(1) ESA Regs; reg 27(1) ESA Regs 2013
7 **ESA** Reg 30 ESA Regs; reg 26 ESA Regs 2013
UC Reg 39(1) UC Regs
8 R(IB) 8/04
9 **ESA** Regs 20, 25 and 26 ESA Regs; regs 16, 22 and 26 ESA Regs 2013
UC Regs 39(6) and 40(5) and Schs 8 and 9 UC Regs
10 Memo DMG 1/13, para 9
11 Regs 26, 44 and 46 ESA Regs; regs 22, 38 and 40 ESA Regs 2013; paras 42049-58 DMG
12 **ESA** Reg 19 ESA Regs; reg 15 ESA Regs 2013
UC Regs 39 and 42 UC Regs
13 **ESA** Reg 19(4) ESA Regs; reg 15(4) ESA Regs 2013
UC Reg 42(2) UC Regs
14 **ESA** Reg 19(5) ESA Regs; reg 15(5) ESA Regs 2013
UC Reg 39(4) UC Regs
15 *AF v SSWP (ESA)* [2011] UKUT 61 (AAC); *SAG v Department for Social Development (ESA)* [2011] NICom 171
16 CIB/14534/1996
17 CIB/2620/2000
18 CIB/14587/1996; CIB/14722/1996; CIB/13161/1996; CIB/13508/1996
19 CIB/14722/1996
20 CSIB/12/1996
21 **ESA** Reg 29 ESA Regs; reg 25 ESA Regs 2013
UC Sch 8 paras 4 and 5 UC Regs
22 *Charlton v SSWP* [2009] EWCA Civ 42, 6 February 2009; *JW v SSWP* [2011] UKUT 416 (AAC). CSIB/33/2004 is disapproved in *Charlton*, but not on the point it makes about risk arising from apprehension.
23 Regs 36-39 ESA Regs; regs 34-36 ESA Regs 2013
24 **ESA** Reg 34(3) ESA Regs; reg 30(3) ESA Regs 2013
UC Reg 42(2) UC Regs
25 **ESA** Reg 34(6) ESA Regs; reg 30(6) ESA Regs 2013
UC Reg 40(3) UC Regs
26 **ESA** Reg 34 ESA Regs; reg 30 ESA Regs 2013
UC Reg 41 UC Regs
27 **ESA** Reg 35 ESA Regs; reg 31 ESA Regs 2013
UC Sch 9 UC Regs
28 Memo DMG 1/13, para 9
29 **ESA** Reg 22 ESA Regs; reg 18 ESA Regs 2013
UC Reg 43 UC Regs
30 Reg 24 ESA Regs; reg 18 ESA Regs 2013
31 Medical Service, *Training and Development ESA Handbook*, Med-ESAHB-001, p118
32 **ESA** Reg 23 ESA Regs; reg 19 ESA Regs 2013
UC Reg 44 UC Regs
33 R(IS) 9/51

2. Challenging a decision

34 **ESA** Reg 19 ESA Regs; reg 15 ESA Regs 2013
UC Reg 39 UC Regs
35 para 06041 DMG
36 s20 SSA 1998; R(S) 3/84
37 CIB/407/1998; CIB/1149/1998; R(M) 1/93; CIB/3074/2003
38 CIB/511/2005
39 s20(3) SSA 1998
40 House of Commons, *Hansard*, Written Answers, 16 December 2013, col 486W
41 Reg 30(3) ESA Regs; reg 26(3) ESA Regs 2013
42 Reg 5(4) ESA Regs; reg 6(5) ESA Regs 2013 provide that the assessment phase applies pending the decision of the First-tier Tribunal.
43 Reg 3(j) SS(C&P) Regs; reg 79 UC,PIP,JSA&ESA(C&P) Regs
44 Reg 147A(2) and (4) ESA Regs; reg 87(2) and (4) ESA Regs 2013
45 Reg 147A(6) and (7) ESA Regs; reg 87(7) and (8) ESA Regs 2013

46 This is because the DWP will have made a determination that you do not have limited capability for work, and not merely treated you as not having limited capability for work, so reg 30(3) ESA Regs and reg 26(3) ESA Regs 2013 should apply.

47 Reg 147A(5) ESA Regs; reg 87(5) ESA Regs 2013

48 Reg 3(j) SS(C&P) Regs; reg 7 UC,PIP,JSA&ESA(C&P) Regs; Memo DMG 33/10, para 52

49 Memo DMG 51/10; reg 3(5G) and (5H) SS&CS(DA) Regs; reg 16(3) UC,PIP,JSA&ESA(DA) Regs

3. **Periods of limited capability for work, waiting days and linking rules**
50 Reg 2, definition of 'period of limited capability for work', ESA Regs
51 Sch 2 para 2 WRA 2007; reg 144 ESA Regs; reg 85 ESA Regs 2013
52 Regs 2 and 145 ESA Regs; regs 2 and 86 ESA Regs 2013
53 Paras 1-3 Sch 1 WRA 2007

4. **Work you can do while claiming**
54 Reg 40 ESA Regs; reg 37 ESA Regs 2013
55 Regs 40 and 44 ESA Regs; regs 37 and 38 ESA Regs 2013
56 Reg 40(4) ESA Regs; reg 37(4) ESA Regs 2013
57 CIB/5298/1997; CIB/6777/1999
58 Regs 40 and 45 ESA Regs; regs 37 and 39 ESA Regs 2013
59 Reg 46 ESA Regs; reg 40 ESA Regs 2013
60 Reg 45 ESA Regs; reg 39 ESA Regs 2013
61 Regs 40(1) and (2)(f) and 45 ESA Regs; regs 37(2)(f) and 39 ESA Regs 2013

Chapter 48

Jobseeking and other conditions

This chapter covers:
1. The jobseeking conditions (p1024)
2. Available for work (p1025)
3. Actively seeking work (p1038)
4. The jobseeker's agreement (p1043)
5. Special rules for laid-off and short-time workers (p1047)
6. Participating in interviews (p1048)

If you come under the universal credit system (see p19), the rules in this chapter do not apply to you. Instead, see Chapter 50 for information about your responsibilities and the work-related requirements.

Key facts

- To qualify for jobseeker's allowance (JSA), you must usually satisfy jobseeking conditions – ie, you must be available for work, actively seek work and have a current jobseeker's agreement. The DWP calls this a 'claimant commitment'.
- In some cases, there are special rules to help you satisfy the jobseeking conditions. These include if you are a lone parent, have a disability, have experienced or been threatened with domestic violence, are 16 or 17, or are laid off or on short-time work.
- You may be able to place some restrictions on the work you are available to do, but you must usually prove that you still have a reasonable prospect of getting a job.
- If you do not satisfy the jobseeking conditions, you may be sanctioned. If this happens, your JSA might be paid at a reduced (or nil) rate for a certain period. However, you may qualify for hardship payments.
- There are a number of things you must do after you have been awarded JSA. These include 'signing on', and attending and participating in regular interviews.

Part 8: Work
Chapter 48: Jobseeking and other conditions
1. The jobseeking conditions

1. The jobseeking conditions

To qualify for jobseeker's allowance (JSA), you must usually satisfy three jobseeking conditions. You must:
- be available for work; *and*
- actively seek work; *and*
- have a current jobseeker's agreement with the DWP.

You can be treated as available for work (see p1027), as actively seeking work (see p1041) and as signing a jobseeker's agreement (see p1044). There are also special rules to help you satisfy the jobseeking conditions if:
- you are in full-time training or study (see below);
- you have a disability (see p1035);
- you are a lone parent (see p1026);
- you are 16 or 17 (see p893);
- you have experienced or been threatened with domestic violence (see p1030);
- you are a laid-off or short-time worker (see p1047).

Note: the DWP calls your jobseeker's agreement a 'claimant commitment'. All the rules about jobseeker's agreements must be satisfied. These are not the same as for claimant commitments under the universal credit system (see p19).

If you do not satisfy the jobseeking conditions, or there is doubt about whether you do, you may be able to get hardship payments (see Chapter 55).

Employment officers

Employment officers work in Jobcentre Plus offices. They are sometimes called personal advisers or work coaches. Their job is to agree with you the steps you are willing to take to get back to work, keep a check on those steps, and offer practical help and advice. You cannot apply for a revision or supersession of, or appeal against, their decisions.

Full-time training and study

If you are studying full time, you are treated as unavailable for work and you, therefore, cannot qualify for JSA. There are exceptions (see p1032). **Note:** even if none of the exceptions apply, you might be able to get JSA while studying full or part time, or while waiting to go back on your course having taken approved time out because of an illness or caring responsibilities that have now ended (see Chapter 44).

Getting a training allowance

Provided you are not a child or qualifying young person for child benefit purposes (see p551), if you are receiving training and getting a specified type of training allowance, you can get income-based JSA without having to satisfy the jobseeking conditions.[1] For these purposes, 'training' does not include training for people aged 16–24 provided by the Secretary of State, the Skills Funding Agency, the Welsh Ministers or by Skills Development Scotland, Scottish Enterprise or Highlands and Islands Enterprise. However, if you are receiving this type of training you might qualify for income support (see p30).

2. Available for work

To qualify for jobseeker's allowance (JSA), you must be available for work. The general rule is that to be available for work you must be:[2]

- 'willing and able' to take up work 'immediately' (see p1026); *and*
- available at any time of the day and on any day of the week; *and*
- prepared to take a job that would involve working for *at least* 40 hours a week; *and*
- prepared to work for *less than* 40 hours a week if required to do so. In practice, this means that you must be prepared to work part time.

However, you may be able to place restrictions on your availability for work (see p1033) such as the number of hours, days and times you are available. **Note:** if your entitlement to JSA ends because you failed to comply with the requirement to be available for work, you may be sanctioned when you claim JSA again (see p1097).

You do not have to be available for work if:[3]

- you are participating in a specified scheme for assisting people to obtain employment and you count as a full-time student, or it is the first week after you are released from detention in prison, a remand centre or youth custody. However, you are likely to be required to take specific steps to improve your changes of getting work while participating; *or*
- in some cases, you are getting a training allowance (see p1024).

In some circumstances:

- you can be treated as being available for work even if you are not (see p1027);
- you can qualify for joint-claim JSA even if you or your partner (but not both of you) are not available for work (see p47).

If you are not available or treated as available for work, you cannot get JSA under the normal rules, but you may be able to get hardship payments (see Chapter 55).

Your availability for work is considered at an initial interview when you first claim JSA (see p56 and p703). Your jobseeker's agreement (the DWP calls this a 'claimant commitment') contains details of your 'pattern of availability' (ie, the particular days and times that you are available for work) as well as any other restrictions you may place on your availability.

Part 8: Work
Chapter 48: Jobseeking and other conditions
2. Available for work

Note: the DWP can decide that you are not available for work without having to show that you have turned down a job.[4] However, the fact that you turn down a job does not necessarily mean that you are not available.

If you are a lone parent

Even if you are a lone parent and have childcare responsibilities, you must be available for work to qualify for JSA. However, some special rules can apply.

- You only need to be able to take up a job on one week's (or, in some cases, 28 days') notice (see below).
- You may be treated as available for work if:
  - you have a five-year-old child who is not at school full time (see p1028); *or*
  - you are looking after a child under 16:
    - when your child is sick (see p1032); *or*
    - during the school holidays and at times when s/he is excluded from school and not receiving education provided by the local authority (see p1028).
- You may be able to restrict your availability for work:
  - in any way, if you are the subject of a parenting order or have entered into a parenting contract in respect of a child under 16 (see p1034); *or*
  - to less than 40 hours a week (see p1036); *or*
  - to your child's normal school hours, if you have a child under 13 (see p1037).

Willing and able to take up work immediately

Being **willing** to work is essentially a test of your attitude – your desire and willingness to work. What you do in practice to display this willingness is usually dealt with under the rules for actively seeking work.

You must be prepared to take up work as an employed person – being only available for self-employment is not sufficient.[5] However, this means that you do not count as being unavailable for work if you refuse to work as a self-employed person.

In order to be **able** to work it must be lawful for you to work in Great Britain.[6] Your immigration status may affect this – eg, if a condition of your entry is that you do not work. In addition, there must be nothing to prevent you from receiving job offers (eg, because you are away from home for more than a short time) and nothing to prevent you from acting on them straight away (eg, because you have other commitments that you cannot easily abandon).

Being able to take up work **immediately** means that you must usually be able to start work without any delay, with little more than the time needed to get washed and dressed and have breakfast.[7] You can be allowed more time than this in the following situations. You only need to be available for work:

- **on one week's notice** if you are doing voluntary work or have caring responsibilities (see p1027 for what counts).[8] You must be willing and able to attend an interview in connection with opportunities for work on 48 hours' notice. However, if you have caring responsibilities for a child under 16 and you can show these make it unreasonable for you to take up a job or attend an interview within these periods, you only have to be available on **28 days' notice** and be willing and able to attend an interview on seven days' notice;

- **on 24 hours' notice** if you are providing a paid or unpaid service, but do not qualify as a carer or a volunteer.[9] This includes services you provide for family or friends on a non-commercial basis, such as giving someone a regular lift to work in your car.[10] It could also include activities that are of service to the community in general (eg, offenders working in the community as part of their punishment) and tribunal members (eg, of the First-tier Tribunal and employment tribunals);
- **after your notice period** has passed if you are working part time. This applies if you have a duty to give your employer notice that you are leaving work under employment law.[11] If you must, under the terms of your contract, give longer notice, argue that the longer notice period should apply.

Note: if the DWP agrees that you are only available to work at certain times, you are *not* required to be able to take up employment at times when you are not available.[12] However, you must be willing and able to take up the offer as soon as you reach the next period in your pattern of availability (the days and times you are available).

Definitions[13]

'**Voluntary work**' is work which is done for a charity or other not-for-profit organisation or for anyone other than your partner or a child who is included in your claim, for which you receive no payment other than for your reasonable expenses.

'**Caring responsibilities**' means responsibility for looking after a member of your household (see p215 for the meaning of household) or a close relative who is a child under 16, someone over pension age or someone who needs care because of her/his mental or physical condition.

'**Close relative**' means partner, parent, step-parent, parent-in-law, parent of a civil partner, grandparent, son, stepson, son-in-law, son of a civil partner, daughter, stepdaughter, daughter-in-law, daughter of a civil partner, brother, sister, grandchild or the partner of any of these.

Treated as available for work

Even if you are not actually available for work, you can be treated as if you are for periods during your claim. You must still satisfy the other conditions of entitlement to JSA. Remember that special rules allow you to count as available for work for up to 13 weeks of being laid off or on short-time working (see p1048).

Part 8: Work
Chapter 48: Jobseeking and other conditions
2. Available for work

General rules

You are treated as available for work:[14]

- during any part of a week at the beginning of your claim if, in respect of all the days concerned, you satisfy some specified rules for being available for work;[15]
- during any part week at the end of your claim;
- if you are sick for a two-week period or are temporarily absent from Great Britain for the purpose of getting NHS hospital treatment (see pp50 and 695);
- if you were recently found not to have limited capability for work, but only if your time limit for claiming JSA is extended because you were not told promptly enough that your entitlement to income support (IS), employment and support allowance (ESA) or incapacity benefit (IB) had ended so you could not claim JSA in time. You are treated as available for work during the period for which the time limit is extended.

Lone parents

You are treated as available for work in any week in which you are the lone parent of a five-year-old child who is not in full-time education.[16] This only applies if:

- the child is included in your claim (see p210);
- the child is not required by law to be in full-time education; *and*
- it would be unreasonable for you to make other arrangements for the care of the child.

Looking after a child under 16

You are treated as available for work if you are looking after a child under 16 and:[17]

- you are a member of a couple and looking after the child while your partner is temporarily absent from the UK (for a maximum of eight weeks). The child must be included in your claim (see p210); *or*
- the person who normally looks after the child is ill, temporarily away from home or looking after her/his partner or another child who is ill (for a maximum of eight weeks). You must be looking after the child full time; *or*
- you have caring responsibilities for the child (see p1027 for what counts) and you are looking after her/him:
  – during the school holidays or other similar vacation. This only applies if it would be unreasonable to make other arrangements; *or*
  – at a time when s/he is excluded from school and is not receiving education provided by the local authority. This only applies if there are no other arrangements it would be reasonable for you to make.

Studying and training

In some situations in which you would not normally count as being available for work while studying, special rules apply. You count as available:[18]

- for one period of up to two weeks in any 12 months when you are a full-time student (see p905) on an employment-related course which has been approved in advance by your employment officer (EO). See below for more generous rules if you are on a 'qualifying course';
- if you are attending a compulsory residential course as part of an Open University course (for up to one week for each course);
- if you are attending a residential training programme run by the Venture Trust (for one programme only for a maximum of four weeks in any 12-month period).

Note: some people getting a training allowance do not have to satisfy the jobseeking conditions (see p1024). If you are participating in a specified scheme for assisting people to obtain employment (see p1093) and count as a full-time student, you do not have to be available for work.[19] However, you are likely to be required to take specific steps while participating.

Special rules apply if you are attending a 'qualifying course' with the approval of an EO. You can get JSA while attending a qualifying course if:[20]

- you are aged 25 or over; *and*
- you had been 'receiving benefit' (see below) during a jobseeking period (see p49 and p693) for at least two years at the time the course starts. When working out whether you have been 'receiving benefit' for two years, the rules for linking jobseeking periods apply (see p49 and p693); *and*
- an EO approves your attendance; *and*
- you satisfy the special conditions for being treated as available for and actively seeking work (see below and p1042).

Once you have started the course, the course becomes compulsory. This means that if you abandon it without a good reason or are dismissed because of misconduct, you could be sanctioned (see Chapter 51).

Qualifying courses and receiving benefit[21]

A **'qualifying course'** is a course of further education which is employment-related and lasts no more than 12 consecutive months. A course of a higher standard than this can also be a qualifying course if your EO agrees.

'Receiving benefit' means getting benefit as an unemployed person (eg, JSA) or national insurance (NI) credits for unemployment, or under the rules that apply if you are a man born before 6 October 1954 who has not yet reached 65 (see p858).

If you are on a qualifying course, you are treated as being available for work in any week:[22]

- which falls entirely or partly in term time, so long as you provide written evidence within five days of its being requested, confirming that you are

Part 8: Work
Chapter 48: Jobseeking and other conditions
2. Available for work

attending and making satisfactory progress on the course. This must be signed by you and by the college or educational establishment;
- in which you are taking exams relating to the course; *or*
- which falls entirely in a vacation, if you are willing and able to take up any casual employment immediately. **'Casual employment'** means employment that you can leave without giving notice or, if you must give notice, that you can leave before the end of the vacation.

Temporary absence from Great Britain

You are treated as available for work when you are temporarily absent from Great Britain and you are:[23]
- taking a child or qualifying young person who is included in your claim (see p210) abroad temporarily (for a maximum of eight weeks) for specified medical treatment;[24] *or*
- attending a job interview (for a maximum of seven days). You must tell your EO in advance and confirm it in writing if required to do so; *or*
- a member of a couple and the pensioner, enhanced pensioner, higher pensioner, disability or severe disability premium is being paid for your partner (see Chapter 12) and you are both away from Great Britain (for a maximum of four weeks); *or*
- abroad for the purpose of getting NHS hospital treatment (see p50 and p695); *or*
- a member of a joint-claim couple on the date of your claim and on the day your partner makes the claim for JSA, you are:
  - in Northern Ireland (for a maximum of four weeks) but only if you are unlikely to be away for more than 52 weeks; *or*
  - attending a job interview (for a maximum of seven days).

If you are looking after a child because your partner is temporarily absent from the UK, see p1028.

Domestic violence

If you notify the DWP that you have experienced, or been threatened with, domestic violence from your partner, your former partner or a family member (see p1031 for who counts), you are treated as available for work for four weeks from the date of notification.[25] This only applies if you are not living at the same address as the person and if the domestic violence (or threat of domestic violence) took place within the 26 weeks before you notify the DWP.

The four-week period is extended to 13 weeks if you provide 'relevant evidence' during the four weeks from a person acting in an official capacity. You are only treated as available for work under this rule once in any 12-month period. The four and 13 weeks run on whether or not you are entitled to JSA for the whole period. However, you can ask for the 13-week period to be suspended provided this is within 12 months of the date you notified the DWP about the domestic violence.

Definitions

'Domestic violence' means any incident or pattern of incidents of controlling behaviour, coercive behaviour, violence or abuse, including physical, sexual, psychological, financial or emotional abuse, regardless of your gender or sexuality.

A **'family member'** for these purposes means the following members of your family, or the family of your partner or your former partner: grandparent, grandchild, parent, parent-in-law, son, son-in-law, daughter, daughter-in-law, step-parent, stepson, stepdaughter, brother, brother-in-law, sister, sister-in-law, or the partner of any of these.

A **'person acting in an official capacity'** means a healthcare professional, a police officer, a registered social worker, your employer or your trade union representative. It also means any public, voluntary or charitable body with which you have had direct contact in connection with domestic violence.

'Relevant evidence' is written evidence that shows that your circumstances are consistent with those of a person who has experienced or been threatened with domestic violence in the 26 weeks before you notified the DWP, and that you have made contact with a person acting in an official capacity about an incident that occured in those 26 weeks.

Commmunity activities

You are treated as available for work:[26]

- if you are required to attend a court or tribunal as a justice of the peace, juror, witness or party to any proceedings (but not if you come within the definition of 'prisoner' – see p962) (for a maximum of eight weeks). You must have notified your EO beforehand;[27]

  Note: if you are selected as a juror, you must attend court when asked to do so. However, if this is for more than eight weeks and you lose JSA, this is not necessarily made up by the court. You may be able to claim IS instead of JSA.

- if you are engaged in crewing or launching a lifeboat, are carrying out duties as a part-time firefighter or are engaged during an emergency as a member of an organised group which is helping to save lives, prevent injury or a serious threat to the health of others or protect property;[28]

- if you are on annual training as a member of a territorial or reserve force (for a maximum of 15 days in any calendar year);

- for one period of up to two weeks in any 12 months when you are attending a residential work camp in Great Britain organised by a charity, local authority or voluntary organisation for the benefit of the community or the environment.[29]

Part 8: Work
Chapter 48: Jobseeking and other conditions
2. Available for work

Other

You are treated as available for work:[30]

- if you have been discharged from detention in prison, a remand centre or a youth custody institution, but only if you have not been required to participate in a specified scheme for assisting people to obtain employment (see p1093) (for one week from the date of discharge). If you have been required to participate in a scheme, you are instead exempt from being available for work (see p1025);[31]

- during temporary police detention (legal custody in Scotland) of up to 96 hours, but not if you come within the definition of 'prisoner' (see p962);

- if you are dealing with circumstances arising from:
  - a domestic emergency affecting you or a close friend or close relative (see p1027 for who counts). This could apply for instance if you are looking after one of your children who is ill; *or*
  - the death or serious illness of a close friend or close relative; *or*
  - the death of someone for whom you had caring responsibilities (see p1027 for what counts); *or*
  - the funeral of a close friend or close relative.

You are only treated as available during the time it takes to deal with the matter and only for up to a week at a time, and on no more than four occasions in any 12-month period. However, if you have caring responsibilities for a child under 16, you can be treated as available for up to eight weeks in either of the first two situations (or a combination of these) on one occasion in any 12-month period. If this applies, you can then only be treated as being available for up to a week on three more occasions in the 12-month period.[32]

Treated as unavailable for work

Even if you are (or can be treated as) available for work, you are nevertheless treated as unavailable for work if:[33]

- you are a full-time student (see p905 for who counts), *unless* you are:[34]
  - on a qualifying course (see p1029); *or*
  - on an employment-related course or a residential training programme run by the Venture Trust (see p1029); *or*
  - a lone parent, or a member of a couple who are both students, you (or your partner) are responsible for a child (see p212) and it is the summer vacation. You must satisfy all the normal rules on being available for work or be treated as being available for work because you are on an employment-related course or a residential training programme run by the Venture Trust (see p1029);

Note: you do not have to be available for work if you are participating in a specified scheme for assisting people to obtain employment, but you are likely to be required to take specific steps while participating;[35]

- you are on temporary release from prison;
- you are receiving maternity allowance or statutory maternity pay;
- you are on paternity or adoption leave;
- it is during any part of a week at the beginning of your claim. You are treated as unavailable for work unless you satisfy specified rules for being treated as available for that period (see the general rules on p1028).

Unavailable for part of a week

On occasion, you might be **unavailable for work for a short period** during a benefit week – eg, because you are away from home.

If this happens and you have put restrictions on the times that you are available (see p1036):[36]

- your JSA is not affected if the period during which you are *not* available comes entirely outside your 'pattern of availability' – ie, the particular days and times that you are available for work; *or*
- you lose JSA for the whole of that benefit week if all or part of the period during which you are not available comes within your pattern of availability.

If this happens and you have *not* put any restrictions on the times you are available, you may lose benefit for that week because you are not available to take up work immediately.[37] For this reason, it is best to avoid signing a jobseeker's agreement with totally unrestricted times that you are available.

If you are arrested and held by the police for a short time but then released, you can be treated as available for work for up to 96 hours while you are detained (see p1032).

If you are doing **voluntary work** and have placed restrictions on the total number of hours you are available to work (see p1036), any voluntary work you do (see p1027 for what counts) within your pattern of availability must be ignored for the purpose of deciding if you are available, so long as you are willing and able to rearrange the voluntary work within:[38]

- one week's notice, in order to take up any job whose hours fall within your pattern of availability;
- 48 hours' notice, to attend an interview in connection with an opportunity for work at a time that falls within your pattern of availability.

There is a similar rule in certain cases if you are a part-time student (see p911).

Restrictions on availability for work

You can restrict your availability for work in any way if the restrictions are reasonable in light of your physical or mental condition and, in some cases, if you have specified caring responsibilities for a child under 16. See p1034 for further information.

Part 8: Work
Chapter 48: Jobseeking and other conditions
2. Available for work

If you can prove that you still have a reasonable prospect of securing employment (see below), you can place some restrictions on the work you are available to do. These are:[39]

- the type of work for which you are available (see p1035);
- the number of hours, days and times you are available (see p1036);
- the terms and conditions of employment for which you are available, including the rate of pay (see p1037);
- the location of the job (see p1038).

Any restrictions are entered in your jobseeker's agreement. If you and the DWP have not agreed in advance that there are certain types of work which you cannot, or are unwilling to, do, it may prove difficult to justify turning down such a job if it is offered to you later.

A 'reasonable prospect' of securing employment

Except if you can restrict your availability in any way (see below), or you can restrict your availability to your child's normal school hours (see p1037), you must show that you have a reasonable prospect of securing employment despite any restrictions you are allowed to place on your availability.[40] If you impose more than one type of restriction, the cumulative effect on your job prospects is considered. The DWP must consider all the evidence and, in particular:[41]

- your skills, qualifications and experience; *and*
- the type and number of job vacancies within daily travelling distance of your home; *and*
- the length of time you have been unemployed; *and*
- the job applications that you have made and their outcome; *and*
- whether you are willing to move home to take up a job, but only where you are placing restrictions on the type of job you are prepared to do.

Your job prospects may be poor. However, if you do not put any restrictions on the work you will take, you are accepted as being available for work. Therefore, think carefully about whether it is sensible to apply restrictions.

Restricting your availability in any way

You can restrict your availability for work in any way if:[42]

- the restrictions are reasonable in light of your physical or mental condition (see p1035); *or*
- you have caring responsibilities (see p1027 for what counts) for a child under 16 and you are the subject of a parenting order or have entered into a parenting contract in respect of the child under specific provisions. The restrictions must be reasonable in light of the terms of the order or contract.

This means that you can restrict the type of work for which you are available, as well as the number of hours, the days and times, the terms and conditions of employment, the location of the job, and any other matter whatsoever. If the restrictions you impose are reasonable ones in light of your physical or mental condition, or the terms of the order or contract, you do not have to show that you have reasonable prospects of securing employment (see p1034).

Physical or mental condition

If you want to restrict your availability for work because of your physical or mental condition, you are normally expected to provide medical evidence. However, if you have no prospects of work at all, you should consider whether you are capable of work. If not, it may be in your interest to claim ESA or pension credit (PC) instead of JSA.

If you also place restrictions on your availability for work that are *not* connected with your physical or mental condition, you must show that you have a reasonable prospect of securing employment (see p1034) with all your restrictions. Therefore, think carefully before placing additional restrictions on your availability.

The type of work

The general rule is that you must be available for any type of employment, but you are allowed to place restrictions on the sort of jobs for which you are available, provided you have a reasonable prospect of securing employment (see p1034).[43] In addition, special rules allow you to make restrictions:
- during your 'permitted period' if you have one (see below);
- if you are a laid-off or short-time worker (see p1047);
- because of a sincerely held religious belief or conscientious objection (see p1036).

Permitted periods

If you have previously done work of a particular type (a 'usual occupation'), you can be allowed a 'permitted period' of one to 13 weeks from the date you claim JSA during which you are allowed to be available only for vacancies in your usual occupation or which pay at least what you would normally receive, or both.[44] Any other restrictions you place on your availability must be consistent with the conditions of work that are normal in your usual occupation.

Usual occupation

The term **'usual occupation'** is not defined in the rules. The DWP says that if you have followed an occupation for a long time, this can count as your usual occupation, and also that a new occupation may count as your usual occupation if you intend to follow that type of work in future.[45]

Part 8: Work
Chapter 48: Jobseeking and other conditions
2. Available for work

Not everyone is allowed a permitted period. Whether you are allowed one and, if so, how long it lasts, are matters that you and your adviser discuss at your initial interview. It should be entered in your jobseeker's agreement.[46] The DWP must consider:[47]

- your usual occupation and any relevant skills or qualifications you may have; *and*
- the length of time you have spent training for or have worked in that occupation, and the length of time since you have worked in the occupation; *and*
- the availability and location of jobs in that area of work.

Religious or conscientious objection

You do not have to be available for work that offends a sincerely held religious belief or a sincere conscientious objection – eg, a job in a company associated with live animal exports if you have a conscientious objection to these.[48] You must still have reasonable prospects of securing employment despite those restrictions (see p1034).[49]

The number of hours, days and times

You are allowed to restrict the total number of hours you are available, provided you are available for at least 40 hours a week and:[50]

- you have agreed with the DWP a pattern of availability (ie, the particular days and times that you are available for work) and this has been recorded in your jobseeker's agreement;[51] *and*
- you still have reasonable prospects of securing employment despite the restrictions (see p1034) and they do not *considerably* reduce your prospects of securing employment.

You are allowed to restrict the total number of hours you are available to *less* than 40 in some situations if you have caring responsibilities or if you are a lone parent. If you are a short-time or laid-off worker, see p1048.

Note: you must be prepared to work for the maximum number of hours for which you are available, or for a lower number.

Caring responsibilities

If you have caring responsibilities (see p1027 for what counts), you can restrict the total hours you are available to less than 40 hours a week if:[52]

- you are available for employment for at least 16 hours a week and for as many hours as your caring responsibilities permit. When deciding whether you are available for as many hours as your caring responsibilities permit, the DWP must consider relevant factors, including the particular hours and days you spend caring, whether your caring responsibilities are shared with someone else, and the age and physical and mental condition of the person for whom you care; *and*

- you have a reasonable chance of securing employment (see p1034) despite the restricted hours. You do not have to show this if you have caring responsibilities for a child under 16 and an EO decides that you would not satisfy this condition because of the type and number of job vacancies within daily travelling distance of your home.

If you are a carer and you cannot make yourself available for work at least 16 hours a week, you might be able to claim IS or, if you are at least the qualifying age (see p78), PC rather than JSA.

If you are a lone parent

If you are a lone parent and a child who is included in your claim (see p210) is under 13, you only need to be available for work during your child's normal school hours.[53] This means that you can restrict the total number of hours, days and times you are available. You do not have to show that you still have reasonable prospects of securing employment. **Note:** you also count as a person with caring responsibilities, so you may be able to restrict the total number of hours further.

The terms and conditions of employment

You can make restrictions on the terms and conditions of employment for which you are available (including the rate of pay – but see p1038), provided you can show you still have reasonable prospects of securing employment despite those restrictions (see p1034).[54]

The rate of pay

You can restrict the rate of pay:

- during your permitted period (see p1035), if you have one, to the rate you are accustomed to receiving in your usual occupation;[55]
- for six months from the date you claimed JSA, as long as you still have reasonable prospects of securing employment (see p1034).[56]

Any restrictions you may place on the rate of pay should be agreed at your initial interview. These should be recorded in your jobseeker's agreement.

What should you remember?

1. It is *vital* that the wage or salary you say you are willing to accept should not be higher than the going rate for the jobs you have said you are looking for.

2. You should not be expected to work for a rate of pay below the national minimum wage (see p1649).

Part 8: Work
Chapter 48: Jobseeking and other conditions
3. Actively seeking work

The location of the job

You can make restrictions on the localities within which you are available for work, as long as you can show you still have reasonable prospects of securing employment in the selected areas (see p1034).[57]

The rules on minimum working conditions

The rules about minimum working conditions (see Appendix 12) can affect your claim for JSA if you are looking for work. The DWP should not object to your placing a restriction on your availability for work – ie, that you will not accept a job if the terms do not comply with the legal requirements, such as if an employer is offering a job at less than the minimum wage. You can try to argue that the rule that says you must still have reasonable prospects of finding work despite the restriction (see p1034) does not apply as the DWP should assume that all employers will obey the law.

3. **Actively seeking work**

To qualify for jobseeker's allowance (JSA), you must actively seek work. Special rules apply if you have been allowed a 'permitted period' (see p1041).

You do not have to actively seek work if you are participating in:[58]

- New Enterprise Allowance; *or*
- a specified scheme for assisting people to obtain employment (see p1093) and either you count as a full-time student or it is the first week after you are released from detention in prison, a remand centre or youth custody.

However, you are likely to be required to take specific steps to improve your changes of getting a job while participating. Some people getting a training allowance (see p1024) do not have to actively seek work.

In some cases you can be treated as if you are actively seeking work even if you are not (see p1041). In some cases you can qualify for joint-claim JSA even if you or your partner (but not both of you) are not actively seeking work (see p47).

Note: if your entitlement to JSA ends because you failed to comply with the requirement to actively seek work, you may be sanctioned when you claim JSA again (see p1097).

What you must do

To be actively seeking work:

- you must take, in each benefit week, such 'steps' as you can reasonably be expected to have to take in order to have the best prospects of securing employment;[59]

- you are expected to take more than two steps during a week unless taking fewer steps is all that it is reasonable for you to do.[60] **Note:** it is possible that, in some weeks, there may be no steps that you could reasonably be expected to take.[61]

The normal actively seeking work rule is adapted to cover any part-week at the beginning of your claim. You satisfy the test provided you take reasonable steps in the part-week to ensure you have the best chance of getting a job.[62]

Your jobseeker's agreement (the DWP calls this a 'claimant commitment') says what steps you have agreed to take to find work, but you do not necessarily have to take all the steps each week to prove you are actively seeking work.[63] The test for whether you have been actively seeking work is what you *did*, not what you did not do. However, bear in mind that the DWP says that looking for work should be a full-time job and may expect you to spend a considerable amount of time actively seeking work.

You might not count as actively seeking work if it is considered that you should be taking more steps or ones that give you a better chance of finding work. You may be asked at an interview to change the steps you will take to find work. Your adviser may propose a change in your jobseeker's agreement (see p1046).

For information about how you prove that you are actively seeking work, see p1041.

What counts as a 'step'

Steps are not limited to applying for job vacancies. Anything you do that might lead to your applying for or being offered employment should count as a step.

What counts as a step?

Steps include:[64]

- applying for jobs in writing, personally or by phone, as well as seeking information from advertisements, advertisers, agencies or employers;
- calling or visiting employers to see if they are recruiting;
- registering with an agency or appointing someone else to help you find work – eg, an agent if you are looking for work in the entertainment field;
- preparing a CV;
- asking a previous employer for a reference;
- preparing a list of, or looking for information about, employers who may be able to offer you a job as well as looking for information about an occupation with a view to finding a job in that occupation;
- getting specialist advice following referral by an employment officer (EO) on how to improve your chances of finding a job – eg, from a disability employment adviser.

There are many other things that could count as steps – eg, searching for jobs on the Jobcentre Plus website and making enquiries about jobs via the internet or by email. Remember to keep a record as proof.

Part 8: Work
Chapter 48: Jobseeking and other conditions
3. Actively seeking work

When the DWP decides whether you have been actively seeking work, it must disregard a step if (unless there are reasons beyond your control) you:[65]
- act in a violent or abusive manner; *or*
- spoil an application if the step is completing a job application; *or*
- undermine your prospects of getting a job by your behaviour or appearance.

Deciding what steps are reasonable

When the DWP decides whether the steps you took in a particular week were reasonable, all the circumstances in your individual case must be considered, including:[66]
- your skills, qualifications and abilities;
- any physical or mental limitations you may have;
- how long you have been unemployed, and your work experience;
- the steps you have taken in previous weeks and how those steps have improved your chances of finding a job;
- the availability and location of job vacancies;
- any time you have spent:
  - launching or crewing a lifeboat or acting as a part-time firefighter, undertaking duties as a member of the Territorial Army or reserve forces, attending an Outward Bound course or taking part in an organised group helping in an emergency;
  - undertaking voluntary work and the extent to which it may have improved your chances of finding a paid job;
  - improving your chances of finding a job by training to use aids to overcome any physical or mental disabilities you may have or, if you are blind, training to use a guide dog;
  - as a part-time student on an employment-related course or time you have spent on a government-sponsored employment or training programme for which no training allowance is paid, if this is for less than three days a week;
- any circumstances that have resulted in your being treated as being available for work (see p1027);
- whether you have applied for, taken part in or accepted a place on a course funded by the government or European Union, which is designed to help you select, train for, obtain or retain employment or self-employment;
- if you are homeless, the steps which you needed to take and did take to find a home. It should be accepted that being homeless may limit the steps you can take to look for work and that you need time to look for somewhere to live.

If your chances of getting work are poor, there may only be a limited number of steps you can take each week, but it may be reasonable for the DWP to expect you to pursue all of them every week. If your chances of getting work are good, there may be many steps you could take each week but it would not be reasonable for the DWP to expect you to take all of them.[67]

Proving you are actively seeking work

It is important to keep careful records of the steps you take to get a job. The DWP may give you a form on which to do this.

How do you prove you are actively seeking work?

1. Make a note every time you do anything that might count as a 'step' towards actively seeking work. Include the dates and times, who you spoke to and what was said. You must be able to give details of the steps you have taken (eg, at your interview when you sign on), so it is extremely important that you keep records of your attempts to get a job.

2. Keep copies of any letters or emails you send, and of any advertisements to which you reply.

3. Tell the EO if you have difficulty reading or writing, or with the English language. You can get a friend or relative to help you compile your record (and to help you look for jobs). The DWP may be prepared to accept an oral report. You could keep a written record in your first language and take an interpreter or ask for an interpreter to be provided by the DWP.

4. Sometimes your activities to seek work may be looked at more intensively than normal, so ensure that your activities are always sufficient. Do not rely on the fact that they have not been challenged by the Jobcentre up to now.

Actively seeking work during your 'permitted period'

If you have been allowed a permitted period (see p1035), you count as actively seeking work during that period even if you are only looking for jobs in your normal line of work or at your normal level of pay, or both.[68] If you have been self-employed in your usual occupation at any time within the 12 months before you claim JSA, you count as actively seeking work if you are seeking self-employment in that occupation.

Treated as actively seeking work

Even if you are not actively seeking work, you can be treated as if you are.

- You can count as actively seeking work while you are laid off or on short-time working (see p1048).
- You are allowed two weeks (longer in some circumstances) during which time you are regarded as actively seeking work while away from home (see p1042).
- Other situations in which you can be treated as actively seeking work generally mirror those where you are treated as 'available for work' and have the same maximum lengths (see pp1027–32).[69] However, in most cases, you are only considered to be actively seeking work if the situation affects you for at least three days in the 'benefit week' (see p295 for the definition). There are differences.
  - You are treated as actively seeking work in any week which is part of a period in which you are taking active steps to set yourself up as self-employed under

Part 8: Work
Chapter 48: Jobseeking and other conditions
3. Actively seeking work

a scheme to assist people to do so (for up to eight weeks).[70] This can only apply once in any period of entitlement to JSA. The scheme must be provided or funded by a specified government agency. **Note:** if you are participating in New Enterprise Allowance, you do not have to actively seek work.[71]

– You are not treated as actively seeking work just because you have caring responsibilities for a child under 16 and are looking after her/him during the school holidays or at a time when s/he is excluded from school, see p1028. It is not known if this is an error or the intention.

– You are treated as actively seeking work for any week in which you spend at least three days on a government-sponsored employment or training course or programme for which you are not paid a training allowance.[72] This does not apply if you are on Work Experience. **Note:** if you are participating in a specified scheme for assisting people to obtain employment and either count as a full-time student or it is the first week after you are released from detention in prison, a remand centre or youth custody, you do not have to actively seek work, but you are likely to be required to take specific steps while participating.[73]

• If you are attending a 'qualifying course' with the approval of an EO (see p1029) and are treated as being available for work, you are also treated as actively seeking work.[74] If this is in any week that falls entirely in a vacation, you must take such steps as can reasonably be expected in order to have the best prospects of securing 'casual employment' (see p1030 for the meaning).

Absence from home

While you are on JSA, you can be treated as actively seeking work while away from home – eg, on holiday.[75] You still have to be available for work, so you are expected to give an assurance that you are willing and able to cut your absence short if notified of a job. In any 12-month period, you can be away from home for up to:[76]

• three weeks, if during each week you spend at least three days on an Outward Bound course; *or*

• if you are blind, two weeks, plus up to four other weeks spent attending training in the use of guide dogs for at least three days a week; *or*

• two weeks, in any other case.

If you are away for longer than this and so cannot be treated as actively seeking work, you must show that you are looking for work while you are away.

You must usually be in Great Britain to qualify for JSA. To see if you can get JSA while temporarily away, see p1580, and to see if you can be treated as available for work, see p1030. If you are unemployed and want to look for work in a European Economic Area country, see p1582 to see if you can be paid your contribution-based JSA. Even if you cannot get JSA while you are away, you might be able to get national insurance credits (see p851).

What should you do before you go away?

1. Inform the DWP before you go away. You can be required to give notice in writing.

2. You must be available for work and be able to receive information about job offers. You must, therefore, provide details of how you can be contacted or how you plan to contact the DWP while you are away.[77]

3. Check with your Jobcentre Plus office when you must sign on when you return home (see p1049). This could be a day that is not your usual signing day. If you do not sign on when you are supposed to, you may lose benefit for the whole of the period you were away unless you can show you had a 'good reason' for failing to sign on (see p1051).

4. The jobseeker's agreement

To qualify for jobseeker's allowance (JSA) you must agree and sign a 'jobseeker's agreement'. The DWP calls this a 'claimant commitment'. It enables the DWP to monitor and direct your search for a job and gives you a chance to put any agreed restrictions on your availability for work on record. It is discussed with you during your initial interview (see p56 and p703).

Some people getting a training allowance do not have to have a current jobseeker's agreement (see p1024). In some cases, you can qualify for joint-claim JSA even if you or your partner (but not both of you) do not have a current jobseeker's agreement (see p47).

Until you have agreed the contents of the jobseeker's agreement with your employment officer (EO), your claim for JSA is not passed to a decision maker to decide whether you are entitled to JSA. However, see below for situations when you can be treated as having signed an agreement. If a decision on your claim is delayed or JSA is refused because you have not entered into a jobseeker's agreement, you may be able to get hardship payments (see Chapter 55).

The agreement is not valid until it has been signed by you and the EO.[78] It can be in electronic form and can be signed by an electronic signature.[79] You must be given a copy.[80] To find out when your agreement can be backdated, see p1046. For what happens if you cannot agree, see p1045.

Note: the DWP calls your jobseeker's agreement a '**claimant commitment**' and you are asked to confirm that you understand it acts as your jobseeker's agreement. However, all the rules about jobseeker's agreements described in this section continue to apply. If you claim contribution-based JSA under the universal credit system (see p19), the rules for claimant commitments are different (see p1064).

If you are in any doubt about which rules apply to you, ask the DWP and seek advice – eg, from your local welfare rights service, law centre or CAB.

Part 8: Work
Chapter 48: Jobseeking and other conditions
4. The jobseeker's agreement

What is in the jobseeker's agreement

A jobseeker's agreement *must* contain specific information, such as your name and the date of the agreement. It must also include:[81]

- the type of job you are looking for – ie, the type of work you are going to actively seek. If you are allowed to place restrictions on the type of work for which you are available, these are entered in a separate box;[82]
- unless you say that you are prepared to work at any time, the total number of hours that you are available for work each week, with a breakdown of what hours you are available on each day. This is known as your 'pattern of availability'. For information on restricting the number of hours and the times for which you are available, see p1036;
- how quickly you must be available for work (see p1026), and other restrictions you are placing on the work for which you are available – eg, the level of pay or the distance you are prepared to travel;
- the steps you are to take to seek work or to improve your chances of work – eg, attending relevant courses;
- if you have been allowed a 'permitted period' (see p1035), the dates on which it starts and ends;
- a statement of your rights if you and the EO cannot agree on what should be in the agreement.

It also advises you to keep a record of what you do to find work and states that if you do not do enough, your JSA might be affected.

Your jobseeker's agreement is not binding on you or the DWP; there is no penalty if you fail to keep it.[83] However, the contents of the agreement and whether you have abided by it are very important evidence if there is ever a dispute about whether you are available for or actively seeking work, and also if you are ever accused of refusing a suitable job offer. If you have done everything in your jobseeker's agreement, argue that you should not be accused of not actively seeking work.[84]

Treated as signing a jobseeker's agreement

The rules that treat you as signing a jobseeker's agreement are mainly to deal with situations where there is an unavoidable delay between the date you claim JSA and the date of your initial interview (see p56 and p703), and so enable JSA to be put into payment prior to the interview.[85] You can be treated as signing a jobseeker's agreement in other situations including:

- for as long as you are treated as being available for work because of circumstances that arose between your date of claim and your interview;

- if there are circumstances affecting the normal procedures for claiming, awarding or paying JSA (eg, a computer failure at the DWP, a strike by staff or severe weather), which make it impracticable or difficult for you to comply with them;[86]
- during the period of up to 13 weeks during which you are treated as available for work because you have experienced, or been threatened with, domestic violence (see p1030), if you have not signed a jobseeker's agreement before the period begins.

Disputes about a jobseeker's agreement

Your EO is not allowed to sign your jobseeker's agreement unless s/he is satisfied that you will qualify as being available for and actively seeking work if you comply with its terms.[87] If s/he thinks you are placing unreasonable restrictions on your availability for work, or that the steps you propose to take to actively seek work are not sufficient, s/he will not sign an agreement based on your proposals.

If this situation arises, the EO may refer a proposed jobseeker's agreement (including one proposed by you) to a decision maker. If you ask your EO to do so, s/he must refer the proposed agreement to a decision maker immediately.[88] You should immediately apply for hardship payments (see Chapter 55).

The decision maker decides:[89]

- whether it is reasonable to expect you to comply with the jobseeker's agreement; *and*
- whether you would qualify as being available for and actively seeking work if you were to comply with it.

The decision maker may also direct the EO to enter into a jobseeker's agreement on whatever terms the decision maker considers appropriate and may also order that, if the agreement is entered into, it should be backdated.[90]

The decision maker must make a decision within 14 days of the agreement being referred, unless to do so would be impracticable, and must notify you of the decision.[91] If you are happy with the decision, you must see your EO and sign the agreement. If you are unhappy with it, you can ask for the decision to be revised or superseded, or appeal to the First-tier Tribunal (see Chapters 58 and 59). **Note:** you are likely to have to apply for a revision before you can appeal.

What happens if you refuse to sign your jobseeker's agreement?

If the decision maker decides in your favour, your jobseeker's agreement is normally backdated and you are paid arrears of JSA from the date of your claim. However, if the decision maker decides against you, you are unlikely to get any backdating. You therefore risk losing benefit if you refuse to sign the jobseeker's agreement and insist on it being referred to a decision maker.

Part 8: Work
Chapter 48: Jobseeking and other conditions
4. The jobseeker's agreement

Rather than refusing to sign the jobseeker's agreement proposed by your EO, it may be better to sign it and then write to the DWP saying that you would like to change it. You should not lose JSA, provided you comply with the original agreement while the variation is being considered. It is important you make it clear that you intend to do so.

Backdating the jobseeker's agreement

A jobseeker's agreement is automatically backdated to the first day you claimed JSA, as long as you and your EO can agree about what it should contain and it is not referred to a decision maker.[92] This includes any date to which your claim has been backdated (see p1146).

If the agreement is referred to a decision maker, it is only backdated if s/he makes a direction ordering this.[93] S/he must consider all the relevant circumstances including:[94]

- whether it was reasonable for you to refuse to accept the agreement proposed by the EO; *and*
- whether the terms of any alternative agreement that you may have proposed are reasonable; *and*
- whether you have subsequently said that you would be prepared to accept the agreement proposed by the EO; *and*
- the date on which you were first prepared to enter into an agreement that the decision maker considers to be reasonable; *and*
- the fact that the first opportunity you had to sign a jobseeker's agreement was later than the date of your claim for JSA.

Changing your jobseeker's agreement

The terms of your jobseeker's agreement can be changed by agreement between you and your EO. Any change must be in writing and signed by you and the EO.[95] This can be in electronic form and can be signed by an electronic signature.[96]

Both you and the EO can propose changes at any time. Put your proposals in writing, giving full details of the changes you want to make and your reasons. Explain how your proposals give you a reasonable chance of finding a job.

An EO cannot agree to a change unless s/he considers that the terms mean that you satisfy the jobseeking conditions.[97] If you and the EO:

- agree the proposed changes, you must be given a copy of the new jobseeker's agreement;[98]
- do not agree the proposed changes, these can be referred to a decision maker.[99] They *must* be referred to a decision maker if you request this.

When a referral to a decision maker is made

When a proposed change to a jobseeker's agreement is referred to a decision maker, your existing agreement remains in force until a decision is made.

Payment of your JSA might be suspended if you do not stick to the terms of the agreement if this causes a doubt about whether you are available for or actively seeking work.

If the decision maker believes that both your and the EO's proposals are reasonable and you would qualify as being available for and actively seeking work, the DWP says s/he should change the agreement along the lines you propose.[100]

The decision maker can direct a change of the jobseeker's agreement, the terms and when the new agreement takes effect.[101] The terms can be those that either you or the EO have proposed, or terms prepared by the decision maker her/himself. If a change you proposed is accepted and it makes the terms of the agreement less restrictive, argue that the new agreement should take effect from the date on which you proposed the change.[102]

If you fail to sign the new agreement within 21 days of the date a change in your jobseeker's agreement is directed, the decision maker can bring the agreement to an end.[103] If this happens, you no longer get JSA, including during any revision or appeal period, unless you qualify for hardship payments (see Chapter 55).

If you are unhappy with the decision maker's decision, you can request a revision or appeal to the First-tier Tribunal (see Chapters 58 and 59). You are likely to have to apply for a revision before you can appeal. If your appeal is eventually allowed, the original jobseeker's agreement revives and you are owed arrears, even if the First-tier or Upper Tribunal directs another change in the agreement.[104]

5. Special rules for laid-off and short-time workers

If, because of 'temporary adverse industrial conditions', you have a job but:[105]
- your work and wages have been suspended, you count as being **laid off** – eg, you are a farm worker whose work is suspended because of a food safety scare;
- your hours of work have been reduced, you count as being on **short-time working** – eg, you are a secretary in a solicitor's office whose hours are reduced because the property market is flat and there is no conveyancing to be done.

You must be available for and actively seeking work to qualify for jobseeker's allowance (JSA). Special rules allow you to be treated as available for and actively seeking work for up to 13 weeks if you have been laid off or put on short-time working, even though you are still subject to your normal employment contract and so have a duty to return to work or to working full time as soon as your employer wants you to do so.

Part 8: Work
Chapter 48: Jobseeking and other conditions
6. Participating in interviews

Availability for work

You are treated as available for work for the first 13 weeks of a period of being laid off or of short-time working, provided:[106]

- you are willing and able to:
  - return immediately to the job from which you were laid off or to full-time working in the job in which you are being kept on short time; *and*
  - take up immediately (subject to the rules on p1026) any 'casual employment' that is within daily travelling distance of your home. If you are a short-time worker, this only has to be during the hours when you are not working in your normal job; *and*
- in the case of short-time working only, the weekly total of the number of hours during which you are working and the number of hours during which you are available for casual employment is at least 40 hours (unless you are restricting your hours of availability to less than 40 because of a physical or mental condition or because of caring responsibilities – see p1035 and p1036).

Definitions

A '**week**' for this purpose means any period of seven consecutive days.[107]

'**Casual employment**' is work that the employer is prepared for you to leave without giving any notice.[108]

You are not entitled to a 'permitted period' (see p1035) unless you lose your job completely during the first 13 weeks of being laid off or being on short time.[109] In this case, you may be allowed a permitted period, but it must end by a date no more than 13 weeks after the start of your JSA claim.

Actively seeking work

You are treated as actively seeking work during any benefit week (see p295) in which you are subject to the special rules on availability described above for at least three days. You must take all the steps that you can reasonably be expected to take which give you the best prospects of finding casual employment.[110]

6. Participating in interviews

In order for the DWP to check that you have satisfied the jobseeking conditions and that you continue to qualify for jobseeker's allowance (JSA), you must participate in regular interviews and sign on regularly at the Jobcentre Plus office (see p1051). If you:

- do not participate in an interview, your entitlement to JSA may end or you may be given a sanction (see p1053 and p1054);
- fail to sign on, your entitlement to JSA may end (see p1051).

When you first claim JSA, you must attend an initial interview (see pp56 and 703). If you fail to do so, your date of claim is affected.

Your travel expenses to and from the Jobcentre Plus office to participate in interviews are generally not reimbursed. However, you may be able to have your travel expenses reimbursed if you are given an appointment for an interview on a day other than the day you normally sign on, or if you have to attend a different office on your normal signing-on day and you incur additional costs. If you are signing on by post but are required to attend for an interview, you may also be entitled to a refund of travel costs.

The requirement to participate

While you are getting JSA, you (and, if you are a joint-claim couple, both of you) must normally participate in regular interviews, usually at the Jobcentre Plus office.[111] You can be required to provide information about your circumstances, your availability for work and how you have been actively seeking work.[112] You can be notified of the manner, time and place of an interview by phone, post or electronic means.[113]

Note: your entitlement to JSA can end if you fail to participate in an interview (see p1053) or you can be sanctioned (see p1054).

Regular interviews and signing on

While you are getting JSA you (and, if you are a joint-claim couple, both of you) must normally attend the Jobcentre Plus office to participate in a regular interview (generally every fortnight). Take your records of your attempts to find work with you. The aims of the interview are to:

- keep a regular check on what you are doing to find work and make sure that your jobseeker's agreement (the DWP calls this a 'claimant commitment') remains up to date and relevant;
- discuss any difficulties you are experiencing and identify any help and support that the DWP can give you;
- check whether there have been any relevant changes in your circumstances;
- decide if you should be sent after a job vacancy, or required to participate in a training or employment scheme – eg, Work Experience or the Work Programme (see p707).

You may be referred to an employment officer (EO) for a more in-depth interview if what you say raises a doubt about whether you remain entitled to JSA.

At the interview, you must sign a declaration (known as **'signing on'**) that:[114]

- you have been available for and actively seeking work or could be treated as if you were and, for most 16/17-year-olds, that you have been actively seeking suitable training (see p894). See p1041 for information about proving you are actively seeking work; *and*

Part 8: Work
Chapter 48: Jobseeking and other conditions
6. Participating in interviews

- there has been no change in your circumstances that might affect the amount of, or your right to, JSA (other than those you may have already notified to the DWP).

Note: if you fail to sign on, your entitlement to JSA can end (see p1051) or you may be sanctioned under the rules that apply to interviews (see p1054).

You are normally told your regular signing day and time at the start of your claim.

Generally, you must sign on every fortnight. This is the case even if you are paid weekly. You can also be instructed to sign on more frequently (see p1050). Your travel expenses to and from the Jobcentre Plus office to sign on are *not* reimbursed. If this causes you hardship, ask if you can sign on by post (see below).

Have you been told that you are not entitled to jobseeker's allowance?
If you are told that you are not entitled to JSA, you can argue that you no longer have to sign on – eg, while you are appealing against the decision.[115] However, if your appeal is successful, in order to be paid arrears you must show that you have satisfied the jobseeking conditions since the last time that you signed on, which can often be difficult. So it is always best to continue to sign on to protect your position.

Signing on by post

The DWP might allow you to sign on by post – eg, if you live a long way from the Jobcentre Plus office, or you have a mental or physical disability which restricts your mobility. Even so:

- you must attend and participate in interviews (see p1052). You could try to get an interview arranged with a visiting EO nearer your home, if attending at the Jobcentre Plus office would result in your being away from home for a long time;
- you must send a signed declaration and show that you are available for and actively seeking work. If this is not received at the time specified by the DWP, your entitlement to JSA ends unless you can show a 'good reason' for the delay (see p1051). If you cannot show this, you must make a fresh claim for JSA.

More frequent signing on

You may be required to sign on and participate in interviews more frequently than once every two weeks if the Jobcentre Plus office thinks you need more help to find work, if you are suspected of fraud or if you have no fixed abode. Because decisions about how often you have to sign on are made by EOs, you do not have a right of appeal. However, you can ask for the frequency to be altered – eg, if your circumstances change or the cost of travel causes hardship.

Failure to sign on

Your entitlement to JSA ends if you do not provide a signed declaration on the day you were notified to do so, unless you can show a 'good reason' within five working days of your failure.[116] You must be given five days before a decision is made to end your entitlement.[117] 'Good reason' is not defined in the rules, but for information about what may count, see p1107.

If you fail to sign on because you did not show up at the Jobcentre Plus office for an interview, you may instead lose your entitlement or be sanctioned under the rules about failure to participate in an interview (see p1052).

If you contact the Jobcentre Plus office within five days of the date you failed to sign on but cannot show a good reason, or you do not contact the Jobcentre Plus office within those five days, your entitlement to JSA ends and you must make a fresh claim. You lose JSA for the whole period between the date on which your entitlement ends and the date on which you are treated as having claimed again. The date on which your entitlement to JSA ends is the *earliest* of the following days:[118]

- the day after the last day for which you have provided information that shows you continue to be entitled to JSA – eg, at your regular fortnightly interview. In many cases, this means the day after the last day on which you signed on;
- the day on which you should have signed on.

The date on which you are treated as having claimed JSA again is normally the first day on which you contact the Jobcentre Plus office again. See p1053 to see if your new claim can be backdated. The rules are the same as for failing to attend an interview.

The effect of this is that if you fail to sign on you may lose JSA for the full period for which you would have been paid if you had signed on at the right time. In addition, you lose JSA for the days between the day you missed signing on and the day you next contact the Jobcentre Plus office.

How can you minimise your loss?

1. Go to the Jobcentre Plus office within five days of your failure to participate in an interview or to sign on.

2. Explain why you did not participate in the interview or why you did not sign on – eg, if you did not receive notice that you were supposed to attend, or you have a good reason.

3. If a decision is made to stop your entitlement or to sanction you, ask for the decision to be revised, or appeal against it. You are likely to have to apply for a revision before you can appeal.

4. To protect your position, make a new claim for JSA as soon as possible. Ask for it to be backdated under the special rule on p1053 or the normal rules (if relevant).

Part 8: Work
Chapter 48: Jobseeking and other conditions
6. Participating in interviews

5. If you have missed signing on, ask the Jobcentre Plus office to accept the information you would have provided on your signing-on day. If this is accepted, the decision maker should revise the decision that stopped your benefit so that you are paid up to the date you failed to sign on.[119]

Further interviews

If you remain unemployed for a period of time, you must participate in a number of interviews. If you fail to do so, your entitlement to JSA can end (see p1053) or you can be sanctioned (see p1054).

Some interviews take place at regular intervals. However, you can be required to participate in an interview at any time – eg, if the DWP thinks you need more help with your search for work or there is a question about whether you fulfil the jobseeking conditions.

At the interview, an EO reviews your situation, the type of work you are looking for and the steps you are taking to find it. You may be asked to agree to a change of your jobseeker's agreement (see p1046) to record any change in the type of work for which you are looking or steps you will take to find it.

Failure to participate in an interview

Your entitlement to JSA can end if you do not participate in an interview (eg, you miss the appointment or you turn up but refuse to answer questions) when you are required to do so (see p1053). However, in some cases, your entitlement to JSA does not end – instead, you are sanctioned (see p1054). You may be able to get hardship payments (see Chapter 55). If you fail to sign on because you miss an interview, you may lose your entitlement to JSA for this reason (see p1051). See p1051 for ideas about how to minimise your loss.

Notification of your regular interviews is normally given when you first claim JSA. Notification of interviews can be in writing, by telephone or by electronic means.[120] If you can show you did not receive the notification, this means that you have not failed to participate and, therefore, your entitlement to JSA should not end, nor should you be sanctioned. The law normally assumes that when a letter has been sent correctly addressed and with the full postage paid, it will be received. So if notification was sent to you, you need to put forward a good case to show why this assumption should not be made – eg, you have always responded properly to other notifications when these were received from the Jobcentre Plus office or there are problems with your postal address.[121]

Note:
- If you fail to attend and participate in your initial interview (ie, when you claim JSA), you might not be awarded JSA or your date of claim might be affected.

- If the requirement to attend or participate is for a training or employment scheme or programme, your entitlement does not end, but you can be sanctioned under other rules (see p1091).[122]

When your entitlement to jobseeker's allowance ends

If you are given notice by an EO that you must participate in an interview on a specified date, unless you contact the EO within five working days (see below) your entitlement to JSA ends if you fail to participate in the interview:[123]

- at the right time – eg, you attend on the right day, but are late. This only applies if, on a previous occasion, you failed to participate in an interview and the DWP gave or sent you a written notice warning you that, if you failed to participate the next time you are required to do so, your entitlement to JSA could cease or you could be sanctioned; *or*
- on the right day. The rules do not make any provision for you to be given a warning in the way that they do for the situation where you fail to participate in an interview at the right time.

Your entitlement to JSA can only end if you do not contact the EO within five working days of the date you failed to participate in an interview.[124] However, you may be sanctioned if you cannot show a good reason (see p1054).

If you contact the EO, but not within five days of the date you failed to participate in an interview, your entitlement to JSA ends and you must make a fresh claim. You lose JSA for the whole period between the date on which your entitlement ends and the date on which you are treated as having claimed again. The date on which your entitlement to JSA ends is the *earliest* of the following days:[125]

- the day after the last day for which you have provided information that shows you continue to be entitled to JSA – eg, at your regular fortnightly interview. In many cases, this means the day after the last day on which you signed on; or
- the day on which you should have participated in an interview.

The date on which you are treated as having claimed JSA again is normally the first day on which you contact the Jobcentre Plus office again. However, if this was the same day as the failure to participate in an interview, you are treated as having made your fresh claim on the *following* day.[126] See below to see if your new claim can be backdated.

Backdating your new claim

If your entitlement to JSA has ceased because you failed to participate in an interview and you have to make a new claim, it may be possible to get your new claim backdated and so avoid some, or all, of the loss of JSA. Your claim can be backdated under any of the normal rules (see p1146). It can also be backdated under a special rule: your claim can be backdated to the day after your entitlement to JSA ended if you are not normally required to attend at the Jobcentre Plus office (eg, you are allowed to sign on by post), you did not receive the notice to attend and you make a new claim for JSA immediately after you are informed that you had failed to attend.[127]

When you are sanctioned

Your entitlement to JSA does not end if you fail to participate in an interview when required, but you contact the EO within five working days. However, you may be sanctioned unless you can show a 'good reason'. See p1093 for further information about sanctions for failing to participate in interviews and p1107 for what may count as a good reason.

Notes

1. The jobseeking conditions
1 Regs 1(3) and 170 JSA Regs

2. Available for work
2 s6(1) JSA 1995; regs 6, 7(1) and (2) and 10 JSA Regs
3 Reg 7 JSA(SAPOE) Regs
4 R(U) 44/53
5 s6(1) JSA 1995
6 *Shaukat Ali v CAO*, appendix to R(U) 1/85
7 *Secretary of State for Social Security v David*, 15 December 2000 (CA), reported as R(JSA) 3/01
8 Regs 4 and 5(1)-(1B) and (6) JSA Regs
9 Reg 5(2) JSA Regs
10 C(U) 96/1994
11 Reg 5(3) JSA Regs
12 Reg 5(4) JSA Regs
13 Reg 4 JSA Regs
14 Reg 14(1)(i), (j), (l), (ll) and (o) JSA Regs
15 Reg 14(2A) JSA Regs; R(JSA) 2/07
16 Reg 17B JSA Regs
17 Reg 14(1)(e), (g), (t) or (u) JSA Regs
18 Reg 14(1)(a), (f) and (k) JSA Regs
19 Reg 7 JSA(SAPOE) Regs
20 Reg 17A(2), (3) and (5) JSA Regs
21 Reg 17A(7) and (8) JSA Regs
22 Reg 17A(3) and (7) JSA Regs
23 Reg 14(1)(c), (m), (n), (nn), (p) and (q) JSA Regs

24 Reg 14(4) JSA Regs
25 Reg 14A JSA Regs; Art 11(2) WRA 2012 (No.11)O
26 Reg 14(1)(b), (d), (r) and (v) JSA Regs
27 Reg 14(2B) JSA Regs
28 Reg 14(5) JSA Regs
29 Reg 4 JSA Regs
30 Reg 14(1)(h) and (s) and (2) JSA Regs
31 CJSA/5944/1999
32 Reg 14(2ZA) and (2ZB) JSA Regs
33 Reg 15 JSA Regs
34 Regs 14(1)(a) and (k), 15(1)(a), (2) and (3) and 17A(1) JSA Regs
35 Reg 7 JSA(SAPOE) Regs
36 Reg 7(3) JSA Regs
37 *Secretary of State for Social Security v David*, 15 December 2000 (CA), reported as R(JSA) 3/01
38 Reg 12 JSA Regs
39 s6(3) JSA 1995; regs 6, 7, 8, 13 and 13A JSA Regs
40 Reg 10 JSA Regs
41 Reg 10(1) JSA Regs
42 Reg 13(3) and (3A) JSA Regs
43 Reg 8 JSA Regs
44 s6(5), (7) and (8) JSA 1995; reg 16 JSA Regs
45 paras 21399 and 21403-04 DMG
46 Reg 31(f) JSA Regs
47 Reg 16(2) JSA Regs
48 para 21451 DMG

Chapter 48

Jobseeking and other conditions

49 Reg 13(2) JSA Regs
50 Reg 7(2) JSA Regs
51 R(JSA) 2/07
52 Regs 4 and 13(4)-(7) JSA Regs
53 Reg 13A JSA Regs
54 Reg 8 JSA Regs
55 Reg 16(1) JSA Regs
56 Regs 8 and 9 JSA Regs
57 Reg 8 JSA Regs

3. Actively seeking work
58 Reg 7 JSA(SAPOE) Regs
59 s7(1) JSA 1995
60 Reg 18(1) JSA Regs
61 CJSA/2162/2001
62 Reg 18A JSA Regs
63 CJSA/1814/2007
64 Reg 18(2) JSA Regs
65 Reg 18(4) JSA Regs
66 Reg 18(3) JSA Regs
67 paras 21616-20 DMG
68 Reg 20 JSA Regs
69 Regs 19 and 21B JSA Regs
70 Reg 19(1)(r) and (3) JSA Regs
71 Reg 7 JSA(SAPOE) Regs
72 Reg 19(1)(q) JSA Regs
73 Reg 7 JSA(SAPOE) Regs
74 Reg 21A JSA Regs
75 Reg 19(1)(p) JSA Regs
76 Reg 19(2) JSA Regs
77 R(U) 4/66

4. The jobseeker's agreement
78 s9(3) JSA 1995
79 s9(3A) JSA 1995
80 s9(4) JSA 1995
81 s9(1) JSA 1995; reg 31 JSA Regs
82 HS v SSWP [2009] UKUT 177 (AAC);
     [2010] AACR 10
83 CJSA/1814/2007
84 CJSA/2162/2001
85 Reg 34 JSA Regs
86 CJSA/935/1999
87 s9(5) JSA 1995
88 s9(6) JSA 1995
89 s9(6)(a) and (b) JSA 1995
90 s9(7)(b) and (c) JSA 1995
91 s9(7)(a) and (8)(b) JSA 1995; reg 33 JSA
     Regs
92 Reg 35 JSA Regs
93 s9(7)(c) JSA 1995
94 s9(8)(a) JSA 1995; reg 32 JSA Regs
95 s10(1) and (2) JSA 1995
96 s10(2A) JSA 1995
97 s10(4) JSA 1995
98 s10(3) JSA 1995
99 s10(5) JSA 1995

100 s10(7)(a) JSA 1995; reg 39 JSA Regs;
      para 21951 DMG
101 s10(6)(b) and (d) JSA 1995
102 R(JSA) 2/07
103 s10(6)(c) JSA 1995; reg 38 JSA Regs
104 CJSA/4435/1998

5. Special rules for laid-off and short-time workers
105 Reg 4 JSA Regs
106 Reg 17(1)-(3) JSA Regs
107 Reg 17(5) JSA Regs
108 Reg 4 JSA Regs
109 Reg 17(4) JSA Regs
110 Reg 21 JSA Regs

6. Participating in interviews
111 s8 JSA 1995; regs 23 and 23A JSA Regs
112 Reg 24(1)-(5A) JSA Regs
113 Regs 23 and 23A JSA Regs
114 s8 JSA 1995; regs 24(6) and (10) and
      65A JSA Regs
115 CJSA/1080/2002
116 Regs 25(1)(c) and (1A) and 27 JSA
      Regs; SSWP v Michael Ferguson [2003]
      EWCA Civ 536, reported as R(JSA) 6/03
117 DL v SSWP(JSA) [2013] UKUT 295 (AAC)
118 Reg 26 JSA Regs; SSWP v Michael
      Ferguson [2003] EWCA Civ
      536, reported as R(JSA) 6/03; R(JSA) 2/
      04
119 R(JSA) 2/04
120 Regs 23 and 23A JSA Regs
121 Regs 23 and 23A JSA Regs;
      s7 Interpretation Act 1978; R(JSA) 1/04
122 Reg 25(1A) JSA Regs
123 s8(2) JSA 1995; reg 25(1)(a) and (b) and
      (1A) JSA Regs
124 DL v SSWP(JSA) [2013] UKUT 295 (AAC)
125 Reg 26 JSA Regs; SSWP v Michael
      Ferguson [2003] EWCA Civ
      536, reported as R(JSA) 6/03; R(JSA) 2/
      04
126 Reg 6(4C) SS(C&P) Regs
127 Reg 6(4B) SS(C&P) Regs

1055

Chapter 49

Claimant responsibilities

This chapter covers:
1. Work-focused interviews (below)
2. Taking part in an interview (p1060)
3. Work-related activity (p1061)

This chapter covers your responsibilities if you do not come under the universal credit (UC) system, other than the jobseeking conditions for jobseeker's allowance (see Chapter 48). If you come under the UC system, see Chapter 50.

Key facts
- You and your partner may have to take part in work-focused interviews for income support (IS), jobseeker's allowance, employment and support allowance (ESA), incapacity benefit, severe disablement allowance or carer's allowance.
- If you only qualify for IS because you are a lone parent and you do not have any children under three, or you are entitled to ESA and you are not in the support group, you may be required to undertake some work-related activity.
- If you do not take part in work-focused interviews or undertake work-related activity, you may be sanctioned. Your benefit is then paid at a reduced (or nil) rate. However, you may qualify for hardship payments.

1. Work-focused interviews

If you are getting specified benefits, you (or, in some cases, your partner) can be required to take part in work-focused interviews. These are intended to help and encourage you to keep in contact with the employment market and eventually begin full-time paid work. Claimants who are not required to attend an interview can still take part in the schemes on a voluntary basis. At the interview, job opportunities, training and rehabilitation are discussed. **Note:** some income support (IS) claimants who are lone parents, and employment and support allowance (ESA) claimants, may also have to undertake work-related activity (see p1061).

There are currently a number of schemes under which you can be required to take part in work-focused interviews.

- Interviews for ESA and benefits for incapacity (see below) – ie, if you are incapable of work and entitled to IS, incapacity benefit (IB) or severe disablement allowance (SDA).
- Interviews for lone parents entitled to IS (see p1058).
- Jobcentre Plus interviews for certain IS claimants (see p1059).
- Interviews for the partners of those entitled to IS, income-based jobseeker's allowance (JSA) (but not joint-claim JSA), income-related ESA, IB, SDA or carer's allowance (CA) (see p1059).

If you (or your partner) do not take part, you could be sanctioned and your benefit paid at a reduced rate (see p1099). Under the Jobcentre Plus rules, if you fail to take part when you claim IS, you may be treated as not having made a claim (see p1059).

There have been many changes to the rules for work-focused interviews since the requirement to take part in them was introduced. You may still come under one of the earlier sets of rules. However, this section only covers the current rules. See previous editions of this *Handbook* for details of the old schemes.

Note: you do not have to take part in work-focused interviews under these rules if you are getting any type of JSA. However, you may have to participate in interviews under other rules, and you must satisfy jobseeking conditions (see Chapter 48).

Interviews for employment and support allowance and benefits for incapacity

If these rules apply, you can be required to take part in work-focused interviews in order to continue to receive the full rate of your benefit.[1] Unless you are exempt (see p1058), you come under these rules if you are entitled to ESA, IB, IS on the grounds of incapacity for work or SDA. This includes if you have been awarded ESA in advance (see p70).[2] These rules can also apply if you make a new claim for IB, IS on the grounds of incapacity for work or SDA, although, in most cases, new claims for these are not now possible and you must claim ESA instead.

Note:

- There are no limits on the frequency or timing of interviews.
- The requirement to take part in an interview can be deferred to another date if it is considered that an interview would not be of assistance or appropriate.[3] There is no right of appeal about this.
- If you fail to take part in a work-focused interview without 'good cause', you may be sanctioned and your benefit is paid at a reduced rate (see pp1099–1101).

In certain circumstances, if you are entitled to ESA, you may be required to undertake work-related activity as well as attend work-focused interviews (see p1061).

Exemptions

You do not have to take part in work-focused interviews if:[4]
- you are at least the qualifying age for pension credit (PC – see p78); *or*
- you are a lone parent and responsible for a child under one who is a member of your household; *or*
- for IB, IS and SDA, you are incapable of work because you have a severe condition; *or*
- for ESA:
  - the decision maker has decided that you have, or are treated as having, limited capability for work-related activity – ie, you are in the support group (see p621); *or*
  - the decision maker thinks that an interview would not be (or would not have been) of assistance because you are (or were likely to be) starting or returning to work; *or*
  - you are only entitled to contributory ESA at a nil rate.

Work-focused interviews for lone parents

Some lone parents whose youngest child is aged one or over must take part in work-focused interviews under the Jobcentre Plus rules for IS claimants (see below). Otherwise, unless you are exempt, you must take part in work-focused interviews under the rules described in this section if you are entitled to IS and you are a lone parent responsible for and living in the same household as a child.[5] This applies even if you are claiming IS on a basis other than that you are a lone parent – eg, you are also a carer on CA.

Note:
- The requirement to take part in an interview can be waived or deferred to another date if it is considered that it would not be of assistance or appropriate.[6] There is no right of appeal about this.
- If you fail to take part in a work-focused interview and cannot show 'good cause', you may be sanctioned and your IS is paid at a reduced rate (see p1099).

In certain circumstances, you may be required to undertake work-related activity as well as attend work-focused interviews (see p1061).

Exemptions

You are not required to take part in a work-focused interview under these rules if you are:[7]
- under 18; *or*
- responsible for a child aged under one who is a member of your household; *or*

- already subject to the Jobcentre Plus rules for other IS claimants (see below) or the rules for ESA and benefits for incapacity (see p1057).

Jobcentre Plus interviews for income support

Unless the rules for ESA and benefits for incapacity (see p1057) apply to you, the Jobcentre Plus rules apply to most claims for IS (including claims from some lone parents). Unless you are exempt, you are required to take part in a work-focused interview:

- when you make a new claim for IS. **Note:** this does not apply if you are a lone parent responsible for a child under five or a lone parent under 18;[8]
- as a condition of continuing to receive the full rate of IS. In this case, interviews are triggered by certain events, such as stopping or starting part-time work, but in any case occur at least every three years.[9]

The requirement to take part in an interview can be waived or deferred to another date if it is considered that an interview would not be of assistance or appropriate.[10] There is no right of appeal about this. If you fail to take part in an interview when you claim IS, you are treated as not having made a claim and are therefore not entitled to benefit.[11] If, when you claim IS, your interview is deferred to another date, you are paid IS in the meantime and, if you fail to take part in the interview, your entitlement to IS is terminated.[12] Otherwise, if you are entitled to IS and you fail to take part in a work-focused interview and cannot show 'good cause', you may be sanctioned and your IS is paid at a reduced rate (see p1099).

Note:
- If you are a lone parent on IS, whether you come under this scheme or the lone parents' scheme on p1058 depends on when you first claimed IS.[13]
- In certain circumstances, if you are a lone parent entitled to IS, you may be required to undertake work-related activity as well as attend work-focused interviews (see p1061).

Exemptions

You are not required to take part in an interview if you are a lone parent responsible for a child under one.[14]

Work-focused interviews for partners

If you are a member of a couple and you are entitled to a specified benefit (see below), your partner may be required to take part in a work-focused interview. This applies if:[15]

- you and your partner are both aged 18 or over but under the qualifying age for PC (see p78); *and*
- you have been continuously entitled to a specified benefit for 26 weeks or more; *and*
- the benefit is paid to you at a higher rate because of your partner – eg, you get the couple rate of income-based JSA or get an increase for an adult with CA.

* * *

Specified benefits

The '**specified benefits**' are IS, income-based JSA (but not joint-claim JSA), ESA, IB, SDA and CA.[16]

* * *

Note:

- Your partner must take part in one work-focused interview as a condition of your receiving the full amount of your benefit. However, if you are claiming income-based JSA and you or your partner are responsible for a child aged one or over who is a member of your household, your partner must take part in further interviews every six months.[17]
- The requirement to take part in an interview can be waived or deferred to another date if it is considered that it would not be of assistance or appropriate.[18] There is no right of appeal about this.
- If your partner fails to take part in a work-focused interview and cannot show 'good cause', you may be sanctioned and your benefit is paid at a reduced rate (see p1099).

Exemptions

Your partner is not required to take part in a work-focused interview under these rules if:[19]

- s/he is entitled to one of the specified benefits in her/his own right; *or*
- you or your partner are responsible for a child under one who is a member of your household.

* * *

2. **Taking part in an interview**

Work-focused interviews normally take place at the local DWP or Jobcentre Plus office. However, an interview can take place in your home if the DWP thinks that going to the office would cause undue inconvenience or endanger your health.[20] There is no right of appeal against this decision.

'**Taking part**' means that you must:[21]

- turn up at the time and place notified;
- 'participate in discussions' with your personal adviser about your employability and about any activity you are willing to do (or have done) which may enhance your employment prospects. **Note:** this does not apply if it is your partner who is required to take part in an interview and, under the Jobcentre Plus rules, this only applies if you are a lone parent;
- answer questions about your educational qualifications, employment history, any current work and your future hopes for working, vocational training, employment skills and abilities and medical conditions that affect your chances of getting a job, and your caring or childcare responsibilities;

- except for ESA (where action plans are drawn up for your 'work-related activity' – see below) and for work-focused interviews for partners, discuss and assist in completing an 'action plan'. Under the Jobcentre Plus rules, this only applies if you are a lone parent. The action plan includes any action you and the personal adviser agree is reasonable and you are willing to take. There is nothing to say you must take the steps in the action plan, although this is likely to change in the future. See CPAG's online service and *Welfare Rights Bulletin* for updates;
- discuss your progress, any action you 'might have taken' under the action plan, how the action plan might be amended and any further support that might be available to you in further interviews.

Under the Jobcentre Plus rules (see p1059), if you are under 18, 'taking part' also requires you to attend an interview with a person specified by the DWP – eg, someone at the place where the local authority provides careers advice.[22]

3. Work-related activity

Unless you are exempt (see p1062), you can be required to undertake some 'work-related activity' if you are required to take part in work-focused interviews and you are entitled to:[23]
- income support (IS), the only reason you are entitled is because you are a lone parent and you do not have any children under three; *or*
- employment and support allowance (ESA).

Note: the IS rules for lone parents described below are based on draft regulations, due to come into force on 6 April 2014. See CPAG's online service and *Welfare Rights Bulletin* for updates.

You may be required to undertake the work-related activity by the DWP as well as by advisers contracted by the DWP – eg, in the Work Programme (an employment initiative that includes back-to-work support for ESA claimants). If you fail to take part in work-related activity without 'good cause', you may be sanctioned (see p1103).

The main features are as follows.
- 'Work-related activity' is activity that makes it more likely that you will get a job or remain in work.[24] The exact activity is at the discretion of your personal adviser. For ESA, it specifically includes work experience and work placements. However, the DWP says you cannot be required to undertake work experience; this is voluntary.[25] So if you do not undertake work experience, you should *not* be sanctioned.

- Any requirement to undertake work-related activity must be 'reasonable', taking into account your circumstances.[26] A requirement as to the time at or by which you must undertake work-related activity can be lifted if the decision maker considers it would be (or would have been) unreasonable to require you to undertake the activity at or by that time.[27]
- You cannot be required to apply for a job, undertake work (as an employee or otherwise) or (for ESA) undergo medical treatment.[28]
- All work-related activity must be recorded in an 'action plan', which must be in writing and specify the activity you are required to undertake.[29] An action plan must be reconsidered if you request it, and a written decision issued following the request.[30]

If you are a lone parent, you can only be required to undertake work-related activity during your child's normal school hours.[31] For ESA, the child must be under 13. **Note:** for IS, you can also required to undertake work-related activity during periods in which you have entrusted someone over 18 to supervise your child on a temporary basis (other than for healthcare) – eg, a babysitter or member of your family.

Exemptions

You cannot be required to undertake work-related activity if:[32]
- you are a lone parent who is responsible for a child under three; *or*
- you are exempt from the requirement to take part in work-focused interviews; *or*
- for IS, as well as being a lone parent, you come within any of the other groups of people who can claim IS (see p26); *or*
- for ESA, you are entitled to carer's allowance (see Chapter 25), or your ESA includes a carer premium (p237).

Notes

1. **Work-focused interviews**
   1 SS(IBWFI) Regs; regs 54-62 ESA Regs
   2 Reg 54(2) ESA Regs
   3 Reg 5 SS(IBWFI) Regs; reg 59 ESA Regs
   4 **ESA** Regs 54(2) and 60 ESA Regs
     Other benefits Reg 3(4)-(6) SS(IBWFI) Regs
   5 Regs 2-2ZB SS(WFILP) Regs

   6 Regs 5 and 6 SS(WFILP) Regs
   7 Reg 4 SS(WFILP) Regs
   8 Regs 2(1) and 3(1)(a)(i) SS(JPI) Regs
   9 Regs 4, 4ZA and 4A SS(JPI) Regs
   10 Regs 6 and 7 SS(JPI) Regs
   11 Reg 12(2)(a) SS(JPI) Regs
   12 Regs 7(3) and 12(2)(b) SS(JPI) Regs
   13 Regs 4ZA and 4A SS(JPI) Regs

Chapter 49

Claimant responsibilities

14 s2A(2A)(b) SSAA 1992; reg 8 SS(JPI)
Regs
15 s2AA SSAA 1992; regs 2, 'definition of
partner', and 3 SS(JPIP) Regs
16 s2AA(2) SSAA 1992
17 Reg 3A SS(JPIP) Regs
18 Regs 5 and 6 SS(JPIP) Regs
19 s2AA SSAA 1992; regs 3, 3A and 7
SS(JPIP) Regs

2. Taking part in an interview
20 Reg 10(2) SS(JPI) Regs; reg 2C(3)
SS(WFILP) Regs; reg 6(2) SS(IBWFI)
Regs; reg 56(2) ESA Regs; reg 9(2)
SS(JPIP) Regs
21 Reg 11(2)-(2B) SS(JPI) Regs; reg 3
SS(WFILP) Regs; regs 6 and 7 SS(IBWFI)
Regs; regs 57 and 58 ESA Regs; reg
10(1) and (2) SS(JPIP) Regs
22 Regs 3(3) and 11(3) SS(JPI) Regs

3. Work-related activity
23 **IS** s2D SSAA 1992; regs 2(1) and 11
IS(WRA) Regs (draft)
ESA s13 WRA 2007; regs 3(1) and 9
ESA(WRA) Regs
24 **IS** s2D(9) SSAA 1992
ESA s13(7) and (8) WRA 2007
25 para 4 Memo DMG 41/12
26 **IS** Reg 2(3)(a) IS(WRA) Regs (draft)
ESA Reg 3(4)(a) ESA(WRA) Regs
27 **IS** Reg 4 IS(WRA) Regs (draft)
ESA Reg 6 ESA(WRA) Regs
28 **IS** Reg 2(3)(b) IS(WRA) Regs (draft)
ESA Reg 3(4)(b) ESA(WRA) Regs
29 **IS** Reg 3 IS(WRA) Regs (draft)
ESA Reg 5 ESA(WRA) Regs
30 **IS** Reg 5 IS(WRA) Regs (draft)
ESA Reg 7 ESA(WRA) Regs
31 **IS** Reg 10 IS(WRA) Regs (draft)
ESA Reg 3(5) ESA(WRA) Regs
32 **IS** Reg 2(2) IS(WRA) Regs (draft)
ESA Reg 3(2) ESA(WRA) Regs

8

Chapter 50

Claimant responsibilities: the universal credit system

This chapter covers:
1. The claimant commitment (below)
2. The work-related requirements (p1066)
3. The requirements you must meet (p1073)

This chapter covers your responsibilities if you come under the universal credit (UC) system. If you do not come under the UC system, see Chapters 48 and 49.

Key facts

- If you come under the universal credit (UC) system, to qualify for UC, contribution-based jobseeker's allowance or contributory employment and support allowance, you must accept a 'claimant commitment'.
- There are work-related requirements, some or all of which you may have to meet. These are: **work-focused interviews**, **work preparation**, **work search** and **work availability**.
- If you do not meet the work-related requirements, you may be sanctioned. Your benefit is then paid at a reduced (or nil) rate. However, you may qualify for UC hardship payments.

1. The claimant commitment

If you come under the universal credit (UC) system (see p19), you must accept a claimant commitment to qualify for UC, contribution-based jobseeker's allowance (JSA) and contributory employment and support allowance (ESA).[1] The claimant commitment is a record of your responsibilities while you are receiving benefit.[2] **Note:** if you are claiming UC jointly with your partner and one of you refuses to accept a claimant commitment, you cannot qualify for UC even if the other does accept a claimant commitment.[3]

You can qualify for UC, contribution-based JSA or contributory ESA without accepting a claimant commitment if the DWP considers that:[4]

- you cannot accept one because you lack the capacity to do so – eg, if you need an appointee to make your benefit claim for you; *or*
- there are exceptional circumstances in which it would be unreasonable to expect you to accept one. The DWP says this includes if you are in hospital and likely to be there for weeks, if there is a domestic emergency, or if the Jobcentre Plus office is closed because of an emergency – eg, a fire or flood.[5]

Your claimant commitment must include:[6]
- the work-related requirements you must meet (see p1073); *and*
- any other information the DWP thinks is appropriate to include.

Accepting your claimant commitment

Your claimant commitment is prepared by the DWP and is in such form as it thinks fit.[7] If no, or not all, work-related requirements are to be imposed on you, the government intends that your first claimant commitment is accepted as part of the normal claims process. Otherwise, your claimant commitment is drawn up by your personal adviser during a face-to-face discussion. **Note:** your claimant commitment can be reviewed and updated as the DWP thinks fit (see p1066).

You must accept the most up-to-date version of your claimant commitment using the method specified by the DWP. This could be electronically (eg, online), by telephone or in writing.[8] Be sure to use the method specified or you might not count as accepting the claimant commitment.

The DWP specifies a time within which you must accept your claimant commitment. If you accept it within that time, you are usually treated as accepting it on the date of your claim (or any date to which it has been backdated).[9] However, if you are awarded UC or ESA without making a claim, you are treated as accepting it on the first day of the first assessment period (for UC) or the first benefit week (for ESA) of your benefit award.

The time within which you must accept your claimant commitment (including one that has been updated) can be extended, if:
- for UC and JSA, you ask the DWP to review any action proposed by the decision maker as a work search or work availability requirement, or whether there should be any limitations on these;[10]
- for ESA, you ask for an extension.[11]

In both cases, the DWP must be satisfied that your request is reasonable.
Note:
- The government intends to give you a 'cooling-off' period if you refuse to accept a claimant commitment, to give you the chance to reconsider.[12]
- If you are not happy with your claimant commitment, you may be able to get it reviewed (see p1066).

Part 8: Work
Chapter 50: Claimant responsibilities: the universal credit system
2. The work-related requirements

Reviewing your claimant commitment

Your claimant commitment can be reviewed and updated as the DWP thinks fit.[13] This will be done on an ongoing basis to record clearly the expectations placed on you, when these have changed and the consequences for failing to comply with them.

When should you ask for a review?

There is nothing to prevent you from asking for your claimant commitment to be reviewed and updated. However, you risk losing benefit if you refuse to accept a claimant commitment. Rather than refusing to accept the claimant commitment that has been proposed, it is better to accept it and then write to the DWP saying you would like it to be reviewed. You should not lose benefit, provided you comply with the work-related requirements that have been imposed on you while a review is being considered. It is important to make it clear that you intend to do so.

2. **The work-related requirements**

If you are entitled to universal credit (UC) or if you come under the UC system (see p19) and you are entitled to contribution-based jobseeker's allowance (JSA) or contributory employment and support allowance (ESA), you must normally meet work-related requirements.[14] If you do not meet these, you may be sanctioned and your benefit may be paid at a reduced (or nil) rate (see Chapter 52). **Note:** if you are entitled to UC and also to contribution-based JSA or contributory ESA, you only have to meet one set of work-related requirements – those for UC.[15]

The work-related requirements are:
- work-focused interviews (see p1067);
- work preparation (see p1067);
- work search (see p1068); *and*
- work availability (see p1070).

You may have to meet work-related requirements even if you are in paid work.

Your claimant commitment sets out the work-related requirements you must meet and the specific actions you must take to satisfy these. They can be adjusted to reflect your personal circumstances – eg, if you are a lone parent, a carer or have an illness or disability.

Note: there are situations when no work-related requirements can be imposed on you (see p1073).

The work-focused interview requirement

If a work-focused interview requirement is imposed on you, you must take part in one or more work-focused interviews – ie, interviews relating to work or work preparation.[16] You may also have to participate in other interviews for any purpose connected to the work-related requirements (see p1072).

The purpose of the interviews is to make it more likely that you will find or remain in work.

A work-focused interview should:[17]

- assess your prospects for obtaining or remaining in work ('paid work' for UC);
- assist or encourage you to obtain or remain in work ('paid work' for UC);
- identify activities you can undertake and opportunities for training, education or rehabilitation that will make it more likely that you will obtain or remain in work ('paid work' for UC);
- for UC, determine whether you are in gainful self-employment or whether you are in a 'start-up period';
- identify work opportunities that are relevant to your needs and abilities.

The DWP tells you when and where a work-focused interview is to take place. **Note:** if you do not attend or do not take part in a work-focused interview, you may be sanctioned and your benefit may be paid at a reduced (or nil) rate (see Chapter 52).

Obtaining paid work
'Paid work' means work done for payment or for which you expect to be paid.[18] For UC, it does not include work for a charity or voluntary organisation, or as a volunteer, if the only payment you get (or expect to get) is your expenses. For UC and JSA, **'obtaining paid work'** includes obtaining more paid work, or better paid work.[19] 'Obtaining paid work' is not defined for ESA.

The work preparation requirement

If a work preparation requirement is imposed on you, you must take 'particular action' specified by the DWP that makes it more likely that you will obtain paid work, more paid work or better paid work.[20] **Note:** there are situations when no work-related requirements can be imposed on you (see p1073) and when only a work-focused interview requirement can be imposed on you (see p1077).

Particular action
'Particular action' includes: attending a skills assessment, improving personal presentation, participating in training or in an employment programme, undertaking

Part 8: Work
Chapter 50: Claimant responsibilities: the universal credit system
2. The work-related requirements

work experience or a work placement (including Mandatory Work Activity) and developing a business plan.[21]

If you have limited capability for work, 'particular action' also includes taking part in a work-focused health-related assessment – ie, an assessment by a healthcare professional, including how far your capability for work can be improved by taking steps in respect of your physical or mental condition.

The DWP can specify the amount of time you must spend doing any 'particular action'.[22] **Note:** if you fail to meet this requirement, you may be sanctioned and your benefit may be paid at a reduced (or nil) rate (see Chapter 52).

The work search requirement

If a work search requirement is imposed on you, you are expected to take 'all reasonable action' (see p1068) to obtain paid work (see p1067 for what counts), more paid work or better paid work. You must also take any 'particular action' specified by the DWP.[23] **Note:** for ESA, a work search requirement can *never* be imposed on you.

Particular action

'**Particular action**' includes carrying out work searches, applying for jobs, creating and maintaining an online profile, registering with an employment agency and seeking references.[24]

The DWP can specify the amount of time you must spend doing any 'particular action'.[25]

Note:
- If you are told to apply for a particular job vacancy, you are treated as failing to meet the work search requirement if you do not participate in an interview for the vacancy.[26]
- If you fail to meet the work search requirement, you may be sanctioned and your benefit may be paid at a reduced (or nil) rate (see Chapter 52).

All reasonable action

In general, you are expected to look for work regardless of its type or salary, provided it is within 90 minutes travel time of your home.[27] However, you may be able to persuade the DWP that certain limitations should apply to the work you are available for and seeking to do (see p1071).

To count as taking 'all reasonable action' to find paid work, more paid work or better paid work, you must take action that gives you the best prospects of obtaining work. The DWP looks at the time you spend looking for work and the quality of action you have taken – eg, contacting employers, registering with employment agencies and investigating opportunities for self-employment.[28] In each week you must normally seek work for:[29]

- at least the weekly number of hours you are expected to work (your 'expected hours' – see below) – normally 35 a week, minus any deductions the DWP allows (see below); *or*
- a lower number of hours than your 'expected hours', provided the DWP is satisfied that you have taken all reasonable action despite the lower hours of work search.

The DWP can agree deductions from your expected hours of work search for time you spend:[30]

- carrying out paid work; *or*
- carrying out voluntary work. This must not be for more than 50 per cent of your expected hours; *or*
- carrying out a work preparation requirement or 'voluntary work preparation' (ie, action that is agreed with the DWP that you take on a voluntary basis to make it more likely you will obtain paid work, more work or better paid work); *or*
- dealing with temporary childcare responsibilities, a domestic emergency, funeral arrangements or other temporary circumstances.

Examples

Kathy is claiming contribution-based JSA. She is looking for shop work. To get relevant experience, she volunteers in a local charity shop for 10 hours a week. Her 'expected hours' (see below) are 35 hours a week. However, she need only spend 25 hours a week looking for work because the DWP agrees to deduct the 10 hours during which she is doing voluntary work.

Jim and Bill are joint UC claimants. Jim spends a lot of time caring for Bill who is on long-term sick leave. All of the work-related requirements are imposed on Jim. No work-related requirements are imposed on Bill. Jim counts as a 'relevant carer' and his 'expected hours' (see below) are 16 hours a week (the hours the DWP is satisfied are compatible with his caring responsibilities). He is therefore meant to look for work for 16 hours a week. Jim only looked for work for 10 hours this week. This is because he was offered and accepted a job working 18 hours a week, starting next week. The decision maker agrees that he has taken all reasonable action despite the lower hours.

Your expected hours

You are normally expected to work 35 hours a week (your 'expected hours'). However, your expected hours can be lower if:[31]

- you are a 'relevant carer', a 'responsible carer' or a 'responsible foster parent' (see p1075 for the definitions) and the DWP is satisfied that you have

Part 8: Work
Chapter 50: Claimant responsibilities: the universal credit system
2. The work-related requirements

reasonable prospects of obtaining paid work, more paid work or better paid work. Your expected hours are the number that the DWP thinks is compatible with your caring responsibilities;
- you are a 'responsible carer' or, for JSA only, a 'responsible foster carer' for a child under 13. Your expected hours are the number that the DWP thinks is compatible with your child's normal school hours (including travelling time to and from school). 'Responsible foster carer' is not defined, but it is presumed this is meant to apply if you are a 'responsible foster parent' (see p1075);
- you have a 'physical or mental impairment'. Your expected hours are the number that the DWP thinks is reasonable in the light of your impairment.

The work availability requirement

If a work availability requirement is imposed on you, you must be available for work. **Note:** for ESA, a work availability requirement can *never* be imposed on you.

To meet the work availability requirement, you must be able and willing immediately to:
- take up paid work (see p1067 for what counts), more paid work or better paid work;[32] *and*
- attend an interview in connection with getting paid work.[33]

Note: if you are someone who does not have to meet a work search requirement for a period (see p1079), or a work availability requirement because your earnings are sufficient (see p1080), you can count as able and willing to take up paid work or attend an interview immediately (see below) once the circumstances that exempt you from the requirement no longer apply.[34]

You may be able to persuade the DWP that certain limitations should apply to the work you are available for and seeking to do. See p1071 for further information.

If you fail to be available for work, you may be sanctioned and your benefit may be paid at a reduced (or nil) rate (see Chapter 52).

Note: for JSA, you are treated as *not* having met the work availability requirement if you are a prisoner on temporary release under specified provisions.[35] For UC, you continue to count as a prisoner in this situation (see p962).

Able and willing to take up work or attend an interview immediately

For information about what may count as being able and willing to take up work immediately, see p1026. The issues are the same as for JSA jobseeking conditions.

Although the rules normally permit no delay, you can in some situations be allowed more time. If the DWP is satisfied that you need longer, you can be allowed:[36]
- up to **one week** to take up work if you are doing voluntary work;

- taking into account alternative care arrangements, up to **one month** to take up work if you are a 'responsible carer' or a 'relevant carer' (see p1075 for the definitions);
- until **after your notice period** has passed if you are working and you have a duty under employment law to give your employer notice that you are leaving work.

In all the situations above, you can also be given **up to 48 hours' notice to attend an interview** in connection with obtaining work.

Limitations on availability and search for work

You may be able to persuade the DWP that certain limitations should apply to the work you are available for and seeking to do. They can be applied to:[37]
- the type of work;
- the number of hours a week, or the times, you can work;
- the rate of pay;
- the location of the work.

The rules specify some limitations you may be allowed to place (see below). The decision maker can also specify limitations in individual cases. For example, the decision maker may agree that you should not have to seek work of a particular type if it offends a sincerely held religious belief or a sincere conscientious objection – eg, a job in a slaughterhouse if you are a vegetarian.

Limitations may be either indefinite or for a limited period.

The type of work

Limitations can be placed on your availability for work and your search for work in the following circumstances.
- If you have previously done work of a particular type, you can limit your work search and work availability to work of a similar type for up to three months if the DWP is satisfied that you still have a reasonable prospect of getting work despite the limitation (see p1034 for ideas about what might be considered).[38] Ensure you understand the period you have been allowed.
- If you have a 'physical or mental impairment' that has a substantial adverse effect on your ability to do work of a particular type, you do not have to be available for or look for work of that type.[39]

The number of hours

You are normally expected to be available for and to search for work for the weekly number of hours you are expected to work (your 'expected hours') – usually 35 hours a week. **Remember:** if you are a 'relevant carer', a 'responsible carer' or a 'responsible foster parent' (see p1075 for the definitions), or you have

Part 8: Work
Chapter 50: Claimant responsibilities: the universal credit system
2. The work-related requirements

a 'physical or mental impairment', your 'expected hours' can be lower.[40] See p1069 for further information.

The rate of pay

If you have previously done work at a particular rate of pay, you can limit your work search and work availability to work for a similar rate of pay for up to three months if the DWP is satisfied that you still have a reasonable prospect of getting work despite the limitation (see p1034 for ideas about what might be considered).[41] Ensure you understand the period you have been allowed.

The location of the work

There are limitations on the location of the work you must search for and be available to do.
• You only have to be available for work, and to look for work, in locations that are no more than 90 minutes travel time from your home.[42]
• If you have a 'physical or mental impairment' that has a substantial adverse effect on your ability to do work in particular locations, you do not have to be available for work or to look for work there.[43]

The effect of the rules on minimum working conditions

The rules about minimum working conditions (see Appendix 12) can affect your claim for UC or JSA if you are looking for work. It should be possible for you to claim that a limitation should apply to the work you are available to do – ie, that you will not accept a job if terms do not comply with the legal requirements (eg, if an employer is offering a job at less than the minimum wage).

Interviews

The DWP can require you to participate in an interview for any purpose connected to work-related requirements (called 'connected requirements') – ie, to:[44]
• impose a work-related requirement on you; *or*
• verify that you have complied with a work-related requirement; *or*
• assist you to comply with a work-related requirement.

These requirements are likely to include a requirement to take part in regular interviews and to 'sign on'.

At the interview, you may be asked to provide evidence and information. You may also be asked to report any changes in your circumstances that are relevant to the imposition of work-related requirements on you and your compliance with them.

3. The requirements you must meet

In many cases, you must meet *all* the work-related requirements (see below). However:

- in some cases, work-related requirements cannot be imposed on you (see below); *or*
- you may only have to meet a work-focused interview requirement (see p1077); *or*
- you may only have to meet a work-focused interview requirement and a work preparation requirement (see p1078); *or*
- you may not have to meet a work search requirement or a work availability requirement for a period (see p1079 and p1080).

All work-related requirements

Unless you are covered by any of the exceptions described on pp1073–80, for universal credit (UC) and jobseeker's allowance (JSA) the decision maker *must* impose a work search requirement and a work availability requirement on you. S/he can also impose a work-focused interview requirement or a work preparation requirement, or both.[45]

Even if you would otherwise be covered by any of the exceptions described below, for UC you must meet all of the work-related requirements if you are a European Economic Area (EEA) 'jobseeker' (ie, you are an EEA national looking for work in the UK – see p1535) or you are someone who has retained your 'worker' status while you are involuntarily unemployed and registered as a jobseeker (see p1538).[46] You must also meet all the work-related requirements if you are a family member of an EEA jobseeker.

No work-related requirements

No work-related requirements *at all* can be imposed on you in some situations. These are generally when the DWP cannot reasonably expect you to work or prepare for work over a sustained period, or if you are already earning all that it is reasonable to expect you to earn. No work-related requirements can be imposed on you if:

- you are a recent victim of domestic violence (see p1074). **Note:** for contribution-based JSA, this is the *only* situation when no work-related requirements can be imposed on you; *or*
- for UC and contributory employment and support allowance (ESA), you fit into a specified group – ie:
  - you are looking after children or have other responsibilities (see p1074);
  - you are sick or disabled (see p1075);

Part 8: Work
Chapter 50: Claimant responsibilities: the universal credit system
3. The requirements you must meet

– for UC only, you are in work (see p1076);
– in other situations (see p1077).

Any requirements that have been imposed previously cease.[47]

Domestic violence

All work-related requirements that have been imposed on you cease to have effect for 13 weeks if you notify the DWP that you have experienced, or been threatened with, domestic violence from your partner, your former partner or a family member.[48] In addition, no new work-related requirements can be imposed on you during this period.

You must satisfy all of the following conditions.

- This rule must not have applied to you in the 12 months before you notify the DWP.
- You must not be living at the same address as the person when you notify the DWP.
- The domestic violence (or threat of domestic violence) must have taken place within the six months before you notify the DWP.
- As soon as possible, and no later than one month after you notify the DWP, you must provide evidence from a person acting in an official capacity that shows that your circumstances are consistent with those of a person who has experienced, or been threatened with, domestic violence in the six months before you notified the DWP, and that you have made contact with a person acting in an official capacity about an incident that occured in that six-month period.

See p1031 for who counts as a 'family member' and a 'person acting in an official capacity' and for what counts as domestic violence. The rules are the same as for the JSA jobseeking conditions.

Looking after children and other responsibilities

If you are getting UC or contributory ESA, no work-related requirements can be imposed on you if:[49]

- you have 'regular and substantial caring responsibilities for a severely disabled person' (see p1075); or
- you have caring responsibilities for one or more severely disabled people for at least 35 hours a week, but do not satisfy the qualifying conditions for carer's allowance (CA). For UC, this only applies if the decision maker is satisfied that it would be unreasonable for you to meet a work search requirement and a work availability requirement, even if these were limited; or
- for UC, you are the 'responsible carer' (see p1075) of a child under one; or
- for ESA, you are not a member of a couple and you are responsible for a child under one – eg, you are a lone parent. The rules do not define when you count as responsible for a child; or

- you are the 'responsible foster parent' (see below) of a child under one; *or*
- you are pregnant and there are 11 weeks or less before the week your baby is due; *or*
- you had a baby not more than 15 weeks ago (including if this was a still birth); *or*
- you are an 'adopter' (see below) and it is not more than 12 months (for UC) or 52 weeks (for ESA) since your child was placed with you for adoption. You can elect for the 12 months (or 52 weeks) to start in the 14 days before your child was expected to be placed with you.

Definitions

You are an **'adopter'** if you have been matched with a child for adoption and you are, or are intended to be, the 'responsible carer' of the child.[50] This does not apply if you are the foster parent or a close relative of the child.

You have **'regular and substantial caring responsibilities for a severely disabled person'** if you satisfy the qualifying conditions for CA (see Chapter 25), or you would do but for the fact that your earnings are higher than £100 a week (see p541).[51] This does not apply if you receive earnings from those caring responsibilities. You do not have to be getting CA.

You are a **'relevant carer'** if:[52]
- you are the parent of a child, have caring responsibilites for her/him but are not the 'responsible carer'; *or*
- you have caring responsibilities for someone who has a 'physical or mental impairment' which means s/he needs such care.

You are a **'responsible carer'** for UC if you are a single claimant who is responsible for a child under 16 (see p210) – eg, you are a lone parent. You are a 'responsible carer' for JSA and ESA if you are the only person responsible for the child. If you are a member of a couple, you are a 'responsible carer' if you and your partner are responsible for a child under 16 (see p210) and you and your partner have nominated you as responsible for the child.[53] Only one of you can be nominated.

You are a **'responsible foster parent'** if you are the child's only foster parent, or if you are a member of a couple who are foster parents and you and your partner have nominated you as the 'responsible foster parent'.[54] Only one of you can be nominated.

A person is **'severely disabled'** if s/he is a person to whom attendance allowance, the highest or middle rate of disability living allowance care component, the daily living component of personal independence payment, armed forces independence payment or constant attendance allowance in respect of an industrial or war disablement (see p679) is payable.[55]

Sick and disabled people

If you are getting UC or contributory ESA, no work-related requirements can be imposed on you if:[56]

Part 8: Work
Chapter 50: Claimant responsibilities: the universal credit system
3. The requirements you must meet

- you have both limited capability for work and limited capability for work-related activity (see Chapter 47); *or*
- for ESA, you are entitled to ESA, but it is paid at a nil rate – eg, because you are getting an occupational pension.

You are in work

If you are getting UC, no work-related requirements can be imposed on you if you are working and you are:[57]

- a single claimant and your average weekly earnings are at least your individual earnings threshold (see below); *or*
- a member of a couple and your combined average weekly earnings are at least your joint earnings threshold; *or*
- an apprentice and your average weekly earnings are at least the amount you would be paid at the rate of the national minimum wage (see Appendix 12) for 30 hours work (or, if lower, for your weekly 'expected hours' – see p1069).

Your average weekly earnings are calculated using your gross actual or estimated earned income – ie, before income tax, national insurance contributions and pension contributions have been deducted.[58] **Note:** if you are self-employed and are treated as having minimum earnings in an assessment period (see p329), you are treated as having weekly earnings equal to your individual earnings threshold for each week in that period.[59]

See below for how to work out your earnings threshold.

Earnings thresholds

To work out your:

- **individual earnings threshold**, multiply the amount you would earn at the hourly rate of the national minimum wage (see Appendix 12) by the relevant number of hours for you (see below);[60]
- **joint earnings threshold** if you are a member of a couple, work out the sum of your and your partner's individual earnings thresholds and add these together.[61] However, if you are claiming as a single person (see p192), your joint earnings threshold is the sum of your individual threshold and the amount someone would be paid at the rate of the minimum wage for 35 hours work.

For your individual threshold, the **relevant hours** are:[62]

- 16 hours a week, but only if (even though you are exempt from any work-related requirements under this rule) you would otherwise be someone who only has to meet a work-focused interview requirement (see p1077) or a work-focused interview requirement and a work preparation requirement (see p1078); *or*

- the hours you are expected to work each week (your 'expected hours') – usually 35 a week. A lower number of hours can apply (see p1069).

Examples

James is a lone parent and his son is two years old. He is a UC claimant who would otherwise be someone who only has to meet a work-focused interview requirement. He works 10 hours a week and is paid £12 an hour, so earns £120 a week. His individual earnings threshold is 16 hours x £6.31 = £100.96. His earnings therefore exceed his individual earnings threshold. No work-related requirements can be imposed on him.

Raj and Sunita are joint UC claimants. They have three children, one of whom is under 13. They agree that Sunita should be the 'responsible carer'. Raj's 'expected hours' are 35 a week. The decision maker has agreed that Sunita's 'expected hours' are 21 a week as these are compatible with their child's school hours (see p1069). Raj works 30 hours a week and earns £9 an hour (£270 a week). His individual earnings threshold is 35 hours x £6.31 = £220.85. Sunita works 15 hours a week and earns £7 an hour (£105 a week). Her individual earnings threshold is 21 hours x £6.31 = £132.51. Their joint earnings threshold is therefore £220.85 + £132.51 = £353.36. Their joint earnings (£375) therefore exceed their joint earnings threshold. No work-related requirements can be imposed on either of them.

Others

If you are getting UC or contributory ESA, no work-related requirements can be imposed on you if:[63]

- for UC, you are at least the qualifying age for pension credit (see p78). This is only relevant if you are a member of a couple and your partner is not yet that age; *or*
- you are in full-time non-advanced education or training and you have no parental support (see p897 for what this means). For ESA, this also applies if you have been been enrolled or accepted for the education or training. You must be under 21, or have reached 21 while on the course; *or*
- for UC, you are eligible for UC while in education and you have student income for your course which is taken into account when calculating your UC (see p919).

Work-focused interview requirement only

A work-focused interview requirement, and no other work-related requirements, can be imposed on you if you are getting UC or contributory ESA and you are someone who is only expected to stay in touch with the labour market and to begin to think about going back to work, or taking up more or better paid work. This applies if you are:[64]

Part 8: Work
Chapter 50: Claimant responsibilities: the universal credit system
3. The requirements you must meet

- for UC, the 'responsible carer' (see p1075) of or, for ESA, a single person who is responsible for, a child aged at least one but under three; *or*
- the 'responsible foster parent' (p1075) of a:
  - child aged at least one but under 16; *or*
  - qualifying young person and the decision maker is satisfied that s/he has care needs which make it unreasonable for you to have to meet a work search requirement or a work availability requirement even if these were limited (for UC), or a work preparation requirement (for ESA); *or*
- a foster parent, but *not* the 'responsible foster parent' (see p1075), of a child under 16 or a qualifying young person, and the decision maker is satisfied that the child or young person has care needs which make it unreasonable for you to have to meet a work search requirement or a work availability requirement even if these were limited (for UC), or a work preparation requirement (for ESA); *or*
- a foster parent, you do not have a child or qualifying young person placed with you currently, but intend to have one placed with you and:
  - for UC, you have been in any of the situations described above applying to foster parents within the past eight weeks; *or*
  - for ESA, you have been the 'responsible foster parent' of a child aged at least one but under 16 within the past eight weeks; *or*
- you have become a 'friend or family carer' (see below) for a child under 16 in the past 12 months, and you are her/his 'responsible carer' (see p1075).

Note: if your child is under one, no work-related requirements can be imposed on you (see p1073).

Friend or family carer[65]
You are a **'friend or family carer'** if you are responsible for a child under 16 (see p210) but are not her/his parent or step-parent. You must be taking care of the child because:
– s/he has no parents, or has parents who are unable to care for her/him; *or*
– it is likely that s/he would otherwise be looked after by a local authority because there are concerns about her/his welfare.

Note: if you have been getting UC or ESA on the basis that you have to meet additional work-related requirements but you now fit into one of the groups above, any requirements previously imposed on you cease.[66]

Work-focused interview and work preparation requirement only

A work-focused interview requirement *and* a work preparation requirement, but no other work-related requirements, may be imposed on you if you are only expected to prepare for a move into paid work, more paid work or better paid work – eg, by participating in a training or employment scheme. Unless you do not have to meet any work-related requirements (see p1073) or only have to meet a work-focused interview requirement (see p1077), this applies if you are entitled to contributory ESA or UC and you have limited capability for work (see Chapter 47).[67] For UC it also applies if you are the 'responsible carer' (see p1074) of a child aged three or four.[68] You are not, however, expected to look for work. **Note:**

- If you have limited capability for work-related activity, no work-related requirements at all can be imposed on you.
- If you have been getting UC on the basis that you have to meet additional work-related requirements, any requirements previously imposed cease.[69]

No work search requirement

If you are getting contribution-based JSA or UC, a work search requirement cannot be imposed on you for a period (but you may have to meet other work-related requirements) if:[70]

- you are unfit for work. This usually applies for a maximum of 14 days and no more than twice in any 12-month period. For UC, it can apply if you are unfit more than twice, or for longer than this. For the first seven days, you must provide a declaration that you are unfit for work. For any further days, you must provide a fit note from your doctor. For UC only, this only applies if requested by the DWP; or
- you are attending a court or tribunal as a witness or party to the proceedings; or
- you qualify for JSA or UC while you are temporarily absent from Great Britain (see p1580 and p1584) because you are attending an interview (for JSA only), or receiving, or taking your child under 16 (or for UC, your partner or a qualifying young person) for, medical treatment or convalescence; or
- it is less than six months since the death of your partner or child under 16 (or, for UC, a qualifying young person). You must have been the child's parent, or you or your partner must have been responsible for the child or qualifying young person; or
- you are receiving and participating in a structured recovery-orientated course of treatment for alcohol or drug addiction (for up to six months); or
- you are subject to protection arrangements under s82 of the Serious Organised Crime and Police Act 2005 (for up to three months); or
- for UC only, you are a prisoner (see p962); or
- for UC, you are engaged in an activity that the DWP approves as being a public duty. This is not defined, but should include, for example, being on jury service, crewing a lifeboat or carrying out duties as a part-time firefighter. For JSA, see p1080; or

Part 8: Work
Chapter 50: Claimant responsibilities: the universal credit system
3. The requirements you must meet

- the decision maker is satisfied that it would be unreasonable for you to have to meet a work search requirement, even if this were limited, because you are taking action to make it more likely that you will get work, more work or better paid work, have temporary childcare responsibilities, there are other temporary circumstances or, for JSA, you are carrying out a public duty. For UC, you might not have to be available for work either. Temporary circumstances include anything that makes it unreasonable for you to have to seek work – eg, temporary caring responsibilities for a relative, or a flood, fire or other disaster at your home. For UC, dealing with domestic emergencies and funeral arrangements are specifically included.

In addition, for UC only, a work search requirement cannot be imposed on you (but you may have to meet other work-related requirements) if your weekly earnings (or, if you are a member of a couple, your joint weekly earnings) are such that the DWP is satisfied that a work search requirement should not be imposed at the present time. No work availability requirement can be imposed either.[71] **Note:** if your earnings are above a threshold, *no* work-related requirements can be imposed on you (see p1076).

Note:
- For ESA, a work search requirement can never be imposed on you.
- You can count as being available for work if you are able and willing to take up paid work or attend an interview immediately (see p1070) once the circumstances that exempt you from a work search requirement no longer apply.[72]

No work availability requirement

For UC only, a work availability requirement cannot be imposed on you (but you may have to meet other work-related requirements) if your weekly earnings (or, if you are a member of a couple, your joint weekly earnings) are such that the DWP is satisfied that a work availability requirement should not be imposed at the present time.[73] No work search requirement can be imposed either. You must be able and willing to take up paid work or attend an interview immediately (see p1070) once this circumstance no longer applies.[74] **Note:** if your earnings are above a threshold, *no* work-related requirement can be imposed on you (see p1076).

Notes

1. The claimant commitment
1 **UC** s4(1)(e) WRA 2012
JSA s1(2)(b) JSA 1995
ESA s1(3)(aa) WRA 2007
2 **UC** s14(1) WRA 2012
JSA s6A(1) JSA 1995
ESA s11A(1) WRA 2007
3 s3(2) WRA 2012
4 **UC** Reg 16 UC Regs
JSA Reg 8 JSA Regs 2013
ESA Reg 45 ESA Regs 2013
5 para J1026 ADM
6 **UC** s14(1) and (4) WRA 2012
JSA s6A(1) and (4) JSA 1995
ESA s11A(1) and (4) WRA 2007
7 **UC** s14(2) and (3) WRA 2012
JSA s6A(2) and (3) JSA 1995
ESA s11A(2) and (3) WRA 2007
8 **UC** s14(5) WRA 2012; reg 15 UC Regs
JSA s6A(5) JSA 1995; reg 7 JSA Regs 2013
ESA s11A(5) WRA 2007; reg 44 ESA Regs 2013
9 **UC** Reg 15(1) and (2) UC Regs
JSA Reg 7(1) JSA Regs 2013
ESA Reg 44(1) and (2) ESA Regs 2013
10 **UC** Reg 15(3) UC Regs
JSA Reg 7(2) JSA Regs 2013
11 Reg 44(3) ESA Regs 2013
12 Explanatory Memorandum to the draft UC Regs, para 213
13 **UC** s14(2) WRA 2012
JSA s6A(2) JSA 1995
ESA s11A(2) WRA 2007

2. The work-related requirements
14 **UC** s13 WRA 2012
JSA ss6 and 6F JSA 1995
ESA s11 WRA 2007
15 **JSA** Reg 5(2) JSA Regs 2013
ESA Reg 42(2) ESA Regs 2013
16 **UC** s15 WRA 2012
JSA s6B JSA 1995
ESA s11B WRA 2007
17 **UC** Regs 87 and 93 UC Regs
JSA Reg 10 JSA Regs 2013
ESA Reg 46 ESA Regs 2013
18 **UC** Reg 2(1) UC Regs
All R(IS) 5/95; *Fiory v CAO*, 20 June 1995

19 **UC** Reg 87 UC Regs
JSA Reg 3(7) JSA Regs 2013
20 **UC** s16(1) WRA 2012
JSA s6C(1) JSA 1995
ESA s11C(1) WRA 2007
21 **UC** s16(3)-(6) WRA 2012
JSA s6C(3) JSA 1995
ESA s11C(3)-(6) WRA 2007
22 **UC** s16(2) WRA 2012
JSA s6C(2) JSA 1995
ESA s11C(2) WRA 2007
23 **UC** s17(1) WRA 2012
JSA s6D(1) JSA 1995
24 **UC** s17(3) WRA 2012
JSA s6D(3) JSA 1995
25 **UC** s17(2) WRA 2012
JSA s6D(2) JSA 1995
26 **UC** Reg 94 UC Regs
JSA Reg 11 JSA Regs 2013
27 **UC** Reg 97(3) UC Regs
JSA Reg 14(2) JSA Regs 2013
28 para J3052 ADM
29 **UC** Reg 95(1) UC Regs
JSA Reg 12(1) JSA Regs 2013
30 **UC** Reg 95(2)-(4) UC Regs
JSA Regs 4(1) and 12(2) and (3) JSA Regs 2013
31 **UC** Reg 88 UC Regs
JSA Reg 9 JSA Regs 2013
32 **UC** s18(1) and (2) WRA 2012
JSA s6E(1) and (2) JSA 1995
33 **UC** Reg 96(1) UC Regs
JSA Reg 13(1) JSA Regs 2013
34 **UC** Reg 99(1)(b) UC Regs
JSA Reg 16(1)(b) JSA Regs 2013
35 Reg 13(1)(b) JSA Regs 2013
36 **UC** Reg 96(2)-(5) UC Regs
JSA Regs 2 and 13(2)-(5) JSA Regs 2013
37 **UC** s17(4) and (5) WRA 2012
JSA s6D(4) and (5) JSA 1995
38 **UC** Reg 97(4) and (5) UC Regs
JSA Reg 14(3) JSA Regs 2013
39 **UC** Reg 97(6) UC Regs
JSA Reg 14(4) JSA Regs 2013
40 **UC** Reg 97(2) UC Regs
JSA Reg 14(5) JSA Regs 2013
41 **UC** Reg 97(4) and (5) UC Regs
JSA Reg 14(3) JSA Regs 2013
42 **UC** Reg 97(3) UC Regs
JSA Reg 14(2) JSA Regs 2013

43 **UC** Reg 97(6) UC Regs
   JSA Reg 14(4) JSA Regs 2013
44 **UC** s23 WRA 2012
   JSA s6G JSA 1995
   ESA s11G WRA 2007

3. The requirements you must meet
45 **UC** s22 WRA 2012
   JSA s6F JSA 1995
46 Reg 92 UC Regs
47 **UC** s19(5) WRA 2012
   JSA Reg 15(1)(a) JSA Regs 2013
   ESA s11D(3) WRA 2007
48 **UC** Reg 98 UC Regs
   JSA Reg 15 JSA Regs 2013
   ESA Reg 49 ESA Regs 2013
49 **UC** s19(2)(b) and (c) WRA 2012; reg
   89(1)(b)-(d) and (f) UC Regs
   ESA s11D(2)(b) and (c) WRA 2007; reg
   47(1)(a)-(c), (f) and (g) ESA Regs 2013
50 **UC** Reg 89(3) UC Regs
   ESA Reg 47(5) ESA Regs 2013
51 **UC** Reg 30 UC Regs
   ESA Reg 47(2) and (3) ESA Regs 2013
52 **UC** Reg 85 UC Regs
   JSA Reg 4(1) JSA Regs 2013
53 **UC** s19(6) WRA 2012; reg 86 UC Regs
   JSA Reg 4(1) JSA Regs 2013
   ESA Reg 41(1) ESA Regs 2013
54 **UC** Regs 85 and 86 UC Regs
   JSA Reg 4(1) JSA Regs 2013
   ESA Reg 41 ESA Regs 2013
55 **UC** Reg 89(2) UC Regs
   ESA Reg 47(5) ESA Regs 2013
56 **UC** s19(2)(a) WRA 2012
   ESA s11D(2)(a) WRA 2007; reg 47(1)(e)
   ESA Regs 2013
57 Reg 90 UC Regs
58 Reg 90(6) UC Regs
59 Reg 90(5) UC Regs
60 Reg 90(2) UC Regs
61 Reg 90(3) UC Regs
62 Regs 88 and 90(2) UC Regs
63 **UC** s19 WRA 2012; reg 89 UC Regs
   ESA s11D WRA 2007; reg 47 ESA Regs
   2013
64 **UC** s20 WRA 2012; reg 91 UC Regs
   ESA s11E WRA 2007; reg 48 ESA Regs
   2013
65 **UC** Reg 91(3) UC Regs
   ESA Reg 48(3) ESA Regs 2013
66 **UC** s20(3) WRA 2012
   ESA s11E(3) WRA 2007
67 **UC** s21 WRA 2012
   ESA s11F WRA 2007
68 Reg 91A UC Regs
69 s21(4) WRA 2012

70 **UC** Reg 99(3)-(5B) UC Regs
   JSA Regs 4(1) and 16 JSA Regs 2013
71 Reg 99(6) UC Regs
72 **UC** Reg 99(1)(b), (2A)–(2C), (5A) and
   (5B) UC Regs
   JSA Reg 16(1)(b) JSA Regs 2013
73 Reg 99(6) UC Regs
74 Reg 99(1)(b) UC Regs

Chapter 51

Sanctions

This chapter covers:
1. Jobseeker's allowance sanctions (below)
2. Other sanctions (p1099)
3. General rules about sanctions (p1104)

The rules in this chapter do not apply if you come under the universal credit system. For these, see Chapter 52.

Key facts
- If you are getting jobseeker's allowance, you can be given a sanction – eg, if you leave work or a training scheme or employment programme voluntarily or because of misconduct, if you do not accept a job or scheme or programme place, or if you stop being available for work or stop actively seeking work.
- You can be given a sanction if you are getting some other benefits if you do not take part in work-focused interviews.
- If you are getting employment and support allowance or, in some cases, if you are a lone parent getting income support, you may be given a sanction if you do not take part in work-related activity.
- You may be able to avoid a sanction if you can show that you have a good cause or a good reason for your actions.
- If you are given a sanction, your benefit is paid at a reduced (or nil) rate for a period.
- Special rules apply if you are aged 16 or 17.
- You may qualify for hardship payments if you have been given a sanction.
- You can apply for a revision or supersession, or appeal against a sanction decision. You are likely to have to apply for a revision before you can appeal.

1. Jobseeker's allowance sanctions

If you are entitled to any type of jobseeker's allowance (JSA), you can be sanctioned for a period – eg, if you are dismissed from a job for misconduct or leave a job without a good reason, or if you fail to attend a training scheme or employment programme. There are high level sanctions (see p1085) and low level sanctions (see p1091) and sanctions for ceasing to be available for work and ceasing to actively seek work (see p1097).

If you are sanctioned, JSA is paid at a reduced (or nil) rate during a fixed period. For information about the amount of JSA payable if you are sanctioned, see p1085. While you are being sanctioned, you might be able to get hardship payments (see Chapter 55).

Some special rules apply if you are aged 16 or 17 (see p897).

High level sanctions   *Sanction period: 13, 26 or 156 weeks*
Losing a job because of misconduct (p1088)
Leaving a job voluntarily (p1088)
Failing to apply for or accept a job (p1088)
'Neglecting to avail' yourself of a job
opportunity (p1089)
Failing to participate in Mandatory Work Activity
(p1091)

Low level sanctions   *Sanction period: four or 13 weeks*
Failing to participate in interviews (p1093)
Failing to participate in a specified scheme for
assisting people to obtain employment (p1093)
Failing to carry out a jobseeker's direction
(p1095)
Other training scheme or employment
programme sanctions (p1096)

Ceasing to be available for or to actively seek work   *Sanction period: four or 13 weeks*
(p1097)

Once a sanction period has begun, it continues unbroken until the sanction period comes to an end. If you take a job or training for a short period but then claim again during the period of the sanction, you are still caught by the sanction.
Note:
- The days in your sanction period count towards your 182 days of entitlement to contribution-based JSA even if you are not actually paid any benefit.
- You are treated as being on income-based JSA if you are not being paid it because of a sanction, so you remain entitled to maximum housing benefit.[1]
- If you disagree that you should be sanctioned or disagree with the sanction period, you can challenge the decision (see p1111).

Additional rules apply if you have been sanctioned because of a benefit offence (see p1258).

The benefit reduction

JSA is paid at a reduced (or nil) rate during the sanction period.[2] The amount of the reduction depends on whether or not you are a member of a joint-claim couple (see p46). **Note:** special rules apply if you are aged 16 or 17 (see p899). If you are a:[3]

- single person, a member of a couple (other than a joint-claim couple) or a member of a joint-claim couple and both of you are given a sanction, your JSA is reduced by 100 per cent of the amount of JSA that is payable to you – ie, you are not paid any JSA during the sanction period;
- member of a joint-claim couple and only one of you is given a sanction, your JSA is paid at the rate of:
  - contribution-based JSA, if the person who has not been given a sanction qualifies for it; *or*
  - hardship payments, if you and your partner qualify (see p1199); *or*
  - in any other case, income-based JSA calculated as if the person who has not been given the sanction is a single person. However, any income or capital either of you have is taken into account in the calculation.

In this situation, the joint-claim JSA is paid to the person who has not been sanctioned.[4]

If your JSA is paid at a reduced (or nil) rate, you might be able to get hardship payments (see Chapter 55). Check to see whether you (or your partner) qualify for income support, income-related employment and support allowance or pension credit instead of JSA. If you are a member of a couple (other than a joint-claim couple), your partner might be able to claim JSA instead of you.

High level sanctions

You can be given a high level sanction if you:[5]

- lose a job because of 'misconduct' (see p1088); *or*
- leave a job voluntarily without a good reason (see p1088); *or*
- refuse or fail to apply for or accept a job without a good reason (see p1088); *or*
- 'neglect to avail' yourself of a job without a good reason(see p1089); *or*
- fail to participate in Mandatory Work Activity without a good reason (see p1091).

We refer to these as 'sanctionable actions' in this *Handbook*. The DWP may refer to these as 'sanctionable failures'.[6]

A 'job' for these purposes does not include self-employment or employment while participating in an employment programme (see p1096 for what counts).[7] When considering whether you should be sanctioned, the decision maker should only look at your last employment preceding your claim and your subsequent actions.[8]

For information about the amount of JSA you are paid, see p1085. **Note:** special rules may apply if you are aged 16 or 17 (see p897).

Length of the sanction period

If you are given a high level sanction, it is usually imposed for 13 weeks. However, it can be imposed for:[9]

- 26 weeks, if you have been given a high level sanction once previously (but see below) for a sanctionable action of yours – ie, not your partner's; *or*
- 156 weeks (three years), if you have been given a high level sanction at least twice previously (but see below) for a sanctionable action of yours (ie, not your partner's), the most recent of which was for 26 or 156 weeks.

In both cases, the previous sanctionable action must have taken place more than two weeks, but less than 52 weeks, before your current sanctionable action. The 52 weeks run from the date of the previous sanctionable action, not from the date of the decision imposing the previous sanction, which could be some time later.

For when your sanction period could be reduced, see p1087.

If the previous sanctionable action was that you lost a job because of misconduct (see p1088), you left a job voluntarily (see p1088) or you 'neglected to avail' yourself of a job (see p1089) and this happened before your date of claim (see p57 and p704), this action does not count for the purposes of determining the sanction period for any later sanctionable action.[10] Your sanction period may be reduced in similar circumstances (see p1087).

If you stop claiming JSA before the end of your sanction period, the sanction is applied if you claim JSA again. Your JSA is paid at a reduced (or nil) rate for the amount of the sanction period that is still outstanding.[11] However, if:

- you are a member of a joint-claim couple, this rule only applies if the sanction on the previous award was imposed because of a 'sanctionable action' of yours (or your current partner's) – eg, the sanction was not imposed on a former partner if you are now claiming as a member of a different couple;[12]
- the DWP is satisfied that since the date of your most recent sanctionable action, you have been in employment for a period of at least 26 weeks, or for more than one period totalling at least 26 weeks, the sanction is not applied if you claim JSA again.[13] 'Employment' for these purposes includes self-employment, provided your income is more than your applicable amount (see Chapter 12).

Note: if you are given a 26- or 156-week sanction but later a previous (13-, 26- or 156-week) sanction is removed (eg, by the First-tier Tribunal), ask a decision maker to reduce the sanction period.[14] If s/he fails to do so, appeal. If you have already appealed against the later sanction, the Tribunal should take the removal of the previous sanction into account.[15]

Reduced sanction periods

If you are sanctioned because, before the day you claim JSA, you lost a job because of misconduct (see p1088), you left a job voluntarily (see p1088) or you 'neglected to avail' yourself of a job (see p1089):[16]

- unless the job was only due to last for a 'limited period' (see below), your sanction period is reduced to take account of days on which you did not claim JSA. The sanction period that would normally apply is reduced by the number of days between the date of the sanctionable action and your date of claim (see p57 and p704);
- if the job was only due to last for a 'limited period' (see below) that ends on or before the end of the sanction period that would normally apply, the sanction period is the number of days starting with the day after the date of the sanctionable action and ending on the day the job would have ended, reduced by the number of days between the date of the sanctionable action and your date of claim (see p57 and p704).

In both cases, if the result is that your sanction period is reduced to nothing, you are not sanctioned.[17]

Limited period

A 'limited period' is a specific term of time that is either fixed or which can be ascertained before it begins by reference to some relevant circumstance.[18]

Examples

Rita quits her job on 3 May. It was only due to last until 5 July. She claims JSA on 10 May. She cannot show a good reason for leaving her job so is sanctioned. This is the first time she has been sanctioned so a 13-week sanction period would normally apply.

The period starting on 4 May (the day after the date of the sanctionable action) and ending on 5 July (the day the job would have ended) is 63 days.

The number of days between 3 May (the date of the sanctionable action) and 10 May (her date of claim) is six days.

63 days – 6 days = 57 days. Rita is therefore sanctioned for 57 days (eight weeks and one day).

Tom is dismissed from a permanent job because of misconduct on 2 September. He claims JSA on 8 October. He failed to participate in Mandatory Work Activity three months ago, and was given a 13-week high level sanction. He is sanctioned for the second time and a 26-week sanction period would normallly apply.

26 weeks x 7 days = 182 days.

• •

The number of days between 2 September (the date of the sanctionable action) and 8 October (his date of claim) is 35 days.
182 days – 35 days = 147 days. Tom is therefore sanctioned for 147 days (21 weeks).

• •

When the sanction period starts

The sanction period normally starts on the first day of the benefit week after the last benefit week in which you were paid JSA.[19] However, if you have not been paid any JSA since the sanctionable action, the sanction period starts on the first day of the benefit week in which it took place.

Losing a job because of misconduct

You can be given a high level sanction if you lose your job because of misconduct.[20] This includes if you are suspended from work for misconduct or if you resigned rather than being dismissed.[21] You cannot be sanctioned for misconduct in self-employment. For information about:
• what may count as misconduct, see p1105;
• whether misconduct caused the loss of employment, see p1106.

Leaving your job voluntarily

You can be given a high level sanction if you leave your job 'voluntarily' without a 'good reason' (see p1107).[22] A sanction can only be imposed if:
• you were in employment (not self-employment); *and*
• you were not in a 'trial period' (see p1090).

The decision maker has to show that you left your employment voluntarily. To avoid a sanction, you must then show that you had a good reason for leaving. For information about:
• whether you left voluntarily, see p1106;
• what may happen if you take retirement, see p1107.

Refusing or failing to apply for or to accept a job

You can be given a high level sanction if you are notified by an employment officer (EO) of a job vacancy and you do not apply for it or refuse to accept it when offered to you.[23] This does not apply if you can show you have a good reason (see p1107). **Note:** the decision maker cannot apply this sanction if the job was vacant because of a stoppage of work caused by a trade dispute.[24]

Note: if you repeatedly fail to take jobs that are offered to you, a decision maker may also decide that you are not available for or actively seeking work and refuse you JSA altogether. You may then be sanctioned when you claim JSA again (see p1097).

Notification of a job vacancy

To be sanctioned, you must have been notified of a job vacancy by an EO. This may be orally, in writing or by other means (eg, by text or email). No sanction should be imposed if you did not receive the notification. Your reading a job advert that is simply displayed in a Jobcentre Plus office or on the Jobcentre Plus website does not, by itself, amount to being notified by the EO. However, if you identify a vacancy yourself and then discuss it with an EO, the DWP may say that you have been notified.[25] You must be given sufficient information to enable you to pursue the vacancy or to make an informed decision about whether to pursue it.[26]

If you are notified of a vacancy and are unsure about what your financial situation would be, check the amount of benefits and tax credits for which you would qualify if you took the job – eg, working tax credit and housing benefit. If you need help with the calculations, get advice. Remember that it may be difficult to show you have a good reason for refusing a job because of your income or the rate of pay.

Have you been notified of a job that you are not qualified to do?
In some cases, you may be notified of a vacancy for a job that you think is unsuitable for you or for which you think you are not qualified. In this situation, to avoid the risk of being sanctioned, it may be best to apply for the job and let the employer be the one to say you are not suitable.

8

Treated as refusing to apply for or to accept a job

The DWP may treat you as having refused to apply for or accept a job if:[27]

- you do not complete the job application form properly or you give inappropriate answers to questions on the form. However, if you submit your application to the DWP and it does not pass this on to a potential employer, you can argue that you did not fail to apply for the job; *or*
- you do not attend or are late for a job interview, or you go to the wrong place through your own negligence; *or*
- you behave in such a way that you lose the chance of getting the job. This should only apply to things you actually said or did (or refused to do) and should not apply just because a prospective employer disliked your appearance or manner; *or*
- you accept a job but fail to start it or impose unreasonable conditions so that the offer is withdrawn.

You can be expected to apply for and accept temporary work. You cannot escape a sanction on the grounds that a job is temporary.

'Neglecting to avail' yourself of a job

You can be given a high level sanction if you fail to take up ('neglect to avail' yourself of) a reasonable opportunity of employment without a good reason (see p1107).[28] You do not have to be notified of a vacancy by an EO for this sanction to apply.

In practice, this sanction usually applies in situations where you do not return to work with a former employer after what was originally intended to be a temporary break – eg, if you decide not to resume work after maternity leave or you refuse an offer of alternative employment in a redundancy situation.

The DWP is likely to apply a sanction if, for example, you knew you had a reasonable chance of getting the job and did not take the necessary steps to get it. However, it cannot apply the sanction if:

- the job was vacant because of a stoppage of work caused by a trade dispute;[29] *or*
- the 'opportunity' is for further work with an employer you have been working for during a trial period (see below).

Trial periods

In certain circumstances, you may take a job for a trial period and leave it without the risk of being sanctioned for leaving voluntarily or for 'neglecting to avail' yourself of a reasonable opportunity of employment (see p1088 and p1089).[30] The rules lay down both a minimum and a maximum length for the trial period. You *must* leave the employment within the specified times to avoid being sanctioned. You do not have to have agreed with the DWP that you were taking up the employment on a trial basis. If you leave shortly before or after the trial period and are sanctioned, see p1087 to see if your sanction period can be reduced.

Trial period

A '**trial period**' is the period of eight weeks starting with the beginning of your fifth week and ending at the end of your 12th week in a job. Weeks in which you work for fewer than 16 hours are ignored.[31] The DWP includes periods when you are not actually working but you are required by your contract to be in a certain place in order to carry out a job.[32] Periods when you are off work sick or on holiday, even if you are paid, do not count when calculating the number of hours. To be sure you are covered by this rule, you must work at least some of the fifth week and leave before you have worked all of the 12th. In calculating the fifth and the 12th weeks, the 'week' starts on the day you begin work and ends at midnight seven days later.[33]

The trial period rule applies if, for at least 13 weeks before the day you begin employment, you have not:[34]

- worked (including as a self-employed person); *or*

- been a full-time student (see p905) or in 'relevant education' (see p903). You do not count as a full-time student if you were in receipt of a training allowance.[35]

If you are dismissed or you leave the job as an alternative to being dismissed, you might still be sanctioned if this was because of misconduct.

Note: if you do not claim JSA for more than 12 consecutive weeks (ie, until after the trial period), a new 'jobseeking period' (see p693) begins when you next claim. This means:

- you have to serve a further three waiting days (see p697) before getting JSA; *and*
- you may not qualify for contribution-based JSA if you no longer satisfy the contribution conditions.

Failing to participate in Mandatory Work Activity

You can be given a high level sanction if you fail to participate in Mandatory Work Activity without a good reason (see p1107).[36] Mandatory Work Activity is a scheme that provides four weeks of work (or work-related activity) of up to 30 hours a week, with a view to assisting you improve your prospects of getting employment. You can only be required to participate in it if you are required to meet the jobseeking conditions (see Chapter 48) and you are 18 or over.[37]

You must be given notice in writing.[38] The notice must give you specified information, including the day on which your participation will begin, what you must do to participate and the consequences of failing to do so. If you were not given proper notice, you can argue that you cannot be sanctioned if you failed to participate in the scheme.[39]

What information should you be given about Mandatory Work Activity?[40]

1. Before a notice requiring you to participate is given, you should be provided with enough information about the scheme and the criteria for being placed on it to enable you to make an informed decision about whether or not to participate.

2. If you are required to participate in Mandatory Work Activity, the written notice must specify what you must do to participate in it. This should include the hours, where you are to participate and the likely nature of the tasks you will be expected to do. You cannot simply be told that you must carry out any activities required by the scheme provider.

You have failed to participate if you fail to do what has been required.[41] The requirement to participate ceases if your award of JSA ends or you are given written notice that you are no longer required to participate.[42]

Low level sanctions

You can be given a low level sanction if you:[43]
- fail to participate in an interview without a good reason (see p1093); *or*
- fail to participate in a specified scheme for assisting people to obtain employment without a good reason(see p1093); *or*
- fail to carry out a jobseeker's direction without a good reason (see p1095); *or*
- 'neglect to avail' yourself of a place on a training scheme or employment programme without a good reason (see p1096); *or*
- fail to apply for or accept a place on a training scheme or employment programme without a good reason (see p1096); *or*
- give up a place on a training scheme or employment programme or fail to attend if given a place without a good reason (see p1096); *or*
- lose a place on a training scheme or employment programme through misconduct (see p1096).

We refer to these as 'sanctionable actions' in this *Handbook*. The DWP may refer to these as 'sanctionable failures'.[44]

For information about the amount of JSA you are paid, see p1085.

Note:
- Special rules may apply if you are 16 or 17 years old (see p897).
- You can also be given a low level sanction if you ceased to be available for work or ceased to actively seek work (see p1097).

Length of the sanction period

If you are given this type of low level sanction, it is imposed for:[45]
- four weeks; *or*
- 13 weeks, if you have been given one or more of this type of low level sanctions for a sanctionable action of yours (ie, not your partner's), the most recent of which took place more than two weeks, but less than 52 weeks, before your current sanctionable action.

The 52 weeks run from the date of the previous sanctionable action, not from the date of the decision imposing the previous sanction, which could be some time later.

If you stop claiming JSA before the end of your sanction period, the sanction is applied if you claim JSA again. Your JSA is paid at a reduced (or nil) rate for the amount of the sanction period that is still outstanding.[46] However, if:
- you are a member of a joint-claim couple, this rule only applies if the sanction on the previous award was imposed because of a sanctionable action of yours (or your current partner's) – eg, the sanction was not imposed on a former partner if you are now claiming as a member of a different couple;[47]
- the DWP is satisfied that since the date of your most recent sanctionable action, you have been in employment for a period of at least 26 weeks, or for

more than one period totalling at least 26 weeks, the sanction is not applied if you claim JSA again.[48] 'Employment' for these purposes includes self-employment, provided your income is more than your applicable amount (see Chapter 12).

Note: if you are given a 13-week sanction but later the previous (four-week or 13-week) sanction is removed (eg, by the First-tier Tribunal), ask a decision maker to reduce the sanction period.[49] If s/he fails to do so, appeal. If you have already appealed against the later sanction, the Tribunal should take the removal of the previous sanction into account.[50]

When the sanction period starts
The sanction period normally starts on the first day of the benefit week after the last benefit week in which you were paid JSA.[51] However, if you have not been paid any JSA since the sanctionable action, the sanction period starts on the first day of the benefit week in which it took place.

Failure to participate in an interview
You can be given a low level sanction if, without a good reason (see p1107), you do not participate in an interview when required to do so.[52] In practice, this means you can be sanctioned if you are given notice by an EO that you must participate in an interview on a specified date and you fail to participate:[53]
- at the right time – eg, you attend on the right day but are late. This only applies if there was a previous occasion on which you failed to participate in an interview at the right time and the EO gave or sent you a written notice warning you that, if you failed to participate the next time you were required to do so, your entitlement to JSA could cease or you could be sanctioned; or
- on the right day, you contact the EO within five working days but cannot show a good reason (see p1107) for the failure.

You may be able to participate in an interview without having to attend in person – eg, the EO may allow the interview to take place by telephone.[54] For information about the notification you must be given, see p1052.
Note:
- In some cases, if you fail to participate in an interview, your entitlement to JSA could end (see p1053) – eg, if you do not contact the EO within five working days.
- If you attend and participate in an interview but do not sign on, your entitlement to JSA could end (see p1051).
- If the requirement to attend and participate is for a training or employment scheme or programme, your entitlement does not end, and these sanction rules do not apply. However, you can be sanctioned under other rules (see pp1094–96).[55]

Schemes for assisting people to obtain employment

You can be given a low level sanction if you fail to participate in a specified scheme for assisting people to obtain employment without a good reason (see p1107).[56]

Specified schemes[57]

The Work Programme: up to two years of back-to-work support to assist those at risk of becoming long-term unemployed.

Skills Conditionality: skills training.

The sector-based work academy: up to six weeks of pre-employment training, a work experience placement for an agreed period and a guaranteed job interview or support in the application process. **Note:** it is understood that it is voluntary to agree to participate in the sector-based work academy, but if you agree it becomes compulsory and you can be sanctioned. However, the government says that sanctions should not be applied except in cases of misconduct.

New Enterprise Allowance: self-employment support.

Full-time Training Flexibility: training for 16 to 30 hours a week for those on JSA continuously for at least 26 weeks.

Day One Support for Young People:13 weeks of a work placement for the benefit of the community for up to 30 hours a week and up to 10 hours a week supported work search for those aged 18 to 24 with less than six months' work history since leaving full-time education. 'Work history' includes employment, voluntary work, internships and work experience.

Community work placements: up to 30 weeks of work placements for the benefit of the community and work-related activity, to assist those who require further support to get and sustain employment.

Traineeships: a government-funded course providing work preparation training, a work experience placement and, if needed, English and Maths tuition for up to six months for those with limited educational qualifications and work history, aged 16 to 23 (or to 24 if subject to a learning difficulty assessment).[58]

Derbyshire Mandatory Youth Activity Programme

Schemes may be added to or deleted from the above list, so get advice if you are in doubt about whether a scheme is specified. Remember that even if a scheme is not specified, other sanction rules may apply (see p1096). **Note:** new pilot schemes are expected by the end of 2014. If you are required to participate in one of them, you will be expected to attend a local centre for 35 hours a week for up to six months to receive support and supervision while you search for, and apply for, jobs. Two others will be aimed at 18–21-year-olds. See CPAG's online service and *Welfare Rights Bulletin* for updates.

You must be given notice in writing.[59] The notice must give you specified information, including the day on which your participation will begin, what you must do to participate and the consequences of failing to do so. If you were not given proper notice, you can argue that you cannot be sanctioned if you failed to participate in the scheme.[60] **Note:** scheme providers can notify you that you are required to participate in a particular scheme, but they cannot decide to sanction you if you do not do so. Only a DWP decision maker can do this.

Before a notice requiring you to participate is given, you should be provided with enough information about the scheme and the criteria for being placed on it to enable you to make an informed decision about whether or not to participate.[61] If you are required to participate in a scheme, the written notice must specify what you must do to participate in it. This should include the hours, where you are to participate and the likely nature of the tasks you will be expected to do. You cannot simply be told that you must carry out any activities required by the scheme provider.

The requirement to participate:[62]

- is suspended if you are no longer required to meet the jobseeking conditions; *or*
- ceases if your award of JSA ends or you are given written notice that you are no longer required to participate.

Note: before 12 February 2013, there were sanctions for failing to participate in the Employment, Skills and Enterprise Scheme, which included, for example, the Work Programme, the sector-based work academy and Community Action. However, the rules for this scheme were found to be unlawful[63] and the government amended them.[64] This was intended to prevent your being entitled to repayment of any JSA that was not paid to you as a result of being sanctioned for failing to participate.[65] However, it may still be possible to argue that you should not have been sanctioned and that any JSA that has been withheld should be repaid to you – eg, if you were not notified properly (see above). If this applies to you, you should appeal if you can. See pp7–8 of CPAG's *Welfare Rights Bulletin* 237 for further information.

Jobseeker's direction sanctions

You can be given a low level sanction if you refuse or fail to carry out a reasonable jobseeker's direction, without a good reason (see p1107).[66]

Jobseeker's direction

A **'jobseeker's direction'** is a direction given by your EO aimed at assisting you to find a job or increase your chances of employment.[67]

A jobseeker's direction might, for example, direct you to apply for a specific job vacancy, to use the DWP job-posting and job-matching service (Universal Jobmatch), to attend a training or employment scheme, or to improve your appearance or behaviour in order to present yourself better to potential employers. You can be given an opportunity to take the action voluntarily before any direction is given. It must be clear that you are being given a jobseeker's direction.

A jobseeker's direction can be given at any time and more than once. It states the time within which you are expected to comply with it, and checks are made to ensure that you have done so. Each refusal to carry out a direction could result in your being sanctioned.

Is a jobseeker's direction 'reasonable'?

A jobseeker's direction must be reasonable. It would not be reasonable, for example, if it would not help you find a job or increase your chances of being employed, was at odds with your sincere conscientious or religious beliefs or if it might unlawfully discriminate against you on grounds such as gender, disability, religion or nationality.

Any jobseeker's direction must be relevant to *your* needs and to the circumstances of the local labour market. If the EO accepts that a jobseeker's direction was unreasonable, or could not be carried out in the time required, s/he cancels it.

Other training scheme and employment programme sanctions

If you are required to attend a training scheme or employment programme, you can be given a low level sanction if you:[68]

- lose your place because of 'misconduct'. See the information on p1105. References to an employer should be read as references to your scheme or programme provider; *or*
- give up or fail to attend without a good reason (see p1107). You are treated as failing to attend if you have been absent without authorisation, even if the absence is only for one day.[69] You might be treated as failing to attend if you arrive late and are not allowed to attend;[70] *or*
- are informed by an EO of a place and refuse or fail to apply for or accept it without a good reason (see p1107). See the information in the section about refusing or failing to apply for or accept a job on p1088. References to an employer should be read as references to your scheme or programme provider; *or*
- 'neglect to avail' yourself of a reasonable opportunity of a place without a good reason (see p1107). You do not have to be notified by an EO for this sanction to apply.

Training schemes and employment programmes

A **'training scheme'** is any scheme or course designed to help you gain skills, knowledge or experience that will make it more likely that you will obtain work, or be able to do so.[71]

An **'employment programme'** is any programme or scheme designed to assist you to prepare for, or move into, work.[72]

If you refuse to start a scheme or programme once you have received your official referral letter, or if you leave a scheme or programme without a good reason, you can be sanctioned under these rules. However, if you refused to participate in meetings about what arrangements might be most suitable for you before receiving your official referral letter, you might be sanctioned instead under the rules about failing to participate in interviews (see p1093).

Note: the government says it is voluntary to agree to join Work Experience (work placements of two to eight weeks, or 12 weeks if you are offered an apprenticeship). However, if you agree, the rules above can apply, although the government says that sanctions should only be applied if you leave as a result of misconduct.

Ceasing to be available for or to actively seek work

If you were previously entitled to JSA (including as a member of a joint-claim couple) and that entitlement ended in the last 13 weeks because you did not comply with the requirement to be available for or to actively seek work, you can be given a sanction if you make a new claim for JSA (other than a claim for joint-claim JSA) or, if your benefit was only suspended, when payment resumes.[73]

If you make a new claim for joint-claim JSA or your benefit was only suspended and payment resumes, you can be given a sanction if you (or your partner) were previously entitled to JSA and that entitlement ended in the last 13 weeks because you (or s/he) failed to comply with the requirement to be available for or to actively seek work.[74]

We refer to these as 'sanctionable actions' in this *Handbook*. The DWP may refer to these as 'sanctionable failures'.[75]

For information about the amount of JSA you are paid, see p1085. **Note:** special rules may apply if you are 16 or 17 years old (see p897).

Note: even if a previous entitlement to JSA ended in the circumstances above, you cannot be given a sanction for this reason if:[76]
- you were treated as available for work (see p1027) or as actively seeking work (p1041); *and*
- the reason you were treated as available for work or actively seeking work no longer applied, and as a result your entitlement to JSA ended because you failed to comply with the requirement to be available for or to actively seek work; *and*
- the DWP considers that, in your circumstances, it is not appropriate to sanction you.

Length of the sanction period

If you are given a sanction because a previous entitlement to JSA ended when you (or your partner) ceased to be available for work or to actively seek work, a sanction is normally imposed for:[77]

- four weeks if entitlement has only ended once for this reason; *or*
- 13 weeks, if entitlement has ended two or more times for this reason and the most recent time is two weeks or more, but less than 52 weeks since the time before.

The four- or 13-week period is reduced by the days during which you were not paid JSA – ie, the period starting on the first day of the benefit week following the benefit week in which you were last paid JSA and ending with the day before your date of claim (see p57 and p704) or, if your JSA was suspended because there was a question about whether you were available for or actively seeking work, ending with the day before the suspension ends.[78]

If you are sanctioned but you stop claiming JSA before the end of your sanction period, the sanction is applied if you claim JSA again. Your JSA is paid at a reduced (or nil) rate for the amount of the sanction period that is still outstanding.[79] However, if:

- you are a member of a joint-claim couple, this rule only applies if the sanction on the previous award was imposed because of a sanctionable action of yours (or your current partner's) – eg, the sanction was not imposed on a former partner if you are now claiming as a member of a different couple;[80]
- the DWP is satisfied that since the date of your most recent sanctionable action, you have been in employment for a period of at least 26 weeks, or for more than one period totalling at least 26 weeks, the sanction is not applied if you claim JSA again. Employment for these purposes includes self-employment, provided your income is more than your applicable amount (see Chapter 12).[81]

Note: if you are given a 13-week sanction but later the previous (four-week or 13-week) sanction is removed (eg, by the First-tier Tribunal), ask a decision maker to reduce the sanction period.[82] If s/he fails to do so, appeal. If you have already appealed against the later sanction, the Tribunal should take the removal of the previous sanction into account.[83]

When the sanction period starts

The sanction period starts on your date of claim (see p57 and p704) or, if your JSA was suspended because there was a question about whether you were available for or actively seeking work, on the date the suspension ends.[84]

---

2. **Other sanctions**

You can be given a sanction if:

- you are entitled to a specified benefit and you (or in some cases, your partner) fail to take part in a work-focused interview without a good cause (see p1099);

- you fail to take part in work-related activity when required to do so while entitled to employment and support allowance (ESA) or income support (IS) (see p1103). For IS, this only applies if the only reason you are on IS is because you are a lone parent and if you do not have any children under three.

Work-focused interview sanctions

There are currently a number of schemes under which you can be required to take part in work-focused interviews while you are entitled to benefit – ie, if you:
- are incapable of work and are entitled to IS, incapacity benefit (IB), severe disablement allowance (SDA) or ESA (see p1057); *or*
- are entitled to IS and are a lone parent (see p1058); *or*
- come under the Jobcentre Plus rules for certain IS claimants (see p1059); *or*
- you are the partner of someone entitled to IS, income-based jobseeker's allowance (JSA) (but not joint-claim JSA), income-related ESA, IB, SDA or carer's allowance (CA) (see p1059).

If you (or your partner) fail to take part without good cause, you are given a sanction and your benefit is paid at a reduced rate. For what may count as 'good cause', see below. **Note:**
- What the benefit reduction is, and how long it lasts, depends on the benefit you are getting and the rules under which you are required to take part.
- If you are getting ESA and you experience hardship as a result of a sanction, you may qualify for hardship payments (see p1202).

For ESA, you have a right of appeal against a decision imposing a sanction.[85] For other benefits, you can appeal against a decision that you did not take part in an interview and a decision that you have not shown good cause for your failure within five working days.[86] Decisions may also be revised or superseded (see Chapter 58). If you are given a sanction because your partner fails to take part in an interview, both you and your partner are notified of the decision and both of you have the right to appeal against the decision on failure to take part and on good cause.[87]

Note: under the Jobcentre Plus rules that apply to some IS claimants (see p1059), when you make a new claim for IS, you are required to attend an initial work-focused interview. If the decision maker decides that you did not take part, unless you have good cause for not doing so (see below), you are treated as not having made a claim and hence are not entitled to any benefit.[88]

Good cause for failing to take part

To avoid a sanction, you (or your partner) must show 'good cause' for failing to take part in a work-focused interview within five working days of:
- the date on which the interview was to take place (for a partner of someone on a specified benefit);[89]

- the date you are notified by the DWP that you failed to participate in the interview (in all other cases).[90]

You must be given at least five days to show good cause before any decision to impose a sanction is made.[91] However, for benefits other than ESA, you may still be able to demonstrate good cause up to a month after the decision that you did not participate was notified to you, if the facts you rely on could not have been brought to the DWP's attention within five days.[92] There is no equivalent rule for ESA. However, it is understood that the DWP views it as unnecessary to have attempted to show good cause within five days.[93]

When deciding whether you have good cause for benefits other than ESA, the decision maker considers all the circumstances, but in particular must take into account:[94]

- any misunderstanding on your part because of learning, literacy or language difficulties, or misleading information given by the DWP;
- attending a doctor or dentist appointment or accompanying a person for whom you are caring, where the appointment could not reasonably have been rearranged;
- difficulties with transport where no reasonable alternative was available;
- the customs and practices of your religion that prevented you attending at the fixed time;
- attending a job interview;
- the need to pursue employment opportunities for your self-employment;
- if you or a dependent child or a person for whom you are caring had an accident, illness or relapse;
- attending the funeral of a close friend or relative;
- a disability that makes attendance impracticable;
- any other relevant matter. This depends on the facts in your case, but might include things like emergencies and problems with caring arrangements.

'Good cause' is not defined in the ESA rules. However, the decision maker should consider factors that are broadly the same as those above.[95]

The benefit reduction

The amount by which your benefit is reduced depends on the benefit you are claiming and the rules that apply to you. For ESA, see below. For incapacity benefits, see p1101. For other benefits, see p1101.

Employment and support allowance

If you are entitled to ESA and you are given a sanction, the benefit reduction is 100 per cent of the personal allowance that applies for a single person who qualifies for ESA that includes a work-related activity component or a support component (ie, the personal allowance for main phase ESA) – currently £72.40 a week.[96] Your weekly benefit cannot be reduced by more than this amount and you must be left with at least 10 pence a week. This means that you are paid any other amounts to which you are entitled – ie, a component, amounts for a partner, premiums and housing costs.

Note: if you experience hardship as a result of the reduction, you may qualify for hardship payments. See Chapter 55 for further information.

Examples

Bernie is getting ESA of £101.15 a week, including a work-related activity component. When he is sanctioned, his benefit is reduced by £72.40 a week and he is paid £28.75 a week for the duration of the sanction period.

Lisa is a single claimant aged 23 living in rented accommodation. She has only been claiming income-related ESA for 10 weeks, so is getting £57.35 a week. When she is sanctioned her benefit is reduced to 10 pence a week for the duration of the sanction period.

Incapacity benefits

If you are entitled to IB, SDA or IS on the grounds of disability and are given a sanction, the benefit reduction is 50 per cent of the equivalent of the value of the ESA work-related activity component for the first four weeks of the reduction (currently £14.37 a week), then 100 per cent of the value (currently £28.75 a week) for each following week.[97] Your weekly benefit cannot be reduced by more than these amounts and you must be left with at least 10 pence a week.

Other benefits

Unless you are getting ESA, IB, SDA or IS on the grounds of disability, if you are given a sanction, the benefit reduction is £14.48 a week.[98] This also applies if it is your partner who fails to take part in an interview.[99] Your weekly benefit cannot be reduced by more than this amount. You must be left with at least 10 pence a week. If your benefit is reduced because your partner fails to take part in an interview and you are getting more than one of the specified benefits (see p1060), income-based JSA is the first benefit to be reduced, followed by income-related ESA, IS, IB, SDA and then CA.[100]

Note: your IS cannot be reduced under these rules if you are a lone parent and if, in the two weeks before your current failure to take part in a work-focused interview, it has been reduced because you failed to take part in a work-focused interview or in work-related activity.[101]

Length of the sanction period

The length of the sanction period depends on the benefit you are claiming and the rules you come under. For ESA, see p1102. For other benefits, see p1103.

Employment and support allowance

For ESA, the sanction period is normally one week for each seven-day period during which you fail to take part in an interview or agree a date when you will do so with the DWP – ie, it lasts until you comply. However, see below for when this indefinite period can end. You are also given a further fixed-period sanction as follows:[102]

- one week, if it is the first time you have been sanctioned; *or*
- two weeks, if you failed to take part in an interview two weeks or more after, but within 52 weeks of, a previous failure to take part that resulted in a sanction; *or*
- four weeks, if you failed to take part in an interview two weeks or more after, but within 52 weeks of, a previous failure to take part that resulted in a two- or four-week sanction.

The previous sanction must relate to your failure to take part in an interview on or after 3 December 2012. If you failed to take part in an interview before this date, see p1037 of the 2012/13 edition of this *Handbook* for information.

Note:

- If, within one week after you failed to take part in an interview, you take part in one, or agree a date when you will do so, your ESA is only reduced for the fixed period above (one, two or four weeks).[103]
- A sanction ceases to apply if you are no longer someone required to take part in work-focused interviews.[104]

Examples

Sandra does not take part in a work-focused interview and is sanctioned. This is the first time she has failed to take part in an interview. After two days, she agrees to take part in an interview. Her benefit is paid at a reduced rate for a fixed period of one week.

Allison does not take part in a work-focused interview on 1 June 2014. This is the second time she has been sanctioned: she failed to take part in an interview 15 weeks ago. Her ESA starts to be paid at a reduced rate. Three weeks later, she takes part in an interview. The ongoing sanction ends, but her ESA continues to be paid at a reduced rate for a further fixed period of two weeks.

If you are given a two- or four-week sanction but later the previous (one-week or two-week) sanction is removed (eg, by the First-tier Tribunal), ask a decision maker to reduce the fixed sanction period.[105] If s/he fails to do so, appeal. If you have already appealed against the later sanction, the Tribunal should take the removal of the previous sanction into account.[106]

Other benefits

For benefits other than ESA, you are sanctioned for an indefinite period. However, the sanction ceases to apply if:[107]

- you (or your partner) take part in a work-focused interview; *or*
- for IS, you take part in work-related activity; *or*
- you (or your partner) are no longer required to take part in work-focused interviews under the relevant scheme or you reach the qualifying age for pension credit (see p78).

In addition, if you are sanctioned because your partner failed to take part in a work-focused interview, the sanction ceases to apply if you cease to be partners, or you cease to get additional benefit for her/him.[108]

Work-related activity sanctions

If you are entitled to IS or ESA, you can be required to undertake work-related activity (see p1061). **Note:** the IS rules for lone parents described below are based on draft regulations, due to come into force on 6 April 2014. See CPAG's online service and *Welfare Rights Bulletin* for updates. For IS, you can only be required to do so if the only reason you are on IS is because you are a lone parent and if you do not have any children under three. If you fail to do so without good cause, you are given a sanction and your benefit is paid at a reduced rate. You must be given at least five days to show good cause – ie, you must show good cause within five working days of the date you are notified by the DWP that you failed to take part.[109] **Note:** the rules described in this section only apply if you do *not* come under the universal credit (UC) system. If you come under the UC system and are entitled to contributory ESA, different rules apply (see p1115).

The rules for what might count as good cause and the amount of the benefit reduction are the same as for work-focused interview sanctions (see p1099 and p1100).[110] **Note:**

- For IS:
  - when deciding whether you have good cause, the circumstances listed on p1099 must be taken into account, as well as the availability of childcare;[111]
  - your IS cannot be reduced under these rules if it has been reduced because you failed to take part in a work-focused interview, and this was two weeks or less before you failed to take part in work-related activity.
- For ESA, if you experience hardship as a result of a sanction, you may qualify for hardship payments (see Chapter 55).

You have a right of appeal against a decision imposing a sanction. You are likely to have to apply for a revision before you can appeal.

Length of the sanction period

For **ESA**, the sanction period is normally one week for each seven-day period during which you fail to:[112]
- undertake the work-related activity set out in your action plan (see p1062); *or*
- undertake alternative work-related activity notified by the DWP; *or*
- make an agreement with the DWP to undertake the work-related activity set out in your action plan or alternative work-related activity on an agreed date.

A further fixed period is added (see p1101 – the rules are the same as for ESA work-focused interview sanctions). Your ESA cannot be paid at a reduced rate if you are no longer someone required to undertake work-related activity or the DWP decides it is no longer appropriate to require you to undertake it at that time.[113]

For **IS**, the sanction period lasts until either you meet a requirement to undertake work-related activity or a work-focused interview, or you are no longer required to do so.[114]

3. **General rules about sanctions**

There are a number of rules and issues that are common to some or all of the benefits and types of sanction.

Deciding whether you should be sanctioned

A decision maker decides whether you should be sanctioned, often some time after the incident that led to the sanction (the 'sanctionable action') took place. Do not presume that because you have not yet been informed of any sanction that your previous action has been excused.

If there is a possibility that you will be sanctioned, make sure you give full details of your side of the story. If you:
- left or were dismissed from a job and it appears there may have been misconduct or you may have left voluntarily without a good reason, your former employer is asked for a statement. You should be given an adequate chance to comment on what s/he says. Your remarks may be passed to her/him for further comments. Make sure you explain why you disagree with the allegation of misconduct or why you had a good reason for leaving. If you are going to an employment tribunal (eg, to claim unfair dismissal), you should say so. Discuss your reply with whoever is advising you on this, as you may be asked questions at the employment tribunal hearing by your former employer about what you have said;
- refused to apply for or accept a job, what the potential employer says might be taken into account. Make sure you explain what enquiries you made about the nature of the job, and your reasons for not applying for or accepting it.

For training scheme and employment programme-related sanctions (including sanctions for failing to participate in specified schemes for assisting people to obtain employment), your scheme or programme provider refers your case to a decision maker. Before a sanction is imposed, you should be given an adequate chance to comment on any statements made against you.

What is misconduct?

For jobseeker's allowance (JSA), you can be given a high level sanction if you lose your job because of your misconduct (see p1088). **Note:** the information below about misconduct is also relevant if you come under the universal credit system (see p19) and you cease paid work or lose pay because of misconduct.

'**Misconduct**' is not defined in the rules. However, bear the following in mind.

- You are guilty of misconduct only if your actions or omissions are 'blameworthy'. This does not mean that it has to be established that you did anything dishonest or that you deliberately did something wrong; serious carelessness or negligence may be enough.[115]
- Everyone makes mistakes or is inefficient from time to time. So, for example, if you are a naturally slow worker who, despite making every effort, cannot produce the output required by your employer, you are not guilty of misconduct even if the poor performance may justify your dismissal.
- The misconduct must have some connection with your employment but it does not have to take place during working hours to count. However, a sanction cannot be imposed if the actions or omissions took place before your employment began – eg, you gave inaccurate information about yourself when applying for the job.[116]
- Some behaviour is clearly misconduct – eg, dishonesty (whether or not connected with your work) if it causes your employer to dismiss you because s/he no longer trusts you.[117]
- Some behaviour is not necessarily misconduct.
  - Bad timekeeping and failing to report in time that you are sick might amount to misconduct – eg, if you were persistently late or failed to report that you were sick on a number of occasions.
  - A refusal to carry out a reasonable instruction by an employer is not misconduct if you had a good reason for refusing or your refusal was due to a genuine misunderstanding.[118]
  - Breaking rules covering personal conduct might be misconduct, depending on the seriousness of the breach. A breach of a trivial rule might not be misconduct.[119]
  - You should not be sanctioned for losing a job because of misconduct if you are dismissed for 'whistleblowing' – ie, for disclosing wrongful behaviour which it was in the public interest to disclose.[120]

– Refusing to work overtime is misconduct if you were under a duty to work overtime when required and the request to do it was reasonable.

Although evidence from your employer is taken into account, the fact that s/he did not describe your actions as 'misconduct' does not guarantee that you can escape a sanction. However, this should go heavily in your favour.

Whether misconduct caused the loss of employment

Your misconduct need not be the only cause of the loss of your employment, but it must be an immediate and substantial reason for your losing your job.[121] If your misconduct was not the real reason for your dismissal (eg, your employer used this as an excuse to dismiss you, but really only wanted to reduce staff numbers), you should not be sanctioned.

It is not relevant that your dismissal was unreasonable or an overreaction on your employer's part. However, seek advice to see whether you might have a case for unfair dismissal at an employment tribunal.

If there was misconduct, the exact way in which you lost your employment is not important. You may be summarily dismissed, be dismissed with notice or resign as an alternative to possible dismissal.[122]

Did you leave voluntarily?

For JSA, you can be given a high level sanction if you leave your job 'voluntarily' without a good reason (see p1088). **Note:** the information below about leaving a job voluntarily is also relevant if you come under the UC system (see p19) and you cease paid work or lose pay voluntarily.

'**Voluntarily**' is not defined in the rules, but the DWP says it means that you have brought the situation about by your own acts and of your own free will.[123] You have not left your employment voluntarily if you had no choice in the matter or there is convincing evidence (eg, medical evidence from your GP) that you were not responsible for your actions.

You are likely to be treated as giving up your job voluntarily if:

- you resign giving notice. However, if you resign because you genuinely believe that your employer is about to end your employment or because you were given the 'choice' of resignation or dismissal, you have not left your job voluntarily. However, the DWP may then consider whether you lost your job through misconduct (see p1088);
- your employer gives you notice to end your employment but then cancels or suspends it, allowing you to continue in the same employment but you decide not to continue in the employment. If it is clear that you have a genuine choice to remain, you are likely to be treated as leaving voluntarily.[124] However, the circumstances may be such as to amount to a 'good reason'.

You have not left your job voluntarily if:

- you volunteer, or accept your employer's proposal, for redundancy.[125] This only applies if there is a redundancy situation at your workplace – eg, if a whole factory or department is closing down or if there is a cut in the number of people needed to carry out certain tasks. This is the case even if you were offered, or you could have applied for, alternative jobs with the same employer. However, if you refuse other work, you might be sanctioned for another reason – eg, refusing employment or 'neglecting to avail' yourself of an opportunity of employment (see pp1088–89). **Note:** if you take early retirement, see p1107);

- your employer ends your contract of employment.[126] A change in your terms or conditions by your employer can mean that s/he has ended your existing contract of employment – eg, if a change is imposed without your agreement and the new terms are less favourable than before. If you leave your employment as a result, try to argue that you have not left your job voluntarily but have been dismissed, or that you had a good reason for leaving.

Taking retirement

If you take retirement, you might be regarded as having left your job voluntarily.[127] Under employment law, your employer cannot usually make you retire at any particular age, so taking retirement is something you do of your own choice. However, you might be able to show you have a good reason if, for example, you can show that the work was getting too much for you because of your age or your health.

Employers sometimes have special early retirement schemes allowing you to take your occupational pension at an earlier age than normal that run for a limited period, often in order to deal with a redundancy situation. In this case, you come under the special rules about redundancy (see p1106). Employers often try to avoid using the word 'redundancy' and you may have to prove to the decision maker that a redundancy situation existed.

If you take early retirement under some other special scheme, you cannot show you have a good reason merely because your action was in your employer's interest.[128]

Good reason

In a number of situations, a sanction cannot be imposed if you have a good reason for your actions. '**Good reason**' is not defined in the rules, but what may count is set out in guidance.[129] **Note:** if you appeal against the sanction decision, the guidance is not binding on the First-tier Tribunal; it must make up its own mind about what counts as a good reason.

The factors that may mean you have a good reason depend on the sanction. It is up to you to show you have a good reason, but the decision maker should take all the circumstances into account. You must show that you acted reasonably. You should be given sufficent time to explain your reasons and to provide relevant evidence. The DWP says you should be given at least five days, but you may be given less time than this if you can be contacted by telephone or electronic means.

For ideas about what might count as a good reason, see below. **Note:** there are some special rules for 16/17-year-olds (see p898).

Note: If you are sanctioned for refusing or failing to apply for or accept a job (see p1088), neglecting to avail yourself of a job (see p1089) or not carrying out a jobseeker's direction (see p1095), you cannot show a good reason if your reason relates to the time it took (or would normally take) to travel from your home to your place of employment or a place mentioned in a jobseeker's direction, and back home again, if this was (or is normally) less than one hour and 30 minutes either way.[130] This does not apply if the time is unreasonable in the light of your health or your caring responsibilities (see p1027 for the meaning).

Circumstances that should be taken into account

The decision maker should take all of your circumstances into account when deciding whether you have a 'good reason'. Argue that this should include the following.

- Any restrictions or limitations you have been allowed to place on your availability for work, having regard to any discrepancy between these and the requirements of the job, although minor differences might not count. Although you do not necessarily have a good reason for refusing to apply for a job covered by your restrictions or limitations, it is a very significant factor to take into account.[131]
- Any condition of yours or personal circumstances that suggest that a particular job, or scheme or programme, or carrying out a jobseeker's direction, would be likely to cause you unreasonable physical or mental stress or significant harm to your health.
- A disease or physical/mental disability that meant you were unable to attend a scheme or programme, or your health (or that of others) would have been at risk if you had done so.
- You misunderstood what you had to do because of language, learning or literacy difficulties, or because you were misled by the DWP.
- You (or someone for whom you care) were attending a medical, dental or other important appointment which would have been unreasonable to rearrange.
- You are the victim of domestic violence or of bullying or harassment.
- A sincerely held religious or conscientious objection.[132]
- Caring responsibilities that make it unreasonable for you to do the job, attend an interview, participate in the scheme or programme or carry out a jobseeker's direction. This should include whether suitable childcare would have been (or was) reasonably available;

- You are homeless.
- Any transport difficulties.
- Excessive travelling time involved between your home and the place of work or the scheme or programme or a place mentioned in a jobseeker's direction (but see p1108 for when this does not count as a good reason).
- Unreasonably high expenses (eg, for childcare or travel) that were (or would be) unavoidable if you had taken the job or carried out the jobseeker's direction.

Account should also be taken of any other factor that appears relevant. See, in particular, below for when the terms of a job on offer break the laws on minimum working conditions.

Refusing a job

You may be able to show you have a good reason for refusing a job, for example, if:

- the travelling time to or from the job was more than one hour and 30 minutes;
- you are within your 'permitted period' (see p1035) and have restricted the type of work for which you are available to your usual occupation or to at least your usual rate of pay, and you refuse a job that does not meet these conditions;
- you have been laid off or are on short-time working, have been accepted as available only for casual employment (see p1048), and you refuse to take some other type of work;
- you come under the rules that exempt you from having to be able to start work immediately, and you refuse to take a job which you would have to start immediately (see p1026).

Note: you cannot be given a sanction if you refuse a job because it is vacant because of a trade dispute.[133]

The effect of minimum working conditions

Employers are required to provide certain minimum working conditions and pay a minimum wage (see Appendix 12). Try to argue that you have a good reason for not applying for any job where the terms do not comply with the legal requirements. Make sure that this is the case, particularly where the Working Time Regulations are concerned, as there are many exceptions and opt-outs that might apply. If the terms offered break the rules about the hour limit on the average working week, it is possible that the DWP might suggest that you agree to an 'individual opt-out'. Argue that this would be unreasonable, as the working time rules are intended to protect the health and safety of workers. Argue that you have a good reason for refusing a job if you do so because it does not pay at least the national minimum wage that applies to you. The DWP has accepted this in the past and should continue to do so.[134]

Leaving a job, training scheme or employment programme

If the conditions of a job or of a training scheme or employment programme are poor, if possible you should try to sort out any problems (eg, by raising them with your employer or the scheme or programme provider, or using any grievance procedure) rather than leaving immediately, and to look for another job seriously before giving one up. You may have difficulty showing you have a good reason if you do not do so.

Note: in some cases, you cannot be given a sanction if you leave a job in specified circumstances – eg, because you are laid off or are on short time working. The decision maker should take into account:

- any caring responsibilities you have which made it unreasonable for you to stay in your job and whether suitable childcare was (or could have been) available; *and*
- any childcare expenses you had to pay as a result of being in the job, if they amounted to an unreasonably high proportion of the income you received.

You may be able to show you have a good reason for leaving a job in the following situations.

- Your chances of getting other employment, including self-employment, were good and, in addition, there were strong reasons for leaving your job and you acted reasonably in doing so.[135]
- You genuinely did not know or were mistaken about the conditions of the job (eg, it was beyond your physical or mental capacity, or was harmful to your health), you gave it a fair trial before leaving and it was reasonable for you to leave when you did.[136]
- You left your job for personal or domestic reasons – eg, you gave up work to look after a sick relative.[137] Explain why you left your job before looking for alternative employment. It could be helpful to show that you tried to negotiate an arrangement with your employer to resolve the problem – eg, for a reduction in your hours or time off work.
- You left your job to move with your partner who has taken a job elsewhere.[138] Relevant factors may include how important it was to your partner's career to make the move and how good your chances are of finding work in the new area.
- Your employer made a change in the terms and conditions of your employment that does not amount to your contract of employment ending. You are expected to use any grievance procedure first.
  If you leave your job because your employer cuts your wages unilaterally, you might not be able to show you have a good reason. However, a cut in pay can mean your existing contract of employment has ended and, therefore, you have been dismissed rather than having left your job.
- You left your job because of a firm offer of alternative employment, but claimed benefit because the offer fell through. However, the DWP may say

you do not have a good reason if the offer was cancelled before you left your previous employment or you changed your mind and did not take the new job and you could have stayed in the existing employment, or did not ask your employer if you could stay.

You may be able to show you have a good reason for leaving a training scheme or employment programme in the following situations.

- You gave up a place and your continued participation would have put your health and safety at risk.
- The travelling time to or from the scheme or programme was excessive.
- You had caring responsibilities, no one else was available to provide the care, and it was not practical to make other arrangements.
- You were attending court as a party to the proceedings, a witness or a juror.
- You were arranging or attending the funeral of a close relative or a close friend.
- You had to deal with a domestic emergency.
- You were engaged in activities of benefit to the community – eg, crewing or launching a lifeboat, working as a part-time firefighter or doing work as part of an organised group for the benefit of others in an emergency.

Note: these reasons may also enable you to show you have a good reason for failing to participate in the scheme or programme.

The effect of minimum working conditions

Employers are required to provide certain minimum working conditions and pay the minimum wage (see Appendix 12).

Is your employer not complying with the legal requirements?

1. Do everything possible to resolve problems before giving up your job.

2. If all else fails or if you think that the hours you are expected to work or the amount of pay you receive is intolerable, you might decide to give up work. The laws about minimum working conditions could help to show that you have a good reason for doing so. Point out that the intention of the Working Time Regulations is to protect the health and safety of workers, so conditions that do not comply with them should be regarded as unacceptable.

3. You are likely to have difficulty showing you have a good reason for leaving a job just because the pay is low. However, in the past, the DWP has said that this does not apply if you left your job because you tried to get your employer to pay the national minimum wage and your employer was not doing so.

Challenging a sanction decision

If you disagree with a sanction decision, you can apply for a revision or supersession, or appeal against it in the usual way (but see p1099 for special rules about work-focused interview sanctions). You are likely to have to apply for a revision before you can appeal.

You can challenge:

- the decision to give you a sanction – eg, whether you failed to do something, whether you did what you are alleged to have done, whether you have been properly notified of any requirements or whether you have a good reason; *and*
- the length of the sanction period – eg, if there is a dispute about the number of times you have been sanctioned.

Although you cannot appeal against an EO's decision to issue a jobseeker's direction, if you are sanctioned for failing to comply with one (see p1095), you can challenge this on the basis that the direction that led to the sanction was not reasonable or that you have a good reason for not complying with it.

Is it worth appealing?

1. It is often worth appealing to the First-tier Tribunal.

2. An appeal gives you a chance to challenge your former employer's (or the scheme or programme provider's) version of events. Note that employers can be invited to attend appeal hearings, but rarely do so.

3. Attend the appeal hearing if you can. Explain your case fully and, if relevant, the good reasons for what you did or failed to do. If you do not attend the appeal hearing and fresh allegations are made against you, the Tribunal should consider an adjournment to allow you to attend or to answer the allegations in writing.

Relationship with unfair dismissal and other proceedings

Sometimes the same facts have to be considered by other bodies – eg, employment tribunals and the criminal courts. The questions and legal tests that other bodies use may not be the same as those which apply to benefits.

DWP decision makers, the First-tier Tribunal and employment tribunals are independent of each other; decisions by one are not binding on the other. This means:

- a finding by an employment tribunal that a dismissal was fair does not prevent a decision maker or the First-tier Tribunal from concluding that you did not lose your job through misconduct;[139]
- although the First-tier Tribunal normally accepts a criminal conviction as proof that you have done what is alleged, it must go on to consider whether this was connected with your employment, whether it amounts to misconduct and whether the misconduct was the reason why you lost your employment;
- the decision maker or the First-tier Tribunal does not have to wait for the outcome of other proceedings before making a decision, but they are more likely to do so if there is a conflict of evidence.[140]

Notes

1. Jobseeker's allowance sanctions

1 Reg 2(3)(a) HB Regs; reg 2(3)(a) HB(SPC) Regs
2 ss19(1), 19A(1) and 19B(1-3) JSA 1995; reg 70 JSA Regs
3 Reg 70(1) and (3) JSA Regs
4 ss19(7), 19A(10) and 19B(8) JSA 1995
5 s19(2) JSA 1995; reg 70B JSA Regs
6 Reg 75(5) JSA Regs
7 Reg 75(4) JSA Regs
8 CJSA/3304/1999
9 Reg 69(1) and (2) JSA Regs
10 Reg 69(3) JSA Regs
11 Reg 70C JSA Regs
12 Reg 70C(1)(e) JSA Regs
13 Reg 70C(4) JSA Regs
14 Reg 3(6) SS&CS(DA) Regs
15 CJSA/2375/2000
16 Reg 69(4) JSA Regs
17 Reg 70A(1) JSA Regs
18 Reg 69(5) JSA Regs
19 Reg 69(6) JSA Regs
20 s19(2)(a) JSA 1995
21 R(U) 10/71; R(U) 2/76
22 s19(2)(b) JSA 1995
23 s19(2)(c) JSA 1995
24 s20(1) JSA 1995
25 para 34399 DMG
26 R(U) 32/52
27 para 34400 DMG; CJSA/2082/2002; CJSA/2692/1999
28 s19(2)(d) JSA 1995
29 s20(1) JSA 1995
30 s20(3) JSA 1995
31 Reg 74(4) JSA Regs
32 para 34237 DMG
33 Reg 75(3) JSA Regs
34 Reg 74 JSA Regs
35 Reg 1(3), definition of 'full-time student', JSA Regs
36 s19(2)(e) JSA 1995; reg 70B JSA Regs
37 s17A(4) JSA 1995; reg 3 JSA(MWAS) Regs
38 Reg 4 JSA(MWAS) Regs
39 PL v SSWP (JSA) [2013] UKUT 227 (AAC)
40 R (Reilly and another) v SSWP [2013] UKSC 68, 30 October 2013
41 Reg 6 JSA(MWAS) Regs
42 Regs 5 and 6 JSA(MWAS) Regs
43 s19A(2) JSA 1995

44 Reg 75(5) JSA Regs
45 Reg 69A(1) and (2) JSA Regs
46 Reg 70C JSA Regs
47 Reg 70C(1)(e) JSA Regs
48 Reg 70C(4) JSA Regs
49 Reg 3(6) SS&CS(DA) Regs
50 CJSA/2375/2000
51 Reg 69A(3) JSA Regs
52 s19A(2)(a) JSA 1995
53 Reg 70A(2)-(4) JSA Regs
54 Memo DMG 37/12, para 50
55 Reg 70A(5), definition of 'relevant notification', JSA Regs
56 s19A(2)(b) JSA 1995
57 Reg 3 JSA(SAPOE) Regs
58 defined in s139A Learning and Skills Act 2000
59 Reg 5 JSA(SAPOE) Regs
60 PL v SSWP(JSA) [2013] UKUT 227 (AAC)
61 R (Reilly and another) v SSWP [2013] UKSC 68, 30 October 2013
62 Reg 6 JSA(SAPOE) Regs
63 The Court of Appeal quashed the Jobseeker's Allowance (Employment, Skills and Enterprise Scheme) Regulations 2011 in R (Reilly and Another) v SSWP [2013] UKSC 68, 30 October 2013
64 The Jobseeker's (Back to Work Schemes) Act 2013
65 Judicial review proceedings have been issued challenging the legality of the Jobseeker's (Back to Work Schemes) Act 2013
66 s19A(2)(c) JSA 1995
67 s19A(11) JSA 1995
68 s19A(2)(d)-(g) JSA 1995
69 para 34688 DMG
70 R(JSA) 2/06
71 Reg 75(1)(b) JSA Regs
72 Reg 75(1)(a) JSA Regs
73 s19B(1) and (5) JSA 1995; reg 69B JSA Regs
74 s19B(2), (3) and (5) JSA 1995; reg 69B JSA Regs
75 Reg 75(5) JSA Regs
76 Reg 69B(5) JSA Regs
77 Reg 69B(6) JSA Regs
78 Reg 69B(7) JSA Regs
79 Reg 70C JSA Regs

80 Reg 70C(1)(e) JSA Regs
81 Reg 70C(4) JSA Regs
82 Reg 3(6) SS&CS(DA) Regs
83 CJSA/2375/2000
84 Reg 69B(8) JSA Regs

2. **Other sanctions**

85 There is no specific appeal provision, but the DWP confirmed there is a normal right of appeal against such a decision: email from DWP to CPAG, 21 January 2008.
86 Reg 15 SS(JPI) Regs; reg 9 SS(WFLIP) Regs; reg 10 SS(IBWFI) Regs; reg 14 SS(JPIP) Regs
87 Reg 14 SS(JPIP) Regs
88 Reg 12(2)(a) SS(JPI) Regs
89 Reg 10(3) SS(JPIP) Regs
90 Reg 61(1) ESA Regs; reg 8(1) SS(IBWFI) Regs; reg 11(4) SS(JPI) Regs; reg 7(1)(b) SS(WFILP) Regs
91 *DL v SSWP (JSA)* [2013] UKUT 295 (AAC)
92 Reg 12(12) SS(JPI) Regs; reg 7(2) SS(WFILP) Regs; reg 9(11) SS(IBWFI) Regs; reg 11(11) SS(JPIP) Regs
93 The DWP has confirmed that it is not necessary to have attempted to show good cause within five days: email from DWP to CPAG, 21 January 2008.
94 Reg 8 SS(IBWFI) Regs; reg 13 SS(JPIP) Regs; reg 7(5) SS(WFILP) Regs; reg 14 SS(JPI) Regs
95 paras 53029 and 53052-53 DMG
96 Reg 63 ESA Regs
97 Reg 9 SS(IBWFI) Regs
98 Reg 12(2)(c)-(8) SS(JPI) Regs; reg 8 SS(WFILP) Regs
99 Reg 11 SS(JPIP) Regs
100 Reg 11(4) SS(JPIP) Regs
101 Reg 12A SS(JPIP) Regs; reg 7(5A) and (5B) SS(WFILP) Regs
102 Reg 63(6)-(8) and (11) ESA Regs
103 Reg 63(9) and (10) ESA Regs
104 Reg 64(2) ESA Regs
105 Reg 3(5C) and (6A) SS&CS(DA) Regs
106 CJSA/2375/2000
107 Reg 12(9), (9A) and (12) SS(JPI) Regs; reg 9(8) and (11) SS(IBWFI) Regs; regs 7(2) and 8(3) and (4) SS(WFILP) Regs; regs 11(9) and (11) and 12 SS(JPIP) Regs
108 Reg 12 SS(JPIP) Regs
109 Reg 8(1) ESA(WRA) Regs; reg 6(1) IS(WRA) Regs (draft); *DL v SSWP (JSA)* [2013] UKUT 295 (AAC)
110 **IS** Reg 8 IS(WRA) Regs (draft)
     ESA Reg 8 ESA(WRA) Regs; regs 63 and 64 ESA Regs; Memo DMG 41/12
111 Reg 7 IS(WRA) Regs (draft)

112 Reg 63(6)-(11) ESA Regs
113 Reg 64(1)(b) and (c) ESA Regs
114 Reg 9 IS(WRA) Regs (draft)

3. **General rules about sanctions**

115 R(U) 8/57, para 6
116 R(U) 26/56; R(U) 1/58
117 R(U) 10/53
118 R(U) 14/56
119 R(U) 24/56
120 *AA v SSWP (JSA)* [2012] UKUT 100 (AAC); [2012] AACR 42
121 R(U) 1/57; R(U) 14/57; CU/34/1992
122 R(U) 2/76
123 para 34241 DMG; para K3203 ADM
124 para 34256 DMG; para K3236 ADM
125 **JSA** s19(3) JSA 1995; reg 71 JSA Regs; R(U) 3/91
     UC/JSA under UC Reg 113(1)(f) UC Regs; reg 28(1)(f) and (2) JSA Regs 2013
126 R(U) 25/52
127 R(U) 26/51; R(U) 20/64; R(U) 4/70; R(U) 1/81
128 R(U) 3/81
129 Chapter K2 ADM
130 Reg 72 JSA Regs
131 *HS v SSWP* [2009] UKUT 177 (AAC); [2010] AACR 10
132 R(JSA) 7/03 discusses the meaning of 'conscientious objection' in this context.
133 s21(1) JSA 1995
134 para 34437 DMG
135 R(U) 4/73
136 R(U) 3/73
137 R(U) 14/52
138 R(U) 19/52; R(U) 4/87; CJSA/2507/2005
139 R(U) 2/74
140 R(U) 10/54

Chapter 52

Sanctions: the universal credit system

This chapter covers:
1. Sanctions under the universal credit system (below)
2. High level sanctions (p1122)
3. Medium level sanctions (p1122)
4. Low level sanctions (p1127)
5. Lowest level sanctions (p1129)

This chapter covers the rules on sanctions under the universal credit system. It does not cover the rules for any other sanctions. For these, see Chapter 51.

Key facts
- You can be given a sanction in a number of situations, including if you leave work, a training scheme or employment programme, if you lose pay voluntarily or because of misconduct, if you do not accept a job or place on a scheme or programme, if you fail to take part in work-focused interviews, and if you stop being available for work or actively seeking work.
- You may be able to avoid a sanction if you can show that you have a good reason for your actions.
- If you are given a sanction, your benefit is paid at a reduced (or nil) rate for a period.
- Special rules apply if you are aged 16 or 17.
- You may qualify for universal credit hardship payments if you have been given a sanction.
- You can apply for a revision or supersession, or appeal against a sanction decision. You are likely to have to apply for a revision before you can appeal.

---

1. Sanctions under the universal credit system

If you come under the universal credit (UC) system (see p19) and you are entitled to UC, contribution-based jobseeker's allowance (JSA) or contributory

Part 8: Work
Chapter 52: Sanctions: the universal credit system
1. Sanctions under the universal credit system

employment and support allowance (ESA), you can be sanctioned for a period – eg, if you are dismissed from a job for misconduct or leave a job voluntarily, if you fail to attend a training scheme or employment programme, if you stop being available for or stop seeking work, or if you do not participate in a work-focused interview. See the chart below. **Note:** in some cases, you cannot be given a sanction if you can show you had a good reason for your actions. For what may count as a 'good reason', see p1107. The issues are the same as for other sanctions.

If you are sanctioned, your UC, JSA or ESA is paid at a reduced (or nil) rate during a 'sanction period'. For information about the amount of benefit payable, see p1117. If you experience hardship as a result of a sanction, you might be able to get UC hardship payments (see Chapter 55). Some special rules apply if you are aged 16 or 17. For information about challenging a sanction decision, see p1111. The issues are the same as for other sanctions.

High level sanctions (UC and JSA only)
Failing to participate in Mandatory Work Activity (p1124)
Failing to apply for or to accept paid work (p1124)
Ceasing paid work or losing pay for specified reasons (p1125)

Sanction period: 91, 182 or 1,095 days

Medium level sanctions (UC and JSA only)
Failing to be available for paid work or to take all reasonable action to get paid work

Sanction period: 28 or 91 days

Low level sanctions (UC, JSA and ESA)
Failing to meet a work-focused interview requirement
Failing to comply with a requirement connected to a work-related requirement
Failing to meet a work preparation requirement
Failing to take a particular action to get paid work (UC and JSA only)

Sanction period: until compliance with the requirement, plus a fixed period: seven, 14 or 28 days

Lowest level sanctions (UC and ESA only)
Failing to meet a work-focused interview requirement

Sanction period: until compliance with the requirement

The number of days your benefit is reduced (the 'sanction period') is worked out for each sanction you are given. If you are given more than one sanction, the sanction periods run consecutively, but the total number of days for all the sanctions outstanding at any particular time cannot be more than 1,095 days.[1]

Note: if you are entitled to UC, the reduction is applied to UC, even if the sanction was in respect of your JSA or ESA claim. See p1122 for information about applying sanctions to other benefits.

The benefit reduction

If you are given a sanction, your benefit is paid at a reduced (or nil) rate until the sanction period ends. The reduction for each assessment period (or, for JSA and ESA, benefit week) is calculated as follows.[2]

- **Step one:** take the number of days in the assessment period (or for JSA and ESA, the benefit week) or, if lower, the total number of outstanding days in the sanction period. Deduct any days in the assessment period (or benefit week) for which the sanction period has been suspended because you have also been given a sanction for a benefit offence (see p1258).
- **Step two:** multiply the number of days in Step one by the relevant daily reduction rate (see below).

For UC, the amount in Step two is adjusted so it is not more than your standard allowance (see p250) or, if you are a joint claimant and only one of you has been sanctioned, so that it is not more than 50 per cent of your standard allowance. The reduction in your UC is made after the 'benefit cap' has been applied, if relevant (see p1169).

The daily reduction rates

Universal credit

For UC, the daily reduction rate is normally the amount of standard allowance that applies to you multiplied by 12 and divided by 365 (the 'high rate').[3] However, the daily reduction is 40 per cent of this amount (the 'low rate') if, at the end of the assessment period:[4]

- you do not have to meet any work-related requirements (see p1073) because you:
  - are the responsible carer or foster parent of a child under one;
  - are pregnant and there are 11 weeks or less before the week your baby is due;
  - had a baby not more than 15 weeks ago (including if the baby was stillborn);
  - are adopting a child and it is no more than 52 weeks since the child was placed with you; *or*
- you only have to meet a work-focused interview requirement (see p1077); *or*
- you are 16 or 17 years old.

Part 8: Work
Chapter 52: Sanctions: the universal credit system
1. Sanctions under the universal credit system

The daily reduction rate is nil if, at the end of the assessment period, you are someone who does not have to meet any work-related requirements because you have limited capability for work and work-related activity (see p1073).[5]

If you are a member of a couple and are a joint claimant and only one of you is given a sanction, the daily rate that applies to you is divided by two.[6]

The daily reduction rates are rounded down to the nearest 10 pence.

Daily reduction rates

	High rate £ per day	Low rate £ per day
Single		
Under 25	8.10	3.20
25 or over	10.30	4.10
Couple		
Both under 25	12.80	5.10
Either 25 or over	16.20	6.40

Note: you may still be entitled to some UC during the assessment period – ie, if you qualify for elements for children or any other elements such as for childcare or housing costs.

Example

Jim is aged 35. He and his partner are getting UC as joint claimants. They live in rented accommodation. Jim was given a 182-day high level sanction. His partner was not sanctioned. There are 150 days outstanding in Jim's sanction period. It is a 30-day assessment period.

Step one: the relevant number of days is 30, as this is lower than the number of outstanding days in Jim's sanction period.

Step two: The daily rate is £8.10 (£16.20 ÷ 2). The reduction is therefore 30 x £8.10 = £243. 50 per cent of Jim's standard allowance is £246.97 (£493.95 ÷ 2). This is higher than the reduction.

Jim and his partner's UC is therefore reduced by £243 over the assessment period. They continue to get the amount to which they are entitled that exceeds £243, including the help they get with their rent.

Jobseeker's allowance

For JSA, the daily reduction rate is the weekly amount of JSA to which you are entitled multiplied by 52 and divided by 365, rounded down to the nearest 10 pence.[7] The daily reduction rates are therefore as follows. If you are:

- under 25: £8.10;
- 25 or over: £10.30.

Example

Mary is a JSA claimant aged 24. She is given a 28-day medium level sanction. She takes a job for a short period but when she claims JSA again, there are five days outstanding in the sanction period.

Step one: the relevant number of days is five as this is lower than the number of days in the benefit week.

Step two: 5 x £8.10 = £40.50

Mary's JSA for the benefit week is reduced by £40.50. She is paid the remainder (£16.85). The following benefit week, she is paid the full rate of JSA (£57.35) because the sanction period has ended.

Employment and support allowance

For ESA, the daily reduction rate is normally the weekly amount of ESA to which you are entitled (not including any component) multiplied by 52 and divided by 365, rounded down to the nearest 10 pence (the 'high rate').[8]

The daily reduction rate is 40 per cent of the amount above (the 'low rate') if, at the end of the benefit week:[9]

- you are a lone parent responsible for a child under one or the responsible foster parent of a child under one (see p1075);
- you are pregnant and there are 11 weeks or less before the week your baby is due;
- you had a baby not more than 15 weeks ago (including if the baby was stillborn);
- you are adopting a child and it is no more than 52 weeks since the child was placed with you (see p1075);
- you only have to meet a work-focused interview requirement.

The daily reduction is nil if, at the end of the benefit week, you do not have to meet any work-related requirements because you have limited capability for work and for work-related activity (see p1073).[10]

Note: if you are getting a reduced rate of ESA because you have been disqualified from receiving ESA for any of the reasons on p617 (eg, because of misconduct or failure to accept treatment), the daily reduction rates are also reduced.

Daily reduction rates

	High rate £ per day	Low rate £ per day
Entitled to main phase ESA	10.30	4.10
Under 25, not entitled to main phase ESA	8.10	3.20
25 or over	10.30	4.10

Part 8: Work
Chapter 52: Sanctions: the universal credit system
1. Sanctions under the universal credit system

Reduced rate ESA due to disqualification:		
Entitled to main phase ESA	8.20	3.20
Under 25, not entitled to main phase ESA	6.50	2.60
25 or over	8.20	3.20

Example

Julie is getting main phase ESA of £101.15, including a work-related activity component. She fails to participate in a work-focused interview for the second time in 365 days and is given a low level sanction. She participates in an interview three days into the benefit week, so the indefinite sanction period ends. However, the sanction period continues for a further 14 days. Her sanction period is therefore 2 days + 14 days = 16 days.

For the first benefit week the reduction is calculated as follows.

Step one: the relevant number of days is seven (the number of days in the benefit week).

Step two: 7 x £10.30 = £72.10

Julie's ESA is reduced by £72.10 for two benefit weeks. She is paid the remainder (£29.05). For the third benefit week, the reduction is calculated as follows.

Step one: the relevant number of days is two (the number of days in the sanction period still outstanding).

Step two: 2 x £10.30 = £20.60

Julie's ESA for the week is reduced by £20.60. She is paid the remainder (£80.55). For the following weeks, she is paid as normal.

When the sanction period starts and ends

For all levels of sanction, the sanction period starts for:[11]
- UC, on the first day of the assessment period in which the decision is made to give you a sanction or, if your UC is not paid at a reduced rate for the sanction during that period, from the first day of the next assessment period;
- JSA, if you have not been paid any JSA for the benefit week in which the sanctionable action took place, on the first day of that benefit week. If you have been paid JSA in that benefit week, the sanction period starts on the first day of the benefit week after you were last paid JSA;
- for ESA, if you have not been paid any ESA for the benefit week in which the decision maker decides you should be sanctioned, on the first day of that benefit week. If you have been paid ESA in that benefit week, the sanction period starts on the first day of the benefit week after you were last paid ESA.

However, if your benefit is already being paid at a reduced rate because of a previous sanction, it is not reduced for a new sanction until the previous reduction ends.

Once a sanction period has begun, it continues unbroken until the sanction period comes to an end.[12] For example, if you take a job for a short period but then claim UC (or JSA or ESA) again during the period of the sanction (whether on your own or as a joint claimant), you are still caught by the sanction, but only for any outstanding sanction period. If your UC (or JSA or ESA) entitlement ends before the decision maker has decided to give you a sanction, but the decision to do so is made when you are again entitled to the benefit, the sanction period is treated as starting on the day before your previous entitlement ended.[13] **Note:** see below for special rules if you no longer come under the UC system.

A sanction is **terminated** if, since the date of the most recent sanctionable action, you have been in paid work for (or for periods that total) at least 26 weeks.[14] You count as in paid work if:

- for UC, your weekly earnings during the 26 weeks are at least the amount of your individual earnings threshold (see p1076). This includes if you are treated as having a minimum amount of self-employed earnings under the rules described on p329;
- for JSA, your weekly earnings are at least what you would earn for the number of hours you are expected to work (see p1069) at the weekly minimum wage for a person of your age;
- for ESA, your weekly earnings are at least 16 times the weekly minimum wage for a person of your age.

A sanction is **suspended** for any period during which you are sanctioned for a benefit offence (see p1258).[15]

Note:
- The days in your sanction period count towards your days of entitlement to contribution-based JSA or contributory ESA, even if you are not actually paid any benefit.
- If you disagree that you should be sanctioned or with the sanction period, you can challenge the decision (see p1111). The issues are the same as for other sanctions.

If you no longer come under the universal credit system

Special rules apply if you are given a sanction under the UC system and you subsequently no longer come under that system – eg, your entitlement to UC ends and when you need to claim benefit again, you are living in an area where UC has not yet been introduced. In this case, if you were claiming:

- JSA or ESA, the sanction period ends on the first day you become entitled to income support (IS), or when the UC system rules cease to apply to your JSA or ESA award;[16] *or*
- UC, the sanction period ends on the first day you become entitled to IS, income-based JSA, income-related ESA, housing benefit, working tax credit or child tax credit.[17]

Part 8: Work
Chapter 52: Sanctions: the universal credit system
2. High level sanctions

Applying a sanction to another benefit

If you are given a JSA or ESA sanction under the UC system and you become entitled to UC, the reduction is made to your UC.[18] This applies whether or not you are still entitled to JSA or ESA. The reduction is made for the remainder of the JSA or ESA sanction period. Any days between the day your entitlement to JSA or ESA ends and the day your entitlement to UC starts are deducted from the period.

If your UC is being paid at a reduced rate because of a sanction, your entitlement to UC ends, you still come under the UC system and you are entitled to JSA or ESA, the reduction is then made to your JSA or ESA.[19] The reduction is made for the remainder of the UC sanction period. Any days between the day your entitlement to UC ends and the day your entitlement to JSA or ESA starts are deducted from the period.

Special rules apply if you were given a sanction while entitled to JSA (or ESA) before you came under the UC system. In this case, if you are now entitled to:
- JSA (or ESA) under the UC system, but not UC, you are treated as if you were given a JSA (or ESA) sanction under the UC system;[20]
- UC, you are treated as if you were given a UC sanction.[21]

In both cases, the reduction is made for the remainder of the former JSA (or ESA) sanction period, minus any days between the day your former JSA (or ESA) entitlement ended (if relevant) and your current UC, JSA or ESA entitlement starts.

2. **High level sanctions**

If you are entitled to universal credit (UC) or jobseeker's allowance (JSA), you can be given a high level sanction if you:[22]
- fail to participate in Mandatory Work Activity without a good reason (see p1124); *or*
- fail to apply for a particular vacancy or accept an offer of paid work, more paid work or better paid work without a good reason (see p1124); *or*
- cease paid work or lose pay voluntarily without a good reason or because of 'misconduct' (see p1125).

We refer to them as 'sanctionable actions' in this *Handbook*. The DWP may refer to these as 'sanctionable failures'.

For information about the amount of UC or JSA you are paid, see p1117.

Length of the sanction period

If you are given a high level JSA sanction or, if you are 18 or over, a UC sanction, it is usually imposed for 91 days. However it is imposed for:[23]

* 182 days if you have been given a 91-day high level sanction previously (but see below); *or*
* 1,095 days (three years) if you have been given a 182- or a 1,095-day high level sanction previously (but see below).

If you are given a high level UC sanction and you are 16 or 17 years old, a fixed sanction period is imposed of:[24]

* 14 days; *or*
* 28 days, if you have been given a 14- or 28-day high level sanction previously (but see below).

For all claimants, the previous sanctionable action must have taken place 364 days or less before your current sanctionable action. For JSA, a high level UC sanction, and for UC a high level JSA sanction which has been applied to your UC, also counts for this purpose.[25] Previous sanctionable actions that took place in the 13 days before your current sanctionable action are disregarded.[26] For JSA, this includes sanctionable actions that resulted in a UC sanction.

If the previous sanctionable action was that you did not accept an offer of paid work or ceased paid work, lost pay voluntarily or because of misconduct and this took place before you made your claim, it does not count for the purpose of determining the sanction period for any later sanctionable action.[27] Your sanction period may be reduced in the same circumstances (see below).

Note:

* If, when you did not come under the UC system, you were given a JSA sanction and you are then given another sanction under the UC system, the previous sanctionable action can count when the new sanction period is determined.[28]
* If you are given a sanction but later a previous sanction is removed (eg, by the First-tier Tribunal), ask a decision maker to reduce the sanction period.[29] If s/he fails to do so, appeal. If you have already appealed against the later sanction, the Tribunal should take the removal of the previous sanction into account.[30]

Reduced sanction periods

If you are given a high level sanction because, before the date of your claim, you failed to accept paid work, ceased paid work or lost pay voluntarily or because of misconduct, your sanction period is reduced to take account of days when you did not claim UC (or JSA). In this case, your sanction period is the shorter of the following.[31]

* Unless the job was only due to last for a limited period, the sanction period that would normally apply is reduced by the number of days between the date of your current sanctionable action and your date of claim (see p193 and p704).
* If the job was only due to last for a limited period, the sanction period is the number of days starting with the day after the date of your current sanctionable

Part 8: Work
Chapter 52: Sanctions: the universal credit system
2. High level sanctions

action and ending on the day the paid work would have ended, reduced by the number of days between the date of your current sanctionable action and your date of claim (see p193 and p704).

In practical terms, this means that, if the job was only meant to last for a limited period and you claim UC (or JSA) after it would have ended, your benefit is not paid at a reduced (or nil) rate.[32] 'Limited period' is not defined.

Example
Glynis quits her job on 7 October. It was only due to last until 1 November. She claims JSA on 15 November. She is given a high level sanction for the second time in 365 days so a 182-day sanction period would normally apply. However, her job was only due to last for a limited period.
The number of days from 8 October to 1 November is 25 days.
The number of days between 7 October and 15 November is 38 days. This is higher than the number of days from 8 October to 1 November (25 days). Glynis's sanction period is therefore reduced to nil and her JSA is not paid at a reduced rate.

Failing to undertake Mandatory Work Activity

You can be given a high level sanction if you do not meet a work preparation requirement to undertake Mandatory Work Activity without a good reason.[33] Mandatory Work Activity is a scheme that provides four weeks of work, or work-related activity of up to 30 hours a week, with a view to assisting you to improve your prospect of getting employment.[34]

The rules do not say what notice must be given, but any work preparation requirement should be recorded in your claimant commitment or, if it is not, you should be notified by other means.[35] The rules do not say when you may count as not meeting a requirement to undertake Mandatory Work Activity.[36] However, the DWP says this includes failing to attend or participate in the scheme, as well as failing to take part in, or meet expected standards of, any activity.[37]

Failing to apply for or to accept paid work

You can be given a high level sanction if, without a good reason:[38]
- you are told to apply for a particular vacancy for paid work (under a work search requirement) and do not do so, or you fail to take up paid work when it is offered to you (under a work availability requirement). **Note:** if the vacancy was available because of a strike, you cannot be sanctioned;[39] *or*
- you failed to take up an offer of paid work before your claim for UC (or JSA). For UC, you must be subject to all the work-related requirements (see p1073) when you are awarded UC. For both UC and JSA, this only applies if the number of days between the date you failed to take up the offer and your date

of claim for UC (or JSA) is more than the sanction period that would otherwise apply.

For when the DWP might treat you as having refused to apply for or accept paid work, see p1089. The issues are similar to those for JSA sanctions that are not under the UC system. **Note:**

- You only have to be available for work and to look for work in locations that are no more than 90 minutes from your home.[41] So you may find it difficult to show you have a good reason if your travel time is shorter than this.
- You may be able to show that you have a good reason for refusing a job if you have previously done work of a particular type or at a particular rate of pay, you have been allowed to limit your work search to looking for work of a similar type or rate of pay (see p1071 and p1072), and you refuse a job that does not meet these conditions.

Ceasing paid work or losing pay

You can be given a high level sanction if you cease paid work (see above) or lose pay:[42]

- 'voluntarily' without a good reason. This applies even if:
  - for UC, when this happened no work-related requirements could be imposed on you because you were earning a sufficient amount (see p1076 for the earnings thresholds) and this results in your now being subject to all the work-related requirements; *or*
  - this happened before your claim for UC (or JSA). For UC, you must be someone subject to all the work-related requirements when you are awarded UC. However, for both UC and JSA, no reduction in your benefit can be made if the number of days between the date you ceased work or lost pay and your date of claim for UC (or JSA) is more than the sanction period that would otherwise apply; *or*
- because of misconduct. You can be sanctioned if you are suspended from work for misconduct or if you resigned rather than be dismissed.[43]

The issues are similar to those for JSA sanctions that are not under the UC system. For information about:

- whether you left work or lost pay voluntarily, see p1106;
- what may happen if you take retirement, see p1107;

Part 8: Work
Chapter 52: Sanctions: the universal credit system
3. Medium level sanctions

- what may count as misconduct, see p1105;
- whether misconduct caused the loss of work or pay, see p1106.

When you cannot be sanctioned

For UC only, you cannot be given a sanction (even if you cease paid work or lose pay voluntarily or because of misconduct) if your weekly earnings (or, if you are a joint claimant, your joint earnings) are sufficiently high that the DWP is satisfied that a work search requirement and a work availability requirement should not be imposed on you at the present time.[44]

For both UC and JSA, you cannot be given a sanction (even if you cease paid work or lose pay voluntarily) if:[45]

- you volunteer or accept your employer's proposal for redundancy. The issues are the same as for JSA if you do not come under the UC system (see p1107); *or*
- you are allowed to limit the number of hours you are available for work and are looking for work (see p1069), you take up paid work (or more hours of paid work) and you cease that paid work (or doing the higher hours) or lose pay within a trial period. 'Trial period' is not defined in the rules, but the DWP says it is a period of 56 days starting on the 29th day and ending on the 84th day on which you took up paid work (or more hours). You can argue that anything that can reasonably be described as a trial period should count;[46] *or*
- you ceased paid work or lost pay because of a strike; *or*
- you ceased paid work as a member of the armed forces, or lost pay in that capacity; *or*
- you have been laid off or kept on short time work by your employer for at least four consecutive weeks (or for six weeks in a 13-week period). You must have applied for redundancy pay within a specified time.[47]

3. **Medium level sanctions**

If you are entitled to universal credit (UC) or jobseeker's allowance (JSA), you can be given a medium level sanction if, for no good reason, you:[48]

- do not take all reasonable action to get paid work, more paid work or better paid work (under a work search requirement – see p1068); *or*
- are not available for work (under the work availability requirement – see p1070).

We refer to them as 'sanctionable actions' in this *Handbook*. The DWP may refer to these as 'sanctionable failures'.

For information about the amount of UC or JSA you are paid, see p1117.

Length of the sanction period

If you are given a medium level JSA sanction or, if you are 18 or over, a UC sanction, it is usually imposed for 28 days. However, it is imposed for 91 days, if you have previously been given a 28-day or 91-day medium level sanction (but see below).[49]

If you are given a medium level UC sanction and are 16 or 17 years old, a fixed sanction period applies of:[50]

- seven days; or
- 14 days, if you have been given a seven- or 14-day medium level sanction previously (but see below).

For all claimants, the previous sanctionable action must have taken place 364 days or less before your current sanctionable action. For JSA, a medium level UC sanction, and for UC, a medium level JSA sanction which has been applied to your UC, also counts for these purposes.[51] Previous sanctionable actions that took place in the 13 days before your current sanctionable action are disregarded.[52] For JSA, this includes sanctionable actions that resulted in a UC sanction.

Note:

- If, when you did not come under the UC system, you were given a JSA sanction and you are then given another sanction under the UC system, the previous sanctionable action can count when the new sanction period is determined.[53]
- If you are given a sanction but later a previous sanction is removed (eg, by the First-tier Tribunal), ask a decision maker to reduce the sanction period.[54] If s/he fails to do so, appeal. If you have already appealed against the later sanction, the Tribunal should take the removal of the previous sanction into account.[55]

---

4. Low level sanctions

If you are entitled to universal credit (UC), jobseeker's allowance (JSA) or employment and support allowance (ESA), you can be given a low level sanction if, without a good reason, you:[56]

- fail to meet a work-focused interview requirement (see p1067); *or*
- fail to comply with a connected requirement to participate in interviews, provide evidence, confirm compliance (eg, by signing on) or report a change in your circumstances that is relevant to whether work-related requirements can be imposed on you or to your compliance with a work-related requirement – eg, if you have lost your job or lost pay; *or*
- fail to meet a work preparation requirement (see p1067) – eg, you refuse to participate in the Work Programme or to go on a training scheme or employment programme; *or*

Part 8: Work
Chapter 52: Sanctions: the universal credit system
4. Low level sanctions

- for UC and JSA only, fail to take any particular action specified by the DWP to get paid work, more paid work or better paid work (see p1068).

We refer to them as 'sanctionable actions' in this *Handbook*. The DWP may refer to these as 'sanctionable failures'.

For ESA, to be sanctioned, you must be someone who can be required to meet a work preparation requirement and a work-focused interview requirement (see p1078). For UC, you must be someone who can be required to meet all the work-related requirements, or only to meet a work preparation requirement (or a work preparation and a work-focused interview requirement).

For information about the amount of UC, JSA or ESA you are paid, see p1117.

Length of the sanction period

If you are given a low level UC, JSA or ESA sanction, it is imposed in two stages. Firstly, it lasts for an unspecified number of days starting on the date your sanctionable action took place and ending on the earliest of the following: [57]

- the day before the date you meet a 'compliance condition' specified by the DWP; *or*
- for UC and ESA only, the day before the date you no longer have to meet any work-related requirements (see p1073); *or*
- the day before the date you are no longer required to take particular action specified in a work preparation requirement; *or*
- the date your entitlement to UC (or JSA or ESA) ends. For UC, this does not apply if this is because you cease to be, or become, a member of a couple.

Compliance condition

A **'compliance condition'** is:[58]

– a condition that you stop a sanctionable action – eg, if you failed to participate in an employment programme, a condition that you must participate; *or*

– a condition relating to your future compliance with a work-related requirement (or a requirement connected to one) – eg, if you failed to participate in a work-focused interview, a condition that you must arrange to attend and participate in another one.

In addition, a fixed-period sanction is imposed:

- for UC (if you are at least 18 years old), JSA or ESA, usually for seven days. However the period is:[59]
  – 14 days, if you have been given a seven-day low level sanction previously (but see p1129); *or*
  – 28 days, if you have been given a 14-day or 28-day low level sanction previously (but see p1129); *or*
- for UC, if you are 16 or 17 years old, for seven days if you have been given a low level sanction previously (but see p1129).[60]

For all claimants, the previous sanctionable action must have taken place 364 days or less before your current sanctionable action. For UC, a low level JSA or ESA sanction that has been applied to your UC, and for JSA, a low level UC or ESA sanction, and for ESA, a low level UC or JSA sanction, also count for these purposes.[61] Previous sanctionable actions that took place in the 13 days before your current sanctionable action are disregarded.[62] For JSA, this includes sanctionable actions that resulted in a UC or ESA sanction. For ESA, this includes sanctionable actions that resulted in a UC or JSA sanction.

Note:

- If, when you did not come under the UC system, you were given a JSA or ESA sanction and you are then given another sanction under the UC system, the previous sanctionable action can count when the new sanction period is determined.[63]
- If you are given a sanction but later a previous sanction is removed (eg, by the First-tier Tribunal), ask a decision maker to reduce the sanction period.[64] If s/he fails to do so, appeal. If you have already appealed against the later sanction, the Tribunal should take the removal of the previous sanction into account.[65]

5. Lowest level sanctions

For universal credit (UC) and employment and support allowance (ESA) only, you can be given a lowest level sanction if you are someone who can only be required to meet a work-focused interview requirement (see p1077) and you fail to participate in a work-focused interview without a good reason.[66] We refer to this as a 'sanctionable action' in this *Handbook*. The DWP may refer to it as a 'sanctionable failure'.

For information about the amount of UC or ESA you are paid, see p1085.

Length of the sanction period

If you are given a lowest level sanction, it is imposed for an unspecified number of days starting on the date your sanctionable action took place and ending on the earliest of the following:[67]

- the day before the date you meet a 'compliance condition' specified by the DWP (see p1128); *or*
- the day before the date you no longer have to meet any work-related requirements (see p1073); *or*
- the date your entitlement to UC (or ESA) ends. For UC, this does not apply if this is because you cease to be, or become, a member of a couple.

Notes

1. Sanctions under the universal credit system

1 **UC** Reg 101(1)-(3) UC Regs
   JSA Reg 18(1)-(3) JSA Regs 2013
   ESA Reg 51(1)-(3) ESA Regs 2013
2 **UC** Regs 101(5) and 110 UC Regs
   JSA Regs 17 and 26 JSA Regs 2013
   ESA Regs 50 and 58 ESA Regs 2013
3 Reg 111(1) UC Regs
4 Reg 111(2) UC Regs
5 Reg 111(3) UC Regs
6 Reg 111(5) UC Regs
7 Reg 27 JSA Regs 2013
8 Reg 59 ESA Regs 2013
9 Reg 60(1) ESA Regs 2013
10 Reg 60(2) ESA Regs 2013
11 **UC** Reg 106 UC Regs
   JSA Reg 22 JSA Regs 2013
   ESA Reg 54 ESA Regs 2013
12 **UC** Reg 107(1) UC Regs
   JSA Reg 23(1) JSA Regs 2013
   ESA Reg 55(1) ESA Regs 2013
13 **UC** Reg 107(2) UC Regs
   JSA Reg 23(2) and (3) JSA Regs 2013
   ESA Reg 55(2) and (3) ESA Regs 2013
14 **UC** Reg 109 UC Regs
   JSA Reg 25 JSA Regs 2013
   ESA Reg 57 ESA Regs 2013
15 **UC** Reg 108 UC Regs
   JSA Reg 24 JSA Regs 2013
   ESA Reg 46 ESA Regs 2013
16 Art 20 WRA(No.9)O
17 Reg 34 UC(TP) Regs
18 **UC** Reg 112 and Sch 11 paras 1 and 2
   UC Regs
   JSA Reg 6 JSA Regs 2013
   ESA Reg 43 ESA Regs 2013
19 **JSA** Reg 30 JSA Regs 2013
   ESA Reg 61 ESA Regs 2013
20 Arts 14, 15, 17 and 18 WRA(No.9)O
21 Regs 30 and 32 UC(TP) Regs

2. High level sanctions

22 **UC** s26 WRA 2012; reg 114 UC Regs
   JSA s6J JSA 1995; reg 29 JSA Regs 2013
23 **UC** Regs 102 and 112 and Sch 11 para 3
   UC Regs
   JSA Reg 19 JSA Regs 2013
24 Reg 102(2)(b) UC Regs

25 **UC** Sch 11 para 3 UC Regs
   JSA Reg 19 JSA Regs 2013
26 **UC** Reg 101(4) UC Regs
   JSA Reg 18(4) JSA Regs 2013
27 **UC** Reg 102(3) and (5) UC Regs
   JSA Regs 17 and 19(2) JSA Regs 2013
28 Reg 33 UC(TP) Regs; Arts 17-19
   WRA(No.9)O
29 Reg 14 UC,PIP,JSA&ESA(DA) Regs
30 CJSA/2375/2000
31 **UC** Reg 102(4) and (5) UC Regs
   JSA Regs 17 and 19(3) JSA Regs 2013
32 **UC** Reg 113(1)(e) UC Regs
   JSA Reg 28(1)(c) JSA Regs 2013
33 **UC** s26(2)(a) WRA 2012; reg 114 UC
   Regs
   JSA s6J(2)(a) JSA 1995; reg 29 JSA Regs
   2013
34 Reg 114(2) UC Regs; reg 29(2) JSA Regs
   2013
35 para J305 ADM
36 Reg 6 JSA(MWAS) Regs is no longer in
   force under the UC system.
37 para K3038 ADM
38 **UC** s26(2)(b) and (c) and (4)(a) WRA
   2012; reg 113(1)(e) UC Regs
   JSA s6J(2)(b) and (c) and (3)(a) JSA
   1995; reg 28(1)(c) JSA Regs 2013
39 **UC** Reg 113(1)(a) UC Regs
   JSA Reg 28(1)(a) JSA Regs 2013
40 **UC** s17(1) WRA 2012; regs 2(1) and 87
   UC Regs
   JSA s6D JSA 1995; reg 3(7) JSA Regs
   2013
   Both R(IS) 5/95; *Fiory v CAO*, 20 June
   1995
41 **UC** Reg 97(3) UC Regs
   JSA Reg 14(2) JSA Regs 2013
42 **UC** s26(2)(d), (3) and (4) WRA 2012;
   reg 113(1)(e) UC Regs
   JSA s6J(2)(d) and (3) JSA 1995; reg
   28(1)(c) JSA Regs 2013
43 R(U) 10/71; R(U) 2/76
44 Reg 113(1)(g) UC Regs
45 **UC** Reg 113(1)(b)-(d) and (f) and (2) UC
   Regs
   JSA Reg 28(1)(b) and (d)-(f) and (2) JSA
   Regs 2013
46 para K3213 ADM
47 s148 Employment Rights Act 1996

3. Medium level sanctions
48 **UC** s27 WRA 2012; reg 103(1) UC Regs
    JSA s6K JSA 1995; reg 17 JSA Regs 2013
49 **UC** Regs 103 and 112 and Sch 11 para 3
    UC Regs
    JSA Reg 20 JSA Regs 2013
50 Reg 103(2)(b) UC Regs
51 **UC** Sch 11 para 3 UC Regs
    JSA Reg 20 JSA Regs 2013
52 **UC** Reg 101(4) UC Regs
    JSA Reg 18(4) JSA Regs 2013
53 Reg 33 UC(TP) Regs; Arts 17-19
    WRA(No.9)O
54 Reg 14 UC,PIP,JSA&ESA(DA) Regs
55 CJSA/2375/2000

4. Low level sanctions
56 **UC** s27 WRA 2012; reg 104(1) UC Regs
    JSA s6K JSA 1995; reg 17 JSA Regs 2013
    ESA s11J WRA 2007; reg 50 ESA Regs
    2013
57 **UC** Reg 104(2)(a) and (3)(a) UC Regs
    JSA Reg 21(2) JSA Regs 2013
    ESA Reg 52(a) ESA Regs 2013
58 **UC** s27(6) and (7) WRA 2012
    JSA s6K(6) and (7) JSA 1995
    ESA s11J(5) and (6) WRA 2007
59 **UC** Regs 104(2)(b) and 112 and Sch 11
    para 3 UC Regs
    JSA Reg 21(3) JSA Regs 2013
    ESA Reg 52(b) ESA Regs 2013
60 Reg 104(3)(b) UC Regs
61 **UC** Sch 11 para 3 UC Regs
    JSA Reg 21 JSA Regs 2013
    ESA Reg 52 ESA Regs 2013
62 **UC** Reg 101(4) UC Regs
    JSA Reg 18(4) JSA Regs 2013
    ESA Reg 51(4) ESA Regs 2013
63 Regs 31 and 33 UC(TP) Regs; Arts 16-19
    WRA(No.9)O
64 Reg 14 UC,PIP,JSA&ESA(DA) Regs
65 CJSA/2375/2000

5. Lowest level sanctions
66 **UC** s27 WRA 2012; reg 105 UC Regs
    ESA s11J WRA 2007; reg 50 ESA Regs
    2013
67 **UC** Reg 105(2) UC Regs
    ESA Reg 53 ESA Regs 2013

Part 9

Claiming benefits and getting paid

Chapter 53

Claims and decisions

This chapter covers:
1. Making a claim (below)
2. What you must provide when you claim (p1138)
3. If you claim the wrong benefit (p1144)
4. Backdating your claim (p1144)
5. Decisions (p1150)

This chapter covers the general rules on claims, backdating and decisions. See the chapter about the benefit you are claiming for the specific rules about that benefit. This chapter does *not* cover the rules for statutory sick pay (see Chapter 39) and statutory maternity, adoption and paternity pay (see Chapter 38), payments of budgeting loans from the social fund (see p765), the health benefits in Chapter 30, the other payments in Chapter 40, or discretionary housing payments (see Chapter 21).

References in this chapter to HM Revenue and Customs only apply to claims and decisions about child benefit and guardian's allowance. For information about tax credit claims and decisions, see Chapter 65.

Key facts
- To be entitled to a benefit, you must usually make a claim for it.
- Depending on the benefit concerned, claims are made by telephone, using a claim form, online, or in person at an office.
- You must usually provide a national insurance number and any other evidence considered reasonable.
- Once you have made a valid claim, a decision must be made by a decision maker at the DWP, a local authority or HM Revenue and Customs.
- If you want more information about a decision, you can ask for an explanation. In some cases, you can also ask for written reasons for a decision.

1. Making a claim

In most cases, to be entitled to benefit, you must make a claim for it. If you cannot claim for yourself, an 'appointee' can claim on your behalf (see p1137).

Part 9: Claiming benefits and getting paid
Chapter 53: Claims and decisions
1. Making a claim

How to make a claim

Each benefit has its own rules for how to make a claim and the ways you can do so. See the chapter in this *Handbook* about the benefit you want to claim. In general, you may be able to make your claim in writing, including online, or by telephone. If you claim online or by telephone, you may still be sent a written statement to sign and return.

You may be encouraged to make your claim, or to start your claim, online or by telephone. In many cases, the number you must use is free of charge if you use a landline, but not always free if you use a mobile.

Universal credit (UC) can normally only be claimed by completing an online form – there is no paper claim form. However, the DWP may accept claims made by telephone,[1] or you may be able to get face-to-face help if completing a form online is difficult for you.

Is a telephone or online claim difficult for you?

If the benefit you want to claim is normally started by telephone or online, and this is either impractical or impossible for you, tell the DWP, the local authority or HM Revenue and Customs (HMRC) and ask to claim in an alternative way. For example:
– if speaking in English is difficult, an interpreter can be arranged;
– another person may be able to make the call on your behalf, especially if you are there to help;
– if you cannot claim by telephone, you may be able to claim online;
– if you cannot claim by telephone or online, a face-to-face interview could take place at the Jobcentre Plus or local authority office. HMRC does not offer this facility, but you can ask for help from its Mobile Advisory Service (from May 2014);
– a home visit could be arranged;
– you may be able to claim in person at an 'alternative office' (see below);
– except for UC, a claim form could be completed and sent.

Alternative offices

The DWP has made arrangements to enable you to get help with making a claim for some benefits from an 'alternative office'. You can claim carer's allowance, disability living allowance, income support (IS), employment and support allowance (ESA), pension credit (PC) and retirement pension by sending your claim to, or by making it in person in writing at, an alternative office. If you are at least the qualifying age for PC (see p78), you can also claim attendance allowance, bereavement benefits and winter fuel payments at these offices.[2] **Note:** these arrangements do not apply to claims for contributory ESA if you come under the UC system (see p19).

Alternative offices[3]
'Alternative offices' can include: designated DWP offices, designated local authority housing benefit (HB) offices and, in England only, designated county councils. Also included are some local advice centres. If you want to claim at an alternative office, ask if it has been designated to accept your claim.

'Tell Us Once'

If you are registering a birth or a death to the registrar at a local authority, you may be able to get help with claims for benefit (eg, with child benefit) under the 'Tell Us Once' arrangements. This is a scheme that allows you to tell the government once about a death or a birth. Check with your local authority (at the registrar's office or on its website) to see whether it offers this service. Under Tell Us Once, you are given a reference number after registering a death, which the DWP uses to access the relevant details when you telephone to make a claim for bereavement benefits. After registering a birth, the registrar includes details on your completed application form for child benefit, so you do not need to send the birth certificate to the Child Benefit Office.

Appointees

Someone else (eg, a friend or relative), called an 'appointee', can be authorised to act on your behalf if s/he is aged at least 18 and you cannot claim for yourself – eg, you have a mental illness or a learning disability.[4] The appointee takes on all your rights and responsibilities as a claimant – eg, s/he must notify changes in your circumstances. Normally, this only applies from the date the appointment is agreed, but if someone acts on your behalf before becoming your official appointee, her/his actions can be validated in retrospect by her/his appointment.[5] A person must normally apply to be an appointee in writing. If you are an appointee for a claimant who dies, it is best to reapply for appointee status in order to settle any outstanding benefit matters.[6] An executor under a will can also pursue an outstanding claim or appeal on behalf of a deceased claimant, even if the decision was made before the formal grant of probate.[7]

For HB, if a person is unable to manage her/his own affairs, the local authority must accept a claim made by someone formally appointed to act legally on her/his behalf. If no one has been appointed, the local authority can appoint someone. See p125 for further information.

If someone has already been made an appointee by the local authority for HB purposes, the DWP can, by agreement, make her/him an appointee without a written application, and vice versa.[8]

Part 9: Claiming benefits and getting paid
Chapter 53: Claims and decisions
2. What you must provide when you claim

Amending or withdrawing your claim

For benefits other than child benefit or guardian's allowance, you can amend your claim at any time before a decision is made by writing to or telephoning the office handling it.[9] If you claimed online, you can also amend your claim online if you are registered for this with the DWP or local authority and do so in the approved way.[10] The decision maker may also accept other methods of notification in a particular case, but does not have to. Your claim is treated as being amended from the date it was initially made.

For child benefit and guardian's allowance, you must amend your claim in writing, and HMRC has the discretion to treat your claim as amended from the date it was initially made.[11] This includes amending your claim online, if you do so in the approved way.[12]

You can withdraw your claim at any time before a decision is made.[13] Notice to withdraw your claim takes effect from the day it is received. In practice, you should also be allowed to withdraw a claim for a benefit you have already been awarded in respect of a future period, and your award will be superseded (see p1281). You can do this because there is a principle that you should not be forced to continue receiving benefit when you have indicated that you no longer wish to do so.[14]

2. **What you must provide when you claim**

When you claim benefit, you must normally:
- satisfy the national insurance (NI) number requirement (see below); *and*
- provide proof of your identity, if required (see p1140).

You must also ensure your claim is valid (see p1140). Even if you have satisfied all the requirements and the DWP, local authority or HM Revenue and Customs (HMRC) accepts your claim is valid, you may be asked to provide additional information and evidence before a decision is made on your claim (see p1152).

The national insurance number requirement

When you claim benefit you must usually satisfy the NI number requirement by:[15]
- providing an NI number and information or evidence to show that it is yours; *or*
- providing evidence or information to enable the DWP (or the local authority or HMRC) to trace your NI number, if you do not know it; *or*
- applying for an NI number if you do not have one and providing sufficient information and evidence to allow one to be allocated to you. This does not necessarily mean that you must be allocated an NI number. In general, you

will have done enough if you have supplied all the information you could reasonably have been expected to when you made your application.[16]

If you are claiming a means-tested benefit, including universal credit (UC), as a couple (see p205), your partner must usually also satisfy the NI number requirement.[17] However, see below for when s/he is exempt.

Note:
- If you do not need to make a claim for the benefit (eg, for retirement pension or, in some circumstances, a bereavement payment), the NI number requirement should not apply.
- If you cannot satisfy the NI number requirement straight away, you may be able to claim a short-term advance of benefit (see p1167).
- If you are refused benefit because you have not satisifed the NI number requirement, you can appeal against that decision.[18] You may have to apply for a revision of the decision before you can appeal (see p1271).

Exemptions

You are exempt from the NI number requirement if the benefit is:
- disability living allowance and you are under 16;[19]
- housing benefit (HB) and you live in a hostel.[20]

Partners and children

If you are claiming for your partner, s/he must usually satisfy the NI number requirement, even if s/he is a 'person subject to immigration control' and no extra benefit will be paid for her/him.[21] However (except for UC), a special rule applies in some cases, which exempts your partner from the NI number requirement if you are the benefit claimant and:[22]
- your partner is a 'person subject to immigration control' because s/he does not have leave to enter or remain in the UK – eg, s/he is an asylum seeker or an overstayer (see p1500); *and*
- s/he has not previously been given an NI number; *and*
- if you are claiming income support (IS), jobseeker's allowance (JSA), employment and support allowance (ESA) or pension credit (PC), your partner is not entitled to the benefit and, if you are claiming HB, s/he is not 'habitually resident' (see p1520).

In practice, information is still requested about an NI number application for your partner, but an NI number will be refused.[23] The rule ensures that your benefit claim can still be allowed.

If your claim includes a 'person subject to immigration control', there can be consequences for her/his immigration status (see Chapter 69).

If a child (including a qualifying young person – see p551) is included in your claim for UC or HB, s/he does not need to satisfy the NI number requirement.[24] If

Part 9: Claiming benefits and getting paid
Chapter 53: Claims and decisions
2. What you must provide when you claim

a child or qualifying young person can still be included in your award of IS or income-based JSA (see p210), s/he does not need to satisfy the NI number requirement.[25]

Proof of identity

You may be asked to produce further documents or evidence that prove your identity. If you are claiming for your partner, you must also prove her/his identity.

In an online claim for UC, the DWP attempts to verify your identity online. If it cannot, you may be asked for proof of your identity.

You can prove your identity with a passport, a national identity card issued by a European Economic Area member state, or a letter issued by the Home Office acknowledging your application for asylum. You could also produce your birth certificate, full driving licence, a travel pass with a photograph, a local council rent card or tenancy agreement, or even paid fuel or telephone bills.

Note:
- Provide details of any other people who can confirm what you have stated – eg, your solicitor or other legal representative or official organisation.
- You should not be refused benefit simply because you do not have any documents, especially if it is unreasonable for you to have or obtain them. Ask the decision maker to make a decision on your claim and you can then appeal, if necessary. You may have to apply for a revision before you can appeal (see p1271).

In some cases, the decision maker may refuse to accept evidence that you are who you say you are. Some claimants may have particular difficulty supplying evidence. Press the decision maker to be clear about what is required and why, and complain if you consider any requests for information are unreasonable (see p1381). Seek advice if you think you have experienced discrimination – eg, from the Equality and Human Rights Commission (www.equalityhumanrights.com).

Making sure your claim is valid

To be entitled to benefit, you must make a valid claim – ie, you must claim in the correct way (see p1136) and your claim must not be 'defective'. What is and is not a valid claim should not, in general, be decided in an overly technical way.[26] The DWP or HMRC should inform you if your claim is defective. It must then give you the opportunity to correct the defect.

Note: the rules about valid claims for HB are covered on p122.

For JSA only, most people have to attend an interview to count as having made a valid claim (see p1141). For other benefits, or for JSA if you do not have to attend an interview, if you claimed by telephone, see p1141 for information about valid and defective claims. If you claimed in writing, see p1141.

If your claim is valid, it is then referred to a decision maker to decide whether you are entitled to benefit (see p1150). Before making a decision, the decision maker can ask you to provide further information to support your claim or, in some cases, ask you to attend a medical examination.

Claims for jobseeker's allowance if you must attend an interview

In order to make a valid claim for JSA, you must usually attend an interview, at which a properly completed claim form is signed. Your claim is then treated as having been made on the date you first notified your intention to claim (usually, when you made the appointment for the interview) or the first date you are claiming for if this is later.[27]

If you fail to attend the interview without good cause or do not submit a properly completed form at or before the interview, you are treated as not having made a valid claim until the date you do so. The DWP has the discretion to allow you up to one month from the date you first notified your intention to claim to rectify the situation.[28]

Claims by telephone

A claim made by telephone is only valid if you provide all the information the decision maker needs to decide your claim during the telephone call. If you do not do this, your claim is defective. You are given a chance to remedy the defect.[29] For ESA and PC only, you must also approve a written statement of your circumstances if you are asked to do this.[30]

For benefits other than IS and JSA (and for contribution-based JSA if you come under the UC system – see p19), if you supply the necessary information within a month of being notified of the defect, your claim is treated as having been made on the date of your initial telephone claim. The decision maker can extend this one-month period if s/he thinks it is reasonable.[31]

For IS and JSA, if you do not have to attend an interview to complete your claim, you must supply the necessary information within a month of first telephoning to make a claim.[32]

Claims in writing

To be valid, written claims for IS, JSA, ESA or personal independence payment (PIP) must be made on an approved form.[33] For other benefits (except UC), the decision maker may decide to treat any letter or other written communication as being a valid written claim.[34] However, in practice, if you claim other than on the approved form, you are likely to be sent a form to complete. If you properly complete and return this form within one month (or longer, if the decision maker considers it reasonable) of its being sent to you, you count as having made a valid claim on the date of your first letter or other written communication.[35]

If you initially made your claim in writing on the approved form (this includes claiming online if you are able to do so for the particular benefit), it may be treated

Part 9: Claiming benefits and getting paid
Chapter 53: Claims and decisions
2. What you must provide when you claim

as defective if it is not completed in accordance with the instructions on the form.[36] For benefits other than IS or JSA (and for contribution-based JSA if you come under the UC system – see p19), you have one month from the date you are notified of the defect to provide the necesary information, or longer if considered reasonable.[37]

For IS and JSA, if you do not have to attend an interview to complete your claim (see p1141), you have one month from the date on which you first notified the DWP of your intention to claim to provide the properly completed form and any necessary information.[38]

Note:

- If you claim online, the system may not allow you to submit it if the essential information is not entered. While this means there will be fewer defective claims, if your claim is not accepted, you should try to claim in another way as soon as you can, otherwise you will lose benefit.
- A written claim for IS or JSA may also be defective if you do not supply the information or evidence required (see below).
- A written claim for PC, child benefit or guardian's allowance may also be defective if you do not make it on the approved form. To correct the defect, you must return the properly completed form within one month of your first written contact (or longer if considered reasonable).[39]

Evidence requirement for income support and jobseeker's allowance

In order for your claim for IS or JSA to be valid, unless you are exempt (see below), you may have to:[40]

- complete your claim form according to the instructions on the form; *and*
- produce all the information and evidence required by the claim form to verify your claim.

This is known as the evidence requirement or 'onus of proof' rule. If you do not satisfy this rule, your claim is defective.

If you come under the UC system (see p19), the evidence requirement does not apply to your new claim for contribution-based JSA.[41] However, you may still be asked to provide further information and evidence before a decision is made on your claim (see p1152).

If you do not fill in the form properly or provide all the information and evidence required, the DWP must notify you that your claim is defective and contact you to put things right.[42] It might telephone or write to you or, in the case of IS, visit you to get the information or evidence. However, it might simply return your claim form. You should provide the information or evidence or complete the form and return it to your local office within one month of your initial contact (or of someone contacting the DWP on your behalf). If you do not, you might lose benefit. See p1144 for when your claim can be backdated. In any case, if the DWP does not accept that your claim is valid, you should be given a decision saying so, and you can appeal against that decision.[43] You are likely to have to apply for a revision before you can appeal (see p1271).

Exemptions from the evidence requirement

You are exempt from the evidence requirement if:[44]

- you could not complete the form or get the information or evidence required because of a physical, mental, learning or communication difficulty. You must also show that it is not reasonably practicable for you to find someone to help you complete the form or get the proof on your behalf. However, you can argue that someone else is not expected to take the initiative in offering you assistance;[45] *or*
- the information or evidence required does not exist; *or*
- you could not get the information or evidence required without serious risk of physical or mental harm. You must also show that it is not reasonably practicable to get it in another way; *or*
- you could only get the information or evidence required from a third party and it is not reasonably practicable to get it from her/him; *or*
- the decision maker thinks sufficient proof has been provided to show that you are not entitled to IS or JSA (eg, because your capital or income is too high), so it would be inappropriate to require further information or evidence.

If you are unable to complete your claim form or provide the required information or evidence for one of the reasons listed above, notify the office handling your claim as soon as possible, ideally explaining this on the claim form or by telephoning or visiting the office. The DWP says that notice must be given within one month of the date when you first contacted it. Explain your circumstances fully. You can provide supporting letters – eg, from a social worker or a solicitor. If the DWP accepts you are exempt from the evidence requirement, it might:

- help you to fill in the form; *or*
- give you longer to complete it; *or*
- collect evidence or information on your behalf; *or*
- tell you that you do not have to provide the information.

Remember that the decision maker can ask you for further information or evidence even after s/he has accepted your claim as valid (see p1152). However, if s/he eventually decides you are entitled to benefit, you should still be paid from your date of claim.

If your claim is not accepted as valid

If your claim is not accepted as valid, you should be given a decision saying so. You have the right of appeal against this.[46] You may have to apply for a revision before you can appeal (see p1271). If your claim is finally accepted as valid, the

Part 9: Claiming benefits and getting paid
Chapter 53: Claims and decisions
4. Backdating your claim

decision maker must make a decision on your entitlement to benefit.[47] See p1150 for further information about decisions.

3. If you claim the wrong benefit

If you claim a benefit by mistake when you are entitled to another benefit, your claim can sometimes be treated as a claim for the right benefit. This might be a way round the strict backdating rules, as your claim for the benefit you should have claimed is treated as having been made on the date you claimed the wrong benefit.

For which claims can interchange in this way, see below and the chapter about the benefit you should have claimed.

A claim for:[48]

- employment and support allowance (ESA) can be treated as a claim for maternity alllowance and vice versa;
- widows' benefits or bereavement benefits can be treated as a claim for retirement pension and vice versa;
- income support can be treated as a claim for carer's allowance;
- any of attendance allowance (AA), disability living allowance (DLA) or an increase in disablement pension for constant attendance (see p679) can be treated as a claim for any of the others;
- personal independence payment (PIP) can be treated as a claim for either DLA or AA and vice versa, but only if it appears that you are not entitled to the benefit that you actually claimed;[49]
- child benefit can be treated as a claim for guardian's allowance and vice versa.[50]

Note:

- The decision maker does not have to accept your claim for one benefit as a claim for another. You cannot appeal if this is refused. Your only remedy is to seek a judicial review (see p1351).[51]
- For all benefits, except universal credit (UC), income support (IS), jobseeker's allowance (JSA), ESA and PIP, there is a general power to treat any written document as a claim for benefit, which could arguably include if you filled in the wrong claim form.[52]
- A claim for UC cannot be treated as a claim for another means-tested benefit, or vice versa.

4. Backdating your claim

In general, you should claim benefit as soon as you think you qualify. There are strict time limits for making a claim.[53] If you miss the time limit, the date of your claim can sometimes be backdated for up to three months (12 months for retirement pension, six months for housing benefit (HB) if you are not yet the qualifying age for pension credit – PC). See the relevant chapter for details. The backdating period is longer for some benefits if you are reclaiming following the award of a 'qualifying benefit' (see p1149). **Note:**

- If you want your claim to be backdated you must ask for this to happen, otherwise it will not be considered.[54]
- Some benefits can be backdated without special reasons (see p1146).
- Claims for attendance allowance (AA), disability living allowance (DLA) and personal independence payment (PIP) can never be backdated.[55]
- Claims for income support (IS) and jobseeker's allowance (JSA) can only be backdated in limited circumstances (see p1146).
- Special rules apply if you are claiming backdated JSA because your entitlement stopped when you failed to attend an interview (see p1052) or sign on (see p1051).
- If you claim the wrong benefit, your claim can sometimes be treated as a claim for the benefit you should have claimed (see p1144).
- Different rules apply to HB (see p128).
- Claims for universal credit (UC) can only be backdated in limited circumstances (see p194).

If you are prevented from receiving backdated benefit because of an error of the DWP or, in child benefit and guardian's allowance cases, HM Revenue and Customs (HMRC), write and request an ex gratia payment or extra-statutory payment as compensation (see p1382). The intervention of an MP or the Ombudsman (see p1387) may help.

If you satisfy the conditions for getting benefit, it should be paid from your date of claim, even if backdating is refused. If backdating is refused, you can appeal (see Chapter 59). You may have to apply for a revision before you can appeal (see p1271). Payment should not be held up because you are challenging a decision on backdating.

Do you come under the universal credit system?

If you come under the UC system (see p19), you cannot make a new claim for IS, income-based JSA, income-related employment and support allowance (ESA), HB (unless it is for 'exempt accommodation' – see p474)[56] or tax credits, but must claim UC. Once you are entitled to UC, you cannot be entitled to any of these means-tested benefits (except HB in exempt accomodation), PC or tax credits.

If you would otherwise come under the UC system, you may be able to use the backdating rules explained in this section to make a new claim for JSA or ESA from a date before UC was introduced in your area, and so avoid having to claim UC.[57] If you live in an area where UC has been introduced but you could claim IS, income-related ESA or tax credits, you do not meet the 'personal conditions' for claiming UC (see p20) and so could claim any of

Part 9: Claiming benefits and getting paid
Chapter 53: Claims and decisions
4. Backdating your claim

these benefits instead of UC. If appropriate, request that these are backdated. **Note:** these rules are expected to change during the lifetime of this *Handbook*. See CPAG's online service and *Welfare Rights Bulletin* for updates.

Benefits that can be backdated without special reasons

Claims for some benefits can be backdated for up to three months. Retirement pension and bereavement payment (but see p519 if you are over pension age) can be backdated for up to 12 months without needing to have special reasons.[58] If you want benefit for a period before the date you make your claim, you must show that you would have qualified for the benefit had you claimed at the time.

> *Benefits that can be backdated without special reasons*
> Bereavement benefits (see p532), carer's allowance (CA – see p545), child benefit (see p566), contributory and income-related ESA (see p629), guardian's allowance (see p641), HB if you are at least the qualifying age for PC (see p128), industrial injuries benefits (see p685), maternity allowance (see p722), PC (see p87) and retirement pension (see p758).
> Also included are incapacity benefit (IB), although new claims are now only possible in very limited circumstances (see Chapter 31), and increases to IB and severe disablement allowance for an adult (see pp680–83 of the 2013/14 edition of this *Handbook* for details).

There are exceptions to the rules.
- The time limit for claiming a bereavement payment can be extended in some cases – eg, when you did not know your partner had died (see p533).
- If you are claiming backdated child benefit or guardian's allowance after being awarded refugee status, see p1512.
- If you miss the time limit for claiming disablement benefit for occupational deafness or occupational asthma (see p672) or, if you have to make a claim to qualify, bereavement payment (see p519), you may lose your right to benefit altogether.

Backdating income support and jobseeker's allowance

Your claim for IS or JSA can be backdated for up to one or three months in particular circumstances, if these circumstances mean that it was not reasonable for you to claim sooner, or for longer periods after an award of a qualifying benefit.

Note: you may be paid less arrears if you claim because of a new interpretation of the law (see p1296).

If a person has been formally appointed by a court or the DWP to act on your behalf, your appointee (see p1137), not you, must show that it was not reasonable to expect her/him to claim sooner than s/he did.[59]

If someone is informally acting on your behalf, you must show that s/he was acting for you. You must also show that it was reasonable for you to delegate responsibility for your claim and that you took care to ensure the person helping you claimed properly.[60]

If you are claiming late, it is important to explain why.

Why are you claiming late?

1. If you can, provide evidence or information that backs up why you are making a late claim – eg, a copy of the letter from your adviser or information from your employer which misled you (see p1148).

2. If you have been misled, misinformed or given insufficient advice by an officer of the DWP, explain how and when this happened and, where possible, give the name and a description of the officer concerned.

3. Where relevant, explain why there was no one else who could have helped you make your claim.

One month's backdating

The decision maker must backdate your claim for up to one month if one or more of the following applies (or has applied), and because of this you could not reasonably have been expected to make your claim any earlier.[61]

- The office where you are supposed to claim was closed (eg, because of a strike) and there were no other arrangements for claims to be made.
- You could not get to the DWP office because there were difficulties with the type of transport you normally use and there was no reasonable alternative.
- There were adverse postal conditions – eg, bad weather, a postal strike, or the Post Office failed to act under its agreement to deliver under-stamped mail to the DWP.[62]
- You (or your partner) stopped getting another benefit, but you (or your partner) were not informed before your entitlement ceased, so you could not claim IS or JSA in time. **Note:** if you come under the UC system (see p19), this only applies if you stopped getting contributory ESA but were not informed before your entitlement ceased.
- For joint-claim JSA, your partner failed to attend her/his initial interview at Jobcentre Plus.
- You claimed IS or JSA in your own right within one month of separating from your partner.
- A close relative of yours died in the month before your claim. '**Close relative**' means your partner, parent, son, daughter, brother or sister.
- You were unable to notify the DWP of your intention to make a claim because the telephone lines to the office were busy or not working.
- If you come under the UC system, you could not make an online claim for contribution-based JSA because the DWP's computer system was not working.

Part 9: Claiming benefits and getting paid
Chapter 53: Claims and decisions
4. Backdating your claim

Three months' backdating

Your claim can be backdated for up to three months if you can show it was not reasonable to expect you to claim earlier than you did for one of the following reasons.[63] If more than one reason applies to you, the combined effect of all of them must be considered in deciding whether it was reasonable to expect you to claim earlier.[64]

- You were given information by an officer of the DWP or HMRC and, as a result, thought your claim would not succeed. **Note:** once you come under the UC system (see p19), the information you are given must be from a DWP officer to allow your JSA claim to be backdated for this reason. The information that is relevant includes if:
  - you were given incorrect information or the wrong claim form and this led you to claim the wrong benefit;
  - someone with authority to act on your behalf was given incorrect information;[65]
  - you were told your claim would not be accepted;[66]
  - you were told you did not have to fill in a claim form;[67]
  - the refusal of, or failure to respond to,[68] an earlier claim for the same[69] or a different[70] benefit led you to believe that you were not entitled;
  - the information was incomplete and had not included advice on claiming when it should have done.[71]

  'Officer' includes anyone carrying out public functions at the benefit office – eg, a security guard.[72] It does not matter if the information you received was correct or reasonable on the basis of any information that you gave to the officer about your circumstances, as long as the officer's advice caused you to think that a claim would fail.[73]
- You were given advice in writing by a Citizens Advice Bureau or other advice worker, a solicitor or other professional adviser (eg, an accountant), a doctor or a local authority and, as a result, thought your claim would not succeed. 'Advice in writing' includes leaflets, emails[74] or information on a website, provided it is directed at claimants in your position. Your claim should be backdated if you are given written confirmation of advice that was originally given to you orally,[75] provided this is done before the decision maker decides whether you are entitled to backdating.[76] The written advice must also be given to you; it is not enough for your adviser to record a note of oral advice unless you are provided with a copy.[77]
- You or your partner were given written information about your income or capital by your employer or former employer, or a bank or building society, and, as a result, you thought your claim would not succeed.
- You could not get to the DWP office because of bad weather.

In addition, your claim can be backdated for up to three months if any of the following conditions apply and it was not 'reasonably practicable' for you to seek help from anyone else to make your claim.[78] If you are mentally ill, this does not necessarily mean you cannot be expected to seek assistance.[79] However, another person is not expected to take the initiative in offering assistance.[80] The conditions are:

- you have learning, language or literacy difficulties; *or*
- you are deaf or blind *or* were sick or disabled (but not if you are claiming JSA); *or*
- you were caring for someone who is sick or disabled; *or*
- you were dealing with a domestic emergency that affected you.

Backdating after an award of a qualifying benefit

If your claim for benefit is refused, it can be backdated if you reclaim it after an award of a 'qualifying benefit'.

Note:

- More generous rules apply for CA (see p545).
- Different rules apply for Sure Start maternity grants and funeral expenses payments (see p770 and p772).
- This rule does not apply to backdating claims for ESA, HB or, if you come under the UC system (see p19), JSA.

Generally, a '**qualifying benefit**' is any benefit (except PIP) awarded to you or someone else, which gives you entitlement to another benefit, or makes another benefit payable at a higher rate. PIP is only a qualifying benefit for entitlement to CA.[81]

You can get backdating if:[82]

- your original claim (eg, for PC) is refused while you (or your dependent child or your partner) are waiting to hear about a qualifying benefit – eg, AA for your partner; *and*
- the qualifying benefit was claimed no later than 10 days after your original claim; *and*
- the qualifying benefit is then awarded; *and*
- you make a further claim (eg, for PC) within three months of the decision awarding the qualifying benefit and you are now entitled because of the award of the qualifying benefit.

In these circumstances, benefit is backdated to the date of your original claim or the date on which the qualifying benefit was first payable, whichever is later.

An additional rule applies to IS and income-based JSA only. If you have been awarded either of these benefits but that award is terminated, a further claim for IS/income-based JSA can be backdated either to the date of the termination, or the date when a qualifying benefit was first awarded (whichever date is the later) if:[83]

Part 9: Claiming benefits and getting paid
Chapter 53: Claims and decisions
5. Decisions

- you or a member of your family (or a person being cared for) claim a qualifying benefit; *and*
- you make a further claim for IS/income-based JSA within three months of the qualifying benefit being awarded.

Note:
- The qualifying benefit rule also applies if the claim for the qualifying benefit was originally refused, but you were awarded it later on revision, supersession or appeal.[84]
- If you lost entitlement to benefit (eg, CA), or payment of it stopped because the award of a qualifying benefit (eg, DLA) was terminated or reduced, your benefit is backdated if you reclaim within three months of the reinstatement of the qualifying benefit. This also applies if you lost entitlement to a benefit (eg, you lost your IS because your income increased) but a claim for a qualifying benefit had not yet been decided and, had it been awarded, you would have been entitled again. In this case, your benefit is backdated if you claim within three months of the date the qualifying benefit is awarded.[85]
- If you lost entitlement to benefit or payment of it was stopped because AA or DLA stopped being paid because the person entitled to it was in hospital, a care home or other special accommodation, your benefit is backdated if you reclaim it within three months of the AA or DLA starting to be paid again.[86] **Note:** this rule does not apply when PIP stops in these circumstances.

If you are already entitled to some IS, JSA, ESA, PC, HB or UC, you might be entitled to it at a higher rate once you, a family member or a non-dependant becomes entitled to another benefit. See p1294 for getting extra backdating of the increase in this situation.

5. **Decisions**

Decisions about entitlement to benefits are made by officers of the DWP, the local authority or HM Revenue and Customs (HMRC) – called 'decision makers' in this *Handbook* (see below). A decision must be made once you have made a valid claim for benefit (see p1151). Decisions may also be made once you are awarded benefit – eg, if there was a mistake about the facts or your circumstances change (see p1153).
Note:
- If it is taking too long for a decision to be made, see p1155.
- If you need information about a decision, you can ask for an explanation or for written reasons for the decision (see p1156).
- If there is an accidental error in a decision, it can be corrected (see p1155).

- If you disagree with a decision, you may be able to apply for a revision or a supersession of the decision, or appeal against it (see Chapters 58 and 59). You may have to apply for a revision before you can appeal (see p1271).

Decision makers

In this *Handbook*, those who make decisions about benefits and the social fund are referred to as **'decision makers'**. In practice, decisions about:
- benefits and the social fund, other than child benefit, guardian's allowance and housing benefit (HB), are made by officers of the DWP;
- child benefit and guardian's allowance are made by officers of HMRC;
- HB are made by officers of the local authority.

Note: the DWP refers to personal independence payment (PIP) decision makers as 'case managers', although, in practice, their role is the same.

Some issues (eg, whether you have or can be treated as having limited capability for work or are terminally ill for benefit purposes) are decided by the DWP, even if the main benefit decision is made by another authority – eg, the local authority.[87]

You may have to meet someone at your local Jobcentre Plus office to discuss your jobseeking conditions (see Chapter 48) or claimant responsibilities (see Chapters 49 and 50). In practice, the person you meet is extremely unlikely to be a decision maker, although s/he may make recommendations to the decision maker – eg, about whether your benefit should be sanctioned.

Making a decision on a claim

Once you have made a valid claim for benefit (see p1140), your claim is referred to a decision maker to decide whether you are entitled. A decision maker must normally make a decision on the claim,[88] but may sometimes withhold making a decision if there is a 'test case' pending (see p1297).

The decision maker may request further information, in addition to what you have already provided, before making a decision (see p1152). If you do not provide this information, the decision maker might draw adverse conclusions and make a decision based on these.
- If your claim involves medical issues, in most cases the decision maker can refer you to a 'healthcare professional' (see p1152) for a medical examination and a report. If you fail to have an examination without 'good cause' when asked to, the decision maker must decide your claim against you.[89] **Note:** if your claim concerns limited capability for work, under separate rules you can be required to supply information or evidence or attend a medical (see Chapter 47).
- If you are claiming PIP, you can be referred to a 'health professional' (see p1152).[90] For details of what you can be asked to do, see p738.

Part 9: Claiming benefits and getting paid
Chapter 53: Claims and decisions
5. Decisions

- The decision maker can refer national insurance contribution issues to HMRC (see p1154).
- If your disablement benefit claim involves whether you may have a prescribed disease or have a disablement or the extent of any injury you have from an industrial accident, the decision maker can refer the issue to a healthcare professional (see below) for a report.[91]
- If there is a questions about the facts of your claim and special expertise is needed, the decision maker can get assistance from experts.[92]

Healthcare professionals and health professionals

A **'healthcare professional'** is a registered medical practitioner (eg, a doctor), registered nurse, or registered occupational therapist or physiotherapist, or for disability living allowance mobility component for a severe visual impairment only, a registered optometrist or orthoptist.[93]

The rules for who counts as a **'health professional'** for PIP are not set out in regulations. Guidance states that paramedics are included, along with doctors, registered nurses, occupational therapists and physiotherapists.[94]

If you think a decision is wrong, you may be able to apply for a revision or supersession, or appeal against it (see Chapters 58 and 59). You may have to apply for a revision before you can appeal (see p1271). If you claimed the wrong benefit based on incorrect advice from an employee of the DWP, local authority or HMRC, see p1382 for information about seeking compensation.

Further information to support your claim

Even if your claim has been accepted as valid, you may still be required to provide additional documentation and evidence.[95] You may be able to claim travelling expenses for this.[96] You must provide the information or evidence within one month of the request (within seven days of the request for jobseeker's allowance (JSA) only). A decision maker can allow you longer than this if reasonable. If you do not provide the information, the decision maker is likely to decide your claim in the way most adverse to you.

It is best to send evidence and documents to the office handling the claim. For certain benefits, a designated local authority or English county council office or other 'alternative office' (see p1136) may also be able to accept evidence and documents. If a local authority has used information on your claim for HB and has passed it to the DWP because it is relevant to your claim for another benefit, in most cases the DWP must use that information without checking it further.[97]

If you are asked to provide evidence which you do not have, ask what other evidence would be acceptable. Ask the DWP, the local authority or HMRC to explain what is required and why, and complain if you think any requests for information are unreasonable.

1. Writing to the DWP, the local authority or HMRC is the best way to have your case dealt with. It ensures there is a record of what you said and enables you to cover all the points you want to make.

2. Always keep a copy of the letters, forms and other documents you send, as well as copies of those sent to you. This may help you or your adviser to challenge decisions.

3. It is often necessary to telephone the DWP, the local authority or HMRC. If you do this, make a note of the date and what is said. If the information is important, follow up the phone call with a letter confirming what was said.

4. If you need to visit an office (eg, because your case cannot be dealt with by telephone) and you cannot get there (eg, because of your age, health or a disability), an officer may be able to make a home visit. If you are refused a visit and are not satisfied with the reason you are given, ask to speak to a supervisor or the customer services manager.

Making a decision after benefit is awarded

Decisions may be made after you are awarded benefit (eg, if there was a mistake about the facts or your circumstances change) by a revision (see pp1270–81) or a supersession (see pp1281–94). You can be required to supply information or evidence if the decision maker needs this to make her/his decision, and payment of your benefit could be suspended or your award terminated if you fail to do so (see p1175). The same points apply as when providing further information for a decision to be made on your claim (see p1152).

If you think a decision made after your benefit is awarded is wrong, you may be able to apply for a revision or supersession, or appeal against it (see Chapters 58 and 59). You may have to apply for a revision before you can appeal (see p1271).

Decisions made with limited information

The decision maker can make a decision in certain circumstances, even if s/he is waiting for you to provide more evidence or information.

A decision is always made on the basis that the evidence or information needed is adverse to you if:[98]

- for income support (IS) and JSA only, it is needed to decide:
  - whether you should be paid benefit (or less benefit) because you (or a member of your family) are involved in a trade dispute (see p971). **Note:** this does not apply for JSA if you come under the universal credit (UC) system (see p19); *or*
  - whether you are in relevant education (see p903);

Part 9: Claiming benefits and getting paid
Chapter 53: Claims and decisions
5. Decisions

- for IS, employment and support allowance (ESA), social fund payments and pension credit (PC) only, it is needed to decide whether you are entitled to a severe disability premium (additional amount for PC).

For retirement pension, if you deferred claiming your pension, but when you did claim you had not yet elected whether to take a lump sum or an increased pension, the decision maker can choose whether or not to decide your claim immediately.[99] If s/he does make a decision on your claim, s/he must revise it when you make the election (see p1279).

For PIP, if you are in a care home and evidence or information is required to decide whether the cost of your accommodation is borne out of local or public funds, the DWP makes a decision on the evidence or information it has, provided it has made 'reasonable enquiries'.[100]

If further evidence or information is needed to decide what housing costs you can be paid in your IS, ESA or PC (see Chapter 20), a decision is made on the basis of the evidence or information the decision maker already has.[101] A similar rule for UC housing costs (see Chapter 22) gives the decision maker the discretion to make a decision if further evidence or information is needed.[102]

Special procedure

Certain questions are dealt with by a special procedure. These are to do with contributions and a person's employment – eg:[103]
- whether you were an 'employed earner' for the purposes of paying contributions or entitlement to industrial injuries disablement benefit; *or*
- whether you were liable to pay a particular class of contributions or have paid contributions for a particular period; *or*
- the amount of contributions you were liable to pay.

The decision maker refers these matters to HMRC for a decision, which is then binding on the decision maker.[104] The decision maker can continue to deal with other issues relating to your claim, but can defer making a decision on it. The decision maker should also refer matters to HMRC if s/he decides your claim on the basis of facts which do not appear to be under dispute – eg, if it appears you do not satisfy the contribution conditions for the benefit, but you apply for a revision or supersession of the decision, or appeal against it because, for example, you think your contribution record is wrong.

When HMRC makes a decision, you can appeal against it.[105] The appeals process is similar to appealing against an HMRC decision on your entitlement to statutory payments (see Chapter 60).

The First-tier Tribunal can also require the DWP to refer matters that are HMRC's responsibility, but which are relevant to a benefit appeal, to HMRC for a decision.[106] The DWP may revise the decision on your claim as a result. If not, the matter goes back to the First-tier Tribunal.

Note: the decision maker can make arrangements for some issues concerning whether you can be credited with earnings or contributions to be decided by HMRC.[107] You can appeal to the First-tier Tribunal against these decisions in the same way as against DWP decisions (see Chapter 59).

Delays

HMRC has a 22-day target for dealing with child benefit (and tax credits) claims, published in half-yearly performance briefings.[108] The DWP no longer publishes official targets, although a suggestion of how long claims should take to be processed can be found in its business plan – eg, 95 per cent of attendance allowance claims within 48 days and 90 per cent of JSA claims within 16 days).[109] There are no actual rules on target times, although all claims should be dealt with as soon as is reasonably practicable. Local authorities must make a decision on your claim for HB within 14 days or, if that is not reasonably practicable, as soon as possible after that.[110]

Is there a delay?

1. If you have been waiting more than the relevant time for a decision, check that your claim has been received. If it has not, if possible let the office have a copy or fill out a new form and refer to the claim form you sent earlier.

2. If the DWP, the local authority or HMRC deny receiving your claim, you may have to claim again and ask for it to be backdated if possible.

3. If your claim has been received but not dealt with, ask why. If you are not satisfied with the explanation for the delay, complain (see Chapter 61). In extreme cases, it might be possible to apply for judicial review (see p1351).

4. If a decision cannot be made on your claim straight away, ask the office to make a short-term advance of benefit if these are payable for the benefit you have claimed (see p1167), or an interim payment of child benefit or guardian's allowance (see p1169). If the benefit is HB and you are a private or housing association tenant, in most cases you *must* be given a 'payment on account' (see p139).

5. If your claim is for a non-means-tested benefit, you may be able to claim a means-tested benefit while a decision is being made. The amount paid to you may be deducted from arrears of other benefits that you subsequently receive, or you may be asked to repay the amount.[111]

6. You may be able to get help from your local authority for any short-term needs in a crisis (see p829).

Correcting a decision

Unless the benefit is child benefit or guardian's allowance, if the decision maker makes an accidental error in her/his decision (eg, a typing error or mathematical miscalculation), this can be corrected.[112] You must be sent or given written notice

Part 9: Claiming benefits and getting paid
Chapter 53: Claims and decisions
5. Decisions

of the correction as soon as practicable. To see how the time limit for applying for an 'any grounds' revision of the decision can be extended when a decision has been corrected, see p1273.

Information about decisions

You must be given written notice of a decision against which you can appeal (see p1307 for which decisions). This is sometimes called a 'decision notice'. You must be informed of:[113]

• your right to appeal against the decision; *and*
• your right to a written statement of reasons for the decision, if this is not already included (see below).

Note: you are also told whether you must apply for a revision before you can appeal against the decision (see p1271).

You may want to know more about a decision or want a breakdown of how your benefit has been calculated. You can ask for an explanation to find out more about a decision. **Note:** you do not have to ask for an explanation or a written statement of reasons in order to apply for a revision or a supersession, or to appeal.

Explanations

You can ask for an explanation of any decision maker's decision. Contact the office that made the decision.

At the end of the explanation, you should be asked whether you are happy with the decision. If you are not happy, say so. The decision maker should then advise you about your right to apply for a revision (see p1270) or to appeal (see Chapter 59). S/he may refer to this as a dispute or a request for a reconsideration.

Explanations are usually given orally. You may have a right to request a written statement of reasons for a decision if it is one against which you can appeal (see p1156).

The time limit for applying for a revision or appealing is very strict. It runs from the date you are sent or given the decision with which you disagree (*not* the date of the explanation) and can only be extended in limited circumstances (see p1273 and p1310). Therefore, ensure you apply for a revision or appeal within the time limit, even if an explanation for the decision has not yet been given to you. **Note:** you may have to apply for a revision before you can appeal (see p1271).

Written reasons

You may want to see the reasons for a decision in writing. You have a right to a written statement of reasons for a decision against which you can appeal, if this has not already been provided with the decision. You must ask for the written statement of reasons within one month of the date of the decision maker's notification of the decision. The decision maker must then provide the statement within 14 days, or as soon as practicable afterwards.[114]

Note: your time limit for applying for a revision or appealing is extended if you ask for a written statement of reasons, but only if these have not already been provided. See p1273 and p1310 for further information.

Month

'**Month**' means a complete calendar month running from the day after the day you have been sent or given a decision.[115] For example, a decision sent on 24 July has a time limit that expires at the end of 24 August.

The DWP says that a written statement of reasons is provided automatically with decisions about PIP, bereavement benefits, ESA, maternity allowance, retirement pension, UC, and social fund funeral payments, cold weather payments and Sure Start maternity grants. Even for other benefits that are not listed here, if you are in any doubt about whether there is a statement of reasons for the decision, you should apply for a revision or appeal within the time limit.

Although you may believe that a written statement of reasons has not been included with your decision or that what has been provided is inadequate, the DWP, the local authority or HMRC could disagree. In these cases, the decision maker is likely to argue that your time limit for applying for a revision or appealing cannot be extended.

If you are in any doubt, you should assume that the time limit for applying for a revision or appealing has *not* been extended. If you miss the time limit in this situation, argue that the rules that allow a late application for a revision or a late appeal apply (see p1274 and p1353). You may also be able to apply for an 'any time' revision (see p1275). **Note:** you may have to apply for a revision before you can appeal (see p1271).

If you disagree with a decision maker's decision

If you think a decision maker's decision is wrong, you may be able to:
- apply for a revision of the decision (see p1270); *or*
- apply for a supersession of the decision (see p1281).

In some cases, you also have an immediate right to appeal to the First-tier Tribunal (see Chapter 59). However, you may have apply for a revision first (see p1271).

The time limits for applying for what is known as an 'any grounds' revision or appealing are strict – normally only one month from the date on the decision letter (see p1273 and p1310).

Part 9: Claiming benefits and getting paid
Chapter 53: Claims and decisions
Notes

Notes

1. Making a claim
1 Reg 8 UC,PIP,JSA&ESA(C&P) Regs
2 Regs 4(6A)-(6CC), 4D and 4H SS(C&P) Regs
3 Regs 4(6B), 4D(3A) and (4) and 4H(3) SS(C&P) Regs
4 **CB/GA** Reg 28 CB&GA(Admin) Regs
UC/PIP/JSA&ESA under UC Reg 57 UC,PIP,JSA&ESA(C&P) Regs
Other benefits Reg 33 SS(C&P) Regs
5 R(SB) 5/90
6 CIS/642/1994
7 CIS/379/1992
8 **HB** Reg 82(5) HB Regs; reg 63(5) HB(SPC) Regs
UC/PIP/JSA&ESA under UC Reg 57(6) UC,PIP,JSA&ESA(C&P) Regs
Other benefits Reg 33(1A) SS(C&P) Regs
9 **HB** Reg 87(1) and (3) HB Regs; reg 68(1) and (3) HB(SPC) Regs
UC/PIP/JSA&ESA under UC Reg 30 UC,PIP,JSA&ESA(C&P) Regs
Other benefits Reg 5(1) SS(C&P) Regs
10 **HB** Reg 83A and Sch 11 HB Regs; reg 64A and Sch 10 HB(SPC) Regs
UC/PIP/JSA&ESA under UC Regs 2, 3 and Sch 2 UC,PIP,JSA&ESA(C&P) Regs
Other benefits Reg 4ZC and Sch 9ZC SS(C&P) Regs
11 Reg 8 CB&GA(Admin) Regs
12 Reg 2 and Sch 2 CB&GA(Admin) Regs
13 **HB** Reg 87(4)-(6) HB Regs; reg 68(4)-(6) HB(SPC) Regs
CB/GA Reg 9 CB&GA(Admin) Regs
UC/PIP/JSA&ESA under UC Reg 31 UC,PIP,JSA&ESA(C&P) Regs
Other benefits Reg 5(2) SS(C&P) Regs
14 CJSA/3979/1999; CJSA/1332/2001; CDLA/1589/2005; HB G10/2008

2. What you must provide when you claim
15 s1(1A) and (1B) SSAA 1992
16 CH/4085/2007
17 s1(1A) SSAA 1992
18 CH/1231/2004; CH/4085/2007
19 Reg 1A SS(DLA) Regs
20 Reg 4(a) HB Regs; reg 4(a) HB(SPC) Regs
21 SSWP v Wilson [2006] EWCA Civ 882, reported as R(H) 7/06
22 **IS** Reg 2A IS Regs
JSA Reg 2A JSA Regs
ESA Reg 2A ESA Regs
PC Reg 1A SPC Regs
HB Reg 4(c) HB Regs; reg 4C HB(SPC) Regs
23 HB A4/2009
24 **HB** Reg 4(b) HB Regs; reg 4(b) HB(SPC) Regs
UC Reg 5 UC,PIP,JSA&ESA(C&P) Regs
25 **IS** Reg 2A(a) IS Regs, which has continued effect in these cases due to the transitional protection in reg 1(3) SS(WTCCTC)(CA) Regs
JSA Reg 2A(a) JSA Regs, which has continued effect in these cases due to the transitional protection in reg 1(7) SS(WTCCTC)(CA) Regs
26 Novitskaya v London Borough of Brent and Another [2009] EWCA Civ 1260
27 **UC/PIP/JSA&ESA under UC** Regs 19 and 20 UC,PIP,JSA&ESA(C&P) Regs
Other benefits Regs 4(6)(a) and 6(4ZB), (4ZC), (4A)(a) and (4AA) SS(C&P) Regs
28 **UC/PIP/JSA&ESA under UC** Reg 20(3) UC,PIP,JSA&ESA(C&P) Regs
Other benefits Reg 6(4AB) SS(C&P) Regs
29 **UC/PIP/JSA&ESA under UC** Regs 8(4) and (5), 11(4) and (5), 13 and 23 UC,PIP,JSA&ESA(C&P) Regs
Other benefits Regs 4(11)-(13), 4D(6A)-(6E) and 4G SS(C&P) Regs
30 Regs 4D(6B) and 4G(2) SS(C&P) Regs; reg 13(2) UC,PIP,JSA&ESA(C&P) Regs
31 **UC/PIP/JSA&ESA under UC** Regs 8(5) and (6), 11(5) and (6), 13(4) and (5) and 23(3) and (4) UC,PIP,JSA&ESA(C&P) Regs
Other benefits Regs 4(7) and (13), 4D(6D) and (6E) and 4G(4) and (5) SS(C&P) Regs
32 Regs 4(7A) and (7B) and 6(1A) and (4A)(b) SS(C&P) Regs

33 **UC/PIP/JSA&ESA under UC** Regs
11(1)(a), 15(1) and 21(1)
UC,PIP,JSA&ESA(C&P) Regs
Other benefits Regs
4(1A) and 4H(2) SS(C&P)Regs
34 **CB/GA** Reg 5 CB&GA(Admin) Regs
Other benefits Regs 4(1) and 4D(2)
SS(C&P) Regs
35 **CB/GA** Reg 10 CB&GA(Admin) Regs
Other benefits Reg 4(7ZA) SS(C&P)
Regs
36 **CB/GA** Reg 10 CB&GA(Admin) Regs
UC/PIP/JSA&ESA under UC Regs
8(3), 11(3), 15(2) and 21(3) UC, PIP,
JSA&ESA(C&P) Regs
Other benefits Regs 4(1A), (8)
and (9), 4D(2) and 4H(2) SS(C&P) Regs
37 **CB/GA** Reg 10 CB&GA(Admin) Regs
UC/PIP/JSA&ESA under UC Regs 8(5)
and (6), 11(5) and (6), 15(3) and (4)
and 21(4) and (5)
UC,PIP,JSA&ESA(C&P) Regs
Other benefits Regs 4(7), 4D(10) and
(11), and 4H(6) and (7) SS(C&P) Regs
38 Regs 4(7A) and (7B) and 6(1A) and
(4A)(b) SS(C&P) Regs
39 Reg 4D(2) and (10) SS(C&P) Regs; reg
10 CB&GA(Admin) Regs
40 Reg 4(1A) SS(C&P) Regs
41 Regs 19-24 UC,PIP,JSA&ESA(C&P) Regs;
DWP, *Explanatory Memorandum to the
Social Security Advisory Committee*, 13
June 2012, p21
42 Reg 4(7A) and (7B) SS(C&P) Regs
43 Sch 2 SS&CS(DA) Regs does not include
such decisions in the list of decisions
against which no appeal lies.
44 Reg 4(1B) SS(C&P) Regs
45 CIS/2057/1998
46 Sch 2 SS&CS(DA) Regs, Sch 3
UC,PIP,JSA&ESA(DA) Regs and Sch 2
CB&GA(DA) Regs do not include such
decisions in the list of decisions against
which no appeal lies.
47 s8 SSA 1998

3. **If you claim the wrong benefit**
48 Reg 9 and Sch 1 SS(C&P) Regs; reg 25
UC,PIP,JSA&ESA(C&P) Regs
49 Reg 25(3) and (4)
UC,PIP,JSA&ESA(C&P) Regs
50 Reg 11 CB&GA(Admin) Regs
51 R(A) 3/81
52 **PC** Reg 4D(2) SS(C&P) Regs
CB/GA Reg 5(1)(b) CB&GA(Admin)
Regs
Other benefits Reg 4(1) SS(C&P) Regs

4. **Backdating your claim**
53 **HB** Reg 83(12) and (12A) HB Regs; reg
64(1) and (1A) HB(SPC) Regs
CB/GA Reg 6 CB&GA(Admin) Regs
UC/PIP/JSA&ESA under UC Regs 26-
29 UC,PIP,JSA&ESA(C&P) Regs
Other benefits Reg 19 and Sch 4
SS(C&P) Regs
54 R(SB) 9/84
55 ss65(4) and (6) and 76 SSCBA 1992; reg
27 UC,PIP,JSA&ESA(C&P) Regs
56 Reg 15 UC(TP) Regs
57 Art 5(1) WRA(No.9)O; Art 4(5)
WRA(No.11)O; Art 4(5) WRA(No.13)O;
Art 4(5)WRA(No.14)O; Art 4(5)
WRA(No.16)O
58 **CB/GA** Reg 6 CB&GA(Admin) Regs
UC/PIP/JSA&ESA under UC Reg 28
UC,PIP,JSA&ESA(C&P) Regs
Other benefits Reg 19(2) and (3) and
Sch 4 SS(C&P) Regs
59 R(SB) 17/83; R(IS) 5/91; CIS/812/1992
60 R(P) 2/85
61 **UC/PIP/JSA&ESA under UC** Reg
29(4) and (5) UC,PIP,JSA&ESA(C&P)
Regs
Other benefits Reg 19(6) and (7)
SS(C&P) Regs
62 CIS/4901/2002
63 **UC/PIP/JSA&ESA under UC** Reg
29(2) and (3) UC,PIP,JSA&ESA(C&P)
Regs
Other benefits Reg 19(4) and (5)
SS(C&P) Regs
64 CIS/2484/1999
65 CJSA/4573/1999
66 CJSA/4066/1998
67 CIS/610/1998
68 CJSA/3084/2004
69 CIS/4354/1999
70 CIS/4490/1998
71 CJSA/0580/2003
72 CIS/610/1998
73 CIS/3994/1998; CSIS 815/2004
74 CIS/5430/1999
75 CJSA/1136/1998
76 CIS/5430/1999
77 CIS/5430/1999
78 **UC/PIP/JSA&ESA under UC** Reg
29(3) UC,PIP,JSA&ESA(C&P) Regs
Other benefits Reg 19(5) SS(C&P)
Regs; C12/98 (IS)
79 C12/98 (IS)
80 CIS/2057/1998
81 Reg 6(22) SS(C&P) Regs (PIP does not
count for the general rule, as it is not
defined as a 'relevant benefit' for the
purpose of this regulation.)

Part 9: Claiming benefits and getting paid
Chapter 53: Claims and decisions
Notes

82 Reg 6(16)-(26) SS(C&P) Regs
83 Reg 6(30) SS(C&P) Regs
84 Reg 6(26) and (33) SS(C&P) Regs
85 Reg 6(19) SS(C&P) Regs
86 Reg 6(19)-(21A) SS(C&P) Regs

5. Decisions

87 **UC/PIP/JSA&ESA under UC** Reg 40
UC,PIP,JSA&ESA(DA) Regs
Other benefits Reg 11 SS&CS(DA)
Regs
88 R(SB) 29/83; CIS/807/1992; R(H) 3/05
89 s19 SSA 1998
90 s80 WRA 2012; regs 8-10 SS(PIP) Regs
91 Reg 12 SS&CS(DA) Regs
92 **HB** Sch 7 para 5 CSPSSA 2000
Other benefits s11(2) SSA 1998
93 s39(1) SSA 1998; reg 3 Social Security
(Disability Living Allowance)
(Amendment) Regulations 2010,
No.1651
94 DWP, *PIP Assessment Guide*, 4 July 2013,
p112
95 **JSA** Reg 24 JSA Regs; reg 31 JSA Regs
2013
HB Reg 86 HB Regs; reg 67 HB(SPC)
Regs
CB/GA Reg 7 CB&GA(Admin) Regs
UC/PIP&ESA under UC Reg 37
UC,PIP,JSA&ESA(C&P) Regs
Other benefits Reg 7 SS(C&P) Regs
96 ss180 and 180A SSAA 1992
97 The Social Security (Claims and
Information) Regulations 2007,
No.2911
98 **UC/PIP&ESA under UC** Reg 39
UC,PIP,JSA&ESA(DA) Regs
Other benefits Regs 13(2) and
(3) and 15 SS&CS(DA) Regs
99 Reg 13A SS&CS(DA) Regs
100 Reg 39(5) UC,PIP,JSA&ESA(DA) Regs
101 Reg 13(1) SS&CS(DA) Regs
102 Reg 39(4) UC,PIP,JSA&ESA(DA) Regs
103 s8 SSC(TF)A 1999
104 **UC/PIP&ESA under UC** Reg 42
UC,PIP,JSA&ESA(DA) Regs
Other benefits s10A SSA 1998; reg
11A SS&CS(DA) Regs
105 s11 SSC(TF)A 1999
106 **UC/PIP&ESA under UC** Reg 43
UC,PIP,JSA&ESA(DA) Regs
Other benefits s24A SSA 1998; reg
38A SS&CS(DA) Regs
107 s17 SSC(TF)A 1999; Sch 3 para 17 SSA
1998; the National Insurance
Contribution Credits (Transfer of
Functions) Order 2009, No.1377

108 Via www.gov.uk/government/
collections/briefings
109 Published as a result of a Freedom of
Information request. Can be located by
an internet search for 'DWP
Operations Business Plan 2013/14'.
110 Reg 89 HB Regs; reg 70 HB(SPC) Regs
111 s74 SSAA 1992; regs 7-10 SS(PAOR)
Regs
112 **HB** Reg 10A HB&CTB(DA) Regs
UC/PIP/JSA&ESA under UC Reg 38
UC,PIP,JSA&ESA(DA) Regs
Other benefits Reg 9A SS&CS(DA)
Regs
113 **HB** Reg 10(1) HB&CTB(DA) Regs
CB/GA Reg 26(1) CB&GA(DA) Regs
UC/PIP/JSA&ESA under UC Reg 51
UC,PIP,JSA&ESA(DA) Regs
Other benefits Reg 28(1) SS&CS(DA)
Regs
114 **HB** Regs 2 and 10(1)(b) and (2)
HB&CTB(DA) Regs
CB/GA Regs 3 and 26(1)(b) and (2)
CB&GA(DA) Regs
UC/PIP/JSA&ESA under UC Regs 3
and 51 UC,PIP,JSA&ESA(DA) Regs
Other benefits Regs 2 and 28(1)(b)
and (2) SS&CS(DA) Regs
115 R(IB) 4/02

Chapter 54

Getting paid

This chapter covers:
1. Who is paid (p1162)
2. How and when you are paid (p1162)
3. Overlapping benefits (p1165)
4. Short-term advances (p1167)
5. The benefit cap (p1169)
6. Change of circumstances after you claim (p1174)
7. When payments can be suspended (p1175)
8. When your benefit entitlement is terminated (p1177)
9. Deductions and payments to third parties (p1178)
10. Recovery of benefits from compensation payments (p1191)

This chapter covers the general rules for benefits. See the chapter about the benefit you are claiming for specific rules about that benefit. This chapter does *not* cover the rules for statutory sick pay (see Chapter 39) and statutory maternity, paternity and adoption pay (see Chapter 38), payments from the social fund (see Chapter 37), the health benefits in Chapter 30, the other types of financial help in Chapter 40, or discretionary housing payments (see p467).

References in this chapter to HM Revenue and Customs (HMRC) only apply to child benefit and guardian's allowance. HMRC also administers tax credits. For information about payment of tax credits, see Chapter 65 .

Key facts
- How, when and how often your benefit is paid depends on the benefit you have claimed. The DWP, local authority or HM Revenue and Customs (HMRC) decides how benefit is paid to you. There is no right of appeal.
- The DWP and HMRC usually pay your benefit by direct credit transfer into a bank or similar account.
- If your claim or payment of your benefit is delayed, you may be able to get a short-term advance, or an interim payment (known as a 'payment on account') of housing benefit.
- A 'benefit cap' may be applied to the total amount of benefit you receive if it is above a certain level.
- You must report certain changes in your circumstances.

Part 9: Claiming benefits and getting paid
Chapter 54: Getting paid
2. How and when you are paid

- Deductions can be made from your benefit. In certain circumstances, payment of your benefit can be suspended. In addition, your benefit might not be paid, or might be paid at a reduced rate, as a result of a sanction or a penalty.

1. Who is paid

Payment is usually made directly to you, but there are some circumstances when payments can be made to other people or organisations on your behalf.

- If you are unable to manage your own money or if you die, your benefit is paid to a person appointed to act on your behalf – called an 'appointee' (see p1137).[1]
- You can choose to have child benefit, guardian's allowance, joint-claim jobseeker's allowance (JSA) or universal credit (UC) paid to your partner.
- Your benefit (except housing benefit – HB) can be paid to someone else if it is in the interests of you or your partner, or any of your children for whom you are getting benefit.[2] This includes paying your UC housing costs for rent to someone to then make payments to your landlord.
- If you are claiming income support (IS), income-based JSA, income-related employment and support allowance (ESA), pension credit (PC) or UC and are getting help with your housing costs for a mortgage (see Chapter 20), these are usually paid directly to your lender on your behalf (see p1180).
- Your HB can be paid directly to your landlord (or the person to whom you pay rent) on your behalf in certain circumstances (see p133). Your UC housing costs for rent are not paid directly to your landlord, unless the DWP thinks the 'alternative payment arrangements' should apply (see p194).
- If you are claiming IS, JSA, ESA, PC or UC and have certain types of debt, payments can be made to your creditors on your behalf (see p1178).[3]

2. How and when you are paid

How and when your benefit is paid depends on the benefit you have claimed. The DWP, local authority or HM Revenue and Customs (HMRC) decides how your benefit is paid to you and there is no right of appeal about the way in which you are paid. For how and when housing benefit is paid, see p132.

Note:

- You are usually paid your benefit by direct credit transfer into a bank or similar account (see p1163).
- If you cannot open or manage an acount, payment can sometimes be made by 'simple payment' or, for child benefit and guardian's allowance, by cheque (see p1163).

- If you have claimed universal credit (UC), you can check your payments online. If you are unable to do this, ask the DWP for help in accessing your online account. It may be able to do this by telephone, or possibly in person at a Jobcentre Plus office.

Direct payment

Payment by direct credit transfer into a bank account, building society account or similar account (including a Post Office card account and some credit union accounts) is the usual method of payment for new benefit claims. This is called 'direct payment'. If this is not suitable for you, you may be able to get your benefit paid by 'simple payment', or your child benefit or guardian's allowance paid by cheque (see below).

You can request that your benefit is paid into an account held in your name, into your partner's or appointee's account, or into a joint account with your partner or appointee.[4]

If you experience difficulty accessing your money as a result of these arrangements, complain to the DWP or HMRC. You could contact your MP.

If someone collects your benefit for you

It should be possible, if necessary, to arrange for someone else to be able to access your account in order to collect your benefit for you. If you already have a bank or building society account, ask the bank or building society about this. If you use a Post Office card account, a second card can be issued to the person who collects your benefit.

If you lose your card or forget your PIN

If you lose your bank card or forget your PIN, contact the bank for a replacement card or to change the PIN, and issue you with a new one as soon as possible. If you cannot access your benefit, contact the office that pays your benefit for advice about what to do.

If you use a Post Office card account and you lose your card or forget your PIN, call the customer service helpline number on 0845 722 3344 (textphone 0845 722 3355). You should get a replacement card or PIN within four working days. If you cannot access your benefit in the meantime, contact the office that pays your benefit for advice.

If all else fails, you may be able to get a payment from your local authority while the problem is sorted out. These can be paid if there is a crisis (see p829). If you cannot get access to your benefit, and the DWP or HMRC refuses to remedy the situation, seek advice (see Appendix 2).

Payment by 'simple payment' or cheque

If you cannot open or manage an account, it should be possible for your DWP benefits to be paid by a 'simple payment' card at a PayPoint outlet. The DWP does

Part 9: Claiming benefits and getting paid
Chapter 54: Getting paid
2. How and when you are paid

not issue cheques. If you are to be paid by simple payment, the DWP sends you a letter and information pack about simple payment, and identifies two PayPoint outlets near your home which you could use. You must produce your simple payment card, a memorable date agreed with the DWP and proof of your identity to get your benefit at the PayPoint outlet. If someone regularly gets your benefit for you, s/he can be issued with her/his own simple payment card. For more information, see www.gov.uk/simple-payment.

If you lose your simple payment card, telephone 0800 032 5872. There is also a simple payment telephone helpline on 0845 600 0046 (textphone 0800 032 5864). Phone this if you forget your memorable date.

If you cannot open or manage an account, the local authority (for housing benefit) or HMRC (for child benefit and guardian's allowance) may arrange to pay you by another method, including by cheque.

When you are paid

When and how often your benefit is paid depends on the benefit you have claimed.[5] You are sometimes paid in advance and sometimes in arrears. Some benefits have specific paydays; for others, the day you are paid depends on your national insurance (NI) number. See the chapter for the benefit you are claiming.

Last two numbers of your NI number	Day of payment
00–19	Monday
20–39	Tuesday
40–59	Wednesday
60–79	Thursday
80–89	Friday

Missing payments

If you are entitled to benefit, you must be paid it.[6] If your benefit is not paid into your account, your simple payment card does not allow you to collect your benefit or you are not issued with a cheque, the DWP or HMRC must rectify this.

If there is a long delay, the DWP or HMRC may refer to a rule that says that your entitlement to payment is lost 12 months after the date it was due to be paid into your account. However, this should not apply if you have not been paid.[7] If necessary, seek advice (see Appendix 2).

Emergencies

If you have lost all your money or there has been a crisis, it is possible to get help at any time. Your local police station should have a contact number for DWP staff on call outside normal office hours.

If you are unable to contact the DWP, or it does not help, you may be able to get a payment from your local authority in a crisis (see p829) or from the social services department (see p837). The police station should have a contact number.

If you need money urgently, you should provide as much information as you can to support your claim. It may help if you can get an advice agency or third party (eg, a health visitor, social worker, doctor or MP) to support you.

3. Overlapping benefits

The 'overlapping benefit' rules mean that sometimes you cannot be paid more than one non-means-tested benefit in full at the same time. These rules may also apply if:

- more than one person is claiming an increase for the same child or adult (see p1167);
- you are getting child benefit, guardian's allowance or an increase in your non-means-tested benefit for your child (see p1167);
- you are entitled to an increase in your non-means-tested benefit for an adult who is getting one or more of certain benefits her/himself (see p1167).

Disability living allowance (DLA) care component, the daily living component of personal independence payment (PIP) , attendance allowance (AA) and armed forces independence payments overlap with each other and with constant attendance allowance.[8] Otherwise AA, DLA, PIP, disablement benefit (see p677), reduced earnings allowance (see p679) and retirement allowance (see p683) can be received in addition to any of the other benefits described in this *Handbook* – eg, you can receive employment and support allowance (ESA), both components of DLA or of PIP and disablement benefit all at once.

Earnings-replacement benefits

Some benefits compensate you for your inability to work because of unemployment, sickness, pregnancy or old age. These are 'earnings-replacement' benefits. You cannot usually receive more than one of the following earnings-replacement benefits at a time.

- Contributory benefits:
  - contribution-based jobseeker's allowance;
  - incapacity benefit;
  - contributory ESA;

     – maternity allowance, which counts as contributory for the purposes of this
       rule;
     – retirement pension;
     – bereavement allowance or widow's pension;
     – widowed parent's allowance or widowed mother's allowance .
- Non-contributory benefits:
     – severe disablement allowance;
     – carer's allowance (CA).

If more than one of the earnings-replacement benefits listed above is payable to
you:[9]
- a contributory benefit is paid in preference to a non-contributory benefit. This
  is then topped up by any balance of a non-contributory benefit due;
- if the above does not apply, weekly benefits are paid and topped up by any
  balance of a daily benefit (unless you make an application to receive the daily
  benefit in full). See the chapter in this *Handbook* about the benefit you are
  claiming to see if it is a daily or a weekly benefit;
- if neither of the above bullet points apply, the highest rate benefit is paid or, if
  the rates are the same, one benefit is paid.

Other adjustments

If you are getting a training allowance paid by a government department or
training agency, your earnings-replacement benefit is reduced by the amount of
the training allowance.[10]
    You cannot usually get more than one retirement pension at a time. However,
there are special rules if you are a widow or widower entitled to both a Category A
(see p748) and a Category B retirement pension (see p748) and your Category A
pension would be paid at a reduced rate because you have not paid sufficient
contributions (see p866). In this situation, your basic Category A pension is
increased by whichever is less of either:[11]
- the amount of the shortfall between your Category A pension and the full
  Category A pension of £113.10; *or*
- the amount of your Category B pension,

You are also entitled to an additional pension on your own contribution record
and one on that of your spouse or civil partner up to the maximum additional
pension a person could theoretically receive on one contribution record.[12]

Earnings-related additions to non-means-tested benefits

Additional pensions under the additional state pension scheme (see p760) and
graduated retirement benefit (see p750) do not themselves overlap with non-
means-tested benefits. However, if *two or more* such benefits are payable with an
additional pension and graduated retirement benefit, the benefits are calculated

as if the additional pension or graduated retirement benefit is part of the benefit, and the overlapping benefit rule is then applied to the benefits.[13]

There are exceptions to this rule if you are a Category B retirement pensioner whose own contribution record would entitle you to a Category A retirement pension. See p278 of the 2008/09 edition of this *Handbook*.

An age addition paid with retirement pension overlaps with another age addition.[14]

Increases in non-means-tested benefits for adults

An increase in a non-means-tested benefit for an adult overlaps with certain earnings-replacement benefits (see p1165) or training allowances which are payable to that adult – eg, an increase of retirement pension for your partner is not paid if s/he is being paid CA in her/his own right.[15] If the increase is less than or equal to the benefit payable to the adult, the increase is not paid. If the increase is greater than the basic benefit, you get the difference. This does not apply if the adult is not residing with you and is employed by you to care for a child.

Increases in non-means-tested benefits for children

Only one person can receive child benefit or an increase in a non-means-tested benefit for the same child.

The standard rate of child benefit (see p561) does not overlap with any other benefit. However, if you receive the higher amount payable for your eldest child (see p561), any other non-means-tested benefit (except DLA, PIP or guardian's allowance) or increase paid for the same child is reduced by £3.30.[16] All increases for children overlap with guardian's allowance and are reduced by the amount of guardian's allowance you get for the child.[17]

4. Short-term advances

You may be able to get an advance payment of your benefit award, called a short-term advance, if there is a delay in dealing with your claim or in paying your benefit and, because of the delay, you are in 'financial need'. See p1168 for exceptions.

Financial need

'Financial need' means that because you have not received your benefit, there is a serious risk of damage to the health or safety of you or a member of your family. '**Family**' means your partner and any children for whom you or your partner are responsible (see p210).[18]

Part 9: Claiming benefits and getting paid
Chapter 54: Getting paid
4. Short-term advances

If you are in financial need because of a **delay in dealing with your claim**, you may be able to get a short-term advance if the decison maker considers it likely that you are entitled to the benefit, and:

- you have made a claim, but the claim has not yet been decided; *or*
- you are not required to make a claim for the benefit, but you have not yet been awarded it.

If you are in financial need because of a **delay in paying your benefit**, you may be able to get a short-term advance if you have been awarded the benefit, and:

- you are waiting for your first payment; *or*
- you have received your first payment, but it was for a shorter period than subsequent payments will be paid for, and you are waiting for your next payment; *or*
- you have had a change of circumstances which will increase your entitlement, but your benefit has not yet been increased and paid to you; *or*
- you are entitled to a payment but it is 'impracticable' to pay all or some of it on the date on which it is due.

Note:
- There is no right of appeal against a refusal to award a short-term advance.[19] The only legal remedy is judicial review (see p1351). You could contact your MP to see if s/he can help to get the decision reconsidered. You may be able to get help in a crisis from your local authority (see p829). You could also try using the emergency service (see p1165).
- A short-term advance is recovered by deductions from subsequent payments of your benefit. The same method of recovery is used as for recovery of overpayments described on p1230. You must be notified of your liability to have the advance repaid in this way (or, if not, of your liability to repay the short-term advance).[20] If you need a longer period than the decision maker has allowed to repay, tell her/him and explain why. You can appeal the decision to deduct the repayments from subsequent payments of your benefit.[21]

Exceptions

You cannot get a short-term advance of:[22]
- housing benefit (HB). If your HB is delayed and you are a private or housing association tenant, you might be able to get a 'payment on account' (see p139);
- attendance allowance;
- disability living allowance;
- personal independence payment;
- child benefit (see p1169);
- guardian's allowance (see p1169);
- statutory sick pay, statutory maternity pay, statutory paternity pay or statutory adoption pay.

Interim payments of child benefit and guardian's allowance

If your claim for child benefit or guardian's allowance is delayed, instead of a short-term advance you can ask HM Revenue and Customs (HMRC) for an interim payment. HMRC does not make an interim payment if you have an appeal pending. An interim payment can be made if it seems that you may be entitled to benefit and:[23]

- there is a delay in your making a claim; *or*
- you have claimed but not in the correct way – eg, you have filled in the form incorrectly; *or*
- you have claimed correctly, but it is not possible for the claim to be dealt with immediately; *or*
- you have been awarded benefit, but it is not possible to pay you immediately, other than by an interim payment.

Note:
- There is no right of appeal against a refusal to award you an interim payment. The only legal remedy is judicial review. You could contact your MP to see if s/he can help to get the decision reconsidered. You may be able to get help in a crisis from your local authority (see p829). You could also try using the emergency service (see p1165).
- An interim payment can be deducted from any later payment of the benefit, and if it is more than your actual entitlement, the overpayment can be recovered. You should be notified of this in advance.[24]

5. The benefit cap

A 'benefit cap' may limit the total amount you can be paid from certain specified benefits.[25] See p1170 and p1171 for the benefits that are taken into account when deciding whether the cap applies.

If the total amount of your benefits is capped, the cap is applied:
- by reducing the amount of your housing benefit (HB) (see p1170); *or*
- by reducing the amount of your universal credit (UC) (see p1171).

If you are not entitled to HB or UC, the cap is not applied. The benefit cap is also not applied to your HB if you are at least the qualifying age for pension credit (PC – see p78) and you (and your partner, if you are in a couple) are not getting income support (IS), income-based jobseeker's allowance (JSA) or income-related employment and support allowance (ESA).

There are other exceptions to when the cap is applied (see p1172) and, in some circumstances, the cap is not applied immediately (see p1172).

You can appeal (see Chapter 59) against having the benefit cap applied through your HB.[26] However, there is no right of appeal against a decision to apply the

Part 9: Claiming benefits and getting paid
Chapter 54: Getting paid
5. The benefit cap

benefit cap through UC. Instead, you must ask for a revision or a supersession (see Chapter 58).

Can you avoid having your benefits capped?

1. If you are not getting HB for people below the qualifying age for PC or UC, the cap does not apply.

2. If you or your partner are working and get working tax credit (WTC), the cap does not apply (see p1172).

3. If you or your partner (or, in some cases, your child) are entitled to a one of the disability benefits listed on p1173, the cap does not apply.

4. If you or your partner have been working recently, there may be a 'grace period' in which the cap does not apply (see p1172).

5. If the cap would be applied through your UC, you are exempt from the cap if you and/ or your partner work, provided your combined earnings are high enough (see p1171).

6. If you get HB, the cap is likely to apply because the amount of your HB may be relatively high. If the amount of your HB decreases (eg, because you have moved to cheaper accommodation), this may mean that the cap no longer applies.

When the benefit cap applies

The benefit cap only applies if:

- you get HB for people below the qualifying age for PC, or you get UC; *and*
- none of the exceptions apply (see p1172); *and*
- the total amount of certain specified benefits you (and your partner, if you are a member of a couple) receive is above a certain level (see below for HB and p1171 for UC).

When calculating the amount of benefit you receive, the general rule is that your full benefit entitlement is taken into account. Deductions for repayment of overpayments, payments to third parties, council tax debts, fines and sanctions are generally ignored (but see below for some exceptions if the cap is applied through your HB and you get child tax credit (CTC), widowed mother's allowance or widowed parent's allowance).[27]

If you get housing benefit

If you get HB, unless there is an exception (see p1172) the cap applies once your (and, if you are in a couple, your partner's) weekly entitlement to certain specified benefits exceeds £500 a week if you are claiming as a couple or as a lone parent, or £350 a week if you are claiming as a single person.

For when you count a a couple, see p205. You count as a lone parent if you are not part of a couple and are responsible for a child. For when you count as responsible for a child, see p212.

The '**specified benefits**' are:

- IS;
- JSA;
- ESA, if neither you nor your partner are in the support group;
- HB, except for 'specified accommodation'. This means 'exempt accommodation' (see p416) or accommodation provided by a housing association, charity, voluntary organisation or English county council to meet your need for care, support or supervision; temporary accommodation provided by one of these bodies or a local authority because you have left home because of domestic violence; or a local authority hostel where you get care, support or supervision;
- bereavement allowance;
- carer's allowance (CA);
- child benefit;
- guardian's allowance;
- CTC (but if you are repaying an overpayment from the previous tax year, the amount of CTC taken into account is reduced by the amount deducted for the repayment);
- incapacity benefit;
- maternity allowance (MA);
- severe disablement allowance;
- widowed mother's/parent's allowance (after the £15 disregard);
- widow's pension.

The local authority does not have to decide whether or not to apply the cap, unless it is told by the DWP that the cap may apply in your case or that you have had a change in your benefit entitlement. However, it can decide to apply the cap on the basis of information or evidence suggesting that it should do so.[29]

If you get universal credit

If you get UC, unless there is an exception (see p1172), the cap applies once your (and your partner's) monthly entitlement to specified benefits exceeds £2,167 a month for couples or lone parents, and £1,517 a month otherwise. Your benefit payments are converted into monthly amounts for this calculation. For when you count a a couple, see p205. You count as a lone parent if you are not part of a couple and are responsible for a child. For when you count as responsible for a child, see p212.

The '**specified benefits**' are:

- UC;[31]
- JSA;

Part 9: Claiming benefits and getting paid
Chapter 54: Getting paid
5. The benefit cap

- ESA, if neither you nor your partner are in the support group;
- bereavement allowance;
- CA;
- child benefit;
- guardian's allowance;
- MA;
- widowed mother's allowance;
- widowed parent's allowance;
- widow's pension.

When the benefit cap does not apply

There are a number of situations in which the benefit cap does not apply. Generally, these exceptions apply to:
- work or recent work, including a 'grace period' after stopping work (see below);
- entitlement to a particular disability benefit (see p1173).

Work-related exceptions
If the benefit cap should be applied through your HB, it is not applied if:[32]
- you or your partner are entitled to WTC. This includes if you have claimed WTC but have a nil award because of your income (see p1440); *or*
- you are within a 'grace period' after finishing work (see below).

The benefit cap is not applied for a 'grace period' of 39 weeks if:[33]
- you or your partner were previously in work (either employed or self-employed) for at least 50 weeks out of the 52 weeks before the last day of work; *and*
- in that 50 weeks, the person in work was not entitled to IS, JSA or ESA.

The grace period begins on the day after the last day of work.
   You count as still in work while on maternity, paternity or adoption leave, or while receiving statutory sick pay (SSP).[34]
   If the benefit cap should be applied through your UC, it is not applied if:[35]
- you or your partner are working (either employed or self-employed) and have net monthly earnings of at least £430 in your UC monthly assessment period. Your partner's earnings are added to yours; *or*
- you are within a nine-month 'grace period' (see below).

The benefit cap is not applied for a 'grace period' of nine consecutive months, if:[36]
- your earnings (or your and your partner's combined earnings) from employed or self-employed work are now less than £430 a month but, immediately

before the first day on which this applies, your earnings (or your combined earnings) had been at least £430 a month in each of the preceding 12 months; *or*

- before your current period of entitlement to UC, you stopped paid employed or self-employed work and, before you stopped work, your earnings (or your and your partner's combined earnings) had been at least £430 a month in each of the preceding 12 months.

The grace period begins on the most recent day on which either condition applies. For how earnings from work are calculated for UC, see Chapter 16.

Although not explicitly stated in the UC rules, it is arguable that you count as still in work while on maternity, paternity or adoption leave, or while receiving SSP. If you are in this position, seek advice.

Disability benefits
The benefit cap does not apply if you or your partner get:
- ESA that includes the support component;
- UC that includes the limited capability for work-related activity component;
- attendance allowance (or you are entitled to it but are not paid while you are in hospital or a care home);
- disability living allowance (DLA), personal independence payment (PIP) or armed forces independence payment. This exemption also applies if the person entitled is a child for whom you or your partner are responsible. The exemption continues while the person entitled to it is in hospital or a care home;
- industrial injuries disablement benefit, reduced earnings allowance or retirement allowance;
- a war pension (or are entitled to it but are not paid while you are in hospital or a care home).

How the benefit cap is applied

If the cap is applied through your HB, the local authority reduces your HB by the amount by which the total amount of the specified benefits you receive (see p1170) exceeds the cap – ie, by the amount it exceeds £500 week if you are a couple or lone parent, or £350 week otherwise. You must be left with at least 50 pence a week HB, so that you can still access discretionary housing payments and other passported payments.[37]

If the cap is applied through your UC, the DWP reduces your UC by the amount by which the total amount of the specified benefits you receive exceeds the cap – ie, by the amount it exceeds £2,167 a month if you are a couple or lone parent, or £1,517 a month otherwise. However, if you are entitled to the childcare costs element in your UC (see p253) and this is more than the amount by which your specified benefits exceed the cap (the 'excess'), your UC is not reduced. If it is

Part 9: Claiming benefits and getting paid
Chapter 54: Getting paid
6. Change of circumstances after you claim

not more than the excess, your UC is reduced, but the excess is reduced by your childcare costs element before the reduction is applied.[38]

6. Change of circumstances after you claim

You have a duty to report certain changes in your circumstances. The DWP or HM Revenue and Customs (HMRC) should inform you of the main kinds of changes that you must report, but might not list them all. It is also your duty to report *any* change in your circumstances that you might reasonably be expected to know might affect your right to, the amount of, or the payment of, your benefit.[39] For the rules on changes of circumstances that apply to housing benefit, see pp139–43.

You must notify changes promptly to the DWP or HMRC office handling your claim. This might be at a benefit delivery centre or other benefit processing unit (for income support – IS), a central or regional unit (eg, for disability living allowance (DLA) or personal independence payment – PIP) or a local Jobcentre Plus office. Check the information sent to you about your benefit award, but seek advice if you are in doubt. The rules say that the office handling your claim for child benefit or guardian's allowance includes the HMRC child benefit office (see Appendix 1), or any office specified by HMRC.

You must notify the changes in writing or by telephone.[40] It is best to notify changes in writing so that you have a record of what you have reported. If you report a change by telephone, note the time and date of your call and confirm what was said in writing. Keep a copy of any letters you send. If you give the original to an officer, ask her/him to stamp your copy to confirm s/he has received the original.

There are additional ways you can report a change of circumstances.

- For child benefit and guardian's allowance, you may be able to report the change in person,[41] either at the HMRC child benefit office or another office specified by HMRC. However, it is always better to do so in writing.
- Except for child benefit and guardian's allowance, if the change is a birth or a death, there is a special rule (sometimes called 'Tell Us Once'). You can report such a change in person at a local authority (and, in England, a county council) office specified for that purpose. If the change is a death, you can notify it by telephone to the DWP if a number has been specified for that purpose.[42] Check with your local authority for the Tell Us Once arrangements in your area (eg, at the registry office) or via www.gov.uk.

Note:
- If you do not promptly report a change which you have a duty to notify, any resulting overpayment may be recoverable from you (see Chapter 56).

- If you are considered to have acted 'knowingly' or dishonestly, you may also be guilty of an offence, which may lead to prosecution or a benefit penalty. Even if you have not committed an offence, a civil penalty may be applied (see Chapter 57).

7. When payments can be suspended

Payment of part or all of your benefit can be suspended in certain circumstances. This includes if you do not provide further information or evidence or fail to have a medical examination to help decide if you are still entitled to benefit (or are getting it at the correct rate). It is important that you provide all the information that is required and attend the medical examination. Your entitlement to benefit could be terminated if you fail to do so (see p1177).

Suspension while an appeal is pending

Your benefit can be suspended if the DWP, the local authority or HM Revenue and Customs (HMRC) is appealing (or considering an appeal) against:[43]
- a decision of the First-tier Tribunal, Upper Tribunal or court to award you benefit; *or*
- a decision of the Upper Tribunal or court about someone else's case if the issue in the appeal could affect your claim. For housing benefit (HB) only, the other case must also be about a HB issue.

The DWP, the local authority or HMRC must give you written notice that it intends to request the statement of reasons from the First-tier Tribunal, or that it intends to apply for leave to appeal or to appeal. It must do this as soon as is 'reasonably practicable'.[44]

The decision maker must then do one of these things within the usual time limits for doing so (see Chapter 59).

If s/he does not, the suspended benefit must be paid to you.[45] The suspended benefit must also be paid to you if the decision maker withdraws an application for leave to appeal, withdraws the appeal or is refused leave to appeal and it is not possible for her/him to renew the application for leave to appeal.

Suspension for not providing information and evidence

You can be required to supply information or evidence if the decision maker needs this to determine whether your award of benefit should be revised or superseded (see p1270 and p1281).[46]

Payment of your benefit can be suspended if you do not provide the information and evidence, and:[47]
- your benefit has been suspended in the circumstances described above; *or*

Part 9: Claiming benefits and getting paid
Chapter 54: Getting paid
7. When payments can be suspended

- you apply for a revision or supersession (see p1270 and p1281); *or*
- you do not provide certificates, documents, evidence and other information about the facts of your case as required;[48] *or*
- your entitlement to benefit is conditional on your being incapable of work or having limited capability for work.

You must be notified in writing if the decision maker wants you to provide information or evidence. Within 14 days (one month for child benefit, guardian's allowance and HB; seven days for contribution-based jobseeker's allowance (JSA) if you come under the universal credit (UC) system – see p19) of being sent the request, you must:

- supply the information or evidence.[49] You can be given more time than this if you satisfy the decision maker that this is necessary; *or*
- satisfy the decision maker that the information does not exist or you cannot obtain it.[50]

If the decision maker has not already done so, your benefit can be suspended if you do not provide the information or evidence within the relevant time limit.[51] See below for whether your entitlement to benefit can be terminated.

Suspension for not taking part in a medical examination

Most benefits can be suspended if you do not take part in a medical examination on two consecutive occasions without 'good cause'.[52] This applies if:

- the decision maker is looking at whether you should still be getting a benefit (or whether you are getting it at the correct rate); *or*
- you apply for a revision or a supersession and the decision maker thinks a medical examination is necessary in order to make a decision.

This rule does not apply if the issue is whether you have limited capability for work. For information on these medicals and the consequences of failing to take part in them, see p1010. This rule does not apply to personal independence payment. However, if you do not take part in a medical, the DWP may still suspend your benefit because of a doubt about your entitlement (see below).
See p1177 for whether your entitlement to benefit can be terminated.

Suspension in other circumstances

Your benefit can also be suspended if:[53]

- a question has arisen about your entitlement.[54] In this case, all or part of the benefit due to you can be suspended pending a revision, supersession or appeal of the decision about your entitlement;
- you have been getting JSA and a question has arisen about whether you are meeting your jobseeking conditions. Your JSA must be suspended until this

matter is resolved. **Note:** this does not apply to contribution-based JSA if you come under the UC system (see p19);[55]
- it looks as though your award of benefit should be superseded or revised;[56]
- the DWP or HMRC thinks you are being (or may have been) overpaid.[57] All or part of your benefit may be withheld during an investigation;
- you are not living at the last address you notified;[58] for child benefit and guardian's allowance, the bank account or other account details which you have given to HMRC are incorrect;[59]
- for HB, a recoverable overpayment may have occurred.[60]

Challenging decisions to suspend benefit

The decision maker may be willing to continue to pay your benefit, or at least some of it, if you can show that you will experience hardship otherwise. If you receive a letter telling you that your benefit has been suspended, reply and explain how the suspension affects you and ask for it to be reconsidered. It may be wise to get advice first (see Appendix 2).

You cannot appeal to the First-tier Tribunal against the decision to suspend your benefit. The only ways to change the decision are to negotiate to get your benefit reinstated or to challenge the decision in the courts by judicial review (see p1351). You could also ask for a short-term advance of benefit (see p1167). Seek advice.

8. When your benefit entitlement is terminated

Your entitlement to benefit can be terminated if:
- your benefit was suspended in full, you are then required to provide information or evidence to determine whether the decision awarding you benefit should be revised or superseded, and you fail to do so within one month of the request;[61] *or*
- your benefit was suspended in full because you did not provide information or evidence required to determine whether the decision awarding you benefit should be revised or superseded and it is more than one month since your benefit was suspended.[62]

The termination of your entitlement to benefit takes effect from the date payment was suspended (or an earlier date if you ceased to be entitled for another reason).[63]

Your entitlement to most benefits can also be terminated if you do not take part in a medical examination and it is more than one month since your benefit was suspended on this ground.[64] This is discretionary.

Part 9: Claiming benefits and getting paid
Chapter 54: Getting paid
9. Deductions and payments to third parties

If you disagree with a decision to terminate your benefit, you can ask for a revision (see p1270) or appeal (see Chapter 59).[65] It is likely that you will have to ask for a revision before you can appeal.

9. **Deductions and payments to third parties**

Your benefits are usually paid directly to you, but there are some circumstances when money can be deducted and paid to a third party on your behalf. The majority of these deductions can usually only be made from income support (IS), income-based jobseeker's allowance (JSA), income-related employment and support allowance (ESA), pension credit (PC) and universal credit (UC). In limited circumstances, they can also be made from contribution-based JSA and contributory ESA or from some other benefits.

What deductions can be made

Amounts can be deducted from your benefit (usually from , IS, income-based JSA, income-related ESA, PC or UC) to pay for:[66]
- housing costs paid to your lender under the mortgage payment scheme (see p1180);
- other housing costs (see p1181);
- rent arrears (see p1182);
- residential accommodation charges (see p1183);
- hostel payments (see p1183);
- fuel (see p1183);
- water charges (p1184);
- council tax arrears (see p1184);
- fines (see p1184);
- repayment of eligible loans (see p1185);
- child support maintenance (see p1185);
- integration loans paid to refugees and others (see p1185); *and*
- repayment of tax credit overpayments and self-assessment tax debts (see p1187).

Note: in addition to the deductions described in this chapter, you may also have deductions made for the recovery of budgeting loans from the social fund (see p769), overpayments (see p1226) and for penalties for fraud (Chapter 57). Your benefit may also be reduced because the DWP has applied a sanction (see Chapters 51 or 52) or because it is recovering a hardship payment (see Chapter 55).

Deductions from contribution-based jobseeker's allowance and contributory employment and support allowance

Deductions can be made from your contribution-based JSA or your contributory ESA for the payments listed above if you have an 'underlying entitlement' to income-based JSA or income-related ESA – ie, were you not entitled to contribution-based JSA or contributory ESA, you would be entitled to income-based JSA or income-related ESA at the same rate.[67]

Deductions can also be made from contribution-based JSA and contributory ESA even if you have no underlying entitlement to income-based JSA or income-related ESA for council tax arrears, fines and child support maintenance arrears.

If you come under the UC system (see p19), these rules do not apply. Deductions for child support maintenance can be made from your contribution-based JSA or contributory ESA (see p1187).

Deductions can also be made from your contribution-based JSA or contributory ESA for mortgage payments if your income-based JSA, income-related ESA or your UC is insufficient to cover the deductions (see p1180).

Deductions from other benefits

Deductions can only be made from other benefits to repay eligible loans (see p1185) and child support maintenance that you owe (see p1185).

When deductions can be made

Deductions and direct payments to third parties can only be made if you or your partner are liable to make the payments.[68] If there is a doubt about whether you or your partner are liable, deductions should only be made if there is evidence that you are liable – eg, the bill is in your name or your partner's name.

Agreeing to the deductions

Your written consent is required before deductions for tax credit overpayments and self-assessment tax debts can be made from your **IS, income-based JSA, income-related ESA** and **PC**. Your consent is also required before deductions are made for arrears of housing costs paid to your lender, rent arrears, service charges for fuel and water, fuel costs (including arrears), water charges (including arrears) and repayment of integration loans if:[69]

- you (or your partner) do not get child tax credit (CTC) and the total to be deducted for these payments exceeds 25 per cent of your family's applicable amount (see Chapter 12) or, in the case of PC, 25 per cent of your minimum guarantee (see p79). Housing costs included in your applicable amount should not be taken into account when calculating the 25 per cent;
- you (or your partner) get CTC, and the total to be deducted for these payments exceeds 25 per cent of your CTC and child benefit and, for benefits other than ESA, your family's applicable amount (see Chapter 12) or, in the case of PC, your minimum guarantee (see p79). Any housing costs included in your

Part 9: Claiming benefits and getting paid
Chapter 54: Getting paid
9. Deductions and payments to third parties

applicable amount should not be taken into account when calculating the 25 per cent.

The DWP can make deductions without your agreement if they are made for:
- council tax arrears;
- fines;
- child support maintenance;
- current housing costs;
- nursing home charges or hostel charges not included in housing benefit (HB).

Consent is not needed for these deductions even if the total amount deducted exceeds the 25 per cent referred to above.[70]

Your consent is required before direct payments (including for arrears) are made for fuel costs and water charges from your **UC** if the total amount deducted for these payments exceeds five times 5 per cent of your UC standard allowance and child elements (see Chapter 13).[71]

Otherwise, the DWP can make deductions from your UC without your consent.

The deductions

Deductions are made at the DWP office before you receive your regular benefit payment. If you want to have deductions made to help you clear any arrears or debts, ask the DWP office dealing with your claim. If you disagree with a decision about deductions, you can appeal (see Chapter 59).

The mortgage payment scheme

When you claim IS, income-based JSA, income-related ESA, PC or UC, you may get help with your housing costs. This can include help with mortgage interest payments or interest on loans for repairs and improvements (see Chapter 20 or Chapter 22). **Note:** these loans are included in UC as owner-occupier payments. The general rules for payment of housing costs are as follows.
- Housing costs are usually paid directly to your lender four weeks in arrears (monthly in arrears for UC).[72]
- Payment is not made directly to your lender if your lender is not covered by, or has opted out of, the mortgage payments scheme.[73] The DWP should tell you if this is the case and you must then pay your own mortgage.
- If you receive PC and you are only entitled to the savings credit, not to the guarantee credit, direct payments are only made if a written request has been made by you or the DWP considers that it is in the best interests of you or your family.[74]

The amount paid to your lender is deducted from your total IS, income-based JSA, income-related ESA, PC or UC entitlement.[75] If you are on JSA or ESA and the amount of your income-based JSA or income-related ESA is insufficient to cover the deduction, deductions can be made from your contribution-based JSA or contributory ESA. If you are on UC but the amount is insufficient to cover the deduction, deductions can also be made from your contribution-based JSA or contributory ESA.

You must make up any difference between what the DWP pays to your lender and the amount you owe. If you do not have enough benefit to meet the full cost, all but 10 pence of your benefit (1 pence for UC) is paid and you must pay the rest yourself.[76]

If you are in mortgage arrears, no amount towards the arrears can be deducted from your benefit if deductions are made under the mortgage payment scheme.

Except in the case of PC, if you have a mortgage protection policy, the amount deducted and paid to your lender is reduced by the amount of payment from the policy. The reduction is the amount of income from the insurance policy which is taken into account.[77]

If an overpayment of mortgage interest is paid to your lender, see p1214.

Other housing costs

The amount in your IS, income-based JSA, income-related ESA, PC or UC for your mortgage interest is usually paid directly to your lender under the mortgage payment scheme (see p1180).[78] If this applies to you (or would apply if your lender had not opted out of the scheme), the deductions described here only cover payments for debts of other types of housing costs – eg, service charges and, in some cases, rent. For IS, income-based JSA, income-related ESA and PC, see p444; for UC see p475. **Note:** rent payments covered by UC are not included in these rules.[79] For the amount of the deductions, see p1188.

If your current **IS, income-based JSA, income-related ESA or PC** includes money for these other housing costs and you are in debt for such costs (excluding payments for ground rent or rent charge payments, unless paid with your service charges or for a tent[80]), deductions can be made from your IS, JSA, ESA or PC both to clear the debt and to meet current payments. Deductions are made if it would be 'in the interests' of you or your family to do so.

For **IS, income-based JSA, income-related ESA and PC**, you only qualify for direct deductions if you owe more than half of the annual total of the relevant housing cost. This condition can be waived if it is in the 'overriding interests' of you or your family that deductions start as soon as possible – eg, repossession of your home is imminent.[81]

In the case of mortgage payments, the decision maker must be satisfied that there are arrears.[82] You must have paid less than eight weeks' full payments in the last 12 weeks.[83] The amount of mortgage interest taken into account is the amount after deductions for non-dependants (see p450).

For **UC**, the rules are slightly different. To have UC deductions for other housing costs (in practice, this usually means service charges), you must be in debt with your other housing costs. Your earnings (or your combined earnings

Part 9: Claiming benefits and getting paid
Chapter 54: Getting paid
9. Deductions and payments to third parties

with your partner) must also be below the UC work allowance that applies to you (see p188). If your earnings (or combined earnings) equal or exceed the work allowance for three monthly assessment periods, the deduction must stop.[84]

Rent arrears

If you are in arrears with your rent (including any inclusive water, fuel and service charges) while on housing benefit (HB), or are £100 or more in arrears of hostel payments, an amount can be deducted from your **IS, income-based JSA, income-related ESA or PC** and paid directly to your landlord. This can also apply if you are in approved premises under s13 of the Offender Management Act 2007 and have built up arrears of service charges rather than rent arrears.[85] For the amount of the deductions, see p1188.

Rent arrears do not include the amount of any non-dependant deductions (see p116), but can cover any water charges or service charges payable with your rent and not met by HB. Fuel charges included in your rent cannot be covered by direct deductions if they change more than twice a year.

To qualify for direct deductions, your rent arrears must be at least four times your full weekly rent. If you have not paid your full rent for eight weeks or more, direct deductions can be made automatically if your landlord asks the DWP to make them.[86] If your arrears relate to a shorter period, deductions can only be made if it is in the overriding interests of your family to do so.[87] In either case, the decision maker must be satisfied that you are in rent arrears. Even if you are, you can ask her/him not to make direct deductions – eg, if you are claiming compensation from your landlord because of the state of repair of your home.[88] Once your arrears are paid off, direct payments can continue for any fuel and water charges included in your rent.[89]

If you are in debt with your rent (including water, service and other charges included in it), deductions can be made from your **UC** if:[90]

* you are entitled to UC housing costs for rent payments or occupy exempt accommodation and get HB for that (p472); *and*
* you occupy the accommodation to which the rent applies; *and*
* your earnings (or if you make a joint claim with your partner, your combined earnings) for the previous UC monthly assessment period (see p186) are below the level of the work allowance that applies to you (see p188). If your earnings (or joint earnings) equal or exceed the work allowance for three monthly assessment periods, the deduction must stop.

The DWP can make a monthly deduction from your UC equivalent to 5 per cent of the standard allowance (see p250) that applies in your case and pay it to your landlord. **Note:** ongoing payments of rent (ie, other than arrears) are paid directly to your landlord, but are not regarded as a deduction from your benefit and so are not included in these rules.

Residential accommodation charges

Deductions can be made from your **IS, JSA, ESA or PC** to meet your accommodation charges if you have failed to budget for them and it is considered to be in your interests for deductions to be made.[91] **Note:** this rule does not apply to UC. For the amount of the deduction, see p1188.

Hostel payments

If you (or your partner) live in a hostel or approved premises under s13 of the Offender Management Act 2007, you have claimed HB to meet your accommodation costs and your payments cover fuel, meals, water charges, laundry and/or cleaning of your room, part of your **IS, JSA, ESA or PC** can be paid directly to the hostel for these items.[92] For the amount of the deduction, see p1188.

If you are in arrears for your hostel payments, deductions can be made under the rule about rent arrears (see p1182). **Note:** these rules do not apply to UC.

Fuel

If you are in debt with your mains gas or electricity, an amount can be deducted from your **IS, income-based JSA, income-related ESA and PC** each week and paid to the fuel company in instalments – usually once a quarter.[93] This is called 'fuel direct'. In return, the fuel company agrees not to disconnect you. For the amount of the deduction, see p1188. Deductions can be made if:[94]

- the amount you owe is £72.40 or more (including reconnection or disconnection charges if you have been disconnected); *and*
- you continue to need the fuel supply; *and*
- it is in your, or your family's, interests to have deductions made.

An amount is deducted for the fuel you use each week (your current consumption) as well as for the arrears you owe. The amount deducted for current consumption is whatever is necessary to meet your current weekly fuel costs. This is adjusted if the cost increases or decreases. Deductions for current consumption can be continued after the debt has been cleared.[95]

If you are in debt for any mains gas or mains electricity (including reconnection or disconnection charges), deductions can be made from your UC if your earnings (or, if you are claiming jointly with your partner, your combined earnings) for the previous monthly UC assessment period (see p186) are below the level of the work allowance that applies in your case (see p188).[96] If your earnings equal or exceed the work allowance for three monthly assessment periods, the deduction must stop.

The DWP can make deductions from your UC and pay it to the fuel company. It can deduct a monthly amount equal to 5 per cent of your standard allowance (see p250), plus an additional amount that the DWP considers to be equal to the average monthly fuel costs, except if you are paying for that by other means – eg, a prepayment meter.

Part 9: Claiming benefits and getting paid
Chapter 54: Getting paid
9. Deductions and payments to third parties

Water charges

If you get into debt with charges for water and sewerage, direct deductions can be made from your **IS, income-based JSA, income-related ESA and PC**.[97] Debt includes any disconnection, reconnection and legal charges. For the amount of the deductions, see p1188. If you pay your landlord for water with your rent, deductions are made under the arrangements for rent arrears (see p1182).[98]

Deductions can be made if you failed to budget and it is in the interests of you or your family to make deductions.[99] If you are in debt to two water companies, you can only have a deduction for arrears made to one at a time. Your debts for water charges should be cleared before your debts for sewerage costs, but the amount paid for current consumption can include both water and sewerage charges.[100]

If you are in debt with charges for water and sewerage (including reconnection charges), deductions may be made from your **UC** if your earnings (or, if you are claiming jointly with your partner, your combined earnings) for the previous monthly UC assessment period (see p186) are below the level of the work allowance that applies in your case (see p188).[101] If your earnings equal or exceed the work allowance for three monthly assessment periods, the deduction must stop.

The DWP can make deductions from your UC and pay it to the water company. It can deduct a monthly amount equal to 5 per cent of your standard allowance (see p250), plus an additional amount that the DWP considers necessary to meet your continuing monthly water costs.

Council tax arrears

Deductions for council tax can be made from **IS, JSA, ESA, PC or UC** (and for community charge arrears from IS, JSA or PC) if the local authority gets a liability order from a magistrates' court (in Scotland, a summary warrant or decree from a sheriff court) and applies to the DWP for recovery to be made in this way.[102] Deductions can be made for arrears and any unpaid costs or penalties imposed. For the amount of the deductions, see p1188.

Fines

Magistrates' courts (any court in Scotland) can apply to the DWP for a fine, costs or compensation order to be deducted from your **IS, JSA, ESA, PC or UC**.[103] Only one court application can be dealt with at a time. If a second application is made, it is not dealt with until the first debt is paid. For the amount of the deductions, see p1188.

Deductions from your benefit can only be made if you are 18 or over and you have defaulted on payments.

Repayment of eligible loans

Deductions can be made from your **IS, JSA, ESA, PC or UC and (if necessary) your retirement pension or carer's allowance (CA)** towards repaying 'eligible' loans if you have not kept up with the repayments.[104] This applies only to loans made by certain not-for-profit lenders, such as community development financial institutions, credit unions and charities. For the amount of the deductions, see p1188.

The loan must be unsecured, not made for business purposes and not made by a credit card.

Except for UC, when taking out the loan, you must have given your agreement that, were your repayments to fall behind, your lender could send your details to the DWP so that deductions could be made from your benefit.

Deductions can be made from **IS, JSA, ESA and PC** if you have failed to make payments for at least 13 weeks and have not started making them again. They can only be made if your lender has agreed that no interest or other charges will be added from the point the deductions start, and if you do not already have deductions being made to repay a benefit overpayment or social fund loan. Only one deduction for repayment of certain loans can be made.

Deductions can be made from your **UC** if your loan repayments are in arrears. The lender need not have agreed not to add interest or other charges. The amount of the deduction is 5 per cent of your standard allowance (see p250). If your UC award is not enough to allow the deduction to be made, it may be made from your contribution-based JSA or contributory ESA.

Repayment of integration loans

Deductions can be made from your benefit to repay an integration loan – ie, loans paid to refugees and people granted humanitarian protection and their dependants.[105] You must have been told when repayment will start and that it will be by deduction from your benefit. For the amount of the deduction, see p1188.

The amount of the deduction is 5 per cent of your standard allowance (see p250).

Child support maintenance

The rules that apply to deductions depend on which child support rules the child maintenance is payable under. Child support cases are dealt with under one of three sets of rules:

- the 1993 rules, if child support was applied for between 1993 and 3 March 2003;
- the 2003 rules, if child support was applied for on or after 3 March 2003 and the 2012 rules do not apply;

Part 9: Claiming benefits and getting paid
Chapter 54: Getting paid
9. Deductions and payments to third parties

- the 2012 rules, if a new application for child support is made on or after 25 November 2013 (some new cases began to be dealt with under these rules from 10 December 2012). **Note:** the government intends to transfer existing cases to these rules, and to complete this process by 2017.

For full details of which set of rules apply, including on conversion from one set to another, see CPAG's *Child Support Handbook*.

1993 rules

Under the 1993 rules, deductions can be made from a non-resident parent's **IS, income-based JSA, income-related ESA, PC or UC** as a contribution towards the maintenance of her/his child(ren). Currently, the deduction is a standard amount of £7.30 a week or, for UC, a monthly amount equal to 5 per cent of the non-resident parent's standard allowance (see p250).

If you are a non-resident parent and have children from two or more different relationships, only one deduction can be made and the deduction is apportioned between the people who care for them.[106]

The deduction does not apply if you:[107]

- are aged under 18; *or*
- would qualify for a family premium (see p228) or have 'day-to-day care' of any child (see CPAG's *Child Support Handbook* for details of 'day-to-day care'); *or*
- receive one or more of the following:
  - maternity allowance;
  - statutory sick pay or statutory maternity pay;
  - attendance allowance, disability living allowance, personal independence payment or armed force independence payment;
  - CA;
  - industrial injuries disablement benefit or a war disablement pension;
  - an Armed Forces Compensation Scheme payment or a payment from the Independent Living Funds.

If one of the above benefits is not paid solely because of overlapping benefit rules or an inadequate contribution record, you are still exempt from deductions.

A deduction of half the above standard amount may be made if deductions are also being made for debts of other payments (see p1189).[108] **Note:** at the time this *Handbook* was written, this did not apply to UC.

Deductions may also be made from your **contribution-based JSA or contributory ESA** for arrears of child support maintenance (unless you come under the UC system – see p19).[109]

2003 and 2012 rules

If you are a non-resident parent on benefit and liable to pay child support maintenance at the flat rate, a deduction of £5 a week under the 2003 rules, or £7 a week under the 2012 rules, can be made from your:[110]

- IS, including if your partner is liable;
- income-based JSA, including if your partner is liable;
- income-related ESA, including if your partner is liable;
- PC, including if your partner is liable;
- UC, including if your partner is liable;
- bereavement allowance;
- CA;
- contributory ESA;
- industrial injuries benefit;
- contribution-based JSA;
- retirement pension;
- war widow's or war disablement pension;
- widowed mother's allowance and widowed parent's allowance;
- widow's pension;
- training allowance (other than Work-Based Learning for Young People or Skillseekers).

The whole of the child support may be deducted from the benefits listed above.[111] If more than one partner in a couple or polygamous marriage is liable to pay maintenance at the flat rate, it is deducted from any IS, income-based JSA, income-related ESA, PC or UC they jointly receive, with the deduction paid equally. So for example, if both partners in a couple are non-resident parents liable for child support at a flat rate of £5, they each pay £2.50.[112]

Deductions can also be made for any arrears of child support from any of the above benefits, except IS, income-based JSA, income-related ESA and PC (received by the non-resident parent or her/his partner). However, if you come under the UC system (see p19), deductions for arrears can only be made from your contribution-based JSA or contributory ESA, and only if you have not been awarded UC. The deduction for arrears in all cases is £1 per week.[113]

Repayment of tax credit overpayments and self-assessment tax debts

If you have a recoverable overpayment of tax credits, or a debt of income tax arising from a self-assessment, it can be paid to HM Revenue and Customs (HMRC) by deductions from your benefit. Your written consent is required. You may withdraw the consent.[114] **Note:** these rules do not apply to UC. However, if your entitlement to tax credits has stopped and you are entitled to UC in the same tax year, and you have an outstanding tax credit overpayment, the DWP intends to recover the overpayment by making deductions from your UC.[115]

Part 9: Claiming benefits and getting paid
Chapter 54: Getting paid
9. Deductions and payments to third parties

How much can be deducted

If deductions are being made under the rules described in this chapter from your IS, income-based JSA, income-related ESA or PC (or contribution-based JSA if you have an underlying entitlement to income-based JSA, or contributory ESA if you have an underlying entitlement to income-related ESA – see p1179), the maximum deductions are shown below. If deductions are made from your UC, they are made at a fixed rate of 5 per cent of your standard allowance (see p250).

Type of arrears	Deduction for arrears	Deduction for ongoing cost
Mortgage direct payments*	Nil	Current weekly cost
Housing costs*	£3.65 each housing debt (maximum of £10.95)	Current weekly cost
Rent arrears/hostel payments	£3.65	Nil (met by HB)
Fuel	£3.65 each fuel debt (maximum of £7.30 payable)	Estimated amount of current consumption
Water charges	£3.65 (adjusted every 26 weeks)	Estimated costs
Council tax	£3.65	Nil
Community charge	£3.65 (single person) £5.70 (couple)	Not applicable
Fines	Nil	£5 (lower amount £3.65)
Repayment of eligible loans	Nil	£3.65
Repayment of integration loans	Nil	£3.65
Child support maintenance	Nil	£5 (2003 rules); £7 (2012 rules); £7.30 (1993 rules)
Residential accommodation charges	Nil	The accommodation allowance (for those in local authority homes); all but £24.40 of your IS, JSA, ESA or PC (for those in private or voluntary homes)
Repayment of tax credit overpayments and self-assessment tax debts	Nil	Maximum £10.95
Hostel charges	Nil	Weekly amount assessed by local authority

*If you have more than one type of housing cost (ie, one under the mortgage payment scheme and one under other housing costs) and these are not met in full because of a restriction on the amount that can be covered (see p448) or a non-dependant deduction (see p450), the direct payment to meet the current weekly costs is reduced by multiplying the amount of the restriction and/or deduction by the amount of the item of housing costs to be paid directly and then dividing by the amount of total housing costs.[116] This ensures that the deductions are shared proportionately between different housing costs.

More than one deduction

More than one deduction can be made from your **IS, income-based JSA, income-related ESA** and **PC**. You must be left with at least 10 pence of benefit.[117]
Note:

- The maximum amount that can be deducted for arrears (excluding community charge arrears) and for current child support maintenance under the 1993 rules is £10.86 a week.[118]
- If the combined cost of deductions for arrears and current consumption for fuel, rent, water charges, housing costs arrears and repayment of certain loans is more than 25 per cent of your total applicable amount (see p220) or, for PC, more than 25 per cent of your minimum guarantee(see p79) before housing costs, the deductions cannot be made without your consent.[119]
- Most deductions are taken into account when calculating the total amount of deductions, including all those mentioned in the priority rules (see below), as well as those for sanctions (see Chapter 51 or Chapter 52), benefit offences (p1258) and to recover overpayments of JSA, ESA or UC). Deductions for ongoing costs (as opposed to arrears) of fuel or water charges are ignored. Deductions of more than the limit may still be made for other housing costs (ie, those not covered by the mortgage payment scheme), rent arrears or fuel debts, if the DWP considers it would be in your best interests.

If there is no underlying entitlement to income-based JSA or income-related ESA, the maximum amount that can be deducted in total (for debts) from contribution-based JSA or contributory ESA for council tax, fines and child support maintenance arrears or, for JSA only, community charge arrears, is one-third of the weekly amount of JSA or ESA for a person of your age.

More than one deduction can be made from your **UC**, provided you are left with at least one pence of UC. There is a limit to the total number of certain deductions that can be made. No more than three of the following deductions from UC may be made at any one time:[120]

- other housing costs – ie, those not covered by the mortgage payment scheme;
- rent arrears;

Part 9: Claiming benefits and getting paid
Chapter 54: Getting paid
9. Deductions and payments to third parties

- fuel debts;
- water charges;
- child support maintenance under the 1993 rules;
- repayment of eligible loans;
- repayment of integration loans;
- council tax and community charge arrears;
- fines, costs and compensation orders.

The total amount payable for fuel debts and water charges combined cannot exceed an amount equal to five times 5 per cent of your standard allowance plus any child elements to which you are entitled (see Chapter 13) without your consent.[121]

Also, the total amount of deductions from UC cannot exceed eight times 5 per cent of the standard allowance that applies in your case (p250).[122] The priority rules (below) apply to ensure that certain deductions are made.

Priority between deductions

If you have more debts or current charges than can be met from your benefit (see p1188), for **IS, income-based JSA, income-related ESA and PC**, they are paid in the following order of priority:[123]
- housing costs not covered by the mortgage payment scheme;
- rent arrears (and related charges);
- fuel charges;
- water charges;
- council tax and community charge arrears;
- unpaid fines, costs and compensation orders;
- payments for child support maintenance under the 1993 rule (payments due under the 2003 and 2012 rules are always payable);
- repayment of integration loans;
- repayment of eligible loans;
- repayment of tax credit overpayments and self-assessment tax debts.

If you owe both gas and electricity arrears, the DWP chooses which one to pay first, depending on your circumstances. If you have arrears for both council tax and community charge, only one application can be dealt with at a time and the earliest debt should be dealt with first.[124]

If you have been overpaid benefit or given a social fund loan, you may have to repay these through deductions from your benefit.[125] You should argue that these deductions should take a lower priority.

For **UC**, an order of priority applies if your UC is 'insufficient' to meet all the deductions that apply to it. Your award of UC is 'insufficient' if the total amount of certain deductions would be more than eight times 5 per cent of the standard allowance that applies to you (see p250). The deductions are paid in the following order of priority:[126]

- housing costs not covered by the mortgage payment scheme;
- rent arrears;
- fuel;
- council tax and community charge arrears;
- fines;
- water charges;
- child support maintenance under the 1993 rules;
- child support maintenance under the 2003 or 2012 rules ;
- repayment of social fund payments;
- recovery of hardship payments;
- penalties for benefit offences instead of prosecution;
- recovery of overpayments of benefits or tax credits caused by fraud;
- loss of benefit for benefit offences;
- recovery of overpayments of benefits or tax credits not caused by fraud;
- repayment of integration loans;
- repayment of eligible loans;
- fines, costs and compensation orders if the amount of the deduction is more than £3.65 a week.

10. Recovery of benefits from compensation payments

If you are seeking compensation from someone (a defendant) through the courts (eg, because you have been unfairly dismissed or because you have had a personal injury), you might be awarded damages to compensate you for your loss. However, if, as the result of a defendant's action, you have had to claim benefit, the amount of damages awarded is reduced by the amount of benefit you received.

Employment cases

In an employment case such as wrongful or unfair dismissal, your claim for compensation for loss of earnings may be reduced by the amount of benefit (eg, jobseeker's allowance – JSA) you received.[127] Seek specialist employment law advice. Also, the DWP is able to recover payments of JSA, income support or income-related employment and support allowance from your employer by deductions from your compensation if it is an unfair dismissal or protective award case dealt with in an employment tribunal. In such cases, the DWP sends a 'recoupment notice' to the employer, and a copy to you, setting out the benefit to be deducted before the compensation is paid to you. You may give notice to the DWP that you do not accept the amount recouped within 21 days of the

Part 9: Claiming benefits and getting paid
Chapter 54: Getting paid
10. Recovery of benefits from compensation payments

recoupment notice (or longer if allowed), and can appeal to the First-tier Tribunal against the decision that the DWP makes in response.[128]

Personal injury cases

If you are paid compensation for an accident, injury or disease after 6 October 1997, those compensating you can reduce the amount paid to you when you have received benefit in respect of the same loss. They must then pay the money back to the Compensation Recovery Unit (CRU), which is part of the DWP. It does not matter whether the payment is voluntary, with or without legal proceedings, or by order of a court. A reduction is not made if the compensation is paid for pain and suffering, because benefits are not paid for this.

The CRU can only recover the benefit in the right-hand column of the table on p1193, and only if you were paid it as a consequence of the accident, injury or disease.

Note: the CRU can also recover, under a similar scheme with its own rules, certain lump-sum payments made by the DWP to you or a dependant.[129] The lump-sum payments that can be recovered are those made by the DWP for lung diseases under the Pneumoconiosis etc. (Workers' Compensation Act) 1979 (or as compensation if you have had a claim under that Act rejected) or payments under the Diffuse Mesothelioma Scheme.

Details of the procedures to be followed and other advice can be obtained from the CRU (see Appendix 1). A guide to the procedures, *Recovery of Benefits or Lump-sum Payments and NHS Charges*, is available at www.dwp.gov.uk/cru.

Which benefits can be recovered

The recoverable benefit consists of all benefits paid to you 'in consequence' of the injury or disease from which you have suffered during the 'relevant period'.

> #### The relevant period
> The '**relevant period**' is usually the period of five years from the date:[130]
> – of your accident or injury if you are claiming compensation for an accident or injury; *or*
> – you first claimed a recoverable benefit because of the disease if you are claiming compensation in respect of a disease.
> The relevant period ends if those compensating you make a final payment of compensation or an agreement is made under which compensation already paid is accepted as being in final payment.[131]

Before you are paid compensation, those compensating you must apply to the DWP for a 'certificate of recoverable benefits'.[132] This tells them which benefits are recoverable.

Those compensating you become liable to pay the DWP for the total amount of recoverable benefit 14 days after the certificate is issued.[133] It is the compensator's obligation, not yours, and so if the compensator fails to pay, the CRU cannot pursue you for the money. The compensator remains liable even if it fails to apply for a certificate.[134]

Offsetting against your compensation

Before the compensator pays your compensation, it can deduct the recoverable benefits paid during the relevant period from certain types of compensation.[135]

Compensation	Recoverable benefits
Loss of earnings	Disability working allowance, disablement benefit, employment and support allowance (ESA), incapacity benefit, income support, invalidity allowance, invalidity pension, jobseeker's allowance, reduced earnings allowance, severe disablement allowance, sickness benefit, statutory sick pay (paid before 6 April 1994), unemployment benefit, unemployability supplement, universal credit
Cost of care	Attendance allowance, disability living allowance care component, disablement benefit paid for constant attendance (see p679) or exceptionally severe disablement (see p679), personal independence payment (PIP) daily living component
Loss of mobility	Mobility allowance, disability living allowance mobility component, personal independence payment mobility component

Example
Gary receives a £30,000 compensation payment consisting of £15,000 for loss of earnings, £5,000 for pain and suffering, and £10,000 for the cost of care. By the time the award is made he has received £20,000 of ESA and £5,000 PIP daily living component. The award for loss of earnings is reduced to nil. Gary will receive the full award for pain and suffering, but his award for the cost of care is reduced by £5,000. The compensator is liable to pay the DWP recoverable benefits of £25,000, and pays Gary a net award of £10,000 (£5,000 pain and suffering plus £5,000 care).

Any compensation reduced by this method is treated as being paid to you. Those compensating you must give you a statement showing how the payment has been calculated, even if the recovery of benefits reduces a particular type of

Part 9: Claiming benefits and getting paid
Chapter 54: Getting paid
10. Recovery of benefits from compensation payments

compensation to nil. If the recoverable benefit exceeds the compensation paid to you for a particular loss, those compensating you still have to pay the balance to the DWP.

Exempt payments

The recovery rules apply to all claims, no matter how small. However, certain compensation payments are exempt.[136] These include:

- payments under the Fatal Accidents Act 1996, the Vaccine Damage Payments Act 1979 and the NHS industrial injury scheme;
- payments under the Pneumoconiosis Compensation Scheme and certain payments for loss of hearing;
- criminal injuries compensation;
- contractual sick pay and redundancy payments;
- payments from insurance companies from policies agreed before the accident; *and*
- payments from certain trusts – eg, the Macfarlane Trust, Eileen Trust, MFET Ltd, The Caxton Foundation, UK Asbestos Trust and the EL Scheme Trust.

Challenging a recovery decision

A decision maker may look at a certificate of recoverable benefit again if s/he is satisfied that it was issued in ignorance of, or based on a mistake about, a material fact, or if there was an error in its preparation – eg, a miscalculation.[137] You and those compensating you can both appeal against the certificate but not until the compensation payment has been made and the benefit paid back to the DWP.[138] Appeals are heard by the First-tier Tribunal (see p1303).[139] Further appeals can be made to the Upper Tribunal in the usual way (see p1329).[140]

Notes

1. Who is paid
1 **HB** Reg 94(2) HB Regs; reg 75(2) HB(SPC) Regs
CB/GA Regs 27 and 28 CB&GA(Admin) Regs
UC/PIP/JSA&ESA under UC Regs 57 and 58 UC,PIP,JSA&ESA(C&P) Regs
Other benefits Regs 30 and 33 SS(C&P) Regs
2 **CB/GA** Reg 34 CB&GA(Admin) Regs
UC/PIP/JSA&ESA under UC Reg 58 UC,PIP,JSA&ESA(C&P) Regs
Other benefits Reg 34(1) and (2) SS(C&P) Regs
3 Reg 35 SS(C&P) Regs; reg 60 UC,PIP,JSA&ESA(C&P) Regs

2. How and when you are paid
4 **CB/GA** Reg 16 CB&GA(Admin) Regs
UC/PIP/JSA&ESA under UC Reg 46 UC,PIP,JSA&ESA(C&P) Regs
Other benefits Reg 21 SS(C&P) Regs
5 **CB/GA** Regs 16-20 CB&GA(Admin) Regs
UC/PIP/JSA&ESA under UC Reg 51 UC,PIP,JSA&ESA(C&P) Regs
Other benefits Regs 22-26C SS (C&P) Regs
6 **HB** Reg 91 HB regs; reg 72 HB (SPC) Regs
CB/GA Reg 18 CB&GA(Admin) Regs
UC/PIP/JSA&ESA under UC Reg 45 UC,PIP,JSA&ESA(C&P) Regs
Other benefits Reg 20 SS(C&P) Regs
7 **CB/GA** Reg 25 CB&GA(Admin) Regs
UC/PIP/JSA&ESA under UC Reg 55 UC,PIP,JSA&ESA(C&P) Regs
Other benefits Reg 38(1)(bb) SS(C&P) Regs
CDLA/2609/2002 commented on the way a similar rule applied to payment by giro/order book.

3. Overlapping benefits
8 Reg 6 SS(OB) Regs
9 Reg 4(5) SS(OB) Regs
10 Reg 6 SS(OB) Regs
11 s52(2) SSCBA 1992
12 s16(1), (2) and (6) SSCBA 1992; reg 2 SS(MAP) Regs

13 Reg 4 (2)(f) and (4) SS(OB) Regs
14 Reg 4(3) SS(OB) Regs
15 Reg 10 SS(OB) Regs
16 Reg 8 SS(OB) Regs
17 Reg 7 SS(OB) Regs

4. Short-term advances
18 Reg 7 SS(PAB) Regs
19 Sch 2 para 20A SS&CS(DA) Regs
20 Reg 8 SS(PAB) Regs
21 Sch 2 para 20A SS&CS(DA) Regs allows a right of appeal against decisons on deductions under reg 10 SS(PAB) Regs
22 Reg 3, definition of 'benefit', SS(PAB) Regs
23 Reg 22 CB&GA(Admin) Regs
24 Regs 3 and 4 SS(PAOR) Regs

5. The benefit cap
25 ss96 and 97 WRA 2012
26 Under Sch 2 para 8AA SSA 1998 there is no right of appeal for UC, but at time of writing the relevant rule for HB appeals at Sch 7 para 6 CSPSSA 2000 had not been amended.
27 Regs 75C HB Regs; reg 80 UC Regs
28 Regs 75A, 75C and 75G HB Regs
29 Reg 75B HB Regs
30 Reg 79 UC Regs
31 Reg 20 UC(TP) Regs
32 Reg 75E HB Regs; HB Circular A15/2013
33 Reg 75E(3) HB Regs
34 Reg 75E(4) HB Regs
35 Reg 82(1) UC Regs
36 Reg 82(2) UC Regs
37 Reg 75D HB Regs
38 Reg 81 UC Regs

6. Change of circumstances after you claim

39 **JSA** Reg 24 JSA Regs
CB/GA Reg 23 CB&GA(Admin) Regs
UC/PIP/JSA&ESA under UC Reg 38 UC,PIP,JSA&ESA(C&P) Regs
Other benefits Reg 32 SS(C&P) Regs

40 **JSA** Reg 24(7) JSA Regs
UC/PIP/JSA&ESA under UC Reg 38(5) UC,PIP,JSA&ESA(C&P) Regs
Regs 2, 3 and 5 SS(NCC) Regs, which apply for fraud, allow notification by telephone (unless it is specifically required to be in writing).
Other benefits Reg 32(1B) SS(C&P) Regs

41 Reg 23(5) CB&GA(Admin) Regs

42 Reg 32ZZA SS(C&P) Regs; reg 24 JSA Regs
UC/PIP/JSA&ESA under UC Reg 39 UC, PIP, JSA&ESA (C&P) Regs

7. When payments can be suspended

43 **HB** Reg 11(2)(b) HB&CTB(DA) Regs
CB/GA Sch 7 para 13(2) CSPSSA 2000
UC/PIP/JSA&ESA under UC Reg 44(2)(b) and (c) UC,PIP,JSA&ESA(DA) Regs
Other benefits s21(2)(c) and (d) SSA 1998; reg 16(3)(b) SS&CS(DA) Regs

44 **HB** Reg 11(3) HB&CTB(DA) Regs
CB/GA Reg 18(4) and (5) CB&GA(DA) Regs
UC/PIP/JSA&ESA under UC Reg 44(5) UC,PIP,JSA&ESA(DA) Regs
Other benefits Reg 16(4) SS&CS(DA) Regs

45 **HB** Reg 12(1)(b) HB&CTB(DA) Regs
CB/GA Reg 21 CB&GA(DA) Regs
UC/PIP/JSA&ESA under UC Reg 46(c) UC,PIP,JSA&ESA(DA) Regs
Other benefits Reg 20(2) and (3) SS&CS(DA) Regs

46 **HB** Reg 86(1) HB Regs; reg 67(1) HB(SPC) Regs
CB/GA Reg 23 CB&GA(Admin) Regs
UC/PIP/JSA&ESA under UC Reg 38(2) UC,PIP,JSA&ESA(C&P) Regs; reg 45 UC,PIP,JSA&ESA(DA) Regs
Other benefits Reg 32(1) SS(C&P) Regs

47 **HB** Reg 13 HB&CTB(DA) Regs
CB/GA Reg 19 CB&GA(DA) Regs
UC/PIP/JSA&ESA under UC Reg 45(6) UC,PIP,JSA&ESA(DA) Regs
Other benefits Reg 17(2) SS&CS(DA) Regs

48 **HB** Reg 86(1) HB Regs; reg 67(1) HB(SPC) Regs
CB/GA Reg 23 CB&GA(Admin) Regs
UC/PIP/JSA&ESA under UC Reg 38(2) UC,PIP,JSA&ESA(C&P) Regs
Other benefits Reg 32(1) SS(C&P) Regs

49 **HB** Reg 13(4)(a) HB&CTB(DA) Regs
CB/GA Reg 19(2) CB&GA(DA) Regs
UC/PIP/JSA&ESA under UC Reg 45(4)(a) UC,PIP,JSA&ESA(DA) Regs
Other benefits Reg 17(4)(a) SS&CS(DA) Regs

50 **HB** Reg 13(4)(b) HB&CTB(DA) Regs
CB/GA Reg 19(2)(b) CB&GA(DA) Regs
UC/PIP/JSA&ESA under UC Reg 45(4)(b) UC,PIP,JSA&ESA(DA) Regs
Other benefits Reg 17(4)(b) SS&CS(DA) Regs

51 **HB** Reg 13(4) HB&CTB(DA) Regs
CB/GA Reg 19(5) CB&GA(DA) Regs
UC/PIP/JSA&ESA under UC Reg 45(6) UC,PIP,JSA&ESA(DA) Regs
Other benefits Reg 17(5) SS&CS(DA) Regs

52 s24 SSA 1998; reg 19(2) SS&CS(DA) Regs

53 **HB** Sch 7 para 13(2)(a) CSPSSA 2000
CB/GA Reg 18(2) CB&GA(DA) Regs
Other benefits ss21(2)(a) and (b), 22 and 24 SSA 1998

54 **HB** Reg 11(2)(a)(i) HB&CTB(DA) Regs
CB/GA Reg 18(2)(a) CB&GA(DA) Regs
UC/PIP/JSA&ESA under UC Reg 44(2)(a)(i) UC,PIP,JSA&ESA(DA) Regs
Other benefits Reg 16(3)(a)(i) SS&CS(DA) Regs

55 Reg 16(2) SS&CS(DA) Regs; reg 44(2) UC,PIP,JSA&ESA(C&P) Regs does not include this provision.

56 **HB** Reg 11(2)(a)(ii) HB&CTB(DA) Regs
CB/GA Reg 18(2)(b) CB&GA(DA) Regs
UC/PIP/JSA&ESA under UC Reg 44(2)(a)(ii) UC,PIP,JSA&ESA(DA) Regs
Other benefits Reg 16(3)(a)(ii) SS&CS(DA) Regs

57 **CB/GA** Reg 18(2)(c) CB&GA(DA) Regs
UC/PIP/JSA&ESA under UC Reg 44(2)(a)(iii) UC,PIP,JSA&ESA(DA) Regs
Other benefits Reg 16(3)(a)(iii) SS&CS(DA) Regs

58 **CB/GA** Reg 18(2)(d) CB&GA (DA) Regs
UC/PIP/JSA&ESA under UC Reg 44(2)(a)(iv) UC,PIP,JSA&ESA(DA) Regs
Other benefits Reg 16(3)(a)(iv) SS&CS(DA) Regs

59 Reg 18(e) CB&GA(DA)Regs

60 Reg 11(2)(c) HB&CTB(DA) Regs

106 **UC/PIP/JSA&ESA under UC** Sch 7
para 2 UC,PIP,JSA&ESA(C&P) Regs
Other benefits Sch 9 para 7A SS(C&P)
Regs; reg 28(3) CS(MASC) Regs;
107 Reg 28(1) and Sch 4 CS(MASC) Regs
108 s43 CSA 1991; Sch 9 paras 7A and 7B
SS(C&P) Regs
109 Schs 9 para 7B SS(C&P) Regs
110 **UC/PIP/JSA&ESA under UC** Sch 7
paras 1 and 2 UC,PIP,JSA&ESA(C&P)
Regs;
Other benefits Sch 9B para 2 SS(C&P)
Regs; Memo DMG/25/13; Memo ADM
08/13; Sch 1 para 4(l)(b) and (c) CSA
1991; reg 4(1) and (2) CS(MCSC) Regs
111 **UC/PIP/JSA&ESA under UC** Sch 7
para 2 UC,PIP,JSA&ESA(C&P) Regs
Other benefits Sch 9B para 2 SS(C&P)
Regs
112 **UC/PIP/JSA&ESA under UC** Sch 7
para 5 UC,PIP,JSA&ESA(C&P) Regs
Other benefits Sch 9B paras 4-6
SS(C&P) Regs
113 **UC/PIP/JSA&ESA under UC** Sch 7
para 3 UC,PIP,JSA&ESA(C&P) Regs
Other benefits Sch 9B para 3 SS (C&P)
Regs
114 Sch 9 para 7E SS(C&P) Regs
115 Reg 17 and Sch para 9 UC(TP) Regs
116 Sch 9 para 3(2A) SS(C&P) Regs
117 Sch 9 para 2(2) SS(C&P) Regs
118 Sch 9 para 8 SS(C&P) Regs
119 Sch 9 paras 5(5), 6(6), 7(8) and 8(2)
SS(C&P) Regs
120 Sch 6 para 3(1) and (2)
UC,PIP,JSA&ESA(C&P) Regs
121 Sch 6 para 3(3) UC,PIP,JSA&ESA(C&P)
Regs
122 Sch 6 para 4 UC,PIP,JSA&ESA(C&P)
Regs
123 Sch 9 para 9 SS(C&P) Regs
124 Reg 4 CC(DIS) Regs; reg 8 CT(DIS) Regs
125 Regs 15 and 16 SS(PAOR) Regs; reg 3
SF(RDB) Regs
126 Sch 6 para 5 UC,PIP,JSA&ESA(C&P)
Regs

**10. Recovery of benefits from
compensation payments**
127 *Nabi v British Leyland (UK) Ltd* [1980] 1
WLR 529 (CA)
128 The Employment Protection
(Recoupment of Jobseeker's Allowance
and Income Support) Regulations
1996, No.2349
129 The Social Security (Recovery of
Benefits) (Lump Sum Payments)
Regulations 2008, No.1596

130 s3 SS(RB)A 1997
131 s3(4) SS(RB)A 1997
132 s4 SS(RB)A 1997
133 s6(4) SS(RB)A 1997
134 s7 SS(RB)A 1997
135 s8 and Sch 2 SS(RB)A 1997
136 s1 and Sch 1 SS(RB)A 1997; reg 2 SS(RB)
Regs
137 s10 SS(RB)A 1997
138 s11 SS(RB)A 1997
139 s12 SS(RB)A 1997
140 s13 SS(RB)A 1997; reg 13 SS(RB)App
Regs

Chapter 55

* *

Hardship payments

This chapter covers:
1. Hardship payments of jobseeker's allowance (below)
2. Hardship payments of employment and support allowance (p1202)
3. Hardship payments of universal credit (p1203)
4. Deciding hardship (p1205)
5. Claiming hardship payments (p1209)
6. Challenging a hardship payment decision (p1209)
7. Tax, other benefits and the benefit cap (p1210)

Key facts

- Hardship payments are reduced-rate payments of jobseeker's allowance (JSA), employment and support allowance (ESA) and universal credit (UC) that are made in limited circumstances, including if you have been sanctioned.
- You or your partner or children must be experiencing hardship. In some cases for JSA, you must be in a 'vulnerable group'.
- You must apply for hardship payments and demonstrate on a regular basis that you are experiencing hardship.
- Hardship payments of JSA are currently not recoverable. Hardship payments of ESA are not recoverable. Hardship payments of UC are recoverable.

1. Hardship payments of jobseeker's allowance

You may be able to get hardship payments of income-based jobseeker's allowance (JSA) if your JSA is being paid at a reduced (or nil) rate. At the time this *Handbook* was written, hardship payments of JSA were not recoverable.[1] However, they may be recoverable in future. See CPAG's online service and *Welfare Rights Bulletin* for updates.

Note: if you come under the universal credit (UC) system (see p19), there are no JSA hardship payments. If you are sanctioned while getting JSA and experience hardship, you need to claim UC to get hardship payments of UC.

Part 9: Claiming benefits and getting paid
Chapter 55: Hardship payments
1. Hardship payments of jobseeker's allowance

When you can get hardship payments

You can qualify for hardship payments of income-based JSA in a number of situations (see below). You cannot qualify for hardship payments if you or your partner are entitled to income support (IS) or income-related employment and support allowance (ESA), or come within one of the groups of people who can claim IS (see Chapter 3).[2] In this case, you or your partner can claim IS or income-related ESA instead of hardship payments. If you or your partner are at least the qualifying age for pension credit (PC – see p78), you (or your partner) might qualify for PC instead of hardship payments.

If, after receiving hardship payments, you are awarded full income-based JSA, IS, income-related ESA or PC for the same period, the income-based JSA, IS, income-related ESA or PC is reduced by the amount of hardship payments you were paid.[3]

At the beginning of a claim

You qualify for hardship payments at the beginning of a claim for JSA if you are waiting for a decision about whether you (or if you are a member of a joint-claim couple, you or your partner) satisfy the 'jobseeking conditions' (see p1024).[4] If there is any other reason for the delay in deciding your claim, you are not eligible under this rule.

You normally cannot start receiving hardship payments until the 15th day after your date of claim, but if you are in a vulnerable group (see p1207), they start sooner.[5] You get hardship payments until the decision maker makes a decision on your claim, provided you (or if you are a member of a joint-claim couple, both of you) continue to satisfy the other conditions for getting income-based JSA.

The jobseeking conditions are not satisfied

If a decision maker decides that you (or if you are a member of a joint-claim couple, you or your partner) do not satisfy the 'jobseeking conditions' (see p1024), you only qualify for hardship payments if you are in a vulnerable group (see p1207).[6] This does not apply if you (or if you are a joint-claim couple, either of you) are treated as unavailable for work for one of the reasons listed on p1032.

You get hardship payments indefinitely from the day the decision maker decides that you do not satisfy the jobseeking conditions. You (or if you are a member of a joint-claim couple, both of you) must continue to satisfy the other conditions for getting income-based JSA.

Jobseeker's allowance is suspended

You can qualify for hardship payments if your JSA is suspended because there is doubt about whether you (or if you are a member of a joint-claim couple, you or your partner) are meeting the 'jobseeking conditions' (see p1024).[7]

If you are in a vulnerable group (see p1207), you get hardship payments from the date that the suspension begins.

If you are not in a vulnerable group, you cannot get hardship payments until the 15th day of the suspension.[8] If you are subject to successive 14-day suspensions (eg, at each signing day the employment officer doubts that you took sufficient steps to find work) and so never reach the 15th day of any suspension period, seek advice as this may be unlawful.

You get hardship payments until the decision maker makes a decision, provided you satisfy the other conditions for getting income-based JSA. If you are a member of a joint-claim couple, both of you must satisfy these conditions (or one of you if the other is in an exempt group – see p48). If the decision maker eventually decides that you do not satisfy the jobseeking conditions, you can only continue to get hardship payments if you are in a vulnerable group (see p1200).

Jobseeker's allowance is not paid because of a sanction

If you are sanctioned (see p1083), you can qualify for hardship payments.[9]

If you are in a vulnerable group (see p1207), you get hardship payments from the first day of the period when JSA is not paid. If you are not in a vulnerable group, you cannot get hardship payments until the 15th day of the period. The DWP says that if during a sanction period another sanction is imposed for a different reason, you cannot get hardship payments for the first 14 days of the period of the new sanction.[10] If this happens, you should appeal. **Note:** you are likely to have to ask for a revision before you can appeal.

Hardship payments continue until the end of the period provided:
- if you are a single person or a member of a couple (but not a joint-claim couple), you satisfy the other conditions for getting income-based JSA; *or*
- if you are a member of a joint-claim couple, you both satisfy the other conditions for getting income-based JSA, or one of you does and the other is in an exempt group (see p48).

The rules about your age

You cannot usually qualify for hardship payments until you are 18. However, if you are 16 or 17, you can qualify if you come into any of the categories of 16/17-year-olds who can qualify for income-based JSA (see p888). If you have been sanctioned, you do not need to claim hardship payments because you continue to get income-based JSA, although at a reduced rate (see p899).

The amount of hardship payments

The weekly amount of hardship payments you get depends on your needs. Your personal allowance, premiums and housing costs are calculated as for income-based JSA. The usual disregards for capital and income are applied when calculating your hardship payments. However, your applicable amount is normally reduced by 40 per cent of:[11]

Part 9: Claiming benefits and getting paid
Chapter 55: Hardship payments
2. Hardship payments of employment and support allowance

- if you are not a member of a couple, the appropriate personal allowance for a single person of your age;
- if you are a member of a couple (other than a joint-claim couple), the appropriate personal allowance for a single person:
  - aged under 25, if both of you are aged 16 or 17, or if one of you is between 18 and 25 years old and the other is a 16/17-year-old who would not be eligible for income-based JSA in her/his own right;
  - aged 25 or over in all other cases, provided one of you is 18 or over;
- if you are a joint-claim couple, the appropriate personal allowance for a single person aged 25 or over.

The reduction is only 20 per cent if you or your partner, or a child included in your claim (see p210) is pregnant or 'seriously ill' (not defined).

Consider whether there are other benefits or tax credits you (or your partner) could claim. Also check whether you qualify for any passported benefits (see p63).

2. Hardship payments of employment and support allowance

You may be able to get hardship payments of income-related employment and support allowance (ESA) if your ESA is being paid at a reduced (or nil) rate because you have been sanctioned, or under the loss of benefit for benefit offences rules. Hardship payments of ESA are not recoverable.

Note:
- If you come under the universal credit (UC) system (see p19), there are no ESA hardship payments. If you are sanctioned while getting ESA and experience hardship, you need to claim UC to get hardship payments of UC.
- Different hardship rules apply if you would be disqualified from receiving ESA (eg, because you have limited capability for work through your own misconduct, or you have failed to accept treatment without 'good cause') (see p617).

When you can get hardship payments

You can qualify for hardship payments of income-related ESA if:[12]
- your ESA is being paid at a reduced (or nil) rate:
  - because you have been sanctioned for failing to take part in a work-focused interview (see p1057), or for failing to undertake work-related activity (see p1061); or
  - under the loss of benefit for benefit offences rules (see p1260); and

• you, your partner or a child or qualifying young person for whom you or your partner are responsible (see p212) would experience hardship if payments were not made.

You must satisfy the rules for entitlement to income-related ESA (see Chapter 5).

The amount of hardship payments

The weekly amount of hardship payments you get is 60 per cent of the ESA personal allowance that applies for a single person whose ESA includes a work-related activity component or a support component (ie, the personal allowance for main phase ESA), rounded to the nearest five pence.[13] This is currently 60 per cent of £72.40 = £43.45 a week. This is paid in addition to any amounts of ESA you can be paid, despite the reduction for the sanction – eg, a component (if you qualify), as well as premiums and housing costs, if relevant.

3. Hardship payments of universal credit

You may be able to get hardship payments of universal credit (UC) if your UC is being paid at a reduced (or nil) rate because you have been sanctioned or under the loss of benefit for benefit offences rules. Hardship payments of UC are recoverable (see p1205).

Note: if you come under the UC system (see p19) and your jobseeker's allowance (JSA) or employment and support allowance (ESA) is paid at a reduced (or nil) rate and you experience hardship, you need to claim UC and apply for hardship payments of UC.

When you can get hardship payments

If you (or your partner) are **sanctioned**, you can qualify for hardship payments of UC if:[14]

• you are 18 or over and are given a sanction (or your partner is 18 or over and has been given a sanction) and, as a result, your UC has been paid at a reduced (or nil) rate using the 'high rate' daily reduction (see p1117); *and*

• if you (or if you are a joint claimant, your partner) were given a low level sanction, you (or your partner, or both of you if both of you have been sanctioned) have complied with any condition specified by the DWP – eg, you have now taken part in a work-focused interview or have agreed to attend training. In this case, you can only get hardship payments for the fixed part of your sanction period; *and*

• you (or your partner) apply for hardship payments in the approved manner, or in a way that the DWP accepts is sufficient, and provide any information or evidence required by the DWP; *and*

Part 9: Claiming benefits and getting paid
Chapter 55: Hardship payments
3. Hardship payments of universal credit

- you (and your partner) accept that the hardship payments are recoverable; *and*
- the DWP is satisfied that:
  - you (and your partner) have met all the work-related requirements that were imposed on you in the seven days before you applied for hardship payments; *and*
  - you (and your partner) are experiencing hardship.

Note: if you are aged 16 or 17, or your partner is sanctioned and s/he is 16 or 17, you cannot qualify for hardship payments. This is because, while you are sanctioned, your UC continues to be paid, although at a reduced rate (see p1117).

If your UC has been **reduced because of a benefit offence** (see p1260), you can qualify for hardship payments of UC if:[15]

- you (and your partner) meet all the conditions of entitlement to UC; *and*
- you (or your partner) apply for hardship payments in the approved manner, or in a way that the DWP accepts is sufficient, and provide any information or evidence required by the DWP; *and*
- you (and your partner) accept that the hardship payments are recoverable; *and*
- the DWP is satisfied that you (and your partner) are experiencing hardship.

Note: you can qualify under these rules even if you (or your partner) are aged 16 or 17.

The amount and period of hardship payments

Each hardship payment is made for the period starting on the date you satisfy all the conditions for getting one (for sanctions) or the date of your application (for benefit offences) and ending on the day before your next normal UC payday.[16] If the period is seven days or less, a hardship payment is made until the end of the next assessment period, or if sooner, the last day in respect of which your UC is paid at a reduced (or nil) rate. This means you must apply for a hardship payment for each assessment period you need one.

The amount of hardship payments is worked out as follows.[17]

- **Step one:** determine the amount of the reduction made from your UC for the sanction (see p1117) or the benefit offence (see p1260) in the assessment period before the one in which you apply for hardship payments.
- **Step two:** multiply the amount in Step one by 12 and divide by 365. Take 60 per cent of this amount, rounding to the nearest penny.
- **Step three:** multiply the amount in Step two by the number of days for which hardship payments can be made to you.

Example
Dan is a single claimant aged 40. He was given a 91-day medium level sanction. His UC was reduced for 30 days in the previous assessment period. He applies for hardship payments four days into the current (31-day) assessment period.

Step one: the relevant amount is £309 (£10.30 daily reduction x 30 days).

Step two: £309 x 12 ÷ 365 = £10.16. 60% × £10.16 = £6.10

Step three: the number of days for which Dan can be paid hardship payments during his current assessment period is 27 days (31– 4).

£6.10 x 27 = £164.70

Dan's hardship payments for that assessment period = £164.70. He gets these in addition to any UC he can be paid – eg, if he qualifies for a housing costs element.

If Dan is still experiencing hardship, he can apply for hardship payments on the day he receives his next payment of UC to ensure he gets hardship payments for each day in the previous assessment period.

Recovery of hardship payments

Hardship payments of UC are usually recoverable.[18] However, hardship payments:
- are *not* recoverable during any assessment period in which you (and your partner, if you are a joint claimant) are someone who does not have to meet any work-related requirements because your earnings are the same as or above your earnings threshold (see p1076); *and*
- *stop* being recoverable if, since the last day on which your UC was paid at a reduced (or nil) rate , you have earned at least the amount of your individual earnings threshold (see p1076) (or, if you are a joint claimant, your and your partner's combined individual earnings thresholds) for a period of at least 26 weeks, or for more than one period that totals at least 26 weeks.

Hardship payments can normally only be recovered from the person to whom they were paid. However, if you are a joint claimant, an amount paid to your partner is treated as paid to you, and vice versa.[19]

The same methods of recovery for overpayments on p1230 can be used to recover hardship payments.[20]

4. Deciding hardship

'Hardship' is not defined in the rules. The DWP says that it means 'severe suffering or privation' (meaning 'a lack of the necessities of life').[21]

When you apply for hardship payments, ensure you explain anything that is causing you hardship, or which makes it more likely that you will experience hardship. This includes health, disability, pregnancy, and any special needs you and your partner and children have.

When deciding whether or not you are experiencing hardship, there are things the decision maker must consider. For jobseeker's allowance (JSA) see p1206, for employment and support allowance (ESA) see p1208 and for universal credit (UC) see p1208.

In all cases, the decision maker looks at the resources that are available to you.

Do you have available resources?

1. The decision maker normally takes into account income and capital that is disregarded when calculating your benefit – eg, disability living allowance (DLA) and savings below £6,000 (see p343).

2. You should only be treated as having resources that are likely to be actually available to you. For example, you may have savings in a bank account but they are subject to a notice period for withdrawal and so you may face hardship until you get access to your capital.

3. You should not be treated as having resources if these are only available on credit, or you would have to sell any of your possessions.

If your claim is refused, consider applying for a revision or appealing (see Chapters 58 and 59). **Note:** you are likely to have to apply for a revision before you can appeal (see p1305).

Jobseeker's allowance

For JSA, even if you come within one of the situations when hardship payments can be made, you cannot get them unless the decision maker is satisfied that you are in a vulnerable group or that you or your partner would experience hardship if payments were not made.[22] Hardship payments can be made sooner if you are in a vulnerable group. In some situations, you can only get hardship payments if you are in a vulnerable group.

When deciding whether or not you would experience hardship, the decision maker must consider:[23]

- whether you or your partner, or a child included in your claim (see p210), qualify for a disability premium or the disabled child or severely disabled child element of child tax credit (CTC);
- the resources likely to be available to you or your partner, or a child included in your claim (see p210), if no hardship payments are made, how far these fall short of your reduced applicable amount and the length of time this is likely to be the case. Also included are any resources that may be available from others in your household (eg, your parents). The decision maker cannot take into account any CTC or child benefit paid to you or your partner for a child (see p210) or who is a member of your household (see p215).[24] See above for what might be taken into account;
- whether there is a 'substantial risk' that you or your partner, or a child included in your claim (see p210), would be without essential items (eg, food, clothes, heating or accommodation) or whether they would be available at considerably reduced levels and, if so, for how long.

Vulnerable groups

You are in a vulnerable group if:[25]

- you or your partner are **pregnant** and would experience hardship if no payment were made;
- you or your partner are **responsible for a child under 16 or a qualifying young person** who would experience hardship if no payment were made. See p212 for when you count as responsible for a child or young person. **Note:** if you are a lone parent and are responsible for a child under five, or you are a lone parent under 18, you can claim IS and cannot claim hardship payments;
- your income-based JSA includes a **disability premium** or would include one if your claim were to succeed and the person for whom the premium is paid would experience hardship if no payment were made;
- you or your partner have a **chronic medical condition** and as a result your (or your partner's) functional capacity is 'limited or restricted by physical impairment', and the decision maker is satisfied that:
  - it has lasted or is likely to last for at least 26 weeks; *and*
  - if no payment were made, the health of the person with the condition will decline further than that of a 'normal healthy adult' within the next two weeks and the person would experience hardship;
- you or your partner:
  - are **caring for someone** who:
    - is getting attendance allowance (AA), the highest or middle rate of the care component of DLA, either rate of the daily living component of personal independence payment (PIP) or armed forces independence payment. If the person has claimed one of these benefits, you count as being in a vulnerable group for up to 26 weeks from the date of the claim or until the claim is decided, whichever is first; *or*
    - has been awarded AA, the highest or middle rate of DLA care component, the daily living component of PIP or armed forces independence payment but it is not yet in payment; *and*
  - would not be able to continue caring if no hardship payment were made. You do not have to show that the person you are caring for would experience hardship.
  The care must be provided for a considerable portion of each week.
  This rule does not apply if the person who is being cared for is in a care home, an Abbeyfield Home or an independent hospital;[26]
- you or your partner are a **16/17-year-old** who can claim income-based JSA (see p888) and would experience hardship if no payment were made (or if you are a joint-claim couple, you both would experience hardship);
- you or your partner are a 16/17-year-old claiming JSA on the basis of a **severe hardship direction** (see p892). You do not have to show that you would experience hardship. However, you do not count as being in a vulnerable

group if the person subject to the direction does not satisfy the jobseeking conditions; *or*

- you (or if you are a joint-claim couple, at least one of you) are under 21 at the date of your hardship statement and within the last three years were **being looked after by the local authority** under the Children Act 1989, were someone the local authority had a duty to keep in touch with under that Act, or you qualified for advice and assistance from the local authority under that Act. Remember that if you are 16 or 17 and were being looked after by a local authority when you reached 16, you usually cannot claim income-based JSA. Instead, your local authority should support and accommodate you. See p886 for further information and exceptions to the rule.

Employment and support allowance

For ESA, when deciding whether or not you would experience hardship, the decision maker must consider:[27]

- whether you or your partner, or a child included in your claim (see p210) qualify for a severe disability premium or an enhanced disability premium, or the disabled child or severely disabled child element of CTC;
- the resources likely to be available to your household (see p215) if no hardship payments are made, and how far these fall short of the amount of hardship payments to which you would be entitled. Also included are any resources that may be available from people who are not members of your household. For ESA sanctions, the decision maker cannot take into account any CTC or child benefit paid to you or your partner for a child who is included in your claim (see p210) or who is a member of your household (see p215).[28] See p1206 for information about what might be taken into account;
- whether there is a 'substantial risk' that you or your household (see p215) would be without essential items (eg, food, clothes, heating or accommodation) or whether they would be available at considerably reduced levels.

The decision maker must also consider the length of time any of the factors above are likely to continue.[29]

Universal credit

The decision maker only considers you to be in hardship if:[30]

- because your UC has been reduced as a result of a sanction (see p1115), or under the loss of benefit for benefit offences rules (see p1256), you (and your partner) cannot meet your immediate and most basic and essential needs, or those of a child or qualifying young person for whom you (or your partner) are responsible. '**Needs**' means accommodation, heating, food and hygiene – eg, products to keep you and your home clean, or nappies for your baby; *and*

- you (and your partner) have made every effort to get alternative sources of support to meet (or partly meet) the needs (eg, from a charity) and to cease to incur any expenditure not relating to basic and essential needs. The DWP says that this should not include expenditure on things you need to help you look for work, such as a telephone and access to the internet, or to maintain your child(ren)'s access to education.

See p1206 for information about what resources might be taken into account.

5. Claiming hardship payments

You must apply for hardship payments in the approved manner, or in such other form as the DWP accepts is sufficient. You must provide information and evidence if required.[31] For jobseeker's allowance (JSA), the DWP calls this a 'hardship statement'.

Although you cannot receive JSA or employment and support allowance (ESA) hardship payments until you have made your application, there is no general rule to prevent you from receiving these for a period before the date on which you made it. A special rule applies if you qualify for hardship payments because you are waiting for a decision at the beginning of your JSA claim (see p1200).

The likelihood of being able to convince the decision maker that you are experiencing hardship increases over time. You should apply for hardship payments at any time you are without the normal payment of JSA, ESA or universal credit (UC). Note, however, that for UC, because of the way the amount of your hardship payments are calculated (see p1204), if you apply for hardship payments in the first assessment period in which you are sanctioned (ie, before you have actually been paid UC at a reduced rate), you cannot qualify for hardship payments.

Note: for JSA, while you are receiving hardship payments, you (or if you are a joint-claim couple, one of you) normally must make a 'hardship declaration' at the Jobcentre Plus office each time you sign on, to confirm that you are still in hardship.[32]

6. Challenging a hardship payment decision

If you are refused hardship payments, you can appeal to the First-tier Tribunal (see Chapter 59). You are likely to have to apply for a revision before you can appeal. To help you challenge the decision, ask for a written statement of reasons for the decision if this has not already been provided (see p1156).

Part 9: Claiming benefits and getting paid
Chapter 55: Hardship payments
7. Tax, other benefits and the benefit cap

Remember to tell the DWP if your circumstances worsen while you are seeking a revision or appealing. Ask it to consider whether hardship payments can now be paid based on your new circumstances.

7. **Tax, other benefits and the benefit cap**

Hardship payments of jobseeker's allowance (JSA) are taxable in the same way as income-based JSA (see p61). Hardship payments of employment and support allowance (ESA) and universal credit (UC) are not taxable.

Claiming other benefits or tax credits

If you have a partner, consider whether s/he could claim income support, income-based JSA, income-related ESA or pension credit instead of you. If so, continue to claim JSA or ESA hardship payments until her/his claim has been decided (to cover the period while the claim is being processed). However, let the DWP know that this is what you are doing so that there is no overpayment. If your partner's claim for benefit is accepted, your entitlement to hardship payments ends. You may wish to claim national insurance (NI) credits (see p851), although for JSA you cannot be awarded NI credits for any week in which the only income-based JSA you are paid comprises hardship payments.[33]

If your partner counts as being in full-time paid work for working tax credit (WTC) purposes (see p165), check if you might be better off claiming WTC.

Passported benefits

JSA (and ESA and UC) hardship payments are a type of income-based JSA (or of income-related ESA or of UC) and you are still entitled to full housing benefit (HB) and other passported benefits in the usual way. You may also be entitled to a council tax reduction from your local authority (see p827). **Note:** if you are entitled to UC, you can only qualify for HB if this is for 'exempt accommodation'.

Notes

1. **Hardship payments of jobseeker's allowance**
   1 s19C(2)(f) JSA 1995 (not yet in force); s71ZH(1)(b)-(d) SSAA 1992
   2 Regs 140(3) and 146A(3) JSA Regs
   3 Regs 146 and 146H JSA Regs; reg 5(2) Case 1 SS(PAOR) Regs
   4 Regs 141(2), 142(2), 146C(2) and 146D(2) JSA Regs
   5 Regs 141(3), 142(2), 146C(3) and 146D(2) JSA Regs
   6 Regs 141(4) and 146C(4) JSA Regs
   7 Regs 141(5), 142(3), 146C(5) and 146D(3) JSA Regs
   8 Regs 142(4), and 146D(4) JSA Regs
   9 Regs 141(6), 142(5), 146C(6) and 146D(5) JSA Regs
   10 para 35304 DMG
   11 Regs 145 and 146G JSA Regs

2. **Hardship payments of employment and support allowance**
   12 Regs 2(1), definition of 'hardship payment', 64A(a)-(c) and 64B ESA Regs; reg 16A(1) SS(LB) Regs
   13 Reg 64D ESA Regs; reg 16C SS(LB) Regs

3. **Hardship payments of universal credit**
   14 Reg 116(1)(a), (b) and (e)-(g) UC Regs
   15 Reg 16D(1) and (2)(a) and 16E(c) SS(LB) Regs
   16 Reg 117 UC Regs; reg 16F SS(LB) Regs
   17 Regs 6 and 118 UC Regs; reg 16G SS(LB) Regs
   18 s71ZH(1)(a) SSAA 1992; s28(2)(f) WRA 2012; reg 119 UC Regs; reg 16H SS(LB) Regs
   19 s71ZH(4) SSAA 1992
   20 s71ZH(5) SSAA 1992

4. **Deciding hardship**
   21 para 35155 DMG
   22 Regs 140(1) and (2) and 146A(1) and (2) JSA Regs
   23 Regs 140(5) and 146A(6) JSA Regs
   24 Reg 140(6) JSA Regs
   25 Regs 140(1) and 146A(1) JSA Regs
   26 Regs 140(4) and 146A(4) JSA Regs
   27 Reg 64C ESA Regs; reg 16A(2) SS(LB) Regs

   28 Reg 64C(2) ESA Regs
   29 Reg 64C(1)(e) ESA Regs; reg 16A(2)(e) SS(LB) Regs
   30 Reg 116(2) and (3) UC Regs; reg 16D(2)(b)-(d) and (3) SS(LB) Regs; Chapter L1 ADM

5. **Claiming hardship payments**
   31 **JSA** Regs 143 and 146E JSA Regs
   ESA Reg 64A(d) and (e) ESA Regs; reg 16B SS(LB) Regs
   UC Reg 116(1)(c) and (d) UC Regs; reg 16E(a) and (b) SS(LB) Regs
   32 Regs 144 and 146F JSA Regs

7. **Tax, other benefits and the benefit cap**
   33 Reg 8A(5)(d) and (dd) SS(CR) Regs

Chapter 56

· ·

Overpayments

This chapter covers :

For overpayments of tax credits, see Chapter 66.

References in this chapter to HM Revenue and Customs apply to overpayments of child benefit and guardian's allowance.

Key facts

- If you are paid more benefit than you are entitled to, this is called an overpayment.
- There are some situations when overpaid benefit must be repaid, regardless of how it was caused.
- In other situations, except for housing benefit (HB), the general rule is that you must repay the overpayment if it arose because you did not disclose something or you misrepresented something, regardless of whether this was your fault.
- All overpayments of HB are recoverable, except those caused by official error and which you could not have reasonably known were overpayments.
- The DWP, HM Revenue and Customs and local authorities have the discretion not to recover an overpayment in certain situations.

1. Introduction

An 'overpayment' occurs when you are paid more benefit than you should have been paid. If you are told that you must repay an overpayment, you should do the following.

- Use the relevant chapter in this *Handbook* to check whether or not you were entitled to some or all of the amount that the DWP, HM Revenue and Customs or local authority says is an overpayment.

- If some or all of the amount should not have been paid, check whether:
  - the overpayment is one that is always recoverable (see below);
  - the overpayment is one which is sometimes recoverable. If so, check whether all of the three conditions that allow the overpayment to be recovered are met (see p1218, p1219 and p1223), and also whether the overpayment can be reduced under the rules described on p1224;
  - any HB has been overpaid. If so, check whether this was caused by official error and whether or not the overpayment is recoverable (see p1233). If so, check whether it can be recovered from you (p1236) and whether any amount can be offset against the sum claimed (see p1237).
- If you are not the person whose benefit was overpaid, check whether the overpayment can be recovered from you (see p1225 and p1236).
- Consider whether it is worth asking for the overpayment not to be recovered. For overpayments of HB, see p1238, and for other benefits, see p1227.
- If an overpayment is being recovered, check that the method of recovery used is correct and whether you should ask for the money to be recovered in a different way. For overpayments of HB, see p1238, and for other benefits, see p1227.

Note: for benefits other than HB, if you are overpaid and this was because you made an incorrect statement or failed to provide information, you may also have to pay a penalty (p1249). This applies regardless of whether the overpayment is one where it must be shown that it was caused by a failure to disclose or a misrepresentation (see p1217) in order to recover it. If it is considered that an overpayment was made because of fraud, in addition to the overpayment being recovered, you may be prosecuted or given the option of paying a penalty instead of going to court. See Chapter 57 for further information.

2. Overpayments that are always recoverable

Except for overpayments of housing benefit (HB – see p1232), the following overpayments are always recoverable.

- You have been paid too much income support (IS), income-based jobseeker's allowance (JSA), income-related employment and support allowance (ESA) or pension credit (PC) because other income due to you was paid late (see p1214).
- Too much mortgage interest has been paid directly to your lender (see p1214).
- Too much benefit has been paid into your bank account by mistake (see p1215).
- You come under the universal credit (UC) system (see p19) and you have been paid too much UC, contribution-based JSA or contributory ESA (see p1215).

Part 9: Claiming benefits and getting paid
Chapter 56: Overpayments
2. Overpayments that are always recoverable

Although the above overpayments are always recoverable, you may still be able to argue that you were entitled to some or all of the amount or that some or all of the overpayment does not fall into one of the above categories. The decision maker in the DWP, HM Revenue and Customs (HMRC) or local authority also has the discretion not to recover in certain circumstances (see p1227).

You receive other income late

You may receive too much IS, income-based JSA, income-related ESA or PC because money owing to you does not arrive on time. When you get your arrears, you must repay the IS, income-based JSA, income-related ESA or PC that you would not have been entitled to had the other income been paid on time.[1] This is to prevent a duplication of payment.

This applies to any income that affects the amount of IS, income-based JSA, income-related ESA or PC, including:[2]

* earnings;
* other social security benefits. **Note:** arrears of some benefits are treated as capital and ignored for 52 weeks (see Chapters 17 and 18);
* benefits paid by other European Economic Area member states.[3]

Note: you can appeal about whether an overpayment has occurred and how it has been calculated.[4] In most cases you must apply for a revision before you can appeal (see p1305). You cannot appeal against the decision to recover any overpayment that has occurred, but you can ask the DWP to exercise its discretion not to recover it (see p1227).

See p1226 for how the overpayment can be recovered.

Too much mortgage interest has been paid to your lender

If you are getting help with your housing costs in your IS, income-based JSA, income-related ESA or PC (see Chapter 21), your mortgage interest is usually paid directly to your lender. Any overpayment of mortgage interest paid must be returned to the DWP by your lender if it arose because:[5]

* you ceased to be entitled to IS, income-based JSA, income-related ESA or PC and the DWP asks for repayment within four weeks of your entitlement ceasing; *or*
* the DWP did not reduce your mortgage interest payments, even though you were entitled to less money because there was a reduction in the amount of your outstanding loan, the standard interest rate (see p446) or your actual mortgage interest rate. If you have a deferred interest mortgage, the relevant interest rate is the one you are liable to pay, not the one charged by your lender. If the DWP pays the latter rate by mistake, any resulting overpayment cannot be recovered.[6]

In this case, your mortgage account should simply be corrected. However, if you come off IS, income-based JSA, income-related ESA or PC and the interest is recovered, your account will be in arrears unless you have started to make payments yourself.

In practice, the DWP often stops paying your lender your ongoing mortgage interest until it has recovered the overpayment, rather than asking it to return what was overpaid. The DWP should not do this if you are put into arrears as a result.[7] If you go into arrears, seek advice immediately to avoid losing your home.

You can appeal to the First-tier Tribunal (see p1304) if, for example, you dispute the amount being recovered.[8] Usually, you must apply for a revision first (see p1305). You can ask the DWP to use its discretion not to ask your lender to repay the overpayment.

Note: if your mortgage interest has been overpaid, but not in the circumstances described above that make it automatically recoverable, the DWP may also be able to recover it under the rules described on p1217.[9]

Too much benefit has been credited to your account

Your benefit may be paid by direct credit transfer into a bank or building society account. If you are credited with too much money because of the direct credit transfer system itself, the excess can be recovered in certain circumstances.[10]

The overpayment can only be recovered if it was caused by the direct credit transfer system and:[11]
- you were notified in writing before you agreed to your benefit being paid into a bank or other account that any excess benefit could be recovered; *and*
- it has been certified that you were paid excess benefit because of the direct credit transfer system.

If the excess benefit cannot be recovered under the rules described above, it might still be recoverable under the rules described on p1217, or those for recovery following late payment of income (see p1214).

You can appeal to the First-tier Tribunal against a decision to recover excess benefit credited to your bank or other account.[12]

Even if the overpayment is recoverable, you can ask the DWP or HMRC to use its discretion not to recover it (see p1227).

Overpayments of universal credit, contribution-based jobseeker's allowance and contributory employment and support allowance if you come under the universal credit system

If you come under the UC system (see p19) and you are overpaid UC, contribution-based JSA or contributory ESA , any amount of overpaid benefit can be recovered,

Part 9: Claiming benefits and getting paid
Chapter 56: Overpayments
2. Overpayments that are always recoverable

regardless of the cause of the overpayment.[13] See p1226 for how the overpayment can be recovered.

Note:

- If you are overpaid, the amount that is recovered can be reduced (see below).
- Generally, a decision cannot be made that your benefit is recoverable unless the decision(s) awarding you too much benefit has been changed (see p1218).[14]
- The overpayment can usually be recovered from the person to whom it is paid, but see p1217 for more details.
- You can challenge a decision that you have been overpaid by applying for a revision and, if this is refused, by appealing (see p1304).
- You can ask the DWP to exercise its discretion not to recover the overpayment (see p1227).

The amount recovered

The amount recovered is the difference between what you received and the amount to which you were entitled after the decisions awarding you benefit have been changed.[15] However, this amount can be reduced in the following circumstances.

Offsetting universal credit

If you were overpaid JSA or ESA, the amount of the overpayment that can be recovered may be reduced by the amount of any UC you could have received. For this to happen, you must have made a claim for UC. The overpaid amount is reduced by the amount of UC you would have got had:[16]

- you notified any change of circumstances that affected your JSA/ESA entitlement (other than a change of dwelling) to the DWP at the time it occurred; *or*
- you not misrepresented or failed to disclose something before the award of JSA/ESA; *or*
- a mistake by the decision maker not occurred.

You are overpaid universal credit because of a mistake about your capital

If you are overpaid UC because of a mistake about your savings for a period of more than three months, the amount that can be recovered is reduced to take into account the fact that you would have been spending your capital had you not been receiving UC.

At the end of each period of three months for which you have been overpaid, the amount of capital you are regarded as having is reduced by the amount of UC that you were overpaid in these three months.[17] The overpayment for the next three months is then calculated as if you had this reduced amount of capital.

You are overpaid because you moved home

If you are overpaid the housing element of UC because you have moved home but payments continue being made for your previous home, the decision maker may reduce the amount to be recovered by an amount equal to what you would have received in respect of your new home.[18]

S/he can only do this if the payments for your previous home are made to the same person as payments for your new home.[19] If the decision maker reduces the amount to be recovered in this way, the reduction in the overpaid amount is treated as if it were paid in respect of your new home.[20]

From whom can an overpayment be recovered

If you come under the UC suystem, an overpayment of UC, contribution-based JSA or contributory ESA is usually recoverable from the person to whom it was paid. However, it can be recovered from someone else in the following circumstances.[21]

- If the overpaid amount was paid to an appointee or to someone other than you because it was not in your interests to pay you directly (see p1162), the overpayment can also be recovered from you, the claimant.
- If an overpaid amount was paid to a third party under the rules about deductions and payments to third parties (see p1178), the amount is recoverable from you, the claimant. However, amounts paid to the third party in excess of the amounts allowed by those rules are only recoverable from the third party.
- If the overpaid amount includes an amount for housing costs paid to another person (eg, your landlord) and:
  - the overpayment occurred because someone failed to disclose or misrepresented a material fact (see p1219 and p1223), it is recoverable from that person, not the person to whom it was paid;
  - the overpayment occurred because you moved home, it is recoverable from you as well as from the person to whom it was paid;
  - the overpayment did not occur for either of the above two reasons, it is recoverable from you, the claimant, not the person to whom it was paid.

3. Overpayments that are sometimes recoverable

This section applies to all overpayments of benefit except:
- those described on p1213;
- overpayments of housing benefit (see p1232).

Some overpayments can only be recovered if all the following conditions are met.[22]
- The decision awarding you benefit has been changed (see p1218).

Part 9: Claiming benefits and getting paid
Chapter 56: Overpayments
3. Overpayments that are sometimes recoverable

- You either did not disclose, or you misrepresented, a relevant material fact (see p1219).
- The overpayment was caused by your failure to disclose, or your misrepresentation of, that fact (see p1219).

If you have been overpaid and all the above conditions do not apply to the whole of the overpayment, only that part of the overpayment to which all the above conditions apply is recoverable from you. For example, if you were paid too much benefit over a two-year period, but you made a full disclosure of the relevant fact after the first year, the overpayment made after that disclosure was not caused by your failure to disclose and is, therefore, not recoverable from you.

Example

Seamus was receiving income support as a carer. The person he was caring for stopped getting disability living allowance in 2008. Seamus informed the DWP of this in 2009, but the DWP continued to pay Seamus his income support until 2012. This overpayment from 2009 is not recoverable.

Note:
- The DWP has sometimes claimed that it can recover overpayments outside these rules (ie, even when all the above conditions are not met) under 'common law', but it is not allowed to do so (see p1230).
- Even if an overpayment can be recovered, in some situations amounts must be deducted from the recoverable sum (see p1224).
- This type of overpayment can sometimes be recovered from you, even if you are not the claimant (see p1225).
- You can appeal against a decision that the overpayment is recoverable from you (see p1226). Usually, you must apply for a revision first (see p1305).
- Even if an overpayment is recoverable under these rules, you can ask the DWP or HM Revenue and Customs (HMRC) to use its discretion not to recover it (see p1227).

The decision awarding you benefit has been changed

Once you have been awarded benefit, if the decision is then considered to be incorrect, it must be changed before any overpayment is recoverable. If the decision is not changed, any overpayment is not recoverable.[23] The only exception to this rule is when the circumstances of the overpayment mean that no decision needs to be revised in order for an overpayment to exist.[24] This would be the case if you were actually paid more than the amount which the original decision awarded to you.

During the period when you were overpaid, there may have been more than one decision awarding you benefit or setting the amount of benefit to which you are entitled. Unless *all* these decisions are changed, *all* of the overpayment cannot be recovered.[25] The new decision should state the new amount payable (if any).[26]

A decision to change your benefit award should have been made by a decision maker, who can change a decision by carrying out a revision or a supersession (see p1270 and p1281).

There are therefore two decisions: one changing a previous decision about your benefit, and one that the overpayment is recoverable. Unless both decisions are made and notified to you, it is not possible to recover the overpayment from you.[27] **Note:** notification of both decisions might be included in one decision letter, but it must be clear that both have been made – eg, the letter must be clear enough to allow you to know that it has been decided that your entitlement has changed *and* that the resultant overpayment is recoverable.[28] It is also possible that your benefit award for the past period has been changed, but not notified to you until you are also notified that the overpayment is recoverable.[29]

If the decisions have not been changed and the new decisions notified (or it appears that they may not have been), you should appeal to the First-tier Tribunal (see p1303) against the decision that the overpayment is recoverable. The First-tier Tribunal should decide that the decision that the overpayment is recoverable is 'of no effect' – ie, the overpayment cannot be recovered because there is no valid decision. The DWP or HMRC may try again to recover the overpayment by making and notifying the correct decisions.[30] However, sometimes the First-tier Tribunal will go further and say that an overpayment is not recoverable, in which case the First-tier Tribunal's decision will be final (unless the DWP or HMRC appeals or the decision can be altered in some other way – see p1329 and p1270).

You failed to disclose or you misrepresented a material fact

For an overpayment to be recoverable you must have:
- failed to disclose a relevant material fact (see below); *or*
- misrepresented a relevant material fact (see p1221).

Failure to disclose

You count as having 'failed to disclose' a relevant material fact (see p1223) if:[31]
- you knew about a fact (see p1220);
- you had a legal duty to disclose that fact (see p1220); *and*
- you did not comply with that legal duty (see p1220).

If the DWP or HMRC decides that you have been overpaid and that the overpayment is recoverable from you because you have failed to disclose a material fact, check whether you had a legal duty to disclose that fact and whether you have complied with that duty.

Part 9: Claiming benefits and getting paid
Chapter 56: Overpayments
3. Overpayments that are sometimes recoverable

Knowledge of a fact

If you did not know about a fact, including if it was a change in your circumstances, you have not 'failed' to disclose it.[32] You cannot fail to disclose something you did not know about unless:

- there was a reason why you should have been aware of it;[33] *or*
- it was reasonable for you to make enquiries which would have revealed the information to you;[34] *or*
- you had been aware of it, but simply forgot.[35]

Legal duty to disclose

There are two different types of legal duty to disclose in the benefit system: a specific duty and a general duty.

You have a 'specific duty to disclose' a fact which you know about (see below) and which you were clearly told by the DWP or HMRC you must disclose – eg, in your benefit award letter or in the notes which accompanied it.

You do not have a specific legal duty to disclose something unless the instruction is clear and there is no room for doubt about whether or not you are required to report it.[36]

If you were not clearly told that you must report a certain fact, this specific duty to disclose does not apply. However, you still have a 'general duty to disclose' the fact if it was a change in your circumstances since the decision awarding you benefit and you could reasonably have been expected to know that your benefit might be affected.[37]

What you can reasonably be expected to know depends on the details of your case. For example, if you were told by the DWP or a lawyer that your benefit would not be affected, or if you were too ill to have realised that it might be, it is arguable that you could not reasonably have been expected to have known that your benefit might be affected.[38] If there is no obvious connection between the fact and the overpaid benefit, argue that it was not reasonable to expect you to know that your benefit might be affected.

Complying with your duty to disclose

Generally, to make a valid disclosure, you must disclose the fact to the 'relevant office' in sufficiently clear terms so that how it affects your claim can be examined.

How do you comply with your legal duty to disclose?

1. If you have a specific duty to disclose (see above), the 'relevant office' is the one that handles the benefit you are claiming.[39] This may be a benefit delivery centre (eg, for income support – IS) or a central office – eg, for disability living allowance (DLA). For special rules on reporting a birth or death (sometimes called 'Tell Us Once'), see p1174.

2. If you have a general duty to disclose (see p1220), the 'relevant office' is any DWP office or, in jobseeker's allowance (JSA) cases, a specified DWP office. However, it is always best to tell the office handling your claim if you can. For child benefit and guardian's allowance,

you can disclose changes in your circumstances to the Child Benefit Office, or any office specified to you by HMRC.[40] Again, it is best to ensure that you tell HMRC, as it administers your claim. You only count as having failed to disclose once the time by which it was reasonably practicable for you to have done so has passed. For example, if it was impossible for you to make the disclosure earlier than you did, you have not failed to comply with the general duty to disclose.

3. If the office already knew about the fact and you were aware of this, it is arguable that you have not failed to disclose. Even if you were not aware that the office already knew, it may be possible to argue that its knowledge means that any failure on your part did not actually cause the overpayment. This is especially so if the evidence shows that the office would not have acted any differently even if you had reported the fact to it.[41]

4. You can usually notify changes in writing or by telephone, but it is best to do so in writing.[42]

5. If you filled in a form while giving information, whether you count as having failed to disclose depends not just on what you said on the form, but also on whether you gave the necessary information in another way.[43] If you do not complete a form correctly, but give the relevant information in the wrong place, you have disclosed the facts.[44]

6. If you made a statement in person or by telephone but the decision maker says there is no record of this, s/he must show, 'on the balance of probabilities', that there would be a record of the conversation at the local office if it had taken place. In order to do this, the decision maker must give the First-tier Tribunal information on: the instructions that should have applied for recording and attaching information to your file; whether the appropriate administrative arrangements were in place to enable these to be carried out; and to what extent in practice these instructions are carried out.[45]

7. You should usually make the disclosure yourself, unless you have an appointee acting for you (see p1137).[46] If someone else discloses the fact on your behalf, it must be made to the correct office with your knowledge and you must believe that there is no need to repeat the disclosure yourself. However, if someone else makes the disclosure to an office not handling your claim, but s/he reasonably believes that the information will be passed to the correct office, this may count as disclosure.[47]

8. Once you have made a proper disclosure to the office handling your claim, you are not expected to repeat it.[48] However, if you give the information to a different office and subsequently become aware that it has not been acted on, you are obliged to take further steps to make a proper disclosure.[49] A short time may elapse before you can reasonably be expected to realise that the original information has not been acted on.[50]

Misrepresentation

Misrepresentation occurs if you have provided information that is inaccurate – eg, you gave a wrong answer to a specific question on the claim form. It does not apply if you have not given information, unless this was deliberately intended to mislead.[51] The following apply.

Part 9: Claiming benefits and getting paid
Chapter 56: Overpayments
3. Overpayments that are sometimes recoverable

- It does not matter whether a reasonable person would also have given the information inaccurately. No 'failure' on your part needs to be shown.[52]
- It does not matter if you honestly believed the information you gave to be correct – once it is shown to be incorrect, you have misrepresented it. However, you have not misrepresented if you added the phrase 'not to my knowledge' to your statement.[53]
- A written statement may be qualified by an oral one. If you fill in a form incorrectly but explain the situation to an officer when handing in the form, the explanation must be taken into account when deciding whether what is stated on the form is misrepresentation.[54] Similarly, if you give incorrect information in one document but correct information in another, there may not be misrepresentation.[55] However, if you have declared a fact on a previous claim but inadvertently give incorrect information on a later claim, you have misrepresented it. The decision maker is not required to check for you.[56]
- If you are incapable of managing your affairs but nevertheless sign a claim form which is incorrectly completed, you cannot argue later that you were not capable of making a true representation of your circumstances.[57] However, it is arguable that benefit cannot be recovered from you if you:[58]
  - have a disability or you cannot read or write English very well; *and*
  - thought you were signing something different from what you were, or you did not understand the effect of your signature; *and*
  - took precautions to understand what you were signing – eg, you checked the form for accuracy before you signed it.[59]
- If you sign a declaration on a claim form that states: 'I declare that the information I have given is correct and complete', but you left out relevant information because you were unaware of it, this is not misrepresentation unless you knew (or ought reasonably to have known) the information was incomplete.[60]

Note:

- If you did not declare a fact because you were unaware of it, signing the declaration does not amount to a misrepresentation because all you are declaring is that you have correctly disclosed those facts *which were known to you*.[61]
- If you were told by the DWP or HMRC that certain facts are irrelevant to your claim, signing the declaration cannot be a misrepresentation if you fail to disclose those facts.[62]
- If someone else disclosed a fact to an office not handling your claim but s/he reasonably believed it would be passed to the correct office, it may be that disclosure has been made, and therefore your signing the declaration does not amount to a misrepresentation.[63]

A material fact

Overpayments can only usually be recovered if you failed to disclose (see below), or you misrepresented (see p1221), a 'material fact'. A **'material fact'** is one which influences how much benefit you should be paid.[64] Sometimes there can be a difference between a statement of your honest opinion and a statement of a material fact.[65] For example, it may well be that a statement about the distance you can walk should be taken merely as your honest opinion of your ability, rather than as a statement of fact.[66] If the decision maker has simply come to a different conclusion about the facts than you, you can argue that an overpayment should not be recovered.[67]

Facts	Conclusions about the facts
You have arthritis	You have limited capability for work
A friend is sharing your flat	You are living together as husband and wife or civil partners
You have a bad back	Your mobility is severely restricted most of the time

Your failure to disclose or your misrepresentation has caused the overpayment

An overpayment is only recoverable if it was caused by your failure to disclose (see p1219) or your misrepresentation (see p1221) of a material fact (see above).

You may be able to argue that the overpayment was not caused by your failure to disclose or your misrepresentation.

- If the relevant office has been given the correct information to decide your claim by someone else, but does not act on it, you could argue that the overpayment did not arise because of your failure.[68] If one office of the DWP fails to inform another about *other* changes in your circumstances (eg, an increase in your earnings), this does not prevent the overpayment resulting from your failure to disclose the information yourself to the second office.[69]

- If the relevant office has obtained information from another source which leads it to think you might be being overpaid but it does not suspend your benefit while it makes enquiries to establish this for certain, it is still possible that the cause of the overpayment is your failure to disclose or your misrepresentation.[70]

- In any case, if you have not disclosed a relevant fact to the relevant office and you then sign a declaration that you have reported the relevant facts (eg, when you sign on), this will be a misrepresentation.

- If what you say on your claim form is obviously incorrect and the decision maker does not check this, the overpayment will have been caused by official error, not your misrepresentation, and it is not recoverable.[71]

Part 9: Claiming benefits and getting paid
Chapter 56: Overpayments
3. Overpayments that are sometimes recoverable

The amount that is recovered

You should check that the amount of the overpayment is correct by:

- checking the period of the overpayment;
- working out the total amount of benefit you were paid over the period;
- working out the correct amount of benefit you should have received during the period;
- deducting this from the total amount of benefit you were paid.

No interest charges may be added to the amount of the overpayment.

The amount of the overpayment is the difference between what you were paid and what you should have been paid.[72] The decision maker works out what you should have been paid using the information you originally gave her/him, plus any facts you misrepresented or did not disclose.

If you have been overpaid, the decision maker should deduct from the overpayment any IS, income-based JSA, income-related employment and support allowance (ESA) or pension credit (PC) to which you or your partner would have been entitled had benefit been paid correctly.[73]

If additional facts are needed to prove you were underpaid IS, income-based JSA, ESA, PC or universal credit (UC), you cannot offset the underpayment of those benefits against the overpayment.[74] However, if you have been getting one of those benefits, you can ask the DWP to revise or supersede your award (see p1270 and p1281). It could then withhold any arrears owed to you to reduce the overpayment.

If you were overpaid IS, income-based JSA, income-related ESA or PC because you had too much capital (see p343), the overpayment is calculated taking account of the fact that, had you received no benefit, you would have had to use your capital to meet everyday expenses. For each 13-week period, the DWP assumes your capital is reduced by the amount of overpaid benefit.[75] This is known as the 'diminishing capital' rule, and if your capital goes below the capital limit, any subsequent overpayment is not recoverable. However, if there are any increases or decreases in your actual capital during the overpayment period, these are also taken into account.[76]

Example
Nina received IS of £100 a week for a period of 30 weeks. She has capital of £20,000. After 13 weeks, the diminishing capital rule means that she is treated as having spent 13 x £100 = £1,300 and her capital is deemed to be £18,700. After a further 13 weeks, her capital is deemed to be £17,400.
After 26 weeks, Nina has paid £5,000 towards her credit card arrears after the credit card company threatened her with court proceedings. As long as obtaining benefit was not the significant purpose for making this payment (see p359), her capital is now deemed to be £12,400.

Although your capital is treated as reducing for these purposes, if you reclaim benefit, your full capital counts (see p362).

In addition to checking that the overpayment has been calculated correctly, you should claim any other benefits or tax credits to which you may be entitled and ask for these to be backdated (see p1144 for benefits and p1446 for tax credits) so you can repay the overpayment. Do not delay making the claims or you could lose out.

If you were overpaid a benefit which overlaps with another benefit you claimed but were not paid (see p1165), ask for a revision or supersession of that benefit and ask for it to be paid instead (see p1270).

If you were overpaid a benefit but, in fact, were entitled to another, check whether the claim for the benefit you were overpaid can be treated as a claim for the other (see p1144).

Example

Maxine should not have been receiving IS because her partner is in full-time paid work. However, she is caring for her aunt who is disabled and receiving attendance allowance. Maxine should ask the DWP to treat her claim for IS as a claim for carer's allowance (CA) and offset arrears of CA against the IS she has been overpaid.

From whom can an overpayment be recovered

An overpayment can be recovered from you if it was caused by your failing to disclose or misrepresenting a material fact (see p1219).[77] The DWP or HMRC may try to argue that it can recover the overpayment from you even if you are *not* the claimant or were not otherwise paid the benefit. However, it is arguable that it is only a claimant (or appointee – see below) who can fail to disclose.[78]

If you are an appointee (see p1137), the overpayment can be recovered from you or the claimant (or both of you), depending on your individual circumstances and the facts of the case – ie, which one of you misrepresented or failed to disclose a material fact. The DWP or HMRC should issue a decision that deals with the liability of both the appointee and the claimant.[79] However:

- if the overpaid benefit has not been given to you, the claimant, the overpayment cannot be recovered from you, unless you contributed to the misrepresentation or you did not disclose a material fact;
- the overpayment cannot be recovered from an appointee if s/he used 'due care and diligence' in making the representation.

Having power of attorney is not the same as being an appointee. Unless you are an appointee, a benefit overpayment caused by your actions cannot be recovered from the claimant. However, such an overpayment may be recoverable from you.[80] Seek advice if you are in this situation.

Part 9: Claiming benefits and getting paid
Chapter 56: Overpayments
4. Recovery of overpaid benefit

An overpayment can be recovered from a claimant's estate if s/he dies.[81] Recovery can only begin once a grant either of probate or of letters of administration has been made. [82]

Challenging an overpayment decision

If a decision is made that an overpayment is recoverable from you because it was caused by your failure to disclose a material fact or because you misrepresented a material fact (whether or not you are the claimant), you can appeal if you disagree:[83]

- that an overpayment has occurred; *or*
- that an overpayment can be recovered – ie, because the required conditions are not met; *or*
- with the amount to be recovered.

Do not pay back any of the money until your appeal has been decided. If you do so and then successfully appeal, the DWP or HMRC should reimburse you. If it does not do so, you may be entitled to recover the money in court proceedings because you repaid the money on the basis of a mistake. Write to the DWP or HMRC and explain that you do not intend to repay any of the money until your appeal has been decided. If the DWP or HMRC is already making deductions from your benefit (see p769), ask it to stop doing so straight away.

Note: even if the final decision is that an overpayment of a particular amount is recoverable, the decision maker has the discretion not to recover, so it is sometimes still worth asking that nothing be recovered (see p1227).

4. **Recovery of overpaid benefit**

Note: this section does *not* apply to recovery of overpayments of housing benefit (HB – see p1232).

If an overpayment can be recovered (see p1213 and p1217), the DWP or HM Revenue and Customs (HMRC) must decide whether to recover it (see p1227) and, if so, on the method of recovery. The method of recovery depends on the type of overpayment. If you come under the universal credit (UC) system and have been overpaid UC, contribution-based jobseeker's allowance (JSA) or contributory employment and support allowance (ESA), see p19. For all other overpayments, see p1227.

Note: except when seeking to recover overpaid benefit through the courts, there is no time limit within which the DWP or HMRC must begin recovery action.

The discretion to recover

Even if an overpayment is recoverable, the DWP and HMRC have the discretion not to recover all or part of it. The DWP has two policies that set out the situations when recovery is not made.

- Guidance for overpayments of UC, contribution-based JSA and contributory ESA if you come under the UC system (see p1215) states that the DWP can use its discretion not to recover an overpayment if it would cause you hardship.[84] You can also ask the DWP not to recover if the reason why you were overpaid was because of a mistake on the part of the DWP.[85]
- Guidance for all other overpayments emphasises that recovery is not pursued only in exceptional cases.[86] However, the DWP and HMRC can use their discretion to decide not to recover the overpayment, particularly if you acted in good faith and recovery would cause you hardship or be detrimental to your health or the health of your family.

If you agree to repay the overpayment or you do not ask for recovery not to be made, in almost all cases the DWP or HMRC recover the overpayment from you. If an overpayment is recoverable from you, but repaying it is difficult, or you think there is a reason why recovery should not take place, contact the DWP/HMRC debt management section. The details should be on the letters you receive about the overpayment. Each case is decided on its merits. You should emphasise that you acted in good faith, point out any misleading advice you received (particularly from the DWP or HMRC) and how repaying would cause you hardship. To demonstrate hardship on financial grounds, you must usually provide full income and expenditure details for you and your family.

If the DWP or HMRC refuses to use its discretion not to recover, you cannot appeal against this decision. Your only possible legal recourse is judicial review (see p1351), but it may also help to involve your MP. The First-tier Tribunal cannot 'write off' part of the overpayment, even if there are mitigating circumstances. It can only decide if it is recoverable and, if so, how much is repayable.

If you have been underpaid in the past but cannot now get arrears (eg, because of the rules on backdating – see p1144), ask the DWP or HMRC to reduce the amount to be recovered by this sum if it will not write it off altogether.

Methods of recovery: general rules

This section applies to all recoverable overpayments except overpayments of UC, and contribution-based JSA or contributory ESA if you come under the UC system. For these, see p1230.

Deductions from benefit

Recoverable overpayments can usually be paid back through deductions from most of the benefits in this *Handbook*. One exception is that, although

Part 9: Claiming benefits and getting paid
Chapter 56: Overpayments
4. Recovery of overpaid benefit

overpayments of child benefit or guardian's allowance can be recovered by deductions from either of these benefits,[87] overpayments of other benefits cannot be deducted from them.[88] In addition, no deductions can be made from HB, except for HB or council tax benefit overpayments.[89] Except in the case of income support (IS), income-based JSA, income-related ESA and pension credit (PC), deductions can only be made from the benefit of the person who must repay the overpayment.

Overpayments can also be recovered from arrears of benefit you are owed, except arrears of a benefit that has been suspended (see p1175).[90]

If you are a member of a couple, overpayments of IS, income-based JSA, income-related ESA and PC can be recovered from either of your benefits, provided you are married or living together as husband and wife (or are civil partners or living together as if you were civil partners).[91]

If an overpayment of IS, income-based JSA, income-related ESA or PC occurred because of a duplication of payment, the DWP usually deducts it from the arrears owing to you.[92] However, if it does not do so, you can still be asked to repay even if you have spent the money.

Note: overpaid benefit cannot be recovered by making deductions from tax credits.

Maximum deductions from benefit

The maximum weekly amounts that can be deducted from IS, income-based JSA, contribution-based JSA (if you would be entitled to income-based JSA at the same rate), income-related ESA, contributory ESA (if you would be entitled to income-related ESA at the same rate) and PC are:[93]

- £18.25 if you have agreed to pay a penalty (see p1256), admitted fraud or been found guilty of fraud; *or*
- £10.95 in any other case.

The deduction can be increased by half of any:[94]

- £5, £10 or £20 earnings disregard (see p267); *or*
- charitable income paid on a regular basis subject to a disregard (see p279); *or*
- benefit subject to a £10 disregard (see p267).

If you have been overpaid contribution-based JSA but are not entitled to income-based JSA, the maximum deduction is one-third of the personal allowance for someone of your age (see p222).[95]

The above amounts are maximum amounts. The DWP might be persuaded to deduct less, especially if you have other direct deductions made from your benefit.

If an overpayment is being recovered from a benefit other than IS, income-based JSA, income-related ESA or PC, the rules limiting the maximum payment that can be deducted do not apply. See p1231 if the overpayment is being recovered from your UC.[96] For recovery from all other benefits, the DWP usually wants to deduct one-third of your weekly benefit. However, you can argue that your rate of repayment should be less than this.

Deductions from earnings

If you work for an organisation with 10 or more employees, an overpayment can be recovered by your employer deducting amounts from your earnings.[97] If this happens, you and your employer should be sent a notice setting out that deductions from your earnings are to be made and the rules for calculating how much to deduct.[98] You must inform the DWP if you leave your employment and you must give the DWP details of any new employment.[99] Failure to notify the DWP of these issues is a criminal offence.[100] Your employer should inform you, in writing, of how much the deductions are and how they were calculated no later than the day on which you are given a payment which has had a deduction made from it (or, if that is impractical, no later than the following pay day).[101]

The maximum that can be deducted each week is worked out as a percentage of your net earnings – ie, earnings after income tax, Class 1 national insurance contributions and pension contributions have been deducted.[102]

Maximum deductions from earnings

Net weekly earnings	Deduction
Less than £100	Nil
£100 to £160.00	3%
£160.01 to £220	5%
£220.01 to £270	7%
£270.01 to £375	11%
£375.01 to £520	15%
£520.01 over	20%

Net monthly earnings	Deduction
Less than £430	Nil
£430.01 to £690	3%
£690.01 to £950	5%
£950.01 to £1,160	7%
£1,160.01 to £1,615	11%
£1,615.01 to £2,240	15%
£2,240.01 or over	20%

If you would be left with less than 60 per cent of your net earnings after the deductions (eg, because amounts are being deducted from your wages or salary for other things), the deduction should be reduced so that you are left with 60 per cent of your net earnings.[103] There are rules on the order of priority in which deductions should be made.[104] **Note:** the decision maker can reduce the

Part 9: Claiming benefits and getting paid
Chapter 56: Overpayments
4. Recovery of overpaid benefit

amount to be deducted below the above percentages by issuing a new notice to your employer with the reduced amount.[105]

Recovery through the courts

Recoverable overpayments of benefit may be recovered by enforcement proceedings in the county court in England or Wales or the sheriff court in Scotland.[106] The DWP or HMRC may use these proceedings if you are no longer claiming benefit.

Once there is a decision from a decision maker, the First-tier Tribunal or Upper Tribunal, the court must enforce it, unless you persuade it to delay enforcement (known as a 'stay of execution') while you appeal against the relevant decision. If you are in this situation, seek advice.

Note: recovery action through the courts in England and Wales must be taken within six years of the decision to recover or, if later, any written acknowledgement of the overpayment or voluntary repayment.[107] In Scotland, the DWP regards the time limit as being 20 years from the date of the decision to recover (or, if there was no such decision, five years from the decision that there was an overpayment).[108] Seek advice about how these limits apply to you.

Can the DWP rely on common law?

In the past, the DWP has claimed to be entitled to recover overpayments of benefit under 'common law', even if the overpayment was entirely caused by official error. However, it is now clear that it cannot recover in this way. This means that, if the DWP cannot recover an overpayment under the rules described in this chapter (see p1217) because, for example, it was not caused by misrepresentation or a failure to disclose, it cannot reclaim it through the courts.[109]

Methods of recovery: universal credit, contribution-based jobseeker's allowance and contributory employment and support allowance

This section applies to the recovery of overpayments of UC, and contribution-based JSA or contributory ESA if you come under the UC system (see p1215).

Note: the methods of recovery described in this section can also be used to collect or recover court costs incurred in recovering overpayments, short-term advances (see p1167), budgeting advances of UC (see p197), hardship payments of UC (see p1199), financial penalties for benefit offences (see p1256), civil penalties for incorrect statements (see p1249) and overpayments of tax credits if you are now receiving UC (see p1464).

Deductions from benefit

Overpayments of UC, and contribution-based JSA or contributory ESA if you come under the UC system, can be recovered through deductions from all the benefits in this *Handbook* except IS, HB, social fund payments, child benefit and guardian's allowance.[110]

Maximum deductions from universal credit

Note: the maximum amounts below apply to *all* overpayments being recovered by deductions from your UC – eg, an overpayment of IS that occured before you came under the UC system.[111]

If an overpayment is being recovered from your UC, the maximum amount that can be deducted each month is the highest of:[112]

- if you or your partner are found guilty of an offence, or have accepted a caution or agreed to pay a penalty in connection with the overpayment (see p1248) (these rates also apply for recovery of UC hardship payments):
  - £99.71 if you are single and under 25;
  - £125.87 if you are single and 25 or over;
  - £156.52 if you and your partner are both under 25;
  - £197.58 if you or your partner are 25 or over;
- if you have some earned income:
  - £62.32 if you are single and under 25;
  - £78.67 if you are single and 25 or over;
  - £97.82 if you and your partner are both under 25;
  - £123.49 if you or your partner are 25 or over;
- in all other cases:
  - £37.39 if you are single and under 25;
  - £47.20 if you are single and 25 or over;
  - £58.69 if you and your partner are both under 25;
  - £74.09 if you or your partner are 25 or over.

You must be left with at least one pence of UC each month after the deduction.[113] The above maximum amounts do not apply if:

- you are being paid arrears of UC (other than if they are as a result of payments being restored following a suspension of your benefit), so the whole of the arrears can be used to recover an overpayment;[114] *or*
- the overpayment is of UC housing costs to cover rent and it is being recovered from someone else other than you, the claimant – eg, your landlord.[115]

Maximum deductions from jobseeker's allowance or employment and support allowance

The maximum weekly deduction that can be made to recover an overpayment from your JSA is an amount equal to 40 per cent of your JSA.[116]

The maximum weekly deduction that can be made to recover an overpayment from your ESA is 40 per cent of the basic allowance that applies to you (see p619).[117]

Part 9: Claiming benefits and getting paid
Chapter 56: Overpayments
5. Overpayments of housing benefit

In both cases, if the 40 per cent figure is not a multiple of five pence, the amount is rounded up to the next highest multiple of five pence.

Maximum deductions from pension credit

The maximum weekly amount that can be deducted from PC to repay an overpayment under these rules is:[118]

- £18.25 if the overpayment is one in respect of which you were found guilty of an offence, you were cautioned or you agreed to pay a penalty as an alternative to prosecution; *or*
- £10.95 in all other cases.

You must be left with at least 10 pence of PC after any deductions.

Deductions from earnings

Overpayments can be recovered by your employer deducting amounts from your wages or salary.[119] The rules are the same as the general rules (see p1229).

Recovery through the courts

The rules for recovering overpayments through the courts are similar to those for the recovery of HB (see p1241).[120]

5. **Overpayments of housing benefit**

Note: council tax benefit (CTB) was abolished from 1 April 2013. However, it is possible that there will be decisions after this date about CTB overpayments made before this date. You may also still be repaying an overpayment of CTB. The rules on calculating the amount and the recoverability of overpayments of CTB were similar to those for housing benefit (HB). For further details, see p1094 of the 2012/13 edition of this *Handbook*.

If you have been overpaid income support (IS), income-based jobseeker's allowance (JSA) or income-related employment and support allowance (ESA), you may also have been overpaid HB. This is because your automatic passport to maximum HB ceases when you are no longer entitled to those benefits. If you are in this situation, inform the local authority dealing with your HB claim.

What is an overpayment

An 'overpayment' is an amount of HB which has been paid and to which the local authority decides you were not entitled under the HB rules.[121] Being 'paid' includes payment to you, your landlord or someone else, including HB credited to your local authority rent account (see p132).[122]

When an overpayment can be recovered

An overpayment can only be recovered if the local authority has taken all the following five steps.

- **Step one:** decide whether the overpayment is legally recoverable (see below).
- **Step two:** decide from whom recovery can be made, and whether recovery should be made (see p1236).
- **Step three:** work out how much of the overpayment is repayable and for what period (see p1237).
- **Step four:** decide how the overpayment should be recovered and at what rate (see p1238).
- **Step five:** notify you of all the above decisions about the overpayment (see p1242) and give you an opportunity to request further information or a review (see p131).

Step one: is the overpayment recoverable

All overpayments of HB are recoverable except, in certain circumstances, those caused by 'official error' (see below). An overpayment may be recoverable even if it was caused by an innocent mistake on your part or was someone else's fault. Remember that, in most cases, the local authority has the discretion to decide whether or not to recover an overpayment (see p1238).

Note: if an overpayment was included in a debt relief order, it is not recoverable. Similarly if you are subject to a bankruptcy order, any overpayment notified to you as recoverable before the order was made is not recoverable. However, after the order ceases to have effect, any overpayment caused by fraud (see p1253) becomes recoverable.

Overpayments that are always recoverable

An overpayment is always recoverable if:

- it is the result of the local authority's over-estimating your HB when making a payment on account (see p139). When the local authority decides how much HB you should get, it must recover any excess you were paid from future HB payments.[123] However, if you stop getting HB before the local authority decides, the overpayment can only be recovered under the other rules described in this section;
- it is a future payment that has been credited to your rent account. In this case, the overpayment can be recovered even if it was made as a result of an 'official error'.[124] If an overpayment of HB caused by an official error has been credited to your account for a *past* period, see below.

Overpayments caused by official error

An overpayment that does not fall into the above category is *not* recoverable if you can show that:[125]

Part 9: Claiming benefits and getting paid
Chapter 56: Overpayments
5. Overpayments of housing benefit

- it was caused by an 'official error'; *and*
- no 'relevant person' caused the official error to be made; *and*
- no 'relevant person' could reasonably have been expected to realise that an overpayment was being made.

Official error

An **'official error'** is a mistake (either an act or omission) by:[126]

– the local authority responsible for HB; *or*

– an officer of the authority; *or*

– a person acting for that authority; *or*

– an officer of the DWP or HM Revenue and Customs (HMRC) acting as such.

An 'official error' includes:
- a mistake made by the local authority in calculating your entitlement;
- a failure by the local authority to reduce your HB when you inform it of a change of circumstances. It is always best to notify changes in writing to the office you have been told to report changes to, and keep a copy. If you have reported a move into work to the DWP by telephone under the arrangements where it passes this on to the local authority (see p139) and have provided all the information and evidence needed, any overpayment that occurs is due to official error. However, if you have not provided all that is needed, the local authority does not treat any overpayment as official error;[127]
- a failure by another department of the local authority to pass on details of a change of circumstances, when it promised to do so. This is an official error because the definition does not require the mistake to be made by the HB office. If you have not been given a particular office to report a change to, you may have fulfilled your duty by reporting the change to any local authority office, and there may be an official error if that office fails to pass it to the HB office;[128]
- similar mistakes by someone carrying out HB functions on behalf of the local authority – eg, a private agency to whom work has been contracted;
- a mistake made by the DWP in calculating your entitlement to IS, income-based JSA or income-related ESA which results in an incorrect calculation of your entitlement to HB. However, it is not an official error if the local authority failed to check your entitlement with the DWP, unless it has information that shows the award is wrong or fraudulent;[129]
- a failure by the DWP to pass on information to the local authority;[130]
- incorrect advice given to you by an officer of the local authority, the DWP or HMRC, provided s/he is acting as an officer at the time (rather than as a friend giving you informal advice).

The list above is not exhaustive. The official error does not have to be the sole cause of the overpayment. However, even if an official error has occurred, if the substantial cause of the overpayment was something that you did or failed to do, the overpayment is likely to be recoverable.[131]

An overpayment is not recoverable if you can show that the official error was not partially or wholly caused by a 'relevant person'.

Relevant person

A **'relevant person'** is:
- the HB claimant; *or*
- a person acting on the claimant's behalf, either because s/he is unable to deal with her/his affairs or because s/he has asked the authority in writing to deal with her/him on her/his behalf; *or*
- a person to whom the payment was made, including a different person acting on the claimant's behalf or a landlord.

The relevant person must have caused the *error*, not the overpayment.[132]

The local authority might say it only needs to show that *any* relevant person caused the official error, but it does not have to pursue that person for the overpayment.[133] If a relevant person caused the official error, the overpayment is recoverable. However, you may still be able to argue that it is not recoverable from you – eg, it was caused by a failure to disclose a relevant fact, but it was not you who failed to disclose. See p1236 for information about from whom overpayments can be recovered.

Even if the official error was not caused by a relevant person, an overpayment is still recoverable if any relevant person knew, or ought reasonably to have known, that an overpayment had been made. The test is whether or not you could reasonably have been be expected to *know* (not merely suspect) that an overpayment had occurred. Much depends on what could reasonably have been expected of you given the information available to you, in particular the extent to which the local authority advised you about the scheme, your duties and obligations (especially your duty to notify changes of circumstances).[134]

If you or another relevant person could only have realised that there was an overpayment at some point during the period of the overpayment, the overpayment is only recoverable from that date.

The local authority's discretion to recover

Except for certain payments on account (see p139), the local authority has a discretion whether or not to recover an overpayment.[135]

Part 9: Claiming benefits and getting paid
Chapter 56: Overpayments
5. Overpayments of housing benefit

Is repaying an overpayment difficult?

1. If you think that repaying an overpayment will cause you difficulty, contact your local authority and ask it to consider not recovering it.

2. If appropriate, point out that you acted in good faith, or that recovery will cause you hardship. You may need to supply details of your income and expenditure.

3. Although you cannot appeal against a decision to recover a recoverable overpayment, in exceptional circumstance you may be able to chanllenge the decision by judicial review in the courts. A local authority policy of always recovering all recoverable overpayments could be challenged by judicial review (see p1351).

4. If you think the overpayment might not be recoverable from you, consider challenging the decision either by asking for a revision (see Chapter 58) or making an appeal (see Chapter 59).

5. If the overpayment was caused by someone else, you could suggest that recovery is made from her/him. If this is your landlord, see below.

You may be asked to repay a non-recoverable overpayment on a voluntary basis. You are under no legal obligation to do so.

Step two: from whom can the overpayment be recovered

The general rule is that a **recoverable overpayment** can be recovered from the person to whom it was paid (except some overpayments paid to your landlord – see p1237).[136] However, this does not apply if someone else misrepresented or failed to disclose a material fact, or if someone else should have realised that there was an overpayment at the time.

An overpayment can be recovered from someone other than the person to whom it was paid, including the claimant, if:[137]

- the overpayment was caused by misrepresentation or failure to disclose a material fact. These terms are not specifically defined for HB, but are likely to be the same as for the sort of overpayments described on p1217. In this case, it must be recovered from the person who misrepresented or failed to disclose the fact, not the person to whom it was paid; *or*
- the overpayment was caused by an official error (see p1233) and you, the claimant (or someone acting on your behalf) or any other person to whom the HB was paid could reasonably have been expected to realise that there was an overpayment at the time. In this case, it must be recovered from whomever should have realised, not the person to whom it was paid; *or*
- neither of the above two bullet points apply, in which case the overpayment is also recoverable from the claimant. The overpayment may, therefore, be recovered from you, the claimant, as well as the person to whom it was paid.

If you are the claimant and the overpayment is recoverable from you, no matter how it was caused, the local authority can also recover the overpayment by deducting any HB paid to your partner, provided you were a couple both at the time of the overpayment and when the deduction is made.[138]

If you think you have been wrongly chosen under these rules (eg, because you did not fail to disclose a material fact), you can appeal to the First-tier Tribunal. However, if the overpayment can be recovered from you under these rules, you cannot appeal simply because you think the local authority should recover from another person instead.[139]

In the event of the death of the person from whom recovery is being sought, the local authority may consider recovering any outstanding overpayment from that person's estate.[140]

Recovery from your landlord

If a recoverable overpayment has been paid to your landlord, in general s/he can be required to pay it back, as s/he is the person to whom the overpayment was made. This does not apply if someone else misrepresented or failed to disclose a material fact, or if someone else should have realised there was an overpayment at the time (see p1219). If your benefit has been calculated using the local housing allowance, your landlord cannot be required to pay back more than s/he received – any amount above this may be recoverable from you.[141]

An overpayment can be recovered from another person, including you as the claimant, in certain circumstances.

An overpayment cannot be recovered from your landlord if:[142]
- s/he was receiving the payment; *and*
- s/he wrote to the local authority notifying it of the possible overpayment; *and*
- the overpayment was not caused by your ceasing to live in the property as your home; *and*
- there are grounds to take action for fraud (see p1253) or the overpayment was caused by a deliberate failure to report a relevant change of circumstances; *and*
- s/he has not colluded with you or otherwise contributed to the overpayment.

Step three: how much is repayable and for what period

Check the amount of an overpayment to ensure the local authority has calculated it correctly. The local authority should distinguish between parts of an overpayment that are recoverable and those that are not. To calculate the amount of the overpayment, it should:
- determine the period over which you have been paid too much benefit;
- identify the period(s) over which it is entitled to recover;
- work out the total amount of HB you were paid over the period(s) during which it can recover;
- work out the correct amount of HB you should have received during the period(s) of the overpayment. The local authority must award you the amount

Part 9: Claiming benefits and getting paid
Chapter 56: Overpayments
5. Overpayments of housing benefit

of HB you would have received if it had been aware of your true circumstances (even if the overpayment occurred before the rules were changed in October 2000). If necessary, it should ask you for any required information or evidence to do this. However, the local authority does not include a change of your address when doing this;[143]

- deduct the HB you should have been paid from what you were paid.[144]

The local authority must not add any interest charges to the amount of the overpayment.[145]

Deductions from the overpayment

As well as any amount of HB which you should have been paid, the local authority must consider deducting other amounts from the overpayment (this is known as 'offsetting'). These are:

- if you are a council tenant, extra rent paid into your rent account. If you have been getting HB during the overpayment period and, for some reason, have paid more into your rent account than you should have paid according to your original (incorrect) benefit assessment, the extra rent you have paid can be deducted from any overpayment made during that period. The local authority might not apply this rule if you paid extra rent to repay rent arrears;[146]
- reductions under the 'diminishing capital rule' (see below).

No other amounts can be deducted.

If you were overpaid HB because you had too much capital, the overpayment is calculated taking into account the fact that, had you received no HB, you would have used your capital. This is known as the **'diminishing capital rule'**. It only applies if:[147]

- you were overpaid for more than 13 weeks; *and either*
- the overpayment was caused by a misrepresentation of, or a failure to disclose, the amount of your capital (see p1219); *or*
- the overpayment was caused by an error (other than an 'official error' – see p1234) about your capital (or that of a member of your family).

For each 13-week period, the local authority assumes that your capital is reduced by the amount of overpaid HB.[148] Although your capital is treated as reducing for these purposes, if you reclaim benefit, your full capital counts (see p344).

Step four: how is the overpayment recovered

A local authority can decide how much, if any, of a **recoverable overpayment** it will recover. This is similar to the discretion which the DWP or HMRC has to recover overpayments (see p1227).

If the local authority decides to recover, it can ask for the whole amount or recover it by instalments. When an overpayment is recovered from your landlord, note how this affects your liability to pay rent (see p1243). Overpayments of HB can be recovered:

- from payments of HB (see below);
- from other benefits (see p1240);
- by adjusting your rent account if you are a local authority tenant (see p1241);
- by your employer deducting amounts from your wages or salary (see p1229);
- through the courts (see p1241).

The methods used and the rates of recovery should be consistent between groups of claimants. For example, council tenants should not be required to repay an overpayment in a lump sum if private tenants can repay by instalments.

Note: except when seeking to recover overpaid benefit through the courts, there is no time limit within which a local authority must begin recovery action.

Recovery from housing benefit payments

A local authority can recover an overpayment by deducting amounts from HB payable to any person from whom an overpayment can be recovered (see p1225).[149] As well as yourself, this could be your partner (see below) or your landlord (see below). Deductions can be made from both future payments of HB and any arrears that are owing.

If you have moved home, the local authority may be able to recover an overpayment of HB from your previous home by adjusting the HB paid at your new home. It can decide to do this if:[150]

- the overpayment occurred after you moved, and occurred because you were no longer living at your previous home; *and*
- the same local authority that paid you the overpayment is paying your HB at your new home.

In these circumstances, the local authority can deduct all the weekly HB owing to you for your new home to recover the overpayment, for however many weeks you were overpaid at your previous home.

Recovery from your partner

If you were the claimant and the overpayment, no matter how it was caused, is recoverable from you, the local authority can also recover it by deductions from any HB later awarded to your partner, provided you were a couple at the time of the overpayment and when the deduction is made.[151]

Recovery from a landlord

The local authority may recover the overpayment from:

- HB paid to your landlord if s/he is claiming HB her/himself;[152]
- HB paid directly to your landlord on your behalf.[153] The notification of the overpayment (see p1242) should make it clear from whom the authority is recovering;

Part 9: Claiming benefits and getting paid
Chapter 56: Overpayments
5. Overpayments of housing benefit

- HB paid directly to your landlord on behalf of other claimants.[154]

When HB is recovered from a landlord in this way, there are special rules on how this affects your liability to pay rent (see p1243).

The rate of recovery

The same weekly rates apply as those for IS, income-based JSA and income-related ESA (see p1228).[155]

The rate of recovery can be increased by up to half of any amount of earned income which is being disregarded. However, this cannot be done if the £5 or £10 disregard applies in your case (see p267 and p309).[156] Amounts of income disregarded for childcare costs cannot be used to increase the rate of recovery in this way.

However, you can argue that the rate will cause you hardship and a lesser amount should be recovered instead.

Recovery from other benefits

The local authority can ask the DWP to recover an overpayment of HB by making deductions from most of the benefits in this *Handbook* (except guardian's allowance and, arguably, child benefit).[157] If the overpayment is recoverable from your partner (see p1236), it can be recovered by deductions from her/his IS, income-based JSA, income-related ESA, pension credit, universal credit or personal independence payment.

An overpayment can also be recovered from benefits paid to your landlord personally.[158]

Deductions can only be made if:[159]
- a recoverable overpayment has been made as a result of a misrepresentation of, or failure to disclose (see p1219), a material fact by you, on your behalf or by or on behalf of another person to whom HB has been paid; *and*
- the local authority is unable to recover that overpayment from any HB; *and*
- the person who is to repay the overpayment is receiving a sufficient amount of at least one of the relevant benefits to allow deductions to be made.

There are no rules limiting the maximum amount that can be deducted. However, you can argue that your rate of repayment should be reasonable. If you are on IS, income-based JSA or income-related ESA, argue that the weekly maximums for these benefits should apply (see p1228). Ask the DWP to use its discretion to reduce the amounts if the deductions will cause you hardship.

If deductions stop because you are no longer entitled to a particular benefit, or the amount to which you are entitled is insufficient for deductions to be made, the DWP notifies the local authority which, once again, becomes responsible for any further recovery action.

Adjusting your rent account

If you are a local authority tenant, the local authority can recover an overpayment by adding it as a debt to your rent account. If a local authority recovers overpaid HB in this way, the overpayment should be separately identified and you should be informed that the amount being recovered does not represent rent arrears.[160]

If the local authority is seeking to evict you because you have rent arrears, you should obtain advice. It cannot argue you owe it rent arrears if you have only been overpaid HB. Local authorities are reminded in DWP guidance that overpayments of HB paid to their own tenants are not rent arrears and should not be treated as such.[161]

An overpayment cannot be recovered in this way if you have a private or housing association landlord. However, an overpayment can be recovered from your landlord (see p1239). If the local authority recovers from your landlord, you might count as being in rent arrears (see p1221).

Deductions from earnings

The local authority can order your employer to deduct amounts from your wages or salary in order to recover the overpayment.[162] The rules for this are explained on p1229.

Court action

If a local authority cannot use any of the methods of recovery listed on p1238 and you cannot agree on repayments, it can try to recover the money you owe through the county court (sheriff court in Scotland) if it thinks you can afford to make repayments. You have one month to ask for a revision or appeal against a decision that an overpayment is recoverable. This should be borne in mind when local authorities are deciding when to start proceedings.

A local authority should not use court proceedings to recover an overpayment if it has not followed the correct procedure (see p1233) – eg, if it has not issued the correct notification.[163]

A local authority can:

- sue you for the debt created by the overpayment. If the correct procedure (see p1233) has not been followed, you can use this as a defence.[164] You may also be able to claim compensation in certain circumstances (see p1233). However, you cannot say that you should have received more HB – you must seek a review instead;[165] *or*
- use the special rules to register the overpayment as a debt which can then be recovered using a court procedure.[166] Seek advice if you think the local authority is not entitled to do this.

Note: recovery action through the courts in England and Wales must be taken within six years of the decision to recover or, if later, any written acknowledgement of the overpayment or voluntary repayment.[167] In Scotland, the DWP regards the

Part 9: Claiming benefits and getting paid
Chapter 56: Overpayments
5. Overpayments of housing benefit

time limit as being 20 years from the date of the decision to recover (or, if there was no such decision, five years from the decision that there was an overpayment). Seek advice about how these limits apply to your case.[168]

If the local authority is successful in its court proceedings against you, you may have to pay legal costs and interest, as well as the overpayment. Remember that court procedures often require you to take action within a very short period of time. If the local authority is threatening to use court proceedings, seek urgent advice.

Step five: notification of an overpayment

If the local authority decides that a recoverable overpayment has occurred, it must write to the person from whom recovery is being sought (see p1236) within 14 days if possible, notifying her/him of this.[169]

What should be in the notification

This notification must state:[170]

– that there is an overpayment which is legally recoverable;

– the reason why there is a recoverable overpayment;

– the amount of the recoverable overpayment;

– how the amount of the overpayment was calculated;

– the benefit weeks to which the overpayment relates;

– if recovery is to be made from future benefit, how much the deduction will be;

– if recovery is to be made from your landlord by deductions from someone else's HB, your identity and the claimant whose HB will be deducted;[171]

– your right to ask for a further written explanation of any of the decisions the local authority has made about the overpayment, how you can do this and the time limit for doing so;

– that you have a right to ask the local authority to reconsider any of the decisions it has made about the overpayment, how you can do this and the time limit for doing so.

It may also include any other relevant matters.

Guidance states that the local authority should issue a single notification to all relevant parties (eg, landlord and tenant), saying from whom the overpayment is recoverable and from whom it is not.[172]

If you write and ask the local authority for a more detailed written explanation of any of the decisions it has made about an overpayment, it must send you this within 14 days or, if this is not reasonably practicable, as soon as possible.[173]

If a notification sent to you is a clear decision that there is an overpayment which is recoverable from you, but does not contain all the matters above, it is only valid if the omissions do not put you at a disadvantage.[174] If, for example, it does not set out your right to apply for a revision so that you do not do so until it is too late, you will have been put at a disadvantage and so can argue that the overpayment is not recoverable. However, if the decision is not about recoverability and is only about the fact that you have been overpaid, you can argue that there is no decision saying that you must repay the overpayment.[175]

No recovery should be sought until after you have been notified and the one-month time period for asking for a revision or appealing has passed.[176]

The effect of recovery from your landlord

If you are a private or housing association tenant, an overpayment of HB recovered from your landlord (see p1239) could mean that s/he tries to obtain money from you. The landlord could argue that you are in rent arrears as a result and could seek possession of your home.

Whether or not HB was paid directly to your landlord, s/he may still try to argue that, even if you owe no rent, you nevertheless owe a debt under common law. This is probably not correct. If s/he threatens to sue you, seek advice straight away.

If you are a local authority tenant, these rules do not apply. However, the local authority can recover an overpayment of HB by making deductions from your rent account (see p1240).

If you were overpaid HB after 4 November 1997 and HB was paid directly to your landlord, the following rules apply.

- If you are overpaid, and the local authority recovers the overpayment from your landlord by making deductions from direct payments of other tenants' HB (see p1239), the other tenants are treated as having paid the amount of the deduction towards their rent.[177]

- If you are overpaid, and the local authority recovers the overpayment from your landlord by making deductions from direct payments of your HB, you are treated as having paid the amount of the deduction towards your rent if your landlord is convicted of an offence or agrees to pay a penalty (see p1256) in relation to that overpayment.[178] If the local authority decides to recover under this rule, it must notify both your landlord and you that you are to be treated as having paid your rent.[179]

In these situations, your landlord cannot argue that you are in arrears of rent. It is also much easier to argue that your landlord cannot sue you under common law for a debt.

The law does not make clear what happens in other cases where deductions are made from your HB. If you are in this position, you could argue that the rules do not say what happens in your case and so the same rules apply as before the law was introduced. If this is right, you should be treated as having paid your rent. However, because there is a risk of losing your home if your landlord were to seek possession, you should seek advice immediately.

If you were overpaid HB before 4 November 1997, see the different rules on pp1119–20 of the *Welfare Benefits Handbook* 2000/01 and seek advice.

Challenging an overpayment decision

You can apply for a revision or appeal (see Chapters 58 and 59) if you want to dispute:

- the decision that you have been overpaid HB;
- the amount of the overpayment;
- the decision that it is a recoverable overpayment;
- that the overpayment is to be recovered from you under the rules set out on p1236.

Do not pay back any of the money until your challenge has been dealt with. Local authority guidance states that overpayments should not be recovered while under appeal.[180] If the local authority is already making deductions from your HB (see p1237) or deductions are being made from your other benefits (see p1240), ask it to stop this straight away

Notes

2. Overpayments that are always recoverable
1 s74 SSAA 1992
2 Reg 7(1) SS(PAOR) Regs
3 R(SB) 3/91
4 See for example, the appeals in R(SB) 28/85 and R(IS) 6/02
5 Sch 9A para 11 SS(C&P) Regs
6 *R v Secretary of State for Social Security ex parte Craigie* [2000] EWCA Civ 329, 15 December (CA)
7 *R v Secretary of State for Social Security ex parte Golding* [1996] 1 July, unreported (CA)
8 CIS/5206/1995
9 CIS/5206/1995
10 s71(4) SSAA 1992; reg 11 SS(PAOR) Regs; reg 35 CB&GA(Admin) Regs
11 Reg 11 SS(PAOR) Regs; reg 35 CB&GA(Admin) Regs
12 Sch 2 para 20(d) SS&CS(DA) Regs
13 s71ZB(1) WRA 2012; Art 5(3A) WRA(No. 8)O

14 s71ZB(3) SSAA 1992
15 Reg 16 SS(OR) Regs
16 Reg 8(3) SS(OR) Regs
17 Reg 7 SS(OR) Regs
18 Reg 9(1)(a) and (b) and (2) SS(OR) Regs
19 Reg 9(1)(c) SS(OR) Regs
20 Reg 9(3) SS(OR) Regs
21 Reg 4 SS(OR) Regs

3. Overpayments that are sometimes recoverable
22 s71(1) and (5A) SSAA 1992; R(SB) 34/83
23 s71(5A) SSAA 1992; CIS/3228/2003; R(IS) 13/05. See CPC/3743/2006 for when not all the overpayment period has been covered by the change of the award.
24 Reg 12 SS(PAOR) Regs
25 CSIS/45/1990
26 CIS/3228/2003
27 R(SB) 7/91
28 *LL v SSWP* [2013] UKUT 208 (AAC)

29 This was the case in *Hamilton v Department for Social Development* [2010] NICA, but it is clear from *SSWP v AD(IS)* [2011] UKUT 184 (AAC) that whether this is the case depends on the specific decision-making history in your case.

30 R(SB) 7/91; R(IS) 13/05. But see CIS/3228/2003 in cases where a decision changing the award is defective but has been certified.

31 *B v SSWP* [2005] EWCA Civ 929, reported as R(IS) 9/06. The effect of the decision is that recovery is under reg 32 SS(C&P) Regs and, presumably, under the equivalent rules in reg 24 JSA Regs and reg 23 CB&GA(Admin) Regs.

32 R(SB) 21/82

33 R(SB) 54/83; CSB/296/1985

34 CG/190/1999

35 R(SB) 21/82

36 *Hooper v SSWP* [2007] EWCA Civ 495, reported as R(IB) 4/07. See also official guidance in Memo DMG 26/07.

37 Reg 32(1B) SS(C&P) Regs

38 CSB/510/1987; CIS/545/1992; CIS/1769/1999. These decisions arose from the old test of failure to disclose and it is not clear they apply now. However, the point seems to have been adopted in *DG v SSWP* [2009] UKUT 120 (AAC).

39 R(SB) 15/87; *Hinchy v SSWP*, 3 March 2005 (HL), reported as R(IS) 7/05

40 Reg 23(5) CB&GA(Admin) Regs

41 CG/5631/1999; CIS/1887/2002; *WA v SSWP* [2009] UKUT 132 (AAC); *GJ v SSWP (IS)* [2010] UKUT 107 (AAC)

42 Reg 32(1B) SS(C&P) Regs requires notification in writing or by telephone, unless the DWP specifically requires otherwise.

43 R(SB) 18/85

44 CWSB/2/1985

45 CSB/347/1983; R(SB) 10/85

46 R(SB) 15/87

47 CDLA/6336/1999

48 R(SB) 15/87; CIS/3529/2008

49 R(SB) 54/83

50 CSB/393/1985

51 CIS/5117/1998

52 R(SB) 9/85

53 *Jones and Sharples v CAO* [1994] 1 All ER 225 (CA); R(SB) 9/85

54 R(SB) 18/85

55 R(SB) 2/91

56 R(SB) 3/90

57 *Sheriff v CAO, The Times*, 10 May 1995 (CA), reported as R(IS) 14/96

58 CG/4494/1999 suggests the principle may apply in social security; R(IS) 4/06 is more doubtful, but does not rule it out.

59 CIS/3846/2001

60 *Jones and Sharples v CAO* [1994] 1 All ER 225 (CA); *Franklin v CAO, The Times*, 29 December 1995 (CA); CIS/674/1994; CIS/583/1994; CIS/674/1994

61 *Franklin v CAO, The Times*, 29 December 1995 (CA)

62 CIS/583/1994

63 CDLA/6336/1999

64 R(SB) 2/92

65 CDLA/5803/1999

66 CDLA/1823/2004

67 R(S) 4/86; R(I) 3/75

68 CIS/159/1990; CS/11700/1996; CSIS/7/1994; CG/5631/1999; *GJ v SSWP (IS)* [2010] UKUT 107 (AAC)

69 *Duggan v CAO, The Times*, 18 December 1989 (CA); CG/662/1998; CG/4494/1999; *Hinchy v SSWP* [2003] EWCA Civ 138 (CA)

70 *JM v SSWP (IS)* [2011] UKUT 15 (AAC)

71 CIS/222/1991

72 R(SB) 20/84; R(SB) 24/87

73 Reg 13(1)(b) and (1A) SS(PAOR) Regs

74 *Commock v CAO*, reported as an appendix to R(SB) 6/90; CSIS/8/1995

75 Reg 14 SS(PAOR) Regs

76 CIS/5825/1999

77 s71(3) SSAA 1992

78 *B v SSWP* [2005] EWCA Civ 929, reported as R(IS) 9/06, which says that overpayments for failure to disclose are recoverable because of a breach of duty by a claimant of reg 32 SS(C&P) Regs; CIS/1996/2006; CIS/2125/2006

79 R(IS) 5/03. This tribunal of commissioners' decision was intended to resolve the conflict between the earlier CIS/332/1993 and R(IS) 5/00, and preferred the latter.

80 CA/1014/1999; CSDLA/1282/2001

81 *Secretary of State for Social Services v Solly* [1974] 3 All ER 922; R(SB) 21/82

82 CIS/1423/1997

83 s12 SSAA 1998

4. Recovery of overpaid benefit

84 www.gov.uk/government/publications/what-happens-if-you-are-overpaid-universal-credit-jobseekers-allowance-or-employment-and-support-allowance

85 When the Welfare Reform Bill (which introduced these rules) was being debated, the minister said it was the intention not to recover many overpayments which had been caused by official error- see House of Commons, *Hansard*, 19 May 2011, col 1019

86 *Guidance on the Application of Secretary of State Discretion* at: www.cpag.org.uk/overpayments-adviser-tools

87 Reg 42A CB&GA(Admin) Regs

88 Reg 16(1) and (2) SS(PAOR) Regs

89 Regs 15 and 16 SS(PAOR) Regs

90 Reg 16(3) SS(PAOR) Regs

91 Reg 17 SS(PAOR) Regs

92 s74(2)(b) SSAA 1992

93 Reg 16(4), (4A), (5) and (6) SS(PAOR) Regs

94 Reg 16(6) SS(PAOR) Regs

95 Reg 16(5A) SS(PAOR) Regs

96 Reg 16(7A) and (7B) SS(PAOR) Regs

97 Reg 18 SS(OR) Regs

98 Reg 19 SS(OR) Regs

99 Reg 23 SS(OR) Regs

100 Reg 30 SS(OR) Regs

101 Reg 21 SS(OR) Regs

102 Reg 20(3) SS(OR) Regs

103 Regs 17(1) and 20(7) SS(OR) Regs

104 Reg 29 SS(OR) Regs

105 Reg 25 SS(OR) Regs

106 s71(10) SSAA 1992

107 s9(1) Limitation Act 1980

108 DWP, *Benefit Overpayment Recovery Guide* (draft), based on the provisions of the Prescription and Limitation (Scotland) Act 1973

109 *CPAG v SSWP* [2010] UKSC 54, 8 December 2010, upholding the decision of the Court of Appeal in *CPAG, R (on the application of) v SSWP* [2009] EWCA Civ 1058, 14 October 2009

110 Reg 10 SS(OR) Regs

111 Reg 16(7A) and (7B) SS(PAOR) Regs

112 Reg 11 SS(OR) Regs

113 Reg 11(7) SS(OR) Regs

114 Reg 11(8) SS(OR) Regs

115 Reg 11(9) SS(OR) Regs

116 Reg 12 SS(OR) Regs

117 Reg 13 SS(OR) Regs

118 Reg 14 SS(OR) Regs (the maximum amounts recoverable per week stated in this rule are calculated by reference to percentages of a monthly figure of UC – we assume these are converted to weekly figures)

119 Reg 29A SS(PAOR) Regs

120 s71ZE SSAA 1992

5. Overpayments of housing benefit

121 Reg 99 HB Regs; reg 80 HB(SPC) Regs

122 Reg 99 HB Regs; reg 80 HB(SPC) Regs

123 Reg 93(3) HB Regs; reg 74(3) HB(SPC) Regs

124 Reg 100(4) HB Regs; reg 81(4) HB(SPC) Regs

125 Reg 100(2) HB Regs; reg 81(2) HB(SPC) Regs

126 Reg 100(3) HB Regs; reg 81(3) HB(SPC) Regs

127 HB/CTB Circular A23/2009

128 CH/2567/2007; HB/CTB Circular A15/2009

129 CH/571/2003; CH/5485/2002

130 CH/939/2004; see also *R on the application of Sier v Cambridge CC* [2001], unreported (QBD), as upheld by the Court of Appeal [2001] EWCA Civ 1523, 8 October 2001; CH/3761/2005

131 *Duggan v CAO, The Times*, 18 December 1989 (CA); *R on the application of Sier v Cambridge CC* [2001] unreported (QBD), as upheld by the Court of Appeal [2001] EWCA Civ 1523, 8 October 2001; CH/571/2003; CH/3761/2005

132 *R on the application of Sier v Cambridge CC* [2001] (QBD), as upheld by the Court of Appeal [2001] EWCA Civ 1523, 8 October 2001

133 *Warwick DC v Freeman* [1994] 27 HLR 616 (CA); CH/4918/2003

134 *R v Liverpool City Council ex parte Griffiths* [1990] 22 HLR 312; CH/2554/2002; CH/2567/2007

135 s75(1) SSAA 1992

136 s75(3)(a) SSAA 1992

137 Reg 101(2) HB Regs; reg 82(2) HB(SPC) Regs

138 Reg 101(2)(b)(ii) and (4) HB Regs; reg 82(2)(b)(ii) and (4) HB(SPC) Regs

139 RH 6/06

140 *HB/CTB Overpayments Guide*, para 4.115

141 Reg 101(2A) HB Regs; reg 82(2A) HB(SPC) Regs

142 Reg 101(1) HB Regs; reg 82(1) HB(SPC) Regs

Chapter 56

Overpayments

143 Reg 104 HB Regs; reg 85 HB(SPC) Regs; *Adan v London Borough of Hounslow and SSWP* [2004] EWCA Civ 101, 19 February 2004, reported as R(H) 5/04; CH/4943/2001; HB/CTB Circular A13/2006

144 Reg 104(1) HB Regs; reg 85 HB(SPC) Regs

145 *R v Kensington and Chelsea RBC ex parte Brandt* [1995] 28 HLR 528 at 537 (QBD)

146 Reg 104(3) HB Regs; reg 85(3) HB(SPC) Regs

147 Reg 103 HB Regs; reg 84 HB(SPC) Regs

148 Reg 103(1)(a) and (b) HB Regs; reg 84(1)(a) and (b) HB(SPC) Regs

149 Reg 102 HB Regs; reg 83 HB(SPC) Regs; s75 SSAA 1992

150 Reg 104A HB Regs; reg 85A HB(SPC) Regs

151 Reg 101(2)(b)(ii) and (4) HB Regs; reg 83(2)(b)(ii) and (4) HB(SPC) Regs

152 s75(5)(a) SSAA 1992; reg 106 HB Regs; reg 87 HB(SPC) Regs

153 s75(5)(b) SSAA 1992; reg 106 HB Regs; reg 87 HB(SPC) Regs

154 s75(5)(c) SSAA 1992; reg 106 HB Regs; reg 87 HB(SPC) Regs

155 Reg 102 HB Regs; reg 83 HB(SPC) Regs; HB/CTB Circular A42/00

156 Reg 102(4) HB Regs; reg 83(4) HB(SPC) Regs

157 Reg 105(1)(a) HB Regs

158 s75(5)(a) SSAA 1992; reg 106 HB Regs; reg 87 HB(SPC) Regs

159 Regs 102 and 105 HB Regs; regs 83 and 86 HB(SPC) Regs

160 *R v Haringey LBC ex parte Azad Ayub* [1992] 25 HLR 566 (QBD)

161 paras A7.360 GM

162 Reg 106A HB Regs; reg 87A HB(SPC) Regs

163 *Warwick DC v Freeman* [1994] 27 HLR 616 (CA)

164 *Warwick DC v Freeman* [1994] 27 HLR 616 (CA)

165 *Plymouth CC v Gigg* [1997] 30 HLR 284 (CA)

166 s75(7) SSAA 1992

167 s9(1) Limitation Act 1980

168 DWP, *Benefit Overpayment Recovery Guide* (draft), based on the provisions of the Prescription and Limitation (Scotland) Act 1973

169 Reg 90(1)(b) HB Regs; reg 71(1)(b) HB(SPC) Regs

170 Sch 9 paras 2, 3, 6 and 15 HB Regs; Sch 8 paras 2, 3, 6 and 15 HB(SPC) Regs; para A7.222 GM

171 Sch 9 para 15(2) HB Regs; Sch 8 para 15(2) HB(SPC) Regs

172 HB/CTB Circular A13/2006

173 Reg 90(4) HB Regs; reg 71(4) HB(SPC) Regs

174 *Haringey LBC v Awaritefe* [1999] 32 HLR 517 (CA)

175 CH/1395/2006

176 para A7.230-233 GM; HB/CTB Circular A13/2006

177 s75(6) SSAA 1992

178 s75(6) SSAA 1992; reg 107 HB Regs; reg 88 HB(SPC) Regs

179 Reg 107(3) HB Regs; reg 88(3) HB(SPC) Regs

180 *Overpayments Guide*, paras 4.391 and 6.50; *Housing Benefit and Council Tax Benefit General Information Bulletin* HB/CTB G18/2010

9

Chapter 57

Fraud and penalties

This chapter covers:
1. Civil penalties (p1249)
2. Investigating benefit claims (p1250)
3. Prosecution of offences (p1253)
4. Financial penalties for benefit offences (p1256)
5. Sanctions for benefit offences (p1258)

This chapter covers the rules on fraud for all the benefits administered by the DWP, housing benefit, child benefit and guardian's allowance. For information on tax credits and fraud, see Chapter 67. This chapter does not cover the rules for statutory sick, maternity, paternity and adoption pay.

Key facts

- When you claim benefit, you must give correct and complete information to the DWP, HM Revenue and Customs (HMRC) or the local authority. You might commit an offence if you deliberately mislead the agency dealing with your claim.
- You must report changes in your circumstances that could affect your entitlement. You may commit an offence if you do not notify the relevant office of such changes promptly.
- You may receive a fine (known as a 'civil penalty') if you provide incorrect information and you are considered to have acted negligently, or if you have not notified a change of circumstances and do not have a reasonable excuse.
- If the DWP, HMRC or local authority believes you have committed fraud, you may be prosecuted. Alternatively, you may be given the option of paying a financial penalty. Your benefit could be stopped or reduced ('sanctioned'), even if you are not prosecuted.
- If you are accused of fraud, seek urgent advice before taking any action or making any statements.

1. Civil penalties

You can be given a civil penalty if you are overpaid benefit because of negligence or a failure on your behalf. A civil penalty can be given if you are not considered to have committed fraud, but have acted carelessly in relation to your claim. Civil penalties are different from the financial penalties imposed for benefit offences (see p1256).

Note: you cannot be given a civil penalty if you have been sent a notice about a penalty for a benefit offence or if you have been charged or accepted a formal caution for a benefit offence.

A civil penalty of £50 may given if:[1]

- you 'negligently' (see below) make an incorrect statement or representation, or negligently give incorrect information or evidence, about a claim for or an award of a benefit, and you do not take 'reasonable steps' (see below) to correct the error; *or*
- you do not provide information or evidence, or you fail to notify a 'relevant change of circumstances' (see below), and you do not have a 'reasonable excuse' (see below); *and*
- your negligence or failure results in your being overpaid benefit of more than £65.[2]

Definitions

A **'relevant change of circumstances'** is one that affects entitlement to benefit.[3]

Other terms used are not defined in the legislation, but their meaning may be clarified by caselaw over time. The DWP has produced guidance on the meaning of the following.[4]

'Negligently' is acting carelessly, not paying attention to or disregarding the importance of anything that needs to be done relating to your claim.

'Reasonable steps' is doing something which is sensible or practicable to correct an error.

'Reasonable excuse' is credible reasons or justification for failing to do something or doing it late.

The penalty can be recovered in the same way as an overpayment (see p1230).[5] If you are claiming jointly with your partner and the penalty is for negligently making or giving incorrect statements, representations, information or evidence, it can be recovered from your partner instead of you, unless s/he was not (and could not reasonably be expected to be) aware of the error.

You can appeal against the imposition of a civil penalty – eg, you can argue that you did not behave negligently or that you had a 'reasonable excuse' for not declaring a change in your circumstances. **Note:** if you receive a decision that you have been overpaid because you have failed to disclose a change of circumstances, consider whether you also want to appeal against that decision and/or the decision that the overpayment is recoverable from you (see Chapter 56).

Part 9: Claiming benefits and getting paid
Chapter 57: Fraud and penalties
2. Investigating benefit claims

2. Investigating benefit claims

The DWP, HM Revenue and Customs (HMRC) or local authority may start an investigation into your benefit claim for a variety of reasons. It does not have to tell you straight away about the enquiries it is making. It usually waits until it has collected more information and then asks you to attend an interview to explain matters.

Note: the government has announced that, from October 2014, the separate services in the DWP, HMRC and local authorities will start to be replaced by a single service within the DWP that will investigate all benefit and tax credit fraud. See CPAG's online services and *Welfare Rights Bulletin* for updates.

Collecting information

In order to prevent fraud, the DWP can ask for information from a wide variety of sources. Not all information is confidential, but there are special rules allowing the release of information to the DWP from:

- HMRC;[6]
- government departments – eg, on issues about passports, immigration, emigration, nationality and prisoners;[7]
- the Registration Service, which is under an additional duty to report particulars of deaths to the DWP for social security purposes and to HMRC;[8]
- local authorities.[9]

Local authorities may also be supplied with information held by the DWP or HMRC, and may share information with other local authorities.[10]

Local authorities, HMRC and the DWP can require information about redirected post and have undelivered social security post returned to them.[11]

All information acquired is confidential to the bodies concerned with the administration of benefit, including private companies contracted to carry out such functions. Unauthorised disclosure of this information is a criminal offence.[12]

Are you unhappy about the use of your personal information?
The Data Protection Act 1998 restricts the use of accessible personal data held on computer or in a relevant filing system in written form. If a local authority, the DWP or HMRC makes a request for information under either the provisions above or the investigative powers below which you think is inappropriate or unreasonable, you can refer the matter to the Information Commissioner.

Powers of investigation

As 'authorised officers', fraud investigators have certain powers to obtain information.[13]

In local authorities, authorised officers normally investigate housing benefit (HB) fraud, but if an investigation into HB has begun, the local authority can also investigate fraudulent claims for income support, jobseeker's allowance, employment and support allowance, pension credit and incapacity benefit.[14] **Note:** council tax benefit was abolished from April 2013 but investigations can still be carried out into previous awards.

'**Authorised officers**' can be:
- officials of any government department (not just the DWP or HMRC);
- employees of local authorities carrying out HB functions; *or*
- employees of organisations that perform contracted-out HB functions.

Authorised officers should use a code of practice when obtaining information.[15] Information that is the subject of 'legal privilege' (ie, confidential communication between a legal adviser and her/his client) cannot be requested.[16]

Authorised officers have powers to enter, at a reasonable time, premises which they have reasonable grounds for suspecting are:[17]
- a person's place of employment;
- where a trade or business is carried out or documents relating to it are kept;
- where a personal or occupational pension scheme is administered or documents relating to it are kept;
- where someone operating a compensatory scheme for an industrial accident or disease may be found;
- where a person on whose behalf a compensatory payment for an industrial accident or disease may be found.

This may include someone's home. The authorised officer must show a certificate of appointment if asked for it. S/he can question anyone on the premises, and require, if reasonable, any documents or copies of documents.

Authorised officers cannot come into your home without your permission (except if you run a business from your home) and they cannot detain you. They cannot make you give information or answer questions in such a way as to confess that you, or your partner, are guilty of an offence.[18]

All fraud investigators (not just authorised officers) can use ongoing surveillance to investigate social security fraud – eg, observing people entering or leaving premises. Any surveillance must be authorised by an officer of the appropriate level.

Fraud investigators are bound by codes of practice under the Police and Criminal Evidence Act 1984.[19] If these are breached, this may restrict the use of evidence they have obtained.[20] If you think the officers have acted unfairly, seek advice.

Part 9: Claiming benefits and getting paid
Chapter 57: Fraud and penalties
2. Investigating benefit claims

Interviews

Fraud investigators may carry out interviews to get information. If you are suspected of fraud, officers should carry out a formal interview, known as an 'interview under caution'. You should always be cautioned before the interview if there are grounds to suspect that you have committed an offence. If the fraud officer fails to do so, the interview may not be admissible in court. If you do not understand the caution, its meaning should be explained to you.

You do not have to answer any questions put to you, but if you do not answer questions after being cautioned, this might be taken as a sign of guilt. If you are interviewed under caution and you decide not to answer questions, you could instead prepare a written statement to give to the investigators.

You might not be told why the interview is happening. If you have not been informed of the purpose of a fraud interview, a court may rule that the interview is inadmissible as evidence.

A formal interview is taped. A transcript of the tape is produced for use at any trial or appeal hearing.

Are you suspected of fraud?

1. If you think fraud officers may interview you, seek advice before you attend the interview. Free legal advice may be available from a solicitor.

2. Take someone (eg, a solicitor, adviser or friend) to the interview with you. Although s/he cannot speak for you, s/he can support you and take notes.

3. Although it can be very distressing to be accused of committing an offence, remain calm and listen carefully to the questions you are asked. If you do not understand anything, ask for clarification. You must answer the questions yourself. Think carefully about the implications of the answers you give.

4. If you think you can explain why the situation has arisen, you should mention it at the interview, as any explanation you give later is less likely to be believed if you are prosecuted.[21] If you can explain matters, your benefit is less likely to be taken away.

5. Do not confess to something that you did not do just to finish the interview or to prevent your benefit from being stopped.

The effect of a fraud investigation on your benefit

If the DWP, HMRC or local authority have doubts about your entitlement to benefit, other procedures may also be applied at the same time as a fraud investigation.

- In some circumstances, your benefit may be suspended (see p1175) – eg, if there are doubts about your entitlement or if there is a possibility that you are being overpaid.

- You may be asked to provide information and evidence about your claim. If you do not do so within a specified time limit, your claim can be terminated (see p1177). If you still believe that you are entitled to benefit, make a new claim.

If a fraud investigation is taking a long time to complete, your benefit may also be suspended for a long time. However, the DWP, HMRC or local authority should not withhold your benefit indefinitely without making a decision on whether or not you are entitled to it. Complain if you think an investigation is taking too long (see p1383). If that brings no results, seek legal advice about forcing the DWP, HMRC or local authority to make a decision.

The decision on whether you should be prosecuted is separate from a decision to recover an overpayment of benefit (see Chapter 53).The two processes are independent and have different tests. Therefore:

- a decision or appeal on your claim does not have to be delayed while you wait for the outcome of a criminal prosecution;[22]
- a court fine does not prevent the DWP, HMRC or local authority from taking action to recover an overpayment. If you have made payments under a compensation order made by a court to the DWP, HMRC or local authority, it cannot also recover that amount as an overpayment.[23]

Acquittal in a fraud case does not necessarily mean that the decision on your benefit entitlement was wrong. Whatever the result of an investigation or prosecution, the DWP, HMRC or local authority may take more time assessing your future claims because it may check your circumstances more thoroughly. Complain if it takes too long to make a decision (see p1383). You should not be prevented from making a fresh claim during a fraud investigation if your circumstances have changed. You could also apply for a short-term advance of benefit (see p1167) or help from local authority discretionary funds (see p829).

3. Prosecution of offences

Benefit offences can broadly be divided into two categories, based on the severity of the penalty you can potentially be given. For information about:

- making false representations in order to claim benefit, see p1254; and
- making dishonest representations in order to claim benefit, see p1255.

In more serious cases in England and Wales, you may be charged with the criminal offences of theft or fraud, and in Scotland with common law offences.[24] These offences carry more severe penalties.

If found guilty, you can be fined or imprisoned, or both. Any fine that you have to pay is in addition to any overpayment that is found to be recoverable

Part 9: Claiming benefits and getting paid
Chapter 57: Fraud and penalties
3. Prosecution of offences

from you (see Chapter 56). Your benefits can also be sanctioned for a period (see p1258).

Note: from April 2012 in England and Wales, the DWP's Prosecution Division merged with the Crown Prosecution Service, which also conducts prosecutions on behalf of many local authorities. In Scotland, prosecutions are conducted by the Procurator Fiscal.

False representations

Making false representations in order to claim benefit is the less serious of the benefit offences. You commit this offence if you:

- make a statement which you know to be false or give information or produce documents that you know to be false (or knowingly cause or allow someone else to do so) in order to claim a benefit or payment for yourself or someone else, or for any other purpose relating to the benefit rules.[25] It does not have to be shown that you intended to obtain benefit to which you were not entitled;[26]
- fail to notify the DWP, HM Revenue and Customs (HMRC) or local authority promptly of a change of circumstances which you know affects your entitlement to benefit or another payment. This also applies to appointees and other third parties receiving benefit on your behalf, and landlords receiving direct payments of housing benefit (HB). You count as notifying a change promptly if you do so as soon as reasonably practicable after the change occurs;[27]
- cause or allow another person to fail to notify a change of circumstances to the DWP, HMRC or local authority promptly which you know affects her/his entitlement to benefit or other payment.[28]

You do not 'know' something if you are merely careless about whether or not something is true, or if you fail to find out.[29] You will not have committed an offence if you do not notify a change of circumstances that did not affect your entitlement to benefit or if there was already no entitlement to benefit.[30]

The maximum penalty for these offences is a £5,000 fine or three months in prison, or both.[31]

Duty to report a change in circumstances

The rules on fraud and your duty to report a change of circumstances are different from the general rules on reporting a change of circumstances outlined on p1174. For fraud purposes, you only commit an offence if you do not report promptly a change that you know affects your benefit.[32] However, to avoid potential allegations of fraud or prosecution, you should report *all* changes promptly, in writing or by telephone. **Note:** for some benefits, you may be allowed to report a change other than in writing or by telephone. For child benefit and guardian's allowance, you must report any change in writing unless HMRC says otherwise. In all cases, it is advisable to report the change in a way that allows you to show that you have done so – eg, in writing, dated and retain a copy or get a receipt.

Except for child benefit and guardian's allowance, there is a special rule if the change is a birth or a death (sometimes called 'Tell Us Once'). You can report such a change in person at a local authority (and, in England, county council) office, if an office has been specified for reporting these changes. You can notify a death by telephone if a number has been specified for that purpose.[33]

For an offence to have been committed, you must have acted 'knowingly' when failing to report a change of circumstances. To have acted 'knowingly', you must have been aware of where the change must be reported and the manner in which it must be reported.[34]

Duties of advisers and other third parties

If you are an adviser, you are not under a duty to notify the DWP, HMRC or local authority about a claimant's change of circumstances, provided you have fully advised her/him of the law and her/his requirement to notify changes in her/his circumstances and provide truthful information. In order to commit an offence of allowing or causing someone to fail to notify a change of circumstances, or knowingly allowing or causing someone to give false information, there must be some sort of implied permission given to the person to fail to report the change or give false information.[35] You do not 'allow' someone to do something unless you can stop them doing it.[36] You should do nothing to help facilitate a misrepresentation or failure to notify a change of circumstances – eg, help to complete a claim or review form which you know is inaccurate.

Dishonest representations

Making dishonest representations in order to claim benefit is the more serious of the benefit offences. You commit this offence if you make any of the false representations on p1254 in order to claim benefit and you act dishonestly ('knowingly' in Scotland) in doing so.[37] This means that you did something that most people would consider dishonest and that you must have known it was dishonest.[38]

The maximum penalty if you are convicted in a magistrates' court (sheriff court in Scotland) is a £5,000 fine or six months in prison (12 months in Scotland[39]), or both. If you are convicted in the Crown Court (High Court in Scotland), you can receive an unlimited fine or seven years in prison, or both.[40]

Prosecutions

Not all cases in which there is evidence to justify a prosecution are taken to court. Instead, you may be given the chance to pay a penalty (see p1257). In some cases, no fraud action is taken at all. The factors taken into account include the strength of the evidence, the amount of benefit involved, whether an offence was planned

Part 9: Claiming benefits and getting paid
Chapter 57: Fraud and penalties
4. Financial penalties for benefit offences

and your personal circumstances. **Note:** you may have sanctions imposed on certain benefits, even if you are not prosecuted (see p1258).

There are time limits for bringing a prosecution for making false representations in order to claim benefit (see p1254). A prosecution must be started either within three months of the date the DWP, HMRC or local authority (or, in Scotland, the Procurator Fiscal) thinks it has sufficient evidence to prosecute you, or within 12 months of the date you committed the offence, whichever is later.[41]

There are no time limits for bringing a prosecution for making dishonest representations in order to claim benefit (see p1255) .

Are you being prosecuted?

If you are being prosecuted, get advice. You may be entitled to free legal help from a solicitor and representation in court. Check carefully that the DWP, HMRC or local authority is able to prove all the parts of the offence with which you are charged. Do not plead guilty until you have obtained advice.

4. **Financial penalties for benefit offences**

The DWP, HM Revenue and Customs (HMRC) or local authority may offer you the option of paying a financial penalty under civil law instead of being prosecuted under criminal law. These financial penalties are not the same as the civil penalties described on p1249. **Note:** your benefit can still be sanctioned if you accept a penalty (see p1258).

For offences committed wholly after 7 May 2012, the amount of the penalty is 50 per cent of the overpayment (or £350 if you were not overpaid), subject to a minimum of £350 and a maximum of £2,000.[42] If an offence was committed partly or wholly before 8 May 2012, the amount of the penalty is 30 per cent of the overpayment. The overpayment must have been caused by an offence you committed on or after 18 December 1997.[43]

The penalty is added to the overpayment of benefit and is recoverable in the same way as the overpayment (see p1226 and p1238).[44]

Formal cautions

The DWP no longer offers cautions for offences committed wholly or partly after 1 April 2012. Penalties may be offered instead.[45] For more details about formal cautions, see the 2012/13 edition of this *Handbook*.

The option of paying a penalty

You can be offered the option of paying a penalty if:[46]

- an overpayment has been found to be recoverable from you, or, for offences committed wholly after 7 May 2012, would have been if an award had been made. The DWP, HMRC or local authority must have revised or superseded your award of benefit and issued a decision that an overpayment is recoverable (see Chapter 56); *and*

- the overpayment was due to an act or omission on your part. This must have occurred on or after 18 December 1997;[47] *and*

- there are grounds for prosecuting you for an offence relating to the overpayment.

The DWP, HMRC or local authority issues you with a notice setting out how the scheme works and giving you information about how to agree to pay a penalty and how to notify your withdrawal of your agreement.[48] If you are not issued with a proper notice, it may not be possible to enforce the penalty.

The notice is sent with an invitation to an interview to discuss accepting the penalty. The interview should not be carried out by the same officer who interviewed you under caution (see p1252).[49] The interview is only about whether to offer you a penalty. You cannot use it to add to or alter any statement you made about the alleged offence in an interview under caution. If you are unable to decide whether or not to accept the penalty at the interview, you should be allowed five days to make up your mind.[50]

What happens if you accept a penalty?

1. If you agree to pay a penalty, you cannot be prosecuted for any offence relating to the overpayment.[51] However, you can still be prosecuted in the future if you commit another offence or one relating to a different overpayment.

2. If it is found on revision, supersession or appeal that the overpayment is not due or not recoverable, any penalty you have paid must be repaid to you.[52] This does not change the fact that you have agreed to pay a penalty in exchange for immunity from prosecution, so you still cannot be prosecuted for the offence.

3. If the amount of the overpayment is changed following a revision, supersession or appeal, the agreement is cancelled, so you lose your immunity from prosecution, and any penalty you have paid must be repaid to you. However, if you make a fresh agreement to accept a penalty, you are again immune from prosecution and the amount of penalty you have already paid can be offset against the new penalty rather than being repaid to you.[53]

If you do not accept the penalty, the DWP, HMRC or local authority may pass the case to the Crown Prosecution Service or Procurator Fiscal to consider whether to prosecute you.

Part 9: Claiming benefits and getting paid
Chapter 57: Fraud and penalties
5. Sanctions for benefit offences

Changing your mind

If you agree to pay a penalty, you can change your mind, provided you notify the DWP, HMRC or local authority within 14 days (28 days for offences committed partly or wholly before 8 May 2012) in the manner it specifies.[54] If you decide not to accept the penalty, you lose your immunity from prosecution, but you do not have to pay the penalty. If you have already paid any part of it, this must be refunded to you.

Should you agree to pay a penalty?

1. Seek advice and consider your options carefully.

2. If you are not prosecuted, your case does not go to court and you cannot get a prison sentence.

3. If you accept a penalty, your benefit may still be sanctioned (see p1258).

4. You may be invited to pay a penalty when there is insufficient evidence to prosecute you. The fraud officer can only recommend that your case be considered for prosecution. The Crown Prosecution Service, Procurator Fiscal, HMRC or local authority legal department decides whether or not to prosecute (see p1253). You are not automatically prosecuted if you refuse to accept a penalty.

5. If you are prosecuted and found guilty, you might be offered a caution or community service rather than a fine. On the other hand, you could get a large fine or even a prison sentence.

6. A penalty may be a substantial amount of money. For minor offences, the amount of the fine could be less.

---

5. **Sanctions for benefit offences**

Sanctions can be imposed on certain benefits, known as 'sanctionable benefits' (see p1259), if:[55]

- you are convicted of one or more benefit offence in a set of proceedings; *or*
- you agree to pay a penalty for a benefit offence instead of being prosecuted (see p1256).

A sanction can be imposed for a specified period (see p1261).

Under what is sometimes referred to as the 'one-strike rule' (because it can apply after just one offence), a conviction is not always required.

If you are convicted of a benefit offence and have already committed another offence(s), a longer sanction may be imposed under the 'two-strikes rule' instead. This applies if:[56]

- you are convicted of one or more benefit offences in a set of proceedings; *and*

- within five years of the date you committed the offence(s), you committed an earlier benefit offence, including an offence for which you accepted a financial penalty or formal caution; *and*
- the later offence has not previously been taken into account and the earlier offence has not previously been taken into account as an earlier offence under the two-strikes rule. Neither offence must have been taken into account in relation to a reduction in a joint claim for jobseeker's allowance (JSA) or a family member's benefit under these 'loss of benefit for benefit offences' rules.[57]

The benefit offence(s) must have been committed after 1 April 2010 (for the one-strike rule) or on or after 1 April 2002 (for the two-strikes rule) and be:[58]
- in connection with a 'disqualifying' benefit (see below); *or*
- to attempt, conspire or aid the committing of a benefit offence.

Disqualifying benefits[59]

All social security benefits and tax credits are **'disqualifying'** benefits for the purposes listed above, except statutory sick pay, statutory maternity pay, statutory adoption pay, statutory paternity pay and maternity allowance.

See p1260 for details of the sanctions that can be applied.

Which benefits can be sanctioned

Sanctions can be imposed on 'sanctionable benefits'. These are all the disqualifying benefits above *except*:[60]
- attendance allowance;
- bereavement payment;
- child benefit;
- child tax credit (CTC);
- Christmas bonus;
- disability living allowance;
- guardian's allowance;
- industrial injuries constant attendance and exceptional severe disablement allowances;
- joint-claim JSA, but note that it can still be removed or reduced;[61]
- personal independence payment;
- graduated retirement benefit;
- retirement pension;
- social fund payments;
- war pensions constant attendance allowance, exceptional severe disablement allowance and mobility supplement;

Part 9: Claiming benefits and getting paid
Chapter 57: Fraud and penalties
5. Sanctions for benefit offences

- working tax credit (WTC). However, under separate rules, you lose your WTC if you have committed a benefit offence on or after 5 April 2012 (see p1261).

The above benefits cannot therefore be sanctioned.

The sanctions

Usually, sanctionable benefits (see p1259) are not paid during a specified sanction period (see p1261). In some cases, however, your benefit may be paid at a reduced rate.

- **Income support (IS), income-based JSA, joint-claim JSA, pension credit (PC) and housing benefit (HB)** are usually reduced by 40 per cent of the appropriate personal allowance for a single person of the offender's age (see p222), or 20 per cent if you or a member of your family are pregnant or seriously ill.[62] However:
  - joint-claim JSA is not paid at all if the sanctions for benefit offences rules apply to both of you, or to one of you and the other has been given an employment, training or employment programme-related sanction (see Chapter 51);
  - unless you are in a 'vulnerable group' (see p1206), no income-based JSA can be paid at the reduced rate until the 15th day of the sanction period and only if a decision maker is satisfied you face hardship.[63] If you are in a vulnerable group, income-based JSA can be paid at the reduced rate from the first day of the sanction period;[64]
  - HB is unaffected if you or a member of your family are entitled to IS, income-based JSA, income-related employment and support allowance (ESA) or PC during the sanction period.
- **Income-related ESA** is reduced by 100 per cent of the appropriate personal allowance for a single person of the offender's age (see p222), or 40 per cent if you or a member of your family is subject to no work-related requirements (see p1079), or 20 per cent if you or a member of your family are pregnant or seriously ill.[65] You may be able to get hardship payments if your income-related ESA is reduced in this way (see p1202).
- **Universal credit (UC)** is reduced by the applicable daily standard allowance for you (50 per cent of it for a joint claim) multiplied by the number of days in the assessment period (or the remaining number of days if less).[66] However, the total reduction in any assessment period cannot be more than the applicable monthly standard allowance. The daily standard allowance is calculated by multiplying the monthly standard allowance by 12, dividing by 365 and rounding down to the nearest 10 pence. The daily standard allowance is reduced by 40 per cent (20 per cent for a joint claim) if you (or your partner if you have a joint claim) are:
  - not subject to any work-related requirements because you are the responsible carer of a child or foster child under the age of one, have adopted a child in

the last 12 months, or it is 11 weeks or less before your expected week of childbirth or 15 weeks or less since you gave birth; *or*
– subject to the work-focused interview requirement only.
If your UC is reduced, you may be able to get hardship payments in the same way as when you are sanctioned for not meeting your claimant responsibilities, except that there are no restrictions for 16/17-year-olds (see p1203).[67]

The sanction period

The sanction period under the one-strike rule (see p1258) is **three years** if:[68]
* you are convicted for serious fraud or conspiracy to defraud; *or*
* the overpayment is at least £50,000; *or*
* you are given a sentence of at least a year; *or*
* the offence is committed over a period of at least two years.

The sanction period under the one-strike rule is **13 weeks** if you are convicted in less serious cases and **four weeks** if you pay a penalty as an alternative to prosecution (see p1256).[69]

Sanction periods under the two-strikes rule are **26 weeks** (except for serious fraud, for which the sanction period is three years) or **three years** if the earlier offence is within five years of a previous one.[70]

Note: while benefits are sanctioned, an underlying entitlement remains in place to ensure the link between benefits and other entitlements (eg, free school lunches and free prescriptions) remains.

Loss of working tax credit for a benefit offence

You are disqualified from being paid WTC for a set period of time if you have committed a benefit offence.[71] You do not need to have been convicted.
You are disqualified from WTC if:
* you commit a benefit offence concerning a 'disqualifying benefit' (see p1259) on or after 5 April 2012; *and*
* you would be entitled to WTC if it were not for this rule, either as a single person or as part of a joint claim. If you have a joint claim, but only one of you is disqualified from WTC, WTC remains payable, but the amount is reduced by 50 per cent.[72]

The 'one-strike' and 'two-strikes' rules and the definition of a sanctionable offence that apply to sanctionable benefits (see p1258) apply. The sanction periods are also the same (see p1260).
Note: you are not disqualified from receiving CTC under this rule.

Part 9: Claiming benefits and getting paid
Chapter 57: Fraud and penalties
Notes

Notes

1. Civil penalties
1   ss115C-115D SSAA 1992; SS(CP) Regs
2   para 09420 DMG
3   s115D(6) SSAA 1992
4   paras 09425-30 DMG
5   Reg 3 SS(OR) Regs

2. Investigating benefit claims
6   s127 WRA 2012
7   s122B SSAA 1992
8   ss124, 124A, 124B and 125 SSAA 1992
9   ss122D and 122E SSAA 1992
10 ss122C and 122E SSAA 1992
11 ss182A and 182B SSAA 1992
12 s123 and Sch 4 SSAA 1992
13 ss109A, 109B and 109C SSAA 1992
14 s109A(2) SSAA 1992; SS(LAIP) Regs
15 DWP, *Social Security Fraud Act 2001 Code of Practice on Obtaining Information*, available from www.gov.uk
16 s109B(5)(b) SSAA 1992; DWP, *Social Security Fraud Act 2001 Code of Practice on Obtaining Information*, s2.11
17 s109C SSAA 1992
18 ss109B(5) and 109C(6) SSAA 1992
19 s67(9) PACEA 1984
20 s78(1) PACEA 1984; *DHSS v McKee* [1995] 6 *Bulletin of NI Law* 17 (NI Crown Court)
21 s34 CJPOA 1994
22 *Mote v SSWP and Chichester District Council* [2007] EWCA Civ 1324, 14 December 2007, reported as R(IS) 4/08
23 CIS/683/1994

3. Prosecution of offences
24 *Osinuga v Director of Public Prosecution* [1997] 30 HLR 853 (DC)
25 s112(1) SSAA 1992
26 *Clear v Smith* [1981] 1 WLR 399 (DC)
27 s112(1A)-(1F) SSAA 1992
28 s112(1B) and (1F) SSAA 1992
29 *Taylor's Central Garages v Roper* [1951] 115 JPR 445
30 *R v Passmore* [2007] EWCA Crim 2053; *R v Laku* [2008] EWCA Crim 1745
31 s112(2) SSAA 1992
32 Regs 4 and 5 SS(NCC) Regs; reg 4 CB&GA(Admin) Regs

33 Regs 3(1A), 4(1A) and 5(1ZZA) SS(NCC) Regs
34 *Coventry City Council v Vassell* [2011] EWHC 1542 (Admin)
35 *R v Chainey* [1914] 1 KB 137 at 142 (DC)
36 *R v Tilley* [2009] EWCA Crim 1426
37 s111A SSAA 1992
38 *R v Ghosh* [1982] QB 1053 at 1064D-G (CA)
39 s45 Criminal Proceedings etc (Reform) (Scotland) Act 2007
40 s111A(3) SSAA 1992
41 s116(2), (2A) and (7) SSAA 1992; *Bennett v SSWP* [2012] EWHC 371 (Admin)

4. Financial penalties for benefit offences
42 s115A(3)-(3A) SSAA 1992
43 s25(7) SSA(F)A 1997; Art 2(1)(b) SSA(F)AO No.5
44 s115A(4)(a) SSAA 1992
45 DWP, *Fraud Guide: staff guide - cautions*, October 2012, Introduction, para 14, available at www.gov.uk
46 s115A(1)-(1A) SSAA 1992
47 s25(7) SSA(F)A 1997; art 2(1)(b) SSA(F)AO No.5
48 s115A(2) SSAA 1992
49 DWP, *Fraud Guide: staff guide - administrative penalties on or after 8 May 2012*, December 2012, s03, para 25, available from www.gov.uk
50 DWP, *Fraud Guide: staff guide – administrative penalties on or after 8 May 2012*, December 2012, s03, para 80
51 s115A(4)(b) SSAA 1992
52 s115A(6) SSAA 1992
53 s115A(7) SSAA 1992
54 s115A(5) SSAA 1992

5. Sanctions for benefit offences
55 s6B(1) SSFA 2001
56 s7(1) SSFA 2001
57 s7(1)(c)-(d) SSFA 2001
58 ss6B(13) and 7(8), definition of 'benefit offence', SSFA 2001
59 s6A(1), definition of 'disqualifying benefit', SSFA 2001; reg 19A, definition of 'disqualifying benefit', SS(LB) Regs

60 s6A(1), definition of 'sanctionable
   benefit', SSFA 2001; reg 19 SS(LB) Regs
61 s8 SSFA 2001
62 ss6B, 7, 8 and 9 SSFA 2001; regs 3, 3A,
   5-10, 17 and 18 SS(LB) Regs
63 Reg 7 SS(LB) Regs
64 Reg 6 SS(LB) Regs
65 Reg 3ZA SS(LB) Regs
66 Reg 3ZB SS(LB) Regs
67 Regs 16D-16H SS(LB) Regs
68 s6B(11A)(a) and (14) SSFA 2001
69 s6B(11A)(b) and (c) SSFA 2001
70 s7(6A) SSFA 2001
71 ss36A-B TCA 2002
72 Reg 3 Loss of Tax Credit Regulations
   2013, No.715

Part 10

Getting a benefit decision changed

Chapter 58

Revisions and supersessions

This chapter covers:
1. Getting a decision changed (below)
2. Revisions (p1270)
3. Supersessions (p1281)
4. Revisions and supersessions after a 'qualifying benefit' award (p1294)
5. The 'anti-test case rule' (p1296)

This chapter covers the rules for benefits and the social fund payments in Chapter 37, except budgeting loans. It does *not* cover the rules for statutory sick pay and statutory maternity, adoption and paternity pay (see Chapter 60), the health benefits in Chapter 30, the other types of financial help in Chapter 40 or discretionary housing payments (see Chapter 21).

References in this chapter to HM Revenue and Customs (HMRC) only apply to decisions about child benefit and guardian's allowance. HMRC also makes decisions about tax credits. For information about tax credit decisions, see Chapter 68.

Key facts

- If you think a decision is wrong, or is no longer correct, you can ask the decision maker to change it by applying for a revision or a supersession.
- In some cases, you must show grounds for a revision or a supersession.
- In some cases, you do not need to show grounds for a revision, but you must ask for one within a set time limit.
- In many cases, you can also challenge a decision by appealing to the First-tier Tribunal, but you are likely to have to apply for a revision of the decision first.
- The date a revision or a supersession takes effect is important. This is the date from when you are paid arrears if you are entitled to more benefit, or have been overpaid if you are entitled to less benefit.

1. Getting a decision changed

If you are getting benefit but you cease to satisfy the conditions of entitlement or if the amount of benefit to which you are entitled should be reduced or increased,

Part 10: Getting a benefit decision changed
Chapter 58: Revisions and supersessions
1. Getting a decision changed

the decision awarding you benefit can be changed. Likewise, if a decision maker's decision is wrong (eg, because s/he got the facts or the law wrong), it can be changed. Decisions can be changed either by:
- a revision (see pp1270–81); or
- a supersession (see pp1281–94).

In some cases, this can only be done if one of the grounds for revision or supersession applies (see p1275 and p1282). You can apply for a revision or a supersession, or the decision maker can decide to do one. Claims for benefit or questions about your entitlement can be treated as applications for a revision or a supersession.[1]

Note: in many cases, you also have a right of appeal to the First-tier Tribunal (see Chapter 59). However, you are likely to have to apply for a revision before you can appeal (see p1271).

The time limits for applying for what is known as an 'any grounds' revision or appealing are strict – normally only one month (see p1273 and p1310). For information about how an application for a revision could affect your appeal rights and the time limit for appealing, see p1271, p1314 and p1310.

You can apply for a revision or a supersession of a decision that you cannot appeal to the First-tier Tribunal (see p1308 for which decisions). If you are still dissatisfied, seek advice about whether you can apply for judicial review (see p1351).

Getting a decision changed: checklist

1. To get more information about a decision, ask for an explanation or a written statement of reasons if this has not already been provided (see p1156).

2. Decide whether to apply for a revision or a supersession, or to appeal. Get advice as soon as possible (see Appendix 2).

3. If you decide to appeal, check whether you must apply for a revision before you can do so (see p1271).

4. Ensure you keep within the time limit (see p1273 for revisions and p1310 for appeals).

Information about a decision

If you are trying to get arrears going back several years, it can be difficult to identify the grounds for a revision or supersession. If you are the one who wants the revision or supersession, the onus is on you to show that there are grounds. You can obtain information held by the DWP, the local authority or HM Revenue and Customs (HMRC) by making a 'subject access request' under the Data Protection Act 1998. See the Information Commissioner's website at www.ico.gov.uk for details.

In some cases the DWP, the local authority or HMRC may say it has destroyed old papers relating to your claim. Check to see if your papers have simply been stored (archived), rather than actually destroyed. You can try to argue that missing papers should be presumed to contain information that is favourable to your case. However, this is unlikely to be accepted unless you can show that the papers were destroyed deliberately to thwart your case.[2]

The risks of revision and supersession

Following a revision or a supersession, the original decision may remain the same or be changed to either increase *or* decrease the amount of your benefit, or take away your entitlement altogether. Seek advice before you apply for a revision or supersession if you are concerned about what could happen in your case. There are particular issues if you apply for a revision or supersession of a disability living allowance (DLA) or a personal independence payment (PIP) decision (see below). However, you must always notify changes in your circumstances that you are told you must report, as well as changes you might reasonably be expected to know might affect your right to, the amount of, or payment of, your benefit. Bear the following in mind.

- Although s/he does not have to do so, the decision maker can consider issues even if these are not raised by your application for a revision or supersession.[3] So, you may apply for a revision or supersession in the hope that your benefit will be increased, but the outcome could be that you get less benefit.
- If a revision or supersession reduces the amount of benefit to which you are entitled, it may mean that you have been overpaid. See Chapter 56 for information about overpayments and when they can be recovered.

Disability living allowance and personal independence payment

Get advice if you want to apply for a revision or supersession because you have not been awarded one component of DLA or PIP when you are already in receipt of the other, or if you are not happy with the rate you have been awarded of one component of DLA or PIP when you are satisfied with the rate you have been awarded of the other. In these circumstances, although s/he does not have to do so, the decision maker may consider:

- the component which is not the subject of the revision or supersession;
- reducing the length of the period for which you have been awarded a component, even if it was originally awarded for an indefinite period.

Note: if you report a change of circumstances after 6 October 2013 that is relevant to the rate of DLA to which you are entitled, you are likely to be invited to claim PIP (see p605). Your entitlement to DLA will then end, even if you do not claim PIP.

Part 10: Getting a benefit decision changed
Chapter 58: Revisions and supersessions
2. Revisions

Providing evidence and information

When considering whether to carry out a revision or a supersession, the decision maker decides what further evidence is needed to come to a decision, and how to collect this. The DWP can ask you to have a medical examination (see p1151).

The decision maker can ask you for more evidence or information if s/he thinks this is needed to consider all the issues raised by your application for a revision or supersession.[4] You must provide this information within one month of the request. The decision maker can allow longer than this. If you do not provide the information, your application is decided on the basis of the information and evidence the decision maker already has.

Remember, in some cases if you fail to provide information in a specified time period or have a medical examination, payment of your benefit could be suspended, which may lead to your entitlement being terminated (see p1175).

If a decision is changed

If a decision is changed in your favour, you can receive arrears of benefit. You usually get more arrears with a revision than a supersession (see p1281 and p1287). For this reason, it is best to apply for a revision if you can. If you are in any doubt about how you would be better off, seek advice. **Note:** if you were overpaid, the decision maker decides whether or not to recover the overpayment (see Chapter 56). There is no limit on how far back an overpayment can be recovered.

2. **Revisions**

If you think a decision maker's decision is wrong, you can apply for a revision.[5] The decision maker must then look at the decision again to see if it can be changed. The DWP, the local authority and HM Revenue and Customs (HMRC) often refer to your request as a dispute or a request for a reconsideration. However, you should use the term 'revision'.

In some cases, if you can show grounds, you can apply for a revision even if the decision was made a long time ago (an 'anytime' revision – see p1275). Revisions can, therefore, be a way around the strict time limit for appealing to the First-tier Tribunal (see p1310).

Note: in most cases, you *must* apply for a revision of a decision before you can appeal against it (see p1271).

When a decision can be revised

You can ask for a decision maker's decision to be revised or the decision maker can decide to do this.[6] There are two types of revision:
* 'any grounds' revisions where you do not have to show that specific grounds apply (see p1273); *and*

10

- 'any time' revisions where you must show specific grounds (see p1275).

Note:
- If you want to apply for an 'any grounds' revision of a decision about employment and support allowance (ESA), attendance allowance (AA), disability living allowance (DLA) or personal independence payment (PIP) because you (or the person on whose behalf you are claiming) are terminally ill, you must state this explicitly.[7] If you do not do so, the decision maker cannot revise the decision on this ground.
- A First-tier Tribunal's or an Upper Tribunal's decision cannot be revised. In some cases you can apply for a supersession of these. Otherwise you must appeal to a court (see Chapter 59).

If you want to appeal against a decision

For benefits other than housing benefit (HB), if you want to appeal against a decision to the First-tier Tribunal, you can only do so if you have applied for a revision of the decision and:
- for child benefit and guardian's allowance, HMRC has decided not to revise it. HMRC's intention is that if it revises the decision, you can appeal against the original decision as revised. Note: the rules on child benefit and guardian's allowance are based on draft regulations, due to come into force on 6 April 2014. See CPAG's online service and *Welfare Rights Bulletin* for updates;[8] *or*
- for other benefits, the DWP has considered whether to revise it.[9] This only applies if you are given proper written notice.

The DWP and HMRC call this **'mandatory reconsideration'**.
For benefits other than child benefit and guardian's allowance, you only have to apply for a revision of a decision before you can appeal against it if:[10]
- you are given a written notice of the decision; *and*
- the notice of the decision:
  - includes a statement that you only have a right of appeal against the decision if the DWP has considered an application for a revision of the decision; *and*
  - informs you of the time limit for applying for an 'any grounds' revision; *and*
  - if the notice does not include a written statement of reasons for the decision, informs you that you can ask for one, within one month of being notified of the decision (see p1156). If you ask for a written statement of reasons, one must be provided within 14 days, or as soon as practicable after. Note: your time limit for applying for an 'any grounds' revision is extended if you ask for a written statement of reasons (see p1274).

If the notice of the decision does not tell you that you only have a right of appeal if the DWP has considered an application for a revision of the decision, you do not have to apply for a revision before you can appeal to the First-tier Tribunal.

Part 10: Getting a benefit decision changed
Chapter 58: Revisions and supersessions
2. Revisions

For where to send your appeal, see p1309 and the time limit for doing so, see p1310.

Note: you do *not* have to apply for a revision of local authority decisions about HB before you can appeal.

Applying for a revision before an appeal

If you have to apply for a revision before you can appeal, it is always best to apply in writing, although you can apply orally. If you apply by telephone, all calls should be recorded, but this may not always happen. See p1280 for information about applying for a revision and p1273 for the time limit for applying for an 'any grounds' revision. There is no time limit for applying for an 'any time' revision, but you must show grounds. It is important to follow up your application to ensure that it has been received.

You are provided with a notice of the result of your application for a revision – called a '**mandatory reconsideration notice**'. You can then appeal to the First-tier Tribunal. The notice is proof that the DWP or HMRC has accepted and considered your application for a revision. You must send a copy of it to the First-tier Tribunal when you appeal (see p1311). Although the First-tier Tribunal can waive this requirement, this is discretionary.[11] If you do not have a mandatory reconsideration notice, try to provide the Tribunal with as much evidence as you can that you have applied for a revision, and that the DWP (or HMRC) has considered your application.

Note:
- If you are required to apply for a revision before you can appeal but you fail to do so, your right to appeal is affected.
- If you appeal against a decision, but you should have applied for a revision first, the DWP can (but does not have to) treat your appeal as an application for a revision.[12] If the DWP has not treated your appeal as an application for a revision, apply for a revision as soon as possible, explaining why your application is late if relevant.
- There is an absolute time limit for applying for an 'any grounds' revision (see p1274). There is no time limit for applying for an 'any time' revision (see p1275).
- If you send or deliver your appeal to the First-tier Tribunal when you should have applied for a revision first, the First-tier Tribunal should return your appeal to you and advise you to apply for a revision.
- The DWP says that if the decision maker refuses to consider your application for an 'any grounds' revision because it was made outside the time limit for doing so (see p1274), s/he should go on to consider whether there are grounds for an 'any time' revision, and if there are no grounds, whether to do a supersession.[13]
- If the decision maker refuses to accept your application for an 'any grounds' revision of a decision (eg, because it was made outside the absolute

time limit for doing so), the DWP and HMRC intention is that you do not have a right of appeal against the decision.[14]

Bear in mind that it is the First-tier Tribunal that decides if you have a right of appeal, not the DWP or HMRC. However, the only way to be sure you have a right of appeal is to apply for a revision where you are required to do so, and to do this in time. If the Tribunal says you do not have a right of appeal, your only remedy is judicial review.

'Any grounds' revisions

You can apply for a revision on any grounds if you do so within a strict time limit, normally one month (see below).[15] We call these 'any grounds' revisions in this *Handbook*. You do not have to show specific grounds; it is enough if you simply think a decision is wrong. However, you should still explain why you disagree with the decision and provide information and evidence to support this.

In addition, if the decision maker commences action within one month of the date you are sent or given a decision, for benefits other than HB, s/he can decide to revise it her/himself, on any grounds.[16] For HB, a decision maker can also decide to revise a decision her/himself but only if, within one month of the date you are sent or given it, s/he has information which shows that there was a mistake about the facts of your case or the decision was made in ignorance of relevant facts.[17]

A decision maker can only revise a decision on 'any grounds' on the basis of your circumstances at the time:[18]

- the decision took effect; *or*
- in the case of advance awards for benefits other than HB, the decision was made.

If your circumstances have since changed, instead make a fresh claim or ask for the decision to be superseded (see p1281).

Note:

- In many cases, you *must* apply for a revision of a decision before you can appeal against it (see p1271).
- The decision maker may decide to revise a decision after you appeal against it. Your appeal could lapse if s/he revises the decision, even if you do not get everything you want and you have to appeal again (see p1314).

Time limit for seeking an any grounds revision

If you want an any grounds revision you must apply for one:

- in the case of a **Sure Start maternity grant** or a **social fund funeral expenses payment**, within one month of the date you were sent or given the decision or within the time limit for claiming the payment if this is later;[19]

Part 10: Getting a benefit decision changed
Chapter 58: Revisions and supersessions
2. Revisions

- in the case of a **cold weather payment** or a **winter fuel payment**, within one month of the date you were notified of the decision. For these purposes, you are generally assumed to have been notified seven days after the decision was made, but there are exceptions;[20]
- in the case of **HB**, within one month of the date you were sent or given the decision.[21] If a written statement of reasons has not already been included with the decision, days between the date your request for the statement is received by the local authority and the date on which it is provided to you are ignored when calculating the one month;[22]
- in all **other cases:**[23]
  - within one month of the date you were sent or given the decision; *or*
  - within one month and 14 days of the date you were sent or given the decision, if you requested a written statement of reasons (see p1156) and it is provided within the month; *or*
  - within 14 days of a written statement of reasons being provided, if you requested one within one month of the date you were sent or given the decision, but it is not provided within that one-month period.

For benefits (other than a Sure Start maternity grant or a social fund funeral expenses payment, child benefit or guardian's allowance), if an accidental error in a decision has been corrected (see p1155), any day falling before the day on which the correction is notified to you is ignored when calculating the one-month period.[24]

Late requests for an any grounds revision

You can apply for an 'any grounds' revision outside the time limit in limited circumstances, so long as this is within an absolute time limit.

The absolute time limit
For most benefits, you must apply for an 'any grounds' revision within 13 months of the date you were notified of the decision.[25]
For PIP and, if you come under the universal credit (UC) system (see p19), contribution-based JSA, contributory ESA and UC, you must apply for an 'any grounds' revision within 13 months of the latest date by which your application for a revision should have been received (see p1273).[26]

If you requested a written statement of reasons (see p1156):
- for **HB**, days between the date you requested the statement and the date on which it was provided are ignored in calculating the 13 months; *or*
- for **other benefits**, if the statement of reasons is provided:
  - within one month of the date you were notified of the decision, the 13 months are extended by 14 days; *or*

– during a period later than one month after the date you were notified of the decision, the 13 months are extended by 14 days, plus the number of days in that period.

Your application outside the time limit must contain:[27]
- sufficient details about the decision with which you disagree for it to be identified. Say which benefit you are disagreeing about and the date the DWP, the local authority or HMRC sent you the decision; *and*
- a summary of your reasons for applying for a revision late. You must show that:[28]
  – it is reasonable to grant your application; *and*
  – there are special circumstances. The special circumstances must mean that it was not practicable for you to apply for a revision within the time limit. Any special circumstances can count. The longer you have delayed applying for a revision, the more compelling the special circumstances must be.

Unless you are applying for a revision because you must do so before you can appeal, other than for child benefit and guardian's allowance (the DWP calls this 'mandatory reconsideration' – see p1271), or the decision you want to be revised is about PIP, or, if you come under the UC system, contribution-based JSA, contributory ESA or UC, in addition:
- you must also show your application for a revision has merit;[29]
- when deciding whether it is reasonable to grant your application, the decision maker cannot take account of the fact that:[30]
  – a court or the Upper Tribunal has interpreted the law in a different way than previously understood and applied;
  – you (or anyone acting for you) misunderstood or were unaware of the relevant law, including the time limits for applying for a revision.

You cannot appeal against the decision maker's refusal to let you apply for a revision outside the time limit.[31] The only remedy is judicial review. However, see if you can make a late appeal against the original decision.

'Any time' revisions

If you can show there are specific grounds, you can apply for a revision at any time (called an 'any time' revision in this *Handbook*). There is no time limit for applying for an any time revision. In practice, if you apply for a revision and it is within one month of your being sent or given the decision, the DWP, the local authority or HMRC treats your application as one for an any grounds revision (see p1273). If a decision maker refuses to do an any time revision, see p1281.

The main grounds for revision

There are a number of grounds for an any time revision. The main ones are where there has been:

Part 10: Getting a benefit decision changed
Chapter 58: Revisions and supersessions
2. Revisions

- an official error (see below);
- a mistake about or ignorance of facts (see p1277);
- an award of a 'qualifying benefit' (see p1278);
- an appeal against a decision (see p1278).

Other grounds for revision are summarised on pp1279–80.

Official error

A decision can be revised at any time if there was an official error.[32] For **benefits, other than child benefit and guardian's allowance**, this means:[33]

- an error made by an officer of the DWP; *or*
- for HB only, errors made by the local authority or by a person authorised to carry out any function of the local authority or providing services relating to HB; *or*
- other than for HB, errors made by a person employed by someone providing services to the DWP; *or*
- other than for HB, PIP and, if you come under the UC system (see p19), contribution-based JSA, contributory ESA and UC, errors made by an employee of a local authority (or a person acting on behalf of, and employed by someone providing services to, a local authority).

For **child benefit and guardian's allowance**, it means an error made by an officer of HMRC or a person employed by someone providing services to HMRC.[34]

The following can count as official errors.

- The decision maker made an error of law – ie, s/he got the law wrong. If the decision maker was only shown to have made an error of law after a later decision of the Upper Tribunal or a court, this ground does not apply.[35] In this case, you could make a fresh claim (or apply for a supersession), but the 'anti-test case rule' could apply (see p1296).
- There is specific evidence that the decision maker had (or, in the case of HB, the local authority had), but which s/he failed to take into account even though it was relevant. You should argue this applies even if the evidence does not conclusively prove your entitlement, so long as it raised a strong possibility that you were entitled.
- There is documentary or other written evidence of your entitlement that the DWP, the local authority or HMRC had, but failed to give to the decision maker dealing with your claim when the earlier decision was made.
- The decision maker failed to ask you about something that was relevant to your claim. However, the decision maker is likely to say that it is *not* an official error if s/he fails to keep your claim constantly under review or to raise issues that you should have raised, or if s/he fails to make enquiries into things that do not appear to be at issue.[36]

If someone else (eg, you, your partner or your representative) caused or materially contributed to the error, it does not count as an official error. This includes if the way your claim form was completed contributed to the error.[37]

Mistake about or ignorance of facts

An any time revision can be done if there was a mistake about the facts of your case or the decision was made in ignorance of relevant facts, but only if, as a result of the mistake or ignorance about the facts, the decision was more favourable to you than it would have been – eg, you were awarded too much benefit.[38] If you have been overpaid, the decision maker may seek to recover the overpayment (see Chapter 56). **Note:** there must have been a mistake about or ignorance of facts, not conclusions or opinions about the facts. See p1223 for some examples.

The rules are different if there was a mistake about, or ignorance of, facts relating to a 'disability determination', a 'limited capability for work determination' or an 'incapacity determination'.[39] In this case, it must be shown that, at the time the decision that you were entitled to a benefit was made (eg, DLA or income-related ESA), you (or the person being paid the benefit) knew, or could reasonably have been expected to know, about the fact and that it was relevant to your benefit. If the benefit is a qualifying benefit for another benefit (see p1278) and revision of the decision means your entitlement to the other benefit is affected, the decision about the other benefit takes effect on the same date.[40]

Disability, limited capability for work and incapacity determinations[41]

A **'disability determination'** is a decision about whether you satisfy the disability conditions for AA or DLA, are disabled for the purposes of severe disablement allowance (SDA), or whether the existence or extent of your disablement is sufficient for you to be entitled to industrial injuries disablement benefit or to be paid at the same rate as that paid immediately before the decision that you were entitled to benefit. It does *not* include decisions about PIP.

A **'limited capability for work determination'** is a decision about whether you have limited capability for work (see Chapter 47) or can be treated as having limited capability for work under specified rules. This does not apply if you come under the UC system (see p19).

An **'incapacity determination'** is a decision about your incapacity for work under the personal capability assessment, whether you can be treated as incapable of work, or whether there are exceptional circumstances – eg, for incapacity benefit or SDA purposes. See p683 of the 2013/14 edition of this *Handbook*.

Note: if the mistake about or ignorance of facts means you should be entitled to *more* benefit:

Part 10: Getting a benefit decision changed
Chapter 58: Revisions and supersessions
2. Revisions

- a decision can be superseded on this ground (see p1283), but arrears might be limited;
- a decision can be revised on any ground if you apply in time (see p1273);
- for benefits other than HB, if the decision maker starts action within one month of the date you are sent a decision, s/he can decide to revise it her/himself, on any grounds;[42]
- for HB, a decision can be revised if, within one month of your being sent or given it, the local authority has information that shows there was a mistake about the facts of your case or the decision was made in ignorance of relevant facts.[43]

Awards of a 'qualifying benefit'

A 'qualifying benefit' is, in general, any benefit which gives you entitlement to another benefit, or makes another benefit payable at a higher rate. If you are awarded a benefit (eg, IS, income-related ESA or HB), and for a period which includes the date that award took effect **you (or your partner, or a child included in your claim** – see p210) are awarded a 'qualifying benefit' (eg, DLA or carer's allowance) or the qualifying benefit is increased, the decision awarding you benefit can be revised.[44]

A decision to end your entitlement to HB because your (or your partner's or child's) qualifying benefit ceases can also be revised at any time. This only applies if the qualifying benefit is later reinstated following a revision, supersession or appeal.[45]

For IS, JSA, ESA and pension credit (PC) only, if you have a non-dependant living with you (see p235) and since you were awarded IS, income-based JSA, income-related ESA or PC, **your non-dependant has been awarded a qualifying benefit** for a period that includes the date your award took effect and this means that you are now entitled to a severe disability premium (for IS, JSA or ESA) or a severe disability additional amount (for PC), the decision awarding benefit can be revised.[46]

See p1294 for further information. If you are only entitled to a benefit once a qualifying benefit is awarded, see p127 and p1149.

A decision that has been appealed

If you appealed against a decision, and you:

- appealed within the time limit or were allowed a late appeal (see p1310 and p1353) and the appeal has not yet been determined, a decision maker can look at the decision again and carry out a revision.[47] This includes if the First-tier Tribunal has adjourned the hearing or if the Upper Tribunal has sent a case back to the First-tier Tribunal to make a new decision; *or*
- make a fresh claim or seek a supersession when your circumstances change (eg, because the First-tier Tribunal cannot, in general, take changes into account – see p1324) and as a result a new decision about your entitlement is made, a

decision maker can revise the new decision once the appeal against the first decision has been determined. This only applies if you appealed against a decision to the First-tier Tribunal (or, for HB only, to the Upper Tribunal or a court);[48] *and*
- a fresh claim is decided or the decision is superseded before your appeal is determined; *and*
- the appeal is then determined; *and*
- the decision maker would have made her/his decision differently if s/he had been aware of the appeal decision at the time her/his decision was made.

Note: if you have appealed against a decision, your appeal could lapse if a decision maker revises the decision, even if you do not get everything you want (see p1314).

Other grounds for revision

There are many other situations when a decision maker can do an any time revision. This includes if the decision is one against which you have no right of appeal (see p1308 for which decisions).[49]

Other decisions that can be revised at any time include those:
- to reduce your HB (or your UC) under the 'benefit cap' rules (see p1169);[50]
- to award you ESA if, when you first claimed ESA, you were not entitled because you were not treated as having limited capability for work (eg, because you had been found to be capable of work within the last six months), from a later date you were awarded ESA and it is now accepted that you did have limited capability for work for the earlier period;[51]
- to refuse you PIP because you are resident in a care home and the costs of any qualifying services provided for you are borne out of public funds, the decision was made with incomplete evidence and after the decision, any of the costs of the qualifying services are recovered from you;[52]
- that are made in consequence of a determination containing an error to which you did not contribute that, because you did not return your questionnaire or you failed to participate in your assessment consultation (see p736 and p738), you do not satisfy the disability conditions for the daily living component or the mobility component of PIP;[53]
- where your maximum rent (for HB) or the amount of rent for the purposes of the housing costs element (for UC) increases because of a rent officer redetermination, or because a local housing allowance rate or broad rental market area has been amended because of a rent officer's error, or for HB only, if (in Scotland) an order or notice that your landlord is not entitled to charge rent for your property is revoked following an appeal;[54]
- about retirement pension, PC or HB, where you or your partner deferred claiming a pension, then change your option from a higher pension to a lump sum (or, for retirement pension only, vice versa).[55]

10

Part 10: Getting a benefit decision changed
Chapter 58: Revisions and supersessions
2. Revisions

Note: the list on p1279 is not exhaustive. There are a number of other decisions that can be revised at any time.[56]

How to apply for a revision

Apply for a revision to the office specified on the notice of the decision with which you disagree or, for JSA if you do not come under the UC system (see p19), the office where you have to sign on.[57] For benefits (other than child benefit, guardian's allowance, HB and if you come under the UC system, contribution-based JSA, contributory ESA and UC), if you are a person who is, or would be, required to attend a work-focused interview as a condition of getting benefit, you can also apply to the Jobcentre Plus office. The DWP, the local authority or HMRC can treat an application for a supersession as an application for a revision.[58]

For **HB**, you must apply for a revision in writing.[59] A late application for a revision must also be in writing.[60]

For **benefits other than HB**, you do not have to ask for a revision in writing, although it is always best to do so. This ensures that the decision maker understands that you are asking for a revision, not just seeking an explanation or complaining about the rules.

When you apply for a revision, you should include any information and evidence that supports your case and that might enable the decision maker to revise the decision in your favour. This may mean you can avoid an appeal.

Example

Stan is awarded IS, but the DWP says he is not entitled to help with his housing costs. He telephones the benefit office and complains that he has not got enough money to live on. The benefit office takes no action because it thinks Stan is simply letting off steam, not seeking a revision. Stan should have made it clear he wanted a revision. He can still ask for one but only if he is within the time limit (see p1273).

A decision maker does not have to consider any issues other than those raised by your application for a revision or which caused her/him to act on her/his own initiative.[61] You should, therefore, ensure you:

- tell the decision maker all the points about the decision with which you disagree;
- provide any information or evidence that supports your case. This includes, for example, medical evidence from a GP, consultant or other health worker if this is relevant. If the benefit is AA, DLA or PIP, evidence or information from your carer or a diary of your walking, supervision or care needs over a period may be useful.

The decision maker may ask you for further information or evidence to help her/ him make a decision (see p1270). Check that your application has been received to ensure that you do not miss the time limit for seeking an any grounds revision or affect your right of appeal.

The revised decision

After a decision maker considers a revision, s/he can decide there are:
- grounds for revision and that the original decision was correct or should be changed; *or*
- no grounds for revision and refuse to change the original decision.

When a revision takes effect

The date a revision takes effect is important. This is the date from which you are paid arrears if you are entitled to more benefit, or have been overpaid if you are entitled to less benefit. In all cases, a revision takes effect from:
- the date the decision being revised took (or would have taken) effect[62] – eg, your date of claim or the date a supersession took effect; *or*
- the correct date, if the date on which the decision being revised took effect was found to be wrong.[63]

It is important to make it clear that you want payment for the past period. You might get less backdating if the 'anti-test case rule' applies (see p1296).

Challenging a revision

If a decision is revised or the decision maker refuses to revise a decision, you are notified of this in writing. If the original decision is one against which you have a right of appeal (see p1307 for which decisions), you can appeal to the First-tier Tribunal against the revised decision (or in the case of a refusal to do an any grounds revision, against the original decision). For benefits other than child benefit and guardian's allowance, your time limit for appealing (see p1310) runs from the date you are sent or given the notification.[64] **Note:** this is also likely to be the time limit for child benefit and guardian's allowance from 6 April 2014, but at the time of writing the rules had not yet been amended.

If a decision maker refuses to do an any time revision (see p1275) (eg, because s/he does not accept that an official error was made), you cannot appeal against the refusal.[65] However, you could make a late request for an any grounds revision, if you are still within the absolute time limit for this, or see if you can appeal against the original decision.

3. Supersessions

If your circumstances have changed since a decision was made, you can seek a supersession.[66] You can also seek a supersession if you think a decision is wrong, but you must show there are grounds (see p1282).

Part 10: Getting a benefit decision changed
Chapter 58: Revisions and supersessions
3. Supersessions

You can seek a supersession even if the decision was made a long time ago, but the arrears of benefit you are paid can be limited (see p1287 for when a supersession takes effect). It is usually better to try for a revision or appeal if you can.

When a decision can be superseded

You can ask for a decision maker's decision (and in some cases a First-tier Tribunal's or an Upper Tribunal's decision) to be superseded or the decision maker can decide to do this her/himself.[67] However, there must be grounds for a supersession.

Note: if a decision could be revised, it cannot be superseded unless there are grounds for supersession that are not covered by the revision rules.[68]

The main grounds for supersession

There are a large number of grounds for supersession. The main grounds are:
- change of circumstances (see below);
- mistakes about or ignorance of facts (see p1283);
- where a decision is legally wrong (see p1284);
- capability for work and disability conditions (see p1284);
- where a qualifying benefit has been awarded (see p1285).

Other grounds for supersession are summarised on pp1285–86.

Change of circumstances

A decision can be superseded if:[69]
- your circumstances have changed since it had effect; *or*
- in the case of advance awards (other than for housing benefit – HB), your circumstances have changed since it was made; *or*
- it is anticipated that your circumstances will change.

The change must mean that the decision may no longer be correct – ie, it must be what is known as a 'relevant change of circumstances'. If the change means that you could be entitled to more benefit, there is a strict time limit for reporting the change in order to get all the arrears of benefit to which you are entitled (see p1287 for when a supersession takes effect).

The decision maker might say that a change of circumstances you have reported is a change that could not possibly result in a supersession and so refuse to consider a supersession. If this happens, see p1293.

Note:
- An amendment to the law counts as a change of circumstances, but a decision of a court or the Upper Tribunal that the law has been wrongly interpreted does not.[70]

10

- A new medical opinion is not a change of circumstances, but a new medical report following an examination might give evidence of such a change.[71]
- For income support (IS), jobseeker's allowance (JSA) and employment and support allowance (ESA), the repayment of a student loan does not count as a relevant change of circumstance.[72] This does not apply if you come under the universal credit (UC) system (see p19).
- For ESA, incapacity benefit (IB), attendance allowance (AA), disability living allowance (DLA), personal independence payment (PIP) and UC, you or the person claiming on your behalf must state explicitly that you are terminally ill in the application for a supersession for this to count as a relevant change of circumstances.[73]
- In respect of your assessed income period for pension credit (PC), the only change of circumstances that is relevant is that the period has ended for one of the reasons listed on p91.[74]
- In deciding whether there has been a change of circumstances, it is necessary to compare the circumstances as they were at the time the decision took effect and as they were at the time the supersession would take effect.[75]

You must always report any change in your circumstances which you are told you must report, as well as changes you might reasonably be expected to know might affect your right to, the amount of, or payment of, your benefit (see p1174).

Change of circumstances after benefit is refused

If you were correctly refused benefit but your circumstances are now different, you *cannot* seek a supersession on the grounds of a change of circumstances. You must instead make a fresh claim (unless you are seeking a supersession because there has been a 'recrudescence' of a prescribed disease – see p673).[76] Even if you are appealing against the decision refusing or stopping your benefit, make a fresh claim when your circumstances change and appeal if you are still refused. If you do not, you could lose out. This is because if you appeal to the First-tier Tribunal against a decision refusing benefit or terminating your award, the tribunal cannot take a change of circumstances into account if it happens after the decision with which you disagree (see p1324).

Mistake about or ignorance of facts

A decision can be superseded if there was a mistake about the facts of your case or if it was made in ignorance of relevant facts, and in the case of a decision maker's decision:[77]

- for HB, a revision on the same ground cannot be done. Note that the local authority can revise a decision if, within one month of your being sent or given it, it has information that shows that there was a mistake about the facts of your case or the decision was made in ignorance of relevant facts;[78] *or*

Part 10: Getting a benefit decision changed
Chapter 58: Revisions and supersessions
3. Supersessions

• for other benefits, the time limit for seeking an 'any grounds' revision (or any longer period allowed) has passed (see p1273).

In practice, this ground for supersession only applies if, as a result of a mistake or ignorance about the facts, a decision was less favourable to you than it would have been (eg, you were awarded too little benefit) and you have missed the time limit for seeking an any grounds revision. If a decision is more favourable to you than it would have been (ie, you were being overpaid), a decision maker can instead do an 'any time' revision (see p1277).

Note:
• There must have been a mistake about the facts or the decision maker must not have had all the facts, but it does not matter how the mistake came about or whether you could have produced evidence sooner than you did or failed to give the information on your claim form.
• The mistake or ignorance must be in respect of facts, not conclusions or opinions about the facts. See p1223 for some examples.

Decisions that are legally wrong

A decision can be superseded if it was made by a decision maker and was legally wrong (known as an error of law) and:[79]
• for HB a revision on the same ground cannot be done; or
• for other benefits, the time limit for seeking an any grounds revision (or any longer period allowed) has passed (see p1273).

In many cases, if there has been an error of law, an any time revision on grounds of official error is also possible (see p1276). If the new decision is to your advantage, revision is the better option as full arrears of benefit are payable.

Note: if you think a decision of the First-tier Tribunal or the Upper Tribunal is legally wrong, you need to appeal against it.

Capability for work and disability conditions

A decision can be superseded if it is a decision to award you ESA, UC or national insurance (NI) credits on the basis that you have, or are treated as having, limited capability for work (see Chapter 47), or it is a decision to award you PIP. The decision can be superseded if:
• since the decision was made:[80]
  – a healthcare professional (see p1152 for who counts) approved by the Secretary of State has provided medical evidence – eg, on your capability for work (or on whether you satisfy the disability conditions for PIP); or
  – the decision maker has decided that you can be treated as having limited capability for work (or, for UC, for work and work-related activity) under specified provisions.
The rules allow the decision maker to consider your entitlement to ESA, UC, NI credits or PIP. However, this entitlement should only end if s/he decides on

the basis of the evidence that you no longer have limited capability for work, or no longer satisfy the conditions for PIP;[81] *or*
- it is a decision to award you PIP and there has been a determination that, because you did not return your questionnaire or you failed to participate in your assessment consultation (see p736 and p738), you do not satisfy the disability conditions for the daily living component or the mobility component.[82]

If you have told the decision maker that your condition has not improved since your last assessment or you have a variable condition, you can argue that reference should be made to earlier assessments and decisions on your claim.[83]

Note: a decision might still be superseded on the grounds of a change of circumstances.

Awards of qualifying benefits

A 'qualifying benefit' is, in general, any benefit which gives you entitlement to another benefit, or makes another benefit payable at a higher rate. If you are awarded a benefit (eg, IS, ESA or HB) but, from a later date than the entitlement began, **you or your partner (or a child included in your claim** – see p210) **become entitled to a qualifying benefit** (eg, DLA, PIP or carer's allowance (CA)) or the qualifying benefit is increased, the decision awarding you benefit can be superseded.[84]

For IS, income-based JSA, income-related ESA and PC only, if you have a non-dependant living with you (see p235) and since you were awarded the benefit, **your non-dependant has been awarded a qualifying benefit** for a period beginning after the date your award took effect, and this means that you are now entitled to a severe disability premium (for IS, JSA or ESA) or a severe disability additional amount (for PC), the decision awarding you benefit can be superseded.[85]

See p1294 for further information. If you are only entitled to a benefit once a qualifying benefit is awarded, see p127 and p1149.

Other grounds for supersession

There are many other situations when a decision maker can do a supersession. This includes if the decision is one against which you have no right of appeal (see p1308 for which decisions).[86]

Other decisions that can be superseded include those:
- where your maximum rent (for HB) or the amount of rent for the purposes of the UC housing costs element decreases because of a rent officer redetermination. Note that for HB, a decrease in your maximum rent because a local housing allowance rate or a broad rental market area has been amended because of a rent officer's error is dealt with as a change of circumstances;[87]
- which reduced your HB under the 'benefit cap' rules (see p1169), or increased or reduced the reduction;[88]

Part 10: Getting a benefit decision changed
Chapter 58: Revisions and supersessions
3. Supersessions

- about PC and HB, where you or your partner deferred claiming a pension and you are paid a lump sum or repay it because you change your option to a pension increase;[89]
- of the First-tier Tribunal or the Upper Tribunal made while a test case was pending, where the test case is eventually decided in your favour (see p1347).[90]

The list above is not exhaustive. There are many other decisions that can be superseded.[91]

How to apply for a supersession

Apply for a supersession to the office that made the decision with which you disagree. The following can be treated as an application for a supersession:[92]
- an application for a revision;
- a notification of a change in circumstances;
- a claim for benefit or a question about your entitlement.

For HB, you *must* ask the local authority for a supersession in writing.[93] For other benefits, you do not have to ask for a supersession in writing although it is always best to do so.

The decision maker does not have to consider any issue other than those raised by your application for a supersession or which caused her/him to act on her/his own initiative.[94] You should, therefore, ensure you:
- tell the decision maker all the points with which you disagree;
- provide any information or evidence that supports your case. This includes medical evidence from a GP or consultant or health worker if this is relevant. If the benefit is AA, DLA or PIP, evidence or information from your carer or a diary of your walking, supervision or care needs over a period may be useful.

The decision maker may ask you for further information or evidence to help her/him make a decision (see p1270).

The new decision

After a decision maker carries out a supersession, s/he makes a new decision. S/he can decide that:
- the original decision should continue; *or*
- the original decision should be replaced, what the new decision should be and when it should take effect.

For information about challenging a decision, see p1293. If the decision maker refuses to consider a supersession, see p1293.

When a supersession takes effect: general rule

If a decision is superseded, the date the new decision (the supersession) takes effect is important. This is the date from which you are paid arrears if you are entitled to more benefit, or the date from which you have been overpaid if you are entitled to less benefit. It is important to make it clear that you want payment for a past period.

There is a general rule that applies in many cases. This is that if a decision is superseded, the new decision takes effect from the date you applied for the supersession.[95] However, if the decision maker decides to do one on her/his own, the new decision takes effect from the date the decision is made. **Note:**

- There are many exceptions when the general rule does *not* apply (see below).
- For how the 'anti-test case rule' may affect the amount of backdated benefit you can receive, see p1296.

When a supersession takes effect: exceptions

There are a large number of exceptions when the general rule does *not* apply. For these, the date a supersession takes effect depends on the ground for the supersession. For the exceptions, see below and the chapter in this *Handbook* about the benefit you are claiming.

Changes in your circumstances

If the ground for supersession is a change in your circumstances, when the supersession takes effect usually depends on whether or not it is advantageous to you. For HB, see below. For PIP, see p1288. For other benefits, see p1289. For benefits under the UC system, see p1290.

Note:

- If a supersession is advantageous to you, you must usually notify the decision maker of the change within one month or you could lose out. For UC you must notify before the end of the assessment period in which the change takes place.
- If a supersession is not advantageous to you, you may have been overpaid. The DWP, the local authority or HMRC might seek to recover the overpayment.

There are also some special rules that apply in particular situations, including the following.

- For benefits other than child benefit and guardian's allowance, if there has been a **change in the legislation** that affects your benefit, the supersession takes effect from the date the legislation takes effect.[96]
- For IS, income-based JSA, income-related ESA and PC, if your **carer** (or your partner's carer) **has stopped being paid CA**, the supersession takes effect from the day after the last day for which CA was paid, so long as this was to someone other than you or your partner. This means that if you are now entitled to the severe disability premium with your IS, income-based JSA or income-related

Part 10: Getting a benefit decision changed
Chapter 58: Revisions and supersessions
3. Supersessions

ESA (or the severe disability additional amount with PC), this can be backdated to when the carer stopped getting CA for looking after you (or your partner).[97]

- For ESA, if the change is that **you are terminally ill** (you must state this in the application for a supersession), the supersession takes effect from the date you became terminally ill.[98] This also applies for UC.

Housing benefit

For HB, the supersession usually takes effect from the Monday after the week in which the change occurs.[99] However, if the change is one you are required to notify to the local authority (other than, if you get PC, one of the types of change covered by the exceptions to the rules described on p143) and the supersession is *advantageous* to you, the change must be notified within one month of its taking place.[100] The one-month period can be extended in certain circumstances (see p1290). If your application for an extension is refused, see p1291 for when the supersession takes effect.

For further information on when changes in circumstances take effect and exceptions to this rule, see p142.

Personal independence payment

For PIP, the supersession usually takes effect as follows.

- If the decision maker decides to do a supersession her/himself and the decision is *advantageous* to you, it usually takes effect from the date on which s/he first took action with a view to doing a supersession.[101]
- If you apply for the supersession and it is *advantageous* to you, it usually takes effect on the date the change takes place, or is expected to take place.[102] However, if the change means you are now entitled to a particular rate of benefit, the supersession takes effect from the day you satisfy the conditions of entitlement for that rate.[103] In both cases, you must notify the DWP of the change within one month.

The one-month period can be extended in certain circumstances (see p1290). If your application for an extension is refused, see p1291 for when the supersession takes effect.

If the decision maker decides to do a supersession her/himself or you apply for a supersession and it is *not advantageous* to you, the supersession usually takes effect from the date on which the change takes place or is expected to take place.[104] If the decision is one you were required to notify, this does not apply for certain decisions about the disability conditions for PIP. In this case, the supersession takes effect from the date you (or the person being paid the benefit) ought to have notified the change if you (or the person being paid the benefit) failed to notify the change when you knew that you should have, or could reasonably be expected to have known that you should have, done so.[105] If you could not have been reasonably expected to know that you should have reported the change, the supersession takes effect from the date you applied for the supersession, or if the decision maker decides to do a supersession on her/his own, the date the decision is made.[106] So if your condition is found to have improved in the past, and you could not have been expected to report this, you will not have been overpaid benefit.

Other benefits

For other benefits, if the supersession is *advantageous* to you, it takes effect as follows.

- If the decision maker decides to do a supersession her/himself, it usually takes effect from:[107]
  - for AA and DLA, the date on which s/he first took action with a view to doing a supersession; *or*
  - for other benefits, the start of the benefit week in which s/he first took action with a view to doing a supersession.
- If you apply for the supersession and the decision is about AA or DLA and:[108]
  - the change means you are now entitled to a particular rate of benefit, the supersession takes effect from the day you satisfy the conditions of entitlement to that rate. You must notify the DWP of the change within one month of doing so;
  - the change makes a difference to whether benefit is payable to you (eg, you leave hospital or a care home), the supersession takes effect from the day of the change. You must notify the DWP of the change within one month.
- If you apply for the supersession and the decision is not about AA or DLA, the supersession takes effect from the date of the change, so long as the DWP or HMRC is notified of the change within one month.[109]

To see if the one-month period can be extended, see p1290. If your application for an extension is refused, see p1291 for when the supersession takes effect.

If the decision maker decides to do a supersession her/himself or you apply for a supersession and it is *not advantageous* to you, the supersession usually takes effect from the date of the change of circumstances.[110] If the decision is one you were required to notify, this does not apply to certain decisions about disability, limited capability or incapacity for work. In this case, a supersession takes effect from the date you (or the person being paid the benefit) ought to have notified the change.[111] However, this only applies if you (or the person being paid the benefit) failed to notify the change when you knew that you should have, or could reasonably be expected to have known that you should have, done so. If this is not the case and the change related to a disability determination, the general rule on p1287 applies – ie, the supersession takes effect from the date you applied for it or the date the decision was made. So if your condition is found to have improved in the past, and you could not have been expected to report this, you will not have been overpaid benefit. If the benefit is a qualifying benefit

Part 10: Getting a benefit decision changed
Chapter 58: Revisions and supersessions
3. Supersessions

(see p1285) and the supersession means your entitlement to another benefit is affected, the decision about the other benefit takes effect on the same date.[112]

Benefits under the universal credit system

If you come under the UC system (see p19), the supersession for contribution-based JSA, contributory ESA and UC usually takes effect as follows.

- If the decision maker decides to do a supersession her/himself and the decision is *advantageous* to you, it usually takes effect from the start of the assessment period (for UC) or the start of the benefit week (for JSA and ESA) in which s/he first took action with a view to doing a supersession.[113]
- If you apply for the supersession and it is *advantageous* to you, it usually takes effect from:
  - for UC, the start of the assessment period in which the change takes place or is expected to take place, so long as the DWP is notified of the change within that assessment period;[114]
  - for JSA and ESA, the start of the benefit week in which the change takes place or is expected to take place, so long as the DWP is notified of the change within one month.[115]

To see if the period in which you must report a change can be extended, see below. If your application for an extension is refused, see p1291 for when the supersession takes effect.

If the decision maker decides to do a supersession her/himself or you apply for a supersession and it is *not advantageous* to you, the supersession usually takes effect from the start of the assessment period in which (for UC) or the start of the benefit week in which (for JSA and ESA) the change takes place or is expected to take place.[116] If the decision is one you were required to notify, this does not apply for certain decisions about limited capability for work. In this case, the supersession takes effect from the date you (or the person being paid the benefit) ought to have notified the change if you (or the person being paid the benefit) failed to notify the change when you knew that you should have, or could reasonably be expected to have known that you should have, done so.[117] If you could not have been reasonably expected to know that you should have reported the change, the supersession takes effect from the date you applied for the supersession, or if the decision maker decides to do a supersession on her/his own, the date the decision is made.[118] So if your condition is found to have improved in the past, and you could not have been expected to report this, you will not have been overpaid benefit.

Late notification of a change of circumstances

If the supersession is *advantageous* to you and you fail to notify a change within the one-month periods above (or for UC within the assessment period), you can apply for an extension of time in limited circumstances.[119] The time limit can be extended to a maximum of 13 months. Your application must contain:[120]

- details of the relevant change of circumstances; *and*
- the reasons why you failed to notify the change in time. You must show that:[121]
  - it is reasonable to grant your request; *and*
  - the change of circumstances is relevant to the decision you want changed; *and*
  - there are special circumstances that mean it was not practicable for you to notify the change within the time limit. The longer you have delayed, the more compelling the special circumstances have to be.

When deciding whether it is reasonable to grant your application, the decision maker cannot take account of the fact that:[122]

- a court or the Upper Tribunal has interpreted the law in a different way than previously understood and applied;
- you (or anyone acting for you) misunderstood or were unaware of the relevant law, including the time limits for applying for a supersession.

If your application for an extension of time is refused, arrears are limited. The supersession takes effect:

- for AA or DLA, from the date you applied for the supersession;[123] *or*
- for IS, JSA, ESA and PC:[124]
  - if you are paid in arrears, from the start of the benefit week in which you notified the change; *or*
  - if you are paid in advance and you notified the change on the first day of the benefit week, from that day. Otherwise it takes effect from the start of the benefit week following the week in which you notified the change; *or*
- for HB, usually from the Monday after the date when you notified the change (see p142);[125] *or*
- for UC, from the start of the assessment period in which you notified the change;[126]
- for other benefits, from when you notified the change.[127]

Mistake about or ignorance of facts

If there has been a mistake about or ignorance of facts, the general rule on p1287 usually applies. So even if you are entitled to more benefit, arrears are limited. There are exceptions including the following.

If the First-tier Tribunal or the Upper Tribunal made the original decision in ignorance of relevant facts or made a mistake about the facts and, as a result, it was more *advantageous* to you than it would otherwise have been, the supersession takes effect from the date the Tribunal's decision took effect.[128] However, if you come under the UC system (see p19), the supersession takes effect from the start of the assessment period (for UC) or the start of the benefit week (for contributory

Part 10: Getting a benefit decision changed
Chapter 58: Revisions and supersessions
3. Supersessions

ESA) in which the Tribunal's decision took effect.[129] If this means that you have been overpaid, the decision maker may seek to recover the overpayment. However, if the decision related to a disability determination or an incapacity determination (see p1277 for the definitions), this only happens if you (or the person being paid the benefit) knew, or could reasonably have been expected to know, the fact in question and that it was relevant to the decision. If you come under the UC system, this also applies for contributory ESA and UC if it is a decision about your limited capability for work under the work capability assessment or whether you can be treated as having limited capability for work.[130] **Note:** if you do not come under the UC system, this exception does not apply to ESA.

For HB, if a decision maker's decision was made in ignorance of facts or there was a mistake about the facts and the new decision is *advantageous* to you, the supersession takes effect from the start of the benefit week in which:[131]

- you applied for the supersession; *or*
- if you did not apply for a supersession, the local authority first had sufficient information to show that the original decision was made in ignorance of, or based on a mistake about, the facts.

The list above is not exhaustive. There are other exceptions to the general rule.[132]

Awards of qualifying benefits

If you are entitled to a benefit at a higher rate because you or your partner (or a child included in your claim) or a non-dependant were awarded a qualifying benefit, the supersession takes effect on the date of entitlement to the qualifying benefit or to an increase in its rate. For IS, JSA, ESA and PC only, if you had a non-dependant living with you while you were waiting for a decision on your claim for a qualifying benefit, and a severe disability premium (additional amount with PC) can now be included, the supersession takes effect from the date the non-dependant can be ignored (or ceased to live with you). See pp1294–96 for further information.

Test cases

If a decision about your benefit is being superseded because of a decision by the Upper Tribunal or a court in another case (a test case), the supersession is effective from the date of the Upper Tribunal's or court's decision, even if you did not realise it was relevant to your case until some time later.[133] This could help you get considerable arrears of benefit. See p1296 for the 'anti-test case rule'.

If, while an appeal against the initial decision in a test case was pending:

- for benefits other than HB, a decision was made on your claim for benefit or to make a revision or a supersession, but your benefit was suspended and the test case is eventually decided against you (in whole or in part), the supersession takes effect from the date the earlier decision took effect;[134]

- you appealed to the First-tier Tribunal or the Upper Tribunal, it determined your appeal as if the test case had been decided in the way most unfavourable to you and the test case eventually goes in your favour (see p1347), the supersession takes effect from the date it would have taken effect had the tribunal made its decision in accordance with the decision in the test case.[135] For IS, JSA, ESA and PC, it takes effect from the start of the benefit week (or for UC the start of the assessment period) in which it it would have taken effect had the Tribunal made its decision in accordance with the decision in the test case.[136]

Other grounds for supersession

There are a large number of other exceptions to the general rule. These include if:

- your maximum rent (for HB) or your rent for the purposes of the housing costs element (for UC) has decreased because of a rent officer redetermination;[137]
- for ESA (and UC), a healthcare professional (see p1152 for who counts) approved by the Secretary of State has provided medical evidence on your capability for work or a decision maker has decided that you can be treated as having limited capability for work or work-related activity;[138]
- for PC and HB, you or your partner deferred claiming a pension and you are paid a lump sum or change your option to a pension increase;[139]
- entitlement to a benefit depends on your NI contribution record, and the decision needed to be changed because additional contributions have been added to the record.[140]

The list above is *not* exhaustive. There are many other exceptions to the general rule.[141]

Challenging a supersession

Following your application for a supersession, or a decision maker deciding to do a supersession on her/his own, a new decision is issued in writing. If you do not get all that you wanted from the supersession, you can seek a revision of the new decision. If the decision is one against which you have a right of appeal (see p1307), you can appeal to the First-tier Tribunal. If you have a right of appeal against the decision, you must be told about this. **Note:** you are likely to have to apply for a revision of the decision before you can appeal (see p1271).

If the decision maker has said there are no grounds for a supersession, you must show why there are, and say what you think the new decision should be. If the decision maker has done a supersession, but you do not agree that s/he had grounds for this, you should explain why.

If a decision maker refuses to consider a supersession

When you apply for a supersession, a decision maker must make a decision if your application for a supersession contains a ground for supersession that is

Part 10: Getting a benefit decision changed
Chapter 58: Revisions and supersessions
4. Revisions and supersessions after a 'qualifying benefit' award

potentially relevant to the amount of benefit you can be paid or the length of time you can be paid it. There are two possibilities.

- The decision maker agrees that there is a reason to change your award. For example, you are claiming HB and notify the decision maker that your non-dependant has moved out and so are entitled to more benefit. In this situation, the decision maker does a supersession.
- The decision maker does not think there is a reason to change your award. For example, you are getting DLA care component at the lowest rate, feel your condition has deteriorated and want to claim middle rate instead. However, the decision maker thinks you do not qualify for the middle rate. In this situation, the decision maker issues a decision refusing to do a supersession.

In either situation, you can seek a revision of the decision maker's decision or appeal against it.[142] The only situations in which a decision maker does not have to make a decision are if an application has not been made properly and, therefore, cannot possibly lead to a supersession, or if an application is transparently not on a potentially relevant ground for supersession or is otherwise misconceived. In these cases, there is no decision against which you can seek a revision or appeal, but you may be able to apply for a judicial review.

4. Revisions and supersessions after a 'qualifying benefit' award

There are special revision and supersession rules, known as 'qualifying benefit rules'. A 'qualifying benefit' is, in general, any benefit which gives you entitlement to another benefit, or makes another benefit payable at a higher rate. The rules help, for example, where, because of delays in assessing entitlement to a qualifying benefit – eg, attendance allowance (AA), disability living allowance (DLA), personal independence payment (PIP), carer's allowance (CA) or child benefit:

- you did not get certain premiums paid with your means-tested benefit (eg, disability, enhanced disability, severe disability, disabled child or carer premium), additional amounts paid with your pension credit (PC), elements paid with your universal credit (UC) or allowances for your children. For income support (IS), jobseeker's allowance (JSA), employment and support allowance (ESA) and PC only, this includes where there are delays in assessing your non-dependant's entitlement to a qualifying benefit (see p1295); *or*
- a non-dependant deduction was made from your means-tested benefit.

These rules can help you get arrears of benefit, even if the qualifying benefit was awarded some time ago, and you did not report the change in your circumstances at the time.[143]

Note: you can only apply for a revision or supersession on this ground if you are already entitled to IS, JSA, ESA, PC, HB or UC.[144] It is, therefore, essential to make a claim for these at the same time as the claim for a qualifying benefit. If you only qualify for one of these when the qualifying benefit is awarded, see p1296.

You or a family member are awarded a qualifying benefit or an increased rate

If you, or your partner or a child included in your claim (see p210), are awarded a qualifying benefit or an increase in its rate, and arrears of the qualifying benefit are payable, your award of IS, JSA, ESA, PC, HB or UC can be increased on revision or supersession and arrears paid for the same length of time.[145] This applies if:

- you are now entitled to premiums/components/elements/additional amounts (or if the qualifying benefit is child benefit, to allowances for your children paid with your benefit); *or*
- no non-dependant deduction should now be made from your means-tested benefit because you are now entitled to AA, the care component of DLA or the daily living component of PIP.

Note: for IS, JSA, ESA and PC only, if you had a non-dependant living with you while you were waiting for a decision on your claim for a qualifying benefit, your IS, JSA, ESA or PC award can be superseded to include the severe disability premium (additional amount), from the date s/he can be ignored (or from the date s/he ceased to reside with you) if this is after the date from which the qualifying benefit is payable.[146]

Example

Gus has been getting IS and HB for two months. His IS does not include any premiums and, because his uncle lives with him and his partner, Tanya, a non-dependant deduction is being made from his HB. He claims DLA, and Tanya claims CA on 15 July. Six months later, Gus is awarded DLA highest rate care component and Tanya is awarded CA, both payable from 15 July. Gus is now entitled to the disability, enhanced disability and carer premiums with his IS and a non-dependant deduction should not be made from his HB. His IS and HB awards are superseded and he is paid arrears, backdated to 15 July.

Your non-dependant is awarded a qualifying benefit or an increased rate

For IS, JSA, ESA and PC only, if you have a non-dependant living with you and, but for this, a severe disability premium (additional amount for PC) would be paid, your award of IS, income-based JSA, income-related ESA or PC can be increased on revision or supersession to include this premium (additional amount) from the date the non-dependant is awarded a qualifying benefit.[147]

Part 10: Getting a benefit decision changed
Chapter 58: Revisions and supersessions
5. The 'anti-test case rule'

If you only qualify when the qualifying benefit is awarded

If you make an unsuccessful claim for a benefit, and only qualify when the qualifying benefit is awarded, you should make a second claim as soon as you hear about the qualifying benefit. See p1149 for further information.

If you only qualify for HB when the qualifying benefit is awarded, see p127. If you lose benefit because of the way the rules operate, ask the local authority for compensation.

Remember, if you only claim for the first time *after* you hear about the qualifying benefit:
- for IS, JSA or UC, you can only get arrears if you satisfy the backdating rules for the benefit;
- for ESA and PC and (if you are at least the qualifying age for PC (see p78) and not getting IS, income-based JSA, income-related ESA or UC) HB, your claim can only be backdated for up to three months;
- for HB if you are under the qualifying age for PC or either you or your partner are getting IS, income-based JSA, income-related ESA or UC, your claim can only be backdated for up to six months, and only if you can show 'good cause' for your late claim (see p128).

See p1149 for a similar rule that helps you get extra backdating if your entitlement to CA depends on whether you or the person for whom you care are entitled to a qualifying benefit.

5. **The 'anti-test case rule'**

Special rules apply when a case is going through the appeals system that will determine a point of social security law (a test case). A rule (the 'anti-test case rule') says that some court and Upper Tribunal decisions should be ignored when decision makers are considering your entitlement to benefit for periods before the court or Tribunal decisions were given. If the anti-test case rule applies, you get arrears of benefit backdated only to the date of the decision in the test case.

How the anti-test case rule operates

If the Upper Tribunal or a court decides in an appeal that a decision maker in a totally different case (the test case) has made an error of law (see p1330 for what counts), and you make a claim, or apply for a revision or a supersession (whether before or after the test case decision), your decision maker must decide any part of *your* claim (or revision or supersession) which relates to the period *before* the test case decision as if the decision that was under appeal in the test case had been found by the Upper Tribunal or court in question not to have been wrong.[148] **Note:**

- The anti-test case rule only applies if the test case is the first authoritative decision on the issue, and not merely a later decision confirming an earlier decision.[149]
- The test case decision only has to be disregarded for the period before it was made if it found the decision maker to have been wrong, not if it found her/him to be right.

You can avoid the anti-test case rule by appealing rather than seeking a revision or supersession if the rules allow you to do so. In many cases, you have to seek a revision before you can appeal (see p1271). However, if you do not have to apply for a revision, if you think the anti-test case rule might apply and you are still within the absolute time limit for appealing, it may be better to appeal first (applying for an extension of time to appeal if necessary) and only ask for a revision or supersession if you cannot appeal.

What happens while a test case is pending

If an appeal (a test case) is pending against a decision of the Upper Tribunal or a court, the decision maker can postpone making a decision on your claim or request for a supersession or revision.[150] This prevents you appealing until a decision is made in the test case. If you already have a decision in your favour, the decision maker can suspend payment of your benefit (see p1175). If the decision on your claim or request for a revision or supersession is postponed, once a decision has been made in the test case, the decision maker makes the decision in your case.[151]

If you would be entitled to benefit even if the test case were decided against you, the decision maker can make a decision.[152] This is done on the assumption that the test case has been decided in the way that is most unfavourable to you. However, this does mean that you are at least paid something while you wait for the result of the test case. Then, if the decision in the test case is in your favour, the decision maker revises her/his decision.

If you have already appealed to the First-tier Tribunal, see p1347.

Part 10: Getting a benefit decision changed
Chapter 58: Revisions and supersessions
Notes

Notes

1. Getting a decision changed

1 R(I) 50/56
2 R(IS) 11/92
3 **HB** Sch 7 paras 3(2) and 4(3) CSPSSA 2000
Other benefits ss9(2) and 10(2) SSA 1998
4 **HB** Regs 4(5) and 7(5) HB&CTB(DA) Regs
CB/GA Regs 7(2) and (3) and 14(3) CB&GA(DA) Regs
UC/PIP/JSA&ESA under UC Regs 20(2) and (3) and 33(2) and (3) UC,PIP,JSA&ESA(DA) Regs
Other benefits Regs 3(2) and 6(4) SS&CS(DA) Regs

2. Revisions

5 **HB** Sch 7 para 3 CSPSSA 2000
Other benefits s9 SSA 1998
6 **HB** Sch 7 para 3(1) CSPSSA 2000; reg 4 HB&CTB(DA) Regs
CB/GA s9(1) SSA 1998; regs 5, 8, 10 and 11 CB&GA(DA) Regs
UC/PIP/JSA&ESA under UC s9(1) SSA 1998; regs 5 and 8 UC,PIP,JSA&ESA(DA) Regs
Other benefits s9(1) SSA 1998; reg 3 SS&CS(DA) Regs
7 Reg 3(9)(b) and (c) SS&CS(DA) Regs; reg 5(2)(c) UC,PIP,JSA&ESA(DA) Regs
8 s12(1), (2) and (3D) SSA 1998
9 s12(2)(b) and (3A)-(3C) SSA 1998
10 **UC/PIP/JSA&ESA under UC** Reg 7 UC,PIP,JSA&ESA(DA) Regs
Other benefits Reg 3ZA SS&CS(DA) Regs
11 r7 TP(FTT) Rules
12 **UC/PIP/JSA&ESA under UC** Reg 7(5) UC,PIP,JSA&ESA(DA) Regs
Other benefits Reg 3ZA(5) SS&CS(DA) Regs
13 para A3046 ADM
14 para A3015 ADM
15 **CB/GA** Reg 5(2)(b) CB&GA(DA) Regs
UC/PIP/JSA&ESA under UC Reg 5(1)(b) UC,PIP,JSA&ESA(DA) Regs
Other benefits Reg 3(1)(b) SS&CS(DA) Regs

16 **CB/GA** Reg 5(2)(a) CB&GA(DA) Regs
UC/PIP/JSA&ESA under UC Reg 5(1)(a) UC,PIP,JSA&ESA(DA) Regs
Other benefits Reg 3(1)(a) SS&CS(DA) Regs
17 Reg 4(1)(b) HB&CTB(DA) Regs
18 **HB** Reg 4(10) HB&CTB(DA) Regs
CB/GA Reg 5(3) CB&GA(DA) Regs
UC/PIP/JSA&ESA under UC Reg 5(2)(a) UC,PIP,JSA&ESA(DA) Regs
Other benefits Reg 3(9)(a) SS&CS(DA) Regs; Sch 2 para 25A(1)(b) and (c) ESA(TP)(EA) No.2 Regs
19 Reg 3(3) SS&CS(DA) Regs
20 Regs 1(3), definition of 'date of notification', and 3(1)(b) SS&CS(DA) Regs
21 Regs 2 and 4(1)(a) HB&CTB(DA) Regs
22 Reg 4(4) HB&CTB(DA) Regs
23 **CB/GA** Regs 3 and 5(2)(b) CB&GA(DA) Regs
UC/PIP/JSA&ESA under UC Regs 2, 3(2) and 5(1)(b) UC,PIP,JSA&ESA(DA) Regs
Other benefits Regs 1(3), 2(b) and 3(1)(b) SS&CS(DA) Regs
24 **HB** Reg 10A(3) HB&CTB(DA) Regs
UC/PIP/JSA&ESA under UC Reg 38(4) UC,PIP,JSA&ESA(DA) Regs
Other benefits Reg 9A(3) SS&CS(DA) Regs
25 **HB** Regs 4(4) and 5(3)(b) HB&CTB(DA) Regs
CB/GA Reg 6(3)(c) CB&GA(DA) Regs
Other benefits Reg 4 SS&CS(DA) Regs
26 Reg 6 UC,PIP,JSA&ESA(DA) Regs
27 **HB** Reg 5(3)(a) HB&CTB(DA) Regs
CB/GA Reg 6(3)(a) and (b) CB&GA(DA) Regs
UC/PIP/JSA&ESA under UC Reg 6(3) UC,PIP,JSA&ESA(DA) Regs
Other benefits Reg 4(3)(a) SS&CS(DA) Regs

10

28 **HB** Reg 5(4)(a) and (c) HB&CTB(DA)
Regs
CB/GA Reg 6(4)(a) and (c) CB&GA(DA)
Regs
UC/PIP/JSA&ESA under UC Reg 6(4)
and (5) UC,PIP,JSA&ESA(DA) Regs
Other benefits Reg 4(4)(a) and (c)
SS&CS(DA) Regs

29 **HB** Reg 5(4)(b) and (6) HB&CTB(DA)
Regs
CB/GA Reg 6(4)(b) and (5)
CB&GA(DA) Regs
Other benefits Reg 4(4)(b) and (5)
SS&CS(DA) Regs

30 **HB** Reg 5(5) HB&CTB(DA) Regs
CB/GA Reg 6(6) CB&GA(DA) Regs
Other benefits Reg 4(6) SS&CS(DA)
Regs

31 R(TC) 1/05

32 **HB** Reg 4(2)(a) HB&CTB(DA) Regs
CB/GA Reg 10(2)(a) CB&GA(DA) Regs
UC/PIP/JSA&ESA under UC Regs 8
and 9(a) UC,PIP,JSA&ESA(DA) Regs
Other benefits Reg 3(5)(a)
SS&CS(DA) Regs

33 **HB** Reg 1(2) HB&CTB(DA) Regs
UC/PIP/JSA&ESA under UC Reg 2
UC,PIP,JSA&ESA(DA) Regs
Other benefits Reg 1(3) SS&CS(DA)
Regs

34 Reg 10(3) CB&GA(DA) Regs

35 **HB** Reg 1(2) HB&CTB(DA) Regs
CB/GA Reg 10(3) CB&GA(DA) Regs
UC/PIP/JSA&ESA under UC Reg 2
UC,PIP,JSA&ESA(DA) Regs
Other benefits Reg 1(3) SS&CS(DA)
Regs

36 CIS/34/2006

37 CDLA/393/2006

38 **HB** Reg 4(2)(b) HB&CTB(DA) Regs
CB/GA Reg 10(2)(b) CB&GA(DA) Regs
UC/PIP/JSA&ESA under UC Regs 8
and 9(b) UC,PIP,JSA&ESA(DA) Regs
Other benefits Reg 3(5)(b) and (d)
SS&CS(DA) Regs

39 Regs 3(5)(c)and 7A(1) SS&CS(DA) Regs

40 Reg 7A(2) SS&CS(DA) Regs

41 Reg 7A SS&CS(DA) Regs

42 **CB/GA** Reg 5(2)(a) CB&GA(DA) Regs
UC/PIP/JSA&ESA under UC Reg
5(1)(a) UC,PIP,JSA&ESA(DA) Regs
Other benefits Reg 3(1)(a)
SS&CS(DA) Regs

43 Reg 4(1)(b) HB&CTB(DA) Regs

44 **HB** Reg 4(7B) HB&CTB(DA) Regs
CB/GA Reg 11 CB&GA(DA) Regs
UC/PIP/JSA&ESA under UC Regs 8
and 12 UC,PIP,JSA&ESA(DA) Regs
Other benefits Reg 3(7) SS&CS(DA)
Regs

45 Reg 4(7C) HB&CTB(DA) Regs

46 Reg 3(7ZA) SS&CS(DA) Regs

47 **HB** Reg 4(1)(c) HB&CTB(DA) Regs
CB/GA Reg 8(2) CB&GA(DA) Regs
UC/PIP/JSA&ESA under UC Regs 8
and 11(1) UC,PIP,JSA&ESA(DA) Regs
Other benefits Reg 3(4A) SS&CS(DA)
Regs

48 **HB** Reg 4(7) HB&CTB(DA) Regs
CB/GA Reg 8(3) CB&GA(DA) Regs
UC/PIP/JSA&ESA under UC Regs 8
and 11(2) UC,PIP,JSA&ESA(DA) Regs
Other benefits Reg 3(5A) SS&CS(DA)
Regs

49 **HB** Reg 4(6) HB&CTB(DA) Regs
CB/GA Reg 9 CB&GA(DA) Regs
UC/PIP/JSA&ESA under UC Regs 8
and 10 UC,PIP,JSA&ESA(DA) Regs
Other benefits Reg 3(8) SS&CS(DA)
Regs

50 **HB** Reg 4(7H) HB&CTB(DA) Regs
UC/PIP/JSA&ESA under UC Regs 8
and 19(1) UC,PIP,JSA&ESA(DA) Regs

51 **UC/PIP/JSA&ESA under UC** Regs 8
and 15(3) UC,PIP,JSA&ESA(DA) Regs
Other benefits Reg 3(5D) SS&CS(DA)
Regs

52 Regs 8 and 18(2) UC,PIP,JSA&ESA(DA)
Regs

53 Regs 8 and 18(3) UC,PIP,JSA&ESA(DA)
Regs

54 **HB** Reg 4(3), (7E) and (7F)
HB&CTB(DA) Regs; reg 18A(1) and (3)
HB Regs; reg 18A(1) and (3) HB(SPC)
Regs
UC/PIP/JSA&ESA under UC Regs 8
and 19(2) UC,PIP,JSA&ESA(DA) Regs

55 **RP** Reg 3(7E) SS&CS(DA) Regs
PC Reg 3(7D) SS&CS(DA) Regs
HB Reg 4(7D) HB&CTB(DA) Regs

56 **HB** Reg 4(7A) HB&CTB(DA) Regs
UC/PIP/JSA&ESA under UC Regs 8,
13, 14, 15(2), (4) and (5), 16, 17 and 18
UC,PIP,JSA&ESA(DA) Regs
Other benefits Reg 3(5C), (5E)-(5I),
(6), (6A), (6B), (7A), (7EA), (7EB), (8B),
(8C) and (8D) SS&CS(DA) Regs

10

Part 10: Getting a benefit decision changed
Chapter 58: Revisions and supersessions
Notes

57 **HB** Reg 4(8) HB&CTB(DA) Regs
CB/GA Reg 2(1), definition of
'appropriate office', CB&GA(DA) Regs
UC/PIP/JSA&ESA under UC Reg 2
UC,PIP,JSA&ESA(DA) Regs
Other benefits Reg 3(11) SS&CS(DA)
Regs
58 **HB** Reg 4(9) HB&CTB(DA) Regs
CB/GA Reg 7(1) CB&GA(DA) Regs
UC/PIP/JSA&ESA under UC Reg
20(1) UC,PIP,JSA&ESA(DA) Regs
Other benefits Reg 3(10) SS&CS(DA)
Regs
59 Reg 4(8) HB&CTB(DA) Regs
60 Reg 5(2) HB&CTB(DA) Regs
61 **HB** Sch 7 para 3(2) CSPSSA 2000
Other benefits s9(2) SSA 1998
62 **HB** Sch 7 para 3(3) CSPSSA 2000
Other benefits s9(3) SSA 1998
63 **HB** Reg 6 HB&CTB(DA) Regs
CB/GA Reg 12 CB&GA(DA) Regs
UC/PIP and JSA/ESA under UC Reg
21 UC,PIP,JSA&ESA(DA) Regs
Other benefits Reg 5(1) SS&CS(DA)
Regs
64 **HB** Sch 7 para 3(5) CSPSSA 2000; r23
and Sch 1 TP(FT) Rules
Other benefits s9(5) SSA 1998; r23
and Sch 1 TP(FT) Rules
65 R(IS) 15/04; *Beltekian v Westminster City
Council and Another* [2004] EWCA Civ
1784 reported as R(H) 8/05; *AS v SSWP
(CSM)* [2012] UKUT 448 (AAC)

3. **Supersessions**
66 **HB** Sch 7 para 4 CSPSSA 2000
Other benefits s10 SSA 1998
67 **HB** Reg 7(2) HB&CTB(DA) Regs
CB/GA Reg 13(1) CB&GA(DA) Regs
UC/PIP/JSA&ESA under UC Reg 22
UC,PIP,JSA&ESA(DA) Regs
Other benefits Reg 6(2) SS&CS(DA)
Regs
68 **HB** Reg 7(4) HB&CTB(DA) Regs
CB/GA Reg 15 CB&GA(DA) Regs
UC/PIP/JSA&ESA under UC Reg 32
UC,PIP,JSA&ESA(DA) Regs
Other benefits Reg 6(3) SS&CS(DA)
Regs

69 **HB** Regs 7(2)(a) and (3) and 7A(4)
HB&CTB(DA) Regs
CB/GA Reg 13(2)(a) CB&GA(DA) Regs
UC/PIP/JSA&ESA under UC Reg 23
UC,PIP,JSA&ESA(DA) Regs
Other benefits Reg 6(2)(a)
SS&CS(DA) Regs; Sch 2 para 25A(2)
ESA(TP)(EA) No.2 Regs
All *Wood v SSWP* [2003] EWCA Civ 53
reported as R(DLA) 1/03
70 *CAO v McKiernon*, 8 July 1993 (CA)
71 *Cooke v Secretary of State for Social
Security* [2001] reported as R(DLA) 6/01;
R(S) 4/86; R(IS) 2/98; CIB/7899/1996;
CIS/856/1994
72 Reg 6(6)(a) SS&CS(DA) Regs
73 Reg 6(6)(c) SS&CS(DA) Regs; reg 23(2)
UC,PIP,JSA&ESA(DA) Regs
74 Reg 6(8) SS&CS(DA) Regs
75 CSDLA/637/2006; CSDLA/822/2006
76 **HB** Sch 7 para 2 CSPSSA 2000
Other benefits s8(2) SSA 1998; reg
12A SS&CS(DA) Regs
77 **HB** Reg 7(2)(b) and (d) HB&CTB(DA)
Regs
CB/GA Reg 13(2)(b) and (c)(i)
CB&GA(DA) Regs
UC/PIP/JSA&ESA under UC Regs 24
and 31(a) UC,PIP,JSA&ESA(DA) Regs
Other benefits Reg 6(2)(b) and (c)
SS&CS(DA) Regs
78 Reg 4(1)(b) HB&CTB(DA) Regs
79 **HB** Reg 7(2)(b) HB&CTB(DA) Regs
CB/GA Reg 13(2)(b) CB&GA(DA) Regs
UC/PIP/JSA&ESA under UC Reg 24
UC,PIP,JSA&ESA(DA) Regs
Other benefits Reg 6(2)(b)
SS&CS(DA) Regs
80 Regs 6(2)(r) and 7A(1) SS&CS(DA) Regs;
reg 26(1) UC,PIP,JSA&ESA(DA) Regs;
CIB/4033/2003; R(IB) 2/05
81 CSIB/377/2003; CIB/1509/2004 ; R(IB)
5/05; *JB v SSWP (IB)* [2010] UKUT 246
(AAC); *ST v SSWP (ESA)* [2012] UKUT
469 (AAC)
82 s80(5) and (6) WRA 2012; reg 26(2)
UC,PIP,JSA&ESA(DA) Regs
83 CIB/1972/2000; CIB/3179/2000; CIB/
3985/2001; *ST v SSWP (ESA)* [2012]
UKUT 469 (AAC)
84 **HB** Reg 7(2)(i) HB&CTB(DA) Regs
CB/GA Reg 13(2)(e) CB&GA(DA) Regs
UC/PIP/JSA&ESA under UC Reg 23
UC,PIP,JSA&ESA(DA) Regs. Note that for
these benefits, this is dealt with as a
change of circumstances.
Other benefits Reg 6(2)(e)
SS&CS(DA) Regs

85 Reg 6(2)(ee) SS&CS(DA) Regs
86 **HB** Reg 7(2)(e) HB&CTB(DA) Regs
    CB/GA Reg 13(2)(d) CB&GA(DA) Regs
    UC/PIP/JSA&ESA under UC Reg 25
    UC,PIP,JSA&ESA(DA) Regs
    Other benefits Reg 6(2)(d)
    SS&CS(DA) Regs
87 Reg 7(2)(c) HB&CTB(DA) Regs; reg
    18A(2) HB Regs; reg 18A(2) HB(SPC)
    Regs; reg 30 UC,PIP,JSA&ESA(DA) Regs
88 Reg 7(2)(r) HB&CTB(DA) Regs
89 **PC** Reg 6(2)(o) SS&CS(DA) Regs
    HB Reg 7(2)(j) HB&CTB(DA) Regs
90 **HB** Reg 7(2)(d)(ii) HB&CTB(DA) Regs
    CB/GA Reg 13(2)(c)(ii) CB&GA(DA)
    Regs
    UC/PIP/JSA&ESA under UC Reg
    31(b) UC,PIP,JSA&ESA(DA) Regs
    Other benefits Reg 6(2)(c)(ii)
    SS&CS(DA) Regs
91 **HB** Regs 7(2)(g), (h), (q) and (r) and
    7A(2) and (3) HB&CTB(DA) Regs
    UC/PIP/JSA&ESA under UC Regs 27,
    28 and 29 UC,PIP,JSA&ESA(DA) Regs
    Other benefits Reg 6(2)(f), (fa), (h),
    (j), (k), (l), (m), (n), (p), (q) and (s)
    SS&CS(DA) Regs
92 **HB** Reg 7(6) HB&CTB(DA) Regs
    CB/GA Reg 14(1) CB&GA(DA) Regs
    UC/PIP/JSA&ESA under UC Reg
    33(1) UC,PIP,JSA&ESA(DA) Regs
    Other benefits Reg 6(5) SS&CS(DA)
    Regs
    All R(I) 50/56
93 Reg 7(7) HB&CTB(DA) Regs
94 **HB** Sch 7 para 4(3) CSPSSA 2000
    Other benefits s10(2) SSA 1998
95 **HB** Sch 7 para 4(5) CSPSSA 2000
    Other benefits s10(5) SSA 1998
96 **HB** Reg 8(10) HB&CTB(DA) Regs
    UC/PIP/JSA&ESA under UC Reg
    35(1) and Sch 1 paras 32 and 33
    UC,PIP,JSA&ESA(DA) Regs
    Other benefits Reg 7(9)(a)(ii), (30)
    and (30A) SS&CS(DA) Regs
97 Reg 7(2)(bc) SS&CS(DA) Regs
98 Reg 7(2)(be) SS&CS(DA) Regs; reg
    35(1) and Sch 1 paras 9 and 28
    UC,PIP,JSA&ESA(DA) Regs
99 Reg 8(2) HB&CTB(DA) Regs
100 Reg 8(3) HB&CTB(DA) Regs
101 Sch 1 para 18 UC,PIP,JSA&ESA(DA) Regs
102 Sch 1 para 12 UC,PIP,JSA&ESA(DA) Regs
103 Sch 1 para 15 UC,PIP,JSA&ESA(DA) Regs
104 Sch 1 para 12 UC,PIP,JSA&ESA(DA) Regs
105 Sch 1 paras 16, 17 and 19
    UC,PIP,JSA&ESA(DA) Regs

106 s10(5) SSA 1998; Sch 1 para 13
    UC,PIP,JSA&ESA(DA) Regs
107 **CB/GA** Reg 16(4) CB&GA(DA) Regs
    Other benefits Reg 7(2)(bb) and
    (9)(a) SS&CS(DA) Regs
108 Reg 7(9) SS&CS(DA) Regs; *SSWP v DA*
    [2009] UKUT 214 (AAC)
109 **CB/GA** Reg 16(3)(a) CB&GA(DA) Regs
    Other benefits Reg 7(2)(a)
    SS&CS(DA) Regs
110 **CB/GA** Reg 16(5) CB&GA(DA) Regs
    Other benefits Reg 7(2)(c)(iv) and
    (v) SS&CS(DA) Regs
111 Regs 7(2)(c)(ii) and 7A(1) SS&CS(DA)
    Regs
112 Reg 7A(2) SS&CS(DA) Regs
113 Sch 1 paras 10 and 29
    UC,PIP,JSA&ESA(DA) Regs
114 Sch 1 para 20 UC,PIP,JSA&ESA(DA) Regs
115 Sch 1 para 1 UC,PIP,JSA&ESA(DA) Regs
116 Sch 1 paras 1 and 20
    UC,PIP,JSA&ESA(DA) Regs
117 Sch 1 paras 7, 8, 11, 23, 24 and 30
    UC,PIP,JSA&ESA(DA) Regs
118 s10(5) SSA 1998; Sch 1 paras 2 and 25
    UC,PIP,JSA&ESA(DA) Regs
119 **HB** Reg 9 HB&CTB(DA) Regs
    CB/GA Reg 17 CB&GA(DA) Regs
    UC/PIP/JSA&ESA under UC Reg 36
    UC,PIP,JSA&ESA(DA) Regs
    Other benefits Reg 8 SS&CS(DA) Regs
120 **HB** Reg 9(2) HB&CTB(DA) Regs
    CB/GA Reg 17(3) CB&GA(DA) Regs
    UC/PIP/JSA&ESA under UC Reg
    36(3) UC,PIP,JSA&ESA(DA) Regs
    Other benefits Reg 8(3) SS&CS(DA)
    Regs
121 **HB** Reg 9(3) and (4) HB&CTB(DA) Regs
    CB/GA Reg 17(4) and (5) CB&GA(DA)
    Regs
    UC/PIP/JSA&ESA under UC Reg
    36(4)-(6) UC,PIP,JSA&ESA(DA) Regs
    Other benefits Reg 8(4) and (5)
    SS&CS(DA) Regs
122 **HB** Reg 9(5) HB&CTB(DA) Regs
    CB/GA Reg 17(6) CB&GA(DA) Regs
    UC/PIP/JSA&ESA under UC Reg
    36(7) UC,PIP,JSA&ESA(DA) Regs
    Other benefits Reg 8(6) SS&CS(DA)
    Regs
123 Reg 7(9)(d) SS&CS(DA) Regs
124 Reg 7(2)(b)(i) and (ii) SS&CS(DA)
    Regs; Sch 1 para 6 UC,PIP,JSA&ESA(DA)
    Regs
125 Reg 8(3) HB&CTB(DA) Regs
126 Sch 1 para 21 UC,PIP,JSA&ESA(DA) Regs

10

Part 10: Getting a benefit decision changed
Chapter 58: Revisions and supersessions
Notes

127 **CB/GA** Reg 16(3)(b) CB&GA(DA) Regs
UC/PIP/JSA&ESA under UC Sch 1
para 14 UC,PIP,JSA&ESA(DA) Regs
Other benefits Reg 7(2)(b)(iii)
SS&CS(DA) Regs

128 **HB** Reg 8(7) HB&CTB(DA) Regs
CB/GA Reg 16(7) CB&GA(DA) Regs
UC/PIP/JSA&ESA under UC Reg
37(1) and (2) UC,PIP,JSA&ESA(DA) Regs
Other benefits Reg 7(5) SS&CS(DA)
Regs

129 Reg 37 (1) and (3) UC,PIP,JSA&ESA(DA)
Regs

130 **UC/ESA** Regs 2 and 37 (1) and (3)
UC,PIP,JSA&ESA(DA) Regs
Other benefits Reg 7(5) SS&CS(DA)
Regs

131 Reg 8(4) HB&CTB(DA) Regs

132 Sch 3A para 12, Sch 3B para 7 and Sch
3C para 8 SS&CS(DA) Regs; reg 35(2)-
(4) UC,PIP,JSA&ESA(DA) Regs

133 **HB** Reg 8(8) HB&CTB(DA) Regs
CB/GA Reg 16(9) CB&GA(DA) Regs
UC/PIP/JSA&ESA under UC Reg
35(5) UC,PIP,JSA&ESA(DA) Regs
Other benefits Reg 7(6) SS&CS(DA)
Regs
All MP v SSWP (DLA) [2010] UKUT 130
(AAC)

134 **CB/GA** Reg 16(9A) CB&GA(DA) Regs
UC/PIP/JSA&ESA under UC Reg
37(5) and (6) UC,PIP,JSA&ESA(DA) Regs
Other benefits Reg 7(6A) SS&CS(DA)
Regs

135 **HB** Reg 8(11) HB&CTB(DA) Regs
CB/GA Reg 16(8) CB&GA(DA) Regs
PIP Reg 37(4)(a) UC,PIP,JSA&ESA(DA)
Regs
Other benefits Reg 7(33) SS&CS(DA)
Regs

136 Sch 3A para 12, Sch 3B para 7 and Sch
3C para 8 SS&CS(DA) Regs; reg
37(4)(b) and (c) UC,PIP,JSA&ESA(DA)
Regs

137 Reg 8(2) and (6) HB&CTB(DA) Regs; reg
35(14) UC,PIP,JSA&ESA(DA) Regs

138 Reg 7(38)-(40) SS&CS(DA) Regs; reg
35(6)-(9) UC,PIP,JSA&ESA(DA) Regs

139 **PC** Reg 7(7A) SS&CS(DA) Regs
HB Reg 8(14A) HB&CTB(DA) Regs

140 Reg 7(8A) SS&CS(DA) Regs; reg 33(13)
UC,PIP,JSA&ESA(DA) Regs

141 **HB** Reg 8(6A), (9), (14D), (14C),
(14F) and (15) HB&CTB(DA) Regs
UC/PIP/JSA&ESA under UC Reg
35(10)-(12) UC,PIP,JSA&ESA(DA) Regs
Other benefits Reg 7(8), (8ZA), (8ZB),
(10)-(13), (24), (25), (28), (29), (29A)-
(29C) and (34)-(37) SS&CS(DA) Regs

142 Wood v SSWP [2003] EWCA Civ 53,
reported as R(DLA) 1/03

4. Revisions and supersessions after a 'qualifying benefit' award

143 HR v Wakefield DC [2009] UKUT 72
(AAC)

144 **IS/JSA/ESA/PC/UC** s8(2) SSA 1998
HB Sch 7 para 2 CSPSSA 2000

145 **IS/JSA/ESA/PC** Regs 3(7), 6(2)(e)
and 7(7) SS&CS(DA) Regs
HB Regs 4(7B) and (7C), 7(2)(i)
and 8(14) HB&CTB(DA) Regs; CIS/
1178/2001
UC/PIP/JSA&ESA under UC Regs 12,
21 and 23 and Sch 1 para 31
UC,PIP,JSA&ESA(DA) Regs

146 Reg 7(7)(b) SS&CS(DA) Regs

147 Regs 3(7ZA), 6(2)(ee) and
7(7) SS&CS(DA) Regs

5. The 'anti-test case rule'

148 **HB** Sch 7 para 18 CSPSSA 2000
Other benefits s27 SSA 1998
All CAO and Another v Bate [1996] 2 All
ER 790 (HL)

149 R(FC) 3/98; R(I) 1/03

150 **HB** Sch 7 para 16 CSPSSA 2000
Other benefits s25 SSA 1998

151 **HB** Sch 7 para 18(2) CSPSSA 2000
Other benefits s27(2) SSA 1998

152 **HB** Sch 7 para 16(3) and (4) CSPSSA
2000; reg 15 HB&CTB(DA) Regs
CB/GA s25(3) and (4) SSA 1998; reg 22
CB&GA(DA) Regs
UC/PIP/JSA&ESA under UC s25(3)
and (4) SSA 1998; reg 53
UC,PIP,JSA&ESA(DA) Regs
Other benefits s25(3) and (4) SSA
1998; reg 21 SS&CS(DA) Regs

10

Chapter 59

· ·

Appeals

This chapter covers:
1. Appealing to the First-tier Tribunal (p1304)
2. Appealing to the Upper Tribunal (p1329)
3. Procedural rules (p1341)
4. Appealing to the courts (p1348)
5. Time limits (p1352)
6. Presenting your case (p1355)

This chapter covers the rules for appeals about benefits, the social fund payments in Chapter 37 (except budgeting loans) and national insurance (NI) credits. It does *not* cover the rules for statutory sick pay and statutory maternity, adoption and paternity pay (see Chapter 60), the health benefits in Chapter 30 or the other types of financial help in Chapter 40, discretionary housing payments (see Chapter 21) or NI contributions.

References in this chapter to HM Revenue and Customs (HMRC) only apply to decisions about child benefit and guardian's allowance. HMRC also makes decisions about tax credits. For information about getting a tax credits decision changed, see Chapter 68.

Key facts

- If you disagree with certain decisions made by the DWP, the local authority or HM Revenue and Customs, you can appeal to the First-tier Tribunal.
- For benefits other than housing benefit, in most cases you have to apply for a revision before you can appeal to the First-tier Tribunal.
- If your appeal to the First-tier Tribunal is unsuccessful, you might be able to appeal to the Upper Tribunal. If your appeal to the Upper Tribunal is unsuccessful, you might be able to appeal to a court.
- Occasionally, if you cannot appeal, you may be able to challenge a decision by a judicial review.
- The time limits for appealing are very strict.
- Appeals can take time. If your circumstances change while you are waiting for your appeal to be heard, you may need to make a fresh claim for benefit or seek a supersession.

Part 10: Getting a benefit decision changed
Chapter 59: Appeals
1. Appealing to the First-tier Tribunal

1. Appealing to the First-tier Tribunal

The appeals against decision makers' decisions described in this chapter are dealt with by a judge (and in some cases members) of the First-tier Tribunal (Social Security and Child Support) – referred to as the First-tier Tribunal in this *Handbook* (except in Chapter 60), who has been assigned to its Social Entitlement Chamber. The administration of the work of all tribunals is the responsibility of HM Courts and Tribunals Service (HMCTS), part of the Ministry of Justice. HMCTS officials deal with the day-to-day work of the First-tier Tribunal.

There are **procedural rules** that the First-tier Tribunal must follow (covered on pp1341–48). The overriding objective of the rules is to enable the First-tier Tribunal to deal with cases fairly and justly.[1] The Tribunal can do a number of things, including to extend or shorten time limits and to postpone or adjourn hearings. If a test case or lead case is pending that deals with issues raised in your appeal, you may find that your appeal is delayed (see p1347).

Revision, supersession or appeal?

1. You are likely to have to apply for a revision before you can appeal (see p1305), but you get two bites at the cherry, because if your application for a revision is turned down, you can still appeal against the original decision.

2. There is no time limit for applying for an 'any time' revision (see p1275). You can ask for one even if the time limit for applying for an 'any grounds' revision or appealing has expired. However, you cannot appeal against a refusal to do an any time revision (see p1281).

3. In most cases, there is no time limit for applying for a supersession – eg, if there has been a mistake about the facts or if a test case is decided in your favour but you do not become aware of this until some time after. However, you generally get less arrears of benefit if you apply for a supersession rather than a revision or by appealing, even if you are successful. See pp1287–93 for information about when a supersession takes effect.

4. If you apply for a revision or a supersession instead of appealing and the 'anti-test case' rule (see p1296) applies to you, the arrears of benefit you get could be limited.

5. In some cases, you should seek advice before you appeal. Because the First-tier Tribunal looks at your case afresh, there is a risk you could lose benefit. For example, if your appeal is about a benefit that can be paid at different rates (eg, disability living allowance (DLA) or industrial injuries disablement benefit), the rate could go down. If you are appealing about an overpayment, the amount could increase.

Appeal rights

You can appeal to the First-tier Tribunal against some decisions of the DWP, the local authority or HM Revenue and Customs (HMRC). For information about:

- whether you must apply for a revision before you can appeal, see p1305 and p1271;
- how to appeal, see p1309;
- where to send your appeal, see p1309;
- the time limit for appealing, see p1310. This is strict;
- making sure your appeal is valid, see p1311. If not, it might not go ahead.

Applying for a revision before you can appeal

For benefits other than housing benefit (HB), in most cases, if you want to appeal against a decision to the First-tier Tribunal, you can only do so if you have applied for a revision of the decision and:

- for child benefit and guardian's allowance, HMRC has decided not to revise it. HMRC's intention is that if it revises the decision, you can appeal against the original decision as revised. **Note:** the rules on child benefit and guardian's allowance are based on draft regulations, due to come into force on 6 April 2014. See CPAG's online service and *Welfare Rights Bulletin* for updates;[2] *or*
- for other benefits, the DWP has considered whether to revise the decision. This only applies if you have been given proper written notice.[3]

The DWP and HMRC call this **'mandatory reconsideration'**. For further information, see pp1271–73. The DWP (or HMRC) gives you notice of the result (called a **'mandatory reconsideration notice'**). You must send a copy of it to the First-tier Tribunal when you appeal (see p1311).

Note: you do not have to apply for a revision of local authority decisions about HB before you can appeal; you can appeal straight away.

Appeals: checklist

1. Check whether you must apply for a revision (a 'mandatory reconsideration') before you can appeal.

2. To get more information about a decision, ask for a written statement of reasons if this has not already been provided (see p1156).

3. If you must apply for a revision before you can appeal, do so within the time limit (see p1273). If your application is late, explain why fully. If you miss the absolute time limit, check if there are grounds for an 'any time' revision (see p1275).

4. When you get the decision maker's 'mandatory reconsideration notice' (see p1272), appeal within the time limit (see p1310).

Note:

- If you are required to apply for a revision before you can appeal but you fail to do so, your right of appeal is affected.
- If you appeal against a decision, but you should have applied for a revision first, the DWP can (but does not have to) treat your appeal as an application for

Part 10: Getting a benefit decision changed
Chapter 59: Appeals
1. Appealing to the First-tier Tribunal

a revision.[4] If the DWP has not treated your appeal as an application for a revision, apply for a revision as soon as possible, explaining why your application is late if relevant.

- The DWP says that if the decision maker refuses to consider your application for an 'any grounds' revision because it was made outside the time limit for doing so (see p1274), s/he should go on to consider whether there are grounds for an 'any time' revision, and if there are no grounds, whether to do a supersession.[5]
- There is an absolute time limit for applying for an any grounds revision (see p1274). There is no time limit for applying for an 'any time' revision (see p1275).
- If you send or deliver your appeal to the First-tier Tribunal when you should have applied for a revision first, the First-tier Tribunal should return your appeal to you and advise you to apply for a revision.
- If the decision maker refuses to accept your application for an 'any grounds' revision of a decision (eg, because it was made outside the absolute time limit for doing so), the DWP and HMRC intention is that you do not have a right of appeal against the decision.[6]

Bear in mind that it is the First-tier Tribunal who decides if you have a right of appeal, not the DWP (or HMRC). However, the only way to be sure you have a right of appeal is to apply for a revision where you are required to do so, and to do this in time. If the Tribunal says you do not have a right of appeal, your only remedy is judicial review.

Who can appeal

You can appeal to the First-tier Tribunal if you are the claimant. However, certain other people can also appeal.

- If you are appealing about a **benefit other than HB**, you have a right to appeal if you are:[7]
  - a claimant;
  - an appointee claiming on someone's behalf (see p1137);
  - claiming attendance allowance (AA), DLA or personal independence payment (PIP) on behalf of someone who is terminally ill, even if this is without her/his knowledge;
  - a person from whom an ordinary overpayment of a benefit or a regulated social fund payment or a duplication of payment of income support (IS), income-based jobseeker's allowance (JSA), income-related employment and support allowance (ESA) or pension credit (PC) can be recovered (see Chapter 56). This is the case even if you were not the person who claimed the benefit that was overpaid;[8]
  - someone from whom a short-term or budgeting advance, or hardship payments, can be recovered;

Chapter 59

Appeals

- the partner of a claimant, if the decision concerns whether *you* failed to take part in a work-focused interview without good cause;[9]
- a person appointed by the DWP or HMRC to proceed with a claim for benefit made by someone who has since died or to make a claim for (and who has now claimed) benefit for someone who has died.[10]
- If you are appealing about **HB**, you have a right to appeal if you are a person affected by the decision – ie, your rights, duties or obligations are affected by the decision, and you are:[11]
  - a claimant;
  - someone acting for a claimant who is unable to act for her/himself – eg, an appointee (see p1137);
  - someone from whom the local authority decides an overpayment can be recovered (including a landlord or agent);[12] *or*
  - a landlord or agent, if the decision concerns whether or not to make a direct payment of HB to you.

In all cases, if the person who appealed dies, the DWP, the local authority or HMRC can appoint someone else to proceed with the appeal.[13]

Decisions you can appeal

You can appeal to the First-tier Tribunal against most decisions taken by the Secretary of State for Work and Pensions (the DWP), a local authority officer or an officer of HMRC (known as decision makers – see p1150).[14] You can appeal against an original decision (even if you have first applied for a revision) or a decision made after a supersession.

You must be given a written notice of any decision against which you can appeal.[15] The notice must give you information about your right to appeal against the decision and your right to request a written statement of reasons for it if this has not been included. For benefits other than child benefit and guardian's allowance, if you have to apply for a revision before you can appeal, it must also include information about this (see p1305).

Sometimes, a decision maker refuses to make a decision on your claim. If this happens, it effectively prevents you having the right to appeal. However, a decision maker must make a decision on every valid claim.[16] You can then appeal (applying for a revision first if required) and the First-tier Tribunal decides whether the decision is correct. **Note:** if the decision maker does not accept that a claim made on the correct claim form is valid, you should be given a decision saying so. You can appeal to the First-tier Tribunal and ask it to decide if your claim is valid.[17]

A decision maker can sometimes postpone making a decision if there is a test case pending (see p1297).

1307

Part 10: Getting a benefit decision changed
Chapter 59: Appeals
1. Appealing to the First-tier Tribunal

Examples of decisions you can appeal
All benefits
Whether you are entitled to a benefit.

Whether an overpayment is recoverable (unless it is an overpayment that is always recoverable – see p1215).

Whether your claim has been validly made or can be backdated.

Whether benefit is payable under the overlapping benefit rules.[18]

Whether you should be given a sanction, whether you had good cause or a good reason for your actions or your failure to take action.

Whether you have limited capability for work or limited capability for work-related activity.

Whether you satisfy the habitual residence test.

Whether you satisfy the disability conditions for benefit.

Whether you can be paid hardship payments.

Jobseeker's allowance and universal credit only
Whether you are available for or actively seeking work.

Whether you have left a job voluntarily or have lost it through misconduct.

Whether you have given up or lost your place on a training scheme or employment programme.

For JSA, whether a jobseeker's agreement is reasonable or you had a good reason for refusing or failing to carry out a jobseeker's direction.

Decisions you cannot appeal

You cannot appeal to the First-tier Tribunal against some decisions.[19] You *can* ask for an 'any time' revision or a supersession of a decision against which you do not have a right of appeal, whatever your reason for thinking it is wrong.[20] However, if the decision maker refuses to revise or supersede the decision, your only legal remedy is to apply for judicial review (see p1351).

Examples of decisions you cannot appeal
Who should be the claimant when a couple is unable to decide.

Who should be entitled to child benefit when two people whose claims have equal priority cannot agree.

Whether a claim for one benefit can be treated as a claim for (or in addition to) another benefit.

Whether to demand recovery of an overpayment, and the amount of weekly deductions.

Whether to suspend payment of benefit.

Whether to appoint a person as an appointee (see p1137).

Whether to make a short-term advance, a budgeting advance or a payment on account.

Chapter 59

Appeals

How to appeal

You must appeal in writing. This is known as a 'notice of appeal'. Remember: other than for HB, in most cases, you must apply for a revision before you can appeal (see p1305).

You must appeal within a strict time limit (see p1310). See p1311 to find out what information your notice of appeal must contain.

Appeal forms

For **HB**, use the form approved by your local authority.[21]

For **benefits other than child benefit and guardian's allowance**, if you must send your appeal direct to the First-tier Tribunal, the appeal form (SSCS1) is in the leaflet *Notice of Appeal Against a Decision of the Department for Work and Pensions*, available from www.gov.uk. Otherwise, the appeal form is in leaflet GL24, *If You Think Our Decision is Wrong*, available at www.gov.uk.

Note: at the time of writing, details of the appeal form for child benefit and guardian's allowance were not available. See CPAG's online service and *Welfare Rights Bulletin* for updates.

You should use the appropriate form wherever possible. If you do not use the appropriate form, your appeal can be accepted provided it is in writing and includes all the information required (see p1311) but there is no guarantee of this.

Note: if you want the First-tier Tribunal to deal with your appeal quickly, make this clear when you appeal, explaining why. If you have to send or deliver your notice of appeal to the decision maker, you could write to the First-tier Tribunal, asking it to intervene.

Where to send your appeal

You must send or deliver your notice of appeal:
- direct to the First-tier Tribunal unless the notice of the decision says you must send it to the decision maker.[22] This is sometimes called 'direct lodgement'. The address to use is on the appeal form;
- if the notice of the decision says you must send your appeal to the decision maker, you must send it to the office of the local authority (or the DWP or HMRC) that sent you the decision.[23] Your appeal is then passed to the First-tier Tribunal.

Note: it is unlikely that many decisions about benefits other than HB will tell you to send your appeal to the decision maker. However, unless the benefit is child benefit, guardian's allowance, personal independence payment or, if you come under the universal credit (UC) system (see p19), contribution-based JSA, contributory ESA or UC, if the decision you dispute was sent to you before 28 October 2013, you usually have to send your appeal to the decision maker.

Part 10: Getting a benefit decision changed
Chapter 59: Appeals
1. Appealing to the First-tier Tribunal

The time limit for appealing

The time limit for appealing is very strict. The First-tier Tribunal can extend it (see p1353) but there is an absolute time limit within which you must appeal (see p1353).

If you must send or deliver your appeal direct to the First-tier Tribunal and you had to apply for a revision first (see p1305), your appeal, including all the information described on p1311, must arrive at the First-tier Tribunal within one month after you are sent the result of your application for a revision – a 'mandatory reconsideration notice' (see p1272).[24]

Month

'**Month**' means a complete calendar month running from the day after the day you have been sent or given a decision.[25] For example, a decision sent on 24 July has an appeal time limit that expires at the end of 24 August.

When calculating time, if something has to be done by a certain day, it must be done by 5pm that day. If a time limit ends on a day other than a working day, you have until the next working day to meet the time limit.[26]

If you did not have to apply for a revision before you could appeal, or the notice of the decision says you must send your appeal to the decision maker, the rules are as follows.

Your appeal, including all the information described on p1311, must arrive at the relevant office (see p1309 – this could be the First-tier Tribunal or the office that sent you the decision) by the latest of the following:[27]

- one month after the date the written decision was sent to you; *or*
- if you ask for a written statement of reasons for the decision (where one has not already been given to you – see p1156), 14 days after the latest of:
  - the end of that month – ie, if the written statement of reasons is provided within the one-month period, you get one month plus 14 days to appeal; *or*
  - the date the written statement of reasons is provided.

Remember, you must ask for a written statement of reasons within one month of being given notice of a decision.

Note: at the time this *Handbook* was written, the rules for child benefit and guardian's allowance were not yet known, but are likely to be the same as for other benefits. See CPAG's online service and *Welfare Rights Bulletin* for updates.

If you did not have to apply for a revision before you could appeal, but you did so anyway and the decision maker revises the decision, the one-month time limit runs from the date you are sent the new decision.[28] For benefits other than child benefit and guardian's allowance, if you applied for an 'any grounds' revision and the decision maker refused to do a revision, you must appeal within one month after the date you are sent notice of the refusal.[29]

If the decision maker refuses to do an 'any time' revision and says you cannot appeal, you should appeal against the original decision within the time limit (if this has not already passed) or if this is not possible, seek advice.

If you miss the time limit

If you miss the time limit, your appeal is still treated as made in time if neither the decision maker nor any other person with a right of appeal against the decision (or anyone who has been added as a party to the appeal – eg, the other parent if you are disputing who counts as responsible for your child) does not object.[30] However, if you had to send or deliver your appeal to the First-tier Tribunal, this only applies if the Tribunal does not direct otherwise.

If the decision maker (or other person) does object, the First-tier Tribunal can still extend your time limit.[31] There is no guarantee that it will do so, so keep within the time limit wherever possible. There is an **absolute time limit** for appealing after which you *cannot* appeal. See p1353 for further information.

Note:

- The First-tier Tribunal decides whether your appeal has been made within the time limit, *not* the DWP, the local authority or HMRC. If you think your appeal has been made within the time limit, explain why when you appeal.
- If you miss the time limit, the decision maker objects to your appeal being treated as made in time and the First-tier Tribunal does not extend it, you can appeal to the Upper Tribunal against the decision not to extend the time limit.[32]
- The First-tier Tribunal can also shorten time limits, but should only do this if this will enable it to deal with your appeal fairly and justly (see p1352).
- If you are appealing a decision about HB (and, in some cases, a DWP decision sent to you before 28 October 2013) and are required to provide information you did not include with your appeal, your time limit can be extended under separate rules (see p1312).

Making sure your appeal is valid

For your appeal to be valid, your notice of appeal must contain all the information required. Even if you do not use the correct appeal form your appeal can still be valid. The First-tier Tribunal decides whether your appeal is valid, *not* the DWP, the local authority or HMRC.

You must sign your notice of appeal.[33] If you have provided written notice that you have appointed a representative, s/he can sign it on your behalf.[34]

Your notice of appeal must be in English or Welsh. You must provide:[35]

- your name and address and that of your representative, if you have one;
- the address where documents can be sent or delivered – eg, to you or your representative;

Part 10: Getting a benefit decision changed
Chapter 59: Appeals
1. Appealing to the First-tier Tribunal

- if you have to send or deliver your appeal direct to the First-tier Tribunal (see p1309):
  - the name and address of any person who had a right of appeal against the decision (see p1306);
  - a copy of the 'mandatory reconsideration notice' (see p1272) or, if you did not have to apply for a revision before the appeal, a copy of the decision you want to appeal. **Note:** if you do not have a copy of the mandatory reconsideration notice (eg, because you were not sent one), the First-tier Tribunal can waive this requirement, but this is discretionary. Try to provide the Tribunal with as much evidence as you can that you have applied for a revision, and that the decision maker has considered your application;[36]
  - any statement of reasons for the decision that you have;
  - any documents in support of your appeal that you have not already supplied;
- if you have to send or deliver your appeal to the office that sent you the decision (see p1309), details about the decision with which you disagree, sufficient for it to be identified;
- a summary of your reasons for believing the decision is wrong (your grounds for appeal). Do not simply say you think the decision is wrong, but explain why.

Examples
'The decision says I have been overpaid income support because I failed to disclose that my wife had started working part time, but I wrote to you as soon as she started work and told you what her take-home pay would be.'
'HMRC says I should not get child benefit for my son because he left school in June. This decision is wrong because my son stayed on at school to do his A levels.'
'You say I cannot get DLA care component. This decision is wrong because you have not taken into account the amount of help I need due to incontinence problems.'

It is also helpful to include information and evidence that supports your appeal because a decision maker may look at the decision again before the appeal hearing and might revise it.

What happens if you do not provide sufficient information
If you are appealing about HB and you do not include the information required on your appeal form or in your appeal letter, the local authority can ask you to provide the information you left out.[37] If you used an appeal form, this is returned to you to complete. Be sure to provide the information within the time allowed, otherwise you might not have made your appeal within the time limit.
Your time limit for appealing (see p1310) is extended by:[38]
- 14 days from the date your appeal form is returned to you for completion, if the completed form is received back within 14 days;

- 14 days from the date you are asked for further information, if you provide this within 14 days of the request;
- the length of time you are given to complete the form or provide information, if this is longer than 14 days.

If you fail to complete the form properly or provide the information required in time, your appeal, along with any relevant documents and evidence, is forwarded to the First-tier Tribunal. A judge then considers whether your appeal is valid and can go ahead.[39] **Note:** if you complete and return the form or provide the information:

- after the expiry of the time limit, but before your appeal is forwarded to the First-tier Tribunal, the decision maker should accept that your appeal is valid and then consider whether to object to it being treated as made in time (see p1353);[40]
- before the judge makes a decision, any further details you provide must be taken into account.[41]

If your appeal is not accepted as valid, try to make a late appeal (see p1353).

Note: the rules above also apply for appeals against DWP decisions, sent to you before 28 October 2013 (including late appeals), about benefits other than PIP or, if you come under the UC system (see p19), contribution-based JSA, contributory ESA and UC.[42]

What happens after you appeal

The DWP, the local authority or HMRC prepares the appeal papers – known as the decision maker's response. See p1314 for what it must contain. It sends a copy to you (and your representative if you have one).[43] A copy is also forwarded to the First-tier Tribunal. This must be done as soon as reasonably practicable. **Note:** from 1 October 2014, the decision maker will have to do this within 28 days.

You might find that your appeal is not dealt with if there is a test case or a lead case pending that deals with the same issues (see p1347).

You are entitled to have your appeal heard within a reasonable period of time, so the decision maker should prepare the response and send it to the First-tier Tribunal without delay.[44] Following a complaint, an Ombudsman said the local authority should forward an appeal to the First-tier Tribunal within 28 days.[45] The decision maker can still consider revising the decision pending the appeal being heard.

Has your appeal been held up by the decision maker?

You cannot usually bypass the normal procedures. However, note the following.

1. If you had to send or deliver your appeal to the office that sent you the decision and the decision maker does not forward your appeal within a reasonable period, forward a copy of it to the First-tier Tribunal yourself.

Part 10: Getting a benefit decision changed
Chapter 59: Appeals
1. Appealing to the First-tier Tribunal

2. Although you cannot usually expect the First-tier Tribunal to deal with your appeal before the decision maker has had a chance to prepare her/his response, it is free to allow matters to be handled differently if circumstances require it.[46]
3. Ask the First-tier Tribunal to make a direction requiring the decision maker to provide documents, information and evidence (see p1342) by a specified date, or a direction setting a hearing date.[47]

Note: in some circumstances, the First-tier Tribunal can bar the decision maker from taking any further part in the appeal (see p1344), in which case your appeal could be decided without a response being made.

When your appeal can lapse

After you appeal, a decision maker may look at the decision you are appealing about again and might revise it – eg, on the basis of any, information or evidence you provided with your appeal form. This is the case even if you already applied for, and the decision maker considered, a revision before you could appeal. If the decision maker revises the decision, your appeal could lapse, even if you do not get everything you want, and you have to appeal again.[48]

Your appeal lapses if the revised decision is more advantageous to you than the original decision – eg, the decision:[49]

- awards you benefit at a higher rate or for a longer period;
- lifts a refusal or disqualification of benefit or a sanction (in whole or in part);
- reverses a decision to pay benefit to a third party (see p1178);
- means you gain financially from the revised decision;
- says an overpayment of benefit is not recoverable or that less should be recovered.

If the revised decision is not more advantageous to you, your appeal must go ahead, but against the revised decision.[50] You have one month from the date the decision is sent or given to you to make further representations.[51] At the end of that period (or earlier if you agree in writing), your appeal proceeds unless the decision is revised again and is now more advantageous to you.[52]

If your appeal lapses, you must make a fresh appeal. You do not have to apply for another revision before you can appeal in this situation. Your time limit for appealing (see p1310) runs from the date the revised decision is sent to you.[53] **Note:** at the time this *Handbook* was written, the time limit for child benefit and guardian's allowance was not yet known, but is likely to be the same. See CPAG's online service and *Welfare Rights Bulletin* for updates.

The decision maker's response

The DWP, the local authority or HMRC must prepare a bundle of papers relevant to your appeal (called the 'decision maker's response') and forward this to the

First-tier Tribunal as soon as reasonably practicable.[54] **Note:** from 1 October 2014, the decision maker must do this within 28 days. You and your representative (if any) are normally both sent a copy.[55] However, check with your representative as this might not always happen.[56]

The response must include the reasons why the decision maker opposes your appeal.[57] The decision maker must also provide:[58]

- a copy of any written record of, and statement of reasons for, the decision with which you disagree;
- copies of all relevant documents s/he has that may be relevant, unless the First-tier Tribunal directs otherwise. If your appeal involves a medical issue or one about your disability, a record of medical examinations you have had in connection with your claim is usually included; *and*
- if you had to send your appeal to the decision maker, a copy of your appeal form (or letter) along with all the documents you provided with it, and unless already provided to the First-tier Tribunal, the name and address of your representative (if any).

Read through the whole response carefully to find out the case being made against you. Be sure to take it with you to the hearing.

The enquiry form

When the HMCTS regional office (see Appendix 1) receives your appeal papers, it sends you a questionnaire (called an enquiry form) asking you whether you want an oral hearing and, if so, when you and your representative (if you have one) are available to attend, if you have not already provided this information – eg, on your appeal form. If you want an oral hearing, you must state this. **Note:** you should always consult your representative before completing and returning the appeal form and the enquiry form.

You should return the enquiry form within 14 days. If you do not return the enquiry form in time, the First-tier Tribunal can strike out your appeal (see p1343) or automatically deal with your appeal at a paper hearing (see p1319). However, you are entitled to receive a ruling on the merits of your appeal, so the Tribunal should only strike it out on this ground in exceptional cases.[59]

For further information about oral and paper hearings, see p1317. Bear in mind that your appeal must be dealt with at an oral hearing, unless both you and the DWP, the local authority or HMRC have consented or both of you have not objected to the appeal being dealt with without one.

Note: if you had to send or deliver your appeal direct to the First-tier Tribunal, the appeal form has questions about whether or not you want an oral hearing and when you and your representative are available to attend.

Part 10: Getting a benefit decision changed
Chapter 59: Appeals
1. Appealing to the First-tier Tribunal

Providing other information

Make sure that everything you want to say in support of your appeal has been put in writing and that there are no other documents which you would like the First-tier Tribunal to see. Note the following.

- It is always good to provide a written submission and additional evidence or information to support your appeal (known as a 'reply') – eg, independent medical evidence or supporting statements from witnesses.
- You (or your representative) must provide your reply within one month after the date you were sent the decision maker's response.[60] The First-tier Tribunal can give you longer (or shorter) than one month.[61] There is no guarantee that you will be given longer, so keep within the time limit wherever possible.

Note: the First-tier Tribunal might issue directions requiring you (or the DWP, the local authority or HMRC) to provide a submission or further information or documents within a specific period. You (or the decision maker) can also apply to the First-tier Tribunal and ask it to issue directions. If you are given a direction, it is important that you comply with it. If you do not, your appeal can be struck out (see p1343). See p1342 for further information about directions.

Withdrawing an appeal

If you change your mind about appealing, you can withdraw your appeal.[62]

- If you had to send or deliver your appeal to the office that made the decision (see p1309) and it has not yet been passed to the First-tier Tribunal, write to that office, saying that you do not wish your appeal to go ahead. Your authorised representative can write on your behalf.
- In any other case, you must give written notice to the First-tier Tribunal that you want to withdraw your appeal. The Tribunal may notify you that you can only do so if it agrees. You can also withdraw your appeal once the hearing has started, but only if the Tribunal agrees.

If you tell the First-tier Tribunal that you want to withdraw your appeal before the hearing (eg, you telephone the Tribunal office), but then you fail to confirm this in writing, the clerk to the First-tier Tribunal can waive the requirement to provide written notice.[63] You can ask the Tribunal to reconsider the clerk's decision – eg, if you did not send written notice because you changed your mind and no longer wanted to withdraw your appeal. You must apply in writing within 14 days after the date you are sent notice of the decision. The First-tier Tribunal can give you longer (or shorter) than this. There is no guarantee you will be given longer, so keep within the time limit wherever possible.

If you withdraw your appeal but then decide that you want it to go ahead, you can apply for it to be reinstated.[64] You must apply in writing. Your application must be received by the First-tier Tribunal within one month after the date it received notice that you wanted to withdraw your appeal or, if you withdrew your appeal at an oral hearing, within one month after the date of the hearing. The First-tier Tribunal can give you longer (or shorter) than one month. There is no guarantee that you will be given longer, so keep within the time limit wherever possible.

Oral or paper hearings

Your appeal must be dealt with at an **oral hearing**, unless:[65]
- both you and the DWP (or the local authority or HMRC) have consented or both of you have not objected to the appeal being dealt with at a paper hearing; *and*
- the First-tier Tribunal considers it can decide the matter without an oral hearing. It should explain this in its statement of reasons if you ask for one.

If either you or the DWP (or the local authority or HMRC) have stated that you want an oral hearing, there must be one. If you want an oral hearing, state this on the appeal form or the enquiry form (see p1315) as the case may be. Otherwise, the First-tier Tribunal presumes that you do not object to a paper hearing.

If there is not an oral hearing, the First-tier Tribunal makes its decision by looking at what you said on your appeal form, any evidence or other information you provided to support your appeal and the decision maker's response. This is known as a **paper hearing**.

Have you opted for a paper hearing?
1. If you opt for a paper hearing, your appeal could still be dealt with at an oral hearing if the DWP (or the local authority or HMRC) wants one or the First-tier Tribunal decides there should be an oral hearing because it can only deal with your appeal fairly and justly by doing so (eg, it needs to ask you questions about the facts of your case) or if during a paper hearing it is uncertain whether or not anyone asked for an oral hearing.[66]
2. If you get unexpected notice of an oral hearing, contact HMCTS to check the reasons for this. You should attend the hearing.
3. If you opt for a paper hearing but then decide you want an oral hearing, you may be able to change your mind. You must tell the First-tier Tribunal before it makes its decision.

Why choose an oral hearing?

You may not want to attend an oral hearing – eg, because you are worried about speaking for yourself or about the cost or difficulty in attending. You can seek advice before you decide what to do, but remember the following.
- You are more likely to win your appeal if you attend an oral hearing, particularly if it concerns a medical issue or your disability, or if the facts of your case are in dispute.

Part 10: Getting a benefit decision changed
Chapter 59: Appeals
1. Appealing to the First-tier Tribunal

- If you attend an oral hearing, you can explain your side of the story.
- You can ask someone to represent you at the hearing (see p1342) – your chances of winning are likely to be higher if you do.[67] You can also take a friend, relative or adviser with you for support.
- If you are disabled, the First-tier Tribunal may help to meet the costs of special transport so you can get to the hearing.
- The First-tier Tribunal aims to provide a qualified interpreter if you need one. If you do, tell it in advance of the hearing. If a qualified interpreter is not available, the Tribunal might allow a relative to act as your interpreter if s/he understands that s/he should simply translate accurately and tell your answers in your own words, without comment or explanation.[68]
- You, an interpreter (if needed) and any witnesses may be able to get expenses paid – eg, you can claim for travel (including the extra costs involved for disabled people), meals, loss of earnings and childcare costs.[69]

Note: if you or your representative cannot be physically present at an oral hearing (eg, because of a disability), one might be arranged at a venue where you can (called a 'domiciliary hearing' – see p1319), or you might be able to be present – eg, via a video link or telephone.[70]

The oral hearing

You must be given reasonable notice of the oral hearing – at least 14 days' notice, unless you agree to less notice than this or there are urgent or exceptional circumstances.[71] If you have not been given the correct notice (you can argue that this includes the decision maker's response as well as the time and date of the hearing[72]), you can object to the hearing going ahead. If the First-tier Tribunal decides to proceed with the hearing, you should attend and explain why your case will be prejudiced (eg, you did not have an adequate time to prepare it) and ask for an adjournment (see p1345).

The First-tier Tribunal can go ahead with an the oral hearing even if you are not there if it:[73]

- is satisfied that you were notified of the hearing, or that reasonable steps have been taken to notify you; *and*
- thinks that it is in the interests of justice.

For further information about decisions on appeals in the absence of the claimant, see pp5–7 of CPAG's *Welfare Rights Bulletin* 236, October 2013.

An appeal is heard in public unless the First-tier Tribunal thinks it should be in private.[74] The Tribunal can exclude people from hearings in some circumstances. If you want your hearing to be in private, ask for this to be considered. In practice, it is extremely rare for members of the public to attend.

The First-tier Tribunal can **postpone or adjourn a hearing** (see p1345).

The paper hearing

You are not sent notice of a paper hearing. The First-tier Tribunal makes its decision in your absence and you are then notified of its decision.

If you opt for a paper hearing, think about sending the First-tier Tribunal your arguments about your appeal in writing and any information and evidence you can get to support your appeal (called a 'reply'). If you intend to send a reply, state this clearly on the appeal form or enquiry form and state how long it may take to provide it. See p1355 for information about how to present your case.

You must provide your reply within one month after the date you were sent the decision maker's response.[75] If you need longer than this to provide a reply, ask HMCTS for an extension. If your paper hearing takes place before the month is up and you could (and would) have provided further evidence within that period, you can challenge the First-tier Tribunal's decision on the ground that it made an error of law.[76]

Domiciliary hearings

Most appeal venues have access for disabled people, and the First-tier Tribunal may meet the cost of special transport to get there or arrange the hearing at another venue. However, if you are unable to attend a hearing at the venue, it is possible to hold the hearing in your home – a 'domiciliary hearing', although the First-tier Tribunal may say this is not necessary if you can use special transport.[77] Include a letter from your doctor with your request, confirming that you are unable to travel at all – eg, even by private ambulance. You can argue that you can appeal against a decision to refuse you a domiciliary hearing.[78] Alternatively, if the refusal meant that the way your appeal was dealt with was unfair, you may be able to appeal against the First-tier Tribunal's decision on your appeal.[79] **Note:** you may be able to be present via a video link, telephone or other means of instantaneous two-way electronic communication.[80] Contact HMCTS to see if this can be arranged.

10

At the hearing

The following may be present at the hearing.
- A **judge** and up to two other **members**. They hear and decide your appeal. The judge makes a note of what is said by everyone at the hearing. To see which members decide your appeal, see p1320.
- An **expert** (the First-tier Tribunal may call her/him an 'assessor'), if your appeal involves issues that require expertise not available to the Tribunal.[81] If s/he provides a written report, it should be sent to every party involved in the appeal. The expert cannot take part in making the decision.
- The **clerk to the First-tier Tribunal**. S/he is there in an administrative capacity – eg, to pay expenses. The clerk cannot take part in making the decision and should not express any views on the case.

Part 10: Getting a benefit decision changed
Chapter 59: Appeals
1. Appealing to the First-tier Tribunal

- A **presenting officer**. S/he represents the decision maker. S/he explains the reasons for the decision, but is not there to defend it at all costs and may provide information which helps your case. Presenting officers often only attend if an appeal is considered complicated.

You can have a **representative** with you at the hearing.[82] If you have one, see p1342 for information about the notice you must send or give the First-tier Tribunal. You can also be accompanied by someone at the hearing – eg, a friend or relative. The First-tier Tribunal can give permission for her/him to act as your representative or assist you in presenting your case.[83]

The judge and members

Those who decide a particular kind of appeal are as follows.[84]

- **A judge, a doctor and a person with experience of disability** decide AA, DLA and PIP appeals. If your appeal only raises issues of law, so a doctor and a person with experience of disability are not needed, a judge can hear your appeal (or a judge and a member whose experience and qualifications are needed to make the decision).
- **A judge and a doctor** decide appeals about:
  - whether you have limited capability for work under the work capability assessment or have limited capability for work-related activity;
  - industrial injuries benefits (see Chapter 32) or severe disablement allowance (SDA).

  However, if your appeal only raises issues of law so a doctor is not needed, a judge can hear your appeal (or a judge and a member whose experience and qualifications are needed to make the decision).
- **A judge** decides all other appeals on her/his own.

The judge must be legally qualified. S/he always acts as the chair of the hearing.

Unless your appeal is about AA, DLA or PIP, an extra judge can be included in specified cases, an accountant may be included (if the examination of financial accounts is required) or there can be an additional doctor (if there are complex medical issues). However, there can never be more than two members, plus a judge.

If the group deciding your appeal is composed incorrectly, you can appeal to the Upper Tribunal and argue that this was an error of law.[85] **Note:**

- If your appeal is meant to be heard by two or more members but some of these are absent, the hearing can still go ahead, but only if you and the DWP (or the local authority or HMRC) agree.[86]
- If you have both a DLA and an ESA appeal, they should not be heard together or consecutively by the same members. They should be heard completely separately, by entirely different members.[87]

- You cannot argue that a doctor should not decide your appeal even if s/he regularly provides medical reports about benefit claimants to the DWP.[88] You *can* argue that the First-tier Tribunal should not rely on evidence from a DWP doctor with whom any of the members hearing your appeal sit at other times; this depends on how often and how recently this has happened.[89]

Procedure at an oral hearing

When the First-tier Tribunal is ready to hear your case, you (and your representative if you have one) are taken in with any presenting officer. There are no strict rules of procedure. The judge decides how the hearing is conducted.[90] The First-tier Tribunal's overriding objective is that your appeal is dealt with fairly and justly.[91] This includes ensuring that you are able to participate fully.

What happens at the oral hearing?

1. The judge should introduce everyone present.

2. The judge (and members) often start by asking you (and the presenting officer) questions. Be prepared for some searching questions.

3. The presenting officer, if any, may be asked to summarise the decision maker's case.

4. You should be given the opportunity to explain your case. It is the First-tier Tribunal's job to help you to say everything you want by putting you at your ease and asking the right questions. If you think there are mistakes in the papers, point them out. You can call witnesses and ask questions of the presenting officer's witnesses. If you forget to say something when it is your turn to speak, do not hesitate to add it at the end of the hearing. See p1355 for help with preparing for your appeal and presenting your case.

5. The First-tier Tribunal considers all the facts, evidence and law before it makes a decision. It should not bargain with you by 'offering' to allow part of your appeal if you agree to drop other parts – eg, by offering you one component of DLA if you agree not to argue for the other.[92]

Medical examination at the oral hearing

The First-tier Tribunal cannot carry out physical examinations unless your appeal relates to the assessment of your disablement for SDA or industrial injuries disablement benefit, or whether you have a prescribed disease or injury.[93] Studying X-ray evidence does not count as a physical examination, so you can ask the Tribunal to consider this.[94] The First-tier Tribunal should let you know during the hearing if it thinks a physical examination is not necessary so you can make representations.[95]

You are examined by the medical member(s) of the Tribunal.[96] You can have someone with you as a chaperone or if, for instance, you need help undressing. Make sure you tell the medical member(s) if you are in pain or discomfort. It is also a good idea to provide a full list of any medicines you are taking. After the

Part 10: Getting a benefit decision changed
Chapter 59: Appeals
1. Appealing to the First-tier Tribunal

examination, you should be invited to make further representations to the First-tier Tribunal if you wish.

Is your ability to walk tested?

There is no 'walking test' or physical test for the DLA or PIP mobility component, but the First-tier Tribunal may take its observation of you into account.[97] However, it should not attach undue weight to its observations[98] and you should be given the opportunity to comment on the observations. Remind the First-tier Tribunal that what it sees may only be relevant to your condition on that day and not in general.[99] It should check, for instance, whether you have just taken medication or have been resting for some time in the waiting area.

Appeals about disability, incapacity or limited capability for work

Tell the First-tier Tribunal how your disability or limited capability for work affects you at work or in your daily life at home. You should be completely straightforward, neither underplaying nor overplaying your symptoms. If you feel better on some days than others, explain how and how often, and say whether you are being seen on a good day or a bad day.

The First-tier Tribunal listens and asks you questions. It considers all of the medical and other relevant evidence, and tries to draw out the evidence about your disabilities, with the help of questioning from the doctor member(s). This may confirm the opinions expressed in medical reports with which you disagree, or it may support your view. See p1358 for information about medical evidence.

The First-tier Tribunal should not feel restricted to accepting the medical evidence about you given in written reports.[100] If there is conflict between what is said in a report and what you have said in writing (eg, on your claim form), it should not accept the evidence in the report without first listening to what you have to say about how your condition affects you.[101] Ensure that you explain any inconsistencies. The Tribunal should be particularly careful not to automatically accept the findings in medical reports produced with the assistance of a computer programme.[102]

The First-tier Tribunal can adjourn the hearing and refer you to a healthcare professional approved by the DWP (eg, a doctor or a nurse – see p1152) for a medical examination and report if your appeal concerns:[103]

- whether you are entitled to AA, DLA or PIP, the appropriate rate of benefit or the period for which you are entitled; *or*
- whether you are entitled to SDA; *or*
- whether you are incapable of work or have limited capability for work or for work-related activity; *or*
- the extent of your disablement for SDA or industrial injuries disablement benefit purposes; *or*

- whether you have a loss of faculty as a result of an industrial accident (see p673).

The medical examination may take place in your home or at a DWP medical examination centre.

A report may also be requested from your GP or other medical adviser.

The written decision to adjourn for a report should make clear why the First-tier Tribunal adjourned and what sort of medical evidence is being sought.

Note: athough you cannot be compelled to undergo a medical examination, the First-tier Tribunal might draw negative conclusions if you refuse.

What the First-tier Tribunal considers

The job of the First-tier Tribunal is to decide whether the decision you are appealing about was correct. It must look at the law and issues afresh, taking into account any new evidence or information you (and the DWP, the local authority or HMRC) provide. **Note:**

- The First-tier Tribunal considers all the evidence.[104] It decides what weight the evidence should be given, taking account of any possible deficiencies, when deciding whether the facts are proved.[105] It should decide your appeal in an investigative way, but the members should not make their own enquiries into the facts of your case before the hearing.[106]
- The First-tier Tribunal should consider an issue if it is in the appeal papers or in any representations you make, or if the evidence should lead it to believe it is relevant to your appeal.[107]
- You (or the DWP, the local authority or HMRC) can raise an issue at the hearing.[108] However, the First-tier Tribunal might then adjourn to give the other side a chance to address the point.
- You do not necessarily have to raise an issue with the Tribunal for it to be something it should consider, even if you have a representative. However, the issue must be one which in some way obviously demands attention.[109] If you have a representative, the First-tier Tribunal may decide not to investigate matters that s/he does not raise on your behalf.[110]
- The First-tier Tribunal does not have to consider issues that are 'not raised by' your appeal.[111] However, it can consider issues even if neither you nor the DWP, the local authority or HMRC raises them.[112] The First-tier Tribunal should exercise its discretion fairly.

If you are appealing about not being awarded one component of DLA or PIP when you are already in receipt of the other, or you ask for a higher rate of DLA, PIP or AA than you are already getting, the First-tier Tribunal does not have to consider issues which are not the subject of your appeal. However, it may decide to consider both components of DLA or PIP, or to consider whether you should get a lower rate of DLA, PIP or AA than you are already getting. You should be given

Part 10: Getting a benefit decision changed
Chapter 59: Appeals
1. Appealing to the First-tier Tribunal

notice of this, and a chance to prepare your case properly and make representations or to consider withdrawing your appeal.[113] Ask for the hearing to be adjourned if you need time or want someone to advise or represent you. If your appeal is being dealt with at a paper hearing, you should be given the opportunity to attend an oral hearing or to withdraw your appeal.[114] You should be given an explanation of why the Tribunal decided to use its discretion in this way in the statement of reasons for its decision.[115]

Note: if you are concerned about what might happen in your appeal, you can withdraw it at any time before the First-tier Tribunal makes its decision (see p1316). You need permission if you ask to withdraw your appeal at the hearing.

Faulty revisions and supersessions

If your appeal involves a revision or a supersession decision which is faulty, the First-tier Tribunal can remedy any defect and make any decision that the decision maker could have taken.[116] This includes where the decision maker:

- carried out a supersession but failed to state the grounds or to identify the correct grounds for doing so; *or*
- carried out a supersession when s/he should have conducted a revision (and, in some cases, vice versa).

In addition, the First-tier Tribunal can decide that an 'any time' revision should be done where no decision has been made on the matter by a decision maker (either to revise the decision or refuse to do so) – ie, if you are appealing because the decision maker refused to carry out a supersession.[117]

If errors in the decision making are extensive, try to argue that the First-tier Tribunal should adjourn the hearing, point out the errors to the decision maker and invite her/him to reconsider, rather than making any corrections itself.[118]

Changes of circumstances after you appeal

When the First-tier Tribunal hears your appeal, it considers whether the decision with which you disagree was correct for the period up to and including the date it was made. If your circumstances change after the decision, it cannot take this into account.[119]

Any evidence you get after the decision with which you disagree could still be relevant to your appeal. If the evidence relates to the period before the decision you are disputing was made, or to a past event that was relevant to the decision, it must be taken into account.[120] In some situations, events that happen after the date of the decision can throw light on the situation at or before that date, in which case evidence of such events may also be taken into account – eg, if the Tribunal needs to decide if an improvement in your health was likely to happen.

What you should do if your circumstances change

It is important, as a general rule, for you to consider making a fresh claim (or to consider seeking a supersession) every time your circumstances change, and appeal if you are unhappy with the subsequent decision. This is particularly so if your appeal is about:

- whether you have limited capability for work, have limited capability for work-related activity or qualify for AA, DLA or PIP or the rate of AA, DLA or PIP to which you are entitled and your condition has worsened;
- whether you satisfy the 'habitual residence test' (see Chapter 70); or
- how much income or capital you have, and this changes.

If you wait until the First-tier Tribunal makes its decision and this goes against you, you could lose out. You can only get arrears from the date your circumstances changed if a fresh claim (or the effect of a supersession) can be backdated. This is only possible in limited circumstances.

Example

Ravi has been getting DLA mobility component. A decision maker decides his condition has improved so he is no longer virtually unable to walk, and stops his DLA. He appeals. While waiting for his appeal hearing, his condition deteriorates, he makes a fresh claim and is awarded DLA mobility component. When the First-tier Tribunal hears his appeal against the original decision, it upholds the decision maker's decision. However, because Ravi made a fresh claim when his circumstances changed, he has not lost out.

If you make a fresh claim (or seek a supersession), you can ask the decision maker to wait until your appeal has been determined before making a decision. However, if the decision maker decides the fresh claim (or supersession) and you disagree with the decision:

- you can appeal against the new decision. Consider whether it is in your interests to ask for all of the appeals to be heard together by the First-tier Tribunal;[121] or
- whether or not you appeal against the new decision, you can ask the decision maker to revise it once your first appeal is determined (see p1278).

Example

Henry claims PC but the decision maker says he does not satisfy the habitual residence test and refuses his claim. He appeals against the decision and makes a fresh claim for PC on 7 April 2014. The fresh claim is refused. Henry wins his appeal. Because he did not appeal the new decision, the First-tier Tribunal can only award PC up to 7 April 2014. However, the decision maker does an 'any time' revision and awards PC from that date.

The decision

You may be told the First-tier Tribunal's decision at the hearing and you are given a **decision notice** confirming it. If it is not given at the hearing or you opted for a

Part 10: Getting a benefit decision changed
Chapter 59: Appeals
1. Appealing to the First-tier Tribunal

paper hearing, the decision notice is sent to you later. It may include a summary of the First-tier Tribunal's reasons for its decision. You *must* be informed of:[122]
- your right to request a statement of reasons for the First-tier Tribunal's decision (see below); *and*
- the conditions for appealing to the Upper Tribunal, including the time limit for doing so.

Note:
- If the First-tier Tribunal is unable to come to a unanimous decision, it makes a majority decision. The judge has the casting vote.[123]
- A decision can be corrected, superseded, reviewed or set aside (see p1327). You (or the DWP, the local authority or HMRC) can also appeal against it to the Upper Tribunal.

Record of proceedings

A record of the First-tier Tribunal proceedings is made by the judge that indicates the evidence taken and submissions made, as well as any procedural applications.[124] You can apply for a typed copy. If you are considering an appeal to the Upper Tribunal, it is a good idea to get a copy. If you foresee disputes about what happened at the hearing, keep your own notes.

The record is kept by the First-tier Tribunal for six months from the date of its decision or for six months from various other specific dates. You must apply in writing for a copy within the six-month period. The First-tier Tribunal can give you longer (or shorter) than this. There is no guarantee that you will be given longer, so keep within the time limit wherever possible. Bear in mind that if you apply after the six-month period, the record may have been destroyed.

The statement of reasons

The First-tier Tribunal may give the reasons for its decision at the oral hearing, or give or send you a written statement of reasons, prepared by the judge.[125] If you are not provided with a written statement of reasons, you have a right to apply for one.[126] **Note:** the judge may say that the decision notice is to stand as the written statement of reasons, so check the decision notice carefully.

You must generally have a statement of reasons if you lose your appeal and want to appeal to the Upper Tribunal. It may otherwise be difficult to show that the First-tier Tribunal made an error of law (see p1330).

Your request for a statement of reasons must be:[127]
- in writing; *and*
- received by the First-tier Tribunal within one month (see p1310) of your being sent or given its decision notice. The First-tier Tribunal can give you longer (or shorter) than this.[128] There is no guarantee that you will be given longer, so keep within the time limit wherever possible.

If you request a written statement of reasons, this must be sent to you within one month or as soon as it is reasonably practicable after that.[129]

Note:
- If you mistakenly ask the First-tier Tribunal for permission to appeal to the Upper Tribunal instead of asking for a statement of reasons, it should treat this as a request for a statement of reasons.[130]
- If the judge refuses wrongly to provide a statement of reasons, you may have grounds for appeal to the Upper Tribunal.
- If there is a long delay in getting a statement of reasons, you could apply for permission to appeal to the Upper Tribunal. The Upper Tribunal can require the First-tier Tribunal to provide reasons for its decision.[131]

The DWP (or the local authority or HMRC) can also ask for a statement of reasons. If this happens, it usually means it is considering appealing to the Upper Tribunal.

After the hearing

If you have won your appeal, the DWP (or the local authority or HMRC) should carry out the First-tier Tribunal's decision straight away. It can do this on the basis of the decision notice (see p1325). However, if either you or the DWP, the local authority or HMRC apply for permission to appeal to the Upper Tribunal, the First-tier Tribunal may be able to suspend the effect of its decision until the application is determined (either by the First-tier or Upper Tribunal), and then until any review of, or appeal against, the decision is determined.[132] This could be useful – eg, if you are seeking permission to appeal against a decision that an overpayment is recoverable from you.

If the DWP (or the local authority or HMRC) disagrees with the decision, it might consider appealing against it to the Upper Tribunal. In this case, you are not normally paid while it decides what to do. See p1175 for what the DWP (or the local authority or HMRC) must do before it can suspend your benefit. If the DWP (or the local authority or HMRC) decides to appeal, you are not normally paid until the Upper Tribunal decides the case.[133] However, you can ask the DWP, the local authority or HMRC to pay you if you are left in financial hardship.

If you disagree with the First-tier Tribunal's decision

If you disagree with the First-tier Tribunal's decision, you cannot simply ask it to look at the decision again – eg, if you have additional evidence. However:
- if the decision contains a clerical mistake or other accidental slip or omission, this can be **corrected** by the First-tier Tribunal. This only applies if it is a genuine error such as a typing or spelling mistake or a mathematical miscalculation, not an error of law on an important issue in your appeal – eg, a change of the date of onset of an industrial disease. **Note:** the Tribunal cannot

Part 10: Getting a benefit decision changed
Chapter 59: Appeals
1. Appealing to the First-tier Tribunal

use this rule to amend or add to its reasons for the decision, but can amend these if it reviews its decision (see p1334);[134]
- the decision can be **superseded** by the DWP (or the local authority or HMRC), if there are grounds (see p1281). However, if the First-tier Tribunal made a mistake about the law, you must appeal to the Upper Tribunal;
- you (or the DWP, the local authority or HMRC) can **appeal to the Upper Tribunal** against the decision (see p1329);
- if you (or the DWP, the local authority or HMRC) seek permission to appeal to the Upper Tribunal against a decision, the First-tier Tribunal can **review** it (see p1334);
- the decision can be **set aside**, which means the decision is cancelled and your appeal is heard again (see below).

If you are considering an appeal to the Upper Tribunal, remember to ask for the First-tier Tribunal's statement of reasons (if one has not yet been provided) within the one-month time limit (see p1326). You should do so even if you are first going to apply for the First-tier Tribunal's decision to be set aside.

Setting aside a decision on procedural grounds

A decision of the First-tier Tribunal can only be set aside on procedural grounds if the judge thinks it is 'in the interests of justice' to do so and:[135]
- you, your representative or the DWP (or the local authority or HMRC):
  - were not sent or did not receive appeal papers or other relevant documents, at an appropriate time – eg, in sufficient time before the hearing; *or*
  - were not present at the oral hearing. However, if you (or they) chose not to attend, it might not be 'in the interests of justice' to set the decision aside; *or*
- the First-tier Tribunal was not sent appeal papers or other relevant documents at an appropriate time – eg, in sufficient time before the hearing; *or*
- there was some other procedural irregularity.

You must apply in writing to the First-tier Tribunal. The application must be received no later than one month after the date you are sent the decision notice (see p1325).[136] The First-tier Tribunal can give you longer (or shorter) than this.[137] There is no guarantee that you will be given longer, so keep within the time limit wherever possible. **Note:** the rules do not say what the time limit is if you are given the decision notice at the hearing.
Note:
- Applications are normally decided without a hearing.[138] Make sure you give a full explanation of your reasons when you apply. If you could not attend the hearing (eg, because you were ill), provide evidence of this – eg, a note from your doctor. If your application is late, explain the reasons for this.

- If the First-tier Tribunal's decision is set aside, your appeal is heard again and a new decision is made. You should be given the opportunity to ask for an oral hearing, even if your appeal was originally decided at a paper hearing.[139]
- If a decision is wrongly set aside, any subsequent rehearing by the First-tier Tribunal is invalid.[140]

Note: in some circumstances, a decision can also be set aside when you (or the DWP, the local authority or HMRC) seek the permission of the First-tier Tribunal to appeal to the Upper Tribunal and you agree the First-tierTribunal made an 'error of law' (see p1330).

If the decision is not set aside

The First-tier Tribunal can treat your application for a decision to be set aside as an application for permission to appeal to the Upper Tribunal, or as an application for a correction of the decision.[141]

If the First-tier Tribunal refuses to set aside a decision, you can appeal to the Upper Tribunal against the refusal.[142] It might be better to try to appeal to the Upper Tribunal against the original decision. If your application for the First-tier Tribunal's decision to be set aside is refused, the time limit for appealing to the Upper Tribunal can run from the date you are sent notice of this.[143] However, this only applies where you applied for the decision to be set aside within the one-month time limit (or any longer period allowed by the First-tier Tribunal).

Setting aside a decision by agreement

The First-tier Tribunal's decision *must* be set aside if an application is made for permission to appeal to the Upper Tribunal, and you and the DWP (or the local authority or HMRC) agree that the First-tier Tribunal made an 'error of law' (see p1330).[144] Bear in mind that the First-tier Tribunal does not send copies of applications for permission to appeal to the other party. If you think that the DWP (or the local authority or HMRC) might agree that the First-tier Tribunal made an error of law, you should send a copy of your application to them. However, there is no guarantee that it will take any action on this.

---

2. Appealing to the Upper Tribunal

You have a right of appeal against any decision of the First-tier Tribunal (other than an excluded decision) to the Administrative Appeals Chamber of the Upper Tribunal (called the Upper Tribunal in this *Handbook*).[145] Your appeal is dealt with by a judge (or judges).

Excluded decisions[146]

'Excluded decisions' are certain decisions taken by the First-tier Tribunal when it considers a review (see p1334) – ie, decisions:

Part 10: Getting a benefit decision changed
Chapter 59: Appeals
2. Appealing to the Upper Tribunal

- to review, or not to review, an earlier decision;
- to take no action, or not to take any particular action, in the light of a review of an earlier decision;
- to set aside an earlier decision on review (the decision that is set aside is also excluded);
- to refer, or not to refer, a matter to the Upper Tribunal.

There are **procedural rules** that the Upper Tribunal must follow (see pp1341–48). The overriding objective of the rules is to enable the Upper Tribunal to deal with cases fairly and justly.[147] The Upper Tribunal can do a number of things, including to extend or shorten time limits and to adjourn or postpone hearings.

If a test case is pending that deals with issues raised in your appeal, you may find that your appeal is delayed (see p1347).

Some Upper Tribunal decisions can be made by approved legally qualified HM Courts and Tribunals Service (HMCTS) staff (called 'registrars').[148] You can ask an Upper Tribunal judge to reconsider a registrar's decision. You must apply in writing within 14 days after the date you are sent notice of the decision. The Upper Tribunal can give you longer (or shorter) than this. There is no guarantee you will be given longer, so keep within the time limit wherever possible.

Appeal rights

There is only one possible ground for appeal: that the First-tier Tribunal has made an 'error of law' (see below).[149] You must first apply for, and obtain, permission to appeal and there is a strict time limit for applying (see p1334). The DWP, the local authority and HM Revenue and Customs (HMRC) have the same right of appeal as you.

If you have evidence not known by the First-tier Tribunal, it might enable you to ask the DWP (or the local authority or HMRC) for a supersession of the First-tier Tribunal's decision (see p1281) and you can do so while your appeal is pending. Bear in mind that the amount of arrears you can get with a supersession is usually limited, so you need to continue with your appeal at the same time.

Note: you can also apply for a judicial review by the Upper Tribunal of a decision of the First-tier Tribunal against which you do not have a right of appeal. If you are in any doubt about whether you should appeal against a decision or apply for a judicial review, see p1340.

Error of law

The First-tier Tribunal made an error of law if:[150]

- it got the law wrong or misinterpreted it – eg, it misunderstood the particular benefit rule concerned. **Note:** if the First-tier Tribunal sets out the reasons for its decision in the decision notice (see p1325) and these indicate that it did not apply the law correctly, the decision notice is likely to be a more reliable

statement of the First-tier Tribunal's reasons than a later conflicting explanation in a statement of reasons;[151]
- there is no evidence to support its decision;
- it gave you a physical examination when it was not permitted to do so (see p1321) and based its decision on evidence obtained from that examination;[152]
- the facts it found are such that, had it acted reasonably and interpreted the law correctly, it could not have made the decision it did. This argument can be used where the facts are inconsistent with the decision – eg, the First-tier Tribunal finds that a man and a woman live in separate households, but decides they are living together as husband and wife;[153]
- it took things into account which it should not have, or refused or failed to take into account things which it should have taken into account. However, the First-tier Tribunal has not necessarily made an error of law if it fails to take account of evidence that was not before it at the hearing – ie, if you (or the DWP, the local authority or HMRC) only produce evidence when your appeal is before the Upper Tribunal;
- there is a breach of the rules of natural justice. This includes where:
  - the procedure followed by the First-tier Tribunal leads to unfairness. Whether or not this is so depends on the facts of the case, but examples include if:
    - the person presenting the DWP (or local authority or HMRC) case (the presenting officer) is allowed to be in the room with the Tribunal before you go in;[154] *or*
    - you are not allowed to call witnesses to support you; *or*
    - the First-tier Tribunal has unreasonably refused to postpone or adjourn a hearing (see p1345) even though you notified it that you could not attend and had a good reason; *or*
    - the First-tier Tribunal failed to act on a request for an interpretor and as a result the Tribunal was unable to understand your evidence correctly;[155] *or*
    - the standard of interpretation is not adequate and the First-tier Tribunal does not take appropriate action;[156] *or*
    - the First-tier Tribunal pressures you into giving up your right to a fair hearing – eg, it bargains with you by 'offering' you one component of disability living allowance (DLA) if you agree not to argue for the other;[157]
  - you did not get notice of the hearing through no fault of your own and the result is that you lost without having a chance to put your case properly, even if you could have applied for the First-tier Tribunal's decision to be set aside instead;[158]
  - you (or the DWP, the local authority or HMRC) asked for an oral hearing but one did not take place;[159]
  - you did not receive the decision maker's response or receive it in sufficient time before the hearing, or advance notice of documentary evidence that

Part 10: Getting a benefit decision changed
Chapter 59: Appeals
2. Appealing to the Upper Tribunal

you had not seen before, and were not given an opportunity to read it properly;[160]
– the First-tier Tribunal removed your entitlement to benefit at a paper hearing without warning you or giving you the chance to make representations;[161]
• it does not give proper findings of fact. The First-tier Tribunal must find sufficient facts to support its decision.[162] It can rely on the summary of the facts given in the decision maker's response (see p1314), but only if these are not in dispute and s/he has covered all relevant issues.[163] If you and the DWP (or the local authority or HMRC) disagree about the facts, the First-tier Tribunal must explain which version it prefers and why;
• it does not provide adequate reasons for its decision.[164] The First-tier Tribunal must not simply say what its decision was. It must give sufficient reasons so that you can see why, on the evidence, it reached the conclusion it did. It should refer to the main items of evidence on which it has relied. However, the First-tier Tribunal has not necessarily erred in law for failing to mention every item of evidence put forward. If a delay in writing the reasons indicates that they are unreliable as an accurate statement of the First-tier Tribunal's reasoning, you can argue the reasons are inadequate.[165] **Note:** the First-tier Tribunal does not have to give its reasons for refusing to adjourn an appeal hearing.[166] However, the refusal to adjourn may be so obviously unfair as to constitute an error of law.

Note: the First-tier Tribunal has *not* erred in law simply because a different judge (and members) or the Upper Tribunal might have come to a different conclusion.[167] An appeal to the Upper Tribunal is *not* another opportunity to argue about the facts of the case.[168]

How to appeal to the Upper Tribunal

You must first obtain permission to appeal to the Upper Tribunal.[169] This means you must show that the First-tier Tribunal has possibly made an error of law (see p1330) and you have the beginnings of a case. There is a strict time limit for applying for permission to appeal. If you wish to appeal you:
• must usually have the First-tier Tribunal's statement of reasons (see p1326). You may find it difficult to show that it made an error of law without one;
• first have to apply to the First-tier Tribunal for permission to appeal. If it refuses (or rejects) your application, you can then apply for permission directly to the Upper Tribunal.

Applying to the First-tier Tribunal

You must apply for permission to appeal, in the first instance, to the First-tier Tribunal.[170] You should first apply for a statement of reasons for its decision (see p1326).
Your application for permission to appeal must:[171]

- be in writing; *and*
- contain details of your grounds for appeal (ie, the error(s) of law you think the First-tier Tribunal made) and sufficient information about its decision for it to be identified. If you are making a late application, you must also give your reasons for this; *and*
- state the result you are seeking – eg, say what you think the First-tier Tribunal's decision should have been, or how it should have dealt with your appeal.

Bear in mind that the person considering your application might not be the judge who decided your appeal.[172] Applications for permission to appeal are normally decided without a hearing so make sure you give a full explanation of your grounds for appeal when you apply.[173]

If you do not have a statement of reasons for the First-tier Tribunal's decision (eg, because you did not apply for one, or one has not been provided):[174]

- the First-tier Tribunal must treat your application for permission to appeal as an application for a statement of reasons. Then, unless it decides to give you permission to appeal, you must seek permission to appeal again – eg, once the statement of reasons is provided. If a statement is refused because you did not apply in time, see p1334; *and*
- if your application for a statement of reasons is (or has been) refused because of a delay in making the application (ie, you missed the one-month time limit or any longer period allowed), the First-tier Tribunal can admit your application for permission to appeal, but only if it thinks it is in the interests of justice to do so. It then goes on to decide whether or not to give you permission.

You must be sent a record of the decision on your application for permission as soon as practicable.[175] If your application (or a ground for appeal) is refused, you must also be sent a statement of reasons for the refusal and notice of your right to make a fresh application to the Upper Tribunal for permission to appeal (see p1335), along with information about how to apply, and the time limit for doing so. You should study the First-tier Tribunal's reasons for refusing your application carefully; be prepared to re-think your arguments before applying to the Upper Tribunal.

Note:

- If you (or the DWP, the local authority or HMRC) apply for permission to appeal to the Upper Tribunal, the First-tier Tribunal can:
  – review its decision (see p1334); *or*
  – treat the application for permission to appeal as an application for the decision to be corrected or set aside.[176]
- If you and the DWP (or the local authority or HMRC) agree that the First-tier Tribunal made an error of law, its decision *must* be set aside (see p1329).

Part 10: Getting a benefit decision changed
Chapter 59: Appeals
2. Appealing to the Upper Tribunal

The time limit for applying

Your application for permission to appeal must be received by the First-tier Tribunal no later than one month (see p1310) after the latest of the following dates – ie, the date you were sent:[177]

*   the decision notice; *or*
*   a written statement of reasons (see p1326) for the First-tier Tribunal's decision. See p1333 for how your application is dealt with if you do not have a statement of reasons; *or*
*   notice that, following a review, the reasons for the First-tier Tribunal's decision were amended, or the decision was corrected; *or*
*   notice that an application for the First-tier Tribunal's decision to be set aside was unsuccessful.

The First-tier Tribunal can extend (or shorten) your time limit for applying for permission to appeal to the Upper Tribunal.[178] There is no guarantee that you will be given longer, so keep within the one-month time limit wherever possible. If your time limit is not extended, the First-tier Tribunal must reject your application.[179] If your application is rejected, you can still apply to the Upper Tribunal for permission, but see p1354 for the special rules that apply.

When the First-tier Tribunal can review its decision

When the First-tier Tribunal receives an application for permission to appeal to the Upper Tribunal, it must first consider whether to review its decision.[180] You do not have a right to apply for a review yourself, but if you do, your application can be treated as an application for permission to appeal.[181]

The First-tier Tribunal can only review a decision if it is satisfied that there was an error of law in the decision (see p1330).[182] In considering a review, it can give you an opportunity to make a submission.[183] If it *does* review the decision, it can:[184]

*   correct accidental errors in the decision or the record of the decision; *and*
*   amend the reasons given for the decision – eg, if it considered matters, but inadvertently did not include them in the statement of reasons. However, the First-tier Tribunal should not add reasons which it had not fully considered before it made its decision;[185] *and*
*   set aside the decision. If it does this, it must either make a new decision or refer your appeal to the Upper Tribunal for it to make a decision.

You must be notified in writing of the outcome of the review and your right of appeal (if any).[186] If the First-tier Tribunal has taken any action and you were not given an opportunity to comment before the review, you must also be notified that you can apply for the action to be cancelled and for the decision to be reviewed again.

If the First-tier Tribunal decides not to review its decision, or reviews it but takes no action (or no action on a part of the decision), it must consider whether to give you permission to appeal to the Upper Tribunal against the decision (or the part of the decision on which no action was taken).[187]

Applying to the Upper Tribunal

Before you can apply to the Upper Tribunal, you must first apply to the First-tier Tribunal for permission to appeal.[188] If the First-tier Tribunal refuses you permission to appeal or rejects your application (eg, because your application was late), you may make a fresh application to the Upper Tribunal. You must apply in writing.

Forms

Use Form UT1 (Social Entitlement), available from the regional office of HMCTS, the Upper Tribunal Office (see Appendix 1) or at http://hmctsformfinder.justice.gov.uk/HMCTS/FormFinder.do.

Your application must include:[189]
- your name and address and the name and address of your representative (if any). You must also give the address where documents can be sent or delivered;
- details of the decision you want to appeal;
- the grounds for your appeal – ie, the error(s) of law you think the First-tier Tribunal made;
- if your application is late, a request for your time limit for appealing to be extended and the reasons why you are applying late;
- whether you want your application to be dealt with at an oral hearing;
- copies of the First-tier Tribunal's decision, its statement of reasons (if you have one – see below) and the notice of its refusal or rejection of your application for permission. If your application to the First-tier Tribunal was rejected because it (or your application for a statement of reasons) was late, you must also include the reasons why.

The Upper Tribunal can waive any irregularities in your application for permission to appeal.[190] If your application to the First-tier Tribunal for permission to appeal was rejected, either because it was late or your application for a statement of reasons was late, the Upper Tribunal can only allow your application if it thinks it is in the interests of justice to do so.[191]

Do you have a statement of reasons?

If you do not have a statement of reasons for the First-tier Tribunal's decision, you are not prevented from applying to the Upper Tribunal for permission to appeal. However, you must still show that the First-tier Tribunal made an error of law (see p1330) without it – eg,

Part 10: Getting a benefit decision changed
Chapter 59: Appeals
2. Appealing to the Upper Tribunal

if what is said in the decision notice is sufficient to do so.[192] The failure of the First-tier Tribunal to provide a statement of reasons where it has a duty to do so is, in itself, an error of law.[193]

You can send your application by post, fax or document exchange, or deliver it in person. You can also send it by other methods (eg, email) if you have been given permission in advance by the Upper Tribunal.[194]

The Upper Tribunal Office obtains the file of your appeal papers from the regional office of HMCTS. The Upper Tribunal considers these as well as what you say in your application before reaching a decision. The DWP (or the local authority or HMRC) normally plays no part in the procedure at this stage. However, the Upper Tribunal sometimes asks the DWP (or the local authority or HMRC) to make a submission in cases of particular difficulty. If this happens, you are given an opportunity to reply.

You are sent a written notice of the Upper Tribunal's decision on your application for permission to appeal, including the reasons for the decision.[195] You cannot appeal against a refusal to grant you permission to appeal to the Upper Tribunal, but you might be able to apply for the decision to be set aside (see p1339) or to a court for judicial review (see p1351).[196]

The time limit for applying

Your application for permission to appeal must be received by the Upper Tribunal no later than one month (see p1310 for the definition) after the date the First-tier Tribunal's refusal (or rejection) was sent to you.[197] The Upper Tribunal can extend (or shorten) your time limit for applying for permission to appeal.[198] There is no guarantee that you will be given longer, so keep within the one-month time limit wherever possible. See p1354 for further information about late appeals to the Upper Tribunal.

If you get permission to appeal

If you have been given permission to appeal by the First-tier Tribunal, you must send a 'notice of appeal' to the Upper Tribunal so that it is received within one month after you are sent notice of the permission.[199] You are sent a form on which to do this. The Upper Tribunal can extend (or shorten) the time limit.[200] There is no guarantee that you will be given longer, so keep within the time limit wherever possible. **Note:** if you send your notice of appeal late and your time limit is not extended, your appeal is rejected and does not go ahead.

As well as the notice of appeal, you must send a copy of the notice telling you that you have been given permission to appeal, a copy of the First-tier Tribunal's decision and its statement of reasons (if you have one), along with your details and your reasons for appealing against the decision. If you are sending the notice of appeal late, you must also include a request for an extension of time and the reasons why your notice is late.

Where you have applied for permission to appeal directly to the Upper Tribunal on Form UT1, unless you are told otherwise, your application is treated as a notice of appeal. In this case, you do not have to send in another.[201]

Remember that the Upper Tribunal may be able to suspend the effect of the First-tier Tribunal's decision pending your appeal being decided (see p1341). This can be useful – eg, if you are appealing about whether an overpayment of benefit can be recovered.

Withdrawing an appeal

If you change your mind about appealing, you can withdraw your appeal.[202] However, once you have been given permission to appeal, you must have the consent of the Upper Tribunal. You must give notice to the Upper Tribunal that you want to withdraw your appeal:

* in writing; *or*
* at an oral hearing.

If you withdraw your appeal but then decide that you want it to go ahead, you can apply for it to be reinstated.[203] You must apply in writing. Your application must be received by the Upper Tribunal within one month after the date it received written notice that you wanted to withdraw your appeal, or if you withdraw your appeal at an oral hearing, within one month after the date of the hearing. The Upper Tribunal can give you longer (or shorter) than one month. There is no guarantee that you will be given longer, so keep within the time limit wherever possible.

The written procedure

The Upper Tribunal Office sends you a copy of the appeal file. You and the DWP (or the local authority or HMRC) are asked for responses and are told the timetable for providing them.[204]

The decision maker is usually asked to provide a response first. You are given the chance to reply. You are usually given one month in which to do so, although the Upper Tribunal may extend (or shorten) the time limit.[205] There is no guarantee that you will be given longer, so keep within the time limit wherever possible. If you have nothing to add and do not want to reply at any stage, tell the Upper Tribunal Office.

You may find the decision maker supports your appeal. In this case, the Upper Tribunal may give its decision without reasons if you consent to this.[206]

The Upper Tribunal decides whether or not there should be an oral hearing of the appeal.[207] It must take your views (and those of the DWP, the local authority or HMRC) into account. It normally only holds an oral hearing if the case involves

Part 10: Getting a benefit decision changed
Chapter 59: Appeals
2. Appealing to the Upper Tribunal

complicated issues of law that cannot easily be resolved by written argument. It can decide to hold an oral hearing even if you have not asked for one. If there is no oral hearing, the Upper Tribunal reaches a decision on the basis of written responses and other documents.

Note: because of the length of time you usually have to wait before your case is dealt with, you should make a fresh claim for benefit (or seek a supersession) if, for example, your circumstances change. However, see p1324 (the issues are similar to those for appeals to the First-tier Tribunal).

Oral hearings

Oral hearings are usually held in Cardiff, Edinburgh, Leeds, London or Manchester but can be held in other locations, subject to the needs of the case. A hearing closer to your home can exceptionally be held if you have difficulty travelling because of a disability. A judge decides whether or not to hold a local hearing based on, for instance, medical evidence and why a local hearing is needed.

You must be given at least 14 days' notice of the hearing, although you may get less notice than this if you agree, or your appeal is urgent or there are exceptional circumstances.[208] Your fares are paid in advance.

You and your representative may be able to participate in the oral hearing via a video link – eg, if your disability makes it difficult for you to travel, or to avoid travel costs and time.[209] Video conferencing facilities are available in a number of areas outside London. You may also be able to participate in the hearing by telephone or other means of instantaneous two-way electronic communication. Ask the Upper Tribunal Office if this can be arranged.

What happens at the hearing

Usually, one judge hears your appeal. However, if there is a 'question of law of special difficulty', an important point of principle or practice, or it is otherwise appropriate, two or three judges may hear your appeal,[210] but the procedure is the same. **Note:**

- The Upper Tribunal may ask you to provide a summary of the arguments you are going to make (a 'skeleton argument') in advance of the hearing. If it does, you must provide one.[211]
- The hearing is more formal than that before the First-tier Tribunal, but the judge lets you say everything you want to. Judges usually intervene a lot and ask questions so be prepared to argue your case without your script.
- A full set of Upper Tribunal (and commissioners') decisions (see p1359) and the statute law (see p1359) are available for your use.
- The DWP (or the local authority or HMRC) is usually represented by a lawyer, so you should also consider obtaining representation.

The decision

There are two stages to an Upper Tribunal decision.

- First, the Upper Tribunal decides if the First-tier Tribunal made an error of law. If it decides that it did, the First-tier Tribunal's decision is normally set aside and no longer has any effect. In a few cases, the Upper Tribunal may decide that the error of law made by the First-tier Tribunal had no practical effect on the outcome of your appeal and so the decision does not have to be set aside.
- Second, the Upper Tribunal decides how to deal with the case.[212]
  - If the Upper Tribunal agrees that the First-tier Tribunal's decision was wrong, the case is often sent back to the First-tier Tribunal to hear your appeal again and make a new decision. The Upper Tribunal can give directions on how to reconsider the issues.
  - If the Upper Tribunal thinks the First-tier Tribunal's statement of reasons for its decision contains all the material facts, or it has been able to make any necessary extra findings of fact, the Upper Tribunal makes the final decision.

The Upper Tribunal's decision is usually given in writing, but may be given orally at the hearing.[213] Detailed reasons for the decision are given. You must be sent a decision notice as soon as is reasonably practicable, as well as notice of your right of appeal, how to appeal and the time limit for doing so.

If you disagree with the Upper Tribunal's decision

If you disagree with the Upper Tribunal's decision, you cannot simply ask it to look at the decision again – eg, if you have additional points to make. However:

- the Upper Tribunal may **correct** any clerical mistake or other accidental slip or omission in a decision or record of a decision;[214]
- the Upper Tribunal may **set aside** its decision on procedural grounds.[215] A decision can be set aside if the Upper Tribunal thinks it is in the interests of justice *and*:
  - you, your representative or the DWP (or the local authority or HMRC) were not sent papers or other relevant documents, or did not receive them at an appropriate time, or the Upper Tribunal was not sent them at an appropriate time; *or*
  - you, your representative or the DWP (or the local authority or HMRC) were not present at the hearing; *or*
  - there has been some other procedural irregularity.

You must apply in writing for a decision to be set aside. Your application must be received by the Upper Tribunal no later than one month after you were sent notice of the decision. The Upper Tribunal can extend (or shorten) this time limit. There is no guarantee that you will be given longer, so keep within the time limit wherever possible;[216]

Part 10: Getting a benefit decision changed
Chapter 59: Appeals
2. Appealing to the Upper Tribunal

- the decision can be **superseded** by the DWP (or the local authority or HMRC) if there are grounds – eg, if there was a mistake about, or ignorance of, the facts (see p1281). However, if the Upper Tribunal made a mistake about the law, you must appeal to a court;
- you or the DWP (or the local authority or HMRC) can **appeal** to the Court of Appeal (in Scotland, the Court of Session) – see p1348;
- if you (or the DWP, the local authority or HMRC) seek permission to appeal to the Court of Appeal (or in Scotland, the Court of Session), the Upper Tribunal can **review** its decision (see p1350).

Note: the Upper Tribunal can treat an application for a decision to be corrected, set aside or reviewed, or for permission to appeal against a decision as an application for any other of these.[217]

Judicial review in the Upper Tribunal

Occasionally, you can challenge decisions of the First-tier Tribunal by applying for a judicial review by the Upper Tribunal. You cannot usually apply for a judicial review if you have a right of appeal to the Upper Tribunal against the decision. You may need the services of a solicitor or legal advice centre to apply for a judicial review. Before making *any* application, seek advice about what you might have to pay (see p1363).

In **England and Wales**, you can apply for a judicial review of a First-tier Tribunal decision if it is a decision against which you have no right of appeal to the Upper Tribunal *and*:[218]

- it is a decision made under any of the First-tier Tribunal procedural rules; *or*
- it is a decision to review (or not to review) a decision following an application for permission to appeal to the Upper Tribunal (see p1334) or a decision as to what action to take in the light of the review.

You must first apply for permission in writing and must include specified information.[219] You can use Form JR1 which is available from the Upper Tribunal office or at http://hmctsformfinder.justice.gov.uk/HMCTS/FormFinder.do. You must apply promptly. In any event, your application must be received by the Upper Tribunal by the latest of the following:[220]

- three months after the date of the decision, action or omission you are seeking to challenge; *or*
- one month after the date you were sent written reasons for the First-tier Tribunal's decision; *or*
- one month after the date you were sent notice that an application to set aside the decision (see p1328) was unsuccessful, provided the application was made within the time limit (or longer period allowed).

In **Scotland**, you can challenge a decision of the First-tier Tribunal by a judicial review if it is a procedural decision or ruling, including procedural omissions or oversights.[221] You must first apply to the Court of Session. If specified conditions are satisfied, your case is then transferred to the Upper Tribunal.[222] You must apply promptly.

Note: if you are in any doubt about whether you have a right of appeal against a decision you want to challenge, you can apply both for permission to appeal and for a judicial review. The Upper Tribunal decides which is the proper route.

3. Procedural rules

There are procedural rules that the First-tier Tribunal and the Upper Tribunal must follow. The overriding objective is to enable the First-tier Tribunal and the Upper Tribunal to deal with cases fairly and justly.[223] This includes avoiding delay (provided the issues can be considered properly), avoiding unnecessary formality, seeking flexibility in the proceedings and ensuring that all the parties can participate fully. It also involves dealing with appeals in ways that are proportionate to the importance of the case, the complexity of the issues, the potential costs and the resources of the parties. All parties must help the First-tier Tribunal and the Upper Tribunal further the objective and co-operate with it. This involves ensuring, as far as possible, that your case is ready by the time of the hearing.[224]

Both the First-tier Tribunal and the Upper Tribunal can do a number of things to further the overriding objective.[225] This includes directions (see p1342), striking out an appeal (see p1343) or barring people from taking part (see p1344) and adjourning or postponing a hearing (see p1345). This also includes:

- extending or shortening any time limits (see p1352);
- summonsing witnesses to attend a hearing, answer questions and produce documents. If someone fails to comply, the First-tier Tribunal can refer the matter to the Upper Tribunal. The Upper Tribunal can punish the person for contempt of court.[226] **Note:** you cannot be required to give evidence or produce any document that you could not be compelled to give by a court;[227]
- suspending the effect of its decision while considering an application for permission to appeal, or any appeal against or review of that decision. The Upper Tribunal can also suspend the effect of a decision of the First-tier Tribunal while an application for permission to appeal against the decision is being considered, and pending the appeal being determined.[228]

The Upper Tribunal can require the First-tier Tribunal to provide reasons for its decision, or other information or documents relating to the appeal.[229] **Note:** if you have a representative, you must notify the First-tier Tribunal and Upper Tribunal.

Directions

The First-tier Tribunal and the Upper Tribunal might issue directions requiring you (or the DWP, the local authority or HMRC) to provide a submission, further information or documents.[230] The Tribunal must send you and the decision maker (and anyone affected by the direction) notice of any direction it issues, unless it thinks there is a good reason not to do so.[231] You can challenge a direction (eg, if you think insufficient time has been given to comply with it) by applying for another direction to amend, suspend or set aside the first one.[232]

You or the decision maker can also apply to the First-tier Tribunal or the Upper Tribunal to ask it to issue directions. This can be useful, for example, if you are having trouble getting documents or information from the decision maker. You can apply in writing, or orally at the hearing.[233] In either case, you must give reasons for your application.

If you are given a direction, it is important that you comply with it. If you (or the DWP, the local authority or HMRC) fail to comply with a requirement or a direction, the First-tier Tribunal and the Upper Tribunal can take any action it thinks is 'just' – eg, it can:[234]

- waive the requirement;
- require you (or the DWP, the local authority or HMRC) to remedy the failure;
- strike out the appeal (see p1343) (or bar the DWP, the local authority or HMRC from taking further part – see p1344). *You* can be barred from taking further part in an appeal to the Upper Tribunal if the DWP (or the local authority or HMRC) appealed;
- conclude that the information or evidence was adverse to you.

If you miss the deadline in a direction, try to provide what has been requested as soon as possible. The Tribunal may still consider the information or evidence – eg, if you provide it at the hearing.[235] However, remember that the Tribunal can decide *not* to consider evidence if it is late or if it would otherwise be unfair to do so.[236]

Representatives

You can have a representative to help you with your appeal and to be with you at the hearing.[237] S/he can explain the procedures, present your case to the First-tier Tribunal or the Upper Tribunal and ensure the Tribunal is aware of all the relevant issues and the law. You must send or give the Tribunal written notice of your representative's name and address or s/he must do this on your behalf. For the First-tier Tribunal only, this does not apply if you provide this notice to the DWP (or the local authority or HMRC) before your appeal is forwarded to it. If your representative is providing the notice, s/he should also provide an authorisation signed by you. **Note:** even if your representative acted for you in your appeal to the First-tier Tribunal, you must still authorise her/him to act for you in your appeal to the Upper Tribunal.

Even if you have not previously notified the First-tier Tribunal or Upper Tribunal that you have a representative, someone can attend the hearing with you (eg, a friend or relative) and act as your representative, or assist you at the hearing, if the Tribunal agrees.

Once you have given notice that you have a representative, s/he is presumed to be acting for you unless you give notice in writing that this is no longer the case.[238] Your representative must be sent any documents required to be sent to you; these then do not have to be sent to you.[239] However, do not presume this always happens. If you receive documents, check that your representative has also received them.

When your appeal can be struck out

Your appeal to the First-tier Tribunal or the Upper Tribunal can be struck out, in whole or in part. This cancels your appeal, or part of your appeal, and it does not go ahead. This only applies if you fail to comply with a direction (see below for when you can get your appeal reinstated) or in a limited number of other circumstances.

If you fail to comply with a direction

If you fail to comply with a direction given to you by the First-tier Tribunal or the Upper Tribunal (see p1342) – eg, you fail to provide information or documents required by the Tribunal:[240]

- your appeal is **struck out automatically** if you were notified in the direction that a failure to comply *would* lead to your appeal being struck out;
- there is **discretion to strike out** your appeal if you were notified in the direction that a failure to comply with it *could* lead to your appeal being struck out. Before deciding to do so, the Tribunal should consider carefully why the direction was given and whether it can still make a fair and just decision – eg, without the information you were supposed to provide.[241]

In both cases, you can apply for your appeal to be reinstated.

Getting your appeal reinstated

If your appeal is struck out because you failed to comply with a direction given to you by the First-tier Tribunal or the Upper Tribunal, you may be able to get it reinstated.[242] You must apply in writing. Your application must be received by the Tribunal within one month of your being sent notice that your appeal was struck out. The Tribunal can give you longer (or shorter) than one month. There is no guarantee that you will be given longer, so keep within the time limit wherever possible. You should explain why you think your appeal should not have been struck out – eg, why you think you did comply with the direction, or why you were unable to do so or to comply in time.

Other circumstances

Your appeal *must* be struck out if **the First-tier Tribunal or the Upper Tribunal does not have 'jurisdiction'** to deal with it – eg, you do not have a right to appeal against the decision or you have appealed to the wrong Tribunal.[243] If the Tribunal no longer has jurisdiction because of a change of circumstances, this rule only applies if your appeal has not been transferred to another court or Tribunal.

There is *discretion* to strike out your appeal if:[244]

- you **failed to co-operate with the First-tier Tribunal or the Upper Tribunal** to such an extent that it cannot deal with your appeal fairly and justly; *or*
- for appeals to the First-tier Tribunal only, if it considers your appeal has **no reasonable prospect of success**. The Tribunal should only do so if the result of the appeal is clear and incontestable. It should generally not do so if the facts of the case are in dispute.[245]

In all cases:

- you must be given an opportunity to comment. You should always take this opportunity and explain why you think your appeal should not be struck out – eg, why you had a good reason for failing to co-operate with the Tribunal or why you think you have a chance of winning your appeal;
- you cannot apply for your appeal to be reinstated, but may be able to challenge the decision to strike it out.

Challenging a decision

If the First-tier Tribunal strikes out your appeal or refuses to reinstate your appeal after it has been struck out, you may be able to make a fresh appeal against the decision maker's decision.[246] See p1310 for the time limit for appealing and p1352 for late appeals. Otherwise, you can appeal to the Upper Tribunal against the First-tier Tribunal's decision to strike out your appeal or to refuse to reinstate it.[247]

Being barred from taking part in an appeal

The decision maker and any person (other than you) who is taking part in the appeal because s/he has a right of appeal against the decision you are challenging (see p1306) or s/he has been added as a party to the appeal by the Tribunal (eg, the other parent if you are disputing who counts as responsible for your child) can be barred from taking further part in the appeal in the same circumstances in which your appeal can be struck out.[248] In practice, this is likely to apply mainly if the decision maker (or other person with a right of appeal):

- fails to comply with a direction; *or*
- fails to co-operate with the First-tier Tribunal or the Upper Tribunal to such an extent that it cannot deal with your appeal fairly and justly.

The decision maker (or other person) can apply for the bar to be lifted in the same circumstances in which you can apply for an appeal to be reinstated (see p1343). If the decision maker (or other person) is barred from taking further part in your appeal, and the bar has not been lifted, the First-tier Tribunal or the Upper Tribunal does not have to consider any response or other submission made by her/him.[249] In addition, the Tribunal can decide any or all of the issues against her/him without further consideration. However, the decision maker (or person) who has been barred from taking part in an appeal still has a right of appeal against the Tribunal's decision and a right to apply for a statement of reasons for the decision.[250]

Note: if the DWP (or the local authority or HMRC) appeals to the Upper Tribunal, *you* could be barred from taking further part in the appeal under the rules above.

Postponements and adjournments

The First-tier Tribunal and the Upper Tribunal can postpone or adjourn a hearing.[251] In the First-tier Tribunal, the decision can be made by the judge. However, if the issue arises at a hearing and the Tribunal consists of more than one member, the judge should consult the other member(s).[252] The decision must be recorded properly. You may be able to appeal against the decision.

Remember that if you do not attend a hearing, the Tribunal can hear the appeal without you (see p1318).[253] Your appeal to the First-tier Tribunal is less likely to succeed if you do not attend. **Note:** oral hearings at the Upper Tribunal are more concerned with legal arguments than evidence of facts, so if you have a representative, an oral hearing is likely to go ahead if s/he can attend, even if you are unable to do so.

Your case might be postponed or adjourned if there is a test case or lead case pending which deals with the same issues as your appeal (see p1347).

Getting a hearing postponed

If the hearing date is inconvenient or you want more time to prepare your case, you can ask for the hearing to be postponed to another date. You should apply in writing to the relevant tribunal before the hearing date, saying why you want your appeal to be postponed. Make it clear that you do not want the hearing to go ahead in your absence. You should apply as soon as you decide that you want a postponement. The Tribunal can postpone your oral hearing even if this is not requested. Bear the following in mind.

• Do *not* presume that a postponement will be granted. Telephone before the hearing is due to take place to check if it has been agreed. Be ready to attend the hearing if it goes ahead. If you have a representative, s/he should warn you that your application might not be successful.[254]

- If you do not attend the hearing, the judge conducting the hearing should consider whether it should be adjourned, even if you have been refused a postponement.[255]

Getting a hearing adjourned

If a hearing (either oral or paper) is underway, it can be adjourned – eg, if you or the DWP (or the local authority or HMRC) asks for an adjournment, or if the First-tier Tribunal or the Upper Tribunal itself thinks this is the best course (eg, if more evidence is required or you need time to consider statute law or caselaw). The First-tier Tribunal should consider the benefit of an adjournment (eg whether further evidence would be helpful), why you (or the DWP, the local authority or HMRC) are not ready to go ahead and what the impact of an adjournment would be on the other party and the tribunal system.[256] It should adjourn a hearing:

- if you are not there and there is doubt about whether you received notice of the oral hearing;[257] *or*
- if you have advised it that you cannot attend, have a good reason for not attending and have asked for another hearing date;[258] *or*
- if you are unable to attend the hearing (eg, you are in prison or hospital) but your evidence could play an important part in it reaching a decision;[259] *or*
- if you want to be represented at the oral hearing, but your representative is not available on the date it has been listed and has made a reasonable request for a postponement. Your representative should explain why s/he cannot attend and why no one else can represent you in her/his place;[260] *or*
- if you need to get a representative – eg, because it is difficult for you to represent yourself or the decision with which you disagree concerns a large overpayment;[261] *or*
- to enable you to get additional evidence which you could not until then have reasonably been expected to realise was needed.[262]

You should consider asking for an adjournment if the First-tier Tribunal says it is going to consider whether you should get a lower rate of benefit than you are getting currently, to allow you to prepare your case and make representations.

If a hearing is not postponed or adjourned

If the hearing is not postponed or adjourned and the First-tier Tribunal makes a decision with which you disagree, you can try to appeal to the Upper Tribunal or, in limited circumstances, apply for the decision to be set aside (see p1328). If the Upper Tribunal makes a decision with which you disagree, you can try to appeal to the Court of Appeal (in Scotland, the Court of Session) or, in limited circumstances, to apply for the decision to be set aside (see p1339).

• •

Test cases and lead cases

Sometimes appeals to the First-tier Tribunal or the Upper Tribunal are made by more than one person about the same issues of fact or law. When this happens, there are procedural rules that can mean appeals dealing with the same issues may be delayed until a decision has been made in a test case or a lead case.

Test cases

If a case is pending against a decision of the Upper Tribunal or a court that deals with issues raised in your case (a 'test case'), the DWP (or the local authority or HMRC) can suspend payment of your benefit or even postpone making a decision about your claim (see p1297). This means you will not be able to appeal until a decision is made about the test case.

However, for benefits other than housing benefit, if a test case is pending and you have already appealed to the First-tier Tribunal or Upper Tribunal (your appeal is then known as a 'look-alike' case), the decision maker can serve notice requiring the First-tier Tribunal or the Upper Tribunal in *your* appeal:[263]
- not to make a decision and to refer your case back to her/him; *or*
- to deal with your appeal by either:
  - postponing making a decision until the test case is decided; *or*
  - deciding your appeal as if the test case had been decided in the way most unfavourable to you, but only if this is in your interests. If this happens, and the test case eventually goes in your favour, the decision maker has to make a new decision superseding the decision of the First-tier Tribunal or Upper Tribunal in the light of the decision in the test case.[264]

If the decision on your appeal has been postponed, once a decision has been made in the test case, the decision is made on your appeal.

Lead cases

If appeals are made to the First-tier Tribunal by more than one person about the same issues of fact or law (eg, a number of appeals about service charges from a tenants in the same block of flats), the First-tier Tribunal can specify one or more of the appeals as a 'lead case' and postpone making a decision on all the other related appeals.[265] When it makes its decision in the lead cases(s), the decision applies to (ie, is binding on) all the other related appeals. You must be sent a copy of the decision.

If your appeal is not the lead case, you can apply to the First-tier Tribunal for a direction that the decision does not apply to, and is not binding on, your appeal. You must apply in writing within one month after the date you are sent a copy of the decision. The First-tier Tribunal can give you longer (or shorter) than this. There is no guarantee that you will be given longer, so keep within the time limit wherever possible.

Part 10: Getting a benefit decision changed
Chapter 59: Appeals
4. Appealing to the courts

Consent orders

If all the parties (eg, you and the DWP, the local authority or HMRC) agree what the solution to your dispute should be, you can ask the judge in the First-tier Tribunal or the Upper Tribunal to make a 'consent order' and to make any other appropriate provision you have agreed.[266] This procedure is unlikely to be relevant in most cases and is only likely to be of use if you are effectively giving up your appeal, but the DWP (or the local authority or HMRC) promises you something in return for this. The Tribunal only deals with your appeal in this way if it considers it appropriate. It may simply make a decision on your appeal in the usual way. In any case, the decision maker can often revise the decision with which you disagree. **Note:** if you are appealing to the First-tier Tribunal, your appeal could lapse if s/he revises the decision (see p1314).

If a consent order is made, there does not have to be a hearing and no reasons for the order need to be given. Seek independent advice *before* agreeing to a consent order.

---

4. **Appealing to the courts**

You might consider taking your case to a court if you want to:
- appeal against a decision of the Upper Tribunal (see below); *or*
- apply for a judicial review (see p1351).

Appeals from the Upper Tribunal

You may appeal against a decision of the Upper Tribunal (other than an excluded decision) to the Court of Appeal (in Scotland, the Court of Session). You can only do this if the Upper Tribunal made an error of law (see p1330) and you must first obtain permission to appeal.[267] The DWP, the local authority and HM Revenue and Customs (HMRC) have the same rights of appeal as you.

Excluded decisions[268]
'**Excluded decisions**' are decisions taken by the Upper Tribunal refusing to grant permission to appeal against a decision of the First-tier Tribunal and certain decisions taken when it considers a review (see p1350) – ie, decisions:
– to review, or not to review, an earlier decision;
– to take no action, or not to take any particular action, in the light of a review of an earlier decision;
– to set aside an earlier decision on review (the decision that is set aside is also excluded).

Permission to appeal to the Court of Appeal or the Court of Session cannot be given unless the Upper Tribunal or the Court considers that:[269]

- the appeal would raise some important point of principle or practice; *or*
- there is some other compelling reason for the Court to hear the appeal.

The procedure in the Court is strict, formal and far less flexible than the procedure before the First-tier Tribunal or Upper Tribunal.

The DWP (or the local authority or HMRC) is represented by a solicitor and a barrister. You should consider obtaining legal advice from a solicitor before appealing. See p1352 for information about meeting the cost of going to court. **Note:** before making any application, seek advice about whether you could be liable for the other side's costs.

How to appeal

You apply for permission to appeal, in the first instance, to the Upper Tribunal. Your application must:[270]
- be in writing; *and*
- contain sufficient information about the Upper Tribunal's decision for it to be identified; *and*
- state the error(s) of law you think the Upper Tribunal made. These must be identified clearly;[271] *and*
- if your application is late, include a request for an extension of time and the reasons why the application was not made in time; *and*
- state the result you are seeking – eg, what you think the Upper Tribunal's decision should have been.

Your application must be received by the Upper Tribunal within three months after the date you were sent:[272]
- written notice of the decision; *or*
- notice that the reasons for the decision have been amended, or the decision has been corrected, following a review; *or*
- notice that an application for a set-aside has been refused. This only applies if the application for a set-aside was made within the time limit (or any longer period allowed).

The Upper Tribunal can extend (or shorten) your time limit for applying for permission to appeal to the Court.[273] There is no guarantee that you will be given longer, so keep within the time limit wherever possible. If your time limit is not extended, the Upper Tribunal must refuse your application.[274]

You must be sent a record of the decision on your application for permission as soon as practicable.[275] If your application (or a ground for appeal) is refused, you must also be sent a statement of reasons for the refusal and notice of your right to apply to the Court for permission, along with information about how to apply and the time limit for doing so.

Part 10: Getting a benefit decision changed
Chapter 59: Appeals
4. Appealing to the courts

When the Upper Tribunal can review its decision

When the Upper Tribunal receives an application for permission to appeal to the Court of Appeal (or Court of Session), it can review its decision if:[276]

- when it made the decision, it overlooked a legal provision, or a Court or Upper Tribunal decision it should have followed, which could have had a 'material effect' on the decision; *or*
- since the Upper Tribunal decision, a Court has made a decision which the Upper Tribunal must follow. This only applies if the Court's decision could have had a 'material effect' on the Upper Tribunal's decision had it been made at the time.

If the Upper Tribunal *does* review the decision it can:[277]

- correct accidental errors in the decision or the record of the decision; *and*
- amend the reasons given for the decision; *and*
- set aside the decision. If it does this, it must make a new decision.

You must be notified in writing of the outcome of the review and your right of appeal (if any).[278] If the Upper Tribunal has taken any action and you were not given an opportunity to comment before the review, you must also be notified that you can apply for the outcome to be set aside and for the decision to be reviewed again.

If the Upper Tribunal does not review its decision, or reviews it but takes no action (or no action on a part of the decision), it must consider whether to give you permission to appeal to the Court against the decision (or the part of the decision on which no action was taken).[279]

If the Upper Tribunal refuses permission to appeal

If the Upper Tribunal refuses you permission to appeal, you can make a fresh application to the Court of Appeal (in England and Wales) or the Court of Session (in Scotland).[280] The Upper Tribunal's statement of reasons for the refusal tells you the relevant court and the time limit for applying.[281] The time limit is very short so you should lodge your application with the court as soon as possible.

Generally, in **England and Wales**, the Court of Appeal first considers your application for permission to appeal without an oral hearing. If permission is refused, you can ask for the decision to be reconsidered at a hearing by writing to the Court Office, but you must do this within seven days.[282] However, if the Court of Appeal considers that your application is totally without merit, it can make an order stating you cannot do this.[283]

If the Court of Appeal refuses you permission to appeal after an oral hearing, you cannot appeal further, or apply for a judicial review.

In **Scotland**, the procedures for appealing to the Court of Session are similar to those for England and Wales but there are a number of differences. The Court of Session hears applications for permission to appeal in open court rather than making the decision simply by reading the papers. The DWP (or the local authority or HMRC) may agree that the application for permission and the appeal itself are heard at the same time.

If you get permission to appeal

If you are given permission to appeal by the Upper Tribunal or the Court, you must serve a notice of appeal on the relevant parties. There are strict time limits for doing this. Seek advice immediately if you are in this position. The DWP solicitor will accept the notice of appeal on behalf of the DWP. The solicitor to HMRC will accept on behalf of HMRC (see Appendix 1 for the addresses). Ask your local authority who will accept the notice of appeal on its behalf.

Applying for judicial review

Occasionally it is possible to challenge decisions with which you disagree by a judicial review in the High Court (the Court of Session in Scotland). Judicial review is a means of challenging the decisions of any form of Tribunal, government department or local authority. For example, you can apply for a judicial review of a decision:

- made by a decision maker, if it is a decision against which you do not have a right of appeal (see p1308); *or*
- made by the DWP refusing you payment of a budgeting loan; *or*
- made by a local authority about discretionary housing payments.

You cannot usually go to the Court for a judicial review if you have another independent means of appeal, such as to the First-tier Tribunal or the Upper Tribunal. You need the services of a solicitor or legal advice centre to apply for judicial review. **Note:**

- In England and Wales, you must apply to the High Court promptly. In any event, you must apply within three months of the decision you want to challenge.[284]
- In Scotland, you apply to the Court of Session. There is no time limit but you should make your application as soon as possible.[285]

You can apply for judicial review of some decisions of the Upper Tribunal, but only if the case would raise some important point of principle or practice, or there is some other compelling reason for the Court to hear it. **Note:** if the application is for judicial review of a decision to refuse permission to appeal against a First-tier Tribunal decision, you must apply no more than 16 days after you were notified of the Upper Tribunal's decision.[286] Your application is decided on the papers. If it is refused, you cannot ask for it to be reconsidered at an oral hearing.

In some cases, you may be able to apply to the Upper Tribunal for a judicial review instead of the Court (see p1340). In Scotland, you must first apply to the Court of Session and it transfers your case to the Upper Tribunal if relevant.

Meeting the cost of going to court

Free legal help from a solicitor is currently available for appeals on a point of law in the Supreme Court, the Court of Appeal, the High Court and the Court of Session, and you should consider obtaining legal advice and representation for these. You usually have to pay court fees unless you are eligible for free legal help or you are exempt from paying court fees – eg, because of your financial circumstances. If you want to be represented by a lawyer, and do not have free legal help, you also have to pay her/his fees and, if you lose your case, your opponent's costs (before making any application to a court, seek advice about whether you could be liable for your opponent's costs).

5. Time limits

Any of the time limits given to you by the First-tier Tribunal or the Upper Tribunal can be extended or shortened.[287] The rules do not specify when this should (or must) be done. However, the overriding objective of *all* the tribunal rules is to enable the First-tier Tribunal and the Upper Tribunal to deal with appeals fairly and justly (see p1341).[288]

Shortening time limits

The First-tier Tribunal and the Upper Tribunal may shorten your and the DWP's, the local authority's or HM Revenue and Customs' (HMRC's) time limits if it thinks that, for your appeal to be dealt with fairly and justly, delay should be avoided, provided the issues can be considered properly.[289] You might want to ask for the DWP's (or the local authority's or HMRC's) time limits (eg, to apply for permission to appeal) to be shortened if your situation is urgent or your circumstances are exceptional.

Extending time limits

If you know you have missed (or are going to miss) a time limit, you should ask for it to be extended by the First-tier Tribunal or the Upper Tribunal. Other than if you are appealing to the First-tier Tribunal, there is no limit on how far a time limit can be extended, even if it ran out a long time ago. The First-tier Tribunal and the Upper Tribunal do not have to extend any particular time limit so there is no guarantee that you will be given more time. You should, therefore, keep within the time limits wherever possible.

Always ask in writing for a time limit to be extended and apply in advance if you can. Give the reasons why you are (or are going to be) late in meeting the time limit, as well as any special circumstances which mean your time limit should be extended so that your appeal can be dealt with fairly and justly (see p1354 for some ideas).

Late appeals to the First-tier Tribunal

If you miss the time limit for appealing to the First-tier Tribunal (see p1310), but are within the absolute time limit for appealing (see below), the First-tier Tribunal can extend the time limit.[290] There is no guarantee that you will be given longer.

The absolute time limit for appealing

Your appeal to the First-tier Tribunal cannot be allowed outside an absolute time limit. This is 12 months from the date your time limit for appealing expired.[291] At the time this *Handbook* was written this did not apply to appeals about child benefit or guardian's allowance that must be sent or delivered direct to the First-tier Tribunal. See CPAG's online service and *Welfare Rights Bulletin* for updates.

If you had to send or deliver your appeal to the office that sent you the decision and the decision maker thinks your appeal has been made outside the 12-month limit, s/he must refer your appeal to the First-tier Tribunal immediately.[292]

The First-tier Tribunal decides whether your appeal has been made within the time limit, not the DWP, the local authority or HMRC.

If the First-tier Tribunal decides that you cannot appeal because your appeal was made outside the absolute time limit for appealing but you think your appeal was made in time, you can appeal to the Upper Tribunal against the decision.[293]

In addition to the information you must provide on your appeal form, you must include the reasons why your appeal is late (see p1309).[294] Also, give details of any special circumstances that mean it would be fair and just for the First-tier Tribunal to extend the time limit. See p1354 for some ideas about what may be relevant.

Note: your appeal must be treated as having been made within the time limit if neither the decision maker nor any person with a right of appeal against the decision (or anyone who has been added as a party to the appeal – eg, the other parent if you are disputing who counts as responsible for your child) objects.[295] However, if you had to send or deliver your appeal to the First-tier Tribunal, this only applies if the Tribunal does not direct otherwise.

When the decision maker might not object to a late appeal

Additional rules apply for appeals about housing benefit (HB). Under these rules, the decision maker does not object to your appeal being treated as having been made in time if s/he is satisfied that it is in the interests of justice to do so.[296] For these purposes, it is not in the interests of justice unless it was not practicable for you to appeal in time because:[297]

- you, your partner or a dependant died or had a serious illness;
- you are not resident in the UK;
- normal postal services were disrupted; *or*
- there are other special circumstances that are 'wholly exceptional'.

The longer you have delayed appealing, the more compelling the special circumstances must be.[298] When deciding whether it is in the interests of justice, account cannot be taken of the fact that:[299]

- a court or the Upper Tribunal has interpreted the law in a different way than was previously understood and applied;
- you (or anyone acting for you) misunderstood or were unaware of the relevant law, including the time limits for appealing.

If the decision maker *does* object to your appeal being treated as made within the time limit, s/he must refer it to the First-tier Tribunal immediately. The Tribunal then decides if your time limit can be extended.

Note: these rules also apply for appeals against decisions sent to you before 28 October 2013, other than decisions about child benefit, guardian's allowance, personal independence payment and, if you come under the universal credit (UC) system, contribution-based jobseeker's allowance, contributory employment and support allowance and UC.[300]

Late appeals to the Upper Tribunal

The one-month time limit for applying to the First-tier Tribunal for permission to appeal to the Upper Tribunal (see p1334) can be extended. There is no absolute time limit for applying.

If your application is refused or rejected, you can apply directly to the Upper Tribunal for permission to appeal. If you apply outside the one-month limit for doing so (see p1336), the time limit can be extended. There is no absolute time limit for applying.

Note: if your application to the First-tier Tribunal for permission to appeal was rejected because it was late or your application for a statement of reasons was late, the Upper Tribunal can only allow your application if it thinks it is in the interests of justice to do so.[301]

The decision whether or not to allow a late appeal to the Upper Tribunal must be made bearing in mind the merits of the appeal and the consequences for you (and the DWP, the local authority or HMRC). If you are refused permission, you do not have a right of appeal against the decision, but you might be able to apply for a judicial review.

Reasons why a time limit should be extended

The overriding objective of the procedural rules is to enable the First-tier Tribunal and the Upper Tribunal to deal with appeals fairly and justly (see p1341). Your reasons and circumstances need to show it would be fair and just to extend a time limit. What may or may not be such a reason or circumstance cannot be defined in advance, but the following are all relevant.

- **The reasons for the delay.** Explain these as clearly and as fully as possible. Do not worry if some or all of the delay is your fault. Any explanation is better than none at all. Even if you knew the time limit, but simply ignored it, it may be possible to say something favourable. Say if things have been difficult at home or you were confused by the rules or just assumed that the DWP (or the local authority or HMRC) were the experts and had got it right until, for example, you were advised otherwise or read an article in a newspaper. Reasons for the delay could include the fact that:

- you did not receive the decision;
- you made a reasonable mistake in calculating the time limit;
- you posted your appeal in time but it went astray in the post;
- you were ill;
- a mistake was made by your advisers. It should not make any difference that you might be able to sue them for negligence;
- you were given wrong advice or otherwise misled by the DWP (or the local authority or HMRC) – eg, you were discouraged from appealing by a decision maker who advised you incorrectly that an appeal would be doomed to fail. If you lose money because you are refused a late appeal, consider claiming compensation (see p1382).

- **The length of the delay.** The usual approach is that time limits have to be kept to, and there has to be good reason for not doing so. Short delays are likely to be easier to justify than long delays, but a good reason is still needed.
- **The merits of your appeal.** The more likely your appeal is to succeed, the greater the injustice in refusing to extend the time limit. A strong case is particularly useful if there has been a very long delay and a time limit is usually extended where there has been a 'clear error', which would have long-term continuing effects unless corrected.[302]
- **The amount of money at stake.** Even if there has been no clear error, a time limit may be extended if there is a lot of money at stake.[303]
- **A decision in a test case.** A decision in a test case, establishing that an earlier decision was incorrect, can amount to a reason to extend a time limit, in some circumstances.[304] Such appeals often involve large sums of money and (given the test case) a clear error in the decision which is being appealed against.

6. Presenting your case

Appeals to the First-tier Tribunal are taken on all sorts of issues – disputes about facts or the law or both – so the advice given here can only be general. You usually need to think about both the facts and the law because they are connected.

Sorting out the facts

You are likely to know more than anyone else about the facts of your case. Your key task is to pass your knowledge on to the First-tier Tribunal. It rehears your case completely, so fresh facts and arguments can be put by either side.

Part 10: Getting a benefit decision changed
Chapter 59: Appeals
6. Presenting your case

Remember to:

- check through the appeal papers carefully to work out what evidence the decision maker used in support of the decision. This helps you decide what evidence you need to win your case;
- study the decision maker's evidence and think about your arguments – eg, to show how the decision maker may have got the wrong impression;
- gather evidence and information to back up your arguments. Send it to the First-tier Tribunal as soon as possible before your oral hearing. Otherwise, it might decide to adjourn your appeal (see p1345) or even decide not to take the evidence or information into account. The First-tier Tribunal sends a copy to the DWP, the local authority or HM Revenue and Customs (HMRC), which might then decide to support your appeal;
- ask any witnesses who support your case to attend the hearing. The First-tier Tribunal has the power to refuse to hear witnesses who are not relevant, but it should always be fair to you and generally allow witnesses to speak, even if it looks like they may have nothing useful to say.[305] Bear in mind that the First-tier Tribunal can summons witnesses.[306]

Evidence

Evidence includes:

- oral evidence – what you (and any witnesses or others) actually say at the hearing; *and*
- written evidence – any documents you (or the DWP, the local authority or HMRC) provide, including medical evidence.

The First-tier Tribunal can issue directions (see p1342) on how you (or the DWP, the local authority or HMRC) should provide evidence and submissions or on whether witnesses should give evidence – eg, orally at a hearing, or by making a written submission or a witness statement within a set period of time.[307] It can accept evidence from you (or the DWP, the local authority or HMRC) even if it was not available to a previous decision maker.[308]

The DWP (or the local authority or HMRC) might use video evidence – eg, if you are appealing about entitlement to employment and support allowance or disability living allowance. You cannot prevent the DWP (or the local authority or HMRC) doing so.[309] However, insist you are given proof that the surveillance was properly authorised and time to view and consider the evidence in advance of the hearing and, if relevant, that the person who made the video is called as a witness.

Oral evidence

You and the presenting officer are likely to be questioned at the hearing. Witnesses can also give oral evidence at the hearing. You or the DWP (or the local authority or HMRC) can call witnesses, although the First-tier Tribunal can limit the number.[310] The First-tier Tribunal cannot dismiss oral evidence without a proper explanation of why it has done so.[311]

You are usually expected to give your own oral evidence at the hearing, if you can. Your representative is generally not allowed to give oral evidence for you. However, s/he can assist the First-tier Tribunal in gathering evidence from you (eg, by asking you questions)[312] and can give her/his *own* evidence based on her/his observations.[313]

You, your representative and the presenting officer can report what other people have said – called hearsay evidence. The First-tier Tribunal must carefully weigh up its value, given that the person who originally made the statement is not present at the hearing.[314]

If s/he is at the hearing, the presenting officer puts the DWP's (or the local authority's or HMRC's) case but is not necessarily the person who actually made the decision on your claim. Unless giving her/his own evidence (eg, because s/he was directly involved in the decision on your claim), any factual statements s/he makes are hearsay evidence.[315]

Written evidence

Written evidence includes letters, medical and other reports, wage slips, bank statements, birth certificates and anything else that helps prove the facts. If, for example, the DWP (or the local authority or HMRC) says you failed to disclose an increase in your earnings and you have been overpaid, you could explain to the First-tier Tribunal how and when you did so. It is even better to produce a copy of the letter you sent informing it of the change. It is not unknown for the DWP (or the local authority or HMRC) to fail to include copies of relevant documents in the decision maker's response. Check the response carefully and submit copies of any missing documents to the Tribunal as soon as you can. If you do not have copies, insist that the decision maker provides these. The Tribunal can issue a direction requiring the decision maker to do so (see p1342).

Most evidence relied on by the DWP (or the local authority or HMRC) is written and you can point out that you have not had the opportunity of questioning the witnesses. You are not entitled to insist on the presence of any particular witness,[316] although you could ask the First-tier Tribunal to issue a direction for her/him to attend a hearing. You should argue that the First-tier Tribunal should not place any weight on the written evidence of, for instance, an interviewing officer if you are disputing the interview, or an investigating officer if you are disputing what s/he heard or saw. **Note:** you and the DWP (or the local authority or HMRC) cannot rely on the evidence of an anonymous witness without the consent of the First-tier Tribunal, and consent should only be given in exceptional circumstances.[317]

Part 10: Getting a benefit decision changed
Chapter 59: Appeals
6. Presenting your case

Medical evidence

You can ask your doctor to provide medical evidence, or ask an advice agency to write to your doctor. Your doctor may charge for such evidence, but an advice agency or solicitor might be able to get a report free. Your medical evidence should deal with the points in dispute and also with the dates relevant to the decision with which you disagree. If your doctor does not know about the effect of your disability on your everyday life, tell her/him about it and ask her/him to confirm that this is consistent with the degree of your disability. Your evidence, or that of a friend or relative, may also be of use.

If you obtain a medical report, send it to the First-tier Tribunal in advance of the hearing, with a copy of the letter to your doctor as this helps to show that s/he is expressing her/his own opinion about your case. You could also ask your doctor to supply a copy of her/his notes about you over the last few years.

Note:

- The First-tier Tribunal can refer you for an examination and obtain a report if it thinks this is necessary. If the lack of a report is causing you difficulties at the hearing, you could remind the Tribunal of its power to obtain one.
- If your opinion about the effect of your ill health or disabilities is contradicted by evidence from a doctor, you should:
  - point out how long the doctor has known you and what s/he knows about your day-to-day living activities or walking ability. If a doctor does not know you or how you are affected by your condition (eg, if s/he only gave you a very short examination), this should be taken into account;
  - seek further medical evidence to support your view in advance of the hearing if you foresee any conflict of evidence.
- You can argue that the First-tier Tribunal should not rely on evidence from a DWP doctor with whom any of the members hearing your appeal sit at other times. This depends on how often and on how recently this has happened.[318]

Checking the law

If you know what the law says, you know what facts you have to prove. The primary sources of social security law are statute law and caselaw decided by the Upper Tribunal and courts. It is easy to find both, once you know what you are looking for. The footnotes in this *Handbook* point you in the right direction. There are also a number of books that explain the law and refer you to relevant legislation and cases (see Appendix 3).

Look carefully at the decision maker's response (see p1314), as this refers to the statute law and caselaw which s/he thinks is relevant. The DWP (or the local authority or HMRC) does not always get the law right and you should emphasise a point that it has overlooked or got wrong.

Statute law

Statute law consists of Acts of Parliament and regulations (and rules for procedure in the First-tier Tribunal and Upper Tribunal). The Acts set out the main framework and empower the making of regulations and rules covering the details. These regulations and rules are known as statutory instruments.

The best way to look up the relevant statute law is to read one of the annotated volumes of legislation listed in Appendix 3. Remember that, in rare cases, the books do not contain all the regulations and rules that are relevant. Many Acts, regulations and rules are also available at www.legislation.gov.uk. The legislation is often amended, so you must confirm that those in the annotated volumes of legislation (or obtained individually or online) are up to date.

If you are trying to discover the current law or chase up a reference, unless your appeal is an old one and the law has changed since the relevant time, you can refer to *The Law Relating to Social Security* – known as the 'Blue Volumes'. These are currently available at www.dwp.gov.uk/law-volumes. However, it is understood that social security legislation is to be moved to www.legislation.gov.uk in the near future, so it is important to ensure that the 'Blue Volumes' you are using are up to date.

Benefit law is complicated and the staff who administer benefits are issued with guidance manuals and circulars. The DWP (or the local authority or HMRC) and the First-tier Tribunal and Upper Tribunal are only bound by what the law says, not by the guidance. Nevertheless, it is sometimes useful to check the guidance. See Appendix 3 for a list of what is available.

If the statute law is ambiguous

If the statute law is ambiguous, the First-tier Tribunal, the Upper Tribunal and the courts can look at statements made to Parliament by ministers when the law was first made.[319] You can check the House of Commons' and House of Lords' official reports (known as *Hansard*) to see what was said in Parliament when the law was first introduced, and the transcripts of debates in the Delegated Legislation Committee at www.parliament.uk/business/publications/hansard. Another source of information is the Social Security Advisory Committee (http://ssac.independent.gov.uk).

Caselaw

The decision maker's response often refers to decisions of the Upper Tribunal and the courts (known as 'caselaw'). You should also use caselaw to support your appeal if possible. To help you decide which cases to use, see p1361.

Note: before 3 November 2008, decisions now made by the Upper Tribunal were made by social security commissioners.

Identifying Upper Tribunal and commissioners' decisions

All Upper Tribunal decisions have file numbers – eg, CDLA/2195/2008.

- The last numbers indicate the year in which the appeal was lodged.

Part 10: Getting a benefit decision changed
Chapter 59: Appeals
6. Presenting your case

• The second letters indicate the benefit involved in the decision. An extra 'S' after the 'C' denotes a Scottish case, as in CSIB/721/2004.

Upper Tribunal decisions that are published on the Upper Tribunal website are given a 'citation number' – eg, *SW v SSWP (IB)* [2010] UKUT 73 (AAC).

• First, the parties to the appeal are identified. The benefit claimant is identified by initials. The first name (or initials) is the party who appealed and the second, the other party.
• Next is the year the decision was given (in square brackets).
• The final number is the appeal number.
• Since 2010, letters to indicate the type of benefit involved in the decision are included.

Significant decisions are highlighted on the Upper Tribunal website. The most important Upper Tribunal decisions are chosen to be reported.

Reported decisions are given a new number. All reported decisions:

• from 1951 to 2010 begin with an 'R' – eg, CU/255/1984 became R(U) 3/86. The second letter(s) denote(s) the type of benefit. The last numbers indicate the year in which the decision was published.
• from 2010, begin with the citation number (see above). This is followed by the year the decision is reported (in square brackets), then the letters AACR (meaning Administrative Appeals Chamber Reports) and the reported decision number – eg, *Torbay BC v RF (HB)* [2010] UKUT 7 (AAC); [2010] AACR 26.

Identifying court decisions

Court decisions are identified by the names of the parties involved in the appeal. The first name is usually the party who has appealed and the second name is the other party. In judicial review cases, the case citation begins with 'R'.

Examples of court decisions

Hockenjos v Secretary of State for Social Security [2004] EWCA Civ 1749, 21 December 2004 is a decision of the England and Wales Court of Appeal Civil Division.

R v South Tyneside MBC ex parte Tooley [1997] QBD and *R (Reynolds) v Secretary of State for Work and Pensions* [2002] EWHC Admin 426 are decisions following applications for judicial review.

Precedent

When the Upper Tribunal or a court decides an appeal, the decision sets a precedent, which a decision maker or the First-tier Tribunal deciding a similar case must follow.[320] Unreported decisions must be followed in the same way as reported ones.[321] **Note:** commissioners' decisions also set a precedent.

If there is an irreconcilable conflict between two or more decisions, the **First-tier Tribunal** has to choose which decision to follow.[322]

- It normally follows a reported decision of the Upper Tribunal (or a commissioner) in preference to an unreported one.
- It must follow an Upper Tribunal decision made by a three-judge panel (or the decision of a Tribunal of commissioners) in preference to a decision of a single judge (or commissioner).
- Decisions of the Supreme Court, House of Lords, the Court of Appeal, the Court of Session or the Court of Justice of the European Union take precedence over all decisions of the Upper Tribunal (and commissioners).[323]

The **Upper Tribunal** has more freedom than the First-tier Tribunal.
- It does not have to follow an Upper Tribunal decision made by a single judge (or the decision of a single commissioner) if satisfied that the earlier decision was wrong.[324]
- It follows an Upper Tribunal decision made by a three-judge panel (and the decision of a tribunal of commissioners) unless there are compelling reasons not to. If the judge thinks it may be wrong, s/he can ask the President of the Administrative Appeals Chamber for the case to be transferred to another three-judge panel in the Upper Tribunal to reconsider the point.
- If an appeal is heard by a three-judge panel in the Upper Tribunal, the panel does not have to follow the decision of another similarly composed panel (or tribunal of commissioners), but usually does so.[325]

Which cases to use

Caselaw can seem less precise than statute law, and frequently cases seem to contradict each other. Very often there are small differences in the facts of the cases, which justify the different results. To find cases relevant to your own, you can use the footnotes in this *Handbook* or any of the publications listed in Appendix 3. Bear the following in mind.
- Find cases where the facts are similar to yours. If cases appear to be against you, look at the facts of those cases and see whether any differences justify a different decision in your case (known as 'distinguishing' cases). One distinction may simply be that what seemed reasonable in the 1950s does not seem fair in the 2010s.[326]
- Most appeals before April 1987 were decided when there was a right of appeal to commissioners on questions of fact as well as law, so the First-tier Tribunal may not necessarily be erring in law if it takes a different view from a commissioner in a pre-April 1987 decision.
- Ensure that the caselaw is still relevant to the decision you are appealing. A case might only apply to a previous version of the law – ie, if there have been amendments to the statute law since it was decided.
- Check the decisions referred to in the decision maker's response (see p1314) as sometimes they rely on only part of a decision and fail to mention another part which is more favourable to you.

10

Part 10: Getting a benefit decision changed
Chapter 59: Appeals
6. Presenting your case

Obtaining Upper Tribunal, commissioners' and court decisions

Many **Upper Tribunal and commissioners' decisions** are available at www.administrativeappeals.Tribunals.gov.uk/Decisions/decisions.htm, at www.bailii.org and on the Rightsnet website at www.rightsnet.org.uk. Decisions may also be obtained from the Upper Tribunal Office (see Appendix 1). Some are available free of charge.

Reported decisions are published from time to time in bound volumes, which are sometimes available in law libraries. The bound volumes of decisions from 2010 onwards are called Administrative Appeal Chamber Reports and contain reports of social security cases as well as those from other jurisdictions.

Summaries of reported Upper Tribunal and commissioners' decisions, most highlighted decisions and important court decisions are published in CPAG's *Welfare Rights Bulletin*. It is important to use the full decision, not just the summary, at the appeal hearing.

If an unreported decision is to be used at a hearing in the First-tier Tribunal by the DWP (or the local authority or HMRC), a copy should be supplied to you. Similarly, if you wish to use one, you should supply copies to everyone, preferably by sending one to the First-tier Tribunal in advance of the hearing.

Many **court decisions** are available online. A useful link to these is at www.bailii.org. In addition, where there has been an appeal against an Upper Tribunal (or a commissioner's) decision, it is usually reported.

At the hearing

Each case is different and hearings are informal, so there is no set pattern for presenting cases. If you want to make a presentation on your appeal, make this clear to the First-tier Tribunal as soon as possible – eg, before the hearing starts. **Note:** send any detailed submissions and medical reports *before* the hearing.

How should you present your case?

1. You can use a written submission at the hearing and read directly from it. However, the First-tier Tribunal usually asks questions, so be prepared to talk about your case without the script.

2. Make it clear at the beginning which parts of the decision maker's response are in dispute and the parts with which you agree. It is then usually best to set out the facts and to call any witnesses before turning to legal arguments.

3. It is the First-tier Tribunal's job to help you to say everything you want by putting you at your ease and asking the right questions. However, you must also be prepared for some searching questions. If you forget to say something when it is your turn to speak, do not hesitate to add it at the end of the hearing.

Advice and representation

There are a number of agencies which can advise you and help you prepare your case for the hearing (see Appendix 2). Some can also represent you at hearings if you think that someone else would put your case better than you. Remember that many non-lawyer advisers know more about social security law than lawyers, and their advice and representation are usually free.

Meeting the costs of going to the First-tier or Upper Tribunal

Free legal help is available in limited cases. However, for an appeal to the First-tier Tribunal:

- you cannot get free legal help to cover **preparatory work**, such as obtaining medical reports and writing submissions. If you have a solicitor acting for you in an industrial injury or personal injury claim, s/he may have medical and other reports and evidence which you can use for your benefit appeal;
- you cannot *normally* get free legal help from a lawyer to cover **representation**. You may be able to get free legal help in very exceptional cases (see below). If you are not eligible for free advice and assistance, or you want to be represented by a lawyer at an oral hearing, you are likely to have to pay.

You may be able to get free help from a Citizens Advice Bureau or advice centre.

If you are resident in Scotland, free legal help is currently available for **appeals to the Upper Tribunal**. This includes help preparing for paper as well as oral hearings. This may be subject to change. If you are resident in England or Wales, free legal help is available for advice and assistance with appealing to the Upper Tribunal, including applications for permission to appeal that are made direct to the Upper Tribunal (but not applications for permission made to the First-tier Tribunal). However, free legal help from a lawyer for representation at an appeal hearing in the Upper Tribunal is only available in very exceptional cases (see below). If you are granted funding, you must send a copy of the funding notice (in Scotland, the legal aid certificate) to the Upper Tribunal Office as soon as practicable.[327] You must also let the other parties involved in your appeal know that you have been granted funding.

You may qualify for help from a lawyer to cover representation at the First-tier Tribunal or the Upper Tribunal in very exceptional cases. This only applies if it is necessary to make these services available to you because a failure to do so would be a breach of your Human Rights or your EU rights.[328]

Legal aid is available for a **judicial review** by the Upper Tribunal (see p1340).

Notes

1. **Appealing to the First-tier Tribunal**
   1 r2(2) TP(FT) Rules
   2 s12(1), (2) and (3D) SSA 1998
   3 s12(2)(b) and (3A)-(3C) SSA 1998; reg
     3ZA SS&CS(DA) Regs; reg 7
     UC,PIP,JSA&ESA(DA) Regs
   4 **UC/PIP/JSA&ESA under UC** Reg 7(5)
     UC,PIP,JSA&ESA(DA) Regs
     Other benefits Reg 3ZA(5)
     SS&CS(DA) Regs
   6 para A3015 ADM
   5 para A3046 ADM
   7 **CB/GA**Reg 24 CB&GA(DA) Regs
     UC/PIP/JSA&ESA under UC s12 SSA
     1998; reg 49 UC,PIP,JSA&ESA(DA) Regs
     Other benefits s12 SSA 1998; reg 25
     SS&CS(DA) Regs
   8 s12(4) SSA 1998
   9 Reg 14 SS(JPIP) Regs
   10 **CB/GA** Regs 29 and 31 CB&GA(Admin)
     Regs
     UC/PIP/JSA&ESA under UC Reg 56
     UC,PIP,JSA&ESA(C&P) Regs; reg 49(a)
     UC,PIP,JSA&ESA(DA) Regs
     Other benefits Reg 30(1), (5) and (6)-
     (6B) SS(C&P) Regs
   11 Sch 7 para 6(3) and (6) CSPSSA
     2000; reg 3 HB&CTB(DA) Regs; *Wirral
     MBC v Salisbury Independent Living Ltd*
     [2012] EWCA Civ 84
   12 R(H) 3/04; R(H) 10/07
   13 **HB/CTB** Reg 21 HB&CTB(DA) Regs
     CB/GA Reg 33 CB&GA(DA) Regs
     UC/PIP/JSA&ESA under UC Reg
     56(1) UC,PIP,JSA&ESA(C&P) Regs
     Other benefits Reg 30(1) SS&CS(DA)
     Regs
   14 **HB** Sch 7 para 6 CSPSSA 2000
     CB/GA s12 and Schs 2 and 3 SSA 1998;
     reg 25(2) CB&GA(DA) Regs
     UC/PIP/JSA&ESA under UC s12 and
     reg 50(1) and Sch 2
     UC,PIP,JSA&ESA(DA) Regs
     Other benefits s12 and Schs 2 and 3
     SSA 1998; reg 26 SS&CS(DA) Regs

15 **HB** Reg 10 HB&CTB(DA) Regs
   CB/GA Reg 26 CB&GA(DA) Regs
   UC/PIP/JSA&ESA under UC Reg 51
   UC,PIP,JSA&ESA(DA) Regs
   Other benefits Regs 3ZA and 28
   SS&CS(DA) Regs
16 R(SB) 29/83; R(SB) 12/89; CIS/807/
   1992; R(H) 3/05
17 R(IS) 6/04
18 *SSWP v Adams* [2003] EWCA Civ 796, 18
   June 2003, reported as R(G) 1/03
19 **HB** Sch 7 para 6(2) CSPSSA 2000; reg
   16 and Sch HB&CTB(DA) Regs
   CB/GA Sch 2 SSA 1998; reg 25 and Sch
   2 CB&GA(DA) Regs
   UC/PIP/JSA&ESA under UC Reg
   50(2) and Sch 3 UC,PIP,JSA&ESA(DA)
   Regs
   Other benefits Sch 2 SSA 1998; reg 27
   and Sch 2 SS&CS(DA) Regs
20 **HB** Regs 4(6) and 7(2)(e) HB&CTB(DA)
   Regs
   CA/GA Regs 9 and 13(2)(d)
   CB&GA(DA) Regs
   UC/PIP/JSA&ESA under UC Regs 10
   and 25 UC,PIP,JSA&ESA(DA) Regs
   Other benefits Regs 3(8) and 6(2)(d)
   SS&CG(DA) Regs
21 Reg 20(1) HB&CTB(DA) Regs
22 r22(1) TP(FT) Rules
23 **HB** Reg 20(1) HB&CTB(DA) Regs; r23
   TP(FT) Rules
   Other benefits r23(1) TP(FT) Rules;
   reg 8 SSCSVDOP(DA)(A) Regs
24 r22(2)(d)(i) TP(FT) Rules
25 CIB/3937/2000; *SSWP v SC (SF)* [2013]
   UKUT 607 (AAC)
26 r12 TP(FT) Rules
27 rr12, 22(2)d)(ii) and 23(2) and Sch 1
   TP(FT) Rules
28 s9(5) SSA 1998; Sch 7 para 3(5) CSPSSA
   2000
29 Sch 1 TP(FT) Rules
30 rr22(8)(a) and 23(4) and (5) TP(FT)
   Rules
31 r5(3)(a) TP(FT) Rules
32 *LS v Lambeth LB (HB)* [2010] UKUT 461
   (AAC); [2011] AACR 27
33 rr22(3) and 23(6) TP(FT) Rules
34 r11(5) TP(FT) Rules

10

90 Practice Statement, *Composition of Tribunals in Social Security and Child Support Cases in the Social Entitlement Chamber on or after 1 August 2013*, 31 July 2013, para 12
91 r2 TP(FT) Rules
92 CSDLA/606/2003
93 s20(3) SSA 1998; r25(2) TP(FT) Rules; R(DLA) 5/03
94 R(IB) 2/06
95 CI/3384/2006
96 Practice Statement, *Composition of Tribunals in Social Security and Child Support Cases in the Social Entitlement Chamber on or after 1 August 2013*, 31 July 2013, para 14
97 r25(4) TP(FT) Rules
98 R(DLA) 1/95, qualified by CM/2/1994; *GL v SSWP* [2008] UKUT 36 (AAC)
99 R(DLA) 8/06
100 CM/527/1992; CIB/3074/2003
101 CIB/5586/1999
102 CIB/476/2005; CIB/511/2005
103 s20(2) SSA 1998; r25(3) and Sch 2 TP(FT) Rules
104 CDLA/2014/2004
105 *Walsall MBC v PL* [2009] UKUT 27 (AAC)
106 *GL v SSWP* [2008] UKUT 36 (AAC)
107 *Mongan v Department for Social Development* [2005] NICA 16, 13 April 2005, reported as R3/05 (DLA)
108 CH/1229/2002
109 *Mooney v SSWP* [2004] SLT 1141, 23 April 2004, reported as R(DLA) 5/04; *Mongan v Department for Social Development* [2005] NICA 16, 13 April 2005, reported as R3/05 (DLA); *SSWP v Hooper* [2007] EWCA Civ 495, reported as R(IB) 4/07
110 CSDLA/336/2000; CSIB/160/2000; R(H) 1/02
111 **HB** Sch 7 para 6(9)(a) CSPSSA 2000
Other benefits s12(8)(a) SSA 1998
112 CH/1229/2002; R(IB) 2/04; *AP-H v SSWP (DLA)* [2010] UKUT 183 (AAC)
113 CI/531/2000; CDLA/1000/2001; CH/1229/2002; R(IB) 2/04; CDLA/884/2008
114 CDLA/4184/2004
115 R(IB) 2/04
116 R(IB) 2/04; CH/3009/2002
117 CDLA/1707/2005
118 R(IB) 2/04; R(IB) 7/04; CIS/1675/2004
119 **HB** Sch 7 para 6(9)(b) CSPSSA 2000
Other benefits s12(8)(b) SSA 1998; R(DLA) 4/05
120 R(DLA) 2/01; R(DLA) 3/01; CJSA/2375/2000

121 R(SB) 4/85
122 r33 TP(FT) Rules
123 Art 8 First-tier Tribunal and Upper Tribunal (Composition of Tribunal) Order 2008, No.2835
124 Practice Statement, *Record of Proceedings in Social Security and Child Support Cases in the Social Entitlement Chamber on or after 3 November 2008*, 30 October 2008
125 r34(2) TP(FT) Rules
126 r34(3) TP(FT) Rules; CCS/1664/2001
127 r34(4) TP(FT) Rules; CIB/3937/2000
128 r5(3)(a) TP(FT) Rules
129 r34(5) TP(FT) Rules
130 r38(7)(a) TP(FT) Rules
131 r5(3)(n) TP(UT) Rules
132 r5(3)(l) TP(FT) Rules
133 **HB** Sch 7 para 13 CSPSSA 2000; reg 11 HB&CTB(DA) Regs
CB/GA Reg 18 CB&GA(DA) Regs
UC/PIP/JSA&ESA under UC Reg 44 UC,PIP,JSA&ESA(DA) Regs
Other benefits s21 SSA 1998; reg 16 SS&CS(DA) Regs
134 r36 TP(FT) Rules; CI/3887/1999; CSDLA/168/2008; *AS v SSWP (ESA)* [2011] UKUT 159 (AAC)
135 r37(1) and (2) TP(FT) Rules
136 r37(3) TP(FT) Rules
137 r5(3)(a) TP(FT) Rules
138 r27(2) TP(FT) Rules; CSB/172/1990
139 CIB/4193/2003
140 CI/79/1990; CIS/373/1994
141 r41 TP(FT) Rules
142 *LS v Lambeth LB (HB)* [2010] UKUT 461 (AAC); [2011] AACR 27
143 r38(3) and (4) TP(FT) Rules
144 **HB** Sch 7 para 7(3) CSPSSA 2000
Other benefits s13(3) SSA 1998

2. **Appealing to the Upper Tribunal**
145 s11 TCEA 2007; *LS v Lambeth LB (HB)* [2010] UKUT 461 (AAC); [2011] AACR 27
146 s11(5)(d) and (e) TCEA 2007
147 r2 TP(UT) Rules
148 r4 TP(UT) Rules; Practice Statement, *Delegation of Functions to Staff on or after 3 November 2008*, 30 October 2008
149 s11 TCEA 2007
150 R(A) 1/72; R(SB) 11/83; R(IS) 11/99; R(I) 2/06
151 CIS/2345/2001; CH/4065/2001
152 CDLA/433/1999
153 CDLA/7980/1995; CH/5221/2001; CH/396/2002; CIB/2977/2002

10

230 rr5, 6 and 15 TP(FT) Rules; rr5, 6 and 15 TP(UT) Rules; *SR v Bristol CC* [2008] UKUT 7 (AAC)
231 r6(4) TP(FT) Rules; r5(4) TP(UT) Rules
232 r6(5) TP(FT) Rules; r6(5) TP(UT) Rules
233 r6(2) and (3) TP(FT) Rules; r6(2) and (3) TP(UT) Rules
234 r7 TP(FT) Rules; r7 TP(UT) Rules
235 CIB/4253/2004
236 r15(2)(b) TP(FT) Rules; r15(2)(b) TP(UT) Rules
237 r11 TP(FT) Rules; r11 TP(UT) Rules; CIB/1009/2004; CIB/2058/2004
238 r11(6)(b) TP(FT) Rules; r11(4)(b) TP(UT) Rules
239 r11(6)(a) TP(FT) Rules; r11(4)(a) TP(UT) Rules; *MP v SSWP (DLA)* [2010] UKUT 103 (AAC)
240 r8(1), (3)(a) and (5) TP(FT) Rules; r8(1), (3)(a) and (5) TP(UT) Rules
241 *DTM v Kettering BC (CTB)* [2013] UKUT 625 (AAC)
242 r8(5) and (6) TP(FT) Rules; r8(5) and (6) TP(UT) Rules
243 r8(2) and (4) TP(FT) Rules; r8(2) and (4) TP(UT) Rules
244 r8(3)(b) and (c) and (4) TP(FT) Rules; r8(3)(b) TP(UT) Rules
245 *AW v IC and Blackpool CC* [2013] UKUT 30 (AAC)
246 R(IS) 5/94
247 *LS v Lambeth LB (HB)* [2010] UKUT 461 (AAC); [2011] AACR 27
248 rr1(3), definition of 'respondent', and 8(7) TP(FT) Rules; rr1(3), definition of 'respondent', and 8(7) TP(UT) Rules
249 r8(8) TP(FT) Rules; r8(8) TP(UT) Rules
250 *ZB v SSWP (CSM)* [2013] UKUT 367 (AAC)
251 r5(3)(h) TP(FT) Rules; r5(3)(h) TP(UT) Rules; *MA v SSWP* [2009] UKUT 211 (AAC)
252 *GC v SSWP (ESA)* [2012] UKUT 60 (AAC)
253 r31 TP(FT) Rules; r38 TP(UT) Rules
254 CDLA/1290/2004
255 CDLA/3680/1997
256 *MA v SSWP* [2009] UKUT 211 (AAC)
257 CDLA/5413/1999
258 CIS/566/1991; CS/99/1993
259 CIS/2292/2000
260 CIS/6002/1997; *R v Social Security Commissioner ex parte Angora Bibi* [2000] 23 May 2000, unreported (HC); CIB/1009/2004; CIB/2058/2004
261 CIS/3338/2001
262 *MH v Pembrokeshire (HB)* [2010] UKUT 28 (AAC)
263 s26 SSA 1998

264 s26(5) SSA 1998
265 rr5(3)(b) and 18 TP(FT) Rules
266 r32 TP(FT) Rules; r39 TP(UT) Rules

4. Appealing to the courts
267 s13 TCEA 2007
268 s13(8)(c)-(e) TCEA 2007
269 s13(6) and (6A) TCEA 2007; Appeals from the Upper Tribunal to the Court of Appeal Order 2008, No.2834; r41.59 Rules of the Court of Session 1994
270 r44(1), (6)(a) and (7) TP(UT) Rules
271 *Fryer-Kelsey v SSWP* [2005] EWCA Civ 511, 21 April 2005, reported as R(IB) 6/05
272 r44(2), (3) and (5) TP(UT) Rules
273 r5(3)(a) TP(UT) Rules
274 r44(6) TP(UT) Rules
275 r45(3)-(5) TP(UT) Rules
276 s10 TCEA 2007; r45(1) TP(UT) Rules
277 s10(4) and (5) TCEA 2007
278 r46(2) and (3) TP(UT) Rules
279 r45(2) TP(UT) Rules
280 s13(3)-(5) TCEA 2007
281 r45(4)(b) TP(UT) Rules
282 Practice Direction 52C, para 15.3
283 r52.3(4A) Civil Procedure Rules
284 r54.5 Civil Procedure Rules
285 See *Hanlon v Traffic Commission* [1988] SLT 802 and *Perfect Swivel v Dundee District Licensing Board* (No.2) [1993] SLT 112
286 r54.7A Civil Procedure Rules

5. Time limits
287 r5(3)(a) TP(FT) Rules; r5(3)(a) TP(UT) Rules
288 r2 TP(FT) Rules; r2 TP(UT) Rules
289 r2(2)(e) TP(FT) Rules; r2(2)(e) TP(UT) Rules
290 r5(3)(a) and (aa) TP(FT) Rules
291 rr22(8)(a) and 23(4) and (5) TP(FT) Rules
292 r23(7)(b) TP(FT) Rules
293 *LS v Lambeth LB (HB)* [2010] UKUT 461 (AAC); [2011] AACR 27
294 rr22(6) and 23(3) TP(FT) Rules
295 rr22(8)(a) and 23(4) and (5) TP(FT) Rules
296 Reg 19(5A) HB&CTB(DA) Regs
297 Reg 19(6) and (7) HB&CTB(DA) Regs
298 Reg 19(8) HB&CTB(DA) Regs
299 Reg 19(9) HB&CTB(DA) Regs
300 Reg 8 Social Security, Child Support, Vaccine Damage and Other Payments (Decisions and Appeals) (Amendment) Regulations 2013, No.2380
301 r21(7)(b) TP(UT) Rules

302 R(M) 1/87; R(I) 5/91
303 R(M) 1/87
304 CIS/147/1995

6. Presenting your case
305 R(SB) 6/82
306 r16 TP(FT) Rules
307 r15(1)(e) and (f) TP(FT) Rules
308 r15(2) TP(FT) Rules
309 R(DLA) 4/02; CIS/1481/2006; *DG v
   SSWP (DLA)* [2011] UKUT 14 (AAC)
310 r15(1)(d) TP(FT) Rules; CDLA/2014/
   2004
311 R(SB) 33/85; R(SB) 12/89
312 CIB/2058/2004
313 r11(5) TP(FT) Rules; CDLA/1138/2003;
   CDLA/2462/2003
314 CIS/4901/2002
315 *Walsall MBC v PL* [2009] UKUT 27 (AAC)
316 R(SB) 1/81
317 *JM v SSWP* [2012] UKUT 472 (AAC)
318 *SSWP v Cunningham* [2004] 6 August,
   ScotCS 211, reported as R(DLA) 7/
   04; R(DLA) 3/07
319 *Pepper v Hart* [1992] 3 WLR 1032, *The
   Times,* 30 November 1992
320 R(I) 12/75; *Dorset Healthcare Trust v MH*
   [2009] UKUT 4 (AAC)
321 R(SB) 22/86
322 R(I) 12/75; *Dorset Healthcare Trust v MH*
   [2009] UKUT 4 (AAC)
323 *CSBO v Leary,* reported as R(SB) 6/85;
   see generally CS/140/1991
324 R(G) 3/62; R(U) 4/88
325 R(U) 4/88
326 *Nancollas v Insurance Officer* [1985] 1 All
   ER 833 (CA), also reported as R(I) 7/85
327 r18 TP(UT) Rules
328 s10 Legal Aid, Sentencing and
   Punishment of Offenders Act 2012

10

Chapter 60

Challenging decisions on statutory payments

This chapter covers:
1. Information from your employer (p1371)
2. Involving HM Revenue and Customs (p1371)
3. Appealing against the decision (p1374)
4. Appeals to the Upper Tribunal (p1377)
5. Appeals to the courts (p1378)
6. Payment if your challenge is successful (p1379)

This chapter explains the rules for challenging decisions on entitlement to statutory sick pay, statutory maternity pay, statutory paternity pay and statutory adoption pay. These rules do not apply to challenging decisions on other benefits (except some decisions on national insurance contributions – see p842).

In this chapter, when the term First-tier Tribunal is used, it means the First-tier Tribunal (Tax) and when the term Upper Tribunal is used, it means the Upper Tribunal (Tax and Chancery).

Key facts

* Statutory sick pay, statutory maternity pay, statutory paternity pay and statutory adoption pay are normally paid by your employer (in some cases, your ex-employer) and your employer should make the initial decision on your entitlement.
* If you disagree with your employer's decision, or your employer has failed to make a decision, you can ask HM Revenue and Customs (HMRC) to decide whether you are entitled.
* You and your employer can appeal against an HMRC decision. You can request that your appeal be decided either by an HMRC review or by the First-tier Tribunal. If you disagree with the HMRC review decision, you can still ask the First-tier Tribunal to consider your appeal.
* If you disagree with the First-tier Tribunal's decision, you might be able to appeal to the Upper Tribunal. If you disagree with the Upper Tribunal's decision, you might be able to appeal to a court.

Future changes

At the time of writing, HMRC was reviewing its procedures for dealing with disputes about entitlement to statutory payments. See CPAG's online service and *Welfare Rights Bulletin* for updates.

1. Information from your employer

If you have taken the necessary steps to request statutory sick pay (SSP), statutory maternity pay (SMP), statutory paternity pay (SPP) or statutory adoption pay (SAP) from your employer (see p800 and p820), but your employer decides it is not liable to pay you (or your employer has been paying you SSP, but it decides your period of entitlement has, or is due to, come to an end), it should provide you with details of its decision and the reasons within certain time limits. This also applies to a former employer for SMP, SPP and SAP.[1]

For SSP, your employer should normally provide this information on Form SSP1 or on its own computerised form if it contains the same information. For SMP, ordinary SPP, additional SPP and SAP, it is normally given on Form SMP1, OSPP1, ASPP1 or SAP1 respectively. The employer should also return to you certain evidence you have provided to establish your entitlement – eg, Form MATB1 for SMP (see p800).

For SSP and SMP, you can also request a written statement from your employer detailing, in respect of the period before your request, its view on the:[2]

- days (or for SMP, weeks) you are entitled to SSP or SMP, and the reason why SSP or SMP is not payable for other days (or for SMP, other weeks);
- daily rate of SSP, or the weekly rate of SMP, to which you are entitled.

For SMP, you also have the right to request this information from a former employer. If your request is reasonable, your employer (or former employer) should provide this information within a reasonable time.

2. Involving HM Revenue and Customs

If you disagree with your employer's decision on your entitlement to statutory sick pay (SSP), statutory maternity pay (SMP), statutory paternity pay (SPP) or statutory adoption pay (SAP), or if your employer has failed to make a decision,

Part 10: Getting a benefit decision changed
Chapter 60: Challenging decisions on statutory payments
2. Involving HM Revenue and Customs

you can request that HM Revenue and Customs (HMRC) makes a formal decision on your entitlement.[3] There are time limits for doing so (see below).

It can take some time to get a final decision on your entitlement, so you should consider whether there are other benefits or tax credits which you can claim in the interim (see Chapter 1). If you claim employment and support allowance (ESA – see Chapters 5 and 28) while waiting for a decision on your SSP, or maternity allowance (MA – see Chapter 34) while waiting for a SMP decision, the DWP does not normally make a decision on your entitlement to ESA or MA until HMRC has made a decision on your entitlement to SSP or SMP (because you will not qualify for ESA if you are entitled to SSP, nor for MA if you are entitled to SMP). For this reason, the DWP can request that HMRC makes a formal decision on your entitlement to SSP or SMP, if you have not already requested this yourself. Despite this, it is important not to delay a claim for ESA or MA as you may lose some weeks' benefit if the final decision is that you do not qualify for SSP or SMP.

Note: if you are considering challenging your employer's decision on your entitlement to a statutory payment, consider how this might affect your employment. You may wish to consult an employment adviser to discuss this.

Applying for a decision

Forms
You should normally apply on Form SSP14 (for SSP), SMP14 (for SMP), SPP14 (for ordinary and additional SPP) or SAP14 (for SAP), which can be obtained from the Statutory Payments Disputes Team (see Appendix 1). Send your application to the Statutory Payments Disputes Team.

Your application to HMRC must be made within six months of the earliest date for which your entitlement to SSP, SMP, SPP or SAP is in dispute.[4] If problems obtaining the correct form mean you would otherwise miss the six-month deadline, you should apply for a decision by letter. Your letter *must* contain details of the period in respect of which your entitlement to SSP, SMP, SPP or SAP is at issue and the grounds (if any) on which your employer is refusing payment.[5]

If possible, send a copy of the SSP1, SMP1, OSPP1, ASPP1 or SAP1 form your employer has given you and evidence of your entitlement – eg, a medical certificate if you have been sick for more than seven days, a MATB1 form, or the 'matching certificate' from the adoption agency. However, do not delay your application if you do not have this information.

Chapter 60

Requests for further information

On receiving your application, HMRC may contact you for further information and is likely to send a form to your employer to complete.

HMRC can require your employer to provide certain information and can impose a financial penalty on your employer if your employer fails do so. For example, if your employer has not notified you of its decision on your entitlement to SSP, SMP, SPP or SAP within the time limits, HMRC can impose a penalty, with added penalties for each day it fails to comply. However, in this situation, if your employer does not comply, press HMRC to make its own decision on your entitlement.

HMRC can request information from you if it is making a decision on your entitlement to SSP or SMP, or from you or your spouse/partner if it is making a decision on your entitlement to SPP or SAP.[6]

HMRC can impose a financial penalty on you for not providing information or documents that you have been reasonably required to provide to decide your entitlement.[7] However, this is only likely to happen if HMRC believes that you have acted fraudulently or have been negligent.

HM Revenue and Customs' decision

In order to try to resolve the dispute, HMRC may send both you and your employer a written opinion on your entitlement to SSP, SMP, SPP or SAP before it issues a formal decision on your application. If you disagree with this, write to HMRC, explaining why you disagree. HMRC may give you a deadline to object to its written opinion before it issues a formal decision. HMRC considers any new information you or your employer have provided and should then issue a formal decision on your entitlement.

In some cases, HMRC sends the formal decision without first issuing a written opinion. The formal decision is legally binding on the employer (see p1379 for the time limits for complying). However, both you and your employer have a right to appeal against the formal decision (see p1374).

Varying or superseding a decision

HMRC can change one of its own decisions by varying or superseding it.[8] It can **vary** its decision if it believes that the decision was wrong at the time it was made. The new decision may take effect from the date that the original decision would have had effect if the reason for the variation had been known. If you or your employer have appealed against a decision, HMRC may vary that decision at any time before the appeal is determined. If HMRC varies its decision, it must tell you and your employer of the new decision in writing.

HMRC can **supersede** an earlier decision if the decision has become incorrect for any reason – eg, if your circumstances have changed. The new decision will take effect from the date of your change in circumstances.

Part 10: Getting a benefit decision changed
Chapter 60: Challenging decisions on statutory payments
3. Appealing against the decision

If HMRC varies or supersedes an earlier decision, either you or your employer can appeal against the new decision.

---

3. **Appealing against the decision**

Both you and your employer can appeal against a decision by HM Revenue and Customs (HMRC).[9] This section assumes that you are the appellant, but the same rules apply if your employer has appealed.

Your appeal should be made in writing to HMRC and should include your reasons for appealing.[10] Send your appeal to the Statutory Payments Disputes Team (see Appendix 1).

Your appeal should reach HMRC within 30 days of the date on which HMRC's decision was issued (but see below for when this time limit can be extended).[11]

You can request that your appeal either be decided by the First-tier Tribunal or by HMRC conducting a review. To do so, in addition to sending your written appeal to HMRC, you should notify:[12]

- the First-tier Tribunal in writing, that you want it to consider your appeal (see p1376); *or*
- HMRC in writing, that you want it to conduct a review. (If HMRC conducts a review and you disagree with its decision you can still apply to the First-tier Tribunal for a decision on your appeal, provided you apply within the time limits on p1376.)

If, having made your appeal, you do not ask either the First-tier Tribunal to consider your appeal or HMRC to review its decision, HMRC can write to you, offering to review its decision (called an 'HMRC-initiated review' in this chapter). Before HMRC initiates a review, it may try to settle the appeal (see below). However, until HMRC has issued a notification offering you a review, you can still notify the First-tier Tribunal that you want it to decide your appeal or inform HMRC yourself that you want it to conduct a review.

Note:

- HMRC can try to settle an appeal with the consent of all the parties at any time before the determination of the appeal. If, before the appeal is decided, an agreement is reached between HMRC and you (if you have appealed) or your employer (if your employer has appealed), the matter is treated as settled by agreement and the appeal lapses.[13]
- You can withdraw your appeal at any time before it is decided by notifying HMRC and your employer that you wish to do so. Your employer and HMRC have 30 days to object and, if no objection is made, your appeal will lapse.[14]
- The 30-day time limit for appealing can be extended by HMRC, provided you request this in writing, you have a reasonable excuse for not having made your appeal within the time limit and your appeal was made without unreasonable

delay.[15] If HMRC does not accept your late appeal, you can apply to the First-tier Tribunal for permission to appeal late (see p1376). If the First-tier Tribunal refuses the application, you can appeal to the Upper Tribunal.

Review by HM Revenue and Customs

Initial view on entitlement

If you have asked for your appeal to be decided by an HMRC review, or if HMRC has initiated a review, HMRC first must notify you of its initial view on your entitlement. This is not necessarily the same as its original decision on your entitlement.

If you have requested an HMRC review, HMRC should send you its initial view on your entitlement within 30 days, beginning with the date it receives your written request for a review, or longer if this is reasonable.[16] The same rules apply if it is your employer who has initiated the review.

If HMRC has initiated the review, HMRC should send its initial view on your entitlement with its offer of a review.[17] You then have 30 days starting on the date of HMRC's letter to inform in writing:[18]

- HMRC, that you want it to conduct the review (see below); *or*
- the First-tier Tribunal, that you want it to decide your appeal (see p1376). In some circumstances, the First-tier Tribunal can consider your appeal even if you apply after the 30-day time limit (see p1376).

If HMRC has initiated the review but you neither accept the offer of a review nor notify the First-tier Tribunal that you want it to consider your appeal within the above time limit, HMRC will proceed as if you have agreed to its initial view on your entitlement and will treat the matter as settled by agreement. Notification of this should be sent to you and your employer, and your appeal lapses.[19]

The review

After HMRC has issued its initial view on your entitlement (and, for HMRC-initiated reviews, provided you have accepted HMRC's offer of a review), a review should be carried out by an HMRC decision maker who was not involved in making the original decision. If you disagree with HMRC's initial view, it is important to write to explain why.

The decision maker must consider any information you provide, if you provide it at a stage that gives her/him a reasonable opportunity to do so.[20]

HMRC should notify you of its review decision and the reasons for it within 45 days beginning with the date it:[21]

- notified you of its initial view of the matter, if you requested the review; *or*
- received your acceptance of its offer of a review, if HMRC initiated the review.

In either case, these time limits can be changed if you agree.

Part 10: Getting a benefit decision changed
Chapter 60: Challenging decisions on statutory payments
3. Appealing against the decision

If HMRC does not notify you of its review decision within this time limit, its decision is taken to be the same as its initial view on your entitlement and HMRC must inform you of this.[22]

If you or your employer do not agree with HMRC's review decision, you may notify the First-tier Tribunal that you want it to consider your appeal. The time limit for doing so is 30 days, beginning with the date of either:[23]

- HMRC's letter notifying you of its review decision; or
- if HMRC did not notify you of its review decision within the time limit, the date of its letter telling you it has adopted its initial view on your entitlement as its decision.

In the latter situation, you can appeal before receiving HMRC's letter, provided your appeal is made after the expiry of the time limit for making the review decision.

If you do not notify the First-tier Tribunal within the time limit, your appeal can only be considered by the First-tier Tribunal if it gives permission (see below).[24]

Appeals to the First-tier Tribunal

You can request that the First-tier Tribunal considers your appeal if:[25]

- you have appealed against HMRC's original decision on your entitlement and want your appeal to be decided by the First-tier Tribunal, rather than by an HMRC review (see p1374);
- you have appealed and, because you did not inform the First-tier Tribunal or HMRC of how you wanted your appeal decided, HMRC has initiated a review (see p1375). Rather than accept the offer of a review, you can notify the First-tier Tribunal that you want it to decide your appeal. See above for the time limits for notifying the Tribunal, and below if you miss the time limit;
- you requested that your appeal be decided by a HMRC review or accepted HMRC's offer of a review, but either you do not agree with the review decision or HMRC has not notified you of its review decision within the time limits. You can notify the First-tier Tribunal that you want it to determine your appeal. See above for the time limits for notifying the First-tier Tribunal and below if you miss the time limit;
- you missed the time limit for appealing against HMRC's original decision on your entitlement and HMRC does not agree to accept your late appeal (but see below).

Time limits

If you either miss one of the time limits for notifying the First-tier Tribunal that you want it to determine your appeal, or you miss the time limit for appealing against HMRC's original decision on your entitlement (and HMRC does not agree to accept your late appeal), you can still ask the First-tier Tribunal to consider your appeal but it must give its permission for the time limit to be extended. Although there are no specific rules about when the time limit can be extended,[26] the overriding objective of the rules is to enable tribunals to deal with cases fairly and justly.[27] Whether the First-tier Tribunal extends the time limit depends on the circumstances of your case. Explain your circumstances when you apply for permission (see p1354 for guidance). As you cannot be certain of success, it is important to keep within the time limits if you can.

Notifying the First-tier Tribunal

To request that the First-tier Tribunal considers your appeal, your written notice must contain certain information, including the details of the decision you are appealing against, the result you want and the grounds on which you are relying to make the appeal. If you are making a late application, you must also give your grounds for doing so.[28]

Use the 'Notice of Appeal (tax)' form, available from www.justice.gov.uk (click on link for tax tribunal) or telephone 0845 223 8080 (typetalk: 18001 0845 223 8080). Your notice should be sent to the First-tier Tribunal (Tax) (see Appendix 1). You must include a copy of the written record of the decision which you are appealing against and any statement giving the reasons for that decision (eg, the notification HMRC sent informing you of its decision), unless you do not have this information and cannot reasonably obtain it.

How the First-tier Tribunal decides your case

The First-tier Tribunal allocates your case to be considered in one of four ways.[29] Further details of the procedures can be obtained from the First-tier Tribunal (Tax) leaflet *Making an Appeal*, available from www.justice.gov.uk (search for 'making an appeal to the tax chamber').

The First-tier Tribunal can confirm the decision of HMRC or change HMRC's decision.[30] The Tribunal must send you a notice informing you of its decision, which may include its full written findings and the reasons for its decision.[31] If you disagree with the decision of the First-tier Tribunal, you may be able to appeal against it to the Upper Tribunal (see below).

In certain circumstances, you can apply for the First-tier Tribunal's decision to be 'set aside' (there is a time limit for doing so), or the First-tier Tribunal can correct its own decision.[32] The First-tier Tribunal can also review its decision if you have applied for permission to appeal to the Upper Tribunal.[33]

4. Appeals to the Upper Tribunal

You and your employer can appeal to the Upper Tribunal (Tax and Chancery Chamber) against a decision of the First-tier Tribunal, but only on the grounds that the First-tier Tribunal has made an 'error of law' (see p1330).[34] The rules for

Part 10: Getting a benefit decision changed
Chapter 60: Challenging decisions on statutory payments
5. Appeals to the courts

making an appeal are almost the same as those for making an appeal to the Upper Tribunal (Administrative Appeals Chamber), described in Chapter 59, (although there are differences in the procedure for lodging an appeal and in the time limit for applying). You must first apply for permission to appeal; your application should be made to the First-tier Tribunal (Tax) and must normally be received no later than 56 days after the latest of the dates listed on p1334 (usually the date the First-tier Tribunal sent you its full written reasons for the decision). In some circumstances, the First-tier Tribunal can give permission for you to appeal later than this.[35]

If you have not been sent the First-tier Tribunal's full written findings and reasons, you must obtain these before applying for permission to appeal. Write to the First-tier Tribunal to request these – your request must be received within 28 days of the date it sent you its decision notice. In some circumstances, this time limit can be extended.[36]

If the First-tier Tribunal refuses permission for you to appeal, or only gives permission on limited grounds, you can apply to the Upper Tribunal for permission (see Appendix 1). Use Form FTC1, available from www.justice.gov.uk (search for 'FTC1').

See p1336 for the time limits for applying.[37] If, without a hearing, the Upper Tribunal refuses you permission to appeal, or to appeal late, or gives permission to appeal subject to conditions or on limited grounds, you may apply for this decision to be reconsidered at a hearing. An application to do so must be made in writing and be received by the Upper Tribunal within 14 days of the date it sent you notice of its decision, although the Upper Tribunal has discretion to extend this time limit.[38] However, the Upper Tribunal has the power to make an order for costs (expenses in Scotland), so before making any application seek advice about whether you could be liable for costs if you lose your case.

See Chapter 59 for other information on the procedures of the Upper Tribunal.

5. Appeals to the courts

You and your employer can appeal against the decision of the Upper Tribunal to the Court of Appeal (the Court of Session in Scotland) if the Upper Tribunal made an 'error of law' – ie, it interpreted the law incorrectly.[39]

You must apply for permission to appeal, which is only granted if certain conditions are met (see p1348). Your application should normally be made to the Upper Tribunal within one month of the date it sent you written reasons for its decision. This time limit can be extended with the permission of the Upper Tribunal.[40] See p1348 for further details on appealing to the courts.

Seek advice from a solicitor, law centre or legal advice centre if you are considering appealing against the decision of the Upper Tribunal.

6. Payment if your challenge is successful

If it is decided that your employer should pay you a statutory payment, your employer should pay you within a certain time limit. If your employer has appealed or is within the time limit to do so, your employer does not have to pay you until a final decision is given on appeal, or until the time limit for the appeal or a further appeal has passed. If no appeal against the decision has been made (or if the matter has been finally determined), your employer should pay you on or before the first payday after either:[41]

- the day the employer is notified that the appeal has been finally disposed of; *or*
- the day the employer receives notification that leave to appeal has been refused, and there is no further opportunity to apply for leave; *or*
- in any other case, the day the time limit for appeal expires.

If, because of your employer's payroll methods, it is not practical for you to be paid at this time, your employer should pay you on or before your next payday after this date.

If your employer does not pay

If your employer does not pay you within the above time limit, HMRC should pay you (although HMRC states it will first contact your employer to try to get it to pay).[42] Write to HMRC's Statutory Payments Disputes Team (see Appendix 1) asking for payment. This applies even if your employer is insolvent, but only for payment owed for the period before the date of insolvency. For any period that falls after the date of insolvency, HMRC, rather than your employer, is automatically liable to pay you any statutory payment for which you are eligible.[43]

10

Notes

1. **Information from your employer**
   1 **SSP** s130 SSAA 1992; reg 15 SSP Regs
   SMP s132 SSAA 1992; reg 25A SMP Regs
   OSPP&SAP Reg 11 SPPSAP(A) Regs
   ASPP Reg 11 ASPP(BAAO)(A) Regs
   2 **SSP** s14(3) SSAA 1992
   SMP s15(2) SSAA 1992

2. **Involving HM Revenue and Customs**
   3 s8 SSC(TF)A 1999
   4 **SSP&SMP** Reg 3 SSP&SMP(D) Regs
   OSSP&SAP Reg 13 SPPSAP(A) Regs
   ASPP Reg 13 ASPP(BAAO)(A) Regs
   5 **SSP&SMP** Reg 3 SSP&SMP(D) Regs
   OSSP&SAP Reg 13 SPPSAP(A) Regs
   ASPP Reg 13 ASPP(BAAO)(A) Regs

Part 10: Getting a benefit decision changed
Chapter 60: Challenging decisions on statutory payments
Notes

6 **SSP** Reg 14 SSP Regs
SMP Reg 25 SMP Regs
OSPP&SAP Reg 14 SPPSAP(A) Regs
ASPP Reg 14 ASPP(BAAO)(A) Regs
7 **SSP&SAP** s113A SSAA 1992
SPP&SAP s11(1) and (2) Employment
Act 2002
8 s10 SSC(TF)A 1999; regs 5 and 6
SSC(DA) Regs

3. **Appealing against the decision**
9 s11(2)(a) SSC(TF)A 1999
10 s12 SSC(TF)A 1999
11 s12(1) SSC(TF)A 1999
12 ss 49A, 49B, 49D and 49I TMA
1970; reg 7 SSC(DA) Regs
13 s49A(4) TMA 1970; reg 11 SSC(DA)
Regs
14 Reg 11(5) SSC(DA) Regs
15 s49 TMA 1970; reg 9 SSC(DA) Regs
16 s49B(2) and (5) TMA 1970
17 s49C(2) TMA 1970
18 ss49C(3) and (8) and 49H TMA 1970
19 s49C(4) TMA 1970; reg 11 SSC(DA)
Regs
20 s49E(4) TMA 1970
21 s49E(6) and (7) TMA 1970
22 s49E(8) and (9) TMA 1970
23 s49G TMA 1970
24 s49G(3) TMA 1970
25 ss49D, 49G and 49H TMA 1970
26 s49(2)(b) TMA 1970; r20(4) TP(FT)(TC)
Rules
27 r2 TP(FT)(TC) Rules
28 r20 TP(FT)(TC) Rules
29 r23 TP(FT)(TC) Rules
30 Reg 10 SSC(DA) Regs
31 r35 TP(FT)(TC) Rules
32 rr37 and 38 TP(FT)(TC) Rules
33 r41 TP(FT)(TC) Rules

4. **Appeals to the Upper Tribunal**
34 s11 TCEA 2007; reg 12(2) SSC(DA) Regs
35 r39 TP(FT)(TC) Rules
36 rr5(3)(a) and 35(4) and (5) TP(FT)(TC)
Rules
37 r21(3)(b) TP(UT) Rules
38 rr5(3)(a) and 22(3)-(5) TP(UT) Rules

5. **Appeals to the courts**
39 s13(2) TCEA 2007; reg 12(2) SSC(DA)
Regs
40 r44 TP(UT) Rules

6. **Payment if your challenge is successful**
41 **SSP** Reg 9 SSP Regs
SMP Reg 29 SMP Regs
OSPP&SAP Reg 42 SPPSAP(G) Regs
ASPP Reg 34 ASPP(G) Regs
42 **SSP** s151(6) SSCBA 1992; reg 9A SSP
Regs
SMP s164(9)(b) SSCBA 1992; reg 7
SMP Regs
OSPP&SAP ss171ZD(3) and 171ZM(3)
SSCBA 1992; reg 43 SPPSAP(G) Regs
ASPP s171ZED(3) SSCBA 1992; reg 35
ASPP(G) Regs
43 **SSP** Reg 9B SSP Regs
SMP Reg 7(3) and (4) SMP Regs
OSPP&SAP Reg 43(2) and (3)
SPPSAP(G) Regs
ASPP Reg 35(2) and (3) ASPP(G) Regs

10

Chapter 61

Complaints

This chapter covers:
1. Grounds for a complaint (below)
2. Compensation payments (p1382)
3. Complaining about the DWP (p1383)
4. Complaining about HM Revenue and Customs (p1384)
5. Complaining about a local authority (p1385)
6. Complaining about HM Courts and Tribunals Service (p1386)
7. Using your MP (p1387)
8. Complaining to the Ombudsman (p1387)
9. Legal action (p1389)

Key facts
- A complaint can be made about any government or local authority department.
- You can complain about a delay in dealing with your claim, poor administration, the behaviour of staff, or the way in which a particular policy or practice has impacted on you.
- If your complaint is not resolved, you may be able to complain to an Ombudsman or Adjudicator.

10

1. Grounds for a complaint

If you are dissatisfied with how you have been treated by a government or local authority department, you can complain. This is a different from when you disagree with a decision about your benefit or tax credit. In this case, you can usually apply for a revision or appeal (see Chapters 58, 59 and 68).

You can complain about matters such as delays (see p1382), discourtesy, poor administration, the behaviour of staff, bad advice and the way in which a particular department's policy or practice impacts on you. You may be able to complain about other issues if you are unhappy about how your claim has been handled or how you have been treated.

Delays

All benefit authorities should act promptly to process your claim. If they do not do so, you can complain and possibly obtain compensation (see below).

A local authority should process your housing benefit claim within 14 days, provided you have given it all the information asked for.[1] Many do not. Complaining may be one way to get your claim processed more quickly, although threatening legal action may be more effective (see p139). The Ombudsman (see p1388) often orders compensation to be paid where there have been long delays that are not the claimant's fault.

HM Revenue and Customs has no official targets for processing tax credit claims.

DWP offices have target times for dealing with claims, but they are not always able to meet these. If there is a delay that has resulted in or from maladministration, you may be entitled to compensation in the form of interest.

2. Compensation payments

You should expect prompt, courteous and efficient service from staff dealing with your claim. If you are dissatisfied with the way your claim has been administered, you can seek compensation. **Note:** compensation payments are discretionary.

The DWP, HM Revenue and Customs (HMRC) and local authorities sometimes pay compensation if you can show that you have lost out through their error or delay and the loss cannot be made good by a revision, supersession or appeal (see Chapters 58 and 59) or by backdating your claim. For instance, if you did not claim carer's allowance because you were misled by the DWP and you could not have the benefit backdated for more than three months, you can claim compensation.

The DWP should automatically consider whether compensation should be paid if you are owed arrears of benefit, but you should still write to your local DWP office and ask. If you do not get a sympathetic response, ask your MP (see p1387) to write on your behalf or to take up your case with the social security minister.

The DWP uses a guide, *Financial Redress for Maladministration*, to help it decide when and how much compensation (known as 'extra-statutory' or ex gratia payments) should be paid. The guide is available from the DWP website (see Appendix 1). HMRC has a code of practice, *Complaints* (C/FS), which sets out when it makes compensatory or consolatory payments.

You should ask for a payment equal to the money you have lost, but you can also ask for additional amounts to cover interest on arrears and any extra expenses you had, and to compensate you for any hardship or distress experienced because of the mistake. If your loss was as a clear result of incorrect advice or negligence

10

on the part of the agency, you may be able to bring a court action for damages. Seek legal advice if this is the case.

3. Complaining about the DWP

The DWP has complaint procedures for each of its agencies. These are:
- the Pension Service;
- Jobcentre Plus;
- the Child Support Agency (CSA);
- the Child Maintenance Service (CMS);
- the Disability and Carers Service;
- the Debt Management organisation.

Note: although the Pension Service and the Disability and Carers Service merged on 1 April 2008, they remain two distinct organisations for complaint purposes.

The DWP does not deal with complaints about contracted providers – eg, Work Programme providers and those carrying out medical assessments on behalf of the DWP. If you want to complain about a provider, use its internal complaints procedure. If you are still not satisfied, you can complain to the Independent Case Examiner (see p1384) and the Parliamentary and Health Service Ombudsman (see p1388).

If you want to complain about the CSA or CMS, see CPAG's *Child Support Handbook*.

Ask your local office for any written information on the standards and levels of service that you can expect, including targets for the time it should take to deal with your claim. The DWP website also has information about standards and complaints. All DWP agencies should also be able to provide you with written details about how to complain.

The DWP's preferred method of dealing with complaints is by telephone. If the DWP cannot contact you by phone, it should respond in writing. You can also request that any response is made in writing. All 'tier two' complaints (see below) should receive a written response.

If you are unhappy about how a particular DWP agency has dealt with your case, first contact the office that dealt with your claim. You should receive a response within 15 days.

If you are still dissatisfied, your complaint is passed to a complaints resolution manager. This is referred to as a 'tier one' complaint. S/he should contact you by telephone within 48 hours of receiving your complaint and keep you updated about its progress. Your complaint should be dealt with within 15 days.

If you remain dissatisfied, you can ask for your complaint to be passed to a more senior DWP officer. The DWP refers to this as a 'tier two' complaint. If you

Part 10: Getting a benefit decision changed
Chapter 61: Complaints
4. Complaining about HM Revenue and Customs

are still not satisfied, you can complain to the Independent Case Examiner (see below). You may also have grounds to make a complaint to the Ombudsman.

Further details on the complaints procedure for each agency can be found on the DWP website (see Appendix 1).

Complaining to the Independent Case Examiner

The Independent Case Examiner's Office (ICE) deals with complaints about DWP agencies and its contracted providers.

A complaint can only be made to the ICE if you have already completed the complaints procedure of the particular agency concerned. This usually means that you have had a response to a tier-2 complaint. A complaint should be made to the ICE no later than six months after the final response from the agency you are complaining about.

Complaints can be made in writing (including email) or by telephone (see Appendix 1). An appointed representative can act on your behalf. The complaint form can be downloaded from the ICE website. You must give all the relevant information, including the agency you are complaining about.

The ICE will first consider whether or not it can accept the complaint. If it can, it attempts to settle it by suggesting ways in which you and the agency concerned can come to an agreement. If this fails, the ICE prepares a formal report, setting out how the complaint arose and how it believes it should be settled. The ICE considers whether there has been maladministration. It cannot deal with matters of law or cases that are subject to judicial review or other legal procedures, or cases under appeal.

If you are unhappy with the way the ICE dealt with your case, first use the ICE internal complaints process. If you remain unhappy, ask your MP to consider referring your concerns to the Parliamentary and Health Service Ombudsman (see p1388).

4. **Complaining about HM Revenue and Customs**

If you want to complain about how HM Revenue and Customs (HMRC) has dealt with your tax credit, child benefit or guardian's allowance claim, or with your national insurance credits or contributions, first raise the complaint with the office dealing with your case, or the named contact person on the letters you have received.

If you are not happy with the response, ask for it to be passed to an HMRC complaints handler. If you are dissatisfied with her/his response, you can ask that your complaint be reviewed by another complaints handler.

If you are not happy with HMRC's reply, you can ask the Adjudicator to look into it (see below).

HMRC's complaints procedure is set out in its factsheet, *Complaints* (C/FS), available on its website (see Appendix 1).

Complaining to the Adjudicator

The Adjudicator's Office investigates complaints about HMRC and is similar in nature to the Independent Case Examiner (see p1384). Complaints can be made about delays, inappropriate staff behaviour, misleading advice or any other form of maladministration. The Adjudicator cannot, however, investigate disputes about matters of law. The Adjudicator only investigates a complaint if you have first exhausted the HMRC internal complaints procedure. A complaint should be made within six months of the final correspondence with HMRC.[2]

The Adjudicator can recommend that compensation be paid. HMRC has undertaken to follow her/his recommendations in all but exceptional circumstances.

Is it worth complaining?

In 2012/13, the Adjudicator upheld 64 per cent of complaints it received about benefits and tax credits. The majority of these were about overpayments, and resulted in write-offs and recommended compensation in excess of £800,000.

If you are unhappy with the Adjudicator's response, ask your MP to put your complaint to the Parliamentary and Health Service Ombudsman (see p1388). As well as looking at your complaint about HMRC, the Ombudsman may also look into the way in which the Adjudicator has investigated your complaint. Further information about the Adjudicator can be found on the Adjudicator's Office website (see Appendix 1).

5. Complaining about a local authority

If you are unhappy about the actions of your local authority and wish to make a complaint, ask for a copy of its complaints policy. Local authorities are required to have an effective complaints procedure, which should be made available to the public. If you are unable to obtain the policy or there is no formal complaints procedure, write to the supervisor of the person dealing with your claim, making it clear why you are dissatisfied. If you do not receive a satisfactory reply, take up the matter with someone more senior in the department and, ultimately, the principal officer. Send a copy of the letter to your ward councillor and to the councillor who chairs the relevant committee responsible (eg, for housing benefit)

Part 10: Getting a benefit decision changed
Chapter 61: Complaints
6. Complaining about HM Courts and Tribunals Service

– local authority officers are always accountable to the councillors. If this does not produce results, or if the delay is causing you severe hardship, consider a complaint to the Ombudsman (see p1388) or court action.

Government departments also monitor local authorities, so you could contact your MP or write to the relevant minister – eg, the Secretary of State for Work and Pensions.

If you want to make a complaint about an elected member of a council, you must write to the local authority.

In England, the Localism Act requires all local authorities to promote and maintain high standards of conduct by elected members. However, they can choose whether or not to set up standards committees to consider complaints about the conduct of councillors. The practice may therefore vary and you should ask your local authority for its procedure for complaints against members.

In Wales and Scotland, elected members of a council are subject to a code of conduct. Complaints about Scottish councillors can be made to the Commissioner for Ethical Standards in Public Life in Scotland who can refer cases to the Standards Commission for Scotland (see Appendix 1). Complaints about Welsh councillors can be made to the Public Services Ombudsman for Wales (see Appendix 1).

6. Complaining about HM Courts and Tribunals Service

Complaints about the administration of your appeal

HM Courts and Tribunals Service (HMCTS) provides administrative support to the First-tier Tribunal and Upper Tribunal. If you are dissatisfied with the administration of your appeal, complain to HMCTS. Raise your complaint initially with the person who has been dealing with your appeal. Her/his name and telephone number should be on all the correspondence you have received. You should receive a response to your complaint within 10 working days. If you are not happy with the response, write to the senior manager at the same office and ask for a review. You should receive a response within 10 working days.

If you think the matter has still not been resolved satisfactorily, appeal to the Complaints, Correspondence and Litigation Team (CCLT) at HMCTS (the senior manager who dealt with your complaint should give you contact details). This is not an independent appeal, but an internal review of how the complaint has been handled. It is the final stage of the internal complaints procedure. HMCTS aims to respond within 15 days.

If you are dissatisfied with the CCLT response, you can complain to the Parliamentary and Health Service Ombudsman in England and Wales or the Scottish Public Services Ombudsman (see p1388).

The leaflet *Unhappy With Our Service: what can you do?* (EX343) is available from the HMCTS website at www.justice.gov.uk/complaints/hm-courts-and-tribunal-service.

Complaints about the conduct of panel members

If you are unhappy about the way in which you were treated by a tribunal member (eg, because s/he was discourteous or racist), raise the matter initially by writing to the tribunal judge of the region in which the appeal was heard. You should receive an acknowledgement of your complaint within five working days of its being received. The judge then investigates the complaint.

If the complaint is about the conduct of the regional judge, it should be made to the President of HMCTS. If your complaint is about the President, it should be made to the Lord Chancellor.

The leaflet *The Tribunal Complaints Procedure* (JCI03) is available at the Judicial Conduct Investigations Office website (see Appendix 1).

7. Using your MP

If you are not satisfied with the reply from the officers to whom you have written, you may wish to take up the matter with your MP.

Most MPs have 'surgeries' in their areas where they meet constituents to discuss problems. You can get the details from your MP's website or local library. You can either go to the surgery or write to your MP with details of your complaint. To find out who your MP is, contact the House of Commons Information Office on 020 7219 4272 or go to http://findyourmp.parliament.uk.

Your MP will probably want to write to the benefit authority for an explanation of what has happened. If you wish to make a complaint to the relevant Ombudsman, you must usually do so through your MP. This does not apply if you are complaining to the Ombudsman about a local authority.

8. Complaining to the Ombudsman

The role of the Ombudsman is to investigate complaints of maladministration by government departments, including avoidable delays, failure to advise about appeal rights, refusal to answer reasonable questions or respond to correspondence, discourteousness, racism or sexism. The Parliamentary and Health Service Ombudsman deals with complaints about central government departments and the Local Government Ombudsman (in England) or the Public

Part 10: Getting a benefit decision changed
Chapter 61: Complaints
8. Complaining to the Ombudsman

Services Ombudsman (in Scotland and Wales) hears complaints about local government.

Should you ask for compensation first?

It is probably better to pursue a compensation payment before making a complaint to the Ombudsman. This is because, if the Ombudsman does not uphold your complaint, the particular benefit authority is likely to resist compensating you. Wherever possible, get and keep receipts for expenses such as postage, phone calls, travel and professional advice to help prove the cost of any delay or maladministration.

The Ombudsman does not usually investigate a complaint unless you have exhausted the internal complaints procedure. However, if the authority is not acting on your complaint, or there are unreasonable delays, this delay may also form part of your complaint. The time limit for lodging a complaint with the Ombudsman is normally 12 months from the date you were notified of the matter complained about. However, a delay in bringing a complaint does not necessarily prevent a complaint being heard if there are good reasons for the delay.

The Ombudsman can look at documents on your claim held by benefit authorities. You may be interviewed to check any facts. The Ombudsman can recommend financial compensation if you have been unfairly treated or experienced a loss as a result of the maladministration.

A public body, such as the DWP or a local authority, is required to follow the recommendations of a complaints panel unless there are good reasons not to. If it has failed to do so, you may have grounds to complain to the Ombudsman and, in some circumstances, may have grounds for a judicial review.

The Parliamentary and Health Service Ombudsman

The Parliamentary and Health Service Ombudsman deals with complaints about all central government departments. This includes the DWP, HM Revenue and Customs, HM Courts and Tribunals Service and any agencies carrying out functions on behalf of these departments. In order to make a complaint, you must write to your MP, who then refers the complaint to the Ombudsman. See p1387 for how to contact your MP. Remember, the Ombudsman can only investigate complaints of maladministration and not complaints about entitlement, which should be dealt with by the First-tier Tribunal.

The Local Government Ombudsman/Public Services Ombudsman

If you have tried to sort out your complaint with the local authority but you are still not satisfied with the outcome, you can apply to the Local Government Ombudsman (in England) or the Public Services Ombudsman (in Wales and

0

Scotland). The Ombudsman can investigate any cases of maladministration by local authorities, but not matters of entitlement, which are dealt with by the First-tier Tribunal.

You can complain to the Ombudsman either in writing (including online) or by telephone (see Appendix 1). Straightforward cases can be dealt with in about three months. A complaint may make the authority review its procedures, which could benefit other claimants.

One outcome of your complaint may be a 'local settlement'. This is where the local authority agrees to take some action that the Ombudsman considers is a satisfactory response to your complaint and the investigation is discontinued. If you are unhappy with the way in which the Ombudsman has dealt with your complaint, seek legal advice as quickly as possible.

9. Legal action

It is not possible to sue a benefit authority for negligence in the way it decides your claim.[3] Instead, if a decision is wrong, you can apply for a revision or supersession, or appeal against it. However, you can seek compensation through the courts if there has been:

- 'misadvice' – ie, if an employee of a benefit authority or HM Courts and Tribunals Service gives wrong advice which leads to some financial loss for you;
- unpaid benefit – ie, if your benefit claim has been determined, but you have not been paid;
- a breach of human rights.

Although it is possible to seek compensation through the courts, it should never be your first course of action and should only ever be considered after seeking legal advice.

If a benefit authority refuses to process your claim, you may have grounds for a judicial review. Seek legal advice.

Notes

1. Grounds for a complaint
1 Reg 89(2) HB Regs; reg 70(2) HB(SPC)
   Regs

4. Complaining about HM Revenue and Customs
2 For further details, see CPAG's *Tax Credits and Complaints* factsheet at www.cpag.org.uk/content/tax-credits-and-complaints.

9. Legal action
3 *Jones v Department of Employment* [1989] QB 1 (CA)

Chapter 62

Discrimination and human rights

This chapter covers:
1. European law and discrimination between men and women (below)
2. The Human Rights Act (p1394)

Key facts

- If the benefit rules treat you and others in a similar situation worse than another group of people, this may be unlawful under European law or under the Human Rights Act 1998.
- If the less favourable treatment is based on your sex, the European Equal Treatment Directive 79/7 may help you.
- If the less favourable treatment is based on your sex, race, colour, language, religion, political or other opinion, national or social origin, association with a national minority, property, birth or other status, or on another ground, the Human Rights Act may help you.
- The Human Rights Act can help you if the benefit rules breach some of its other provisions, including the right to a fair trial, the right to a private and family life and the right to peaceful enjoyment of your possessions.

1. European law and discrimination between men and women

Social security benefits are not governed by British law alone. Regulations and Directives made by the European Union (EU) apply in the UK and throughout the European Economic Area (EEA) – eg, to ensure that (subject to limited exceptions) social security benefits, occupational pensions, pay and other benefits from employment are received on an equal basis by both men and women. This chapter deals only with the European Equal Treatment Directive (Directive 79/7). This prevents discrimination in social security between men and women. For other EU provisions, see Chapter 72.

Part 10: Getting a benefit decision changed
Chapter 62: Discrimination and human rights
1. European law and discrimination between men and women

British courts (including decision makers, the First-tier Tribunal and the Upper Tribunal) must apply EU law as well as domestic British law and, although British law has been amended to take these Directives into account, the EU rules override the British rules where the two still conflict.[1] Cases involving points of EU law that are not clear may be referred to the Court of Justice of the European Union (CJEU) in Luxembourg for a ruling. The CJEU is not the same as the European Court of Human Rights, which is an institution of the Council of Europe and operates from Strasbourg.

This *Handbook* cannot cover the subject comprehensively. What follows is an outline of the general principles and what they mean in practical terms for people claiming benefits. If you think you may benefit from the principle of equal treatment, seek advice (see Appendix 2).

The principle of equal treatment

The 'principle of equal treatment' is that there must be no direct or indirect discrimination whatsoever on the ground of your sex, particularly in respect of your marital or family status.[2]

However, this principle is subject to a number of limitations and exceptions. To work out whether there is discrimination against you, you must ask three questions.

- Is the benefit you are claiming (or your liability to pay contributions) covered by Directive 79/7 (see p1393)?
- Are you personally covered by Directive 79/7 (see p1393)?
- Do any of the exceptions apply in your case (see p1394)?

Discrimination

'Discrimination' means treating one person less favourably than another. It can also encompass failing to treat different groups differently without justification.[3]

'Indirect discrimination' occurs when a rule appears to apply equally to both men and women but, in practice, can be satisfied by fewer members of one sex than the other and where that rule cannot be justified for reasons other than discrimination based on sex.

For example, a rule saying that applicants for a job have to be at least 1.9m tall would be indirectly discriminatory even though it applied equally to women and men. This is because, in practice, fewer women than men are likely to qualify. Such a rule would be unlawful unless the employer could show a good, non-discriminatory reason for employing only tall people.

Note: you cannot argue that a rule discriminates against you just because it differentiates between married (or cohabiting) people and single people.[4] On the other hand, a rule which differentiates between married men and married women or single men and single women is directly discriminatory on grounds of sex.

10

Which benefits are covered

The principle of equal treatment applies to schemes for state benefits that are designed to protect against specific 'risks'.

The risks[5]

Sickness, invalidity, old age, accidents at work and occupational diseases, and unemployment.

The benefits covered are:
- most contributory benefits;
- certain non-contributory benefits, such as carer's allowance, severe disablement allowance and industrial injuries benefits;[6]
- in some cases, benefits that are intended to supplement or replace the benefits referred to above – eg, income-based jobseeker's allowance (JSA), pension credit and both types of employment and support allowance (ESA).[7]

Income support and housing benefit are not covered by Directive 79/7, so discrimination arguments about these benefits must be brought under alternative provisions – eg, the Human Rights Act (see p1394).

Note: certain risks are specifically excluded – in particular, positive discrimination for maternity allowances and the different pension ages for men and women. Widows' and widowers' benefits and family benefits (eg, child benefit and child tax credit) are also excluded from the scope of the Directive.

Who is covered

You are personally covered if you are a member of the working population. If you are not a member of the working population, you cannot use the principle of equal treatment to stop the government discriminating against you, even if the benefit which you are claiming is covered.

The working population

You count as a member of the 'working population' if you:[8]
– are an employed worker;
– are self-employed;
– are seeking employment;
– were employed or self-employed, but your job has been interrupted by illness, accident or involuntary unemployment;
– were employed or self-employed, but you have retired or become unable to work because of invalidity.

Part 10: Getting a benefit decision changed
Chapter 62: Discrimination and human rights
2. The Human Rights Act

You must have been either working or actively looking for work when you became affected by one of the risks on p1393.[9] So, for example, you are not covered if:

- you have been so ill or disabled since before you reached the age of 16 that you have never been able to contemplate working or looking for work; *or*
- you stopped working for a reason not included in the list of risks on p1393 (eg, because you were pregnant) and before you began to look for work again you became too ill to work.

The risks do not have to be experienced by you personally – eg, if you gave up work to look after your severely disabled mother, you count as a member of the working population because your work was interrupted by invalidity, even though it was your mother's, not your own.[10]

Exceptions to the principle of equal treatment

In some cases, the government can discriminate against you.
Discriminatory rules which may be lawful are those which:[11]

- set a different age for men and women to become entitled to retirement pensions. This also covers rules that deal with the possible consequences for other benefits of having different pension ages;
- allow people who have looked after children to claim retirement pensions and other benefits on advantageous terms;
- allow special treatment for people who, before 22 December 1984, opted 'not to acquire rights or incur obligations under a statutory scheme'. This is intended to cover the rules on married women's reduced national insurance contributions (see p846).

Equal treatment and benefits

Over the years, many cases have been argued in the courts. The main areas of dispute concerned:

- the difference in pension age between men and women;
- shared care of children between mothers and fathers;
- discrimination in the income-based JSA rules;
- the anti-test case rules (see p1296); *and*
- gender recognition.

For detailed information, see pp1243–47 of the 2012/13 edition of this *Handbook*.

2. **The Human Rights Act**

The Human Rights Act 1998 incorporates into UK law most of the Articles of the European Convention on Human Rights. All legislation must be applied, *so far as it is possible to do so*, in a way which is compatible with this Convention.[12] This duty applies to all social security decision makers – eg, Secretary of State decision makers, the First-tier Tribunal and the Upper Tribunal.[13]

The First-tier Tribunal, Upper Tribunal or court must take into account any relevant caselaw of the European Court of Human Rights (ECtHR) when deciding an appeal in which a human rights issue arises.[14] However, if there is a conflict between a UK court and the ECtHR, the decision of the UK court should generally be followed.[15]

Relevant Articles of the Convention

The Articles of the Convention most likely to be relevant in social security are:
- Article 6(1): right to a fair and public hearing within a reasonable time by an independent and impartial tribunal;
- Article 8: right to respect for private and family life, home and correspondence;
- Article 1 of the First Protocol: right to peaceful enjoyment of possessions and the right not to be deprived of them;
- Article 14: prohibition of discrimination (although you cannot rely on this alone; it can only be used if it is linked to the enjoyment of one of the other rights under the Convention).

In addition, Article 2 of the First Protocol (right to education) could be relevant. For detailed information, see pp1247–51 of the 2012/13 edition of this *Handbook*.

Note: Article 14 will often be needed in social security cases to supplement the other Articles because of the difficulty of bringing social security within those Articles.

Using the Human Rights Act

For most social security cases, there are no special courts or procedures that need to be used if you want to bring a challenge that relies on the Human Rights Act. Arguments using the Act can, therefore, be used at the First-tier Tribunal and the Upper Tribunal, and the ordinary time limits for bringing such challenges apply (see Chapter 59).[16] In addition, guidance has been issued concerning social security appeals, which recommends the following.[17]
- You should raise any Human Rights Act challenge as early as possible – eg, in your grounds for appeal.
- Your grounds for appeal need to:
  - identify the rule, regulation or practice which you allege breaches the Act and the Article(s) of the Convention;
  - set out the Articles of the Convention which you claim have been breached, and explain why; *and*
  - set out the relevant supporting caselaw (and provide copies of the cases).

Part 10: Getting a benefit decision changed
Chapter 62: Discrimination and human rights
Notes

· ·

If you fail to do the above and merely state that the decision is in breach of the Human Rights Act, you are unlikely to succeed. Raising a Human Rights Act argument for the first time at your appeal hearing, when it could have reasonably been raised in advance, will almost certainly lead to an adjournment of the appeal.

Note: challenges in social security using the Human Rights Act and the Convention are difficult and need specialist input. If you have a case in which a Human Rights Act argument arises, seek specialist advice (see Appendix 2).

Notes

· ·

1. European law and discrimination between men and women
1 s2 ECA 1972
2 Art 4(1) Directive 79/7/EEC
3 *Burnip v Birmingham CC and SSWP and others* [2012] EWCA Civ; [2013] AACR 7
4 R(SB) 6/91
5 Art 3(1)(a) Directive 79/7/EEC
6 *Thomas v Secretary of State for Social Security*, C-328/91 [1993] ECR, unreported
7 Art 3(1)(b) Directive 79/7/EEC; R(JSA) 3/02; *Hockenjos v Secretary of State for Social Security* [2001] EWCA Civ 624 (CA); CPC/4177/2005
8 Art 2 Directive 79/7/EEC
9 *Achterberg-te Riele and Others v Sociale Verzekeringsbank*, C-48/88, C-106-107/88 [1989]
10 *Drake v CAO*, C-150/85 [1986] ECR, unreported
11 Art 7(1) Directive 79/7/EEC

2. The Human Rights Act
12 s3(1) HRA 1998
13 See definition of 'public authority' in s6(3) HRA 1998
14 s2(1) HRA 1998
15 *Leeds CC v Price* [2006] UKHL 10
16 s7(5) HRA 1998
17 President's Protocol No.6, *Handling Questions Under the Human Rights Act 1998*, 14 July 2000

Part 11

General rules for tax credits

Chapter 63

Tax credit amounts

This chapter covers:
1. The relevant period (below)
2. The maximum amount of child tax credit (p1400)
3. The maximum amount of working tax credit (p1402)
4. How to calculate the amount of tax credit (p1410)
5. Change of circumstances (p1415)

Key facts

- The amount of tax credits to which you are entitled depends on your family circumstances and your income.
- There are no limits on the amount of savings or other capital that you can have.
- If you are entitled to income support (IS), income-based jobseeker's allowance (JSA), income-related employment and support allowance (ESA) or pension credit (PC), you are automatically entitled to the maximum amount of tax credits that you could receive.
- If you are not entitled to IS, income-based JSA, income-related ESA or PC, you may receive less than your maximum amount of tax credits, depending on the level of your income.
- Your maximum amount of child tax credit depends on how many children you have, and whether any child in your family has a disability.
- The amount of working tax credit depends on whether you are single with no dependants, a lone parent, or a member of a couple, the hours you work, whether you (or your partner) are disabled, and whether you have eligible childcare costs.

1. The relevant period

The amount of tax credits you can receive is based on your entitlement during a 'relevant period'. Tax credit awards are calculated using a maximum *annual* amount that you could receive. If you claim at the beginning of the new tax year, your award is usually calculated on the basis that you will be entitled to tax

Part 11: General rules for tax credits
Chapter 63: Tax credit amounts
2. The maximum amount of child tax credit

credits for the whole of that tax year (6 April to 5 April), and your relevant period is therefore one year.[1] Your annual entitlement is calculated and then paid to you over the course of that year.

If you claim tax credits after the beginning of a tax year, your award is calculated for a period beginning with the date on which you make your claim and ending at the end of that tax year, unless you can have your claim backdated to an earlier period (see p1446). Similarly, if your circumstances change in the course of the year, and your award is amended, a new relevant period begins. The new relevant period is calculated on the basis that it will end at the end of the tax year.[2] In both of these cases, you are entitled to tax credits for less than a year, and so only a proportion of the annual amount can be paid.

In order to work out your maximum amount of tax credits, therefore, you must know the length of your relevant period.

Relevant period

A 'relevant period' for child tax credit (CTC) is the number of days in a period of an award during which your maximum amount remains the same.[3]

A 'relevant period' for working tax credit (WTC) is the number of days in a period during which the elements making up your maximum amount of tax credit (apart from the childcare element) remain the same and your average weekly childcare charge does not change by £10 or more or reduce to nil.[4]

If you are entitled to both CTC and WTC, a 'relevant period' is one during which both of the above conditions are satisfied.[5]

---

2. **The maximum amount of child tax credit**

The maximum amount of child tax credit (CTC) you can get is calculated by adding together the 'elements' that apply to you.[6] The amount of each element is set at a yearly rate. The annual rate is converted to a daily rate by dividing by the number of days in the tax year (365 in 2014/15) and rounding *up* to the nearest penny. To calculate entitlement, the daily rate of each element is then multiplied by the number of days in the relevant period. The effect of this is that entitlement in a whole year is always slightly higher than the annual rates listed on p1401 – eg, the family element (£1.50 x 365) works out as £547.50 in 2014/15. If you are entitled to CTC for a period of less than a year, or if your entitlement changes part way through the year, the amount of each of these elements is adjusted so that the correct proportion of your annual maximum amount is paid to you.[7] How entitlement is calculated when entitlement changes part way through a tax year is explained on p1415.

Element	Daily rate	Annual rate
Family element	£1.50	£545
Child element	£7.54	£2,750
Disabled child element	£8.49	£3,100
Severely disabled child element	£3.44	£1,255

- One family element is payable for your family (see p174 for who counts). The amount is not affected by how many children you have, or their ages, or whether you are a lone parent or one of a couple.
- You get a child element for each child in your family (see p151 for when a child or young person counts as a member of your family).
- You get a disabled child element for any child in your family who gets disability living allowance (DLA), or young person who gets personal independence payment (PIP), or who is registered blind or who has been taken off the register in the last 28 weeks. The element still applies if DLA or PIP has stopped because your child or young person is in hospital.[8] It is paid in addition to the child element for that child.
- You get a severely disabled child element for each child in your family who gets the highest rate of the care component of DLA, or for each young person who gets the enhanced rate for daily living of PIP. The element still applies if DLA or PIP has stopped because your child or young person is in hospital.[9] It is paid in addition to the child element and disabled child element for that child.
- A qualifying young person who is entitled to armed forces independence payment is entitled to the disabled child element and severely disabled child element.

Note: the legislation only refers to a 'child element', payable at different annual rates if the child is disabled or severely disabled. In practice, HM Revenue and Customs (HMRC) refers to a 'disabled child element' and a 'severely disabled child element', paid in addition to the basic child element. This means that the 'disabled child element' works out as £8.50 per day, rather than £8.49 as calculated according to the legislation.

Example

Tracy is a lone parent with two children aged five and three. The annual elements used when calculating her maximum amount are as follows:

Family element	£545
Child element for three-year-old child	£2,750
Child element for five-year-old child	£2,750

Part 11: General rules for tax credits
Chapter 63: Tax credit amounts
3. The maximum amount of working tax credit

3. The maximum amount of working tax credit

The maximum amount of working tax credit (WTC) you get is calculated by adding together the 'elements' that apply to you.[10] The amount of each element, except the childcare element, is set at a yearly rate. The annual rate is converted to a daily rate by dividing by the number of days in the tax year (365 in 2014/15) and rounding up to the nearest penny. To calculate entitlement, the daily rate of each element is then multiplied by the number of days in the relevant period. The effect of this is that entitlement in a whole year is always slightly higher than the annual rates listed below – eg, the basic element works out as £1,941.80 in 2014/15. The amount of the childcare element is set using your average *weekly* childcare costs.[11] See p1405 for how your childcare element is calculated.

If you are entitled to WTC for a period of less than a year, or if your entitlement changes part way through the year, the amount of the elements is adjusted so that the correct proportion of your annual maximum amount is paid.[12] See p1415 for how your entitlement is calculated when it changes part way through a tax year.

Element	Daily rate	Annual rate
Basic element	£5.32	£1,940
Lone parent element	£5.46	£1,990
Couple element	£5.46	£1,990
30-hour element	£2.20	£800
Disabled worker element	£8.05	£2,935
Severe disability element	£3.44	£1,255
Childcare element. For this, see p1405.		

Basic element

One basic element is paid with each award of WTC. To be entitled to this element, you must be engaged in 'qualifying remunerative work'. In this *Handbook* we call this 'full-time paid work' (see p165).[13] Unless you qualify for the basic element of WTC, you cannot qualify for any of the other elements.[14]

Lone parent element

You get the lone parent element if you claim as a single person and are responsible for a child or qualifying young person.[15]

Couple element

You get the couple element if you are a couple making a joint claim (see p1438).[16] You still make a joint claim but you cannot get the couple element if your partner is serving a prison sentence of more than 12 months or is a 'person subject to immigration control' (see p1500), unless you or your partner are responsible for a child or qualifying young person.[17] You can only have one couple element included in your maximum amount.[18] For when you count as a couple, see p1438.

30-hour element

You get a 30-hour element if you are:[19]
- a single claimant who works for at least 30 hours a week; *or*
- making a joint claim and either or both of you work for at least 30 hours a week; *or*
- making a joint claim, responsible for a child or qualifying young person, and:
  - you are both working; *and*
  - one of you works at least 16 hours a week; *and*
  - your joint hours of work total at least 30 hours a week.

You can only have one 30-hour element included in your maximum amount.[20]

Disabled worker element

You get a disabled worker element if you:[21]
- work at least 16 hours a week; *and*
- have a disability which puts you at a disadvantage in getting a job; *and*
- receive, or have recently received, a qualifying benefit for sickness or disability.

If you are claiming as a couple, at least one of you must satisfy all these conditions – ie, the element is not payable if only you are working and your partner is disabled.

If both you and your partner meet all these conditions, two disabled worker elements can be paid.[22]

Having 'a disability which puts you at a disadvantage in getting a job' means you must meet any one of the conditions listed in Appendix 9. For initial claims only (where there has been no entitlement to the disabled worker element in the preceding two years), this can include undergoing a period of rehabilitation as a result of an illness or accident, but only for the remainder of the tax year in which you claim.

In order to count as receiving a 'qualifying benefit', you must satisfy one of the following conditions. A disabled worker element can be included in your maximum amount in a new claim or added to an existing tax credit award at any time during the tax year if you report a change (see p1415). You must:
- for at least one day in the 182 days immediately preceding your claim, have been in receipt of:
  - incapacity benefit (IB) at the long-term or short-term higher rate; *or*
  - severe disablement allowance (SDA); *or*

11

Part 11: General rules for tax credits
Chapter 63: Tax credit amounts
3. The maximum amount of working tax credit

- employment and support allowance (ESA) for at least 28 weeks (including linked periods); *or*
- credits for limited capability for work following the end of the entitlement period of contributory ESA, for at least 28 weeks (including periods on ESA and linked periods); *or*
- ESA or credits (as above), together with IB, SDA or statutory sick pay (SSP) for at least 28 weeks (including linked periods); *or*
- for at least one day in the 182 days immediately preceding your claim, have been in receipt of a disability premium paid for you with income support (IS), income-based jobseeker's allowance (JSA), housing benefit, or a higher pensioner premium with IS or JSA; *or*
- have received for at least 140 days forming a single period of incapacity for work (see p814) or limited capability for work (see Chapter 47) (the last of which must have fallen within the 56 days of the date of the claim) SSP, occupational sick pay, ESA, or credits for limited capability for work for a period of 20 weeks; *and*
  - have a disability at the date of the claim which is likely to last for at least six months (or for the rest of your life if your death is expected within that time); *and*
  - have gross earnings that are less than they were before the disability began by at least the greater of 20 per cent and £15 a week; *or*
- have undertaken 'training for work' for at least one day in the 56 days immediately preceding the claim *and* were receiving one of the benefits or credits listed in the first bullet point within the 56 days before that training started. 'Training for work' means training provided under the Employment and Training Act 1973, or, in Scotland, the Enterprise and New Towns (Scotland) Act 1990, or training which you attend for 16 hours or more a week if its primary purpose is teaching occupational or vocational skills;[23] *or*
- receive disability living allowance (DLA), personal independence payment (PIP), attendance allowance (AA), armed forces independence payment or a mobility supplement or constant attendance allowance payable with a war pension or industrial injuries disablement benefit. If your qualifying benefit stops, you are no longer entitled to the disability element on these grounds;[24] *or*
- have an invalid carriage or similar vehicle.

Renewals or linked claims

If you make a further claim for WTC within 56 days of the day your previous award ended, *and* in that earlier claim you qualified for the disabled worker element under any of the first four bullet points above, you are treated as though you still meet those conditions and can continue to receive the disabled worker element in your new award. You must also still have a disability which puts you at a disadvantage in getting a job (see Appendix 9 – note that for renewals and new claims within two years of a previous entitlement to the disabled worker element this must be under Part 1[25]).

You can still benefit from this linking rule if your income was too high for you to receive any WTC within the previous 56 days, provided your maximum amount of WTC would have included the disabled worker element on one of the grounds on pp1403–04.[26]

Severe disability element

You get a severe disability element if you receive the highest rate of the care component of DLA, the enhanced rate of the daily living component of PIP, the higher rate of AA, or armed forces independence payment (including if payment of these has been suspended because you are in hospital).[27] If you have a partner who meets this condition, a severe disability element can be included for her/him, whether or not s/he is in work.

If both you and your partner meet the condition, two severe disability elements can be paid.[28]

Childcare element

Your maximum amount of WTC can include a childcare element to help meet the cost of 'relevant childcare' (see p1407).[29] This element is 70 per cent of your actual childcare costs of up to £175 a week for one child or £300 a week for two or more children – ie, up to £122.50 or £210 a week.[30]

To get the childcare element of WTC, you or your partner must be 'responsible for' at least one child.[31] You do not have to be the child's parent. 'Responsible for' has the same meaning for WTC as it does for child tax credit (CTC) (see p153).[32]

The childcare element is part of the maximum WTC calculation and cannot be claimed on its own or as part of CTC.[33]

You must be:[34]
- a lone parent working at least 16 hours a week; *or*
- a member of a couple; *and*
  - you are both working at least 16 hours a week; *or*
  - one of you is working at least 16 hours a week and the other is incapacitated (see p1406); *or*
  - one of you is working at least 16 hours a week and the other is entitled to carer's allowance (including an underlying entitlement); *or*
  - one of you is working at least 16 hours a week and the other is in hospital or in prison (serving a sentence or remanded in custody).

You are still entitled to the childcare element during periods throughout which you are treated as in work for WTC purposes – eg, during the first 39 weeks of maternity leave or the four-week run-on period (see p170).[35]

Part 11: General rules for tax credits
Chapter 63: Tax credit amounts
3. The maximum amount of working tax credit

Incapacitated

You or your partner are treated as '**incapacitated**' if you (or your partner, if s/he is the one who is not working):[36]

- get IB or SDA; *or*
- have been getting contributory ESA for at least 28 weeks; *or*
- get contributory ESA after a period on SSP, which adds up to at least 28 weeks, provided you satisfied the national insurance (NI) contribution conditions for contributory ESA (the 28 weeks can have been in one period or in periods that can be linked together); *or*
- get ESA after being transferred from IB or SDA; *or*
- are entitled to credits for limited capability for work only because your contributory ESA has stopped after 52 weeks; *or*
- get AA, DLA, PIP or armed forces independence payment (or an equivalent award paid as an increase under the war pensions or industrial injuries disablement scheme), or would get it but for the fact that you are in hospital; *or*
- get industrial injuries disablement benefit with constant attendance allowance; *or*
- have an award of housing benefit which includes a disability premium or a childcare earnings disregard, because the non-working member of the couple is incapacitated; *or*
- were treated as incapacitated solely on the basis of being paid council tax benefit on 31 March 2013 that included a disability premium because the non-working member of the couple was incapacitated, but only if your entitlement to WTC remains continuous from 1 April 2013); *or*
- have an invalid carriage or similar vehicle.

You can claim the childcare element for a new baby as well as for any other children for whom you are responsible while you are on statutory maternity, paternity or adoption leave (for the first 39 weeks only), or while you are paid maternity allowance. See p170 for these and other situations when you are treated as being in full-time work.

Relevant childcare charges can be for any child in your family up to the last day of the week in which 1 September falls, following the child's 15th birthday or her/his 16th birthday if s/he is disabled.[37]

Disabled child

'**Disabled child**' means a child or qualifying young person who:[38]

- receives DLA, PIP or armed forces independence payment, including if payment has been suspended because s/he is a hospital inpatient; *or*
- is registered blind; *or*
- has ceased to be registered blind in the 28 weeks immediately preceding the WTC claim.

Relevant childcare

In England, in order to be 'relevant childcare' the childcare must be:[39]
- provided by a childcare provider correctly registered by Ofsted;
- provided to a child who is three or four years old by a school under the direction of the school's governing body (or equivalent) on school premises or premises that may be inspected as part of an inspection of the school by the Chief Inspector;
- out-of-school-hours childcare or supervised activity-based childcare provided for a child aged between five and 15 years (16 if disabled) by a school on the school premises or premises that may be inspected as part of an inspection of the school by the Chief Inspector;
- provided by a domiciliary worker or nurse from an agency registered under the Domiciliary Care Agencies Regulations 2002 in the child's home;
- provided by a foster parent who is also registered with Ofsted, but not in respect of the child who is being fostered by that foster parent.

In Wales, in order to be 'relevant childcare', the childcare must be:[40]
- provided by a childcare provider registered by the Care and Social Services Inspectorate Wales;
- provided by an approved foster parent, who is providing daycare or childminding for a child aged eight or over, but not for a child who is being fostered by that foster parent. If the child is under eight, the foster parent must also be registered by the Care and Social Services Inspectorate Wales;
- out-of-school-hours childcare provided by a school on the school premises or by a local authority;
- provided by a person approved under the Tax Credits (Approval of Child Care Providers) (Wales) Scheme 2007 in the child's home or, if several children are being looked after, in one of the children's homes;
- provided by a domiciliary worker or nurse from an agency registered under the Domiciliary Care Agencies (Wales) Regulations 2004 in the child's home.

In Scotland, in order to be 'relevant childcare', the childcare must be:[41]
- provided by a childcare provider registered by the Care Inspectorate;
- in an out-of-school-hours childcare club registered by the Care Inspectorate;
- provided in the child's home by, or introduced through, a childcare agency, sitter service or nanny agency registered by the Care Inspectorate.

For Crown servants working abroad, relevant childcare also includes a childcare provider approved under a Ministry of Defence accreditation scheme abroad.

You cannot claim help with the costs of childcare provided in your own home if that care is provided by a relative of your child.

'**Relative**' means parent, grandparent, aunt or uncle, brother or sister, whether related by blood, marriage, civil partnership or 'affinity'.[42] By 'affinity', we

11

Part 11: General rules for tax credits
Chapter 63: Tax credit amounts
3. The maximum amount of working tax credit

understand that HM Revenue and Customs (HMRC) means people who are related through a partner, rather than a spouse or civil partner. For example, if childcare is provided in your home by your partner's mother, she is related to the child by affinity, even if your partner is not the child's parent, and so you cannot claim for the cost of paying her.

You can claim help with the costs of childcare provided by a relative away from your home, but s/he must also be a registered or approved childminder. In practice, it is unlikely that a childminder would be able to remain registered for long if only looking after a child to whom s/he was related – contact the relevant agency for advice in this situation. If approved under the Tax Credits (Approval of Child Care Providers) (Wales) Scheme 2007, s/he must also care for at least one other child who is not related to her/him.[43]

You can only claim for charges that you pay. If you receive childcare vouchers from your employer, you cannot claim for the amount covered by the voucher, so you should seek advice on whether you are better off accepting vouchers in exchange for part of your salary. You cannot claim the childcare element for free early years' entitlement or for charges in respect of the child's compulsory education or, in England, for childcare during school hours for a child of compulsory school age. If you will not be making payments for childcare until some time after you have claimed WTC, you cannot receive a childcare element for these until you start making the payments. If you have made an arrangement with a childcare provider to pay childcare costs, you can notify HMRC of these up to a week before the childcare is provided.[44]

The amount of the childcare element

Step one: work out your relevant period

Add the number of days in your relevant period (see p1399). If you are making a claim for tax credits before the beginning of a new tax year, your award is usually based on entitlement at the same rate for a whole tax year, and your relevant period is one year. The tax year 2014/15 has 365 days.

Step two: calculate your relevant childcare charge

Your 'relevant childcare charge' is your average weekly charge. The way in which your average weekly charge is calculated depends on whether you pay for childcare weekly, monthly or at some other interval, and on whether the amount you pay varies over time.[45]

- If you pay for childcare on a weekly basis and the charge is a fixed weekly amount, add together the charges in the most recent four weeks before the claim and divide by four.
- If you pay for childcare on a weekly basis, have paid for childcare for at least 52 weeks and the charge varies over time, add together the charges in the 52 weeks before the claim and divide by 52.

- If you pay on a monthly basis and the charge is a fixed monthly amount, multiply that monthly amount by 12 and divide the total by 52.
- If you pay on a monthly basis and the charge varies from month to month, add together the charges for the last 12 months and divide the total by 52.
- If there is insufficient information for HMRC to establish your average weekly charge by any of the above methods, the charge is calculated on the basis of information you provide about your childcare costs, using any method which, in its opinion, is reasonable.
- If you have entered into an agreement to pay for childcare that will be provided during the period of your award, your average weekly childcare costs are calculated on the basis of your own written estimate of these. In practice, you provide this estimate on your tax credit claim form.
- If you are only paying childcare costs for a fixed period (eg, over the summer holidays), your relevant childcare charge can be averaged and paid over that period rather than over the whole year.

When you have calculated your average weekly childcare charges by one of these methods, round the figure up to the nearest whole pound.

Step three: calculate your childcare costs for the relevant period
The weekly amount from Step two is converted to an amount covering your relevant period. Multiply the weekly charge by 52 to calculate the annual amount. Divide this figure by the number of days in the current tax year to find the daily rate, and then multiply this daily rate by the number of days in your relevant period. This gives your childcare costs for the relevant period.[46]

Step four: calculate your maximum eligible childcare costs for the relevant period
Divide the maximum eligible weekly childcare costs that apply to you by seven, to find the daily rate. The maximum eligible weekly amount is £175 for one child, and £300 for two or more children. Round this figure up to the nearest penny and then multiply this daily rate by the number of days in the relevant period.

Step five: calculate the childcare element for the relevant period
Take the lower of the two figures from Steps three and four, and calculate 70 per cent of that figure. Round the amount up to the nearest penny. This gives your childcare element for the relevant period.

Example

Tracy pays a fixed amount of £200 every week in eligible childcare costs for her two children. Her childcare element for the whole of the tax year is calculated as follows.

Step one
Tracy's relevant period is one year (365 days).

Part 11: General rules for tax credits
Chapter 63: Tax credit amounts
4. How to calculate the amount of tax credit

Step two
Her relevant childcare charge is £200. (This is her average weekly charge.)

Step three
£200 x 52 = £10,400
(£10,400 ÷ 365) x 365 = £10,400

Step four
The maximum weekly eligible childcare cost for Tracy is £300, as she has two children.
The daily rate is £300 ÷ 7 = £42.86 (rounded up to the nearest penny).
The annual rate is £42.86 x 365 = £15,643.90

Step five
The lower figure from Steps three and four is her actual costs of £10,400.
Childcare element is 70% x £10,400 = £7,280
Tracy's childcare element for the relevant period (in this case, one whole tax year) is £7,280.

---

4. How to calculate the amount of tax credit

If you are receiving certain benefits

If you or your partner are entitled to income support (IS), income-based jobseeker's allowance (JSA), income-related employment and support allowance (ESA) or pension credit (PC), you are automatically entitled to the maximum amount of child tax credit (CTC) or working tax credit (WTC). **Note:** this does not apply to WTC during the four-week 'run-on' period after stopping work (see p1720).[47] You calculate the maximum amount by adding together the elements of each tax credit for which you qualify over your relevant period, as described on pp1400–09. Your maximum amount is not subject to any reduction during the period you are receiving IS, income-based JSA, income-related ESA or PC, regardless of your income in the rest of the current or previous tax year (but see Chapter 66 if an overpayment is being recovered from your award).

If you are not receiving certain benefits

If you or your partner are *not* receiving IS, income-based JSA, income-related ESA or PC, your entitlement is worked out as described below. **Note:** the rates, taper, disregard and thresholds apply to entitlement in 2014/15. To calculate tax credits entitlement for earlier years, see previous editions of this *Handbook*.

Step one: work out your relevant period

Add the number of days in your relevant period (see p1399). If you are making a claim for tax credits at the beginning of a new tax year, your award is based on entitlement at the same rate for a whole tax year, and your relevant period is one year. The tax year 2014/15 has 365 days.

Step two: calculate your maximum entitlement for the relevant period

First, identify the different elements of each tax credit for which you are eligible. Take the daily rate (see pxx) of each element apart from the childcare element of WTC.

Multiply this daily rate by the number of days in the relevant period. Add the adjusted amounts of each element together. Next, calculate your childcare element for the relevant period as described on p1408.

Add the childcare element for the relevant period to the other elements for the relevant period to find your maximum entitlement for the relevant period.

Step three: work out your relevant income

The income used in the tax credit calculation is your 'relevant income' (see Chapter 64).

HM Revenue and Customs (HMRC) begins by using your previous tax year's income.

At the end of the tax year, it compares your previous year's income with your current year's income. If your income has not changed, the current year's income is used. If your income has changed by less than a disregarded amount, your entitlement is still based on the previous year's income. If your income has changed by more than a disregarded amount, your entitlement is based on the current year's income after the disregard. Your relevant income is calculated as follows.[48]

- If your current year's income is more than your previous year's income but the difference is £5,000 or less, your previous year's income is used.
- If your current year's income is more than your previous year's income but the difference is more than £5,000, your current year's income minus £5,000 is used.
- If your current year's income is less than your previous year's income but the difference is £2,500 or less, your current year's income is used.
- If your current year's income is less than your previous year's income and the difference is more than £2,500, your current year's income plus £2,500 is used.

Divide this income by the number of days in the tax year to which your claim for tax credits relates (365 in 2014/15) to find the daily rate, then multiply this by the

Part 11: General rules for tax credits
Chapter 63: Tax credit amounts
4. How to calculate the amount of tax credit

number of days in the relevant period. Round this amount down to the nearest penny. This is your relevant income. See p1418 for more on relevant income, including if your tax credit award is finalised during the year because you become entitled to universal credit.

Step four: compare your income with the threshold

Find the annual threshold that applies to you.
- If you are entitled to WTC only, the annual threshold is £6,420.
- If you are entitled to WTC *and* CTC, the annual threshold is £6,420.
- If you are entitled to CTC only, and not to WTC, the annual threshold is £16,010.

Divide the threshold that applies to you by the number of days in the current tax year, then multiply this figure by the number of days in the relevant period. Round this amount up to the nearest penny. This figure is your threshold for the relevant period.

Step five: calculate tax credit entitlement for the relevant period

- If your income is less than the threshold that applies to you, you are entitled to receive the maximum amount of tax credits.
- If your income is greater than the threshold that applies to you, subtract the threshold figure from your relevant income to find your excess income. Calculate 41 per cent of this excess income and round this figure down to the nearest penny. Finally, reduce your maximum amount of tax credits by this amount.
- The different elements of your maximum tax credits are tapered away in a set order.
  - First, the elements of WTC, except for the childcare element are reduced.
  - Next, the childcare element is reduced.
  - Third, the child elements of CTC plus any disabled or severely disabled child elements for your children are reduced.
  - Finally, the family element is reduced.

If you are entitled to CTC only, or to WTC only, and the calculation results in entitlement of less than £26, no tax credit award is made. If you are entitled to both CTC and WTC and the total entitlement is less than £26, no award is made.[49]

To find out the amount of your weekly payment, divide the above total by the number of days in your relevant period to find the daily rate and then multiply this daily rate by seven. If your tax credits are paid four-weekly, multiply the daily rate by 28 to calculate the amount of your payments.

Example

Tracy claims tax credits at the beginning of the tax year 2014/15. During the tax year 2013/14 she worked 20 hours a week and earned £8 an hour, gross. During the tax year 2014/15, she continues to work the same hours, with a small rise in pay. Tracy's entitlement to tax credits is calculated as follows.

Step one: work out the relevant period

Tracy's relevant period is 365 days.

Step two: calculate her maximum entitlement for the relevant period

CTC	Family element	£547.50
	Child element for three-year-old child	£2,752.10
	Child element for five-year-old child	£2,752.10
WTC	Basic element	£1,941.80
	Lone parent element	£1,992.90
	Childcare element	£7,280.00
Total maximum amount of tax credits		**£17,266.40**

Note: although Tracy's annual period is one year, the figures for each element do not equal the annual amount of each element. For example, the annual amount of the family element is £545, but the calculation above shows Tracy's family element during her relevant period of one year as being £547.50. This is because when the annual amount has been divided by 365 and the figure produced is *rounded up* to the nearest penny before being multiplied by the number of days in the tax year, this rounding up has the effect of increasing Tracy's annual maximum amount.

Step three: work out her relevant income

Tracy earned £8,342.85 during the tax year 2013/14. (She is paid £8 an hour, gross, and works 20 hours a week.) This total is calculated as follows:

$((£8 \times 20) \div 7) \times 365 = £8,342.85$

She continues at the same hours, with a small rise in pay during the tax year 2014/15. This total is calculated as follows:

$((£8.10 \times 20) \div 7) \times 365 = £8,447.14$

During the year in which tax credits are paid (2014/15), as the increase is below the disregard, her income for the year 2013/14 is used.

Tracy's income for the relevant period is therefore:

$(£8,342.85 \div 365) \times 365 = £8,342.85$, rounded down to the nearest penny.

Step four: compare her income with the threshold for the relevant period

As Tracy will receive both WTC and CTC, her annual threshold figure is £6,420. The threshold for the relevant period is therefore:

$(£6,420 \div 365) \times 365 = £6,420$, rounded up to the nearest penny.

Part 11: General rules for tax credits
Chapter 63: Tax credit amounts
4. How to calculate the amount of tax credit

Step five: calculate tax credit entitlement for the relevant period

Tracy has excess income of £1,922.85 (income of £8,342.85 minus the threshold figure of £6,420).

Apply the taper of 41 per cent to this excess income:

41% x £1,922.85 = £788.36

Tracy's maximum tax credits (£17,266.40) are reduced by this amount. Her total tax credit entitlement is:

£17,266.40 – £788.36 = £16,478.04

The reduction is first applied to the elements of her WTC apart from the childcare element – ie, the basic element of £1,941.80 plus the lone parent element of £1,992.90 = £3,934.70

£3,934.70 – £788.36 = £3,146.34

Tracy's tax credit entitlement for the tax year 2014/15 is:

WTC (not including childcare element)	£3,146.34
Childcare element	£7,280.00
CTC	£6,051.70
Total tax credits	**£16,478.04**

To find the weekly rate of payment, this figure is divided by 365 (the number of days in Tracy's relevant period) and multiplied by 7.

(£16,478.04 ÷ 365) x 7 = £316.02

Calculating the amount of tax credits: a quick way

For a rough projection of an award, you can use the annual rates as follows.

Step one: calculate maximum tax credits

Add together the annual rates of CTC and WTC elements to which you are entitled. For the childcare element, multiply 70 per cent of the weekly cost by 52 to give an annual amount.

Step two: work out relevant income

This is either your income in the previous tax year, or an estimate of your current year's income after a disregard, if it has increased or decreased by more than the disregarded amounts (see Chapter 64).

Step three: compare income with threshold

The threshold is £6,420 if you are eligible for WTC only, or to WTC and CTC. The threshold is £16,010 if you are eligible for CTC only – ie, you are not working sufficient hours to qualify for WTC.

If your income is below the threshold, the maximum tax credit in Step one is payable.

If your income is above the threshold, the difference is used for Step four.

Step four: work out tax credits payable

The maximum amount of tax credits in Step one is reduced by 41 per cent of your income above the threshold in Step three. This gives an annual figure for a complete tax year, which can be misleading as circumstances may change. It may be more helpful to divide by 52 to give a weekly income figure.

Note: a new calculation must be made if your circumstances change or if your income goes up or down by more than you estimated.

Example

As in the previous examples, Tracy, is a lone parent with two children, working 20 hours a week, earning £8 an hour, paying £200 a week for childcare.

Step one:
Maximum CTC = £545 (family element) + £5,500 (2 x child elements £2,750) = £6,045
Maximum WTC = £1,940 (basic element) + £1,990 (lone parent element) + £7,280 (childcare element £200 x 70% x 52 weeks) = £11,210
Total = £17,255

Step two:
Relevant income = £8,320 (£8 x 20 x 52 weeks in 2013/14)

Step three:
£8,320 (income) – £6,420 (threshold) = £1,900

Step four:
£17,255 (maximum tax credits) – £779 (£1,900 x 41%) = £16,476 tax credits payable for complete tax year
= £316.85 per week.

5. Change of circumstances

There are three different ways in which a change in your circumstances can affect your entitlement to tax credits.

- If your circumstances change in a way that affects your maximum entitlement, a new relevant period begins. For example, if a disability benefit which gives entitlement to a disability element is awarded to you or someone included in your claim, this changes your maximum amount of tax credit and starts a new relevant period.
- Other changes, such as becoming single or part of a couple, bring your award to an end. You must make a fresh claim for tax credits, if you remain entitled. This also starts a new relevant period.

Part 11: General rules for tax credits
Chapter 63: Tax credit amounts
Notes

- Finally, some changes that do not affect your maximum entitlement and do not bring your existing award to an end affect the amount of tax credit which is payable to you. For example, if your existing award has been based on your current tax year's income and you have a significant rise in your income during that tax year, you may be overpaid tax credit unless you report the change at once, enabling your award to be recalculated.

See p1450 for more information about how these changes affect your award.

In any of these circumstances, your tax credit award will need to be recalculated. This is done by working through Steps one to five as described on pp1411–12, for each relevant period.

Example

Tracy claims disability living allowance (DLA) for her five-year-old child and this is awarded (middle rate of the care component) from day 201 of the tax year 2014/15. She therefore has two relevant periods during this tax year. The first is 200 days long, and the second, from the date her daughter is awarded DLA, 165 days long. Two calculations have to be done, as in the previous example but for the first relevant period, multiply daily rates by 200. For the second relevant period, the daily rate of the disabled child element is included and then multiply daily rates by 165. The first relevant period works out as £9,029.07 (or approximately £316.02 a week). The second relevant period works out as £8,849.43 (or approximately £375.45 a week).

Notes

1. The relevant period
1 s5(1) TCA 2002
2 s5(2) TCA 2002
3 Reg 8(2) TC(ITDR) Regs
4 Reg 7(2) TC(ITDR) Regs
5 Reg 8(2) TC(ITDR) Regs

2. The maximum amount of child tax credit
6 Reg 7 CTC Regs
7 Regs 7 and 8 TC(ITDR) Regs
8 Reg 8(1) and (2) CTC Regs
9 Reg 8(1) and (3) CTC Regs

3. The maximum amount of working tax credit
10 Reg 20 WTC(EMR) Regs
11 Reg 15 WTC(EMR) Regs
12 Regs 7 and 8 TC(ITDR) Regs
13 Reg 4 WTC(EMR) Regs
14 Reg 3(2) WTC(EMR) Regs
15 Reg 12 WTC(EMR) Regs
16 Reg 11(1) WTC(EMR) Regs
17 Reg 11 WTC(EMR) Regs
18 Reg 3 WTC(EMR) Regs
19 Reg 10 WTC(EMR) Regs
20 Reg 3 WTC(EMR) Regs
21 Reg 9 WTC(EMR) Regs

4. **How to calculate the amount of tax credit**

11

Chapter 64

Income: tax credits

This chapter covers:
1. Relevant income (below)
2. Whose income counts (p1421)
3. What income counts (p1421)
4. Notional income (p1433)

Key facts
- The amount of tax credits to which you are entitled depends on how much income you have.
- In general, most taxable income is taken into account and non-taxable income is ignored, but there are exceptions.
- The assessment is based on income for a full tax year, 6 April to 5 April.
- The amount to which you are entitled changes if your income increases or decreases by more than a certain amount in the current year compared with the previous year.
- Your savings or other capital are not taken into account, and you are eligible for tax credits whatever the level of your capital. However, interest and other income earned from savings or capital do count.
- If you are employed, HMRC may check your award with 'real time information' on earnings provided by your employer when you are paid.

1. Relevant income

Tax credits are calculated using your 'relevant income'. The assessment is always based on income over a full tax year (6 April to 5 April) except during a time when you are getting income support (IS), income-based jobseeker's allowance (JSA), income-related employment and support allowance (ESA) or pension credit (PC). If the tax credit award only runs for part of the year, the full year's income is reduced on a pro rata basis (see p1411). Your relevant income is *either*:
- your income in the complete tax year before your claim (previous year's income); *or*
- your income in the complete tax year of your claim (current year's income) after a disregard.

Note: while you are on IS, income-based JSA, income-related ESA or PC, you are entitled to maximum tax credits without any income test, so the level of your income in the previous or current year does not matter. When your benefit stops, the tax credit award is again based on relevant income.

If your tax credit award is finalised during the tax year because you become entitled to universal credit (UC), your current year's income is based on your income in the part of the year up to the date you become entitled to UC. Your income from 6 April to the date your tax credit award ends is divided by the number of days in that part of the year, and multiplied by the number of days in the tax year (then rounded down to the nearest pound).[1] The result is compared with your previous year's income, applying the disregards. During 2014/15, this is only likely to happen if you form a couple with someone who is entitled to UC (see p19).

Previous year's income

Tax credit awards are initially based on your income in the tax year before the year for which you are claiming. This is referred to as the 'previous year's income'. So, for a tax credits claim made from 6 April 2014, the previous year is 2013/14. The claim form only asks for your income in the previous tax year. Your tax credit entitlement is finalised at the end of the year by comparing this figure with your income in the year of the award (current year's income – see below). Your income can decrease by up to £2,500 compared with the previous year or increase by up to £5,000 without it affecting your final entitlement. If your income has not changed by more than these amounts, your final tax credit entitlement is still based on the previous year's income. Changes of less than these disregarded amounts do not affect your award until the following year.

Before 2012/13, there was no disregard for a decrease in income, so any drop in income meant that the lower current year's income was used.

The disregard for an increase in income has been changed several times:
- awards in 2011/12 to 2012/13 – £10,000 disregarded;
- awards in 2006/07 to 2010/11 – £25,000 disregarded;
- awards up to 2005/06 – £2,500 disregarded.

If you do not tell HM Revenue and Customs (HMRC) about any change in your income, your award continues to be based on the previous year's income until the end of the tax year.

Current year's income

Your final tax credit entitlement is based on a comparison of the previous year's income with your income in the year for which you are claiming, known as the 'current year's income'. So for a tax credits claim made from 6 April 2014, the current year is 2014/15. An annual amount for a complete tax year is required,

Part 11: General rules for tax credits
Chapter 64: Income: tax credits
1. Relevant income

which you may not know for certain until the end of the tax year, but you can provide an estimate during the year. At the end of the tax year, HMRC finalises your entitlement by comparing your previous year's income with your current year's income. This process is called the 'annual review'. If your income has decreased by more than £2,500 or increased by more than £5,000, your entitlement is based on your current's year income, after the disregarded amount.

If your income in the current year (2014/15):[2]

- has not changed since the previous year, the current year's income is used;
- has fallen by £2,500 or less, the previous year's income is used;
- has fallen by more than £2,500, the current year's income plus £2,500 is used;
- has increased by £5,000 or less, the previous year's income is used;
- has increased by more than £5,000, the current year's income minus £5,000 is used.

If you tell HMRC during the year about an increase in income of more than £5,000 compared with the previous year, your award can be revised based on an estimate of the current year's income less a disregard of £5,000. This is advisable if you want to reduce the risk of overpayments at the end of the year.

If you expect your income in the current year to decrease by more than £2,500 compared with the previous year, tell HMRC. It will adjust your award basing it on your estimate plus £2,500. Tell HMRC quickly if you later think your estimate was too low so it can readjust your award. If you do not, you could end up with an overpayment.

You can phone the Tax Credit Helpline or write to the Tax Credit Office with details of your current year's income. There is no special form to fill in so make sure you provide full details of *all* your (and your partner's) relevant income for the current year. At the end of the year, HMRC carries out an annual review and you are usually required to declare your income for the year that has just ended.

Examples

From 6 April 2013 to 5 April 2014, Izzy worked part time and earned a total of £8,000. Since then she has worked full time and earns £12,500 in the current year of the award, from 6 April 2014 to 5 April 2015. Her tax credit award is initially based on income of £8,000. Because her income increased by just £4,500 in the current year (ie, below the £5,000 disregard), her final entitlement is also based on an income of £8,000.

From 6 April 2013 to 5 April 2014, Marsha and Bill, who are claiming as a couple, had a total income of £27,000. In the current year of the award, from 6 April 2014 to 5 April 2015, Marsha stops work and they earn £11,000 between them. Their tax credit award is initially based on the previous year's income of £27,000. Because their income decreased by £16,000 in the current year (£27,000 − £11,000), their final entitlement is based on income of £13,500 (£11,000 + £2,500). For the next year, 6 April 2015 to 5 April 2016, their award will initially be based on an income of £11,000.

Estimating income

There are no special rules for how to estimate income. Using, for instance, payslips and benefit award letters, work out how much income you have already received in the current year and estimate how much you will receive for the remainder of the year. Tax credits are always worked out using annual income, so you must include all income received or estimated for the whole tax year, 6 April to 5 April, even if you are asking for an award to be adjusted part way through the year.

If you are self-employed, HMRC's Self Assessment Helpline (tel: 0300 200 3310; textphone: 0300 200 3319) can advise you how to work out your business profits. You need to estimate your profits for the accounting period that ends in the current tax year. This might be different from your current earnings, particularly if your accounting year end is early in the tax year.

You should always make it clear that you are using an estimate; there is a box to tick on the claim form and annual declaration to do this.

2. Whose income counts

If you are a member of a couple (see p1438), your partner's income is added to yours.[3] Otherwise, only your own income counts.[3]

If you were previously part of a couple, but have separated and are now a single claimant, only your individual income in the previous and current year counts in your new single award, not that of your former partner. In your old award as a couple, your joint income in the previous and current year counts – ie, including the remainder of the tax year after you separated.[4] The income in the complete tax year is used and then apportioned on a pro rata basis for the period of the claim (see p1411).

If you were a single claimant but are now in a couple, your joint income in the previous and current year counts in the new joint claim, even if you were not in a couple in the previous year.[5]

Children's income

Children's income is ignored. However, if you have transferred money under a trust to your child and tax rules treat that income as still belonging to you, it may also be treated as yours for tax credits.[6]

3. What income counts

In general, taxable social security benefits are taken into account, and gross earnings (before tax and national insurance (NI)) and business profits are taken into account less your pension contributions. Most other income, such as

Part 11: General rules for tax credits
Chapter 64: Income: tax credits
3. What income counts

pensions and interest on savings, is added together and taken into account only if the total is more than £300 a year. The rules specify what income must be taken into account and what is disregarded.

If you have a special exemption from income tax, your income is calculated as though you were liable for tax.[7] People such as foreign military personnel, officials of international organisations or consular staff may have such an exemption.

Types of income

Income taken into account falls into certain categories and within each category certain amounts may be disregarded. There is also a general list of income that is disregarded (see p1431).

The income taken into account in the assessment is worked out as follows.[8]

Add together your income, or your joint income if you are a couple, from:

- social security benefits (see p1423);
- income from employment (see p1424);
- taxable profits from self-employment (see p1426);
- student income (see p1427);
- miscellaneous income (see p1428).

Add together your income, or your joint income if you are a couple, from:

- pension income (see p1428);
- income from investments (see p1429);
- income from property (see p1430);
- foreign income (see p1430);
- notional income (see p1433).

If the total income in the last group of five categories is £300 or less, it is ignored completely; otherwise, deduct £300 and add the remainder to your income from the first group of five categories. **Note:** couples share one £300 disregard.[9]

This gives you the total income that is taken into account – subject to any disregards described later in this chapter.

11

Example
Mr and Mrs Killean renew their claim for child tax credit (CTC) and working tax credit (WTC) from April 2014. HM Revenue and Customs (HMRC) assesses their claim on their joint income for the year 6 April 2013 to 5 April 2014. In 2013/14 Mrs Killean earned £13,500 before tax and NI contributions. Mr Killean received contributory employment and support allowance (ESA) totalling £4,700 and an occupational pension of £500. Income taken into account is:
Employment income = £13,500
ESA = £4,700
Occupational pension = £200 (ie, £500 less £300 disregard)
Total income = £18,400

Benefits

Generally, benefits are taken into account if they are taxable, and ignored if they are not.

Disregarded benefits

The following benefits are disregarded:[10]
- armed forces independence payment;
- attendance allowance;
- bereavement payment;
- child benefit;
- Christmas bonus;
- council tax reduction;
- disability living allowance;
- discretionary housing payment;
- guardian's allowance;
- housing benefit (HB);
- income support (IS), except to strikers;
- income-based jobseeker's allowance (JSA) (even though this is taxable);
- income-related ESA including a transitional addition;[11]
- industrial injuries benefit (except industrial death benefit);
- maternity allowance;
- pension credit (guarantee and savings credit);[12]
- personal independence payment;
- severe disablement allowance;
- short-term lower rate incapacity benefit (IB);
- social fund payments;
- transitional long-term IB (paid if you transferred from invalidity benefit in 1995) but no longer disregarded when converted to ESA;
- any payment to compensate for the loss of IS, JSA or HB;
- any payment in lieu of milk tokens or vitamins;
- increases for a child[13] or adult[14] paid with any of the above.

Tax credits themselves are disregarded. Statutory sick pay (SSP), statutory maternity pay (SMP), statutory adoption pay (SAP) and statutory paternity pay (SPP) are treated as employment income (see p1424). Retirement pensions, widowed mother's allowance, widowed parent's allowance, widow's pension, industrial death benefit and war pensions are treated as pension income (see p1428). Universal credit (UC) is not included as income, but the intention is that once you have started to receive UC, you cannot claim tax credits.[15]

Benefits taken into account

Any benefits not in the list above are taken into account in full. These include:
- bereavement allowance;

Part 11: General rules for tax credits
Chapter 64: Income: tax credits
3. What income counts

- carer's allowance (CA);
- contribution-based JSA;[16]
- contributory ESA including a transitional addition;
- long-term IB (except the non-taxable transitional long-term IB – see p1423);
- increases for a child or adult (even if not taxable) paid with any of the above.

It is the amount of benefit payable that is taken into account. Arrears of benefit or any ex gratia payment in connection with a benefit are taken into account as income for the year in which the payment of arrears is made.[17]

Each year the DWP should give you a statement of the taxable benefits you received in the previous tax year. You can ask the local benefit office for a replacement if you did not get one. If you get any increase for a child paid with CA or IB (or widowed mother's or widowed parent's allowance), this is not included in the statement but is taken into account as income, so you should include it when completing your tax credit claim form.

Employment income

For tax credits, it is your 'gross' taxable pay that is taken into account.[18] This means your pay before any income tax or NI contributions are deducted, but after pension contributions are deducted.

Income counts whether received in the UK or elsewhere, unless it has been classed as not taxable because it cannot be transferred to or realised in the UK.[19]

What counts as employment income

'Employment income' means the following income received in the tax year:[20]
- any earnings from an office or employment, including:[21]
  - wages;
  - holiday pay;
  - occupational sick pay;
  - fees;
  - bonuses;
  - commission;
  - overtime pay;
  - tips or gratuities;
  - goods or assets that can be converted into money – eg, gifts of drink, clothes and fuel;
  - payments made on your behalf – eg, rent paid by your employer directly to your landlord;
  - earnings from 'permitted work' (see p1019) – note that there is no income test while you are receiving income-related ESA, but this does not mean the earnings are disregarded when applying the income test for other periods;
- taxable expenses (see p1425 for expenses that do not count as earnings);[22]

- any taxable cash voucher, non-cash voucher or credit token – eg, company credit card.[23] Vouchers spent on allowable expenses are ignored;[24]
- taxable payments in connection with the termination of your employment or with a change in your duties or wages, including non-statutory and statutory redundancy payments, pay in lieu of notice and employment tribunal awards for unfair dismissal. With the exception of pay in lieu of notice (except in some cases involving damages for breach of contract or practice),[25] the first £30,000 of the total of such payments is ignored;[26]
- SSP;[27]
- SMP above £100 a week. The first £100 a week is ignored;[28]
- ordinary and additional SPP and SAP above £100 a week;[29]
- strike pay from your trade union (even though this is non-taxable);[30]
- the cash equivalent of the benefit of a company car for private use and car fuel benefits if you earn £8,500 or more or you are a company director.[31] Other expenses in connection with the car are ignored.[32] However, if you are a disabled employee with an adapted or automatic company car, the car is exempt from income tax and ignored for tax credits;[33]
- payments for agreeing to restrict your future conduct or activities;[34]
- taxable income from an employee share scheme;[35]
- payment for work done while sentenced or on remand in prison (but note this does not count as remunerative work).[36]

The taxable value of goods and vouchers is shown on Form P9D or P11D, given to you by your employer at the end of the tax year.

Payments not counted as earnings

Some payments do not count as earnings and are disregarded in the tax credits assessment. Insofar as they are exempt from income tax, ignore the following:[37]

- expenses incurred 'wholly, exclusively and necessarily' in the course of your employment.[38] **Note:** if you are a volunteer with a charity or voluntary organisation, all your expenses are ignored.[39] If you earn less than £8,500 a year, generally all your expenses are ignored.[40] However, any that are taxable are taken into account – eg, 'round-sum' expense allowances payable irrespective of how you might spend it;[41]
- certain other expenses – eg, for travel and subsistence, mileage allowance, car parking expenses, fixed deductions for work tools and tax-free mobile phone;[42]
- homeworkers' additional household expenses;[43]
- childcare vouchers or credit tokens for 'relevant childcare' (see p1407) (but any childcare element in your WTC is based on the lower subsidised childcare costs);[44]
- certain other vouchers – eg, for staff canteens, sports and recreation facilities and small gifts;[45]

11

Part 11: General rules for tax credits
Chapter 64: Income: tax credits
3. What income counts

- certain professional fees – eg, to approved professional bodies, for indemnity insurance or registration under the protection of vulnerable groups scheme;[46]
- any charity payments under a payroll giving scheme[47] (deduct from earnings or from a benefit or pension);[48]
- payment for work-related training, individual learning account training and retraining expenses when leaving employment;[49]
- job grant, return-to-work credit, in-work credit and other DWP payments from certain former employment schemes.[50]

Some groups of workers have special income tax exemptions. The following are ignored as earnings for tax credits:

- certain armed forces' allowances – eg, for travel to and from leave, food, certain operational allowances, council tax relief, continuity of education and reserve forces' training;[51]
- free coal to miners, or former miners, or cash in lieu;[52]
- if you are an actor or performer, the tax-free amount of agents' fees;[53]
- expenses for mainland transfers for offshore oil and gas workers;[54]
- Crown employees' foreign service allowance;[55]
- expenses of a minister of religion, including a rent deduction;[56]
- European Commission daily subsistence allowance to seconded national experts.[57]

Deduct pension contributions

Deduct any contributions you make to a personal or occupational pension approved by HMRC.[58]

If you pay contributions through your employer, your P60 or P45 should show your wages after the contributions have been deducted, so there is no further deduction to make.

If you pay the pension contributions directly, deduct the gross annual contributions. Because tax relief is given on personal pension contributions, your actual contributions are less than the gross amount included in the pension plan. It is the higher gross amount that you should deduct from your employment income. Your pension provider should supply you with annual statements of contributions received.

If you have no income from employment but are still making pension contributions, deduct the contributions from any other income you may have.

Income from self-employment

Your taxable profits from any 'trade', 'profession' or 'vocation' are taken into account for the relevant year.[59] If you have a business partner, it is taxable profits from your share of the business income that count.[60] This includes trading outside the UK. It also includes profits from renting out property if this is conducted as a business. (If property income comes from a 'trade', income counts without the

£300 disregard that would otherwise apply to such income.) If renting property is not conducted as a business, see p1430.

Taxable profits are shown on your tax return for the relevant year. If you have not yet submitted a tax return, the notes that accompany the tax credit claim form (TC600) explain how to work out your profit. You should deduct allowable business expenses from annual turnover to arrive at a profit figure. HMRC's Self Assessment Helpline (tel: 0300 200 3310; textphone: 0300 200 3319) should be able to give advice. See also p1421. **Note:** the provision allowing artists, farmers and market gardeners to average out fluctuating profits across two tax years does not apply; it is the actual taxable profit in the relevant year that counts.[61]

Business losses

If your business is run on a commercial basis and has made a loss, your income is nil for that tax year unless you have other income that counts in the assessment. If you do have other income, you should deduct the amount of the loss from that income (from joint income if you are claiming as a couple).[62] If you do not have enough income to offset the full amount, any left over can be carried forward and deducted from profits of the same trade in the next and later tax years.

Deduct pension contributions

Deduct the gross amount of any contributions you make to an approved personal pension scheme or a retirement annuity (see p1426).

Student income

The following income is taken into account:[63]
- adult dependants' grant;
- in Scotland, lone parents' grant;
- professional and career development loan, but only any amount applied for or paid in respect of living expenses for the period supported by the loan.[64]

Other kinds of student support are disregarded – eg:
- student loans;
- supplementary grants (other than those above);
- tuition fees;
- postgraduate maintenance grant;
- young student's bursary, health bursary, social work bursary, English opportunity bursary and other bursaries;
- education maintenance allowance;[65]
- hardship funds;
- 16–19 bursary fund payments;
- care-to-learn grant;
- childcare grant;
- parents' learning allowance.

Part 11: General rules for tax credits
Chapter 64: Income: tax credits
3. What income counts

Note: unlike means-tested benefits, students are not excluded from WTC and CTC. Provided you satisfy the eligibility rules, you can qualify.

Miscellaneous income

Any income that does not fit into any of the other nine categories on p1422 is taken into account if it is taxable under the HMRC 'sweep-up' provisions in Part 5 of the Income Tax (Trading and Other Income) Act 2005.[66] This includes copyright royalties if your writing does not amount to a trade or profession.

Pension income

Pension income taken into account

The following pension income is taken into account. The first £300 a year is ignored from the total of your pension and any income from savings, investments, property or foreign or notional income.

- **State retirement pensions and graduated retirement benefit.**[67] (Note: the Christmas bonus and winter fuel payment are ignored.) HMRC says that, as well as your pension, it takes into account any additional state pension, and any increase for an adult or child paid with your pension.[68] Include as income any lump sum to which you become entitled through deferring your state pension.
- **Personal and occupational pensions.**[69] It is the gross amount before tax is deducted that counts. Your pension provider should give you a certificate each year showing how much pension was paid and how much tax deducted. If you retired because of work-related illness or disability caused by injury on duty, only count the amount of pension that you would have been paid if you had retired on non-work-related ill-health grounds. Any extra amount paid is ignored.[70] Tax-free lump sums paid under a personal pension scheme, retirement annuity contract or tax-exempt pension scheme are ignored completely.[71] If you cash in a small pension or the fund is too small to pay a pension (within the 'trivial commutation' limit – your pension provider can advise on this), the lump sum you get counts. If you get a winding-up lump sum when your occupational pension scheme winds up, this counts.
- **Widow's pension, widowed mother's and widowed parent's allowance,** including any increases for a child or adult dependant.[72]
- **Industrial death benefit.**[73]
- **Survivor's guaranteed income payment and child's payment** under the Armed Forces Compensation Scheme.[74]

Pension income disregarded

Ignore the following **war pensions:**[75]

- war disablement pension including constant attendance allowance and mobility supplement;

- annuity or additional pension to holders of the Victoria Cross, George Cross and certain other medals;
- wounds, injury or disablement pensions to members of the armed forces – eg, guaranteed income payment;
- death in service pensions for service in the armed forces or war injuries. If the death in service pension is overlapped by another pension, ignore an equivalent amount from the other pension;
- armed forces independence payment.[76]

Investment income

There is no capital limit in the tax credit assessment as there is with means-tested benefits. The value of your savings is ignored completely. However, taxable *income* from savings and investments is taken into account. For example, the amount of savings in a bank account is ignored, but the interest on those savings is taken into account.

Investment income is taken into account as described below. The first £300 a year is ignored from the total of your investment income and any income from pensions or property, or foreign or notional income.

Investment income taken into account

Take into account the following amounts before tax is deducted:[77]

- interest on invested money, including outside the UK – eg, interest on savings in a bank account;[78]
- dividends from shares of a company resident in the UK (including the tax credit payable by the company with the dividend);[79]
- income from government stocks and bonds;[80]
- taxable payments from a life assurance policy, life annuity contract or capital redemption policy;[81]
- discounts on securities – ie, the profit from trading in securities such as government stocks and bonds;[82]
- payments from a trust;[83]
- payments from the estate of a deceased person;[84]
- interest arising from a debt owed to you.[85]

Investment income disregarded

Certain investment income is disregarded:

- interest, dividend or bonus from an individual savings account (ISA);[86]
- interest under a certified Save As You Earn (SAYE) scheme;[87]
- income from savings certificates and tax reserve certificates;[88]
- tax-exempt annual payments made by an individual in the UK not for commercial reasons – eg, from a covenant;[89]
- winnings from betting, pools, lotteries and games with prizes;[90]
- certain compensation payments to World War Two victims;[91]

Part 11: General rules for tax credits
Chapter 64: Income: tax credits
3. What income counts

- interest on damages awarded through the courts for personal injuries, or periodical payments of personal injury damages or from the Thalidomide Trust;[92]
- annuity payments under a Criminal Injuries Compensation Scheme award;[93]
- interest on the first £30,000 of a home income plan loan taken out before 9 March 1999 to buy a life annuity;[94]
- interest on compensation to a child under 18 for the loss of a parent;[95]
- payments from the variant Creutzfeldt-Jakob disease government-funded trust, the Macfarlane Trusts, Independent Living Funds and the Eileen Trust. These are disregarded for the lifetime of the disabled person or a partner who receives the payment or inherits from the estate, or for two years if paid to or inherited by a parent;[96]
- capital element of a purchased life annuity;[97]
- tax-free health and employment insurance or immediate-needs annuity payments.[98]

Property income

The capital value of property is ignored but rental income is taken into account unless this is exempt from tax under the 'rent-a-room' scheme.[99] This scheme allows you to rent furnished accommodation in your own home earning up to £4,250 a year tax free.[100]

If you are not within the 'rent-a-room' scheme (eg, you rent out a property that you do not live in yourself), the amount of rent taken into account is the same as that agreed for income tax purposes. You can deduct expenses wholly and exclusively incurred in running the property – eg, repairs, council tax (if you, rather than your tenant, are liable to pay), water charges, insurance premiums and mortgage interest (but not capital repayments of a mortgage).[101] You can offset any losses against property income in the following tax year.

The first £300 a year is ignored from the total of your property income and any pensions, investment income, foreign or notional income.

If you rent property as a business (eg, you run a hotel or guesthouse), count this as income from self-employment (see p1426).[102]

Income from property outside the UK counts as 'foreign income' (see below).

Income from outside the UK

Although earnings from abroad are taken into account in the same way as UK earnings, other 'foreign income' (eg, from pensions, property or investments, other than taxable gains from an overseas insurer, which fall within the definition of 'investment income') is taken into account subject to the following rules.[103]

The following are disregarded:[104]

- a banking charge or commission for converting currency to sterling;[105]

- social security payments from outside the UK that are equivalent to tax-free UK benefits (see p1423);
- certain pensions or compensation for victims of Nazi persecution;
- one-tenth of the amount of any overseas pension or of a pension payable in the UK by the governments of certain countries;
- tax-free lump-sum payments under an overseas pension scheme;
- personal injury damages from a court outside the UK;
- certain education allowances payable to workers in the public sector of some countries outside the UK;
- property losses in one tax year that can be offset against property income in the following year;[106]
- maintenance payments;
- income that you are prevented from transferring to the UK by law or by the government of the country where the income arises or because you cannot get foreign currency in that country. Other income that remains abroad is counted.[107]

The first £300 a year is disregarded from the total of your foreign income and any pensions, investment, property or notional income.

Income from outside the UK is still taken into account even if you would normally have tax relief on that income in the UK to avoid double taxation in both countries (such income is treated as though it were taxable in the UK in the normal way).[108]

Converting currency

If your income is in another currency, HMRC converts it to sterling using a 12-month average of exchange rates for the tax year in which the income is paid.[109] If your tax credit award is based on an estimate of current year's income, the rate of conversion will be adjusted once the exchange rate average is available at the end of the tax year. These rates are published on the HMRC website (see Appendix 1).

General income disregards

All of the following income is disregarded in the tax credit assessment.[110]

Employment and training programmes

Ignore the following income:
- travelling expenses, a living away from home allowance and a training grant if you are participating in training under s2 of the Employment and Training Act 1973 or, in Scotland, under s2 of the Enterprise and New Towns (Scotland) Act 1990, or attending a course at an employment rehabilitation centre (where these are not taxable as profits);[111]
- if you are aged 25 or over and getting JSA while on a 'qualifying course', a discretionary payment to help meet your special needs;[112]

Part 11: General rules for tax credits
Chapter 64: Income: tax credits
3. What income counts

- a payment to a disabled person under s2 of the Employment and Training Act 1973 or s15 of the Disabled Persons (Employment) Act 1944 to assist disabled people to get or keep employment;[113]
- education maintenance allowance;[114]
- certain DWP payments from former employment programmes.

See also p1426 for other disregarded payments.

Maintenance and children

Any maintenance you receive from an ex-partner, or that your partner receives from her/his ex-partner, is ignored, whether it is paid under a court order or not. Any maintenance for a child or qualifying young person which you receive from her/his parent (if the parent is not currently your partner) is also ignored.[115]

If you *pay* maintenance, you cannot deduct this from income.

If you foster a child placed with you by a local authority or independent fostering provider, all your income from foster care (eg, the fostering allowance) is ignored, provided the annual amount is no more than £10,000 plus £200 a week for each child under 11 and £250 a week for each child aged 11 or over. If your fostering income is over this limit, only the taxable amount is taken into account – ie, the amount above this limit or the actual net profit.[116] There is a similar disregard for local authority payments if a child or adult is placed with you under an adult placement scheme or staying put care for care leavers, or you are a kinship carer of a looked-after child.[117]

Note: a foster child or looked-after child may not count as a member of your family for tax credits, so you may not get CTC for her/him (see p155).

An adoption allowance,[118] or special guardianship payment for a child who is a member of your household is ignored completely. For a child who lives with you under a residence order, a residence order allowance and any payments made by a local authority under s17 of the Children Act 1989 or, in Scotland, under s22 of the Children (Scotland) Act 1995 or s50 of the Children Act 1975 are ignored.[119]

Other income

The following is ignored from your income:

- any contribution you make to an approved personal or occupational pension scheme (see p1426);[120]
- payments for fares to hospital;[121]
- payments to assist prison visits;[122]
- community care direct payments;[123]
- payments under the Supporting People programme;[124]
- asylum support payments or vouchers for a former asylum seeker or dependant;[125]
- trade union provident benefits – eg, sickness or accident benefit or funeral payment;[126]

- payment for expenses incurred if you are an unpaid volunteer with a charity or voluntary organisation;[127]
- jury or witness payments if this is not compensation for loss of earnings or loss of benefit;[128]
- a payment to you for someone you are caring for temporarily made by a health authority, local authority, voluntary organisation, clinical commissioning group, the NHS Commissioning Board, or by the person her/himself under the local authority's financial assessment. This disregard only applies if the payment would be tax free under HMRC's 'rent-a-room' scheme (see p1430);[129]
- any payment under an insurance policy taken out to insure against the risk of being unable to maintain mortgage repayments or other payments on a loan secured on your home. However, any payment you get above the amount you use to maintain the repayments, plus the premiums on that policy or buildings insurance premiums required as a condition of the mortgage, count as your income;[130]
- any payment under an insurance policy taken out to insure against the risk of being unable to maintain repayments under a hire purchase, regulated or conditional sale agreement. However, any payment above the amount you use to maintain the repayments and the premiums on that policy counts as your income;[131]
- the gross amount of any 'gift aid' donation to charity;[132]
- a sports award for anything other than living expenses. Living expenses count as your income. Ignore parts of the award for dietary supplements and living-away-from-home accommodation costs.[133]

4. Notional income

Sometimes you are treated as though you have income that you do not actually have. This is called '**notional income**'.[134] There are four kinds of notional income:

- income you have deprived yourself of to get or increase tax credits;
- income that would be available to you if you applied for it;
- a reasonable rate for work you have done for less than the going rate;
- income you are treated as having through certain provisions for preventing tax avoidance or when tax law treats capital as income and charges it to income tax.

Deprivation of income

You are treated as having income you have deprived yourself of for the purpose of getting a tax credit or a higher tax credit.[135] See p359 for details of when this rule might affect you (the basic rules are similar to those that apply to deprivation of capital for benefits).

Part 11: General rules for tax credits
Chapter 64: Income: tax credits
Notes

Failing to apply for income

You are treated as having income that would become available to you if you applied for it.[136] This does not include:
- income under a trust set up from a personal injury payment;
- income from a personal pension scheme;
- interest on damages awarded through the courts for personal injury;
- a rehabilitation allowance;
- Category A or B retirement pension;
- graduated retirement benefit;
- shared additional pension.

Cheap or unpaid labour

If you work or provide a service for less than the going rate, you are treated as getting a reasonable rate for the job if the person has the means to pay.[137]

This does not affect you if you are a volunteer and HM Revenue and Customs is satisfied that it is reasonable for you to provide your services free of charge. Nor does it apply if you are on an approved employment or training programme.

Sometimes carers looking after disabled people have been expected to charge the person they care for under a similar provision affecting means-tested benefits. If you are in this position, see p290 for more details.

Preventing tax avoidance and treatment of capital as income

If income is treated as yours under certain prevention of tax avoidance provisions or where tax law treats capital as income, it also counts as your income for tax credits.[138]

Notes

11

1. Relevant income
1 Reg 17 and Sch UC(TP) Regs 2013
2 s7(3)(a), (b) and (e) TCA 2002; reg 5 TC(ITDR) Regs

2. Whose income counts
3 s7(5) TCA 2002
4 *PD v HMRC* [2010] UKUT 159 (AAC)
5 R(TC) 1/08
6 Reg 14(2)(b)(vii) TC(DCI) Regs

3. What income counts
7 Reg 3(6) TC(DCI) Regs
8 Reg 3(1) TC(DCI) Regs
9 Reg 3(1) Step 1 TC(DCI) Regs
10 Reg 7(3) TC(DCI) Regs
11 A transitional addition is part of the ESA applicable amount under reg 67(1)(d) ESA Regs, inserted by Sch 2 para 52 ESA(TP)(EA)(No.2) Regs

12 PC paid under SPCA 2002 is by definition not counted as social security income under reg 7(1) TC(DCI) Regs

13 Reg 7(4) TC(DCI) Regs

14 Regulations make no mention of the treatment of increases for adults. However, these are non-taxable if paid with a non-taxable benefit and the intention is that tax credits follow suit. See HMRC *Employment Income Manual*, para 76102.

15 Reg 7(1) TC(DCI) Regs (universal credit is paid under the WRA 2012)

16 s674 IT(EP)A 2003

17 Reg 7(1)(c) and (d) TC(DCI) Regs

18 Reg 4 TC(DCI) Regs

19 Reg 3(3)-(5) TC(DCI) Regs

20 Reg 4 TC(DCI) Regs

21 Regs 2(2) and 4(1)(a) TC(DCI) Regs; HMRC, *Employment Income Manual*, para 00520

22 Reg 4(1)(b) TC(DCI) Regs

23 Reg 4(1)(c)-(e) TC(DCI) Regs

24 ss362-63 IT(EP)A 2003; reg 4(4) Table 1 para 11D and (5) TC(DCI) Regs

25 HMRC, *Employment Income Manual*, paras 12975-79

26 Reg 4(1)(f) TC(DCI) Regs

27 Reg 4(1)(g) TC(DCI) Regs

28 Reg 4(1)(h) TC(DCI) Regs

29 Reg 4(1)(h) TC(DCI) Regs

30 Reg 4(1)(k) TC(DCI) Regs

31 Reg 4(1)(i) TC(DCI) Regs

32 Reg 4(4) Table 1 paras 14B, 14C and 14D TC(DCI) Regs

33 Reg 4(4) Table 1 para 2B TC(DCI) Regs

34 Reg 4(1)(j) TC(DCI) Regs

35 Reg 4(1)(l) TC(DCI) Regs

36 Reg 4(1)(m) TC(DCI) Regs; reg 4(2)(g) WTC(EMR) Regs

37 Reg 4(4) TC(DCI) Regs; for a full list see para 04200 TCTM

38 Reg 4(5) TC(DCI) Regs; s336 IT(EP)A 2003

39 Reg 19 Table 7 para 1 TC(DCI) Regs

40 ss216-17 IT(EP)A 2003

41 Reg 4(1)(b) TC(DCI) Regs; HMRC, *Employment Income Manual*, para 05100

42 Regs 4(4) Table 1 paras 1, 2A, 2C, 4, 6, 11F, 13, and 20, and 4(5) TC(DCI) Regs; ss231, 337, 338, 367, 370, 371, 373, 376 and 377 IT(EP)A 2003

43 Reg 4(4) Table 1 paras 17 and 19 TC(DCI) Regs

44 Reg 4(4) Table 1 para 15 TC(DCI) Regs

45 Reg 4(4) Table 1 paras 5, 8, 11E and 14 TC(DCI) Regs

46 Regs 4(4) Table 1 para 21 and 4(5) TC(DCI) Regs; ss343 and 346 IT(EP)A 2003

47 Reg 4(5) TC(DCI) Regs; s713 IT(EP)A 2003

48 Regs 5(3) and 7(5A) TC(DCI) Regs

49 Reg 4(4) Table 1 paras 11C and 18 TC(DCI) Regs

50 Reg 4(4) Table 1 para 16 TC(DCI) Regs

51 Reg 4(4) Table 1 paras 3, 3A, 3B, 3C and 7 TC(DCI) Regs

52 Regs 4(4) Table 1 para 9 and 5(2) Table 2 para 11 TC(DCI) Regs

53 Reg 4(5) TC(DCI) Regs; s352 IT(EP)A 2003

54 Reg 4(4) Table 1 para 11A TC(DCI) Regs

55 Reg 4(4) Table 1 para 11B TC(DCI) Regs

56 Reg 4(5) TC(DCI) Regs; s351 IT(EP)A 2003

57 Reg 4(4) Table 1 para 11 TC(DCI) Regs

58 Reg 3(7)(c) TC(DCI) Regs

59 Reg 6(a) TC(DCI) Regs

60 Reg 6(b) TC(DCI) Regs

61 Reg 6 TC(DCI) Regs

62 Reg 3(1) Step 4 TC(DCI) Regs

63 Reg 8 TC(DCI) Regs

64 Reg 19(c) Table 8 para 2 TC(DCI) Regs

65 Reg 19 Table 6 para 5(a) TC(DCI) Regs

66 Reg 18 TC(DCI) Regs

67 Reg 5(1)(a) TC(DCI) Regs

68 para 04301 TCTM; HMRC, *Employment Income Manual*, para 76102

69 Reg 5(1)(b)-(o) TC(DCI) Regs

70 Reg 5(2) Table 2 para 9 TC(DCI) Regs

71 Reg 5(2) Table 2 para 10 TC(DCI) Regs

72 Reg 5(1)(a) TC(DCI) Regs

73 Reg 5(1)(a) TC(DCI) Regs

74 Reg 5(1)(b) TC(DCI) Regs; HMRC, *Employment Income Manual*, para 74306

75 Reg 5(2) Table 2 paras 1-8 TC(DCI) Regs

76 Reg 19 Table 7 para 17 TC(DCI) Regs

77 Reg 10(1) TC(DCI) Regs

78 Reg 10(1)(a) TC(DCI) Regs

79 Reg 10(1)(d) TC(DCI) Regs

80 Reg 10(1)(c) TC(DCI) Regs

81 Reg 10(1)(e) TC(DCI) Regs

82 Reg 10(1)(b) TC(DCI) Regs

83 Reg 10(1)(a) TC(DCI) Regs

84 Reg 10(1)(a) TC(DCI) Regs

85 Reg 10(1)(a) TC(DCI) Regs

86 Reg 10(2)(a) Table 4 paras 1(a) and (b) TC(DCI) Regs

87 Reg 10(2)(a) Table 4 para 3 TC(DCI) Regs

88 Reg 10(2)(c) TC(DCI) Regs

89 Reg 10(2)(e) TC(DCI) Regs

90 Reg 10(2)(a) Table 4 para 4 TC(DCI) Regs

11

Part 11: General rules for tax credits
Chapter 64: Income: tax credits
Notes

91 Reg 10(2)(a) Table 4 paras 5-7 TC(DCI) Regs
92 Reg 10(2)(a) Table 4 para 8 TC(DCI) Regs; para 4608 TCTM
93 Reg 10(2)(a) Table 4 para 9 TC(DCI) Regs
94 Reg 10(2)(a) Table 4 para 10 TC(DCI) Regs
95 Reg 10(2)(a) Table 4 para 11 TC(DCI) Regs
96 Reg 10(2)(b) Table 5 TC(DCI) Regs
97 Reg 10(2)(a) Table 4 para 12 TC(DCI) Regs
98 Reg 10(2)(a) Table 4 para 13 TC(DCI) Regs
99 Reg 11 TC(DCI) Regs
100 See HMRC, *Help Sheet* (HS 223)
101 para 04006 TCTM; HMRC, *Property Income Manual*, paras 2020-40 and 2105
102 para 04006 TCTM
103 Reg 12(1) TC(DCI) Regs
104 Reg 12(3) TC(DCI) Regs
105 Reg 3(7)(a) TC(DCI) Regs
106 Reg 12(4) TC(DCI) Regs
107 Reg 3(3) TC(DCI) Regs
108 Reg 3(5A) TC(DCI) Regs
109 Reg 3(6A) TC(DCI) Regs
110 Reg 19 TC(DCI) Regs
111 Reg 19 Table 7 para 2(a)-(c) TC(DCI) Regs
112 Reg 19 Table 8 para 1 TC(DCI) Regs
113 Reg 19 Table 6 para 2 TC(DCI) Regs
114 Reg 19 Table 6 para 5 TC(DCI) Regs
115 Reg 19 Table 6 para 10 TC(DCI) Regs
116 Reg 19 Table 6 para 9 TC(DCI) Regs
117 Reg 19 Table 6 para 9 TC(DCI) Regs, The Qualifying Care Relief (Specified Social Care Schemes) Order 2011 No.712; s806A ITTOIA 2005
118 Reg 19 Table 6 para 11(a) TC(DCI) Regs
119 Reg 19 Table 6 para 11(a) and (b) TC(DCI) Regs
120 Reg 3(7)(c) TC(DCI) Regs
121 Reg 19 Table 6 para 12 TC(DCI) Regs
122 Reg 19 Table 6 para 13 TC(DCI) Regs
123 Reg 19 Table 6 para 14 TC(DCI) Regs
124 Reg 19 Table 6 para 14A TC(DCI) Regs
125 Reg 19 Table 6 para 15 TC(DCI) Regs
126 Reg 19 Table 6 para 16 TC(DCI) Regs
127 Reg 19 Table 7 para 1 TC(DCI) Regs
128 Reg 19 Table 8 para 6 TC(DCI) Regs
129 Reg 19 Table 8 paras 3 and 4 TC(DCI) Regs
130 Reg 19 Table 8 para 5(a) TC(DCI) Regs
131 Reg 19 Table 8 para 5(b) TC(DCI) Regs
132 Reg 3(7)(b) TC(DCI) Regs
133 Reg 19 Table 8 para 7 TC(DCI) Regs

4. Notional income
134 Reg 13 TC(DCI) Regs
135 Reg 15 TC(DCI) Regs
136 Reg 16 TC(DCI) Regs
137 Reg 17 TC(DCI) Regs
138 Reg 14 TC(DCI) Regs

Chapter 65

Claims, decisions and getting paid: tax credits

This chapter covers:
1. Who should claim (p1438)
2. How and when to make a claim (p1440)
3. How your claim is dealt with (p1445)
4. Backdating your claim (p1446)
5. Getting paid (p1447)
6. Changes of circumstances (p1450)
7. Annual reviews (p1455)
8. Contacting HM Revenue and Customs (p1458)

Key facts

- Tax credits are administered and paid by HM Revenue and Customs. Claims are dealt with by the Tax Credit Office.
- Tax credit claims are dealt with differently from social security benefits. Tax credits are dealt with over a tax year, using annual income, and entitlement is finalised at the end of the tax year.
- Tax credit claims can usually only be backdated for 31 days.
- Your award of tax credits may be affected by changes in your circumstances or income.
- Tax credit claims are finalised between April and July each year. This annual review also acts as a renewal claim for the new tax year.

Future changes

Tax credits will eventually be replaced by universal credit (UC). You cannot get tax credits and UC at the same time. If you do not come under the UC system (see p19), you can still make a new claim for tax credits. If UC has been introduced in your area and you are already getting tax credits, you can renew your tax credits claim. You will be transferred to UC at some point, although this is not expected to happen during 2014/15. See CPAG's online service and *Welfare Rights Bulletin* for updates.

1437

Part 11: General rules for tax credits
Chapter 65: Claims, decisions and getting paid: tax credits
1. Who should claim

1. Who should claim

You must be at least 16 years old to claim tax credits.[1]

If you are a member of a married couple or registered civil partnership, or live with someone as if you were married or civil partners, you must claim jointly with your partner. This is known as a 'joint claim'.[2] Both partners must claim the tax credits jointly, but there are special rules about who receives payment of the different tax credits. HM Revenue and Customs (HMRC) has the discretion to treat a claim by one member of a couple as having also been made by the other member, but usually only uses this power to accept renewal claims by telephone.[3]

If you are a single person, you make a single claim.

If you made a joint claim and are no longer part of a couple, or if you made a single claim and are now part of a couple, your entitlement ends. You must make a new claim.[4] You should tell the Tax Credit Office (TCO) as soon as possible. If you do not, you could be overpaid. You could also incur a financial penalty if you fail to notify the change within one month.[5] When you contact the TCO to report that your joint claim has ended, your new single claim can be made in the same telephone call without the need to fill in a new claim form.[6] If you report that a single claim has ended and you are now part of a couple, you will need to complete a new claim form and request backdating or you will lose out on tax credits. In either case, your new claim can only be backdated for 31 days.

You cannot claim tax credits if you or your partner are entitled to universal credit (UC – see p19).[7]

Couples

You and your partner count as a 'couple' if you are:[8]
- a man and woman and are:
  - married, unless you are separated and this is under a court order or is likely to be permanent (see p1439); *or*
  - not married and are 'living together as husband and wife' (see p1439); *or*
- the same sex as your partner and are:
  - registered as civil partners, unless you are separated and this is under a court order or is likely to be permanent (see p1439); *or*
  - not civil partners and are living together as if you are – ie, you would be regarded as 'living together as husband and wife' if you were a different sex from your partner (see p1439).[9]

Note: from 29 March 2014 in England and Wales and at some point in 2014 in Scotland, marriage is/will be extended to same-sex couples. At the time of writing, tax credit legislation had not been amended to reflect this change, so references to a married couple only apply to a man and a woman. See CPAG's online service and *Welfare Rights Bulletin* for updates.

If you are entitled to tax credits and become part of a couple with someone who is entitled to UC (see p19), your tax credit award ends and you are treated as making a joint UC claim.[10]

Married couples and civil partners

You must claim tax credits jointly with your partner if you are married to her/him or you are registered as civil partners. You still count as a couple for tax credits purposes if you are a man and a woman who are married, or a same-sex couple who are registered civil partners, and are still in a relationship but are not living together – eg, because of work or housing reasons. You continue to count as a couple while you and your partner are temporarily separated. It does not matter how long the temporary separation lasts (but see below if you or your partner go abroad).

If you and your partner are permanently separated or are separated under a court order, claim tax credits as a single person immediately. This is the case even if you are still living under the same roof and whether or not you are taking steps to divorce your partner or dissolve your civil partnership.[11] The test is whether you are 'separated in circumstances in which the separation is likely to be permanent' and this depends on your (and your partner's) intentions.[12] The focus is on the state of the relationship, not exclusively whether you are living in the 'same household', which differs from the rule for means-tested benefits (see p205).[13] If you and your partner are having a trial separation and there is at least a 50 per cent chance of reconciliation, HMRC is likely to say you still count as a couple.[14]

Special rules apply if you are a member of a polygamous unit.[15]

Living together as a couple

You must claim tax credits jointly with your partner if you are living together as if you are married or civil partners. In determining whether or not you count as living together as a couple, HMRC is likely to consider the same factors the DWP does for means-tested benefits.[16] See p206 and p209 for more information about the situations when you might count as living together as a couple.

If you and your partner stop living together, claim tax credits as a single person immediately. However, if you and your partner are only temporarily living apart (eg, one of you is in hospital or in respite care), you may still be treated as a couple.

Note: decision makers often apply too narrow an interpretation of the test. For example, there is no rule that says that if your partner stays with you for three nights or more a week you are *automatically* to be treated as a couple living together.

If you or your partner go abroad

If you or your partner go abroad, either permanently or for more than a set period of time and cannot be treated as being in the UK (see p1585), you cease to satisfy

Part 11: General rules for tax credits
Chapter 65: Claims, decisions and getting paid: tax credits
2. How and when to make a claim

the residence conditions. In this case, you must terminate your joint claim. Failure to do this may result in a penalty (see p1476). The person still in the UK may be able to make a new claim as a single person.

Challenging a decision

In some cases you may have to prove that you are a couple – eg, if you want to claim working tax credit instead of income support and you are not in full-time paid work yourself, but your partner is. In other cases you may have to prove that you are not a couple – eg, if your former partner's income is being taken into account when working out your tax credits. HMRC often relies on information it obtains from credit reference agencies, but in the event of an appeal, it must usually produce all the evidence it used to make the decision, and such information on its own is unlikely to be sufficient to justify a 'living together' decision.[17]

If you think a decision about whether or not you count as a couple is wrong and it affects your tax credits, consider appealing. It is possible that the DWP, the local authority and HMRC might reach different conclusions about whether you are a couple. If so, appeal *all* the decisions with which you disagree.

Appointees

The following people can make a claim on your behalf if you are unable to make the claim yourself:[18]

- a receiver appointed by the Court of Protection with power to make a claim for tax credits on your behalf;
- in Scotland, a tutor, curator or other guardian acting or appointed in terms of the law who is administering your estate;
- in Northern Ireland, a controller appointed by the High Court with power to make a tax credit claim on your behalf;
- a person who is your 'appointee' (see p1137) for social security purposes; *or*
- if none of the above applies, a person aged 18 or over who applies to HMRC in writing to act on your behalf and is appointed by HMRC in that capacity.

2. **How and when to make a claim**

You must claim tax credits in writing on Form TC600. You have no entitlement to tax credits unless you make a claim.[19] You claim both child tax credit (CTC) and working tax credit (WTC) on one claim form. HM Revenue and Customs (HMRC) has discretion to accept an application not made on the correct claim form but in practice this rarely happens.[20] There are specific circumstances where a claim may be accepted by other means.

- If you have been getting additional amounts for your children in your income support (IS) and your entitlement to IS ends (eg, because you are a lone parent and have been moved onto jobseeker's allowance (JSA) when your youngest child reached the age of five), the DWP can pass the required information to HMRC to allow a 'deemed claim' for CTC and you do not have to fill in a separate claim form.[21]
- If you are starting work after being on JSA or IS as a lone parent, you can claim tax credits at your local Jobcentre Plus office as part of the 'In and Out of Work Project', which can also include telephone claims.
- If you were claiming tax credits as a couple and notify the Tax Credit office (TCO) that you are no longer a couple, your new single claim can be accepted by telephone.
- If you are renewing a claim, this may be done by telephone or automatically in specific cases (see p1445).

You can get a claim form by contacting the Tax Credit Helpline on 0345 300 3900 (textphone: 0345 300 3909), which may also ask you questions about your identity and eligibility for tax credits. Once you have passed the identification process, the Helpline must send a claim form if you request one, even if entitlement is in doubt.[22] If you cannot prove your identity over the telephone, you may be required to attend an interview. Some Citizens Advice Bureaux may also have a supply of claim forms. Even if you are advised by the Helpline that you are not entitled to tax credits, still request a claim form and make a claim if you think you are eligible. There will then be a decision on which to base an appeal.

Send the completed claim form directly to the TCO in the pre-paid envelope provided with the claim form (Comben House, Farriers Way, Netherton, Merseyside L75 1AX) or to any other office specified in writing by HMRC (such as the TCO address in Appendix 1).[23] Keep a copy of your claim form in case queries arise.

If you have sent your claim form to the TCO and you later realise that the details on it need to be amended, contact the TCO as soon as possible. You can amend or withdraw your claim at any time before the claim has been decided.[24]

When to claim

You should claim tax credits as soon as you think you are eligible. You cannot make a claim for tax credits in advance of the tax year for which you are claiming.[25] The general rule is that a claim for tax credits runs from the date it is received by the TCO until the end of the tax year in which the claim is made.[26] If you were entitled to tax credits before the date your claim is received by the TCO, your claim can be backdated for a period of up to 31 days. Backdating of WTC is possible for a longer period if you are a disabled worker and only become entitled to WTC following an award of a qualifying benefit (see p1446).

Part 11: General rules for tax credits
Chapter 65: Claims, decisions and getting paid: tax credits
2. How and when to make a claim

Once a claim for tax credits has been made, it can be renewed at the end of that tax year (see p1445).

You cannot make a new claim for tax credits if you or your partner are entitled to universal credit (UC), even if your claim could be backdated to a date before you were entitled to UC.[27]

Should you protect your claim?[28]

Tax credits are always based on annual income. HMRC bases the initial award on your (and your partner's) *previous* tax year's income (see p1419). If your income in the previous year was too high to qualify for tax credits, but you think your income in the current year may be substantially lower and you will qualify (eg, if you are self-employed with a fluctuating income, or your income is going to fall because your work is seasonal, you are going on maternity leave or you might be made redundant), you may wish to consider making a claim, including a request for it to be backdated if relevant.

This is known as a 'protective claim' and you are given a 'nil award'.[29] This means that you are eligible for tax credits and your claim is in the system, but you are currently not paid anything because your previous year's income was too high. This protects your position because once your current year's income is known, HMRC can then amend the nil award to make a payment for the whole period of your claim, rather than requiring you to make a new claim, which can only be backdated 31 days. The nil award can be amended during the year or at the end of the tax year, and the new award runs from your original date of claim (or the date to which your claim was backdated).

Information to support your claim

Your claim must contain all the information requested on the claim form, unless HMRC decides otherwise.[30] If you do not supply all the requested information, a decision may not be made on your claim until the required information is provided, or your claim may be rejected as not validly made. There is no right of appeal against a decision not to accept an incomplete claim, and the only remedy is judicial review.[31] If you need advice about the information required, contact the Helpline (see p1458).

National insurance number requirement

Your claim must include the following for each person who makes a claim:[32]

- your (and your partner's if you are claiming as a couple) national insurance (NI) number plus information or evidence establishing that the number is yours (or your partner's); *or*
- information or evidence to enable HMRC to find your (and your partner's) NI number; *or*
- an application for an NI number, with the necessary evidence or information to allow one to be allocated (this does not necessarily mean that you must actually be allocated an NI number).

You do not need to meet the above NI number requirement if HMRC believes you have a 'reasonable excuse'.[33] 'Reasonable excuse' is not defined, but HMRC says it will vary from case to case and discretion must be used fairly.[34] There is no right of appeal against a decision that you do not have a reasonable excuse for not meeting the NI number requirement, and the only remedy is judicial review.[35] The NI number requirement does not need to be satisfied for someone (usually one member of a couple) who is a 'person subject to immigration control' because s/he does not have leave to enter or remain in the UK (see p1500) and who has not been given an NI number.[36] If your claim is rejected because the NI number requirement has not been met, you can appeal to the First-tier Tribunal on the grounds that the NI number requirement does not apply because you or your partner fall into this category of person subject to immigration control.[37] However, the NI number requirement does apply to other people who have limited leave to enter or remain in the UK but who are still subject to immigration control. If someone has not been given an NI number, you can argue this is a reasonable excuse. **Note:** entitlement to tax credits is affected by your immigration status (see p1561).

Child benefit reference number

The tax credit claim form asks for the child benefit reference number for any child(ren) for whom you are claiming. You should leave the box blank if you do not know it. There is no legal requirement to claim child benefit in order to be entitled to CTC. If you do not have a child benefit reference number (eg, because you are waiting for your child benefit claim to be processed), do not delay claiming CTC. Child benefit can be backdated three months, but CTC can only be backdated 31 days, and it usually takes longer than this for a child benefit claim to be made and processed. HMRC has confirmed that tax credit claims will not be rejected because the child benefit reference number is missing.[38] It may take longer to confirm the identity of the child, and that you are responsible for the child. In this case, the tax credit award will be made from the date of claim, with up to 31 days' backdating. As long as your tax credit claim is received within 31 days of the date of birth of a new baby, or the date you became responsible for a child, it will be awarded from that date, even if it takes longer than this to process.

Income

If you are receiving IS, income-based JSA, income-related employment and support allowance (ESA) or pension credit (PC) when you claim tax credits, you must tick a box to confirm this on the claim form. You do not need to provide any other income details.[39] HMRC expects you to know which type of JSA or ESA you are getting.[40]

Otherwise, when you make a claim for tax credits, you must provide a figure for your income during the previous tax year. If you are part of a couple and making a joint claim, your award is based on your joint income during the

Part 11: General rules for tax credits
Chapter 65: Claims, decisions and getting paid: tax credits
2. How and when to make a claim

previous tax year. This applies even in situations in which you may not have been living as a couple in the previous year, so income before the relationship began still counts as joint income.[41] The notes that accompany the claim form include a working sheet to help you calculate your income. For details of what counts as income, see Chapter 64.

If you think that your current tax year's income is going to be substantially different to the previous tax year's income, you must still complete the claim form with details of your previous tax year's income. When HMRC makes a decision on your claim, you will be sent an award notice informing you how to notify it of your estimated income for the current year. You can also request that your award be adjusted at any time during the year of the award. Where appropriate, HMRC will then adjust your award of tax credits, using your estimated figure of your current year's income (see p1452).

If you worked as an employee throughout the previous tax year, your P60 for that year has details of your taxable income. If you received any payments in kind from your employer, you should have details of these on Form P9D or P11D, which your employer should give you. If you were self-employed throughout the previous tax year, you can use your tax return as the basis for your taxable income. If you were in receipt of taxable social security benefits, you should be able to get a statement of taxable benefit income from the DWP.

Note: if your previous year's income was too high to receive tax credits, but you think your current year's income may be less, you should make a protective claim for tax credits if you meet the qualifying conditions (see p1442).

Bank account details

You are required to provide details of a bank, building society or Post Office card account into which the tax credits can be paid. This is because entitlement depends on having a bank or other account.[42] See p1448 if you do not have an account.

Further information and evidence

HMRC might need further information or evidence before making a decision on a claim, renewal or revision. The information or evidence can be required from you or from your employer or childcare provider. If material is required, HMRC gives notice to provide it within a specified time limit. In all cases, this must be at least 30 days.[43] The basic rule is that you can be required to provide any further information or evidence that HMRC considers necessary. If you do not provide the material requested, you might be refused tax credits. If you provide incorrect information or fail to comply with requirements to provide information or evidence, you may be given a financial penalty or, if you are considered to have acted fraudulently, a fine or imprisonment, or both (see Chapter 67).

Renewing your claim

From 6 April each year, HMRC reviews all tax credit awards, including nil awards and awards that ended before 5 April. This review process and your response form the basis of the renewal of your claim for the following year. Your response to the annual review is treated as a claim for the new tax year, unless you state that you wish to withdraw your claim. Tax credits continue to be paid on a provisional basis during the annual review (see p1449). Your claim may be renewed automatically if you have been on IS, income-based JSA, income-related ESA or PC throughout the previous tax year and are still in receipt of one of these benefits. Your claim may be withdrawn automatically by HMRC if you have a nil award and do not state that you wish your claim to continue. See p1455 for more on the annual review.

Note: your claim can be renewed until you are transferred to UC.

Withdrawing your claim

If you no longer wish to claim tax credits, you can withdraw your claim during the annual review (see p1455). However, if you have been receiving 'provisional payments' (see p1449) since the start of the new tax year, these become overpayments if there is no renewal claim. If you have a nil award because your income is too high for an award to be made, HMRC seeks to withdraw your claim. HMRC will write to you at least 35 days before the annual review to notify you that your claim will not be renewed unless you respond within 30 days that you want your claim to continue.[44] Renewing a nil award protects your future entitlement and may prove valuable if income drops unexpectedly later in the year.[45]

---

3. How your claim is dealt with

Once you have made a valid claim for tax credits (see p1440), HM Revenue and Customs (HMRC) must make a decision on whether you are entitled to either of the tax credits and, if so, at what rate.[46] HMRC may first require you, or your partner if you are making a joint claim, to provide any information or evidence that it needs to make a decision.[47]

You can amend, either verbally or in writing, the details you provided when making your claim at any time until HMRC makes its initial decision and your date of claim will remain the same.[48]

An '**initial decision**' (see p1446) is made at the start of your claim and is based on an estimate of your tax credit award for the whole year (6 April to 5 April) or the remainder of the year if you claim during the year. You are notified of the initial decision and your award on Form TC602. You are asked to check the details on your award notice using a checklist (TC602(SN)). Contact the Tax Credit Office

Part 11: General rules for tax credits
Chapter 65: Claims, decisions and getting paid: tax credits
4. Backdating your claim

if any of the details shown on the award notice are wrong or have changed. If you do not and an overpayment results, HMRC may expect you to pay it back (see p1468).

A **'revised decision'** may be made during the tax year – eg, following certain changes of circumstances (see p1450). Decisions can be revised at any time during the tax year, and as many times as is required. Each revised decision is notified on a tax credits award notice, Form TC602.

A **'final decision'** is made after the end of the tax year in which your claim was made, as part of the annual review (see p1457). It is based on your circumstances during the year and is the decision that confirms what your entitlement actually was. You are sent a tax credits award notice, Form TC602. A final decision can only be changed in limited circumstances (see p1484).

Unless the decision on your award is changed, either on revision or appeal, the initial decision and the final decision are the only decisions on your claim that you will receive.

If you think an initial decision, revised decision or final decision is wrong, you can appeal (see Chapter 68).

Initial decisions

On receiving your application for tax credits, HMRC must make an initial decision on whether you are entitled to tax credits, and if so, the amount. The claim form does not distinguish between child tax credit and working tax credit, so HMRC must decide your entitlement for both.

The main evidence normally used relates to your income in the *previous* tax year to the one in which you make your claim and to your circumstances (eg, if you have children or if you are working) in the *current* tax year – ie, the one in which you make your claim. So, for an initial decision for 2014/15, the current year is 2014/15 and the previous year is 2013/14. See Chapter 64 for more details about income.

You must be notified of the initial decision. The notice must include the date on which it is given and your right to an appeal or, as expected from April 2014, a review before you can appeal.[49] If you had already claimed tax credits in the previous year, your initial decision for the coming year may be included in the annual review (see p1455).[50] The initial decision sets out the amount of tax credits you are due to receive until the final decision is made, unless it is changed on revision or appeal.

4. Backdating your claim

In general, your claim for tax credits can be backdated for up to 31 days (but see p1447), provided you would have satisfied the rules of entitlement throughout the 31-day period.[51] You do not need any reason for backdating. Although HM Revenue and Customs looks at your claim form for evidence of possible backdating, it is best to ask for your claim to be backdated to when you think your entitlement began (subject to the 31-day limit). The claim form does not ask about backdating, so request it separately in writing and follow up by telephone.

A renewal claim can be backdated for longer periods, depending on when you make your annual declaration (see p1456).

If you were entitled to tax credits but no payment was made because you failed to provide sufficient details of an account into which tax credits could be paid and you subsequently provide the necessary details, your payment can be backdated for up to three months from the date you supply the information.[52]

A new claim for working tax credit (WTC) can be backdated for more than 31 days if you have a disability and you have been waiting to hear about a disability benefit. If your claim includes the disabled worker element (see p1403) and you claim within 31 days of being awarded a qualifying disability benefit, usually disability living allowance (DLA) or personal independence payment (PIP), your WTC claim can be backdated to the date your DLA or PIP was awarded, provided you were working at least 16 hours throughout the period and did not qualify for WTC under any other route.[53]

A new claim for child tax credit (CTC) cannot be backdated for more than 31 days, even if a disability benefit has been awarded for the child. If your income is too high to receive CTC unless a disability element is included, you should make a 'protective claim' (see p1442). If you have an existing award of WTC or CTC and want to be awarded the disability or severe disability elements following an award of a qualifying disability benefit, see p1452.

See p1512 for backdating if you are granted refugee status.

5. Getting paid

Who is paid

If you make a joint claim, child tax credit (CTC) and the childcare element of working tax credit (WTC) are paid into the account of the 'main carer' of the children, as nominated on the claim form.[54] The **'main carer'** can be either you or your partner, depending on who you both agree should be paid. If you and your partner are living at the same address and either you do not identify who should be paid, or you cannot agree, HM Revenue and Customs (HMRC) decides. If you and your partner are not currently living at the same address or one of you is temporarily absent, HMRC decides which of you will be paid.[55] If the main carer changes following an award of tax credits, HMRC can make the payments to that person instead if it considers it reasonable.[56]

Part 11: General rules for tax credits
Chapter 65: Claims, decisions and getting paid: tax credits
5. Getting paid

If you claim WTC as part of a joint claim and one of you is working, the payment (apart from any amount for childcare) is made to the person who is in full-time paid work (see Chapter 9). If you are both in full-time paid work, you can decide who will receive the payment. If you cannot agree, HMRC decides. If you both agree, write to the Tax Credit Office (TCO) requesting that payment be made to the other person.[57]

If you make a joint claim and your partner dies, you receive any outstanding amount of tax credits that would have been paid to your partner up to the date of death, after which you must make a new claim as a single person.[58]

If an appointee (see p1137) has claimed tax credits on your behalf, payment is normally made to the appointee.[59]

How and when payments are made

HMRC makes payments of tax credits by direct credit transfer into a bank, building society (or similar) or Post Office card account.[60] You can request that the payments are made into your account every week or every four weeks, but HMRC has the discretion to make payments weekly or four-weekly as it sees fit. CTC and the childcare element of WTC must be paid at the same time and at the same intervals.[61]

If you are entitled to less than £2 tax credits a week, your award may be paid as a lump sum.[62]

If it is not considered appropriate for payments to be made into an account, HMRC can decide on the manner and timing of payment by other means.[63] If you do not provide account details, HMRC should write to you, requesting that you supply the information within four weeks, after which your payments may be postponed.[64] If you then require an authority from HMRC to open an account, you have three weeks from the date it supplies you with this to provide details of your account. If you do not provide details of an account within three months of your payments being postponed (or by the end of the relevant tax year if this is earlier), your entitlement may cease from the date payments were postponed. These periods can be extended if there are exceptional circumstances or you have a 'reasonable excuse' for not being able to provide the details within the time limits.[65] If you lose or forget your PIN, see p1163.

Payments of tax credits may be reduced if an overpayment is being recovered. See Chapter 66 for more information.

Urgent payments

There is no provision in the tax credits legislation for payments to be made before a decision has been made on entitlement. However, once a decision has been made to award tax credits, there is detailed staff guidance on making payments urgently when requested by you or via the MP Hotline. Urgent payments should be made where you or your children are experiencing hardship, especially in cases of domestic violence, identity fraud, immediate risk of eviction, or other individual circumstances. These payments are variously referred to in the *Tax Credits Manual* as 'manual payments', 'interim payments' and 'user-requested payments'. Payment can be made by the next day into an account or by cashcheque.[66]

When payment is postponed

Payment of tax credits may be postponed if:[67]

- there is an appeal pending against a decision of the First-tier Tribunal, Upper Tribunal or a court either in your case or in another case that might affect your award (including if HMRC is waiting to receive a decision or statement of reasons, or considering whether to make a further appeal or request a statement of reasons); *or*
- you have failed to provide account details; *or*
- details of your account or address appear to be incorrect; *or*
- you have failed to respond to a request for information or evidence by a specified date.

If your income drops during the year, your tax credits may be increased and you may appear to be due some arrears of tax credits for the earlier part of the year. HMRC refers to this as a 'potential payment', and it may be held back until the end of the year when your final income is known. If the underpayment is confirmed at the end of the tax year, it must be paid to you.[68]

Provisional payments

Your claim is renewed by the annual review process from April to July, during which time your tax credits continue to be paid on a provisional basis.[69]

Provisional payments continue at the start of the new tax year while you are waiting to renew your claim and have not had a final decision on the previous year, or, if you have renewed your claim but not yet received an initial decision, on the new tax year.

If HMRC does not have up-to-date income details, these payments are based on the assumption that your income for the tax year just ended increased in line with average earnings.[70] If your income increased by more than this, you may be overpaid until the review is complete. Therefore, it is best to provide income details as soon as possible and not wait for the annual review. If you withdraw or fail to renew your claim, any provisional payments since the start of the year will become an overpayment because there is no claim for the new tax year.

Part 11: General rules for tax credits
Chapter 65: Claims, decisions and getting paid: tax credits
6. Changes of circumstances

6. Changes of circumstances

Changes in your family circumstances, childcare charges or income during your award may lead to changes in your entitlement. If changes do affect your entitlement, this can be altered either soon after the change has occurred, or at the end of the year when the final decision is made and HM Revenue and Customs (HMRC) makes a final check on your details. However, certain changes must be notified to the Tax Credit Office (TCO) within one month or you may incur a penalty. Some other changes which increase your entitlement should be notified within one month if your increased award is to be backdated in full.

Once an initial decision has been made, there are three types of change which can affect your entitlement to tax credits:
- changes that must be notified to the TCO (see below);
- changes that affect your maximum entitlement to tax credits (see p1451);
- changes in income (see p1452).

Following any change of circumstances that must be notified or that affect your maximum entitlement, the way your tax credits are calculated changes.[71] The changes mean that either your entitlement to tax credits has ceased or that a new 'relevant period' is started from the time the change is treated as taking effect. A new relevant period means that a new calculation of your entitlement is made. See p1399 for more on the relevant period and details of the calculation.

Changes that must be notified

Some changes must be notified to the TCO within one month of the date of the change or the date you became aware of the change, if this was later. The notification must be 'given' to the appropriate office (see p1454).[72] If you do not do this, HMRC may impose a financial penalty on you (see p1476). You must notify the TCO within one month if:
- you were claiming as a single person but are now part of a couple. Your tax credit entitlement comes to an end from the time the change occurred, and you must make a new claim;
- you were claiming as a couple but are no longer part of that couple. Your entitlement comes to an end from the date the change occurred, and you must make a new claim;
- you or your partner leave the UK permanently or for more than eight weeks (12 if due to illness or bereavement) and cannot be treated as being in the UK (see p1585). Entitlement comes to an end and you must make a new claim. If your partner is not treated as being in the UK, you must make a new claim as a single person (and when s/he comes back, claim again as a couple);
- for child tax credit (CTC) only, you lose your right to reside in the UK (see p1525);

- there has been a decrease of £10 a week or more over four consecutive weeks in your or your partner's average weekly childcare charge (as calculated on p1408) or the childcare costs have stopped. This change takes effect on the day after the four consecutive weeks. If you have been awarded childcare costs for a fixed period that was known when the costs were awarded, the change takes effect from the week following the end of the period of the award, instead of the usual four-week period;[73]
- you or your partner stop normally working at least 16 or 30 hours a week (see p165 for rules about work). You can still count as being in work in some situations – eg, in some cases of illness or maternity. If you stop work, you may get a four-week run-on of working tax credit (WTC – see p172). For a couple, you do not need to report a change in which partner is working, as long as this does not affect your entitlement or maximum rate;[74]
- you are a couple with children, and you and your partner stop normally working a combined total of 24 or 30 hours a week;
- you or your partner cease to be responsible for one or more of your children (see p153 for when you count as responsible);
- a child for whom you or your partner are responsible dies (see p151 for who counts as a child);
- a child for whom you or your partner are responsible stops counting as a child or qualifying young person, other than by reaching age 20 (see p151 for who counts as a child). In this case, you must notify the TCO within one month of the date the change actually occurred, rather than when you became aware of the change.

Changes that affect your maximum entitlement

In addition to the changes outlined above, there are other changes in your circumstances that affect your maximum entitlement to tax credits – ie, they affect the tax credit elements to which you are entitled (see Chapter 63).

You do not have to notify the TCO of these changes when they occur. Some changes can be notified up to a week in advance (see p1454). However, most changes which *increase* your entitlement are only backdated for a maximum of one month from the time that you make the notification.[75] The only exception concerns one of the disability elements (see p1452). Changes that *decrease* your entitlement always take effect from the date of change, irrespective of when you notify the TCO. Delaying notifying these changes can, therefore, lead to your being underpaid or overpaid. Note that overpayments are usually recovered from you (see Chapter 66).

The changes to which these rules apply include:
- you have a new baby, or another child joins your family;

11

Part 11: General rules for tax credits
Chapter 65: Claims, decisions and getting paid: tax credits
6. Changes of circumstances

- your child is staying on in full-time non-advanced education after 31 August following his/her 16th birthday (HMRC considers this to be a change, as the default position is that CTC will stop unless you notify it of this);
- you or your partner start normally working at least 16, 24 or 30 hours a week;
- your childcare costs increase by £10 or more a week for at least four weeks in a row. The change takes effect from the first week in which your costs increase.[76] You can report an increase of £10 or more a week as soon as one occurs, provided you expect it to last for at least four weeks. For how your childcare costs are calculated, see p1408.

Changes in entitlement to one of the disability elements

The disabled worker and severe disability elements of WTC can be backdated for more than one month if you notify the TCO that you have been awarded a qualifying disability benefit, usually disability living allowance (DLA) or personal independence payment (PIP), within one month of that award being made.[77] The elements can be backdated to the date the disability benefit was awarded. This includes after an appeal or supersession from a previous tax year. If the award means that you become entitled to WTC for the first time, see p1446.

A similar rule applies to CTC entitlement. If a child for whom you are responsible is awarded DLA or a young person is awarded PIP, you are entitled to the disabled child element. If the child is awarded DLA care component at the highest rate or PIP at the enhanced rate for daily living, you are entitled to the severely disabled child element in your CTC award. The elements can be backdated for more than one month, to the date DLA or PIP was awarded, if you notify the TCO of the award of DLA or PIP within one month of the DLA or PIP decision.[78] This includes after an appeal or supersession from a previous tax year. However, it is not possible to backdate a new claim for CTC in this way, because you would have been eligible anyway provided you were responsible for the child. If your income is too high to receive CTC unless the disabled child or severely disabled child element is awarded, make a 'protective claim' (see p1442).

11 Changes in income

The initial decision on your award of tax credit is usually based on your previous year's income. Your award can be changed to reflect:

- an expected fall in your annual income of more than £2,500 compared with the previous year – eg, if your earnings fall during the year. A fall of less than £2,500 is disregarded during the year; *and*
- an expected rise in your annual income of more than £5,000 compared with the previous year – eg, if your earnings increase during the year. A rise of less than £5,000 is disregarded during the year.

You are not required to report a change in income during the year and a penalty cannot be imposed on you if you fail to do so, unless it is a formal request for information (see p1475). However, it is often worth reporting a change in income when it occurs to avoid overpayments or underpayments. Remember that HMRC always requires a figure for your annual income in the complete tax year, so you should be careful to keep an in-year estimate accurate and up to date.

If you expect your annual income to fall by more than £2,500

- If you notify the TCO of an estimated decrease in your annual income of more than £2,500 during the year, your tax credit payments may be increased. However, the first £2,500 of the decrease is disregarded, so it is only any decrease over that amount that makes a difference. HMRC adds £2,500 onto the current year's income and bases your award on the result. For example, if your 2013/14 income was £10,000 and your 2014/15 income is £6,000, your tax credits award is based on £8,500.[79]
- An increase in tax credits means that if you get housing benefit (HB), the amount could be reduced because tax credits count as income.
- At the end of the year, it may be that your income did not fall as you predicted and, as a result, you have been overpaid tax credits, which you may have to repay. For example, if your 2013/14 income was £9,000 and you ask for your tax credits to be based on an estimate that your 2014/15 income will be £6,000 but, at the end of 2014/15, your actual income is £8,000, your tax credit award should not have been increased and you will have been overpaid.
- HB takes into account the amount of tax credits you actually *receive*. If you have been overpaid tax credits, HB is *not* increased for the period during which you should have received a lower amount of tax credits. Not only will you usually have to repay the overpaid tax credits, you may have lost out on the additional HB which you would have been able to claim had you been receiving a lower award of tax credits.
- If you do not notify the TCO of a fall in income of more than £2,500 during the year, your tax credit entitlement is not adjusted until the final decision at the end of the year. In this instance, you will have been underpaid tax credits for the year, and this should be paid to you as a lump sum. This lump sum counts as capital for HB and is ignored for 52 weeks after you have received it.[80] You will not, therefore, have been overpaid HB as a result of receiving these arrears and you will not have been overpaid or lost out on tax credits.

If you expect your annual income to rise by more than £5,000

- If you notify the TCO that you expect your income to increase by more than £5,000 during the year, your tax credit award is decreased. This may mean that you prevent an overpayment of tax credits building up further during the year (see Chapter 66). Your HB (if you are entitled to any) can then be increased to take account of the lower award of tax credits.
- If you do not notify the TCO of an expected rise in your income during the year, you will keep being paid the 'extra' tax credits during the year and will incur an overpayment. The overpaid tax credits are usually recoverable from

Part 11: General rules for tax credits
Chapter 65: Claims, decisions and getting paid: tax credits
6. Changes of circumstances

you by a reduction in the tax credits you are paid in the following year, in which case your HB in that year is likely to increase.

- There is no penalty for incurring an overpayment of tax credits on the basis of an increase in income.
- All this, however, does not mean that you are better off building up such an overpayment. You will not know for sure exactly how much you have been overpaid and at what rate it will be recovered from you until the final decision at the end of the year. Although the reduced tax credit entitlement in the following year may increase your HB, your increased earnings will also have the effect of reducing these benefits, and any further fluctuations in your income could complicate matters further.

Notifying changes of circumstances

You can notify any changes in your circumstances either orally or in writing. The notification must be given to an 'appropriate office', defined as Comben House, Farriers Way, Netherton, Merseyside L75 1AX or any other office specified in writing by HMRC – eg, the TCO address on your award notice (see Appendix 1).[81] This could include the Jobcentre Plus office dealing with your tax credits claim as part of the 'In and Out of Work Project' or the Child Benefit Office as part of the 'Tell Us Once' initiative, but only if this has been specified in writing by HMRC. If you did notify the DWP or another part of HMRC of a change which affects your tax credit entitlement and this was not passed on and resulted in an underpayment or overpayment, you should raise this in your dispute (see p1467). In practice, to be safe, you should ensure that the TCO has been informed. HMRC encourages claimants to telephone the Helpline with queries or to report a change (see p1458). However, it is advisable to confirm the notification in writing to the TCO and to keep a copy so you have a record of what you have said and when you said it.

Notification must be given by the person who claimed the tax credit. In joint claim cases, it can be given by either member of the couple.[82]

Some changes of circumstances can be notified up to a week in advance. These are if:[83]

- you have accepted an offer of work and expect to start work within seven days;
- you have arranged childcare and will incur childcare costs during the current tax year;
- your weekly childcare costs are going to change by £10 a week or more.

You can also notify in advance if you expect your child to stay on in full-time, non-advanced education or approved training from 1 September after her/his 16th birthday.[84]

You can amend the notification at any time before the initial award is revised, in which case the amended notification is taken as being notified at the time that your original notification was sent.[85]

If you notify a change of circumstances, HMRC should send you a new award notice (if the change affected your award) within 30 days.[86] If you do not receive one within 30 days, HMRC's leaflet asks you to call the Helpline again. However, provided you can prove the original notification was made, this is not part of your responsibilities (see p1468).

7. Annual reviews

The annual review is the process by which HM Revenue and Customs (HMRC) finalises your entitlement for the year that has just ended, and makes an initial decision on your award for the year that has just begun. Responding to the annual review is how you renew your claim for tax credits for the new tax year.

If you claimed tax credits for the tax year 2013/14, HMRC should write to you between April and July 2014, enclosing an annual review form (TC603R). This is referred to in the legislation as the 'final notice'.[87] Unless you have been receiving income support (IS), income-based jobseeker's allowance (JSA), income-related employment and support allowance (ESA) or pension credit (PC) throughout 2013/14 and are still getting one of those benefits, or have a nil award, you should also receive an annual declaration (Form TC603D – see p1456).

If you made more than one claim for tax credits during the previous tax year (eg, because you separated from your partner and made a new claim as a single person), you receive a separate annual review form and annual declaration form, if required, for each claim. If you are sent more than one set of forms covering different claims, reply to each separately, even if they ask for the same information. If an annual declaration is required, one member of a couple can make this by telephone on behalf of her/his partner; if it is in writing both partners must sign it.[88] If a couple separate during the renewal period, a declaration by one partner allows the claim to be renewed up to the date of separation.[89] Both members of a separated couple are expected to make signed declarations for the previous year to allow the award for that year to be finalised. However, if only one signs the declaration, the award can be finalised, based on the information held by HMRC about the other member.[90]

If you are sent an annual review form, but not an annual declaration form, you are asked to check that all the details about your claim for the previous year are correct and to notify the Tax Credit Office (TCO) of any changes in your circumstances. You are then deemed to have confirmed that all the details in the form are correct.[91] The final decision on the award for 2013/14 and an initial decision on the award for 2014/15 are as set out on the annual review form. However, always check the form and the notes accompanying it carefully to see whether you need to return the forms or report a change or error.

If the details on the forms sent to you about your claim and income are not correct and you fail to reply within the time allowed, you may not receive the

Part 11: General rules for tax credits
Chapter 65: Claims, decisions and getting paid: tax credits
7. Annual reviews

correct amount of tax credit. If you are overpaid as a result, you may have to repay the overpayment. If you fail to notify certain changes of circumstances promptly, you may be given a penalty (see p1476).

If your tax credit award ends because you become entitled to universal credit (UC), the annual review may be carried out during the tax year, and you must declare your income in the part of the year up to the date your tax credit entitlement ends.[92] During 2014/15, this is only likely to happen if you form a couple with someone who is entitled to UC (see p19).

The annual declaration

You may receive an annual declaration form (TC603D) that asks for details of your income in the previous tax year. Anyone who was not on IS, income-based JSA, income-related ESA or PC throughout 2013/14 and who does not have a nil award should get an annual declaration form.

Responses must usually be on a form provided by HMRC (Form TC603RD). Alternatively, you can call the Helpline. If you are unable to respond to the annual declaration (eg, because of illness), responses can be accepted from receivers and people who are appointees for tax credit or benefit purposes.[93]

If you are sent an annual declaration form, you must always respond to it on or before the date specified – usually 31 July, unless it was issued after 1 July, in which case you must be given at least 30 days. If you are returning the annual declaration form by post, this is the date it must be received by the TCO. If you respond in writing but do not use the annual declaration form, HMRC has discretion whether to accept it.[94] Alternatively, you can make your annual declaration by telephone on or before the deadline. If you do not respond to the annual declaration, your tax credit payments will stop, you may have to repay any tax credit paid since 6 April and you may have to pay a penalty. You must also tell the TCO of any changes in your personal circumstances from those set out in the annual review form.

If you do not know your total income for the period in question, do not delay making your annual declaration. Instead, provide an estimate and send details of your actual income as soon as you can. The annual declaration form allows for this, and there is a box to tick to show that you have given an estimate. You must provide your actual income figure on or before a second deadline, usually 31 January at the latest. The annual declaration form notifies you that if you do not do so, you are treated as having declared that your final income was as estimated, and your estimate is used to finalise your entitlement.[95] Responding to the annual declaration, if required, is how your claim is renewed for the new tax year, and failure to meet the deadline can mean that you lose out on tax credits.

- If you make your annual declaration on or before the 31 July deadline, your renewal claim is backdated to 6 April 2014.[96]

- If you do not make your annual declaration on or before 31 July, HMRC sends you a notice that your payments of tax credits have ceased. If you make your annual declaration within 30 days following the date on the notice, your renewal claim is backdated to 6 April 2014.[97] This statutory 30-day period has been extended to 60 days as a matter of policy in recent years.
- If neither of the above apply, but you make your annual declaration on or before 31 January 2015 and have 'good cause' for making a late declaration, your renewal claim is backdated to 6 April 2014.[98] 'Good cause' is not defined, but HMRC says it will look at each case on its individual merits. It will consider whether you were not able to complete the form because of exceptional circumstances and could not make arrangements for someone else to handle your affairs.[99]
- If you make your annual declaration late without good cause, or after 31 January in any case, this should be treated as a new claim and it can only be backdated for 31 days.[100]

Note: if you are not accepted as having good cause for making a late declaration, HMRC's view is that there is no right of appeal against this decision. However, this is disputed and so you should appeal and ask the First-tier Tribunal to accept it.[101]

The above rules allowing a late declaration to serve as a renewal do not apply if your previous claim was on the basis that you were:[102]

- single and you are now a member of a couple; *or*
- a member of a couple and you are now single.

The final decision

After the annual review has been completed, HMRC must make a final decision on whether you were entitled to tax credits for the tax year in question and, if so, the amount of your entitlement for that year.[103] The final decision can therefore establish that:

- the initial decision was correct and you received the right amount;
- you were underpaid tax credits;
- you were overpaid tax credits.

If you are underpaid tax credits, HMRC must pay you, usually in a lump sum.[104] If you are overpaid, HMRC asks you to pay back the overpayment (see Chapter 66). You do not have the right of appeal against a decision that an overpayment is to be recovered from you, although you can ask HMRC not to recover it (see p1467).

If you do not agree that you have been paid too much tax credit, it is important that you appeal against the lower award notified to you in the final decision.

The final decision is made in two main stages.

- The annual review forms are issued to gather information and evidence about what your income and circumstances were in the year.

Part 11: General rules for tax credits
Chapter 65: Claims, decisions and getting paid: tax credits
8. Contacting HM Revenue and Customs

- The information from the annual review is used to make a final decision on your entitlement for the year.

HMRC aims to deal with your review within eight weeks of receiving your declaration.[105] If you did not have an annual declaration form to complete, the final decision is as set out in your annual review form (unless, having read your annual review form, you find that you have a change of circumstances to report, in which case HMRC sends you details of your new award after it has dealt with the reported change).

A final decision must not be made before you have been given the chance to respond to the annual review and make your annual declaration on or before the deadline (usually 31 July). Once you have made your annual declaration, HMRC may make a final decison before the deadline. However, you can still change your declaration on or before the deadline, in which case HMRC may revise the final decision.[106] If you do not make your annual declaration on or before the deadline, the final decision can be made after that date, based on the information held by HMRC at that time.[107] If you have given an estimate, HMRC may make a final decision, but can revise it if you give details of your actual income on or before the second deadline (usually 31 January).

HMRC also sends you an initial decision notice (TC602), setting out your award for the tax year 2014/15.

If your tax credit award ends because you become entitled to UC, the final decision may be made during the tax year. During 2014/15, this is only likely to happen if you form a couple with someone who is entitled to UC.

8. **Contacting HM Revenue and Customs**

Telephoning the Tax Credit Helpline (tel: 0345 300 3900; textphone: 0345 300 3909) is HM Revenue and Customs' (HMRC's) preferred method of contact. Be ready to give your name, address and national insurance (NI) number. Always keep a note of the date and time of your call, with a brief note of what is said and, if possible, the name and title of the person you speak to. HMRC aims to record all calls made to the Helpline, but a small number may not be recorded because of technical difficulties.[108] In the event of a dispute, you can request the recording of your call. If the recording is not available, and you can show that you made a call on a certain date, HMRC has agreed that you should be given the benefit of the doubt about what was said.[109] It is best to follow up your call with a letter confirming the information you have provided and the advice given by the Helpline. Write to the Tax Credit Office at the address on the award notice and include your name, address, NI number and the date. Always keep a copy of your letter. If you are appealing, disputing recovery of an overpayment or making a complaint, it is best to use the relevant form or put it in writing. HMRC's policy is to retain images of claim forms, documents and recordings of telephone calls for five years plus the tax year or from the date of the last decision on that claim.[110]

If things go wrong

It is not possible to sue HMRC for negligence in the way your claim is decided.[111] If a decision is wrong, you can request a revision or appeal against it. If you are given wrong advice by an employee of HMRC, you may be able to seek compensation either through the courts or through the internal complaints procedure (see p1384). If you are given wrong information by HMRC or the DWP which led to an overpayment, this may be grounds for recovery to be waived (see p1467).

If your claim has been received but not dealt with, ask why. If you are not satisfied with the explanation, make a complaint to HMRC (see Chapter 61). You can also complain if, for example, you have been treated badly or your case has been mishandled. In some cases, you can seek a judicial review (see p1351). If you are unhappy with the way HMRC handles your complaint, you can take it to the Adjudicator's Office and if still unhappy, to the Parliamentary Ombudsman (see p1385).

Notes

1. Who should claim
1 s3(3) TCA 2002
2 s3(3)(a) and (8) TCA 2002
3 Reg 13(3) TC(CN) Regs
4 s3(4) TCA 2002
5 s32(3) TCA 2002; reg 21(2)(a) TC(CN) Regs
6 HMRC, *Departmental Report 2008*, p38
7 Reg 15 UC(TP) Regs
8 s3(5A) TCA 2002; reg 2(1), definition of 'couple', WTC(EMR) Regs
9 s48(2) TCA 2002
10 Reg 16 UC(TP) Regs; reg 9(8) UC,PIP,JSA&ESA(C&P) Regs
11 *HMRC v PD (TC)* [2012] UKUT 230 (AAC)
12 s3(5A)(a)(ii) and (c)(ii) TCA 2002
13 *DG v HMRC (TC)* [2013] UKUT 631 (AAC)
14 R(TC) 2/06
15 TC(PM) Regs
16 *Crake and Butterworth v SBC* [1982] 1 All ER 498; R(SB) 17/81; CTC/3864/2004

17 See CPAG's *Welfare Rights Bulletin* 235 and *TM v HMRC (TC)* [2013] UKUT 444 (AAC)
18 Regs 17 and 18 TC(CN) Regs

2. How and when to make a claim
19 s3(1) TCA 2002
20 Reg 5(2) TC(CN) Regs
21 Reg 4 TCA(TP)O
22 HMRC Benefits and Credits Consultation Group minutes, 30 May 2012, available at www.hmrc.gov.uk/taxcredits/meetings.htm
23 Reg 2 TC(CN) Regs
24 Reg 5(7) TC(CN) Regs
25 Reg 9 TC(CN) Regs
26 s5(2) TCA 2002; reg 4 TC(CN) Regs
27 Reg 15 UC(TP) Regs
28 See 'Protect your right to tax credits by claiming early' at www.hmrc.gov.uk/taxcredits/start/claiming/backdate-ahead/protect-claim.htm
29 s14(3) TCA 2002

Part 11: General rules for tax credits
Chapter 65: Claims, decisions and getting paid: tax credits
Notes

30 Reg 5(3) TC(CN) Regs
31 *ZM and AB v HMRC (TC)* [2013] UKUT 547 (AAC)
32 Reg 5(4) TC(CN) Regs
33 Reg 5(6) TC(CN) Regs
34 para 06110 TCTM
35 *ZM and AB v HMRC (TC)* [2013] UKUT 0547 (AAC)
36 Reg 5(8) TC(CN) Regs
37 *ZM and AB v HMRC (TC)* [2013] UKUT 547 (AAC)
38 HMRC reply to CPAG email, 11 April 2012
39 s7(2) TCA 2002; Form TC600, Part 5; reg 4 TC(ITDR) Regs
40 HMRC leaflet, *Why Do Overpayments Happen* (WTC8), pp4-5
41 s7(5)(a) TCA 2002; R(TC) 1/08
42 Reg 14 TC(PC) Regs
43 ss14, 15, 16, 17,18,19 and 22 TCA 2002; regs 30-33 TC(CN) Regs
44 Reg 12(8) TC(CN) Regs
45 s14(3) TCA 2002

3. How your claim is dealt with
46 s14(1) TCA 2002
47 s14(2) TCA 2002
48 Regs 5 and 6 TC(CN) Regs
49 s23 TCA 2002
50 s23(3) TCA 2002

4. Backdating your claim
51 Reg 7 TC(CN) Regs
52 Reg 14(2) TC(PC) Regs
53 Reg 8 TC(CN) Regs

5. Getting paid
54 Reg 3 TC(PC) Regs
55 Reg 3(3) TC(PC) Regs
56 Reg 3(6) TC(PC) Regs
57 Reg 4 TC(PC) Regs
58 Reg 5 TC(PC) Regs
59 Reg 6 TC(PC) Regs
60 Reg 13(1) TC(PC) Regs
61 Reg 8(2), (2A) and (2B) TC(PC) Regs
62 Reg 10 TC(PC) Regs
63 Regs 9 and 13 TC(PC) Regs
64 Reg 11(2A) TC(PC) Regs
65 Reg 14 (3) and (4A-4E) TC(PC) Regs; para 0212200 TCM
66 para 0212160 TCM
67 Reg 11 TC(PC) Regs
68 Reg 12(3) TC(PC) Regs
69 s24(4) TCA 2002; reg 7 TC(PC) Regs
70 Reg 12(4) TC(PC) Regs

6. Changes of circumstances
71 Regs 7(2) and 8(2) TC(ITDR) Regs
72 ss6(3) and 32(3) TCA 2002; regs 2, 21 and 22 TC(CN) Regs
73 Reg 16(5) WTC(EMR) Regs
74 *JL v HMRC (TC)* [2013] UKUT 325 (AAC)
75 Regs 20 and 25 TC(CN) Regs
76 Reg 16(5)(a) WTC(EMR) Regs
77 Reg 26 TC(CN) Regs
78 Reg 26A TC(CN) Regs
79 s7(3)(d) TCA 2002; reg 5(b) TC(ITDR) Regs
80 Sch 6(9) HB Regs
81 Regs 2 and 22 TC(CN) Regs
82 Reg 23 TC(CN) Regs
83 Reg 27 TC(CN) Regs
84 Reg 27(2B) TC(CN) Regs
85 Reg 24 TC (CN) Regs
86 HMRC leaflet, *What Happens If We've Paid You Too Much Tax Credit?* (COP 26)

7. Annual reviews
87 s17(1) TCA 2002
88 Reg 34 TC(CN) Regs
89 Reg 13 TC (CN) Regs
90 s18(3) TCA 2002
91 s17(2)(b) and (6)(b) TCA 2002
92 Reg 17 and Sch UC(TP) Regs
93 Regs 34-36 TC(CN) Regs
94 *SG v HMRC (TC)* [2011] UKUT 199 (AAC)
95 s17(8) TCA 2002; reg 33(b) TC(CN) Regs
96 Reg 11(3)(a) TC(CN) Regs
97 Reg 11(3)(b) TC(CN) Regs
98 Reg 11(3)(c) TC(CN) Regs
99 para 0136160 TCM
100 Reg 11(3)(d) TC(CN) Regs
101 *SG v HMRC (TC)* [2011] UKUT 199 (AAC), in particular para 84
102 Reg 11(4) TC(CN) Regs
103 s18 TCA 2002
104 s30 TCA 2002
105 HMRC leaflet, *Renewing Your Tax Credits: getting it right* (TC603RD)
106 s18(5) TCA 2002
107 s18(8) TCA 2002

8. Contacting HM Revenue and Customs
108 Response to Freedom of Information request, www.hmrc.gov.uk/freedom/tc-helpline.htm, 12 January 2009
109 HMRC Benefits and Credits Consultation Group minutes, 4 December 2008
110 *AG v HMRC (TC)* [2013] UKUT 530 (AAC)
111 *Jones v Department of Employment* [1989] QB1 (CA)

Chapter 66

Overpayments of tax credits

This chapter covers:
1. What is an overpayment of tax credits (below)
2. Recovery of overpayments (p1463)
3. Disputing recovery (p1467)
4. Interest on overpayments (p1471)

Key facts

- The rules on the recovery of tax credit overpayments are different from those that apply to most social security benefits.
- All tax credit overpayments are recoverable, however they are caused, but HM Revenue and Customs (HMRC) has the discretion to decide whether or not to recover.
- There are rules on the amount that may be recovered and guidance on the way in which HMRC should recover an overpayment.
- There is no right of appeal to an independent tribunal about a decision on whether or not to recover an overpayment of tax credits. However, you can ask HMRC to use its discretion not to recover.
- If you do not accept that you were overpaid, you can appeal against the decision about your entitlement. From April 2014, it is expected that you must first apply for a review and be notified of the outcome before you can appeal.

1. What is an overpayment of tax credits

The main rules are the same for child tax credit (CTC) and working tax credit (WTC).[1] If you (and your partner if you are making a joint claim) are paid more tax credit for a tax year than you are entitled to, the extra amount is regarded as an overpayment. HM Revenue and Customs (HMRC) can decide to adjust your award during the year of your current tax credit award to prevent an overpayment building up (an **'in-year overpayment'**) and/or recover all or some of the overpayment from you after the end of the tax year (an **'end-of-year overpayment'**). There is no right of appeal against the decison to recover the overpayment, although you can appeal against the decision about your

Part 11: General rules for tax credits
Chapter 66: Overpayments of tax credits
1. What is an overpayment of tax credits

entitlement to tax credits. This means that by challenging the decision on your entitlement, you are arguing that you were not overpaid (or by as much), and were correctly entitled to the amount you received (or part of it).

When an overpayment occurs

The most likely cause of an overpayment is if:
- your income rose by more than the disregarded amount (see p1452) in the current year, compared with the previous tax year – eg, your income rises by more than £5,000 in 2014/15, compared with 2013/14;[2]
- you did not tell the Tax Credit Office (TCO) in time about a change of circumstances that reduces your entitlement (see p1450);
- the information you gave to the TCO was incorrect;
- HMRC failed to act on information you provided, or made a mistake;
- none of the above applies, but an overpayment occurred anyway because of the way the rules on income and changes in circumstances work.

In-year overpayments

In-year overpayments arise during the year of your current tax credit award. Decisions on in-year overpayments can be made during the course of the tax year concerned in the following circumstances.[3]
- If HMRC thinks that there is likely to be an overpayment, it can adjust the award (or an award of another tax credit) to reduce or wipe out the overpayment. This may mean that your award is reduced for the rest of the year.
- If an award is terminated on the grounds that you did not satisfy the basic conditions for entitlement, HMRC may decide that the amount already paid to you, or some of it, is to be regarded as an overpayment. The basic conditions of entitlement are, for CTC, that you are responsible for a child (see p151) and, for WTC, that you are engaged in full-time work (see p165).

End-of-year overpayments

End-of-year overpayments are overpayments that are identified at or after the end of the tax year concerned – ie, after your award for that year has been finalised. HMRC can decide that there has been an end-of-year overpayment when it makes:[4]
- a final decision (see p1457);
- an enquiry decision (see p1487);
- a decision on discovery (see p1487).

Notification of overpayments

HMRC must change the decision on your entitlement and notify you of the new decision.[5] Remember that you have the right of appeal against any decision about the amount of your entitlement to tax credit (see p1489). If you think that the new decision on your entitlement is wrong and that, therefore, you have not been overpaid as much as HMRC says, or that you have not been overpaid at all, appeal against the new decision on your entitlement.

You may only find out about an in-year overpayment when HMRC writes to you to say that your entitlement has changed and your payment has been adjusted. If HMRC is going to recover an end-of-year overpayment from you, it must also give you notice of that, how much it is and how it is to be recovered from you. It usually does this at the same time as it writes to you about the final decision on your entitlement for the tax year. There is no right of appeal against the decision to recover an overpayment.[6] For what you can do, see p1467.

2. Recovery of overpayments

HM Revenue and Customs (HMRC) can recover all or part of any overpayment.[7] It usually recovers the overpayment by:
- adjusting (ie, reducing) your current award; *or*
- requiring you to repay the overpayment.

However, it does not have to recover an overpayment and should exercise discretion. The official policy is in the HMRC leaflet *What Happens If We've Paid You Too Much Tax Credit?* (COP26), which can be obtained from the Tax Credits Helpline on 0345 300 3900 or from www.hmrc.gov.uk. An overpayment may be written off, in whole or in part, if HMRC has made a mistake or failed to act, and you have acted correctly in connection with your claim.[8] The guidance also allows for recovery to be waived in exceptional circumstances or if it would cause hardship (see p1468).

You must be given notice that you must repay an end-of-year overpayment. The notice must also say how much the overpayment is, and how it is to be recovered from you.[9]

HMRC usually begins recovery immediately after notification of the overpayment, and does not ask you if recovering an overpayment will cause you hardship or if you think it should not be recovered from you. It is, therefore, important to contact the Tax Credit Office (TCO) if you do not think the overpayment should be recovered from you. HMRC refers to this as a 'dispute' (see p1467). Recovery is not suspended during the dispute process, but if the dispute is found in your favour, you should be given a refund of the amount already recovered.

If you do not agree that you have been overpaid, you should appeal against the decision about your entitlement (see Chapter 68). Recovery is suspended if you have appealed against the decision on your entitlement that gave rise to the alleged overpayment.[10] From April 2014, it is expected that you will have to apply

Part 11: General rules for tax credits
Chapter 66: Overpayments of tax credits
2. Recovery of overpayments

for a review (referred to by HMRC as 'mandatory reconsideration') before you can appeal. HMRC has confirmed that recovery should also be suspended during the mandatory reconsideration stage.[11]

Overpayments and award notices

For every overpayment, there should be a revised decision on your entitlement, which is sent as an award notice. The tax credit award notices can be very complicated. You should be sent a checklist (Form TC602(SN)) with your award notice with information used in the calculation for you to check. You can request an award calculation notice (Form TC647) from HMRC, which gives more details about how your payment has been worked out. If it is still unclear, you can write to the TCO (its address will be at the top of the award notice) requesting an individual explanation. However, you should not delay sending in your dispute form while you are waiting for the explanation, as a dispute should usually be made within three months. You can send further details once you have received the full explanation.

If you still do not receive a satisfactory response, consider taking up the matter with your MP or making a complaint (see Chapter 61).

From whom can an overpayment be recovered

In-year overpayments are recovered from you by reducing the ongoing tax credit award. An end-of-year overpayment can be recovered from the person(s) to whom the tax credit award was made. This means:[12]
- if you made a claim as a single person, the overpayment can be recovered from you;
- if you made a joint claim with your partner, the overpayment can be recovered from one or both of you. If you have separated from your partner, HMRC's practice is first to ask you both to repay the overpayment equally. If you wish, you and your ex-partner may agree to each pay different amounts. Although HMRC has the power to ask one person to repay the whole amount, guidance states that usually each person will be asked to repay a maximum of half the overpayment, unless one partner has acted fraudulently or negligently and the other is seen to be an 'innocent partner'.[13]

How the overpayment is recovered

You must be notified of the new decision on your entitlement that gave rise to the overpayment.[14] For end-of-year overpayments, HMRC must notify you (and your partner, if it is a joint overpayment) of the amount to be repaid, and how the overpayment is to be repaid.[15]

HMRC can require you to repay:[16]

- by deductions from ongoing payments of any tax credit (see below). This is HMRC's preferred method of repayment. The amount that is deducted is usually limited;
- directly to HMRC. You should receive a notice showing the full amount to be repaid. You are offered a standard repayment period of 12 monthly instalments, although up to 10 years may be negotiated;
- with your agreement, by deductions from certain benefits paid by the DWP (see p1187);[17]
- with your agreement, via PAYE by altering your tax code to allow deductions from your wages.[18]

If your tax credit entitlement has ended and you are now getting universal credit (UC), deductions for an outstanding tax credit overpayment may be made from your UC award (see p1230).[19]

Deductions from ongoing awards

HMRC can adjust your payments so that you receive less money and so, in effect, repay the overpayment. It only does this if you have an ongoing award as the same household in which the overpayment arose. For example, it will not make a deduction from an ongoing award if you were overpaid as a single person and are now claiming as a couple. However, it is expected that HMRC will use this method to recover old debts from ongoing awards from October 2014. You should be notified of the amount being deducted. The amount by which HMRC can reduce your payments to recover an end-of-year overpayment is limited by law. The *maximum* amounts by which HMRC can reduce your tax credit award to recover an end-of-year overpayment are:[20]

- 10 per cent of the award if you are receiving the maximum tax credits to which you could be entitled – ie, with no reduction for income;
- 100 per cent of the award if you receive only the family element of child tax credit (CTC);
- 25 per cent of the award if neither of the above apply.

Note: these are maximum amounts, although HMRC applies them automatically. If you accept that you should repay but cannot afford to repay at these rates, ask HMRC to accept repayment at a lower rate. In order to persuade HMRC, you may need to show why it would cause you hardship (see p1468) to pay at the maximum rate.

The law only deals with end-of-year overpayments but HMRC has, in practice, taken the same approach with in-year overpayments.[21]

However, the government has announced that it will stop tax credit payments during the year where, due to a change of circumstances, you have already received your full annual entitlement.[22] This is effectively recovery at 100 per cent and could cause severe hardship for some claimants. Guidance is expected, but

Part 11: General rules for tax credits
Chapter 66: Overpayments of tax credits
2. Recovery of overpayments

HMRC will consider adjusting recovery or making payments on hardship grounds.[23]

Revised notices of overpayments, changing the method of recovery, can be issued at any time.[24]

Direct payment to HM Revenue and Customs

If you are no longer entitled to tax credits, or one tax credit award has ended and another started because of a change in your household (eg, you started or stopped being part of a couple), you must repay your overpayment by direct payments to HMRC. HMRC will suspend direct recovery if you are already repaying another overpayment (at the 10 per cent or 25 per cent rate described on p1465) through your current tax credit award – but you may need to ask for this.[25] The notice to pay (TC610) asks you to contact HMRC to pay in full or negotiate repayment. If the overpayment has not been repaid and you have not contacted HMRC within 42 days, a reminder letter will be sent, followed by a more strongly worded warning letter. If you fail to respond to this letter, HMRC may use a debt collection agency or start legal proceedings to recover the debt.

Other methods of recovery

HMRC may recover tax credit overpayments by deductions from specified benefits with your written consent (see p1187).[26] If you are getting UC, a tax credit overpayment may be treated as an overpayment of UC and can be recovered by deductions from UC without your consent (see p1230).[27] HMRC may recover tax credit from your wages via PAYE, but only with your agreement.[28] If HMRC is not satisfied with recovery using the methods described above, it will consider taking legal action. Further action will follow if HMRC considers that you are refusing to repay, or neglecting to keep to an agreement to repay. All the circumstances will be taken into account before taking such action, but HMRC may:[29]

- seize and sell your personal possessions. However, this power is generally not used, and unless you let HMRC officials or agents into your property, they cannot enter your home and seize your personal possessions without a warrant from the court; *or*
- take court action against you, including bankruptcy proceedings.

Negotiating repayment

If you have difficulty repaying, HMRC may agree to your repaying the overpayment over a longer period than normal by making an instalment plan. In cases of hardship or if your mental health is a factor (see p1468), the overpayment may be written off. Contact the Tax Credit Payment Helpline on 0345 302 1429 (textphone 0345 300 3909), or write to HMRC at the address on the Notice to Pay. Usually you are asked to pay something straight away, and the rest over a later period. HMRC takes into account all the relevant circumstances, including your income, savings, other debts and outgoings. Usually you must show how the repayments will cause you hardship by providing evidence of your income and expenditure and showing, for example, how you will be unable to meet your essential living expenses, or providing evidence of your mental health problems.

3. **Disputing recovery**

You can 'dispute' HMRC's decision to recover an overpayment if you think it failed to meet its responsibilities or if there were exceptional circumstances why you were unable to meet your responsibilities as set out in HMRC leaflet *What Happens If We've Paid You Too Much Tax Credit?* (COP26). To dispute recovery, complete Form TC846 (available at www.hmrc.gov.uk or by contacting the helpline) or write to the TCO. HMRC does not recover all or part of the overpayment if it accepts that it has not met its responsibilities (see p1468) and you have met yours. Recovery of the overpayment usually begins immediately and is not suspended during the dispute, although if your dispute is successful you should be given a refund of the amount already recovered. There is no legal time limit for disputing recovery, but HMRC expects you to do so within three months of notification of the overpayment or the outcome of an appeal on the decision that gave rise to the overpayment.[30] HMRC says it will consider exceptions to this if you could not reasonably have been expected to act within three months – eg, if you were in hospital. It is arguable that a late dispute should also be allowed if you have been waiting for an explanation of the overpayment. HMRC retains discretion. However, too rigid an application of this time limit may be unlawful.

What should you do?

1. If you do not agree that you have been overpaid and you think that you were entitled to all or part of the amount of tax credit you received, appeal the entitlement decision that gave rise to the alleged overpayment, using Form WTC/AP. Recovery of the overpayment is suspended until the outcome of the appeal is known. From April 2014, it is intended that you must first apply for a review on Form WTC/AP. After you have been notified of the outcome, appeal directly to the First-tier Tribunal.

2. If you have been overpaid because your claim should have ended, but you would have been entitled to some or all of the amount you received if you had claimed correctly, ask for the overpayment to be reduced by offsetting your notional entitlement (see p1469).

3. If you accept that you were overpaid, but you do not think you should have to repay some or all of the money because you met your responsibilities and some or all of the overpayment was caused by HMRC's mistake or failure, you should dispute the decision to recover, using Form TC846. If there were exceptional circumstances that meant you were unable to meet your responsibilities, tell HMRC about this on Form TC846. The dispute is an internal HMRC process. Recovery continues during the dispute. You can ask for a review of the outcome, and make a complaint if you are still unhappy.

Part 11: General rules for tax credits
Chapter 66: Overpayments of tax credits
3. Disputing recovery

4. If you cannot afford to repay, ask for the rate of recovery to be reduced, or written off altogether on hardship grounds. Form TC846 does not allow you to raise this in the dispute, so raise this separately via the Payment Helpline or in writing to the address on your Notice to Pay.

5. If you have mental health problems and recovery may cause you distress, supply evidence of this in writing and ask for the overpayment to be written off in line with HMRC guidance.

6. If you are still unhappy with the decision to recover, consider applying for judicial review or making a complaint.

The responsibilities test

The way in which HMRC exercises its discretion whether or not to recover tax credit overpayments is set out in its leaflet *What Happens If We've Paid You Too Much Tax Credit?* (COP26), which is used if you dispute recovery. If an overpayment has been caused by mistake or failure to act by HMRC (referred to as failing to meet its 'responsibilities'), it may decide not to recover all or part of the overpayment.

However, for the overpayment not to be recovered, you must also show that you have acted correctly in relation to your claim for tax credits – ie, you have met your responsibilities. Your **'responsibilities'** are not defined in the law, but the official guidance is that HMRC will not ask you to repay an overpayment if it accepts that:[31]

- the overpayment was caused by HMRC failing to meet its responsibilities; *and*
- you have met all of your responsibilities.

If HMRC thinks it has met all its responsibilities but you have not met all of yours, it will normally recover the overpayment. If it thinks that both itself and you have failed to meet responsibilities, it will look at the circumstances and may write off parts of the overpayment. An overpayment can still occur even though both you and HMRC have met these reponsibilities, in which case HMRC is still likely to seek recovery.

HMRC regards its responsibilities as:

- giving you correct advice based on your information;
- accurately recording your information and paying the correct amount;
- putting right mistakes you tell it about and sending you a corrected award notice;
- accurately recording your notification of changes in your circumstances;
- sending you a new award notice within 30 days of having all the necessary information.

HMRC regards your responsibilities as:

- providing accurate, complete and up-to-date information;

- reporting changes of circumstances throughout the year;
- using the checklist (TC602(SN)) sent with your award notice to tell it if anything is wrong or incomplete;
- checking that your payments match the amount given on the award notice;
- reporting any errors on your award notice, normally within one month.

If there were exceptional circumstances which meant that you were unable to meet your responsibilities at the time, such as illness, explain this and HMRC may write off the overpayment. Remember that it is best to dispute the decision to recover the overpayment on Form TC846 (see p1466).

Reducing the overpayment

According to official guidance, HMRC may reduce ('offset') the amount of the overpayment by the amount of any tax credit to which you would have been entitled had you claimed correctly – ie, by your 'notional entitlement'. This is referred to in HMRC guidance as 'offsetting notional entitlement' and is applied if the overpayment was caused by:[32]
- your ceasing to count as a single claimant and becoming part of a couple (you will need details of your partner's income); or
- your ceasing to count as part of a couple and claiming instead as a single claimant.

In either case, you must make a new claim and have some tax credit entitlement following the change in your status.

HMRC may contact you about this but, as this cannot be guaranteed, you should contact it yourself if you think you may benefit from offsetting. Offsetting can be applied to in-year or end-of-year overpayments. It is understood that HMRC will not refund overpayments already repaid, but may offset notional entitlement on old cases if there is still an overpayment outstanding, or if you still have a review, dispute or complaint outstanding about the overpayment. Offsetting may not be applied if your claim was incorrect from the start, or if you made a deliberate error or false statement. In such cases, HMRC may also consider imposing a penalty. If HMRC refuses to offset your overpayment, ask it to consider any factors you think are relevant, including if there has been no actual loss to the public purse, the volatility of the relationship and whether you made a 'genuine error' or not. Although the guidance only refers to single/couple claims, you should request offsetting notional entitlement in other circumstances – eg, if you were overpaid because you left the UK for more than the permitted period but you would have been entitled to tax credits on your return. In some cases, refusals by HMRC to offset may be challenged by judicial review in the courts. Seek further advice.[33]

Part 11: General rules for tax credits
Chapter 66: Overpayments of tax credits
3. Disputing recovery

Hardship and mental health

Hardship is not defined, but HMRC leaflet *What Happens If We've Paid You Too Much Tax Credit* (COP26) refers to financial hardship in terms of family circumstances that lead to extra living costs, such as looking after someone who is chronically ill or disabled, and inability to pay for essential living expenses such as rent, gas or electricity. In cases of hardship, HMRC may put recovery on hold, reduce the amount being recovered by extending the period over which the overpayment is repaid, partially remit or, in exceptional circumstances, write off the overpayment altogether. Other guidance suggests that consideration will also be given to reducing or writing off your overpayment if you are unemployed and have no savings or assets, or if you are on incapacity benefit (IB) or employment and support allowance (ESA) and have little prospect of gaining employment.[34]

The situation may be kept under review, depending on your circumstances – ie, if there is a chance that your ability to repay will increase. It is in your interest to show how repayment will leave you in hardship.

The guidance also states that if you have a mental health problem, HMRC will deal with your case carefully and sympathetically to avoid causing you distress. It may require a letter from a healthcare professional or mental health social worker explaining the nature of your illness, prognosis and prospects for recovery. If your mental health problem existed at the time the overpayment occurred, this may be considered to be exceptional circumstances and so HMRC should consider writing off the overpayment. If you have a mental health problem at the time the overpayment is being recovered, HMRC may decide not to continue with the recovery.[35]

These decisions are discretionary and there is no right of appeal against them. Explain your circumstances and ask HMRC to exercise its discretion in your favour. The guidance on hardship and mental health applies whether you are repaying directly or by deductions from an ongoing award, but it may not be commonly known to all helpline staff. There is a special payment helpline on 0345 302 1429 to discuss hardship. You may also write with a financial statement to the HMRC office dealing with repayment. You should not use Form TC846 (see p1466) if you want more time to repay. If you remain unhappy with the decision, see p1467 for what you can do.

Taking your dispute further

The only legal challenge to a decision on recovering an overpayment (ie, either after a dispute or an attempt to negotiate repayment) is by judicial review in the courts. Usually, this is only possible in extreme cases – eg, if HMRC insists on your repaying an overpayment that was clearly caused by an error or failure on its part, you met all your responsibilities and it is urgent that HMRC changes its decision. For more about judicial review, see p1351.

The only other way of persuading HMRC to change its mind is by making a complaint. You first need to use HMRC's own complaints procedure. If you remain dissatisfied, you can complain to the Adjudicator's Office and then to the Parliamentary Ombudsman via your MP (see Appendix 1 for the addresses and Chapter 61 for details about making a complaint). Both can recommend action and order financial compensation, but are likely to take time to complete their investigations. You may wish to involve your MP at an earlier stage of your complaint, as this can produce quicker results.

4. Interest on overpayments

Interest may be added to an overpayment being recovered from you (and/or your partner, if you have a joint claim) if HMRC considers that the overpayment is due to 'fraud or neglect' on the part of you (and/or your partner).[36]
   Interest is added 30 days after whichever of the following dates apply:[37]
- if you (or your partner) were treated during the tax year concerned as being overpaid as a result of your award being terminated because you did not satisfy the basic conditions of entitlement (see p1462), the date of the decision terminating the award; or
- if the above did not apply, the date in the final notice that you were given to confirm your actual income for the tax year.

When added to the overpayment, the interest is treated as if it were part of the overpayment. This means that it is subject to the same rules as the overpayment itself.[38]

How much interest is added

The amount of interest added to the penalty is 6.5 per cent a year or, if it is different from the average lending rate of the main banks, the bank lending rate plus 2.5 per cent.[39]

Challenging an interest decision

You can appeal a decision adding interest to an overpayment (see Chapter 68). For example, you might wish to argue that you did not act fraudulently or negligently, or that the amount of the interest is wrong. You (and/or your partner, if s/he is subject to the decision) must be given notice of a decision adding interest to an overpayment. The notice must be dated and include details of your right of appeal against the decision.[40]

Part 11: General rules for tax credits
Chapter 66: Overpayments of tax credits
Notes

Notes

1. **What is an overpayment of tax credits**
   1 s28 TCA 2002
   2 Reg 5 TC(ITDR) Regs
   3 s28(5) and (6) TCA 2002
   4 s28(1) TCA 2002
   5 s23 TCA 2002
   6 ss29(1) and (2) and 38 TCA 2002

2. **Recovery of overpayments**
   7 s28(1) TCA 2002
   8 HMRC leaflet, *What Happens If We've
      Paid You Too Much Tax Credit?* (COP26)
   9 ss28(1) and 29 TCA 2002
   10 HMRC leaflet, *How HMRC Handle Tax
      Credits Overpayments;* Benefits and
      Credits Consultation Group minutes
      November 2013
   11 HMRC Benefits and Credits Consultation
      Group email to CPAG, 20 January 2014
   12 s28(3) and (4) TCA 2002
   13 HMRC leaflets, *How HMRC Handle Tax
      Credits Overpayments* and *What Happens
      If We've Paid You Too Much Tax Credit?*
      (COP 26), p11
   14 s23 TCA 2002
   15 s29 TCA 2002
   16 s29(3)-(5) TCA 2002
   17 Sch 9 (7E) SS(C&P) Regs
   18 s29(5) TCA 2002
   19 Reg 17 and Sch UC(TP) Regs
   20 Reg 12A TC(PC) Regs; HMRC leaflet,
      *What Happens If We've Paid You Too
      Much Tax Credit?* (COP 26)
   21 Tax Credits Consultation Group
      minutes, 17 July 2007
   22 2013 Autumn Statement, para 1.317
   23 para 0216120 TCM
   24 s29(2) TCA 2002
   25 HMRC leaflets, *How HMRC Handle Tax
      Credits Overpayments* and *What Happens
      If We've Paid You Too Much Tax Credit?*
      (COP 26), p9
   26 Sch 9 (7E)(3) SS(C&P) Regs
   27 Reg 17 and Sch UC(TP) Regs
   28 s684 (7A) IT(EP)A 2003
   29 s29(3) TCA 2002 (overpayment of tax
      credits may be treated as if it were
      outstanding tax); HMRC leaflet, *How
      HMRC Handle Tax Credits Overpayments*

3. **Disputing recovery**
   30 HMRC leaflet, *What Happens If We've
      Paid You Too Much Tax Credit?* (COP26)
   31 HMRC leaflet, *What Happens If We've
      Paid You Too Much Tax Credit?* (COP 26)
   32 *Pre-Budget Report 2009;* HMRC
      statement at www.hmrc.gov.uk/
      pbr2009/individuals.htm; HMRC
      leaflet, *What Happens If We've Paid You
      Too Much Tax Credit?* (COP 26), p2
   33 For the pre-January 2010 position, see
      CPAG's *Welfare Rights Bulletin* 211, p4
   34 HMRC leaflet, *How HMRC Handle Tax
      Credits Overpayments*
   35 HMRC leaflet, *How HMRC Handle Tax
      Credits Overpayments*

4. **Interest on overpayments**
   36 s37(1) TCA 2002
   37 s37(2)-(3) TCA 2002
   38 s37(6) TCA 2002
   39 Reg 4 TC(IR) Regs
   40 ss37(4) and 38(1)(d) TCA 2002

11

Chapter 67

Investigations, penalties and fraud: tax credits

This chapter covers:
1. Investigating claims (below)
2. Penalties (p1476)
3. Prosecution for fraud (p1480)

Key facts

- HM Revenue and Customs has wide powers to investigate your tax credits claim and require information from you.
- In certain circumstances, including if you supply incorrect information or do not comply with other requirements, a financial penalty may be imposed.
- If you are considered to have acted fraudulently, you may be fined, imprisoned, or both.

1. Investigating claims

HM Revenue and Customs (HMRC) can require you to supply information and evidence to help it check whether your claim is correct and to investigate fraud. HMRC refers to investigations into the accuracy of awards as 'examinations' and 'enquiries'. Examinations are carried out on some claims *during* the year in order to check that they are correct. Enquiries may be carried out *after* the year concerned to check that you were paid the correct amount. More serious investigations into fraud may also be carried out.

HMRC might ask you to provide things like bank statements or your rent book. It usually explains why it needs these and gives you reasonable time to produce them. You can seek advice (eg, from a welfare rights adviser or a solicitor) and can be accompanied at meetings you have with HMRC.

Not all investigations are fraud investigations. Fraud investigations tend only to happen in the more serious cases and, in such cases, HMRC has additional powers (see p1475).

1473

Part 11: General rules for tax credits
Chapter 67: Investigations, penalties and fraud: tax credits
1. Investigating claims

Examining your claim

During the course of your award, or sometimes before your claim is decided, HMRC may telephone or write to you requiring information or evidence. It may request a meeting with you in connection with your claim. Normally, it writes to you to say that it is examining your claim. If the examination is started before your claim is decided, usually you are not paid before it is completed. If it starts while you are already receiving tax credits, usually you continue to be paid while the examination is being carried out.

If you prefer, HMRC can deal with someone else on your behalf – eg, an adviser, accountant or a relative. HMRC requires a signed letter from you confirming this is what you want (or use Form TC689). However, you are still treated as responsible for the information provided.

HMRC may request a meeting to discuss the examination with you. You do not have to attend, but remember that HMRC has powers to seek information or evidence (see p1475). HMRC says you can have an interpreter at a meeting if required.[1] At the meeting, HMRC takes notes – it should let you have a copy later. If you do not co-operate with the examination (eg, you refuse to provide information), your claim might be refused or your award stopped, and you may be subject to a penalty (see p1476).

In some cases, HMRC may ask you to sign the notes as an accurate record of the meeting. You do not have to sign this. Signed notes may be used by HMRC as evidence, so be sure that you point out anything you disagree with in the notes before signing. If HMRC finds your claim is incorrect or that you have not notified a change of circumstances that you must report, it might ask you to confirm the information by signing a certificate of full disclosure. Be sure you are satisfied of the accuracy of the information in this, as HMRC takes a very serious view if you sign it when you know it is wrong.

You cannot stop an examination taking place, but if you are unhappy with the way you are being treated, you can make a complaint (see Chapter 61).

Enquiries

After your tax credit award is finalised at the end of the tax year, HMRC may carry out an enquiry into the award. Usually, this is not until the following May or June, at the earliest. There is a deadline by which HMRC must have initiated the enquiry (see p1487). HMRC must write to you about this.

If you prefer, HMRC can deal with someone else on your behalf – eg, an adviser, accountant or a relative. HMRC requires a signed letter from you to confirm this is what you want. However, you are still treated as responsible for the information provided.

HMRC may request a meeting with you. The same points apply as for examinations (see above).

You can stop the enquiry by requesting HMRC to complete it by making a decision on your tax credit entitlement for the year in question. If HMRC wishes to continue making the enquiry, it passes your request to the First-tier Tribunal. You can also appeal to the First-tier Tribunal if you are unhappy with the decision following the enquiry. For more details on when the First-tier Tribunal deals with requests and decisions about enquiries, see p1487.

Powers to seek information

HMRC can require you (and/or your partner if you have a joint claim) to provide information or evidence during the course of your award, if it believes your award may be wrong (for an examination). It can also require information or evidence after your award has been finalised (for an enquiry).

It can also do this if it is necessary for a decision on an initial claim (see Chapter 65), a revision during an award (see Chapter 68), or a final notice and final decision (see Chapter 65).[2] You must be given at least 30 days to provide the information.[3] HMRC does not have to suspect you of fraud in order to require information or evidence from you.

It is important that you co-operate with requests for information or evidence as far as you can. Even though you may not be the subject of a fraud investigation, HMRC might refuse your claim, suspend your payments or reduce your award (possibly to nil), and there are a number of circumstances in which you can be given a financial penalty or even prosecuted if you refuse to supply information and evidence, or you supply material which you know is incorrect (see p1476). It is important that you are as truthful as possible when responding.

HMRC can also require your employer or childcare provider to provide information. They must be given at least 30 days to provide it. If they are subject to these requirements, they can also be subject to penalties (see p1476). They can be required to provide information and evidence relating to your claim or, for the purpose of a revision during an award or an enquiry (see p1484 and p1489), your award.[4]

If fraud is suspected

If you are suspected of fraud, HMRC may undertake a civil investigation with a view to charging a financial penalty (see p1476). In serious cases it undertakes a criminal investigation with a view to prosecuting you (see p1480). Fraud investigations in serious cases are normally carried out by the Special Compliance Office of HMRC. If fraud is suspected, HMRC usually explains to you why your claim is being investigated and that you can seek professional advice from someone who can attend any meetings you have with HMRC. It is advisable to seek professional advice (eg, from a solicitor) if you are investigated on suspicion of fraud. If you are being investigated, seek advice as quickly as possible. You are likely to be interviewed under caution.

Part 11: General rules for tax credits
Chapter 67: Investigations, penalties and fraud: tax credits
2. Penalties

In addition to the powers described above, HMRC has specific powers when investigating fraud.[5] If HMRC has 'reasonable grounds' for suspecting fraud, a court can make an order requiring that documents containing relevant evidence be delivered by you (or any other person who has them) to HMRC within the time specified in the court order.

If a court is satisfied that there are 'reasonable grounds' for suspecting serious fraud, it can issue a warrant giving HMRC authority to enter and search premises for evidence within 14 days. HMRC can only apply for a warrant if it is satisfied that asking the person in possession of the evidence to deliver it might 'seriously prejudice' the investigation. Under the warrant, HMRC can remove anything that there is 'reasonable cause' to believe may be required as evidence, and search any person on the premises where there is reasonable cause to believe s/he is in possession of such evidence.[6]

2. **Penalties**

HM Revenue and Customs (HMRC) can impose a financial penalty on you if you have:[7]

- fraudulently or negligently made an incorrect statement or declaration, or supplied incorrect information or evidence; *or*
- failed to comply with requirements.

Despite the use of the word 'fraudulently', these penalties are civil penalties; you do not have to be prosecuted for a criminal offence. If you do not think a penalty should be imposed (eg, because you had a reasonable excuse for not declaring a change in circumstances or you could not obtain the information asked for), tell HMRC. If a penalty is imposed, HMRC contacts you. It must state the date of the penalty and the amount. HMRC says that it is always willing to discuss the amount of the penalty and the reasons for it with you.[8] You can appeal against the imposition of a penalty (see p1494).

In making its decision, HMRC considers things like how much you have co-operated (it may reduce the amount of your penalty if you have co-operated in the investigation) and the seriousness of the changes that need to be made. In certain circumstances, these rules can also apply in the same way to your employer or your childcare provider (see p1475).

Incorrect statements and information

HMRC can impose a financial penalty of up to £3,000 (it does not have to impose the maximum) on you if you have acted fraudulently or negligently and you have:[9]

- made an incorrect statement or declaration in connection with a claim, a notification of a change of circumstances (see p1450) or in a response to a final notice (see p1457); *or*
- given incorrect information or evidence in connection with an initial decision (see p1446), a requirement to provide information or evidence during the course of your award, a revision during an award (see p1484), a final decision (see p1457) or an enquiry (see p1487).

There is no definition of 'negligence' but, in practice, HMRC considers things like what you could reasonably be expected to have known and how careful you were.[10]

Penalties for incorrect statements and information

The maximum penalty is £3,000, although HMRC need not impose the maximum. In practice, it sets it at 30 per cent of the amount over-claimed, 50 per cent for a second incorrect declaration, or 100 per cent for a third, subject to the £3,000 maximum. You must be notified of the penalty, including the date on which it is given, and your right of appeal. The penalty is payable 30 days after the date you were notified of it.[11] The amount of the penalty may be increased by the addition of interest (see p1479).

If you are a member of a joint-claim couple (see p1438), the penalty may be imposed or partly imposed on your partner, unless s/he could not reasonably have been expected to have been aware that you had fraudulently or negligently made an incorrect statement or provided incorrect information or evidence. However, even if the penalty is imposed or partly imposed on your partner, the total penalty for the same incorrect statement cannot amount to more than £3,000.

If you are acting for someone else in connection with her/his claim and you fraudulently or negligently make an incorrect statement, the penalty applies to you.

Failing to comply

HMRC can impose a financial penalty on you of up to £300 (it does not have to impose the maximum):[12]

- if you fail to provide information or evidence for a decision on an initial claim (see p1446), a requirement to provide information or evidence during the course of your award, a revision during an award (see p1484), a final decision (see p1457) or for an enquiry (see p1487); *or*
- if you fail to comply with a requirement about a final notice (see p1455); *or*
- if you fail to notify a specified change of circumstances within one month of the change or, except in the last case below, of the date you became aware of the change if that is later.[13] These are if:

Part 11: General rules for tax credits
Chapter 67: Investigations, penalties and fraud: tax credits
2. Penalties

- there is a decrease of £10 a week or more over four consecutive weeks in your or your partner's childcare costs, or if the childcare costs have stopped; *or*
- you have stopped being counted as a single claimant; *or*
- you were claiming as a couple but are no longer part of that couple. This includes if you or your partner leave the UK permanently or go abroad for more than a set period (see p1585); *or*
- you (or your partner) lose your right to reside in the UK or stop being treated as being in the UK; *or*
- your (or your partner's) hours of work fall to less than 16 or 30 hours a week, or you and your partner's combined total falls below 24 hours a week; *or*
- you have a joint claim and get the 30-hour element of working tax credit because your joint hours total at least 30 hours a week, but these have now fallen to less than 30 hours a week; *or*
- you or your partner cease to be responsible for one or more of your children (see p153 for when you count as responsible); *or*
- a child for whom you (or your partner) are responsible dies (see p153 for when you count as responsible for a child); *or*
- a child for whom you (or your partner) are responsible stops being counted as a child (other than by reaching her/his 20th birthday), including if s/he were due to continue counting as a child by remaining in full-time education or training, but did not do so (see p151 for who counts as a child).

A penalty is not imposed if you had 'reasonable excuse' for not telling HMRC about the change. Tell HMRC if you think this applies. However, HMRC does not accept the fact that you did not know you had to inform it as a reasonable excuse.[14]

Penalties for failing to comply

The maximum penalty for failing to comply is £300. If the penalty is for failing to provide information or evidence, there is a further daily penalty of up to £60 a day for each further day you continue to fail to comply. You must be notified of the penalty, including the date on which it is given, and your right of appeal. The penalty is payable 30 days after the date you were notified of it.[15] The amount of the penalty may be increased by the addition of interest (see p1479).

However, if the penalty is for failing to provide information or evidence, or for a failure concerning a final notice, HMRC cannot apply the penalty itself. Instead, it must write to the HM Courts and Tribunals Service, which then summons you to the First-tier Tribunal to decide whether the penalty should be applied.[16] You can appeal against the First-tier Tribunal's decision to the Upper Tribunal (see p1494).

Once you have provided the information or evidence, a penalty cannot be imposed on you. You have not failed to provide information or evidence if you did so within any time that HMRC has allowed you to, or if you had a 'reasonable excuse' for the failure, or if, having had a reasonable excuse, you later provided the information or evidence without unreasonable delay.

If you are a member of a couple and a £300 penalty has been imposed for failing to comply with a requirement about a final notice or for failing to report the specified change of circumstances, the total of that penalty applied to either or both of you is a maximum of £300.

Interest added to penalties

If a penalty is imposed on you, HMRC can apply interest to it. Although it does not have to apply interest, it can do so even if you are not considered to have acted fraudulently or negligently – ie, if the penalty is for failing to comply. The amount of the interest becomes part of the penalty and is recoverable in the same way as the penalty itself.[17]

The amount of interest added to the penalty is 6.5 per cent a year or, if that is different from the average lending rate of the main banks, the bank lending rate plus 2.5 per cent.[18]

You can appeal against the penalty itself and the amount of the penalty. However, the way the law is written suggests that there is no right of appeal about the addition of interest.[19]

Separately from the above rules, if HMRC considers that an overpayment has arisen because of 'fraud or neglect' on your part (or, if you are a member of a couple, on the part of one or both of you), it can decide to apply interest to all or some of the overpayment (see p1471).

Recovery of penalties

HMRC has discretion about whether to impose a penalty and, subject to the maximum amounts, the amount. Also, although the penalty itself can only be altered on appeal, HMRC has discretion about whether to insist that you pay all or some of the penalty.[20] If you tried your best to fulfil all your obligations, or if the penalty would cause you hardship, tell HMRC and ask it to exercise its discretion not to recover all or some of the penalty.

If HMRC decides that a penalty may be imposed on you, it tries to come to an agreement with you which involves your offering to pay the agreed amount. If you agree, it sends you a final letter setting out the agreement, which HMRC regards as a legally binding contract. It may be best to try to come to an agreement, because if HMRC is not able to reach such an agreement with you, it may use its legal powers to recover the penalty. However, if you think you may want to challenge the penalty (see p1480), check whether the contract means that HMRC will not actually issue a decision imposing the penalty. If you do not have a decision, you cannot challenge it on an appeal. If HMRC uses its legal powers to recover a penalty, it can:

Part 11: General rules for tax credits
Chapter 67: Investigations, penalties and fraud: tax credits
3. Prosecution for fraud

- seize and sell your personal possessions. However, unless you let them into your property or they are are otherwise easily able to get in, authorised officers cannot enter your home and seize your personal possessions unless they have a warrant from the court; *or*
- take court action against you, including bankruptcy proceedings.[21]

Challenging a penalty

You can tell HMRC that you disagree with the penalty and/or the addition of interest to it – eg, when it contacts you to tell you that you are liable for a penalty. In some cases, it may warn you about a possible penalty before a formal decision is made. It can remove the penalty and/or the interest. Once a formal decision has been made, you can appeal, including against the amount of the penalty (but not against any addition of interest). However, it is expected that you will first have to request a review from HMRC (see Chapter 68).

Note: subject to the maximum, the First-tier Tribunal that considers your appeal can increase as well as decrease the amount.

For more information on appeals, see p1489 and for more on penalty appeals, see p1494.

Have you been given a penalty?

1. Explain to HMRC why you think a penalty should not be imposed – eg, if you acted with reasonable care or had a reasonable excuse for failing to report a change in circumstances.

2. If you get a decision imposing a penalty, you can appeal against it and the First-tier Tribunal reconsiders the decision.

3. If you accept that a penalty can be imposed, you can still negotiate with HMRC about the amount. You could argue that the maximum amount should not be imposed in your case – eg, because you acted innocently and to the best of your knowledge or abilities.

4. You can come to an agreement with HMRC about repaying a penalty, but check whether this means that a formal decision imposing a penalty will still be issued. If a decision is not issued, you do not have the right of appeal against the penalty.

11

---

3. **Prosecution for fraud**

You are regarded as having committed the offence of fraud if you knowingly take part in fraudulent activity in order to get a tax credit for you or anyone else. If you are prosecuted and then convicted by a court, you are liable to be fined or imprisoned, or both.[22]

Fines and imprisonment

If a court convicts you of fraud in connection with tax credits and:[23]

- you are convicted in a moderately serious case, usually in a magistrates' court (sheriff court in Scotland), you are liable to a maximum of six months' imprisonment or a maximum fine of £5,000, or both; *or*
- you are convicted in a very serious case, usually in the Crown Court (High Court in Scotland), you are liable to a maximum of seven years' imprisonment or a fine of an unlimited amount, or both.

Note: at some point the above rules will change.[24]

- If your offence is in connection with no more than £20,000 of tax credits, you may be tried only in the magistrates' court (sheriff court in Scotland). If you are convicted, you are liable to a maximum of 51 weeks' (England and Wales) or six months' (Scotland and Northern Ireland) imprisonment, or a maximum fine of £5,000.
- If the offence is in connection with more than £20,000 of tax credits, you may be tried in either the magistrates' court (sheriff court) or the Crown Court (High Court). If you are convicted in the magistrates' court/sheriff court, you are liable to a maximum of 12 months' imprisonment (six months in Northern Ireland) or a maximum fine of £5,000, or both. If you are convicted in the Crown Court/High Court, you are liable to a maximum of seven years' imprisonment or a fine of an unlimited amount, or both.

See CPAG's online service and *Welfare Rights Bulletin* for updates.

Will you be prosecuted?

Whether or not you will be prosecuted is a discretionary decision. Not all cases of fraud end in prosecution. HM Revenue and Customs (HMRC) may investigate your claim under civil investigation procedures – ie, without a view to prosecuting you, but with a view to charging a penalty (see p1476). If you are being investigated by the Special Compliance Office *without* a view to prosecuting you, you are usually told about this. However, this does not mean that HMRC cannot change its mind and decide that a prosecution should be made.

The factors that it may take into account are likely to include the strength of the evidence, the amount of tax credits involved, whether an offence was planned and your personal circumstances.

Official HMRC policy indicates that criminal investigations are more likely if:[25]

- there is organised or systematic fraud, including conspiracy;
- false statements are made or false documents given during a civil investigation;
- deliberate concealment, deception, conspiracy or corruption is suspected;
- false or forged documents have been used;

Part 11: General rules for tax credits
Chapter 67: Investigations, penalties and fraud: tax credits
Notes

• the person involved has committed previous offences or there is a repeated course of unlawful conduct or previous civil action;
• there is a link to suspected wider criminality.

Note: this is not a complete list and ultimately everything depends on the circumstances of your case.

What should you do if you are prosecuted?
1. The most important thing to do is to get advice. You may be entitled to legal help and have a solicitor or barrister represent you in court.
2. Check carefully that HMRC can prove all the parts of the offence with which you are charged. Do not plead guilty until you have obtained advice.

Notes

1. Investigating claims
1 HMRC leaflet WTC/FS4, available at www.hmrc.gov.uk/taxcredits/forms-and-leaflets/leaflets.htm.
2 ss14(2),15(2),16(3),17, 19(2) and 22 TCA 2002
3 Reg 32 TC(CN) Regs
4 ss14(2)(b),15(2)(b),16(3)(b) and 19(2)(b) TCA 2002; regs 30 and 31 TC(CN) Regs
5 s36 TCA 2002
6 s36(2) TCA 2002

2. Penalties
7 ss31 and 32 TCA 2002
8 Sch 2 TCA 2002; HMRC leaflet, *Tax Credits Penalties* (WTC7), available at www.hmrc.gov.uk/taxcredits/forms-and-leaflets/leaflets.htm
9 s31 TCA 2002
10 HMRC leaflet, *Tax Credits Penalties* (WTC7), available at www.hmrc.gov.uk/taxcredits/forms-and-leaflets/leaflets.htm
11 Sch 2 para 1 TCA 2002; HMRC leaflet, *Tax Credits Penalties* (WTC7), available at www.hmrc.gov.uk/taxcredits/forms-and-leaflets/leaflets.htm

12 s32 TCA 2002
13 ss3(4), 6(3) and 32(3) TCA 2002; reg 21(2) TC(CN) Regs
14 s32(5)(b) TCA 2002; para 10170 CCM
15 Sch 2 para 1 TCA 2002
16 Sch 2 paras 1 and 3 TCA 2002
17 s37(5) and (6) TCA 2002
18 Reg 4 TC(IR) Regs
19 ss37(5)-(6) and 38 TCA 2002
20 Sch 2 paras 1 and 5 TCA 2002
21 Sch 2 para 7 TCA 2002

3. Prosecution for fraud
22 s35(1) TCA 2002
23 s35(2) TCA 2002
24 s124 WRA 2012
25 HMRC criminal investigation policy, available at www.hmrc.gov.uk/prosecutions/crim-inv-policy.htm

Chapter 68

Revisions and appeals: tax credits

This chapter covers:
1. Revisions (p1484)
2. Appeals (p1489)
3. Appealing to the Upper Tribunal (p1494)
4. Appealing to the courts (p1495)

Tax credit appeals are heard by the First-tier Tribunal Social Entitlement Chamber, which also deals with social security benefits, and are administered by HM Courts and Tribunals Service. Chapter 59 covers appeals for social security benefits. This chapter refers you to this chapter when the tax credit rules are the same as the benefit rules.

Key facts
- Decisions on tax credit entitlement can be changed by a revision by HM Revenue and Customs (HMRC) or by an appeal to an independent tribunal (the First-tier Tribunal).
- If you are overpaid tax credits, the decision on your entitlement can be changed by revision or appeal, but the decision to recover an overpayment cannot be changed in this way. Instead, you can ask HMRC to use its discretion not to recover all or part of the overpayment and use the complaints procedures if necessary.
- HMRC can only revise your tax credit award if certain grounds are met.
- You must appeal within 30 days after the date of the decision.
- When you appeal, HMRC will usually want to 'settle' the appeal with you. If it is not settled, your appeal goes forward to the First-tier Tribunal.
- It is expected that, from April 2014, you must apply for a review and receive a 'mandatory reconsideration notice' before you can appeal.

Part 11: General rules for tax credits
Chapter 68: Revisions and appeals: tax credits
1. Revisions

1. Revisions

A decision may be revised by HM Revenue and Customs (HMRC). The circumstances in which a revision can be made depend on whether the decision with which you disagree is:

- an 'initial decision' on a claim (see below);
- a 'final decision' after the tax year has ended following an annual review (see p1486); *or*
- a decision of the First-tier Tribunal (see p1494).

The process of revision is where HMRC decides to change a decision – eg, after notification of a change of circumstances. If you disagree with a decision, including a revised decision, you should appeal. From April 2014, it is expected that you must first apply for a review and receive a 'mandatory reconsideration notice' before you can appeal.

Revising an initial decision during an award

When you claim a tax credit, HMRC must decide whether to make an award and the rate at which to award it.[1] This is called an 'initial decision'. If you disagree with it, you have the right to appeal (see p1489). HMRC may revise the decision as described below. Your award can also be revised if your circumstances change.

Your claim is refused or award stopped

If your claim has been turned down altogether or your award has been terminated, you do not have the option to ask for the decision to be revised. You must appeal within 30 days if you want the decision to be changed. If you do not appeal or your appeal is unsuccessful, you need to make a fresh claim to get any further tax credit in that tax year.[2]

No award because your income is too high

If your income in the previous year is too high to qualify for a tax credit, but you satisfy the other qualifying conditions, you are awarded a tax credit at a nil rate. This nil-rate award can be revised if your income is estimated to be lower in the current year.[3]

When an initial decision may be revised

The initial decision can be revised if:

- your circumstances have changed so that you should get an additional or higher element (see p1485); *or*
- HMRC has reasonable grounds for believing that you are entitled to a different rate of tax credit or that you are not entitled to a tax credit at all (see p1485); *or*
- there has been an official error (see p1486).

Changes in circumstances that increase entitlement to a tax credit element

If you notify the Tax Credit Office (TCO) that your circumstances have changed so that you should be getting an element you were not getting before, HMRC must decide whether to amend your award and, if so, how.[4] For example, if you report that you have had a new baby, your child tax credit (CTC) award can be revised to include another child element. HMRC may request further information or evidence before making a revised decision.

If you notify the TCO of the change within one month, the increase in the award can be fully backdated.[5] There are specific rules dealing with the date from which an award is recalculated if there is a change in childcare charges or childcare provided (see p1451).

The increase in the award cannot be backdated for more than one month before the date you provide notification of the change, except in the following cases relating to the disabled and severely disabled child elements of CTC and the disabled worker and severe disability elements of working tax credit (WTC).

- If you claim and are awarded disability living allowance (DLA) for a child, or personal independence payment (PIP) for a qualifying young person, tell the TCO within one month of the decision that DLA or PIP has been awarded so that the disabled child element or severely disabled child element of CTC is fully backdated.[6] The same should apply if you get DLA or PIP on appeal, or the highest rate following a supersession.[7]
- If you are already getting WTC when you claim one of the benefits that would entitle you to a disabled worker element or severe disability element in WTC (eg, DLA or PIP – see p1403), notify the TCO within one month of being awarded the benefit, so that the element can be fully backdated.[8]

If you disagree with a revised decision, you can appeal to the First-tier Tribunal (see p1489). A revised decision may be revised again following another change, or on 'reasonable grounds' (see below) or because of official error (see p1488).

Reasonable grounds

HMRC has the power to amend or terminate an award if it has 'reasonable grounds for believing' that you are:[9]

- entitled to a different rate of tax credit; *or*
- not entitled to WTC or not entitled to CTC.

This could happen, for example, because you tell the TCO about an income change or wrong information is used in deciding your claim. Or it could happen following an examination into your claim (see p1474).

If the rate of tax credit is changed, HMRC revises your award, taking into account any change in circumstances from the date it arose unless:

- it is a change that increases entitlement to tax credit elements, which can only be backdated for up to one month (see above);

Part 11: General rules for tax credits
Chapter 68: Revisions and appeals: tax credits
1. Revisions

- childcare charges go down by £10 a week or more. In this case, there is a four-week run-on at the same rate before the award is reduced (see p1450);[10]
- there is a four-week run-on because you stop work or reduce your hours below 16, 24 or 30 a week (see p172).

Decisions can only be revised in this way during the period of the award, not after an award has been terminated, nor after a final decision has been made.[11]

Example
Pauline provides an estimate of her income for the current year and this has decreased by more than £2,500 compared with the previous year's income on which the award was based. The initial decision can be revised and her award recalculated based on the current year's income plus £2,500. The estimate she provides must be sufficient to give HMRC reasonable grounds for believing that her entitlement should change.

HMRC is not obliged to revise even when there are grounds. It could leave changes to be dealt with at the annual review – eg, if it is late in the year and the change is minor.[12]

If you disagree with the revised decision, you can appeal (see p1489).

Official error

An initial decision can be revised in your favour if it is incorrect because of an official error (see p1488).[13]

Revising a final decision

After 5 April, HMRC carries out the annual review (see p1455) for the year just ended and makes a final decision on your entitlement for that year. It sends you an annual review form which details the circumstances on which the award was based and usually an annual declaration form, giving your income for the tax year just passed.

If HMRC sends you an annual declaration form, you must complete and return it by the deadline given (31 July in most cases). HMRC finalises your entitlement for the year just passed. A final decision is conclusive unless it is changed on appeal or in the following circumstances.

- If you change your statement about your income or circumstances before the deadline, the final decision can be changed (see p1487).
- Once a final decision is made, there is a period during which HMRC can enquire into your entitlement (see p1487).
- Outside the period of enquiry, a final decision can be revised on 'discovery' of certain information about your tax liability or in relation to fraud or neglect (see p1487). There is a deadline for such revisions.

- A final decision can be revised in your favour because of official error (see p1488).

Changing your statement

If you reply to the annual review notice but then wish to change your statement, you may do so. If it is on or before the deadline given in the notice for replying (31 July in most cases), but HMRC has already made a final decision, the final decision may be revised.[14]

If HMRC only had an estimate of your income for the current year (eg, because you are self-employed and have not yet finalised your accounts), you will have a later deadline (usually 31 January) in which to give details of your actual income for that year. If you do so, HMRC must make a new final decision.[15] It can revise the new decision if you change your statement on or before the later deadline.[16] If you do not give further details of actual income, HMRC must nevertheless make a new final decision once the later deadline is passed.

Revision on enquiry

HMRC does not need any particular grounds to enquire into entitlement, and some claims are selected for enquiry at random.[17] It must begin its enquiry by giving you written notice. An enquiry can only be opened into entitlement for a particular tax year after the final decision for that year has been made, and within a limited period of time. This is known as the enquiry window, which begins immediately after the final decision, and ends a year after the deadline by which you were to reply to the annual review notice, or a year after the later deadline for self-employed people or others to supply actual income details where only an estimate had been provided.[18] If you are required to submit an income tax return, the enquiry must begin by the day your tax return becomes final.

When the enquiry is completed, HMRC makes a fresh decision on whether you are entitled and how much the award should be.

Only one enquiry into entitlement can be conducted for any one tax year.[19]

For more details, see p1474.

If you disagree with an enquiry decision

If you disagree with the decision, you have the right to appeal (see p1489). Alternatively, it may be revised if it is incorrect because of an official error (see p1488).[20] HMRC may also revise an enquiry decision by a 'revision on discovery' (see below).

Revision on discovery

Discovery is a power to revise entitlement in earlier years. If it is too late to 'enquire' into your entitlement, HMRC can still revise a final decision, but only in specific circumstances, and there are further time limits by when such a revision must take place. A final decision or an enquiry decision may be revised outside

Part 11: General rules for tax credits
Chapter 68: Revisions and appeals: tax credits
1. Revisions

the period allowed for an enquiry if HMRC has 'reasonable grounds for believing' that tax credit entitlement is wrong:

* because of a revision of your income tax liability. The revision of your tax credit entitlement must take place within a year of your income tax liability being revised;[21] *or*
* for reasons attributable to fraud or neglect (see below).

There is nothing to stop HMRC going through this process more than once.[22] If a final decision, enquiry decision or discovery decision has been revised for official error, that too can be further revised in this way.[23]

Fraud or neglect

A decision can be revised using the discovery power if HMRC has reasonable grounds for believing that an incorrect decision on tax credit entitlement is attributable to fraud or neglect.[24] The fraud or neglect may be on your part, or your partner's if it is a joint claim, or on the part of anyone acting for you (see p1440).

Your tax credit entitlement in a tax year cannot be revised on this ground after five years from the end of the tax year – eg, a tax credit award for 2008/09 (or earlier) cannot be revised after 5 April 2014.[25]

If you disagree with a discovery decision

You have the right of appeal (see p1489). Alternatively, the decision may be revised if it is incorrect because of an official error.

Official error

An initial decision, final decision, enquiry decision or discovery decision can be revised in your favour if it is incorrect because of an official error.[26] The decision can be revised at any time up to five years after the date of the decision.

> *Official error*
> 'Official error' means an error relating to a tax credit made by an HMRC or DWP officer or a person providing tax credit services for them. If you, or someone acting for you, contributed to the error, it is *not* an official error. An error of law can be an official error, but not if it is only shown to be an error of law because of a later Upper Tribunal or court decision.

How to request a revision

If your circumstances change, there are rules on how HMRC should be notified (see p1454). In other cases, there are no set rules to follow. If you disagree with a decision, you should usually follow the appeal procedure (see p1489) rather than ask HMRC to use one of its powers to revise a decision. If you are outside the absolute time limit for appeals and want a decision to be revised on grounds of official error, you should request this in writing. If HMRC refuses to revise a decision on official error grounds, it is arguable that there is a right of appeal against this decision.[27]

Keep a copy of any letter you send to HMRC. If you call the Tax Credit Helpline, keep a log of your calls: the date and time you made the call, the information provided and what was agreed.

What happens after you request a revision

Before making its decision, HMRC may ask you to provide more information or evidence if it considers it needs this to help with the decision.[28] HMRC may contact your employer if it also needs information from her/him.[29]

It is important that you respond to a request for information by the date given in the letter. If you do not provide the required information, you may have to pay a penalty of up to £300 and, if you still do not comply, a further daily penalty of up to £60 a day could be imposed. See p1476 for how these penalties are applied.

HMRC must give notice of the decision to you, and to your partner if it is a joint claim. This must include details of your right to appeal.[30]

2. Appeals

Tax credit appeals are heard by the same First-tier Tribunal that deals with social security benefits and are administered by HM Courts and Tribunals Service (HMCTS).[31] Many of the rules are the same as those for social security benefits (see Chapter 59). This chapter refers you to Chapter 59 where the tax credit rules are the same as the benefit rules.

Note: at the time of writing, draft legislation had been laid to introduce, from 6 April 2014, a new requirement to ask HMRC to 'review' a decision before you can appeal.[32] Your application for a review must be received within 30 days of the decision. A late application may be accepted within 13 months if HMRC is satisfied that there were special circumstances that meant it was not practicable for you to apply for a review within the time limit, and it is reasonable to grant the extension. The longer the delay, the more compelling the reasons should be. If an application to extend the time limit is refused, you cannot ask for this to be reviewed again, and you do not have a right of appeal against the original decision. The review must be carried out as soon as is reasonably practical, and HMRC must notify you of the outcome. You must receive a 'mandatory reconsideration notice' before you can appeal.[33] See CPAG's online service and *Welfare Rights Bulletin* for updates.

Part 11: General rules for tax credits
Chapter 68: Revisions and appeals: tax credits
2. Appeals

Who can appeal

The following people have the right of appeal:[34]

- you, the tax credit claimant. For joint claimants, both or either of you can make the appeal. If only one appeals, the First-tier Tribunal decision still applies to both, provided you are both given the right to a hearing;[35]
- for appeals about penalties, the person subject to the penalty;
- an appointee, if you are unable to make the appeal yourself (see p1440). If you do not have an appointee, the person (who must be 18 or over) who is to act on your behalf in the appeal should write to HM Revenue and Customs (HMRC) asking to be appointed;
- another person with the power to make a tax credit claim for you – ie, a receiver appointed by the Court of Protection, a judicial factor or guardian.[36]

Decisions you can appeal

You can appeal against:[37]

- an initial decision;
- a final decision;
- a revised decision (for change in circumstances, on reasonable grounds or for official error);
- an enquiry decision;
- a discovery decision;
- a decision imposing a penalty;
- a decision charging interest on an overpayment;
- a decision to reject a claim because the NI number requirement has not been met, but only on the grounds that it does not apply to you because you or your partner are a person subject to immigration control who requires leave to enter or remain in the UK and does not have it.

If you have made a late annual declaration (see p1456), it is arguable that you have the right of appeal against a decision that you do not have good cause for a late declaration.[38] If you have requested a revision on the grounds of official error (see p1488), it is arguable that you have the right of appeal against a refusal to revise.[39]

Decisions you cannot appeal

You cannot appeal against:

- a decision to reject a claim which is not made on the approved form, or does not contain all the information requested on the form;
- a decision to reject a claim because a claimant has not met the NI number requirement and does not have a reasonable excuse;
- a decision to recover all or part of an overpayment;
- a decision about the rate or method of recovery of an overpayment;
- a decision to postpone payments (see p1449).

There is a dispute process for decisions to recover overpayments. If HMRC decides you have been overpaid tax credits, it can recover all or part of them at its discretion, and you cannot appeal against the decision. You can, however, appeal against the amount of the award. In some cases, HMRC may use its discretion not to recover an overpayment, or to reduce the amount – eg, if recovery would cause hardship (see p1468). Complain to HMRC if you are unhappy with the way your claim has been handled, and if your complaint is not resolved to your satisfaction you can ask the Adjudicator to look into it (see p1384).

Time limit for appealing

Your appeal, including the details specified below, must be given to HMRC within 30 days after the date given on the decision letter.[40]

You may not get a separate initial or final decision notice if the annual review notice states what the decision will be and the date on which it will be made, usually 31 July. This may apply if your award is made up of just the family element of child tax credit (CTC) and your circumstances have not changed. In this case, your appeal must be made within 30 days after the date the annual review notice gives as the date on which the decision is made – eg, by 30 August if the decision date is given as 31 July.

Late appeals

A decision on a case in 2013 held that amendments to the rules unintentionally removed the power to accept a late appeal in tax credit cases.[41] At the time of writing, draft legislation had been made to restore the power for HMRC to accept a late appeal, up to one year after the original time limit has expired in special circumstances (see p1352).[42] The draft legislation also says that late appeals made on or after 1 April 2013 can be treated as made in time if HMRC agrees. See CPAG's online service and *Welfare Rights Bulletin* for updates.

How to appeal

You can appeal on the form in HMRC leaflet WTC/AP, *What To Do If You Think Your Child Tax Credit/Working Tax Credit Is Wrong*. Alternatively, you can write a letter, but you must include:[43]

- sufficient information to identify you – eg, your name and NI number;
- sufficient information to identify the decision being appealed – eg, the date of the decision and whether it is about CTC or working tax credit (WTC);
- the grounds of your appeal – ie, why the decision is wrong;
- your signature (or a signature on your behalf – eg, from an appointee).

Send your appeal to HMRC at the address given on the decision notice.

From April 2014, it is expected that you must use Form WTC/AP to apply for a review and, when notified of the outcome, send your appeal directly to HMCTS, enclosing the 'mandatory reconsideration' notice.

Part 11: General rules for tax credits
Chapter 68: Revisions and appeals: tax credits
2. Appeals

Suggestions for how to prepare your appeal and present your case are given in Chapter 59. Information in that chapter applies equally to tax credit appeals.

What happens after you appeal

Settling the appeal

HMRC may want to settle the appeal without going to the First-tier Tribunal. You can point out to HMRC where you think its decision is wrong and supply information or arguments you want it to consider. HMRC may offer you terms on which to settle the appeal. Your appeal can only be settled with your consent. If you do not agree, the appeal must proceed to the First-tier Tribunal.

If you agree to settle the appeal, HMRC must write to you setting out the terms of the agreement – eg, giving a new amount for your award. Your appeal then lapses unless you write to HMRC within 30 days from the date of the written notice of agreement saying you have changed your mind and wish to proceed with your appeal.[44]

If you are asked to settle the appeal, check first whether the proposed agreement gives you everything to which you think you are entitled. Seek advice if you are not sure whether to agree. If in doubt, you should exercise your right to continue with the appeal.

From April 2014, it is expected that the 'settlement' process is less likely to arise due to there being a review stage before you appeal.

Asking for a hearing

If your appeal is not settled, HMRC prepares the appeal papers (its 'submission'). It sends a copy to you and a copy to your representative and forwards your appeal to HMCTS. HMCTS sends you an enquiry form asking whether you want an oral hearing or not. Return the form within 14 days of the date it was issued.

For information and issues to consider when deciding whether to opt for an oral hearing, see p1317.

You are entitled to have your appeal heard within a reasonable period of time.

If HMRC does not forward your appeal, you can forward a copy of the appeal yourself. Although the First-tier Tribunal does not normally accept an appeal made directly in this way, it can do so and can require HMRC to produce a submission.[45] You can also complain to HMRC (see p1384) and consider taking up the issue with your MP (see p1387). Before you do, check that the decision is one that carries a right of appeal (see p1490).

Appeal not heard by the end of the year

If your appeal has not been heard by the time you get HMRC's final decision on your entitlement after the end of the year, you should put in another appeal against the final decision.[46]

When your appeal can be struck out

Your appeal may be struck out in certain circumstances. The rules are the same as those for benefits, explained on p1343.

Withdrawing an appeal

You can ask to withdraw the appeal if you decide not to go ahead with it. You can tell HMRC in writing or telephone the helpline or, if your appeal has already been forwarded, by writing to HMCTS. See p1316 for more details of withdrawing and reinstating an appeal if you change your mind.

The hearing

The First-tier Tribunal holds an oral hearing if you have asked for one. Otherwise there is a paper hearing in your absence (see p1317). For information on asking for the hearing to be postponed or adjourned to a later date, see p1345. The tax credit rules are the same as those for benefits, except that there are no special 'test case' provisions for tax credits that can block your appeal or affect its outcome (although payment can be postponed while there is an appeal pending in another case that could affect your own award).[47] The rules on 'lead cases' described on p1347 do apply to tax credits.

First-tier Tribunal procedures

Chapter 59 describes First-tier Tribunal procedures for benefits. See pp1319–29 and pp1341–48 for details. The tax credit rules are the same, with the following exceptions.
- **Medical examination.** The First-tier Tribunal cannot refer you to a doctor for a medical examination.[48] However, if your appeal concerns a disability question it may be important to get your own medical evidence (see p1358).
- **Change in circumstances after you appeal.** These rules apply to tax credits in the same way as they do to benefits except:
  - wherever Chapter 59 refers to 'supersession' this should read 'revision' for tax credits;
  - if you reclaim or ask for a revision because of a change in circumstances after you appeal, there is no specific provision for a decision maker to revisit her/his decision on that claim/revision once the appeal has been heard on the grounds that s/he would have made a different decision had s/he known what the First-tier Tribunal's decision would be.
- **After the hearing.** If HMRC is considering an appeal to the Upper Tribunal or has decided to appeal, you are normally not paid until the Upper Tribunal decides the case. HMRC can 'postpone' payment in these circumstances, without notifying you of its intention.[49]

Part 11: General rules for tax credits
Chapter 68: Revisions and appeals: tax credits
3. Appealing to the Upper Tribunal

- **If you disagree with the First-tier Tribunal's decision.** The First-tier Tribunal decision cannot be 'superseded' (because supersessions do not apply to tax credits) but it can be revised in any of the ways described in this chapter except for official error (see p1484).
  If the First-tier Tribunal made an error of law, you can appeal to the Upper Tribunal as you can in benefit appeals. For tax credits, HMRC is not prevented from revising the First-tier Tribunal's decision on 'reasonable grounds', which could also include an error of law (if it is still within the tax year of the award).
- **When a decision can be set aside.** If you appeal to the Upper Tribunal, there is no provision obliging the First-tier Tribunal to set aside the decision if both you and HMRC agree the First-tier Tribunal made an error of law.[50]

Penalty appeals

You have the right to appeal against a decision imposing a penalty. For information on penalties, see p1476. From April 2014, it is expected that you must first apply for a review of the decision and receive a 'mandatory reconsideration notice' before you can appeal against a penalty.

For most types of penalty, HMRC has the power to make its own decision on imposing one. You can appeal against this decision to the First-tier Tribunal in the normal way, with any further appeal going to the Upper Tribunal under the usual rules.[51] However, to impose a penalty of up to £300 for failing to provide required information or evidence, HMRC cannot make the decision itself but must take 'proceedings' to the First-tier Tribunal. You have an opportunity to attend a hearing where the First-tier Tribunal decides whether to apply a penalty. Your right of appeal then lies with the Upper Tribunal.[52] In any case, the First-tier or Upper Tribunal also has the power to increase a penalty, within the maximum amount allowed.

In these penalty appeals to the Upper Tribunal (ie, where the decision was made by the First-tier Tribunal under penalty proceedings), you can appeal on a question of law *or* on the amount of the penalty.[53] The usual time limits and procedures for applying for permission to appeal apply.

---

3. **Appealing to the Upper Tribunal**

You can appeal to the Upper Tribunal against a decision of the First-tier Tribunal if the First-tier Tribunal made an error of law. In some penalty appeals, you can also appeal about the amount of the penalty (see above).

Chapter 59 explains what an error of law is and how to appeal (see p1330). The rules for tax credits are the same as those for benefits described in Chapter 59, except that if you disagree with the Upper Tribunal decision it cannot be 'superseded', but it can be revised in any of the ways described above, except for revision because of official error (see p1484).

4. Appealing to the courts

You can appeal to the Court of Appeal (in England and Wales) or to the Court of Session (in Scotland) against a decision of the Upper Tribunal, but only if there has been an error of law (see Chapter 59).

Notes

1. Revisions
1   s14(1) TCA 2002
2   s3(2) TCA 2002
3   s14(3) TCA 2002
4   s15(1) TCA 2002
5   Reg 25 TC(CN) Regs; reg 16(5)(a) WTC(EMR) Regs
6   Reg 26A TC(CN) Regs
7   Email to CPAG from HMRC, 8 February 2010
8   Reg 26(3) TC(CN) Regs
9   s16(1) TCA 2002
10 Reg 16(5)(b) WTC(EMR) Regs
11 s16(1) TCA 2002
12 CTC/2662/2005; CTC/3981/2005
13 s21 TCA 2002
14 s18(5) TCA 2002
15 s18(6) TCA 2002
16 s18(9) TCA 2002
17 s19(1) TCA 2002
18 s19(4) TCA 2002
19 s19(11) TCA 2002
20 s21 TCA 2002
21 s20(1) and (3) TCA 2002
22 s20(6)(a) TCA 2002
23 s20(6)(b) TCA 2002
24 s20(4) TCA 2002
25 s20(5) TCA 2002
26 s21 TCA 2002; reg 3 TC(OE) Regs
27 *JI v HMRC (TC)* [2013] UKUT 199 (AAC), para 50
28 ss15(2)(b),16(3)(b) and 19(2)(b) TCA 2002
29 Reg 30 TC(CN) Regs
30 s23 TCA 2002

2. Appeals
31 s63(2) TCA 2002
32 The Tax Credits, Child Benefit and Guardian's Allowance Reviews and Appeals Order 2014 (draft)
33 s102 WRA 2012
34 s12 SSA 1998, as applied by reg 4 TC(A) Regs under the power in s63(8) TCA 2002
35 CTC/2612/2005
36 Reg 3 TC(A)(No.2) Regs
37 s38 TCA 2002
38 *SG v HMRC (TC)* [2011] UKUT 199 (AAC)
39 *JI v HMRC (TC)* [2013] UKUT 199 (AAC)
40 ss23(2) and 39(1) TCA 2002
41 *JI v HMRC (TC)* [2013] UKUT 0199 (AAC); see also CPAG's *Welfare Rights Bulletin* 234
42 The Tax Credits (Late Appeals) Order 2014 (draft)
43 Reg 2 TC(NA) Regs
44 s54 TMA 1970, as applied by reg 3 TC(A) Regs
45 rr2, 5 and 7 TP(FT) Rules
46 CTC/2662/2005; CTC/3981/2005
47 Reg 11 TC(PC) Regs
48 The power to refer to a doctor in s20 SSA 1998 does not apply to tax credits.

Part 11: General rules for tax credits
Chapter 68: Revisions and appeals: tax credits
Notes

49 Reg 11 TC(PC) Regs
50 s13(3) SSA 1998, as applied by reg 5(2)
    TC(A) Regs under the power in s63(8)
    TCA 2002
51 s38 TCA 2002
52 s63 and Sch 2 para 4(1) TCA 2002
53 Sch 2 para 4(1) TCA 2002

11

Part 12

Immigration and residence rules for benefits and tax credits

Chapter 69

Coming from abroad: immigration status

This chapter covers:
1. Immigration status (below)
2. Benefits and tax credits affected by immigration status (p1503)
3. Partners and children (p1507)
4. National insurance numbers and contributions (p1509)
5. Asylum seekers and refugees (p1511)

You should check this chapter if you, your partner and child are not all European Economic Area (EEA) nationals. If you are all EEA nationals, the rules in this chapter do not apply to you. In either case, you must satisfy the residence requirements in Chapter 70.

Key facts
- Your immigration status may mean that you are not entitled to some benefits and tax credits, although there are limited exceptions.
- The immigration status of your partner can affect the amount you are paid. If your partner's or child's leave in the UK is on condition that s/he does not have recourse to public funds, your claim could affect her/his right to remain in the UK.

1. Immigration status

It is important to know your immigration status, and that of anyone included in your claim, before making a claim for a benefit or tax credit. This is because your immigration status affects your right to benefits and tax credits and being paid an increased amount for someone included in your claim can affect her/his right to remain in the UK if her/his leave is on condition that s/he has 'no recourse to public funds'. If you are unsure about your immigration status, or that of anyone included in your claim, you should seek specialist advice from your local law

Part 12: Immigration and residence rules for benefits and tax credits
Chapter 69: Coming from abroad: immigration status
1. Immigration status

centre, Citizens Advice Bureau or other advice agency that gives immigration advice.

Who is a 'person subject to immigration control'

Most people, apart from British citizens, are subject to immigration control. However, for benefit and tax credit purposes, the term 'person subject to immigration control' has a specific meaning. It is this meaning that is referred to when the phrase 'person subject to immigration control' is used in this *Handbook*.

You are defined as a **'person subject to immigration control'** if you are not a European Economic Area (EEA) national and you:[1]

- require leave to enter or remain in the UK, but do not have it (see below);
- have leave to enter or remain on condition that you do not have recourse to public funds (see p1501);
- have leave to enter or remain given as a result of a maintenance undertaking (see p1502);
- have leave to enter or remain solely because you are appealing a decision to refuse to vary your previous leave (see p1503).

If you are defined as a 'person subject to immigration control', you are excluded from many benefits and tax credits (see p1503). There are, however, some limited exceptions (see p1504, p1505 and p1506).

Note:

- You cannot be a person subject to immigration control if you are an EEA national (this includes British citizens) as the definition only applies to non-EEA nationals. See p1590 for a list of EEA states.
- If you are not an EEA national but you have a 'right to reside' under European Union (EU) law (see p1525), you cannot be refused benefit on the basis of your immigration status. If this applies to you, you do not require leave to enter or remain.[2] Therefore, even if you have been given leave to enter or remain subject to a condition that you do not have recourse to public funds or as a result of a maintenance undertaking, this does not exclude you from benefits.

You require leave to enter or remain, but do not have it

You are a 'person subject to immigration control' if you require leave to enter or remain but do not have it.[3]

If you are not an EEA national, you require leave to enter or remain in the UK unless you are:

- a person with the right of abode or certificate of partiality;
- a person with a right of residence in EU law. This applies if, for example, you are:
  - a family member of an EEA or Swiss national who has a right to reside in the UK (see p1542);[4]

- a Swiss national with a right to reside. Swiss nationals, in general, have the same residence rights as EEA nationals and do not require leave to enter or, if they have a right to reside, leave to remain in the UK;[5]
- the primary carer of a British citizen who is in the UK, and it is necessary for you to have a right to reside in the UK so that s/he can continue to reside within the EU.[6] **Note:** having a right to reside on this basis does not entitle you to any of the benefits that require a right to reside (see p1520), but you can still be entitled to other benefits that do not require a right to reside, such as personal independence payment (PIP) or carer's allowance (CA).

Examples of when you require leave to enter or remain but do not have it include if you:
- are an asylum seeker with temporary admission;
- have overstayed your limited leave to enter or remain;
- have entered the UK illegally;
- are subject to a deportation order.

Note: there are close links between the benefit authorities and the Home Office UK Border Agency. Making a claim for benefit could alert the immigration authorities to your presence and status in the UK. Get specialist immigration advice before claiming if you are unsure about your immigration status.

You are prohibited from having recourse to public funds

You are a 'person subject to immigration control' if you have leave to enter or remain in the UK on condition that you do not have recourse to 'public funds'.[7]

Most people admitted to the UK with time-limited leave, such as spouses/civil partners, students or visitors, are given limited leave to stay on condition they do not have recourse to public funds.

Public funds

'**Public funds**' are defined in the Immigration Rules as:[8]
- attendance allowance;
- CA;
- child benefit;
- child tax credit;
- council tax benefit and council tax reduction;
- disability living allowance;
- income-related employment and support allowance;
- housing benefit (HB);
- income support;
- income-based jobseeker's allowance;
- pension credit;
- PIP;

12

Part 12: Immigration and residence rules for benefits and tax credits
Chapter 69: Coming from abroad: immigration status
1. Immigration status

- severe disablement allowance;
- social fund payments;
- universal credit;
- working tax credit.

Homelessness assistance and housing provided under specific provisions are also defined as public funds.

Only the benefits and tax credits listed in the Immigration Rules are public funds. Therefore, if you get any other benefit, you are not in breach of the 'no recourse to public funds' condition.

If you have recourse to public funds when your leave is subject to a condition that you do not do so, you have breached one of the conditions of your leave. This may affect your right to remain in the UK; you could be liable to be deported, have further leave refused and/or be prosecuted for committing a criminal offence.[9]

However, if you are subject to a 'no recourse to public funds' condition, you are defined as a 'person subject to immigration control' and (unless you are covered by one of the exceptions – see p1504, p1505 and p1506) you are not entitled to the benefits and tax credits defined as public funds (see p1503).

If you do come within one of the exceptions, there is no problem with you claiming and receiving that public fund benefit as you are not regarded as having recourse to public funds under the Immigration Rules.[10]

Note: you are regarded as having recourse to public funds if someone else's benefit is increased because of your presence – eg, if the amount of your partner's HB is greater because you are included in her/his claim. If this happens, you will have breached the condition not to have recourse to public funds. Seek specialist advice before making a claim.

Your leave was given as a result of a maintenance undertaking

If your leave to enter or remain was given as a result of a maintenance undertaking, you are a 'person subject to immigration control'.[11] For example, if an elderly relative is seeking to join family in the UK, it is usual to require a maintenance undertaking.

A 'maintenance undertaking' means a written undertaking given by another person under the Immigration Rules to be responsible for your maintenance and accommodation.[12] There are specific Home Office forms on which an undertaking can be given. However, no official form need be used, provided the undertaking is sufficiently formal and definite.[13] The document must contain a promise or agreement that the other person will maintain and accommodate you in the future. If it merely contains a statement about her/his present abilities and intentions, it does not amount to an undertaking.[14] Your leave is considered to be 'as a result of a maintenance undertaking' if this was a factor in granting it. It does not need to have been the only, or even a major, factor.[15] However, if the maintenance undertaking was not relevant to your being granted leave, its existence does not make you a person subject to immigration control. If you are in doubt about whether you have leave given as a result of an undertaking, seek specialist advice.

You are appealing a refusal to vary previous leave

If you have leave solely because you have appealed against a decision to refuse an application to vary the leave you previously had, you can be considered to be a 'person subject to immigration control'. It is arguable that this does not apply in all cases.[16] If you are refused benefit in these circumstances, you should obtain specialist advice.

Example

Sayf is granted three years' discretionary leave. Just before this expires he applies for a further period of discretionary leave. His application is refused and he immediately appeals against this decision. His previous discretionary leave is extended while the appeal is pending, but it may be argued that he is now a 'person subject to immigration control'.

2. Benefits and tax credits affected by immigration status

The general rule is that if you are defined as a 'person subject to immigration control' (see p1500) you are excluded from council tax reduction[17] and the following benefits and tax credits:[18]

- attendance allowance (AA);
- carer's allowance (CA);
- child benefit;
- child tax credit (CTC);
- disability living allowance (DLA);
- income-related employment and support allowance (ESA);
- ESA in youth;[19]
- housing benefit (HB);
- incapacity benefit (IB) for incapacity in youth;[20]
- income-based jobseeker's allowance (JSA);
- income support (IS);
- pension credit (PC);
- personal independence payment (PIP);
- severe disablement allowance (SDA);
- social fund payments;

12

Part 12: Immigration and residence rules for benefits and tax credits
Chapter 69: Coming from abroad: immigration status
2. Benefits and tax credits affected by immigration status

- universal credit (UC);
- working tax credit (WTC).

However, there are limited exceptions when some people subject to immigration control can claim means tested benefits (see below), some can claim non-means tested benefits (see p1505) and some can claim tax credits (see p1506).

A person subject to immigration control is only excluded from the above benefits and tax credits and can therefore claim any other benefit. For example, if you have paid sufficient national insurance contributions, you can claim any of the contributory benefits – eg, retirement pensions, contribution-based JSA and contributory ESA. You can also claim benefits that depend on previous employment – eg, maternity allowance (MA) or industrial injuries benefits. **Note:** the government intends to make it a condition of entitlement to contributory ESA, contribution-based JSA, MA and statutory sick, maternity, paternity and adoption pay that you are entitled to work in the UK.[21] See CPAG's online service and *Welfare Rights Bulletin* for updates.

Exceptions

Means-tested benefits
The relevant benefits are:
- IS;
- income-based JSA;
- income-related ESA;
- PC;
- HB;
- UC.

If you are a 'person subject to immigration control' (see p1500), this does not exclude you from entitlement to the means-tested benefits listed above if you:[22]
- are a national of Macedonia or Turkey and you are lawfully present in the UK – eg, during a period in which you have leave to enter or remain in the UK. Asylum seekers with temporary admission have been accepted as being lawfully present.[23] However, in order to be entitled to means-tested benefits, you must still satisfy the residence tests. Having temporary admission does not give you a right to reside (see p1525), so unless you have a right to reside on another basis, you will not be entitled to means-tested benefits;[24] or
- have leave to enter or remain given as a result of a maintenance undertaking and have been resident in the UK for at least five years (beginning on either the date of your entry to the UK or the signing of the maintenance undertaking, whichever is later). If there are gaps in your residence as a result of your going to live for a period in another country, the periods of residency in the UK can be added together to make the five years.[25] However, depending on your

12

circumstances, you may not have ceased to be resident during the short periods of absence and each absence must be considered individually (see p1519);[26] *or*

- have leave to enter or remain given as a result of a maintenance undertaking and the person (or, if more than one, all the people) who gave the undertaking has died; *or*
- applied for asylum before 3 April 2000, have not had a decision on that application, and are covered by the transitional protection rules.[27] See Chapter 58 of the 2011/12 edition of this *Handbook* for these rules.

Social fund payments
If you are defined as a 'person subject to immigration control', this does not exclude you from entitlement to social fund payments if you are in any of the exempt categories for means-tested or non-means-tested benefits listed on p1504 and below.[28] However, you must meet the other conditions of entitlement, including (except for winter fuel payments) being in receipt of a qualifying benefit.

Non-means-tested benefits
The relevant benefits are:

- AA;
- CA;
- child benefit;
- DLA;
- ESA in youth;
- IB for incapacity in youth;
- PIP;
- SDA.

If you are a 'person subject to immigration control' (see p1500), this does not exclude you from the non-contributory benefits listed above if:[29]

- you have leave to enter or remain given as a result of a maintenance undertaking; *or*
- you are a member of a European Economic Area national's (see p1590) (including a British citizen's) family;[30] *or*
- you are a national of Algeria, Morocco, San Marino, Tunisia or Turkey and either you are currently lawfully working in Great Britain, or you have ceased lawfully working in Great Britain for a reason such as pregnancy, childcare, illness or accident, or because you have reached retirement age.[31] You are lawfully working if your work does not breach any conditions attached to your leave or, if you are an asylum seeker, you have permission to work from the UK Border Agency; *or*
- you are living with a family member (see p1592) who is someone listed in the above bullet point; *or*

Part 12: Immigration and residence rules for benefits and tax credits
Chapter 69: Coming from abroad: immigration status
2. Benefits and tax credits affected by immigration status

- for DLA, PIP, AA and child benefit only, you are covered by a reciprocal agreement. In practice, this is most helpful for child benefit and, in particular, if you are covered by the agreement with former Yugoslavia which applies to Bosnia-Herzegovina, Kosovo, Macedonia, Montenegro, and Serbia.[32] See p1517 for more information about reciprocal agreements; *or*
- you have been receiving that benefit continuously since 4 February 1996 (6 October 1996 for child benefit). If this applies, you should not request a revision or supersession of your award as you will bring your entitlement to an end.

Tax credits

If you are a 'person subject to immigration control' (see p1500), this does not exclude you from getting CTC or WTC if:[33]

- you have leave to enter or remain given as a result of a maintenance undertaking and you have been resident in the UK for at least five years (beginning on the date of either your entry to the UK or the signing of the maintenance undertaking, whichever is later); *or*
- you have leave to enter or remain given as a result of a maintenance undertaking and the person (or, if more than one, all the people) who gave the undertaking has died; *or*
- (CTC only) you are a national of Algeria, Morocco, San Marino, Tunisia or Turkey and either you are lawfully working in the UK, or you have ceased lawfully working for a reason such as pregnancy, childcare, illness or accident, or because you have reached retirement age.[34] You are lawfully working if your work does not breach any conditions attached to your leave, or, if you are an asylum seeker, you have permission to work from the UK Border Agency; *or*
- (WTC only) you are a national of Macedonia or Turkey and you are lawfully present in the UK. This is most likely to enable you to get benefits if you have leave to enter or remain as you are lawfully present during that period of leave; *or*
- (CTC only) you claim CTC on or after 6 April 2004 and immediately before this you were entitled to an increase in your IS or income-based JSA for a child because you fell into either the group of people in the first bullet point or the last bullet point on p1504 as not excluded from means-tested benefits – ie, you are Turkish and lawfully present, or you claimed asylum before 3 April 2000 and are covered by the transitional protection rules.[35] This only applies if you are transferring to CTC from an IS or JSA claim that included amounts for a child. It does not apply if you have not been receiving IS or income-based JSA for a child.

Note: if you are a person subject to immigration control, but your partner is not (or s/he falls into one of the above groups), you can make a joint claim for tax credits (see p1509).

3. Partners and children

Some benefits and tax credits have special rules that apply if any partner or child who lives with you is subject to immigration control. These rules vary, so check the rules for the benefit or tax credit you want to claim.

Means-tested benefits

Income support, income-based jobseeker's allowance and income-related employment and support allowance

If your partner is a 'person subject to immigration control' (see p1500), s/he is included in your claim for income support (IS), income-based jobseeker's allowance (JSA), including if you are a joint-claim couple, or income-related employment and support allowance (ESA). However, you are only paid a personal allowance at the single person's rate, unless s/he comes into one of the groups that can get the means-tested benefits listed on p1504, in which case, you are paid at the couple rate.[36]

In all cases, your partner is still treated as part of your household and part of your claim. Therefore, her/his work, income and capital can all affect your benefit entitlement. Her/his presence means you cannot claim IS as a lone parent (see p27) and may mean you are not entitled to a severe disability premium (see p233).

Premiums are payable if either you or your partner satisfy the qualifying conditions (see p226) and should be paid at the couple rate.

Note: if your partner's leave to enter or remain in the UK is on condition that s/he does not have recourse to public funds, receiving an additional (or a couple rate of a) premium for her/him could be regarded as having recourse to public funds and affect her/his right to remain in the UK. Seek specialist advice before making a claim. However, we have no experience of claimants' partners being refused further leave because of this.

Pension credit

If your partner is a 'person subject to immigration control' (whether or not s/he is in one of the exempt groups listed on p1504), s/he is treated as not being part of your household.[37] This means that you are paid as a single person and your partner's income and capital do not affect your claim. If you would otherwise be entitled to the additional amount for severe disability, your partner's presence may mean you are not entitled to it as the DWP may count her/him as 'normally residing with' you for this purpose (see p233).[38]

12

Part 12: Immigration and residence rules for benefits and tax credits
Chapter 69: Coming from abroad: immigration status
3. Partners and children

Housing benefit

If your partner and/or child for whom you are responsible is a 'person subject to immigration control', this does not affect the amount you are paid. Your partner is included in your claim and your applicable amount includes the couple rate of the personal allowance and any premiums to which either of you are entitled. Similarly, your child is included in your claim and your applicable amount includes a personal allowance for each child, together with any premiums for which s/he qualifies.

Note: if your partner's and/or child's leave is on condition that s/he does not have recourse to public funds, a claim for housing benefit could result in additional public funds being paid as a result of her/his presence. This could affect her/his right to remain in the UK (see p1501). Seek specialist advice before making a claim.

Universal credit

If your partner is a 'person subject to immigration control' (see p1500), and is not in one of the groups who can get universal credit (UC) listed on p1503, you must claim UC as a single person.[39] Your award is based on the maximum amount for a single person, but your partner's income and capital are taken into account (see p184).[40]

Non-means-tested benefits

Contributory benefits are not affected by your immigration status, or that of your partner or child. Note: the government intends to make it a condition of entitlement to contributory ESA, contribution-based JSA, maternity allowance and statutory sick, maternity, paternity and adoption pay that you are entitled to work in the UK.[41] See CPAG's online service and *Welfare Rights Bulletin* for updates.

Only the claimant's immigration status affects entitlement to non-contributory benefits. Therefore, for **child benefit**, if you are not a 'person subject to immigration control' or you are but you are in one of the exempt groups (see p1505), you can claim for any child for whom you are responsible, regardless of the child's immigration status.

Similarly, if your child is not a person subject to immigration control, or s/he is but is in one of the exempt groups on p1505, s/he can claim **disability living allowance** even if you are a person subject to immigration control.

Tax credits

If your partner is a 'person subject to immigration control' and you are not, or you are but are in one of the exempt groups on p1506, your joint claim for tax credits (see p1438) is treated as if your partner were not subject to immigration control. You are therefore entitled to working tax credit (WTC) and child tax credit

(CTC).[42] However, unless you or your partner are responsible for a child, or your partner is a national of Macedonia or Turkey and is lawfully present in the UK, your WTC does not include the couple element.[43]

There are no immigration status conditions for children for tax credits. Consequently, any child for whom you are responsible is included in your claim and your CTC and/or WTC includes amounts for her/him.

If your partner's leave is on condition that s/he does not have recourse to public funds, s/he is not regarded as having recourse by making a joint tax credits claim with you. This means that you and your partner can make the joint claim without it affecting her/his right to remain in the UK. If a joint claim includes a child whose leave is on condition that s/he does not have recourse to public funds, any tax credits awarded in respect of that child are also not regarded as recourse.[44]

If your claim for CTC or WTC is not a joint claim as described above (ie, in which one partner is a person subject to immigration control) and it includes an amount for a child whose leave prevents her/him from having recourse to public funds, this may be regarded as recourse and could affect her/his right to remain in the UK. Seek specialist advice before making a claim. However, we have no experience of children being refused further leave because of this.

---

4. National insurance numbers and contributions

The national insurance number requirement

In general, in order to be entitled to any social security benefit or tax credit, you (and any partner who is included in your claim) must satisfy the national insurance (NI) number requirement (see p1138) when you make a claim for benefit. It also applies when someone who will be included in your existing award of benefit joins your family – eg, if your spouse joins you from abroad. Your partner must, unless s/he is exempt (see p1510), satisfy the NI number requirement even if you are not going to receive any extra benefit for her/him because s/he is a 'person subject to immigration control' (see p1500). For the rules on when you are paid for your partner, see p1507.

Any child or young person who is included in your housing benefit (HB) or universal credit (UC) claim does not have to satisfy the NI number requirement.[45] However if s/he is the claimant s/he must satisfy the NI number requirement.[46]

Part 12: Immigration and residence rules for benefits and tax credits
Chapter 69: Coming from abroad: immigration status
5. Asylum seekers and refugees

Who is exempt

If you are the benefit claimant, your partner does not have to satisfy the NI number requirement if:[47]

- s/he is a 'person subject to immigration control' because s/he requires leave to enter or remain in the UK, but does not have it (see p1500); and
- s/he has not previously been given an NI number; and
- you are claiming income support, income-based jobseeker's allowance, income-related employment and support allowance or pension credit and your partner is not entitled to that benefit her/himself, or you are claiming HB and your partner fails the 'habitual residence test' (see p1521). However, in practice it is difficult to see who could satisfy the first bullet point and not satisfy this.

You are still asked for information about an NI number application for your partner, even though s/he is exempt. An NI number will be refused, but this does not prevent you from being entitled to benefits or tax credits or council tax reduction.

Note: this exemption does not apply to UC. If your partner is a 'person subject to immigration control' because s/he requires leave, you must claim UC as a single person (see p184) and your partner is not required to have an NI number.

Tax credits

The NI number requirement for tax credits is similar to the requirement for benefits (and includes the same exemption for partners) except that the requirement does not apply if the Tax Credit Office is satisfied that you (and/or your partner if it is a joint claim) have 'reasonable excuse' for not complying with the requirement – eg, if you are unable to prove your identity because the Home Office has all your documents and you can prove this, for instance, with a letter from your solicitor.[48]

National insurance contributions

If you have worked and paid contributions in a country with which the UK has a reciprocal agreement (see p1517), these can be taken into account when working out your entitlement to UK contributory benefits.[49] You may also be able to make up a shortfall in your contribution record by making voluntary contributions (see p846). Seek advice to check if this is worth doing.

5. **Asylum seekers and refugees**

Asylum seekers

You are referred to as an **'asylum seeker'** while you are waiting for a Home Office decision on an application for refugee status. If you are a non-European Economic

Area national seeking asylum in the UK, unless you have leave on some other basis or you do not require it (eg, because you are joining your family member who has a right to reside in the UK), you come within the definition of a 'person subject to immigration control'. This is because you are someone who requires leave but does not have it (see p1500). You are therefore excluded from the social security benefits listed on p1503 unless you are in one of the exempt groups on p1504, p1505 or 1506.

If benefit can be paid for you either because you are in an exempt group or because your partner can include you in her/his claim, this does affect your asylum application. You can receive any benefit defined as a 'public fund' (see p1501) because asylum seekers do not have a 'no recourse to public funds' restriction.

If you are excluded from claiming social security benefits because you are a 'person subject to immigration control', you may be entitled to alternative forms of state support. If you are destitute, you may be eligible for asylum support from the UK Border Agency. **Note:** asylum support is taken into account as income when calculating any housing benefit your partner claims, but it is not taken into account as income for income support (IS), income-based jobseeker's allowance (JSA) or income-related employment and support allowance (ESA) and universal credit (UC).[50]

However, any IS, income-based JSA, income-related ESA or UC your partner receives is taken into account as income when calculating your asylum support.

If you are not eligible for asylum support or benefits, ask your local authority for help. If you have children, you may be eligible for support under the Children Act 1989 or Children (Scotland) Act 1995. If you are sick or disabled, you may be eligible for help under the National Assistance Act 1948. Seek independent legal advice if you are refused.

For more information about asylum support and other support for asylum seekers, see CPAG's *Benefits for Migrants Handbook*.

Refugees and other leave granted after an asylum application

If you are granted either refugee leave, humanitarian protection, discretionary leave or indefinite leave granted under the 'case resolution exercise', you are no longer a 'person subject to immigration control'. Therefore, during this period of leave, your immigration status does not affect your entitlement to benefit and you can claim all benefits, provided you meet the usual rules of entitlement. However, if you are granted another form of leave that is subject to the condition that you do not have 'recourse to public funds', you are defined as a 'person subject to immigration control' and excluded from the benefits and tax credits listed on p1503, unless you come within an exempt group (see p1504, p1505 and p1506).

Part 12: Immigration and residence rules for benefits and tax credits
Chapter 69: Coming from abroad: immigration status
5. Asylum seekers and refugees

If you are granted refugee leave or humanitarian protection, you can be joined by certain family members under family reunion provisions. A family member who comes to the UK under these provisions is not, during her/his period of leave, a 'person subject to immigration control' and can claim all benefits, provided s/he meets the usual rules of entitlement.

If you are granted refugee status, humanitarian protection, or discretionary leave, you are exempt from the habitual residence test (see p1521).

Income support for refugees studying English

Refugees who are studying English are entitled to IS (see p30). If you have been granted refugee leave (not humanitarian protection or discretionary leave), you can claim IS for up to nine months while you are studying if you:[51]

- attend, for more than 15 hours a week, a course for the purpose of learning English so you may obtain employment; *and*
- have been in Great Britain for not more than 12 months on the date the course began.

Backdating tax credits, child benefit and guardian's allowance

If you have been granted refugee leave (not humanitarian protection or discretionary leave), you can claim tax credits, child benefit and guardian's allowance and have them backdated to the date of your asylum application (or, for tax credits, 6 April 2003 if this is later).[52] Generally, with tax credits you are required to reclaim each year. However, under the special backdating rules for refugees, the claim is treated as having been renewed each April.[53]

You must claim backdated tax credits within one month, and child benefit and guardian's allowance within three months, of receiving the Home Office letter granting you leave as a refugee.[54] If the Home Office letter is sent to a solicitor acting for you, the three- or one-month period starts from the date your solicitor receives the letter.[55]

The amount of tax credits paid is reduced by the amount of asylum support you received for your essential living needs over the period.[56]

In many cases, the amount of asylum support is greater than the rate of tax credits and therefore cancels out any entitlement to tax credits over the backdated period. However, if you did not receive asylum support or your tax credit entitlement exceeds the amount of asylum support paid (eg, if you worked sufficient hours to qualify for working tax credit), you can be entitled to an amount of backdated tax credits.

The amount of child benefit and guardian's allowance paid is not reduced by any asylum support you may have received.

Integration loans

If you (or someone upon whom you are dependent) are granted refugee leave or humanitarian protection and you are aged 18 or over, you may be eligible for an integration loan.[57] This is a discretionary loan of at least £100, paid for expenses associated with your integration into UK society, including for employment, education and housing. Claims are decided by the UK Border Agency and so these loans are not covered in this *Handbook*. Details and an application form are available on the UK Border Agency website (www.ukba.homeoffice.gov.uk).

Notes

1. Immigration status

1 s115(9) IAA 1999
2 s7 IA 1988
3 s115(9)(a) IAA 1999
4 s7 IA 1988
5 *The Agreement Between the European Community and its Member States, of the one part, and the Swiss Confederation, of the other, on the Free Movement of Persons*, Luxembourg, 21 June 1999, Cm 5639; reg 2 I(EEA) Regs defines Switzerland as an EEA state; reg 11 provides that no EEA national requires leave to enter the UK.
6 Reg 15A(4A) I(EEA) Regs; *Zambrano*, C-34/09 [2011] ECR, IO1177; *Dereci and Others*, C-256/11 [2011] ECR I-11315
7 s115(9)(b) IAA 1999
8 para 6 Immigration Rules, HC395
9 s24(1)(b)(ii) IA 1971
10 para 6B Immigration Rules, HC395
11 s115(9)(c) IAA 1999
12 s115(10) IAA 1999
13 *R (Begum) v Social Security Commissioner* [2003] EWHC 3380 (Admin)
14 *Ahmed v SSWP* [2005] EWCA Civ 535
15 CIS/3508/2001
16 s115(9)(d) IAA 1999 referred to Sch 4 para 17 IAA 1999, which was repealed by Sch 9 para 1 NIAA 2002. It may be that the reference should be read as if to s3C(2) IA 1971 (s17(2) Interpretation Act 1978).

2. Benefits and tax credits affected by immigration status

17 Sch para 22 CTRS(DS)E Regs; reg 13 CTRS(PR)E Regs; reg 19 CTR(SPC)S Regs; reg 19 CTR(S) Regs; reg 27 CTRSPR(W) Regs; Sch para 20 CTRS(DS)W Regs
18 s115 IAA 1999; s42 TCA 2002; reg 3 TC(Imm) Regs
19 Reg 11(1)(b) ESA Regs; reg 12(1)(b) ESA Regs 2013
20 Reg 16(1)(b) SS(IB) Regs
21 ss61-63 WRA 2012
22 Reg 2(1) and Part 1 of Sch SS(IA)CA Regs
23 *Szoma v SSWP* [2005] UKHL 64, 27 October 2005
24 *Yesiloz v London Borough of Camden Anor* [2009] EWCA Civ 415
25 R(IS) 2/02
26 CPC/1005/2005
27 Reg 12 SS(IA)CA Regs; reg 12 SS(PFA)MA Regs
28 Reg 2 SS(IA)CA Regs
29 Reg 2(2), (3) and (4)(b) and Sch Part II SS(IA)CA Regs; reg 2(1)(a)(ib) SS(AA) Regs; reg 9(1)(ia) SS(ICA) Regs; reg 16(d)(ii) SS(PIP) Regs; reg 2(1)(a)(ib) SS(DLA) Regs; reg 11(1)(b) and (3) ESA Regs; reg 12(1)(b) and (3) ESA Regs 2013; reg 16(1)(b) and (5) SS(IB) Regs
30 *JFP v DSD (DLA)* [2012] NI Com 267 which declined to follow the more restrictive approach of CDLA/708/2007
31 *Zoulika Krid v Caisse Nationale d'Assurance Vieillesse des Travailleurs Salariés (CNAVTS)*, C-103/94 [1995] ECR I-00719, para 26

Part 12: Immigration and residence rules for benefits and tax credits
Chapter 69: Coming from abroad: immigration status
Notes

32 The Family Allowances, National Insurance and Industrial Injuries (Yugoslavia) Order, 1958, No.1263
33 Reg 3 TC(Imm) Regs
34 *Zoulika Krid v Caisse Nationale d'Assurance Vieillesse des Travailleurs Salariés (CNAVTS), C-103/94 [1995] ECR I-00719, para 26*
35 Reg 5 TC(Imm) Regs. Macedonia is not listed here as it only ratified the European Social Charter on 31 March 2005 – ie, after 6 March 2005.

53 Reg 3(6)(b) TC(Imm) Regs
54 **CB/GA** Reg 6(2)(d) CB and GA(Admin) Regs
   TC Reg 3(5) TC(Imm) Regs
55 *Tkachuk v SSWP* [2007] EWCA Civ 515; CIS/3797/2003
56 Reg 3(9) TC(Imm) Regs
57 s13 The Asylum and Immigration (Treatment of Claimants, etc) Act 2004, No.19; The Integration Loans for Refugees and Others Regulations 2007, No.1598

3. Partners and children
36 **IS** Reg 21(3) and Sch 7 para 16A IS Regs
   JSA Reg 85(4) and Sch 5 para 13A JSA Regs
   ESA Reg 69 and Sch 5 para 10 ESA Regs
37 Reg 5(1)(h) SPC Regs
38 para 38946 DMG
39 Reg 3(3) UC Regs
40 Regs 18(2), 22(3) and 36(3) UC Regs
41 ss61-63 WRA 2012
42 Reg 3(2) TC(Imm) Regs
43 Reg 11(4) and (5) WTC(EMR) Regs
44 para 6B Immigration Rules, HC395. The TC(Imm) Regs are made under s42 TCA 2002.

4. National insurance numbers and contributions
45 **HB** Reg 4(b) HB Regs; reg 4(b) HB(SPC) Regs
   UC Reg 5 UC,PIP,JSA&ESA(C&P) Regs
46 *Westminster CC v AT and SSWP* [2013] UKUT 321 (AAC)
47 **IS** Reg 2A IS Regs
   JSA Reg 2A JSA Regs
   ESA Reg 2A ESA Regs
   PC Reg 1A SPC Regs
   HB Reg 4(c) HB Regs; reg 4(c) HB(SPC) Regs
   TC Reg 5(8) TC(CN) Regs
48 Reg 5(6) TC(CN) Regs
49 Under orders made in powers conferred by s179 SSAA 1992

5. Asylum seekers and refugees
50 **IS** Sch 9 para 21 IS Regs
   JSA Sch 7 para 22 JSA Regs
   ESA Sch 8 para 22 ESA Regs
   HB Sch 5 para 23 HB Regs
   UC Reg 66 UC Regs
51 Reg 4ZA(3)(b) and Sch 1B para 18 IS Regs
52 **CB/GA** Reg 6(d) CB&GA(Admin) Regs
   TC Regs 3(4)-(9) and 4 TC(Imm) Regs

Chapter 70

Coming from abroad: residence rules

This chapter covers:

This chapter describes the residence and presence rules that affect your entitlement while you are in Great Britain. If you go abroad, see Chapter 71.

If you or your partner are not a European Economic Area (EEA) national, before using this chapter check Chapter 69 for information on how your immigration status can affect your entitlement to benefits and tax credits.

If you are an EEA national, the European Union co-ordination rules may help you to satisfy the residence and presence tests when you are in the UK. These rules are outlined in Chapter 72.

Key facts

- Different types of residence conditions apply to many benefits and tax credits. These are: **residence, ordinary residence, right to reside** and **habitual residence.**
- Entitlement to some benefits and tax credits also depends on your being **present** in Great Britain and/or having been present for a certain period of time (known as **'past presence'**).
- The rules on residence and presence vary between different benefits and tax credits. If you satisfy the conditions for one benefit or tax credit, it does not mean you necessarily satisfy the conditions for another.

Part 12: Immigration and residence rules for benefits and tax credits
Chapter 70: Coming from abroad: residence rules
1. Introduction

1. Introduction

Many benefits have residence and/or presence conditions. The rules vary between different benefits and tax credits. Whether you meet the conditions depends on how long you have been in Great Britain, your nationality, your immigration status, and whether you are covered by the provisions of European law.

Although many presence and residence rules refer to Great Britain rather than the UK, there is a reciprocal agreement between Britain and Northern Ireland, which means that, generally, you can satisfy the residence conditions if you move between Great Britain and Northern Ireland.

There are residence conditions for the following benefits and tax credits:
- attendance allowance (see p1555);
- carer's allowance (see p1555);
- child benefit (see p1554);
- child tax credit (see p1561);
- disability living allowance (see p1555);
- contributory employment and support allowance (ESA) in youth (see p1555);
- income-related ESA (see p1552);
- guardian's allowance (see p1557);
- housing benefit (see p1552);
- incapacity benefit in youth (see p1555);
- income support (see p1552);
- income-based jobseeker's allowance (JSA) (see p1552);
- pension credit (see p1552);
- personal independence payment (see p1555);
- Category D retirement pension (see p1560);
- severe disablement allowance (see p1555);
- universal credit (see p1552);
- working tax credit (see p1561).

Council tax reduction also has residence conditions.

Contributory benefits, such as contribution-based JSA, contributory ESA and retirement pension (except Category D), as well as the employment-related benefits (maternity allowance and industrial injuries benefits) do not have residence conditions. However, they do have presence requirements, which mean that if you go abroad, some benefits cease and others are not increased unless exceptions apply (see Chapter 71). Industrial injuries benefits also have conditions related to your presence in Great Britain at the time you had your accident or contracted your disease. There are no residence or presence requirements for statutory sick pay, statutory maternity pay, statutory paternity pay or statutory adoption pay paid by your employer.

Which rules apply

If you are covered by European Union (EU) law, these more generous provisions apply. If they do not apply, but you are covered by a reciprocal agreement, these apply. If you are not covered by either EU law or a reciprocal agreement, UK law applies.

The **UK benefits and tax credits legislation** contains rules about the residence and presence conditions that you must satisfy to be entitled to certain benefits. These rules are set out in this chapter.

EU law (legislation and caselaw) applies in the UK and throughout the European Economic Area (EEA). In general, for EU law to apply, you must be an EEA national (see p1590) or the family member of an EEA national and your circumstances must involve more than one EEA state – eg, you are a French national living in the UK.

There are two main areas of EU law which affect benefit and tax credit entitlement that are covered in this *Handbook*. Firstly, if you or your family member are an EEA national, EU law may give you a right of residence that enables you to satisfy the right to reside requirement (see p1525). Secondly, if you are covered by the co-ordination rules (see p1592), these can help you get benefits or tax credits in the UK – eg, by enabling you to count periods of residence in any EEA state to satisfy the past presence requirements (see p1518) for UK benefits.

Note: it is not usually necessary to understand how the co-ordination rules may affect you in order to know whether you have a right of residence in EU law, or vice versa. However, it can be helpful to know if you are covered by the co-ordination rules (see p1592) if you would not otherwise satisfy a requirement to be present, have been present for a past period or be ordinarily resident.

Reciprocal agreements exist between the UK and some other countries and can assist in similar ways to EU law.

Reciprocal agreements with the UK

EEA member states: Austria, Belgium, Croatia, Cyprus, Denmark, Finland, France, Germany, Iceland, Ireland, Italy, Luxembourg, Malta, Netherlands, Norway, Portugal, Slovenia, Spain and Sweden. In general, the reciprocal agreement applies if the EU co-ordination rules do not apply.

Non-EEA member states: Barbados, Bermuda, Bosnia-Herzegovina, Canada, Guernsey, Isle of Man, Israel, Jamaica, Jersey, Kosova, Macedonia, Mauritius, Montenegro, New Zealand, Philippines, Serbia, Turkey and the United States of America.

There are 'association' and 'co-operation' agreements with Algeria, Morocco, San Marino, Slovenia, Tunisia and Turkey.

12

Part 12: Immigration and residence rules for benefits and tax credits
Chapter 70: Coming from abroad: residence rules
2. The different residence and presence tests

The scope of the reciprocal agreements differs greatly, in terms of the people covered, the benefits covered and the provisions made. It is therefore crucial to check the individual agreement. You can find the agreements in the *Law Relating to Social Security* at www.dwp.gov.uk.

2. The different residence and presence tests

The presence and residence conditions you are required to satisfy vary between the different benefits and tax credits. You may be required to satisfy tests for your:

- presence (see below);
- past presence (see below);
- residence (see p1519);
- ordinary residence (see p1519);
- habitual residence (see p1520);
- right to reside (see p1520).

Presence

You must usually be present in Great Britain at the time you make your benefit or tax credit claim, and continue to be present. There are specific rules that allow you to be treated as present during temporary absences (see Chapter 71). The European Union (EU) co-ordination rules can also mean that you do not need to be present (see pp1551–62 and pp1571–86).

Being present means being physically present in Great Britain. If a benefit authority (ie, the DWP, HM Revenue and Customs or local authority) wants to disqualify you from benefit because you were absent from Great Britain, it must show you were absent throughout that day. This means that on the day you leave Great Britain and the day you arrive in Great Britain you count as present.

Past presence

For some benefits (see below), in addition to being present at the time you make your claim, you must also have been present for a period of time before you become entitled. The requirement depends on the benefit you are claiming and, for some benefits, when you make your claim (see pp1551–62).

If you are covered by the EU co-ordination rules (see p1592), these can assist either by exempting you from the requirement or by enabling you to count periods of time in another European Economic Area state. See pp1551–62 and, for an overview of the co-ordination rules, see Chapter 72.

The benefits that have a past presence requirement are:

- attendance allowance (AA);
- carer's allowance (CA);
- disability living allowance (DLA);

- employment and support allowance (ESA) in youth;
- incapacity benefit (IB) in youth;
- income-based jobseeker's allowance (JSA), but note that the test is not one of past presence but of 'living in' (see p1552);
- personal independence payment (PIP);
- severe disablement allowance (SDA).

Residence

The requirement to be simply 'resident', rather than 'ordinarily resident' or 'habitually resident', is only a condition for Category D retirement pension. However, it is a necessary part of being ordinarily resident (see below) or habitually resident (see p1520). Residence is more than mere physical presence in a country and you can be resident without being present – eg, if you are away for a short holiday. You are usually resident in the country in which you have your home for the time being.[1] You can remain resident during a temporary absence, depending on your circumstances, including the length of your absence, your intentions to return, your accommodation, and where your family and your personal belongings are.

Ordinary residence

The benefits and tax credits that have an ordinary residence requirement are:
- AA (if claimed before 8 April 2013 until the award is terminated, revised or superseded);
- CA (if claimed before 8 April 2013 until the award is terminated, revised or superseded);
- child benefit;
- child tax credit (CTC);
- DLA (if claimed before 8 April 2013 until the award is terminated, revised or superseded);
- ESA in youth;
- IB in youth;
- Category D retirement pension;
- SDA;
- social fund funeral payment;
- working tax credit.

The term 'ordinary residence' is not defined in the legislation, and caselaw has confirmed that the words should have their natural and ordinary meaning.[2] You are ordinarily resident in a country if you have a home there that you have adopted for a settled purpose and where you live for the time being (whether for a short or long duration).[3] There are some exceptions to the requirement and if you are covered by the EU co-ordination rules, these may assist you in satisfying it (see

Part 12: Immigration and residence rules for benefits and tax credits
Chapter 70: Coming from abroad: residence rules
2. The different residence and presence tests

pp1551–62). In practice, claims are rarely refused on the basis of ordinary residence.

Habitual residence

The benefits that have a habitual residence requirement are:
- AA;
- CA;
- DLA;
- income-related ESA;
- housing benefit (HB);
- income support (IS);
- income-based JSA;
- pension credit (PC);
- PIP;
- universal credit (UC).

For the benefits listed above, you must satisfy (or be in a group that is exempt from) the habitual residence test (see p1521).
Note:
- You are also excluded from council tax reduction if you do not satisfy (and are not exempt from) the habitual residence test.[4]
- If your claim for AA, CA or DLA began before 8 April 2013, you must be ordinarily, rather than habitually, resident until your award is revised or superseded.[5]

Right to reside

The benefits and tax credits that have a right to reside requirement are:
- child benefit;
- CTC;
- income-related ESA;
- HB;
- IS;
- income-based JSA;
- PC;
- UC.

For the benefits and tax credits listed above, you must satisfy the right to reside requirement, unless, for means-tested benefits only, you are in group that is exempt from the habitual residence test (see p1523). For details of the right to reside test, see p1525. For who has a right to reside, see p1527.
Note: you are also excluded from council tax reduction if you do not satisfy the right to reside requirement.[6]

3. Habitual residence

The requirement to be habitually resident applies to:[7]
- attendance allowance (AA);
- carer's allowance (CA);
- disability living allowance (DLA);
- housing benefit (HB);
- income support (IS);
- income-based jobseeker's allowance (JSA);
- income-related employment and support allowance (ESA);
- pension credit (PC);
- personal independence payment (PIP);
- universal credit (UC).

To be entitled to one of the above benefits, you must be habitually resident in the '**common travel area**' (ie, the UK, Ireland, the Channel Islands and the Isle of Man) or in one of the groups that is exempt from the test.
Note:
- You are also excluded from council tax reduction if you do not satisfy (and are not exempt from) the habitual residence test.[8]
- For AA, CA and DLA, the habitual residence test only applies to new claims made, or awards that are revised or superseded, on or after 8 April 2013.[9] If your claim began before this date, the previous requirement to be ordinarily resident continues to apply until your award is revised or superseded.

The habitual residence test

To satisfy the habitual residence test, you must:
- be 'habitually resident in fact' (see p1524);
- for IS, income-based JSA, income-related ESA, PC, HB and UC, have a right to reside (see p1525); *and*
- for new claims for income-based JSA from 1 January 2014 , you must have been living for the past three months (see p1552) in the common travel area.

Some groups of people are exempt from the habitual residence test (see p1523). If you are in one of these groups and you claim a means-tested benefit, you are treated as satisfying the test. Your residence is not examined further and, provided you meet the other conditions of entitlement, you are eligible for benefit. Whether or not you are exempt from the habitual residence test is not always considered. If you fall into one of these groups, make it clear to the DWP or local authority that you are exempt, particularly if you might not otherwise be accepted as habitually resident.

Part 12: Immigration and residence rules for benefits and tax credits
Chapter 70: Coming from abroad: residence rules
3. Habitual residence

In practice, for means-tested benefits, the DWP or local authority first considers your right to reside. If you satisfy this requirement, it then considers whether you are 'habitually resident in fact' and (for income-based JSA) whether you have been living here for the past three months.

The habitual residence test applies to the benefit claimant. If you are making a joint claim for UC, both partners must satisfy it. If your partner fails the test, you must claim UC as a single person. Your award is based on the maximum amount for a single person, but your partner's income and capital are taken into account (see p192).[10] For other means-tested benefits, if you are the claimant and you satisfy (or are exempt from) the habitual residence test, whether or not your partner satisfies it does not affect your entitlement, unless you are a joint-claim couple for JSA. In this case, if you satisfy the test, but your partner does not, you are entitled to JSA without your partner making a joint claim with you and you are paid as a couple (see p46).

If you fail the habitual residence test

If you fail the habitual residence test, you are not paid any benefit.

- For IS, income-based JSA, income-related ESA and HB, you are classed as a 'person from abroad'. This means for IS, income-based JSA and income-related ESA, you have an applicable amount of nil[11] and for HB, you are treated as not liable for rent.[12]
- For PC and UC, you are treated as not present in Great Britain.[13]
- For AA, CA, DLA and PIP you have failed to meet the prescribed residence requirements.[14]

Have you failed the habitual residence test?

1. If you are refused benefit because you have failed the habitual residence test, consider challenging this decision (see Chapters 58 and 59). You may want to contact a local advice agency for help with this.

2. While challenging the decision, you should make a further claim. If that claim is refused, you should also challenge that decision and make another further claim and so on. This is because when the decision refusing your initial claim is looked at again, the decision maker (or First-tier Tribunal) cannot take account of things that have changed since the decision was made. So, if the decision maker considers that you were not habitually resident at the time benefit was originally refused, but you are now (because you have been resident for an appreciable period of time), s/he cannot take this into account when looking again at the decision in your case. However, s/he can take it into account if you had completed an appreciable period of residence before the date of the decision on your second, or subsequent, claim. Sometimes, the benefit authorities say you cannot make another claim while your appeal (or request to have the first decision looked at again) is pending. This is wrong. Seek specialist advice if you are in this situation.

3. Check whether you fall into one of the exempt categories (see p1523).

4. If you are not in one of the exempt categories, establish which part of the test the decision maker considers you have failed.

5. Remember that the habitual residence test applies to the claimant, so even if you have been found not to be habitually resident, your partner may satisfy the test and should make the claim. You can still challenge the refusal of your claim.

6. Remember that if you were receiving IS, income-based JSA, income-related ESA or PC at the time, you are exempt from the habitual residence test for HB. If the DWP decides that you are not habitually resident, the local authority must consider the issue for itself when it makes its own decision and not just follow the DWP's decision.

7. Although the onus of proof is on the benefit authorities to establish that you are *not* habitually resident,[15] produce as much evidence as possible to show that you *are*.

Who is exempt from the habitual residence test

You are exempt from the habitual residence test for means-tested benefits if you:[16]

- are a European Economic Area (EEA) national and are a 'worker' (see p1536), including if you have retained this status;
- are an EEA national and a 'self-employed person' (see p1540), including if you have retained this status;
- are a family member (see p1542) of someone in either of the above two groups;
- are an EEA national with a permanent right of residence as a retired or permanently incapacitated worker or self-employed person, or you are a family member of such a person (see p1550);
- are a Croatian national subject to worker authorisation and working in accordance with the conditions of your authorisation document;
- are a refugee;
- have discretionary leave, leave granted under the 'destitute domestic violence' concession or temporary protection granted under the displaced persons' provisions;
- have humanitarian protection granted under the Immigration Rules;
- have been deported, expelled or legally removed from another country to the UK and you are not a 'person subject to immigration control' (see p1500);
- (for HB only) receive income-based JSA (and either you have been receiving both HB and income-based JSA since 31 March 2014 or you have a right to reside other than those excluded for HB – see p1526), IS, income-related ESA or PC;
- (for income-related ESA only) are being transferred from an award of IS which was transitionally protected from the requirement to have a right to reside.

The above exempt groups do not apply to AA, CA, DLA and PIP. However, for these benefits, you are treated as habitually resident (as well as treated as present, see p1571 and p1573) if you are abroad in your capacity as a serving member of the forces, or you are living with someone who is and s/he is your

Part 12: Immigration and residence rules for benefits and tax credits
Chapter 70: Coming from abroad: residence rules
3. Habitual residence

spouse, civil partner, son, stepson, daughter, stepdaughter, father, stepfather, father-in-law, mother, stepmother or mother-in-law.[17]

Establishing you are 'habitually resident in fact'

You must be habitually resident in the 'common travel area' – ie, the UK, Channel Islands, the Isle of Man and the Republic of Ireland.

There is no definition of 'habitual residence' in the legislation. However, there is a considerable amount of caselaw on its meaning and from this certain principles have emerged.

- There is no comprehensive list of factors that are relevant, so all the facts of your situation should be considered.[18]
- To be habitually resident, you must be resident (see p1519). It is not enough merely to intend to reside in the future.[19]
- You must have a settled intention to reside in the common travel area. It does not need to be permanent; it is enough if you intend to make the common travel area your home for the time being.[20] You must provide evidence of your intention, including your reasons for coming to the common travel area, the strength of your ties (or your 'centre of interest') and the viability of your residence here. Factors that could be relevant include arranging or seeking employment, education or training, joining and/or bringing your family, arranging accommodation, bringing possessions, registering with a doctor, joining clubs and associations, and breaking ties with the place of your previous residence. The viability of your continued residence, although a relevant factor, is not an additional requirement.[21]
- In most cases, you must have an 'appreciable period' of actual residence. How long this period must be is not fixed and depends on your circumstances.[22] Benefit authorities must not set a standard period of time for which all claimants must be resident before they can become habitually resident and any such policy should be challenged by judicial review (see p1351). There is an extensive body of caselaw on what constitutes an appreciable period of residence. Periods of between one and three months are frequently cited,[23] but too much weight should not be put on any one decision, nor should any general rule about a specific time period be derived from it.[24] The stronger your settled intention to make your home in the common travel area for the time being, the shorter your period of actual residence needs to be before you can be accepted as habitually resident (and vice versa).[25]

You may not need an appreciable period of actual residence, or the period may be very short, if you are:

- – a returning resident. This applies if you have been habitually resident in the common travel area previously, you left in circumstances which meant you ceased to be habitually resident and you then return to live in the common travel area again. The decision on how long a period of residence you need to have in order to resume your previous habitual residence depends on the circumstances in which you left, your links with the common travel area while you were away and the circumstances of your return.[26] You can be found to be habitually resident on the day of your return;

– covered by the co-ordination rules (see p1592) and are claiming income-based JSA, income-related ESA or PC (since these are listed as special non-contributory benefits – see p1595). If this applies, you cannot be denied benefit solely because you have not satisfied an 'appreciable period' of residence. Your period of residence is one of the factors that should be taken into account in assessing habitual residence, but it is not an absolute requirement and may be outweighed by other factors.[27]

- A temporary absence, such as a holiday, should not mean that you cease to be habitually resident. This should be accepted if you have a definite date of return.[28]
- When deciding whether you are habitually resident, benefit authorities must consider the whole period up to the date the decision is made, since the time between the date of your claim and the decision may mean you have been resident for an appreciable period.[29]

4. Right to reside

The right to reside requirement applies to:
- income support (IS);
- income-based jobseeker's allowance (JSA);
- income-related employment and support allowance (ESA);
- pension credit (PC);
- housing benefit (HB);
- child benefit;
- child tax credit (CTC);
- universal credit (UC).

Note: you are also excluded from council tax reduction if you do not have a right to reside.[30]

Means-tested benefits

You must have a right to reside in order to satisfy the habitual residence test for IS, income-based JSA, income-related ESA, PC, HB and UC. If you (or your partner for UC) do not satisfy the habitual residence test because you do not have a right to reside, see p1522.

Part 12: Immigration and residence rules for benefits and tax credits
Chapter 70: Coming from abroad: residence rules
4. Right to reside

The right to reside requirement was introduced as part of the habitual residence test for means-tested benefits on 1 May 2004. If you have been receiving IS, income-based JSA, PC, HB or CTB since 30 April 2004, you do not need a right to reside in order to continue to receive that benefit.[31] Also, you do not need a right to reside for a new claim for one of these benefits (or, from 31 October 2011, for a new claim for income-related ESA), provided the periods of entitlement are continuous since 30 April 2004. You do not need a right to reside for a new claim for income-related ESA if it is linked to a previous period of entitlement by the 12-week linking rule (see p1018), provided this earlier period of entitlement began on or after 31 October 2011.

Example
Delphine is French. She came to the UK in 2003 with her baby and claimed IS as a lone parent while living with friends. In 2008, she had another child, moved into a rented flat and made a new claim for HB. In 2011, she started work and so her IS stopped, but she continued to get HB as she had a low income. In 2012, she left her job as her child was seriously ill and she claimed IS as a carer. In April 2014, Delphine became sick and claimed income-related ESA instead of IS.
Delphine does not need to pass the right to reside test for any of these new benefit claims because she has been receiving one of the five benefits for each day from 30 April 2004.

If you received transitionally protected IS on the grounds of incapacity and are then transferred to income-related ESA, you are exempt from the habitual residence test from the date you are transferred to ESA (see p662).[32]

The type of residence right you need

Any right of residence in the common travel area (see p1521) enables you to satisfy the right to reside requirement for each of the means-tested benefits, unless your only right of residence is as:[33]
- a European Economic Area (EEA) national with a right of residence during your first three months in the UK;
- a family member of the above;
- the primary carer of a British citizen who is dependent on you and would have to leave the European Union (EU) if you were required to leave (see p1547). **Note:** this exclusion is arguably unlawful and although legal challenges have not yet been successful,[34] future ones may be. See CPAG's online service and *Welfare Rights Bulletin* for updates;
- (except for income-based JSA and UC) an EEA jobseeker;
- except for income-based JSA and UC) a family member of an EEA jobseeker.

These restrictions mean that if your only right to reside is as an EEA jobseeker, you will not satisfy the right to reside test for any of the means-tested benefits *except* for income-based JSA and UC. However, if you receive income-based JSA, you are

12

exempt from the habitual residence test for HB if either you have a right to reside other than one of those listed on p1526, or you have been receiving both income-based JSA and HB since 31 March 2014 (see p1523).

Note: it may be arguable that income-related ESA is a benefit designed to facilitate access to the labour market and that it is therefore unlawful to exclude people whose only right to reside is as a jobseeker.[35] Seek specialist advice if this affects you.

Child benefit and child tax credit

If you do not have a right to reside for child benefit and CTC, you are treated as not present in Great Britain and, therefore, are not entitled to these benefits.[36] If you are making a joint claim for CTC, you and your partner must both have a right to reside. If one of you has a right to reside, s/he can make a claim as a single person.

The right to reside requirement was introduced on 1 May 2004. You do not need a right to reside to continue to receive child benefit or CTC if you have been receiving it since this date.

If you are claiming CTC and you (or your partner if it is a joint claim) lose your right to reside, this is a change of circumstances that you must notify to HM Revenue and Customs within one month (see p1450). The other partner may be able to claim as a single person.

If you do not have a right to reside but you are covered by the EU co-ordination rules (see p1592), you may be able to argue that the right to reside test is unlawful for child benefit. **Note:** this argument was found to apply by the Northern Ireland Chief Commissioner, but the decision is not binding in Great Britain and is currently being appealed.[37]

Get specialist advice if you want to rely on this argument and see CPAG's online service and *Welfare Rights Bulletin* for updates.

The type of residence right you need

Any right of residence in the UK enables you to satisfy the requirement for child benefit and CTC *except* a right to reside as the primary carer of a British citizen who is dependent on you and would have to leave the EU if you were required to leave (see p1547).[38]

Note: this exclusion is arguably unlawful and although legal challenges have not yet been successful,[39] future challenges may be. See CPAG's online service and *Welfare Rights Bulletin* for updates.

5. Who has a right to reside

Whether or not you have a right to reside can depend on your nationality, immigration status, and the circumstances of you and your family members. You

Part 12: Immigration and residence rules for benefits and tax credits
Chapter 70: Coming from abroad: residence rules
5. Who has a right to reside

may have a right of residence under UK law or one that stems directly from European Union (EU) law. You may have more than one right of residence, or you may not have any.

Any residence right is sufficient to satisfy the right to reside requirement, unless it is specifically excluded (see p1526 and p1527).

You have a right to reside if you are:

- a British citizen;
- an Irish citizen. Irish citizens have a right to reside in Ireland, which is part of the common travel area;
- a Commonwealth citizen with a right of abode;
- a person with leave to enter or remain. You have a right to reside during your period of leave. Any form of leave counts – eg, indefinite leave, refugee leave, humanitarian protection, discretionary leave and limited leave granted under the Immigration Rules, such as a spouse or a visitor. **Note:** if you have leave which is subject to a condition that you do not have recourse to public funds, or indefinite leave granted as the result of a maintenance undertaking, you are a 'person subject to immigration control' (see p1500) and, therefore, likely to be excluded from benefits on that basis.

These are just examples of some people whose right to reside is clear. It is not an exhaustive list.

If you are a European Economic Area (EEA) national, or the family member or primary carer of an EEA national, your residence rights are more complex. Check the rest of this section to see if you have a right to reside. The majority of claimants affected by the right to reside requirement are EEA nationals and their family members and the rest of this section focuses on their residence rights.

European Economic Area nationals, their family members and carers

In practice, the right to reside requirement mainly affects EEA nationals. The residence rights of EEA nationals, their family members and carers can be complex, as both EU law and UK law must be considered, and both are subject to a considerable amount of interpretation through caselaw.

EU Directive 2004/38 sets out most (but not all) of the situations in which an EEA national or her/his family member has a right to reside in the UK. This has been in force since 30 April 2006 and was extended to cover nationals of Norway, Iceland and Liechtenstein from 1 March 2009.[40]

Swiss nationals and their family members are covered by a separate agrement which provides similar rights.[41]

The Immigration (European Economic Area) Regulations 2006 ('the EEA Regulations') apply to all EEA nationals (except British citizens – see p1530) and Swiss nationals.[42] These give similar rights of residence to those contained in the

Directive. Where these rules conflict with, or do not completely incorporate, Directive 2004/38, you can rely on whichever is more favourable to you.

If you are a family member of a British citizen, see p1544.

How to check your right to reside

Use the following steps to check whether you have a right to reside.

- **Step one: are you an EEA national with a right to reside based on your current or previous employment, self-employment, jobseeking, or self-sufficiency (including while a student)?** You have a right to reside if you:
    - are a 'qualified person'. You are a 'qualified person' if you are a:[43]
        - jobseeker (see p1535);
        - worker (see p1536), including if you have retained this status (see p1537);
        - self-employed person (see p1540), including if you have retained this status (see p1541);
        - self-sufficient person (see p1541);
        - student (see p1542); *or*
    - have a permanent right of residence (see p1548). This will normally be after five years of 'legal residence' but, in limited circumstances, can be acquired before five years.
- **Step two: are you a 'family member' (see p1542) of someone covered in Step one?** You have a right to reside even if you are not an EEA national yourself.
- **Step three: do you have a 'derivative right to reside' – ie, through someone else's right to reside, but not as her/his family member?** Certain primary carers and children have a 'derivative right to reside'. See p1547 for more details.

Note:
- You can have more than one right to reside at a time.[44] For example, you may be both a self-employed person and also the family member of someone with a permanent right of residence.
- If you are an EEA national or family member of an EEA national, you also have an initial right of residence for the first three months that you are in the UK. However, if this is your only right to reside, this does not entitle you to means-tested benefits (see p1534).
- If you are an A8, A2 or Croatian national (see p1530), or a family member of an A8, A2 or Croatian national, see p1531 for additional restrictions that can affect whether you have a right to reside.

Part 12: Immigration and residence rules for benefits and tax credits
Chapter 70: Coming from abroad: residence rules
5. Who has a right to reside

British citizens

If you are a British citizen, including if you also hold another nationality, you have an automatic right to reside in the UK. If you are the family member of a British citizen, see p1544. If you are the primary carer of a British citizen, see p1547.

A8, A2 and Croatian nationals

A8, A2 states and Croatia

The A8 states are: Czech Republic, Estonia, Hungary, Latvia, Lithuania, Poland, Slovakia and Slovenia.

These states joined the EU on 1 May 2004.

The restrictions applied until 30 April 2011.

The A2 states are: Bulgaria and Romania.

These states joined the EU on 1 January 2007.

The restrictions applied until 31 December 2013.

Croatia joined the EU on 1 July 2013.

The restrictions are currently in force until 30 June 2018.

The treaties under which the above 'accession' states joined the EU allowed existing member states to limit access to their labour markets for nationals of these states. The UK government imposed restrictions on the residence rights of workers and jobseekers from these states. All these restrictions can only be imposed for a maximum of seven years from the date the states joined the EU.

Most Croatian nationals have, and A8 and A2 nationals had, certain restrictions on their residence rights as jobseekers, workers or people who retain worker status. These restrictions on Croatian nationals have applied since 1 July 2013 and apply until 30 June 2018, but may be extended for a further two years. The restrictions on A2 nationals applied between 1 January 2007 and 31 December 2013 and on A8 nationals between 1 May 2004 and 30 April 2011. **Note:** although the restrictions on A2 and A8 nationals have now ended, in certain circumstances you may still need to know what the restrictions were and how they operated. This is because the residence rights you or your family member had in the past can affect current or future residence rights.

While in force, the restrictions apply unless you come within one of the exempt groups. If you are a Croatian national and not exempt, you must obtain an 'accession worker authorisation document' (in most cases, an accession worker registration certificate, specifying the employer you can work for) before taking up employment, and then work in accordance with it.[45] If you are an A2 national who was subject to restrictions, you were required to obtain an accession worker authorisation document (in most cases, an accession worker card specifying the employer you can work for) before taking up employment, and then work in

12

accordance with it.[46] If you are an A8 national who was subject to restrictions, you had to work for an 'authorised employer'.[47]

Broadly speaking, this meant you had to register each job you took with the Worker Registration Scheme (but see below for the precise meaning as it can affect your residence rights).

Restrictions on residence rights

If you are a **Croatian national** subject to worker authorisation, your residence rights are restricted until 30 June 2018 as follows.[48]

*   You do not have a right to reside as a jobseeker.
*   You are only defined as a 'worker' if you have an accession worker authorisation document and are working in accordance with it.
*   You cannot retain your worker status when you stop work in the ways other workers can (see p1537).

If you are an **A2 national** who was subject to restrictions, you were required to obtain an accession worker authorisation document and your residence rights were restricted between 1 January 2007 to 31 December 2013 in the same way as Croatian nationals above.[49]

If you are an **A8 national** who was subject to restrictions, you had to work for an 'authorised employer' (see below),[50] and your residence rights were restricted between 1 May 2004 and 30 April 2011 as follows.[51]

*   You did not have a right to reside as a jobseeker.
*   You were only defined as a 'worker' if you were working for an authorised employer.
*   You could not retain your worker status when you stopped work in the ways other workers can (see p1537). However, if you lost your job within the first month of employment, you could retain your status in those ways, but only until the end of the month.

Authorised employer

You were working for an **'authorised employer'** if you:[52]
– were within the first month of employment;
– applied for a worker's registration certificate within the first month of work, but did not yet have a certificate or refusal;
– had a valid worker's registration certificate for that employer;
– had been legally working (see p1533) for that employer since 30 April 2004;
– began work at an agricultural camp between 1 May 2004 and 31 December 2004 and before 1 May 2004 you had been issued with leave under the Immigration Act 1971 as a seasonal worker at such a camp.

If you only applied for a registration certificate after the first month of work, you only count as working for an authorised employer from the date it was issued. It does not apply retrospectively.[53]

Part 12: Immigration and residence rules for benefits and tax credits
Chapter 70: Coming from abroad: residence rules
5. Who has a right to reside

The restrictions do not affect other residence rights you may have as an EEA national – eg, as a self-employed or self-sufficient person.[54]

Croatian and A2 nationals not subject to worker authorisation

Note: the requirement for A2 nationals to be subject to worker authorisation ended on 31 December 2013.

If you are a Croatian national, you are not (or an A2 national before 31 December 2013 you were not) subject to worker authorisation if you:[55]

- have (or had on 30 June 2013 (Croatian) or 31 December 2006 (A2)) leave to enter or remain with no restriction on employment;
- were legally working (see p1533) in the UK for 12 months, without breaks of more than 30 days (in total), up to and including 31 December 2006 (A2) or 30 June 2013 (Croatian);
- have legally worked for 12 months (beginning before or after 31 December 2006 (A2) or 30 June 2013 (Croatian)), disregarding any breaks of less than 30 days (in total);
- are a posted worker – ie, you are working in the UK providing services on behalf of an employer who is not established in the UK;
- are a member of a diplomatic mission (or the family member of such a person) or a person otherwise entitled to diplomatic immunity;
- have dual nationality with the UK or another (non-A2/Croatian) EEA state;
- are the spouse/civil partner (or, Croatian only, unmarried or same-sex partner) of a UK national or of a person settled in the UK;
- are the spouse/civil partner (or, Croatian only, unmarried or same-sex partner) or child under 18 of a person with leave to enter or remain in the UK that allows employment;
- have a permanent right of residence (see p1548);
- are a student with a registration certificate, which states that you cannot work more than 20 hours a week (unless it is part of vocational training or during vacations) and you comply with this. If the certificate confirms you can work during the four months after the course ends, the exemption continues for this period;
- are a family member of an EEA national who has a right to reside, unless the EEA national is an A2 (or, Croatian only, a Croatian) national subject to worker authorisation (or, A2 only, the only reason s/he is not an A2 national subject to worker authorisation is because s/he is covered by the group below);
- are a family member of an A2 (or, if you are Croatian, a Croatian) national subject to worker authorisation who has a right to reside (for an A2 national only, as a worker, student, self-employed or self-sufficient person). If you are a Croatian national (or an A2 national relying on an A2 worker), you are a 'family member' if you are the descendant and either under 21 or dependent, or the spouse/civil partner or (Croatians only) the unmarried or same-sex partner; *or*

- are a 'highly skilled person' – ie, you:[56]
  - met the points based criteria set out in the Immigration Rules for entering the UK on this basis; or
  - have a qualification at degree level or higher in the UK, or Higher National Diploma in Scotland and, within 12 months of this award, you apply for a registration certificate confirming your unconditional access to the labour market.

A8 nationals who were not required to register
If you are an A8 national, you were not required to register if you:[57]
- had leave to enter or remain on 30 April 2004 which had no restriction on employment;
- were legally working (see below) in the UK for 12 months, without breaks of more than 30 days (in total), up to and including 30 April 2004;
- had legally worked for 12 months (beginning before or after 30 April 2004), disregarding any breaks of less than 30 days (in total);
- were the spouse/civil partner or child under 18 of a person with leave to enter or remain in the UK that allowed employment;
- had dual nationality with the UK or another (non-A8/A2) EEA state or Switzerland;
- were a family member of another EEA or Swiss national who had a right to reside under the EEA Regulations (other than an A8/A2 national subject to registration/authorisation if her/his only right to reside was for the first three months in the UK);
- were the member of a diplomatic mission (or the family member of such a person) or a person otherwise entitled to diplomatic immunity;
- were a posted worker – ie, you were working in the UK providing services on behalf of an employer who is not established in the UK.

Legally working
If you are a Croatian national (or an A2 national before 1 January 2014), you are 'legally working' if:[58]
- you are/were working in accordance with your worker authorisation document; or
- you are/were working during a period when you are within one of the exempt groups on p1532 (other than posted workers); or
- the work was done before 1 July 2013 (for Croatian nationals) or before 1 January 2007 (for A2 nationals), either in accordance with any leave you had under the Immigration Act 1971 or when you did not require leave. The Court of Appeal has held that this does not apply to work done with permission from the Home Office while you were an asylum seeker.[59]

If you are an A8 national, you were 'legally working' before 1 May 2011 if:[60]

12

Part 12: Immigration and residence rules for benefits and tax credits
Chapter 70: Coming from abroad: residence rules
5. Who has a right to reside

- you were working for an authorised employer (see p1531); *or*
- you were working during a period when you were within one of the exempt groups on p1533 (other than if you were the spouse/civil partner or child of a person whose leave to enter or remain in the UK allowed employment); *or*
- the work was done before 1 May 2004 either in accordance with any leave you had under the Immigration Act 1971 or when you did not require leave. The Court of Appeal has held that this does not apply to work done with permission from the Home Office while you were an asylum seeker.[61]

If you are a Croatian national and your employment ends, you stop legally working, stop being a 'worker' and, unless you are in an exempt group, you cannot retain your worker status. However, if you are still under a contract of employment, you continue to be legally working and a worker – eg, if you are on maternity leave, holiday leave, sick leave or compassionate leave (including if the leave is unpaid).[62]

The same applied to A2 nationals between 1 January 2007 and 31 December 2013 and A8 nationals between 1 May 2004 and 30 April 2011. If you stop working after these end dates, your rights are the same as for other non-accession state EEA nationals and the relevant question is whether you are still a 'worker' or can retain 'worker' status (see p1537). However, it may still be relevant to know whether you were legally working before these dates in order to establish whether you had completed your 12 months of legal work or whether you were a 'worker' at a particular time as it can affect your residence rights and those of your family members.

Initial right of residence

All EEA nationals have an unconditional right to enter any member state. They also have an initial right of residence for the first three months of their stay in the UK.[63] This is given whether or not you are working or seeking work, but it is subject to your not becoming an unreasonable burden on the social assistance system of the UK.[64]

You also have a right of residence if you are not an EEA national, but are a family member of an EEA national who has an initial right of residence for three months.[65]

If your only right of residence is on the basis of this initial three-month period, you are not entitled to **income support (IS)**, **income-based jobseeker's allowance (JSA)**, **income-related employment and support allowance (ESA)**, **pension credit (PC)**, **housing benefit (HB)** and **universal credit (UC)**. However, you can have one or more rights of residence (eg, as the family member of a worker and/or as a jobseeker) in addition to your initial right of residence. If this is the case, provided it is not a residence right that is excluded for the means-tested benefit you want to claim, you can satisfy the right to reside requirement and are therefore entitled to benefit (see p1525).

Note: the requirement for income-based JSA claims for you to have been 'living in' the common travel area for the past three months is a separate part of the habitual residence test (see p1552) and unrelated to this initial right of residence.

Jobseekers

If you are an EEA national, you have a right to reside as a jobseeker if:[66]
- you are in the UK and you can provide evidence that you are seeking employment and have a 'genuine chance of being engaged'; *and*
- (EEA Regulations only) you entered the UK in order to seek employment or you are present in the UK seeking employment immediately after having a right to reside as a worker (except if you retained worker status while involuntarily unemployed see p1538), a student, a self-employed or self-sufficient person.

Note: if you are refused benefit on the basis of the second bullet, you should challenge the decision on the basis that the UK EEA Regulations interpret the category of jobseeker more narrowly than the European Court of Justice.[67]

You should be accepted as seeking employment and having a genuine chance of being engaged if you are 'signing on' and are awarded either JSA or national insurance (NI) credits (see p850), since both show you have been accepted as being available for work (see p1025) and actively seeking work (see p1038). If you come under the UC system (see p19), you should be accepted as being a jobseeker if you meet all the work-related requirements (see p1073). There would only be a few unusual circumstances in which you would satisfy these conditions and not be accepted as having a genuine chance of being engaged.[68]

There is no time limit on how long you can have a right to reside as a jobseeker. It continues for as long as you can provide evidence that you are looking for work and have a genuine chance of being engaged.[69] From 1 January 2014, after six months, the EEA Regulations require that evidence that you provide must be 'compelling'.[70] However, there is no such requirement under European law.

If you have a right to reside as a jobseeker, you satisfy the right to reside requirement for income-based JSA, UC, child benefit and child tax credit (CTC). You do not satisfy the right to reside requirement for IS, income-related ESA, PC and HB and must have some other right to reside for these. Remember that, unless you are exempt from the habitual residence test (see p1523), in order to get income-based JSA, you must have been living here for the past three months (see p1552) and be 'habitually resident in fact' (see p1521).

If you are a Croatian national subject to worker authorisation (see p1531), you do not have a right to reside as a jobseeker. Similarly, before 1 January 2014, if you are an A2 national who was subject to worker authorisation, or before 1 May 2011, if you were an A8 national who was required to register your work (see p1533), you did not have a right to reside as a jobseeker (see p1531).

Part 12: Immigration and residence rules for benefits and tax credits
Chapter 70: Coming from abroad: residence rules
5. Who has a right to reside

If you are the family member (see p1542) of a jobseeker, you have a right to reside. However, this is only sufficient to satisfy the right to reside requirement for income-based JSA (which, in turn can 'passport' you to HB), child benefit and CTC.

Note: if your only right to reside is as a jobseeker or family member of a jobseeker, you are not exempt from the UC work-related requirements, even if you would otherwise come within one of the exempt groups (see p1073).[71] This may be unlawful and may be subject to legal challenge. See CPAG's online service and *Welfare Rights Bulletin* for updates.

Workers

If you are an EEA national and a 'worker', you have a right to reside.[72] You satisfy the right to reside requirement for the relevant benefits and you are exempt from the habitual residence test (see p1523).

Note: if you are a **Croatian** national who is subject to worker authorisation (see p1531), you only count as a 'worker' if you have an accession worker authorisation document and are working in accordance with it. Similarly, before 1 January 2014, if you were an **A2 national** who was subject to worker authorisation (see p1532), you only counted as a 'worker' if you had a worker authorisation card and were working in accordance with it and, before 1 May 2011, if you were an **A8 national** who was required to register, you only counted as a 'worker' if you were working for an 'authorised employer' (see p1531).

You count as a 'worker' if:
- you are in an employment relationship. This means you must:[73]
  – provide services;
  – work in return for remuneration;
  – work under the direction of another person;
- the work you do entails activities that are 'genuine and effective', rather than 'marginal and ancillary'.

12

Is your work genuine and effective?
All the relevant factors must be taken into account when deciding whether your work is genuine and effective, including the following.

1. The duration of the employment. The longer the period of time your employment lasts, the more likely it is that you have established worker status. However, someone working as a steward at Wimbledon for two weeks was held to be a worker.[74]

2. The number of hours worked. There is no minimum threshold. Someone working 10 hours a week was held to be a worker,[75] as was an au pair working 13 hours a week for a modest wage plus board and lodging.[76] The European Court of Justice (ECJ) has held that 5.5 hours' work was potentially capable of making someone a worker.[77]

3. The level of your earnings. There must be some remuneration (although it can be in kind, such as board and lodgings[78]) and voluntary work does not result in worker status.[79] The work can be low paid. Provided the work done is genuine and effective, even if your earnings are so low that you need to subsidise your wages with benefits, this is irrelevant to the question of whether or not you are a worker.[80]

4. The regularity of the work. The more regular and less erratic the work, the more likely it is that worker status will be established. Agency work is not necessarily marginal and ancillary. It is possible to be a worker while undertaking work through an agency,[81] or while working 'cash in hand' without tax and NI being deducted.[82]

Note: although guidance to decision makers advises that someone is automatically a worker if s/he has been earning a threshold weekly income (£153) for three months, it confirms that, in all other cases, an individual assessment must be made, taking the above factors into account.

You only cease to be a worker when the employment relationship ends. While you are still under a contract of employment, you continue to be a worker. Consequently, you are still a worker if you are a woman on maternity leave (including unpaid maternity leave),[83] or if you are on holiday leave or sick leave (including if it is unpaid).[84]

If you have ceased to be a worker, you may retain your worker status in certain circumstances (see below).

Retaining worker status

You can retain the status of 'worker', even though you are no longer working if:[85]
- you are involuntarily unemployed and registered as a jobseeker (see p1538);
- you are temporarily unable to work because of an illness or accident (see p1539);
- you are undertaking vocational training (see p1539).

However, before arguing that you have retained your worker status, check whether you have ceased to be a worker (see above). For example, if you are off work on unpaid sick leave but you can return to your job when you are better, you are still a worker and so you do not need to argue that you have retained your worker status.

Note: if you are a **Croatian** national subject to worker authorisation (see p1532), you cannot retain your worker status in the ways described in this section. Similarly if, before 1 January 2014, you were an **A2 national** subject to worker authorisation (see p1532), or before 1 May 2011, you were an **A8 national** who was required to register (see p1533), you could not retain your worker status in the ways described in this section. However, if you were an A8 national required

Part 12: Immigration and residence rules for benefits and tax credits
Chapter 70: Coming from abroad: residence rules
5. Who has a right to reside

to register and you stopped working during the first month of employment, you could retain your worker status in the ways described in this section for the remainder of that month.[86]

You are involuntarily unemployed and registered as a jobseeker

To retain worker status on this basis you must:[87]
- be recorded as involuntarily unemployed; *and*
- registered as a jobseeker with Jobcentre Plus; *and*
- provide evidence that you are seeking employment and have a genuine chance of being engaged.

In addition:
- you must have entered the UK in order to seek employment; *or*
- you must be present in the UK seeking employment immediately after having a right to reside as a worker (except if you retained your worker status while involuntarily unemployed, a student, or a self-employed or self-sufficient person.

If you are refused benefit on the basis of the last two bullets, you should challenge the decision on the basis that this is not a requirement under EU law.[88]

You are 'involuntarily unemployed' if you are seeking, and are available to take up, a job. This depends on your remaining in the labour market. The circumstances in which you left your last job are just one factor in determining this, and your actions and circumstances since leaving work are taken into account.[89]

The best way to 'register as a jobseeker' is to claim JSA and keep signing on, even if you are not entitled to JSA. If you are looking for work and claim IS, income-related ESA or PC, you should be accepted as having registered as a jobseeker if you declared that you are looking for work – eg, on your claim form or habitual residence questionnaire.[90]

If you were employed for more than a year, you can retain your worker status on this basis indefinitely.[91]

However, from 1 January 2014, after six months, the UK EEA Regulations require you to provide 'compelling' evidence that you are continuing to seek employment and have a genuine chance of being engaged.[92] This requirement may be unlawful as there is no such requirement under the EU Directive.

If you were employed for less than a year, the EEA Regulations limit the period during which you can retain your worker status while registered as a jobseeker to a maximum of six months.[93] However, arguably the EU Directive allows you to retain worker status beyond six months if you continue to provide evidence that you are seeking employment and have a genuine chance of being engaged.[94]

Note: if your only right to reside is on the basis that you have retained your worker status while involuntarily unemployed and registered as a jobseeker, you are not exempt from the UC work-related requirements, even if you would

12

otherwise fall within one of those exempt groups (see p1073).[95] Arguably this exclusion is unlawful and may be subject to legal challenge. See CPAG's online service and *Welfare Rights Bulletin* for updates.

You are temporarily unable to work because of an illness or accident

To retain your worker status, your inability to work must be temporary. This simply means not permanent.[96] This can apply if you have a permanent health condition that fluctuates and causes temporary periods when you are unable to work.[97] You are considered temporarily unable to work if there is a realistic prospect of your being able to work again in the forseeable future.[98] You do not need to have claimed ESA or another benefit on grounds of incapacity, nor do you need to pass the test of incapacity for work or limited capability for work. The test is whether you are unable to do the work you were doing or, if it follows a period in which you were seeking work, the sort of work you were seeking.[99] Your inability to work must be caused by an illness or accident which *you* have – ie, you are not covered if you are unable to work because you are looking after a child who is ill.[100]

If you are unable to work because of pregnancy, see p1540.

You are undertaking vocational training

You retain your worker status if you are undertaking a vocational training course. Unless you are involuntarily unemployed, the training must be related to your previous employment. If it is not, you must be accepted as 'involuntarily unemployed'. You should be accepted as 'involuntarily unemployed' if there is no employment available to you that is equivalent to your last employment.[101]

Moving between groups and gaps

You can retain your worker status if you are in one of the groups on p1537 and continue to do so if you move into another category.[102] For example, you may have been involuntarily unemployed and registered as a jobseeker, then you became ill and were temporarily unable to work, and then you got better and embarked on vocational training. You retain your worker status throughout.

You may be able to retain your worker status if there is a gap between ceasing work and registering as a jobseeker by claiming JSA.[103] If the delay is more than a few days, all your circumstances including the reasons for the gap and what you did during it should be considered to establish if there was undue delay[104] and whether you withdrew from the labour market during that period.[105] Arguably, you should also be able to retain your worker status if there is a gap between your ceasing work and being temporarily unable to work because of illness or an accident, since there is no requirement that the illness or accident be the reason for your ceasing work. You should also still retain your worker status during a

Part 12: Immigration and residence rules for benefits and tax credits
Chapter 70: Coming from abroad: residence rules
5. Who has a right to reside

short gap between two different circumstances applying, provided you remain in the labour market during that time.

Pregnancy and childbirth

If you have established worker (or self-employed) status and you are now not working because of pregnancy or childbirth, you may still count as a worker or self-employed person, or you may be able to retain your worker or self employed status.

You do not cease to be a worker while you are still under a contract of employment, so you are still a worker while on maternity leave, whether or not it is paid. This also applies to Croatian nationals from 1 July 2013, A2 nationals (including before 1 January 2014) and A8 nationals (including before 1 May 2011) who have established worker status.[106] You can still be a self-employed person if you stop work for a period of maternity leave, but intend to resume your self-employment.[107]

You can retain your worker or self-employed status if you have a pregnancy-related illness that prevents you from working (see p1537).[108]

The Supreme Court has referred questions to the Court of Justice of the European Community (CJEU) about whether a worker can retain her worker status if she gives up work because of the physical constraints of the late stages of pregnancy and the aftermath of childbirth.[109]

See CPAG's online service and *Welfare Rights Bulletin* for updates. If your circumstances are similar, seek advice.

Self-employed people

If you are an EEA national and a 'self-employed person', you have a right to reside and therefore satisfy the right to reside requirement for each of the relevant benefits (see p1525). You are also exempt from the habitual residence test (see p1523).

If you are a Croatian national and you are self-employed, you have the same rights as other EEA nationals; there are no additional restrictions. This was also true of A2 nationals who were self-employed between 1 January 2007 and 31 December 2013 and A8 nationals who were self-employed between 1 May 2004 and 30 April 2011.

You are a self-employed person if you provide services in return for remuneration, but not under the direction of another person. The work you do must entail activities that are 'genuine and effective' rather than 'marginal and ancillary' (see p1536).[110]

You count as self-employed when you are establishing yourself in order to pursue your self-employed activity.[111] You must provide evidence of the steps you have taken or the ways in which you have set yourself up as self-employed. It will help if you have registered with HM Revenue and Customs as self-employed.

However, if you have not registered, this will not necessarily mean you cannot be accepted as self-employed.[112]

If you stop working, you do not necessarily cease to be self-employed. You may be in a temporary lull and it is accepted that you can continue to be self-employed during such times, depending on your particular circumstances and the evidence you provide – eg, the amount of work you have coming in, any steps you are taking to develop your business or find new work, marketing and business administration. Account must also be taken of your motives and intentions.[113] You continue to be self-employed if you take a period of maternity leave, but intend to return to work afterwards.[114]

If you have ceased to be self-employed, you may be able to retain your self-employed status in certain circumstances (see below). If you have ceased to be self-employed because of your pregnancy, see p1540.

Retaining self-employed status

Like workers, if you have established self-employed status, you can retain it when you have stopped working if you are temporarily unable to work as the result of an illness or accident (see p1537).[115] **Note:** unlike retaining worker status, there are no restrictions on retaining your self-employed status if you are a Croatian national (or an A2 national before 1 January 2014 or an A8 national before 1 May 2011).

If you have ceased self-employment because of pregnancy, you may be able to retain your self-employed status (see p1540).

You do not retain self-employed status if you are involuntarily unemployed and registered as a jobseeker or if you are doing vocational training.[116]

Before arguing that you have retained your self-employed status, check whether you can still count as self-employed. If this applies, the question of whether you retain that status does not arise.

Remember that, even if you cannot retain your status as a self-employed person, unless you are a Croatian national subject to worker authorisation, you may have a right to reside as a jobseeker and be able to get JSA, UC, child benefit and CTC on that basis (see p1535).

Self-sufficient people

You have a right of residence as a self-sufficient person if you have:[117]
- sufficient resources for yourself, and any family members who do not have an independent right to reside, so that you will not become an unreasonable burden on the social assistance system of the UK; *and*
- comprehensive sickness insurance.

The UK government cannot set a fixed amount that is regarded as 'sufficient resources' and must take account of your personal situation.[118] You have 'sufficient resources' if they:[119]

Part 12: Immigration and residence rules for benefits and tax credits
Chapter 70: Coming from abroad: residence rules
5. Who has a right to reside

- exceed the maximum level you (and your family) can have to be eligible for 'social assistance' (see below); *or*
- do not exceed that level, but the decision maker considers that you still have sufficient resources, taking into account your (and your family's) personal situation.[120]

The 'maximum level' is the equivalent of your means-tested benefit applicable amount, including any premiums. Your resources also include your accommodation, so if your resources are more than your applicable amount plus your rent, you should be self-sufficient. You may also be self-sufficient if your resources are more than your applicable amount and you are provided with free and stable accommodation by friends or family.[121]

You cannot automatically be regarded as not self-sufficient just because you make a claim for a means-tested benefit. All your circumstances, including the likely duration of your claim, must be assessed to determine whether or not your benefit claim makes you an unreasonable burden on the social assistance system of the UK.[122]

The source of the resources does not matter.[123]

The requirement to have comprehensive sickness insurance cover is satisfied if you have private health insurance.[124] It is also satisfied if the UK can be reimbursed by another state for any NHS costs you incur while in the UK. This usually applies if you are covered by the EU co-ordination rules (see p1592) and another state continues to be your 'competent state' (see p1596).[125] If neither of these applies, seek specialist advice as other arguments may be possible, depending on your circumstances.

Students

You have a right to reside as a student if you are an EEA national and you:[126]
- are enrolled as a student in a government-accredited college;
- provide an assurance at the start of your studies that you have sufficient resources for yourself and your family members not to become a burden on the UK social assistance system during your period of residence (see p1541);
- have comprehensive sickness insurance (see p1541).

Family members

You have a right to reside if you are a 'family member' (see p1543) of an EEA national who has a right to reside (other than a 'derivative right to reside'). This applies whether or not you are an EEA national yourself. You have a right to reside for as long as the EEA national has a right to reside and for as long as you remain her/his family member.

Note:
- If your only right to reside is as the family member of an EEA national who has a right to reside on the basis of an initial right of residence for three months,

this does not enable you to satisfy the right to reside requirement for IS, income-based JSA, income-related ESA, PC, HB and UC (see p1526).

- If your only right to reside is as the family member of an EEA national who has a right to reside as a jobseeker, this does not enable you to satisfy the right to reside requirement for IS, income-related ESA, PC and HB (see p1525).

Family members[127]

You are a **'family member'** if you are the:

- spouse or civil partner of an EEA national;
- child, grandchild or great-grandchild of an EEA national, or her/his spouse/civil partner, and you are under 21;
- child, grandchild or great-grandchild of an EEA national, or her/his spouse/civil partner, and you are her/his dependant;
- parent, grandparent or great-grandparent of an EEA national, or her/his spouse/civil partner, and you are her/his dependant.

You remain a spouse or civil partner even if you are separated. You only cease to be a spouse or civil partner on divorce or termination of the civil partnership.[128]

'Dependence' is not defined in the legislation, but caselaw has established a number of principles.[129] To be dependent, you must receive support from the other person. It is irrelevant if there are alternative sources of support available. The support must be 'material', although not necessarily financial, and must contribute towards your basic necessities.

If you only became dependent on the EEA national in the UK, this does not prevent you from being classed as a family member, unless you are an extended family member (see p1544), in which case you must have already been dependent in the country from where you have come.[130]

Are you unable to prove your right to reside?

If you are relying on your family member for your right to reside and you cannot prove what they are doing (eg, if you have separated from your spouse and have no evidence that s/he is a worker), you should ask the benefit authority to investigate if this is possible – eg, by using the database of NI contributions to establish that your spouse is a worker. If it does not do so and you appeal, you can argue that it has not shown that you do not have a right to reside.[131]

Extended family members

If you do not count as a family member under the above rules, but you have a relative in the UK who is an EEA national, you may count as her/his 'extended family member' (see p1544). However, even if you are defined as an 'extended

Part 12: Immigration and residence rules for benefits and tax credits
Chapter 70: Coming from abroad: residence rules
5. Who has a right to reside

family member', you are not treated as a 'family member' (and cannot acquire a right to reside from your relative) unless you have been issued with an EEA family permit, a registration certificate or a residence card (see p1551). If you do not have this documentation, you are not treated as a family member.[132]

Extended family member

You are an **'extended family member'** if you are the:[133]

– partner of an EEA national and you are in a durable relationship with her/him; *or*

– relative of an EEA national and would satisfy the requirements of the Immigration Rules for indefinite leave as her/his dependent relative if s/he were present and settled in the UK; *or*

– relative of an EEA national or her/his spouse/civil partner and:
  – you have serious health problems that require her/his care; *or*
  – you previously lived with, or were dependent on, the EEA national in a country other than the UK and either you are accompanying her/him to, or wish to join her/him in, the UK, or you have joined her/him in the UK and continue to be dependent on her/him or to be a member of her/his household.

Family members of British citizens

British citizens do not automatically give residence rights to their family members.

If you are a family member of a British citizen, you have a right to reside on the basis of EU law as her/his family member if s/he has lived with a right to reside (eg, as a worker) in *another* EEA state. On her/his return to the UK, s/he has the same rights as other EEA nationals and can confer rights on you.

The EEA Regulations contain these rights, but interpret them more restrictively than the ECJ has done.

- If you are the spouse or civil partner of a British citizen, the EEA Regulations state that you must have lived together in the other EEA state. This conflicts with an ECJ decision, which held that you can have residence rights as a family member if you became a family member either before or after entering the member state.[134]

- The EEA Regulations only treat a British national as an EEA national if s/he was a worker or self-employed person (and not if s/he had another right of residence – eg, as a self-sufficient person) in the other EEA state and if s/he had transferred her/his 'centre of life' there (taking into account the period of residence, the location of her/his principle residence and degree of integration in that country).[135] The condition to have transferred your centre of life is not required if, on 1 January 2014, you had and continue to have a permanent right to reside or a residence document confirming your right to reside (or an outstanding application for, or were appealing against a refusal of, such a document). This condition is not required under EU law.

- The EEA Regulations only give you a right to reside as a family member of a British person who has returned to the UK if s/he currently has a right to reside under these Regulations. However, the ECJ has decided that it was not necessary for someone who had been a worker in another EEA state and then returned to her/his own state to carry out an economic activity in order for her/his family member to have a right of residence.[136]

Seek specialist advice if any of these restrictions affect you.

If you are the family member of someone who has both British and another EEA nationality, before 16 October 2012 you had the same rights as family members of other EEA nationals.[137] If you had already acquired such a right before this date, it continues in limited circumstances. See the 2013/14 edition of this *Handbook* for more details.

A dual British/other EEA national does not have rights under EU law if s/he has lived all her/his life in the UK and you cannot derive any rights from her/him.[138]

Family members who retain their right to reside

In general, if you are the family member of an EEA national who has a right to reside, you lose your right to reside if s/he ceases to be your family member or to have a right to reside. However, there are some exceptions which mean you can retain your right to reside if the EEA national dies or leaves the UK, or if your marriage or civil partnership ends. These rights are in EU Directive 2004/38, but they are not exactly reproduced in the UK EEA Regulations. The benefit authorities accept the rights set out in the EEA Regulations (the first list below), but do not always accept those in the Directive (the second list on p1546). If you only have a right to reside under the Directive and are refused benefit, you should appeal and seek specialist advice.

You retain your right to reside under the EEA Regulations if you are a family member of a 'qualified person' (see p1529) or a person with a permanent right to reside (see p1548) *and:*[139]

- that person dies and you are:
  - not an EEA national, but if you were, you would be a worker, or a self-employed or self-sufficient person (or you are the family member of such a non-EEA national) and you resided in the UK with a right to reside under the Regulations for at least a year immediately before s/he died; *or*
  - the child or grandchild of the qualified person (or her/his spouse or civil partner) and in education immediately before the death and you remain in education; *or*
  - a parent with custody of a child in the previous bullet point; *or*
- that person leaves the UK and you are:
  - the child or grandchild of the qualified person (or her/his spouse or civil partner) and in education immediately before s/he left the UK and you remain in education; *or*

Part 12: Immigration and residence rules for benefits and tax credits
Chapter 70: Coming from abroad: residence rules
5. Who has a right to reside

- a parent with custody of a child in the previous bullet point; *or*
- your marriage or civil partnership to that person is terminated and you are not an EEA national, but if you were, you would be a worker, or a self-employed or self-sufficient person (or you are the family member of such a non-EEA national) and you were residing in the UK with a right to reside under the Regulations at the date of the termination and:
  - the marriage/civil partnership had, prior to the termination, lasted for at least three years with you both residing in the UK for at least one of those years; *or*
  - you have custody of the qualified person's child; *or*
  - you have a right of access to the qualified person's child which a court has said must take place in the UK; *or*
  - your continued right of residence in the UK is warranted by particularly difficult circumstances, such as your (or another family member's) being subject to domestic violence during the period of the marriage/civil partnership.

You have a right to reside on this basis for as long as the conditions apply to you,[140] until you can acquire a permanent right of residence (see p1548).[141]

It is arguable that you retain your right to reside under EU Directive 2004/38 if you are a family member of an EU national who has a right to reside as a worker, self-employed or self-sufficient person or a student, *and*:

- the EU national dies and you:[142]
  - are an EU national; *or*
  - have lived in the UK as her/his family member for at least a year before her/his death and you are a non-EU national; *or*
- the EU national leaves the UK and you are:[143]
  - an EU national; *or*
  - the child or grandchild of the EU national and in education; *or*
  - the parent with custody of a child in education; *or*
- your marriage or civil partnership to the EU national is terminated and:[144]
  - you are an EU national; *or*
  - the marriage/civil partnership had, prior to the termination, lasted for at least three years with you both residing in the UK for at least one of those years; *or*
  - you have custody of the EU national's child; *or*
  - you have a right of access to the EU national's child, which a court has said must take place in the UK; *or*
  - your continued right of residence in the UK is warranted by particularly difficult circumstances, such as your being subject to domestic violence during the period of the marriage/civil partnership.

Before acquiring a permanent right to reside following your retaining your right to reside under the Directive, you must show that you are a worker, or a self-

12

employed or self-sufficient person, or you are the family member of such a person.[145]

Note: you may have a right to reside if you are the family member of someone who has acquired a permanent right of residence (see p1548).

Derivative right to reside

Some people have a right to reside based on someone else's right to reside, but not through being her/his family member.

You have a 'derivative right to reside' on this basis if you are:[146]
- the child of an EEA national who was a 'worker' in the UK (see p1536) while you were living in the UK, and you are currently in education;[147] *or*
- the primary carer of a child in the above bullet point and the child would be unable to continue her/his education if you were required to leave (see below);[148] *or*
- the primary carer of a self-sufficient child who is an EEA national, who would be unable to remain here if you were required to leave;[149] *or*
- a dependent child of a primary carer in either the second or third bullet points above and s/he would be prevented from residing in the UK if you were required to leave and you do not have leave to enter or remain in the UK; *or*
- the primary carer of a British citizen residing in the UK who would be unable to reside in the UK or another EEA state if you were required to leave (see below).[150]

You may be accepted as having a right to reside as the primary carer even if you share that responsibility with someone else who does not already have a right to reside. If this applies, the consequences of your being required to leave are considered on the basis that both you and the other carer are required to leave.[151]

From 8 November 2012, if your only right of residence is as the primary carer of a dependent British citizen who would otherwise have to leave the whole of the EEA (the last bullet above), you do not satisfy the right to reside requirement for any benefits or CTC (see p1526 and p1527). Note: this is arguably unlawful and although legal challenges have not yet been successful,[152] future ones may be. See CPAG's online service and *Welfare Rights Bulletin* for updates.

Note: periods with a right to reside under any of the above bullet points do not count towards the period of residence required for acquiring a permanent right to reside (see p1548).

Child in education

To have a right to reside as a worker's child in education and as a primary carer of a child in education, the child must have been in the UK while the parent was a worker in the UK. The child need not have entered education while the parent was a worker.[153] The EEA Regulations say that the child must have been in

Part 12: Immigration and residence rules for benefits and tax credits
Chapter 70: Coming from abroad: residence rules
5. Who has a right to reside

education while the parent was in the UK, but this is not supported by caselaw. If you are refused benefit for this reason, appeal and seek advice.

These rights also apply if the worker was an A8 national working, before 1 May 2011, for an authorised employer (see p1531), even if it was for less than 12 months.[154] As the first month of work an A8 national did was always for an authorised employer, her/his child who was in the UK during that first month of work and who is now in education can also have these rights.[155] These rights also apply in the same way if the worker was a Croatian or (before 1 January 2014) an A2 national working in accordance with her/his worker authorisation document.

Your right to reside as a primary carer of a worker's child in education ends when the child reaches 18, unless s/he continues to need your presence and care in order to be able to pursue and complete her/his education.[156] 'Education' does not include nursery education[157] or pre-school education since the rights arise when a child enters compulsory education at around the age of five.[158] However, it may arguably extend to a child under five in a school reception class.[159]

If you are the primary carer of a child of a self-employed EEA national, you are not currently accepted as deriving a right to reside from that child.[160] However, this may change as further caselaw develops. See CPAG's online service and *Welfare Rights Bulletin* for updates.

People with a permanent right of residence

From 30 April 2006, you have a permanent right of residence if you have 'resided legally' (see p1549) in the UK for a 'continuous period of five years' (see below).[161] Once you have this permanent right of residence, you do not need to satisfy any other conditions – eg, you do not need to also be a worker or other qualified person.

Once acquired, you only lose your permanent right of residence if you are absent from the UK for more than two consecutive years.[162]

A continuous period of five years
When calculating whether you have five years' continuous residence, temporary absences from the UK are not counted if:[163]
– they are not more than a total of six months a year; *or*
– they comprise one absence of up to 12 consecutive months for important reasons, such as pregnancy and childbirth, serious illness, study or vocational training, or a posting abroad; *or*
– they are for compulsory military service.
Although these periods relate to absences from the UK, it is arguable that temporary gaps between periods of legal residence when you remain in the UK should be treated in the same way.[164]
If you have one or more temporary absences from the UK, you can count the time spent abroad as part of your five continuous years.[165]

What counts as 'resided legally'

You have 'resided legally' in any period during which you had a right of residence as a:

- 'worker' (see p1536) (including if you retain your worker status – see p1537);
- 'self-employed person' (see p1540) (including if you retain your self-employed status – see p1541);
- 'self-sufficient person' (see p1541);
- 'student' (see p1542);
- 'family member' (see p1542) of any of the above.

If you have a continuous period of five years' residence on the basis of being in one or more of the above groups, you have a right of permanent residence under both EU Directive 2004/38 and the UK EEA Regulations. However, if you need to rely on periods when you were not in one of these groups, the specific provisions in each can be relevant.

Under the EEA Regulations, you must have resided continuously in accordance with these Regulations, other than with a 'derivative right to reside' (see p1547)[166] or, for periods before 30 April 2006, in accordance with previous regulations.[167] **Note:** the legislation before 30 April 2006 did not provide residence rights for jobseekers and, therefore, periods of residence as a jobseeker can only be used towards your five years from 30 April 2006.

Under EU Directive 2004/38, you must have 'resided legally for a continuous period of five years'.[168] This means that you had a residence right under the Directive or under any of the earlier EU legislation that the Directive replaced.[169] This covers all the five groups listed above. You are not counted as having 'resided legally' during periods when your right to reside was as the primary carer of either a worker's child in education or a self-sufficient child,[170] or when your right of residence was only in accordance with UK law – eg, a period during which you had leave to remain under the Immigration Rules.[171]

If you are an A8, A2 or a Croatian national, you count as having 'resided legally' during periods before your state joined the EU if you would have fallen into one of the five groups above or you would have resided in accordance with the EEA Regulations were it not for the fact that you were not an EU national at that time.[172] Once your state joined the EU, the periods when you count as having resided legally are as above, except they are subject to the additional restrictions for A8, A2 and Croatian nationals (see p1531).

Family members

If you are the family member (see p1542) of a person with a permanent right of residence, you have a right to reside for as long as you remain a family member.[173] After five years of being the family member of an EEA national with a permanent right of residence, you acquire a permanent right of residence yourself. Under the EEA Regulations, you can also add periods as a family member of a person with a

Part 12: Immigration and residence rules for benefits and tax credits
Chapter 70: Coming from abroad: residence rules
5. Who has a right to reside

permanent right of residence to other periods of residence as a qualified person (see p1529) to make up your five years, and so acquire a permanent right of residence.[174]

Retired and incapacitated people

If you were a 'worker' (see p1536) or self-employed person (see p1540) and you are now retired or permanently incapacitated, you can acquire a permanent right of residence before five years in the following circumstances. If you are covered, you are exempt from the habitual residence test (see p1523).

You have a permanent right to reside if you:[175]
- are a worker or self-employed person and you:
  - have reached retirement age or taken early retirement and you either:
    - have a spouse or civil partner who is a UK national (or who lost that nationality by marrying you); or
    - have worked in the UK for the preceding year and resided in the UK continuously for more than three years; or
  - stopped working in the UK because of a permanent incapacity and:
    - you have a spouse or civil partner who is a UK national (or who lost that nationality by marrying you); or
    - you have resided in the UK continuously for more than two years; or
    - the incapacity was because of an accident at work or occupational disease that resulted in benefit entitlement; or
  - have worked and resided in the UK continuously for three years and then work in another member state and return to the UK at least once a week; or
- are the family member of and live (anywhere in the UK[176]) with a worker or self-employed person in any of the above groups; or
- are the family member of a worker or self-employed person who died while still working and who did not acquire a permanent right of residence under one of the above groups and:
  - s/he had lived in the UK for two years; or
  - the death resulted from an accident at work or an occupational disease; or
  - you lost your UK nationality as a result of marrying her/him.

Periods count as periods of employment if you were involuntarily unemployed (subject to the same limitations that apply to those retaining worker status in this way – see p1538) or not working because of illness or an accident. [177]

Other rights of residence under European Union law

If none of the usual ways in which you may have a right of residence under EU law in the UK (see pp1527–50) apply to you, it may be possible to argue that you should still have a right of residence despite not meeting any of the specific conditions.

If you are an EU national, you may be able to argue that you have a right to reside under Article 21 of the Treaty on the Functioning of the European Union. Arguments that you have a right of residence despite not meeting the usual conditions are complex and you should seek specialist advice. Always check whether you have a right of residence under one of the other routes first.

Residence documents

To have a right of residence as an 'extended family member' (see p1543), you must have a residence document. If you have some other right of residence, you can also obtain a residence document, but it is not necessary. **Note:** a residence document does not, in itself, give you a right to reside – eg, if your right to reside has ended.[178]

You can be issued with the following residence documents.

- A **registration certificate** if you are an EEA national with a right of residence provided under the EEA Regulations.[179]
- A **residence card** if you are a non-EEA national and you have a right to reside as the family member of an EEA 'qualified person' (see p1529) or an EEA national with a permanent right of residence.[180]
- A **derivative residence card** if you are an EEA national with a derivative right to reside – eg, as the primary carer of a worker's child in education.[181]
- A **document certifying permanent right of residence** if you are an EEA national with a permanent right of residence, or a **permanent residence card** if you are a non-EEA national with a permanent right of residence.[182]
- Before 30 April 2006, EEA nationals and their family members may have been issued with **residence permits**. These were valid for a five-year period. From 30 April 2006, these documents should be treated as if they were the equivalent type of document issued after that date – eg, one of the first three documents in the above bullet points.[183]
- **Family permits** are only issued for entry to the UK if you are a non-EEA family member of an EEA national and do not have any of the other residence documentation.

Forms and further information, including about application fees, are available on the UK Border Agency website.

12

---

6. Rules for individual benefits and tax credits

This section explains the residence and presence rules for each benefit. These include:

- which, if any, residence and presence tests apply;

Part 12: Immigration and residence rules for benefits and tax credits
Chapter 70: Coming from abroad: residence rules
6. Rules for individual benefits and tax credits

- how, if you are living in the UK, you may be assisted by the European Union (EU) co-ordination rules.

For the rules on being paid while you are abroad, see Chapter 71.

Means-tested benefits

To be entitled to income support (IS), income-based jobseeker's allowance (JSA), income-related employment and support allowance (ESA), pension credit (PC) and universal credit (UC), you (and your partner for UC) must:
- be present in Great Britain (see p1518);[184] *and*
- be habitually resident (see p1521), including having a right to reside (see p1525), and, for income-based JSA only, have been living for the past three months, in the 'common travel area' – ie, the UK, Republic of Ireland, Channel Islands and the Isle of Man (unless you are exempt, see p1523).[185]

The requirement to be living in the common travel area only applies to income-based JSA claims made on or after 1 January 2014.[186] The three months do not have to be continuous so you may satisfy this condition even if you have had temporary absences from the common travel area. **Note:** if you are covered by the co-ordination rules (see p1592) and have moved to the UK from another EEA state, you may be able to use periods of residence there to satisfy this condition (see p1598).

In certain circumstances, the rules treat you as present in Great Britain during a temporary absence, so you can continue to receive these benefits while you are abroad for limited periods (see Chapter 71).

If you come under the UC system and meet the personal conditions (see p20), you must satisfy additional residence and presence rules. You must:
- be a British citizen; *and*
- have resided in the UK throughout the two years before the date of your claim; *and*
- not have left the UK for a continuous period of more than four weeks during the above period.

If your partner fails the habitual residence test, you must claim UC as a single person (and your partner does not need a national insurance (NI) number). Your award is based on the maximum amount for a single person, but your partner's income and capital are taken into account.

To be entitled to housing benefit (HB), you must be habitually resident (see p1521), including having a right to reside (see p1525) in the 'common travel area' (unless you are exempt).[187]

There is no requirement to be present in Great Britain for HB. However, you must be liable to make payments in respect of a dwelling in Great Britain, which you occupy as your home.[188] There are rules that treat you as occupying your

12

home, including during a temporary absence from it.[189] If you are going abroad, these rules determine whether you can be entitled to HB while you are away (see p103).

If your partner is abroad

If you have a partner who is abroad, you can continue to receive benefit that includes an amount for her/him for a limited period depending on your circumstances (see Chapter 71).

If this does not apply, or at the end of the limited period:

- your applicable amount for IS, income-based JSA and income-related ESA no longer includes an amount for your partner;
- you cease to be entitled for UC as joint claimants. You must claim as a single person. Your award is based on the maximum amount for a single person, but your partner's income and capital are taken into account until you have been, or you expect to be, apart for six months (as then you cease to be treated as a couple).[190]

Your partner's capital, income and work are still taken into account when working out how much of the above benefits you get. This is because s/he is still treated as being part of your household, despite temporarily living away from you, unless you are in any of the situations listed on p208.[191]

Your partner's absence is from *you*, not from the family home, so these rules can apply even if your partner has never lived in your current home. The length of the absence is calculated from when it started to when it is likely to finish.

Where questions of 'intention' are involved (eg, when deciding whether you or your partner intend to resume living with your family), the intention must be 'unqualified'. This means it must not depend on a factor over which you have no control – eg, the right of entry to the UK being granted by the Home Office[192] or the offer of a suitable job.[193]

If your child is abroad

If you have a child who is abroad, your benefit entitlement could be affected as s/he is treated as part of your household, despite temporarily living away from you, unless s/he does not count as being a member of your household because of one of the reasons on p214.[194]

For IS, income-based JSA and UC, your child is only included in your applicable amount for a limited period while s/he is abroad (see Chapter 71).

Bereavement benefits

You do not need to satisfy any residence or presence rules to be entitled to bereavement benefits. There is one exception, which only applies to a bereavement payment.

Part 12: Immigration and residence rules for benefits and tax credits
Chapter 70: Coming from abroad: residence rules
6. Rules for individual benefits and tax credits

If you are absent from Great Britain when you claim a bereavement payment, you can only be entitled if:[195]
- your late spouse/civil partner was in Great Britain when s/he died; *or*
- you were in Great Britain on the date of the death of your spouse or civil partner; *or*
- neither of the above two bullets apply, but you returned to Great Britain within four weeks of the death of your late spouse or civil partner; *or*
- your late spouse's/civil partner's NI contribution record is sufficient for you to satisfy the contribution conditions for widowed parent's allowance and bereavement allowance; *or*
- your spouse/civil partner died while abroad in another European Economic Area (EEA) state and the EU co-ordination rules apply to you (see p1592); *or*
- your spouse/civil partner died while abroad in a state which has a reciprocal agreement with the UK that covers your entitlement to a bereavement payment.

According to official guidance, the DWP takes the view that if you and your late spouse/civil partner were outside Great Britain when s/he died and you do not return to Great Britain within four weeks of the death (and none of the last three bullets above apply), you are disqualified from a bereavement payment, even if you claim within the time limit (see p519) when you are back in Great Britain.[196] It is arguable that this approach is incorrect and you should only be disqualified if you are absent from Great Britain when you make your claim (and none of the above bullets apply). Seek advice if this affects you.

European Union co-ordination rules

If the EU co-ordination rules apply to you (see p1592) you can rely on NI contributions paid by your late spouse/civil partner in other EEA states to calculate your entitlement to bereavement benefits (see p1598).

If your late spouse/civil partner died in another EEA state, s/he can be treated as having died in the UK for the purposes of entitlement to a bereavement payment if the UK is your 'competent state' (see p1596).[197]

Reciprocal agreements

If you have lived and worked in a country with which the UK has a reciprocal agreement (see p1570), you may be able to count periods of insurance paid in that country towards your bereavement benefit entitlement.

Child benefit

To be entitled to child benefit, you and your child(ren) must be present in Great Britain (see p1518).[198]

You are treated as not present and, therefore, not eligible for child benefit if:[199]
- you are not ordinarily resident in the UK (see p1519); *or*

- you do not have a right to reside in the UK (see p1520) and your claim for child benefit was made after 1 May 2004.

Note: you do not need to have a right to reside if you claimed child benefit before 1 May 2004 and you have been receiving it since that date.
    You are treated as present if you are:[200]
- a Crown servant posted overseas; *and*
    - you are, or immediately before your posting abroad you were, ordinarily resident in the UK; *or*
    - immediately before your posting you were in the UK in connection with that posting; *or*
- the partner of a Crown servant posted overseas and in the same country as her/him or temporarily absent from that country under the same exceptions that enable child benefit to continue during a temporary absence from Great Britain (see p1572);
- a person who is in the UK as a result of your being deported or legally removed from another country.

You and/or your child can be treated as present for limited periods during a temporary absence (see p1572).
    While you are treated as present, you continue to satisfy that condition of entitlement. This means that you can continue to receive child benefit if it is already being paid and you can also make a fresh claim during your, or your child's, absence. If you, or your child, spend longer abroad than the permitted periods (see p1572), you (or s/he) will cease to satisfy the presence condition and your entitlement to child benefit will end.

European Union co-ordination rules
If the EU co-ordiantion rules apply to you (see p1592), you may be able to be paid child benefit for a child who is resident in another EEA country without her/him needing to satisfy the rules on temporary absences. See p1599 for more details. If you are covered by the co-ordination rules, but do not have a right to reside, see p1527 for a potential argument that you should still be entitled to child benefit.

Disability and carers' benefits
For **attendance allowance (AA), carer's allowance (CA), disability living allowance (DLA) and personal independence payment (PIP)**, you must satisfy the presence, past presence and habitual residence tests. This means you must:[201]
- be present in Great Britain at the time of your claim;
- have been present in Great Britain for at least 104 weeks in the last 156 weeks (the 'past presence test'). See p1518, but see also p1556;
- be habitually resident in the common travel area (see p1521).

Part 12: Immigration and residence rules for benefits and tax credits
Chapter 70: Coming from abroad: residence rules
6. Rules for individual benefits and tax credits

However, if you were entitled to AA, DLA or CA on 7 April 2013, the rules that applied when you claimed (which are the same as those described below for ESA in youth) continue to apply until your benefit award is terminated unless:[202]

- your benefit award is revised or superseded. You must then be habitually resident rather than ordinarily resident in Great Britain; *or*
- your benefit award continues until 7 April 2015. In this case, you must have been present for at least 104 weeks in the last 156 weeks, rather than 26 weeks in the last 52.

For **ESA in youth, incapacity benefit (IB) in youth and severe disablement allowance (SDA)**, you must satisfy the presence, past presence and ordinary residence tests. This means to be entitled to each of these benefits you must:[203]

- be present in Great Britain at the time of claim (see p1518);
- have been present in Great Britain for not less than 26 weeks in the last 52 weeks (the 'past presence' test). See p1518, but see also below;
- be ordinarily resident in Great Britain (see p1519).

For ESA in youth, IB in youth and SDA, once you pass the residence and presence tests, you do not need to satisfy them again while you are in the same period of limited capability for work or incapacity for work.[204]

When you can be treated as present

You are treated as being present during certain absences (see p1571). Any period when you are treated as present can be counted to satisfy both the presence and the past presence tests.

Exceptions to the past presence test

If you are claiming the DLA care component for a baby under six months old, there is a shorter 13-week past presence test. If covered by this, it continues to apply until your child's first birthday. If your child becomes entitled to DLA at between six months and 36 months, the past presence test is 26 weeks in the last 156 weeks.

For AA, DLA and PIP, the 104-week (or 26-week or 13-week) past presence test does not apply if you are terminally ill (see p510).[205]

European Union co-ordination rules

The EU co-ordination rules can make it easier to claim AA, CA, DLA and PIP in the UK and can also enable you to make a new claim if you live in another EEA state.

The past presence test does not apply to AA, CA, DLA and PIP if:[206]

- you are habitually resident in Great Britain; *and*
- you are covered by the co-ordination rules (see p1592); *and*
- you can demonstrate 'a genuine and sufficient link to the UK social security system' (see p1557).

If you are covered by the co-ordination rules (see p1592), but are not *exempt* from the past presence test because you are not accepted as having 'a genuine and sufficient link to the UK social security system', you may be able to count periods of residence in another EEA member state to *satisfy* the past presence test for these benefits (and also for ESA in youth) (see p1598).

If you are covered by the co-ordination rules (see p1592), you can only be entitled to AA, CA, DLA care component and the daily living component of PIP if the UK is your 'competent state' (see p1596).[207] This might not be the case if you (or your family member who brings you within the co-ordination rules) receive a pension from another member state.[208] See CPAG's *Benefits for Migrants Handbook* for further details.

Factors that are relevant to demonstrate that you have a 'genuine and sufficient link to the UK social security system' include if you have worked in the UK, have spent a significant part of your life in the UK, are receiving a UK contributory benefit, or you are dependent on a family member who has worked in the UK and/or receives a UK contributory benefit.[209] You must show that you have a 'genuine and sufficient link to the UK social security system' for the purpose of the benefit you are claiming, taking all your circumstances into account.[210]

Contributory employment and support allowance

To be entitled to contributory ESA, you must be in Great Britain.[211] The rules on when you can be paid during a temporary absence are covered in Chapter 71. There are no residence conditions, unless you are claiming contributory ESA in youth (see p1555).

European Union co-ordination rules

If the EU co-ordination rules apply to you (see p1592) and the UK is your 'competent state' (see p1596), you can, if necessary, rely on NI contributions paid in another EEA state to entitle you to contributory ESA in the UK. You may be able to continue to receive a sickness or invalidity benefit from another EEA state if the co-ordination rules apply to you.

Reciprocal agreements

If you have lived and worked in a country with which the UK has a reciprocal agreement (see p1570), you may be able to count periods of insurance paid in that country towards your entitlement to contributory ESA in the UK.

Guardian's allowance

Entitlement to guardian's allowance depends on entitlement to child benefit, so you must meet the conditions for child benefit set out on p1554.

A further condition of entitlement to guardian's allowance is that at least one of the child's parents must:[212]

Part 12: Immigration and residence rules for benefits and tax credits
Chapter 70: Coming from abroad: residence rules
6. Rules for individual benefits and tax credits

- have been born in the UK; *or*
- have, at some time after reaching the age of 16, spent a total of 52 weeks in any two-year period in Great Britain.

In order to satisfy the second condition above, you are treated as being present in Great Britain during any absence abroad which is due to your employment as a serving member of the forces, an airman or airwoman, mariner or continental shelf worker.

European Union co-ordination rules

If the EU co-ordination rules apply to you (see p1592), you may be able to be paid guardian's allowance for a child resident in another EEA country.

If the EU co-ordination rules apply to you (see p1592), time spent in other EEA states can count toward the time spent in Great Britain to help meet the second of the two conditions above (see p1598). It may also be arguable that this requirement should not apply if you have a 'genuine and sufficient link to the UK social security system' (see p1556).[213]

Industrial injuries benefits

To be entitled to any of the industrial injury benefits, you must have:

- been in Great Britain when the accident at work happened;[214] *or*
- been engaged in Great Britain in the employment that caused the disease (even if you have also been engaged outside Great Britain in that employment);[215] *or*
- been paying UK NI contributions, either at Class 1 rate or at Class 2 rate as a volunteer development worker when the accident at work happened or you contracted the disease. Benefit is not payable until you return to Great Britain.[216]

There are exceptions, which mean that you can qualify for benefit in respect of an accident which happens, or a disease which is contracted, outside Great Britain while you are:[217]

- employed as a mariner or airman or airwoman;
- employed as an apprentice pilot on board a ship or vessel;
- on board an aircraft on a test flight starting in Great Britain in the course of your employment.

In these cases, there are also more generous rules for defining when accidents arise 'out of and in the course of' your employment, and for complying with time limits under benefit rules.[218]

European Union co-ordination rules

If the EU co-ordination rules apply to you (see p1592) and the UK is your 'competent state' (see p1596), you can, if necessary, rely on periods of employment and NI paid in other EEA states in order to qualify for industrial injuries benefits in the UK (see p1598).

If you have an accident while travelling abroad in another member state, this can be deemed to have occurred in the state liable to pay industrial injuries benefits.[219] If you have worked in two or more EEA states in a job that gave you a prescribed industrial disease, you only get benefit from the member state in which you last worked in that job.[220]

Contribution-based jobseeker's allowance

To be entitled to contribution-based JSA, you must be in Great Britain.[221] The rules on when you can be paid during a temporary absence are covered in Chapter 71. There are no residence conditions.

European Union co-ordination rules

If the EU co-ordination rules apply to you (see p1592) and the UK is your 'competent state' (see p1596), you can, if necessary, rely on NI contributions paid in another EEA state to entitle you to contribution-based JSA in the UK. See p1598 for more details.

If you are coming to, or returning to, the UK to look for work and have been insured in another EEA member state, you may be able to get the other state's unemployment benefit for up to three months if:[222]

- you were getting it immediately before coming to the UK;
- you have been registered as available for work for four weeks (or less if that state's rules allow) in that member state;
- you claim JSA within seven days after you were last registered in the other member state; *and*
- if you do not come under the UC system (see p19), you satisfy the JSA jobseeking conditions (see p1024) or, if you come under the UC system, you accept a claimant commitment and you meet any work-related requirements that have been imposed on you (see p1064).

The three months can be extended to a maximum of six months if the state from which you are claiming the unemployment benefit agrees.[223]

Reciprocal agreements

If you have lived and worked in a country with which the UK has a reciprocal agreement (see p1517), you may be able to count periods of insurance paid in that country towards your entitlement to contribution-based JSA.

Maternity allowance

Entitlement to maternity allowance (MA) is based on past employment. There are no residence requirements, but you are disqualified if you are absent from Great

Part 12: Immigration and residence rules for benefits and tax credits
Chapter 70: Coming from abroad: residence rules
6. Rules for individual benefits and tax credits

Britain.[224] See p1576 for the rules allowing you to be paid during a temporary absence.

European Union co-ordination rules

If the EU co-ordiantion rules apply to you (see p1592) and the UK is your 'competent state' (see p1596), you can, if necessary, rely on periods of employment in other EEA states in order to qualify for MA in the UK. See p1598 for more details.

Retirement pensions

Retirement pensions, other than Category D retirement pension, do not have any residence or presence conditions.[225] They can be paid without time limit, whether or not you are present in Great Britain. The exception to this is the annual uprating, which is only paid while you are abroad in certain circumstances (see p1583).

To be entitled to Category D retirement pension, you must:
- have been resident in Great Britain for at least 10 years in any continuous period of 20 years ending on or after your 80th birthday; *and*
- have been ordinarily resident (see p1519) in Great Britain on either:
  - your 80th birthday; *or*
  - the date on which you claimed Category D pension, if later.

European Union co-ordination rules

If the co-ordination rules apply to you (see p1592) and the UK is your 'competent state' (see p1596), you can, if necessary, rely on NI contributions paid, or for Category D retirement pension, periods of residence completed, in other EEA states to calculate your entitlement to retirement pensions in the UK (see p1598). However, your award may be reduced to reflect the proportion of years of contributions paid, or periods of residence completed, in the UK out of the total years of contributions paid or periods of residence completed in all states.[226] The requirement to be ordinarily resident for Category D retirement pension may not apply to you if you can show that you have a 'genuine and sufficient link to the UK social security system' (see p1556).[227]

Reciprocal agreements

If you have lived and worked in a country with which the UK has a reciprocal agreement (see p1517), you may be able to count periods of residence or insurance paid in that country towards your UK retirement pension entitlement.

Social fund funeral payments

To qualify for a funeral payment:
- the deceased must have been ordinarily resident (see p1519) in the UK;[228]

- the funeral must take place in the UK. However, it can take place in any EEA state if you or your partner are:[229]
  - an EEA national and a 'worker', including if you have retained this status (see p1536);
  - an EEA national and a 'self-employed person', including if you have retained this status (see p1540);
  - a 'family member' of one of the above (see p1542);
  - an EEA national with a permanent right of residence as a retired or permanently incapacitated worker or self-employed person, or you are the family member of such a person (see p1550);
  - a person with any other right of residence in the UK under EU law – eg, with a permanent right of residence following five years' residence (see p1548).[230]

Tax credits

To be entitled to **child tax credit** (CTC), you (and your partner if you are making a joint claim) must:[231]
- be present in the UK (see p1518); *and*
- be ordinarily resident in the UK (see p1519); *and*
- have a right to reside in the UK (see p1520).

To be entitled to **working tax credit** (WTC), you (and your partner if you are making a joint claim) must be:[232]
- present in the UK (see p1518); *and*
- ordinarily resident in the UK (see p1519).

There are, however, some exceptions.[233] You do not need a right to reside for CTC if you claimed it before 1 May 2004 and you have been receiving it since this date.

Although there are exceptions to the requirement to be ordinarily resident, in practice claims are rarely refused on this basis.

For the rules on when you can be treated as present for either eight or 12 weeks during a temporary absence, or while you or your partner are a Crown servant posted overseas, see p1585.

While you are treated as present, you continue to satisfy the conditions of entitlement to tax credits. This means that you can continue to receive tax credits that are already in payment and can make a fresh or renewal claim during your absence. If you spend longer abroad than the permitted periods, you cease to satisfy the presence condition and your tax credit entitlement ends.

Being absent (other than a temporary absence of less than eight or 12 weeks – see p1585) or losing your right to reside are both changes that you must notify to HM Revenue and Customs (HMRC) within one month. If you do not, HMRC may impose a penalty (see Chapter 67) and may also recover any overpaid tax credits (see Chapter 66).

Part 12: Immigration and residence rules for benefits and tax credits
Chapter 70: Coming from abroad: residence rules
Notes

Couples

If you are a member of a couple and make a joint tax credit claim, you must both satisfy the residence requirements. Your entitlement to tax credits as a couple ends if either you or your partner:

- are abroad for longer than a permitted temporary absence;
- (for CTC only) lose the right to reside;
- cease to be ordinarily resident.

The person who continues to satisfy the residence rules can make a fresh claim for CTC and/or WTC as a single person, provided s/he is entitled on that basis.

You must notify HMRC if you or your partner have ceased to satisfy the residence or presence requirements within one month (see p1450). If you fail to do so, HMRC may recover any overpaid tax credits (see Chapter 66) and impose a penalty (see Chapter 67). When the partner returns to the UK, or becomes ordinarily resident or acquires a right to reside, you must terminate the single person claim and claim again as a couple.

If you or your partner are abroad (even for a temporary absence of less than eight or 12 weeks) and you (or s/he) were the only partner in full-time work, you may lose entitlement to WTC if the requirement to be in full-time work is no longer satisfied (see p165). This is a change that you must notify to HMRC within one month. If you do not, HMRC may impose a penalty as well as recovering any overpaid tax credits.

European Union co-ordination rules

If the EU co-ordination rules apply to you (see p1592), you may be able to be paid CTC for a partner or child resident in another EEA country. See p1599 for more details.

Notes

2. The different residence and presence tests
1 R(IS) 6/96 (para 19); R(P) 2/67
2 R(M)1/85
3 *R v Barnet London Borough Council ex parte Shah* [1983] 2 AC 309

4 Sch para 21 CTRS(DS)E Regs; reg 12 CTRS(PR)E Regs; reg 16 CTR(SPC)S Regs; reg 16 CTR(S) Regs; reg 12 CTRSPR(W) Regs; Sch para 19 CTRS(DS)W Regs

5   Reg 1(2),(3) and (4) SS(DLA,AA&CA)(A)
    Regs
6   Sch para 21 CTRS(DS)E Regs; reg 12
    CTRS(PR)E Regs; reg 16 CTR(SPC)S
    Regs; reg 16 CTR(S) Regs; reg 12
    CTRSPR(W) Regs; Sch para 19
    CTRS(DS)W Regs

3. Habitual residence

7   **IS** Regs 21 and 21AA IS Regs
    JSA Regs 85 and 85A JSA Regs
    ESA Regs 69 and 70 ESA Regs
    PC Reg 2 SPC Regs
    HB Reg 10 HB Regs; reg 10 HB(SPC)
    Regs
    UC Reg 9 UC Regs
    AA Reg 2(1)(a)(i) SS(AA) Regs
    DLA Reg 2(1)(a)(i) SS(DLA) Regs
    PIP Reg 16(c) SS(PIP) Regs
    CA Reg 9(1)(a) SS(ICA) Regs
8   Reg 21 CTRS(DS)E Regs; reg 12
    CTRS(PR)E Regs; reg 16 CTR(SPC)S
    Regs; reg 16 CTR(S) Regs; reg 12
    CTRSPR(W) Regs; Sch para 19
    CTRS(DS)W Regs
9   Reg 1(2),(3) and (4) SS(DLA,AA&CA)(A)
    Regs
10 Regs 3(3), 18(2), 22(3) and 36(3) UC
    Regs
11 **IS** Regs 21 and 21AA and Sch 7 para 17
    IS Regs
    JSA Regs 85 and 85A and Sch 5 para 14
    JSA Regs
    ESA Regs 69 and 70 and Sch 5 para 11
    ESA Regs
12 Reg 10(1) HB Regs; reg 10(1) HB(SPC)
    Regs
13 **PC** Reg 2 SPC Regs
    UC Reg 9 UC Regs
14 **AA** s35(1) SSA 1975; reg 2(1) SS(AA)
    Regs
    DLA s71(6) SSCBA 1992; reg 2(1)
    SS(DLA) Regs
    PIP s77(3) WRA 2012; reg 16 SS(PIP)
    Regs
    CA s70(4) SSCBA 1992; reg 9(1) SS(ICA)
    Regs
15 R(IS) 6/96
16 **IS** Reg 21AA(4) IS Regs
    JSA Reg 85A(4) JSA Regs
    ESA Reg 70(4) ESA Regs
    PC Reg 2(4) SPC Regs
    HB Reg 10(3B) HB Regs; reg 10(4A)
    HB(SPC) Regs; Housing Benefit
    (Habitual Residence) Amendment
    Regulations 2014, No.539
    UC Reg 9(4) UC Regs

17 **AA** Reg 2(3A) SS(AA) Regs
    DLA Reg 2(3A) SS(DLA) Regs
    PIP Reg 20 SS(PIP) Regs
    CA Reg 9(3) SS(ICA) Regs
18 R(IS) 6/96, paras 17 and 20; CIS/13498/
    96, para 17
19 CIS/15927/1996
20 *R v Barnet London Borough Council ex
    parte Shah* [1983] 2 AC 309, at 344; CIS/
    13498/1996
21 R(IS) 2/00; CIS/4474/2003
22 *Nessa v Chief Adjudication Officer* [1999]
    UKHL 41
23 CIS/4474/2003
24 CIS/1972/2003
25 CIS 1304/97; CJSA 5394/98
26 CIS/1304/1997; CJSA/5394/1998
27 Art 70 EU Reg 883/04; Art 10a EU Reg
    1408/71; *Robin Swaddling v Adjudication
    Officer*, C-90/97 [1999] ECR I-01075
28 CIS/12703/1996
29 R(IS) 2/00; CIS/11481/1995

4. Right to reside

30 Reg 21 CTRS(DS)E Regs; reg 12 CTRS
    (PR)E Regs; reg 16 CTR(SPC)S Regs; reg
    16 CTR(S) Regs; reg 12 CTRSPR(W)
    Regs; Sch para 19 CTRS(DS)W Regs
31 Reg 6 SS(HR)A Regs; reg 11 SS(PA)A
    Regs
32 Reg 70(4)(l) ESA Regs
33 **IS** Reg 21AA(2) and (3) IS Regs
    JSA Reg 85A(2) and (3) JSA Regs
    ESA Reg 70(2) and (3) ESA Regs
    PC Reg 2(2) and (3) SPC Regs
    HB Reg 10(3) and (3A) HB Regs; reg
    10(3) and (4) HB(SPC) Regs
    UC Reg 9(3) UC Regs
34 *R (HC) v SSWP* [2013] EWHC 3874
    (Admin)
35 *Vatsouras* (C-22/08) *and Koupatantze*
    (C-23/08) *v Arbeitsgemeinschaft (ARGE)
    Nürnberg 900* [2009] ECR I-04585
36 **CB** Reg 23(4) CB Regs
    TC Reg 3(5) TC(R) Regs
37 *AS v HMRC (CB)* [2013] NICom 15, 25
    March 2013
38 **CB** Reg 23(4) CB Regs
    TC Reg 3(5) TC(R) Regs
39 *R (HC) v SSWP* [2013] EWHC 3874
    (Admin)

12

Part 12: Immigration and residence rules for benefits and tax credits
Chapter 70: Coming from abroad: residence rules
Notes

5. Who has a right to reside

40 Decision of the EEA Joint Committee No.158/2007

41 Swiss nationals: *Agreement between the European Community and its Member States, of the one part, and the Swiss Confederation, of the other, on the Free Movement of Persons*, 21 June 1999, Cmd 5639. In force from 1 June 2002.

42 Reg 2(1) I(EEA) Regs

43 Regs 6 and 14(1) I(EEA) Regs. The same groups are covered in Arts 7 and 14 EU Dir 2004/38 but the term 'qualified person' is not used in the Directive.

44 *SSWP v JB (JSA)* [2011] UKUT 96 (AAC)

45 Reg 8 AC(IWA) Regs

46 Reg 9 A(IWA) Regs

47 Reg 9 A(IWA) Regs

48 Regs 4 and 5 AC(IWA) Regs

49 Reg 6 A(IWA) Regs; reg 7B EEA Regs

50 Reg 7 A(IWR) Regs

51 Reg 5 A(IWR) Regs; reg 7A I(EEA) Regs

52 Reg 7 A(IWR) Regs

53 *SSWP v ZA* [2009] UKUT 294 (AAC); *Szpak v SSWP* [2013] EWCA Civ 46

54 CIS/1042/2008; *SSWP v JB* [2011] UKUT 96 (AAC)

55 Reg 2 AC(IWA) Regs; reg 2 A(IWA) Regs

56 Reg 4 A(IWA) Regs; reg 3 AC(IWA) Regs

57 Reg 2 A(IWR) Regs

58 Reg 2(5) AC(IWA) Regs; reg 2(12) A(IWA) Regs

59 *Miskovic and Another v SSWP* [2011] EWCA Civ 16

60 Reg 2(7) A(IWR) Regs

61 *Miskovic and Another v SSWP* [2011] EWCA Civ 16

62 *BS v SSWP* [2009] UKUT 16 (AAC)

63 Reg 13(1) I(EEA) Regs; Art 6(1) EU Dir 2004/38

64 Reg 13(3)(b) I(EEA) Regs; Art 14(1) EU Dir 2004/38

65 Reg 13(2) I(EEA) Regs; Art 6(2) EU Dir 2004/38

66 Art 45 TFEU; Arts 14 and 24 EU Dir 2004/38; reg 6 I(EEA) Regs

67 Art 45 TFEU; *The Queen v Immigration Appeal Tribunal, ex parte Gustaff Desiderius Antonissen*, C-292/89 [1991] ECR I-00745

68 R(IS) 8/08

69 *The Queen v Immigration Appeal Tribunal, ex parte Gustaff Desiderius Antonissen*, C-292/89 [1991] ECR I-00745

70 Reg 6(7) I(EEA) Regs; sch 3 para 1 I(EEA)A Regs

71 Reg 92 UC Regs

72 Regs 6(1) and 14 I(EEA) Regs; Arts 7(1) and 14 EU Dir 2004/38

73 *Deborah Lawrie-Blum v Land Baden-Württemberg*, 66/86 [1986] ECR 02121

74 *Barry v London Borough of Southwark* [2008] EWCA Civ 1440

75 *Ingrid Rinner-Kühn v FWW Spezial-Gebäudereinigung GmbH & Co. KG*, 171/88 [1989] ECR 02743

76 R(IS) 12/98

77 *Hava Genc v Land Berlin*, C-14/09 [2010] ECR I-00931

78 *Udo Steymann v Staatssecretaris van Justitie*, 196/87 [1988] ECR 06159

79 CIS/1837/2006; CIS/868/2008

80 *I Bettray v Staatssecretaris van Justitie*, C-344/87 [1989] ECR 01621; *Hava Genc v Land Berlin*, C-14/09 [2010] ECR I-00931

81 CIS/1502/2007

82 *JA v SSWP (ESA)* [2012] UKUT 122 (AAC)

83 CIS/4237/2007

84 *BS v SSWP* [2009] UKUT 16 (AAC)

85 Art 7(3) EU Dir 2004/38; reg 6(2),(2A) and (5)-(7) I(EEA) Regs

86 Reg 5(4) A(IWR) Regs; reg 7A(4) I(EEA) Regs

87 Art 7(3)(b) and (c) EU Dir 2004/38; reg 6 I(EEA) Regs

88 Art 7(3)(c) EU Dir 2004/38

89 CH/3314/2005, para 11; *SSWP v MK* [2013] UKUT 0163 (AAC)

90 *SSWP v Elmi* [2011] EWCA Civ 1403

91 Art 7(3)(b) EU Dir 2004/38; reg 6(2)(b) I(EEA) Regs

92 Reg 6(7) I(EEA) Regs

93 Reg 6(2)(ba), (2A), (5) and (6) I(EEA) Regs

94 Art 7(3)(c) EU Dir 2004/38

95 Reg 92 UC Regs

96 *SSHD v FB* [2010] UKUT 447 (IAC)

97 CIS/3890/2005

98 *De Brito v SSHD* [2012] EWCA Civ 709; *Konodyba v RB of K&C* [2012] EWCA Civ 982; *Samin v SSHD* [2012] EWCA Civ 1468

99 CIS/4304/2007

100 CIS/3182/2005

101 *SSWP v EM* [2009] UKUT 146 (AAC)

102 CIS/4304/2007; *SSWP v IR* [2009] UKUT 11 (AAC)

103 CIS/1934/2006

104 *SSWP v MK* [2013] UKUT 0163 (AAC)

105 *SSWP v IR* [2009] UKUT 11 (AAC)

106 CIS/4237/2007

107 CIS/1042/2008

108 CIS/731/2007

109 *Jessy Saint-Prix v SSWP* [2012] UKSC 49; referred to CJEU as C-507/12

110 *Aldona Malgorzata Jany and Others v Staatssecretaris van Justitie, C-268/99* [2001] ECR I-08615
111 Reg 4(1)(b) I(EEA) Regs; R(IS) 6/00
112 *TG v SSWP* [2009] UKUT 58 (AAC)
113 *SSWP v JS (IS)* [2010] UKUT 240 (AAC)
114 CIS/1042/2008
115 Art 7(3) EU Dir 2004/38; reg 6(3) I(EEA) Regs
116 *Tilianu v SSWP* [2010] EWCA Civ 1397
117 Art 7(1) EU Dir 2004/38; regs 4(1)(c), 6(1) and 14(1) I(EEA) Regs
118 Art 8(4) EU Dir 2004/38
119 Reg 4(4) I(EEA) Regs
120 With effect from 2 June 2011
121 *SG v Tameside MBC (HB)* [2010] UKUT 243 (AAC)
122 *Pensionsversicherungsanstalt v Brey*, C-140/12 [2013] ECR, not yet reported
123 *Commission of the European Communities v Kingdom Belgium, C-408/03* [2006] ECR I-02647; *Zhu and Chen v SSHD*, C-200/02 [2004] ECR I-09925
124 *W(China) and Another v SSHD* [2006] EWCA Civ 1494
125 *SG v Tameside MBC (HB)* [2010] UKUT 243 (AAC); *VP v SSWP (JSA)* [2014] UKUT 0032 (AAC)
126 Art 7(1) EU Dir 2004/38; regs 4(1)(d), 6(1) and 14(1) I(EEA) Regs
127 Art 2(2) EU Dir 2004/38; reg 7(1) I(EEA) Regs
128 *Aissatou Diatta v Land Berlin, 267/83* [1985] ECR 00567
129 CIS/2100/2007which considers the findings of *Centre Public d'Aide Sociale de Courcelles v Lebon, 316/85* [1987] ECR 02811, *Zhu and Chen v SSHD*, C-200/02 [2004] ECR I-09925 and *Jia v Migrationsverket,* C-1/05 [2007] ECR I-00001
130 *Pedro v SSWP* [2009] EWCA Civ 1358; *Jia v Migrationsverket,* C-1/05 [2007] ECR I-00001; *SSHD v Rahman and others,* C-83/11 [2012] ECR, not yet reported
131 *Kerr v DSDNI* [2004] UKHL 23, paras 62-65
132 CPC/3588/2006; *SS v SSWP (ESA)* [2010] UKUT 8 (AAC)
133 Regs 7(3) and 8 I(EEA) Regs. The same groups are covered in Art 3 EU Dir 2004/38, but the term is not used.
134 *Blaise Baheten Metock and Others v Minister for Justice, Equality and Law Reform*, C-127/08 [2008] ECR I-06241
135 Reg 9(2) and (3) I(EEA) Regs

136 *Minister voor Vreemdelingenzaken en Integratie v Eind*, C-291/05 [2007] ECR I-10719
137 *AA v SSWP* [2009] UKUT 249 (AAC); *HG v SSWP (SPC)* [2011] UKUT 382 (AAC)
138 *McCarthy v SSHD,* C-434-09 [2011] ECR I-03375
139 Reg 10 I(EEA) Regs
140 Reg 14(3) I(EEA) Regs
141 Reg 10(8) I(EEA) Regs
142 Art 12 EU Dir 2004/38
143 Art 12 EU Dir 2004/38
144 Art 13 EU Dir 2004/38
145 Arts 12(2) and 13(1) EU Dir 2004/38
146 Reg 15A I(EEA) Regs
147 See also *London Borough of Harrow v Nimco Hassan Ibrahim and SSHD*, C-310/08 [2010] ECR I-01065; *Maria Teixeira v London Borough of Lambeth and SSHD,* C-480/08 [2010] ECR I-01107; *GBC Echternach and A Moritz v Minister van Onderwijs en Wetenschappen,* joined cases 389/87 and 390/87 [1989] ECR 00723; *Baumbast and R v SSHD,* C-413/99 [2002] ECR I-07091
148 See also *London Borough of Harrow v Nimco Hassan Ibrahim and SSHD*, C-310/08 [2010] ECR I-01065; *Maria Teixeira v London Borough of Lambeth and SSHD,* C-480/08 [2010] ECR I-01107; *GBC Echternach and A Moritz v Minister van Onderwijs en Wetenschappen,* joined cases 389/87 and 390/87 [1989] ECR 00723; *Baumbast and R v SSHD,* C-413/99 [2002] ECR I-07091
149 See also *Zhu and Chen v SSHD*, C-200/02 [2004] ECR I-09925
150 See also *Zambrano v ONEm*, C-34/09 [2011] ECR I-01177; *Dereci and Others v Bundesministerium für Inneres,* C-256/11 [2011] ECR I-11315
151 Reg 15A(7)-(9) I(EEA) Regs. See also *MA v DSD (JSA)* [2011] NICom 205
152 *R (HC) v SSWP* [2013] EWHC 3874 (Admin)
153 *Maria Teixeira v London Borough of Lambeth and SSHD,* C-480/08 [2010] ECR I-01107, para 74
154 *SSWP v JS (IS)* [2010] UKUT 347 (AAC)
155 *DJ v SSWP* [2013] UKUT 0113 (AAC)
156 *Maria Teixeira v London Borough of Lambeth and SSHD,* C-480/08 [2010] ECR I-01107, para 87; see also *Alarape and Tijani v SSHD,* C-529/11 [2013] ECR, not yet reported
157 Reg 15A(6)(a) I(EEA) Regs; CIS/3960/2007
158 *SSWP v IM (IS)* [2011] UKUT 231 AAC

12

Part 12: Immigration and residence rules for benefits and tax credits
Chapter 70: Coming from abroad: residence rules
Notes

159 *Shabani v SSHD* [2013] UKUT 00315 (IAC)
160 Joined cases of *Czop*, C-147/11 *and Punakova*, C-148/11 [2012] ECR, not yet reported
161 Art 16 EU Dir 2004/38; reg 15 I(EEA) Regs
162 Art 16(4) EU Dir 2004/38; reg 15(2) I(EEA) Regs
163 Art 16(3) EU Dir 2004/38; reg 3 I(EEA) Regs
164 Following *SSWP v Dias*, C-325/09 [2011] ECR I-06387
165 *Idezuna v SSHD* [2011] UKUT 474 (IAC); *Babajanov v SSHD* [2013] UKUT 00513 (IAC)
166 Reg 15(1) and (1A) I(EEA) Regs
167 Sch 4 para 6 I(EEA) Regs
168 *SSWP v Taous Lassal*, C-162/09 [2010] ECR I-09217; *SSWP v Dias*, C-325-09 [2011] ECR I-06387
169 Sch 4 para 6 I(EEA) Regs; *SSWP v Taous Lassal*, C-162/09 [2010] ECR I-09217; *SSWP v Dias*, C-325-09 [2011] ECR I-06387; *Oakafor and others v SSHD* [2011] EWCA Civ 499; *Alarape and Tijani v SSHD*, C-529/11 [2013] ECR not yet reported; *Bee and another v SSHD* [2013] UKUT 00083 (IAC)
170 *Oakafor and others v SSHD* [2011] EWCA Civ 499; *Alarape and Tijani v SSHD*, C-529/11 [2013] ECR not yet reported; *Bee and another v SSHD* [2013] UKUT 00083 (IAC)
171 *Ziolkowski* (C-425/10) *and Szeja* (C-425/10) *v Land Berlin* [2011] ECR , not yet reported
172 *Ziolkowski* (C-425/10) *and Szeja* (C-425/10) *v Land Berlin* [2011] ECR, not yet reported; Sch 4 para 6(3) I(EEA) Regs
173 Reg 14(2) I(EEA) Regs
174 Reg 15(1)(a) and (b) I(EEA) Regs
175 Regs 5 and 15 I(EEA) Regs; Art 17 EU Dir 2004/38
176 *PM (EEA – spouse - 'residing with')* Turkey [2011] UKUT 89 (IAC)
177 Regs 5(7), 6(2), 7A(3) and 7B(3) I(EEA) Regs
178 *SSWP v Dias*, C-325/09 [2011] ECR I006387; *EM and KN v SSWP* [2009] UKUT 44 (AAC)
179 Reg 16 I(EEA) Regs
180 Reg 17 I(EEA) Regs
181 Reg 18A I(EEA) Regs
182 Reg 18 I(EEA) Regs
183 Reg 31(2) and Sch 4 para 2 I(EEA) Regs

6. Rules for individual benefits and tax credits
184 **IS** s124(1) SSCBA 1992
  JSA s1(2)(i) JSA 1995
  ESA s1(3)(d) WRA 2007
  PC s1(2)(a) SPCA 2002
  UC s4(1)(c) WRA 2012
185 **IS** Regs 21-21AA IS Regs
  JSA Regs 85-85A JSA Regs
  ESA Regs 69-70 ESA Regs
  PC Reg 2 SPC Regs
  UC Reg 9 UC Regs
186 Reg 3 JSA(HR)A Regs
187 Reg 10 HB Regs; reg 10 HB(SPC) Regs
188 s130(1)(a) SSCBA 1992
189 Reg 7 HB Regs; reg 7 HB(SPC) Regs
190 Regs 3, 18(2), 22(3) and 36(3) UC Regs
191 **IS** Reg 16 IS Regs
  JSA Reg 78 JSA Regs
  ESA Reg 156 ESA Regs
  PC Reg 5 SPC Regs
  HB Reg 21 HB Regs; reg 21 HB(SPC) Regs
  UC Regs 3(3) and (6), 18(2), 22(3) and 36(3) UC Regs
192 CIS/508/1992; CIS/13805/1996
193 CIS/484/1993
194 **IS** Reg 16 IS Regs
  JSA Reg 78 JSA regs
  ESA Reg 156 ESA Regs
  PC Reg 5 SPC Regs
  HB Reg 21 HB Regs; reg 21 HB(SPC) Regs
  UC Reg 4(7) UC Regs
195 s113 SSCBA 1992; reg 4(1) and (2B) SSB(PA) Regs
196 para 073081 DMG, Example 2
197 Arts 5, 42 and 43 EU Reg 883/04
198 s146 SSCBA 1992
199 Reg 23 CB Regs
200 Regs 23, 30 and 31 CB Regs
201 **AA** Reg 2 SS(AA) Regs
  DLA Reg 2 SS(DLA) Regs
  PIP Reg 16 SS(PIP) Regs
  CA Reg 9 SS(ICA) Regs
202 Reg 1 SS(DLA,AA&CA)(A) Regs
203 **ESA** Reg 11 ESA Regs; reg 12 ESA Regs 2013
  AA Reg 2 SS(AA) Regs
  DLA Reg 2 SS(DLA) Regs
  CA Reg 9 SS(ICA) Regs
  IB Reg 16 SS(IB) Regs
  SDA Reg 3 SS(SDA) Regs
204 **ESA** Reg 11(4) ESA Regs; reg 12(4) ESA Regs 2013
  IB Reg 16(6) SS(IB) Regs
  SDA Reg 3(3) SS(SDA) Regs

12

205 **AA** Reg 2(3) SS(AA) Regs
DLA Reg 2(4) SS(DLA) Regs
PIP Reg 21 SS(PIP) Regs
206 **AA** Reg 2A SS(AA) Regs
DLA Reg 2A SS(DLA) Regs
PIP Reg 22 SS(PIP) Regs
CA Reg 9A SS(ICA) Regs
207 ss65(7), 70(4A) and 72(7B) SSCBA; s84 WRA 2012
208 Arts 23-32 EU Reg 883/04
209 *Stewart v SSWP*, C-503/09 [2011] ECR, I-06497
210 *SSWP v JG (IS)* [2013]UKUT 0298 (AAC); *SSWP v JG (RP)* [2013] UKUT 0300 (AAC)
211 ss1(3)(d)and 18(4)(a) WRA 2007
212 Reg 9 GA(Gen) Regs
213 *Stewart v SSWP*, C-503/09 [2011] ECR I-06497
214 s94(5) SSCBA 1992
215 Reg 14 SS(IIPD) Regs
216 Reg 10C(5) and (6) SSB(PA) Regs
217 Reg 2 SS(II)(AB) Regs 1975; SS(II)(MB) Regs
218 Regs 3, 4, 6 and 8 SS(II)(MB) Regs; regs 3 and 6 SS(II)(AB) Regs
219 Art 5 EU Reg 883/04
220 Art 38 EU Reg 883/04
221 s1(2)(i) JSA 1995
222 Art 64 EU Reg 883/04
223 Art 64(3) EU Reg 883/04
224 s113(1) SSCBA 1992
225 s113 SSCBA 1992; reg 4(1) SSB(PA) Regs
226 Art 52 EU Reg 883/04
227 *Stewart v SSWP*, C-503/09 [2011] ECR, I-06497; *SSWP v JG (RP)* [2013] UKUT 300 (AAC)
228 Reg 7(5) SFM&FE Regs
229 Reg 7(9) and (10) SFM&FE Regs
230 *John O'Flynn v Adjudication Officer*, C-237/94 [1996] ECR I-02617 (R(IS) 4/98)
231 s3(3) TCA 2002; reg 3(1) and (5) TC(R) Regs
232 s3(3) TCA 2002; reg 3(1) TC(R) Regs
233 Reg 3 TC(R) Regs

12

Chapter 71

Going abroad

This chapter covers:
1. Introduction (below)
2. UK law (p1569)
3. European Union co-ordination rules and reciprocal agreements (p1570)
4. Rules for individual benefits and tax credits (see p1571)

Key facts
- Most benefits and tax credits are affected if you, or your partner or child, go abroad.
- In certain circumstances, you can continue to receive benefit for a set number of weeks while you are away for a temporary period.
- You may be entitled to receive UK benefits for a longer (or indefinite) period if you go to another European Economic Area state.

1. Introduction

Most benefits and tax credits are affected if you, or your partner or child, go abroad. Some can always be paid abroad, some can only be paid in certain circumstances and for limited periods, and some have rules affecting the amount that can be paid if you are abroad.

Your entitlement abroad depends on:
- the benefit or tax credit you are claiming (see p1571);
- the reason why you are going abroad;
- whether your absence is temporary or permanent;
- the length of time you are going abroad for;
- the country you are going to;
- whether you are covered by the European Union (EU) co-ordination rules;
- whether you are covered by a reciprocal agreement.

Which rules apply

The **UK benefit and tax credit legislation** contains rules about how your absence affects your entitlement (see p1569).

The **EU co-ordination rules** can be more generous if you are going to, or have a family member living in, another European Economic Area (EEA) member state (see p1570).

Reciprocal agreements exist between the UK and some other countries and can assist in similar ways to the EU co-ordination rules (see p1517).

If you are covered by the EU co-ordination rules, these more generous provisions apply. If they do not apply, but you are covered by a reciprocal agreement, those provisions apply. If you are not covered by either, you must rely on UK law.

2. UK law

Ordinary residence

In order to receive some benefits and tax credits (listed on p1519), you must be 'ordinarily resident' in Great Britain (see p1519). If, by going abroad, you cease to be ordinarily resident, your entitlement also ceases. However, if your absence abroad is temporary and you intend to return to the UK, your ordinary residence is not usually affected.[1] In pratice, it is very rare that ceasing to be ordinarily resident is the reason why your entitlement ends when you go abroad. It is more likely that your entitlement ends simply because you are absent (see below). If you receive a decision that your entitlement to a benefit or tax credit has ended because you have ceased to be ordinarily resident, ask for the decision to be looked at again and seek specialist advice.

Presence and absence

Most benefits require you to be **present** in Great Britain (or, for tax credits, the UK). There are rules that allow you to be treated as present and therefore still entitled to the benefit or tax credit in specified circumstances during a temporary absence. Some benefits also have a rule that disqualifies you from entitlement if you are **absent** from Great Britain. There are specified exemptions to this rule for each benefit.

'Presence' means being physically present in Great Britain and 'absence' means not physically present in Great Britain. If the DWP, HM Revenue and Customs or a local authority wants to disqualify you from benefit because you were absent from Great Britain, it must show you were absent throughout that day. This means that, on the day you leave Great Britain and the day you arrive in Great Britain, you count as present.

Temporary absence

In specified circumstances, you can be treated as present, and therefore entitled to benefit, during a temporary absence.

Part 12: Immigration and residence rules for benefits and tax credits
Chapter 71: Going abroad
3. European Union co-ordination rules and reciprocal agreements

For tax credits, child benefit (for your, not the child's absence), attendance allowance, disability living allowance and personal independence payment, you are defined as temporarily absent from the UK if, at the beginning of the period of absence, you are unlikely to be absent for more than 52 weeks.[2]

For all other benefits, temporary absence is not defined and you must demonstrate that your absence will be temporary.[3] Provide full details of why you are going abroad, how long you intend to be away, and what you intend to do while abroad. **Note:** although your intentions are relevant, they are not decisive.[4] Remember that the nature of an absence can change over time. If you are temporarily absent at the beginning of a period, it does not mean that it will remain temporary. If your circumstances change while you are abroad (eg, you go abroad for one reason and decide to stay abroad for a different purpose), your absence may no longer be regarded as temporary.[5] There is no set period for a temporary absence. However, as a general rule, absences of more than 12 months are not temporary unless there are exceptional circumstances.[6] If the purpose of the trip abroad is obviously temporary (eg, for a holiday, to visit friends or relatives or for a particular course of medical treatment) and you buy a return ticket, the DWP should view it as temporary.

3. European Union co-ordination rules and reciprocal agreements

European Union co-ordination rules

If you are a European Economic Area (EEA) national (see p1590) (including a British citizen) or a family member of an EEA national and you are going to another EEA state, you may benefit from the European Union (EU) co-ordination rules (see p1591). These can help you to be paid your benefits or tax credits when you go abroad for longer than would be the case under UK law. They can also enable you to be paid benefit for a family member living in another EEA state. See p1571 for information on individual benefits and tax credits and see Chapter 72 for further information on the co-ordination rules.

Reciprocal agreements

The UK has agreements with several EEA and non-EEA countries. For a list of these and further information, see p1517.

Chapter 71

Going abroad

4. Rules for individual benefits and tax credits

Bereavement benefits

In general, bereavement benefits are payable while you are abroad (but see bereavement payment below). However, your benefit is not uprated each year if you have ceased to be ordinarily resident in Great Britain on the day before the annual uprating takes place,[7] unless you have gone to another European Economic Area (EEA) state and you are covered by the European Union (EU) co-ordination rules (see p1592) or can rely on a reciprocal agreement.

If you are absent from Great Britain when you claim a bereavement payment, you are only entitled in limited circumstances. See p1553 for further details.

European Union co-ordination rules

If the EU co-ordination rules apply to you (see p1594) and you go to stay or live in another EEA state, you can be paid your bereavement allowance and widowed parent's allowance without any time limit. The amounts are uprated each year. If your late spouse/civil partner died in another EEA state, s/he can be treated as having died in the UK for bereavement payment purposes if the UK is your 'competent state' (see p1596).[8]

See Chapter 72 for more information.

Carer's allowance

Provided you satisfy the residence condition (see p1572), you are treated as present and can continue to receive carer's allowance (CA) during an absence from Great Britain if:[9]

- the absence is, and was when it began, for a temporary purpose and does not exceed four weeks. You must be accompanied by the disabled person for whom you are caring, unless you qualify for CA during a break from caring (see p540 for the rules on this); or
- the absence is temporary and for the specific purpose of caring for the disabled person who is also absent from Great Britain and who continues to receive attendance allowance (AA), disability living allowance (DLA) care component, the highest or middle rate of the personal independence payment (PIP) daily living component, armed forces independence payment or constant attendance allowance; or
- you are abroad as an airwoman/man, mariner or continental shelf worker; or
- you are abroad as a serving member of the armed forces, or you are living with your spouse, civil partner, son, daughter, stepson, stepdaughter, father, father-in-law, stepfather, mother, mother-in-law or stepmother who is a serving member of the armed forces.

Part 12: Immigration and residence rules for benefits and tax credits
Chapter 71: Going abroad
4. Rules for individual benefits and tax credits

You must satisfy the habitual residence test unless you were entitled to CA on 7 April 2013, in which case you must be ordinarily resident until your award is terminated, revised or superseded.[10] If you must satisfy the habitual residence test, you are treated as habitually resident (in addition to being treated as present) if you are in the last group above.

You can continue to be paid an increase in your CA for your spouse/civil partner or dependent adult while s/he is abroad, provided you continue to be entitled to CA and reside with her/him. **Note:** you can be treated as residing together during a temporary absence from each other.[11]

European Union co-ordination rules

The rules for getting your CA paid in another EEA state under the co-ordination rules are the same as for AA, DLA care component and PIP daily living component (see p1573).

If the EU co-ordination rules apply to you (see p1592) and you remain in the UK, you may be able to continue to be paid an addition for an adult or child who goes to stay or live in another EEA state. See p1599 for more information.

Child benefit

You and your child can be treated as present in Great Britain during a temporary absence (see p1569).

Provided you are ordinarily resident, you continue to be entitled to child benefit for:[12]
- the first eight weeks; or
- the first 12 weeks of any period of absence, or any extension to that period, which is in connection with:
  - the treatment of an illness or disability of you, your partner, a child for whom you are responsible, or another relative of you or your partner; or
  - the death of your partner, a child or qualifying young person for whom you or your partner are responsible, or another relative of you or your partner.

Relative

'**Relative**' means brother, sister, parent, grandparent, great-grandparent, child, grandchild or great-grandchild.[13]

Your child is treated as present during a temporary absence for:[14]
- the first 12 weeks; or
- any period during which s/he is absent for the specific purpose of being treated for an illness or disability which began before her/his absence began; or
- any period when s/he is in Northern Ireland; or
- any period during which s/he is absent because s/he is:

- receiving full-time education at a school or college in another EEA member state or in Switzerland; *or*
- engaged in an educational exchange or visit made with the written approval of the school or college which s/he normally attends; *or*
- a child who normally lives with a Crown servant posted overseas who is either in the same country as her/him or is absent from that country for one of the reasons in the above two bullet points.[15]

If a child is born outside the UK during the eight- or 12-week period in which you could be treated as present in Great Britain, s/he is treated as being in the UK for up to 12 weeks from the start of your absence.[16]

While you and your child are present, or treated as present, you can continue to receive child benefit that was already in payment and can also make a fresh claim during your, or her/his, absence.

European Union co-ordination rules

Child benefit is classed as a 'family benefit' under the EU co-ordination rules (see p1594). If these rules apply to you (see p1592):

- you can be paid child benefit for a child resident in another EEA country. S/he does not have to be in education; *and/or*
- you can be paid child benefit if you are an EEA national and you go to stay or live in another EEA country. Your benefit is uprated in the normal way.

See p1599 for more information.

Disability benefits

You can be treated as present in Great Britain, and therefore continue to be entitled to AA, DLA or PIP, during a temporary absence (see p1569 for how this is defined) abroad:[17]

- for the first 13 weeks;
- for the first 26 weeks if the absence is solely in connection with medical treatment for your illness or disability that began before you left Great Britain;
- if you are an airwoman/man, mariner or continental shelf worker;
- while you are a serving member of the armed forces, or you are living with your spouse, civil partner, son, daughter, stepson, stepdaughter, father, father-in-law, stepfather, mother, mother-in-law or stepmother who is a serving member of the armed forces.

You must be ordinarily resident (see p1519) if you were entitled to AA or DLA on 7 April 2013 until either that award is terminated, revised or superseded. In all other cases, you must be habitually resident (see p1521). You are treated as habitually resident if you are in the group in the last bullet point above.

Part 12: Immigration and residence rules for benefits and tax credits
Chapter 71: Going abroad
4. Rules for individual benefits and tax credits

If you were already abroad on 8 April 2013 but continued to be entitled to AA or DLA because your absence is temporary and for the specific purpose of being treated for an illness or disability that began before you left Great Britain, and the DWP has agreed you should be treated as present, you continue to be treated as present in Great Britain until either you return or your award is revised or superseded.[18]

European Union co-ordination rules

If you move to another EEA member state, you can continue to be paid (or make a new claim for) AA, PIP, daily living component or DLA care component (and carer's allowance – CA) without having to satisfy the presence, past presence and habitual residence tests (see p1555) if:[19]

- you are habitually resident in another EEA state or Switzerland; *and*
- you are covered by the co-ordination rules (see p1592); *and*
- you can demonstrate a genuine and sufficient link to the UK social security system.

You can continue to be paid for as long as the UK continues to be your 'competent state' (see p1596).[20]

When demonstrating that you have 'genuine and sufficient link to the UK social security system', relvant factors include whether you have worked in the UK, whether you have spent a significant part of your life in the UK, whether you are receiving a UK contributory benefit and whether you are dependent on a family member who has worked in the UK and/or who receives a UK contributory benefit.[21]

The above provision has only been in force since April 2013. Before 1 June 1992, you could be paid your benefit in another EEA state. If you had an award of AA, DLA care component or CA on or after 8 March 2001 and a decision was made to stop your entitlement because you went to another EEA state, the DWP can restore your entitlement and pay arrears from 18 October 2007 (or the date your payment was stopped, if this is later).[22] You can only get arrears before 18 October 2007 in very limited circumstances.[23] See CPAG's *Benefits for Migrants Handbook* for more details.

DLA mobility component is listed as, and PIP mobility component is treated by the DWP as, a special non-contributory benefit and is therefore not 'exportable'.[24] You can only be paid these in the state where you are resident.[25]

Employment and support allowance

You cannot normally get employment and support allowance (ESA) if you are not in Great Britain.[26] However, provided you meet the other conditions of entitlement, if you were entitled to ESA immediately before leaving Great Britain and are temporarily absent, you can continue to be entitled:[27]

- **indefinitely** if:

- your absence is for NHS treatment at a hospital or other institution outside Great Britain; *or*
- you are living with your spouse, civil partner, son, daughter, stepson, stepdaughter, father, father-in-law, stepfather, mother, mother-in-law or stepmother who is a serving member of the armed forces;
• for the first **four weeks** if your absence is unlikely to exceed 52 weeks;
• for the first **26 weeks** if your absence is unlikely to exceed 52 weeks and is solely in connection with arrangements made to treat:
  - your disease or disablement which is directly related to your limited capability for work which began before you left Great Britain; *or*
  - the disease or disablement of a dependent child who you are accompanying.

The treatment must be carried out by, or under the supervision of, a person qualified to provide medical treatment, physiotherapy or similar treatment.

If your partner is abroad

If you are the claimant and you stay in Great Britain, your income-related ESA includes an amount for your partner for:[28]
• the first four weeks; *or*
• the first 26 weeks if s/he is accompanying a child abroad for treatment in line with the 26-week rule above.

If both you and your partner are abroad, your income-related ESA includes an amount for your partner for the first 26 weeks if both of you are accompanying a child abroad for treatment in line with the 26-week rule above.[29]

After this four- or 26-week period, your benefit is reduced because your applicable amount is calculated as if you have no partner. However, your partner is still treated as part of your household and therefore her/his work, income and capital affects your income-related ESA entitlement unless you are no longer treated as a couple (see p208).[30]

European Union co-ordination rules

If the co-ordination rules apply to you (see p1592) and the UK is your 'competent state' (see p1596), you can generally continue to be paid contributory ESA if you go to live in another EEA state.

If the UK continues to pay your contributory ESA while you are resident in another EEA state, the DWP continues to assess your limited capability for work and work-related activity. However, any checks and medicals take place in the state in which you live and the reports are sent to the DWP.[31]

Income-related ESA is listed as a 'special non-contributory benefit' (see p1595) and is therefore not exportable.

12

Part 12: Immigration and residence rules for benefits and tax credits
Chapter 71: Going abroad
4. Rules for individual benefits and tax credits

Guardian's allowance

Entitlement to guardian's allowance depends on entitlement to child benefit, so you can be paid guardian's allowance abroad for the same period as child benefit (see p1572).

However, your guardian's allowance is not uprated each year if you have ceased to be ordinarily resident in Great Britain on the day before the annual uprating takes place,[32] unless you have gone to another EEA state and you are covered by the EU co-ordination rules (see below) or you can rely on a reciprocal agreement.

European Union co-ordination rules

Guardian's allowance is classed as a 'family benefit' under the EU co-ordination rules (see p1594). If these rules apply to you (see p1592):
- you may be able to be paid guardian's allowance for a child resident in another EEA country; *and/or*
- you may be able to be paid guardian's allowance if you are an EEA national and you go to stay or live in another EEA country. Your benefit is uprated in the normal way.

See p1599 for more details.

Housing benefit

There is no requirement to be present in Great Britain to be entitled to housing benefit (HB). However, you must be liable to make payments in respect of a dwelling in Great Britain which you occupy as your home.[33] There are rules that treat you as occupying your home,[34] including during a temporary absence. If you are going abroad, these rules determine whether you can be entitled to HB while you are away (see p103).

If your partner or child is abroad

Whether or not you have amounts included in your HB for your partner or child who is abroad depends on whether s/he is treated as part of your household (see p208 and p214).

Incapacity benefit, severe disablement allowance and maternity allowance

If you are temporarily absent from Great Britain, you can continue to be paid incapacity benefit (IB), severe disablement allowance (SDA) and maternity allowance (MA) if:[35]
- you are receiving AA, DLA, PIP or armed forces independence payment (see p1573); *or*

- the DWP agrees. You can then receive the benefit for the first 26 weeks of your temporary absence; *or*
- you are the spouse, civil partner, son, stepson, daughter, stepdaughter, father, stepfather, father-in-law, mother, stepmother, or mother-in-law of a serving member of the armed forces and you are abroad only because you are living with her/him.

In addition:

- when you left Great Britain you must have been continuously incapable of work for six months and have been continuously incapable since your departure; *or*
- your absence from Great Britain must be for the specific purpose of being treated for an incapacity which began before you left Great Britain; *or*
- for IB only, the incapacity for work is the result of a personal injury caused by an accident at work (see p668) and your absence from Great Britain is for the specific purpose of receiving treatment for it.

If you are due to have a medical examination, this can be arranged abroad.

Note: IB and SDA have now been replaced by ESA. If you lose entitlement to IB or SDA by going abroad, you will not be entitled to contributory ESA on your return if you do not satisfy the contribution conditions at that time.

You can continue to be paid an increase for your spouse/civil partner or dependent adult in your IB or SDA while s/he is abroad if you are entitled to IB/SDA and you are residing with her/him. **Note:** you can be treated as residing together during a temporary absence from each other.[36]

European Union co-ordination rules

Long-term IB and SDA are classed as 'invalidity benefits' under the EU co-ordination rules (see p1594). If these rules apply to you (see p1592) and the UK is your 'competent state' (see p1596), you can export your IB and SDA if you go to live in another EEA state. Provided you continue to satisfy the rules of entitlement, benefit is paid without any time limit and at the same rate as if you were still in the UK, including your annual uprating.

The state from which you claim benefit is the one that determines your degree of invalidity, but any checks and medicals take place in the state in which you are living. The reports are then sent to the paying state.[37]

If the EU co-ordination rules apply to you and you remain in the UK, you may be able to continue to be paid an increase for an adult or child if s/he goes to stay or live in another EEA state (see p1599).

MA is classed as a 'maternity benefit' under the EU co-ordination rules (see p1594). If these rules apply to you (see p1592) and the UK is your competent state (see p1596), you can be paid MA if you go to stay or live in another EEA country.[38] See p1598 for more details.

12

Part 12: Immigration and residence rules for benefits and tax credits
Chapter 71: Going abroad
4. Rules for individual benefits and tax credits

Income support

You cannot normally get income support (IS) if you are not in Great Britain.[39] However, IS can be paid when you are temporarily absent from Great Britain, provided you meet the other conditions of entitlement:[40]

- **indefinitely** if your absence is for NHS treatment at a hospital or other institution outside Great Britain;
- during the first **four weeks** of your absence if it is unlikely to exceed 52 weeks and either:
  - you are in Northern Ireland; *or*
  - you and your partner are both abroad and s/he satisfies the conditions for one of the pensioner premiums, the disability premium or the severe disability premium (see p226); *or*
  - you are claiming IS on the grounds of being incapable of work and are abroad for the sole purpose of receiving treatment for that incapacity. The treatment must be carried out by, or under the supervision of, a person qualified to provide medical treatment, physiotherapy or similar treatment; *or*
  - you are incapable of work; *and*
    - you have been continuously incapable for the previous 28 weeks and you are terminally ill or receiving the highest rate of DLA care component, the enhanced rate of the daily living component of PIP or armed forces idependence payment; *or*
    - you have been continuously incapable for 364 days; *or*
  - you fall within one of the groups of people who can claim IS (see p26) *other than* if you are:
    - a person in 'relevant education'; *or*
    - involved in a trade dispute, or have returned to work for 15 days or less following the dispute; *or*
    - entitled to statutory sick pay; *or*
    - appealing a decision that you are not incapable of work; *or*
    - incapable of work and not covered by one of the groups of people incapable of work listed above;
- during the first **eight weeks** of your absence if it is unlikely to exceed 52 weeks and is solely in connection with arrangements made for the treatment of a disease or disablement of a child or qualifying young person. The treatment must be carried out by, or under the supervision of, a person qualified to provide medical treatment, physiotherapy or similar treatment and the child or young person must be a member of your family (see p210).

If your partner is abroad

If you are the IS claimant and you stay in Great Britain, your IS applicable amount includes an amount for your partner who is abroad for:[41]

- the first four weeks; *or*
- the first eight weeks if s/he meets the conditions of the eight-week rule above.

If both you and your partner are abroad, your IS includes amounts for your partner for the first eight weeks if both you and your partner meet the conditions of the eight-week rule above.[42]

After this four- or eight-week period, your benefit is reduced because your applicable amount is calculated as if you have no partner. However, your partner is still treated as part of your household and therefore her/his work, income and capital affect your IS entitlement unless you are no longer treated as a couple (see p208).[43]

If your child is abroad

If you were getting an amount in your IS for your child before s/he went abroad, you can continue to be paid for her/him for:[44]

- the first four weeks; *or*
- the first eight weeks if your child meets the conditions of the eight-week rule above.

European Union co-ordination rules

IS is not classified as a social security benefit under the EU co-ordination rules (see p1594). This means that the EU co-ordination rules cannot assist you and, if you go to another EEA state, you can only be paid under the UK rules above.

Industrial injuries benefits

Disablement benefit and retirement allowance are not affected if you go abroad.[45]

Constant attendance allowance and exceptionally severe disablement allowance are payable for the first six months of a temporary absence, or a longer period that the DWP may allow.[46]

Reduced earnings allowance (REA) can be paid while you are temporarily absent abroad for the first three months, or longer if the DWP allows, if:[47]

- your absence from Great Britain is *not* in connection with employment, trade or business; *and*
- your claim was made before you left Great Britain; *and*
- you were entitled to REA before going abroad.

Note: REA has now been abolished. If you break your claim, you may no longer be eligible for benefit.

Part 12: Immigration and residence rules for benefits and tax credits
Chapter 71: Going abroad
4. Rules for individual benefits and tax credits

European Union co-ordination rules

Industrial injuries benefits, with the exception of retirement allowance, are classed as 'benefits for accidents at work and occupational diseases' under the EU co-ordination rules (see p1594) and are therefore fully 'exportable'. If these rules apply to you (see p1592) and you go to stay or live in another EEA state, you can be paid without any time limit and they are fully uprated each year. See p1598 for more details.

Jobseeker's allowance

You cannot normally get jobseeker's allowance (JSA) if you are not in Great Britain.[48] However, provided you meet the other conditions of entitlement, JSA can be paid when you are temporarily absent from Great Britain:[49]

- **indefinitely** if you are entitled to JSA immediately before leaving Great Britain and your absence is for NHS treatment at a hospital or other institution outside Great Britain;
- for up to **four weeks** if you are entitled to JSA immediately before leaving Great Britain and:
  - your absence is unlikely to exceed 52 weeks, you continue to satisfy the conditions of entitlement and you are in Northern Ireland; *or*
  - (except if you come under the UC system – see p19) the absence is unlikely to exceed 52 weeks, you continue to satisfy the conditions of entitlement and your partner satisfies the conditions for one of the pensioner premiums, the disability premium or the severe disability premium (see p226); *or*
  - (except if you come under the UC system – see p19) you are in receipt of a training allowance in the circumstances set out on p1024;[50]
- for up to **eight weeks** if you are entitled to JSA immediately before leaving Great Britain and your absence is unlikely to exceed 52 weeks and is solely in connection with arrangements made for the treatment of a disease or disablement of a child or qualifying young person. The treatment must be carried out by, or under the supervision of, a person qualified to provide medical treatment, physiotherapy or similar treatment and the child or young person must be a member of your family (see p210);
- for an absence of up to **seven days** if you are attending a job interview and you notified the employment officer (EO) before you left (in writing if required). On your return, you must satisfy the EO that you attended the interview as stated;
- for an absence of up to **15 days** for the purpose of training as a member of the territorial or reserve forces.

You can be treated as available for work and actively seeking work or, if you come under the UC system (see p19), you are exempt from the work search requirement and are treated as 'able and willing immediately to take up work' during certain temporary absences abroad. These are similar to, but more limited than, those listed above (see p1027, p1041 and p1079).[51]

Joint-claim jobseeker's allowance if your partner is abroad

If you are a joint-claim couple (see p46) and your partner is temporarily absent from Great Britain **on the date you make your claim**, you are paid as a couple for:[52]

- an absence of up to **seven days** if your partner is attending a job interview;
- up to **four weeks** if your partner is:
  - in Northern Ireland and the absence is unlikely to exceed 52 weeks; *or*
  - in receipt of a training allowance in the circumstances set out on p1024.

After this period, your JSA is reduced because your applicable amount is calculated as if you have no partner.[53] However, your partner is still treated as part of your household, and therefore her/his work, income and capital affect your income-based JSA entitlement unless you are no longer treated as a couple (see p208).[54]

If you are a joint-claim couple and your partner goes abroad **after you claimed JSA**, you continue to be paid as a joint-claim couple:[55]

- for up to **four weeks** if you are entitled to joint-claim JSA immediately before s/he leaves Great Britain and either:
  - her/his absence is unlikely to exceed 52 weeks, you continue to satisfy the conditions of entitlement, and your partner satisfies the conditions for one of the pensioner premiums, the disability premium or the severe disability premium (see p226); *or*
  - her/his absence is unlikely to exceed 52 weeks, you both continue to satisfy the conditions of entitlement, and your partner is in Northern Ireland; *or*
  - your partner is in receipt of a training allowance in the circumstances set out on p1024;[56]
- for an absence of up to **seven days** if your partner is attending a job interview and has notified the EO before leaving (in writing if required). On her/his return, s/he must satisfy the EO that s/he attended the interview as stated.

Income-based jobseeker's allowance if your partner is abroad

If you are the income-based JSA claimant and you stay in Great Britain, your applicable amount includes an amount for your partner while s/he is abroad for:[57]

- the first **four weeks** of a temporary absence; *or*
- the first **eight weeks** if your partner meets the conditions of the eight-week rule on p1580.

If both you and your partner are abroad, your applicable amount includes an amount for your partner for the first eight weeks if both you and your partner meet the conditions of the eight-week rule on p1580.[58]

Part 12: Immigration and residence rules for benefits and tax credits
Chapter 71: Going abroad
4. Rules for individual benefits and tax credits

After this four- or eight-week period, your benefit is reduced because your applicable amount is calculated as if you have no partner. However, your partner is still treated as part of your household, and therefore her/his work, income and capital affect your income-based JSA entitlement unless you are no longer treated as a couple (see p208).[59]

Income-based jobseeker's allowance if your child is abroad

If you were getting JSA for your child before s/he went abroad, you can continue to be paid for her/him for:[60]
* the **first four weeks**; *or*
* the **first eight weeks** if your child meets the conditions of the eight-week rule on p1580.

European Union co-ordination rules

Contribution-based JSA is classed as an 'unemployment benefit' under the EU co-ordination rules (see p1594). If these rules apply to you (see p1592) and the UK is your 'competent state' (see p1596), you can be paid contribution-based JSA for up to three months if:[61]
* you satisfied the conditions for contribution-based JSA for at least four weeks before you left the UK unless authorised by the DWP to go abroad before you have claimed for four weeks; *and*
* you register as unemployed in the EEA state you go to within seven days and comply with its procedures.

Income-based JSA is classed as a 'special non-contributory benefit' under the EU co-ordination rules (see p1595) and therefore cannot be 'exported'. This means that the EU co-ordination rules cannot assist you. You can only be paid income-based JSA abroad under the UK rules on p1580.

Pension credit

You cannot normally get pension credit (PC) if you are not in Great Britain.[62] However, provided you meet the other conditions of entitlement, PC can be paid when you are temporarily absent from Great Britain:[63]
* **indefinitely** if your absence is for NHS treatment at a hospital or other institution outside Great Britain; *or*
* **for up to 13 weeks** if your absence is unlikely to exceed 52 weeks.

If your partner is abroad

If you are entitled to PC and your partner is abroad, your PC only includes an amount for her/him if s/he is covered by the situations above. After this, s/he is not treated as part of your household and you are paid as a single person.[64] Your partner can also cease to be treated as part of your household in the circumstances on p208.[65]

European Union co-ordination rules

PC is classed as a 'special non-contributory benefit' under the EU co-ordination rules (see p1595) and therefore cannot be 'exported'. This means that the EU co-ordination rules cannot assist you. You can only be paid PC abroad under the UK rules on p1582.

Retirement pension

With the exception of Category D retirement pension, all retirement pensions are payable without time limit while you are abroad.[66] However, your benefit is not uprated each year if you have ceased to be ordinarily resident on the day before the annual uprating takes place,[67] unless you have gone to another EEA state and you are covered by the EU co-ordination rules (see below), or you can rely on a reciprocal agreement.

For the residence requirements for Category D retirement pension, see p1560.

Note: you cannot 'de-retire' if you are not ordinarily resident in Great Britain (see p1519).[68]

You can continue to be paid an adult dependant increase in your Category A retirement pension for your spouse/civil partner or dependent adult while s/he is abroad if:[69]

* you are entitled to the pension; *and*
* you are residing with her/him. You can be treated as residing together during a temporary absence from each other.[70]

European Union co-ordination rules

Retirement pensions are classed as 'old age benefits' under the EU co-ordination rules (see p1594). If these rules apply to you (see p1592) and the UK is your 'competent state' (see p1596), you can 'export' your retirement pension if you go to live in another EEA state. It is paid without time limit and at the same rate as if you were still in the UK, including your annual uprating.

If the EU co-ordination rules apply and you remain in the UK, you may be able to continue to be paid an increase for an adult or child if s/he goes to stay or live in another EEA state. See p1599 for more details.

Statutory maternity, paternity, adoption and sick pay

There are no presence or residence rules for statutory maternity pay (SMP), statutory paternity pay (SPP), statutory adoption pay (SAP) or statutory sick pay (SSP). You remain entitled to these benefits if you go abroad, provided you meet the normal rules of entitlement, including being an employee (see Chapters 38 and 39).[71]

Part 12: Immigration and residence rules for benefits and tax credits
Chapter 71: Going abroad
4. Rules for individual benefits and tax credits

Even while employed abroad, you count as an employee in certain circumstances, including if:[72]

- your employer is required to pay secondary Class 1 NI contributions for you; *or*
- you are a continental shelf worker or, in certain circumstances, an airwoman/man or mariner; *or*
- you are employed in another EEA state and, had you been employed in Great Britain, you would have been considered an employee, and the UK is the competent state under the EU co-ordination rules (see p1596).

Your employer is not required to pay you SSP, SMP, SPP or SAP if:[73]

- your employer is not required by law to pay employer's Class 1 NI contributions (even if those contributions are in fact made) because, at the time they become payable, your employer:
  – is not resident or present in Great Britain; *or*
  – has (or is treated as having) a place of business in Great Britain; *or*
- because of an international treaty or convention your employer is exempt from the Social Security Acts or those Acts are not enforceable against your employer.

European Union co-ordination rules

It is arguable that SSP is a sickness benefit and SPP and SMP are maternity/paternity benefits under the co-ordination rules (see p1594). However, given the generosity of the above UK rules, it is unlikely that you will need to rely on the EU co-ordination rules.

Universal credit

You cannot normally be paid UC if you (and your partner if it is a joint claim) are not in Great Britain.[74] However, provided you meet the other conditions of entitlement, UC can be paid when you are temporarily absent from Great Britain for:[75]

- **a month** if your absence is not expected to exceed and does not exceed one month; *or*
- **two months** if your absence is in connection with the death of your partner or child, or a close relative of yours or of your partner or child, and it would be unreasonable for you to return to Great Britain within the first month; *or*
- **six months** if your absence is not expected to exceed and does not exceed six months and you are a mariner or continental shelf work; *or*
- **six months** if your absence is not expected to exceed and does not exceed six months and is solely in connection with the medically approved care, convalesence or treatment of you, your partner or child.

You are automatically exempt from the work search requirement and also treated as 'able and willing immediately to take up work' during the period that you are temporarily absent and in the last group listed above (see p1079).[76]

If your partner is abroad

If you have a joint claim for UC and you both go abroad, this does not affect your entitlement during the period when one of the situations listed on p1584 applies to *both* of you. After this time, if you both remain abroad your entitlement ends.

If you stay in Great Britain while your partner is abroad, her/his absence does not affect your entitlement during the one-, two- or six-month period if one of the circumstances listed above applies to her/him. After this time, you cease to be entitled as joint claimants. If your partner has been, or is expected to be, apart from you for six months, you stop being treated as a couple and you may then be entitled as a single person.[77] If you have been apart for less than six months, you must claim as a single person. However, although your award is then based on the maximum amount for a single person, your partner's income and capital are taken into account until you have been apart (or expect to be apart) for six months (as you then cease to be treated as a couple).[78]

If your child is abroad

If your child is abroad, you cease to be entitled for her/him if her/his absence abroad is, or is expected to be, longer than the one-, two- or six-month period allowed in the circumstances set out above (the circumstances must apply to your child).[79]

European Union co-ordination rules

The DWP considers that UC is not a social security benefit under the EU co-ordination rules (see p1594). This means that the EU co-ordination rules cannot assist you and, if you go to another EEA state, you can only be paid under the UK rules above.

Tax credits

Provided you are ordinarily resident (see p1569), you can be treated as present and, therefore, entitled to child tax credit (CTC) and working tax credit (WTC) during a 'temporary absence' (see p1569) for:[80]
- the first **eight weeks**; *or*
- the first **12 weeks** of any period of absence, or any extension to that period of absence, which is in connection with:
  - the treatment of an illness or disability of you, your partner, a child for whom you are responsible, or another relative of either you or your partner; *or*

Part 12: Immigration and residence rules for benefits and tax credits
Chapter 71: Going abroad
4. Rules for individual benefits and tax credits

- the death of your partner, a child or qualifying young person for whom you or your partner are responsible, or another relative (see below) of yours or your partner.

Relative

'**Relative**' means brother, sister, parent, grandparent, grandchild or great-grandparent or child.[81]

You are also treated as present if you are:[82]
- a Crown servant posted overseas and:
  - you are, or immediately before your posting abroad you were, ordinarily resident in the UK; *or*
  - immediately before your posting you were in the UK in connection with that posting; *or*
- the partner of a Crown servant posted overseas and in the same country as her/him or temporarily absent from that country under the same exceptions that enable tax credits to continue during a temporary absence from Great Britain.

While you are treated as present in any of the ways above, you can continue to receive any tax credits that are already in payment and can make a fresh or renewal claim during your absence.

If you (or your partner if you are making a joint claim) spend longer abroad than the permitted periods, you cease to satisfy the presence condition and therefore your tax credit entitlement ends. If you do not notify this to HM Revenue and Customs within one month (see p1450), you may be overpaid (see Chapter 66) and could be subject to a penalty (see Chapter 67).

See p1562 for considerations if you are making a joint claim as a couple.

European Union co-ordination rules

CTC is classed as a 'family benefit' under the EU co-ordination rules (see p1594). If these rules apply to you (see p1592), you can be paid CTC:
- for a child resident in another EEA country; *and/or*
- if you are an EEA national and you go to stay or live in another EEA country.

See p1599 for more details.

Chapter 71

Going abroad

Notes

2. UK law

1 *R v Barnet LBC ex parte Shah* [1983] 2 AC 309, HL, Lord Scarman at p342D
2 **CB** Reg 24(2) CB Regs
   AA Reg 2(3C) SS(AA) Regs
   DLA Reg 2(3C) SS(DLA) Regs
   PIP Reg 17(2) SS(PIP) Regs
   TC Reg 4(2) TC(R) Regs
3 *Chief Adjudication Officer v Ahmed and others*, 16 March 1994, CA, the *Guardian*, 15 April 1994, reported as R(S)1/96
4 *Chief Adjudication Officer v Ahmed and others*, 16 March 1994, CA, the *Guardian*, 15 April 1994, reported as R(S)1/96
5 R(S) 1/85
6 R(U) 16/62

4. Rules for individual benefits and tax credits

7 Reg 5 SSB(PA) Regs
8 Arts 5, 42 and 43 EU Reg 883/04
9 Reg 9(2) and (3) SS(ICA) Regs
10 Reg 1(2), (3) and (4) SS(DLA,AA&CA)(A) Regs
11 Reg 13 SSB(PA) Regs; Sch 2 para 7 SSB(Dep) Regs; reg 2(4) SSB(PRT)Regs
12 Reg 24 CB Regs
13 Reg 24(1) CB Regs
14 Reg 21 CB Regs
15 Reg 32 CB Regs
16 Reg 21(2) CB Regs
17 **AA** Reg 2(2), (3B) and (3C) SS(AA) Regs
   DLA Reg 2(2), (3B) and (3C) SS(DLA) Regs
   PIP Regs 17-20 SS(PIP) Regs
18 Reg 5 SS(DLA,AA&CA)(A) Regs
19 **AA** Reg 2B SS(AA) Regs
   DLA Reg 2B SS(DLA) Regs
   CA Reg 9B SS(ICA) Regs
   PIP Reg 23 SS(PIP) Regs
20 **AA** s65(7) SSCBA 1992
   DLA s72(7B) SSCBA 1992
   CA s70(4A) SSCBA 1992
   PIP s84 WRA 2012
21 *Stewart v SSWP*, C-503/09 [2011] ECR, I-06497; *SSWP v JG* [2013] UKUT 298 (AAC); *SSWP v JG* [2013] UKUT 300 (AAC)

22 Reg 6(35)-(37) SS(C&P) Regs; reg 7(9A) SS&CS(DA) Regs
23 *CK & JK v SSWP* [2013] UKUT 218 (AAC); see also *BD v SSWP* [2013] UKUT 216 (AAC)
24 *Bartlett and others v SSWP*, C-537/09 [2011] ECR, I-03417
25 Art 70 EU Reg 883/04; *Robin Swaddling v AO*, C-90/97 [1999] ECR I-01075
26 ss1(3)(d) and 18(4)(a) WRA 2007
27 Regs 151-55 ESA Regs; regs 88-92 ESA Regs 2013
28 Reg 156 and Sch 5 paras 6 and 7 ESA Regs
29 Reg 156 and Sch 5 para 7 ESA Regs
30 Reg 156 ESA Regs
31 Arts 5, 46 and 82 EU Reg 883/04; Arts 27 and 46 EU Reg 987/2009
32 Reg 5 SSB(PA) Regs
33 s130(1)(a) SSCBA 1992
34 Reg 7 HB Regs; reg 7 HB(SPC) Regs
35 Reg 2 SSB(PA) Regs
36 Reg 13 SSB(PA) Regs; reg 14 SS(IB-ID) Regs; reg 2(4) SSB(PRT)Regs
37 Arts 5 and 46 EU Reg 883/04; Art 87 EU Reg 987/2009
38 Arts 7 and 21 EU Reg 883/04
39 s124(1) SSCBA 1992
40 Reg 4 IS Regs
41 Reg 21 and Sch 7 paras 11 and 11A IS Regs
42 Reg 21 and Sch 7 para 11A IS Regs
43 Reg 16 IS Regs
44 Reg 16(5) IS Regs
45 Reg 9(3) SSB(PA) Regs
46 Reg 9(4) SSB(PA) Regs
47 Reg 9(5) SSB(PA) Regs
48 s1(2)(i) JSA 1995
49 s21 and Sch 1 para 11 JSA 1995; reg 50 JSA Regs; reg 41 JSA Regs 2013
50 Regs 50(4) and 170 JSA Regs
51 Regs 14 and 19 JSA Regs; reg 16 JSA Regs 2013
52 Regs 50(6B), 86C and 170 and Sch 5A para 7 JSA Regs
53 Sch 5A para 7 JSA Regs
54 Reg 78 JSA Regs
55 Reg 50(3) and (6C) and Sch 5A para 7 JSA Regs
56 Regs 50(4) and 170 JSA Regs

12

57 Reg 85 and Sch 5 paras 10 and 11 JSA
    Regs
58 Reg 85 and Sch 5 para 11 JSA Regs
59 Reg 78 JSA Regs
60 Reg 78(5) JSA Regs
61 Art 64 EU Reg 883/04
62 s1(2)(a) SPCA 2002
63 Regs 3 and 4 SPC Regs
64 Regs 4 and 5 SPC Regs
65 Reg 5 SPC Regs
66 s113 SSCBA 1992; reg 4(1) SSB(PA)
    Regs
67 Reg 4(3) SSB(PA) Regs
68 Reg 6 SSB(PA) Regs
69 Reg 13 SSB(PA) Regs; reg 10 SSB(Dep)
    Regs
70 Reg 2(4) SSB(PRT) Regs
71 **SMP** Reg 2A SMP(PAM) Regs
    SAP/SPP Reg 4 SPPSAP(PAM) Regs
    SSP Reg 10 SSP(MAPA) Regs
72 Art 6 EU Reg 883/04
    SMP s171(1) SSCBA 1992; regs 2, 2A, 7
    and 8 SMP(PAM) Regs
    SAP/SPP ss171ZJ(2) and 171ZS(2)
    SSCBA 1992; regs 3, 4, 8 and 9
    SPPSAP(PAM) Regs
    SSP s163(1) SSCBA 1992; reg 16 SSP
    Regs; regs 5-10 SSP(MAPA) Regs
73 **SMP** Reg 3 SMP(PAM) Regs; reg 17(3)
    SMP Regs
    SAP/SPP Reg 2 SPPSAP(PAM) Regs; reg
    32(3) SPPSAP(G) Regs; reg 24(4)
    ASPP(G) Regs
    SSP Reg 16(2) SSP Regs
74 s3 and 4(1)(c) WRA 2012
75 Reg 11 UC Regs
76 Reg 99(1)-(3) UC Regs
77 Reg 3(6) UC Regs
78 Regs 3, 18, 22 and 36 UC Regs
79 Reg 4(7) UC Regs
80 Reg 4 TC(R) Regs
81 Reg 2(1) TC(R) Regs
82 Reg 3, 5 and 6 TC(R) Regs

12

Chapter 72

* *

European Union co-ordination rules

This chapter covers:
1. Introduction (below)
2. Who is covered (p1592)
3. Which benefits are covered (p1594)
4. Principles of co-ordination (p1596)

Key facts

- If you are a European Economic Area (EEA) national, or the family member of an EEA national, and your circumstances involve more than one EEA state, you may be able to benefit from the European Union co-ordination rules.
- The co-ordination rules can help you qualify for benefits in the UK. You can count periods of residence and employment in another EEA state, and insurance contributions paid in another EEA state, to help you meet the conditions of entitlement of the UK benefit you want to claim.
- The co-ordination rules also allow you to be paid a UK benefit in another EEA state for longer than the UK rules allow, and to be paid a benefit by another EEA state while you are in the UK.

---

1. Introduction

If you are a European Economic Area (EEA) national (see p1590) or a family member of an EEA national, you may be able to benefit from European Union (EU) law.

There are two main areas of EU law that affect benefit and tax credit entitlement that are covered in this *Handbook*: the residence rights which enable you to satisfy the right to reside requirement outlined in Chapter 70 and the social security co-ordination rules, which are summarised in this chapter.

The co-ordination rules can help you qualify for benefits in the UK – eg, by enabling you to count periods of residence, insurance and employment in any EEA state to meet the conditions of entitlement. They can also help you be paid a

Part 12: Immigration and residence rules for benefits and tax credits
Chapter 72: European Union co-ordination rules
1. Introduction

UK benefit in another EEA state for longer than you would be able to do under UK law alone.

European Union law

EU legislation and caselaw apply in the UK and throughout the EEA. In general, for EU law to apply, you must be an EEA national or the family member of an EEA national and your circumstances must involve more than one EEA state – eg, if you have moved between states, you live in one and work in another, or you live in one but are the national of another.[1]

Member states of the European Union

Austria	Estonia	Italy	Portugal
Belgium	Finland	Latvia	Romania
Bulgaria	France	Lithuania	Slovakia
Croatia	Germany	Luxembourg	Slovenia
Cyprus	Greece	Malta	Spain
Czech Republic	Hungary	The Netherlands	Sweden
Denmark	Ireland	Poland	United Kingdom

Member states of the European Economic Area
The EEA consists of the EU countries plus Iceland, Liechtenstein and Norway.
From 1 June 2002, an agreement with Switzerland means that, in general, Swiss nationals are treated the same as EEA nationals. Any references to EEA nationals therefore also includes Swiss nationals.[2]

EU law has been extended to countries outside the EU which are covered by the EEA Agreement. In general, EEA nationals are covered by EU law to much the same extent as nationals of EU states.

EU law applies in all the above countries and extends beyond the actual territory of the member states. It also applies to countries 'for whose external relations a member state is responsible'. Therefore, Spain includes not only the mainland, but also the Balearic and the Canary Islands. Portugal includes Madeira and the Azores. However, there are certain exceptions to this general rule. In particular, in the UK, Gibraltar is covered, but not the Isle of Man and the Channel Islands.

Note: the restrictions that were applied to nationals of states that joined the EU in 2004 (the 'A8 states'), in 2007 (the 'A2 states') and on 1 July 2013 (Croatia) (see p1531) only affect entitlement to benefits and tax credits which have a right to reside requirement (see p1520). Other provisions of EU law, including the co-ordination rules, apply to nationals of these states in the same way as they apply to other EEA nationals.

The co-ordination rules

EU law co-ordinates all the social security systems within the EEA. The intention is that people should not lose out on social security protection simply because they move to another member state.

The co-ordination rules contain the following principles.

- **The single state principle.** You can generally only claim benefit from one member state (see p1596).
- **Equal treatment of people.** Discrimination on nationality grounds in terms of access to, the rate of, and payment of, the benefits covered is prohibited (see p1598).
- **Equal treatment of benefits, income, facts or events.** If receipt of a benefit or a fact or an event has a legal consequence in one member state, this must be recognised in the same way by other member states (see p1598).
- **Aggregation.** Periods of residence, insurance and employment in any EEA state can be used towards entitlement to benefit in another (see p1598).
- **Exportability of certain benefits.** You can continue to be paid certain benefits if you go to another member state (see p1598).
- **Administrative co-operation.** Member states undertake to co-operate in the administration of the co-ordination rules.

The current co-ordination rules succeed, but do not repeal, the previous set of rules (referred to in this *Handbook* as the 'old co-ordiantion rules'). See p1593 for who is covered by the old rules.

Using the co-ordination rules

In order to rely on the co-ordination rules, you must check:

- whether you are covered by the current or the old co-ordination rules (see p1593);
- whether you are personally covered (see p1592);
- whether the benefit you want to claim is covered and into which category it falls (see p1594);
- which state is the 'competent state' (see p1596);
- the principle you want to use – eg, 'exporting' a benefit or aggregating periods of insurance (see p1598);
- the individual benefit and tax credit rules in Chapter 70 for your entitlement in the UK or in Chapter 71 if you want to be paid when you or your family are in another EEA state.

The co-ordination rules are complex and this chapter only provides an overview. For more information, see CPAG's *Benefits for Migrants Handbook*.

12

Part 12: Immigration and residence rules for benefits and tax credits
Chapter 72: European Union co-ordination rules
2. Who is covered

2. **Who is covered**

In order to be covered by the co-ordination rules, you must fall within their 'personal scope'.

You are within the personal scope of the co-ordination rules if:[3]

- you have been 'subject to the legislation of one or more member states' (see below) and you are:
  - a European Economic Area (EEA) national; *or*
  - a refugee; *or*
  - a stateless person; *or*
- a family member (see below) or a survivor (in the UK this means a widow, widower or surviving civil partner[4]) of one of the above.

For the co-ordination rules to apply, there must also be more than one member state involved. This usually means that you must have moved between EEA states, or you live in one and work in another, or you live in one and are the national of another.[5]

Subject to the legislation of a member state

You have been '**subject to the legislation of a member state**' if you have worked in and paid (or should have paid) national insurance (NI) contributions to, or received any social security or special non-contributory benefit (see p1594 for what these are) from, that state. You may also be subject to the legislation if you are potentially eligible for any social security benefit or special non-contributory benefit.

'**Legislation**' is defined as 'in respect of each member state, laws, regulations and other statutory provisions and all other implementing measures relating to the social security branches covered by Article 3(1) of the Regulation.'[6]

The '**social security branches**' referred to in this definition include UK benefits which are intended to assist you in the event of one of the risks on p1594.

Family members

Family members of someone covered by the co-ordination rules can also rely on the rules that cover that person (which can vary depending on the type of benefit claimed).

Family members

You are a '**member of the family**' of a person covered by the co-ordination rules if you are:[7]

- a person defined or recognised as a member of the family, or designated as a member of the household, by the legislation under which benefits are provided; *or*

– if the legislation under which benefits are provided does not make a distinction between members of the family and other people to whom the legislation applies, the person's spouse or child either under the age of 'majority' (18 in England and Wales; 16 in Scotland) or older but dependent on the person covered.

If under the legislation you are only considered a member of the family or member of the household if you are living in the same household as the person, this condition is considered satisfied if you are mainly dependent on her/him.

The **'legislation under which benefits are provided'** should cover the legislation for the particular benefit you are claiming. However, it may be arguable that a broader category of social security legislation should apply. See specialist advice if this affects you.

When the old co-ordination rules apply

There are two sets of co-ordination rules. The current rules[8] apply to the majority of benefit claimants. However, the old co-ordination rules[9] apply to you if:

- you are getting a benefit that you qualified for under the old co-ordination rules. Your claim is determined under the rules that were applicable at the time it was made. This depends on your nationality (see below). The old rules continue to apply to you for up to 10 years, provided your circumstances do not change. This transitional period is intended to protect anyone who might otherwise have lost benefit under the new rules. However, you can ask to be transferred and considered under the new rules if this would be better for you. If so, the new rules take effect from the start of the following month;[10] *or*
- you are a 'third-country national' other than a refugee (ie, you are not an EEA national yourself), you are legally resident in the UK,[11] you have been employed or self-employed and you have paid (or should have paid) NI contributions, or you have been a student.

When did the current co-ordination rules take effect?

The current co-ordination rules apply to nationals (and their family members) of:

– the European Union member states, refugees and stateless people from 1 May 2010;

– Switzerland from 1 April 2012;

– Iceland, Liechtenstein and Norway from 1 June 2012.

12

Note: as most claims are now covered by the current co-ordination rules, this *Handbook* does not include the old ones. For information on these, see the 2012/13 edition.

Part 12: Immigration and residence rules for benefits and tax credits
Chapter 72: European Union co-ordination rules
3. Which benefits are covered

3. **Which benefits are covered**

The benefits to which the co-ordination rules apply are referred to as being within the '**material scope**' of the rules.

Individual benefits are not directly referred to. Instead, the rules have broad categories of benefits (eg, 'old age' or 'maternity') designed to cover certain 'risks'. Any social security benefit designed to provide assistance in the event of a particular risk falls into that particular category of benefit. Each member state must list the benefits it considers are designed to assist with that risk.

Benefits are also divided into the following types, depending on the conditions of eligibility:

- social security benefits (see below);
- special non-contributory benefits (see p1595);
- social and medical assistance (see p1596).

Those benefits deemed to be social security benefits have the most rights and special non-contributory benefits provide fewer rights. Social and medical assistance are not covered by the co-ordination rules.

Social security benefits

Risk	UK benefit
Sickness	Attendance allowance (AA) (but see p1595)
	Carer's allowance (CA) (but see p1595)
	Disability living allowance (DLA) care component (but see p1595)
	Personal independence payment (PIP) daily living component
	Statutory sick pay
	Contributory employment and support allowance (ESA) in the assessment phase (but see p1595)
Maternity	Maternity allowance
	Statutory maternity pay
Paternity	Statutory paternity pay
Invalidity	AA, DLA care and mobility component and CA if you were in receipt of benefit before 1 June 1992. If you claimed after this date, see the note below
	Long-term incapacity benefit
	Severe disablement allowance
	Contributory ESA after the assessment phase
	Arguably, contributory ESA during the assessment phase (see p1595)
	Additional pension

Old age	Graduated retirement benefit
	Winter fuel payments
	Increments – eg, to pensions
	Increases of retirement pension for an adult
	Age addition in pensions
Pre-retirement	None
Survivors	Bereavement benefits
Death grants	Bereavement payment
Accidents at work and	Industrial injuries disablement benefit
occupational diseases	Constant attendance allowance
	Exceptionally severe disablement allowance
	Reduced earnings allowance
Unemployment	Contribution-based jobseeker's allowance (JSA)
Family benefits (see p1599)	Child benefit
	Child tax credit
	Increases in other benefits for an adult or a child
	Guardian's allowance

Note: AA, CA and DLA care component have been categorised as assisting with different risks at different times. Until 1 June 1992 they were categorised as invalidity benefits. They were then categorised as special non-contributory benefits until this was held to be wrong[12] and they were then re-categorised as sickness benefits. For the relevance of this if you want to be paid one of these benefits in another European Economic Area state, see p1574.

The mobility component of DLA has been listed as, and the mobility component of PIP is treated by the DWP as, a special non-contributory benefit.

Note:
- If you have a long-term or permanent disability, it is arguable that contributory ESA during the assessment phase, as well as after, should be regarded as an invalidity benefit.[13] However, in most cases it makes no difference to when it can be paid.
- For rules on 'exporting' family benefits, see p1599.
- The DWP considers that universal credit is not a social security benefit nor a special non-contributory benefit.[14]

Special non-contributory benefits

The UK government has only listed pension credit, income-related ESA, income-based JSA and DLA mobility component as special non-contributory benefits.[15] However, it is expected that the mobility component of PIP will also be listed as a special non-contributory benefit and the DWP is currently treating it as such.

Part 12: Immigration and residence rules for benefits and tax credits
Chapter 72: European Union co-ordination rules
4. Principles of co-ordination

Special non-contributory benefits can only be paid in the state in which you are resident.[16] See below for details of when you count as resident. However, although you cannot 'export' special non-contributory benefits, all the other co-ordination principles apply.

Social and medical assistance

The UK does not specify which benefits it considers to be social assistance and consequently excluded from the co-ordination rules.

4. **Principles of co-ordination**

The single competent state

If you are covered by the co-ordination rules (see p1592), you are subject to the legislation of one member state only.[17] This means that, in general, you can only claim a particular type of benefit from one state and are only liable to pay national insurance (NI) contributions to one. The '**competant state**' is the one responsible for paying your benefit and to which you are liable to pay NI contributions.[18] In general, this is the one in which you are:[19]

- employed or self-employed;
- resident and from which you receive an unemployment benefit;
- a conscripted member of the armed forces or someone doing compulsory civilian service;
- a civil servant.

There are exceptions to this general rule – eg, in particular, regarding the payment of sickness benefits if you (or your family member who brings you within the co-ordination rules) receive a pension from a member state other than the one in which you live.[20]

Note: you are treated as still employed or self-employed if, as a result of that activity, you are receiving cash benefits (other than for the risks of invalidity, sickness, old age, being a survivor or accidents at work).[21]

If you work simultaneously in two or more states, you are subject to the legislation of the state where you reside if you pursue a substantial part (generally at least 25 per cent) of your activities there.[22]

If your employer's business is normally in one member state, but you are sent to another state to work and it is anticipated that the posting will last for no more than 24 months, you remain subject to the legislation of the first state. Similarly, if you are self-employed in one state and go to another state to provide similar

12

services, you remain subject to the legislation of the first state, provided you do not anticipate being abroad for more than 24 months.[23]

If none of the bullet points on p1596 apply, the competent state is the state in which you are resident.[24]

'**Residence**' in this context means habitually resident. If there is a difference of views between two states or institutions about where you are resident, they must agree where your centre of interest is, taking into account all your circumstances, including:[25]

- the duration and continuity of your presence in the states concerned;
- your personal situation including:
  - the nature and specific characteristics of any activity pursued, in particular the place where such activity is habitually pursued, the stability of the activity, and the duration of any work contract;
  - your family status and family ties;
  - any unpaid activity, such as voluntary work;
  - if you are a student, the source of your income;
  - your housing situation, in particular how permanent it is;
  - the state in which you are deemed to reside for tax purposes.

If there is still a dispute, consideration must be given to your intentions, especially the reasons why you moved. This will be decisive in establishing your actual place of residence.

When the UK remains the competent state

If you are subject to the legislation of the UK, either because you last worked in the UK or you are resident in the UK, you remain subject to this until:[26]

- you start to work in another member state;
- (unless you last worked in the UK) you receive a pension from another member state and request that the UK cease to be your competent state;[27]
- in some circumstances, you move to another member state and become resident there (see below).

Note: these general rules can be supplemented by other rules specific to the category of benefit being paid.[28]

The point at which the UK stops being responsible for paying your benefits if you move to another state is not always clear and most of the caselaw has considered the old co-ordination rules, which differ in some respects from the current ones. However, in general, if you continue to be entitled to a UK benefit when you move to another state, the UK remains the competent state for paying that benefit until either you become employed/self-employed in the other state or, in certain circumstances, you start to receive a benefit from it.[29]

Part 12: Immigration and residence rules for benefits and tax credits
Chapter 72: European Union co-ordination rules
4. Principles of co-ordination

Equal treatment

If you are covered by the co-ordination rules, you are entitled to the same benefits under the legislation of the 'competent state' (see p1596) as a national of that state.[30] Equal treatment is one of the fundamental rights of European Union (EU) law, and the principle of non-discrimination prohibits discrimination based on your nationality. Both direct discrimination and, if it cannot be justified as proportionate and in pursuit of a legitimate aim, indirect discrimination are prohibited. See CPAG's *Benefits for Migrants Handbook* for further information.

The co-ordination rules also provide for the 'equal treatment of benefits, income, facts or events'.[31] This rule is designed to ensure that if the competent state regards the receipt of a particular benefit or income, or the occurrence of certain facts or events, as producing certain legal effects, it should regard the receipt of an equivalent benefit or income from another state, or the occurrence of particular facts or events in another state, as producing the same effect. For example, a person getting attendance allowance (AA) is entitled to have a disability premium included in her/his housing benefit applicable amount. Therefore, a person getting a benefit equivalent to AA from another state but who is resident in the UK should also receive a disability premium.

Aggregation

The principle of **'aggregation'** enables you to add together periods of NI contributions, residence or employment/self-employment completed under the legislation of other member states to satisfy the requirements of a benefit.[32] This may be necessary if your entitlement to benefit depends on your fulfilling a certain period of residence, employment or insurance. For example, if you want to claim a UK contribution-based benefit, such as contributory employment and support allowance, but you have not paid sufficient NI contributions, you can rely on contributions paid in other EEA states to satisfy the UK contribution rules. What constitutes a period of residence, employment or insurance is determined by the legislation of the member state in which it took place.[33]

Example
Sancha is a Portuguese national who worked for many years in Portugal. She leaves her job in Portugal and moves to the UK. She works for two weeks before being made redundant. Sancha is expecting a baby in two months' time and claims maternity allowance (MA). She is entitled to MA because she can rely on her periods of employment in Portugal to satisfy the condition of having worked for 26 out of the last 66 weeks.

Exporting benefits

The co-ordination rules allow you to 'export' certain benefits to another state if you cease to be resident in the member state in which your entitlement arose.

This means that certain benefits may not be reduced, modified, suspended, withdrawn or confiscated just because you go to live in a different state.[34] The rules for exporting vary according to the benefit concerned: some are fully exportable, some may be exportable on a temporary basis, and some are not exportable at all.

Check the individual benefit rules in Chapter 71 to see whether the benefit can be exported. If it can, you should contact the office that pays your benefit well in advance, so that arrangements can be made to pay you in the other state.

Under the co-ordination rules, all benefits categorised as social security benefits are exportable. See p1594 for a list of the UK benefits covered.

The following benefits are **fully exportable** and can be exported indefinitely:
- invalidity benefits;
- old age benefits;
- survivors' cash benefits;
- pensions for accidents at work or occupational diseases;
- death grants.

The following benefits can be **exported for a limited period** or subject to certain restrictions:
- unemployment benefits;
- sickness, maternity and paternity benefits (although, in most cases, these are exportable in a similar way to the fully exportable benefits).[35]

Special non-contributory benefits (see p1595) cannot be exported. They are paid only in the state in which you are resident.[36]

Family benefits

Under the co-ordination rules, family benefits in the UK include child benefit, child tax credit (CTC), guardian's allowance and child dependants' additions in other benefits.

For the definition of family member, see p1592.

You can export family benefits without any time limit and they are uprated in the normal way. You can also be paid for family members living in another member state.[37]

Generally, you are entitled to receive family benefits from your competent state, determined in the usual way. However, if you are receiving a pension, you claim any family benefits from the state which is the competent state for paying your pension.[38]

If there is entitlement (which, in most cases, requires a claim to have been made) to family benefits in separate states, there are detailed rules to determine which state has priority to pay. These rules prevent family benefits being claimed from more than one state for the same person for the same period.[39] If the state

Part 12: Immigration and residence rules for benefits and tax credits
Chapter 72: European Union co-ordination rules
Notes

with priority pays family benefits at a lower rate than a state with lower priority, the latter pays a 'top-up' to supplement the amount paid by the priority state. However, this top-up need not be paid for children residing in another state where entitlement to the family benefit is based on residence only (rather than based on employment or receipt of pension).[40]

Overlapping benefit rules

A general principle of the co-ordination rules is that you should not use one period of compulsory insurance to obtain more than one benefit.[41] In general, you are only insured in one EEA member state for any one period, so you cannot use insurance from that period to obtain entitlement to benefits of the same kind from two states. Usually, benefits are adjusted to ensure that either only one state (the 'competent state' – see p1596) pays the benefit, taking into account periods of insurance in other states, or that the benefit is paid pro rata according to the lengths of the periods of insurance in different member states.

In certain cases, however, you may be paid both the full level of a UK benefit and a proportion of a benefit from another member state, accrued as a result of having paid insurance contributions there. Member states are not allowed to apply provisions preventing the overlapping of their own benefits with those of other member states if it would reduce what you would have received from your years of contributions in the first member state alone.[42]

Notes

1. Introduction
1 *Petit*, C-153/91 [1992] ECR I-04973; Art 3(1) EU Dir 2004/38
2 *The Agreement between the European Community and its Member States, of the one part, and the Swiss Confederation, of the other, on the Free Movement of Persons*, Luxembourg, 21 June 1999, Cmd 5639 (in force 1 June 2002). Note also that reg 2 I(EEA) Regs defines Switzerland as an EEA state.

2. Who is covered
3 Art 2 EU Reg 883/04
4 Art 1(g) EU Reg 1408/71
5 *Petit*, C-153/91 [1992] ECR I-04973
6 Art 1(l) EU Reg 883/04

7 Arts 1(i) and 2 EU Reg 883/04
8 EU Reg 883/04
9 EU Reg 1408/71
10 Art 87(8) EU Reg 883/04
11 Art 1 EU Reg 859/2003

3. Which benefits are covered
12 *Commission of the European Communities v European Parliament and Council of the European Union*, C-299/05 [2007] ECR I-08695
13 *Stewart v SSWP*, C-503/09 [2011] ECR I-06497
14 SSAC, *Universal Credit and Related Regulations Report and Government Response*, December 2012

12

12

Appendices

Appendix 1

Useful addresses

The Tribunals Service

The President of the Social Entitlement Chamber
5th Floor
Fox Court
14 Gray's Inn Road
London WC1X 8HN
Tel: 0203 206 0619
www.justice.gov.uk/about/hmcts

The President (Northern Ireland)
Cleaver House
3 Donegall Square North
Belfast BT1 5GA
Tel: 028 9051 8500
www.dsdni.gov.uk/taser-appeals_service

Tribunal areas

Birmingham
Admin Support Centre
PO Box 14620
Birmingham B16 6FR
Tel: 0300 123 0736
ASCBirmingham@hmcts.gsi.gov.uk

Cardiff
Eastgate House
Newport Road
Cardiff CF24 0YP
Tel: 0300 123 1142
SSCSA-Cardiff@hmcts.gsi.gov.uk

Glasgow
Wellington House
134–136 Wellington Street
Glasgow G2 2XL
Tel: 0141 354 8400
SSCSA-Glasgow@hmcts.gsi.gov.uk

Leeds
York House
York Place
Leeds LS1 2ED
Tel: 0300 123 1142
SSCSA-Leeds@hmcts.gsi.gov.uk

Liverpool
36 Dale Street
Liverpool L2 5UZ
Tel: 0300 123 1142
SSCSA-Liverpool@hmcts.gsi.gov.uk

Newcastle
Manor View House
Kings Manor
Newcastle-upon-Tyne
NE1 6PA
Tel: 0300 123 1142
SSCSA-Newcastle@hmcts.gsi.gov.uk

Sutton
Copthall House
9 The Pavement
Grove Road
Sutton SM1 1DA
Tel: 0300 123 1142
SSCSA-Sutton@hmcts.gsi.gov.uk

First-Tier Tribunal (Tax)
HM Courts and Tribunals Service
Temple Court
35 Bull Street
Birmingham B4 6EQ
Tel: 0845 223 8080
www.justice.gov.uk/tribunals/tax
taxappeals@tribunals.gsi.gov.uk

The Upper Tribunal (Administrative Appeals Chamber)

England
5th Floor
7 Rolls Buildings
Fetter Lane
London EC4A 1NL
Tel: 020 7071 5662
www.justice.gov.uk/tribunals/aa
adminappeals@hmcts.gsi.gov.uk

Scotland
George House
126 George Street
Edinburgh EH2 4HH
Tel: 0131 271 4310
ossc@ossc-scotland.org.uk

Northern Ireland
Bedford House
16–22 Bedford Street
Belfast BT2 7FD
Tel: 028 9072 4883

Wales
Civil Justice Centre
2 Park Street
Cardiff CF10 1ET
Tel: 029 2066 2257

The Upper Tribunal (Tax and Chancery Chamber)

England and Wales
45 Bedford Square
London WC1B 3DN
Tel: 020 7612 9700
financeandtaxappeals@
tribunals.gsi.gov.uk

Scotland
George House
126 George Street
Edinburgh EH2 4HH

HM Revenue and Customs (tax credits)

Tax Credit Office
Tax Credit Office
Preston PR1 4AT
www.hmrc.gov.uk/taxcredits

Tax Credit Helpline
Tel: 0345 300 3900
Textphone: 0345 300 3909
Advice line for advisers and
intermediaries: 0345 300 3946

HM Revenue and Customs (child benefit and guardian's allowance)

Child benefit
Child Benefit Office
PO Box 1
Newcastle upon Tyne NE88 1AA
Tel: 0300 200 3100
Textphone: 0300 200 3103

Advice line for advisers and
intermediatries: 0300 200 3102
www.hmrc.gov.uk/childbenefit

Guardian's allowance
PO Box 1
Newcastle upon Tyne NE88 1AA
Tel: 0300 200 3101
Textphone: 0300 200 3103
www.gov.uk/guardians-allowance

HM Revenue and Customs (Office of the Solicitor)
South West Wing
Bush House
Strand
London WC2B 4RD

HM Revenue and Customs (national insurance)
National Insurance Contributions Office
Benton Park View
Newcastle upon Tyne NE98 1ZZ
Tel: 0300 200 3500
www.hmrc.gov.uk/ni

HM Revenue and Customs (Statutory Payments Disputes Team)
Room BP2301
Benton Park View
Longbenton
Newcastle upon Tyne NE98 1YS
Tel: 0191 225 5221

Department for Work and Pensions
Caxton House
Tothill Street
London SW1H 9NA
www.gov.uk/dwp

Department for Work and Pensions (Office of the Solicitor)
DWP Litigation Division
Caxton House
Tothill Street
London SW1H 9NA

Department for Work and Pensions (Overseas Medical Benefits Section)
Tyneview Park
Newcastle upon Tyne NE98 1BA
Tel: 0191 218 1999

Disability and Carers Service

Attendance Allowance Unit
Warbreck House
Warbreck Hill
Blackpool FY2 0YE
Tel: 0345 605 6055
Textphone: 0845 604 5312
attendance.allowanceenquiries@
dwp.gsi.gov.uk

Disability Living Allowance Unit

Claimants aged 16 years and over:
Disability Benefits Centre
Warbreck House
Warbreck Hill
Blackpool FY2 0YE
Tel: 08457 12 34 56
Textphone: 08457 22 44 33
dcpu.customer-services@
dwp.gsi.gov.uk

Claimants aged under 16 years:
Disability Benefits Centre 4
Post Handling Site B
Wolverhampton WV99 1BY
Tel: 08457 12 34 56
Textphone: 08457 22 44 33
midlands-dbc-customer-services@
dwp.gsi.gov.uk

Personal Independence Payment Unit
PIP new claims
Post Handling Site B
Wolverhampton WV99 1AH
Claims: 0800 917 2222 (textphone 0800 917 7777)
Helpline: 0845 850 3322 (textphone 0845 601 6677)

Carer's Allowance Unit
Palatine House
Lancaster Road
Preston PR1 1HB
Tel: 0845 608 4321
Textphone: 0845 604 5312
cau.customer-services@dwp.gsi.gov.uk
www.gov.uk/carers-allowance-unit

Exporting benefits overseas
Exportability Team
Room C216
Pension, Disability and Carers Service
Warbreck House
Warbreck Hill Road
Blackpool FY2 0YE
exportability.team@dwp.gsi.gov.uk

Jobcentre Plus (income support, jobseeker's allowance, employment and support allowance and incapacity benefit)

New benefit claims
Tel: 0800 055 6688
Textphone: 0800 023 4888
www.gov.uk/contact-jobcentre-plus

Enquiries about ongoing claims and to report bereavement
Tel: 0345 608 8545
Tel: 0345 600 3018 (Welsh speakers)
Textphone: 0345 608 8551
www.gov.uk/contact-jobcentre-plus

The Pension Service
Tel: 0800 731 7898 (new claims)
Tel: 0845 60 60 265 (enquiries or to report a change of circumstances)
www.gov.uk/contact-pension-service

Winter fuel payments
Winter Fuel Payment Centre
Mail Handling Site A
Wolverhampton WV98 1LR
Tel: 08459 15 15 15
Textphone: 0845 601 5613
www.gov.uk/winter-fuel-payment

International Pension Centre
The Pension Service 11
Mail Handling Site A
Wolverhampton WV98 1LW
Tel: 0191 218 7777
Textphone: 0191 218 7280
www.gov.uk/international-pension-centre

NHS Business Services Authority (help with health costs)
Tel: 0300 330 1343 (low income scheme)
Tel: 0300 330 1341 (medical and maternity exemption certificates)
Tel: 0300 330 1347 (NHS tax credit exemption certificates)
www.nhsbsa.nhs.uk/healthcosts

Department for Education
Sanctuary Buildings
20 Great Smith Street
London SW1P 3BT
Tel: 0370 000 2288
www.education.gov.uk

Compensation Recovery Unit

England, Scotland and Wales
Durham House
Washington NE38 7SF
www.gov.uk/government/collections/cru

Northern Ireland
Magnet House
81–93 York Street
Belfast BT15 1SS
Tel: 028 9054 5890
www.dsdni.gov.uk/ssa_cru

Local Government Ombudsman
England
PO Box 4771
Coventry CV4 0EH
Tel: 0300 061 0614
www.lgo.org.uk

Scottish Public Services Ombudsman
4 Melville Street
Edinburgh EH3 7NS
Tel: 0800 377 7330
www.spso.org.uk

Public Services Ombudsman for Wales
1 Ffordd yr Hen Gae
Pencoed CF35 5LJ
Tel: 0300 790 0203
www.ombudsman-wales.org.uk

The Parliamentary and Health Service Ombudsman
Millbank Tower
Millbank
London SW1P 4QP
Tel: 0345 015 4033
www.ombudsman.org.uk
phso.enquiries@ombudsman.org.uk

The Adjudicator
Judy Clements
Adjudicator's Office
PO Box 10280
Nottingham NG2 9PF
Tel: 0300 057 1111
www.adjudicatorsoffice.gov.uk

Independent Case Examiner
The Independent Case Examiner
PO Box 209
Bootle L20 7WA
Tel: 0845 606 0777
ice@dwp.gsi.gov.uk
www.ind-case-exam.org.uk

Judicial Conduct Investigations Office
81–82 Queens Building
Royal Courts of Justice
Strand
London WC2A 2LL
Tel: 020 7073 4719
inbox@jcio.gsi.gov.uk
www.gov.uk/complain-judge-magistrate-tribunal-coroner

Standards Commission for Scotland
Room T2.21 Scottish Parliament
Edinburgh EH99 1SP
Tel: 0131 348 6666
enquiries@standardscommission.org.uk
www.standardscommission scotland.org.uk

Commissioner for Ethical Standards in Public Life in Scotland
39 Drumsheugh Gardens
Edinburgh EH3 7SW
Tel: 0300 011 0550
info@ethicalstandards.org.uk
www.publicstandards commissioner.org.uk

Appendix 2
Information and advice

Independent advice and representation

If you want advice or information on a benefit or tax credit issue, the following may be able to assist.

- Citizens Advice Bureaux (CABx). You can find out where your local CAB is from the Citizens Advice website at www.citizensadvice.org.uk (England and Wales) or www.cas.org.uk (Scotland).
- Law centres. You can find your nearest law centre at www.lawcentres.org.uk.
- Other independent advice centres.
- Local authority welfare rights services.
- Local organisations for particular groups of claimants may offer help. For instance, there are unemployed centres, pensioners' groups and centres for people with disabilities.
- Civil Legal Advice (tel: 0845 345 4345 or www.gov.uk/civil-legal-advice). Note, however, that help with welfare benefits is limited to appeals in the Upper Tribunal and higher courts.

Advice from CPAG

Unfortunately, CPAG is unable to deal with enquiries directly from members of the public, but if you are an adviser you can phone or email for help with advising your client.

Advisers in England, Wales and Northern Ireland can call from 10am to 12pm and from 2pm to 4pm (Monday to Friday) on 020 7833 4627. Email advice is now limited to possible judicial review cases and enquiries that are specifically about child benefit, tax credits or other HMRC-administered benefits. Our email address is advice@cpag.org.uk.

Organisations based in Scotland can contact CPAG in Scotland at Unit 9, Ladywell, 94 Duke Street, Glasgow G4 0UW or email advice@cpagscotland.org.uk. A phone line is open for advisers in Scotland from 10am to 4pm (Monday to Thursday) and from 10am to 12pm (Friday) on 0141 552 0552.

For more information, see www.cpag.org.uk/advisers.

Advice from the DWP

The phone book should list contact details for your local DWP office. See also Appendix 1 of this *Handbook* for contact details for the DWP and HM Revenue and Customs (HMRC).

Finding help online

Information about benefits and tax credits, including a selection of leaflets and forms, is available on the www.gov.uk website and the HMRC website at www.hmrc.gov.uk.

CPAG's website (www.cpag.org.uk) has articles, briefings and factsheets on benefit issues.

The rightsnet website (aimed at advisers) at www.rightsnet.org.uk has details of new legislation, some caselaw and guidance. It also has links to other useful sites.

Most Acts and regulations can be found on the government information website at www.legislation.gov.uk.

You can find commssioners' and Upper Tribunal decisions at www.justice.gov.uk.

Appendix 3

Useful publications

Caselaw and legislation

The Law Relating to Social Security
All the legislation but without any commentary. Known as the 'Blue Book'.
Available at www.dwp.gov.uk/law-volumes (it is expected that this will transfer
to www.legislation.gov.uk sometime in 2014).

Social Security Legislation, Volume I: Non-Means-Tested Benefits, D Bonner, I Hooker
and R White (Sweet & Maxwell)
Legislation with commentary. 2014/15 edition (October 2014): £104 for the main
volume, reduced to £99 for CPAG members who order from CPAG before 30 June
2014, or at full price from July.

*Social Security Legislation, Volume II: Income Support, Jobseeker's Allowance and the
Social Fund*, J Mesher, P Wood, R Poynter, N Wikeley and D Bonner (Sweet &
Maxwell)
Legislation with commentary. 2014/15 edition (October 2014): £104 for the main
volume, reduced to £99 for CPAG members who order from CPAG before 30 June
2014, or at full price from July.

*Social Security Legislation, Volume III: Administration, Adjudication and the European
Dimension*, M Rowland and R White (Sweet & Maxwell)
Legislation with commentary. 2014/15 edition (October 2014): £104 for the main
volume, reduced to £99 for CPAG members who order from CPAG before 30 June
2014, or at full price from July.

*Social Security Legislation, Volume IV: Tax Credits and HMRC-Administered Social
Security Benefits*, N Wikeley and D Williams (Sweet & Maxwell)
Legislation with commentary. 2014/15 edition (October 2014): £104 for the main
volume, reduced to £99 for CPAG members who order from CPAG before 30 June
2014, or at full price from July.

Social Security Legislation, Volume V: Universal Credit, P Wood, R Poynter and N Wikeley (Sweet & Maxwell)
Legislation with commentary. 2014/15 edition (October 2014): £104 for the main volume, reduced to £99 for CPAG members who order from CPAG before 30 June 2014, or at full price from July.

Social Security Legislation – updating supplement to Volumes I – V, (Sweet & Maxwell)
The spring 2015 update to the 2014/15 main volumes: £66.

Work Capability Assessment Caselaw Pack (MNP Training)
1st edition (Spring 2014): £64.50 (printed book), £52.50 (USB).

Child Support: The Legislation, E Jacobs (CPAG)
Legislation with detailed commentary. 11th edition main volume (October 2013): £89.

CPAG's Housing Benefit and Council Tax Reduction Legislation, L Findlay, R Poynter, S Wright, C George and M Williams (CPAG)
Legislation with detailed commentary. 2014/15 (27th) edition (Winter 2014): £109 including Supplement; £105 per set if ordered from CPAG before 30 June 2014. The 26th edition (2013/14) is still available, £107 per set.

Official guidance

Decision Makers Guide
Available at www.gov.uk/government/collections/decision-makers-guide-staff-guide.

Advice for Decision Making: staff guide
Available at www.gov.uk/government/publications/advice-for-decision-making-staff-guide.

Housing Benefit Guidance Manual
Available at www.gov.uk/government/collections/housing-benefit-claims-processing-and-good-practice-for-local-authority-staff.

DWP Health and Work Guidance
Available at www.gov.uk/government/collections/healthcare-practitioners-guidance-and-information-from-dwp.

Work Capability Assessment (WCA) Handbook
Available at www.gov.uk/government/publications/work-capability-assessment-handbook-for-healthcare-professionals.

Tax Credit Technical Manual
Available at www.hmrc.gov.uk/manuals.

Budgeting Loan Guide
Available at www.gov.uk/government/publications/budgeting-loan-guide-for-decision-makers-reviewing-officers-and-further-reviewing-officers.

Leaflets

DWP leaflets are available free from your local DWP or Jobcentre Plus office. To order large numbers of leaflets: telephone 0845 850 0479, or email: ion-pass@xerox.com. Leaflets on housing benefit are available from your local authority.

Periodicals

Welfare Rights Bulletin (CPAG, bi-monthly)
Covers developments in social security law, including Upper Tribunal decisions, and updates this *Handbook* between editions. The annual subscription is £34 but it is sent automatically to CPAG Rights members.

Articles on social security can also be found in *Legal Action* (Legal Action Group), *The Adviser* (Citizens Advice) and the *Journal of Social Security Law* (Sweet & Maxwell).

Other publications

CPAG's Welfare Benefits and Tax Credits Online
Includes the full text of the *Welfare Benefits and Tax Credits Handbook* updated throughout the year. Annual subscription: £55 + VAT per user (bulk discounts available). More information at www.cpag.org.uk/bookshop.

Universal Credit: what you need to know
£11 (2nd edition, July 2013)

Personal Independence Payment: what you need to know
£12 (1st edition, September 2013)

Winning Your Benefit Appeal: what you need to know
£12 (1st edition, December 2013)

Child Support Handbook
£30 (22nd edition, summer 2014) (£10 for claimants)

Debt Advice Handbook
£26 (11th edition, autumn 2014)

Fuel Rights Handbook
£25 (17th edition, autumn 2014)

Benefits for Students in Scotland Handbook
£18 (12th edition, autumn 2014)
Available free online at: http://onlineservices.cpag.org.uk

Council Tax Handbook
£18 (10th edition, March 2014)

Benefits for Migrants Handbook
£25 (6th edition, summer 2014)

Children's Handbook Scotland: a benefits guide for children living away from their parents
£16 (7th edition, summer 2014)
Available free online at: http://onlineservices.cpag.org.uk

Guide to Housing Benefit 2014-17
£35 (May 2014)

Help with Housing Costs: universal credit and council tax rebates 2014/15
£35 (1st edition, May 2014)

Disability Rights Handbook 2014/15
£32.50 (May 2014)

Children in Need: local authority support for children and families
£50 (2nd edition, November 2013)

Disabled Children: a legal handbook
£45 (2nd edition, spring 2014)

Tribunal Practice and Procedure
£55 (3rd edition, autumn 2014)

Big Book of Benefits and Mental Health
£20 (14th edition, April 2014)

For CPAG and most other publications contact:
CPAG, 94 White Lion Street, London N1 9PF, tel: 020 7837 7979, fax: 020 7837 6414, email: bookorders@cpag.org.uk. Order forms are available at www.cpag.org.uk/bookshop. Postage and packing: free for online subscriptions and orders up to £10 in value; for order value £10.01–£100 add a flat rate charge of £3.99; for order value £100.01–£400 add £6.99; for order value £400+ add £10.99.

Appendix 4

Statutory maternity pay, statutory paternity pay (birth) and maternity allowance

Baby is expected during the week beginning Sunday	Latest start date of employment for SMP	15th week before the EWC begins Sunday+	Earliest week for SMP or MA begins Sunday++	66-week test period for MA begins Sunday
6.4.14	6.7.13	22.12.13	19.1.14	30.12.12
13.4.14	13.7.13	29.12.13	26.1.14	6.1.13
20.4.14	20.7.13	5.1.14	2.2.14	13.1.13
27.4.14	27.7.13	12.1.14	9.2.14	20.1.13
4.5.14	3.8.13	19.1.14	16.2.14	27.1.13
11.5.14	10.8.13	26.1.14	23.2.14	3.2.13
18.5.14	17.8.13	2.2.14	2.3.14	10.2.13
25.5.14	24.8.13	9.2.14	9.3.14	17.2.13
1.6.14	31.8.13	16.2.14	16.3.14	24.2.13
8.6.14	7.9.13	23.2.14	23.3.14	3.3.13
15.6.14	14.9.13	2.3.14	30.3.14	10.3.13
22.6.14	21.9.13	9.3.14	6.4.14	17.3.13
29.6.14	28.9.13	16.3.14	13.4.14	24.3.13
6.7.14	5.10.13	23.3.14	20.4.14	31.3.13
13.7.14	12.10.13	30.3.14	27.4.14	7.4.13
20.7.14	19.10.13	6.4.14	4.5.14	14.4.13
27.7.14	26.10.13	13.4.14	11.5.14	21.4.13
3.8.14	2.11.13	20.4.14	18.5.14	28.4.13
10.8.14	9.11.13	27.4.14	25.5.14	5.5.13
17.8.14	16.11.13	4.5.14	1.6.14	12.5.13
24.8.14	23.11.13	11.5.14	8.6.14	19.5.13
31.8.14	30.11.13	18.5.14	15.6.14	26.5.13
7.9.14	7.12.13	25.5.14	22.6.14	2.6.13
14.9.14	14.12.13	1.6.14	29.6.14	9.6.13
21.9.14	21.12.13	8.6.14	6.7.14	16.6.13

A

Baby is expected during the week beginning Sunday	Latest start date of employment for SMP	15th week before the EWC begins Sunday+	Earliest week for SMP or MA begins Sunday++	66-week test period for MA begins Sunday
28.9.14	28.12.13	15.6.14	13.7.14	23.6.13
5.10.14	4.1.14	22.6.14	20.7.14	30.6.13
12.10.14	11.1.14	29.6.14	27.7.14	7.7.13
19.10.14	18.1.14	6.7.14	3.8.14	14.7.13
26.10.14	25.1.14	13.7.14	10.8.14	21.7.13
2.11.14	1.2.14	20.7.14	17.8.14	28.7.13
9.11.14	8.2.14	27.7.14	24.8.14	4.8.13
16.11.14	15.2.14	3.8.14	31.8.14	11.8.13
23.11.14	22.2.14	10.8.14	7.9.14	18.8.13
30.11.14	1.3.14	17.8.14	14.9.14	25.8.13
7.12.14	8.3.14	24.8.14	21.9.14	1.9.13
14.12.14	15.3.14	31.8.14	28.9.14	8.9.13
21.12.14	22.3.14	7.9.14	5.10.14	15.9.13
28.12.14	29.3.14	14.9.14	12.10.14	22.9.13
4.1.15	5.4.14	21.9.14	19.10.14	29.9.13
11.1.15	12.4.14	28.9.14	26.10.14	6.10.13
18.1.15	19.4.14	5.10.14	2.11.14	13.10.13
25.1.15	26.4.14	12.10.14	9.11.14	20.10.13
1.2.15	3.5.14	19.10.14	16.11.14	27.10.13
8.2.15	10.5.14	26.10.14	23.11.14	3.11.13
15.2.15	17.5.14	2.11.14	30.11.14	10.11.13
22.2.15	24.5.14	9.11.14	7.12.14	17.11.13
1.3.15	31.5.14	16.11.14	14.12.14	24.11.13
8.3.15	7.6.14	23.11.14	21.12.14	1.12.13
15.3.15	14.6.14	30.11.14	28.12.14	8.12.13
22.3.15	21.6.14	7.12.14	4.1.15	15.12.13
29.3.15	28.6.14	14.12.14	11.1.15	22.12.13
5.4.15	5.7.14	21.12.14	18.1.15	29.12.13
12.4.15	12.7.14	28.12.14	25.1.15	5.1.14
19.4.15	19.7.14	4.1.15	1.2.15	12.1.14
26.4.15	26.7.14	11.1.15	8.2.15	19.1.14
3.5.15	2.8.14	18.1.15	15.2.15	26.1.14
10.5.15	9.8.14	25.1.15	22.2.15	2.2.14
17.5.15	16.8.14	1.2.15	1.3.15	9.2.14
24.5.15	23.8.14	8.2.15	8.3.15	16.2.14
31.5.15	30.8.14	15.2.15	15.3.15	23.2.14
7.6.15	6.9.14	22.2.15	22.3.15	2.3.14
14.6.15	13.9.14	1.3.15	29.3.15	9.3.14
21.6.15	20.9.14	8.3.15	5.4.15	16.3.14
28.6.15	27.9.14	15.3.15	12.4.15	23.3.14

Baby is expected during the week beginning Sunday	Latest start date of employment for SMP	15th week before the EWC begins Sunday+	Earliest week for SMP or MA begins Sunday++	66-week test period for MA begins Sunday
5.7.15	4.10.14	22.3.15	19.4.15	30.3.14
12.7.15	11.10.14	29.3.15	26.4.15	6.4.14
19.7.15	18.10.14	5.4.15	3.5.15	13.4.14
26.7.15	25.10.14	12.4.15	10.5.15	20.4.14
2.8.15	1.11.14	19.4.15	17.5.15	27.4.14
9.8.15	8.11.14	26.4.15	24.5.15	4.5.14
16.8.15	15.11.14	3.5.15	31.5.15	11.5.14
23.8.15	22.11.14	10.5.15	7.6.15	18.5.14
30.8.15	29.11.14	17.5.15	14.6.15	25.5.14
6.9.15	6.12.14	24.5.15	21.6.15	1.6.14
13.9.15	13.12.14	31.5.15	28.6.15	8.6.14
20.9.15	20.12.14	7.6.15	5.7.15	15.6.14
27.9.15	27.12.14	14.6.15	12.7.15	22.6.14
4.10.15	3.1.15	21.6.15	19.7.15	29.6.14
11.10.15	10.1.15	28.6.15	26.7.15	6.7.14
18.10.15	17.1.15	5.7.15	2.8.15	13.7.14
25.10.15	24.1.15	12.7.15	9.8.15	20.7.14
1.11.15	31.1.15	19.7.15	16.8.15	27.7.14
8.11.15	7.2.15	26.7.15	23.8.15	3.8.14
15.11.15	14.2.15	2.8.15	30.8.15	10.8.14
22.11.15	21.2.15	9.8.15	6.9.15	17.8.14
29.11.15	28.2.15	16.8.15	13.9.15	24.8.14
6.12.15	7.3.15	23.8.15	20.9.15	31.8.14
13.12.15	14.3.15	30.8.15	27.9.15	7.9.14
20.12.15	21.3.15	6.9.15	4.10.15	14.9.14
27.12.15	28.3.15	13.9.15	11.10.15	21.9.14

+ EWC is the expected week of childbirth. The 15th week before the EWC is relevant to the continuous employment rule and the earnings condition for SMP and SPP (birth). See Chapter 38.
++ This is the 11th week before the baby is due (unless your baby is born earlier. See Chapters 34 and 38 for possible exceptions).

Appendix 5

Pension age for women born between 6 April 1950 and 5 December 1953

Date of birth	Pension age (in years/months)*	Date pension age reached
06.04.50 – 05.05.50	60.1 – 60.0	06.05.2010
06.05.50 – 05.06.50	60.2 – 60.1	06.07.2010
06.06.50 – 05.07.50	60.3 – 60.2	06.09.2010
06.07.50 – 05.08.50	60.4 – 60.3	06.11.2010
06.08.50 – 05.09.50	60.5 – 60.4	06.01.2011
06.09.50 – 05.10.50	60.6 – 60.5	06.03.2011
06.10.50 – 05.11.50	60.7 – 60.6	06.05.2011
06.11.50 – 05.12.50	60.8 – 60.7	06.07.2011
06.12.50 – 05.01.51	60.9 – 60.8	06.09.2011
06.01.51 – 05.02.51	60.10 – 60.9	06.11.2011
06.02.51 – 05.03.51	60.11 – 60.10	06.01.2012
06.03.51 – 05.04.51	61.0 – 60.11	06.03.2012
06.04.51 – 05.05.51	61.1 – 61.0	06.05.2012
06.05.51 – 05.06.51	61.2 – 61.1	06.07.2012
06.06.51 – 05.07.51	61.3 – 61.2	06.09.2012
06.07.51 – 05.08.51	61.4 – 61.3	06.11.2012
06.08.51 – 05.09.51	61.5 – 61.4	06.01.2013
06.09.51 – 05.10.51	61.6 – 61.5	06.03.2013
06.10.51 – 05.11.51	61.7 – 61.6	06.05.2013
06.11.51 – 05.12.51	61.8 – 61.7	06.07.2013
06.12.51 – 05.01.52	61.9 – 61.8	06.09.2013
06.01.52 – 05.02.52	61.10 – 61.9	06.11.2013
06.02.52 – 05.03.52	61.11 – 61.10	06.01.2014
06.03.52 – 05.04.52	62.0 – 61.11	06.03.2014
06.04.52 – 05.05.52	62.1 – 62.0	06.05.2014
06.05.52 – 05.06.52	62.2 – 62.1	06.07.2014

A

Date of birth	Pension age (in years/months)*	Date pension age reached
06.06.52 – 05.07.52	62.3 – 62.2	06.09.2014
06.07.52 – 05.08.52	62.4 – 62.3	06.11.2014
06.08.52 – 05.09.52	62.5 – 62.4	06.01.2015
06.09.52 – 05.10.52	62.6 – 62.5	06.03.2015
06.10.52 – 05.11.52	62.7 – 62.6	06.05.2015
06.11.52 – 05.12.52	62.8 – 62.7	06.07.2015
06.12.52 – 05.01.53	62.9 – 62.8	06.09.2015
06.01.53 – 05.02.53	62.10 – 62.9	06.11.2015
06.02.53 – 05.03.53	62.11 – 62.10	06.01.2016
06.03.53 – 05.04.53	63.0 – 62.11	06.03.2016
06.04.53 – 05.05.53	63.3 – 63.2	06.07.2016
06.05.53 – 05.06.53	63.6 – 63.5	06.11.2016
06.06.53 – 05.07.53	63.9 – 63.8	06.03.2017
06.07.53 – 05.08.53	64.0 – 63.11	06.07.2017
06.08.53 – 05.09.53	64.3 – 64.2	06.11.2017
06.09.53 – 05.10.53	64.6 – 64.5	06.03.2018
06.10.53 – 05.11.53	64.9 – 64.8	06.07.2018
06.11.53 – 05.12.53	65.0 – 64.11	06.11.2018

* For example, '60.1–60.0' means you would be aged between 60 and 60 years and one month, depending on your date of birth, when you reach pension age.

Appendix 6

Prescribed degrees of disablement

Schedule 2 to the Social Security (General Benefit) Regulations 1982 SI No.1408

Description of injury	Degree of disablement %
1 Loss of both hands or amputation at higher sites	100
2 Loss of a hand and a foot	100
3 Double amputation through leg or thigh, or amputation through leg or thigh on one side and loss of other foot	100
4 Loss of sight to such an extent as to render the claimant unable to perform any work for which eyesight is essential	100
5 Very severe facial disfiguration	100
6 Absolute deafness	100
7 Forequarter or hindquarter amputation	100
Amputation cases – upper limbs (either arm)	
8 Amputation through shoulder joint	90
9 Amputation below shoulder with stump less than 20.5 cms from tip of acromion	80
10 Amputation from 20.5 cms from tip of acromion to less than 11.5 cms below tip of olecranon	70
11 Loss of a hand or of the thumb and 4 fingers of 1 hand or amputation from 11.5 cms below tip of olecranon	60

Description of injury	Degree of disablement %
12 Loss of thumb	30
13 Loss of thumb and its metacarpal bone	40
14 Loss of 4 fingers of 1 hand	50
15 Loss of 3 fingers of 1 hand	30
16 Loss of 2 fingers of 1 hand	20
17 Loss of terminal phalanx of thumb	20
Amputation cases – lower limbs	
18 Amputation of both feet resulting in end-bearing stumps	90
19 Amputation through both feet proximal to the metatarso-phalangeal joint	80
20 Loss of all toes to both feet through the metatarso-phalangeal joint	40
21 Loss of all toes of both feet proximal to the proximal inter-phalangeal joint	30
22 Loss of all toes of both feet distal to the proximal inter-phalangeal joint	20
23 Amputation at hip	90
24 Amputation below hip with stump not exceeding 13 cms in length measured from tip of great trochanter	80

A

Appendix 6: Prescribed degrees of disablement

Description of injury	Degree of disablement %
25 Amputation below hip and above knee with stump exceeding 13 cms in length measured from tip of great trochanter, or at knee not resulting in end-bearing stump	70
26 Amputation at knee resulting in end-bearing stump or below knee with stump not exceeding 9 cms	60
27 Amputation below knee with stump exceeding 9 cms but not exceeding 13 cms	50
28 Amputation below knee with stump exceeding 13 cms	40
29 Amputation of 1 foot resulting in end-bearing stump	30
30 Amputation through 1 foot proximal to the metatarso-phalangeal joint	30
31 Loss of all toes of 1 foot through the metatarso-phalangeal joint	20
Other injuries	
32 Loss of 1 eye, without complications, the other being normal	40
33 Loss of vision of 1 eye, without complications or disfigurement of the eyeball, the other being normal	30
Loss of fingers of right or left hand	
Index finger:	
34 Whole	14
35 2 phalanges	11
36 1 phalanx	9

Description of injury	Degree of disablement %
37 Guillotine amputation of tip without loss of bone	5
Middle finger:	
38 Whole	12
39 2 phalanges	9
40 1 phalanx	7
41 Guillotine amputation of tip without loss of bone	4
Ring or little finger:	
42 Whole	7
43 2 phalanges	6
44 1 phalanx	5
45 Guillotine amputation of tip without loss of bone	2
Loss of toes of right or left foot	
Great toe:	
46 Through metatarso-phalangeal joint	14
47 Part, with some loss of bone	3
Any other toe:	
48 Through metatarso-phalangeal joint	3
49 Part, with some loss of bone	1
2 toes of 1 foot, excluding great toe:	
50 Through metatarso-phalangeal joint	5
51 Part, with some loss of bone	2
3 toes of 1 foot, excluding great toe:	
52 Through metatarso-phalangeal joint	6
53 Part, with some loss of bone	3
4 toes of 1 foot, excluding great toe:	
54 Through metatarso-phalangeal joint	9
55 Part, with some loss of bone	3

The degree of disablement due to occupational deafness is assessed using tables and a formula to be found in reg 34 and Sch 3 Social Security (Industrial Injuries) (Prescribed Diseases) Regulations 1985, as amended.

A

Appendix 7

Prescribed industrial diseases

Part I of Schedule 1 to the Social Security (Industrial Injuries) (Prescribed Diseases) Regulations 1985 as amended

Prescribed disease or injury A – Conditions due to physical agents	Occupation Any occupation involving:
A1 Leukaemia (other than chronic lymphatic leukaemia) or cancer of the bone, female breast, testis or thyroid.	Exposure to electro-magnetic radiations (other than radiant heat), or to ionising particles, where the dose is sufficient to double the condition.
A2 Cataract.	Frequent or prolonged exposure to radiation from red-hot or white-hot material.
A3 Dysbarism, including decompression sickness, barotrauma and osteonecrosis.	Subjection to compressed or rarified air or from molten or red-hot material.
A4 Task-specific focal dystonia of the hand or forearm.	Prolonged periods of handwriting, typing or other repetitive movements of the fingers, hand or arm.
A5 Subcutaneous cellulitis of the hand.	Manual labour causing severe or prolonged friction or pressure on the hand.
A6 Bursitis or subcutaneous cellulites arising at or about the knee due to severe or prolonged external friction or pressure at or about the knee.	Manual labour causing severe or prolonged external friction or pressure at or about the knee.
A7 Bursitis or subcutaneous cellulites arising at or about the elbow due to severe or prolonged external friction or pressure at or about the elbow (beat elbow).	Manual labour causing severe or prolonged external friction or pressure at or about the elbow.
A8 Traumatic inflammation of the tendons of the hand or forearm, or of the associated tendon sheaths.	Manual labour, or frequent or repeated movements of the hand or wrist.

Prescribed disease or injury
A10 Sensorineural hearing loss amounting to at least 50dB in each ear, being the average of hearing losses at 1, 2 and 3 kHz frequencies, and being due in the case of at least one ear to occupational noise (occupational deafness).

Occupation
Any occupation involving the use of, or work wholly or mainly in the immediate vicinity of the use of, a:

(a) band saw, circular saw or cutting disc to cut metal in the metal founding or forging industries, circular saw to cut products in the manufacture of steel, powered (other than hand powered) grinding tool on metal (other than sheet metal or plate metal), pneumatic percussive tool on metal, pressurised air arc tool to gouge metal, burner or torch to cut or dress steel based products, skid transfer bank, knock out and shake out grid in a foundry, machine (other than a power press machine) to forge metal including a machine used to drop stamp metal by means of closed or open dies or drop hammers, machine to cut or shape or clean metal nails, or plasma spray gun to spray molten metal;

(b) pneumatic percussive tool to drill rock in a quarry, on stone in a quarry works, used underground, for mining coal, for sinking a shaft, or for tunnelling in civil engineering works;

(c) vibrating metal moulding box in the concrete products industry, or circular saw to cut concrete masonry blocks;

(d) machine in the manufacture of textiles for weaving man-made or natural fibres (including mineral fibres), high speed false twisting of fibres, or the mechanical cleaning of bobbins;

(e) multi-cutter moulding machine on wood, planing machine on wood, automatic or semi-automatic lathe on wood, multiple cross-cut machine on wood, automatic shaping machine on wood, double-end tenoning machine on wood, vertical spindle moulding machine (including a high speed routing machine) on wood, edge banding machine on wood, bandsawing machine (with a blade width of not less than 75 millimetres) on wood including one operated by moving the blade towards the material being cut, or chain saw on wood;

A

Prescribed disease or injury

Occupation

(f) jet of water (or a mixture of water and abrasive material) at a pressure above 680 bar, or jet channelling process to burn stone in a quarry;

(g) machine in a ship's engine room, or gas turbine for performance testing on a test bed, installation testing of a replacement engine in an aircraft, or acceptance testing of an Armed Service fixed wing combat aircraft;

(h) machine in the manufacture of glass containers or hollow ware for automatic moulding, automatic blow moulding, or automatic glass pressing and forming;

(i) spinning machine using compressed air to produce glass wool or mineral wool;

(j) continuous glass toughening furnace;

(k) firearm by a police firearms training officer;

(l) shot-blaster to carry abrasives in air for cleaning.

A11(a) Intense blanching of the skin, with a sharp demarcation line between affected and non-affected skin, where the blanching is cold-induced, episodic, occurs throughout the year and affects the skin of the distal with the middle and proximal phalanges, or distal with the middle phalanx (or in the case of a thumb the distal with the proximal phalanx), of–

(i) in the case of a person with 5 fingers (including thumb) on one hand, any 3 of those fingers, or

(ii) in the case of a person with only 4 such fingers, any 2 of those fingers, or

(iii) in the case of a person with less than 4 such fingers, any one of them or, as the case may be, the one remaining finger, where none of the person's fingers was subject to any degree of cold-induced, episodic blanching of the skin prior to the person's employment in an occupation described in the second column in relation to this paragraph, or

(a) The use of hand-held chain saws on wood; *or*

(b) the use of hand-held rotary tools in grinding or in the sanding or polishing of metal, or the holding of material being ground, or metal being sanded or polished by rotary tools; *or*

(c) the use of hand-held percussive metal-working tools, or the holding of metal being worked upon by percussive tools, in riveting, caulking, chipping, hammering, fettling or swaging; *or*

(d) the use of hand-held powered percussive drills or hand-held powered percussive hammers in mining, quarrying, demolition, or on roads or footpaths, including road construction; *or*

(e) the holding of material being worked upon by pounding machines in shoe manufacture.

Prescribed disease or injury	Occupation
(b) significant, demonstrable reduction in both sensory perception and manipulative dexterity with continuous numbness or continuous tingling all present at the same time in the distal phalanx of any finger (including thumb) where none of the person's fingers was subject to any degree of reduction in sensory perception, manipulative dexterity, numbness or tingling prior to the person's employment in an occupation described in the second column in relation to this paragraph, where the symptoms in paragraph (a) or paragraph (b) were caused by vibration.	

A12 Carpal tunnel syndrome.

(a) The use, at the time the symptoms first develop, of hand-held powered tools whose internal parts vibrate so as to transmit that vibration to the hand; *or*
(b) repeated palmar flexion and dorsiflexion of the wrist for at least 20 hours per week for a period or periods amounting in aggregate to at least 12 months in the 24 months prior to the onset of the symptoms, where 'repeated' means once or more often in every 30 seconds.

A13 Osteoarthritis of the hip.

Work in agriculture as a farmer or farm worker for a period of, or periods which amount in aggregate to, 10 years or more.

A14 Osteoarthritis of the knee

Work underground in a coal mine for a period of, or periods which amount in aggregate to, at least 10 years in any one or more of the following occupations:
(a) before 1 Januray 1986 as a coal miner; or
(b) on or after 1 Januray 1986 as a–
　(i) face worker working on a non-mechanised coal face;*
　(ii) development worker;
　(iii) face-salvage worker;
　(iv) conveyor belt cleaner; or
　(v) conveyor belt attendant.
*'A non-mechanised coal face' means a coal face without either powered roof supports or a power loader machine which simultaneously cuts and loads the coal or without both.
Work wholly or mainly fitting or laying carpets or other floors (other than concrete floors) for a period of, or periods which amount in aggregate to, 20 years or more.

Prescribed disease or injury	*Occupation*
B – Conditions due to biological agents	Any occupation involving:

B1 Anthrax.

    (a) Contact with anthrax spores, including contact with animals infected by anthrax; *or*

    (b) handling, loading, unloading or transport of animals of a type susceptible to infection with anthrax or of the products or residues of such animals.

B2 Glanders.

    Contact with equine animals or their carcasses.

B3 Infection by leptospira.

    (a) Work in places which are, or are liable to be, infested by rats, field mice or voles, or other small mammals; *or*

    (b) work at dog kennels or the care or handling of dogs; *or*

    (c) contact with bovine animals or pigs or their meat products.

B4 Ankylostomiasis.

    Contact with a source of ankylostomiasis.

B5 Tuberculosis.

    Contact with a source of tuberculous infection.

B6 Extrinsic allergic alveolitis (including farmer's lung).

    Exposure to moulds or fungal spores or heterologous proteins by reason of employment in:

    (a) agriculture, horticulture, forestry, cultivation of edible fungi or malt-working; *or*

    (b) loading or unloading or handling in storage mouldy vegetable matter or edible fungi; *or*

    (c) caring for or handling birds; *or*

    (d) handling bagasse.

B7 Infection by organisms of the genus brucella.

    Contact with:

    (a) animals infected by brucella, or their carcasses or parts thereof, or their untreated products; *or*

    (b) laboratory specimens or vaccines of, or containing, brucella.

B8*(a)* Infection by hepatitis A virus.

    Contact with raw sewage.

(b) Infection by hepatitis B or C virus.

    Contact with:

    (a) human blood or human blood products; *or*

    (b) any other source of hepatitis B or C virus.

B9 Infection by Streptococcus suis.

    Contact with pigs infected by Streptococcus suis, or with the carcasses, products or residues of pigs so infected.

B10*(a)* Avian chlamydiosis.

    Contact with birds infected with chlamydia psittaci, or with the remains or untreated products of such birds.

(b) Ovine chlamydiosis.

    Contact with sheep infected with chlamydia psittaci, or with the remains or untreated products of such sheep.

Prescribed disease or injury	Occupation
B11 Q fever.	Contact with animals, their remains or their untreated products.
B12 Orf.	Contact with sheep, goats or with the carcasses of sheep or goats.
B13 Hydatidosis.	Contact with dogs.
B14 Lyme disease.	Exposure to deer or other mammals of a type liable to harbour ticks harbouring Borrelia bacteria.
B15 Anaphylaxis.	Employment as a healthcare worker having contact with products made with natural rubber latex.

C – Conditions due to chemical agents	Any occupation involving:
C1(*a*) Anaemia with a haemoglobin concentration of 9g/dl or less, and a blood film showing punctate basophilia. (*b*) Peripheral neuropathy. (*c*) Central nervous system toxicity.	The use or handling of, or exposure to the fumes, dust or vapour of, lead or a compound of lead, or a substance containing lead.
C2 Central nervous system toxicity characterised by parkinsonism.	The use or handling of, or exposure to the fumes, dust or vapour of, manganese or a compound of manganese, or a substance containing manganese.
C3(*a*) Phossy Jaw.	Work involving the use or handling of, or exposure to, white phosphorus.
(*b*) Peripheral polyneuropathy with pyramidal involvement of the central nervous system, caused by organic compounds of phosphorus which inhibit the enzyme neuropathy target esterase.	Work involving the use or handling of, or exposure to, organic compounds of phosphorus.
C4 Primary carcinoma of the bronchus or lung.	Exposure to the fumes, dust or vapour of arsenic, a compound of arsenic or a substance containing arsenic.
C5(*a*) Central nervous system toxicity characterised by tremor and neuropsychiatric disease.	Exposure to mercury or inorganic compounds of mercury for a period of, or periods which amount in aggregate to, 10 years or more.
(*b*) Central nervous system toxicity characterised by combined cerebellar and cortical degeneration.	Exposure to methylmercury.
C6 Peripheral neuropathy.	The use or handling of, or exposure to carbon disulphide (also called carbon disulfide).
C7 Acute non-lymphatic leukaemia.	Exposure to benzene.
C12(*a*) Peripheral neuropathy. (*b*) Central nervous system toxicity.	Exposure to methyl bromide (also called bromomethane).
C13 Cirrhosis of the liver.	Exposure to chlorinated naphthalene.
C16(*a*) Neurotoxicity. (*b*) Cardiotoxicity.	Exposure to the dust of gonioma kamassi.
C17 Chronic beryllium disease.	Inhalation of beryllium or a compound of beryllium.

Prescribed disease or injury

C18 Emphysema.

C19*(a)* Peripheral neuropath.
(b) Central nervous system toxicity.

C20 Dystrophy of the cornea (including ulceration of the corneal surface) of the eye.

C21 Primary carcinoma of the skin.

C22*(a)* Primary carcinoma of the mucous membrane of the nose or paranasal sinuses.
(b) Primary carcinoma of a bronchus or lung.

C23 Primary neoplasm of the epithelial lining of the urinary tract (renal pelvis, ureter, bladder and urethra), including papilloma carcinoma-in-situ and invasive carcinoma.

C24*(a)* Angiosarcoma of the liver.
(b) Osteolysis of the terminal phalanges of the fingers.
(c) Sclerodermatous thickening of the skin of the hand.
(d) Liver fibrosis, due to exposure to vinyl chloride monomer.

C24A Raynaud's phenomenon due to exposure to vinyl chloride monomer.

Occupation

Inhalation of cadmium fumes for a period of, or periods which amount in aggregate to, 20 years or more.

Exposure to acrylamide.

Exposure to quinone or hydroquinone.

Exposure to arsenic or arsenic compounds, tar, pitch, bitumen, mineral oil (including paraffin) or soot.

Work before 1950 in the refining of nickel involving exposure to oxides, sulphides or water-soluble compounds of nickel.

(a) The manufacture of 1-naphtylamine, 2-naphthylamine, benzidine, auramine, magenta or 4 aminobiphenyl (also called biphenyl-4-ylamine);
(b) work in the process of manufacturing methylenebis-orthochloroanile (also called MbOCA) for a period of, or periods which amount in aggregate to, 12 months or more;
(c) exposure to 2-naphtylamine, benzidine, 4-aminobiphenyl (also called MbOCA) for a period of, or periods which amount in aggregate to, 12 months or more;
(d) exposure to orthotoluidine, 4-chloro-2-methylaniline or salts of those compounds; *or*
(e) exposure for a period of, or periods which amount in aggregate to, 5 years or more, to coal tar pitch volatiles produced in aluminium smelting involving the Sodeberg process (that is to say, the method of producing aluminium by electrolysis in which the anode consists of a paste of petroleum coke and mineral oil which is baked in situ).

Exposure to vinyl chloride monomer in the manufacture of polyvinyl chloride.

Exposure to vinyl chloride monomer in the manufacture of polyvinyl chloride before 1st January 1984.

Prescribed disease or injury	Occupation
C25 Vitiligo.	The use or handling of, or exposure to, para-tertiary-butylphenol (also called 4-tert-butylphenol), para-tertiary-butylcatechol (also called 4-tert-butylcatechol), para-amyl-phenol (also called p-pentyl phenol isomers), hydroquinone monobenzyl ether of hydroquinone (also called 4-benzyloxyphenol), mono-benzyl ether of hydroquinone (also called 4-benzyloxyphenol) or mono-butyl ether of hydroquinone (also called 4-butoxyphenol).
C26(a) Liver toxicity. (b) Kidney toxicity.	The use of or handling of, or exposure to, carbon tetrachloride (also called tetrachloromethane).
C27 Liver toxicity.	The use of or handling of, or exposure to the fumes of, or vapour containing, trichloromethane (also called chloroform).
C29 Peripheral neuropathy.	The use of or handling of, or exposure to, n-hexane or n-butyl methyl ketone.
C30(a) Dermatitis. (b) Ulceration of the mucous membrane or the epidermis.	The use or handling of, or exposure to, chromic acid, chromates or dichromates.
C31 Bronchiolitis obliterans.	The use or handling of, or exposure to, diacetyl (also called butanedione or 2,3-butanedione) in the manufacture of– (a) diacetyl; or (b) food favouring containing diacetyl; or (c) food to which food flavouring containing diacetyl is added.
C32 Carcinoma of the nasal cavity or associated air sinuses (nasal carcinoma).	(a) The manufacture of inorganic chromates; or (b) work in hexavalent chrome plating.
D – Miscellaneous conditions	Any occupation involving:
D1 Pneumoconiosis.	[Occupations specified in reg 2(b) of, and Part II of Schedule 1 to, the Social Security (Industrial Injuries) (Prescribed Diseases) Regulations 1985 which are too numerous to set out here. They are all occupations involving exposure to dust, such as mining, quarrying, sand blasting, grinding, making china or earthenware, boiler-sealing and other work involving the use of stone, asbestos, etc.]
D2 Byssinosis.	Work in any room where any process up to and including the weaving process is performed in a factory in which the spinning or manipulation of raw or waste cotton or of flax, or the weaving of cotton or flax, is carried on.

A

Prescribed disease or injury

Occupation

D3 Diffuse mesothelioma (primary neoplasm of the mesothelium of the pleura or of the pericardium or of the peritoneum).

Exposure to asbestos, asbestos dust or any admixture of asbestos at a level above that commonly found in the environment at large.

D4 Allergic rhinitis which is due to exposure to any of the following agents:
(a) isocyanates;
(b) platinum salts;
(c) fumes or dusts arising from the manufacture, transport or use of hardening agents (including epoxy resin curing agents) based on phthalic anhydride, tetrachlorophthalic anhydride, trimellitic anhydride or triethylenetetramine;
(d) fumes arising from the use of rosin as a soldering flux;
(e) proteolytic enzymes;
(f) animals including insects and other anthropods used for the purposes of research or education or in laboratories;
(g) dusts arising from the sowing, cultivation, harvesting, drying, handling, milling, transport or storage of barley, oats, rye, wheat or maize, or the handling, milling, transport or storage of meal or flour made therefrom;
(h) antibiotics;
(i) cimetidine;
(j) wood dust;
(k) ispaghula;
(l) castor bean dust;
(m) ipecacuanha;
(n) azodice-bonamide;
(o) animals including insects and other arthropods or their larval forms, used for the purposes of pest control or fruit cultivation, or the larval forms of animals used for the purposes of research, education or in laboratories;
(p) glutaraldehyde;
(q) persulphate salts or henna;
(r) crustaceans or fish or products arising from these in the food processing industry;
(s) reactive dyes;
(t) soya bean;
(u) tea dust;
(v) green coffee bean dust;
(w) fumes from stainless steel welding;
(x) products made with natural rubber latex.

Exposure to any of the agents set out in column 1 of this paragraph.

Prescribed disease or injury	Occupation
D5 Non-infective dermatitis of external origin (excluding dermatitis due to ionising particles or electro-magnetic radiant heat).	Exposure to dust, liquid or vapour or any other external agent except chromic acid, chromates or bi-chromates capable of irritating the skin (including friction or heat but excluding ionising particles or electromagnetic radiations other than radiant heat).
D6 Carcinoma of the nasal cavity or associated air sinuses (nasal carcinoma).	(a) Attendance for work in or about a building where wooden goods are; *or* (b) attendance for work in a building used for the manufacture of footwear or components of footwear made wholly or partly of leather or fibre board; *or* (c) attendance for work at a place used wholly or mainly for the repair of footwear made wholly or partly of leather or fibre board.
D7 Asthma which is due to exposure to any of the following agents: (a) isocyanates; (b) platinum salts; (c) fumes or dusts arising from the manufacture, transport or use of hardening agents (including epoxy resin curing agents) based on phthalic anhydride, tetrachlorophthalic anhydride, trimellitic anhydride or triethylenetetramine; (d) fumes arising from the use of rosin as a soldering flux; (e) proteolytic enzymes; (f) animals including insects and other anthropods used for the purposes of research or education or in laboratories; (g) dusts arising from the sowing, cultivation, harvesting, drying, handling, milling, transport or storage of barley, oats, rye, wheat or maize, or the handling, milling, transport or storage of meal or flour made therefrom; (h) antibiotics; (i) cimetidine; (j) wood dust; (k) ispaghula; (l) castor bean dust; (m) ipecacuanha; (n) azodicarbonamide;	Exposure to any of the agents set out in column 1 of this paragraph.

A

Prescribed disease or injury
(o) animals including insects and other arthropods or their larval forms, used for the purposes of pest control or fruit cultivation, or the larval forms of animals used for the purposes of research, education or in laboratories;
(p) glutaraldehyde;
(q) persulphate salts or henna;
(r) crustaceans or fish or products arising from these in the food processing industry;
(s) reactive dyes;
(t) soya bean;
(u) tea dust;
(v) green coffee bean dust;
(w) fumes from stainless steel welding;
(wa) products made with natural rubber latex;
(x) any other sensitising agent (occupational asthma).

D8 Primary carcinoma of the lung where there is accompanying evidence of asbestosis.

Occupation

(a) The working or handling of asbestos or any admixture of asbestos; or
(b) the manufacture or repair of asbestos textiles or other articles containing or composed of asbestos; or
(c) the cleaning of any machinery or plant used in any of the foregoing operations and of any chambers, fixtures and appliances for the collection of asbestos dust; or
(d) substantial exposure to the dust arising from any of the foregoing operations.

D8A Primary carcinoma of the lung.

Exposure to asbestos in the course of–
(a) the manufacture of asbestos textiles; or
(b) spraying asbestos; or
(c) asbestos insulation work; or
(d) applying or removing materials containing asbestos in the course of shipbuilding,
where all or any of the exposure occurs before 1st January 1975, for a period of, or periods which amount in aggregate to, five years or more, or otherwise, for a period of, or periods which amount in aggregate to, ten years or more.

Prescribed disease or injury	*Occupation*
D9 Unilateral or bilateral diffuse pleural thickening with obliteration of the costophrenic angle.	(a) The working or handling of asbestos; or any admixture of asbestos; *or*
	(b) the manufacture or repair of asbestos textiles or other articles containing or composed of asbestos; *or*
	(c) the cleaning of any machinery or plant used in any of the foregoing operations and appliances for the collection of asbestos dust; *or*
	(d) substantial exposure to the dust arising from any of the foregoing operations.
D10 Primary carcinoma of the lung.	(a) Work underground in a tin mine; *or*
	(b) exposure to bis(chloromethyl) ether produced during the manufacture of chloromethyl methyl ether; *or*
	(c) exposure to zinc chromate, calcium chromate or strontium chromate in their pure forms; *or*
	(d) employment wholly or mainly as a coke oven worker–
	(i) for a period of, or periods which amount in aggregate to, 15 years or more;
	(ii) in top oven work, for a period of, or periods which amount in aggregate to, 5 years or more; *or*
	(iii) in a combination of top oven work and other coke oven work for a total aggregate period of 15 years or more, where one year working in top oven work is treated as equivalent to 3 years in other coke oven work.
D11 Primary carcinoma of the lung where there is accompanying evidence of silicosis.	Exposure to silica dust in the course of:
	(a) the manufacture of glass or pottery;
	(b) tunnelling in or quarrying sandstone or granite;
	(c) mining metal ores;
	(d) slate quarrying or the manufacture of artefacts from slate;
	(e) mining clay;
	(f) using silicous materials as abrasives;
	(g) cutting stone;
	(h) stone masonry; *or*
	(i) work in a foundry.

Prescribed disease or injury

Occupation

D12 Except in the circumstances specified in regulation 2(d):
(a) chronic bronchitis; *or*
(b) emphysema; *or*
(c) both, where there is evidence of a forced expiratory volume in one second (measured from the position of maximum inspiration with the claimant making maximum effort) which is:
  (i) at least one litre below the appropriate mean value predicted, obtained from the following prediction formulae which give the mean values predicted in litres: For a man, where the measurement is made without back-extrapolation, (3.62 x Height in metres) – (0.031 x Age in years) – 1.41; or, where the measurement is made with back-extrapolation, (3.71 x Height in metres) – (0.032 x Age in years) – 1.44. For a woman, where the measurement is made without back-extrapolation, (3.29 x Height in metres) – (0.029 x Age in years) – 1.42; or where the measurement is made with back-extrapolation, (3.37 x Height in metres) – (0.030 x Age in years) – 1.46; or
  (ii) less than one litre.

Exposure to coal dust (whether before or after 5th July 1948) by reason of working–
(a) underground in a coal mine for a period or periods amounting in aggregate to at least 20 years;
(b) on the surface of a coal mine as a screen worker for a period or periods amounting in aggregate to at least 40 years before 1st January 1983; or
(c) both underground in a coal mine, and on the surface as a screen worker before 1st January 1983, where 2 years working as a surface screen worker is equivalent to 1 year working underground, amounting in aggregate to at least the equivalent of 20 years underground.

Any such period or periods shall include a period or periods of incapacity while engaged in such an occupation.

D13 Primary cacinoma of the nasopharynx

Exposure to wood dust in the course of the processing of wood or the manufacture or repair of wood products, for a period or periods which amount in aggregate to at least 10 years.

Appendix 8

Upper and lower earnings limits

Year	Lower earnings limit (£)	Primary threshold (£)	Upper earnings limit (£)
1990/91	46.00		350.00
1991/92	52.00		390.00
1992/93	54.00		405.00
1993/94	56.00		420.00
1994/95	57.00		430.00
1995/96	58.00		440.00
1996/97	61.00		455.00
1997/98	62.00		465.00
1998/99	64.00		485.00
1999/00	66.00		500.00
2000/01	67.00	76.00	535.00
2001/02	72.00	87.00	575.00
2002/03	75.00	89.00	585.00
2003/04	77.00	89.00	595.00
2004/05	79.00	91.00	610.00
2005/06	82.00	94.00	630.00
2006/07	84.00	97.00	645.00
2007/08	87.00	100.00	670.00
2008/09	90.00	105.00	770.00
2009/10	95.00	110.00	844.00
2010/11	97.00	110.00	844.00
2011/12	102.00	139.00	817.00
2012/13	107.00	146.00	817.00
2013/14	109.00	149.00	797.00
2014/15	111.00	153.00	805.00

Appendix 9

Disability which puts a person at a disadvantage in getting a job

Schedule 1 Regulation 9(1) to the Working Tax Credit (Entitlement and Maximum Rate) Regulations 2002

PART 1

1. When standing he cannot keep his balance unless he continually holds onto something.

2. Using any crutches, walking frame, walking stick, prosthesis or similar walking aid which he habitually uses, he cannot walk a continuous distance of 100 metres along level ground without stopping or without suffering severe pain.

3. He can use neither of his hands behind his back as in the process of putting on a jacket or of tucking a shirt into trousers.

4. He can extend neither of his arms in front of him so as to shake hands with another person without difficulty.

5. He can put neither of his hands up to his head without difficulty so as to put on a hat.

6. Due to lack of manual dexterity he cannot, with one hand, pick up a coin which is not more than $2\frac{1}{2}$ centimetres in diameter.

7. He is not able to use his hands or arms to pick up a full jug of 1 litre capacity and pour from it into a cup, without difficulty.

8. He can turn neither of his hands sideways through 180 degrees.

9. He–

   (a) is registered as blind or registered as partially sighted in a register compiled by a local authority under section 24(9)(g) of the National Assistance Act 1948;

   (b) has been certified as blind or as partially sighted and, in consequence, registered as blind or partially sighted in a register maintained by or on behalf of a council constituted under section 2 of the Local Government etc. (Scotland) Act 1994; or

(c) has been certified as blind or partially sighted and in consequence is registered as blind or partially sighted in a register maintained by or on behalf of a Health and Social Services Board in Northern Ireland.

10. He cannot see to read 16 point print at a distance greater than 20 centimetres, if appropriate, wearing the glasses he normally uses.

11. He cannot hear a telephone ring when he is in the same room as the telephone, if appropriate, using a hearing aid he normally uses.

12. In a quiet room he has difficulty in hearing what someone talking in a loud voice at a distance of 2 metres says, if appropriate, using a hearing aid he normally uses.

13. People who know him well have difficulty in understanding what he says.

14. When a person he knows well speaks to him, he has difficulty in understanding what that person says.

15. At least once a year during waking hours he is in a coma or has a fit in which he loses consciousness.

16. He has a mental illness for which he receives regular treatment under the supervision of a medically qualified person.

17. Due to mental disability he is often confused or forgetful.

18. He cannot do the simplest addition and subtraction.

19. Due to mental disability he strikes people or damages property or is unable to form normal social relationships.

20. He cannot normally sustain an 8 hour working day or a five day working week due to a medical condition or intermittent or continuous severe pain.

PART 2 (INITIAL CLAIMS ONLY)

21. As a result of an illness or accident he is undergoing a period of habilitation or rehabilitation.

Appendix 10

Limited capability for work assessment

Schedule 2 Employment and Support Allowance Regulations 2008 and Schedule 6 Universal Credit Regulations 2013

Activity	Descriptors	Points
Part 1: Physical disabilities		

1. Mobilising unaided by another person with or without a walking stick, manual wheelchair or other aid if such aid is normally or could reasonably be worn or used.	(a) Cannot, unaided by another person, either:
	  (i) mobilise more than 50 metres on level ground without stopping in order to avoid significant discomfort or exhaustion; or
	  (ii) repeatedly mobilise 50 metres within a reasonable timescale because of significant discomfort or exhaustion.
		15

	(b) Cannot, unaided by another person, mount or descend two steps even with the support of a handrail.	9

	(c) Cannot, unaided by another person, either:
	  (i) mobilise more than 100 metres on level ground without stopping in order to avoid significant discomfort or exhaustion; or
	  (ii) repeatedly mobilise 100 metres within a reasonable timescale because of significant discomfort or exhaustion.
		9

	(d) Cannot, unaided by another person, either:
	  (i) mobilise more than 200 metres on level ground without stopping in order to avoid significant discomfort or exhaustion; or
	  (ii) repeatedly mobilise 200 metres within a reasonable timescale because of significant discomfort or exhaustion.
		6

	(e) None of the above applies.	0

A

Activity	Descriptors	Points
2. Standing and sitting.	(a) Cannot move between one seated position and another seated position which are located next to one another without receiving physical assistance from another person.	15
	(b) Cannot, for the majority of the time, remain at a work station: (i) standing unassisted by another person (even if free to move around); or (ii) sitting (even in an adjustable chair); or (iii) a combination of paragraphs (i) and (ii), for more than 30 minutes, before needing to move away in order to avoid significant discomfort or exhaustion.	9
	(c) Cannot, for the majority of the time, remain at a work station either: (i) standing unassisted by another person (even if free to move around); or (ii) sitting (even in an adjustable chair); or (iii) a combination of paragraphs (i) and (ii), for more than an hour before needing to move away in order to avoid significant discomfort or exhaustion.	6
	(d) None of the above applies.	0
3. Reaching.	(a) Cannot raise either arm as if to put something in the top pocket of a coat or jacket.	15
	(b) Cannot raise either arm to top of head as if to put on a hat.	9
	(c) Cannot raise either arm above head height as if to reach for something.	6
	(d) None of the above applies.	0
4. Picking up and moving or transferring by the use of the upper body and arms.	(a) Cannot pick up and move a 0.5 litre carton full of liquid.	15
	(b) Cannot pick up and move a one litre carton full of liquid.	9
	(c) Cannot transfer a light but bulky object such as an empty cardboard box.	6
	(d) None of the above applies.	0
5. Manual dexterity.	(a) Cannot press a button (such as a telephone keypad) with either hand or cannot turn the pages of a book with either hand.	15
	(b) Cannot pick up a £1 coin or equivalent with either hand.	15
	(c) Cannot use a pen or pencil to make a meaningful mark with either hand.	9
	(d) Cannot single-handedly use a suitable keyboard or mouse.	9
	(e) None of the above applies.	0

Activity	Descriptors	Points
6. Making self understood through speaking, writing, typing, or other means which are normally or could reasonably be used, unaided by another person.	(a) Cannot convey a simple message, such as the presence of a hazard.	15
	(b) Has significant difficulty conveying a simple message to strangers.	15
	(c) Has some difficulty conveying a simple message to strangers.	6
	(d) None of the above applies.	0
7. Understanding communication by: (i) verbal means (such as hearing or lip reading) alone; (ii) non-verbal means (such as reading 16 point print or Braille) alone; or (iii) a combination of (i) and (ii), using any aid that is normally or could reasonably be used, unaided by another person.	(a) Cannot understand a simple message, such as the location of a fire escape, due to sensory impairment.	15
	(b) Has significant difficulty understanding a simple message from a stranger due to sensory impairment.	15
	(c) Has some difficulty understanding a simple message from a stranger due to sensory impairment.	6
	(d) None of the above applies.	0
8. Navigation and maintaining safety using a guide dog or other aid if either or both are normally used or could reasonably be used.	(a) Unable to navigate around familiar surroundings, without being accompanied by another person, due to sensory impairment.	15
	(b) Cannot safely complete a potentially hazardous task such as crossing the road, without being accompanied by another person, due to sensory impairment.	15
	(c) Unable to navigate around unfamiliar surroundings, without being accompanied by another person, due to sensory impairment.	9
	(d) None of the above applies.	0
9. Absence or loss of control whilst conscious leading to extensive evacuation of the bowel and/or bladder, other than enuresis (bed-wetting), despite the wearing or use of any aids or adaptations which are normally or could reasonably be worn or used.	(a) At least once a month experiences: (i) loss of control leading to extensive evacuation of the bowel and/or voiding of the bladder; or (ii) substantial leakage of the contents of a collecting device, sufficient to require cleaning and a change in clothing.	15
	(b) The majority of the time is at risk of loss of control leading to extensive evacuation of the bowel and/or voiding of the bladder, sufficient to require cleaning and a change in clothing, if not able to reach a toilet quickly.	6
	(c) Neither of the above applies.	0

Activity	Descriptors	Points
10. Consciousness during waking moments	(a) At least once a week, has an involuntary episode of lost or altered consciousness resulting in significantly disrupted awareness or concentration.	15
	(b) At least once a month, has an involuntary episode of lost or altered consciousness resulting in significantly disrupted awareness or concentration.	6
	(c) Neither of the above applies.	0

Part 2: Mental, cognitive and intellectual function assessment

Activity	Descriptors	Points
11. Learning tasks.	(a) Cannot learn how to complete a simple task, such as setting an alarm clock.	15
	(b) Cannot learn anything beyond a simple task, such as setting an alarm clock.	9
	(c) Cannot learn anything beyond a moderately complex task, such as the steps involved in operating a washing machine to clean clothes.	6
	(d) None of the above applies.	0
12. Awareness of everyday hazards (such as boiling water or sharp objects).	(a) Reduced awareness of everyday hazards leads to a significant risk of: (i) injury to self or others; or (ii) damage to property or possessions, such that the claimant requires supervision for the majority of the time to maintain safety.	15
	(b) Reduced awareness of everyday hazards leads to a significant risk of: (i) injury to self or others; or (ii) damage to property or possessions, such that the claimant frequently requires supervision to maintain safety.	9
	(c) Reduced awareness of everyday hazards leads to a significant risk of: (i) injury to self or others; or (ii) damage to property or possessions, such that the claimant occasionally requires supervision to maintain safety.	6
	(d) None of the above applies.	0
13. Initiating and completing personal action (which means planning, organisation, problem solving, prioritising or switching tasks).	(a) Cannot, due to impaired mental function, reliably initiate or complete at least two sequential personal actions.	15
	(b) Cannot, due to impaired mental function, reliably initiate or complete at least two sequential personal actions for the majority of the time.	9

Activity	Descriptors	Points
	(c) Frequently cannot, due to impaired mental function, reliably initiate or complete at least two sequential personal actions.	6
	(d) None of the above applies.	0
14. Coping with change.	(a) Cannot cope with any change to the extent that day to day life cannot be managed.	15
	(b) Cannot cope with minor planned change (such as a pre-arranged change to the routine time scheduled for a lunch break), to the extent that, overall, day to day life is made significantly more difficult.	9
	(c) Cannot cope with minor unplanned change (such as the timing of an appointment on the day it is due to occur), to the extent that, overall, day to day life is made significantly more difficult.	6
	(d) None of the above applies.	0
15. Getting about.	(a) Cannot get to any place outside the claimant's home with which the claimant is familiar.	15
	(b) Is unable to get to a specified place with which the claimant is familiar, without being accompanied by another person.	9
	(c) Is unable to get to a specified place with which the claimant is unfamiliar without being accompanied by another person.	6
	(d) None of the above applies.	0
16. Coping with social engagement due to cognitive impairment or mental disorder.	(a) Engagement in social contact is always precluded due to difficulty relating to others or significant distress experienced by the claimant.	15
	(b) Engagement in social contact with someone unfamiliar to the claimant is always precluded due to difficulty relating to others or significant distress experienced by the claimant.	9
	(c) Engagement in social contact with someone unfamiliar to the claimant is not possible for the majority of the time due to difficulty relating to others or significant distress experienced by the claimant.	6
	(d) None of the above applies.	0

Activity	Descriptors	Points
17. Appropriateness of behaviour with other people, due to cognitive impairment or mental disorder.	(a) Has, on a daily basis, uncontrollable episodes of aggressive or disinhibited behaviour that would be unreasonable in any workplace.	15
	(b) Frequently has uncontrollable episodes of aggressive or disinhibited behaviour that would be unreasonable in any workplace.	9
	(c) Occasionally has uncontrollable episodes of aggressive or disinhibited behaviour that would be unreasonable in any workplace.	6
	(d) None of the above applies.	0

Appendix 11

Limited capability for work-related activity assessment

Schedule 3 Employment and Support Allowance Regulations 2008 and Schedule 7 Universal Credit Regulations 2013

Activity	Descriptors
1. Mobilising unaided by another person with or without a walking stick, manual wheelchair or other aid if such aid is normally or could reasonably be worn or used.	Cannot either: (a) mobilise more than 50 metres on level ground without stopping in order to avoid significant discomfort or exhaustion; or (b) repeatedly mobilise 50 metres within a reasonable timescale because of significant discomfort or exhaustion.
2. Transferring from one seated position to another.	Cannot move between one seated position and another seated position located next to one another without receiving physical assistance from another person.
3. Reaching.	Cannot raise either arm as if to put something in the top pocket of a coat or jacket.
4. Picking up and moving or transferring by the use of the upper body and arms (excluding standing, sitting, bending or kneeling and all other activities specified in this Schedule).	Cannot pick up and move a 0.5 litre carton full of liquid.
5. Manual dexterity.	Cannot press a button (such as a telephone keypad) with either hand or cannot turn the pages of a book with either hand.
6. Making self understood through speaking, writing, typing, or other means which are normally, or could reasonably be, used unaided by another person.	Cannot convey a simple message, such as the presence of a hazard.

Activity	Descriptors
7. Understanding communication by: (i) verbal means (such as hearing or lip reading) alone; (ii) non-verbal means (such as reading 16 point print or Braille) alone; or (iii) a combination of (i) and (ii), using any aid that is normally, or could reasonably, be used unaided by another person.	Cannot understand a simple message, such as the location of a fire escape, due to sensory impairment.
8. Absence or loss of control whilst conscious leading to extensive evacuation of the bowel and/or voiding of the bladder, other than enuresis (bed-wetting), despite the wearing or use of any aids or adaptations which are normally or could reasonably be worn or used.	At least once a week experiences: (a) loss of control leading to extensive evacuation of the bowel and/or voiding of the bladder; or (b) substantial leakage of the contents of a collecting device sufficient to require the individual to clean themselves and change clothing.
9. Learning tasks.	Cannot learn how to complete a simple task, such as setting an alarm clock, due to cognitive impairment or mental disorder.
10. Awareness of hazard.	Reduced awareness of everyday hazards, due to cognitive impairment or mental disorder, leads to a significant risk of: (a) injury to self or others; or (b) damage to property or possessions, such that the claimant requires supervision for the majority of the time to maintain safety.
11. Initiating and completing personal action (which means planning, organisation, problem solving, prioritising or switching tasks).	Cannot, due to impaired mental function, reliably initiate or complete at least two sequential personal actions.
12. Coping with change.	Cannot cope with any change, due to cognitive impairment or mental disorder, to the extent that day to day life cannot be managed.
13. Coping with social engagement, due to cognitive impairment or mental disorder.	Engagement in social contact is always precluded due to difficulty relating to others or significant distress experienced by the claimant.

Activity	Descriptors
14. Appropriateness of behaviour with other people, due to cognitive impairment or mental disorder.	Has, on a daily basis, uncontrollable episodes of aggressive or disinhibited behaviour that would be unreasonable in any workplace.
15. Conveying food or drink to the mouth.	(a) Cannot convey food or drink to the claimant's own mouth without receiving physical assistance from someone else; (b) Cannot convey food or drink to the claimant's own mouth without repeatedly stopping or experiencing breathlessness or severe discomfort; (c) Cannot convey food or drink to the claimant's own mouth without receiving regular prompting given by someone else in the claimant's presence; or (d) Owing to a severe disorder of mood or behaviour, fails to convey food or drink to the claimant's own mouth without receiving: (i) physical assistance from someone else; or (ii) regular prompting given by someone else in the claimant's presence.
16. Chewing or swallowing food or drink.	(a) Cannot chew or swallow food or drink; (b) Cannot chew or swallow food or drink without repeatedly stopping or experiencing breathlessness or severe discomfort; (c) Cannot chew or swallow food or drink without repeatedly receiving regular prompting given by someone else in the claimant's presence; or (d) Owing to a severe disorder of mood or behaviour, fails to: (i) chew or swallow food or drink; or (ii) chew or swallow food or drink without regular prompting given by someone else in the claimant's presence.

Appendix 12

Minimum working conditions

Employers are required to provide certain minimum working conditions. These rules are relevant to the universal credit and jobseeker's allowance rules about sanctions and being available for and looking for work. A brief summary of the rules follows.

The Working Time Regulations
These regulations are designed to protect the health and safety of workers. The main rules are:
- a limit on the hours in the average working week;
- minimum annual holiday entitlement;
- entitlement to breaks from work (both daily breaks and a longer break once a week) and to rest periods while at work;
- special protection for night workers.

This *Handbook* cannot cover the detailed rules nor the complicated system of exceptions to them. Seek specialist advice if you think your employer is breaking these rules.

The National Minimum Wage Act
This Act provides that the minimum hourly rate of pay in any job should be:
- if you are aged 21 or over, £6.31;
- if you are aged 18–20, £5.03;
- if you are under age 18 and not of compulsory school age, £3.72;
- if you are in the first year of employment or are under 19, and you are employed under a contract of apprenticeship (or treated as if you are), £2.68.

Note: these amounts are due to increase in October 2014. See CPAG's online service and *Welfare Rights Bulletin* for updates.

A

Appendix 13

••

Personal independence payment assessment

Schedule 1 Social Security (Personal Independence Payment) Regulations 2013

Part 1: Interpretation

1. In this Schedule–
"aided" means with–
(a) the use of an aid or appliance; or
(b) supervision, prompting or assistance;
"assistance" means physical intervention by another person and does not include speech;
"assistance dog" means a dog trained to guide or assist a person with a sensory impairment;
"basic verbal information" means information in C's native language conveyed verbally in a simple sentence;
"basic written information" means signs, symbols and dates written or printed standard size text in C's native language;
"bathe" includes get into or out of an unadapted bath or shower;
"communication support" means support from a person trained or experienced in communicating with people with specific communication needs, including interpreting verbal information into a non-verbal form and vice versa;
"complex budgeting decisions" means decisions involving–
(a) calculating household and personal budgets;
(b) managing and paying bills; and
(c) planning future purchases;
"complex verbal information" means information in C's native language conveyed verbally in either more than one sentence or one complicated sentence;
"complex written information" means more than one sentence of written or printed standard size text in C's native language;
"cook" means heat food at or above waist height;
"dress and undress" includes put on and take off socks and shoes;

"engage socially" means–
  (a) interact with others in a contextually and socially appropriate manner;
  (b) understand body language; and
  (c) establish relationships;
"manage incontinence" means manage involuntary evacuation of the bowel or bladder, including use a collecting device or self-catheterisation, and clean oneself afterwards;
"manage medication or therapy" means take medication or undertake therapy, where a failure to do so is likely to result in a deterioration in C's health;
"medication" means medication to be taken at home which is prescribed or recommended by a registered–
  (a) doctor;
  (b) nurse; or
  (c) pharmacist;
"monitor health" means–
  (a) detect significant changes in C's health condition which are likely to lead to a deterioration in C's health; and
  (b) take action advised by a–
    (i) registered doctor;
    (ii) registered nurse; or
    (iii) health professional who is regulated by the Health Professions Council, without which C's health is likely to deteriorate;
"orientation aid" means a specialist aid designed to assist disabled people to follow a route safely;
"prepare", in the context of food, means make food ready for cooking or eating;
"prompting" means reminding, encouraging or explaining by another person;
"psychological distress" means distress related to an enduring mental health condition or an intellectual or cognitive impairment;
"read" includes read signs, symbols and words but does not include read Braille;
"simple budgeting decisions" means decisions involving–
  (a) calculating the cost of goods; and
  (b) calculating change required after a purchase;
"simple meal" means a cooked one-course meal for one using fresh ingredients;
"social support" means support from a person trained or experienced in assisting people to engage in social situations;
"stand" means stand upright with at least one biological foot on the ground;
"supervision" means the continuous presence of another person for the purpose of ensuring C's safety;
"take nutrition" means–
  (a) cut food into pieces, convey food and drink to one's mouth and chew and swallow food and drink; or
  (b) take nutrition by using a therapeutic source;

"therapeutic source" means parenteral or enteral tube feeding, using a rate-limiting device such as a delivery system or feed pump;

"therapy" means therapy to be undertaken at home which is prescribed or recommended by a–

(a) registered–

(i) doctor;

(ii) nurse; or

(iii) pharmacist; or

(b) health professional regulated by the Health Professions Council;

"toilet needs" means–

(a) getting on and off an unadapted toilet;

(b) evacuating the bladder and bowel; and

(c) cleaning oneself afterwards; and

"unaided" means without–

(a) the use of an aid or appliance; or

(b) supervision, prompting or assistance.

Part 2: Daily living activities

Activity	Descriptors	Points
1. Preparing food.	a. Can prepare and cook a simple meal unaided.	0
	b. Needs to use an aid or appliance to be able to either prepare or cook a simple meal.	2
	c. Cannot cook a simple meal using a conventional cooker but is able to do so using a microwave.	2
	d. Needs prompting to be able to either prepare or cook a simple meal.	2
	e. Needs supervision or assistance to either prepare or cook a simple meal.	4
	f. Cannot prepare and cook food.	8
2. Taking nutrition.	a. Can take nutrition unaided.	0
	b. Needs–	2
	(i) to use an aid or appliance to be able to take nutrition; or	
	(ii) supervision to be able to take nutrition; or	
	(iii) assistance to be able to cut up food.	
	c. Needs a therapeutic source to be able to take nutrition.	2
	d. Needs prompting to be able to take nutrition.	4
	e. Needs assistance to be able to manage a therapeutic source to take nutrition.	6
	f. Cannot convey food and drink to their mouth and needs another person to do so.	10

Activity	Descriptors	Points

3. Managing therapy or monitoring a health condition.	a. Either–
	  (i) does not receive medication or therapy or need to monitor a health condition; or
	  (ii) can manage medication or therapy or monitor a health condition unaided.
		0

	b. Needs either–
	  (i) to use an aid or appliance to be able to manage medication; or
	  (ii) supervision, prompting or assistance to be able to manage medication or monitor a health condition.
		1

	c. Needs supervision, prompting or assistance to be able to manage therapy that takes no more than 3.5 hours a week.	2
	d. Needs supervision, prompting or assistance to be able to manage therapy that takes more than 3.5 but no more than 7 hours a week.	4
	e. Needs supervision, prompting or assistance to be able to manage therapy that takes more than 7 but no more than 14 hours a week.	6
	f. Needs supervision, prompting or assistance to be able to manage therapy that takes more than 14 hours a week.	8
4. Washing and bathing.	a. Can wash and bathe unaided.	0
	b. Needs to use an aid or appliance to be able to wash or bathe.	2
	c. Needs supervision or prompting to be able to wash or bathe.	2
	d. Needs assistance to be able to wash either their hair or body below the waist.	2
	e. Needs assistance to be able to get in or out of a bath or shower.	3
	f. Needs assistance to be able to wash their body between the shoulders and waist.	4
	g. Cannot wash and bathe at all and needs another person to wash their entire body.	8
5. Managing toilet needs or incontinence.	a. Can manage toilet needs or incontinence unaided.	0
	b. Needs to use an aid or appliance to be able to manage toilet needs or incontinence.	2
	c. Needs supervision or prompting to be able to manage toilet needs.	2
	d. Needs assistance to be able to manage toilet needs.	4

A

Activity	Descriptors	Points
	e. Needs assistance to be able to manage incontinence of either bladder or bowel.	6
	f. Needs assistance to be able to manage incontinence of both bladder and bowel.	8
6. Dressing and undressing.	a. Can dress and undress unaided.	0
	b. Needs to use an aid or appliance to be able to dress or undress.	2
	c. Needs either– (i) prompting to be able to dress, undress or determine appropriate circumstances for remaining clothed; or (ii) prompting or assistance to be able to select appropriate clothing.	2
	d. Needs assistance to be able to dress or undress their lower body.	2
	e. Needs assistance to be able to dress or undress their upper body.	4
	f. Cannot dress or undress at all.	8
7. Communicating verbally.	a. Can express and understand verbal information unaided.	0
	b. Needs to use an aid or appliance to be able to speak or hear.	2
	c. Needs communication support to be able to express or understand complex verbal information.	4
	d. Needs communication support to be able to express or understand basic verbal information.	8
	e. Cannot express or understand verbal information at all even with communication support.	12
8. Reading and understanding signs, symbols and words.	a. Can read and understand basic and complex written information either unaided or using spectacles or contact lenses.	0
	b. Needs to use an aid or appliance, other than spectacles or contact lenses, to be able to read or understand either basic or complex written information.	2
	c. Needs prompting to be able to read or understand complex written information.	2
	d. Needs prompting to be able to read or understand basic written information.	4
	e. Cannot read or understand signs, symbols or words at all.	8

Activity	Descriptors	Points
9. Engaging with other people face to face.	a. Can engage with other people unaided.	0
	b. Needs prompting to be able to engage with other people.	2
	c. Needs social support to be able to engage with other people.	4
	d. Cannot engage with other people due to such engagement causing either – (i) overwhelming psychological distress to the claimant; or (ii) the claimant to exhibit behaviour which would result in a substantial risk of harm to the claimant or another person.	8
10. Making budgeting decisions.	a. Can manage complex budgeting decisions unaided.	0
	b. Needs prompting or assistance to be able to make complex budgeting decisions.	2
	c. Needs prompting or assistance to be able to make simple budgeting decisions.	4
	d. Cannot make any budgeting decisions at all.	6

Part 3: Mobility activities

1. Planning and following journeys.	a. Can plan and follow the route of a journey unaided.	0
	b. Needs prompting to be able to undertake any journey to avoid overwhelming psychological distress to the claimant.	4
	c. Cannot plan the route of a journey.	8
	d. Cannot follow the route of an unfamiliar journey without another person, assistance dog or orientation aid.	10
	e. Cannot undertake any journey because it would cause overwhelming psychological distress to the claimant.	10
	f. Cannot follow the route of a familiar journey without another person, an assistance dog or an orientation aid.	12
2. Moving around.	a. Can stand and then move more than 200 metres, either aided or unaided.	0
	b. Can stand and then move more than 50 metres but no more than 200 metres, either aided or unaided.	4
	c. Can stand and then move unaided more than 20 metres but no more than 50 metres.	8

A

Activity	Descriptors	Points
	d. Can stand and then move using an aid or appliance more than 20 metres but no more than 50 metres.	10
	e. Can stand and then move more than 1 metre but no more than 20 metres, either aided or unaided.	12
	f. Cannot, either aided or unaided–	12
	(i) stand; or	
	(ii) move more than 1 metre.	

Appendix 14

Abbreviations used in the notes

AAC	Administrative Appeals Chamber	HLR	Housing Law Reports
AACR	Administrative Appeals Chamber Reports	IAC	Immigration and Asylum Chamber
AC	Appeal Cases	ICR	Industrial Cases Reports
All ER	All England Reports	JPR	Justice of the Peace Reports
Art(s)	Article(s)	KB	King's Bench
CA	Court of Appeal	NICA	Northern Ireland Court of Appeal
CCLR	Community Care Law Reports	NICom	Northern Ireland Social Security Commissioner
CJEU	Court of Justice of the European Union	para(s)	paragraph(s)
CLY	Current Law Year Book	QB	Queen's Bench Reports
CPR	Civil Procedure Rules	QBD	Queen's Bench Division
CS	Court of Session	r(r)	rule(s)
CSIH	Court of Session, Inner House	Reg(s)	Regulation(s)
CSOH	Court of Session, Outer House	s(s)	section(s)
		SC	Supreme Court
		Sch(s)	Schedule(s)
DC	Divisional Court	SCLR	Scottish Civil Law Reports
Dir	Directive	ScotCS	Scottish Court of Session
ECJ	European Court of Justice	SLT	Scots Law Times
ECR	European Court Reports	SSAC	Social Security Advisory Committee
ECtHR	European Court of Human Rights	TCC	Tax and Chancery Chamber
EWCA Civ	England and Wales Court of Appeal (Civil Division)	TFEU	The Treaty on the Functioning of the European Union
EWCA Crim	England and Wales Court of Appeal (Criminal Division)	UKHL	United Kingdom House of Lords
EWHC	England and Wales High Court	UKSC	United Kingdom Supreme Court
FLR	Family Law Reports	UKUT	United Kingdom Upper Tibunal
HC	High Court		
HL	House of Lords	WLR	Weekly Law Reports

Acts of Parliament

CA 1989	Children Act 1989
C(LC)A 2000	Children (Leaving Care) Act 2000
C(S)A 1995	Children (Scotland) Act 1995
CJPOA 1994	Criminal Justice and Public Order Act 1994
CMOPA 2008	Child Maintenance and Other Payments Act 2008
CPA 2004	Civil Partnership Act 2004
CSA 1991	Child Support Act 1991
CSA 1995	Child Support Act 1995
CSPSSA 2000	Child Support, Pensions and Social Security Act 2000
ECA 1972	European Communities Act 1972
ETA 1973	Employment and Training Act 1973
GRA 2004	Gender Recognition Act 2004
HRA 1998	Human Rights Act 1998
IA 1971	Immigration Act 1971
IA 1988	Immigration Act 1988
IAA 1999	Immigration and Asylum Act 1999
IT(EP)A 2003	Income Tax (Earnings and Pensions) Act 2003
ITTOIA 2005	Income Tax (Trading and Other Income) Act 2005
JSA 1995	Jobseekers Act 1995
MCA 1973	Matrimonial Causes Act 1973
NHSA 2006	National Health Service Act 2006
NHS(S)A 1978	National Health Service (Scotland) Act 1978
NHS(W)A 2006	National Health Service (Wales) Act 2006
NHSCCA 1990	National Health Service and Community Care Act 1990
NIA 1965	National Insurance Act 1965
NIAA 2002	Nationality, Immigration and Asylum Act 2002
PA 1995	Pensions Act 1995
PA 2007	Pensions Act 2007
PSA 1993	Pension Schemes Act 1993
SPCA 2002	State Pension Credit Act 2002
SSA 1975	Social Security Act 1975
SSA 1998	Social Security Act 1998
SSA(F)A 1997	Social Security Administration (Fraud) Act 1997
SSAA 1992	Social Security Administration Act 1992
SSCBA 1992	Social Security Contributions and Benefits Act 1992
SSC(TF)A 1999	Social Security Contributions (Transfer of Functions etc) Act 1999
SSFA 2001	Social Security Fraud Act 2001
SS(RB)A 1997	Social Security (Recovery of Benefits) Act 1997
TCA 2002	Tax Credits Act 2002
TCEA 2007	Tribunals, Courts and Enforcement Act 2007
TMA 1970	Taxes Management Act 1970
WRA 2007	Welfare Reform Act 2007
WRA 2009	Welfare Reform Act 2009
WRA 2012	Welfare Reform Act 2012
WRPA 1999	Welfare Reform and Pensions Act 1999

A

Regulations and other statutory instruments

Each set of regulations has a statutory instrument (SI) number and a date. You ask for them by giving their date and number.

A(IWA) Regs	The Accession (Immigration and Worker Authorisation) Regulations 2006 No.3317
A(IWR) Regs	The Accession (Immigration and Worker Registration) Regulations 2004 No.1219
AC(IWA) Regs	The Accession of Croatia (Immigration and Worker Authorisation) Regulations 2013 No.1460
ASPP(BAAO)(A) Regs	The Additional Statutory Paternity Pay (Birth, Adoption and Adoptions from Overseas)(Administration) Regulations 2010 No.154
ASPP(AO) Regs	The Additional Statutory Paternity Pay (Adoptions from Overseas) Regulations 2010 No.1057
ASPP(G) Regs	The Additional Statutory Paternity Pay (General) Regulations 2010 No.1056
ASPP(WR) Regs	The Additional Statutory Paternity Pay (Weekly Rates) Regulations 2010 No.1060
C(LC)SSB Regs	The Children (Leaving Care) Social Security Benefits Regulations 2001 No.3074
C(LC)SSB(S) Regs	The Children (Leaving Care) Social Security Benefits (Scotland) Regulations 2004 No.747
C(LC)(W) Regs	The Children (Leaving Care) (Wales) Regulations 2001 No.2189 (W151)
CB Regs	The Child Benefit (General) Regulations 2006 No.223
CB(R) Regs	The Child Benefit (Rates) Regulations 2006 No.965
CB&GA(AA) Regs	The Child Benefit and Guardian's Allowance (Administrative Arrangements) Regulations 2003 No.494
CB&GA(Admin) Regs	The Child Benefit and Guardian's Allowance (Administration) Regulations 2003 No.492
CB&GA(DA) Regs	The Child Benefit and Guardian's Allowance (Decisions and Appeals) Regulations 2003 No.916
CC(DIS) Regs	The Community Charges (Deductions from Income Support) (No.2) Regulations 1990 No.545
CL(E) Regs	The Care Leavers (England) Regulations 2010 No.2571
CPP&CR(E) Regs	The Care Planning, Placement and Case Review (England) Regulations 2010 No.959
CS(MASC) Regs	The Child Support (Maintenance Assessments and Special Cases) Regulations 1992 No.1815
CS(MCSC) Regs	The Child Support (Maintenance Calculations and Special Cases) Regulations 2000 No.2001/155
CT(DIS) Regs	The Council Tax (Deductions from Income Support) Regulations 1993 No.494
CTC Regs	The Child Tax Credit Regulations 2002 No.2007
CTR(S) Regs	The Council Tax Reduction (Scotland) Regulations 2012 No.303
CTR(SPC)S Regs	The Council Tax Reduction (State Pension Credit) (Scotland) Regulations 2012 No.319

A

CTRS(DS)E Regs	The Council Tax Reduction Schemes (Default Scheme) (England) Regulations 2012 No.2886
CTRS(DS)W Regs	The Council Tax Reduction Schemes (Default Scheme) (Wales) Regulations 2012 No.3145 (W317)
CTRS(PR)E Regs	The Council Tax Reduction Schemes (Prescribed Requirements) (England) Regulations 2012 No.2885
CTRSPR(W) Regs	The Council Tax Reduction Schemes and Prescribed Requirements (Wales) Regulations 2012 No.3144 (W316)
DFA Regs	Discretionary Financial Assistance Regulations 2001 No.1167
ESA Regs	The Employment and Support Allowance Regulations 2008 No.794
ESA Regs 2013	The Employment and Support Allowance Regulations 2013 No.379
ESA(TP) Regs	The Employment and Support Allowance (Transitional Provisions) Regulations 2008 No.795
ESA(TP)(EA)(No.2) Regs	The Employment and Support Allowance (Transitional Provisions, Housing Benefit and Council Tax Benefit) (Existing Awards) (No.2) Regulations 2010 No.1907
ESA(WRA) Regs	The Employment and Support Allowance (Work-Related Activity) Regulations 2011 No.1349
F(DIS) Regs	The Fines (Deductions from Income Support) Regulations 1992 No.2182
GA(Gen) Regs	The Guardian's Allowance (General) Regulations 2003 No.495
HB Regs	The Housing Benefit Regulations 2006 No.213
HB(SPC) Regs	The Housing Benefit (Persons who have Attained the Qualifying Age for State Pension Credit) Regulations 2006 No.214
HB&CTB(CP) Regs	The Housing Benefit and Council Tax Benefit (Consquential Provisions) Regulations 2006 No.217
HB&CTB(DA) Regs	The Housing Benefit and Council Tax Benefit (Decisions and Appeals) Regulations 2001 No.1002
HB&CTB(WPD) Regs	The Housing Benefit and Council Tax Benefit (War Pension Disregards) Regulations 2007 No.1619
HSS(DHSF)(W) Regs	The Healthy Start Scheme (Description of Healthy Start Food) (Wales) Regulations 2006 No.3108
HSS&WF(A) Regs	The Healthy Start Scheme and Welfare Food (Amendment) Regulations 2005 No.3262
I(EEA) Regs	The Immigration (European Economic Area) Regulations 2006 No.1003
I(EEA)A Regs	The Immigration (European Economic Area) (Amendment) (No.2) Regulations 2013 No.3032
IS Regs	The Income Support (General) Regulations 1987 No.1967
IS(AT) Regs	The Income Support (General) Amendment and Transitional Regualtions 1995 No.2287
IS(JSACA) Regs	The Income Support (General)(Jobseeker's Allowance Consequential Amendments) Regulations 1996 No.206

IS(PCP) Regs	The Income Support (Prescribed Categories of Person) Regulations 2009 No.3152
JSA Regs	The Jobseeker's Allowance Regulations 1996 No.207
JSA Regs 2013	The Jobseeker's Allowance Regulations 2013 No.378
JSA(HR)A Regs	The Jobseeker's Allowance (Habitual Residence) Amendment Regulations 2013 No.3196
JSA(MWAS) Regs	The Jobseeker's Allowance (Mandatory Work Activity Scheme) Regulations 2011 No.688
JSA(SAPOE) Regs	The Jobseeker's Allowance (Schemes for Assisting Persons to Obtain Employment) Regulations 2013 No.276
NHS(CDA) Regs	The National Health Service (Charges for Drugs and Appliances) Regulations 2000 No.620
NHS(DC) Regs	The National Health Service (Dental Charges) Regulations 2005 No.3477
NHS(DC)(S) Regs	The National Health Service (Dental Charges) (Scotland) Regulations 2003 No.158
NHS(DC)(W) Regs	The National Health Service (Dental Charges) (Wales) Regulations 2006 No.491
NHS(FP&CDA)(S) Regs	The National Health Service (Free Prescriptions and Charges for Drugs and Appliances) (Scotland) Regulations 2011 No.55
NHS(FP&CDA)(W) Regs	The National Health Service (Free Prescriptions and Charges for Drugs and Appliances) (Wales) Regulations 2007 No.121
NHS(GOS) Regs	The National Health Service (General Ophthalmic Services) Regulations 1986 No.975
NHS(OCP) Regs	The National Health Service (Optical Charges and Payments) Regulations 1997 No.818
NHS(OCP) Regs 2013	The National Health Service (Optical Charges and Payments) Regulations 2013 No.461
NHS(OCP)(S) Regs	The National Health Service (Optical Charges and Payments) (Scotland) Regulations 1998 No.642
NHS(TERC) Regs	The National Health Service (Travelling Expenses and Remission of Charges) Regulations 2003 No.2382
NHS(TERC)(S) Regs	The National Health Service (Travelling Expenses and Remission of Charges) (Scotland) (No.2) Regulations 2003 No.460
NHS(TERC)(W) Regs	The National Health Service (Travelling Expenses and Remission of Charges Regulations) (Wales) 2007 No.1104
OSPP(A)ASPP(A)& SAP(AO)(PAM) Regs	The Ordinary Statutory Paternity Pay (Adoption), Additional Statutory Paternity Pay (Adoption) and Statutory Adoption Pay (Adoptions from Overseas) (Persons Abroad and Mariners) Regulations 2010 No.150
PAL Regs	The Paternity and Adoption Leave Regulations 2002 No.2788
PIP(TP) Regs	The Personal Independence Payment (Transitional Provisions) Regulations 2013 No.387

POS Regs	The Primary Ophthalmic Services Regulations 2008 No.1186
RO(HBF)O	The Rent Officers (Housing Benefit Functions) Order 1997 No.1984
RO(HBF)(S)O	The Rent Officers (Housing Benefit Functions) (Scotland) Order 1997 No.144
RO(UCF)O	The Rent Officers (Universal Credit Functions) Order 2013 No.382
SF(AM) Regs	The Social Fund (Applications and Miscellaneous Provisions) Regulations 2008 No.2265
SF(AR) Regs	The Social Fund (Application for Review) Regulations 1988 No.34
SF(RDB) Regs	The Social Fund (Recovery by Deductions from Benefits) Regulations 1988 No.35
SFCWP Regs	The Social Fund Cold Weather Payments (General) Regulations 1988 No.1724
SFM&FE Regs	The Social Fund Maternity and Funeral Expenses (General) Regulations 2005 No.3061
SFWFP Regs	The Social Fund Winter Fuel Payment Regulations 2000 No.729
SMP Regs	The Statutory Maternity Pay(General) Regulations 1986 No.1960
SMP(ME) Regs	The Statutory Maternity Pay (Medical Evidence) Regulations 1987 No.235
SMP(PAM) Regs	The Statutory Maternity Pay (Persons Abroad and Mariners) Regulations 1987 No.418
SMPSS(MA) Regs	The Statutory Maternity Pay, Social Security (Maternity Allowance) and Social Security (Overlapping Benefits) (Amendment) Regulations 2006 No.2379
SPC Regs	The State Pension Credit Regulations 2002 No.1792
SPC(CTMP) Regs	The State Pension Credit (Consequential, Transitional and Miscellaneous Provisions) Regulations 2002 No.3019
SPP(A)&SAP(AO)(No.2) Regs	The Statutory Paternity Pay (Adoption) and Statutory Adoption Pay (Adoptions from Overseas) (No.2) Regulations 2003 No.1194
SPPSAP(A) Regs	The Statutory Paternity Pay and Statutory Adoption Pay (Administration) Regulations 2002 No.2820
SPPSAP(G) Regs	The Statutory Paternity Pay and Statutory Adoption Pay (General) Regulations 2002 No.2822
SPPSAP(PAM) Regs	The Statutory Paternity Pay and Statutory Adoption Pay (Persons Abroad and Mariners) Regulations 2002 No.2821
SPPSAP(WR) Regs	The Statutory Paternity Pay and Statutory Adoption Pay (Weekly Rates) Regulations 2002 No.2818
SS(AA) Regs	The Social Security (Attendance Allowance) Regulations 1991 No.2740
SS(CatE) Regs	The Social Security (Categorisation of Earners) Regulations 1978 No.1689

SS(CCPC) Regs	Social Security (Contribution Credits for Parents and Carers) Regulations 2009 No.19
SS(Con) Regs	The Social Security (Contributions) Regulations 2001 No.1004
SS(C&P) Regs	The Social Security (Claims and Payments) Regulations 1987 No.1968
SS(CP)Regs	The Social Security (Civil Penalties) Regulations 2012 No.1990
SS(Cr) Regs	The Social Security (Credits) Regulations 1975 No.556
SS(CTCNIN)Regs	The Social Security (Crediting and Treatment of Contributions, and National Insurance Numbers) Regulations 2001 No.769
SS(DLA) Regs	The Social Security (Disability Living Allowance) Regulations 1991 No.2890
SS(DLA,AA&CA)(A) Regs	The Social Security (Disability Living Allowance, Attendance Allowance and Carer's Allowance) (Amendment) Regulations 2013 No.389
SS(DRPSAPGRB)(MP) Regs	The Social Security (Deferral of Retirement Pension, Shared Additional Pension and Graduated Retirement Benefit)(Miscellaneous Provisions) Regulations 2005 No.2677
SS(EEEIIP) Regs	The Social Security (Employed Earners' Employment for Industrial Injuries Purposes) Regulations 1975 No.467
SS(EF) Regs	The Social Security (Earnings Factor) Regulations 1979 No.676
SS(GB) Regs	The Social Security (General Benefits) Regulations 1982 No.1408
SS(GRB) No.2 Regs	The Social Security (Graduated Retirement Benefit) (No.2) Regulations 1978 No.393
SS(HCSA)(A&M) Regs	The Social Security (Housing Costs Special Arrangements) (Amendment and Modification) Regulations 2008 No.3195
SS(HIP) Regs	The Social Security (Hospital In-Patients) Regulations 2005 No.3360
SS(HR)A Regs	The Social Security (Habitual Residence) Amendment Regulations 2004 No.1232
SS(IA)CA Regs	The Social Security (Immigration and Asylum) Consequential Amendments Regulations 2000 No.636
SS(IB) Regs	The Social Security (Incapacity Benefit) Regulations 1994 No.2946
SS(IB)MA Regs	The Social Security (Incapacity Benefit) Miscellaneous Amendments Regulations 2000 No.3120
SS(IB)(T) Regs	The Social Security (Incapacity Benefit) (Transitional) Regulations 1995 No.310
SS(IB-ID) Regs	The Social Security (Incapacity Benefit – Increases for Dependants) Regulations 1994 No.2945
SS(IBWFI) Regs	The Social Security (Incapacity Benefit Work-focused Interviews) Regulations 2008 No.2928
SS(ICA) Regs	The Social Security (Invalid Care Allowance) Regulations 1976 No.409

A

SS(IFW) Regs	The Social Security (Incapacity for Work) (General) Regulations 1995 No.311
SS(II)(AB) Regs	The Social Security (Industrial Injuries) (Airmen's Benefits) Regulations 1975 No.469
SS(II)(MB) Regs	The Social Security (Industrial Injuries) (Mariners' Benefits) Regulations 1975 No.470
SS(II&D)MP Regs	The Social Security (Industrial Injuries and Diseases) Miscellaneous Provisions Regulations 1986 No.1561
SS(IIPD) Regs	The Social Security (Industrial Injuries) (Prescribed Diseases) Regulations 1985 No.967
SS(II)(RE) Regs	The Social Security (Industrial Injuries) (Regular Employment) Regulations 1990 No.256
SS(JPI) Regs	The Social Security (Jobcentre Plus Interviews) Regulations 2002 No.1703
SS(JPIP) Regs	Social Security (Jobcentre Plus Interviews for Partners) Regulations 2003 No.1886
SS(LB) Regs	The Social Security (Loss of Benefit) Regulations 2001 No.4022
SS(LP) Regs	The Social Security (Lone Parents and Miscellaneous Amendments) Regulations 2012 No.874
SS(LPMA) Regs	The Social Security (Lone Parents and Miscellaneous Amendments) Regulations 2008 No.3051
SS(MA)(No.5) Regs 2009	The Social Security (Miscellaneous Amendments) (No.5) Regulations 2009 No.3228
SS(MA)(No.5) Regs 2010	The Social Security (Miscellaneous Amendments) (No.5) Regulations 2010 No.2429
SS(MAP) Regs	The Social Security (Maximum Additional Pension) Regulations 1978 No.949
SS(MatA) Regs	The Social Security (Maternity Allowance) Regulations 1987 No.416
SS(MatA)(E) Regs	The Social Security (Maternity Allowance) (Earnings) Regulations 2000 No.688
SS(MatA)(WA) Regs	The Social Security (Maternity Allowance) (Work Abroad) Regulations 1987 No.417
SS(ME) Regs	The Social Security (Medical Evidence) Regulations 1976 No.615
SS(NCC) Regs	The Social Security (Notification of Change of Circumstances) Regulations 2001 No.3252
SS(OB) Regs	The Social Security (Overlapping Benefits) Regulations 1979 No.597
SS(OR) Regs	The Social Security (Overpayments and Recovery) Regulations 2013 No.384
SS(PA)A Regs	Social Security (Persons from Abroad) Amendment Regulations 2006 No.1026
SS(PAB) Regs	The Social Security (Payments on Account of Benefit) Regulations 2013 No.383
SS(PAOR) Regs	The Social Security (Payments on Account, Overpayments and Recovery) Regulations 1988 No.664
SS(PFA)MA Regs	The Social Security (Persons From Abroad) Miscellaneous Amendment Regulations 1996 No.30

SS(PIP) Regs	The Social Security (Personal Independence Payment) Regulations 2013 No.377
SS(RB) Regs	The Social Security (Recovery of Benefits) Regulations 1997 No.2205
SS(RB)App Regs	The Social Security (Recovery of Benefits) (Appeals) Regulations 1997 No.2237
SS(SDA) Regs	The Social Security (Severe Disablement Allowances) Regulations 1984 No.1303
SS(STB)(T) Regs	The Social Security (Short-term Benefits) (Transitional) Regulations 1974 No.2192
SS(WB&RP) Regs	The Social Security (Widow's Benefit and Retirement Pensions) Regulations 1979 No.642
SS(WBRP&OB)(T) Regs	The Social Security (Widow's Benefit, Retirement Pensions and Other Benefits) (Transitional) Regulations 1979 No.643
SS(WFILP) Regs	The Social Security (Work-focused Interviews for Lone Parents) and Miscellaneous Amendments Regulations 2000 No.1926
SS(WTCCTC)(CA) Regs	The Social Security (Working Tax Credit and Child Tax Credit)(Consequential Amendments) Regulations 2003 No.455
SSA(F)AO No.5	The Social Security Administration (Fraud) Act 1997 (Commencement No.5) Order 1997 No.2766
SSB(CE) Regs	The Social Security Benefit (Computation of Earnings) Regulations 1996 No.2745
SSB(Dep) Regs	The Social Security Benefit (Dependency) Regulations 1977 No.343
SSB(MW&WSP) Regs	The Social Security (Benefit) (Married Women and Widows' Special Provisions) Regulations 1974 No.2010
SSB(PA) Regs	The Social Security Benefit (Persons Abroad) Regulations 1975 No.563
SSB(PRT) Regs	The Social Security Benefit (Persons Residing Together) Regulations 1977 No.956
SSC(DA) Regs	The Social Security Contributions (Decisions and Appeals) Regulations 1999 No.1027
SSCBA(AAO) Regs	The Social Security Contributions and Benefits Act 1992 (Application of Parts 12ZA and 12ZB to Adoptions from Overseas) Regulations 2003 No.499
SSCBA(MHMFIB) Regs	The Social Security Contributions and Benefits Act 1992 (Modifications for Her Majesty's Forces and Incapacity Benefit) Regulations 2003 No.737
SSCP(TCA) Regs	The Social Security Commissioners (Procedure) (Tax Credit Appeals) Regulations 2002 No.3237
SS&CS(DA) Regs	The Social Security and Child Support (Decisions and Appeals) Regulations 1999 No.991
SSCSVDOP(DA)(A) Regs	The Social Security, Child Support, Vaccine Damage and Other Payments (Decisions and Appeals) (Amendment) Regulations 2013 SI No.2380
SSFA(PM) Regs	The Social Security and Family Allowances (Polygamous Marriages) Regulations 1975 No.561

SSP Regs	The Statutory Sick Pay (General) Regulations 1982 No.894
SSP(MAPA) Regs	The Statutory Sick Pay (Mariners, Airmen and Persons Abroad) Regulations 1982 No.1349
SSP(ME) Regs	The Statutory Sick Pay (Medical Evidence) Regulations 1985 No.1604
SSP&SMP(D) Regs	The Statutory Sick Pay and Statutory Maternity Pay (Decisions) Regulations 1999 No.776
TC(A) Regs	The Tax Credits (Appeals) Regulations 2002 No.2926
TC(CN) Regs	The Tax Credits (Claims and Notifications) Regulations 2002 No.2014
TC(DCI) Regs	The Tax Credits (Definition and Calculation of Income) Regulations 2002 No.2006
TC(Imm) Regs	The Tax Credits (Immigration) Regulations 2003 No.653
TC(IR) Regs	The Tax Credits (Interest Rate) Regulations 2003 No.123
TC(ITDR) Regs	The Tax Credits (Income Thresholds and Determination of Rates) Regulations 2002 No.2008
TC(NA)Regs	The Tax Credits (Notice of Appeal) Regulations 2002 No.3119
TC(OE) Regs	The Tax Credits (Official Error) Regulations 2003 No.692
TC(PC) Regs	The Tax Credits (Payments by the Commissioners) Regulations 2002 No.2173
TC(PM) Regs	The Tax Credits (Polygamous Marriages) Regulations 2003 No.742
TC(R) Regs	The Tax Credits (Residence) Regulations 2003 No.654
TCA(No.3)O	The Tax Credits Act 2002 (Commencement No.3 and Transitional Provisions and Savings) Order 2003 No.938
TCA(TP)O	The Tax Credits Act 2002 (Transitional Provisions) Order 2010 No.644
TP(FT) Rules	The Tribunal Procedure (First-tier Tribunal) (Social Entitlement Chamber) Rules 2008 No.2685
TP(FT)(TC) Rules	The Tribunal Procedure (First-tier Tribunal) (Tax Chamber) Rules 2009 No.273
TP(UT) Rules	The Tribunal Procedure (Upper Tribunal) Rules 2008 No.2698
UC Regs	The Universal Credit Regulations 2013 No.376
UC,PIP,JSA&ESA(C&P) Regs	The Universal Credit, Personal Independence Payment, Jobseeker's Allowance and Employment and Support Allowance (Claims and Payments) Regulations 2013 No.380
UC,PIP,JSA&ESA(DA) Regs	The Universal Credit, Personal Independence Payment, Jobseeker's Allowance and Employment and Support Allowance (Decisions and Appeals) Regulations 2013 No.381
UC(TP) Regs	The Universal Credit (Transitional Provisions) Regulations 2013 No.386
WF Regs	The Welfare Food Regulations 1996 No.1434

A

WRA(No.8)O	The Welfare Reform Act 2012 (Commencement No.8 and Savings and Transitional Provisions) Order 2013 No.358
WRA(No.9)O	The Welfare Reform Act 2012 (Commencement No.9 and Transitional and Transitory Provisions and Commencement No.8 and Savings and Transitional Provisions (Amendment)) Order 2013 No.983
WRA(No.11)O	The Welfare Reform Act 2012 (Commencement No.11 and Transitional and Transitory Provisions and Commencement No.9 and Transitional and Transitory Provisions (Amendment)) Order 2013 No.1511
WRA(No.13)O	The Welfare Reform Act 2012 (Commencement No.13 and Transitional and Transitory Provisions) Order 2013 No.2657
WRA(No.14)O	The Welfare Reform Act 2012 (Commencement No.14 and Transitional and Transitory Provisions) Order 2013 No.2846
WRA(No.16)O	The Welfare Reform Act 2012 (Commencement No.16 and Transitional and Transitory Provisions) Order 2014 No.209
WRPA(No.9)O	The Welfare Reform and Pensions Act 1999 (Commencement No.9, Transitional Provisions and Savings) Order 2000 No.2958
WTC(EMR) Regs	The Working Tax Credit (Entitlement and Maximum Rate) Regulations 2002 No.2005

Other information

ADM	*Advice for Decision Making*, vols A1-V8
CBTM	*Child Benefit Technical Manual*
CCM	*Claimant Compliance Manual* (HMRC guidance on investigation of tax credit claims)
DMG	*Decision Makers Guide*, vols 1-14
GM	*Housing Benefit/Council Tax Benefit Guidance Manual*
BLG	*Social Fund Budgeting Loan Guide*
SF Dir	*Social Fund Directive*
TCM	*Tax Credits Manual*
TCTM	*Tax Credits Technical Manual*

References like CIS/142/1990 and R(IS) 1/07 are references to commissioners' decisions.

References like CH/426/2008 [2009] UKUT 34 (AAC) are references to decisions of the Upper Tribunal

Index

· ·

How to use this Index

Because the Handbook is divided into separate sections covering the different benefits, many entries in the index have several references, each to a different section. Where this occurs, we use the following abbreviations to show to which benefit each reference relates.

AA	Attendance allowance	I-JSA	Income-based jobseeker's
CA	Carer's allowance		allowance
C-ESA	Contributory employment and	JSA	Jobseeker's allowance
	support allowance	MA	Maternity allowance
C-JSA	Contribution-based jobseeker's	NI	National insurance
	allowance	PC	Pension credit
CTC	Child tax credit	PIP	Personal independence payment
DLA	Disability living allowance	SAP	Statutory adoption pay
ESA	Employment and support allowance	SDA	Severe disablement allowance
HB	Housing benefit	SMP	Statutory maternity pay
IB	Incapacity benefit	SPP	Statutory paternity pay
IIDB	Industrial injuries disablement	SSP	Statutory sick pay
	benefit	UC	Universal credit
IS	Income support	WTC	Working tax credit
I-ESA	Income-related employment and		
	support allowance		

Entries against the bold headings direct you to the general information on the subject, or where the subject is covered most fully. Sub-entries are listed alphabetically and direct you to specific aspects of the subject.

NI credits 852
overlapping benefits 724, 1166
overpayments 1212
passport to other benefits 724
payment 722
period of payment 714, 718
prisoners 959
residence rules 1559
revisions 1267, 1270
SSP 820
statutory shared parental pay 714
supersessions 1267, 1281
test period 715
treated as in full-time work
    WTC 170
treatment as income
    means-tested benefits over PC age 312
    means-tested benefits under PC age
        274
    UC 333
    WTC/CTC 1423
who can claim 714
maternity allowance period 714
working during MA period 716
maternity grant
see: Sure Start maternity grant
maternity leave
childcare costs
    HB 271
failure to return to work
    JSA 1090
treated as in full-time work
    WTC 171
treated as not in full-time work
    HB/PC 996
    IS/JSA/ESA 995
maternity pay
see: statutory maternity pay
maternity pay period
definition 794
working during period 792
maximum amount
elements 250
standard allowance 250
UC 187, 249
maximum benefit
CTC 1400
HB 108
WTC 1402
maximum rent
local housing allowance 401
local reference rent 413
pre-Jan '96 rules 420
social sector tenants 406
meals
deductions from benefit
    HB 115

medical assessments
DLA 598
medical certificates
fit for work 813
SSP 813, 822
medical evidence
appeals 1322, 1358
DLA 596
limited capability for work 1014
    C-ESA 628
    I-ESA 73
PIP 738
SSP 822
medical examination
AA 513
appeals 1321
DLA 601
ESA 1010
expenses 1010
failure to attend 1176
    AA 513
    DLA 601
healthcare professional 1152
limited capability for work 1010
PIP 738
right payment programme
    DLA 604
SSP 813
work capability assessments 1010
medical treatment
absence from home
    HB 104
child abroad
    IS/JSA/ESA 215
    JSA 1030
excluded from HB 114
housing costs
    IS/I-JSA/I-ESA/PC 433
Member of Parliament
complaints to MP 1387
mental illness
appointees 1137
DLA care component 589
limited capability for work 1006
not treated as couple if compulsory
    patient
    IS/I-JSA/I-ESA/PC 209
PIP 727
prisoners detained in hospital
    means-tested benefits 963
    non-means-tested benefits 958, 963
    UC 963
recovery of overpayments
    WTC/CTC 1470
mental stress
good reason for refusing a job 1108
mesne profits
HB 97